D0252814

THE
HOLY BIBLE

CONTAINING THE

OLD AND NEW TESTAMENTS

TRANSLATED OUT OF THE ORIGINAL TONGUES
AND WITH THE FORMER TRANSLATIONS
DILIGENTLY COMPARED & REVISED

KING JAMES VERSION

AMERICAN BIBLE SOCIETY
NEW YORK

THE
HOLY BIBLE

King James Version

The work of the American Bible Society is made possible by contributions from supporters. If you would like to help spread the Gospel through Scripture distribution and engagement in the USA and around the world, we would be grateful for your donation.

You can mail your gift to the American Bible Society at the address below. Credit card contributions can be made at our secure website, www.americanbible.org, or through our toll-free number 1-866-895-4448.

American Bible Society/1865 Broadway/NewYork, NY 10023

ISBN 9781585161515

Printed in the United States of America
Eng. Bible KJV053-100028
ABS-9/13-20,000-849,000-NA3(23)

THE BOOKS OF THE OLD AND NEW TESTAMENTS

THE OLD TESTAMENT

THE NEW TESTAMENT

HELPS FOR THE READER

TABLE OF PRONUNCIATION MARKS

ā *as in* day, legate
ă " am, accept
ä " arm
ȧ " ask, sofa
ǣ = ĕ, end
a͡u *as in* author
c = k, cat
ç = s, cell
c̦ = sh, ocean
ch = k, chorus
Çn = N
ē *as in* evil, equip
ĕ " end, moment
ẽ " her
e̦ = ā, obey

g *as in* go
ġ = j, gem
ī *as in* ice
ĭ " ill
ï = ē, machine
ĩ *as in* firm
i̦ = y, union
Ṃn = N
ō *as in* old
ŏ " not, connect
ô " order
ȯ " come
o͡i " oil

Pt = T
ș = z, has
ș = sh, sure
ș = zh, vision
ț = sh, nation
ū *as in* use, unite
ŭ " up, circus
û " burn
ṳ " rude
ȳ = ī, fly
y̆ = ĭ, hymn

The less common proper names are marked according to the table above; in such names unmarked vowels are silent. The accents (′ ′) and the short hyphen (-) divide the word into syllables; the lighter accent (′) indicating a lesser stress. The long hyphen (–) divides compound words.

The pronunciation indicated in this book and the system of marks used are based upon Webster's New International Dictionary by courtesy of its publishers, G. & C. Merriam Company, Springfield, Mass.

THE FIRST BOOK OF MOSES, CALLED

GENESIS

CHAPTER 1

IN the beginning God created the
heaven and the earth.
2 And the earth was without form, and
void; and darkness *was* upon the face
of the deep. And the Spirit of God
moved upon the face of the waters.
3 And God said, Let there be light: and
there was light.
4 And God saw the light, that *it was*
good: and God divided the light from the
darkness.
5 And God called the light Day, and the
darkness he called Night. And the evening and the morning were the first day.
6 ℂ And God said, Let there be a firmament in the midst of the waters, and
let it divide the waters from the waters.
7 And God made the firmament, and
divided the waters which *were* under the
firmament from the waters which *were*
above the firmament: and it was so.
8 And God called the firmament Heav-
en. And the evening and the morning
were the second day.
9 ℂ And God said, Let the waters under the heaven be gathered together
unto one place, and let the dry *land* appear: and it was so.
10 And God called the dry *land* Earth;
and the gathering together of the waters
called he Seas: and God saw that *it was*
good.
11 And God said, Let the earth bring
forth grass, the herb yielding seed, *and*
the fruit tree yielding fruit after his kind,
whose seed *is* in itself, upon the earth:
and it was so.
12 And the earth brought forth grass,
and herb yielding seed after his kind,
and the tree yielding fruit, whose seed
was in itself, after his kind: and God
saw that *it was* good.
13 And the evening and the morning
were the third day.
14 ℂ And God said, Let there be lights
in the firmament of the heaven to divide
the day from the night; and let them be
for signs, and for seasons, and for days,
and years:
15 And let them be for lights in the
firmament of the heaven to give light
upon the earth: and it was so.
16 And God made two great lights; the
greater light to rule the day, and the
lesser light to rule the night: *he made*
the stars also.
17 And God set them in the firmament
of the heaven to give light upon the
earth,
18 And to rule over the day and over
the night, and to divide the light from
the darkness: and God saw that *it was*
good.
19 And the evening and the morning
were the fourth day.
20 And God said, Let the waters bring
forth abundantly the moving creature
that hath life, and fowl *that* may fly
above the earth in the open firmament
of heaven.
21 And God created great whales, and
every living creature that moveth, which
the waters brought forth abundantly,
after their kind, and every winged fowl
after his kind: and God saw that *it was*
good.
22 And God blessed them, saying, Be
fruitful, and multiply, and fill the waters
in the seas, and let fowl multiply in the
earth.
23 And the evening and the morning
were the fifth day.
24 ℂ And God said, Let the earth
bring forth the living creature after his
kind, cattle, and creeping thing, and
beast of the earth after his kind: and it
was so.
25 And God made the beast of the earth
after his kind, and cattle after their kind,
and every thing that creepeth upon the
earth after his kind: and God saw that
it was good.
26 ℂ And God said, Let us make man
in our image, after our likeness: and let
them have dominion over the fish of the
sea, and over the fowl of the air, and
over the cattle, and over all the earth,
and over every creeping thing that
creepeth upon the earth.
27 So God created man in his *own*
image, in the image of God created he
him; male and female created he them.

28 And God blessed them, and God said unto them, Be fruitful, and multiply, and replenish the earth, and subdue it: and have dominion over the fish of the sea, and over the fowl of the air, and over every living thing that moveth upon the earth.

29 ¶ And God said, Behold, I have given you every herb bearing seed, which *is* upon the face of all the earth, and every tree, in the which *is* the fruit of a tree yielding seed; to you it shall be for meat.

30 And to every beast of the earth, and to every fowl of the air, and to every thing that creepeth upon the earth, wherein *there is* life, *I have given* every green herb for meat: and it was so.

31 And God saw every thing that he had made, and, behold, *it was* very good. And the evening and the morning were the sixth day.

CHAPTER 2

THUS the heavens and the earth were finished, and all the host of them.

2 And on the seventh day God ended his work which he had made; and he rested on the seventh day from all his work which he had made.

3 And God blessed the seventh day, and sanctified it: because that in it he had rested from all his work which God created and made.

4 ¶ These *are* the generations of the heavens and of the earth when they were created, in the day that the LORD God made the earth and the heavens,

5 And every plant of the field before it was in the earth, and every herb of the field before it grew: for the LORD God had not caused it to rain upon the earth, and *there was* not a man to till the ground.

6 But there went up a mist from the earth, and watered the whole face of the ground.

7 And the LORD God formed man *of* the dust of the ground, and breathed into his nostrils the breath of life; and man became a living soul.

8 ¶ And the LORD God planted a garden eastward in Ē′den; and there he put the man whom he had formed.

9 And out of the ground made the LORD God to grow every tree that is pleasant to the sight, and good for food; the tree of life also in the midst of the garden, and the tree of knowledge of good and evil.

10 And a river went out of Ē′den to water the garden; and from thence it was parted, and became into four heads.

11 The name of the first *is* Pī′sŏn: that *is* it which compasseth the whole land of Hăv′ĭ-lăh, where *there is* gold;

12 And the gold of that land *is* good: there *is* bdellium and the onyx stone.

13 And the name of the second river *is* Gī′hŏn: the same *is* it that compasseth the whole land of Ethiopia.

14 And the name of the third river *is* Hĭd′dē-kĕl: that *is* it which goeth toward the east of Assyria. And the fourth river *is* Eū-phrā′tēs.

15 And the LORD God took the man, and put him into the garden of Ē′den to dress it and to keep it.

16 And the LORD God commanded the man, saying, Of every tree of the garden thou mayest freely eat:

17 But of the tree of the knowledge of good and evil, thou shalt not eat of it: for in the day that thou eatest thereof thou shalt surely die.

18 ¶ And the LORD God said, *It is* not good that the man should be alone; I will make him a help meet for him.

19 And out of the ground the LORD God formed every beast of the field, and every fowl of the air; and brought *them* unto Adam to see what he would call them: and whatsoever Adam called every living creature, that *was* the name thereof.

20 And Adam gave names to all cattle, and to the fowl of the air, and to every beast of the field; but for Adam there was not found a help meet for him.

21 And the LORD God caused a deep sleep to fall upon Adam, and he slept; and he took one of his ribs, and closed up the flesh instead thereof.

22 And the rib, which the LORD God had taken from man, made he a woman, and brought her unto the man.

23 And Adam said, This *is* now bone of my bones, and flesh of my flesh: she shall be called Woman, because she was taken out of man.

24 Therefore shall a man leave his father and his mother, and shall cleave unto his wife: and they shall be one flesh.

25 And they were both naked, the man
and his wife, and were not ashamed.

CHAPTER 3

NOW the serpent was more subtile
than any beast of the field which the
LORD God had made. And he said unto
the woman, Yea, hath God said, Ye shall
not eat of every tree of the garden?
2 And the woman said unto the serpent,
We may eat of the fruit of the trees of
the garden:
3 But of the fruit of the tree which *is* in
the midst of the garden, God hath said,
Ye shall not eat of it, neither shall ye
touch it, lest ye die.
4 And the serpent said unto the woman,
Ye shall not surely die:
5 For God doth know that in the day
ye eat thereof, then your eyes shall be
opened, and ye shall be as gods, knowing good and evil.
6 And when the woman saw that the
tree *was* good for food, and that it *was*
pleasant to the eyes, and a tree to be
desired to make *one* wise, she took of
the fruit thereof, and did eat, and gave
also unto her husband with her; and he
did eat.
7 And the eyes of them both were
opened, and they knew that they *were*
naked; and they sewed fig leaves together, and made themselves aprons.
8 And they heard the voice of the LORD
God walking in the garden in the cool of
the day: and Adam and his wife hid
themselves from the presence of the
LORD God amongst the trees of the
garden.
9 And the LORD God called unto Adam,
and said unto him, Where *art* thou?
10 And he said, I heard thy voice in the
garden, and I was afraid, because I *was*
naked; and I hid myself.
11 And he said, Who told thee that thou
wast naked? Hast thou eaten of the
tree, whereof I commanded thee that
thou shouldest not eat?
12 And the man said, The woman
whom thou gavest *to be* with me, she
gave me of the tree, and I did eat.
13 And the LORD God said unto the
woman, What *is* this *that* thou hast
done? And the woman said, The serpent beguiled me, and I did eat.
14 And the LORD God said unto the
serpent, Because thou hast done this,
thou *art* cursed above all cattle, and
above every beast of the field; upon thy
belly shalt thou go, and dust shalt thou
eat all the days of thy life:
15 And I will put enmity between thee
and the woman, and between thy seed
and her seed; it shall bruise thy head,
and thou shalt bruise his heel.
16 Unto the woman he said, I will
greatly multiply thy sorrow and thy conception; in sorrow thou shalt bring forth
children; and thy desire *shall be* to thy
husband, and he shall rule over thee.
17 And unto Adam he said, Because
thou hast hearkened unto the voice of
thy wife, and hast eaten of the tree, of
which I commanded thee, saying, Thou
shalt not eat of it: cursed *is* the ground
for thy sake; in sorrow shalt thou eat
of it all the days of thy life;
18 Thorns also and thistles shall it
bring forth to thee; and thou shalt eat
the herb of the field;
19 In the sweat of thy face shalt thou
eat bread, till thou return unto the
ground; for out of it wast thou taken: for
dust thou *art*, and unto dust shalt thou
return.
20 And Adam called his wife's name
Eve; because she was the mother of all
living.
21 Unto Adam also and to his wife did
the LORD God make coats of skins, and
clothed them.
22 ¶ And the LORD God said, Behold,
the man is become as one of us, to know
good and evil: and now, lest he put forth
his hand, and take also of the tree of
life, and eat, and live for ever:
23 Therefore the LORD God sent him
forth from the garden of Ē'den, to till
the ground from whence he was taken.
24 So he drove out the man: and he
placed at the east of the garden of Ē'den
cherubim, and a flaming sword which
turned every way, to keep the way of the
tree of life.

CHAPTER 4

AND Adam knew Eve his wife; and she
conceived, and bare Cain, and said,
I have gotten a man from the LORD.
2 And she again bare his brother Abel.
And Abel was a keeper of sheep, but
Cain was a tiller of the ground.
3 And in process of time it came to
pass, that Cain brought of the fruit of the
ground an offering unto the LORD.
4 And Abel, he also brought of the

firstlings of his flock and of the fat
thereof. And the LORD had respect unto
Abel and to his offering:
5 But unto Cain and to his offering he
had not respect. And Cain was very
wroth, and his countenance fell.
6 And the LORD said unto Cain, Why
art thou wroth? and why is thy countenance fallen?
7 If thou doest well, shalt thou not be
accepted? and if thou doest not well, sin
lieth at the door: and unto thee *shall be*
his desire, and thou shalt rule over him.
8 And Cain talked with Abel his
brother: and it came to pass, when they
were in the field, that Cain rose up
against Abel his brother, and slew him.
9 ¶ And the LORD said unto Cain,
Where *is* Abel thy brother? And he said,
I know not: *Am* I my brother's keeper?
10 And he said, What hast thou done?
the voice of thy brother's blood crieth
unto me from the ground.
11 And now *art* thou cursed from the
earth, which hath opened her mouth to
receive thy brother's blood from thy
hand.
12 When thou tillest the ground, it
shall not henceforth yield unto thee her
strength; a fugitive and a vagabond
shalt thou be in the earth.
13 And Cain said unto the LORD, My
punishment *is* greater than I can bear.
14 Behold, thou hast driven me out this
day from the face of the earth; and from
thy face shall I be hid; and I shall be a
fugitive and a vagabond in the earth;
and it shall come to pass, *that* every one
that findeth me shall slay me.
15 And the LORD said unto him, Therefore whosoever slayeth Cain, vengeance
shall be taken on him sevenfold. And
the LORD set a mark upon Cain, lest any
finding him should kill him.
16 ¶ And Cain went out from the presence of the LORD, and dwelt in the land
of Nod, on the east of Ē'den.
17 And Cain knew his wife; and she
conceived, and bare Enoch: and he
builded a city, and called the name of the
city, after the name of his son, Enoch.
18 And unto Enoch was born Ī'răd:
and Ī'răd begat Mē-hū'jā-ĕl: and Mē-
hū'jā-ĕl begat Mē-thū'sā-ĕl: and Mē-
thū'sā-ĕl begat Lā'mĕch.
19 ¶ And Lā'mĕch took unto him two
wives: the name of the one *was* Ā'dȧh,
and the name of the other Zĭl'lȧh.
20 And Ā'dȧh bare Jā'băl: he was the
father of such as dwell in tents, and *of*
such as have cattle.
21 And his brother's name *was* Jubal:
he was the father of all such as handle
the harp and organ.
22 And Zĭl'lȧh, she also bare Tū'băl-
cāin, an instructor of every artificer in
brass and iron: and the sister of Tū'-
băl-cāin *was* Nā'ȧ-mȧh.
23 And Lā'mĕch said unto his wives,
Ā'dȧh and Zĭl'lȧh, hear my voice; ye
wives of Lā'mĕch, hearken unto my
speech: for I have slain a man to my
wounding, and a young man to my hurt.
24 If Cain shall be avenged sevenfold,
truly Lā'mĕch seventy and sevenfold.
25 ¶ And Adam knew his wife again;
and she bare a son, and called his name
Seth: For God, *said she*, hath appointed
me another seed instead of Abel, whom
Cain slew.
26 And to Seth, to him also there was
born a son; and he called his name
Ē'nŏs: then began men to call upon the
name of the LORD.

CHAPTER 5

THIS *is* the book of the generations
of Adam. In the day that God
created man, in the likeness of God
made he him;
2 Male and female created he them;
and blessed them, and called their name
Adam, in the day when they were
created.
3 ¶ And Adam lived a hundred and
thirty years, and begat *a son* in his own
likeness, after his image; and called his
name Seth:
4 And the days of Adam after he had
begotten Seth were eight hundred years:
and he begat sons and daughters:
5 And all the days that Adam lived were
nine hundred and thirty years: and he
died.
6 And Seth lived a hundred and five
years, and begat Ē'nŏs:
7 And Seth lived after he begat Ē'nŏs
eight hundred and seven years, and
begat sons and daughters:
8 And all the days of Seth were nine
hundred and twelve years: and he died.
9 ¶ And Ē'nŏs lived ninety years, and
begat Cā-ī'năn:
10 And Ē'nŏs lived after he begat
Cā-ī'năn eight hundred and fifteen
years, and begat sons and daughters:

11 And all the days of Ē′nŏs were nine hundred and five years: and he died.

12 ¶ And Cā-ī′năn lived seventy years, and begat Mȧ-hā′lȧ-lē′ĕl:

13 And Cā-ī′năn lived after he begat Mȧ-hā′lȧ-lē′ĕl eight hundred and forty years, and begat sons and daughters:

14 And all the days of Cā-ī′năn were nine hundred and ten years: and he died.

15 ¶ And Mȧ-hā′lȧ-lē′ĕl lived sixty and five years, and begat Jā′rĕd:

16 And Mȧ-hā′lȧ-lē′ĕl lived after he begat Jā′rĕd eight hundred and thirty years, and begat sons and daughters:

17 And all the days of Mȧ-hā′lȧ-lē′ĕl were eight hundred ninety and five years: and he died.

18 ¶ And Jā′rĕd lived a hundred sixty and two years, and he begat Enoch:

19 And Jā′rĕd lived after he begat Enoch eight hundred years, and begat sons and daughters:

20 And all the days of Jā′rĕd were nine hundred sixty and two years: and he died.

21 ¶ And Enoch lived sixty and five years, and begat Mē-thū′sē-lȧh:

22 And Enoch walked with God after he begat Mē-thū′sē-lȧh three hundred years, and begat sons and daughters:

23 And all the days of Enoch were three hundred sixty and five years:

24 And Enoch walked with God: and he *was* not; for God took him.

25 And Mē-thū′sē-lȧh lived a hundred eighty and seven years, and begat Lā′mĕch:

26 And Mē-thū′sē-lȧh lived after he begat Lā′mĕch seven hundred eighty and two years, and begat sons and daughters:

27 And all the days of Mē-thū′sē-lȧh were nine hundred sixty and nine years: and he died.

28 ¶ And Lā′mĕch lived a hundred eighty and two years, and begat a son:

29 And he called his name Noah, saying, This *same* shall comfort us concerning our work and toil of our hands, because of the ground which the LORD hath cursed.

30 And Lā′mĕch lived after he begat Noah five hundred ninety and five years, and begat sons and daughters:

31 And all the days of Lā′mĕch were seven hundred seventy and seven years: and he died.

32 And Noah was five hundred years old: and Noah begat Shĕm, Ham, and Jā′phĕth.

CHAPTER 6

AND it came to pass, when men began to multiply on the face of the earth, and daughters were born unto them,

2 That the sons of God saw the daughters of men that they *were* fair; and they took them wives of all which they chose.

3 And the LORD said, My Spirit shall not always strive with man, for that he also *is* flesh: yet his days shall be a hundred and twenty years.

4 There were giants in the earth in those days; and also after that, when the sons of God came in unto the daughters of men, and they bare *children* to them, the same *became* mighty men which *were* of old, men of renown.

5 ¶ And God saw that the wickedness of man *was* great in the earth, and *that* every imagination of the thoughts of his heart *was* only evil continually.

6 And it repented the LORD that he had made man on the earth, and it grieved him at his heart.

7 And the LORD said, I will destroy man whom I have created from the face of the earth; both man, and beast, and the creeping thing, and the fowls of the air; for it repenteth me that I have made them.

8 But Noah found grace in the eyes of the LORD.

9 ¶ These *are* the generations of Noah: Noah was a just man *and* perfect in his generations, *and* Noah walked with God.

10 And Noah begat three sons, Shĕm, Ham, and Jā′phĕth.

11 The earth also was corrupt before God; and the earth was filled with violence.

12 And God looked upon the earth, and, behold, it was corrupt; for all flesh had corrupted his way upon the earth.

13 And God said unto Noah, The end of all flesh is come before me; for the earth is filled with violence through them; and, behold, I will destroy them with the earth.

14 ¶ Make thee an ark of gopher wood; rooms shalt thou make in the ark, and shalt pitch it within and without with pitch.

15 And this *is the fashion* which thou

shalt make it *of:* The length of the ark
shall be three hundred cubits, the
breadth of it fifty cubits, and the height
of it thirty cubits.
16 A window shalt thou make to the
ark, and in a cubit shalt thou finish it
above; and the door of the ark shalt
thou set in the side thereof; *with* lower,
second, and third *stories* shalt thou
make it.
17 And, behold, I, even I, do bring a
flood of waters upon the earth to destroy all flesh, wherein *is* the breath of
life, from under heaven; *and* every thing
that *is* in the earth shall die.
18 But with thee will I establish my
covenant; and thou shalt come into the
ark, thou, and thy sons, and thy wife,
and thy sons' wives with thee.
19 And of every living thing of all
flesh, two of every *sort* shalt thou bring
into the ark, to keep *them* alive with
thee; they shall be male and female.
20 Of fowls after their kind, and of
cattle after their kind, of every creeping
thing of the earth after his kind; two of
every *sort* shall come unto thee, to keep
them alive.
21 And take thou unto thee of all food
that is eaten, and thou shalt gather *it* to
thee; and it shall be for food for thee,
and for them.
22 Thus did Noah; according to all that
God commanded him, so did he.

CHAPTER 7

AND the LORD said unto Noah, Come
thou and all thy house into the ark;
for thee have I seen righteous before me
in this generation.
2 Of every clean beast thou shalt take
to thee by sevens, the male and his
female: and of beasts that *are* not clean
by two, the male and his female.
3 Of fowls also of the air by sevens, the
male and the female; to keep seed alive
upon the face of all the earth.
4 For yet seven days, and I will cause
it to rain upon the earth forty days and
forty nights; and every living substance
that I have made will I destroy from off
the face of the earth.
5 And Noah did according unto all that
the LORD commanded him.
6 And Noah *was* six hundred years old
when the flood of waters was upon the
earth.
7 ¶ And Noah went in, and his sons,
and his wife, and his sons' wives with
him, into the ark, because of the waters
of the flood.
8 Of clean beasts, and of beasts that
are not clean, and of fowls, and of every
thing that creepeth upon the earth,
9 There went in two and two unto Noah
into the ark, the male and the female, as
God had commanded Noah.
10 And it came to pass after seven
days, that the waters of the flood were
upon the earth.
11 ¶ In the six hundredth year of
Noah's life, in the second month, the
seventeenth day of the month, the same
day were all the fountains of the great
deep broken up, and the windows of
heaven were opened.
12 And the rain was upon the earth
forty days and forty nights.
13 In the selfsame day entered Noah,
and Shĕm, and Ham, and Jā'phĕth, the
sons of Noah, and Noah's wife, and the
three wives of his sons with them, into
the ark;
14 They, and every beast after his kind,
and all the cattle after their kind, and
every creeping thing that creepeth upon
the earth after his kind, and every fowl
after his kind, every bird of every sort.
15 And they went in unto Noah into
the ark, two and two of all flesh, wherein
is the breath of life.
16 And they that went in, went in male
and female of all flesh, as God had commanded him: and the LORD shut him in.
17 And the flood was forty days upon
the earth; and the waters increased, and
bare up the ark, and it was lifted up
above the earth.
18 And the waters prevailed, and were
increased greatly upon the earth; and
the ark went upon the face of the waters.
19 And the waters prevailed exceedingly upon the earth; and all the high
hills, that *were* under the whole heaven,
were covered.
20 Fifteen cubits upward did the waters
prevail; and the mountains were covered.
21 And all flesh died that moved upon
the earth, both of fowl, and of cattle, and
of beast, and of every creeping thing
that creepeth upon the earth, and every
man:
22 All in whose nostrils *was* the breath
of life, of all that *was* in the dry *land*,
died.

God have Noah make ark (to destroy evil world) bring N's family, creatures 2 of sort

23 And every living substance was destroyed which was upon the face of the ground, both man, and cattle, and the creeping things, and the fowl of the heaven; and they were destroyed from the earth: and Noah only remained *alive,* and they that *were* with him in the ark.

24 And the waters prevailed upon the earth a hundred and fifty days.

CHAPTER 8

AND God remembered Noah, and every living thing, and all the cattle that *was* with him in the ark: and God made a wind to pass over the earth, and the waters assuaged.

2 The fountains also of the deep and the windows of heaven were stopped, and the rain from heaven was restrained.

3 And the waters returned from off the earth continually: and after the end of the hundred and fifty days the waters were abated.

4 And the ark rested in the seventh month, on the seventeenth day of the month, upon the mountains of Ăr′ȧ-răt.

5 And the waters decreased continually until the tenth month: in the tenth *month,* on the first *day* of the month, were the tops of the mountains seen.

6 ¶ And it came to pass at the end of forty days, that Noah opened the window of the ark which he had made:

7 And he sent forth a raven, which went forth to and fro, until the waters were dried up from off the earth.

8 Also he sent forth a dove from him, to see if the waters were abated from off the face of the ground.

9 But the dove found no rest for the sole of her foot, and she returned unto him into the ark; for the waters *were* on the face of the whole earth. Then he put forth his hand, and took her, and pulled her in unto him into the ark.

10 And he stayed yet other seven days; and again he sent forth the dove out of the ark.

11 And the dove came in to him in the evening, and, lo, in her mouth *was* an olive leaf plucked off: so Noah knew that the waters were abated from off the earth.

12 And he stayed yet other seven days, and sent forth the dove, which returned not again unto him any more.

13 ¶ And it came to pass in the six hundredth and first year, in the first *month,* the first *day* of the month, the waters were dried up from off the earth: and Noah removed the covering of the ark, and looked, and, behold, the face of the ground was dry.

14 And in the second month, on the seven and twentieth day of the month, was the earth dried.

15 ¶ And God spake unto Noah, saying,

16 Go forth of the ark, thou, and thy wife, and thy sons, and thy sons' wives with thee.

17 Bring forth with thee every living thing that *is* with thee, of all flesh, *both* of fowl, and of cattle, and of every creeping thing that creepeth upon the earth; that they may breed abundantly in the earth, and be fruitful, and multiply upon the earth.

18 And Noah went forth, and his sons, and his wife, and his sons' wives with him:

19 Every beast, every creeping thing, and every fowl, *and* whatsoever creepeth upon the earth, after their kinds, went forth out of the ark.

20 ¶ And Noah builded an altar unto the LORD; and took of every clean beast, and of every clean fowl, and offered burnt offerings on the altar.

21 And the LORD smelled a sweet savor; and the LORD said in his heart, I will not again curse the ground any more for man's sake; for the imagination of man's heart *is* evil from his youth: neither will I again smite any more every thing living, as I have done.

22 While the earth remaineth, seedtime and harvest, and cold and heat, and summer and winter, and day and night shall not cease.

CHAPTER 9

AND God blessed Noah and his sons, and said unto them, Be fruitful, and multiply, and replenish the earth.

2 And the fear of you and the dread of you shall be upon every beast of the earth, and upon every fowl of the air, upon all that moveth *upon* the earth, and upon all the fishes of the sea; into your hand are they delivered.

3 Every moving thing that liveth shall be meat for you; even as the green herb have I given you all things.

4 But flesh with the life thereof, *which*
is the blood thereof, shall ye not eat.
5 And surely your blood of your lives
will I require: at the hand of every beast
will I require it, and at the hand of man;
at the hand of every man's brother will I
require the life of man.
6 Whoso sheddeth man's blood, by man
shall his blood be shed: for in the image
of God made he man.
7 And you, be ye fruitful, and multiply;
bring forth abundantly in the earth, and
multiply therein.
8 ¶ And God spake unto Noah, and
to his sons with him, saying,
9 And I, behold, I establish my covenant with you, and with your seed after
you;
10 And with every living creature that
is with you, of the fowl, of the cattle, and
of every beast of the earth with you;
from all that go out of the ark, to every
beast of the earth.
11 And I will establish my covenant
with you; neither shall all flesh be cut
off any more by the waters of a flood;
neither shall there any more be a flood
to destroy the earth.
12 And God said, This *is* the token of
the covenant which I make between
me and you, and every living creature
that *is* with you, for perpetual generations:
13 I do set my bow in the cloud, and it
shall be for a token of a covenant between me and the earth.
14 And it shall come to pass, when I
bring a cloud over the earth, that the
bow shall be seen in the cloud:
15 And I will remember my covenant,
which *is* between me and you and every
living creature of all flesh; and the
waters shall no more become a flood to
destroy all flesh.
16 And the bow shall be in the cloud;
and I will look upon it, that I may remember the everlasting covenant between God and every living creature of
all flesh that *is* upon the earth.
17 And God said unto Noah, This *is*
the token of the covenant, which I have
established between me and all flesh
that *is* upon the earth.
18 ¶ And the sons of Noah, that went
forth of the ark, were Shĕm, and Ham,
and Jā′phĕth: and Ham *is* the father of
Cā′năan.
19 These *are* the three sons of Noah:
and of them was the whole earth over-
spread.
20 And Noah began *to be* a husbandman, and he planted a vineyard:
21 And he drank of the wine, and was
drunken; and he was uncovered within
his tent.
22 And Ham, the father of Cā′năan,
saw the nakedness of his father, and
told his two brethren without.
23 And Shĕm and Jā′phĕth took a garment, and laid *it* upon both their shoulders, and went backward, and covered
the nakedness of their father; and their
faces *were* backward, and they saw not
their father's nakedness.
24 And Noah awoke from his wine, and
knew what his younger son had done
unto him.
25 And he said, Cursed *be* Cā′năan; a
servant of servants shall he be unto his
brethren.
26 And he said, Blessed *be* the LORD
God of Shĕm; and Cā′năan shall be his
servant.
27 God shall enlarge Jā′phĕth, and he
shall dwell in the tents of Shĕm; and
Cā′năan shall be his servant.
28 ¶ And Noah lived after the flood
three hundred and fifty years.
29 And all the days of Noah were nine
hundred and fifty years: and he died.

CHAPTER 10

NOW these *are* the generations of the
sons of Noah; Shĕm, Ham, and
Jā′phĕth: and unto them were sons born
after the flood.
2 The sons of Jā′phĕth; Gō′mĕr, and
Mā′gŏg, and Măd′ā-ī, and Jā′văn, and
Tū′băl, and Mē′shĕch, and Tī′răs.
3 And the sons of Gō′mĕr; Ăsh′kē-năz,
and Rī′phăth, and Tō-gär′mȧh.
4 And the sons of Jā′văn; Ē-lī′shȧh,
and Tär′shĭsh, Kĭt′tĭm, and Dō′dȧ-nĭm.
5 By these were the isles of the Ġĕn′-
tīleș divided in their lands; every one
after his tongue, after their families, in
their nations.
6 ¶ And the sons of Ham; Cŭsh, and
Mĭz′rā-ĭm, and Phŭt, and Cā′năan.
7 And the sons of Cŭsh; Sē′bȧ, and
Hăv′ĭ-lăh, and Săb′tȧh, and Rā′ȧ-mȧh,
and Săb′tē-chȧ: and the sons of Rā′ȧ-
mȧh; Shē′bȧ, and Dē′dăn.
8 And Cŭsh begat Nimrod: he began to
be a mighty one in the earth.
9 He was a mighty hunter before the

LORD: wherefore it is said, Even as
Nimrod the mighty hunter before the
LORD.
10 And the beginning of his kingdom
was Bā'bĕl, and Ĕr'ĕch, and Ăc'căd, and
Căl'nĕh, in the land of Shī'När.
11 Out of that land went forth Ăssh'ŭr,
and builded Nĭn'ē-vĕh, and the city
Rē-hō'bŏth, and Cā'lȧh,
12 And Rē'sĕn between Nĭn'ē-vĕh
and Cā'lȧh: the same *is* a great city.
13 And Mĭz'rā-ĭm begat Lū'dĭm, and
Ăn'ȧ-mĭm, and Lē-hā'bĭm, and Năph-
tū'hĭm,
14 And Păth-rŭ'sĭm, and Căs'lū-hĭm,
(out of whom came Phĭ-lĭs'tĭm,) and
Căph'tō-rĭm.
15 ℂ And Cā'năan begat Sī'dŏn his
firstborn, and Heth,
16 And the Jĕb'ū-sīte, and the Ăm'ō-
rīte, and the Gĭr'gȧ-sīte,
17 And the Hī'vīte, and the Ärk'īte, and
the Sī'nīte,
18 And the Är'văd-īte, and the Zĕm'ȧ-
rīte, and the Hā'măth-īte: and afterward
were the families of the Cā'năan-ītes
spread abroad.
19 And the border of the Cā'năan-ītes
was from Sī'dŏn, as thou comest to
Gē'rär, unto Gā'zȧ; as thou goest unto
Sŏd'ŏm, and Gō-mŏr'rȧh, and Ăd'mȧh,
and Zē-bō'ĭm, even unto Lā'shȧ.
20 These *are* the sons of Hăm, after
their families, after their tongues, in
their countries, *and* in their nations.
21 ℂ Unto Shĕm also, the father of all
the children of Ē'bĕr, the brother of
Jā'phĕth the elder, even to him were
children born.
22 The children of Shĕm; Ē'lăm, and
Ăssh'ŭr, and Är-phăx'ăd, and Lŭd, and
Ā'răm.
23 And the children of Ā'răm; Ŭz, and
Hŭl, and Gē'thĕr, and Măsh.
24 And Är-phăx'ăd begat Sā'lȧh; and
Sā'lȧh begat Ē'bĕr.
25 And unto Ē'bĕr were born two sons:
the name of one *was* Pē'lĕg; for in his
days was the earth divided; and his
brother's name *was* Jŏk'tăn.
26 And Jŏk'tăn begat Ăl-mō'dăd, and
Shē'lĕph, and Hā'zär-mā'vĕth, and
Jē'rȧh,
27 And Hȧ-dō'răm, and Ū'zăl, and
Dĭk'lȧh,
28 And Ō'băl, and Ȧ-bĭm'ā-ĕl, and
Shē'bȧ,
29 And Ō'phĭr, and Hăv'ĭ-lăh, and
Jō'băb: all these *were* the sons of
Jŏk'tăn.
30 And their dwelling was from Mē'-
shȧ, as thou goest unto Sē'phär, a mount
of the east.
31 These *are* the sons of Shĕm, after
their families, after their tongues, in
their lands, after their nations.
32 These *are* the families of the sons
of Noah, after their generations, in their
nations: and by these were the nations
divided in the earth after the flood.

CHAPTER 11

AND the whole earth was of one language, and of one speech.
2 And it came to pass, as they journeyed from the east, that they found a
plain in the land of Shī'när; and they
dwelt there.
3 And they said one to another, Go to,
let us make brick, and burn them
thoroughly. And they had brick for
stone, and slime had they for mortar.
4 And they said, Go to, let us build us
a city, and a tower, whose top *may
reach* unto heaven; and let us make us
a name, lest we be scattered abroad
upon the face of the whole earth.
5 And the LORD came down to see the
city and the tower, which the children
of men builded.
6 And the LORD said, Behold, the
people *is* one, and they have all one
language; and this they begin to do: and
now nothing will be restrained from
them, which they have imagined to do.
7 Go to, let us go down, and there confound their language, that they may not
understand one another's speech.
8 So the LORD scattered them abroad
from thence upon the face of all the
earth: and they left off to build the city.
9 Therefore is the name of it called
Bā'bĕl; because the LORD did there confound the language of all the earth: and
from thence did the LORD scatter them
abroad upon the face of all the earth.
10 ℂ These *are* the generations of
Shĕm: Shĕm *was* a hundred years old,
and begat Är-phăx'ăd two years after
the flood:
11 And Shĕm lived after he begat
Är-phăx'ăd five hundred years, and begat sons and daughters.
12 And Är-phăx'ăd lived five and
thirty years, and begat Sā'lȧh:
13 And Är-phăx'ăd lived after he begat

Sā'lȧh four hundred and three years,
and begat sons and daughters.
14 And Sā'lȧh lived thirty years, and
begat Ē'bĕr:
15 And Sā'lȧh lived after he begat
Ē'bĕr four hundred and three years, and
begat sons and daughters.
16 And Ē'bĕr lived four and thirty
years, and begat Pē'lĕg:
17 And Ē'bĕr lived after he begat
Pē'lĕg four hundred and thirty years,
and begat sons and daughters.
18 And Pē'lĕg lived thirty years, and
begat Rē'ū:
19 And Pē'lĕg lived after he begat
Rē'ū two hundred and nine years, and
begat sons and daughters.
20 And Rē'ū lived two and thirty years,
and begat Sē'rŭg:
21 And Rē'ū lived after he begat Sē'-
rŭg two hundred and seven years, and
begat sons and daughters.
22 And Sē'rŭg lived thirty years, and
begat Nā'hŏr:
23 And Sē'rŭg lived after he begat
Nā'hŏr two hundred years, and begat
sons and daughters.
24 And Nā'hŏr lived nine and twenty
years, and begat Tē'rȧh:
25 And Nā'hŏr lived after he begat
Tē'rȧh a hundred and nineteen years,
and begat sons and daughters.
26 And Tē'rȧh lived seventy years, and
begat Abram, Nā'hŏr, and Hā'răn.
27 ¶ Now these *are* the generations of
Tē'rȧh: Tē'rȧh begat Abram, Nā'hŏr,
and Hā'răn; and Hā'răn begat Lot.
28 And Hā'răn died before his father
Tē'rȧh in the land of his nativity, in Ûr
of the Chăl'dēeş.
29 And Abram and Nā'hŏr took them
wives: the name of Abram's wife *was*
Sā'raī; and the name of Nā'hŏr's wife,
Mĭl'cȧh, the daughter of Hā'răn, the
father of Mĭl'cȧh, and the father of
Ĭs'cȧh.
30 But Sā'raī was barren; she *had* no
child.
31 And Tē'rȧh took Abram his son, and
Lot the son of Hā'răn his son's son, and
Sā'raī his daughter-in-law, his son
Abram's wife; and they went forth with
them from Ûr of the Chăl'dēeş, to go into
the land of Cā'năan; and they came unto
Hā'răn, and dwelt there.
32 And the days of Tē'rȧh were two
hundred and five years: and Tē'rȧh
died in Hā'răn.

CHAPTER 12

NOW the LORD had said unto Abram,
Get thee out of thy country, and
from thy kindred, and from thy father's
house, unto a land that I will show thee:
2 And I will make of thee a great
nation, and I will bless thee, and make
thy name great; and thou shalt be a
blessing:
3 And I will bless them that bless thee,
and curse him that curseth thee: and in
thee shall all families of the earth be
blessed.
4 So Abram departed, as the LORD had
spoken unto him; and Lot went with him:
and Abram *was* seventy and five years
old when he departed out of Hā'răn.
5 And Abram took Sā'raī his wife, and
Lot his brother's son, and all their substance that they had gathered, and the
souls that they had gotten in Hā'răn;
and they went forth to go into the land
of Cā'năan; and into the land of Cā'-
năan they came.
6 ¶ And Abram passed through the
land unto the place of Sī'chĕm, unto the
plain of Mō'rĕh. And the Cā'năan-īte
was then in the land.
7 And the LORD appeared unto Abram,
and said, Unto thy seed will I give this
land: and there builded he an altar unto
the LORD, who appeared unto him.
8 And he removed from thence unto a
mountain on the east of Beth-el, and
pitched his tent, *having* Beth-el on the
west, and Hā'ī on the east: and there he
builded an altar unto the LORD, and
called upon the name of the LORD.
9 And Abram journeyed, going on still
toward the south.
10 ¶ And there was a famine in the
land: and Abram went down into Egypt
to sojourn there; for the famine *was*
grievous in the land.
11 And it came to pass, when he was
come near to enter into Egypt, that he
said unto Sā'raī his wife, Behold now, I
know that thou *art* a fair woman to look
upon:
12 Therefore it shall come to pass,
when the Egyptians shall see thee, that
they shall say, This *is* his wife: and they
will kill me, but they will save thee alive.
13 Say, I pray thee, thou *art* my sister:
that it may be well with me for thy sake;
and my soul shall live because of thee.
14 ¶ And it came to pass, that, when

Abram was come into Egypt, the Egyptians beheld the woman that she *was*
very fair.
15 The princes also of Phā′raōh saw
her, and commended her before Phā′-
raōh: and the woman was taken into
Phā′raōh's house.
16 And he entreated Abram well for
her sake: and he had sheep, and oxen,
and he asses, and menservants, and
maidservants, and she asses, and
camels.
17 And the LORD plagued Phā′raōh
and his house with great plagues, because of Sā′raī, Abram's wife.
18 And Phā′raōh called Abram, and
said, What *is* this *that* thou hast done
unto me? why didst thou not tell me
that she *was* thy wife?
19 Why saidst thou, She *is* my sister?
so I might have taken her to me to wife:
now therefore behold thy wife, take *her*,
and go thy way.
20 And Phā′raōh commanded *his* men
concerning him: and they sent him away,
and his wife, and all that he had.

CHAPTER 13

AND Abram went up out of Egypt, he,
and his wife, and all that he had,
and Lot with him, into the south.
2 And Abram *was* very rich in cattle,
in silver, and in gold.
3 And he went on his journeys from
the south even to Beth-el, unto the
place where his tent had been at the
beginning, between Beth-el and Hā′ī;
4 Unto the place of the altar, which he
had made there at the first: and there
Abram called on the name of the LORD.
5 ℂ And Lot also, which went with
Abram, had flocks, and herds, and tents.
6 And the land was not able to bear
them, that they might dwell together:
for their substance was great, so that
they could not dwell together.
7 And there was a strife between the
herdmen of Abram's cattle and the
herdmen of Lot's cattle: and the Cā′-
năan-īte and the Pĕr′ĭz-zīte dwelt then
in the land.
8 And Abram said unto Lot, Let there
be no strife, I pray thee, between me
and thee, and between my herdmen and
thy herdmen; for we *be* brethren.
9 *Is* not the whole land before thee?
separate thyself, I pray thee, from me:
if *thou wilt take* the left hand, then I will
go to the right; or if *thou depart* to the
right hand, then I will go to the left.
10 And Lot lifted up his eyes, and beheld all the plain of Jordan, that it *was*
well watered every where, before the
LORD destroyed Sŏd′ŏm and Gō-mŏr′-
răh, *even* as the garden of the LORD,
like the land of Egypt, as thou comest
unto Zō′ăr.
11 Then Lot chose him all the plain of
Jordan; and Lot journeyed east: and
they separated themselves the one from
the other.
12 Abram dwelt in the land of Cā′năan,
and Lot dwelt in the cities of the plain,
and pitched *his* tent toward Sŏd′ŏm.
13 But the men of Sŏd′ŏm *were*
wicked and sinners before the LORD
exceedingly.
14 ℂ And the LORD said unto Abram,
after that Lot was separated from him,
Lift up now thine eyes, and look from
the place where thou art northward, and
southward, and eastward, and westward:
15 For all the land which thou seest,
to thee will I give it, and to thy seed for
ever.
16 And I will make thy seed as the dust
of the earth: so that if a man can number the dust of the earth, *then* shall thy
seed also be numbered.
17 Arise, walk through the land in the
length of it and in the breadth of it; for
I will give it unto thee.
18 Then Abram removed *his* tent, and
came and dwelt in the plain of Măm′rē,
which *is* in Hē′brŏn, and built there an
altar unto the LORD.

CHAPTER 14

AND it came to pass in the days of
Ăm′ră-phĕl king of Shī′năr, Ă′rĭ-
ŏch king of Ĕl-lā′săr, Chĕd′ŏr-lā-ō′mĕr
king of Ē′lăm, and Tī′dăl king of nations;
2 *That these* made war with Bē′ră king
of Sŏd′ŏm, and with Bĭr′shă king of
Gō-mŏr′răh, Shī′năb king of Ăd′măh,
and Shĕm-ē′bĕr king of Zē-bōī′ĭm, and
the king of Bē′lă, which is Zō′ăr.
3 All these were joined together in the
vale of Sĭd′dĭm, which is the salt sea.
4 Twelve years they served Chĕd′ŏr-
lā-ō′mĕr, and in the thirteenth year they
rebelled.
5 And in the fourteenth year came
Chĕd′ŏr-lā-ō′mĕr, and the kings that
were with him, and smote the Rĕph′ā-ĭm

in Ăsh′tē-rŏth Kär-nā′ĭm, and the Zū′-
zĭm in Ham, and the Ē′mĭm in Shā′vĕh
Kĭr′ĭ-ȧ-thā′ĭm,
6 And the Hō′rītes in their mount Sē′ĭr,
unto Ĕl-pā′răn, which *is* by the wilderness.
7 And they returned, and came to
Ĕn-mĭsh′păt, which *is* Kā′dĕsh, and
smote all the country of the Ăm′ȧ-
lĕk-ītes, and also the Ăm′ō-rītes, that
dwelt in Hăz′ē-zŏn-tā′mȧr.
8 And there went out the king of Sŏd′-
ȯm, and the king of Gō-mŏr′rȧh, and the
king of Ăd′mȧh, and the king of Zē-
bôi′ĭm, and the king of Bē′lȧ, (the same
is Zō′ȧr;) and they joined battle with
them in the vale of Sĭd′dĭm;
9 With Chĕd′ŏr-lā-ō′mẽr the king of
Ē′lăm, and with Tī′dăl king of nations,
and Ăm′rȧ-phĕl king of Shī′när, and
Ăr′ĭ-ŏch king of Ĕl-lā′sär; four kings
with five.
10 And the vale of Sĭd′dĭm *was full of*
slime pits; and the kings of Sŏd′ȯm and
Gō-mŏr′rȧh fled, and fell there; and
they that remained fled to the mountain.
11 And they took all the goods of
Sŏd′ȯm and Gō-mŏr′rȧh, and all their
victuals, and went their way.
12 And they took Lot, Abram's brother's son, who dwelt in Sŏd′ȯm, and his
goods, and departed.
13 ¶ And there came one that had
escaped, and told Abram the Hebrew;
for he dwelt in the plain of Măm′rē the
Ăm′ō-rīte, brother of Ĕsh′cŏl, and
brother of Ā′nẽr: and these *were* confederate with Abram.
14 And when Abram heard that his
brother was taken captive, he armed his
trained *servants*, born in his own house,
three hundred and eighteen, and pursued *them* unto Dan.
15 And he divided himself against
them, he and his servants, by night, and
smote them, and pursued them unto
Hō′bȧh, which *is* on the left hand of
Damascus.
16 And he brought back all the goods,
and also brought again his brother Lot,
and his goods, and the women also, and
the people.
17 ¶ And the king of Sŏd′ȯm went out
to meet him, after his return from the
slaughter of Chĕd′ŏr-lā-ō′mẽr and of
the kings that *were* with him, at the valley of Shā′vĕh, which *is* the king's dale.
18 And Mĕl-chĭz′ē-dĕk king of Sā′lĕm
brought forth bread and wine: and he
was the priest of the most high God.
19 And he blessed him, and said,
Blessed be Abram of the most high God,
possessor of heaven and earth:
20 And blessed be the most high God,
which hath delivered thine enemies into
thy hand. And he gave him tithes of all.
21 And the king of Sŏd′ȯm said unto
Abram, Give me the persons, and take
the goods to thyself.
22 And Abram said to the king of
Sŏd′ȯm, I have lifted up mine hand unto
the LORD, the most high God, the possessor of heaven and earth,
23 That I will not *take* from a thread
even to a shoe-latchet, and that I will
not take any thing that *is* thine, lest
thou shouldest say, I have made Abram
rich:
24 Save only that which the young men
have eaten, and the portion of the men
which went with me, Ā′nẽr, Ĕsh′cŏl, and
Măm′rē; let them take their portion.

CHAPTER 15

AFTER these things the word of the
LORD came unto Abram in a
vision, saying, Fear not, Abram: I *am*
thy shield, *and* thy exceeding great
reward.
2 And Abram said, Lord GOD, what
wilt thou give me, seeing I go childless,
and the steward of my house *is* this
Ĕl′ĭ-ē′zẽr of Damascus?
3 And Abram said, Behold, to me thou
hast given no seed: and, lo, one born in
my house is mine heir.
4 And, behold, the word of the LORD
came unto him, saying, This shall not be
thine heir; but he that shall come forth
out of thine own bowels shall be thine
heir.
5 And he brought him forth abroad, and
said, Look now toward heaven, and tell
the stars, if thou be able to number
them: and he said unto him, So shall
thy seed be.
6 And he believed in the LORD; and
he counted it to him for righteousness.
7 And he said unto him, I *am* the LORD
that brought thee out of Ûr of the Chăl′-
dēeṣ, to give thee this land to inherit it.
8 And he said, Lord GOD, whereby
shall I know that I shall inherit it?
9 And he said unto him, Take me a
heifer of three years old, and a she goat
of three years old, and a ram of three

years old, and a turtledove, and a young pigeon.

10 And he took unto him all these, and divided them in the midst, and laid each piece one against another: but the birds divided he not.

11 And when the fowls came down upon the carcasses, Abram drove them away.

12 And when the sun was going down, a deep sleep fell upon Abram; and, lo, a horror of great darkness fell upon him.

13 And he said unto Abram, Know of a surety that thy seed shall be a stranger in a land *that is* not theirs, and shall serve them; and they shall afflict them four hundred years;

14 And also that nation, whom they shall serve, will I judge: and afterward shall they come out with great substance.

15 And thou shalt go to thy fathers in peace; thou shalt be buried in a good old age.

16 But in the fourth generation they shall come hither again: for the iniquity of the Ăm'ō-rītes *is* not yet full.

17 And it came to pass, that, when the sun went down, and it was dark, behold a smoking furnace, and a burning lamp that passed between those pieces.

18 In that same day the LORD made a covenant with Abram, saying, Unto thy seed have I given this land, from the river of Egypt unto the great river, the river Eū-phrā'tēs̱:

19 The Kē'nītes, and the Kē'nĭz-zītes, and the Kăd'mŏn-ītes,

20 And the Hĭt'tītes, and the Pĕr'ĭz-zītes, and the Rĕph'ā-ĭm,

21 And the Ăm'ō-rītes, and the Cā'năan-ītes, and the Gĭr'gȧ-shītes, and the Jĕb'ū-s̱ītes.

CHAPTER 16

NOW Sā'raī, Abram's wife, bare him no children: and she had a handmaid, an Egyptian, whose name *was* Hā'gȧr.

2 And Sā'raī said unto Abram, Behold now, the LORD hath restrained me from bearing: I pray thee, go in unto my maid; it may be that I may obtain children by her. And Abram hearkened to the voice of Sā'raī.

3 And Sā'raī, Abram's wife, took Hā'gȧr her maid the Egyptian, after Abram had dwelt ten years in the land of Cā'năan, and gave her to her husband Abram to be his wife.

4 ¶ And he went in unto Hā'gȧr, and she conceived: and when she saw that she had conceived, her mistress was despised in her eyes.

5 And Sā'raī said unto Abram, My wrong *be* upon thee: I have given my maid into thy bosom; and when she saw that she had conceived, I was despised in her eyes: the LORD judge between me and thee.

6 But Abram said unto Sā'raī, Behold, thy maid *is* in thy hand; do to her as it pleaseth thee. And when Sā'raī dealt hardly with her, she fled from her face.

7 ¶ And the angel of the LORD found her by a fountain of water in the wilderness, by the fountain in the way to Shu̱r.

8 And he said, Hā'gȧr, Sā'raī's maid, whence camest thou? and whither wilt thou go? And she said, I flee from the face of my mistress Sā'raī.

9 And the angel of the LORD said unto her, Return to thy mistress, and submit thyself under her hands.

10 And the angel of the LORD said unto her, I will multiply thy seed exceedingly, that it shall not be numbered for multitude.

11 And the angel of the LORD said unto her, Behold, thou *art* with child, and shalt bear a son, and shalt call his name Ĭsh'mā-ĕl; because the LORD hath heard thy affliction.

12 And he will be a wild man; his hand *will be* against every man, and every man's hand against him: and he shall dwell in the presence of all his brethren.

13 And she called the name of the LORD that spake unto her, Thou God seest me: for she said, Have I also here looked after him that seeth me?

14 Wherefore the well was called Bē'ĕr-lȧ-haī'-roî: behold, *it is* between Kā'dĕsh and Bē'rĕd.

15 ¶ And Hā'gȧr bare Abram a son: and Abram called his son's name, which Hā'gȧr bare, Ĭsh'mā-ĕl.

16 And Abram *was* fourscore and six years old, when Hā'gȧr bare Ĭsh'mā-ĕl to Abram.

CHAPTER 17

AND when Abram was ninety years old and nine, the LORD appeared to Abram, and said unto him, I *am* the

Almighty God; walk before me, and be
thou perfect.
2 And I will make my covenant between me and thee, and will multiply
thee exceedingly.
3 And Abram fell on his face: and God
talked with him, saying,
4 As for me, behold, my covenant *is*
with thee, and thou shalt be a father of
many nations.
5 Neither shall thy name any more be
called Abram, but thy name shall be
Abraham; for a father of many nations
have I made thee.
6 And I will make thee exceeding fruitful, and I will make nations of thee, and
kings shall come out of thee.
7 And I will establish my covenant between me and thee and thy seed after
thee in their generations, for an everlasting covenant, to be a God unto thee
and to thy seed after thee.
8 And I will give unto thee, and to thy
seed after thee, the land wherein thou
art a stranger, all the land of Cā'năan,
for an everlasting possession; and I will
be their God.
9 ℂ And God said unto Abraham, Thou
shalt keep my covenant therefore, thou,
and thy seed after thee in their generations.
10 This *is* my covenant, which ye shall
keep, between me and you and thy seed
after thee; Every man child among you
shall be circumcised.
11 And ye shall circumcise the flesh of
your foreskin; and it shall be a token of
the covenant betwixt me and you.
12 And he that is eight days old shall
be circumcised among you, every man
child in your generations, he that is born
in the house, or bought with money of
any stranger, which *is* not of thy seed.
13 He that is born in thy house, and he
that is bought with thy money, must
needs be circumcised: and my covenant
shall be in your flesh for an everlasting
covenant.
14 And the uncircumcised man child
whose flesh of his foreskin is not circumcised, that soul shall be cut off from his
people; he hath broken my covenant.
15 ℂ And God said unto Abraham, As
for Sā'raī thy wife, thou shalt not call
her name Sā'raī, but Sarah *shall* her
name *be*.
16 And I will bless her, and give thee a
son also of her: yea, I will bless her, and
she shall be *a mother* of nations; kings
of people shall be of her.
17 Then Abraham fell upon his face,
and laughed, and said in his heart, Shall
a child be born unto him that is a hundred years old? and shall Sarah, that is
ninety years old, bear?
18 And Abraham said unto God, O that
Ĭsh'mā-ĕl might live before thee!
19 And God said, Sarah thy wife shall
bear thee a son indeed; and thou shalt
call his name Isaac: and I will establish
my covenant with him for an everlasting
covenant, *and* with his seed after him.
20 And as for Ĭsh'mā-ĕl, I have heard
thee: Behold, I have blessed him, and
will make him fruitful, and will multiply
him exceedingly; twelve princes shall
he beget, and I will make him a great
nation.
21 But my covenant will I establish
with Isaac, which Sarah shall bear unto
thee at this set time in the next year.
22 And he left off talking with him, and
God went up from Abraham.
23 ℂ And Abraham took Ĭsh'mā-ĕl his
son, and all that were born in his house,
and all that were bought with his money,
every male among the men of Abraham's
house; and circumcised the flesh of their
foreskin in the selfsame day, as God had
said unto him.
24 And Abraham *was* ninety years old
and nine, when he was circumcised in
the flesh of his foreskin.
25 And Ĭsh'mā-ĕl his son *was* thirteen
years old, when he was circumcised in
the flesh of his foreskin.
26 In the selfsame day was Abraham
circumcised, and Ĭsh'mā-ĕl his son.
27 And all the men of his house, born
in the house, and bought with money
of the stranger, were circumcised with
him.

CHAPTER 18

AND the LORD appeared unto him in
the plains of Măm'rē: and he sat
in the tent door in the heat of the day;
2 And he lifted up his eyes and looked,
and, lo, three men stood by him: and
when he saw *them*, he ran to meet them
from the tent door, and bowed himself
toward the ground,
3 And said, My Lord, if now I have
found favor in thy sight, pass not away,
I pray thee, from thy servant:
4 Let a little water, I pray you, be

fetched, and wash your feet, and rest
yourselves under the tree:
5 And I will fetch a morsel of bread,
and comfort ye your hearts; after that
ye shall pass on: for therefore are ye
come to your servant. And they said,
So do, as thou hast said.
6 And Abraham hastened into the tent
unto Sarah, and said, Make ready
quickly three measures of fine meal,
knead *it*, and make cakes upon the
hearth.
7 And Abraham ran unto the herd, and
fetched a calf tender and good, and gave
it unto a young man; and he hasted to
dress it.
8 And he took butter, and milk, and
the calf which he had dressed, and set
it before them; and he stood by them
under the tree, and they did eat.
9 ¶ And they said unto him, Where *is*
Sarah thy wife? And he said, Behold,
in the tent.
10 And he said, I will certainly return
unto thee according to the time of life;
and, lo, Sarah thy wife shall have a son.
And Sarah heard *it* in the tent door,
which *was* behind him.
11 Now Abraham and Sarah *were* old
and well stricken in age; *and* it ceased
to be with Sarah after the manner of
women.
12 Therefore Sarah laughed within
herself, saying, After I am waxed old
shall I have pleasure, my lord being old
also?
13 And the LORD said unto Abraham,
Wherefore did Sarah laugh, saying,
Shall I of a surety bear a child, which
am old?
14 Is any thing too hard for the LORD?
At the time appointed I will return unto
thee, according to the time of life, and
Sarah shall have a son.
15 Then Sarah denied, saying, I
laughed not; for she was afraid. And he
said, Nay; but thou didst laugh.
16 ¶ And the men rose up from thence,
and looked toward Sŏd′ŏm: and Abraham went with them to bring them on
the way.
17 And the LORD said, Shall I hide
from Abraham that thing which I do;
18 Seeing that Abraham shall surely
become a great and mighty nation, and
all the nations of the earth shall be
blessed in him?
19 For I know him, that he will command his children and his household
after him, and they shall keep the way
of the LORD, to do justice and judgment;
that the LORD may bring upon Abraham
that which he hath spoken of him.
20 And the LORD said, Because the
cry of Sŏd′ŏm and Gō-mŏr′rah is great,
and because their sin is very grievous,
21 I will go down now, and see whether
they have done altogether according to
the cry of it, which is come unto me; and
if not, I will know.
22 And the men turned their faces
from thence, and went toward Sŏd′ŏm:
but Abraham stood yet before the LORD.
23 ¶ And Abraham drew near, and
said, Wilt thou also destroy the righteous with the wicked?
24 Peradventure there be fifty righteous within the city: wilt thou also destroy and not spare the place for the
fifty righteous that *are* therein?
25 That be far from thee to do after
this manner, to slay the righteous with
the wicked; and that the righteous
should be as the wicked, that be far
from thee: Shall not the Judge of all the
earth do right?
26 And the LORD said, If I find in
Sŏd′ŏm fifty righteous within the city,
then I will spare all the place for their
sakes.
27 And Abraham answered and said,
Behold now, I have taken upon me to
speak unto the Lord, which *am but* dust
and ashes:
28 Peradventure there shall lack five
of the fifty righteous: wilt thou destroy
all the city for *lack of* five? And he said,
If I find there forty and five, I will not
destroy *it*.
29 And he spake unto him yet again,
and said, Peradventure there shall be
forty found there. And he said, I will
not do *it* for forty's sake.
30 And he said *unto him*, Oh let not
the Lord be angry, and I will speak: Peradventure there shall thirty be found
there. And he said, I will not do *it*, if I
find thirty there.
31 And he said, Behold now, I have
taken upon me to speak unto the Lord:
Peradventure there shall be twenty
found there. And he said, I will not
destroy *it* for twenty's sake.
32 And he said, Oh let not the Lord be
angry, and I will speak yet but this once:
Peradventure ten shall be found there.

And he said, I will not destroy *it* for ten's sake.

33 And the LORD went his way, as soon as he had left communing with Abraham: and Abraham returned unto his place.

CHAPTER 19

AND there came two angels to Sŏd′ŏm at even; and Lot sat in the gate of Sŏd′ŏm: and Lot seeing *them* rose up to meet them; and he bowed himself with his face toward the ground;

2 And he said, Behold now, my lords, turn in, I pray you, into your servant's house, and tarry all night, and wash your feet, and ye shall rise up early, and go on your ways. And they said, Nay; but we will abide in the street all night.

3 And he pressed upon them greatly; and they turned in unto him, and entered into his house; and he made them a feast, and did bake unleavened bread, and they did eat.

4 ¶ But before they lay down, the men of the city, *even* the men of Sŏd′ŏm, compassed the house round, both old and young, all the people from every quarter:

5 And they called unto Lot, and said unto him, Where *are* the men which came in to thee this night? bring them out unto us, that we may know them.

6 And Lot went out at the door unto them, and shut the door after him,

7 And said, I pray you, brethren, do not so wickedly.

8 Behold now, I have two daughters which have not known man; let me, I pray you, bring them out unto you, and do ye to them as *is* good in your eyes: only unto these men do nothing; for therefore came they under the shadow of my roof.

9 And they said, Stand back. And they said *again*, This one *fellow* came in to sojourn, and he will needs be a judge: now will we deal worse with thee than with them. And they pressed sore upon the man, *even* Lot, and came near to break the door.

10 But the men put forth their hand, and pulled Lot into the house to them, and shut to the door.

11 And they smote the men that *were* at the door of the house with blindness, both small and great: so that they wearied themselves to find the door.

12 ¶ And the men said unto Lot, Hast thou here any besides? son-in-law, and thy sons, and thy daughters, and whatsoever thou hast in the city, bring *them* out of this place:

13 For we will destroy this place, because the cry of them is waxen great before the face of the LORD; and the LORD hath sent us to destroy it.

14 And Lot went out, and spake unto his sons-in-law, which married his daughters, and said, Up, get you out of this place; for the LORD will destroy this city. But he seemed as one that mocked unto his sons-in-law.

15 ¶ And when the morning arose, then the angels hastened Lot, saying, Arise, take thy wife, and thy two daughters, which are here; lest thou be consumed in the iniquity of the city.

16 And while he lingered, the men laid hold upon his hand, and upon the hand of his wife, and upon the hand of his two daughters; the LORD being merciful unto him: and they brought him forth, and set him without the city.

17 ¶ And it came to pass, when they had brought them forth abroad, that he said, Escape for thy life; look not behind thee, neither stay thou in all the plain; escape to the mountain, lest thou be consumed.

18 And Lot said unto them, Oh, not so, my Lord:

19 Behold now, thy servant hath found grace in thy sight, and thou hast magnified thy mercy, which thou hast showed unto me in saving my life; and I cannot escape to the mountain, lest some evil take me, and I die:

20 Behold now, this city *is* near to flee unto, and it *is* a little one: O, let me escape thither, (*is* it not a little one?) and my soul shall live.

21 And he said unto him, See, I have accepted thee concerning this thing also, that I will not overthrow this city, for the which thou hast spoken.

22 Haste thee, escape thither; for I cannot do any thing till thou be come thither. Therefore the name of the city was called Zō′ăr.

23 ¶ The sun was risen upon the earth when Lot entered into Zō′ăr.

24 Then the LORD rained upon Sŏd′ŏm and upon Gō-mŏr′răh brimstone and fire from the LORD out of heaven;

25 And he overthrew those cities, and

all the plain, and all the inhabitants of
the cities, and that which grew upon the
ground.
26 ℂ But his wife looked back from
behind him, and she became a pillar of
salt.
27 ℂ And Abraham gat up early in the
morning to the place where he stood before the LORD:
28 And he looked toward Sŏd′ŏm and
Gō-mŏr′rȧh, and toward all the land of
the plain, and beheld, and, lo, the smoke
of the country went up as the smoke of
a furnace.
29 ℂ And it came to pass, when God
destroyed the cities of the plain, that
God remembered Abraham, and sent
Lot out of the midst of the overthrow,
when he overthrew the cities in the
which Lot dwelt.
30 ℂ And Lot went up out of Zō′ȧr,
and dwelt in the mountain, and his two
daughters with him; for he feared to
dwell in Zō′ȧr: and he dwelt in a cave,
he and his two daughters.
31 And the firstborn said unto the
younger, Our father *is* old, and *there is*
not a man in the earth to come in unto
us after the manner of all the earth:
32 Come, let us make our father drink
wine, and we will lie with him, that we
may preserve seed of our father.
33 And they made their father drink
wine that night: and the firstborn went
in, and lay with her father; and he perceived not when she lay down, nor when
she arose.
34 And it came to pass on the morrow,
that the firstborn said unto the younger,
Behold, I lay yesternight with my father:
let us make him drink wine this night
also; and go thou in, *and* lie with him,
that we may preserve seed of our father.
35 And they made their father drink
wine that night also: and the younger
arose, and lay with him; and he perceived not when she lay down, nor
when she arose.
36 Thus were both the daughters of
Lot with child by their father.
37 And the firstborn bare a son, and
called his name Mō′ăb: the same *is*
the father of the Mō′ăb-ītes unto this
day.
38 And the younger, she also bare a
son, and called his name Bĕn′-ăm′mi:
the same *is* the father of the children of
Ammon unto this day.

CHAPTER 20

AND Abraham journeyed from thence
toward the south country, and
dwelt between Kā′dĕsh and Shụr, and
sojourned in Gē′rär.
2 And Abraham said of Sarah his wife,
She *is* my sister: and Ȧ-bĭm′ē-lĕch king
of Gē′rär sent, and took Sarah.
3 But God came to Ȧ-bĭm′ē-lĕch in a
dream by night, and said to him, Behold, thou *art but* a dead man, for the
woman which thou hast taken; for she
is a man's wife.
4 But Ȧ-bĭm′ē-lĕch had not come near
her: and he said, LORD, wilt thou slay
also a righteous nation?
5 Said he not unto me, She *is* my sister? and she, even she herself said, He
is my brother: in the integrity of my
heart and innocency of my hands have I
done this.
6 And God said unto him in a dream,
Yea, I know that thou didst this in the
integrity of thy heart; for I also withheld
thee from sinning against me: therefore suffered I thee not to touch her.
7 Now therefore restore the man *his*
wife; for he *is* a prophet, and he shall
pray for thee, and thou shalt live: and if
thou restore *her* not, know thou that
thou shalt surely die, thou, and all that
are thine.
8 Therefore Ȧ-bĭm′ē-lĕch rose early in
the morning, and called all his servants, and told all these things in their
ears: and the men were sore afraid.
9 Then Ȧ-bĭm′ē-lĕch called Abraham,
and said unto him, What hast thou done
unto us? and what have I offended thee,
that thou hast brought on me and on my
kingdom a great sin? thou hast done
deeds unto me that ought not to be done.
10 And Ȧ-bĭm′ē-lĕch said unto Abraham, What sawest thou, that thou hast
done this thing?
11 And Abraham said, Because I
thought, Surely the fear of God *is* not in
this place; and they will slay me for my
wife's sake.
12 And yet indeed *she is* my sister; she
is the daughter of my father, but not the
daughter of my mother; and she became
my wife.
13 And it came to pass, when God
caused me to wander from my father's
house, that I said unto her, This *is* thy
kindness which thou shalt show unto

me; at every place whither we shall
come, say of me, He *is* my brother.
14 And Ȧ-bĭm′ē-lĕch took sheep, and
oxen, and menservants, and womenservants, and gave *them* unto Abraham,
and restored him Sarah his wife.
15 And Ȧ-bĭm′ē-lĕch said, Behold, my
land *is* before thee: dwell where it
pleaseth thee.
16 And unto Sarah he said, Behold, I
have given thy brother a thousand
pieces of silver: behold, he *is* to thee a
covering of the eyes, unto all that *are*
with thee, and with all *other:* thus she
was reproved.
17 ¶ So Abraham prayed unto God:
and God healed Ȧ-bĭm′ē-lĕch, and his
wife, and his maidservants; and they
bare *children*.
18 For the LORD had fast closed up all
the wombs of the house of Ȧ-bĭm′ē-
lĕch, because of Sarah, Abraham's wife.

CHAPTER 21

AND the LORD visited Sarah as he
had said, and the LORD did unto
Sarah as he had spoken.
2 For Sarah conceived, and bare Abraham a son in his old age, at the set time
of which God had spoken to him.
3 And Abraham called the name of his
son that was born unto him, whom
Sarah bare to him, Isaac.
4 And Abraham circumcised his son
Isaac being eight days old, as God had
commanded him.
5 And Abraham was a hundred years
old, when his son Isaac was born unto
him.
6 ¶ And Sarah said, God hath made
me to laugh, *so that* all that hear will
laugh with me.
7 And she said, Who would have said
unto Abraham, that Sarah should have
given children suck? for I have borne
him a son in his old age.
8 And the child grew, and was weaned:
and Abraham made a great feast the
same day that Isaac was weaned.
9 ¶ And Sarah saw the son of Hā′gȧr
the Egyptian, which she had borne unto
Abraham, mocking.
10 Wherefore she said unto Abraham,
Cast out this bondwoman and her son:
for the son of this bondwoman shall not
be heir with my son, *even* with Isaac.
11 And the thing was very grievous in
Abraham's sight because of his son.
12 ¶ And God said unto Abraham, Let
it not be grievous in thy sight because
of the lad, and because of thy bondwoman; in all that Sarah hath said unto
thee, hearken unto her voice; for in
Isaac shall thy seed be called.
13 And also of the son of the bondwoman will I make a nation, because he
is thy seed.
14 And Abraham rose up early in the
morning, and took bread, and a bottle of
water, and gave *it* unto Hā′gȧr, putting
it on her shoulder, and the child, and
sent her away: and she departed, and
wandered in the wilderness of Bē′ẽr-
shē′bȧ.
15 And the water was spent in the
bottle, and she cast the child under one
of the shrubs.
16 And she went, and sat her down
over against *him* a good way off, as it
were a bowshot: for she said, Let me
not see the death of the child. And she
sat over against *him*, and lifted up her
voice, and wept.
17 And God heard the voice of the lad;
and the angel of God called to Hā′gȧr
out of heaven, and said unto her, What
aileth thee, Hā′gȧr? fear not; for God
hath heard the voice of the lad where
he *is*.
18 Arise, lift up the lad, and hold him
in thine hand; for I will make him a
great nation.
19 And God opened her eyes, and she
saw a well of water; and she went, and
filled the bottle with water, and gave the
lad drink.
20 And God was with the lad; and he
grew, and dwelt in the wilderness, and
became an archer.
21 And he dwelt in the wilderness of
Pā′răn: and his mother took him a wife
out of the land of Egypt.
22 ¶ And it came to pass at that time,
that Ȧ-bĭm′ē-lĕch and Phī′chŏl the
chief captain of his host spake unto
Abraham, saying, God *is* with thee in
all that thou doest:
23 Now therefore swear unto me here
by God, that thou wilt not deal falsely
with me, nor with my son, nor with my
son's son: *but* according to the kindness
that I have done unto thee, thou shalt
do unto me, and to the land wherein
thou hast sojourned.
24 And Abraham said, I will swear.
25 And Abraham reproved Ȧ-bĭm′ē-

lĕch because of a well of water, which Ȧ-bĭm'ē-lĕch's servants had violently taken away.

26 And Ȧ-bĭm'ē-lĕch said, I wot not who hath done this thing: neither didst thou tell me, neither yet heard I *of it*, but to-day.

27 And Abraham took sheep and oxen, and gave them unto Ȧ-bĭm'ē-lĕch; and both of them made a covenant.

28 And Abraham set seven ewe lambs of the flock by themselves.

29 And Ȧ-bĭm'ē-lĕch said unto Abraham, What *mean* these seven ewe lambs which thou hast set by themselves?

30 And he said, For *these* seven ewe lambs shalt thou take of my hand, that they may be a witness unto me, that I have digged this well.

31 Wherefore he called that place Bē'ĕr–shē'bȧ; because there they sware both of them.

32 Thus they made a covenant at Bē'ĕr–shē'bȧ: then Ȧ-bĭm'ē-lĕch rose up, and Phī'chŏl the chief captain of his host, and they returned into the land of the Phĭ-lĭs'tĭnes.

33 ¶ And *Abraham* planted a grove in Bē'ĕr–shē'bȧ, and called there on the name of the LORD, the everlasting God.

34 And Abraham sojourned in the Phĭ-lĭs'tĭneş' land many days.

CHAPTER 22

AND it came to pass after these things, that God did tempt Abraham, and said unto him, Abraham: and he said, Behold, *here* I *am*.

2 And he said, Take now thy son, thine only *son* Isaac, whom thou lovest, and get thee into the land of Mō-rī'ăh; and offer him there for a burnt offering upon one of the mountains which I will tell thee of.

3 ¶ And Abraham rose up early in the morning, and saddled his ass, and took two of his young men with him, and Isaac his son, and clave the wood for the burnt offering, and rose up, and went unto the place of which God had told him.

4 Then on the third day Abraham lifted up his eyes, and saw the place afar off.

5 And Abraham said unto his young men, Abide ye here with the ass; and I and the lad will go yonder and worship, and come again to you.

6 And Abraham took the wood of the burnt offering, and laid *it* upon Isaac his son; and he took the fire in his hand, and a knife; and they went both of them together.

7 And Isaac spake unto Abraham his father, and said, My father: and he said, Here *am* I, my son. And he said, Behold the fire and the wood: but where *is* the lamb for a burnt offering?

8 And Abraham said, My son, God will provide himself a lamb for a burnt offering: so they went both of them together.

9 And they came to the place which God had told him of; and Abraham built an altar there, and laid the wood in order, and bound Isaac his son, and laid him on the altar upon the wood.

10 And Abraham stretched forth his hand, and took the knife to slay his son.

11 And the Angel of the LORD called unto him out of heaven, and said, Abraham, Abraham: and he said, Here *am* I.

12 And he said, Lay not thine hand upon the lad, neither do thou any thing unto him: for now I know that thou fearest God, seeing thou hast not withheld thy son, thine only *son*, from me.

13 And Abraham lifted up his eyes, and looked, and behold behind *him* a ram caught in a thicket by his horns: and Abraham went and took the ram, and offered him up for a burnt offering in the stead of his son.

14 And Abraham called the name of that place Jehovah–jī'rĕh: as it is said *to* this day, In the mount of the LORD it shall be seen.

15 ¶ And the Angel of the LORD called unto Abraham out of heaven the second time,

16 And said, By myself have I sworn, saith the LORD, for because thou hast done this thing, and hast not withheld thy son, thine only *son*,

17 That in blessing I will bless thee, and in multiplying I will multiply thy seed as the stars of the heaven, and as the sand which *is* upon the seashore; and thy seed shall possess the gate of his enemies;

18 And in thy seed shall all the nations of the earth be blessed; because thou hast obeyed my voice.

19 So Abraham returned unto his young men, and they rose up and went together to Bē'ĕr–shē'bȧ; and Abraham dwelt at Bē'ĕr–shē'bȧ.

20 ¶ And it came to pass after these

things, that it was told Abraham, saying,
Behold, Mĭl'cȧh, she hath also borne
children unto thy brother Nā'hŏr;
21 Huz his firstborn, and Bŭz his
brother, and Kĕm'ū-ĕl the father of
Ā'răm,
22 And Chē'sĕd, and Hā'zō, and Pĭl'-
dăsh, and Jĭd'lăph, and Bē-thū'ĕl.
23 And Bē-thū'ĕl begat Rē-bĕk'ȧh:
these eight Mĭl'cȧh did bear to Nā'hŏr,
Abraham's brother.
24 And his concubine, whose name
was Reu'mȧh, she bare also Tē'bȧh, and
Gā'hăm, and Thā'hăsh, and Mā'ȧ-chȧh.

CHAPTER 23

AND Sarah was a hundred and seven
and twenty years old: *these were*
the years of the life of Sarah.
2 And Sarah died in Kĭr'jăth–är'bȧ;
the same *is* Hē'brȯn in the land of Cā'-
năan: and Abraham came to mourn for
Sarah, and to weep for her.
3 ¶ And Abraham stood up from before his dead, and spake unto the sons
of Heth, saying,
4 I *am* a stranger and a sojourner with
you: give me a possession of a buryingplace with you, that I may bury my dead
out of my sight.
5 And the children of Heth answered
Abraham, saying unto him,
6 Hear us, my lord: thou *art* a mighty
prince among us: in the choice of our
sepulchres bury thy dead; none of us
shall withhold from thee his sepulchre,
but that thou mayest bury thy dead.
7 And Abraham stood up, and bowed
himself to the people of the land, *even*
to the children of Heth.
8 And he communed with them, saying, If it be your mind that I should bury
my dead out of my sight, hear me, and
entreat for me to Ē'phrŏn the son of
Zō'här,
9 That he may give me the cave of
Măch-pē'lȧh, which he hath, which *is* in
the end of his field; for as much money
as it is worth he shall give it me for a
possession of a buryingplace amongst
you.
10 And Ē'phrŏn dwelt among the children of Heth: and Ē'phrŏn the Hĭt'tīte
answered Abraham in the audience of
the children of Heth, *even* of all that
went in at the gate of his city, saying,
11 Nay, my lord, hear me: the field
give I thee, and the cave that *is* therein,
I give it thee; in the presence of the
sons of my people give I it thee: bury
thy dead.
12 And Abraham bowed down himself
before the people of the land.
13 And he spake unto Ē'phrŏn in the
audience of the people of the land, saying, But if thou *wilt give it,* I pray thee,
hear me: I will give thee money for the
field; take *it* of me, and I will bury my
dead there.
14 And Ē'phrŏn answered Abraham,
saying unto him,
15 My lord, hearken unto me: the land
is worth four hundred shekels of silver;
what *is* that betwixt me and thee? bury
therefore thy dead.
16 And Abraham hearkened unto
Ē'phrŏn; and Abraham weighed to
Ē'phrŏn the silver, which he had named
in the audience of the sons of Heth, four
hundred shekels of silver, current
money with the merchant.
17 ¶ And the field of Ē'phrŏn, which
was in Măch-pē'lȧh, which *was* before
Măm'rē, the field, and the cave which
was therein, and all the trees that *were*
in the field, that *were* in all the borders
round about, were made sure
18 Unto Abraham for a possession in
the presence of the children of Heth,
before all that went in at the gate of his
city.
19 And after this, Abraham buried
Sarah his wife in the cave of the field of
Măch-pē'lȧh before Măm'rē: the same
is Hē'brȯn in the land of Cā'năan.
20 And the field, and the cave that *is*
therein, were made sure unto Abraham
for a possession of a buryingplace by
the sons of Heth.

CHAPTER 24

AND Abraham was old, *and* well
stricken in age: and the LORD had
blessed Abraham in all things.
2 And Abraham said unto his eldest
servant of his house, that ruled over all
that he had, Put, I pray thee, thy hand
under my thigh:
3 And I will make thee swear by the
LORD, the God of heaven, and the God
of the earth, that thou shalt not take a
wife unto my son of the daughters of the
Cā'năan-ītes, among whom I dwell:
4 But thou shalt go unto my country,
and to my kindred, and take a wife unto
my son Isaac.

5 And the servant said unto him, Peradventure the woman will not be willing to follow me unto this land: must I needs bring thy son again unto the land from whence thou camest?

6 And Abraham said unto him, Beware thou that thou bring not my son thither again.

7 ¶ The LORD God of heaven, which took me from my father's house, and from the land of my kindred, and which spake unto me, and that sware unto me, saying, Unto thy seed will I give this land; he shall send his angel before thee, and thou shalt take a wife unto my son from thence.

8 And if the woman will not be willing to follow thee, then thou shalt be clear from this my oath: only bring not my son thither again.

9 And the servant put his hand under the thigh of Abraham his master, and sware to him concerning that matter.

10 ¶ And the servant took ten camels of the camels of his master, and departed; for all the goods of his master *were* in his hand: and he arose, and went to Mĕs'ō-pō-tā'mĭ-ȧ, unto the city of Nā'hŏr.

11 And he made his camels to kneel down without the city by a well of water at the time of the evening, *even* the time that women go out to draw *water*.

12 And he said, O LORD God of my master Abraham, I pray thee, send me good speed this day, and show kindness unto my master Abraham.

13 Behold, I stand *here* by the well of water; and the daughters of the men of the city come out to draw water:

14 And let it come to pass, that the damsel to whom I shall say, Let down thy pitcher, I pray thee, that I may drink; and she shall say, Drink, and I will give thy camels drink also: *let the same be* she *that* thou hast appointed for thy servant Isaac; and thereby shall I know that thou hast showed kindness unto my master.

15 ¶ And it came to pass, before he had done speaking, that, behold, Rē-bĕk'ȧh came out, who was born to Bē-thū'ĕl, son of Mĭl'cȧh, the wife of Nā'hŏr, Abraham's brother, with her pitcher upon her shoulder.

16 And the damsel *was* very fair to look upon, a virgin, neither had any man known her: and she went down to the well, and filled her pitcher, and came up.

17 And the servant ran to meet her, and said, Let me, I pray thee, drink a little water of thy pitcher.

18 And she said, Drink, my lord: and she hasted, and let down her pitcher upon her hand, and gave him drink.

19 And when she had done giving him drink, she said, I will draw *water* for thy camels also, until they have done drinking.

20 And she hasted, and emptied her pitcher into the trough, and ran again unto the well to draw *water*, and drew for all his camels.

21 And the man wondering at her held his peace, to wit whether the LORD had made his journey prosperous or not.

22 And it came to pass, as the camels had done drinking, that the man took a golden earring of half a shekel weight, and two bracelets for her hands of ten *shekels* weight of gold;

23 And said, Whose daughter *art* thou? tell me, I pray thee: is there room *in* thy father's house for us to lodge in?

24 And she said unto him, I *am* the daughter of Bē-thū'ĕl the son of Mĭl'cȧh, which she bare unto Nā'hŏr.

25 She said moreover unto him, We have both straw and provender enough, and room to lodge in.

26 And the man bowed down his head, and worshipped the LORD.

27 And he said, Blessed *be* the LORD God of my master Abraham, who hath not left destitute my master of his mercy and his truth: I *being* in the way, the LORD led me to the house of my master's brethren.

28 And the damsel ran, and told *them of* her mother's house these things.

29 ¶ And Rē-bĕk'ȧh had a brother, and his name *was* Lā'băn: and Lā'băn ran out unto the man, unto the well.

30 And it came to pass, when he saw the earring, and bracelets upon his sister's hands, and when he heard the words of Rē-bĕk'ȧh his sister, saying, Thus spake the man unto me, that he came unto the man; and, behold, he stood by the camels at the well.

31 And he said, Come in, thou blessed of the LORD; wherefore standest thou without? for I have prepared the house, and room for the camels.

32 ¶ And the man came into the house: and he ungirded his camels, and gave

straw and provender for the camels, and
water to wash his feet, and the men's
feet that *were* with him.
33 And there was set *meat* before him
to eat: but he said, I will not eat, until I
have told mine errand. And he said,
Speak on.
34 And he said, I *am* Abraham's
servant.
35 And the LORD hath blessed my
master greatly, and he is become great:
and he hath given him flocks, and herds,
and silver, and gold, and menservants,
and maidservants, and camels, and
asses.
36 And Sarah my master's wife bare a
son to my master when she was old: and
unto him hath he given all that he hath.
37 And my master made me swear,
saying, Thou shalt not take a wife to my
son of the daughters of the Cā'năan-
ītes, in whose land I dwell:
38 But thou shalt go unto my father's
house, and to my kindred, and take a
wife unto my son.
39 And I said unto my master, Peradventure the woman will not follow me.
40 And he said unto me, The LORD, before whom I walk, will send his angel
with thee, and prosper thy way; and
thou shalt take a wife for my son of my
kindred, and of my father's house:
41 Then shalt thou be clear from *this*
my oath, when thou comest to my kindred; and if they give not thee *one*, thou
shalt be clear from my oath.
42 And I came this day unto the well,
and said, O LORD God of my master
Abraham, if now thou do prosper my
way which I go:
43 Behold, I stand by the well of water;
and it shall come to pass, that when the
virgin cometh forth to draw *water*, and
I say to her, Give me, I pray thee, a little
water of thy pitcher to drink;
44 And she say to me, Both drink thou,
and I will also draw for thy camels: *let*
the same *be* the woman whom the LORD
hath appointed out for my master's son.
45 And before I had done speaking in
mine heart, behold, Rē-bĕk'ȧh came
forth with her pitcher on her shoulder;
and she went down unto the well, and
drew *water:* and I said unto her, Let me
drink, I pray thee.
46 And she made haste, and let down
her pitcher from her *shoulder*, and said,
Drink, and I will give thy camels drink
also: so I drank, and she made the camels drink also.
47 And I asked her, and said, Whose
daughter *art* thou? And she said, The
daughter of Bē-thū'ĕl, Nā'hŏr's son,
whom Mĭl'cȧh bare unto him: and I put
the earring upon her face, and the bracelets upon her hands.
48 And I bowed down my head, and
worshipped the LORD, and blessed the
LORD God of my master Abraham,
which had led me in the right way to
take my master's brother's daughter
unto his son.
49 And now, if ye will deal kindly and
truly with my master, tell me: and if not,
tell me; that I may turn to the right hand,
or to the left.
50 Then Lā'băn and Bē-thū'ĕl answered and said, The thing proceedeth
from the LORD: we cannot speak unto
thee bad or good.
51 Behold, Rē-bĕk'ȧh *is* before thee;
take *her*, and go, and let her be thy
master's son's wife, as the LORD hath
spoken.
52 And it came to pass, that, when
Abraham's servant heard their words,
he worshipped the LORD, *bowing himself* to the earth.
53 And the servant brought forth jewels
of silver, and jewels of gold, and raiment, and gave *them* to Rē-bĕk'ȧh: he
gave also to her brother and to her
mother precious things.
54 And they did eat and drink, he and
the men that *were* with him, and tarried
all night; and they rose up in the morning, and he said, Send me away unto
my master.
55 And her brother and her mother
said, Let the damsel abide with us *a
few* days, at the least ten; after that she
shall go.
56 And he said unto them, Hinder me
not, seeing the LORD hath prospered my
way; send me away that I may go to my
master.
57 And they said, We will call the damsel, and inquire at her mouth.
58 And they called Rē-bĕk'ȧh, and
said unto her, Wilt thou go with this
man? And she said, I will go.
59 And they sent away Rē-bĕk'ȧh their
sister, and her nurse, and Abraham's
servant, and his men.
60 And they blessed Rē-bĕk'ȧh, and
said unto her, Thou *art* our sister; be

thou *the mother* of thousands of mil-
lions, and let thy seed possess the gate
of those which hate them.
61 ℂ And Rē-bĕk'ȧh arose, and her
damsels, and they rode upon the camels,
and followed the man: and the servant
took Rē-bĕk'ȧh, and went his way.
62 And Isaac came from the way of the
well Lȧ-haī'-rôi; for he dwelt in the
south country.
63 And Isaac went out to meditate in
the field at the eventide: and he lifted
up his eyes, and saw, and, behold, the
camels *were* coming.
64 And Rē-bĕk'ȧh lifted up her eyes,
and when she saw Isaac, she lighted off
the camel.
65 For she *had* said unto the servant,
What man *is* this that walketh in the
field to meet us? And the servant *had*
said, It *is* my master: therefore she took
a veil, and covered herself.
66 And the servant told Isaac all things
that he had done.
67 And Isaac brought her into his
mother Sarah's tent, and took Rē-
bĕk'ȧh, and she became his wife; and he
loved her: and Isaac was comforted
after his mother's *death*.

CHAPTER 25

THEN again Abraham took a wife,
and her name *was* Kĕ-tụ'răh.
2 And she bare him Zĭm'răn, and Jŏk'-
shăn, and Mē'dăn, and Mĭd'ĭ-ăn, and
Ĭsh'băk, and Shụ'ăh.
3 And Jŏk'shăn begat Shē'bȧ, and
Dē'dăn. And the sons of Dē'dăn were
Ăs-shụ'rĭm, and Lē-tū'shĭm, and Lē-
ŭm'mĭm.
4 And the sons of Mĭd'ĭ-ăn; Ē'phȧh,
and Ē'phẽr, and Hā'nŏch, and Ȧ-bī'-
dȧh, and Ĕl-dā'ȧh. All these *were* the
children of Kĕ-tụ'răh.
5 ℂ And Abraham gave all that he had
unto Isaac.
6 But unto the sons of the concubines,
which Abraham had, Abraham gave
gifts, and sent them away from Isaac
his son, while he yet lived, eastward,
unto the east country.
7 And these *are* the days of the years
of Abraham's life which he lived, a
hundred threescore and fifteen years.
8 Then Abraham gave up the ghost,
and died in a good old age, an old man,
and full *of years;* and was gathered to
his people.
9 And his sons Isaac and Ĭsh'mā-ĕl
buried him in the cave of Măch-pē'lȧh,
in the field of Ē'phrŏn the son of Zō'här
the Hĭt'tīte, which *is* before Măm'rē;
10 The field which Abraham purchased
of the sons of Heth: there was Abraham
buried, and Sarah his wife.
11 ℂ And it came to pass after the
death of Abraham, that God blessed his
son Isaac; and Isaac dwelt by the well
Lȧ-haī'-rôi.
12 ℂ Now these *are* the generations of
Ĭsh'mā-ĕl, Abraham's son, whom Hā'-
gȧr the Egyptian, Sarah's handmaid,
bare unto Abraham:
13 And these *are* the names of the sons
of Ĭsh'mā-ĕl, by their names, according
to their generations: the firstborn of
Ĭsh'mā-ĕl, Nē-bā'jŏth; and Kē'dȧr, and
Ăd'bē-ĕl, and Mĭb'săm,
14 And Mĭsh'mȧ, and Dū'mȧh, and
Măs'sȧ,
15 Hā'dȧr, and Tē'mȧ, Jē'tŭr, Nā'-
phĭsh, and Kĕd'ē-mȧh:
16 These *are* the sons of Ĭsh'mā-ĕl, and
these *are* their names, by their towns,
and by their castles; twelve princes according to their nations.
17 And these *are* the years of the life of
Ĭsh'mā-ĕl, a hundred and thirty and
seven years: and he gave up the ghost
and died, and was gathered unto his
people.
18 And they dwelt from Hăv'ĭ-lăh unto
Shụr, that *is* before Egypt, as thou goest
toward Assyria: *and* he died in the presence of all his brethren.
19 ℂ And these *are* the generations of
Isaac, Abraham's son: Abraham begat
Isaac:
20 And Isaac was forty years old when
he took Rē-bĕk'ȧh to wife, the daughter
of Bē-thū'ĕl the Syrian of Pā'dăn-
ā'răm, the sister to Lā'băn the Syrian.
21 And Isaac entreated the LORD for
his wife, because she *was* barren: and
the LORD was entreated of him, and
Rē-bĕk'ȧh his wife conceived.
22 And the children struggled together
within her; and she said, If *it be* so, why
am I thus? And she went to inquire of
the LORD.
23 And the LORD said unto her, Two
nations *are* in thy womb, and two manner of people shall be separated from
thy bowels; and *the one* people shall be
stronger than *the other* people; and the
elder shall serve the younger.

24 ℭ And when her days to be delivered were fulfilled, behold, *there*
were twins in her womb.
25 And the first came out red, all over
like a hairy garment; and they called his
name Ē′sȃu.
26 And after that came his brother out,
and his hand took hold on Ē′sȃu's heel;
and his name was called Jacob: and
Isaac *was* threescore years old when she
bare them.
27 And the boys grew: and Ē′sȃu was
a cunning hunter, a man of the field; and
Jacob *was* a plain man, dwelling in
tents.
28 And Isaac loved Ē′sȃu, because he
did eat of *his* venison: but Rē-běk′ȧh
loved Jacob.
29 ℭ And Jacob sod pottage: and
Ē′sȃu came from the field, and he *was*
faint:
30 And Ē′sȃu said to Jacob, Feed me,
I pray thee, with that same red *pottage;*
for I *am* faint: therefore was his name
called Ē′dŏm.
31 And Jacob said, Sell me this day thy
birthright.
32 And Ē′sȃu said, Behold, I *am* at the
point to die: and what profit shall this
birthright do to me?
33 And Jacob said, Swear to me this
day; and he sware unto him: and he sold
his birthright unto Jacob.
34 Then Jacob gave Ē′sȃu bread and
pottage of lentils; and he did eat and
drink, and rose up, and went his way.
Thus Ē′sȃu despised *his* birthright.

CHAPTER 26

AND there was a famine in the land,
besides the first famine that was
in the days of Abraham. And Isaac
went unto Ȧ-bĭm′ē-lĕch king of the Phĭ-
lĭs′tĭnes unto Gē′rär.
2 And the LORD appeared unto him,
and said, Go not down into Egypt; dwell
in the land which I shall tell thee of.
3 Sojourn in this land, and I will be
with thee, and will bless thee; for unto
thee, and unto thy seed, I will give all
these countries, and I will perform the
oath which I sware unto Abraham thy
father;
4 And I will make thy seed to multiply
as the stars of heaven, and will give unto
thy seed all these countries; and in thy
seed shall all the nations of the earth be
blessed:
5 Because that Abraham obeyed my
voice, and kept my charge, my commandments, my statutes, and my laws.
6 ℭ And Isaac dwelt in Gē′rär.
7 And the men of the place asked *him*
of his wife; and he said, She *is* my
sister: for he feared to say, *She is* my
wife; lest, *said he,* the men of the place
should kill me for Rē-běk′ȧh; because
she *was* fair to look upon.
8 And it came to pass, when he had
been there a long time, that Ȧ-bĭm′ē-
lĕch king of the Phĭ-lĭs′tĭneş looked out
at a window, and saw, and, behold,
Isaac *was* sporting with Rē-běk′ȧh his
wife.
9 And Ȧ-bĭm′ē-lĕch called Isaac, and
said, Behold, of a surety she *is* thy wife:
and how saidst thou, She *is* my sister?
And Isaac said unto him, Because I said,
Lest I die for her.
10 And Ȧ-bĭm′ē-lĕch said, What *is* this
thou hast done unto us? one of the
people might lightly have lain with thy
wife, and thou shouldest have brought
guiltiness upon us.
11 And Ȧ-bĭm′ē-lĕch charged all *his*
people, saying, He that toucheth this
man or his wife shall surely be put to
death.
12 Then Isaac sowed in that land, and
received in the same year a hundredfold: and the LORD blessed him.
13 And the man waxed great, and went
forward, and grew until he became very
great:
14 For he had possession of flocks, and
possession of herds, and great store of
servants: and the Phĭ-lĭs′tĭneş envied
him.
15 For all the wells which his father's
servants had digged in the days of Abraham his father, the Phĭ-lĭs′tĭneş had
stopped them, and filled them with
earth.
16 And Ȧ-bĭm′ē-lĕch said unto Isaac,
Go from us; for thou art much mightier
than we.
17 ℭ And Isaac departed thence, and
pitched his tent in the valley of Gē′rär,
and dwelt there.
18 And Isaac digged again the wells of
water, which they had digged in the
days of Abraham his father; for the
Phĭ-lĭs′tĭneş had stopped them after the
death of Abraham: and he called their
names after the names by which his
father had called them.

19 And Isaac's servants digged in the valley, and found there a well of springing water.

20 And the herdmen of Gē′rär did strive with Isaac's herdmen, saying, The water *is* ours: and he called the name of the well Ē′sĕk; because they strove with him.

21 And they digged another well, and strove for that also: and he called the name of it Sĭt′nȧh.

22 And he removed from thence, and digged another well; and for that they strove not: and he called the name of it Rē-hō′bōth; and he said, For now the LORD hath made room for us, and we shall be fruitful in the land.

23 And he went up from thence to Bē′ẽr–shē′bȧ.

24 And the LORD appeared unto him the same night, and said, I *am* the God of Abraham thy father: fear not, for I *am* with thee, and will bless thee, and multiply thy seed for my servant Abraham's sake.

25 And he builded an altar there, and called upon the name of the LORD, and pitched his tent there: and there Isaac's servants digged a well.

26 ¶ Then Ȧ-bĭm′ē-lĕch went to him from Gē′rär, and Ȧ-hŭz′zăth one of his friends, and Phī′chŏl the chief captain of his army.

27 And Isaac said unto them, Wherefore come ye to me, seeing ye hate me, and have sent me away from you?

28 And they said, We saw certainly that the LORD was with thee: and we said, Let there be now an oath betwixt us, *even* betwixt us and thee, and let us make a covenant with thee;

29 That thou wilt do us no hurt, as we have not touched thee, and as we have done unto thee nothing but good, and have sent thee away in peace: thou *art* now the blessed of the LORD.

30 And he made them a feast, and they did eat and drink.

31 And they rose up betimes in the morning, and sware one to another: and Isaac sent them away, and they departed from him in peace.

32 And it came to pass the same day, that Isaac's servants came, and told him concerning the well which they had digged, and said unto him, We have found water.

33 And he called it Shē′bȧh: therefore the name of the city *is* Bē′ẽr–shē′bȧ unto this day.

34 ¶ And Ē′sa͡u was forty years old when he took to wife Judith the daughter of Bē-ē′rī the Hĭt′tīte, and Băsh′ē-măth the daughter of Ē′lŏn the Hĭt′tīte:

35 Which were a grief of mind unto Isaac and to Rē-bĕk′ȧh.

CHAPTER 27

AND it came to pass, that when Isaac was old, and his eyes were dim, so that he could not see, he called Ē′sa͡u his eldest son, and said unto him, My son: and he said unto him, Behold, *here am* I.

2 And he said, Behold now, I am old, I know not the day of my death:

3 Now therefore take, I pray thee, thy weapons, thy quiver and thy bow, and go out to the field, and take me *some* venison;

4 And make me savory meat, such as I love, and bring *it* to me, that I may eat; that my soul may bless thee before I die.

5 And Rē-bĕk′ȧh heard when Isaac spake to Ē′sa͡u his son. And Ē′sa͡u went to the field to hunt *for* venison, *and* to bring *it*.

6 ¶ And Rē-bĕk′ȧh spake unto Jacob her son, saying, Behold, I heard thy father speak unto Ē′sa͡u thy brother, saying,

7 Bring me venison, and make me savory meat, that I may eat, and bless thee before the LORD before my death.

8 Now therefore, my son, obey my voice according to that which I command thee.

9 Go now to the flock, and fetch me from thence two good kids of the goats; and I will make them savory meat for thy father, such as he loveth:

10 And thou shalt bring *it* to thy father, that he may eat, and that he may bless thee before his death.

11 And Jacob said to Rē-bĕk′ȧh his mother, Behold, Ē′sa͡u my brother *is* a hairy man, and I *am* a smooth man:

12 My father peradventure will feel me, and I shall seem to him as a deceiver; and I shall bring a curse upon me, and not a blessing.

13 And his mother said unto him, Upon me *be* thy curse, my son: only obey my voice, and go fetch me *them*.

14 And he went, and fetched, and brought *them* to his mother: and his mother made savory meat, such as his father loved.

15 And Rē-bĕk'ăh took goodly raiment
of her eldest son Ē'sȃu, which *were* with
her in the house, and put them upon
Jacob her younger son:
16 And she put the skins of the kids of
the goats upon his hands, and upon the
smooth of his neck:
17 And she gave the savory meat and
the bread, which she had prepared, into
the hand of her son Jacob.
18 ℂ And he came unto his father, and
said, My father: and he said, Here *am*
I; who *art* thou, my son?
19 And Jacob said unto his father, I *am*
Ē'sȃu thy firstborn; I have done according as thou badest me: arise, I pray thee,
sit and eat of my venison, that thy soul
may bless me.
20 And Isaac said unto his son, How *is*
it that thou hast found *it* so quickly, my
son? And he said, Because the LORD
thy God brought *it* to me.
21 And Isaac said unto Jacob, Come
near, I pray thee, that I may feel thee,
my son, whether thou *be* my very son
Ē'sȃu or not.
22 And Jacob went near unto Isaac his
father; and he felt him, and said, The
voice *is* Jacob's voice, but the hands *are*
the hands of Ē'sȃu.
23 And he discerned him not, because
his hands were hairy, as his brother
Ē'sȃu's hands: so he blessed him.
24 And he said, *Art* thou my very son
Ē'sȃu? And he said, I *am*.
25 And he said, Bring *it* near to me,
and I will eat of my son's venison, that
my soul may bless thee. And he brought
it near to him, and he did eat: and he
brought him wine, and he drank.
26 And his father Isaac said unto him,
Come near now, and kiss me, my son.
27 And he came near, and kissed him:
and he smelled the smell of his raiment,
and blessed him, and said, See, the
smell of my son *is* as the smell of a field
which the LORD hath blessed:
28 Therefore God give thee of the dew
of heaven, and the fatness of the earth,
and plenty of corn and wine:
29 Let people serve thee, and nations
bow down to thee: be lord over thy
brethren, and let thy mother's sons bow
down to thee: cursed *be* every one that
curseth thee, and blessed *be* he that
blesseth thee.
30 ℂ And it came to pass, as soon as
Isaac had made an end of blessing
Jacob, and Jacob was yet scarce gone out
from the presence of Isaac his father,
that Ē'sȃu his brother came in from his
hunting.
31 And he also had made savory meat,
and brought it unto his father, and said
unto his father, Let my father arise, and
eat of his son's venison, that thy soul
may bless me.
32 And Isaac his father said unto him,
Who *art* thou? And he said, I *am* thy
son, thy firstborn, Ē'sȃu.
33 And Isaac trembled very exceedingly, and said, Who? where *is* he that
hath taken venison, and brought *it* me,
and I have eaten of all before thou
camest, and have blessed him? yea, *and*
he shall be blessed.
34 And when Ē'sȃu heard the words of
his father, he cried with a great and exceeding bitter cry, and said unto his
father, Bless me, *even* me also, O my
father.
35 And he said, Thy brother came with
subtilty, and hath taken away thy
blessing.
36 And he said, Is not he rightly named
Jacob? for he hath supplanted me these
two times: he took away my birthright;
and, behold, now he hath taken away my
blessing. And he said, Hast thou not
reserved a blessing for me?
37 And Isaac answered and said unto
Ē'sȃu, Behold, I have made him thy
lord, and all his brethren have I given to
him for servants; and with corn and
wine have I sustained him: and what
shall I do now unto thee, my son?
38 And Ē'sȃu said unto his father, Hast
thou but one blessing, my father? bless
me, *even* me also, O my father. And
Ē'sȃu lifted up his voice, and wept.
39 And Isaac his father answered and
said unto him, Behold, thy dwelling shall
be the fatness of the earth, and of the
dew of heaven from above;
40 And by thy sword shalt thou live,
and shalt serve thy brother: and it shall
come to pass when thou shalt have the
dominion, that thou shalt break his yoke
from off thy neck.
41 ℂ And Ē'sȃu hated Jacob because
of the blessing wherewith his father
blessed him: and Ē'sȃu said in his heart,
The days of mourning for my father are
at hand; then will I slay my brother
Jacob.
42 And these words of Ē'sȃu her elder

son were told to Rē-bĕk′ȧh: and she
sent and called Jacob her younger son,
and said unto him, Behold, thy brother
Ē′saȗ, as touching thee, doth comfort
himself, *purposing* to kill thee.
43 Now therefore, my son, obey my
voice; and arise, flee thou to Lā′băn my
brother to Hā′răn;
44 And tarry with him a few days, until
thy brother's fury turn away;
45 Until thy brother's anger turn away
from thee, and he forget *that* which thou
hast done to him: then I will send, and
fetch thee from thence: why should I be
deprived also of you both in one day?
46 And Rē-bĕk′ȧh said to Isaac, I am
weary of my life because of the daughters of Heth: if Jacob take a wife of the
daughters of Heth, such as these *which*
are of the daughters of the land, what
good shall my life do me?

CHAPTER 28

AND Isaac called Jacob, and blessed
him, and charged him, and said
unto him, Thou shalt not take a wife
of the daughters of Cā′năan.
2 Arise, go to Pā′dăn-ā′răm, to the
house of Bē-thū′ĕl thy mother's father;
and take thee a wife from thence of
the daughters of Lā′băn thy mother's
brother.
3 And God Almighty bless thee, and
make thee fruitful, and multiply thee,
that thou mayest be a multitude of
people;
4 And give thee the blessing of Abraham, to thee, and to thy seed with thee;
that thou mayest inherit the land wherein thou art a stranger, which God gave
unto Abraham.
5 And Isaac sent away Jacob: and he
went to Pā′dăn-ā′răm unto Lā′băn, son
of Bē-thū′ĕl the Syrian, the brother of
Rē-bĕk′ȧh, Jacob's and Ē′saȗ's mother.
6 ℭ When Ē′saȗ saw that Isaac had
blessed Jacob, and sent him away to
Pā′dăn-ā′răm, to take him a wife from
thence; and that as he blessed him he
gave him a charge, saying, Thou shalt
not take a wife of the daughters of
Cā′năan;
7 And that Jacob obeyed his father and
his mother, and was gone to Pā′dăn-
ā′răm;
8 And Ē′saȗ seeing that the daughters
of Cā′năan pleased not Isaac his father;
9 Then went Ē′saȗ unto Ĭsh′mā-ĕl, and
took unto the wives which he had Mā-
hȧ-lăth the daughter of Ĭsh′mā-ĕl Abraham's son, the sister of Nē-bā′jŏth, to
be his wife.
10 ℭ And Jacob went out from Bē′ẽr-
shē′bȧ, and went toward Hā′răn.
11 And he lighted upon a certain place,
and tarried there all night, because the
sun was set; and he took of the stones of
that place, and put *them for* his pillows,
and lay down in that place to sleep.
12 And he dreamed, and behold a lad-
der set up on the earth, and the top of it
reached to heaven: and behold the angels of God ascending and descending
on it.
13 And, behold, the LORD stood above
it, and said, I *am* the LORD God of
Abraham thy father, and the God of
Isaac: the land whereon thou liest, to
thee will I give it, and to thy seed;
14 And thy seed shall be as the dust of
the earth; and thou shalt spread abroad
to the west, and to the east, and to the
north, and to the south: and in thee and
in thy seed shall all the families of the
earth be blessed.
15 And, behold, I *am* with thee, and
will keep thee in all *places* whither thou
goest, and will bring thee again into this
land; for I will not leave thee, until I
have done *that* which I have spoken to
thee of.
16 ℭ And Jacob awaked out of his
sleep, and he said, Surely the LORD is
in this place; and I knew *it* not.
17 And he was afraid, and said, How
dreadful *is* this place! this *is* none other
but the house of God, and this *is* the
gate of heaven.
18 And Jacob rose up early in the morning, and took the stone that he had put
for his pillows, and set it up *for* a pillar,
and poured oil upon the top of it.
19 And he called the name of that place
Beth-el: but the name of that city *was*
called Lŭz at the first.
20 And Jacob vowed a vow, saying, If
God will be with me, and will keep me
in this way that I go, and will give me
bread to eat, and raiment to put on,
21 So that I come again to my father's
house in peace; then shall the LORD be
my God:
22 And this stone, which I have set *for*
a pillar, shall be God's house: and of all
that thou shalt give me I will surely give
the tenth unto thee.

CHAPTER 29

THEN Jacob went on his journey, and came into the land of the people of the east.

2 And he looked, and behold a well in the field, and, lo, there *were* three flocks of sheep lying by it; for out of that well they watered the flocks: and a great stone *was* upon the well's mouth.

3 And thither were all the flocks gathered: and they rolled the stone from the well's mouth, and watered the sheep, and put the stone again upon the well's mouth in his place.

4 And Jacob said unto them, My brethren, whence *be* ye? And they said, Of Hā'răn *are* we.

5 And he said unto them, Know ye Lā'băn the son of Nā'hŏr? And they said, We know *him*.

6 And he said unto them, *Is* he well? And they said, *He is* well: and, behold, Rachel his daughter cometh with the sheep.

7 And he said, Lo, *it is* yet high day, neither *is it* time that the cattle should be gathered together: water ye the sheep, and go *and* feed *them*.

8 And they said, We cannot, until all the flocks be gathered together, and *till* they roll the stone from the well's mouth; then we water the sheep.

9 ¶ And while he yet spake with them, Rachel came with her father's sheep: for she kept them.

10 And it came to pass, when Jacob saw Rachel the daughter of Lā'băn his mother's brother, and the sheep of Lā'băn his mother's brother, that Jacob went near, and rolled the stone from the well's mouth, and watered the flock of Lā'băn his mother's brother.

11 And Jacob kissed Rachel, and lifted up his voice, and wept.

12 And Jacob told Rachel that he *was* her father's brother, and that he *was* Rē-bĕk'ȧh's son: and she ran and told her father.

13 And it came to pass, when Lā'băn heard the tidings of Jacob his sister's son, that he ran to meet him, and embraced him, and kissed him, and brought him to his house. And he told Lā'băn all these things.

14 And Lā'băn said to him, Surely thou *art* my bone and my flesh. And he abode with him the space of a month.

15 ¶ And Lā'băn said unto Jacob, Because thou *art* my brother, shouldest thou therefore serve me for nought? tell me, what *shall* thy wages *be*?

16 And Lā'băn had two daughters: the name of the elder *was* Lē'ȧh, and the name of the younger *was* Rachel.

17 Lē'ȧh *was* tender eyed; but Rachel was beautiful and well-favored.

18 And Jacob loved Rachel; and said, I will serve thee seven years for Rachel thy younger daughter.

19 And Lā'băn said, *It is* better that I give her to thee, than that I should give her to another man: abide with me.

20 And Jacob served seven years for Rachel; and they seemed unto him *but* a few days, for the love he had to her.

21 ¶ And Jacob said unto Lā'băn, Give *me* my wife, for my days are fulfilled, that I may go in unto her.

22 And Lā'băn gathered together all the men of the place, and made a feast.

23 And it came to pass in the evening, that he took Lē'ȧh his daughter, and brought her to him; and he went in unto her.

24 And Lā'băn gave unto his daughter Lē'ȧh Zĭl'pȧh his maid *for* a handmaid.

25 And it came to pass, that in the morning, behold, it *was* Lē'ȧh: and he said to Lā'băn, What *is* this thou hast done unto me? did not I serve with thee for Rachel? wherefore then hast thou beguiled me?

26 And Lā'băn said, It must not be so done in our country, to give the younger before the firstborn.

27 Fulfil her week, and we will give thee this also for the service which thou shalt serve with me yet seven other years.

28 And Jacob did so, and fulfilled her week: and he gave him Rachel his daughter to wife also.

29 And Lā'băn gave to Rachel his daughter Bĭl'hȧh his handmaid to be her maid.

30 And he went in also unto Rachel, and he loved also Rachel more than Lē'ȧh, and served with him yet seven other years.

31 ¶ And when the LORD saw that Lē'ȧh *was* hated, he opened her womb: but Rachel *was* barren.

32 And Lē'ȧh conceived, and bare a son; and she called his name Reuben: for she said, Surely the LORD hath looked

upon my affliction; now therefore my
husband will love me.
33 And she conceived again, and bare a
son; and said, Because the LORD hath
heard that I *was* hated, he hath therefore given me this *son* also: and she
called his name Simeon.
34 And she conceived again, and bare
a son; and said, Now this time will my
husband be joined unto me, because I
have borne him three sons: therefore
was his name called Levi.
35 And she conceived again, and bare
a son; and she said, Now will I praise
the LORD: therefore she called his name
Judah; and left bearing.

CHAPTER 30

AND when Rachel saw that she bare
Jacob no children, Rachel envied
her sister; and said unto Jacob, Give
me children, or else I die.
2 And Jacob's anger was kindled
against Rachel; and he said, *Am* I in
God's stead, who hath withheld from
thee the fruit of the womb?
3 And she said, Behold my maid Bĭl'-
hăh, go in unto her; and she shall bear
upon my knees, that I may also have
children by her.
4 And she gave him Bĭl'hăh her handmaid to wife: and Jacob went in unto
her.
5 And Bĭl'hăh conceived, and bare
Jacob a son.
6 And Rachel said, God hath judged
me, and hath also heard my voice, and
hath given me a son: therefore called
she his name Dan.
7 And Bĭl'hăh Rachel's maid conceived
again, and bare Jacob a second son.
8 And Rachel said, With great wres-
tlings have I wrestled with my sister,
and I have prevailed: and she called
his name Năph'tȧ-lī.
9 When Lē'ăh saw that she had left
bearing, she took Zĭl'păh her maid, and
gave her Jacob to wife.
10 And Zĭl'păh Lē'ăh's maid bare Jacob
a son.
11 And Lē'ăh said, A troop cometh:
and she called his name Gad.
12 And Zĭl'păh Lē'ăh's maid bare Jacob
a second son.
13 And Lē'ăh said, Happy am I, for
the daughters will call me blessed: and
she called his name Ăsh'ẽr.
14 ℂ And Reuben went in the days of
wheat harvest, and found mandrakes in
the field, and brought them unto his
mother Lē'ăh. Then Rachel said to
Lē'ăh, Give me, I pray thee, of thy son's
mandrakes.
15 And she said unto her, *Is it* a small
matter that thou hast taken my husband? and wouldest thou take away my
son's mandrakes also? And Rachel
said, Therefore he shall lie with thee
to-night for thy son's mandrakes.
16 And Jacob came out of the field in
the evening, and Lē'ăh went out to meet
him, and said, Thou must come in unto
me; for surely I have hired thee with
my son's mandrakes. And he lay with
her that night.
17 And God hearkened unto Lē'ăh, and
she conceived, and bare Jacob the fifth
son.
18 And Lē'ăh said, God hath given me
my hire, because I have given my maid-
en to my husband: and she called his
name Ĭs'sȧ-chär.
19 And Lē'ăh conceived again, and
bare Jacob the sixth son.
20 And Lē'ăh said, God hath endued
me *with* a good dowry; now will my husband dwell with me, because I have
borne him six sons: and she called his
name Zĕb'ū-lŭn.
21 And afterward she bare a daughter,
and called her name Dinah.
22 ℂ And God remembered Rachel,
and God hearkened to her, and opened
her womb.
23 And she conceived, and bare a son;
and said, God hath taken away my
reproach:
24 And she called his name Joseph;
and said, The LORD shall add to me
another son.
25 ℂ And it came to pass, when Rachel
had borne Joseph, that Jacob said unto
Lā'băn, Send me away, that I may go
unto mine own place, and to my country.
26 Give *me* my wives and my children,
for whom I have served thee, and let me
go: for thou knowest my service which
I have done thee.
27 And Lā'băn said unto him, I pray
thee, if I have found favor in thine eyes,
tarry: for I have learned by experience
that the LORD hath blessed me for thy
sake.
28 And he said, Appoint me thy wages,
and I will give *it*.
29 And he said unto him, Thou know-

est how I have served thee, and how thy
cattle was with me.
30 For *it was* little which thou hadst
before I *came*, and it is *now* increased
unto a multitude; and the LORD hath
blessed thee since my coming: and now,
when shall I provide for mine own house
also?
31 And he said, What shall I give thee?
And Jacob said, Thou shalt not give me
any thing: if thou wilt do this thing for
me, I will again feed *and* keep thy flock.
32 I will pass through all thy flock
to-day, removing from thence all the
speckled and spotted cattle, and all the
brown cattle among the sheep, and the
spotted and speckled among the goats:
and *of such* shall be my hire.
33 So shall my righteousness answer
for me in time to come, when it shall
come for my hire before thy face: every
one that *is* not speckled and spotted
among the goats, and brown among the
sheep, that shall be counted stolen with
me.
34 And Lā'băn said, Behold, I would it
might be according to thy word.
35 And he removed that day the he
goats that were ring-streaked and
spotted, and all the she goats that were
speckled and spotted, *and* every one
that had *some* white in it, and all the
brown among the sheep, and gave *them*
into the hand of his sons.
36 And he set three days' journey betwixt himself and Jacob: and Jacob fed
the rest of Lā'băn's flocks.
37 ℂ And Jacob took him rods of green
poplar, and of the hazel and chestnut
tree; and pilled white streaks in them,
and made the white appear which *was*
in the rods.
38 And he set the rods which he had
pilled before the flocks in the gutters in
the watering troughs when the flocks
came to drink, that they should conceive when they came to drink.
39 And the flocks conceived before the
rods, and brought forth cattle ring-
streaked, speckled, and spotted.
40 And Jacob did separate the lambs,
and set the faces of the flocks toward
the ring-streaked, and all the brown in
the flock of Lā'băn; and he put his own
flocks by themselves, and put them not
unto Lā'băn's cattle.
41 And it came to pass, whensoever
the stronger cattle did conceive, that
Jacob laid the rods before the eyes of
the cattle in the gutters, that they might
conceive among the rods.
42 But when the cattle were feeble, he
put *them* not in: so the feebler were
Lā'băn's, and the stronger Jacob's.
43 And the man increased exceedingly,
and had much cattle, and maidservants,
and menservants, and camels, and
asses.

CHAPTER 31

AND he heard the words of Lā'băn's
sons, saying, Jacob hath taken away
all that *was* our father's; and of *that*
which *was* our father's hath he gotten
all this glory.
2 And Jacob beheld the countenance of
Lā'băn, and, behold, it *was* not toward
him as before.
3 And the LORD said unto Jacob, Return unto the land of thy fathers, and to
thy kindred; and I will be with thee.
4 And Jacob sent and called Rachel
and Lē'ăh to the field unto his flock,
5 And said unto them, I see your father's countenance, that it *is* not toward
me as before; but the God of my father
hath been with me.
6 And ye know that with all my power
I have served your father.
7 And your father hath deceived me,
and changed my wages ten times; but
God suffered him not to hurt me.
8 If he said thus, The speckled shall be
thy wages; then all the cattle bare
speckled: and if he said thus, The ring-
streaked shall be thy hire; then bare all
the cattle ring-streaked.
9 Thus God hath taken away the cattle
of your father, and given *them* to me.
10 And it came to pass at the time that
the cattle conceived, that I lifted up
mine eyes, and saw in a dream, and, behold, the rams which leaped upon the
cattle *were* ring-streaked, speckled, and
grizzled.
11 And the angel of God spake unto
me in a dream, *saying*, Jacob: and I
said, Here *am* I.
12 And he said, Lift up now thine eyes,
and see, all the rams which leap upon
the cattle *are* ring-streaked, speckled,
and grizzled: for I have seen all that
Lā'băn doeth unto thee.
13 I *am* the God of Beth-el, where
thou anointedst the pillar, *and* where
thou vowedst a vow unto me: now arise,

get thee out from this land, and return
unto the land of thy kindred.
14 And Rachel and Lē′ȧh answered and
said unto him, *Is there* yet any portion or
inheritance for us in our father's house?
15 Are we not counted of him strangers? for he hath sold us, and hath quite
devoured also our money.
16 For all the riches which God hath
taken from our father, that *is* ours, and
our children's: now then, whatsoever
God hath said unto thee, do.
17 ¶ Then Jacob rose up, and set his
sons and his wives upon camels;
18 And he carried away all his cattle,
and all his goods which he had gotten,
the cattle of his getting, which he had
gotten in Pā′dăn–ā′răm, for to go to
Isaac his father in the land of Cā′năan.
19 And Lā′băn went to shear his sheep:
and Rachel had stolen the images that
were her father's.
20 And Jacob stole away unawares to
Lā′băn the Syrian, in that he told him
not that he fled.
21 So he fled with all that he had; and
he rose up, and passed over the river,
and set his face *toward* the mount
Gĭl′ē-ăd.
22 And it was told Lā′băn on the third
day, that Jacob was fled.
23 And he took his brethren with him,
and pursued after him seven days' journey; and they overtook him in the mount
Gĭl′ē-ăd.
24 And God came to Lā′băn the Syrian
in a dream by night, and said unto him,
Take heed that thou speak not to Jacob
either good or bad.
25 ¶ Then Lā′băn overtook Jacob.
Now Jacob had pitched his tent in the
mount: and Lā′băn with his brethren
pitched in the mount of Gĭl′ē-ăd.
26 And Lā′băn said to Jacob, What
hast thou done, that thou hast stolen
away unawares to me, and carried away
my daughters, as captives *taken* with
the sword?
27 Wherefore didst thou flee away
secretly, and steal away from me; and
didst not tell me, that I might have sent
thee away with mirth, and with songs,
with tabret, and with harp?
28 And hast not suffered me to kiss
my sons and my daughters? thou hast
now done foolishly in *so* doing.
29 It is in the power of my hand to do
you hurt: but the God of your father
spake unto me yesternight, saying, Take
thou heed that thou speak not to Jacob
either good or bad.
30 And now, *though* thou wouldest
needs be gone, because thou sore long-
edst after thy father's house, *yet* wherefore hast thou stolen my gods?
31 And Jacob answered and said to
Lā′băn, Because I was afraid: for I said,
Peradventure thou wouldest take by
force thy daughters from me.
32 With whomsoever thou findest thy
gods, let him not live: before our brethren discern thou what *is* thine with me,
and take *it* to thee. For Jacob knew not
that Rachel had stolen them.
33 And Lā′băn went into Jacob's tent,
and into Lē′ȧh's tent, and into the two
maidservants' tents; but he found *them*
not. Then went he out of Lē′ȧh's tent,
and entered into Rachel's tent.
34 Now Rachel had taken the images,
and put them in the camel's furniture,
and sat upon them. And Lā′băn
searched all the tent, but found *them*
not.
35 And she said to her father, Let it not
displease my lord that I cannot rise up
before thee; for the custom of women *is*
upon me. And he searched, but found
not the images.
36 ¶ And Jacob was wroth, and chode
with Lā′băn: and Jacob answered and
said to Lā′băn, What *is* my trespass?
what *is* my sin, that thou hast so hotly
pursued after me?
37 Whereas thou hast searched all my
stuff, what hast thou found of all thy
household stuff? set *it* here before my
brethren and thy brethren, that they
may judge betwixt us both.
38 This twenty years *have* I *been* with
thee; thy ewes and thy she goats have
not cast their young, and the rams of
thy flock have I not eaten.
39 That which was torn *of beasts* I
brought not unto thee; I bare the loss of
it; of my hand didst thou require it,
whether stolen by day, or stolen by
night.
40 *Thus* I was; in the day the drought
consumed me, and the frost by night;
and my sleep departed from mine eyes.
41 Thus have I been twenty years in
thy house: I served thee fourteen years
for thy two daughters, and six years for
thy cattle; and thou hast changed my
wages ten times.

42 Except the God of my father, the God of Abraham, and the fear of Isaac, had been with me, surely thou hadst sent me away now empty. God hath seen mine affliction and the labor of my hands, and rebuked *thee* yesternight.

43 ¶ And Lā′băn answered and said unto Jacob, *These* daughters *are* my daughters, and *these* children *are* my children, and *these* cattle *are* my cattle, and all that thou seest *is* mine: and what can I do this day unto these my daughters, or unto their children which they have borne?

44 Now therefore come thou, let us make a covenant, I and thou; and let it be for a witness between me and thee.

45 And Jacob took a stone, and set it up *for* a pillar.

46 And Jacob said unto his brethren, Gather stones; and they took stones, and made a heap: and they did eat there upon the heap.

47 And Lā′băn called it Jē′gär–sā′hȧ-dū′thȧ: but Jacob called it Găl′ē-ĕd.

48 And Lā′băn said, This heap *is* a witness between me and thee this day. Therefore was the name of it called Găl′ē-ĕd,

49 And Mĭz′päh; for he said, The LORD watch between me and thee, when we are absent one from another.

50 If thou shalt afflict my daughters, or if thou shalt take *other* wives beside my daughters, no man *is* with us; see, God *is* witness betwixt me and thee.

51 And Lā′băn said to Jacob, Behold this heap, and behold *this* pillar, which I have cast betwixt me and thee;

52 This heap *be* witness, and *this* pillar *be* witness, that I will not pass over this heap to thee, and that thou shalt not pass over this heap and this pillar unto me, for harm.

53 The God of Abraham, and the God of Nā′hŏr, the God of their father, judge betwixt us. And Jacob sware by the fear of his father Isaac.

54 Then Jacob offered sacrifice upon the mount, and called his brethren to eat bread: and they did eat bread, and tarried all night in the mount.

55 And early in the morning Lā′băn rose up, and kissed his sons and his daughters, and blessed them: and Lā′băn departed, and returned unto his place.

CHAPTER 32

AND Jacob went on his way, and the angels of God met him.

2 And when Jacob saw them, he said, This *is* God's host: and he called the name of that place Mā′hȧ-nā′ĭm.

3 And Jacob sent messengers before him to Ē′saȗ his brother unto the land of Sē′ĭr, the country of Ē′dŏm.

4 And he commanded them, saying, Thus shall ye speak unto my lord Ē′saȗ; Thy servant Jacob saith thus, I have sojourned with Lā′băn, and stayed there until now:

5 And I have oxen, and asses, flocks, and menservants, and womenservants: and I have sent to tell my lord, that I may find grace in thy sight.

6 ¶ And the messengers returned to Jacob, saying, We came to thy brother Ē′saȗ, and also he cometh to meet thee, and four hundred men with him.

7 Then Jacob was greatly afraid and distressed: and he divided the people that *was* with him, and the flocks, and herds, and the camels, into two bands;

8 And said, If Ē′saȗ come to the one company, and smite it, then the other company which is left shall escape.

9 ¶ And Jacob said, O God of my father Abraham, and God of my father Isaac, the LORD which saidst unto me, Return unto thy country, and to thy kindred, and I will deal well with thee:

10 I am not worthy of the least of all the mercies, and of all the truth, which thou hast showed unto thy servant; for with my staff I passed over this Jordan; and now I am become two bands.

11 Deliver me, I pray thee, from the hand of my brother, from the hand of Ē′saȗ: for I fear him, lest he will come and smite me, *and* the mother with the children.

12 And thou saidst, I will surely do thee good, and make thy seed as the sand of the sea, which cannot be numbered for multitude.

13 ¶ And he lodged there that same night; and took of that which came to his hand a present for Ē′saȗ his brother;

14 Two hundred she goats and twenty he goats, two hundred ewes and twenty rams,

15 Thirty milch camels with their colts, forty kine and ten bulls, twenty she asses and ten foals.

16 And he delivered *them* into the hand
of his servants, every drove by themselves; and said unto his servants, Pass
over before me, and put a space betwixt
drove and drove.
17 And he commanded the foremost,
saying, When Ē'sau my brother meeteth thee, and asketh thee, saying, Whose
art thou? and whither goest thou? and
whose *are* these before thee?
18 Then thou shalt say, *They be* thy
servant Jacob's; it *is* a present sent
unto my lord Ē'sau: and, behold, also
he *is* behind us.
19 And so commanded he the second,
and the third, and all that followed the
droves, saying, On this manner shall ye
speak unto Ē'sau, when ye find him.
20 And say ye moreover, Behold, thy
servant Jacob *is* behind us. For he said,
I will appease him with the present that
goeth before me, and afterward I will
see his face; peradventure he will accept of me.
21 So went the present over before
him; and himself lodged that night in
the company.
22 And he rose up that night, and took
his two wives, and his two womenservants, and his eleven sons, and
passed over the ford Jăb'bŏk.
23 And he took them, and sent them
over the brook, and sent over that he had.
24 ¶ And Jacob was left alone; and
there wrestled a man with him until the
breaking of the day.
25 And when he saw that he prevailed
not against him, he touched the hollow
of his thigh; and the hollow of Jacob's
thigh was out of joint, as he wrestled
with him.
26 And he said, Let me go, for the day
breaketh. And he said, I will not let
thee go, except thou bless me.
27 And he said unto him, What *is* thy
name? And he said, Jacob.
28 And he said, Thy name shall be
called no more Jacob, but Is'rā-ĕl: for
as a prince hast thou power with God
and with men, and hast prevailed.
29 And Jacob asked *him,* and said,
Tell *me,* I pray thee, thy name. And he
said, Wherefore *is* it *that* thou dost ask
after my name? And he blessed him
there.
30 And Jacob called the name of the
place Pē-nī'ĕl: for I have seen God face
to face, and my life is preserved.
31 And as he passed over Pē-nū'ĕl the
sun rose upon him, and he halted upon
his thigh.
32 Therefore the children of Is'rā-ĕl
eat not *of* the sinew which shrank,
which *is* upon the hollow of the thigh,
unto this day; because he touched the
hollow of Jacob's thigh in the sinew
that shrank.

CHAPTER 33

AND Jacob lifted up his eyes, and
looked, and, behold, Ē'sau came,
and with him four hundred men. And
he divided the children unto Lē'ah, and
unto Rachel, and unto the two handmaids.
2 And he put the handmaids and their
children foremost, and Lē'ah and her
children after, and Rachel and Joseph
hindermost.
3 And he passed over before them, and
bowed himself to the ground seven
times, until he came near to his brother.
4 And Ē'sau ran to meet him, and embraced him, and fell on his neck, and
kissed him: and they wept.
5 And he lifted up his eyes, and saw
the women and the children, and said,
Who *are* those with thee? And he said,
The children which God hath graciously
given thy servant.
6 Then the handmaidens came near,
they and their children, and they bowed
themselves.
7 And Lē'ah also with her children
came near, and bowed themselves: and
after came Joseph near and Rachel, and
they bowed themselves.
8 And he said, What *meanest* thou by
all this drove which I met? And he said,
These are to find grace in the sight of
my lord.
9 And Ē'sau said, I have enough, my
brother; keep that thou hast unto thyself.
10 And Jacob said, Nay, I pray thee, if
now I have found grace in thy sight, then
receive my present at my hand: for
therefore I have seen thy face, as though
I had seen the face of God, and thou
wast pleased with me.
11 Take, I pray thee, my blessing that
is brought to thee; because God hath
dealt graciously with me, and because I
have enough. And he urged him, and
he took *it.*
12 And he said, Let us take our jour-

ney, and let us go, and I will go before
thee.
13 And he said unto him, My lord
knoweth that the children *are* tender,
and the flocks and herds with young *are*
with me; and if men should overdrive
them one day, all the flock will die.
14 Let my lord, I pray thee, pass over
before his servant; and I will lead on
softly, according as the cattle that goeth
before me and the children be able to
endure, until I come unto my lord unto
Sē′ĭr.
15 And Ē′saû said, Let me now leave
with thee *some* of the folk that *are* with
me. And he said, What needeth it? let
me find grace in the sight of my lord.
16 ℂ So Ē′saû returned that day on
his way unto Sē′ĭr.
17 And Jacob journeyed to Sŭc′cōth,
and built him a house, and made booths
for his cattle: therefore the name of the
place is called Sŭc′cōth.
18 ℂ And Jacob came to Shā′lĕm, a
city of Shē′chĕm, which *is* in the land of
Cā′năan, when he came from Pā′dăn–
ā′răm; and pitched his tent before the
city.
19 And he bought a parcel of a field,
where he had spread his tent, at the
hand of the children of Hā′mŏr, Shē′-
chĕm's father, for a hundred pieces of
money.
20 And he erected there an altar, and
called it Ĕl′–Ē-lō′hĕ–Ĭş′rā-ĕl.

CHAPTER 34

AND Dinah the daughter of Lē′áh,
which she bare unto Jacob, went out
to see the daughters of the land.
2 And when Shē′chĕm the son of Hā′-
mŏr the Hī′vīte, prince of the country,
saw her, he took her, and lay with her,
and defiled her.
3 And his soul clave unto Dinah the
daughter of Jacob, and he loved the
damsel, and spake kindly unto the damsel.
4 And Shē′chĕm spake unto his father
Hā′mŏr, saying, Get me this damsel to
wife.
5 And Jacob heard that he had defiled
Dinah his daughter: now his sons were
with his cattle in the field: and Jacob
held his peace until they were come.
6 ℂ And Hā′mŏr the father of Shē′-
chĕm went out unto Jacob to commune
with him.
7 And the sons of Jacob came out of
the field when they heard *it:* and the
men were grieved, and they were very
wroth, because he had wrought folly in
Ĭş′rā-ĕl in lying with Jacob's daughter;
which thing ought not to be done.
8 And Hā′mŏr communed with them,
saying, The soul of my son Shē′chĕm
longeth for your daughter: I pray you
give her him to wife.
9 And make ye marriages with us, *and*
give your daughters unto us, and take
our daughters unto you.
10 And ye shall dwell with us: and the
land shall be before you; dwell and
trade ye therein, and get you possessions therein.
11 And Shē′chĕm said unto her father
and unto her brethren, Let me find
grace in your eyes, and what ye shall
say unto me I will give.
12 Ask me never so much dowry and
gift, and I will give according as ye shall
say unto me: but give me the damsel to
wife.
13 And the sons of Jacob answered
Shē′chĕm and Hā′mŏr his father deceitfully, and said, because he had
defiled Dinah their sister:
14 And they said unto them, We cannot do this thing, to give our sister to
one that is uncircumcised; for that *were*
a reproach unto us:
15 But in this will we consent unto you:
If ye will be as we *be,* that every male
of you be circumcised;
16 Then will we give our daughters
unto you, and we will take your daughters to us, and we will dwell with you,
and we will become one people.
17 But if ye will not hearken unto us,
to be circumcised; then will we take our
daughter, and we will be gone.
18 And their words pleased Hā′mŏr
and Shē′chĕm Hā′mŏr's son.
19 And the young man deferred not to
do the thing, because he had delight in
Jacob's daughter: and he *was* more
honorable than all the house of his
father.
20 ℂ And Hā′mŏr and Shē′chĕm his
son came unto the gate of their city, and
communed with the men of their city,
saying,
21 These men *are* peaceable with us;
therefore let them dwell in the land, and
trade therein; for the land, behold, *it is*
large enough for them; let us take their

daughters to us for wives, and let us give them our daughters.

22 Only herein will the men consent unto us for to dwell with us, to be one people, if every male among us be circumcised, as they *are* circumcised.

23 *Shall* not their cattle and their substance and every beast of theirs *be* ours? only let us consent unto them, and they will dwell with us.

24 And unto Hā'mŏr and unto Shē'chĕm his son hearkened all that went out of the gate of his city; and every male was circumcised, all that went out of the gate of his city.

25 ¶ And it came to pass on the third day, when they were sore, that two of the sons of Jacob, Simeon and Levi, Dinah's brethren, took each man his sword, and came upon the city boldly, and slew all the males.

26 And they slew Hā'mŏr and Shē'chĕm his son with the edge of the sword, and took Dinah out of Shē'chĕm's house, and went out.

27 The sons of Jacob came upon the slain, and spoiled the city, because they had defiled their sister.

28 They took their sheep, and their oxen, and their asses, and that which *was* in the city, and that which *was* in the field,

29 And all their wealth, and all their little ones, and their wives took they captive, and spoiled even all that *was* in the house.

30 And Jacob said to Simeon and Levi, Ye have troubled me to make me to stink among the inhabitants of the land, among the Cā'năan-ītes and the Pĕr'ĭz-zītes: and I *being* few in number, they shall gather themselves together against me, and slay me; and I shall be destroyed, I and my house.

31 And they said, Should he deal with our sister as with a harlot?

CHAPTER 35

AND God said unto Jacob, Arise, go up to Beth-el, and dwell there: and make there an altar unto God, that appeared unto thee when thou fleddest from the face of Ē'sâu thy brother.

2 Then Jacob said unto his household, and to all that *were* with him, Put away the strange gods that *are* among you, and be clean, and change your garments:

3 And let us arise, and go up to Beth-el; and I will make there an altar unto God, who answered me in the day of my distress, and was with me in the way which I went.

4 And they gave unto Jacob all the strange gods which *were* in their hand, and *all their* earrings which *were* in their ears; and Jacob hid them under the oak which *was* by Shē'chĕm.

5 And they journeyed: and the terror of God was upon the cities that *were* round about them, and they did not pursue after the sons of Jacob.

6 ¶ So Jacob came to Lŭz which *is* in the land of Cā'năan, that *is*, Beth-el, he and all the people that *were* with him.

7 And he built there an altar, and called the place Ĕl'-bĕth'-ĕl; because there God appeared unto him, when he fled from the face of his brother.

8 But Deborah Rē-bĕk'ăh's nurse died, and she was buried beneath Beth-el under an oak: and the name of it was called Ăl'lŏn-băch'ŭth.

9 ¶ And God appeared unto Jacob again, when he came out of Pā'dăn-ā'răm, and blessed him.

10 And God said unto him, Thy name *is* Jacob: thy name shall not be called any more Jacob, but Ĭṣ'rā-ĕl shall be thy name; and he called his name Ĭṣ'rā-ĕl.

11 And God said unto him, I *am* God Almighty: be fruitful and multiply; a nation and a company of nations shall be of thee, and kings shall come out of thy loins;

12 And the land which I gave Abraham and Isaac, to thee I will give it, and to thy seed after thee will I give the land.

13 And God went up from him in the place where he talked with him.

14 And Jacob set up a pillar in the place where he talked with him, *even* a pillar of stone: and he poured a drink offering thereon, and he poured oil thereon.

15 And Jacob called the name of the place where God spake with him, Beth-el.

16 ¶ And they journeyed from Beth-el; and there was but a little way to come to Ĕph'răth: and Rachel travailed, and she had hard labor.

17 And it came to pass, when she was in hard labor, that the midwife said unto her, Fear not; thou shalt have this son also.

18 And it came to pass, as her soul was in departing, (for she died,) that she called his name Bĕn–ō′nī: but his father called him Benjamin.

19 And Rachel died, and was buried in the way to Ĕph′răth, which *is* Beth-lehem.

20 And Jacob set a pillar upon her grave: that *is* the pillar of Rachel's grave unto this day.

21 ℭ And Ĭs̱′rā-ĕl journeyed, and spread his tent beyond the tower of Ē′dȧr.

22 And it came to pass, when Ĭs̱′rā-ĕl dwelt in that land, that Reuben went and lay with Bĭl′hȧh his father's concubine: and Ĭs̱′rā-ĕl heard *it*. Now the sons of Jacob were twelve:

23 The sons of Lē′ȧh; Reuben, Jacob's firstborn, and Simeon, and Levi, and Judah, and Ĭs′sȧ-ehär, and Zĕb′ū-lŭn:

24 The sons of Rachel; Joseph, and Benjamin:

25 And the sons of Bĭl′hȧh, Rachel's handmaid; Dan, and Năph′tȧ-lī:

26 And the sons of Zĭl′pȧh, Lē′ȧh's handmaid; Gad, and Ăsh′ēr. These *are* the sons of Jacob, which were born to him in Pā′dăn–ā′răm.

27 ℭ And Jacob came unto Isaac his father unto Măm′rē, unto the city of Är′bȧ, which *is* Hē′brŏn, where Abraham and Isaac sojourned.

28 And the days of Isaac were a hundred and fourscore years.

29 And Isaac gave up the ghost, and died, and was gathered unto his people, *being* old and full of days: and his sons Ē′saû and Jacob buried him.

CHAPTER 36

NOW these *are* the generations of Ē′saû, who *is* Ē′dŏm.

2 Ē′saû took his wives of the daughters of Cā′năan; Ā′dȧh the daughter of Ē′lŏn the Hĭt′tīte, and Ȧ-hŏl′ĭ-bā′mȧh the daughter of Ā′nȧh the daughter of Zĭb′ē-ŏn the Hī′vīte;

3 And Băsh′ē-măth Ĭsh′mā-ĕl's daughter, sister of Nē-bā′jŏth.

4 And Ā′dȧh bare to Ē′saû Ĕl′ĭ-phăz, and Băsh′ē-măth bare Reṳ′ĕl;

5 And Ȧ-hŏl′ĭ-bā′mȧh bare Jē′ŭsh, and Jā′ȧ-lăm, and Kō′rȧh: these *are* the sons of Ē′saû, which were born unto him in the land of Cā′năan.

6 And Ē′saû took his wives, and his sons, and his daughters, and all the persons of his house, and his cattle, and all his beasts, and all his substance, which he had got in the land of Cā′năan; and went into the country from the face of his brother Jacob.

7 For their riches were more than that they might dwell together; and the land wherein they were strangers could not bear them because of their cattle.

8 Thus dwelt Ē′saû in mount Sē′ïr: Ē′saû *is* Ē′dŏm.

9 ℭ And these *are* the generations of Ē′saû the father of the Ē′dŏm-ītes in mount Sē′ïr:

10 These *are* the names of Ē′saû's sons; Ĕl′ĭ-phăz the son of Ā′dȧh the wife of Ē′saû, Reṳ′ĕl the son of Băsh′ē-măth the wife of Ē′saû.

11 And the sons of Ĕl′ĭ-phăz were Tē′măn, Ō′mȧr, Zē′phō, and Gā′tăm, and Kē′năz.

12 And Tĭm′nȧ was concubine to Ĕl′ĭ-phăz Ē′saû's son; and she bare to Ĕl′ĭ-phăz Ăm′ȧ-lĕk: these *were* the sons of Ā′dȧh Ē′saû's wife.

13 And these *are* the sons of Reṳ′ĕl; Nā′hăth, and Zē′rȧh, Shăm′mȧh, and Mĭz′zȧh: these were the sons of Băsh′ē-măth Ē′saû's wife.

14 ℭ And these were the sons of Ȧ-hŏl′ĭ-bā′mȧh, the daughter of Ā′nȧh the daughter of Zĭb′ē-ŏn, Ē′saû's wife: and she bare to Ē′saû Jē′ŭsh, and Jā′ȧ-lăm, and Kō′rȧh.

15 ℭ These *were* dukes of the sons of Ē′saû: the sons of Ĕl′ĭ-phăz the firstborn *son* of Ē′saû; duke Tē′măn, duke Ō′mȧr, duke Zē′phō, duke Kē′năz,

16 Duke Kō′rȧh, duke Gā′tăm, *and* duke Ăm′ȧ-lĕk: these *are* the dukes *that came* of Ĕl′ĭ-phăz in the land of Ē′dŏm: these *were* the sons of Ā′dȧh.

17 ℭ And these *are* the sons of Reṳ′ĕl Ē′saû's son; duke Nā′hăth, duke Zē′rȧh, duke Shăm′mȧh, duke Mĭz′zȧh: these *are* the dukes *that came* of Reṳ′ĕl in the land of Ē′dŏm: these *are* the sons of Băsh′ē-măth Ē′saû's wife.

18 ℭ And these *are* the sons of Ȧ-hŏl′ĭ-bā′mȧh Ē′saû's wife; duke Jē′ŭsh, duke Jā′ȧ-lăm, duke Kō′rȧh: these *were* the dukes *that came* of Ȧ-hŏl′ĭ-bā′mȧh the daughter of Ā′nȧh, Ē′saû's wife.

19 These *are* the sons of Ē′saû, who *is* Ē′dŏm, and these *are* their dukes.

20 ℭ These *are* the sons of Sē′ïr the Hō′rīte, who inhabited the land; Lō′tăn, and Shō′băl, and Zĭb′ē-ŏn, and Ā′nȧh,

21 And Dī'shŏn, and Ē'zĕr, and Dī'-
shăn: these *are* the dukes of the Hō'-
rītes, the children of Sē'ĭr in the land of
Ē'dŏm.
22 And the children of Lō'tăn were
Hō'rī and Hē'măm; and Lō'tăn's sister
was Tĭm'nȧ.
23 And the children of Shō'băl *were*
these; Ăl'văn, and Măn'ȧ-hăth, and
Ē'băl, Shē'phō, and Ō'năm.
24 And these *are* the children of Zĭb'ē-
ŏn; both Ā'jȧh, and Ā'nȧh: this *was that*
Ā'nȧh that found the mules in the wilderness, as he fed the asses of Zĭb'ē-ŏn
his father.
25 And the children of Ā'nȧh *were*
these; Dī'shŏn, and Ȧ-hŏl'ĭ-bā'mȧh the
daughter of Ā'nȧh.
26 And these *are* the children of Dī'-
shŏn; Hĕm'dăn, and Ĕsh'băn, and
Ĭth'răn, and Chē'răn.
27 The children of Ē'zĕr *are* these;
Bĭl'hăn, and Zā'ȧ-văn, and Ā'kăn.
28 The children of Dī'shăn *are* these;
Ŭz, and Ā'răn.
29 These *are* the dukes *that came* of
the Hō'rītes; duke Lō'tăn, duke Shō'-
băl, duke Zĭb'ē-ŏn, duke Ā'nȧh,
30 Duke Dī'shŏn, duke Ē'zĕr, duke
Dī'shăn: these *are* the dukes *that came*
of Hō'rī, among their dukes in the land
of Sē'ĭr.
31 ℂ And these *are* the kings that
reigned in the land of Ē'dŏm, before
there reigned any king over the children
of Ī̦ṣ'rā-ĕl.
32 And Bē'lȧ the son of Bē'ŏr reigned
in Ē'dŏm: and the name of his city *was*
Dĭn'hȧ-băh.
33 And Bē'lȧ died, and Jō'băb the son
of Zē'rȧh of Bŏz'rȧh reigned in his stead.
34 And Jō'băb died, and Hū'shăm of
the land of Tĕm'ȧ-nī reigned in his
stead.
35 And Hū'shăm died, and Hā'dăd the
son of Bē'dăd, who smote Mĭd'ĭ-ăn in
the field of Mō'ăb, reigned in his stead:
and the name of his city *was* Ā'vĭth.
36 And Hā'dăd died, and Săm'lȧh of
Măs'rē-kȧh reigned in his stead.
37 And Săm'lȧh died, and Saul of Rē-
hō'bŏth *by* the river reigned in his stead.
38 And Saul died, and Bā'ăl-hā'năn the
son of Ăch'bŏr reigned in his stead.
39 And Bā'ăl-hā'năn the son of Ăch'-
bŏr died, and Hā'dȧr reigned in his
stead: and the name of his city *was* Pā'ū;
and his wife's name *was* Mē-hĕt'ȧ-bĕl,
the daughter of Mā'trĕd, the daughter of
Mĕz'ā-hăb.
40 And these *are* the names of the
dukes *that came* of Ē'saū, according to
their families, after their places, by
their names; duke Tĭm'nȧh, duke Ăl'-
vȧh, duke Jē'thĕth,
41 Duke Ȧ-hŏl'ĭ-bā'mȧh, duke Ē'lȧh,
duke Pī'nŏn,
42 Duke Kē'năz, duke Tē'măn, duke
Mĭb'zăr,
43 Duke Măg'dĭ-ĕl, duke Ī'răm: these
be the dukes of Ē'dŏm, according to
their habitations in the land of their
possession: he *is* Ē'saū the father of
the Ē'dŏm-ītes.

CHAPTER 37

AND Jacob dwelt in the land wherein
his father was a stranger, in the
land of Cā'năan.
2 These *are* the generations of Jacob.
Joseph, *being* seventeen years old, was
feeding the flock with his brethren; and
the lad *was* with the sons of Bĭl'hȧh,
and with the sons of Zĭl'pȧh, his father's
wives: and Joseph brought unto his
father their evil report.
3 Now Ī̦ṣ'rā-ĕl loved Joseph more than
all his children, because he *was* the son
of his old age: and he made him a coat
of *many* colors.
4 And when his brethren saw that their
father loved him more than all his brethren, they hated him, and could not speak
peaceably unto him.
5 ℂ And Joseph dreamed a dream, and
he told *it* his brethren: and they hated
him yet the more.
6 And he said unto them, Hear, I pray
you, this dream which I have dreamed:
7 For, behold, we *were* binding sheaves
in the field, and, lo, my sheaf arose, and
also stood upright; and, behold, your
sheaves stood round about, and made
obeisance to my sheaf.
8 And his brethren said to him, Shalt
thou indeed reign over us? or shalt thou
indeed have dominion over us? And
they hated him yet the more for his
dreams, and for his words.
9 ℂ And he dreamed yet another
dream, and told it his brethren, and said,
Behold, I have dreamed a dream more;
and, behold, the sun and the moon and
the eleven stars made obeisance to me.
10 And he told *it* to his father, and to
his brethren: and his father rebuked

him, and said unto him, What *is* this dream that thou hast dreamed? Shall I and thy mother and thy brethren indeed come to bow down ourselves to thee to the earth?

11 And his brethren envied him; but his father observed the saying.

12 ℂ And his brethren went to feed their father's flock in Shē′chĕm.

13 And Ĭs′rā-ĕl said unto Joseph, Do not thy brethren feed *the flock* in Shē′chĕm? come, and I will send thee unto them. And he said to him, Here *am I*.

14 And he said to him, Go, I pray thee, see whether it be well with thy brethren, and well with the flocks; and bring me word again. So he sent him out of the vale of Hē′brŏn, and he came to Shē′chĕm.

15 ℂ And a certain man found him, and, behold, *he was* wandering in the field: and the man asked him, saying, What seekest thou?

16 And he said, I seek my brethren: tell me, I pray thee, where they feed *their flocks*.

17 And the man said, They are departed hence; for I heard them say, Let us go to Dō′thăn. And Joseph went after his brethren, and found them in Dō′thăn.

18 And when they saw him afar off, even before he came near unto them, they conspired against him to slay him.

19 And they said one to another, Behold, this dreamer cometh.

20 Come now therefore, and let us slay him, and cast him into some pit, and we will say, Some evil beast hath devoured him; and we shall see what will become of his dreams.

21 And Reuben heard *it*, and he delivered him out of their hands; and said, Let us not kill him.

22 And Reuben said unto them, Shed no blood, *but* cast him into this pit that *is* in the wilderness, and lay no hand upon him; that he might rid him out of their hands, to deliver him to his father again.

23 ℂ And it came to pass, when Joseph was come unto his brethren, that they stripped Joseph out of his coat, *his* coat of *many* colors that *was* on him;

24 And they took him, and cast him into a pit: and the pit *was* empty, *there was* no water in it.

25 And they sat down to eat bread: and they lifted up their eyes and looked, and, behold, a company of Ĭsh′mā-ĕl-ītes came from Gĭl′ē-ăd, with their camels bearing spicery and balm and myrrh, going to carry *it* down to Egypt.

26 And Judah said unto his brethren, What profit *is it* if we slay our brother, and conceal his blood?

27 Come, and let us sell him to the Ĭsh′mā-ĕl-ītes, and let not our hand be upon him; for he *is* our brother *and* our flesh: and his brethren were content.

28 Then there passed by Mĭd′ĭ-ăn-ītes merchantmen; and they drew and lifted up Joseph out of the pit, and sold Joseph to the Ĭsh′mā-ĕl-ītes for twenty *pieces* of silver: and they brought Joseph into Egypt.

29 ℂ And Reuben returned unto the pit; and, behold, Joseph *was* not in the pit; and he rent his clothes.

30 And he returned unto his brethren, and said, The child *is* not; and I, whither shall I go?

31 And they took Joseph's coat, and killed a kid of the goats, and dipped the coat in the blood;

32 And they sent the coat of *many* colors, and they brought *it* to their father; and said, This have we found: know now whether it *be* thy son's coat or no.

33 And he knew it, and said, *It is* my son's coat; an evil beast hath devoured him; Joseph is without doubt rent in pieces.

34 And Jacob rent his clothes, and put sackcloth upon his loins, and mourned for his son many days.

35 And all his sons and all his daughters rose up to comfort him; but he refused to be comforted; and he said, For I will go down into the grave unto my son mourning. Thus his father wept for him.

36 And the Mĭd′ĭ-ăn-ītes sold him into Egypt unto Pŏt′ĭ-phär, an officer of Phā′raōh's, *and* captain of the guard.

CHAPTER 38

AND it came to pass at that time, that Judah went down from his brethren, and turned in to a certain Ȧ-dŭl′lăm-īte, whose name *was* Hī′răh.

2 And Judah saw there a daughter of a certain Cā′năan-īte, whose name *was* Shū′ăh; and he took her, and went in unto her.

3 And she conceived, and bare a son; and he called his name Ẽr.

4 And she conceived again, and bare a son; and she called his name Ō′năn.

5 And she yet again conceived, and bare a son; and called his name Shē′lȧh: and he was at Chē′zĭb, when she bare him.

6 And Judah took a wife for Ẽr his firstborn, whose name *was* Tā′mȧr.

7 And Ẽr, Judah's firstborn, was wicked in the sight of the LORD; and the LORD slew him.

8 And Judah said unto Ō′năn, Go in unto thy brother's wife, and marry her, and raise up seed to thy brother.

9 And Ō′năn knew that the seed should not be his; and it came to pass, when he went in unto his brother's wife, that he spilled *it* on the ground, lest that he should give seed to his brother.

10 And the thing which he did displeased the LORD: wherefore he slew him also.

11 Then said Judah to Tā′mȧr his daughter-in-law, Remain a widow at thy father's house, till Shē′lȧh my son be grown: for he said, Lest peradventure he die also, as his brethren *did*. And Tā′mȧr went and dwelt in her father's house.

12 ℂ And in process of time the daughter of Shụ′ȧh Judah's wife died; and Judah was comforted, and went up unto his sheepshearers to Tĭm′năth, he and his friend Hī′rȧh the Ȧ-dŭl′lăm-īte.

13 And it was told Tā′mȧr, saying, Behold, thy father-in-law goeth up to Tĭm′năth to shear his sheep.

14 And she put her widow's garments off from her, and covered her with a veil, and wrapped herself, and sat in an open place, which *is* by the way to Tĭm′năth; for she saw that Shē′lȧh was grown, and she was not given unto him to wife.

15 When Judah saw her, he thought her *to be* a harlot; because she had covered her face.

16 And he turned unto her by the way, and said, Go to, I pray thee, let me come in unto thee; (for he knew not that she *was* his daughter-in-law:) and she said, What wilt thou give me, that thou mayest come in unto me?

17 And he said, I will send *thee* a kid from the flock. And she said, Wilt thou give *me* a pledge, till thou send *it?*

18 And he said, What pledge shall I give thee? And she said, Thy signet, and thy bracelets, and thy staff that *is* in thine hand. And he gave *it* her, and came in unto her, and she conceived by him.

19 And she arose, and went away, and laid by her veil from her, and put on the garments of her widowhood.

20 And Judah sent the kid by the hand of his friend the Ȧ-dŭl′lăm-īte, to receive *his* pledge from the woman's hand: but he found her not.

21 Then he asked the men of that place, saying, Where *is* the harlot, that *was* openly by the wayside? And they said, There was no harlot in this *place*.

22 And he returned to Judah, and said, I cannot find her; and also the men of the place said, *that* there was no harlot in this *place*.

23 And Judah said, Let her take *it* to her, lest we be shamed: behold, I sent this kid, and thou hast not found her.

24 ℂ And it came to pass about three months after, that it was told Judah, saying, Tā′mȧr thy daughter-in-law hath played the harlot; and also, behold, she *is* with child by whoredom. And Judah said, Bring her forth, and let her be burnt.

25 When she *was* brought forth she sent to her father-in-law, saying, By the man, whose these *are*, *am* I with child: and she said, Discern, I pray thee, whose *are* these, the signet, and bracelets, and staff.

26 And Judah acknowledged *them*, and said, She hath been more righteous than I; because that I gave her not to Shē′lȧh my son. And he knew her again no more.

27 ℂ And it came to pass in the time of her travail, that, behold, twins *were* in her womb.

28 And it came to pass, when she travailed, that *the one* put out *his* hand: and the midwife took and bound upon his hand a scarlet thread, saying, This came out first.

29 And it came to pass, as he drew back his hand, that, behold, his brother came out: and she said, How hast thou broken forth? *this* breach *be* upon thee: therefore his name was called Phā′rēz.

30 And afterward came out his brother, that had the scarlet thread upon his hand: and his name was called Zā′rȧh.

CHAPTER 39

AND Joseph was brought down to Egypt; and Pŏt′ĭ-phăr, an officer of Phā′raōh, captain of the guard, an Egyptian, bought him of the hands of the Ĭsh′mā-ĕl-ītes, which had brought him down thither.

2 And the LORD was with Joseph, and he was a prosperous man; and he was in the house of his master the Egyptian.

3 And his master saw that the LORD *was* with him, and that the LORD made all that he did to prosper in his hand.

4 And Joseph found grace in his sight, and he served him: and he made him overseer over his house, and all *that* he had he put into his hand.

5 And it came to pass from the time *that* he had made him overseer in his house, and over all that he had, that the LORD blessed the Egyptian's house for Joseph's sake; and the blessing of the LORD was upon all that he had in the house, and in the field.

6 And he left all that he had in Joseph's hand; and he knew not aught he had, save the bread which he did eat. And Joseph was a goodly person, and well-favored.

7 ℂ And it came to pass after these things, that his master's wife cast her eyes upon Joseph; and she said, Lie with me.

8 But he refused, and said unto his master's wife, Behold, my master wotteth not what *is* with me in the house, and he hath committed all that he hath to my hand;

9 *There is* none greater in this house than I; neither hath he kept back any thing from me but thee, because thou *art* his wife: how then can I do this great wickedness, and sin against God?

10 And it came to pass, as she spake to Joseph day by day, that he hearkened not unto her, to lie by her, *or* to be with her.

11 And it came to pass about this time, that *Joseph* went into the house to do his business; and *there was* none of the men of the house there within.

12 And she caught him by his garment, saying, Lie with me: and he left his garment in her hand, and fled, and got him out.

13 And it came to pass, when she saw that he had left his garment in her hand, and was fled forth,

14 That she called unto the men of her house, and spake unto them, saying, See, he hath brought in a Hebrew unto us to mock us; he came in unto me to lie with me, and I cried with a loud voice:

15 And it came to pass, when he heard that I lifted up my voice and cried, that he left his garment with me, and fled, and got him out.

16 And she laid up his garment by her, until his lord came home.

17 And she spake unto him according to these words, saying, The Hebrew servant, which thou hast brought unto us, came in unto me to mock me:

18 And it came to pass, as I lifted up my voice and cried, that he left his garment with me, and fled out.

19 And it came to pass, when his master heard the words of his wife, which she spake unto him, saying, After this manner did thy servant to me; that his wrath was kindled.

20 And Joseph's master took him, and put him into the prison, a place where the king's prisoners *were* bound: and he was there in the prison.

21 ℂ But the LORD was with Joseph, and showed him mercy, and gave him favor in the sight of the keeper of the prison.

22 And the keeper of the prison committed to Joseph's hand all the prisoners that *were* in the prison; and whatsoever they did there, he was the doer *of it*.

23 The keeper of the prison looked not to any thing *that was* under his hand; because the LORD was with him, and *that* which he did, the LORD made *it* to prosper.

CHAPTER 40

AND it came to pass after these things, *that* the butler of the king of Egypt and *his* baker had offended their lord the king of Egypt.

2 And Phā′raōh was wroth against two *of* his officers, against the chief of the butlers, and against the chief of the bakers.

3 And he put them in ward in the house of the captain of the guard, into the prison, the place where Joseph *was* bound.

4 And the captain of the guard charged Joseph with them, and he served them: and they continued a season in ward.

5 ℂ And they dreamed a dream both

of them, each man his dream in one
night, each man according to the interpretation of his dream, the butler and
the baker of the king of Egypt, which
were bound in the prison.
6 And Joseph came in unto them in the
morning, and looked upon them, and,
behold, they *were* sad.
7 And he asked Phā'raōh's officers that
were with him in the ward of his lord's
house, saying, Wherefore look ye *so*
sadly to-day?
8 And they said unto him, We have
dreamed a dream, and *there is* no interpreter of it. And Joseph said unto them,
Do not interpretations *belong* to God?
tell me *them,* I pray you.
9 And the chief butler told his dream to
Joseph, and said to him, In my dream,
behold, a vine *was* before me;
10 And in the vine *were* three branches:
and it *was* as though it budded, *and* her
blossoms shot forth; and the clusters
thereof brought forth ripe grapes:
11 And Phā'raōh's cup *was* in my hand:
and I took the grapes, and pressed them
into Phā'raōh's cup, and I gave the cup
into Phā'raōh's hand.
12 And Joseph said unto him, This
is the interpretation of it: The three
branches *are* three days:
13 Yet within three days shall Phā'raōh
lift up thine head, and restore thee unto
thy place; and thou shalt deliver Phā'-
raōh's cup into his hand, after the former
manner when thou wast his butler.
14 But think on me when it shall be
well with thee, and show kindness, I
pray thee, unto me, and make mention
of me unto Phā'raōh, and bring me out
of this house:
15 For indeed I was stolen away out of
the land of the Hebrews: and here also
have I done nothing that they should
put me into the dungeon.
16 When the chief baker saw that the
interpretation was good, he said unto
Joseph, I also *was* in my dream, and,
behold, *I had* three white baskets on
my head:
17 And in the uppermost basket *there*
was of all manner of bakemeats for
Phā'raōh; and the birds did eat them
out of the basket upon my head.
18 And Joseph answered and said, This
is the interpretation thereof: The three
baskets *are* three days:
19 Yet within three days shall Phā'raōh
lift up thy head from off thee, and shall
hang thee on a tree; and the birds shall
eat thy flesh from off thee.
20 ¶ And it came to pass the third day,
which was Phā'raōh's birthday, that he
made a feast unto all his servants: and
he lifted up the head of the chief butler
and of the chief baker among his
servants.
21 And he restored the chief butler unto
his butlership again; and he gave the
cup into Phā'raōh's hand:
22 But he hanged the chief baker: as
Joseph had interpreted to them.
23 Yet did not the chief butler remember Joseph, but forgat him.

CHAPTER 41

AND it came to pass at the end of two
full years, that Phā'raōh dreamed:
and, behold, he stood by the river.
2 And, behold, there came up out of
the river seven well-favored kine and
fat-fleshed; and they fed in a meadow.
3 And, behold, seven other kine came
up after them out of the river, ill-
favored and lean-fleshed; and stood by
the *other* kine upon the brink of the
river.
4 And the ill-favored and lean-fleshed
kine did eat up the seven well-favored
and fat kine. So Phā'raōh awoke.
5 And he slept and dreamed the second
time: and, behold, seven ears of corn
came up upon one stalk, rank and good.
6 And, behold, seven thin ears and
blasted with the east wind sprung up
after them.
7 And the seven thin ears devoured
the seven rank and full ears. And Phā'-
raōh awoke, and, behold, *it was* a
dream.
8 And it came to pass in the morning
that his spirit was troubled; and he sent
and called for all the magicians of Egypt,
and all the wise men thereof: and Phā'-
raōh told them his dream; but *there was*
none that could interpret them unto
Phā'raōh.
9 ¶ Then spake the chief butler unto
Phā'raōh, saying, I do remember my
faults this day:
10 Phā'raōh was wroth with his servants, and put me in ward in the captain
of the guard's house, *both* me and the
chief baker:
11 And we dreamed a dream in one
night, I and he; we dreamed each man

according to the interpretation of his
dream.
12 And *there was* there with us a young
man, a Hebrew, servant to the captain
of the guard; and we told him, and he
interpreted to us our dreams; to each
man according to his dream he did interpret.
13 And it came to pass, as he interpreted to us, so it was; me he restored
unto mine office, and him he hanged.
14 ℂ Then Phā′raōh sent and called
Joseph, and they brought him hastily
out of the dungeon: and he shaved *himself,* and changed his raiment, and came
in unto Phā′raōh.
15 And Phā′raōh said unto Joseph, I
have dreamed a dream, and *there is*
none that can interpret it: and I have
heard say of thee, *that* thou canst understand a dream to interpret it.
16 And Joseph answered Phā′raōh,
saying, *It is* not in me: God shall give
Phā′raōh an answer of peace.
17 And Phā′raōh said unto Joseph, In
my dream, behold, I stood upon the
bank of the river:
18 And, behold, there came up out of
the river seven kine, fat-fleshed and
well-favored; and they fed in a meadow:
19 And, behold, seven other kine came
up after them, poor and very ill-favored
and lean-fleshed, such as I never saw in
all the land of Egypt for badness:
20 And the lean and the ill-favored kine
did eat up the first seven fat kine:
21 And when they had eaten them up,
it could not be known that they had
eaten them; but they *were* still ill-favored, as at the beginning. So I awoke.
22 And I saw in my dream, and, behold,
seven ears came up in one stalk, full
and good:
23 And, behold, seven ears, withered,
thin, *and* blasted with the east wind,
sprung up after them:
24 And the thin ears devoured the
seven good ears: and I told *this* unto the
magicians; but *there was* none that
could declare *it* to me.
25 ℂ And Joseph said unto Phā′raōh,
The dream of Phā′raōh *is* one: God hath
showed Phā′raōh what he *is* about to do.
26 The seven good kine *are* seven
years; and the seven good ears *are* seven
years: the dream *is* one.
27 And the seven thin and ill-favored
kine that came up after them *are* seven
years; and the seven empty ears blasted
with the east wind shall be seven years
of famine.
28 This *is* the thing which I have
spoken unto Phā′raōh: What God *is*
about to do he showeth unto Phā′raōh.
29 Behold, there come seven years of
great plenty throughout all the land of
Egypt:
30 And there shall arise after them
seven years of famine; and all the plenty
shall be forgotten in the land of Egypt;
and the famine shall consume the land;
31 And the plenty shall not be known
in the land by reason of that famine following; for it *shall be* very grievous.
32 And for that the dream was doubled
unto Phā′raōh twice; *it is* because the
thing *is* established by God, and God
will shortly bring it to pass.
33 Now therefore let Phā′raōh look out
a man discreet and wise, and set him
over the land of Egypt.
34 Let Phā′raōh do *this,* and let him
appoint officers over the land, and take
up the fifth part of the land of Egypt in
the seven plenteous years.
35 And let them gather all the food of
those good years that come, and lay up
corn under the hand of Phā′raōh, and
let them keep food in the cities.
36 And that food shall be for store to
the land against the seven years of
famine, which shall be in the land of
Egypt; that the land perish not through
the famine.
37 ℂ And the thing was good in the
eyes of Phā′raōh, and in the eyes of all
his servants.
38 And Phā′raōh said unto his servants,
Can we find *such a one* as this *is,* a man
in whom the Spirit of God *is*?
39 And Phā′raōh said unto Joseph,
Forasmuch as God hath showed thee
all this, *there is* none so discreet and
wise as thou *art:*
40 Thou shalt be over my house, and
according unto thy word shall all my
people be ruled: only in the throne will
I be greater than thou.
41 And Phā′raōh said unto Joseph, See,
I have set thee over all the land of Egypt.
42 And Phā′raōh took off his ring from
his hand, and put it upon Joseph's hand,
and arrayed him in vestures of fine
linen, and put a gold chain about his
neck;
43 And he made him to ride in the

second chariot which he had; and they
cried before him, Bow the knee: and he
made him *ruler* over all the land of
Egypt.
44 And Phā'raōh said unto Joseph, I
am Phā'raōh, and without thee shall no
man lift up his hand or foot in all the
land of Egypt.
45 And Phā'raōh called Joseph's name
Zăph'năth-pā'ă-nē'ăh; and he gave him
to wife Ăs'ē-năth the daughter of Pŏt'ĭ-
phē'răh priest of Ŏn. And Joseph went
out over *all* the land of Egypt.
46 ℂ And Joseph *was* thirty years old
when he stood before Phā'raōh king of
Egypt. And Joseph went out from the
presence of Phā'raōh, and went throughout all the land of Egypt.
47 And in the seven plenteous years
the earth brought forth by handfuls.
48 And he gathered up all the food of
the seven years, which were in the land
of Egypt, and laid up the food in the
cities: the food of the field, which *was*
round about every city, laid he up in the
same.
49 And Joseph gathered corn as the
sand of the sea, very much, until he left
numbering; for *it was* without number.
50 And unto Joseph were born two
sons, before the years of famine came:
which Ăs'ē-năth the daughter of Pŏt'ĭ-
phē'răh priest of Ŏn bare unto him.
51 And Joseph called the name of the
firstborn Mă-năs'sĕh: For God, *said he,*
hath made me forget all my toil, and all
my father's house.
52 And the name of the second called
he Ē'phră-ĭm: For God hath caused me
to be fruitful in the land of my affliction.
53 ℂ And the seven years of plenteousness, that was in the land of Egypt,
were ended.
54 And the seven years of dearth began
to come, according as Joseph had said:
and the dearth was in all lands; but in
all the land of Egypt there was bread.
55 And when all the land of Egypt was
famished, the people cried to Phā'raōh
for bread: and Phā'raōh said unto all
the Egyptians, Go unto Joseph; what he
saith to you, do.
56 And the famine was over all the face
of the earth: and Joseph opened all the
storehouses, and sold unto the Egyptians; and the famine waxed sore in the
land of Egypt.
57 And all countries came into Egypt
to Joseph for to buy *corn;* because that
the famine was *so* sore in all lands.

CHAPTER 42

NOW when Jacob saw that there was
corn in Egypt, Jacob said unto his
sons, Why do ye look one upon another?
2 And he said, Behold, I have heard
that there is corn in Egypt: get you down
thither, and buy for us from thence;
that we may live, and not die.
3 ℂ And Joseph's ten brethren went
down to buy corn in Egypt.
4 But Benjamin, Joseph's brother,
Jacob sent not with his brethren; for he
said, Lest peradventure mischief befall
him.
5 And the sons of Ĭş'rā-ĕl came to buy
corn among those that came: for the
famine was in the land of Cā'năan.
6 And Joseph *was* the governor over
the land, *and* he *it was* that sold to all
the people of the land: and Joseph's
brethren came, and bowed down themselves before him *with* their faces to the
earth.
7 And Joseph saw his brethren, and
he knew them, but made himself strange
unto them, and spake roughly unto
them; and he said unto them, Whence
come ye? And they said, From the land
of Cā'năan to buy food.
8 And Joseph knew his brethren, but
they knew not him.
9 And Joseph remembered the dreams
which he dreamed of them, and said
unto them, Ye *are* spies; to see the
nakedness of the land ye are come.
10 And they said unto him, Nay, my
lord, but to buy food are thy servants
come.
11 We *are* all one man's sons; we *are*
true *men;* thy servants are no spies.
12 And he said unto them, Nay, but
to see the nakedness of the land ye are
come.
13 And they said, Thy servants *are*
twelve brethren, the sons of one man in
the land of Cā'năan; and, behold, the
youngest *is* this day with our father, and
one *is* not.
14 And Joseph said unto them, That
is it that I spake unto you, saying, Ye
are spies:
15 Hereby ye shall be proved: By the
life of Phā'raōh ye shall not go forth
hence, except your youngest brother
come hither.

16 Send one of you, and let him fetch
your brother, and ye shall be kept in
prison, that your words may be proved,
whether *there be any* truth in you: or
else by the life of Phā′raōh surely ye
are spies.
17 And he put them all together into
ward three days.
18 And Joseph said unto them the
third day, This do, and live; *for* I fear
God:
19 If ye *be* true *men,* let one of your
brethren be bound in the house of your
prison: go ye, carry corn for the famine
of your houses:
20 But bring your youngest brother
unto me; so shall your words be verified,
and ye shall not die. And they did so.
21 ¶ And they said one to another.
We *are* verily guilty concerning our
brother, in that we saw the anguish of
his soul, when he besought us, and we
would not hear; therefore is this distress
come upon us.
22 And Reuben answered them, saying, Spake I not unto you saying, Do
not sin against the child; and ye would
not hear? therefore, behold, also his
blood is required.
23 And they knew not that Joseph
understood *them;* for he spake unto
them by an interpreter.
24 And he turned himself about from
them, and wept; and returned to them
again, and communed with them, and
took from them Simeon, and bound him
before their eyes.
25 ¶ Then Joseph commanded to fill
their sacks with corn, and to restore
every man's money into his sack, and to
give them provision for the way: and
thus did he unto them.
26 And they laded their asses with the
corn, and departed thence.
27 And as one of them opened his sack
to give his ass provender in the inn, he
espied his money; for, behold, it *was* in
his sack's mouth.
28 And he said unto his brethren, My
money is restored; and, lo, *it is* even in
my sack: and their heart failed *them,*
and they were afraid, saying one to another, What *is* this *that* God hath done
unto us?
29 ¶ And they came unto Jacob their
father unto the land of Cā′năan, and
told him all that befell unto them;
saying,
30 The man, *who is* the lord of the land,
spake roughly to us, and took us for
spies of the country.
31 And we said unto him, We *are* true
men; we are no spies:
32 We *be* twelve brethren, sons of our
father; one *is* not, and the youngest *is*
this day with our father in the land of
Cā′năan.
33 And the man, the lord of the country, said unto us, Hereby shall I know
that ye *are* true *men;* leave one of your
brethren *here* with me, and take *food*
for the famine of your households, and
be gone:
34 And bring your youngest brother
unto me: then shall I know that ye *are*
no spies, but *that* ye *are* true *men: so*
will I deliver you your brother, and ye
shall traffic in the land.
35 ¶ And it came to pass as they emptied their sacks, that, behold, every
man's bundle of money *was* in his sack:
and when *both* they and their father saw
the bundles of money, they were afraid.
36 And Jacob their father said unto
them, Me have ye bereaved *of my chil-*
dren: Joseph *is* not, and Simeon *is* not,
and ye will take Benjamin *away:* all
these things are against me.
37 And Reuben spake unto his father,
saying, Slay my two sons, if I bring him
not to thee: deliver him into my hand,
and I will bring him to thee again.
38 And he said, My son shall not go
down with you; for his brother is dead,
and he is left alone: if mischief befall
him by the way in the which ye go, then
shall ye bring down my gray hairs with
sorrow to the grave.

CHAPTER 43

AND the famine *was* sore in the land.
2 And it came to pass, when they
had eaten up the corn which they had
brought out of Egypt, their father said
unto them, Go again, buy us a little food.
3 And Judah spake unto him, saying,
The man did solemnly protest unto us,
saying, Ye shall not see my face, except
your brother *be* with you.
4 If thou wilt send our brother with us,
we will go down and buy thee food:
5 But if thou wilt not send *him,* we will
not go down: for the man said unto us,
Ye shall not see my face, except your
brother *be* with you.
6 And Ĭş′rā-ēl said, Wherefore dealt

ye *so* ill with me, *as* to tell the man whether ye had yet a brother?

7 And they said, The man asked us straitly of our state, and of our kindred, saying, *Is* your father yet alive? have ye *another* brother? and we told him according to the tenor of these words: Could we certainly know that he would say, Bring your brother down?

8 And Judah said unto Ĭş′rā-ĕl his father, Send the lad with me, and we will arise and go; that we may live, and not die, both we, and thou, *and* also our little ones.

9 I will be surety for him; of my hand shalt thou require him: if I bring him not unto thee, and set him before thee, then let me bear the blame for ever:

10 For except we had lingered, surely now we had returned this second time.

11 And their father Ĭş′rā-ĕl said unto them, If *it must be* so now, do this; take of the best fruits in the land in your vessels, and carry down the man a present, a little balm, and a little honey, spices and myrrh, nuts and almonds:

12 And take double money in your hand; and the money that was brought again in the mouth of your sacks, carry *it* again in your hand; peradventure it *was* an oversight.

13 Take also your brother, and arise, go again unto the man:

14 And God Almighty give you mercy before the man, that he may send away your other brother, and Benjamin. If I be bereaved *of my children,* I am bereaved.

15 ¶ And the men took that present, and they took double money in their hand, and Benjamin; and rose up, and went down to Egypt, and stood before Joseph.

16 And when Joseph saw Benjamin with them, he said to the ruler of his house, Bring *these* men home, and slay, and make ready; for *these* men shall dine with me at noon.

17 And the man did as Joseph bade; and the man brought the men into Joseph's house.

18 And the men were afraid, because they were brought into Joseph's house; and they said, Because of the money that was returned in our sacks at the first time are we brought in; that he may seek occasion against us, and fall upon us, and take us for bondmen, and our asses.

19 And they came near to the steward of Joseph's house, and they communed with him at the door of the house,

20 And said, O sir, we came indeed down at the first time to buy food:

21 And it came to pass, when we came to the inn, that we opened our sacks, and, behold, *every* man's money *was* in the mouth of his sack, our money in full weight: and we have brought it again in our hand.

22 And other money have we brought down in our hands to buy food: we cannot tell who put our money in our sacks.

23 And he said, Peace *be* to you, fear not: your God, and the God of your father, hath given you treasure in your sacks: I had your money. And he brought Simeon out unto them.

24 And the man brought the men into Joseph's house, and gave *them* water, and they washed their feet; and he gave their asses provender.

25 And they made ready the present against Joseph came at noon: for they heard that they should eat bread there.

26 ¶ And when Joseph came home, they brought him the present which *was* in their hand into the house, and bowed themselves to him to the earth.

27 And he asked them of *their* welfare, and said, *Is* your father well, the old man of whom ye spake? *Is* he yet alive?

28 And they answered, Thy servant our father *is* in good health, he *is* yet alive. And they bowed down their heads, and made obeisance.

29 And he lifted up his eyes, and saw his brother Benjamin, his mother's son, and said, *Is* this your younger brother, of whom ye spake unto me? And he said, God be gracious unto thee, my son.

30 And Joseph made haste; for his bowels did yearn upon his brother: and he sought *where* to weep; and he entered into *his* chamber, and wept there.

31 And he washed his face, and went out, and refrained himself, and said, Set on bread.

32 And they set on for him by himself, and for them by themselves, and for the Egyptians, which did eat with him, by themselves: because the Egyptians might not eat bread with the Hebrews; for that *is* an abomination unto the Egyptians.

33 And they sat before him, the firstborn according to his birthright, and the

youngest according to his youth: and the
men marveled one at another.
34 And he took *and sent* messes unto
them from before him: but Benjamin's
mess was five times so much as any of
theirs. And they drank, and were
merry with him.

CHAPTER 44

AND he commanded the steward of
his house, saying, Fill the men's
sacks *with* food, as much as they can
carry, and put every man's money in
his sack's mouth.
2 And put my cup, the silver cup, in the
sack's mouth of the youngest, and his
corn money. And he did according to
the word that Joseph had spoken.
3 As soon as the morning was light, the
men were sent away, they and their
asses.
4 *And* when they were gone out of the
city, *and* not *yet* far off Joseph said
unto his steward, Up, follow after the
men; and when thou dost overtake them,
say unto them, Wherefore have ye
rewarded evil for good?
5 *Is* not this *it* in which my lord drinketh, and whereby indeed he divineth?
ye have done evil in so doing.
6 ℂ And he overtook them, and he
spake unto them these same words.
7 And they said unto him, Wherefore
saith my lord these words? God forbid
that thy servants should do according to
this thing:
8 Behold, the money, which we found
in our sacks' mouths, we brought again
unto thee out of the land of Cā′năan:
how then should we steal out of thy
lord's house silver or gold?
9 With whomsoever of thy servants it
be found, both let him die, and we also
will be my lord's bondmen.
10 And he said, Now also *let* it *be* according unto your words: he with whom
it is found shall be my servant; and ye
shall be blameless.
11 Then they speedily took down every
man his sack to the ground, and opened
every man his sack.
12 And he searched, *and* began at the
eldest, and left at the youngest: and the
cup was found in Benjamin's sack.
13 Then they rent their clothes, and
laded every man his ass, and returned
to the city.
14 ℂ And Judah and his brethren
came to Joseph's house; for he *was* yet
there: and they fell before him on the
ground.
15 And Joseph said unto them, What
deed *is* this that ye have done? wot ye
not that such a man as I can certainly
divine?
16 And Judah said, What shall we say
unto my lord? what shall we speak? or
how shall we clear ourselves? God hath
found out the iniquity of thy servants:
behold, we *are* my lord's servants, both
we, and *he* also with whom the cup is
found.
17 And he said, God forbid that I
should do so: *but* the man in whose hand
the cup is found, he shall be my servant;
and as for you, get you up in peace unto
your father.
18 ℂ Then Judah came near unto him,
and said, O my lord, let thy servant, I
pray thee, speak a word in my lord's
ears, and let not thine anger burn
against thy servant: for thou *art* even as
Phā′raōh.
19 My lord asked his servants, saying,
Have ye a father, or a brother?
20 And we said unto my lord, We have
a father, an old man, and a child of his
old age, a little one; and his brother is
dead, and he alone is left of his mother,
and his father loveth him.
21 And thou saidst unto thy servants,
Bring him down unto me, that I may set
mine eyes upon him.
22 And we said unto my lord, The lad
cannot leave his father: for *if* he should
leave his father, *his father* would die.
23 And thou saidst unto thy servants,
Except your youngest brother come
down with you, ye shall see my face no
more.
24 And it came to pass when we came
up unto thy servant my father, we told
him the words of my lord.
25 And our father said, Go again, *and*
buy us a little food.
26 And we said, We cannot go down:
if our youngest brother be with us, then
will we go down: for we may not see the
man's face, except our youngest brother
be with us.
27 And thy servant my father said unto
us, Ye know that my wife bare me two
sons:
28 And the one went out from me, and
I said, Surely he is torn in pieces; and I
saw him not since:

29 And if ye take this also from me, and mischief befall him, ye shall bring down my gray hairs with sorrow to the grave.

30 Now therefore when I come to thy servant my father, and the lad *be* not with us; seeing that his life is bound up in the lad's life;

31 It shall come to pass, when he seeth that the lad *is* not *with us,* that he will die: and thy servants shall bring down the gray hairs of thy servant our father with sorrow to the grave.

32 For thy servant became surety for the lad unto my father, saying, If I bring him not unto thee, then I shall bear the blame to my father for ever.

33 Now therefore, I pray thee, let thy servant abide instead of the lad a bondman to my lord; and let the lad go up with his brethren.

34 For how shall I go up to my father, and the lad *be* not with me? lest peradventure I see the evil that shall come on my father.

CHAPTER 45

THEN Joseph could not refrain himself before all them that stood by him; and he cried, Cause every man to go out from me. And there stood no man with him, while Joseph made himself known unto his brethren.

2 And he wept aloud: and the Egyptians and the house of Phā'raōh heard.

3 And Joseph said unto his brethren, I *am* Joseph; doth my father yet live? And his brethren could not answer him; for they were troubled at his presence.

4 And Joseph said unto his brethren, Come near to me, I pray you. And they came near. And he said, I *am* Joseph your brother, whom ye sold into Egypt.

5 Now therefore be not grieved, nor angry with yourselves, that ye sold me hither: for God did send me before you to preserve life.

6 For these two years *hath* the famine *been* in the land: and yet *there are* five years, in the which *there shall* neither *be* earing nor harvest.

7 And God sent me before you to preserve you a posterity in the earth, and to save your lives by a great deliverance.

8 So now *it was* not you *that* sent me hither, but God: and he hath made me a father to Phā'raōh, and lord of all his house, and a ruler throughout all the land of Egypt.

9 Haste ye, and go up to my father, and say unto him, Thus saith thy son Joseph, God hath made me lord of all Egypt: come down unto me, tarry not:

10 And thou shalt dwell in the land of Gō'shĕn, and thou shalt be near unto me, thou, and thy children, and thy children's children, and thy flocks, and thy herds, and all that thou hast:

11 And there will I nourish thee; for yet *there are* five years of famine; lest thou, and thy household, and all that thou hast, come to poverty.

12 And, behold, your eyes see, and the eyes of my brother Benjamin, that *it is* my mouth that speaketh unto you.

13 And ye shall tell my father of all my glory in Egypt, and of all that ye have seen; and ye shall haste and bring down my father hither.

14 And he fell upon his brother Benjamin's neck, and wept; and Benjamin wept upon his neck.

15 Moreover he kissed all his brethren, and wept upon them: and after that his brethren talked with him.

16 ℂ And the fame thereof was heard in Phā'raōh's house, saying, Joseph's brethren are come: and it pleased Phā'raōh well, and his servants.

17 And Phā'raōh said unto Joseph, Say unto thy brethren, This do ye; lade your beasts, and go, get you unto the land of Cā'năan;

18 And take your father and your households, and come unto me: and I will give you the good of the land of Egypt, and ye shall eat the fat of the land.

19 Now thou art commanded, this do ye; take you wagons out of the land of Egypt for your little ones, and for your wives, and bring your father, and come.

20 Also regard not your stuff; for the good of all the land of Egypt *is* yours.

21 And the children of Iș'rā-ĕl did so: and Joseph gave them wagons, according to the commandment of Phā'raōh, and gave them provision for the way.

22 To all of them he gave each man changes of raiment; but to Benjamin he gave three hundred *pieces* of silver, and five changes of raiment.

23 And to his father he sent after this *manner;* ten asses laden with the good things of Egypt, and ten she asses laden with corn and bread and meat for his father by the way.

24 So he sent his brethren away, and they departed: and he said unto them, See that ye fall not out by the way.

25 ¶ And they went up out of Egypt, and came into the land of Cā′năan unto Jacob their father,

26 And told him, saying, Joseph *is* yet alive, and he *is* governor over all the land of Egypt. And Jacob's heart fainted, for he believed them not.

27 And they told him all the words of Joseph, which he had said unto them: and when he saw the wagons which Joseph had sent to carry him, the spirit of Jacob their father revived.

28 And Ĭs′rā-ēl said, *It is* enough; Joseph my son *is* yet alive: I will go and see him before I die.

CHAPTER 46

AND Ĭs′rā-ĕl took his journey with all that he had, and came to Bē′ẽr-shē′bȧ, and offered sacrifices unto the God of his father Isaac.

2 And God spake unto Ĭs′rā-ĕl in the visions of the night, and said, Jacob, Jacob. And he said, Here *am* I.

3 And he said, I *am* God, the God of thy father: fear not to go down into Egypt; for I will there make of thee a great nation.

4 I will go down with thee into Egypt; and I will also surely bring thee up *again:* and Joseph shall put his hand upon thine eyes.

5 And Jacob rose up from Bē′ẽr-shē′bȧ: and the sons of Ĭs′rā-ĕl carried Jacob their father, and their little ones, and their wives, in the wagons which Phā′raōh had sent to carry him.

6 And they took their cattle, and their goods, which they had gotten in the land of Cā′năan, and came into Egypt, Jacob, and all his seed with him:

7 His sons, and his sons' sons with him, his daughters, and his sons' daughters, and all his seed brought he with him into Egypt.

8 ¶ And these *are* the names of the children of Ĭs′rā-ĕl, which came into Egypt, Jacob and his sons: Reuben, Jacob's firstborn.

9 And the sons of Reuben; Hā′nŏch, and Phăl′lụ, and Hĕz′rŏn, and Cär′mī.

10 ¶ And the sons of Simeon; Jē-mū′ĕl, and Jā′mĭn, and Ō′hăd and Jā′chĭn, and Zō′här, and Shā′ŭl the son of a Cā′năan-ĭt-ĭsh woman.

11 ¶ And the sons of Levi; Gẽr′shŏn, Kō′hăth, and Mē-rā′rī.

12 ¶ And the sons of Judah; Ẽr, and Ō′năn, and Shē′lȧh, and Phā′rēz, and Zā′rȧh: but Ẽr and Ō′năn died in the land of Cā′năan. And the sons of Phā′rēz were Hĕz′rŏn and Hā′mŭl.

13 ¶ And the sons of Ĭs′sȧ-chär; Tō′lȧ, and Phū′vȧh, and Jōb, and Shĭm′rŏn.

14 ¶ And the sons of Zĕb′ū-lŭn; Sē′rĕd, and Ē′lŏn, and Jăh′lē-ĕl.

15 These *be* the sons of Lē′ȧh, which she bare unto Jacob in Pā′dăn-ā′răm, with his daughter Dinah: all the souls of his sons and his daughters *were* thirty and three.

16 ¶ And the sons of Gad; Zĭph′ĭ-ŏn, and Hăg′gī, Shụ′nī, and Ĕz′bŏn, Ē′rī, and Ăr′ō-dī, and Ȧ-rē′lī.

17 ¶ And the sons of Ăsh′ẽr; Jĭm′nȧh, and Ĭsh′ū-ȧh, and Ĭs′ū-ī, and Bē-rī′ȧh, and Sē′rȧh their sister: and the sons of Bē-rī′ȧh; Hē′bẽr, and Măl′chĭ-ĕl.

18 These *are* the sons of Zĭl′pȧh, whom Lā′băn gave to Lē′ȧh his daughter; and these she bare unto Jacob, *even* sixteen souls.

19 The sons of Rachel Jacob's wife; Joseph, and Benjamin.

20 ¶ And unto Joseph in the land of Egypt were born Mȧ-năs′sĕh and Ē′phrā-ĭm, which Ăs′ē-năth the daughter of Pŏt′ĭ-phẽ′rȧh priest of Ŏn bare unto him.

21 ¶ And the sons of Benjamin *were* Bē′lȧh, and Bē′chẽr, and Ăsh′bĕl, Gē′rȧ, and Nā′ȧ-măn, Ē′hī, and Rŏsh, Mŭp′pĭm, and Hŭp′pĭm, and Ärd.

22 These *are* the sons of Rachel, which were born to Jacob: all the souls *were* fourteen.

23 ¶ And the sons of Dan; Hū′shĭm.

24 ¶ And the sons of Năph′tȧ-lī; Jăh′zē-ĕl, and Gū′nī, and Jē′zẽr, and Shĭl′lĕm.

25 These *are* the sons of Bĭl′hȧh, which Lā′băn gave unto Rachel his daughter, and she bare these unto Jacob: all the souls *were* seven.

26 All the souls that came with Jacob into Egypt, which came out of his loins, besides Jacob's sons' wives, all the souls *were* threescore and six;

27 And the sons of Joseph, which were borne him in Egypt, *were* two souls: all the souls of the house of Jacob, which came into Egypt, *were* threescore and ten.

28 ℂ And he sent Judah before him
unto Joseph, to direct his face unto
Gō'shĕn; and they came into the land
of Gō'shĕn.
29 And Joseph made ready his chariot,
and went up to meet Ĭṣ'rā-ĕl his father,
to Gō'shĕn, and presented himself unto
him; and he fell on his neck, and wept
on his neck a good while.
30 And Ĭṣ'rā-ĕl said unto Joseph, Now
let me die, since I have seen thy face,
because thou *art* yet alive.
31 And Joseph said unto his brethren,
and unto his father's house, I will go up,
and show Phā'raōh, and say unto him,
My brethren, and my father's house,
which *were* in the land of Cā'năan, are
come unto me;
32 And the men *are* shepherds, for their
trade hath been to feed cattle; and they
have brought their flocks, and their
herds, and all that they have.
33 And it shall come to pass, when
Phā'raōh shall call you, and shall say,
What *is* your occupation?
34 That ye shall say, Thy servants'
trade hath been about cattle from our
youth even until now, both we, *and*
also our fathers: that ye may dwell in the
land of Gō'shĕn; for every shepherd *is*
an abomination unto the Egyptians.

CHAPTER 47

THEN Joseph came and told Phā'-
raōh, and said, My father and my
brethren, and their flocks, and their
herds, and all that they have, are come
out of the land of Cā'năan; and, behold,
they *are* in the land of Gō'shĕn.
2 And he took some of his brethren,
even five men, and presented them
unto Phā'raōh.
3 And Phā'raōh said unto his brethren,
What *is* your occupation? And they said
unto Phā'raōh, Thy servants *are* shepherds, both we, *and* also our fathers.
4 They said moreover unto Phā'raōh,
For to sojourn in the land are we come;
for thy servants have no pasture for their
flocks; for the famine *is* sore in the land
of Cā'năan: now therefore, we pray thee,
let thy servants dwell in the land of
Gō'shĕn.
5 And Phā'raōh spake unto Joseph,
saying, Thy father and thy brethren are
come unto thee:
6 The land of Egypt *is* before thee; in
the best of the land make thy father and
brethren to dwell; in the land of Gō'shĕn
let them dwell: and if thou knowest *any*
men of activity among them, then make
them rulers over my cattle.
7 And Joseph brought in Jacob his
father, and set him before Phā'raōh: and
Jacob blessed Phā'raōh.
8 And Phā'raōh said unto Jacob, How
old *art* thou?
9 And Jacob said unto Phā'raōh, The
days of the years of my pilgrimage *are*
a hundred and thirty years: few and evil
have the days of the years of my life
been, and have not attained unto the
days of the years of the life of my fathers
in the days of their pilgrimage.
10 And Jacob blessed Phā'raōh, and
went out from before Phā'raōh.
11 ℂ And Joseph placed his father
and his brethren, and gave them a possession in the land of Egypt, in the best
of the land, in the land of Răm'ē-sēṣ, as
Phā'raōh had commanded.
12 And Joseph nourished his father,
and his brethren, and all his father's
household, with bread, according to
their families.
13 ℂ And *there was* no bread in all the
land; for the famine *was* very sore, so
that the land of Egypt and *all* the land
of Cā'năan fainted by reason of the
famine.
14 And Joseph gathered up all the
money that was found in the land of
Egypt, and in the land of Cā'năan, for
the corn which they bought: and Joseph
brought the money into Phā'raōh's
house.
15 And when money failed in the land
of Egypt, and in the land of Cā'năan,
all the Egyptians came unto Joseph,
and said, Give us bread: for why should
we die in thy presence? for the money
faileth.
16 And Joseph said, Give your cattle;
and I will give you for your cattle, if
money fail.
17 And they brought their cattle unto
Joseph: and Joseph gave them bread *in
exchange* for horses, and for the flocks,
and for the cattle of the herds, and for
the asses; and he fed them with bread
for all their cattle for that year.
18 When that year was ended, they
came unto him the second year, and
said unto him, We will not hide *it* from
my lord, how that our money is spent;
my lord also hath our herds of cattle;

there is not aught left in the sight of my lord, but our bodies, and our lands:

19 Wherefore shall we die before thine eyes, both we and our land? buy us and our land for bread, and we and our land will be servants unto Phā′raōh: and give *us* seed, that we may live, and not die, that the land be not desolate.

20 And Joseph bought all the land of Egypt for Phā′raōh; for the Egyptians sold every man his field, because the famine prevailed over them: so the land became Phā′raōh's.

21 And as for the people, he removed them to cities from *one* end of the borders of Egypt even to the *other* end thereof.

22 Only the land of the priests bought he not; for the priests had a portion *assigned them* of Phā′raōh, and did eat their portion which Phā′raōh gave them: wherefore they sold not their lands.

23 Then Joseph said unto the people, Behold, I have bought you this day and your land for Phā′raōh: lo, *here is* seed for you, and ye shall sow the land.

24 And it shall come to pass in the increase, that ye shall give the fifth *part* unto Phā′raōh, and four parts shall be your own, for seed of the field, and for your food, and for them of your households, and for food for your little ones.

25 And they said, Thou hast saved our lives: let us find grace in the sight of my lord, and we will be Phā′raōh's servants.

26 And Joseph made it a law over the land of Egypt unto this day, *that* Phā′raōh should have the fifth *part;* except the land of the priests only, *which* became not Phā′raōh's.

27 ¶ And Ĭṣ′rā-ĕl dwelt in the land of Egypt, in the country of Gō′shĕn; and they had possessions therein, and grew, and multiplied exceedingly.

28 And Jacob lived in the land of Egypt seventeen years: so the whole age of Jacob was a hundred forty and seven years.

29 And the time drew nigh that Ĭṣ′rā-ĕl must die: and he called his son Joseph, and said unto him, If now I have found grace in thy sight, put, I pray thee, thy hand under my thigh, and deal kindly and truly with me; bury me not, I pray thee, in Egypt:

30 But I will lie with my fathers, and thou shalt carry me out of Egypt, and bury me in their buryingplace. And he said, I will do as thou hast said.

31 And he said, Swear unto me. And he sware unto him. And Ĭṣ′rā-ĕl bowed himself upon the bed's head.

CHAPTER 48

AND it came to pass after these things, that *one* told Joseph, Behold, thy father *is* sick: and he took with him his two sons, Mȧ-năs′sĕh and Ē′phrā-ĭm.

2 And *one* told Jacob, and said, Behold, thy son Joseph cometh unto thee: and Ĭṣ′rā-ĕl strengthened himself, and sat upon the bed.

3 And Jacob said unto Joseph, God Almighty appeared unto me at Lŭz in the land of Cā′năan, and blessed me,

4 And said unto me, Behold, I will make thee fruitful, and multiply thee, and I will make of thee a multitude of people; and will give this land to thy seed after thee *for* an everlasting possession.

5 ¶ And now thy two sons, Ē′phrā-ĭm and Mȧ-năs′sĕh, which were born unto thee in the land of Egypt, before I came unto thee into Egypt, *are* mine; as Reuben and Simeon, they shall be mine.

6 And thy issue, which thou begettest after them, shall be thine, *and* shall be called after the name of their brethren in their inheritance.

7 And as for me, when I came from Pā′dăn, Rachel died by me in the land of Cā′năan in the way, when yet *there was* but a little way to come unto Ĕph′răth: and I buried her there in the way of Ĕph′răth; the same *is* Beth-lehem.

8 And Ĭṣ′rā-ĕl beheld Joseph's sons, and said, Who *are* these?

9 And Joseph said unto his father, They *are* my sons, whom God hath given me in this *place*. And he said, Bring them, I pray thee, unto me, and I will bless them.

10 Now the eyes of Ĭṣ′rā-ĕl were dim for age, *so that* he could not see. And he brought them near unto him; and he kissed them, and embraced them.

11 And Ĭṣ′rā-ĕl said unto Joseph, I had not thought to see thy face: and, lo, God hath showed me also thy seed.

12 And Joseph brought them out from between his knees, and he bowed himself with his face to the earth.

13 And Joseph took them both, Ē′phrā-ĭm in his right hand toward Ĭṣ′rā-ĕl's

left hand, and Mȧ-năs′sĕh in his left hand toward Ĭş′rā-ĕl's right hand, and brought *them* near unto him.

14 And Ĭş′rā-ĕl stretched out his right hand, and laid *it* upon Ē′phrā-ĭm's head, who *was* the younger, and his left hand upon Mȧ-năs′sĕh's head, guiding his hands wittingly; for Mȧ-năs′sĕh *was* the firstborn.

15 ℂ And he blessed Joseph, and said, God, before whom my fathers Abraham and Isaac did walk, the God which fed me all my life long unto this day,

16 The Angel which redeemed me from all evil, bless the lads; and let my name be named on them, and the name of my fathers Abraham and Isaac; and let them grow into a multitude in the midst of the earth.

17 And when Joseph saw that his father laid his right hand upon the head of Ē′phrā-ĭm, it displeased him: and he held up his father's hand, to remove it from Ē′phrā-ĭm's head unto Mȧ-năs′sĕh's head.

18 And Joseph said unto his father, Not so, my father: for this *is* the firstborn; put thy right hand upon his head.

19 And his father refused, and said, I know *it*, my son, I know *it*: he also shall become a people, and he also shall be great: but truly his younger brother shall be greater than he, and his seed shall become a multitude of nations.

20 And he blessed them that day, saying, In thee shall Ĭş′rā-ĕl bless, saying, God make thee as Ē′phrā-ĭm and as Mȧ-năs′sĕh: and he set Ē′phrā-ĭm before Mȧ-năs′sĕh.

21 And Ĭş′rā-ĕl said unto Joseph, Behold, I die; but God shall be with you, and bring you again unto the land of your fathers.

22 Moreover I have given to thee one portion above thy brethren, which I took out of the hand of the Ăm′ō-rīte with my sword and with my bow.

CHAPTER 49

AND Jacob called unto his sons, and said, Gather yourselves together, that I may tell you *that* which shall befall you in the last days.

2 Gather yourselves together, and hear, ye sons of Jacob; and hearken unto Ĭş′rā-ĕl your father.

3 ℂ Reuben, thou *art* my firstborn, my might, and the beginning of my strength, the excellency of dignity, and the excellency of power:

4 Unstable as water, thou shalt not excel; because thou wentest up to thy father's bed; then defiledst thou *it*: he went up to my couch.

5 ℂ Simeon and Levi *are* brethren; instruments of cruelty *are in* their habitations.

6 O my soul, come not thou into their secret; unto their assembly, mine honor, be not thou united: for in their anger they slew a man, and in their self-will they digged down a wall.

7 Cursed *be* their anger, for *it was* fierce; and their wrath, for it was cruel: I will divide them in Jacob, and scatter them in Ĭş′rā-ĕl.

8 ℂ Judah, thou *art he* whom thy brethren shall praise: thy hand *shall be* in the neck of thine enemies; thy father's children shall bow down before thee.

9 Judah *is* a lion's whelp: from the prey, my son, thou art gone up: he stooped down, he couched as a lion, and as an old lion; who shall rouse him up?

10 The sceptre shall not depart from Judah, nor a lawgiver from between his feet, until Shī′lōh come; and unto him *shall* the gathering of the people *be*.

11 Binding his foal unto the vine, and his ass's colt unto the choice vine; he washed his garments in wine, and his clothes in the blood of grapes:

12 His eyes *shall be* red with wine, and his teeth white with milk.

13 ℂ Zĕb′ū-lŭn shall dwell at the haven of the sea; and he *shall be* for a haven of ships; and his border *shall be* unto Zī′dŏn.

14 ℂ Ĭs′sȧ-chär *is* a strong ass couching down between two burdens:

15 And he saw that rest *was* good, and the land that *it was* pleasant; and bowed his shoulder to bear, and became a servant unto tribute.

16 ℂ Dan shall judge his people, as one of the tribes of Ĭş′rā-ĕl.

17 Dan shall be a serpent by the way, an adder in the path, that biteth the horse heels, so that his rider shall fall backward.

18 I have waited for thy salvation, O LORD.

19 ℂ Gad, a troop shall overcome him: but he shall overcome at the last.

20 ℂ Out of Ăsh′ẽr his bread *shall be* fat, and he shall yield royal dainties.

21 ¶ Năph′tă-lī *is* a hind let loose: he giveth goodly words.

22 ¶ Joseph *is* a fruitful bough, *even* a fruitful bough by a well; *whose* branches run over the wall:

23 The archers have sorely grieved him, and shot *at him,* and hated him:

24 But his bow abode in strength, and the arms of his hands were made strong by the hands of the mighty *God* of Jacob; (from thence *is* the shepherd, the stone of Ĭş′rā-ĕl;)

25 *Even* by the God of thy father, who shall help thee; and by the Almighty, who shall bless thee with blessings of heaven above, blessings of the deep that lieth under, blessings of the breasts, and of the womb:

26 The blessings of thy father have prevailed above the blessings of my progenitors unto the utmost bound of the everlasting hills: they shall be on the head of Joseph, and on the crown of the head of him that was separate from his brethren.

27 ¶ Benjamin shall raven *as* a wolf: in the morning he shall devour the prey, and at night he shall divide the spoil.

28 ¶ All these *are* the twelve tribes of Ĭş′rā-ĕl: and this *is it* that their father spake unto them, and blessed them; every one according to his blessing he blessed them.

29 And he charged them, and said unto them, I am to be gathered unto my people: bury me with my fathers in the cave that *is* in the field of Ē′phrŏn the Hĭt′tīte,

30 In the cave that *is* in the field of Măch-pē′lȧh, which *is* before Măm′rē, in the land of Că′năan, which Abraham bought with the field of Ē′phrŏn the Hĭt′tīte for a possession of a buryingplace.

31 There they buried Abraham and Sarah his wife; there they buried Isaac and Rē-bĕk′ȧh his wife; and there I buried Lē′ȧh.

32 The purchase of the field and of the cave that *is* therein *was* from the children of Heth.

33 And when Jacob had made an end of commanding his sons, he gathered up his feet into the bed, and yielded up the ghost, and was gathered unto his people.

CHAPTER 50

AND Joseph fell upon his father's face, and wept upon him, and kissed him.

2 And Joseph commanded his servants the physicians to embalm his father: and the physicians embalmed Ĭş′rā-ĕl.

3 And forty days were fulfilled for him; for so are fulfilled the days of those which are embalmed: and the Egyptians mourned for him threescore and ten days.

4 And when the days of his mourning were past, Joseph spake unto the house of Phā′raōh, saying, If now I have found grace in your eyes, speak, I pray you, in the ears of Phā′raōh, saying,

5 My father made me swear, saying, Lo, I die: in my grave which I have digged for me in the land of Că′năan, there shalt thou bury me. Now therefore let me go up, I pray thee, and bury my father, and I will come again.

6 And Phā′raōh said, Go up, and bury thy father, according as he made thee swear.

7 ¶ And Joseph went up to bury his father: and with him went up all the servants of Phā′raōh, the elders of his house, and all the elders of the land of Egypt,

8 And all the house of Joseph, and his brethren, and his father's house: only their little ones, and their flocks, and their herds, they left in the land of Gō′shĕn.

9 And there went up with him both chariots and horsemen: and it was a very great company.

10 And they came to the threshingfloor of Ā′tăd, which *is* beyond Jordan; and there they mourned with a great and very sore lamentation: and he made a mourning for his father seven days.

11 And when the inhabitants of the land, the Că′năan-ītes, saw the mourning in the floor of Ā′tăd, they said, This *is* a grievous mourning to the Egyptians: wherefore the name of it was called Ā′bĕl–mĭz′rā-ĭm, which *is* beyond Jordan.

12 And his sons did unto him according as he commanded them:

13 For his sons carried him into the land of Că′năan, and buried him in the cave of the field of Măch-pē′lȧh, which Abraham bought with the field for a possession of a buryingplace of Ē′phrŏn the Hĭt′tīte, before Măm′rē.

14 ¶ And Joseph returned into Egypt, he, and his brethren, and all that went up with him to bury his father, after he had buried his father.

15 ¶ And when Joseph's brethren saw that their father was dead, they said, Joseph will peradventure hate us, and will certainly requite us all the evil which we did unto him.

16 And they sent a messenger unto Joseph, saying, Thy father did command before he died, saying,

17 So shall ye say unto Joseph, Forgive, I pray thee now, the trespass of thy brethren, and their sin; for they did unto thee evil: and now, we pray thee, forgive the trespass of the servants of the God of thy father. And Joseph wept when they spake unto him.

18 And his brethren also went and fell down before his face; and they said, Behold, we *be* thy servants.

19 And Joseph said unto them, Fear not: for *am* I in the place of God?

20 But as for you, ye thought evil against me; *but* God meant it unto good, to bring to pass, as *it is* this day, to save much people alive.

21 Now therefore fear ye not: I will nourish you, and your little ones. And he comforted them, and spake kindly unto them.

22 ¶ And Joseph dwelt in Egypt, he, and his father's house: and Joseph lived a hundred and ten years.

23 And Joseph saw Ē'phrā-ĭm's children of the third *generation:* the children also of Mā'chĭr the son of Mȧ-năs'sĕh were brought up upon Joseph's knees.

24 And Joseph said unto his brethren, I die; and God will surely visit you, and bring you out of this land unto the land which he sware to Abraham, to Isaac, and to Jacob.

25 And Joseph took an oath of the children of Ĭş'rā-ĕl, saying, God will surely visit you, and ye shall carry up my bones from hence.

26 So Joseph died, *being* a hundred and ten years old: and they embalmed him, and he was put in a coffin in Egypt.

THE SECOND BOOK OF MOSES, CALLED

EXODUS

CHAPTER 1

NOW these *are* the names of the children of Ĭş'rā-ĕl, which came into Egypt; every man and his household came with Jacob.

2 Reuben, Simeon, Levi, and Judah,

3 Ĭs'sȧ-chär, Zĕb'ū-lŭn, and Benjamin,

4 Dan, and Năph'tȧ-lī, Gad, and Ăsh'ẽr.

5 And all the souls that came out of the loins of Jacob were seventy souls: for Joseph was in Egypt *already*.

6 And Joseph died, and all his brethren, and all that generation.

7 ¶ And the children of Ĭş'rā-ĕl were fruitful, and increased abundantly, and multiplied, and waxed exceeding mighty; and the land was filled with them.

8 Now there arose up a new king over Egypt, which knew not Joseph.

9 And he said unto his people, Behold, the people of the children of Ĭş'rā-ĕl *are* more and mightier than we:

10 Come on, let us deal wisely with them; lest they multiply, and it come to pass, that, when there falleth out any war, they join also unto our enemies, and fight against us, and *so* get them up out of the land.

11 Therefore they did set over them taskmasters to afflict them with their burdens. And they built for Phā'raōh treasure cities, Pī'thŏm and Rā'ăm-sēş.

12 But the more they afflicted them, the more they multiplied and grew. And they were grieved because of the children of Ĭş'rā-ĕl.

13 And the Egyptians made the children of Ĭş'rā-ĕl to serve with rigor:

14 And they made their lives bitter with hard bondage, in mortar, and in brick, and in all manner of service in the field: all their service, wherein they made them serve, *was* with rigor.

15 ¶ And the king of Egypt spake to the Hebrew midwives, of which the name of the one *was* Shĭph'rȧh, and the name of the other Pū'ȧh;

16 And he said, When ye do the office

of a midwife to the Hebrew women, and see *them* upon the stools, if it *be* a son, then ye shall kill him; but if it *be* a daughter, then she shall live.

17 But the midwives feared God, and did not as the king of Egypt commanded them, but saved the men children alive.

18 And the king of Egypt called for the midwives, and said unto them, Why have ye done this thing, and have saved the men children alive?

19 And the midwives said unto Phā′raōh, Because the Hebrew women *are* not as the Egyptian women; for they *are* lively, and are delivered ere the midwives come in unto them.

20 Therefore God dealt well with the midwives: and the people multiplied, and waxed very mighty.

21 And it came to pass, because the midwives feared God, that he made them houses.

22 And Phā′raōh charged all his people, saying, Every son that is born ye shall cast into the river, and every daughter ye shall save alive.

CHAPTER 2

AND there went a man of the house of Levi, and took *to wife* a daughter of Levi.

2 And the woman conceived, and bare a son: and when she saw him that he *was* a goodly *child,* she hid him three months.

3 And when she could not longer hide him, she took for him an ark of bulrushes, and daubed it with slime and with pitch, and put the child therein; and she laid *it* in the flags by the river's brink.

4 And his sister stood afar off, to wit what would be done to him.

5 ℂ And the daughter of Phā′raōh came down to wash *herself* at the river; and her maidens walked along by the river's side: and when she saw the ark among the flags, she sent her maid to fetch it.

6 And when she had opened *it,* she saw the child: and, behold, the babe wept. And she had compassion on him, and said, This *is one* of the Hebrews' children.

7 Then said his sister to Phā′raōh's daughter, Shall I go and call to thee a nurse of the Hebrew women, that she may nurse the child for thee?

8 And Phā′raōh's daughter said to her, Go. And the maid went and called the child's mother.

9 And Phā′raōh's daughter said unto her, Take this child away, and nurse it for me, and I will give *thee* thy wages. And the woman took the child, and nursed it.

10 And the child grew, and she brought him unto Phā′raōh's daughter, and he became her son. And she called his name Moses: and she said, Because I drew him out of the water.

11 ℂ And it came to pass in those days, when Moses was grown, that he went out unto his brethren, and looked on their burdens: and he spied an Egyptian smiting a Hebrew, one of his brethren.

12 And he looked this way and that way, and when he saw that *there was* no man, he slew the Egyptian, and hid him in the sand.

13 And when he went out the second day, behold, two men of the Hebrews strove together: and he said to him that did the wrong, Wherefore smitest thou thy fellow?

14 And he said, Who made thee a prince and a judge over us? intendest thou to kill me, as thou killedst the Egyptian? And Moses feared, and said, Surely this thing is known.

15 Now when Phā′raōh heard this thing, he sought to slay Moses. But Moses fled from the face of Phā′raōh, and dwelt in the land of Mĭd′ĭ-ăn: and he sat down by a well.

16 Now the priest of Mĭd′ĭ-ăn had seven daughters: and they came and drew *water,* and filled the troughs to water their father's flock.

17 And the shepherds came and drove them away: but Moses stood up and helped them, and watered their flock.

18 And when they came to Reu′ĕl their father, he said, How *is it that* ye are come so soon to-day?

19 And they said, An Egyptian delivered us out of the hand of the shepherds, and also drew *water* enough for us, and watered the flock.

20 And he said unto his daughters, And where *is* he? why *is* it *that* ye have left the man? call him, that he may eat bread.

21 And Moses was content to dwell with the man: and he gave Moses Zĭp-pō′rah his daughter.

22 And she bare *him* a son, and he
called his name Gẽr′shŏm: for he said,
I have been a stranger in a strange land.
23 ¶ And it came to pass in process of
time, that the king of Egypt died: and
the children of Ĭş′rā-ĕl sighed by reason
of the bondage, and they cried, and their
cry came up unto God by reason of the
bondage.
24 And God heard their groaning, and
God remembered his covenant with
Abraham, with Isaac, and with Jacob.
25 And God looked upon the children
of Ĭş′rā-ĕl, and God had respect unto
them.

CHAPTER 3

NOW Moses kept the flock of Jethro
his father-in-law, the priest of
Mĭd′ĭ-ăn: and he led the flock to the
back side of the desert, and came to the
mountain of God, *even* to Hō′rĕb.
2 And the Angel of the LORD appeared
unto him in a flame of fire out of the
midst of a bush: and he looked, and,
behold, the bush burned with fire, and
the bush *was* not consumed.
3 And Moses said, I will now turn
aside, and see this great sight, why the
bush is not burnt.
4 And when the LORD saw that he
turned aside to see, God called unto
him out of the midst of the bush, and
said, Moses, Moses. And he said, Here
am I.
5 And he said, Draw not nigh hither:
put off thy shoes from off thy feet; for
the place whereon thou standest *is* holy
ground.
6 Moreover he said, I *am* the God of
thy father, the God of Abraham, the
God of Isaac, and the God of Jacob.
And Moses hid his face; for he was
afraid to look upon God.
7 ¶ And the LORD said, I have surely
seen the affliction of my people which
are in Egypt, and have heard their cry
by reason of their taskmasters; for I
know their sorrows;
8 And I am come down to deliver them
out of the hand of the Egyptians, and to
bring them up out of that land unto a
good land and a large, unto a land flowing with milk and honey; unto the place
of the Că′năan-ītes, and the Hĭt′tītes,
and the Ăm′ō-rītes, and the Pĕr′ĭz-zītes,
and the Hī′vītes, and the Jĕb′ū-şītes.
9 Now therefore, behold, the cry of the
children of Ĭş′rā-ĕl is come unto me:
and I have also seen the oppression
wherewith the Egyptians oppress them.
10 Come now therefore, and I will send
thee unto Phā′raōh, that thou mayest
bring forth my people the children of
Ĭş′rā-ĕl out of Egypt.
11 ¶ And Moses said unto God, Who
am I, that I should go unto Phā′raōh,
and that I should bring forth the children of Ĭş′rā-ĕl out of Egypt?
12 And he said, Certainly I will be with
thee; and this *shall be* a token unto thee,
that I have sent thee: When thou hast
brought forth the people out of Egypt,
ye shall serve God upon this mountain.
13 And Moses said unto God, Behold,
when I come unto the children of Ĭş′-
rā-ĕl, and shall say unto them, The God
of your fathers hath sent me unto you;
and they shall say to me, What *is* his
name? what shall I say unto them?
14 And God said unto Moses, I AM
THAT I AM: and he said, Thus shalt
thou say unto the children of Ĭş′rā-ĕl,
I AM hath sent me unto you.
15 And God said moreover unto Moses,
Thus shalt thou say unto the children of
Ĭş′rā-ĕl, The LORD God of your fathers,
the God of Abraham, the God of Isaac,
and the God of Jacob, hath sent me
unto you: this *is* my name for ever, and
this *is* my memorial unto all generations.
16 Go, and gather the elders of Ĭş′rā-ĕl
together, and say unto them, The LORD
God of your fathers, the God of Abraham, of Isaac, and of Jacob, appeared
unto me, saying, I have surely visited
you, and *seen* that which is done to you
in Egypt:
17 And I have said, I will bring you up
out of the affliction of Egypt unto the
land of the Că′năan ītes, and the Hĭt′-
tītes, and the Ăm′ō-rītes, and the Pĕr′-
ĭz-zītes, and the Hī′vītes, and the Jĕb′ū-
şītes, unto a land flowing with milk and
honey.
18 And they shall hearken to thy voice:
and thou shalt come, thou and the elders
of Ĭş′rā-ĕl, unto the king of Egypt, and
ye shall say unto him, The LORD God of
the Hebrews hath met with us: and now
let us go, we beseech thee, three days'
journey into the wilderness, that we
may sacrifice to the LORD our God.
19 ¶ And I am sure that the king of
Egypt will not let you go, no, not by a
mighty hand.

20 And I will stretch out my hand, and
smite Egypt with all my wonders which
I will do in the midst thereof: and after
that he will let you go.
21 And I will give this people favor in
the sight of the Egyptians: and it shall
come to pass, that, when ye go, ye shall
not go empty:
22 But every woman shall borrow of
her neighbor, and of her that sojourneth
in her house, jewels of silver, and jewels
of gold, and raiment: and ye shall put
them upon your sons, and upon your
daughters; and ye shall spoil the
Egyptians.

CHAPTER 4

AND Moses answered and said, But,
behold, they will not believe me,
nor hearken unto my voice: for they
will say, The LORD hath not appeared
unto thee.
2 And the LORD said unto him, What *is*
that in thine hand? And he said, A rod.
3 And he said, Cast it on the ground.
And he cast it on the ground, and it became a serpent; and Moses fled from
before it.
4 And the LORD said unto Moses, Put
forth thine hand, and take it by the tail.
And he put forth his hand, and caught it,
and it became a rod in his hand:
5 That they may believe that the LORD
God of their fathers, the God of Abraham, the God of Isaac, and the God of
Jacob, hath appeared unto thee.
6 ¶ And the LORD said furthermore
unto him, Put now thine hand into thy
bosom. And he put his hand into his
bosom: and when he took it out, behold,
his hand *was* leprous as snow.
7 And he said, Put thine hand into thy
bosom again. And he put his hand into
his bosom again; and plucked it out of
his bosom, and, behold, it was turned
again as his *other* flesh.
8 And it shall come to pass, if they will
not believe thee, neither hearken to the
voice of the first sign, that they will believe the voice of the latter sign.
9 And it shall come to pass, if they will
not believe also these two signs, neither
hearken unto thy voice, that thou shalt
take of the water of the river, and pour
it upon the dry *land:* and the water
which thou takest out of the river shall
become blood upon the dry *land.*
10 ¶ And Moses said unto the LORD,
O my Lord, I *am* not eloquent, neither
heretofore, nor since thou hast spoken
unto thy servant; but I *am* slow of
speech, and of a slow tongue.
11 And the LORD said unto him, Who
hath made man's mouth? or who maketh the dumb, or deaf, or the seeing, or
the blind? have not I the LORD?
12 Now therefore go, and I will be with
thy mouth, and teach thee what thou
shalt say.
13 And he said, O my Lord, send, I
pray thee, by the hand *of him whom*
thou wilt send.
14 And the anger of the LORD was
kindled against Moses, and he said, *Is*
not Aaron the Lē'vīte thy brother? I
know that he can speak well. And also,
behold, he cometh forth to meet thee:
and when he seeth thee, he will be glad
in his heart.
15 And thou shalt speak unto him, and
put words in his mouth: and I will be
with thy mouth, and with his mouth, and
will teach you what ye shall do.
16 And he shall be thy spokesman unto
the people: and he shall be, *even* he
shall be to thee instead of a mouth, and
thou shalt be to him instead of God.
17 And thou shalt take this rod in thine
hand, wherewith thou shalt do signs.
18 ¶ And Moses went and returned to
Jethro his father-in-law, and said unto
him, Let me go, I pray thee, and return
unto my brethren which *are* in Egypt,
and see whether they be yet alive. And
Jethro said to Moses, Go in peace.
19 And the LORD said unto Moses in
Mĭd'ĭ-ăn, Go, return into Egypt: for all
the men are dead which sought thy
life.
20 And Moses took his wife and his
sons, and set them upon an ass, and he
returned to the land of Egypt: and
Moses took the rod of God in his hand.
21 And the LORD said unto Moses,
When thou goest to return into Egypt,
see that thou do all those wonders before Phā'raōh, which I have put in thine
hand: but I will harden his heart, that
he shall not let the people go.
22 And thou shalt say unto Phā'raōh,
Thus saith the LORD, Ĭṣ'rā-ĕl *is* my son,
even my firstborn:
23 And I say unto thee, Let my son go,
that he may serve me: and if thou refuse
to let him go, behold, I will slay thy son,
even thy firstborn.

24 ℂ And it came to pass by the way in
the inn, that the LORD met him, and
sought to kill him.
25 Then Zĭp-pō′rȧh took a sharp stone,
and cut off the foreskin of her son, and
cast *it* at his feet, and said, Surely a
bloody husband *art* thou to me.
26 So he let him go: then she said, A
bloody husband *thou art*, because of the
circumcision.
27 ℂ And the LORD said to Aaron, Go
into the wilderness to meet Moses. And
he went, and met him in the mount of
God, and kissed him.
28 And Moses told Aaron all the words
of the LORD who had sent him, and all
the signs which he had commanded
him.
29 ℂ And Moses and Aaron went and
gathered together all the elders of the
children of Ĭṣ′rā-ĕl:
30 And Aaron spake all the words
which the LORD had spoken unto Moses,
and did the signs in the sight of the
people.
31 And the people believed: and when
they heard that the LORD had visited
the children of Ĭṣ′rā-ĕl, and that he had
looked upon their affliction, then they
bowed their heads and worshipped.

CHAPTER 5

AND afterward Moses and Aaron went
in, and told Phā′raōh, Thus saith
the LORD God of Ĭṣ′rā-ĕl, Let my people
go, that they may hold a feast unto me
in the wilderness.
2 And Phā′raōh said, Who *is* the LORD,
that I should obey his voice to let Ĭṣ′-
rā-ĕl go? I know not the LORD, neither
will I let Ĭṣ′rā-ĕl go.
3 And they said, The God of the Hebrews hath met with us: let us go, we
pray thee, three days' journey into the
desert, and sacrifice unto the LORD our
God; lest he fall upon us with pestilence,
or with the sword.
4 And the king of Egypt said unto them,
Wherefore do ye, Moses and Aaron, let
the people from their works? get you
unto your burdens.
5 And Phā′raōh said, Behold, the people of the land now *are* many, and ye
make them rest from their burdens.
6 And Phā′raōh commanded the same
day the taskmasters of the people, and
their officers, saying,
7 Ye shall no more give the people
straw to make brick, as heretofore: let
them go and gather straw for themselves.
8 And the tale of the bricks, which they
did make heretofore, ye shall lay upon
them; ye shall not diminish *aught* thereof: for they *be* idle; therefore they cry,
saying, Let us go *and* sacrifice to our
God.
9 Let there more work be laid upon the
men, that they may labor therein; and let
them not regard vain words.
10 ℂ And the taskmasters of the people went out, and their officers, and they
spake to the people, saying, Thus saith
Phā′raōh, I will not give you straw.
11 Go ye, get you straw where ye can
find it: yet not aught of your work shall
be diminished.
12 So the people were scattered abroad
throughout all the land of Egypt to
gather stubble instead of straw.
13 And the taskmasters hasted *them*,
saying, Fulfil your works, *your* daily
tasks, as when there was straw.
14 And the officers of the children of
Ĭṣ′rā-ĕl, which Phā′raōh's taskmasters
had set over them, were beaten, *and*
demanded, Wherefore have ye not fulfilled your task in making brick both
yesterday and to-day, as heretofore?
15 ℂ Then the officers of the children
of Ĭṣ′rā-ĕl came and cried unto Phā′-
raōh, saying, Wherefore dealest thou
thus with thy servants?
16 There is no straw given unto thy
servants, and they say to us, Make
brick: and, behold, thy servants *are*
beaten; but the fault *is* in thine own
people.
17 But he said, Ye *are* idle, *ye are* idle:
therefore ye say, Let us go *and* do sacrifice to the LORD.
18 Go therefore now, *and* work; for
there shall no straw be given you, yet
shall ye deliver the tale of bricks.
19 And the officers of the children of
Ĭṣ′rā-ĕl did see *that* they *were* in evil
case, after it was said, Ye shall not min-
ish *aught* from your bricks of your daily
task.
20 ℂ And they met Moses and Aaron,
who stood in the way, as they came forth
from Phā′raōh:
21 And they said unto them, The LORD
look upon you, and judge; because ye
have made our savor to be abhorred in
the eyes of Phā′raōh, and in the eyes of

his servants, to put a sword in their hand to slay us.

22 And Moses returned unto the LORD, and said, Lord, wherefore hast thou *so* evil entreated this people? why *is* it *that* thou hast sent me?

23 For since I came to Phā′raōh to speak in thy name, he hath done evil to this people; neither hast thou delivered thy people at all.

CHAPTER 6

THEN the LORD said unto Moses, Now shalt thou see what I will do to Phā′raōh: for with a strong hand shall he let them go, and with a strong hand shall he drive them out of his land.

2 And God spake unto Moses, and said unto him, I *am* the LORD:

3 And I appeared unto Abraham, unto Isaac, and unto Jacob, by *the name of* God Almighty; but by my name JEHOVAH was I not known to them.

4 And I have also established my covenant with them, to give them the land of Cā′năan, the land of their pilgrimage, wherein they were strangers.

5 And I have also heard the groaning of the children of Ĭş′rā-ĕl, whom the Egyptians keep in bondage; and I have remembered my covenant.

6 Wherefore say unto the children of Ĭş′rā-ĕl, I *am* the LORD, and I will bring you out from under the burdens of the Egyptians, and I will rid you out of their bondage, and I will redeem you with a stretched out arm, and with great judgments:

7 And I will take you to me for a people, and I will be to you a God: and ye shall know that I *am* the LORD your God, which bringeth you out from under the burdens of the Egyptians.

8 And I will bring you in unto the land, concerning the which I did swear to give it to Abraham, to Isaac, and to Jacob; and I will give it you for a heritage: I *am* the LORD.

9 ℂ And Moses spake so unto the children of Ĭş′rā-ĕl: but they hearkened not unto Moses for anguish of spirit, and for cruel bondage.

10 And the LORD spake unto Moses, saying,

11 Go in, speak unto Phā′raōh king of Egypt, that he let the children of Ĭş′rā-ĕl go out of his land.

12 And Moses spake before the LORD, saying, Behold, the children of Ĭş′rā-ĕl have not hearkened unto me; how then shall Phā′raōh hear me, who *am* of uncircumcised lips?

13 And the LORD spake unto Moses and unto Aaron, and gave them a charge unto the children of Ĭş′rā-ĕl, and unto Phā′raōh king of Egypt, to bring the children of Ĭş′rā-ĕl out of the land of Egypt.

14 ℂ These *be* the heads of their fathers' houses: The sons of Reuben the firstborn of Ĭş′rā-ĕl; Hā′nŏch, and Păl′lū, Hĕz′rŏn, and Cär′mī: these *be* the families of Reuben.

15 And the sons of Simeon; Jē-mū′ĕl, and Jā′mĭn, and Ō′hăd, and Jā′chĭn, and Zō′här, and Shā′ŭl the son of a Cā′năanīt′ĭsh woman: these *are* the families of Simeon.

16 ℂ And these *are* the names of the sons of Levi according to their generations; Gēr′shŏn, and Kō′hăth, and Mē-rā′rī: and the years of the life of Levi *were* a hundred thirty and seven years.

17 The sons of Gēr′shŏn; Lĭb′nī, and Shĭm′ī, according to their families.

18 And the sons of Kō′hăth; Ăm′răm, and Ĭz′här, and Hē′brŏn, and Ŭz-zī′ĕl: and the years of the life of Kō′hăth *were* a hundred thirty and three years.

19 And the sons of Mē-rā′rī; Mā′hȧ-lī and Mū′shī: these *are* the families of Levi according to their generations.

20 And Ăm′răm took him Jŏch′ē-bĕd his father's sister to wife; and she bare him Aaron and Moses: and the years of the life of Ăm′răm *were* a hundred and thirty and seven years.

21 ℂ And the sons of Ĭz′här; Kō′rȧh, and Nē′phĕg, and Zĭch′rī.

22 And the sons of Ŭz-zī′ĕl; Mĭsh′ā-ĕl, and Ĕl-zā′phăn, and Zĭth′rī.

23 And Aaron took him Ē-lĭsh′ē-bä, daughter of Ȧm-mĭn′ȧ-dăb, sister of Nā-ăsh′ŏn, to wife; and she bare him Nā′dăb and Ȧ-bī′hū, Ĕl′ē-ā′zȧr and Ĭth′ȧ-mär.

24 And the sons of Kō′rȧh; Ăs′sĭr, and Ĕl-kā′nȧh, and Ȧ-bī′ȧ-săph: these *are* the families of the Kôr′hītes.

25 And Ĕl′ē-ā′zȧr Aaron's son took him *one* of the daughters of Pū′tĭ-ĕl to wife; and she bare him Phĭn′ē-hăs: these *are* the heads of the fathers of the Lē′vītes according to their families.

26 These *are* that Aaron and Moses, to whom the LORD said, Bring out the chil-

dren of Ĭş'rā-ĕl from the land of Egypt
according to their armies.
27 These *are* they which spake to Phā'-
raōh king of Egypt, to bring out the children of Ĭş'rā-ĕl from Egypt: these *are* that
Moses and Aaron.
28 ¶ And it came to pass on the day
when the LORD spake unto Moses in the
land of Egypt,
29 That the LORD spake unto Moses,
saying, I *am* the LORD: speak thou unto
Phā'raōh king of Egypt all that I say
unto thee.
30 And Moses said before the LORD,
Behold, I *am* of uncircumcised lips, and
how shall Phā'raōh hearken unto me?

CHAPTER 7

AND the LORD said unto Moses, See,
I have made thee a god to Phā'-
raōh; and Aaron thy brother shall be thy
prophet.
2 Thou shalt speak all that I command
thee; and Aaron thy brother shall speak
unto Phā'raōh, that he send the children
of Ĭş'rā-ĕl out of his land.
3 And I will harden Phā'raōh's heart,
and multiply my signs and my wonders
in the land of Egypt.
4 But Phā'raōh shall not hearken unto
you, that I may lay my hand upon Egypt,
and bring forth mine armies, *and* my
people the children of Ĭş'rā-ĕl, out of the
land of Egypt by great judgments.
5 And the Egyptians shall know that I
am the LORD, when I stretch forth mine
hand upon Egypt, and bring out the children of Ĭş'rā-ĕl from among them.
6 And Moses and Aaron did as the
LORD commanded them, so did they.
7 And Moses *was* fourscore years old,
and Aaron fourscore and three years old,
when they spake unto Phā'raōh.
8 ¶ And the LORD spake unto Moses
and unto Aaron, saying,
9 When Phā'raōh shall speak unto you,
saying, Show a miracle for you: then
thou shalt say unto Aaron, Take thy rod,
and cast *it* before Phā'raōh, *and* it shall
become a serpent.
10 ¶ And Moses and Aaron went in
unto Phā'raōh, and they did so as the
LORD had commanded: and Aaron cast
down his rod before Phā'raōh, and before his servants, and it became a serpent.
11 Then Phā'raōh also called the wise
men and the sorcerers: now the magicians of Egypt, they also did in like manner with their enchantments.
12 For they cast down every man his
rod, and they became serpents: but
Aaron's rod swallowed up their rods.
13 And he hardened Phā'raōh's heart,
that he hearkened not unto them; as the
LORD had said.
14 ¶ And the LORD said unto Moses,
Phā'raōh's heart *is* hardened, he refuseth to let the people go.
15 Get thee unto Phā'raōh in the morning; lo, he goeth out unto the water; and
thou shalt stand by the river's brink
against he come; and the rod which was
turned to a serpent shalt thou take in
thine hand.
16 And thou shalt say unto him, The
LORD God of the Hebrews hath sent me
unto thee, saying, Let my people go, that
they may serve me in the wilderness:
and, behold, hitherto thou wouldest not
hear.
17 Thus saith the LORD, In this thou
shalt know that I *am* the LORD: behold,
I will smite with the rod that *is* in mine
hand upon the waters which *are* in
the river, and they shall be turned to
blood.
18 And the fish that *is* in the river shall
die, and the river shall stink; and the
Egyptians shall loathe to drink of the
water of the river.
19 ¶ And the LORD spake unto Moses,
Say unto Aaron, Take thy rod, and
stretch out thine hand upon the waters
of Egypt, upon their streams, upon their
rivers, and upon their ponds, and upon
all their pools of water, that they may
become blood; and *that* there may be
blood throughout all the land of Egypt,
both in *vessels of* wood, and in *vessels
of* stone.
20 And Moses and Aaron did so, as the
LORD commanded; and he lifted up the
rod, and smote the waters that *were* in
the river, in the sight of Phā'raōh, and
in the sight of his servants; and all the
waters that *were* in the river were
turned to blood.
21 And the fish that *was* in the river
died; and the river stank, and the Egyptians could not drink of the water of the
river; and there was blood throughout
all the land of Egypt.
22 And the magicians of Egypt did so
with their enchantments: and Phā'-
raōh's heart was hardened, neither did

he hearken unto them; as the LORD had
said.
23 And Phā'raōh turned and went into
his house, neither did he set his heart to
this also.
24 And all the Egyptians digged round
about the river for water to drink; for
they could not drink of the water of the
river.
25 And seven days were fulfilled, after
that the LORD had smitten the river.

CHAPTER 8

AND the LORD spake unto Moses, Go
unto Phā'raōh, and say unto him,
Thus saith the LORD, Let my people go,
that they may serve me.
2 And if thou refuse to let *them* go, behold, I will smite all thy borders with
frogs:
3 And the river shall bring forth frogs
abundantly, which shall go up and come
into thine house, and into thy bedchamber, and upon thy bed, and into the
house of thy servants, and upon thy
people, and into thine ovens, and into
thy kneadingtroughs:
4 And the frogs shall come up both on
thee, and upon thy people, and upon all
thy servants.
5 ¶ And the LORD spake unto Moses,
Say unto Aaron, Stretch forth thine hand
with thy rod over the streams, over the
rivers, and over the ponds, and cause
frogs to come up upon the land of Egypt.
6 And Aaron stretched out his hand
over the waters of Egypt; and the frogs
came up, and covered the land of Egypt.
7 And the magicians did so with their
enchantments, and brought up frogs
upon the land of Egypt.
8 ¶ Then Phā'raōh called for Moses
and Aaron, and said, Entreat the LORD,
that he may take away the frogs from
me, and from my people; and I will let
the people go, that they may do sacrifice
unto the LORD.
9 And Moses said unto Phā'raōh, Glory
over me: when shall I entreat for thee,
and for thy servants, and for thy people,
to destroy the frogs from thee and thy
houses, *that* they may remain in the
river only?
10 And he said, To-morrow. And he
said, *Be it* according to thy word; that
thou mayest know that *there is* none like
unto the LORD our God.
11 And the frogs shall depart from thee,
and from thy houses, and from thy servants, and from thy people; they shall remain in the river only.
12 And Moses and Aaron went out from
Phā'raōh: and Moses cried unto the
LORD because of the frogs which he had
brought against Phā'raōh.
13 And the LORD did according to the
word of Moses; and the frogs died out
of the houses, out of the villages, and
out of the fields.
14 And they gathered them together
upon heaps; and the land stank.
15 But when Phā'raōh saw that there
was respite, he hardened his heart, and
hearkened not unto them; as the LORD
had said.
16 ¶ And the LORD said unto Moses,
Say unto Aaron, Stretch out thy rod,
and smite the dust of the land, that it
may become lice throughout all the
land of Egypt.
17 And they did so; for Aaron stretched
out his hand with his rod, and smote the
dust of the earth, and it became lice in
man, and in beast; all the dust of the
land became lice throughout all the land
of Egypt.
18 And the magicians did so with their
enchantments to bring forth lice, but
they could not: so there were lice upon
man, and upon beast.
19 Then the magicians said unto Phā'-
raōh, This *is* the finger of God: and Phā'-
raōh's heart was hardened, and he
hearkened not unto them; as the LORD
had said.
20 ¶ And the LORD said unto Moses,
Rise up early in the morning, and stand
before Phā'raōh; lo, he cometh forth to
the water; and say unto him, Thus saith
the LORD, Let my people go, that they
may serve me.
21 Else, if thou wilt not let my people
go, behold, I will send swarms of flies
upon thee, and upon thy servants, and
upon thy people, and into thy houses:
and the houses of the Egyptians shall be
full of swarms of flies, and also the
ground whereon they *are*.
22 And I will sever in that day the land
of Gō'shĕn, in which my people dwell,
that no swarms of flies shall be there; to
the end thou mayest know that I *am* the
LORD in the midst of the earth.
23 And I will put a division between my
people and thy people: to-morrow shall
this sign be.

24 And the LORD did so; and there
came a grievous swarm of flies into the
house of Phā'raōh, and *into* his servants' houses, and into all the land of
Egypt: the land was corrupted by reason
of the swarm of flies.
25 ℂ And Phā'raōh called for Moses
and for Aaron, and said, Go ye, sacrifice
to your God in the land.
26 And Moses said, It is not meet so to
do; for we shall sacrifice the abomination of the Egyptians to the LORD our
God: lo, shall we sacrifice the abomination of the Egyptians before their eyes,
and will they not stone us?
27 We will go three days' journey into
the wilderness, and sacrifice to the LORD
our God, as he shall command us.
28 And Phā'raōh said, I will let you go,
that ye may sacrifice to the LORD your
God in the wilderness; only ye shall not
go very far away: entreat for me.
29 And Moses said, Behold, I go out
from thee, and I will entreat the LORD
that the swarms of flies may depart from
Phā'raōh, from his servants, and from
his people, to-morrow: but let not Phā'-
raōh deal deceitfully any more in not
letting the people go to sacrifice to the
LORD.
30 And Moses went out from Phā'raōh,
and entreated the LORD.
31 And the LORD did according to the
word of Moses; and he removed the
swarms of flies from Phā'raōh, from his
servants, and from his people; there
remained not one.
32 And Phā'raōh hardened his heart at
this time also, neither would he let the
people go.

CHAPTER 9

THEN the LORD said unto Moses,
Go in unto Phā'raōh, and tell him,
Thus saith the LORD God of the Hebrews, Let my people go, that they may
serve me.
2 For if thou refuse to let *them* go, and
wilt hold them still,
3 Behold, the hand of the LORD is upon
thy cattle which *is* in the field, upon the
horses, upon the asses, upon the camels,
upon the oxen, and upon the sheep:
there shall be a very grievous murrain.
4 And the LORD shall sever between
the cattle of Ĭş'rā-ĕl and the cattle of
Egypt: and there shall nothing die of all
that is the children's of Ĭş'rā-ĕl.
5 And the LORD appointed a set time,
saying, To-morrow the LORD shall do
this thing in the land.
6 And the LORD did that thing on the
morrow, and all the cattle of Egypt died:
but of the cattle of the children of Ĭş'-
rā-ĕl died not one.
7 And Phā'raōh sent, and, behold, there
was not one of the cattle of the Ĭş'rā-
ĕl-ītes dead. And the heart of Phā'raōh
was hardened, and he did not let the
people go.
8 ℂ And the LORD said unto Moses
and unto Aaron, Take to you handfuls
of ashes of the furnace, and let Moses
sprinkle it toward the heaven in the
sight of Phā'raōh.
9 And it shall become small dust in all
the land of Egypt, and shall be a boil
breaking forth *with* blains upon man,
and upon beast, throughout all the land
of Egypt.
10 And they took ashes of the furnace,
and stood before Phā'raōh; and Moses
sprinkled it up toward heaven; and it
became a boil breaking forth *with* blains
upon man, and upon beast.
11 And the magicians could not stand
before Moses because of the boils; for
the boil was upon the magicians, and
upon all the Egyptians.
12 And the LORD hardened the heart
of Phā'raōh, and he hearkened not unto
them; as the LORD had spoken unto
Moses.
13 ℂ And the LORD said unto Moses,
Rise up early in the morning, and stand
before Phā'raōh, and say unto him,
Thus saith the LORD God of the Hebrews, Let my people go, that they may
serve me.
14 For I will at this time send all my
plagues upon thine heart, and upon thy
servants, and upon thy people; that thou
mayest know that *there is* none like me
in all the earth.
15 For now I will stretch out my hand,
that I may smite thee and thy people
with pestilence; and thou shalt be cut
off from the earth.
16 And in very deed for this *cause* have
I raised thee up, for to show *in* thee my
power; and that my name may be declared throughout all the earth.
17 As yet exaltest thou thyself against
my people, that thou wilt not let them
go?
18 Behold, to-morrow about this time

I will cause it to rain a very grievous
hail, such as hath not been in Egypt
since the foundation thereof even until
now.
19 Send therefore now, *and* gather thy
cattle, and all that thou hast in the field;
for upon every man and beast which
shall be found in the field, and shall not
be brought home, the hail shall come
down upon them, and they shall die.
20 He that feared the word of the LORD
among the servants of Phā′raōh made
his servants and his cattle flee into the
houses:
21 And he that regarded not the word
of the LORD left his servants and his
cattle in the field.
22 ℂ And the LORD said unto Moses,
Stretch forth thine hand toward heaven,
that there may be hail in all the land of
Egypt, upon man, and upon beast, and
upon every herb of the field, throughout
the land of Egypt.
23 And Moses stretched forth his rod
toward heaven: and the LORD sent
thunder and hail, and the fire ran along
upon the ground; and the LORD rained
hail upon the land of Egypt.
24 So there was hail, and fire mingled
with the hail, very grievous, such as
there was none like it in all the land of
Egypt since it became a nation.
25 And the hail smote throughout all
the land of Egypt all that *was* in the
field, both man and beast; and the hail
smote every herb of the field, and brake
every tree of the field.
26 Only in the land of Gō′shĕn, where
the children of Ĭṣ′rā-ĕl *were*, was there
no hail.
27 ℂ And Phā′raōh sent, and called
for Moses and Aaron, and said unto
them, I have sinned this time: the LORD
is righteous, and I and my people *are*
wicked.
28 Entreat the LORD (for *it is* enough)
that there be no *more* mighty thunderings and hail; and I will let you go, and
ye shall stay no longer.
29 And Moses said unto him, As soon
as I am gone out of the city, I will spread
abroad my hands unto the LORD; *and*
the thunder shall cease, neither shall
there be any more hail; that thou mayest
know how that the earth *is* the LORD'S.
30 But as for thee and thy servants, I
know that ye will not yet fear the LORD
God.
31 And the flax and the barley was
smitten: for the barley *was* in the ear,
and the flax *was* bolled.
32 But the wheat and the rye were not
smitten: for they *were* not grown up.
33 And Moses went out of the city from
Phā′raōh, and spread abroad his hands
unto the LORD: and the thunders and
hail ceased, and the rain was not poured
upon the earth.
34 And when Phā′raōh saw that the
rain and the hail and the thunders were
ceased, he sinned yet more, and hardened his heart, he and his servants.
35 And the heart of Phā′raōh was hardened, neither would he let the children
of Ĭṣ′rā-ĕl go; as the LORD had spoken
by Moses.

CHAPTER 10

AND the LORD said unto Moses, Go
in unto Phā′raōh: for I have hardened his heart, and the heart of his servants, that I might show these my signs
before him:
2 And that thou mayest tell in the ears
of thy son, and of thy son's son, what
things I have wrought in Egypt, and my
signs which I have done among them;
that ye may know how that I *am* the
LORD.
3 And Moses and Aaron came in unto
Phā′raōh, and said unto him, Thus saith
the LORD God of the Hebrews, How
long wilt thou refuse to humble thyself
before me? let my people go, that they
may serve me.
4 Else, if thou refuse to let my people
go, behold, to-morrow will I bring the
locusts into thy coast:
5 And they shall cover the face of the
earth, that one cannot be able to see the
earth: and they shall eat the residue of
that which is escaped, which remaineth
unto you from the hail, and shall eat
every tree which groweth for you out of
the field:
6 And they shall fill thy houses, and
the houses of all thy servants, and the
houses of all the Egyptians; which
neither thy fathers, nor thy fathers'
fathers have seen, since the day that
they were upon the earth unto this day.
And he turned himself, and went out
from Phā′raōh.
7 And Phā′raōh's servants said unto
him, How long shall this man be a snare
unto us? let the men go, that they may

serve the LORD their God: knowest
thou not yet that Egypt is destroyed?
8 And Moses and Aaron were brought
again unto Phā'raōh: and he said unto
them, Go, serve the LORD your God:
but who *are* they that shall go?
9 And Moses said, We will go with our
young and with our old, with our sons
and with our daughters, with our flocks
and with our herds will we go; for we
must hold a feast unto the LORD.
10 And he said unto them, Let the
LORD be so with you, as I will let you
go, and your little ones: look *to it;* for
evil *is* before you.
11 Not so: go now ye *that are* men, and
serve the LORD; for that ye did desire.
And they were driven out from Phā'-
raōh's presence.
12 ¶ And the LORD said unto Moses,
Stretch out thine hand over the land of
Egypt for the locusts, that they may
come up upon the land of Egypt, and eat
every herb of the land, *even* all that the
hail hath left.
13 And Moses stretched forth his rod
over the land of Egypt, and the LORD
brought an east wind upon the land all
that day, and all *that* night; *and* when it
was morning, the east wind brought the
locusts.
14 And the locusts went up over all the
land of Egypt, and rested in all the
coasts of Egypt: very grievous *were
they;* before them there were no such
locusts as they, neither after them shall
be such.
15 For they covered the face of the
whole earth, so that the land was darkened; and they did eat every herb of the
land, and all the fruit of the trees which
the hail had left: and there remained not
any green thing in the trees, or in the
herbs of the field, through all the land of
Egypt.
16 ¶ Then Phā'raōh called for Moses
and Aaron in haste; and he said, I have
sinned against the LORD your God, and
against you.
17 Now therefore forgive, I pray thee,
my sin only this once, and entreat the
LORD your God, that he may take away
from me this death only.
18 And he went out from Phā'raōh, and
entreated the LORD.
19 And the LORD turned a mighty
strong west wind, which took away the
locusts, and cast them into the Red sea;
there remained not one locust in all the
coasts of Egypt.
20 But the LORD hardened Phā'raōh's
heart, so that he would not let the children of Is'ra-ĕl go.
21 ¶ And the LORD said unto Moses,
Stretch out thine hand toward heaven,
that there may be darkness over the
land of Egypt, even darkness *which*
may be felt.
22 And Moses stretched forth his hand
toward heaven; and there was a thick
darkness in all the land of Egypt three
days:
23 They saw not one another, neither
rose any from his place for three days:
but all the children of Is'rā-ĕl had light
in their dwellings.
24 ¶ And Phā'raōh called unto Moses,
and said, Go ye, serve the LORD; only
let your flocks and your herds be stayed:
let your little ones also go with you.
25 And Moses said, Thou must give us
also sacrifices and burnt offerings, that
we may sacrifice unto the LORD our
God.
26 Our cattle also shall go with us;
there shall not a hoof be left behind; for
thereof must we take to serve the LORD
our God; and we know not with what we
must serve the LORD, until we come
thither.
27 ¶ But the LORD hardened Phā'-
raōh's heart, and he would not let
them go.
28 And Phā'raōh said unto him, Get
thee from me, take heed to thyself, see
my face no more; for in *that* day thou
seest my face thou shalt die.
29 And Moses said, Thou hast spoken
well, I will see thy face again no more.

CHAPTER 11

AND the LORD said unto Moses, Yet
will I bring one plague *more* upon
Phā'raōh, and upon Egypt; afterward he
will let you go hence: when he shall let
you go, he shall surely thrust you out
hence altogether.
2 Speak now in the ears of the people,
and let every man borrow of his neighbor, and every woman of her neighbor,
jewels of silver, and jewels of gold.
3 And the LORD gave the people favor
in the sight of the Egyptians. Moreover,
the man Moses *was* very great in the
land of Egypt, in the sight of Phā'raōh's
servants, and in the sight of the people.

4 And Moses said, Thus saith the LORD, About midnight will I go out into the midst of Egypt:

5 And all the firstborn in the land of Egypt shall die, from the firstborn of Phā′raōh that sitteth upon his throne, even unto the firstborn of the maidservant that *is* behind the mill; and all the firstborn of beasts.

6 And there shall be a great cry throughout all the land of Egypt, such as there was none like it, nor shall be like it any more.

7 But against any of the children of Ĭṣ′rā-ĕl shall not a dog move his tongue, against man or beast: that ye may know how that the LORD doth put a difference between the Egyptians and Ĭṣ′rā-ĕl.

8 And all these thy servants shall come down unto me, and bow down themselves unto me, saying, Get thee out, and all the people that follow thee: and after that I will go out. And he went out from Phā′raōh in a great anger.

9 And the LORD said unto Moses, Phā′raōh shall not hearken unto you; that my wonders may be multiplied in the land of Egypt.

10 And Moses and Aaron did all these wonders before Phā′raōh: and the LORD hardened Phā′raōh's heart, so that he would not let the children of Ĭṣ′rā-ĕl go out of his land.

CHAPTER 12

AND the LORD spake unto Moses and Aaron in the land of Egypt, saying,

2 This month *shall be* unto you the beginning of months: it *shall be* the first month of the year to you.

3 ℂ Speak ye unto all the congregation of Ĭṣ′rā-ĕl, saying, In the tenth *day* of this month they shall take to them every man a lamb, according to the house of *their* fathers, a lamb for a house:

4 And if the household be too little for the lamb, let him and his neighbor next unto his house take *it* according to the number of the souls; every man according to his eating shall make your count for the lamb.

5 Your lamb shall be without blemish, a male of the first year: ye shall take *it* out from the sheep, or from the goats:

6 And ye shall keep it up until the fourteenth day of the same month: and the whole assembly of the congregation of Ĭṣ′rā-ĕl shall kill it in the evening.

7 And they shall take of the blood, and strike *it* on the two side posts and on the upper doorpost of the houses, wherein they shall eat it.

8 And they shall eat the flesh in that night, roast with fire, and unleavened bread; *and* with bitter *herbs* they shall eat it.

9 Eat not of it raw, nor sodden at all with water, but roast *with* fire; his head with his legs, and with the purtenance thereof.

10 And ye shall let nothing of it remain until the morning; and that which remaineth of it until the morning ye shall burn with fire.

11 ℂ And thus shall ye eat it; *with* your loins girded, your shoes on your feet, and your staff in your hand; and ye shall eat it in haste: it *is* the LORD's passover.

12 For I will pass through the land of Egypt this night, and will smite all the firstborn in the land of Egypt, both man and beast; and against all the gods of Egypt I will execute judgment: I *am* the LORD.

13 And the blood shall be to you for a token upon the houses where ye *are:* and when I see the blood, I will pass over you, and the plague shall not be upon you to destroy *you,* when I smite the land of Egypt.

14 And this day shall be unto you for a memorial; and ye shall keep it a feast to the LORD throughout your generations: ye shall keep it a feast by an ordinance for ever.

15 Seven days shall ye eat unleavened bread; even the first day ye shall put away leaven out of your houses: for whosoever eateth leavened bread from the first day until the seventh day, that soul shall be cut off from Ĭṣ′rā-ĕl.

16 And in the first day *there shall be* a holy convocation, and in the seventh day there shall be a holy convocation to you; no manner of work shall be done in them, save *that* which every man must eat, that only may be done of you.

17 And ye shall observe *the feast of* unleavened bread; for in this selfsame day have I brought your armies out of the land of Egypt: therefore shall ye observe this day in your generations by an ordinance for ever.

18 ℂ In the first *month,* on the four-

teenth day of the month at even, ye shall
eat unleavened bread, until the one and
twentieth day of the month at even.
19 Seven days shall there be no leaven
found in your houses: for whosoever eateth that which is leavened, even that
soul shall be cut off from the congregation of Ĭs̱'rā-ĕl, whether he be a stranger,
or born in the land.
20 Ye shall eat nothing leavened; in all
your habitations shall ye eat unleavened
bread.
21 ¶ Then Moses called for all the
elders of Ĭs̱'rā-ĕl, and said unto them,
Draw out and take you a lamb according
to your families, and kill the passover.
22 And ye shall take a bunch of hyssop,
and dip *it* in the blood that *is* in the basin, and strike the lintel and the two side
posts with the blood that *is* in the basin;
and none of you shall go out at the door
of his house until the morning.
23 For the LORD will pass through to
smite the Egyptians; and when he seeth
the blood upon the lintel, and on the two
side posts, the LORD will pass over the
door, and will not suffer the destroyer to
come in unto your houses to smite *you.*
24 And ye shall observe this thing for
an ordinance to thee and to thy sons for
ever.
25 And it shall come to pass, when ye
be come to the land which the LORD will
give you, according as he hath promised,
that ye shall keep this service.
26 And it shall come to pass, when your
children shall say unto you, What mean
ye by this service?
27 That ye shall say, It *is* the sacrifice
of the LORD's passover, who passed
over the houses of the children of Ĭs̱'-
rā-ĕl in Egypt, when he smote the Egyptians, and delivered our houses. And
the people bowed the head and worshipped.
28 And the children of Ĭs̱'rā-ĕl went
away, and did as the LORD had commanded Moses and Aaron, so did they.
29 ¶ And it came to pass, that at midnight the LORD smote all the firstborn
in the land of Egypt, from the firstborn
of Phā'raōh that sat on his throne unto
the firstborn of the captive that *was* in
the dungeon; and all the firstborn of
cattle.
30 And Phā'raōh rose up in the night,
he, and all his servants, and all the
Egyptians; and there was a great cry in
Egypt: for *there was* not a house where
there was not one dead.
31 ¶ And he called for Moses and
Aaron by night, and said, Rise up, *and*
get you forth from among my people,
both ye and the children of Ĭs̱'rā-ĕl; and
go, serve the LORD, as ye have said.
32 Also take your flocks and your
herds, as ye have said, and be gone; and
bless me also.
33 And the Egyptians were urgent upon
the people, that they might send them
out of the land in haste; for they said,
We *be* all dead *men.*
34 And the people took their dough before it was leavened, their kneadingtroughs being bound up in their clothes
upon their shoulders.
35 And the children of Ĭs̱'rā-ĕl did according to the word of Moses; and they
borrowed of the Egyptians jewels of silver, and jewels of gold, and raiment:
36 And the LORD gave the people favor
in the sight of the Egyptians, so that
they lent unto them *such things as they
required:* and they spoiled the Egyptians.
37 ¶ And the children of Ĭs̱'rā-ĕl journeyed from Răm'ē-sēs̱ to Sŭc'cōth,
about six hundred thousand on foot *that
were* men, beside children.
38 And a mixed multitude went up also
with them; and flocks, and herds, *even*
very much cattle.
39 And they baked unleavened cakes
of the dough which they brought forth
out of Egypt, for it was not leavened; because they were thrust out of Egypt, and
could not tarry, neither had they prepared for themselves any victuals.
40 ¶ Now the sojourning of the children of Ĭs̱'rā-ĕl, who dwelt in Egypt,
was four hundred and thirty years.
41 And it came to pass at the end of the
four hundred and thirty years, even the
selfsame day it came to pass, that all the
hosts of the LORD went out from the land
of Egypt.
42 It *is* a night to be much observed
unto the LORD for bringing them out
from the land of Egypt: this *is* that night
of the LORD to be observed of all the
children of Ĭs̱'rā-ĕl in their generations.
43 ¶ And the LORD said unto Moses
and Aaron, This *is* the ordinance of the
passover: There shall no stranger eat
thereof:
44 But every man's servant that is

bought for money, when thou hast circumcised him, then shall he eat thereof.
45 A foreigner and a hired servant shall
not eat thereof.
46 In one house shall it be eaten; thou
shalt not carry forth aught of the flesh
abroad out of the house; neither shall ye
break a bone thereof.
47 All the congregation of Ĭṣ′rā-ĕl shall
keep it.
48 And when a stranger shall sojourn
with thee, and will keep the passover to
the LORD, let all his males be circumcised, and then let him come near and
keep it; and he shall be as one that is
born in the land: for no uncircumcised
person shall eat thereof.
49 One law shall be to him that is
homeborn, and unto the stranger that
sojourneth among you.
50 Thus did all the children of Ĭṣ′rā-ĕl;
as the LORD commanded Moses and
Aaron, so did they.
51 And it came to pass the selfsame
day, *that* the LORD did bring the children of Ĭṣ′rā-ĕl out of the land of Egypt
by their armies.

CHAPTER 13

AND the LORD spake unto Moses,
saying,
2 Sanctify unto me all the firstborn,
whatsoever openeth the womb among
the children of Ĭṣ′rā-ĕl, *both* of man and
of beast: it *is* mine.
3 ¶ And Moses said unto the people,
Remember this day, in which ye came
out from Egypt, out of the house of
bondage; for by strength of hand the
LORD brought you out from this *place:*
there shall no leavened bread be
eaten.
4 This day came ye out in the month
Ā′bĭb.
5 ¶ And it shall be when the LORD
shall bring thee into the land of the Cā′-
năan-ītes, and the Hĭt′tītes, and the
Ăm′ō-rītes, and the Hī′vītes, and the
Jĕb′ū-ṣītes, which he sware unto thy
fathers to give thee, a land flowing with
milk and honey, that thou shalt keep
this service in this month.
6 Seven days thou shalt eat unleavened
bread, and in the seventh day *shall be*
a feast to the LORD.
7 Unleavened bread shall be eaten
seven days; and there shall no leavened
bread be seen with thee, neither shall
there be leaven seen with thee in all thy
quarters.
8 ¶ And thou shalt show thy son in
that day, saying, *This is done* because
of that *which* the LORD did unto me
when I came forth out of Egypt.
9 And it shall be for a sign unto thee
upon thine hand, and for a memorial between thine eyes, that the LORD's law
may be in thy mouth: for with a strong
hand hath the LORD brought thee out of
Egypt.
10 Thou shalt therefore keep this ordinance in his season from year to year.
11 ¶ And it shall be when the LORD
shall bring thee into the land of the Cā′-
năan-ītes, as he sware unto thee and to
thy fathers, and shall give it thee,
12 That thou shalt set apart unto the
LORD all that openeth the matrix, and
every firstling that cometh of a beast
which thou hast; the male *shall be* the
LORD's.
13 And every firstling of an ass thou
shalt redeem with a lamb; and if thou
wilt not redeem it, then thou shalt break
his neck: and all the firstborn of man
among thy children shalt thou redeem.
14 ¶ And it shall be when thy son asketh thee in time to come, saying, What
is this? that thou shalt say unto him, By
strength of hand the LORD brought us
out from Egypt, from the house of
bondage:
15 And it came to pass, when Phā′raōh
would hardly let us go, that the LORD
slew all the firstborn in the land of
Egypt, both the firstborn of man, and
the firstborn of beast: therefore I sacrifice to the LORD all that openeth the
matrix, being males; but all the firstborn
of my children I redeem.
16 And it shall be for a token upon thine
hand, and for frontlets between thine
eyes: for by strength of hand the LORD
brought us forth out of Egypt.
17 ¶ And it came to pass, when Phā′-
raōh had let the people go, that God led
them not *through* the way of the land of
the Phĭ-lĭs′tīneṣ, although that *was* near;
for God said, Lest peradventure the people repent when they see war, and they
return to Egypt:
18 But God led the people about,
through the way of the wilderness of the
Red sea: and the children of Ĭṣ′rā-ĕl
went up harnessed out of the land of
Egypt.

19 And Moses took the bones of Joseph
with him: for he had straitly sworn the
children of Ĭṣ′rā-ĕl, saying, God will
surely visit you; and ye shall carry up
my bones away hence with you.
20 ¶ And they took their journey from
Sŭc′cŏth, and encamped in Ē′thăm, in
the edge of the wilderness.
21 And the LORD went before them by
day in a pillar of a cloud, to lead them
the way; and by night in a pillar of fire,
to give them light; to go by day and
night.
22 He took not away the pillar of the
cloud by day, nor the pillar of fire by
night, *from* before the people.

CHAPTER 14

AND the LORD spake unto Moses,
saying,
2 Speak unto the children of Ĭṣ′rā-ĕl,
that they turn and encamp before Pī′-
hȧ-hī′rŏth, between Mĭg′dŏl and the
sea, over against Bā′ăl-zē′phŏn: before
it shall ye encamp by the sea.
3 For Phā′raōh will say of the children
of Ĭṣ′rā-ĕl, They *are* entangled in the
land, the wilderness hath shut them in.
4 And I will harden Phā′raōh's heart,
that he shall follow after them; and I
will be honored upon Phā′raōh, and upon all his host; that the Egyptians may
know that I *am* the LORD. And they
did so.
5 ¶ And it was told the king of Egypt
that the people fled: and the heart of
Phā′raōh and of his servants was turned
against the people, and they said, Why
have we done this, that we have let Ĭṣ′-
rā-ĕl go from serving us?
6 And he made ready his chariot, and
took his people with him:
7 And he took six hundred chosen
chariots, and all the chariots of Egypt,
and captains over every one of them.
8 And the LORD hardened the heart of
Phā′raōh king of Egypt, and he pursued
after the children of Ĭṣ′rā-ĕl: and the
children of Ĭṣ′rā-ĕl went out with a high
hand.
9 But the Egyptians pursued after
them, all the horses *and* chariots of Phā′-
raōh, and his horsemen, and his army,
and overtook them encamping by the
sea, beside Pī′-hȧ-hī′rŏth, before Bā′-
ăl-zē′phŏn.
10 ¶ And when Phā′raōh drew
nigh, the children of Ĭṣ′rā-ĕl lifted up
their eyes, and, behold, the Egyptians
marched after them; and they were sore
afraid: and the children of Ĭṣ′rā-ĕl cried
out unto the LORD.
11 And they said unto Moses, Because
there were no graves in Egypt, hast thou
taken us away to die in the wilderness?
wherefore hast thou dealt thus with us,
to carry us forth out of Egypt?
12 *Is* not this the word that we did tell
thee in Egypt, saying, Let us alone, that
we may serve the Egyptians? For *it had
been* better for us to serve the Egyptians, than that we should die in the
wilderness.
13 ¶ And Moses said unto the people,
Fear ye not, stand still, and see the salvation of the LORD, which he will show
to you to-day: for the Egyptians whom
ye have seen to-day, ye shall see them
again no more for ever.
14 The LORD shall fight for you, and ye
shall hold your peace.
15 ¶ And the LORD said unto Moses,
Wherefore criest thou unto me? speak
unto the children of Ĭṣ′rā-ĕl, that they
go forward:
16 But lift thou up thy rod, and stretch
out thine hand over the sea, and divide
it: and the children of Ĭṣ′rā-ĕl shall go
on dry *ground* through the midst of the
sea.
17 And I, behold, I will harden the
hearts of the Egyptians, and they shall
follow them: and I will get me honor
upon Phā′raōh, and upon all his host,
upon his chariots, and upon his horsemen.
18 And the Egyptians shall know that I
am the LORD, when I have gotten me
honor upon Phā′raōh, upon his chariots,
and upon his horsemen.
19 ¶ And the Angel of God, which
went before the camp of Ĭṣ′rā-ĕl, removed and went behind them; and the
pillar of the cloud went from before
their face, and stood behind them:
20 And it came between the camp of
the Egyptians and the camp of Ĭṣ′rā-ĕl;
and it was a cloud and darkness *to
them,* but it gave light by night *to these:*
so that the one came not near the other
all the night.
21 And Moses stretched out his hand
over the sea; and the LORD caused the
sea to go *back* by a strong east wind all
that night, and made the sea dry *land,*
and the waters were divided.

22 And the children of Ĭş′rā-ĕl went into the midst of the sea upon the dry *ground:* and the waters *were* a wall unto them on their right hand, and on their left.

23 ¶ And the Egyptians pursued, and went in after them to the midst of the sea, *even* all Phā′raōh's horses, his chariots, and his horsemen.

24 And it came to pass, that in the morning watch the LORD looked unto the host of the Egyptians through the pillar of fire and of the cloud, and troubled the host of the Egyptians,

25 And took off their chariot wheels, that they drave them heavily: so that the Egyptians said, Let us flee from the face of Ĭş′rā-ĕl; for the LORD fighteth for them against the Egyptians.

26 ¶ And the LORD said unto Moses, Stretch out thine hand over the sea, that the waters may come again upon the Egyptians, upon their chariots, and upon their horsemen.

27 And Moses stretched forth his hand over the sea, and the sea returned to his strength when the morning appeared; and the Egyptians fled against it; and the LORD overthrew the Egyptians in the midst of the sea.

28 And the waters returned, and covered the chariots, and the horsemen, *and* all the host of Phā′raōh that came into the sea after them; there remained not so much as one of them.

29 But the children of Ĭş′rā-ĕl walked upon dry *land* in the midst of the sea; and the waters *were* a wall unto them on their right hand, and on their left.

30 Thus the LORD saved Ĭş′rā-ĕl that day out of the hand of the Egyptians; and Ĭş′rā-ĕl saw the Egyptians dead upon the seashore.

31 And Ĭş′rā-ĕl saw that great work which the LORD did upon the Egyptians: and the people feared the LORD, and believed the LORD, and his servant Moses.

CHAPTER 15

THEN sang Moses and the children of Ĭş′rā-ĕl this song unto the LORD, and spake, saying, I will sing unto the LORD, for he hath triumphed gloriously: the horse and his rider hath he thrown into the sea.

2 The LORD *is* my strength and song, and he is become my salvation: he *is* my God, and I will prepare him a habitation; my father's God, and I will exalt him.

3 The LORD *is* a man of war: the LORD *is* his name.

4 Phā′raōh's chariots and his host hath he cast into the sea: his chosen captains also are drowned in the Red sea.

5 The depths have covered them: they sank into the bottom as a stone.

6 Thy right hand, O LORD, is become glorious in power: thy right hand, O LORD, hath dashed in pieces the enemy.

7 And in the greatness of thine excellency thou hast overthrown them that rose up against thee: thou sentest forth thy wrath, *which* consumed them as stubble.

8 And with the blast of thy nostrils the waters were gathered together, the floods stood upright as a heap, *and* the depths were congealed in the heart of the sea.

9 The enemy said, I will pursue, I will overtake, I will divide the spoil; my lust shall be satisfied upon them; I will draw my sword, my hand shall destroy them.

10 Thou didst blow with thy wind, the sea covered them: they sank as lead in the mighty waters.

11 Who *is* like unto thee, O LORD, among the gods? who *is* like thee, glorious in holiness, fearful *in* praises, doing wonders?

12 Thou stretchedst out thy right hand, the earth swallowed them.

13 Thou in thy mercy hast led forth the people *which* thou hast redeemed: thou hast guided *them* in thy strength unto thy holy habitation.

14 The people shall hear, *and* be afraid: sorrow shall take hold on the inhabitants of Păl′ĕs-tī′nȧ.

15 Then the dukes of Ē′dŏm shall be amazed; the mighty men of Mō′ăb, trembling shall take hold upon them; all the inhabitants of Cā′năan shall melt away.

16 Fear and dread shall fall upon them; by the greatness of thine arm they shall be *as* still as a stone; till thy people pass over, O LORD, till the people pass over, *which* thou hast purchased.

17 Thou shalt bring them in, and plant them in the mountain of thine inheritance, *in* the place, O LORD, *which* thou hast made for thee to dwell in; *in* the Sanctuary, O LORD, *which* thy hands have established.

18 The LORD shall reign for ever and
ever.
19 For the horse of Phā'raōh went in
with his chariots and with his horsemen
into the sea, and the LORD brought
again the waters of the sea upon them;
but the children of Ĭş'rā-ĕl went on dry
land in the midst of the sea.
20 ¶ And Miriam the prophetess, the
sister of Aaron, took a timbrel in her
hand; and all the women went out after
her with timbrels and with dances.
21 And Miriam answered them, Sing
ye to the LORD, for he hath triumphed
gloriously: the horse and his rider hath
he thrown into the sea.
22 So Moses brought Ĭş'rā-ĕl from the
Red sea, and they went out into the wilderness of Shụr; and they went three
days in the wilderness, and found no
water.
23 ¶ And when they came to Mā'rȧh,
they could not drink of the waters of
Mā'rȧh, for they *were* bitter: therefore
the name of it was called Mā'rȧh.
24 And the people murmured against
Moses, saying, What shall we drink?
25 And he cried unto the LORD; and
the LORD showed him a tree, *which*
when he had cast into the waters, the
waters were made sweet: there he made
for them a statute and an ordinance,
and there he proved them,
26 And said, If thou wilt diligently
hearken to the voice of the LORD thy
God, and wilt do that which is right in
his sight, and wilt give ear to his commandments, and keep all his statutes, I
will put none of these diseases upon
thee, which I have brought upon the
Egyptians: for I *am* the LORD that
healeth thee.
27 ¶ And they came to Ē'lĭm, where
were twelve wells of water, and threescore and ten palm trees: and they encamped there by the waters.

CHAPTER 16

AND they took their journey from
Ē'lĭm, and all the congregation of
the children of Ĭş'rā-ĕl came unto the
wilderness of Sin, which *is* between
Ē'lĭm and Sī'naī, on the fifteenth day of
the second month after their departing
out of the land of Egypt.
2 And the whole congregation of the
children of Ĭş'rā-ĕl murmured against
Moses and Aaron in the wilderness:
3 And the children of Ĭş'rā-ĕl said unto
them, Would to God we had died by the
hand of the LORD in the land of Egypt,
when we sat by the fleshpots, *and* when
we did eat bread to the full: for ye have
brought us forth into this wilderness, to
kill this whole assembly with hunger.
4 ¶ Then said the LORD unto Moses,
Behold, I will rain bread from heaven
for you; and the people shall go out and
gather a certain rate every day, that I
may prove them, whether they will walk
in my law, or no.
5 And it shall come to pass, that on the
sixth day they shall prepare *that* which
they bring in; and it shall be twice as
much as they gather daily.
6 And Moses and Aaron said unto all
the children of Ĭş'rā-ĕl, At even, then ye
shall know that the LORD hath brought
you out from the land of Egypt:
7 And in the morning, then ye shall
see the glory of the LORD; for that he
heareth your murmurings against the
LORD: and what *are* we, that ye murmur
against us?
8 And Moses said, *This shall be,* when
the LORD shall give you in the evening
flesh to eat, and in the morning bread to
the full; for that the LORD heareth your
murmurings which ye murmur against
him: and what *are* we? your murmurings
are not against us, but against the LORD.
9 ¶ And Moses spake unto Aaron, Say
unto all the congregation of the children
of Ĭş'rā-ĕl, Come near before the LORD:
for he hath heard your murmurings.
10 And it came to pass, as Aaron spake
unto the whole congregation of the children of Ĭş'rā-ĕl, that they looked toward
the wilderness, and, behold, the glory of
the LORD appeared in the cloud.
11 ¶ And the LORD spake unto Moses,
saying,
12 I have heard the murmurings of the
children of Ĭş'rā-ĕl: speak unto them,
saying, At even ye shall eat flesh, and
in the morning ye shall be filled with
bread; and ye shall know that I *am* the
LORD your God.
13 And it came to pass, that at even the
quails came up, and covered the camp:
and in the morning the dew lay round
about the host.
14 And when the dew that lay was gone
up, behold, upon the face of the wilderness *there lay* a small round thing, *as*
small as the hoar frost on the ground.

15 And when the children of Ĭş′rā-ĕl saw *it,* they said one to another, It *is* manna: for they wist not what it *was.* And Moses said unto them, This *is* the bread which the LORD hath given you to eat.

16 ¶ This *is* the thing which the LORD hath commanded, Gather of it every man according to his eating, an omer for every man, *according to* the number of your persons; take ye every man for *them* which *are* in his tents.

17 And the children of Ĭş′rā-ĕl did so, and gathered, some more, some less.

18 And when they did mete *it* with an omer, he that gathered much had nothing over, and he that gathered little had no lack; they gathered every man according to his eating.

19 And Moses said, Let no man leave of it till the morning.

20 Notwithstanding they hearkened not unto Moses; but some of them left of it until the morning, and it bred worms, and stank: and Moses was wroth with them.

21 And they gathered it every morning, every man according to his eating: and when the sun waxed hot, it melted.

22 ¶ And it came to pass, *that* on the sixth day they gathered twice as much bread, two omers for one *man:* and all the rulers of the congregation came and told Moses.

23 And he said unto them, This *is that* which the LORD hath said, To-morrow *is* the rest of the holy sabbath unto the LORD: bake *that* which ye will bake *to-day,* and seethe that ye will seethe; and that which remaineth over lay up for you to be kept until the morning.

24 And they laid it up till the morning, as Moses bade: and it did not stink, neither was there any worm therein.

25 And Moses said, Eat that to-day; for to-day *is* a sabbath unto the LORD: to-day ye shall not find it in the field.

26 Six days ye shall gather it; but on the seventh day, *which is* the sabbath, in it there shall be none.

27 ¶ And it came to pass, *that* there went out *some* of the people on the seventh day for to gather, and they found none.

28 And the LORD said unto Moses, How long refuse ye to keep my commandments and my laws?

29 See, for that the LORD hath given you the sabbath, therefore he giveth you on the sixth day the bread of two days: abide ye every man in his place, let no man go out of his place on the seventh day.

30 So the people rested on the seventh day.

31 And the house of Ĭş′rā-ĕl called the name thereof Manna: and it *was* like coriander seed, white; and the taste of it *was* like wafers *made* with honey.

32 ¶ And Moses said, This *is* the thing which the LORD commandeth, Fill an omer of it to be kept for your generations; that they may see the bread wherewith I have fed you in the wilderness, when I brought you forth from the land of Egypt.

33 And Moses said unto Aaron, Take a pot, and put an omer full of manna therein, and lay it up before the LORD, to be kept for your generations.

34 As the LORD commanded Moses, so Aaron laid it up before the Testimony, to be kept.

35 And the children of Ĭş′rā-ĕl did eat manna forty years, until they came to a land inhabited: they did eat manna, until they came unto the borders of the land of Cā′năan.

36 Now an omer *is* the tenth *part* of an ē′phäh.

CHAPTER 17

AND all the congregation of the children of Ĭş′rā-ĕl journeyed from the wilderness of Sin, after their journeys, according to the commandment of the LORD, and pitched in Rĕph′ĭ-dĭm: and *there was* no water for the people to drink.

2 Wherefore the people did chide with Moses, and said, Give us water that we may drink. And Moses said unto them, Why chide ye with me? wherefore do ye tempt the LORD?

3 And the people thirsted there for water; and the people murmured against Moses, and said, Wherefore *is* this *that* thou hast brought us up out of Egypt, to kill us and our children and our cattle with thirst?

4 And Moses cried unto the LORD, saying, What shall I do unto this people? they be almost ready to stone me.

5 And the LORD said unto Moses, Go on before the people, and take with thee of the elders of Ĭş′rā-ĕl; and thy rod,

wherewith thou smotest the river, take
in thine hand, and go.
6 Behold, I will stand before thee there
upon the rock in Hō'rĕb; and thou shalt
smite the rock, and there shall come
water out of it, that the people may
drink. And Moses did so in the sight of
the elders of Ĭs'rā-ĕl.
7 And he called the name of the place
Măs'sȧh, and Mĕr'ĭ-băh, because of the
chiding of the children of Ĭs'rā-ĕl, and
because they tempted the LORD, saying,
Is the LORD among us, or not?
8 ¶ Then came Ăm'ȧ-lĕk, and fought
with Ĭs'rā-ĕl in Rĕph'ĭ-dĭm.
9 And Moses said unto Joshua, Choose
us out men, and go out, fight with Ăm'ȧ-
lĕk: to-morrow I will stand on the top of
the hill with the rod of God in mine
hand.
10 So Joshua did as Moses had said to
him, and fought with Ăm'ȧ-lĕk: and
Moses, Aaron, and Hûr went up to the
top of the hill.
11 And it came to pass, when Moses
held up his hand, that Ĭs'rā-ĕl prevailed:
and when he let down his hand, Ăm'ȧ-
lĕk prevailed.
12 But Moses' hands *were* heavy; and
they took a stone, and put *it* under him,
and he sat thereon; and Aaron and Hûr
stayed up his hands, the one on the one
side and the other on the other side; and
his hands were steady until the going
down of the sun.
13 And Joshua discomfited Ăm'ȧ-lĕk
and his people with the edge of the
sword.
14 And the LORD said unto Moses,
Write this *for* a memorial in a book, and
rehearse *it* in the ears of Joshua: for I
will utterly put out the remembrance of
Ăm'ȧ-lĕk from under heaven.
15 And Moses built an altar, and called
the name of it Jehovah–nĭs'sī:
16 For he said, Because the LORD hath
sworn *that* the LORD *will have* war with
Ăm'ȧ-lĕk from generation to generation.

CHAPTER 18

WHEN Jethro, the priest of Mĭd'-
ĭ-ăn, Moses' father-in-law, heard
of all that God had done for Moses, and
for Ĭs'rā-ĕl his people, *and* that the LORD
had brought Ĭs'rā-ĕl out of Egypt;
2 Then Jethro, Moses' father-in-law,
took Zĭp-pō'rȧh, Moses' wife, after he
had sent her back,
3 And her two sons; of which the name
of the one *was* Gĕr'shŏm; for he said, I
have been an alien in a strange land:
4 And the name of the other *was* Ĕl'ĭ-ē'-
zĕr; for the God of my father, *said he*,
was mine help, and delivered me from
the sword of Phā'raōh:
5 And Jethro, Moses' father-in-law,
came with his sons and his wife unto
Moses into the wilderness, where he
encamped at the mount of God:
6 And he said unto Moses, I thy father-
in-law Jethro am come unto thee, and
thy wife, and her two sons with her.
7 ¶ And Moses went out to meet his
father-in-law, and did obeisance, and
kissed him; and they asked each other
of *their* welfare; and they came into the
tent.
8 And Moses told his father-in-law all
that the LORD had done unto Phā'raōh
and to the Egyptians for Ĭs'rā-ĕl's sake,
and all the travail that had come upon
them by the way, and *how* the LORD delivered them.
9 And Jethro rejoiced for all the goodness which the LORD had done to Ĭs'-
rā-ĕl, whom he had delivered out of the
hand of the Egyptians.
10 And Jethro said, Blessed *be* the
LORD, who hath delivered you out of the
hand of the Egyptians, and out of the
hand of Phā'raōh, who hath delivered
the people from under the hand of the
Egyptians.
11 Now I know that the LORD *is* greater
than all gods: for in the thing wherein
they dealt proudly *he was* above them.
12 And Jethro, Moses' father-in-law,
took a burnt offering and sacrifices for
God: and Aaron came, and all the elders
of Ĭs'rā-ĕl, to eat bread with Moses'
father-in-law before God.
13 ¶ And it came to pass on the morrow, that Moses sat to judge the people:
and the people stood by Moses from the
morning unto the evening.
14 And when Moses' father-in-law saw
all that he did to the people, he said,
What *is* this thing that thou doest to the
people? Why sittest thou thyself alone,
and all the people stand by thee from
morning unto even?
15 And Moses said unto his father-in-
law, Because the people come unto me
to inquire of God:
16 When they have a matter, they come
unto me; and I judge between one and

another, and I do make *them* know the
statutes of God, and his laws.
17 And Moses' father-in-law said unto
him, The thing that thou doest *is* not
good.
18 Thou wilt surely wear away, both
thou, and this people that *is* with thee:
for this thing *is* too heavy for thee; thou
art not able to perform it thyself alone.
19 Hearken now unto my voice, I will
give thee counsel, and God shall be with
thee: Be thou for the people to God-
ward, that thou mayest bring the causes
unto God:
20 And thou shalt teach them ordinances and laws, and shalt show them
the way wherein they must walk, and
the work that they must do.
21 Moreover thou shalt provide out of
all the people able men, such as fear
God, men of truth, hating covetousness;
and place *such* over them, *to be* rulers
of thousands, *and* rulers of hundreds,
rulers of fifties, and rulers of tens:
22 And let them judge the people at
all seasons: and it shall be, *that* every
great matter they shall bring unto thee,
but every small matter they shall judge:
so shall it be easier for thyself, and they
shall bear *the burden* with thee.
23 If thou shalt do this thing, and God
command thee *so,* then thou shalt be
able to endure, and all this people shall
also go to their place in peace.
24 So Moses hearkened to the voice of
his father-in-law, and did all that he had
said.
25 And Moses chose able men out of
all Ĭṣ′rā-ĕl, and made them heads over
the people, rulers of thousands, rulers
of hundreds, rulers of fifties, and rulers
of tens.
26 And they judged the people at all
seasons: the hard causes they brought
unto Moses, but every small matter
they judged themselves.
27 ℂ And Moses let his father-in-law
depart; and he went his way into his
own land.

CHAPTER 19

IN the third month, when the children
of Ĭṣ′rā-ĕl were gone forth out of the
land of Egypt, the same day came they
into the wilderness of Sī′naī.
2 For they were departed from Rĕph′ĭ-
dĭm, and were come *to* the desert of
Sī′naī, and had pitched in the wilderness; and there Ĭṣ′rā-ĕl camped before
the mount.
3 And Moses went up unto God, and
the LORD called unto him out of the
mountain, saying, Thus shalt thou say
to the house of Jacob, and tell the children of Ĭṣ′rā-ĕl;
4 Ye have seen what I did unto the
Egyptians, and *how* I bare you on eagles'
wings, and brought you unto myself.
5 Now therefore, if ye will obey my
voice indeed, and keep my covenant,
then ye shall be a peculiar treasure unto
me above all people: for all the earth *is*
mine:
6 And ye shall be unto me a kingdom
of priests, and a holy nation. These *are*
the words which thou shalt speak unto
the children of Ĭṣ′rā-ĕl.
7 ℂ And Moses came and called for
the elders of the people, and laid before
their faces all these words which the
LORD commanded him.
8 And all the people answered together,
and said, All that the LORD hath spoken
we will do. And Moses returned the
words of the people unto the LORD.
9 And the LORD said unto Moses, Lo,
I come unto thee in a thick cloud, that
the people may hear when I speak with
thee, and believe thee for ever. And
Moses told the words of the people unto
the LORD.
10 ℂ And the LORD said unto Moses,
Go unto the people, and sanctify them
to-day and to-morrow, and let them
wash their clothes,
11 And be ready against the third day:
for the third day the LORD will come
down in the sight of all the people upon
mount Sī′naī.
12 And thou shalt set bounds unto the
people round about, saying, Take heed
to yourselves, *that ye* go *not* up into the
mount, or touch the border of it: whosoever toucheth the mount shall be surely
put to death:
13 There shall not a hand touch it, but
he shall surely be stoned, or shot
through; whether *it be* beast or man, it
shall not live: when the trumpet sound-
eth long, they shall come up to the
mount.
14 ℂ And Moses went down from the
mount unto the people, and sanctified
the people; and they washed their
clothes.
15 And he said unto the people, Be

ready against the third day: come not at *your* wives.

16 ¶ And it came to pass on the third day in the morning, that there were thunders and lightnings, and a thick cloud upon the mount, and the voice of the trumpet exceeding loud; so that all the people that *was* in the camp trembled.

17 And Moses brought forth the people out of the camp to meet with God; and they stood at the nether part of the mount.

18 And mount Sī′naī was altogether on a smoke, because the LORD descended upon it in fire: and the smoke thereof ascended as the smoke of a furnace, and the whole mount quaked greatly.

19 And when the voice of the trumpet sounded long, and waxed louder and louder, Moses spake, and God answered him by a voice.

20 And the LORD came down upon mount Sī′naī, on the top of the mount: and the LORD called Moses *up* to the top of the mount; and Moses went up.

21 And the LORD said unto Moses, Go down, charge the people, lest they break through unto the LORD to gaze, and many of them perish.

22 And let the priests also, which come near to the LORD, sanctify themselves, lest the LORD break forth upon them.

23 And Moses said unto the LORD, The people cannot come up to mount Sī′naī: for thou chargedst us, saying, Set bounds about the mount, and sanctify it.

24 And the LORD said unto him, Away, get thee down, and thou shalt come up, thou, and Aaron with thee: but let not the priests and the people break through to come up unto the LORD, lest he break forth upon them.

25 So Moses went down unto the people, and spake unto them.

CHAPTER 20

AND God spake all these words, saying,

2 I *am* the LORD thy God, which have brought thee out of the land of Egypt, out of the house of bondage.

3 Thou shalt have no other gods before me.

4 Thou shalt not make unto thee any graven image, or any likeness *of any thing* that *is* in heaven above, or that *is* in the earth beneath, or that *is* in the water under the earth:

5 Thou shalt not bow down thyself to them, nor serve them: for I the LORD thy God *am* a jealous God, visiting the iniquity of the fathers upon the children unto the third and fourth *generation* of them that hate me;

6 And showing mercy unto thousands of them that love me, and keep my commandments.

7 Thou shalt not take the name of the LORD thy God in vain: for the LORD will not hold him guiltless that taketh his name in vain.

8 Remember the sabbath day, to keep it holy.

9 Six days shalt thou labor, and do all thy work:

10 But the seventh day *is* the sabbath of the LORD thy God: *in it* thou shalt not do any work, thou, nor thy son, nor thy daughter, thy manservant, nor thy maidservant, nor thy cattle, nor thy stranger that *is* within thy gates:

11 For *in* six days the LORD made heaven and earth, the sea, and all that in them *is*, and rested the seventh day: wherefore the LORD blessed the sabbath day, and hallowed it.

12 ¶ Honor thy father and thy mother: that thy days may be long upon the land which the LORD thy God giveth thee.

13 Thou shalt not kill.

14 Thou shalt not commit adultery.

15 Thou shalt not steal.

16 Thou shalt not bear false witness against thy neighbor.

17 Thou shalt not covet thy neighbor's house, thou shalt not covet thy neighbor's wife, nor his manservant, nor his maidservant, nor his ox, nor his ass, nor any thing that *is* thy neighbor's.

18 ¶ And all the people saw the thunderings, and the lightnings, and the noise of the trumpet, and the mountain smoking: and when the people saw *it*, they removed, and stood afar off.

19 And they said unto Moses, Speak thou with us, and we will hear: but let not God speak with us, lest we die.

20 And Moses said unto the people, Fear not: for God is come to prove you, and that his fear may be before your faces, that ye sin not.

21 And the people stood afar off, and Moses drew near unto the thick darkness where God *was*.

22 ¶ And the LORD said unto Moses,
Thus thou shalt say unto the children of
Iṣ'rā-ĕl, Ye have seen that I have talked
with you from heaven.
23 Ye shall not make with me gods of
silver, neither shall ye make unto you
gods of gold.
24 ¶ An altar of earth thou shalt make
unto me, and shalt sacrifice thereon thy
burnt offerings, and thy peace offerings,
thy sheep, and thine oxen: in all places
where I record my name I will come
unto thee, and I will bless thee.
25 And if thou wilt make me an altar of
stone, thou shalt not build it of hewn
stone: for if thou lift up thy tool upon it,
thou hast polluted it.
26 Neither shalt thou go up by steps
unto mine altar, that thy nakedness be
not discovered thereon.

CHAPTER 21

NOW these *are* the judgments which
thou shalt set before them.
2 If thou buy a Hebrew servant, six
years he shall serve: and in the seventh
he shall go out free for nothing.
3 If he came in by himself, he shall go
out by himself: if he were married, then
his wife shall go out with him.
4 If his master have given him a wife,
and she have borne him sons or daughters; the wife and her children shall be
her master's, and he shall go out by
himself.
5 And if the servant shall plainly say,
I love my master, my wife, and my children; I will not go out free:
6 Then his master shall bring him unto
the judges; he shall also bring him to
the door, or unto the doorpost; and his
master shall bore his ear through with
an awl; and he shall serve him for ever.
7 ¶ And if a man sell his daughter to
be a maidservant, she shall not go out
as the menservants do.
8 If she please not her master, who
hath betrothed her to himself, then shall
he let her be redeemed: to sell her unto
a strange nation he shall have no power,
seeing he hath dealt deceitfully with her.
9 And if he have betrothed her unto his
son, he shall deal with her after the
manner of daughters.
10 If he take him another *wife*, her
food, her raiment, and her duty of marriage, shall he not diminish.
11 And if he do not these three unto
her, then shall she go out free without
money.
12 ¶ He that smiteth a man, so that he
die, shall be surely put to death.
13 And if a man lie not in wait, but God
deliver *him* into his hand; then I will appoint thee a place whither he shall flee.
14 But if a man come presumptuously
upon his neighbor, to slay him with
guile; thou shalt take him from mine
altar, that he may die.
15 ¶ And he that smiteth his father, or
his mother, shall be surely put to death.
16 ¶ And he that stealeth a man, and
selleth him, or if he be found in his
hand, he shall surely be put to death.
17 ¶ And he that curseth his father, or
his mother, shall surely be put to death.
18 ¶ And if men strive together, and
one smite another with a stone, or with
his fist, and he die not, but keepeth *his*
bed:
19 If he rise again, and walk abroad
upon his staff, then shall he that smote
him be quit: only he shall pay *for* the
loss of his time, and shall cause *him* to
be thoroughly healed.
20 ¶ And if a man smite his servant,
or his maid, with a rod, and he die under
his hand; he shall be surely punished.
21 Notwithstanding, if he continue a
day or two, he shall not be punished:
for he *is* his money.
22 ¶ If men strive, and hurt a woman
with child, so that her fruit depart *from
her*, and yet no mischief follow: he shall
be surely punished, according as the
woman's husband will lay upon him;
and he shall pay as the judges *deter-
mine*.
23 And if *any* mischief follow, then
thou shalt give life for life,
24 Eye for eye, tooth for tooth, hand
for hand, foot for foot,
25 Burning for burning, wound for
wound, stripe for stripe.
26 ¶ And if a man smite the eye of his
servant, or the eye of his maid, that it
perish; he shall let him go free for his
eye's sake.
27 And if he smite out his manservant's tooth, or his maidservant's tooth;
he shall let him go free for his tooth's
sake.
28 ¶ If an ox gore a man or a woman,
that they die: then the ox shall be surely
stoned, and his flesh shall not be eaten;
but the owner of the ox *shall be* quit.

29 But if the ox were wont to push with
his horn in time past, and it hath been
testified to his owner, and he hath not
kept him in, but that he hath killed a
man or a woman; the ox shall be stoned,
and his owner also shall be put to death.
30 If there be laid on him a sum of
money, then he shall give for the ransom
of his life whatsoever is laid upon him.
31 Whether he have gored a son, or
have gored a daughter, according to this
judgment shall it be done unto him.
32 If the ox shall push a manservant or
a maidservant; he shall give unto their
master thirty shekels of silver, and the
ox shall be stoned.
33 ℂ And if a man shall open a pit, or
if a man shall dig a pit, and not cover it,
and an ox or an ass fall therein;
34 The owner of the pit shall make *it*
good, *and* give money unto the owner of
them; and the dead *beast* shall be his.
35 ℂ And if one man's ox hurt another's, that he die; then they shall sell
the live ox, and divide the money of it;
and the dead *ox* also they shall divide.
36 Or if it be known that the ox hath
used to push in time past, and his owner
hath not kept him in; he shall surely pay
ox for ox; and the dead shall be his own.

CHAPTER 22

IF a man shall steal an ox, or a sheep,
and kill it, or sell it; he shall restore
five oxen for an ox, and four sheep for a
sheep.
2 ℂ If a thief be found breaking up,
and be smitten that he die, *there shall*
no blood *be shed* for him.
3 If the sun be risen upon him, *there*
shall be blood *shed* for him; *for* he
should make full restitution: if he have
nothing, then he shall be sold for his
theft.
4 If the theft be certainly found in his
hand alive, whether it be ox, or ass, or
sheep; he shall restore double.
5 ℂ If a man shall cause a field or vineyard to be eaten, and shall put in his
beast, and shall feed in another man's
field; of the best of his own field, and of
the best of his own vineyard, shall he
make restitution.
6 ℂ If fire break out, and catch in
thorns, so that the stacks of corn, or the
standing corn, or the field, be consumed
therewith; he that kindled the fire shall
surely make restitution.
7 ℂ If a man shall deliver unto his
neighbor money or stuff to keep, and it
be stolen out of the man's house; if the
thief be found, let him pay double.
8 If the thief be not found, then the
master of the house shall be brought
unto the judges, *to see* whether he have
put his hand unto his neighbor's goods.
9 For all manner of trespass, *whether*
it be for ox, for ass, for sheep, for raiment, *or* for any manner of lost thing,
which *another* challengeth to be his, the
cause of both parties shall come before
the judges; *and* whom the judges shall
condemn, he shall pay double unto his
neighbor.
10 If a man deliver unto his neighbor
an ass, or an ox, or a sheep, or any
beast, to keep; and it die, or be hurt,
or driven away, no man seeing *it:*
11 *Then* shall an oath of the LORD be
between them both, that he hath not put
his hand unto his neighbor's goods; and
the owner of it shall accept *thereof,* and
he shall not make *it* good.
12 And if it be stolen from him, he shall
make restitution unto the owner thereof.
13 If it be torn in pieces, *then* let him
bring it *for* witness, *and* he shall not
make good that which was torn.
14 ℂ And if a man borrow *aught* of his
neighbor, and it be hurt, or die, the
owner thereof *being* not with it, he shall
surely make *it* good.
15 *But* if the owner thereof *be* with it,
he shall not make *it* good: if it *be* a hired
thing, it came for his hire.
16 ℂ And if a man entice a maid that
is not betrothed, and lie with her, he
shall surely endow her to be his wife.
17 If her father utterly refuse to give
her unto him, he shall pay money according to the dowry of virgins.
18 ℂ Thou shalt not suffer a witch to
live.
19 ℂ Whosoever lieth with a beast
shall surely be put to death.
20 ℂ He that sacrificeth unto *any* god,
save unto the LORD only, he shall be
utterly destroyed.
21 ℂ Thou shalt neither vex a stranger,
nor oppress him: for ye were strangers
in the land of Egypt.
22 ℂ Ye shall not afflict any widow, or
fatherless child.
23 If thou afflict them in any wise, and
they cry at all unto me, I will surely hear
their cry;

24 And my wrath shall wax hot, and I will kill you with the sword; and your wives shall be widows, and your children fatherless.

25 ¶ If thou lend money to *any of* my people *that is* poor by thee, thou shalt not be to him as a usurer, neither shalt thou lay upon him usury.

26 If thou at all take thy neighbor's raiment to pledge, thou shalt deliver it unto him by that the sun goeth down:

27 For that *is* his covering only, it *is* his raiment for his skin: wherein shall he sleep? and it shall come to pass, when he crieth unto me, that I will hear; for I *am* gracious.

28 ¶ Thou shalt not revile the gods, nor curse the ruler of thy people.

29 ¶ Thou shalt not delay *to offer* the first of thy ripe fruits, and of thy liquors: the firstborn of thy sons shalt thou give unto me.

30 Likewise shalt thou do with thine oxen, *and* with thy sheep: seven days it shall be with his dam; on the eighth day thou shalt give it me.

31 ¶ And ye shall be holy men unto me: neither shall ye eat *any* flesh *that is* torn of beasts in the field; ye shall cast it to the dogs.

CHAPTER 23

THOU shalt not raise a false report: put not thine hand with the wicked to be an unrighteous witness.

2 ¶ Thou shalt not follow a multitude to *do* evil; neither shalt thou speak in a cause to decline after many to wrest *judgment:*

3 ¶ Neither shalt thou countenance a poor man in his cause.

4 ¶ If thou meet thine enemy's ox or his ass going astray, thou shalt surely bring it back to him again.

5 If thou see the ass of him that hateth thee lying under his burden, and wouldest forbear to help him, thou shalt surely help with him.

6 Thou shalt not wrest the judgment of thy poor in his cause.

7 Keep thee far from a false matter; and the innocent and righteous slay thou not: for I will not justify the wicked.

8 ¶ And thou shalt take no gift: for the gift blindeth the wise, and perverteth the words of the righteous.

9 ¶ Also thou shalt not oppress a stranger: for ye know the heart of a stranger, seeing ye were strangers in the land of Egypt.

10 And six years thou shalt sow thy land, and shalt gather in the fruits thereof:

11 But the seventh *year* thou shalt let it rest and lie still; that the poor of thy people may eat: and what they leave the beasts of the field shall eat. In like manner thou shalt deal with thy vineyard, *and* with thy oliveyard.

12 Six days thou shalt do thy work, and on the seventh day thou shalt rest: that thine ox and thine ass may rest, and the son of thy handmaid, and the stranger, may be refreshed.

13 And in all *things* that I have said unto you be circumspect: and make no mention of the name of other gods, neither let it be heard out of thy mouth.

14 ¶ Three times thou shalt keep a feast unto me in the year.

15 Thou shalt keep the feast of unleavened bread: (thou shalt eat unleavened bread seven days, as I commanded thee, in the time appointed of the month Ā'bĭb; for in it thou camest out from Egypt: and none shall appear before me empty:)

16 And the feast of harvest, the firstfruits of thy labors, which thou hast sown in the field: and the feast of ingathering, *which is* in the end of the year, when thou hast gathered in thy labors out of the field.

17 Three times in the year all thy males shall appear before the Lord GOD.

18 Thou shalt not offer the blood of my sacrifice with leavened bread; neither shall the fat of my sacrifice remain until the morning.

19 The first of the firstfruits of thy land thou shalt bring into the house of the LORD thy God. Thou shalt not seethe a kid in his mother's milk.

20 ¶ Behold, I send an Angel before thee, to keep thee in the way, and to bring thee into the place which I have prepared.

21 Beware of him, and obey his voice, provoke him not; for he will not pardon your transgressions: for my name *is* in him.

22 But if thou shalt indeed obey his voice, and do all that I speak; then I will be an enemy unto thine enemies, and an adversary unto thine adversaries.

23 For mine Angel shall go before thee,

and bring thee in unto the Ăm′ō-rītes, and the Hĭt′tītes, and the Pĕr′ĭz-zītes, and the Cā′năan-ītes, the Hī′vītes, and the Jĕb′ū-ṣītes; and I will cut them off.

24 Thou shalt not bow down to their gods, nor serve them, nor do after their works: but thou shalt utterly overthrow them, and quite break down their images.

25 And ye shall serve the LORD your God, and he shall bless thy bread, and thy water; and I will take sickness away from the midst of thee.

26 ¶ There shall nothing cast their young, nor be barren, in thy land: the number of thy days I will fulfil.

27 I will send my fear before thee, and will destroy all the people to whom thou shalt come; and I will make all thine enemies turn their backs unto thee.

28 And I will send hornets before thee, which shall drive out the Hī′vīte, the Cā′năan-īte, and the Hĭt′tīte, from before thee.

29 I will not drive them out from before thee in one year; lest the land become desolate, and the beast of the field multiply against thee.

30 By little and little I will drive them out from before thee, until thou be increased, and inherit the land.

31 And I will set thy bounds from the Red sea even unto the sea of the Phĭ-lĭs′tīneṣ, and from the desert unto the river: for I will deliver the inhabitants of the land into your hand; and thou shalt drive them out before thee.

32 Thou shalt make no covenant with them, nor with their gods.

33 They shall not dwell in thy land, lest they make thee sin against me: for if thou serve their gods, it will surely be a snare unto thee.

CHAPTER 24

AND he said unto Moses, Come up unto the LORD, thou, and Aaron, Nā′dăb, and Ȧ-bī′hū, and seventy of the elders of Ĭṣ′rā-ĕl; and worship ye afar off.

2 And Moses alone shall come near the LORD: but they shall not come nigh; neither shall the people go up with him.

3 ¶ And Moses came and told the people all the words of the LORD, and all the judgments: and all the people answered with one voice, and said, All the words which the LORD hath said will we do.

4 And Moses wrote all the words of the LORD, and rose up early in the morning, and builded an altar under the hill, and twelve pillars, according to the twelve tribes of Ĭṣ′rā-ĕl.

5 And he sent young men of the children of Ĭṣ′rā-ĕl, which offered burnt offerings, and sacrificed peace offerings of oxen unto the LORD.

6 And Moses took half of the blood, and put *it* in basins; and half of the blood he sprinkled on the altar.

7 And he took the book of the covenant, and read in the audience of the people: and they said, All that the LORD hath said will we do, and be obedient.

8 And Moses took the blood, and sprinkled *it* on the people, and said, Behold the blood of the covenant, which the LORD hath made with you concerning all these words.

9 ¶ Then went up Moses, and Aaron, Nā′dăb, and Ȧ-bī′hū, and seventy of the elders of Ĭṣ′rā-ĕl;

10 And they saw the God of Ĭṣ′rā-ĕl: and *there was* under his feet as it were a paved work of a sapphire stone, and as it were the body of heaven in *his* clearness.

11 And upon the nobles of the children of Ĭṣ′rā-ĕl he laid not his hand: also they saw God, and did eat and drink.

12 ¶ And the LORD said unto Moses, Come up to me into the mount, and be there: and I will give thee tables of stone, and a law, and commandments which I have written; that thou mayest teach them.

13 And Moses rose up, and his minister Joshua; and Moses went up into the mount of God.

14 And he said unto the elders, Tarry ye here for us, until we come again unto you: and, behold, Aaron and Hûr *are* with you: if any man have any matters to do, let him come unto them.

15 And Moses went up into the mount, and a cloud covered the mount.

16 And the glory of the LORD abode upon mount Sī′naī, and the cloud covered it six days: and the seventh day he called unto Moses out of the midst of the cloud.

17 And the sight of the glory of the LORD *was* like devouring fire on the top

of the mount in the eyes of the children of Ĭṣ′rā-ĕl.

18 And Moses went into the midst of the cloud, and gat him up into the mount: and Moses was in the mount forty days and forty nights.

CHAPTER 25

AND the LORD spake unto Moses, saying,

2 Speak unto the children of Ĭṣ′rā-ĕl, that they bring me an offering: of every man that giveth it willingly with his heart ye shall take my offering.

3 And this *is* the offering which ye shall take of them; gold, and silver, and brass,

4 And blue, and purple, and scarlet, and fine linen, and goats' *hair*,

5 And rams' skins dyed red, and badgers' skins, and shittim wood,

6 Oil for the light, spices for anointing oil, and for sweet incense,

7 Onyx stones, and stones to be set in the ĕph′ŏd, and in the breastplate.

8 And let them make me a sanctuary; that I may dwell among them.

9 According to all that I show thee, *after* the pattern of the tabernacle, and the pattern of all the instruments thereof, even so shall ye make *it*.

10 ¶ And they shall make an ark *of* shittim wood: two cubits and a half *shall be* the length thereof, and a cubit and a half the breadth thereof, and a cubit and a half the height thereof.

11 And thou shalt overlay it with pure gold, within and without shalt thou overlay it, and shalt make upon it a crown of gold round about.

12 And thou shalt cast four rings of gold for it, and put *them* in the four corners thereof; and two rings *shall be* in the one side of it, and two rings in the other side of it.

13 And thou shalt make staves *of* shittim wood, and overlay them with gold.

14 And thou shalt put the staves into the rings by the sides of the ark, that the ark may be borne with them.

15 The staves shall be in the rings of the ark: they shall not be taken from it.

16 And thou shalt put into the ark the testimony which I shall give thee.

17 And thou shalt make a mercy seat *of* pure gold: two cubits and a half *shall be* the length thereof, and a cubit and a half the breadth thereof.

18 And thou shalt make two cherubim *of* gold, *of* beaten work shalt thou make them, in the two ends of the mercy seat.

19 And make one cherub on the one end, and the other cherub on the other end: *even* of the mercy seat shall ye make the cherubim on the two ends thereof.

20 And the cherubim shall stretch forth *their* wings on high, covering the mercy seat with their wings, and their faces *shall look* one to another; toward the mercy seat shall the faces of the cherubim be.

21 And thou shalt put the mercy seat above upon the ark; and in the ark thou shalt put the testimony that I shall give thee.

22 And there I will meet with thee, and I will commune with thee from above the mercy seat, from between the two cherubim which *are* upon the ark of the testimony, of all *things* which I will give thee in commandment unto the children of Ĭṣ′rā-ĕl.

23 ¶ Thou shalt also make a table *of* shittim wood: two cubits *shall be* the length thereof, and a cubit the breadth thereof, and a cubit and a half the height thereof.

24 And thou shalt overlay it with pure gold, and make thereto a crown of gold round about.

25 And thou shalt make unto it a border of a handbreadth round about, and thou shalt make a golden crown to the border thereof round about.

26 And thou shalt make for it four rings of gold, and put the rings in the four corners that *are* on the four feet thereof.

27 Over against the border shall the rings be for places of the staves to bear the table.

28 And thou shalt make the staves *of* shittim wood, and overlay them with gold, that the table may be borne with them.

29 And thou shalt make the dishes thereof, and spoons thereof, and covers thereof, and bowls thereof, to cover withal: *of* pure gold shalt thou make them.

30 And thou shalt set upon the table showbread before me always.

31 ¶ And thou shalt make a candlestick *of* pure gold: *of* beaten work shall the candlestick be made: his shaft, and

his branches, his bowls, his knops, and his flowers, shall be of the same.

32 And six branches shall come out of the sides of it; three branches of the candlestick out of the one side, and three branches of the candlestick out of the other side:

33 Three bowls made like unto almonds, *with* a knop and a flower in one branch; and three bowls made like almonds in the other branch, *with* a knop and a flower: so in the six branches that come out of the candlestick.

34 And in the candlestick *shall be* four bowls made like unto almonds, *with* their knops and their flowers.

35 And *there shall be* a knop under two branches of the same, and a knop under two branches of the same, and a knop under two branches of the same, according to the six branches that proceed out of the candlestick.

36 Their knops and their branches shall be of the same: all of it *shall be* one beaten work *of* pure gold.

37 And thou shalt make the seven lamps thereof: and they shall light the lamps thereof, that they may give light over against it.

38 And the tongs thereof, and the snuffdishes thereof, *shall be of* pure gold.

39 *Of* a talent of pure gold shall he make it, with all these vessels.

40 And look that thou make *them* after their pattern, which was showed thee in the mount.

CHAPTER 26

MOREOVER thou shalt make the tabernacle *with* ten curtains *of* fine twined linen, and blue, and purple, and scarlet: *with* cherubim of cunning work shalt thou make them.

2 The length of one curtain *shall be* eight and twenty cubits, and the breadth of one curtain four cubits: and every one of the curtains shall have one measure.

3 The five curtains shall be coupled together one to another; and *other* five curtains *shall be* coupled one to another.

4 And thou shalt make loops of blue upon the edge of the one curtain from the selvedge in the coupling; and likewise shalt thou make in the uttermost edge of *another* curtain, in the coupling of the second.

5 Fifty loops shalt thou make in the one curtain, and fifty loops shalt thou make in the edge of the curtain that *is* in the coupling of the second; that the loops may take hold one of another.

6 And thou shalt make fifty taches of gold, and couple the curtains together with the taches: and it shall be one tabernacle.

7 ¶ And thou shalt make curtains *of* goats' *hair* to be a covering upon the tabernacle: eleven curtains shalt thou make.

8 The length of one curtain *shall be* thirty cubits, and the breadth of one curtain four cubits: and the eleven curtains *shall be all* of one measure.

9 And thou shalt couple five curtains by themselves, and six curtains by themselves, and shalt double the sixth curtain in the forefront of the tabernacle.

10 And thou shalt make fifty loops on the edge of the one curtain *that is* outmost in the coupling, and fifty loops in the edge of the curtain which coupleth the second.

11 And thou shalt make fifty taches of brass, and put the taches into the loops, and couple the tent together, that it may be one.

12 And the remnant that remaineth of the curtains of the tent, the half curtain that remaineth, shall hang over the back side of the tabernacle.

13 And a cubit on the one side, and a cubit on the other side of that which remaineth in the length of the curtains of the tent, it shall hang over the sides of the tabernacle, on this side and on that side, to cover it.

14 And thou shalt make a covering for the tent *of* rams' skins dyed red, and a covering above *of* badgers' skins.

15 ¶ And thou shalt make boards for the tabernacle *of* shittim wood standing up.

16 Ten cubits *shall be* the length of a board, and a cubit and a half *shall be* the breadth of one board.

17 Two tenons *shall there be* in one board, set in order one against another: thus shalt thou make for all the boards of the tabernacle.

18 And thou shalt make the boards for the tabernacle, twenty boards on the south side southward.

19 And thou shalt make forty sockets of silver under the twenty boards; two sockets under one board for his two

tenons, and two sockets under another
board for his two tenons.
20 And for the second side of the tabernacle on the north side *there shall be*
twenty boards,
21 And their forty sockets *of* silver;
two sockets under one board, and two
sockets under another board.
22 And for the sides of the tabernacle
westward thou shalt make six boards.
23 And two boards shalt thou make for
the corners of the tabernacle in the two
sides.
24 And they shall be coupled together
beneath, and they shall be coupled together above the head of it unto one
ring: thus shall it be for them both; they
shall be for the two corners.
25 And they shall be eight boards, and
their sockets *of* silver, sixteen sockets;
two sockets under one board, and two
sockets under another board.
26 ¶ And thou shalt make bars *of*
shittim wood; five for the boards of the
one side of the tabernacle,
27 And five bars for the boards of the
other side of the tabernacle, and five
bars for the boards of the side of the
tabernacle, for the two sides westward.
28 And the middle bar in the midst of
the boards shall reach from end to end.
29 And thou shalt overlay the boards
with gold, and make their rings *of* gold
for places for the bars: and thou shalt
overlay the bars with gold.
30 And thou shalt rear up the tabernacle according to the fashion thereof
which was showed thee in the mount.
31 ¶ And thou shalt make a veil *of*
blue, and purple, and scarlet, and fine
twined linen of cunning work: with
cherubim shall it be made.
32 And thou shalt hang it upon four
pillars of shittim *wood* overlaid with
gold: their hooks *shall be of* gold, upon
the four sockets of silver.
33 ¶ And thou shalt hang up the veil
under the taches, that thou mayest
bring in thither within the veil the ark of
the testimony: and the veil shall divide
unto you between the holy *place* and the
most holy.
34 And thou shalt put the mercy seat
upon the ark of the testimony in the
most holy *place*.
35 And thou shalt set the table without
the veil, and the candlestick over against
the table on the side of the tabernacle
toward the south: and thou shalt put the
table on the north side.
36 And thou shalt make a hanging for
the door of the tent, *of* blue, and purple,
and scarlet, and fine twined linen,
wrought with needlework.
37 And thou shalt make for the hanging five pillars *of* shittim *wood*, and
overlay them with gold, *and* their hooks
shall be of gold: and thou shalt cast five
sockets of brass for them.

CHAPTER 27

AND thou shalt make an altar *of*
shittim wood, five cubits long, and
five cubits broad; the altar shall be foursquare: and the height thereof *shall be*
three cubits.
2 And thou shalt make the horns of it
upon the four corners thereof: his horns
shall be of the same: and thou shalt
overlay it with brass.
3 And thou shalt make his pans to receive his ashes, and his shovels, and his
basins, and his fleshhooks, and his firepans: all the vessels thereof thou shalt
make *of* brass.
4 And thou shalt make for it a grate of
network *of* brass; and upon the net shalt
thou make four brazen rings in the four
corners thereof.
5 And thou shalt put it under the compass of the altar beneath, that the net
may be even to the midst of the altar.
6 And thou shalt make staves for the
altar, staves *of* shittim wood, and overlay them with brass.
7 And the staves shall be put into the
rings, and the staves shall be upon the
two sides of the altar, to bear it.
8 Hollow with boards shalt thou make
it: as it was showed thee in the mount,
so shall they make *it*.
9 ¶ And thou shalt make the court of
the tabernacle: for the south side southward *there shall be* hangings for the
court *of* fine twined linen of a hundred
cubits long for one side:
10 And the twenty pillars thereof and
their twenty sockets *shall be of* brass;
the hooks of the pillars and their fillets
shall be of silver.
11 And likewise for the north side in
length *there shall be* hangings of a hundred *cubits* long, and his twenty pillars
and their twenty sockets *of* brass; the
hooks of the pillars and their fillets *of*
silver.

12 ¶ And *for* the breadth of the court on the west side *shall be* hangings of fifty cubits: their pillars ten, and their sockets ten.

13 And the breadth of the court on the east side eastward *shall be* fifty cubits.

14 The hangings of one side *of the gate shall be* fifteen cubits: their pillars three, and their sockets three.

15 And on the other side *shall be* hangings fifteen *cubits:* their pillars three, and their sockets three.

16 ¶ And for the gate of the court *shall be* a hanging of twenty cubits, *of* blue, and purple, and scarlet, and fine twined linen, wrought with needlework: *and* their pillars *shall be* four, and their sockets four.

17 All the pillars round about the court *shall be* filleted with silver; their hooks *shall be of* silver, and their sockets *of* brass.

18 ¶ The length of the court *shall be* a hundred cubits, and the breadth fifty every where, and the height five cubits *of* fine twined linen, and their sockets *of* brass.

19 All the vessels of the tabernacle in all the service thereof, and all the pins thereof, and all the pins of the court, *shall be of* brass.

20 ¶ And thou shalt command the children of Ĭş'rā-ĕl, that they bring thee pure oil olive beaten for the light, to cause the lamp to burn always.

21 In the tabernacle of the congregation without the veil, which *is* before the testimony, Aaron and his sons shall order it from evening to morning before the LORD: *it shall be* a statute for ever unto their generations on the behalf of the children of Ĭş'rā-ĕl.

CHAPTER 28

AND take thou unto thee Aaron thy brother, and his sons with him, from among the children of Ĭş'rā-ĕl, that he may minister unto me in the priest's office, *even* Aaron, Nā'dăb and Ȧ-bī'hū, Ĕl'ē-ā'zȧr and Ĭth'ȧ-mär, Aaron's sons.

2 And thou shalt make holy garments for Aaron thy brother, for glory and for beauty.

3 And thou shalt speak unto all *that are* wise-hearted, whom I have filled with the spirit of wisdom, that they may make Aaron's garments to consecrate him, that he may minister unto me in the priest's office.

4 And these *are* the garments which they shall make; a breastplate, and an ĕph'ŏd, and a robe, and a broidered coat, a mitre, and a girdle: and they shall make holy garments for Aaron thy brother, and his sons, that he may minister unto me in the priest's office.

5 And they shall take gold, and blue, and purple, and scarlet, and fine linen.

6 ¶ And they shall make the ĕph'ŏd *of* gold, *of* blue, and *of* purple, *of* scarlet, and fine twined linen, with cunning work.

7 It shall have the two shoulderpieces thereof joined at the two edges thereof; and *so* it shall be joined together.

8 And the curious girdle of the ĕph'ŏd, which *is* upon it, shall be of the same, according to the work thereof; *even of* gold, *of* blue, and purple, and scarlet, and fine twined linen.

9 And thou shalt take two onyx stones, and grave on them the names of the children of Ĭş'rā-ĕl:

10 Six of their names on one stone, and *the other* six names of the rest on the other stone, according to their birth.

11 With the work of an engraver in stone, *like* the engravings of a signet, shalt thou engrave the two stones with the names of the children of Ĭş'rā-ĕl: thou shalt make them to be set in ouches of gold.

12 And thou shalt put the two stones upon the shoulders of the ĕph'ŏd *for* stones of memorial unto the children of Ĭş'rā-ĕl: and Aaron shall bear their names before the LORD upon his two shoulders for a memorial.

13 ¶ And thou shalt make ouches *of* gold;

14 And two chains *of* pure gold at the ends; *of* wreathed work shalt thou make them, and fasten the wreathed chains to the ouches.

15 ¶ And thou shalt make the breastplate of judgment with cunning work; after the work of the ĕph'ŏd thou shalt make it; *of* gold, *of* blue, and *of* purple, and *of* scarlet, and *of* fine twined linen, shalt thou make it.

16 Foursquare it shall be *being* doubled; a span *shall be* the length thereof, and a span *shall be* the breadth thereof.

17 And thou shalt set in it settings of stones, *even* four rows of stones: *the*

first row *shall be* a sardius, a topaz, and a carbuncle: *this shall be* the first row.

18 And the second row *shall be* an emerald, a sapphire, and a diamond.

19 And the third row a ligure, an agate, and an amethyst.

20 And the fourth row a beryl, and an onyx, and a jasper: they shall be set in gold in their inclosings.

21 And the stones shall be with the names of the children of Ĭs̱'rā-ēl, twelve, according to their names, *like* the engravings of a signet; every one with his name shall they be according to the twelve tribes.

22 ¶ And thou shalt make upon the breastplate chains at the ends *of* wreathed work *of* pure gold.

23 And thou shalt make upon the breastplate two rings of gold, and shalt put the two rings on the two ends of the breastplate.

24 And thou shalt put the two wreathed *chains* of gold in the two rings *which are* on the ends of the breastplate.

25 And *the other* two ends of the two wreathed *chains* thou shalt fasten in the two ouches, and put *them* on the shoulderpieces of the ĕph'ŏd before it.

26 ¶ And thou shalt make two rings of gold, and thou shalt put them upon the two ends of the breastplate in the border thereof, which *is* in the side of the ĕph'ŏd inward.

27 And two *other* rings of gold thou shalt make, and shalt put them on the two sides of the ĕph'ŏd underneath, toward the forepart thereof, over against the *other* coupling thereof, above the curious girdle of the ĕph'ŏd.

28 And they shall bind the breastplate by the rings thereof unto the rings of the ĕph'ŏd with a lace of blue, that *it* may be above the curious girdle of the ĕph'ŏd, and that the breastplate be not loosed from the ĕph'ŏd.

29 And Aaron shall bear the names of the children of Ĭs̱'rā-ēl in the breastplate of judgment upon his heart, when he goeth in unto the holy *place*, for a memorial before the LORD continually.

30 ¶ And thou shalt put in the breastplate of judgment the Ū'rĭm and the Thŭm'mĭm; and they shall be upon Aaron's heart, when he goeth in before the LORD: and Aaron shall bear the judgment of the children of Ĭs̱'rā-ēl upon his heart before the LORD continually.

31 ¶ And thou shalt make the robe of the ĕph'ŏd all *of* blue.

32 And there shall be a hole in the top of it, in the midst thereof: it shall have a binding of woven work round about the hole of it, as it were the hole of an habergeon, that it be not rent.

33 ¶ And *beneath* upon the hem of it thou shalt make pomegranates *of* blue, and *of* purple, and *of* scarlet, round about the hem thereof; and bells of gold between them round about:

34 A golden bell and a pomegranate, a golden bell and a pomegranate, upon the hem of the robe round about.

35 And it shall be upon Aaron to minister: and his sound shall be heard when he goeth in unto the holy *place* before the LORD, and when he cometh out, that he die not.

36 ¶ And thou shalt make a plate *of* pure gold, and grave upon it, *like* the engravings of a signet, HOLINESS TO THE LORD.

37 And thou shalt put it on a blue lace, that it may be upon the mitre; upon the forefront of the mitre it shall be.

38 And it shall be upon Aaron's forehead, that Aaron may bear the iniquity of the holy things, which the children of Ĭs̱'rā-ēl shall hallow in all their holy gifts; and it shall be always upon his forehead, that they may be accepted before the LORD.

39 ¶ And thou shalt embroider the coat of fine linen, and thou shalt make the mitre *of* fine linen, and thou shalt make the girdle *of* needlework.

40 ¶ And for Aaron's sons thou shalt make coats, and thou shalt make for them girdles, and bonnets shalt thou make for them, for glory and for beauty.

41 And thou shalt put them upon Aaron thy brother, and his sons with him; and shalt anoint them, and consecrate them, and sanctify them, that they may minister unto me in the priest's office.

42 And thou shalt make them linen breeches to cover their nakedness; from the loins even unto the thighs they shall reach:

43 And they shall be upon Aaron, and upon his sons, when they come in unto the tabernacle of the congregation, or when they come near unto the altar to minister in the holy *place;* that they bear not iniquity, and die: *it shall be* a

statute for ever unto him and his seed after him.

CHAPTER 29

AND this *is* the thing that thou shalt do unto them to hallow them, to minister unto me in the priest's office: Take one young bullock, and two rams without blemish,

2 And unleavened bread, and cakes unleavened tempered with oil, and wafers unleavened anointed with oil: *of* wheaten flour shalt thou make them.

3 And thou shalt put them into one basket, and bring them in the basket, with the bullock and the two rams.

4 And Aaron and his sons thou shalt bring unto the door of the tabernacle of the congregation, and shalt wash them with water.

5 And thou shalt take the garments, and put upon Aaron the coat, and the robe of the ĕph'ŏd, and the ĕph'ŏd, and the breastplate, and gird him with the curious girdle of the ĕph'ŏd:

6 And thou shalt put the mitre upon his head, and put the holy crown upon the mitre.

7 Then shalt thou take the anointing oil, and pour *it* upon his head, and anoint him.

8 And thou shalt bring his sons, and put coats upon them.

9 And thou shalt gird them with girdles, Aaron and his sons, and put the bonnets on them: and the priest's office shall be theirs for a perpetual statute: and thou shalt consecrate Aaron and his sons.

10 And thou shalt cause a bullock to be brought before the tabernacle of the congregation; and Aaron and his sons shall put their hands upon the head of the bullock.

11 And thou shalt kill the bullock before the LORD, *by* the door of the tabernacle of the congregation.

12 And thou shalt take of the blood of the bullock, and put *it* upon the horns of the altar with thy finger, and pour all the blood beside the bottom of the altar.

13 And thou shalt take all the fat that covereth the inwards, and the caul *that is* above the liver, and the two kidneys, and the fat that *is* upon them, and burn *them* upon the altar.

14 But the flesh of the bullock, and his skin, and his dung, shalt thou burn with fire without the camp: it *is* a sin offering.

15 ¶ Thou shalt also take one ram; and Aaron and his sons shall put their hands upon the head of the ram.

16 And thou shalt slay the ram, and thou shalt take his blood, and sprinkle *it* round about upon the altar.

17 And thou shalt cut the ram in pieces, and wash the inwards of him, and his legs, and put *them* unto his pieces, and unto his head.

18 And thou shalt burn the whole ram upon the altar: it *is* a burnt offering unto the LORD: it *is* a sweet savor, an offering made by fire unto the LORD.

19 ¶ And thou shalt take the other ram; and Aaron and his sons shall put their hands upon the head of the ram.

20 Then shalt thou kill the ram, and take of his blood, and put *it* upon the tip of the right ear of Aaron, and upon the tip of the right ear of his sons, and upon the thumb of their right hand, and upon the great toe of their right foot, and sprinkle the blood upon the altar round about.

21 And thou shalt take of the blood that *is* upon the altar, and of the anointing oil, and sprinkle *it* upon Aaron, and upon his garments, and upon his sons, and upon the garments of his sons with him: and he shall be hallowed, and his garments, and his sons, and his sons' garments with him.

22 Also thou shalt take of the ram the fat and the rump, and the fat that covereth the inwards, and the caul *above* the liver, and the two kidneys, and the fat that *is* upon them, and the right shoulder; for it *is* a ram of consecration:

23 And one loaf of bread, and one cake of oiled bread, and one wafer out of the basket of the unleavened bread that *is* before the LORD:

24 And thou shalt put all in the hands of Aaron, and in the hands of his sons; and shalt wave them *for* a wave offering before the LORD.

25 And thou shalt receive them of their hands, and burn *them* upon the altar for a burnt offering, for a sweet savor before the LORD: it *is* an offering made by fire unto the LORD.

26 And thou shalt take the breast of the ram of Aaron's consecration, and wave it *for* a wave offering before the LORD: and it shall be thy part.

27 And thou shalt sanctify the breast of the wave offering, and the shoulder of

the heave offering, which is waved, and
which is heaved up, of the ram of the
consecration, *even* of *that* which *is* for
Aaron, and of *that* which is for his sons:
28 And it shall be Aaron's and his sons'
by a statute for ever from the children
of Ĭṣ'rā-ĕl; for it *is* a heave offering: and
it shall be a heave offering from the
children of Ĭṣ'rā-ĕl of the sacrifice of
their peace offerings, *even* their heave
offering unto the LORD.
29 ¶ And the holy garments of Aaron
shall be his sons' after him, to be
anointed therein, and to be consecrated
in them.
30 *And* that son that is priest in his
stead shall put them on seven days,
when he cometh into the tabernacle of
the congregation to minister in the holy
place.
31 ¶ And thou shalt take the ram of
the consecration, and seethe his flesh in
the holy place.
32 And Aaron and his sons shall eat the
flesh of the ram, and the bread that *is* in
the basket, *by* the door of the tabernacle
of the congregation.
33 And they shall eat those things
wherewith the atonement was made, to
consecrate *and* to sanctify them: but a
stranger shall not eat *thereof*, because
they *are* holy.
34 And if aught of the flesh of the consecrations, or of the bread, remain unto
the morning, then thou shalt burn the
remainder with fire: it shall not be eaten,
because it *is* holy.
35 And thus shalt thou do unto Aaron,
and to his sons, according to all *things*
which I have commanded thee: seven
days shalt thou consecrate them.
36 And thou shalt offer every day a
bullock *for* a sin offering for atonement:
and thou shalt cleanse the altar, when
thou hast made an atonement for it, and
thou shalt anoint it, to sanctify it.
37 Seven days thou shalt make an
atonement for the altar, and sanctify it;
and it shall be an altar most holy: whatsoever toucheth the altar shall be holy.
38 ¶ Now this *is that* which thou shalt
offer upon the altar; two lambs of the
first year day by day continually.
39 The one lamb thou shalt offer in the
morning; and the other lamb thou shalt
offer at even:
40 And with the one lamb a tenth deal
of flour mingled with the fourth part of
a hin of beaten oil; and the fourth part
of a hin of wine *for* a drink offering.
41 And the other lamb thou shalt offer
at even, and shalt do thereto according
to the meat offering of the morning, and
according to the drink offering thereof,
for a sweet savor, an offering made by
fire unto the LORD.
42 *This shall be* a continual burnt offering throughout your generations *at* the
door of the tabernacle of the congregation before the LORD, where I will meet
you, to speak there unto thee.
43 And there I will meet with the children of Ĭṣ'rā-ĕl, and *the tabernacle* shall
be sanctified by my glory.
44 And I will sanctify the tabernacle of
the congregation, and the altar: I will
sanctify also both Aaron and his sons, to
minister to me in the priest's office.
45 ¶ And I will dwell among the children of Ĭṣ'rā-ĕl, and will be their God.
46 And they shall know that I *am* the
LORD their God, that brought them forth
out of the land of Egypt, that I may dwell
among them: I *am* the LORD their God.

CHAPTER 30

AND thou shalt make an altar to burn
incense upon: *of* shittim wood shalt
thou make it.
2 A cubit *shall be* the length thereof,
and a cubit the breadth thereof; foursquare shall it be: and two cubits *shall*
be the height thereof: the horns thereof
shall be of the same.
3 And thou shalt overlay it with pure
gold, the top thereof, and the sides
thereof round about, and the horns
thereof; and thou shalt make unto it a
crown of gold round about.
4 And two golden rings shalt thou make
to it under the crown of it, by the two
corners thereof, upon the two sides of it
shalt thou make *it;* and they shall be
for places for the staves to bear it
withal.
5 And thou shalt make the staves *of*
shittim wood, and overlay them with
gold.
6 And thou shalt put it before the veil
that *is* by the ark of the testimony, before the mercy seat that *is* over the
testimony, where I will meet with thee.
7 And Aaron shall burn thereon sweet
incense every morning: when he dress-
eth the lamps, he shall burn incense
upon it.

8 And when Aaron lighteth the lamps at even, he shall burn incense upon it, a perpetual incense before the LORD throughout your generations.

9 Ye shall offer no strange incense thereon, nor burnt sacrifice, nor meat offering; neither shall ye pour drink offering thereon.

10 And Aaron shall make an atonement upon the horns of it once in a year with the blood of the sin offering of atonements; once in the year shall he make atonement upon it throughout your generations: it *is* most holy unto the LORD.

11 ¶ And the LORD spake unto Moses, saying,

12 When thou takest the sum of the children of Ĭş′rā-ĕl after their number, then shall they give every man a ransom for his soul unto the LORD, when thou numberest them; that there be no plague among them, when *thou* numberest them.

13 This they shall give, every one that passeth among them that are numbered, half a shekel after the shekel of the sanctuary: (a shekel *is* twenty gē′rȧhs:) a half shekel *shall be* the offering of the LORD.

14 Every one that passeth among them that are numbered, from twenty years old and above, shall give an offering unto the LORD.

15 The rich shall not give more, and the poor shall not give less, than half a shekel, when *they* give an offering unto the LORD, to make an atonement for your souls.

16 And thou shalt take the atonement money of the children of Ĭş′rā-ĕl, and shalt appoint it for the service of the tabernacle of the congregation; that it may be a memorial unto the children of Ĭş′rā-ĕl before the LORD, to make an atonement for your souls.

17 ¶ And the LORD spake unto Moses, saying,

18 Thou shalt also make a laver *of* brass, and his foot *also of* brass, to wash *withal:* and thou shalt put it between the tabernacle of the congregation and the altar, and thou shalt put water therein.

19 For Aaron and his sons shall wash their hands and their feet thereat:

20 When they go into the tabernacle of the congregation, they shall wash with water, that they die not; or when they come near to the altar to minister, to burn offering made by fire unto the LORD:

21 So they shall wash their hands and their feet, that they die not: and it shall be a statute for ever to them, *even* to him and to his seed throughout their generations.

22 ¶ Moreover the LORD spake unto Moses, saying,

23 Take thou also unto thee principal spices, of pure myrrh five hundred *shekels,* and of sweet cinnamon half so much, *even* two hundred and fifty *shekels,* and of sweet calamus two hundred and fifty *shekels,*

24 And of cassia five hundred *shekels,* after the shekel of the sanctuary, and of oil olive a hin:

25 And thou shalt make it an oil of holy ointment, an ointment compound after the art of the apothecary: it shall be a holy anointing oil.

26 And thou shalt anoint the tabernacle of the congregation therewith, and the ark of the testimony,

27 And the table and all his vessels, and the candlestick and his vessels, and the altar of incense,

28 And the altar of burnt offering with all his vessels, and the laver and his foot.

29 And thou shalt sanctify them, that they may be most holy: whatsoever toucheth them shall be holy.

30 And thou shalt anoint Aaron and his sons, and consecrate them, that *they* may minister unto me in the priest's office.

31 And thou shalt speak unto the children of Ĭş′rā-ĕl, saying, This shall be a holy anointing oil unto me throughout your generations.

32 Upon man's flesh shall it not be poured, neither shall ye make *any other* like it, after the composition of it: it *is* holy, *and* it shall be holy unto you.

33 Whosoever compoundeth *any* like it, or whosoever putteth *any* of it upon a stranger, shall even be cut off from his people.

34 ¶ And the LORD said unto Moses, Take unto thee sweet spices, stacte, and onycha, and galbanum; *these* sweet spices with pure frankincense: of each shall there be a like *weight:*

35 And thou shalt make it a perfume, a confection after the art of the apothecary, tempered together, pure *and* holy:

36 And thou shalt beat *some* of it very small, and put of it before the testimony in the tabernacle of the congregation, where I will meet with thee: it shall be unto you most holy.
37 And *as for* the perfume which thou shalt make, ye shall not make to yourselves according to the composition thereof: it shall be unto thee holy for the LORD.
38 Whosoever shall make like unto that, to smell thereto, shall even be cut off from his people.

CHAPTER 31

AND the LORD spake unto Moses, saying,
2 See, I have called by name Bĕ-zăl'ē-ĕl the son of Ū'rī, the son of Hûr, of the tribe of Judah:
3 And I have filled him with the spirit of God, in wisdom, and in understanding, and in knowledge, and in all manner of workmanship,
4 To devise cunning works, to work in gold, and in silver, and in brass,
5 And in cutting of stones, to set *them*, and in carving of timber, to work in all manner of workmanship.
6 And I, behold, I have given with him Ȧ-hō'lĭ-ăb, the son of Ȧ-hĭs'ȧ-măch, of the tribe of Dan: and in the hearts of all that are wise-hearted I have put wisdom, that they may make all that I have commanded thee;
7 The tabernacle of the congregation, and the ark of the testimony, and the mercy seat that *is* thereupon, and all the furniture of the tabernacle,
8 And the table and his furniture, and the pure candlestick with all his furniture, and the altar of incense,
9 And the altar of burnt offering with all his furniture, and the laver and his foot,
10 And the clothes of service, and the holy garments for Aaron the priest, and the garments of his sons, to minister in the priest's office,
11 And the anointing oil, and sweet incense for the holy *place:* according to all that I have commanded thee shall they do.
12 ¶ And the LORD spake unto Moses, saying,
13 Speak thou also unto the children of Ĭş'rā-ĕl, saying, Verily my sabbaths ye shall keep: for it *is* a sign between me and you throughout your generations; that *ye* may know that I *am* the LORD that doth sanctify you.
14 Ye shall keep the sabbath therefore; for it *is* holy unto you. Every one that defileth it shall surely be put to death: for whosoever doeth *any* work therein, that soul shall be cut off from among his people.
15 Six days may work be done; but in the seventh *is* the sabbath of rest, holy to the LORD: whosoever doeth *any* work in the sabbath day, he shall surely be put to death.
16 Wherefore the children of Ĭş'rā-ĕl shall keep the sabbath, to observe the sabbath throughout their generations, *for* a perpetual covenant.
17 It *is* a sign between me and the children of Ĭş'rā-ĕl for ever: for *in* six days the LORD made heaven and earth, and on the seventh day he rested, and was refreshed.
18 ¶ And he gave unto Moses, when he had made an end of communing with him upon mount Sī'naī, two tables of testimony, tables of stone, written with the finger of God.

CHAPTER 32

AND when the people saw that Moses delayed to come down out of the mount, the people gathered themselves together unto Aaron, and said unto him, Up, make us gods, which shall go before us; for *as for* this Moses, the man that brought us up out of the land of Egypt, we wot not what is become of him.
2 And Aaron said unto them, Break off the golden earrings, which *are* in the ears of your wives, of your sons, and of your daughters, and bring *them* unto me.
3 And all the people brake off the golden earrings which *were* in their ears, and brought *them* unto Aaron.
4 And he received *them* at their hand, and fashioned it with a graving tool, after he had made it a molten calf: and they said, These *be* thy gods, O Ĭş'rā-ĕl, which brought thee up out of the land of Egypt.
5 And when Aaron saw *it*, he built an altar before it; and Aaron made proclamation, and said, To-morrow *is* a feast to the LORD.
6 And they rose up early on the morrow, and offered burnt offerings, and brought peace offerings; and the people

sat down to eat and to drink, and rose
up to play.
7 ¶ And the LORD said unto Moses,
Go, get thee down; for thy people, which
thou broughtest out of the land of Egypt,
have corrupted *themselves:*
8 They have turned aside quickly out
of the way which I commanded them:
they have made them a molten calf, and
have worshipped it, and have sacrificed
thereunto, and said, These *be* thy gods,
O Ĭṣ'rā-ĕl, which have brought thee up
out of the land of Egypt.
9 And the LORD said unto Moses, I
have seen this people, and, behold, it *is*
a stiffnecked people:
10 Now therefore let me alone, that my
wrath may wax hot against them, and
that I may consume them: and I will
make of thee a great nation.
11 And Moses besought the LORD his
God, and said, LORD, why doth thy
wrath wax hot against thy people, which
thou hast brought forth out of the land
of Egypt with great power, and with a
mighty hand?
12 Wherefore should the Egyptians
speak, and say, For mischief did he
bring them out, to slay them in the
mountains, and to consume them from
the face of the earth? Turn from thy
fierce wrath, and repent of this evil
against thy people.
13 Remember Abraham, Isaac, and
Ĭṣ'rā-ĕl, thy servants, to whom thou
swarest by thine own self, and saidst
unto them, I will multiply your seed as
the stars of heaven, and all this land that
I have spoken of will I give unto your
seed, and they shall inherit *it* for ever.
14 And the LORD repented of the evil
which he thought to do unto his people.
15 ¶ And Moses turned, and went
down from the mount, and the two tables
of the testimony *were* in his hand: the
tables *were* written on both their sides;
on the one side and on the other *were*
they written.
16 And the tables *were* the work of
God, and the writing *was* the writing of
God, graven upon the tables.
17 And when Joshua heard the noise
of the people as they shouted, he said
unto Moses, *There is* a noise of war in
the camp.
18 And he said, *It is* not the voice of
them that shout for mastery, neither *is*
it the voice of *them that* cry for being
overcome; *but* the noise of *them that*
sing do I hear.
19 ¶ And it came to pass, as soon as
he came nigh unto the camp, that he
saw the calf, and the dancing: and
Moses' anger waxed hot, and he cast
the tables out of his hands, and brake
them beneath the mount.
20 And he took the calf which they had
made, and burnt *it* in the fire, and
ground *it* to powder, and strewed *it* upon the water, and made the children of
Ĭṣ'rā-ĕl drink *of it.*
21 And Moses said unto Aaron, What
did this people unto thee, that thou hast
brought so great a sin upon them?
22 And Aaron said, Let not the anger
of my lord wax hot: thou knowest the
people, that they *are set* on mischief.
23 For they said unto me, Make us
gods, which shall go before us: for *as for*
this Moses, the man that brought us up
out of the land of Egypt, we wot not what
is become of him.
24 And I said unto them, Whosoever
hath any gold, let them break *it* off. So
they gave *it* me: then I cast it into the
fire, and there came out this calf.
25 ¶ And when Moses saw that the
people *were* naked, (for Aaron had
made them naked unto *their* shame
among their enemies,)
26 Then Moses stood in the gate of the
camp, and said, Who *is* on the LORD's
side? *let him come* unto me. And all the
sons of Levi gathered themselves together unto him.
27 And he said unto them, Thus saith
the LORD God of Ĭṣ'rā-ĕl, Put every man
his sword by his side, *and* go in and out
from gate to gate throughout the camp,
and slay every man his brother, and
every man his companion, and every
man his neighbor.
28 And the children of Levi did according to the word of Moses: and there fell
of the people that day about three thousand men.
29 For Moses had said, Consecrate
yourselves to-day to the LORD, even
every man upon his son, and upon his
brother; that he may bestow upon you a
blessing this day.
30 ¶ And it came to pass on the morrow, that Moses said unto the people,
Ye have sinned a great sin: and now I
will go up unto the LORD; peradventure
I shall make an atonement for your sin.

31 And Moses returned unto the LORD, and said, Oh, this people have sinned a great sin, and have made them gods of gold.

32 Yet now, if thou wilt forgive their sin—; and if not, blot me, I pray thee, out of thy book which thou hast written.

33 And the LORD said unto Moses, Whosoever hath sinned against me, him will I blot out of my book.

34 Therefore now go, lead the people unto *the place* of which I have spoken unto thee: behold, mine Angel shall go before thee: nevertheless, in the day when I visit, I will visit their sin upon them.

35 And the LORD plagued the people, because they made the calf, which Aaron made.

CHAPTER 33

AND the LORD said unto Moses, Depart, *and* go up hence, thou and the people which thou hast brought up out of the land of Egypt, unto the land which I sware unto Abraham, to Isaac, and to Jacob, saying, Unto thy seed will I give it:

2 And I will send an Angel before thee; and I will drive out the Cā'năan-īte, the Ăm'ō-rīte, and the Hĭt'tīte and the Pĕr'ĭz-zīte, the Hī'vīte, and the Jĕb'ū-şīte:

3 Unto a land flowing with milk and honey: for I will not go up in the midst of thee; for thou *art* a stiffnecked people: lest I consume thee in the way.

4 ¶ And when the people heard these evil tidings, they mourned: and no man did put on him his ornaments.

5 For the LORD had said unto Moses, Say unto the children of Ĭş'rā-ēl, Ye *are* a stiffnecked people: I will come up into the midst of thee in a moment, and consume thee: therefore now put off thy ornaments from thee, that I may know what to do unto thee.

6 And the children of Ĭş'rā-ĕl stripped themselves of their ornaments by the mount Hō'rĕb.

7 And Moses took the tabernacle, and pitched it without the camp, afar off from the camp, and called it the Tabernacle of the congregation. And it came to pass, *that* every one which sought the LORD went out unto the tabernacle of the congregation, which *was* without the camp.

8 And it came to pass, when Moses went out unto the tabernacle, *that* all the people rose up, and stood every man *at* his tent door, and looked after Moses, until he was gone into the tabernacle.

9 And it came to pass, as Moses entered into the tabernacle, the cloudy pillar descended, and stood *at* the door of the tabernacle, and *the Lord* talked with Moses.

10 And all the people saw the cloudy pillar stand *at* the tabernacle door: and all the people rose up and worshipped, every man *in* his tent door.

11 And the LORD spake unto Moses face to face, as a man speaketh unto his friend. And he turned again into the camp; but his servant Joshua, the son of Nŭn, a young man, departed not out of the tabernacle.

12 ¶ And Moses said unto the LORD, See, thou sayest unto me, Bring up this people: and thou hast not let me know whom thou wilt send with me. Yet thou hast said, I know thee by name, and thou hast also found grace in my sight.

13 Now therefore, I pray thee, if I have found grace in thy sight, show me now thy way, that I may know thee, that I may find grace in thy sight: and consider that this nation *is* thy people.

14 And he said, My presence shall go *with thee,* and I will give thee rest.

15 And he said unto him, If thy presence go not *with me,* carry us not up hence.

16 For wherein shall it be known here that I and thy people have found grace in thy sight? *is it* not in that thou goest with us? So shall we be separated, I and thy people, from all the people that *are* upon the face of the earth.

17 And the LORD said unto Moses, I will do this thing also that thou hast spoken: for thou hast found grace in my sight, and I know thee by name.

18 And he said, I beseech thee, show me thy glory.

19 And he said, I will make all my goodness pass before thee, and I will proclaim the name of the LORD before thee; and will be gracious to whom I will be gracious, and will show mercy on whom I will show mercy.

20 And he said, Thou canst not see my face: for there shall no man see me, and live.

21 And the LORD said, Behold, *there is*

a place by me, and thou shalt stand upon a rock:

22 And it shall come to pass, while my glory passeth by, that I will put thee in a cleft of the rock, and will cover thee with my hand while I pass by:

23 And I will take away mine hand, and thou shalt see my back parts; but my face shall not be seen.

CHAPTER 34

AND the LORD said unto Moses, Hew thee two tables of stone like unto the first: and I will write upon *these* tables the words that were in the first tables, which thou brakest.

2 And be ready in the morning, and come up in the morning unto mount Sī'naī, and present thyself there to me in the top of the mount.

3 And no man shall come up with thee, neither let any man be seen throughout all the mount; neither let the flocks nor herds feed before that mount.

4 ¶ And he hewed two tables of stone like unto the first; and Moses rose up early in the morning, and went up unto mount Sī'naī, as the LORD had commanded him, and took in his hand the two tables of stone.

5 And the LORD descended in the cloud, and stood with him there, and proclaimed the name of the LORD.

6 And the LORD passed by before him, and proclaimed, The LORD, The LORD God, merciful and gracious, long-suffering, and abundant in goodness and truth,

7 Keeping mercy for thousands, forgiving iniquity and transgression and sin, and that will by no means clear *the guilty;* visiting the iniquity of the fathers upon the children, and upon the children's children, unto the third and to the fourth *generation.*

8 And Moses made haste, and bowed his head toward the earth, and worshipped.

9 And he said, If now I have found grace in thy sight, O Lord, let my Lord, I pray thee, go among us; for it *is* a stiffnecked people; and pardon our iniquity and our sin, and take us for thine inheritance.

10 ¶ And he said, Behold, I make a covenant: before all thy people I will do marvels, such as have not been done in all the earth, nor in any nation: and all the people among which thou *art* shall see the work of the LORD: for it *is* a terrible thing that I will do with thee.

11 Observe thou that which I command thee this day: behold, I drive out before thee the Ăm'ō-rīte, and the Cā'năan-īte, and the Hĭt'tīte, and the Pĕr'ĭz-zīte, and the Hī'vīte, and the Jĕb'ū-sīte.

12 Take heed to thyself, lest thou make a covenant with the inhabitants of the land whither thou goest, lest it be for a snare in the midst of thee:

13 But ye shall destroy their altars, break their images, and cut down their groves:

14 For thou shalt worship no other god: for the LORD, whose name *is* Jealous, *is* a jealous God.

15 Lest thou make a covenant with the inhabitants of the land, and they go a whoring after their gods, and do sacrifice unto their gods, and *one* call thee, and thou eat of his sacrifice;

16 And thou take of their daughters unto thy sons, and their daughters go a whoring after their gods, and make thy sons go a whoring after their gods.

17 Thou shalt make thee no molten gods.

18 ¶ The feast of unleavened bread shalt thou keep. Seven days thou shalt eat unleavened bread, as I commanded thee, in the time of the month Ā'bĭb: for in the month Ā'bĭb thou camest out from Egypt.

19 All that openeth the matrix *is* mine; and every firstling among thy cattle, *whether* ox or sheep, *that is male.*

20 But the firstling of an ass thou shalt redeem with a lamb: and if thou redeem *him* not, then shalt thou break his neck. All the firstborn of thy sons thou shalt redeem. And none shall appear before me empty.

21 ¶ Six days thou shalt work, but on the seventh day thou shalt rest: in earing time and in harvest thou shalt rest.

22 ¶ And thou shalt observe the feast of weeks, of the firstfruits of wheat harvest, and the feast of ingathering at the year's end.

23 ¶ Thrice in the year shall all your men children appear before the LORD GOD, the God of Ĭṣ'rā-ĕl.

24 For I will cast out the nations before thee, and enlarge thy borders: neither shall any man desire thy land, when

thou shalt go up to appear before the LORD thy God thrice in the year.

25 Thou shalt not offer the blood of my sacrifice with leaven; neither shall the sacrifice of the feast of the passover be left unto the morning.

26 The first of the firstfruits of thy land thou shalt bring unto the house of the LORD thy God. Thou shalt not seethe a kid in his mother's milk.

27 And the LORD said unto Moses, Write thou these words: for after the tenor of these words I have made a covenant with thee and with Ĭṣ'rā-ĕl.

28 And he was there with the LORD forty days and forty nights; he did neither eat bread, nor drink water. And he wrote upon the tables the words of the covenant, the ten commandments.

29 ¶ And it came to pass, when Moses came down from mount Sī'naī with the two tables of testimony in Moses' hand, when he came down from the mount, that Moses wist not that the skin of his face shone while he talked with him.

30 And when Aaron and all the children of Ĭṣ'rā-ĕl saw Moses, behold, the skin of his face shone; and they were afraid to come nigh him.

31 And Moses called unto them; and Aaron and all the rulers of the congregation returned unto him: and Moses talked with them.

32 And afterward all the children of Ĭṣ'rā-ĕl came nigh: and he gave them in commandment all that the LORD had spoken with him in mount Sī'naī.

33 And *till* Moses had done speaking with them, he put a veil on his face.

34 But when Moses went in before the LORD to speak with him, he took the veil off, until he came out. And he came out, and spake unto the children of Ĭṣ'rā-ĕl *that* which he was commanded.

35 And the children of Ĭṣ'rā-ĕl saw the face of Moses, that the skin of Moses' face shone: and Moses put the veil upon his face again, until he went in to speak with him.

CHAPTER 35

AND Moses gathered all the congregation of the children of Ĭṣ'rā-ĕl together, and said unto them, These *are* the words which the LORD hath commanded, that *ye* should do them.

2 Six days shall work be done, but on the seventh day there shall be to you a holy day, a sabbath of rest to the LORD: whosoever doeth work therein shall be put to death.

3 Ye shall kindle no fire throughout your habitations upon the sabbath day.

4 ¶ And Moses spake unto all the congregation of the children of Ĭṣ'rā-ĕl, saying, This *is* the thing which the LORD commanded, saying,

5 Take ye from among you an offering unto the LORD: whosoever *is* of a willing heart, let him bring it, an offering of the LORD; gold, and silver, and brass,

6 And blue, and purple, and scarlet, and fine linen, and goats' *hair,*

7 And rams' skins dyed red, and badger's skins, and shittim wood,

8 And oil for the light, and spices for anointing oil, and for the sweet incense,

9 And onyx stones, and stones to be set for the ĕph'ŏd, and for the breastplate.

10 And every wise-hearted among you shall come, and make all that the LORD hath commanded;

11 The tabernacle, his tent, and his covering, his taches, and his boards, his bars, his pillars, and his sockets;

12 The ark, and the staves thereof, *with* the mercy seat, and the veil of the covering;

13 The table, and his staves, and all his vessels, and the showbread;

14 The candlestick also for the light, and his furniture, and his lamps, with the oil for the light;

15 And the incense altar, and his staves, and the anointing oil, and the sweet incense, and the hanging for the door at the entering in of the tabernacle;

16 The altar of burnt offering, with his brazen grate, his staves, and all his vessels, the laver and his foot;

17 The hangings of the court, his pillars, and their sockets, and the hanging for the door of the court;

18 The pins of the tabernacle, and the pins of the court, and their cords;

19 The clothes of service, to do service in the holy *place,* the holy garments for Aaron the priest, and the garments of his sons, to minister in the priest's office.

20 ¶ And all the congregation of the children of Ĭṣ'rā-ĕl departed from the presence of Moses.

21 And they came, every one whose heart stirred him up, and every one whom his spirit made willing, *and* they brought the LORD's offering to the work

of the tabernacle of the congregation, and for all his service, and for the holy garments.

22 And they came, both men and women, as many as were willing-hearted, *and* brought bracelets, and earrings, and rings, and tablets, all jewels of gold: and every man that offered, *offered* an offering of gold unto the LORD.

23 And every man, with whom was found blue, and purple, and scarlet, and fine linen, and goats' *hair,* and red skins of rams, and badgers' skins, brought *them.*

24 Every one that did offer an offering of silver and brass brought the LORD'S offering: and every man, with whom was found shittim wood for any work of the service, brought *it.*

25 And all the women that were wise-hearted did spin with their hands, and brought that which they had spun, *both* of blue, and of purple, *and* of scarlet, and of fine linen.

26 And all the women whose heart stirred them up in wisdom spun goats' *hair.*

27 And the rulers brought onyx stones, and stones to be set, for the ĕph′ŏd, and for the breastplate;

28 And spice, and oil for the light, and for the anointing oil, and for the sweet incense.

29 The children of Ĭṣ′rā-ĕl brought a willing offering unto the LORD, every man and woman, whose heart made them willing to bring for all manner of work, which the LORD had commanded to be made by the hand of Moses.

30 ¶ And Moses said unto the children of Ĭṣ′rā-ĕl, See, the LORD hath called by name Bē-zăl′ē-ĕl the son of Ū′rī, the son of Hûr, of the tribe of Judah;

31 And he hath filled him with the spirit of God, in wisdom, in understanding, and in knowledge, and in all manner of workmanship;

32 And to devise curious works, to work in gold, and in silver, and in brass,

33 And in the cutting of stones, to set *them,* and in carving of wood, to make any manner of cunning work.

34 And he hath put in his heart that he may teach, *both* he, and Ȧ-hō′lĭ-ăb, the son of Ȧ-hĭs′ȧ-măch, of the tribe of Dan.

35 Them hath he filled with wisdom of heart, to work all manner of work, of the engraver, and of the cunning workman, and of the embroiderer, in blue, and in purple, in scarlet, and in fine linen, and of the weaver, *even* of them that do any work, and of those that devise cunning work.

CHAPTER 36

THEN wrought Bē-zăl′ē-ĕl and Ȧ-hō′lĭ-ăb, and every wise-hearted man, in whom the LORD put wisdom and understanding to know how to work all manner of work for the service of the sanctuary, according to all that the LORD had commanded.

2 And Moses called Bē-zăl′ē-ĕl and Ȧ-hō′lĭ-ăb, and every wise-hearted man, in whose heart the LORD had put wisdom, *even* every one whose heart stirred him up to come unto the work to do it:

3 And they received of Moses all the offering, which the children of Ĭṣ′rā-ĕl had brought for the work of the service of the sanctuary, to make it *withal.* And they brought yet unto him free offerings every morning.

4 And all the wise men, that wrought all the work of the sanctuary, came every man from his work which they made;

5 ¶ And they spake unto Moses, saying, The people bring much more than enough for the service of the work, which the LORD commanded to make.

6 And Moses gave commandment, and they caused it to be proclaimed throughout the camp, saying, Let neither man nor woman make any more work for the offering of the sanctuary. So the people were restrained from bringing.

7 For the stuff they had was sufficient for all the work to make it, and too much.

8 ¶ And every wise-hearted man among them that wrought the work of the tabernacle made ten curtains *of* fine twined linen, and blue, and purple, and scarlet: *with* cherubim of cunning work made he them.

9 The length of one curtain *was* twenty and eight cubits, and the breadth of one curtain four cubits: the curtains *were* all of one size.

10 And he coupled the five curtains one unto another: and *the other* five curtains he coupled one unto another.

11 And he made loops of blue on the edge of one curtain from the selvedge in the coupling: likewise he made in the

uttermost side of *another* curtain, in the coupling of the second.

12 Fifty loops made he in one curtain, and fifty loops made he in the edge of the curtain which *was* in the coupling of the second: the loops held one *curtain* to another.

13 And he made fifty taches of gold, and coupled the curtains one unto another with the taches: so it became one tabernacle.

14 ¶ And he made curtains *of* goats' *hair* for the tent over the tabernacle: eleven curtains he made them.

15 The length of one curtain *was* thirty cubits, and four cubits *was* the breadth of one curtain: the eleven curtains *were* of one size.

16 And he coupled five curtains by themselves, and six curtains by themselves.

17 And he made fifty loops upon the uttermost edge of the curtain in the coupling, and fifty loops made he upon the edge of the curtain which coupleth the second.

18 And he made fifty taches *of* brass to couple the tent together, that it might be one.

19 And he made a covering for the tent *of* rams' skins dyed red, and a covering *of* badgers' skins above *that*.

20 ¶ And he made boards for the tabernacle *of* shittim wood, standing up.

21 The length of a board *was* ten cubits, and the breadth of a board one cubit and a half.

22 One board had two tenons, equally distant one from another: thus did he make for all the boards of the tabernacle.

23 And he made boards for the tabernacle; twenty boards for the south side southward:

24 And forty sockets of silver he made under the twenty boards; two sockets under one board for his two tenons, and two sockets under another board for his two tenons.

25 And for the other side of the tabernacle, *which is* toward the north corner, he made twenty boards,

26 And their forty sockets of silver; two sockets under one board, and two sockets under another board.

27 And for the sides of the tabernacle westward he made six boards.

28 And two boards made he for the corners of the tabernacle in the two sides.

29 And they were coupled beneath, and coupled together at the head thereof, to one ring: thus he did to both of them in both the corners.

30 And there were eight boards; and their sockets *were* sixteen sockets of silver, under every board two sockets.

31 ¶ And he made bars of shittim wood; five for the boards of the one side of the tabernacle,

32 And five bars for the boards of the other side of the tabernacle, and five bars for the boards of the tabernacle for the sides westward.

33 And he made the middle bar to shoot through the boards from the one end to the other.

34 And he overlaid the boards with gold, and made their rings *of* gold *to be* places for the bars, and overlaid the bars with gold.

35 ¶ And he made a veil *of* blue, and purple, and scarlet, and fine twined linen: *with* cherubim made he it of cunning work.

36 And he made thereunto four pillars *of* shittim *wood*, and overlaid them with gold: their hooks *were of* gold; and he cast for them four sockets of silver.

37 ¶ And he made a hanging for the tabernacle door *of* blue, and purple, and scarlet, and fine twined linen, of needlework;

38 And the five pillars of it with their hooks: and he overlaid their chapiters and their fillets with gold: but their five sockets *were of* brass.

CHAPTER 37

AND Bē-zăl'ē-ĕl made the ark *of* shittim wood: two cubits and a half *was* the length of it, and a cubit and a half the breadth of it, and a cubit and a half the height of it:

2 And he overlaid it with pure gold within and without, and made a crown of gold to it round about.

3 And he cast for it four rings of gold, *to be set* by the four corners of it; even two rings upon the one side of it, and two rings upon the other side of it.

4 And he made staves *of* shittim wood, and overlaid them with gold.

5 And he put the staves into the rings by the sides of the ark, to bear the ark.

6 ¶ And he made the mercy seat *of* pure gold: two cubits and a half *was* the

length thereof, and one cubit and a half
the breadth thereof.
7 And he made two cherubim *of* gold,
beaten out of one piece made he them,
on the two ends of the mercy seat;
8 One cherub on the end on this side,
and another cherub on the *other* end on
that side: out of the mercy seat made he
the cherubim on the two ends thereof.
9 And the cherubim spread out *their*
wings on high, *and* covered with their
wings over the mercy seat, with their
faces one to another; *even* to the
mercy seat-ward were the faces of the
cherubim.
10 ¶ And he made the table *of* shittim
wood: two cubits *was* the length thereof.
and a cubit the breadth thereof, and a
cubit and a half the height thereof:
11 And he overlaid it with pure gold,
and made thereunto a crown of gold
round about.
12 Also he made thereunto a border of
a handbreadth round about; and made
a crown of gold for the border thereof
round about.
13 And he cast for it four rings of gold,
and put the rings upon the four corners
that *were* in the four feet thereof.
14 Over against the border were the
rings, the places for the staves to bear
the table.
15 And he made the staves *of* shittim
wood, and overlaid them with gold, to
bear the table.
16 And he made the vessels which
were upon the table, his dishes, and his
spoons, and his bowls, and his covers to
cover withal, *of* pure gold.
17 ¶ And he made the candlestick *of*
pure gold: *of* beaten work made he the
candlestick; his shaft, and his branch,
his bowls, his knops, and his flowers,
were of the same:
18 And six branches going out of the
sides thereof; three branches of the
candlestick out of the one side thereof,
and three branches of the candlestick
out of the other side thereof:
19 Three bowls made after the fashion
of almonds in one branch, a knop and a
flower; and three bowls made like almonds in another branch, a knop and a
flower: so throughout the six branches
going out of the candlestick.
20 And in the candlestick *were* four
bowls made like almonds, his knops,
and his flowers:
21 And a knop under two branches
of the same, and a knop under two
branches of the same, and a knop under
two branches of the same, according to
the six branches going out of it.
22 Their knops and their branches
were of the same: all of it *was* one
beaten work *of* pure gold.
23 And he made his seven lamps, and
his snuffers, and his snuffdishes, *of*
pure gold.
24 *Of* a talent of pure gold made he it,
and all the vessels thereof.
25 ¶ And he made the incense altar
of shittim wood: the length of it *was* a
cubit, and the breadth of it a cubit; *it*
was foursquare; and two cubits *was* the
height of it; the horns thereof were of
the same.
26 And he overlaid it with pure gold,
both the top of it, and the sides thereof
round about, and the horns of it: also he
made unto it a crown of gold round
about.
27 And he made two rings of gold for it
under the crown thereof, by the two corners of it, upon the two sides thereof, to
be places for the staves to bear it withal.
28 And he made the staves *of* shittim
wood, and overlaid them with gold.
29 ¶ And he made the holy anointing
oil, and the pure incense of sweet spices,
according to the work of the apothecary.

CHAPTER 38

AND he made the altar of burnt offering *of* shittim wood: five cubits *was*
the length thereof, and five cubits the
breadth thereof; *it was* foursquare; and
three cubits the height thereof.
2 And he made the horns thereof on
the four corners of it; the horns thereof
were of the same: and he overlaid it
with brass.
3 And he made all the vessels of the
altar, the pots, and the shovels, and the
basins, *and* the fleshhooks, and the firepans: all the vessels thereof made he *of*
brass.
4 And he made for the altar a brazen
grate of network, under the compass
thereof, beneath unto the midst of it.
5 And he cast four rings for the four
ends of the grate of brass, *to be* places
for the staves.
6 And he made the staves *of* shittim
wood, and overlaid them with brass.
7 And he put the staves into the rings

on the sides of the altar, to bear it
withal; he made the altar hollow with
boards.
8 ¶ And he made the laver *of* brass,
and the foot of it *of* brass, of the looking-
glasses of *the women* assembling, which
assembled *at* the door of the tabernacle
of the congregation.
9 ¶ And he made the court: on the
south side southward the hangings of
the court *were of* fine twined linen, a
hundred cubits:
10 Their pillars *were* twenty, and their
brazen sockets twenty; the hooks of the
pillars and their fillets *were of* silver.
11 And for the north side *the hangings*
were a hundred cubits, their pillars
were twenty, and their sockets of brass
twenty; the hooks of the pillars and
their fillets *of* silver.
12 And for the west side *were* hangings
of fifty cubits, their pillars ten, and their
sockets ten; the hooks of the pillars and
their fillets *of* silver.
13 And for the east side eastward fifty
cubits.
14 The hangings of the one side *of the*
gate were fifteen cubits; their pillars
three, and their sockets three.
15 And for the other side of the court
gate, on this hand and that hand, *were*
hangings of fifteen cubits; their pillars
three, and their sockets three.
16 All the hangings of the court round
about *were* of fine twined linen.
17 And the sockets for the pillars *were*
of brass; the hooks of the pillars and
their fillets *of* silver; and the overlaying
of their chapiters *of* silver; and all the
pillars of the court *were* filleted with
silver.
18 And the hanging for the gate of the
court *was* needlework, *of* blue, and purple, and scarlet, and fine twined linen:
and twenty cubits *was* the length, and
the height in the breadth *was* five cubits,
answerable to the hangings of the court.
19 And their pillars *were* four, and
their sockets *of* brass four; their hooks
of silver, and the overlaying of their
chapiters and their fillets *of* silver.
20 And all the pins of the tabernacle,
and of the court round about, *were of*
brass.
21 ¶ This is the sum of the tabernacle,
even of the tabernacle of testimony, as
it was counted, according to the commandment of Moses, *for* the service of
the Lē′vītes, by the hand of Ĭth′ȧ-mär,
son to Aaron the priest.
22 And Bē-zăl′ē-ĕl the son of Ū′rī, the
son of Hûr, of the tribe of Judah, made
all that the LORD commanded Moses.
23 And with him *was* Ȧ-hō′lĭ-ăb, son
of Ȧ-hĭs′ȧ-măch, of the tribe of Dan, an
engraver, and a cunning workman, and
an embroiderer in blue, and in purple,
and in scarlet, and fine linen.
24 All the gold that was occupied for
the work in all the work of the holy
place, even the gold of the offering, was
twenty and nine talents, and seven hundred and thirty shekels, after the shekel
of the sanctuary.
25 And the silver of them that were
numbered of the congregation *was* a
hundred talents, and a thousand seven
hundred and threescore and fifteen
shekels, after the shekel of the sanctuary:
26 A bē′käh for every man, *that is,* half
a shekel, after the shekel of the sanctuary, for every one that went to be
numbered, from twenty years old and
upward, for six hundred thousand and
three thousand and five hundred and
fifty *men.*
27 And of the hundred talents of silver
were cast the sockets of the sanctuary,
and the sockets of the veil; a hundred
sockets of the hundred talents, a talent
for a socket.
28 And of the thousand seven hundred
seventy and five *shekels* he made hooks
for the pillars, and overlaid their chapiters, and filleted them.
29 And the brass of the offering *was*
seventy talents, and two thousand and
four hundred shekels.
30 And therewith he made the sockets
to the door of the tabernacle of the congregation, and the brazen altar, and the
brazen grate for it, and all the vessels of
the altar,
31 And the sockets of the court round
about, and the sockets of the court gate,
and all the pins of the tabernacle, and
all the pins of the court round about.

CHAPTER 39

AND of the blue, and purple, and
scarlet, they made clothes of service, to do service in the holy *place,* and
made the holy garments for Aaron; as
the LORD commanded Moses.
2 And he made the ĕph′ŏd *of* gold, blue,

and purple, and scarlet, and fine twined linen.

3 And they did beat the gold into thin plates, and cut *it into* wires, to work *it* in the blue, and in the purple, and in the scarlet, and in the fine linen, *with* cunning work.

4 They made shoulderpieces for it, to couple *it* together: by the two edges was it coupled together.

5 And the curious girdle of his ĕph'ŏd, that *was* upon it, *was* of the same, according to the work thereof; *of* gold, blue, and purple, and scarlet, and fine twined linen; as the LORD commanded Moses.

6 ¶ And they wrought onyx stones inclosed in ouches of gold, graven, as signets are graven, with the names of the children of Ĭş'rā-ĕl.

7 And he put them on the shoulders of the ĕph'ŏd, *that they should be* stones for a memorial to the children of Ĭş'rā-ĕl; as the LORD commanded Moses.

8 ¶ And he made the breastplate *of* cunning work, like the work of the ĕph'ŏd; *of* gold, blue, and purple, and scarlet, and fine twined linen.

9 It was foursquare; they made the breastplate double: a span *was* the length thereof, and a span the breadth thereof, *being* doubled.

10 And they set in it four rows of stones: *the first* row *was* a sardius, a topaz, and a carbuncle: this *was* the first row.

11 And the second row, an emerald, a sapphire, and a diamond.

12 And the third row, a ligure, an agate, and an amethyst.

13 And the fourth row, a beryl, an onyx, and a jasper: *they were* inclosed in ouches of gold in their inclosings.

14 And the stones *were* according to the names of the children of Ĭş'rā-ĕl, twelve according to their names, *like* the engravings of a signet, every one with his name, according to the twelve tribes.

15 And they made upon the breastplate chains at the ends, *of* wreathed work *of* pure gold.

16 And they made two ouches *of* gold, and two gold rings, and put the two rings in the two ends of the breastplate.

17 And they put the two wreathed chains of gold in the two rings on the ends of the breastplate.

18 And the two ends of the two wreathed chains they fastened in the two ouches, and put them on the shoulderpieces of the ĕph'ŏd, before it.

19 And they made two rings of gold, and put *them* on the two ends of the breastplate, upon the border of it, which *was* on the side of the ĕph'ŏd inward.

20 And they made two *other* golden rings, and put them on the two sides of the ĕph'ŏd underneath, toward the forepart of it, over against the *other* coupling thereof, above the curious girdle of the ĕph'ŏd.

21 And they did bind the breastplate by his rings unto the rings of the ĕph'ŏd with a lace of blue, that it might be above the curious girdle of the ĕph'ŏd, and that the breastplate might not be loosed from the ĕph'ŏd; as the LORD commanded Moses.

22 ¶ And he made the robe of the ĕph'ŏd *of* woven work, all *of* blue.

23 And *there was* a hole in the midst of the robe, as the hole of an habergeon, *with* a band round about the hole, that it should not rend.

24 And they made upon the hems of the robe pomegranates *of* blue, and purple, and scarlet, *and* twined *linen.*

25 And they made bells *of* pure gold, and put the bells between the pomegranates upon the hem of the robe, round about between the pomegranates;

26 A bell and a pomegranate, a bell and a pomegranate, round about the hem of the robe to minister *in;* as the LORD commanded Moses.

27 ¶ And they made coats *of* fine linen *of* woven work for Aaron, and for his sons,

28 And a mitre *of* fine linen, and goodly bonnets *of* fine linen, and linen breeches *of* fine twined linen,

29 And a girdle *of* fine twined linen, and blue, and purple, and scarlet, *of* needlework; as the LORD commanded Moses.

30 ¶ And they made the plate of the holy crown *of* pure gold, and wrote upon it a writing, *like to* the engravings of a signet, HOLINESS TO THE LORD.

31 And they tied unto it a lace of blue, to fasten *it* on high upon the mitre; as the LORD commanded Moses.

32 ¶ Thus was all the work of the tabernacle of the tent of the congregation finished: and the children of Ĭş'rā-ĕl

did according to all that the LORD commanded Moses, so did they.

33 ¶ And they brought the tabernacle unto Moses, the tent, and all his furniture, his taches, his boards, his bars, and his pillars, and his sockets;

34 And the covering of rams' skins dyed red, and the covering of badgers' skins, and the veil of the covering;

35 The ark of the testimony, and the staves thereof, and the mercy seat;

36 The table, *and* all the vessels thereof, and the showbread;

37 The pure candlestick, *with* the lamps thereof, *even with* the lamps to be set in order, and all the vessels thereof, and the oil for light;

38 And the golden altar, and the anointing oil, and the sweet incense, and the hanging for the tabernacle door;

39 The brazen altar, and his grate of brass, his staves, and all his vessels, the laver and his foot;

40 The hangings of the court, his pillars, and his sockets, and the hanging for the court gate, his cords, and his pins, and all the vessels of the service of the tabernacle, for the tent of the congregation;

41 The clothes of service to do service in the holy *place,* and the holy garments for Aaron the priest, and his sons' garments, to minister in the priest's office.

42 According to all that the LORD commanded Moses, so the children of Is′rā-ĕl made all the work.

43 And Moses did look upon all the work, and, behold, they had done it as the LORD had commanded, even so had they done it: and Moses blessed them.

CHAPTER 40

AND the LORD spake unto Moses, saying,

2 On the first day of the first month shalt thou set up the tabernacle of the tent of the congregation.

3 And thou shalt put therein the ark of the testimony, and cover the ark with the veil.

4 And thou shalt bring in the table, and set in order the things that are to be set in order upon it; and thou shalt bring in the candlestick, and light the lamps thereof.

5 And thou shalt set the altar of gold for the incense before the ark of the testimony, and put the hanging of the door to the tabernacle.

6 And thou shalt set the altar of the burnt offering before the door of the tabernacle of the tent of the congregation.

7 And thou shalt set the laver between the tent of the congregation and the altar, and shalt put water therein.

8 And thou shalt set up the court round about, and hang up the hanging at the court gate.

9 And thou shalt take the anointing oil, and anoint the tabernacle, and all that *is* therein, and shalt hallow it, and all the vessels thereof: and it shall be holy.

10 And thou shalt anoint the altar of the burnt offering, and all his vessels, and sanctify the altar: and it shall be an altar most holy.

11 And thou shalt anoint the laver and his foot, and sanctify it.

12 And thou shalt bring Aaron and his sons unto the door of the tabernacle of the congregation, and wash them with water.

13 And thou shalt put upon Aaron the holy garments, and anoint him, and sanctify him; that he may minister unto me in the priest's office.

14 And thou shalt bring his sons, and clothe them with coats:

15 And thou shalt anoint them, as thou didst anoint their father, that they may minister unto me in the priest's office: for their anointing shall surely be an everlasting priesthood throughout their generations.

16 Thus did Moses: according to all that the LORD commanded him, so did he.

17 ¶ And it came to pass in the first month in the second year, on the first *day* of the month, *that* the tabernacle was reared up.

18 And Moses reared up the tabernacle, and fastened his sockets, and set up the boards thereof, and put in the bars thereof, and reared up his pillars.

19 And he spread abroad the tent over the tabernacle, and put the covering of the tent above upon it; as the LORD commanded Moses.

20 ¶ And he took and put the testimony into the ark, and set the staves on the ark, and put the mercy seat above upon the ark:

21 And he brought the ark into the tabernacle, and set up the veil of the

covering, and covered the ark of the testimony; as the LORD commanded Moses.

22 ¶ And he put the table in the tent of the congregation, upon the side of the tabernacle northward, without the veil.

23 And he set the bread in order upon it before the LORD; as the LORD had commanded Moses.

24 ¶ And he put the candlestick in the tent of the congregation, over against the table, on the side of the tabernacle southward.

25 And he lighted the lamps before the LORD; as the LORD commanded Moses.

26 ¶ And he put the golden altar in the tent of the congregation before the veil:

27 And he burnt sweet incense thereon; as the LORD commanded Moses.

28 ¶ And he set up the hanging *at* the door of the tabernacle.

29 And he put the altar of burnt offering *by* the door of the tabernacle of the tent of the congregation, and offered upon it the burnt offering and the meat offering; as the LORD commanded Moses.

30 ¶ And he set the laver between the tent of the congregation and the altar, and put water there, to wash *withal*.

31 And Moses and Aaron and his sons washed their hands and their feet thereat:

32 When they went into the tent of the congregation, and when they came near unto the altar, they washed; as the LORD commanded Moses.

33 And he reared up the court round about the tabernacle and the altar, and set up the hanging of the court gate. So Moses finished the work.

34 ¶ Then a cloud covered the tent of the congregation, and the glory of the LORD filled the tabernacle.

35 And Moses was not able to enter into the tent of the congregation, because the cloud abode thereon, and the glory of the LORD filled the tabernacle.

36 And when the cloud was taken up from over the tabernacle, the children of Ĭş′rā-ĕl went onward in all their journeys:

37 But if the cloud were not taken up, then they journeyed not till the day that it was taken up.

38 For the cloud of the LORD *was* upon the tabernacle by day, and fire was on it by night, in the sight of all the house of Ĭş′rā-ĕl, throughout all their journeys.

THE THIRD BOOK OF MOSES, CALLED

LEVITICUS

CHAPTER 1

AND the LORD called unto Moses, and spake unto him out of the tabernacle of the congregation, saying,

2 Speak unto the children of Ĭş′rā-ĕl, and say unto them, If any man of you bring an offering unto the LORD, ye shall bring your offering of the cattle, *even* of the herd, and of the flock.

3 If his offering *be* a burnt sacrifice of the herd, let him offer a male without blemish: he shall offer it of his own voluntary will at the door of the tabernacle of the congregation before the LORD.

4 And he shall put his hand upon the head of the burnt offering; and it shall be accepted for him to make atonement for him.

5 And he shall kill the bullock before the LORD: and the priests, Aaron's sons, shall bring the blood, and sprinkle the blood round about upon the altar that *is* *by* the door of the tabernacle of the congregation.

6 And he shall flay the burnt offering, and cut it into his pieces.

7 And the sons of Aaron the priest shall put fire upon the altar, and lay the wood in order upon the fire:

8 And the priests, Aaron's sons, shall lay the parts, the head, and the fat, in order upon the wood that *is* on the fire which *is* upon the altar:

9 But his inwards and his legs shall he wash in water: and the priest shall burn all on the altar, *to be* a burnt sacrifice, an offering made by fire, of a sweet savor unto the LORD.

10 ¶ And if his offering *be* of the flocks,

namely, of the sheep, or of the goats,
for a burnt sacrifice; he shall bring it a
male without blemish.
11 And he shall kill it on the side of the
altar northward before the LORD: and
the priests, Aaron's sons, shall sprinkle
his blood round about upon the altar.
12 And he shall cut it into his pieces,
with his head and his fat: and the
priest shall lay them in order on the
wood that *is* on the fire which *is* upon
the altar:
13 But he shall wash the inwards and
the legs with water: and the priest shall
bring *it* all, and burn *it* upon the altar:
it *is* a burnt sacrifice, an offering made
by fire, of a sweet savor unto the
LORD.
14 ¶ And if the burnt sacrifice for his
offering to the LORD *be* of fowls, then he
shall bring his offering of turtledoves, or
of young pigeons.
15 And the priest shall bring it unto the
altar, and wring off his head, and burn
it on the altar; and the blood thereof
shall be wrung out at the side of the altar:
16 And he shall pluck away his crop
with his feathers, and cast it beside the
altar on the east part, by the place of the
ashes.
17 And he shall cleave it with the wings
thereof, *but* shall not divide *it* asunder:
and the priest shall burn it upon the
altar, upon the wood that *is* upon the
fire: it *is* a burnt sacrifice, an offering
made by fire, of a sweet savor unto the
LORD.

CHAPTER 2

AND when any will offer a meat offering unto the LORD, his offering
shall be *of* fine flour; and he shall pour
oil upon it, and put frankincense
thereon.
2 And he shall bring it to Aaron's sons
the priests: and he shall take thereout
his handful of the flour thereof, and of
the oil thereof, with all the frankincense
thereof; and the priest shall burn the
memorial of it upon the altar, *to be* an
offering made by fire, of a sweet savor
unto the LORD:
3 And the remnant of the meat offering
shall be Aaron's and his sons': *it is* a
thing most holy of the offerings of the
LORD made by fire.
4 ¶ And if thou bring an oblation of a
meat offering baked in the oven, *it shall*
be unleavened cakes of fine flour mingled with oil, or unleavened wafers
anointed with oil.
5 ¶ And if thy oblation *be* a meat offering *baked* in a pan, it shall be *of* fine
flour unleavened, mingled with oil.
6 Thou shalt part it in pieces, and pour
oil thereon: it *is* a meat offering.
7 ¶ And if thy oblation *be* a meat offering *baked* in the frying pan, it shall be
made *of* fine flour with oil.
8 And thou shalt bring the meat offering that is made of these things unto
the LORD: and when it is presented
unto the priest, he shall bring it unto the
altar.
9 And the priest shall take from the
meat offering a memorial thereof, and
shall burn *it* upon the altar: *it is* an offering made by fire, of a sweet savor unto
the LORD.
10 And that which is left of the meat
offering *shall be* Aaron's and his sons':
it is a thing most holy of the offerings of
the LORD made by fire.
11 No meat offering, which ye shall
bring unto the LORD, shall be made with
leaven: for ye shall burn no leaven, nor
any honey, in any offering of the LORD
made by fire.
12 ¶ As for the oblation of the firstfruits, ye shall offer them unto the LORD:
but they shall not be burnt on the altar
for a sweet savor.
13 And every oblation of thy meat offering shalt thou season with salt; neither
shalt thou suffer the salt of the covenant of thy God to be lacking from thy
meat offering: with all thine offerings
thou shalt offer salt.
14 And if thou offer a meat offering of
thy firstfruits unto the LORD, thou shalt
offer for the meat offering of thy firstfruits green ears of corn dried by the
fire, *even* corn beaten out of full ears.
15 And thou shalt put oil upon it, and
lay frankincense thereon: it *is* a meat
offering.
16 And the priest shall burn the memorial of it, *part* of the beaten corn
thereof, and *part* of the oil thereof, with
all the frankincense thereof: *it is* an
offering made by fire unto the LORD.

CHAPTER 3

AND if his oblation *be* a sacrifice of
peace offering, if he offer *it* of the
herd, whether *it be* a male or female, he

shall offer it without blemish before the LORD.

2 And he shall lay his hand upon the head of his offering, and kill it *at* the door of the tabernacle of the congregation: and Aaron's sons the priests shall sprinkle the blood upon the altar round about.

3 And he shall offer of the sacrifice of the peace offering an offering made by fire unto the LORD; the fat that covereth the inwards, and all the fat that *is* upon the inwards,

4 And the two kidneys, and the fat that *is* on them, which *is* by the flanks, and the caul above the liver, with the kidneys, it shall he take away.

5 And Aaron's sons shall burn it on the altar upon the burnt sacrifice, which *is* upon the wood that *is* on the fire: *it is* an offering made by fire, of a sweet savor unto the LORD.

6 ¶ And if his offering for a sacrifice of peace offering unto the LORD *be* of the flock, male or female, he shall offer it without blemish.

7 If he offer a lamb for his offering, then shall he offer it before the LORD.

8 And he shall lay his hand upon the head of his offering, and kill it before the tabernacle of the congregation: and Aaron's sons shall sprinkle the blood thereof round about upon the altar.

9 And he shall offer of the sacrifice of the peace offering an offering made by fire unto the LORD; the fat thereof, *and* the whole rump, it shall he take off hard by the backbone; and the fat that covereth the inwards, and all the fat that *is* upon the inwards,

10 And the two kidneys, and the fat that *is* upon them, which *is* by the flanks, and the caul above the liver, with the kidneys, it shall he take away.

11 And the priest shall burn it upon the altar: *it is* the food of the offering made by fire unto the LORD.

12 ¶ And if his offering *be* a goat, then he shall offer it before the LORD.

13 And he shall lay his hand upon the head of it, and kill it before the tabernacle of the congregation: and the sons of Aaron shall sprinkle the blood thereof upon the altar round about.

14 And he shall offer thereof his offering, *even* an offering made by fire unto the LORD; the fat that covereth the inwards, and all the fat that *is* upon the inwards,

15 And the two kidneys, and the fat that *is* upon them, which *is* by the flanks, and the caul above the liver, with the kidneys, it shall he take away.

16 And the priest shall burn them upon the altar: *it is* the food of the offering made by fire for a sweet savor: all the fat *is* the LORD's.

17 *It shall be* a perpetual statute for your generations throughout all your dwellings, that ye eat neither fat nor blood.

CHAPTER 4

AND the LORD spake unto Moses, saying,

2 Speak unto the children of Is'rā-ĕl, saying, If a soul shall sin through ignorance against any of the commandments of the LORD *concerning things* which ought not to be done, and shall do against any of them:

3 If the priest that is anointed do sin according to the sin of the people; then let him bring for his sin, which he hath sinned, a young bullock without blemish unto the LORD for a sin offering.

4 And he shall bring the bullock unto the door of the tabernacle of the congregation before the LORD; and shall lay his hand upon the bullock's head, and kill the bullock before the LORD.

5 And the priest that is anointed shall take of the bullock's blood, and bring it to the tabernacle of the congregation:

6 And the priest shall dip his finger in the blood, and sprinkle of the blood seven times before the LORD, before the veil of the sanctuary.

7 And the priest shall put *some* of the blood upon the horns of the altar of sweet incense before the LORD, which *is* in the tabernacle of the congregation; and shall pour all the blood of the bullock at the bottom of the altar of the burnt offering, which *is at* the door of the tabernacle of the congregation.

8 And he shall take off from it all the fat of the bullock for the sin offering; the fat that covereth the inwards, and all the fat that *is* upon the inwards,

9 And the two kidneys, and the fat that *is* upon them, which *is* by the flanks, and the caul above the liver, with the kidneys, it shall he take away,

10 As it was taken off from the bullock

of the sacrifice of peace offerings: and the priest shall burn them upon the altar of the burnt offering.

11 And the skin of the bullock, and all his flesh, with his head, and with his legs, and his inwards, and his dung,

12 Even the whole bullock shall he carry forth without the camp unto a clean place, where the ashes are poured out, and burn him on the wood with fire: where the ashes are poured out shall he be burnt.

13 ¶ And if the whole congregation of Ĭṣ′rā-ĕl sin through ignorance, and the thing be hid from the eyes of the assembly, and they have done *somewhat against* any of the commandments of the LORD *concerning things* which should not be done, and are guilty;

14 When the sin, which they have sinned against it, is known, then the congregation shall offer a young bullock for the sin, and bring him before the tabernacle of the congregation.

15 And the elders of the congregation shall lay their hands upon the head of the bullock before the LORD; and the bullock shall be killed before the LORD.

16 And the priest that is anointed shall bring of the bullock's blood to the tabernacle of the congregation:

17 And the priest shall dip his finger *in some* of the blood, and sprinkle *it* seven times before the LORD, *even* before the veil.

18 And he shall put *some* of the blood upon the horns of the altar which *is* before the LORD, that *is* in the tabernacle of the congregation, and shall pour out all the blood at the bottom of the altar of the burnt offering, which *is at* the door of the tabernacle of the congregation.

19 And he shall take all his fat from him, and burn *it* upon the altar.

20 And he shall do with the bullock as he did with the bullock for a sin offering, so shall he do with this: and the priest shall make an atonement for them, and it shall be forgiven them.

21 And he shall carry forth the bullock without the camp, and burn him as he burned the first bullock: it *is* a sin offering for the congregation.

22 ¶ When a ruler hath sinned, and done *somewhat* through ignorance *against* any of the commandments of the LORD his God *concerning things* which should not be done, and is guilty;

23 Or if his sin, wherein he hath sinned, come to his knowledge; he shall bring his offering, a kid of the goats, a male without blemish:

24 And he shall lay his hand upon the head of the goat, and kill it in the place where they kill the burnt offering before the LORD: it *is* a sin offering.

25 And the priest shall take of the blood of the sin offering with his finger, and put *it* upon the horns of the altar of burnt offering, and shall pour out his blood at the bottom of the altar of burnt offering.

26 And he shall burn all his fat upon the altar, as the fat of the sacrifice of peace offerings: and the priest shall make an atonement for him as concerning his sin, and it shall be forgiven him.

27 ¶ And if any one of the common people sin through ignorance, while he doeth *somewhat against* any of the commandments of the LORD, *concerning things* which ought not to be done, and be guilty;

28 Or if his sin, which he hath sinned, come to his knowledge; then he shall bring his offering, a kid of the goats, a female without blemish, for his sin which he hath sinned.

29 And he shall lay his hand upon the head of the sin offering, and slay the sin offering in the place of the burnt offering.

30 And the priest shall take of the blood thereof with his finger, and put *it* upon the horns of the altar of burnt offering, and shall pour out all the blood thereof at the bottom of the altar.

31 And he shall take away all the fat thereof, as the fat is taken away from off the sacrifice of peace offerings; and the priest shall burn *it* upon the altar for a sweet savor unto the LORD; and the priest shall make an atonement for him, and it shall be forgiven him.

32 And if he bring a lamb for a sin offering, he shall bring it a female without blemish.

33 And he shall lay his hand upon the head of the sin offering, and slay it for a sin offering in the place where they kill the burnt offering.

34 And the priest shall take of the blood of the sin offering with his finger, and put *it* upon the horns of the altar of burnt offering, and shall pour out all the blood thereof at the bottom of the altar:

35 And he shall take away all the fat thereof, as the fat of the lamb is taken away from the sacrifice of the peace offerings; and the priest shall burn them upon the altar, according to the offerings made by fire unto the LORD: and the priest shall make an atonement for his sin that he hath committed, and it shall be forgiven him.

CHAPTER 5

AND if a soul sin, and hear the voice of swearing, and *is* a witness, whether he hath seen or known *of it;* if he do not utter *it,* then he shall bear his iniquity.

2 Or if a soul touch any unclean thing, whether *it be* a carcass of an unclean beast, or a carcass of unclean cattle, or the carcass of unclean creeping things, and *if* it be hidden from him; he also shall be unclean, and guilty.

3 Or if he touch the uncleanness of man, whatsoever uncleanness *it be* that a man shall be defiled withal, and it be hid from him; when he knoweth *of it,* then he shall be guilty.

4 Or if a soul swear, pronouncing with *his* lips to do evil, or to do good, whatsoever *it be* that a man shall pronounce with an oath, and it be hid from him; when he knoweth *of it,* then he shall be guilty in one of these.

5 And it shall be, when he shall be guilty in one of these *things,* that he shall confess that he hath sinned in that *thing:*

6 And he shall bring his trespass offering unto the LORD for his sin which he hath sinned, a female from the flock, a lamb, or a kid of the goats, for a sin offering; and the priest shall make an atonement for him concerning his sin.

7 And if he be not able to bring a lamb, then he shall bring for his trespass, which he hath committed, two turtledoves, or two young pigeons, unto the LORD; one for a sin offering, and the other for a burnt offering.

8 And he shall bring them unto the priest, who shall offer *that* which *is* for the sin offering first, and wring off his head from his neck, but shall not divide *it* asunder:

9 And he shall sprinkle of the blood of the sin offering upon the side of the altar; and the rest of the blood shall be wrung out at the bottom of the altar: it *is* a sin offering.

10 And he shall offer the second *for* a burnt offering, according to the manner: and the priest shall make an atonement for him for his sin which he hath sinned, and it shall be forgiven him.

11 ¶ But if he be not able to bring two turtledoves, or two young pigeons, then he that sinned shall bring for his offering the tenth part of an ē′phȧh of fine flour for a sin offering; he shall put no oil upon it, neither shall he put *any* frankincense thereon: for it *is* a sin offering.

12 Then shall he bring it to the priest, and the priest shall take his handful of it, *even* a memorial thereof, and burn *it* on the altar, according to the offerings made by fire unto the LORD: it *is* a sin offering.

13 And the priest shall make an atonement for him as touching his sin that he hath sinned in one of these, and it shall be forgiven him: and *the remnant* shall be the priest's, as a meat offering.

14 ¶ And the LORD spake unto Moses, saying,

15 If a soul commit a trespass, and sin through ignorance, in the holy things of the LORD; then he shall bring for his trespass unto the LORD a ram without blemish out of the flocks, with thy estimation by shekels of silver, after the shekel of the sanctuary, for a trespass offering:

16 And he shall make amends for the harm that he hath done in the holy thing, and shall add the fifth part thereto, and give it unto the priest: and the priest shall make an atonement for him with the ram of the trespass offering, and it shall be forgiven him.

17 ¶ And if a soul sin, and commit any of these things which are forbidden to be done by the commandments of the LORD; though he wist *it* not, yet is he guilty, and shall bear his iniquity.

18 And he shall bring a ram without blemish out of the flock, with thy estimation, for a trespass offering, unto the priest: and the priest shall make an atonement for him concerning his ignorance wherein he erred and wist *it* not, and it shall be forgiven him.

19 It *is* a trespass offering: he hath certainly trespassed against the LORD.

CHAPTER 6

AND the LORD spake unto Moses, saying,

2 If a soul sin, and commit a trespass

against the LORD, and lie unto his neighbor in that which was delivered him to
keep, or in fellowship, or in a thing
taken away by violence, or hath deceived his neighbor;
3 Or have found that which was lost,
and lieth concerning it, and sweareth
falsely; in any of all these that a man
doeth, sinning therein:
4 Then it shall be, because he hath
sinned, and is guilty, that he shall restore that which he took violently away,
or the thing which he hath deceitfully
gotten, or that which was delivered him
to keep, or the lost thing which he found,
5 Or all that about which he hath sworn
falsely; he shall even restore it in the
principal, and shall add the fifth part
more thereto, *and* give it unto him to
whom it appertaineth, in the day of his
trespass offering.
6 And he shall bring his trespass offering unto the LORD, a ram without blemish out of the flock, with thy estimation,
for a trespass offering, unto the priest:
7 And the priest shall make an atonement for him before the LORD: and it
shall be forgiven him for any thing of all
that he hath done in trespassing therein.
8 ¶ And the LORD spake unto Moses,
saying,
9 Command Aaron and his sons, saying, This *is* the law of the burnt offering:
It *is* the burnt offering, because of the
burning upon the altar all night unto the
morning, and the fire of the altar shall
be burning in it.
10 And the priest shall put on his linen
garment, and his linen breeches shall he
put upon his flesh, and take up the ashes
which the fire hath consumed with the
burnt offering on the altar, and he shall
put them beside the altar.
11 And he shall put off his garments,
and put on other garments, and carry
forth the ashes without the camp unto
a clean place.
12 And the fire upon the altar shall be
burning in it; it shall not be put out: and
the priest shall burn wood on it every
morning, and lay the burnt offering in
order upon it; and he shall burn thereon
the fat of the peace offerings.
13 The fire shall ever be burning upon
the altar; it shall never go out.
14 ¶ And this *is* the law of the meat
offering: The sons of Aaron shall offer it
before the LORD, before the altar.
15 And he shall take of it his handful,
of the flour of the meat offering, and of
the oil thereof, and all the frankincense
which *is* upon the meat offering, and
shall burn *it* upon the altar *for* a sweet
savor, *even* the memorial of it, unto the
LORD.
16 And the remainder thereof shall
Aaron and his sons eat: with unleavened
bread shall it be eaten in the holy place;
in the court of the tabernacle of the congregation they shall eat it.
17 It shall not be baked with leaven. I
have given it *unto them for* their portion
of my offerings made by fire; it *is* most
holy, as *is* the sin offering, and as the
trespass offering.
18 All the males among the children of
Aaron shall eat of it. *It shall be* a statute
for ever in your generations concerning
the offerings of the LORD made by fire:
every one that toucheth them shall be
holy.
19 ¶ And the LORD spake unto Moses,
saying,
20 This *is* the offering of Aaron and of
his sons, which they shall offer unto the
LORD in the day when he is anointed;
the tenth part of an ē′phăh of fine flour
for a meat offering perpetual, half of
it in the morning, and half thereof at
night.
21 In a pan it shall be made with oil;
and when it is baked, thou shalt bring it
in: *and* the baked pieces of the meat
offering shalt thou offer *for* a sweet savor
unto the LORD.
22 And the priest of his sons that is
anointed in his stead shall offer it: *it is*
a statute for ever unto the LORD; it shall
be wholly burnt.
23 For every meat offering for the priest
shall be wholly burnt: it shall not be
eaten.
24 ¶ And the LORD spake unto Moses,
saying,
25 Speak unto Aaron and to his sons,
saying, This *is* the law of the sin offering:
In the place where the burnt offering is
killed shall the sin offering be killed before the LORD: it *is* most holy.
26 The priest that offereth it for sin
shall eat it: in the holy place shall it be
eaten, in the court of the tabernacle of
the congregation.
27 Whatsoever shall touch the flesh
thereof shall be holy: and when there is
sprinkled of the blood thereof upon any

garment, thou shalt wash that whereon it was sprinkled in the holy place.

28 But the earthen vessel wherein it is sodden shall be broken: and if it be sodden in a brazen pot, it shall be both scoured, and rinsed in water.

29 All the males among the priests shall eat thereof: it *is* most holy.

30 And no sin offering, whereof *any* of the blood is brought into the tabernacle of the congregation to reconcile *withal* in the holy *place*, shall be eaten: it shall be burnt in the fire.

CHAPTER 7

LIKEWISE this *is* the law of the trespass offering: it *is* most holy.

2 In the place where they kill the burnt offering shall they kill the trespass offering: and the blood thereof shall he sprinkle round about upon the altar.

3 And he shall offer of it all the fat thereof; the rump, and the fat that covereth the inwards,

4 And the two kidneys, and the fat that *is* on them, which *is* by the flanks, and the caul *that is* above the liver, with the kidneys, it shall he take away:

5 And the priest shall burn them upon the altar *for* an offering made by fire unto the LORD: it *is* a trespass offering.

6 Every male among the priests shall eat thereof: it shall be eaten in the holy place: it *is* most holy.

7 As the sin offering *is*, so *is* the trespass offering: *there is* one law for them: the priest that maketh atonement therewith shall have *it*.

8 And the priest that offereth any man's burnt offering, *even* the priest shall have to himself the skin of the burnt offering which he hath offered.

9 And all the meat offering that is baked in the oven, and all that is dressed in the frying pan, and in the pan, shall be the priest's that offereth it.

10 And every meat offering, mingled with oil, and dry, shall all the sons of Aaron have, one *as much* as another.

11 And this *is* the law of the sacrifice of peace offerings, which he shall offer unto the LORD.

12 If he offer it for a thanksgiving, then he shall offer with the sacrifice of thanksgiving unleavened cakes mingled with oil, and unleavened wafers anointed with oil, and cakes mingled with oil, of fine flour, fried.

13 Besides the cakes, he shall offer *for* his offering leavened bread with the sacrifice of thanksgiving of his peace offerings.

14 And of it he shall offer one out of the whole oblation *for* a heave offering unto the LORD, *and* it shall be the priest's that sprinkleth the blood of the peace offerings.

15 And the flesh of the sacrifice of his peace offerings for thanksgiving shall be eaten the same day that it is offered; he shall not leave any of it until the morning.

16 But if the sacrifice of his offering *be* a vow, or a voluntary offering, it shall be eaten the same day that he offereth his sacrifice; and on the morrow also the remainder of it shall be eaten:

17 But the remainder of the flesh of the sacrifice on the third day shall be burnt with fire.

18 And if *any* of the flesh of the sacrifice of his peace offerings be eaten at all on the third day, it shall not be accepted, neither shall it be imputed unto him that offereth it: it shall be an abomination, and the soul that eateth of it shall bear his iniquity.

19 And the flesh that toucheth any unclean *thing* shall not be eaten; it shall be burnt with fire: and as for the flesh, all that be clean shall eat thereof.

20 But the soul that eateth *of* the flesh of the sacrifice of peace offerings, that *pertain* unto the LORD, having his uncleanness upon him, even that soul shall be cut off from his people.

21 Moreover the soul that shall touch any unclean *thing, as* the uncleanness of man, or *any* unclean beast, or any abominable unclean *thing*, and eat of the flesh of the sacrifice of peace offerings, which *pertain* unto the LORD, even that soul shall be cut off from his people.

22 ¶ And the LORD spake unto Moses, saying,

23 Speak unto the children of Ĭṣ′rā-ĕl, saying, Ye shall eat no manner of fat, of ox, or of sheep, or of goat.

24 And the fat of the beast that dieth of itself, and the fat of that which is torn with beasts, may be used in any other use: but ye shall in no wise eat of it.

25 For whosoever eateth the fat of the beast, of which men offer an offering made by fire unto the LORD, even the

soul that eateth *it* shall be cut off from his people.

26 Moreover ye shall eat no manner of blood, *whether it be* of fowl or of beast, in any of your dwellings.

27 Whatsoever soul *it be* that eateth any manner of blood, even that soul shall be cut off from his people.

28 ℂ And the LORD spake unto Moses, saying,

29 Speak unto the children of Ĭs̱'rā-ĕl, saying, He that offereth the sacrifice of his peace offerings unto the LORD, shall bring his oblation unto the LORD of the sacrifice of his peace offerings.

30 His own hands shall bring the offerings of the LORD made by fire, the fat with the breast; it shall he bring, that the breast may be waved *for* a wave offering before the LORD.

31 And the priest shall burn the fat upon the altar: but the breast shall be Aaron's and his sons'.

32 And the right shoulder shall ye give unto the priest *for* a heave offering of the sacrifices of your peace offerings.

33 He among the sons of Aaron, that offereth the blood of the peace offerings, and the fat, shall have the right shoulder for *his* part.

34 For the wave breast and the heave shoulder have I taken of the children of Ĭs̱'rā-ĕl from off the sacrifices of their peace offerings, and have given them unto Aaron the priest and unto his sons, by a statute for ever, from among the children of Ĭs̱'rā-ĕl.

35 ℂ This *is the portion* of the anointing of Aaron, and of the anointing of his sons, out of the offerings of the LORD made by fire, in the day *when* he presented them to minister unto the LORD in the priest's office;

36 Which the LORD commanded to be given them of the children of Ĭs̱'rā-ĕl, in the day that he anointed them, *by* a statute for ever throughout their generations.

37 This *is* the law of the burnt offering, of the meat offering, and of the sin offering, and of the trespass offering, and of the consecrations, and of the sacrifice of the peace offerings;

38 Which the LORD commanded Moses in mount Sī'naī, in the day that he commanded the children of Ĭs̱'rā-ĕl to offer their oblations unto the LORD, in the wilderness of Sī'naī.

CHAPTER 8

AND the Lord spake unto Moses, saying,

2 Take Aaron and his sons with him, and the garments, and the anointing oil, and a bullock for the sin offering, and two rams, and a basket of unleavened bread;

3 And gather thou all the congregation together unto the door of the tabernacle of the congregation.

4 And Moses did as the LORD commanded him; and the assembly was gathered together unto the door of the tabernacle of the congregation.

5 And Moses said unto the congregation, This *is* the thing which the LORD commanded to be done.

6 And Moses brought Aaron and his sons, and washed them with water.

7 And he put upon him the coat, and girded him with the girdle, and clothed him with the robe, and put the ĕph'ŏd upon him, and he girded him with the curious girdle of the ĕph'ŏd, and bound *it* unto him therewith.

8 And he put the breastplate upon him: also he put in the breastplate the Ū'rĭm and the Thŭm'mĭm.

9 And he put the mitre upon his head; also upon the mitre, *even* upon his forefront, did he put the golden plate, the holy crown; as the LORD commanded Moses.

10 And Moses took the anointing oil, and anointed the tabernacle and all that *was* therein, and sanctified them.

11 And he sprinkled thereof upon the altar seven times, and anointed the altar and all his vessels, both the laver and his foot, to sanctify them.

12 And he poured of the anointing oil upon Aaron's head, and anointed him, to sanctify him.

13 And Moses brought Aaron's sons, and put coats upon them, and girded them with girdles, and put bonnets upon them; as the LORD commanded Moses.

14 And he brought the bullock for the sin offering: and Aaron and his sons laid their hands upon the head of the bullock for the sin offering.

15 And he slew *it;* and Moses took the blood, and put *it* upon the horns of the altar round about with his finger, and purified the altar, and poured the blood at the bottom of the altar, and sanctified it, to make reconciliation upon it.

16 And he took all the fat that *was*
upon the inwards, and the caul *above*
the liver, and the two kidneys, and
their fat, and Moses burned *it* upon the
altar.
17 But the bullock, and his hide, his
flesh, and his dung, he burnt with fire
without the camp; as the LORD commanded Moses.
18 ℭ And he brought the ram for the
burnt offering: and Aaron and his sons
laid their hands upon the head of the
ram.
19 And he killed *it;* and Moses sprinkled the blood upon the altar round
about.
20 And he cut the ram into pieces; and
Moses burnt the head, and the pieces,
and the fat.
21 And he washed the inwards and the
legs in water; and Moses burnt the
whole ram upon the altar: it *was* a burnt
sacrifice for a sweet savor, *and* an offering made by fire unto the LORD; as the
LORD commanded Moses.
22 ℭ And he brought the other ram,
the ram of consecration: and Aaron and
his sons laid their hands upon the head
of the ram.
23 And he slew *it;* and Moses took of
the blood of it, and put *it* upon the tip of
Aaron's right ear, and upon the thumb
of his right hand, and upon the great toe
of his right foot.
24 And he brought Aaron's sons, and
Moses put of the blood upon the tip of
their right ear, and upon the thumbs of
their right hands, and upon the great
toes of their right feet: and Moses
sprinkled the blood upon the altar round
about.
25 And he took the fat, and the rump,
and all the fat that *was* upon the inwards, and the caul *above* the liver, and
the two kidneys, and their fat, and the
right shoulder:
26 And out of the basket of unleavened
bread, that *was* before the LORD, he
took one unleavened cake, and a cake of
oiled bread, and one wafer, and put
them on the fat, and upon the right
shoulder:
27 And he put all upon Aaron's hands,
and upon his sons' hands, and waved
them *for* a wave offering before the
LORD.
28 And Moses took them from off their
hands, and burnt *them* on the altar upon
the burnt offering: they *were* consecrations for a sweet savor: it *is* an offering
made by fire unto the LORD.
29 And Moses took the breast, and
waved it *for* a wave offering before the
LORD: *for* of the ram of consecration it
was Moses' part; as the LORD commanded Moses.
30 And Moses took of the anointing
oil, and of the blood which *was* upon the
altar, and sprinkled *it* upon Aaron, *and*
upon his garments, and upon his sons,
and upon his sons' garments with him;
and sanctified Aaron, *and* his garments,
and his sons, and his sons' garments
with him.
31 ℭ And Moses said unto Aaron and
to his sons, Boil the flesh *at* the door of
the tabernacle of the congregation; and
there eat it with the bread that *is* in the
basket of consecrations, as I commanded, saying, Aaron and his sons
shall eat it.
32 And that which remaineth of the
flesh and of the bread shall ye burn with
fire.
33 And ye shall not go out of the door
of the tabernacle of the congregation *in*
seven days, until the days of your consecration be at an end: for seven days
shall he consecrate you.
34 As he hath done this day, *so* the
LORD hath commanded to do, to make
an atonement for you.
35 Therefore shall ye abide *at* the door
of the tabernacle of the congregation day
and night seven days, and keep the
charge of the LORD, that ye die not: for
so I am commanded.
36 So Aaron and his sons did all things
which the LORD commanded by the
hand of Moses.

CHAPTER 9

AND it came to pass on the eighth day,
that Moses called Aaron and his
sons, and the elders of Ĭş'rā-ĕl;
2 And he said unto Aaron, Take thee a
young calf for a sin offering, and a ram
for a burnt offering, without blemish,
and offer *them* before the LORD.
3 And unto the children of Ĭş'rā-ĕl thou
shalt speak, saying, Take ye a kid of the
goats for a sin offering; and a calf and a
lamb, *both* of the first year, without
blemish, for a burnt offering;
4 Also a bullock and a ram for peace
offerings, to sacrifice before the LORD;

and a meat offering mingled with oil: for to-day the LORD will appear unto you.

5 ¶ And they brought *that* which Moses commanded before the tabernacle of the congregation: and all the congregation drew near and stood before the LORD.

6 And Moses said, This *is* the thing which the LORD commanded that ye should do: and the glory of the LORD shall appear unto you.

7 And Moses said unto Aaron, Go unto the altar, and offer thy sin offering, and thy burnt offering, and make an atonement for thyself, and for the people: and offer the offering of the people, and make an atonement for them; as the LORD commanded.

8 ¶ Aaron therefore went unto the altar, and slew the calf of the sin offering, which *was* for himself.

9 And the sons of Aaron brought the blood unto him: and he dipped his finger in the blood, and put *it* upon the horns of the altar, and poured out the blood at the bottom of the altar:

10 But the fat, and the kidneys, and the caul above the liver of the sin offering, he burnt upon the altar; as the LORD commanded Moses.

11 And the flesh and the hide he burnt with fire without the camp.

12 And he slew the burnt offering; and Aaron's sons presented unto him the blood, which he sprinkled round about upon the altar.

13 And they presented the burnt offering unto him, with the pieces thereof, and the head: and he burnt *them* upon the altar.

14 And he did wash the inwards and the legs, and burnt *them* upon the burnt offering on the altar.

15 ¶ And he brought the people's offering, and took the goat, which *was* the sin offering for the people, and slew it, and offered it for sin, as the first.

16 And he brought the burnt offering, and offered it according to the manner.

17 And he brought the meat offering, and took a handful thereof, and burnt *it* upon the altar, besides the burnt sacrifice of the morning.

18 He slew also the bullock and the ram *for* a sacrifice of peace offerings, which *was* for the people: and Aaron's sons presented unto him the blood, which he sprinkled upon the altar round about,

19 And the fat of the bullock and of the ram, the rump, and that which covereth *the inwards*, and the kidneys, and the caul *above* the liver:

20 And they put the fat upon the breasts, and he burnt the fat upon the altar:

21 And the breasts and the right shoulder Aaron waved *for* a wave offering before the LORD; as Moses commanded.

22 And Aaron lifted up his hand toward the people, and blessed them; and came down from offering of the sin offering, and the burnt offering, and peace offerings.

23 And Moses and Aaron went into the tabernacle of the congregation, and came out, and blessed the people: and the glory of the LORD appeared unto all the people.

24 And there came a fire out from before the LORD, and consumed upon the altar the burnt offering and the fat: *which* when all the people saw, they shouted, and fell on their faces.

CHAPTER 10

AND Nā'dăb and Ȧ-bī'hū, the sons of Aaron, took either of them his censer, and put fire therein, and put incense thereon, and offered strange fire before the LORD, which he commanded them not.

2 And there went out fire from the LORD, and devoured them, and they died before the LORD.

3 Then Moses said unto Aaron, This *is it* that the LORD spake, saying, I will be sanctified in them that come nigh me, and before all the people I will be glorified. And Aaron held his peace.

4 And Moses called Mĭsh'ā-ĕl and Ĕl-zā'phăn, the sons of Ŭz-zī'ĕl the uncle of Aaron, and said unto them, Come near, carry your brethren from before the sanctuary out of the camp.

5 So they went near, and carried them in their coats out of the camp; as Moses had said.

6 And Moses said unto Aaron, and unto Ĕl'ē-ā'zăr and unto Ĭth'ă-mär, his sons, Uncover not your heads, neither rend your clothes; lest ye die, and lest wrath come upon all the people: but let your brethren, the whole house of Ĭş'rā-ĕl,

bewail the burning which the LORD hath kindled.

7 And ye shall not go out from the door of the tabernacle of the congregation, lest ye die: for the anointing oil of the LORD *is* upon you. And they did according to the word of Moses.

8 ℂ And the LORD spake unto Aaron, saying,

9 Do not drink wine nor strong drink, thou, nor thy sons with thee, when ye go into the tabernacle of the congregation, lest ye die: *it shall be* a statute for ever throughout your generations:

10 And that ye may put difference between holy and unholy, and between unclean and clean;

11 And that ye may teach the children of Ĭṣ′rā-ĕl all the statutes which the LORD hath spoken unto them by the hand of Moses.

12 ℂ And Moses spake unto Aaron, and unto Ĕl′ē-ā′zär and unto Ĭth′ȧ-mär, his sons that were left, Take the meat offering that remaineth of the offerings of the LORD made by fire, and eat it without leaven beside the altar: for it *is* most holy.

13 And ye shall eat it in the holy place, because it *is* thy due, and thy sons' due, of the sacrifices of the LORD made by fire: for so I am commanded.

14 And the wave breast and heave shoulder shall ye eat in a clean place; thou, and thy sons, and thy daughters with thee: for *they be* thy due, and thy sons' due, *which* are given out of the sacrifices of peace offerings of the children of Ĭṣ′rā-ĕl.

15 The heave shoulder and the wave breast shall they bring with the offerings made by fire of the fat, to wave *it for* a wave offering before the LORD; and it shall be thine, and thy sons' with thee, by a statute for ever; as the LORD hath commanded.

16 ℂ And Moses diligently sought the goat of the sin offering, and, behold, it was burnt: and he was angry with Ĕl′ē-ā′zär and Ĭth′ȧ-mär, the sons of Aaron *which were* left *alive,* saying,

17 Wherefore have ye not eaten the sin offering in the holy place, seeing it *is* most holy, and *God* hath given it you to bear the iniquity of the congregation, to make atonement for them before the LORD?

18 Behold, the blood of it was not brought in within the holy *place:* ye should indeed have eaten it in the holy *place,* as I commanded.

19 And Aaron said unto Moses, Behold, this day have they offered their sin offering and their burnt offering before the LORD; and such things have befallen me: and *if* I had eaten the sin offering to-day, should it have been accepted in the sight of the LORD?

20 And when Moses heard *that,* he was content.

CHAPTER 11

AND the LORD spake unto Moses and to Aaron, saying unto them,

2 Speak unto the children of Ĭṣ′rā-ĕl, saying, These *are* the beasts which ye shall eat among all the beasts that *are* on the earth.

3 Whatsoever parteth the hoof, and is cloven-footed, *and* cheweth the cud, among the beasts, that shall ye eat.

4 Nevertheless, these shall ye not eat of them that chew the cud, or of them that divide the hoof: *as* the camel, because he cheweth the cud, but divideth not the hoof; he *is* unclean unto you.

5 And the coney, because he cheweth the cud, but divideth not the hoof; he *is* unclean unto you.

6 And the hare, because he cheweth the cud, but divideth not the hoof; he *is* unclean unto you.

7 And the swine, though he divide the hoof, and be cloven-footed, yet he cheweth not the cud; he *is* unclean to you.

8 Of their flesh shall ye not eat, and their carcass shall ye not touch; they *are* unclean to you.

9 ℂ These shall ye eat of all that *are* in the waters: whatsoever hath fins and scales in the waters, in the seas, and in the rivers, them shall ye eat.

10 And all that have not fins and scales in the seas, and in the rivers, of all that move in the waters, and of any living thing which *is* in the waters, they *shall be* an abomination unto you:

11 They shall be even an abomination unto you; ye shall not eat of their flesh, but ye shall have their carcasses in abomination.

12 Whatsoever hath no fins nor scales in the waters, that *shall be* an abomination unto you.

13 ℂ And these *are they which* ye shall

have in abomination among the fowls;
they shall not be eaten, they *are* an
abomination: the eagle, and the ossifrage, and the ospray,
14 And the vulture, and the kite after
his kind;
15 Every raven after his kind;
16 And the owl, and the nighthawk, and
the cuckoo, and the hawk after his kind,
17 And the little owl, and the cormorant, and the great owl,
18 And the swan, and the pelican, and
the gier-eagle,
19 And the stork, the heron after her
kind, and the lapwing, and the bat.
20 All fowls that creep, going upon *all*
four, *shall be* an abomination unto you.
21 Yet these may ye eat of every flying
creeping thing that goeth upon *all* four,
which have legs above their feet, to leap
withal upon the earth;
22 *Even* these of them ye may eat; the
locust after his kind, and the bald locust
after his kind, and the beetle after his
kind, and the grasshopper after his kind.
23 But all *other* flying creeping things,
which have four feet, *shall be* an abomination unto you.
24 And for these ye shall be unclean:
whosoever toucheth the carcass of them
shall be unclean until the even.
25 And whosoever beareth *aught* of the
carcass of them shall wash his clothes,
and be unclean until the even.
26 *The carcasses* of every beast which
divideth the hoof, and *is* not cloven-
footed, nor cheweth the cud, *are* unclean
unto you: every one that toucheth them
shall be unclean.
27 And whatsoever goeth upon his
paws, among all manner of beasts that
go on *all* four, those *are* unclean unto
you: whoso toucheth their carcass shall
be unclean until the even.
28 And he that beareth the carcass of
them shall wash his clothes, and be unclean until the even: they *are* unclean
unto you.
29 ¶ These also *shall be* unclean unto
you among the creeping things that
creep upon the earth; the weasel, and
the mouse, and the tortoise after his
kind,
30 And the ferret, and the chameleon,
and the lizard, and the snail, and the
mole.
31 These *are* unclean to you among all
that creep: whosoever doth touch them,
when they be dead, shall be unclean
until the even.
32 And upon whatsoever *any* of them,
when they are dead, doth fall, it shall be
unclean; whether *it be* any vessel of
wood, or raiment, or skin, or sack, whatsoever vessel *it be*, wherein *any* work is
done, it must be put into water, and it
shall be unclean until the even; so it
shall be cleansed.
33 And every earthen vessel, whereinto *any* of them falleth, whatsoever
is in it shall be unclean; and ye shall
break it.
34 Of all meat which may be eaten,
that on which *such* water cometh shall
be unclean: and all drink that may be
drunk in every *such* vessel shall be
unclean.
35 And every *thing* whereupon *any
part* of their carcass falleth shall be unclean; *whether it be* oven, or ranges for
pots, they shall be broken down: *for*
they *are* unclean, and shall be unclean
unto you.
36 Nevertheless a fountain or pit,
wherein there is plenty of water, shall
be clean: but that which toucheth their
carcass shall be unclean.
37 And if *any part* of their carcass fall
upon any sowing seed which is to be
sown, it *shall be* clean.
38 But if *any* water be put upon the
seed, and *any part* of their carcass fall
thereon, it *shall be* unclean unto you.
39 And if any beast, of which ye may
eat, die; he that toucheth the carcass
thereof shall be unclean until the even.
40 And he that eateth of the carcass of
it shall wash his clothes, and be unclean
until the even: he also that beareth the
carcass of it shall wash his clothes, and
be unclean until the even.
41 And every creeping thing that creepeth upon the earth *shall be* an abomination; it shall not be eaten.
42 Whatsoever goeth upon the belly,
and whatsoever goeth upon *all* four, or
whatsoever hath more feet among all
creeping things that creep upon the
earth, them ye shall not eat; for they *are*
an abomination.
43 Ye shall not make yourselves abominable with any creeping thing that
creepeth, neither shall ye make yourselves unclean with them, that ye should
be defiled thereby.
44 For I *am* the LORD your God: ye

shall therefore sanctify yourselves, and ye shall be holy; for I *am* holy: neither shall ye defile yourselves with any manner of creeping thing that creepeth upon the earth.

45 For I *am* the LORD that bringeth you up out of the land of Egypt, to be your God: ye shall therefore be holy, for I *am* holy.

46 This *is* the law of the beasts, and of the fowl, and of every living creature that moveth in the waters, and of every creature that creepeth upon the earth:

47 To make a difference between the unclean and the clean, and between the beast that may be eaten and the beast that may not be eaten.

CHAPTER 12

AND the LORD spake unto Moses, saying,

2 Speak unto the children of Īs̱′rā-ĕl, saying, If a woman have conceived seed, and borne a man child, then she shall be unclean seven days; according to the days of the separation for her infirmity shall she be unclean.

3 And in the eighth day the flesh of his foreskin shall be circumcised.

4 And she shall then continue in the blood of her purifying three and thirty days; she shall touch no hallowed thing, nor come into the sanctuary, until the days of her purifying be fulfilled.

5 But if she bear a maid child, then she shall be unclean two weeks, as in her separation: and she shall continue in the blood of her purifying threescore and six days.

6 And when the days of her purifying are fulfilled, for a son, or for a daughter, she shall bring a lamb of the first year for a burnt offering, and a young pigeon, or a turtledove, for a sin offering, unto the door of the tabernacle of the congregation, unto the priest:

7 Who shall offer it before the LORD, and make an atonement for her; and she shall be cleansed from the issue of her blood. This *is* the law for her that hath borne a male or a female.

8 And if she be not able to bring a lamb, then she shall bring two turtles, or two young pigeons; the one for the burnt offering, and the other for a sin offering: and the priest shall make an atonement for her, and she shall be clean.

CHAPTER 13

AND the LORD spake unto Moses and Aaron, saying,

2 When a man shall have in the skin of his flesh a rising, a scab, or bright spot, and it be in the skin of his flesh *like* the plague of leprosy; then he shall be brought unto Aaron the priest, or unto one of his sons the priests:

3 And the priest shall look on the plague in the skin of the flesh: and *when* the hair in the plague is turned white, and the plague in sight *be* deeper than the skin of his flesh, it *is* a plague of leprosy: and the priest shall look on him, and pronounce him unclean.

4 If the bright spot *be* white in the skin of his flesh, and in sight *be* not deeper than the skin, and the hair thereof be not turned white; then the priest shall shut up *him that hath* the plague seven days:

5 And the priest shall look on him the seventh day: and, behold, *if* the plague in his sight be at a stay, *and* the plague spread not in the skin; then the priest shall shut him up seven days more:

6 And the priest shall look on him again the seventh day: and, behold, *if* the plague *be* somewhat dark, *and* the plague spread not in the skin, the priest shall pronounce him clean: it *is but* a scab: and he shall wash his clothes, and be clean.

7 But if the scab spread much abroad in the skin, after that he hath been seen of the priest for his cleansing, he shall be seen of the priest again:

8 And *if* the priest see that, behold, the scab spreadeth in the skin, then the priest shall pronounce him unclean: it *is* a leprosy.

9 ¶ When the plague of leprosy is in a man, then he shall be brought unto the priest;

10 And the priest shall see *him:* and, behold, *if* the rising *be* white in the skin, and it have turned the hair white, and *there be* quick raw flesh in the rising;

11 It *is* an old leprosy in the skin of his flesh, and the priest shall pronounce him unclean, and shall not shut him up: for he *is* unclean.

12 And if a leprosy break out abroad in the skin, and the leprosy cover all the skin of *him that hath* the plague from his head even to his foot, wheresoever the priest looketh;

13 Then the priest shall consider: and, behold, *if* the leprosy have covered all his flesh, he shall pronounce *him* clean *that hath* the plague: it is all turned white: he *is* clean.

14 But when raw flesh appeareth in him, he shall be unclean.

15 And the priest shall see the raw flesh, and pronounce him to be unclean: *for* the raw flesh *is* unclean: it *is* a leprosy.

16 Or if the raw flesh turn again, and be changed unto white, he shall come unto the priest;

17 And the priest shall see him: and, behold, *if* the plague be turned into white; then the priest shall pronounce *him* clean *that hath* the plague: he *is* clean.

18 ¶ The flesh also, in which, *even* in the skin thereof, was a boil, and is healed,

19 And in the place of the boil there be a white rising, or a bright spot, white, and somewhat reddish, and it be showed to the priest;

20 And if, when the priest seeth it, behold, it *be* in sight lower than the skin, and the hair thereof be turned white; the priest shall pronounce him unclean: it *is* a plague of leprosy broken out of the boil.

21 But if the priest look on it, and, behold, *there be* no white hairs therein, and *if* it *be* not lower than the skin, but *be* somewhat dark; then the priest shall shut him up seven days:

22 And if it spread much abroad in the skin, then the priest shall pronounce him unclean: it *is* a plague.

23 But if the bright spot stay in his place, *and* spread not, it *is* a burning boil; and the priest shall pronounce him clean.

24 ¶ Or if there be *any* flesh, in the skin whereof *there is* a hot burning, and the quick *flesh* that burneth have a white bright spot, somewhat reddish, or white;

25 Then the priest shall look upon it: and, behold, *if* the hair in the bright spot be turned white, and it *be in* sight deeper than the skin; it *is* a leprosy broken out of the burning: wherefore the priest shall pronounce him unclean: it *is* the plague of leprosy.

26 But if the priest look on it, and, behold, *there be* no white hair in the bright spot, and it *be* no lower than the *other* skin, but *be* somewhat dark; then the priest shall shut him up seven days:

27 And the priest shall look upon him the seventh day: *and* if it be spread much abroad in the skin, then the priest shall pronounce him unclean: it *is* the plague of leprosy.

28 And if the bright spot stay in his place, *and* spread not in the skin, but it *be* somewhat dark; it *is* a rising of the burning, and the priest shall pronounce him clean: for it *is* an inflammation of the burning.

29 ¶ If a man or woman have a plague upon the head or the beard;

30 Then the priest shall see the plague: and, behold, if it *be* in sight deeper than the skin, and *there be* in it a yellow thin hair; then the priest shall pronounce him unclean: it *is* a dry scall, *even* a leprosy upon the head or beard.

31 And if the priest look on the plague of the scall, and, behold, it *be* not in sight deeper than the skin, and *that there is* no black hair in it; then the priest shall shut up *him that hath* the plague of the scall seven days:

32 And in the seventh day the priest shall look on the plague: and, behold, *if* the scall spread not, and there be in it no yellow hair, and the scall *be* not in sight deeper than the skin;

33 He shall be shaven, but the scall shall he not shave; and the priest shall shut up *him that hath* the scall seven days more:

34 And in the seventh day the priest shall look on the scall: and, behold, *if* the scall be not spread in the skin, nor *be* in sight deeper than the skin; then the priest shall pronounce him clean: and he shall wash his clothes, and be clean.

35 But if the scall spread much in the skin after his cleansing;

36 Then the priest shall look on him: and, behold, if the scall be spread in the skin, the priest shall not seek for yellow hair; he *is* unclean.

37 But if the scall be in his sight at a stay, and *that* there is black hair grown up therein; the scall is healed, he *is* clean: and the priest shall pronounce him clean.

38 ¶ If a man also or a woman have in the skin of their flesh bright spots, *even* white bright spots;

39 Then the priest shall look: and, be-

hold, *if* the bright spots in the skin of
their flesh *be* darkish white, it *is* a
freckled spot *that* groweth in the skin:
he *is* clean.
40 And the man whose hair is fallen off
his head, he *is* bald; *yet is* he clean.
41 And he that hath his hair fallen
off from the part of his head toward
his face, he *is* forehead bald; *yet is* he
clean.
42 And if there be in the bald head, or
bald forehead, a white reddish sore; it
is a leprosy sprung up in his bald head,
or his bald forehead.
43 Then the priest shall look upon it:
and, behold, *if* the rising of the sore *be*
white reddish in his bald head, or in his
bald forehead, as the leprosy appeareth
in the skin of the flesh;
44 He is a leprous man, he *is* unclean:
the priest shall pronounce him utterly
unclean; his plague *is* in his head.
45 And the leper in whom the plague *is,*
his clothes shall be rent, and his head
bare, and he shall put a covering upon
his upper lip, and shall cry, Unclean,
unclean.
46 All the days wherein the plague
shall be in him he shall be defiled; he *is*
unclean: he shall dwell alone; without
the camp *shall* his habitation *be.*
47 ¶ The garment also that the plague
of leprosy is in, *whether it be* a woolen
garment, or a linen garment;
48 Whether *it be* in the warp, or woof,
of linen, or of woolen; whether in a skin,
or in any thing made of skin;
49 And if the plague be greenish or reddish in the garment, or in the skin, either
in the warp, or in the woof, or in any
thing of skin; it *is* a plague of leprosy,
and shall be showed unto the priest:
50 And the priest shall look upon the
plague, and shut up *it that hath* the
plague seven days:
51 And he shall look on the plague on
the seventh day: if the plague be spread
in the garment, either in the warp, or in
the woof, or in a skin, *or* in any work
that is made of skin; the plague *is* a
fretting leprosy; it *is* unclean.
52 He shall therefore burn that garment, whether warp or woof, in woolen
or in linen, or any thing of skin, wherein
the plague is: for it *is* a fretting leprosy;
it shall be burnt in the fire.
53 And if the priest shall look, and, behold, the plague be not spread in the
garment, either in the warp, or in the
woof, or in any thing of skin;
54 Then the priest shall command that
they wash *the thing* wherein the plague
is, and he shall shut it up seven days
more:
55 And the priest shall look on the
plague, after that it is washed: and, behold, *if* the plague have not changed his
color, and the plague be not spread, it
is unclean; thou shalt burn it in the fire;
it *is* fret inward, *whether* it *be* bare
within or without.
56 And if the priest look, and, behold,
the plague *be* somewhat dark after the
washing of it; then he shall rend it out
of the garment, or out of the skin, or out
of the warp, or out of the woof:
57 And if it appear still in the garment,
either in the warp, or in the woof, or in
any thing of skin; it *is* a spreading
plague: thou shalt burn that wherein
the plague *is* with fire.
58 And the garment, either warp, or
woof, or whatsoever thing of skin *it be,*
which thou shalt wash, if the plague be
departed from them, then it shall be
washed the second time, and shall be
clean.
59 This *is* the law of the plague of
leprosy in a garment of woolen or linen,
either in the warp, or woof, or any thing
of skins, to pronounce it clean, or to pronounce it unclean.

CHAPTER 14

AND the LORD spake unto Moses,
saying,
2 This shall be the law of the leper in
the day of his cleansing: He shall be
brought unto the priest:
3 And the priest shall go forth out of the
camp; and the priest shall look, and,
behold, *if* the plague of leprosy be
healed in the leper;
4 Then shall the priest command to
take for him that is to be cleansed two
birds alive *and* clean, and cedar wood,
and scarlet, and hyssop:
5 And the priest shall command that
one of the birds be killed in an earthen
vessel over running water.
6 As for the living bird, he shall take it,
and the cedar wood, and the scarlet, and
the hyssop, and dip them and the living bird in the blood of the bird *that*
was killed over the running water:
7 And he shall sprinkle upon him that

is to be cleansed from the leprosy seven times, and shall pronounce him clean, and shall let the living bird loose into the open field.

8 And he that is to be cleansed shall wash his clothes, and shave off all his hair, and wash himself in water, that he may be clean: and after that he shall come into the camp, and shall tarry abroad out of his tent seven days.

9 But it shall be on the seventh day, that he shall shave all his hair off his head and his beard and his eyebrows, even all his hair he shall shave off: and he shall wash his clothes, also he shall wash his flesh in water, and he shall be clean.

10 And on the eighth day he shall take two he lambs without blemish, and one ewe lamb of the first year without blemish, and three tenth deals of fine flour *for* a meat offering, mingled with oil, and one log of oil:

11 And the priest that maketh *him* clean shall present the man that is to be made clean, and those things, before the LORD, *at* the door of the tabernacle of the congregation:

12 And the priest shall take one he lamb, and offer him for a trespass offering, and the log of oil, and wave them *for* a wave offering before the LORD:

13 And he shall slay the lamb in the place where he shall kill the sin offering and the burnt offering, in the holy place: for as the sin offering *is* the priest's, *so is* the trespass offering: it *is* most holy:

14 And the priest shall take *some* of the blood of the trespass offering, and the priest shall put *it* upon the tip of the right ear of him that is to be cleansed, and upon the thumb of his right hand, and upon the great toe of his right foot.

15 And the priest shall take *some* of the log of oil, and pour *it* into the palm of his own left hand:

16 And the priest shall dip his right finger in the oil that *is* in his left hand, and shall sprinkle of the oil with his finger seven times before the LORD:

17 And of the rest of the oil that *is* in his hand shall the priest put upon the tip of the right ear of him that is to be cleansed, and upon the thumb of his right hand, and upon the great toe of his right foot, upon the blood of the trespass offering:

18 And the remnant of the oil that *is* in the priest's hand he shall pour upon the head of him that is to be cleansed: and the priest shall make an atonement for him before the LORD.

19 And the priest shall offer the sin offering, and make an atonement for him that is to be cleansed from his uncleanness; and afterward he shall kill the burnt offering:

20 And the priest shall offer the burnt offering and the meat offering upon the altar: and the priest shall make an atonement for him, and he shall be clean.

21 And if he *be* poor, and cannot get so much; then he shall take one lamb *for* a trespass offering to be waved, to make an atonement for him, and one tenth deal of fine flour mingled with oil for a meat offering, and a log of oil;

22 And two turtledoves, or two young pigeons, such as he is able to get; and the one shall be a sin offering, and the other a burnt offering.

23 And he shall bring them on the eighth day for his cleansing unto the priest, unto the door of the tabernacle of the congregation, before the LORD.

24 And the priest shall take the lamb of the trespass offering, and the log of oil, and the priest shall wave them *for* a wave offering before the LORD:

25 And he shall kill the lamb of the trespass offering, and the priest shall take *some* of the blood of the trespass offering, and put *it* upon the tip of the right ear of him that is to be cleansed, and upon the thumb of his right hand, and upon the great toe of his right foot.

26 And the priest shall pour of the oil into the palm of his own left hand:

27 And the priest shall sprinkle with his right finger *some* of the oil that *is* in his left hand seven times before the LORD:

28 And the priest shall put of the oil that *is* in his hand upon the tip of the right ear of him that is to be cleansed, and upon the thumb of his right hand, and upon the great toe of his right foot, upon the place of the blood of the trespass offering:

29 And the rest of the oil that *is* in the priest's hand he shall put upon the head of him that is to be cleansed, to make an atonement for him before the LORD.

30 And he shall offer the one of the turtledoves, or of the young pigeons, such as he can get;

31 *Even* such as he is able to get, the
one *for* a sin offering, and the other *for* a
burnt offering, with the meat offering:
and the priest shall make an atonement
for him that is to be cleansed before the
LORD.
32 This *is* the law *of him* in whom *is* the
plague of leprosy, whose hand is not
able to get *that which pertaineth* to his
cleansing.
33 ℭ And the LORD spake unto Moses
and unto Aaron, saying,
34 When ye be come into the land of
Cā′năan, which I give to you for a possession, and I put the plague of leprosy
in a house of the land of your possession;
35 And he that owneth the house shall
come and tell the priest, saying, It seemeth to me *there is* as it were a plague in
the house:
36 Then the priest shall command that
they empty the house, before the priest
go *into it* to see the plague, that all that
is in the house be not made unclean:
and afterward the priest shall go in to
see the house:
37 And he shall look on the plague,
and, behold, *if* the plague *be* in the walls
of the house with hollow streaks, greenish or reddish, which in sight *are* lower
than the wall;
38 Then the priest shall go out of the
house to the door of the house, and shut
up the house seven days:
39 And the priest shall come again the
seventh day, and shall look: and, behold, *if* the plague be spread in the walls
of the house;
40 Then the priest shall command that
they take away the stones in which the
plague *is*, and they shall cast them into
an unclean place without the city:
41 And he shall cause the house to be
scraped within round about, and they
shall pour out the dust that they scrape
off without the city into an unclean
place:
42 And they shall take other stones,
and put *them* in the place of those
stones; and he shall take other mortar,
and shall plaster the house.
43 And if the plague come again, and
break out in the house, after that he hath
taken away the stones, and after he
hath scraped the house, and after it is
plastered;
44 Then the priest shall come and look,
and, behold, *if* the plague be spread in
the house, it *is* a fretting leprosy in the
house: it *is* unclean.
45 And he shall break down the house,
the stones of it, and the timber thereof,
and all the mortar of the house; and he
shall carry *them* forth out of the city into
an unclean place.
46 Moreover, he that goeth into the
house all the while that it is shut up
shall be unclean until the even.
47 And he that lieth in the house shall
wash his clothes; and he that eateth in
the house shall wash his clothes.
48 And if the priest shall come in, and
look *upon it*, and, behold, the plague
hath not spread in the house, after the
house was plastered; then the priest
shall pronounce the house clean, because the plague is healed.
49 And he shall take to cleanse the
house two birds, and cedar wood, and
scarlet, and hyssop:
50 And he shall kill the one of the
birds in an earthen vessel over running
water:
51 And he shall take the cedar wood,
and the hyssop, and the scarlet, and the
living bird, and dip them in the blood of
the slain bird, and in the running water,
and sprinkle the house seven times:
52 And he shall cleanse the house with
the blood of the bird, and with the running water, and with the living bird, and
with the cedar wood, and with the hyssop, and with the scarlet:
53 But he shall let go the living bird out
of the city into the open fields, and make
an atonement for the house: and it shall
be clean.
54 This *is* the law for all manner of
plague of leprosy, and scall,
55 And for the leprosy of a garment,
and of a house,
56 And for a rising, and for a scab, and
for a bright spot:
57 To teach when *it is* unclean, and
when *it is* clean: this *is* the law of
leprosy.

CHAPTER 15

AND the LORD spake unto Moses and
to Aaron, saying,
2 Speak unto the children of Ĭş′rā-ĕl,
and say unto them, When any man hath
a running issue out of his flesh, *because
of* his issue he *is* unclean.
3 And this shall be his uncleanness in
his issue: whether his flesh run with his

issue, or his flesh be stopped from his issue, it *is* his uncleanness.

4 Every bed, whereon he lieth that hath the issue, is unclean: and every thing, whereon he sitteth, shall be unclean.

5 And whosoever toucheth his bed shall wash his clothes, and bathe *himself* in water, and be unclean until the even.

6 And he that sitteth on *any* thing whereon he sat that hath the issue shall wash his clothes, and bathe *himself* in water, and be unclean until the even.

7 And he that toucheth the flesh of him that hath the issue shall wash his clothes, and bathe *himself* in water, and be unclean until the even.

8 And if he that hath the issue spit upon him that is clean; then he shall wash his clothes, and bathe *himself* in water, and be unclean until the even.

9 And what saddle soever he rideth upon that hath the issue shall be unclean.

10 And whosoever toucheth any thing that was under him shall be unclean until the even: and he that beareth *any of* those things shall wash his clothes, and bathe *himself* in water, and be unclean until the even.

11 And whomsoever he toucheth that hath the issue, and hath not rinsed his hands in water, he shall wash his clothes, and bathe *himself* in water, and be unclean until the even.

12 And the vessel of earth, that he toucheth which hath the issue, shall be broken: and every vessel of wood shall be rinsed in water.

13 And when he that hath an issue is cleansed of his issue, then he shall number to himself seven days for his cleansing, and wash his clothes, and bathe his flesh in running water, and shall be clean.

14 And on the eighth day he shall take to him two turtledoves, or two young pigeons, and come before the LORD unto the door of the tabernacle of the congregation, and give them unto the priest:

15 And the priest shall offer them, the one *for* a sin offering, and the other *for* a burnt offering; and the priest shall make an atonement for him before the LORD for his issue.

16 And if any man's seed of copulation go out from him, then he shall wash all his flesh in water, and be unclean until the even.

17 And every garment, and every skin, whereon is the seed of copulation, shall be washed with water, and be unclean until the even.

18 The woman also with whom man shall lie *with* seed of copulation, they shall *both* bathe *themselves* in water, and be unclean until the even.

19 ¶ And if a woman have an issue, *and* her issue in her flesh be blood, she shall be put apart seven days: and whosoever toucheth her shall be unclean until the even.

20 And every thing that she lieth upon in her separation shall be unclean: every thing also that she sitteth upon shall be unclean.

21 And whosoever toucheth her bed shall wash his clothes, and bathe *himself* in water, and be unclean until the even.

22 And whosoever toucheth any thing that she sat upon shall wash his clothes, and bathe *himself* in water, and be unclean until the even.

23 And if it *be* on *her* bed, or on any thing whereon she sitteth, when he toucheth it, he shall be unclean until the even.

24 And if any man lie with her at all, and her flowers be upon him, he shall be unclean seven days; and all the bed whereon he lieth shall be unclean.

25 And if a woman have an issue of her blood many days out of the time of her separation, or if it run beyond the time of her separation; all the days of the issue of her uncleanness shall be as the days of her separation: she *shall be* unclean.

26 Every bed whereon she lieth all the days of her issue shall be unto her as the bed of her separation: and whatsoever she sitteth upon shall be unclean, as the uncleanness of her separation.

27 And whosoever toucheth those things shall be unclean, and shall wash his clothes, and bathe *himself* in water, and be unclean until the even.

28 But if she be cleansed of her issue, then she shall number to herself seven days, and after that she shall be clean.

29 And on the eighth day she shall take unto her two turtles, or two young pigeons, and bring them unto the priest, to the door of the tabernacle of the congregation.

30 And the priest shall offer the one

for a sin offering, and the other *for* a burnt offering; and the priest shall make an atonement for her before the LORD for the issue of her uncleanness.

31 Thus shall ye separate the children of Ĭş'rā-ĕl from their uncleanness; that they die not in their uncleanness, when they defile my tabernacle that *is* among them.

32 This *is* the law of him that hath an issue, and *of him* whose seed goeth from him, and is defiled therewith;

33 And of her that is sick of her flowers, and of him that hath an issue, of the man, and of the woman, and of him that lieth with her that is unclean.

CHAPTER 16

AND the LORD spake unto Moses after the death of the two sons of Aaron, when they offered before the LORD, and died;

2 And the LORD said unto Moses, Speak unto Aaron thy brother, that he come not at all times into the holy *place* within the veil before the mercy seat, which *is* upon the ark; that he die not: for I will appear in the cloud upon the mercy seat.

3 Thus shall Aaron come into the holy *place;* with a young bullock for a sin offering, and a ram for a burnt offering.

4 He shall put on the holy linen coat, and he shall have the linen breeches upon his flesh, and shall be girded with a linen girdle, and with the linen mitre shall he be attired: these *are* holy garments; therefore shall he wash his flesh in water, and *so* put them on.

5 And he shall take of the congregation of the children of Ĭş'rā-ĕl two kids of the goats for a sin offering, and one ram for a burnt offering.

6 And Aaron shall offer his bullock of the sin offering, which *is* for himself, and make an atonement for himself, and for his house.

7 And he shall take the two goats, and present them before the LORD *at* the door of the tabernacle of the congregation.

8 And Aaron shall cast lots upon the two goats; one lot for the LORD, and the other lot for the scapegoat.

9 And Aaron shall bring the goat upon which the LORD's lot fell, and offer him *for* a sin offering.

10 But the goat, on which the lot fell to be the scapegoat, shall be presented alive before the LORD, to make an atonement with him, *and* to let him go for a scapegoat into the wilderness.

11 And Aaron shall bring the bullock of the sin offering, which *is* for himself, and shall make an atonement for himself, and for his house, and shall kill the bullock of the sin offering which *is* for himself:

12 And he shall take a censer full of burning coals of fire from off the altar before the LORD, and his hands full of sweet incense beaten small, and bring *it* within the veil:

13 And he shall put the incense upon the fire before the LORD, that the cloud of the incense may cover the mercy seat that *is* upon the testimony, that he die not:

14 And he shall take of the blood of the bullock, and sprinkle *it* with his finger upon the mercy seat eastward; and before the mercy seat shall he sprinkle of the blood with his finger seven times.

15 ¶ Then shall he kill the goat of the sin offering, that *is* for the people, and bring his blood within the veil, and do with that blood as he did with the blood of the bullock, and sprinkle it upon the mercy seat, and before the mercy seat:

16 And he shall make an atonement for the holy *place*, because of the uncleanness of the children of Ĭş'rā-ĕl, and because of their transgressions in all their sins: and so shall he do for the tabernacle of the congregation, that remaineth among them in the midst of their uncleanness.

17 And there shall be no man in the tabernacle of the congregation when he goeth in to make an atonement in the holy *place*, until he come out, and have made an atonement for himself, and for his household, and for all the congregation of Ĭş'rā-ĕl.

18 And he shall go out unto the altar that *is* before the LORD, and make an atonement for it; and shall take of the blood of the bullock, and of the blood of the goat, and put *it* upon the horns of the altar round about.

19 And he shall sprinkle of the blood upon it with his finger seven times, and cleanse it, and hallow it from the uncleanness of the children of Ĭş'rā-ĕl.

20 ¶ And when he hath made an end of reconciling the holy *place*, and the

tabernacle of the congregation, and the
altar, he shall bring the live goat:
21 And Aaron shall lay both his hands
upon the head of the live goat, and confess over him all the iniquities of the
children of Ĭṣ′rā-ĕl, and all their transgressions in all their sins, putting them
upon the head of the goat, and shall
send *him* away by the hand of a fit man
into the wilderness:
22 And the goat shall bear upon him all
their iniquities unto a land not inhabited: and he shall let go the goat in
the wilderness.
23 And Aaron shall come into the
tabernacle of the congregation, and
shall put off the linen garments, which
he put on when he went into the holy
place, and shall leave them there:
24 And he shall wash his flesh with water in the holy place, and put on his garments, and come forth, and offer his
burnt offering, and the burnt offering of
the people, and make an atonement for
himself, and for the people.
25 And the fat of the sin offering shall
he burn upon the altar.
26 And he that let go the goat for the
scapegoat shall wash his clothes, and
bathe his flesh in water, and afterward
come into the camp.
27 And the bullock *for* the sin offering,
and the goat *for* the sin offering, whose
blood was brought in to make atonement in the holy *place,* shall *one* carry
forth without the camp; and they shall
burn in the fire their skins, and their
flesh, and their dung.
28 And he that burneth them shall
wash his clothes, and bathe his flesh in
water, and afterward he shall come into
the camp.
29 ℂ And *this* shall be a statute for
ever unto you: *that* in the seventh
month, on the tenth *day* of the month,
ye shall afflict your souls, and do no
work at all, *whether it be* one of your
own country, or a stranger that sojourneth among you:
30 For on that day shall *the priest*
make an atonement for you, to cleanse
you, *that* ye may be clean from all your
sins before the LORD.
31 It *shall be* a sabbath of rest unto
you, and ye shall afflict your souls, by a
statute for ever.
32 And the priest, whom he shall
anoint, and whom he shall consecrate to
minister in the priest's office in his
father's stead, shall make the atonement, and shall put on the linen clothes,
even the holy garments:
33 And he shall make an atonement for
the holy sanctuary, and he shall make
an atonement for the tabernacle of the
congregation, and for the altar: and he
shall make an atonement for the priests,
and for all the people of the congregation.
34 And this shall be an everlasting
statute unto you, to make an atonement
for the children of Ĭṣ′rā-ĕl for all their
sins once a year. And he did as the
LORD commanded Moses.

CHAPTER 17

AND the LORD spake unto Moses,
saying,
2 Speak unto Aaron, and unto his sons,
and unto all the children of Ĭṣ′rā-ĕl, and
say unto them; This *is* the thing which
the LORD hath commanded, saying,
3 What man soever *there be* of the
house of Ĭṣ′rā-ĕl, that killeth an ox, or
lamb, or goat, in the camp, or that killeth *it* out of the camp,
4 And bringeth it not unto the door of
the tabernacle of the congregation, to
offer an offering unto the LORD before
the tabernacle of the LORD; blood shall
be imputed unto that man; he hath shed
blood; and that man shall be cut off
from among his people:
5 To the end that the children of Ĭṣ′-
rā-ĕl may bring their sacrifices, which
they offer in the open field, even that
they may bring them unto the LORD,
unto the door of the tabernacle of the
congregation, unto the priest, and offer
them *for* peace offerings unto the LORD.
6 And the priest shall sprinkle the
blood upon the altar of the LORD *at* the
door of the tabernacle of the congregation, and burn the fat for a sweet savor
unto the LORD.
7 And they shall no more offer their
sacrifices unto devils, after whom they
have gone a whoring. This shall be a
statute for ever unto them throughout
their generations.
8 ℂ And thou shalt say unto them,
Whatsoever man *there be* of the house
of Ĭṣ′rā-ĕl, or of the strangers which sojourn among you, that offereth a burnt
offering or sacrifice,
9 And bringeth it not unto the door of

the tabernacle of the congregation, to
offer it unto the LORD; even that man
shall be cut off from among his people.
10 ¶ And whatsoever man *there be* of
the house of Ĭs'rā-ĕl, or of the strangers
that sojourn among you, that eateth any
manner of blood; I will even set my face
against that soul that eateth blood, and
will cut him off from among his people.
11 For the life of the flesh *is* in the
blood; and I have given it to you upon
the altar to make an atonement for your
souls: for it *is* the blood *that* maketh an
atonement for the soul.
12 Therefore I said unto the children of
Ĭs'rā-ĕl, No soul of you shall eat blood,
neither shall any stranger that sojourneth among you eat blood.
13 And whatsoever man *there be* of the
children of Ĭs'rā-ĕl, or of the strangers
that sojourn among you, which hunteth
and catcheth any beast or fowl that may
be eaten; he shall even pour out the
blood thereof, and cover it with dust.
14 For *it is* the life of all flesh; the blood
of it *is* for the life thereof: therefore I
said unto the children of Ĭs'rā-ĕl, Ye
shall eat the blood of no manner of
flesh; for the life of all flesh *is* the blood
thereof: whosoever eateth it shall be
cut off.
15 And every soul that eateth that
which died *of itself*, or that which was
torn *with beasts, whether it be* one of
your own country, or a stranger, he shall
both wash his clothes, and bathe *himself* in water, and be unclean until the
even: then shall he be clean.
16 But if he wash *them* not, nor bathe
his flesh; then he shall bear his iniquity.

CHAPTER 18

AND the LORD spake unto Moses,
saying,
2 Speak unto the children of Ĭs'rā-ĕl,
and say unto them, I *am* the LORD your
God.
3 After the doings of the land of Egypt,
wherein ye dwelt, shall ye not do: and
after the doings of the land of Cā'năan,
whither I bring you, shall ye not do:
neither shall ye walk in their ordinances.
4 Ye shall do my judgments, and keep
mine ordinances, to walk therein: I *am*
the LORD your God.
5 Ye shall therefore keep my statutes,
and my judgments: which if a man do,
he shall live in them: I *am* the LORD.
6 ¶ None of you shall approach to any
that is near of kin to him, to uncover
their nakedness: I *am* the LORD.
7 The nakedness of thy father, or the
nakedness of thy mother, shalt thou not
uncover: she *is* thy mother; thou shalt
not uncover her nakedness.
8 The nakedness of thy father's wife
shalt thou not uncover: it *is* thy father's
nakedness.
9 The nakedness of thy sister, the
daughter of thy father, or daughter of
thy mother, *whether she be* born at
home, or born abroad, *even* their nakedness thou shalt not uncover.
10 The nakedness of thy son's daughter, or of thy daughter's daughter, *even*
their nakedness thou shalt not uncover:
for theirs *is* thine own nakedness.
11 The nakedness of thy father's wife's
daughter, begotten of thy father, she *is*
thy sister, thou shalt not uncover her
nakedness.
12 Thou shalt not uncover the nakedness of thy father's sister: she *is* thy
father's near kinswoman.
13 Thou shalt not uncover the nakedness of thy mother's sister: for she *is*
thy mother's nearest kinswoman.
14 Thou shalt not uncover the nakedness of thy father's brother, thou shalt
not approach to his wife: she *is* thine
aunt.
15 Thou shalt not uncover the nakedness of thy daughter-in-law: she *is* thy
son's wife; thou shalt not uncover her
nakedness.
16 Thou shalt not uncover the nakedness of thy brother's wife: it *is* thy
brother's nakedness.
17 Thou shalt not uncover the nakedness of a woman and her daughter,
neither shalt thou take her son's daughter, or her daughter's daughter, to uncover her nakedness; *for* they *are* her
near kinswomen: it *is* wickedness.
18 Neither shalt thou take a wife to her
sister, to vex *her*, to uncover her nakedness, besides the other in her life *time*.
19 Also thou shalt not approach unto a
woman to uncover her nakedness, as
long as she is put apart for her uncleanness.
20 Moreover thou shalt not lie carnally
with thy neighbor's wife, to defile thyself with her.
21 And thou shalt not let any of thy
seed pass through *the fire* to Mō'lĕch,

neither shalt thou profane the name of
thy God: I *am* the LORD.
22 Thou shalt not lie with mankind, as
with womankind: it *is* abomination.
23 Neither shalt thou lie with any
beast to defile thyself therewith: neither
shall any woman stand before a beast
to lie down thereto: it *is* confusion.
24 Defile not ye yourselves in any of
these things: for in all these the nations are defiled which I cast out before
you:
25 And the land is defiled: therefore I
do visit the iniquity thereof upon it, and
the land itself vomiteth out her inhabitants.
26 Ye shall therefore keep my statutes
and my judgments, and shall not commit *any* of these abominations; *neither*
any of your own nation, nor any stranger that sojourneth among you:
27 (For all these abominations have
the men of the land done, which *were*
before you, and the land is defiled;)
28 That the land spew not you out also,
when ye defile it, as it spewed out the
nations that *were* before you.
29 For whosoever shall commit any of
these abominations, even the souls that
commit *them* shall be cut off from
among their people.
30 Therefore shall ye keep mine ordinance, that *ye* commit not *any one* of
these abominable customs, which were
committed before you, and that ye defile
not yourselves therein: I *am* the LORD
your God.

CHAPTER 19

AND the LORD spake unto Moses,
saying,
2 Speak unto all the congregation of
the children of Is'rā-ĕl, and say unto
them, Ye shall be holy: for I the LORD
your God *am* holy.
3 ¶ Ye shall fear every man his mother, and his father, and keep my sabbaths: I *am* the LORD your God.
4 ¶ Turn ye not unto idols, nor make
to yourselves molten gods: I *am* the
LORD your God.
5 ¶ And if ye offer a sacrifice of peace
offerings unto the LORD, ye shall offer
it at your own will.
6 It shall be eaten the same day ye
offer it, and on the morrow: and if aught
remain until the third day, it shall be
burnt in the fire.
7 And if it be eaten at all on the third
day, it *is* abominable; it shall not be
accepted.
8 Therefore *every one* that eateth it
shall bear his iniquity, because he hath
profaned the hallowed thing of the
LORD; and that soul shall be cut off from
among his people.
9 ¶ And when ye reap the harvest of
your land, thou shalt not wholly reap
the corners of thy field, neither shalt
thou gather the gleanings of thy harvest.
10 And thou shalt not glean thy vineyard, neither shalt thou gather *every*
grape of thy vineyard; thou shalt leave
them for the poor and stranger: I *am* the
LORD your God.
11 ¶ Ye shall not steal, neither deal
falsely, neither lie one to another.
12 ¶ And ye shall not swear by my
name falsely, neither shalt thou profane
the name of thy God: I *am* the LORD.
13 ¶ Thou shalt not defraud thy
neighbor, neither rob *him:* the wages of
him that is hired shall not abide with
thee all night until the morning.
14 ¶ Thou shalt not curse the deaf, nor
put a stumblingblock before the blind,
but shalt fear thy God: I *am* the LORD.
15 ¶ Ye shall do no unrighteousness
in judgment; thou shalt not respect the
person of the poor, nor honor the person
of the mighty: *but* in righteousness
shalt thou judge thy neighbor.
16 ¶ Thou shalt not go up and down
as a talebearer among thy people; neither shalt thou stand against the blood
of thy neighbor: I *am* the LORD.
17 ¶ Thou shalt not hate thy brother
in thine heart: thou shalt in any wise
rebuke thy neighbor, and not suffer sin
upon him.
18 ¶ Thou shalt not avenge, nor bear
any grudge against the children of thy
people, but thou shalt love thy neighbor
as thyself: I *am* the LORD.
19 ¶ Ye shall keep my statutes. Thou
shalt not let thy cattle gender with a
diverse kind: thou shalt not sow thy
field with mingled seed: neither shall a
garment mingled of linen and woolen
come upon thee.
20 ¶ And whosoever lieth carnally
with a woman, that *is* a bondmaid,
betrothed to a husband, and not at all
redeemed, nor freedom given her; she
shall be scourged: they shall not be put
to death, because she was not free.

21 And he shall bring his trespass offering unto the LORD, unto the door of the tabernacle of the congregation, *even* a ram for a trespass offering.

22 And the priest shall make an atonement for him with the ram of the trespass offering before the LORD for his sin which he hath done; and the sin which he hath done shall be forgiven him.

23 ¶ And when ye shall come into the land, and shall have planted all manner of trees for food, then ye shall count the fruit thereof as uncircumcised: three years shall it be as uncircumcised unto you: it shall not be eaten of.

24 But in the fourth year all the fruit thereof shall be holy to praise the LORD *withal*.

25 And in the fifth year shall ye eat of the fruit thereof, that it may yield unto you the increase thereof: I *am* the LORD your God.

26 ¶ Ye shall not eat *any thing* with the blood: neither shall ye use enchantment, nor observe times.

27 Ye shall not round the corners of your heads, neither shalt thou mar the corners of thy beard.

28 Ye shall not make any cuttings in your flesh for the dead, nor print any marks upon you: I *am* the LORD.

29 ¶ Do not prostitute thy daughter, to cause her to be a whore; lest the land fall to whoredom, and the land become full of wickedness.

30 ¶ Ye shall keep my sabbaths, and reverence my sanctuary: I *am* the LORD.

31 ¶ Regard not them that have familiar spirits, neither seek after wizards, to be defiled by them: I *am* the LORD your God.

32 ¶ Thou shalt rise up before the hoary head, and honor the face of the old man, and fear thy God: I *am* the LORD.

33 ¶ And if a stranger sojourn with thee in your land, ye shall not vex him.

34 *But* the stranger that dwelleth with you shall be unto you as one born among you, and thou shalt love him as thyself; for ye were strangers in the land of Egypt: I *am* the LORD your God.

35 ¶ Ye shall do no unrighteousness in judgment, in meteyard, in weight, or in measure.

36 Just balances, just weights, a just ē'phäh, and a just hin, shall ye have: I *am* the LORD your God, which brought you out of the land of Egypt.

37 Therefore shall ye observe all my statutes, and all my judgments, and do them: I *am* the LORD.

CHAPTER 20

AND the LORD spake unto Moses, saying,

2 Again, thou shalt say to the children of Ĭṣ'rā-ĕl, Whosoever *he be* of the children of Ĭṣ'rā-ĕl, or of the strangers that sojourn in Ĭṣ'rā-ĕl, that giveth *any* of his seed unto Mō'lĕch; he shall surely be put to death: the people of the land shall stone him with stones.

3 And I will set my face against that man, and will cut him off from among his people; because he hath given of his seed unto Mō'lĕch, to defile my sanctuary, and to profane my holy name.

4 And if the people of the land do any ways hide their eyes from the man, when he giveth of his seed unto Mō'lĕch, and kill him not;

5 Then I will set my face against that man, and against his family, and will cut him off, and all that go a whoring after him, to commit whoredom with Mō'lĕch, from among their people.

6 ¶ And the soul that turneth after such as have familiar spirits, and after wizards, to go a whoring after them, I will even set my face against that soul, and will cut him off from among his people.

7 ¶ Sanctify yourselves therefore, and be ye holy: for I *am* the LORD your God.

8 And ye shall keep my statutes, and do them: I *am* the LORD which sanctify you.

9 ¶ For every one that curseth his father or his mother shall be surely put to death: he hath cursed his father or his mother; his blood *shall be* upon him.

10 ¶ And the man that committeth adultery with *another* man's wife, *even he* that committeth adultery with his neighbor's wife, the adulterer and the adulteress shall surely be put to death.

11 And the man that lieth with his father's wife hath uncovered his father's nakedness: both of them shall surely be put to death; their blood *shall be* upon them.

12 And if a man lie with his daughter-in-law, both of them shall surely be put to death: they have wrought confusion; their blood *shall be* upon them.

13 If a man also lie with mankind, as he lieth with a woman, both of them have committed an abomination: they shall surely be put to death; their blood *shall be* upon them.

14 And if a man take a wife and her mother, it *is* wickedness: they shall be burnt with fire, both he and they; that there be no wickedness among you.

15 And if a man lie with a beast, he shall surely be put to death; and ye shall slay the beast.

16 And if a woman approach unto any beast, and lie down thereto, thou shalt kill the woman, and the beast: they shall surely be put to death; their blood *shall be* upon them.

17 And if a man shall take his sister, his father's daughter, or his mother's daughter, and see her nakedness, and she see his nakedness; it *is* a wicked thing; and they shall be cut off in the sight of their people: he hath uncovered his sister's nakedness; he shall bear his iniquity.

18 And if a man shall lie with a woman having her sickness, and shall uncover her nakedness; he hath discovered her fountain, and she hath uncovered the fountain of her blood: and both of them shall be cut off from among their people.

19 And thou shalt not uncover the nakedness of thy mother's sister, nor of thy father's sister; for he uncovereth his near kin: they shall bear their iniquity.

20 And if a man shall lie with his uncles's wife, he hath uncovered his uncle's nakedness: they shall bear their sin; they shall die childless.

21 And if a man shall take his brother's wife, it *is* an unclean thing: he hath uncovered his brother's nakedness; they shall be childless.

22 ¶ Ye shall therefore keep all my statutes, and all my judgments, and do them: that the land, whither I bring you to dwell therein, spew you not out.

23 And ye shall not walk in the manners of the nation, which I cast out before you: for they committed all these things, and therefore I abhorred them.

24 But I have said unto you, Ye shall inherit their land, and I will give it unto you to possess it, a land that floweth with milk and honey: I *am* the LORD your God, which have separated you from *other* people.

25 Ye shall therefore put difference between clean beasts and unclean, and between unclean fowls and clean: and ye shall not make your souls abominable by beast, or by fowl, or by any manner of living thing that creepeth on the ground, which I have separated from you as unclean.

26 And ye shall be holy unto me: for I the LORD *am* holy, and have severed you from *other* people, that ye should be mine.

27 ¶ A man also or woman that hath a familiar spirit, or that is a wizard, shall surely be put to death: they shall stone them with stones; their blood *shall be* upon them.

CHAPTER 21

AND the LORD said unto Moses, Speak unto the priests the sons of Aaron, and say unto them, There shall none be defiled for the dead among his people:

2 But for his kin, that is near unto him, *that is*, for his mother, and for his father, and for his son, and for his daughter, and for his brother,

3 And for his sister a virgin, that is nigh unto him, which hath had no husband; for her may he be defiled.

4 *But* he shall not defile himself, *being* a chief man among his people, to profane himself.

5 They shall not make baldness upon their head, neither shall they shave off the corner of their beard, nor make any cuttings in their flesh.

6 They shall be holy unto their God, and not profane the name of their God: for the offerings of the LORD made by fire, *and* the bread of their God, they do offer: therefore they shall be holy.

7 They shall not take a wife *that is* a whore, or profane; neither shall they take a woman put away from her husband: for he *is* holy unto his God.

8 Thou shalt sanctify him therefore; for he offereth the bread of thy God: he shall be holy unto thee: for I the LORD, which sanctify you, *am* holy.

9 ¶ And the daughter of any priest, if she profane herself by playing the whore, she profaneth her father: she shall be burnt with fire.

10 And *he that is* the high priest among his brethren, upon whose head the anointing oil was poured, and that is consecrated to put on the garments,

shall not uncover his head, nor rend his
clothes;
11 Neither shall he go in to any dead
body, nor defile himself for his father,
or for his mother;
12 Neither shall he go out of the sanctuary, nor profane the sanctuary of his
God; for the crown of the anointing oil
of his God *is* upon him: I *am* the LORD.
13 And he shall take a wife in her
virginity.
14 A widow, or a divorced woman, or
profane, *or* a harlot, these shall he not
take: but he shall take a virgin of his
own people to wife.
15 Neither shall he profane his seed
among his people: for I the LORD do
sanctify him.
16 ¶ And the LORD spake unto Moses,
saying,
17 Speak unto Aaron, saying, Whosoever *he be* of thy seed in their generations that hath *any* blemish, let him not
approach to offer the bread of his God.
18 For whatsoever man *he be* that hath
a blemish, he shall not approach: a blind
man, or a lame, or he that hath a flat
nose, or any thing superfluous,
19 Or a man that is broken-footed, or
broken-handed,
20 Or crookbacked, or a dwarf, or that
hath a blemish in his eye, or be scurvy,
or scabbed, or hath his stones broken;
21 No man that hath a blemish of the
seed of Aaron the priest shall come nigh
to offer the offerings of the LORD made
by fire: he hath a blemish; he shall not
come nigh to offer the bread of his God.
22 He shall eat the bread of his God,
both of the most holy, and of the holy.
23 Only he shall not go in unto the veil,
nor come nigh unto the altar, because he
hath a blemish; that he profane not my
sanctuaries: for I the LORD do sanctify
them.
24 And Moses told *it* unto Aaron, and
to his sons, and unto all the children of
Ĭş′rā-ĕl.

CHAPTER 22

AND the LORD spake unto Moses,
saying,
2 Speak unto Aaron and to his sons,
that they separate themselves from the
holy things of the children of Ĭş′rā-ĕl,
and that they profane not my holy name
in those things which they hallow unto
me: I *am* the LORD.
3 Say unto them, Whosoever *he be* of
all your seed among your generations,
that goeth unto the holy things, which
the children of Ĭş′rā-ĕl hallow unto the
LORD, having his uncleanness upon him,
that soul shall be cut off from my presence: I *am* the LORD.
4 What man soever of the seed of Aaron
is a leper, or hath a running issue; he
shall not eat of the holy things, until he
be clean. And whoso toucheth any thing
that is unclean *by* the dead, or a man
whose seed goeth from him;
5 Or whosoever toucheth any creeping
thing, whereby he may be made unclean, or a man of whom he may take
uncleanness, whatsoever uncleanness
he hath;
6 The soul which hath touched any
such shall be unclean until even, and
shall not eat of the holy things, unless
he wash his flesh with water.
7 And when the sun is down, he
shall be clean, and shall afterward eat
of the holy things; because it *is* his
food.
8 That which dieth of itself, or is torn
with beasts, he shall not eat to defile
himself therewith: I *am* the LORD.
9 They shall therefore keep mine ordinance, lest they bear sin for it, and die
therefore, if they profane it: I the LORD
do sanctify them.
10 There shall no stranger eat *of* the
holy thing: a sojourner of the priest, or
a hired servant, shall not eat *of* the holy
thing.
11 But if the priest buy *any* soul with
his money, he shall eat of it, and he that
is born in his house: they shall eat of his
meat.
12 If the priest's daughter also be *married* unto a stranger, she may not eat of
an offering of the holy things.
13 But if the priest's daughter be a
widow, or divorced, and have no child,
and is returned unto her father's house,
as in her youth, she shall eat of her
father's meat: but there shall no stranger eat thereof.
14 ¶ And if a man eat *of* the holy thing
unwittingly, then he shall put the fifth
part thereof unto it, and shall give *it*
unto the priest with the holy thing.
15 And they shall not profane the holy
things of the children of Ĭş′rā-ĕl, which
they offer unto the LORD;
16 Or suffer them to bear the iniquity

of trespass, when they eat their holy things: for I the LORD do sanctify them.
17 ¶ And the LORD spake unto Moses, saying,
18 Speak unto Aaron, and to his sons, and unto all the children of Is′rā-ĕl, and say unto them, Whatsoever *he be* of the house of Is′rā-ĕl, or of the strangers in Is′rā-ĕl, that will offer his oblation for all his vows, and for all his freewill offerings, which they will offer unto the LORD for a burnt offering;
19 *Ye shall offer* at your own will a male without blemish, of the beeves, of the sheep, or of the goats.
20 *But* whatsoever hath a blemish, *that* shall ye not offer: for it shall not be acceptable for you.
21 And whosoever offereth a sacrifice of peace offerings unto the LORD to accomplish *his* vow, or a freewill offering in beeves or sheep, it shall be perfect to be accepted; there shall be no blemish therein.
22 Blind, or broken, or maimed, or having a wen, or scurvy, or scabbed, ye shall not offer these unto the LORD, nor make an offering by fire of them upon the altar unto the LORD.
23 Either a bullock or a lamb that hath any thing superfluous or lacking in his parts, that mayest thou offer *for* a freewill offering; but for a vow it shall not be accepted.
24 Ye shall not offer unto the LORD that which is bruised, or crushed, or broken, or cut; neither shall ye make *any offering thereof* in your land.
25 Neither from a stranger's hand shall ye offer the bread of your God of any of these; because their corruption *is* in them, *and* blemishes *be* in them: they shall not be accepted for you.
26 ¶ And the LORD spake unto Moses, saying,
27 When a bullock, or a sheep, or a goat, is brought forth, then it shall be seven days under the dam; and from the eighth day and thenceforth it shall be accepted for an offering made by fire unto the LORD.
28 And *whether it be* cow or ewe, ye shall not kill it and her young both in one day.
29 And when ye will offer a sacrifice of thanksgiving unto the LORD, offer *it* at your own will.
30 On the same day it shall be eaten up; ye shall leave none of it until the morrow: I *am* the LORD.
31 Therefore shall ye keep my commandments, and do them: I *am* the LORD.
32 Neither shall ye profane my holy name; but I will be hallowed among the children of Is′rā-ĕl: I *am* the LORD which hallow you,
33 That brought you out of the land of Egypt, to be your God: I *am* the LORD.

CHAPTER 23

AND the LORD spake unto Moses, saying,
2 Speak unto the children of Is′rā-ĕl, and say unto them, *Concerning* the feasts of the LORD, which ye shall proclaim *to be* holy convocations, *even* these *are* my feasts.
3 Six days shall work be done: but the seventh day *is* the sabbath of rest, a holy convocation; ye shall do no work *therein:* it *is* the sabbath of the LORD in all your dwellings.
4 ¶ These *are* the feasts of the LORD, *even* holy convocations, which ye shall proclaim in their seasons.
5 In the fourteenth *day* of the first month at even *is* the LORD's passover.
6 And on the fifteenth day of the same month *is* the feast of unleavened bread unto the LORD: seven days ye must eat unleavened bread.
7 In the first day ye shall have a holy convocation: ye shall do no servile work therein.
8 But ye shall offer an offering made by fire unto the LORD seven days: in the seventh day *is* a holy convocation: ye shall do no servile work *therein.*
9 ¶ And the LORD spake unto Moses, saying,
10 Speak unto the children of Is′rā-ĕl, and say unto them, When ye be come into the land which I give unto you, and shall reap the harvest thereof, then ye shall bring a sheaf of the firstfruits of your harvest unto the priest:
11 And he shall wave the sheaf before the LORD, to be accepted for you: on the morrow after the sabbath the priest shall wave it.
12 And ye shall offer that day when ye wave the sheaf a he lamb without blemish of the first year for a burnt offering unto the LORD.
13 And the meat offering thereof *shall*

be two tenth deals of fine flour mingled with oil, an offering made by fire unto the LORD *for* a sweet savor: and the drink offering thereof *shall be* of wine, the fourth *part* of a hin.

14 And ye shall eat neither bread, nor parched corn, nor green ears, until the selfsame day that ye have brought an offering unto your God: *it shall be* a statute for ever throughout your generations in all your dwellings.

15 ¶ And ye shall count unto you from the morrow after the sabbath, from the day that ye brought the sheaf of the wave offering; seven sabbaths shall be complete:

16 Even unto the morrow after the seventh sabbath shall ye number fifty days; and ye shall offer a new meat offering unto the LORD.

17 Ye shall bring out of your habitations two wave loaves of two tenth deals: they shall be of fine flour; they shall be baked with leaven; *they are* the firstfruits unto the LORD.

18 And ye shall offer with the bread seven lambs without blemish of the first year, and one young bullock, and two rams: they shall be *for* a burnt offering unto the LORD, with their meat offering, and their drink offerings, *even* an offering made by fire, of sweet savor unto the LORD.

19 Then ye shall sacrifice one kid of the goats for a sin offering, and two lambs of the first year for a sacrifice of peace offerings.

20 And the priest shall wave them with the bread of the firstfruits *for* a wave offering before the LORD, with the two lambs: they shall be holy to the LORD for the priest.

21 And ye shall proclaim on the selfsame day, *that* it may be a holy convocation unto you: ye shall do no servile work *therein: it shall be* a statute for ever in all your dwellings throughout your generations.

22 ¶ And when ye reap the harvest of your land, thou shalt not make clean riddance of the corners of thy field when thou reapest, neither shalt thou gather any gleaning of thy harvest: thou shalt leave them unto the poor, and to the stranger: I *am* the LORD your God.

23 ¶ And the LORD spake unto Moses, saying,

24 Speak unto the children of Ĭş'rā-ĕl, saying, In the seventh month, in the first *day* of the month, shall ye have a sabbath, a memorial of blowing of trumpets, a holy convocation.

25 Ye shall do no servile work *therein:* but ye shall offer an offering made by fire unto the LORD.

26 ¶ And the LORD spake unto Moses, saying,

27 Also on the tenth *day* of this seventh month *there shall be* a day of atonement: it shall be a holy convocation unto you; and ye shall afflict your souls, and offer an offering made by fire unto the LORD.

28 And ye shall do no work in that same day: for it *is* a day of atonement, to make an atonement for you before the LORD your God.

29 For whatsoever soul *it be* that shall not be afflicted in that same day, he shall be cut off from among his people.

30 And whatsoever soul *it be* that doeth any work in that same day, the same soul will I destroy from among his people.

31 Ye shall do no manner of work: *it shall be* a statute for ever throughout your generations in all your dwellings.

32 It *shall be* unto you a sabbath of rest, and ye shall afflict your souls: in the ninth *day* of the month at even, from even unto even, shall ye celebrate your sabbath.

33 ¶ And the LORD spake unto Moses, saying,

34 Speak unto the children of Ĭş'rā-ĕl, saying, The fifteenth day of this seventh month *shall be* the feast of tabernacles *for* seven days unto the LORD.

35 On the first day *shall be* a holy convocation: ye shall do no servile work *therein.*

36 Seven days ye shall offer an offering made by fire unto the LORD; on the eighth day shall be a holy convocation unto you, and ye shall offer an offering made by fire unto the LORD: it *is* a solemn assembly; *and* ye shall do no servile work *therein.*

37 These *are* the feasts of the LORD, which ye shall proclaim *to be* holy convocations, to offer an offering made by fire unto the LORD, a burnt offering, and a meat offering, a sacrifice, and drink offerings, every thing upon his day:

38 Beside the sabbaths of the LORD, and beside your gifts, and beside all

your vows, and beside all your freewill offerings, which ye give unto the LORD.

39 Also in the fifteenth day of the seventh month, when ye have gathered in the fruit of the land, ye shall keep a feast unto the LORD seven days: on the first day *shall be* a sabbath, and on the eighth day *shall be* a sabbath.

40 And ye shall take you on the first day the boughs of goodly trees, branches of palm trees, and the boughs of thick trees, and willows of the brook; and ye shall rejoice before the LORD your God seven days.

41 And ye shall keep it a feast unto the LORD seven days in the year: *it shall be* a statute for ever in your generations; ye shall celebrate it in the seventh month.

42 Ye shall dwell in booths seven days; all that are Ĭş′rā-ĕl-ītes born shall dwell in booths:

43 That your generations may know that I made the children of Ĭş′rā-ĕl to dwell in booths, when I brought them out of the land of Egypt: I *am* the LORD your God.

44 And Moses declared unto the children of Ĭş′rā-ĕl the feasts of the LORD.

CHAPTER 24

AND the LORD spake unto Moses, saying,

2 Command the children of Ĭş′rā-ĕl, that they bring unto thee pure oil olive beaten for the light, to cause the lamps to burn continually.

3 Without the veil of the testimony, in the tabernacle of the congregation, shall Aaron order it from the evening unto the morning before the LORD continually: *it shall be* a statute for ever in your generations.

4 He shall order the lamps upon the pure candlestick before the LORD continually.

5 ¶ And thou shalt take fine flour, and bake twelve cakes thereof: two tenth deals shall be in one cake.

6 And thou shalt set them in two rows, six on a row, upon the pure table before the LORD.

7 And thou shalt put pure frankincense upon *each* row, that it may be on the bread for a memorial, *even* an offering made by fire unto the LORD.

8 Every sabbath he shall set it in order before the LORD continually, *being* *taken* from the children of Ĭş′rā-ĕl by an everlasting covenant.

9 And it shall be Aaron's and his sons'; and they shall eat it in the holy place: for it *is* most holy unto him of the offerings of the LORD made by fire by a perpetual statute.

10 ¶ And the son of an Ĭş′rā-ĕl-īt′ĭsh woman, whose father *was* an Egyptian, went out among the children of Ĭş′rā-ĕl: and this son of the Ĭş′rā-ĕl-īt′ĭsh *woman* and a man of Ĭş′rā-ĕl strove together in the camp;

11 And the Ĭş′rā-ĕl-īt′ĭsh woman's son blasphemed the name *of the LORD*, and cursed. And they brought him unto Moses: (and his mother's name *was* Shē′lō-mĭth, the daughter of Dĭb′rī, of the tribe of Dan:)

12 And they put him in ward, that the mind of the LORD might be showed them.

13 And the LORD spake unto Moses, saying,

14 Bring forth him that hath cursed without the camp; and let all that heard *him* lay their hands upon his head, and let all the congregation stone him.

15 And thou shalt speak unto the children of Ĭş′rā-ĕl, saying, Whosoever curseth his God shall bear his sin.

16 And he that blasphemeth the name of the LORD, he shall surely be put to death, *and* all the congregation shall certainly stone him: as well the stranger, as he that is born in the land, when he blasphemeth the name *of the LORD*, shall be put to death.

17 ¶ And he that killeth any man shall surely be put to death.

18 And he that killeth a beast shall make it good; beast for beast.

19 And if a man cause a blemish in his neighbor; as he hath done, so shall it be done to him;

20 Breach for breach, eye for eye, tooth for tooth: as he hath caused a blemish in a man, so shall it be done to him *again*.

21 And he that killeth a beast, he shall restore it: and he that killeth a man, he shall be put to death.

22 Ye shall have one manner of law, as well for the stranger, as for one of your own country: for I *am* the LORD your God.

23 ¶ And Moses spake to the children of Ĭş′rā-ĕl, that they should bring forth

him that had cursed out of the camp, and stone him with stones: and the children of Ĭs′rā-ĕl did as the LORD commanded Moses.

CHAPTER 25

AND the LORD spake unto Moses in mount Sī′naī, saying,

2 Speak unto the children of Ĭs′rā-ĕl, and say unto them, When ye come into the land which I give you, then shall the land keep a sabbath unto the LORD.

3 Six years thou shalt sow thy field, and six years thou shalt prune thy vineyard, and gather in the fruit thereof;

4 But in the seventh year shall be a sabbath of rest unto the land, a sabbath for the LORD: thou shalt neither sow thy field, nor prune thy vineyard.

5 That which groweth of its own accord of thy harvest thou shalt not reap, neither gather the grapes of thy vine undressed: *for* it is a year of rest unto the land.

6 And the sabbath of the land shall be meat for you; for thee, and for thy servant, and for thy maid, and for thy hired servant, and for thy stranger that sojourneth with thee,

7 And for thy cattle, and for the beast that *are* in thy land, shall all the increase thereof be meat.

8 ¶ And thou shalt number seven sabbaths of years unto thee, seven times seven years; and the space of the seven sabbaths of years shall be unto thee forty and nine years.

9 Then shalt thou cause the trumpet of the jubilee to sound on the tenth *day* of the seventh month, in the day of atonement shall ye make the trumpet sound throughout all your land.

10 And ye shall hallow the fiftieth year, and proclaim liberty throughout *all* the land unto all the inhabitants thereof: it shall be a jubilee unto you; and ye shall return every man unto his possession, and ye shall return every man unto his family.

11 A jubilee shall that fiftieth year be unto you: ye shall not sow, neither reap that which groweth of itself in it, nor gather *the grapes* in it of thy vine undressed.

12 For it *is* the jubilee; it shall be holy unto you: ye shall eat the increase thereof out of the field.

13 In the year of this jubilee ye shall return every man unto his possession.

14 And if thou sell aught unto thy neighbor, or buyest *aught* of thy neighbor's hand, ye shall not oppress one another:

15 According to the number of years after the jubilee thou shalt buy of thy neighbor, *and* according unto the number of years of the fruits he shall sell unto thee:

16 According to the multitude of years thou shalt increase the price thereof, and according to the fewness of years thou shalt diminish the price of it: for *according* to the number *of the years* of the fruits doth he sell unto thee.

17 Ye shall not therefore oppress one another; but thou shalt fear thy God: for I *am* the LORD your God.

18 ¶ Wherefore ye shall do my statutes, and keep my judgments, and do them; and ye shall dwell in the land in safety.

19 And the land shall yield her fruit, and ye shall eat your fill, and dwell therein in safety.

20 And if ye shall say, What shall we eat the seventh year? behold, we shall not sow, nor gather in our increase:

21 Then I will command my blessing upon you in the sixth year, and it shall bring forth fruit for three years.

22 And ye shall sow the eighth year, and eat *yet* of old fruit until the ninth year; until her fruits come in ye shall eat *of* the old *store*.

23 ¶ The land shall not be sold for ever: for the land *is* mine; for ye *are* strangers and sojourners with me.

24 And in all the land of your possession ye shall grant a redemption for the land.

25 ¶ If thy brother be waxen poor, and hath sold away *some* of his possession, and if any of his kin come to redeem it, then shall he redeem that which his brother sold.

26 And if the man have none to redeem it, and himself be able to redeem it;

27 Then let him count the years of the sale thereof, and restore the overplus unto the man to whom he sold it; that he may return unto his possession.

28 But if he be not able to restore *it* to him, then that which is sold shall remain in the hand of him that hath bought it until the year of jubilee: and

in the jubilee it shall go out, and he
shall return unto his possession.
29 And if a man sell a dwelling house in
a walled city, then he may redeem it
within a whole year after it is sold; *within* a full year may he redeem it.
30 And if it be not redeemed within the
space of a full year, then the house that
is in the walled city shall be established
for ever to him that bought it throughout
his generations: it shall not go out in the
jubilee.
31 But the houses of the villages which
have no wall round about them shall be
counted as the fields of the country:
they may be redeemed, and they shall
go out in the jubilee.
32 Notwithstanding the cities of the
Lē′vītes, *and* the houses of the cities of
their possession, may the Lē′vītes redeem at any time.
33 And if a man purchase of the Lē′-
vītes, then the house that was sold, and
the city of his possession, shall go out in
the year of jubilee: for the houses of the
cities of the Lē′vītes *are* their possession
among the children of Ĭș′rā-ĕl.
34 But the field of the suburbs of their
cities may not be sold; for it *is* their perpetual possession.
35 ℂ And if thy brother be waxen poor,
and fallen in decay with thee; then thou
shalt relieve him: *yea, though he be* a
stranger, or a sojourner; that he may
live with thee.
36 Take thou no usury of him, or
increase: but fear thy God; that thy
brother may live with thee.
37 Thou shalt not give him thy money
upon usury, nor lend him thy victuals
for increase.
38 I *am* the LORD your God, which
brought you forth out of the land of
Egypt, to give you the land of Cā′năan,
and to be your God.
39 ℂ And if thy brother *that dwelleth*
by thee be waxen poor, and be sold unto
thee; thou shalt not compel him to serve
as a bondservant:
40 *But* as a hired servant, *and* as a sojourner, he shall be with thee, *and* shall
serve thee unto the year of jubilee:
41 And *then* shall he depart from thee,
both he and his children with him, and
shall return unto his own family, and
unto the possession of his fathers shall
he return.
42 For they *are* my servants, which I
brought forth out of the land of Egypt:
they shall not be sold as bondmen.
43 Thou shalt not rule over him with
rigor; but shalt fear thy God.
44 Both thy bondmen, and thy bondmaids, which thou shalt have, *shall be*
of the heathen that are round about you;
of them shall ye buy bondmen and
bondmaids.
45 Moreover, of the children of the
strangers that do sojourn among you, of
them shall ye buy, and of their families
that *are* with you, which they begat in
your land: and they shall be your
possession.
46 And ye shall take them as an inheritance for your children after you, to
inherit *them for* a possession; they shall
be your bondmen for ever: but over your
brethren the children of Ĭș′rā-ĕl, ye shall
not rule one over another with rigor.
47 ℂ And if a sojourner or stranger
wax rich by thee, and thy brother *that
dwelleth* by him wax poor, and sell himself unto the stranger *or* sojourner by
thee, or to the stock of the stranger's
family:
48 After that he is sold he may be redeemed again; one of his brethren may
redeem him:
49 Either his uncle, or his uncle's son,
may redeem him, or *any* that is nigh of
kin unto him of his family may redeem
him; or if he be able, he may redeem
himself.
50 And he shall reckon with him that
bought him from the year that he was
sold to him unto the year of jubilee: and
the price of his sale shall be according
unto the number of years, according to
the time of a hired servant shall it be
with him.
51 If *there be* yet many years *behind*,
according unto them he shall give again
the price of his redemption out of the
money that he was bought for.
52 And if there remain but few years
unto the year of jubilee, then he shall
count with him, *and* according unto his
years shall he give him again the price
of his redemption.
53 *And* as a yearly hired servant shall
he be with him: *and the other* shall not
rule with rigor over him in thy sight.
54 And if he be not redeemed in these
years, then he shall go out in the year
of jubilee, *both* he, and his children with
him.

55 For unto me the children of Ĭş′rā-ĕl *are* servants; they *are* my servants whom I brought forth out of the land of Egypt: I *am* the LORD your God.

CHAPTER 26

YE shall make you no idols nor graven image, neither rear you up a standing image, neither shall ye set up *any* image of stone in your land, to bow down unto it: for I *am* the LORD your God.

2 ¶ Ye shall keep my sabbaths, and reverence my sanctuary: I *am* the LORD.

3 ¶ If ye walk in my statutes, and keep my commandments, and do them;

4 Then I will give you rain in due season, and the land shall yield her increase, and the trees of the field shall yield their fruit.

5 And your threshing shall reach unto the vintage, and the vintage shall reach unto the sowing time: and ye shall eat your bread to the full, and dwell in your land safely.

6 And I will give peace in the land, and ye shall lie down, and none shall make *you* afraid: and I will rid evil beasts out of the land, neither shall the sword go through your land.

7 And ye shall chase your enemies, and they shall fall before you by the sword.

8 And five of you shall chase a hundred, and a hundred of you shall put ten thousand to flight: and your enemies shall fall before you by the sword.

9 For I will have respect unto you, and make you fruitful, and multiply you, and establish my covenant with you.

10 And ye shall eat old store, and bring forth the old because of the new.

11 And I will set my tabernacle among you: and my soul shall not abhor you.

12 And I will walk among you, and will be your God, and ye shall be my people.

13 I *am* the LORD your God, which brought you forth out of the land of Egypt, that ye should not be their bondmen; and I have broken the bands of your yoke, and made you go upright.

14 ¶ But if ye will not hearken unto me, and will not do all these commandments;

15 And if ye shall despise my statutes, or if your soul abhor my judgments, so that ye will not do all my commandments, *but* that ye break my covenant:

16 I also will do this unto you; I will even appoint over you terror, consumption, and the burning ague, that shall consume the eyes, and cause sorrow of heart: and ye shall sow your seed in vain, for your enemies shall eat it.

17 And I will set my face against you, and ye shall be slain before your enemies: they that hate you shall reign over you; and ye shall flee when none pursueth you.

18 And if ye will not yet for all this hearken unto me, then I will punish you seven times more for your sins.

19 And I will break the pride of your power; and I will make your heaven as iron, and your earth as brass:

20 And your strength shall be spent in vain: for your land shall not yield her increase, neither shall the trees of the land yield their fruits.

21 ¶ And if ye walk contrary unto me, and will not hearken unto me; I will bring seven times more plagues upon you according to your sins.

22 I will also send wild beasts among you, which shall rob you of your children, and destroy your cattle, and make you few in number; and your *high* ways shall be desolate.

23 And if ye will not be reformed by me by these things, but will walk contrary unto me;

24 Then will I also walk contrary unto you, and will punish you yet seven times for your sins.

25 And I will bring a sword upon you, that shall avenge the quarrel of *my* covenant: and when ye are gathered together within your cities, I will send the pestilence among you; and ye shall be delivered into the hand of the enemy.

26 *And* when I have broken the staff of your bread, ten women shall bake your bread in one oven, and they shall deliver *you* your bread again by weight: and ye shall eat, and not be satisfied.

27 And if ye will not for all this hearken unto me, but walk contrary unto me;

28 Then I will walk contrary unto you also in fury; and I, even I, will chastise you seven times for your sins.

29 And ye shall eat the flesh of your sons, and the flesh of your daughters shall ye eat.

30 And I will destroy your high places, and cut down your images, and cast your carcasses upon the carcasses of your idols, and my soul shall abhor you.

31 And I will make your cities waste, and bring your sanctuaries unto desolation, and I will not smell the savor of your sweet odors.
32 And I will bring the land into desolation: and your enemies which dwell therein shall be astonished at it.
33 And I will scatter you among the heathen, and will draw out a sword after you: and your land shall be desolate, and your cities waste.
34 Then shall the land enjoy her sabbaths, as long as it lieth desolate, and ye *be* in your enemies' land; *even* then shall the land rest, and enjoy her sabbaths.
35 As long as it lieth desolate it shall rest; because it did not rest in your sabbaths, when ye dwelt upon it.
36 And upon them that are left *alive* of you I will send a faintness into their hearts in the lands of their enemies; and the sound of a shaken leaf shall chase them; and they shall flee, as fleeing from a sword; and they shall fall when none pursueth.
37 And they shall fall one upon another, as it were before a sword, when none pursueth: and ye shall have no power to stand before your enemies.
38 And ye shall perish among the heathen, and the land of your enemies shall eat you up.
39 And they that are left of you shall pine away in their iniquity in your enemies' lands; and also in the iniquities of their fathers shall they pine away with them.
40 If they shall confess their iniquity, and the iniquity of their fathers, with their trespass which they trespassed against me, and that also they have walked contrary unto me;
41 And *that* I also have walked contrary unto them, and have brought them into the land of their enemies; if then their uncircumcised hearts be humbled, and they then accept of the punishment of their iniquity:
42 Then will I remember my covenant with Jacob, and also my covenant with Isaac, and also my covenant with Abraham will I remember; and I will remember the land.
43 The land also shall be left of them, and shall enjoy her sabbaths, while she lieth desolate without them: and they shall accept of the punishment of their iniquity; because, even because they despised my judgments, and because their soul abhorred my statutes.
44 And yet for all that, when they be in the land of their enemies, I will not cast them away, neither will I abhor them, to destroy them utterly, and to break my covenant with them: for I *am* the LORD their God.
45 But I will for their sakes remember the covenant of their ancestors, whom I brought forth out of the land of Egypt in the sight of the heathen, that I might be their God: I *am* the LORD.
46 These *are* the statutes and judgments and laws, which the LORD made between him and the children of Ĭṣ′rā-ĕl in mount Sī′naī by the hand of Moses.

CHAPTER 27

AND the LORD spake unto Moses, saying,
2 Speak unto the children of Ĭṣ′rā-ĕl, and say unto them, When a man shall make a singular vow, the persons *shall be* for the LORD by thy estimation.
3 And thy estimation shall be of the male from twenty years old even unto sixty years old, even thy estimation shall be fifty shekels of silver, after the shekel of the sanctuary.
4 And if it *be* a female, then thy estimation shall be thirty shekels.
5 And if *it be* from five years old even unto twenty years old, then thy estimation shall be of the male twenty shekels, and for the female ten shekels.
6 And if *it be* from a month old even unto five years old, then thy estimation shall be of the male five shekels of silver, and for the female thy estimation *shall be* three shekels of silver.
7 And if *it be* from sixty years old and above; if *it be* a male, then thy estimation shall be fifteen shekels, and for the female ten shekels.
8 But if he be poorer than thy estimation, then he shall present himself before the priest, and the priest shall value him; according to his ability that vowed shall the priest value him.
9 And if *it be* a beast, whereof men bring an offering unto the LORD, all that *any man* giveth of such unto the LORD shall be holy.
10 He shall not alter it, nor change it, a good for a bad, or a bad for a good: and

if he shall at all change beast for beast, then it and the exchange thereof shall be holy.

11 And if *it be* any unclean beast, of which they do not offer a sacrifice unto the LORD, then he shall present the beast before the priest:

12 And the priest shall value it, whether it be good or bad: as thou valuest it, *who art* the priest, so shall it be.

13 But if he will at all redeem it, then he shall add a fifth *part* thereof unto thy estimation.

14 ¶ And when a man shall sanctify his house *to be* holy unto the LORD, then the priest shall estimate it, whether it be good or bad: as the priest shall estimate it, so shall it stand.

15 And if he that sanctified it will redeem his house, then he shall add the fifth *part* of the money of thy estimation unto it, and it shall be his.

16 And if a man shall sanctify unto the LORD *some part* of a field of his possession, then thy estimation shall be according to the seed thereof: a homer of barley seed *shall be valued* at fifty shekels of silver.

17 If he sanctify his field from the year of jubilee, according to thy estimation it shall stand.

18 But if he sanctify his field after the jubilee, then the priest shall reckon unto him the money according to the years that remain, even unto the year of the jubilee, and it shall be abated from thy estimation.

19 And if he that sanctified the field will in any wise redeem it, then he shall add the fifth *part* of the money of thy estimation unto it, and it shall be assured to him.

20 And if he will not redeem the field, or if he have sold the field to another man, it shall not be redeemed any more.

21 But the field, when it goeth out in the jubilee, shall be holy unto the LORD, as a field devoted; the possession thereof shall be the priest's.

22 And if *a man* sanctify unto the LORD a field which he hath bought, which *is* not of the fields of his possession;

23 Then the priest shall reckon unto him the worth of thy estimation, *even* unto the year of the jubilee: and he shall give thine estimation in that day, *as* a holy thing unto the LORD.

24 In the year of the jubilee the field shall return unto him of whom it was bought, *even* to him to whom the possession of the land *did belong*.

25 And all thy estimations shall be according to the shekel of the sanctuary: twenty gē′rahs shall be the shekel.

26 ¶ Only the firstling of the beasts, which should be the LORD's firstling, no man shall sanctify it; whether *it be* ox, or sheep: it *is* the LORD's.

27 And if *it be* of an unclean beast, then he shall redeem *it* according to thine estimation, and shall add a fifth *part* of it thereto: or if it be not redeemed, then it shall be sold according to thy estimation.

28 Notwithstanding, no devoted thing, that a man shall devote unto the LORD of all that he hath, *both* of man and beast, and of the field of his possession, shall be sold or redeemed: every devoted thing *is* most holy unto the LORD.

29 None devoted, which shall be devoted of men, shall be redeemed; *but* shall surely be put to death.

30 And all the tithe of the land, *whether* of the seed of the land, *or* of the fruit of the tree, *is* the LORD's: *it is* holy unto the LORD.

31 And if a man will at all redeem *aught* of his tithes, he shall add thereto the fifth *part* thereof.

32 And concerning the tithe of the herd, or of the flock, *even* of whatsoever passeth under the rod, the tenth shall be holy unto the LORD.

33 He shall not search whether it be good or bad, neither shall he change it: and if he change it at all, then both it and the change thereof shall be holy; it shall not be redeemed.

34 These *are* the commandments, which the LORD commanded Moses for the children of Ĭş′rā-ĕl in mount Sī′naī.

THE FOURTH BOOK OF MOSES, CALLED

NUMBERS

CHAPTER 1

AND the LORD spake unto Moses in the wilderness of Sī′naī, in the tabernacle of the congregation, on the first *day* of the second month, in the second year after they were come out of the land of Egypt, saying,

2 Take ye the sum of all the congregation of the children of Ĭs′rā-ĕl, after their families, by the house of their fathers, with the number of *their* names, every male by their polls;

3 From twenty years old and upward, all that are able to go forth to war in Ĭs′rā-ĕl: thou and Aaron shall number them by their armies.

4 And with you there shall be a man of every tribe; every one head of the house of his fathers.

5 ¶ And these *are* the names of the men that shall stand with you: of *the tribe of* Reuben; Ē-lī′zŭr the son of Shĕd′ē-ŭr.

6 Of Simeon; Shē-lū′mĭ-ĕl the son of Zū′rĭ-shăd′daī.

7 Of Judah; Năh′shŏn the son of Ăm-mĭn′ā-dăb.

8 Of Ĭs′sā-chär; Nē-thăn′ē-ĕl the son of Zū′är.

9 Of Zĕb′ū-lŭn; Ē-lī′ăb the son of Hē′lŏn.

10 Of the children of Joseph: of Ē′phrā-ĭm; Ē-lĭsh′ā-mä the son of Ăm-mī′hŭd: of Mā-năs′sĕh; Gā-mā′lĭ-ĕl the son of Pē-däh′zŭr.

11 Of Benjamin; Ăb′ĭ-dăn the son of Gĭd′ē-ō′nī.

12 Of Dan; Ā′hī-ē′zĕr the son of Ăm′mĭ-shăd′daī.

13 Of Ăsh′ĕr; Pā′gĭ-ĕl the son of Ŏc′răn.

14 Of Gad; Ē-lī′ā-săph the son of Deū′ĕl.

15 Of Năph′tā-lī; Ā-hī′rā the son of Ē′năn.

16 These *were* the renowned of the congregation, princes of the tribes of their fathers, heads of thousands in Ĭs′rā-ĕl.

17 ¶ And Moses and Aaron took these men which are expressed by *their* names:

18 And they assembled all the congregation together on the first *day* of the second month, and they declared their pedigrees after their families, by the house of their fathers, according to the number of the names, from twenty years old and upward, by their polls.

19 As the LORD commanded Moses, so he numbered them in the wilderness of Sī′naī.

20 And the children of Reuben, Ĭs′rā-ĕl's eldest son, by their generations, after their families, by the house of their fathers, according to the number of the names, by their polls, every male from twenty years old and upward, all that were able to go forth to war;

21 Those that were numbered of them, *even* of the tribe of Reuben, *were* forty and six thousand and five hundred.

22 ¶ Of the children of Simeon, by their generations, after their families, by the house of their fathers, those that were numbered of them, according to the number of the names, by their polls, every male from twenty years old and upward, all that were able to go forth to war;

23 Those that were numbered of them, *even* of the tribe of Simeon, *were* fifty and nine thousand and three hundred.

24 ¶ Of the children of Gad, by their generations, after their families, by the house of their fathers, according to the number of the names, from twenty years old and upward, all that were able to go forth to war;

25 Those that were numbered of them, *even* of the tribe of Gad, *were* forty and five thousand six hundred and fifty.

26 ¶ Of the children of Judah, by their generations, after their families, by the house of their fathers, according to the number of the names, from twenty years old and upward, all that were able to go forth to war;

27 Those that were numbered of them, *even* of the tribe of Judah, *were* threescore and fourteen thousand and six hundred.

28 ¶ Of the children of Ĭs′sā-chär, by their generations, after their families, by

the house of their fathers, according to the number of the names, from twenty years old and upward, all that were able to go forth to war;

29 Those that were numbered of them, *even* of the tribe of Ĭs′sȧ-chär, *were* fifty and four thousand and four hundred.

30 ¶ Of the children of Zĕb′ū-lŭn, by their generations, after their families, by the house of their fathers, according to the number of the names, from twenty years old and upward, all that were able to go forth to war;

31 Those that were numbered of them, *even* of the tribe of Zĕb′ū-lŭn, *were* fifty and seven thousand and four hundred.

32 ¶ Of the children of Joseph, *namely,* of the children of Ē′phrā-ĭm, by their generations, after their families, by the house of their fathers, according to the number of the names, from twenty years old and upward, all that were able to go forth to war;

33 Those that were numbered of them, *even* of the tribe of Ē′phrā-ĭm, *were* forty thousand and five hundred.

34 ¶ Of the children of Mȧ-năs′sĕh, by their generations, after their families, by the house of their fathers, according to the number of the names, from twenty years old and upward, all that were able to go forth to war;

35 Those that were numbered of them, *even* of the tribe of Mȧ-năs′sĕh, *were* thirty and two thousand and two hundred.

36 ¶ Of the children of Benjamin, by their generations, after their families, by the house of their fathers, according to the number of the names, from twenty years old and upward, all that were able to go forth to war;

37 Those that were numbered of them, *even* of the tribe of Benjamin, *were* thirty and five thousand and four hundred.

38 ¶ Of the children of Dan, by their generations, after their families, by the house of their fathers, according to the number of the names, from twenty years old and upward, all that were able to go forth to war;

39 Those that were numbered of them, *even* of the tribe of Dan, *were* threescore and two thousand and seven hundred.

40 ¶ Of the children of Ăsh′ẽr, by their generations, after their families, by the house of their fathers, according to the number of the names, from twenty years old and upward, all that were able to go forth to war;

41 Those that were numbered of them, *even* of the tribe of Ăsh′ẽr, *were* forty and one thousand and five hundred.

42 ¶ Of the children of Năph′tȧ-lī, throughout their generations, after their families, by the house of their fathers, according to the number of the names, from twenty years old and upward, all that were able to go forth to war;

43 Those that were numbered of them, *even* of the tribe of Năph′tȧ-lī, *were* fifty and three thousand and four hundred.

44 These *are* those that were numbered, which Moses and Aaron numbered, and the princes of Ĭş′rā-ĕl, *being* twelve men: each one was for the house of his fathers.

45 So were all those that were numbered of the children of Ĭş′rā-ĕl, by the house of their fathers, from twenty years old and upward, all that were able to go forth to war in Ĭş′rā-ĕl;

46 Even all they that were numbered were six hundred thousand and three thousand and five hundred and fifty.

47 ¶ But the Lē′vītes after the tribe of their fathers were not numbered among them.

48 For the LORD had spoken unto Moses, saying,

49 Only thou shalt not number the tribe of Levi, neither take the sum of them among the children of Ĭş′rā-ĕl:

50 But thou shalt appoint the Lē′vītes over the tabernacle of testimony, and over all the vessels thereof, and over all things that *belong* to it: they shall bear the tabernacle, and all the vessels thereof; and they shall minister unto it, and shall encamp round about the tabernacle.

51 And when the tabernacle setteth forward, the Lē′vītes shall take it down; and when the tabernacle is to be pitched, the Lē′vītes shall set it up: and the stranger that cometh nigh shall be put to death.

52 And the children of Ĭş′rā-ĕl shall pitch their tents, every man by his own camp, and every man by his own standard, throughout their hosts.

53 But the Lē′vītes shall pitch round about the tabernacle of testimony, that there be no wrath upon the congregation of the children of Ĭş′rā-ēl: and the Lē′vītes shall keep the charge of the tabernacle of testimony.

54 And the children of Ĭş′rā-ēl did according to all that the LORD commanded Moses, so did they.

CHAPTER 2

AND the LORD spake unto Moses and unto Aaron, saying,

2 Every man of the children of Ĭş′rā-ēl shall pitch by his own standard, with the ensign of their father's house: far off about the tabernacle of the congregation shall they pitch.

3 And on the east side toward the rising of the sun shall they of the standard of the camp of Judah pitch throughout their armies: and Näh′shŏn the son of Ȧm-mĭn′ȧ-dăb *shall be* captain of the children of Judah.

4 And his host, and those that were numbered of them, *were* threescore and fourteen thousand and six hundred.

5 And those that do pitch next unto him *shall be* the tribe of Ĭs′sȧ-ehär: and Nē-thăn′ē-ĕl the son of Zū′ȧr *shall be* captain of the children of Ĭs′sȧ-ehär.

6 And his host, and those that were numbered thereof, *were* fifty and four thousand and four hundred.

7 *Then* the tribe of Zĕb′ū-lŭn: and Ē-lī′ăb the son of Hē′lŏn *shall be* captain of the children of Zĕb′ū-lŭn.

8 And his host, and those that were numbered thereof, *were* fifty and seven thousand and four hundred.

9 All that were numbered in the camp of Judah *were* a hundred thousand and fourscore thousand and six thousand and four hundred, throughout their armies: these shall first set forth.

10 ¶ On the south side *shall be* the standard of the camp of Reuben according to their armies: and the captain of the children of Reuben *shall be* Ē-lī′zŭr the son of Shĕd′ē-ŭr.

11 And his host, and those that were numbered thereof, *were* forty and six thousand and five hundred.

12 And those which pitch by him *shall be* the tribe of Simeon: and the captain of the children of Simeon *shall be* Shē-lū′mĭ-ēl the son of Zū′rĭ-shăd′daī.

13 And his host, and those that were numbered of them, *were* fifty and nine thousand and three hundred.

14 Then the tribe of Gad: and the captain of the sons of Gad *shall be* Ē-lī′ȧ-săph the son of Reu′ĕl.

15 And his host, and those that were numbered of them, *were* forty and five thousand and six hundred and fifty.

16 All that were numbered in the camp of Reuben *were* a hundred thousand and fifty and one thousand and four hundred and fifty, throughout their armies: and they shall set forth in the second rank.

17 ¶ Then the tabernacle of the congregation shall set forward with the camp of the Lē′vītes in the midst of the camp: as they encamp, so shall they set forward, every man in his place by their standards.

18 ¶ On the west side *shall be* the standard of the camp of Ē′phrā-ĭm according to their armies: and the captain of the sons of Ē′phrā-ĭm *shall be* Ē-lĭsh′ȧ-mä the son of Ȧm-mī′hŭd.

19 And his host, and those that were numbered of them, *were* forty thousand and five hundred.

20 And by him *shall be* the tribe of Mȧ-năs′sĕh: and the captain of the children of Mȧ-năs′sĕh *shall be* Gȧ-mā′lĭ-ēl the son of Pē-däh′zŭr.

21 And his host, and those that were numbered of them, *were* thirty and two thousand and two hundred.

22 Then the tribe of Benjamin: and the captain of the sons of Benjamin *shall be* Ăb′ĭ-dăn the son of Gĭd′ē-ō′nī.

23 And his host, and those that were numbered of them, *were* thirty and five thousand and four hundred.

24 All that were numbered of the camp of Ē′phrā-ĭm *were* a hundred thousand and eight thousand and a hundred, throughout their armies: and they shall go forward in the third rank.

25 ¶ The standard of the camp of Dan *shall be* on the north side by their armies: and the captain of the children of Dan *shall be* Ā′hī-ē′zĕr the son of Ăm′mĭ-shăd′daī.

26 And his host, and those that were numbered of them, *were* threescore and two thousand and seven hundred.

27 And those that encamp by him *shall be* the tribe of Ăsh′ĕr: and the captain of the children of Ăsh′ĕr *shall be* Pā′gĭ-ēl the son of Ŏc′răn.

28 And his host, and those that were

numbered of them, *were* forty and one
thousand and five hundred.
29 ¶ Then the tribe of Năph'tȧ-lī: and
the captain of the children of Năph'tȧ-lī
shall be Ȧ-hī'rȧ the son of Ē'năn.
30 And his host, and those that were
numbered of them, *were* fifty and three
thousand and four hundred.
31 All they that were numbered in the
camp of Dan *were* a hundred thousand
and fifty and seven thousand and six
hundred: they shall go hindmost with
their standards.
32 ¶ These *are* those which were numbered of the children of Ĭṣ'rā-ĕl by the
house of their fathers: all those that
were numbered of the camps throughout their hosts *were* six hundred thousand and three thousand and five hundred and fifty.
33 But the Lē'vītes were not numbered
among the children of Ĭṣ'rā-ĕl; as the
LORD commanded Moses.
34 And the children of Ĭṣ'rā-ĕl did
according to all that the LORD commanded Moses: so they pitched by their
standards, and so they set forward,
every one after their families, according
to the house of their fathers.

CHAPTER 3

THESE also *are* the generations of
Aaron and Moses, in the day *that*
the LORD spake with Moses in mount
Sī'naī.
2 And these *are* the names of the sons
of Aaron; Nā'dăb the firstborn, and
Ȧ-bī'hū, Ĕl'ē-ā'zȧr, and Ĭth'ȧ-mär.
3 These *are* the names of the sons of
Aaron, the priests which were anointed,
whom he consecrated to minister in the
priest's office.
4 And Nā'dăb and Ȧ-bī'hū died before
the LORD, when they offered strange
fire before the LORD, in the wilderness
of Sī'naī, and they had no children: and
Ĕl'ē-ā'zȧr and Ĭth'ȧ-mär ministered in
the priest's office in the sight of Aaron
their father.
5 ¶ And the LORD spake unto Moses,
saying,
6 Bring the tribe of Levi near, and present them before Aaron the priest, that
they may minister unto him.
7 And they shall keep his charge, and
the charge of the whole congregation
before the tabernacle of the congregation, to do the service of the tabernacle.
8 And they shall keep all the instruments of the tabernacle of the congregation, and the charge of the children of
Ĭṣ'rā-ĕl, to do the service of the tabernacle.
9 And thou shalt give the Lē'vītes unto
Aaron and to his sons: they *are* wholly
given unto him out of the children
of Ĭṣ'rā-ĕl.
10 And thou shalt appoint Aaron and
his sons, and they shall wait on their
priest's office: and the stranger that
cometh nigh shall be put to death.
11 And the LORD spake unto Moses,
saying,
12 And I, behold, I have taken the Lē'-
vītes from among the children of Ĭṣ'rā-ĕl
instead of all the firstborn that openeth
the matrix among the children of Ĭṣ'-
rā-ĕl: therefore the Lē'vītes shall be
mine;
13 Because all the firstborn *are* mine;
for on the day that I smote all the firstborn in the land of Egypt I hallowed unto me all the firstborn in Ĭṣ'rā-ĕl, both
man and beast: mine they shall be: I *am*
the LORD.
14 ¶ And the LORD spake unto Moses
in the wilderness of Sī'naī, saying,
15 Number the children of Levi after
the house of their fathers, by their families: every male from a month old and
upward shalt thou number them.
16 And Moses numbered them according to the word of the LORD, as he was
commanded.
17 And these were the sons of Levi by
their names; Gĕr'shŏn, and Kō'hăth,
and Mē-rā'rī.
18 And these *are* the names of the sons
of Gĕr'shŏn by their families; Lĭb'nī,
and Shĭm'ē-ī.
19 And the sons of Kō'hăth by their
families; Ăm'răm, and Ĭz'ē-här, Hē'-
brŏn, and Ŭz-zī'ĕl.
20 And the sons of Mē-rā'rī by their
families; Mäh'lī, and Mū'shī. These
are the families of the Lē'vītes according to the house of their fathers.
21 Of Gĕr'shŏn *was* the family of the
Lĭb'nītes, and the family of the Shĭ'-
mītes: these *are* the families of the
Gĕr'shŏn-ītes.
22 Those that were numbered of them,
according to the number of all the males,
from a month old and upward, *even*
those that were numbered of them *were*
seven thousand and five hundred.

23 The families of the Gẽr′shŏn-ītes shall pitch behind the tabernacle westward.

24 And the chief of the house of the father of the Gẽr′shŏn-ītes *shall be* Ē-lī′ȧ-săph the son of Lā′ĕl.

25 And the charge of the sons of Gẽr′shŏn in the tabernacle of the congregation *shall be* the tabernacle, and the tent, the covering thereof, and the hanging for the door of the tabernacle of the congregation,

26 And the hangings of the court, and the curtain for the door of the court, which *is* by the tabernacle, and by the altar round about, and the cords of it, for all the service thereof.

27 ℭ And of Kō′hăth *was* the family of the Ăm′răm-ītes, and the family of the Ĭz′ē-här-ītes, and the family of the Hē′brȯn-ītes, and the family of the Ŭz-zī′ĕl-ītes: these *are* the families of the Kō′hăth-ītes.

28 In the number of all the males, from a month old and upward, *were* eight thousand and six hundred, keeping the charge of the sanctuary.

29 The families of the sons of Kō′hăth shall pitch on the side of the tabernacle southward.

30 And the chief of the house of the father of the families of the Kō′hăth-ītes *shall be* Ĕl′ĭ-zā′phăn the son of Ŭz-zī′ĕl.

31 And their charge *shall be* the ark, and the table, and the candlestick, and the altars, and the vessels of the sanctuary wherewith they minister, and the hanging, and all the service thereof.

32 And Ĕl′ē-ā′zȧr the son of Aaron the priest *shall be* chief over the chief of the Lē′vītes, *and have* the oversight of them that keep the charge of the sanctuary.

33 ℭ Of Mē-rā′rī *was* the family of the Măh′lītes, and the family of the Mū′shītes: these *are* the families of Mē-rā′rī.

34 And those that were numbered of them, according to the number of all the males, from a month old and upward, *were* six thousand and two hundred.

35 And the chief of the house of the father of the families of Mē-rā′rī *was* Zū′rĭ-ĕl the son of Ăb′ĭ-hāil: *these* shall pitch on the side of the tabernacle northward.

36 And *under* the custody and charge of the sons of Mē-rā′rī *shall be* the boards of the tabernacle, and the bars thereof, and the pillars thereof, and the sockets thereof, and all the vessels thereof, and all that serveth thereto,

37 And the pillars of the court round about, and their sockets, and their pins, and their cords.

38 ℭ But those that encamp before the tabernacle toward the east, *even* before the tabernacle of the congregation eastward, *shall be* Moses, and Aaron and his sons, keeping the charge of the sanctuary for the charge of the children of Ĭs̱′rā-ĕl; and the stranger that cometh nigh shall be put to death.

39 All that were numbered of the Lē′vītes, which Moses and Aaron numbered at the commandment of the LORD, throughout their families, all the males from a month old and upward, *were* twenty and two thousand.

40 ℭ And the LORD said unto Moses, Number all the firstborn of the males of the children of Ĭs̱′rā-ĕl from a month old and upward, and take the number of their names.

41 And thou shalt take the Lē′vītes for me (I *am* the LORD) instead of all the firstborn among the children of Ĭs̱′rā-ĕl; and the cattle of the Lē′vītes instead of all the firstlings among the cattle of the children of Ĭs̱′rā-ĕl.

42 And Moses numbered, as the LORD commanded him, all the firstborn among the children of Ĭs̱′rā-ĕl.

43 And all the firstborn males by the number of names, from a month old and upward, of those that were numbered of them, were twenty and two thousand two hundred and threescore and thirteen.

44 ℭ And the LORD spake unto Moses, saying,

45 Take the Lē′vītes instead of all the firstborn among the children of Ĭs̱′rā-ĕl, and the cattle of the Lē′vītes instead of their cattle; and the Lē′vītes shall be mine: I *am* the LORD.

46 And for those that are to be redeemed of the two hundred and threescore and thirteen of the firstborn of the children of Ĭs̱′rā-ĕl, which are more than the Lē′vītes;

47 Thou shalt even take five shekels apiece by the poll, after the shekel of the sanctuary shalt thou take *them:* (the shekel *is* twenty gē′rȧhs:)

48 And thou shalt give the money,

wherewith the odd number of them is to be redeemed, unto Aaron and to his sons.

49 And Moses took the redemption money of them that were over and above them that were redeemed by the Lē′vītes:

50 Of the firstborn of the children of Ĭş′rā-ĕl took he the money; a thousand three hundred and threescore and five *shekels*, after the shekel of the sanctuary:

51 And Moses gave the money of them that were redeemed unto Aaron and to his sons, according to the word of the LORD, as the LORD commanded Moses.

CHAPTER 4

AND the LORD spake unto Moses and unto Aaron, saying,

2 Take the sum of the sons of Kō′hăth from among the sons of Levi, after their families, by the house of their fathers,

3 From thirty years old and upward even until fifty years old, all that enter into the host, to do the work in the tabernacle of the congregation.

4 This *shall be* the service of the sons of Kō′hăth in the tabernacle of the congregation, *about* the most holy things.

5 ¶ And when the camp setteth forward, Aaron shall come, and his sons, and they shall take down the covering veil, and cover the ark of testimony with it:

6 And shall put thereon the covering of badgers' skins, and shall spread over *it* a cloth wholly of blue, and shall put in the staves thereof.

7 And upon the table of showbread they shall spread a cloth of blue, and put thereon the dishes, and the spoons, and the bowls, and covers to cover withal: and the continual bread shall be thereon:

8 And they shall spread upon them a cloth of scarlet, and cover the same with a covering of badgers' skins, and shall put in the staves thereof.

9 And they shall take a cloth of blue, and cover the candlestick of the light, and his lamps, and his tongs, and his snuffdishes, and all the oil vessels thereof, wherewith they minister unto it:

10 And they shall put it and all the vessels thereof within a covering of badgers' skins, and shall put *it* upon a bar.

11 And upon the golden altar they shall spread a cloth of blue, and cover it with a covering of badgers' skins, and shall put to the staves thereof:

12 And they shall take all the instruments of ministry, wherewith they minister in the sanctuary, and put *them* in a cloth of blue, and cover them with a covering of badgers' skins, and shall put *them* on a bar.

13 And they shall take away the ashes from the altar, and spread a purple cloth thereon:

14 And they shall put upon it all the vessels thereof, wherewith they minister about it, *even* the censers, the fleshhooks, and the shovels, and the basins, all the vessels of the altar; and they shall spread upon it a covering of badgers' skins, and put to the staves of it.

15 And when Aaron and his sons have made an end of covering the sanctuary, and all the vessels of the sanctuary, as the camp is to set forward; after that, the sons of Kō′hăth shall come to bear *it:* but they shall not touch *any* holy thing, lest they die. These *things are* the burden of the sons of Kō′hăth in the tabernacle of the congregation.

16 ¶ And to the office of Ĕl′ē-ā′zăr the son of Aaron the priest *pertaineth* the oil for the light, and the sweet incense, and the daily meat offering, and the anointing oil, *and* the oversight of all the tabernacle, and of all that therein *is,* in the sanctuary, and in the vessels thereof.

17 ¶ And the LORD spake unto Moses and unto Aaron, saying,

18 Cut ye not off the tribe of the families of the Kō′hăth-ītes from among the Lē′vītes:

19 But thus do unto them, that they may live, and not die, when they approach unto the most holy things: Aaron and his sons shall go in, and appoint them every one to his service and to his burden:

20 But they shall not go in to see when the holy things are covered, lest they die.

21 ¶ And the LORD spake unto Moses, saying,

22 Take also the sum of the sons of Gēr′shŏn, throughout the houses of their fathers, by their families;

23 From thirty years old and upward until fifty years old shalt thou number them; all that enter in to perform the

service, to do the work in the tabernacle of the congregation.
24 This *is* the service of the families of
the Gĕr'shŏn-ītes, to serve, and for
burdens:
25 And they shall bear the curtains of
the tabernacle, and the tabernacle of the
congregation, his covering, and the covering of the badgers' skins that *is* above
upon it, and the hanging for the door of
the tabernacle of the congregation,
26 And the hangings of the court, and
the hanging for the door of the gate of
the court, which *is* by the tabernacle and
by the altar round about, and their
cords, and all the instruments of their
service, and all that is made for them:
so shall they serve.
27 At the appointment of Aaron and his
sons shall be all the service of the sons
of the Gĕr'shŏn-ītes, in all their burdens,
and in all their service: and ye shall
appoint unto them in charge all their
burdens.
28 This *is* the service of the families of
the sons of Gĕr'shŏn in the tabernacle
of the congregation: and their charge
shall be under the hand of Ĭth'ă-mär the
son of Aaron the priest.
29 ¶ As for the sons of Mē-rā'rī, thou
shalt number them after their families,
by the house of their fathers;
30 From thirty years old and upward
even unto fifty years old shalt thou number them, every one that entereth into
the service, to do the work of the tabernacle of the congregation.
31 And this *is* the charge of their burden, according to all their service in the
tabernacle of the congregation; the
boards of the tabernacle, and the bars
thereof, and the pillars thereof, and
sockets thereof,
32 And the pillars of the court round
about, and their sockets, and their pins,
and their cords, with all their instruments, and with all their service: and by
name ye shall reckon the instruments
of the charge of their burden.
33 This *is* the service of the families of
the sons of Mē-rā'rī, according to all
their service, in the tabernacle of the
congregation, under the hand of Ĭth'ă-
mär the son of Aaron the priest.
34 ¶ And Moses and Aaron and the
chief of the congregation numbered the
sons of the Kō'hăth-ītes after their families, and after the house of their fathers,
35 From thirty years old and upward
even unto fifty years old, every one that
entereth into the service, for the work
in the tabernacle of the congregation:
36 And those that were numbered of
them by their families were two thousand seven hundred and fifty.
37 These *were* they that were numbered of the families of the Kō'hăth-
ītes, all that might do service in the
tabernacle of the congregation, which
Moses and Aaron did number according
to the commandment of the LORD by the
hand of Moses.
38 And those that were numbered of
the sons of Gĕr'shŏn, throughout their
families, and by the house of their
fathers,
39 From thirty years old and upward
even unto fifty years old, every one that
entereth into the service, for the work
in the tabernacle of the congregation,
40 Even those that were numbered of
them, throughout their families, by the
house of their fathers, were two thousand and six hundred and thirty.
41 These *are* they that were numbered
of the families of the sons of Gĕr'shŏn,
of all that might do service in the tabernacle of the congregation, whom Moses
and Aaron did number according to the
commandment of the LORD.
42 ¶ And those that were numbered of
the families of the sons of Mē-rā'rī,
throughout their families, by the house
of their fathers,
43 From thirty years old and upward
even unto fifty years old, every one that
entereth into the service, for the work
in the tabernacle of the congregation,
44 Even those that were numbered of
them after their families, were three
thousand and two hundred.
45 These *be* those that were numbered
of the families of the sons of Mē-rā'rī,
whom Moses and Aaron numbered
according to the word of the LORD by
the hand of Moses.
46 All those that were numbered of the
Lē'vītes, whom Moses and Aaron and
the chief of Ĭş'rā-ĕl numbered, after
their families, and after the house of
their fathers,
47 From thirty years old and upward
even unto fifty years old, every one that
came to do the service of the ministry,
and the service of the burden in the
tabernacle of the congregation,

48 Even those that were numbered of
them, were eight thousand and five hundred and fourscore.
49 According to the commandment of
the LORD they were numbered by the
hand of Moses, every one according to
his service, and according to his burden:
thus were they numbered of him, as the
LORD commanded Moses.

CHAPTER 5

AND the LORD spake unto Moses,
saying,
2 Command the children of Ĭş′rā-ĕl,
that they put out of the camp every
leper, and every one that hath an issue,
and whosoever is defiled by the dead:
3 Both male and female shall ye put
out, without the camp shall ye put them;
that they defile not their camps, in the
midst whereof I dwell.
4 And the children of Ĭş′rā-ĕl did so,
and put them out without the camp: as
the LORD spake unto Moses, so did the
children of Ĭş′rā-ĕl.
5 ¶ And the LORD spake unto Moses,
saying,
6 Speak unto the children of Ĭş′rā-ĕl,
When a man or woman shall commit any
sin that men commit, to do a trespass
against the LORD, and that person be
guilty;
7 Then they shall confess their sin
which they have done: and he shall recompense his trespass with the principal thereof, and add unto it the fifth *part*
thereof, and give *it* unto *him* against
whom he hath trespassed.
8 But if the man have no kinsman to
recompense the trespass unto, let the
trespass be recompensed unto the
LORD, *even* to the priest; beside the
ram of the atonement, whereby an
atonement shall be made for him.
9 And every offering of all the holy
things of the children of Ĭş′rā-ĕl, which
they bring unto the priest, shall be his.
10 And every man's hallowed things
shall be his: whatsoever any man giveth
the priest, it shall be his.
11 ¶ And the LORD spake unto Moses,
saying,
12 Speak unto the children of Ĭş′rā-ĕl,
and say unto them, If any man's wife go
aside, and commit a trespass against
him,
13 And a man lie with her carnally, and
it be hid from the eyes of her husband,
and be kept close, and she be defiled,
and *there be* no witness against her,
neither she be taken *with the manner;*
14 And the spirit of jealousy come upon
him, and he be jealous of his wife, and
she be defiled; or if the spirit of jealousy
come upon him, and he be jealous of his
wife, and she be not defiled:
15 Then shall the man bring his wife
unto the priest, and he shall bring her
offering for her, the tenth *part* of an
ē′phăh of barley meal; he shall pour no
oil upon it, nor put frankincense thereon; for it *is* an offering of jealousy, an
offering of memorial, bringing iniquity
to remembrance.
16 And the priest shall bring her near,
and set her before the LORD:
17 And the priest shall take holy water
in an earthen vessel; and of the dust
that is in the floor of the tabernacle
the priest shall take, and put *it* into the
water:
18 And the priest shall set the woman
before the LORD, and uncover the woman's head, and put the offering of memorial in her hands, which *is* the jealousy offering: and the priest shall have
in his hand the bitter water that causeth
the curse:
19 And the priest shall charge her by
an oath, and say unto the woman, If no
man have lain with thee, and if thou hast
not gone aside to uncleanness *with another* instead of thy husband, be thou
free from this bitter water that causeth
the curse:
20 But if thou hast gone aside *to another* instead of thy husband, and if
thou be defiled, and some man have lain
with thee besides thine husband:
21 Then the priest shall charge the
woman with an oath of cursing, and the
priest shall say unto the woman, The
LORD make thee a curse and an oath
among thy people, when the LORD doth
make thy thigh to rot, and thy belly to
swell;
22 And this water that causeth the
curse shall go into thy bowels, to make
thy belly to swell, and *thy* thigh to rot.
And the woman shall say, Amen, amen.
23 And the priest shall write these
curses in a book, and he shall blot *them*
out with the bitter water:
24 And he shall cause the woman to
drink the bitter water that causeth the
curse: and the water that causeth the

curse shall enter into her, *and become*
bitter.
25 Then the priest shall take the jealousy offering out of the woman's hand,
and shall wave the offering before the
LORD, and offer it upon the altar:
26 And the priest shall take a handful
of the offering, *even* the memorial
thereof, and burn *it* upon the altar, and
afterward shall cause the woman to
drink the water.
27 And when he hath made her to drink
the water, then it shall come to pass,
that if she be defiled, and have done
trespass against her husband, that the
water that causeth the curse shall enter
into her, *and become* bitter, and her
belly shall swell, and her thigh shall rot:
and the woman shall be a curse among
her people.
28 And if the woman be not defiled,
but be clean; then she shall be free, and
shall conceive seed.
29 This *is* the law of jealousies, when
a wife goeth aside *to another* instead of
her husband, and is defiled;
30 Or when the spirit of jealousy cometh upon him, and he be jealous over
his wife, and shall set the woman before
the LORD, and the priest shall execute
upon her all this law.
31 Then shall the man be guiltless
from iniquity, and this woman shall bear
her iniquity.

CHAPTER 6

AND the LORD spake unto Moses,
saying,
2 Speak unto the children of Iş'rā-ĕl,
and say unto them, When either man or
woman shall separate *themselves* to
vow a vow of a Nazarite, to separate
themselves unto the LORD;
3 He shall separate *himself* from wine
and strong drink, and shall drink no
vinegar of wine, or vinegar of strong
drink, neither shall he drink any liquor
of grapes, nor eat moist grapes, or
dried.
4 All the days of his separation shall he
eat nothing that is made of the vine
tree, from the kernels even to the husk.
5 All the days of the vow of his separation there shall no razor come upon
his head: until the days be fulfilled, in
the which he separateth *himself* unto
the LORD, he shall be holy, *and* shall let
the locks of the hair of his head grow.
6 All the days that he separateth *him-*
self unto the LORD he shall come at no
dead body.
7 He shall not make himself unclean
for his father, or for his mother, for his
brother, or for his sister, when they die:
because the consecration of his God *is*
upon his head.
8 All the days of his separation he *is*
holy unto the LORD.
9 And if any man die very suddenly by
him, and he hath defiled the head of his
consecration; then he shall shave his
head in the day of his cleansing, on the
seventh day shall he shave it.
10 And on the eighth day he shall bring
two turtles, or two young pigeons, to the
priest, to the door of the tabernacle of
the congregation:
11 And the priest shall offer the one for
a sin offering, and the other for a burnt
offering, and make an atonement for
him, for that he sinned by the dead, and
shall hallow his head that same day.
12 And he shall consecrate unto the
LORD the days of his separation, and
shall bring a lamb of the first year for a
trespass offering: but the days that were
before shall be lost, because his separation was defiled.
13 ¶ And this *is* the law of the Nazarite: when the days of his separation are
fulfilled, he shall be brought unto the
door of the tabernacle of the congregation:
14 And he shall offer his offering unto
the LORD, one he lamb of the first
year without blemish for a burnt offering, and one ewe lamb of the first year
without blemish for a sin offering, and
one ram without blemish for peace
offerings,
15 And a basket of unleavened bread,
cakes of fine flour mingled with oil, and
wafers of unleavened bread anointed
with oil, and their meat offering, and
their drink offerings.
16 And the priest shall bring *them* before the LORD, and shall offer his sin
offering, and his burnt offering:
17 And he shall offer the ram *for* a sacrifice of peace offerings unto the LORD,
with the basket of unleavened bread:
the priest shall offer also his meat offering, and his drink offering.
18 And the Nazarite shall shave the
head of his separation *at* the door of the
tabernacle of the congregation, and shall

take the hair of the head of his separation, and put *it* in the fire which *is* under the sacrifice of the peace offerings.
19 And the priest shall take the sodden shoulder of the ram, and one unleavened cake out of the basket, and one unleavened wafer, and shall put *them* upon the hands of the Nazarite, after *the hair of* his separation is shaven:
20 And the priest shall wave them *for* a wave offering before the LORD: this *is* holy for the priest, with the wave breast and heave shoulder: and after that the Nazarite may drink wine.
21 This *is* the law of the Nazarite who hath vowed, *and of* his offering unto the LORD for his separation, besides *that* that his hand shall get: according to the vow which he vowed, so he must do after the law of his separation.
22 ¶ And the LORD spake unto Moses, saying,
23 Speak unto Aaron and unto his sons, saying, On this wise ye shall bless the children of Ĭş'rā-ĕl, saying unto them,
24 The LORD bless thee, and keep thee:
25 The LORD make his face shine upon thee, and be gracious unto thee:
26 The LORD lift up his countenance upon thee, and give thee peace.
27 And they shall put my name upon the children of Ĭş'rā-ĕl, and I will bless them.

CHAPTER 7

AND it came to pass on the day that Moses had fully set up the tabernacle, and had anointed it, and sanctified it, and all the instruments thereof, both the altar and all the vessels thereof, and had anointed them, and sanctified them;
2 That the princes of Ĭş'rā-ĕl, heads of the house of their fathers, who *were* the princes of the tribes, and were over them that were numbered, offered:
3 And they brought their offering before the LORD, six covered wagons, and twelve oxen; a wagon for two of the princes, and for each one an ox: and they brought them before the tabernacle.
4 And the LORD spake unto Moses, saying,
5 Take *it* of them, that they may be to do the service of the tabernacle of the congregation; and thou shalt give them unto the Lē'vītes, to every man according to his service.
6 And Moses took the wagons and the oxen, and gave them unto the Lē'vītes.
7 Two wagons and four oxen he gave unto the sons of Gĕr'shŏn, according to their service:
8 And four wagons and eight oxen he gave unto the sons of Mē-rā'rī, according unto their service, under the hand of Ĭth'ȧ-mär the son of Aaron the priest.
9 But unto the sons of Kō'hăth he gave none: because the service of the sanctuary belonging unto them *was that* they should bear upon their shoulders.
10 ¶ And the princes offered for dedicating of the altar in the day that it was anointed, even the princes offered their offering before the altar.
11 And the LORD said unto Moses, They shall offer their offering, each prince on his day, for the dedicating of the altar.
12 ¶ And he that offered his offering the first day was Näh'shŏn the son of Ȧm-mĭn'ȧ-dăb, of the tribe of Judah:
13 And his offering *was* one silver charger, the weight whereof *was* a hundred and thirty *shekels*, one silver bowl of seventy shekels, after the shekel of the sanctuary; both of them *were* full of fine flour mingled with oil for a meat offering:
14 One spoon of ten *shekels* of gold, full of incense:
15 One young bullock, one ram, one lamb of the first year, for a burnt offering:
16 One kid of the goats for a sin offering:
17 And for a sacrifice of peace offerings, two oxen, five rams, five he goats, five lambs of the first year: this *was* the offering of Näh'shŏn the son of Ȧm-mĭn'ȧ-dăb.
18 ¶ On the second day Nē-thăn'ē-ĕl the son of Zū'ār, prince of Ĭs'sȧ-chär, did offer:
19 He offered *for* his offering one silver charger, the weight whereof *was* a hundred and thirty *shekels*, one silver bowl of seventy shekels, after the shekel of the sanctuary; both of them full of fine flour mingled with oil for a meat offering:
20 One spoon of gold of ten *shekels*, full of incense:
21 One young bullock, one ram, one

lamb of the first year, for a burnt
offering:
22 One kid of the goats for a sin
offering:
23 And for a sacrifice of peace offerings, two oxen, five rams, five he goats,
five lambs of the first year: this *was*
the offering of Nē-thăn′ē-ĕl the son of
Zū′ȧr.
24 ¶ On the third day Ē-lī′ăb the son
of Hē′lŏn, prince of the children of
Zĕb′ū-lŭn, *did offer:*
25 His offering *was* one silver charger,
the weight whereof *was* a hundred and
thirty *shekels,* one silver bowl of seventy
shekels, after the shekel of the sanctuary; both of them full of fine flour
mingled with oil for a meat offering:
26 One golden spoon of ten *shekels,*
full of incense:
27 One young bullock, one ram, one
lamb of the first year, for a burnt
offering:
28 One kid of the goats for a sin
offering:
29 And for a sacrifice of peace offerings,
two oxen, five rams, five he goats, five
lambs of the first year: this *was* the
offering of Ē-lī′ăb the son of Hē′lŏn.
30 ¶ On the fourth day Ē-lī′zŭr the
son of Shĕd′ē-ŭr, prince of the children
of Reuben, *did offer:*
31 His offering *was* one silver charger
of the weight of a hundred and thirty
shekels, one silver bowl of seventy
shekels, after the shekel of the sanctuary; both of them full of fine flour mingled with oil for a meat offering:
32 One golden spoon of ten *shekels,*
full of incense:
33 One young bullock, one ram, one
lamb of the first year, for a burnt
offering:
34 One kid of the goats for a sin
offering:
35 And for a sacrifice of peace offerings,
two oxen, five rams, five he goats, five
lambs of the first year: this *was* the
offering of Ē-lī′zŭr the son of Shĕd′ē-ŭr.
36 ¶ On the fifth day Shē-lū′mĭ-ĕl the
son of Zū′rĭ-shăd′daī, prince of the children of Simeon, *did offer:*
37 His offering *was* one silver charger,
the weight whereof *was* a hundred and
thirty *shekels,* one silver bowl of seventy
shekels, after the shekel of the sanctuary; both of them full of fine flour
mingled with oil for a meat offering:
38 One golden spoon of ten *shekels,*
full of incense:
39 One young bullock, one ram, one
lamb of the first year, for a burnt
offering:
40 One kid of the goats for a sin
offering:
41 And for a sacrifice of peace offerings, two oxen, five rams, five he goats,
five lambs of the first year: this *was* the
offering of Shē-lū′mĭ-ĕl the son of
Zū′rĭ-shăd′daī.
42 ¶ On the sixth day Ē-lī′ȧ-săph the
son of Deū′ĕl, prince of the children of
Gad, *offered:*
43 His offering *was* one silver charger
of the weight of a hundred and thirty
shekels, a silver bowl of seventy shekels, after the shekel of the sanctuary;
both of them full of fine flour mingled
with oil for a meat offering:
44 One golden spoon of ten *shekels,*
full of incense:
45 One young bullock, one ram, one
lamb of the first year, for a burnt
offering:
46 One kid of the goats for a sin
offering:
47 And for a sacrifice of peace offerings,
two oxen, five rams, five he goats, five
lambs of the first year: this *was* the
offering of Ē-lī′ȧ-săph the son of
Deū′ĕl.
48 ¶ On the seventh day Ē-lĭsh′ȧ-mä
the son of Ȧm-mī′hŭd, prince of the
children of Ē′phrā-ĭm, *offered:*
49 His offering *was* one silver charger,
the weight whereof *was* a hundred and
thirty *shekels,* one silver bowl of seventy shekels, after the shekel of the
sanctuary; both of them full of fine flour
mingled with oil for a meat offering:
50 One golden spoon of ten *shekels,*
full of incense:
51 One young bullock, one ram, one
lamb of the first year, for a burnt
offering:
52 One kid of the goats for a sin
offering:
53 And for a sacrifice of peace offerings,
two oxen, five rams, five he goats,
five lambs of the first year: this *was* the
offering of Ē-lĭsh′ȧ-mä the son of
Ȧm-mī′hŭd.
54 ¶ On the eighth day *offered* Gȧ-
mā′lĭ-ĕl the son of Pē-dăh′zŭr, prince
of the children of Mȧ-năs′sĕh:
55 His offering *was* one silver charger

of the weight of a hundred and thirty
shekels, one silver bowl of seventy shekels, after the shekel of the sanctuary;
both of them full of fine flour mingled
with oil for a meat offering:
56 One golden spoon of ten *shekels,*
full of incense:
57 One young bullock, one ram, one
lamb of the first year, for a burnt
offering:
58 One kid of the goats for a sin
offering:
59 And for a sacrifice of peace offerings, two oxen, five rams, five he goats,
five lambs of the first year: this *was* the
offering of Gȧ-mā'lĭ-ĕl the son of
Pē-däh'zŭr.
60 ¶ On the ninth day Ăb'ĭ-dăn the
son of Gĭd'ē-ō'nī, prince of the children
of Benjamin, *offered:*
61 His offering *was* one silver charger,
the weight whereof *was* a hundred and
thirty *shekels,* one silver bowl of seventy shekels, after the shekel of the
sanctuary; both of them full of fine
flour mingled with oil for a meat offering:
62 One golden spoon of ten *shekels,*
full of incense:
63 One young bullock, one ram, one
lamb of the first year, for a burnt
offering:
64 One kid of the goats for a sin
offering:
65 And for a sacrifice of peace offerings, two oxen, five rams, five he goats,
five lambs of the first year: this *was* the
offering of Ăb'ĭ-dăn the son of Gĭd'-
ē-ō'nī.
66 ¶ On the tenth day Ā'hī-ē'zēr the
son of Ăm'mĭ-shăd'daī, prince of the
children of Dan, *offered:*
67 His offering *was* one silver charger,
the weight whereof *was* a hundred and
thirty *shekels,* one silver bowl of seventy shekels, after the shekel of the
sanctuary; both of them full of fine flour
mingled with oil for a meat offering:
68 One golden spoon of ten *shekels,*
full of incense:
69 One young bullock, one ram, one
lamb of the first year, for a burnt
offering:
70 One kid of the goats for a sin
offering:
71 And for a sacrifice of peace offerings,
two oxen, five rams, five he goats, five
lambs of the first year: this *was* the
offering of Ā'hī-ē'zēr the son of Ăm'-
mĭ-shăd'daī.
72 ¶ On the eleventh day Pā'gĭ-ĕl the
son of Ŏc'răn, prince of the children of
Ȧsh'ēr, *offered:*
73 His offering *was* one silver charger,
the weight whereof *was* a hundred and
thirty *shekels,* one silver bowl of seventy shekels, after the shekel of the
sanctuary; both of them full of fine flour
mingled with oil for a meat offering:
74 One golden spoon of ten *shekels,*
full of incense:
75 One young bullock, one ram, one
lamb of the first year, for a burnt
offering:
76 One kid of the goats for a sin
offering:
77 And for a sacrifice of peace offerings, two oxen, five rams, five he
goats, five lambs of the first year: this
was the offering of Pā'gĭ-ĕl the son of
Ŏc'răn.
78 ¶ On the twelfth day Ȧ-hī'rȧ the
son of Ē'năn, prince of the children of
Năph'tȧ-lī, *offered:*
79 His offering *was* one silver charger,
the weight whereof *was* a hundred and
thirty *shekels,* one silver bowl of seventy shekels, after the shekel of the
sanctuary; both of them full of fine flour
mingled with oil for a meat offering:
80 One golden spoon of ten *shekels,*
full of incense:
81 One young bullock, one ram, one
lamb of the first year, for a burnt
offering:
82 One kid of the goats for a sin
offering:
83 And for a sacrifice of peace offerings, two oxen, five rams, five he goats,
five lambs of the first year: this *was* the
offering of Ȧ-hī'rȧ the son of Ē'năn.
84 This *was* the dedication of the altar,
in the day when it was anointed, by the
princes of Īş'rā-ĕl: twelve chargers of
silver, twelve silver bowls, twelve
spoons of gold:
85 Each charger of silver *weighing* a
hundred and thirty *shekels,* each bowl
seventy: all the silver vessels *weighed*
two thousand and four hundred *shekels,*
after the shekel of the sanctuary:
86 The golden spoons *were* twelve, full
of incense, *weighing* ten *shekels* apiece,
after the shekel of the sanctuary: all the
gold of the spoons *was* a hundred and
twenty *shekels.*

87 All the oxen for the burnt offering
were twelve bullocks, the rams twelve,
the lambs of the first year twelve, with
their meat offering: and the kids of the
goats for sin offering twelve.
88 And all the oxen for the sacrifice of
the peace offerings *were* twenty and
four bullocks, the rams sixty, the he
goats sixty, the lambs of the first year
sixty. This *was* the dedication of the
altar, after that it was anointed.
89 And when Moses was gone into the
tabernacle of the congregation to speak
with him, then he heard the voice of one
speaking unto him from off the mercy
seat that *was* upon the ark of testimony,
from between the two cherubim: and he
spake unto him.

CHAPTER 8

AND the LORD spake unto Moses,
saying,
2 Speak unto Aaron, and say unto him,
When thou lightest the lamps, the seven
lamps shall give light over against the
candlestick.
3 And Aaron did so; he lighted the
lamps thereof over against the candlestick, as the LORD commanded Moses.
4 And this work of the candlestick *was
of* beaten gold; unto the shaft thereof,
unto the flowers thereof, *was* beaten
work: according unto the pattern which
the LORD had showed Moses, so he
made the candlestick.
5 ¶ And the LORD spake unto Moses,
saying,
6 Take the Lē'vītes from among the
children of Ĭş'rā-ĕl, and cleanse them.
7 And thus shalt thou do unto them, to
cleanse them: Sprinkle water of purifying upon them, and let them shave all
their flesh, and let them wash their
clothes, and *so* make themselves clean.
8 Then let them take a young bullock
with his meat offering, *even* fine flour
mingled with oil, and another young
bullock shalt thou take for a sin offering.
9 And thou shalt bring the Lē'vītes before the tabernacle of the congregation:
and thou shalt gather the whole assembly of the children of Ĭş'rā-ĕl together.
10 And thou shalt bring the Lē'vītes
before the LORD: and the children of
Ĭş'rā-ĕl shall put their hands upon the
Lē'vītes:
11 And Aaron shall offer the Lē'vītes
before the LORD *for* an offering of the
children of Ĭş'rā-ĕl, that they may execute the service of the LORD.
12 And the Lē'vītes shall lay their
hands upon the heads of the bullocks:
and thou shalt offer the one *for* a sin
offering, and the other *for* a burnt offering, unto the LORD, to make an atonement for the Lē'vītes.
13 And thou shalt set the Lē'vītes before Aaron, and before his sons, and
offer them *for* an offering unto the
LORD.
14 Thus shalt thou separate the Lē'-
vītes from among the children of Ĭş'rā-ĕl:
and the Lē'vītes shall be mine.
15 And after that shall the Lē'vītes go
in to do the service of the tabernacle of
the congregation: and thou shalt cleanse
them, and offer them *for* an offering.
16 For they *are* wholly given unto me
from among the children of Ĭş'rā-ĕl; instead of such as open every womb, *even
instead of* the firstborn of all the children of Ĭş'rā-ĕl, have I taken them unto
me.
17 For all the firstborn of the children
of Ĭş'rā-ĕl *are* mine, *both* man and beast:
on the day that I smote every firstborn
in the land of Egypt I sanctified them
for myself.
18 And I have taken the Lē'vītes for
all the firstborn of the children of
Ĭş'rā-ĕl.
19 And I have given the Lē'vītes *as* a
gift to Aaron and to his sons from among
the children of Ĭş'rā-ĕl, to do the service of the children of Ĭş'rā-ĕl in the
tabernacle of the congregation, and to
make an atonement for the children of
Ĭş'rā-ĕl: that there be no plague among
the children of Ĭş'rā-ĕl, when the children of Ĭş'rā-ĕl come nigh unto the
sanctuary.
20 And Moses, and Aaron, and all the
congregation of the children of Ĭş'rā-ĕl,
did to the Lē'vītes according unto all
that the LORD commanded Moses concerning the Lē'vītes, so did the children
of Ĭş'rā-ĕl unto them.
21 And the Lē'vītes were purified, and
they washed their clothes; and Aaron
offered them *as* an offering before the
LORD; and Aaron made an atonement
for them to cleanse them.
22 And after that went the Lē'vītes in
to do their service in the tabernacle of
the congregation before Aaron, and before his sons: as the LORD had com-

manded Moses concerning the Lē′vītes,
so did they unto them.
23 ¶ And the LORD spake unto Moses,
saying,
24 This *is it* that *belongeth* unto the
Lē′vītes: from twenty and five years
old and upward they shall go in to wait
upon the service of the tabernacle of the
congregation:
25 And from the age of fifty years they
shall cease waiting upon the service
thereof, and shall serve no more:
26 But shall minister with their brethren in the tabernacle of the congregation, to keep the charge, and shall do no
service. Thus shalt thou do unto the
Lē′vītes touching their charge.

CHAPTER 9

AND the LORD spake unto Moses in
the wilderness of Sī′naī, in the first
month of the second year after they were
come out of the land of Egypt, saying,
2 Let the children of Ĭş′rā-ĕl also keep
the passover at his appointed season.
3 In the fourteenth day of this month,
at even, ye shall keep it in his appointed
season: according to all the rites of it,
and according to all the ceremonies
thereof, shall ye keep it.
4 And Moses spake unto the children
of Ĭş′rā-ĕl, that they should keep the
passover.
5 And they kept the passover on the
fourteenth day of the first month at even
in the wilderness of Sī′naī: according
to all that the LORD commanded Moses,
so did the children of Ĭş′rā-ĕl.
6 ¶ And there were certain men, who
were defiled by the dead body of a man,
that they could not keep the passover
on that day: and they came before
Moses and before Aaron on that day.
7 And those men said unto him, We
are defiled by the dead body of a man:
wherefore are we kept back, that we
may not offer an offering of the LORD in
his appointed season among the children of Ĭş′rā-ĕl?
8 And Moses said unto them, Stand
still, and I will hear what the LORD will
command concerning you.
9 ¶ And the LORD spake unto Moses,
saying,
10 Speak unto the children of Ĭş′rā-ĕl,
saying, If any man of you or of your
posterity shall be unclean by reason of
a dead body, or *be* in a journey afar off,
yet he shall keep the passover unto the
LORD.
11 The fourteenth day of the second
month at even they shall keep it, *and*
eat it with unleavened bread and bitter
herbs.
12 They shall leave none of it unto the
morning, nor break any bone of it:
according to all the ordinances of the
passover they shall keep it.
13 But the man that *is* clean, and is not
in a journey, and forbeareth to keep the
passover, even the same soul shall be
cut off from among his people: because
he brought not the offering of the LORD
in his appointed season, that man shall
bear his sin.
14 And if a stranger shall sojourn
among you, and will keep the passover
unto the LORD; according to the ordinance of the passover, and according to
the manner thereof, so shall he do: ye
shall have one ordinance, both for the
stranger, and for him that was born in
the land.
15 ¶ And on the day that the tabernacle was reared up the cloud covered
the tabernacle, *namely,* the tent of the
testimony: and at even there was upon
the tabernacle as it were the appearance
of fire, until the morning.
16 So it was alway: the cloud covered
it *by day,* and the appearance of fire by
night.
17 And when the cloud was taken up
from the tabernacle, then after that the
children of Ĭş′rā-ĕl journeyed: and in
the place where the cloud abode, there
the children of Ĭş′rā-ĕl pitched their
tents.
18 At the commandment of the LORD
the children of Ĭş′rā-ĕl journeyed, and
at the commandment of the LORD they
pitched: as long as the cloud abode upon the tabernacle they rested in their
tents.
19 And when the cloud tarried long
upon the tabernacle many days, then
the children of Ĭş′rā-ĕl kept the charge
of the LORD, and journeyed not.
20 And *so* it was, when the cloud was a
few days upon the tabernacle; according to the commandment of the LORD
they abode in their tents, and according
to the commandment of the LORD they
journeyed.
21 And *so* it was, when the cloud abode
from even unto the morning, and *that*

the cloud was taken up in the morning, then they journeyed: whether *it was* by day or by night that the cloud was taken up, they journeyed.

22 Or *whether it were* two days, or a month, or a year, that the cloud tarried upon the tabernacle, remaining thereon, the children of Ĭṣ′rā-ĕl abode in their tents, and journeyed not: but when it was taken up, they journeyed.

23 At the commandment of the LORD they rested in their tents, and at the commandment of the LORD they journeyed: they kept the charge of the LORD, at the commandment of the LORD by the hand of Moses.

CHAPTER 10

AND the LORD spake unto Moses, saying,

2 Make thee two trumpets of silver; of a whole piece shalt thou make them: that thou mayest use them for the calling of the assembly, and for the journeying of the camps.

3 And when they shall blow with them, all the assembly shall assemble themselves to thee at the door of the tabernacle of the congregation.

4 And if they blow *but* with one *trumpet*, then the princes, *which are* heads of the thousands of Ĭṣ′rā-ĕl, shall gather themselves unto thee.

5 When ye blow an alarm, then the camps that lie on the east parts shall go forward.

6 When ye blow an alarm the second time, then the camps that lie on the south side shall take their journey: they shall blow an alarm for their journeys.

7 But when the congregation is to be gathered together, ye shall blow, but ye shall not sound an alarm.

8 And the sons of Aaron, the priests, shall blow with the trumpets; and they shall be to you for an ordinance for ever throughout your generations.

9 And if ye go to war in your land against the enemy that oppresseth you, then ye shall blow an alarm with the trumpets; and ye shall be remembered before the LORD your God, and ye shall be saved from your enemies.

10 Also in the day of your gladness, and in your solemn days, and in the beginnings of your months, ye shall blow with the trumpets over your burnt offerings, and over the sacrifices of your peace offerings; that they may be to you for a memorial before your God: I *am* the LORD your God.

11 ¶ And it came to pass on the twentieth *day* of the second month, in the second year, that the cloud was taken up from off the tabernacle of the testimony.

12 And the children of Ĭṣ′rā-ĕl took their journeys out of the wilderness of Sī′naī; and the cloud rested in the wilderness of Pā′răn.

13 And they first took their journey according to the commandment of the LORD by the hand of Moses.

14 ¶ In the first *place* went the standard of the camp of the children of Judah according to their armies: and over his host *was* Näh′shŏn the son of Ȧm-mĭn′ȧ-dăb.

15 And over the host of the tribe of the children of Ĭs′sȧ-chär *was* Nē-thăn′ē-ĕl the son of Zū′ȧr.

16 And over the host of the tribe of the children of Zĕb′ū-lŭn *was* Ē-lĭ′ăb the son of Hē′lŏn.

17 And the tabernacle was taken down; and the sons of Gẽr′shŏn and the sons of Mē-rā′rī set forward, bearing the tabernacle.

18 ¶ And the standard of the camp of Reuben set forward according to their armies: and over his host *was* Ē-lĭ′zŭr the son of Shĕd′ē-ŭr.

19 And over the host of the tribe of the children of Simeon *was* Shē-lū′mĭ-ĕl the son of Zū′rĭ-shăd′daī.

20 And over the host of the tribe of the children of Gad *was* Ē-lĭ′ȧ-săph the son of Deū′ĕl.

21 And the Kō′hăth-ītes set forward, bearing the sanctuary: and *the other* did set up the tabernacle against they came.

22 ¶ And the standard of the camp of the children of Ē′phrā-ĭm set forward according to their armies: and over his host *was* Ē-lĭsh′ȧ-mä the son of Ȧm-mī′hŭd.

23 And over the host of the tribe of the children of Mȧ-năs′sĕh *was* Gȧ-mā′lĭ-ĕl the son of Pē-däh′zŭr.

24 And over the host of the tribe of the children of Benjamin *was* Ăb′ĭ-dăn the son of Gĭd′ē-ō′nī.

25 ¶ And the standard of the camp of the children of Dan set forward, *which was* the rearward of all the camps throughout their hosts: and over his

host *was* Ā'hī-ē'zēr the son of Ăm'-
mĭ-shăd'daī.
26 And over the host of the tribe of the
children of Ăsh'ēr *was* Pā'gĭ-ēl the son
of Ŏc'răn.
27 And over the host of the tribe of the
children of Năph'tȧ-lī *was* Ȧ-hī'rȧ the
son of Ē'năn.
28 Thus *were* the journeyings of the
children of Ĭş'rā-ēl according to their
armies, when they set forward.
29 ℂ And Moses said unto Hō'băb,
the son of Rȧ-gū'ēl the Mĭd'ĭ-ăn-īte,
Moses' father-in-law, We are journeying unto the place of which the LORD
said, I will give it you: come thou with
us, and we will do thee good: for the
LORD hath spoken good concerning
Ĭş'rā-ēl.
30 And he said unto him, I will not go;
but I will depart to mine own land, and
to my kindred.
31 And he said, Leave us not, I pray
thee; forasmuch as thou knowest how
we are to encamp in the wilderness, and
thou mayest be to us instead of eyes.
32 And it shall be, if thou go with us,
yea, it shall be, that what goodness the
LORD shall do unto us, the same will we
do unto thee.
33 ℂ And they departed from the
mount of the LORD three days' journey:
and the ark of the covenant of the LORD
went before them in the three days'
journey, to search out a resting place for
them.
34 And the cloud of the LORD *was* upon
them by day, when they went out of the
camp.
35 And it came to pass, when the ark
set forward, that Moses said, Rise up,
LORD, and let thine enemies be scattered; and let them that hate thee flee
before thee.
36 And when it rested, he said, Return,
O LORD, unto the many thousands of
Ĭş'rā-ēl.

CHAPTER 11

AND *when* the people complained, it
displeased the LORD: and the
LORD heard *it;* and his anger was kindled; and the fire of the LORD burnt
among them, and consumed *them that
were* in the uttermost parts of the camp.
2 And the people cried unto Moses;
and when Moses prayed unto the LORD,
the fire was quenched.
3 And he called the name of the place
Tăb'ē-rȧh: because the fire of the LORD
burnt among them.
4 ℂ And the mixed multitude that *was*
among them fell a lusting: and the children of Ĭş'rā-ēl also wept again, and
said, Who shall give us flesh to eat?
5 We remember the fish, which we did
eat in Egypt freely; the cucumbers, and
the melons, and the leeks, and the
onions, and the garlic:
6 But now our soul *is* dried away: *there
is* nothing at all, besides this manna,
before our eyes.
7 And the manna *was* as coriander
seed, and the color thereof as the color
of bdellium.
8 *And* the people went about, and gathered *it*, and ground *it* in mills, or beat *it*
in a mortar, and baked *it* in pans, and
made cakes of it: and the taste of it was
as the taste of fresh oil.
9 And when the dew fell upon the camp
in the night, the manna fell upon it.
10 ℂ Then Moses heard the people
weep throughout their families, every
man in the door of his tent: and the
anger of the LORD was kindled greatly;
Moses also was displeased.
11 And Moses said unto the LORD,
Wherefore hast thou afflicted thy servant? and wherefore have I not found
favor in thy sight, that thou layest the
burden of all this people upon me?
12 Have I conceived all this people?
have I begotten them, that thou shouldest say unto me, Carry them in thy
bosom, as a nursing father beareth the
sucking child, unto the land which thou
swarest unto their fathers?
13 Whence should I have flesh to give
unto all this people? for they weep unto
me, saying, Give us flesh, that we may
eat.
14 I am not able to bear all this people
alone, because *it is* too heavy for me.
15 And if thou deal thus with me, kill
me, I pray thee, out of hand, if I have
found favor in thy sight; and let me not
see my wretchedness.
16 ℂ And the LORD said unto Moses,
Gather unto me seventy men of the
elders of Ĭş'rā-ēl, whom thou knowest
to be the elders of the people, and officers over them; and bring them unto
the tabernacle of the congregation, that
they may stand there with thee.
17 And I will come down and talk with

thee there: and I will take of the spirit
which *is* upon thee, and will put *it* upon
them; and they shall bear the burden of
the people with thee, that thou bear *it*
not thyself alone.
18 And say thou unto the people, Sanctify yourselves against to-morrow, and
ye shall eat flesh: for ye have wept in
the ears of the LORD, saying, Who shall
give us flesh to eat? for *it was* well with
us in Egypt: therefore the LORD will
give you flesh, and ye shall eat.
19 Ye shall not eat one day, nor two
days, nor five days, neither ten days, nor
twenty days;
20 *But* even a whole month, until it
come out at your nostrils, and it be
loathsome unto you: because that ye
have despised the LORD which *is* among
you, and have wept before him, saying,
Why came we forth out of Egypt?
21 And Moses said, The people, among
whom I *am, are* six hundred thousand
footmen; and thou hast said, I will give
them flesh, that they may eat a whole
month.
22 Shall the flocks and the herds be
slain for them, to suffice them? or shall
all the fish of the sea be gathered together for them, to suffice them?
23 And the LORD said unto Moses, Is
the LORD's hand waxed short? thou
shalt see now whether my word shall
come to pass unto thee or not.
24 ¶ And Moses went out, and told the
people the words of the LORD, and gathered the seventy men of the elders of
the people, and set them round about
the tabernacle.
25 And the LORD came down in a cloud,
and spake unto him, and took of the
spirit that *was* upon him, and gave *it*
unto the seventy elders: and it came to
pass, that, when the spirit rested upon
them, they prophesied, and did not
cease.
26 But there remained two *of the* men
in the camp, the name of the one *was*
Ĕl'dăd, and the name of the other Mē'-
dăd: and the spirit rested upon them;
and they *were* of them that were written,
but went not out unto the tabernacle:
and they prophesied in the camp.
27 And there ran a young man, and
told Moses, and said, Ĕl'dăd and Mē'-
dăd do prophesy in the camp.
28 And Joshua the son of Nŭn, the
servant of Moses, *one* of his young men,
answered, and said, My lord Moses, forbid them.
29 And Moses said unto him, Enviest
thou for my sake? would God that all the
LORD's people were prophets, *and* that
the LORD would put his Spirit upon
them.
30 And Moses gat him into the camp,
he and the elders of Ĭṣ'rā-ĕl.
31 ¶ And there went forth a wind from
the LORD, and brought quails from the
sea, and let *them* fall by the camp, as it
were a day's journey on this side, and as
it were a day's journey on the other side,
round about the camp, and as it were
two cubits *high* upon the face of the
earth.
32 And the people stood up all that
day, and all *that* night, and all the next
day, and they gathered the quails: he
that gathered least gathered ten homers:
and they spread *them* all abroad for
themselves round about the camp.
33 And while the flesh *was* yet between
their teeth, ere it was chewed, the
wrath of the LORD was kindled against
the people, and the LORD smote the
people with a very great plague.
34 And he called the name of that
place Kĭb'rŏth-hăt-tā'ȧ-vȧh: because
there they buried the people that lusted.
35 *And* the people journeyed from
Kĭb'rŏth-hăt-tā'ȧ-vȧh unto Hȧ-zē'rŏth;
and abode at Hȧ-zē'rŏth.

CHAPTER 12

AND Miriam and Aaron spake against
Moses because of the Ethiopian
woman whom he had married: for he
had married an Ethiopian woman.
2 And they said, Hath the LORD indeed
spoken only by Moses? hath he not
spoken also by us? And the LORD heard
it.
3 (Now the man Moses *was* very meek,
above all the men which *were* upon the
face of the earth.)
4 And the LORD spake suddenly unto
Moses, and unto Aaron, and unto
Miriam, Come out ye three unto the
tabernacle of the congregation. And
they three came out.
5 And the LORD came down in the
pillar of the cloud, and stood *in* the
door of the tabernacle, and called
Aaron and Miriam: and they both came
forth.
6 And he said, Hear now my words: If

there be a prophet among you, *I* the LORD will make myself known unto him in a vision, *and* will speak unto him in a dream.

7 My servant Moses *is* not so, who *is* faithful in all mine house.

8 With him will I speak mouth to mouth, even apparently, and not in dark speeches; and the similitude of the LORD shall he behold: wherefore then were ye not afraid to speak against my servant Moses?

9 And the anger of the LORD was kindled against them; and he departed.

10 And the cloud departed from off the tabernacle; and, behold, Miriam *became* leprous, *white* as snow: and Aaron looked upon Miriam, and, behold, *she was* leprous.

11 And Aaron said unto Moses, Alas, my lord, I beseech thee, lay not the sin upon us, wherein we have done foolishly, and wherein we have sinned.

12 Let her not be as one dead, of whom the flesh is half consumed when he cometh out of his mother's womb.

13 And Moses cried unto the LORD, saying, Heal her now, O God, I beseech thee.

14 ¶ And the LORD said unto Moses, If her father had but spit in her face, should she not be ashamed seven days? let her be shut out from the camp seven days, and after that let her be received in *again*.

15 And Miriam was shut out from the camp seven days: and the people journeyed not till Miriam was brought in *again*.

16 And afterward the people removed from Hȧ-zē'rŏth, and pitched in the wilderness of Pā'răn.

CHAPTER 13

AND the LORD spake unto Moses, saying,

2 Send thou men, that they may search the land of Cā'năan, which I give unto the children of Ĭs'rā-ĕl: of every tribe of their fathers shall ye send a man, every one a ruler among them.

3 And Moses by the commandment of the LORD sent them from the wilderness of Pā'răn: all those men *were* heads of the children of Ĭs'rā-ĕl.

4 And these *were* their names: Of the tribe of Reuben, Shăm-mū'ȧ the son of Zăc'cŭr.

5 Of the tribe of Simeon, Shā'phăt the son of Hō'rī.

6 Of the tribe of Judah, Caleb the son of Jē-phŭn'nĕh.

7 Of the tribe of Ĭs'sȧ-chär, Ī'găl the son of Joseph.

8 Of the tribe of Ē'phrā-ĭm, Ō-shē'ȧ the son of Nŭn.

9 Of the tribe of Benjamin, Păl'tī the son of Rā'phū.

10 Of the tribe of Zĕb'ū-lŭn, Găd'dī-ĕl the son of Sō'dī.

11 Of the tribe of Joseph, *namely*, of the tribe of Mȧ-năs'sĕh, Găd'dī the son of Sū'sī.

12 Of the tribe of Dan, Ăm'mī-ĕl the son of Gē-măl'lī.

13 Of the tribe of Ăsh'ĕr, Sē'thŭr the son of Mī'chā-ĕl.

14 Of the tribe of Năph'tȧ-lī, Näh'bī the son of Vŏph'sī.

15 Of the tribe of Gad, Gē-ū'ĕl the son of Mā'chī.

16 These *are* the names of the men which Moses sent to spy out the land. And Moses called Ō-shē'ȧ the son of Nŭn, Jē-hŏsh'ū-ȧ.

17 ¶ And Moses sent them to spy out the land of Cā'năan, and said unto them, Get you up this *way* southward, and go up into the mountain:

18 And see the land, what it *is;* and the people that dwelleth therein, whether they *be* strong or weak, few or many;

19 And what the land *is* that they dwell in, whether it *be* good or bad; and what cities *they be* that they dwell in, whether in tents, or in strongholds;

20 And what the land *is*, whether it *be* fat or lean, whether there be wood therein, or not. And be ye of good courage, and bring of the fruit of the land. Now the time *was* the time of the first ripe grapes.

21 ¶ So they went up, and searched the land from the wilderness of Zĭn unto Rē'hŏb, as men come to Hā'măth.

22 And they ascended by the south, and came unto Hē'brŏn; where Ȧ-hī'măn, Shē'shaī, and Tăl'maī, the children of Ā'năk, *were*. (Now Hē'brŏn was built seven years before Zō'ăn in Egypt.)

23 And they came unto the brook of Ĕsh'cŏl, and cut down from thence a branch with one cluster of grapes, and they bare it between two upon a staff; and *they brought* of the pomegranates, and of the figs.

24 The place was called the brook Ĕsh′cŏl, because of the cluster of grapes which the children of Ĭs̱′rā-ĕl cut down from thence.

25 And they returned from searching of the land after forty days.

26 ¶ And they went and came to Moses, and to Aaron, and to all the congregation of the children of Ĭs̱′rā-ĕl, unto the wilderness of Pā′răn, to Kā′dĕsh; and brought back word unto them, and unto all the congregation, and showed them the fruit of the land.

27 And they told him, and said, We came unto the land whither thou sentest us, and surely it floweth with milk and honey; and this *is* the fruit of it.

28 Nevertheless the people *be* strong that dwell in the land, and the cities *are* walled, *and* very great: and moreover we saw the children of Ā′năk there.

29 The Ăm′ȧ-lĕk-ītes dwell in the land of the south: and the Hĭt′tītes, and the Jĕb′ū-s̱ītes, and the Ăm′ō-rītes, dwell in the mountains: and the Cā′năan-ītes dwell by the sea, and by the coast of Jordan.

30 And Caleb stilled the people before Moses, and said, Let us go up at once, and possess it; for we are well able to overcome it.

31 But the men that went up with him said, We be not able to go up against the people; for they *are* stronger than we.

32 And they brought up an evil report of the land which they had searched unto the children of Ĭs̱′rā-ĕl, saying, The land, through which we have gone to search it, *is* a land that eateth up the inhabitants thereof; and all the people that we saw in it *are* men of a great stature.

33 And there we saw the giants, the sons of Ā′năk, *which come* of the giants: and we were in our own sight as grasshoppers, and so we were in their sight.

CHAPTER 14

AND all the congregation lifted up their voice, and cried; and the people wept that night.

2 And all the children of Ĭs̱′rā-ĕl murmured against Moses and against Aaron: and the whole congregation said unto them, Would God that we had died in the land of Egypt! or would God we had died in this wilderness!

3 And wherefore hath the LORD brought us unto this land, to fall by the sword, that our wives and our children should be a prey? were it not better for us to return into Egypt?

4 And they said one to another, Let us make a captain, and let us return into Egypt.

5 Then Moses and Aaron fell on their faces before all the assembly of the congregation of the children of Ĭs̱′rā-ĕl.

6 ¶ And Joshua the son of Nŭn, and Caleb the son of Jē-phŭn′nĕh, *which were* of them that searched the land, rent their clothes:

7 And they spake unto all the company of the children of Ĭs̱′rā-ĕl, saying, The land, which we passed through to search it, *is* an exceeding good land.

8 If the LORD delight in us, then he will bring us into this land, and give it us; a land which floweth with milk and honey.

9 Only rebel not ye against the LORD, neither fear ye the people of the land; for they *are* bread for us: their defense is departed from them, and the LORD *is* with us: fear them not.

10 But all the congregation bade stone them with stones. And the glory of the LORD appeared in the tabernacle of the congregation before all the children of Ĭs̱′rā-ĕl.

11 ¶ And the LORD said unto Moses, How long will this people provoke me? and how long will it be ere they believe me, for all the signs which I have showed among them?

12 I will smite them with the pestilence, and disinherit them, and will make of thee a greater nation and mightier than they.

13 ¶ And Moses said unto the LORD, Then the Egyptians shall hear *it*, (for thou broughtest up this people in thy might from among them;)

14 And they will tell *it* to the inhabitants of this land: *for* they have heard that thou LORD *art* among this people, that thou LORD art seen face to face, and *that* thy cloud standeth over them, and *that* thou goest before them, by daytime in a pillar of a cloud, and in a pillar of fire by night.

15 ¶ Now *if* thou shalt kill *all* this people as one man, then the nations which have heard the fame of thee will speak, saying,

16 Because the LORD was not able to

bring this people into the land which he
sware unto them, therefore he hath slain
them in the wilderness.
17 And now, I beseech thee, let the
power of my LORD be great, according
as thou hast spoken, saying,
18 The LORD *is* long-suffering, and of
great mercy, forgiving iniquity and
transgression, and by no means clearing *the guilty*, visiting the iniquity of the
fathers upon the children unto the third
and fourth *generation*.
19 Pardon, I beseech thee, the iniquity
of this people according unto the greatness of thy mercy, and as thou hast forgiven this people, from Egypt even until
now.
20 And the LORD said, I have pardoned
according to thy word:
21 But *as* truly *as* I live, all the earth
shall be filled with the glory of the
LORD.
22 Because all those men which have
seen my glory, and my miracles, which
I did in Egypt and in the wilderness,
and have tempted me now these ten
times, and have not hearkened to my
voice;
23 Surely they shall not see the land
which I sware unto their fathers, neither
shall any of them that provoked me
see it:
24 But my servant Caleb, because he
had another spirit with him, and hath
followed me fully, him will I bring into
the land whereinto he went; and his
seed shall possess it.
25 (Now the Ăm'ȧ-lĕk-ītes and the
Cā'năan-ītes dwelt in the valley.) To-
morrow turn you, and get you into the
wilderness by the way of the Red
sea.
26 ¶ And the LORD spake unto Moses
and unto Aaron, saying,
27 How long *shall I bear with* this evil
congregation, which murmur against
me? I have heard the murmurings of
the children of Ĭs'rā-ĕl, which they murmur against me.
28 Say unto them, *As truly as* I live,
saith the LORD, as ye have spoken in
mine ears, so will I do to you:
29 Your carcasses shall fall in this
wilderness, and all that were numbered
of you, according to your whole number,
from twenty years old and upward,
which have murmured against me,
30 Doubtless ye shall not come into the
land, *concerning* which I sware to make
you dwell therein, save Caleb the son of
Jē-phŭn'nĕh, and Joshua the son of
Nŭn.
31 But your little ones, which ye said
should be a prey, them will I bring in,
and they shall know the land which ye
have despised.
32 But *as for* you, your carcasses, they
shall fall in this wilderness.
33 And your children shall wander in
the wilderness forty years, and bear
your whoredoms, until your carcasses
be wasted in the wilderness.
34 After the number of the days in
which ye searched the land, *even* forty
days, each day for a year, shall ye bear
your iniquities, *even* forty years, and ye
shall know my breach of promise.
35 I the LORD have said, I will surely
do it unto all this evil congregation, that
are gathered together against me: in
this wilderness they shall be consumed,
and there they shall die.
36 And the men which Moses sent to
search the land, who returned, and made
all the congregation to murmur against
him, by bringing up a slander upon the
land,
37 Even those men that did bring up
the evil report upon the land, died by the
plague before the LORD.
38 But Joshua the son of Nŭn, and
Caleb the son of Jē-phŭn'nĕh, *which
were* of the men that went to search the
land, lived *still*.
39 And Moses told these sayings unto
all the children of Ĭs'rā-ĕl: and the people mourned greatly.
40 ¶ And they rose up early in the
morning, and gat them up into the top
of the mountain, saying, Lo, we *be here*,
and will go up unto the place which
the LORD hath promised: for we have
sinned.
41 And Moses said, Wherefore now do
ye transgress the commandment of the
LORD? but it shall not prosper.
42 Go not up, for the LORD *is* not
among you; that ye be not smitten before your enemies.
43 For the Ăm'ȧ-lĕk-ītes and the Cā'-
năan-ītes *are* there before you, and ye
shall fall by the sword: because ye are
turned away from the LORD, therefore
the LORD will not be with you.
44 But they presumed to go up unto
the hilltop: nevertheless the ark of the

covenant of the LORD, and Moses, departed not out of the camp.
45 Then the Ăm′ȧ-lĕk-ītes came down,
and the Cā′năan-ītes which dwelt in that
hill, and smote them, and discomfited
them, *even* unto Hôr′mȧh.

CHAPTER 15

AND the LORD spake unto Moses,
saying,
2 Speak unto the children of Ĭş′rā-ĕl,
and say unto them, When ye be come
into the land of your habitations, which
I give unto you,
3 And will make an offering by fire
unto the LORD, a burnt offering, or a
sacrifice in performing a vow, or in a
freewill offering, or in your solemn
feasts, to make a sweet savor unto the
LORD, of the herd, or of the flock:
4 Then shall he that offereth his offering unto the LORD bring a meat offering
of a tenth deal of flour, mingled with the
fourth *part* of a hin of oil.
5 And the fourth *part* of a hin of wine
for a drink offering shalt thou prepare
with the burnt offering or sacrifice, for
one lamb.
6 Or for a ram, thou shalt prepare *for*
a meat offering two tenth deals of flour,
mingled with the third *part* of a hin of oil.
7 And for a drink offering thou shalt
offer the third *part* of a hin of wine, *for*
a sweet savor unto the LORD.
8 And when thou preparest a bullock
for a burnt offering, or *for* a sacrifice in
performing a vow, or peace offerings
unto the LORD;
9 Then shall he bring with a bullock a
meat offering of three tenth deals of
flour, mingled with half a hin of oil.
10 And thou shalt bring for a drink
offering half a hin of wine, *for* an offering made by fire, of a sweet savor unto
the LORD.
11 Thus shall it be done for one bullock, or for one ram, or for a lamb, or a
kid.
12 According to the number that ye
shall prepare, so shall ye do to every one
according to their number.
13 All that are born of the country shall
do these things after this manner, in
offering an offering made by fire, of a
sweet savor unto the LORD.
14 And if a stranger sojourn with you,
or whosoever *be* among you in your
generations, and will offer an offering
made by fire, of a sweet savor unto the
LORD; as ye do, so he shall do.
15 One ordinance *shall be both* for you
of the congregation, and also for the
stranger that sojourneth *with you,* an
ordinance for ever in your generations:
as ye *are,* so shall the stranger be before
the LORD.
16 One law and one manner shall be
for you, and for the stranger that sojourneth with you.
17 ℂ And the LORD spake unto Moses,
saying,
18 Speak unto the children of Ĭş′rā-ĕl,
and say unto them, When ye come into
the land whither I bring you,
19 Then it shall be, that, when ye eat
of the bread of the land, ye shall offer
up a heave offering unto the LORD.
20 Ye shall offer up a cake of the first
of your dough *for* a heave offering: as
ye do the heave offering of the threshingfloor, so shall ye heave it.
21 Of the first of your dough ye shall
give unto the LORD a heave offering in
your generations.
22 ℂ And if ye have erred, and not
observed all these commandments,
which the LORD hath spoken unto
Moses,
23 *Even* all that the LORD hath commanded you by the hand of Moses, from
the day that the LORD commanded
Moses, and henceforward among your
generations:
24 Then it shall be, if *aught* be committed by ignorance without the knowledge of the congregation, that all the
congregation shall offer one young bullock for a burnt offering, for a sweet
savor unto the LORD, with his meat
offering, and his drink offering, according to the manner, and one kid of the
goats for a sin offering.
25 And the priest shall make an atonement for all the congregation of the children of Ĭş′rā-ĕl, and it shall be forgiven
them; for it *is* ignorance: and they shall
bring their offering, a sacrifice made
by fire unto the LORD, and their sin offering before the LORD, for their ignorance:
26 And it shall be forgiven all the congregation of the children of Ĭş′rā-ĕl, and
the stranger that sojourneth among
them; seeing all the people *were* in
ignorance.
27 ℂ And if any soul sin through igno-

rance, then he shall bring a she goat of
the first year for a sin offering.
28 And the priest shall make an atonement for the soul that sinneth ignorantly, when he sinneth by ignorance before the LORD, to make an atonement for
him; and it shall be forgiven him.
29 Ye shall have one law for him that
sinneth through ignorance, *both for*
him that is born among the children of
Ĭs'rā-ĕl, and for the stranger that sojourneth among them.
30 ¶ But the soul that doeth *aught*
presumptuously, *whether he be* born in
the land, or a stranger, the same reproacheth the LORD; and that soul shall
be cut off from among his people.
31 Because he hath despised the word
of the LORD, and hath broken his commandment, that soul shall utterly be
cut off; his iniquity *shall be* upon him.
32 ¶ And while the children of Ĭs'rā-ĕl
were in the wilderness, they found a
man that gathered sticks upon the sabbath day.
33 And they that found him gathering
sticks brought him unto Moses and
Aaron, and unto all the congregation.
34 And they put him in ward, because
it was not declared what should be done
to him.
35 And the LORD said unto Moses, The
man shall be surely put to death: all the
congregation shall stone him with stones
without the camp.
36 And all the congregation brought
him without the camp, and stoned him
with stones, and he died; as the LORD
commanded Moses.
37 ¶ And the LORD spake unto Moses,
saying,
38 Speak unto the children of Ĭs'rā-ĕl,
and bid them that they make them
fringes in the borders of their garments,
throughout their generations, and that
they put upon the fringe of the borders
a ribband of blue:
39 And it shall be unto you for a fringe,
that ye may look upon it, and remember
all the commandments of the LORD, and
do them; and that ye seek not after your
own heart and your own eyes, after
which ye use to go a whoring:
40 That ye may remember, and do all
my commandments, and be holy unto
your God.
41 I *am* the LORD your God, which
brought you out of the land of Egypt,
to be your God: I *am* the LORD your
God.

CHAPTER 16

NOW Kō'răh, the son of Ĭz'hār, the
son of Kō'hăth, the son of Levi,
and Dā'thăn and Ȧ-bī'răm, the sons of
Ē-lī'ăb, and Ŏn, the son of Pē'lĕth, sons
of Reuben, took *men:*
2 And they rose up before Moses, with
certain of the children of Ĭs'rā-ĕl, two
hundred and fifty princes of the assembly, famous in the congregation, men of
renown:
3 And they gathered themselves together against Moses and against
Aaron, and said unto them, *Ye take* too
much upon you, seeing all the congregation *are* holy, every one of them, and
the LORD *is* among them: wherefore
then lift ye up yourselves above the congregation of the LORD?
4 And when Moses heard *it,* he fell
upon his face:
5 And he spake unto Kō'răh and unto
all his company, saying, Even to-morrow the LORD will show who *are* his,
and *who is* holy; and will cause *him* to
come near unto him: even *him* whom he
hath chosen will he cause to come near
unto him.
6 This do; Take you censers, Kō'răh,
and all his company;
7 And put fire therein, and put incense
in them before the LORD to-morrow:
and it shall be *that* the man whom the
LORD doth choose, he *shall be* holy: *ye*
take too much upon you, ye sons of Levi.
8 And Moses said unto Kō'răh, Hear,
I pray you, ye sons of Levi:
9 *Seemeth it but* a small thing unto
you, that the God of Ĭs'rā-ĕl hath separated you from the congregation of
Ĭs'rā-ĕl, to bring you near to himself to
do the service of the tabernacle of the
LORD, and to stand before the congregation to minister unto them?
10 And he hath brought thee near *to*
him, and all thy brethren the sons of
Levi with thee: and seek ye the priesthood also?
11 For which cause *both* thou and all
thy company *are* gathered together
against the LORD: and what *is* Aaron,
that ye murmur against him?
12 ¶ And Moses sent to call Dā'thăn
and Ȧ-bī'răm, the sons of Ē-lī'ăb; which
said, We will not come up:

13 *Is it* a small thing that thou hast
brought us up out of a land that floweth
with milk and honey, to kill us in the
wilderness, except thou make thyself
altogether a prince over us?
14 Moreover, thou hast not brought us
into a land that floweth with milk and
honey, or given us inheritance of fields
and vineyards: wilt thou put out the
eyes of these men? we will not come up.
15 And Moses was very wroth, and
said unto the LORD, Respect not thou
their offering: I have not taken one ass
from them, neither have I hurt one of
them.
16 And Moses said unto Kō′rȧh, Be
thou and all thy company before the
LORD, thou, and they, and Aaron, to-
morrow:
17 And take every man his censer, and
put incense in them, and bring ye before
the LORD every man his censer, two
hundred and fifty censers; thou also,
and Aaron, each *of you* his censer.
18 And they took every man his censer, and put fire in them, and laid incense thereon, and stood in the door of
the tabernacle of the congregation with
Moses and Aaron.
19 And Kō′rȧh gathered all the congregation against them unto the door of
the tabernacle of the congregation: and
the glory of the LORD appeared unto all
the congregation.
20 And the LORD spake unto Moses
and unto Aaron, saying,
21 Separate yourselves from among
this congregation, that I may consume
them in a moment.
22 And they fell upon their faces, and
said, O God, the God of the spirits of
all flesh, shall one man sin, and wilt
thou be wroth with all the congregation?
23 ¶ And the LORD spake unto Moses,
saying,
24 Speak unto the congregation, saying, Get you up from about the tabernacle of Kō′rȧh, Dā′thăn, and Ȧ-bī′răm.
25 And Moses rose up and went unto
Dā′thăn and Ȧ-bī′răm; and the elders of
Ĭs̩′rā-ĕl followed him.
26 And he spake unto the congregation, saying, Depart, I pray you, from
the tents of these wicked men, and
touch nothing of theirs, lest ye be consumed in all their sins.
27 So they gat up from the tabernacle
of Kō′rȧh, Dā′thăn, and Ȧ-bī′răm, on
every side: and Dā′thăn and Ȧ-bī′răm
came out, and stood in the door of their
tents, and their wives, and their sons,
and their little children.
28 And Moses said, Hereby ye shall
know that the LORD hath sent me to do
all these works; for *I have* not *done
them* of mine own mind.
29 If these men die the common death
of all men, or if they be visited after the
visitation of all men; *then* the LORD
hath not sent me.
30 But if the LORD make a new thing,
and the earth open her mouth, and swallow them up, with all that *appertain*
unto them, and they go down quick into
the pit; then ye shall understand that
these men have provoked the LORD.
31 ¶ And it came to pass, as he had
made an end of speaking all these
words, that the ground clave asunder
that *was* under them:
32 And the earth opened her mouth,
and swallowed them up, and their
houses, and all the men that *appertained* unto Kō′rȧh, and all *their* goods.
33 They, and all that *appertained* to
them, went down alive into the pit, and
the earth closed upon them: and they
perished from among the congregation.
34 And all Ĭs̩′rā-ĕl that *were* round
about them fled at the cry of them: for
they said, Lest the earth swallow us up
also.
35 And there came out a fire from the
LORD, and consumed the two hundred
and fifty men that offered incense.
36 ¶ And the LORD spake unto Moses,
saying,
37 Speak unto Ĕl′ē-ā′zȧr the son of
Aaron the priest, that he take up the
censers out of the burning, and scatter
thou the fire yonder; for they are
hallowed.
38 The censers of these sinners against
their own souls, let them make them
broad plates *for* a covering of the altar:
for they offered them before the LORD,
therefore they are hallowed: and they
shall be a sign unto the children of
Ĭs̩′rā-ĕl.
39 And Ĕl′ē-ā′zȧr the priest took the
brazen censers, wherewith they that
were burnt had offered; and they were
made broad *plates for* a covering of the
altar:
40 *To be* a memorial unto the children
of Ĭs̩′rā-ĕl, that no stranger, which *is* not

of the seed of Aaron, come near to offer
incense before the LORD; that he be not
as Kō'rȧh, and as his company: as the
LORD said to him by the hand of Moses.
41 ¶ But on the morrow all the congregation of the children of Ĭṣ'rā-ĕl murmured against Moses and against Aaron,
saying, Ye have killed the people of the
LORD.
42 And it came to pass, when the congregation was gathered against Moses
and against Aaron, that they looked toward the tabernacle of the congregation: and, behold, the cloud covered it,
and the glory of the LORD appeared.
43 And Moses and Aaron came before
the tabernacle of the congregation.
44 ¶ And the LORD spake unto Moses,
saying,
45 Get you up from among this congregation, that I may consume them as
in a moment. And they fell upon their
faces.
46 ¶ And Moses said unto Aaron, Take
a censer, and put fire therein from off
the altar, and put on incense, and go
quickly unto the congregation, and make
an atonement for them: for there is
wrath gone out from the LORD; the
plague is begun.
47 And Aaron took as Moses commanded, and ran into the midst of the
congregation; and, behold, the plague
was begun among the people: and he
put on incense, and made an atonement
for the people.
48 And he stood between the dead and
the living; and the plague was stayed.
49 Now they that died in the plague
were fourteen thousand and seven hundred, besides them that died about the
matter of Kō'rȧh.
50 And Aaron returned unto Moses
unto the door of the tabernacle of the
congregation: and the plague was
stayed.

CHAPTER 17

AND the LORD spake unto Moses,
saying,
2 Speak unto the children of Ĭṣ'rā-ĕl,
and take of every one of them a rod
according to the house of *their* fathers,
of all their princes according to the
house of their fathers, twelve rods:
write thou every man's name upon his
rod.
3 And thou shalt write Aaron's name
upon the rod of Levi: for one rod *shall*
be for the head of the house of their
fathers.
4 And thou shalt lay them up in the
tabernacle of the congregation before
the testimony, where I will meet with
you.
5 And it shall come to pass, *that* the
man's rod, whom I shall choose, shall
blossom: and I will make to cease from
me the murmurings of the children of
Ĭṣ'rā-ĕl, whereby they murmur against
you.
6 ¶ And Moses spake unto the children of Ĭṣ'rā-ĕl, and every one of their
princes gave him a rod apiece, for each
prince one, according to their fathers'
houses, *even* twelve rods: and the rod
of Aaron *was* among their rods.
7 And Moses laid up the rods before
the LORD in the tabernacle of witness.
8 And it came to pass, that on the morrow Moses went into the tabernacle of
witness; and, behold, the rod of Aaron
for the house of Levi was budded, and
brought forth buds, and bloomed blossoms, and yielded almonds.
9 And Moses brought out all the rods
from before the LORD unto all the children of Ĭṣ'rā-ĕl: and they looked, and
took every man his rod.
10 ¶ And the LORD said unto Moses,
Bring Aaron's rod again before the testimony, to be kept for a token against the
rebels; and thou shalt quite take away
their murmurings from me, that they
die not.
11 And Moses did *so:* as the LORD
commanded him, so did he.
12 And the children of Ĭṣ'rā-ĕl spake
unto Moses, saying, Behold, we die, we
perish, we all perish.
13 Whosoever cometh any thing near
unto the tabernacle of the LORD shall
die: shall we be consumed with dying?

CHAPTER 18

AND the LORD said unto Aaron, Thou
and thy sons and thy father's house
with thee shall bear the iniquity of the
sanctuary: and thou and thy sons with
thee shall bear the iniquity of your
priesthood.
2 And thy brethren also of the tribe of
Levi, the tribe of thy father, bring thou
with thee, that they may be joined unto
thee, and minister unto thee: but thou

and thy sons with thee *shall minister*
before the tabernacle of witness.
3 And they shall keep thy charge, and
the charge of all the tabernacle: only
they shall not come nigh the vessels of
the sanctuary and the altar, that neither
they, nor ye also, die.
4 And they shall be joined unto thee,
and keep the charge of the tabernacle of
the congregation, for all the service of
the tabernacle: and a stranger shall not
come nigh unto you.
5 And ye shall keep the charge of the
sanctuary, and the charge of the altar;
that there be no wrath any more upon
the children of Ĭş′rā-ĕl.
6 And I, behold, I have taken your
brethren the Lē′vītes from among the
children of Ĭş′rā-ĕl: to you *they are*
given *as* a gift for the LORD, to do the
service of the tabernacle of the congregation.
7 Therefore thou and thy sons with
thee shall keep your priest's office for
every thing of the altar, and within the
veil; and ye shall serve: I have given
your priest's office *unto you as* a service
of gift: and the stranger that cometh
nigh shall be put to death.
8 ℂ And the LORD spake unto Aaron,
Behcld, I also have given thee the charge
of mine heave offerings of all the hallowed things of the children of Ĭş′rā-ĕl;
unto thee have I given them by reason
of the anointing, and to thy sons, by an
ordinance for ever.
9 This shall be thine of the most holy
things, *reserved* from the fire: every
oblation of theirs, every meat offering of
theirs, and every sin offering of theirs,
and every trespass offering of theirs,
which they shall render unto me, *shall
be* most holy for thee and for thy sons.
10 In the most holy *place* shalt thou
eat it; every male shall eat it: it shall be
holy unto thee.
11 And this *is* thine; the heave offering
of their gift, with all the wave offerings
of the children of Ĭş′rā-ĕl: I have given
them unto thee, and to thy sons and to
thy daughters with thee, by a statute for
ever: every one that is clean in thy
house shall eat of it.
12 All the best of the oil, and all the
best of the wine, and of the wheat, the
firstfruits of them which they shall offer
unto the LORD, them have I given thee.
13 *And* whatsoever is first ripe in the
land, which they shall bring unto the
LORD, shall be thine; every one that is
clean in thine house shall eat *of* it.
14 Every thing devoted in Ĭş′rā-ĕl shall
be thine.
15 Every thing that openeth the matrix
in all flesh, which they bring unto the
LORD, *whether it be* of men or beasts,
shall be thine: nevertheless the firstborn of man shalt thou surely redeem,
and the firstling of unclean beasts shalt
thou redeem.
16 And those that are to be redeemed
from a month old shalt thou redeem,
according to thine estimation, for the
money of five shekels, after the shekel
of the sanctuary, which *is* twenty
gē′rȧhs.
17 But the firstling of a cow, or the
firstling of a sheep, or the firstling of a
goat, thou shalt not redeem; they *are*
holy: thou shalt sprinkle their blood upon the altar, and shalt burn their fat *for*
an offering made by fire, for a sweet
savor unto the LORD.
18 And the flesh of them shall be thine,
as the wave breast and as the right
shoulder are thine.
19 All the heave offerings of the holy
things, which the children of Ĭş′rā-ĕl
offer unto the LORD, have I given thee,
and thy sons and thy daughters with
thee, by a statute for ever: it *is* a covenant of salt for ever before the LORD
unto thee and to thy seed with thee.
20 ℂ And the LORD spake unto Aaron,
Thou shalt have no inheritance in their
land, neither shalt thou have any part
among them: I *am* thy part and thine
inheritance among the children of
Ĭş′rā-ĕl.
21 And, behold, I have given the children of Levi all the tenth in Ĭş′rā-ĕl for
an inheritance, for their service which
they serve, *even* the service of the
tabernacle of the congregation.
22 Neither must the children of Ĭş′-
rā-ĕl henceforth come nigh the tabernacle of the congregation, lest they bear
sin, and die.
23 But the Lē′vītes shall do the service
of the tabernacle of the congregation,
and they shall bear their iniquity: *it
shall be* a statute for ever throughout
your generations, that among the children of Ĭş′rā-ĕl they have no inheritance.
24 But the tithes of the children of
Ĭş′rā-ĕl, which they offer *as* a heave

offering unto the LORD, I have given to
the Lē′vītes to inherit: therefore I have
said unto them, Among the children of
Īṣ′rā-ĕl they shall have no inheritance.
25 ℂ And the LORD spake unto Moses,
saying,
26 Thus speak unto the Lē′vītes, and
say unto them, When ye take of the
children of Īṣ′rā-ĕl the tithes which I
have given you from them for your inheritance, then ye shall offer up a heave
offering of it for the LORD, *even* a tenth
part of the tithe.
27 And *this* your heave offering shall
be reckoned unto you, as though *it were*
the corn of the threshingfloor, and as
the fulness of the winepress.
28 Thus ye also shall offer a heave
offering unto the LORD of all your tithes,
which ye receive of the children of
Īṣ′rā-ĕl; and ye shall give thereof the
LORD's heave offering to Aaron the
priest.
29 Out of all your gifts ye shall offer
every heave offering of the LORD, of all
the best thereof, *even* the hallowed part
thereof out of it.
30 Therefore thou shalt say unto them,
When ye have heaved the best thereof
from it, then it shall be counted unto the
Lē′vītes as the increase of the threshingfloor, and as the increase of the winepress.
31 And ye shall eat it in every place, ye
and your households: for it *is* your reward for your service in the tabernacle
of the congregation.
32 And ye shall bear no sin by reason
of it, when ye have heaved from it the
best of it: neither shall ye pollute the
holy things of the children of Īṣ′rā-ĕl,
lest ye die.

CHAPTER 19

AND the LORD spake unto Moses and
unto Aaron, saying,
2 This *is* the ordinance of the law which
the LORD hath commanded, saying,
Speak unto the children of Īṣ′rā-ĕl, that
they bring thee a red heifer without
spot, wherein *is* no blemish, *and* upon
which never came yoke.
3 And ye shall give her unto Ĕl′ē-ā′zăr
the priest, that he may bring her forth
without the camp, and *one* shall slay her
before his face:
4 And Ĕl′ē-ā′zăr the priest shall take of
her blood with his finger, and sprinkle
of her blood directly before the tabernacle of the congregation seven times.
5 And *one* shall burn the heifer in his
sight; her skin, and her flesh, and her
blood, with her dung, shall he burn:
6 And the priest shall take cedar wood,
and hyssop, and scarlet, and cast *it* into
the midst of the burning of the heifer.
7 Then the priest shall wash his
clothes, and he shall bathe his flesh in
water, and afterward he shall come into
the camp, and the priest shall be unclean until the even.
8 And he that burneth her shall wash
his clothes in water, and bathe his flesh
in water, and shall be unclean until the
even.
9 And a man *that is* clean shall gather
up the ashes of the heifer, and lay *them*
up without the camp in a clean place,
and it shall be kept for the congregation
of the children of Īṣ′rā-ĕl for a water of
separation: it *is* a purification for sin.
10 And he that gathereth the ashes of
the heifer shall wash his clothes, and be
unclean until the even: and it shall be
unto the children of Īṣ′rā-ĕl, and unto
the stranger that sojourneth among
them, for a statute for ever.
11 ℂ He that toucheth the dead body
of any man shall be unclean seven days.
12 He shall purify himself with it on
the third day, and on the seventh day he
shall be clean: but if he purify not himself the third day, then the seventh day
he shall not be clean.
13 Whosoever toucheth the dead body
of any man that is dead, and purifieth
not himself, defileth the tabernacle of
the LORD; and that soul shall be cut off
from Īṣ′rā-ĕl: because the water of separation was not sprinkled upon him, he
shall be unclean; his uncleanness *is* yet
upon him.
14 This *is* the law, when a man dieth in
a tent: all that come into the tent, and
all that *is* in the tent, shall be unclean
seven days.
15 And every open vessel, which hath
no covering bound upon it, *is* unclean.
16 And whosoever toucheth one that is
slain with a sword in the open fields, or
a dead body, or a bone of a man, or a
grave, shall be unclean seven days.
17 And for an unclean *person* they shall
take of the ashes of the burnt heifer of
purification for sin, and running water
shall be put thereto in a vessel:

18 And a clean person shall take hyssop, and dip *it* in the water, and sprinkle *it* upon the tent, and upon all the vessels, and upon the persons that were there, and upon him that touched a bone, or one slain, or one dead, or a grave:

19 And the clean *person* shall sprinkle upon the unclean on the third day, and on the seventh day: and on the seventh day he shall purify himself, and wash his clothes, and bathe himself in water, and shall be clean at even.

20 But the man that shall be unclean, and shall not purify himself, that soul shall be cut off from among the congregation, because he hath defiled the sanctuary of the LORD: the water of separation hath not been sprinkled upon him; he *is* unclean.

21 And it shall be a perpetual statute unto them, that he that sprinkleth the water of separation shall wash his clothes; and he that toucheth the water of separation shall be unclean until even.

22 And whatsoever the unclean *person* toucheth shall be unclean; and the soul that toucheth *it* shall be unclean until even.

CHAPTER 20

THEN came the children of Ĭṣ′rā-ĕl, *even* the whole congregation, into the desert of Zĭn in the first month: and the people abode in Kā′dĕsh; and Miriam died there, and was buried there.

2 And there was no water for the congregation: and they gathered themselves together against Moses and against Aaron.

3 And the people chode with Moses, and spake, saying, Would God that we had died when our brethren died before the LORD!

4 And why have ye brought up the congregation of the LORD into this wilderness, that we and our cattle should die there?

5 And wherefore have ye made us to come up out of Egypt, to bring us in unto this evil place? it *is* no place of seed, or of figs, or of vines, or of pomegranates; neither *is* there any water to drink.

6 And Moses and Aaron went from the presence of the assembly unto the door of the tabernacle of the congregation, and they fell upon their faces: and the glory of the LORD appeared unto them.

7 ¶ And the LORD spake unto Moses, saying,

8 Take the rod, and gather thou the assembly together, thou and Aaron thy brother, and speak ye unto the rock before their eyes; and it shall give forth his water, and thou shalt bring forth to them water out of the rock: so thou shalt give the congregation and their beasts drink.

9 And Moses took the rod from before the LORD, as he commanded him.

10 And Moses and Aaron gathered the congregation together before the rock, and he said unto them, Hear now, ye rebels; must we fetch you water out of this rock?

11 And Moses lifted up his hand, and with his rod he smote the rock twice: and the water came out abundantly, and the congregation drank, and their beasts *also*.

12 ¶ And the LORD spake unto Moses and Aaron, Because ye believed me not, to sanctify me in the eyes of the children of Ĭṣ′rā-ĕl, therefore ye shall not bring this congregation into the land which I have given them.

13 This *is* the water of Mĕr′ĭ-bäh; because the children of Ĭṣ′rā-ĕl strove with the LORD, and he was sanctified in them.

14 ¶ And Moses sent messengers from Kā′dĕsh unto the king of Ē′dŏm, Thus saith thy brother Ĭṣ′rā-ĕl, Thou knowest all the travail that hath befallen us:

15 How our fathers went down into Egypt, and we have dwelt in Egypt a long time; and the Egyptians vexed us, and our fathers:

16 And when we cried unto the LORD, he heard our voice, and sent an angel, and hath brought us forth out of Egypt: and, behold, we *are* in Kā′dĕsh, a city in the uttermost of thy border.

17 Let us pass, I pray thee, through thy country: we will not pass through the fields, or through the vineyards, neither will we drink *of* the water of the wells: we will go by the king's *high* way, we will not turn to the right hand nor to the left, until we have passed thy borders.

18 And Ē′dŏm said unto him, Thou shalt not pass by me, lest I come out against thee with the sword.

19 And the children of Ĭṣ′rā-ĕl said

unto him, We will go by the high way: and if I and my cattle drink of thy water, then I will pay for it: I will only, without *doing* any thing *else*, go through on my feet.

20 And he said, Thou shalt not go through. And Ē′dŏm came out against him with much people, and with a strong hand.

21 Thus Ē′dŏm refused to give Ĭṣ′rā-ĕl passage through his border: wherefore Ĭṣ′rā-ĕl turned away from him.

22 ¶ And the children of Ĭṣ′rā-ĕl, *even* the whole congregation, journeyed from Kā′dĕsh, and came unto mount Hôr.

23 And the LORD spake unto Moses and Aaron in mount Hôr, by the coast of the land of Ē′dŏm, saying,

24 Aaron shall be gathered unto his people: for he shall not enter into the land which I have given unto the children of Ĭṣ′rā-ĕl, because ye rebelled against my word at the water of Mĕr′ĭ-bäh.

25 Take Aaron and Ĕl′ē-ā′zȧr his son, and bring them up unto mount Hôr:

26 And strip Aaron of his garments, and put them upon Ĕl′ē-ā′zȧr his son: and Aaron shall be gathered *unto his people*, and shall die there.

27 And Moses did as the LORD commanded: and they went up into mount Hôr in the sight of all the congregation.

28 And Moses stripped Aaron of his garments, and put them upon Ĕl′ē-ā′zȧr his son; and Aaron died there in the top of the mount: and Moses and Ĕl′ē-ā′zȧr came down from the mount.

29 And when all the congregation saw that Aaron was dead, they mourned for Aaron thirty days, *even* all the house of Ĭṣ′rā-ĕl.

CHAPTER 21

AND *when* king Ā′răd the Cā′năan-īte, which dwelt in the south, heard tell that Ĭṣ′rā-ĕl came by the way of the spies; then he fought against Ĭṣ′rā-ĕl, and took *some* of them prisoners.

2 And Ĭṣ′rā-ĕl vowed a vow unto the LORD, and said, If thou wilt indeed deliver this people into my hand, then I will utterly destroy their cities.

3 And the LORD hearkened to the voice of Ĭṣ′rā-ĕl, and delivered up the Cā′năan-ītes; and they utterly destroyed them and their cities: and he called the name of the place Hôr′mȧh.

4 ¶ And they journeyed from mount Hôr by the way of the Red sea, to compass the land of Ē′dŏm: and the soul of the people was much discouraged because of the way.

5 And the people spake against God, and against Moses, Wherefore have ye brought us up out of Egypt to die in the wilderness? for *there is* no bread, neither *is there any* water; and our soul loatheth this light bread.

6 And the LORD sent fiery serpents among the people, and they bit the people; and much people of Ĭṣ′rā-ĕl died.

7 ¶ Therefore the people came to Moses, and said, We have sinned, for we have spoken against the LORD, and against thee; pray unto the LORD, that he take away the serpents from us. And Moses prayed for the people.

8 And the LORD said unto Moses, Make thee a fiery serpent, and set it upon a pole: and it shall come to pass, that every one that is bitten, when he looketh upon it, shall live.

9 And Moses made a serpent of brass, and put it upon a pole; and it came to pass, that if a serpent had bitten any man, when he beheld the serpent of brass, he lived.

10 ¶ And the children of Ĭṣ′rā-ĕl set forward, and pitched in Ō′bŏth.

11 And they journeyed from Ō′bŏth, and pitched at Ī′jē-ăb′ȧ-rĭm, in the wilderness which *is* before Mō′ăb, toward the sunrising.

12 ¶ From thence they removed, and pitched in the valley of Zā′rĕd.

13 From thence they removed, and pitched on the other side of Är′nŏn, which *is* in the wilderness that cometh out of the coasts of the Ăm′ō-rītes: for Är′nŏn *is* the border of Mō′ăb, between Mō′ăb and the Ăm′ō-rītes.

14 Wherefore it is said in the book of the wars of the LORD, What he did in the Red sea, and in the brooks of Är′nŏn,

15 And at the stream of the brooks that goeth down to the dwelling of Är, and lieth upon the border of Mō′ăb.

16 And from thence *they went* to Bē′ĕr: that *is* the well whereof the LORD spake unto Moses, Gather the people together, and I will give them water.

17 ¶ Then Ĭṣ′rā-ĕl sang this song, Spring up, O well; sing ye unto it:

18 The princes digged the well, the nobles of the people digged it, by *the*

direction of the lawgiver, with their
staves. And from the wilderness *they
went* to Măt′tȧ-nȧh:
19 And from Măt′tȧ-nȧh to Nȧ-hā′-
lĭ-ĕl: and from Nȧ-hā′lĭ-ĕl to Bā′mŏth:
20 And from Bā′mŏth *in* the valley,
that *is* in the country of Mō′ăb, to the
top of Pĭṣ′gȧh, which looketh toward
Jē-shī′mŏn.
21 ℭ And Ĭṣ′rā-ĕl sent messengers
unto Sī′hŏn king of the Ăm′ō-rītes,
saying,
22 Let me pass through thy land: we
will not turn into the fields, or into the
vineyards; we will not drink *of* the waters of the well: *but* we will go along by
the king's *high* way, until we be past
thy borders.
23 And Sī′hŏn would not suffer Ĭṣ′rā-ĕl
to pass through his border: but Sī′hŏn
gathered all his people together, and
went out against Ĭṣ′rā-ĕl into the wilderness: and he came to Jā′hăz, and fought
against Ĭṣ′rā-ĕl.
24 And Ĭṣ′rā-ĕl smote him with the
edge of the sword, and possessed his
land from Är′nŏn unto Jăb′bŏk, even
unto the children of Ammon: for the
border of the children of Ammon *was*
strong.
25 And Ĭṣ′rā-ĕl took all these cities:
and Ĭṣ′rā-ĕl dwelt in all the cities of the
Ăm′ō-rītes, in Hĕsh′bŏn, and in all the
villages thereof.
26 For Hĕsh′bŏn *was* the city of Sī′hŏn
the king of the Ăm′ō-rītes, who had
fought against the former king of Mō′ăb,
and taken all his land out of his hand,
even unto Är′nŏn.
27 Wherefore they that speak in proverbs say, Come into Hĕsh′bŏn, let the
city of Sī′hŏn be built and prepared:
28 For there is a fire gone out of Hĕsh′-
bŏn, a flame from the city of Sī′hŏn: it
hath consumed Är of Mō′ăb, *and* the
lords of the high places of Är′nŏn.
29 Woe to thee, Mō′ăb! thou art undone, O people of Chē′mŏsh: he hath
given his sons that escaped, and his
daughters, into captivity unto Sī′hŏn
king of the Ăm′ō-rītes.
30 We have shot at them; Hĕsh′bŏn is
perished even unto Dī′bŏn, and we have
laid them waste even unto Nō′phȧh,
which *reacheth* unto Mĕd′ē-bȧ.
31 ℭ Thus Ĭṣ′rā-ĕl dwelt in the land of
the Ăm′ō-rītes.
32 And Moses sent to spy out Jā′ȧ-zĕr,
and they took the villages thereof, and
drove out the Ăm′ō-rītes that *were* there.
33 ℭ And they turned and went up
by the way of Bā′shăn: and Og the
king of Bā′shăn went out against them,
he, and all his people, to the battle at
Ĕd′rē-ī.
34 And the LORD said unto Moses,
Fear him not: for I have delivered him
into thy hand, and all his people, and his
land; and thou shalt do to him as thou
didst unto Sī′hŏn king of the Ăm′ō-rītes,
which dwelt at Hĕsh′bŏn.
35 So they smote him, and his sons, and
all his people, until there was none left
him alive: and they possessed his land.

CHAPTER 22

AND the children of Ĭṣ′rā-ĕl set forward, and pitched in the plains of
Mō′ăb on this side Jordan *by* Jĕr′ī-chō.
2 ℭ And Bā′lăk the son of Zĭp′pŏr saw
all that Ĭṣ′rā-ĕl had done to the Ăm′ō-
rītes.
3 And Mō′ăb was sore afraid of the
people, because they *were* many: and
Mō′ăb was distressed because of the
children of Ĭṣ′rā-ĕl.
4 And Mō′ăb said unto the elders of
Mĭd′ĭ-ăn, Now shall this company lick
up all *that are* round about us, as the ox
licketh up the grass of the field. And
Bā′lăk the son of Zĭp′pŏr *was* king of the
Mō′ăb-ītes at that time.
5 He sent messengers therefore unto
Bā′lȧam the son of Bē′ŏr to Pē′thŏr,
which *is* by the river of the land of the
children of his people, to call him, saying, Behold, there is a people come out
from Egypt: behold, they cover the face
of the earth, and they abide over against
me:
6 Come now therefore, I pray thee,
curse me this people; for they *are* too
mighty for me: peradventure I shall prevail, *that* we may smite them, and *that*
I may drive them out of the land: for I
wot that he whom thou blessest *is*
blessed, and he whom thou cursest is
cursed.
7 And the elders of Mō′ăb and the
elders of Mĭd′ĭ-ăn departed with the
rewards of divination in their hand; and
they came unto Bā′lȧam, and spake
unto him the words of Bā′lăk.
8 And he said unto them, Lodge here
this night, and I will bring you word
again, as the LORD shall speak unto me:

and the princes of Mō'ăb abode with
Bā'lȧam.
9 And God came unto Bā'lȧam, and
said, What men *are* these with thee?
10 And Bā'lȧam said unto God, Bā'lăk
the son of Zĭp'pŏr, king of Mō'ăb, hath
sent unto me, *saying*,
11 Behold, *there is* a people come out
of Egypt, which covereth the face of the
earth: come now, curse me them; peradventure I shall be able to overcome
them, and drive them out.
12 And God said unto Bā'lȧam, Thou
shalt not go with them; thou shalt not
curse the people: for they *are* blessed.
13 And Bā'lȧam rose up in the morning, and said unto the princes of Bā'lăk,
Get you into your land: for the LORD
refuseth to give me leave to go with
you.
14 And the princes of Mō'ăb rose up,
and they went unto Bā'lăk, and said,
Bā'lȧam refuseth to come with us.
15 ¶ And Bā'lăk sent yet again princes,
more, and more honorable than they.
16 And they came to Bā'lȧam, and said
to him, Thus saith Bā'lăk the son of Zĭp'-
pŏr, Let nothing, I pray thee, hinder
thee from coming unto me:
17 For I will promote thee unto very
great honor, and I will do whatsoever
thou sayest unto me: come therefore, I
pray thee, curse me this people.
18 And Bā'lȧam answered and said
unto the servants of Bā'lăk, If Bā'lăk
would give me his house full of silver
and gold, I cannot go beyond the word
of the LORD my God, to do less or more.
19 Now therefore, I pray you, tarry ye
also here this night, that I may know
what the LORD will say unto me more.
20 And God came unto Bā'lȧam at
night, and said unto him, If the men
come to call thee, rise up, *and* go with
them; but yet the word which I shall say
unto thee, that shalt thou do.
21 And Bā'lȧam rose up in the morning, and saddled his ass, and went with
the princes of Mō'ăb.
22 ¶ And God's anger was kindled because he went: and the angel of the
LORD stood in the way for an adversary
against him. Now he was riding upon
his ass, and his two servants *were* with
him.
23 And the ass saw the angel of the
LORD standing in the way, and his
sword drawn in his hand: and the ass
turned aside out of the way, and went
into the field: and Bā'lȧam smote the
ass, to turn her into the way.
24 But the angel of the LORD stood in
a path of the vineyards, a wall *being* on
this side, and a wall on that side.
25 And when the ass saw the angel of
the LORD, she thrust herself unto the
wall, and crushed Bā'lȧam's foot against
the wall: and he smote her again.
26 And the angel of the LORD went
further, and stood in a narrow place,
where *was* no way to turn either to the
right hand or to the left.
27 And when the ass saw the angel of
the LORD, she fell down under Bā'lȧam:
and Bā'lȧam's anger was kindled, and
he smote the ass with a staff.
28 And the LORD opèned the mouth of
the ass, and she said unto Bā'lȧam,
What have I done unto thee, that thou
hast smitten me these three times?
29 And Bā'lȧam said unto the ass, Because thou hast mocked me: I would
there were a sword in mine hand, for
now would I kill thee.
30 And the ass said unto Bā'lȧam, *Am*
not I thine ass, upon which thou hast
ridden ever since I *was* thine unto this
day? was I ever wont to do so unto thee?
And he said, Nay.
31 Then the LORD opened the eyes of
Bā'lȧam, and he saw the angel of the
LORD standing in the way, and his sword
drawn in his hand: and he bowed down
his head, and fell flat on his face.
32 And the angel of the LORD said unto
him, Wherefore hast thou smitten thine
ass these three times? Behold, I went
out to withstand thee, because *thy* way
is perverse before me:
33 And the ass saw me, and turned
from me these three times: unless she
had turned from me, surely now also I
had slain thee, and saved her alive.
34 And Bā'lȧam said unto the angel of
the LORD, I have sinned; for I knew not
that thou stoodest in the way against
me: now therefore, if it displease thee,
I will get me back again.
35 And the angel of the LORD said unto
Bā'lȧam, Go with the men: but only the
word that I shall speak unto thee, that
thou shalt speak. So Bā'lȧam went with
the princes of Bā'lăk.
36 ¶ And when Bā'lăk heard that Bā'-
lȧam was come, he went out to meet him
unto a city of Mō'ăb, which *is* in the

border of Är'nŏn, which *is* in the utmost coast.
37 And Bā'lăk said unto Bā'lȧam, Did
I not earnestly send unto thee to call
thee? wherefore camest thou not unto
me? am I not able indeed to promote
thee to honor?
38 And Bā'lȧam said unto Bā'lăk, Lo,
I am come unto thee: have I now any
power at all to say any thing? the word
that God putteth in my mouth, that shall
I speak.
39 And Bā'lȧam went with Bā'lăk, and
they came unto Kĭr'jăth–hū'zŏth.
40 And Bā'lăk offered oxen and sheep,
and sent to Bā'lȧam, and to the princes
that *were* with him.
41 And it came to pass on the morrow,
that Bā'lăk took Bā'lȧam, and brought
him up into the high places of Bā'ăl,
that thence he might see the utmost
part of the people.

CHAPTER 23

AND Bā'lȧam said unto Bā'lăk, Build
me here seven altars, and prepare
me here seven oxen and seven rams.
2 And Bā'lăk did as Bā'lȧam had
spoken; and Bā'lăk and Bā'lȧam offered
on *every* altar a bullock and a ram.
3 And Bā'lȧam said unto Bā'lăk, Stand
by thy burnt offering, and I will go: peradventure the LORD will come to meet
me; and whatsoever he showeth me I
will tell thee. And he went *to* a high
place.
4 And God met Bā'lȧam: and he said
unto him, I have prepared seven altars,
and I have offered upon *every* altar a
bullock and a ram.
5 And the LORD put a word in Bā'lȧam's mouth, and said, Return unto
Bā'lăk, and thus thou shalt speak.
6 And he returned unto him, and, lo,
he stood by his burnt sacrifice, he, and
all the princes of Mō'ăb.
7 And he took up his parable, and said,
Bā'lăk the king of Mō'ăb hath brought
me from Ā'răm, out of the mountains of
the east, *saying,* Come, curse me Jacob,
and come, defy Ĭṣ'rā-ĕl.
8 How shall I curse, *whom* God hath
not cursed? or how shall I defy, *whom*
the LORD hath not defied?
9 For from the top of the rocks I see
him, and from the hills I behold him:
lo, the people shall dwell alone, and
shall not be reckoned among the nations.
10 Who can count the dust of Jacob,
and the number of the fourth *part* of
Ĭṣ'rā-ĕl? Let me die the death of the
righteous, and let my last end be like
his!
11 And Bā'lăk said unto Bā'lȧam, What
hast thou done unto me? I took thee to
curse mine enemies, and, behold, thou
hast blessed *them* altogether.
12 And he answered and said, Must I
not take heed to speak that which the
LORD hath put in my mouth?
13 And Bā'lăk said unto him, Come, I
pray thee, with me unto another place,
from whence thou mayest see them:
thou shalt see but the utmost part of
them, and shalt not see them all: and
curse me them from thence.
14 ℭ And he brought him into the
field of Zō'phĭm, to the top of Pĭṣ'gȧh,
and built seven altars, and offered a
bullock and a ram on *every* altar.
15 And he said unto Bā'lăk, Stand here
by thy burnt offering, while I meet *the
LORD* yonder.
16 And the LORD met Bā'lȧam, and
put a word in his mouth, and said, Go
again unto Bā'lăk, and say thus.
17 And when he came to him, behold,
he stood by his burnt offering, and the
princes of Mō'ăb with him. And Bā'lăk
said unto him, What hath the LORD
spoken?
18 And he took up his parable, and
said, Rise up, Bā'lăk, and hear; hearken
unto me, thou son of Zĭp'pŏr:
19 God *is* not a man, that he should lie;
neither the son of man, that he should
repent: hath he said, and shall he not do
it? or hath he spoken, and shall he not
make it good?
20 Behold, I have received *commandment* to bless: and he hath blessed; and
I cannot reverse it.
21 He hath not beheld iniquity in
Jacob, neither hath he seen perverseness in Ĭṣ'rā-ĕl: the LORD his God *is*
with him, and the shout of a king *is*
among them.
22 God brought them out of Egypt; he
hath as it were the strength of a unicorn.
23 Surely *there is* no enchantment
against Jacob, neither *is there* any divination against Ĭṣ'rā-ĕl: according to this
time it shall be said of Jacob and of
Ĭṣ'rā-ĕl, What hath God wrought!
24 Behold, the people shall rise up as a
great lion, and lift up himself as a young

lion: he shall not lie down until he eat
of the prey, and drink the blood of the
slain.
25 ¶ And Bā'lăk said unto Bā'lȧam,
Neither curse them at all, nor bless
them at all.
26 But Bā'lȧam answered and said
unto Bā'lăk, Told not I thee, saying, All
that the LORD speaketh, that I must do?
27 ¶ And Bā'lăk said unto Bā'lȧam,
Come, I pray thee, I will bring thee unto
another place; peradventure it will
please God that thou mayest curse me
them from thence.
28 And Bā'lăk brought Bā'lȧam unto
the top of Pē'ŏr, that looketh toward
Jē-shī'mŏn.
29 And Bā'lȧam said unto Bā'lăk, Build
me here seven altars, and prepare me
here seven bullocks and seven rams.
30 And Bā'lăk did as Bā'lȧam had said,
and offered a bullock and a ram on
every altar.

CHAPTER 24

AND when Bā'lȧam saw that it
pleased the LORD to bless Ĭş'rā-ēl,
he went not, as at other times, to seek
for enchantments, but he set his face
toward the wilderness.
2 And Bā'lȧam lifted up his eyes, and
he saw Ĭş'rā-ēl abiding *in his tents* according to their tribes; and the Spirit of
God came upon him.
3 And he took up his parable, and said,
Bā'lȧam the son of Bē'ŏr hath said, and
the man whose eyes are open hath said:
4 He hath said, *which* heard the words
of God, which saw the vision of the
Almighty, falling *into a trance*, but having his eyes open:
5 How goodly are thy tents, O Jacob,
and thy tabernacles, O Ĭş'rā-ēl!
6 As the valleys are they spread forth,
as gardens by the river's side, as the
trees of lignaloes which the LORD hath
planted, *and* as cedar trees beside the
waters.
7 He shall pour the water out of his
buckets, and his seed *shall be* in many
waters, and his king shall be higher
than Ā'găg, and his kingdom shall be
exalted.
8 God brought him forth out of Egypt;
he hath as it were the strength of a unicorn: he shall eat up the nations his enemies, and shall break their bones, and
pierce *them* through with his arrows.
9 He couched, he lay down as a lion,
and as a great lion: who shall stir him
up? Blessed *is* he that blesseth thee,
and cursed *is* he that curseth thee.
10 ¶ And Bā'lăk's anger was kindled
against Bā'lȧam, and he smote his hands
together: and Bā'lăk said unto Bā'lȧam,
I called thee to curse mine enemies,
and, behold, thou hast altogether blessed
them these three times.
11 Therefore now flee thou to thy place:
I thought to promote thee unto great
honor; but, lo, the LORD hath kept thee
back from honor.
12 And Bā'lȧam said unto Bā'lăk,
Spake I not also to thy messengers
which thou sentest unto me, saying,
13 If Bā'lăk would give me his house
full of silver and gold, I cannot go beyond the commandment of the LORD,
to do *either* good or bad of mine own
mind; *but* what the LORD saith, that will
I speak?
14 And now, behold, I go unto my people: come *therefore, and* I will advertise
thee what this people shall do to thy
people in the latter days.
15 ¶ And he took up his parable, and
said, Bā'lȧam the son of Bē'ŏr hath said,
and the man whose eyes are open hath
said:
16 He hath said, which heard the words
of God, and knew the knowledge of the
Most High, *which* saw the vision of the
Almighty, falling *into a trance*, but having his eyes open:
17 I shall see him, but not now: I shall
behold him, but not nigh: there shall
come a Star out of Jacob, and a Sceptre
shall rise out of Ĭş'rā-ēl, and shall smite
the corners of Mō'ăb, and destroy all
the children of Shĕth.
18 And Ē'dŏm shall be a possession,
Sē'ĭr also shall be a possession for his
enemies; and Ĭş'rā-ēl shall do valiantly.
19 Out of Jacob shall come he that
shall have dominion, and shall destroy
him that remaineth of the city.
20 ¶ And when he looked on Ăm'ȧ-lĕk,
he took up his parable, and said,
Ăm'ȧ-lĕk *was* the first of the nations;
but his latter end *shall be* that he perish
for ever.
21 And he looked on the Kē'nītes, and
took up his parable, and said, Strong is
thy dwelling place, and thou puttest thy
nest in a rock.
22 Nevertheless the Kē'nīte shall be

wasted, until Ăş'shŭr shall carry thee
away captive.
23 And he took up his parable, and
said, Alas, who shall live when God doeth this!
24 And ships *shall come* from the coast
of Chĭt'tĭm, and shall afflict Ăş'shŭr, and
shall afflict Ē'bĕr, and he also shall perish for ever.
25 And Bā'laam rose up, and went and
returned to his place: and Bā'lăk also
went his way.

CHAPTER 25

AND Īş'rā-ĕl abode in Shĭt'tĭm, and
the people began to commit whoredom with the daughters of Mō'ăb.
2 And they called the people unto the
sacrifices of their gods: and the people
did eat, and bowed down to their gods.
3 And Īs'rā-ĕl joined himself unto
Bā'āl–pē'ŏr: and the anger of the LORD
was kindled against Īş'rā-ĕl.
4 And the LORD said unto Moses, Take
all the heads of the people, and hang
them up before the LORD against the
sun, that the fierce anger of the LORD
may be turned away from Īş'rā-ĕl.
5 And Moses said unto the judges of
Īş'rā-ĕl, Slay ye every one his men that
were joined unto Bā'āl–pē'ŏr.
6 ¶ And, behold, one of the children
of Īş'rā-ĕl came and brought unto his
brethren a Mĭd'ĭ-ăn-ĭt'ĭsh woman in the
sight of Moses, and in the sight of all the
congregation of the children of Īs'rā-ĕl,
who *were* weeping *before* the door of the
tabernacle of the congregation.
7 And when Phĭn'ē-hăs, the son of
Ĕl'ē-ā'zar, the son of Aaron the priest,
saw *it,* he rose up from among the
congregation, and took a javelin in his
hand;
8 And he went after the man of Īş'rā-ĕl
into the tent, and thrust both of them
through, the man of Īş'rā-ĕl, and the
woman through her belly. So the plague
was stayed from the children of Īş'rā-ĕl.
9 And those that died in the plague
were twenty and four thousand.
10 ¶ And the LORD spake unto Moses,
saying,
11 Phĭn'ē-hăs, the son of Ĕl'ē-ā'zar,
the son of Aaron the priest, hath turned
my wrath away from the children of
Īş'rā-ĕl, while he was zealous for my
sake among them, that I consumed not
the children of Īş'rā-ĕl in my jealousy.
12 Wherefore say, Behold, I give unto
him my covenant of peace:
13 And he shall have it, and his seed
after him, *even* the covenant of an everlasting priesthood; because he was
zealous for his God, and made an atonement for the children of Īş'rā-ĕl.
14 Now the name of the Īş'rā-ĕl-īte
that was slain, *even* that was slain with
the Mĭd'ĭ-ăn-ĭt'ĭsh woman, *was* Zĭm'rī,
the son of Sā'lū, a prince of a chief
house among the Sĭm'ē-ŏn-ītes.
15 And the name of the Mĭd'ĭ-ăn-ĭt'ĭsh
woman that was slain *was* Cŏz'bī, the
daughter of Zûr: he *was* head over a
people, *and* of a chief house in Mĭd'ĭ-ăn.
16 ¶ And the LORD spake unto Moses,
saying,
17 Vex the Mĭd'ĭ-ăn-ītes, and smite
them:
18 For they vex you with their wiles,
wherewith they have beguiled you in the
matter of Pē'ŏr, and in the matter of
Cŏz'bī, the daughter of a prince of
Mĭd'ĭ-ăn, their sister, which was slain
in the day of the plague for Pē'ŏr's
sake.

CHAPTER 26

AND it came to pass after the plague,
that the LORD spake unto Moses
and unto Ĕl'ē-ā'zar the son of Aaron the
priest, saying,
2 Take the sum of all the congregation
of the children of Īş'rā-ĕl, from twenty
years old and upward, throughout their
fathers' house, all that are able to go to
war in Īş'rā-ĕl.
3 And Moses and Ĕl'ē-ā'zar the priest
spake with them in the plains of Mō'ăb
by Jordan *near* Jĕr'ĭ-chō, saying,
4 *Take the sum of the people,* from
twenty years old and upward; as the
LORD commanded Moses and the children of Īş'rā-ĕl, which went forth out of
the land of Egypt.
5 ¶ Reuben, the eldest son of Īş'rā-ĕl:
the children of Reuben; Hā'nŏch, *of
whom cometh* the family of the Hā'-
nŏch-ītes: of Păl'lū, the family of the
Păl'lū-ītes:
6 Of Hĕz'rŏn, the family of the Hĕz'-
rŏn-ītes: of Cär'mī, the family of the
Carmites.
7 These *are* the families of the Reubenites: and they that were numbered
of them were forty and three thousand
and seven hundred and thirty.

8 And the sons of Păl'lū; Ē-lī'ăb.
9 And the sons of Ē-lī'ăb; Nĕm'ū-ĕl,
and Dā'thăn, and Ȧ-bī'răm. This *is that*
Dā'thăn and Ȧ-bī'răm, *which were*
famous in the congregation, who strove
against Moses and against Aaron in the
company of Kō'rȧh, when they strove
against the LORD:
10 And the earth opened her mouth,
and swallowed them up together with
Kō'rȧh, when that company died, what
time the fire devoured two hundred and
fifty men: and they became a sign.
11 Notwithstanding the children of
Kō'rȧh died not.
12 ℂ The sons of Simeon after their
families: of Nĕm'ū-ĕl, the family of the
Nĕm'ū-ĕl-ītes: of Jā'mĭn, the family of
the Jā'mĭn-ītes: of Jā'chĭn, the family of
the Jā'chĭn-ītes:
13 Of Zē'rȧh, the family of the Zär'-
hītes: of Shā'ŭl, the family of the
Shā'ŭl-ītes.
14 These *are* the families of the Sĭm'ē-
ŏn-ītes, twenty and two thousand and
two hundred.
15 ℂ The children of Gad after their
families: of Zē'phŏn, the family of the
Zē'phŏn-ītes: of Hăg'gī, the family of the
Hăg'gītes: of Shụ'nī, the family of the
Shụ'nītes:
16 Of Ŏz'nī, the family of the Ŏz'nītes:
of Ē'rī, the family of the Ē'rītes:
17 Of Ā'rŏd, the family of the Ā'rŏd-
ītes: of Ȧ-rē'lī, the family of the Ȧ-rē'-
lītes.
18 These *are* the families of the children of Gad according to those that were
numbered of them, forty thousand and
five hundred.
19 ℂ The sons of Judah *were* Ĕr and
Ō'năn: and Ĕr and Ō'năn died in the
land of Cā'năan.
20 And the sons of Judah after their
families were; of Shē'lȧh, the family of
the Shē'lăn-ītes: of Phā'rĕz, the family
of the Phär'zītes: of Zē'rȧh, the family
of the Zär'hītes.
21 And the sons of Phā'rĕz were; of
Hĕz'rŏn, the family of the Hĕz'rŏn-ītes:
of Hā'mŭl, the family of the Hā'-
mŭl-ītes.
22 These *are* the families of Judah
according to those that were numbered
of them, threescore and sixteen thousand and five hundred.
23 ℂ *Of* the sons of Ĭs'sȧ-chär after
their families: *of* Tō'lȧ, the family of the
Tō'lȧ-ītes: of Pū'ȧ, the family of the
Pū'nītes:
24 Of Jā'shŭb, the family of the Jā'-
shŭb-ītes: of Shĭm'rŏn, the family of the
Shĭm'rŏn-ītes.
25 These *are* the families of Ĭs'sȧ-chär
according to those that were numbered
of them, threescore and four thousand
and three hundred.
26 ℂ *Of* the sons of Zĕb'ū-lŭn after
their families: of Sē'rĕd, the family of
the Sardites: of Ē'lŏn, the family of the
Ē'lŏn-ītes: of Jäh'lē-ĕl, the family of the
Jäh'lē-ĕl-ītes.
27 These *are* the families of the Zĕb'ū-
lŭn-ītes according to those that were
numbered of them, threescore thousand
and five hundred.
28 ℂ The sons of Joseph after their families *were* Mȧ-năs'sĕh and Ē'phrā-ĭm.
29 Of the sons of Mȧ-năs'sĕh: of
Mā'chĭr, the family of the Mā'chĭr-ītes:
and Mā'chĭr begat Gĭl'ē-ăd: of Gĭl'ē-ăd
come the family of the Gĭl'ē-ăd-ītes.
30 These *are* the sons of Gĭl'ē-ăd: *of*
Jē-ē'zĕr, the family of the Jē-ē'zĕr-ītes:
of Hē'lĕk, the family of the Hē'lĕk-ītes:
31 And *of* Ăs'rĭ-ĕl, the family of the
Ăs'rĭ-ĕl-ītes: and *of* Shē'chĕm, the family of the Shē'chĕm-ītes:
32 And *of* Shē-mī'dȧ, the family of the
Shē-mī'dȧ-ītes: and *of* Hē'phĕr, the
family of the Hē'phĕr-ītes.
33 ℂ And Zē-lŏ'phē-hăd the son of
Hē'phĕr had no sons, but daughters:
and the names of the daughters of Zē-
lŏ'phē-hăd *were* Mäh'lȧh, and Noah,
Hŏg'lȧh, Mĭl'cȧh, and Tĭr'zȧh.
34 These *are* the families of Mȧ-
năs'sĕh, and those that were numbered
of them, fifty and two thousand and
seven hundred.
35 ℂ These *are* the sons of Ē'phrā-ĭm
after their families: of Shụ-thē'lȧh, the
family of the Shụ-thăl'hītes: of Bē'chĕr,
the family of the Băch'rītes: of Tā'hăn,
the family of the Tā'hăn-ītes.
36 And these *are* the sons of Shụ-
thē'lȧh: of Ē'răn, the family of the
Ē'răn-ītes.
37 These *are* the families of the sons
of Ē-phrā'ĭm according to those that
were numbered of them, thirty and two
thousand and five hundred. These *are*
the sons of Joseph after their families.
38 ℂ The sons of Benjamin after their
families: of Bē'lȧ, the family of the Bē'-
lȧ-ītes: of Ăsh'bĕl, the family of the

Ăsh′bĕl-ītes: of Ȧ-hī′răm, the family of
the Ȧ-hī′răm-ītes:
39 Of Shu̟′phăm, the family of the Shu̟′-
phăm-ītes: of Hū′phăm, the family of
the Hū′phăm-ītes.
40 And the sons of Bē′lȧ were Ärd and
Nā′ȧ-măn: *of Ard,* the family of the
Är′dītes: *and* of Nā′ȧ-măn, the family of
the Nā′ȧ-mītes.
41 These *are* the sons of Benjamin after
their families: and they that were numbered of them *were* forty and five thousand and six hundred.
42 ¶ These *are* the sons of Dan after
their families: of Shu̟′hăm, the family of
the Shu̟′hăm-ītes. These *are* the families of Dan after their families.
43 All the families of the Shu̟′hăm-ītes,
according to those that were numbered
of them, *were* threescore and four thousand and four hundred.
44 ¶ *Of* the children of Ăsh′ẽr after
their families: of Jĭm′nȧ, the family of
the Jĭm′nītes: of Jĕs′ū-ī, the family of
the Jĕs′ū-ītes: of Bē-rī′ăh, the family of
the Bē-rī′ītes.
45 Of the sons of Bē-rī′ăh: of Hē′bẽr,
the family of the Hē′bẽr-ītes: of Măl′-
chĭ-ĕl, the family of the Măl′chĭ-ĕl-ītes.
46 And the name of the daughter of
Ăsh′ẽr *was* Sarah.
47 These *are* the families of the sons of
Ăsh′ẽr according to those that were
numbered of them; *who were* fifty and
three thousand and four hundred.
48 ¶ *Of* the sons of Năph′tȧ-lī after
their families: of Jăh′zē-ĕl, the family of
the Jăh′zē-ĕl-ītes: of Gū′nī, the family
of the Gū′nītes:
49 Of Jē′zẽr, the family of the Jē′zẽr-
ītes: of Shĭl′lĕm, the family of the
Shĭl′lĕm-ītes.
50 These *are* the families of Năph′tȧ-lī
according to their families: and they
that were numbered of them *were* forty
and five thousand and four hundred.
51 These *were* the numbered of the
children of Ĭs̱′rā-ĕl, six hundred thousand and a thousand seven hundred and
thirty.
52 ¶ And the LORD spake unto Moses,
saying,
53 Unto these the land shall be divided
for an inheritance according to the number of names.
54 To many thou shalt give the more
inheritance, and to few thou shalt give
the less inheritance: to every one shall
his inheritance be given according to
those that were numbered of him.
55 Notwithstanding the land shall be
divided by lot: according to the names of
the tribes of their fathers they shall
inherit.
56 According to the lot shall the possession thereof be divided between
many and few.
57 ¶ And these *are* they that were
numbered of the Lē′vītes after their
families: of Gẽr′shŏn, the family of the
Gẽr′shŏn-ītes: of Kō′hăth, the family of
the Kō′hăth-ītes: of Mē-rā′rī, the family
of the Mē-rā′rītes.
58 These *are* the families of the Lē′-
vītes: the family of the Lĭb′nītes, the
family of the Hē′brȯn-ītes, the family of
the Mäh′lītes, the family of the Mū′-
shītes, the family of the Kō′răth-ītes.
And Kō′hăth begat Ăm′răm.
59 And the name of Ăm′răm's wife *was*
Jŏch′ē-bĕd, the daughter of Levi, whom
her mother bare to Levi in Egypt: and
she bare unto Ăm′răm, Aaron and
Moses, and Miriam their sister.
60 And unto Aaron was born Nā′dăb
and Ȧ-bī′hū, Ĕl′ē-ā′zȧr and Ĭth′ȧ-mär.
61 And Nā′dăb and Ȧ-bī′hū died, when
they offered strange fire before the
LORD.
62 And those that were numbered of
them were twenty and three thousand,
all males from a month old and upward:
for they were not numbered among the
children of Ĭs̱′rā-ĕl, because there was
no inheritance given them among the
children of Ĭs̱′rā-ĕl.
63 ¶ These *are* they that were numbered by Moses and Ĕl′ē-ā′zȧr the priest,
who numbered the children of Ĭs̱′rā-ĕl
in the plains of Mō′ăb by Jordan *near*
Jĕr′ĭ-chō.
64 But among these there was not a
man of them whom Moses and Aaron
the priest numbered, when they numbered the children of Ĭs̱′rā-ĕl in the wilderness of Sī′naī.
65 For the LORD had said of them, They
shall surely die in the wilderness. And
there was not left a man of them, save
Caleb the son of Jē-phŭn′nĕh, and
Joshua the son of Nŭn.

CHAPTER 27

THEN came the daughters of Zē-lō′-
phē-hăd, the son of Hē′phẽr, the
son of Gĭl′ē-ăd, the son of Mā′chīr, the

son of Mȧ-năs′sĕh, of the families of
Mȧ-năs′sĕh the son of Joseph: and
these *are* the names of his daughters;
Māh′lȧh, Noah, and Hŏg′lȧh, and Mĭl′-
cȧh, and Tĭr′zȧh.
2 And they stood before Moses, and
before Ĕl′ē-ā′zȧr the priest, and before
the princes and all the congregation, *by*
the door of the tabernacle of the congregation, saying,
3 Our father died in the wilderness,
and he was not in the company of them
that gathered themselves together
against the LORD in the company of
Kō′rȧh; but died in his own sin, and had
no sons.
4 Why should the name of our father
be done away from among his family,
because he hath no son? Give unto us
therefore a possession among the brethren of our father.
5 And Moses brought their cause before the LORD.
6 ¶ And the LORD spake unto Moses,
saying,
7 The daughters of Zē-lō′phē-hăd
speak right: thou shalt surely give them
a possession of an inheritance among
their father's brethren; and thou shalt
cause the inheritance of their father to
pass unto them.
8 And thou shalt speak unto the children of Ĭs′rā-ĕl, saying, If a man die,
and have no son, then ye shall cause his
inheritance to pass unto his daughter.
9 And if he have no daughter, then ye
shall give his inheritance unto his
brethren.
10 And if he have no brethren, then ye
shall give his inheritance unto his
father's brethren.
11 And if his father have no brethren,
then ye shall give his inheritance unto
his kinsman that is next to him of his
family, and he shall possess it: and it
shall be unto the children of Ĭs′rā-ĕl a
statute of judgment, as the LORD commanded Moses.
12 ¶ And the LORD said unto Moses,
Get thee up into this mount Ăb′ȧ-rĭm,
and see the land which I have given
unto the children of Ĭs′rā-ĕl.
13 And when thou hast seen it, thou
also shalt be gathered unto thy people,
as Aaron thy brother was gathered.
14 For ye rebelled against my commandment in the desert of Zĭn, in the
strife of the congregation, to sanctify me
at the water before their eyes: that *is*
the water of Mĕr′ĭ-bāh in Kā′dĕsh in
the wilderness of Zĭn.
15 ¶ And Moses spake unto the LORD,
saying,
16 Let the LORD, the God of the spirits
of all flesh, set a man over the congregation,
17 Which may go out before them, and
which may go in before them, and which
may lead them out, and which may
bring them in; that the congregation of
the LORD be not as sheep which have
no shepherd.
18 ¶ And the LORD said unto Moses,
Take thee Joshua the son of Nŭn, a man
in whom *is* the spirit, and lay thine hand
upon him;
19 And set him before Ĕl′ē-ā′zȧr the
priest, and before all the congregation;
and give him a charge in their sight.
20 And thou shalt put *some* of thine
honor upon him, that all the congregation of the children of Ĭs′rā-ĕl may be
obedient.
21 And he shall stand before Ĕl′ē-ā′zȧr
the priest, who shall ask *counsel* for him
after the judgment of Ū′rĭm before the
LORD: at his word shall they go out, and
at his word they shall come in, *both* he,
and all the children of Ĭs′rā-ĕl with him,
even all the congregation.
22 And Moses did as the LORD commanded him: and he took Joshua, and
set him before Ĕl′ē-ā′zȧr the priest, and
before all the congregation:
23 And he laid his hands upon him, and
gave him a charge, as the LORD commanded by the hand of Moses.

CHAPTER 28

AND the LORD spake unto Moses,
saying,
2 Command the children of Ĭs′rā-ĕl,
and say unto them, My offering, *and*
my bread for my sacrifices made by
fire, *for* a sweet savor unto me, shall ye
observe to offer unto me in their due
season.
3 And thou shalt say unto them, This
is the offering made by fire which ye
shall offer unto the LORD; two lambs of
the first year without spot day by day,
for a continual burnt offering.
4 The one lamb shalt thou offer in the
morning, and the other lamb shalt thou
offer at even;
5 And a tenth *part* of an ē′phȧh of flour

for a meat offering, mingled with the
fourth *part* of a hin of beaten oil.
6 *It is* a continual burnt offering, which
was ordained in mount Sī'naī for a sweet
savor, a sacrifice made by fire unto the
LORD.
7 And the drink offering thereof *shall*
be the fourth *part* of a hin for the one
lamb: in the holy *place* shalt thou cause
the strong wine to be poured unto the
LORD *for* a drink offering.
8 And the other lamb shalt thou offer
at even: as the meat offering of the
morning, and as the drink offering thereof, thou shalt offer *it*, a sacrifice made by
fire, of a sweet savor unto the LORD.
9 ¶ And on the sabbath day two lambs
of the first year without spot, and two
tenth deals of flour *for* a meat offering,
mingled with oil, and the drink offering
thereof:
10 *This is* the burnt offering of every
sabbath, beside the continual burnt
offering, and his drink offering.
11 ¶ And in the beginnings of your
months ye shall offer a burnt offering
unto the LORD; two young bullocks, and
one ram, seven lambs of the first year
without spot;
12 And three tenth deals of flour *for* a
meat offering, mingled with oil, for one
bullock; and two tenth deals of flour *for*
a meat offering, mingled with oil, for one
ram;
13 And a several tenth deal of flour
mingled with oil *for* a meat offering
unto one lamb; *for* a burnt offering of a
sweet savor, a sacrifice made by fire
unto the LORD.
14 And their drink offerings shall be
half a hin of wine unto a bullock, and
the third *part* of a hin unto a ram, and a
fourth *part* of a hin unto a lamb: this *is*
the burnt offering of every month
throughout the months of the year.
15 And one kid of the goats for a sin
offering unto the LORD shall be offered,
beside the continual burnt offering, and
his drink offering.
16 And in the fourteenth day of the
first month *is* the passover of the LORD.
17 And in the fifteenth day of this
month *is* the feast: seven days shall unleavened bread be eaten.
18 In the first day *shall be* a holy convocation; ye shall do no manner of servile work *therein:*
19 But ye shall offer a sacrifice made
by fire *for* a burnt offering unto the
LORD; two young bullocks, and one ram,
and seven lambs of the first year: they
shall be unto you without blemish.
20 And their meat offering *shall be of*
flour mingled with oil: three tenth deals
shall ye offer for a bullock, and two
tenth deals for a ram;
21 A several tenth deal shalt thou offer
for every lamb, throughout the seven
lambs:
22 And one goat *for* a sin offering, to
make an atonement for you.
23 Ye shall offer these beside the burnt
offering in the morning, which *is* for a
continual burnt offering.
24 After this manner ye shall offer
daily, throughout the seven days, the
meat of the sacrifice made by fire, of a
sweet savor unto the LORD: it shall be
offered beside the continual burnt offering, and his drink offering.
25 And on the seventh day ye shall
have a holy convocation; ye shall do no
servile work.
26 ¶ Also in the day of the firstfruits,
when ye bring a new meat offering unto
the LORD, after your weeks *be out*, ye
shall have a holy convocation; ye shall
do no servile work:
27 But ye shall offer the burnt offering
for a sweet savor unto the LORD; two
young bullocks, one ram, seven lambs
of the first year;
28 And their meat offering of flour
mingled with oil, three tenth deals unto
one bullock, two tenth deals unto one
ram,
29 A several tenth deal unto one lamb,
throughout the seven lambs;
30 *And* one kid of the goats, to make
an atonement for you.
31 Ye shall offer *them* beside the continual burnt offering, and his meat offering, (they shall be unto you without
blemish,) and their drink offerings.

CHAPTER 29

AND in the seventh month, on the first
day of the month, ye shall have a
holy convocation; ye shall do no servile
work: it is a day of blowing trumpets
unto you.
2 And ye shall offer a burnt offering for
a sweet savor unto the LORD; one young
bullock, one ram, *and* seven lambs of the
first year without blemish:
3 And their meat offering *shall be of*

flour mingled with oil, three tenth deals
for a bullock, *and* two tenth deals for a
ram,
4 And one tenth deal for one lamb,
throughout the seven lambs:
5 And one kid of the goats *for* a sin
offering, to make an atonement for you:
6 Beside the burnt offering of the
month, and his meat offering, and the
daily burnt offering, and his meat offering, and their drink offerings, according
unto their manner, for a sweet savor, a
sacrifice made by fire unto the LORD.
7 ¶ And ye shall have on the tenth *day*
of this seventh month a holy convocation; and ye shall afflict your souls: ye
shall not do any work *therein:*
8 But ye shall offer a burnt offering
unto the LORD *for* a sweet savor; one
young bullock, one ram, *and* seven
lambs of the first year; they shall be
unto you without blemish.
9 And their meat offering *shall be of*
flour mingled with oil, three tenth deals
to a bullock, *and* two tenth deals to one
ram,
10 A several tenth deal for one lamb,
throughout the seven lambs:
11 One kid of the goats *for* a sin offering; beside the sin offering of atonement, and the continual burnt offering,
and the meat offering of it, and their
drink offerings.
12 ¶ And on the fifteenth day of the
seventh month ye shall have a holy convocation; ye shall do no servile work,
and ye shall keep a feast unto the LORD
seven days:
13 And ye shall offer a burnt offering, a
sacrifice made by fire, of a sweet savor
unto the LORD; thirteen young bullocks,
two rams, *and* fourteen lambs of the
first year; they shall be without blemish:
14 And their meat offering *shall be of*
flour mingled with oil, three tenth deals
unto every bullock of the thirteen bullocks, two tenth deals to each ram of the
two rams,
15 And a several tenth deal to each
lamb of the fourteen lambs:
16 And one kid of the goats *for* a sin
offering; beside the continual burnt
offering, his meat offering, and his drink
offering.
17 ¶ And on the second day *ye shall*
offer twelve young bullocks, two rams,
fourteen lambs of the first year without
spot:
18 And their meat offering and their
drink offerings for the bullocks, for the
rams, and for the lambs, *shall be* according to their number, after the manner:
19 And one kid of the goats *for* a sin
offering; beside the continual burnt
offering, and the meat offering thereof,
and their drink offerings.
20 ¶ And on the third day eleven bullocks, two rams, fourteen lambs of the
first year without blemish:
21 And their meat offering and their
drink offerings for the bullocks, for the
rams, and for the lambs, *shall be* according to their number, after the
manner:
22 And one goat *for* a sin offering; beside the continual burnt offering, and his
meat offering, and his drink offering.
23 ¶ And on the fourth day ten bullocks, two rams, *and* fourteen lambs of
the first year without blemish:
24 Their meat offering and their drink
offerings for the bullocks, for the rams,
and for the lambs, *shall be* according to
their number, after the manner:
25 And one kid of the goats *for* a sin
offering; beside the continual burnt
offering, his meat offering, and his drink
offering.
26 ¶ And on the fifth day nine bullocks, two rams, *and* fourteen lambs of
the first year without spot:
27 And their meat offering and their
drink offerings for the bullocks, for the
rams, and for the lambs, *shall be* according to their number, after the manner:
28 And one goat *for* a sin offering; beside the continual burnt offering, and
his meat offering, and his drink offering.
29 ¶ And on the sixth day eight bullocks, two rams, *and* fourteen lambs of
the first year without blemish:
30 And their meat offering and their
drink offerings for the bullocks, for the
rams, and for the lambs, *shall be* according to their number, after the
manner:
31 And one goat *for* a sin offering; beside the continual burnt offering, his
meat offering, and his drink offering.
32 ¶ And on the seventh day seven
bullocks, two rams, *and* fourteen lambs
of the first year without blemish:
33 And their meat offering and their
drink offerings for the bullocks, for the
rams, and for the lambs, *shall be* according to their number, after the manner:

34 And one goat *for* a sin offering; beside the continual burnt offering, his
meat offering, and his drink offering.
35 ¶ On the eighth day ye shall have
a solemn assembly: ye shall do no servile work *therein:*
36 But ye shall offer a burnt offering, a
sacrifice made by fire, of a sweet savor
unto the LORD: one bullock, one ram,
seven lambs of the first year without
blemish:
37 Their meat offering and their drink
offerings for the bullock, for the ram,
and for the lambs, *shall be* according to
their number, after the manner:
38 And one goat *for* a sin offering; beside the continual burnt offering, and
his meat offering, and his drink offering.
39 These *things* ye shall do unto the
LORD in your set feasts, beside your
vows, and your freewill offerings, for
your burnt offerings, and for your meat
offerings, and for your drink offerings,
and for your peace offerings.
40 And Moses told the children of
Ĭs′rā-ĕl according to all that the LORD
commanded Moses.

CHAPTER 30

AND Moses spake unto the heads of
the tribes concerning the children
of Ĭs′rā-ĕl, saying, This *is* the thing
which the LORD hath commanded.
2 If a man vow a vow unto the LORD,
or swear an oath to bind his soul with a
bond; he shall not break his word, he
shall do according to all that proceedeth
out of his mouth.
3 If a woman also vow a vow unto the
LORD, and bind *herself* by a bond, *being*
in her father's house in her youth;
4 And her father hear her vow, and her
bond wherewith she hath bound her
soul, and her father shall hold his peace
at her; then all her vows shall stand, and
every bond wherewith she hath bound
her soul shall stand.
5 But if her father disallow her in the
day that he heareth, not any of her vows,
or of her bonds wherewith she hath
bound her soul, shall stand; and the
LORD shall forgive her, because her
father disallowed her.
6 And if she had at all a husband, when
she vowed, or uttered aught out of her
lips, wherewith she bound her soul;
7 And her husband heard *it,* and held
his peace at her in the day that he heard
it: then her vows shall stand, and her
bonds wherewith she bound her soul
shall stand.
8 But if her husband disallowed her on
the day that he heard *it,* then he shall
make her vow which she vowed, and
that which she uttered with her lips,
wherewith she bound her soul, of none
effect; and the LORD shall forgive her.
9 But every vow of a widow, and of her
that is divorced, wherewith they have
bound their souls, shall stand against
her.
10 And if she vowed in her husband's
house, or bound her soul by a bond with
an oath;
11 And her husband heard *it,* and held
his peace at her, *and* disallowed her not:
then all her vows shall stand, and every
bond wherewith she bound her soul
shall stand.
12 But if her husband hath utterly
made them void on the day he heard
them; then whatsoever proceeded out
of her lips concerning her vows, or concerning the bond of her soul, shall not
stand: her husband hath made them
void; and the LORD shall forgive her.
13 Every vow, and every binding oath
to afflict the soul, her husband may establish it, or her husband may make it
void.
14 But if her husband altogether hold
his peace at her from day to day; then
he establisheth all her vows, or all her
bonds, which *are* upon her: he confirmeth them, because he held his peace
at her in the day that he heard *them.*
15 But if he shall any ways make them
void after that he hath heard *them;* then
he shall bear her iniquity.
16 These *are* the statutes, which the
LORD commanded Moses, between a
man and his wife, between the father
and his daughter, *being yet* in her youth
in her father's house.

CHAPTER 31

AND the LORD spake unto Moses,
saying,
2 Avenge the children of Ĭs′rā-ĕl of the
Mĭd′ĭ-ăn-ītes: afterward shalt thou be
gathered unto thy people.
3 And Moses spake unto the people,
saying, Arm some of yourselves unto
the war, and let them go against the
Mĭd′ĭ-ăn-ītes, and avenge the LORD
of Mĭd′ĭ-ăn.

4 Of every tribe a thousand, throughout all the tribes of Ĭs̱′rā-ĕl, shall ye send to the war.

5 So there were delivered out of the thousands of Ĭs̱′rā-ĕl, a thousand of *every* tribe, twelve thousand armed for war.

6 And Moses sent them to the war, a thousand of *every* tribe, them and Phĭn′ē-hăs the son of Ĕl′ē-ā′zȧr the priest, to the war, with the holy instruments, and the trumpets to blow in his hand.

7 And they warred against the Mĭd′ĭ-ăn-ītes, as the LORD commanded Moses; and they slew all the males.

8 And they slew the kings of Mĭd′ĭ-ăn, beside the rest of them that were slain; *namely,* Ē′vī, and Rē′kĕm, and Zûr, and Hûr, and Rē′bȧ, five kings of Mĭd′ĭ-ăn: Bā′lȧam also the son of Bē′ŏr they slew with the sword.

9 And the children of Ĭs̱′rā-ĕl took *all* the women of Mĭd′ĭ-ăn captives, and their little ones, and took the spoil of all their cattle, and all their flocks, and all their goods.

10 And they burnt all their cities wherein they dwelt, and all their goodly castles, with fire.

11 And they took all the spoil, and all the prey, *both* of men and of beasts.

12 And they brought the captives, and the prey, and the spoil, unto Moses and Ĕl′ē-ā′zȧr the priest, and unto the congregation of the children of Ĭs̱′rā-ĕl, unto the camp at the plains of Mō′ăb, which *are* by Jordan *near* Jĕr′ĭ-chō.

13 ¶ And Moses, and Ĕl′ē-ā′zȧr the priest, and all the princes of the congregation, went forth to meet them without the camp.

14 And Moses was wroth with the officers of the host, *with* the captains over thousands, and captains over hundreds, which came from the battle.

15 And Moses said unto them, Have ye saved all the women alive?

16 Behold, these caused the children of Ĭs̱′rā-ĕl, through the counsel of Bā′lȧam, to commit trespass against the LORD in the matter of Pē′ŏr, and there was a plague among the congregation of the LORD.

17 Now therefore kill every male among the little ones, and kill every woman that hath known man by lying with him.

18 But all the women children, that have not known a man by lying with him, keep alive for yourselves.

19 And do ye abide without the camp seven days: whosoever hath killed any person, and whosoever hath touched any slain, purify *both* yourselves and your captives on the third day, and on the seventh day.

20 And purify all *your* raiment, and all that is made of skins, and all work of goats' *hair,* and all things made of wood.

21 ¶ And Ĕl′ē-ā′zȧr the priest said unto the men of war which went to the battle, This *is* the ordinance of the law which the LORD commanded Moses;

22 Only the gold, and the silver, the brass, the iron, the tin, and the lead,

23 Every thing that may abide the fire, ye shall make *it* go through the fire, and it shall be clean: nevertheless it shall be purified with the water of separation: and all that abideth not the fire ye shall make go through the water.

24 And ye shall wash your clothes on the seventh day, and ye shall be clean, and afterward ye shall come into the camp.

25 ¶ And the LORD spake unto Moses, saying,

26 Take the sum of the prey that was taken, *both* of man and of beast, thou, and Ĕl′ē-ā′zȧr the priest, and the chief fathers of the congregation:

27 And divide the prey into two parts; between them that took the war upon them, who went out to battle, and between all the congregation.

28 And levy a tribute unto the LORD of the men of war which went out to battle: one soul of five hundred, *both* of the persons, and of the beeves, and of the asses, and of the sheep:

29 Take *it* of their half, and give *it* unto Ĕl′ē-ā′zȧr the priest, *for* a heave offering of the LORD.

30 And of the children of Ĭs̱′rā-ĕl's half, thou shalt take one portion of fifty, of the persons, of the beeves, of the asses, and of the flocks, of all manner of beasts, and give them unto the Lē′vītes, which keep the charge of the tabernacle of the LORD.

31 And Moses and Ĕl′ē-ā′zȧr the priest did as the LORD commanded Moses.

32 And the booty, *being* the rest of the prey which the men of war had caught,

was six hundred thousand and seventy
thousand and five thousand sheep,
33 And threescore and twelve thousand beeves,
34 And threescore and one thousand
asses,
35 And thirty and two thousand persons in all, of women that had not known
man by lying with him.
36 And the half, *which was* the portion
of them that went out to war, was in
number three hundred thousand and
seven and thirty thousand and five hundred sheep:
37 And the LORD's tribute of the sheep
was six hundred and threescore and
fifteen.
38 And the beeves *were* thirty and six
thousand; of which the LORD's tribute
was threescore and twelve.
39 And the asses *were* thirty thousand
and five hundred; of which the LORD's
tribute *was* threescore and one.
40 And the persons *were* sixteen thousand; of which the LORD's tribute *was*
thirty and two persons.
41 And Moses gave the tribute, *which
was* the LORD's heave offering, unto
Ĕl′ē-ā′zȧr the priest, as the LORD commanded Moses.
42 And of the children of Ĭş′rā-ĕl's half,
which Moses divided from the men that
warred,
43 (Now the half *that pertained unto*
the congregation was three hundred
thousand and thirty thousand *and* seven
thousand and five hundred sheep,
44 And thirty and six thousand beeves,
45 And thirty thousand asses and five
hundred,
46 And sixteen thousand persons,)
47 Even of the children of Ĭş′rā-ĕl's
half, Moses took one portion of fifty,
both of man and of beast, and gave them
unto the Lē′vītes, which kept the charge
of the tabernacle of the LORD; as the
LORD commanded Moses.
48 ¶ And the officers which *were* over
thousands of the host, the captains of
thousands, and captains of hundreds,
came near unto Moses:
49 And they said unto Moses, Thy servants have taken the sum of the men of
war which *are* under our charge, and
there lacketh not one man of us.
50 We have therefore brought an oblation for the LORD, what every man hath
gotten, of jewels of gold, chains, and
bracelets, rings, earrings, and tablets,
to make an atonement for our souls before the LORD.
51 And Moses and Ĕl′ē-ā′zȧr the priest
took the gold of them, *even* all wrought
jewels.
52 And all the gold of the offering that
they offered up to the LORD, of the captains of thousands, and of the captains
of hundreds, was sixteen thousand
seven hundred and fifty shekels.
53 (*For* the men of war had taken spoil,
every man for himself.)
54 And Moses and Ĕl′ē-ā′zȧr the priest
took the gold of the captains of thousands and of hundreds, and brought it
into the tabernacle of the congregation,
for a memorial for the children of Ĭş′rā-ĕl before the LORD.

CHAPTER 32

NOW the children of Reuben and the
children of Gad had a very great
multitude of cattle: and when they saw
the land of Jā′zĕr, and the land of
Gĭl′ē-ăd, that, behold, the place *was* a
place for cattle;
2 The children of Gad and the children of Reuben came and spake unto
Moses, and to Ĕl′ē-ā′zȧr the priest, and
unto the princes of the congregation,
saying,
3 Ăt′ȧ-rŏth, and Dī′bŏn, and Jā′zĕr,
and Nĭm′rȧh, and Hĕsh′bŏn, and Ĕl′ē-ā′lĕh, and Shē′băm, and Nē′bō, and
Bē′ŏn,
4 *Even* the country which the LORD
smote before the congregation of Ĭş′rā-ĕl, *is* a land for cattle, and thy servants have cattle:
5 Wherefore, said they, if we have
found grace in thy sight, let this land be
given unto thy servants for a possession,
and bring us not over Jordan.
6 ¶ And Moses said unto the children
of Gad and to the children of Reuben,
Shall your brethren go to war, and shall
ye sit here?
7 And wherefore discourage ye the
heart of the children of Ĭş′rā-ĕl from going over into the land which the LORD
hath given them?
8 Thus did your fathers, when I sent
them from Kā′dĕsh-bär′nē-ȧ to see the
land.
9 For when they went up unto the valley of Ĕsh′cŏl, and saw the land, they
discouraged the heart of the children of

Iș'rā-ĕl, that they should not go into the
land which the LORD had given them.
10 And the LORD's anger was kindled
the same time, and he sware, saying,
11 Surely none of the men that came
up out of Egypt, from twenty years old
and upward, shall see the land which I
sware unto Abraham, unto Isaac, and
unto Jacob; because they have not
wholly followed me:
12 Save Caleb the son of Jē-phŭn'nĕh
the Kē'nĕz-īte, and Joshua the son of
Nŭn; for they have wholly followed the
LORD.
13 And the LORD's anger was kindled
against Iș'rā-ĕl, and he made them wander in the wilderness forty years, until
all the generation, that had done evil in
the sight of the LORD, was consumed.
14 And, behold, ye are risen up in your
fathers' stead, an increase of sinful
men, to augment yet the fierce anger of
the LORD toward Iș'rā-ĕl.
15 For if ye turn away from after him,
he will yet again leave them in the wilderness; and ye shall destroy all this
people.
16 ¶ And they came near unto him,
and said, We will build sheepfolds here
for our cattle, and cities for our little
ones:
17 But we ourselves will go ready
armed before the children of Iș'rā-ĕl,
until we have brought them unto their
place: and our little ones shall dwell in
the fenced cities, because of the inhabitants of the land.
18 We will not return unto our houses,
until the children of Iș'rā-ĕl have inherited every man his inheritance:
19 For we will not inherit with them on
yonder side Jordan, or forward; because
our inheritance is fallen to us on this
side Jordan eastward.
20 ¶ And Moses said unto them, If ye
will do this thing, if ye will go armed before the LORD to war,
21 And will go all of you armed over
Jordan before the LORD, until he hath
driven out his enemies from before him,
22 And the land be subdued before the
LORD: then afterward ye shall return,
and be guiltless before the LORD, and
before Iș'rā-ĕl; and this land shall be
your possession before the LORD.
23 But if ye will not do so, behold, ye
have sinned against the LORD: and be
sure your sin will find you out.
24 Build you cities for your little ones,
and folds for your sheep; and do that
which hath proceeded out of your mouth.
25 And the children of Gad and the
children of Reuben spake unto Moses,
saying, Thy servants will do as my lord
commandeth.
26 Our little ones, our wives, our
flocks, and all our cattle, shall be there
in the cities of Gĭl'ē-ăd:
27 But thy servants will pass over,
every man armed for war, before the
LORD to battle, as my lord saith.
28 So concerning them Moses commanded Ĕl'ē-ā'zär the priest, and
Joshua the son of Nŭn, and the chief
fathers of the tribes of the children of
Iș'rā-ĕl:
29 And Moses said unto them, If the
children of Gad and the children of Reuben will pass with you over Jordan,
every man armed to battle, before the
LORD, and the land shall be subdued
before you; then ye shall give them the
land of Gĭl'ē-ăd for a possession:
30 But if they will not pass over with
you armed, they shall have possessions
among you in the land of Cā'năan.
31 And the children of Gad and the
children of Reuben answered, saying,
As the LORD hath said unto thy servants, so will we do.
32 We will pass over armed before the
LORD into the land of Cā'năan, that the
possession of our inheritance on this
side Jordan *may be* ours.
33 And Moses gave unto them, *even*
to the children of Gad, and to the children of Reuben, and unto half the tribe
of Mȧ-năs'sĕh the son of Joseph, the
kingdom of Sī'hŏn king of the Ăm'ō-
rītes, and the kingdom of Og king of
Bā'shăn, the land, with the cities thereof in the coasts, *even* the cities of the
country round about.
34 ¶ And the children of Gad built
Dī'bŏn, and Ăt'ȧ-rŏth, and Ȧ-rō'ēr,
35 And Ăt'rŏth, Shō'phăn, and Jā'ȧ-
zēr, and Jŏg-bē'hăh,
36 And Bĕth'-nĭm'rȧh, and Bĕth'-hā'-
răn, fenced cities; and folds for sheep.
37 And the children of Reuben built
Hĕsh'bŏn, and El'ē-ā'lĕh, and Kir'ja-
thā'im,
38 And Nē'bō, and Bā'ăl-mē'ŏn, (their
names being changed,) and Shĭb'mȧh:
and gave other names unto the cities
which they builded.

39 And the children of Mā′chĭr the son
of Mȧ-năs′sĕh went to Gĭl′ē-ăd, and
took it, and dispossessed the Ăm′ō-rīte
which *was* in it.
40 And Moses gave Gĭl′ē-ăd unto Mā′-
chĭr the son of Mȧ-năs′sĕh; and he
dwelt therein.
41 And Jā′ĭr the son of Mȧ-năs′sĕh
went and took the small towns thereof,
and called them Hā′vŏth-jā′ĭr.
42 And Nō′bȧh went and took Kē′nȧth,
and the villages thereof, and called it
Nō′bȧh, after his own name.

CHAPTER 33

THESE *are* the journeys of the children of Ĭs′rā-ĕl, which went forth
out of the land of Egypt with their
armies under the hand of Moses and
Aaron.
2 And Moses wrote their goings out
according to their journeys by the commandment of the LORD: and these *are*
their journeys according to their goings
out.
3 And they departed from Răm′ē-sēs
in the first month, on the fifteenth day
of the first month; on the morrow after
the passover the children of Ĭs′rā-ĕl
went out with a high hand in the sight
of all the Egyptians.
4 For the Egyptians buried all *their*
firstborn, which the LORD had smitten
among them: upon their gods also the
LORD executed judgments.
5 And the children of Ĭs′rā-ĕl removed
from Răm′ē-sēs, and pitched in Sŭc′-
cŏth.
6 And they departed from Sŭc′cŏth,
and pitched in Ē′thăm, which *is* in the
edge of the wilderness.
7 And they removed from Ē′thăm, and
turned again unto Pī′–hȧ-hī′rŏth, which
is before Bā′ăl–zē′phŏn: and they
pitched before Mĭg′dŏl.
8 And they departed from before Pī′–
hȧ-hī′rŏth, and passed through the midst
of the sea into the wilderness, and went
three days' journey in the wilderness of
Ē′thăm, and pitched in Mā′rȧh.
9 And they removed from Mā′rȧh, and
came unto Ē′lĭm: and in Ē′lĭm *were*
twelve fountains of water, and threescore and ten palm trees; and they
pitched there.
10 And they removed from Ē′lĭm, and
encamped by the Red sea.
11 And they removed from the Red
sea, and encamped in the wilderness of
Sin.
12 And they took their journey out of
the wilderness of Sin, and encamped in
Dŏph′kȧh.
13 And they departed from Dŏph′kȧh,
and encamped in Ā′lŭsh.
14 And they removed from Ā′lŭsh, and
encamped at Rĕph′ĭ-dĭm, where was no
water for the people to drink.
15 And they departed from Rĕph′ĭ-dĭm,
and pitched in the wilderness of Sī′naī.
16 And they removed from the desert
of Sī′naī, and pitched at Kĭb′rŏth–hȧt-
tā′ȧ-vȧh.
17 And they departed from Kĭb′rŏth–
hȧt-tā′ȧ-vȧh, and encamped at Hȧ-
zē′rŏth.
18 And they departed from Hȧ-zē′-
rŏth, and pitched in Rĭth′mȧh.
19 And they departed from Rĭth′mȧh,
and pitched at Rĭm′mŏn–pā′rĕz.
20 And they departed from Rĭm′mŏn–
pā′rĕz, and pitched in Lĭb′nȧh.
21 And they removed from Lĭb′nȧh,
and pitched at Rĭs′sȧh.
22 And they journeyed from Rĭs′sȧh,
and pitched in Kē′hē-lā′thȧh.
23 And they went from Kē′hē-lā′thȧh,
and pitched in mount Shā′phĕr.
24 And they removed from mount
Shā′phĕr, and encamped in Hȧ-rā′dȧh.
25 And they removed from Hȧ-rā′dȧh,
and pitched in Măk-hē′lŏth.
26 And they removed from Măk-hē′-
lŏth, and encamped at Tā′hăth.
27 And they departed from Tā′hăth,
and pitched at Tā′rȧh.
28 And they removed from Tā′rȧh, and
pitched in Mĭth′cȧh.
29 And they went from Mĭth′cȧh, and
pitched in Hăsh-mō′nȧh.
30 And they departed from Hăsh-
mō′nȧh, and encamped at Mō-sē′rŏth.
31 And they departed from Mō-sē′rŏth,
and pitched in Bē′nē–jā′ȧ-kăn.
32 And they removed from Bē′nē–
jā′ȧ-kăn, and encamped at Hôr′–hȧ-
gĭd′găd.
33 And they went from Hôr′–hȧ-gĭd′-
găd, and pitched in Jŏt′bȧ-thȧh.
34 And they removed from Jŏt′bȧ-
thȧh, and encamped at Ē-brō′nȧh.
35 And they departed from Ē-brō′nȧh,
and encamped at Ē′zĭ-ŏn–gā′bĕr.
36 And they removed from Ē′zĭ-ŏn–
gā′bĕr, and pitched in the wilderness of
Zĭn, which *is* Kā′dĕsh.

37 And they removed from Kā′děsh,
and pitched in mount Hôr, in the edge of
the land of Ē′dŏm.
38 And Aaron the priest went up into
mount Hôr at the commandment of the
LORD, and died there, in the fortieth
year after the children of Ĭş′rā-ĕl were
come out of the land of Egypt, in the
first *day* of the fifth month.
39 And Aaron *was* a hundred and
twenty and three years old when he died
in mount Hôr.
40 And king Ā′răd the Cā′năan-īte,
which dwelt in the south in the land of
Cā′năan, heard of the coming of the
children of Ĭş′rā-ĕl.
41 And they departed from mount
Hôr, and pitched in Zăl-mō′nȧh.
42 And they departed from Zăl-mō′nȧh,
and pitched in Pū′nŏn.
43 And they departed from Pū′nŏn,
and pitched in Ō′bŏth.
44 And they departed from Ō′bŏth, and
pitched in Ī′jē–ăb′ȧ-rĭm, in the border
of Mō′ăb.
45 And they departed from Ī′ĭm, and
pitched in Dī′bŏn–găd′.
46 And they removed from Dī′bŏn–
găd′, and encamped in Ăl′mŏn–dĭb′lȧ-
thā′ĭm.
47 And they removed from Ăl′mŏn–
dĭb′lȧ-thā′ĭm, and pitched in the mountains of Ăb′ȧ-rĭm, before Nē′bō.
48 And they departed from the mountains of Ăb′ȧ-rĭm, and pitched in the
plains of Mō′ăb by Jordan *near*
Jĕr′ĭ-chō.
49 And they pitched by Jordan, from
Bĕth′–jĕs′ĭ-mŏth *even* unto Ā′bĕl–shĭt′-
tĭm in the plains of Mō′ăb.
50 ¶ And the LORD spake unto Moses
in the plains of Mō′ăb by Jordan *near*
Jĕr′ĭ-chō, saying,
51 Speak unto the children of Ĭş′rā-ĕl,
and say unto them, When ye are passed
over Jordan into the land of Cā′năan;
52 Then ye shall drive out all the inhabitants of the land from before you,
and destroy all their pictures, and destroy all their molten images, and quite
pluck down all their high places:
53 And ye shall dispossess *the inhabitants of* the land, and dwell therein:
for I have given you the land to possess it.
54 And ye shall divide the land by lot
for an inheritance among your families;
and to the more ye shall give the more
inheritance, and to the fewer ye shall
give the less inheritance: every man's
inheritance shall be in the place where
his lot falleth; according to the tribes of
your fathers ye shall inherit.
55 But if ye will not drive out the inhabitants of the land from before you;
then it shall come to pass, that those
which ye let remain of them *shall be*
pricks in your eyes, and thorns in your
sides, and shall vex you in the land
wherein ye dwell.
56 Moreover it shall come to pass, *that*
I shall do unto you, as I thought to do
unto them.

CHAPTER 34

AND the LORD spake unto Moses,
saying,
2 Command the children of Ĭş′rā-ĕl,
and say unto them, When ye come into
the land of Cā′năan; (this *is* the land
that shall fall unto you for an inheritance, *even* the land of Cā′năan with the
coasts thereof:)
3 Then your south quarter shall be
from the wilderness of Zĭn along by the
coast of Ē′dŏm, and your south border
shall be the outmost coast of the salt sea
eastward:
4 And your border shall turn from the
south to the ascent of Ăk-răb′bĭm, and
pass on to Zĭn: and the going forth thereof shall be from the south to Kā′děsh-
bär′nē-ȧ, and shall go on to Hā′zär–
ăd′där, and pass on to Ăz′mŏn:
5 And the border shall fetch a compass
from Ăz′mŏn unto the river of Egypt,
and the goings out of it shall be at the
sea.
6 And *as for* the western border, ye
shall even have the great sea for a border: this shall be your west border.
7 And this shall be your north border:
from the great sea ye shall point out for
you mount Hôr:
8 From mount Hôr ye shall point out
your border unto the entrance of Hā′-
măth; and the goings forth of the border
shall be to Zē′dăd:
9 ¶ And the border shall go on to
Zĭph′rŏn, and the goings out of it shall
be at Hā′zär–ē′năn: this shall be your
north border.
10 And ye shall point out your east
border from Hā′zär–ē′năn to Shē′phăm:
11 And the coast shall go down from
Shē′phăm to Rĭb′lȧh, on the east side of

Ā'ĭn; and the border shall descend, and
shall reach unto the side of the sea of
Chĭn'nē-rĕth eastward:
12 And the border shall go down to
Jordan, and the goings out of it shall be
at the salt sea: this shall be your land
with the coasts thereof round about.
13 And Moses commanded the chil-
dren of Ĭș'rā-ĕl, saying, This *is* the land
which ye shall inherit by lot, which the
LORD commanded to give unto the nine
tribes, and to the half tribe:
14 For the tribe of the children of Reuben according to the house of their
fathers, and the tribe of the children of
Gad according to the house of their
fathers, have received *their inheritance;*
and half the tribe of Mȧ-năs'sĕh have
received their inheritance:
15 The two tribes and the half tribe
have received their inheritance on this
side Jordan *near* Jĕr'ĭ-chō eastward,
toward the sunrising.
16 And the LORD spake unto Moses,
saying,
17 These *are* the names of the men
which shall divide the land unto you:
Ĕl'ē-ā'zȧr the priest, and Joshua the
son of Nŭn.
18 And ye shall take one prince of every
tribe, to divide the land by inheritance.
19 And the names of the men *are* these:
Of the tribe of Judah, Caleb the son of
Jē-phŭn'nĕh.
20 And of the tribe of the children of
Simeon, Shē-mū'ĕl the son of Ăm-
mī'hŭd.
21 Of the tribe of Benjamin, Ē-lī'dăd
the son of Chĭs'lŏn.
22 And the prince of the tribe of the
children of Dan, Bŭk'kī the son of
Jŏg'lī.
23 The prince of the children of Joseph,
for the tribe of the children of Mȧ-
năs'sĕh, Hăn'nĭ-ĕl the son of Ē'phŏd.
24 And the prince of the tribe of the
children of Ē'phrā-ĭm, Kĕm'ū-ĕl the
son of Shĭph'tăn.
25 And the prince of the tribe of the
children of Zĕb'ū-lŭn, Ĕ'lĭ-zā'phăn the
son of Pär'năch.
26 And the prince of the tribe of the
children of Ĭs'sȧ-chär, Păl'tĭ-ĕl the son
of Ăz'zăn.
27 And the prince of the tribe of the
children of Ăsh'ēr, Ȧ-hī'hŭd the son of
Shē-lō'mī.
28 And the prince of the tribe of the
children of Năph'tȧ-lī, Pĕd'ȧ-hĕl the
son of Ȧm-mī'hŭd.
29 These *are they* whom the LORD
commanded to divide the inheritance
unto the children of Ĭș'rā-ĕl in the land
of Cā'năan.

CHAPTER 35

AND the LORD spake unto Moses in
the plains of Mō'ăb by Jordan *near*
Jĕr'ĭ-chō, saying,
2 Command the children of Ĭș'rā-ĕl,
that they give unto the Lē'vītes, of the
inheritance of their possession, cities to
dwell in; and ye shall give *also* unto the
Lē'vītes suburbs for the cities round
about them.
3 And the cities shall they have to dwell
in; and the suburbs of them shall be for
their cattle, and for their goods, and for
all their beasts.
4 And the suburbs of the cities, which
ye shall give unto the Lē'vītes, *shall
reach* from the wall of the city and outward a thousand cubits round about.
5 And ye shall measure from without
the city on the east side two thousand
cubits, and on the south side two thousand cubits, and on the west side two
thousand cubits, and on the north side
two thousand cubits; and the city *shall
be* in the midst: this shall be to them the
suburbs of the cities.
6 And among the cities which ye shall
give unto the Lē'vītes *there shall be* six
cities for refuge, which ye shall appoint
for the manslayer, that he may flee
thither: and to them ye shall add forty
and two cities.
7 *So* all the cities which ye shall give
to the Lē'vītes *shall be* forty and eight
cities: them *shall ye give* with their
suburbs.
8 And the cities which ye shall give
shall be of the possession of the children
of Ĭș'rā-ĕl: from *them that have* many
ye shall give many; but from *them that
have* few ye shall give few: every one
shall give of his cities unto the Lē'vītes
according to his inheritance which he
inheriteth.
9 ¶ And the LORD spake unto Moses,
saying,
10 Speak unto the children of Ĭș'rā-ĕl,
and say unto them, When ye be come
over Jordan into the land of Cā'năan,
11 Then ye shall appoint you cities to
be cities of refuge for you; that the slayer

may flee thither, which killeth any person at unawares.
12 And they shall be unto you cities for
refuge from the avenger; that the manslayer die not, until he stand before the
congregation in judgment.
13 And of these cities which ye shall
give, six cities shall ye have for refuge.
14 Ye shall give three cities on this side
Jordan, and three cities shall ye give in
the land of Cā'năan, *which* shall be
cities of refuge.
15 These six cities shall be a refuge,
both for the children of Ĭs̱'rā-ĕl, and for
the stranger, and for the sojourner
among them; that every one that killeth
any person unawares may flee thither.
16 And if he smite him with an instrument of iron, so that he die, he *is* a murderer: the murderer shall surely be put
to death.
17 And if he smite him with throwing
a stone, wherewith he may die, and he
die, he *is* a murderer: the murderer shall
surely be put to death.
18 Or *if* he smite him with a hand
weapon of wood, wherewith he may die,
and he die, he *is* a murderer: the murderer shall surely be put to death.
19 The revenger of blood himself shall
slay the murderer: when he meeteth
him, he shall slay him.
20 But if he thrust him of hatred, or
hurl at him by laying of wait, that he die;
21 Or in enmity smite him with his
hand, that he die: he that smote *him*
shall surely be put to death; *for* he *is* a
murderer: the revenger of blood shall
slay the murderer, when he meeteth
him.
22 But if he thrust him suddenly without enmity, or have cast upon him any
thing without laying of wait,
23 Or with any stone, wherewith a man
may die, seeing *him* not, and cast *it* upon
him, that he die, and *was* not his enemy,
neither sought his harm:
24 Then the congregation shall judge
between the slayer and the revenger of
blood according to these judgments:
25 And the congregation shall deliver
the slayer out of the hand of the revenger of blood, and the congregation
shall restore him to the city of his refuge, whither he was fled: and he shall
abide in it unto the death of the high
priest, which was anointed with the holy
oil.
26 But if the slayer shall at any time
come without the border of the city of
his refuge, whither he was fled;
27 And the revenger of blood find him
without the borders of the city of his
refuge, and the revenger of blood kill the
slayer; he shall not be guilty of blood:
28 Because he should have remained
in the city of his refuge until the death of
the high priest: but after the death of the
high priest the slayer shall return into
the land of his possession.
29 So these *things* shall be for a statute
of judgment unto you throughout your
generations in all your dwellings.
30 Whoso killeth any person, the murderer shall be put to death by the mouth
of witnesses: but one witness shall not
testify against any person *to cause him*
to die.
31 Moreover ye shall take no satisfaction for the life of a murderer, which *is*
guilty of death: but he shall be surely
put to death.
32 And ye shall take no satisfaction for
him that is fled to the city of his refuge,
that he should come again to dwell in the
land, until the death of the priest.
33 So ye shall not pollute the land
wherein ye *are:* for blood it defileth the
land: and the land cannot be cleansed
of the blood that is shed therein, but by
the blood of him that shed it.
34 Defile not therefore the land which
ye shall inhabit, wherein I dwell: for I
the LORD dwell among the children of
Ĭs̱'rā-ĕl.

CHAPTER 36

AND the chief fathers of the families
of the children of Gĭl'ē-ăd, the son
of Mā'chĭr, the son of Mȧ-năs'sĕh, of the
families of the sons of Joseph, came
near, and spake before Moses, and before the princes, the chief fathers of the
children of Ĭs̱'rā-ĕl:
2 And they said, The LORD commanded
my lord to give the land for an inheritance by lot to the children of Ĭs̱'rā-ĕl:
and my lord was commanded by the
LORD to give the inheritance of Zē-lō'-
phē-hăd our brother unto his daughters.
3 And if they be married to any of the
sons of the *other* tribes of the children
of Ĭs̱'rā-ĕl, then shall their inheritance
be taken from the inheritance of our
fathers, and shall be put to the inheritance of the tribe whereunto they are

received: so shall it be taken from the
lot of our inheritance.
4 And when the jubilee of the children
of Ĭş'rā-ĕl shall be, then shall their inheritance be put unto the inheritance of
the tribe whereunto they are received:
so shall their inheritance be taken away
from the inheritance of the tribe of our
fathers.
5 And Moses commanded the children
of Ĭş'rā-ĕl according to the word of the
LORD, saying, The tribe of the sons of
Joseph hath said well.
6 This *is* the thing which the LORD doth
command concerning the daughters of
Zē-lō'phē-hăd, saying, Let them marry
to whom they think best; only to the
family of the tribe of their father shall
they marry.
7 So shall not the inheritance of the
children of Ĭş'rā-ĕl remove from tribe to
tribe: for every one of the children of
Ĭş'rā-ĕl shall keep himself to the inheritance of the tribe of his fathers.
8 And every daughter, that possesseth
an inheritance in any tribe of the children of Ĭş'rā-ĕl, shall be wife unto one
of the family of the tribe of her father,
that the children of Ĭş'rā-ĕl may enjoy
every man the inheritance of his fathers.
9 Neither shall the inheritance remove
from *one* tribe to another tribe; but
every one of the tribes of the children
of Ĭş'rā-ĕl shall keep himself to his own
inheritance.
10 Even as the LORD commanded
Moses, so did the daughters of Zē-lō'-
phē-hăd:
11 For Māh'lȧh, Tĭr'zȧh, and Hŏg'lȧh,
and Mĭl'cȧh, and Noah, the daughters
of Zē-lō'phē-hăd, were married unto
their father's brothers' sons:
12 *And* they were married into the
families of the sons of Mȧ-năs'sĕh the
son of Joseph, and their inheritance remained in the tribe of the family of their
father.
13 These *are* the commandments and
the judgments, which the LORD commanded, by the hand of Moses, unto the
children of Ĭş'rā-ĕl in the plains of
Mō'ăb by Jordan *near* Jĕr'ĭ-chō.

THE FIFTH BOOK OF MOSES, CALLED

DEUTERONOMY

CHAPTER 1

THESE *be* the words which Moses
spake unto all Ĭş'rā-ĕl on this side
Jordan in the wilderness, in the plain
over against the Red *sea*, between
Pā'răn, and Tō'phĕl, and Lā'băn, and
Hȧ-zē'rŏth, and Dĭz'ȧ-hăb.
2 (*There are* eleven days' *journey* from
Hō'rĕb by the way of mount Sē'ĭr unto
Kā'dĕsh–bär'nē-ȧ.)
3 And it came to pass in the fortieth
year, in the eleventh month, on the first
day of the month, *that* Moses spake
unto the children of Ĭş'rā-ĕl, according
unto all that the LORD had given him in
commandment unto them;
4 After he had slain Sī'hŏn the king of
the Ăm'ō-rītes, which dwelt in Hĕsh'-
bŏn, and Og the king of Bā'shăn, which
dwelt at Ăs'tȧ-rŏth in Ĕd'rē-ī:
5 On this side Jordan, in the land of
Mō'ăb, began Moses to declare this
law, saying,
6 The LORD our God spake unto us in
Hō'rĕb, saying, Ye have dwelt long
enough in this mount:
7 Turn you, and take your journey, and
go to the mount of the Ăm'ō-rītes, and
unto all *the places* nigh thereunto, in
the plain, in the hills, and in the vale,
and in the south, and by the sea side, to
the land of the Cā'năan-ītes, and unto
Lebanon, unto the great river, the river
Eū-phrā'tēş.
8 Behold, I have set the land before
you: go in and possess the land which
the LORD sware unto your fathers,
Abraham, Isaac, and Jacob, to give unto
them and to their seed after them.
9 ¶ And I spake unto you at that time,
saying, I am not able to bear you myself
alone:
10 The LORD your God hath multiplied
you, and, behold, ye *are* this day as the
stars of heaven for multitude.
11 (The LORD God of your fathers
make you a thousand times so many

more as ye *are*, and bless you, as he hath promised you!)

12 How can I myself alone bear your cumbrance, and your burden, and your strife?

13 Take you wise men, and understanding, and known among your tribes, and I will make them rulers over you.

14 And ye answered me, and said, The thing which thou hast spoken *is* good *for us* to do.

15 So I took the chief of your tribes, wise men, and known, and made them heads over you, captains over thousands, and captains over hundreds, and captains over fifties, and captains over tens, and officers among your tribes.

16 And I charged your judges at that time, saying, Hear *the causes* between your brethren, and judge righteously between *every* man and his brother, and the stranger *that is* with him.

17 Ye shall not respect persons in judgment; *but* ye shall hear the small as well as the great; ye shall not be afraid of the face of man; for the judgment *is* God's: and the cause that is too hard for you, bring *it* unto me, and I will hear it.

18 And I commanded you at that time all the things which ye should do.

19 ¶ And when we departed from Hō'rĕb, we went through all that great and terrible wilderness, which ye saw by the way of the mountain of the Ăm'ō-rītes, as the LORD our God commanded us; and we came to Kā'dĕsh-bär'nē-ȧ.

20 And I said unto you, Ye are come unto the mountain of the Ăm'ō-rītes, which the LORD our God doth give unto us.

21 Behold, the LORD thy God hath set the land before thee: go up *and* possess *it*, as the LORD God of thy fathers hath said unto thee; fear not, neither be discouraged.

22 ¶ And ye came near unto me every one of you, and said, We will send men before us, and they shall search us out the land, and bring us word again by what way we must go up, and into what cities we shall come.

23 And the saying pleased me well; and I took twelve men of you, one of a tribe:

24 And they turned and went up into the mountain, and came unto the valley of Ĕsh'cŏl, and searched it out.

25 And they took of the fruit of the land in their hands, and brought *it* down unto us, and brought us word again, and said, *It is* a good land which the LORD our God doth give us.

26 Notwithstanding ye would not go up, but rebelled against the commandment of the LORD your God:

27 And ye murmured in your tents, and said, Because the LORD hated us, he hath brought us forth out of the land of Egypt, to deliver us into the hand of the Ăm'ō-rītes, to destroy us.

28 Whither shall we go up? our brethren have discouraged our heart, saying, The people *is* greater and taller than we; the cities *are* great and walled up to heaven; and moreover we have seen the sons of the Ăn'ȧ-kĭm there.

29 Then I said unto you, Dread not, neither be afraid of them.

30 The LORD your God which goeth before you, he shall fight for you, according to all that he did for you in Egypt before your eyes;

31 And in the wilderness, where thou hast seen how that the LORD thy God bare thee, as a man doth bear his son, in all the way that ye went, until ye came into this place.

32 Yet in this thing ye did not believe the LORD your God,

33 Who went in the way before you, to search you out a place to pitch your tents *in*, in fire by night, to show you by what way ye should go, and in a cloud by day.

34 And the LORD heard the voice of your words, and was wroth, and sware, saying,

35 Surely there shall not one of these men of this evil generation see that good land, which I sware to give unto your fathers,

36 Save Caleb the son of Jē-phŭn'nĕh; he shall see it, and to him will I give the land that he hath trodden upon, and to his children, because he hath wholly followed the LORD.

37 Also the LORD was angry with me for your sakes, saying, Thou also shalt not go in thither.

38 *But* Joshua the son of Nŭn, which standeth before thee, he shall go in thither: encourage him: for he shall cause Ĭş'rā-ĕl to inherit it.

39 Moreover your little ones, which ye said should be a prey, and your children, which in that day had no knowledge

between good and evil, they shall go in
thither, and unto them will I give it, and
they shall possess it.
40 But *as for* you, turn you, and take
your journey into the wilderness by the
way of the Red sea.
41 Then ye answered and said unto me,
We have sinned against the LORD, we
will go up and fight, according to all that
the LORD our God commanded us. And
when ye had girded on every man his
weapons of war, ye were ready to go up
into the hill.
42 And the LORD said unto me, Say
unto them, Go not up, neither fight; for
I *am* not among you; lest ye be smitten
before your enemies.
43 So I spake unto you; and ye would
not hear, but rebelled against the commandment of the LORD, and went presumptuously up into the hill.
44 And the Ăm′ō-rītes, which dwelt in
that mountain, came out against you,
and chased you, as bees do, and destroyed you in Sē′ĭr, *even* unto Hôr′mȧh.
45 And ye returned and wept before
the LORD; but the LORD would not
hearken to your voice, nor give ear unto
you.
46 So ye abode in Kā′dĕsh many days,
according unto the days that ye abode
there.

CHAPTER 2

THEN we turned, and took our journey into the wilderness by the way
of the Red sea, as the LORD spake unto
me: and we compassed mount Sē′ĭr
many days.
2 And the LORD spake unto me, saying,
3 Ye have compassed this mountain
long enough: turn you northward.
4 And command thou the people, saying, Ye *are* to pass through the coast of
your brethren the children of Ē′sa͡u,
which dwell in Sē′ĭr; and they shall be
afraid of you: take ye good heed unto
yourselves therefore:
5 Meddle not with them; for I will not
give you of their land, no, not so much
as a footbreadth; because I have given
mount Sē′ĭr unto Ē′sa͡u *for* a possession.
6 Ye shall buy meat of them for money,
that ye may eat; and ye shall also buy
water of them for money, that ye may
drink.
7 For the LORD thy God hath blessed
thee in all the works of thy hand: he
knoweth thy walking through this great
wilderness: these forty years the LORD
thy God *hath been* with thee; thou hast
lacked nothing.
8 And when we passed by from our
brethren the children of Ē′sa͡u, which
dwelt in Sē′ĭr, through the way of the
plain from Ē′lȧth, and from Ē′zĭ-ŏn-
gā′bẽr, we turned and passed by the
way of the wilderness of Mō′ăb.
9 And the LORD said unto me, Distress
not the Mō′ăb-ītes, neither contend with
them in battle: for I will not give thee of
their land *for* a possession; because I
have given Är unto the children of Lot
for a possession.
10 The Ē′mĭm dwelt therein in times
past, a people great, and many, and
tall, as the Ăn′ȧ-kĭm;
11 Which also were accounted giants,
as the Ăn′ȧ-kĭm; but the Mō′ăb-ītes call
them Ē′mĭm.
12 The Hō′rĭm also dwelt in Sē′ĭr beforetime; but the children of Ē′sa͡u succeeded them, when they had destroyed
them from before them, and dwelt in
their stead; as Ĭṣ′rā-ĕl did unto the land
of his possession, which the LORD gave
unto them.
13 Now rise up, *said I*, and get you
over the brook Zē′rĕd. And we went
over the brook Zē′rĕd.
14 And the space in which we came
from Kā′dĕsh–bär′nē-ȧ, until we were
come over the brook Zē′rĕd, *was* thirty
and eight years; until all the generation
of the men of war were wasted out from
among the host, as the LORD sware unto
them.
15 For indeed the hand of the LORD
was against them, to destroy them from
among the host, until they were consumed.
16 ¶ So it came to pass, when all the
men of war were consumed and dead
from among the people,
17 That the LORD spake unto me,
saying,
18 Thou art to pass over through Är,
the coast of Mō′ăb, this day:
19 And *when* thou comest nigh over
against the children of Ammon, distress
them not, nor meddle with them: for I
will not give thee of the land of the children of Ammon *any* possession; because
I have given it unto the children of Lot
for a possession.
20 (That also was accounted a land of

giants: giants dwelt therein in old time;
and the Ammonites call them Zăm-zŭm'mĭm;
21 A people great, and many, and tall,
as the Ăn'ȧ-kĭm; but the LORD destroyed them before them; and they succeeded them, and dwelt in their stead:
22 As he did to the children of Ē'saû,
which dwelt in Sē'ĭr, when he destroyed the Hō'rĭm from before them; and they succeeded them, and dwelt in their stead even unto this day:
23 And the Ā'vĭm which dwelt in Hȧ-zē'rĭm, *even* unto Ăz'zȧh, the Căph'tō-rĭm, which came forth out of Căph'tŏr, destroyed them, and dwelt in their stead.)
24 ℂ Rise ye up, take your journey,
and pass over the river Är'nŏn: behold, I have given into thine hand Sī'hŏn the Ăm'ō-rīte, king of Hĕsh'bŏn, and his land: begin to possess *it*, and contend with him in battle.
25 This day will I begin to put the
dread of thee and the fear of thee upon the nations *that are* under the whole heaven, who shall hear report of thee, and shall tremble, and be in anguish because of thee.
26 ℂ And I sent messengers out of the
wilderness of Kĕd'ē-mŏth unto Sī'hŏn king of Hĕsh'bŏn with words of peace, saying,
27 Let me pass through thy land: I will
go along by the high way, I will neither turn unto the right hand nor to the left.
28 Thou shalt sell me meat for money,
that I may eat; and give me water for money, that I may drink: only I will pass through on my feet:
29 (As the children of Ē'saû which
dwell in Sē'ĭr, and the Mō'ăb-ītes which dwell in Är, did unto me:) until I shall pass over Jordan into the land which the LORD our God giveth us.
30 But Sī'hŏn king of Hĕsh'bŏn would
not let us pass by him: for the LORD thy God hardened his spirit, and made his heart obstinate, that he might deliver him into thy hand, as *appeareth* this day.
31 And the LORD said unto me, Behold,
I have begun to give Sī'hŏn and his land before thee: begin to possess, that thou mayest inherit his land.
32 Then Sī'hŏn came out against us, he
and all his people, to fight at Jā'hăz.
33 And the LORD our God delivered
him before us; and we smote him, and his sons, and all his people.
34 And we took all his cities at that
time, and utterly destroyed the men, and the women, and the little ones, of every city, we left none to remain:
35 Only the cattle we took for a prey
unto ourselves, and the spoil of the cities which we took.
36 From Ȧ-rō'ēr, which *is* by the brink
of the river of Är'nŏn, and *from* the city that *is* by the river, even unto Gĭl'ē-ăd, there was not one city too strong for us: the LORD our God delivered all unto us:
37 Only unto the land of the children
of Ammon thou camest not, *nor* unto any place of the river Jăb'bŏk, nor unto the cities in the mountains, nor unto whatsoever the LORD our God forbade us.

CHAPTER 3

THEN we turned, and went up the way to Bā'shăn: and Og the king of Bā'shăn came out against us, he and all his people, to battle at Ĕd'rē-ī.
2 And the LORD said unto me, Fear him
not: for I will deliver him, and all his people, and his land, into thy hand; and thou shalt do unto him as thou didst unto Sī'hŏn king of the Ăm'ō-rītes, which dwelt at Hĕsh'bŏn.
3 So the LORD our God delivered into
our hands Og also, the king of Bā'shăn, and all his people: and we smote him until none was left to him remaining.
4 And we took all his cities at that time,
there was not a city which we took not from them, threescore cities, all the region of Är'gŏb, the kingdom of Og in Bā'shan.
5 All these cities *were* fenced with high
walls, gates, and bars; beside unwalled towns a great many.
6 And we utterly destroyed them, as we
did unto Sī'hŏn king of Hĕsh'bŏn, utterly destroying the men, women, and children, of every city.
7 But all the cattle, and the spoil of
the cities, we took for a prey to ourselves.
8 And we took at that time out of the
hand of the two kings of the Ăm'ō-rītes the land that *was* on this side Jordan, from the river of Är'nŏn unto mount Hermon;

9 (*Which* Hermon the Sī-dō′nĭ-ănş call
Sĭ′rĭ-ŏn; and the Ăm′ō-rītes call it
Shē′nĭr;)
10 All the cities of the plain, and all
Gĭl′ē-ăd, and all Bā′shăn, unto Săl′chăh
and Ĕd′rē-ī, cities of the kingdom of Og
in Bā′shăn.
11 For only Og king of Bā′shăn remained of the remnant of giants; behold,
his bedstead *was* a bedstead of iron; *is*
it not in Răb′băth of the children of Ammon? nine cubits *was* the length thereof, and four cubits the breadth of it, after
the cubit of a man.
12 And this land, *which* we possessed
at that time, from Ȧ-rō′ēr, which *is* by
the river Är′nŏn, and half mount Gĭl′-
ē-ăd, and the cities thereof, gave I unto
the Reubenites and to the Gadites.
13 And the rest of Gĭl′ē-ăd, and all
Bā′shăn, *being* the kingdom of Og, gave
I unto the half tribe of Mȧ-năs′sĕh; all
the region of Är′gŏb, with all Bā′shăn,
which was called the land of giants.
14 Jā′ĭr the son of Mȧ-năs′sĕh took all
the country of Är′gŏb unto the coasts of
Gē-shụ′rī and Mā-ăch′ȧ-thī; and called
them after his own name, Bā′shăn–
hā′vŏth–jā′ĭr, unto this day.
15 And I gave Gĭl′ē-ăd unto Mā′chĭr.
16 And unto the Reubenites and unto
the Gadites I gave from Gĭl′ē-ăd even
unto the river Är′nŏn half the valley,
and the border even unto the river
Jăb′bŏk, *which is* the border of the children of Ammon;
17 The plain also, and Jordan, and the
coast *thereof,* from Chĭn′nē-rĕth even
unto the sea of the plain, *even* the salt
sea, under Ăsh′dŏth–pĭş′gȧh eastward.
18 ¶ And I commanded you at that
time, saying, The LORD your God hath
given you this land to possess it: ye shall
pass over armed before your brethren
the children of Ĭş′rā-ĕl, all *that are* meet
for the war.
19 But your wives, and your little ones,
and your cattle, (*for* I know that ye have
much cattle,) shall abide in your cities
which I have given you;
20 Until the LORD have given rest unto
your brethren, as well as unto you, and
until they also possess the land which
the LORD your God hath given them beyond Jordan: and *then* shall ye return
every man unto his possession, which I
have given you.
21 ¶ And I commanded Joshua at that
time, saying, Thine eyes have seen all
that the LORD your God hath done unto
these two kings: so shall the LORD do
unto all the kingdoms whither thou
passest.
22 Ye shall not fear them: for the LORD
your God he shall fight for you.
23 And I besought the LORD at that
time, saying,
24 O LORD God, thou hast begun to
show thy servant thy greatness, and thy
mighty hand: for what God *is there* in
heaven or in earth, that can do according
to thy works, and according to thy
might?
25 I pray thee, let me go over, and see
the good land that *is* beyond Jordan,
that goodly mountain, and Lebanon.
26 But the LORD was wroth with me for
your sakes, and would not hear me: and
the LORD said unto me, Let it suffice
thee; speak no more unto me of this
matter.
27 Get thee up into the top of Pĭş′gȧh,
and lift up thine eyes westward, and
northward, and southward, and eastward, and behold *it* with thine eyes: for
thou shalt not go over this Jordan.
28 But charge Joshua, and encourage
him, and strengthen him: for he shall go
over before this people, and he shall
cause them to inherit the land which
thou shalt see.
29 So we abode in the valley over
against Bĕth′–pē′ŏr.

CHAPTER 4

NOW therefore hearken, O Ĭş′rā-ĕl,
unto the statutes and unto the
judgments, which I teach you, for to do
them, that ye may live, and go in and
possess the land which the LORD God
of your fathers giveth you.
2 Ye shall not add unto the word which
I command you, neither shall ye diminish *aught* from it, that ye may keep the
commandments of the LORD your God
which I command you.
3 Your eyes have seen what the LORD
did because of Bā′ăl–pē′ŏr: for all the
men that followed Bā′ăl–pē′ŏr, the LORD
thy God hath destroyed them from
among you.
4 But ye that did cleave unto the LORD
your God *are* alive every one of you this
day.
5 Behold, I have taught you statutes
and judgments, even as the LORD my

God commanded me, that ye should do so in the land whither ye go to possess it.

6 Keep therefore and do *them;* for this *is* your wisdom and your understanding in the sight of the nations, which shall hear all these statutes, and say, Surely this great nation *is* a wise and understanding people.

7 For what nation *is there so* great, who *hath* God *so* nigh unto them, as the LORD our God *is* in all *things that* we call upon him *for?*

8 And what nation *is there so* great, that hath statutes and judgments *so* righteous as all this law, which I set before you this day?

9 Only take heed to thyself, and keep thy soul diligently, lest thou forget the things which thine eyes have seen, and lest they depart from thy heart all the days of thy life: but teach them thy sons, and thy sons' sons;

10 *Specially* the day that thou stoodest before the LORD thy God in Hō'rĕb, when the LORD said unto me, Gather me the people together, and I will make them hear my words, that they may learn to fear me all the days that they shall live upon the earth, and *that* they may teach their children.

11 And ye came near and stood under the mountain; and the mountain burned with fire unto the midst of heaven, with darkness, clouds, and thick darkness.

12 And the LORD spake unto you out of the midst of the fire: ye heard the voice of the words, but saw no similitude; only *ye heard* a voice.

13 And he declared unto you his covenant, which he commanded you to perform, *even* ten commandments; and he wrote them upon two tables of stone.

14 ¶ And the LORD commanded me at that time to teach you statutes and judgments, that ye might do them in the land whither ye go over to possess it.

15 Take ye therefore good heed unto yourselves; for ye saw no manner of similitude on the day *that* the LORD spake unto you in Hō'rĕb out of the midst of the fire;

16 Lest ye corrupt *yourselves,* and make you a graven image, the similitude of any figure, the likeness of male or female,

17 The likeness of any beast that *is* on the earth, the likeness of any winged fowl that flieth in the air,

18 The likeness of any thing that creepeth on the ground, the likeness of any fish that *is* in the waters beneath the earth:

19 And lest thou lift up thine eyes unto heaven, and when thou seest the sun, and the moon, and the stars, *even* all the host of heaven, shouldest be driven to worship them, and serve them, which the LORD thy God hath divided unto all nations under the whole heaven.

20 But the LORD hath taken you, and brought you forth out of the iron furnace, *even* out of Egypt, to be unto him a people of inheritance, as *ye are* this day.

21 Furthermore the LORD was angry with me for your sakes, and sware that I should not go over Jordan, and that I should not go in unto that good land, which the LORD thy God giveth thee *for* an inheritance:

22 But I must die in this land, I must not go over Jordan: but ye shall go over, and possess that good land.

23 Take heed unto yourselves, lest ye forget the covenant of the LORD your God, which he made with you, and make you a graven image, *or* the likeness of any *thing,* which the LORD thy God hath forbidden thee.

24 For the LORD thy God *is* a consuming fire, *even* a jealous God.

25 ¶ When thou shalt beget children, and children's children, and ye shall have remained long in the land, and shall corrupt *yourselves,* and make a graven image, *or* the likeness of any *thing,* and shall do evil in the sight of the LORD thy God, to provoke him to anger;

26 I call heaven and earth to witness against you this day, that ye shall soon utterly perish from off the land whereunto ye go over Jordan to possess it; ye shall not prolong *your* days upon it, but shall utterly be destroyed.

27 And the LORD shall scatter you among the nations, and ye shall be left few in number among the heathen, whither the LORD shall lead you.

28 And there ye shall serve gods, the work of men's hands, wood and stone, which neither see, nor hear, nor eat, nor smell.

29 But if from thence thou shalt seek the LORD thy God, thou shalt find *him,* if thou seek him with all thy heart and with all thy soul.

30 When thou art in tribulation, and all

these things are come upon thee, *even* in the latter days, if thou turn to the LORD thy God, and shalt be obedient unto his voice;

31 (For the LORD thy God *is* a merciful God;) he will not forsake thee, neither destroy thee, nor forget the covenant of thy fathers, which he sware unto them.

32 For ask now of the days that are past, which were before thee, since the day that God created man upon the earth, and *ask* from the one side of heaven unto the other, whether there hath been *any such thing* as this great thing *is*, or hath been heard like it?

33 Did *ever* people hear the voice of God speaking out of the midst of the fire, as thou hast heard, and live?

34 Or hath God assayed to go *and* take him a nation from the midst of *another* nation, by temptations, by signs, and by wonders, and by war, and by a mighty hand, and by a stretched out arm, and by great terrors, according to all that the LORD your God did for you in Egypt before your eyes?

35 Unto thee it was showed, that thou mightest know that the LORD he *is* God; *there is* none else beside him.

36 Out of heaven he made thee to hear his voice, that he might instruct thee: and upon earth he showed thee his great fire; and thou heardest his words out of the midst of the fire.

37 And because he loved thy fathers, therefore he chose their seed after them, and brought thee out in his sight with his mighty power out of Egypt;

38 To drive out nations from before thee greater and mightier than thou *art*, to bring thee in, to give thee their land *for* an inheritance, as *it is* this day.

39 Know therefore this day, and consider *it* in thine heart, that the LORD he *is* God in heaven above, and upon the earth beneath: *there is* none else.

40 Thou shalt keep therefore his statutes, and his commandments, which I command thee this day, that it may go well with thee, and with thy children after thee, and that thou mayest prolong *thy* days upon the earth, which the LORD thy God giveth thee, for ever.

41 ¶ Then Moses severed three cities on this side Jordan toward the sunrising;

42 That the slayer might flee thither, which should kill his neighbor unawares, and hated him not in times past; and that fleeing unto one of these cities he might live:

43 *Namely*, Bē'zĕr in the wilderness, in the plain country, of the Reubenites; and Rā'mŏth in Gĭl'ē-ăd, of the Gadites; and Gō'lăn in Bā'shăn, of the Mȧ-năs'sītes.

44 ¶ And this *is* the law which Moses set before the children of Ĭs'rā-ĕl:

45 These *are* the testimonies, and the statutes, and the judgments, which Moses spake unto the children of Ĭs'rā-ĕl, after they came forth out of Egypt,

46 On this side Jordan, in the valley over against Bĕth'–pē'ŏr, in the land of Sī'hŏn king of the Ăm'ō-rītes, who dwelt at Hĕsh'bŏn, whom Moses and the children of Ĭs'rā-ĕl smote, after they were come forth out of Egypt:

47 And they possessed his land, and the land of Og king of Bā'shăn, two kings of the Ăm'ō-rītes, which *were* on this side Jordan toward the sunrising;

48 From Ȧ-rō'ĕr, which *is* by the bank of the river Är'nŏn, even unto mount Sī'ŏn, which *is* Hermon,

49 And all the plain on this side Jordan eastward, even unto the sea of the plain, under the springs of Pĭs'gȧh.

CHAPTER 5

AND Moses called all Ĭs'rā-ĕl, and said unto them, Hear, O Ĭs'rā-ĕl, the statutes and judgments which I speak in your ears this day, that ye may learn them, and keep and do them.

2 The LORD our God made a covenant with us in Hō'rĕb.

3 The LORD made not this covenant with our fathers, but with us, *even* us, who *are* all of us here alive this day.

4 The LORD talked with you face to face in the mount out of the midst of the fire,

5 (I stood between the LORD and you at that time, to show you the word of the LORD: for ye were afraid by reason of the fire, and went not up into the mount,) saying,

6 ¶ I *am* the LORD thy God, which brought thee out of the land of Egypt, from the house of bondage.

7 Thou shalt have none other gods before me.

8 Thou shalt not make thee *any* graven image, *or* any likeness *of any thing* that *is* in heaven above, or that *is* in the earth

beneath, or that *is* in the waters beneath the earth:

9 Thou shalt not bow down thyself unto them, nor serve them: for I the LORD thy God *am* a jealous God, visiting the iniquity of the fathers upon the children unto the third and fourth *generation* of them that hate me,

10 And showing mercy unto thousands of them that love me and keep my commandments.

11 Thou shalt not take the name of the LORD thy God in vain: for the LORD will not hold *him* guiltless that taketh his name in vain.

12 Keep the sabbath day to sanctify it, as the LORD thy God hath commanded thee.

13 Six days thou shalt labor, and do all thy work:

14 But the seventh day *is* the sabbath of the LORD thy God: *in it* thou shalt not do any work, thou, nor thy son, nor thy daughter, nor thy manservant, nor thy maidservant, nor thine ox, nor thine ass, nor any of thy cattle, nor thy stranger that *is* within thy gates; that thy manservant and thy maidservant may rest as well as thou.

15 And remember that thou wast a servant in the land of Egypt, and *that* the LORD thy God brought thee out thence through a mighty hand and by a stretched out arm: therefore the LORD thy God commanded thee to keep the sabbath day.

16 ¶ Honor thy father and thy mother, as the LORD thy God hath commanded thee; that thy days may be prolonged, and that it may go well with thee, in the land which the LORD thy God giveth thee.

17 Thou shalt not kill.

18 Neither shalt thou commit adultery.

19 Neither shalt thou steal.

20 Neither shalt thou bear false witness against thy neighbor.

21 Neither shalt thou desire thy neighbor's wife, neither shalt thou covet thy neighbor's house, his field, or his manservant, or his maidservant, his ox, or his ass, or any *thing* that *is* thy neighbor's.

22 ¶ These words the LORD spake unto all your assembly in the mount out of the midst of the fire, of the cloud, and of the thick darkness, with a great voice; and he added no more. And he wrote them in two tables of stone, and delivered them unto me.

23 And it came to pass, when ye heard the voice out of the midst of the darkness, (for the mountain did burn with fire,) that ye came near unto me, *even* all the heads of your tribes, and your elders;

24 And ye said, Behold, the LORD our God hath showed us his glory and his greatness, and we have heard his voice out of the midst of the fire: we have seen this day that God doth talk with man, and he liveth.

25 Now therefore why should we die? for this great fire will consume us: if we hear the voice of the LORD our God any more, then we shall die.

26 For who *is there of* all flesh, that hath heard the voice of the living God speaking out of the midst of the fire, as we *have,* and lived?

27 Go thou near, and hear all that the LORD our God shall say; and speak thou unto us all that the LORD our God shall speak unto thee; and we will hear *it,* and do *it.*

28 And the LORD heard the voice of your words, when ye spake unto me; and the LORD said unto me, I have heard the voice of the words of this people, which they have spoken unto thee: they have well said all that they have spoken.

29 Oh that there were such a heart in them, that they would fear me, and keep all my commandments always, that it might be well with them, and with their children for ever!

30 Go say to them, Get you into your tents again.

31 But as for thee, stand thou here by me, and I will speak unto thee all the commandments, and the statutes, and the judgments, which thou shalt teach them, that they may do *them* in the land which I give them to possess it.

32 Ye shall observe to do therefore as the LORD your God hath commanded you: ye shall not turn aside to the right hand or to the left.

33 Ye shall walk in all the ways which the LORD your God hath commanded you, that ye may live, and *that it may be* well with you, and *that* ye may prolong *your* days in the land which ye shall possess.

CHAPTER 6

NOW these *are* the commandments, the statutes, and the judgments, which the LORD your God commanded to teach you, that ye might do *them* in the land whither ye go to possess it:

2 That thou mightest fear the LORD thy God, to keep all his statutes and his commandments, which I command thee, thou, and thy son, and thy son's son, all the days of thy life; and that thy days may be prolonged.

3 ¶ Hear therefore, O Ĭṣ′rā-ĕl, and observe to do *it;* that it may be well with thee, and that ye may increase mightily, as the LORD God of thy fathers hath promised thee, in the land that floweth with milk and honey.

4 Hear, O Ĭṣ′rā-ĕl: The LORD our God *is* one LORD:

5 And thou shalt love the LORD thy God with all thine heart, and with all thy soul, and with all thy might.

6 And these words, which I command thee this day, shall be in thine heart:

7 And thou shalt teach them diligently unto thy children, and shalt talk of them when thou sittest in thine house, and when thou walkest by the way, and when thou liest down, and when thou risest up.

8 And thou shalt bind them for a sign upon thine hand, and they shall be as frontlets between thine eyes.

9 And thou shalt write them upon the posts of thy house, and on thy gates.

10 And it shall be, when the LORD thy God shall have brought thee into the land which he sware unto thy fathers, to Abraham, to Isaac, and to Jacob, to give thee great and goodly cities, which thou buildedst not,

11 And houses full of all good *things,* which thou filledst not, and wells digged, which thou diggedst not, vineyards and olive trees, which thou plantedst not; when thou shalt have eaten and be full;

12 *Then* beware lest thou forget the LORD, which brought thee forth out of the land of Egypt, from the house of bondage.

13 Thou shalt fear the LORD thy God, and serve him, and shalt swear by his name.

14 Ye shall not go after other gods, of the gods of the people which *are* round about you;

15 (For the LORD thy God *is* a jealous God among you;) lest the anger of the LORD thy God be kindled against thee, and destroy thee from off the face of the earth.

16 ¶ Ye shall not tempt the LORD your God, as ye tempted *him* in Măs′sȧh.

17 Ye shall diligently keep the commandments of the LORD your God, and his testimonies, and his statutes, which he hath commanded thee.

18 And thou shalt do *that which is* right and good in the sight of the LORD; that it may be well with thee, and that thou mayest go in and possess the good land which the LORD sware unto thy fathers,

19 To cast out all thine enemies from before thee, as the LORD hath spoken.

20 *And* when thy son asketh thee in time to come, saying, What *mean* the testimonies, and the statutes, and the judgments, which the LORD our God hath commanded you?

21 Then thou shalt say unto thy son, We were Phā′raōh's bondmen in Egypt; and the LORD brought us out of Egypt with a mighty hand:

22 And the LORD showed signs and wonders, great and sore, upon Egypt, upon Phā′raōh, and upon all his household, before our eyes:

23 And he brought us out from thence, that he might bring us in, to give us the land which he sware unto our fathers.

24 And the LORD commanded us to do all these statutes, to fear the LORD our God, for our good always, that he might preserve us alive, as *it is* at this day.

25 And it shall be our righteousness, if we observe to do all these commandments before the LORD our God, as he hath commanded us.

CHAPTER 7

WHEN the LORD thy God shall bring thee into the land whither thou goest to possess it, and hath cast out many nations before thee, the Hĭt′tītes, and the Gĭr′gȧ-shītes, and the Ăm′ō-rītes, and the Cā′năan-ītes, and the Pĕr′ĭz-zītes, and the Hī′vītes, and the Jĕb′ū-ṣītes, seven nations greater and mightier than thou;

2 And when the LORD thy God shall deliver them before thee; thou shalt smite them, *and* utterly destroy them; thou shalt make no covenant with them, nor show mercy unto them:

3 Neither shalt thou make marriages

with them; thy daughter thou shalt not
give unto his son, nor his daughter shalt
thou take unto thy son.
4 For they will turn away thy son from
following me, that they may serve other
gods: so will the anger of the LORD be
kindled against you, and destroy thee
suddenly.
5 But thus shall ye deal with them; ye
shall destroy their altars, and break
down their images, and cut down their
groves, and burn their graven images
with fire.
6 For thou *art* a holy people unto the
LORD thy God: the LORD thy God hath
chosen thee to be a special people unto
himself, above all people that *are* upon
the face of the earth.
7 The LORD did not set his love upon
you, nor choose you, because ye were
more in number than any people; for ye
were the fewest of all people:
8 But because the LORD loved you, and
because he would keep the oath which
he had sworn unto your fathers, hath
the LORD brought you out with a mighty
hand, and redeemed you out of the
house of bondmen, from the hand of
Phā'raōh king of Egypt.
9 Know therefore that the LORD thy
God, he *is* God, the faithful God, which
keepeth covenant and mercy with them
that love him and keep his commandments to a thousand generations;
10 And repayeth them that hate him to
their face, to destroy them: he will not
be slack to him that hateth him, he will
repay him to his face.
11 Thou shalt therefore keep the commandments, and the statutes, and the
judgments, which I command thee this
day, to do them.
12 ¶ Wherefore it shall come to pass,
if ye hearken to these judgments, and
keep and do them, that the LORD thy
God shall keep unto thee the covenant
and the mercy which he sware unto thy
fathers:
13 And he will love thee, and bless
thee, and multiply thee: he will also
bless the fruit of thy womb, and the fruit
of thy land, thy corn, and thy wine, and
thine oil, the increase of thy kine, and
the flocks of thy sheep, in the land which
he sware unto thy fathers to give thee.
14 Thou shalt be blessed above all people: there shall not be male or female
barren among you, or among your cattle.
15 And the LORD will take away
from thee all sickness, and will put
none of the evil diseases of Egypt,
which thou knowest, upon thee; but
will lay them upon all *them* that hate
thee.
16 And thou shalt consume all the people which the LORD thy God shall deliver thee; thine eye shall have no pity
upon them: neither shalt thou serve
their gods; for that *will be* a snare unto
thee.
17 If thou shalt say in thine heart,
These nations *are* more than I; how can
I dispossess them?
18 Thou shalt not be afraid of them:
but shalt well remember what the LORD
thy God did unto Phā'raōh, and unto all
Egypt;
19 The great temptations which thine
eyes saw, and the signs, and the wonders, and the mighty hand, and the
stretched out arm, whereby the LORD
thy God brought thee out: so shall the
LORD thy God do unto all the people of
whom thou art afraid.
20 Moreover the LORD thy God will
send the hornet among them, until they
that are left, and hide themselves from
thee, be destroyed.
21 Thou shalt not be affrighted at them:
for the LORD thy God *is* among you, a
mighty God and terrible.
22 And the LORD thy God will put out
those nations before thee by little and
little: thou mayest not consume them at
once, lest the beasts of the field increase
upon thee.
23 But the LORD thy God shall deliver
them unto thee, and shall destroy them
with a mighty destruction, until they be
destroyed.
24 And he shall deliver their kings into
thine hand, and thou shalt destroy their
name from under heaven: there shall no
man be able to stand before thee, until
thou have destroyed them.
25 The graven images of their gods
shall ye burn with fire: thou shalt not
desire the silver or gold *that is* on them,
nor take *it* unto thee, lest thou be snared
therein: for it *is* an abomination to the
LORD thy God.
26 Neither shalt thou bring an abomination into thine house, lest thou be a
cursed thing like it: *but* thou shalt utterly
detest it, and thou shalt utterly abhor
it; for it *is* a cursed thing.

CHAPTER 8

ALL the commandments which I command thee this day shall ye observe
to do, that ye may live, and multiply,
and go in and possess the land which
the LORD sware unto your fathers.
2 And thou shalt remember all the
way which the LORD thy God led thee
these forty years in the wilderness,
to humble thee, *and* to prove thee, to
know what *was* in thine heart, whether
thou wouldest keep his commandments,
or no.
3 And he humbled thee, and suffered
thee to hunger, and fed thee with manna, which thou knewest not, neither did
thy fathers know; that he might make
thee know that man doth not live by
bread only, but by every *word* that proceedeth out of the mouth of the LORD
doth man live.
4 Thy raiment waxed not old upon thee,
neither did thy foot swell, these forty
years.
5 Thou shalt also consider in thine
heart, that, as a man chasteneth his son,
so the LORD thy God chasteneth thee.
6 Therefore thou shalt keep the commandments of the LORD thy God, to
walk in his ways, and to fear him.
7 For the LORD thy God bringeth thee
into a good land, a land of brooks of
water, of fountains and depths that
spring out of valleys and hills;
8 A land of wheat, and barley, and
vines, and fig trees, and pomegranates;
a land of oil olive, and honey;
9 A land wherein thou shalt eat bread
without scarceness, thou shalt not lack
any *thing* in it; a land whose stones *are*
iron, and out of whose hills thou mayest
dig brass.
10 When thou hast eaten and art full,
then thou shalt bless the LORD thy God
for the good land which he hath given
thee.
11 Beware that thou forget not the
LORD thy God, in not keeping his commandments, and his judgments, and his
statutes, which I command thee this day:
12 Lest *when* thou hast eaten and art
full, and hast built goodly houses, and
dwelt *therein;*
13 And *when* thy herds and thy flocks
multiply, and thy silver and thy gold is
multiplied, and all that thou hast is
multiplied;
14 Then thine heart be lifted up, and
thou forget the LORD thy God, which
brought thee forth out of the land of
Egypt, from the house of bondage;
15 Who led thee through that great and
terrible wilderness, *wherein were* fiery
serpents, and scorpions, and drought,
where *there was* no water; who brought
thee forth water out of the rock of flint;
16 Who fed thee in the wilderness with
manna, which thy fathers knew not, that
he might humble thee, and that he
might prove thee, to do thee good at thy
latter end;
17 And thou say in thine heart, My
power and the might of *mine* hand hath
gotten me this wealth.
18 But thou shalt remember the LORD
thy God: for *it is* he that giveth thee
power to get wealth, that he may establish his covenant which he sware unto
thy fathers, as *it is* this day.
19 And it shall be, if thou do at all forget the LORD thy God, and walk after
other gods, and serve them, and worship them, I testify against you this day
that ye shall surely perish.
20 As the nations which the LORD destroyeth before your face, so shall ye
perish; because ye would not be obedient unto the voice of the LORD your God.

CHAPTER 9

HEAR, O Ĭş'rā-ĕl: Thou *art* to pass
over Jordan this day, to go in to
possess nations greater and mightier
than thyself, cities great and fenced up
to heaven,
2 A people great and tall, the children
of the Ăn'ȧ-kĭm, whom thou knowest,
and *of whom* thou hast heard *say*, Who
can stand before the children of Ā'năk!
3 Understand therefore this day, that
the LORD thy God *is* he which goeth over
before thee; *as* a consuming fire he shall
destroy them, and he shall bring them
down before thy face: so shalt thou drive
them out, and destroy them quickly, as
the LORD hath said unto thee.
4 Speak not thou in thine heart, after
that the LORD thy God hath cast them
out from before thee, saying, For my
righteousness the LORD hath brought
me in to possess this land: but for the
wickedness of these nations the LORD
doth drive them out from before thee.
5 Not for thy righteousness, or for the
uprightness of thine heart, dost thou go

to possess their land: but for the wickedness of these nations the LORD thy God doth drive them out from before thee, and that he may perform the word which the LORD sware unto thy fathers, Abraham, Isaac, and Jacob.

6 Understand therefore, that the LORD thy God giveth thee not this good land to possess it for thy righteousness; for thou *art* a stiffnecked people.

7 ¶ Remember, *and* forget not, how thou provokedst the LORD thy God to wrath in the wilderness: from the day that thou didst depart out of the land of Egypt, until ye came unto this place, ye have been rebellious against the LORD.

8 Also in Hō'rĕb ye provoked the LORD to wrath, so that the LORD was angry with you to have destroyed you.

9 When I was gone up into the mount to receive the tables of stone, *even* the tables of the covenant which the LORD made with you, then I abode in the mount forty days and forty nights; I neither did eat bread nor drink water:

10 And the LORD delivered unto me two tables of stone written with the finger of God; and on them *was written* according to all the words which the LORD spake with you in the mount, out of the midst of the fire, in the day of the assembly.

11 And it came to pass at the end of forty days and forty nights, *that* the LORD gave me the two tables of stone, *even* the tables of the covenant.

12 And the LORD said unto me, Arise, get thee down quickly from hence; for thy people which thou hast brought forth out of Egypt have corrupted *themselves;* they are quickly turned aside out of the way which I commanded them; they have made them a molten image.

13 Furthermore the LORD spake unto me, saying, I have seen this people, and, behold, it *is* a stiffnecked people:

14 Let me alone, that I may destroy them, and blot out their name from under heaven: and I will make of thee a nation mightier and greater than they.

15 So I turned and came down from the mount, and the mount burned with fire: and the two tables of the covenant *were* in my two hands.

16 And I looked, and, behold, ye had sinned against the LORD your God, *and* had made you a molten calf: ye had turned aside quickly out of the way which the LORD had commanded you.

17 And I took the two tables, and cast them out of my two hands, and brake them before your eyes.

18 And I fell down before the LORD, as at the first, forty days and forty nights: I did neither eat bread nor drink water, because of all your sins which ye sinned, in doing wickedly in the sight of the LORD, to provoke him to anger.

19 For I was afraid of the anger and hot displeasure, wherewith the LORD was wroth against you to destroy you. But the LORD hearkened unto me at that time also.

20 And the LORD was very angry with Aaron to have destroyed him: and I prayed for Aaron also the same time.

21 And I took your sin, the calf which ye had made, and burnt it with fire, and stamped it, *and* ground *it* very small, *even* until it was as small as dust: and I cast the dust thereof into the brook that descended out of the mount.

22 And at Tăb'ē-rȧh, and at Măs'sȧh, and at Kĭb'rŏth–hăt-tā'ȧ-vȧh, ye provoked the LORD to wrath.

23 Likewise when the LORD sent you from Kā'dĕsh–bär'nē-ȧ, saying, Go up and possess the land which I have given you; then ye rebelled against the commandment of the LORD your God, and ye believed him not, nor hearkened to his voice.

24 Ye have been rebellious against the LORD from the day that I knew you.

25 Thus I fell down before the LORD forty days and forty nights, as I fell down *at the first;* because the LORD had said he would destroy you.

26 I prayed therefore unto the LORD, and said, O LORD GOD, destroy not thy people and thine inheritance, which thou hast redeemed through thy greatness, which thou hast brought forth out of Egypt with a mighty hand.

27 Remember thy servants, Abraham, Isaac, and Jacob; look not unto the stubbornness of this people, nor to their wickedness, nor to their sin:

28 Lest the land whence thou broughtest us out say, Because the LORD was not able to bring them into the land which he promised them, and because he hated them, he hath brought them out to slay them in the wilderness.

29 Yet they *are* thy people and thine inheritance, which thou broughtest out

by thy mighty power and by thy
stretched out arm.

CHAPTER 10

AT that time the LORD said unto me,
Hew thee two tables of stone like
unto the first, and come up unto me into
the mount, and make thee an ark of
wood.
2 And I will write on the tables the
words that were in the first tables which
thou brakest, and thou shalt put them
in the ark.
3 And I made an ark *of* shittim wood,
and hewed two tables of stone like unto
the first, and went up into the mount,
having the two tables in mine hand.
4 And he wrote on the tables, according
to the first writing, the ten commandments, which the LORD spake unto you
in the mount, out of the midst of the fire,
in the day of the assembly: and the
LORD gave them unto me.
5 And I turned myself and came down
from the mount, and put the tables in
the ark which I had made; and there
they be, as the LORD commanded me.
6 ¶ And the children of Ĭs′rā-ĕl took
their journey from Bē-ē′rŏth of the children of Jā′ȧ-kăn to Mō-sē′rȧ: there
Aaron died, and there he was buried;
and Ĕl′ē-ā′zȧr his son ministered in the
priest's office in his stead.
7 From thence they journeyed unto
Gŭd-gō′dȧh; and from Gŭd-gō′dȧh to
Jŏt′bȧth, a land of rivers of waters.
8 ¶ At that time the LORD separated
the tribe of Levi, to bear the ark of the
covenant of the LORD, to stand before
the LORD to minister unto him, and to
bless in his name, unto this day.
9 Wherefore Levi hath no part nor inheritance with his brethren; the LORD
is his inheritance, according as the LORD
thy God promised him.
10 And I stayed in the mount, according
to the first time, forty days and forty
nights; and the LORD hearkened unto
me at that time also, *and* the LORD
would not destroy thee.
11 And the LORD said unto me, Arise,
take *thy* journey before the people, that
they may go in and possess the land,
which I sware unto their fathers to give
unto them.
12 ¶ And now, Ĭs′rā-ĕl, what doth the
LORD thy God require of thee, but to
fear the LORD thy God, to walk in all his
ways, and to love him, and to serve the
LORD thy God with all thy heart and
with all thy soul,
13 To keep the commandments of the
LORD, and his statutes, which I command thee this day for thy good?
14 Behold, the heaven and the heaven
of heavens *is* the LORD's thy God, the
earth *also*, with all that therein *is*.
15 Only the LORD had a delight in thy
fathers to love them, and he chose their
seed after them, *even* you above all
people, as *it is* this day.
16 Circumcise therefore the foreskin
of your heart, and be no more stiffnecked.
17 For the LORD your God *is* God of
gods, and Lord of lords, a great God, a
mighty, and a terrible, which regardeth
not persons, nor taketh reward:
18 He doth execute the judgment of
the fatherless and widow, and loveth the
stranger, in giving him food and raiment.
19 Love ye therefore the stranger: for
ye were strangers in the land of Egypt.
20 Thou shalt fear the LORD thy God;
him shalt thou serve, and to him shalt
thou cleave, and swear by his name.
21 He *is* thy praise, and he *is* thy God,
that hath done for thee these great and
terrible things, which thine eyes have
seen.
22 Thy fathers went down into Egypt
with threescore and ten persons; and
now the LORD thy God hath made thee
as the stars of heaven for multitude.

CHAPTER 11

THEREFORE thou shalt love the
LORD thy God, and keep his charge,
and his statutes, and his judgments,
and his commandments, alway.
2 And know ye this day: for *I speak*
not with your children which have not
known, and which have not seen the
chastisement of the LORD your God, his
greatness, his mighty hand, and his
stretched out arm,
3 And his miracles, and his acts, which
he did in the midst of Egypt unto Phā′-
raōh the king of Egypt, and unto all his
land;
4 And what he did unto the army of
Egypt, unto their horses, and to their
chariots; how he made the water of the
Red sea to overflow them as they pursued after you, and *how* the LORD hath
destroyed them unto this day;

5 And what he did unto you in the wilderness, until ye came into this place;
6 And what he did unto Dā'thăn and
Ȧ-bī'răm, the sons of Ē-lī'ăb, the son of
Reuben: how the earth opened her
mouth, and swallowed them up, and
their households, and their tents, and
all the substance that *was* in their possession, in the midst of all Ĭş'rā-ĕl:
7 But your eyes have seen all the great
acts of the LORD which he did.
8 Therefore shall ye keep all the commandments which I command you this
day, that ye may be strong, and go in
and possess the land, whither ye go to
possess it;
9 And that ye may prolong *your* days
in the land, which the LORD sware unto
your fathers to give unto them and to
their seed, a land that floweth with milk
and honey.
10 ¶ For the land, whither thou goest
in to possess it, *is* not as the land of
Egypt, from whence ye came out, where
thou sowedst thy seed, and wateredst *it*
with thy foot, as a garden of herbs:
11 But the land, whither ye go to possess it, *is* a land of hills and valleys, *and*
drinketh water of the rain of heaven:
12 A land which the LORD thy God
careth for: the eyes of the LORD thy God
are always upon it, from the beginning
of the year even unto the end of the
year.
13 ¶ And it shall come to pass, if ye
shall hearken diligently unto my commandments which I command you this
day, to love the LORD your God, and to
serve him with all your heart and with
all your soul,
14 That I will give *you* the rain of your
land in his due season, the first rain and
the latter rain, that thou mayest gather
in thy corn, and thy wine, and thine oil.
15 And I will send grass in thy fields
for thy cattle, that thou mayest eat and
be full.
16 Take heed to yourselves, that your
heart be not deceived, and ye turn aside,
and serve other gods, and worship them;
17 And *then* the LORD's wrath be kindled against you, and he shut up the
heaven, that there be no rain, and that
the land yield not her fruit; and *lest* ye
perish quickly from off the good land
which the LORD giveth you.
18 ¶ Therefore shall ye lay up these
my words in your heart and in your soul,
and bind them for a sign upon your
hand, that they may be as frontlets between your eyes.
19 And ye shall teach them your children, speaking of them when thou sittest in thine house, and when thou walkest by the way, when thou liest down,
and when thou risest up.
20 And thou shalt write them upon the
doorposts of thine house, and upon thy
gates:
21 That your days may be multiplied,
and the days of your children, in the
land which the LORD sware unto your
fathers to give them, as the days of
heaven upon the earth.
22 ¶ For if ye shall diligently keep all
these commandments which I command
you, to do them, to love the LORD your
God, to walk in all his ways, and to
cleave unto him;
23 Then will the LORD drive out all
these nations from before you, and
ye shall possess greater nations and
mightier than yourselves.
24 Every place whereon the soles of
your feet shall tread shall be yours: from
the wilderness and Lebanon, from the
river, the river Eū-phrā'tēs̱, even unto
the uttermost sea shall your coast be.
25 There shall no man be able to stand
before you: *for* the LORD your God shall
lay the fear of you and the dread of you
upon all the land that ye shall tread
upon, as he hath said unto you.
26 ¶ Behold, I set before you this day
a blessing and a curse;
27 A blessing, if ye obey the commandments of the LORD your God, which I
command you this day:
28 And a curse, if ye will not obey the
commandments of the LORD your God,
but turn aside out of the way which I
command you this day, to go after other
gods, which ye have not known.
29 And it shall come to pass, when the
LORD thy God hath brought thee in unto
the land whither thou goest to possess
it, that thou shalt put the blessing upon
mount Gĕr'ĭ-zĭm, and the curse upon
mount Ē'băl.
30 *Are* they not on the other side Jordan, by the way where the sun goeth
down, in the land of the Cā'năan-ītes,
which dwell in the champaign over
against Gĭl'găl, beside the plains of
Mō'rĕh?
31 For ye shall pass over Jordan to go

in to possess the land which the LORD
your God giveth you, and ye shall possess it, and dwell therein.
32 And ye shall observe to do all the
statutes and judgments which I set before you this day.

CHAPTER 12

THESE *are* the statutes and judgments, which ye shall observe to do
in the land, which the LORD God of thy
fathers giveth thee to possess it, all the
days that ye live upon the earth.
2 Ye shall utterly destroy all the places,
wherein the nations which ye shall possess served their gods, upon the high
mountains, and upon the hills, and
under every green tree:
3 And ye shall overthrow their altars,
and break their pillars, and burn their
groves with fire; and ye shall hew down
the graven images of their gods, and
destroy the names of them out of that
place.
4 Ye shall not do so unto the LORD your
God.
5 But unto the place which the LORD
your God shall choose out of all your
tribes to put his name there, *even* unto
his habitation shall ye seek, and thither
thou shalt come:
6 And thither ye shall bring your burnt
offerings, and your sacrifices, and your
tithes, and heave offerings of your hand,
and your vows, and your freewill offerings, and the firstlings of your herds and
of your flocks:
7 And there ye shall eat before the
LORD your God, and ye shall rejoice in
all that ye put your hand unto, ye and
your households, wherein the LORD thy
God hath blessed thee.
8 Ye shall not do after all *the things*
that we do here this day, every man
whatsoever *is* right in his own eyes.
9 For ye are not as yet come to the rest
and to the inheritance, which the LORD
your God giveth you.
10 But *when* ye go over Jordan, and
dwell in the land which the LORD your
God giveth you to inherit, and *when* he
giveth you rest from all your enemies
round about, so that ye dwell in safety;
11 Then there shall be a place which
the LORD your God shall choose to cause
his name to dwell there; thither shall ye
bring all that I command you; your burnt
offerings, and your sacrifices, your
tithes, and the heave offering of your
hand, and all your choice vows which ye
vow unto the LORD:
12 And ye shall rejoice before the LORD
your God, ye, and your sons, and your
daughters, and your menservants, and
your maidservants, and the Lē'vīte that
is within your gates; forasmuch as he
hath no part nor inheritance with you.
13 Take heed to thyself that thou offer
not thy burnt offerings in every place
that thou seest:
14 But in the place which the LORD
shall choose in one of thy tribes, there
thou shalt offer thy burnt offerings, and
there thou shalt do all that I command
thee.
15 Notwithstanding, thou mayest kill
and eat flesh in all thy gates, whatsoever thy soul lusteth after, according to
the blessing of the LORD thy God which
he hath given thee: the unclean and the
clean may eat thereof, as of the roebuck,
and as of the hart.
16 Only ye shall not eat the blood; ye
shall pour it upon the earth as water.
17 ¶ Thou mayest not eat within thy
gates the tithe of thy corn, or of thy
wine, or of thy oil, or the firstlings of thy
herds or of thy flock, nor any of thy vows
which thou vowest, nor thy freewill
offerings, or heave offering of thine hand:
18 But thou must eat them before the
LORD thy God in the place which the
LORD thy God shall choose, thou, and
thy son, and thy daughter, and thy manservant, and thy maidservant, and the
Lē'vīte that *is* within thy gates: and thou
shalt rejoice before the LORD thy God
in all that thou puttest thine hands unto.
19 Take heed to thyself that thou forsake not the Lē'vīte as long as thou
livest upon the earth.
20 ¶ When the LORD thy God shall
enlarge thy border, as he hath promised
thee, and thou shalt say, I will eat flesh,
because thy soul longeth to eat flesh;
thou mayest eat flesh, whatsoever thy
soul lusteth after.
21 If the place which the LORD thy God
hath chosen to put his name there be
too far from thee, then thou shalt kill of
thy herd and of thy flock, which the
LORD hath given thee, as I have commanded thee, and thou shalt eat in thy
gates whatsoever thy soul lusteth after.
22 Even as the roebuck and the hart is
eaten, so thou shalt eat them: the un-

clean and the clean shall eat *of* them
alike.
23 Only be sure that thou eat not the
blood: for the blood *is* the life; and thou
mayest not eat the life with the flesh.
24 Thou shalt not eat it; thou shalt
pour it upon the earth as water.
25 Thou shalt not eat it; that it may go
well with thee, and with thy children
after thee, when thou shalt do *that which*
is right in the sight of the LORD.
26 Only thy holy things which thou
hast, and thy vows, thou shalt take, and
go unto the place which the LORD shall
choose:
27 And thou shalt offer thy burnt offerings, the flesh and the blood, upon the
altar of the LORD thy God: and the
blood of thy sacrifices shall be poured
out upon the altar of the LORD thy God,
and thou shalt eat the flesh.
28 Observe and hear all these words
which I command thee, that it may go
well with thee, and with thy children
after thee for ever, when thou doest
that which is good and right in the sight
of the LORD thy God.
29 ¶ When the LORD thy God shall
cut off the nations from before thee,
whither thou goest to possess them, and
thou succeedest them, and dwellest in
their land;
30 Take heed to thyself that thou be
not snared by following them, after
that they be destroyed from before thee;
and that thou inquire not after their
gods, saying, How did these nations
serve their gods? even so will I do likewise.
31 Thou shalt not do so unto the LORD
thy God: for every abomination to the
LORD which he hateth have they done
unto their gods; for even their sons and
their daughters they have burnt in the
fire to their gods.
32 What thing soever I command you,
observe to do it: thou shalt not add
thereto, nor diminish from it.

CHAPTER 13

IF there arise among you a prophet, or
a dreamer of dreams, and giveth thee
a sign or a wonder,
2 And the sign or the wonder come to
pass, whereof he spake unto thee, saying, Let us go after other gods, which
thou hast not known, and let us serve
them;
3 Thou shalt not hearken unto the
words of that prophet, or that dreamer
of dreams: for the LORD your God prov-
eth you, to know whether ye love the
LORD your God with all your heart and
with all your soul.
4 Ye shall walk after the LORD your
God, and fear him, and keep his commandments, and obey his voice, and ye
shall serve him, and cleave unto him.
5 And that prophet, or that dreamer of
dreams, shall be put to death; because
he hath spoken to turn *you* away from
the LORD your God, which brought you
out of the land of Egypt, and redeemed
you out of the house of bondage, to
thrust thee out of the way which the
LORD thy God commanded thee to walk
in. So shalt thou put the evil away from
the midst of thee.
6 ¶ If thy brother, the son of thy
mother, or thy son, or thy daughter, or
the wife of thy bosom, or thy friend,
which *is* as thine own soul, entice thee
secretly, saying, Let us go and serve
other gods, which thou hast not known,
thou, nor thy fathers;
7 *Namely*, of the gods of the people
which *are* round about you, nigh unto
thee, or far off from thee, from the *one*
end of the earth even unto the *other* end
of the earth;
8 Thou shalt not consent unto him, nor
hearken unto him; neither shall thine
eye pity him, neither shalt thou spare,
neither shalt thou conceal him:
9 But thou shalt surely kill him; thine
hand shall be first upon him to put him
to death, and afterward the hand of all
the people.
10 And thou shalt stone him with
stones, that he die; because he hath
sought to thrust thee away from the
LORD thy God, which brought thee out
of the land of Egypt, from the house of
bondage.
11 And all Ĭṣ'rā-ĕl shall hear, and fear,
and shall do no more any such wickedness as this is among you.
12 ¶ If thou shalt hear *say* in one of
thy cities, which the LORD thy God hath
given thee to dwell there, saying,
13 *Certain* men, the children of Bē'-
lĭ-ăl, are gone out from among you, and
have withdrawn the inhabitants of their
city, saying, Let us go and serve other
gods, which ye have not known;
14 Then shalt thou inquire, and make

search, and ask diligently; and, behold, *if it be* truth, *and* the thing certain, *that* such abomination is wrought among you;
15 Thou shalt surely smite the inhabitants of that city with the edge of the sword, destroying it utterly, and all that *is* therein, and the cattle thereof, with the edge of the sword.
16 And thou shalt gather all the spoil of it into the midst of the street thereof, and shalt burn with fire the city, and all the spoil thereof every whit, for the LORD thy God: and it shall be a heap for ever; it shall not be built again.
17 And there shall cleave nought of the cursed thing to thine hand: that the LORD may turn from the fierceness of his anger, and show thee mercy, and have compassion upon thee, and multiply thee, as he hath sworn unto thy fathers;
18 When thou shalt hearken to the voice of the LORD thy God, to keep all his commandments which I command thee this day, to do *that which is* right in the eyes of the LORD thy God.

CHAPTER 14

YE *are* the children of the LORD your God: ye shall not cut yourselves, nor make any baldness between your eyes for the dead.
2 For thou *art* a holy people unto the LORD thy God, and the LORD hath chosen thee to be a peculiar people unto himself, above all the nations that *are* upon the earth.
3 ¶ Thou shalt not eat any abominable thing.
4 These *are* the beasts which ye shall eat: the ox, the sheep, and the goat,
5 The hart, and the roebuck, and the fallow deer, and the wild goat, and the pygarg, and the wild ox, and the chamois.
6 And every beast that parteth the hoof, and cleaveth the cleft into two claws, *and* cheweth the cud among the beasts, that ye shall eat.
7 Nevertheless these ye shall not eat, of them that chew the cud, or of them that divide the cloven hoof; *as* the camel, and the hare, and the coney: for they chew the cud, but divide not the hoof; *therefore* they *are* unclean unto you.
8 And the swine, because it divideth the hoof, yet cheweth not the cud, it *is* unclean unto you: ye shall not eat of their flesh, nor touch their dead carcass.
9 ¶ These ye shall eat, of all that *are* in the waters: all that have fins and scales shall ye eat:
10 And whatsoever hath not fins and scales ye may not eat; it *is* unclean unto you.
11 ¶ *Of* all clean birds ye shall eat.
12 But these *are they* of which ye shall not eat: the eagle, and the ossifrage, and the ospray,
13 And the glede, and the kite, and the vulture after his kind,
14 And every raven after his kind,
15 And the owl, and the nighthawk, and the cuckoo, and the hawk after his kind,
16 The little owl, and the great owl, and the swan,
17 And the pelican, and the gier-eagle, and the cormorant,
18 And the stork, and the heron after her kind, and the lapwing, and the bat.
19 And every creeping thing that flieth *is* unclean unto you: they shall not be eaten.
20 *But of* all clean fowls ye may eat.
21 ¶ Ye shall not eat *of* any thing that dieth of itself: thou shalt give it unto the stranger that *is* in thy gates, that he may eat it; or thou mayest sell it unto an alien: for thou *art* a holy people unto the LORD thy God. Thou shalt not seethe a kid in his mother's milk.
22 Thou shalt truly tithe all the increase of thy seed, that the field bringeth forth year by year.
23 And thou shalt eat before the LORD thy God, in the place which he shall choose to place his name there, the tithe of thy corn, of thy wine, and of thine oil, and the firstlings of thy herds and of thy flocks; that thou mayest learn to fear the LORD thy God always.
24 And if the way be too long for thee, so that thou art not able to carry it; *or* if the place be too far from thee, which the LORD thy God shall choose to set his name there, when the LORD thy God hath blessed thee:
25 Then shalt thou turn *it* into money, and bind up the money in thine hand, and shalt go unto the place which the LORD thy God shall choose:
26 And thou shalt bestow that money for whatsoever thy soul lusteth after, for oxen, or for sheep, or for wine, or for strong drink, or for whatsoever thy soul

desireth: and thou shalt eat there before
the LORD thy God, and thou shalt rejoice, thou, and thine household.
27 And the Lē′vīte that *is* within thy
gates; thou shalt not forsake him: for he
hath no part nor inheritance with thee.
28 ¶ At the end of three years thou
shalt bring forth all the tithe of thine increase the same year, and shalt lay *it* up
within thy gates:
29 And the Lē′vīte, (because he hath
no part nor inheritance with thee,) and
the stranger, and the fatherless, and the
widow, which *are* within thy gates, shall
come, and shall eat and be satisfied;
that the LORD thy God may bless thee
in all the work of thine hand which thou
doest.

CHAPTER 15

AT the end of *every* seven years thou
shalt make a release.
2 And this *is* the manner of the release:
Every creditor that lendeth *aught* unto
his neighbor shall release *it;* he shall not
exact *it* of his neighbor, or of his brother;
because it is called the LORD's release.
3 Of a foreigner thou mayest exact *it*
again: but *that* which is thine with thy
brother thine hand shall release;
4 Save when there shall be no poor
among you; for the LORD shall greatly
bless thee in the land which the LORD
thy God giveth thee *for* an inheritance
to possess it:
5 Only if thou carefully hearken unto
the voice of the LORD thy God, to observe to do all these commandments
which I command thee this day.
6 For the LORD thy God blesseth thee,
as he promised thee: and thou shalt lend
unto many nations, but thou shalt not
borrow; and thou shalt reign over many
nations, but they shall not reign over
thee.
7 ¶ If there be among you a poor man
of one of thy brethren within any of thy
gates in thy land which the LORD thy
God giveth thee, thou shalt not harden
thine heart, nor shut thine hand from
thy poor brother:
8 But thou shalt open thine hand wide
unto him, and shalt surely lend him
sufficient for his need, *in that* which he
wanteth.
9 Beware that there be not a thought in
thy wicked heart, saying, The seventh
year, the year of release, is at hand; and
thine eye be evil against thy poor
brother, and thou givest him nought;
and he cry unto the LORD against thee,
and it be sin unto thee.
10 Thou shalt surely give him, and
thine heart shall not be grieved when
thou givest unto him: because that for
this thing the LORD thy God shall bless
thee in all thy works, and in all that thou
puttest thine hand unto.
11 For the poor shall never cease out
of the land: therefore I command thee,
saying, Thou shalt open thine hand wide
unto thy brother, to thy poor, and to thy
needy, in thy land.
12 ¶ *And* if thy brother, a Hebrew
man, or a Hebrew woman, be sold unto
thee, and serve thee six years; then in
the seventh year thou shalt let him go
free from thee.
13 And when thou sendest him out free
from thee, thou shalt not let him go away
empty:
14 Thou shalt furnish him liberally out
of thy flock, and out of thy floor, and out
of thy winepress: *of that* wherewith the
LORD thy God hath blessed thee thou
shalt give unto him.
15 And thou shalt remember that thou
wast a bondman in the land of Egypt,
and the LORD thy God redeemed thee:
therefore I command thee this thing
to-day.
16 And it shall be, if he say unto thee,
I will not go away from thee; because he
loveth thee and thine house, because he
is well with thee;
17 Then thou shalt take an awl, and
thrust *it* through his ear unto the door,
and he shall be thy servant for ever.
And also unto thy maidservant thou
shalt do likewise.
18 It shall not seem hard unto thee,
when thou sendest him away free from
thee; for he hath been worth a double
hired servant *to thee,* in serving thee six
years: and the LORD thy God shall bless
thee in all that thou doest.
19 ¶ All the firstling males that come
of thy herd and of thy flock thou shalt
sanctify unto the LORD thy God: thou
shalt do no work with the firstling of thy
bullock, nor shear the firstling of thy
sheep.
20 Thou shalt eat *it* before the LORD
thy God year by year in the place which
the LORD shall choose, thou and thy
household.

21 And if there be *any* blemish therein, *as if it be* lame, or blind, *or have* any ill blemish, thou shalt not sacrifice it unto the LORD thy God.

22 Thou shalt eat it within thy gates: the unclean and the clean *person shall eat it* alike, as the roebuck, and as the hart.

23 Only thou shalt not eat the blood thereof; thou shalt pour it upon the ground as water.

CHAPTER 16

OBSERVE the month of Ā'bĭb, and keep the passover unto the LORD thy God: for in the month of Ā'bĭb the LORD thy God brought thee forth out of Egypt by night.

2 Thou shalt therefore sacrifice the passover unto the LORD thy God, of the flock and the herd, in the place which the LORD shall choose to place his name there.

3 Thou shalt eat no leavened bread with it; seven days shalt thou eat unleavened bread therewith, *even* the bread of affliction; for thou camest forth out of the land of Egypt in haste: that thou mayest remember the day when thou camest forth out of the land of Egypt all the days of thy life.

4 And there shall be no leavened bread seen with thee in all thy coast seven days; neither shall there *any thing* of the flesh, which thou sacrificedst the first day at even, remain all night until the morning.

5 Thou mayest not sacrifice the passover within any of thy gates, which the LORD thy God giveth thee:

6 But at the place which the LORD thy God shall choose to place his name in, there thou shalt sacrifice the passover at even, at the going down of the sun, at the season that thou camest forth out of Egypt.

7 And thou shalt roast and eat *it* in the place which the LORD thy God shall choose: and thou shalt turn in the morning, and go unto thy tents.

8 Six days thou shalt eat unleavened bread: and on the seventh day *shall be* a solemn assembly to the LORD thy God: thou shalt do no work *therein*.

9 ¶ Seven weeks shalt thou number unto thee: begin to number the seven weeks from *such time as* thou beginnest *to put* the sickle to the corn.

10 And thou shalt keep the feast of weeks unto the LORD thy God with a tribute of a freewill offering of thine hand, which thou shalt give *unto the LORD thy God,* according as the LORD thy God hath blessed thee:

11 And thou shalt rejoice before the LORD thy God, thou, and thy son, and thy daughter, and thy manservant, and thy maidservant, and the Lē'vīte that *is* within thy gates, and the stranger, and the fatherless, and the widow, that *are* among you, in the place which the LORD thy God hath chosen to place his name there.

12 And thou shalt remember that thou wast a bondman in Egypt: and thou shalt observe and do these statutes.

13 ¶ Thou shalt observe the feast of tabernacles seven days, after that thou hast gathered in thy corn and thy wine:

14 And thou shalt rejoice in thy feast, thou, and thy son, and thy daughter, and thy manservant, and thy maidservant, and the Lē'vīte, the stranger, and the fatherless, and the widow, that *are* within thy gates.

15 Seven days shalt thou keep a solemn feast unto the LORD thy God in the place which the LORD shall choose: because the LORD thy God shall bless thee in all thine increase, and in all the works of thine hands, therefore thou shalt surely rejoice.

16 ¶ Three times in a year shall all thy males appear before the LORD thy God in the place which he shall choose; in the feast of unleavened bread, and in the feast of weeks, and in the feast of tabernacles: and they shall not appear before the LORD empty:

17 Every man *shall give* as he is able, according to the blessing of the LORD thy God which he hath given thee.

18 ¶ Judges and officers shalt thou make thee in all thy gates, which the LORD thy God giveth thee, throughout thy tribes: and they shall judge the people with just judgment.

19 Thou shalt not wrest judgment; thou shalt not respect persons, neither take a gift: for a gift doth blind the eyes of the wise, and pervert the words of the righteous.

20 That which is altogether just shalt thou follow, that thou mayest live, and inherit the land which the LORD thy God giveth thee.

21 ¶ Thou shalt not plant thee a grove of any trees near unto the altar of the LORD thy God, which thou shalt make thee.

22 Neither shalt thou set thee up *any* image; which the LORD thy God hateth.

CHAPTER 17

THOU shalt not sacrifice unto the LORD thy God *any* bullock, or sheep, wherein is blemish, *or* any evil-favoredness: for that *is* an abomination unto the LORD thy God.

2 ¶ If there be found among you, within any of thy gates which the LORD thy God giveth thee, man or woman, that hath wrought wickedness in the sight of the LORD thy God, in transgressing his covenant,

3 And hath gone and served other gods, and worshipped them, either the sun, or moon, or any of the host of heaven, which I have not commanded;

4 And it be told thee, and thou hast heard *of it*, and inquired diligently, and, behold, *it be* true, *and* the thing certain, *that* such abomination is wrought in Iṣ′rā-ĕl:

5 Then shalt thou bring forth that man or that woman, which have committed that wicked thing, unto thy gates, *even* that man or that woman, and shalt stone them with stones, till they die.

6 At the mouth of two witnesses, or three witnesses, shall he that is worthy of death be put to death; *but* at the mouth of one witness he shall not be put to death.

7 The hands of the witnesses shall be first upon him to put him to death, and afterward the hands of all the people. So thou shalt put the evil away from among you.

8 ¶ If there arise a matter too hard for thee in judgment, between blood and blood, between plea and plea, and between stroke and stroke, *being* matters of controversy within thy gates: then shalt thou arise, and get thee up into the place which the LORD thy God shall choose;

9 And thou shalt come unto the priests the Lē′vītes, and unto the judge that shall be in those days, and inquire; and they shall show thee the sentence of judgment:

10 And thou shalt do according to the sentence, which they of that place which the LORD shall choose shall show thee; and thou shalt observe to do according to all that they inform thee:

11 According to the sentence of the law which they shall teach thee, and according to the judgment which they shall tell thee, thou shalt do: thou shalt not decline from the sentence which they shall show thee, *to* the right hand, nor *to* the left.

12 And the man that will do presumptuously, and will not hearken unto the priest that standeth to minister there before the LORD thy God, or unto the judge, even that man shall die: and thou shalt put away the evil from Iṣ′rā-ĕl.

13 And all the people shall hear, and fear, and do no more presumptuously.

14 ¶ When thou art come unto the land which the LORD thy God giveth thee, and shalt possess it, and shalt dwell therein, and shalt say, I will set a king over me, like as all the nations that *are* about me;

15 Thou shalt in any wise set *him* king over thee, whom the LORD thy God shall choose: *one* from among thy brethren shalt thou set king over thee: thou mayest not set a stranger over thee, which *is* not thy brother.

16 But he shall not multiply horses to himself, nor cause the people to return to Egypt, to the end that he should multiply horses: forasmuch as the LORD hath said unto you, Ye shall henceforth return no more that way.

17 Neither shall he multiply wives to himself, that his heart turn not away: neither shall he greatly multiply to himself silver and gold.

18 And it shall be, when he sitteth upon the throne of his kingdom, that he shall write him a copy of this law in a book out of *that which is* before the priests the Lē′vītes:

19 And it shall be with him, and he shall read therein all the days of his life; that he may learn to fear the LORD his God, to keep all the words of this law and these statutes, to do them:

20 That his heart be not lifted up above his brethren, and that he turn not aside from the commandment, *to* the right hand, or *to* the left: to the end that he may prolong *his* days in his kingdom, he, and his children, in the midst of Iṣ′rā-ĕl.

CHAPTER 18

THE priests the Lē′vītes, *and* all the tribe of Levi, shall have no part nor inheritance with Is̩′rā-ēl: they shall eat the offerings of the LORD made by fire, and his inheritance.

2 Therefore shall they have no inheritance among their brethren: the LORD *is* their inheritance, as he hath said unto them.

3 ¶ And this shall be the priest's due from the people, from them that offer a sacrifice, whether *it be* ox or sheep; and they shall give unto the priest the shoulder, and the two cheeks, and the maw.

4 The firstfruit *also* of thy corn, of thy wine, and of thine oil, and the first of the fleece of thy sheep, shalt thou give him.

5 For the LORD thy God hath chosen him out of all thy tribes, to stand to minister in the name of the LORD, him and his sons for ever.

6 ¶ And if a Lē′vīte come from any of thy gates out of all Is̩′rā-ĕl, where he sojourned, and come with all the desire of his mind unto the place which the LORD shall choose;

7 Then he shall minister in the name of the LORD his God, as all his brethren the Lē′vītes *do*, which stand there before the LORD.

8 They shall have like portions to eat, besides that which cometh of the sale of his patrimony.

9 ¶ When thou art come into the land which the LORD thy God giveth thee, thou shalt not learn to do after the abominations of those nations.

10 There shall not be found among you *any one* that maketh his son or his daughter to pass through the fire, *or* that useth divination, *or* an observer of times, or an enchanter, or a witch,

11 Or a charmer, or a consulter with familiar spirits, or a wizard, or a necromancer.

12 For all that do these things *are* an abomination unto the LORD: and because of these abominations the LORD thy God doth drive them out from before thee.

13 Thou shalt be perfect with the LORD thy God.

14 For these nations, which thou shalt possess, hearkened unto observers of times, and unto diviners: but as for thee, the LORD thy God hath not suffered thee so *to do*.

15 ¶ The LORD thy God will raise up unto thee a Prophet from the midst of thee, of thy brethren, like unto me; unto him ye shall hearken;

16 According to all that thou desiredst of the LORD thy God in Hō′rĕb in the day of the assembly, saying, Let me not hear again the voice of the LORD my God, neither let me see this great fire any more, that I die not.

17 And the LORD said unto me, They have well *spoken that* which they have spoken.

18 I will raise them up a Prophet from among their brethren, like unto thee, and will put my words in his mouth; and he shall speak unto them all that I shall command him.

19 And it shall come to pass, *that* whosoever will not hearken unto my words which he shall speak in my name, I will require *it* of him.

20 But the prophet, which shall presume to speak a word in my name, which I have not commanded him to speak, or that shall speak in the name of other gods, even that prophet shall die.

21 And if thou say in thine heart, How shall we know the word which the LORD hath not spoken?

22 When a prophet speaketh in the name of the LORD, if the thing follow not, nor come to pass, that *is* the thing which the LORD hath not spoken, *but* the prophet hath spoken it presumptuously: thou shalt not be afraid of him.

CHAPTER 19

WHEN the LORD thy God hath cut off the nations, whose land the LORD thy God giveth thee, and thou succeedest them, and dwellest in their cities, and in their houses;

2 Thou shalt separate three cities for thee in the midst of thy land, which the LORD thy God giveth thee to possess it.

3 Thou shalt prepare thee a way, and divide the coasts of thy land, which the LORD thy God giveth thee to inherit, into three parts, that every slayer may flee thither.

4 ¶ And this *is* the case of the slayer, which shall flee thither, that he may live: Whoso killeth his neighbor ignorantly, whom he hated not in time past;

5 As when a man goeth into the wood with his neighbor to hew wood, and his hand fetcheth a stroke with the axe to

cut down the tree, and the head slippeth
from the helve, and lighteth upon his
neighbor, that he die; he shall flee unto
one of those cities, and live:
6 Lest the avenger of the blood pursue
the slayer, while his heart is hot, and
overtake him, because the way is long,
and slay him; whereas he *was* not
worthy of death, inasmuch as he hated
him not in time past.
7 Wherefore I command thee, saying,
Thou shalt separate three cities for thee.
8 And if the LORD thy God enlarge thy
coast, as he hath sworn unto thy fathers,
and give thee all the land which he
promised to give unto thy fathers;
9 If thou shalt keep all these commandments to do them, which I command
thee this day, to love the LORD thy God,
and to walk ever in his ways; then shalt
thou add three cities more for thee, beside these three:
10 That innocent blood be not shed in
thy land, which the LORD thy God giveth
thee *for* an inheritance, and *so* blood be
upon thee.
11 ¶ But if any man hate his neighbor,
and lie in wait for him, and rise up
against him, and smite him mortally that
he die, and fleeth into one of these cities;
12 Then the elders of his city shall send
and fetch him thence, and deliver him
into the hand of the avenger of blood,
that he may die.
13 Thine eye shall not pity him, but
thou shalt put away *the guilt of* innocent
blood from Ĭş'rā-ĕl, that it may go well
with thee.
14 ¶ Thou shalt not remove thy neighbor's landmark, which they of old time
have set in thine inheritance, which thou
shalt inherit in the land that the LORD
thy God giveth thee to possess it.
15 ¶ One witness shall not rise up
against a man for any iniquity, or for any
sin, in any sin that he sinneth: at the
mouth of two witnesses, or at the mouth
of three witnesses, shall the matter be
established.
16 ¶ If a false witness rise up against
any man to testify against him *that
which is* wrong;
17 Then both the men, between whom
the controversy *is*, shall stand before
the LORD, before the priests and the
judges, which shall be in those days;
18 And the judges shall make diligent
inquisition: and, behold, *if* the witness
be a false witness, *and* hath testified
falsely against his brother;
19 Then shall ye do unto him, as he
had thought to have done unto his
brother: so shalt thou put the evil away
from among you.
20 And those which remain shall hear,
and fear, and shall henceforth commit
no more any such evil among you.
21 And thine eye shall not pity; *but* life
shall go for life, eye for eye, tooth for
tooth, hand for hand, foot for foot.

CHAPTER 20

WHEN thou goest out to battle
against thine enemies, and seest
horses, and chariots, *and* a people more
than thou, be not afraid of them: for the
LORD thy God *is* with thee, which
brought thee up out of the land of Egypt.
2 And it shall be, when ye are come
nigh unto the battle, that the priest shall
approach and speak unto the people,
3 And shall say unto them, Hear, O
Ĭş'rā-ĕl, ye approach this day unto battle against your enemies: let not your
hearts faint, fear not, and do not tremble, neither be ye terrified because of
them;
4 For the LORD your God *is* he that
goeth with you, to fight for you against
your enemies, to save you.
5 ¶ And the officers shall speak unto
the people, saying, What man *is there*
that hath built a new house, and hath
not dedicated it? let him go and return
to his house, lest he die in the battle,
and another man dedicate it.
6 And what man *is he* that hath planted
a vineyard, and hath not *yet* eaten of it?
let him *also* go and return unto his
house, lest he die in the battle, and another man eat of it.
7 And what man *is there* that hath betrothed a wife, and hath not taken her?
let him go and return unto his house,
lest he die in the battle, and another man
take her.
8 And the officers shall speak further
unto the people, and they shall say,
What man *is there that is* fearful and
faint-hearted? let him go and return unto his house, lest his brethren's heart
faint as well as his heart.
9 And it shall be, when the officers have
made an end of speaking unto the people, that they shall make captains of the
armies to lead the people.

10 ¶ When thou comest nigh unto a city to fight against it, then proclaim peace unto it.

11 And it shall be, if it make thee answer of peace, and open unto thee, then it shall be, *that* all the people *that is* found therein shall be tributaries unto thee, and they shall serve thee.

12 And if it will make no peace with thee, but will make war against thee, then thou shalt besiege it:

13 And when the LORD thy God hath delivered it into thine hands, thou shalt smite every male thereof with the edge of the sword:

14 But the women, and the little ones, and the cattle, and all that is in the city, *even* all the spoil thereof, shalt thou take unto thyself; and thou shalt eat the spoil of thine enemies, which the LORD thy God hath given thee.

15 Thus shalt thou do unto all the cities *which are* very far off from thee, which *are* not of the cities of these nations.

16 But of the cities of these people, which the LORD thy God doth give thee *for* an inheritance, thou shalt save alive nothing that breatheth:

17 But thou shalt utterly destroy them; *namely*, the Hĭt'tītes, and the Ăm'ō-rītes, the Cā'năan-ītes, and the Pĕr'ĭz-zītes, the Hī'vītes, and the Jĕb'ū-ṣītes; as the LORD thy God hath commanded thee:

18 That they teach you not to do after all their abominations, which they have done unto their gods; so should ye sin against the LORD your God.

19 ¶ When thou shalt besiege a city a long time, in making war against it to take it, thou shalt not destroy the trees thereof by forcing an axe against them: for thou mayest eat of them, and thou shalt not cut them down (for the tree of the field *is* man's *life*) to employ *them* in the siege:

20 Only the trees which thou knowest that they *be* not trees for meat, thou shalt destroy and cut them down; and thou shalt build bulwarks against the city that maketh war with thee, until it be subdued.

CHAPTER 21

IF *one* be found slain in the land which the LORD thy God giveth thee to possess it, lying in the field, *and* it be not known who hath slain him:

2 Then thy elders and thy judges shall come forth, and they shall measure unto the cities which *are* round about him that is slain:

3 And it shall be, *that* the city *which is* next unto the slain man, even the elders of that city shall take a heifer, which hath not been wrought with, *and* which hath not drawn in the yoke;

4 And the elders of that city shall bring down the heifer unto a rough valley, which is neither eared nor sown, and shall strike off the heifer's neck there in the valley.

5 And the priests the sons of Levi shall come near; for them the LORD thy God hath chosen to minister unto him, and to bless in the name of the LORD; and by their word shall every controversy and every stroke be *tried:*

6 And all the elders of that city, *that are* next unto the slain *man*, shall wash their hands over the heifer that is beheaded in the valley:

7 And they shall answer and say, Our hands have not shed this blood, neither have our eyes seen *it*.

8 Be merciful, O LORD, unto thy people Ĭṣ'rā-ĕl, whom thou hast redeemed, and lay not innocent blood unto thy people of Ĭṣ'rā-ĕl's charge. And the blood shall be forgiven them.

9 So shalt thou put away the *guilt of* innocent blood from among you, when thou shalt do *that which is* right in the sight of the LORD.

10 ¶ When thou goest forth to war against thine enemies, and the LORD thy God hath delivered them into thine hands, and thou hast taken them captive,

11 And seest among the captives a beautiful woman, and hast a desire unto her, that thou wouldest have her to thy wife;

12 Then thou shalt bring her home to thine house; and she shall shave her head, and pare her nails;

13 And she shall put the raiment of her captivity from off her, and shall remain in thine house, and bewail her father and her mother a full month: and after that thou shalt go in unto her, and be her husband, and she shall be thy wife.

14 And it shall be, if thou have no delight in her, then thou shalt let her go whither she will; but thou shalt not sell her at all for money, thou shalt not make

merchandise of her, because thou hast
humbled her.
15 ¶ If a man have two wives, one beloved, and another hated, and they have
borne him children, *both* the beloved
and the hated; and *if* the firstborn son
be hers that was hated:
16 Then it shall be, when he maketh
his sons to inherit *that* which he hath,
that he may not make the son of the beloved firstborn before the son of the
hated, *which is indeed* the firstborn:
17 But he shall acknowledge the son of
the hated *for* the firstborn, by giving
him a double portion of all that he hath:
for he *is* the beginning of his strength;
the right of the firstborn *is* his.
18 ¶ If a man have a stubborn and
rebellious son, which will not obey the
voice of his father, or the voice of his
mother, and *that*, when they have chastened him, will not hearken unto them:
19 Then shall his father and his mother
lay hold on him, and bring him out unto
the elders of his city, and unto the gate
of his place;
20 And they shall say unto the elders
of his city, This our son *is* stubborn and
rebellious, he will not obey our voice; *he*
is a glutton, and a drunkard.
21 And all the men of his city shall
stone him with stones, that he die: so
shalt thou put evil away from among
you; and all Is'rā-ĕl shall hear, and fear.
22 ¶ And if a man have committed a
sin worthy of death, and he be to be
put to death, and thou hang him on a
tree:
23 His body shall not remain all night
upon the tree, but thou shalt in any wise
bury him that day; (for he that is hanged
is accursed of God;) that thy land be not
defiled, which the LORD thy God giveth
thee *for* an inheritance.

CHAPTER 22

THOU shalt not see thy brother's ox
or his sheep go astray, and hide thyself from them: thou shalt in any case
bring them again unto thy brother.
2 And if thy brother *be* not nigh unto
thee, or if thou know him not, then thou
shalt bring it unto thine own house, and
it shall be with thee until thy brother
seek after it, and thou shalt restore it to
him again.
3 In like manner shalt thou do with his
ass; and so shalt thou do with his raiment; and with all lost things of thy
brother's, which he hath lost, and thou
hast found, shalt thou do likewise: thou
mayest not hide thyself.
4 ¶ Thou shalt not see thy brother's
ass or his ox fall down by the way, and
hide thyself from them: thou shalt surely
help him to lift *them* up again.
5 ¶ The woman shall not wear that
which pertaineth unto a man, neither
shall a man put on a woman's garment:
for all that do so *are* abomination unto
the LORD thy God.
6 ¶ If a bird's nest chance to be before
thee in the way in any tree, or on the
ground, *whether they be* young ones, or
eggs, and the dam sitting upon the
young, or upon the eggs, thou shalt not
take the dam with the young:
7 *But* thou shalt in any wise let the dam
go, and take the young to thee; that it
may be well with thee, and *that* thou
mayest prolong *thy* days.
8 ¶ When thou buildest a new house,
then thou shalt make a battlement for
thy roof, that thou bring not blood upon
thine house, if any man fall from thence.
9 ¶ Thou shalt not sow thy vineyard
with divers seeds: lest the fruit of thy
seed which thou hast sown, and the
fruit of thy vineyard, be defiled.
10 ¶ Thou shalt not plow with an ox
and an ass together.
11 ¶ Thou shalt not wear a garment of
divers sorts, *as* of woolen and linen
together.
12 ¶ Thou shalt make thee fringes
upon the four quarters of thy vesture,
wherewith thou coverest *thyself*.
13 ¶ If any man take a wife, and go in
unto her, and hate her,
14 And give occasions of speech against
her, and bring up an evil name upon her,
and say, I took this woman, and when I
came to her, I found her not a maid:
15 Then shall the father of the damsel,
and her mother, take and bring forth
the tokens of the damsel's virginity unto
the elders of the city in the gate:
16 And the damsel's father shall say
unto the elders, I gave my daughter unto this man to wife, and he hateth her;
17 And, lo, he hath given occasions of
speech *against her*, saying, I found not
thy daughter a maid; and yet these *are*
the tokens of my daughter's virginity.
And they shall spread the cloth before
the elders of the city.

18 And the elders of that city shall take
that man and chastise him;
19 And they shall amerce him in a hundred *shekels* of silver, and give *them* unto the father of the damsel, because he hath brought up an evil name upon a virgin of Ĭş'rā-ĕl: and she shall be his wife; he may not put her away all his days.
20 But if this thing be true, *and the tokens of* virginity be not found for the damsel:
21 Then they shall bring out the damsel to the door of her father's house, and the men of her city shall stone her with stones that she die; because she hath wrought folly in Ĭş'rā-ĕl, to play the whore in her father's house: so shalt thou put evil away from among you.
22 ℂ If a man be found lying with a woman married to a husband, then they shall both of them die, *both* the man that lay with the woman, and the woman: so shalt thou put away evil from Ĭş'rā-ĕl.
23 ℂ If a damsel *that is* a virgin be betrothed unto a husband, and a man find her in the city, and lie with her;
24 Then ye shall bring them both out unto the gate of that city, and ye shall stone them with stones that they die; the damsel, because she cried not, *being* in the city; and the man, because he hath humbled his neighbor's wife: so thou shalt put away evil from among you.
25 ℂ But if a man find a betrothed damsel in the field, and the man force her, and lie with her; then the man only that lay with her shall die:
26 But unto the damsel thou shalt do nothing; *there is* in the damsel no sin *worthy* of death: for as when a man riseth against his neighbor, and slayeth him, even so *is* this matter:
27 For he found her in the field, *and* the betrothed damsel cried, and *there was* none to save her.
28 ℂ If a man find a damsel *that is* a virgin, which is not betrothed, and lay hold on her, and lie with her, and they be found;
29 Then the man that lay with her shall give unto the damsel's father fifty *shekels* of silver, and she shall be his wife; because he hath humbled her, he may not put her away all his days.
30 ℂ A man shall not take his father's wife, nor discover his father's skirt.

CHAPTER 23

HE that is wounded in the stones, or hath his privy member cut off, shall not enter into the congregation of the LORD.
2 A bastard shall not enter into the congregation of the LORD; even to his tenth generation shall he not enter into the congregation of the LORD.
3 An Ammonite or Mō'ăb-īte shall not enter into the congregation of the LORD; even to their tenth generation shall they not enter into the congregation of the LORD for ever:
4 Because they met you not with bread and with water in the way, when ye came forth out of Egypt; and because they hired against thee Bā'lāam the son of Bē'ŏr of Pē'thŏr of Mĕs'ō-pō-tā'mĭ-ȧ, to curse thee.
5 Nevertheless, the LORD thy God would not hearken unto Bā'lāam; but the LORD thy God turned the curse into a blessing unto thee, because the LORD thy God loved thee.
6 Thou shalt not seek their peace nor their prosperity all thy days for ever.
7 ℂ Thou shalt not abhor an Ē'dŏm-īte; for he *is* thy brother: thou shalt not abhor an Egyptian; because thou wast a stranger in his land.
8 The children that are begotten of them shall enter into the congregation of the LORD in their third generation.
9 ℂ When the host goeth forth against thine enemies, then keep thee from every wicked thing.
10 ℂ If there be among you any man, that is not clean by reason of uncleanness that chanceth him by night, then shall he go abroad out of the camp, he shall not come within the camp:
11 But it shall be, when evening cometh on, he shall wash *himself* with water: and when the sun is down, he shall come into the camp *again*.
12 ℂ Thou shalt have a place also without the camp, whither thou shalt go forth abroad:
13 And thou shalt have a paddle upon thy weapon; and it shall be, when thou wilt ease thyself abroad, thou shalt dig therewith, and shalt turn back and cover that which cometh from thee:
14 For the LORD thy God walketh in the midst of thy camp, to deliver thee, and to give up thine enemies before

thee; therefore shall thy camp be holy: that he see no unclean thing in thee, and turn away from thee.

15 ¶ Thou shalt not deliver unto his master the servant which is escaped from his master unto thee:

16 He shall dwell with thee, *even* among you, in that place which he shall choose in one of thy gates, where it liketh him best: thou shalt not oppress him.

17 ¶ There shall be no whore of the daughters of Ĭṣ′rā-ĕl, nor a sodomite of the sons of Ĭṣ′rā-ĕl.

18 Thou shalt not bring the hire of a whore, or the price of a dog, into the house of the LORD thy God for any vow: for even both these *are* abomination unto the LORD thy God.

19 ¶ Thou shalt not lend upon usury to thy brother; usury of money, usury of victuals, usury of any thing that is lent upon usury:

20 Unto a stranger thou mayest lend upon usury; but unto thy brother thou shalt not lend upon usury: that the LORD thy God may bless thee in all that thou settest thine hand to in the land whither thou goest to possess it.

21 ¶ When thou shalt vow a vow unto the LORD thy God, thou shalt not slack to pay it: for the LORD thy God will surely require it of thee; and it would be sin in thee.

22 But if thou shalt forbear to vow, it shall be no sin in thee.

23 That which is gone out of thy lips thou shalt keep and perform; *even* a freewill offering, according as thou hast vowed unto the LORD thy God, which thou hast promised with thy mouth.

24 ¶ When thou comest into thy neighbor's vineyard, then thou mayest eat grapes thy fill at thine own pleasure; but thou shalt not put *any* in thy vessel.

25 When thou comest into the standing corn of thy neighbor, then thou mayest pluck the ears with thine hand; but thou shalt not move a sickle unto thy neighbor's standing corn.

CHAPTER 24

WHEN a man hath taken a wife, and married her, and it come to pass that she find no favor in his eyes, because he hath found some uncleanness in her: then let him write her a bill of divorcement, and give *it* in her hand, and send her out of his house.

2 And when she is departed out of his house, she may go and be another man's *wife*.

3 And *if* the latter husband hate her, and write her a bill of divorcement, and giveth *it* in her hand, and sendeth her out of his house; or if the latter husband die, which took her *to be* his wife;

4 Her former husband, which sent her away, may not take her again to be his wife, after that she is defiled; for that *is* abomination before the LORD: and thou shalt not cause the land to sin, which the LORD thy God giveth thee *for* an inheritance.

5 ¶ When a man hath taken a new wife, he shall not go out to war, neither shall he be charged with any business: *but* he shall be free at home one year, and shall cheer up his wife which he hath taken.

6 ¶ No man shall take the nether or the upper millstone to pledge: for he taketh *a man*'s life to pledge.

7 ¶ If a man be found stealing any of his brethren of the children of Ĭṣ′rā-ĕl, and maketh merchandise of him, or selleth him; then that thief shall die; and thou shalt put evil away from among you.

8 ¶ Take heed in the plague of leprosy, that thou observe diligently, and do according to all that the priests the Lē′vītes shall teach you: as I commanded them, *so* ye shall observe to do.

9 Remember what the LORD thy God did unto Miriam by the way, after that ye were come forth out of Egypt.

10 ¶ When thou dost lend thy brother any thing, thou shalt not go into his house to fetch his pledge.

11 Thou shalt stand abroad, and the man to whom thou dost lend shall bring out the pledge abroad unto thee.

12 And if the man *be* poor, thou shalt not sleep with his pledge:

13 In any case thou shalt deliver him the pledge again when the sun goeth down, that he may sleep in his own raiment, and bless thee: and it shall be righteousness unto thee before the LORD thy God.

14 ¶ Thou shalt not oppress a hired servant *that is* poor and needy, *whether he be* of thy brethren, or of thy strangers that *are* in thy land within thy gates:

15 At his day thou shalt give *him* his hire, neither shall the sun go down upon

it; for he *is* poor, and setteth his heart upon it: lest he cry against thee unto the LORD, and it be sin unto thee.

16 The fathers shall not be put to death for the children, neither shall the children be put to death for the fathers: every man shall be put to death for his own sin.

17 ¶ Thou shalt not pervert the judgment of the stranger, *nor* of the fatherless; nor take a widow's raiment to pledge:

18 But thou shalt remember that thou wast a bondman in Egypt, and the LORD thy God redeemed thee thence: therefore I command thee to do this thing.

19 ¶ When thou cuttest down thine harvest in thy field, and hast forgot a sheaf in the field, thou shalt not go again to fetch it: it shall be for the stranger, for the fatherless, and for the widow: that the LORD thy God may bless thee in all the work of thine hands.

20 When thou beatest thine olive tree, thou shalt not go over the boughs again: it shall be for the stranger, for the fatherless, and for the widow.

21 When thou gatherest the grapes of thy vineyard, thou shalt not glean *it* afterward: it shall be for the stranger, for the fatherless, and for the widow.

22 And thou shalt remember that thou wast a bondman in the land of Egypt: therefore I command thee to do this thing.

CHAPTER 25

IF there be a controversy between men, and they come unto judgment, that *the judges* may judge them; then they shall justify the righteous, and condemn the wicked.

2 And it shall be, if the wicked man *be* worthy to be beaten, that the judge shall cause him to lie down, and to be beaten before his face, according to his fault, by a certain number.

3 Forty stripes he may give him, *and* not exceed: lest, *if* he should exceed, and beat him above these with many stripes, then thy brother should seem vile unto thee.

4 ¶ Thou shalt not muzzle the ox when he treadeth out *the corn*.

5 ¶ If brethren dwell together, and one of them die, and have no child, the wife of the dead shall not marry without unto a stranger: her husband's brother shall go in unto her, and take her to him to wife, and perform the duty of a husband's brother unto her.

6 And it shall be, *that* the firstborn which she beareth shall succeed in the name of his brother *which is* dead, that his name be not put out of Ĭṣ′rā-ĕl.

7 And if the man like not to take his brother's wife, then let his brother's wife go up to the gate unto the elders, and say, My husband's brother refuseth to raise up unto his brother a name in Ĭṣ′rā-ĕl, he will not perform the duty of my husband's brother.

8 Then the elders of his city shall call him, and speak unto him: and *if* he stand *to it,* and say, I like not to take her;

9 Then shall his brother's wife come unto him in the presence of the elders, and loose his shoe from off his foot, and spit in his face, and shall answer and say, So shall it be done unto that man that will not build up his brother's house.

10 And his name shall be called in Ĭṣ′rā-ĕl, The house of him that hath his shoe loosed.

11 ¶ When men strive together one with another, and the wife of the one draweth near for to deliver her husband out of the hand of him that smiteth him, and putteth forth her hand, and taketh him by the secrets:

12 Then thou shalt cut off her hand, thine eye shall not pity *her*.

13 ¶ Thou shalt not have in thy bag divers weights, a great and a small:

14 Thou shalt not have in thine house divers measures, a great and a small:

15 *But* thou shalt have a perfect and just weight, a perfect and just measure shalt thou have: that thy days may be lengthened in the land which the LORD thy God giveth thee.

16 For all that do such things, *and* all that do unrighteously, *are* an abomination unto the LORD thy God.

17 ¶ Remember what Ăm′ȧ-lĕk did unto thee by the way, when ye were come forth out of Egypt;

18 How he met thee by the way, and smote the hindmost of thee, *even* all *that were* feeble behind thee, when thou *wast* faint and weary; and he feared not God.

19 Therefore it shall be, when the LORD thy God hath given thee rest from all

thine enemies round about, in the land which the LORD thy God giveth thee *for* an inheritance to possess it, *that* thou shalt blot out the remembrance of Ăm'a-lĕk from under heaven; thou shalt not forget *it*.

CHAPTER 26

AND it shall be, when thou *art* come in unto the land which the LORD thy God giveth thee *for* an inheritance, and possessest it, and dwellest therein;

2 That thou shalt take of the first of all the fruit of the earth, which thou shalt bring of thy land that the LORD thy God giveth thee, and shalt put *it* in a basket, and shalt go unto the place which the LORD thy God shall choose to place his name there.

3 And thou shalt go unto the priest that shall be in those days, and say unto him, I profess this day unto the LORD thy God, that I am come unto the country which the LORD sware unto our fathers for to give us.

4 And the priest shall take the basket out of thine hand, and set it down before the altar of the LORD thy God.

5 And thou shalt speak and say before the LORD thy God, A Syrian ready to perish *was* my father; and he went down into Egypt, and sojourned there with a few, and became there a nation, great, mighty, and populous:

6 And the Egyptians evil entreated us, and afflicted us, and laid upon us hard bondage:

7 And when we cried unto the LORD God of our fathers, the LORD heard our voice, and looked on our affliction, and our labor, and our oppression:

8 And the LORD brought us forth out of Egypt with a mighty hand, and with an outstretched arm, and with great terribleness, and with signs, and with wonders:

9 And he hath brought us into this place, and hath given us this land, *even* a land that floweth with milk and honey.

10 And now, behold, I have brought the firstfruits of the land, which thou, O LORD, hast given me. And thou shalt set it before the LORD thy God, and worship before the LORD thy God:

11 And thou shalt rejoice in every good *thing* which the LORD thy God hath given unto thee, and unto thine house, thou, and the Lē'vīte, and the stranger that *is* among you.

12 ¶ When thou hast made an end of tithing all the tithes of thine increase the third year, *which is* the year of tithing, and hast given *it* unto the Lē'vīte, the stranger, the fatherless, and the widow, that they may eat within thy gates, and be filled;

13 Then thou shalt say before the LORD thy God, I have brought away the hallowed things out of *mine* house, and also have given them unto the Lē'vīte, and unto the stranger, to the fatherless, and to the widow, according to all thy commandments which thou hast commanded me: I have not transgressed thy commandments, neither have I forgotten *them*:

14 I have not eaten thereof in my mourning, neither have I taken away *aught* thereof for *any* unclean *use*, nor given *aught* thereof for the dead: *but* I have hearkened to the voice of the LORD my God, *and* have done according to all that thou hast commanded me.

15 Look down from thy holy habitation, from heaven, and bless thy people Ĭş'rā-ĕl, and the land which thou hast given us, as thou swarest unto our fathers, a land that floweth with milk and honey.

16 ¶ This day the LORD thy God hath commanded thee to do these statutes and judgments: thou shalt therefore keep and do them with all thine heart, and with all thy soul.

17 Thou hast avouched the LORD this day to be thy God, and to walk in his ways, and to keep his statutes, and his commandments, and his judgments, and to hearken unto his voice:

18 And the LORD hath avouched thee this day to be his peculiar people, as he hath promised thee, and that *thou* shouldest keep all his commandments;

19 And to make thee high above all nations which he hath made, in praise, and in name, and in honor; and that thou mayest be a holy people unto the LORD thy God, as he hath spoken.

CHAPTER 27

AND Moses with the elders of Ĭş'rā-ĕl commanded the people, saying, Keep all the commandments which I command you this day.

2 And it shall be, on the day when ye

shall pass over Jordan unto the land
which the LORD thy God giveth thee,
that thou shalt set thee up great stones,
and plaster them with plaster:
3 And thou shalt write upon them all
the words of this law, when thou art
passed over, that thou mayest go in unto
the land which the LORD thy God giveth
thee, a land that floweth with milk and
honey; as the LORD God of thy fathers
hath promised thee.
4 Therefore it shall be when ye be gone
over Jordan, *that* ye shall set up these
stones, which I command you this day,
in mount Ē'băl, and thou shalt plaster
them with plaster.
5 And there shalt thou build an altar
unto the LORD thy God, an altar of
stones: thou shalt not lift up *any* iron
tool upon them.
6 Thou shalt build the altar of the LORD
thy God of whole stones: and thou shalt
offer burnt offerings thereon unto the
LORD thy God:
7 And thou shalt offer peace offerings,
and shalt eat there, and rejoice before
the LORD thy God.
8 And thou shalt write upon the stones
all the words of this law very plainly.
9 ¶ And Moses and the priests the
Lē'vītes spake unto all Ĭs'rā-ĕl, saying,
Take heed, and hearken, O Ĭs'rā-ĕl;
this day thou art become the people of
the LORD thy God.
10 Thou shalt therefore obey the voice
of the LORD thy God, and do his commandments and his statutes, which I
command thee this day.
11 ¶ And Moses charged the people
the same day, saying,
12 These shall stand upon mount
Gĕr'ĭ-zĭm to bless the people, when
ye are come over Jordan; Simeon, and
Levi, and Judah, and Ĭs'sā-chär, and
Joseph, and Benjamin:
13 And these shall stand upon mount
Ē'băl to curse; Reuben, Gad, and
Ăsh'ẽr, and Zĕb'ū-lŭn, Dan, and Năph'-
tā-lī.
14 ¶ And the Lē'vītes shall speak, and
say unto all the men of Ĭs'rā-ĕl with a
loud voice,
15 Cursed *be* the man that maketh *any*
graven or molten image, an abomination unto the LORD, the work of the
hands of the craftsman, and putteth *it*
in a secret place: and all the people shall
answer and say, Amen.
16 Cursed *be* he that setteth light by
his father or his mother: and all the people shall say, Amen.
17 Cursed *be* he that removeth his
neighbor's landmark: and all the people
shall say, Amen.
18 Cursed *be* he that maketh the blind
to wander out of the way: and all the
people shall say, Amen.
19 Cursed *be* he that perverteth the
judgment of the stranger, fatherless,
and widow: and all the people shall say,
Amen.
20 Cursed *be* he that lieth with his
father's wife; because he uncovereth
his father's skirt: and all the people shall
say, Amen.
21 Cursed *be* he that lieth with any
manner of beast: and all the people shall
say, Amen.
22 Cursed *be* he that lieth with his sister, the daughter of his father, or the
daughter of his mother: and all the people shall say, Amen.
23 Cursed *be* he that lieth with his
mother-in-law: and all the people shall
say, Amen.
24 Cursed *be* he that smiteth his neighbor secretly: and all the people shall
say, Amen.
25 Cursed *be* he that taketh reward to
slay an innocent person: and all the
people shall say, Amen.
26 Cursed *be* he that confirmeth not *all*
the words of this law to do them: and
all the people shall say, Amen.

CHAPTER 28

AND it shall come to pass, if thou
shalt hearken diligently unto the
voice of the LORD thy God, to observe
and to do all his commandments which
I command thee this day, that the LORD
thy God will set thee on high above all
nations of the earth:
2 And all these blessings shall come on
thee, and overtake thee, if thou shalt
hearken unto the voice of the LORD thy
God.
3 Blessed *shalt* thou *be* in the city, and
blessed *shalt* thou *be* in the field.
4 Blessed *shall be* the fruit of thy body,
and the fruit of thy ground, and the fruit
of thy cattle, the increase of thy kine,
and the flocks of thy sheep.
5 Blessed *shall be* thy basket and thy
store.
6 Blessed *shalt* thou *be* when thou

comest in, and blessed *shalt* thou *be*
when thou goest out.
7 The LORD shall cause thine enemies
that rise up against thee to be smitten
before thy face: they shall come out
against thee one way, and flee before
thee seven ways.
8 The LORD shall command the blessing upon thee in thy storehouses, and
in all that thou settest thine hand unto;
and he shall bless thee in the land which
the LORD thy God giveth thee.
9 The LORD shall establish thee a holy
people unto himself, as he hath sworn
unto thee, if thou shalt keep the commandments of the LORD thy God, and
walk in his ways.
10 And all people of the earth shall see
that thou art called by the name of the
LORD; and they shall be afraid of thee.
11 And the LORD shall make thee
plenteous in goods, in the fruit of thy
body, and in the fruit of thy cattle, and
in the fruit of thy ground, in the land
which the LORD sware unto thy fathers
to give thee.
12 The LORD shall open unto thee his
good treasure, the heaven to give the
rain unto thy land in his season, and to
bless all the work of thine hand: and
thou shalt lend unto many nations, and
thou shalt not borrow.
13 And the LORD shall make thee the
head, and not the tail; and thou shalt be
above only, and thou shalt not be beneath; if that thou hearken unto the
commandments of the LORD thy God,
which I command thee this day, to observe and to do *them*:
14 And thou shalt not go aside from
any of the words which I command thee
this day, *to* the right hand, or *to* the left,
to go after other gods to serve them.
15 ¶ But it shall come to pass, if thou
wilt not hearken unto the voice of the
LORD thy God, to observe to do all his
commandments and his statutes which
I command thee this day; that all these
curses shall come upon thee, and overtake thee:
16 Cursed *shalt* thou *be* in the city, and
cursed *shalt* thou *be* in the field.
17 Cursed *shall be* thy basket and thy
store.
18 Cursed *shall be* the fruit of thy body,
and the fruit of thy land, the increase of
thy kine, and the flocks of thy sheep.
19 Cursed *shalt* thou *be* when thou
comest in, and cursed *shalt* thou *be*
when thou goest out.
20 The LORD shall send upon thee
cursing, vexation, and rebuke, in all that
thou settest thine hand unto for to do,
until thou be destroyed, and until thou
perish quickly; because of the wickedness of thy doings, whereby thou hast
forsaken me.
21 The LORD shall make the pestilence
cleave unto thee, until he have consumed thee from off the land, whither
thou goest to possess it.
22 The LORD shall smite thee with a
consumption, and with a fever, and with
an inflammation, and with an extreme
burning, and with the sword, and with
blasting, and with mildew; and they
shall pursue thee until thou perish.
23 And thy heaven that *is* over thy
head shall be brass, and the earth that
is under thee *shall be* iron.
24 The LORD shall make the rain of thy
land powder and dust: from heaven
shall it come down upon thee, until thou
be destroyed.
25 The LORD shall cause thee to be
smitten before thine enemies: thou shalt
go out one way against them, and flee
seven ways before them; and shalt be
removed into all the kingdoms of the
earth.
26 And thy carcass shall be meat unto
all fowls of the air, and unto the beasts
of the earth, and no man shall fray *them*
away.
27 The LORD will smite thee with the
botch of Egypt, and with the emerods,
and with the scab, and with the itch,
whereof thou canst not be healed.
28 The LORD shall smite thee with
madness, and blindness, and astonishment of heart:
29 And thou shalt grope at noonday,
as the blind gropeth in darkness, and
thou shalt not prosper in thy ways: and
thou shalt be only oppressed and spoiled
evermore, and no man shall save *thee*.
30 Thou shalt betroth a wife, and another man shall lie with her: thou shalt
build a house, and thou shalt not dwell
therein: thou shalt plant a vineyard, and
shalt not gather the grapes thereof.
31 Thine ox *shall be* slain before thine
eyes, and thou shalt not eat thereof:
thine ass *shall be* violently taken away
from before thy face, and shall not be
restored to thee: thy sheep *shall be*

given unto thine enemies, and thou
shalt have none to rescue *them.*
32 Thy sons and thy daughters *shall be*
given unto another people, and thine
eyes shall look, and fail *with longing* for
them all the day long: and *there shall be*
no might in thine hand.
33 The fruit of thy land, and all thy
labors, shall a nation which thou knowest not eat up; and thou shalt be only
oppressed and crushed alway:
34 So that thou shalt be mad for the
sight of thine eyes which thou shalt see.
35 The LORD shall smite thee in the
knees, and in the legs, with a sore botch
that cannot be healed, from the sole of
thy foot unto the top of thy head.
36 The LORD shall bring thee, and thy
king which thou shalt set over thee,
unto a nation which neither thou nor thy
fathers have known; and there shalt
thou serve other gods, wood and stone.
37 And thou shalt become an astonishment, a proverb, and a byword, among
all nations whither the LORD shall lead
thee.
38 Thou shalt carry much seed out into
the field, and shalt gather *but* little
in; for the locust shall consume it.
39 Thou shalt plant vineyards, and
dress *them,* but shalt neither drink *of*
the wine, nor gather *the grapes;* for the
worms shall eat them.
40 Thou shalt have olive trees throughout all thy coasts, but thou shalt not
anoint *thyself* with the oil; for thine
olive shall cast *his fruit.*
41 Thou shalt beget sons and daughters, but thou shalt not enjoy them; for
they shall go into captivity.
42 All thy trees and fruit of thy land
shall the locust consume.
43 The stranger that *is* within thee
shall get up above thee very high; and
thou shalt come down very low.
44 He shall lend to thee, and thou shalt
not lend to him: he shall be the head,
and thou shalt be the tail.
45 Moreover all these curses shall
come upon thee, and shall pursue thee,
and overtake thee, till thou be destroyed; because thou hearkenedst not
unto the voice of the LORD thy God, to
keep his commandments and his statutes which he commanded thee.
46 And they shall be upon thee for a
sign and for a wonder, and upon thy
seed for ever.
47 Because thou servedst not the LORD
thy God with joyfulness, and with gladness of heart, for the abundance of all
things;
48 Therefore shalt thou serve thine
enemies, which the LORD shall send
against thee, in hunger, and in thirst,
and in nakedness, and in want of all
things: and he shall put a yoke of iron
upon thy neck, until he have destroyed
thee.
49 The LORD shall bring a nation
against thee from far, from the end of
the earth, *as swift* as the eagle flieth; a
nation whose tongue thou shalt not
understand;
50 A nation of fierce countenance,
which shall not regard the person of the
old, nor show favor to the young:
51 And he shall eat the fruit of thy
cattle, and the fruit of thy land, until
thou be destroyed: which *also* shall not
leave thee *either* corn, wine, or oil, *or*
the increase of thy kine, or flocks of thy
sheep, until he have destroyed thee.
52 And he shall besiege thee in all thy
gates, until thy high and fenced walls
come down, wherein thou trustedst,
throughout all thy land: and he shall besiege thee in all thy gates throughout all
thy land, which the LORD thy God hath
given thee.
53 And thou shalt eat the fruit of thine
own body, the flesh of thy sons and of
thy daughters, which the LORD thy God
hath given thee, in the siege, and in the
straitness, wherewith thine enemies
shall distress thee:
54 *So that* the man *that is* tender among
you, and very delicate, his eye shall be
evil toward his brother, and toward the
wife of his bosom, and toward the remnant of his children which he shall leave:
55 So that he will not give to any of
them of the flesh of his children whom
he shall eat: because he hath nothing
left him in the siege, and in the straitness, wherewith thine enemies shall
distress thee in all thy gates.
56 The tender and delicate woman
among you, which would not adventure
to set the sole of her foot upon the
ground for delicateness and tenderness,
her eye shall be evil toward the husband
of her bosom, and toward her son, and
toward her daughter,
57 And toward her young one that
cometh out from between her feet, and

toward her children which she shall
bear: for she shall eat them for want of
all *things* secretly in the siege and straitness, wherewith thine enemy shall distress thee in thy gates.
58 If thou wilt not observe to do all the
words of this law that are written in this
book, that thou mayest fear this glorious
and fearful name, THE LORD THY
GOD;
59 Then the LORD will make thy
plagues wonderful, and the plagues of
thy seed, *even* great plagues, and of
long continuance, and sore sicknesses,
and of long continuance.
60 Moreover, he will bring upon thee
all the diseases of Egypt, which thou
wast afraid of; and they shall cleave
unto thee.
61 Also every sickness, and every
plague, which *is* not written in the book
of this law, them will the LORD bring
upon thee, until thou be destroyed.
62 And ye shall be left few in number,
whereas ye were as the stars of heaven
for multitude; because thou wouldest
not obey the voice of the LORD thy God.
63 And it shall come to pass, *that* as the
LORD rejoiced over you to do you good,
and to multiply you; so the LORD will
rejoice over you to destroy you, and to
bring you to nought; and ye shall be
plucked from off the land whither thou
goest to possess it.
64 And the LORD shall scatter thee
among all people, from the one end of
the earth even unto the other; and there
thou shalt serve other gods, which neither thou nor thy fathers have known,
even wood and stone.
65 And among these nations shalt thou
find no ease, neither shall the sole of thy
foot have rest: but the LORD shall give
thee there a trembling heart, and failing
of eyes, and sorrow of mind:
66 And thy life shall hang in doubt before thee; and thou shalt fear day and
night, and shalt have none assurance of
thy life:
67 In the morning thou shalt say,
Would God it were even! and at even
thou shalt say, Would God it were morning! for the fear of thine heart wherewith thou shalt fear, and for the sight of
thine eyes which thou shalt see.
68 And the LORD shall bring thee into
Egypt again with ships, by the way
whereof I spake unto thee, Thou shalt
see it no more again: and there ye shall
be sold unto your enemies for bondmen
and bondwomen, and no man shall buy
you.

CHAPTER 29

THESE *are* the words of the covenant, which the LORD commanded
Moses to make with the children of
Ĭş′rā-ĕl in the land of Mō′ăb, besides
the covenant which he made with them
in Ho′rĕb.
2 ℭ And Moses called unto all Ĭş′ra-ĕl,
and said unto them, Ye have seen all
that the LORD did before your eyes in
the land of Egypt unto Phā′raōh, and
unto all his servants, and unto all his
land;
3 The great temptations which thine
eyes have seen, the signs, and those
great miracles:
4 Yet the LORD hath not given you a
heart to perceive, and eyes to see, and
ears to hear, unto this day.
5 And I have led you forty years in the
wilderness: your clothes are not waxen
old upon you, and thy shoe is not waxen
old upon thy foot.
6 Ye have not eaten bread, neither have
ye drunk wine or strong drink: that ye
might know that I *am* the LORD your
God.
7 And when ye came unto this place,
Sī′hŏn the king of Hĕsh′bŏn, and Og the
king of Bā′shăn, came out against us
unto battle, and we smote them:
8 And we took their land, and gave it
for an inheritance unto the Reubenites,
and to the Gadites, and to the half tribe
of Mȧ-năs′sĕh.
9 Keep therefore the words of this
covenant and do them, that ye may
prosper in all that ye do.
10 ℭ Ye stand this day all of you before
the LORD your God; your captains of
your tribes, your elders, and your
officers, *with* all the men of Ĭş′rā-ĕl,
11 Your little ones, your wives, and thy
stranger that *is* in thy camp, from the
hewer of thy wood unto the drawer of
thy water:
12 That thou shouldest enter into covenant with the LORD thy God, and into
his oath, which the LORD thy God maketh with thee this day:
13 That he may establish thee to-day
for a people unto himself, and *that* he
may be unto thee a God, as he hath said

unto thee, and as he hath sworn unto
thy fathers, to Abraham, to Isaac, and
to Jacob.
14 Neither with you only do I make
this covenant and this oath;
15 But with *him* that standeth here
with us this day before the LORD our
God, and also with *him* that *is* not here
with us this day:
16 (For ye know how we have dwelt in
the land of Egypt; and how we came
through the nations which ye passed by;
17 And ye have seen their abominations, and their idols, wood and stone,
silver and gold, which *were* among
them:)
18 Lest there should be among you
man, or woman, or family, or tribe,
whose heart turneth away this day from
the LORD our God, to go *and* serve the
gods of these nations; lest there should
be among you a root that beareth gall
and wormwood;
19 And it come to pass, when he heareth the words of this curse, that he bless
himself in his heart, saying, I shall have
peace, though I walk in the imagination
of mine heart, to add drunkenness to
thirst:
20 The LORD will not spare him, but
then the anger of the LORD and his
jealousy shall smoke against that man,
and all the curses that are written in this
book shall lie upon him, and the LORD
shall blot out his name from under
heaven.
21 And the LORD shall separate him
unto evil out of all the tribes of Ĭs̩'rā-ĕl,
according to all the curses of the covenant that are written in this book of the
law:
22 So that the generation to come of
your children that shall rise up after
you, and the stranger that shall come
from a far land, shall say, when they
see the plagues of that land, and the sicknesses which the LORD hath laid upon it;
23 *And that* the whole land thereof *is*
brimstone, and salt, *and* burning, *that* it
is not sown, nor beareth, nor any grass
groweth therein, like the overthrow of
Sŏd'ŏm and Gō-mŏr'răh, Ăd'măh and
Zē-bō'ĭm, which the LORD overthrew in
his anger, and in his wrath:
24 Even all nations shall say, Wherefore hath the LORD done thus unto this
land? what *meaneth* the heat of this
great anger?
25 Then men shall say, Because they
have forsaken the covenant of the LORD
God of their fathers, which he made
with them when he brought them forth
out of the land of Egypt:
26 For they went and served other
gods, and worshipped them, gods whom
they knew not, and *whom* he had not
given unto them:
27 And the anger of the LORD was
kindled against this land, to bring upon
it all the curses that are written in this
book:
28 And the LORD rooted them out of
their land in anger, and in wrath, and in
great indignation, and cast them into
another land, as *it is* this day.
29 The secret *things belong* unto the
LORD our God: but those *things which
are* revealed *belong* unto us and to our
children for ever, that *we* may do all the
words of this law.

CHAPTER 30

AND it shall come to pass, when all
these things are come upon thee,
the blessing and the curse, which I have
set before thee, and thou shalt call *them*
to mind among all the nations, whither
the LORD thy God hath driven thee,
2 And shalt return unto the LORD thy
God, and shalt obey his voice according
to all that I command thee this day, thou
and thy children, with all thine heart,
and with all thy soul;
3 That then the LORD thy God will
turn thy captivity, and have compassion
upon thee, and will return and gather
thee from all the nations, whither the
LORD thy God hath scattered thee.
4 If *any* of thine be driven out unto the
outmost *parts* of heaven, from thence
will the LORD thy God gather thee, and
from thence will he fetch thee:
5 And the LORD thy God will bring thee
into the land which thy fathers possessed, and thou shalt possess it; and
he will do thee good, and multiply thee
above thy fathers.
6 And the LORD thy God will circumcise thine heart, and the heart of thy
seed, to love the LORD thy God with all
thine heart, and with all thy soul, that
thou mayest live.
7 And the LORD thy God will put all
these curses upon thine enemies, and
on them that hate thee, which persecuted thee.

8 And thou shalt return and obey the voice of the LORD, and do all his commandments which I command thee this day.

9 And the LORD thy God will make thee plenteous in every work of thine hand, in the fruit of thy body, and in the fruit of thy cattle, and in the fruit of thy land, for good: for the LORD will again rejoice over thee for good, as he rejoiced over thy fathers:

10 If thou shalt hearken unto the voice of the LORD thy God, to keep his commandments and his statutes *which are* written in this book of the law, *and* if thou turn unto the LORD thy God with all thine heart, and with all thy soul.

11 ¶ For this commandment which I command thee this day, it *is* not hidden from thee, neither *is* it far off.

12 It *is* not in heaven, that thou shouldest say, Who shall go up for us to heaven, and bring it unto us, that we may hear it, and do it?

13 Neither *is* it beyond the sea, that thou shouldest say, Who shall go over the sea for us, and bring it unto us, that we may hear it, and do it?

14 But the word *is* very nigh unto thee, in thy mouth, and in thy heart, that thou mayest do it.

15 ¶ See, I have set before thee this day life and good, and death and evil;

16 In that I command thee this day to love the LORD thy God, to walk in his ways, and to keep his commandments, and his statutes, and his judgments, that thou mayest live and multiply: and the LORD thy God shall bless thee in the land whither thou goest to possess it.

17 But if thine heart turn away, so that thou wilt not hear, but shalt be drawn away, and worship other gods, and serve them;

18 I denounce unto you this day, that ye shall surely perish, *and that* ye shall not prolong *your* days upon the land, whither thou passest over Jordan to go to possess it.

19 I call heaven and earth to record this day against you, *that* I have set before you life and death, blessing and cursing: therefore choose life, that both thou and thy seed may live:

20 That thou mayest love the LORD thy God, *and* that thou mayest obey his voice, and that thou mayest cleave unto him: for he *is* thy life, and the length of thy days: that thou mayest dwell in the land which the LORD sware unto thy fathers, to Abraham, to Isaac, and to Jacob, to give them.

CHAPTER 31

AND Moses went and spake these words unto all Ĭş'rā-ĕl.

2 And he said unto them, I *am* a hundred and twenty years old this day; I can no more go out and come in: also the LORD hath said unto me, Thou shalt not go over this Jordan.

3 The LORD thy God, he will go over before thee, *and* he will destroy these nations from before thee, and thou shalt possess them: *and* Joshua, he shall go over before thee, as the LORD hath said.

4 And the LORD shall do unto them as he did to Sī'hŏn and to Og, kings of the Ăm'ō-rītes, and unto the land of them, whom he destroyed.

5 And the LORD shall give them up before your face, that ye may do unto them according unto all the commandments which I have commanded you.

6 Be strong and of a good courage, fear not, nor be afraid of them: for the LORD thy God, he *it is* that doth go with thee; he will not fail thee, nor forsake thee.

7 ¶ And Moses called unto Joshua, and said unto him in the sight of all Ĭş'rā-ĕl, Be strong and of a good courage: for thou must go with this people unto the land which the LORD hath sworn unto their fathers to give them; and thou shalt cause them to inherit it.

8 And the LORD, he *it is* that doth go before thee; he will be with thee, he will not fail thee, neither forsake thee: fear not, neither be dismayed.

9 ¶ And Moses wrote this law, and delivered it unto the priests the sons of Levi, which bare the ark of the covenant of the LORD, and unto all the elders of Ĭş'rā-ĕl.

10 And Moses commanded them, saying, At the end of *every* seven years, in the solemnity of the year of release, in the feast of tabernacles,

11 When all Ĭş'rā-ĕl is come to appear before the LORD thy God in the place which he shall choose, thou shalt read this law before all Ĭş'rā-ĕl in their hearing.

12 Gather the people together, men, and women, and children, and thy stranger that *is* within thy gates, that they

may hear, and that they may learn, and fear the LORD your God, and observe to do all the words of this law:

13 And *that* their children, which have not known *any thing*, may hear, and learn to fear the LORD your God, as long as ye live in the land whither ye go over Jordan to possess it.

14 ℂ And the LORD said unto Moses, Behold, thy days approach that thou must die: call Joshua, and present yourselves in the tabernacle of the congregation, that I may give him a charge. And Moses and Joshua went, and presented themselves in the tabernacle of the congregation.

15 And the LORD appeared in the tabernacle in a pillar of a cloud: and the pillar of the cloud stood over the door of the tabernacle.

16 ℂ And the LORD said unto Moses, Behold, thou shalt sleep with thy fathers; and this people will rise up, and go a whoring after the gods of the strangers of the land, whither they go *to be* among them, and will forsake me, and break my covenant which I have made with them.

17 Then my anger shall be kindled against them in that day, and I will forsake them, and I will hide my face from them, and they shall be devoured, and many evils and troubles shall befall them; so that they will say in that day, Are not these evils come upon us, because our God *is* not among us?

18 And I will surely hide my face in that day for all the evils which they shall have wrought, in that they are turned unto other gods.

19 Now therefore write ye this song for you, and teach it the children of Ĭṣ′rā-ĕl: put it in their mouths, that this song may be a witness for me against the children of Ĭṣ′rā-ĕl.

20 For when I shall have brought them into the land which I sware unto their fathers, that floweth with milk and honey; and they shall have eaten and filled themselves, and waxen fat; then will they turn unto other gods, and serve them, and provoke me, and break my covenant.

21 And it shall come to pass, when many evils and troubles are befallen them, that this song shall testify against them as a witness; for it shall not be forgotten out of the mouths of their seed: for I know their imagination which they go about, even now, before I have brought them into the land which I sware.

22 ℂ Moses therefore wrote this song the same day, and taught it the children of Ĭṣ′rā-ĕl.

23 And he gave Joshua the son of Nŭn a charge, and said, Be strong and of a good courage: for thou shalt bring the children of Ĭṣ′rā-ĕl into the land which I sware unto them: and I will be with thee.

24 ℂ And it came to pass, when Moses had made an end of writing the words of this law in a book, until they were finished,

25 That Moses commanded the Lē′vītes, which bare the ark of the covenant of the LORD, saying,

26 Take this book of the law, and put it in the side of the ark of the covenant of the LORD your God, that it may be there for a witness against thee.

27 For I know thy rebellion, and thy stiff neck: behold, while I am yet alive with you this day, ye have been rebellious against the LORD; and how much more after my death?

28 ℂ Gather unto me all the elders of your tribes, and your officers, that I may speak these words in their ears, and call heaven and earth to record against them.

29 For I know that after my death ye will utterly corrupt *yourselves*, and turn aside from the way which I have commanded you; and evil will befall you in the latter days; because ye will do evil in the sight of the LORD, to provoke him to anger through the work of your hands.

30 And Moses spake in the ears of all the congregation of Ĭṣ′rā-ĕl the words of this song, until they were ended.

CHAPTER 32

GIVE ear, O ye heavens, and I will speak; and hear, O earth, the words of my mouth.

2 My doctrine shall drop as the rain, my speech shall distil as the dew, as the small rain upon the tender herb, and as the showers upon the grass:

3 Because I will publish the name of the LORD: ascribe ye greatness unto our God.

4 *He is* the Rock, his work *is* perfect: for all his ways *are* judgment: a God of truth and without iniquity, just and right *is* he.

5 They have corrupted themselves,
their spot *is* not *the spot* of his children:
they are a perverse and crooked generation.
6 Do ye thus requite the LORD, O foolish people and unwise? *is* not he thy
father *that* hath bought thee? hath he
not made thee, and established thee?
7 ¶ Remember the days of old, consider the years of many generations: ask
thy father, and he will show thee; thy
elders, and they will tell thee.
8 When the Most High divided to the
nations their inheritance, when he separated the sons of Adam, he set the
bounds of the people according to the
number of the children of Ĭṣ'rā-ĕl.
9 For the LORD's portion *is* his people;
Jacob *is* the lot of his inheritance.
10 He found him in a desert land, and
in the waste howling wilderness; he led
him about, he instructed him, he kept
him as the apple of his eye.
11 As an eagle stirreth up her nest,
fluttereth over her young, spreadeth
abroad her wings, taketh them, beareth
them on her wings:
12 *So* the LORD alone did lead him,
and *there was* no strange god with him.
13 He made him ride on the high places
of the earth, that he might eat the increase of the field; and he made him to
suck honey out of the rock, and oil out
of the flinty rock;
14 Butter of kine, and milk of sheep,
with fat of lambs, and rams of the breed
of Bā'shăn, and goats, with the fat of
kidneys of wheat; and thou didst drink
the pure blood of the grape.
15 ¶ But Jĕsh'ū-rŭn waxed fat, and
kicked: thou art waxen fat, thou art
grown thick, thou art covered *with fatness;* then he forsook God *which* made
him, and lightly esteemed the Rock of
his salvation.
16 They provoked him to jealousy with
strange *gods,* with abominations provoked they him to anger.
17 They sacrificed unto devils, not to
God; to gods whom they knew not, to
new *gods that* came newly up, whom
your fathers feared not.
18 Of the Rock *that* begat thee thou art
unmindful, and hast forgotten God that
formed thee.
19 And when the LORD saw *it,* he abhorred *them,* because of the provoking
of his sons, and of his daughters.

20 And he said, I will hide my face from
them, I will see what their end *shall be:*
for they *are* a very froward generation,
children in whom *is* no faith.
21 They have moved me to jealousy
with *that which is* not God; they have
provoked me to anger with their vanities: and I will move them to jealousy
with *those which are* not a people; I will
provoke them to anger with a foolish
nation.
22 For a fire is kindled in mine anger,
and shall burn unto the lowest hell, and
shall consume the earth with her increase, and set on fire the foundations
of the mountains.
23 I will heap mischiefs upon them; I
will spend mine arrows upon them.
24 *They shall be* burnt with hunger,
and devoured with burning heat, and
with bitter destruction: I will also send
the teeth of beasts upon them, with the
poison of serpents of the dust.
25 The sword without, and terror within, shall destroy both the young man
and the virgin, the suckling *also* with
the man of gray hairs.
26 I said, I would scatter them into
corners, I would make the remembrance
of them to cease from among men:
27 Were it not that I feared the wrath
of the enemy, lest their adversaries
should behave themselves strangely,
and lest they should say, Our hand *is*
high, and the LORD hath not done all
this.
28 For they *are* a nation void of counsel, neither *is there any* understanding
in them.
29 O that they were wise, *that* they
understood this, *that* they would consider their latter end!
30 How should one chase a thousand,
and two put ten thousand to flight, except their Rock had sold them, and the
LORD had shut them up?
31 For their rock *is* not as our Rock,
even our enemies themselves *being*
judges.
32 For their vine *is* of the vine of
Sŏd'ŏm, and of the fields of Gō-mŏr'rȧh:
their grapes *are* grapes of gall, their
clusters *are* bitter:
33 Their wine *is* the poison of dragons,
and the cruel venom of asps.
34 *Is* not this laid up in store with me,
and sealed up among my treasures?
35 To me *belongeth* vengeance, and

recompense; their foot shall slide in *due*
time: for the day of their calamity *is* at
hand, and the things that shall come
upon them make haste.
36 For the LORD shall judge his people,
and repent himself for his servants,
when he seeth that *their* power is gone,
and *there is* none shut up, or left.
37 And he shall say, Where *are* their
gods, *their* rock in whom they trusted,
38 Which did eat the fat of their sacrifices, *and* drank the wine of their drink
offerings? let them rise up and help you,
and be your protection.
39 See now that I, *even* I, *am* he, and
there is no god with me: I kill, and I
make alive; I wound, and I heal: neither
is there any that can deliver out of my
hand.
40 For I lift up my hand to heaven, and
say, I live for ever.
41 If I whet my glittering sword, and
mine hand take hold on judgment; I
will render vengeance to mine enemies,
and will reward them that hate me.
42 I will make mine arrows drunk with
blood, and my sword shall devour flesh;
and that with the blood of the slain and
of the captives, from the beginning of
revenges upon the enemy.
43 Rejoice, O ye nations, *with* his people: for he will avenge the blood of his
servants, and will render vengeance to
his adversaries, and will be merciful
unto his land, *and* to his people.
44 ¶ And Moses came and spake all
the words of this song in the ears of the
people, he, and Hō-shē'ȧ the son of Nŭn.
45 And Moses made an end of speaking all these words to all Ĭs'rā-ĕl:
46 And he said unto them, Set your
hearts unto all the words which I testify
among you this day, which ye shall command your children to observe to do, all
the words of this law.
47 For it *is* not a vain thing for you;
because it *is* your life: and through this
thing ye shall prolong *your* days in the
land, whither ye go over Jordan to possess it.
48 And the LORD spake unto Moses
that selfsame day, saying,
49 Get thee up into this mountain
Ăb'ȧ-rĭm, *unto* mount Nē'bō, which *is*
in the land of Mō'ăb, that *is* over against
Jĕr'ĭ-chō; and behold the land of
Cā'năan, which I give unto the children
of Ĭs'rā-ĕl for a possession:
50 And die in the mount whither thou
goest up, and be gathered unto thy
people; as Aaron thy brother died in
mount Hôr, and was gathered unto his
people:
51 Because ye trespassed against me
among the children of Ĭs'rā-ĕl at the
waters of Mĕr'ĭ-bȧh–Kā'dĕsh, in the
wilderness of Zĭn; because ye sanctified
me not in the midst of the children of
Ĭs'rā-ĕl.
52 Yet thou shalt see the land before
thee; but thou shalt not go thither unto
the land which I give the children of
Ĭs'rā-ĕl.

CHAPTER 33

AND this *is* the blessing, wherewith
Moses the man of God blessed the
children of Ĭs'rā-ĕl before his death.
2 And he said, The LORD came from
Sī'naī, and rose up from Sē'ïr unto them;
he shined forth from mount Pā'răn, and
he came with ten thousands of saints:
from his right hand *went* a fiery law for
them.
3 Yea, he loved the people; all his
saints *are* in thy hand: and they sat
down at thy feet; *every one* shall receive
of thy words.
4 Moses commanded us a law, *even*
the inheritance of the congregation of
Jacob.
5 And he was king in Jĕsh'ū-rŭn, when
the heads of the people *and* the tribes of
Ĭs'rā-ĕl were gathered together.
6 ¶ Let Reuben live, and not die; and
let *not* his men be few.
7 ¶ And this *is the blessing* of Judah:
and he said, Hear, LORD, the voice of
Judah, and bring him unto his people:
let his hands be sufficient for him; and
be thou a help *to him* from his enemies.
8 ¶ And of Levi he said, *Let* thy Thŭm'mĭm and thy Ū'rĭm *be* with thy holy one,
whom thou didst prove at Măs'sȧh, *and*
with whom thou didst strive at the waters of Mĕr'ĭ-bȧh;
9 Who said unto his father and to his
mother, I have not seen him; neither did
he acknowledge his brethren, nor knew
his own children: for they have observed
thy word, and kept thy covenant.
10 They shall teach Jacob thy judgments, and Ĭs'rā-ĕl thy law: they shall
put incense before thee, and whole
burnt sacrifice upon thine altar.

11 Bless, LORD, his substance, and
accept the work of his hands: smite
through the loins of them that rise
against him, and of them that hate him,
that they rise not again.
12 ¶ *And* of Benjamin he said, The
beloved of the LORD shall dwell in
safety by him; *and the LORD* shall
cover him all the day long, and he shall
dwell between his shoulders.
13 ¶ And of Joseph he said, Blessed
of the LORD *be* his land, for the precious
things of heaven, for the dew, and for
the deep that coucheth beneath,
14 And for the precious fruits *brought
forth* by the sun, and for the precious
things put forth by the moon,
15 And for the chief things of the
ancient mountains, and for the precious
things of the lasting hills,
16 And for the precious things of the
earth and fulness thereof, and *for* the
good will of him that dwelt in the bush:
let *the blessing* come upon the head of
Joseph, and upon the top of the head
of him that was separated from his
brethren.
17 His glory *is like* the firstling of his
bullock, and his horns *are like* the horns
of unicorns: with them he shall push the
people together to the ends of the earth:
and they *are* the ten thousands of
Ē′phrā-ĭm, and they *are* the thousands
of Mȧ-năs′sĕh.
18 ¶ And of Zĕb′ū-lŭn he said, Rejoice, Zĕb′ū-lŭn, in thy going out;
and, Ĭs′sȧ-chär, in thy tents.
19 They shall call the people unto the
mountain; there they shall offer sacrifices of righteousness: for they shall
suck *of* the abundance of the seas, and
of treasures hid in the sand.
20 ¶ And of Gad he said, Blessed *be*
he that enlargeth Gad: he dwelleth as a
lion, and teareth the arm with the crown
of the head.
21 And he provided the first part for
himself, because there, *in* a portion of
the lawgiver, *was he* seated; and he
came with the heads of the people, he
executed the justice of the LORD, and
his judgments with Ĭs′rā-ĕl.
22 ¶ And of Dan he said, Dan *is* a
lion's whelp: he shall leap from Bā′shăn.
23 ¶ And of Năph′tȧ-lī he said, O
Năph′tȧ-lī, satisfied with favor, and full
with the blessing of the LORD, possess
thou the west and the south.
24 ¶ And of Ăsh′ĕr he said, *Let* Ăsh′ĕr
be blessed with children; let him be
acceptable to his brethren, and let him
dip his foot in oil.
25 Thy shoes *shall be* iron and brass;
and as thy days, *so shall* thy strength
be.
26 ¶ *There is* none like unto the God
of Jĕsh′ū-rŭn, *who* rideth upon the
heaven in thy help, and in his excellency
on the sky.
27 The eternal God *is thy* refuge, and
underneath *are* the everlasting arms:
and he shall thrust out the enemy from
before thee; and shall say, Destroy
them.
28 Ĭs′rā-ĕl then shall dwell in safety
alone: the fountain of Jacob *shall be*
upon a land of corn and wine; also his
heavens shall drop down dew.
29 Happy *art* thou, O Ĭs′rā-ĕl: who *is*
like unto thee, O people saved by the
LORD, the shield of thy help, and who *is*
the sword of thy excellency! and thine
enemies shall be found liars unto thee;
and thou shalt tread upon their high
places.

CHAPTER 34

AND Moses went up from the plains
of Mō′ăb unto the mountain of
Nē′bō, to the top of Pĭs′gȧh, that *is*
over against Jĕr′ĭ-chō: and the LORD
showed him all the land of Gĭl′ē-ăd,
unto Dan,
2 And all Năph′tȧ-lī, and the land of
Ē′phrā-ĭm, and Mȧ-năs′sĕh, and all the
land of Judah, unto the utmost sea,
3 And the south, and the plain of the
valley of Jĕr′ĭ-chō, the city of palm
trees, unto Zō′ȧr.
4 And the LORD said unto him, This *is*
the land which I sware unto Abraham,
unto Isaac, and unto Jacob, saying, I
will give it unto thy seed: I have caused
thee to see *it* with thine eyes, but thou
shalt not go over thither.
5 ¶ So Moses the servant of the LORD
died there in the land of Mō′ăb, according to the word of the LORD.
6 And he buried him in a valley in the
land of Mō′ăb, over against Bĕth′-pē′ŏr:
but no man knoweth of his sepulchre
unto this day.
7 ¶ And Moses *was* a hundred and
twenty years old when he died: his eye
was not dim, nor his natural force
abated.

8 ¶ And the children of Ĭş′rā-ĕl wept for Moses in the plains of Mō′ăb thirty days: so the days of weeping *and* mourning for Moses were ended.

9 ¶ And Joshua the son of Nŭn was full of the spirit of wisdom; for Moses had laid his hands upon him: and the children of Ĭş′rā-ĕl hearkened unto him, and did as the LORD commanded Moses.

10 ¶ And there arose not a prophet since in Ĭş′rā-ĕl like unto Moses, whom the LORD knew face to face,

11 In all the signs and the wonders which the LORD sent him to do in the land of Egypt, to Phā′raōh, and to all his servants, and to all his land,

12 And in all that mighty hand, and in all the great terror which Moses showed in the sight of all Ĭş′rā-ĕl.

THE BOOK OF JOSHUA

CHAPTER 1

NOW after the death of Moses the servant of the LORD, it came to pass, that the LORD spake unto Joshua the son of Nŭn, Moses' minister, saying,

2 Moses my servant is dead; now therefore arise, go over this Jordan, thou, and all this people, unto the land which I do give to them, *even* to the children of Ĭş′rā-ĕl.

3 Every place that the sole of your foot shall tread upon, that have I given unto you, as I said unto Moses.

4 From the wilderness and this Lebanon even unto the great river, the river Eū-phrā′tēş, all the land of the Hĭt′tītes, and unto the great sea toward the going down of the sun, shall be your coast.

5 There shall not any man be able to stand before thee all the days of thy life: as I was with Moses, *so* I will be with thee: I will not fail thee, nor forsake thee.

6 Be strong and of a good courage: for unto this people shalt thou divide for an inheritance the land, which I sware unto their fathers to give them.

7 Only be thou strong and very courageous, that thou mayest observe to do according to all the law, which Moses my servant commanded thee: turn not from it *to* the right hand or *to* the left, that thou mayest prosper whithersoever thou goest.

8 This book of the law shall not depart out of thy mouth; but thou shalt meditate therein day and night, that thou mayest observe to do according to all that is written therein: for then thou shalt make thy way prosperous, and then thou shalt have good success.

9 Have not I commanded thee? Be strong and of a good courage; be not afraid, neither be thou dismayed: for the LORD thy God *is* with thee whithersoever thou goest.

10 ¶ Then Joshua commanded the officers of the people, saying,

11 Pass through the host, and command the people, saying, Prepare you victuals; for within three days ye shall pass over this Jordan, to go in to possess the land, which the LORD your God giveth you to possess it.

12 ¶ And to the Reubenites, and to the Gadites, and to half the tribe of Mȧ-năs′sĕh, spake Joshua, saying,

13 Remember the word which Moses the servant of the LORD commanded you, saying, The LORD your God hath given you rest, and hath given you this land.

14 Your wives, your little ones, and your cattle, shall remain in the land which Moses gave you on this side Jordan; but ye shall pass before your brethren armed, all the mighty men of valor, and help them;

15 Until the LORD have given your brethren rest, as *he hath given* you, and they also have possessed the land which the LORD your God giveth them: then ye shall return unto the land of your possession, and enjoy it, which Moses the LORD's servant gave you on this side Jordan toward the sunrising.

16 ¶ And they answered Joshua, saying, All that thou commandest us we will do, and whithersoever thou sendest us, we will go.

17 According as we hearkened unto Moses in all things, so will we hearken

unto thee: only the LORD thy God be with thee, as he was with Moses.

18 Whosoever *he be* that doth rebel against thy commandment, and will not hearken unto thy words in all that thou commandest him, he shall be put to death: only be strong and of a good courage.

CHAPTER 2

AND Joshua the son of Nŭn sent out of Shĭt'tĭm two men to spy secretly, saying, Go view the land, even Jĕr'ĭ-chō. And they went, and came into a harlot's house, named Rā'hăb, and lodged there.

2 And it was told the king of Jĕr'ĭ-chō, saying, Behold, there came men in hither to-night of the children of Ĭş'rā-ĕl to search out the country.

3 And the king of Jĕr'ĭ-chō sent unto Rā'hăb, saying, Bring forth the men that are come to thee, which are entered into thine house: for they be come to search out all the country.

4 And the woman took the two men, and hid them, and said thus, There came men unto me, but I wist not whence they *were:*

5 And it came to pass *about the time* of shutting of the gate, when it was dark, that the men went out; whither the men went, I wot not: pursue after them quickly; for ye shall overtake them.

6 But she had brought them up to the roof of the house, and hid them with the stalks of flax, which she had laid in order upon the roof.

7 And the men pursued after them the way to Jordan unto the fords: and as soon as they which pursued after them were gone out, they shut the gate.

8 ℂ And before they were laid down, she came up unto them upon the roof;

9 And she said unto the men, I know that the LORD hath given you the land, and that your terror is fallen upon us, and that all the inhabitants of the land faint because of you.

10 For we have heard how the LORD dried up the water of the Red sea for you, when ye came out of Egypt; and what ye did unto the two kings of the Ăm'ō-rītes, that *were* on the other side Jordan, Sī'hŏn and Og, whom ye utterly destroyed.

11 And as soon as we had heard *these things,* our hearts did melt, neither did there remain any more courage in any man, because of you: for the LORD your God, he *is* God in heaven above, and in earth beneath.

12 Now therefore, I pray you, swear unto me by the LORD, since I have showed you kindness, that ye will also show kindness unto my father's house, and give me a true token:

13 And *that* ye will save alive my father, and my mother, and my brethren, and my sisters, and all that they have, and deliver our lives from death.

14 And the men answered her, Our life for yours, if ye utter not this our business. And it shall be, when the LORD hath given us the land, that we will deal kindly and truly with thee.

15 Then she let them down by a cord through the window: for her house *was* upon the town wall, and she dwelt upon the wall.

16 And she said unto them, Get you to the mountain, lest the pursuers meet you; and hide yourselves there three days, until the pursuers be returned: and afterward may ye go your way.

17 And the men said unto her, We *will be* blameless of this thine oath which thou hast made us swear.

18 Behold, *when* we come into the land, thou shalt bind this line of scarlet thread in the window which thou didst let us down by: and thou shalt bring thy father, and thy mother, and thy brethren, and all thy father's household, home unto thee.

19 And it shall be, *that* whosoever shall go out of the doors of thy house into the street, his blood *shall be* upon his head, and we *will be* guiltless: and whosoever shall be with thee in the house, his blood *shall be* on our head, if *any* hand be upon him.

20 And if thou utter this our business, then we will be quit of thine oath which thou hast made us to swear.

21 And she said, According unto your words, so *be* it. And she sent them away, and they departed: and she bound the scarlet line in the window.

22 And they went, and came unto the mountain, and abode there three days, until the pursuers were returned: and the pursuers sought *them* throughout all the way, but found *them* not.

23 ℂ So the two men returned, and descended from the mountain, and passed over, and came to Joshua the

son of Nŭn, and told him all *things* that befell them:

24 And they said unto Joshua, Truly the LORD hath delivered into our hands all the land; for even all the inhabitants of the country do faint because of us.

CHAPTER 3

AND Joshua rose early in the morning; and they removed from Shĭt'tĭm, and came to Jordan, he and all the children of Ĭṣ'rā-ĕl, and lodged there before they passed over.

2 And it came to pass after three days, that the officers went through the host;

3 And they commanded the people, saying, When ye see the ark of the covenant of the LORD your God, and the priests the Lē'vītes bearing it, then ye shall remove from your place, and go after it.

4 Yet there shall be a space between you and it, about two thousand cubits by measure: come not near unto it, that ye may know the way by which ye must go: for ye have not passed *this* way heretofore.

5 And Joshua said unto the people, Sanctify yourselves: for to-morrow the LORD will do wonders among you.

6 And Joshua spake unto the priests, saying, Take up the ark of the covenant, and pass over before the people. And they took up the ark of the covenant, and went before the people.

7 ¶ And the LORD said unto Joshua, This day will I begin to magnify thee in the sight of all Ĭṣ'rā-ĕl, that they may know that, as I was with Moses, *so* I will be with thee.

8 And thou shalt command the priests that bear the ark of the covenant, saying, When ye are come to the brink of the water of Jordan, ye shall stand still in Jordan.

9 ¶ And Joshua said unto the children of Ĭṣ'rā-ĕl, Come hither, and hear the words of the LORD your God.

10 And Joshua said, Hereby ye shall know that the living God *is* among you, and *that* he will without fail drive out from before you the Cā'năan-ītes, and the Hĭt'tītes, and the Hī'vītes, and the Pĕr'ĭz-zītes, and the Gĭr'gȧ-shītes, and the Ăm'ō-rītes, and the Jĕb'ū-sītes.

11 Behold, the ark of the covenant of the Lord of all the earth passeth over before you into Jordan.

12 Now therefore take you twelve men out of the tribes of Ĭṣ'rā-ĕl, out of every tribe a man.

13 And it shall come to pass, as soon as the soles of the feet of the priests that bear the ark of the LORD, the Lord of all the earth, shall rest in the waters of Jordan, *that* the waters of Jordan shall be cut off *from* the waters that come down from above; and they shall stand upon a heap.

14 ¶ And it came to pass, when the people removed from their tents, to pass over Jordan, and the priests bearing the ark of the covenant before the people;

15 And as they that bare the ark were come unto Jordan, and the feet of the priests that bare the ark were dipped in the brim of the water, (for Jordan overfloweth all his banks all the time of harvest,)

16 That the waters which came down from above stood *and* rose up upon a heap very far from the city Adam, that *is* beside Zăr'ē-tăn; and those that came down toward the sea of the plain, *even* the salt sea, failed, *and* were cut off: and the people passed over right against Jĕr'ĭ-chō.

17 And the priests that bare the ark of the covenant of the LORD stood firm on dry ground in the midst of Jordan, and all the Ĭṣ'rā-ĕl-ītes passed over on dry ground, until all the people were passed clean over Jordan.

CHAPTER 4

AND it came to pass, when all the people were clean passed over Jordan, that the LORD spake unto Joshua, saying,

2 Take you twelve men out of the people, out of every tribe a man,

3 And command ye them, saying, Take you hence out of the midst of Jordan, out of the place where the priests' feet stood firm, twelve stones, and ye shall carry them over with you, and leave them in the lodging place, where ye shall lodge this night.

4 Then Joshua called the twelve men, whom he had prepared of the children of Ĭṣ'rā-ĕl, out of every tribe a man:

5 And Joshua said unto them, Pass over before the ark of the LORD your God into the midst of Jordan, and take you up every man of you a stone upon his shoulder, according unto the number of the tribes of the children of Ĭṣ'rā-ĕl:

6 That this may be a sign among you, *that* when your children ask *their fathers* in time to come, saying, What *mean* ye by these stones?

7 Then ye shall answer them, That the waters of Jordan were cut off before the ark of the covenant of the LORD; when it passed over Jordan, the waters of Jordan were cut off: and these stones shall be for a memorial unto the children of Ĭṣ'rā-ĕl for ever.

8 And the children of Ĭṣ'rā-ĕl did so as Joshua commanded, and took up twelve stones out of the midst of Jordan, as the LORD spake unto Joshua, according to the number of the tribes of the children of Ĭṣ'rā-ĕl, and carried them over with them unto the place where they lodged, and laid them down there.

9 And Joshua set up twelve stones in the midst of Jordan, in the place where the feet of the priests which bare the ark of the covenant stood: and they are there unto this day.

10 ¶ For the priests which bare the ark stood in the midst of Jordan, until every thing was finished that the LORD commanded Joshua to speak unto the people, according to all that Moses commanded Joshua: and the people hasted and passed over.

11 And it came to pass, when all the people were clean passed over, that the ark of the LORD passed over, and the priests, in the presence of the people.

12 And the children of Reuben, and the children of Gad, and half the tribe of Mȧ-năs'sĕh, passed over armed before the children of Ĭṣ'rā-ĕl, as Moses spake unto them:

13 About forty thousand prepared for war passed over before the LORD unto battle, to the plains of Jĕr'ĭ-chō.

14 ¶ On that day the LORD magnified Joshua in the sight of all Ĭṣ'rā-ĕl; and they feared him, as they feared Moses, all the days of his life.

15 And the LORD spake unto Joshua, saying,

16 Command the priests that bear the ark of the testimony, that they come up out of Jordan.

17 Joshua therefore commanded the priests, saying, Come ye up out of Jordan.

18 And it came to pass, when the priests that bare the ark of the covenant of the LORD were come up out of the midst of Jordan, *and* the soles of the priests' feet were lifted up unto the dry land, that the waters of Jordan returned unto their place, and flowed over all his banks, as *they did* before.

19 ¶ And the people came up out of Jordan on the tenth *day* of the first month, and encamped in Gĭl'găl, in the east border of Jĕr'ĭ-chō.

20 And those twelve stones, which they took out of Jordan, did Joshua pitch in Gĭl'găl.

21 And he spake unto the children of Ĭṣ'rā-ĕl, saying, When your children shall ask their fathers in time to come, saying, What *mean* these stones?

22 Then ye shall let your children know, saying, Ĭṣ'rā-ĕl came over this Jordan on dry land.

23 For the LORD your God dried up the waters of Jordan from before you, until ye were passed over, as the LORD your God did to the Red sea, which he dried up from before us, until we were gone over:

24 That all the people of the earth might know the hand of the LORD, that it *is* mighty: that ye might fear the LORD your God for ever.

CHAPTER 5

AND it came to pass, when all the kings of the Ăm'o-rītes, which *were* on the side of Jordan westward, and all the kings of the Cā'năan-ītes, which *were* by the sea, heard that the LORD had dried up the waters of Jordan from before the children of Ĭṣ'rā-ĕl, until we were passed over, that their heart melted, neither was there spirit in them any more, because of the children of Ĭṣ'rā-ĕl.

2 ¶ At that time the LORD said unto Joshua, Make thee sharp knives, and circumcise again the children of Ĭṣ'rā-ĕl the second time.

3 And Joshua made him sharp knives, and circumcised the children of Ĭṣ'rā-ĕl at the hill of the foreskins.

4 And this *is* the cause why Joshua did circumcise: All the people that came out of Egypt, *that were* males, *even* all the men of war, died in the wilderness by the way, after they came out of Egypt.

5 Now all the people that came out were circumcised; but all the people

that were born in the wilderness by the way as they came forth out of Egypt, *them* they had not circumcised.

6 For the children of Ĭṣ′rā-ĕl walked forty years in the wilderness, till all the people *that were* men of war, which came out of Egypt, were consumed, because they obeyed not the voice of the LORD: unto whom the LORD sware that he would not show them the land, which the LORD sware unto their fathers that he would give us, a land that floweth with milk and honey.

7 And their children, *whom* he raised up in their stead, them Joshua circumcised: for they were uncircumcised, because they had not circumcised them by the way.

8 And it came to pass, when they had done circumcising all the people, that they abode in their places in the camp, till they were whole.

9 And the LORD said unto Joshua, This day have I rolled away the reproach of Egypt from off you. Wherefore the name of the place is called Gĭl′găl unto this day.

10 ¶ And the children of Ĭṣ′rā-ĕl encamped in Gĭl′găl, and kept the passover on the fourteenth day of the month at even in the plains of Jĕr′ĭ-chō.

11 And they did eat of the old corn of the land on the morrow after the passover, unleavened cakes, and parched *corn* in the selfsame day.

12 ¶ And the manna ceased on the morrow after they had eaten of the old corn of the land; neither had the children of Ĭṣ′rā-ĕl manna any more; but they did eat of the fruit of the land of Cā′năan that year.

13 ¶ And it came to pass, when Joshua was by Jĕr′ĭ-chō, that he lifted up his eyes and looked, and, behold, there stood a man over against him with his sword drawn in his hand: and Joshua went unto him, and said unto him, *Art* thou for us, or for our adversaries?

14 And he said, Nay; but *as* captain of the host of the LORD am I now come. And Joshua fell on his face to the earth, and did worship, and said unto him, What saith my lord unto his servant?

15 And the captain of the LORD's host said unto Joshua, Loose thy shoe from off thy foot; for the place whereon thou standest *is* holy. And Joshua did so.

CHAPTER 6

NOW Jĕr′ĭ-chō was straitly shut up because of the children of Ĭṣ′rā-ĕl: none went out, and none came in.

2 And the LORD said unto Joshua, See, I have given into thine hand Jĕr′ĭ-chō, and the king thereof, *and* the mighty men of valor.

3 And ye shall compass the city, all *ye* men of war, *and* go round about the city once. Thus shalt thou do six days.

4 And seven priests shall bear before the ark seven trumpets of rams' horns: and the seventh day ye shall compass the city seven times, and the priests shall blow with the trumpets.

5 And it shall come to pass, that when they make a long *blast* with the ram's horn, *and* when ye hear the sound of the trumpet, all the people shall shout with a great shout; and the wall of the city shall fall down flat, and the people shall ascend up every man straight before him.

6 ¶ And Joshua the son of Nŭn called the priests, and said unto them, Take up the ark of the covenant, and let seven priests bear seven trumpets of rams' horns before the ark of the LORD.

7 And he said unto the people, Pass on, and compass the city, and let him that is armed pass on before the ark of the LORD.

8 ¶ And it came to pass, when Joshua had spoken unto the people, that the seven priests bearing the seven trumpets of rams' horns passed on before the LORD, and blew with the trumpets: and the ark of the covenant of the LORD followed them.

9 ¶ And the armed men went before the priests that blew with the trumpets, and the rearward came after the ark, *the priests* going on, and blowing with the trumpets.

10 And Joshua had commanded the people, saying, Ye shall not shout, nor make any noise with your voice, neither shall *any* word proceed out of your mouth, until the day I bid you shout; then shall ye shout.

11 So the ark of the LORD compassed the city, going about *it* once: and they came into the camp, and lodged in the camp.

12 ¶ And Joshua rose early in the morning, and the priests took up the ark of the LORD.

13 And seven priests bearing seven trumpets of rams' horns before the ark of the LORD went on continually, and blew with the trumpets: and the armed men went before them; but the rearward came after the ark of the LORD, *the priests* going on, and blowing with the trumpets.

14 And the second day they compassed the city once, and returned into the camp. So they did six days.

15 And it came to pass on the seventh day, that they rose early about the dawning of the day, and compassed the city after the same manner seven times: only on that day they compassed the city seven times.

16 And it came to pass at the seventh time, when the priests blew with the trumpets, Joshua said unto the people, Shout; for the LORD hath given you the city.

17 ¶ And the city shall be accursed, *even* it, and all that *are* therein, to the LORD: only Rā′hăb the harlot shall live, she and all that *are* with her in the house, because she hid the messengers that we sent.

18 And ye, in any wise keep *yourselves* from the accursed thing, lest ye make *yourselves* accursed, when ye take of the accursed thing, and make the camp of Ĭṣ′rā-ĕl a curse, and trouble it.

19 But all the silver, and gold, and vessels of brass and iron, *are* consecrated unto the LORD: they shall come into the treasury of the LORD.

20 So the people shouted when *the priests* blew with the trumpets: and it came to pass, when the people heard the sound of the trumpet, and the people shouted with a great shout, that the wall fell down flat, so that the people went up into the city, every man straight before him, and they took the city.

21 And they utterly destroyed all that *was* in the city, both man and woman, young and old, and ox, and sheep, and ass, with the edge of the sword.

22 But Joshua had said unto the two men that had spied out the country, Go into the harlot's house, and bring out thence the woman, and all that she hath, as ye sware unto her.

23 And the young men that were spies went in, and brought out Rā′hăb, and her father, and her mother, and her brethren, and all that she had; and they brought out all her kindred, and left them without the camp of Ĭṣ′rā-ĕl.

24 And they burnt the city with fire, and all that *was* therein: only the silver, and the gold, and the vessels of brass and of iron, they put into the treasury of the house of the LORD.

25 And Joshua saved Rā′hăb the harlot alive, and her father's household, and all that she had; and she dwelleth in Ĭṣ′rā-ĕl *even* unto this day; because she hid the messengers, which Joshua sent to spy out Jĕr′ĭ-chō.

26 ¶ And Joshua adjured *them* at that time, saying, Cursed *be* the man before the LORD, that riseth up and buildeth this city Jĕr′ĭ-chō: he shall lay the foundation thereof in his firstborn, and in his youngest *son* shall he set up the gates of it.

27 So the LORD was with Joshua; and his fame was *noised* throughout all the country.

CHAPTER 7

BUT the children of Ĭṣ′rā-ĕl committed a trespass in the accursed thing: for Ā′chăn, the son of Cär′mī, the son of Zăb′dī, the son of Zē′răh, of the tribe of Judah, took of the accursed thing: and the anger of the LORD was kindled against the children of Ĭṣ′rā-ĕl.

2 And Joshua sent men from Jĕr′ĭ-chō to Ā′ī, which *is* beside Bĕth′-ā′vĕn, on the east side of Beth-el, and spake unto them, saying, Go up and view the country. And the men went up and viewed Ā′ī.

3 And they returned to Joshua, and said unto him, Let not all the people go up; but let about two or three thousand men go up and smite Ā′ī; *and* make not all the people to labor thither; for they *are but* few.

4 So there went up thither of the people about three thousand men; and they fled before the men of Ā′ī.

5 And the men of Ā′ī smote of them about thirty and six men: for they chased them *from* before the gate *even* unto Shĕb′ă-rĭm, and smote them in the going down: wherefore the hearts of the people melted, and became as water.

6 ¶ And Joshua rent his clothes, and fell to the earth upon his face before the ark of the LORD until the eventide, he and the elders of Ĭṣ′rā-ĕl, and put dust upon their heads.

7 And Joshua said, Alas, O Lord GOD, wherefore hast thou at all brought this people over Jordan, to deliver us into the hand of the Ăm'ō-rītes, to destroy us? would to God we had been content, and dwelt on the other side Jordan!

8 O Lord, what shall I say, when Ĭṣ'rā-ĕl turneth their backs before their enemies!

9 For the Cā'năan-ītes and all the inhabitants of the land shall hear *of it,* and shall environ us round, and cut off our name from the earth: and what wilt thou do unto thy great name?

10 ¶ And the LORD said unto Joshua, Get thee up; wherefore liest thou thus upon thy face?

11 Ĭṣ'rā-ĕl hath sinned, and they have also transgressed my covenant which I commanded them: for they have even taken of the accursed thing, and have also stolen, and dissembled also, and they have put *it* even among their own stuff.

12 Therefore the children of Ĭṣ'rā-ĕl could not stand before their enemies, *but* turned *their* backs before their enemies, because they were accursed: neither will I be with you any more, except ye destroy the accursed from among you.

13 Up, sanctify the people, and say, Sanctify yourselves against to-morrow: for thus saith the LORD God of Ĭṣ'rā-ĕl, *There is* an accursed thing in the midst of thee, O Ĭṣ'rā-ĕl: thou canst not stand before thine enemies, until ye take away the accursed thing from among you.

14 In the morning therefore ye shall be brought according to your tribes: and it shall be, *that* the tribe which the LORD taketh shall come according to the families *thereof;* and the family which the LORD shall take shall come by households; and the household which the LORD shall take shall come man by man.

15 And it shall be, *that* he that is taken with the accursed thing shall be burnt with fire, he and all that he hath: because he hath transgressed the covenant of the LORD, and because he hath wrought folly in Ĭṣ'rā-ĕl.

16 ¶ So Joshua rose up early in the morning, and brought Ĭṣ'rā-ĕl by their tribes; and the tribe of Judah was taken:

17 And he brought the family of Judah; and he took the family of the Zär'hītes: and he brought the family of the Zär'hītes man by man; and Zăb'dī was taken:

18 And he brought his household man by man; and Ā'chăn, the son of Cär'mī, the son of Zăb'dī, the son of Zē'rȧh, of the tribe of Judah, was taken.

19 And Joshua said unto Ā'chăn, My son, give, I pray thee, glory to the LORD God of Ĭṣ'rā-ĕl, and make confession unto him; and tell me now what thou hast done; hide *it* not from me.

20 And Ā'chăn answered Joshua, and said, Indeed I have sinned against the LORD God of Ĭṣ'rā-ĕl, and thus and thus have I done:

21 When I saw among the spoils a goodly Babylonish garment, and two hundred shekels of silver, and a wedge of gold of fifty shekels weight, then I coveted them, and took them; and, behold, they *are* hid in the earth in the midst of my tent, and the silver under it.

22 ¶ So Joshua sent messengers, and they ran unto the tent; and, behold, *it was* hid in his tent, and the silver under it.

23 And they took them out of the midst of the tent, and brought them unto Joshua, and unto all the children of Ĭṣ'rā-ĕl, and laid them out before the LORD.

24 And Joshua, and all Ĭṣ'rā-ĕl with him, took Ā'chăn the son of Zē'rȧh, and the silver, and the garment, and the wedge of gold, and his sons, and his daughters, and his oxen, and his asses, and his sheep, and his tent, and all that he had: and they brought them unto the valley of Ā'chŏr.

25 And Joshua said, Why hast thou troubled us? the LORD shall trouble thee this day. And all Ĭṣ'rā-ĕl stoned him with stones, and burned them with fire, after they had stoned them with stones.

26 And they raised over him a great heap of stones unto this day. So the LORD turned from the fierceness of his anger. Wherefore the name of that place was called, The valley of Ā'chŏr, unto this day.

CHAPTER 8

AND the LORD said unto Joshua, Fear not, neither be thou dismayed: take all the people of war with thee, and arise, go up to Ā'ī: see, I have given into thy hand the king of Ā'ī, and his people, and his city, and his land:

2 And thou shalt do to Ā'ī and her king as thou didst unto Jĕr'ī-chō and her king: only the spoil thereof, and the cattle thereof, shall ye take for a prey unto yourselves: lay thee an ambush for the city behind it.

3 ¶ So Joshua arose, and all the people of war, to go up against Ā'ī: and Joshua chose out thirty thousand mighty men of valor, and sent them away by night.

4 And he commanded them, saying, Behold, ye shall lie in wait against the city, *even* behind the city: go not very far from the city, but be ye all ready:

5 And I, and all the people that *are* with me, will approach unto the city: and it shall come to pass, when they come out against us, as at the first, that we will flee before them,

6 (For they will come out after us,) till we have drawn them from the city; for they will say, They flee before us, as at the first: therefore we will flee before them.

7 Then ye shall rise up from the ambush, and seize upon the city: for the LORD your God will deliver it into your hand.

8 And it shall be, when ye have taken the city, *that* ye shall set the city on fire: according to the commandment of the LORD shall ye do. See, I have commanded you.

9 ¶ Joshua therefore sent them forth; and they went to lie in ambush, and abode between Beth-el and Ā'ī, on the west side of Ā'ī: but Joshua lodged that night among the people.

10 And Joshua rose up early in the morning, and numbered the people, and went up, he and the elders of Ĭṣ'rā-ĕl, before the people to Ā'ī.

11 And all the people, *even the people* of war that *were* with him, went up, and drew nigh, and came before the city, and pitched on the north side of Ā'ī: now *there was* a valley between them and Ā'ī.

12 And he took about five thousand men, and set them to lie in ambush between Beth-el and Ā'ī, on the west side of the city.

13 And when they had set the people, *even* all the host that *was* on the north of the city, and their liers in wait on the west of the city, Joshua went that night into the midst of the valley.

14 ¶ And it came to pass, when the king of Ā'ī saw *it*, that they hasted and rose up early, and the men of the city went out against Ĭṣ'rā-ĕl to battle, he and all his people, at a time appointed, before the plain; but he wist not that *there were* liers in ambush against him behind the city.

15 And Joshua and all Ĭṣ'rā-ĕl made as if they were beaten before them, and fled by the way of the wilderness.

16 And all the people that *were* in Ā'ī were called together to pursue after them: and they pursued after Joshua, and were drawn away from the city.

17 And there was not a man left in Ā'ī or Beth-el, that went not out after Ĭṣ'rā-ĕl: and they left the city open, and pursued after Ĭṣ'rā-ĕl.

18 And the LORD said unto Joshua, Stretch out the spear that *is* in thy hand toward Ā'ī; for I will give it into thine hand. And Joshua stretched out the spear that *he had* in his hand toward the city.

19 And the ambush arose quickly out of their place, and they ran as soon as he had stretched out his hand: and they entered into the city, and took it, and hasted and set the city on fire.

20 And when the men of Ā'ī looked behind them, they saw, and, behold, the smoke of the city ascended up to heaven, and they had no power to flee this way or that way: and the people that fled to the wilderness turned back upon the pursuers.

21 And when Joshua and all Ĭṣ'rā-ĕl saw that the ambush had taken the city, and that the smoke of the city ascended, then they turned again, and slew the men of Ā'ī.

22 And the other issued out of the city against them; so they were in the midst of Ĭṣ'rā-ĕl, some on this side, and some on that side: and they smote them, so that they let none of them remain or escape.

23 And the king of Ā'ī they took alive, and brought him to Joshua.

24 And it came to pass, when Ĭṣ'rā-ĕl had made an end of slaying all the inhabitants of Ā'ī in the field, in the wilderness wherein they chased them, and when they were all fallen on the edge of the sword, until they were consumed, that all the Ĭṣ'rā-ĕl-ītes returned unto Ā'ī, and smote it with the edge of the sword.

25 And *so* it was, *that* all that fell that
day, both of men and women, *were*
twelve thousand, *even* all the men of Ā'ī.
26 For Joshua drew not his hand back,
wherewith he stretched out the spear,
until he had utterly destroyed all the
inhabitants of Ā'ī.
27 Only the cattle and the spoil of that
city Ĭş'rā-ĕl took for a prey unto themselves, according unto the word of the
LORD which he commanded Joshua.
28 And Joshua burnt Ā'ī, and made it a
heap for ever, *even* a desolation unto
this day.
29 And the king of Ā'ī he hanged on a
tree until eventide: and as soon as the
sun was down, Joshua commanded that
they should take his carcass down from
the tree, and cast it at the entering of
the gate of the city, and raise thereon a
great heap of stones, *that remaineth*
unto this day.
30 ℂ Then Joshua built an altar unto
the LORD God of Ĭş'rā-ĕl in mount
Ē'băl,
31 As Moses the servant of the LORD
commanded the children of Ĭş'rā-ĕl, as
it is written in the book of the law of
Moses, an altar of whole stones, over
which no man hath lifted up *any* iron:
and they offered thereon burnt offerings
unto the LORD, and sacrificed peace
offerings.
32 ℂ And he wrote there upon the
stones a copy of the law of Moses, which
he wrote in the presence of the children
of Ĭş'rā-ĕl.
33 And all Ĭş'rā-ĕl, and their elders,
and officers, and their judges, stood on
this side the ark and on that side before
the priests the Lē'vītes, which bare the
ark of the covenant of the LORD, as well
the stranger, as he that was born among
them; half of them over against mount
Gĕr'ĭ-zĭm, and half of them over against
mount Ē'băl; as Moses the servant of
the LORD had commanded before, that
they should bless the people of Ĭş'rā-ĕl.
34 And afterward he read all the words
of the law, the blessings and cursings,
according to all that is written in the
book of the law.
35 There was not a word of all that
Moses commanded, which Joshua read
not before all the congregation of Ĭş'-
rā'ĕl, with the women, and the little
ones, and the strangers that were conversant among them.

CHAPTER 9

AND it came to pass, when all the
kings which *were* on this side Jordan, in the hills, and in the valleys, and
in all the coasts of the great sea over
against Lebanon, the Hĭt'tīte, and the
Ăm'ō-rīte, the Cā'năan-īte, the Pĕr'ĭz-
zīte, the Hī'vīte, and the Jĕb'ū-şīte,
heard *thereof;*
2 That they gathered themselves together, to fight with Joshua and with Ĭş'-
rā-ĕl, with one accord.
3 ℂ And when the inhabitants of
Gĭb'ē-ŏn heard what Joshua had done
unto Jĕr'ĭ-chō and to Ā'ī,
4 They did work wilily, and went and
made as if they had been ambassadors,
and took old sacks upon their asses, and
wine bottles, old, and rent, and bound up;
5 And old shoes and clouted upon their
feet, and old garments upon them; and
all the bread of their provision was dry
and mouldy.
6 And they went to Joshua unto the
camp at Gĭl'găl, and said unto him, and
to the men of Ĭş'rā-ĕl, We be come from
a far country: now therefore make ye a
league with us.
7 And the men of Ĭş'rā-ĕl said unto the
Hī'vītes, Peradventure ye dwell among
us; and how shall we make a league
with you?
8 And they said unto Joshua, We *are*
thy servants. And Joshua said unto
them, Who *are* ye? and from whence
come ye?
9 And they said unto him, From a very
far country thy servants are come, because of the name of the LORD thy God:
for we have heard the fame of him, and
all that he did in Egypt,
10 And all that he did to the two kings
of the Ăm'ō-rītes, that *were* beyond
Jordan, to Sī'hŏn king of Hĕsh'bŏn, and
to Og king of Bā'shăn, which *was* at
Ăsh'tá-rŏth.
11 Wherefore our elders and all the
inhabitants of our country spake to us,
saying, Take victuals with you for the
journey, and go to meet them, and say
unto them, We *are* your servants: therefore now make ye a league with us.
12 This our bread we took hot *for* our
provision out of our houses on the day
we came forth to go unto you; but now,
behold, it is dry, and it is mouldy:
13 And these bottles of wine, which we

filled, *were* new; and, behold, they be rent: and these our garments and our shoes are become old by reason of the very long journey.

14 And the men took of their victuals, and asked not *counsel* at the mouth of the LORD.

15 And Joshua made peace with them, and made a league with them, to let them live: and the princes of the congregation sware unto them.

16 ¶ And it came to pass at the end of three days after they had made a league with them, that they heard that they *were* their neighbors, and *that* they dwelt among them.

17 And the children of Ĭs′rā-ĕl journeyed, and came unto their cities on the third day. Now their cities *were* Gĭb′ē-ȯn, and Chē-phī′rȧh, and Bē-ē′rŏth, and Kĭr′jăth–jē′ȧ-rĭm.

18 And the children of Ĭs′rā-ĕl smote them not, because the princes of the congregation had sworn unto them by the LORD God of Ĭs′rā-ĕl. And all the congregation murmured against the princes.

19 But all the princes said unto all the congregation, We have sworn unto them by the LORD God of Ĭs′rā-ĕl: now therefore we may not touch them.

20 This we will do to them; we will even let them live, lest wrath be upon us, because of the oath which we sware unto them.

21 And the princes said unto them, Let them live; but let them be hewers of wood and drawers of water unto all the congregation; as the princes had promised them.

22 ¶ And Joshua called for them, and he spake unto them, saying, Wherefore have ye beguiled us, saying, We *are* very far from you; when ye dwell among us?

23 Now therefore ye *are* cursed, and there shall none of you be freed from being bondmen, and hewers of wood and drawers of water for the house of my God.

24 And they answered Joshua, and said, Because it was certainly told thy servants, how that the LORD thy God commanded his servant Moses to give you all the land, and to destroy all the inhabitants of the land from before you, therefore we were sore afraid of our lives because of you, and have done this thing.

25 And now, behold, we *are* in thine hand: as it seemeth good and right unto thee to do unto us, do.

26 And so did he unto them, and delivered them out of the hand of the children of Ĭs′rā-ĕl, that they slew them not.

27 And Joshua made them that day hewers of wood and drawers of water for the congregation, and for the altar of the LORD, even unto this day, in the place which he should choose.

CHAPTER 10

NOW it came to pass, when Ȧ-dō′nī–zē′dĕk king of Jerusalem had heard how Joshua had taken Ā′ī, and had utterly destroyed it; as he had done to Jĕr′ĭ-chō and her king, so he had done to Ā′ī and her king; and how the inhabitants of Gĭb′ē-ȯn had made peace with Ĭs′rā-ĕl, and were among them;

2 That they feared greatly, because Gĭb′ē-ȯn *was* a great city, as one of the royal cities, and because it *was* greater than Ā′ī, and all the men thereof *were* mighty.

3 Wherefore Ȧ-dō′nī–zē′dĕk king of Jerusalem sent unto Hō′hăm king of Hē′brȯn, and unto Pī′rȧm king of Jär′mŭth, and unto Jȧ-phī′ȧ king of Lā′chĭsh, and unto Dē′bĭr king of Ĕg′lŏn, saying,

4 Come up unto me, and help me, that we may smite Gĭb′ē-ȯn: for it hath made peace with Joshua and with the children of Ĭs′rā-ĕl.

5 Therefore the five kings of the Ăm′ō-rītes, the king of Jerusalem, the king of Hē′brȯn, the king of Jär′mŭth, the king of Lā′chĭsh, the king of Ĕg′lŏn, gathered themselves together, and went up, they and all their hosts, and encamped before Gĭb′e-on, and made war against it.

6 ¶ And the men of Gĭb′ē-ȯn sent unto Joshua to the camp to Gĭl′găl, saying, Slack not thy hand from thy servants; come up to us quickly, and save us, and help us: for all the kings of the Ăm′ō-rītes that dwell in the mountains are gathered together against us.

7 So Joshua ascended from Gĭl′găl, he, and all the people of war with him, and all the mighty men of valor.

8 ¶ And the LORD said unto Joshua, Fear them not: for I have delivered them into thine hand; there shall not a man of them stand before thee.

9 Joshua therefore came unto them

suddenly, *and* went up from Gĭl′găl all
night.
10 And the LORD discomfited them before Is′rā-ĕl, and slew them with a great
slaughter at Gĭb′ē-ŏn, and chased them
along the way that goeth up to Bĕth′–
hō′rŏn, and smote them to Ȧ-zē′kȧh,
and unto Măk-kē′dȧh.
11 And it came to pass, as they fled
from before Ĭṣ′rā-ĕl, *and* were in the going down to Bĕth′–hō′rŏn, that the LORD
cast down great stones from heaven upon them unto Ȧ-zē′kȧh, and they died:
they were more which died with hailstones than *they* whom the children of
Ĭṣ′rā-ĕl slew with the sword.
12 ¶ Then spake Joshua to the LORD
in the day when the LORD delivered up
the Ăm′ō-rītes before the children of
Ĭṣ′rā-ĕl, and he said in the sight of
Ĭṣ′rā-ĕl, Sun, stand thou still upon
Gĭb′ē-ŏn; and thou, Moon, in the valley
of Ăj′ȧ-lŏn.
13 And the sun stood still, and the
moon stayed, until the people had
avenged themselves upon their enemies.
Is not this written in the book of Jā′shĕr?
So the sun stood still in the midst of
heaven, and hasted not to go down about
a whole day.
14 And there was no day like that before it or after it, that the LORD hearkened unto the voice of a man: for the
LORD fought for Ĭṣ′rā-ĕl.
15 ¶ And Joshua returned, and all
Ĭṣ′rā-ĕl with him, unto the camp to
Gĭl′găl.
16 But these five kings fled, and hid
themselves in a cave at Măk-kē′dȧh.
17 And it was told Joshua, saying, The
five kings are found hid in a cave at
Măk-kē′dȧh.
18 And Joshua said, Roll great stones
upon the mouth of the cave, and set men
by it for to keep them:
19 And stay ye not, *but* pursue after
your enemies, and smite the hindmost
of them; suffer them not to enter into
their cities: for the LORD your God hath
delivered them into your hand.
20 And it came to pass, when Joshua
and the children of Ĭṣ′rā-ĕl had made an
end of slaying them with a very great
slaughter, till they were consumed, that
the rest *which* remained of them entered
into fenced cities.
21 And all the people returned to the
camp to Joshua at Măk-kē′dȧh in peace:
none moved his tongue against any of
the children of Ĭṣ′rā-ĕl.
22 Then said Joshua, Open the mouth
of the cave, and bring out those five
kings unto me out of the cave.
23 And they did so, and brought forth
those five kings unto him out of the
cave, the king of Jerusalem, the king of
Hē′brŏn, the king of Jär′mŭth, the king
of Lā′chĭsh, *and* the king of Ĕg′lŏn.
24 And it came to pass, when they
brought out those kings unto Joshua,
that Joshua called for all the men of
Ĭṣ′rā-ĕl, and said unto the captains of
the men of war which went with him,
Come near, put your feet upon the necks
of these kings. And they came near, and
put their feet upon the necks of them.
25 And Joshua said unto them, Fear
not, nor be dismayed, be strong and of
good courage: for thus shall the LORD
do to all your enemies against whom ye
fight.
26 And afterward Joshua smote them,
and slew them, and hanged them on five
trees: and they were hanging upon the
trees until the evening.
27 And it came to pass at the time of
the going down of the sun, *that* Joshua
commanded, and they took them down
off the trees, and cast them into the cave
wherein they had been hid, and laid
great stones in the cave's mouth, *which
remain* until this very day.
28 ¶ And that day Joshua took Măk-
kē′dȧh, and smote it with the edge of the
sword, and the king thereof he utterly
destroyed, them, and all the souls that
were therein; he let none remain: and
he did to the king of Măk-kē′dȧh as he
did unto the king of Jĕr′ĭ-chō.
29 Then Joshua passed from Măk-
kē′dȧh, and all Ĭṣ′rā-ĕl with him, unto
Lĭb′nȧh, and fought against Lĭb′nȧh:
30 And the LORD delivered it also, and
the king thereof, into the hand of Ĭṣ′-
rā-ĕl; and he smote it with the edge of
the sword, and all the souls that *were*
therein; he let none remain in it; but did
unto the king thereof as he did unto the
king of Jĕr′ĭ-chō.
31 ¶ And Joshua passed from Lĭb′nȧh,
and all Ĭṣ′rā-ĕl with him, unto Lā′chĭsh,
and encamped against it, and fought
against it:
32 And the LORD delivered Lā′chĭsh
into the hand of Ĭṣ′rā-ĕl, which took it on
the second day, and smote it with the

edge of the sword, and all the souls that
were therein, according to all that he
had done to Lĭb′nȧh.
33 ¶ Then Hō′răm king of Gē′zĕr
came up to help Lā′ɕhish; and Joshua
smote him and his people, until he had
left him none remaining.
34 ¶ And from Lā′ɕhĭsh Joshua passed
unto Ĕg′lŏn, and all Ĭs′rā-ĕl with him;
and they encamped against it, and
fought against it:
35 And they took it on that day, and
smote it with the edge of the sword, and
all the souls that *were* therein he utterly
destroyed that day, according to all that
he had done to Lā′ɕhĭsh.
36 And Joshua went up from Ĕg′lŏn,
and all Ĭs′rā-ĕl with him, unto Hē′brȯn;
and they fought against it:
37 And they took it, and smote it with
the edge of the sword, and the king
thereof, and all the cities thereof, and all
the souls that *were* therein; he left none
remaining, according to all that he had
done to Ĕg′lŏn; but destroyed it utterly, and all the souls that *were* therein.
38 ¶ And Joshua returned, and all
Ĭs′rā-ĕl with him, to Dē′bĭr; and fought
against it:
39 And he took it, and the king thereof,
and all the cities thereof; and they smote
them with the edge of the sword, and
utterly destroyed all the souls that *were*
therein; he left none remaining: as he
had done to Hē′brȯn, so he did to Dē′bĭr,
and to the king thereof; as he had done
also to Lĭb′nȧh, and to her king.
40 ¶ So Joshua smote all the country
of the hills, and of the south, and of the
vale, and of the springs, and all their
kings: he left none remaining, but utterly destroyed all that breathed, as the
LORD God of Ĭs′rā-ĕl commanded.
41 And Joshua smote them from Kā′-
dĕsh–bär′nē-ȧ even unto Gā′zȧ, and all
the country of Gō′shĕn, even unto
Gĭb′ē-ȯn.
42 And all these kings and their land
did Joshua take at one time, because the
LORD God of Ĭs′rā-ĕl fought for Ĭs′rā-ĕl.
43 And Joshua returned, and all
Ĭs′rā ĕl with him, unto the camp to
Gĭl′găl.

CHAPTER 11

AND it came to pass, when Jā′bĭn
king of Hā′zŏr had heard *those
things,* that he sent to Jō′băb king of
Mā′dŏn, and to the king of Shĭm′rŏn,
and to the king of Ăɕh′shȧph,
2 And to the kings that *were* on the
north of the mountains, and of the plains
south of ɕhĭn′nē-rŏth, and in the valley,
and in the borders of Dor on the west,
3 *And to* the Că′năan-īte on the east
and on the west, and *to* the Ăm′ō-rīte,
and the Hĭt′tīte, and the Pĕr′ĭz-zīte, and
the Jĕb′ū-sīte in the mountains, and *to*
the Hī′vīte under Hermon in the land of
Mĭz′pĕh.
4 And they went out, they and all their
hosts with them, much people, even as
the sand that *is* upon the seashore in
multitude, with horses and chariots very
many.
5 And when all these kings were met
together, they came and pitched together at the waters of Mē′rŏm, to fight
against Ĭs′rā-ĕl.
6 ¶ And the LORD said unto Joshua,
Be not afraid because of them: for to-
morrow about this time will I deliver
them up all slain before Ĭs′rā-ĕl: thou
shalt hough their horses, and burn their
chariots with fire.
7 So Joshua came, and all the people of
war with him, against them by the waters of Mē′rŏm suddenly; and they fell
upon them.
8 And the LORD delivered them into the
hand of Ĭs′rā-ĕl, who smote them, and
chased them unto great Zī′dȯn, and unto
Mĭs′rē-phŏth–mā′ĭm, and unto the valley of Mĭz′pĕh eastward; and they smote
them, until they left them none remaining.
9 And Joshua did unto them as the
LORD bade him: he houghed their
horses, and burnt their chariots with fire.
10 ¶ And Joshua at that time turned
back, and took Hā′zŏr, and smote the
king thereof with the sword: for Hā′zŏr
beforetime was the head of all those
kingdoms.
11 And they smote all the souls that
were therein with the edge of the sword,
utterly destroying *them:* there was not
any left to breathe: and he burnt Hā′zŏr
with fire.
12 And all the cities of those kings, and
all the kings of them, did Joshua take,
and smote them with the edge of the
sword, *and* he utterly destroyed them,
as Moses the servant of the LORD
commanded.
13 But *as for* the cities that stood still

in their strength, Ĭş'rā-ĕl burned none
of them, save Hā'zŏr only; *that* did
Joshua burn.
14 And all the spoil of these cities, and
the cattle, the children of Ĭş'rā-ĕl took
for a prey unto themselves; but every
man they smote with the edge of the
sword, until they had destroyed them,
neither left they any to breathe.
15 ¶ As the LORD commanded Moses
his servant, so did Moses command
Joshua, and so did Joshua; he left nothing undone of all that the LORD commanded Moses.
16 So Joshua took all that land, the
hills, and all the south country, and all
the land of Gō'shĕn, and the valley, and
the plain, and the mountain of Ĭş'rā-ĕl,
and the valley of the same;
17 *Even* from the mount Hā'lăk, that
goeth up to Sē'ĭr, even unto Bā'ăl–găd
in the valley of Lebanon under mount
Hermon: and all their kings he took, and
smote them, and slew them.
18 Joshua made war a long time with
all those kings.
19 There was not a city that made
peace with the children of Ĭş'rā-ĕl,
save the Hī'vītes the inhabitants of Gĭb'-
ē-ŏn: all *other* they took in battle.
20 For it was of the LORD to harden
their hearts, that they should come
against Ĭş'rā-ĕl in battle, that he might
destroy them utterly, *and* that they might
have no favor, but that he might destroy
them, as the LORD commanded Moses.
21 ¶ And at that time came Joshua,
and cut off the Ăn'ă-kĭm from the mountains, from Hē'brŏn, from Dē'bĭr, from
Ā'năb, and from all the mountains of
Judah, and from all the mountains
of Ĭş'rā-ĕl: Joshua destroyed them utterly with their cities.
22 There was none of the Ăn'ă-kĭm
left in the land of the children of Ĭş'rā-ĕl:
only in Gā'ză, in Gath, and in Ashdod,
there remained.
23 So Joshua took the whole land,
according to all that the LORD said unto
Moses; and Joshua gave it for an inheritance unto Ĭş'rā-ĕl according to
their divisions by their tribes. And the
land rested from war.

CHAPTER 12

NOW these *are* the kings of the land,
which the children of Ĭş'rā-ĕl
smote, and possessed their land on the
other side Jordan toward the rising of
the sun, from the river Är'nŏn unto
mount Hermon, and all the plain on the
east:
2 Sī'hŏn king of the Ăm'ō-rītes, who
dwelt in Hĕsh'bŏn, *and* ruled from
Ă-rō'ĕr, which *is* upon the bank of the
river Är'nŏn, and from the middle of
the river, and from half Gĭl'ē-ăd, even
unto the river Jăb'bŏk, *which is* the border of the children of Ammon;
3 And from the plain to the sea of
Chĭn'nē-rŏth on the east, and unto the
sea of the plain, *even* the salt sea on
the east, the way to Bĕth'–jĕsh'ĭ-mŏth;
and from the south, under Ăsh'dŏth–
pĭş'gäh:
4 ¶ And the coast of Og king of Bā'-
shăn, *which was* of the remnant of the
giants, that dwelt at Ăsh'tă-rŏth and
at Ĕd'rē-ī,
5 And reigned in mount Hermon, and
in Săl'căh, and in all Bā'shăn, unto the
border of the Gĕsh'ū-rītes and the
Mā-ăch'ă-thītes, and half Gĭl'ē-ăd, the
border of Sī'hŏn king of Hĕsh'bŏn.
6 Them did Moses the servant of the
LORD and the children of Ĭş'rā-ĕl smite:
and Moses the servant of the LORD gave
it *for* a possession unto the Reubenites,
and the Gadites, and the half tribe of
Mă-năs'sĕh.
7 ¶ And these *are* the kings of the
country which Joshua and the children
of Ĭş'rā-ĕl smote on this side Jordan on
the west, from Bā'ăl–găd in the valley of
Lebanon even unto the mount Hā'lăk,
that goeth up to Sē'ĭr; which Joshua
gave unto the tribes of Ĭş'rā-ĕl *for* a
possession according to their divisions;
8 In the mountains, and in the valleys,
and in the plains, and in the springs, and
in the wilderness, and in the south
country; the Hĭt'tītes, the Ăm'ō-rītes,
and the Cā'năan-ītes, the Pĕr'ĭz-zītes,
the Hī'vītes, and the Jĕb'ū-şītes:
9 ¶ The king of Jĕr'ĭ-chō, one; the
king of Ā'ī, which *is* beside Beth-el, one;
10 The king of Jerusalem, one; the
king of Hē'brŏn, one;
11 The king of Jär'mŭth, one; the king
of Lā'chĭsh, one;
12 The king of Ĕg'lŏn, one; the king of
Gē'zĕr, one;
13 The king of Dē'bĭr, one; the king of
Gē'dĕr, one;
14 The king of Hôr'măh, one; the king
of Ā'răd, one;

15 The king of Lĭb'nȧh, one; the king
of Ȧ-dŭl'lăm, one;
16 The king of Măk-kē'dȧh, one; the
king of Beth-el, one;
17 The king of Tȧp-pū'ȧh, one; the
king of Hē'phĕr, one;
18 The king of Ā'phĕk, one; the king
of Lȧ-shā'rŏn, one;
19 The king of Mā'dŏn, one; the king
of Hā'zŏr, one;
20 The king of Shĭm'rŏn-mē'rŏn, one;
the king of Ȧch'shȧph, one;
21 The king of Tā'ȧ-năch, one; the
king of Mē-gĭd'dō, one;
22 The king of Kē'dĕsh, one; the king
of Jŏk'nē-ăm of Căr'mĕl, one;
23 The king of Dor in the coast of Dor,
one; the king of the nations of Gĭl'găl,
one;
24 The king of Tĭr'zȧh, one: all the
kings thirty and one.

CHAPTER 13

NOW Joshua was old *and* stricken
in years; and the LORD said unto
him, Thou art old *and* stricken in years,
and there remaineth yet very much land
to be possessed.
2 This *is* the land that yet remaineth:
all the borders of the Phĭ-lĭs'tīneṣ, and
all Gē-shu'rī,
3 From Sī'hôr, which *is* before Egypt,
even unto the borders of Ĕk'rŏn northward, *which* is counted to the Cā'-
năan-īte: five lords of the Phĭ-lĭs'tīneṣ;
the Gā'zăth-ītes, and the Ăsh'dŏth-ītes,
the Ĕsh'kȧ-lŏn-ītes, the Gĭt'tītes, and
the Ĕk'rŏn-ītes; also the Ā'vītes:
4 From the south, all the land of the
Cā'năan-ītes, and Mē-ā'rȧh that *is* beside the Sī-dō'nĭ-ans, unto Ā'phĕk, to
the borders of the Ăm'ō-rītes:
5 And the land of the Gĭb'lītes, and all
Lebanon toward the sunrising, from
Bā'ăl-găd under mount Hermon unto
the entering into Hā'măth.
6 All the inhabitants of the hill country
from Lebanon unto Mĭs'rē-phŏth-mā'-
ĭm, *and* all the Sī-dō'nĭ-ănṣ, them will I
drive out from before the children of
Ĭṣ'rā-ĕl: only divide thou it by lot unto
the Ĭṣ'rā-ĕl-ītes for an inheritance, as I
have commanded thee.
7 Now therefore divide this land for an
inheritance unto the nine tribes, and the
half tribe of Mȧ-năs'sĕh,
8 With whom the Reubenites and the
Gadites have received their inheritance,
which Moses gave them, beyond Jordan
eastward, *even* as Moses the servant of
the LORD gave them;
9 From Ȧ-rō'ĕr, that *is* upon the bank
of the river Ăr'nŏn, and the city that *is*
in the midst of the river, and all the
plain of Mĕd'ē-bȧ unto Dī'bŏn;
10 And all the cities of Sī'hŏn king of
the Ăm'ō-rītes, which reigned in Hĕsh'-
bŏn, unto the border of the children of
Ammon;
11 And Gĭl'ē-ăd, and the border of the
Gĕsh'ū-rītes and Mā-ăch'ȧ-thītes, and
all mount Hermon, and all Bā'shăn unto
Săl'cȧh;
12 All the kingdom of Og in Bā'shăn,
which reigned in Ăsh'tȧ-rŏth and in
Ĕd'rē-ī, who remained of the remnant
of the giants: for these did Moses smite,
and cast them out.
13 Nevertheless the children of Ĭṣ'rā-ĕl
expelled not the Gĕsh'ū-rītes, nor the
Mā-ăch'ȧ-thītes: but the Gĕsh'ū-rītes
and the Mā-ăch'ȧ-thītes dwell among
the Ĭṣ'rā-ĕl-ītes until this day.
14 Only unto the tribe of Levi he
gave none inheritance; the sacrifices of
the LORD God of Ĭṣ'rā-ĕl made by fire
are their inheritance, as he said unto
them.
15 ¶ And Moses gave unto the tribe
of the children of Reuben *inheritance*
according to their families.
16 And their coast was from Ȧ-ro'ĕr,
that *is* on the bank of the river Ăr'nŏn,
and the city that *is* in the midst of the
river, and all the plain by Mĕd'ē-bȧ;
17 Hĕsh'bŏn, and all her cities that *are*
in the plain; Dī'bŏn, and Bā'mŏth-bā'ăl,
and Bĕth'-bā'ăl-mē'ŏn,
18 And Jȧ-hā'zȧ, and Kĕd'ē-mŏth, and
Mĕph'ȧ-ăth,
19 And Kĭr'jȧ-thā'ĭm, and Sĭb'mȧh,
and Zā'rĕth-shā'hăr in the mount of
the valley,
20 And Bĕth'-pē'ŏr, and Ăsh'dŏth-
pĭs'gȧh, and Bĕth'-jĕsh'ĭ-mŏth,
21 And all the cities of the plain, and
all the kingdom of Sī'hŏn king of the
Ăm'ō-rītes, which reigned in Hĕsh'bŏn,
whom Moses smote with the princes of
Mĭd'ĭ-ăn, Ē'vī, and Rē'kĕm, and Zûr,
and Hûr, and Rē'bȧ, *which were* dukes
of Sī'hŏn, dwelling in the country.
22 ¶ Bā'laam also the son of Bē'ŏr,
the soothsayer, did the children of
Ĭṣ'rā-ĕl slay with the sword among them
that were slain by them.

23 And the border of the children of
Reuben was Jordan, and the border
thereof. This *was* the inheritance of the
children of Reuben after their families,
the cities and the villages thereof.
24 And Moses gave *inheritance* unto
the tribe of Gad, *even* unto the children
of Gad according to their families.
25 And their coast was Jā'zēr, and all
the cities of Gĭl'ē-ăd, and half the land
of the children of Ammon, unto Ȧ-rō'ēr
that *is* before Răb'bȧh;
26 And from Hĕsh'bŏn unto Rā'măth–
mĭz'pĕh, and Bĕt'ō-nĭm; and from Mā'-
hȧ-nā'ĭm unto the border of Dē'bĭr;
27 And in the valley, Bĕth'–ā'răm, and
Bĕth'–nĭm'rȧh, and Sŭc'cōth, and Zā'-
phŏn, the rest of the kingdom of Sī'hŏn
king of Hĕsh'bŏn, Jordan and *his* border, *even* unto the edge of the sea of
Chĭn'nē-rĕth on the other side Jordan
eastward.
28 This *is* the inheritance of the children of Gad after their families, the
cities, and their villages.
29 ¶ And Moses gave *inheritance*
unto the half tribe of Mȧ-năs'sĕh: and
this was *the possession* of the half tribe
of the children of Mȧ-năs'sĕh by their
families.
30 And their coast was from Mā'hȧ-
nā'ĭm, all Bā'shăn, all the kingdom of
Og king of Bā'shăn, and all the towns of
Jā'ĭr, which *are* in Bā'shăn, threescore
cities:
31 And half Gĭl'ē-ăd, and Ăsh'tȧ-rŏth,
and Ĕd'rē-ī, cities of the kingdom of Og
in Bā'shăn, *were pertaining* unto the
children of Mā'chĭr the son of Mȧ-năs'-
sĕh, *even* to the one half of the children
of Mā'chĭr by their families.
32 These *are the countries* which
Moses did distribute for inheritance in
the plains of Mō'ăb, on the other side
Jordan, by Jĕr'ī-chō, eastward.
33 But unto the tribe of Levi Moses
gave not *any* inheritance: the LORD God
of Ĭs'rā-ĕl *was* their inheritance, as he
said unto them.

CHAPTER 14

AND these *are the countries* which the
children of Ĭs'rā-ĕl inherited in the
land of Cā'năan, which Ĕl'ē-ā'zȧr the
priest, and Joshua the son of Nŭn, and
the heads of the fathers of the tribes of
the children of Ĭs'rā-ĕl, distributed for
inheritance to them.
2 By lot *was* their inheritance, as the
LORD commanded by the hand of
Moses, for the nine tribes, and *for* the
half tribe.
3 For Moses had given the inheritance
of two tribes and a half tribe on the
other side Jordan: but unto the Lē'vītes
he gave none inheritance among them.
4 For the children of Joseph were two
tribes, Mȧ-năs'sĕh and Ē'phrā-ĭm:
therefore they gave no part unto the
Lē'vītes in the land, save cities to dwell
in, with their suburbs for their cattle and
for their substance.
5 As the LORD commanded Moses, so
the children of Ĭs'rā-ĕl did, and they
divided the land.
6 ¶ Then the children of Judah came
unto Joshua in Gĭl'găl: and Caleb the
son of Jē-phŭn'nĕh the Kē'nĕz-īte said
unto him, Thou knowest the thing that
the LORD said unto Moses the man of
God concerning me and thee in Kā'-
dĕsh–bär'nē-ȧ.
7 Forty years old *was* I when Moses
the servant of the LORD sent me from
Kā'dĕsh–bär'nē-ȧ to espy out the land;
and I brought him word again as *it was*
in mine heart.
8 Nevertheless my brethren that went
up with me made the heart of the people
melt: but I wholly followed the LORD my
God.
9 And Moses sware on that day, saying,
Surely the land whereon thy feet have
trodden shall be thine inheritance, and
thy children's for ever, because thou
hast wholly followed the LORD my God.
10 And now, behold, the LORD hath
kept me alive, as he said, these forty
and five years, even since the LORD
spake this word unto Moses, while *the
children of* Ĭs'rā-ĕl wandered in the
wilderness: and now, lo, I *am* this day
fourscore and five years old.
11 As yet I *am as* strong this day as *I
was* in the day that Moses sent me: as
my strength *was* then, even so *is* my
strength now, for war, both to go out,
and to come in.
12 Now therefore give me this mountain, whereof the LORD spake in that
day; for thou heardest in that day how
the Ăn'ȧ-kĭm *were* there, and *that* the
cities *were* great *and* fenced: if so be the
LORD *will be* with me, then I shall be
able to drive them out, as the LORD said.
13 And Joshua blessed him, and gave

unto Caleb the son of Jē-phŭn′nĕh Hē′brŏn for an inheritance.

14 Hē′brŏn therefore became the inheritance of Caleb the son of Jē-phŭn′nĕh the Kē′nĕz-īte unto this day; because that he wholly followed the LORD God of Ĭs′rā-ĕl.

15 And the name of Hē′brŏn before *was* Kĭr′jăth-är′bȧ; *which Arba was* a great man among the Ăn′ȧ-kĭm. And the land had rest from war.

CHAPTER 15

THIS then was the lot of the tribe of the children of Judah by their families; *even* to the border of Ē′dŏm the wilderness of Zĭn southward *was* the uttermost part of the south coast.

2 And their south border was from the shore of the salt sea, from the bay that looketh southward:

3 And it went out to the south side to Mā′ȧ-lĕh-ȧ-crăb′bĭm, and passed along to Zĭn, and ascended up on the south side unto Kā′dĕsh-bär′nē-ȧ, and passed along to Hĕz′rŏn, and went up to Ȧ′där, and fetched a compass to Kär′kā-ȧ:

4 *From thence* it passed toward Ăz′mŏn, and went out unto the river of Egypt; and the goings out of that coast were at the sea: this shall be your south coast.

5 And the east border *was* the salt sea, *even* unto the end of Jordan. And *their* border in the north quarter *was* from the bay of the sea at the uttermost part of Jordan:

6 And the border went up to Bĕth′-hŏg′lȧ, and passed along by the north of Bĕth′-ăr′ȧ-bȧh; and the border went up to the stone of Bō′hăn the son of Reuben:

7 And the border went up toward Dē′bĭr from the valley of Ā′chŏr, and so northward, looking toward Gĭl′găl, that *is* before the going up to Ȧ-dŭm′mĭm, which *is* on the south side of the river: and the border passed toward the waters of Ĕn-shē′mĕsh, and the goings out thereof were at Ĕn-rō′gĕl:

8 And the border went up by the valley of the son of Hĭn′nŏm unto the south side of the Jĕb′ū-şīte; the same *is* Jerusalem: and the border went up to the top of the mountain that *lieth* before the valley of Hĭn′nŏm westward, which *is* at the end of the valley of the giants northward:

9 And the border was drawn from the top of the hill unto the fountain of the water of Nĕph-tō′ȧh, and went out to the cities of mount Ē′phrŏn; and the border was drawn to Bā′ȧ-lȧh, which *is* Kĭr′jăth-jē′ȧ-rĭm:

10 And the border compassed from Bā′ȧ-lȧh westward unto mount Sē′ĭr, and passed along unto the side of mount Jē′ȧ-rĭm, which *is* Chĕs′ȧ-lŏn, on the north side, and went down to Bĕth′-shē′mĕsh, and passed on to Tĭm′nȧh:

11 And the border went out unto the side of Ĕk′rŏn northward: and the border was drawn to Shĭc′rŏn, and passed along to mount Bā′ȧ-lȧh, and went out unto Jăb′nē-ĕl; and the goings out of the border were at the sea.

12 And the west border *was* to the great sea, and the coast *thereof*. This *is* the coast of the children of Judah round about according to their families.

13 ℂ And unto Caleb the son of Jē-phŭn′nĕh he gave a part among the children of Judah, according to the commandment of the LORD to Joshua, *even* the city of Är′bȧ the father of Ā′năk, which *city is* Hē′brŏn.

14 And Caleb drove thence the three sons of Ā′năk, Shē′shaī, and Ȧ-hī′măn, and Tăl′maī, the children of Ā′năk.

15 And he went up thence to the inhabitants of Dē′bĭr: and the name of Dē′bĭr before *was* Kĭr′jăth-sē′phĕr.

16 ℂ And Caleb said, He that smiteth Kĭr′jăth-sē′phĕr, and taketh it, to him will I give Ăch′sȧh my daughter to wife.

17 And Ŏth′nĭ-ĕl the son of Kē′năz, the brother of Caleb, took it: and he gave him Ăch′sȧh his daughter to wife.

18 And it came to pass, as she came *unto him*, that she moved him to ask of her father a field: and she lighted off *her* ass; and Caleb said unto her, What wouldest thou?

19 Who answered, Give me a blessing; for thou hast given me a south land; give me also springs of water. And he gave her the upper springs, and the nether springs.

20 This *is* the inheritance of the tribe of the children of Judah according to their families.

21 And the uttermost cities of the tribe of the children of Judah toward the coast of Ē′dŏm southward were Kăb′zē-ĕl, and Ē′dĕr, and Jā′gŭr,

22 And Kī'nȧh, and Dī-mō'nȧh, and
Ăd'ȧ-dȧh,
23 And Kē'dĕsh, and Hā'zŏr, and
Ĭth'năn,
24 Zīph, and Tē'lĕm, and Bē'ȧ-lōth,
25 And Hā'zŏr, Hȧ-dăt'tȧh, and Kē-
rī-ōth, *and* Hĕz'rŏn, which *is* Hā'zŏr,
26 Ā'măm, and Shē'mȧ, and Mŏl'ȧ-
dȧh,
27 And Hā'zär-găd'dȧh, and Hĕsh'-
mŏn, and Bĕth'-pā'lĕt,
28 And Hā'zär-shṳ'ăl, and Bē'ĕr-
shē'bȧ, and Bīz-jŏth'jȧh,
29 Bā'ȧ-lȧh, and Ī'ĭm, and Ā'zĕm,
30 And Ĕl-tō'lăd, and Chē'sĭl, and
Hôr'mȧh,
31 And Zĭk'lăg, and Măd-măn'nȧh,
and Săn-săn'nȧh,
32 And Lē-bā'ŏth, and Shĭl'hĭm, and
Ā'ĭn, and Rĭm'mŏn: all the cities *are*
twenty and nine, with their villages:
33 *And* in the valley, Ĕsh'tā-ŏl, and
Zō'rē-ȧh, and Ăsh'nȧh,
34 And Zȧ-nō'ȧh, and Ĕn-găn'nĭm,
Tȧp-pū'ȧh, and Ē'năm,
35 Jär'mŭth, and Ȧ-dŭl'lăm, Sō'cōh,
and Ȧ-zē'kȧh,
36 And Shȧ-rā'ĭm, and Ăd'ĭ-thā'ĭm,
and Gē-dē'rȧh, and Gĕd'ē-rō-thā'ĭm;
fourteen cities with their villages:
37 Zē'năn, and Hȧ-dăsh'ȧh, and
Mĭg'dăl-găd',
38 And Dĭl'ē-ăn, and Mĭz'pĕh, and
Jŏk'thē-ĕl,
39 Lā'chĭsh, and Bŏz'kăth, and Ĕg'lŏn,
40 And Căb'bŏn, and Läh'măm, and
Kĭth'lĭsh,
41 And Gē-dē'rŏth, Bĕth'-dā'gŏn, and
Nā'ȧ-mȧh, and Măk-kē'dȧh; sixteen
cities with their villages:
42 Lĭb'nȧh, and Ē'thĕr, and Ā'shăn,
43 And Jĭph'tȧh, and Ăsh'nȧh, and
Nē'zĭb,
44 And Kē-ī'lȧh, and Ăch'zĭb, and Mȧ-
rē'shȧh; nine cities with their villages:
45 Ĕk'rŏn, with her towns and her
villages:
46 From Ĕk'rŏn even unto the sea,
all that *lay* near Ashdod, with their
villages:
47 Ashdod, with her towns and her villages; Gā'zȧ, with her towns and her villages, unto the river of Egypt, and the
great sea, and the border *thereof:*
48 ℂ And in the mountains, Shā'mĭr,
and Jăt'tĭr, and Sō'cōh,
49 And Dăn'nȧh, and Kĭr'jăth-săn'-
nȧh, which *is* Dē'bĭr,
50 And Ā'năb, and Ĕsh'tē-mōh, and
Ā'nĭm,
51 And Gō'shĕn, and Hō'lŏn, and Gī'-
lōh; eleven cities with their villages:
52 Ăr'ăb, and Dū'mȧh, and Ĕsh'ē-ăn,
53 And Jā'nŭm, and Bĕth'-tȧp'pū-ȧh,
and Ȧ-phē'kȧh,
54 And Hŭm'tȧh, and Kĭr'jăth-är'bȧ,
which *is* Hē'brŏn, and Zī'ŏr; nine cities
with their villages:
55 Mā'ŏn, Cär'mĕl, and Zīph, and
Jŭt'tȧh,
56 And Jĕz'rē-ĕl, and Jŏk'dē-ăm, and
Zȧ-nō'ȧh,
57 Cain, Gĭb'ē-ȧh, and Tĭm'nȧh; ten
cities with their villages:
58 Hăl'hŭl, Bĕth'-zûr', and Gē'dŏr,
59 And Mā'ȧ-răth, and Bĕth'-ā'nŏth,
and Ĕl'tē-kŏn; six cities with their
villages:
60 Kĭr'jăth-bā'ăl, which *is* Kĭr'jăth-
jē'ȧ-rĭm, and Răb'bȧh; two cities with
their villages.
61 In the wilderness, Bĕth'-är'ȧ-bȧh,
Mĭd'dĭn, and Sē-cā'cȧh,
62 And Nĭb'shăn, and the city of Salt,
and Ĕn-gē'dī; six cities with their
villages.
63 ℂ As for the Jĕb'ū-sītes the inhabitants of Jerusalem, the children of Judah could not drive them out: but the
Jĕb'ū-sītes dwell with the children of
Judah at Jerusalem unto this day.

CHAPTER 16

AND the lot of the children of Joseph
fell from Jordan by Jĕr'ĭ-chō, unto
the water of Jĕr'ĭ-chō on the east, to the
wilderness that goeth up from Jĕr'ĭ-chō
throughout mount Beth-el,
2 And goeth out from Beth-el to Lŭz,
and passeth along unto the borders of
Är'chī to Ăt'ȧ-rŏth,
3 And goeth down westward to the
coast of Jăph'lē-tī, unto the coast of
Bĕth'-hō'rŏn the nether, and to Gē'zĕr:
and the goings out thereof are at the sea.
4 So the children of Joseph, Mȧ-năs'-
sĕh and Ē'phrā-ĭm, took their inheritance.
5 ℂ And the border of the children of
Ē'phrā-ĭm according to their families
was *thus:* even the border of their inheritance on the east side was Ăt'ȧ-rŏth-
ăd'där, unto Bĕth'-hō'rŏn the upper;
6 And the border went out toward the
sea to Mĭch'mē-thȧh on the north side;
and the border went about eastward

unto Tā'ȧ-năth–shī'lōh, and passed by
it on the east to Jȧ-nō'hȧh;
7 And it went down from Jȧ-nō'hȧh to
Ăt'ȧ-rŏth, and to Nā'ȧ-răth, and came to
Jĕr'ī-chō, and went out at Jordan.
8 The border went out from Tȧp-pū'ȧh
westward unto the river Kā'nȧh; and
the goings out thereof were at the sea.
This *is* the inheritance of the tribe of
the children of Ē'phrā-ĭm by their
families.
9 And the separate cities for the children of Ē'phrā-ĭm *were* among the inheritance of the children of Mȧ-năs'sĕh,
all the cities with their villages.
10 And they drave not out the Cā'năan-
ītes that dwelt in Gē'zēr: but the Cā'-
năan-ītes dwell among the Ē'phrā-ĭm-
ītes unto this day, and serve under
tribute.

CHAPTER 17

THERE was also a lot for the tribe of
Mȧ-năs'sĕh; for he *was* the firstborn
of Joseph; *to wit,* for Mā'chĭr the firstborn of Mȧ-năs'sĕh, the father of
Gĭl'ē-ăd: because he was a man of war,
therefore he had Gĭl'ē-ăd and Bā'shăn.
2 There was also *a lot* for the rest of
the children of Mȧ-năs'sĕh by their
families; for the children of Ā'bĭ-ē'zēr,
and for the children of Hē'lĕk, and for
the children of Ăs'rĭ-ĕl, and for the children of Shē'chĕm, and for the children
of Hē'phēr, and for the children of
Shē-mī'dȧ: these *were* the male children of Mȧ-năs'sĕh the son of Joseph
by their families.
3 ¶ But Zē-lō'phē-hăd, the son of
Hē'phēr, the son of Gĭl'ē-ăd, the son of
Mā'chĭr, the son of Mȧ-năs'sĕh, had no
sons, but daughters: and these *are* the
names of his daughters, Măh'lȧh, and
Noah, Hŏg'lȧh, Mĭl'cȧh, and Tĭr'zȧh.
4 And they came near before Ĕl'ē-ā'zȧr
the priest, and before Joshua the son of
Nŭn, and before the princes, saying,
The LORD commanded Moses to give us
an inheritance among our brethren.
Therefore, according to the commandment of the LORD, he gave them an inheritance among the brethren of their
father.
5 And there fell ten portions to Mȧ-
năs'sĕh, besides the land of Gĭl'ē-ăd
and Bā'shăn, which *were* on the other
side Jordan;
6 Because the daughters of Mȧ-năs'sĕh
had an inheritance among his sons: and
the rest of Mȧ-năs'sĕh's sons had the
land of Gĭl'ē-ăd.
7 ¶ And the coast of Mȧ-năs'sĕh was
from Ăsh'ēr to Mĭch'mē-thȧh, that *lieth*
before Shē'chĕm; and the border went
along on the right hand unto the inhabitants of Ĕn–tăp'pū-ăh.
8 *Now* Mȧ-năs'sĕh had the land of
Tȧp-pū'ȧh: but Tȧp-pū'ȧh on the border of Mȧ-năs'sĕh *belonged* to the children of Ē'phrā-ĭm;
9 And the coast descended unto the
river Kā'nȧh, southward of the river:
these cities of Ē'phrā-ĭm *are* among the
cities of Mȧ-năs'sĕh: the coast of Mȧ-
năs'sĕh also *was* on the north side of
the river, and the outgoings of it were
at the sea:
10 Southward *it was* Ē'phrā-ĭm's, and
northward *it was* Mȧ-năs'sĕh's, and the
sea is his border; and they met together
in Ăsh'ēr on the north, and in Ĭs'sȧ-chär
on the east.
11 And Mȧ-năs'sĕh had in Ĭs'sȧ-chär
and in Ăsh'ēr Bĕth'–shē'ăn and her
towns, and Ĭb'lē-ăm and her towns, and
the inhabitants of Dor and her towns,
and the inhabitants of Ĕn'–dôr and her
towns, and the inhabitants of Tā'ȧ-
năch and her towns, and the inhabitants
of Mē-gĭd'dō and her towns, *even* three
countries.
12 Yet the children of Mȧ-năs'sĕh
could not drive out *the inhabitants of*
those cities; but the Cā'năan-ītes would
dwell in that land.
13 Yet it came to pass, when the children of Ĭṣ'rā-ĕl were waxen strong, that
they put the Cā'năan-ītes to tribute; but
did not utterly drive them out.
14 And the children of Joseph spake
unto Joshua, saying, Why hast thou
given me *but* one lot and one portion to
inherit, seeing I *am* a great people, forasmuch as the LORD hath blessed me
hitherto?
15 And Joshua answered them, If thou
be a great people, *then* get thee up to
the wood *country*, and cut down for thyself there in the land of the Pĕr'ĭz-zītes
and of the giants, if mount Ē'phrā-ĭm
be too narrow for thee.
16 And the children of Joseph said,
The hill is not enough for us: and all the
Cā'năan-ītes that dwell in the land of
the valley have chariots of iron, *both*
they who *are* of Bĕth'–shē'ăn and her

towns, and *they* who *are* of the valley of Jĕz′rē-ĕl.

17 And Joshua spake unto the house of Joseph, *even* to Ē′phrā-ĭm and to Mȧ-năs′sĕh, saying, Thou *art* a great people, and hast great power: thou shalt not have one lot *only:*

18 But the mountain shall be thine; for it *is* a wood, and thou shalt cut it down: and the outgoings of it shall be thine: for thou shalt drive out the Cā′năan-ītes, though they have iron chariots, *and* though they *be* strong.

CHAPTER 18

AND the whole congregation of the children of Ĭş′rā-ĕl assembled together at Shī′lōh, and set up the tabernacle of the congregation there: and the land was subdued before them.

2 And there remained among the children of Ĭş′rā-ĕl seven tribes, which had not yet received their inheritance.

3 And Joshua said unto the children of Ĭş′rā-ĕl, How long *are* ye slack to go to possess the land, which the LORD God of your fathers hath given you?

4 Give out from among you three men for *each* tribe: and I will send them, and they shall rise, and go through the land, and describe it according to the inheritance of them; and they shall come *again* to me.

5 And they shall divide it into seven parts: Judah shall abide in their coast on the south, and the house of Joseph shall abide in their coasts on the north.

6 Ye shall therefore describe the land *into* seven parts, and bring *the description* hither to me, that I may cast lots for you here before the LORD our God.

7 But the Lē′vītes have no part among you; for the priesthood of the LORD *is* their inheritance: and Gad, and Reuben, and half the tribe of Mȧ-năs′sĕh, have received their inheritance beyond Jordan on the east, which Moses the servant of the LORD gave them.

8 ¶ And the men arose, and went away: and Joshua charged them that went to describe the land, saying, Go and walk through the land, and describe it, and come again to me, that I may here cast lots for you before the LORD in Shī′lōh.

9 And the men went and passed through the land, and described it by cities into seven parts in a book, and came *again* to Joshua to the host at Shī′lōh.

10 ¶ And Joshua cast lots for them in Shī′lōh before the LORD: and there Joshua divided the land unto the children of Ĭş′rā-ĕl according to their divisions.

11 ¶ And the lot of the tribe of the children of Benjamin came up according to their families: and the coast of their lot came forth between the children of Judah and the children of Joseph.

12 And their border on the north side was from Jordan; and the border went up to the side of Jĕr′ĭ-chō on the north side, and went up through the mountains westward; and the goings out thereof were at the wilderness of Bĕth′–ā′vĕn.

13 And the border went over from thence toward Lŭz, to the side of Lŭz, which *is* Beth-el, southward; and the border descended to Ăt′ȧ-rŏth–ā′dăr, near the hill that *lieth* on the south side of the nether Bĕth′–hō′rŏn.

14 And the border was drawn *thence,* and compassed the corner of the sea southward, from the hill that *lieth* before Bĕth′–hō′rŏn southward; and the goings out thereof were at Kĭr′jăth–bā′ăl, which *is* Kĭr′jăth–jē′ȧ-rĭm, a city of the children of Judah: this *was* the west quarter.

15 And the south quarter *was* from the end of Kĭr′jăth–jē′ȧ-rĭm, and the border went out on the west, and went out to the well of waters of Nĕph-tō′ȧh:

16 And the border came down to the end of the mountain that *lieth* before the valley of the son of Hĭn′nŏm, *and* which *is* in the valley of the giants on the north, and descended to the valley of Hĭn′nŏm, to the side of Jĕb′ū-sī on the south, and descended to Ĕn–rō′gĕl,

17 And was drawn from the north, and went forth to Ĕn–shē′mĕsh, and went forth toward Gē-lĭ′lŏth, which *is* over against the going up of Ȧ-dŭm′mĭm, and descended to the stone of Bō′hăn the son of Reuben,

18 And passed along toward the side over against Ăr′ȧ-bȧh northward, and went down unto Ăr′ȧ-bȧh:

19 And the border passed along to the side of Bĕth′–hŏg′lȧh northward: and the outgoings of the border were at the north bay of the salt sea at the south end of Jordan: this *was* the south coast.

20 And Jordan was the border of it on
the east side. This *was* the inheritance
of the children of Benjamin, by the
coasts thereof round about, according
to their families.
21 Now the cities of the tribe of the
children of Benjamin according to their
families were Jĕr'ĭ-chō, and Bĕth'-
hŏg'lȧh, and the valley of Kē'zĭz,
22 And Bĕth'-ăr'ȧ-bȧh, and Zĕm'ȧ-
rā'ĭm, and Beth-el,
23 And Ā'vĭm, and Pa'rah, and
Ŏph'rȧh,
24 And Chē'phär-hä-ăm'mō-naī, and
Ŏph'nī, and Gā'bȧ; twelve cities with
their villages:
25 Gĭb'ē-ŏn, and Rā'mȧh, and Bē-ē'-
rŏth,
26 And Mĭz'pĕh, and Chē-phī'rȧh, and
Mō'zȧh,
27 And Rē'kĕm, and Ĭr'pē-ēl, and
Tăr'ȧ-läh,
28 And Zē'lȧh, Ē'lĕph, and Jĕb'ū-sī,
which *is* Jerusalem, Gĭb'ē-ăth, *and*
Kĭr'jăth; fourteen cities with their villages. This *is* the inheritance of the
children of Benjamin according to their
families.

CHAPTER 19

AND the second lot came forth to
Simeon, *even* for the tribe of the
children of Simeon according to their
families: and their inheritance was within the inheritance of the children of
Judah.
2 And they had in their inheritance
Bē'ĕr-shē'bȧ, or Shē'bȧ, and Mŏl'ȧ-dȧh,
3 And Hā'zär-shu'ăl, and Bā'lȧh, and
Ā'zĕm,
4 And Ĕl-tō'lăd, and Bĕth'ŭl, and
Hôr'mȧh,
5 And Zĭk'lăg, and Bĕth'-mär'cȧ-bŏth,
and Hā'zär-su'sȧh,
6 And Bĕth'-lē-bā'ŏth, and Shȧ-ru'-
hĕn; thirteen cities and their villages:
7 Ā'ĭn, Rĕm'mŏn, and Ē'thĕr, and
Ā'shăn; four cities and their villages:
8 And all the villages that *were* round
about these cities to Bā'ȧ-lăth-bē'ĕr,
Rā'măth of the south. This *is* the inheritance of the tribe of the children of
Simeon according to their families.
9 Out of the portion of the children of
Judah *was* the inheritance of the children of Simeon: for the part of the children of Judah was too much for them:
therefore the children of Simeon had
their inheritance within the inheritance
of them.
10 ¶ And the third lot came up for the
children of Zĕb'ū-lŭn according to their
families: and the border of their inheritance was unto Sā'rĭd:
11 And their border went up toward the
sea, and Măr'ȧ-läh, and reached to
Dăb'bȧ-shĕth, and reached to the river
that *is* before Jŏk'nē-ăm;
12 And turned from Sā'rĭd eastward
toward the sunrising unto the border of
Chĭs'lŏth-tā'bŏr, and then goeth out to
Dăb'ē-răth, and goeth up to Jȧ-phī'ȧ,
13 And from thence passeth on along
on the east to Gĭt'täh-hē'phĕr, to Ĭt'-
tȧh-kā'zĭn, and goeth out to Rĕm'mŏn-
mĕth'ō-är to Nē'ȧh;
14 And the border compasseth it on the
north side to Hăn'nȧ-thŏn: and the outgoings thereof are in the valley of Jĭph'-
thȧh-ĕl':
15 And Kăt'tăth, and Nȧ-hăl'lăl, and
Shĭm'rŏn, and Ĭd'ȧ-lȧh, and Beth-lehem: twelve cities with their villages.
16 This *is* the inheritance of the children of Zĕb'ū-lŭn according to their
families, these cities with their villages.
17 ¶ *And* the fourth lot came out to
Ĭs'sȧ-chär, for the children of Ĭs'sȧ-chär
according to their families.
18 And their border was toward Jĕz'-
rē-ĕl, and Chē-sŭl'lŏth, and Shu'nĕm,
19 And Hăph'rā-ĭm, and Shī'hŏn, and
Ȧ-nā'hȧ-răth,
20 And Răb'bĭth, and Kĭsh'ĭ-ŏn, and
Ā'bĕz,
21 And Rē'mĕth, and Ĕn-găn'nĭm, and
Ĕn-hăd'dȧh, and Bĕth'-păz'zĕz;
22 And the coast reacheth to Tā'bŏr,
and Shā'hȧ-zī'mȧh, and Bĕth'-shē'-
mĕsh; and the outgoings of their border
were at Jordan: sixteen cities with their
villages.
23 This *is* the inheritance of the tribe
of the children of Ĭs'sȧ-chär according
to their families, the cities and their
villages.
24 ¶ And the fifth lot came out for
the tribe of the children of Ăsh'ĕr according to their families.
25 And their border was Hĕl'kăth, and
Hā'lī, and Bē'tĕn, and Ăch'shȧph,
26 And Ȧ-lăm'mē-lĕch, and Ā'măd,
and Mĭsh'ē-ăl; and reacheth to Cär'mĕl
westward, and to Shī'hôr-lĭb'năth;
27 And turneth toward the sunrising to
Bĕth'-dā'gŏn, and reacheth to Zĕb'ū-

lŭn, and to the valley of Jĭph′thȧh–ĕl′
toward the north side of Bĕth′–ē′mĕk,
and Nē-ī′ĕl, and goeth out to Cā′bŭl on
the left hand,
28 And Hē′brȯn, and Rē′hŏb, and Hăm′-
mŏn, and Kā′nȧh, *even* unto great
Zī′dŏn;
29 And *then* the coast turneth to Rā′-
mȧh, and to the strong city Tȳre; and
the coast turneth to Hō′sȧh; and the
outgoings thereof are at the sea from
the coast to Ăch′zĭb:
30 Ŭm′mȧh also, and Ā′phĕk, and
Rē′hŏb: twenty and two cities with their
villages.
31 This *is* the inheritance of the tribe
of the children of Ăsh′ẽr according to
their families, these cities with their
villages.
32 ℂ The sixth lot came out to the
children of Năph′tȧ-lī, *even* for the
children of Năph′tȧ-lī according to their
families.
33 And their coast was from Hē′lĕph,
from Ăl′lŏn to Zā′ȧ-năn′nĭm, and Ăd′ȧ-
mī, Nē′kĕb, and Jăb′nē-ĕl, unto Lā′kŭm;
and the outgoings thereof were at Jordan:
34 And *then* the coast turneth westward
to Ăz′nŏth–tā′bŏr, and goeth out from
thence to Hŭk′kŏk, and reacheth to
Zĕb′ū-lŭn on the south side, and reacheth to Ăsh′ẽr on the west side, and to
Judah upon Jordan toward the sunrising.
35 And the fenced cities *are* Zĭd′dĭm,
Zẽr, and Hăm′măth, Răk′kăth, and
Chĭn′nē-rĕth,
36 And Ăd′ȧ-mȧh, and Rā′mȧh, and
Hā′zŏr,
37 And Kē′dĕsh, and Ĕd′rē-ī, and
Ĕn–hā′zŏr,
38 And Ī′rŏn, and Mĭg′dăl–ĕl′, Hō′rĕm,
and Bĕth′–ā′năth, and Bĕth′–shē′mĕsh;
nineteen cities with their villages.
39 This *is* the inheritance of the tribe
of the children of Năph′tȧ-lī according
to their families, the cities and their
villages.
40 ℂ *And* the seventh lot came out for
the tribe of the children of Dan according to their families.
41 And the coast of their inheritance
was Zō′rȧh, and Ĕsh′tā-ŏl, and Īr′–
shē′mĕsh,
42 And Shā′ȧ-lăb′bĭn, and Ăj′ȧ-lŏn,
and Jĕth′lȧh,
43 And Ē′lŏn, and Thĭm′nȧ-thăh, and
Ĕk′rŏn,
44 And Ĕl′tē-kĕh, and Gĭb′bē-thŏn,
and Bā′ȧ-lȧth,
45 And Jē′hŭd, and Bĕn′ē–bē′răk, and
Găth′–rĭm′mȯn,
46 And Mē′–jăr′kŏn, and Răk′kŏn,
with the border before Jā′phō.
47 And the coast of the children of Dan
went out *too little* for them: therefore
the children of Dan went up to fight
against Lē′shĕm, and took it, and smote
it with the edge of the sword, and possessed it, and dwelt therein, and called
Lē′shĕm, Dan, after the name of Dan
their father.
48 This *is* the inheritance of the tribe
of the children of Dan according to their
families, these cities with their villages.
49 ℂ When they had made an end of
dividing the land for inheritance by
their coasts, the children of Ĭṣ′rā-ĕl gave
an inheritance to Joshua the son of Nŭn
among them:
50 According to the word of the LORD
they gave him the city which he asked,
even Tĭm′năth–sē′rȧh in mount Ē′phrā-
ĭm: and he built the city, and dwelt
therein.
51 These *are* the inheritances, which
Ĕl′ē-ā′zȧr the priest, and Joshua the
son of Nŭn, and the heads of the fathers
of the tribes of the children of Ĭṣ′rā-ĕl,
divided for an inheritance by lot in
Shī′lōh before the LORD, at the door of
the tabernacle of the congregation. So
they made an end of dividing the
country.

CHAPTER 20

THE LORD also spake unto Joshua,
saying,
2 Speak to the children of Ĭṣ′rā-ĕl, saying, Appoint out for you cities of refuge,
whereof I spake unto you by the hand
of Moses:
3 That the slayer that killeth *any* person unawares *and* unwittingly may flee
thither: and they shall be your refuge
from the avenger of blood.
4 And when he that doth flee unto one
of those cities shall stand at the entering
of the gate of the city, and shall declare
his cause in the ears of the elders of that
city, they shall take him into the city
unto them, and give him a place, that he
may dwell among them.
5 And if the avenger of blood pursue
after him, then they shall not deliver the
slayer up into his hand; because he

smote his neighbor unwittingly, and hated him not beforetime.

6 And he shall dwell in that city, until he stand before the congregation for judgment, *and* until the death of the high priest that shall be in those days: then shall the slayer return, and come unto his own city, and unto his own house, unto the city from whence he fled.

7 ¶ And they appointed Kē′dĕsh in Galilee in mount Năph′tȧ-lī, and Shē′chĕm in mount Ē′phrā-ĭm, and Kïr′jăth-är′bȧ, which *is* Hē′brȯn, in the mountain of Judah.

8 And on the other side Jordan by Jĕr′ĭ-chō eastward, they assigned Bē′zẽr in the wilderness upon the plain out of the tribe of Reuben, and Rā′mŏth in Gĭl′ē-ăd out of the tribe of Gad, and Gō′lăn in Bā′shăn out of the tribe of Mȧ-năs′sĕh.

9 These were the cities appointed for all the children of Ĭş′rā-ĕl, and for the stranger that sojourneth among them, that whosoever killeth *any* person at unawares might flee thither, and not die by the hand of the avenger of blood, until he stood before the congregation.

CHAPTER 21

THEN came near the heads of the fathers of the Lē′vītes unto Ĕl′ē-ā′zȧr the priest, and unto Joshua the son of Nŭn, and unto the heads of the fathers of the tribes of the children of Ĭş′rā-ĕl;

2 And they spake unto them at Shī′lŏh in the land of Cā′năan, saying, The LORD commanded by the hand of Moses to give us cities to dwell in, with the suburbs thereof for our cattle.

3 And the children of Ĭş′rā-ĕl gave unto the Lē′vītes out of their inheritance, at the commandment of the LORD, these cities and their suburbs.

4 And the lot came out for the families of the Kō′hăth-ītes: and the children of Aaron the priest, *which were* of the Lē′vītes, had by lot out of the tribe of Judah, and out of the tribe of Simeon, and out of the tribe of Benjamin, thirteen cities.

5 And the rest of the children of Kō′hăth *had* by lot out of the families of the tribe of Ē′phrā-ĭm, and out of the tribe of Dan, and out of the half tribe of Mȧ-năs′sĕh, ten cities.

6 And the children of Gẽr′shŏn *had* by lot out of the families of the tribe of Ĭs′sȧ-chär, and out of the tribe of Ȧsh′ẽr, and out of the tribe of Năph′tȧ-lī, and out of the half tribe of Mȧ-năs′sĕh in Bā′shăn, thirteen cities.

7 The children of Mē-rā′rī by their families *had* out of the tribe of Reuben, and out of the tribe of Gad, and out of the tribe of Zĕb′ū-lŭn, twelve cities.

8 And the children of Ĭş′rā-ĕl gave by lot unto the Lē′vītes these cities with their suburbs, as the LORD commanded by the hand of Moses.

9 ¶ And they gave out of the tribe of the children of Judah, and out of the tribe of the children of Simeon, these cities which are *here* mentioned by name,

10 Which the children of Aaron, *being* of the families of the Kō′hăth-ītes, *who were* of the children of Levi, had: for theirs was the first lot.

11 And they gave them the city of Är′bȧ the father of Ā′năk, which *city is* Hē′brȯn, in the hill *country* of Judah, with the suburbs thereof round about it.

12 But the fields of the city, and the villages thereof, gave they to Caleb the son of Jē-phŭn′nĕh for his possession.

13 ¶ Thus they gave to the children of Aaron the priest Hē′brȯn with her suburbs, *to be* a city of refuge for the slayer; and Lĭb′nȧh with her suburbs,

14 And Jăt′tïr with her suburbs, and Ĕsh′tē-mō′ȧ with her suburbs,

15 And Hō′lŏn with her suburbs, and Dē′bïr with her suburbs,

16 And Ā′ĭn with her suburbs, and Jŭt′tȧh with her suburbs, *and* Bĕth′-shē′mĕsh with her suburbs; nine cities out of those two tribes.

17 And out of the tribe of Benjamin, Gĭb′ē-ŏn with her suburbs, Gē′bȧ with her suburbs,

18 Ăn′ȧ-thŏth with her suburbs, and Ăl′mŏn with her suburbs; four cities.

19 All the cities of the children of Aaron, the priests, *were* thirteen cities with their suburbs.

20 ¶ And the families of the children of Kō′hăth, the Lē′vītes which remained of the children of Kō′hăth, even they had the cities of their lot out of the tribe of Ē′phrā-ĭm.

21 For they gave them Shē′chĕm with her suburbs in mount Ē′phrā-ĭm, *to be*

a city of refuge for the slayer; and Gē′zĕr with her suburbs,
22 And Kĭb-zā′ĭm with her suburbs, and Bĕth′–hō′rŏn with her suburbs; four cities.
23 And out of the tribe of Dan, Ĕl′tē-kĕh with her suburbs, Gĭb′bē-thŏn with her suburbs,
24 Āi′jȧ-lŏn with her suburbs, Găth′–rĭm′mȯn with her suburbs; four cities.
25 And out of the half tribe of Mȧ-năs′sĕh, Tā′năch with her suburbs, and Găth′–rĭm′mȯn with her suburbs; two cities.
26 All the cities *were* ten with their suburbs for the families of the children of Kō′hăth that remained.
27 ¶ And unto the children of Gẽr′shŏn, of the families of the Lē′vītes, out of the *other* half tribe of Mȧ-năs′sĕh *they gave* Gō′lăn in Bā′shăn with her suburbs, *to be* a city of refuge for the slayer; and Bē-ĕsh′–tē-rȧh with her suburbs; two cities.
28 And out of the tribe of Ĭs′sȧ-chär, Kī′shŏn with her suburbs, Dăb′ȧ-rĕh with her suburbs,
29 Jär′mŭth with her suburbs, Ĕn–găn′nĭm with her suburbs; four cities.
30 And out of the tribe of Ăsh′ẽr, Mī′shăl with her suburbs, Ăb′dŏn with her suburbs,
31 Hĕl′kăth with her suburbs, and Rē′hŏb with her suburbs; four cities.
32 And out of the tribe of Năph′tȧ-lī, Kē′dĕsh in Galilee with her suburbs, *to be* a city of refuge for the slayer; and Hăm′mŏth–dôr′ with her suburbs, and Kär′tăn with her suburbs; three cities.
33 All the cities of the Gẽr′shŏn-ītes according to their families *were* thirteen cities with their suburbs.
34 ¶ And unto the families of the children of Mē-rā′rī, the rest of the Lē′vītes, out of the tribe of Zĕb′ū-lŭn, Jŏk′nē-ăm with her suburbs, and Kär′tȧh with her suburbs,
35 Dĭm′năh with her suburbs, Nā′hȧ-lăl with her suburbs; four cities.
36 And out of the tribe of Reuben, Bē′zẽr with her suburbs, and Jȧ-hā′zȧh with her suburbs,
37 Kĕd′ē-mŏth with her suburbs, and Mĕph′ȧ-ăth with her suburbs; four cities.
38 And out of the tribe of Gad, Rā′mŏth in Gĭl′ē-ăd with her suburbs, *to be* a city of refuge for the slayer; and Mā′hȧ-nā′ĭm with her suburbs,
39 Hĕsh′bŏn with her suburbs, Jā′zẽr with her suburbs; four cities in all.
40 So all the cities for the children of Mē-rā′rī by their families, which were remaining of the families of the Lē′vītes, were *by* their lot twelve cities.
41 All the cities of the Lē′vītes within the possession of the children of Ĭṣ′rā-ĕl *were* forty and eight cities with their suburbs.
42 These cities were every one with their suburbs round about them: thus *were* all these cities.
43 ¶ And the LORD gave unto Ĭṣ′rā-ĕl all the land which he sware to give unto their fathers; and they possessed it, and dwelt therein.
44 And the LORD gave them rest round about, according to all that he sware unto their fathers: and there stood not a man of all their enemies before them; the LORD delivered all their enemies into their hand.
45 There failed not aught of any good thing which the LORD had spoken unto the house of Ĭṣ′rā-ĕl; all came to pass.

CHAPTER 22

THEN Joshua called the Reubenites, and the Gadites, and the half tribe of Mȧ-năs′sĕh,
2 And said unto them, Ye have kept all that Moses the servant of the LORD commanded you, and have obeyed my voice in all that I commanded you:
3 Ye have not left your brethren these many days unto this day, but have kept the charge of the commandment of the LORD your God.
4 And now the LORD your God hath given rest unto your brethren, as he promised them: therefore now return ye, and get you unto your tents, *and* unto the land of your possession, which Moses the servant of the LORD gave you on the other side Jordan.
5 But take diligent heed to do the commandment and the law, which Moses the servant of the LORD charged you, to love the LORD your God, and to walk in all his ways, and to keep his commandments, and to cleave unto him, and to serve him with all your heart and with all your soul.
6 So Joshua blessed them, and sent

them away: and they went unto their
tents.
7 ¶ Now to the *one* half of the tribe
of Mȧ-năs′sĕh Moses had given *posses-*
sion in Bā′shăn: but unto the *other*
half thereof gave Joshua among their
brethren on this side Jordan westward. And when Joshua sent them
away also unto their tents, then he
blessed them,
8 And he spake unto them, saying,
Return with much riches unto your
tents, and with very much cattle, with
silver, and with gold, and with brass,
and with iron, and with very much raiment: divide the spoil of your enemies
with your brethren.
9 ¶ And the children of Reuben and
the children of Gad and the half tribe of
Mȧ-năs′sĕh returned, and departed
from the children of Ĭṣ′rā-ĕl out of Shī′-
lōh, which *is* in the land of Cā′năan, to
go unto the country of Gĭl′ē-ăd, to the
land of their possession, whereof they
were possessed, according to the word
of the LORD by the hand of Moses.
10 ¶ And when they came unto the
borders of Jordan, that *are* in the land
of Cā′năan, the children of Reuben and
the children of Gad and the half tribe of
Mȧ-năs′sĕh built there an altar by Jordan, a great altar to see to.
11 ¶ And the children of Ĭṣ′rā-ĕl heard
say, Behold, the children of Reuben and
the children of Gad and the half tribe of
Mȧ-năs′sĕh have built an altar over
against the land of Cā′năan, in the borders of Jordan, at the passage of the
children of Ĭṣ′rā-ĕl.
12 And when the children of Ĭṣ′rā-ĕl
heard *of it,* the whole congregation of
the children of Ĭṣ′rā-ĕl gathered themselves together at Shī′lōh, to go up to
war against them.
13 And the children of Ĭṣ′rā-ĕl sent
unto the children of Reuben, and to the
children of Gad, and to the half tribe of
Mȧ-năs′sĕh, into the land of Gĭl′ē-ăd,
Phĭn′ē-hăs the son of Ĕl′ē-ā′zȧr the
priest,
14 And with him ten princes, of each
chief house a prince throughout all the
tribes of Ĭṣ′rā-ĕl; and each one *was* a
head of the house of their fathers among
the thousands of Ĭṣ′rā-ĕl.
15 ¶ And they came unto the children
of Reuben, and to the children of Gad,
and to the half tribe of Mȧ-năs′sĕh, unto
the land of Gĭl′ē-ăd, and they spake
with them, saying,
16 Thus saith the whole congregation
of the LORD, What trespass *is* this that
ye have committed against the God
of Ĭṣ′rā-ĕl, to turn away this day from
following the LORD, in that ye have
builded you an altar, that ye might rebel
this day against the LORD?
17 *Is* the iniquity of Pē′ŏr too little for
us, from which we are not cleansed
until this day, although there was a
plague in the congregation of the LORD,
18 But that ye must turn away this day
from following the LORD? and it will be,
seeing ye rebel to-day against the LORD,
that to-morrow he will be wroth with
the whole congregation of Ĭṣ′rā-ĕl.
19 Notwithstanding, if the land of your
possession *be* unclean, *then* pass ye
over unto the land of the possession of
the LORD, wherein the LORD's tabernacle dwelleth, and take possession
among us: but rebel not against the
LORD, nor rebel against us, in building
you an altar besides the altar of the
LORD our God.
20 Did not Ā′chăn the son of Zē′rȧh
commit a trespass in the accursed thing,
and wrath fell on all the congregation of
Ĭṣ′rā-ĕl? and that man perished not
alone in his iniquity.
21 ¶ Then the children of Reuben and
the children of Gad and the half tribe of
Mȧ-năs′sĕh answered, and said unto
the heads of the thousands of Ĭṣ′rā-ĕl,
22 The LORD God of gods, the LORD
God of gods, he knoweth, and Ĭṣ′rā-ĕl he
shall know; if *it be* in rebellion, or if in
transgression against the LORD, (save
us not this day,)
23 That we have built us an altar to
turn from following the LORD, or if to
offer thereon burnt offering or meat
offering, or if to offer peace offerings
thereon, let the LORD himself require *it;*
24 And if we have not *rather* done it for
fear of *this* thing, saying, In time to
come your children might speak unto
our children, saying, What have ye to do
with the LORD God of Ĭṣ′rā-ĕl?
25 For the LORD hath made Jordan a
border between us and you, ye children
of Reuben and children of Gad; ye have
no part in the LORD: so shall your children make our children cease from fearing the LORD.
26 Therefore we said, Let us now

prepare to build us an altar, not for burnt offering, nor for sacrifice:

27 But *that* it *may be* a witness between us, and you, and our generations after us, that we might do the service of the LORD before him with our burnt offerings, and with our sacrifices, and with our peace offerings; that your children may not say to our children in time to come, Ye have no part in the LORD.

28 Therefore said we, that it shall be, when they should *so* say to us or to our generations in time to come, that we may say *again,* Behold the pattern of the altar of the LORD, which our fathers made, not for burnt offerings, nor for sacrifices; but it *is* a witness between us and you.

29 God forbid that we should rebel against the LORD, and turn this day from following the LORD, to build an altar for burnt offerings, for meat offerings, or for sacrifices, besides the altar of the LORD our God that *is* before his tabernacle.

30 ¶ And when Phĭn′ē-hăs the priest, and the princes of the congregation and heads of the thousands of Ĭş′rā-ĕl which *were* with him, heard the words that the children of Reuben and the children of Gad and the children of Mȧ-năs′sĕh spake, it pleased them.

31 And Phĭn′ē-hăs the son of Ĕl′ē-ā′zȧr the priest said unto the children of Reuben, and to the children of Gad, and to the children of Mȧ-năs′sĕh, This day we perceive that the LORD *is* among us, because ye have not committed this trespass against the LORD: now ye have delivered the children of Ĭş′rā-ĕl out of the hand of the LORD.

32 ¶ And Phĭn′ē-hăs the son of Ĕl′ē-ā′zȧr the priest, and the princes, returned from the children of Reuben, and from the children of Gad, out of the land of Gĭl′ē-ăd, unto the land of Cā′năan, to the children of Ĭş′rā-ĕl, and brought them word again.

33 And the thing pleased the children of Ĭş′rā-ĕl; and the children of Ĭş′rā-ĕl blessed God, and did not intend to go up against them in battle, to destroy the land wherein the children of Reuben and Gad dwelt.

34 And the children of Reuben and the children of Gad called the altar *Ed:* for it *shall be* a witness between us that the LORD *is* God.

CHAPTER 23

AND it came to pass, a long time after that the LORD had given rest unto Ĭş′rā-ĕl from all their enemies round about, that Joshua waxed old *and* stricken in age.

2 And Joshua called for all Ĭş′rā-ĕl, *and* for their elders, and for their heads, and for their judges, and for their officers, and said unto them, I am old *and* stricken in age:

3 And ye have seen all that the LORD your God hath done unto all these nations because of you; for the LORD your God *is* he that hath fought for you.

4 Behold, I have divided unto you by lot these nations that remain, to be an inheritance for your tribes, from Jordan, with all the nations that I have cut off, even unto the great sea westward.

5 And the LORD your God, he shall expel them from before you, and drive them from out of your sight; and ye shall possess their land, as the LORD your God hath promised unto you.

6 Be ye therefore very courageous to keep and to do all that is written in the book of the law of Moses, that ye turn not aside therefrom *to* the right hand or *to* the left;

7 That ye come not among these nations, these that remain among you; neither make mention of the name of their gods, nor cause to swear *by them,* neither serve them, nor bow yourselves unto them:

8 But cleave unto the LORD your God, as ye have done unto this day.

9 For the LORD hath driven out from before you great nations and strong: but *as for* you, no man hath been able to stand before you unto this day.

10 One man of you shall chase a thousand: for the LORD your God, he *it is* that fighteth for you, as he hath promised you.

11 Take good heed therefore unto yourselves, that ye love the LORD your God.

12 Else, if ye do in any wise go back, and cleave unto the remnant of these nations, *even* these that remain among you, and shall make marriages with them, and go in unto them, and they to you:

13 Know for a certainty that the LORD your God will no more drive out *any of* these nations from before you; but they

shall be snares and traps unto you, and
scourges in your sides, and thorns in
your eyes, until ye perish from off this
good land which the LORD your God
hath given you.
14 And, behold, this day I *am* going
the way of all the earth: and ye know in
all your hearts and in all your souls, that
not one thing hath failed of all the good
things which the LORD your God spake
concerning you; all are come to pass
unto you, *and* not one thing hath failed
thereof.
15 Therefore it shall come to pass, *that*
as all good things are come upon you,
which the LORD your God promised
you; so shall the LORD bring upon you
all evil things, until he have destroyed
you from off this good land which the
LORD your God hath given you.
16 When ye have transgressed the
covenant of the LORD your God, which
he commanded you, and have gone and
served other gods, and bowed yourselves to them; then shall the anger of
the LORD be kindled against you, and
ye shall perish quickly from off the
good land which he hath given unto
you.

CHAPTER 24

AND Joshua gathered all the tribes of
Ĭṣ'rā-ĕl to Shē'chĕm, and called for
the elders of Ĭṣ'rā-ĕl, and for their
heads, and for their judges, and for
their officers; and they presented themselves before God.
2 And Joshua said unto all the people,
Thus saith the LORD God of Ĭṣ'rā-ĕl,
Your fathers dwelt on the other side of
the flood in old time, *even* Tē'rȧh,
the father of Abraham, and the father
of Nā'chôr: and they served other
gods.
3 And I took your father Abraham from
the other side of the flood, and led him
throughout all the land of Cā'năan,
and multiplied his seed, and gave him
Isaac.
4 And I gave unto Isaac Jacob and
Ē'saû: and I gave unto Ē'saû mount
Sē'ĭr, to possess it; but Jacob and his
children went down into Egypt.
5 I sent Moses also and Aaron, and I
plagued Egypt, according to that which
I did among them: and afterward I
brought you out.
6 And I brought your fathers out of
Egypt: and ye came unto the sea; and
the Egyptians pursued after your fathers
with chariots and horsemen unto the
Red sea.
7 And when they cried unto the LORD,
he put darkness between you and the
Egyptians, and brought the sea upon
them, and covered them; and your eyes
have seen what I have done in Egypt:
and ye dwelt in the wilderness a long
season.
8 And I brought you into the land of
the Ăm'ō-rītes, which dwelt on the other
side Jordan; and they fought with you:
and I gave them into your hand, that ye
might possess their land; and I destroyed them from before you.
9 Then Bā'lăk the son of Zĭp'pôr, king
of Mō'ăb, arose and warred against
Ĭṣ'rā-ĕl, and sent and called Bā'laam
the son of Bē'ôr to curse you:
10 But I would not hearken unto Bā'-
laam, therefore he blessed you still: so
I delivered you out of his hand.
11 And ye went over Jordan, and came
unto Jĕr'ĭ-chō: and the men of Jĕr'ĭ-chō
fought against you, the Ăm'ō-rītes, and
the Pĕr'ĭz-zītes, and the Cā'năan-ītes,
and the Hĭt'tītes, and the Gĭr'gȧ-shītes,
the Hī'vītes, and the Jĕb'ū-ṣītes; and I
delivered them into your hand.
12 And I sent the hornet before you,
which drave them out from before you,
even the two kings of the Ăm'ō-rītes;
but not with thy sword, nor with thy
bow.
13 And I have given you a land for
which ye did not labor, and cities which
ye built not, and ye dwell in them; of the
vineyards and oliveyards which ye
planted not do ye eat.
14 ¶ Now therefore fear the LORD,
and serve him in sincerity and in truth;
and put away the gods which your
fathers served on the other side of the
flood, and in Egypt; and serve ye the
LORD.
15 And if it seem evil unto you to serve
the LORD, choose you this day whom ye
will serve; whether the gods which your
fathers served that *were* on the other
side of the flood, or the gods of the
Ăm'ō-rītes, in whose land ye dwell: but
as for me and my house, we will serve
the LORD.
16 And the people answered and said,
God forbid that we should forsake the
LORD, to serve other gods;

17 For the LORD our God, he *it is* that
brought us up and our fathers out of the
land of Egypt, from the house of bondage, and which did those great signs in
our sight, and preserved us in all the
way wherein we went, and among all
the people through whom we passed:
18 And the LORD drave out from before
us all the people, even the Ăm'ō-rītes
which dwelt in the land: *therefore* will
we also serve the LORD; for he *is* our
God.
19 And Joshua said unto the people, Ye
cannot serve the LORD: for he *is* a holy
God; he *is* a jealous God; he will not
forgive your transgressions nor your
sins.
20 If ye forsake the LORD, and serve
strange gods, then he will turn and do
you hurt, and consume you, after that
he hath done you good.
21 And the people said unto Joshua,
Nay; but we will serve the LORD.
22 And Joshua said unto the people,
Ye *are* witnesses against yourselves
that ye have chosen you the LORD, to
serve him. And they said, *We are* witnesses.
23 Now therefore put away, *said he*,
the strange gods which *are* among you,
and incline your heart unto the LORD
God of Ĭş'rā-ĕl.
24 And the people said unto Joshua,
The LORD our God will we serve, and
his voice will we obey.
25 So Joshua made a covenant with
the people that day, and set them a
statute and an ordinance in Shē'chĕm.
26 ¶ And Joshua wrote these words
in the book of the law of God, and took
a great stone, and set it up there under
an oak, that *was* by the sanctuary of the
LORD.
27 And Joshua said unto all the people, Behold, this stone shall be a witness
unto us; for it hath heard all the words
of the LORD which he spake unto us: it
shall be therefore a witness unto you,
lest ye deny your God.
28 So Joshua let the people depart,
every man unto his inheritance.
29 ¶ And it came to pass after these
things, that Joshua the son of Nŭn, the
servant of the LORD, died, *being* a hundred and ten years old.
30 And they buried him in the border
of his inheritance in Tĭm'năth–sē'rȧh,
which *is* in mount Ē'phrā-ĭm, on the
north side of the hill of Gā'ăsh.
31 And Ĭş'rā-ĕl served the LORD all the
days of Joshua, and all the days of the
elders that overlived Joshua, and which
had known all the works of the LORD,
that he had done for Ĭş'rā-ĕl.
32 ¶ And the bones of Joseph, which
the children of Ĭş'rā-ĕl brought up out
of Egypt, buried they in Shē'chĕm, in a
parcel of ground which Jacob bought of
the sons of Hā'mŏr the father of Shē'-
chĕm for a hundred pieces of silver; and
it became the inheritance of the children
of Joseph.
33 And Ĕl'ē-ā'zȧr the son of Aaron
died; and they buried him in a hill *that
pertained to* Phĭn'ē-hăs his son, which
was given him in mount Ē'phrā-ĭm.

THE BOOK OF JUDGES

CHAPTER 1

NOW after the death of Joshua it
came to pass, that the children of
Ĭş'rā-ĕl asked the LORD, saying, Who
shall go up for us against the Cā'năan-
ītes first, to fight against them?
2 And the LORD said, Judah shall go
up: behold, I have delivered the land
into his hand.
3 And Judah said unto Simeon his
brother, Come up with me into my lot,
that we may fight against the Cā'năan-
ītes; and I likewise will go with thee
into thy lot. So Simeon went with
him.
4 And Judah went up; and the LORD
delivered the Cā'năan-ītes and the
Pĕr'ĭz-zītes into their hand: and they
slew of them in Bē'zĕk ten thousand
men.
5 And they found Ȧ-dō'nī–bē'zĕk in
Bē'zĕk: and they fought against him,
and they slew the Cā'năan-ītes and the
Pĕr'ĭz-zītes.
6 But Ȧ-dō'nī–bē'zĕk fled; and they

pursued after him, and caught him, and
cut off his thumbs and his great toes.
7 And Ȧ-dō′nĭ-bē′zĕk said, Threescore and ten kings, having their thumbs
and their great toes cut off, gathered
their meat under my table: as I have
done, so God hath requited me. And
they brought him to Jerusalem, and
there he died.
8 Now the children of Judah had fought
against Jerusalem, and had taken it, and
smitten it with the edge of the sword,
and set the city on fire.
9 ¶ And afterward the children of Judah went down to fight against the Cā′-
năan-ītes, that dwelt in the mountain,
and in the south, and in the valley.
10 And Judah went against the Cā′-
năan-ītes that dwelt in Hē′brȯn: now
the name of Hē′brȯn before *was* Kĭr′-
jăth-är′bȧ: and they slew Shē′shaī, and
Ȧ-hī′măn, and Tăl′maī.
11 And from thence he went against
the inhabitants of Dē′bĭr: and the name
of Dē′bĭr before *was* Kĭr′jăth-sē′phĕr:
12 And Caleb said, He that smiteth
Kĭr′jăth-sē′phĕr, and taketh it, to him
will I give Ăch′sȧh my daughter to wife.
13 And Ŏth′nĭ-ĕl the son of Kē′năz,
Caleb's younger brother, took it: and
he gave him Ăch′sȧh his daughter to
wife.
14 And it came to pass, when she came
to him, that she moved him to ask of
her father a field: and she lighted from
off *her* ass; and Caleb said unto her,
What wilt thou?
15 And she said unto him, Give me a
blessing: for thou hast given me a south
land; give me also springs of water. And
Caleb gave her the upper springs and
the nether springs.
16 ¶ And the children of the Kē′nīte,
Moses' father-in-law, went up out of the
city of palm trees with the children of
Judah into the wilderness of Judah,
which *lieth* in the south of Ā′răd; and
they went and dwelt among the people.
17 And Judah went with Simeon his
brother, and they slew the Cā′năan-ītes
that inhabited Zē′phăth, and utterly
destroyed it. And the name of the city
was called Hôr′mȧh.
18 Also Judah took Gā′zȧ with the
coast thereof, and Ăs′kē-lŏn with the
coast thereof, and Ĕk′rŏn with the coast
thereof.
19 And the LORD was with Judah; and
he drave out *the inhabitants of* the
mountain; but could not drive out the
inhabitants of the valley, because they
had chariots of iron.
20 And they gave Hē′brȯn unto Caleb,
as Moses said: and he expelled thence
the three sons of Ā′năk.
21 And the children of Benjamin did
not drive out the Jĕb′ū-ṣītes that inhabited Jerusalem; but the Jĕb′ū-ṣītes
dwell with the children of Benjamin in
Jerusalem unto this day.
22 ¶ And the house of Joseph, they
also went up against Beth-el: and the
LORD *was* with them.
23 And the house of Joseph sent to
descry Beth-el. (Now the name of the
city before *was* Lŭz.)
24 And the spies saw a man come forth
out of the city, and they said unto him,
Show us, we pray thee, the entrance
into the city, and we will show thee
mercy.
25 And when he showed them the entrance into the city, they smote the city
with the edge of the sword; but they let
go the man and all his family.
26 And the man went into the land of
the Hĭt′tītes, and built a city, and called
the name thereof Lŭz: which *is* the name
thereof unto this day.
27 ¶ Neither did Mȧ-năs′sĕh drive
out *the inhabitants of* Bĕth′-shē′ăn and
her towns, nor Tā′ȧ-năch and her towns,
nor the inhabitants of Dor and her
towns, nor the inhabitants of Ĭb′lē-ăm
and her towns, nor the inhabitants of
Mē-gĭd′dō and her towns: but the Cā′-
năan-ītes would dwell in that land.
28 And it came to pass, when Ĭṣ′rā-ĕl
was strong, that they put the Cā′năan-
ītes to tribute, and did not utterly drive
them out.
29 ¶ Neither did Ē′phrā-ĭm drive out
the Cā′năan-ītes that dwelt in Gē′zĕr;
but the Cā′năan-ītes dwelt in Gē′zĕr
among them.
30 ¶ Neither did Zĕb′ū-lŭn drive out
the inhabitants of Kĭt′rŏn, nor the inhabitants of Nā′hȧ-lŏl; but the Cā′năan-
ītes dwelt among them, and became
tributaries.
31 ¶ Neither did Ăsh′ĕr drive out the
inhabitants of Ăc′chō, nor the inhabitants of Zī′dŏn, nor of Äh′lăb, nor of
Ăch′zĭb, nor of Hĕl′bȧh, nor of Ā′phĭk,
nor of Rē′hŏb:
32 But the Ăsh′ĕr-ītes dwelt among the

Cā′năan-ītes, the inhabitants of the
land: for they did not drive them out.
33 ¶ Neither did Năph′tȧ-lī drive out
the inhabitants of Bĕth′–shē′mĕsh, nor
the inhabitants of Bĕth′–ā′năth; but he
dwelt among the Cā′năan-ītes, the inhabitants of the land: nevertheless, the
inhabitants of Bĕth′–shē′mĕsh and of
Bĕth′–ā′năth became tributaries unto
them.
34 And the Ăm′ō-rītes forced the children of Dan into the mountain: for they
would not suffer them to come down to
the valley:
35 But the Ăm′ō-rītes would dwell in
mount Hē′rēs in Āi′jȧ-lŏn, and in Shā-
ăl′bĭm: yet the hand of the house of
Joseph prevailed, so that they became
tributaries.
36 And the coast of the Ăm′ō-rītes *was*
from the going up to Ăk-răb′bĭm, from
the rock, and upward.

CHAPTER 2

AND an Angel of the LORD came up
from Gĭl′găl to Bō′chĭm, and said,
I made you to go up out of Egypt, and
have brought you unto the land which I
sware unto your fathers; and I said, I
will never break my covenant with you.
2 And ye shall make no league with the
inhabitants of this land; ye shall throw
down their altars: but ye have not
obeyed my voice; why have ye done this?
3 Wherefore I also said, I will not drive
them out from before you; but they shall
be *as thorns* in your sides, and their gods
shall be a snare unto you.
4 And it came to pass, when the Angel
of the LORD spake these words unto all
the children of Ĭs′rā-ĕl, that the people
lifted up their voice, and wept.
5 And they called the name of that
place Bō′chĭm: and they sacrificed there
unto the LORD.
6 ¶ And when Joshua had let the people go, the children of Ĭs′rā-ĕl went
every man unto his inheritance to possess the land.
7 And the people served the LORD all
the days of Joshua, and all the days of
the elders that outlived Joshua, who had
seen all the great works of the LORD,
that he did for Ĭs′rā-ĕl.
8 And Joshua the son of Nŭn, the servant of the LORD, died, *being* a hundred
and ten years old.
9 And they buried him in the border of
his inheritance in Tĭm′năth–hē′rēs, in
the mount of Ē′phrā-ĭm, on the north
side of the hill Gā′ăsh.
10 And also all that generation were
gathered unto their fathers: and there
arose another generation after them,
which knew not the LORD, nor yet the
works which he had done for Ĭs′rā-ĕl.
11 ¶ And the children of Ĭs′rā-ĕl did
evil in the sight of the LORD, and served
Bā′ȧ-lĭm:
12 And they forsook the LORD God of
their fathers, which brought them out of
the land of Egypt, and followed other
gods, of the gods of the people that *were*
round about them, and bowed themselves unto them, and provoked the
LORD to anger.
13 And they forsook the LORD, and
served Bā′ăl and Ăsh′tȧ-rŏth.
14 ¶ And the anger of the LORD was
hot against Ĭs′rā-ĕl, and he delivered
them into the hands of spoilers that
spoiled them, and he sold them into the
hands of their enemies round about, so
that they could not any longer stand before their enemies.
15 Whithersoever they went out, the
hand of the LORD was against them for
evil, as the LORD had said, and as the
LORD had sworn unto them: and they
were greatly distressed.
16 ¶ Nevertheless the LORD raised up
judges, which delivered them out of the
hand of those that spoiled them.
17 And yet they would not hearken unto their judges, but they went a whoring
after other gods, and bowed themselves
unto them: they turned quickly out of
the way which their fathers walked in,
obeying the commandments of the
LORD; *but* they did not so.
18 And when the LORD raised them up
judges, then the LORD was with the
judge, and delivered them out of the
hand of their enemies all the days of the
judge: for it repented the LORD because
of their groanings by reason of them
that oppressed them and vexed them.
19 And it came to pass, when the judge
was dead, *that* they returned, and corrupted *themselves* more than their
fathers, in following other gods to serve
them, and to bow down unto them; they
ceased not from their own doings, nor
from their stubborn way.
20 ¶ And the anger of the LORD was
hot against Ĭs′rā-ĕl; and he said, Be-

cause that this people hath transgressed my covenant which I commanded their fathers, and have not hearkened unto my voice;

21 I also will not henceforth drive out any from before them of the nations which Joshua left when he died:

22 That through them I may prove Ĭṣ′rā-ĕl, whether they will keep the way of the LORD to walk therein, as their fathers did keep *it*, or not.

23 Therefore the LORD left those nations, without driving them out hastily; neither delivered he them into the hand of Joshua.

CHAPTER 3

NOW these *are* the nations which the LORD left, to prove Ĭṣ′rā-ĕl by them, *even* as many of *Israel* as had not known all the wars of Că′năan;

2 Only that the generations of the children of Ĭṣ′rā-ĕl might know to teach them war, at the least such as before knew nothing thereof;

3 *Namely*, five lords of the Phĭ-lĭs′tĭneṣ, and all the Că′năan-ītes, and the Sī-dō′nĭ-ănṣ, and the Hī′vītes that dwelt in mount Lebanon, from mount Bā′ăl–hĕr′mŏn unto the entering in of Hā′măth.

4 And they were to prove Ĭṣ′rā-ĕl by them, to know whether they would hearken unto the commandments of the LORD, which he commanded their fathers by the hand of Moses.

5 ¶ And the children of Ĭṣ′rā-ĕl dwelt among the Că′năan-ītes, Hĭt′tītes, and Ăm′ō-rītes, and Pĕr′ĭz-zītes, and Hī′vītes, and Jĕb′ū-ṣītes:

6 And they took their daughters to be their wives, and gave their daughters to their sons, and served their gods.

7 And the children of Ĭṣ′rā-ĕl did evil in the sight of the LORD, and forgat the LORD their God, and served Bā′ȧ-lĭm and the groves.

8 ¶ Therefore the anger of the LORD was hot against Ĭṣ′rā-ĕl, and he sold them into the hand of Chū′shăn–rĭsh′ȧ-thā′ĭm king of Mĕs′ō-pō-tā′mĭ-ȧ: and the children of Ĭṣ′rā-ĕl served Chū′shăn–rĭsh′ȧ-thā′ĭm eight years.

9 And when the children of Ĭṣ′rā-ĕl cried unto the LORD, the LORD raised up a deliverer to the children of Ĭṣ′rā-ĕl, who delivered them, *even* Ŏth′nĭ-ĕl the son of Kē′năz, Caleb's younger brother.

10 And the Spirit of the LORD came upon him, and he judged Ĭṣ′rā-ĕl, and went out to war: and the LORD delivered Chū′shăn–rĭsh′ȧ-thā′ĭm king of Mĕs′ō-pō-tā′mĭ-ȧ into his hand; and his hand prevailed against Chū′shăn–rĭsh′ȧ-thā′ĭm.

11 And the land had rest forty years: and Ŏth′nĭ-ĕl the son of Kē′năz died.

12 ¶ And the children of Ĭṣ′rā-ĕl did evil again in the sight of the LORD: and the LORD strengthened Ĕg′lŏn the king of Mō′ăb against Ĭṣ′rā-ĕl, because they had done evil in the sight of the LORD.

13 And he gathered unto him the children of Ammon and Ăm′ȧ-lĕk, and went and smote Ĭṣ′rā-ĕl, and possessed the city of palm trees.

14 So the children of Ĭṣ′rā-ĕl served Ĕg′lŏn the king of Mō′ăb eighteen years.

15 But when the children of Ĭṣ′rā-ĕl cried unto the LORD, the LORD raised them up a deliverer, Ē′hŭd the son of Gē′rȧ, a Benjamite, a man left-handed: and by him the children of Ĭṣ′rā-ĕl sent a present unto Ĕg′lŏn the king of Mō′ăb

16 But Ē′hŭd made him a dagger which had two edges, of a cubit length; and he did gird it under his raiment upon his right thigh.

17 And he brought the present unto Ĕg′lŏn king of Mō′ăb: and Ĕg′lŏn *was* a very fat man.

18 And when he had made an end to offer the present, he sent away the people that bare the present.

19 But he himself turned again from the quarries that *were* by Gĭl′găl, and said, I have a secret errand unto thee, O king: who said, Keep silence. And all that stood by him went out from him.

20 And Ē′hŭd came unto him; and he was sitting in a summer parlor, which he had for himself alone. And Ē′hŭd said, I have a message from God unto thee. And he arose out of *his* seat.

21 And Ē′hŭd put forth his left hand, and took the dagger from his right thigh, and thrust it into his belly:

22 And the haft also went in after the blade; and the fat closed upon the blade, so that he could not draw the dagger out of his belly; and the dirt came out.

23 Then Ē′hŭd went forth through the porch, and shut the doors of the parlor upon him, and locked them.

24 When he was gone out, his servants came; and when they saw that, behold,

the doors of the parlor *were* locked, they
said, Surely he covereth his feet in his
summer chamber.
25 And they tarried till they were
ashamed: and, behold, he opened not
the doors of the parlor; therefore they
took a key, and opened *them:* and, behold, their lord *was* fallen down dead on
the earth.
26 And Ē'hŭd escaped while they tarried, and passed beyond the quarries,
and escaped unto Sē-ī'răth.
27 And it came to pass, when he was
come, that he blew a trumpet in the
mountain of Ē'phrā-ĭm, and the children
of Ĭṣ'rā-ĕl went down with him from the
mount, and he before them.
28 And he said unto them, Follow after
me: for the LORD hath delivered your
enemies the Mō'ăb-ītes into your hand.
And they went down after him, and took
the fords of Jordan toward Mō'ăb, and
suffered not a man to pass over.
29 And they slew of Mō'ăb at that time
about ten thousand men, all lusty, and
all men of valor; and there escaped not
a man.
30 So Mō'ăb was subdued that day
under the hand of Ĭṣ'rā-ĕl. And the land
had rest fourscore years.
31 ¶ And after him was Shăm'găr the
son of Ā'năth, which slew of the Phĭ-lĭs'-
tĭneṣ six hundred men with an oxgoad:
and he also delivered Ĭṣ'rā-ĕl.

CHAPTER 4

AND the children of Ĭṣ'rā-ĕl again did
evil in the sight of the LORD, when
Ē'hŭd was dead.
2 And the LORD sold them into the
hand of Jā'bĭn king of Cā'năan, that
reigned in Hā'zôr; the captain of whose
host *was* Sĭs'ĕr-ȧ, which dwelt in Hȧ-
rō'shĕth of the Ġĕn'tīles.
3 And the children of Ĭṣ'rā-ĕl cried
unto the LORD: for he had nine hundred
chariots of iron; and twenty years he
mightily oppressed the children of
Ĭṣ'rā-ĕl.
4 ¶ And Deborah, a prophetess, the
wife of Lăp'ĭ-dŏth, she judged Ĭṣ'rā-ĕl
at that time.
5 And she dwelt under the palm tree
of Deborah, between Rā'mȧh and Beth-
el in mount Ē'phrā-ĭm: and the children
of Ĭṣ'rā-ĕl came up to her for judgment.
6 And she sent and called Bā'răk the
son of Ȧ-bĭn'ō-ăm out of Kē'dĕsh-
năph'tȧ-lī, and said unto him, Hath not
the LORD God of Ĭṣ'rā-ĕl commanded,
saying, Go and draw toward mount
Tā'bŏr, and take with thee ten thousand
men of the children of Năph'tȧ-lī and of
the children of Zĕb'ū-lŭn?
7 And I will draw unto thee, to the river
Kī'shŏn, Sĭs'ĕr-ȧ the captain of Jā'bĭn's
army, with his chariots and his multitude; and I will deliver him into thine
hand.
8 And Bā'răk said unto her, If thou wilt
go with me, then I will go: but if thou
wilt not go with me, *then* I will not go.
9 And she said, I will surely go with
thee: notwithstanding the journey that
thou takest shall not be for thine honor;
for the LORD shall sell Sĭs'ĕr-ȧ into the
hand of a woman. And Deborah arose,
and went with Bā'răk to Kē'dĕsh.
10 ¶ And Bā'răk called Zĕb'ū-lŭn and
Năph'tȧ-lī to Kē'dĕsh; and he went up
with ten thousand men at his feet: and
Deborah went up with him.
11 Now Hē'bĕr the Kē'nīte, *which was*
of the children of Hō'băb the father-in-
law of Moses, had severed himself from
the Kē'nītes, and pitched his tent unto
the plain of Zā'ȧ-nā'ĭm, which *is* by
Kē'dĕsh.
12 And they showed Sĭs'ĕr-ȧ that Bā'-
răk the son of Ȧ-bĭn'ō-ăm was gone up
to mount Tā'bŏr.
13 And Sĭs'ĕr-ȧ gathered together all
his chariots, *even* nine hundred chariots
of iron, and all the people that *were* with
him, from Hȧ-rō'shĕth of the Ġĕn'tīles
unto the river of Kī'shŏn.
14 And Deborah said unto Bā'răk, Up;
for this *is* the day in which the LORD
hath delivered Sĭs'ĕr-ȧ into thine hand:
is not the LORD gone out before thee?
So Bā'răk went down from mount
Tā'bŏr, and ten thousand men after
him.
15 And the LORD discomfited Sĭs'ĕr-ȧ,
and all *his* chariots, and all *his* host,
with the edge of the sword before Bā'-
răk; so that Sĭs'ĕr-ȧ lighted down off
his chariot, and fled away on his feet.
16 But Bā'răk pursued after the chariots, and after the host, unto Hȧ-rō'-
shĕth of the Ġĕn'tīles: and all the host
of Sĭs'ĕr-ȧ fell upon the edge of the
sword; *and* there was not a man left.
17 Howbeit Sĭs'ĕr-ȧ fled away on his
feet to the tent of Jā'ĕl the wife of Hē'-
bĕr the Kē'nīte: for *there was* peace

between Jā′bĭn the king of Hā′zŏr and
the house of Hē′bẽr the Kē′nīte.
18 ℂ And Jā′ĕl went out to meet
Sĭs′ẽr-ȧ, and said unto him, Turn in,
my lord, turn in to me; fear not. And
when he had turned in unto her into
the tent, she covered him with a mantle.
19 And he said unto her, Give me, I
pray thee, a little water to drink; for I
am thirsty. And she opened a bottle of
milk, and gave him drink, and covered
him.
20 Again he said unto her, Stand in the
door of the tent, and it shall be, when
any man doth come and inquire of thee,
and say, Is there any man here? that
thou shalt say, No.
21 Then Jā′ĕl Hē′bẽr's wife took a nail
of the tent, and took a hammer in her
hand, and went softly unto him, and
smote the nail into his temples, and
fastened it into the ground: for he was
fast asleep and weary. So he died.
22 And, behold, as Bā′răk pursued
Sĭs′ẽr-ȧ, Jā′ĕl came out to meet him,
and said unto him, Come, and I will
show thee the man whom thou seekest.
And when he came into her *tent*, behold, Sĭs′ẽr-ȧ lay dead, and the nail *was*
in his temples.
23 So God subdued on that day Jā′bĭn
the king of Cā′năan before the children
of Ĭs′rā-ĕl.
24 And the hand of the children of
Ĭs′rā-ĕl prospered, and prevailed against
Jā′bĭn the king of Cā′năan, until they
had destroyed Jā′bĭn king of Cā′năan.

CHAPTER 5

THEN sang Deborah and Bā′răk
the son of Ȧ-bĭn′ō-ăm on that day,
saying,
2 Praise ye the LORD for the avenging
of Ĭs′rā-ĕl, when the people willingly
offered themselves.
3 Hear, O ye kings; give ear, O ye
princes; I, *even* I, will sing unto the
LORD; I will sing *praise* to the LORD God
of Ĭs′rā-ĕl.
4 LORD, when thou wentest out of
Sē′ïr, when thou marchedst out of the
field of Ē′dŏm, the earth trembled, and
the heavens dropped, the clouds also
dropped water.
5 The mountains melted from before
the LORD, *even* that Sī′naī from before
the LORD God of Ĭs′rā-ĕl.
6 In the days of Shăm′gär the son of
Ā′năth, in the days of Jā′ĕl, the highways were unoccupied, and the travelers
walked through byways.
7 *The inhabitants of* the villages
ceased, they ceased in Ĭs′rā-ĕl, until
that I Deborah arose, that I arose a
mother in Ĭs′rā-ĕl.
8 They chose new gods; then *was* war
in the gates: was there a shield or spear
seen among forty thousand in Ĭs′rā-ĕl?
9 My heart *is* toward the governors of
Ĭs′rā-ĕl, that offered themselves willingly among the people. Bless ye the
LORD.
10 Speak, ye that ride on white asses,
ye that sit in judgment, and walk by the
way.
11 *They that are delivered* from the
noise of archers in the places of drawing water, there shall they rehearse the
righteous acts of the LORD, *even* the
righteous acts *toward the inhabitants*
of his villages in Ĭs′rā-ĕl: then shall the
people of the LORD go down to the gates.
12 Awake, awake, Deborah: awake,
awake, utter a song: arise, Bā′răk, and
lead thy captivity captive, thou son of
Ȧ-bĭn′ō-ăm.
13 Then he made him that remaineth
have dominion over the nobles among
the people: the LORD made me have
dominion over the mighty.
14 Out of Ē′phră-ĭm *was there* a root
of them against Ăm′ȧ-lĕk; after thee,
Benjamin, among thy people; out of
Mā′chĭr came down governors, and out
of Zĕb′ū-lŭn they that handle the pen of
the writer.
15 And the princes of Ĭs′sȧ-chär *were*
with Deborah; even Ĭs′sȧ-chär, and also
Bā′răk: he was sent on foot into the valley. For the divisions of Reuben *there*
were great thoughts of heart.
16 Why abodest thou among the sheepfolds, to hear the bleatings of the flocks?
For the divisions of Reuben *there were*
great searchings of heart.
17 Gĭl′ē-ăd abode beyond Jordan: and
why did Dan remain in ships? Ăsh′ẽr
continued on the seashore, and abode in
his breaches.
18 Zĕb′ū-lŭn and Năph′tȧ-lī *were* a
people *that* jeoparded their lives unto
the death in the high places of the field.
19 The kings came *and* fought; then
fought the kings of Cā′năan in Tā′ȧ-
năch by the waters of Mē-gĭd′dō; they
took no gain of money.

20 They fought from heaven; the stars
in their courses fought against Sĭs′ẽr-ȧ.
21 The river of Kī′shŏn swept them
away, that ancient river, the river Kī′-
shŏn. O my soul, thou hast trodden
down strength.
22 Then were the horsehoofs broken
by the means of the prancings, the
prancings of their mighty ones.
23 Curse ye Mē′rŏz, said the angel of
the LORD, curse ye bitterly the inhabitants thereof; because they came not to
the help of the LORD, to the help of the
LORD against the mighty.
24 Blessed above women shall Jā′ĕl
the wife of Hē′bẽr the Kē′nīte be;
blessed shall she be above women in
the tent.
25 He asked water, *and* she gave *him*
milk; she brought forth butter in a
lordly dish.
26 She put her hand to the nail, and
her right hand to the workmen's hammer; and with the hammer she smote
Sĭs′ẽr-ȧ, she smote off his head, when
she had pierced and stricken through
his temples.
27 At her feet he bowed, he fell, he lay
down: at her feet he bowed, he fell:
where he bowed, there he fell down
dead.
28 The mother of Sĭs′ẽr-ȧ looked out
at a window, and cried through the lattice, Why is his chariot *so* long in
coming? why tarry the wheels of his
chariots?
29 Her wise ladies answered her, yea,
she returned answer to herself,
30 Have they not sped? have they *not*
divided the prey; to every man a damsel
or two; to Sĭs′ẽr-ȧ a prey of divers colors,
a prey of divers colors of needlework, of
divers colors of needlework on both
sides, *meet* for the necks of *them that
take* the spoil?
31 So let all thine enemies perish, O
LORD: but *let* them that love him *be* as
the sun when he goeth forth in his
might. And the land had rest forty
years.

CHAPTER 6

AND the children of Ĭṣ′rā-ĕl did evil
in the sight of the LORD: and the
LORD delivered them into the hand of
Mĭd′ĭ-ăn seven years.
2 And the hand of Mĭd′ĭ-ăn prevailed
against Ĭṣ′rā-ĕl: *and* because of the
Mĭd′ĭ-ăn-ītes the children of Ĭṣ′rā-ĕl
made them the dens which *are* in the
mountains, and caves, and strongholds.
3 And *so* it was, when Ĭṣ′rā-ĕl had
sown, that the Mĭd′ĭ-ăn-ītes came up,
and the Ăm′ȧ-lĕk-ītes, and the children
of the east, even they came up against
them;
4 And they encamped against them,
and destroyed the increase of the earth,
till thou come unto Gā′zȧ, and left no
sustenance for Ĭṣ′rā-ĕl, neither sheep,
nor ox, nor ass.
5 For they came up with their cattle
and their tents, and they came as grasshoppers for multitude; *for* both they
and their camels were without number:
and they entered into the land to destroy it.
6 And Ĭṣ′rā-ĕl was greatly impoverished because of the Mĭd′ĭ-ăn-ītes; and
the children of Ĭṣ′rā-ĕl cried unto the
LORD.
7 ℂ And it came to pass, when the
children of Ĭṣ′rā-ĕl cried unto the LORD
because of the Mĭd′ĭ-ăn-ītes,
8 That the LORD sent a prophet unto
the children of Ĭṣ′rā-ĕl, which said unto
them, Thus saith the LORD God of
Ĭṣ′rā-ĕl, I brought you up from Egypt,
and brought you forth out of the house
of bondage;
9 And I delivered you out of the hand
of the Egyptians, and out of the hand of
all that oppressed you, and drave them
out from before you, and gave you their
land;
10 And I said unto you, I *am* the LORD
your God; fear not the gods of the Ăm′-
ō-rītes, in whose land ye dwell: but ye
have not obeyed my voice.
11 ℂ And there came an angel of the
LORD, and sat under an oak which *was*
in Ŏph′răh, that *pertained* unto Jō′ăsh
the Ā′bĭ-ĕz′rīte: and his son Gideon
threshed wheat by the winepress, to
hide *it* from the Mĭd′ĭ-ăn-ītes.
12 And the angel of the LORD appeared
unto him, and said unto him, The LORD
is with thee, thou mighty man of valor.
13 And Gideon said unto him, O my
Lord, if the LORD be with us, why then
is all this befallen us? and where *be* all
his miracles which our fathers told us
of, saying, Did not the LORD bring us up
from Egypt? but now the LORD hath
forsaken us, and delivered us into the
hands of the Mĭd′ĭ-ăn-ītes.

14 And the LORD looked upon him, and said, Go in this thy might, and thou shalt save Ĭş'rā-ĕl from the hand of the Mĭd'ĭ-ăn-ītes: have not I sent thee?

15 And he said unto him, O my Lord, wherewith shall I save Ĭş'rā-ĕl? behold, my family *is* poor in Mȧ-năs'sĕh, and I *am* the least in my father's house.

16 And the LORD said unto him, Surely I will be with thee, and thou shalt smite the Mĭd'ĭ-ăn-ītes as one man.

17 And he said unto him, If now I have found grace in thy sight, then show me a sign that thou talkest with me.

18 Depart not hence, I pray thee, until I come unto thee, and bring forth my present, and set *it* before thee. And he said, I will tarry until thou come again.

19 ¶ And Gideon went in, and made ready a kid, and unleavened cakes of an ē'phȧh of flour: the flesh he put in a basket, and he put the broth in a pot, and brought *it* out unto him under the oak, and presented *it*.

20 And the angel of God said unto him, Take the flesh and the unleavened cakes, and lay *them* upon this rock, and pour out the broth. And he did so.

21 ¶ Then the angel of the LORD put forth the end of the staff that *was* in his hand, and touched the flesh and the unleavened cakes; and there rose up fire out of the rock, and consumed the flesh and the unleavened cakes. Then the angel of the LORD departed out of his sight.

22 And when Gideon perceived that he *was* an angel of the LORD, Gideon said, Alas, O Lord GOD! for because I have seen an angel of the LORD face to face.

23 And the LORD said unto him, Peace *be* unto thee; fear not: thou shalt not die.

24 Then Gideon built an altar there unto the LORD, and called it Jehovah-shā'lŏm: unto this day it *is* yet in Ŏph'rȧh of the Ā'bĭ-ĕz'rītes.

25 ¶ And it came to pass the same night, that the LORD said unto him, Take thy father's young bullock, even the second bullock of seven years old, and throw down the altar of Bā'ăl that thy father hath, and cut down the grove that *is* by it:

26 And build an altar unto the LORD thy God upon the top of this rock, in the ordered place, and take the second bullock, and offer a burnt sacrifice with the wood of the grove which thou shalt cut down.

27 Then Gideon took ten men of his servants, and did as the LORD had said unto him: and *so* it was, because he feared his father's household, and the men of the city, that he could not do *it* by day, that he did *it* by night.

28 ¶ And when the men of the city arose early in the morning, behold, the altar of Bā'ăl was cast down, and the grove was cut down that *was* by it, and the second bullock was offered upon the altar *that was* built.

29 And they said one to another, Who hath done this thing? And when they inquired and asked, they said, Gideon the son of Jō'ăsh hath done this thing.

30 Then the men of the city said unto Jō'ăsh, Bring out thy son, that he may die: because he hath cast down the altar of Bā'ăl, and because he hath cut down the grove that *was* by it.

31 And Jō'ăsh said unto all that stood against him, Will ye plead for Bā'ăl? will ye save him? he that will plead for him, let him be put to death whilst *it is yet* morning: if he *be* a god, let him plead for himself, because *one* hath cast down his altar.

32 Therefore on that day he called him Jĕr'ŭb-bā'ăl, saying, Let Bā'ăl plead against him, because he hath thrown down his altar.

33 ¶ Then all the Mĭd'ĭ-ăn-ītes and the Ăm'ȧ-lĕk-ītes and the children of the east were gathered together, and went over, and pitched in the valley of Jĕz'rē-ĕl.

34 But the Spirit of the LORD came upon Gideon, and he blew a trumpet; and Ā'bĭ-ē'zĕr was gathered after him.

35 And he sent messengers throughout all Mȧ-năs'sĕh; who also was gathered after him: and he sent messengers unto Ăsh'ĕr, and unto Zĕb'ū-lŭn, and unto Năph'tȧ-lī; and they came up to meet them.

36 ¶ And Gideon said unto God, If thou wilt save Ĭş'rā-ĕl by mine hand, as thou hast said,

37 Behold, I will put a fleece of wool in the floor; *and* if the dew be on the fleece only, and *it be* dry upon all the earth *besides*, then shall I know that thou wilt save Ĭş'rā-ĕl by mine hand, as thou hast said.

38 And it was so: for he rose up early

on the morrow, and thrust the fleece together, and wringed the dew out of the
fleece, a bowlful of water.
39 And Gideon said unto God, Let not
thine anger be hot against me, and I
will speak but this once: let me prove, I
pray thee, but this once with the fleece;
let it now be dry only upon the fleece,
and upon all the ground let there be dew.
40 And God did so that night: for it was
dry upon the fleece only, and there was
dew on all the ground.

CHAPTER 7

THEN Jĕr′ŭb-bā′ăl, who *is* Gideon,
and all the people that *were* with
him, rose up early, and pitched beside
the well of Hā′rŏd: so that the host of
the Mĭd′ĭ-ăn-ītes were on the north side
of them, by the hill of Mō′rĕh, in the
valley.
2 And the LORD said unto Gideon, The
people that *are* with thee *are* too many
for me to give the Mĭd′ĭ-ăn-ītes into
their hands, lest Ĭş′rā-ĕl vaunt themselves against me, saying, Mine own
hand hath saved me.
3 Now therefore go to, proclaim in the
ears of the people, saying, Whosoever
is fearful and afraid, let him return and
depart early from mount Gĭl′ē-ăd. And
there returned of the people twenty and
two thousand; and there remained ten
thousand.
4 And the LORD said unto Gideon, The
people *are* yet *too* many; bring them
down unto the water, and I will try them
for thee there: and it shall be, *that* of
whom I say unto thee, This shall go
with thee, the same shall go with thee;
and of whomsoever I say unto thee, This
shall not go with thee, the same shall
not go.
5 So he brought down the people unto
the water: and the LORD said unto Gideon, Every one that lappeth of the water
with his tongue, as a dog lappeth, him
shalt thou set by himself; likewise every
one that boweth down upon his knees to
drink.
6 And the number of them that lapped,
putting their hand to their mouth, were
three hundred men: but all the rest of
the people bowed down upon their
knees to drink water.
7 And the LORD said unto Gideon, By
the three hundred men that lapped will
I save you, and deliver the Mĭd′ĭ-ăn-ītes
into thine hand: and let all the *other*
people go every man unto his place.
8 So the people took victuals in their
hand, and their trumpets: and he sent
all *the rest of* Ĭş′rā-ĕl every man unto
his tent, and retained those three hundred men: and the host of Mĭd′ĭ-ăn was
beneath him in the valley.
9 ¶ And it came to pass the same
night, that the LORD said unto him,
Arise, get thee down unto the host; for I
have delivered it into thine hand.
10 But if thou fear to go down, go thou
with Phū′rȧh thy servant down to the
host:
11 And thou shalt hear what they say;
and afterward shall thine hands be
strengthened to go down unto the host.
Then went he down with Phū′rȧh his
servant unto the outside of the armed
men that *were* in the host.
12 And the Mĭd′ĭ-ăn-ītes and the Ăm′-
ȧ-lĕk-ītes and all the children of the east
lay along in the valley like grasshoppers
for multitude; and their camels *were*
without number, as the sand by the sea
side for multitude.
13 And when Gideon was come, behold, *there was* a man that told a dream
unto his fellow, and said, Behold, I
dreamed a dream, and, lo, a cake of barley bread tumbled into the host of
Mĭd′ĭ-ăn, and came unto a tent, and
smote it that it fell, and overturned it,
that the tent lay along.
14 And his fellow answered and said,
This *is* nothing else save the sword of
Gideon the son of Jō′ăsh, a man of
Ĭş′rā-ĕl: *for* into his hand hath God delivered Mĭd′ĭ-ăn, and all the host.
15 ¶ And it was *so*, when Gideon
heard the telling of the dream, and the
interpretation thereof, that he worshipped, and returned into the host of
Ĭş′rā-ĕl, and said, Arise; for the LORD
hath delivered into your hand the host
of Mĭd′ĭ-ăn.
16 And he divided the three hundred
men *into* three companies, and he put a
trumpet in every man's hand, with
empty pitchers, and lamps within the
pitchers.
17 And he said unto them, Look on me,
and do likewise: and, behold, when I
come to the outside of the camp, it shall
be *that*, as I do, so shall ye do.
18 When I blow with a trumpet, I and
all that *are* with me, then blow ye the

trumpets also on every side of all the
camp, and say, *The sword* of the LORD,
and of Gideon.
19 ¶ So Gideon, and the hundred men
that *were* with him, came unto the outside of the camp in the beginning of the
middle watch; and they had but newly
set the watch: and they blew the trumpets, and brake the pitchers that *were*
in their hands.
20 And the three companies blew the
trumpets, and brake the pitchers, and
held the lamps in their left hands, and
the trumpets in their right hands to
blow *withal*: and they cried, The sword
of the LORD, and of Gideon.
21 And they stood every man in his
place round about the camp: and all the
host ran, and cried, and fled.
22 And the three hundred blew the
trumpets, and the LORD set every man's
sword against his fellow, even throughout all the host: and the host fled to
Bĕth′-shĭt′tȧh in Zĕr′ē-răth, *and* to the
border of Ā′bĕl-mē-hō′lȧh, unto Tăb′-
bȧth.
23 And the men of Ĭṣ′rā-ĕl gathered
themselves together out of Năph′tȧ-lī,
and out of Ăsh′ēr, and out of all Mȧ-năs′-
sĕh, and pursued after the Mĭd′ĭ-ăn-
ītes.
24 ¶ And Gideon sent messengers
throughout all mount Ē′phrā-ĭm, saying,
Come down against the Mĭd′ĭ-ăn-ītes,
and take before them the waters unto
Bĕth′-bā′rȧh and Jordan. Then all the
men of Ē′phrā-ĭm gathered themselves
together, and took the waters unto
Bĕth′-bā′rȧh and Jordan.
25 And they took two princes of the
Mĭd′ĭ-ăn-ītes, Ō′rĕb and Zē′ĕb; and
they slew Ō′rĕb upon the rock Ō′rĕb,
and Zē′ĕb they slew at the winepress of
Zē′ĕb, and pursued Mĭd′ĭ-ăn, and
brought the heads of Ō′rĕb and Zē′ĕb to
Gideon on the other side Jordan.

CHAPTER 8

AND the men of Ē′phrā-ĭm said unto
him, Why hast thou served us thus,
that thou calledst us not, when thou
wentest to fight with the Mĭd′ĭ-ăn-ītes?
And they did chide with him sharply.
2 And he said unto them, What have I
done now in comparison of you? *Is* not
the gleaning of the grapes of Ē′phrā-ĭm
better than the vintage of Ā′bĭ-ē′zēr?
3 God hath delivered into your hands
the princes of Mĭd′ĭ-ăn, Ō′rĕb and
Zē′ĕb: and what was I able to do in comparison of you? Then their anger was
abated toward him, when he had said
that.
4 ¶ And Gideon came to Jordan, *and*
passed over, he, and the three hundred
men that *were* with him, faint, yet pursuing *them*.
5 And he said unto the men of Sŭc′-
cōth, Give, I pray you, loaves of bread
unto the people that follow me; for they
be faint, and I am pursuing after Zē′bȧh
and Zăl-mŭn′nȧ, kings of Mĭd′ĭ-ăn.
6 ¶ And the princes of Sŭc′cōth said,
Are the hands of Zē′bȧh and Zăl-mŭn′nȧ
now in thine hand, that we should give
bread unto thine army?
7 And Gideon said, Therefore when
the LORD hath delivered Zē′bȧh and
Zăl-mŭn′nȧ into mine hand, then I will
tear your flesh with the thorns of the
wilderness and with briers.
8 ¶ And he went up thence to Pē-
nū′ĕl, and spake unto them likewise:
and the men of Pē-nū′ĕl answered him
as the men of Sŭc′cōth had answered
him.
9 And he spake also unto the men of
Pē-nū′ĕl, saying, When I come again in
peace, I will break down this tower.
10 ¶ Now Zē′bȧh and Zăl-mŭn′nȧ
were in Kär′kŏr, and their hosts with
them, about fifteen thousand *men*, all
that were left of all the hosts of the children of the east: for there fell a hundred
and twenty thousand men that drew
sword.
11 ¶ And Gideon went up by the way
of them that dwelt in tents on the east
of Nō′bȧh and Jŏg′bē-hăh, and smote
the host: for the host was secure.
12 And when Zē′bȧh and Zăl-mŭn′nȧ
fled, he pursued after them, and took
the two kings of Mĭd′ĭ-ăn, Zē′bȧh and
Zăl-mŭn′nȧ, and discomfited all the
host.
13 ¶ And Gideon the son of Jō′ăsh
returned from battle before the sun *was*
up,
14 And caught a young man of the men
of Sŭc′cōth, and inquired of him: and
he described unto him the princes of
Sŭc′cōth, and the elders thereof, *even*
threescore and seventeen men.
15 And he came unto the men of Sŭc′-
cōth, and said, Behold Zē′bȧh and Zăl-
mŭn′nȧ, with whom ye did upbraid me,

saying, *Are* the hands of Zē′bȧh and
Zăl-mŭn′nȧ now in thine hand, that we
should give bread unto thy men *that*
are weary?
16 And he took the elders of the city,
and thorns of the wilderness, and briers,
and with them he taught the men of
Sŭc′cŏth.
17 And he beat down the tower of
Pē-nū′ĕl, and slew the men of the
city.
18 ¶ Then said he unto Zē′bȧh and
Zăl-mŭn′nȧ, What manner of men *were*
they whom ye slew at Tā′bŏr? And they
answered, As thou *art*, so *were* they;
each one resembled the children of a
king.
19 And he said, They *were* my brethren, *even* the sons of my mother: *as* the
LORD liveth, if ye had saved them alive,
I would not slay you.
20 And he said unto Jē′thĕr his firstborn, Up, *and* slay them. But the youth
drew not his sword: for he feared, because he *was* yet a youth.
21 Then Zē′bȧh and Zăl-mŭn′nȧ said,
Rise thou, and fall upon us: for as the
man *is, so is* his strength. And Gideon
arose, and slew Zē′bȧh and Zăl-mŭn′nȧ,
and took away the ornaments that *were*
on their camels' necks.
22 ¶ Then the men of Ĭş′rā-ĕl said
unto Gideon, Rule thou over us, both
thou, and thy son, and thy son's son also:
for thou hast delivered us from the hand
of Mĭd′ĭ-ăn.
23 And Gideon said unto them, I will
not rule over you, neither shall my son
rule over you: the LORD shall rule over
you.
24 ¶ And Gideon said unto them, I
would desire a request of you, that ye
would give me every man the earrings
of his prey. (For they had golden earrings, because they *were* Ĭsh′mā-ĕl-ītes.)
25 And they answered, We will willingly give *them*. And they spread a garment, and did cast therein every man
the earrings of his prey.
26 And the weight of the golden earrings that he requested was a thousand
and seven hundred *shekels* of gold; besides ornaments, and collars, and purple raiment that *was* on the kings of
Mĭd′ĭ-ăn, and besides the chains that
were about their camels' necks.
27 And Gideon made an ĕph′ŏd thereof, and put it in his city, *even* in Ŏph′-
rȧh: and all Ĭş′rā-ĕl went thither a whoring after it: which thing became a snare
unto Gideon, and to his house.
28 ¶ Thus was Mĭd′ĭ-ăn subdued before the children of Ĭş′rā-ĕl, so that they
lifted up their heads no more. And the
country was in quietness forty years in
the days of Gideon.
29 ¶ And Jĕr′ŭb-bā′ăl the son of Jō′-
ăsh went and dwelt in his own house.
30 And Gideon had threescore and ten
sons of his body begotten: for he had
many wives.
31 And his concubine that *was* in Shē′-
chĕm, she also bare him a son, whose
name he called Ȧ-bĭm′ē-lĕch.
32 ¶ And Gideon the son of Jō′ăsh
died in a good old age, and was buried
in the sepulchre of Jō′ăsh his father, in
Ŏph′rȧh of the Ā′bĭ–ĕz′rītes.
33 And it came to pass, as soon as
Gideon was dead, that the children of
Ĭş′rā-ĕl turned again, and went a whoring after Bā′ȧ-lĭm, and made Bā′ăl–
bē′rĭth their god.
34 And the children of Ĭş′rā-ĕl remembered not the LORD their God, who had
delivered them out of the hands of all
their enemies on every side:
35 Neither showed they kindness to
the house of Jĕr′ŭb-bā′ăl, *namely*,
Gideon, according to all the goodness
which he had showed unto Ĭş′rā-ĕl.

CHAPTER 9

AND Ȧ-bĭm′ē-lĕch the son of Jĕr′ŭb-
bā′ăl went to Shē′chĕm unto his
mother's brethren, and communed with
them, and with all the family of the
house of his mother's father, saying,
2 Speak, I pray you, in the ears of all
the men of Shē′chĕm, Whether *is* better
for you, either that all the sons of Jĕr′-
ŭb-bā′ăl, *which are* threescore and ten
persons, reign over you, or that one
reign over you? remember also that I *am*
your bone and your flesh.
3 And his mother's brethren spake of
him in the ears of all the men of Shē′-
chem all these words: and their hearts
inclined to follow Ȧ-bĭm′ē-lĕch; for they
said, He *is* our brother.
4 And they gave him threescore and
ten *pieces* of silver out of the house of
Bā′ăl–bē′rĭth, wherewith Ȧ-bĭm′ē-lĕch
hired vain and light persons, which followed him.
5 And he went unto his father's house

at Ŏph'rȧh, and slew his brethren the
sons of Jĕr'ŭb-bā'ăl, *being* threescore
and ten persons, upon one stone: notwithstanding, yet Jō'thăm the youngest
son of Jĕr'ŭb-bā'ăl was left; for he hid
himself.
6 And all the men of Shē'chĕm gathered together, and all the house of
Mĭl'lō, and went and made Ȧ-bĭm'ē-
lĕch king, by the plain of the pillar that
was in Shē'chĕm.
7 ¶ And when they told *it* to Jō'thăm,
he went and stood in the top of mount
Gĕr'ĭ-zĭm, and lifted up his voice, and
cried, and said unto them, Hearken
unto me, ye men of Shē'chĕm, that God
may hearken unto you.
8 The trees went forth *on a time* to
anoint a king over them; and they said
unto the olive tree, Reign thou over us.
9 But the olive tree said unto them,
Should I leave my fatness, wherewith
by me they honor God and man, and go
to be promoted over the trees?
10 And the trees said to the fig tree,
Come thou, *and* reign over us.
11 But the fig tree said unto them,
Should I forsake my sweetness, and my
good fruit, and go to be promoted over
the trees?
12 Then said the trees unto the vine,
Come thou, *and* reign over us.
13 And the vine said unto them,
Should I leave my wine, which cheereth
God and man, and go to be promoted
over the trees?
14 Then said all the trees unto the
bramble, Come thou, *and* reign over us.
15 And the bramble said unto the trees,
If in truth ye anoint me king over you,
then come *and* put your trust in my
shadow; and if not, let fire come out of
the bramble, and devour the cedars of
Lebanon.
16 Now therefore, if ye have done truly
and sincerely, in that ye have made
Ȧ-bĭm'ē-lĕch king, and if ye have dealt
well with Jĕr'ŭb-bā'ăl and his house,
and have done unto him according to
the deserving of his hands:
17 (For my father fought for you, and
adventured his life far, and delivered
you out of the hand of Mĭd'ĭ-ăn:
18 And ye are risen up against my
father's house this day, and have slain
his sons, threescore and ten persons,
upon one stone, and have made Ȧ-bĭm'-
ē-lĕch, the son of his maidservant, king
over the men of Shē'chĕm, because he
is your brother:)
19 If ye then have dealt truly and sincerely with Jĕr'ŭb-bā'ăl and with his
house this day, *then* rejoice ye in
Ȧ-bĭm'ē-lĕch, and let him also rejoice
in you:
20 But if not, let fire come out from
Ȧ-bĭm'ē-lĕch, and devour the men of
Shē'chĕm, and the house of Mĭl'lō; and
let fire come out from the men of Shē'-
chĕm, and from the house of Mĭl'lō, and
devour Ȧ-bĭm'ē-lĕch.
21 And Jō'thăm ran away, and fled,
and went to Bē'ĕr, and dwelt there, for
fear of Ȧ-bĭm'ē-lĕch his brother.
22 ¶ When Ȧ-bĭm'ē-lĕch had reigned
three years over Ĭș'rā-ĕl,
23 Then God sent an evil spirit between Ȧ-bĭm'ē-lĕch and the men of
Shē'chĕm; and the men of Shē'chĕm
dealt treacherously with Ȧ-bĭm'ē-lĕch:
24 That the cruelty *done* to the threescore and ten sons of Jĕr'ŭb-bā'ăl might
come, and their blood be laid upon
Ȧ-bĭm'ē-lĕch their brother, which slew
them, and upon the men of Shē'chĕm,
which aided him in the killing of his
brethren.
25 And the men of Shē'chĕm set liers
in wait for him in the top of the mountains, and they robbed all that came
along that way by them: and it was told
Ȧ-bĭm'ē-lĕch.
26 And Gā'ăl the son of Ē'bĕd came
with his brethren, and went over to
Shē'chĕm: and the men of Shē'chĕm
put their confidence in him.
27 And they went out into the fields,
and gathered their vineyards, and trode
the grapes, and made merry, and went
into the house of their god, and did eat
and drink, and cursed Ȧ-bĭm'ē-lĕch.
28 And Gā'ăl the son of Ē'bĕd said,
Who *is* Ȧ-bĭm'ē-lĕch, and who *is* Shē'-
chĕm, that we should serve him? *is* not
he the son of Jĕr'ŭb-bā'ăl? and Zē'bŭl
his officer? serve the men of Hā'mŏr the
father of Shē'chĕm: for why should we
serve him?
29 And would to God this people were
under my hand! then would I remove
Ȧ-bĭm'ē-lĕch. And he said to Ȧ-bĭm'ē-
lĕch, Increase thine army, and come
out.
30 ¶ And when Zē'bŭl the ruler of the
city heard the words of Gā'ăl the son of
Ē'bĕd, his anger was kindled.

31 And he sent messengers unto Ȧ-bĭm'ē-lĕch privily, saying, Behold, Gā'ăl the son of Ē'bĕd and his brethren be come to Shē'chĕm; and, behold, they fortify the city against thee.

32 Now therefore up by night, thou and the people that *is* with thee, and lie in wait in the field:

33 And it shall be, *that* in the morning, as soon as the sun is up, thou shalt rise early, and set upon the city: and, behold, *when* he and the people that *is* with him come out against thee, then mayest thou do to them as thou shalt find occasion.

34 ¶ And Ȧ-bĭm'ē-lĕch rose up, and all the people that *were* with him, by night, and they laid wait against Shē'chĕm in four companies.

35 And Gā'ăl the son of Ē'bĕd went out, and stood in the entering of the gate of the city: and Ȧ-bĭm'ē-lĕch rose up, and the people that *were* with him, from lying in wait.

36 And when Gā'ăl saw the people, he said to Zē'bŭl, Behold, there come people down from the top of the mountains. And Zē'bŭl said unto him, Thou seest the shadow of the mountains as *if they were* men.

37 And Gā'ăl spake again and said, See, there come people down by the middle of the land, and another company come along by the plain of Mē-ŏn'ē-nĭm.

38 Then said Zē'bŭl unto him, Where *is* now thy mouth, wherewith thou saidst, Who *is* Ȧ-bĭm'ē-lĕch, that we should serve him? *is* not this the people that thou hast despised? go out, I pray now, and fight with them.

39 And Gā'ăl went out before the men of Shē'chĕm, and fought with Ȧ-bĭm'ē-lĕch.

40 And Ȧ-bĭm'ē-lĕch chased him, and he fled before him, and many were overthrown *and* wounded, *even* unto the entering of the gate.

41 And Ȧ-bĭm'ē-lĕch dwelt at Ȧ-ru'-mah: and Zē'bŭl thrust out Gā'ăl and his brethren, that they should not dwell in Shē'chĕm.

42 And it came to pass on the morrow, that the people went out into the field; and they told Ȧ-bĭm'ē-lĕch.

43 And he took the people, and divided them into three companies, and laid wait in the field, and looked, and, behold, the people *were* come forth out of the city; and he rose up against them, and smote them.

44 And Ȧ-bĭm'ē-lĕch, and the company that *was* with him, rushed forward, and stood in the entering of the gate of the city: and the two *other* companies ran upon all *the people* that *were* in the fields, and slew them.

45 And Ȧ-bĭm'ē-lĕch fought against the city all that day; and he took the city, and slew the people that *was* therein, and beat down the city, and sowed it with salt.

46 ¶ And when all the men of the tower of Shē'chĕm heard *that,* they entered into a hold of the house of the god Bē'rĭth.

47 And it was told Ȧ-bĭm'ē-lĕch, that all the men of the tower of Shē'chĕm were gathered together.

48 And Ȧ-bĭm'ē-lĕch gat him up to mount Zăl'mŏn, he and all the people that *were* with him; and Ȧ-bĭm'ē-lĕch took an axe in his hand, and cut down a bough from the trees, and took it, and laid *it* on his shoulder, and said unto the people that *were* with him, What ye have seen me do, make haste, *and* do as I *have done.*

49 And all the people likewise cut down every man his bough, and followed Ȧ-bĭm'ē-lĕch, and put *them* to the hold, and set the hold on fire upon them; so that all the men of the tower of Shē'chĕm died also, about a thousand men and women.

50 ¶ Then went Ȧ-bĭm'ē-lĕch to Thē'bĕz, and encamped against Thē'bĕz, and took it.

51 But there was a strong tower within the city, and thither fled all the men and women, and all they of the city, and shut *it* to them, and gat them up to the top of the tower.

52 And Ȧ-bĭm'ē-lĕch came unto the tower, and fought against it, and went hard unto the door of the tower to burn it with fire.

53 And a certain woman cast a piece of a millstone upon Ȧ-bĭm'ē-lĕch's head, and all to brake his skull.

54 Then he called hastily unto the young man his armor-bearer, and said unto him, Draw thy sword, and slay me, that men say not of me, A woman slew him. And his young man thrust him through, and he died.

55 And when the men of Ĭş'rā-ēl saw

that Ȧ-bĭm'ē-lĕch was dead, they departed every man unto his place.
56 ¶ Thus God rendered the wickedness of Ȧ-bĭm'ē-lĕch, which he did unto his father, in slaying his seventy
brethren:
57 And all the evil of the men of Shē'-
chĕm did God render upon their heads:
and upon them came the curse of Jō'-
thăm the son of Jĕr'ŭb-bā'ăl.

CHAPTER 10

AND after Ȧ-bĭm'ē-lĕch there arose to
defend Ĭs̱'rā-ĕl Tō'lȧ the son of
Pū'ȧh, the son of Dō'dō, a man of
Ĭs'sȧ-chär; and he dwelt in Shā'mĭr in
mount Ē'phrā-ĭm.
2 And he judged Ĭs̱'rā-ĕl twenty and
three years, and died, and was buried
in Shā'mĭr.
3 ¶ And after him arose Jā'ĭr, a Gĭl'-ē-
ăd-īte, and judged Ĭs̱'rā-ĕl twenty and
two years.
4 And he had thirty sons that rode on
thirty ass colts, and they had thirty
cities, which are called Hā'vŏth–jā'ĭr
unto this day, which *are* in the land of
Gĭl'ē-ăd.
5 And Jā'ĭr died, and was buried in
Cā'mŏn.
6 ¶ And the children of Ĭs̱'rā-ĕl did
evil again in the sight of the LORD, and
served Bā'ȧ-lĭm, and Ăsh'tȧ-rŏth, and
the gods of Syria, and the gods of Zī'dŏn,
and the gods of Mō'ăb, and the gods of
the children of Ammon, and the gods of
the Phĭ-lĭs'tīnes̱, and forsook the LORD,
and served not him.
7 And the anger of the LORD was hot
against Ĭs̱'rā-ĕl, and he sold them into
the hands of the Phĭ-lĭs'tīnes̱, and into
the hands of the children of Ammon.
8 And that year they vexed and oppressed the children of Ĭs̱'rā-ĕl: eighteen years, all the children of Ĭs̱'rā-ĕl
that *were* on the other side Jordan in
the land of the Ăm'ō-rītes, which *is* in
Gĭl'ē-ăd.
9 Moreover the children of Ammon
passed over Jordan to fight also against
Judah, and against Benjamin, and
against the house of Ē'phrā-ĭm; so that
Ĭs̱'rā-ĕl was sore distressed.
10 ¶ And the children of Ĭs̱'rā-ĕl cried
unto the LORD, saying, We have sinned
against thee, both because we have
forsaken our God, and also served
Bā'ȧ-lĭm.
11 And the LORD said unto the children
of Ĭs̱'rā-ĕl, *Did* not *I deliver you* from
the Egyptians, and from the Ăm'ō-rītes,
from the children of Ammon, and from
the Phĭ-lĭs'tīnes̱?
12 The Zī-dō'nĭ-ăns̱ also, and the Ăm'-
ȧ-lĕk-ītes, and the Mā'ŏn-ītes, did oppress you; and ye cried to me, and I delivered you out of their hand.
13 Yet ye have forsaken me, and served
other gods: wherefore I will deliver you
no more.
14 Go and cry unto the gods which ye
have chosen; let them deliver you in the
time of your tribulation.
15 ¶ And the children of Ĭs̱'rā-ĕl said
unto the LORD, We have sinned: do
thou unto us whatsoever seemeth good
unto thee; deliver us only, we pray thee,
this day.
16 And they put away the strange gods
from among them, and served the LORD:
and his soul was grieved for the misery
of Ĭs̱'rā-ĕl.
17 Then the children of Ammon were
gathered together, and encamped in
Gĭl'-ē-ăd. And the children of Ĭs̱'rā-ĕl
assembled themselves together, and
encamped in Mĭz'pĕh.
18 And the people *and* princes of
Gĭl'ē-ăd said one to another, What man
is he that will begin to fight against the
children of Ammon? he shall be head
over all the inhabitants of Gĭl'ē-ăd.

CHAPTER 11

NOW Jĕph'thȧh the Gĭl'ē-ăd-īte was
a mighty man of valor, and he *was*
the son of a harlot: and Gĭl'ē-ăd begat
Jĕph'thȧh.
2 And Gĭl'ē-ăd's wife bare him sons;
and his wife's sons grew up, and they
thrust out Jĕph'thȧh, and said unto him,
Thou shalt not inherit in our father's
house; for thou *art* the son of a strange
woman.
3 Then Jĕph'thȧh fled from his brethren, and dwelt in the land of Tŏb: and
there were gathered vain men to Jĕph'-
thȧh, and went out with him.
4 ¶ And it came to pass in process of
time, that the children of Ammon made
war against Ĭs̱'rā-ĕl.
5 And it was so, that when the children
of Ammon made war against Ĭs̱'rā-ĕl,
the elders of Gĭl'ē-ăd went to fetch
Jĕph'thȧh out of the land of Tŏb:
6 And they said unto Jĕph'thȧh, Come,

and be our captain, that we may fight
with the children of Ammon.
7 And Jĕph′thȧh said unto the elders
of Gĭl′ē-ăd, Did not ye hate me, and
expel me out of my father's house? and
why are ye come unto me now when ye
are in distress?
8 And the elders of Gĭl′ē-ăd said unto
Jĕph′thȧh, Therefore we turn again to
thee now, that thou mayest go with us,
and fight against the children of Ammon, and be our head over all the inhabitants of Gĭl′ē-ăd.
9 And Jĕph′thȧh said unto the elders of
Gĭl′ē-ăd, If ye bring me home again to
fight against the children of Ammon,
and the LORD deliver them before me,
shall I be your head?
10 And the elders of Gĭl′ē-ăd said unto
Jĕph′thȧh, The LORD be witness between us, if we do not so according to
thy words.
11 Then Jĕph′thȧh went with the elders of Gĭl′ē-ăd, and the people made
him head and captain over them: and
Jĕph′thȧh uttered all his words before
the LORD in Mĭz′pĕh.
12 ℂ And Jĕph′thȧh sent messengers
unto the king of the children of Ammon,
saying, What hast thou to do with me,
that thou art come against me to fight in
my land?
13 And the king of the children of
Ammon answered unto the messengers
of Jĕph′thȧh, Because Ĭș′rā-ĕl took
away my land, when they came up out
of Egypt, from Är′nŏn even unto Jăb′-
bŏk, and unto Jordan: now therefore
restore those *lands* again peaceably.
14 And Jĕph′thȧh sent messengers
again unto the king of the children of
Ammon:
15 And said unto him, Thus saith
Jĕph′thȧh, Ĭș′rā-ĕl took not away the
land of Mō′ăb, nor the land of the children of Ammon:
16 But when Ĭș′rā-ĕl came up from
Egypt, and walked through the wilderness unto the Red sea, and came to
Kā′dĕsh;
17 Then Ĭș′rā-ĕl sent messengers unto
the king of Ē′dŏm, saying, Let me, I
pray thee, pass through thy land: but
the king of Ē′dŏm would not hearken
thereto. And in like manner they sent
unto the king of Mō′ăb; but he would
not *consent*: and Ĭș′rā-ĕl abode in
Kā′dĕsh.
18 Then they went along through the
wilderness, and compassed the land of
Ē′dŏm, and the land of Mō′ăb, and came
by the east side of the land of Mō′ăb,
and pitched on the other side of Är′nŏn,
but came not within the border of
Mō′ăb: for Är′nŏn *was* the border of
Mō′ăb.
19 And Ĭș′rā-ĕl sent messengers unto
Sī′hŏn king of the Ăm′ō-rītes, the king
of Hĕsh′bŏn; and Ĭș′rā-ĕl said unto him,
Let us pass, we pray thee, through thy
land into my place.
20 But Sī′hŏn trusted not Ĭș′rā-ĕl to
pass through his coast: but Sī′hŏn gathered all his people together, and pitched
in Jā′hăz, and fought against Ĭș′rā-ĕl.
21 And the LORD God of Ĭș′rā-ĕl delivered Sī′hŏn and all his people into
the hand of Ĭș′rā-ĕl, and they smote
them: so Ĭș′rā-ĕl possessed all the land
of the Ăm′ō-rītes, the inhabitants of
that country.
22 And they possessed all the coasts of
the Ăm′ō-rītes, from Är′nŏn even unto
Jăb′bŏk, and from the wilderness even
unto Jordan.
23 So now the LORD God of Ĭș′rā-ĕl
hath dispossessed the Ăm′ō-rītes from
before his people Ĭș′rā-ĕl, and shouldest
thou possess it?
24 Wilt not thou possess that which
Chē′mŏsh thy god giveth thee to possess? So whomsoever the LORD our
God shall drive out from before us,
them will we possess.
25 And now *art* thou any thing better
than Bā′lăk the son of Zĭp′pŏr, king of
Mō′ăb? did he ever strive against Ĭș′-
rā-ĕl, or did he ever fight against them,
26 While Ĭș′rā-ĕl dwelt in Hĕsh′bŏn
and her towns, and in Ȧ-rō′ĕr and her
towns, and in all the cities that *be* along
by the coasts of Är′nŏn, three hundred
years? why therefore did ye not recover
them within that time?
27 Wherefore I have not sinned against
thee, but thou doest me wrong to war
against me: the LORD the Judge be
judge this day between the children
of Ĭș′rā-ĕl and the children of Ammon.
28 Howbeit the king of the children of
Ammon hearkened not unto the words
of Jĕph′thȧh which he sent him.
29 ℂ Then the Spirit of the LORD came
upon Jĕph′thȧh, and he passed over
Gĭl′ē-ăd, and Mȧ-năs′sĕh, and passed
over Mĭz′pĕh of Gĭl′ē-ăd, and from

Mĭz'pĕh of Gĭl'ē-ăd he passed over *unto*
the children of Ammon.
30 And Jĕph'thȧh vowed a vow unto
the LORD, and said, If thou shalt without
fail deliver the children of Ammon
into mine hands,
31 Then it shall be, that whatsoever
cometh forth of the doors of my house to
meet me, when I return in peace from
the children of Ammon, shall surely be
the LORD's, and I will offer it up for a
burnt offering.
32 ℂ So Jĕph'thȧh passed over unto
the children of Ammon to fight against
them; and the LORD delivered them into
his hands.
33 And he smote them from Ȧ-rō'ēr,
even till thou come to Mĭn'nĭth, *even*
twenty cities, and unto the plain of the
vineyards, with a very great slaughter.
Thus the children of Ammon were subdued
before the children of Ĭṣ'rā-ĕl.
34 ℂ And Jĕph'thȧh came to Mĭz'pĕh
unto his house, and, behold, his daughter
came out to meet him with timbrels
and with dances: and she *was his* only
child; beside her he had neither son nor
daughter.
35 And it came to pass, when he saw
her, that he rent his clothes, and said,
Alas, my daughter! thou hast brought
me very low, and thou art one of them
that trouble me: for I have opened my
mouth unto the LORD, and I cannot go
back.
36 And she said unto him, My father,
if thou hast opened thy mouth unto the
LORD, do to me according to that which
hath proceeded out of thy mouth; forasmuch
as the LORD hath taken vengeance
for thee of thine enemies, *even* of the
children of Ammon.
37 And she said unto her father, Let
this thing be done for me: let me alone
two months, that I may go up and down
upon the mountains, and bewail my virginity,
I and my fellows.
38 And he said, Go. And he sent her
away *for* two months: and she went with
her companions, and bewailed her virginity
upon the mountains.
39 And it came to pass at the end of two
months, that she returned unto her
father, who did with her *according* to
his vow which he had vowed: and she
knew no man. And it was a custom in
Ĭṣ'rā-ĕl,
40 *That* the daughters of Ĭṣ'rā-ĕl went
yearly to lament the daughter of Jĕph'thȧh
the Gĭl'ē-ăd-īte four days in a
year.

CHAPTER 12

AND the men of Ē'phrā-ĭm gathered
themselves together, and went
northward, and said unto Jĕph'thȧh,
Wherefore passedst thou over to fight
against the children of Ammon, and
didst not call us to go with thee? we will
burn thine house upon thee with fire.
2 And Jĕph'thȧh said unto them, I and
my people were at great strife with the
children of Ammon; and when I called
you, ye delivered me not out of their
hands.
3 And when I saw that ye delivered *me*
not, I put my life in my hands, and
passed over against the children of Ammon,
and the LORD delivered them into
my hand: wherefore then are ye come
up unto me this day, to fight against me?
4 Then Jĕph'thȧh gathered together
all the men of Gĭl'ē-ăd, and fought with
Ē'phrā-ĭm: and the men of Gĭl'ē-ăd
smote Ē'phrā-ĭm, because they said, Ye
Gĭl'ē-ăd-ītes *are* fugitives of Ē'phrā-ĭm
among the Ē'phrā-ĭm-ītes, *and* among
the Mȧ-năs'sītes.
5 And the Gĭl'ē-ăd-ītes took the passages
of Jordan before the Ē'phrā-ĭm-ītes:
and it was *so,* that when those
Ē'phrā-ĭm-ītes which were escaped said,
Let me go over, that the men of Gĭl'ē-ăd
said unto him, *Art* thou an Ē'phrā-ĭm-īte?
If he said, Nay;
6 Then said they unto him, Say now
Shĭb'bō-lĕth: and he said Sĭb'bō-lĕth:
for he could not frame to pronounce *it*
right. Then they took him, and slew
him at the passages of Jordan: and there
fell at that time of the Ē'phrā-ĭm-ītes
forty and two thousand.
7 And Jĕph'thȧh judged Ĭṣ'rā-ĕl six
years. Then died Jĕph'thȧh the Gĭl'ē-ăd-īte,
and was buried in *one of* the
cities of Gĭl'ē-ăd.
8 ℂ And after him Ĭb'zăn of Beth-lehem
judged Ĭṣ'rā-ĕl.
9 And he had thirty sons, and thirty
daughters, *whom* he sent abroad, and
took in thirty daughters from abroad for
his sons. And he judged Ĭṣ'rā-ĕl seven
years.
10 Then died Ĭb'zăn, and was buried at
Beth-lehem.
11 ℂ And after him Ē'lŏn, a Zĕb'ū-

lŏn-īte, judged Ĭş'rā-ĕl; and he judged
Ĭş'rā-ĕl ten years.
12 And Ē'lŏn the Zĕb'ū-lŏn-īte died,
and was buried in Āi'jȧ-lŏn in the country of Zĕb'ū-lŭn.
13 ¶ And after him Ăb'dŏn the son of
Hĭl'lĕl, a Pĭr'ȧ-thŏn-īte, judged Ĭş'rā-ĕl.
14 And he had forty sons and thirty
nephews, that rode on threescore and
ten ass colts: and he judged Ĭş'rā-ĕl
eight years.
15 And Ăb'dŏn the son of Hĭl'lĕl the
Pĭr'ȧ-thŏn-īte died, and was buried in
Pĭr'ȧ-thŏn in the land of Ē'phrā-ĭm, in
the mount of the Ăm'ȧ-lĕk-ītes.

CHAPTER 13

AND the children of Ĭş'rā-ĕl did evil
again in the sight of the LORD; and
the LORD delivered them into the hand
of the Phĭ-lĭs'tīneş forty years.
2 ¶ And there was a certain man of
Zō'rȧh, of the family of the Dăn'ītes,
whose name *was* Mȧ-nō'ȧh; and his
wife *was* barren, and bare not.
3 And the angel of the LORD appeared
unto the woman, and said unto her, Behold now, thou *art* barren, and bearest
not: but thou shalt conceive, and bear a
son.
4 Now therefore beware, I pray thee,
and drink not wine nor strong drink,
and eat not any unclean *thing:*
5 For, lo, thou shalt conceive, and bear
a son; and no razor shall come on his
head: for the child shall be a Nazarite
unto God from the womb: and he shall
begin to deliver Ĭş'rā-ĕl out of the hand
of the Phĭ-lĭs'tīneş.
6 ¶ Then the woman came and told
her husband, saying, A man of God came
unto me, and his countenance *was* like
the countenance of an angel of God, very
terrible: but I asked him not whence he
was, neither told he me his name:
7 But he said unto me, Behold, thou
shalt conceive, and bear a son; and now
drink no wine nor strong drink, neither
eat any unclean *thing:* for the child shall
be a Nazarite to God from the womb to
the day of his death.
8 ¶ Then Mȧ-nō'ȧh entreated the
LORD, and said, O my Lord, let the man
of God which thou didst send come again
unto us, and teach us what we shall do
unto the child that shall be born.
9 And God hearkened to the voice of
Mȧ-nō'ȧh; and the angel of God came
again unto the woman as she sat in the
field: but Mȧ-nō'ȧh her husband *was*
not with her.
10 And the woman made haste, and
ran, and showed her husband, and said
unto him, Behold, the man hath appeared unto me, that came unto me the
other day.
11 And Mȧ-nō'ȧh arose, and went after
his wife, and came to the man, and said
unto him, *Art* thou the man that spakest
unto the woman? And he said, I *am.*
12 And Mȧ-nō'ȧh said, Now let thy
words come to pass. How shall we order
the child, and *how* shall we do unto
him?
13 And the angel of the LORD said unto
Mȧ-nō'ȧh, Of all that I said unto the
woman let her beware.
14 She may not eat of any *thing* that
cometh of the vine, neither let her drink
wine or strong drink, nor eat any unclean
thing: all that I commanded her let her
observe.
15 ¶ And Mȧ-nō'ȧh said unto the
angel of the LORD, I pray thee, let us
detain thee, until we shall have made
ready a kid for thee.
16 And the angel of the LORD said unto
Mȧ-nō'ȧh, Though thou detain me, I
will not eat of thy bread: and if thou wilt
offer a burnt offering, thou must offer it
unto the LORD. For Mȧ-nō'ȧh knew not
that he *was* an angel of the LORD.
17 And Mȧ-nō'ȧh said unto the angel
of the LORD, What *is* thy name, that
when thy sayings come to pass we may
do thee honor?
18 And the angel of the LORD said unto
him, Why askest thou thus after my
name, seeing it *is* secret?
19 So Mȧ-nō'ȧh took a kid with a meat
offering, and offered *it* upon a rock unto
the LORD: and *the angel* did wondrously;
and Mȧ-nō'ȧh and his wife looked on.
20 For it came to pass, when the flame
went up toward heaven from off the
altar, that the angel of the LORD ascended in the flame of the altar: and
Mȧ-nō'ȧh and his wife looked on *it,* and
fell on their faces to the ground.
21 But the angel of the LORD did no
more appear to Mȧ-nō'ȧh and to his
wife. Then Mȧ-nō'ȧh knew that he *was*
an angel of the LORD.
22 And Mȧ-nō'ȧh said unto his wife,
We shall surely die, because we have
seen God.

23 But his wife said unto him, If the LORD were pleased to kill us, he would not have received a burnt offering and a meat offering at our hands, neither would he have showed us all these *things*, nor would as at this time have told us *such things* as these.

24 ¶ And the woman bare a son, and called his name Samson: and the child grew, and the LORD blessed him.

25 And the Spirit of the LORD began to move him at times in the camp of Dan between Zō'răh and Ĕsh'tā-ŏl.

CHAPTER 14

AND Samson went down to Tĭm'năth, and saw a woman in Tĭm'năth of the daughters of the Phĭ-lĭs'tĭneș.

2 And he came up, and told his father and his mother, and said, I have seen a woman in Tĭm'năth of the daughters of the Phĭ-lĭs'tĭneș: now therefore get her for me to wife.

3 Then his father and his mother said unto him, *Is there* never a woman among the daughters of thy brethren, or among all my people, that thou goest to take a wife of the uncircumcised Phĭ-lĭs'tĭneș? And Samson said unto his father, Get her for me; for she pleaseth me well.

4 But his father and his mother knew not that it *was* of the LORD, that he sought an occasion against the Phĭ-lĭs'tĭneș: for at that time the Phĭ-lĭs'tĭneș had dominion over Ĭș'rā-ĕl.

5 ¶ Then went Samson down, and his father and his mother, to Tĭm'năth, and came to the vineyards of Tĭm'năth: and, behold, a young lion roared against him.

6 And the Spirit of the LORD came mightily upon him, and he rent him as he would have rent a kid, and *he had* nothing in his hand: but he told not his father or his mother what he had done.

7 And he went down, and talked with the woman; and she pleased Samson well.

8 ¶ And after a time he returned to take her, and he turned aside to see the carcass of the lion: and, behold, *there was* a swarm of bees and honey in the carcass of the lion.

9 And he took thereof in his hands, and went on eating, and came to his father and mother, and he gave them, and they did eat: but he told not them that he had taken the honey out of the carcass of the lion.

10 ¶ So his father went down unto the woman: and Samson made there a feast; for so used the young men to do.

11 And it came to pass, when they saw him, that they brought thirty companions to be with him.

12 ¶ And Samson said unto them, I will now put forth a riddle unto you: if ye can certainly declare it me within the seven days of the feast, and find *it* out, then I will give you thirty sheets and thirty change of garments:

13 But if ye cannot declare *it* me, then shall ye give me thirty sheets and thirty change of garments. And they said unto him, Put forth thy riddle, that we may hear it.

14 And he said unto them, Out of the eater came forth meat, and out of the strong came forth sweetness. And they could not in three days expound the riddle.

15 And it came to pass on the seventh day, that they said unto Samson's wife, Entice thy husband, that he may declare unto us the riddle, lest we burn thee and thy father's house with fire: have ye called us to take that we have? *is it* not *so?*

16 And Samson's wife wept before him, and said, Thou dost but hate me, and lovest me not: thou hast put forth a riddle unto the children of my people, and hast not told *it* me. And he said unto her, Behold, I have not told *it* my father nor my mother, and shall I tell *it* thee?

17 And she wept before him the seven days, while their feast lasted: and it came to pass on the seventh day, that he told her, because she lay sore upon him: and she told the riddle to the children of her people.

18 And the men of the city said unto him on the seventh day before the sun went down, What *is* sweeter than honey? and what *is* stronger than a lion? And he said unto them, If ye had not plowed with my heifer, ye had not found out my riddle.

19 ¶ And the Spirit of the LORD came upon him, and he went down to Ăsh'kē-lŏn, and slew thirty men of them, and took their spoil, and gave change of garments unto them which expounded the

riddle. And his anger was kindled, and
he went up to his father's house.
20 But Samson's wife was *given* to his
companion, whom he had used as his
friend.

CHAPTER 15

BUT it came to pass within a while
after, in the time of wheat harvest,
that Samson visited his wife with a kid;
and he said, I will go in to my wife into
the chamber. But her father would not
suffer him to go in.
2 And her father said, I verily thought
that thou hadst utterly hated her; therefore I gave her to thy companion: *is* not
her younger sister fairer than she? take
her, I pray thee, instead of her.
3 ¶ And Samson said concerning them,
Now shall I be more blameless than the
Phĭ-lĭs′tĭneş, though I do them a displeasure.
4 And Samson went and caught three
hundred foxes, and took firebrands, and
turned tail to tail, and put a firebrand in
the midst between two tails.
5 And when he had set the brands on
fire, he let *them* go into the standing
corn of the Phĭ-lĭs′tĭneş, and burnt up
both the shocks, and also the standing
corn, with the vineyards *and* olives.
6 ¶ Then the Phĭ-lĭs′tĭneş said, Who
hath done this? And they answered,
Samson, the son-in-law of the Tĭm′nīte,
because he had taken his wife, and given
her to his companion. And the Phĭ-lĭs′-
tĭneş came up, and burnt her and her
father with fire.
7 ¶ And Samson said unto them,
Though ye have done this, yet will I be
avenged of you, and after that I will
cease.
8 And he smote them hip and thigh
with a great slaughter: and he went
down and dwelt in the top of the rock
Ē′tăm.
9 ¶ Then the Phĭ-lĭs′tĭneş went up,
and pitched in Judah, and spread themselves in Lē′hī.
10 And the men of Judah said, Why
are ye come up against us? And they
answered, To bind Samson are we come
up, to do to him as he hath done to us.
11 Then three thousand men of Judah
went to the top of the rock Ē′tăm, and
said to Samson, Knowest thou not that
the Phĭ-lĭs′tĭneş *are* rulers over us?
what *is* this *that* thou hast done unto us?
And he said unto them, As they did unto
me, so have I done unto them.
12 And they said unto him, We are
come down to bind thee, that we may
deliver thee into the hand of the Phĭ-
lĭs′tĭneş. And Samson said unto them,
Swear unto me, that ye will not fall upon
me yourselves.
13 And they spake unto him, saying,
No; but we will bind thee fast, and deliver thee into their hand: but surely we
will not kill thee. And they bound him
with two new cords, and brought him up
from the rock.
14 ¶ *And* when he came unto Lē′hī,
the Phĭ-lĭs′tĭneş shouted against him:
and the Spirit of the LORD came
mightily upon him, and the cords that
were upon his arms became as flax that
was burnt with fire, and his bands
loosed from off his hands.
15 And he found a new jawbone of an
ass, and put forth his hand, and took it,
and slew a thousand men therewith.
16 And Samson said, With the jawbone
of an ass, heaps upon heaps, with the
jaw of an ass have I slain a thousand
men.
17 And it came to pass, when he had
made an end of speaking, that he cast
away the jawbone out of his hand, and
called that place Rā′măth–lē′hī.
18 ¶ And he was sore athirst, and called
on the LORD, and said, Thou hast given
this great deliverance into the hand of
thy servant: and now shall I die for
thirst, and fall into the hand of the uncircumcised?
19 But God clave a hollow place that
was in the jaw, and there came water
thereout; and when he had drunk, his
spirit came again, and he revived:
wherefore he called the name thereof
Ĕn–hăk′kō-rē, which *is* in Lē′hī unto
this day.
20 And he judged Ĭş′rā-ĕl in the days
of the Phĭ-lĭs′tĭneş twenty years.

CHAPTER 16

THEN went Samson to Gā′zȧ, and
saw there a harlot, and went in
unto her.
2 *And it was told* the Gā′zītes, saying,
Samson is come hither. And they compassed *him* in, and laid wait for him all
night in the gate of the city, and were
quiet all the night, saying, In the morning, when it is day, we shall kill him.

3 And Samson lay till midnight, and arose at midnight, and took the doors of the gate of the city, and the two posts, and went away with them, bar and all, and put *them* upon his shoulders, and carried them up to the top of a hill that *is* before Hē′brȯn.

4 ℂ And it came to pass afterward, that he loved a woman in the valley of Sō′rĕk, whose name *was* Dē-lī′lȧh.

5 And the lords of the Phĭ-lĭs′tĭneş came up unto her, and said unto her, Entice him, and see wherein his great strength *lieth*, and by what *means* we may prevail against him, that we may bind him to afflict him: and we will give thee every one of us eleven hundred *pieces* of silver.

6 ℂ And Dē-lī′lȧh said to Samson, Tell me, I pray thee, wherein thy great strength *lieth*, and wherewith thou mightest be bound to afflict thee.

7 And Samson said unto her, If they bind me with seven green withes that were never dried, then shall I be weak, and be as another man.

8 Then the lords of the Phĭ-lĭs′tĭneş brought up to her seven green withes which had not been dried, and she bound him with them.

9 Now *there were* men lying in wait, abiding with her in the chamber. And she said unto him, The Phĭ-lĭs′tĭneş *be* upon thee, Samson. And he brake the withes, as a thread of tow is broken when it toucheth the fire. So his strength was not known.

10 And Dē-lī′lȧh said unto Samson, Behold, thou hast mocked me, and told me lies: now tell me, I pray thee, wherewith thou mightest be bound.

11 And he said unto her, If they bind me fast with new ropes that never were occupied, then shall I be weak, and be as another man.

12 Dē-lī′lȧh therefore took new ropes, and bound him therewith, and said unto him, The Phĭ-lĭs′tĭneş *be* upon thee, Samson. And *there were* liers in wait abiding in the chamber. And he brake them from off his arms like a thread.

13 And Dē-lī′lȧh said unto Samson, Hitherto thou hast mocked me, and told me lies: tell me wherewith thou mightest be bound. And he said unto her, If thou weavest the seven locks of my head with the web.

14 And she fastened *it* with the pin, and said unto him, The Phĭ-lĭs′tĭneş *be* upon thee, Samson. And he awaked out of his sleep, and went away with the pin of the beam, and with the web.

15 ℂ And she said unto him, How canst thou say, I love thee, when thine heart *is* not with me? Thou hast mocked me these three times, and hast not told me wherein thy great strength *lieth*.

16 And it came to pass, when she pressed him daily with her words, and urged him, *so* that his soul was vexed unto death;

17 That he told her all his heart, and said unto her, There hath not come a razor upon mine head; for I *have been* a Nazarite unto God from my mother's womb: if I be shaven, then my strength will go from me, and I shall become weak, and be like any *other* man.

18 And when Dē-lī′lȧh saw that he had told her all his heart, she sent and called for the lords of the Phĭ-lĭs′tĭneş, saying, Come up this once, for he hath showed me all his heart. Then the lords of the Phĭ-lĭs′tĭneş came up unto her, and brought money in their hand.

19 And she made him sleep upon her knees; and she called for a man, and she caused him to shave off the seven locks of his head; and she began to afflict him, and his strength went from him.

20 And she said, The Phĭ-lĭs′tĭneş *be* upon thee, Samson. And he awoke out of his sleep, and said, I will go out as at other times before, and shake myself. And he wist not that the LORD was departed from him.

21 ℂ But the Phĭ-lĭs′tĭneş took him, and put out his eyes, and brought him down to Gā′zȧ, and bound him with fetters of brass; and he did grind in the prison house.

22 Howbeit the hair of his head began to grow again after he was shaven.

23 Then the lords of the Phĭ-lĭs′tĭneş gathered them together for to offer a great sacrifice unto Dā′gŏn their god, and to rejoice: for they said, Our god hath delivered Samson our enemy into our hand.

24 And when the people saw him, they praised their god: for they said, Our god hath delivered into our hands our enemy, and the destroyer of our country, which slew many of us.

25 And it came to pass, when their

hearts were merry, that they said, Call for Samson, that he may make us sport. And they called for Samson out of the prison house; and he made them sport: and they set him between the pillars.

26 And Samson said unto the lad that held him by the hand, Suffer me that I may feel the pillars whereupon the house standeth, that I may lean upon them.

27 Now the house was full of men and women; and all the lords of the Phĭ-lĭs′tĭneş *were* there; and *there were* upon the roof about three thousand men and women, that beheld while Samson made sport.

28 And Samson called unto the LORD, and said, O Lord GOD, remember me, I pray thee, and strengthen me, I pray thee, only this once, O God, that I may be at once avenged of the Phĭ-lĭs′tĭneş for my two eyes.

29 And Samson took hold of the two middle pillars upon which the house stood, and on which it was borne up, of the one with his right hand, and of the other with his left.

30 And Samson said, Let me die with the Phĭ-lĭs′tĭneş. And he bowed himself with *all his* might; and the house fell upon the lords, and upon all the people that *were* therein. So the dead which he slew at his death were more than *they* which he slew in his life.

31 Then his brethren and all the house of his father came down, and took him, and brought *him* up, and buried him between Zō′răh and Ĕsh′tā-ŏl in the buryingplace of Mȧ-nō′ăh his father. And he judged Ĭş′rā-ĕl twenty years.

CHAPTER 17

AND there was a man of mount Ē′phrā-ĭm, whose name *was* Mī′căh.

2 And he said unto his mother, The eleven hundred *shekels* of silver that were taken from thee, about which thou cursedst, and spakest of also in mine ears, behold, the silver *is* with me; I took it. And his mother said, Blessed *be thou* of the LORD, my son.

3 And when he had restored the eleven hundred *shekels* of silver to his mother, his mother said, I had wholly dedicated the silver unto the LORD from my hand for my son, to make a graven image and a molten image: now therefore I will restore it unto thee.

4 Yet he restored the money unto his mother; and his mother took two hundred *shekels* of silver, and gave them to the founder, who made thereof a graven image and a molten image: and they were in the house of Mī′căh.

5 And the man Mī′căh had a house of gods, and made an ĕph′ŏd, and teraphim, and consecrated one of his sons, who became his priest.

6 In those days *there was* no king in Ĭş′rā-ĕl, *but* every man did *that which was* right in his own eyes.

7 ℭ And there was a young man out of Beth-lehem-judah of the family of Judah, who *was* a Lē′vīte, and he sojourned there.

8 And the man departed out of the city from Beth-lehem-judah to sojourn where he could find *a place:* and he came to mount Ē′phrā-ĭm to the house of Mī′căh, as he journeyed.

9 And Mī′căh said unto him, Whence comest thou? And he said unto him, I *am* a Lē′vīte of Beth-lehem-judah, and I go to sojourn where I may find *a place*.

10 And Mī′căh said unto him, Dwell with me, and be unto me a father and a priest, and I will give thee ten *shekels* of silver by the year, and a suit of apparel, and thy victuals. So the Lē′vīte went in.

11 And the Lē′vīte was content to dwell with the man; and the young man was unto him aş one of his sons.

12 And Mī′căh consecrated the Lē′vīte; and the young man became his priest, and was in the house of Mī′căh.

13 Then said Mī′căh, Now know I that the LORD will do me good, seeing I have a Lē′vīte to *my* priest.

CHAPTER 18

IN those days *there was* no king in Ĭş′rā-ĕl: and in those days the tribe of the Dăn′ītes sought them an inheritance to dwell in; for unto that day *all their* inheritance had not fallen unto them among the tribes of Ĭş′rā-ĕl.

2 And the children of Dan sent of their family five men from their coasts, men of valor, from Zō′răh, and from Ĕsh′tā-ŏl, to spy out the land, and to search it; and they said unto them, Go, search the land: who when they came to mount

Ē′phră-ĭm, to the house of Mī′cȧh, they
lodged there.
3 When they *were* by the house of
Mī′cȧh, they knew the voice of the young
man the Lē′vīte: and they turned in
thither, and said unto him, Who brought
thee hither? and what makest thou in
this *place?* and what hast thou here?
4 And he said unto them, Thus and
thus dealeth Mī′cȧh with me, and hath
hired me, and I am his priest.
5 And they said unto him, Ask counsel, we pray thee, of God, that we may
know whether our way which we go
shall be prosperous.
6 And the priest said unto them, Go in
peace: before the LORD *is* your way
wherein ye go.
7 ¶ Then the five men departed, and
came to Lā′ĭsh, and saw the people that
were therein, how they dwelt careless,
after the manner of the Zī-dō′nĭ-ăns,
quiet and secure; and *there was* no
magistrate in the land, that might put
them to shame in *any* thing; and they
were far from the Zī-dō′nĭ-ăns, and had
no business with *any* man.
8 And they came unto their brethren to
Zō′rȧh and Ĕsh′tā-ŏl: and their brethren
said unto them, What *say* ye?
9 And they said, Arise, that we may go
up against them: for we have seen the
land, and, behold, it *is* very good: and
are ye still? be not slothful to go, *and* to
enter to possess the land.
10 When ye go, ye shall come unto a
people secure, and to a large land: for
God hath given it into your hands; a
place where *there is* no want of any
thing that *is* in the earth.
11 ¶ And there went from thence
of the family of the Dăn′ītes, out of
Zo′rȧh and out of Ĕsh′tā-ŏl, six hundred men appointed with weapons of
war.
12 And they went up, and pitched in
Kĭr′jăth–jē′ȧ-rĭm, in Judah: wherefore
they called that place Mā′hȧ-nĕh–dăn′
unto this day: behold, *it is* behind Kĭr′-
jăth–jē′ȧ-rĭm.
13 And they passed thence unto mount
Ē′phră-ĭm, and came unto the house of
Mī′cȧh.
14 ¶ Then answered the five men that
went to spy out the country of Lā′ĭsh,
and said unto their brethren, Do ye
know that there is in these houses an
ĕph′ŏd, and teraphim, and a graven
image, and a molten image? now therefore consider what ye have to do.
15 And they turned thitherward, and
came to the house of the young man the
Lē′vīte, *even* unto the house of Mī′cȧh,
and saluted him.
16 And the six hundred men appointed
with their weapons of war, which *were*
of the children of Dan, stood by the
entering of the gate.
17 And the five men that went to spy
out the land went up, *and* came in
thither, *and* took the graven image, and
the ĕph′ŏd, and the teraphim, and the
molten image: and the priest stood in the
entering of the gate with the six hundred
men *that were* appointed with weapons
of war.
18 And these went into Mī′cȧh's house,
and fetched the carved image, the
ĕph′ŏd, and the teraphim, and the
molten image. Then said the priest unto them, What do ye?
19 And they said unto him, Hold thy
peace, lay thine hand upon thy mouth,
and go with us, and be to us a father and
a priest: *is it* better for thee to be a priest
unto the house of one man, or that thou
be a priest unto a tribe and a family in
Ĭs′rā-ĕl?
20 And the priest's heart was glad, and
he took the ĕph′ŏd, and the teraphim,
and the graven image, and went in the
midst of the people.
21 So they turned and departed, and
put the little ones and the cattle and the
carriage before them.
22 ¶ *And* when they were a good way
from the house of Mī′cȧh, the men that
were in the houses near to Mī′cȧh's
house were gathered together, and overtook the children of Dan.
23 And they cried unto the children of
Dan. And they turned their faces, and
said unto Mī′cȧh, What aileth thee, that
thou comest with such a company?
24 And he said, Ye have taken away
my gods which I made, and the priest,
and ye are gone away: and what have I
more? and what *is* this *that* ye say unto
me, What aileth thee?
25 And the children of Dan said unto
him, Let not thy voice be heard among
us, lest angry fellows run upon thee, and
thou lose thy life, with the lives of thy
household.
26 And the children of Dan went their
way: and when Mī′cȧh saw that they

were too strong for him, he turned and
went back unto his house.
27 And they took *the things* which
Mī′cȧh had made, and the priest which
he had, and came unto Lā′ĭsh, unto a
people *that were* at quiet and secure:
and they smote them with the edge of
the sword, and burnt the city with fire.
28 And *there was* no deliverer, because
it *was* far from Zī′dŏn, and they had no
business with *any* man; and it was in the
valley that *lieth* by Bĕth′–rē′hŏb. And
they built a city, and dwelt therein.
29 And they called the name of the city
Dan, after the name of Dan their father,
who was born unto Ĭs̱′rā-ĕl: howbeit the
name of the city *was* Lā′ĭsh at the first.
30 ¶ And the children of Dan set up
the graven image: and Jonathan, the
son of Gĕr′shŏm, the son of Mȧ-năs′sĕh,
he and his sons were priests to the tribe
of Dan until the day of the captivity of
the land.
31 And they set them up Mī′cȧh's
graven image, which he made, all the
time that the house of God was in
Shī′lōh.

CHAPTER 19

AND it came to pass in those days,
when *there was* no king in Ĭs̱′rā-ĕl,
that there was a certain Lē′vīte sojourning on the side of mount Ē′phrā-ĭm, who
took to him a concubine out of Beth-
lehem-judah.
2 And his concubine played the whore
against him, and went away from him
unto her father's house to Beth-lehem-
judah, and was there four whole months.
3 And her husband arose, and went
after her, to speak friendly unto her,
and to bring her again, having his servant with him, and a couple of asses: and
she brought him into her father's house;
and when the father of the damsel saw
him, he rejoiced to meet him.
4 And his father-in-law, the damsel's
father, retained him; and he abode with
him three days: so they did eat and
drink, and lodged there.
5 ¶ And it came to pass on the fourth
day, when they arose early in the morning, that he rose up to depart: and the
damsel's father said unto his son-in-
law, Comfort thine heart with a morsel
of bread, and afterward go your way.
6 And they sat down, and did eat and
drink both of them together: for the
damsel's father had said unto the man,
Be content, I pray thee, and tarry all
night, and let thine heart be merry.
7 And when the man rose up to depart,
his father-in-law urged him: therefore
he lodged there again.
8 And he arose early in the morning on
the fifth day to depart: and the damsel's
father said, Comfort thine heart, I pray
thee. And they tarried until afternoon,
and they did eat both of them.
9 And when the man rose up to depart,
he, and his concubine, and his servant,
his father-in-law, the damsel's father,
said unto him, Behold, now the day
draweth toward evening, I pray you
tarry all night: behold, the day groweth
to an end, lodge here, that thine heart
may be merry; and to-morrow get you
early on your way, that thou mayest go
home.
10 But the man would not tarry that
night, but he rose up and departed, and
came over against Jē′bŭs, which *is*
Jerusalem; and *there were* with him two
asses saddled, his concubine also *was*
with him.
11 *And* when they *were* by Jē′bŭs, the
day was far spent; and the servant said
unto his master, Come, I pray thee, and
let us turn in into this city of the Jĕb′ū-
s̱ītes, and lodge in it.
12 And his master said unto him, We
will not turn aside hither into the city of
a stranger, that *is* not of the children of
Ĭs̱′rā-ĕl; we will pass over to Gĭb′ē-ȧh.
13 And he said unto his servant, Come,
and let us draw near to one of these
places to lodge all night, in Gĭb′ē-ȧh, or
in Rā′mȧh.
14 And they passed on and went their
way; and the sun went down upon them
when they were by Gĭb′ē-ȧh, which *belongeth* to Benjamin.
15 And they turned aside thither, to go
in *and* to lodge in Gĭb′ē-ȧh: and when
he went in, he sat him down in a street
of the city: for *there was* no man that
took them into his house to lodging.
16 ¶ And, behold, there came an old
man from his work out of the field at
even, which *was* also of mount Ē′phrā-
ĭm; and he sojourned in Gĭb′ē-ȧh: but
the men of the place *were* Benjamites.
17 And when he had lifted up his eyes,
he saw a wayfaring man in the street of
the city: and the old man said, Whither
goest thou? and whence comest thou?

18 And he said unto him, We *are* passing from Beth-lehem-judah toward the side of mount Ē′phrā-ĭm; from thence *am* I: and I went to Beth-lehem-judah, but I *am now* going to the house of the LORD; and there *is* no man that receiveth me to house.

19 Yet there is both straw and provender for our asses; and there is bread and wine also for me, and for thy handmaid, and for the young man *which is* with thy servants: *there is* no want of any thing.

20 And the old man said, Peace *be* with thee; howsoever, *let* all thy wants *lie* upon me; only lodge not in the street.

21 So he brought him into his house, and gave provender unto the asses: and they washed their feet, and did eat and drink.

22 ¶ *Now* as they were making their hearts merry, behold, the men of the city, certain sons of Bē′lĭ-ăl, beset the house round about, *and* beat at the door, and spake to the master of the house, the old man, saying, Bring forth the man that came into thine house, that we may know him.

23 And the man, the master of the house, went out unto them, and said unto them, Nay, my brethren, *nay,* I pray you, do not *so* wickedly; seeing that this man is come into mine house, do not this folly.

24 Behold, *here is* my daughter a maiden, and his concubine; them I will bring out now, and humble ye them, and do with them what seemeth good unto you: but unto this man do not so vile a thing.

25 But the men would not hearken to him: so the man took his concubine, and brought her forth unto them; and they knew her, and abused her all the night until the morning: and when the day began to spring, they let her go.

26 Then came the woman in the dawning of the day, and fell down at the door of the man's house where her lord *was,* till it was light.

27 And her lord rose up in the morning, and opened the doors of the house, and went out to go his way: and, behold, the woman his concubine was fallen down *at* the door of the house, and her hands *were* upon the threshold.

28 And he said unto her, Up, and let us be going. But none answered. Then the man took her *up* upon an ass, and the man rose up, and gat him unto his place.

29 ¶ And when he was come into his house, he took a knife, and laid hold on his concubine, and divided her, *together* with her bones, into twelve pieces, and sent her into all the coasts of Ĭş′rā-ĕl.

30 And it was so, that all that saw it said, There was no such deed done nor seen from the day that the children of Ĭş′rā-ĕl came up out of the land of Egypt unto this day: consider of it, take advice, and speak *your minds.*

CHAPTER 20

THEN all the children of Ĭş′rā-ĕl went out, and the congregation was gathered together as one man, from Dan even to Bē′ĕr–shē′bȧ, with the land of Gĭl′ē-ăd, unto the LORD in Mĭz′pĕh.

2 And the chief of all the people, *even* of all the tribes of Ĭş′rā-ĕl, presented themselves in the assembly of the people of God, four hundred thousand footmen that drew sword.

3 (Now the children of Benjamin heard that the children of Ĭş′rā-ĕl were gone up to Mĭz′pĕh.) Then said the children of Ĭş′rā-ĕl, Tell *us,* how was this wickedness?

4 And the Lē′vīte, the husband of the woman that was slain, answered and said, I came into Gĭb′ē-ȧh that *belongeth* to Benjamin, I and my concubine, to lodge.

5 And the men of Gĭb′ē-ȧh rose against me, and beset the house round about upon me by night, *and* thought to have slain me: and my concubine have they forced, that she is dead.

6 And I took my concubine, and cut her in pieces, and sent her throughout all the country of the inheritance of Ĭş′rā-ĕl: for they have committed lewdness and folly in Ĭş′rā-ĕl.

7 Behold, ye *are* all children of Ĭş′rā-ĕl; give here your advice and counsel.

8 ¶ And all the people arose as one man, saying, We will not any *of us* go to his tent, neither will we any *of us* turn into his house.

9 But now this *shall be* the thing which we will do to Gĭb′ē-ȧh; *we will go up* by lot against it;

10 And we will take ten men of a hundred throughout all the tribes of Ĭş′rā-ĕl,

and a hundred of a thousand, and a thousand out of ten thousand, to fetch victuals for the people, that they may do, when they come to Gĭb′ē-ȧh of Benjamin, according to all the folly that they have wrought in Ĭş′rā-ĕl.

11 So all the men of Ĭş′rā-ĕl were gathered against the city, knit together as one man.

12 ¶ And the tribes of Ĭş′rā-ĕl sent men through all the tribe of Benjamin, saying, What wickedness *is* this that is done among you?

13 Now therefore deliver *us* the men, the children of Bē′lĭ-ăl, which *are* in Gĭb′ē-ȧh, that we may put them to death, and put away evil from Ĭş′rā-ĕl. But the children of Benjamin would not hearken to the voice of their brethren the children of Ĭş′rā-ĕl:

14 But the children of Benjamin gathered themselves together out of the cities unto Gĭb′ē-ȧh, to go out to battle against the children of Ĭş′rā-ĕl.

15 And the children of Benjamin were numbered at that time out of the cities twenty and six thousand men that drew sword, besides the inhabitants of Gĭb′ē-ȧh, which were numbered seven hundred chosen men.

16 Among all this people *there were* seven hundred chosen men left-handed; every one could sling stones at a hair *breadth*, and not miss.

17 And the men of Ĭş′rā-ĕl, besides Benjamin, were numbered four hundred thousand men that drew sword: all these *were* men of war.

18 ¶ And the children of Ĭş′rā-ĕl arose, and went up to the house of God, and asked counsel of God, and said, Which of us shall go up first to the battle against the children of Benjamin? And the LORD said, Judah *shall go up* first.

19 And the children of Ĭş′rā-ĕl rose up in the morning, and encamped against Gĭb′ē-ȧh.

20 And the men of Ĭş′rā-ĕl went out to battle against Benjamin; and the men of Ĭş′rā-ĕl put themselves in array to fight against them at Gĭb′ē-ȧh.

21 And the children of Benjamin came forth out of Gĭb′ē-ȧh, and destroyed down to the ground of the Ĭş′rā-ĕl-ītes that day twenty and two thousand men.

22 And the people, the men of Ĭş′rā-ĕl, encouraged themselves, and set their battle again in array in the place where they put themselves in array the first day.

23 (And the children of Ĭş′rā-ĕl went up and wept before the LORD until even, and asked counsel of the LORD, saying, Shall I go up again to battle against the children of Benjamin my brother? And the LORD said, Go up against him.)

24 And the children of Ĭş′rā-ĕl came near against the children of Benjamin the second day.

25 And Benjamin went forth against them out of Gĭb′ē-ȧh the second day, and destroyed down to the ground of the children of Ĭş′rā-ĕl again eighteen thousand men; all these drew the sword.

26 ¶ Then all the children of Ĭş′rā-ĕl, and all the people, went up, and came unto the house of God, and wept, and sat there before the LORD, and fasted that day until even, and offered burnt offerings and peace offerings before the LORD.

27 And the children of Ĭş′rā-ĕl inquired of the LORD, (for the ark of the covenant of God *was* there in those days,

28 And Phĭn′ē-hăs, the son of Ĕl′ē-ā′zȧr, the son of Aaron, stood before it in those days,) saying, Shall I yet again go out to battle against the children of Benjamin my brother, or shall I cease? And the LORD said, Go up; for to-morrow I will deliver them into thine hand.

29 And Ĭş′rā-ĕl set liers in wait round about Gĭb′ē-ȧh.

30 And the children of Ĭş′rā-ĕl went up against the children of Benjamin on the third day, and put themselves in array against Gĭb′ē-ȧh, as at other times.

31 And the children of Benjamin went out against the people, *and* were drawn away from the city; and they began to smite of the people, *and* kill, as at other times, in the highways, of which one goeth up to the house of God, and the other to Gĭb′ē-ȧh in the field, about thirty men of Ĭş′rā-ĕl.

32 And the children of Benjamin said, They *are* smitten down before us, as at the first. But the children of Ĭş′rā-ĕl said, Let us flee, and draw them from the city unto the highways.

33 And all the men of Ĭş′rā-ĕl rose up out of their place, and put themselves in array at Bā′ăl–tā′mär: and the liers in wait of Ĭş′rā-ĕl came forth out of their places, *even* out of the meadows of Gĭb′ē-ȧh.

34 And there came against Gĭb′ē-ȧh
ten thousand chosen men out of all
Ĭş′rā-ĕl, and the battle was sore: but
they knew not that evil *was* near them.
35 And the LORD smote Benjamin before
Ĭş′rā-ĕl: and the children of Ĭş′rā-ĕl
destroyed of the Benjamites that day
twenty and five thousand and a hundred
men: all these drew the sword.
36 So the children of Benjamin saw
that they were smitten: for the men of
Ĭş′rā-ĕl gave place to the Benjamites,
because they trusted unto the liers in
wait which they had set beside Gĭb′ē-ȧh.
37 And the liers in wait hasted, and
rushed upon Gĭb′ē-ȧh; and the liers
in wait drew *themselves* along, and
smote all the city with the edge of the
sword.
38 Now there was an appointed sign
between the men of Ĭş′rā-ĕl and the
liers in wait, that they should make a
great flame with smoke rise up out of
the city.
39 And when the men of Ĭş′rā-ĕl retired
in the battle, Benjamin began to smite
and kill of the men of Ĭş′rā-ĕl about
thirty persons: for they said, Surely they
are smitten down before us, as *in* the
first battle.
40 But when the flame began to arise
up out of the city with a pillar of smoke,
the Benjamites looked behind them,
and, behold, the flame of the city
ascended up to heaven.
41 And when the men of Ĭş′rā-ĕl turned
again, the men of Benjamin were
amazed: for they saw that evil was come
upon them.
42 Therefore they turned *their backs*
before the men of Ĭş′rā-ĕl unto the
way of the wilderness; but the battle
overtook them; and them which *came*
out of the cities they destroyed in the
midst of them.
43 *Thus* they inclosed the Benjamites
round about, *and* chased them, *and*
trode them down with ease over against
Gĭb′ē-ȧh toward the sunrising.
44 And there fell of Benjamin eighteen
thousand men; all these *were* men of
valor.
45 And they turned and fled toward the
wilderness unto the rock of Rĭm′mŏn:
and they gleaned of them in the highways
five thousand men; and pursued
hard after them unto Gī′dŏm, and slew
two thousand men of them.
46 So that all which fell that day of
Benjamin were twenty and five thousand
men that drew the sword; all these
were men of valor.
47 But six hundred men turned and
fled to the wilderness unto the rock
Rĭm′mŏn, and abode in the rock Rĭm′mŏn
four months.
48 And the men of Ĭş′rā-ĕl turned again
upon the children of Benjamin, and
smote them with the edge of the sword,
as well the men of *every* city, as the
beast, and all that came to hand: also
they set on fire all the cities that they
came to.

CHAPTER 21

NOW the men of Ĭş′rā-ĕl had sworn
in Mĭz′pĕh, saying, There shall
not any of us give his daughter unto Benjamin
to wife.
2 And the people came to the house of
God, and abode there till even before
God, and lifted up their voices, and wept
sore;
3 And said, O LORD God of Ĭş′rā-ĕl,
why is this come to pass in Ĭş′rā-ĕl, that
there should be to-day one tribe lacking
in Ĭş′rā-ĕl?
4 And it came to pass on the morrow,
that the people rose early, and built
there an altar, and offered burnt offerings
and peace offerings.
5 And the children of Ĭş′rā-ĕl said, Who
is there among all the tribes of Ĭş′rā-ĕl
that came not up with the congregation
unto the LORD? For they had made a
great oath concerning him that came not
up to the LORD to Mĭz′pĕh, saying, He
shall surely be put to death.
6 And the children of Ĭş′rā-ĕl repented
them for Benjamin their brother, and
said, There is one tribe cut off from
Ĭş′rā-ĕl this day.
7 How shall we do for wives for them
that remain, seeing we have sworn by
the LORD, that we will not give them of
our daughters to wives?
8 ¶ And they said, What one *is there*
of the tribes of Ĭş′rā-ĕl that came not up
to Mĭz′pĕh to the LORD? And, behold,
there came none to the camp from
Jā′bĕsh-gĭl′ē-ăd to the assembly.
9 For the people were numbered, and,
behold, *there were* none of the inhabitants
of Jā′bĕsh-gĭl′ē-ăd there.
10 And the congregation sent thither
twelve thousand men of the valiantest,

and commanded them, saying, Go and smite the inhabitants of Jā'bĕsh–gĭl'ē-ăd with the edge of the sword, with the women and the children.

11 And this *is* the thing that ye shall do, Ye shall utterly destroy every male, and every woman that hath lain by man.

12 And they found among the inhabitants of Jā'bĕsh–gĭl'ē-ăd four hundred young virgins, that had known no man by lying with any male: and they brought them unto the camp to Shī'lōh, which *is* in the land of Cā'năan.

13 And the whole congregation sent *some* to speak to the children of Benjamin that *were* in the rock Rĭm'mŏn, and to call peaceably unto them.

14 And Benjamin came again at that time; and they gave them wives which they had saved alive of the women of Jā'bĕsh–gĭl'ē-ăd: and yet so they sufficed them not.

15 And the people repented them for Benjamin, because that the LORD had made a breach in the tribes of Ĭş'rā-ĕl.

16 ¶ Then the elders of the congregation said, How shall we do for wives for them that remain, seeing the women are destroyed out of Benjamin?

17 And they said, *There must be* an inheritance for them that be escaped of Benjamin, that a tribe be not destroyed out of Ĭş'rā-ĕl.

18 Howbeit we may not give them wives of our daughters: for the children of Ĭş'rā-ĕl have sworn, saying, Cursed *be* he that giveth a wife to Benjamin.

19 Then they said, Behold, *there is* a feast of the LORD in Shī'lōh yearly, *in a place* which *is* on the north side of Beth-el, on the east side of the highway that goeth up from Beth-el to Shē'chĕm, and on the south of Lē-bō'nah.

20 Therefore they commanded the children of Benjamin, saying, Go and lie in wait in the vineyards;

21 And see, and, behold, if the daughters of Shī'lōh come out to dance in dances, then come ye out of the vineyards, and catch you every man his wife of the daughters of Shī'lōh, and go to the land of Benjamin.

22 And it shall be, when their fathers or their brethren come unto us to complain, that we will say unto them, Be favorable unto them for our sakes: because we reserved not to each man his wife in the war: for ye did not give unto them at this time, *that* ye should be guilty.

23 And the children of Benjamin did so, and took *them* wives, according to their number, of them that danced, whom they caught: and they went and returned unto their inheritance, and repaired the cities, and dwelt in them.

24 And the children of Ĭş'rā-ĕl departed thence at that time, every man to his tribe and to his family, and they went out from thence every man to his inheritance.

25 In those days *there was* no king in Ĭş'rā-ĕl: every man did *that which was* right in his own eyes.

THE BOOK OF RUTH

CHAPTER 1

NOW it came to pass in the days when the judges ruled, that there was a famine in the land. And a certain man of Beth-lehem-judah went to sojourn in the country of Mō'ăb, he, and his wife, and his two sons.

2 And the name of the man *was* Ē-lĭm'ē-lĕch, and the name of his wife Nā'ō-mī, and the name of his two sons Mäh'lŏn and Chĭl'ĭ-ŏn, Ĕph'răth-ītes of Beth-lehem-judah. And they came into the country of Mō'ăb, and continued there.

3 And Ē-lĭm'ē-lĕch Nā'ō-mī's husband died; and she was left, and her two sons.

4 And they took them wives of the women of Mō'ăb; the name of the one *was* Ôr'päh, and the name of the other Ruth: and they dwelt there about ten years.

5 And Mäh'lŏn and Chĭl'ĭ-ŏn died also both of them; and the woman was left of her two sons and her husband.

6 ¶ Then she arose with her daughters-in-law, that she might return from the country of Mō′ăb: for she had heard in the country of Mō′ăb how that the LORD had visited his people in giving them bread.

7 Wherefore she went forth out of the place where she was, and her two daughters-in-law with her; and they went on the way to return unto the land of Judah.

8 And Nā′ō-mī said unto her two daughters-in-law, Go, return each to her mother's house: the LORD deal kindly with you, as ye have dealt with the dead, and with me.

9 The LORD grant you that ye may find rest, each *of you* in the house of her husband. Then she kissed them; and they lifted up their voice, and wept.

10 And they said unto her, Surely we will return with thee unto thy people.

11 And Nā′ō-mī said, Turn again, my daughters: why will ye go with me? *are* there yet *any more* sons in my womb, that they may be your husbands?

12 Turn again, my daughters, go *your way;* for I am too old to have a husband. If I should say, I have hope, *if* I should have a husband also to-night, and should also bear sons;

13 Would ye tarry for them till they were grown? would ye stay for them from having husbands? nay, my daughters; for it grieveth me much for your sakes that the hand of the LORD is gone out against me.

14 And they lifted up their voice, and wept again: and Ôr′päh kissed her mother-in-law; but Ruth clave unto her.

15 And she said, Behold, thy sister-in-law is gone back unto her people, and unto her gods: return thou after thy sister-in-law.

16 And Ruth said, Entreat me not to leave thee, *or* to return from following after thee: for whither thou goest, I will go; and where thou lodgest, I will lodge: thy people *shall be* my people, and thy God my God:

17 Where thou diest, will I die, and there will I be buried: the LORD do so to me, and more also, *if aught* but death part thee and me.

18 When she saw that she was steadfastly minded to go with her, then she left speaking unto her.

19 ¶ So they two went until they came to Beth-lehem. And it came to pass, when they were come to Beth-lehem, that all the city was moved about them, and they said, *Is* this Nā′ō-mī?

20 And she said unto them, Call me not Nā′ō-mī, call me Mā′rȧ: for the Almighty hath dealt very bitterly with me.

21 I went out full, and the LORD hath brought me home again empty: why *then* call ye me Nā′ō-mī, seeing the LORD hath testified against me, and the Almighty hath afflicted me?

22 So Nā′ō-mī returned, and Ruth the Mō′ăb-īt′ĕss, her daughter-in-law, with her, which returned out of the country of Mō′ăb: and they came to Beth-lehem in the beginning of barley harvest.

CHAPTER 2

AND Nā′ō-mī had a kinsman of her husband's, a mighty man of wealth, of the family of Ē-lĭm′ē-lĕch; and his name *was* Boaz.

2 And Ruth the Mō′ăb-īt′ĕss said unto Nā′ō-mī, Let me now go to the field, and glean ears of corn after *him* in whose sight I shall find grace. And she said unto her, Go, my daughter.

3 And she went, and came, and gleaned in the field after the reapers: and her hap was to light on a part of the field *belonging* unto Boaz, who *was* of the kindred of Ē-lĭm′ē-lĕch.

4 ¶ And, behold, Boaz came from Beth-lehem, and said unto the reapers, The LORD *be* with you. And they answered him, The LORD bless thee.

5 Then said Boaz unto his servant that was set over the reapers, Whose damsel *is* this?

6 And the servant that was set over the reapers answered and said, It *is* the Mō′ăb-īt′ĭsh damsel that came back with Nā′ō-mī out of the country of Mō′ăb:

7 And she said, I pray you, let me glean and gather after the reapers among the sheaves: so she came, and hath continued even from the morning until now, that she tarried a little in the house.

8 Then said Boaz unto Ruth, Hearest thou not, my daughter? Go not to glean in another field, neither go from hence, but abide here fast by my maidens:

9 *Let* thine eyes *be* on the field that they do reap, and go thou after them: have I not charged the young men that

they shall not touch thee? and when thou art athirst, go unto the vessels, and drink of *that* which the young men have drawn.

10 Then she fell on her face, and bowed herself to the ground, and said unto him, Why have I found grace in thine eyes, that thou shouldest take knowledge of me, seeing I *am* a stranger?

11 And Boaz answered and said unto her, It hath fully been showed me, all that thou hast done unto thy mother-in-law since the death of thine husband; and *how* thou hast left thy father and thy mother, and the land of thy nativity, and art come unto a people which thou knewest not heretofore.

12 The LORD recompense thy work, and a full reward be given thee of the LORD God of Ĭṣ′rā-ĕl, under whose wings thou art come to trust.

13 Then she said, Let me find favor in thy sight, my lord; for that thou hast comforted me, and for that thou hast spoken friendly unto thine handmaid, though I be not like unto one of thine handmaidens.

14 And Boaz said unto her, At mealtime come thou hither, and eat of the bread, and dip thy morsel in the vinegar. And she sat beside the reapers: and he reached her parched *corn,* and she did eat, and was sufficed, and left.

15 And when she was risen up to glean, Boaz commanded his young men, saying, Let her glean even among the sheaves, and reproach her not:

16 And let fall also *some* of the handfuls of purpose for her, and leave *them,* that she may glean *them,* and rebuke her not.

17 So she gleaned in the field until even, and beat out that she had gleaned: and it was about an ē′phȧh of barley.

18 ¶ And she took *it* up, and went into the city; and her mother-in-law saw what she had gleaned: and she brought forth, and gave to her that she had reserved after she was sufficed.

19 And her mother-in-law said unto her, Where hast thou gleaned to-day? and where wroughtest thou? blessed be he that did take knowledge of thee. And she showed her mother-in-law with whom she had wrought, and said, The man's name with whom I wrought today *is* Boaz.

20 And Nā′ō-mī said unto her daughter-in-law, Blessed *be* he of the LORD, who hath not left off his kindness to the living and to the dead. And Nā′ō-mī said unto her, The man *is* near of kin unto us, one of our next kinsmen.

21 And Ruth the Mō′ăb-īt′ĕss said, He said unto me also, Thou shalt keep fast by my young men, until they have ended all my harvest.

22 And Nā′ō-mī said unto Ruth her daughter-in-law, *It is* good, my daughter, that thou go out with his maidens, that they meet thee not in any other field.

23 So she kept fast by the maidens of Boaz to glean unto the end of barley harvest and of wheat harvest; and dwelt with her mother-in-law.

CHAPTER 3

THEN Nā′ō-mī her mother-in-law said unto her, My daughter, shall I not seek rest for thee, that it may be well with thee?

2 And now *is* not Boaz of our kindred, with whose maidens thou wast? Behold, he winnoweth barley to-night in the threshingfloor.

3 Wash thyself therefore, and anoint thee, and put thy raiment upon thee, and get thee down to the floor: *but* make not thyself known unto the man, until he shall have done eating and drinking.

4 And it shall be, when he lieth down, that thou shalt mark the place where he shall lie, and thou shalt go in, and uncover his feet, and lay thee down; and he will tell thee what thou shalt do.

5 And she said unto her, All that thou sayest unto me I will do.

6 ¶ And she went down unto the floor, and did according to all that her mother-in-law bade her.

7 And when Boaz had eaten and drunk, and his heart was merry, he went to lie down at the end of the heap of corn: and she came softly, and uncovered his feet, and laid her down.

8 ¶ And it came to pass at midnight, that the man was afraid, and turned himself: and, behold, a woman lay at his feet.

9 And he said, Who *art* thou? And she answered, I *am* Ruth thine handmaid: spread therefore thy skirt over thine handmaid; for thou *art* a near kinsman.

10 And he said, Blessed *be* thou of the LORD, my daughter: *for* thou hast

showed more kindness in the latter end
than at the beginning, inasmuch as thou
followedst not young men, whether poor
or rich.
11 And now, my daughter, fear not; I
will do to thee all that thou requirest:
for all the city of my people doth know
that thou *art* a virtuous woman.
12 And now it is true that I *am thy* near
kinsman: howbeit there is a kinsman
nearer than I.
13 Tarry this night, and it shall be in
the morning, *that* if he will perform unto
thee the part of a kinsman, well; let him
do the kinsman's part: but if he will not
do the part of a kinsman to thee, then
will I do the part of a kinsman to thee,
as the LORD liveth: lie down until the
morning.
14 ¶ And she lay at his feet until the
morning: and she rose up before one
could know another. And he said, Let it
not be known that a woman came into
the floor.
15 Also he said, Bring the veil that *thou*
hast upon thee, and hold it. And when
she held it, he measured six *measures*
of barley, and laid *it* on her: and she
went into the city.
16 And when she came to her mother-
in-law, she said, Who *art* thou, my
daughter? And she told her all that the
man had done to her.
17 And she said, These six *measures*
of barley gave he me; for he said to
me, Go not empty unto thy mother-in-
law.
18 Then said she, Sit still, my daughter,
until thou know how the matter will fall:
for the man will not be in rest, until he
have finished the thing this day.

CHAPTER 4

THEN went Boaz up to the gate, and
sat him down there: and, behold,
the kinsman of whom Boaz spake came
by; unto whom he said, Ho, such a one!
turn aside, sit down here. And he turned
aside, and sat down.
2 And he took ten men of the elders of
the city, and said, Sit ye down here. And
they sat down.
3 And he said unto the kinsman,
Nā′ō-mī, that is come again out of the
country of Mō′ăb, selleth a parcel of
land, which *was* our brother Ē-lĭm′ē-
lĕch's:
4 And I thought to advertise thee, saying, Buy *it* before the inhabitants, and
before the elders of my people. If thou
wilt redeem *it*, redeem *it*: but if thou
wilt not redeem *it*, *then* tell me, that I
may know: for *there is* none to redeem
it besides thee; and I *am* after thee.
And he said, I will redeem *it*.
5 Then said Boaz, What day thou
buyest the field of the hand of Nā′ō-mī,
thou must buy *it* also of Ruth the Mō′-
ăb-īt′ĕss, the wife of the dead, to raise
up the name of the dead upon his
inheritance.
6 ¶ And the kinsman said, I cannot
redeem *it* for myself, lest I mar mine
own inheritance: redeem thou my right
to thyself; for I cannot redeem *it*.
7 Now this *was the manner* in former
time in Īṣ′rā-ĕl concerning redeeming
and concerning changing, for to confirm
all things; a man plucked off his shoe,
and gave *it* to his neighbor: and this *was*
a testimony in Īṣ′rā-ĕl.
8 Therefore the kinsman said unto
Boaz, Buy *it* for thee. So he drew off
his shoe.
9 ¶ And Boaz said unto the elders, and
unto all the people, Ye *are* witnesses
this day, that I have bought all that *was*
Ē-lĭm′ē-lĕch's, and all that *was* Chĭl′ī-
ŏn's and Măh′lŏn's, of the hand of
Nā′ō-mī.
10 Moreover Ruth the Mō′ăb-īt′ĕss,
the wife of Măh′lŏn, have I purchased
to be my wife, to raise up the name of
the dead upon his inheritance, that the
name of the dead be not cut off from
among his brethren, and from the gate
of his place: ye *are* witnesses this day.
11 And all the people that *were* in the
gate, and the elders, said, *We are* witnesses. The LORD make the woman
that is come into thine house like Rachel
and like Lē′ăh, which two did build the
house of Īṣ′rā-ĕl: and do thou worthily
in Ĕph′rȧ-tăh, and be famous in Beth-
lehem:
12 And let thy house be like the house
of Phā′rĕz, whom Tā′mȧr bare unto
Judah, of the seed which the LORD shall
give thee of this young woman.
13 ¶ So Boaz took Ruth, and she was
his wife: and when he went in unto her,
the LORD gave her conception, and she
bare a son.
14 And the women said unto Nā′ō-mī,
Blessed *be* the LORD, which hath not
left thee this day without a kinsman,

that his name may be famous in Ĭṣ′rā-ĕl.
15 And he shall be unto thee a restorer
of *thy* life, and a nourisher of thine old
age: for thy daughter-in-law, which
loveth thee, which is better to thee than
seven sons, hath borne him.
16 And Nā′ō-mī took the child, and
laid it in her bosom, and became nurse
unto it.
17 And the women her neighbors gave
it a name, saying, There is a son born to
Nā′ō-mī; and they called his name
Ō′bĕd: he *is* the father of Jesse, the
father of David.
18 ℂ Now these *are* the generations of
Phā′rĕz: Phā′rĕz begat Hĕz′rŏn,
19 And Hĕz′rŏn begat Răm, and Răm
begat Ȧm-mĭn′ȧ-dăb,
20 And Ȧm-mĭn′ȧ-dăb begat Näh′shŏn,
and Näh′shŏn begat Săl′mŏn,
21 And Săl′mŏn begat Boaz, and Boaz
begat Ō′bĕd,
22 And Ō′bĕd begat Jesse, and Jesse
begat David.

THE FIRST

BOOK OF SAMUEL

OTHERWISE CALLED, THE FIRST BOOK OF THE KINGS

CHAPTER 1

NOW there was a certain man of
Rā′mȧ-thā′ĭm–zō′phĭm, of mount
Ē′phrā-ĭm, and his name *was* Ĕl-kā′nȧh,
the son of Jē-rō′hăm, the son of Ē-lī′hū,
the son of Tō′hū, the son of Zŭph, an
Ĕph′răth-īte:
2 And he had two wives; the name of
the one *was* Hannah, and the name of
the other Pē-nĭn′nȧh: and Pē-nĭn′nȧh
had children, but Hannah had no
children.
3 And this man went up out of his city
yearly to worship and to sacrifice unto
the LORD of hosts in Shī′lōh. And the
two sons of Ē′lī, Hŏph′nī and Phĭn′ē-
hăs, the priests of the LORD, *were* there.
4 ℂ And when the time was that Ĕl-
kā′nȧh offered, he gave to Pē-nĭn′nȧh
his wife, and to all her sons and her
daughters, portions:
5 But unto Hannah he gave a worthy
portion; for he loved Hannah: but the
LORD had shut up her womb.
6 And her adversary also provoked her
sore, for to make her fret, because the
LORD had shut up her womb.
7 And *as* he did so year by year, when
she went up to the house of the LORD,
so she provoked her; therefore she
wept, and did not eat.
8 Then said Ĕl-kā′nȧh her husband to
her, Hannah, why weepest thou? and
why eatest thou not? and why is thy
heart grieved? *am* not I better to thee
than ten sons?
9 ℂ So Hannah rose up after they had
eaten in Shī′lōh, and after they had
drunk. Now Ē′lī the priest sat upon a
seat by a post of the temple of the
LORD.
10 And she *was* in bitterness of soul,
and prayed unto the LORD, and wept
sore.
11 And she vowed a vow, and said, O
LORD of hosts, if thou wilt indeed look
on the affliction of thine handmaid, and
remember me, and not forget thine
handmaid, but wilt give unto thine
handmaid a man child, then I will give
him unto the LORD all the days of his
life, and there shall no razor come upon
his head.
12 And it came to pass, as she continued praying before the LORD, that
Ē′lī marked her mouth.
13 Now Hannah, she spake in her
heart; only her lips moved, but her voice
was not heard: therefore Ē′lī thought
she had been drunken.
14 And Ē′lī said unto her, How long
wilt thou be drunken? put away thy
wine from thee.
15 And Hannah answered and said,
No, my lord, I *am* a woman of a sorrowful spirit: I have drunk neither wine nor
strong drink, but have poured out my
soul before the LORD.
16 Count not thine handmaid for a
daughter of Bē′lī-ăl: for out of the abundance of my complaint and grief have I
spoken hitherto.
17 Then Ē′lī answered and said, Go in

peace: and the God of Ĭṣ′rā-ĕl grant *thee*
thy petition that thou hast asked of him.
18 And she said, Let thine handmaid
find grace in thy sight. So the woman
went her way, and did eat, and her
countenance was no more *sad*.
19 ℂ And they rose up in the morning
early, and worshipped before the LORD,
and returned, and came to their house
to Rā′mȧh: and Ĕl-kā′nȧh knew Hannah his wife; and the LORD remembered
her.
20 Wherefore it came to pass, when
the time was come about after Hannah
had conceived, that she bare a son, and
called his name Samuel, *saying,* Because I have asked him of the LORD.
21 And the man Ĕl-kā′nȧh, and all his
house, went up to offer unto the LORD
the yearly sacrifice, and his vow.
22 But Hannah went not up; for she
said unto her husband, *I will not go up*
until the child be weaned, and *then* I
will bring him, that he may appear before the LORD, and there abide for ever.
23 And Ĕl-kā′nȧh her husband said
unto her, Do what seemeth thee good;
tarry until thou have weaned him; only
the LORD establish his word. So the
woman abode, and gave her son suck
until she weaned him.
24 ℂ And when she had weaned him,
she took him up with her, with three
bullocks, and one ē′phȧh of flour, and a
bottle of wine, and brought him unto the
house of the LORD in Shī′lōh: and the
child *was* young.
25 And they slew a bullock, and
brought the child to Ē′lī.
26 And she said, O my lord, *as* thy soul
liveth, my lord, I *am* the woman that
stood by thee here, praying unto the
LORD.
27 For this child I prayed; and the
LORD hath given me my petition which
I asked of him:
28 Therefore also I have lent him to
the LORD; as long as he liveth he shall
be lent to the LORD. And he worshipped
the LORD there.

CHAPTER 2

AND Hannah prayed, and said, My
heart rejoiceth in the LORD, mine
horn is exalted in the LORD; my mouth
is enlarged over mine enemies; because
I rejoice in thy salvation.
2 *There is* none holy as the LORD: for
there is none besides thee: neither *is*
there any rock like our God.
3 Talk no more so exceeding proudly;
let *not* arrogancy come out of your
mouth: for the LORD *is* a God of knowledge, and by him actions are weighed.
4 The bows of the mighty men *are*
broken, and they that stumbled are
girded with strength.
5 *They that were* full have hired out
themselves for bread; and *they that*
were hungry ceased: so that the barren
hath borne seven; and she that hath
many children is waxed feeble.
6 The LORD killeth, and maketh alive:
he bringeth down to the grave, and
bringeth up.
7 The LORD maketh poor, and maketh
rich: he bringeth low, and lifteth up.
8 He raiseth up the poor out of the
dust, *and* lifteth up the beggar from the
dunghill, to set *them* among princes,
and to make them inherit the throne of
glory: for the pillars of the earth *are* the
LORD's, and he hath set the world upon
them.
9 He will keep the feet of his saints,
and the wicked shall be silent in darkness; for by strength shall no man
prevail.
10 The adversaries of the LORD shall
be broken to pieces; out of heaven
shall he thunder upon them: the LORD
shall judge the ends of the earth; and
he shall give strength unto his king,
and exalt the horn of his anointed.
11 And Ĕl-kā′nȧh went to Rā′mȧh to
his house. And the child did minister
unto the LORD before Ē′lī the priest.
12 ℂ Now the sons of Ē′lī *were* sons of
Bē′lĭ-ăl; they knew not the LORD.
13 And the priest's custom with the
people *was, that,* when any man offered
sacrifice, the priest's servant came,
while the flesh was in seething, with a
fleshhook of three teeth in his hand;
14 And he struck *it* into the pan, or
kettle, or caldron, or pot; all that the
fleshhook brought up the priest took for
himself. So they did in Shī′lōh unto all
the Ĭṣ′rā-ĕl-ītes that came thither.
15 Also before they burnt the fat, the
priest's servant came, and said to the
man that sacrificed, Give flesh to roast
for the priest; for he will not have sodden flesh of thee, but raw.
16 And *if* any man said unto him, Let
them not fail to burn the fat presently,

and *then* take *as much* as thy soul
desireth; then he would answer him,
Nay; but thou shalt give *it me* now: and
if not, I will take *it* by force.
17 Wherefore the sin of the young men
was very great before the LORD: for
men abhorred the offering of the LORD.
18 ℂ But Samuel ministered before
the LORD, *being* a child, girded with a
linen ĕph'ŏd.
19 Moreover his mother made him a
little coat, and brought *it* to him from
year to year, when she came up with
her husband to offer the yearly sacrifice.
20 ℂ And Ē'lī blessed Ĕl-kā'nah and
his wife, and said, The LORD give thee
seed of this woman for the loan which is
lent to the LORD. And they went unto
their own home.
21 And the LORD visited Hannah,
so that she conceived, and bare three
sons and two daughters. And the child
Samuel grew before the LORD.
22 ℂ Now Ē'lī was very old, and heard
all that his sons did unto all Ĭs'rā-ĕl; and
how they lay with the women that
assembled *at* the door of the tabernacle
of the congregation.
23 And he said unto them, Why do ye
such things? for I hear of your evil dealings by all this people.
24 Nay, my sons; for *it is* no good report that I hear: ye make the LORD's
people to transgress.
25 If one man sin against another, the
judge shall judge him: but if a man sin
against the LORD, who shall entreat for
him? Notwithstanding, they hearkened
not unto the voice of their father, because the LORD would slay them.
26 And the child Samuel grew on, and
was in favor both with the LORD, and
also with men.
27 ℂ And there came a man of God
unto Ē'lī, and said unto him, Thus saith
the LORD, Did I plainly appear unto the
house of thy father, when they were in
Egypt in Phā'raōh's house?
28 And did I choose him out of all the
tribes of Ĭs'rā-ĕl *to be* my priest, to offer
upon mine altar, to burn incense, to
wear an ĕph'ŏd before me? and did I
give unto the house of thy father all the
offerings made by fire of the children of
Ĭs'rā-ĕl?
29 Wherefore kick ye at my sacrifice
and at mine offering, which I have commanded *in my* habitation; and honorest
thy sons above me, to make yourselves
fat with the chiefest of all the offerings
of Ĭs'rā-ĕl my people?
30 Wherefore the LORD God of Ĭs'rā-ĕl
saith, I said indeed *that* thy house, and
the house of thy father, should walk before me for ever: but now the LORD
saith, Be it far from me; for them that
honor me I will honor, and they that
despise me shall be lightly esteemed.
31 Behold, the days come, that I will
cut off thine arm, and the arm of thy
father's house, that there shall not be an
old man in thine house.
32 And thou shalt see an enemy *in my*
habitation in all *the wealth* which *God*
shall give Ĭs'rā-ĕl: and there shall not be
an old man in thine house for ever.
33 And the man of thine, *whom* I shall
not cut off from mine altar, *shall be* to
consume thine eyes, and to grieve thine
heart: and all the increase of thine house
shall die in the flower of their age.
34 And this *shall be* a sign unto thee,
that shall come upon thy two sons, on
Hŏph'nī and Phĭn'ē-hăs; in one day
they shall die both of them.
35 And I will raise me up a faithful
priest, *that* shall do according to *that*
which *is* in mine heart and in my mind:
and I will build him a sure house; and
he shall walk before mine anointed for
ever.
36 And it shall come to pass, *that* every
one that is left in thine house shall come
and crouch to him for a piece of silver
and a morsel of bread, and shall say,
Put me, I pray thee, into one of the
priests' offices, that I may eat a piece of
bread.

CHAPTER 3

AND the child Samuel ministered
unto the LORD before Ē'lī. And the
word of the LORD was precious in those
days; *there was* no open vision.
2 And it came to pass at that time, when
Ē'lī *was* laid down in his place, and his
eyes began to wax dim, *that* he could not
see;
3 And ere the lamp of God went out in
the temple of the LORD, where the ark
of God *was,* and Samuel was laid down
to sleep;
4 That the LORD called Samuel: and
he answered, Here *am* I.
5 And he ran unto Ē'lī, and said, Here
am I; for thou calledst me. And he said,

I called not; lie down again. And he went and lay down.

6 And the LORD called yet again, Samuel. And Samuel arose and went to Ē′lī, and said, Here *am* I; for thou didst call me. And he answered, I called not, my son; lie down again.

7 Now Samuel did not yet know the LORD, neither was the word of the LORD yet revealed unto him.

8 And the LORD called Samuel again the third time. And he arose and went to Ē′lī, and said, Here *am* I; for thou didst call me. And Ē′lī perceived that the LORD had called the child.

9 Therefore Ē′lī said unto Samuel, Go, lie down: and it shall be, if he call thee, that thou shalt say, Speak, LORD; for thy servant heareth. So Samuel went and lay down in his place.

10 And the LORD came, and stood, and called as at other times, Samuel, Samuel. Then Samuel answered, Speak; for thy servant heareth.

11 ℂ And the LORD said to Samuel, Behold, I will do a thing in Ĭş′rā-ĕl, at which both the ears of every one that heareth it shall tingle.

12 In that day I will perform against Ē′lī all *things* which I have spoken concerning his house: when I begin, I will also make an end.

13 For I have told him that I will judge his house for ever for the iniquity which he knoweth; because his sons made themselves vile, and he restrained them not.

14 And therefore I have sworn unto the house of Ē′lī, that the iniquity of Ē′lī's house shall not be purged with sacrifice nor offering for ever.

15 ℂ And Samuel lay until the morning, and opened the doors of the house of the LORD. And Samuel feared to show Ē′lī the vision.

16 Then Ē′lī called Samuel, and said, Samuel, my son. And he answered, Here *am* I.

17 And he said, What *is* the thing that *the LORD* hath said unto thee? I pray thee hide *it* not from me: God do so to thee, and more also, if thou hide *any* thing from me of all the things that he said unto thee.

18 And Samuel told him every whit, and hid nothing from him. And he said, It *is* the LORD: let him do what seemeth him good.

19 ℂ And Samuel grew, and the LORD was with him, and did let none of his words fall to the ground.

20 And all Ĭş′rā-ĕl from Dan even to Bē′ĕr–shē′bȧ knew that Samuel *was* established *to be* a prophet of the LORD.

21 And the LORD appeared again in Shī′lōh: for the LORD revealed himself to Samuel in Shī′lōh by the word of the LORD.

CHAPTER 4

AND the word of Samuel came to all Ĭş′rā-ĕl. Now Ĭş′rā-ĕl went out against the Phĭ-lĭs′tīneş to battle, and pitched beside Ĕb′ĕn–ē′zĕr: and the Phĭ-lĭs′tīneş pitched in Ā′phĕk.

2 And the Phĭ-lĭs′tīneş put themselves in array against Ĭş′rā-ĕl: and when they joined battle, Ĭş′rā-ĕl was smitten before the Phĭ-lĭs′tīneş: and they slew of the army in the field about four thousand men.

3 ℂ And when the people were come into the camp, the elders of Ĭş′rā-ĕl said, Wherefore hath the LORD smitten us to-day before the Phĭ-lĭs′tīneş? Let us fetch the ark of the covenant of the LORD out of Shī′lōh unto us, that, when it cometh among us, it may save us out of the hand of our enemies.

4 So the people sent to Shī′lōh, that they might bring from thence the ark of the covenant of the LORD of hosts, which dwelleth *between* the cherubim: and the two sons of Ē′lī, Hŏph′nī and Phĭn′ē-hăs, *were* there with the ark of the covenant of God.

5 And when the ark of the covenant of the LORD came into the camp, all Ĭş′rā-ĕl shouted with a great shout, so that the earth rang again.

6 And when the Phĭ-lĭs′tīneş heard the noise of the shout, they said, What *meaneth* the noise of this great shout in the camp of the Hebrews? And they understood that the ark of the LORD was come into the camp.

7 And the Phĭ-lĭs′tīneş were afraid; for they said, God is come into the camp. And they said, Woe unto us! for there hath not been such a thing heretofore.

8 Woe unto us! who shall deliver us out of the hand of these mighty Gods? these *are* the Gods that smote the Egyptians with all the plagues in the wilderness.

9 Be strong, and quit yourselves like men, O ye Phĭ-lĭs′tīneş, that ye be not

servants unto the Hebrews, as they have been to you: quit yourselves like men, and fight.

10 ℂ And the Phĭ-lĭs′tĭneș fought, and Ĭș′rā-ĕl was smitten, and they fled every man into his tent: and there was a very great slaughter; for there fell of Ĭș′rā-ĕl thirty thousand footmen.

11 And the ark of God was taken; and the two sons of Ē′lī, Hŏph′nī and Phĭn′ē-hăs, were slain.

12 ℂ And there ran a man of Benjamin out of the army, and came to Shī′lōh the same day with his clothes rent, and with earth upon his head.

13 And when he came, lo, Ē′lī sat upon a seat by the wayside watching: for his heart trembled for the ark of God. And when the man came into the city, and told *it*, all the city cried out.

14 And when Ē′lī heard the noise of the crying, he said, What *meaneth* the noise of this tumult? And the man came in hastily, and told Ē′lī.

15 Now Ē′lī was ninety and eight years old; and his eyes were dim, that he could not see.

16 And the man said unto Ē′lī, I *am* he that came out of the army, and I fled to-day out of the army. And he said, What is there done, my son?

17 And the messenger answered and said, Ĭș′rā-ĕl is fled before the Phĭ-lĭs′tĭneș, and there hath been also a great slaughter among the people, and thy two sons also, Hŏph′nī and Phĭn′ē-hăs, are dead, and the ark of God is taken.

18 And it came to pass, when he made mention of the ark of God, that he fell from off the seat backward by the side of the gate, and his neck brake, and he died: for he was an old man, and heavy. And he had judged Ĭș′rā-ĕl forty years.

19 ℂ And his daughter-in-law, Phĭn′ē-hăs′ wife, was with child, *near* to be delivered: and when she heard the tidings that the ark of God was taken, and that her father-in-law and her husband were dead, she bowed herself and travailed; for her pains came upon her.

20 And about the time of her death the women that stood by her said unto her, Fear not; for thou hast borne a son. But she answered not, neither did she regard *it*.

21 And she named the child Ĭ′-chȧ-bŏd, saying, The glory is departed from Ĭș′rā-ĕl: because the ark of God was taken, and because of her father-in-law and her husband.

22 And she said, The glory is departed from Ĭș′rā-ĕl: for the ark of God is taken.

CHAPTER 5

AND the Phĭ-lĭs′tĭneș took the ark of God, and brought it from Ĕb′ĕn-ē′zĕr unto Ashdod.

2 When the Phĭ-lĭs′tĭneș took the ark of God, they brought it into the house of Dā′gŏn, and set it by Dā′gŏn.

3 ℂ And when they of Ashdod arose early on the morrow, behold, Dā′gŏn *was* fallen upon his face to the earth before the ark of the LORD. And they took Dā′gŏn, and set him in his place again.

4 And when they arose early on the morrow morning, behold, Dā′gŏn *was* fallen upon his face to the ground before the ark of the LORD; and the head of Dā′gŏn and both the palms of his hands *were* cut off upon the threshold; only *the stump of* Dā′gŏn was left to him.

5 Therefore neither the priests of Dā′gŏn, nor any that come into Dā′gŏn's house, tread on the threshold of Dā′gŏn in Ashdod unto this day.

6 But the hand of the LORD was heavy upon them of Ashdod, and he destroyed them, and smote them with emerods, *even* Ashdod and the coasts thereof.

7 And when the men of Ashdod saw that *it was* so, they said, The ark of the God of Ĭș′rā-ĕl shall not abide with us: for his hand is sore upon us, and upon Dā′gŏn our god.

8 They sent therefore and gathered all the lords of the Phĭ-lĭs′tĭneș unto them, and said, What shall we do with the ark of the God of Ĭș′rā-ĕl? And they answered, Let the ark of the God of Ĭș′rā-ĕl be carried about unto Gath. And they carried the ark of the God of Ĭș′rā-ĕl about *thither*.

9 And it was *so*, that, after they had carried it about, the hand of the LORD was against the city with a very great destruction: and he smote the men of the city, both small and great, and they had emerods in their secret parts.

10 ℂ Therefore they sent the ark of God to Ĕk′rŏn. And it came to pass, as the ark of God came to Ĕk′rŏn, that the Ĕk′rŏn-ītes cried out, saying, They have brought about the ark of the God of Ĭș′rā-ĕl to us, to slay us and our people.

11 So they sent and gathered together
all the lords of the Phĭ-lĭs′tĭneş, and
said, Send away the ark of the God of
Ĭş′rā-ĕl, and let it go again to his own
place, that it slay us not, and our people:
for there was a deadly destruction
throughout all the city; the hand of God
was very heavy there.
12 And the men that died not were
smitten with the emerods: and the cry of
the city went up to heaven.

CHAPTER 6

AND the ark of the LORD was in the
country of the Phĭ-lĭs′tĭneş seven
months.
2 And the Phĭ-lĭs′tĭneş called for the
priests and the diviners, saying, What
shall we do to the ark of the LORD? tell
us wherewith we shall send it to his
place.
3 And they said, If ye send away the
ark of the God of Ĭş′rā-ĕl, send it not
empty; but in any wise return him a
trespass offering: then ye shall be
healed, and it shall be known to you why
his hand is not removed from you.
4 Then said they, What *shall be* the
trespass offering which we shall return
to him? They answered, Five golden
emerods, and five golden mice, *according
to* the number of the lords of the
Phĭ-lĭs′tĭneş: for one plague *was* on you
all, and on your lords.
5 Wherefore ye shall make images of
your emerods, and images of your mice
that mar the land; and ye shall give
glory unto the God of Ĭş′rā-ĕl: peradventure
he will lighten his hand from off
you, and from off your gods, and from
off your land.
6 Wherefore then do ye harden your
hearts, as the Egyptians and Phā′raōh
hardened their hearts? when he had
wrought wonderfully among them, did
they not let the people go, and they
departed?
7 Now therefore make a new cart, and
take two milch kine, on which there hath
come no yoke, and tie the kine to the
cart, and bring their calves home from
them:
8 And take the ark of the LORD, and
lay it upon the cart; and put the jewels
of gold, which ye return him *for* a
trespass offering, in a coffer by the
side thereof; and send it away, that it
may go.

9 And see, if it goeth up by the way of
his own coast to Bĕth′-shē′mĕsh, *then*
he hath done us this great evil: but if
not, then we shall know that *it is* not his
hand *that* smote us; it *was* a chance
that happened to us.
10 ¶ And the men did so; and took two
milch kine, and tied them to the cart,
and shut up their calves at home:
11 And they laid the ark of the LORD
upon the cart, and the coffer with the
mice of gold and the images of their
emerods.
12 And the kine took the straight way
to the way of Bĕth′-shē′mĕsh, *and* went
along the highway, lowing as they went,
and turned not aside *to* the right hand or
to the left; and the lords of the Phĭ-lĭs′tĭneş
went after them unto the border of
Bĕth′-shē′mĕsh.
13 And *they of* Bĕth′-shē′mĕsh *were*
reaping their wheat harvest in the valley:
and they lifted up their eyes, and
saw the ark, and rejoiced to see *it*.
14 And the cart came into the field of
Joshua, a Bĕth′-shē′mīte, and stood
there, where *there was* a great stone:
and they clave the wood of the cart, and
offered the kine a burnt offering unto
the LORD.
15 And the Lē′vītes took down the ark
of the LORD, and the coffer that *was* with
it, wherein the jewels of gold *were*, and
put *them* on the great stone: and the
men of Bĕth′-shē′mĕsh offered burnt
offerings and sacrificed sacrifices the
same day unto the LORD.
16 And when the five lords of the Phĭ-lĭs′tĭneş
had seen *it*, they returned to
Ĕk′rŏn the same day.
17 And these *are* the golden emerods
which the Phĭ-lĭs′tĭneş returned *for* a
trespass offering unto the LORD; for
Ashdod one, for Gā′zȧ one, for Ăs′kē-lŏn
one, for Gath one, for Ĕk′rŏn one;
18 And the golden mice, *according to*
the number of all the cities of the Phĭ-lĭs′tĭneş
belonging to the five lords, *both*
of fenced cities, and of country villages,
even unto the great *stone of* Abel,
whereon they set down the ark of the
LORD: *which stone remaineth* unto this
day in the field of Joshua, the Bĕth′-shē′mīte.
19 ¶ And he smote the men of Bĕth′-shē′mĕsh,
because they had looked into
the ark of the LORD, even he smote of
the people fifty thousand and three-

score and ten men: and the people lamented, because the LORD had smitten *many* of the people with a great slaughter.

20 And the men of Bĕth′–shē′mĕsh said, Who is able to stand before this holy LORD God? and to whom shall he go up from us?

21 ¶ And they sent messengers to the inhabitants of Kĭr′jăth–jē′ȧ-rĭm, saying, The Phĭ-lĭs′tĭneṣ have brought again the ark of the LORD; come ye down, *and* fetch it up to you.

CHAPTER 7

AND the men of Kĭr′jăth–jē′ȧ-rĭm came, and fetched up the ark of the LORD, and brought it into the house of Ȧ-bĭn′ȧ-dăb in the hill, and sanctified Ĕl′ē-ā′zȧr his son to keep the ark of the LORD.

2 And it came to pass, while the ark abode in Kĭr′jăth–jē′ȧ-rĭm, that the time was long; for it was twenty years: and all the house of Ĭṣ′rā-ĕl lamented after the LORD.

3 ¶ And Samuel spake unto all the house of Ĭṣ′rā-ĕl, saying, If ye do return unto the LORD with all your hearts, *then* put away the strange gods and Ăsh′tȧ-rŏth from among you, and prepare your hearts unto the LORD, and serve him only: and he will deliver you out of the hand of the Phĭ-lĭs′tĭneṣ.

4 Then the children of Ĭṣ′rā-ĕl did put away Bā′ȧ-lĭm and Ăsh′tȧ-rŏth, and served the LORD only.

5 And Samuel said, Gather all Ĭṣ′rā-ĕl to Mĭz′pĕh, and I will pray for you unto the LORD.

6 And they gathered together to Mĭz′pĕh, and drew water, and poured *it* out before the LORD, and fasted on that day, and said there, We have sinned against the LORD. And Samuel judged the children of Ĭṣ′rā-ĕl in Mĭz′pĕh.

7 And when the Phĭ-lĭs′tĭneṣ heard that the children of Ĭṣ′rā-ĕl were gathered together to Mĭz′pĕh, the lords of the Phĭ-lĭs′tĭneṣ went up against Ĭṣ′rā-ĕl. And when the children of Ĭṣ′rā-ĕl heard *it*, they were afraid of the Phĭ-lĭs′tĭneṣ.

8 And the children of Ĭṣ′rā-ĕl said to Samuel, Cease not to cry unto the LORD our God for us, that he will save us out of the hand of the Phĭ-lĭs′tĭneṣ.

9 ¶ And Samuel took a sucking lamb, and offered *it for* a burnt offering wholly unto the LORD: and Samuel cried unto the LORD for Ĭṣ′rā-ĕl; and the LORD heard him.

10 And as Samuel was offering up the burnt offering, the Phĭ-lĭs′tĭnes drew near to battle against Ĭṣ′rā-ĕl: but the LORD thundered with a great thunder on that day upon the Phĭ-lĭs′tĭneṣ, and discomfited them; and they were smitten before Ĭṣ′rā-ĕl.

11 And the men of Ĭṣ′rā-ĕl went out of Mĭz′pĕh, and pursued the Phĭ-lĭs′tĭneṣ, and smote them, until *they came* under Bĕth′–cär′.

12 Then Samuel took a stone, and set *it* between Mĭz′pĕh and Shĕn, and called the name of it Ĕb′ĕn–ē′zĕr, saying, Hitherto hath the LORD helped us.

13 ¶ So the Phĭ-lĭs′tĭneṣ were subdued, and they came no more into the coast of Ĭṣ′rā-ĕl: and the hand of the LORD was against the Phĭ-lĭs′tĭneṣ all the days of Samuel.

14 And the cities which the Phĭ-lĭs′tĭneṣ had taken from Ĭṣ′rā-ĕl were restored to Ĭṣ′rā-ĕl, from Ĕk′rŏn even unto Gath; and the coasts thereof did Ĭṣ′rā-ĕl deliver out of the hands of the Phĭ-lĭs′tĭneṣ. And there was peace between Ĭṣ′rā-ĕl and the Ăm′ō-rītes.

15 And Samuel judged Ĭṣ′rā-ĕl all the days of his life.

16 And he went from year to year in circuit to Beth-el, and Gĭl′găl, and Mĭz′pĕh, and judged Ĭṣ′rā-ĕl in all those places.

17 And his return *was* to Rā′mȧh, for there *was* his house; and there he judged Ĭṣ′rā-ĕl; and there he built an altar unto the LORD.

CHAPTER 8

AND it came to pass, when Samuel was old, that he made his sons judges over Ĭṣ′rā-ĕl.

2 Now the name of his firstborn was Joel; and the name of his second, Ȧ-bī′ȧh: *they were* judges in Bē′ĕr–shē′bȧ.

3 And his sons walked not in his ways, but turned aside after lucre, and took bribes, and perverted judgment.

4 Then all the elders of Ĭṣ′rā-ĕl gathered themselves together, and came to Samuel unto Rā′mȧh,

5 And said unto him, Behold, thou art old, and thy sons walk not in thy ways: now make us a king to judge us like all the nations.

6 ¶ But the thing displeased Samuel,
when they said, Give us a king to judge
us. And Samuel prayed unto the LORD.
7 And the LORD said unto Samuel,
Hearken unto the voice of the people in
all that they say unto thee: for they have
not rejected thee, but they have rejected me, that I should not reign over
them.
8 According to all the works which they
have done since the day that I brought
them up out of Egypt even unto this
day, wherewith they have forsaken me,
and served other gods, so do they also
unto thee.
9 Now therefore hearken unto their
voice: howbeit yet protest solemnly
unto them, and show them the manner
of the king that shall reign over them.
10 ¶ And Samuel told all the words of
the LORD unto the people that asked of
him a king.
11 And he said, This will be the manner of the king that shall reign over you:
He will take your sons, and appoint
them for himself, for his chariots, and
to be his horsemen; and *some* shall run
before his chariots.
12 And he will appoint him captains
over thousands, and captains over
fifties; and *will set them* to ear his
ground, and to reap his harvest, and to
make his instruments of war, and instruments of his chariots.
13 And he will take your daughters *to
be* confectionaries, and *to be* cooks, and
to be bakers.
14 And he will take your fields, and
your vineyards, and your oliveyards,
even the best *of them,* and give *them* to
his servants.
15 And he will take the tenth of your
seed, and of your vineyards, and give to
his officers, and to his servants.
16 And he will take your menservants,
and your maidservants, and your goodliest young men, and your asses, and
put *them* to his work.
17 He will take the tenth of your sheep:
and ye shall be his servants.
18 And ye shall cry out in that day because of your king which ye shall have
chosen you; and the LORD will not hear
you in that day.
19 ¶ Nevertheless the people refused
to obey the voice of Samuel; and they
said, Nay; but we will have a king
over us;
20 That we also may be like all the
nations; and that our king may judge us,
and go out before us, and fight our
battles.
21 And Samuel heard all the words of
the people, and he rehearsed them in
the ears of the LORD.
22 And the LORD said to Samuel,
Hearken unto their voice, and make
them a king. And Samuel said unto the
men of Ĭş'rā-ĕl, Go ye every man unto
his city.

CHAPTER 9

NOW there was a man of Benjamin,
whose name *was* Kish, the son of
Ā'bĭ-ĕl, the son of Zē'rôr, the son of
Bē-chō'răth, the son of Ȧ-phī'ȧh, a
Benjamite, a mighty man of power.
2 And he had a son, whose name *was*
Saul, a choice young man, and a goodly:
and *there was* not among the children of
Ĭş'rā-ĕl a goodlier person than he: from
his shoulders and upward *he was* higher
than any of the people.
3 And the asses of Kish Saul's father
were lost. And Kish said to Saul his
son, Take now one of the servants with
thee, and arise, go seek the asses.
4 And he passed through mount
Ē'phrā-ĭm, and passed through the land
of Shȧ-lī'shȧ, but they found *them* not:
then they passed through the land of
Shā'lĭm, and *there they were* not: and
he passed through the land of the Benjamites, but they found *them* not.
5 *And* when they were come to the land
of Zŭph, Saul said to his servant that
was with him, Come, and let us return;
lest my father leave *caring* for the asses,
and take thought for us.
6 And he said unto him, Behold now,
there is in this city a man of God, and
he is an honorable man; all that he saith
cometh surely to pass: now let us go
thither; peradventure he can show us
our way that we should go.
7 Then said Saul to his servant, But,
behold, *if* we go, what shall we bring the
man? for the bread is spent in our vessels, and *there is* not a present to bring
to the man of God: what have we?
8 And the servant answered Saul again,
and said, Behold, I have here at hand
the fourth part of a shekel of silver: *that*
will I give to the man of God, to tell us
our way.
9 (Beforetime in Ĭş'rā-ĕl, when a man

went to inquire of God, thus he spake, Come, and let us go to the seer: for *he that is* now *called* a Prophet was beforetime called a Seer.)

10 Then said Saul to his servant, Well said; come, let us go. So they went unto the city where the man of God *was*.

11 ¶ *And* as they went up the hill to the city, they found young maidens going out to draw water, and said unto them, Is the seer here?

12 And they answered them, and said, He is; behold, *he is* before you: make haste now, for he came to-day to the city; for *there is* a sacrifice of the people to-day in the high place:

13 As soon as ye be come into the city, ye shall straightway find him, before he go up to the high place to eat: for the people will not eat until he come, because he doth bless the sacrifice; *and* afterward they eat that be bidden. Now therefore get you up; for about this time ye shall find him.

14 And they went up into the city: *and* when they were come into the city, behold, Samuel came out against them, for to go up to the high place.

15 ¶ Now the LORD had told Samuel in his ear a day before Saul came, saying,

16 To-morrow about this time I will send thee a man out of the land of Benjamin, and thou shalt anoint him *to be* captain over my people Ĭş′rā-ēl, that he may save my people out of the hand of the Phĭ-lis′tīneş: for I have looked upon my people, because their cry is come unto me.

17 And when Samuel saw Saul, the LORD said unto him, Behold the man whom I spake to thee of! this same shall reign over my people.

18 Then Saul drew near to Samuel in the gate, and said, Tell me, I pray thee, where the seer's house *is*.

19 And Samuel answered Saul, and said, I *am* the seer: go up before me unto the high place; for ye shall eat with me to-day, and to-morrow I will let thee go, and will tell thee all that *is* in thine heart.

20 And as for thine asses that were lost three days ago, set not thy mind on them; for they are found. And on whom *is* all the desire of Ĭş′rā-ēl? *Is it* not on thee, and on all thy father's house?

21 And Saul answered and said, *Am* not I a Benjamite, of the smallest of the tribes of Ĭş′rā-ēl? and my family the least of all the families of the tribe of Benjamin? wherefore then speakest thou so to me?

22 And Samuel took Saul and his servant, and brought them into the parlor, and made them sit in the chiefest place among them that were bidden, which *were* about thirty persons.

23 And Samuel said unto the cook, Bring the portion which I gave thee, of which I said unto thee, Set it by thee.

24 And the cook took up the shoulder, and *that* which *was* upon it, and set *it* before Saul. And *Samuel* said, Behold that which is left! set *it* before thee, *and* eat: for unto this time hath it been kept for thee since I said, I have invited the people. So Saul did eat with Samuel that day.

25 ¶ And when they were come down from the high place into the city, *Samuel* communed with Saul upon the top of the house.

26 And they arose early: and it came to pass about the spring of the day, that Samuel called Saul to the top of the house, saying, Up, that I may send thee away. And Saul arose, and they went out both of them, he and Samuel, abroad.

27 *And* as they were going down to the end of the city, Samuel said to Saul, Bid the servant pass on before us, (and he passed on,) but stand thou still a while, that I may show thee the word of God.

CHAPTER 10

THEN Samuel took a vial of oil, and poured *it* upon his head, and kissed him, and said, *Is it* not because the LORD hath anointed thee *to be* captain over his inheritance?

2 When thou art departed from me today, then thou shalt find two men by Rachel's sepulchre in the border of Benjamin at Zĕl′zȧh; and they will say unto thee, The asses which thou wentest to seek are found: and, lo, thy father hath left the care of the asses, and sorroweth for you, saying, What shall I do for my son?

3 Then shalt thou go on forward from thence, and thou shalt come to the plain of Tā′bŏr, and there shall meet thee three men going up to God to Beth-el, one carrying three kids, and another

carrying three loaves of bread, and another carrying a bottle of wine:
4 And they will salute thee, and give
thee two *loaves* of bread; which thou
shalt receive of their hands.
5 After that thou shalt come to the hill
of God, where *is* the garrison of the
Phĭ-lĭs′tīneṣ: and it shall come to pass,
when thou art come thither to the city,
that thou shalt meet a company of
prophets coming down from the high
place with a psaltery, and a tabret, and
a pipe, and a harp, before them; and
they shall prophesy:
6 And the Spirit of the LORD will come
upon thee, and thou shalt prophesy with
them, and shalt be turned into another
man.
7 And let it be, when these signs are
come unto thee, *that* thou do as occasion
serve thee; for God *is* with thee.
8 And thou shalt go down before me to
Gĭl′găl; and, behold, I will come down
unto thee, to offer burnt offerings, *and*
to sacrifice sacrifices of peace offerings:
seven days shalt thou tarry, till I come to
thee, and show thee what thou shalt do.
9 ¶ And it was *so,* that, when he had
turned his back to go from Samuel, God
gave him another heart: and all those
signs came to pass that day.
10 And when they came thither to the
hill, behold, a company of prophets met
him; and the Spirit of God came upon
him, and he prophesied among them.
11 And it came to pass, when all that
knew him beforetime saw that, behold,
he prophesied among the prophets, then
the people said one to another, What *is*
this *that* is come unto the son of Kish?
Is Saul also among the prophets?
12 And one of the same place answered
and said, But who *is* their father?
Therefore it became a proverb, *Is* Saul
also among the prophets?
13 And when he had made an end of
prophesying, he came to the high place.
14 ¶ And Saul's uncle said unto him
and to his servant, Whither went ye?
And he said, To seek the asses: and
when we saw that *they were* no where,
we came to Samuel.
15 And Saul's uncle said, Tell me, I
pray thee, what Samuel said unto you.
16 And Saul said unto his uncle, He
told us plainly that the asses were found.
But of the matter of the kingdom, whereof Samuel spake, he told him not.
17 ¶ And Samuel called the people together unto the LORD to Mĭz′pĕh;
18 And said unto the children of
Ĭṣ′rā-ĕl, Thus saith the LORD God of
Ĭṣ′rā-ĕl, I brought up Ĭṣ′rā-ĕl out of
Egypt, and delivered you out of the hand
of the Egyptians, and out of the hand of
all kingdoms, *and* of them that oppressed you:
19 And ye have this day rejected your
God, who himself saved you out of all
your adversities and your tribulations;
and ye have said unto him, *Nay,* but set
a king over us. Now therefore present
yourselves before the LORD by your
tribes, and by your thousands.
20 And when Samuel had caused all
the tribes of Ĭṣ′rā-ĕl to come near, the
tribe of Benjamin was taken.
21 When he had caused the tribe of
Benjamin to come near by their families,
the family of Mā′trī was taken, and Saul
the son of Kish was taken: and when
they sought him, he could not be found.
22 Therefore they inquired of the LORD
further, if the man should yet come
thither. And the LORD answered, Behold, he hath hid himself among the
stuff.
23 And they ran and fetched him
thence: and when he stood among the
people, he was higher than any of the
people from his shoulders and upward.
24 And Samuel said to all the people,
See ye him whom the LORD hath chosen,
that *there is* none like him among all
the people? And all the people shouted,
and said, God save the king.
25 Then Samuel told the people the
manner of the kingdom, and wrote *it* in
a book, and laid *it* up before the LORD.
And Samuel sent all the people away,
every man to his house.
26 ¶ And Saul also went home to
Gĭb′ē-ăh; and there went with him a
band of men, whose hearts God had
touched.
27 But the children of Bē′lĭ-ăl said,
How shall this man save us? And they
despised him, and brought him no
presents. But he held his peace.

CHAPTER 11

THEN Nā′hăsh the Ammonite came
up, and encamped against Jā′bĕsh–
gĭl′ē-ăd: and all the men of Jā′bĕsh said
unto Nā′hăsh, Make a covenant with us,
and we will serve thee.

2 And Nā'hăsh the Ammonite answered them, On this *condition* will I
make *a covenant* with you, that I may
thrust out all your right eyes, and lay it
for a reproach upon all Ĭs'rā-ĕl.
3 And the elders of Jā'bĕsh said unto
him, Give us seven days' respite, that
we may send messengers unto all the
coasts of Ĭs'rā-ĕl: and then, if *there be* no
man to save us, we will come out to thee.
4 ¶ Then came the messengers to
Gĭb'ē-ȧh of Saul, and told the tidings in
the ears of the people: and all the people lifted up their voices, and wept.
5 And, behold, Saul came after the
herd out of the field; and Saul said,
What *aileth* the people that they weep?
And they told him the tidings of the men
of Jā'bĕsh.
6 And the Spirit of God came upon
Saul when he heard those tidings, and
his anger was kindled greatly.
7 And he took a yoke of oxen, and
hewed them in pieces, and sent *them*
throughout all the coasts of Ĭs'rā-ĕl by
the hands of messengers, saying, Whosoever cometh not forth after Saul and
after Samuel, so shall it be done unto his
oxen. And the fear of the LORD fell on
the people, and they came out with one
consent.
8 And when he numbered them in
Bē'zĕk, the children of Ĭs'rā-ĕl were
three hundred thousand, and the men of
Judah thirty thousand.
9 And they said unto the messengers
that came, Thus shall ye say unto the
men of Jā'bĕsh-gĭl'ē-ăd, To-morrow, by
that time the sun be hot, ye shall have
help. And the messengers came and
showed *it* to the men of Jā'bĕsh; and
they were glad.
10 Therefore the men of Jā'bĕsh said,
To-morrow we will come out unto you,
and ye shall do with us all that seemeth
good unto you.
11 And it was *so* on the morrow, that
Saul put the people in three companies;
and they came into the midst of the
host in the morning watch, and slew the
Ammonites until the heat of the day:
and it came to pass, that they which remained were scattered, so that two of
them were not left together.
12 ¶ And the people said unto Samuel,
Who *is* he that said, Shall Saul reign
over us? bring the men, that we may
put them to death.
13 And Saul said, There shall not a man
be put to death this day: for to-day the
LORD hath wrought salvation in Ĭs'rā-ĕl.
14 Then said Samuel to the people,
Come, and let us go to Gĭl'găl, and renew the kingdom there.
15 And all the people went to Gĭl'găl,
and there they made Saul king before
the LORD in Gĭl'găl; and there they
sacrificed sacrifices of peace offerings
before the LORD; and there Saul and all
the men of Ĭs'rā-ĕl rejoiced greatly.

CHAPTER 12

AND Samuel said unto all Ĭs'rā-ĕl, Behold, I have hearkened unto your
voice in all that ye said unto me, and
have made a king over you.
2 And now, behold, the king walketh
before you: and I am old and grayheaded; and, behold, my sons *are* with
you: and I have walked before you from
my childhood unto this day.
3 Behold, here I *am:* witness against
me before the LORD, and before his
anointed: whose ox have I taken? or
whose ass have I taken? or whom have
I defrauded? whom have I oppressed?
or of whose hand have I received *any*
bribe to blind mine eyes therewith? and
I will restore it you.
4 And they said, Thou hast not defrauded us, nor oppressed us, neither
hast thou taken aught of any man's
hand.
5 And he said unto them, The LORD *is*
witness against you, and his anointed *is*
witness this day, that ye have not found
aught in my hand. And they answered,
He is witness.
6 ¶ And Samuel said unto the people,
It is the LORD that advanced Moses and
Aaron, and that brought your fathers up
out of the land of Egypt.
7 Now therefore stand still, that I may
reason with you before the LORD of all
the righteous acts of the LORD, which he
did to you and to your fathers.
8 When Jacob was come into Egypt,
and your fathers cried unto the LORD,
then the LORD sent Moses and Aaron,
which brought forth your fathers out of
Egypt, and made them dwell in this
place.
9 And when they forgat the LORD their
God, he sold them into the hand of
Sĭs'ĕr-ȧ, captain of the host of Hā'zŏr,
and into the hand of the Phĭ-lĭs'tīneș,

and into the hand of the king of Mō'ăb,
and they fought against them.
10 And they cried unto the LORD, and
said, We have sinned, because we have
forsaken the LORD, and have served
Bā'ă-lĭm and Ăsh'tă-rŏth: but now deliver us out of the hand of our enemies,
and we will serve thee.
11 And the LORD sent Jĕr'ŭb-bā'ăl, and
Bē'dăn, and Jĕph'thăh, and Samuel, and
delivered you out of the hand of your
enemies on every side, and ye dwelt
safe.
12 And when ye saw that Nā'hăsh the
king of the children of Ammon came
against you, ye said unto me, Nay; but
a king shall reign over us: when the
LORD your God *was* your king.
13 Now therefore, behold the king
whom ye have chosen, *and* whom ye
have desired! and, behold, the LORD
hath set a king over you.
14 If ye will fear the LORD, and serve
him, and obey his voice, and not rebel
against the commandment of the LORD;
then shall both ye and also the king that
reigneth over you continue following the
LORD your God:
15 But if ye will not obey the voice of
the LORD, but rebel against the commandment of the LORD; then shall the
hand of the LORD be against you, as *it*
was against your fathers.
16 ¶ Now therefore stand and see this
great thing, which the LORD will do before your eyes.
17 *Is it* not wheat harvest to-day? I will
call unto the LORD, and he shall send
thunder and rain; that ye may perceive
and see that your wickedness *is* great,
which ye have done in the sight of the
LORD, in asking you a king.
18 So Samuel called unto the LORD;
and the LORD sent thunder and rain
that day: and all the people greatly
feared the LORD and Samuel.
19 And all the people said unto Samuel,
Pray for thy servants unto the LORD thy
God, that we die not: for we have added
unto all our sins *this* evil, to ask us a
king.
20 ¶ And Samuel said unto the people,
Fear not: ye have done all this wickedness: yet turn not aside from following
the LORD, but serve the LORD with all
your heart;
21 And turn ye not aside: for *then*
should ye go after vain *things,* which
cannot profit nor deliver; for they *are*
vain.
22 For the LORD will not forsake his
people for his great name's sake: because it hath pleased the LORD to make
you his people.
23 Moreover as for me, God forbid that
I should sin against the LORD in ceasing
to pray for you: but I will teach you the
good and the right way:
24 Only fear the LORD, and serve him
in truth with all your heart: for consider
how great *things* he hath done for you.
25 But if ye shall still do wickedly, ye
shall be consumed, both ye and your
king.

CHAPTER 13

SAUL reigned one year; and when he
had reigned two years over Ĭṣ'rā-ĕl,
2 Saul chose him three thousand *men*
of Ĭṣ'rā-ĕl; *whereof* two thousand were
with Saul in Mĭch'măsh and in mount
Beth-el, and a thousand were with
Jonathan in Gĭb'ē-ăh of Benjamin: and
the rest of the people he sent every man
to his tent.
3 And Jonathan smote the garrison of
the Phĭ-lĭs'tĭneṣ that *was* in Gē'bă, and
the Phĭ-lĭs'tĭneṣ heard *of it*. And Saul
blew the trumpet throughout all the land,
saying, Let the Hebrews hear.
4 And all Ĭṣ'rā-ĕl heard say *that* Saul
had smitten a garrison of the Phĭ-lĭs'-
tĭneṣ, and *that* Ĭṣ'rā-ĕl also was had in
abomination with the Phĭ-lĭs'tĭneṣ. And
the people were called together after
Saul to Gĭl'găl.
5 ¶ And the Phĭ-lĭs'tĭneṣ gathered
themselves together to fight with Ĭṣ'-
rā-ĕl, thirty thousand chariots, and six
thousand horsemen, and people as the
sand which *is* on the seashore in multi
tude: and they came up, and pitched in
Mĭch'măsh, eastward from Bĕth'-ā'vĕn.
6 When the men of Ĭṣ'rā-ĕl saw that
they were in a strait, (for the people
were distressed,) then the people did
hide themselves in caves, and in thickets, and in rocks, and in high places, and
in pits.
7 And *some of* the Hebrews went over
Jordan to the land of Gad and Gĭl'ē-ăd.
As for Saul, he *was* yet in Gĭl'găl, and
all the people followed him trembling.
8 ¶ And he tarried seven days, according to the set time that Samuel *had*
appointed: but Samuel came not to

Gĭl′găl; and the people were scattered
from him.
9 And Saul said, Bring hither a burnt
offering to me, and peace offerings. And
he offered the burnt offering.
10 And it came to pass, that as soon as
he had made an end of offering the
burnt offering, behold, Samuel came;
and Saul went out to meet him, that he
might salute him.
11 ¶ And Samuel said, What hast thou
done? And Saul said, Because I saw
that the people were scattered from me,
and *that* thou camest not within the
days appointed, and *that* the Phĭ-lĭs′-
tĭneș gathered themselves together at
Mĭch′măsh;
12 Therefore said I, The Phĭ-lĭs′tĭneș
will come down now upon me to Gĭl′găl,
and I have not made supplication unto
the LORD: I forced myself therefore,
and offered a burnt offering.
13 And Samuel said to Saul, Thou hast
done foolishly: thou hast not kept the
commandment of the LORD thy God,
which he commanded thee: for now
would the LORD have established thy
kingdom upon Ĭș′rā-ĕl for ever.
14 But now thy kingdom shall not continue: the LORD hath sought him a man
after his own heart, and the LORD hath
commanded him *to be* captain over his
people, because thou hast not kept *that*
which the LORD commanded thee.
15 And Samuel arose, and gat him up
from Gĭl′găl unto Gĭb′ē-ȧh of Benjamin.
And Saul numbered the people *that*
were present with him, about six hundred men.
16 And Saul, and Jonathan his son, and
the people *that were* present with them,
abode in Gĭb′ē-ȧh of Benjamin: but the
Phĭ-lĭs′tĭneș encamped in Mĭch′măsh.
17 ¶ And the spoilers came out of the
camp of the Phĭ-lĭs′tĭneș in three companies: one company turned unto the
way *that leadeth to* Ŏph′rȧh, unto the
land of Shụ′ăl:
18 And another company turned the
way *to* Bĕth′-hō′rŏn: and another company turned *to* the way of the border
that looketh to the valley of Zē-bō′ĭm
toward the wilderness.
19 ¶ Now there was no smith found
throughout all the land of Ĭș′rā-ĕl: for
the Phĭ-lĭs′tĭneș said, Lest the Hebrews
make *them* swords or spears:
20 But all the Ĭș′rā-ĕl-ītes went down
to the Phĭ-lĭs′tĭneș, to sharpen every
man his share, and his coulter, and his
axe, and his mattock.
21 Yet they had a file for the mattocks,
and for the coulters, and for the forks,
and for the axes, and to sharpen the
goads.
22 So it came to pass in the day of battle, that there was neither sword nor
spear found in the hand of any of the
people that *were* with Saul and Jonathan: but with Saul and with Jonathan
his son was there found.
23 And the garrison of the Phĭ-lĭs′-
tĭneș went out to the passage of Mĭch′-
măsh.

CHAPTER 14

NOW it came to pass upon a day,
that Jonathan the son of Saul said
unto the young man that bare his armor,
Come, and let us go over to the Phĭ-
lĭs′tĭneș′ garrison, that *is* on the other
side. But he told not his father.
2 And Saul tarried in the uttermost
part of Gĭb′ē-ȧh under a pomegranate
tree which *is* in Mĭg′rŏn: and the people
that *were* with him *were* about six hundred men;
3 And Ȧ-hī′ȧh, the son of Ȧ-hī′tŭb,
Ī′-chȧ-bŏd's brother, the son of Phĭn′ē-
hăs, the son of Ē′lī, the LORD's priest in
Shī′lōh, wearing an ĕph′ŏd. And the
people knew not that Jonathan was
gone.
4 ¶ And between the passages, by
which Jonathan sought to go over unto
the Phĭ-lĭs′tĭneș′ garrison, *there was* a
sharp rock on the one side, and a sharp
rock on the other side: and the name of
the one *was* Bō′zĕz, and the name of the
other Sē′nĕh.
5 The forefront of the one *was* situate
northward over against Mĭch′măsh, and
the other southward over against Gĭb′-
ē-ȧh.
6 And Jonathan said to the young man
that bare his armor, Come, and let us
go over unto the garrison of these uncircumcised: it may be that the LORD
will work for us: for *there is* no restraint
to the LORD to save by many or by
few.
7 And his armor-bearer said unto him,
Do all that *is* in thy heart: turn thee; behold, I *am* with thee according to thy
heart.
8 Then said Jonathan, Behold, we will

pass over unto *these* men, and we will
discover ourselves unto them.
9 If they say thus unto us, Tarry until
we come to you; then we will stand still
in our place, and will not go up unto
them.
10 But if they say thus, Come up unto
us; then we will go up: for the LORD
hath delivered them into our hand; and
this *shall be* a sign unto us.
11 And both of them discovered themselves unto the garrison of the Phĭ-
lĭs′tĭneṣ: and the Phĭ-lĭs′tĭneṣ said, Behold, the Hebrews come forth out of the
holes where they had hid themselves.
12 And the men of the garrison answered Jonathan and his armor-bearer,
and said, Come up to us, and we will
show you a thing. And Jonathan said
unto his armor-bearer, Come up after
me: for the LORD hath delivered them
into the hand of Ĭṣ′rā-ĕl.
13 And Jonathan climbed up upon his
hands and upon his feet, and his armor-
bearer after him: and they fell before
Jonathan; and his armor-bearer slew
after him.
14 And that first slaughter, which
Jonathan and his armor-bearer made,
was about twenty men, within as it were
a half acre of land, *which* a yoke *of oxen
might plow*.
15 And there was trembling in the host,
in the field, and among all the people:
the garrison, and the spoilers, they also
trembled, and the earth quaked: so it
was a very great trembling.
16 And the watchmen of Saul in Gĭb′ē-
ȧh of Benjamin looked; and, behold, the
multitude melted away, and they went
on beating down *one another*.
17 Then said Saul unto the people that
were with him, Number now, and see
who is gone from us. And when they
had numbered, behold, Jonathan and
his armor-bearer *were* not *there*.
18 And Saul said unto Ȧ-hī′ȧh, Bring
hither the ark of God. For the ark of
God was at that time with the children
of Ĭṣ′rā-ĕl.
19 ¶ And it came to pass, while Saul
talked unto the priest, that the noise
that *was* in the host of the Phĭ-lĭs′tĭneṣ
went on and increased: and Saul said
unto the priest, Withdraw thine hand.
20 And Saul and all the people that
were with him assembled themselves,
and they came to the battle: and, behold, every man's sword was against his
fellow, *and there was* a very great dis-
comfiture.
21 Moreover, the Hebrews *that* were
with the Phĭ-lĭs′tĭneṣ before that time,
which went up with them into the camp
from the country round about, even they
also *turned* to be with the Ĭṣ′rā-ĕl-ītes
that *were* with Saul and Jonathan.
22 Likewise all the men of Ĭṣ′rā-ĕl
which had hid themselves in mount
Ē′phrā-ĭm, *when* they heard that the
Phĭ-lĭs′tĭneṣ fled, even they also followed hard after them in the battle.
23 So the LORD saved Ĭṣ′rā-ĕl that
day: and the battle passed over unto
Bĕth′-ā′vĕn.
24 ¶ And the men of Ĭṣ′rā-ĕl were distressed that day: for Saul had adjured
the people, saying, Cursed *be* the man
that eateth *any* food until evening, that
I may be avenged on mine enemies. So
none of the people tasted *any* food.
25 And all *they of* the land came to a
wood; and there was honey upon the
ground.
26 And when the people were come
into the wood, behold, the honey
dropped; but no man put his hand to his
mouth: for the people feared the oath.
27 But Jonathan heard not when his
father charged the people with the oath:
wherefore he put forth the end of the
rod that *was* in his hand, and dipped it
in a honeycomb, and put his hand to his
mouth; and his eyes were enlightened.
28 Then answered one of the people,
and said, Thy father straitly charged the
people with an oath, saying, Cursed *be*
the man that eateth *any* food this day.
And the people were faint.
29 Then said Jonathan, My father hath
troubled the land: see, I pray you, how
mine eyes have been enlightened, because I tasted a little of this honey.
30 How much more, if haply the people
had eaten freely to-day of the spoil of
their enemies which they found? for had
there not been now a much greater
slaughter among the Phĭ-lĭs′tĭneṣ?
31 And they smote the Phĭ-lĭs′tĭneṣ that
day from Mĭch′măsh to Āi′jȧ-lŏn: and
the people were very faint.
32 And the people flew upon the spoil,
and took sheep, and oxen, and calves,
and slew *them* on the ground: and the
people did eat *them* with the blood.
33 ¶ Then they told Saul, saying,

Behold, the people sin against the LORD,
in that they eat with the blood. And he
said, Ye have transgressed: roll a great
stone unto me this day.
34 And Saul said, Disperse yourselves
among the people, and say unto them,
Bring me hither every man his ox, and
every man his sheep, and slay *them*
here, and eat; and sin not against the
LORD in eating with the blood. And all
the people brought every man his ox
with him that night, and slew *them*
there.
35 And Saul built an altar unto the
LORD: the same was the first altar that
he built unto the LORD.
36 ℂ And Saul said, Let us go down
after the Phĭ-lĭs′tīneș by night, and spoil
them until the morning light, and let us
not leave a man of them. And they said,
Do whatsoever seemeth good unto thee.
Then said the priest, Let us draw near
hither unto God.
37 And Saul asked counsel of God,
Shall I go down after the Phĭ-lĭs′tīneș?
wilt thou deliver them into the hand of
Ĭș′rā-ĕl? But he answered him not that
day.
38 And Saul said, Draw ye near hither,
all the chief of the people: and know
and see wherein this sin hath been this
day.
39 For, *as* the LORD liveth, which
saveth Ĭș′rā-ĕl, though it be in Jonathan
my son, he shall surely die. But *there*
was not a man among all the people *that*
answered him.
40 Then said he unto all Ĭș′rā-ĕl, Be ye
on one side, and I and Jonathan my son
will be on the other side. And the people
said unto Saul, Do what seemeth good
unto thee.
41 Therefore Saul said unto the LORD
God of Ĭș′rā-ĕl, Give a perfect *lot*. And
Saul and Jonathan were taken: but the
people escaped.
42 And Saul said, Cast *lots* between me
and Jonathan my son. And Jonathan
was taken.
43 Then Saul said to Jonathan, Tell me
what thou hast done. And Jonathan
told him, and said, I did but taste a little
honey with the end of the rod that *was*
in mine hand, *and*, lo, I must die.
44 And Saul answered, God do so and
more also: for thou shalt surely die,
Jonathan.
45 And the people said unto Saul, Shall
Jonathan die, who hath wrought this
great salvation in Ĭș′rā-ĕl? God forbid:
as the LORD liveth, there shall not one
hair of his head fall to the ground; for
he hath wrought with God this day. So
the people rescued Jonathan, that he
died not.
46 Then Saul went up from following
the Phĭ-lĭs′tīneș: and the Phĭ-lĭs′tīneș
went to their own place.
47 ℂ So Saul took the kingdom over
Ĭș′rā-ĕl, and fought against all his enemies on every side, against Mō′ăb, and
against the children of Ammon, and
against Ē′dŏm, and against the kings of
Zō′bȧh, and against the Phĭ-lĭs′tīneș:
and whithersoever he turned himself,
he vexed *them*.
48 And he gathered a host, and smote
the Ăm′ȧ-lĕk-ītes, and delivered Ĭș′rā-ĕl
out of the hands of them that spoiled
them.
49 Now the sons of Saul were Jonathan,
and Ĭsh′ū-ī, and Mĕl′chī-shụ′ȧ: and the
names of his two daughters *were these;*
the name of the firstborn Mē′răb, and
the name of the younger Mī′chăl:
50 And the name of Saul's wife *was*
Ȧ-hĭn′ō-ăm, the daughter of Ȧ-hĭm′ā-ăz:
and the name of the captain of his host
was Abner, the son of Nĕr, Saul's uncle.
51 And Kish *was* the father of Saul;
and Nĕr the father of Abner *was* the son
of Ā′bĭ-ĕl.
52 And there was sore war against the
Phĭ-lĭs′tīneș all the days of Saul: and
when Saul saw any strong man, or any
valiant man, he took him unto him.

CHAPTER 15

SAMUEL also said unto Saul, The
LORD sent me to anoint thee *to be*
king over his people, over Ĭș′rā-ĕl: now
therefore hearken thou unto the voice of
the words of the LORD.
2 Thus saith the LORD of hosts, I remember *that* which Ăm′ȧ-lĕk did to
Ĭș′rā-ĕl, how he laid *wait* for him in the
way, when he came up from Egypt.
3 Now go and smite Ăm′ȧ-lĕk, and
utterly destroy all that they have, and
spare them not; but slay both man
and woman, infant and suckling, ox
and sheep, camel and ass.
4 And Saul gathered the people together, and numbered them in Tē-lā′ĭm,
two hundred thousand footmen, and ten
thousand men of Judah.

5 And Saul came to a city of Ăm'ȧ-lĕk,
and laid wait in the valley.
6 ¶ And Saul said unto the Kē'nītes,
Go, depart, get you down from among
the Ăm'ȧ-lĕk-ītes, lest I destroy you with
them: for ye showed kindness to all the
children of Ĭs̩'rā-ĕl, when they came up
out of Egypt. So the Kē'nītes departed
from among the Ăm'ȧ-lĕk-ītes.
7 And Saul smote the Ăm'ȧ-lĕk-ītes
from Hăv'ĭ-läh *until* thou comest to
Shu̱r, that *is* over against Egypt.
8 And he took Ā'găg the king of the
Ăm'ȧ-lĕk-ītes alive, and utterly destroyed all the people with the edge of
the sword.
9 But Saul and the people spared
Ā găg, and the best of the sheep, and of
the oxen, and of the fatlings, and the
lambs, and all *that was* good, and would
not utterly destroy them: but every
thing *that was* vile and refuse, that they
destroyed utterly.
10 ¶ Then came the word of the LORD
unto Samuel, saying,
11 It repenteth me that I have set up
Saul *to be* king: for he is turned back
from following me, and hath not performed my commandments. And it
grieved Samuel; and he cried unto the
LORD all night.
12 And when Samuel rose early to
meet Saul in the morning, it was told
Samuel, saying, Saul came to Cär'mĕl,
and, behold, he set him up a place, and
is gone about, and passed on, and gone
down to Gĭl'găl.
13 And Samuel came to Saul: and Saul
said unto him, Blessed *be* thou of the
LORD: I have performed the commandment of the LORD.
14 And Samuel said, What *meaneth*
then this bleating of the sheep in mine
ears, and the lowing of the oxen which I
hear?
15 And Saul said, They have brought
them from the Ăm'ȧ-lĕk-ītes: for the
people spared the best of the sheep and
of the oxen, to sacrifice unto the LORD
thy God; and the rest we have utterly
destroyed.
16 Then Samuel said unto Saul, Stay,
and I will tell thee what the LORD hath
said to me this night. And he said unto
him, Say on.
17 And Samuel said, When thou *wast*
little in thine own sight, *wast* thou not
made the head of the tribes of Ĭs̩'rā-ĕl,
and the LORD anointed thee king over
Ĭs̩'rā-ĕl?
18 And the LORD sent thee on a journey, and said, Go and utterly destroy
the sinners the Ăm'ȧ lĕk-ītes, and fight
against them until they be consumed.
19 Wherefore then didst thou not obey
the voice of the LORD, but didst fly upon
the spoil, and didst evil in the sight of
the LORD?
20 And Saul said unto Samuel, Yea, I
have obeyed the voice of the LORD, and
have gone the way which the LORD sent
me, and have brought Ā'găg the king of
Ăm'ȧ-lĕk, and have utterly destroyed
the Ăm'ȧ-lĕk-ītes.
21 But the people took of the spoil,
sheep and oxen, the chief of the things
which should have been utterly destroyed, to sacrifice unto the LORD thy
God in Gĭl'găl.
22 And Samuel said, Hath the LORD *as*
great delight in burnt offerings and
sacrifices, as in obeying the voice of the
LORD? Behold, to obey *is* better than
sacrifice, *and* to hearken than the fat of
rams.
23 For rebellion *is as* the sin of witchcraft, and stubbornness *is as* iniquity
and idolatry. Because thou hast rejected the word of the LORD, he hath
also rejected thee from *being* king.
24 ¶ And Saul said unto Samuel, I
have sinned: for I have transgressed the
commandment of the LORD, and thy
words: because I feared the people, and
obeyed their voice.
25 Now therefore, I pray thee, pardon
my sin, and turn again with me, that I
may worship the LORD.
26 And Samuel said unto Saul, I will
not return with thee: for thou hast rejected the word of the LORD, and the
LORD hath rejected thee from being
king over Ĭs̩'rā-ĕl.
27 And as Samuel turned about to go
away, he laid hold upon the skirt of his
mantle, and it rent.
28 And Samuel said unto him, The
LORD hath rent the kingdom of Ĭs̩'rā-ĕl
from thee this day, and hath given it to
a neighbor of thine, *that is* better than
thou.
29 And also the Strength of Ĭs̩'rā-ĕl
will not lie nor repent: for he *is* not a
man, that he should repent.
30 Then he said, I have sinned: *yet*
honor me now, I pray thee, before the

elders of my people, and before Ĭṣ′rā-ĕl,
and turn again with me, that I may worship the LORD thy God.
31 So Samuel turned again after Saul;
and Saul worshipped the LORD.
32 ¶ Then said Samuel, Bring ye
hither to me Ā′găg the king of the Ăm′ȧ-
lĕk-ītes. And Ā′găg came unto him delicately. And Ā′găg said, Surely the bitterness of death is past.
33 And Samuel said, As thy sword hath
made women childless, so shall thy
mother be childless among women. And
Samuel hewed Ā′găg in pieces before
the LORD in Gĭl′găl.
34 ¶ Then Samuel went to Rā′mȧh;
and Saul went up to his house to Gĭb′ē-
ȧh of Saul.
35 And Samuel came no more to see
Saul until the day of his death: nevertheless Samuel mourned for Saul: and
the LORD repented that he had made
Saul king over Ĭṣ′rā-ĕl.

CHAPTER 16

AND the LORD said unto Samuel, How
long wilt thou mourn for Saul, seeing I have rejected him from reigning
over Ĭṣ′rā-ĕl? fill thine horn with oil, and
go, I will send thee to Jesse the Beth-
lehemite: for I have provided me a king
among his sons.
2 And Samuel said, How can I go? if
Saul hear *it*, he will kill me. And the
LORD said, Take a heifer with thee, and
say, I am come to sacrifice to the LORD.
3 And call Jesse to the sacrifice, and I
will show thee what thou shalt do: and
thou shalt anoint unto me *him* whom I
name unto thee.
4 And Samuel did that which the LORD
spake, and came to Beth-lehem. And
the elders of the town trembled at his
coming, and said, Comest thou peaceably?
5 And he said, Peaceably: I am come
to sacrifice unto the LORD: sanctify
yourselves, and come with me to the
sacrifice. And he sanctified Jesse and
his sons, and called them to the sacrifice.
6 ¶ And it came to pass, when they
were come, that he looked on Ē-lī′ăb,
and said, Surely the LORD's anointed *is*
before him.
7 But the LORD said unto Samuel,
Look not on his countenance, or on the
height of his stature; because I have
refused him: for *the LORD seeth* not as
man seeth; for man looketh on the outward appearance, but the LORD looketh
on the heart.
8 Then Jesse called Ȧ-bĭn′ȧ-dăb, and
made him pass before Samuel. And he
said, Neither hath the LORD chosen this.
9 Then Jesse made Shăm′mȧh to pass
by. And he said, Neither hath the LORD
chosen this.
10 Again, Jesse made seven of his sons
to pass before Samuel. And Samuel
said unto Jesse, The LORD hath not
chosen these.
11 And Samuel said unto Jesse, Are
here all *thy* children? And he said,
There remaineth yet the youngest, and,
behold, he keepeth the sheep. And
Samuel said unto Jesse, Send and fetch
him: for we will not sit down till he come
hither.
12 And he sent, and brought him in.
Now he *was* ruddy, *and* withal of a
beautiful countenance, and goodly to
look to. And the LORD said, Arise,
anoint him: for this *is* he.
13 Then Samuel took the horn of oil,
and anointed him in the midst of his
brethren: and the Spirit of the LORD
came upon David from that day forward.
So Samuel rose up, and went to Rā′mȧh.
14 ¶ But the Spirit of the LORD departed from Saul, and an evil spirit from
the LORD troubled him.
15 And Saul's servants said unto him,
Behold now, an evil spirit from God
troubleth thee.
16 Let our lord now command thy
servants, *which are* before thee, to seek
out a man, *who is* a cunning player on a
harp: and it shall come to pass, when
the evil spirit from God is upon thee,
that he shall play with his hand, and
thou shalt be well.
17 And Saul said unto his servants,
Provide me now a man that can play
well, and bring *him* to me.
18 Then answered one of the servants,
and said, Behold, I have seen a son of
Jesse the Beth-lehemite, *that is* cunning
in playing, and a mighty valiant man,
and a man of war, and prudent in matters, and a comely person, and the LORD
is with him.
19 ¶ Wherefore Saul sent messengers
unto Jesse, and said, Send me David thy
son, which *is* with the sheep.
20 And Jesse took an ass *laden* with

bread, and a bottle of wine, and a kid, and sent *them* by David his son unto Saul.

21 And David came to Saul, and stood before him: and he loved him greatly; and he became his armor-bearer.

22 And Saul sent to Jesse, saying, Let David, I pray thee, stand before me; for he hath found favor in my sight.

23 And it came to pass, when the *evil* spirit from God was upon Saul, that David took a harp, and played with his hand: so Saul was refreshed, and was well, and the evil spirit departed from him.

CHAPTER 17

NOW the Phĭ-lĭs′tĭneș gathered together their armies to battle, and were gathered together at Shō′chōh, which *belongeth* to Judah, and pitched between Shō′chōh and Ȧ-zē′kȧh, in Ē′phĕs–dăm′mĭm.

2 And Saul and the men of Ĭṣ′rā-ĕl were gathered together, and pitched by the valley of Ē′lȧh, and set the battle in array against the Phĭ-lĭs′tĭneș.

3 And the Phĭ-lĭs′tĭneș stood on a mountain on the one side, and Ĭṣ′rā-ĕl stood on a mountain on the other side: and *there was* a valley between them.

4 ℂ And there went out a champion out of the camp of the Phĭ-lĭs′tĭneș, named Gō-lī′ăth, of Gath, whose height *was* six cubits and a span.

5 And *he had* a helmet of brass upon his head, and he *was* armed with a coat of mail; and the weight of the coat *was* five thousand shekels of brass.

6 And *he had* greaves of brass upon his legs, and a target of brass between his shoulders.

7 And the staff of his spear *was* like a weaver's beam; and his spear's head *weighed* six hundred shekels of iron: and one bearing a shield went before him.

8 And he stood and cried unto the armies of Ĭṣ′rā-ĕl, and said unto them, Why are ye come out to set *your* battle in array? *am* not I a Phĭ-lĭs′tĭne, and ye servants to Saul? choose you a man for you, and let him come down to me.

9 If he be able to fight with me, and to kill me, then will we be your servants: but if I prevail against him, and kill him, then shall ye be our servants, and serve us.

10 And the Phĭ-lĭs′tĭne said, I defy the armies of Ĭṣ′rā-ĕl this day; give me a man, that we may fight together.

11 When Saul and all Ĭṣ′rā-ĕl heard those words of the Phĭ-lĭs′tĭne, they were dismayed, and greatly afraid.

12 ℂ Now David *was* the son of that Ĕph′răth-īte of Beth-lehem-judah, whose name *was* Jesse; and he had eight sons: and the man went among men *for* an old man in the days of Saul.

13 And the three eldest sons of Jesse went *and* followed Saul to the battle: and the names of his three sons that went to the battle *were* Ē-lī′ăb the first-born, and next unto him Ȧ-bĭn′ȧ-dăb, and the third Shăm′mȧh.

14 And David *was* the youngest: and the three eldest followed Saul.

15 But David went and returned from Saul to feed his father's sheep at Beth-lehem.

16 And the Phĭ-lĭs′tĭne drew near morning and evening, and presented himself forty days.

17 And Jesse said unto David his son, Take now for thy brethren an ē′phȧh of this parched *corn*, and these ten loaves, and run to the camp to thy brethren;

18 And carry these ten cheeses unto the captain of *their* thousand, and look how thy brethren fare, and take their pledge.

19 Now Saul, and they, and all the men of Ĭṣ′rā-ĕl, *were* in the valley of Ē′lȧh, fighting with the Phĭ-lĭs′tĭneș.

20 ℂ And David rose up early in the morning, and left the sheep with a keeper, and took, and went, as Jesse had commanded him; and he came to the trench, as the host was going forth to the fight, and shouted for the battle.

21 For Ĭṣ′rā-ĕl and the Phĭ-lĭs′tĭneș had put the battle in array, army against army.

22 And David left his carriage in the hand of the keeper of the carriage, and ran into the army, and came and saluted his brethren.

23 And as he talked with them, behold, there came up the champion, the Phĭ-lĭs′tĭne of Gath, Gō-lī′ăth by name, out of the armies of the Phĭ-lĭs′tĭneș, and spake according to the same words: and David heard *them*.

24 And all the men of Ĭṣ′rā-ĕl, when they saw the man, fled from him, and were sore afraid.

25 And the men of Ĭṣ′rā-ĕl said, Have ye seen this man that is come up? surely to defy Ĭṣ′rā-ĕl is he come up: and it shall be, *that* the man who killeth him, the king will enrich him with great riches, and will give him his daughter, and make his father's house free in Ĭṣ′rā-ĕl.

26 And David spake to the men that stood by him, saying, What shall be done to the man that killeth this Phĭ-lĭs′tīne, and taketh away the reproach from Ĭṣ′rā-ĕl? for who *is* this uncircumcised Phĭ-lĭs′tīne, that he should defy the armies of the living God?

27 And the people answered him after this manner, saying, So shall it be done to the man that killeth him.

28 ¶ And Ē-lĭ′ăb his eldest brother heard when he spake unto the men; and Ē-lĭ′ăb's anger was kindled against David, and he said, Why camest thou down hither? and with whom hast thou left those few sheep in the wilderness? I know thy pride, and the naughtiness of thine heart; for thou art come down that thou mightest see the battle.

29 And David said, What have I now done? *Is there* not a cause?

30 ¶ And he turned from him toward another, and spake after the same manner: and the people answered him again after the former manner.

31 And when the words were heard which David spake, they rehearsed *them* before Saul: and he sent for him.

32 ¶ And David said to Saul, Let no man's heart fail because of him; thy servant will go and fight with this Phĭ-lĭs′tīne.

33 And Saul said to David, Thou art not able to go against this Phĭ-lĭs′tīne to fight with him: for thou *art but* a youth, and he a man of war from his youth.

34 And David said unto Saul, Thy servant kept his father's sheep, and there came a lion, and a bear, and took a lamb out of the flock:

35 And I went out after him, and smote him, and delivered *it* out of his mouth: and when he arose against me, I caught *him* by his beard, and smote him, and slew him.

36 Thy servant slew both the lion and the bear: and this uncircumcised Phĭ-lĭs′tīne shall be as one of them, seeing he hath defied the armies of the living God.

37 David said moreover, The LORD that delivered me out of the paw of the lion, and out of the paw of the bear, he will deliver me out of the hand of this Phĭ-lĭs′tīne. And Saul said unto David, Go, and the LORD be with thee.

38 ¶ And Saul armed David with his armor, and he put a helmet of brass upon his head; also he armed him with a coat of mail.

39 And David girded his sword upon his armor, and he assayed to go; for he had not proved *it*. And David said unto Saul, I cannot go with these: for I have not proved *them*. And David put them off him.

40 And he took his staff in his hand, and chose him five smooth stones out of the brook, and put them in a shepherd's bag which he had, even in a scrip; and his sling *was* in his hand: and he drew near to the Phĭ-lĭs′tīne.

41 And the Phĭ-lĭs′tīne came on and drew near unto David; and the man that bare the shield *went* before him.

42 And when the Phĭ-lĭs′tīne looked about, and saw David, he disdained him: for he was *but* a youth, and ruddy, and of a fair countenance.

43 And the Phĭ-lĭs′tīne said unto David, *Am* I a dog, that thou comest to me with staves? And the Phĭ-lĭs′tīne cursed David by his gods.

44 And the Phĭ-lĭs′tīne said to David, Come to me, and I will give thy flesh unto the fowls of the air, and to the beasts of the field.

45 Then said David to the Phĭ-lĭs′tīne, Thou comest to me with a sword, and with a spear, and with a shield: but I come to thee in the name of the LORD of hosts, the God of the armies of Ĭṣ′rā-ĕl, whom thou hast defied.

46 This day will the LORD deliver thee into mine hand; and I will smite thee, and take thine head from thee; and I will give the carcasses of the host of the Phĭ-lĭs′tīneṣ this day unto the fowls of the air, and to the wild beasts of the earth; that all the earth may know that there is a God in Ĭṣ′rā-ĕl.

47 And all this assembly shall know that the LORD saveth not with sword and spear: for the battle *is* the LORD's, and he will give you into our hands.

48 And it came to pass, when the Phĭ-lĭs′tīne arose, and came and drew nigh to meet David, that David hasted, and

ran toward the army to meet the Phĭ-lĭs′tĭne.

49 And David put his hand in his bag, and took thence a stone, and slang *it*, and smote the Phĭ-lĭs′tĭne in his forehead, that the stone sunk into his forehead; and he fell upon his face to the earth.

50 So David prevailed over the Phĭ-lĭs′tĭne with a sling and with a stone, and smote the Phĭ-lĭs′tĭne, and slew him; but *there was* no sword in the hand of David.

51 Therefore David ran, and stood upon the Phĭ-lĭs′tĭne, and took his sword, and drew it out of the sheath thereof, and slew him, and cut off his head therewith. And when the Phĭ-lĭs′tĭneṣ saw their champion was dead, they fled.

52 And the men of Ĭṣ′rā-ĕl and of Judah arose, and shouted, and pursued the Phĭ-lĭs′tĭneṣ, until thou come to the valley, and to the gates of Ĕk′rŏn. And the wounded of the Phĭ-lĭs′tĭneṣ fell down by the way to Shā′ă-rā′ĭm, even unto Gath, and unto Ĕk′rŏn.

53 And the children of Ĭṣ′rā-ĕl returned from chasing after the Phĭ-lĭs′tĭneṣ, and they spoiled their tents.

54 And David took the head of the Phĭ-lĭs′tĭne, and brought it to Jerusalem; but he put his armor in his tent.

55 ¶ And when Saul saw David go forth against the Phĭ-lĭs′tĭne, he said unto Abner, the captain of the host, Abner, whose son *is* this youth? And Abner said, *As* thy soul liveth, O king, I cannot tell.

56 And the king said, Inquire thou whose son the stripling *is*.

57 And as David returned from the slaughter of the Phĭ-lĭs′tĭne, Abner took him, and brought him before Saul with the head of the Phĭ-lĭs′tĭne in his hand.

58 And Saul said to him, Whose son *art* thou, *thou* young man? And David answered, *I am* the son of thy servant Jesse the Beth-lehemite.

CHAPTER 18

AND it came to pass, when he had made an end of speaking unto Saul, that the soul of Jonathan was knit with the soul of David, and Jonathan loved him as his own soul.

2 And Saul took him that day, and would let him go no more home to his father's house.

3 Then Jonathan and David made a covenant, because he loved him as his own soul.

4 And Jonathan stripped himself of the robe that *was* upon him, and gave it to David, and his garments, even to his sword, and to his bow, and to his girdle.

5 ¶ And David went out whithersoever Saul sent him, *and* behaved himself wisely: and Saul set him over the men of war, and he was accepted in the sight of all the people, and also in the sight of Saul's servants.

6 And it came to pass as they came, when David was returned from the slaughter of the Phĭ-lĭs′tĭne, that the women came out of all cities of Ĭṣ′rā-ĕl, singing and dancing, to meet king Saul, with tabrets, with joy, and with instruments of music.

7 And the women answered *one another* as they played, and said, Saul hath slain his thousands, and David his ten thousands.

8 And Saul was very wroth, and the saying displeased him; and he said, They have ascribed unto David ten thousands, and to me they have ascribed *but* thousands: and *what* can he have more but the kingdom?

9 And Saul eyed David from that day and forward.

10 ¶ And it came to pass on the morrow, that the evil spirit from God came upon Saul, and he prophesied in the midst of the house: and David played with his hand, as at other times: and *there was* a javelin in Saul's hand.

11 And Saul cast the javelin; for he said, I will smite David even to the wall *with it*. And David avoided out of his presence twice.

12 ¶ And Saul was afraid of David, because the LORD was with him, and was departed from Saul.

13 Therefore Saul removed him from him, and made him his captain over a thousand; and he went out and came in before the people.

14 And David behaved himself wisely in all his ways; and the LORD *was* with him.

15 Wherefore when Saul saw that he behaved himself very wisely, he was afraid of him.

16 But all Ĭṣ′rā-ĕl and Judah loved David, because he went out and came in before them.

17 ℂ And Saul said to David, Behold my elder daughter Mē′răb, her will I give thee to wife: only be thou valiant for me, and fight the LORD's battles. For Saul said, Let not mine hand be upon him, but let the hand of the Phĭ-lĭs′tĭneş be upon him.

18 And David said unto Saul, Who *am* I? and what *is* my life, *or* my father's family in Ĭş′rā-ēl, that I should be son-in-law to the king?

19 But it came to pass at the time when Mē′răb Saul's daughter should have been given to David, that she was given unto Ā′drĭ-ēl the Mē-hō′lȧ-thīte to wife.

20 And Mī′chăl Saul's daughter loved David: and they told Saul, and the thing pleased him.

21 And Saul said, I will give him her, that she may be a snare to him, and that the hand of the Phĭ-lĭs′tĭneş may be against him. Wherefore Saul said to David, Thou shalt this day be my son-in-law in *the one of* the twain.

22 ℂ And Saul commanded his servants, *saying,* Commune with David secretly, and say, Behold, the king hath delight in thee, and all his servants love thee: now therefore be the king's son-in-law.

23 And Saul's servants spake those words in the ears of David. And David said, Seemeth it to you a light thing to be a king's son-in-law, seeing that I *am* a poor man, and lightly esteemed?

24 And the servants of Saul told him, saying, On this manner spake David.

25 And Saul said, Thus shall ye say to David, The king desireth not any dowry, but a hundred foreskins of the Phĭ-lĭs′tĭneş, to be avenged of the king's enemies. But Saul thought to make David fall by the hand of the Phĭ-lĭs′tĭneş.

26 And when his servants told David these words, it pleased David well to be the king's son-in-law: and the days were not expired.

27 Wherefore David arose and went, he and his men, and slew of the Phĭ-lĭs′tĭneş two hundred men; and David brought their foreskins, and they gave them in full tale to the king, that he might be the king's son-in-law. And Saul gave him Mī′chăl his daughter to wife.

28 ℂ And Saul saw and knew that the LORD *was* with David, and *that* Mī′chăl Saul's daughter loved him.

29 And Saul was yet the more afraid of David; and Saul became David's enemy continually.

30 Then the princes of the Phĭ-lĭs′tĭneş went forth: and it came to pass, after they went forth, *that* David behaved himself more wisely than all the servants of Saul; so that his name was much set by.

CHAPTER 19

AND Saul spake to Jonathan his son, and to all his servants, that they should kill David.

2 But Jonathan Saul's son delighted much in David: and Jonathan told David, saying, Saul my father seeketh to kill thee: now therefore, I pray thee, take heed to thyself until the morning, and abide in a secret place, and hide thyself:

3 And I will go out and stand beside my father in the field where thou *art,* and I will commune with my father of thee; and what I see, that I will tell thee.

4 ℂ And Jonathan spake good of David unto Saul his father, and said unto him, Let not the king sin against his servant, against David; because he hath not sinned against thee, and because his works *have been* to thee-ward very good:

5 For he did put his life in his hand, and slew the Phĭ-lĭs′tĭne, and the LORD wrought a great salvation for all Ĭş′rā-ēl: thou sawest *it,* and didst rejoice: wherefore then wilt thou sin against innocent blood, to slay David without a cause?

6 And Saul hearkened unto the voice of Jonathan: and Saul sware, *As* the LORD liveth, he shall not be slain.

7 And Jonathan called David, and Jonathan showed him all those things. And Jonathan brought David to Saul, and he was in his presence, as in times past.

8 ℂ And there was war again: and David went out, and fought with the Phĭ-lĭs′tĭneş, and slew them with a great slaughter; and they fled from him.

9 And the evil spirit from the LORD was upon Saul, as he sat in his house with his javelin in his hand: and David played with *his* hand.

10 And Saul sought to smite David even to the wall with the javelin; but he slipped away out of Saul's presence, and he smote the javelin into the wall: and David fled, and escaped that night.

11 Saul also sent messengers unto
David's house, to watch him, and to slay
him in the morning; and Mī'chăl David's
wife told him, saying, If thou save not
thy life to-night, to-morrow thou shalt
be slain.
12 ℂ So Mī'chăl let David down
through a window: and he went, and
fled, and escaped.
13 And Mī'chăl took an image, and laid
it in the bed, and put a pillow of goats'
hair for his bolster, and covered *it* with
a cloth.
14 And when Saul sent messengers to
take David, she said, He *is* sick.
15 And Saul sent the messengers *again*
to see David, saying, Bring him up to
me in the bed, that I may slay him.
16 And when the messengers were
come in, behold, *there was* an image in
the bed, with a pillow of goats' *hair* for
his bolster.
17 And Saul said unto Mī'chăl, Why
hast thou deceived me so, and sent away
mine enemy, that he is escaped? And
Mī'chăl answered Saul, He said unto
me, Let me go; why should I kill thee?
18 ℂ So David fled, and escaped, and
came to Samuel to Rā'măh, and told him
all that Saul had done to him. And he
and Samuel went and dwelt in Nā'ịōth.
19 And it was told Saul, saying, Behold,
David *is* at Nā'ịōth in Rā'măh.
20 And Saul sent messengers to take
David: and when they saw the company
of the prophets prophesying, and
Samuel standing *as* appointed over
them, the Spirit of God was upon the
messengers of Saul, and they also
prophesied.
21 And when it was told Saul, he sent
other messengers, and they prophesied
likewise. And Saul sent messengers
again the third time, and they prophesied also.
22 Then went he also to Rā'măh, and
came to a great well that *is* in Sē'chū:
and he asked and said, Where *are*
Samuel and David? And *one* said, Behold, *they be* at Nā'ịōth in Rā'măh.
23 And he went thither to Nā'ịōth in
Rā'măh: and the Spirit of God was upon
him also, and he went on, and prophesied, until he came to Nā'ịōth in
Rā'măh.
24 And he stripped off his clothes also,
and prophesied before Samuel in like
manner, and lay down naked all that
day and all that night. Wherefore they
say, *Is* Saul also among the prophets?

CHAPTER 20

AND David fled from Nā'ịōth in Rā'-
măh, and came and said before
Jonathan, What have I done? what *is*
mine iniquity? and what *is* my sin before thy father, that he seeketh my life?
2 And he said unto him, God forbid;
thou shalt not die: behold, my father
will do nothing either great or small, but
that he will show it me: and why should
my father hide this thing from me? it *is*
not *so*.
3 And David sware moreover, and said,
Thy father certainly knoweth that I have
found grace in thine eyes; and he saith,
Let not Jonathan know this, lest he be
grieved: but truly, *as* the LORD liveth,
and *as* thy soul liveth, *there is* but a
step between me and death.
4 Then said Jonathan unto David,
Whatsoever thy soul desireth, I will
even do *it* for thee.
5 And David said unto Jonathan, Behold, to-morrow *is* the new moon, and I
should not fail to sit with the king at
meat: but let me go, that I may hide myself in the field unto the third *day* at
even.
6 If thy father at all miss me, then say,
David earnestly asked *leave* of me that
he might run to Beth-lehem his city: for
there is a yearly sacrifice there for all
the family.
7 If he say thus, *It is* well; thy servant
shall have peace: but if he be very
wroth, *then* be sure that evil is determined by him.
8 Therefore thou shalt deal kindly with
thy servant; for thou hast brought thy
servant into a covenant of the LORD
with thee: notwithstanding, if there be
in me iniquity, slay me thyself; for why
shouldest thou bring me to thy father?
9 And Jonathan said, Far be it from
thee: for if I knew certainly that evil
were determined by my father to come
upon thee, then would not I tell it thee?
10 Then said David to Jonathan, Who
shall tell me? or what *if* thy father answer thee roughly?
11 ℂ And Jonathan said unto David,
Come, and let us go out into the field.
And they went out both of them into the
field.
12 And Jonathan said unto David, O

LORD God of Ĭş'rā-ĕl, when I have
sounded my father about to-morrow any
time, *or* the third *day,* and, behold, *if*
there be good toward David, and I then
send not unto thee, and show it thee;
13 The LORD do so and much more to
Jonathan: but if it please my father *to*
do thee evil, then I will show it thee, and
send thee away, that thou mayest go in
peace: and the LORD be with thee, as he
hath been with my father.
14 And thou shalt not only while yet I
live show me the kindness of the LORD,
that I die not:
15 But *also* thou shalt not cut off thy
kindness from my house for ever: no,
not when the LORD hath cut off the enemies of David every one from the face
of the earth.
16 So Jonathan made *a covenant* with
the house of David, *saying,* Let the
LORD even require *it* at the hand of
David's enemies.
17 And Jonathan caused David to
swear again, because he loved him:
for he loved him as he loved his own
soul.
18 Then Jonathan said to David, To-
morrow *is* the new moon: and thou shalt
be missed, because thy seat will be
empty.
19 And *when* thou hast stayed three
days, *then* thou shalt go down quickly,
and come to the place where thou didst
hide thyself when the business was *in*
hand, and shalt remain by the stone
Ē'zĕl.
20 And I will shoot three arrows on the
side *thereof,* as though I shot at a mark.
21 And, behold, I will send a lad, *say-*
ing, Go, find out the arrows. If I expressly say unto the lad, Behold, the
arrows *are* on this side of thee, take
them; then come thou: for *there is* peace
to thee, and no hurt; *as* the LORD liveth.
22 But if I say thus unto the young
man, Behold, the arrows *are* beyond
thee; go thy way: for the LORD hath
sent thee away.
23 And *as touching* the matter which
thou and I have spoken of, behold, the
LORD *be* between thee and me for ever.
24 ℂ So David hid himself in the field:
and when the new moon was come, the
king sat him down to eat meat.
25 And the king sat upon his seat, as
at other times, *even* upon a seat by the
wall: and Jonathan arose, and Abner sat
by Saul's side, and David's place was
empty.
26 Nevertheless Saul spake not any
thing that day: for he thought, Something hath befallen him, he *is* not clean;
surely he *is* not clean.
27 And it came to pass on the morrow,
which was the second *day* of the month,
that David's place was empty: and Saul
said unto Jonathan his son, Wherefore
cometh not the son of Jesse to meat,
neither yesterday, nor to-day?
28 And Jonathan answered Saul,
David earnestly asked *leave* of me *to go*
to Beth-lehem:
29 And he said, Let me go, I pray thee;
for our family hath a sacrifice in the
city; and my brother, he hath commanded me *to be there:* and now, if I
have found favor in thine eyes, let me
get away, I pray thee, and see my brethren. Therefore he cometh not unto the
king's table.
30 Then Saul's anger was kindled
against Jonathan, and he said unto him,
Thou son of the perverse rebellious
woman, do not I know that thou hast
chosen the son of Jesse to thine own
confusion, and unto the confusion of thy
mother's nakedness?
31 For as long as the son of Jesse liveth
upon the ground, thou shalt not be
established, nor thy kingdom. Wherefore now send and fetch him unto me,
for he shall surely die.
32 And Jonathan answered Saul his
father, and said unto him, Wherefore shall he be slain? what hath he
done?
33 And Saul cast a javelin at him to
smite him: whereby Jonathan knew that
it was determined of his father to slay
David.
34 So Jonathan arose from the table in
fierce anger, and did eat no meat the
second day of the month: for he was
grieved for David, because his father
had done him shame.
35 ℂ And it came to pass in the morning, that Jonathan went out into the
field at the time appointed with David,
and a little lad with him.
36 And he said unto his lad, Run, find
out now the arrows which I shoot. *And*
as the lad ran, he shot an arrow beyond
him.
37 And when the lad was come to the
place of the arrow which Jonathan had

shot, Jonathan cried after the lad, and
said, *Is* not the arrow beyond thee?
38 And Jonathan cried after the lad,
Make speed, haste, stay not. And
Jonathan's lad gathered up the arrows,
and came to his master.
39 But the lad knew not any thing: only
Jonathan and David knew the matter.
40 And Jonathan gave his artillery unto
his lad, and said unto him, Go, carry
them to the city.
41 ¶ *And* as soon as the lad was gone,
David arose out of *a place* toward the
south, and fell on his face to the ground,
and bowed himself three times: and
they kissed one another, and wept one
with another, until David exceeded.
42 And Jonathan said to David, Go in
peace, forasmuch as we have sworn
both of us in the name of the LORD, saying, The LORD be between me and thee,
and between my seed and thy seed for
ever. And he arose and departed: and
Jonathan went into the city.

CHAPTER 21

THEN came David to Nŏb to Ȧ-hĭm'-
ē-lĕch the priest: and Ȧ-hĭm'ē-lĕch
was afraid at the meeting of David, and
said unto him, Why *art* thou alone, and
no man with thee?
2 And David said unto Ȧ-hĭm'ē-lĕch the
priest, The king hath commanded me a
business, and hath said unto me, Let no
man know any thing of the business
whereabout I send thee, and what I have
commanded thee: and I have appointed
my servants to such and such a place.
3 Now therefore what is under thine
hand? give *me* five *loaves of* bread in
mine hand, or what there is present.
4 And the priest answered David, and
said, *There is* no common bread under
mine hand, but there is hallowed bread;
if the young men have kept themselves
at least from women.
5 And David answered the priest, and
said unto him, Of a truth women *have
been* kept from us about these three
days, since I came out, and the vessels
of the young men are holy, and *the bread
is* in a manner common, yea, though it
were sanctified this day in the vessel.
6 So the priest gave him hallowed
bread: for there was no bread there but
the showbread, that was taken from before the LORD, to put hot bread in the
day when it was taken away.
7 Now a certain man of the servants of
Saul *was* there that day, detained before
the LORD; and his name *was* Dō'ĕg, an
Ē'dŏm-īte, the chiefest of the herdmen
that *belonged* to Saul.
8 ¶ And David said unto Ȧ-hĭm'ē-lĕch,
And is there not here under thine hand
spear or sword? for I have neither
brought my sword nor my weapons with
me, because the king's business required haste.
9 And the priest said, The sword of
Gō-lī'ăth the Phĭ-lĭs'tīne, whom thou
slewest in the valley of Ē'lȧh, behold, it
is here wrapped in a cloth behind the
ĕph'ŏd: if thou wilt take that, take *it:*
for *there is* no other save that here. And
David said, *There is* none like that; give
it me.
10 ¶ And David arose, and fled that
day for fear of Saul, and went to Ā'chĭsh
the king of Gath.
11 And the servants of Ā'chĭsh said
unto him, *Is* not this David the king of
the land? did they not sing one to another of him in dances, saying, Saul
hath slain his thousands, and David his
ten thousands?
12 And David laid up these words in
his heart, and was sore afraid of Ā'chĭsh
the king of Gath.
13 And he changed his behavior before them, and feigned himself mad in
their hands, and scrabbled on the doors
of the gate, and let his spittle fall down
upon his beard.
14 Then said Ā'chĭsh unto his servants,
Lo, ye see the man is mad: wherefore
then have ye brought him to me?
15 Have I need of madmen, that ye
have brought this *fellow* to play the
madman in my presence? shall this
fellow come into my house?

CHAPTER 22

DAVID therefore departed thence,
and escaped to the cave Ȧ-dŭl'-
lăm: and when his brethren and all his
father's house heard *it,* they went down
thither to him.
2 And every one *that was* in distress,
and every one that *was* in debt, and
every one *that was* discontented, gathered themselves unto him; and he became a captain over them: and there
were with him about four hundred men.
3 ¶ And David went thence to Mĭz'-
pĕh of Mō'ăb: and he said unto the king

of Mō′ăb, Let my father and my mother, I pray thee, come forth, *and be* with you, till I know what God will do for me.

4 And he brought them before the king of Mō′ăb: and they dwelt with him all the while that David was in the hold.

5 ¶ And the prophet Gad said unto David, Abide not in the hold; depart, and get thee into the land of Judah. Then David departed, and came into the forest of Hā′rĕth.

6 ¶ When Saul heard that David was discovered, and the men that *were* with him, (now Saul abode in Gĭb′ē-ȧh under a tree in Rā′mȧh, having his spear in his hand, and all his servants *were* standing about him;)

7 Then Saul said unto his servants that stood about him, Hear now, ye Benjamites; will the son of Jesse give every one of you fields and vineyards, *and* make you all captains of thousands, and captains of hundreds;

8 That all of you have conspired against me, and *there is* none that showeth me that my son hath made a league with the son of Jesse, and *there is* none of you that is sorry for me, or showeth unto me that my son hath stirred up my servant against me, to lie in wait, as at this day?

9 ¶ Then answered Dō′ĕg the Ē′dŏm-īte, which was set over the servants of Saul, and said, I saw the son of Jesse coming to Nŏb, to Ȧ-hĭm′ē-lĕch the son of Ȧ-hī′tŭb.

10 And he inquired of the LORD for him, and gave him victuals, and gave him the sword of Gō-lī′ăth the Phĭ-lĭs′tīne.

11 Then the king sent to call Ȧ-hĭm′ē-lĕch the priest, the son of Ȧ-hī′tŭb, and all his father's house, the priests that *were* in Nŏb: and they came all of them to the king.

12 And Saul said, Hear now, thou son of Ȧ-hī′tŭb. And he answered, Here I *am*, my lord.

13 And Saul said unto him, Why have ye conspired against me, thou and the son of Jesse, in that thou hast given him bread, and a sword, and hast inquired of God for him, that he should rise against me, to lie in wait, as at this day?

14 Then Ȧ-hĭm′ē-lĕch answered the king, and said, And who *is so* faithful among all thy servants as David, which is the king's son-in-law, and goeth at thy bidding, and is honorable in thine house?

15 Did I then begin to inquire of God for him? be it far from me: let not the king impute *any* thing unto his servant, *nor* to all the house of my father: for thy servant knew nothing of all this, less or more.

16 And the king said, Thou shalt surely die, Ȧ-hĭm′ē-lĕch, thou, and all thy father's house.

17 ¶ And the king said unto the footmen that stood about him, Turn, and slay the priests of the LORD; because their hand also *is* with David, and because they knew when he fled, and did not show it to me. But the servants of the king would not put forth their hand to fall upon the priests of the LORD.

18 And the king said to Dō′ĕg, Turn thou, and fall upon the priests. And Dō′ĕg the Ē′dŏm-īte turned, and he fell upon the priests, and slew on that day fourscore and five persons that did wear a linen eph′ŏd.

19 And Nŏb, the city of the priests, smote he with the edge of the sword, both men and women, children and sucklings, and oxen, and asses, and sheep, with the edge of the sword.

20 ¶ And one of the sons of Ȧ-hĭm′ē-lĕch the son of Ȧ-hī′tŭb, named Ȧ-bī′ȧ-thȧr, escaped, and fled after David.

21 And Ȧ-bī′ȧ-thȧr showed David that Saul had slain the LORD's priests.

22 And David said unto Ȧ-bī′ȧ-thȧr, I knew *it* that day, when Dō′ĕg the Ē′dŏm-īte *was* there, that he would surely tell Saul: I have occasioned *the death* of all the persons of thy father's house

23 Abide thou with me, fear not: for he that seeketh my life seeketh thy life: but with me thou *shalt be* in safeguard.

CHAPTER 23

THEN they told David, saying, Behold, the Phĭ-lĭs′tīneş fight against Kē-ī′lȧh, and they rob the threshing-floors.

2 Therefore David inquired of the LORD, saying, Shall I go and smite these Phĭ-lĭs′tīneş? And the LORD said unto David, Go, and smite the Phĭ-lĭs′tīneş, and save Kē-ī′lȧh.

3 And David's men said unto him, Behold, we be afraid here in Judah: how much more then if we come to Kē-ī′lȧh against the armies of the Phĭ-lĭs′tīneş?

4 Then David inquired of the LORD yet
again. And the LORD answered him and
said, Arise, go down to Kē-ī′lȧh; for I will
deliver the Phĭ-lĭs′tīneş into thine hand.
5 So David and his men went to Kē-ī′-
lȧh, and fought with the Phĭ-lĭs′tīneş,
and brought away their cattle, and
smote them with a great slaughter. So
David saved the inhabitants of Kē-ī′lȧh.
6 And it came to pass, when Ȧ-bī′ȧ-
thär the son of Ȧ-hĭm′ē-lĕch fled to
David to Kē-ī′lȧh, *that* he came down
with an ĕph′ŏd in his hand.
7 ¶ And it was told Saul that David
was come to Kē-ī′lȧh. And Saul said,
God hath delivered him into mine hand;
for he is shut in, by entering into a town
that hath gates and bars.
8 And Saul called all the people together to war, to go down to Kē-ī′lȧh,
to besiege David and his men.
9 ¶ And David knew that Saul secretly
practised mischief against him: and he
said to Ȧ-bī′ȧ-thär the priest, Bring
hither the ĕph′ŏd.
10 Then said David, O LORD God of
Ĭş′rā-ĕl, thy servant hath certainly heard
that Saul seeketh to come to Kē-ī′lȧh,
to destroy the city for my sake.
11 Will the men of Kē-ī′lȧh deliver me
up into his hand? will Saul come down,
as thy servant hath heard? O LORD
God of Ĭş′rā-ĕl, I beseech thee, tell thy
servant. And the LORD said, He will
come down.
12 Then said David, Will the men of
Kē-ī′lȧh deliver me and my men into the
hand of Saul? And the LORD said, They
will deliver *thee* up.
13 ¶ Then David and his men, *which*
were about six hundred, arose and departed out of Kē-ī′lȧh, and went whithersoever they could go. And it was told
Saul that David was escaped from Kē-ī′-
lȧh; and he forbare to go forth.
14 And David abode in the wilderness
in strongholds, and remained in a mountain in the wilderness of Zĭph. And Saul
sought him every day, but God delivered
him not into his hand.
15 And David saw that Saul was come
out to seek his life: and David *was* in
the wilderness of Zĭph in a wood.
16 ¶ And Jonathan Saul's son arose,
and went to David into the wood, and
strengthened his hand in God.
17 And he said unto him, Fear not: for
the hand of Saul my father shall not find
thee; and thou shalt be king over
Ĭş′rā-ĕl, and I shall be next unto thee;
and that also Saul my father knoweth.
18 And they two made a covenant before the LORD: and David abode in the
wood, and Jonathan went to his house.
19 ¶ Then came up the Zĭph′ītes to
Saul to Gĭb′ē-ȧh, saying, Doth not David
hide himself with us in strongholds in
the wood, in the hill of Hȧ-chī′lȧh, which
is on the south of Jē-shī′mŏn?
20 Now therefore, O king, come down
according to all the desire of thy soul to
come down; and our part *shall be* to
deliver him into the king's hand.
21 And Saul said, Blessed *be* ye of the
LORD; for ye have compassion on me.
22 Go, I pray you, prepare yet, and
know and see his place where his haunt
is, *and* who hath seen him there: for it
is told me *that* he dealeth very subtilely.
23 See therefore, and take knowledge
of all the lurking places where he hideth
himself, and come ye again to me with
the certainty, and I will go with you: and
it shall come to pass, if he be in the land,
that I will search him out throughout all
the thousands of Judah.
24 And they arose, and went to Zĭph
before Saul: but David and his men *were*
in the wilderness of Mā′ŏn, in the plain
on the south of Jē-shī′mŏn.
25 Saul also and his men went to seek
him. And they told David: wherefore
he came down into a rock, and abode in
the wilderness of Mā′ŏn. And when
Saul heard *that*, he pursued after David
in the wilderness of Mā′ŏn.
26 And Saul went on this side of the
mountain, and David and his men on
that side of the mountain: and David
made haste to get away for fear of Saul;
for Saul and his men compassed David
and his men round about to take them.
27 ¶ But there came a messenger unto
Saul, saying, Haste thee, and come; for
the Phĭ-lĭs′tīneş have invaded the land.
28 Wherefore Saul returned from pursuing after David, and went against the
Phĭ-lĭs′tīneş: therefore they called that
place Sē′lȧ-hȧm-mäh′lē-kŏth.
29 ¶ And David went up from thence,
and dwelt in strongholds at Ĕn-gē′dī.

CHAPTER 24

AND it came to pass, when Saul was
returned from following the Phĭ-
lĭs′tīneş, that it was told him, saying,

Behold, David *is* in the wilderness of Ĕn-gē'dī.

2 Then Saul took three thousand chosen men out of all Ĭṣ'rā-ĕl, and went to seek David and his men upon the rocks of the wild goats.

3 And he came to the sheepcotes by the way, where *was* a cave; and Saul went in to cover his feet: and David and his men remained in the sides of the cave.

4 And the men of David said unto him, Behold the day of which the LORD said unto thee, Behold, I will deliver thine enemy into thine hand, that thou mayest do to him as it shall seem good unto thee. Then David arose, and cut off the skirt of Saul's robe privily.

5 And it came to pass afterward, that David's heart smote him, because he had cut off Saul's skirt.

6 And he said unto his men, The LORD forbid that I should do this thing unto my master, the LORD's anointed, to stretch forth mine hand against him, seeing he *is* the anointed of the LORD.

7 So David stayed his servants with these words, and suffered them not to rise against Saul. But Saul rose up out of the cave, and went on *his* way.

8 David also arose afterward, and went out of the cave, and cried after Saul, saying, My lord the king. And when Saul looked behind him, David stooped with his face to the earth, and bowed himself.

9 ℂ And David said to Saul, Wherefore hearest thou men's words, saying, Behold, David seeketh thy hurt?

10 Behold, this day thine eyes have seen how that the LORD hath delivered thee to-day into mine hand in the cave: and *some* bade *me* kill thee: but *mine eye* spared thee; and I said, I will not put forth mine hand against my lord; for he *is* the LORD's anointed.

11 Moreover, my father, see, yea, see the skirt of thy robe in my hand: for in that I cut off the skirt of thy robe, and killed thee not, know thou and see that *there is* neither evil nor transgression in mine hand, and I have not sinned against thee; yet thou huntest my soul to take it.

12 The LORD judge between me and thee, and the LORD avenge me of thee: but mine hand shall not be upon thee.

13 As saith the proverb of the ancients, Wickedness proceedeth from the wicked: but mine hand shall not be upon thee.

14 After whom is the king of Ĭṣ'rā-ĕl come out? after whom dost thou pursue? after a dead dog, after a flea.

15 The LORD therefore be judge, and judge between me and thee, and see, and plead my cause, and deliver me out of thine hand.

16 ℂ And it came to pass, when David had made an end of speaking these words unto Saul, that Saul said, *Is* this thy voice, my son David? And Saul lifted up his voice, and wept.

17 And he said to David, Thou *art* more righteous than I: for thou hast rewarded me good, whereas I have rewarded thee evil.

18 And thou hast showed this day how that thou hast dealt well with me: forasmuch as when the LORD had delivered me into thine hand, thou killedst me not.

19 For if a man find his enemy, will he let him go well away? wherefore the LORD reward thee good for that thou hast done unto me this day.

20 And now, behold, I know well that thou shalt surely be king, and that the kingdom of Ĭṣ'rā-ĕl shall be established in thine hand.

21 Swear now therefore unto me by the LORD, that thou wilt not cut off my seed after me, and that thou wilt not destroy my name out of my father's house.

22 And David sware unto Saul. And Saul went home; but David and his men gat them up unto the hold.

CHAPTER 25

AND Samuel died; and all the Ĭṣ'rā-ĕl-ītes were gathered together, and lamented him, and buried him in his house at Rā'măh. And David arose, and went down to the wilderness of Pā'răn.

2 And *there was* a man in Mā'ŏn, whose possessions *were* in Cär'mĕl; and the man *was* very great, and he had three thousand sheep, and a thousand goats: and he was shearing his sheep in Cär'mĕl.

3 Now the name of the man *was* Nā'băl, and the name of his wife Ăb'ĭ-gāil; and *she was* a woman of good understanding, and of a beautiful countenance: but the man *was* churlish and evil in his doings; and he *was* of the house of Caleb.

4 ¶ And David heard in the wilderness that Nā'băl did shear his sheep.

5 And David sent out ten young men, and David said unto the young men, Get you up to Cär'mĕl, and go to Nā'băl, and greet him in my name:

6 And thus shall ye say to him that liveth *in prosperity,* Peace *be* both to thee, and peace *be* to thine house, and peace *be* unto all that thou hast.

7 And now I have heard that thou hast shearers: now thy shepherds which were with us, we hurt them not, neither was there aught missing unto them, all the while they were in Cär'mĕl.

8 Ask thy young men, and they will show thee. Wherefore let the young men find favor in thine eyes; for we come in a good day: give, I pray thee, whatsoever cometh to thine hand unto thy servants, and to thy son David.

9 And when David's young men came, they spake to Nā'băl according to all those words in the name of David, and ceased.

10 ¶ And Nā'băl answered David's servants, and said, Who *is* David? and who *is* the son of Jesse? there be many servants nowadays that break away every man from his master.

11 Shall I then take my bread, and my water, and my flesh that I have killed for my shearers, and give *it* unto men, whom I know not whence they *be*?

12 So David's young men turned their way, and went again, and came and told him all those sayings.

13 And David said unto his men, Gird ye on every man his sword. And they girded on every man his sword; and David also girded on his sword: and there went up after David about four hundred men; and two hundred abode by the stuff.

14 ¶ But one of the young men told Ăb'ĭ-gāil, Nā'băl's wife, saying, Behold, David sent messengers out of the wilderness to salute our master; and he railed on them.

15 But the men *were* very good unto us, and we were not hurt, neither missed we any thing, as long as we were conversant with them, when we were in the fields.

16 They were a wall unto us both by night and day, all the while we were with them keeping the sheep.

17 Now therefore know and consider what thou wilt do; for evil is determined against our master, and against all his household: for he *is such* a son of Bē'lĭ-ăl, that *a man* cannot speak to him.

18 ¶ Then Ăb'ĭ-gāil made haste, and took two hundred loaves, and two bottles of wine, and five sheep ready dressed, and five measures of parched *corn,* and a hundred clusters of raisins, and two hundred cakes of figs, and laid *them* on asses.

19 And she said unto her servants, Go on before me; behold, I come after you. But she told not her husband Nā'băl.

20 And it was *so, as* she rode on the ass, that she came down by the covert of the hill, and, behold, David and his men came down against her; and she met them.

21 Now David had said, Surely in vain have I kept all that this *fellow* hath in the wilderness, so that nothing was missed of all that *pertained* unto him: and he hath requited me evil for good.

22 So and more also do God unto the enemies of David, if I leave of all that *pertain* to him by the morning light any that pisseth against the wall.

23 And when Ăb'ĭ-gāil saw David, she hasted, and lighted off the ass, and fell before David on her face, and bowed herself to the ground,

24 And fell at his feet, and said, Upon me, my lord, *upon* me *let this* iniquity *be:* and let thine handmaid, I pray thee, speak in thine audience, and hear the words of thine handmaid.

25 Let not my lord, I pray thee, regard this man of Bē'lĭ-ăl, *even* Nā'băl: for as his name *is,* so *is* he; Nā'băl *is* his name, and folly *is* with him: but I thine handmaid saw not the young men of my lord, whom thou didst send.

26 Now therefore, my lord, *as* the LORD liveth, and *as* thy soul liveth, seeing the LORD hath withholden thee from coming to *shed* blood, and from avenging thyself with thine own hand, now let thine enemies, and they that seek evil to my lord, be as Nā'băl.

27 And now this blessing which thine handmaid hath brought unto my lord, let it even be given unto the young men that follow my lord.

28 I pray thee, forgive the trespass of thine handmaid: for the LORD will certainly make my lord a sure house; because my lord fighteth the battles of the

LORD, and evil hath not been found in
thee *all* thy days.
29 Yet a man is risen to pursue thee,
and to seek thy soul: but the soul of my
lord shall be bound in the bundle of life
with the LORD thy God; and the souls of
thine enemies, them shall he sling out,
as out of the middle of a sling.
30 And it shall come to pass, when the
LORD shall have done to my lord according to all the good that he hath spoken
concerning thee, and shall have appointed thee ruler over Ĭş′rā-ĕl;
31 That this shall be no grief unto thee,
nor offense of heart unto my lord, either
that thou hast shed blood causeless, or
that my lord hath avenged himself: but
when the LORD shall have dealt well
with my lord, then remember thine
handmaid.
32 ℂ And David said to Ăb′ĭ-gāil,
Blessed *be* the LORD God of Ĭş′rā-ĕl,
which sent thee this day to meet me:
33 And blessed *be* thy advice, and
blessed *be* thou, which hast kept me this
day from coming to *shed* blood, and
from avenging myself with mine own
hand.
34 For in very deed, *as* the LORD God
of Ĭş′rā-ĕl liveth, which hath kept me
back from hurting thee, except thou
hadst hasted and come to meet me,
surely there had not been left unto Nā′-
băl by the morning light any that pisseth
against the wall.
35 So David received of her hand *that*
which she had brought him, and said
unto her, Go up in peace to thine house;
see, I have hearkened to thy voice, and
have accepted thy person.
36 ℂ And Ăb′ĭ-gāil came to Nā′băl;
and, behold, he held a feast in his house,
like the feast of a king; and Nā′băl's
heart *was* merry within him, for he *was*
very drunken: wherefore she told him
nothing, less or more, until the morning
light.
37 But it came to pass in the morning,
when the wine was gone out of Nā′băl,
and his wife had told him these things,
that his heart died within him, and he
became *as* a stone.
38 And it came to pass about ten days
after, that the LORD smote Nā′băl, that
he died.
39 ℂ And when David heard that Nā′-
băl was dead, he said, Blessed *be* the
LORD, that hath pleaded the cause of
my reproach from the hand of Nā′băl,
and hath kept his servant from evil: for
the LORD hath returned the wickedness
of Nā′băl upon his own head. And David
sent and communed with Ăb′ĭ-gāil, to
take her to him to wife.
40 And when the servants of David
were come to Ăb′ĭ-gāil to Cär′mĕl, they
spake unto her, saying, David sent us
unto thee, to take thee to him to wife.
41 And she arose, and bowed herself
on *her* face to the earth, and said, Behold, *let* thine handmaid *be* a servant to
wash the feet of the servants of my lord.
42 And Ăb′ĭ-gāil hasted, and arose, and
rode upon an ass, with five damsels of
hers that went after her; and she went
after the messengers of David, and became his wife.
43 David also took Ȧ-hin′ō-ăm of Jĕz′-
rē-ĕl; and they were also both of them
his wives.
44 ℂ But Saul had given Mī′chăl his
daughter, David's wife, to Phăl′tī the
son of Lā′ĭsh, which *was* of Găl′lĭm.

CHAPTER 26

AND the Zĭph′ītes came unto Saul to
Gĭb′ē-ȧh, saying, Doth not David
hide himself in the hill of Hȧ-chī′lȧh,
which is before Jē-shī′mŏn?
2 Then Saul arose, and went down to
the wilderness of Zĭph, having three
thousand chosen men of Ĭş′rā-ĕl with
him, to seek David in the wilderness of
Zĭph.
3 And Saul pitched in the hill of Hȧ-
chī′lȧh, which *is* before Jē-shī′mŏn, by
the way. But David abode in the wilderness, and he saw that Saul came after
him into the wilderness.
4 David therefore sent out spies, and
understood that Saul was come in very
deed.
5 ℂ And David arose, and came to the
place where Saul had pitched: and
David beheld the place where Saul lay,
and Abner the son of Nĕr, the captain of
his host: and Saul lay in the trench, and
the people pitched round about him.
6 Then answered David and said to
Ȧ-hĭm′ē-lĕch the Hĭt′tīte, and to Ȧ-bĭsh′-
ā-ī the son of Zĕr′ụ-ī′ȧh, brother to
Jō′ăb, saying, Who will go down with me
to Saul to the camp? And Ȧ-bĭsh′ā-ī
said, I will go down with thee.
7 So David and Ȧ-bĭsh′ā-ī came to the
people by night: and, behold, Saul lay

sleeping within the trench, and his spear stuck in the ground at his bolster: but Abner and the people lay round about him.

8 Then said Ȧ-bĭsh′ā-ī to David, God hath delivered thine enemy into thine hand this day: now therefore let me smite him, I pray thee, with the spear even to the earth at once, and I will not *smite* him the second time.

9 And David said to Ȧ-bĭsh′ā-ī, Destroy him not: for who can stretch forth his hand against the LORD's anointed, and be guiltless?

10 David said furthermore, *As* the LORD liveth, the LORD shall smite him; or his day shall come to die; or he shall descend into battle, and perish.

11 The LORD forbid that I should stretch forth mine hand against the LORD's anointed: but, I pray thee, take thou now the spear that *is* at his bolster, and the cruse of water, and let us go.

12 So David took the spear and the cruse of water from Saul's bolster; and they gat them away, and no man saw *it*, nor knew *it*, neither awaked: for they *were* all asleep; because a deep sleep from the LORD was fallen upon them.

13 ℂ Then David went over to the other side, and stood on the top of a hill afar off; a great space *being* between them:

14 And David cried to the people, and to Abner the son of Nĕr, saying, Answerest thou not, Abner? Then Abner answered and said, Who *art* thou *that* criest to the king?

15 And David said to Abner, *Art* not thou a *valiant* man? and who *is* like to thee in Ĭş′rā-ĕl? wherefore then hast thou not kept thy lord the king? for there came one of the people in to destroy the king thy lord.

16 This thing *is* not good that thou hast done. *As* the LORD liveth, ye *are* worthy to die, because ye have not kept your master, the LORD's anointed. And now see where the king's spear *is*, and the cruse of water that *was* at his bolster.

17 And Saul knew David's voice, and said, *Is* this thy voice, my son David? And David said, *It is* my voice, my lord, O king.

18 And he said, Wherefore doth my lord thus pursue after his servant? for what have I done? or what evil *is* in mine hand?

19 Now therefore, I pray thee, let my lord the king hear the words of his servant. If the LORD have stirred thee up against me, let him accept an offering: but if *they be* the children of men, cursed *be* they before the LORD; for they have driven me out this day from abiding in the inheritance of the LORD, saying, Go, serve other gods.

20 Now therefore, let not my blood fall to the earth before the face of the LORD: for the king of Ĭş′rā-ĕl is come out to seek a flea, as when one doth hunt a partridge in the mountains.

21 ℂ Then said Saul, I have sinned: return, my son David; for I will no more do thee harm, because my soul was precious in thine eyes this day: behold, I have played the fool, and have erred exceedingly.

22 And David answered and said, Behold the king's spear! and let one of the young men come over and fetch it.

23 The LORD render to every man his righteousness and his faithfulness: for the LORD delivered thee into *my* hand to-day, but I would not stretch forth mine hand against the LORD's anointed.

24 And, behold, as thy life was much set by this day in mine eyes, so let my life be much set by in the eyes of the LORD, and let him deliver me out of all tribulation.

25 Then Saul said to David, Blessed *be* thou, my son David: thou shalt both do great *things*, and also shalt still prevail. So David went on his way, and Saul returned to his place.

CHAPTER 27

AND David said in his heart, I shall now perish one day by the hand of Saul: *there is* nothing better for me than that I should speedily escape into the land of the Phĭ-lĭs′tīneş; and Saul shall despair of me, to seek me any more in any coast of Ĭş′rā-ĕl: so shall I escape out of his hand.

2 And David arose, and he passed over with the six hundred men that *were* with him unto Ā′ehĭsh, the son of Mā′ŏeh, king of Gath.

3 And David dwelt with Ā′ehĭsh at Gath, he and his men, every man with his household, *even* David with his two wives, Ȧ-hĭn′ō-ăm the Jĕz′rē-ĕl-īt′ĕss, and Ăb′ĭ-gāil the Cär′mĕl-īt′ĕss, Nā′băl's wife.

4 And it was told Saul that David was
fled to Gath: and he sought no more
again for him.
5 ℂ And David said unto Ā′chĭsh, If I
have now found grace in thine eyes, let
them give me a place in some town in
the country, that I may dwell there: for
why should thy servant dwell in the
royal city with thee?
6 Then Ā′chĭsh gave him Zĭk′lăg that
day: wherefore Zĭk′lăg pertaineth unto
the kings of Judah unto this day.
7 And the time that David dwelt in the
country of the Phĭ-lĭs′tĭneş was a full
year and four months.
8 ℂ And David and his men went up,
and invaded the Gĕsh′ū-rītes, and the
Gĕz′rītes, and the Ăm′ȧ-lĕk-ītes: for
those *nations were* of old the inhabitants
of the land, as thou goest to Shụr, even
unto the land of Egypt.
9 And David smote the land, and left
neither man nor woman alive, and took
away the sheep, and the oxen, and the
asses, and the camels, and the apparel,
and returned, and came to Ā′chĭsh.
10 And Ā′chĭsh said, Whither have ye
made a road to-day? And David said,
Against the south of Judah, and against
the south of the Jē-răh′mē-ĕl-ītes, and
against the south of the Kē′nītes.
11 And David saved neither man nor
woman alive, to bring *tidings* to Gath,
saying, Lest they should tell on us, saying, So did David, and so *will be* his
manner all the while he dwelleth in the
country of the Phĭ-lĭs′tĭneş.
12 And Ā′chĭsh believed David, saying,
He hath made his people Ĭş′rā-ĕl utterly
to abhor him; therefore he shall be my
servant for ever.

CHAPTER 28

AND it came to pass in those days,
that the Phĭ-lĭs′tĭneş gathered their
armies together for warfare, to fight with
Ĭş′rā-ĕl. And Ā′chĭsh said unto David,
Know thou assuredly, that thou shalt
go out with me to battle, thou and thy
men.
2 And David said to Ā′chĭsh, Surely
thou shalt know what thy servant can
do. And Ā′chĭsh said to David, Therefore will I make thee keeper of mine
head for ever.
3 ℂ Now Samuel was dead, and all
Ĭş′rā-ĕl had lamented him, and buried
him in Rā′măh, even in his own city.
And Saul had put away those that had
familiar spirits, and the wizards, out of
the land.
4 And the Phĭ-lĭs′tĭneş gathered themselves together, and came and pitched
in Shụ′nĕm: and Saul gathered all
Ĭş′rā-ĕl together, and they pitched in
Gĭl-bō′ȧ.
5 And when Saul saw the host of the
Phĭ-lĭs′tĭneş, he was afraid, and his
heart greatly trembled.
6 And when Saul inquired of the
LORD, the LORD answered him not, neither by dreams, nor by Ū′rĭm, nor by
prophets.
7 ℂ Then said Saul unto his servants,
Seek me a woman that hath a familiar
spirit, that I may go to her, and inquire
of her. And his servants said to him,
Behold, *there is* a woman that hath a
familiar spirit at Ĕn′-dôr.
8 And Saul disguised himself, and put
on other raiment, and he went, and two
men with him, and they came to the
woman by night: and he said, I pray
thee, divine unto me by the familiar
spirit, and bring me *him* up, whom I
shall name unto thee.
9 And the woman said unto him,
Behold, thou knowest what Saul hath
done, how he hath cut off those that
have familiar spirits, and the wizards,
out of the land: wherefore then layest
thou a snare for my life, to cause me
to die?
10 And Saul sware to her by the LORD,
saying, *As* the LORD liveth, there shall
no punishment happen to thee for this
thing.
11 Then said the woman, Whom shall
I bring up unto thee? And he said,
Bring me up Samuel.
12 And when the woman saw Samuel,
she cried with a loud voice: and the
woman spake to Saul, saying, Why hast
thou deceived me? for thou *art* Saul.
13 And the king said unto her, Be not
afraid: for what sawest thou? And the
woman said unto Saul, I saw gods
ascending out of the earth.
14 And he said unto her, What form *is*
he of? And she said, An old man cometh
up; and he *is* covered with a mantle.
And Saul perceived that it *was* Samuel,
and he stooped with *his* face to the
ground, and bowed himself.
15 ℂ And Samuel said to Saul, Why
hast thou disquieted me, to bring me up?

And Saul answered, I am sore distressed; for the Phĭ-lĭs′tĭneş make war against me, and God is departed from me, and answereth me no more, neither by prophets, nor by dreams: therefore I have called thee, that thou mayest make known unto me what I shall do.

16 Then said Samuel, Wherefore then dost thou ask of me, seeing the LORD is departed from thee, and is become thine enemy?

17 And the LORD hath done to him, as he spake by me: for the LORD hath rent the kingdom out of thine hand, and given it to thy neighbor, *even* to David:

18 Because thou obeyedst not the voice of the LORD, nor executedst his fierce wrath upon Ăm′ȧ-lĕk, therefore hath the LORD done this thing unto thee this day.

19 Moreover the LORD will also deliver Ĭş′rā-ĕl with thee into the hand of the Phĭ-lĭs′tĭneş: and to-morrow *shalt* thou and thy sons *be* with me: the LORD also shall deliver the host of Ĭş′rā-ĕl into the hand of the Phĭ-lĭs′tĭneş.

20 Then Saul fell straightway all along on the earth, and was sore afraid, because of the words of Samuel; and there was no strength in him; for he had eaten no bread all the day, nor all the night.

21 ¶ And the woman came unto Saul, and saw that he was sore troubled, and said unto him, Behold, thine handmaid hath obeyed thy voice, and I have put my life in my hand, and have hearkened unto thy words which thou spakest unto me.

22 Now therefore, I pray thee, hearken thou also unto the voice of thine handmaid, and let me set a morsel of bread before thee; and eat, that thou mayest have strength, when thou goest on thy way.

23 But he refused, and said, I will not eat. But his servants, together with the woman, compelled him; and he hearkened unto their voice. So he arose from the earth, and sat upon the bed.

24 And the woman had a fat calf in the house; and she hasted, and killed it, and took flour, and kneaded *it*, and did bake unleavened bread thereof:

25 And she brought *it* before Saul, and before his servants; and they did eat. Then they rose up, and went away that night.

CHAPTER 29

NOW the Phĭ-lĭs′tĭneş gathered together all their armies to Ā′phĕk: and the Ĭş′rā-ĕl-ītes pitched by a fountain which *is* in Jĕz′rē-ĕl.

2 And the lords of the Phĭ-lĭs′tĭneş passed on by hundreds, and by thousands: but David and his men passed on in the rearward with Ā′chĭsh.

3 Then said the princes of the Phĭ-lĭs′tĭneş, What *do* these Hebrews *here*? And Ā′chĭsh said unto the princes of the Phĭ-lĭs′tĭneş, *Is* not this David, the servant of Saul the king of Ĭş′rā-ĕl, which hath been with me these days, or these years, and I have found no fault in him since he fell *unto me* unto this day?

4 And the princes of the Phĭ-lĭs′tĭneş were wroth with him; and the princes of the Phĭ-lĭs′tĭneş said unto him, Make this fellow return, that he may go again to his place which thou hast appointed him, and let him not go down with us to battle, lest in the battle he be an adversary to us: for wherewith should he reconcile himself unto his master? *should it* not *be* with the heads of these men?

5 *Is* not this David, of whom they sang one to another in dances, saying, Saul slew his thousands, and David his ten thousands?

6 ¶ Then Ā′chĭsh called David, and said unto him, Surely, *as* the LORD liveth, thou hast been upright, and thy going out and thy coming in with me in the host *is* good in my sight: for I have not found evil in thee since the day of thy coming unto me unto this day: nevertheless the lords favor thee not.

7 Wherefore now return, and go in peace, that thou displease not the lords of the Phĭ-lĭs′tĭneş.

8 ¶ And David said unto Ā′chĭsh, But what have I done? and what hast thou found in thy servant so long as I have been with thee unto this day, that I may not go fight against the enemies of my lord the king?

9 And Ā′chĭsh answered and said to David, I know that thou *art* good in my sight, as an angel of God: notwithstanding, the princes of the Phĭ-lĭs′tĭneş have said, He shall not go up with us to the battle.

10 Wherefore now rise up early in the morning with thy master's servants that

are come with thee: and as soon as ye
be up early in the morning, and have
light, depart.
11 So David and his men rose up early
to depart in the morning, to return into
the land of the Phĭ-lĭs′tĭneş. And the
Phĭ-lĭs′tĭneş went up to Jĕz′rē-ĕl.

CHAPTER 30

AND it came to pass, when David and
his men were come to Zĭk′lăg on
the third day, that the Ăm′ȧ-lĕk-ītes
had invaded the south, and Zĭk′lăg,
and smitten Zĭk′lăg, and burned it
with fire;
2 And had taken the women captives,
that *were* therein: they slew not any,
either great or small, but carried *them*
away, and went on their way.
3 ¶ So David and his men came to the
city, and, behold, *it was* burned with
fire; and their wives, and their sons, and
their daughters, were taken captives.
4 Then David and the people that *were*
with him lifted up their voice and wept,
until they had no more power to weep.
5 And David's two wives were taken
captives, Ȧ-hĭn′ō-ăm the Jĕz′rē-ĕl-īt′ĕss,
and Ăb′ĭ-gāil the wife of Nā′băl the
Cär′mĕl-īte.
6 And David was greatly distressed;
for the people spake of stoning him, because the soul of all the people was
grieved, every man for his sons and for
his daughters: but David encouraged
himself in the LORD his God.
7 And David said to Ȧ-bī′ȧ-thȧr the
priest, Ȧ-hĭm′ē-lĕch's son, I pray thee,
bring me hither the ĕph′ŏd. And Ȧ-bī′ȧ-
thȧr brought thither the ĕph′ŏd to
David.
8 And David inquired at the LORD, saying, Shall I pursue after this troop? shall
I overtake them? And he answered him,
Pursue: for thou shalt surely overtake
them, and without fail recover *all*.
9 So David went, he and the six hundred men that *were* with him, and came
to the brook Bē′sŏr, where those that
were left behind stayed.
10 But David pursued, he and four
hundred men: for two hundred abode
behind, which were so faint that they
could not go over the brook Bē′sŏr.
11 ¶ And they found an Egyptian in
the field, and brought him to David, and
gave him bread, and he did eat; and they
made him drink water;
12 And they gave him a piece of a cake
of figs, and two clusters of raisins: and
when he had eaten, his spirit came again
to him: for he had eaten no bread, nor
drunk *any* water, three days and three
nights.
13 And David said unto him, To whom
belongest thou? and whence *art* thou?
And he said, I *am* a young man of Egypt,
servant to an Ăm′ȧ-lĕk-īte; and my
master left me, because three days
agone I fell sick.
14 We made an invasion *upon* the south
of the Chĕr′ē-thītes, and upon *the coast*
which *belongeth* to Judah, and upon the
south of Caleb; and we burned Zĭk′lăg
with fire.
15 And David said to him, Canst thou
bring me down to this company? And he
said, Swear unto me by God, that thou
wilt neither kill me, nor deliver me into
the hands of my master, and I will bring
thee down to this company.
16 ¶ And when he had brought him
down, behold, *they were* spread abroad
upon all the earth, eating and drinking,
and dancing, because of all the great
spoil that they had taken out of the land
of the Phĭ-lĭs′tĭneş, and out of the land
of Judah.
17 And David smote them from the
twilight even unto the evening of the
next day: and there escaped not a man
of them, save four hundred young men,
which rode upon camels, and fled.
18 And David recovered all that the
Ăm′ȧ-lĕk-ītes had carried away: and
David rescued his two wives.
19 And there was nothing lacking to
them, neither small nor great, neither
sons nor daughters, neither spoil, nor
any *thing* that they had taken to them:
David recovered all.
20 And David took all the flocks and
the herds, *which* they drave before those
other cattle, and said, This *is* David's
spoil.
21 ¶ And David came to the two hundred men, which were so faint that they
could not follow David, whom they had
made also to abide at the brook Bē′sŏr:
and they went forth to meet David, and
to meet the people that *were* with him:
and when David came near to the people, he saluted them.
22 Then answered all the wicked men,
and *men* of Bē′lĭ-ăl, of those that went
with David, and said, Because they went

not with us, we will not give them *aught*
of the spoil that we have recovered, save
to every man his wife and his children,
that they may lead *them* away, and
depart.
23 Then said David, Ye shall not do so,
my brethren, with that which the LORD
hath given us, who hath preserved us,
and delivered the company that came
against us into our hand.
24 For who will hearken unto you in
this matter? but as his part *is* that goeth
down to the battle, so *shall* his part *be*
that tarrieth by the stuff: they shall part
alike.
25 And it was *so* from that day forward,
that he made it a statute and an ordinance for Ĭṣ'rā-ĕl unto this day.
26 ℂ And when David came to Zĭk'lăg,
he sent of the spoil unto the elders of
Judah, *even* to his friends, saying, Behold a present for you of the spoil of the
enemies of the LORD;
27 To *them* which *were* in Beth-el, and
to *them* which *were* in south Rā'mŏth,
and to *them* which *were* in Jăt'tĭr,
28 And to *them* which *were* in Ȧ-rō'ĕr,
and to *them* which *were* in Sĭph'mŏth,
and to *them* which *were* in Ĕsh'tē-
mō'ȧ,
29 And to *them* which *were* in Rā'chăl,
and to *them* which *were* in the cities of
the Jē-răh'mē-ĕl-ītes, and to *them* which
were in the cities of the Kē'nītes,
30 And to *them* which *were* in Hôr'mȧh,
and to *them* which *were* in Chōr-ăsh'ăn,
and to *them* which *were* in Ā'thăch,
31 And to *them* which *were* in Hē'brȯn,
and to all the places where David himself and his men were wont to haunt.

CHAPTER 31

NOW the Phĭ-lĭs'tĭneṣ fought against
Ĭṣ'rā-ĕl: and the men of Ĭṣ'rā-ĕl
fled from before the Phĭ-lĭs'tĭneṣ, and
fell down slain in mount Gĭl-bō'ȧ.
2 And the Phĭ-lĭs'tĭneṣ followed hard
upon Saul and upon his sons; and the
Phĭ-lĭs'tĭneṣ slew Jonathan, and Ȧ-bĭn'-
ȧ-dăb, and Mĕl'chĭ-shụ'ȧ, Saul's sons.
3 And the battle went sore against
Saul, and the archers hit him; and he
was sore wounded of the archers.
4 Then said Saul unto his armor-
bearer, Draw thy sword, and thrust me
through therewith; lest these uncircumcised come and thrust me through, and
abuse me. But his armor-bearer would
not; for he was sore afraid. Therefore
Saul took a sword, and fell upon it.
5 And when his armor-bearer saw that
Saul was dead, he fell likewise upon his
sword, and died with him.
6 So Saul died, and his three sons, and
his armor-bearer, and all his men, that
same day together.
7 ℂ And when the men of Ĭṣ'rā-ĕl that
were on the other side of the valley, and
they that *were* on the other side Jordan,
saw that the men of Ĭṣ'rā-ĕl fled, and
that Saul and his sons were dead, they
forsook the cities, and fled; and the Phĭ-
lĭs'tĭneṣ came and dwelt in them.
8 And it came to pass on the morrow,
when the Phĭ-lĭs'tĭneṣ came to strip the
slain, that they found Saul and his three
sons fallen in mount Gĭl-bō'ȧ.
9 And they cut off his head, and
stripped off his armor, and sent into the
land of the Phĭ-lĭs'tĭneṣ round about, to
publish *it in* the house of their idols, and
among the people.
10 And they put his armor in the house
of Ăsh'tȧ-rŏth: and they fastened his
body to the wall of Bĕth'-shăn'.
11 ℂ And when the inhabitants of Jā'-
bĕsh-gĭl'ē-ăd heard of that which the
Phĭ-lĭs'tĭneṣ had done to Saul,
12 All the valiant men arose, and went
all night, and took the body of Saul and
the bodies of his sons from the wall of
Bĕth'-shăn', and came to Jā'bĕsh, and
burnt them there.
13 And they took their bones, and
buried *them* under a tree at Jā'bĕsh, and
fasted seven days.

THE SECOND

BOOK OF SAMUEL

OTHERWISE CALLED, THE SECOND BOOK OF THE KINGS

CHAPTER 1

NOW it came to pass after the death of Saul, when David was returned from the slaughter of the Ăm′ȧ-lĕk-ītes, and David had abode two days in Zĭk′lăg;

2 It came even to pass on the third day, that, behold, a man came out of the camp from Saul with his clothes rent, and earth upon his head: and *so* it was, when he came to David, that he fell to the earth, and did obeisance.

3 And David said unto him, From whence comest thou? And he said unto him, Out of the camp of Ĭş′rā-ĕl am I escaped.

4 And David said unto him, How went the matter? I pray thee, tell me. And he answered, That the people are fled from the battle, and many of the people also are fallen and dead; and Saul and Jonathan his son are dead also.

5 And David said unto the young man that told him, How knowest thou that Saul and Jonathan his son be dead?

6 And the young man that told him said, As I happened by chance upon mount Gĭl-bō′ȧ, behold, Saul leaned upon his spear; and, lo, the chariots and horsemen followed hard after him.

7 And when he looked behind him, he saw me, and called unto me. And I answered, Here *am* I.

8 And he said unto me, Who *art* thou? And I answered him, I *am* an Ăm′ȧ-lĕk-īte.

9 He said unto me again, Stand, I pray thee, upon me, and slay me: for anguish is come upon me, because my life *is* yet whole in me.

10 So I stood upon him, and slew him, because I was sure that he could not live after that he was fallen: and I took the crown that *was* upon his head, and the bracelet that *was* on his arm, and have brought them hither unto my lord.

11 Then David took hold on his clothes, and rent them; and likewise all the men that *were* with him:

12 And they mourned, and wept, and fasted until even, for Saul, and for Jonathan his son, and for the people of the LORD, and for the house of Ĭş′rā-ĕl; because they were fallen by the sword.

13 ¶ And David said unto the young man that told him, Whence *art* thou? And he answered, I *am* the son of a stranger, an Ăm′ȧ-lĕk-īte.

14 And David said unto him, How wast thou not afraid to stretch forth thine hand to destroy the LORD's anointed?

15 And David called one of the young men, and said, Go near, *and* fall upon him. And he smote him that he died.

16 And David said unto him, Thy blood *be* upon thy head; for thy mouth hath testified against thee, saying, I have slain the LORD's anointed.

17 ¶ And David lamented with this lamentation over Saul and over Jonathan his son:

18 (Also he bade them teach the children of Judah *the use of* the bow: behold, *it is* written in the book of Jā′shẽr:)

19 The beauty of Ĭş′rā-ĕl is slain upon thy high places: how are the mighty fallen!

20 Tell *it* not in Gath, publish *it* not in the streets of Ăs′kē-lŏn; lest the daughters of the Phĭ-lĭs′tĭneş rejoice, lest the daughters of the uncircumcised triumph.

21 Ye mountains of Gĭl-bō′ȧ, *let there be* no dew, neither *let there be* rain, upon you, nor fields of offerings: for there the shield of the mighty is vilely cast away, the shield of Saul, *as though he had* not *been* anointed with oil.

22 From the blood of the slain, from the fat of the mighty, the bow of Jonathan turned not back, and the sword of Saul returned not empty.

23 Saul and Jonathan *were* lovely and pleasant in their lives, and in their death they were not divided: they were swifter than eagles, they were stronger than lions.

24 Ye daughters of Ĭş′rā-ĕl, weep over Saul, who clothed you in scarlet, with *other* delights; who put on ornaments of gold upon your apparel.

25 How are the mighty fallen in the
midst of the battle! O Jonathan, *thou
wast* slain in thine high places.
26 I am distressed for thee, my brother
Jonathan: very pleasant hast thou been
unto me: thy love to me was wonderful,
passing the love of women.
27 How are the mighty fallen, and the
weapons of war perished!

CHAPTER 2

AND it came to pass after this, that
David inquired of the LORD, saying, Shall I go up into any of the cities of
Judah? And the LORD said unto him,
Go up. And David said, Whither shall I
go up? And he said, Unto Hē′brȯn.
2 So David went up thither, and his two
wives also, Ȧ-hĭn′ō-ăm the Jĕz′rē-ĕl-
īt′ĕss, and Ăb′ĭ-gāil Nā′băl's wife the
Cär′mĕl-īte.
3 And his men that *were* with him did
David bring up, every man with his
household: and they dwelt in the cities
of Hē′brȯn.
4 And the men of Judah came, and
there they anointed David king over the
house of Judah. And they told David,
saying, *That* the men of Jā′bĕsh–
gĭl′ē-ăd *were they* that buried Saul.
5 ¶ And David sent messengers unto
the men of Jā′bĕsh–gĭl′ē-ăd, and said
unto them, Blessed *be* ye of the LORD,
that ye have showed this kindness unto
your lord, *even* unto Saul, and have
buried him.
6 And now the LORD show kindness
and truth unto you: and I also will
requite you this kindness, because ye
have done this thing.
7 Therefore now let your hands be
strengthened, and be ye valiant: for your
master Saul is dead, and also the house
of Judah have anointed me king over
them.
8 ¶ But Abner the son of Nĕr, captain
of Saul's host, took Ĭsh′–bō′shĕth the
son of Saul, and brought him over to
Mā′hȧ-nā′ĭm;
9 And made him king over Gĭl′ē-ăd,
and over the Ăsh′ŭr-ītes, and over Jĕz′-
rē–ĕl, and over Ē′phrā-ĭm, and over Benjamin, and over all Ĭş′rā-ĕl.
10 Ĭsh′–bō′shĕth Saul's son *was* forty
years old when he began to reign
over Ĭş′rā-ĕl, and reigned two years.
But the house of Judah followed David.
11 And the time that David was king
in Hē′brȯn over the house of Judah was
seven years and six months.
12 ¶ And Abner the son of Nĕr, and
the servants of Ĭsh′–bō′shĕth the son of
Saul, went out from Mā′hȧ-nā′ĭm to
Gĭb′ē-ȯn.
13 And Jō′ăb the son of Zĕr′ụ-ī′ȧh, and
the servants of David, went out, and
met together by the pool of Gĭb′ē-ȯn:
and they sat down, the one on the one
side of the pool, and the other on the
other side of the pool.
14 And Abner said to Jō′ăb, Let the
young men now arise, and play before
us. And Jō′ăb said, Let them arise.
15 Then there arose and went over by
number twelve of Benjamin, which *pertained* to Ĭsh′–bō′shĕth the son of Saul,
and twelve of the servants of David.
16 And they caught every one his fellow
by the head, and *thrust* his sword in his
fellow's side; so they fell down together:
wherefore that place was called Hĕl′-
kăth–hăz′zū-rĭm, which *is* in Gĭb′ē ȯn.
17 And there was a very sore battle
that day; and Abner was beaten, and
the men of Ĭş′rā-ĕl, before the servants
of David.
18 ¶ And there were three sons of
Zĕr′ụ-ī′ȧh there, Jō′ăb, and Ȧ-bĭsh′ā-ī,
and Ăs′ȧ-hĕl: and Ăs′ȧ-hĕl *was as*
light of foot as a wild roe.
19 And Ăs′ȧ-hĕl pursued after Abner;
and in going he turned not to the right
hand nor to the left from following
Abner.
20 Then Abner looked behind him, and
said, *Art* thou As′ȧ-hĕl? And he answered, I *am*.
21 And Abner said to him, Turn thee
aside to thy right hand or to thy left,
and lay thee hold on one of the young
men, and take thee his armor. But
Ăs′ȧ-hĕl would not turn aside from following of him.
22 And Abner said again to Ăs′ȧ-hĕl,
Turn thee aside from following me:
wherefore should I smite thee to the
ground? how then should I hold up my
face to Jō′ăb thy brother?
23 Howbeit he refused to turn aside:
wherefore Abner with the hinder end of
the spear smote him under the fifth *rib*,
that the spear came out behind him;
and he fell down there, and died in the
same place: and it came to pass, *that* as
many as came to the place where Ăs′ȧ-
hĕl fell down and died stood still.

24 Jō′ăb also and Ȧ-bĭsh′ā-ī pursued
after Abner: and the sun went down
when they were come to the hill of Ăm′-
mȧh, that *lieth* before Gī′ȧh by the way
of the wilderness of Gĭb′ē-ȯn.
25 ℂ And the children of Benjamin
gathered themselves together after
Abner, and became one troop, and stood
on the top of a hill.
26 Then Abner called to Jō′ăb, and
said, Shall the sword devour for ever?
knowest thou not that it will be bitterness in the latter end? how long shall it
be then, ere thou bid the people return
from following their brethren?
27 And Jō′ăb said, *As* God liveth, unless thou hadst spoken, surely then in
the morning the people had gone up
every one from following his brother.
28 So Jō′ăb blew a trumpet, and all
the people stood still, and pursued after
Ĭş′rā-ĕl no more, neither fought they
any more.
29 And Abner and his men walked
all that night through the plain, and
passed over Jordan, and went through
all Bĭth′rŏn, and they came to Mā′hȧ-
nā′ĭm.
30 And Jō′ăb returned from following
Abner: and when he had gathered all
the people together, there lacked of
David's servants nineteen men and
Ă′sȧ-hĕl.
31 But the servants of David had smitten of Benjamin, and of Abner's men, *so
that* three hundred and threescore men
died.
32 ℂ And they took up Ăs′ȧ-hĕl, and
buried him in the sepulchre of his father,
which *was in* Beth-lehem. And Jō′ăb
and his men went all night, and they
came to Hē′brȯn at break of day.

CHAPTER 3

NOW there was long war between the
house of Saul and the house of
David: but David waxed stronger and
stronger, and the house of Saul waxed
weaker and weaker.
2 ℂ And unto David were sons born in
Hē′brȯn: and his firstborn was Amnon,
of Ȧ-hĭn′ō-ăm the Jĕz′rē-ĕl-īt′ĕss;
3 And his second, Chĭl′ē-ăb, of Ăb′ĭ-
gail the wife of Nā′băl the Cär′mĕl-īte;
and the third, Ăb′sȧ-lŏm the son of
Mā′ȧ-cȧh the daughter of Tăl′maī king
of Gē′shŭr;
4 And the fourth, Ăd′ō-nī′jȧh the son of
Hăg′gĭth; and the fifth, Shĕph′ȧ-tī′ȧh the
son of Ăb′ĭ-tăl;
5 And the sixth, Ĭth′rē-ăm, by Ĕg′lȧh
David's wife. These were born to David
in Hē′brȯn.
6 ℂ And it came to pass, while there
was war between the house of Saul and
the house of David, that Abner made
himself strong for the house of Saul.
7 And Saul had a concubine, whose
name *was* Rĭz′păh, the daughter of
Ā-ī′ȧh: and *Ish-bosheth* said to Abner,
Wherefore hast thou gone in unto my
father's concubine?
8 Then was Abner very wroth for the
words of Ĭsh′-bō′shĕth, and said, *Am* I
a dog's head, which against Judah do
show kindness this day unto the house
of Saul thy father, to his brethren, and
to his friends, and have not delivered
thee into the hand of David, that thou
chargest me to-day with a fault concerning this woman?
9 So do God to Abner, and more also,
except, as the LORD hath sworn to
David, even so I do to him;
10 To translate the kingdom from the
house of Saul, and to set up the throne
of David over Ĭş′rā-ĕl and over Judah,
from Dan even to Bē′ĕr-shē′bȧ.
11 And he could not answer Abner a
word again, because he feared him.
12 ℂ And Abner sent messengers to
David on his behalf, saying, Whose *is*
the land? saying *also*, Make thy league
with me, and, behold, my hand *shall be*
with thee, to bring about all Ĭş′rā-ĕl unto
thee.
13 ℂ And he said, Well; I will make a
league with thee: but one thing I require
of thee, that is, Thou shalt not see my
face, except thou first bring Mī′chăl
Saul's daughter, when thou comest to
see my face.
14 And David sent messengers to Ĭsh′-
bō′shĕth Saul's son, saying, Deliver *me*
my wife Mī′chăl, which I espoused to
me for a hundred foreskins of the Phĭ-
lĭs′tīnes.
15 And Ĭsh′-bō′shĕth sent, and took her
from *her* husband, *even* from Phăl′tī-ĕl
the son of Lā′ĭsh.
16 And her husband went with her
along weeping behind her to Bȧ-hū′rĭm.
Then said Abner unto him, Go, return.
And he returned.
17 ℂ And Abner had communication
with the elders of Ĭş′rā-ĕl, saying, Ye

sought for David in times past *to be*
king over you:
18 Now then do *it:* for the LORD hath
spoken of David, saying, By the hand of
my servant David I will save my people
Ĭs̱'rā-ĕl out of the hand of the Phĭ-lĭs'-
tīnes̱, and out of the hand of all their
enemies.
19 And Abner also spake in the ears of
Benjamin: and Abner went also to speak
in the ears of David in Hē'brȯn all that
seemed good to Ĭs̱'rā-ĕl, and that seemed
good to the whole house of Benjamin.
20 So Abner came to David to Hē'brȯn,
and twenty men with him. And David
made Abner and the men that *were* with
him a feast.
21 And Abner said unto David, I will
arise and go, and will gather all Ĭs̱'rā-ĕl
unto my lord the king, that they may
make a league with thee, and that thou
mayest reign over all that thine heart
desireth. And David sent Abner away;
and he went in peace.
22 ¶ And, behold, the servants of
David and Jō'ăb came from *pursuing* a
troop, and brought in a great spoil with
them: but Abner *was* not with David in
Hē'brȯn; for he had sent him away, and
he was gone in peace.
23 When Jō'ăb and all the host that *was*
with him were come, they told Jō'ăb,
saying, Abner the son of Nĕr came to the
king, and he hath sent him away, and he
is gone in peace.
24 Then Jō'ăb came to the king, and
said, What hast thou done? behold,
Abner came unto thee; why *is* it *that*
thou hast sent him away, and he is quite
gone?
25 Thou knowest Abner the son of Nĕr,
that he came to deceive thee, and to
know thy going out and thy coming in,
and to know all that thou doest.
26 And when Jō'ăb was come out from
David, he sent messengers after Abner,
which brought him again from the well
of Sī'rah: but David knew *it* not.
27 And when Abner was returned to
Hē'brȯn, Jō'ăb took him aside in the
gate to speak with him quietly, and
smote him there under the fifth *rib*, that
he died, for the blood of Ăs'ȧ-hĕl his
brother.
28 ¶ And afterward when David heard
it, he said, I and my kingdom *are* guiltless before the LORD for ever from the
blood of Abner the son of Nĕr.
29 Let it rest on the head of Jō'ăb; and
on all his father's house; and let there
not fail from the house of Jō'ăb one that
hath an issue, or that is a leper, or that
leaneth on a staff, or that falleth on the
sword, or that lacketh bread.
30 So Jō'ăb and Ȧ-bĭsh'ā-ī his brother
slew Abner, because he had slain their
brother Ăs'ȧ-hĕl at Gĭb'ē-ŏn in the
battle.
31 ¶ And David said to Jō'ăb, and to
all the people that *were* with him, Rend
your clothes, and gird you with sackcloth, and mourn before Abner. And
king David *himself* followed the bier.
32 And they buried Abner in Hē'brȯn:
and the king lifted up his voice, and
wept at the grave of Abner; and all the
people wept.
33 And the king lamented over Abner,
and said, Died Abner as a fool dieth?
34 Thy hands *were* not bound, nor thy
feet put into fetters: as a man falleth before wicked men, *so* fellest thou. And
all the people wept again over him.
35 And when all the people came to
cause David to eat meat while it was yet
day, David sware, saying, So do God to
me, and more also, if I taste bread, or
aught else, till the sun be down.
36 And all the people took notice *of it*,
and it pleased them: as whatsoever the
king did pleased all the people.
37 For all the people and all Ĭs̱'rā-ĕl
understood that day that it was not of
the king to slay Abner the son of Nĕr.
38 And the king said unto his servants,
Know ye not that there is a prince
and a great man fallen this day in
Ĭs̱'rā-ĕl?
39 And I *am* this day weak, though
anointed king; and these men the sons
of Zĕr'ṳ-ī'ah *be* too hard for me: the
LORD shall reward the doer of evil
according to his wickedness.

CHAPTER 4

AND when Saul's son heard that
Abner was dead in Hē'brȯn, his
hands were feeble, and all the Ĭs̱'rā-
ĕl-ītes were troubled.
2 And Saul's son had two men *that*
were captains of bands: the name of the
one *was* Bā'ȧ-nȧh, and the name of the
other Rē'chăb, the sons of Rĭm'mŏn a
Bē-ē'rŏth-īte, of the children of Benjamin: (for Bē-ē'rŏth also was reckoned
to Benjamin:

3 And the Bē-ĕ'rŏth-ītes fled to Gĭt'tā-
ĭm, and were sojourners there until this
day.)
4 And Jonathan, Saul's son, had a son
that was lame of *his* feet. He was five
years old when the tidings came of Saul
and Jonathan out of Jĕz'rē-ĕl, and his
nurse took him up, and fled: and it came
to pass, as she made haste to flee, that
he fell, and became lame. And his name
was Mē-phĭb'ō-shĕth.
5 And the sons of Rĭm'mŏn the Bē-ĕ'-
rŏth-īte, Rē'chăb and Bā'ȧ-nȧh, went,
and came about the heat of the day to
the house of Ĭsh'-bō'shĕth, who lay on
a bed at noon.
6 And they came thither into the midst
of the house, *as though* they would have
fetched wheat; and they smote him
under the fifth *rib:* and Rē'chăb and
Bā'ȧ-nȧh his brother escaped.
7 For when they came into the house,
he lay on his bed in his bedchamber,
and they smote him, and slew him, and
beheaded him, and took his head, and
gat them away through the plain all
night.
8 And they brought the head of Ĭsh'-
bō'shĕth unto David to Hē'brȯn, and
said to the king, Behold the head of
Ĭsh'-bō'shĕth the son of Saul thine
enemy, which sought thy life; and the
LORD hath avenged my lord the king
this day of Saul, and of his seed.
9 ¶ And David answered Rē'chăb and
Bā'ȧ-nȧh his brother, the sons of Rĭm'-
mŏn the Bē-ĕ'rŏth-īte, and said unto
them, *As* the LORD liveth, who hath
redeemed my soul out of all adversity,
10 When one told me, saying, Behold,
Saul is dead, thinking to have brought
good tidings, I took hold of him, and
slew him in Zĭk'lăg, who *thought* that I
would have given him a reward for his
tidings:
11 How much more, when wicked men
have slain a righteous person in his own
house upon his bed? shall I not therefore now require his blood of your hand,
and take you away from the earth?
12 And David commanded his young
men, and they slew them, and cut off
their hands and their feet, and hanged
them up over the pool in Hē'brȯn. But
they took the head of Ĭsh'-bō'shĕth, and
buried *it* in the sepulchre of Abner in
Hē'brȯn.

CHAPTER 5

THEN came all the tribes of Ĭs̱'rā-ĕl
to David unto Hē'brȯn, and spake,
saying, Behold, we *are* thy bone and thy
flesh.
2 Also in time past, when Saul was
king over us, thou wast he that leddest
out and broughtest in Ĭs̱'rā-ĕl: and the
LORD said to thee, Thou shalt feed my
people Ĭs̱'rā-ĕl, and thou shalt be a captain over Ĭs̱'rā-ĕl.
3 So all the elders of Ĭs̱'rā-ĕl came to
the king to Hē'brȯn; and king David
made a league with them in Hē'brȯn before the LORD: and they anointed David
king over Ĭs̱'rā-ĕl.
4 ¶ David *was* thirty years old when
he began to reign, *and* he reigned forty
years.
5 In Hē'brȯn he reigned over Judah
seven years and six months: and in
Jerusalem he reigned thirty and three
years over all Ĭs̱'rā-ĕl and Judah.
6 ¶ And the king and his men went to
Jerusalem unto the Jĕb'ū-s̱ītes, the inhabitants of the land: which spake unto
David, saying, Except thou take away
the blind and the lame, thou shalt not
come in hither: thinking, David cannot
come in hither.
7 Nevertheless, David took the stronghold of Zion: the same *is* the city of
David.
8 And David said on that day, Whosoever getteth up to the gutter, and smiteth the Jĕb'ū-s̱ītes, and the lame and
the blind, *that are* hated of David's soul,
he shall be chief and captain. Wherefore they said, The blind and the lame
shall not come into the house.
9 So David dwelt in the fort, and called
it the city of David. And David built
round about from Mĭl'lō and inward.
10 And David went on, and grew great,
and the LORD God of hosts *was* with
him.
11 ¶ And Hiram king of Tȳre sent
messengers to David, and cedar trees,
and carpenters, and masons: and they
built David a house.
12 And David perceived that the LORD
had established him king over Ĭs̱'rā-ĕl,
and that he had exalted his kingdom for
his people Ĭs̱'rā-ĕl's sake.
13 ¶ And David took *him* more concubines and wives out of Jerusalem,
after he was come from Hē'brȯn: and

there were yet sons and daughters born to David.

14 And these *be* the names of those that were born unto him in Jerusalem; Shăm-mū'ȧh, and Shō'băb, and Nathan, and Sọlomon,

15 Ĭb'här also, and Ĕl'ĭ-shū'ȧ, and Nē'phĕg, and Jȧ-phī'ȧ,

16 And Ē-lĭsh'ȧ-mä, and Ē-lī'ȧ-dȧ, and Ē-lĭph'ȧ-lĕt.

17 ℂ But when the Phĭ-lĭs'tĭneṣ heard that they had anointed David king over Ĭṣ'rā-ĕl, all the Phĭ-lĭs'tĭneṣ came up to seek David; and David heard *of it,* and went down to the hold.

18 The Phĭ-lĭs'tĭneṣ also came and spread themselves in the valley of Rĕph'ā-ĭm.

19 And David inquired of the LORD, saying, Shall I go up to the Phĭ-lĭs'tĭneṣ? wilt thou deliver them into mine hand? And the LORD said unto David, Go up: for I will doubtless deliver the Phĭ-lĭs'tĭneṣ into thine hand.

20 And David came to Bā'ăl–pē-rā'zĭm, and David smote them there, and said, The LORD hath broken forth upon mine enemies before me, as the breach of waters. Therefore he called the name of that place Bā'ăl–pē-rā'zĭm.

21 And there they left their images, and David and his men burned them.

22 ℂ And the Phĭ-lĭs'tĭneṣ came up yet again, and spread themselves in the valley of Rĕph'ā-ĭm.

23 And when David inquired of the LORD, he said, Thou shalt not go up; *but* fetch a compass behind them, and come upon them over against the mulberry trees.

24 And let it be, when thou hearest the sound of a going in the tops of the mulberry trees, that then thou shalt bestir thyself: for then shall the LORD go out before thee, to smite the host of the Phĭ-lĭs'tĭneṣ.

25 And David did so, as the LORD had commanded him; and smote the Phĭ-lĭs'tĭneṣ from Gē'bȧ until thou come to Gā'zẽr.

CHAPTER 6

AGAIN, David gathered together all the chosen *men* of Ĭṣ'rā-ĕl, thirty thousand.

2 And David arose, and went with all the people that *were* with him from Bā'ȧ-lē of Judah, to bring up from thence the ark of God, whose name is called by the name of the LORD of hosts that dwelleth *between* the cherubim.

3 And they set the ark of God upon a new cart, and brought it out of the house of Ȧ-bĭn'ȧ-dăb that *was* in Gĭb'ē-ȧh: and Ŭz'zȧh and Ȧ-hī'ō, the sons of Ȧ-bĭn'ȧ-dăb, drave the new cart.

4 And they brought it out of the house of Ȧ-bĭn'ȧ-dăb which *was* at Gĭb'ē-ȧh, accompanying the ark of God: and Ȧ-hī'ō went before the ark.

5 And David and all the house of Ĭṣ'rā-ĕl played before the LORD on all manner of *instruments made of* fir wood, even on harps, and on psalteries, and on timbrels, and on cornets, and on cymbals.

6 ℂ And when they came to Nā'chŏn's threshingfloor, Ŭz'zȧh put forth *his hand* to the ark of God, and took hold of it; for the oxen shook *it.*

7 And the anger of the LORD was kindled against Ŭz'zȧh, and God smote him there for *his* error; and there he died by the ark of God.

8 And David was displeased, because the LORD had made a breach upon Ŭz'zȧh: and he called the name of the place Pē'rĕz–ŭz'zȧh to this day.

9 And David was afraid of the LORD that day, and said, How shall the ark of the LORD come to me?

10 So David would not remove the ark of the LORD unto him into the city of David: but David carried it aside into the house of Ō'bĕd–ē'dŏm the Gĭt'tīte.

11 And the ark of the LORD continued in the house of Ō'bĕd–e'dŏm the Gĭt'tīte three months: and the LORD blessed Ō'bĕd–ē'dŏm, and all his household.

12 ℂ And it was told king David, saying, The LORD hath blessed the house of Ō'bĕd–ē'dŏm, and all that *pertaineth* unto him, because of the ark of God. So David went and brought up the ark of God from the house of Ō'bĕd–ē'dŏm into the city of David with gladness.

13 And it was *so,* that when they that bare the ark of the LORD had gone six paces, he sacrificed oxen and fatlings.

14 And David danced before the LORD with all *his* might; and David *was* girded with a linen ĕph'ŏd.

15 So David and all the house of Ĭṣ'rā-ĕl brought up the ark of the LORD with shouting, and with the sound of the trumpet.

16 And as the ark of the LORD came
into the city of David, Mī'chăl Saul's
daughter looked through a window, and
saw king David leaping and dancing before the LORD; and she despised him in
her heart.
17 ℂ And they brought in the ark of
the LORD, and set it in his place, in the
midst of the tabernacle that David had
pitched for it: and David offered burnt
offerings and peace offerings before the
LORD.
18 And as soon as David had made an
end of offering burnt offerings and peace
offerings, he blessed the people in the
name of the LORD of hosts.
19 And he dealt among all the people,
even among the whole multitude of
Ĭş'rā-ĕl, as well to the women as men,
to every one a cake of bread, and a good
piece *of flesh*, and a flagon *of wine*. So
all the people departed every one to his
house.
20 ℂ Then David returned to bless his
household. And Mī'chăl the daughter
of Saul came out to meet David, and
said, How glorious was the king of
Ĭş'rā-ĕl to-day, who uncovered himself
to-day in the eyes of the handmaids of
his servants, as one of the vain fellows
shamelessly uncovereth himself!
21 And David said unto Mī'chăl, *It was*
before the LORD, which chose me before
thy father, and before all his house, to
appoint me ruler over the people of the
LORD, over Ĭş'rā-ĕl: therefore will I play
before the LORD.
22 And I will yet be more vile than
thus, and will be base in mine own sight:
and of the maidservants which thou hast
spoken of, of them shall I be had in
honor.
23 Therefore Mī'chăl the daughter of
Saul had no child unto the day of her
death.

CHAPTER 7

AND it came to pass, when the king
sat in his house, and the LORD had
given him rest round about from all his
enemies;
2 That the king said unto Nathan the
prophet, See now, I dwell in a house of
cedar, but the ark of God dwelleth within curtains.
3 And Nathan said to the king, Go, do
all that *is* in thine heart; for the LORD *is*
with thee.
4 ℂ And it came to pass that night,
that the word of the LORD came unto
Nathan, saying,
5 Go and tell my servant David, Thus
saith the LORD, Shalt thou build me a
house for me to dwell in?
6 Whereas I have not dwelt in *any*
house since the time that I brought up
the children of Ĭş'rā-ĕl out of Egypt,
even to this day, but have walked in a
tent and in a tabernacle.
7 In all *the places* wherein I have
walked with all the children of Ĭş'rā-ĕl
spake I a word with any of the tribes of
Ĭş'rā-ĕl, whom I commanded to feed my
people Ĭş'rā-ĕl, saying, Why build ye
not me a house of cedar?
8 Now therefore so shalt thou say unto
my servant David, Thus saith the LORD
of hosts, I took thee from the sheepcote,
from following the sheep, to be ruler
over my people, over Ĭş'rā-ĕl:
9 And I was with thee whithersoever
thou wentest, and have cut off all thine
enemies out of thy sight, and have made
thee a great name, like unto the name of
the great *men* that *are* in the earth.
10 Moreover I will appoint a place for
my people Ĭş'rā-ĕl, and will plant them,
that they may dwell in a place of their
own, and move no more; neither shall
the children of wickedness afflict them
any more, as beforetime,
11 And as since the time that I commanded judges *to be* over my people
Ĭş'rā-ĕl, and have caused thee to rest
from all thine enemies. Also the LORD
telleth thee that he will make thee a
house.
12 ℂ And when thy days be fulfilled,
and thou shalt sleep with thy fathers, I
will set up thy seed after thee, which
shall proceed out of thy bowels, and I
will establish his kingdom.
13 He shall build a house for my name,
and I will stablish the throne of his kingdom for ever.
14 I will be his father, and he shall be
my son. If he commit iniquity, I will
chasten him with the rod of men, and
with the stripes of the children of men:
15 But my mercy shall not depart away
from him, as I took *it* from Saul, whom I
put away before thee.
16 And thine house and thy kingdom
shall be established for ever before thee:
thy throne shall be established for ever.
17 According to all these words, and

according to all this vision, so did
Nathan speak unto David.
18 ¶ Then went king David in, and sat
before the LORD, and he said, Who *am*
I, O Lord GOD? and what *is* my house,
that thou hast brought me hitherto?
19 And this was yet a small thing in thy
sight, O Lord GOD; but thou hast spoken
also of thy servant's house for a great
while to come. And *is* this the manner
of man, O Lord GOD?
20 And what can David say more unto
thee? for thou, Lord GOD, knowest thy
servant.
21 For thy word's sake, and according
to thine own heart, hast thou done all
these great things, to make thy servant
know *them*.
22 Wherefore thou art great, O LORD
God: for *there is* none like thee, neither
is there any God besides thee, according to all that we have heard with our
ears.
23 And what one nation in the earth *is*
like thy people, *even* like Ĭş′rā-ĕl, whom
God went to redeem for a people to himself, and to make him a name, and to do
for you great things and terrible, for thy
land, before thy people, which thou
redeemedst to thee from Egypt, *from*
the nations and their gods?
24 For thou hast confirmed to thyself
thy people Ĭş′rā-ĕl *to be* a people unto
thee for ever: and thou, LORD, art become their God.
25 And now, O LORD God, the word
that thou hast spoken concerning thy
servant, and concerning his house,
establish *it* for ever, and do as thou hast
said.
26 And let thy name be magnified for
ever, saying, The LORD of hosts *is* the
God over Ĭş′rā-ĕl: and let the house of
thy servant David be established before
thee.
27 For thou, O LORD of hosts, God of
Ĭş′rā-ĕl, hast revealed to thy servant,
saying, I will build thee a house: therefore hath thy servant found in his heart
to pray this prayer unto thee.
28 And now, O Lord GOD, thou *art*
that God, and thy words be true, and
thou hast promised this goodness unto
thy servant:
29 Therefore now let it please thee to
bless the house of thy servant, that it
may continue for ever before thee: for
thou, O Lord GOD, hast spoken *it*: and
with thy blessing let the house of thy
servant be blessed for ever.

CHAPTER 8

AND after this it came to pass, that
David smote the Phĭ-lĭs′tīneş, and
subdued them: and David took Mē′-
thĕg–ăm′mah out of the hand of the
Phĭ-lĭs′tīneş.
2 And he smote Mō′ăb, and measured
them with a line, casting them down to
the ground; even with two lines measured he to put to death, and with one
full line to keep alive. And *so* the Mō′-
ăb-ītes became David's servants, *and*
brought gifts.
3 ¶ David smote also Hăd′ăd-ē′zĕr,
the son of Rē′hŏb, king of Zō′bah, as he
went to recover his border at the river
Eū-phrā′tēş.
4 And David took from him a thousand
chariots, and seven hundred horsemen,
and twenty thousand footmen: and
David houghed all the chariot *horses*,
but reserved of them *for* a hundred
chariots.
5 And when the Syrians of Damascus
came to succor Hăd′ăd-ē′zĕr king of
Zō′bah, David slew of the Syrians two
and twenty thousand men.
6 Then David put garrisons in Syria of
Damascus: and the Syrians became
servants to David, *and* brought gifts.
And the LORD preserved David whithersoever he went.
7 And David took the shields of gold
that were on the servants of Hăd′ăd-ē′-
zĕr, and brought them to Jerusalem.
8 And from Bē′tah, and from Bē-rō′-
thaī, cities of Hăd′ăd-ē′zĕr, king David
took exceeding much brass.
9 ¶ When Tō′ī king of Hā′măth heard
that David had smitten all the host of
Hăd′ăd-ē′zĕr,
10 Then Tō′ī sent Jō′răm his son unto
king David, to salute him, and to bless
him, because he had fought against
Hăd′ăd-ē′zĕr, and smitten him: for
Hăd′ăd-ē′zĕr had wars with Tō′ī. And
Joram brought with him vessels of silver, and vessels of gold, and vessels of
brass:
11 Which also king David did dedicate
unto the LORD, with the silver and gold
that he had dedicated of all nations
which he subdued;
12 Of Syria, and of Mō′ăb, and of the
children of Ammon, and of the Phĭ-lĭs′-

tīnes, and of Ăm′ȧ-lĕk, and of the spoil of Hăd′ăd-ē′zēr, son of Rē′hŏb, king of Zō′bȧh.

13 And David gat *him* a name when he returned from smiting of the Syrians in the valley of salt, *being* eighteen thousand *men*.

14 ¶ And he put garrisons in Ē′dŏm; throughout all Ē′dŏm put he garrisons, and all they of Ē′dŏm became David's servants. And the LORD preserved David whithersoever he went.

15 And David reigned over all Ĭs′rā-ĕl; and David executed judgment and justice unto all his people.

16 And Jō′ăb the son of Zĕr′ụ-ī′ȧh *was* over the host; and Jē-hŏsh′ȧ-phăt the son of Ȧ-hī′lŭd *was* recorder;

17 And Zā′dŏk the son of Ȧ-hī′tŭb, and Ȧ-hĭm′ē-lĕch the son of Ȧ-bī′ȧ-thȧr, *were* the priests; and Sē-rā′ịȧh *was* the scribe;

18 And Bē-nā′ịȧh the son of Jē-hôi′ȧ-dȧ *was over* both the Chĕr′ē-thītes and the Pĕl′ē-thītes; and David's sons were chief rulers.

CHAPTER 9

AND David said, Is there yet any that is left of the house of Saul, that I may show him kindness for Jonathan's sake?

2 And *there was* of the house of Saul a servant whose name *was* Zī′bȧ. And when they had called him unto David, the king said unto him, *Art* thou Zī′bȧ? And he said, Thy servant *is he*.

3 And the king said, *Is* there not yet any of the house of Saul, that I may show the kindness of God unto him? And Zī′bȧ said unto the king, Jonathan hath yet a son, *which is* lame on *his* feet.

4 And the king said unto him, Where *is* he? And Zī′bȧ said unto the king, Behold, he *is* in the house of Mā′chĭr, the son of Ăm′mĭ-ĕl, in Lō′–dē′băr.

5 ¶ Then king David sent, and fetched him out of the house of Mā′chĭr, the son of Ăm′mĭ-ĕl, from Lō′–dē′băr.

6 Now when Mē-phĭb′ō-shĕth, the son of Jonathan, the son of Saul, was come unto David, he fell on his face, and did reverence. And David said, Mē-phĭb′ō-shĕth. And he answered, Behold thy servant!

7 ¶ And David said unto him, Fear not: for I will surely show thee kindness for Jonathan thy father's sake, and will restore thee all the land of Saul thy father; and thou shalt eat bread at my table continually.

8 And he bowed himself, and said, What *is* thy servant, that thou shouldest look upon such a dead dog as I *am*?

9 ¶ Then the king called to Zī′bȧ, Saul's servant, and said unto him, I have given unto thy master's son all that pertained to Saul and to all his house.

10 Thou therefore, and thy sons, and thy servants, shall till the land for him, and thou shalt bring in *the fruits*, that thy master's son may have food to eat: but Mē-phĭb′ō-shĕth thy master's son shall eat bread alway at my table. Now Zī′bȧ had fifteen sons and twenty servants.

11 Then said Zī′bȧ unto the king, According to all that my lord the king hath commanded his servant, so shall thy servant do. As for Mē-phĭb′ō-shĕth, *said the king*, he shall eat at my table, as one of the king's sons.

12 And Mē-phĭb′ō-shĕth had a young son, whose name *was* Mī′chȧ. And all that dwelt in the house of Zī′bȧ *were* servants unto Mē-phĭb′ō-shĕth.

13 So Mē-phĭb′ō-shĕth dwelt in Jerusalem: for he did eat continually at the king's table; and was lame on both his feet.

CHAPTER 10

AND it came to pass after this, that the king of the children of Ammon died, and Hā′nŭn his son reigned in his stead.

2 Then said David, I will show kindness unto Hā′nŭn the son of Nā′hăsh, as his father showed kindness unto me. And David sent to comfort him by the hand of his servants for his father. And David's servants came into the land of the children of Ammon.

3 And the princes of the children of Ammon said unto Hā′nŭn their lord, Thinkest thou that David doth honor thy father, that he hath sent comforters unto thee? hath not David *rather* sent his servants unto thee, to search the city, and to spy it out, and to overthrow it?

4 Wherefore Hā′nŭn took David's servants, and shaved off the one half of their beards, and cut off their garments in the middle, *even* to their buttocks, and sent them away.

5 When they told *it* unto David, he sent
to meet them, because the men were
greatly ashamed: and the king said,
Tarry at Jĕr′ĭ-chō until your beards be
grown, and *then* return.
6 ℂ And when the children of Ammon
saw that they stank before David, the
children of Ammon sent and hired the
Syrians of Bĕth′–rē′hŏb, and the Syrians
of Zō′bȧ, twenty thousand footmen, and
of king Mā′ȧ-cȧh a thousand men, and
of Ĭsh′–tŏb twelve thousand men.
7 And when David heard of *it,* he sent
Jō′ăb, and all the host of the mighty
men.
8 And the children of Ammon came
out, and put the battle in array at the
entering in of the gate: and the Syrians
of Zō′bȧ, and of Rē′hŏb, and Ĭsh′–tŏb,
and Mā′ȧ-cȧh, *were* by themselves in
the field.
9 When Jō′ăb saw that the front of the
battle was against him before and behind, he chose of all the choice *men* of
Ĭş′rā-ĕl, and put *them* in array against
the Syrians:
10 And the rest of the people he delivered into the hand of Ȧ-bĭsh′ā-ī his
brother, that he might put *them* in array
against the children of Ammon.
11 And he said, If the Syrians be too
strong for me, then thou shalt help me:
but if the children of Ammon be too
strong for thee, then I will come and
help thee.
12 Be of good courage, and let us play
the men for our people, and for the cities
of our God: and the LORD do that which
seemeth him good.
13 And Jō′ăb drew nigh, and the people
that *were* with him, unto the battle
against the Syrians: and they fled before him.
14 And when the children of Ammon
saw that the Syrians were fled, then fled
they also before Ȧ-bĭsh′ā-ī, and entered
into the city. So Jō′ăb returned from
the children of Ammon, and came to
Jerusalem.
15 ℂ And when the Syrians saw that
they were smitten before Ĭş′rā-ĕl, they
gathered themselves together.
16 And Hăd′ăr-ē′zĕr sent, and brought
out the Syrians that *were* beyond the
river; and they came to Hē′lăm: and
Shō′băch the captain of the host of
Hăd′ăr-ē′zĕr *went* before them.
17 And when it was told David, he
gathered all Ĭş′rā-ĕl together, and
passed over Jordan, and came to Hē′-
lăm. And the Syrians set themselves in
array against David, and fought with
him.
18 And the Syrians fled before Ĭş′rā-ĕl;
and David slew *the men of* seven hundred chariots of the Syrians, and forty
thousand horsemen, and smote Shō′-
băch the captain of their host, who died
there.
19 And when all the kings *that were*
servants to Hăd′ăr-ē′zĕr saw that they
were smitten before Ĭş′rā-ĕl, they made
peace with Ĭş′rā-ĕl, and served them.
So the Syrians feared to help the children of Ammon any more.

CHAPTER 11

AND it came to pass, after the year
was expired, at the time when
kings go forth *to battle,* that David
sent Jō′ăb, and his servants with him,
and all Ĭş′rā-ĕl; and they destroyed
the children of Ammon, and besieged
Răb′bȧh. But David tarried still at
Jerusalem.
2 ℂ And it came to pass in an eveningtide, that David arose from off his bed,
and walked upon the roof of the king's
house: and from the roof he saw a woman washing herself; and the woman *was*
very beautiful to look upon.
3 And David sent and inquired after
the woman. And *one* said, *Is* not this
Băth′–shē′bȧ, the daughter of Ē-lī′ăm,
the wife of Ū-rī′ȧh the Hĭt′tīte?
4 And David sent messengers, and
took her; and she came in unto him, and
he lay with her; for she was purified
from her uncleanness: and she returned
unto her house.
5 And the woman conceived, and sent
and told David, and said, I *am* with
child.
6 ℂ And David sent to Jō′ăb, *saying,*
Send me Ū-rī′ȧh the Hĭt′tīte. And Jō′ăb
sent Ū-rī′ȧh to David.
7 And when Ū-rī′ȧh was come unto
him, David demanded *of him* how Jō′ăb
did, and how the people did, and how
the war prospered.
8 And David said to Ū-rī′ȧh, Go down
to thy house, and wash thy feet. And
Ū-rī′ȧh departed out of the king's house,
and there followed him a mess *of meat*
from the king.
9 But Ū-rī′ȧh slept at the door of the

king's house with all the servants of his lord, and went not down to his house.

10 And when they had told David, saying, Ū-rī'ah went not down unto his house, David said unto Ū-rī'ah, Camest thou not from *thy* journey? why *then* didst thou not go down unto thine house?

11 And Ū-rī'ah said unto David, The ark, and Iṣ'rā-ēl, and Judah, abide in tents; and my lord Jō'ăb, and the servants of my lord, are encamped in the open fields; shall I then go into mine house, to eat and to drink, and to lie with my wife? *as* thou livest, and *as* thy soul liveth, I will not do this thing.

12 And David said to Ū-rī'ah, Tarry here to-day also, and to-morrow I will let thee depart. So Ū-rī'ah abode in Jerusalem that day, and the morrow.

13 And when David had called him, he did eat and drink before him; and he made him drunk: and at even he went out to lie on his bed with the servants of his lord, but went not down to his house.

14 ¶ And it came to pass in the morning, that David wrote a letter to Jō'ăb, and sent *it* by the hand of Ū-rī'ah.

15 And he wrote in the letter, saying, Set ye Ū-rī'ah in the forefront of the hottest battle, and retire ye from him, that he may be smitten, and die.

16 And it came to pass, when Jō'ăb observed the city, that he assigned Ū-rī'ah unto a place where he knew that valiant men *were*.

17 And the men of the city went out, and fought with Jō'ăb: and there fell *some* of the people of the servants of David; and Ū-rī'ah the Hĭt'tīte died also.

18 ¶ Then Jō'ăb sent and told David all the things concerning the war;

19 And charged the messenger, saying, When thou hast made an end of telling the matters of the war unto the king,

20 And if so be that the king's wrath arise, and he say unto thee, Wherefore approached ye so nigh unto the city when ye did fight? knew ye not that they would shoot from the wall?

21 Who smote Ă-bĭm'ē-lĕch the son of Jĕr'ŭb-bē'shĕth? did not a woman cast a piece of a millstone upon him from the wall, that he died in Thē'bĕz? why went ye nigh the wall? then say thou, Thy servant Ū-rī'ah the Hĭt'tīte is dead also.

22 ¶ So the messenger went, and came and showed David all that Jō'ăb had sent him for.

23 And the messenger said unto David, Surely the men prevailed against us, and came out unto us into the field, and we were upon them even unto the entering of the gate.

24 And the shooters shot from off the wall upon thy servants; and *some* of the king's servants be dead, and thy servant Ū-rī'ah the Hĭt'tīte is dead also.

25 Then David said unto the messenger, Thus shalt thou say unto Jō'ăb, Let not this thing displease thee, for the sword devoureth one as well as another: make thy battle more strong against the city, and overthrow it: and encourage thou him.

26 ¶ And when the wife of Ū-rī'ah heard that Ū-rī'ah her husband was dead, she mourned for her husband.

27 And when the mourning was past, David sent and fetched her to his house, and she became his wife, and bare him a son. But the thing that David had done displeased the LORD.

CHAPTER 12

AND the LORD sent Nathan unto David. And he came unto him, and said unto him, There were two men in one city; the one rich, and the other poor.

2 The rich *man* had exceeding many flocks and herds:

3 But the poor *man* had nothing, save one little ewe lamb, which he had bought and nourished up: and it grew up together with him, and with his children; it did eat of his own meat, and drank of his own cup, and lay in his bosom, and was unto him as a daughter.

4 And there came a traveler unto the rich man, and he spared to take of his own flock and of his own herd, to dress for the wayfaring man that was come unto him; but took the poor man's lamb, and dressed it for the man that was come to him.

5 And David's anger was greatly kindled against the man; and he said to Nathan, *As* the LORD liveth, the man that hath done this *thing* shall surely die:

6 And he shall restore the lamb fourfold, because he did this thing, and because he had no pity.

7 ¶ And Nathan said to David, Thou *art* the man. Thus saith the LORD God of Iṣ'rā-ĕl, I anointed thee king over

Ĭṣ'rā-ĕl, and I delivered thee out of the hand of Saul;

8 And I gave thee thy master's house, and thy master's wives into thy bosom, and gave thee the house of Ĭṣ'rā-ĕl and of Judah; and if *that had been* too little, I would moreover have given unto thee such and such things.

9 Wherefore hast thou despised the commandment of the LORD, to do evil in his sight? thou hast killed Ū-rī'ȧh the Hĭt'tīte with the sword, and hast taken his wife *to be* thy wife, and hast slain him with the sword of the children of Ammon.

10 Now therefore the sword shall never depart from thine house; because thou hast despised me, and hast taken the wife of Ū-rī'ȧh the Hĭt'tīte to be thy wife.

11 Thus saith the LORD, Behold, I will raise up evil against thee out of thine own house, and I will take thy wives before thine eyes, and give *them* unto thy neighbor, and he shall lie with thy wives in the sight of this sun.

12 For thou didst *it* secretly: but I will do this thing before all Ĭṣ'rā-ĕl, and before the sun.

13 And David said unto Nathan, I have sinned against the LORD. And Nathan said unto David, The LORD also hath put away thy sin; thou shalt not die.

14 Howbeit, because by this deed thou hast given great occasion to the enemies of the LORD to blaspheme, the child also *that is* born unto thee shall surely die.

15 ℂ And Nathan departed unto his house. And the LORD struck the child that Ū-rī'ȧh's wife bare unto David, and it was very sick.

16 David therefore besought God for the child; and David fasted, and went in, and lay all night upon the earth.

17 And the elders of his house arose, *and went* to him, to raise him up from the earth: but he would not, neither did he eat bread with them.

18 And it came to pass on the seventh day, that the child died. And the servants of David feared to tell him that the child was dead: for they said, Behold, while the child was yet alive, we spake unto him, and he would not hearken unto our voice: how will he then vex himself, if we tell him that the child is dead?

19 But when David saw that his servants whispered, David perceived that the child was dead: therefore David said unto his servants, Is the child dead? And they said, He is dead.

20 Then David arose from the earth, and washed, and anointed *himself*, and changed his apparel, and came into the house of the LORD, and worshipped: then he came to his own house; and when he required, they set bread before him, and he did eat.

21 Then said his servants unto him, What thing *is* this that thou hast done? thou didst fast and weep for the child, *while it was* alive; but when the child was dead, thou didst rise and eat bread.

22 And he said, While the child was yet alive, I fasted and wept: for I said, Who can tell *whether* God will be gracious to me, that the child may live?

23 But now he is dead, wherefore should I fast? can I bring him back again? I shall go to him, but he shall not return to me.

24 ℂ And David comforted Băth'–shē'bȧ his wife, and went in unto her, and lay with her: and she bare a son, and he called his name Solomon: and the LORD loved him.

25 And he sent by the hand of Nathan the prophet; and he called his name Jĕd'ĭ-dī'ȧh, because of the LORD.

26 ℂ And Jō'ăb fought against Răb'bȧh of the children of Ammon, and took the royal city.

27 And Jō'ăb sent messengers to David, and said, I have fought against Răb'bȧh, and have taken the city of waters.

28 Now therefore gather the rest of the people together, and encamp against the city, and take it: lest I take the city, and it be called after my name.

29 And David gathered all the people together, and went to Răb'bȧh, and fought against it, and took it.

30 And he took their king's crown from off his head, the weight whereof *was* a talent of gold with precious stones: and it was *set* on David's head. And he brought forth the spoil of the city in great abundance.

31 And he brought forth the people that *were* therein, and put *them* under saws, and under harrows of iron, and under axes of iron, and made them pass through the brickkiln: and thus did he unto all the cities of the children of

Ammon. So David and all the people returned unto Jerusalem.

CHAPTER 13

AND it came to pass after this, that Ăb'sȧ-lŏm the son of David had a fair sister, whose name *was* Tā'mȧr; and Amnon the son of David loved her.

2 And Amnon was so vexed, that he fell sick for his sister Tā'mȧr; for she *was* a virgin; and Amnon thought it hard for him to do any thing to her.

3 But Amnon had a friend, whose name *was* Jŏn'ȧ-dăb, the son of Shĭm'ē-ȧh David's brother: and Jŏn'ȧ-dăb *was* a very subtile man.

4 And he said unto him, Why *art* thou, *being* the king's son, lean from day to day? wilt thou not tell me? And Amnon said unto him, I love Tā'mȧr, my brother Ăb'sȧ-lŏm's sister.

5 And Jŏn'ȧ-dăb said unto him, Lay thee down on thy bed, and make thyself sick: and when thy father cometh to see thee, say unto him, I pray thee, let my sister Tā'mȧr come, and give me meat, and dress the meat in my sight, that I may see *it*, and eat *it* at her hand.

6 ¶ So Amnon lay down, and made himself sick: and when the king was come to see him, Amnon said unto the king, I pray thee, let Tā'mȧr my sister come, and make me a couple of cakes in my sight, that I may eat at her hand.

7 Then David sent home to Tā'mȧr, saying, Go now to thy brother Amnon's house, and dress him meat.

8 So Tā'mȧr went to her brother Amnon's house; and he was laid down. And she took flour, and kneaded *it*, and made cakes in his sight, and did bake the cakes.

9 And she took a pan, and poured *them* out before him; but he refused to eat. And Amnon said, Have out all men from me. And they went out every man from him.

10 And Amnon said unto Tā'mȧr, Bring the meat into the chamber, that I may eat of thine hand. And Tā'mȧr took the cakes which she had made, and brought *them* into the chamber to Amnon her brother.

11 And when she had brought *them* unto him to eat, he took hold of her, and said unto her, Come lie with me, my sister.

12 And she answered him, Nay, my brother, do not force me; for no such thing ought to be done in Ĭṣ'rā-ēl: do not thou this folly.

13 And I, whither shall I cause my shame to go? and as for thee, thou shalt be as one of the fools in Ĭṣ'rā-ēl. Now therefore, I pray thee, speak unto the king; for he will not withhold me from thee.

14 Howbeit he would not hearken unto her voice: but, being stronger than she, forced her, and lay with her.

15 ¶ Then Amnon hated her exceedingly; so that the hatred wherewith he hated her *was* greater than the love wherewith he had loved her. And Amnon said unto her, Arise, be gone.

16 And she said unto him, *There is* no cause: this evil in sending me away *is* greater than the other that thou didst unto me. But he would not hearken unto her.

17 Then he called his servant that ministered unto him, and said, Put now this *woman* out from me, and bolt the door after her.

18 And *she had* a garment of divers colors upon her: for with such robes were the king's daughters *that were* virgins appareled. Then his servant brought her out, and bolted the door after her.

19 ¶ And Tā'mȧr put ashes on her head, and rent her garment of divers colors that *was* on her, and laid her hand on her head, and went on crying.

20 And Ăb'sȧ-lŏm her brother said unto her, Hath Amnon thy brother been with thee? but hold now thy peace, my sister: he *is* thy brother; regard not this thing. So Tā'mȧr remained desolate in her brother Ăb'sȧ-lŏm's house.

21 ¶ But when king David heard of all these things, he was very wroth.

22 And Ăb'sȧ-lŏm spake unto his brother Amnon neither good nor bad: for Ăb'sȧ-lŏm hated Amnon, because he had forced his sister Tā'mȧr.

23 ¶ And it came to pass after two full years, that Ăb'sȧ-lŏm had sheepshearers in Bā'ăl–hā'zŏr, which *is* beside Ē'phrā-ĭm: and Ăb'sȧ-lŏm invited all the king's sons.

24 And Ăb'sȧ-lŏm came to the king, and said, Behold now, thy servant hath sheepshearers; let the king, I beseech thee, and his servants go with thy servant.

25 And the king said to Ăb′sȧ-lŏm, Nay, my son, let us not all now go, lest we be chargeable unto thee. And he pressed him: howbeit he would not go, but blessed him.

26 Then said Ăb′sȧ-lŏm, If not, I pray thee, let my brother Amnon go with us. And the king said unto him, Why should he go with thee?

27 But Ăb′sȧ-lŏm pressed him, that he let Amnon and all the king's sons go with him.

28 ¶ Now Ăb′sȧ-lŏm had commanded his servants, saying, Mark ye now when Amnon's heart is merry with wine, and when I say unto you, Smite Amnon; then kill him, fear not: have not I commanded you? be courageous, and be valiant.

29 And the servants of Ăb′sȧ-lŏm did unto Amnon as Ăb′sȧ-lŏm had commanded. Then all the king's sons arose, and every man gat him up upon his mule, and fled.

30 ¶ And it came to pass, while they were in the way, that tidings came to David, saying, Ăb′sȧ-lŏm hath slain all the king's sons, and there is not one of them left.

31 Then the king arose, and tare his garments, and lay on the earth; and all his servants stood by with their clothes rent.

32 And Jŏn′ȧ-dăb, the son of Shĭm′ē-ȧh David's brother, answered and said, Let not my lord suppose *that* they have slain all the young men the king's sons; for Amnon only is dead: for by the appointment of Ăb′sȧ-lŏm this hath been determined from the day that he forced his sister Tā′mȧr.

33 Now therefore let not my lord the king take the thing to his heart, to think that all the king's sons are dead: for Amnon only is dead.

34 But Ăb′sȧ-lŏm fled. And the young man that kept the watch lifted up his eyes, and looked, and, behold, there came much people by the way of the hillside behind him.

35 And Jŏn′ȧ-dăb said unto the king, Behold, the king's sons come: as thy servant said, so it is.

36 And it came to pass, as soon as he had made an end of speaking, that, behold, the king's sons came, and lifted up their voice and wept: and the king also and all his servants wept very sore.

37 ¶ But Ăb′sȧ-lŏm fled, and went to Tăl′maī, the son of Ȧm-mī′hŭd, king of Gē′shŭr. And *David* mourned for his son every day.

38 So Ăb′sȧ-lŏm fled, and went to Gē′shŭr, and was there three years.

39 And *the soul of* king David longed to go forth unto Ăb′sȧ-lŏm: for he was comforted concerning Amnon, seeing he was dead.

CHAPTER 14

NOW Jō′ăb the son of Zĕr′ụ-ī′ȧh perceived that the king's heart *was* toward Ăb′sȧ-lŏm.

2 And Jō′ăb sent to Tē-kō′ȧh, and fetched thence a wise woman, and said unto her, I pray thee, feign thyself to be a mourner, and put on now mourning apparel, and anoint not thyself with oil, but be as a woman that had a long time mourned for the dead:

3 And come to the king, and speak on this manner unto him. So Jō′ăb put the words in her mouth.

4 ¶ And when the woman of Tē-kō′ȧh spake to the king, she fell on her face to the ground, and did obeisance, and said, Help, O king.

5 And the king said unto her, What aileth thee? And she answered, I *am* indeed a widow woman, and mine husband is dead.

6 And thy handmaid had two sons, and they two strove together in the field, and *there was* none to part them, but the one smote the other, and slew him.

7 And behold, the whole family is risen against thine handmaid, and they said, Deliver him that smote his brother, that we may kill him, for the life of his brother whom he slew; and we will destroy the heir also: and so they shall quench my coal which is left, and shall not leave to my husband *neither* name nor remainder upon the earth.

8 And the king said unto the woman, Go to thine house, and I will give charge concerning thee.

9 And the woman of Tē-kō′ȧh said unto the king, My lord, O king, the iniquity *be* on me, and on my father's house: and the king and his throne *be* guiltless.

10 And the king said, Whosoever saith *aught* unto thee, bring him to me, and he shall not touch thee any more.

11 Then said she, I pray thee, let the king remember the LORD thy God, that

thou wouldest not suffer the revengers of blood to destroy any more, lest they destroy my son. And he said, *As* the LORD liveth, there shall not one hair of thy son fall to the earth.

12 Then the woman said, Let thine handmaid, I pray thee, speak *one* word unto my lord the king. And he said, Say on.

13 And the woman said, Wherefore then hast thou thought such a thing against the people of God? for the king doth speak this thing as one which is faulty, in that the king doth not fetch home again his banished.

14 For we must needs die, and *are* as water spilt on the ground, which cannot be gathered up again; neither doth God respect *any* person; yet doth he devise means, that his banished be not expelled from him.

15 Now therefore that I am come to speak of this thing unto my lord the king, *it is* because the people have made me afraid: and thy handmaid said, I will now speak unto the king; it may be that the king will perform the request of his handmaid.

16 For the king will hear, to deliver his handmaid out of the hand of the man *that would* destroy me and my son together out of the inheritance of God.

17 Then thine handmaid said, The word of my lord the king shall now be comfortable: for as an angel of God, so *is* my lord the king to discern good and bad: therefore the LORD thy God will be with thee.

18 Then the king answered and said unto the woman, Hide not from me, I pray thee, the thing that I shall ask thee. And the woman said, Let my lord the king now speak.

19 And the king said, *Is not* the hand of Jō′ăb with thee in all this? And the woman answered and said, *As* thy soul liveth, my lord the king, none can turn to the right hand or to the left from aught that my lord the king hath spoken: for thy servant Jō′ăb, he bade me, and he put all these words in the mouth of thine handmaid:

20 To fetch about this form of speech hath thy servant Jō′ăb done this thing: and my lord *is* wise, according to the wisdom of an angel of God, to know all *things* that *are* in the earth.

21 ℭ And the king said unto Jō′ăb, Behold now, I have done this thing: go therefore, bring the young man Ăb′sȧ-lŏm again.

22 And Jō′ăb fell to the ground on his face, and bowed himself, and thanked the king: and Jō′ăb said, To-day thy servant knoweth that I have found grace in thy sight, my lord, O king, in that the king hath fulfilled the request of his servant.

23 So Jō′ăb arose and went to Gē′shŭr, and brought Ăb′sȧ-lŏm to Jerusalem.

24 And the king said, Let him turn to his own house, and let him not see my face. So Ăb′sȧ-lŏm returned to his own house, and saw not the king's face.

25 ℭ But in all Ĭs̱′rā-ĕl there was none to be so much praised as Ăb′sȧ-lŏm for his beauty: from the sole of his foot even to the crown of his head there was no blemish in him.

26 And when he polled his head, (for it was at every year's end that he polled *it;* because *the hair* was heavy on him, therefore he polled it:) he weighed the hair of his head at two hundred shekels after the king's weight.

27 And unto Ăb′sȧ-lŏm there were born three sons, and one daughter, whose name *was* Tā′mȧr: she was a woman of a fair countenance.

28 ℭ So Ăb′sȧ-lŏm dwelt two full years in Jerusalem, and saw not the king's face.

29 Therefore Ăb′sȧ-lŏm sent for Jō′ăb, to have sent him to the king; but he would not come to him: and when he sent again the second time, he would not come.

30 Therefore he said unto his servants, See, Jō′ăb's field is near mine, and he hath barley there; go and set it on fire. And Ăb′sȧ-lŏm's servants set the field on fire.

31 Then Jō′ăb arose, and came to Ăb′sȧ-lŏm unto *his* house, and said unto him, Wherefore have thy servants set my field on fire?

32 And Ăb′sȧ-lŏm answered Jō′ăb, Behold, I sent unto thee, saying, Come hither, that I may send thee to the king, to say, Wherefore am I come from Gē′shŭr? *it had been* good for me *to have been* there still: now therefore let me see the king's face; and if there be *any* iniquity in me, let him kill me.

33 So Jō′ăb came to the king, and told him: and when he had called for Ăb′sȧ-

lŏm, he came to the king, and bowed
himself on his face to the ground before
the king: and the king kissed Ăb′sȧ-lŏm.

CHAPTER 15

AND it came to pass after this, that
Ăb′sȧ-lŏm prepared him chariots
and horses, and fifty men to run before
him.
2 And Ăb′sȧ-lŏm rose up early, and
stood beside the way of the gate: and it
was *so*, that when any man that had a
controversy came to the king for judgment, then Ăb′sȧ-lŏm called unto him,
and said, Of what city *art* thou? And
he said, Thy servant *is* of one of the
tribes of Ĭs̩′rā-ĕl.
3 And Ăb′sȧ-lŏm said unto him, See,
thy matters *are* good and right; but *there*
is no man *deputed* of the king to hear
thee.
4 Ăb′sȧ-lŏm said moreover, Oh that
I were made judge in the land, that
every man which hath any suit or cause
might come unto me, and I would do
him justice!
5 And it was *so*, that when any man
came nigh *to him* to do him obeisance,
he put forth his hand, and took him, and
kissed him.
6 And on this manner did Ăb′sȧ-lŏm to
all Ĭs̩′rā-ĕl that came to the king for
judgment: so Ăb′sȧ-lŏm stole the hearts
of the men of Ĭs̩′rā-ĕl.
7 ℂ And it came to pass after forty
years, that Ăb′sȧ-lŏm said unto the
king, I pray thee, let me go and pay my
vow, which I have vowed unto the LORD,
in Hē′brŏn.
8 For thy servant vowed a vow while
I abode at Gē′shŭr in Syria, saying, If
the LORD shall bring me again indeed to
Jerusalem, then I will serve the LORD.
9 And the king said unto him, Go
in peace. So he arose, and went to
Hē′brŏn.
10 ℂ But Ăb′sȧ-lŏm sent spies throughout all the tribes of Ĭs̩′rā-ĕl, saying,
As soon as ye hear the sound of the
trumpet, then ye shall say, Ăb′sȧ-lŏm
reigneth in Hē′brŏn.
11 And with Ăb′sȧ-lŏm went two hundred men out of Jerusalem, *that were*
called; and they went in their simplicity,
and they knew not any thing.
12 And Ăb′sȧ-lŏm sent for Ȧ-hĭth′ō-
phĕl the Gī′lō-nīte, David's counselor,
from his city, *even* from Gī′lōh, while he
offered sacrifices. And the conspiracy
was strong; for the people increased
continually with Ăb′sȧ-lŏm.
13 ℂ And there came a messenger to
David, saying, The hearts of the men of
Ĭs̩′rā-ĕl are after Ăb′sȧ-lŏm.
14 And David said unto all his servants
that *were* with him at Jerusalem, Arise,
and let us flee; for we shall not *else*
escape from Ăb′sȧ-lŏm: make speed to
depart, lest he overtake us suddenly,
and bring evil upon us, and smite the
city with the edge of the sword.
15 And the king's servants said unto
the king, Behold, thy servants *are ready*
to do whatsoever my lord the king shall
appoint.
16 And the king went forth, and all his
household after him. And the king left
ten women, *which were* concubines, to
keep the house.
17 And the king went forth, and all the
people after him, and tarried in a place
that was far off.
18 And all his servants passed on beside him; and all the Chĕr′ē-thītes, and
all the Pĕl′ē-thītes, and all the Gĭt′tītes,
six hundred men which came after him
from Gath, passed on before the king.
19 ℂ Then said the king to Ĭt′tā-ī the
Gĭt′tīte, Wherefore goest thou also with
us? return to thy place, and abide with
the king: for thou *art* a stranger, and
also an exile.
20 Whereas thou camest *but* yesterday, should I this day make thee go up
and down with us? seeing I go whither I
may, return thou, and take back thy
brethren: mercy and truth *be* with
thee.
21 And Ĭt′tā-ī answered the king, and
said, *As* the LORD liveth, and *as* my
lord the king liveth, surely in what place
my lord the king shall be, whether in
death or life, even there also will thy
servant be.
22 And David said to Ĭt′tā-ī, Go and
pass over. And Ĭt′tā-ī the Gĭt′tīte passed
over, and all his men, and all the little
ones that *were* with him.
23 And all the country wept with a loud
voice, and all the people passed over;
the king also himself passed over the
brook Kĭd′rŏn, and all the people passed
over, toward the way of the wilderness.
24 ℂ And lo Zā′dŏk also, and all the
Lē′vītes *were* with him, bearing the ark
of the covenant of God: and they set

down the ark of God; and Ȧ-bī′ȧ-thȧr went up, until all the people had done passing out of the city.

25 And the king said unto Zā′dŏk, Carry back the ark of God into the city: if I shall find favor in the eyes of the LORD, he will bring me again, and show me *both* it, and his habitation:

26 But if he thus say, I have no delight in thee; behold, *here am* I, let him do to me as seemeth good unto him.

27 The king said also unto Zā′dŏk the priest, *Art not* thou a seer? return into the city in peace, and your two sons with you, Ȧ-hĭm′ā-ăz thy son, and Jonathan the son of Ȧ-bī′ȧ-thȧr.

28 See, I will tarry in the plain of the wilderness, until there come word from you to certify me.

29 Zā′dŏk therefore and Ȧ-bī′ȧ-thȧr carried the ark of God again to Jerusalem: and they tarried there.

30 ℂ And David went up by the ascent of *mount* Ŏl′ĭ-vĕt, and wept as he went up, and had his head covered, and he went barefoot: and all the people that *was* with him covered every man his head, and they went up, weeping as they went up.

31 ℂ And *one* told David, saying, Ȧ-hĭth′ō-phĕl *is* among the conspirators with Ăb′sȧ-lŏm. And David said, O LORD, I pray thee, turn the counsel of Ȧ-hĭth′ō-phĕl into foolishness.

32 ℂ And it came to pass, that *when* David was come to the top *of the mount,* where he worshipped God, behold, Hū′shaī the Är′chīte came to meet him with his coat rent, and earth upon his head:

33 Unto whom David said, If thou passest on with me, then thou shalt be a burden unto me:

34 But if thou return to the city, and say unto Ăb′sȧ-lŏm, I will be thy servant, O king; *as* I *have been* thy father's servant hitherto, so *will* I now also *be* thy servant: then mayest thou for me defeat the counsel of Ȧ-hĭth′ō-phĕl.

35 And *hast thou* not there with thee Zā′dŏk and Ȧ-bī′ȧ-thȧr the priests? therefore it shall be, *that* what thing soever thou shalt hear out of the king's house, thou shalt tell *it* to Zā′dŏk and Ȧ-bī′ȧ-thȧr the priests.

36 Behold, *they have* there with them their two sons, Ȧ-hĭm′ā-ăz Zā′dŏk's *son,* and Jonathan Ȧ-bī′ȧ-thȧr's *son;* and by them ye shall send unto me every thing that ye can hear.

37 So Hū′shaī David's friend came into the city, and Ăb′sȧ-lŏm came into Jerusalem.

CHAPTER 16

AND when David was a little past the top *of the hill,* behold, Zī′bȧ the servant of Mē-phĭb′ō-shĕth met him, with a couple of asses saddled, and upon them two hundred *loaves* of bread, and a hundred bunches of raisins, and a hundred of summer fruits, and a bottle of wine.

2 And the king said unto Zī′bȧ, What meanest thou by these? And Zī′bȧ said, The asses *be* for the king's household to ride on; and the bread and summer fruit for the young men to eat; and the wine, that such as be faint in the wilderness may drink.

3 And the king said, And where *is* thy master's son? And Zī′bȧ said unto the king, Behold, he abideth at Jerusalem: for he said, To-day shall the house of Ĭṣ′rā-ĕl restore me the kingdom of my father.

4 Then said the king to Zī′bȧ, Behold, thine *are* all that *pertained* unto Mē-phĭb′ō-shĕth. And Zī′bȧ said, I humbly beseech thee *that* I may find grace in thy sight, my lord, O king.

5 ℂ And when king David came to Bȧ-hū′rĭm, behold, thence came out a man of the family of the house of Saul, whose name *was* Shĭm′ē-ī, the son of Gē′rȧ: he came forth, and cursed still as he came.

6 And he cast stones at David, and at all the servants of king David: and all the people and all the mighty men *were* on his right hand and on his left.

7 And thus said Shĭm′ē-ī when he cursed, Come out, come out, thou bloody man, and thou man of Bē′lĭ-ăl.

8 The LORD hath returned upon thee all the blood of the house of Saul, in whose stead thou hast reigned; and the LORD hath delivered the kingdom into the hand of Ăb′sȧ-lŏm thy son: and, behold, thou *art taken* in thy mischief, because thou *art* a bloody man.

9 ℂ Then said Ȧ-bĭsh′ā-ī the son of Zĕr′ụ-ī′ȧh unto the king, Why should this dead dog curse my lord the king? let me go over, I pray thee, and take off his head.

10 And the king said, What have I to do
with you, ye sons of Zĕr′ụ-ī′ȧh? so let
him curse, because the LORD hath said
unto him, Curse David. Who shall then
say, Wherefore hast thou done so?
11 And David said to Ȧ-bĭsh′ā-ī, and to
all his servants, Behold, my son, which
came forth of my bowels, seeketh my
life: how much more now *may this* Benjamite *do it?* let him alone, and let him
curse; for the LORD hath bidden him.
12 It may be that the LORD will look on
mine affliction, and that the LORD will
requite me good for his cursing this
day.
13 And as David and his men went by
the way, Shĭm′ē-ī went along on the
hillside over against him, and cursed as
he went, and threw stones at him, and
cast dust.
14 And the king, and all the people that
were with him, came weary, and refreshed themselves there.
15 ℂ And Ăb′sȧ-lŏm, and all the people the men of Ĭṣ′rā-ĕl, came to Jerusalem, and Ȧ-hĭth′ō-phĕl with him.
16 And it came to pass, when Hū′shaī
the Är′chīte, David's friend, was come
unto Ăb′sȧ-lŏm, that Hū′shaī said unto
Ăb′sȧ-lŏm, God save the king, God save
the king.
17 And Ăb′sȧ-lŏm said to Hū′shaī, *Is*
this thy kindness to thy friend? why
wentest thou not with thy friend?
18 And Hū′shaī said unto Ăb′sȧ-lŏm,
Nay; but whom the LORD, and this people, and all the men of Ĭṣ′rā-ĕl, choose,
his will I be, and with him will I abide.
19 And again, whom should I serve?
should I not *serve* in the presence of his
son? as I have served in thy father's
presence, so will I be in thy presence.
20 ℂ Then said Ăb′sȧ-lŏm to Ȧ-hĭth′ō-
phĕl, Give counsel among you what we
shall do.
21 And Ȧ-hĭth′ō-phĕl said unto Ăb′sȧ-
lŏm, Go in unto thy father's concubines,
which he hath left to keep the house;
and all Ĭṣ′rā-ĕl shall hear that thou art
abhorred of thy father: then shall the
hands of all that *are* with thee be strong.
22 So they spread Ăb′sȧ-lŏm a tent
upon the top of the house; and Ăb′sȧ-
lŏm went in unto his father's concubines
in the sight of all Ĭṣ′rā-ĕl.
23 And the counsel of Ȧ-hĭth′ō-phĕl,
which he counseled in those days, *was*
as if a man had inquired at the oracle of
God: so *was* all the counsel of Ȧ-hĭth′ō-
phĕl both with David and with Ăb′-
sȧ-lŏm.

CHAPTER 17

MOREOVER Ȧ-hĭth′ō-phĕl said unto
Ăb′sȧ-lŏm, Let me now choose out
twelve thousand men, and I will arise
and pursue after David this night:
2 And I will come upon him while he *is*
weary and weak-handed, and will make
him afraid: and all the people that *are*
with him shall flee; and I will smite the
king only:
3 And I will bring back all the people
unto thee: the man whom thou seekest
is as if all returned: *so* all the people
shall be in peace.
4 And the saying pleased Ăb′sȧ-lŏm
well, and all the elders of Ĭṣ′rā-ĕl.
5 Then said Ăb′sȧ-lŏm, Call now Hū′-
shaī the Är′chīte also, and let us hear
likewise what he saith.
6 And when Hū′shaī was come to Ăb′-
sȧ-lŏm, Ăb′sȧ-lŏm spake unto him, saying, Ȧ-hĭth′ō-phĕl hath spoken after this
manner: shall we do *after* his saying?
if not, speak thou.
7 And Hū′shaī said unto Ăb′sȧ-lŏm,
The counsel that Ȧ-hĭth′ō-phĕl hath
given *is* not good at this time.
8 For, said Hū′shaī, thou knowest thy
father and his men, that they *be* mighty
men, and they *be* chafed in their minds,
as a bear robbed of her whelps in the
field: and thy father *is* a man of war, and
will not lodge with the people.
9 Behold, he is hid now in some pit, or
in some *other* place: and it will come to
pass, when some of them be overthrown
at the first, that whosoever heareth it
will say, There is a slaughter among the
people that follow Ăb′sȧ-lŏm.
10 And he also *that is* valiant, whose
heart *is* as the heart of a lion, shall
utterly melt: for all Ĭṣ′rā-ĕl knoweth
that thy father *is* a mighty man, and
they which *be* with him *are* valiant
men.
11 Therefore I counsel that all Ĭṣ′rā-ĕl
be generally gathered unto thee, from
Dan even to Bē′ĕr–shē′bȧ, as the sand
that *is* by the sea for multitude; and
that thou go to battle in thine own person.
12 So shall we come upon him in some
place where he shall be found, and we
will light upon him as the dew falleth on

the ground: and of him and of all the
men that *are* with him there shall not be
left so much as one.
13 Moreover if he be gotten into a city,
then shall all Ĭş'rā-ĕl bring ropes to that
city, and we will draw it into the river,
until there be not one small stone found
there.
14 And Ăb'sȧ-lŏm and all the men of
Ĭş'rā-ĕl said, The counsel of Hū'shaī
the Ăr'chīte *is* better than the counsel
of Ȧ-hĭth'ō-phĕl. For the LORD had
appointed to defeat the good counsel of
Ȧ-hĭth'ō-phĕl, to the intent that the
LORD might bring evil upon Ăb'sȧ-lŏm.
15 ¶ Then said Hū'shaī unto Zā'dŏk
and to Ȧ-bī'ȧ-thär the priests, Thus and
thus did Ȧ-hĭth'ō-phĕl counsel Ăb'sȧ-
lŏm and the elders of Ĭş'rā-ĕl; and thus
and thus have I counseled.
16 Now therefore send quickly, and
tell David, saying, Lodge not this night
in the plains of the wilderness, but
speedily pass over; lest the king be
swallowed up, and all the people that
are with him.
17 Now Jonathan and Ȧ-hĭm'ā-ăz
stayed by Ĕn-rō'gĕl; for they might not
be seen to come into the city: and a
wench went and told them; and they
went and told king David.
18 Nevertheless, a lad saw them, and
told Ăb'sȧ-lŏm: but they went both of
them away quickly, and came to a man's
house in Bȧ-hū'rĭm, which had a well in
his court; whither they went down.
19 And the woman took and spread a
covering over the well's mouth, and
spread ground corn thereon; and the
thing was not known.
20 And when Ăb'sȧ-lŏm's servants came
to the woman to the house, they said,
Where *is* Ȧ-hĭm'ā-ăz and Jonathan?
And the woman said unto them, They be
gone over the brook of water. And when
they had sought and could not find
them, they returned to Jerusalem.
21 And it came to pass, after they were
departed, that they came up out of the
well, and went and told king David, and
said unto David, Arise, and pass quickly
over the water: for thus hath Ȧ-hĭth'ō-
phĕl counseled against you.
22 Then David arose, and all the people
that *were* with him, and they passed
over Jordan: by the morning light there
lacked not one of them that was not
gone over Jordan.
23 ¶ And when Ȧ-hĭth'ō-phĕl saw that
his counsel was not followed, he saddled
his ass, and arose, and gat him home to
his house, to his city, and put his household in order, and hanged himself, and
died, and was buried in the sepulchre of
his father.
24 Then David came to Mā'hȧ-nā'ĭm.
And Ăb'sȧ-lŏm passed over Jordan, he
and all the men of Ĭş'rā-ĕl with him.
25 ¶ And Ăb'sȧ-lŏm made Ăm'ȧ-sȧ
captain of the host instead of Jō'ăb:
which Ăm'ȧ-sȧ *was* a man's son, whose
name *was* Ĭth'rȧ an Ĭş'rā-ĕl-īte, that
went in to Ăb'ĭ-gāil the daughter of
Nā'hăsh, sister to Zĕr'ụ-ī'ȧh Jō'ăb's
mother.
26 So Ĭş'rā-ĕl and Ăb'sȧ-lŏm pitched
in the land of Gĭl'ē-ăd.
27 ¶ And it came to pass, when David
was come to Mā'hȧ-nā'ĭm, that Shō'bī
the son of Nā'hăsh of Răb'bȧh of the
children of Ammon, and Mā'chīr the son
of Ăm'mĭ-ĕl of Lō'-dē'bär, and Bär-zĭl'-
lā-ī the Gĭl'ē-ăd-īte of Rō'gē-lĭm,
28 Brought beds, and basins, and
earthen vessels, and wheat, and barley,
and flour, and parched *corn,* and beans,
and lentils, and parched *pulse,*
29 And honey, and butter, and sheep,
and cheese of kine, for David, and for
the people that *were* with him, to eat: for
they said, The people *is* hungry, and
weary, and thirsty, in the wilderness.

CHAPTER 18

AND David numbered the people that
were with him, and set captains of
thousands and captains of hundreds
over them.
2 And David sent forth a third part of
the people under the hand of Jō'ăb, and
a third part under the hand of Ȧ-bĭsh'ā-ī
the son of Zĕr'ụ-ī'ȧh, Jō'ăb's brother,
and a third part under the hand of
Ĭt'tā-ī the Gĭt'tīte. And the king said
unto the people, I will surely go forth
with you myself also.
3 But the people answered, Thou shalt
not go forth: for if we flee away, they
will not care for us; neither if half of us
die, will they care for us: but now *thou
art* worth ten thousand of us: therefore
now *it is* better that thou succor us out of
the city.
4 And the king said unto them, What
seemeth you best I will do. And the
king stood by the gate side, and all the

people came out by hundreds and by
thousands.
5 And the king commanded Jō'ăb and
Ȧ-bĭsh'ā-ī and Ĭt'tā-ī, saying, *Deal*
gently for my sake with the young man,
even with Ăb'sȧ-lŏm. And all the people
heard when the king gave all the captains charge concerning Ăb'sȧ-lŏm.
6 ℭ So the people went out into the
field against Ĭṣ'rā-ĕl: and the battle was
in the wood of Ē'phrā-ĭm;
7 Where the people of Ĭṣ'rā-ĕl were
slain before the servants of David, and
there was there a great slaughter that
day of twenty thousand *men*.
8 For the battle was there scattered
over the face of all the country: and the
wood devoured more people that day
than the sword devoured.
9 ℭ And Ăb'sȧ-lŏm met the servants
of David. And Ăb'sȧ-lŏm rode upon a
mule, and the mule went under the
thick boughs of a great oak, and his
head caught hold of the oak, and he was
taken up between the heaven and the
earth; and the mule that *was* under him
went away.
10 And a certain man saw *it*, and told
Jō'ăb, and said, Behold, I saw Ăb'sȧ-lŏm
hanged in an oak.
11 And Jō'ăb said unto the man that
told him, And, behold, thou sawest *him*,
and why didst thou not smite him there
to the ground? and I would have given
thee ten *shekels* of silver, and a girdle.
12 And the man said unto Jō'ăb,
Though I should receive a thousand
shekels of silver in mine hand, *yet*
would I not put forth mine hand against
the king's son: for in our hearing the
king charged thee and Ȧ-bĭsh'ā-ī and
Ĭt'tā-ī, saying, Beware that none *touch*
the young man Ăb'sȧ-lŏm.
13 Otherwise I should have wrought
falsehood against mine own life: for
there is no matter hid from the king, and
thou thyself wouldest have set thyself
against *me*.
14 Then said Jō'ăb, I may not tarry
thus with thee. And he took three darts
in his hand, and thrust them through the
heart of Ăb'sȧ-lŏm, while he *was* yet
alive in the midst of the oak.
15 And ten young men that bare Jō'ăb's
armor compassed about and smote
Ăb'sȧ-lŏm, and slew him.
16 And Jō'ăb blew the trumpet, and
the people returned from pursuing after
Ĭṣ'rā-ĕl: for Jō'ăb held back the people.
17 And they took Ăb'sȧ-lŏm, and cast
him into a great pit in the wood, and laid
a very great heap of stones upon him:
and all Ĭṣ'rā-ĕl fled every one to his
tent.
18 ℭ Now Ăb'sȧ-lŏm in his lifetime
had taken and reared up for himself a
pillar, which *is* in the king's dale: for he
said, I have no son to keep my name in
remembrance: and he called the pillar
after his own name: and it is called unto
this day, Ăb'sȧ-lŏm's place.
19 ℭ Then said Ȧ-hĭm'ā-ăz the son of
Zā'dŏk, Let me now run, and bear the
king tidings, how that the LORD hath
avenged him of his enemies.
20 And Jō'ăb said unto him, Thou shalt
not bear tidings this day, but thou shalt
bear tidings another day: but this day
thou shalt bear no tidings, because the
king's son is dead.
21 Then said Jō'ăb to Cū'shī, Go tell
the king what thou hast seen. And
Cū'shī bowed himself unto Jō'ăb, and
ran.
22 Then said Ȧ-hĭm'ā-ăz the son of
Zā'dŏk yet again to Jō'ăb, But howsoever, let me, I pray thee, also run after
Cū'shī. And Jō'ăb said, Wherefore wilt
thou run, my son, seeing that thou hast
no tidings ready?
23 But howsoever, *said he*, let me run.
And he said unto him, Run. Then
Ȧ-hĭm'ā-ăz ran by the way of the plain,
and overran Cū'shī.
24 And David sat between the two
gates: and the watchman went up to the
roof over the gate unto the wall, and
lifted up his eyes, and looked, and behold a man running alone.
25 And the watchman cried, and told
the king. And the king said, If he *be*
alone, *there is* tidings in his mouth.
And he came apace, and drew near.
26 And the watchman saw another
man running: and the watchman called
unto the porter, and said, Behold *another* man running alone. And the king
said, He also bringeth tidings.
27 And the watchman said, Methinketh
the running of the foremost is like the
running of Ȧ-hĭm'a-ăz the son of Zā-
dŏk. And the king said, He *is* a good
man, and cometh with good tidings.
28 And Ȧ-hĭm'ā-ăz called, and said
unto the king, All is well. And he fell
down to the earth upon his face before

the king, and said, Blessed *be* the LORD
thy God, which hath delivered up the
men that lifted up their hand against my
lord the king.
29 And the king said, Is the young man
Ăb′sȧ-lŏm safe? And Ȧ-hĭm′ā-ăz answered, When Jō′ăb sent the king's
servant, and *me* thy servant, I saw a
great tumult, but I knew not what *it was.*
30 And the king said *unto him,* Turn
aside, *and* stand here. And he turned
aside, and stood still.
31 And, behold, Cū′shī came; and
Cū′shī said, Tidings, my lord the king:
for the LORD hath avenged thee this
day of all them that rose up against
thee.
32 And the king said unto Cū′shī, *Is*
the young man Ăb′sȧ-lŏm safe? And
Cū′shī answered, The enemies of my
lord the king, and all that rise against
thee to do *thee* hurt, be as *that* young
man *is.*
33 ℂ And the king was much moved,
and went up to the chamber over the
gate, and wept: and as he went, thus he
said, O my son Ăb′sȧ-lŏm! my son, my
son Ăb′sȧ-lŏm! would God I had died
for thee, O Ăb′sȧ-lŏm, my son, my son!

CHAPTER 19

AND it was told Jō′ăb, Behold, the
king weepeth and mourneth for
Ăb′sȧ-lŏm.
2 And the victory that day was *turned*
into mourning unto all the people: for
the people heard say that day how the
king was grieved for his son.
3 And the people gat them by stealth
that day into the city, as people being
ashamed steal away when they flee in
battle.
4 But the king covered his face, and the
king cried with a loud voice, O my son
Ăb′sȧ-lŏm! O Ăb′sȧ-lŏm, my son, my
son!
5 And Jō′ăb came into the house to the
king, and said, Thou hast shamed this
day the faces of all thy servants, which
this day have saved thy life, and the
lives of thy sons and of thy daughters,
and the lives of thy wives, and the lives
of thy concubines;
6 In that thou lovest thine enemies,
and hatest thy friends. For thou hast
declared this day, that thou regardest
neither princes nor servants: for this
day I perceive, that if Ăb′sȧ-lŏm had
lived, and all we had died this day, then
it had pleased thee well.
7 Now therefore arise, go forth, and
speak comfortably unto thy servants:
for I swear by the LORD, if thou go not
forth, there will not tarry one with thee
this night: and that will be worse unto
thee than all the evil that befell thee
from thy youth until now.
8 Then the king arose, and sat in the
gate. And they told unto all the people,
saying, Behold, the king doth sit in the
gate. And all the people came before
the king: for Ĭṣ′rā-ĕl had fled every man
to his tent.
9 ℂ And all the people were at strife
throughout all the tribes of Ĭṣ′rā-ĕl,
saying, The king saved us out of the
hand of our enemies, and he delivered
us out of the hand of the Phĭ-lĭs′tīneṣ;
and now he is fled out of the land for
Ăb′sȧ-lŏm.
10 And Ăb′sȧ-lŏm, whom we anointed
over us, is dead in battle. Now therefore why speak ye not a word of bringing the king back?
11 ℂ And king David sent to Zā′dŏk
and to Ȧ-bī′ȧ-thȧr the priests, saying,
Speak unto the elders of Judah, saying,
Why are ye the last to bring the king
back to his house? seeing the speech of
all Ĭṣ′rā-ĕl is come to the king, *even* to
his house.
12 Ye *are* my brethren, ye *are* my bones
and my flesh: wherefore then are ye the
last to bring back the king?
13 And say ye to Ăm′ȧ-sȧ, *Art* thou not
of my bone, and of my flesh? God do so
to me, and more also, if thou be not captain of the host before me continually in
the room of Jō′ăb.
14 And he bowed the heart of all the
men of Judah, even as *the heart of* one
man; so that they sent *this word* unto
the king, Return thou, and all thy
servants.
15 So the king returned, and came to
Jordan. And Judah came to Gĭl′găl, to
go to meet the king, to conduct the king
over Jordan.
16 ℂ And Shĭm′ē-ī the son of Gē′rȧ, a
Benjamite, which *was* of Bȧ-hū′rĭm,
hasted and came down with the men of
Judah to meet king David.
17 And *there were* a thousand men of
Benjamin with him, and Zī′bȧ the servant of the house of Saul, and his fifteen
sons and his twenty servants with him;

and they went over Jordan before the king.

18 And there went over a ferryboat to carry over the king's household, and to do what he thought good. And Shĭm′ē-ī the son of Gē′rȧ fell down before the king, as he was come over Jordan;

19 And said unto the king, Let not my lord impute iniquity unto me, neither do thou remember that which thy servant did perversely the day that my lord the king went out of Jerusalem, that the king should take it to his heart.

20 For thy servant doth know that I have sinned: therefore, behold, I am come the first this day of all the house of Joseph to go down to meet my lord the king.

21 But Ȧ-bĭsh′ā-ī the son of Zĕr′ụ-ī′ȧh answered and said, Shall not Shĭm′ē-ī be put to death for this, because he cursed the LORD's anointed?

22 And David said, What have I to do with you, ye sons of Zĕr′ụ-ī′ȧh, that ye should this day be adversaries unto me? shall there any man be put to death this day in Israel? for do not I know that I *am* this day king over Ĭṣ′rā-ēl?

23 Therefore the king said unto Shĭm′ē-ī, Thou shalt not die. And the king sware unto him.

24 ¶ And Mē-phĭb′ō-shĕth the son of Saul came down to meet the king, and had neither dressed his feet, nor trimmed his beard, nor washed his clothes, from the day the king departed until the day he came *again* in peace.

25 And it came to pass, when he was come to Jerusalem to meet the king, that the king said unto him, Wherefore wentest not thou with me, Mē-phĭb′ō-shĕth?

26 And he answered, My lord, O king, my servant deceived me: for thy servant said, I will saddle me an ass, that I may ride thereon, and go to the king; because thy servant *is* lame.

27 And he hath slandered thy servant unto my lord the king; but my lord the king *is* as an angel of God: do therefore *what is* good in thine eyes.

28 For all *of* my father's house were but dead men before my lord the king: yet didst thou set thy servant among them that did eat at thine own table. What right therefore have I yet to cry any more unto the king?

29 And the king said unto him, Why speakest thou any more of thy matters? I have said, Thou and Zī′bȧ divide the land.

30 And Mē-phĭb′ō-shĕth said unto the king, Yea, let him take all, forasmuch as my lord the king is come again in peace unto his own house.

31 ¶ And Bär-zĭl′lā-ī the Gĭl′ē-ăd-īte came down from Rō′gē-lĭm, and went over Jordan with the king, to conduct him over Jordan.

32 Now Bär-zĭl′lā-ī was a very aged man, *even* fourscore years old: and he had provided the king of sustenance while he lay at Mā′hȧ-nā′ĭm; for he *was* a very great man.

33 And the king said unto Bär-zĭl′lā-ī, Come thou over with me, and I will feed thee with me in Jerusalem.

34 And Bär-zĭl′lā-ī said unto the king, How long have I to live, that I should go up with the king unto Jerusalem?

35 I *am* this day fourscore years old: *and* can I discern between good and evil? can thy servant taste what I eat or what I drink? can I hear any more the voice of singing men and singing women? wherefore then should thy servant be yet a burden unto my lord the king?

36 Thy servant will go a little way over Jordan with the king: and why should the king recompense it me with such a reward?

37 Let thy servant, I pray thee, turn back again, that I may die in mine own city, *and be buried* by the grave of my father and of my mother. But behold thy servant Chĭm′hăm; let him go over with my lord the king; and do to him what shall seem good unto thee.

38 And the king answered, Chĭm′hăm shall go over with me, and I will do to him that which shall seem good unto thee: and whatsoever thou shalt require of me, *that* will I do for thee.

39 And all the people went over Jordan. And when the king was come over, the king kissed Bär-zĭl′lā-ī, and blessed him; and he returned unto his own place.

40 Then the king went on to Gĭl′găl, and Chĭm′hăm went on with him: and all the people of Judah conducted the king, and also half the people of Ĭṣ′rā-ēl.

41 ¶ And, behold, all the men of Ĭṣ′rā-ēl came to the king, and said unto the king, Why have our brethren the men of Judah stolen thee away, and have brought the king, and his house-

hold, and all David's men with him,
over Jordan?
42 And all the men of Judah answered
the men of Ĭş'rā-ĕl, Because the king *is*
near of kin to us: wherefore then be ye
angry for this matter? have we eaten at
all of the king's *cost?* or hath he given
us any gift?
43 And the men of Ĭş'rā-ĕl answered
the men of Judah, and said, We have
ten parts in the king, and we have also
more *right* in David than ye: why then
did ye despise us, that our advice should
not be first had in bringing back our
king? And the words of the men of
Judah were fiercer than the words of
the men of Ĭş'rā-ĕl.

CHAPTER 20

AND there happened to be there a
man of Bē'lĭ-ăl, whose name *was*
Shē'bȧ, the son of Bĭch'rī, a Benjamite:
and he blew a trumpet, and said, We
have no part in David, neither have we
inheritance in the son of Jesse: every
man to his tents, O Ĭş'rā-ĕl.
2 So every man of Ĭş'rā-ĕl went up
from after David, *and* followed Shē'bȧ
the son of Bĭch'rī: but the men of Judah
clave unto their king, from Jordan even
to Jerusalem.
3 ¶ And David came to his house at
Jerusalem; and the king took the ten
women *his* concubines, whom he had
left to keep the house, and put them in
ward, and fed them, but went not in
unto them. So they were shut up unto
the day of their death, living in widowhood.
4 ¶ Then said the king to Ăm'ȧ-sȧ,
Assemble me the men of Judah within
three days, and be thou here present.
5 So Ăm'ȧ-sȧ went to assemble *the
men of* Judah: but he tarried longer than
the set time which he had appointed him.
6 And David said to Ȧ-bĭsh'ā-ī, Now
shall Shē'bȧ the son of Bĭch'rī do us
more harm than *did* Ăb'sȧ-lŏm: take
thou thy lord's servants, and pursue
after him, lest he get him fenced cities,
and escape us.
7 And there went out after him Jō'ăb's
men, and the Chĕr'ē-thītes, and the
Pĕl'ē-thītes, and all the mighty men:
and they went out of Jerusalem, to pursue after Shē'bȧ the son of Bĭch'rī.
8 When they *were* at the great stone
which *is* in Gĭb'ē-ŏn, Ăm'ȧ-sȧ went before them. And Jō'ăb's garment that
he had put on was girded unto him, and
upon it a girdle *with* a sword fastened
upon his loins in the sheath thereof; and
as he went forth it fell out.
9 And Jō'ăb said to Ăm'ȧ-sȧ, *Art* thou
in health, my brother? And Jō'ăb took
Ăm'ȧ-sȧ by the beard with the right
hand to kiss him.
10 But Ăm'ȧ-sȧ took no heed to the
sword that *was* in Jō'ăb's hand: so he
smote him therewith in the fifth *rib*,
and shed out his bowels to the ground,
and struck him not again; and he died.
So Jō'ăb and Ȧ-bĭsh'ā-ī his brother
pursued after Shē'bȧ the son of Bĭch'rī.
11 And one of Jō'ăb's men stood by
him, and said, He that favoreth Jō'ăb,
and he that *is* for David, *let him go* after
Jō'ăb.
12 And Ăm'ȧ-sȧ wallowed in blood in
the midst of the highway. And when the
man saw that all the people stood still,
he removed Ăm'ȧ-sȧ out of the highway
into the field, and cast a cloth upon him,
when he saw that every one that came
by him stood still.
13 When he was removed out of the
highway, all the people went on after
Jō'ăb, to pursue after Shē'bȧ the son of
Bĭch'rī.
14 ¶ And he went through all the
tribes of Ĭş'rā-ĕl unto Abel, and to
Bĕth'-mā'ȧ-chȧh, and all the Bē'rītes:
and they were gathered together, and
went also after him.
15 And they came and besieged him in
Abel of Bĕth'-mā'ȧ-chȧh, and they cast
up a bank against the city, and it stood
in the trench: and all the people that
were with Jō'ăb battered the wall, to
throw it down.
16 ¶ Then cried a wise woman out of
the city, Hear, hear; say, I pray you,
unto Jō'ăb, Come near hither, that I may
speak with thee.
17 And when he was come near unto
her, the woman said, *Art* thou Jō'ăb?
And he answered, I *am he.* Then she
said unto him, Hear the words of thine
handmaid. And he answered, I do hear.
18 Then she spake, saying, They were
wont to speak in old time, saying, They
shall surely ask *counsel* at Abel: and so
they ended *the matter*.
19 I *am one of them that are* peaceable
and faithful in Ĭş'rā-ĕl: thou seekest to
destroy a city and a mother in Ĭş'rā-ĕl:

why wilt thou swallow up the inheritance
of the LORD?
20 And Jō'ăb answered and said, Far
be it, far be it from me, that I should
swallow up or destroy.
21 The matter *is* not so: but a man of
mount Ē'phrā-ĭm, Shē'bȧ the son of
Bĭch'rī by name, hath lifted up his hand
against the king, *even* against David:
deliver him only, and I will depart from
the city. And the woman said unto
Jō'ăb, Behold, his head shall be thrown
to thee over the wall.
22 Then the woman went unto all the
people in her wisdom: and they cut off
the head of Shē'bȧ the son of Bĭch'rī,
and cast *it* out to Jō'ăb. And he blew a
trumpet, and they retired from the city,
every man to his tent. And Jō'ăb returned to Jerusalem unto the king.
23 ¶ Now Jō'ăb *was* over all the host of
Ĭş'rā-ĕl: and Bē-nā'ịȧh the son of Jē-
hoi'ȧ-dȧ *was* over the Chĕr'ē-thītes and
over the Pĕl'ē-thītes:
24 And Ȧ-dō'rȧm *was* over the tribute:
and Jē-hŏsh'ȧ-phăt the son of Ȧ-hī'lŭd
was recorder:
25 And Shē'vȧ *was* scribe: and Zā'dŏk
and Ȧ-bī'ȧ-thär *were* the priests:
26 And Ī'rȧ also the Jā'ĭr-īte was a
chief ruler about David.

CHAPTER 21

THEN there was a famine in the days
of David three years, year after
year; and David inquired of the LORD.
And the LORD answered, *It is* for Saul,
and for *his* bloody house, because he
slew the Gĭb'ē-ȯn-ītes.
2 And the king called the Gĭb'ē-ȯn-
ītes, and said unto them; (now the
Gĭb'ē-ȯn-ītes *were* not of the children
of Ĭş'rā-ĕl, but of the remnant of the
Ăm'ō-rītes; and the children of Ĭş'rā-ĕl
had sworn unto them: and Saul sought
to slay them in his zeal to the children
of Ĭş'rā-ĕl and Judah:)
3 Wherefore David said unto the
Gĭb'ē-ȯn-ītes, What shall I do for you?
and wherewith shall I make the atonement, that ye may bless the inheritance
of the LORD?
4 And the Gĭb'ē-ȯn-ītes said unto him,
We will have no silver nor gold of Saul,
nor of his house; neither for us shalt
thou kill any man in Ĭş'rā-ĕl. And he
said, What ye shall say, *that* will I do
for you.
5 And they answered the king, The man
that consumed us, and that devised
against us *that* we should be destroyed
from remaining in any of the coasts of
Ĭş'rā-ĕl,
6 Let seven men of his sons be delivered unto us, and we will hang them
up unto the LORD in Gĭb'ē-ȧh of Saul,
whom the LORD did choose. And the
king said, I will give *them*.
7 But the king spared Mē-phĭb'ō-
shĕth, the son of Jonathan the son of
Saul, because of the LORD's oath that
was between them, between David and
Jonathan the son of Saul.
8 But the king took the two sons of
Rĭz'păh the daughter of Ā-ī'ȧh, whom
she bare unto Saul, Är-mō'nī and Mē-
phĭb'ō-shĕth; and the five sons of Mī'-
chăl the daughter of Saul, whom she
brought up for Ā'drĭ-ĕl the son of Bär-
zĭl'lā-ī the Mē-hō'lȧ-thīte:
9 And he delivered them into the hands
of the Gĭb'ē-ȯn-ītes, and they hanged
them in the hill before the LORD: and
they fell *all* seven together, and were
put to death in the days of harvest, in the
first *days*, in the beginning of barley
harvest.
10 ¶ And Rĭz'păh the daughter of
Ā-ī'ȧh took sackcloth, and spread it for
her upon the rock, from the beginning
of harvest until water dropped upon
them out of heaven, and suffered neither the birds of the air to rest on them
by day, nor the beasts of the field by
night.
11 And it was told David what Rĭz'păh
the daughter of Ā-ī'ȧh, the concubine of
Saul, had done.
12 ¶ And David went and took the
bones of Saul and the bones of Jonathan
his son from the men of Jā'bĕsh-
gĭl'ē-ăd, which had stolen them from
the street of Bĕth'-shăn', where the
Phĭ-lĭs'tĭneş had hanged them, when
the Phĭ-lĭs'tĭneş had slain Saul in
Gĭl-bō'ȧ:
13 And he brought up from thence the
bones of Saul and the bones of Jonathan
his son; and they gathered the bones of
them that were hanged.
14 And the bones of Saul and Jonathan
his son buried they in the country of
Benjamin in Zē'lȧh, in the sepulchre of
Kish his father: and they performed all
that the king commanded. And after
that God was entreated for the land.

15 ℂ Moreover the Phĭ-lĭs′tĭneş had yet war again with Ĭş′rā-ĕl; and David went down, and his servants with him, and fought against the Phĭ-lĭs′tĭneş: and David waxed faint.

16 And Ĭsh′bĭ–bē′nŏb, which *was* of the sons of the giant, the weight of whose spear *weighed* three hundred *shekels* of brass in weight, he being girded with a new *sword*, thought to have slain David.

17 But Ȧ-bĭsh′ā-ī the son of Zĕr′ụ-ī′ȧh succored him, and smote the Phĭ-lĭs′tĭne, and killed him. Then the men of David sware unto him, saying, Thou shalt go no more out with us to battle, that thou quench not the light of Ĭş′rā-ĕl.

18 And it came to pass after this, that there was again a battle with the Phĭ-lĭs′tĭneş at Gob: then Sĭb′bē-ehaī the Hū′shȧth-īte slew Săph, which *was* of the sons of the giant.

19 And there was again a battle in Gob with the Phĭ-lĭs′tĭneş, where Ĕl-hā′năn the son of Jā′ȧ-rē–ôr′ē-ġĭm, a Beth-lehemite, slew *the brother of* Gō-lī′ăth the Gĭt′tīte, the staff of whose spear *was* like a weaver's beam.

20 And there was yet a battle in Gath, where was a man of *great* stature, that had on every hand six fingers, and on every foot six toes, four and twenty in number; and he also was born to the giant.

21 And when he defied Ĭş′rā-ĕl, Jonathan the son of Shĭm′ē-ȧh the brother of David slew him.

22 These four were born to the giant in Gath, and fell by the hand of David, and by the hand of his servants.

CHAPTER 22

AND David spake unto the LORD the words of this song, in the day *that* the LORD had delivered him out of the hand of all his enemies, and out of the hand of Saul:

2 And he said, The LORD *is* my rock, and my fortress, and my deliverer;

3 The God of my rock; in him will I trust: *he is* my shield, and the horn of my salvation, my high tower, and my refuge, my saviour; thou savest me from violence.

4 I will call on the LORD, *who is* worthy to be praised: so shall I be saved from mine enemies.

5 When the waves of death compassed me, the floods of ungodly men made me afraid;

6 The sorrows of hell compassed me about; the snares of death prevented me.

7 In my distress I called upon the LORD, and cried to my God: and he did hear my voice out of his temple, and my cry *did enter* into his ears.

8 Then the earth shook and trembled; the foundations of heaven moved and shook, because he was wroth.

9 There went up a smoke out of his nostrils, and fire out of his mouth devoured: coals were kindled by it.

10 He bowed the heavens also, and came down; and darkness *was* under his feet.

11 And he rode upon a cherub, and did fly: and he was seen upon the wings of the wind.

12 And he made darkness pavilions round about him, dark waters, *and* thick clouds of the skies.

13 Through the brightness before him were coals of fire kindled.

14 The LORD thundered from heaven, and the Most High uttered his voice.

15 And he sent out arrows, and scattered them; lightning, and discomfited them.

16 And the channels of the sea appeared, the foundations of the world were discovered, at the rebuking of the LORD, at the blast of the breath of his nostrils.

17 He sent from above, he took me; he drew me out of many waters:

18 He delivered me from my strong enemy, *and* from them that hated me: for they were too strong for me.

19 They prevented me in the day of my calamity: but the LORD was my stay.

20 He brought me forth also into a large place: he delivered me, because he delighted in me.

21 The LORD rewarded me according to my righteousness; according to the cleanness of my hands hath he recompensed me.

22 For I have kept the ways of the LORD, and have not wickedly departed from my God.

23 For all his judgments *were* before me: and *as for* his statutes, I did not depart from them.

24 I was also upright before him, and have kept myself from mine iniquity.

25 Therefore the LORD hath recompensed me according to my righteousness; according to my cleanness in his eyesight.

26 With the merciful thou wilt show thyself merciful, *and* with the upright man thou wilt show thyself upright.

27 With the pure thou wilt show thyself pure; and with the froward thou wilt show thyself unsavory.

28 And the afflicted people thou wilt save: but thine eyes *are* upon the haughty, *that* thou mayest bring *them* down.

29 For thou *art* my lamp, O LORD: and the LORD will lighten my darkness.

30 For by thee I have run through a troop: by my God have I leaped over a wall.

31 *As for* God, his way *is* perfect; the word of the LORD *is* tried: he *is* a buckler to all them that trust in him.

32 For who *is* God, save the LORD? and who *is* a rock, save our God?

33 God *is* my strength *and* power; and he maketh my way perfect.

34 He maketh my feet like hinds' *feet;* and setteth me upon my high places.

35 He teacheth my hands to war; so that a bow of steel is broken by mine arms.

36 Thou hast also given me the shield of thy salvation: and thy gentleness hath made me great.

37 Thou hast enlarged my steps under me; so that my feet did not slip.

38 I have pursued mine enemies, and destroyed them; and turned not again until I had consumed them.

39 And I have consumed them, and wounded them, that they could not arise: yea, they are fallen under my feet.

40 For thou hast girded me with strength to battle: them that rose up against me hast thou subdued under me.

41 Thou hast also given me the necks of mine enemies, that I might destroy them that hate me.

42 They looked, but *there was* none to save; *even* unto the LORD, but he answered them not.

43 Then did I beat them as small as the dust of the earth: I did stamp them as the mire of the street, *and* did spread them abroad.

44 Thou also hast delivered me from the strivings of my people, thou hast kept me *to be* head of the heathen: a people *which* I knew not shall serve me.

45 Strangers shall submit themselves unto me: as soon as they hear, they shall be obedient unto me.

46 Strangers shall fade away, and they shall be afraid out of their close places.

47 The LORD liveth; and blessed *be* my rock; and exalted be the God of the rock of my salvation.

48 It *is* God that avengeth me, and that bringeth down the people under me,

49 And that bringeth me forth from mine enemies: thou also hast lifted me up on high above them that rose up against me: thou hast delivered me from the violent man.

50 Therefore I will give thanks unto thee, O LORD, among the heathen, and I will sing praises unto thy name.

51 *He is* the tower of salvation for his king: and showeth mercy to his anointed, unto David, and to his seed for evermore.

CHAPTER 23

NOW these *be* the last words of David. David the son of Jesse said, and the man *who was* raised up on high, the anointed of the God of Jacob, and the sweet psalmist of Ĭs̱′rā-ĕl, said,

2 The Spirit of the LORD spake by me, and his word *was* in my tongue.

3 The God of Ĭs̱′rā-ĕl said, the Rock of Ĭs̱′rā-ĕl spake to me, He that ruleth over men *must be* just, ruling in the fear of God.

4 And *he shall be* as the light of the morning, *when* the sun riseth, *even* a morning without clouds; *as* the tender grass *springing* out of the earth by clear shining after rain.

5 Although my house *be* not so with God; yet he hath made with me an everlasting covenant, ordered in all *things,* and sure: for *this is* all my salvation, and all *my* desire, although he make *it* not to grow.

6 ¶ But *the sons* of Bē′lĭ-ăl *shall be* all of them as thorns thrust away, because they cannot be taken with hands:

7 But the man *that* shall touch them must be fenced with iron and the staff of a spear; and they shall be utterly burned with fire in the *same* place.

8 ¶ These *be* the names of the mighty men whom David had: The Tăch′mō-nīte that sat in the seat, chief among the

captains; the same *was* Ăd'ĭ-nō the
Ĕz'nīte: *he lifted up his spear* against
eight hundred, whom he slew at one time.
9 And after him *was* Ĕl'ē-ā'zȧr the son
of Dō'dō the Ȧ-hō'hīte, *one* of the three
mighty men with David, when they defied the Phĭ-lĭs'tīneș *that* were there
gathered together to battle, and the men
of Ĭș'rā-ĕl were gone away:
10 He arose, and smote the Phĭ-lĭs'-
tīneș until his hand was weary, and his
hand clave unto the sword: and the LORD
wrought a great victory that day; and the
people returned after him only to spoil.
11 And after him *was* Shăm'mȧh the
son of Ā'gēe the Hā'rȧ-rīte. And the
Phĭ-lĭs'tīneș were gathered together
into a troop, where was a piece of ground
full of lentils: and the people fled from
the Phĭ-lĭs'tīneș.
12 But he stood in the midst of the
ground, and defended it, and slew the
Phĭ-lĭs'tīneș: and the LORD wrought a
great victory.
13 And three of the thirty chief went
down, and came to David in the harvest
time unto the cave of Ȧ-dŭl'lăm: and the
troop of the Phĭ-lĭs'tīneș pitched in the
valley of Rĕph'ā-ĭm.
14 And David *was* then in a hold, and
the garrison of the Phĭ-lĭs'tīneș *was* then
in Beth-lehem.
15 And David longed, and said, Oh that
one would give me drink of the water of
the well of Beth-lehem, which *is* by the
gate!
16 And the three mighty men brake
through the host of the Phĭ-lĭs'tīneș,
and drew water out of the well of Beth-
lehem, that *was* by the gate, and took
it, and brought *it* to David: nevertheless
he would not drink thereof, but poured
it out unto the LORD.
17 And he said, Be it far from me, O
LORD, that I should do this: *is not this*
the blood of the men that went in jeopardy of their lives? therefore he would
not drink it. These things did these
three mighty men.
18 And Ȧ-bĭsh'ā-ī, the brother of
Jō'ăb, the son of Zĕr'ụ-ī'ȧh, was chief
among three. And he lifted up his spear
against three hundred, *and* slew *them*,
and had the name among three.
19 Was he not most honorable of three?
therefore he was their captain: howbeit
he attained not unto the *first* three.
20 And Bē-nā'ịȧh the son of Jē-
hôi'ȧ-dȧ, the son of a valiant man, of
Kăb'zē-ĕl, who had done many acts, he
slew two lionlike men of Mō'ăb: he went
down also and slew a lion in the midst
of a pit in time of snow.
21 And he slew an Egyptian, a goodly
man: and the Egyptian had a spear in
his hand; but he went down to him with
a staff, and plucked the spear out of the
Egyptian's hand, and slew him with his
own spear.
22 These *things* did Bē-nā'ịȧh the son
of Jē-hôi'ȧ-dȧ, and had the name among
three mighty men.
23 He was more honorable than the
thirty, but he attained not to the *first*
three. And David set him over his guard.
24 Ăs'ȧ-hĕl the brother of Jō'ăb *was*
one of the thirty; Ĕl-hā'năn the son of
Dō'dō of Beth-lehem,
25 Shăm'mȧh the Hā'rŏd-īte, Ē-lī'kȧ
the Hā'rŏd-īte,
26 Hē'lĕz the Păl'tīte, Ī'rȧ the son of
Ĭk'kĕsh the Tē-kō'īte,
27 Ā'bĭ-ē'zĕr the Ăn'ē-thŏth'īte, Mē-
bŭn'naī the Hū'shȧth-īte,
28 Zăl'mŏn the Ȧ-hō'hīte, Mȧ-hăr'ā-ī
the Nē-tŏph'ȧ-thīte,
29 Hē'lĕb the son of Bā'ȧ-nȧh, a Nē-
tŏph'ȧ-thīte, Ĭt'tā-ī the son of Rī'baī out
of Gĭb'ē-ȧh of the children of Benjamin,
30 Bē-nā'ịȧh the Pĭr'ȧ-thŏn-īte, Hĭd'-
dā-ī of the brooks of Gā'ăsh,
31 Ā'bĭ-ăl'bŏn the Är'băth-īte, Ăz-mā'-
vĕth the Bär-hū'mīte,
32 Ē-lī'ȧh-bȧ the Shā'ăl-bō'nīte, of the
sons of Jā'shĕn, Jonathan,
33 Shăm'mȧh the Hā'rȧ-rīte, Ȧ-hī'ăm
the son of Shā'rȧr the Hā'rȧ-rīte,
34 Ē-lĭph'ē-lĕt the son of Ȧ-hăs'baī,
the son of the Mā-ăch'ȧ-thīte, Ē-lī'ăm
the son of Ȧ-hĭth'ō-phĕl the Gī'lō-nīte,
35 Hĕz'rā-ī the Cär'mĕl-īte, Pā'ȧ-raī
the Är'bīte,
36 Ī'găl the son of Nathan of Zō'bȧh,
Bā'nī the Gadite,
37 Zē'lĕk the Ammonite, Nā'hȧ-rī the
Bē-ē'rŏth-īte, armor-bearer to Jō'ăb the
son of Zĕr'ụ-ī'ȧh,
38 Ī'rȧ an Ĭth'rīte, Gā'rĕb an Ĭth'rīte,
39 Ū-rī'ȧh the Hĭt'tīte: thirty and
seven in all.

CHAPTER 24

AND again the anger of the LORD was
kindled against Ĭș'rā-ĕl, and he
moved David against them to say, Go,
number Ĭș'rā-ĕl and Judah.

2 For the king said to Jō'ăb the captain of the host, which *was* with him,
Go now through all the tribes of Ĭṣ'rā-ĕl,
from Dan even to Bē'ĕr-shē'bȧ, and
number ye the people, that I may know
the number of the people.
3 And Jō'ăb said unto the king, Now
the LORD thy God add unto the people,
how many soever they be, a hundredfold, and that the eyes of my lord the
king may see *it:* but why doth my lord
the king delight in this thing?
4 Notwithstanding the king's word prevailed against Jō'ăb, and against the
captains of the host. And Jō'ăb and the
captains of the host went out from the
presence of the king, to number the
people of Ĭṣ'rā-ĕl.
5 ¶ And they passed over Jordan, and
pitched in Ȧ-rō'ĕr, on the right side of
the city that *lieth* in the midst of the
river of Gad, and toward Jā'zĕr:
6 Then they came to Gĭl'ē-ăd, and to
the land of Tăh'tĭm-hŏd'shī; and they
came to Dăn'-jā'ăn, and about to Zī'dŏn,
7 And came to the stronghold of Tȳre,
and to all the cities of the Hī'vītes, and
of the Cā'năan-ītes: and they went out
to the south of Judah, *even* to Bē'ĕr-
shē'bȧ.
8 So when they had gone through all
the land, they came to Jerusalem at the
end of nine months and twenty days.
9 And Jō'ăb gave up the sum of the
number of the people unto the king: and
there were in Ĭṣ'rā-ĕl eight hundred
thousand valiant men that drew the
sword; and the men of Judah *were* five
hundred thousand men.
10 ¶ And David's heart smote him
after that he had numbered the people.
And David said unto the LORD, I have
sinned greatly in that I have done: and
now, I beseech thee, O LORD, take
away the iniquity of thy servant; for I
have done very foolishly.
11 For when David was up in the morning, the word of the LORD came unto
the prophet Gad, David's seer, saying,
12 Go and say unto David, Thus saith
the LORD, I offer thee three *things;*
choose thee one of them, that I may do
it unto thee.
13 So Gad came to David, and told him,
and said unto him, Shall seven years of
famine come unto thee in thy land? or
wilt thou flee three months before thine
enemies, while they pursue thee? or
that there be three days' pestilence in
thy land? now advise, and see what answer I shall return to him that sent me.
14 And David said unto Gad, I am in
a great strait: let us fall now into the
hand of the LORD; for his mercies *are*
great: and let me not fall into the hand
of man.
15 ¶ So the LORD sent a pestilence
upon Ĭṣ'rā-ĕl from the morning even
to the time appointed: and there died
of the people from Dan even to Bē'ĕr-
shē'bȧ seventy thousand men.
16 And when the angel stretched out
his hand upon Jerusalem to destroy it,
the LORD repented him of the evil, and
said to the angel that destroyed the
people, It is enough: stay now thine
hand. And the angel of the LORD was
by the threshingplace of Ȧ-rau'nȧh the
Jĕb'ū-ṣīte.
17 And David spake unto the LORD
when he saw the angel that smote the
people, and said, Lo, I have sinned, and
I have done wickedly: but these sheep,
what have they done? let thine hand, I
pray thee, be against me, and against my
father's house.
18 ¶ And Gad came that day to David,
and said unto him, Go up, rear an altar
unto the LORD in the threshingfloor of
Ȧ-rau'nȧh the Jĕb'ū-ṣīte.
19 And David, according to the saying
of Gad, went up as the LORD commanded.
20 And Ȧ-rau'nȧh looked, and saw the
king and his servants coming on toward
him: and Ȧ-rau'nȧh went out, and
bowed himself before the king on his
face upon the ground.
21 And Ȧ-rau'nȧh said, Wherefore is
my lord the king come to his servant?
And David said, To buy the threshingfloor of thee, to build an altar unto the
LORD, that the plague may be stayed
from the people.
22 And Ȧ-rau'nȧh said unto David, Let
my lord the king take and offer up what
seemeth good unto him: behold, *here be*
oxen for burnt sacrifice, and threshing
instruments and *other* instruments of
the oxen for wood.
23 All these *things* did Ȧ-rau'nȧh, *as* a
king, give unto the king. And Ȧ-rau'nȧh
said unto the king, The LORD thy God
accept thee.
24 And the king said unto Ȧ-rau'nȧh,
Nay; but I will surely buy *it* of thee at a

price: neither will I offer burnt offerings
unto the LORD my God of that which
doth cost me nothing. So David bought
the threshingfloor and the oxen for fifty
shekels of silver.
25 And David built there an altar unto
the LORD, and offered burnt offerings
and peace offerings. So the LORD was
entreated for the land, and the plague
was stayed from Ĭṣ'rā-ēl.

THE FIRST

BOOK OF THE KINGS

COMMONLY CALLED, THE THIRD BOOK OF THE KINGS

CHAPTER 1

NOW king David was old *and*
stricken in years; and they covered
him with clothes, but he gat no heat.
2 Wherefore his servants said unto
him, Let there be sought for my lord the
king a young virgin: and let her stand
before the king, and let her cherish him,
and let her lie in thy bosom, that my
lord the king may get heat.
3 So they sought for a fair damsel
throughout all the coasts of Ĭṣ'rā-ĕl, and
found Ăb'ĭ-shăg a Shụ'nȧm-mīte, and
brought her to the king.
4 And the damsel *was* very fair, and
cherished the king, and ministered to
him: but the king knew her not.
5 ℭ Then Ăd'ō-nī'jȧh the son of Hăg'-
gĭth exalted himself, saying, I will be
king: and he prepared him chariots and
horsemen, and fifty men to run before
him.
6 And his father had not displeased
him at any time in saying, Why hast
thou done so? and he also *was* a very
goodly man; and *his mother* bare him
after Ăb'sȧ-lŏm.
7 And he conferred with Jō'ăb the son
of Zĕr'ụ-ī'ȧh, and with Ȧ-bī'ȧ-thȧr the
priest: and they following Ăd'ō-nī'jȧh
helped *him*.
8 But Zā'dŏk the priest, and Bē-nā'ịȧh
the son of Jē-hôi'ȧ-dȧ, and Nathan the
prophet, and Shĭm'ē-ī, and Rē'ī, and the
mighty men which *belonged* to David,
were not with Ăd'ō-nī'jȧh.
9 And Ăd'ō-nī'jȧh slew sheep and oxen
and fat cattle by the stone of Zō'hē-lĕth,
which *is* by Ĕn-rō'gĕl, and called all his
brethren the king's sons, and all the
men of Judah the king's servants:
10 But Nathan the prophet, and Bē-
nā'ịȧh, and the mighty men, and Solomon his brother, he called not.
11 ℭ Wherefore Nathan spake unto
Băth'-shē'bȧ the mother of Solomon,
saying, Hast thou not heard that Ăd'ō-
nī'jȧh the son of Hăg'gĭth doth reign,
and David our lord knoweth *it* not?
12 Now therefore come, let me, I pray
thee, give thee counsel, that thou mayest
save thine own life, and the life of thy
son Solomon.
13 Go and get thee in unto king David,
and say unto him, Didst not thou, my
lord, O king, swear unto thine handmaid, saying, Assuredly Solomon thy
son shall reign after me, and he shall sit
upon my throne? why then doth Ăd'ō-
nī'jȧh reign?
14 Behold, while thou yet talkest there
with the king, I also will come in after
thee, and confirm thy words.
15 ℭ And Băth'-shē'bȧ went in unto
the king into the chamber: and the king
was very old; and Ăb'ĭ-shăg the Shụ'-
nȧm-mīte ministered unto the king.
16 And Băth'-shē'bȧ bowed, and did
obeisance unto the king. And the king
said, What wouldest thou?
17 And she said unto him, My lord,
thou swarest by the LORD thy God unto
thine handmaid, *saying*, Assuredly
Solomon thy son shall reign after me,
and he shall sit upon my throne.
18 And now, behold, Ăd'ō-nī'jȧh
reigneth; and now, my lord the king,
thou knowest *it* not:
19 And he hath slain oxen and fat cattle and sheep in abundance, and hath
called all the sons of the king, and
Ȧ-bī'ȧ-thȧr the priest, and Jō'ăb the captain of the host: but Solomon thy servant
hath he not called.
20 And thou, my lord, O king, the

eyes of all Ĭṣ′rā-ĕl *are* upon thee, that
thou shouldest tell them who shall sit
on the throne of my lord the king after
him.
21 Otherwise it shall come to pass,
when my lord the king shall sleep with
his fathers, that I and my son Solomon
shall be counted offenders.
22 ¶ And, lo, while she yet talked
with the king, Nathan the prophet also
came in.
23 And they told the king, saying, Behold Nathan the prophet. And when he
was come in before the king, he bowed
himself before the king with his face to
the ground.
24 And Nathan said, My lord, O king,
hast thou said, Ăd′ō-nī′jah shall reign
after me, and he shall sit upon my
throne?
25 For he is gone down this day, and
hath slain oxen and fat cattle and sheep
in abundance, and hath called all the
king's sons, and the captains of the host,
and Ȧ-bī′ȧ-thȧr the priest; and, behold,
they eat and drink before him, and say,
God save king Ăd′ō-nī′jah.
26 But me, *even* me thy servant, and
Zā′dŏk the priest, and Bē-nā′ịah the son
of Jē-hôi′ȧ-dȧ, and thy servant Solomon,
hath he not called.
27 Is this thing done by my lord the
king, and thou hast not showed *it* unto
thy servant, who should sit on the throne
of my lord the king after him?
28 ¶ Then king David answered and
said, Call me Băth′-shē′bȧ. And she
came into the king's presence, and stood
before the king.
29 And the king sware, and said, *As* the
LORD liveth, that hath redeemed my
soul out of all distress,
30 Even as I sware unto thee by the
LORD God of Ĭṣ′rā-ĕl, saying, Assuredly
Solomon thy son shall reign after me,
and he shall sit upon my throne in my
stead; even so will I certainly do this
day.
31 Then Băth′-shē′bȧ bowed with *her*
face to the earth, and did reverence to
the king, and said, Let my lord king
David live for ever.
32 ¶ And king David said, Call me
Zā′dŏk the priest, and Nathan the
prophet, and Bē-nā′ịah the son of Jē-
hôi′ȧ-dȧ. And they came before the
king.
33 The king also said unto them, Take
with you the servants of your lord, and
cause Solomon my son to ride upon
mine own mule, and bring him down to
Gī′hŏn:
34 And let Zā′dŏk the priest and Nathan the prophet anoint him there king
over Ĭṣ′rā-ĕl: and blow ye with the trumpet, and say, God save king Solomon.
35 Then ye shall come up after him,
that he may come and sit upon my
throne; for he shall be king in my stead:
and I have appointed him to be ruler
over Ĭṣ′rā-ĕl and over Judah.
36 And Bē-nā′ịah the son of Jē-hôi′ȧ-dȧ
answered the king, and said, Amen: the
LORD God of my lord the king say so
too.
37 As the LORD hath been with my
lord the king, even so be he with Solomon, and make his throne greater than
the throne of my lord king David.
38 So Zā′dŏk the priest, and Nathan
the prophet, and Bē-nā′ịah the son of
Jē-hôi′ȧ-dȧ, and the Chĕr′ē-thītes, and
the Pĕl′ē-thītes, went down, and caused
Solomon to ride upon king David's mule,
and brought him to Gī′hŏn.
39 And Zā′dŏk the priest took a horn of
oil out of the tabernacle, and anointed
Solomon. And they blew the trumpet;
and all the people said, God save king
Solomon.
40 And all the people came up after
him, and the people piped with pipes,
and rejoiced with great joy, so that the
earth rent with the sound of them.
41 ¶ And Ăd′ō-nī′jah and all the guests
that *were* with him heard *it* as they
had made an end of eating. And when
Jō′ăb heard the sound of the trumpet,
he said, Wherefore *is this* noise of the
city being in an uproar?
42 And while he yet spake, behold,
Jonathan the son of Ȧ-bī′ȧ-thȧr the
priest came: and Ăd′ō-nī′jah said unto
him, Come in; for thou *art* a valiant man,
and bringest good tidings.
43 And Jonathan answered and said to
Ăd′ō-nī′jah, Verily our lord king David
hath made Solomon king.
44 And the king hath sent with him
Zā′dŏk the priest, and Nathan the
prophet, and Bē-nā′ịah the son of
Jē-hôi′ȧ-dȧ, and the Chĕr′ē-thītes, and
the Pĕl′ē-thītes, and they have caused
him to ride upon the king's mule:
45 And Zā′dŏk the priest and Nathan
the prophet have anointed him king in

Gī'hŏn: and they are come up from thence rejoicing, so that the city rang again. This *is* the noise that ye have heard.

46 And also Solomon sitteth on the throne of the kingdom.

47 And moreover the king's servants came to bless our lord king David, saying, God make the name of Solomon better than thy name, and make his throne greater than thy throne. And the king bowed himself upon the bed.

48 And also thus said the king, Blessed *be* the LORD God of Ĭṣ'rā-ĕl, which hath given *one* to sit on my throne this day, mine eyes even seeing *it*.

49 And all the guests that *were* with Ăd'ō-nī'jȧh were afraid, and rose up, and went every man his way.

50 ℂ And Ăd'ō-nī'jȧh feared because of Solomon, and arose, and went, and caught hold on the horns of the altar.

51 And it was told Solomon, saying, Behold, Ăd'ō-nī'jȧh feareth king Solomon: for, lo, he hath caught hold on the horns of the altar, saying, Let king Solomon swear unto me to-day that he will not slay his servant with the sword.

52 And Solomon said, If he will show himself a worthy man, there shall not a hair of him fall to the earth: but if wickedness shall be found in him, he shall die.

53 So king Solomon sent, and they brought him down from the altar. And he came and bowed himself to king Solomon: and Solomon said unto him, Go to thine house.

CHAPTER 2

NOW the days of David drew nigh that he should die; and he charged Solomon his son, saying,

2 I go the way of all the earth: be thou strong therefore, and show thyself a man;

3 And keep the charge of the LORD thy God, to walk in his ways, to keep his statutes, and his commandments, and his judgments, and his testimonies, as it is written in the law of Moses, that thou mayest prosper in all that thou doest, and whithersoever thou turnest thyself:

4 That the LORD may continue his word which he spake concerning me, saying, If thy children take heed to their way, to walk before me in truth with all their heart and with all their soul, there shall not fail thee (said he) a man on the throne of Ĭṣ'rā-ĕl.

5 Moreover thou knowest also what Jō'ăb the son of Zĕr'ṳ-ī'ȧh did to me, *and* what he did to the two captains of the hosts of Ĭṣ'rā-ĕl, unto Abner the son of Nĕr, and unto Ăm'ȧ-sȧ the son of Jē'thĕr, whom he slew, and shed the blood of war in peace, and put the blood of war upon his girdle that *was* about his loins, and in his shoes that *were* on his feet.

6 Do therefore according to thy wisdom, and let not his hoar head go down to the grave in peace.

7 But show kindness unto the sons of Bär-zĭl'lā-ī the Gĭl'ē-ăd-īte, and let them be of those that eat at thy table: for so they came to me when I fled because of Ăb'sȧ-lŏm thy brother.

8 And, behold, *thou hast* with thee Shĭm'ē-ī the son of Gē'rȧ, a Benjamite of Bā-hū'rĭm, which cursed me with a grievous curse in the day when I went to Mā'hȧ-nā'ĭm: but he came down to meet me at Jordan, and I sware to him by the LORD, saying, I will not put thee to death with the sword.

9 Now therefore hold him not guiltless: for thou *art* a wise man, and knowest what thou oughtest to do unto him; but his hoar head bring thou down to the grave with blood.

10 So David slept with his fathers, and was buried in the city of David.

11 And the days that David reigned over Ĭṣ'rā-ĕl *were* forty years: seven years reigned he in Hē'brŏn, and thirty and three years reigned he in Jerusalem.

12 ℂ Then sat Solomon upon the throne of David his father; and his kingdom was established greatly.

13 ℂ And Ăd'ō-nī'jȧh the son of Hăg'gĭth came to Băth'-shē'bȧ the mother of Solomon. And she said, Comest thou peaceably? And he said, Peaceably.

14 He said moreover, I have somewhat to say unto thee. And she said, Say on.

15 And he said, Thou knowest that the kingdom was mine, and *that* all Ĭṣ'rā-ĕl set their faces on me, that I should reign: howbeit the kingdom is turned about, and is become my brother's: for it was his from the LORD.

16 And now I ask one petition of thee,

deny me not. And she said unto him,
Say on.
17 And he said, Speak, I pray thee,
unto Solomon the king, (for he will not
say thee nay,) that he give me Ăb'ĭ-shăg
the Shụ'nȧm-mīte to wife.
18 And Băth'-shē'bȧ said, Well; I will
speak for thee unto the king.
19 ¶ Băth'-shē'bȧ therefore went unto
king Solomon, to speak unto him for
Ăd'ō-nī'jȧh. And the king rose up to
meet her, and bowed himself unto her,
and sat down on his throne, and caused
a seat to be set for the king's mother;
and she sat on his right hand.
20 Then she said, I desire one small
petition of thee; *I pray thee,* say me not
nay. And the king said unto her, Ask on,
my mother; for I will not say thee nay.
21 And she said, Let Ăb'ĭ-shăg the
Shụ'nȧm-mīte be given to Ăd'ō-nī'jȧh
thy brother to wife.
22 And king Solomon answered and
said unto his mother, And why dost thou
ask Ăb'ĭ-shăg the Shụ'nȧm-mīte for
Ăd'ō-nī'jȧh? ask for him the kingdom
also; for he *is* mine elder brother; even
for him, and for Ȧ-bī'ȧ-thȧr the priest,
and for Jō'ăb the son of Zĕr'ụ-ī'ȧh.
23 Then king Solomon sware by the
LORD, saying, God do so to me, and
more also, if Ăd'ō-nī'jȧh have not
spoken this word against his own life.
24 Now therefore, *as* the LORD liveth,
which hath established me, and set me
on the throne of David my father, and
who hath made me a house, as he promised, Ăd'ō-nī'jȧh shall be put to death
this day.
25 And king Solomon sent by the hand
of Bē-nā'ịȧh the son of Jē-hoi'ȧ-dȧ; and
he fell upon him that he died.
26 ¶ And unto Ȧ-bī'ȧ-thȧr the priest
said the king, Get thee to Ăn'ȧ-thŏth,
unto thine own fields; for thou *art*
worthy of death: but I will not at this
time put thee to death, because thou
barest the ark of the Lord GOD before
David my father, and because thou hast
been afflicted in all wherein my father
was afflicted.
27 So Solomon thrust out Ȧ-bī'ȧ-thȧr
from being priest unto the LORD; that
he might fulfil the word of the LORD,
which he spake concerning the house of
Ē'lī in Shī'lōh.
28 ¶ Then tidings came to Jō'ăb: for
Jō'ăb had turned after Ăd'ō-nī'jȧh,
though he turned not after Ăb'sȧ-lŏm.
And Jō'ăb fled unto the tabernacle of
the LORD and caught hold on the horns
of the altar.
29 And it was told king Solomon that
Jō'ăb was fled unto the tabernacle of
the LORD; and, behold, *he is* by the
altar. Then Solomon sent Bē-nā'ịȧh
the son of Jē-hoi'ȧ-dȧ, saying, Go, fall
upon him.
30 And Bē-nā'ịȧh came to the tabernacle of the LORD, and said unto him,
Thus saith the king, Come forth. And
he said, Nay; but I will die here. And
Bē-nā'ịȧh brought the king word again,
saying, Thus said Jō'ăb, and thus he
answered me.
31 And the king said unto him, Do as
he hath said, and fall upon him, and
bury him; that thou mayest take away the
innocent blood, which Jō'ăb shed, from
me, and from the house of my father.
32 And the LORD shall return his blood
upon his own head, who fell upon two
men more righteous and better than he,
and slew them with the sword, my father
David not knowing *thereof, to wit,*
Abner the son of Nēr, captain of the
host of Ĭs'rā-ĕl, and Ăm'ȧ-sȧ the son of
Jē'thēr, captain of the host of Judah.
33 Their blood shall therefore return
upon the head of Jō'ăb, and upon the
head of his seed for ever: but upon
David, and upon his seed, and upon his
house, and upon his throne, shall there
be peace for ever from the LORD.
34 So Bē-nā'ịȧh the son of Jē-hoi'ȧ-dȧ
went up, and fell upon him, and slew
him: and he was buried in his own house
in the wilderness.
35 ¶ And the king put Bē-nā'ịȧh the
son of Jē-hoi'ȧ-dȧ in his room over the
host: and Zā'dŏk the priest did the king
put in the room of Ȧ-bī'ȧ-thȧr.
36 ¶ And the king sent and called for
Shĭm'ē-ī, and said unto him, Build thee
a house in Jerusalem, and dwell there,
and go not forth thence any whither.
37 For it shall be, *that* on the day thou
goest out, and passest over the brook
Kĭd'rŏn, thou shalt know for certain
that thou shalt surely die: thy blood
shall be upon thine own head.
38 And Shĭm'ē-ī said unto the king,
The saying *is* good: as my lord the king
hath said, so will thy servant do. And
Shĭm'ē-ī dwelt in Jerusalem many days.
39 And it came to pass at the end of

three years, that two of the servants of
Shĭm'ē-ī ran away unto Ā'chĭsh son of
Mā'ā-chăh king of Gath. And they told
Shĭm'ē-ī, saying, Behold, thy servants
be in Gath.
40 And Shĭm'ē-ī arose, and saddled his
ass, and went to Gath to Ā'chĭsh to seek
his servants: and Shĭm'ē-ī went, and
brought his servants from Gath.
41 And it was told Solomon that
Shĭm'ē-ī had gone from Jerusalem to
Gath, and was come again.
42 And the king sent and called for
Shĭm'ē-ī, and said unto him, Did I not
make thee to swear by the LORD, and
protested unto thee, saying, Know for a
certain, on the day thou goest out, and
walkest abroad any whither, that thou
shalt surely die? and thou saidst unto
me, The word *that* I have heard *is* good.
43 Why then hast thou not kept the
oath of the LORD, and the commandment that I have charged thee with?
44 The king said moreover to Shĭm'ē-ī,
Thou knowest all the wickedness which
thine heart is privy to, that thou didst to
David my father; therefore the LORD
shall return thy wickedness upon thine
own head;
45 And king Solomon *shall be* blessed,
and the throne of David shall be established before the LORD for ever.
46 So the king commanded Bē-nā'iăh
the son of Jē-hoi'ā-dă; which went out,
and fell upon him, that he died. And the
kingdom was established in the hand of
Solomon.

CHAPTER 3

AND Solomon made affinity with
Phā'raōh king of Egypt, and took
Phā'raōh's daughter, and brought her
into the city of David, until he had made
an end of building his own house, and
the house of the LORD, and the wall of
Jerusalem round about.
2 Only the people sacrificed in high
places, because there was no house
built unto the name of the LORD, until
those days.
3 And Solomon loved the LORD, walking in the statutes of David his father:
only he sacrificed and burnt incense in
high places.
4 And the king went to Gĭb'ē-ŏn to
sacrifice there; for that *was* the great
high place: a thousand burnt offerings
did Solomon offer upon that altar.
5 ¶ In Gĭb'ē-ŏn the LORD appeared
to Solomon in a dream by night: and
God said, Ask what I shall give thee.
6 And Solomon said, Thou hast showed
unto thy servant David my father great
mercy, according as he walked before
thee in truth, and in righteousness, and
in uprightness of heart with thee; and
thou hast kept for him this great kindness, that thou hast given him a son to
sit on his throne, as *it is* this day.
7 And now, O LORD my God, thou hast
made thy servant king instead of David
my father: and I *am but* a little child: I
know not *how* to go out or come in.
8 And thy servant *is* in the midst of thy
people which thou hast chosen, a great
people, that cannot be numbered nor
counted for multitude.
9 Give therefore thy servant an understanding heart to judge thy people, that
I may discern between good and bad:
for who is able to judge this thy so great
a people?
10 And the speech pleased the LORD,
that Solomon had asked this thing.
11 And God said unto him, Because
thou hast asked this thing, and hast not
asked for thyself long life; neither hast
asked riches for thyself, nor hast asked
the life of thine enemies; but hast asked
for thyself understanding to discern
judgment;
12 Behold, I have done according to
thy word: lo, I have given thee a wise
and an understanding heart; so that
there was none like thee before thee,
neither after thee shall any arise like
unto thee.
13 And I have also given thee that
which thou hast not asked, both riches,
and honor: so that there shall not be any
among the kings like unto thee all thy
days.
14 And if thou wilt walk in my ways, to
keep my statutes and my commandments, as thy father David did walk,
then I will lengthen thy days.
15 And Solomon awoke; and behold,
it was a dream. And he came to Jerusalem, and stood before the ark of the
covenant of the LORD, and offered up
burnt offerings, and offered peace offerings, and made a feast to all his servants.
16 ¶ Then came there two women,
that were harlots, unto the king, and
stood before him.
17 And the one woman said, O my

lord, I and this woman dwell in one
house; and I was delivered of a child
with her in the house.
18 And it came to pass the third day
after that I was delivered, that this
woman was delivered also: and we *were*
together; *there was* no stranger with us
in the house, save we two in the house.
19 And this woman's child died in the
night; because she overlaid it.
20 And she arose at midnight, and took
my son from beside me, while thine
handmaid slept, and laid it in her bosom,
and laid her dead child in my bosom.
21 And when I rose in the morning to
give my child suck, behold, it was dead:
but when I had considered it in the
morning, behold, it was not my son,
which I did bear.
22 And the other woman said, Nay;
but the living *is* my son, and the dead *is*
thy son. And this said, No; but the dead
is thy son, and the living *is* my son.
Thus they spake before the king.
23 Then said the king, The one saith,
This *is* my son that liveth, and thy son
is the dead: and the other saith, Nay;
but thy son *is* the dead, and my son *is*
the living.
24 And the king said, Bring me a
sword. And they brought a sword before the king.
25 And the king said, Divide the living
child in two, and give half to the one,
and half to the other.
26 Then spake the woman whose the
living child *was* unto the king, for her
bowels yearned upon her son, and she
said, O my lord, give her the living
child, and in no wise slay it. But the other
said, Let it be neither mine nor thine,
but divide *it*.
27 Then the king answered and said,
Give her the living child, and in no wise
slay it: she *is* the mother thereof.
28 And all Ĭṣ′rā-ĕl heard of the judgment which the king had judged; and
they feared the king: for they saw that
the wisdom of God *was* in him to do
judgment.

CHAPTER 4

SO king Solomon was king over all
Ĭṣ′rā-ĕl.
2 And these *were* the princes which he
had; Ăz′ȧ-rī′ȧh the son of Zā′dŏk the
priest,
3 Ĕl′ĭ-hō′rĕph and Ȧ-hī′ȧh, the sons of
Shī′shȧ, scribes; Jē-hŏsh′ȧ-phăt the son
of Ȧ-hī′lŭd, the recorder.
4 And Bē-nā′ịah the son of Jē-hōi′ȧ-dȧ
was over the host: and Zā′dŏk and
Ȧ-bī′ȧ-thȧr *were* the priests:
5 And Ăz′ȧ-rī′ȧh the son of Nathan *was*
over the officers: and Zā′bŭd the son of
Nathan *was* principal officer, *and* the
king's friend:
6 And Ȧ-hī′shär *was* over the household: and Ăd′ō-nī′răm the son of Abda
was over the tribute.
7 ℂ And Solomon had twelve officers
over all Ĭṣ′rā-ĕl, which provided victuals
for the king and his household: each man
his month in a year made provision.
8 And these *are* their names: The son
of Hûr, in mount Ē′phrā-ĭm:
9 The son of Dē′kär, in Mā′kăz, and
in Shā-ăl′bĭm, and Bĕth′-shē′mĕsh, and
Ē′lŏn-bĕth-hā′năn:
10 The son of Hē′sĕd, in Ȧ-rụ′bōth; to
him *pertained* Sō′chōh, and all the land
of Hē′phẽr:
11 The son of Ȧ-bĭn′ȧ-dăb, in all the
region of Dor; which had Tā′phȧth the
daughter of Solomon to wife:
12 Bā′ȧ-nȧ the son of Ȧ-hī′lŭd; *to him*
pertained Tā′ȧ-năch and Mē-gĭd′dō,
and all Bĕth′-shē′ăn, which *is* by Zär-
tā′nȧh beneath Jĕz′rē-ĕl, from Bĕth′-
shē′ăn to Ā′bĕl-mē-hō′lȧh, *even* unto
the place that is beyond Jŏk′nē-ăm:
13 The son of Gē′bẽr, in Rā′mŏth-
gĭl′ē-ăd; to him *pertained* the towns of
Jā′ĭr the son of Mȧ-năs′sĕh, which *are*
in Gĭl′ē-ăd; to him *also pertained* the
region of Är′gŏb, which *is* in Bā′shăn,
threescore great cities with walls and
brazen bars:
14 Ȧ-hĭn′ȧ-dăb the son of Ĭd′dō *had*
Mā′hȧ-nā′ĭm:
15 Ȧ-hĭm′ā-ăz *was* in Năph′tȧ-lī; he
also took Băs′măth the daughter of
Solomon to wife:
16 Bā′ȧ-nȧh the son of Hū′shaī *was* in
Ăsh′ẽr and in Ā′lŏth:
17 Jē-hŏsh′ȧ-phăt the son of Pȧ-rụ′ȧh,
in Ĭs′sȧ-chär:
18 Shĭm′ē-ī the son of Ē′lȧh, in Benjamin:
19 Gē′bẽr the son of Ū′rī *was* in the
country of Gĭl′ē-ăd, *in* the country of
Sī′hŏn king of the Ăm′ō-rītes, and of
Og king of Bā′shăn; and *he was* the only
officer which *was* in the land.
20 ℂ Judah and Ĭṣ′rā-ĕl *were* many, as
the sand which *is* by the sea in multi-

tude, eating and drinking, and making merry.

21 And Solomon reigned over all kingdoms from the river unto the land of the Phĭ-lĭs′tĭneṣ, and unto the border of Egypt: they brought presents, and served Solomon all the days of his life.

22 ¶ And Solomon's provision for one day was thirty measures of fine flour, and threescore measures of meal,

23 Ten fat oxen, and twenty oxen out of the pastures, and a hundred sheep, besides harts, and roebucks, and fallow deer, and fatted fowl.

24 For he had dominion over all *the region* on this side the river, from Tĭph′sȧh even to Ăz′zȧh, over all the kings on this side the river: and he had peace on all sides round about him.

25 And Judah and Ĭṣ′rā-ĕl dwelt safely, every man under his vine and under his fig tree, from Dan even to Bē′ĕr–shē′bȧ, all the days of Solomon.

26 ¶ And Solomon had forty thousand stalls of horses for his chariots, and twelve thousand horsemen.

27 And those officers provided victuals for king Solomon, and for all that came unto king Solomon's table, every man in his month: they lacked nothing.

28 Barley also and straw for the horses and dromedaries brought they unto the place where *the officers* were, every man according to his charge.

29 ¶ And God gave Solomon wisdom and understanding exceeding much, and largeness of heart, even as the sand that *is* on the seashore.

30 And Solomon's wisdom excelled the wisdom of all the children of the east country, and all the wisdom of Egypt.

31 For he was wiser than all men; than Ē′thăn the Ĕz′rȧ-hīte, and Hē′măn, and Chăl′cŏl, and Där′dȧ, the sons of Mā′hŏl: and his fame was in all nations round about.

32 And he spake three thousand proverbs: and his songs were a thousand and five.

33 And he spake of trees, from the cedar tree that *is* in Lebanon even unto the hyssop that springeth out of the wall: he spake also of beasts, and of fowl, and of creeping things, and of fishes.

34 And there came of all people to hear the wisdom of Solomon, from all kings of the earth, which had heard of his wisdom.

CHAPTER 5

AND Hiram king of Tȳre sent his servants unto Solomon; for he had heard that they had anointed him king in the room of his father: for Hiram was ever a lover of David.

2 And Solomon sent to Hiram, saying,

3 Thou knowest how that David my father could not build a house unto the name of the LORD his God, for the wars which were about him on every side, until the LORD put them under the soles of his feet.

4 But now the LORD my God hath given me rest on every side, *so that there is* neither adversary nor evil occurrent.

5 And, behold, I purpose to build a house unto the name of the LORD my God, as the LORD spake unto David my father, saying, Thy son, whom I will set upon thy throne in thy room, he shall build a house unto my name.

6 Now therefore command thou that they hew me cedar trees out of Lebanon; and my servants shall be with thy servants: and unto thee will I give hire for thy servants according to all that thou shalt appoint: for thou knowest that *there is* not among us any that can skill to hew timber like unto the Sī-dō′nĭ-ănṣ.

7 ¶ And it came to pass, when Hiram heard the words of Solomon, that he rejoiced greatly, and said, Blessed *be* the LORD this day, which hath given unto David a wise son over this great people.

8 And Hiram sent to Solomon, saying, I have considered the things which thou sentest to me for: *and* I will do all thy desire concerning timber of cedar, and concerning timber of fir.

9 My servants shall bring *them* down from Lebanon unto the sea; and I will convey them by sea in floats unto the place that thou shalt appoint me, and will cause them to be discharged there, and thou shalt receive *them:* and thou shalt accomplish my desire, in giving food for my household.

10 So Hiram gave Solomon cedar trees and fir trees *according to* all his desire.

11 And Solomon gave Hiram twenty thousand measures of wheat *for* food to his household, and twenty measures

of pure oil: thus gave Solomon to Hiram
year by year.
12 And the LORD gave Solomon wisdom, as he promised him: and there
was peace between Hiram and Solomon;
and they two made a league together.
13 ¶ And king Solomon raised a levy
out of all Ĭs′rā-ĕl; and the levy was
thirty thousand men.
14 And he sent them to Lebanon, ten
thousand a month by courses: a month
they were in Lebanon, *and* two months
at home: and Ăd′ō-nī′răm *was* over the
levy.
15 And Solomon had threescore and
ten thousand that bare burdens, and
fourscore thousand hewers in the
mountains;
16 Besides the chief of Solomon's
officers which *were* over the work, three
thousand and three hundred, which
ruled over the people that wrought in
the work.
17 And the king commanded, and
they brought great stones, costly stones,
and hewed stones, to lay the foundation
of the house.
18 And Solomon's builders and Hiram's
builders did hew *them*, and the stonesquarers: so they prepared timber and
stones to build the house.

CHAPTER 6

AND it came to pass in the four hundred and eightieth year after the
children of Ĭs′rā-ĕl were come out of the
land of Egypt, in the fourth year of
Solomon's reign over Ĭs′rā-ĕl, in the
month Zĭf, which *is* the second month,
that he began to build the house of the
LORD.
2 And the house which king Solomon
built for the LORD, the length thereof
was threescore cubits, and the breadth
thereof twenty *cubits*, and the height
thereof thirty cubits.
3 And the porch before the temple of
the house, twenty cubits *was* the length
thereof, according to the breadth of
the house; *and* ten cubits *was* the
breadth thereof before the house.
4 And for the house he made windows
of narrow lights.
5 ¶ And against the wall of the house
he built chambers round about, *against*
the walls of the house round about,
both of the temple and of the oracle: and
he made chambers round about.
6 The nethermost chamber *was* five
cubits broad, and the middle *was* six
cubits broad, and the third *was* seven
cubits broad: for without *in the wall* of
the house he made narrowed rests
round about, that *the beams* should not
be fastened in the walls of the house.
7 And the house, when it was in building, was built of stone made ready before it was brought thither: so that there
was neither hammer nor axe *nor* any
tool of iron heard in the house, while it
was in building.
8 The door for the middle chamber *was*
in the right side of the house: and they
went up with winding stairs into the
middle *chamber*, and out of the middle
into the third.
9 So he built the house, and finished
it; and covered the house with beams
and boards of cedar.
10 And *then* he built chambers against
all the house, five cubits high: and they
rested on the house with timber of
cedar.
11 ¶ And the word of the LORD came
to Solomon, saying,
12 *Concerning* this house which thou
art in building, if thou wilt walk in my
statutes, and execute my judgments,
and keep all my commandments to walk
in them; then will I perform my word
with thee, which I spake unto David thy
father:
13 And I will dwell among the children
of Ĭs′rā-ĕl, and will not forsake my
people Ĭs′rā-ĕl.
14 So Solomon built the house, and
finished it.
15 And he built the walls of the house
within with boards of cedar, both the
floor of the house, and the walls of the
ceiling: *and* he covered *them* on the in-
side with wood, and covered the floor
of the house with planks of fir.
16 And he built twenty cubits on the
sides of the house, both the floor and
the walls with boards of cedar: he even
built *them* for it within, *even* for the
oracle, *even* for the most holy *place*.
17 And the house, that *is*, the temple
before it, was forty cubits *long*.
18 And the cedar of the house within
was carved with knops and open flowers:
all *was* cedar; there was no stone seen.
19 And the oracle he prepared in the
house within, to set there the ark of the
covenant of the LORD.

20 And the oracle in the forepart *was* twenty cubits in length, and twenty cubits in breadth, and twenty cubits in the height thereof: and he overlaid it with pure gold; and *so* covered the altar *which was of* cedar.

21 So Solomon overlaid the house within with pure gold: and he made a partition by the chains of gold before the oracle; and he overlaid it with gold.

22 And the whole house he overlaid with gold, until he had finished all the house: also the whole altar that *was* by the oracle he overlaid with gold.

23 ¶ And within the oracle he made two cherubim *of* olive tree, *each* ten cubits high.

24 And five cubits *was* the one wing of the cherub, and five cubits the other wing of the cherub: from the uttermost part of the one wing unto the uttermost part of the other *were* ten cubits.

25 And the other cherub *was* ten cubits: both the cherubim *were* of one measure and one size.

26 The height of the one cherub *was* ten cubits, and so *was it* of the other cherub.

27 And he set the cherubim within the inner house: and they stretched forth the wings of the cherubim, so that the wing of the one touched the *one* wall, and the wing of the other cherub touched the other wall; and their wings touched one another in the midst of the house.

28 And he overlaid the cherubim with gold.

29 And he carved all the walls of the house round about with carved figures of cherubim and palm trees and open flowers, within and without.

30 And the floor of the house he overlaid with gold, within and without.

31 ¶ And for the entering of the oracle he made doors *of* olive tree: the lintel *and* side posts *were* a fifth part *of the wall*.

32 The two doors also *were of* olive tree; and he carved upon them carvings of cherubim and palm trees and open flowers, and overlaid *them* with gold, and spread gold upon the cherubim, and upon the palm trees.

33 So also made he for the door of the temple posts *of* olive tree, a fourth part *of the wall*.

34 And the two doors *were of* fir tree: the two leaves of the one door *were* folding, and the two leaves of the other door *were* folding.

35 And he carved *thereon* cherubim and palm trees and open flowers: and covered *them* with gold fitted upon the carved work.

36 ¶ And he built the inner court with three rows of hewed stone, and a row of cedar beams.

37 ¶ In the fourth year was the foundation of the house of the LORD laid, in the month Zĭf:

38 And in the eleventh year, in the month Bŭl, which *is* the eighth month, was the house finished throughout all the parts thereof, and according to all the fashion of it. So was he seven years in building it.

CHAPTER 7

BUT Solomon was building his own house thirteen years, and he finished all his house.

2 ¶ He built also the house of the forest of Lebanon; the length thereof *was* a hundred cubits, and the breadth thereof fifty cubits, and the height thereof thirty cubits, upon four rows of cedar pillars, with cedar beams upon the pillars.

3 And *it was* covered with cedar above upon the beams, that *lay* on forty-five pillars, fifteen *in* a row.

4 And *there were* windows *in* three rows, and light *was* against light *in* three ranks.

5 And all the doors and posts *were* square, with the windows: and light *was* against light *in* three ranks.

6 ¶ And he made a porch of pillars; the length thereof *was* fifty cubits, and the breadth thereof thirty cubits: and the porch *was* before them: and the *other* pillars and the thick beam *were* before them.

7 ¶ Then he made a porch for the throne where he might judge, *even* the porch of judgment: and *it was* covered with cedar from one side of the floor to the other.

8 ¶ And his house where he dwelt *had* another court within the porch, *which* was of the like work. Solomon made also a house for Phā′raōh's daughter, whom he had taken *to wife*, like unto this porch.

9 All these *were of* costly stones, according to the measures of hewed

stones, sawed with saws, within and without, even from the foundation unto the coping, and *so* on the outside toward the great court.

10 And the foundation *was of* costly stones, *even* great stones, stones of ten cubits, and stones of eight cubits.

11 And above *were* costly stones, after the measures of hewed stones, and cedars.

12 And the great court round about *was* with three rows of hewed stones, and a row of cedar beams, both for the inner court of the house of the LORD, and for the porch of the house.

13 ¶ And king Solomon sent and fetched Hiram out of Tȳre.

14 He *was* a widow's son of the tribe of Năph′tă-lī, and his father *was* a man of Tȳre, a worker in brass: and he was filled with wisdom, and understanding, and cunning to work all works in brass. And he came to king Solomon, and wrought all his work.

15 For he cast two pillars of brass, of eighteen cubits high apiece: and a line of twelve cubits did compass either of them about.

16 And he made two chapiters *of* molten brass, to set upon the tops of the pillars: the height of the one chapiter *was* five cubits, and the height of the other chapiter *was* five cubits:

17 *And* nets of checkerwork, and wreaths of chainwork, for the chapiters which *were* upon the top of the pillars; seven for the one chapiter, and seven for the other chapiter.

18 And he made the pillars, and two rows round about upon the one network, to cover the chapiters that *were* upon the top, with pomegranates: and so did he for the other chapiter.

19 And the chapiters that *were* upon the top of the pillars *were* of lily work in the porch, four cubits.

20 And the chapiters upon the two pillars *had pomegranates* also above, over against the belly which *was* by the network: and the pomegranates *were* two hundred in rows round about upon the other chapiter.

21 And he set up the pillars in the porch of the temple: and he set up the right pillar, and called the name thereof Jā′chin: and he set up the left pillar, and called the name thereof Boaz.

22 And upon the top of the pillars *was* lily work: so was the work of the pillars finished.

23 ¶ And he made a molten sea, ten cubits from the one brim to the other: *it was* round all about, and his height *was* five cubits: and a line of thirty cubits did compass it round about.

24 And under the brim of it round about *there were* knops compassing it, ten in a cubit, compassing the sea round about: the knops *were* cast in two rows, when it was cast.

25 It stood upon twelve oxen, three looking toward the north, and three looking toward the west, and three looking toward the south, and three looking toward the east: and the sea *was set* above upon them, and all their hinder parts *were* inward.

26 And it *was* a handbreadth thick, and the brim thereof was wrought like the brim of a cup, with flowers of lilies: it contained two thousand baths.

27 ¶ And he made ten bases of brass; four cubits *was* the length of one base, and four cubits the breadth thereof, and three cubits the height of it.

28 And the work of the bases *was* on this *manner:* they had borders, and the borders *were* between the ledges:

29 And on the borders that *were* between the ledges *were* lions, oxen, and cherubim: and upon the ledges *there was* a base above: and beneath the lions and oxen *were* certain additions made of thin work.

30 And every base had four brazen wheels, and plates of brass: and the four corners thereof had undersetters: under the laver *were* undersetters molten, at the side of every addition.

31 And the mouth of it within the chapiter and above *was* a cubit: but the mouth thereof *was* round *after* the work of the base, a cubit and a half: and also upon the mouth of it *were* gravings with their borders, foursquare, not round.

32 And under the borders *were* four wheels; and the axletrees of the wheels *were joined* to the base: and the height of a wheel *was* a cubit and half a cubit.

33 And the work of the wheels *was* like the work of a chariot wheel: their axletrees, and their naves, and their felloes, and their spokes, *were* all molten.

34 And *there were* four undersetters to the four corners of one base: *and* the undersetters *were* of the very base itself.

35 And in the top of the base *was there* a round compass of half a cubit high: and on the top of the base the ledges thereof and the borders thereof *were* of the same.

36 For on the plates of the ledges thereof, and on the borders thereof, he graved cherubim, lions, and palm trees, according to the proportion of every one, and additions round about.

37 After this *manner* he made the ten bases: all of them had one casting, one measure, *and* one size.

38 ℂ Then made he ten lavers of brass: one laver contained forty baths: *and* every laver was four cubits: *and* upon every one of the ten bases one laver.

39 And he put five bases on the right side of the house, and five on the left side of the house: and he set the sea on the right side of the house eastward, over against the south.

40 ℂ And Hiram made the lavers, and the shovels, and the basins. So Hiram made an end of doing all the work that he made king Solomon for the house of the LORD:

41 The two pillars, and the *two* bowls of the chapiters that *were* on the top of the two pillars; and the two networks, to cover the two bowls of the chapiters which *were* upon the top of the pillars;

42 And four hundred pomegranates for the two networks, *even* two rows of pomegranates for one network, to cover the two bowls of the chapiters that *were* upon the pillars;

43 And the ten bases, and ten lavers on the bases;

44 And one sea, and twelve oxen under the sea;

45 And the pots, and the shovels, and the basins: and all these vessels, which Hiram made to king Solomon for the house of the LORD, *were of* bright brass.

46 In the plain of Jordan did the king cast them, in the clay ground between Sŭc′cōth and Zär′thăn.

47 And Solomon left all the vessels *unweighed*, because they were exceeding many: neither was the weight of the brass found out.

48 And Solomon made all the vessels that *pertained* unto the house of the LORD: the altar of gold, and the table of gold, whereupon the showbread *was,*

49 And the candlesticks of pure gold, five on the right *side,* and five on the left, before the oracle, with the flowers, and the lamps, and the tongs *of* gold,

50 And the bowls, and the snuffers, and the basins, and the spoons, and the censers *of* pure gold; and the hinges *of* gold, *both* for the doors of the inner house, the most holy *place, and* for the doors of the house, *to wit,* of the temple.

51 So was ended all the work that king Solomon made for the house of the LORD. And Solomon brought in the things which David his father had dedicated; *even* the silver, and the gold, and the vessels, did he put among the treasures of the house of the LORD.

CHAPTER 8

THEN Solomon assembled the elders of Ĭṣ′rā-ĕl, and all the heads of the tribes, the chief of the fathers of the children of Ĭṣ′rā-ĕl, unto king Solomon in Jerusalem, that they might bring up the ark of the covenant of the LORD out of the city of David, which *is* Zion.

2 And all the men of Ĭṣ′rā-ĕl assembled themselves unto king Solomon at the feast in the month Ĕth′ȧ-nĭm, which *is* the seventh month.

3 And all the elders of Ĭṣ′rā-ĕl came, and the priests took up the ark.

4 And they brought up the ark of the LORD, and the tabernacle of the congregation, and all the holy vessels that *were* in the tabernacle, even those did the priests and the Lē′vītes bring up.

5 And king Solomon, and all the congregation of Ĭṣ′rā-ĕl, that were assembled unto him, *were* with him before the ark, sacrificing sheep and oxen, that could not be told nor numbered for multitude.

6 And the priests brought in the ark of the covenant of the LORD unto his place, into the oracle of the house, to the most holy *place, even* under the wings of the cherubim.

7 For the cherubim spread forth *their* two wings over the place of the ark, and the cherubim covered the ark and the staves thereof above.

8 And they drew out the staves, that the ends of the staves were seen out in the holy *place* before the oracle, and they were not seen without: and there they are unto this day.

9 *There was* nothing in the ark save the two tables of stone, which Moses put there at Hō′rĕb, when the LORD made *a*

covenant with the children of Ĭṣ′rā-ĕl,
when they came out of the land of Egypt.
10 And it came to pass, when the priests
were come out of the holy *place,* that
the cloud filled the house of the LORD,
11 So that the priests could not stand
to minister because of the cloud: for the
glory of the LORD had filled the house of
the LORD.
12 ℂ Then spake Solomon, The LORD
said that he would dwell in the thick
darkness.
13 I have surely built thee a house to
dwell in, a settled place for thee to abide
in for ever.
14 And the king turned his face about,
and blessed all the congregation of Ĭṣ′-
rā-ĕl: and all the congregation of Ĭṣ′rā-ĕl
stood;
15 And he said, Blessed *be* the LORD
God of Ĭṣ′rā-ĕl, which spake with his
mouth unto David my father, and hath
with his hand fulfilled *it,* saying,
16 Since the day that I brought forth
my people Ĭṣ′rā-ĕl out of Egypt, I chose
no city out of all the tribes of Ĭṣ′rā-ĕl to
build a house, that my name might be
therein; but I chose David to be over
my people Ĭṣ′rā-ĕl.
17 And it was in the heart of David my
father to build a house for the name of
the LORD God of Ĭṣ′rā-ĕl.
18 And the LORD said unto David my
father, Whereas it was in thine heart to
build a house unto my name, thou didst
well that it was in thine heart.
19 Nevertheless thou shalt not build
the house; but thy son that shall come
forth out of thy loins, he shall build the
house unto my name.
20 And the LORD hath performed his
word that he spake, and I am risen up
in the room of David my father, and sit
on the throne of Ĭṣ′rā-ĕl, as the LORD
promised, and have built a house for the
name of the LORD God of Ĭṣ′rā-ĕl.
21 And I have set there a place for the
ark, wherein *is* the covenant of the
LORD, which he made with our fathers,
when he brought them out of the land
of Egypt.
22 ℂ And Solomon stood before the
altar of the LORD in the presence of all
the congregation of Ĭṣ′rā-ĕl, and spread
forth his hands toward heaven:
23 And he said, LORD God of Ĭṣ′rā-ĕl,
there is no God like thee, in heaven
above, or on earth beneath, who keepest
covenant and mercy with thy servants
that walk before thee with all their heart:
24 Who hast kept with thy servant
David my father that thou promisedst
him: thou spakest also with thy mouth,
and hast fulfilled *it* with thine hand, as
it is this day.
25 Therefore now, LORD God of Ĭṣ′rā-ĕl,
keep with thy servant David my father
that thou promisedst him, saying, There
shall not fail thee a man in my sight to
sit on the throne of Ĭṣ′rā-ĕl; so that thy
children take heed to their way, that
they walk before me as thou hast
walked before me.
26 And now, O God of Ĭṣ′rā-ĕl, let thy
word, I pray thee, be verified, which thou
spakest unto thy servant David my father.
27 But will God indeed dwell on the
earth? behold, the heaven and heaven
of heavens cannot contain thee; how
much less this house that I have builded?
28 Yet have thou respect unto the
prayer of thy servant, and to his supplication, O LORD my God, to hearken
unto the cry and to the prayer, which
thy servant prayeth before thee to-day:
29 That thine eyes may be open toward
this house night and day, *even* toward
the place of which thou hast said, My
name shall be there: that thou mayest
hearken unto the prayer which thy servant shall make toward this place.
30 And hearken thou to the supplication of thy servant, and of thy people
Ĭṣ′rā-ĕl, when they shall pray toward
this place: and hear thou in heaven thy
dwelling place: and when thou hearest,
forgive.
31 ℂ If any man trespass against his
neighbor, and an oath be laid upon him
to cause him to swear, and the oath
come before thine altar in this house:
32 Then hear thou in heaven, and do,
and judge thy servants, condemning the
wicked, to bring his way upon his head;
and justifying the righteous, to give him
according to his righteousness.
33 ℂ When thy people Ĭṣ′rā-ĕl be smitten down before the enemy, because
they have sinned against thee, and shall
turn again to thee, and confess thy
name, and pray, and make supplication
unto thee in this house:
34 Then hear thou in heaven, and forgive the sin of thy people Ĭṣ′rā-ĕl, and
bring them again unto the land which
thou gavest unto their fathers.

35 ¶ When heaven is shut up, and
there is no rain, because they have
sinned against thee; if they pray toward
this place, and confess thy name, and
turn from their sin, when thou afflictest
them:
36 Then hear thou in heaven, and forgive the sin of thy servants, and of thy
people Ĭs'rā-ĕl, that thou teach them the
good way wherein they should walk, and
give rain upon thy land, which thou hast
given to thy people for an inheritance.
37 ¶ If there be in the land famine, if
there be pestilence, blasting, mildew,
locust, *or* if there be caterpillar; if their
enemy besiege them in the land of their
cities; whatsoever plague, whatsoever
sickness *there be;*
38 What prayer and supplication soever
be *made* by any man, *or* by all thy people
Ĭs'rā-ĕl, which shall know every man the
plague of his own heart, and spread forth
his hands toward this house:
39 Then hear thou in heaven thy dwelling place, and forgive, and do, and give
to every man according to his ways,
whose heart thou knowest; (for thou,
even thou only, knowest the hearts of
all the children of men;)
40 That they may fear thee all the days
that they live in the land which thou
gavest unto our fathers.
41 Moreover concerning a stranger,
that *is* not of thy people Ĭs'rā-ĕl, but
cometh out of a far country for thy
name's sake;
42 (For they shall hear of thy great
name, and of thy strong hand, and of
thy stretched out arm;) when he shall
come and pray toward this house:
43 Hear thou in heaven thy dwelling
place, and do according to all that the
stranger calleth to thee for: that all people of the earth may know thy name, to
fear thee, as *do* thy people Ĭs'rā-ĕl; and
that they may know that this house,
which I have builded, is called by thy
name.
44 ¶ If thy people go out to battle
against their enemy, whithersoever thou
shalt send them, and shall pray unto the
LORD toward the city which thou hast
chosen, and *toward* the house that I
have built for thy name:
45 Then hear thou in heaven their
prayer and their supplication, and maintain their cause.
46 If they sin against thee, (for *there is*
no man that sinneth not,) and thou be
angry with them, and deliver them to
the enemy, so that they carry them away
captives unto the land of the enemy, far
or near;
47 *Yet* if they shall bethink themselves
in the land whither they were carried
captives, and repent, and make supplication unto thee in the land of them
that carried them captives saying, We
have sinned, and have done perversely,
we have committed wickedness;
48 And *so* return unto thee with all
their heart, and with all their soul, in
the land of their enemies, which led
them away captive, and pray unto thee
toward their land, which thou gavest
unto their fathers, the city which thou
hast chosen, and the house which I have
built for thy name:
49 Then hear thou their prayer and
their supplication in heaven thy dwelling place, and maintain their cause,
50 And forgive thy people that have
sinned against thee, and all their transgressions wherein they have transgressed against thee, and give them
compassion before them who carried
them captive, that they may have compassion on them:
51 For they *be* thy people, and thine
inheritance, which thou broughtest forth
out of Egypt, from the midst of the furnace of iron:
52 That thine eyes may be open unto
the supplication of thy servant, and unto
the supplication of thy people Ĭs'rā-ĕl,
to hearken unto them in all that they
call for unto thee.
53 For thou didst separate them from
among all the people of the earth, *to be*
thine inheritance, as thou spakest by
the hand of Moses thy servant, when
thou broughtest our fathers out of
Egypt, O Lord GOD.
54 And it was *so*, that when Solomon
had made an end of praying all this
prayer and supplication unto the LORD,
he arose from before the altar of the
LORD, from kneeling on his knees with
his hands spread up to heaven.
55 And he stood, and blessed all the
congregation of Ĭs'rā-ĕl with a loud
voice, saying,
56 Blessed *be* the LORD, that hath given
rest unto his people Ĭs'rā-ĕl, according
to all that he promised: there hath not
failed one word of all his good promise,

which he promised by the hand of Moses his servant.

57 The LORD our God be with us, as he was with our fathers: let him not leave us, nor forsake us:

58 That he may incline our hearts unto him, to walk in all his ways, and to keep his commandments, and his statutes, and his judgments, which he commanded our fathers.

59 And let these my words, wherewith I have made supplication before the LORD, be nigh unto the LORD our God day and night, that he maintain the cause of his servant, and the cause of his people Ĭṣ′rā-ĕl at all times, as the matter shall require:

60 That all the people of the earth may know that the LORD *is* God, *and that there is* none else.

61 Let your heart therefore be perfect with the LORD our God, to walk in his statutes, and to keep his commandments, as at this day.

62 ¶ And the king, and all Ĭṣ′rā-ĕl with him, offered sacrifice before the LORD.

63 And Solomon offered a sacrifice of peace offerings, which he offered unto the LORD, two and twenty thousand oxen, and a hundred and twenty thousand sheep. So the king and all the children of Ĭṣ′rā-ĕl dedicated the house of the LORD.

64 The same day did the king hallow the middle of the court that *was* before the house of the LORD: for there he offered burnt offerings, and meat offerings, and the fat of the peace offerings: because the brazen altar that *was* before the LORD *was* too little to receive the burn offerings, and meat offerings, and the fat of the peace offerings.

65 And at that time Solomon held a feast, and all Ĭṣ′rā-ĕl with him, a great congregation, from the entering in of Hā′măth unto the river of Egypt, before the LORD our God, seven days and seven days, *even* fourteen days.

66 On the eighth day he sent the people away: and they blessed the king, and went unto their tents joyful and glad of heart for all the goodness that the LORD had done for David his servant, and for Ĭṣ′rā-ĕl his people.

CHAPTER 9

AND it came to pass, when Solomon had finished the building of the house of the LORD, and the king's house, and all Solomon's desire which he was pleased to do,

2 That the LORD appeared to Solomon the second time, as he had appeared unto him at Gĭb′ē-ŏn.

3 And the LORD said unto him, I have heard thy prayer and thy supplication, that thou hast made before me: I have hallowed this house, which thou hast built, to put my name there for ever; and mine eyes and mine heart shall be there perpetually.

4 And if thou wilt walk before me, as David thy father walked, in integrity of heart, and in uprightness, to do according to all that I have commanded thee, *and* wilt keep my statutes and my judgments;

5 Then I will establish the throne of thy kingdom upon Ĭṣ′rā-ĕl for ever, as I promised to David thy father, saying, There shall not fail thee a man upon the throne of Ĭṣ′rā-ĕl.

6 *But* if ye shall at all turn from following me, ye or your children, and will not keep my commandments *and* my statutes which I have set before you, but go and serve other gods, and worship them;

7 Then will I cut off Ĭṣ′rā-ĕl out of the land which I have given them; and this house, which I have hallowed for my name, will I cast out of my sight; and Ĭṣ′rā-ĕl shall be a proverb and a byword among all people:

8 And at this house, *which* is high, every one that passeth by it shall be astonished, and shall hiss; and they shall say, Why hath the LORD done thus unto this land, and to this house?

9 And they shall answer, Because they forsook the LORD their God, who brought forth their fathers out of the land of Egypt, and have taken hold upon other gods, and have worshipped them, and served them: therefore hath the LORD brought upon them all this evil.

10 ¶ And it came to pass at the end of twenty years, when Solomon had built the two houses, the house of the LORD, and the king's house,

11 (*Now* Hiram the king of Tȳre had furnished Solomon with cedar trees and fir trees, and with gold, according to all his desire,) that then king Solomon gave Hiram twenty cities in the land of Galilee.

12 And Hiram came out from Tȳre to

see the cities which Solomon had given
him; and they pleased him not.
13 And he said, What cities *are* these
which thou hast given me, my brother?
And he called them the land of Cā'bŭl
unto this day.
14 And Hiram sent to the king sixscore
talents of gold.
15 ¶ And this *is* the reason of the levy
which king Solomon raised; for to build
the house of the LORD, and his own
house, and Mĭl'lō, and the wall of Jerusalem, and Hā'zŏr, and Mē-gĭd'dō, and
Gē'zēr.
16 *For* Phā'raōh king of Egypt had gone
up, and taken Gē'zēr, and burnt it with
fire, and slain the Cā'năan-ītes that
dwelt in the city, and given it *for* a present unto his daughter, Solomon's wife.
17 And Solomon built Gē'zēr, and
Bĕth'-hō'rŏn the nether.
18 And Bā'ăl-ăth, and Tăd'mŏr in the
wilderness, in the land,
19 And all the cities of store that Solomon had, and cities for his chariots, and
cities for his horsemen, and that which
Solomon desired to build in Jerusalem,
and in Lebanon, and in all the land of
his dominion.
20 *And* all the people *that were* left of
the Ăm'ō-rītes, Hĭt'tītes, Pĕr'ĭz-zītes,
Hī'vītes, and Jĕb'ū-ṣītes, which *were*
not of the children of Ĭṣ'rā-ĕl,
21 Their children that were left after
them in the land, whom the children of
Ĭṣ'rā-ĕl also were not able utterly to destroy, upon those did Solomon levy a
tribute of bondservice unto this day.
22 But of the children of Ĭṣ'rā-ĕl did
Solomon make no bondmen: but they
were men of war, and his servants, and
his princes, and his captains, and rulers
of his chariots, and his horsemen.
23 These *were* the chief of the officers
that *were* over Solomon's work, five hundred and fifty, which bare rule over the
people that wrought in the work.
24 ¶ But Phā'raōh's daughter came up
out of the city of David unto her house
which *Solomon* had built for her: then
did he build Mĭl'lō.
25 ¶ And three times in a year did
Solomon offer burnt offerings and peace
offerings upon the altar which he built
unto the LORD, and he burnt incense
upon the altar that *was* before the LORD.
So he finished the house.
26 ¶ And king Solomon made a navy
of ships in Ē'zĭ-ŏn-gē'bĕr, which *is*
beside Ē'lŏth, on the shore of the Red
sea, in the land of Ē'dŏm.
27 And Hiram sent in the navy his
servants, shipmen that had knowledge
of the sea, with the servants of Solomon.
28 And they came to Ō'phīr, and
fetched from thence gold, four hundred
and twenty talents, and brought *it* to
king Solomon.

CHAPTER 10

AND when the queen of Shē'bȧ heard
of the fame of Solomon concerning
the name of the LORD, she came to
prove him with hard questions.
2 And she came to Jerusalem with a
very great train, with camels that bare
spices, and very much gold, and precious
stones: and when she was come to Solomon, she communed with him of all that
was in her heart.
3 And Solomon told her all her questions: there was not *any* thing hid from
the king, which he told her not.
4 And when the queen of Shē'bȧ had
seen all Solomon's wisdom, and the
house that he had built,
5 And the meat of his table, and the
sitting of his servants, and the attendance of his ministers, and their apparel,
and his cupbearers, and his ascent by
which he went up unto the house of the
LORD; there was no more spirit in her.
6 And she said to the king, It was a
true report that I heard in mine own land
of thy acts and of thy wisdom.
7 Howbeit I believed not the words,
until I came, and mine eyes had seen *it;*
and, behold, the half was not told me:
thy wisdom and prosperity exceedeth
the fame which I heard.
8 Happy *are* thy men, happy *are* these
thy servants, which stand continually
before thee, *and* that hear thy wisdom.
9 Blessed be the LORD thy God, which
delighted in thee, to set thee on the
throne of Ĭṣ'rā-ĕl: because the LORD
loved Ĭṣ'rā-ĕl for ever, therefore made
he thee king, to do judgment and justice.
10 And she gave the king a hundred
and twenty talents of gold, and of spices
very great store, and precious stones:
there came no more such abundance of
spices as these which the queen of
Shē'bȧ gave to king Solomon.
11 And the navy also of Hiram, that
brought gold from Ō'phīr, brought in

from Ō'phīr great plenty of almug trees,
and precious stones.
12 And the king made of the almug
trees pillars for the house of the LORD,
and for the king's house, harps also and
psalteries for singers: there came no
such almug trees, nor were seen unto
this day.
13 And king Solomon gave unto the
queen of Shē'bȧ all her desire, whatsoever she asked, besides *that* which Solomon gave her of his royal bounty. So
she turned and went to her own country, she and her servants.
14 ¶ Now the weight of gold that came
to Solomon in one year was six hundred
threescore and six talents of gold,
15 Besides *that he had* of the merchantmen, and of the traffic of the spice merchants, and of all the kings of Arabia,
and of the governors of the country.
16 ¶ And king Solomon made two
hundred targets *of* beaten gold: six hundred *shekels* of gold went to one target.
17 And *he made* three hundred shields
of beaten gold; three pounds of gold
went to one shield: and the king put
them in the house of the forest of
Lebanon.
18 ¶ Moreover, the king made a great
throne of ivory, and overlaid it with the
best gold.
19 The throne had six steps, and the
top of the throne *was* round behind: and
there were stays on either side on the
place of the seat, and two lions stood
beside the stays.
20 And twelve lions stood there on the
one side and on the other upon the six
steps: there was not the like made in
any kingdom.
21 ¶ And all king Solomon's drinking
vessels *were of* gold, and all the vessels
of the house of the forest of Lebanon
were of pure gold; none *were of* silver:
it was nothing accounted of in the days
of Solomon.
22 For the king had at sea a navy of
Thär'shĭsh with the navy of Hiram: once
in three years came the navy of Thär'-
shĭsh, bringing gold, and silver, ivory,
and apes, and peacocks.
23 So king Solomon exceeded all the
kings of the earth for riches and for
wisdom.
24 ¶ And all the earth sought to Solomon, to hear his wisdom, which God had
put in his heart.
25 And they brought every man his
present, vessels of silver, and vessels of
gold, and garments, and armor, and
spices, horses, and mules, a rate year
by year.
26 ¶ And Solomon gathered together
chariots and horsemen: and he had a
thousand and four hundred chariots, and
twelve thousand horsemen, whom he bestowed in the cities for chariots, and
with the king at Jerusalem.
27 And the king made silver *to be* in
Jerusalem as stones, and cedars made
he *to be* as the sycamore trees that *are*
in the vale, for abundance.
28 ¶ And Solomon had horses brought
out of Egypt, and linen yarn: the king's
merchants received the linen yarn at a
price.
29 And a chariot came up and went out
of Egypt for six hundred *shekels* of silver, and a horse for a hundred and fifty:
and so for all the kings of the Hĭt'tītes,
and for the kings of Syria, did they bring
them out by their means.

CHAPTER 11

BUT king Solomon loved many
strange women, together with the
daughter of Phā'raōh, women of the
Mō'ăb-ītes, Ammonites, Ē'dŏm-ītes,
Zī-dō'nĭ-ăns, *and* Hĭt'tītes;
2 Of the nations *concerning* which the
LORD said unto the children of Ĭs'ra-ël,
Ye shall not go in to them, neither shall
they come in unto you: *for* surely they
will turn away your heart after their
gods: Solomon clave unto these in
love.
3 And he had seven hundred wives,
princesses, and three hundred concubines: and his wives turned away his
heart.
4 For it came to pass, when Solomon
was old, *that* his wives turned away his
heart after other gods: and his heart was
not perfect with the LORD his God, as
was the heart of David his father.
5 For Solomon went after Ăsh'tō-rĕth
the goddess of the Zī-dō'nĭ-ăns, and
after Mĭl'cŏm the abomination of the
Ammonites.
6 And Solomon did evil in the sight of
the LORD, and went not fully after the
LORD, as *did* David his father.
7 Then did Solomon build a high place
for Chē'mŏsh, the abomination of Mō'ăb,
in the hill that *is* before Jerusalem, and

for Mō′lĕch, the abomination of the children of Ammon.
8 And likewise did he for all his strange
wives, which burnt incense and sacrificed unto their gods.
9 ¶ And the LORD was angry with
Solomon, because his heart was turned
from the LORD God of Īs̱′rā-ĕl, which
had appeared unto him twice,
10 And had commanded him concerning this thing, that he should not go after
other gods: but he kept not that which
the LORD commanded.
11 Wherefore the LORD said unto Solomon, Forasmuch as this is done of thee,
and thou hast not kept my covenant and
my statutes, which I have commanded
thee, I will surely rend the kingdom from
thee, and will give it to thy servant.
12 Notwithstanding, in thy days I will
not do it for David thy father's sake:
but I will rend it out of the hand of thy
son.
13 Howbeit I will not rend away all the
kingdom; *but* will give one tribe to thy
son for David my servant's sake, and for
Jerusalem's sake which I have chosen.
14 ¶ And the LORD stirred up an
adversary unto Solomon, Hā′dăd the
Ē′dŏm-īte: he *was* of the king's seed in
Ē′dŏm.
15 For it came to pass, when David was
in Ē′dŏm, and Jō′ăb the captain of the
host was gone up to bury the slain, after
he had smitten every male in Ē′dŏm;
16 (For six months did Jō′ăb remain
there with all Īs̱′rā-ĕl, until he had cut
off every male in Ē′dŏm:)
17 That Hā′dăd fled, he and certain
Ē′dŏm-ītes of his father's servants with
him, to go into Egypt; Hā′dăd *being* yet
a little child.
18 And they arose out of Mĭd′ĭ-ăn, and
came to Pā′răn: and they took men with
them out of Pā′răn, and they came to
Egypt, unto Phā′raōh king of Egypt;
which gave him a house, and appointed
him victuals, and gave him land.
19 And Hā′dăd found great favor in the
sight of Phā′raōh, so that he gave him to
wife the sister of his own wife, the sister
of Täh′pē-nēs̱ the queen.
20 And the sister of Täh′pē-nēs̱ bare
him Gē-nū′băth his son, whom Täh′pē-
nēs̱ weaned in Phā′raōh's house: and
Gē-nū′băth was in Phā′raōh's household among the sons of Phā′raōh.
21 And when Hā′dăd heard in Egypt
that David slept with his fathers, and
that Jō′ăb the captain of the host was
dead, Hā′dăd said to Phā′raōh, Let me
depart, that I may go to mine own
country.
22 Then Phā′raōh said unto him, But
what hast thou lacked with me, that,
behold, thou seekest to go to thine own
country? And he answered, Nothing:
howbeit let me go in any wise.
23 ¶ And God stirred him up *another*
adversary, Rē′zŏn the son of Ē-lī′ȧ-dȧh,
which fled from his lord Hăd′ăd-ē′zẽr
king of Zō′bȧh:
24 And he gathered men unto him, and
became captain over a band, when
David slew them *of Zobah:* and they
went to Damascus, and dwelt therein,
and reigned in Damascus.
25 And he was an adversary to Īs̱′rā-ĕl
all the days of Solomon, besides the mischief that Hā′dăd *did:* and he abhorred
Īs̱′rā-ĕl, and reigned over Syria.
26 ¶ And Jĕr′ō-bō′ăm the son of Nē′-
băt, an Ĕph′răth-īte of Zĕr′ē-dȧ, Solomon's servant, whose mother's name
was Zē-rụ′ȧh, a widow woman, even he
lifted up *his* hand against the king.
27 And this *was* the cause that he lifted
up *his* hand against the king: Solomon
built Mĭl′lō, *and* repaired the breaches
of the city of David his father.
28 And the man Jĕr′ō-bō′ăm *was* a
mighty man of valor: and Solomon seeing the young man that he was indus-
trious, he made him ruler over all the
charge of the house of Joseph.
29 And it came to pass at that time
when Jĕr′ō-bō′ăm went out of Jerusalem, that the prophet Ȧ-hī′jȧh the Shī′-
lō-nīte found him in the way; and he had
clad himself with a new garment; and
they two *were* alone in the field:
30 And Ȧ-hī′jȧh caught the new garment that *was* on him, and rent it *in*
twelve pieces:
31 And he said to Jĕr′ō-bō′ăm, Take
thee ten pieces: for thus saith the LORD,
the God of Īs̱′rā-ĕl, Behold, I will rend
the kingdom out of the hand of Solomon,
and will give ten tribes to thee:
32 (But he shall have one tribe for my
servant David's sake, and for Jerusalem's sake, the city which I have chosen
out of all the tribes of Īs̱′rā-ĕl:)
33 Because that they have forsaken me,
and have worshipped Ăsh′tō-rĕth the
goddess of the Zī-dō′nĭ-ăns̱, Chē′mŏsh

the god of the Mō'ăb-ītes, and Mĭl'cŏm
the god of the children of Ammon, and
have not walked in my ways, to do *that*
which is right in mine eyes, and *to keep*
my statutes and my judgments, as *did*
David his father.
34 Howbeit I will not take the whole
kingdom out of his hand: but I will make
him prince all the days of his life for
David my servant's sake, whom I chose,
because he kept my commandments and
my statutes:
35 But I will take the kingdom out of
his son's hand, and will give it unto thee,
even ten tribes.
36 And unto his son will I give one
tribe, that David my servant may have
a light alway before me in Jerusalem,
the city which I have chosen me to put
my name there.
37 And I will take thee, and thou
shalt reign according to all that thy
soul desireth, and shalt be king over
Ĭş'rā-ĕl.
38 And it shall be, if thou wilt hearken
unto all that I command thee, and wilt
walk in my ways, and do *that is* right in
my sight, to keep my statutes and my
commandments, as David my servant
did; that I will be with thee, and build
thee a sure house, as I built for David,
and will give Ĭş'rā-ĕl unto thee.
39 And I will for this afflict the seed of
David, but not for ever.
40 Solomon sought therefore to kill
Jĕr'ō-bō'ăm. And Jĕr'ō-bō'ăm arose,
and fled into Egypt, unto Shī'shăk king
of Egypt, and was in Egypt until the
death of Solomon.
41 ¶ And the rest of the acts of Solomon, and all that he did, and his wisdom, *are* they not written in the book of
the acts of Solomon?
42 And the time that Solomon reigned
in Jerusalem over all Ĭş'rā-ĕl *was* forty
years.
43 And Solomon slept with his fathers,
and was buried in the city of David his
father: and Rē'hō-bō'ăm his son reigned
in his stead.

CHAPTER 12

AND Rē'hō-bō'ăm went to Shē'chĕm:
for all Ĭş'rā-ĕl were come to Shē'-
chĕm to make him king.
2 And it came to pass, when Jĕr'ō-
bō'ăm the son of Nē'băt, who was yet
in Egypt, heard *of it*, (for he was fled
from the presence of king Solomon, and
Jĕr'ō-bō'ăm dwelt in Egypt,)
3 That they sent and called him. And
Jĕr'ō-bō'ăm and all the congregation
of Ĭş'rā-ĕl came, and spake unto Rē'-
hō-bō'ăm, saying,
4 Thy father made our yoke grievous:
now therefore make thou the grievous
service of thy father, and his heavy yoke
which he put upon us, lighter, and we
will serve thee.
5 And he said unto them, Depart yet
for three days, then come again to me.
And the people departed.
6 ¶ And king Rē'hō-bō'ăm consulted
with the old men, that stood before Solomon his father while he yet lived, and
said, How do ye advise that I may answer this people?
7 And they spake unto him, saying, If
thou wilt be a servant unto this people
this day, and wilt serve them, and answer them, and speak good words to
them, then they will be thy servants for
ever.
8 But he forsook the counsel of the old
men, which they had given him, and
consulted with the young men that were
grown up with him, *and* which stood before him:
9 And he said unto them, What counsel
give ye that we may answer this people,
who have spoken to me, saying, Make
the yoke which thy father did put upon
us lighter?
10 And the young men that were grown
up with him spake unto him, saying,
Thus shalt thou speak unto this people
that spake unto thee, saying, Thy father
made our yoke heavy, but make thou *it*
lighter unto us; thus shalt thou say unto
them, My little *finger* shall be thicker
than my father's loins.
11 And now whereas my father did lade
you with a heavy yoke, I will add to your
yoke: my father hath chastised you with
whips, but I will chastise you with scorpions.
12 ¶ So Jĕr'ō-bō'ăm and all the people
came to Rē'hō-bō'ăm the third day, as
the king had appointed, saying, Come to
me again the third day.
13 And the king answered the people
roughly, and forsook the old men's counsel that they gave him;
14 And spake to them after the counsel
of the young men, saying, My father
made your yoke heavy, and I will add to

your yoke: my father *also* chastised you with whips, but I will chastise you with scorpions.

15 Wherefore the king hearkened not unto the people; for the cause was from the LORD, that he might perform his saying, which the LORD spake by Ȧ-hī′jȧh the Shī′lō-nīte unto Jĕr′ō-bō′ăm the son of Nē′băt.

16 ℂ So when all Ĭṣ′rā-ĕl saw that the king hearkened not unto them, the people answered the king, saying, What portion have we in David? neither *have we* inheritance in the son of Jesse: to your tents, O Ĭṣ′rā-ĕl: now see to thine own house, David. So Ĭṣ′rā-ĕl departed unto their tents.

17 But *as for* the children of Ĭṣ′rā-ĕl which dwelt in the cities of Judah, Rē′hō-bō′ăm reigned over them.

18 Then king Rē′hō-bō′ăm sent Ȧ-dō′răm, who *was* over the tribute; and all Ĭṣ′rā-ĕl stoned him with stones, that he died. Therefore king Rē′hō-bō′ăm made speed to get him up to his chariot, to flee to Jerusalem.

19 So Ĭṣ′rā-ĕl rebelled against the house of David unto this day.

20 And it came to pass, when all Ĭṣ′rā-ĕl heard that Jĕr′ō-bō′ăm was come again, that they sent and called him unto the congregation, and made him king over all Ĭṣ′rā-ĕl: there was none that followed the house of David, but the tribe of Judah only.

21 ℂ And when Rē′hō-bō′ăm was come to Jerusalem, he assembled all the house of Judah, with the tribe of Benjamin, a hundred and fourscore thousand chosen men, which were warriors, to fight against the house of Ĭṣ′rā-ĕl, to bring the kingdom again to Rē′hō-bō′ăm the son of Solomon.

22 But the word of God came unto Shē-mā′ịah the man of God, saying,

23 Speak unto Rē′hō-bō′ăm, the son of Solomon, king of Judah, and unto all the house of Judah and Benjamin, and to the remnant of the people, saying,

24 Thus saith the LORD, Ye shall not go up, nor fight against your brethren the children of Ĭṣ′rā-ĕl: return every man to his house; for this thing is from me. They hearkened therefore to the word of the LORD, and returned to depart, according to the word of the LORD.

25 ℂ Then Jĕr′ō-bō′ăm built Shē′chĕm in mount Ē′phrā-ĭm, and dwelt therein; and went out from thence, and built Pē-nū′ĕl.

26 And Jĕr′ō-bō′ăm said in his heart, Now shall the kingdom return to the house of David:

27 If this people go up to do sacrifice in the house of the LORD at Jerusalem, then shall the heart of this people turn again unto their lord, *even* unto Rē′hō-bō′ăm king of Judah, and they shall kill me, and go again to Rē′hō-bō′ăm king of Judah.

28 Whereupon the king took counsel, and made two calves *of* gold, and said unto them, It is too much for you to go up to Jerusalem: behold thy gods, O Ĭṣ′rā-ĕl, which brought thee up out of the land of Egypt.

29 And he set the one in Beth-el, and the other put he in Dan.

30 And this thing became a sin: for the people went *to worship* before the one, *even* unto Dan.

31 And he made a house of high places, and made priests of the lowest of the people, which were not of the sons of Levi.

32 And Jĕr′ō-bō′ăm ordained a feast in the eighth month, on the fifteenth day of the month, like unto the feast that *is* in Judah, and he offered upon the altar. So did he in Beth-el, sacrificing unto the calves that he had made: and he placed in Beth-el the priests of the high places which he had made.

33 So he offered upon the altar which he had made in Beth-el the fifteenth day of the eighth month, *even* in the month which he had devised of his own heart; and ordained a feast unto the children of Ĭṣ′rā-ĕl: and he offered upon the altar, and burnt incense.

CHAPTER 13

AND, behold, there came a man of God out of Judah by the word of the LORD unto Beth-el: and Jĕr′ō-bō′ăm stood by the altar to burn incense.

2 And he cried against the altar in the word of the LORD, and said, O altar, altar, thus saith the LORD; Behold, a child shall be born unto the house of David, Jō-sī′ȧh by name; and upon thee shall he offer the priests of the high places that burn incense upon thee, and men's bones shall be burnt upon thee.

3 And he gave a sign the same day, saying, This *is* the sign which the LORD

hath spoken; Behold, the altar shall be
rent, and the ashes that *are* upon it shall
be poured out.
4 And it came to pass, when king Jĕr′ō-
bō′ăm heard the saying of the man of
God, which had cried against the altar
in Beth-el, that he put forth his hand
from the altar, saying, Lay hold on him.
And his hand, which he put forth against
him, dried up, so that he could not pull
it in again to him.
5 The altar also was rent, and the ashes
poured out from the altar, according to
the sign which the man of God had given
by the word of the LORD.
6 And the king answered and said unto
the man of God, Entreat now the face of
the LORD thy God, and pray for me, that
my hand may be restored me again. And
the man of God besought the LORD, and
the king's hand was restored him again,
and became as *it was* before.
7 And the king said unto the man of
God, Come home with me, and refresh
thyself, and I will give thee a reward.
8 And the man of God said unto the
king, If thou wilt give me half thine
house, I will not go in with thee, neither
will I eat bread nor drink water in this
place:
9 For so was it charged me by the word
of the LORD, saying, Eat no bread, nor
drink water, nor turn again by the same
way that thou camest.
10 So he went another way, and returned not by the way that he came to
Beth-el.
11 ¶ Now there dwelt an old prophet
in Beth-el; and his sons came and told
him all the works that the man of God
had done that day in Beth-el: the words
which he had spoken unto the king,
them they told also to their father.
12 And their father said unto them,
What way went he? For his sons had
seen what way the man of God went,
which came from Judah.
13 And he said unto his sons, Saddle
me the ass. So they saddled him the
ass: and he rode thereon,
14 And went after the man of God, and
found him sitting under an oak: and he
said unto him, *Art* thou the man of God
that camest from Judah? And he said,
I *am*.
15 Then he said unto him, Come home
with me, and eat bread.
16 And he said, I may not return with
thee, nor go in with thee: neither will I
eat bread nor drink water with thee in
this place:
17 For it was said to me by the word
of the LORD, Thou shalt eat no bread
nor drink water there, nor turn again to
go by the way thou camest.
18 He said unto him, I *am* a prophet
also as thou *art;* and an angel spake unto
me by the word of the LORD, saying,
Bring him back with thee into thine
house, that he may eat bread and drink
water. *But* he lied unto him.
19 So he went back with him, and did
eat bread in his house, and drank water.
20 ¶ And it came to pass, as they sat
at the table, that the word of the LORD
came unto the prophet that brought him
back:
21 And he cried unto the man of God
that came from Judah, saying, Thus
saith the LORD, Forasmuch as thou hast
disobeyed the mouth of the LORD, and
hast not kept the commandment which
the LORD thy God commanded thee,
22 But camest back, and hast eaten
bread and drunk water in the place, of
the which *the LORD* did say to thee, Eat
no bread, and drink no water; thy carcass shall not come unto the sepulchre
of thy fathers.
23 ¶ And it came to pass, after he had
eaten bread, and after he had drunk,
that he saddled for him the ass, *to wit,*
for the prophet whom he had brought
back.
24 And when he was gone, a lion met
him by the way, and slew him: and his
carcass was cast in the way, and the ass
stood by it, the lion also stood by the
carcass.
25 And, behold, men passed by, and
saw the carcass cast in the way, and the
lion standing by the carcass: and they
came and told *it* in the city where the
old prophet dwelt.
26 And when the prophet that brought
him back from the way heard *thereof,*
he said, It *is* the man of God, who was
disobedient unto the word of the LORD:
therefore the LORD hath delivered him
unto the lion, which hath torn him, and
slain him, according to the word of the
LORD, which he spake unto him.
27 And he spake to his sons, saying,
Saddle me the ass. And they saddled
him.
28 And he went and found his carcass

cast in the way, and the ass and the lion standing by the carcass: the lion had not eaten the carcass, nor torn the ass.

29 And the prophet took up the carcass of the man of God, and laid it upon the ass, and brought it back: and the old prophet came to the city, to mourn and to bury him.

30 And he laid his carcass in his own grave; and they mourned over him, *saying,* Alas, my brother!

31 And *it* came to pass, after he had buried him, that he spake to his sons, saying, When I am dead, then bury me in the sepulchre wherein the man of God *is* buried; lay my bones beside his bones:

32 For the saying which he cried by the word of the LORD against the altar in Beth-el, and against all the houses of the high places which *are* in the cities of Sȧ-mā′rĭ-ȧ, shall surely come to pass.

33 ¶ After this thing Jĕr′ō-bō′ăm returned not from his evil way, but made again of the lowest of the people priests of the high places: whosoever would, he consecrated him, and he became *one* of the priests of the high places.

34 And this thing became sin unto the house of Jĕr′ō-bō′ăm, even to cut *it* off, and to destroy *it* from off the face of the earth.

CHAPTER 14

AT that time Ȧ-bī′jȧh the son of Jĕr′ō-bō′ăm fell sick.

2 And Jĕr′ō-bō′ăm said to his wife, Arise, I pray thee, and disguise thyself, that thou be not known to be the wife of Jĕr′ō-bō′ăm; and get thee to Shī′lōh: behold, there *is* Ȧ-hī′jȧh the prophet, which told me that *I should be* king over this people.

3 And take with thee ten loaves, and cracknels, and a cruse of honey, and go to him: he shall tell thee what shall become of the child.

4 And Jĕr′ō-bō′ăm's wife did so, and arose, and went to Shī′lōh, and came to the house of Ȧ-hī′jȧh. But Ȧ-hī′jȧh could not see; for his eyes were set by reason of his age.

5 ¶ And the LORD said unto Ȧ-hī′jȧh, Behold, the wife of Jĕr′ō-bō′ăm cometh to ask a thing of thee for her son; for he *is* sick: thus and thus shalt thou say unto her: for it shall be, when she cometh in, that she shall feign herself *to be* another *woman.*

6 And it was *so,* when Ȧ-hī′jȧh heard the sound of her feet, as she came in at the door, that he said, Come in, thou wife of Jĕr′ō-bō′ăm; why feignest thou thyself *to be* another? for I *am* sent to thee *with* heavy *tidings.*

7 Go, tell Jĕr′ō-bō′ăm, Thus saith the LORD God of Ĭş′rā-ĕl, Forasmuch as I exalted thee from among the people, and made thee prince over my people Ĭş′rā-ĕl,

8 And rent the kingdom away from the house of David, and gave it thee: and *yet* thou hast not been as my servant David, who kept my commandments, and who followed me with all his heart, to do *that* only *which was* right in mine eyes;

9 But hast done evil above all that were before thee: for thou hast gone and made thee other gods, and molten images, to provoke me to anger, and hast cast me behind thy back:

10 Therefore, behold, I will bring evil upon the house of Jĕr′ō-bō′ăm, and will cut off from Jĕr′ō-bō′ăm him that pisseth against the wall, *and* him that is shut up and left in Ĭş′rā-ĕl, and will take away the remnant of the house of Jĕr′ō-bō′ăm, as a man taketh away dung, till it be all gone.

11 Him that dieth of Jĕr′ō-bō′ăm in the city shall the dogs eat; and him that dieth in the field shall the fowls of the air eat: for the LORD hath spoken *it.*

12 Arise thou therefore, get thee to thine own house: *and* when thy feet enter into the city, the child shall die.

13 And all Ĭş′rā-ĕl shall mourn for him, and bury him: for he only of Jĕr′ō-bō′ăm shall come to the grave, because in him there is found *some* good thing toward the LORD God of Ĭş′rā-ĕl in the house of Jĕr′ō-bō′ăm.

14 Moreover the LORD shall raise him up a king over Ĭş′rā-ĕl, who shall cut off the house of Jĕr′ō-bō′ăm that day: but what? even now.

15 For the LORD shall smite Ĭş′rā-ĕl, as a reed is shaken in the water, and he shall root up Ĭş′rā-ĕl out of this good land, which he gave to their fathers, and shall scatter them beyond the river, because they have made their groves, provoking the LORD to anger.

16 And he shall give Ĭş′rā-ĕl up because of the sins of Jĕr′ō-bō′ăm, who did sin, and who made Ĭş′rā-ĕl to sin.

17 ¶ And Jĕr′ō-bō′ăm's wife arose,
and departed, and came to Tĭr′zȧh: *and*
when she came to the threshold of the
door, the child died;
18 And they buried him; and all
Ĭş′rā-ĕl mourned for him, according to
the word of the LORD, which he spake
by the hand of his servant Ȧ-hī′jȧh the
prophet.
19 And the rest of the acts of Jĕr′ō-
bō′ăm, how he warred, and how he
reigned, behold, they *are* written in the
book of the Chronicles of the kings of
Ĭş′rā-ĕl.
20 And the days which Jĕr′ō-bō′ăm
reigned *were* two and twenty years: and
he slept with his fathers, and Nā′dăb
his son reigned in his stead.
21 ¶ And Rē′hō-bō′ăm the son of Solomon reigned in Judah. Rē′hō-bō′ăm
was forty and one years old when he
began to reign, and he reigned seventeen years in Jerusalem, the city which
the LORD did choose out of all the tribes
of Ĭş′rā-ĕl, to put his name there. And
his mother's name *was* Nā′ȧ-mȧh an
Ăm′mŏn-īt′ĕss.
22 And Judah did evil in the sight of
the LORD, and they provoked him to
jealousy with their sins which they had
committed, above all that their fathers
had done.
23 For they also built them high places,
and images, and groves, on every high
hill, and under every green tree.
24 And there were also sodomites in
the land: *and* they did according to all
the abominations of the nations which
the LORD cast out before the children
of Ĭş′rā-ĕl.
25 ¶ And it came to pass in the fifth
year of king Rē′hō-bō′ăm, *that* Shī′shăk
king of Egypt came up against Jerusalem:
26 And he took away the treasures of
the house of the LORD, and the treasures
of the king's house; he even took away
all: and he took away all the shields of
gold which Solomon had made.
27 And king Rē′hō-bō′ăm made in
their stead brazen shields, and committed *them* unto the hands of the chief
of the guard, which kept the door of the
king's house.
28 And it was *so*, when the king went
into the house of the LORD, that the
guard bare them, and brought them back
into the guard chamber.
29 ¶ Now the rest of the acts of Rē′-
hō-bō′ăm, and all that he did, *are* they
not written in the book of the Chronicles
of the kings of Judah?
30 And there was war between Rē′-
hō-bō′ăm and Jĕr′ō-bō′ăm all *their*
days.
31 And Rē′hō-bō′ăm slept with his
fathers, and was buried with his fathers
in the city of David. And his mother's
name *was* Nā′ȧ-mȧh an Ăm′mŏn-īt′ĕss.
And Ȧ-bī′jăm his son reigned in his
stead.

CHAPTER 15

NOW in the eighteenth year of king
Jĕr′ō-bō′ăm the son of Nē′băt
reigned Ȧ-bī′jăm over Judah.
2 Three years reigned he in Jerusalem.
And his mother's name *was* Mā′ȧ-chȧh,
the daughter of Ȧ-bĭsh′ȧ-lŏm.
3 And he walked in all the sins of his
father, which he had done before him:
and his heart was not perfect with the
LORD his God, as the heart of David
his father.
4 Nevertheless for David's sake did
the LORD his God give him a lamp in
Jerusalem, to set up his son after him,
and to establish Jerusalem:
5 Because David did *that which was*
right in the eyes of the LORD, and turned
not aside from any *thing* that he commanded him all the days of his life, save
only in the matter of Ū-rī′ȧh the Hĭt′-
tīte.
6 And there was war between Rē′hō-
bō′ăm and Jĕr′ō-bō′ăm all the days of
his life.
7 Now the rest of the acts of Ȧ-bī′jăm,
and all that he did, *are* they not written
in the book of the Chronicles of the
kings of Judah? And there was war between Ȧ-bī′jăm and Jĕr′ō-bō′ăm.
8 And Ȧ-bī′jăm slept with his fathers;
and they buried him in the city of David:
and Ā′sȧ his son reigned in his stead.
9 ¶ And in the twentieth year of Jĕr′ō-
bō′ăm king of Ĭş′rā-ĕl reigned Ā′sȧ
over Judah.
10 And forty and one years reigned he
in Jerusalem. And his mother's name
was Mā′ȧ-chȧh, the daughter of Ȧ-bĭsh′-
ȧ-lŏm.
11 And Ā′sȧ did *that which was* right
in the eyes of the LORD, as *did* David his
father.
12 And he took away the sodomites out

of the land, and removed all the idols
that his fathers had made.
13 And also Mā'ȧ-chȧh his mother,
even her he removed from *being* queen,
because she had made an idol in a grove;
and Ā'sȧ destroyed her idol, and burnt
it by the brook Kĭd'rŏn.
14 But the high places were not removed: nevertheless Ā'sȧ's heart was
perfect with the LORD all his days.
15 And he brought in the things which
his father had dedicated, and the things
which himself had dedicated, into the
house of the LORD, silver, and gold, and
vessels.
16 ¶ And there was war between Ā'sȧ
and Bā'ȧ-shȧ king of Ĭş'rā-ĕl all their
days.
17 And Bā'ȧ-shȧ king of Ĭş'rā-ĕl went
up against Judah, and built Rā'mȧh, that
he might not suffer any to go out or
come in to Ā'sȧ king of Judah.
18 Then Ā'sȧ took all the silver and the
gold *that were* left in the treasures of
the house of the LORD, and the treasures
of the king's house, and delivered them
into the hand of his servants: and king
Ā'sȧ sent them to Bĕn'-hā'dăd, the
son of Tăb'rĭ-mŏn, the son of Hē'zĭ-ŏn,
king of Syria, that dwelt at Damascus,
saying,
19 *There is* a league between me and
thee, *and* between my father and thy
father: behold, I have sent unto thee a
present of silver and gold; come and
break thy league with Bā'ȧ-shȧ king of
Ĭş'rā-ĕl, that he may depart from me.
20 So Bĕn'-hā'dăd hearkened unto
king Ā'sȧ, and sent the captains of the
hosts which he had against the cities of
Ĭş'rā-ĕl, and smote Ī'jŏn, and Dan, and
Ā'bĕl-bĕth-mā'ȧ-chȧh, and all Çĭn'-
nē-rŏth, with all the land of Năph'tȧ-lī.
21 And it came to pass, when Bā'ȧ-shȧ
heard *thereof*, that he left off building
of Rā'mȧh, and dwelt in Tĭr'zȧh.
22 Then king Ā'sȧ made a proclamation throughout all Judah; none *was*
exempted: and they took away the
stones of Rā'mȧh, and the timber thereof, wherewith Bā'ȧ-shȧ had builded;
and king Ā'sȧ built with them Gē'bȧ
of Benjamin, and Mĭz'päh.
23 The rest of all the acts of Ā'sȧ, and
all his might, and all that he did, and
the cities which he built, *are* they not
written in the book of the Chronicles of
the kings of Judah? Nevertheless in the
time of his old age he was diseased in
his feet.
24 And Ā'sȧ slept with his fathers, and
was buried with his fathers in the city
of David his father: and Jē-hŏsh'ȧ-phăt
his son reigned in his stead.
25 ¶ And Nā'dăb the son of Jĕr'ō-
bō'ăm began to reign over Ĭş'rā-ĕl in the
second year of Ā'sȧ king of Judah, and
reigned over Ĭş'rā-ĕl two years.
26 And he did evil in the sight of the
LORD, and walked in the way of his
father, and in his sin wherewith he
made Ĭş'rā-ĕl to sin.
27 ¶ And Bā'ȧ-shȧ the son of Ȧ-hī'jȧh,
of the house of Ĭs'sȧ-chär, conspired
against him; and Bā'ȧ-shȧ smote him at
Gĭb'bē-thŏn, which *belonged* to the
Phĭ-lĭs'tĭneş; for Nā'dăb and all Ĭş'rā-ĕl
laid siege to Gĭb'bē-thŏn.
28 Even in the third year of Ā'sȧ king of
Judah did Bā'ȧ-shȧ slay him, and
reigned in his stead.
29 And it came to pass, when he
reigned, *that* he smote all the house of
Jĕr'ō-bō'ăm; he left not to Jĕr'ō-bō'ăm
any that breathed, until he had destroyed him, according unto the saying
of the LORD, which he spake by his
servant Ȧ-hī'jȧh the Shī'lō-nīte:
30 Because of the sins of Jĕr'ō-bō'ăm
which he sinned, and which he made
Ĭş'rā-ĕl sin, by his provocation wherewith he provoked the LORD God of
Ĭş'rā-ĕl to anger.
31 ¶ Now the rest of the acts of Nā'-
dăb, and all that he did, *are* they not
written in the book of the Chronicles of
the kings of Ĭş'rā-ĕl?
32 And there was war between Ā'sȧ
and Bā'ȧ-shȧ king of Ĭş'rā-ĕl all their
days.
33 In the third year of Ā'sȧ king of
Judah began Bā'ȧ-shȧ the son of Ȧ-hī'-
jȧh to reign over all Ĭş'rā-ĕl in Tĭr'zȧh,
twenty and four years.
34 And he did evil in the sight of the
LORD, and walked in the way of Jĕr'ō-
bō'ăm, and in his sin wherewith he
made Ĭş'rā-ĕl to sin.

CHAPTER 16

THEN the word of the LORD came to
Jē'hū the son of Hȧ-nā'nī against
Bā'ȧ-shȧ, saying,
2 Forasmuch as I exalted thee out of
the dust, and made thee prince over my
people Ĭş'rā-ĕl; and thou hast walked

in the way of Jĕr′ō-bō′ăm, and hast
made my people Ĭs′rā-ĕl to sin, to provoke me to anger with their sins;
3 Behold, I will take away the posterity
of Bā′ȧ-shȧ, and the posterity of his
house; and will make thy house like
the house of Jĕr′ō-bō′ăm the son of
Nē′băt.
4 Him that dieth of Bā′ȧ-shȧ in the
city shall the dogs eat; and him that
dieth of his in the fields shall the fowls
of the air eat.
5 Now the rest of the acts of Bā′ȧ-shȧ,
and what he did, and his might, *are* they
not written in the book of the Chronicles
of the kings of Ĭs′rā-ĕl?
6 So Bā′ȧ-shȧ slept with his fathers,
and was buried in Tĭr′zȧh: and Ē′lȧh his
son reigned in his stead.
7 And also by the hand of the prophet
Jē′hū the son of Hȧ-nā′nī came the
word of the LORD against Bā′ȧ-shȧ, and
against his house, even for all the evil
that he did in the sight of the LORD, in
provoking him to anger with the work
of his hands, in being like the house
of Jĕr′ō-bō′ăm; and because he killed
him.
8 ¶ In the twenty and sixth year of
Ā′sȧ king of Judah began Ē′lȧh the son
of Bā′ȧ-shȧ to reign over Ĭs′rā-ĕl in
Tĭr′zȧh, two years.
9 And his servant Zĭm′rī, captain of
half *his* chariots, conspired against him,
as he was in Tĭr′zȧh, drinking himself
drunk in the house of Är′zȧ steward of
his house in Tĭr′zȧh.
10 And Zĭm′rī went in and smote him,
and killed him, in the twenty and seventh year of Ā′sȧ king of Judah, and
reigned in his stead.
11 ¶ And it came to pass, when he
began to reign, as soon as he sat on his
throne, *that* he slew all the house of
Bā′ȧ-shȧ: he left him not one that pisseth against a wall, neither of his kinsfolk, nor of his friends.
12 Thus did Zĭm′rī destroy all the house
of Bā′ȧ-shȧ, according to the word of the
LORD, which he spake against Bā′ȧ-shȧ
by Jē′hū the prophet,
13 For all the sins of Bā′ȧ-shȧ, and the
sins of Ē′lȧh his son, by which they
sinned, and by which they made Ĭs′rā-ĕl
to sin, in provoking the LORD God of
Ĭs′rā-ĕl to anger with their vanities.
14 Now the rest of the acts of Ē′lȧh,
and all that he did, *are* they not written
in the book of the Chronicles of the kings
of Ĭs′rā-ĕl?
15 ¶ In the twenty and seventh year
of Ā′sȧ king of Judah did Zĭm′rī reign
seven days in Tĭr′zȧh. And the people
were encamped against Gĭb′bē-thŏn,
which *belonged* to the Phĭ-lĭs′tīneș.
16 And the people *that were* encamped
heard say, Zĭm′rī hath conspired, and
hath also slain the king: wherefore all
Ĭs′rā-ĕl made Ŏm′rī, the captain of the
host, king over Ĭs′rā-ĕl that day in the
camp.
17 And Ŏm′rī went up from Gĭb′bē-
thŏn, and all Ĭs′rā-ĕl with him, and they
besieged Tĭr′zȧh.
18 And it came to pass, when Zĭm′rī
saw that the city was taken, that he
went into the palace of the king's house,
and burnt the king's house over him
with fire, and died,
19 For his sins which he sinned in doing evil in the sight of the LORD, in
walking in the way of Jĕr′ō-bō′ăm, and
in his sin which he did, to make Ĭs′rā-ĕl
to sin.
20 Now the rest of the acts of Zĭm′rī,
and his treason that he wrought, *are*
they not written in the book of the
Chronicles of the kings of Ĭs′rā-ĕl?
21 ¶ Then were the people of Ĭs′rā-ĕl
divided into two parts: half of the people followed Tĭb′nī the son of Gī′năth,
to make him king; and half followed
Ŏm′rī.
22 But the people that followed Ŏm′rī
prevailed against the people that followed Tĭb′nī the son of Gī′năth: so
Tĭb′nī died, and Ŏm′rī reigned.
23 ¶ In the thirty and first year of
Ā′sȧ king of Judah began Ŏm′rī to reign
over Ĭs′rā-ĕl, twelve years: six years
reigned he in Tĭr′zȧh.
24 And he bought the hill Sȧ-mā′rĭ-ȧ of
Shē′mĕr for two talents of silver, and
built on the hill, and called the name of
the city which he built, after the name
of Shē′mĕr, owner of the hill, Sȧ-
mā′rĭ-ȧ.
25 ¶ But Ŏm′rī wrought evil in the
eyes of the LORD, and did worse than
all that *were* before him.
26 For he walked in all the way of
Jĕr′ō-bō′ăm the son of Nē′băt, and in
his sin wherewith he made Ĭs′rā-ĕl to
sin, to provoke the LORD God of Ĭs′rā-ĕl
to anger with their vanities.
27 Now the rest of the acts of Ŏm′rī

which he did, and his might that he
showed, *are* they not written in the
book of the Chronicles of the kings of
Ĭs′rā-ĕl?
28 So Ŏm′rī slept with his fathers, and
was buried in Sȧ-mā′rĭ-ȧ: and Ahab his
son reigned in his stead.
29 ¶ And in the thirty and eighth year
of Ā′sȧ king of Judah began Ahab the
son of Ŏm′rī to reign over Ĭs′rā-ĕl: and
Ahab the son of Ŏm′rī reigned over
Ĭs′rā-ĕl in Sȧ-mā′rĭ-ȧ twenty and two
years.
30 And Ahab the son of Ŏm′rī did evil
in the sight of the LORD above all that
were before him.
31 And it came to pass, as if it had been
a light thing for him to walk in the sins
of Jĕr′ō-bō′ăm the son of Nē′băt, that he
took to wife Jĕz′ē-bĕl the daughter of
Ĕth′bā′ăl king of the Zī-dō′nĭ-ăns, and
went and served Bā′ăl, and worshipped
him.
32 And he reared up an altar for Bā′ăl
in the house of Bā′ăl, which he had built
in Sȧ-mā′rĭ-ȧ.
33 And Ahab made a grove; and Ahab
did more to provoke the LORD God of
Ĭs′rā-ĕl to anger than all the kings of
Ĭs′rā-ĕl that were before him.
34 ¶ In his days did Hī′ĕl the Bĕth′-ĕl-īte build Jĕr′ĭ-chō: he laid the foundation thereof in Ȧ-bī′răm his firstborn,
and set up the gates thereof in his
youngest *son* Sē′gŭb, according to the
word of the LORD, which he spake by
Joshua the son of Nŭn.

CHAPTER 17

AND Ē-lī′jȧh the Tĭsh′bīte, *who was*
of the inhabitants of Gĭl′ē-ăd, said
unto Ahab, *As* the LORD God of Ĭs′rā-ĕl
liveth, before whom I stand, there shall
not be dew nor rain these years, but
according to my word.
2 And the word of the LORD came unto
him, saying,
3 Get thee hence, and turn thee eastward, and hide thyself by the brook
Chē′rĭth, that *is* before Jordan.
4 And it shall be, *that* thou shalt drink
of the brook; and I have commanded
the ravens to feed thee there.
5 So he went and did according unto
the word of the LORD: for he went and
dwelt by the brook Chē′rĭth, that *is* before Jordan.
6 And the ravens brought him bread
and flesh in the morning, and bread and
flesh in the evening; and he drank of the
brook.
7 And it came to pass after a while,
that the brook dried up, because there
had been no rain in the land.
8 ¶ And the word of the LORD came
unto him, saying,
9 Arise, get thee to Zăr′ē-phȧth, which
belongeth to Zī′dŏn, and dwell there:
behold, I have commanded a widow
woman there to sustain thee.
10 So he arose and went to Zăr′ē-phȧth.
And when he came to the gate of the
city, behold, the widow woman *was*
there gathering of sticks: and he called
to her, and said, Fetch me, I pray thee,
a little water in a vessel, that I may
drink.
11 And as she was going to fetch *it*, he
called to her, and said, Bring me, I pray
thee, a morsel of bread in thine hand.
12 And she said, *As* the LORD thy God
liveth, I have not a cake, but a handful
of meal in a barrel, and a little oil in a
cruse: and, behold, I *am* gathering two
sticks, that I may go in and dress it for
me and my son, that we may eat it, and
die.
13 And Ē-lī′jȧh said unto her, Fear not;
go *and* do as thou hast said: but make
me thereof a little cake first, and bring
it unto me, and after make for thee and
for thy son.
14 For thus saith the LORD God of
Ĭs′rā-ĕl, The barrel of meal shall not
waste, neither shall the cruse of oil fail,
until the day *that* the LORD sendeth
rain upon the earth.
15 And she went and did according to
the saying of Ē-lī′jȧh: and she, and he,
and her house, did eat *many* days.
16 *And* the barrel of meal wasted not,
neither did the cruse of oil fail, according to the word of the LORD, which he
spake by Ē-lī′jȧh.
17 ¶ And it came to pass after these
things, *that* the son of the woman, the
mistress of the house, fell sick; and his
sickness was so sore, that there was no
breath left in him.
18 And she said unto Ē-lī′jȧh, What
have I to do with thee, O thou man of
God? art thou come unto me to call my
sin to remembrance, and to slay my
son?
19 And he said unto her, Give me thy
son. And he took him out of her bosom,

and carried him up into a loft, where he
abode, and laid him upon his own bed.
20 And he cried unto the LORD, and
said, O LORD my God, hast thou also
brought evil upon the widow with whom
I sojourn, by slaying her son?
21 And he stretched himself upon the
child three times, and cried unto the
LORD, and said, O LORD my God, I
pray thee, let this child's soul come into
him again.
22 And the LORD heard the voice of
Ē-lī'jah; and the soul of the child came
into him again, and he revived.
23 And Ē-lī'jah took the child, and
brought him down out of the chamber
into the house, and delivered him unto
his mother: and Ē-lī'jah said, See, thy
son liveth.
24 ℭ And the woman said to Ē-lī'jah,
Now by this I know that thou *art* a man
of God, *and* that the word of the LORD
in thy mouth *is* truth.

CHAPTER 18

AND it came to pass *after* many days,
that the word of the LORD came to
Ē-lī'jah in the third year, saying, Go,
show thyself unto Ahab; and I will send
rain upon the earth.
2 And Ē-lī'jah went to show himself
unto Ahab. And *there was* a sore famine
in Sa-ma'rĭ-a.
3 And Ahab called Ō'ba-dī'ah, which
was the governor of *his* house. (Now
Ō'ba-dī'ah feared the LORD greatly:
4 For it was *so*, when Jĕz'ē-bĕl cut off
the prophets of the LORD, that Ō'ba-
dī'ah took a hundred prophets, and hid
them by fifty in a cave, and fed them
with bread and water.)
5 And Ahab said unto Ō'ba-dī'ah, Go
into the land, unto all fountains of water, and unto all brooks: peradventure
we may find grass to save the horses
and mules alive, that we lose not all the
beasts.
6 So they divided the land between
them to pass throughout it: Ahab went
one way by himself, and Ō'ba-dī'ah went
another way by himself.
7 ℭ And as Ō'ba-dī'ah was in the way,
behold, Ē-lī'jah met him: and he knew
him, and fell on his face, and said, *Art*
thou that my lord Ē-lī'jah?
8 And he answered him, I *am:* go, tell
thy lord, Behold, Ē-lī'jah *is here*.
9 And he said, What have I sinned,
that thou wouldest deliver thy servant
into the hand of Ahab, to slay me?
10 *As* the LORD thy God liveth, there
is no nation or kingdom, whither my
lord hath not sent to seek thee: and
when they said, *He is* not *there;* he took
an oath of the kingdom and nation, that
they found thee not.
11 And now thou sayest, Go, tell thy
lord, Behold, Ē-lī'jah *is here*.
12 And it shall come to pass, *as soon as*
I am gone from thee, that the Spirit of
the LORD shall carry thee whither I
know not; and *so* when I come and tell
Ahab, and he cannot find thee, he shall
slay me: but I thy servant fear the LORD
from my youth.
13 Was it not told my lord what I did
when Jĕz'ē-bĕl slew the prophets of the
LORD, how I hid a hundred men of the
LORD's prophets by fifty in a cave, and
fed them with bread and water?
14 And now thou sayest, Go, tell thy
lord, Behold, Ē-lī'jah *is here:* and he
shall slay me.
15 And Ē-lī'jah said, *As* the LORD of
hosts liveth, before whom I stand, I will
surely show myself unto him to-day.
16 So Ō'ba-dī'ah went to meet Ahab,
and told him: and Ahab went to meet
Ē-lī'jah.
17 ℭ And it came to pass, when
Ahab saw Ē-lī'jah, that Ahab said unto
him, *Art* thou he that troubleth Ĭs'rā-ĕl?
18 And he answered, I have not troubled Ĭs'rā-ĕl; but thou, and thy father's
house, in that ye have forsaken the commandments of the LORD, and thou hast
followed Bā'a-lĭm.
19 Now therefore send, *and* gather to
me all Ĭs'rā-ĕl unto mount Cär'mĕl, and
the prophets of Bā'ăl four hundred and
fifty, and the prophets of the groves
four hundred, which eat at Jĕz'ē-bĕl's
table.
20 So Ahab sent unto all the children
of Ĭs'rā-ĕl, and gathered the prophets
together unto mount Cär'mĕl.
21 And Ē-lī'jah came unto all the people, and said, How long halt ye between
two opinions? if the LORD *be* God, follow him: but if Bā'ăl, *then* follow him.
And the people answered him not a
word.
22 Then said Ē-lī'jah unto the people,
I, *even* I only, remain a prophet of the
LORD; but Bā'ăl's prophets *are* four
hundred and fifty men.

23 Let them therefore give us two bullocks; and let them choose one bullock
for themselves, and cut it in pieces, and
lay *it* on wood, and put no fire *under:*
and I will dress the other bullock, and
lay *it* on wood, and put no fire *under:*
24 And call ye on the name of your
gods, and I will call on the name of the
LORD: and the God that answereth by
fire, let him be God. And all the people
answered and said, It is well spoken.
25 And Ē-lī′jăh said unto the prophets
of Bā′ăl, Choose you one bullock for
yourselves, and dress *it* first; for ye *are*
many; and call on the name of your
gods, but put no fire *under.*
26 And they took the bullock which
was given them, and they dressed *it,*
and called on the name of Bā′ăl from
morning even until noon, saying, O
Bā′ăl, hear us. But *there was* no voice,
nor any that answered. And they leaped
upon the altar which was made.
27 And it came to pass at noon, that
Ē-lī′jăh mocked them, and said, Cry
aloud: for he *is* a god; either he is talking, or he is pursuing, or he is in a journey, *or* peradventure he sleepeth, and
must be awaked.
28 And they cried aloud, and cut themselves after their manner with knives
and lancets, till the blood gushed out
upon them.
29 And it came to pass, when midday
was past, and they prophesied until the
time of the offering of the *evening* sacrifice, that *there was* neither voice, nor
any to answer, nor any that regarded.
30 And Ē-lī′jăh said unto all the people, Come near unto me. And all the
people came near unto him. And he
repaired the altar of the LORD *that was*
broken down.
31 And Ē-lī′jăh took twelve stones,
according to the number of the tribes of
the sons of Jacob, unto whom the word
of the LORD came, saying, Ĭs′rā-ĕl shall
be thy name:
32 And with the stones he built an altar
in the name of the LORD: and he made a
trench about the altar, as great as would
contain two measures of seed.
33 And he put the wood in order, and
cut the bullock in pieces, and laid *him*
on the wood, and said, Fill four barrels
with water, and pour *it* on the burnt
sacrifice, and on the wood.
34 And he said, Do *it* the second time.
And they did *it* the second time. And he
said, Do *it* the third time. And they did
it the third time.
35 And the water ran round about the
altar; and he filled the trench also with
water.
36 And it came to pass at *the time of*
the offering of the *evening* sacrifice,
that Ē-lī′jăh the prophet came near,
and said, LORD God of Abraham, Isaac,
and of Ĭs′rā-ĕl, let it be known this day
that thou *art* God in Ĭs′rā-ĕl, and *that* I
am thy servant, and *that* I have done
all these things at thy word.
37 Hear me, O LORD, hear me, that
this people may know that thou *art* the
LORD God, and *that* thou hast turned
their heart back again.
38 Then the fire of the LORD fell, and
consumed the burnt sacrifice, and the
wood, and the stones, and the dust, and
licked up the water that *was* in the trench.
39 And when all the people saw *it,* they
fell on their faces: and they said, The
LORD, he *is* the God; the LORD, he *is*
the God.
40 And Ē-lī′jăh said unto them, Take
the prophets of Bā′ăl; let not one of them
escape. And they took them: and Ē-lī′-
jăh brought them down to the brook
Kī′shŏn, and slew them there.
41 ℂ And Ē-lī′jăh said unto Ahab, Get
thee up, eat and drink; for *there is* a
sound of abundance of rain.
42 So Ahab went up to eat and to
drink. And Ē-lī′jăh went up to the top
of Cär′mĕl; and he cast himself down
upon the earth, and put his face between
his knees,
43 And said to his servant, Go up now,
look toward the sea. And he went up,
and looked, and said, *There is* nothing.
And he said, Go again seven times.
44 And it came to pass at the seventh
time, that he said, Behold, there ariseth
a little cloud out of the sea, like a man's
hand. And he said, Go up, say unto
Ahab, Prepare *thy chariot,* and get thee
down, that the rain stop thee not.
45 And it came to pass in the mean
while, that the heaven was black with
clouds and wind, and there was a great
rain. And Ahab rode, and went to
Jĕz′rē-ĕl.
46 And the hand of the LORD was on
Ē-lī′jăh; and he girded up his loins
and ran before Ahab to the entrance of
Jĕz′rē-ĕl.

CHAPTER 19

AND Ahab told Jĕz′ē-bĕl all that Ē-lī′-
jȧh had done, and withal how he
had slain all the prophets with the sword.
2 Then Jĕz′ē-bĕl sent a messenger unto
Ē-lī′jȧh, saying, So let the gods do *to*
me, and more also, if I make not thy
life as the life of one of them by to-
morrow about this time.
3 And when he saw *that,* he arose, and
went for his life, and came to Bē′ẽr-
shē′bȧ, which *belongeth* to Judah, and
left his servant there.
4 ℂ But he himself went a day's journey into the wilderness, and came and
sat down under a juniper tree: and he
requested for himself that he might die;
and said, It is enough; now, O LORD,
take away my life; for I *am* not better
than my fathers.
5 And as he lay and slept under a
juniper tree, behold, then an angel
touched him, and said unto him, Arise
and eat.
6 And he looked, and, behold, *there*
was a cake baked on the coals, and a
cruse of water at his head. And he did
eat and drink, and laid him down again.
7 And the angel of the LORD came
again the second time, and touched him,
and said, Arise *and* eat; because the
journey *is* too great for thee.
8 And he arose, and did eat and drink,
and went in the strength of that meat
forty days and forty nights unto Hō′rĕb
the mount of God.
9 ℂ And he came thither unto a cave,
and lodged there; and, behold, the word
of the LORD *came* to him, and he said
unto him, What doest thou here,
Ē-lī′jȧh?
10 And he said, I have been very
jealous for the LORD God of hosts: for
the children of Ĭs̱′rā-ĕl have forsaken
thy covenant, thrown down thine altars,
and slain thy prophets with the sword;
and I, *even* I only, am left; and they seek
my life, to take it away.
11 And he said, Go forth, and stand
upon the mount before the LORD. And,
behold, the LORD passed by, and a great
and strong wind rent the mountains, and
brake in pieces the rocks before the
LORD; *but* the LORD *was* not in the
wind: and after the wind an earthquake;
but the LORD *was* not in the earthquake:
12 And after the earthquake a fire;
but the LORD *was* not in the fire: and
after the fire a still small voice.
13 And it was *so,* when Ē-lī′jȧh heard
it, that he wrapped his face in his
mantle, and went out, and stood in the
entering in of the cave. And, behold,
there came a voice unto him, and said,
What doest thou here, Ē-lī′jȧh?
14 And he said, I have been very
jealous for the LORD God of hosts: because the children of Ĭs̱′rā-ĕl have forsaken thy covenant, thrown down thine
altars, and slain thy prophets with the
sword; and I, *even* I only, am left; and
they seek my life, to take it away.
15 And the LORD said unto him, Go,
return on thy way to the wilderness of
Damascus: and when thou comest,
anoint Hăz′ā-ĕl *to be* king over Syria:
16 And Jē′hū the son of Nĭm′shī shalt
thou anoint *to be* king over Ĭs̱′rā-ĕl: and
Ē-lī′shȧ the son of Shā′phăt of Ā′bĕl-
mē-hō′lȧh shalt thou anoint *to be*
prophet in thy room.
17 And it shall come to pass, *that* him
that escapeth the sword of Hăz′ā-ĕl
shall Jē′hū slay: and him that escapeth
from the sword of Jē′hū shall Ē-lī′shȧ
slay.
18 Yet I have left *me* seven thousand
in Ĭs̱′rā-ĕl, all the knees which have not
bowed unto Bā′ăl, and every mouth
which hath not kissed him.
19 ℂ So he departed thence, and found
Ē-lī′shȧ the son of Shā′phăt, who *was*
plowing *with* twelve yoke *of oxen* before
him, and he with the twelfth: and
Ē-lī′jȧh passed by him, and cast his
mantle upon him.
20 And he left the oxen, and ran after
Ē-lī′jȧh, and said, Let me, I pray thee,
kiss my father and my mother, and *then*
I will follow thee. And he said unto him,
Go back again: for what have I done to
thee?
21 And he returned back from him,
and took a yoke of oxen, and slew them,
and boiled their flesh with the instruments of the oxen, and gave unto the
people, and they did eat. Then he arose
and went after Ē-lī′jȧh, and ministered
unto him.

CHAPTER 20

AND Bĕn′–hā′dăd the king of Syria
gathered all his host together: and
there were thirty and two kings with
him, and horses, and chariots: and he

went up and besieged Sȧ-mā′rĭ-ȧ, and
warred against it.
2 And he sent messengers to Ahab
king of Ĭş′rā-ĕl into the city, and said
unto him, Thus saith Bĕn′-hā′dăd,
3 Thy silver and thy gold *is* mine; thy
wives also and thy children, *even* the
goodliest, *are* mine.
4 And the king of Ĭş′rā-ĕl answered and
said, My lord, O king, according to thy
saying, I *am* thine, and all that I have.
5 And the messengers came again, and
said, Thus speaketh Bĕn′-hā′dăd, saying, Although I have sent unto thee,
saying, Thou shalt deliver me thy silver, and thy gold, and thy wives, and
thy children;
6 Yet I will send my servants unto thee
to-morrow about this time, and they
shall search thine house, and the houses
of thy servants; and it shall be, *that*
whatsoever is pleasant in thine eyes,
they shall put *it* in their hand, and take
it away.
7 Then the king of Ĭş′rā-ĕl called all
the elders of the land, and said, Mark,
I pray you, and see how this *man* seeketh mischief: for he sent unto me for my
wives, and for my children, and for my
silver, and for my gold; and I denied
him not.
8 And all the elders and all the people
said unto him, Hearken not *unto him*,
nor consent.
9 Wherefore he said unto the messengers of Bĕn′-hā′dăd, Tell my lord the
king, All that thou didst send for to thy
servant at the first I will do: but this
thing I may not do. And the messengers
departed, and brought him word again.
10 And Bĕn′-hā′dăd sent unto him,
and said, The gods do so unto me, and
more also, if the dust of Sȧ-mā′rĭ-ȧ shall
suffice for handfuls for all the people
that follow me.
11 And the king of Ĭş′rā-ĕl answered
and said, Tell *him*, Let not him that
girdeth on *his harness* boast himself as
he that putteth it off.
12 And it came to pass, when *Ben-
hadad* heard this message, as he *was*
drinking, he and the kings in the pavilions, that he said unto his servants,
Set *yourselves in array*. And they set
themselves in array against the city.
13 ¶ And, behold, there came a
prophet unto Ahab king of Ĭş′rā-ĕl, saying, Thus saith the LORD, Hast thou
seen all this great multitude? behold, I
will deliver it into thine hand this day;
and thou shalt know that I *am* the LORD.
14 And Ahab said, By whom? And he
said, Thus saith the LORD, *Even* by the
young men of the princes of the provinces. Then he said, Who shall order
the battle? And he answered, Thou.
15 Then he numbered the young men
of the princes of the provinces, and they
were two hundred and thirty-two: and
after them he numbered all the people,
even all the children of Ĭş′rā-ĕl, *being*
seven thousand.
16 And they went out at noon. But
Bĕn′-hā′dăd *was* drinking himself drunk
in the pavilions, he and the kings, the
thirty and two kings that helped him.
17 And the young men of the princes of
the provinces went out first; and Bĕn′-
hā′dăd sent out, and they told him,
saying, There are men come out of
Sȧ-mā′rĭ-ȧ.
18 And he said, Whether they be
come out for peace, take them alive; or
whether they be come out for war, take
them alive.
19 So these young men of the princes
of the provinces came out of the city,
and the army which followed them.
20 And they slew every one his man:
and the Syrians fled; and Ĭş′rā-ĕl pursued them: and Bĕn′-hā′dăd the king
of Syria escaped on a horse with the
horsemen.
21 And the king of Ĭş′rā-ĕl went out,
and smote the horses and chariots, and
slew the Syrians with a great slaughter.
22 ¶ And the prophet came to the
king of Ĭş′rā-ĕl, and said unto him, Go,
strengthen thyself, and mark, and see
what thou doest: for at the return of the
year the king of Syria will come up
against thee.
23 And the servants of the king of Syria
said unto him, Their gods *are* gods of
the hills; therefore they were stronger
than we; but let us fight against them in
the plain, and surely we shall be
stronger than they.
24 And do this thing, Take the kings
away, every man out of his place, and
put captains in their rooms:
25 And number thee an army, like the
army that thou hast lost, horse for horse,
and chariot for chariot: and we will fight
against them in the plain, *and* surely we
shall be stronger than they. And he

hearkened unto their voice, and did so.
26 And it came to pass at the return of
the year, that Bĕn′-hā′dăd numbered
the Syrians, and went up to Ā′phĕk, to
fight against Ĭṣ′rā-ĕl.
27 And the children of Ĭṣ′rā-ĕl were
numbered, and were all present, and
went against them: and the children of
Ĭṣ′rā-ĕl pitched before them like two
little flocks of kids; but the Syrians filled
the country.
28 ¶ And there came a man of God,
and spake unto the king of Ĭṣ′rā-ĕl, and
said, Thus saith the LORD, Because the
Syrians have said, The LORD *is* God of
the hills, but he *is* not God of the valleys, therefore will I deliver all this
great multitude into thine hand, and ye
shall know that I *am* the LORD.
29 And they pitched one over against
the other seven days. And *so* it was,
that in the seventh day the battle was
joined: and the children of Ĭṣ′rā-ĕl slew
of the Syrians a hundred thousand footmen in one day.
30 But the rest fled to Ā′phĕk, into the
city; and *there* a wall fell upon twenty
and seven thousand of the men *that*
were left. And Bĕn′-hā′dăd fled, and
came into the city, into an inner chamber.
31 ¶ And his servants said unto him,
Behold now, we have heard that the
kings of the house of Ĭṣ′rā-ĕl *are* merciful kings: let us, I pray thee, put sackcloth on our loins, and ropes upon our
heads, and go out to the king of Ĭṣ′-
rā-ĕl: peradventure he will save thy
life.
32 So they girded sackcloth on their
loins, and *put* ropes on their heads, and
came to the king of Ĭṣ′rā-ĕl, and said,
Thy servant Bĕn′-hā′dăd saith, I pray
thee, let me live. And he said, *Is* he yet
alive? he *is* my brother.
33 Now the men did diligently observe
whether *any thing would come* from
him, and did hastily catch *it:* and they
said, Thy brother Bĕn′-hā′dăd. Then
he said, Go ye, bring him. Then Bĕn′-
hā′dăd came forth to him; and he caused
him to come up into the chariot.
34 And *Ben-hadad* said unto him,
The cities, which my father took from
thy father, I will restore; and thou shalt
make streets for thee in Damascus, as
my father made in Sȧ-mā′rĭ-ȧ. Then
said Ahab, I will send thee away with
this covenant. So he made a covenant
with him, and sent him away.
35 ¶ And a certain man of the sons
of the prophets said unto his neighbor
in the word of the LORD, Smite me, I
pray thee. And the man refused to smite
him.
36 Then said he unto him, Because
thou hast not obeyed the voice of the
LORD, behold, as soon as thou art departed from me, a lion shall slay thee.
And as soon as he was departed from
him, a lion found him, and slew him.
37 Then he found another man, and
said, Smite me, I pray thee. And the
man smote him, so that in smiting he
wounded *him.*
38 So the prophet departed, and waited
for the king by the way, and disguised
himself with ashes upon his face.
39 And as the king passed by, he cried
unto the king: and he said, Thy servant
went out into the midst of the battle;
and, behold, a man turned aside, and
brought a man unto me, and said, Keep
this man: if by any means he be missing,
then shall thy life be for his life, or else
thou shalt pay a talent of silver.
40 And as thy servant was busy here
and there, he was gone. And the king
of Ĭṣ′rā-ĕl said unto him, So *shall* thy
judgment *be;* thyself hast decided *it.*
41 And he hasted, and took the ashes
away from his face; and the king of
Ĭṣ′rā-ĕl discerned him that he *was* of the
prophets.
42 And he said unto him, Thus saith
the LORD, Because thou hast let go out
of *thy* hand a man whom I appointed to
utter destruction, therefore thy life shall
go for his life, and thy people for his
people.
43 And the king of Ĭṣ′rā-ĕl went to his
house heavy and displeased, and came
to Sȧ-mā′rĭ-ȧ.

CHAPTER 21

AND it came to pass after these things,
that Nā′bŏth the Jĕz′rē-ĕl-īte had
a vineyard, which *was* in Jĕz′rē-ĕl, hard
by the palace of Ahab king of Sȧ-mā′rĭ-ȧ.
2 And Ahab spake unto Nā′bŏth, saying, Give me thy vineyard, that I may
have it for a garden of herbs, because it
is near unto my house: and I will give
thee for it a better vineyard than it; *or,*
if it seem good to thee, I will give thee
the worth of it in money.

3 And Nā′bŏth said to Ahab, The LORD
forbid it me, that I should give the inheritance of my fathers unto thee.
4 And Ahab came into his house heavy
and displeased because of the word
which Nā′bŏth the Jĕz′rē-ĕl-īte had
spoken to him: for he had said, I will not
give thee the inheritance of my fathers.
And he laid him down upon his bed, and
turned away his face, and would eat no
bread.
5 ¶ But Jĕz′ē-bĕl his wife came to
him, and said unto him, Why is thy
spirit so sad, that thou eatest no bread?
6 And he said unto her, Because I
spake unto Nā′bŏth the Jĕz′rē-ĕl-īte,
and said unto him, Give me thy vineyard for money; or else, if it please thee,
I will give thee *another* vineyard for it:
and he answered, I will not give thee my
vineyard.
7 And Jĕz′ē-bĕl his wife said unto him,
Dost thou now govern the kingdom of
Ĭṣ′rā-ĕl? arise, *and* eat bread, and let
thine heart be merry: I will give thee
the vineyard of Nā′bŏth the Jĕz′rē-
ĕl-īte.
8 So she wrote letters in Ahab's name,
and sealed *them* with his seal, and sent
the letters unto the elders and to the
nobles that *were* in his city, dwelling
with Nā′bŏth.
9 And she wrote in the letters, saying,
Proclaim a fast, and set Nā′bŏth on high
among the people:
10 And set two men, sons of Bē′lĭ-ăl,
before him, to bear witness against him,
saying, Thou didst blaspheme God and
the king. And *then* carry him out, and
stone him, that he may die.
11 And the men of his city, *even* the
elders and the nobles who were the inhabitants in his city, did as Jĕz′ē-bĕl had
sent unto them, *and* as it *was* written
in the letters which she had sent unto
them.
12 They proclaimed a fast, and set
Nā′bŏth on high among the people.
13 And there came in two men, children
of Bē′lĭ-ăl, and sat before him: and the
men of Bē′lĭ-ăl witnessed against him,
even against Nā′bŏth, in the presence of
the people, saying, Nā′bŏth did blaspheme God and the king. Then they
carried him forth out of the city, and
stoned him with stones, that he died.
14 Then they sent to Jĕz′ē-bĕl, saying,
Nā′bŏth is stoned, and is dead.
15 ¶ And it came to pass, when Jĕz′ē-
bĕl heard that Nā′bŏth was stoned, and
was dead, that Jĕz′ē-bĕl said to Ahab,
Arise, take possession of the vineyard
of Nā′bŏth the Jĕz′rē-ĕl-īte, which he
refused to give thee for money: for Nā′-
bŏth is not alive, but dead.
16 And it came to pass, when Ahab
heard that Nā′bŏth was dead, that Ahab
rose up to go down to the vineyard of
Nā′bŏth the Jĕz′rē-ĕl-īte, to take possession of it.
17 ¶ And the word of the LORD came
to Ē-lī′jȧh the Tĭsh′bīte, saying,
18 Arise, go down to meet Ahab king
of Ĭṣ′rā-ĕl, which *is* in Sȧ-mā′rĭ-ȧ: behold, *he is* in the vineyard of Nā′bŏth,
whither he is gone down to possess it.
19 And thou shalt speak unto him,
saying, Thus saith the LORD, Hast thou
killed, and also taken possession? And
thou shalt speak unto him, saying, Thus
saith the LORD, In the place where dogs
licked the blood of Nā′bŏth shall dogs
lick thy blood, even thine.
20 And Ahab said to Ē-lī′jȧh, Hast
thou found me, O mine enemy? And he
answered, I have found *thee:* because
thou hast sold thyself to work evil in the
sight of the LORD.
21 Behold, I will bring evil upon thee,
and will take away thy posterity, and
will cut off from Ahab him that pisseth
against the wall, and him that is shut up
and left in Ĭṣ′rā-ĕl,
22 And will make thine house like the
house of Jĕr′ō-bō′ăm the son of Nē′băt,
and like the house of Bā′ȧ-shȧ the son
of Ȧ-hī′jȧh, for the provocation wherewith thou hast provoked *me* to anger,
and made Ĭṣ′rā-ĕl to sin.
23 And of Jĕz′ē-bĕl also spake the
LORD, saying, The dogs shall eat Jĕz′ē-
bĕl by the wall of Jĕz′rē-ĕl.
24 Him that dieth of Ahab in the city
the dogs shall eat; and him that dieth in
the field shall the fowls of the air eat.
25 ¶ But there was none like unto
Ahab, which did sell himself to work
wickedness in the sight of the LORD,
whom Jĕz′ē-bĕl his wife stirred up.
26 And he did very abominably in following idols, according to all *things* as
did the Ăm′ō-rītes whom the LORD cast
out before the children of Ĭṣ′rā-ĕl.
27 And it came to pass, when Ahab
heard those words, that he rent his
clothes, and put sackcloth upon his

flesh, and fasted, and lay in sackcloth,
and went softly.
28 And the word of the LORD came to
Ē-lī'jah the Tĭsh'bīte, saying,
29 Seest thou how Ahab humbleth
himself before me? because he humbleth himself before me, I will not
bring the evil in his days: *but* in his
son's days will I bring the evil upon his
house.

CHAPTER 22

AND they continued three years without war between Syria and Ĭṣ'rā-ĕl.
2 And it came to pass in the third year,
that Jē-hŏsh'ȧ-phăt the king of Judah
came down to the king of Ĭṣ'rā-ĕl.
3 And the king of Ĭṣ'rā-ĕl said unto his
servants, Know ye that Rā'mŏth in
Gĭl'ē-ăd *is* ours, and we *be* still, *and*
take it not out of the hand of the king
of Syria?
4 And he said unto Jē-hŏsh'ȧ-phăt,
Wilt thou go with me to battle to Rā'-
mŏth–gĭl'ē-ăd? And Jē-hŏsh'ȧ-phăt said
to the king of Ĭṣ'rā-ĕl, I *am* as thou *art,*
my people as thy people, my horses as
thy horses.
5 And Jē-hŏsh'ȧ-phăt said unto the
king of Ĭṣ'rā-ĕl, Inquire, I pray thee, at
the word of the LORD to-day.
6 Then the king of Ĭṣ'rā-ĕl gathered
the prophets together, about four hundred men, and said unto them, Shall I
go against Rā'mŏth–gĭl'ē-ăd to battle,
or shall I forbear? And they said, Go
up; for the Lord shall deliver *it* into the
hand of the king.
7 And Jē-hŏsh'ȧ-phăt said, *Is there*
not here a prophet of the LORD besides,
that we might inquire of him?
8 And the king of Ĭṣ'rā-ĕl said unto
Jē-hŏsh'ȧ-phăt, *There is* yet one man,
Mī-cā'ịah the son of Ĭm'lȧh, by whom
we may inquire of the LORD: but I hate
him; for he doth not prophesy good concerning me, but evil. And Jē-hŏsh'ȧ-
phăt said, Let not the king say so.
9 Then the king of Ĭṣ'rā-ĕl called an
officer, and said, Hasten *hither* Mī-
cā'ịah the son of Ĭm'lȧh.
10 And the king of Ĭṣ'rā-ĕl and Jē-
hŏsh'ȧ-phăt the king of Judah sat each
on his throne, having put on their robes,
in a void place in the entrance of the
gate of Sȧ-mā'rĭ-ȧ; and all the prophets
prophesied before them.
11 And Zĕd'ē-kī'ȧh the son of Chē-
nā'ȧ-năh made him horns of iron: and
he said, Thus saith the LORD, With
these shalt thou push the Syrians, until
thou have consumed them.
12 And all the prophets prophesied so,
saying, Go up to Rā'mŏth–gĭl'ē-ăd, and
prosper: for the LORD shall deliver *it*
into the king's hand.
13 And the messenger that was gone to
call Mī-cā'ịah spake unto him, saying,
Behold now, the words of the prophets
declare good unto the king with one
mouth: let thy word, I pray thee, be like
the word of one of them, and speak *that*
which is good.
14 And Mī-cā'ịah said, *As* the LORD
liveth, what the LORD saith unto me,
that will I speak.
15 ℂ So he came to the king. And the
king said unto him, Mī-cā'ịah, shall we
go against Rā'mŏth–gĭl'ē-ăd to battle,
or shall we forbear? And he answered
him, Go, and prosper: for the LORD shall
deliver *it* into the hand of the king.
16 And the king said unto him, How
many times shall I adjure thee that thou
tell me nothing but *that which is* true in
the name of the LORD?
17 And he said, I saw all Ĭṣ'rā-ĕl scattered upon the hills, as sheep that have
not a shepherd: and the LORD said,
These have no master: let them return
every man to his house in peace.
18 And the king of Ĭṣ'rā-ĕl said unto
Jē-hŏsh'ȧ-phăt, Did I not tell thee that
he would prophesy no good concerning
me, but evil?
19 And he said, Hear thou therefore
the word of the LORD: I saw the LORD
sitting on his throne, and all the host of
heaven standing by him on his right
hand and on his left.
20 And the LORD said, Who shall persuade Ahab, that he may go up and fall
at Rā'mŏth–gĭl'ē-ăd? And one said on
this manner, and another said on that
manner.
21 And there came forth a spirit, and
stood before the LORD, and said, I will
persuade him.
22 And the LORD said unto him,
Wherewith? And he said, I will go forth,
and I will be a lying spirit in the mouth
of all his prophets. And he said, Thou
shalt persuade *him,* and prevail also: go
forth, and do so.
23 Now therefore, behold, the LORD
hath put a lying spirit in the mouth of all

these thy prophets, and the LORD hath
spoken evil concerning thee.
24 But Zĕd′ē-kī′ȧh the son of Chē-
nā′ȧ-näh went near, and smote Mī-
cā′iȧh on the cheek, and said, Which
way went the Spirit of the LORD from
me to speak unto thee?
25 And Mī-cā′iȧh said, Behold, thou
shalt see in that day, when thou shalt go
into an inner chamber to hide thyself.
26 And the king of Ĭs′rā-ĕl said, Take
Mī-cā′iȧh, and carry him back unto
Ā′mŏn the governor of the city, and to
Jō′ăsh the king's son;
27 And say, Thus saith the king, Put
this *fellow* in the prison, and feed him
with bread of affliction and with water
of affliction, until I come in peace.
28 And Mī-cā′iȧh said, If thou return
at all in peace, the LORD hath not spoken
by me. And he said, Hearken, O people, every one of you.
29 So the king of Ĭs′rā-ĕl and Jē-
hŏsh′ȧ-phăt the king of Judah went up
to Rā′mŏth–gĭl′ē-ăd.
30 And the king of Ĭs′rā-ĕl said unto
Jē-hŏsh′ȧ-phăt, I will disguise myself,
and enter into the battle; but put thou
on thy robes. And the king of Ĭs′rā-ĕl
disguised himself, and went into the
battle.
31 But the king of Syria commanded
his thirty and two captains that had rule
over his chariots, saying, Fight neither
with small nor great, save only with the
king of Ĭs′rā-ĕl.
32 And it came to pass, when the captains of the chariots saw Jē-hŏsh′ȧ-phăt,
that they said, Surely it *is* the king of
Ĭs′rā-ĕl. And they turned aside to fight
against him: and Jē-hŏsh′ȧ-phăt cried
out.
33 And it came to pass, when the captains of the chariots perceived that it
was not the king of Ĭs′rā-ĕl, that they
turned back from pursuing him.
34 And a *certain* man drew a bow at a
venture, and smote the king of Ĭs′rā-ĕl
between the joints of the harness:
wherefore he said unto the driver of his
chariot, Turn thine hand, and carry me
out of the host; for I am wounded.
35 And the battle increased that day:
and the king was stayed up in his chariot against the Syrians, and died at even:
and the blood ran out of the wound into
the midst of the chariot.
36 And there went a proclamation
throughout the host about the going
down of the sun, saying, Every man to
his city, and every man to his own
country.
37 ℭ So the king died, and was brought
to Sȧ-mā′rĭ-ȧ; and they buried the king
in Sȧ-mā′rĭ-ȧ.
38 And *one* washed the chariot in the
pool of Sȧ-mā′rĭ-ȧ; and the dogs licked
up his blood; and they washed his
armor; according unto the word of the
LORD which he spake.
39 Now the rest of the acts of Ahab,
and all that he did, and the ivory house
which he made, and all the cities that he
built, *are* they not written in the book of
the Chronicles of the kings of Ĭs′rā-ĕl?
40 So Ahab slept with his fathers; and
Ā′hȧ-zī′ȧh his son reigned in his stead.
41 ℭ And Jē-hŏsh′ȧ-phăt the son of
Ā′sȧ began to reign over Judah in the
fourth year of Ahab king of Ĭs′rā-ĕl.
42 Jē-hŏsh′ȧ-phăt *was* thirty and five
years old when he began to reign; and
he reigned twenty and five years in
Jerusalem. And his mother's name *was*
Ȧ-zū′bȧh the daughter of Shĭl′hī.
43 And he walked in all the ways of
Ā′sȧ his father; he turned not aside from
it, doing *that which was* right in the eyes
of the LORD: nevertheless the high
places were not taken away; *for* the
people offered and burnt incense yet in
the high places.
44 And Jē-hŏsh′ȧ-phăt made peace
with the king of Ĭs′rā-ĕl.
45 Now the rest of the acts of Jē-
hŏsh′ȧ-phăt, and his might that he
showed, and how he warred, *are* they
not written in the book of the Chronicles
of the kings of Judah?
46 And the remnant of the sodomites,
which remained in the days of his father
Ā′sȧ, he took out of the land.
47 *There was* then no king in Ē′dŏm:
a deputy *was* king.
48 Jē-hŏsh′ȧ-phăt made ships of
Thär′shĭsh to go to Ō′phīr for gold: but
they went not; for the ships were broken
at Ē′zĭ-ŏn–gē′bĕr.
49 Then said Ā′hȧ-zī′ȧh the son of
Ahab unto Jē-hŏsh′ȧ-phăt, Let my servants go with thy servants in the ships.
But Jē-hŏsh′ȧ-phăt would not.
50 ℭ And Jē-hŏsh′ȧ-phăt slept with
his fathers, and was buried with his
fathers in the city of David his father: and
Jē-hō′răm his son reigned in his stead.

51 ¶ Ā'hȧ-zī'ȧh the son of Ahab began
to reign over Ĭş'rā-ĕl in Sȧ-mā'rĭ-ȧ the
seventeenth year of Jē-hŏsh'ȧ-phăt
king of Judah, and reigned two years
over Ĭş'rā-ĕl.
52 And he did evil in the sight of the
LORD, and walked in the way of his
father, and in the way of his mother,
and in the way of Jĕr'ō-bō'ăm the son
of Nē'băt, who made Ĭş'rā-ĕl to sin:
53 For he served Bā'ăl, and worshipped him, and provoked to anger the
LORD God of Ĭş'rā-ĕl, according to all
that his father had done.

THE SECOND

BOOK OF THE KINGS

COMMONLY CALLED, THE FOURTH BOOK OF THE KINGS

CHAPTER 1

THEN Mō'ăb rebelled against Ĭş'rā-ĕl after the death of Ahab.
2 And Ā'hȧ-zī'ȧh fell down through a
lattice in his upper chamber that *was* in
Sȧ-mā'rĭ-ȧ, and was sick: and he sent
messengers, and said unto them, Go, inquire of Bā'ăl-zē'bŭb the god of Ĕk'rŏn
whether I shall recover of this disease.
3 But the angel of the LORD said to
Ē-lī'jȧh the Tĭsh'bīte, Arise, go up to
meet the messengers of the king of
Sȧ-mā'rĭ-ȧ, and say unto them, *Is it* not
because *there is* not a God in Ĭş'rā-ĕl,
that ye go to inquire of Bā'ăl-zē'bŭb
the god of Ĕk'rŏn?
4 Now therefore thus saith the LORD,
Thou shalt not come down from that
bed on which thou art gone up, but shalt
surely die. And Ē-lī'jȧh departed.
5 ¶ And when the messengers turned
back unto him, he said unto them, Why
are ye now turned back?
6 And they said unto him, There came
a man up to meet us, and said unto us,
Go, turn again unto the king that sent
you, and say unto him, Thus saith the
LORD, *Is it* not because *there is* not a
God in Ĭş'rā-ĕl, *that* thou sendest to inquire of Bā'ăl-zē'bŭb the god of Ĕk'rŏn?
therefore thou shalt not come down from
that bed on which thou art gone up, but
shalt surely die.
7 And he said unto them, What manner of man *was he* which came up to
meet you, and told you these words?
8 And they answered him, *He was* a
hairy man, and girt with a girdle of
leather about his loins. And he said, It
is Ē-lī'jȧh the Tĭsh'bīte.
9 Then the king sent unto him a captain of fifty with his fifty. And he went
up to him: and, behold, he sat on the
top of a hill. And he spake unto him,
Thou man of God, the king hath said,
Come down.
10 And Ē-lī'jȧh answered and said to
the captain of fifty, If I *be* a man of
God, then let fire come down from
heaven, and consume thee and thy
fifty. And there came down fire from
heaven, and consumed him and his
fifty.
11 Again also he sent unto him another
captain of fifty with his fifty. And he
answered and said unto him, O man of
God, thus hath the king said, Come
down quickly.
12 And Ē-lī'jȧh answered and said
unto them, If I *be* a man of God, let
fire come down from heaven, and consume thee and thy fifty. And the fire of
God came down from heaven, and consumed him and his fifty.
13 ¶ And he sent again a captain of
the third fifty with his fifty. And the
third captain of fifty went up, and came
and fell on his knees before Ē-lī'jȧh,
and besought him, and said unto him,
O man of God, I pray thee, let my life,
and the life of these fifty thy servants,
be precious in thy sight.
14 Behold, there came fire down from
heaven, and burnt up the two captains
of the former fifties with their fifties:
therefore let my life now be precious in
thy sight.
15 And the angel of the LORD said unto
Ē-lī'jȧh, Go down with him: be not
afraid of him. And he arose, and went
down with him unto the king.

16 And he said unto him, Thus saith
the LORD, Forasmuch as thou hast sent
messengers to inquire of Bā′ăl–zē′bŭb
the god of Ĕk′rŏn, *is it* not because *there*
is no God in Ĭṣ′rā-ĕl to inquire of his
word? therefore thou shalt not come
down off that bed on which thou art gone
up, but shalt surely die.
17 ¶ So he died according to the word
of the LORD which Ē-lī′jȧh had spoken.
And Jē-hō′răm reigned in his stead,
in the second year of Jē-hō′răm the son
of Jē-hŏsh′ȧ-phăt king of Judah; because he had no son.
18 Now the rest of the acts of Ā′hȧ-
zī′ȧh which he did, *are* they not written
in the book of the Chronicles of the
kings of Ĭṣ′rā-ĕl?

CHAPTER 2

AND it came to pass, when the LORD
would take up Ē-lī′jȧh into heaven
by a whirlwind, that Ē-lī′jȧh went with
Ē-lī′shȧ from Gĭl′găl.
2 And Ē-lī′jȧh said unto Ē-lī′shȧ, Tarry
here, I pray thee; for the LORD hath
sent me to Beth-el. And Ē-lī′shȧ said
unto him, As the LORD liveth, and *as*
thy soul liveth, I will not leave thee. So
they went down to Beth-el.
3 And the sons of the prophets that
were at Beth-el came forth to Ē-lī′shȧ,
and said unto him, Knowest thou that
the LORD will take away thy master
from thy head to-day? And he said,
Yea, I know *it;* hold ye your peace.
4 And Ē-lī′jȧh said unto him, Ē-lī′shȧ,
tarry here, I pray thee; for the LORD
hath sent me to Jĕr′ĭ-chō. And he said,
As the LORD liveth, and *as* thy soul liveth, I will not leave thee. So they came
to Jĕr′ĭ-chō.
5 And the sons of the prophets that
were at Jĕr′ĭ-chō came to Ē-lī′shȧ, and
said unto him, Knowest thou that the
LORD will take away thy master from
thy head to-day? And he answered,
Yea, I know *it;* hold ye your peace.
6 And Ē-lī′jȧh said unto him, Tarry, I
pray thee, here; for the LORD hath sent
me to Jordan. And he said, *As* the LORD
liveth, and *as* thy soul liveth, I will not
leave thee. And they two went on.
7 And fifty men of the sons of the
prophets went, and stood to view afar
off: and they two stood by Jordan.
8 And Ē-lī′jȧh took his mantle, and
wrapped *it* together, and smote the
waters and they were divided hither
and thither, so that they two went over
on dry ground.
9 ¶ And it came to pass, when they
were gone over, that Ē-lī′jȧh said unto
Ē-lī′shȧ, Ask what I shall do for thee,
before I be taken away from thee. And
Ē-lī′shȧ said, I pray thee, let a double
portion of thy spirit be upon me.
10 And he said, Thou hast asked a
hard thing: *nevertheless,* if thou see me
when I am taken from thee, it shall
be so unto thee; but if not, it shall not
be *so.*
11 And it came to pass, as they still
went on, and talked, that, behold, *there*
appeared a chariot of fire, and horses of
fire, and parted them both asunder; and
Ē-lī′jȧh went up by a whirlwind into
heaven.
12 ¶ And Ē-lī′shȧ saw *it,* and he cried,
My father, my father, the chariot of
Ĭṣ′rā-ĕl, and the horsemen thereof! And
he saw him no more: and he took hold
of his own clothes, and rent them in two
pieces.
13 He took up also the mantle of
Ē-lī′jȧh that fell from him, and went
back, and stood by the bank of Jordan;
14 And he took the mantle of Ē-lī′jȧh
that fell from him, and smote the waters,
and said, Where *is* the LORD God of
Ē-lī′jȧh? And when he also had smitten the waters, they parted hither and
thither: and Ē-lī′shȧ went over.
15 And when the sons of the prophets
which *were* to view at Jĕr′ĭ-chō saw
him, they said, The spirit of Ē-lī′jȧh
doth rest on Ē-lī′shȧ. And they came to
meet him, and bowed themselves to the
ground before him.
16 ¶ And they said unto him, Behold
now, there be with thy servants fifty
strong men; let them go, we pray thee,
and seek thy master: lest peradventure
the Spirit of the LORD hath taken him
up, and cast him upon some mountain,
or into some valley. And he said, Ye
shall not send.
17 And when they urged him till he
was ashamed, he said, Send. They sent
therefore fifty men; and they sought
three days, but found him not.
18 And when they came again to him,
(for he tarried at Jĕr′ĭ-chō,) he said unto
them, Did I not say unto you, Go not?
19 ¶ And the men of the city said unto
Ē-lī′shȧ, Behold, I pray thee, the situa-

tion of this city *is* pleasant, as my lord
seeth: but the water *is* naught, and the
ground barren.
20 And he said, Bring me a new cruse,
and put salt therein. And they brought
it to him.
21 And he went forth unto the spring
of the waters, and cast the salt in there,
and said, Thus saith the LORD, I have
healed these waters; there shall not be
from thence any more death or barren
land.
22 So the waters were healed unto this
day, according to the saying of Ē-lī'shȧ
which he spake.
23 ℂ And he went up from thence unto
Beth-el: and as he was going up by the
way, there came forth little children out
of the city, and mocked him, and said
unto him, Go up, thou bald head; go up,
thou bald head.
24 And he turned back, and looked on
them, and cursed them in the name of
the LORD. And there came forth two
she bears out of the wood, and tare forty
and two children of them.
25 And he went from thence to mount
Cär'mĕl, and from thence he returned
to Sȧ-mā'rĭ-ȧ.

CHAPTER 3

NOW Jē-hō'răm the son of Ahab
began to reign over Ĭṣ'rā-ĕl in
Sȧ-mā'rĭ-ȧ in the eighteenth year of
Jē-hŏsh'ȧ-phăt king of Judah, and
reigned twelve years.
2 And he wrought evil in the sight of
the LORD; but not like his father, and
like his mother: for he put away the
image of Bā'ăl that his father had made.
3 Nevertheless he cleaved unto the
sins of Jĕr'ō-bō'ăm the son of Nē'băt,
which made Ĭṣ'rā-ĕl to sin; he departed
not therefrom.
4 ℂ And Mē'shȧ king of Mō'ăb was a
sheepmaster, and rendered unto the
king of Ĭṣ'rā-ĕl a hundred thousand
lambs, and a hundred thousand rams,
with the wool.
5 But it came to pass, when Ahab was
dead, that the king of Mō'ăb rebelled
against the king of Ĭṣ'rā-ĕl.
6 ℂ And king Jē-hō'răm went out of
Sȧ-mā'rĭ-ȧ the same time, and numbered all Ĭṣ'rā-ĕl.
7 And he went and sent to Jē-hŏsh'ȧ-
phăt the king of Judah, saying, The king
of Mō'ăb hath rebelled against me: wilt
thou go with me against Mō'ăb to
battle? And he said, I will go up: I *am*
as thou *art*, my people as thy people,
and my horses as thy horses.
8 And he said, Which way shall we
go up? And he answered, The way
through the wilderness of Ē'dŏm.
9 So the king of Ĭṣ'rā-ĕl went, and the
king of Judah, and the king of Ē'dŏm:
and they fetched a compass of seven
days' journey: and there was no water
for the host, and for the cattle that followed them.
10 And the king of Ĭṣ'rā-ĕl said, Alas!
that the LORD hath called these three
kings together, to deliver them into the
hand of Mō'ăb!
11 But Jē-hŏsh'ȧ-phăt said, *Is there*
not here a prophet of the LORD, that we
may inquire of the LORD by him? And
one of the king of Ĭṣ'rā-ĕl's servants
answered and said, Here *is* Ē-lī'shȧ the
son of Shā'phăt, which poured water on
the hands of Ē-lī'jȧh.
12 And Jē-hŏsh'ȧ-phăt said, The word
of the LORD is with him. So the king of
Ĭṣ'rā-ĕl and Jē-hŏsh'ȧ-phăt and the
king of Ē'dŏm went down to him.
13 And Ē-lī'shȧ said unto the king of
Ĭṣ'rā-ĕl, What have I to do with thee?
get thee to the prophets of thy father,
and to the prophets of thy mother. And
the king of Ĭṣ'rā-ĕl said unto him, Nay:
for the LORD hath called these three
kings together, to deliver them into the
hand of Mō'ăb.
14 And Ē-lī'shȧ said, *As* the LORD of
hosts liveth, before whom I stand,
surely, were it not that I regard the
presence of Jē-hŏsh'ȧ-phăt the king of
Judah, I would not look toward thee,
nor see thee.
15 But now bring me a minstrel. And
it came to pass, when the minstrel
played, that the hand of the LORD came
upon him.
16 And he said, Thus saith the LORD,
Make this valley full of ditches.
17 For thus saith the LORD, Ye shall
not see wind, neither shall ye see rain;
yet that valley shall be filled with water, that ye may drink, both ye, and your
cattle, and your beasts.
18 And this is *but* a light thing in the
sight of the LORD: he will deliver the
Mō'ăb-ītes also into your hand.
19 And ye shall smite every fenced
city, and every choice city, and shall fell

every good tree, and stop all wells of
water, and mar every good piece of land
with stones.
20 And it came to pass in the morning,
when the meat offering was offered,
that, behold, there came water by the
way of Ē'dŏm, and the country was
filled with water.
21 ¶ And when all the Mō'ăb-ītes
heard that the kings were come up to
fight against them, they gathered all
that were able to put on armor, and
upward, and stood in the border.
22 And they rose up early in the morning, and the sun shone upon the water,
and the Mō'ăb-ītes saw the water on the
other side *as* red as blood:
23 And they said, This *is* blood: the
kings are surely slain, and they have
smitten one another: now therefore,
Mō'ăb, to the spoil.
24 And when they came to the camp
of Ĭṣ'rā-ĕl, the Ĭṣ'rā-ĕl-ītes rose up and
smote the Mō'ăb-ītes, so that they fled
before them: but they went forward
smiting the Mō'ăb-ītes, even in *their*
country.
25 And they beat down the cities, and
on every good piece of land cast every
man his stone, and filled it; and they
stopped all the wells of water, and felled
all the good trees: only in Kĭr'-hăr'ȧ-
sĕth left they the stones thereof; howbeit the slingers went about *it,* and
smote it.
26 ¶ And when the king of Mō'ăb saw
that the battle was too sore for him, he
took with him seven hundred men that
drew swords, to break through *even*
unto the king of Ē'dŏm: but they could
not.
27 Then he took his eldest son that
should have reigned in his stead, and
offered him *for* a burnt offering upon the
wall. And there was great indignation
against Ĭṣ'rā-ĕl: and they departed from
him, and returned to *their own* land.

CHAPTER 4

NOW there cried a certain woman of
the wives of the sons of the prophets unto Ē-lī'shȧ, saying, Thy servant
my husband is dead; and thou knowest
that thy servant did fear the LORD: and
the creditor is come to take unto him my
two sons to be bondmen.
2 And Ē-lī'shȧ said unto her, What
shall I do for thee? tell me, what hast
thou in the house? And she said, Thine
handmaid hath not any thing in the
house, save a pot of oil.
3 Then he said, Go, borrow thee vessels abroad of all thy neighbors, *even*
empty vessels; borrow not a few.
4 And when thou art come in, thou shalt
shut the door upon thee and upon thy
sons, and shalt pour out into all those
vessels, and thou shalt set aside that
which is full.
5 So she went from him, and shut the
door upon her and upon her sons, who
brought *the vessels* to her; and she
poured out.
6 And it came to pass, when the vessels
were full, that she said unto her son,
Bring me yet a vessel. And he said unto
her, *There is* not a vessel more. And
the oil stayed.
7 Then she came and told the man of
God. And he said, Go, sell the oil, and
pay thy debt, and live thou and thy children of the rest.
8 ¶ And it fell on a day, that Ē-lī'shȧ
passed to Shụ'nĕm, where *was* a great
woman; and she constrained him to eat
bread. And *so* it was, *that,* as oft as he
passed by, he turned in thither to eat
bread.
9 And she said unto her husband, Behold now, I perceive that this *is* a holy
man of God, which passeth by us continually.
10 Let us make a little chamber, I pray
thee, on the wall; and let us set for him
there a bed, and a table, and a stool,
and a candlestick: and it shall be, when
he cometh to us, that he shall turn in
thither.
11 And it fell on a day, that he came
thither, and he turned into the chamber,
and lay there.
12 And he said to Gē-hā'zī his servant, Call this Shụ'nȧm-mīte. And when
he had called her, she stood before
him.
13 And he said unto him, Say now unto
her, Behold, thou hast been careful for
us with all this care; what *is* to be done
for thee? wouldest thou be spoken for
to the king, or to the captain of the host?
And she answered, I dwell among mine
own people.
14 And he said, What then *is* to be
done for her? And Gē-hā'zī answered,
Verily she hath no child, and her husband is old.

15 And he said, Call her. And when he
had called her, she stood in the door.
16 And he said, About this season,
according to the time of life, thou shalt
embrace a son. And she said, Nay, my
lord, *thou* man of God, do not lie unto
thine handmaid.
17 And the woman conceived, and bare
a son at that season that Ē-lī'shȧ had
said unto her, according to the time of
life.
18 ¶ And when the child was grown,
it fell on a day, that he went out to his
father to the reapers.
19 And he said unto his father, My
head, my head! And he said to a lad,
Carry him to his mother.
20 And when he had taken him, and
brought him to his mother, he sat on her
knees till noon, and *then* died.
21 And she went up, and laid him on
the bed of the man of God, and shut *the
door* upon him, and went out.
22 And she called unto her husband,
and said, Send me, I pray thee, one of
the young men, and one of the asses,
that I may run to the man of God, and
come again.
23 And he said, Wherefore wilt thou
go to him to-day? *it is* neither new moon,
nor sabbath. And she said, *It shall be*
well.
24 Then she saddled an ass, and said
to her servant, Drive, and go forward;
slack not *thy* riding for me, except I bid
thee.
25 So she went and came unto the man
of God to mount Cär'mĕl. And it came
to pass, when the man of God saw her
afar off, that he said to Gē-hā'zī his
servant, Behold, *yonder is* that Shṳ'-
nȧm-mīte:
26 Run now, I pray thee, to meet her,
and say unto her, *Is it* well with thee?
is it well with thy husband? *is it* well
with the child? And she answered, *It is*
well.
27 And when she came to the man of
God to the hill, she caught him by the
feet: but Gē-hā'zī came near to thrust
her away. And the man of God said,
Let her alone; for her soul *is* vexed within
her: and the LORD hath hid *it* from
me, and hath not told me.
28 Then she said, Did I desire a son of
my lord? did I not say, Do not deceive
me?
29 Then he said to Gē-hā'zī, Gird up
thy loins, and take my staff in thine
hand, and go thy way: if thou meet any
man salute him not; and if any salute
thee, answer him not again: and lay my
staff upon the face of the child.
30 And the mother of the child said,
As the LORD liveth, and *as* thy soul
liveth, I will not leave thee. And he
arose, and followed her.
31 And Gē-hā'zī passed on before
them, and laid the staff upon the face of
the child; but *there was* neither voice,
nor hearing. Wherefore he went again
to meet him, and told him, saying, The
child is not awaked.
32 And when Ē-lī'shȧ was come into
the house, behold, the child was dead,
and laid upon his bed.
33 He went in therefore, and shut the
door upon them twain, and prayed unto
the LORD.
34 And he went up, and lay upon the
child, and put his mouth upon his mouth,
and his eyes upon his eyes, and his
hands upon his hands: and he stretched
himself upon the child; and the flesh of
the child waxed warm.
35 Then he returned, and walked in the
house to and fro; and went up, and
stretched himself upon him: and the
child sneezed seven times, and the
child opened his eyes.
36 And he called Gē-hā'zī, and said,
Call this Shṳ'nȧm-mīte. So he called
her. And when she was come in unto
him, he said, Take up thy son.
37 Then she went in, and fell at his
feet, and bowed herself to the ground,
and took up her son, and went out.
38 ¶ And Ē-lī'shȧ came again to Gĭl'-
găl: and *there was* a dearth in the land;
and the sons of the prophets *were*
sitting before him: and he said unto his
servant, Set on the great pot, and seethe
pottage for the sons of the prophets.
39 And one went out into the field to
gather herbs, and found a wild vine, and
gathered thereof wild gourds his lap
full, and came and shred *them* into the
pot of pottage: for they knew *them* not.
40 So they poured out for the men to
eat. And it came to pass, as they were
eating of the pottage, that they cried out,
and said, O *thou* man of God, *there is*
death in the pot. And they could not eat
thereof.
41 But he said, Then bring meal. And
he cast *it* into the pot; and he said, Pour

out for the people, that they may eat.
And there was no harm in the pot.
42 ¶ And there came a man from
Bā'ăl-shăl'ĭ-shȧ, and brought the man
of God bread of the firstfruits, twenty
loaves of barley, and full ears of corn in
the husk thereof. And he said, Give
unto the people, that they may eat.
43 And his servitor said, What, should
I set this before a hundred men? He
said again, Give the people, that they
may eat: for thus saith the LORD, They
shall eat, and shall leave *thereof*.
44 So he set *it* before them, and they
did eat, and left *thereof*, according to
the word of the LORD.

CHAPTER 5

NOW Nā'ȧ-măn, captain of the host
of the king of Syria, was a great
man with his master, and honorable, because by him the LORD had given deliverance unto Syria: he was also a
mighty man in valor, *but he was* a
leper.
2 And the Syrians had gone out by
companies, and had brought away captive out of the land of Ĭş'rā-ĕl a little
maid; and she waited on Nā'ȧ-măn's
wife.
3 And she said unto her mistress,
Would God my lord *were* with the
prophet that *is* in Sȧ-mā'rĭ-ȧ! for he
would recover him of his leprosy.
4 And *one* went in, and told his lord,
saying, Thus and thus said the maid
that *is* of the land of Ĭş'rā-ĕl.
5 And the king of Syria said, Go to, go,
and I will send a letter unto the king of
Ĭş'rā-ĕl. And he departed, and took
with him ten talents of silver, and six
thousand *pieces* of gold, and ten changes
of raiment.
6 And he brought the letter to the king
of Ĭş'rā-ĕl, saying, Now when this letter
is come unto thee, behold, I have *therewith* sent Nā'ȧ-măn my servant to thee,
that thou mayest recover him of his
leprosy.
7 And it came to pass, when the king
of Ĭş'rā-ĕl had read the letter, that he
rent his clothes, and said, *Am* I God, to
kill and to make alive, that this man doth
send unto me to recover a man of his
leprosy? Wherefore consider, I pray
you, and see how he seeketh a quarrel
against me.
8 ¶ And it was *so*, when Ē-lī'shȧ the
man of God had heard that the king of
Ĭş'rā-ĕl had rent his clothes, that he
sent to the king, saying, Wherefore hast
thou rent thy clothes? let him come now
to me, and he shall know that there is a
prophet in Ĭş'rā-ĕl.
9 So Nā'ȧ-măn came with his horses
and with his chariot, and stood at the
door of the house of Ē-lī'shȧ.
10 And Ē-lī'shȧ sent a messenger unto
him, saying, Go and wash in Jordan
seven times, and thy flesh shall come
again to thee, and thou shalt be clean.
11 But Nā'ȧ-măn was wroth, and went
away, and said, Behold, I thought, He
will surely come out to me, and stand,
and call on the name of the LORD his
God, and strike his hand over the place,
and recover the leper.
12 *Are* not Ăb'ȧ-nȧ and Phär'pär,
rivers of Damascus, better than all the
waters of Ĭş'rā-ĕl? may I not wash in
them, and be clean? So he turned and
went away in a rage.
13 And his servants came near, and
spake unto him, and said, My father, *if*
the prophet had bid thee *do some* great
thing, wouldest thou not have done *it?*
how much rather then, when he saith
to thee, Wash, and be clean?
14 Then went he down, and dipped
himself seven times in Jordan, according to the saying of the man of God: and
his flesh came again like unto the flesh
of a little child, and he was clean.
15 ¶ And he returned to the man of
God, he and all his company, and came,
and stood before him: and he said, Behold, now I know that *there is* no God
in all the earth, but in Ĭş'rā-ĕl: now
therefore, I pray thee, take a blessing of
thy servant.
16 But he said, *As* the LORD liveth, before whom I stand, I will receive none.
And he urged him to take *it;* but he
refused.
17 And Nā'ȧ-măn said, Shall there not
then, I pray thee, be given to thy servant two mules' burden of earth? for thy
servant will henceforth offer neither
burnt offering nor sacrifice unto other
gods, but unto the LORD.
18 In this thing the LORD pardon thy
servant, *that* when my master goeth into
the house of Rĭm'mŏn to worship there,
and he leaneth on my hand, and I bow
myself in the house of Rĭm'mŏn: when I
bow down myself in the house of Rĭm-

mŏn, the LORD pardon thy servant in
this thing.
19 And he said unto him, Go in peace.
So he departed from him a little way.
20 ℭ But Gē-ha'zī, the servant of
Ē-lī'shȧ the man of God, said, Behold,
my master hath spared Nā'ȧ-măn this
Syrian, in not receiving at his hands that
which he brought: but, *as* the LORD
liveth, I will run after him, and take
somewhat of him.
21 So Gē-hā'zī followed after Nā'ȧ-
măn. And when Nā'ȧ-măn saw *him*
running after him, he lighted down from
the chariot to meet him, and said, *Is* all
well?
22 And he said, All *is* well. My master
hath sent me, saying, Behold, even now
there be come to me from mount
Ē'phrā-ĭm two young men of the sons of
the prophets: give them, I pray thee, a
talent of silver, and two changes of
garments.
23 And Nā'ȧ-măn said, Be content,
take two talents. And he urged him,
and bound two talents of silver in two
bags, with two changes of garments, and
laid *them* upon two of his servants; and
they bare *them* before him.
24 And when he came to the tower, he
took *them* from their hand, and bestowed *them* in the house: and he let
the men go, and they departed.
25 But he went in, and stood before his
master. And Ē-lī'shȧ said unto him,
Whence *comest thou*, Gē-hā'zī? And
he said, Thy servant went no whither.
26 And he said unto him, Went not
mine heart *with thee*, when the man
turned again from his chariot to meet
thee? *Is it* a time to receive money, and
to receive garments, and oliveyards,
and vineyards, and sheep, and oxen,
and menservants, and maidservants?
27 The leprosy therefore of Nā'ȧ-măn
shall cleave unto thee, and unto thy
seed for ever. And he went out from
his presence a leper *as white* as snow.

CHAPTER 6

AND the sons of the prophets said
unto Ē-lī'shȧ, Behold now, the
place where we dwell with thee is too
strait for us.
2 Let us go, we pray thee, unto Jordan, and take thence every man a beam,
and let us make us a place there, where
we may dwell. And he answered, Go ye.
3 And one said, Be content, I pray
thee, and go with thy servants. And he
answered, I will go.
4 So he went with them. And when
they came to Jordan, they cut down
wood.
5 But as one was felling a beam, the
axe head fell into the water: and he
cried, and said, Alas, master! for it was
borrowed.
6 And the man of God said, Where fell
it? And he showed him the place. And
he cut down a stick, and cast *it* in
thither; and the iron did swim.
7 Therefore said he, Take *it* up to thee.
And he put out his hand, and took it.
8 ℭ Then the king of Syria warred
against Ĭs̱'rā-ĕl, and took counsel with
his servants, saying, In such and such
a place *shall be* my camp.
9 And the man of God sent unto the
king of Ĭs̱'rā-ĕl, saying, Beware that thou
pass not such a place; for thither the
Syrians are come down.
10 And the king of Ĭs̱'rā-ĕl sent to the
place which the man of God told him
and warned him of, and saved himself
there, not once nor twice.
11 Therefore the heart of the king of
Syria was sore troubled for this thing;
and he called his servants, and said unto
them, Will ye not show me which of us
is for the king of Ĭs̱'rā-ĕl?
12 And one of his servants said, None,
my lord, O king: but Ē-lī'shȧ, the
prophet that *is* in Ĭs̱'rā-ĕl, telleth the
king of Ĭs̱'rā-ĕl the words that thou
speakest in thy bedchamber.
13 ℭ And he said, Go and spy where
he *is*, that I may send and fetch him.
And it was told him, saying, Behold, *he*
is in Dō'thăn.
14 Therefore sent he thither horses,
and chariots, and a great host: and they
came by night, and compassed the
city about.
15 And when the servant of the man of
God was risen early, and gone forth,
behold, a host compassed the city both
with horses and chariots. And his servant said unto him, Alas, my master!
how shall we do?
16 And he answered, Fear not: for they
that *be* with us *are* more than they that
be with them.
17 And Ē-lī'shȧ prayed, and said,
LORD, I pray thee, open his eyes, that
he may see. And the LORD opened the

eyes of the young man; and he saw:
and, behold, the mountain *was* full of
horses and chariots of fire round about
Ē-lī′shȧ.
18 And when they came down to him,
Ē-lī′shȧ prayed unto the LORD, and
said, Smite this people, I pray thee,
with blindness. And he smote them
with blindness according to the word of
Ē-lī′shȧ.
19 ¶ And Ē-lī′shȧ said unto them,
This *is* not the way, neither *is* this the
city: follow me, and I will bring you to
the man whom ye seek. But he led them
to Sȧ-mā′rĭ-ȧ.
20 And it came to pass, when they
were come into Sȧ-mā′rĭ-ȧ, that Ē-lī′-
shȧ said, LORD, open the eyes of these
men, that they may see. And the LORD
opened their eyes, and they saw; and,
behold, *they were* in the midst of
Sȧ-mā′rĭ-ȧ.
21 And the king of Ĭş′rā-ĕl said unto
Ē-lī′shȧ, when he saw them, My father,
shall I smite *them*? shall I smite *them*?
22 And he answered, Thou shalt not
smite *them:* wouldest thou smite those
whom thou hast taken captive with thy
sword and with thy bow? set bread and
water before them, that they may eat
and drink, and go to their master.
23 And he prepared great provision for
them: and when they had eaten and
drunk, he sent them away, and they
went to their master. So the bands of
Syria came no more into the land of
Ĭş′rā-ĕl.
24 ¶ And it came to pass after this,
that Bĕn′-hā′dăd king of Syria gathered
all his host, and went up, and besieged
Sȧ-mā′rĭ-ȧ.
25 And there was a great famine in
Sȧ-mā′rĭ-ȧ: and, behold, they besieged
it, until an ass's head was *sold* for fourscore *pieces* of silver, and the fourth
part of a cab of dove's dung for five
pieces of silver.
26 And as the king of Ĭş′rā-ĕl was passing by upon the wall, there cried a woman
unto him, saying, Help, my lord, O king.
27 And he said, If the LORD do not
help thee, whence shall I help thee? out
of the barnfloor, or out of the winepress?
28 And the king said unto her, What
aileth thee? And she answered, This
woman said unto me, Give thy son, that
we may eat him to-day, and we will eat
my son to-morrow.
29 So we boiled my son, and did eat
him: and I said unto her on the next
day, Give thy son, that we may eat him:
and she hath hid her son.
30 ¶ And it came to pass, when the
king heard the words of the woman,
that he rent his clothes; and he passed
by upon the wall, and the people
looked, and, behold, *he had* sackcloth
within upon his flesh.
31 Then he said, God do so and more
also to me, if the head of Ē-lī′shȧ the
son of Shā′phăt shall stand on him this
day.
32 But Ē-lī′shȧ sat in his house, and
the elders sat with him; and *the king*
sent a man from before him: but ere the
messenger came to him, he said to the
elders, See ye how this son of a murderer hath sent to take away mine head?
look, when the messenger cometh,
shut the door, and hold him fast at the
door: *is* not the sound of his master's
feet behind him?
33 And while he yet talked with them,
behold, the messenger came down unto
him: and he said, Behold, this evil *is* of
the LORD; what should I wait for the
LORD any longer?

CHAPTER 7

THEN Ē-lī′shȧ said, Hear ye the
word of the LORD; Thus saith the
LORD, To-morrow about this time *shall*
a measure of fine flour *be sold* for a
shekel, and two measures of barley for
a shekel, in the gate of Sȧ-mā′rĭ-ȧ.
2 Then a lord on whose hand the king
leaned answered the man of God, and
said, Behold, *if* the LORD would make
windows in heaven, might this thing be?
And he said, Behold, thou shalt see *it*
with thine eyes, but shalt not eat
thereof.
3 ¶ And there were four leprous men
at the entering in of the gate: and they
said one to another, Why sit we here
until we die?
4 If we say, We will enter into the city,
then the famine *is* in the city, and we
shall die there: and if we sit still here,
we die also. Now therefore come, and
let us fall unto the host of the Syrians:
if they save us alive, we shall live; and
if they kill us, we shall but die.
5 And they rose up in the twilight, to
go unto the camp of the Syrians: and
when they were come to the uttermost

part of the camp of Syria, behold, *there*
was no man there.
6 For the LORD had made the host of
the Syrians to hear a noise of chariots,
and a noise of horses, *even* the noise of
a great host: and they said one to another,
Lo, the king of Ĭṣ'rā-ĕl hath hired against
us the kings of the Hĭt'tītes, and the
kings of the Egyptians, to come upon us.
7 Wherefore they arose and fled in the
twilight, and left their tents, and their
horses, and their asses, even the camp
as it *was*, and fled for their life.
8 And when these lepers came to the
uttermost part of the camp, they went
into one tent, and did eat and drink, and
carried thence silver, and gold, and raiment, and went and hid *it;* and came
again, and entered into another tent,
and carried thence *also*, and went and
hid *it*.
9 Then they said one to another, We do
not well: this day *is* a day of good tidings,
and we hold our peace: if we tarry till
the morning light, some mischief will
come upon us: now therefore come, that
we may go and tell the king's household.
10 So they came and called unto the
porter of the city: and they told them,
saying, We came to the camp of the
Syrians, and, behold, *there was* no man
there, neither voice of man, but horses
tied, and asses tied, and the tents as
they *were*.
11 And he called the porters; and they
told *it* to the king's house within.
12 ℂ And the king arose in the night,
and said unto his servants, I will now
show you what the Syrians have done
to us. They know that we *be* hungry;
therefore are they gone out of the camp
to hide themselves in the field, saying,
When they come out of the city, we
shall catch them alive, and get into the
city.
13 And one of his servants answered
and said, Let *some* take, I pray thee,
five of the horses that remain, which are
left in the city, (behold, they *are* as all
the multitude of Ĭṣ'rā-ĕl that are left in
it: behold, *I say*, they *are* even as all the
multitude of the Ĭṣ'rā-ĕl-ītes that are
consumed:) and let us send and see.
14 They took therefore two chariot
horses; and the king sent after the host
of the Syrians, saying, Go and see.
15 And they went after them unto Jordan: and, lo, all the way *was* full of garments and vessels, which the Syrians
had cast away in their haste. And
the messengers returned, and told the
king.
16 And the people went out, and spoiled
the tents of the Syrians. So a measure
of fine flour was *sold* for a shekel, and
two measures of barley for a shekel, according to the word of the LORD.
17 ℂ And the king appointed the lord
on whose hand he leaned to have the
charge of the gate: and the people trode
upon him in the gate, and he died, as
the man of God had said, who spake
when the king came down to him.
18 And it came to pass as the man of
God had spoken to the king, saying,
Two measures of barley for a shekel,
and a measure of fine flour for a shekel,
shall be to-morrow about this time in
the gate of Să-mā'rĭ-ȧ:
19 And that lord answered the man of
God, and said, Now, behold, *if* the LORD
should make windows in heaven, might
such a thing be? And he said, Behold,
thou shalt see it with thine eyes, but
shalt not eat thereof.
20 And so it fell out unto him: for the
people trode upon him in the gate, and
he died.

CHAPTER 8

THEN spake Ē-lī'shȧ unto the woman,
whose son he had restored to life,
saying, Arise, and go thou and thine
household, and sojourn wheresoever
thou canst sojourn: for the LORD hath
called for a famine; and it shall also
come upon the land seven years.
2 And the woman arose, and did after
the saying of the man of God: and she
went with her household, and sojourned
in the land of the Phĭ-lĭs'tĭneṣ seven
years.
3 And it came to pass at the seven
years' end, that the woman returned out
of the land of the Phĭ-lĭs'tĭneṣ: and she
went forth to cry unto the king for her
house and for her land.
4 And the king talked with Gē-hā'zī
the servant of the man of God, saying,
Tell me, I pray thee, all the great things
that E-lī'shȧ hath done.
5 And it came to pass, as he was telling
the king how he had restored a dead
body to life, that, behold, the woman,
whose son he had restored to life, cried
to the king for her house and for her

land. And Gē-hā'zī said, My lord, O
king, this *is* the woman, and this *is* her
son, whom Ē-lī'shȧ restored to life.
6 And when the king asked the woman,
she told him. So the king appointed unto
her a certain officer, saying, Restore all
that *was* hers, and all the fruits of the
field since the day that she left the land,
even until now.
7 ¶ And Ē-lī'shȧ came to Damascus;
and Bĕn'–hā'dăd the king of Syria was
sick; and it was told him, saying, The
man of God is come hither.
8 And the king said unto Hăz'ā-ĕl,
Take a present in thine hand, and go,
meet the man of God, and inquire of the
LORD by him, saying, Shall I recover of
this disease?
9 So Hăz'ā-ĕl went to meet him, and
took a present with him, even of every
good thing of Damascus, forty camels'
burden, and came and stood before him,
and said, Thy son Bĕn'–hā'dăd king of
Syria hath sent me to thee, saying, Shall
I recover of this disease?
10 And Ē-lī'shȧ said unto him, Go, say
unto him, Thou mayest certainly recover:
howbeit the LORD hath showed me that
he shall surely die.
11 And he settled his countenance
steadfastly, until he was ashamed: and
the man of God wept.
12 And Hăz'ā-ĕl said, Why weepeth
my lord? And he answered, Because I
know the evil that thou wilt do unto the
children of Ĭş'rā-ĕl: their strongholds
wilt thou set on fire, and their young
men wilt thou slay with the sword, and
wilt dash their children, and rip up their
women with child.
13 And Hăz'ā-ĕl said, But what, *is* thy
servant a dog, that he should do this
great thing? And Ē-lī'shȧ answered,
The LORD hath showed me that thou
shalt be king over Syria.
14 So he departed from Ē-lī'shȧ, and
came to his master; who said to him,
What said Ē-lī'shȧ to thee? And he answered, He told me *that* thou shouldest
surely recover.
15 And it came to pass on the morrow,
that he took a thick cloth, and dipped *it*
in water, and spread *it* on his face, so
that he died: and Hăz'ā-ĕl reigned in his
stead.
16 ¶ And in the fifth year of Jō'răm
the son of Ahab king of Ĭş'rā-ĕl, Jē-hŏsh'-
ȧ-phăt *being* then king of Judah, Jē-hō'-
răm the son of Jē-hŏsh'ȧ-phăt king of
Judah began to reign.
17 Thirty and two years old was he
when he began to reign; and he reigned
eight years in Jerusalem.
18 And he walked in the way of the
kings of Ĭş'rā-ĕl, as did the house of
Ahab; for the daughter of Ahab was his
wife: and he did evil in the sight of the
LORD.
19 Yet the LORD would not destroy Judah for David his servant's sake, as he
promised him to give him always a light,
and to his children.
20 ¶ In his days Ē'dŏm revolted from
under the hand of Judah, and made a
king over themselves.
21 So Jō'răm went over to Zā'ĭr, and all
the chariots with him: and he rose by
night, and smote the Ē'dŏm-ītes which
compassed him about, and the captains
of the chariots: and the people fled into
their tents.
22 Yet Ē'dŏm revolted from under the
hand of Judah unto this day. Then Lĭb'-
nȧh revolted at the same time.
23 And the rest of the acts of Jō'răm,
and all that he did, *are* they not written
in the book of the Chronicles of the kings
of Judah?
24 And Jō'răm slept with his fathers,
and was buried with his fathers in the
city of David: and Ā'hȧ-zī'ȧh his son
reigned in his stead.
25 ¶ In the twelfth year of Jō'răm the
son of Ahab king of Ĭş'rā-ĕl did Ā'hȧ-
zī'ȧh the son of Jē-hō'răm king of Judah
begin to reign.
26 Two and twenty years old *was* Ā'hȧ-
zī'ȧh when he began to reign; and he
reigned one year in Jerusalem. And his
mother's name *was* Ăth'ȧ-lī'ȧh, the
daughter of Ŏm'rī king of Ĭş'rā-ĕl.
27 And he walked in the way of the
house of Ahab, and did evil in the sight
of the LORD, as *did* the house of Ahab:
for he *was* the son-in-law of the house
of Ahab.
28 ¶ And he went with Jō'răm the son
of Ahab to the war against Hăz'ā-ĕl king
of Syria in Rā'mŏth–gĭl'ē-ăd; and the
Syrians wounded Jō'răm.
29 And king Jō'răm went back to be
healed in Jĕz'rē-ĕl of the wounds which
the Syrians had given him at Rā'mȧh,
when he fought against Hăz'ā-ĕl king of
Syria. And Ā'hȧ-zī'ȧh the son of Jē-
hō'răm king of Judah went down to see

Jō′răm the son of Ahab in Jĕz′rē-ĕl, because he was sick.

CHAPTER 9

AND Ē-lī′shȧ the prophet called one of the children of the prophets, and said unto him, Gird up thy loins, and take this box of oil in thine hand, and go to Rā′mŏth-gĭl′ē-ăd:
2 And when thou comest thither, look out there Jē′hū the son of Jē-hŏsh′ȧ-phăt the son of Nĭm′shī, and go in, and make him arise up from among his brethren, and carry him to an inner chamber;
3 Then take the box of oil, and pour *it* on his head, and say, Thus saith the LORD, I have anointed thee king over Ĭṣ′rā-ĕl. Then open the door, and flee, and tarry not.
4 ¶ So the young man, *even* the young man the prophet, went to Rā′mŏth-gĭl′ē-ăd.
5 And when he came, behold, the captains of the host *were* sitting; and he said, I have an errand to thee, O captain. And Jē′hū said, Unto which of all us? And he said, To thee, O captain.
6 And he arose, and went into the house; and he poured the oil on his head, and said unto him, Thus saith the LORD God of Ĭṣ′rā-ĕl, I have anointed thee king over the people of the LORD, *even* over Ĭṣ′rā-ĕl.
7 And thou shalt smite the house of Ahab thy master, that I may avenge the blood of my servants the prophets, and the blood of all the servants of the LORD, at the hand of Jĕz′ē-bĕl.
8 For the whole house of Ahab shall perish: and I will cut off from Ahab him that pisseth against the wall, and him that is shut up and left in Ĭṣ′rā-ĕl:
9 And I will make the house of Ahab like the house of Jĕr′ō-bō′ăm the son of Nē′băt, and like the house of Bā′ȧ-shȧ the son of Ȧ-hī′jȧh:
10 And the dogs shall eat Jĕz′ē-bĕl in the portion of Jĕz′rē-ĕl, and *there shall be* none to bury *her*. And he opened the door, and fled.
11 ¶ Then Jē′hū came forth to the servants of his lord: and *one* said unto him, *Is* all well? wherefore came this mad *fellow* to thee? And he said unto them, Ye know the man, and his communication.
12 And they said, *It is* false; tell us now. And he said, Thus and thus spake he to me, saying, Thus saith the LORD, I have anointed thee king over Ĭṣ′rā-ĕl.
13 Then they hasted, and took every man his garment, and put *it* under him on the top of the stairs, and blew with trumpets, saying, Jē′hū is king.
14 So Jē′hū the son of Jē-hŏsh′ȧ-phăt the son of Nĭm′shī conspired against Jō′răm. (Now Jō′răm had kept Rā′mŏth-gĭl′ē-ăd, he and all Ĭṣ′rā-ĕl, because of Hăz′ā-ĕl king of Syria.
15 But king Jō′răm was returned to be healed in Jĕz′rē-ĕl of the wounds which the Syrians had given him, when he fought with Hăz′ā-ĕl king of Syria.) And Jē′hū said, If it be your minds, *then* let none go forth *nor* escape out of the city to go to tell *it* in Jĕz′rē-ĕl.
16 So Jē′hū rode in a chariot, and went to Jĕz′rē-ĕl; for Jō′răm lay there. And Ā′hȧ-zī′ȧh king of Judah was come down to see Jō′răm.
17 And there stood a watchman on the tower in Jĕz′rē-ĕl, and he spied the company of Jē′hū as he came, and said, I see a company. And Jō′răm said, Take a horseman, and send to meet them, and let him say, *Is it* peace?
18 So there went one on horseback to meet him, and said, Thus saith the king, *Is it* peace? And Jē′hū said, What hast thou to do with peace? turn thee behind me. And the watchman told, saying, The messenger came to them, but he cometh not again.
19 Then he sent out a second on horseback, which came to them, and said, Thus saith the king, *Is it* peace? And Jē′hū answered, What hast thou to do with peace? turn thee behind me.
20 And the watchman told, saying, He came even unto them, and cometh not again: and the driving *is* like the driving of Jē′hū the son of Nĭm′shī; for he driveth furiously.
21 And Jō′răm said, Make ready. And his chariot was made ready. And Jō′răm king of Ĭṣ′rā-ĕl and Ā′hȧ-zī′ȧh king of Judah went out, each in his chariot, and they went out against Jē′hū, and met him in the portion of Nā′bŏth the Jĕz′rē-ĕl-īte.
22 And it came to pass, when Jō′răm saw Jē′hū, that he said, *Is it* peace, Jē′hū? And he answered, What peace, so long as the whoredoms of thy mother Jĕz′ē-bĕl and her witchcrafts *are so* many?

23 And Jō′răm turned his hands, and
fled, and said to Ā′hȧ-zī′ȧh, *There is*
treachery, O Ā′hȧ-zī′ȧh.
24 And Jē′hū drew a bow with his full
strength, and smote Jē-hō′răm between
his arms, and the arrow went out at his
heart, and he sunk down in his chariot.
25 Then said *Jehu* to Bĭd′kär his captain, Take up, *and* cast him in the portion of the field of Nā′bŏth the Jĕz′rē-
ĕl-īte: for remember how that, when I
and thou rode together after Ahab his
father, the LORD laid this burden upon
him;
26 Surely I have seen yesterday the
blood of Nā′bŏth, and the blood of his
sons, saith the LORD; and I will requite
thee in this plat, saith the LORD. Now
therefore take *and* cast him into the plat
of ground, according to the word of the
LORD.
27 ℭ But when Ā′hȧ-zī′ȧh the king of
Judah saw *this,* he fled by the way of
the garden house. And Jē′hū followed
after him, and said, Smite him also in
the chariot. *And they did so* at the going
up to Gûr, which *is* by Ĭb′lē-ăm. And
he fled to Mē-gĭd′dō, and died there.
28 And his servants carried him in a
chariot to Jerusalem, and buried him in
his sepulchre with his fathers in the city
of David.
29 And in the eleventh year of Jō′răm
the son of Ahab began Ā′hȧ-zī′ȧh to
reign over Judah.
30 ℭ And when Jē′hū was come to
Jĕz′rē-ĕl, Jĕz′ē-bĕl heard *of it;* and she
painted her face, and tired her head,
and looked out at a window.
31 And as Jē′hū entered in at the gate,
she said, *Had* Zĭm′rī peace, who slew
his master?
32 And he lifted up his face to the window, and said, Who *is* on my side? who?
And there looked out to him two *or* three
eunuchs.
33 And he said, Throw her down. So
they threw her down: and *some* of her
blood was sprinkled on the wall, and on
the horses: and he trode her under foot.
34 And when he was come in, he did
eat and drink, and said, Go, see now this
cursed *woman,* and bury her: for she *is*
a king's daughter.
35 And they went to bury her: but they
found no more of her than the skull, and
the feet, and the palms of *her* hands.
36 Wherefore they came again, and
told him. And he said, This *is* the word
of the LORD, which he spake by his servant Ē-lī′jȧh the Tĭsh′bīte, saying, In the
portion of Jĕz′rē-ĕl shall dogs eat the
flesh of Jĕz′ē-bĕl:
37 And the carcass of Jĕz′ē-bĕl shall be
as dung upon the face of the field in the
portion of Jĕz′rē-ĕl; *so* that they shall
not say, This *is* Jĕz′ē-bĕl.

CHAPTER 10

AND Ahab had seventy sons in Sȧ-
mā′rĭ-ȧ. And Jē′hū wrote letters,
and sent to Sȧ-mā′rĭ-ȧ, unto the rulers
of Jĕz′rē-ĕl, to the elders, and to them
that brought up Ahab's *children,* saying,
2 Now as soon as this letter cometh to
you, seeing your master's sons *are* with
you, and *there are* with you chariots and
horses, a fenced city also, and armor;
3 Look even out the best and meetest
of your master's sons, and set *him* on
his father's throne, and fight for your
master's house.
4 But they were exceedingly afraid, and
said, Behold, two kings stood not before
him: how then shall we stand?
5 And he that *was* over the house, and
he that *was* over the city, the elders also,
and the bringers up *of the children,* sent
to Jē′hū, saying, We *are* thy servants,
and will do all that thou shalt bid us; we
will not make any king: do thou *that
which is* good in thine eyes.
6 Then he wrote a letter the second
time to them, saying, If ye *be* mine, and
if ye will hearken unto my voice, take
ye the heads of the men your master's
sons, and come to me to Jĕz′rē-ĕl by
to-morrow this time. Now the king's
sons, *being* seventy persons, *were* with
the great men of the city, which brought
them up.
7 And it came to pass, when the letter
came to them, that they took the king's
sons, and slew seventy persons, and put
their heads in baskets, and sent him
them to Jĕz′rē-ĕl.
8 ℭ And there came a messenger, and
told him, saying, They have brought the
heads of the king's sons. And he said,
Lay ye them in two heaps at the entering
in of the gate until the morning.
9 And it came to pass in the morning,
that he went out, and stood, and said to
all the people, Ye *be* righteous: behold,
I conspired against my master, and slew
him: but who slew all these?

10 Know now that there shall fall unto
the earth nothing of the word of the
LORD, which the LORD spake concerning the house of Ahab: for the LORD hath
done *that* which he spake by his servant
Ē-lī′jȧh.
11 So Jē′hū slew all that remained of
the house of Ahab in Jĕz′rē-ĕl, and all
his great men, and his kinsfolk, and his
priests, until he left him none remaining.
12 ¶ And he arose and departed, and
came to Sȧ-mā′rĭ-ȧ. *And* as he *was* at
the shearing house in the way,
13 Jē′hū met with the brethren of Ā′hȧ-
zī′ȧh king of Judah, and said, Who *are*
ye? And they answered, We *are* the
brethren of Ā′hȧ-zī′ȧh; and we go down
to salute the children of the king and the
children of the queen.
14 And he said, Take them alive. And
they took them alive, and slew them at
the pit of the shearing house, *even* two
and forty men; neither left he any of
them.
15 ¶ And when he was departed thence,
he lighted on Jē-hŏn′ȧ-dăb the son of
Rē′chăb *coming* to meet him: and he
saluted him, and said to him, Is thine
heart right, as my heart *is* with thy
heart? And Jē-hŏn′ȧ-dăb answered, It
is. If it be, give *me* thine hand. And he
gave *him* his hand; and he took him up
to him into the chariot.
16 And he said, Come with me, and see
my zeal for the LORD. So they made him
ride in his chariot.
17 And when he came to Sȧ-mā′rĭ-ȧ, he
slew all that remained unto Ahab in Sȧ-
mā′rĭ-ȧ, till he had destroyed him, according to the saying of the LORD, which
he spake to Ē-lī′jȧh.
18 ¶ And Jē′hū gathered all the people
together, and said unto them, Ahab
served Bā′ăl a little; *but* Jē′hū shall
serve him much.
19 Now therefore call unto me all the
prophets of Bā′ăl, all his servants, and
all his priests; let none be wanting: for I
have a great sacrifice *to do* to Bā′ăl;
whosoever shall be wanting, he shall not
live. But Jē′hū did *it* in subtilty, to the
intent that he might destroy the worshippers of Bā′ăl.
20 And Jē′hū said, Proclaim a solemn
assembly for Bā′ăl. And they proclaimed *it*.
21 And Jē′hū sent through all Ĭş′rā-ĕl:
and all the worshippers of Bā′ăl came,
so that there was not a man left that
came not. And they came into the house
of Bā′ăl; and the house of Bā′ăl was full
from one end to another.
22 And he said unto him that *was* over
the vestry, Bring forth vestments for all
the worshippers of Bā′ăl. And he brought
them forth vestments.
23 And Jē′hū went, and Jē-hŏn′ȧ-dăb
the son of Rē′chăb, into the house of
Bā′ăl, and said unto the worshippers of
Bā′ăl, Search, and look that there be
here with you none of the servants of
the LORD, but the worshippers of Bā′ăl
only.
24 And when they went in to offer sacrifices and burnt offerings, Jē′hū appointed fourscore men without, and said,
If any of the men whom I have brought
into your hands escape, *he that letteth*
him go, his life *shall be* for the life of
him.
25 And it came to pass, as soon as he
had made an end of offering the burnt
offering, that Jē′hū said to the guard and
to the captains, Go in, *and* slay them;
let none come forth. And they smote
them with the edge of the sword; and
the guard and the captains cast *them*
out, and went to the city of the house of
Bā′ăl.
26 And they brought forth the images
out of the house of Bā′ăl, and burned
them.
27 And they brake down the image of
Bā′ăl, and brake down the house of
Bā′ăl, and made it a draught house unto
this day.
28 Thus Jē′hū destroyed Bā′ăl out of
Ĭş′rā-ĕl.
29 ¶ Howbeit, *from* the sins of Jĕr′ō-
bō′ăm the son of Nē′băt, who made Ĭş′-
rā-ĕl to sin, Jē′hū departed not from
after them, *to wit,* the golden calves that
were in Beth-el, and that *were* in Dan.
30 And the LORD said unto Jē′hū, Because thou hast done well in executing
that which is right in mine eyes, *and*
hast done unto the house of Ahab according to all that *was* in mine heart,
thy children of the fourth *generation*
shall sit on the throne of Ĭş′rā-ĕl.
31 But Jē′hū took no heed to walk in
the law of the LORD God of Ĭş′rā-ĕl with
all his heart: for he departed not from
the sins of Jĕr′ō-bō′ăm, which made Ĭş′-
rā-ĕl to sin.
32 ¶ In those days the LORD began to

cut Ĭs̱'rā-ĕl short: and Hăz'ā-ĕl smote
them in all the coasts of Ĭs̱'rā-ĕl;
33 From Jordan eastward, all the land
of Gĭl'ē-ăd, the Gadites, and the Reubenites, and the Mȧ-năs'sītes, from
Ȧ-rō'ẽr, which *is* by the river Ãr'nŏn,
even Gĭl'ē-ăd and Bā'shăn.
34 Now the rest of the acts of Jē'hū,
and all that he did, and all his might,
are they not written in the book of the
Chronicles of the kings of Ĭs̱'rā-ĕl?
35 And Jē'hū slept with his fathers:
and they buried him in Sȧ-mā'rĭ-ȧ. And
Jē-hō'ȧ-hăz his son reigned in his stead.
36 And the time that Jē'hū reigned
over Ĭs̱'rā-ĕl in Sȧ-mā'rĭ-ȧ *was* twenty
and eight years.

CHAPTER 11

AND when Ăth'ȧ-lī'ȧh the mother of
Ā'hȧ-zī'ȧh saw that her son was
dead, she arose and destroyed all the
seed royal.
2 But Jē-hŏsh'ē-bȧ, the daughter of
king Jō'răm, sister of Ā'hȧ-zī'ȧh, took
Jō'ăsh the son of Ā'hȧ-zī'ȧh, and stole
him from among the king's sons *which*
were slain; and they hid him, *even*
him and his nurse, in the bedchamber
from Ăth'ȧ-lī'ȧh, so that he was not
slain.
3 And he was with her hid in the house
of the LORD six years. And Ăth'ȧ-lī'ȧh
did reign over the land.
4 ¶ And the seventh year Jē-hôi'ȧ-dȧ
sent and fetched the rulers over hundreds, with the captains and the guard,
and brought them to him into the house
of the LORD, and made a covenant with
them, and took an oath of them in the
house of the LORD, and showed them
the king's son.
5 And he commanded them, saying,
This *is* the thing that ye shall do; A
third part of you that enter in on the
sabbath shall even be keepers of the
watch of the king's house;
6 And a third part *shall be* at the gate
of Sûr; and a third part at the gate behind the guard: so shall ye keep the
watch of the house, that it be not broken
down.
7 And two parts of all you that go forth
on the sabbath, even they shall keep the
watch of the house of the LORD about
the king.
8 And ye shall compass the king round
about, every man with his weapons in
his hand: and he that cometh within the
ranges, let him be slain: and be ye with
the king as he goeth out and as he cometh in.
9 And the captains over the hundreds
did according to all *things* that Jē-hôi'-
ȧ-dȧ the priest commanded: and they
took every man his men that were to
come in on the sabbath, with them that
should go out on the sabbath, and came
to Jē-hôi'ȧ-dȧ the priest.
10 And to the captains over hundreds
did the priest give king David's spears
and shields, that *were* in the temple of
the LORD.
11 And the guard stood, every man with
his weapons in his hand, round about
the king, from the right corner of the
temple to the left corner of the temple,
along by the altar and the temple.
12 And he brought forth the king's son,
and put the crown upon him, and *gave*
him the testimony; and they made him
king, and anointed him; and they clapped
their hands, and said, God save the
king.
13 ¶ And when Ăth'ȧ-lī'ȧh heard the
noise of the guard *and* of the people, she
came to the people into the temple of
the LORD.
14 And when she looked, behold, the
king stood by a pillar, as the manner
was, and the princes and the trumpeters
by the king, and all the people of the
land rejoiced, and blew with trumpets:
and Ăth'ȧ-lī'ȧh rent her clothes, and
cried, Treason, treason.
15 But Jē-hôi'ȧ-dȧ the priest commanded the captains of the hundreds,
the officers of the host, and said unto
them, Have her forth without the ranges;
and him that followeth her kill with the
sword. For the priest had said, Let her
not be slain in the house of the LORD.
16 And they laid hands on her; and she
went by the way by the which the horses
came into the king's house: and there
was she slain.
17 ¶ And Jē-hôi'ȧ-dȧ made a covenant between the LORD and the king and
the people, that they should be the
LORD's people; between the king also
and the people.
18 And all the people of the land went
into the house of Bā'ăl, and brake it
down; his altars and his images brake
they in pieces thoroughly, and slew
Măt'tăn the priest of Bā'ăl before the

altars. And the priest appointed officers over the house of the LORD.

19 And he took the rulers over hundreds, and the captains, and the guard, and all the people of the land; and they brought down the king from the house of the LORD, and came by the way of the gate of the guard to the king's house. And he sat on the throne of the kings.

20 And all the people of the land rejoiced, and the city was in quiet: and they slew Ăth'ȧ-lī'ăh with the sword *beside* the king's house.

21 Seven years old *was* Jē-hō'ăsh when he began to reign.

CHAPTER 12

IN the seventh year of Jē'hū, Jē-hō'ăsh began to reign; and forty years reigned he in Jerusalem. And his mother's name *was* Zĭb'ĭ-ȧh of Bē'ĕr–shē'bȧ.

2 And Jē-hō'ăsh did *that which was* right in the sight of the LORD all his days wherein Jē-hoi'ȧ-dȧ the priest instructed him.

3 But the high places were not taken away: the people still sacrificed and burnt incense in the high places.

4 ¶ And Jē-hō'ăsh said to the priests, All the money of the dedicated things that is brought into the house of the LORD, *even* the money of every one that passeth *the account,* the money that every man is set at, *and* all the money that cometh into any man's heart to bring into the house of the LORD,

5 Let the priests take *it* to them, every man of his acquaintance: and let them repair the breaches of the house, wheresoever any breach shall be found.

6 But it was *so, that* in the three and twentieth year of king Jē-hō'ăsh the priests had not repaired the breaches of the house.

7 Then king Jē-hō'ăsh called for Jē-hoi'ȧ-dȧ the priest, and the *other* priests, and said unto them, Why repair ye not the breaches of the house? now therefore receive no *more* money of your acquaintance, but deliver it for the breaches of the house.

8 And the priests consented to receive no *more* money of the people, neither to repair the breaches of the house.

9 But Jē-hoi'ȧ-dȧ the priest took a chest, and bored a hole in the lid of it, and set it beside the altar, on the right side as one cometh into the house of the LORD: and the priests that kept the door put therein all the money *that was* brought into the house of the LORD.

10 And it was *so,* when they saw that *there was* much money in the chest, that the king's scribe and the high priest came up, and they put up in bags, and told the money that was found in the house of the LORD.

11 And they gave the money, being told, into the hands of them that did the work, that had the oversight of the house of the LORD: and they laid it out to the carpenters and builders, that wrought upon the house of the LORD,

12 And to masons, and hewers of stone, and to buy timber and hewed stone to repair the breaches of the house of the LORD, and for all that was laid out for the house to repair *it.*

13 Howbeit there were not made for the house of the LORD bowls of silver, snuffers, basins, trumpets, any vessels of gold, or vessels of silver, of the money *that was* brought into the house of the LORD:

14 But they gave that to the workmen, and repaired therewith the house of the LORD.

15 Moreover they reckoned not with the men, into whose hand they delivered the money to be bestowed on workmen: for they dealt faithfully.

16 The trespass money and sin money was not brought into the house of the LORD: it was the priests'.

17 ¶ Then Hăz'ā-ĕl king of Syria went up, and fought against Gath, and took it: and Hăz'ā-ĕl set his face to go up to Jerusalem.

18 And Jē-hō'ăsh king of Judah took all the hallowed things that Jē-hŏsh'ȧ-phăt, and Jē-hō'răm, and Ā'hȧ-zī'ăh, his fathers, kings of Judah, had dedicated, and his own hallowed things, and all the gold that was found in the treasures of the house of the LORD, and in the king's house, and sent *it* to Hăz'ā-ĕl king of Syria: and he went away from Jerusalem.

19 ¶ And the rest of the acts of Jō'ăsh, and all that he did, *are* they not written in the book of the Chronicles of the kings of Judah?

20 And his servants arose, and made a conspiracy, and slew Jō'ăsh in the house of Mĭl'lō, which goeth down to Sĭl'lȧ.

21 For Jŏz'ā-chär the son of Shĭm'ē-ăth, and Jē-hŏz'ā-băd the son of Shō'mĕr,

his servants, smote him, and he died; and they buried him with his fathers in the city of David: and Ăm′ȧ-zī′ȧh his son reigned in his stead.

CHAPTER 13

IN the three and twentieth year of Jō′ăsh the son of Ā′hȧ-zī′ȧh king of Judah, Jē-hō′ȧ-hăz the son of Jē′hū began to reign over Ĭş′rā-ĕl in Sȧ-mā′rĭ-ȧ, *and reigned* seventeen years.

2 And he did *that which was* evil in the sight of the LORD, and followed the sins of Jĕr′ō-bō′ăm the son of Nē′băt, which made Ĭş′rā-ĕl to sin; he departed not therefrom.

3 ¶ And the anger of the LORD was kindled against Ĭş′rā-ĕl, and he delivered them into the hand of Hăz′ā-ĕl king of Syria, and into the hand of Bĕn′–hā′dăd the son of Hăz′ā-ĕl, all *their* days.

4 And Jē-hō′ȧ-hăz besought the LORD, and the LORD hearkened unto him: for he saw the oppression of Ĭş′rā-ĕl, because the king of Syria oppressed them.

5 (And the LORD gave Ĭş′rā-ĕl a saviour, so that they went out from under the hand of the Syrians: and the children of Ĭş′rā-ĕl dwelt in their tents, as beforetime.

6 Nevertheless they departed not from the sins of the house of Jĕr′ō-bō′ăm, who made Ĭş′rā-ĕl sin, *but* walked therein: and there remained the grove also in Sȧ-mā′rĭ-ȧ.)

7 Neither did he leave of the people to Jē-hō′ȧ-hăz but fifty horsemen, and ten chariots, and ten thousand footmen; for the king of Syria had destroyed them, and had made them like the dust by threshing.

8 ¶ Now the rest of the acts of Jē-hō′ȧ-hăz, and all that he did, and his might, *are* they not written in the book of the Chronicles of the kings of Ĭş′rā-ĕl?

9 And Jē-hō′ȧ-hăz slept with his fathers; and they buried him in Sȧ-mā′rĭ-ȧ: and Jō′ăsh his son reigned in his stead.

10 ¶ In the thirty and seventh year of Jō′ăsh king of Judah began Jē-hō′ăsh the son of Jē-hō′ȧ-hăz to reign over Ĭş′rā-ĕl in Sȧ-mā′rĭ-ȧ, *and reigned* sixteen years.

11 And he did *that which was* evil in the sight of the LORD; he departed not from all the sins of Jĕr′ō-bō′ăm the son of Nē′băt, who made Ĭş′rā-ĕl sin: *but* he walked therein.

12 And the rest of the acts of Jō′ăsh, and all that he did, and his might wherewith he fought against Ăm′ȧ-zī′ȧh king of Judah, *are* they not written in the book of the Chronicles of the kings of Ĭş′rā-ĕl?

13 And Jō′ăsh slept with his fathers; and Jĕr′ō-bō′ăm sat upon his throne: and Jō′ăsh was buried in Sȧ-mā′rĭ-ȧ with the kings of Ĭş′rā-ĕl.

14 ¶ Now Ē-lī′shȧ was fallen sick of his sickness whereof he died. And Jō′ăsh the king of Ĭş′rā-ĕl came down unto him, and wept over his face, and said, O my father, my father! the chariot of Ĭş′rā-ĕl, and the horsemen thereof.

15 And Ē-lī′shȧ said unto him, Take bow and arrows. And he took unto him bow and arrows.

16 And he said to the king of Ĭş′rā-ĕl, Put thine hand upon the bow. And he put his hand *upon it:* and Ē-lī′shȧ put his hands upon the king's hands.

17 And he said, Open the window eastward. And he opened *it*. Then Ē-lī′shȧ said, Shoot. And he shot. And he said, The arrow of the LORD's deliverance, and the arrow of deliverance from Syria: for thou shalt smite the Syrians in Ā′phĕk, till thou have consumed *them*.

18 And he said, Take the arrows. And he took *them*. And he said unto the king of Ĭş′rā-ĕl, Smite upon the ground. And he smote thrice, and stayed.

19 And the man of God was wroth with him, and said, Thou shouldest have smitten five or six times; then hadst thou smitten Syria till thou hadst consumed *it:* whereas now thou shalt smite Syria *but* thrice.

20 ¶ And Ē-lī′shȧ died, and they buried him. And the bands of the Mō′ăb-ītes invaded the land at the coming in of the year.

21 And it came to pass, as they were burying a man, that, behold, they spied a band *of men;* and they cast the man into the sepulchre of Ē-lī′shȧ: and when the man was let down, and touched the bones of Ē-lī′shȧ, he revived, and stood up on his feet.

22 ¶ But Hăz′ā-ĕl king of Syria oppressed Ĭş′rā-ĕl all the days of Jē-hō′ȧ-hăz.

23 And the LORD was gracious unto them, and had compassion on them, and had respect unto them, because of his covenant with Abraham, Isaac, and

Jacob, and would not destroy them,
neither cast he them from his presence
as yet.
24 So Hăz′ā-ĕl king of Syria died; and
Bĕn′–ha′dăd his son reigned in his stead.
25 And Jē-hō′ăsh the son of Jē-hō′ȧ-hăz
took again out of the hand of Bĕn′–hā′-
dăd the son of Hăz′ā-ĕl the cities, which
he had taken out of the hand of Jē-hō′-
ȧ-hăz his father by war. Three times
did Jō′ăsh beat him, and recovered the
cities of Ĭș′rā-ĕl.

CHAPTER 14

IN the second year of Jō′ăsh son
of Jē-hō′ȧ-hăz king of Ĭș′rā-ĕl
reigned Ăm′ȧ-zī′ȧh the son of Jō′ăsh
king of Judah.
2 He was twenty and five years old
when he began to reign, and reigned
twenty and nine years in Jerusalem.
And his mother's name *was* Jē′hō-ăd′-
dăn of Jerusalem.
3 And he did *that which was* right in
the sight of the LORD, yet not like David
his father: he did according to all things
as Jō′ăsh his father did.
4 Howbeit the high places were not
taken away: as yet the people did sacrifice and burnt incense on the high places.
5 ¶ And it came to pass, as soon as the
kingdom was confirmed in his hand,
that he slew his servants which had slain
the king his father.
6 But the children of the murderers he
slew not: according unto that which is
written in the book of the law of Moses,
wherein the LORD commanded, saying,
The fathers shall not be put to death for
the children, nor the children be put to
death for the fathers; but every man shall
be put to death for his own sin.
7 He slew of Ē′dŏm in the valley of
salt ten thousand, and took Sē′lȧh by
war, and called the name of it Jŏk′thē-ĕl
unto this day.
8 ¶ Then Ăm′ȧ-zī′ȧh sent messengers
to Jē-hō′ăsh, the son of Jē-hō′ȧ-hăz son
of Jē′hū, king of Ĭș′rā-ĕl, saying, Come,
let us look one another in the face.
9 And Jē-hō′ăsh the king of Ĭș′rā-ĕl
sent to Ăm′ȧ-zī′ȧh king of Judah, saying,
The thistle that *was* in Lebanon sent to
the cedar that *was* in Lebanon, saying,
Give thy daughter to my son to wife: and
there passed by a wild beast that *was* in
Lebanon, and trode down the thistle.
10 Thou hast indeed smitten Ē′dŏm,
and thine heart hath lifted thee up: glory
of this, and tarry at home: for why shouldest thou meddle to *thy* hurt, that thou
shouldest fall, *even* thou, and Judah
with thee?
11 But Ăm′ȧ-zī′ȧh would not hear.
Therefore Jē-hō′ăsh king of Ĭș′rā-ĕl
went up; and he and Ăm′ȧ-zī′ȧh king of
Judah looked one another in the face at
Bĕth′–shē′mĕsh, which *belongeth* to
Judah.
12 And Judah was put to the worse before Ĭș′rā-ĕl; and they fled every man to
their tents.
13 And Jē-hō′ăsh king of Ĭș′rā-ĕl took
Ăm′ȧ-zī′ȧh king of Judah, the son of Jē-
hō′ăsh the son of Ā′hȧ-zī′ȧh, at Bĕth′–
shē′mĕsh, and came to Jerusalem, and
brake down the wall of Jerusalem from
the gate of Ē′phrā-ĭm unto the corner
gate, four hundred cubits.
14 And he took all the gold and silver,
and all the vessels that were found in
the house of the LORD, and in the treasures of the king's house, and hostages,
and returned to Sȧ-mā′rĭ-ȧ.
15 ¶ Now the rest of the acts of Jē-hō′-
ăsh which he did, and his might, and
how he fought with Ăm′ȧ-zī′ȧh king of
Judah, *are* they not written in the book
of the Chronicles of the kings of Ĭș′rā-ĕl?
16 And Jē-hō′ăsh slept with his fathers,
and was buried in Sȧ-mā′rĭ-ȧ with the
kings of Ĭș′rā-ĕl; and Jĕr′ō-bō′ăm his
son reigned in his stead.
17 ¶ And Ăm′ȧ-zī′ȧh the son of Jō′ăsh
king of Judah lived after the death of
Jē-hō′ăsh son of Jē-hō′ȧ-hăz king of Ĭș′-
rā-ĕl fifteen years.
18 And the rest of the acts of Ăm′ȧ-
zī′ȧh, *are* they not written in the book of
the Chronicles of the kings of Judah?
19 Now they made a conspiracy against
him in Jerusalem: and he fled to Lā′-
chĭsh; but they sent after him to Lā′-
chĭsh, and slew him there.
20 And they brought him on horses:
and he was buried at Jerusalem with
his fathers in the city of David.
21 ¶ And all the people of Judah took
Ăz′ȧ-rī′ȧh, which *was* sixteen years old,
and made him king instead of his father
Ăm′ȧ-zī′ȧh.
22 He built Ē′lȧth, and restored it to
Judah, after that the king slept with his
fathers.
23 ¶ In the fifteenth year of Ăm′ȧ-
zī′ȧh the son of Jō′ăsh king of Judah,

Jĕr′ō-bō′ăm the son of Jō′ăsh king
of Ĭṣ′rā-ĕl began to reign in Sȧ-mā′rĭ-ȧ,
and reigned forty and one years.
24 And he did *that which was* evil in
the sight of the LORD: he departed not
from all the sins of Jĕr′ō-bō′ăm the son
of Nē′băt, who made Ĭṣ′rā-ĕl to sin.
25 He restored the coast of Ĭṣ′rā-ĕl
from the entering of Hā′măth unto the
sea of the plain, according to the word
of the LORD God of Ĭṣ′rā-ĕl, which he
spake by the hand of his servant Jonah,
the son of Ȧ-mĭt′taī, the prophet, which
was of Găth′-hē′phĕr.
26 For the LORD saw the affliction of
Ĭṣ′rā-ĕl, *that it was* very bitter: for *there*
was not any shut up, nor any left, nor
any helper for Ĭṣ′rā-ĕl.
27 And the LORD said not that he would
blot out the name of Ĭṣ′rā-ĕl from under
heaven: but he saved them by the hand
of Jĕr′ō-bō′ăm the son of Jō′ăsh.
28 ℂ Now the rest of the acts of Jĕr′ō-
bō′ăm, and all that he did, and his might,
how he warred, and how he recovered
Damascus, and Hā′măth, *which be-*
longed to Judah, for Ĭṣ′rā-ĕl, *are* they
not written in the book of the Chronicles
of the kings of Ĭṣ′rā-ĕl?
29 And Jĕr′ō-bō′ăm slept with his fathers, *even* with the kings of Ĭṣ′rā-ĕl;
and Zăch′ȧ-rī′ȧh his son reigned in his
stead.

CHAPTER 15

IN the twenty and seventh year of
Jĕr′ō-bō′ăm king of Ĭṣ′rā-ĕl began Ăz′ȧ-rī′ȧh son of Ăm′ȧ-zī′ȧh king of
Judah to reign.
2 Sixteen years old was he when he
began to reign, and he reigned two and
fifty years in Jerusalem. And his mother's name *was* Jĕch′ō-lī′ȧh of Jerusalem.
3 And he did *that which was* right in
the sight of the LORD, according to all
that his father Ăm′ȧ-zī′ȧh had done;
4 Save that the high places were not
removed: the people sacrificed and
burnt incense still on the high places.
5 ℂ And the LORD smote the king, so
that he was a leper unto the day of his
death, and dwelt in a several house.
And Jō′thăm the king's son *was* over the
house, judging the people of the land.
6 And the rest of the acts of Ăz′ȧ-rī′ȧh,
and all that he did, *are* they not written
in the book of the Chronicles of the kings
of Judah?
7 So Ăz′ȧ-rī′ȧh slept with his fathers;
and they buried him with his fathers in
the city of David: and Jō′thăm his son
reigned in his stead.
8 ℂ In the thirty and eighth year of
Ăz′ȧ-rī′ȧh king of Judah did Zăch′ȧ-rī′ȧh
the son of Jĕr′ō-bō′ăm reign over Ĭṣ′-
rā-ĕl in Sȧ-mā′rĭ-ȧ six months.
9 And he did *that which was* evil in the
sight of the LORD, as his fathers had
done: he departed not from the sins of
Jĕr′ō-bō′ăm the son of Nē′băt, who
made Ĭṣ′rā-ĕl to sin.
10 And Shăl′lŭm the son of Jā′bĕsh
conspired against him, and smote him
before the people, and slew him, and
reigned in his stead.
11 And the rest of the acts of Zăch′ȧ-
rī′ȧh, behold, they *are* written in the
book of the Chronicles of the kings of
Ĭṣ′rā-ĕl.
12 This *was* the word of the LORD
which he spake unto Jē′hū, saying, Thy
sons shall sit on the throne of Ĭṣ′rā-ĕl
unto the fourth *generation*. And so it
came to pass.
13 ℂ Shăl′lŭm the son of Jā′bĕsh began to reign in the nine and thirtieth
year of Ŭz-zī′ȧh king of Judah; and he
reigned a full month in Sȧ-mā′rĭ-ȧ.
14 For Mĕn′ȧ-hĕm the son of Gā′dī
went up from Tĭr′zȧh, and came to Sȧ-
mā′rĭ-ȧ, and smote Shăl′lŭm the son of
Jā′bĕsh in Sȧ-mā′rĭ-ȧ, and slew him, and
reigned in his stead.
15 And the rest of the acts of Shăl′lŭm,
and his conspiracy which he made, behold, they *are* written in the book of the
Chronicles of the kings of Ĭṣ′rā-ĕl.
16 ℂ Then Mĕn′ȧ-hĕm smote Tĭph′-
sȧh, and all that *were* therein, and the
coasts thereof from Tĭr′zȧh: because
they opened not *to him*, therefore he
smote *it; and* all the women therein that
were with child he ripped up.
17 In the nine and thirtieth year of
Ăz′ȧ-rī′ȧh king of Judah began Mĕn′ȧ-
hĕm the son of Gā′dī to reign over Ĭṣ′-
rā-ĕl *and reigned* ten years in Sȧ-mā′-
rĭ-ȧ.
18 And he did *that which was* evil in the
sight of the LORD: he departed not all
his days from the sins of Jĕr′ō-bō′ăm
the son of Nē′băt, who made Ĭṣ′rā-ĕl to
sin.
19 *And* Pŭl the king of Assyria came
against the land: and Mĕn′ȧ-hĕm gave
Pŭl a thousand talents of silver, that his

hand might be with him to confirm the
kingdom in his hand.
20 And Mĕn'ȧ-hĕm exacted the money
of Ĭṣ'rā-ĕl, *even* of all the mighty men of
wealth, of each man fifty shekels of silver, to give to the king of Assyria. So
the king of Assyria turned back, and
stayed not there in the land.
21 ¶ And the rest of the acts of Mĕn'ȧ-
hĕm, and all that he did, *are* they not
written in the book of the Chronicles of
the kings of Ĭṣ'rā-ĕl?
22 And Mĕn'ȧ-hĕm slept with his fathers; and Pĕk'ȧ-hī'ȧh his son reigned
in his stead.
23 ¶ In the fiftieth year of Ăz'ȧ-rī'ȧh
king of Judah, Pĕk'ȧ-hī'ȧh the son of
Mĕn'ȧ-hĕm began to reign over Ĭṣ'rā-ĕl
in Sȧ-mā'rĭ-ȧ, *and reigned* two years.
24 And he did *that which was* evil in
the sight of the LORD: he departed not
from the sins of Jĕr'ō-bō'ăm the son of
Nē'băt, who made Ĭṣ'rā-ĕl to sin.
25 But Pē'käh the son of Rĕm'ȧ-lī'ȧh,
a captain of his, conspired against him,
and smote him in Sȧ-mā'rĭ-ȧ, in the palace of the king's house, with Är'gŏb and
Ȧ-rī'ĕh, and with him fifty men of the
Gĭl'ē-ăd-ītes: and he killed him, and
reigned in his room.
26 And the rest of the acts of Pĕk'ȧ-
hī'ȧh, and all that he did, behold, they
are written in the book of the Chronicles
of the kings of Ĭṣ'rā-ĕl.
27 ¶ In the two and fiftieth year of
Ăz'ȧ-rī'ȧh king of Judah, Pē'käh the son
of Rĕm'ȧ-lī'ȧh began to reign over Ĭṣ'-
rā-ĕl in Sȧ-mā'rĭ-ȧ, *and reigned* twenty
years.
28 And he did *that which was* evil in
the sight of the LORD: he departed not
from the sins of Jĕr'ō-bō'ăm the son of
Nē'băt, who made Ĭṣ'rā-ĕl to sin.
29 In the days of Pē'käh king of Ĭṣ'-
rā-ĕl came Tĭg'lȧth-pĭ-lē'ṣĕr king of
Assyria, and took Ī'jŏn, and Ā'bĕl-bĕth-
mā'ȧ-cȧh, and Jȧ-nō'ȧh, and Kē'dĕsh,
and Hā'zŏr, and Gĭl'ē-ăd, and Galilee,
all the land of Năph'tȧ-lī, and carried
them captive to Assyria.
30 And Hō-shē'ȧ the son of Ē'lȧh made
a conspiracy against Pē'käh the son of
Rĕm'ȧ-lī'ȧh, and smote him, and slew
him, and reigned in his stead, in the
twentieth year of Jō'thăm the son of
Ŭz-zī'ȧh.
31 And the rest of the acts of Pē'käh,
and all that he did, behold, they *are* written in the book of the Chronicles of the
kings of Ĭṣ'rā-ĕl.
32 ¶ In the second year of Pē'käh the
son of Rĕm'ȧ-lī'ȧh king of Ĭṣ'rā-ĕl began
Jo'thăm the son of Ŭz-zī'ȧh king of Judah to reign.
33 Five and twenty years old was he
when he began to reign, and he reigned
sixteen years in Jerusalem. And his
mother's name *was* Jē-rṳ'shȧ, the daughter of Zā'dŏk.
34 And he did *that which was* right in
the sight of the LORD: he did according to all that his father Ŭz-zī'ȧh had
done.
35 ¶ Howbeit the high places were not
removed: the people sacrificed and
burned incense still in the high places.
He built the higher gate of the house of
the LORD.
36 ¶ Now the rest of the acts of Jō'-
thăm, and all that he did, *are* they not
written in the book of the Chronicles of
the kings of Judah?
37 In those days the LORD began to
send against Judah Rē'zĭn the king of
Syria, and Pē'käh the son of Rĕm'ȧ-
lī'ȧh.
38 And Jō'thăm slept with his fathers,
and was buried with his fathers in the
city of David his father: and Ahaz his
son reigned in his stead.

CHAPTER 16

IN the seventeenth year of Pē'käh the
son of Rĕm'ȧ-lī'ȧh, Ahaz the son of
Jō'thăm king of Judah began to reign.
2 Twenty years old *was* Ahaz when he
began to reign, and reigned sixteen
years in Jerusalem, and did not *that
which was* right in the sight of the LORD
his God, like David his father.
3 But he walked in the way of the kings
of Ĭṣ'rā-ĕl, yea, and made his son to pass
through the fire, according to the abominations of the heathen, whom the LORD
cast out from before the children of
Ĭṣ'rā-ĕl.
4 And he sacrificed and burnt incense
in the high places, and on the hills, and
under every green tree.
5 ¶ Then Rē'zĭn king of Syria, and
Pē'käh son of Rĕm'ȧ-lī'ȧh king of Ĭṣ'-
rā-ĕl, came up to Jerusalem to war: and
they besieged Ahaz, but could not overcome *him*.
6 At that time Rē'zĭn king of Syria recovered Ē'lȧth to Syria, and drave the

Jews from Ē'lȧth: and the Syrians came
to Ē'lȧth, and dwelt there unto this day.
7 So Ahaz sent messengers to Tĭg'lȧth-
pĭ-lē'ṣēr king of Assyria, saying, I *am*
thy servant and thy son: come up, and
save me out of the hand of the king of
Syria, and out of the hand of the king of
Ĭṣ'rā-ĕl, which rise up against me.
8 And Ahaz took the silver and gold
that was found in the house of the LORD,
and in the treasures of the king's house,
and sent *it for* a present to the king of
Assyria.
9 And the king of Assyria hearkened
unto him: for the king of Assyria went
up against Damascus, and took it, and
carried *the people of* it captive to Kīr,
and slew Rē'zĭn.
10 ℂ And king Ahaz went to Damascus
to meet Tĭg'lȧth-pĭ-lē'ṣēr king of Assyria, and saw an altar that *was* at Damascus: and king Ahaz sent to Ū-rī'jȧh
the priest the fashion of the altar, and
the pattern of it, according to all the
workmanship thereof.
11 And Ū-rī'jȧh the priest built an altar
according to all that king Ahaz had sent
from Damascus: so Ū-rī'jȧh the priest
made *it* against king Ahaz came from
Damascus.
12 And when the king was come from
Damascus, the king saw the altar: and
the king approached to the altar, and
offered thereon.
13 And he burnt his burnt offering and
his meat offering, and poured his drink
offering, and sprinkled the blood of his
peace offerings, upon the altar.
14 And he brought also the brazen altar, which *was* before the LORD, from
the forefront of the house, from between
the altar and the house of the LORD, and
put it on the north side of the altar.
15 And king Ahaz commanded Ū-rī'jȧh
the priest, saying, Upon the great altar
burn the morning burnt offering, and the
evening meat offering, and the king's
burnt sacrifice, and his meat offering,
with the burnt offering of all the people
of the land, and their meat offering, and
their drink offerings; and sprinkle upon
it all the blood of the burnt offering,
and all the blood of the sacrifice: and
the brazen altar shall be for me to inquire *by*.
16 Thus did Ū-rī'jȧh the priest, according to all that king Ahaz commanded.
17 ℂ And king Ahaz cut off the borders
of the bases, and removed the laver
from off them; and took down the sea
from off the brazen oxen that *were* under
it, and put it upon a pavement of stones.
18 And the covert for the sabbath that
they had built in the house, and the
king's entry without, turned he from the
house of the LORD for the king of
Assyria.
19 ℂ Now the rest of the acts of Ahaz
which he did, *are* they not written in the
book of the Chronicles of the kings of
Judah?
20 And Ahaz slept with his fathers, and
was buried with his fathers in the city of
David: and Hĕz'ē-kī'ȧh his son reigned
in his stead.

CHAPTER 17

IN the twelfth year of Ahaz king of
Judah began Hō-shē'ȧ the son of
Ē'lȧh to reign in Sȧ-mā'rĭ-ȧ over Ĭṣ'rā-ĕl
nine years.
2 And he did *that which was* evil in the
sight of the LORD, but not as the kings
of Ĭṣ'rā-ĕl that were before him.
3 ℂ Against him came up Shăl'măn-ē'-
ṣēr king of Assyria; and Hō-shē'ȧ became his servant, and gave him presents.
4 And the king of Assyria found conspiracy in Hō-shē'ȧ: for he had sent
messengers to So king of Egypt, and
brought no present to the king of
Assyria, as *he had done* year by year:
therefore the king of Assyria shut him
up, and bound him in prison.
5 ℂ Then the king of Assyria came up
throughout all the land, and went up to
Sȧ-mā'rĭ-ȧ, and besieged it three years.
6 ℂ In the ninth year of Hō-shē'ȧ the
king of Assyria took Sȧ-mā'rĭ-ȧ, and carried Ĭṣ'rā-ĕl away into Assyria, and
placed them in Hā'lȧh and in Hā'bŏr *by*
the river of Gō'zăn, and in the cities of
the Mēdeṣ.
7 For *so* it was, that the children of
Ĭṣ'rā-ĕl had sinned against the LORD
their God, which had brought them up
out of the land of Egypt, from under the
hand of Phā'raōh king of Egypt, and had
feared other gods,
8 And walked in the statutes of the
heathen, whom the LORD cast out from
before the children of Ĭṣ'rā-ĕl, and of
the kings of Ĭṣ'rā-ĕl, which they had
made.
9 And the children of Ĭṣ'rā-ĕl did secretly *those* things that *were* not right

against the LORD their God, and they
built them high places in all their cities,
from the tower of the watchmen to the
fenced city.
10 And they set them up images and
groves in every high hill, and under
every green tree:
11 And there they burnt incense in all
the high places, as *did* the heathen
whom the LORD carried away before
them; and wrought wicked things to
provoke the LORD to anger:
12 For they served idols, whereof the
LORD had said unto them, Ye shall not
do this thing.
13 Yet the LORD testified against Ĭş′-
rā-ĕl, and against Judah, by all the
prophets, *and by* all the seers, saying,
Turn ye from your evil ways, and keep
my commandments *and* my statutes, according to all the law which I commanded your fathers, and which I sent to you
by my servants the prophets.
14 Notwithstanding, they would not
hear, but hardened their necks, like to
the neck of their fathers, that did not
believe in the LORD their God.
15 And they rejected his statutes, and
his covenant that he made with their
fathers, and his testimonies which he
testified against them; and they followed
vanity, and became vain, and went after
the heathen that *were* round about them,
concerning whom the LORD had charged
them, that they should not do like them.
16 And they left all the commandments
of the LORD their God, and made them
molten images, *even* two calves, and
made a grove, and worshipped all the
host of heaven, and served Bā′ăl.
17 And they caused their sons and
their daughters to pass through the fire,
and used divination and enchantments,
and sold themselves to do evil in the
sight of the LORD, to provoke him to
anger.
18 Therefore the LORD was very angry
with Ĭş′rā-ĕl, and removed them out of
his sight: there was none left but the
tribe of Judah only.
19 Also Judah kept not the commandments of the LORD their God, but walked
in the statutes of Ĭş′rā-ĕl which they
made.
20 And the LORD rejected all the seed
of Ĭş′rā-ĕl, and afflicted them, and delivered them into the hand of spoilers,
until he had cast them out of his sight.
21 For he rent Ĭş′rā-ĕl from the house
of David; and they made Jĕr′ō-bō′ăm
the son of Nē′băt king: and Jĕr′ō-bō′ăm
drave Ĭs′rā-ĕl from following the LORD,
and made them sin a great sin.
22 For the children of Ĭş′rā-ĕl walked
in all the sins of Jĕr′ō-bō′ăm which he
did; they departed not from them;
23 Until the LORD removed Ĭş′rā-ĕl out
of his sight, as he had said by all his
servants the prophets. So was Ĭş′rā-ĕl
carried away out of their own land to
Assyria unto this day.
24 ¶ And the king of Assyria brought
men from Babylon, and from Cū′thȧh,
and from Ā′vȧ, and from Hā′măth, and
from Sĕph′är-vā′ĭm, and placed *them* in
the cities of Sȧ-mā′rĭ-ȧ instead of the
children of Ĭş′rā-ĕl: and they possessed
Sȧ-mā′rĭ-ȧ, and dwelt in the cities
thereof.
25 And *so* it was at the beginning of
their dwelling there, *that* they feared
not the LORD: therefore the LORD sent
lions among them, which slew *some* of
them.
26 Wherefore they spake to the king of
Assyria, saying, The nations which thou
hast removed, and placed in the cities of
Sȧ-mā′rĭ-ȧ, know not the manner of the
God of the land: therefore he hath sent
lions among them, and, behold, they
slay them, because they know not the
manner of the God of the land.
27 Then the king of Assyria commanded, saying, Carry thither one of
the priests whom ye brought from
thence; and let them go and dwell there,
and let him teach them the manner of
the God of the land.
28 Then one of the priests whom they
had carried away from Sȧ-mā′rĭ-ȧ came
and dwelt in Beth-el, and taught them
how they should fear the LORD.
29 Howbeit every nation made gods of
their own, and put *them* in the houses of
the high places which the Sȧ-măr′ĭ-tănş
had made, every nation in their cities
wherein they dwelt.
30 And the men of Babylon made Sŭc′-
cōth–bē′nōth, and the men of Cŭth
made Nĕr′găl, and the men of Hā′măth
made A-shī′mȧ,
31 And the Ā′vītes made Nĭb′hăz and
Tär′tăk, and the Sē′phär-vītes burnt
their children in fire to Ȧ-drăm′mē-lĕch
and Ȧ-năm′mē-lĕch, the gods of Sĕph′-
är-vā′ĭm.

32 So they feared the LORD, and made unto themselves of the lowest of them priests of the high places, which sacrificed for them in the houses of the high places.

33 They feared the LORD, and served their own gods, after the manner of the nations whom they carried away from thence.

34 Unto this day they do after the former manners: they fear not the LORD, neither do they after their statutes, or after their ordinances, or after the law and commandment which the LORD commanded the children of Jacob, whom he named Ĭş′rā-ĕl;

35 With whom the LORD had made a covenant, and charged them, saying, Ye shall not fear other gods, nor bow yourselves to them, nor serve them, nor sacrifice to them:

36 But the LORD, who brought you up out of the land of Egypt with great power and a stretched out arm, him shall ye fear, and him shall ye worship, and to him shall ye do sacrifice.

37 And the statutes, and the ordinances, and the law, and the commandment, which he wrote for you, ye shall observe to do for evermore; and ye shall not fear other gods.

38 And the covenant that I have made with you ye shall not forget; neither shall ye fear other gods.

39 But the LORD your God ye shall fear; and he shall deliver you out of the hand of all your enemies.

40 Howbeit they did not hearken, but they did after their former manner.

41 So these nations feared the LORD, and served their graven images, both their children, and their children's children: as did their fathers, so do they unto this day.

CHAPTER 18

NOW it came to pass in the third year of Hō-shē′ȧ son of Ē′lȧh king of Ĭş′rā-ĕl, *that* Hĕz′ē-kī′ȧh the son of Ahaz king of Judah began to reign.

2 Twenty and five years old was he when he began to reign; and he reigned twenty and nine years in Jerusalem. His mother's name also *was* Ā′bī, the daughter of Zăch′ȧ-rī′ȧh.

3 And he did *that which was* right in the sight of the LORD, according to all that David his father did.

4 ℂ He removed the high places, and brake the images, and cut down the groves, and brake in pieces the brazen serpent that Moses had made: for unto those days the children of Ĭş′rā-ĕl did burn incense to it: and he called it Nē-hŭsh′tăn.

5 He trusted in the LORD God of Ĭş′rā-ĕl; so that after him was none like him among all the kings of Judah, nor *any* that were before him.

6 For he clave to the LORD, *and* departed not from following him, but kept his commandments, which the LORD commanded Moses.

7 And the LORD was with him; *and* he prospered whithersoever he went forth: and he rebelled against the king of Assyria, and served him not.

8 He smote the Phĭ-lĭs′tĭneş *even* unto Gā′zȧ, and the borders thereof, from the tower of the watchmen to the fenced city.

9 ℂ And it came to pass in the fourth year of king Hĕz′ē-kī′ȧh, which *was* the seventh year of Hō-shē′ȧ son of Ē′lȧh king of Ĭş′rā-ĕl, *that* Shăl′măn-ē′şĕr king of Assyria came up against Sȧ-mā′rĭ-ȧ, and besieged it.

10 And at the end of three years they took it: *even* in the sixth year of Hĕz′ē-kī′ȧh, that *is* the ninth year of Hō-shē′ȧ king of Ĭş′rā-ĕl, Sȧ-mā′rĭ-ȧ was taken.

11 And the king of Assyria did carry away Ĭş′rā-ĕl unto Assyria, and put them in Hā′lȧh and in Hā′bŏr *by* the river of Gō′zăn, and in the cities of the Mēdeş:

12 Because they obeyed not the voice of the LORD their God, but transgressed his covenant, *and* all that Moses the servant of the LORD commanded, and would not hear *them*, nor do *them*.

13 ℂ Now in the fourteenth year of king Hĕz′ē-kī′ȧh did Sĕn-năch′ĕr-ĭb king of Assyria come up against all the fenced cities of Judah, and took them.

14 And Hĕz′ē-kī′ȧh king of Judah sent to the king of Assyria to Lā′chĭsh, saying, I have offended; return from me: that which thou puttest on me will I bear. And the king of Assyria appointed unto Hĕz′ē-kī′ȧh king of Judah three hundred talents of silver and thirty talents of gold.

15 And Hĕz′ē-kī′ȧh gave *him* all the silver that was found in the house of the LORD, and in the treasures of the king's house.

16 At that time did Hĕz′ē-kī′ȧh cut off
the gold from the doors of the temple
of the LORD, and *from* the pillars which
Hĕz′ē-kī′ȧh king of Judah had overlaid,
and gave it to the king of Assyria.
17 ℂ And the king of Assyria sent Tär′-
tăn and Răb′sȧ-rĭs and Răb′ shȧ kĕh
from Lā′chĭsh to king Hĕz′ē-kī′ȧh with
a great host against Jerusalem: and
they went up and came to Jerusalem.
And when they were come up, they
came and stood by the conduit of the
upper pool, which *is* in the highway of
the fuller's field.
18 And when they had called to the
king, there came out to them Ē-lī′ȧ-kĭm
the son of Hĭl-kī′ȧh, which *was* over the
household, and Shĕb′nȧ the scribe, and
Jō′ȧh the son of Ā′săph the recorder.
19 And Răb′–shȧ-kĕh said unto them,
Speak ye now to Hĕz′ē-kī′ȧh, Thus
saith the great king, the king of Assyria,
What confidence *is* this wherein thou
trustest?
20 Thou sayest, (but *they are but* vain
words,) *I have* counsel and strength for
the war. Now on whom dost thou trust,
that thou rebellest against me?
21 Now, behold, thou trustest upon the
staff of this bruised reed, *even* upon
Egypt, on which if a man lean, it will go
into his hand, and pierce it: so *is* Phā′-
raōh king of Egypt unto all that trust on
him.
22 But if ye say unto me, We trust in
the LORD our God: *is* not that he, whose
high places and whose altars Hĕz′ē-
kī′ȧh hath taken away, and hath said to
Judah and Jerusalem, Ye shall worship
before this altar in Jerusalem?
23 Now therefore, I pray thee, give
pledges to my lord the king of Assyria,
and I will deliver thee two thousand
horses, if thou be able on thy part to set
riders upon them.
24 How then wilt thou turn away the
face of one captain of the least of my
master's servants, and put thy trust on
Egypt for chariots and for horsemen?
25 Am I now come up without the
LORD against this place to destroy it?
The LORD said to me, Go up against
this land, and destroy it.
26 Then said Ē-lī′ȧ-kĭm the son of
Hĭl-kī′ȧh, and Shĕb′nȧ, and Jō′ȧh, unto
Răb′–shȧ-kĕh, Speak, I pray thee, to
thy servants in the Syrian language; for
we understand *it:* and talk not with us
in the Jews' language in the ears of the
people that *are* on the wall.
27 But Răb′–shȧ-kĕh said unto them,
Hath my master sent me to thy master,
and to thee, to speak these words? *hath
he* not *sent me* to the men which sit on
the wall, that they may eat their own
dung, and drink their own piss with
you?
28 Then Răb′–shȧ-kĕh stood and cried
with a loud voice in the Jews' language,
and spake, saying, Hear the word of the
great king, the king of Assyria:
29 Thus saith the king, Let not Hĕz′ē-
kī′ȧh deceive you: for he shall not be
able to deliver you out of his hand:
30 Neither let Hĕz′ē-kī′ȧh make you
trust in the LORD, saying, The LORD
will surely deliver us, and this city shall
not be delivered into the hand of the
king of Assyria.
31 Hearken not to Hĕz′ē-kī′ȧh: for
thus saith the king of Assyria, Make *an
agreement* with me by a present, and
come out to me, and *then* eat ye every
man of his own vine, and every one of
his fig tree, and drink ye every one the
waters of his cistern:
32 Until I come and take you away to
a land like your own land, a land of corn
and wine, a land of bread and vineyards,
a land of oil olive and of honey, that ye
may live, and not die: and hearken not
unto Hĕz′ē-kī′ȧh, when he persuadeth
you, saying, The LORD will deliver us.
33 Hath any of the gods of the nations
delivered at all his land out of the hand
of the king of Assyria?
34 Where *are* the gods of Hā′măth,
and of Är′păd? where *are* the gods of
Sĕph′är-vā′ĭm, Hē′nȧ, and Ī′vȧh? have
they delivered Sȧ-mā′rĭ-ȧ out of mine
hand?
35 Who *are* they among all the gods of
the countries, that have delivered their
country out of mine hand, that the LORD
should deliver Jerusalem out of mine
hand?
36 But the people held their peace, and
answered him not a word: for the king's
commandment was, saying, Answer him
not.
37 Then came Ē-lī′ȧ-kĭm the son of
Hĭl-kī′ȧh, which *was* over the household, and Shĕb′nȧ the scribe, and Jō′ȧh
the son of Ā′săph the recorder, to Hĕz′-
ē-kī′ȧh with *their* clothes rent, and told
him the words of Răb′–shȧ-kĕh.

CHAPTER 19

AND it came to pass, when king Hĕz′ē-kī′ȧh heard *it,* that he rent his clothes, and covered himself with sackcloth, and went into the house of the LORD.

2 And he sent Ē-lī′ȧ-kĭm, which *was* over the household, and Shĕb′nȧ the scribe, and the elders of the priests, covered with sackcloth, to Ī-ṣā′ịȧh the prophet the son of Ā′mŏz.

3 And they said unto him, Thus saith Hĕz′ē-kī′ȧh, This day *is* a day of trouble, and of rebuke, and blasphemy: for the children are come to the birth, and *there is* not strength to bring forth.

4 It may be the LORD thy God will hear all the words of Răb′-shȧ-kĕh, whom the king of Assyria his master hath sent to reproach the living God; and will reprove the words which the LORD thy God hath heard: wherefore lift up *thy* prayer for the remnant that are left.

5 So the servants of king Hĕz′ē-kī′ȧh came to Ī-ṣā′ịȧh.

6 ℂ And Ī-ṣā′ịȧh said unto them, Thus shall ye say to your master, Thus saith the LORD, Be not afraid of the words which thou hast heard, with which the servants of the king of Assyria have blasphemed me.

7 Behold, I will send a blast upon him, and he shall hear a rumor, and shall return to his own land; and I will cause him to fall by the sword in his own land.

8 ℂ So Răb′-shȧ-kĕh returned, and found the king of Assyria warring against Lĭb′nȧh: for he had heard that he was departed from Lā′chĭsh.

9 And when he heard say of Tĭr-hā′kȧh king of Ethiopia, Behold, he is come out to fight against thee; he sent messengers again unto Hĕz′ē-kī′ȧh, saying,

10 Thus shall ye speak to Hĕz′ē-kī′ȧh king of Judah, saying, Let not thy God in whom thou trustest deceive thee, saying, Jerusalem shall not be delivered into the hand of the king of Assyria.

11 Behold, thou hast heard what the kings of Assyria have done to all lands, by destroying them utterly: and shalt thou be delivered?

12 Have the gods of the nations delivered them which my fathers have destroyed; *as* Gō′zăn, and Hā′răn, and Rē′zĕph, and the children of Ē′den which *were* in Thē-lā′sȧr?

13 Where *is* the king of Hā′măth, and the king of Är′păd, and the king of the city of Sĕph′ăr-vā′ĭm, of Hē′nȧ, and Ī′vȧh?

14 ℂ And Hĕz′ē-kī′ȧh received the letter of the hand of the messengers, and read it: and Hĕz′ē-kī′ȧh went up into the house of the LORD, and spread it before the LORD.

15 And Hĕz′ē-kī′ȧh prayed before the LORD, and said, O LORD God of Ĭṣ′rā-ĕl, which dwellest *between* the cherubim, thou art the God, *even* thou alone, of all the kingdoms of the earth; thou hast made heaven and earth.

16 LORD, bow down thine ear, and hear: open, LORD, thine eyes, and see: and hear the words of Sĕn-năch′ĕr-ĭb, which hath sent him to reproach the living God.

17 Of a truth, LORD, the kings of Assyria have destroyed the nations and their lands,

18 And have cast their gods into the fire: for they *were* no gods, but the work of men's hands, wood and stone: therefore they have destroyed them.

19 Now therefore, O LORD our God, I beseech thee, save thou us out of his hand, that all the kingdoms of the earth may know that thou *art* the LORD God, *even* thou only.

20 ℂ Then Ī-ṣā′ịȧh the son of Ā′mŏz sent to Hĕz′ē-kī′ȧh, saying, Thus saith the LORD God of Ĭṣ′rā-ĕl, *That* which thou hast prayed to me against Sĕn-năch′ĕr-ĭb king of Assyria I have heard.

21 This *is* the word that the LORD hath spoken concerning him; The virgin the daughter of Zion hath despised thee, *and* laughed thee to scorn; the daughter of Jerusalem hath shaken her head at thee.

22 Whom hast thou reproached and blasphemed? and against whom hast thou exalted *thy* voice, and lifted up thine eyes on high? *even* against the Holy *One* of Ĭṣ′rā-ĕl.

23 By thy messengers thou hast reproached the Lord, and hast said, With the multitude of my chariots I am come up to the height of the mountains, to the sides of Lebanon, and will cut down the tall cedar trees thereof, *and* the choice fir trees thereof: and I will enter into the lodgings of his borders, *and into* the forest of his Cär′mĕl.

24 I have digged and drunk strange

waters, and with the sole of my feet have
I dried up all the rivers of besieged places.
25 Hast thou not heard long ago *how* I
have done it, *and* of ancient times that
I have formed it? now have I brought it
to pass, that thou shouldest be to lay
waste fenced cities *into* ruinous heaps.
26 Therefore their inhabitants were of
small power, they were dismayed and
confounded; they were *as* the grass of
the field, and *as* the green herb, *as* the
grass on the housetops, and *as corn*
blasted before it be grown up.
27 But I know thy abode, and thy going out, and thy coming in, and thy rage
against me.
28 Because thy rage against me and
thy tumult is come up into mine ears,
therefore I will put my hook in thy nose,
and my bridle in thy lips, and I will turn
thee back by the way by which thou
camest.
29 And this *shall be* a sign unto thee,
Ye shall eat this year such things as
grow of themselves, and in the second
year that which springeth of the same;
and in the third year sow ye, and reap,
and plant vineyards, and eat the fruits
thereof.
30 And the remnant that is escaped of
the house of Judah shall yet again take
root downward, and bear fruit upward.
31 For out of Jerusalem shall go forth
a remnant, and they that escape out of
mount Zion: the zeal of the LORD *of
hosts* shall do this.
32 Therefore thus saith the LORD concerning the king of Assyria, He shall not
come into this city, nor shoot an arrow
there, nor come before it with shield,
nor cast a bank against it.
33 By the way that he came, by the
same shall he return, and shall not
come into this city, saith the LORD.
34 For I will defend this city, to save it,
for mine own sake, and for my servant
David's sake.
35 ℭ And it came to pass that night,
that the angel of the LORD went out,
and smote in the camp of the Assyrians
a hundred fourscore and five thousand:
and when they arose early in the morning, behold, they *were* all dead corpses.
36 So Sĕn-năch′ĕr-ĭb king of Assyria
departed, and went and returned, and
dwelt at Nĭn′ē-vĕh.
37 And it came to pass, as he was worshipping in the house of Nĭs′rŏch his
god, that Ȧ-drăm′mē-lĕch and Shȧ-rē′-
zĕr his sons smote him with the sword:
and they escaped into the land of
Armenia. And Ē′sär-hăd′dŏn his son
reigned in his stead.

CHAPTER 20

IN those days was Hĕz′ē-kī′ȧh sick
unto death. And the prophet Ī-ṣā′-
ịȧh the son of Ā′mŏz came to him, and
said unto him, Thus saith the LORD, Set
thine house in order; for thou shalt die,
and not live.
2 Then he turned his face to the wall,
and prayed unto the LORD, saying,
3 I beseech thee, O LORD, remember
now how I have walked before thee in
truth and with a perfect heart, and have
done *that which is* good in thy sight.
And Hĕz′ē-kī′ȧh wept sore.
4 And it came to pass, afore Ī-ṣā′ịȧh
was gone out into the middle court, that
the word of the LORD came to him,
saying,
5 Turn again, and tell Hĕz′ē-kī′ȧh the
captain of my people, Thus saith the
LORD, the God of David thy father, I
have heard thy prayer, I have seen thy
tears: behold, I will heal thee: on the
third day thou shalt go up unto the
house of the LORD.
6 And I will add unto thy days fifteen
years; and I will deliver thee and this
city out of the hand of the king of
Assyria; and I will defend this city for
mine own sake, and for my servant
David's sake.
7 And Ī-ṣā′ịȧh said, Take a lump of
figs. And they took and laid *it* on the
boil, and he recovered.
8 ℭ And Hĕz′ē-kī′ȧh said unto Ī-ṣā′-
ịȧh, What *shall be* the sign that the LORD
will heal me, and that I shall go up into
the house of the LORD the third day?
9 And Ī-ṣā′ịȧh said, This sign shalt
thou have of the LORD, that the LORD
will do the thing that he hath spoken:
shall the shadow go forward ten degrees, or go back ten degrees?
10 And Hĕz′ē-kī′ȧh answered, It is a
light thing for the shadow to go down
ten degrees: nay, but let the shadow
return backward ten degrees.
11 And Ī-ṣā′ịȧh the prophet cried unto
the LORD: and he brought the shadow
ten degrees backward, by which it had
gone down in the dial of Ahaz.
12 ℭ At that time Bē-rō′dăch-băl′ȧ-

dăn, the son of Băl′ȧ-dăn, king of Babylon, sent letters and a present unto Hĕz′ē-kī′ȧh: for he had heard that Hĕz′ē-kī′ȧh had been sick.

13 And Hĕz′ē-kī′ȧh hearkened unto them, and showed them all the house of his precious things, the silver, and the gold, and the spices, and the precious ointment, and *all* the house of his armor, and all that was found in his treasures: there was nothing in his house, nor in all his dominion, that Hĕz′ē-kī′ȧh showed them not.

14 ¶ Then came Ī-ṣā′ịȧh the prophet unto king Hĕz′ē-kī′ȧh, and said unto him, What said these men? and from whence came they unto thee? And Hĕz′ē-kī′ȧh said, They are come from a far country, *even* from Babylon.

15 And he said, What have they seen in thine house? And Hĕz′ē-kī′ȧh answered, All *the things* that *are* in mine house have they seen: there is nothing among my treasures that I have not showed them.

16 And Ī-ṣā′ịȧh said unto Hĕz′ē-kī′ȧh, Hear the word of the LORD.

17 Behold, the days come, that all that *is* in thine house, and that which thy fathers have laid up in store unto this day, shall be carried unto Babylon: nothing shall be left, saith the LORD.

18 And of thy sons that shall issue from thee, which thou shalt beget, shall they take away; and they shall be eunuchs in the palace of the king of Babylon.

19 Then said Hĕz′ē-kī′ȧh unto Ī-ṣā′ịȧh, Good *is* the word of the LORD which thou hast spoken. And he said, *Is it* not *good*, if peace and truth be in my days?

20 ¶ And the rest of the acts of Hĕz′ē-kī′ȧh, and all his might, and how he made a pool, and a conduit, and brought water into the city, *are* they not written in the book of the Chronicles of the kings of Judah?

21 And Hĕz′ē-kī′ȧh slept with his fathers: and Mȧ-năs′sĕh his son reigned in his stead.

CHAPTER 21

MȦ-NĂS′SĔH *was* twelve years old when he began to reign, and reigned fifty and five years in Jerusalem. And his mother's name *was* Hĕph′zĭ-bȧh.

2 And he did *that which was* evil in the sight of the LORD, after the abominations of the heathen, whom the LORD cast out before the children of Ĭṣ′rā-ĕl.

3 For he built up again the high places which Hĕz′ē-kī′ȧh his father had destroyed; and he reared up altars for Bā′ăl, and made a grove, as did Ahab king of Ĭṣ′rā-ĕl; and worshipped all the host of heaven, and served them.

4 And he built altars in the house of the LORD, of which the LORD said, In Jerusalem will I put my name.

5 And he built altars for all the host of heaven in the two courts of the house of the LORD.

6 And he made his son pass through the fire, and observed times, and used enchantments, and dealt with familiar spirits and wizards: he wrought much wickedness in the sight of the LORD, to provoke *him* to anger.

7 And he set a graven image of the grove that he had made in the house, of which the LORD said to David, and to Solomon his son, In this house, and in Jerusalem, which I have chosen out of all the tribes of Ĭṣ′rā-ĕl, will I put my name for ever:

8 Neither will I make the feet of Ĭṣ′rā-ĕl move any more out of the land which I gave their fathers; only if they will observe to do according to all that I have commanded them, and according to all the law that my servant Moses commanded them.

9 But they hearkened not: and Mȧ-năs′sĕh seduced them to do more evil than did the nations whom the LORD destroyed before the children of Ĭṣ′rā-ĕl.

10 ¶ And the LORD spake by his servants the prophets, saying,

11 Because Mȧ-năs′ṣĕh king of Judah hath done these abominations, *and* hath done wickedly above all that the Ăm′ō-rītes did, which *were* before him, and hath made Judah also to sin with his idols:

12 Therefore thus saith the LORD God of Ĭṣ′rā-ĕl, Behold, I *am* bringing *such* evil upon Jerusalem and Judah, that whosoever heareth of it, both his ears shall tingle.

13 And I will stretch over Jerusalem the line of Sȧ-mā′rĭ-ȧ, and the plummet of the house of Ahab: and I will wipe Jerusalem as *a man* wipeth a dish, wiping *it*, and turning *it* upside down.

14 And I will forsake the remnant of mine inheritance, and deliver them into

the hand of their enemies; and they
shall become a prey and a spoil to all
their enemies;
15 Because they have done *that which*
was evil in my sight, and have provoked
me to anger, since the day their fathers
came forth out of Egypt, even unto this
day.
16 Moreover Mȧ-năs′sĕh shed innocent blood very much, till he had filled
Jerusalem from one end to another; besides his sin wherewith he made Judah
to sin, in doing *that which was* evil in
the sight of the LORD.
17 ¶ Now the rest of the acts of Mȧ-
năs′sĕh, and all that he did, and his sin
that he sinned, *are* they not written in
the book of the Chronicles of the kings
of Judah?
18 And Mȧ-năs′sĕh slept with his
fathers, and was buried in the garden of
his own house, in the garden of Ŭz′zȧ:
and Ā′mŏn his son reigned in his stead.
19 ¶ Ā′mŏn *was* twenty and two years
old when he began to reign, and he
reigned two years in Jerusalem. And
his mother's name *was* Mē-shŭl′lē-
mĕth, the daughter of Hā′rŭz of
Jŏt′bȧh.
20 And he did *that which was* evil in
the sight of the LORD, as his father
Mȧ-năs′sĕh did.
21 And he walked in all the way that
his father walked in, and served the
idols that his father served, and worshipped them:
22 And he forsook the LORD God of
his fathers, and walked not in the way
of the LORD.
23 ¶ And the servants of Ā′mŏn conspired against him, and slew the king
in his own house.
24 And the people of the land slew all
them that had conspired against king
Ā′mŏn; and the people of the land made
Jō-sī′ȧh his son king in his stead.
25 Now the rest of the acts of Ā′mŏn
which he did, *are* they not written in the
book of the Chronicles of the kings of
Judah?
26 And he was buried in his sepulchre
in the garden of Ŭz′zȧ: and Jō-sī′ȧh his
son reigned in his stead.

CHAPTER 22

JŌ-SĪ′ȦH *was* eight years old when he
began to reign, and he reigned thirty
and one years in Jerusalem. And his
mother's name *was* Jē-dī′dȧh, the
daughter of Ȧ-dā′ịah of Bŏs′căth.
2 And he did *that which was* right in
the sight of the LORD, and walked in all
the way of David his father, and turned
not aside to the right hand or to the left.
3 ¶ And it came to pass in the eighteenth year of king Jō-sī′ȧh, *that* the
king sent Shā′phăn the son of Ăz′ȧ-
lī′ȧh, the son of Mē-shŭl′lăm, the scribe,
to the house of the LORD, saying,
4 Go up to Hĭl-kī′ȧh the high priest,
that he may sum the silver which is
brought into the house of the LORD,
which the keepers of the door have
gathered of the people:
5 And let them deliver it into the hand
of the doers of the work, that have the
oversight of the house of the LORD: and
let them give it to the doers of the work,
which *is* in the house of the LORD, to
repair the breaches of the house,
6 Unto carpenters, and builders, and
masons, and to buy timber and hewn
stone to repair the house.
7 Howbeit, there was no reckoning
made with them of the money that was
delivered into their hand, because they
dealt faithfully.
8 ¶ And Hĭl-kī′ȧh the high priest said
unto Shā′phăn the scribe, I have found
the book of the law in the house of the
LORD. And Hĭl-kī′ȧh gave the book to
Shā′phăn, and he read it.
9 And Shā′phăn the scribe came to the
king, and brought the king word again,
and said, Thy servants have gathered
the money that was found in the house,
and have delivered it into the hand of
them that do the work, that have the
oversight of the house of the LORD.
10 And Shā′phăn the scribe showed
the king, saying, Hĭl-kī′ȧh the priest
hath delivered me a book. And Shā′-
phăn read it before the king.
11 And it came to pass, when the king
had heard the words of the book of the
law, that he rent his clothes.
12 And the king commanded Hĭl-kī′ȧh
the priest, and Ȧ-hī′kăm the son of Shā′-
phăn, and Ăch′bŏr the son of Mī-
chā′ịah, and Shā′phăn the scribe, and
Ăs′ȧ-hī′ȧh a servant of the king's, saying,
13 Go ye, inquire of the LORD for me,
and for the people, and for all Judah,
concerning the words of this book that
is found: for great *is* the wrath of the

LORD that is kindled against us, because our fathers have not hearkened unto the words of this book, to do according unto all that which is written concerning us.

14 So Hĭl-kī′ăh the priest, and Ȧ-hī′kăm, and Ăch′bŏr, and Shā′phăn, and Ăs′ȧ-hī′ăh, went unto Huldah the prophetess, the wife of Shăl′lŭm the son of Tĭk′văh, the son of Hăr′hăs, keeper of the wardrobe; (now she dwelt in Jerusalem in the college;) and they communed with her.

15 ¶ And she said unto them, Thus saith the LORD God of Ĭṣ′rā-ĕl, Tell the man that sent you to me,

16 Thus saith the LORD, Behold, I will bring evil upon this place, and upon the inhabitants thereof, *even* all the words of the book which the king of Judah hath read:

17 Because they have forsaken me, and have burned incense unto other gods, that they might provoke me to anger with all the works of their hands; therefore my wrath shall be kindled against this place, and shall not be quenched.

18 But to the king of Judah which sent you to inquire of the LORD, thus shall ye say to him, Thus saith the LORD God of Ĭṣ′rā-ĕl, *As touching* the words which thou hast heard;

19 Because thine heart was tender, and thou hast humbled thyself before the LORD, when thou heardest what I spake against this place, and against the inhabitants thereof, that they should become a desolation and a curse, and hast rent thy clothes, and wept before me; I also have heard *thee*, saith the LORD.

20 Behold therefore, I will gather thee unto thy fathers, and thou shalt be gathered into thy grave in peace; and thine eyes shall not see all the evil which I will bring upon this place. And they brought the king word again.

CHAPTER 23

AND the king sent, and they gathered unto him all the elders of Judah and of Jerusalem.

2 And the king went up into the house of the LORD, and all the men of Judah and all the inhabitants of Jerusalem with him, and the priests, and the prophets, and all the people, both small and great: and he read in their ears all the words of the book of the covenant which was found in the house of the LORD.

3 ¶ And the king stood by a pillar, and made a covenant before the LORD, to walk after the LORD, and to keep his commandments and his testimonies and his statutes with all *their* heart and all *their* soul, to perform the words of this covenant that were written in this book. And all the people stood to the covenant.

4 And the king commanded Hĭl-kī′ăh the high priest, and the priests of the second order, and the keepers of the door, to bring forth out of the temple of the LORD all the vessels that were made for Bā′ăl, and for the grove, and for all the host of heaven: and he burned them without Jerusalem in the fields of Kĭd′rŏn, and carried the ashes of them unto Beth-el.

5 And he put down the idolatrous priests, whom the kings of Judah had ordained to burn incense in the high places in the cities of Judah, and in the places round about Jerusalem; them also that burned incense unto Bā′ăl, to the sun, and to the moon, and to the planets, and to all the host of heaven.

6 And he brought out the grove from the house of the LORD, without Jerusalem, unto the brook Kĭd′rŏn, and burned it at the brook Kĭd′rŏn, and stamped *it* small to powder, and cast the powder thereof upon the graves of the children of the people.

7 And he brake down the houses of the sodomites, that *were* by the house of the LORD, where the women wove hangings for the grove.

8 And he brought all the priests out of the cities of Judah, and defiled the high places where the priests had burned incense, from Gē′bȧ to Bē′ĕr–shē′bȧ, and brake down the high places of the gates that *were* in the entering in of the gate of Joshua the governor of the city, which *were* on a man's left hand at the gate of the city.

9 Nevertheless the priests of the high places came not up to the altar of the LORD in Jerusalem, but they did eat of the unleavened bread among their brethren.

10 And he defiled Tō′phĕth, which *is* in the valley of the children of Hĭn′nŏm, that no man might make his son or his daughter to pass through the fire to Mō′lĕch.

11 And he took away the horses that
the kings of Judah had given to the sun,
at the entering in of the house of the
LORD, by the chamber of Nā′thăn–
mē′lĕch the chamberlain, which *was* in
the suburbs, and burned the chariots of
the sun with fire.
12 And the altars that *were* on the top
of the upper chamber of Ahaz, which the
kings of Judah had made, and the altars
which Mȧ-năs′sĕh had made in the two
courts of the house of the LORD, did the
king beat down, and brake *them* down
from thence, and cast the dust of them
into the brook Kĭd′rŏn.
13 And the high places that *were* before
Jerusalem, which *were* on the right hand
of the mount of corruption, which Solomon the king of Īṣ′rā-ĕl had builded for
Ăsh′tō-rĕth the abomination of the Zī-
dō′nĭ-ănṣ, and for Chē′mŏsh the abomination of the Mō′ăb-ītes, and for Mĭl′-
cŏm the abomination of the children of
Ammon, did the king defile.
14 And he brake in pieces the images,
and cut down the groves, and filled their
places with the bones of men.
15 ¶ Moreover the altar that *was* at
Beth-el, *and* the high place which
Jĕr′ō-bō′ăm the son of Nē′băt, who
made Īṣ′rā-ĕl to sin, had made, both
that altar and the high place he brake
down, and burned the high place, *and*
stamped *it* small to powder, and burned
the grove.
16 And as Jō-sī′ȧh turned himself, he
spied the sepulchres that *were* there in
the mount, and sent, and took the bones
out of the sepulchres, and burned *them*
upon the altar, and polluted it, according to the word of the LORD which the
man of God proclaimed, who proclaimed
these words.
17 Then he said, What title *is* that that
I see? And the men of the city told him,
It is the sepulchre of the man of God,
which came from Judah, and proclaimed these things that thou hast done
against the altar of Beth-el.
18 And he said, Let him alone; let no
man move his bones. So they let his
bones alone, with the bones of the
prophet that came out of Sȧ-mā′rĭ-ȧ.
19 And all the houses also of the high
places that *were* in the cities of Sȧ-
mā′rĭ-ȧ, which the kings of Īṣ′rā-ĕl had
made to provoke *the LORD* to anger,
Jō-sī′ȧh took away, and did to them
according to all the acts that he had
done in Beth-el.
20 And he slew all the priests of the
high places that *were* there upon the
altars, and burned men's bones upon
them, and returned to Jerusalem.
21 ¶ And the king commanded all the
people, saying, Keep the passover unto
the LORD your God, as *it is* written in
the book of this covenant.
22 Surely there was not holden such a
passover from the days of the judges
that judged Īṣ′rā-ĕl, nor in all the days
of the kings of Īṣ′rā-ĕl, nor of the kings
of Judah;
23 But in the eighteenth year of king
Jō-sī′ȧh, *wherein* this passover was
holden to the LORD in Jerusalem.
24 ¶ Moreover the *workers with*
familiar spirits, and the wizards, and
the images, and the idols, and all the
abominations that were spied in the
land of Judah and in Jerusalem, did
Jō-sī′ȧh put away, that he might perform the words of the law, which were
written in the book that Hĭl-kī′ȧh the
priest found in the house of the LORD.
25 And like unto him was there no king
before him, that turned to the LORD
with all his heart, and with all his soul,
and with all his might, according to all
the law of Moses; neither after him
arose there *any* like him.
26 ¶ Notwithstanding, the LORD
turned not from the fierceness of his
great wrath, wherewith his anger was
kindled against Judah, because of all
the provocations that Mȧ-năs′sĕh had
provoked him withal.
27 And the LORD said, I will remove
Judah also out of my sight, as I have
removed Īṣ′rā-ĕl, and will cast off this
city Jerusalem which I have chosen,
and the house of which I said, My name
shall be there.
28 Now the rest of the acts of Jō-sī′ȧh,
and all that he did, *are* they not written
in the book of the Chronicles of the
kings of Judah?
29 ¶ In his days Phā′raōh–nē′chōh
king of Egypt went up against the king
of Assyria to the river Eū-phrā′tēṣ: and
king Jō-sī′ȧh went against him; and he
slew him at Mē-gĭd′dō, when he had
seen him.
30 And his servants carried him in a
chariot dead from Mē-gĭd′dō, and
brought him to Jerusalem, and buried

him in his own sepulchre. And the people of the land took Jē-hō'ȧ-hăz the son
of Jō-sī'ȧh, and anointed him, and made
him king in his father's stead.
31 ℂ Jē-hō'ȧ-hăz *was* twenty and three
years old when he began to reign; and
he reigned three months in Jerusalem.
And his mother's name *was* Hȧ-mū'tăl,
the daughter of Jeremiah of Lĭb'nȧh.
32 And he did *that which was* evil in
the sight of the LORD, according to all
that his fathers had done.
33 And Phā'raōh–nē'ehōh put him in
bands at Rĭb'lȧh in the land of Hā'-
măth, that he might not reign in Jerusalem; and put the land to a tribute of a
hundred talents of silver, and a talent of
gold.
34 And Phā'raōh–nē'ehōh made Ē-lī'ȧ-
kĭm the son of Jō-sī'ȧh king in the room
of Jō-sī'ȧh his father, and turned his
name to Jē-hôi'ȧ-kĭm, and took Jē-
hō'ȧ-hăz away: and he came to Egypt,
and died there.
35 And Jē-hôi'ȧ-kĭm gave the silver
and the gold to Phā'raōh; but he taxed
the land to give the money according
to the commandment of Phā'raōh: he
exacted the silver and the gold of the
people of the land, of every one according to his taxation, to give *it* unto
Phā'raōh–nē'ehōh.
36 ℂ Jē-hôi'ȧ-kĭm *was* twenty and
five years old when he began to reign;
and he reigned eleven years in Jerusalem. And his mother's name *was*
Zē-bū'dȧh, the daughter of Pē-dā'ịȧh of
Rụ'mȧh.
37 And he did *that which was* evil in
the sight of the LORD, according to all
that his fathers had done.

CHAPTER 24

IN his days Nĕb'ū-ehăd-nĕz'zȧr king
of Babylon came up, and Jē-hôi'ȧ-
kĭm became his servant three years:
then he turned and rebelled against
him.
2 And the LORD sent against him bands
of the Ehăl'dēeș, and bands of the
Syrians, and bands of the Mō'ăb-ītes,
and bands of the children of Ammon,
and sent them against Judah to destroy
it, according to the word of the LORD,
which he spake by his servants the
prophets.
3 Surely at the commandment of the
LORD came *this* upon Judah, to remove
them out of his sight, for the sins of
Mȧ-năs'sĕh, according to all that he
did;
4 And also for the innocent blood that
he shed: for he filled Jerusalem with
innocent blood; which the LORD would
not pardon.
5 ℂ Now the rest of the acts of Jē-
hôi'ȧ-kĭm, and all that he did, *are* they
not written in the book of the Chronicles
of the kings of Judah?
6 So Jē-hôi'ȧ-kĭm slept with his fathers: and Jē-hôi'ȧ-ehĭn his son reigned
in his stead.
7 And the king of Egypt came not again
any more out of his land: for the king of
Babylon had taken from the river of
Egypt unto the river Eū-phrā'tēș all
that pertained to the king of Egypt.
8 ℂ Jē-hôi'ȧ-ehĭn *was* eighteen years
old when he began to reign, and he
reigned in Jerusalem three months.
And his mother's name *was* Nē-hŭsh'tȧ,
the daughter of Ĕl-nā'thăn of Jerusalem.
9 And he did *that which was* evil in the
sight of the LORD, according to all that
his father had done.
10 ℂ At that time the servants of
Nĕb'ū-ehăd-nĕz'zȧr king of Babylon
came up against Jerusalem, and the
city was besieged.
11 And Nĕb'ū-ehăd-nĕz'zȧr king of
Babylon came against the city, and his
servants did besiege it.
12 And Jē-hôi'ȧ-ehĭn the king of Judah
went out to the king of Babylon, he, and
his mother, and his servants, and his
princes, and his officers: and the king
of Babylon took him in the eighth year
of his reign.
13 And he carried out thence all the
treasures of the house of the LORD, and
the treasures of the king's house, and
cut in pieces all the vessels of gold
which Solomon king of Ĭș'rā-ĕl had
made in the temple of the LORD, as the
LORD had said.
14 And he carried away all Jerusalem,
and all the princes, and all the mighty
men of valor, *even* ten thousand captives, and all the craftsmen and smiths:
none remained, save the poorest sort of
the people of the land.
15 And he carried away Jē-hôi'ȧ-ehĭn
to Babylon, and the king's mother, and
the king's wives, and his officers, and the
mighty of the land, *those* carried he into
captivity from Jerusalem to Babylon.

16 And all the men of might, *even* seven thousand, and craftsmen and smiths a thousand, all *that were* strong *and* apt for war, even them the king of Babylon brought captive to Babylon.

17 ¶ And the king of Babylon made Măt′tȧ-nī′ȧh his father's brother king in his stead, and changed his name to Zĕd′ē-kī′ȧh.

18 Zĕd′ē-kī′ȧh *was* twenty and one years old when he began to reign, and he reigned eleven years in Jerusalem. And his mother's name *was* Hȧ-mū′tăl, the daughter of Jeremiah of Lĭb′nȧh.

19 And he did *that which was* evil in the sight of the LORD, according to all that Jē-hoi′ȧ-kĭm had done.

20 For through the anger of the LORD it came to pass in Jerusalem and Judah, until he had cast them out from his presence, that Zĕd′ē-kī′ȧh rebelled against the king of Babylon.

CHAPTER 25

AND it came to pass in the ninth year of his reign, in the tenth month, in the tenth *day* of the month, *that* Nĕb′ū-chăd-nĕz′zăr king of Babylon came, he, and all his host, against Jerusalem, and pitched against it; and they built forts against it round about.

2 And the city was besieged unto the eleventh year of king Zĕd′ē-kī′ȧh.

3 And on the ninth *day* of the *fourth* month the famine prevailed in the city, and there was no bread for the people of the land.

4 ¶ And the city was broken up, and all the men of war *fled* by night by the way of the gate between two walls, which *is* by the king's garden: (now the Chăl′dēes *were* against the city round about:) and *the king* went the way toward the plain.

5 And the army of the Chăl′dēeş pursued after the king, and overtook him in the plains of Jĕr′ĭ-chō: and all his army were scattered from him.

6 So they took the king, and brought him up to the king of Babylon to Rĭb′lȧh; and they gave judgment upon him.

7 And they slew the sons of Zĕd′ē-kī′ȧh before his eyes, and put out the eyes of Zĕd′ē-kī′ȧh, and bound him with fetters of brass, and carried him to Babylon.

8 ¶ And in the fifth month, on the seventh *day* of the month, which *is* the nineteenth year of king Nĕb′ū-chăd-nĕz′zăr king of Babylon, came Nĕb′ū-zăr-ā′dăn, captain of the guard, a servant of the king of Babylon, unto Jerusalem:

9 And he burnt the house of the LORD, and the king's house, and all the houses of Jerusalem, and every great *man's* house burnt he with fire.

10 And all the army of the Chăl′dēeş, that *were with* the captain of the guard, brake down the walls of Jerusalem round about.

11 Now the rest of the people that were left in the city, and the fugitives that fell away to the king of Babylon, with the remnant of the multitude, did Nĕb′ū-zăr-ā′dăn the captain of the guard carry away.

12 But the captain of the guard left of the poor of the land *to be* vinedressers and husbandmen.

13 And the pillars of brass that *were* in the house of the LORD, and the bases, and the brazen sea that *was* in the house of the LORD, did the Chăl′dēeş break in pieces, and carried the brass of them to Babylon.

14 And the pots, and the shovels, and the snuffers, and the spoons, and all the vessels of brass wherewith they ministered, took they away.

15 And the firepans, and the bowls, *and* such things as *were* of gold, *in* gold, and of silver, *in* silver, the captain of the guard took away.

16 The two pillars, one sea, and the bases which Solomon had made for the house of the LORD; the brass of all these vessels was without weight.

17 The height of the one pillar *was* eighteen cubits, and the chapiter upon it *was* brass: and the height of the chapiter three cubits; and the wreathed work, and pomegranates upon the chapiter round about, all of brass: and like unto these had the second pillar with wreathed work.

18 ¶ And the captain of the guard took Sē-rā′iȧh the chief priest, and Zĕph′ȧ-nī′ȧh the second priest, and the three keepers of the door:

19 And out of the city he took an officer that was set over the men of war, and five men of them that were in the king's presence, which were found in the city, and the principal scribe of the host, which mustered the people of the land,

and threescore men of the people of the
land *that were* found in the city:
20 And Něb′ū-zär–ā′dăn captain of
the guard took these, and brought them
to the king of Babylon to Rĭb′lȧh:
21 And the king of Babylon smote
them, and slew them at Rĭb′lȧh in the
land of Hā′măth. So Judah was carried
away out of their land.
22 ¶ And *as for* the people that remained in the land of Judah, whom
Něb′ū-chăd-něz′zȧr king of Babylon
had left, even over them he made Gĕd′ȧ-
lī′ȧh the son of Ȧ-hī′kăm, the son of
Shā′phăn, ruler.
23 And when all the captains of the
armies, they and their men, heard that
the king of Babylon had made Gĕd′ȧ-
lī′ȧh governor, there came to Gĕd′ȧ-
lī′ȧh to Mĭz′pāh, even Ĭsh′mā-ĕl the son
of Něth′ȧ-nī′ȧh, and Jō-hā′năn the son
of Cȧ-rē′ȧh, and Sē-rā′ịȧh the son of
Tăn-hū′měth the Nē-tŏph′ȧ-thīte, and
Jā-ăz′ȧ-nī′ȧh the son of a Mā-ăch′ȧ-
thīte, they and their men.
24 And Gĕd′ȧ-lī′ȧh sware to them, and
to their men, and said unto them, Fear
not to be the servants of the Chăl′dēeş:
dwell in the land, and serve the king of
Babylon; and it shall be well with you.
25 But it came to pass in the seventh
month, that Ĭsh′mā-ĕl the son of Něth′ȧ-
nī′ȧh, the son of Ē-lĭsh′ȧ-mä, of the
seed royal, came, and ten men with him,
and smote Gĕd′ȧ-lī′ȧh, that he died, and
the Jews and the Chăl′dēeş that were
with him at Mĭz′pāh.
26 And all the people, both small and
great, and the captains of the armies,
arose, and came to Egypt: for they were
afraid of the Chăl′dēeş.
27 ¶ And it came to pass in the seven
and thirtieth year of the captivity of
Jē-hôi′ȧ-chĭn king of Judah, in the
twelfth month, on the seven and twentieth *day* of the month, *that* Ē′vĭl–mē-
rō′dăch king of Babylon in the year that
he began to reign did lift up the head
of Jē-hôi′ȧ-chĭn king of Judah out of
prison;
28 And he spake kindly to him, and
set his throne above the throne of the
kings that *were* with him in Babylon;
29 And changed his prison garments:
and he did eat bread continually before
him all the days of his life.
30 And his allowance *was* a continual
allowance given him of the king, a daily
rate for every day, all the days of his
life.

THE FIRST BOOK OF THE CHRONICLES

CHAPTER 1

ADAM, Shĕth, Ē′nŏsh,
2 Kē′năn, Mȧ-hā′lȧ-lē′ĕl, Jē′rĕd,
3 Hē′nŏch, Mē-thū′sē-lȧh, Lā′měch,
4 Noah, Shĕm, Ham, and Jā′phĕth.
5 ¶ The sons of Jā′phĕth; Gō′mĕr, and
Mā′gŏg, and Măd′ā-ī, and Jā′văn, and
Tū′băl, and Mē′shěch, and Tī′răs.
6 And the sons of Gō′mĕr; Ăsh′chē-năz,
and Rī′phăth, and Tō-gär′mȧh.
7 And the sons of Jā′văn; Ē-lī′shȧh,
and Tär′shĭsh, Kĭt′tĭm, and Dō′dȧ-nĭm.
8 ¶ The sons of Ham; Cŭsh, and Mĭz′-
rā-ĭm, Pŭt, and Cā′năan.
9 And the sons of Cŭsh; Sē′bȧ, and
Hăv′ĭ-lȧh, and Săb′tȧ, and Rā′ȧ-mȧh,
and Săb′tē-chȧ. And the sons of Rā′ȧ-
mȧh; Shē′bȧ, and Dē′dăn.
10 And Cŭsh begat Nimrod: he
began to be mighty upon the earth.
11 And Mĭz′rā-ĭm begat Lū′dĭm, and Ăn′-
ȧ-mĭm, and Lē-hā′bĭm, and Năph-tū′hĭm,
12 And Păth-rụ′sĭm, and Căs′lū-hĭm,
(of whom came the Phĭ-lĭs′tĭneş,) and
Căph′tō-rĭm.
13 And Cā′năan begat Zī′dŏn his firstborn, and Heth,
14 The Jĕb′ū-şīte also, and the Ăm′ō-
rīte, and the Gĭr′gȧ-shīte,
15 And the Hī′vīte, and the Är′kīte, and
the Sī′nīte,
16 And the Är′văd-īte, and the Zĕm′ȧ-
rīte, and the Hā′măth-īte.
17 ¶ The sons of Shĕm; Ē′lăm, and
Ăssh′ŭr, and Är-phăx′ăd, and Lŭd, and
Ā′răm, and Ŭz, and Hŭl, and Gē′thĕr,
and Mē′shěch.
18 And Är-phăx′ăd begat Shē′lȧh, and
Shē′lȧh begat Ē′bĕr.

19 And unto Ē'bĕr were born two sons:
the name of the one *was* Pē'lĕg; because
in his days the earth was divided: and
his brother's name *was* Jŏk'tăn.
20 And Jŏk'tăn begat Ăl-mō'dăd, and
Shē'lĕph, and Hā'zär-mā'vĕth, and
Jē'rȧh,
21 Hȧ-dō'răm also, and Ū'zăl, and
Dĭk'lăh,
22 And Ē'băl, and Ȧ-bĭm'ā-ĕl, and
Shē'bȧ,
23 And Ō'phĭr, and Hăv'ĭ-lăh, and
Jō'băb. All these *were* the sons of
Jŏk'tăn.
24 ¶ Shĕm, Är-phăx'ăd, Shē'lȧh,
25 Ē'bĕr, Pē'lĕg, Rē'ū,
26 Sē'rŭg, Nā'hŏr, Tē'rȧh,
27 Abram; the same *is* Abraham.
28 The sons of Abraham; Isaac, and
Ĭsh'mā-ĕl.
29 ¶ These *are* their generations: The
firstborn of Ĭsh'mā-ĕl, Nē-bā'ioth; then
Kē'dȧr, and Ăd'bē-ĕl, and Mĭb'săm,
30 Mĭsh'mȧ, and Dū'mȧh, Măs'sȧ,
Hā'dăd, and Tē'mȧ,
31 Jē'tŭr, Nā'phĭsh, and Kĕd'ē-mȧh.
These are the sons of Ĭsh'mā-ĕl.
32 ¶ Now the sons of Kĕ-tụ'răh,
Abraham's concubine: she bare Zĭm'-
răn, and Jŏk'shăn, and Mē'dăn, and
Mĭd'ĭ-ăn, and Ĭsh'băk, and Shụ'ȧh.
And the sons of Jŏk'shăn; Shē'bȧ, and
Dē'dăn.
33 And the sons of Mĭd'ĭ-ăn; Ē'phȧh,
and Ē'phĕr, and Hē'nŏch, and Ȧ-bī'dȧ,
and Ĕl-dā'ȧh. All these *are* the sons of
Kĕ-tụ'răh.
34 And Abraham begat Isaac. The sons
of Isaac; Ē'saû and Ĭs'rā-ĕl.
35 ¶ The sons of Ē'saû; Ĕl'ĭ-phăz,
Reụ'ĕl, and Jē'ŭsh, and Jā'ȧ-lăm, and
Kō'rȧh.
36 The sons of Ĕl'ĭ-phăz; Tē'măn, and
Ō'mȧr, Zē'phī, and Gā'tăm, Kē'năz,
and Tĭm'nȧ, and Ăm'ȧ-lĕk.
37 The sons of Reụ'ĕl; Nā'hăth, Zē'-
rȧh, Shăm'mȧh, and Mĭz'zȧh.
38 And the sons of Sē'ïr; Lō'tăn, and
Shō'băl, and Zĭb'ē-ŏn, and Ā'nȧh, and
Dī'shŏn, and Ē'zȧr, and Dī'shăn.
39 And the sons of Lō'tăn; Hō'rī, and
Hō'măm: and Tĭm'nȧ *was* Lō'tăn's
sister.
40 The sons of Shō'băl; Ȧ-lī'ăn, and
Măn'ȧ-hăth, and Ē'băl, Shē'phī, and
Ō'năm. And the sons of Zĭb'ē-ŏn;
Ā-ī'ȧh, and Ā'nȧh.
41 The sons of Ā'nȧh; Dī'shŏn. And
the sons of Dī'shŏn; Ăm'răm, and Ĕsh'-
băn, and Ĭth'răn, and Chē'răn.
42 The sons of Ē'zĕr; Bĭl'hăn, and Zā'-
văn, *and* Jā'kăn. The sons of Dī'shăn;
Ūz, and Ā'răn.
43 ¶ Now these *are* the kings that
reigned in the land of Ē'dŏm before *any*
king reigned over the children of Ĭs'-
rā-ĕl; Bē'lȧ the son of Bē'ŏr: and the
name of his city *was* Dĭn'hȧ-băh.
44 And when Bē'lȧ was dead, Jō'băb
the son of Zē'rȧh of Bŏz'rȧh reigned in
his stead.
45 And when Jō'băb was dead, Hū'-
shăm of the land of the Tē'măn-ītes
reigned in his stead.
46 And when Hū'shăm was dead, Hā'-
dăd the son of Bē'dăd, which smote
Mĭd'ĭ-ăn in the field of Mō'ăb, reigned
in his stead: and the name of his city
was Ā'vĭth.
47 And when Hā'dăd was dead, Săm'-
lȧh of Măs'rē-kȧh reigned in his stead.
48 And when Săm'lȧh was dead,
Shā'ŭl of Rē-hō'bŏth by the river
reigned in his stead.
49 And when Shā'ŭl was dead, Bā'ăl-
hā'năn the son of Ăch'bŏr reigned in his
stead.
50 And when Bā'ăl-hā'năn was dead,
Hā'dăd reigned in his stead: and the
name of his city *was* Pā'ī; and his
wife's name *was* Mē-hĕt'ȧ-bĕl, the
daughter of Mā'trĕd, the daughter of
Mĕz'ā-hăb.
51 ¶ Hā'dăd died also. And the dukes
of Ē'dŏm were; duke Tĭm'nȧh, duke
Ȧ-lī'ȧh, duke Jē'thĕth,
52 Duke Ȧ-hŏl'ĭ-bā'mȧh, duke Ē'lȧh,
duke Pī'nŏn,
53 Duke Kē'năz, duke Tē'măn, duke
Mĭb'zär,
54 Duke Măg'di-ĕl, duke Ī'răm.
These *are* the dukes of Ē'dŏm.

CHAPTER 2

THESE *are* the sons of Ĭs'rā-ĕl;
Reuben, Simeon, Levi, and Judah,
Ĭs'sȧ-chär, and Zĕb'ū-lŭn,
2 Dan, Joseph, and Benjamin, Năph'-
tȧ-lī, Gad, and Ăsh'ĕr.
3 ¶ The sons of Judah; Ĕr, and Ō'năn,
and Shē'lȧh: *which* three were born unto him of the daughter of Shụ'ȧ the
Cā'năan-īt'ĕss. And Ĕr, the firstborn of
Judah, was evil in the sight of the LORD;
and he slew him.
4 And Tā'mȧr his daughter-in-law bare

him Phā'rez and Zē'rah. All the sons of
Judah *were* five.
5 The sons of Phā'rēz; Hĕz'rŏn, and
Hā'mŭl.
6 And the sons of Zē'rah; Zĭm'rī, and
Ē'thăn, and Hē'măn, and Căl'cŏl, and
Dā'ra: five of them in all.
7 And the sons of Cär'mī; Ā'char, the
troubler of Ĭs'rā-ĕl, who transgressed in
the thing accursed.
8 And the sons of Ē'thăn; Ăz'a-rī'ah.
9 The sons also of Hĕz'rŏn, that were
born unto him; Jē-räh'mē-ĕl, and Răm,
and Chē-lu'baī.
10 And Răm begat Am-mĭn'a-dăb; and
Ăm-mĭn'a-dăb begat Näh'shŏn, prince
of the children of Judah;
11 And Näh'shŏn begat Săl'ma, and
Săl'ma begat Boaz,
12 And Boaz begat Ō'bĕd, and Ō'bĕd
begat Jesse.
13 ¶ And Jesse begat his firstborn
Ē-lī'ăb, and A-bĭn'a-dăb the second,
and Shĭm'ma the third,
14 Nē-thăn'ē-ĕl the fourth, Răd'dā-ī
the fifth,
15 Ō'zĕm the sixth, David the seventh:
16 Whose sisters *were* Zĕr'u-ī'ah, and
Ăb'ĭ-gāil. And the sons of Zĕr'u-ī'ah;
A-bĭsh'ā-ī, and Jō'ăb, and Ăs'a-hĕl,
three.
17 And Ăb'ĭ-gāil bare Ăm'a-sa: and
the father of Ăm'a-sa *was* Jē'thĕr the
Ĭsh'mā-ĕl-īte.
18 ¶ And Caleb the son of Hĕz'rŏn
begat *children* of A-zū'bah *his* wife, and
of Jĕr'ĭ-ŏth: her sons *are* these; Jē'shĕr,
and Shō'băb, and Är'dŏn.
19 And when A-zū'bah was dead,
Caleb took unto him Ĕph'răth, which
bare him Hûr.
20 And Hûr begat Ū'rī, and Ū'rī begat
Bē-zăl'ē-ĕl.
21 ¶ And afterward Hĕz'rŏn went in
to the daughter of Mā'chĭr the father of
Gĭl'ē-ăd, whom he married when he
was threescore years old; and she bare
him Sē'gŭb.
22 And Sē'gŭb begat Jā'ĭr, who had
three and twenty cities in the land of
Gĭl'ē-ăd.
23 And he took Gē'shŭr, and Ā'răm,
with the towns of Jā'ĭr, from them, with
Kē'nath, and the towns thereof, *even*
threescore cities. All these *belonged to*
the sons of Mā'chĭr the father of
Gĭl'ē-ăd.
24 And after that Hĕz'rŏn was dead in
Cā'lĕb-ĕph'ra-täh, then A-bī'ah Hĕz'-
rŏn's wife bare him Ăsh'ŭr the father of
Tē-kō'a.
25 ¶ And the sons of Jē-räh'mē-ĕl the
firstborn of Hĕz'rŏn were, Răm the
firstborn, and Bū'nah, and Ō'rĕn, and
Ō'zĕm, *and* A-hī'jah.
26 Jē-räh'mē-ĕl had also another wife,
whose name *was* Ăt'a-räh; she *was* the
mother of Ō'năm.
27 And the sons of Răm the firstborn
of Jē-räh'mē-ĕl were, Mā'ăz, and Jā'-
mĭn, and Ē'kĕr.
28 And the sons of Ō'năm were,
Shăm'mā-ī, and Jā'da. And the sons of
Shăm'mā-ī; Nā'dăb, and A-bī'shŭr.
29 And the name of the wife of A-bī'-
shŭr *was* Ăb'ĭ-hāil, and she bare him
Äh'băn, and Mō'lĭd.
30 And the sons of Nā'dăb; Sē'lĕd, and
Ăp'pa-ĭm: but Sē'lĕd died without
children.
31 And the sons of Ăp'pa-ĭm; Ĭsh'ī.
And the sons of Ĭsh'ī; Shē'shăn. And
the children of Shē'shăn; Äh'laī.
32 And the sons of Jā'da the brother of
Shăm'mā-ī; Jē'thĕr, and Jonathan: and
Jē'thĕr died without children.
33 And the sons of Jonathan; Pē'lĕth,
and Zā'za. These were the sons of
Jē-räh'mē-ĕl.
34 ¶ Now Shē'shăn had no sons, but
daughters. And Shē'shăn had a servant, an Egyptian, whose name *was*
Jär'ha.
35 And Shē'shăn gave his daughter to
Jär'ha his servant to wife; and she bare
him Ăt'tā-ī.
36 And Ăt'tā-ī begat Nathan, and
Nathan begat Zā'băd,
37 And Zā'băd begat Ĕph'lăl, and
Ĕph'lăl begat Ō'bĕd,
38 And Ō'bĕd begat Jē'hū, and Jē'hū
begat Ăz'a-rī'ah,
39 And Ăz'a-rī'ah begat Hē'lĕz, and
Hē'lĕz begat Ĕl'ē-ā'sah,
40 And Ĕl'ē-ā'sah begat Sĭs'a-maī, and
Sĭs'a-maī begat Shăl'lŭm,
41 And Shăl'lŭm begat Jĕk'a-mī'ah,
and Jĕk'a-mī'ah begat Ē-lĭsh'a-mä.
42 ¶ Now the sons of Caleb the
brother of Jē-räh'mē-ĕl *were*, Mē'sha
his firstborn, which *was* the father of
Zĭph; and the sons of Ma-rē'shah the
father of Hē'bron.
43 And the sons of Hē'bron; Kō'rah,
and Tap-pū'ah, and Rē'kĕm, and
Shē'ma.

44 And Shē′mȧ begat Rā′hăm, the
father of Jôr′kō-ăm: and Rē′kĕm begat
Shăm′mā-ī.
45 And the son of Shăm′mā-ī *was*
Mā′ŏn: and Mā′ŏn *was* the father of
Bĕth′–zûr′.
46 And Ē′phȧh, Caleb's concubine,
bare Hā′răn, and Mō′zȧ, and Gā′zĕz:
and Hā′răn begat Gā′zĕz.
47 And the sons of Jăh′dā-ī; Rē′gĕm,
and Jō′thăm, and Gē′shăm, and Pē′lĕt,
and Ē′phȧh, and Shā′ȧph.
48 Mā′ȧ-chah, Caleb's concubine,
bare Shē′bĕr, and Tĭr′hȧ-năh.
49 She bare also Shā′ȧph the father of
Măd-măn′nȧh, Shē′vȧ the father of
Măch-bē′nȧh, and the father of Gĭb′ē-ȧ:
and the daughter of Caleb *was* Ăch′sȧ.
50 ¶ These were the sons of Caleb the
son of Hûr, the firstborn of Ĕph′rȧ-tăh;
Shō′băl the father of Kĭr′jăth–jē′ȧ-rĭm,
51 Săl′mȧ the father of Beth-lehem,
Hā′rĕph the father of Bĕth′–gā′dĕr.
52 And Shō′băl the father of Kĭr′jăth–
jē′ȧ-rĭm had sons; Hȧ-rō′ĕh, *and* half
of the Mȧ-nā′hĕth-ītes.
53 And the families of Kĭr′jăth–jē′ȧ-
rĭm; the Ĭth′rītes, and the Pū′hītes, and
the Shu̇′mȧth-ītes, and the Mĭsh′rā-
ītes; of them came the Zā′rē-ȧth-ītes,
and the Ĕsh′tȧ-ū′lītes.
54 The sons of Săl′mȧ; Beth-lehem,
and the Nē-tŏph′ȧ-thītes, Ăt′ȧ-rŏth, the
house of Jō′ăb, and half of the Mȧ-nā′-
hĕth-ītes, the Zō′rītes.
55 And the families of the scribes which
dwelt at Jā′bĕz; the Tī′rȧth-ītes, the
Shĭm′ē-ăth-ītes, *and* Sū′chȧth-ītes.
These *are* the Kē′nītes that came of
Hē′măth, the father of the house of
Rē′chăb.

CHAPTER 3

NOW these were the sons of David,
which were born unto him in Hē′-
brȯn; the firstborn Amnon, of Ȧ-hĭn′ō-
ăm the Jĕz′rē-ĕl-īt′ĕss: the second,
Daniel, of Ăb′ĭ-gāil the Cär′mĕl-īt′ĕss:
2 The third, Ăb′sȧ-lŏm the son of
Mā′ȧ-chah the daughter of Tăl′maī king
of Gē′shŭr: the fourth, Ăd′ō-nī′jȧh the
son of Hăg′gĭth:
3 The fifth, Shĕph′ȧ-tī′ȧh of Ăb′ĭ-tăl:
the sixth, Ĭth′rē-ăm by Ĕg′lȧh his wife.
4 *These* six were born unto him in
Hē′brȯn; and there he reigned seven
years and six months: and in Jerusalem
he reigned thirty and three years.
5 And these were born unto him in
Jerusalem; Shĭm′ē-ȧ, and Shō′băb, and
Nathan, and Solomon, four, of Băth′–
shu̇′ȧ the daughter of Ăm′mĭ-ĕl:
6 Ĭb′hār also, and Ē-lĭsh′ȧ-mä, and
Ē-lĭph′ē-lĕt,
7 And Nō′gȧh, and Nē′phĕg, and
Jȧ-phī′ȧ,
8 And Ē-lĭsh′ȧ-mä, and Ē-lī′ȧ-dȧ, and
Ē-lĭph′ē-lĕt, nine.
9 *These were* all the sons of David,
besides the sons of the concubines, and
Tā′mȧr their sister.
10 ¶ And Solomon's son *was* Rē′hō-
bō′ăm, Ȧ-bī′ȧ his son, Ā′sȧ his son,
Jē-hŏsh′ȧ-phăt his son,
11 Jō′răm his son, Ā′hȧ-zī′ȧh his son,
Jō′ăsh his son,
12 Ăm′ȧ-zī′ȧh his son, Ăz′ȧ-rī′ȧh his
son, Jō′thăm his son,
13 Ahaz his son, Hĕz′ē-kī′ȧh his son,
Mȧ-năs′sĕh his son,
14 Ā′mŏn his son, Jō-sī′ȧh his son.
15 And the sons of Jō-sī′ȧh *were*, the
firstborn Jō-hā′năn, the second Jē-
hôi′ȧ-kĭm, the third Zĕd′ē-kī′ȧh, the
fourth Shăl′lŭm.
16 And the sons of Jē-hôi′ȧ-kĭm; Jĕc′ō-
nī′ȧh his son, Zĕd′ē-kī′ȧh his son.
17 ¶ And the sons of Jĕc′ō-nī′ȧh;
Ăs′sĭr, Sȧ-lā′thĭ-ĕl his son,
18 Măl-chī′răm also, and Pē-dā′iȧh,
and Shē-nā′zȧr, Jĕc′ȧ-mī′ȧh, Hŏsh′ȧ-
mȧ, and Nĕd′ȧ-bī′ȧh.
19 And the sons of Pē-dā′iȧh *were*,
Zē-rŭb′bȧ-bĕl, and Shĭm′ē-ī: and the
sons of Zē-rŭb′bȧ-bĕl; Mē-shŭl′lăm,
and Hăn′ȧ-nī′ȧh, and Shē-lō′mĭth their
sister:
20 And Hȧ-shu̇′bȧh, and Ō′hĕl, and
Bĕr′ē-chī′ȧh, and Hăs′ȧ-dī′ȧh, Ju̇′shăb–
hē′sĕd, five.
21 And the sons of Hăn′ȧ-nī′ȧh; Pĕl′-
ȧ-tī′ȧh, and Jē-sā′iȧh: the sons of
Re-phā′iȧh, the sons of Är′năn, the
sons of Ō′bȧ-dī′ȧh, the sons of Shĕch′-
ȧ-nī′ȧh.
22 And the sons of Shĕch′ȧ-nī′ȧh, Shē-
mā′iȧh: and the sons of Shē-mā′iȧh;
Hăt′tŭsh, and Ī′gē-ăl, and Bȧ-rī′ȧh, and
Nē′ȧ-rī′ȧh, and Shā′phăt, six.
23 And the sons of Nē′ȧ-rī′ȧh; Ē-lī′ō-
ē′nā-ī, and Hĕz′ē-kī′ȧh, and Ăz′rī-kăm,
three.
24 And the sons of Ē-lī′ō-ē′nā-ī *were*,
Hō-dā′iȧh, and Ē-lī′ȧ-shĭb, and Pē-
lā′iȧh, and Ăk′kŭb, and Jō-hā′năn, and
Dăl′ā-ī′ȧh, and Ȧ-nā′nī, seven.

CHAPTER 4

THE sons of Judah; Phā'rēz, Hĕz'rŏn,
and Cär'mī, and Hûr, and Shō'băl.
2 And Rē-ā'ịah the son of Shō'băl begat Jā'hăth; and Jā'hăth begat Ȧ-hū'-
maī, and Lā'hăd. These *are* the families
of the Zō'rȧth-ītes.
3 And these *were of* the father of
Ē'tăm; Jĕz'rē-ĕl, and Ĭsh'mȧ, and Ĭd'-
băsh: and the name of their sister *was*
Hăz'ĕ-lĕl-pō'nī:
4 And Pē-nū'ĕl the father of Gē'dŏr,
and Ē'zĕr the father of Hū'shȧh. These
are the sons of Hûr, the firstborn of
Ĕph'rȧ-tăh, the father of Beth-lehem.
5 ¶ And Ăsh'ŭr the father of Tē-kō'ȧ
had two wives, Hē'lăh and Nā'ȧ-rȧh.
6 And Nā'ȧ-rȧh bare him Ȧ-hū'zăm,
and Hē'phĕr, and Tĕm'ē-nī, and Hā'ȧ-
hăsh'tȧ-rī. These *were* the sons of
Nā'ȧ-rȧh.
7 And the sons of Hē'lăh *were,* Zē'-
rĕth, and Jē-zō'ȧr, and Ĕth'năn.
8 And Cŏz begat Ā'nŭb, and Zō-bē'bȧh,
and the families of Ȧ-här'hĕl the son of
Hā'rŭm.
9 ¶ And Jā'bĕz was more honorable
than his brethren: and his mother called
his name Jā'bĕz, saying, Because I bare
him with sorrow.
10 And Jā'bĕz called on the God of
Ĭs'rā-ĕl, saying, Oh that thou wouldest
bless me indeed, and enlarge my coast,
and that thine hand might be with me,
and that thou wouldest keep *me* from
evil, that it may not grieve me! And
God granted him that which he requested.
11 ¶ And Chē'lŭb the brother of
Shụ'ȧh begat Mē'hĭr, which *was* the
father of Ĕsh'tŏn.
12 And Ĕsh'tŏn begat Bĕth'–rā'phȧ,
and Pȧ-sē'ȧh, and Tē-hĭn'nȧh the father
of Ĭr'–nā'hăsh. These *are* the men of
Rē'chȧh.
13 And the sons of Kē'năz; Ŏth'nĭ-ĕl,
and Sē-rā'ịah: and the sons of Ŏth'nĭ-ĕl;
Hā'thăth.
14 And Mē-ŏn'ō-thaī begat Ŏph'rȧh:
and Sē-rā'ịah begat Jō'ăb, the father of
the valley of Chăr'ȧ-shĭm; for they were
craftsmen.
15 And the sons of Caleb the son
of Jē-phŭn'nĕh; Ī'rụ, Ē'lȧh, and Nā'-
ăm: and the sons of Ē'lȧh, even Kē'năz.
16 And the sons of Jē'hȧ-lē'lē-ĕl; Zĭph,
and Zī'phȧh, Tĭr'ĭ-ȧ, and Ȧ-sā'rē-ĕl.
17 And the sons of Ezra *were,* Jē'thĕr,
and Mē'rĕd, and Ē'phĕr, and Jā'lŏn:
and she bare Miriam, and Shăm'mā-ī,
and Ĭsh'bȧh the father of Ĕsh'tē-mō'ȧ.
18 And his wife Jē-hū-dī'jȧh bare Jē'-
rĕd the father of Gē'dŏr, and Hē'bĕr the
father of Sō'chō, and Jē-kū'thĭ-ĕl the
father of Zȧ-nō'ȧh. And these *are* the
sons of Bĭ-thī'ȧh the daughter of Phā'-
raōh, which Mē'rĕd took.
19 And the sons of *his* wife Hō-dī'ȧh
the sister of Nā'hăm, the father of Kē-ī'-
lȧh the Gär'mīte, and Ĕsh'tē-mō'ȧ the
Mā-ăch'ȧ-thīte.
20 And the sons of Shī'mŏn *were,* Amnon, and Rĭn'nȧh, Bĕn'–hā'năn, and
Tī'lŏn. And the sons of Ĭsh'ī *were,* Zō'-
hĕth, and Bĕn'–zō'hĕth.
21 ¶ The sons of Shē'lȧh the son of
Judah *were,* Ēr the father of Lē'cȧh, and
Lā'ȧ-dȧh the father of Mȧ-rē'shȧh, and
the families of the house of them that
wrought fine linen, of the house of
Ăsh'bē-ȧ,
22 And Jō'kĭm, and the men of Chō-
zē'bȧ, and Jō'ăsh, and Sā'rȧph, who had
the dominion in Mō'ăb, and Jȧ-shụ'bī-
lē'hĕm. And *these are* ancient things.
23 These *were* the potters, and those
that dwelt among plants and hedges:
there they dwelt with the king for his
work.
24 ¶ The sons of Simeon *were,*
Nĕm'ū-ĕl, and Jā'mĭn, Jā'rĭb, Zē'rȧh,
and Shā'ŭl:
25 Shăl'lŭm his son, Mĭb'săm his son,
Mĭsh'mȧ his son.
26 And the sons of Mĭsh'mȧ; Hȧ-mū'ĕl
his son, Zăc'chŭr his son, Shĭm'ē-ī his
son.
27 And Shĭm'ē-ī had sixteen sons and
six daughters; but his brethren had not
many children, neither did all their
family multiply, like to the children of
Judah.
28 And they dwelt at Bē'ĕr–shē'bȧ,
and Mŏl'ȧ-dȧh, and Hā'zär–shụ'ăl,
29 And at Bĭl'hȧh, and at Ē'zĕm, and at
Tō'lăd,
30 And at Bē-thū'ĕl, and at Hôr'mȧh,
and at Zĭk'lăg,
31 And at Bĕth'–mär'cȧ-bŏth, and Hā'-
zär–sū'sĭm, and at Bĕth'–bĭr'ē-ī, and at
Shā'ȧ-rā'ĭm. These *were* their cities
unto the reign of David.
32 And their villages *were,* Ē'tăm, and
Ā'ĭn, Rĭm'mŏn, and Tō'chĕn, and
Ā'shăn, five cities:

33 And all their villages that *were*
round about the same cities, unto
Bā'ăl. These *were* their habitations,
and their genealogy.
34 And Mē-shō'băb, and Jăm'lĕch,
and Jō'shăh the son of Ăm'ā-zī'ăh,
35 And Joel, and Jē'hū the son of
Jŏs'ĭ-bī'ăh, the son of Sē-rā'ịăh, the son
of Ā'sĭ-ĕl,
36 And Ē-lī'ō-ē'nā-ī and Jā'ā-kō'băh,
and Jĕsh'ō-hā'ịăh, and Ā-sā'ịăh, and
Ā'dĭ-ĕl, and Je-sim'ī-ĕl, and Bē-nā'ịăh,
37 And Zī'ză the son of Shī'phī, the son
of Ăl'lŏn, the son of Jē-dā'ịăh, the son
of Shĭm'rī, the son of Shē-mā'ịăh;
38 These mentioned by *their* names
were princes in their families: and the
house of their fathers increased greatly.
39 ℂ And they went to the entrance
of Gē'dŏr, *even* unto the east side of
the valley, to seek pasture for their
flocks.
40 And they found fat pasture and
good, and the land *was* wide, and quiet,
and peaceable; for *they* of Ham had
dwelt there of old.
41 And these written by name came in
the days of Hĕz'ē-kī'ăh king of Judah,
and smote their tents, and the habitations that were found there, and destroyed them utterly unto this day, and
dwelt in their rooms: because *there was*
pasture there for their flocks.
42 And *some* of them, *even* of the sons
of Simeon, five hundred men, went to
mount Sē'ïr, having for their captains
Pĕl'ā-tī'ăh, and Nē'ā-rī'ăh, and Rē-
phā'ịăh, and Ŭz-zī'ĕl, the sons of Ĭsh'ī.
43 And they smote the rest of the
Ăm'ā-lĕk-ītes that were escaped, and
dwelt there unto this day.

CHAPTER 5

NOW the sons of Reuben the firstborn of Ĭs'rā-ĕl, (for he *was* the
firstborn; but, forasmuch as he defiled
his father's bed, his birthright was given
unto the sons of Joseph the son of
Ĭs'rā-ĕl: and the genealogy is not to be
reckoned after the birthright.
2 For Judah prevailed above his
brethren, and of him *came* the chief
ruler; but the birthright *was* Joseph's:)
3 The sons, *I say*, of Reuben the firstborn of Ĭs'rā-ĕl *were*, Hā'nŏch, and
Păl'lū, Hĕz'rŏn, and Căr'mī.
4 The sons of Joel; Shē-mā'ịăh his son,
Gog his son, Shĭm'ē-ī his son,
5 Mī'căh his son, Rē-ā'ịă his son,
Bā'ăl his son,
6 Bē-ē'răh his son, whom Tĭl'găth-
pĭl-nē'sēr king of Assyria carried away
captive: he *was* prince of the Reubenites.
7 And his brethren by their families,
when the genealogy of their generations
was reckoned, *were* the chief, Jē-ī'ĕl,
and Zĕch'ā-rī'ăh,
8 And Bē'lă the son of Ā'zăz, the son
of Shē'mă, the son of Joel, who dwelt in
Ā-rō'ēr, even unto Nē'bō and Bā'ăl-
mē'ŏn:
9 And eastward he inhabited unto the
entering in of the wilderness from the
river Eū-phrā'tēs: because their cattle
were multiplied in the land of Gĭl'ē-ăd.
10 And in the days of Saul they made
war with the Hā'găr-ītes, who fell by
their hand: and they dwelt in their
tents throughout all the east *land* of
Gĭl'ē-ăd.
11 ℂ And the children of Gad dwelt
over against them, in the land of Bā'-
shăn unto Săl'căh:
12 Joel the chief, and Shā'phăm the
next, and Jā'ā-naī, and Shā'phăt in
Bā'shăn.
13 And their brethren of the house of
their fathers *were*, Mī'chā-ĕl, and Mē-
shŭl'lăm, and Shē'bă, and Jō'rā-ī, and
Jā'chăn, and Zī'ā, and Hē'bĕr, seven.
14 These *are* the children of Ăb'ī-hāil
the son of Hū'rī, the son of Jā-rō'ăh, the
son of Gĭl'ē-ăd, the son of Mī'chā-ĕl,
the son of Jē-shĭsh'ā-ī, the son of Jăh'dō,
the son of Bŭz;
15 Ā'hī the son of Ăb'dĭ-ĕl, the son of
Gū'nī, chief of the house of their
fathers.
16 And they dwelt in Gĭl'ē-ăd in Bā'-
shăn, and in her towns, and in all the
suburbs of Shăr'ŏn, upon their borders.
17 All these were reckoned by genealogies in the days of Jō'thăm king of
Judah, and in the days of Jĕr'ō-bō'ăm
king of Ĭs'rā-ĕl.
18 ℂ The sons of Reuben, and the
Gadites, and half the tribe of Mā-năs'-
sĕh, of valiant men, men able to bear
buckler and sword, and to shoot with
bow, and skilful in war, *were* four and
forty thousand seven hundred and
threescore, that went out to the war.
19 And they made war with the Hā'-
găr-ītes, with Jē'tŭr, and Nē'phĭsh, and
Nō'dăb.

20 And they were helped against them,
and the Hā'gȧr-ītes were delivered into
their hand, and all that *were* with them:
for they cried to God in the battle, and
he was entreated of them; because they
put their trust in him.
21 And they took away their cattle; of
their camels fifty thousand, and of sheep
two hundred and fifty thousand, and of
asses two thousand, and of men a hundred thousand.
22 For there fell down many slain, because the war *was* of God. And they
dwelt in their steads until the captivity.
23 ¶ And the children of the half tribe
of Mȧ-năs'sĕh dwelt in the land: they
increased from Bā'shăn unto Bā'ăl-
hĕr'mŏn and Sē'nĭr, and unto mount
Hermon.
24 And these *were* the heads of the
house of their fathers, even Ē'phĕr, and
Ĭsh'ī, and Ē'lī-ĕl, and Ăz'rī-ĕl, and
Jeremiah, and Hō'dȧ-vī'ȧh, and Jăh'-
dī-ĕl, mighty men of valor, famous
men, *and* heads of the house of their
fathers.
25 ¶ And they transgressed against
the God of their fathers, and went a
whoring after the gods of the people of
the land, whom God destroyed before
them.
26 And the God of Ĭş'rā-ĕl stirred up
the spirit of Pŭl king of Assyria, and the
spirit of Tĭl'găth-pĭl-nē'şĕr king of
Assyria, and he carried them away, even
the Reubenites, and the Gadites, and
the half tribe of Mȧ-năs'sĕh, and
brought them unto Hā'lȧh, and Hā'bŏr,
and Hā'rȧ, and to the river Gō'zăn, unto
this day.

CHAPTER 6

THE sons of Levi; Gĕr'shŏn, Kō'hăth,
and Mē-rā'rī.
2 And the sons of Kō'hăth; Ăm'răm,
Ĭz'här, and Hē'brŏn, and Ŭz-zī'ĕl.
3 And the children of Ăm'răm; Aaron,
and Moses, and Miriam. The sons also
of Aaron; Nā'dăb and Ȧ-bī'hū, Ĕl'ē-ā'-
zȧr and Ĭth'ȧ-mär.
4 ¶ Ĕl'ē-ā'zȧr begat Phĭn'ē-hăs, Phĭn'-
ē-hăs begat Ȧ-bĭsh'ū-ȧ,
5 And Ȧ-bĭsh'ū-ȧ begat Bŭk'kī, and
Bŭk'kī begat Ŭz'zī,
6 And Ŭz'zī begat Zĕr'ȧ-hī'ȧh, and
Zĕr'ȧ-hī'ȧh begat Mē-rā'ịōth,
7 Mē-rā'ịōth begat Ăm'ȧ-rī'ȧh, and
Ăm'ȧ-rī'ȧh begat Ȧ-hī'tŭb,
8 And Ȧ-hī'tŭb begat Zā'dŏk, and Zā'-
dŏk begat Ȧ-hĭm'ā-ăz,
9 And Ȧ-hĭm'ā-ăz begat Ăz'ȧ-rī'ȧh, and
Ăz'ȧ-rī'ȧh begat Jō-hā'năn,
10 And Jō-hā'năn begat Ăz'ȧ-rī'ȧh; (he
it is that executed the priest's office in
the temple that Solomon built in Jerusalem:)
11 And Ăz'ȧ-rī'ȧh begat Ăm'ȧ-rī'ȧh, and
Ăm'ȧ-rī'ȧh begat Ȧ-hī'tŭb,
12 And Ȧ-hī'tŭb begat Zā'dŏk, and Zā'-
dŏk begat Shăl'lŭm,
13 And Shăl'lŭm begat Hĭl-kī'ȧh, and
Hĭl-kī'ȧh begat Ăz'ȧ-rī'ȧh,
14 And Ăz'ȧ-rī'ȧh begat Sē-rā'ịȧh, and
Sē-rā'ịȧh begat Jē-hŏz'ȧ-dăk,
15 And Jē-hŏz'ȧ-dăk went *into captivity,* when the LORD carried away Judah and Jerusalem by the hand of
Nĕb'ū-chăd-nĕz'zȧr.
16 ¶ The sons of Levi; Gĕr'shŏm, Kō'-
hăth, and Mē-rā'rī.
17 And these *be* the names of the sons
of Gĕr'shŏm; Lĭb'nī, and Shĭm'ē-ī.
18 And the sons of Kō'hăth *were,* Ăm'-
răm, and Ĭz'här, and Hē'brŏn, and
Ŭz-zī'ĕl.
19 The sons of Mē-rā'rī; Măh'lī, and
Mū'shī. And these *are* the families of
the Lē'vītes according to their fathers.
20 Of Gĕr'shŏm; Lĭb'nī his son, Jā'hăth
his son, Zĭm'mȧh his son,
21 Jō'ȧh his son, Ĭd'dō his son, Zē'rȧh
his son, Jē-ăt'ē-raī his son.
22 The sons of Kō'hăth; Ȧm-mĭn'ȧ-dăb
his son, Kō'rȧh his son, Ăs'sĭr his son,
23 Ĕl-kā'nȧh his son, and Ē-bī'ȧ-sȧph
his son, and Ăs'sĭr his son,
24 Tā'hăth his son, Ū'rī-ĕl his son, Ŭz-
zī'ȧh his son, and Shā'ŭl his son.
25 And the sons of Ĕl-kā'nȧh; Ȧ-măs'-
ā-ī, and Ȧ-hī'mŏth.
26 *As for* Ĕl-kā'nȧh: the sons of Ĕl-kā'-
nȧh; Zō'phaī his son, and Nā'hăth his
son,
27 Ē-lī'ăb his son, Jē-rō'hăm his son,
Ĕl-kā'nȧh his son.
28 And the sons of Samuel; the firstborn Văsh'nī, and Ȧ-bī'ȧh.
29 The sons of Mē-rā'rī; Măh'lī, Lĭb'nī
his son, Shĭm'ē-ī his son, Ŭz'zȧ his son,
30 Shĭm'ē-ȧ his son, Hăg-gī'ȧh his son,
Ȧ-sā'ịȧh his son.
31 And these *are they* whom David set
over the service of song in the house of
the LORD, after that the ark had rest.
32 And they ministered before the
dwelling place of the tabernacle of the

congregation with singing, until Solomon had built the house of the LORD in
Jerusalem: and *then* they waited on
their office according to their order.
33 And these *are* they that waited with
their children. Of the sons of the Kō'-
hăth-ītes; Hē'măn a singer, the son of
Joel, the son of Shē-mū'ĕl,
34 The son of Ĕl-kā'nȧh, the son of
Jē-rō'hăm, the son of Ē'lī-ĕl, the son of
Tō'ȧh,
35 The son of Zŭph, the son of Ĕl-kā'-
nȧh, the son of Mā'hăth, the son of
Ȧ-măs'ā-ī,
36 The son of Ĕl-kā'nȧh, the son of
Joel, the son of Ăz'ȧ-rī'ȧh, the son of
Zĕph'ȧ-nī'ȧh,
37 The son of Tā'hăth, the son of Ăs'-
sīr, the son of Ē-bī'ȧ-sȧph, the son of
Kō'rȧh,
38 The son of Ĭz'här, the son of Kō'-
hăth, the son of Levi, the son of Ĭs'rā-ĕl.
39 And his brother, Ā'săph, who stood
on his right hand, *even* Ā'săph the son
of Bĕr'ȧ-chī'ȧh, the son of Shĭm'ē-ȧ,
40 The son of Mī'chā-ĕl, the son of
Bā'ȧ-sē'iȧh, the son of Măl-chī'ȧh,
41 The son of Ĕth'nī, the son of Zē'rȧh,
the son of Ȧ-dā'iȧh,
42 The son of Ē'thăn, the son of Zĭm'-
mȧh, the son of Shĭm'ē-ī,
43 The son of Jā'hăth, the son of Gĕr'-
shŏm, the son of Levi.
44 And their brethren the sons of Mē-
rā'rī *stood* on the left hand: Ē'thăn the
son of Kĭsh'ī, the son of Ăb'dī, the son
of Măl'lŭch,
45 The son of Hăsh'ȧ-bī'ȧh, the son of
Ăm'ȧ-zī'ȧh, the son of Hĭl-kī'ȧh,
46 The son of Ăm'zī, the son of Bā'nī,
the son of Shā'mĕr,
47 The son of Mäh'lī, the son of Mū'-
shī, the son of Mē-rā'rī, the son of Levi.
48 Their brethren also the Lē'vītes
were appointed unto all manner of service of the tabernacle of the house of God.
49 ¶ But Aaron and his sons offered
upon the altar of the burnt offering, and
on the altar of incense, *and were appointed* for all the work of the *place* most
holy, and to make an atonement for Ĭs'-
rā-ĕl, according to all that Moses the
servant of God had commanded.
50 And these *are* the sons of Aaron;
Ĕl'ē-ā'zȧr his son, Phĭn'ē-hăs his son,
Ȧ-bĭsh'ū-ȧ his son,
51 Bŭk'kī his son, Ŭz'zī his son, Zĕr'ȧ-
hī'ȧh his son,
52 Mē-rā'iŏth his son, Ăm'ȧ-rī'ȧh his
son, Ȧ-hī'tŭb his son,
53 Zā'dŏk his son, Ȧ-hĭm'ā-ăz his son.
54 ¶ Now these *are* their dwelling
places throughout their castles in their
coasts, of the sons of Aaron, of the families of the Kō'hăth-ītes: for theirs was
the lot.
55 And they gave them Hē'brŏn in the
land of Judah, and the suburbs thereof
round about it.
56 But the fields of the city, and the
villages thereof, they gave to Caleb the
son of Jē-phŭn'nĕh.
57 And to the sons of Aaron they gave
the cities of Judah, *namely*, Hē'brŏn,
the city of refuge, and Lĭb'nȧh with her
suburbs, and Jăt'tīr, and Ĕsh'tē-mō'ȧ,
with their suburbs,
58 And Hī'lĕn with her suburbs, Dē'-
bīr with her suburbs,
59 And Ā'shăn with her suburbs, and
Bĕth'-shē'mĕsh with her suburbs:
60 And out of the tribe of Benjamin;
Gē'bȧ with her suburbs, and Ăl'ē-mĕth
with her suburbs, and Ăn'ȧ-thŏth with
her suburbs. All their cities throughout
their families *were* thirteen cities.
61 And unto the sons of Kō'hăth, *which
were* left of the family of that tribe, *were
cities given* out of the half tribe, *namely,
out of* the half *tribe* of Mȧ-năs'sĕh, by
lot, ten cities.
62 And to the sons of Gĕr'shŏm throughout their families out of the tribe of
Ĭs'sȧ-chär, and out of the tribe of Ăsh'ĕr,
and out of the tribe of Năph'tȧ-lī, and
out of the tribe of Mȧ-năs'sĕh in Bā'-
shăn, thirteen cities.
63 Unto the sons of Mē-rā'rī *were given*
by lot, throughout their families, out of
the tribe of Reuben, and out of the tribe
of Gad, and out of the tribe of Zĕb'ū-lŭn,
twelve cities.
64 And the children of Ĭs'rā-ĕl gave
to the Lē'vītes *these* cities with their
suburbs.
65 And they gave by lot out of the tribe
of the children of Judah, and out of the
tribe of the children of Simeon, and out
of the tribe of the children of Benjamin,
these cities, which are called by *their*
names.
66 And *the residue* of the families of
the sons of Kō'hăth had cities of their
coasts out of the tribe of Ē'phrā-ĭm.
67 And they gave unto them, *of* the
cities of refuge, Shē'chĕm in mount

Ē'phrā-ĭm with her suburbs; *they gave*
also Gē'zēr with her suburbs,
68 And Jŏk'mē-ăm with her suburbs,
and Bĕth'–hō'rŏn with her suburbs,
69 And Ăj'ȧ-lŏn with her suburbs, and
Găth'–rĭm'mŏn with her suburbs:
70 And out of the half tribe of Mȧ-năs'-
sĕh; Ā'nēr with her suburbs, and Bĭl'-
ē-ăm with her suburbs, for the family of the remnant of the sons of Kō'-
hăth.
71 Unto the sons of Gēr'shŏm *were*
given, out of the family of the half tribe
of Mȧ-năs'sĕh, Gō'lăn in Bā'shăn with
her suburbs, and Ăsh'tȧ-rŏth with her
suburbs:
72 And out of the tribe of Ĭs'sȧ-ɕhär;
Kē'dĕsh with her suburbs, Dăb'ē-răth
with her suburbs,
73 And Rā'mŏth with her suburbs, and
Ā'nĕm with her suburbs:
74 And out of the tribe of Ăsh'ēr; Mā'-
shăl with her suburbs, and Ăb'dŏn with
her suburbs,
75 And Hū'kŏk with her suburbs, and
Rē'hŏb with her suburbs:
76 And out of the tribe of Năph'tȧ-lī;
Kē'dĕsh in Galilee with her suburbs,
and Hăm'mŏn with her suburbs, and
Kĭr'jȧ-thā'ĭm with her suburbs.
77 Unto the rest of the children of Mē-
rā'rī *were given,* out of the tribe of Zĕb'-
ū-lŭn, Rĭm'mŏn with her suburbs, Tā'-
bŏr with her suburbs:
78 And on the other side Jordan by
Jĕr'ĭ-ɕhō, on the east side of Jordan,
were given them, out of the tribe of
Reuben, Bē'zēr in the wilderness with
her suburbs, and Jäh'zȧh with her
suburbs,
79 Kĕd'ē-mŏth also with her suburbs,
and Mĕph'ȧ-ăth with her suburbs:
80 And out of the tribe of Gad; Rā'-
mŏth in Gĭl'ē-ăd with her suburbs, and
Mā'hȧ-nā'ĭm with her suburbs,
81 And Hĕsh'bŏn with her suburbs,
and Jā'zēr with her suburbs.

CHAPTER 7

NOW the sons of Ĭs'sȧ-ɕhär *were,*
Tō'lȧ, and Pū'ȧh, Jā'shŭb, and
Shĭm'rŏm, four.
2 And the sons of Tō'lȧ; Ŭz'zī, and Rē-
phā'ịȧh, and Jē'rī-ĕl, and Jäh'mā-ī, and
Jĭb'săm, and Shē-mū'ĕl, heads of their
father's house, *to wit,* of Tō'lȧ: *they*
were valiant men of might in their generations; whose number *was* in the days
of David two and twenty thousand and
six hundred.
3 And the sons of Ŭz'zī; Ĭz'rȧ-hī'ȧh:
and the sons of Ĭz'rȧ-hī'ȧh; Mī'ɕhā-ĕl,
and Ō'bȧ-dī'ȧh, and Joel, Ī-shī'ȧh, five:
all of them chief men.
4 And with them, by their generations,
after the house of their fathers, *were*
bands of soldiers for war, six and thirty
thousand *men:* for they had many wives
and sons.
5 And their brethren among all the
families of Ĭs'sȧ-ɕhär *were* valiant men
of might, reckoned in all by their genealogies fourscore and seven thousand.
6 ¶ *The sons* of Benjamin; Bē'lȧ, and
Bē'ɕhēr, and Jē-dī'ā-ĕl, three.
7 And the sons of Bē'lȧ; Ĕz'bŏn, and
Ŭz'zī, and Ŭz-zī'ĕl, and Jĕr'ĭ-mŏth, and
Ī'rī, five; heads of the house of *their*
fathers, mighty men of valor; and were
reckoned by their genealogies twenty
and two thousand and thirty and four.
8 And the sons of Bē'ɕhēr; Zē-mī'rȧ,
and Jō'ăsh, and Ĕl'ĭ-ē'zēr, and Ē-lĭ'ō-ē'-
nā-ī, and Ŏm'rī, and Jĕr'ĭ-mŏth, and
Ȧ-bī'ȧh, and Ăn'ȧ-thŏth, and Ăl'ȧ-mĕth.
All these *are* the sons of Bē'ɕhēr.
9 And the number of them, after their
genealogy by their generations, heads of
the house of their fathers, mighty men
of valor, *was* twenty thousand and two
hundred.
10 The sons also of Jē-dī'ā-ĕl; Bĭl'hăn:
and the sons of Bĭl'hăn; Jē'ŭsh, and
Benjamin, and Ē'hŭd, and ɕhē-nā'ȧ-
năh, and Zē'thăn, and Thär'shĭsh, and
Ȧ-hĭsh'ȧ-här.
11 All these the sons of Jē-dī'ā-ĕl, by
the heads of their fathers, mighty men
of valor, *were* seventeen thousand and
two hundred *soldiers,* fit to go out for
war *and* battle.
12 Shŭp'pĭm also, and Hŭp'pĭm, the
children of Ĭr, *and* Hū'shĭm, the sons of
Ā'hēr.
13 ¶ The sons of Năph'tȧ-lī; Jäh'zī-ĕl,
and Gū'nī, and Jē'zēr, and Shăl'lŭm,
the sons of Bĭl'hȧh.
14 ¶ The sons of Mȧ-năs'sĕh; Ăsh'-
rī-ĕl, whom she bare; (*but* his concubine
the Ā'răm-ĭt'ĕss bare Mā'ɕhĭr the father
of Gĭl'ē-ăd:
15 And Mā'ɕhĭr took to wife *the sister*
of Hŭp'pĭm and Shŭp'pĭm, whose sister's name *was* Mā'ȧ-ɕhăh;) and the
name of the second *was* Zē-lō'phē-hăd:
and Zē-lō'phē-hăd had daughters.

16 And Mā'ȧ-chȧh the wife of Mā'chĭr
bare a son, and she called his name Pē'-
rĕsh; and the name of his brother *was*
Shē'rĕsh; and his sons *were* Ū'lăm and
Rā'kĕm.
17 And the sons of Ū'lăm; Bē'dăn.
These *were* the sons of Gĭl'ē-ăd, the son
of Mā'chĭr, the son of Mȧ-năs'sĕh.
18 And his sister Hăm-mŏl'ē-kĕth
bare Ī'shŏd, and Ā'bĭ-ē'zēr, and Mȧ-
hā'lăh.
19 And the sons of Shē-mī'dȧh were,
Ȧ-hī'ăn, and Shē'chĕm, and Lĭk'hī, and
Ȧ-nī'ăm.
20 ℭ And the sons of Ē'phrā-ĭm; Shụ-
thē'lȧh, and Bē'rĕd his son, and Tā'hăth
his son, and Ĕl'ȧ-dȧh his son, and Tā'-
hăth his son,
21 ℭ And Zā'băd his son, and Shụ-
thē'lȧh his son, and Ē'zēr, and Ĕl'ē-ăd,
whom the men of Gath *that were* born
in *that* land slew, because they came
down to take away their cattle.
22 And Ē'phrā-ĭm their father mourned
many days, and his brethren came to
comfort him.
23 ℭ And when he went in to his wife,
she conceived and bare a son, and he
called his name Bē-rī'ȧh, because it
went evil with his house.
24 (And his daughter *was* Shē'rȧh, who
built Bĕth'-hō'rŏn the nether, and the
upper, and Ŭz'zĕn-shē'rȧh.)
25 And Rē'phȧh *was* his son, also Rē'-
shĕph, and Tē'lȧh his son, and Tā'hăn
his son.
26 Lā'ȧ-dăn his son, Ȧm-mī'hŭd his
son, Ē-lĭsh'ȧ-mä his son,
27 Nŏn his son, Jē-hŏsh'ū-ȧh his son.
28 ℭ And their possessions and habitations *were,* Beth-el and the towns thereof, and eastward Nā'ȧ-răn, and westward
Gē'zēr, with the towns thereof; Shē'-
chĕm also and the towns thereof, unto
Gā'zȧ and the towns thereof:
29 And by the borders of the children
of Mȧ-năs'sĕh, Bĕth'-shē'ăn and her
towns, Tā'ȧ-năch and her towns, Mē-
gĭd'dō and her towns, Dor and her
towns. In these dwelt the children of
Joseph the son of Ĭs'rā-ĕl.
30 ℭ The sons of Ăsh'ēr; Ĭm'nȧh, and
Ĭs'ū-ȧh, and Ĭsh'ū-aī, and Bē-rī'ȧh, and
Sē'rȧh their sister.
31 And the sons of Bē-rī'ȧh; Hē'bēr,
and Măl'chĭ-ĕl, who *is* the father of
Bĭr-zā'vĭth.
32 And Hē'bēr begat Jăph'lĕt, and
Shō'mēr, and Hō'thăm, and Shụ'ȧ their
sister.
33 And the sons of Jăph'lĕt; Pā'săch,
and Bĭm'hăl, and Ăsh'văth. These *are*
the children of Jăph'lĕt.
34 And the sons of Shā'mēr; Ā'hī, and
Rōh'gȧh, Jē-hŭb'bȧh, and Ā'răm.
35 And the sons of his brother Hē'lĕm;
Zō'phȧh, and Ĭm'nȧ, and Shē'lĕsh, and
Ā'măl.
36 The sons of Zō'phȧh; Sū'ȧh, and
Här'nē-phēr, and Shụ'ăl, and Bē'rī, and
Ĭm'rȧh,
37 Bē'zēr, and Hŏd, and Shăm'mȧ, and
Shĭl'shȧh, and Ĭth'răn, and Bē-ē'rȧ.
38 And the sons of Jē'thēr; Jē-phŭn'-
nĕh, and Pĭs'păh, and Ā'rȧ.
39 And the sons of Ŭl'lȧ; Ā'rȧh, and
Hăn'ī-ĕl, and Rē-zī'ȧ.
40 All these *were* the children of Ăsh'ēr,
heads of *their* father's house, choice *and*
mighty men of valor, chief of the princes.
And the number throughout the genealogy of them that were apt to the war
and to battle *was* twenty and six thousand men.

CHAPTER 8

NOW Benjamin begat Bē'lȧ his firstborn, Ăsh'bĕl the second, and
Ȧ-hăr'ȧh the third,
2 Nō'hȧh the fourth, and Rā'phȧ the
fifth.
3 And the sons of Bē'lȧ were, Ăd'där,
and Gē'rȧ, and Ȧ-bī'hŭd,
4 And Ȧ-bĭsh'ū-ȧ, and Nā'ȧ-măn, and
Ȧ-hō'ȧh,
5 And Gē'rȧ, and Shē-phū'phăn, and
Hū'răm.
6 And these *are* the sons of Ē'hŭd:
these are the heads of the fathers of the
inhabitants of Gē'bȧ, and they removed
them to Măn'ȧ-hăth:
7 And Nā'ȧ-măn, and Ȧ-hī'ȧh, and
Gē'rȧ, he removed them, and begat
Ŭz'zȧ, and Ȧ-hī'hŭd.
8 And Shā'hȧ-rā'ĭm begat *children* in
the country of Mō'ăb, after he had sent
them away; Hū'shĭm and Bā'ȧ-rȧ *were*
his wives.
9 And he begat of Hō'dĕsh his wife,
Jō'băb, and Zĭb'ī-ȧ, and Mē'shȧ, and
Măl'chăm,
10 And Jē'ŭz, and Shȧ-chī'ȧ, and
Mĭr'mȧ. These *were* his sons, heads of
the fathers.
11 And of Hū'shĭm he begat Ȧ-bī'tŭb,
and Ĕl-pā'ăl.

12 The sons of Ĕl-pā'ăl; Ē'bẽr, and Mī'shăm, and Shā'mĕd, who built Ō'nō, and Lŏd, with the towns thereof:
13 Bē-rī'ah also, and Shē'mȧ, who *were* heads of the fathers of the inhabitants of Ăj'ȧ-lŏn, who drove away the inhabitants of Gath:
14 And Ȧ-hī'ō, Shā'shăk, and Jĕr'ē-mŏth,
15 And Zĕb'ȧ-dī'ȧh, and Ā'răd, and Ā'dẽr,
16 And Mī'chā-ĕl, and Ĭs'pȧh, and Jō'hȧ, the sons of Bē-rī'ȧh;
17 And Zĕb'ȧ-dī'ȧh, and Mē-shŭl'lăm, and Hĕz'ē-kī, and Hē'bẽr,
18 Ĭsh'mē-raī also, and Jĕz-lī'ȧh, and Jō'băb, the sons of Ĕl-pā'ăl;
19 And Jā'kĭm, and Zĭch'rī, and Zăb'dī,
20 And Ĕl'ī-ē'nā-ī, and Zĭl'thaī, and Ē'lī-ĕl,
21 And Ȧ-dā'ịȧh, and Bĕr'ȧ-ī'ȧh, and Shĭm'răth, the sons of Shĭm'hī;
22 And Ĭsh'păn, and Hē'bẽr, and Ē'lī-ĕl,
23 And Ăb'dŏn, and Zĭch'rī, and Hā'năn,
24 And Hăn'ȧ-nī'ȧh, and Ē'lăm, and Ăn'tō-thī'jȧh,
25 And Ĭph'ē-dē'ịȧh, and Pē-nū'ĕl, the sons of Shā'shăk;
26 And Shăm'shē-raī, and Shē'hȧ-rī'ȧh, and Ăth'ȧ-lī'ȧh,
27 And Jăr'ē-sī'ȧh, and Ē-lī'ȧh, and Zĭch'rī, the sons of Jē-rō'hăm.
28 These *were* heads of the fathers, by their generations, chief *men*. These dwelt in Jerusalem.
29 And at Gĭb'ē-ŏn dwelt the father of Gĭb'ē-ŏn; whose wife's name *was* Mā'ȧ-chȧh:
30 And his firstborn son Ăb'dŏn, and Zûr, and Kish, and Bā'ăl, and Nā'dăb,
31 And Gē'dŏr, and Ȧ-hī'ō, and Zā'-chẽr.
32 And Mĭk'lŏth begat Shĭm'ē-ȧh. And these also dwelt with their brethren in Jerusalem, over against them.
33 ¶ And Nĕr begat Kish, and Kish begat Saul, and Saul begat Jonathan, and Măl'chī-shụ'ȧ, and Ȧ-bĭn'ȧ-dăb, and Ĕsh'-bā'ăl.
34 And the son of Jonathan *was* Mĕr'-ĭb-bā'ăl; and Mĕr'ĭb-bā'ăl begat Mī'-cȧh.
35 And the sons of Mī'cȧh *were*, Pī'-thŏn, and Mē'lĕch, and Tā'rē-ȧ, and Ahaz.
36 And Ahaz begat Jē-hō'ȧ-dȧh; and Jē-hō'ȧ-dȧh begat Ăl'ē-mĕth, and Ăz-mā'vĕth, and Zĭm'rī; and Zĭm'rī begat Mō'zȧ;
37 And Mō'zȧ begat Bĭn'ē-ȧ: Rā'phȧ *was* his son, Ĕl'ē-ā'sȧh his son, Ā'zĕl his son.
38 And Ā'zĕl had six sons, whose names *are* these, Ăz'rī-kăm, Bō'chē-rụ, and Ĭsh'mā-ĕl, and Shē'ȧ-rī'ȧh, and Ō'bȧ-dī'ȧh, and Hā'năn. All these *were* the sons of Ā'zĕl.
39 And the sons of Ē'shĕk his brother *were*, Ū'lăm his firstborn, Jē'hŭsh the second, and Ē-lĭph'ē-lĕt the third.
40 And the sons of Ū'lăm were mighty men of valor, archers, and had many sons, and sons' sons, a hundred and fifty. All these *are* of the sons of Benjamin.

CHAPTER 9

SO all Ĭṣ'rā-ĕl were reckoned by genealogies; and, behold, they *were* written in the book of the kings of Ĭṣ'rā-ĕl and Judah, *who* were carried away to Babylon for their transgression.
2 ¶ Now the first inhabitants that *dwelt* in their possessions in their cities *were*, the Ĭṣ'rā-ĕl-ītes, the priests, Lē'-vītes, and the Nĕth'ĭ-nĭm.
3 And in Jerusalem dwelt of the children of Judah, and of the children of Benjamin, and of the children of Ē'phrā-ĭm, and Mȧ-năs'sĕh;
4 Ū'thaī the son of Ȧm-mī'hŭd, the son of Ŏm'rī, the son of Ĭm'rī, the son of Bā'nī, of the children of Phā'rĕz the son of Judah.
5 And of the Shī'lō-nītes; Ȧ-sā'ịȧh the firstborn, and his sons.
6 And of the sons of Zē'rȧh; Jē-ū'ĕl, and their brethren, six hundred and ninety.
7 And of the sons of Benjamin; Săl'lū the son of Mē-shŭl'lăm, the son of Hō'-dȧ-vī'ȧh, the son of Hăs'ē-nū'ȧh,
8 And Ĭb-nē'ịȧh the son of Jē-rō'hăm, and Ē'lȧh the son of Ŭz'zī, the son of Mĭch'rī, and Mē-shŭl'lăm the son of Shĕph'ȧ-tī'ȧh, the son of Reụ'ĕl, the son of Ĭb-nī'jȧh;
9 And their brethren, according to their generations, nine hundred and fifty and six. All these men *were* chief of the fathers in the house of their fathers.
10 ¶ And of the priests; Jē-dā'ịȧh, and Jē-hoi'ȧ-rĭb, and Jā'chĭn,
11 And Ăz'ȧ-rī'ȧh the son of Hĭl-kī'ȧh.

the son of Mē-shŭl′lăm, the son of Zā′-
dŏk, the son of Mē-rā′ịŏth, the son of
Å-hī′tŭb, the ruler of the house of God;
12 And Å-dā′ịah the son of Jē-rō′hăm,
the son of Păsh′ŭr, the son of Măl chī′-
jȧh, and Mā-ăs′ĭ-aī the son of Ā′dĭ-ĕl,
the son of Jăh′zē-rȧh, the son of Mē-
shŭl′lăm, the son of Mē-shĭl′lē-mĭth,
the son of Ĭm′mēr;
13 And their brethren, heads of the
house of their fathers, a thousand and
seven hundred and threescore; very
able men for the work of the service of
the house of God.
14 And of the Lē′vītes; Shē-mā′ịah the
son of Hăs′shŭb, the son of Ăz′rĭ-kăm,
the son of Hăsh′ȧ-bī′ȧh, of the sons of
Mē-rā′rī;
15 And Băk-băk′kȧr, Hē′rĕsh, and Gā′-
lăl, and Măt′tȧ-nī′ȧh the son of Mī′cȧh,
the son of Zĭch′rī, the son of Ā′săph;
16 And Ō′bȧ-dī′ȧh the son of Shē-mā′-
ịah, the son of Gā′lăl, the son of Jē-dū′-
thŭn, and Bĕr′ē-chī′ȧh the son of Ā′sȧ,
the son of Ĕl-kā′nȧh, that dwelt in the
villages of the Nē-tŏph′ȧ-thītes.
17 And the porters *were*, Shăl′lŭm, and
Ăk′kŭb, and Tăl′mŏn, and Å-hī′măn,
and their brethren: Shăl′lŭm *was* the
chief;
18 Who hitherto *waited* in the king's
gate eastward: they *were* porters in the
companies of the children of Levi.
19 And Shăl′lŭm the son of Kō′rē, the
son of Ē-bī′ȧ-sȧph, the son of Kō′rȧh,
and his brethren, of the house of his father, the Kō′rȧh-ītes, *were* over the
work of the service, keepers of the gates
of the tabernacle: and their fathers, *being* over the host of the LORD, *were*
keepers of the entry.
20 And Phĭn′ē-hăs the son of Ĕl′ē-ā′-
zȧr was the ruler over them in time
past, *and* the LORD *was* with him.
21 *And* Zĕch′ȧ-rī′ȧh the son of Mē-
shĕl′ē-mī′ȧh *was* porter of the door of
the tabernacle of the congregation.
22 All these *which were* chosen to be
porters in the gates *were* two hundred
and twelve. These were reckoned by
their genealogy in their villages, whom
David and Samuel the seer did ordain in
their set office.
23 So they and their children *had* the
oversight of the gates of the house of
the LORD, *namely*, the house of the tabernacle, by wards.
24 In four quarters were the porters,
toward the east, west, north, and south.
25 And their brethren, *which were* in
their villages, *were* to come after seven
days from time to time with them.
26 For these Lē′vītes, the four chief
porters, were in *their* set office, and
were over the chambers and treasuries
of the house of God.
27 ℂ And they lodged round about the
house of God, because the charge *was*
upon them, and the opening thereof
every morning *pertained* to them.
28 And *certain* of them had the charge
of the ministering vessels, that they
should bring them in and out by tale.
29 *Some* of them also *were* appointed
to oversee the vessels, and all the
instruments of the sanctuary, and the
fine flour, and the wine, and the oil, and
the frankincense, and the spices.
30 And *some* of the sons of the priests
made the ointment of the spices.
31 And Măt′tĭ-thī′ȧh, *one* of the Lē′-
vītes, who *was* the firstborn of Shăl′lŭm
the Kō′rȧh-īte, had the set office over
the things that were made in the pans.
32 And *other* of their brethren, of the
sons of the Kō′hăth-ītes, *were* over the
showbread, to prepare *it* every sabbath.
33 And these *are* the singers, chief of
the fathers of the Lē′vītes, *who remaining* in the chambers *were* free: for they
were employed in *that* work day and
night.
34 These chief fathers of the Lē′vītes
were chief throughout their generations; these dwelt at Jerusalem.
35 ℂ And in Gĭb′ē-ŏn dwelt the father
of Gĭb′ē-ŏn, Jē-hī′ĕl, whose wife's
name *was* Mā′ȧ-chȧh:
36 And his firstborn son Ăb′dŏn, then
Zûr, and Kish, and Bā′ăl, and Nĕr, and
Nā′dăb,
37 And Gē′dŏr, and Å-hī′ō, and Zĕch′ȧ-
rī′ȧh, and Mĭk′lŏth.
38 And Mĭk′lŏth begat Shĭm′ē-ăm.
And they also dwelt with their brethren
at Jerusalem, over against their brethren.
39 And Nĕr begat Kish; and Kish begat
Saul; and Saul begat Jonathan, and
Măl′chī-shụ′ȧ, and Å-bĭn′ȧ-dăb, and
Ĕsh′-bā′ăl.
40 And the son of Jonathan *was* Mĕr′-
ĭb-bā′ăl: and Mĕr′ĭb-bā′ăl begat Mī′cȧh.
41 And the sons of Mī′cȧh *were*, Pī′-
thŏn, and Mē′lĕch, and Tăh′rē-ȧ, *and
Ahaz*.
42 And Ahaz begat Jā′rȧh; and Jā′rȧh

begat Ăl′ē-mĕth, and Ăz-mā′vĕth, and Zĭm′rī; and Zĭm′rī begat Mō′zȧ;

43 And Mō′zȧ begat Bĭn′ē-ȧ; and Rē-phā′ịah his son, Ĕl′ē-ā′sȧh his son, Ā′zĕl his son.

44 And Ā′zĕl had six sons, whose names *are* these, Ăz′rĭ-kăm, Bō′ѐhē-ru̥, and Ĭsh′mā-ĕl, and Shē′ȧ-rī′ȧh, and Ō′bȧ-dī′ȧh, and Hā′năn. These *were* the sons of Ā′zĕl.

CHAPTER 10

NOW the Phĭ-lĭs′tīneș fought against Ĭș′rā-ĕl; and the men of Ĭș′rā-ĕl fled from before the Phĭ-lĭs′tīneș, and fell down slain in mount Gĭl-bō′ȧ.

2 And the Phĭ-lĭs′tīneș followed hard after Saul, and after his sons; and the Phĭ-lĭs′tīneș slew Jonathan, and Ȧ-bĭn′ȧ-dăb, and Măl′ѐhī-shu̥′ȧ, the sons of Saul.

3 And the battle went sore against Saul, and the archers hit him, and he was wounded of the archers.

4 Then said Saul to his armor-bearer, Draw thy sword, and thrust me through therewith; lest these uncircumcised come and abuse me. But his armor-bearer would not; for he was sore afraid. So Saul took a sword, and fell upon it.

5 And when his armor-bearer saw that Saul was dead, he fell likewise on the sword and died.

6 So Saul died, and his three sons, and all his house died together.

7 And when all the men of Ĭș′rā-ĕl that *were* in the valley saw that they fled, and that Saul and his sons were dead, then they forsook their cities, and fled: and the Phĭ-lĭs′tīneș came and dwelt in them.

8 ¶ And it came to pass on the morrow, when the Phĭ-lĭs′tīneș came to strip the slain, that they found Saul and his sons fallen in mount Gĭl-bō′ȧ.

9 And when they had stripped him, they took his head, and his armor, and sent into the land of the Phĭ-lĭs′tīneș round about, to carry tidings unto their idols, and to the people.

10 And they put his armor in the house of their gods, and fastened his head in the temple of Dā′gŏn.

11 ¶ And when all Jā′bĕsh–gĭl′ē-ăd heard all that the Phĭ-lĭs′tīneș had done to Saul,

12 They arose, all the valiant men, and took away the body of Saul, and the bodies of his sons, and brought them to Jā′bĕsh, and buried their bones under the oak in Jā′bĕsh, and fasted seven days.

13 ¶ So Saul died for his transgression which he committed against the LORD, *even* against the word of the LORD, which he kept not, and also for asking *counsel* of *one that had* a familiar spirit, to inquire *of it;*

14 And inquired not of the LORD: therefore he slew him, and turned the kingdom unto David the son of Jesse.

CHAPTER 11

THEN all Ĭș′rā-ĕl gathered themselves to David unto Hē′brŏn, saying, Behold, we *are* thy bone and thy flesh.

2 And moreover in time past, even when Saul was king, thou *wast* he that leddest out and broughtest in Ĭș′rā-ĕl: and the LORD thy God said unto thee, Thou shalt feed my people Ĭș′rā-ĕl, and thou shalt be ruler over my people Ĭș′rā-ĕl.

3 Therefore came all the elders of Ĭș′rā-ĕl to the king to Hē′brŏn; and David made a covenant with them in Hē′brŏn before the LORD; and they anointed David king over Ĭș′rā-ĕl, according to the word of the LORD by Samuel.

4 ¶ And David and all Ĭș′rā-ĕl went to Jerusalem, which *is* Jē′bŭs; where the Jĕb′ū-șītes *were,* the inhabitants of the land.

5 And the inhabitants of Jē′bŭs said to David, Thou shalt not come hither. Nevertheless David took the castle of Zion, which *is* the city of David.

6 And David said, Whosoever smiteth the Jĕb′ū-șītes first shall be chief and captain. So Jō′ăb the son of Zĕr′u̥-ī′ȧh went first up, and was chief.

7 And David dwelt in the castle; therefore they called it the city of David.

8 And he built the city round about, even from Mĭl′lō round about: and Jō′ăb repaired the rest of the city.

9 So David waxed greater and greater: for the LORD of hosts *was* with him.

10 ¶ These also *are* the chief of the mighty men whom David had, who strengthened themselves with him in his kingdom, *and* with all Ĭș′rā-ĕl, to make him king, according to the word of the LORD concerning Ĭș′rā-ĕl.

11 And this *is* the number of the mighty men whom David had; Jȧ-shō′bē-ăm, a

Hăch'mō-nīte, the chief of the captains:
he lifted up his spear against three hundred slain *by him* at one time.
12 And after him *was* Ĕl'ē-ā'zȧr the son
of Dō'dō, the Ȧ-hō'hīte, who *was one* of
the three mighties.
13 He was with David at Păs'–dăm'mĭm, and there the Phĭ-lĭs'tīneş were
gathered together to battle, where was
a parcel of ground full of barley; and the
people fled from before the Phĭ-lĭs'tīneş.
14 And they set themselves in the
midst of *that* parcel, and delivered it,
and slew the Phĭ-lĭs'tīneş; and the LORD
saved *them* by a great deliverance.
15 ℂ Now three of the thirty captains
went down to the rock of David, into the
cave of Ȧ-dŭl'lăm; and the host of the
Phĭ-lĭs'tīneş encamped in the valley of
Rĕph'ā-ĭm.
16 And David *was* then in the hold,
and the Phĭ-lĭs'tīneş' garrison *was* then
at Beth-lehem.
17 And David longed, and said, Oh
that one would give me drink of the water of the well of Beth-lehem, that *is* at
the gate!
18 And the three brake through the
host of the Phĭ-lĭs'tīneş, and drew water
out of the well of Beth-lehem, that *was*
by the gate, and took *it*, and brought *it*
to David: but David would not drink *of*
it, but poured it out to the LORD,
19 And said, My God forbid it me, that
I should do this thing: shall I drink the
blood of these men that have put their
lives in jeopardy? for with *the jeopardy
of* their lives they brought it: therefore
he would not drink it. These things did
these three mightiest.
20 ℂ And Ȧ-bĭsh'ā-ī the brother of
Jō'ăb, he was chief of the three: for lifting up his spear against three hundred,
he slew *them*, and had a name among
the three.
21 Of the three, he was more honorable than the two, for he was their captain: howbeit he attained not to the *first*
three.
22 Bē-nā'ịah the son of Jē-hôi'ȧ-dȧ,
the son of a valiant man of Kăb'zē-ĕl,
who had done many acts; he slew two
lionlike men of Mō'ăb: also he went down
and slew a lion in a pit in a snowy day.
23 And he slew an Egyptian, a man of
great stature, five cubits high; and in
the Egyptian's hand *was* a spear like a
weaver's beam; and he went down to
him with a staff, and plucked the spear
out of the Egyptian's hand, and slew
him with his own spear.
24 These *things* did Bē-nā'ịah the son
of Jē-hôi'ȧ-dȧ, and had a name among
the three mighties.
25 Behold, he was honorable among
the thirty, but attained not to the *first*
three: and David set him over his guard.
26 ℂ Also the valiant men of the armies
were, Ăs'ȧ-hĕl the brother of Jō'ăb, Ĕl-hā'năn the son of Dō'dō of Beth-lehem,
27 Shăm'mŏth the Hā'rō-rīte, Hē'lĕz
the Pĕl'ō-nīte,
28 Ī'rȧ the son of Ĭk'kĕsh the Tē-kō'īte, Ā'bĭ-ē'zēr the Ăn'tŏth-īte,
29 Sĭb'bē-caī the Hū'shȧth-īte, Ī'lā-ī
the Ȧ-hō'hīte,
30 Mȧ-hăr'ā-ī the Nē-tŏph'ȧ-thīte, Hē'lĕd the son of Bā'ȧ-nȧh the Nē-tŏph'ȧ-thīte,
31 Ĭth'ā-ī the son of Rī'baī of Gĭb'ē-ȧh,
that pertained to the children of Benjamin, Bē-nā'ịah the Pĭr'ȧ-thŏn-īte,
32 Hū'rā-ī of the brooks of Gā'ăsh,
Ā'bĭ-ĕl the Ăr'băth-īte,
33 Ăz-mā'vĕth the Bȧ-hā'rŭm-īte, Ē-lī'ȧh-bȧ the Shā'ăl-bō'nīte,
34 The sons of Hā'shĕm the Gī'zō-nīte,
Jonathan the son of Shā'gē the Hā'rȧ-rīte,
35 Ȧ-hī'ăm the son of Sā'cär the Hā'rȧ-rīte, Ĕl'ī-phăl the son of Ûr,
36 Hē'phēr the Mē-chē'răth-īte, Ȧ-hī'jȧh the Pĕl'ō-nīte,
37 Hĕz'rō the Cär'mĕl-īte, Nā'ȧ-raī the
son of Ĕz'baī,
38 Joel the brother of Nathan, Mĭb'här the son of Hăg'gē-rī,
39 Zē'lĕk the Ammonite, Nā'hȧ-raī the
Bē'rŏth-īte, the armor-bearer of Jō'ăb
the son of Zĕr'ụ-ī'ȧh,
40 Ī'rȧ the Ĭth'rīte, Gā'rĕb the Ĭth'rīte,
41 Ū-rī'ȧh the Hĭt'tīte, Zā'băd the son
of Ăh'laī,
42 Ăd'ī-nȧ the son of Shī'zȧ the Reubenite, a captain of the Reubenites, and
thirty with him,
43 Hā'năn the son of Mā'ȧ-chȧh, and
Jŏsh'ȧ-phăt the Mĭth'nīte,
44 Ŭz-zī'ȧ the Ăsh'tē-răth-īte, Shā'mȧ
and Jē-hī'ĕl the sons of Hō'thăn the
Ȧ-rō'ēr-īte,
45 Jē-dī'ā-ĕl the son of Shĭm'rī, and
Jō'hȧ his brother, the Tī'zīte,
46 Ē'lī-ĕl the Mā'hȧ-vīte, and Jĕr'ī-baī
and Jŏsh'ȧ-vī'ȧh the sons of Ĕl-nā'ăm,
and Ĭth'mäh the Mō'ăb-īte,

47 Ē′lĭ′ĕl, and Ō′bĕd, and Jā′sĭ-ĕl the Mē-sō′bȧ-īte.

CHAPTER 12

NOW these *are* they that came to David to Zĭk′lăg, while he yet kept himself close because of Saul the son of Kish: and they *were* among the mighty men, helpers of the war.

2 *They were* armed with bows, and could use both the right hand and the left in *hurling* stones and *shooting* arrows out of a bow, *even* of Saul's brethren of Benjamin.

3 The chief *was* Ā′hī-ē′zĕr, then Jō′ăsh, the sons of Shē-mā′ȧh the Gĭb′ē-ăth-īte; and Jē′zĭ-ĕl, and Pē′lĕt, the sons of Ăz-mā′vĕth; and Bĕr′ȧ-chȧh, and Jē′hū the Ăn′tŏth-īte,

4 And Ĭs-mā′ịȧh the Gĭb′ē-ŏn-īte, a mighty man among the thirty, and over the thirty; and Jeremiah, and Jȧ-hā′zĭ-ĕl, and Jō-hā′năn, and Jŏs′ȧ-băd the Gē-dē′rȧ-thīte,

5 Ē-lū′zā-ī, and Jĕr′ĭ-mŏth, and Bē′ȧ-lī′ȧh, and Shĕm′ȧ-rī′ȧh, and Shĕph′ȧ-tī′ȧh the Hȧ-rụ′phīte,

6 Ĕl-kā′nȧh, and Jē-sī′ȧh, and Ȧ-zā′rē-ĕl, and Jō-ē′zĕr, and Jȧ-shō′bē-ăm, the Kôr′hītes,

7 And Jō′ē-lȧh, and Zĕb′ȧ-dī′ȧh, the sons of Jē-rō′hăm of Gē′dŏr.

8 And of the Gadites there separated themselves unto David into the hold to the wilderness men of might, *and* men of war *fit* for the battle, that could handle shield and buckler, whose faces *were like* the faces of lions, and *were* as swift as the roes upon the mountains;

9 Ē′zĕr the first, Ō′bȧ-dī′ȧh the second, Ē-lī′ăb the third,

10 Mĭsh-măn′nȧh the fourth, Jeremiah the fifth,

11 Ăt′tā-ī the sixth, Ē′lĭ-ĕl the seventh,

12 Jō-hā′năn the eighth, Ĕl-zā′băd the ninth,

13 Jeremiah the tenth, Măch′bȧ-naī the eleventh.

14 These *were* of the sons of Gad, captains of the host: one of the least *was* over a hundred, and the greatest over a thousand.

15 These *are* they that went over Jordan in the first month, when it had overflown all his banks; and they put to flight all *them* of the valleys, *both* toward the east, and toward the west.

16 And there came of the children of Benjamin and Judah to the hold unto David.

17 And David went out to meet them, and answered and said unto them, If ye be come peaceably unto me to help me, mine heart shall be knit unto you: but if *ye be come* to betray me to mine enemies, seeing *there is* no wrong in mine hands, the God of our fathers look *thereon*, and rebuke *it*.

18 Then the spirit came upon Ȧ-măs′ā-ī, *who was* chief of the captains, *and he said,* Thine *are we,* David, and on thy side, thou son of Jesse: peace, peace *be* unto thee, and peace *be* to thine helpers; for thy God helpeth thee. Then David received them, and made them captains of the band.

19 And there fell *some* of Mȧ-năs′sĕh to David, when he came with the Phĭ-lĭs′tīnes against Saul to battle; but they helped them not: for the lords of the Phĭ-lĭs′tīnes upon advisement sent him away, saying, He will fall to his master Saul to *the jeopardy of* our heads.

20 As he went to Zĭk′lăg, there fell to him of Mȧ-năs′sĕh, Ăd′nȧh, and Jŏz′ȧ-băd, and Jē-dī′ā-ĕl, and Mī′chā-ĕl, and Jŏz′ȧ-băd, and Ē-lī′hū, and Zĭl′thaī, captains of the thousands that *were* of Mȧ-năs′sĕh.

21 And they helped David against the band *of the rovers:* for they *were* all mighty men of valor, and were captains in the host.

22 For at *that* time day by day there came to David to help him, until *it was* a great host, like the host of God.

23 ¶ And these *are* the numbers of the bands *that were* ready armed to the war, *and* came to David to Hē′brŏn, to turn the kingdom of Saul to him, according to the word of the LORD.

24 The children of Judah that bare shield and spear *were* six thousand and eight hundred, ready armed to the war.

25 Of the children of Simeon, mighty men of valor for the war, seven thousand and one hundred.

26 Of the children of Levi four thousand and six hundred.

27 And Jē-hoi′ȧ-dȧ *was* the leader of the Āar′ŏn-ītes, and with him *were* three thousand and seven hundred;

28 And Zā′dŏk, a young man mighty of valor, and of his father's house twenty and two captains.

29 And of the children of Benjamin,

the kindred of Saul, three thousand: for hitherto the greatest part of them had kept the ward of the house of Saul.

30 And of the children of Ē′phrā-ĭm, twenty thousand and eight hundred, mighty men of valor, famous throughout the house of their fathers.

31 And of the half tribe of Mȧ-năs′sĕh eighteen thousand, which were expressed by name, to come and make David king.

32 And of the children of Ĭs′sȧ-chär, *which were men* that had understanding of the times, to know what Ĭs̱′rā-ĕl ought to do; the heads of them *were* two hundred; and all their brethren *were* at their commandment.

33 Of Zĕb′ū-lŭn, such as went forth to battle, expert in war, with all instruments of war, fifty thousand, which could keep rank: *they were* not of double heart.

34 And of Năph′tȧ-lī a thousand captains, and with them with shield and spear thirty and seven thousand.

35 And of the Dăn′ītes expert in war twenty and eight thousand and six hundred.

36 And of Ăsh′ẽr, such as went forth to battle, expert in war, forty thousand.

37 And on the other side of Jordan, of the Reubenites, and the Gadites, and of the half tribe of Mȧ-năs′sĕh, with all manner of instruments of war for the battle, a hundred and twenty thousand.

38 All these men of war, that could keep rank, came with a perfect heart to Hē′brȯn, to make David king over all Ĭs̱′rā-ĕl: and all the rest also of Ĭs̱′rā-ĕl *were* of one heart to make David king.

39 And there they were with David three days, eating and drinking: for their brethren had prepared for them.

40 Moreover they that were nigh them, *even* unto Ĭs′sȧ-chär and Zĕb′ū-lŭn and Năph′tȧ-lī, brought bread on asses, and on camels, and on mules, and on oxen, *and* meat, meal, cakes of figs, and bunches of raisins, and wine, and oil, and oxen, and sheep abundantly: for *there was* joy in Ĭs̱′rā-ĕl.

CHAPTER 13

AND David consulted with the captains of thousands and hundreds, *and* with every leader.

2 And David said unto all the congregation of Ĭs̱′rā-ĕl, If *it seem* good unto you, and *that it be* of the LORD our God, let us send abroad unto our brethren every where, *that are* left in all the land of Ĭs̱′rā-ĕl, and with them *also* to the priests and Lē′vītes *which are* in their cities *and* suburbs, that they may gather themselves unto us:

3 And let us bring again the ark of our God to us: for we inquired not at it in the days of Saul.

4 And all the congregation said that they would do so: for the thing was right in the eyes of all the people.

5 So David gathered all Ĭs̱′rā-ĕl together, from Shī′hôr of Egypt even unto the entering of Hē′măth, to bring the ark of God from Kĭr′jăth-jē′ȧ-rĭm.

6 And David went up, and all Ĭs′rā-ĕl, to Bā′ȧ-lȧh, *that is,* to Kĭr′jăth-jē′ȧ-rĭm, which *belonged* to Judah, to bring up thence the ark of God the LORD, that dwelleth *between* the cherubim, whose name is called *on it.*

7 And they carried the ark of God in a new cart out of the house of Ȧ-bĭn′ȧ-dăb: and Ŭz′zȧ and Ȧ-hī′ō drave the cart.

8 And David and all Ĭs̱′rā-ĕl played before God with all *their* might, and with singing, and with harps, and with psalteries, and with timbrels, and with cymbals, and with trumpets.

9 ¶ And when they came unto the threshingfloor of Chī′dŏn, Ŭz′zȧ put forth his hand to hold the ark; for the oxen stumbled.

10 And the anger of the LORD was kindled against Ŭz′zȧ, and he smote him, because he put his hand to the ark: and there he died before God.

11 And David was displeased, because the LORD had made a breach upon Ŭz′zȧ: wherefore that place is called Pē′rĕz–ŭz′zȧ to this day.

12 And David was afraid of God that day, saying, How shall I bring the ark of God *home* to me?

13 So David brought not the ark *home* to himself to the city of David, but carried it aside into the house of Ō′bĕd-ē′dŏm the Gĭt′tīte.

14 And the ark of God remained with the family of Ō′bĕd–ē′dŏm in his house three months. And the LORD blessed the house of Ō′bĕd–ē′dŏm, and all that he had.

CHAPTER 14

NOW Hiram king of Tȳre sent messengers to David, and timber of cedars, with masons and carpenters, to build him a house.

2 And David perceived that the LORD had confirmed him king over Ĭş'rā-ĕl, for his kingdom was lifted up on high, because of his people Ĭş'rā-ĕl.

3 ℂ And David took more wives at Jerusalem: and David begat more sons and daughters.

4 Now these *are* the names of *his* children which he had in Jerusalem; Shăm-mū'ȧ, and Shō'băb, Nathan, and Solomon,

5 And Ĭb'här, and Ĕl'ĭ-shū'ȧ, and Ĕl-pā'lĕt,

6 And Nō'gȧh, and Nē'phĕg, and Jȧ-phī'ȧ,

7 And Ē-lĭsh'ȧ-mä, and Bē'ē-lī'ȧ-dȧ, and Ē-lĭph'ȧ-lĕt.

8 ℂ And when the Phĭ-lĭs'tĭneş heard that David was anointed king over all Ĭş'rā-ĕl, all the Phĭ-lĭs'tĭneş went up to seek David. And David heard *of it*, and went out against them.

9 And the Phĭ-lĭs'tĭneş came and spread themselves in the valley of Rĕph'ā-ĭm.

10 And David inquired of God, saying, Shall I go up against the Phĭ-lĭs'tĭneş? and wilt thou deliver them into mine hand? And the LORD said unto him, Go up; for I will deliver them into thine hand.

11 So they came up to Bā'ăl–pē-rā'zĭm; and David smote them there. Then David said, God hath broken in upon mine enemies by mine hand like the breaking forth of waters: therefore they called the name of that place Bā'ăl-pē-rā'zĭm.

12 And when they had left their gods there, David gave a commandment, and they were burned with fire.

13 And the Phĭ-lĭs'tĭneş yet again spread themselves abroad in the valley.

14 Therefore David inquired again of God; and God said unto him, Go not up after them; turn away from them, and come upon them over against the mulberry trees.

15 And it shall be, when thou shalt hear a sound of going in the tops of the mulberry trees, *that* then thou shalt go out to battle: for God is gone forth before thee to smite the host of the Phĭ-lĭs'tĭneş.

16 David therefore did as God commanded him: and they smote the host of the Phĭ-lĭs'tĭneş from Gĭb'ē-ŏn even to Gā'zĕr.

17 And the fame of David went out into all lands; and the LORD brought the fear of him upon all nations.

CHAPTER 15

AND *David* made him houses in the city of David, and prepared a place for the ark of God, and pitched for it a tent.

2 Then David said, None ought to carry the ark of God but the Lē'vītes: for them hath the LORD chosen to carry the ark of God, and to minister unto him for ever.

3 And David gathered all Ĭş'rā-ĕl together to Jerusalem, to bring up the ark of the LORD unto his place, which he had prepared for it.

4 And David assembled the children of Aaron, and the Lē'vītes:

5 Of the sons of Kō'hăth; Ū'rĭ-ĕl the chief, and his brethren a hundred and twenty:

6 Of the sons of Mē-rā'rī; Ȧ-sā'ịȧh the chief, and his brethren two hundred and twenty:

7 Of the sons of Gẽr'shŏm; Joel the chief, and his brethren a hundred and thirty:

8 Of the sons of Ĕl'ĭ-zā'phăn; Shē-mā'ịȧh the chief, and his brethren two hundred:

9 Of the sons of Hē'brŏn; Ē'lĭ-ĕl the chief, and his brethren fourscore:

10 Of the sons of Ŭz-zī'ĕl; Ȧm-mĭn'ȧ-dăb the chief, and his brethren a hundred and twelve.

11 And David called for Zā'dŏk and Ȧ-bī'ȧ-thär the priests, and for the Lē'vītes, for Ū'rĭ-ĕl, Ȧ-sā'ịȧh, and Joel, Shē-mā'ịȧh, and Ē'lĭ-ĕl, and Ȧm-mĭn'ȧ-dăb,

12 And said unto them, Ye *are* the chief of the fathers of the Lē'vītes: sanctify yourselves, *both* ye and your brethren, that ye may bring up the ark of the LORD God of Ĭş'rā-ĕl unto *the place that* I have prepared for it.

13 For because ye *did it* not at the first, the LORD our God made a breach upon us, for that we sought him not after the due order.

14 So the priests and the Lē'vītes sanctified themselves to bring up the ark of the LORD God of Ĭş'rā-ĕl.

15 And the children of the Lē'vītes bare the ark of God upon their shoulders with the staves thereon, as Moses com-

manded, according to the word of the
LORD.
16 And David spake to the chief of the
Lē'vītes to appoint their brethren *to be*
the singers with instruments of music,
psalteries and harps and cymbals,
sounding, by lifting up the voice with joy.
17 So the Lē'vītes appointed Hē'măn
the son of Joel; and of his brethren,
Ā'săph the son of Bĕr'e-chī'ah; and of
the sons of Mē-rā'rī their brethren,
Ē'thăn the son of Kū-shā'ịah;
18 And with them their brethren of the
second *degree*, Zĕch'a-rī'ah, Ben, and
Jā-ā'zi-ĕl, and Shē-mĭr'a-mŏth, and Jē-
hī'ĕl, and Ŭn'nī, Ē-lī'ăb, and Bē-nā'ịah,
and Mā'a-sē'ịah, and Măt'tī-thī'ah, and
Ē-lĭph'ē-lĕh, and Mĭk-nē'ịah, and Ō'bĕd-
ē'dŏm, and Jē-ī'ĕl, the porters.
19 So the singers, Hē'măn, Ā'săph, and
Ē'thăn, *were appointed* to sound with
cymbals of brass;
20 And Zĕch'a-rī'ah, and Ā'zi-ĕl, and
Shē-mĭr'a-mŏth, and Jē-hī'ĕl, and Ŭn'-
nī, and Ē-lī'ăb, and Mā'a-sē'ịah, and
Bē-nā'ịah with psalteries on Ăl'a-mŏth;
21 And Măt'tī-thī'ah, and Ē-lĭph'ē-lĕh
and Mĭk-nē'ịah, and Ō'bĕd-ē'dŏm, and
Jē-ī'ĕl, and Ăz'a-zī'ah, with harps on the
Shĕm'ĭ-nĭth to excel.
22 And Chĕn'a-nī'ah, chief of the Lē'-
vītes, *was* for song: he instructed about
the song, because he *was* skilful.
23 And Bĕr'ē-chī'ah and Ĕl-kā'nah
were doorkeepers for the ark.
24 And Shĕb'a-nī'ah, and Jē-hŏsh'a-
phăt, and Nē-thăn'ē-ĕl, and A-măs'ā-ī,
and Zĕch'a-rī'ah, and Bē-nā'ịah, and
Ĕl'ĭ-ē'zĕr, the priests, did blow with the
trumpets before the ark of God: and
Ō'bĕd-ē'dŏm and Jē-hī'ah *were* doorkeepers for the ark.
25 ¶ So David, and the elders of Ĭş'-
rā-ĕl, and the captains over thousands,
went to bring up the ark of the covenant of the LORD out of the house of
Ō'bĕd-ē'dŏm with joy.
26 And it came to pass, when God
helped the Lē'vītes that bare the ark of
the covenant of the LORD, that they offered seven bullocks and seven rams.
27 And David *was* clothed with a robe
of fine linen, and all the Lē'vītes that
bare the ark, and the singers, and Chĕn'-
a-nī'ah the master of the song with the
singers: David also *had* upon him an
ĕph'ŏd of linen.
28 Thus all Ĭş'rā-ĕl brought up the
ark of the covenant of the LORD with
shouting, and with sound of the cornet,
and with trumpets, and with cymbals,
making a noise with psalteries and
harps.
29 ¶ And it came to pass, *as* the ark of
the covenant of the LORD came to the
city of David, that Mī'chăl the daughter
of Saul looking out at a window saw king
David dancing and playing: and she
despised him in her heart.

CHAPTER 16

SO they brought the ark of God, and
set it in the midst of the tent that
David had pitched for it: and they
offered burnt sacrifices and peace offerings before God.
2 And when David had made an end of
offering the burnt offerings and the
peace offerings, he blessed the people in
the name of the LORD.
3 And he dealt to every one of Ĭş'rā-ĕl,
both man and woman, to every one a
loaf of bread, and a good piece of flesh,
and a flagon *of wine*.
4 ¶ And he appointed *certain* of the
Lē'vītes to minister before the ark of the
LORD, and to record, and to thank and
praise the LORD God of Ĭş'rā-ĕl:
5 Ā'săph the chief, and next to him
Zĕch'a-rī'ah, Jē-ī'ĕl, and Shē-mĭr'a-
mŏth, and Jē-hī'ĕl, and Măt'tī-thī'ah,
and Ē-lī'ăb, and Bē-nā'ịah, and Ō'bĕd-
ē'dŏm: and Jē-ī'ĕl with psalteries and
with harps; but Ā'săph made a sound
with cymbals;
6 Bē-nā'ịah also and Ja-hā'zī-ĕl the
priests with trumpets continually before
the ark of the covenant of God.
7 ¶ Then on that day David delivered
first *this psalm* to thank the LORD into
the hand of Ā'săph and his brethren.
8 Give thanks unto the LORD, call upon
his name, make known his deeds among
the people.
9 Sing unto him, sing psalms unto him,
talk ye of all his wondrous works.
10 Glory ye in his holy name: let the
heart of them rejoice that seek the
LORD.
11 Seek the LORD and his strength,
seek his face continually.
12 Remember his marvelous works
that he hath done, his wonders, and the
judgments of his mouth;
13 O ye seed of Ĭş'rā-ĕl his servant,
ye children of Jacob, his chosen ones.

14 He *is* the LORD our God; his judgments *are* in all the earth.
15 Be ye mindful always of his covenant; the word *which* he commanded to a thousand generations;
16 *Even of the covenant* which he made with Abraham, and of his oath unto Isaac;
17 And hath confirmed the same to Jacob for a law, *and* to Ĭṣ′rā-ĕl *for* an everlasting covenant,
18 Saying, Unto thee will I give the land of Cā′năan, the lot of your inheritance;
19 When ye were but few, even a few, and strangers in it.
20 And *when* they went from nation to nation, and from *one* kingdom to another people;
21 He suffered no man to do them wrong: yea, he reproved kings for their sakes,
22 *Saying*, Touch not mine anointed, and do my prophets no harm.
23 Sing unto the LORD, all the earth; show forth from day to day his salvation.
24 Declare his glory among the heathen; his marvelous works among all nations.
25 For great *is* the LORD, and greatly to be praised: he also *is* to be feared above all gods.
26 For all the gods of the people *are* idols: but the LORD made the heavens.
27 Glory and honor *are* in his presence; strength and gladness *are* in his place.
28 Give unto the LORD, ye kindreds of the people, give unto the LORD glory and strength.
29 Give unto the LORD the glory *due* unto his name: bring an offering, and come before him: worship the LORD in the beauty of holiness.
30 Fear before him, all the earth: the world also shall be stable, that it be not moved.
31 Let the heavens be glad, and let the earth rejoice: and let *men* say among the nations, The LORD reigneth.
32 Let the sea roar, and the fulness thereof: let the fields rejoice, and all that *is* therein.
33 Then shall the trees of the wood sing out at the presence of the LORD, because he cometh to judge the earth.
34 O give thanks unto the LORD; for *he is* good; for his mercy *endureth* for ever.
35 And say ye, Save us, O God of our salvation, and gather us together, and deliver us from the heathen, that we may give thanks to thy holy name, *and* glory in thy praise.
36 Blessed *be* the LORD God of Ĭṣ′rā-ĕl for ever and ever. And all the people said, Amen, and praised the LORD.
37 ℂ So he left there before the ark of the covenant of the LORD Ā′săph and his brethren, to minister before the ark continually, as every day's work required:
38 And Ō′bĕd–ē′dŏm with their brethren, threescore and eight; Ō′bĕd–ē′dŏm also the son of Jē-dū′thŭn and Hō′sȧh *to be* porters:
39 And Zā′dŏk the priest, and his brethren the priests, before the tabernacle of the LORD in the high place that *was* at Gĭb′ē-ȯn,
40 To offer burnt offerings unto the LORD upon the altar of the burnt offering continually morning and evening, and *to do* according to all that is written in the law of the LORD, which he commanded Ĭṣ′rā-ĕl;
41 And with them Hē′măn and Jē-dū′thŭn, and the rest that were chosen, who were expressed by name, to give thanks to the LORD, because his mercy *endureth* for ever;
42 And with them Hē′măn and Jē-dū′thŭn with trumpets and cymbals for those that should make a sound, and with musical instruments of God. And the sons of Jē-dū′thŭn *were* porters.
43 And all the people departed every man to his house: and David returned to bless his house.

CHAPTER 17

NOW it came to pass, as David sat in his house, that David said to Nathan the prophet, Lo, I dwell in a house of cedars, but the ark of the covenant of the LORD *remaineth* under curtains.
2 Then Nathan said unto David, Do all that *is* in thine heart; for God *is* with thee.
3 ℂ And it came to pass the same night, that the word of God came to Nathan, saying,
4 Go and tell David my servant, Thus saith the LORD, Thou shalt not build me a house to dwell in:

5 For I have not dwelt in a house since
the day that I brought up Ĭṣ′rā-ĕl unto
this day; but have gone from tent to
tent, and from *one* tabernacle *to another.*
6 Wheresoever I have walked with all
Ĭṣ′rā-ĕl, spake I a word to any of the
judges of Ĭṣ′rā-ĕl, whom I commanded
to feed my people, saying, Why have
ye not built me a house of cedars?
7 Now therefore thus shalt thou say
unto my servant David, Thus saith the
LORD of hosts, I took thee from the
sheepcote, *even* from following the
sheep, that thou shouldest be ruler over
my people Ĭṣ′rā-ĕl:
8 And I have been with thee whithersoever thou hast walked, and have cut
off all thine enemies from before thee,
and have made thee a name like the
name of the great men that *are* in the
earth.
9 Also I will ordain a place for my people Ĭṣ′rā-ĕl, and will plant them, and
they shall dwell in their place, and shall
be moved no more; neither shall the
children of wickedness waste them any
more, as at the beginning,
10 And since the time that I commanded judges *to be* over my people
Ĭṣ′rā-ĕl. Moreover I will subdue all
thine enemies. Furthermore I tell thee,
that the LORD will build thee a house.
11 ¶ And it shall come to pass, when
thy days be expired that thou must go
to be with thy fathers, that I will raise
up thy seed after thee, which shall be
of thy sons; and I will establish his
kingdom.
12 He shall build me a house, and I will
stablish his throne for ever.
13 I will be his father, and he shall be
my son: and I will not take my mercy
away from him, as I took *it* from *him*
that was before thee:
14 But I will settle him in mine house
and in my kingdom for ever: and his
throne shall be established for evermore.
15 According to all these words, and
according to all this vision, so did
Nathan speak unto David.
16 ¶ And David the king came and sat
before the LORD, and said, Who *am* I,
O LORD God, and what *is* mine house,
that thou hast brought me hitherto?
17 And *yet* this was a small thing in
thine eyes, O God; for thou hast *also*
spoken of thy servant's house for a great
while to come, and hast regarded me
according to the estate of a man of high
degree, O LORD God.
18 What can David *speak* more to thee
for the honor of thy servant? for thou
knowest thy servant.
19 O LORD, for thy servant's sake, and
according to thine own heart, hast thou
done all this greatness, in making known
all *these* great things.
20 O LORD, *there is* none like thee,
neither *is there any* God besides thee,
according to all that we have heard with
our ears.
21 And what one nation in the earth *is*
like thy people Ĭṣ′rā-ĕl, whom God went
to redeem *to be* his own people, to make
thee a name of greatness and terribleness, by driving out nations from before
thy people, whom thou hast redeemed
out of Egypt?
22 For thy people Ĭṣ′rā-ĕl didst thou
make thine own people for ever; and
thou, LORD, becamest their God.
23 Therefore now, LORD, let the thing
that thou hast spoken concerning thy
servant and concerning his house be
established for ever, and do as thou
hast said.
24 Let it even be established, that thy
name may be magnified for ever, saying, The LORD of hosts *is* the God of
Ĭṣ′rā-ĕl, *even* a God to Ĭṣ′rā-ĕl: and *let*
the house of David thy servant *be* established before thee.
25 For thou, O my God, hast told thy
servant that thou wilt build him a house:
therefore thy servant hath found *in his*
heart to pray before thee.
26 And now, LORD, thou art God, and
hast promised this goodness unto thy
servant:
27 Now therefore let it please thee to
bless the house of thy servant, that it
may be before thee for ever: for thou
blessest, O LORD, and *it shall be* blessed
for ever.

CHAPTER 18

NOW after this it came to pass, that
David smote the Phĭ-lĭs′tīnes, and
subdued them, and took Gath and her
towns out of the hand of the Phĭ-
lĭs′tīnes.
2 And he smote Mō′ăb; and the Mō′-
ăb-ītes became David's servants, *and*
brought gifts.
3 ¶ And David smote Hăd′ăr-ē′zĕr

king of Zō'bȧh unto Hā'măth, as he went
to stablish his dominion by the river
Eū-phrā'tēṣ.
4 And David took from him a thousand
chariots, and seven thousand horsemen,
and twenty thousand footmen: David
also houghed all the chariot *horses*, but
reserved of them a hundred chariots.
5 And when the Syrians of Damascus
came to help Hăd'ȧr-ē'zēr king of Zō'-
bȧh, David slew of the Syrians two and
twenty thousand men.
6 Then David put *garrisons* in Syria-
damascus; and the Syrians became
David's servants, *and* brought gifts.
Thus the LORD preserved David whithersoever he went.
7 And David took the shields of gold
that were on the servants of Hăd'ȧr-ē'-
zēr, and brought them to Jerusalem.
8 Likewise from Tĭb'hăth, and from
Chŭn, cities of Hăd'ȧr-ē'zēr, brought
David very much brass, wherewith
Solomon made the brazen sea, and the
pillars, and the vessels of brass.
9 ¶ Now when Tō'ụ king of Hā'măth
heard how David had smitten all the
host of Hăd'ȧr-ē'zēr king of Zō'bȧh;
10 He sent Hȧ-dō'răm his son to king
David, to inquire of his welfare, and to
congratulate him, because he had fought
against Hăd'ȧr-ē'zēr, and smitten him;
(for Hăd'ȧr-ē'zēr had war with Tō'ụ;)
and *with him* all manner of vessels of
gold and silver and brass.
11 ¶ Them also king David dedicated
unto the LORD, with the silver and the
gold that he brought from all *these* nations; from Ē'dŏm, and from Mō'ăb,
and from the children of Ammon, and
from the Phĭ-lĭs'tīnes, and from Ăm'ȧ-lĕk.
12 Moreover, Ȧ-bĭsh'ā-ī the son of
Zĕr'ụ-ī'ȧh slew of the Ē'dŏm-ītes in the
valley of salt eighteen thousand.
13 ¶ And he put garrisons in Ē'dŏm;
and all the Ē'dŏm-ītes became David's
servants. Thus the LORD preserved
David whithersoever he went.
14 ¶ So David reigned over all Ĭṣ'-
rā-ēl, and executed judgment and justice among all his people.
15 And Jō'ăb the son of Zĕr'ụ-ī'ȧh *was*
over the host; and Jē-hŏsh'ȧ-phăt the
son of Ȧ-hī'lŭd, recorder;
16 And Zā'dŏk the son of Ȧ-hī'tŭb, and
Ȧ-bĭm'ē-lĕch the son of Ȧ-bī'ȧ-thär,
were the priests; and Shăv'shȧ was
scribe;
17 And Bē-nā'ịȧh the son of Jē-
hōi'ȧ-dȧ *was* over the Chĕr'ē-thītes and
the Pĕl'ē-thītes; and the sons of David
were chief about the king.

CHAPTER 19

NOW it came to pass after this, that
Nā'hăsh the king of the children
of Ammon died, and his son reigned in
his stead.
2 And David said, I will show kindness
unto Hā'nŭn the son of Nā'hăsh, because his father showed kindness to me.
And David sent messengers to comfort
him concerning his father. So the servants of David came into the land of the
children of Ammon to Hā'nŭn, to comfort him.
3 But the princes of the children of
Ammon said to Hā'nŭn, Thinkest thou
that David doth honor thy father, that
he hath sent comforters unto thee? are
not his servants come unto thee for to
search, and to overthrow, and to spy out
the land?
4 Wherefore Hā'nŭn took David's
servants, and shaved them, and cut off
their garments in the midst hard by their
buttocks, and sent them away.
5 Then there went *certain*, and told
David how the men were served; and he
sent to meet them: for the men were
greatly ashamed. And the king said,
Tarry at Jĕr'ĭ-chō until your beards be
grown, and *then* return.
6 ¶ And when the children of Ammon
saw that they had made themselves
odious to David, Hā'nŭn and the children of Ammon sent a thousand talents
of silver to hire them chariots and horsemen out of Mĕs'ō-pō-tā'mĭ-ȧ, and out
of Sȳr'ĭ-ȧ-mā'ȧ-chȧh, and out of Zō'bȧh.
7 So they hired thirty and two thousand
chariots, and the king of Mā'ȧ-chȧh and
his people; who came and pitched before Mĕd'ē-bȧ. And the children of
Ammon gathered themselves together
from their cities, and came to battle.
8 And when David heard *of it*, he sent
Jō'ăb, and all the host of the mighty
men.
9 And the children of Ammon came out,
and put the battle in array before the
gate of the city: and the kings that were
come *were* by themselves in the field.
10 Now when Jō'ăb saw that the battle
was set against him before and behind,
he chose out of all the choice of Ĭṣ'rā-ēl,

and put *them* in array against the
Syrians.
11 And the rest of the people he delivered unto the hand of Ȧ-bĭsh′ā-ī his
brother, and they set *themselves* in
array against the children of Ammon.
12 And he said, If the Syrians be too
strong for me, then thou shalt help me:
but if the children of Ammon be too
strong for thee, then I will help thee.
13 Be of good courage, and let us behave ourselves valiantly for our people,
and for the cities of our God: and let the
LORD do *that which is* good in his sight.
14 So Jō′ăb and the people that *were*
with him drew nigh before the Syrians
unto the battle; and they fled before
him.
15 And when the children of Ammon
saw that the Syrians were fled, they
likewise fled before Ȧ-bĭsh′ā-ī his
brother, and entered into the city. Then
Jō′ăb came to Jerusalem.
16 ¶ And when the Syrians saw that
they were put to the worse before
Ĭs′rā-ĕl, they sent messengers, and drew
forth the Syrians that *were* beyond the
river: and Shō′phăch the captain of the
host of Hăd′ȧr-ē′zĕr *went* before them.
17 And it was told David; and he gathered all Ĭs′rā-ĕl, and passed over Jordan, and came upon them, and set *the
battle* in array against them. So when
David had put the battle in array against
the Syrians, they fought with him.
18 But the Syrians fled before Ĭs′rā-ĕl;
and David slew of the Syrians seven
thousand *men which fought in* chariots,
and forty thousand footmen, and killed
Shō′phăch the captain of the host.
19 And when the servants of Hăd′ȧr-
ē′zĕr saw that they were put to the worse
before Ĭs′ra-ĕl, they made peace with
David, and became his servants: neither
would the Syrians help the children of
Ammon any more.

CHAPTER 20

AND it came to pass, that after the
year was expired, at the time that
kings go out *to battle*, Jō′ăb led forth the
power of the army, and wasted the
country of the children of Ammon, and
came and besieged Răb′bȧh. But David
tarried at Jerusalem. And Jō′ăb smote
Răb′bȧh, and destroyed it.
2 And David took the crown of their
king from off his head, and found it to
weigh a talent of gold, and *there were*
precious stones in it; and it was set upon
David's head: and he brought also exceeding much spoil out of the city.
3 And he brought out the people that
were in it, and cut *them* with saws, and
with harrows of iron, and with axes.
Even so dealt David with all the cities
of the children of Ammon. And David
and all the people returned to Jerusalem.
4 ¶ And it came to pass after this, that
there arose war at Gē′zĕr with the Phi-
lĭs′tĭneș; at which time Sĭb′bē-chaī the
Hū′shȧth-īte slew Sĭp′paī, *that was* of
the children of the giant: and they were
subdued.
5 And there was war again with the
Phĭ-lĭs′tĭneș; and Ĕl-hā′năn the son of
Jā′īr slew Läh′mī the brother of Gō-
lī′ăth the Gĭt′tīte, whose spear staff *was*
like a weaver's beam.
6 And yet again there was war at Gath,
where was a man of *great* stature, whose
fingers and toes *were* four and twenty,
six *on each hand*, and six *on each foot:*
and he also was the son of the giant.
7 But when he defied Ĭs′rā-ĕl, Jonathan the son of Shĭm′ē-ȧ David's brother
slew him.
8 These were born unto the giant in
Gath; and they fell by the hand of David, and by the hand of his servants.

CHAPTER 21

AND Satan stood up against Ĭs′rā-ĕl,
and provoked David to number
Ĭs′rā-ĕl.
2 And David said to Jō′ăb and to the
rulers of the people, Go, number Ĭs′rā-ĕl
from Bē′ĕr–shē′bȧ even to Dan; and
bring the number of them to me, that I
may know *it*.
3 And Jō′ăb answered, The LORD make
his people a hundred times so many
more as they *be:* but, my lord the king,
are they not all my lord's servants? why
then doth my lord require this thing?
why will he be a cause of trespass to
Ĭs′rā-ĕl?
4 Nevertheless the king's word prevailed against Jō′ăb. Wherefore Jō′ăb
departed, and went throughout all
Ĭs′rā-ĕl, and came to Jerusalem.
5 ¶ And Jō′ăb gave the sum of the
number of the people unto David. And
all *they of* Ĭs′rā-ĕl were a thousand
thousand and a hundred thousand men

that drew sword: and Judah *was* four
hundred threescore and ten thousand
men that drew sword.
6 But Levi and Benjamin counted he
not among them: for the king's word was
abominable to Jō'ăb.
7 And God was displeased with this
thing; therefore he smote Ĭṣ'rā-ĕl.
8 And David said unto God, I have
sinned greatly, because I have done this
thing: but now, I beseech thee, do away
the iniquity of thy servant; for I have
done very foolishly.
9 ℂ And the LORD spake unto Gad,
David's seer, saying,
10 Go and tell David, saying, Thus
saith the LORD, I offer thee three
things: choose thee one of them, that I
may do *it* unto thee.
11 So Gad came to David, and said
unto him, Thus saith the LORD, Choose
thee
12 Either three years' famine; or three
months to be destroyed before thy foes,
while that the sword of thine enemies
overtaketh *thee;* or else three days the
sword of the LORD, even the pestilence,
in the land, and the angel of the LORD
destroying throughout all the coasts of
Ĭṣ'rā-ĕl. Now therefore advise thyself
what word I shall bring again to him
that sent me.
13 And David said unto Gad, I am in a
great strait: let me fall now into the
hand of the LORD; for very great *are* his
mercies: but let me not fall into the
hand of man.
14 ℂ So the LORD sent pestilence upon
Ĭṣ'rā-ĕl: and there fell of Ĭṣ'rā-ĕl seventy thousand men.
15 And God sent an angel unto Jerusalem to destroy it: and as he was destroying, the LORD beheld, and he repented him of the evil, and said to the
angel that destroyed, It is enough, stay
now thine hand. And the angel of the
LORD stood by the threshingfloor of
Ôr'năn the Jĕb'ū-ṣīte.
16 And David lifted up his eyes, and
saw the angel of the LORD stand between the earth and the heaven, having
a drawn sword in his hand stretched out
over Jerusalem. Then David and the
elders *of Israel, who were* clothed in
sackcloth, fell upon their faces.
17 And David said unto God, *Is it* not
I *that* commanded the people to be
numbered? even I it is that have sinned
and done evil indeed; but *as for* these
sheep, what have they done? let thine
hand, I pray thee, O LORD my God, be
on me, and on my father's house; but
not on thy people, that they should be
plagued.
18 ℂ Then the angel of the LORD commanded Gad to say to David, that David
should go up, and set up an altar unto
the LORD in the threshingfloor of
Ôr'năn the Jĕb'ū-ṣīte.
19 And David went up at the saying of
Gad, which he spake in the name of the
LORD.
20 And Ôr'năn turned back, and saw
the angel; and his four sons with him hid
themselves. Now Ôr'năn was threshing
wheat.
21 And as David came to Ôr'năn, Ôr'-
năn looked and saw David, and went
out of the threshingfloor, and bowed
himself to David with *his* face to the
ground.
22 Then David said to Ôr'năn, Grant
me the place of *this* threshingfloor, that
I may build an altar therein unto the
LORD: thou shalt grant it me for the full
price: that the plague may be stayed
from the people.
23 And Ôr'năn said unto David, Take
it to thee, and let my lord the king do
that which is good in his eyes: lo, I give
thee the oxen *also* for burnt offerings,
and the threshing instruments for wood,
and the wheat for the meat offering; I
give it all.
24 And king David said to Ôr'năn,
Nay; but I will verily buy it for the full
price: for I will not take *that* which *is*
thine for the LORD, nor offer burnt
offerings without cost.
25 So David gave to Ôr'năn for the
place six hundred shekels of gold by
weight.
26 And David built there an altar unto
the LORD, and offered burnt offerings
and peace offerings, and called upon the
LORD; and he answered him from
heaven by fire upon the altar of burnt
offering.
27 And the LORD commanded the
angel; and he put up his sword again
into the sheath thereof.
28 ℂ At that time when David saw that
the LORD had answered him in the
threshingfloor of Ôr'năn the Jĕb'ū-ṣīte,
then he sacrificed there.
29 For the tabernacle of the LORD,

which Moses made in the wilderness, and the altar of the burnt offering, *were* at that season in the high place at Gĭb′ē-ŏn.

30 But David could not go before it to inquire of God: for he was afraid because of the sword of the angel of the Lord.

CHAPTER 22

THEN David said, This *is* the house of the Lord God, and this *is* the altar of the burnt offering for Ĭs̱′rā-ĕl.

2 And David commanded to gather together the strangers that *were* in the land of Ĭs̱′rā-ĕl; and he set masons to hew wrought stones to build the house of God.

3 And David prepared iron in abundance for the nails for the doors of the gates, and for the joinings; and brass in abundance without weight;

4 Also cedar trees in abundance: for the Zī-do′nĭ-ăns̱ and they of Tȳre brought much cedar wood to David.

5 And David said, Solomon my son *is* young and tender, and the house *that is* to be builded for the Lord *must be* exceeding magnificent, of fame and of glory throughout all countries: I will *therefore* now make preparation for it. So David prepared abundantly before his death.

6 ¶ Then he called for Solomon his son, and charged him to build a house for the Lord God of Ĭs̱′rā-ĕl.

7 And David said to Solomon, My son, as for me, it was in my mind to build a house unto the name of the Lord my God:

8 But the word of the Lord came to me, saying, Thou hast shed blood abundantly, and hast made great wars: thou shalt not build a house unto my name, because thou hast shed much blood upon the earth in my sight.

9 Behold, a son shall be born to thee, who shall be a man of rest; and I will give him rest from all his enemies round about: for his name shall be Solomon, and I will give peace and quietness unto Ĭs̱′rā-ĕl in his days.

10 He shall build a house for my name; and he shall be my son, and I *will be* his father; and I will establish the throne of his kingdom over Ĭs̱′rā-ĕl for ever.

11 Now, my son, the Lord be with thee; and prosper thou, and build the house of the Lord thy God, as he hath said of thee.

12 Only the Lord give thee wisdom and understanding, and give thee charge concerning Ĭs̱′rā-ĕl, that thou mayest keep the law of the Lord thy God.

13 Then shalt thou prosper, if thou takest heed to fulfil the statutes and judgments which the Lord charged Moses with concerning Ĭs̱′rā-ĕl: be strong, and of good courage; dread not, nor be dismayed.

14 Now, behold, in my trouble I have prepared for the house of the Lord a hundred thousand talents of gold, and a thousand thousand talents of silver; and of brass and iron without weight; for it is in abundance: timber also and stone have I prepared; and thou mayest add thereto.

15 Moreover, *there are* workmen with thee in abundance, hewers and workers of stone and timber, and all manner of cunning men for every manner of work.

16 Of the gold, the silver, and the brass, and the iron, *there is* no number. Arise *therefore,* and be doing, and the Lord be with thee.

17 ¶ David also commanded all the princes of Ĭs̱′rā-ĕl to help Solomon his son, *saying,*

18 *Is* not the Lord your God with you? and hath he *not* given you rest on every side? for he hath given the inhabitants of the land into mine hand; and the land is subdued before the Lord, and before his people.

19 Now set your heart and your soul to seek the Lord your God; arise therefore, and build ye the sanctuary of the Lord God, to bring the ark of the covenant of the Lord, and the holy vessels of God, into the house that is to be built to the name of the Lord.

CHAPTER 23

SO when David was old and full of days, he made Solomon his son king over Ĭs̱′rā-ĕl.

2 ¶ And he gathered together all the princes of Ĭs̱′rā-ĕl, with the priests and the Lē′vītes.

3 Now the Lē′vītes were numbered from the age of thirty years and upward: and their number by their polls, man by man, was thirty and eight thousand.

4 Of which, twenty and four thousand
were to set forward the work of the
house of the LORD; and six thousand
were officers and judges:
5 Moreover four thousand *were* porters; and four thousand praised the
LORD with the instruments which I
made, *said David,* to praise *therewith.*
6 And David divided them into courses
among the sons of Levi, *namely,* Gĕr′-
shŏn, Kō′hăth, and Mē-rā′rī.
7 ¶ Of the Gĕr′shŏn-ītes *were* Lā′ȧ-
dăn, and Shĭm′ē-ī.
8 The sons of Lā′ȧ-dăn; the chief *was*
Jē-hī′ĕl, and Zē′thăm, and Joel, three.
9 The sons of Shĭm′ē-ī; Shē-lō′mĭth,
and Hā′zĭ-ĕl, and Hā′răn, three. These
were the chief of the fathers of Lā′ȧ-dăn.
10 And the sons of Shĭm′ē-ī *were,* Jā′-
hăth, Zī′nȧ, and Jē′ŭsh, and Bē-rī′ȧh.
These four *were* the sons of Shĭm′ē-ī.
11 And Jā′hăth was the chief, and Zī′-
zȧh the second: but Jē′ŭsh and Bē-
rī′ȧh had not many sons; therefore they
were in one reckoning, according to
their father's house.
12 ¶ The sons of Kō′hăth; Ăm′răm,
Ĭz′här, Hē′brŏn, and Ŭz-zī′ĕl, four.
13 The sons of Ăm′răm; Aaron, and
Moses: and Aaron was separated, that
he should sanctify the most holy things,
he and his sons for ever, to burn incense
before the LORD, to minister unto him,
and to bless in his name for ever.
14 Now *concerning* Moses the man of
God, his sons were named of the tribe
of Levi.
15 The sons of Moses *were,* Gĕr′shŏm,
and Ĕl′ĭ-ē′zĕr.
16 Of the sons of Gĕr′shŏm, Shē-bū′ĕl
was the chief.
17 And the sons of Ĕl′ĭ-ē′zĕr *were,*
Rē′hȧ-bī′ȧh the chief. And Ĕl′ĭ-ē′zĕr
had none other sons; but the sons of
Rē′hȧ-bī′ȧh were very many.
18 Of the sons of Ĭz′här; Shē-lō′mĭth
the chief.
19 Of the sons of Hē′brŏn; Jē-rī′ȧh the
first, Ăm′ȧ-rī′ȧh the second, Jȧ-hā′zĭ-ĕl
the third, and Jĕk′ȧ-mē′ăm the fourth.
20 Of the sons of Ŭz-zī′ĕl; Mī′cȧh the
first, and Jē-sī′ȧh the second.
21 ¶ The sons of Mē-rā′rī; Măh′lī, and
Mū′shī. The sons of Măh′lī; Ĕl′ē-ā′zȧr,
and Kish.
22 And Ĕl′ē-ā′zȧr died, and had no
sons, but daughters: and their brethren
the sons of Kish took them.
23 The sons of Mū′shī; Măh′lī, and
Ē′dĕr, and Jĕr′ē-mŏth, three.
24 ¶ These *were* the sons of Levi after
the house of their fathers; *even* the chief
of the fathers, as they were counted by
number of names by their polls, that did
the work for the service of the house of
the LORD, from the age of twenty years
and upward.
25 For David said, The LORD God of
Ĭs′rā-ĕl hath given rest unto his people,
that they may dwell in Jerusalem for
ever:
26 And also unto the Lē′vītes: they
shall no *more* carry the tabernacle, nor
any vessels of it for the service thereof.
27 For by the last words of David the
Lē′vītes *were* numbered from twenty
years old and above:
28 Because their office *was* to wait on
the sons of Aaron for the service of the
house of the LORD, in the courts, and in
the chambers, and in the purifying of
all holy things, and the work of the service of the house of God;
29 Both for the showbread, and for the
fine flour for meat offering, and for the
unleavened cakes, and for *that which is*
baked in the pan, and for that which is
fried, and for all manner of measure and
size;
30 And to stand every morning to thank
and praise the LORD, and likewise at
even;
31 And to offer all burnt sacrifices unto
the LORD in the sabbaths, in the new
moons, and on the set feasts, by number, according to the order commanded
unto them, continually before the LORD:
32 And that they should keep the
charge of the tabernacle of the congregation, and the charge of the holy *place,*
and the charge of the sons of Aaron their
brethren, in the service of the house of
the LORD.

CHAPTER 24

NOW *these are* the divisions of the
sons of Aaron. The sons of Aaron;
Nā′dăb and Ȧ-bī′hū, Ĕl′ē-ā′zȧr and
Ĭth′ȧ-mär.
2 But Nā′dăb and Ȧ-bī′hū died before
their father, and had no children: therefore Ĕl′ē-ā′zȧr and Ĭth′ȧ-mär executed
the priest's office.
3 And David distributed them, both
Zā′dŏk of the sons of Ĕl′ē-ā′zȧr, and
Ȧ-hĭm′ē-lĕch of the sons of Ĭth′ȧ-mär,

according to their offices in their
service.
4 And there were more chief men found
of the sons of Ĕl′ē-ā′zär than of the sons
of Ĭth′ȧ-mär; and *thus* were they divided. Among the sons of Ĕl′ē-ā′zär
there were sixteen chief men of the
house of *their* fathers, and eight among
the sons of Ĭth′ȧ-mär according to the
house of their fathers.
5 Thus were they divided by lot, one
sort with another; for the governors of
the sanctuary, and governors *of the
house* of God, were of the sons of Ĕl′ē-
ā′zär, and of the sons of Ĭth′ȧ-mär.
6 And Shē-mā′ịȧh the son of Nē-
thăn′ē-ĕl the scribe, *one* of the Lē′vītes,
wrote them before the king, and the
princes, and Zā′dŏk the priest, and
Ȧ-hĭm′ē-lĕch the son of Ȧ-bī′ȧ-thär, and
before the chief of the fathers of the
priests and Lē′vītes: one principal
household being taken for Ĕl′ē-ā′zär,
and *one* taken for Ĭth′ȧ-mär.
7 Now the first lot came forth to Jē-
hoi′ȧ-rĭb, the second to Jē-dā′ịȧh,
8 The third to Hā′rĭm, the fourth to
Sē-ō′rĭm,
9 The fifth to Măl-chī′jȧh, the sixth to
Mij′ȧ-mĭn,
10 The seventh to Hăk′kŏz, the eighth
to Ȧ-bī′jȧh,
11 The ninth to Jĕsh′ū-ȧh, the tenth
to Shĕc′ȧ-nī′ȧh,
12 The eleventh to Ē-lī′ȧ-shĭb, the
twelfth to Jā′kĭm,
13 The thirteenth to Hŭp′pȧh, the
fourteenth to Jē-shĕb′ē-ăb,
14 The fifteenth to Bĭl′gȧh, the sixteenth to Ĭm′mĕr,
15 The seventeenth to Hē′zĭr, the
eighteenth to Ăph′sēș,
16 The nineteenth to Pĕth′ȧ-hī′ȧh, the
twentieth to Jē-hĕz′ē-kĕl,
17 The one and twentieth to Jā′chĭn,
the two and twentieth to Gā′mŭl,
18 The three and twentieth to Dē-lā′-
ịȧh, the four and twentieth to Mā′ȧ-
zī′ȧh.
19 These *were* the orderings of them
in their service to come into the house
of the LORD, according to their manner,
under Aaron their father, as the LORD
God of Ĭș′rā-ĕl had commanded him.
20 ℂ And the rest of the sons of Levi
were these: Of the sons of Ăm′răm;
Shụ′bā-ĕl: of the sons of Shụ′bā-ĕl;
Jĕh-dē′ịȧh.
21 Concerning Rē′hȧ-bī′ȧh: of the sons
of Rē′hȧ-bī′ȧh, the first *was* Ĭs-shī′ȧh.
22 Of the Ĭz′hăr-ītes; Shē-lō′mŏth: of
the sons of Shē-lō′mŏth; Jā′hăth.
23 And the sons *of Hebron;* Jē-rī′ȧh
the first, Ăm′ȧ-rī′ȧh the second, Jȧ-
hā′zi-ĕl the third, Jĕk′ȧ-mē′ăm the
fourth.
24 *Of* the sons of Ŭz-zī′ĕl; Mī′chȧh:
of the sons of Mī′chȧh; Shā′mĭr.
25 The brother of Mī′chȧh *was*
Ĭs-shī′ȧh: of the sons of Ĭs-shī′ȧh;
Zĕch′ȧ-rī′ȧh.
26 The sons of Mē-rā′rī *were* Mäh′lī
and Mū′shī: the sons of Jā′ȧ-zī′ȧh;
Bē′nō.
27 ℂ The sons of Mē-rā′rī by Jā′ȧ-
zī′ȧh; Bē′nō, and Shō′hăm, and Zăc′cŭr,
and Ĭb′rī.
28 Of Mäh′lī *came* Ĕl′ē-ā′zär, who had
no sons.
29 Concerning Kish: the son of Kish
was Jē-räh′mē-ĕl.
30 The sons also of Mū′shī; Mäh′lī,
and Ē′dĕr, and Jĕr′ĭ-mŏth. These *were*
the sons of the Lē′vītes after the house
of their fathers.
31 These likewise cast lots over against
their brethren the sons of Aaron in the
presence of David the king, and Zā′dŏk,
and Ȧ-hĭm′ē-lĕch, and the chief of the
fathers of the priests and Lē′vītes, even
the principal fathers over against their
younger brethren.

CHAPTER 25

MOREOVER David and the captains of the host separated to
the service of the sons of Ā′săph, and of
Hē′măn, and of Jē-dū′thŭn, who should
prophesy with harps, with psalteries,
and with cymbals: and the number of
the workmen according to their service
was:
2 Of the sons of Ā′săph; Zăc′cŭr, and
Joseph, and Nĕth′ȧ-nī′ȧh, and Ăs′ȧ-rē′-
lȧh, the sons of Ā′săph under the hands
of Ā′săph, which prophesied according
to the order of the king.
3 Of Jē-dū′thŭn: the sons of Jē-dū′-
thŭn; Gĕd′ȧ-lī′ȧh, and Zē′rī, and Jē-
shā′ịȧh, Hăsh′ȧ-bī′ȧh, and Măt′tĭ-thī′ȧh,
six, under the hands of their father
Jē-dū′thŭn, who prophesied with a harp,
to give thanks and to praise the LORD.
4 Of Hē′măn: the sons of Hē′-
măn; Bŭk-kī′ȧh, Măt′tȧ-nī′ȧh, Ŭz-zī′ĕl,
Shē-bū′ĕl, and Jĕr′ĭ-mŏth, Hăn′ȧ-nī′ȧh,

Há-nā′nī, Ē-lī′á-tháh, Gĭd-dăl′tī, and Rō-măm′tĭ–ē′zẽr, Jŏsh′bē-kā′sháh, Măl′lō-thī, Hō′thĭr, *and* Má-hā′zĭ-ōth:

5 All these *were* the sons of Hē′măn the king's seer in the words of God, to lift up the horn. And God gave to Hē′-măn fourteen sons and three daughters.

6 All these *were* under the hands of their father for song *in* the house of the LORD, with cymbals, psalteries, and harps, for the service of the house of God, according to the king's order to Ā′săph, Jē-dū′thŭn, and Hē′măn.

7 So the number of them, with their brethren that were instructed in the songs of the LORD, *even* all that were cunning, was two hundred fourscore and eight.

8 ℂ And they cast lots, ward against *ward*, as well the small as the great, the teacher as the scholar.

9 Now the first lot came forth for Ā′săph to Joseph: the second to Gĕd′á-lī′áh, who with his brethren and sons *were* twelve:

10 The third to Zăc′cŭr, *he*, his sons, and his brethren, *were* twelve:

11 The fourth to Ĭz′rī, *he*, his sons, and his brethren, *were* twelve:

12 The fifth to Nĕth′á-nī′áh, *he*, his sons, and his brethren, *were* twelve:

13 The sixth to Bŭk-kī′áh, *he*, his sons, and his brethren, *were* twelve:

14 The seventh to Jĕsh′á-rē′láh, *he*, his sons, and his brethren, *were* twelve:

15 The eighth to Jē-shā′ịáh, *he*, his sons, and his brethren, *were* twelve:

16 The ninth to Măt′tá-nī′áh, *he*, his sons, and his brethren, *were* twelve:

17 The tenth to Shĭm′ē-ī, *he*, his sons, and his brethren, *were* twelve:

18 The eleventh to Á-zā′rē-ĕl, *he*, his sons, and his brethren, *were* twelve:

19 The twelfth to Hăsh′á-bī′áh, *he*, his sons, and his brethren, *were* twelve:

20 The thirteenth to Shụ′bā-ĕl, *he*, his sons, and his brethren, *were* twelve:

21 The fourteenth to Măt′tĭ-thī′áh, *he*, his sons, and his brethren, *were* twelve:

22 The fifteenth to Jĕr′ē-mōth, *he*, his sons, and his brethren, *were* twelve:

23 The sixteenth to Hăn′á-nī′áh, *he*, his sons, and his brethren, *were* twelve:

24 The seventeenth to Jŏsh′bē-kā′-sháh, *he*, his sons, and his brethren, *were* twelve:

25 The eighteenth to Há-nā′nī, *he*, his sons, and his brethren, *were* twelve:

26 The nineteenth to Măl′lō-thī, *he*, his sons, and his brethren, *were* twelve:

27 The twentieth to Ē-lī′á-tháh, *he*, his sons, and his brethren, *were* twelve:

28 The one and twentieth to Hō′thĭr, *he*, his sons, and his brethren, *were* twelve:

29 The two and twentieth to Gĭd-dăl′tī, *he*, his sons, and his brethren, *were* twelve:

30 The three and twentieth to Má-hā′-zĭ-ōth, *he*, his sons, and his brethren, *were* twelve:

31 The four and twentieth to Rō-măm′tĭ–ē′zẽr, *he*, his sons, and his brethren, *were* twelve.

CHAPTER 26

CONCERNING the divisions of the porters: Of the Kôr′hītes *was* Mē-shĕl′ē-mī′áh the son of Kō′rē, of the sons of Ā′săph.

2 And the sons of Mē-shĕl′ē-mī′áh *were*, Zĕch′á-rī′áh the firstborn, Jē-dī′ā-ĕl the second, Zĕb′á-dī′áh the third, Jăth′nĭ-ĕl the fourth,

3 Ē′lăm the fifth, Jē′hō-hā′năn the sixth, Ē-lĭ′ō-ē′nā-ī the seventh.

4 Moreover the sons of Ō′bẹd–ē′dŏm *were*, Shē-mā′ịáh the firstborn, Jē-hŏz′á-băd the second, Jō′áh the third, and Sā′cär the fourth, and Nē-thăn′ē-ĕl the fifth,

5 Ăm′mĭ-ĕl the sixth, Ĭs′sá-chär the seventh, Pē-ŭl′thaī the eighth: for God blessed him.

6 Also unto Shē-mā′ịáh his son were sons born, that ruled throughout the house of their father: for they *were* mighty men of valor.

7 The sons of Shē-mā′ịáh; Ŏth′nī, and Rē′phā-ĕl, and Ō′bĕd, Ĕl-zā′băd, whose brethren *were* strong men, Ē-lī′hū, and Sĕm′á-chī′áh.

8 All these of the sons of Ō′bĕd–ē′dŏm: they and their sons and their brethren, able men for strength for the service, *were* threescore and two of Ō′bĕd-ē′dŏm.

9 And Mē-shĕl′ē-mī′áh had sons and brethren, strong men, eighteen.

10 Also Hō′sáh, of the children of Mē-rā′rī, had sons; Sĭm′rī the chief, (for *though* he was not the firstborn, yet his father made him the chief;)

11 Hĭl-kī′áh the second, Tĕb′á-lī′áh the third, Zĕch′á-rī′áh the fourth: all

the sons and brethren of Hō'sȧh *were*
thirteen.
12 Among these *were* the divisions of
the porters, *even* among the chief men,
having wards one against another, to
minister in the house of the LORD.
13 ¶ And they cast lots, as well the
small as the great, according to the
house of their fathers, for every gate.
14 And the lot eastward fell to Shĕl'ē-
mī'ȧh. Then for Zĕch'ȧ-rī'ȧh his son, a
wise counselor, they cast lots; and his
lot came out northward.
15 To Ō'bĕd–ē'dŏm southward; and to
his sons the house of Ȧ-sŭp'pĭm.
16 To Shŭp'pĭm and Hō'sȧh *the lot*
came forth westward, with the gate
Shăl'lē-chĕth, by the causeway of the
going up, ward against ward.
17 Eastward *were* six Lē'vītes, northward four a day, southward four a day,
and toward Ȧ-sŭp'pĭm two *and* two.
18 At Pär'bär westward, four at the
causeway, *and* two at Pär'bär.
19 These *are* the divisions of the porters among the sons of Kō'rē, and
among the sons of Mē-rā'rī.
20 ¶ And of the Lē'vītes, Ȧ-hī'jȧh *was*
over the treasures of the house of God,
and over the treasures of the dedicated
things.
21 *As concerning* the sons of Lā'ȧ-dăn;
the sons of the Gĕr'shŏn-īte Lā'ȧ-dăn,
chief fathers, *even* of Lā'ȧ-dăn the
Gĕr'shŏn-īte, *were* Jē-hī'ē-lī.
22 The sons of Jē-hī'ē-lī; Zē'thăm, and
Joel his brother, *which were* over the
treasures of the house of the LORD.
23 Of the Ăm'răm-ītes, *and* the Ĭz'här-
ītes, the Hē'brȯn-ītes, *and* the Ŭz-zī'-
ĕl-ītes:
24 And Shē-bū'ĕl the son of Gĕr'shŏm,
the son of Moses, *was* ruler of the
treasures.
25 And his brethren by Ĕl'ĭ-ē'zēr; Rē-
hȧ-bī'ȧh his son, and Jē-shā'ịȧh his son,
and Jō'răm his son, and Zĭch'rī his son,
and Shē-lō'mĭth his son:
26 Which Shē-lō'mĭth and his brethren
were over all the treasures of the dedicated things, which David the king, and
the chief fathers, the captains over thousands and hundreds, and the captains
of the host, had dedicated.
27 Out of the spoils won in battles did
they dedicate to maintain the house of
the LORD.
28 And all that Samuel the seer, and
Saul the son of Kish, and Abner the son
of Nĕr, and Jō'ăb the son of Zĕr'ụ-ī'ȧh,
had dedicated; *and* whosoever had
dedicated *any thing, it was* under the
hand of Shē-lō'mĭth, and of his brethren.
29 ¶ Of the Ĭz'här-ītes, Chĕn'ȧ-nī'ȧh
and his sons *were* for the outward business over Ĭș'rā-ĕl, for officers and
judges.
30 *And* of the Hē'brȯn-ītes, Hăsh'ȧ-
bī'ȧh and his brethren, men of valor, a
thousand and seven hundred, *were*
officers among them of Ĭș'rā-ĕl on this
side Jordan westward in all the business
of the LORD, and in the service of the
king.
31 Among the Hē'brȯn-ītes *was* Jē-
rī'jȧh the chief, *even* among the Hē'-
brȯn-ītes, according to the generations
of his fathers. In the fortieth year of the
reign of David they were sought for, and
there were found among them mighty
men of valor at Jā'zēr of Gĭl'ē-ăd.
32 And his brethren, men of valor, *were*
two thousand and seven hundred chief
fathers, whom king David made rulers
over the Reubenites, the Gadites, and
the half tribe of Mȧ-năs'sĕh, for every
matter pertaining to God, and affairs of
the king.

CHAPTER 27

NOW the children of Ĭș'rā-ĕl after
their number, *to wit,* the chief
fathers and captains of thousands and
hundreds, and their officers that served
the king in any matter of the courses,
which came in and went out month by
month throughout all the months of the
year, of every course *were* twenty and
four thousand.
2 Over the first course for the first
month *was* Jȧ-shō'bē-ȧm the son of
Zăb'dĭ-ĕl: and in his course *were*
twenty and four thousand.
3 Of the children of Pē'rĕz *was* the
chief of all the captains of the host for
the first month.
4 And over the course of the second
month *was* Dō'daī an Ȧ-hō'hīte, and of
his course *was* Mĭk'lōth also the ruler:
in his course likewise *were* twenty and
four thousand.
5 The third captain of the host for the
third month *was* Bē-nā'ịȧh the son of
Jē-hoi'ȧ-dȧ, a chief priest: and in his
course *were* twenty and four thousand.
6 This *is that* Bē-nā'ịȧh, *who was*

mighty *among* the thirty, and above the
thirty: and in his course *was* Ȧm-mĭz'ȧ-
băd his son.
7 The fourth *captain* for the fourth
month *was* Ăs'ȧ-hĕl the brother of
Jō'ăb, and Zĕb'ȧ-dī'ȧh his son after
him: and in his course *were* twenty and
four thousand.
8 The fifth captain for the fifth month
was Shăm'hŭth the Ĭz'rȧ-hīte: and in his
course *were* twenty and four thousand.
9 The sixth *captain* for the sixth month
was Ī'rȧ the son of Ĭk'kĕsh the Tē-kō'-
īte: and in his course *were* twenty and
four thousand.
10 The seventh *captain* for the seventh
month *was* Hē'lĕz the Pĕl'ō-nite, of the
children of Ē'phrā-ĭm: and in his course
were twenty and four thousand.
11 The eighth *captain* for the eighth
month *was* Sĭb'bē-caī the Hū'shȧth-īte,
of the Zär'hītes: and in his course *were*
twenty and four thousand.
12 The ninth *captain* for the ninth
month *was* Ā'bĭ-ē'zĕr the Ăn'ē-tŏth-īte,
of the Benjamites: and in his course
were twenty and four thousand.
13 The tenth *captain* for the tenth
month *was* Mȧ-hăr'ā-ī the Nē-tŏph'ȧ-
thīte, of the Zär'hītes: and in his course
were twenty and four thousand.
14 The eleventh *captain* for the
eleventh month *was* Bē-nā'iah the Pĭr'ȧ-
thŏn-īte, of the children of Ē'phrā-ĭm:
and in his course *were* twenty and four
thousand.
15 The twelfth *captain* for the twelfth
month *was* Hĕl'dā-ī the Nē-tŏph'ȧ-
thīte, of Ŏth'nĭ-ĕl: and in his course
were twenty and four thousand.
16 ¶ Furthermore over the tribes of
Ĭs'rā-ĕl: the ruler of the Reubenites *was*
Ĕl'ĭ-ē'zĕr the son of Zĭch'rī: of the
Sĭm'ē-ŏn-ītes, Shĕph'ȧ-tī'ȧh the son of
Mā'ȧ-chȧh:
17 Of the Lē'vītes, Hăsh'ȧ-bī'ȧh the son
of Kĕm'ū-ĕl: of the Āar'ŏn-ītes, Zā'dŏk:
18 Of Judah, Ē-lī'hū, *one* of the brethren of David: of Ĭs'sȧ-chär, Ŏm'rī the
son of Mī'chā-ĕl:
19 Of Zĕb'ū-lŭn, Ĭsh-mā'iah the son of
Ō'bȧ-dī'ȧh: of Năph'tȧ-lī, Jĕr'ĭ-mŏth
the son of Ăz'rĭ-ĕl:
20 Of the children of Ē'phrā-ĭm, Hō-
shē'ȧ the son of Ăz'ȧ-zī'ȧh: of the half
tribe of Mȧ-năs'sĕh, Joel the son of
Pē-dā'iah:
21 Of the half *tribe* of Mȧ-năs'sĕh in
Gĭl'ē-ăd, Ĭd'dō the son of Zĕch'ȧ-rī'ȧh:
of Benjamin, Jā-ā'sĭ-ĕl the son of Abner:
22 Of Dan, Ȧ-zā'rē-ĕl the son of Jē-
rō'hăm. These *were* the princes of the
tribes of Ĭs'rā-ĕl.
23 ¶ But David took not the number
of them from twenty years old and
under: because the LORD had said he
would increase Ĭs'rā-ĕl like to the stars
of the heavens.
24 Jō'ăb the son of Zĕr'u-ī'ȧh began to
number, but he finished not, because
there fell wrath for it against Ĭs'rā-ĕl;
neither was the number put in the account of the Chronicles of king David.
25 ¶ And over the king's treasures
was Ăz-mā'vĕth the son of Ā'dĭ-ĕl: and
over the storehouses in the fields, in the
cities, and in the villages, and in the
castles, *was* Jē-hŏn'ȧ-thăn the son of
Ŭz-zī'ȧh:
26 And over them that did the work of
the field for tillage of the ground *was*
Ĕz'rī the son of Chē'lŭb:
27 And over the vineyards *was* Shĭm'-
ē-ī the Rā'măth-īte: over the increase of
the vineyards for the wine cellars *was*
Zăb'dī the Shĭph'mīte:
28 And over the olive trees and the
sycamore trees that *were* in the low
plains *was* Bā'ăl-hā'năn the Gē-dē'rīte:
and over the cellars of oil *was* Jō'ăsh:
29 And over the herds that fed in
Shăr'ŏn *was* Shĭt'raī the Shăr'ŏn-īte:
and over the herds *that were* in the
valleys *was* Shā'phăt the son of Ăd'lā-ī:
30 Over the camels also *was* Ō'bĭl the
Ĭsh'mā-ĕl-īte: and over the asses *was*
Jĕh-dē'iah the Mē-rŏn'ō-thīte:
31 And over the flocks *was* Jā'zĭz the
Hā'gĕr-īte. All these *were* the rulers of
the substance which *was* king David's.
32 Also Jonathan David's uncle was a
counselor, a wise man, and a scribe:
and Jē-hī'ĕl the son of Hăch'mō-nī *was*
with the king's sons:
33 And Ȧ-hĭth'ō-phĕl *was* the king's
counselor: and Hū'shaī the Är'chīte *was*
the king's companion:
34 And after Ȧ-hĭth'ō-phĕl *was* Jē-
hoi'ȧ-dȧ the son of Bē-nā'iah, and
Ȧ-bī'ȧ-thär: and the general of the
king's army *was* Jō'ăb.

CHAPTER 28

AND David assembled all the princes
of Ĭs'rā-ĕl, the princes of the tribes,
and the captains of the companies that

ministered to the king by course, and the captains over the thousands, and captains over the hundreds, and the stewards over all the substance and possession of the king, and of his sons, with the officers, and with the mighty men, and with all the valiant men, unto Jerusalem.

2 Then David the king stood up upon his feet, and said, Hear me, my brethren, and my people: *As for me*, I *had* in mine heart to build a house of rest for the ark of the covenant of the LORD, and for the footstool of our God, and had made ready for the building:

3 But God said unto me, Thou shalt not build a house for my name, because thou *hast been* a man of war, and hast shed blood.

4 Howbeit the LORD God of Ĭṣ′rā-ĕl chose me before all the house of my father to be king over Ĭṣ′rā-ĕl for ever: for he hath chosen Judah *to be* the ruler; and of the house of Judah, the house of my father; and among the sons of my father he liked me to make *me* king over all Ĭṣ′rā-ĕl:

5 And of all my sons, (for the LORD hath given me many sons,) he hath chosen Solomon my son to sit upon the throne of the kingdom of the LORD over Ĭṣ′rā-ĕl.

6 And he said unto me, Solomon thy son, he shall build my house and my courts: for I have chosen him *to be* my son, and I will be his father.

7 Moreover I will establish his kingdom for ever, if he be constant to do my commandments and my judgments, as at this day.

8 Now therefore, in the sight of all Ĭṣ′rā-ĕl the congregation of the LORD, and in the audience of our God, keep and seek for all the commandments of the LORD your God: that ye may possess this good land, and leave *it* for an inheritance for your children after you for ever.

9 ¶ And thou, Solomon my son, know thou the God of thy father, and serve him with a perfect heart and with a willing mind: for the LORD searcheth all hearts, and understandeth all the imaginations of the thoughts: if thou seek him, he will be found of thee; but if thou forsake him, he will cast thee off for ever.

10 Take heed now; for the LORD hath chosen thee to build a house for the sanctuary: be strong, and do *it*.

11 ¶ Then David gave to Solomon his son the pattern of the porch, and of the houses thereof, and of the treasuries thereof, and of the upper chambers thereof, and of the inner parlors thereof, and of the place of the mercy seat,

12 And the pattern of all that he had by the Spirit, of the courts of the house of the LORD, and of all the chambers round about, of the treasuries of the house of God, and of the treasuries of the dedicated things:

13 Also for the courses of the priests and the Lē′vītes, and for all the work of the service of the house of the LORD, and for all the vessels of service in the house of the LORD.

14 *He gave* of gold by weight for *things* of gold, for all instruments of all manner of service; *silver also* for all instruments of silver by weight, for all instruments of every kind of service:

15 Even the weight for the candlesticks of gold, and for their lamps of gold, by weight for every candlestick, and for the lamps thereof: and for the candlesticks of silver by weight, *both* for the candlestick, and *also* for the lamps thereof, according to the use of every candlestick.

16 And by weight *he gave* gold for the tables of showbread, for every table; and *likewise* silver for the tables of silver:

17 Also pure gold for the fleshhooks, and the bowls, and the cups: and for the golden basins *he gave gold* by weight for every basin; and *likewise silver* by weight for every basin of silver:

18 And for the altar of incense refined gold by weight; and gold for the pattern of the chariot of the cherubim, that spread out *their wings*, and covered the ark of the covenant of the LORD.

19 All *this, said David*, the LORD made me understand in writing by *his* hand upon me, *even* all the works of this pattern.

20 And David said to Solomon his son, Be strong and of good courage, and do *it*: fear not, nor be dismayed, for the LORD God, *even* my God, *will be* with thee; he will not fail thee, nor forsake thee, until thou hast finished all the work for the service of the house of the LORD.

21 And, behold, the courses of the

priests and the Lē′vītes, *even they shall be with thee* for all the service of the house of God: and *there shall be* with thee for all manner of workmanship every willing skilful man, for any manner of service: also the princes and all the people *will be* wholly at thy commandment.

CHAPTER 29

FURTHERMORE David the king said unto all the congregation, Solomon my son, whom alone God hath chosen, *is yet* young and tender, and the work *is* great: for the palace *is* not for man, but for the LORD God.

2 Now I have prepared with all my might for the house of my God the gold for *things to be made* of gold, and the silver for *things* of silver, and the brass for *things* of brass, the iron for *things* of iron, and wood for *things* of wood; onyx stones, and *stones* to be set, glistering stones, and of divers colors, and all manner of precious stones, and marble stones in abundance.

3 Moreover, because I have set my affection to the house of my God, I have of mine own proper good, of gold and silver, *which* I have given to the house of my God, over and above all that I have prepared for the holy house,

4 *Even* three thousand talents of gold, of the gold of Ō′phĭr, and seven thousand talents of refined silver, to overlay the walls of the houses *withal:*

5 The gold for *things* of gold, and the silver for *things* of silver, and for all manner of work *to be made* by the hands of artificers. And who *then* is willing to consecrate his service this day unto the LORD?

6 ℂ Then the chief of the fathers and princes of the tribes of Ĭs′rā-ĕl, and the captains of thousands and of hundreds, with the rulers of the king's work, offered willingly,

7 And gave, for the service of the house of God, of gold five thousand talents and ten thousand drams, and of silver ten thousand talents, and of brass eighteen thousand talents, and one hundred thousand talents of iron.

8 And they with whom *precious* stones were found gave *them* to the treasure of the house of the LORD, by the hand of Jē-hī′ĕl the Gĕr′shŏn-īte.

9 Then the people rejoiced, for that they offered willingly, because with perfect heart they offered willingly to the LORD: and David the king also rejoiced with great joy.

10 ℂ Wherefore David blessed the LORD before all the congregation: and David said, Blessed *be* thou, LORD God of Ĭs′rā-ĕl our father, for ever and ever.

11 Thine, O LORD, *is* the greatness, and the power, and the glory, and the victory, and the majesty: for all *that is* in the heaven and in the earth *is thine;* thine *is* the kingdom, O LORD, and thou art exalted as head above all.

12 Both riches and honor *come* of thee, and thou reignest over all; and in thine hand *is* power and might; and in thine hand *it is* to make great, and to give strength unto all.

13 Now therefore, our God, we thank thee, and praise thy glorious name.

14 But who *am* I, and what *is* my people, that we should be able to offer so willingly after this sort? for all things *come* of thee, and of thine own have we given thee.

15 For we *are* strangers before thee, and sojourners, as *were* all our fathers: our days on the earth *are* as a shadow, and *there is* none abiding.

16 O LORD our God, all this store that we have prepared to build thee a house for thine holy name *cometh* of thine hand, and *is* all thine own.

17 I know also, my God, that thou triest the heart, and hast pleasure in uprightness. As for me, in the uprightness of mine heart I have willingly offered all these things: and now have I seen with joy thy people, which are present here, to offer willingly unto thee.

18 O LORD God of Abraham, Isaac, and of Ĭs′rā-ĕl, our fathers, keep this for ever in the imagination of the thoughts of the heart of thy people, and prepare their heart unto thee:

19 And give unto Solomon my son a perfect heart, to keep thy commandments, thy testimonies, and thy statutes, and to do all *these things*, and to build the palace, *for* the which I have made provision.

20 ℂ And David said to all the congregation, Now bless the LORD your God. And all the congregation blessed the LORD God of their fathers, and bowed down their heads, and worshipped the LORD, and the king.

21 And they sacrificed sacrifices unto
the LORD, and offered burnt offerings
unto the LORD, on the morrow after
that day, *even* a thousand bullocks, a
thousand rams, *and* a thousand lambs,
with their drink offerings, and sacrifices
in abundance for all Ĭṣ'rā-ĕl:
22 And did eat and drink before the
LORD on that day with great gladness.
And they made Solomon the son of
David king the second time, and
anointed *him* unto the LORD *to be* the
chief governor, and Zā'dŏk *to be* priest.
23 Then Solomon sat on the throne of
the LORD as king instead of David his
father, and prospered; and all Ĭṣ'rā-ĕl
obeyed him.
24 And all the princes, and the mighty
men, and all the sons likewise of king
David, submitted themselves unto Solomon the king.
25 And the LORD magnified Solomon
exceedingly in the sight of all Ĭṣ'rā-ĕl,
and bestowed upon him *such* royal
majesty as had not been on any king
before him in Ĭṣ'rā-ĕl.
26 ¶ Thus David the son of Jesse
reigned over all Ĭṣ'rā-ĕl.
27 And the time that he reigned over
Ĭṣ'rā-ĕl *was* forty years; seven years
reigned he in Hē'brŏn, and thirty and
three *years* reigned he in Jerusalem.
28 And he died in a good old age, full
of days, riches, and honor: and Solomon
his son reigned in his stead.
29 Now the acts of David the king, first
and last, behold, they *are* written in the
book of Samuel the seer, and in the
book of Nathan the prophet, and in the
book of Gad the seer,
30 With all his reign and his might, and
the times that went over him, and over
Ĭṣ'rā-ĕl, and over all the kingdoms of
the countries.

THE SECOND BOOK OF THE CHRONICLES

CHAPTER 1

AND Solomon the son of David was
strengthened in his kingdom, and
the LORD his God *was* with him, and
magnified him exceedingly.
2 Then Solomon spake unto all Ĭṣ'rā-ĕl,
to the captains of thousands and of hundreds, and to the judges, and to every
governor in all Ĭṣ'rā-ĕl, the chief of the
fathers.
3 So Solomon, and all the congregation
with him, went to the high place that
was at Gĭb'ē-ŏn; for there was the
tabernacle of the congregation of God,
which Moses the servant of the LORD
had made in the wilderness.
4 But the ark of God had David brought
up from Kĭr'jăth–jē'ă-rĭm to *the place
which* David had prepared for it: for he
had pitched a tent for it at Jerusalem.
5 Moreover the brazen altar, that Bē-
zăl'ē-ĕl the son of Ū'rī, the son of Hûr,
had made, he put before the tabernacle
of the LORD: and Solomon and the congregation sought unto it.
6 And Solomon went up thither to the
brazen altar before the LORD, which *was*
at the tabernacle of the congregation,
and offered a thousand burnt offerings
upon it.
7 ¶ In that night did God appear unto
Solomon, and said unto him, Ask what
I shall give thee.
8 And Solomon said unto God, Thou
hast showed great mercy unto David my
father, and hast made me to reign in his
stead.
9 Now, O LORD God, let thy promise
unto David my father be established:
for thou hast made me king over a people
like the dust of the earth in multitude.
10 Give me now wisdom and knowledge, that I may go out and come in before this people: for who can judge this
thy people, *that is so* great?
11 And God said to Solomon, Because
this was in thine heart, and thou hast not
asked riches, wealth, or honor, nor the
life of thine enemies, neither yet hast
asked long life; but hast asked wisdom
and knowledge for thyself, that thou
mayest judge my people, over whom I
have made thee king:
12 Wisdom and knowledge *is* granted
unto thee; and I will give thee riches,

and wealth, and honor, such as none of
the kings have had that *have been* before thee, neither shall there any after
thee have the like.
13 ¶ Then Solomon came *from his
journey* to the high place that *was* at
Gĭb′ē-ŏn to Jerusalem, from before the
tabernacle of the congregation, and
reigned over Ĭṣ′rā-ĕl.
14 And Solomon gathered chariots and
horsemen: and he had a thousand and
four hundred chariots, and twelve thousand horsemen, which he placed in the
chariot cities, and with the king at
Jerusalem.
15 And the king made silver and gold
at Jerusalem *as plenteous* as stones,
and cedar trees made he as the sycamore trees that *are* in the vale for
abundance.
16 And Solomon had horses brought
out of Egypt, and linen yarn: the king's
merchants received the linen yarn at a
price.
17 And they fetched up, and brought
forth out of Egypt a chariot for six hundred *shekels* of silver, and a horse for a
hundred and fifty: and so brought they
out *horses* for all the kings of the Hĭt′-
tītes, and for the kings of Syria, by their
means.

CHAPTER 2

AND Solomon determined to build a
house for the name of the LORD,
and a house for his kingdom.
2 And Solomon told out threescore and
ten thousand men to bear burdens, and
fourscore thousand to hew in the mountain, and three thousand and six hundred to oversee them.
3 ¶ And Solomon sent to Hū′răm the
king of Tȳre, saying, As thou didst deal
with David my father, and didst send
him cedars to build him a house to dwell
therein, *even so deal with me*.
4 Behold, I build a house to the name
of the LORD my God, to dedicate *it* to
him, *and* to burn before him sweet incense, and for the continual showbread,
and for the burnt offerings morning and
evening, on the sabbaths, and on the
new moons, and on the solemn feasts of
the LORD our God. This *is an ordinance*
for ever to Ĭṣ′rā-ĕl.
5 And the house which I build *is* great:
for great *is* our God above all gods.
6 But who is able to build him a house,
seeing the heaven and heaven of heavens cannot contain him? who *am* I then,
that I should build him a house, save
only to burn sacrifice before him?
7 Send me now therefore a man cunning to work in gold, and in silver, and
in brass, and in iron, and in purple,
and crimson, and blue, and that can
skill to grave with the cunning men
that *are* with me in Judah and in
Jerusalem, whom David my father did
provide.
8 Send me also cedar trees, fir trees,
and algum trees, out of Lebanon: for I
know that thy servants can skill to cut
timber in Lebanon; and, behold, my
servants *shall be* with thy servants,
9 Even to prepare me timber in abundance: for the house which I am about to
build *shall be* wonderful great.
10 And, behold, I will give to thy servants, the hewers that cut timber, twenty
thousand measures of beaten wheat,
and twenty thousand measures of barley, and twenty thousand baths of wine,
and twenty thousand baths of oil.
11 ¶ Then Hū′răm the king of Tȳre
answered in writing, which he sent to
Solomon, Because the LORD hath loved
his people, he hath made thee king over
them.
12 Hū′răm said moreover, Blessed *be*
the LORD God of Ĭṣ′rā-ĕl, that made
heaven and earth, who hath given to
David the king a wise son, endued with
prudence and understanding, that might
build a house for the LORD, and a house
for his kingdom.
13 And now I have sent a cunning man,
endued with understanding, of Hū′răm
my father's,
14 The son of a woman of the daughters
of Dan, and his father *was* a man of
Tȳre, skilful to work in gold, and in silver, in brass, in iron, in stone, and in
timber, in purple, in blue, and in fine
linen, and in crimson; also to grave any
manner of graving, and to find out every
device which shall be put to him, with
thy cunning men, and with the cunning
men of my lord David thy father.
15 Now therefore the wheat, and the
barley, the oil, and the wine, which my
lord hath spoken of, let him send unto
his servants:
16 And we will cut wood out of Lebanon, as much as thou shalt need: and
we will bring it to thee in floats by sea to

Jŏp′pȧ; and thou shalt carry it up to
Jerusalem.
17 ¶ And Solomon numbered all the
strangers that *were* in the land of Ĭş′-
ra-ĕl, after the numbering wherewith
David his father had numbered them;
and they were found a hundred and
fifty thousand and three thousand and
six hundred.
18 And he set threescore and ten thousand of them *to be* bearers of burdens,
and fourscore thousand *to be* hewers in
the mountain, and three thousand and
six hundred overseers to set the people
awork.

CHAPTER 3

THEN Solomon began to build the
house of the LORD at Jerusalem in
mount Mō-rī′ăh, where *the LORD* appeared unto David his father, in the
place that David had prepared in the
threshingfloor of Ôr′năn the Jĕb′ū-
şite.
2 And he began to build in the second
day of the second month, in the fourth
year of his reign.
3 ¶ Now these *are the things wherein*
Solomon was instructed for the building
of the house of God. The length by
cubits after the first measure *was* threescore cubits, and the breadth twenty
cubits.
4 And the porch that *was* in the front
of the house, the length *of it was* according to the breadth of the house, twenty
cubits, and the height *was* a hundred
and twenty: and he overlaid it within
with pure gold.
5 And the greater house he ceiled with
fir tree, which he overlaid with fine gold,
and set thereon palm trees and chains.
6 And he garnished the house with
precious stones for beauty: and the gold
was gold of Pär-vā′ĭm.
7 He overlaid also the house, the
beams, the posts, and the walls thereof,
and the doors thereof, with gold; and
graved cherubim on the walls.
8 And he made the most holy house, the
length whereof *was* according to the
breadth of the house, twenty cubits, and
the breadth thereof twenty cubits: and
he overlaid it with fine gold, *amounting*
to six hundred talents.
9 And the weight of the nails *was* fifty
shekels of gold. And he overlaid the
upper chambers with gold.
10 And in the most holy house he made
two cherubim of image work, and overlaid them with gold.
11 ¶ And the wings of the cherubim
were twenty cubits long: one wing *of the*
one cherub was five cubits, reaching to
the wall of the house: and the other wing
was likewise five cubits, reaching to the
wing of the other cherub.
12 And *one* wing of the other cherub
was five cubits, reaching to the wall of
the house: and the other wing *was* five
cubits *also*, joining to the wing of the
other cherub.
13 The wings of these cherubim spread
themselves forth twenty cubits: and
they stood on their feet, and their faces
were inward.
14 ¶ And he made the veil *of* blue, and
purple, and crimson, and fine linen, and
wrought cherubim thereon.
15 Also he made before the house two
pillars of thirty and five cubits high, and
the chapiter that *was* on the top of each
of them *was* five cubits.
16 And he made chains, *as* in the oracle, and put *them* on the heads of the
pillars; and made a hundred pomegranates, and put *them* on the chains.
17 And he reared up the pillars before
the temple, one on the right hand, and
the other on the left; and called the
name of that on the right hand Jā′chĭn,
and the name of that on the left Boaz.

CHAPTER 4

MOREOVER he made an altar of
brass, twenty cubits the length
thereof, and twenty cubits the breadth
thereof, and ten cubits the height thereof.
2 ¶ Also he made a molten sea of ten
cubits from brim to brim, round in compass, and five cubits the height thereof;
and a line of thirty cubits did compass
it round about.
3 And under it *was* the similitude of
oxen, which did compass it round about:
ten in a cubit, compassing the sea round
about. Two rows of oxen *were* cast,
when it was cast.
4 It stood upon twelve oxen, three looking toward the north, and three looking
toward the west, and three looking
toward the south, and three looking toward the east: and the sea *was set*
above upon them, and all their hinder
parts *were* inward.
5 And the thickness of it *was* a hand-

breadth, and the brim of it like the work
of the brim of a cup, with flowers of
lilies; *and* it received and held three
thousand baths.

6 ¶ He made also ten lavers, and put
five on the right hand, and five on the
left, to wash in them: such things as
they offered for the burnt offering they
washed in them; but the sea *was* for the
priests to wash in.

7 And he made ten candlesticks of gold
according to their form, and set *them* in
the temple, five on the right hand, and
five on the left.

8 He made also ten tables, and placed
them in the temple, five on the right
side, and five on the left. And he made
a hundred basins of gold.

9 ¶ Furthermore he made the court
of the priests, and the great court, and
doors for the court, and overlaid the
doors of them with brass.

10 And he set the sea on the right side
of the east end, over against the south.

11 And Hū′răm made the pots, and
the shovels, and the basins. And Hū′-
răm finished the work that he was to
make for king Solomon for the house of
God;

12 *To wit,* the two pillars, and the pommels, and the chapiters *which were* on
the top of the two pillars, and the two
wreaths to cover the two pommels of
the chapiters which *were* on the top of
the pillars;

13 And four hundred pomegranates on
the two wreaths; two rows of pomegranates on each wreath, to cover the
two pommels of the chapiters which
were upon the pillars.

14 He made also bases, and lavers
made he upon the bases;

15 One sea, and twelve oxen under it.

16 The pots also, and the shovels, and
the fleshhooks, and all their instruments, did Hū′răm his father make to
king Solomon for the house of the LORD,
of bright brass.

17 In the plain of Jordan did the king
cast them, in the clay ground between
Sŭc′cōth and Zĕr′ē-dā′thăh.

18 Thus Solomon made all these vessels in great abundance: for the weight
of the brass could not be found out.

19 ¶ And Solomon made all the vessels that *were for* the house of God, the
golden altar also, and the tables whereon
the showbread *was set;*

20 Moreover the candlesticks with
their lamps, that they should burn after
the manner before the oracle, of pure
gold;

21 And the flowers, and the lamps, and
the tongs, *made he of* gold, *and* that perfect gold;

22 And the snuffers, and the basins,
and the spoons, and the censers, *of* pure
gold: and the entry of the house, the
inner doors thereof for the most holy
place, and the doors of the house of the
temple, *were of* gold.

CHAPTER 5

THUS all the work that Solomon
made for the house of the LORD
was finished: and Solomon brought in
all the things that David his father
had dedicated; and the silver, and the
gold, and all the instruments, put he
among the treasures of the house of
God.

2 ¶ Then Solomon assembled the
elders of Ĭş′rā-ĕl, and all the heads of
the tribes, the chief of the fathers of the
children of Ĭs′rā-ĕl, unto Jerusalem, to
bring up the ark of the covenant of the
LORD out of the city of David, which *is*
Zion.

3 Wherefore all the men of Ĭş′rā-ĕl
assembled themselves unto the king in
the feast which *was* in the seventh
month.

4 And all the elders of Ĭş′rā-ĕl came;
and the Lē′vītes took up the ark.

5 And they brought up the ark, and
the tabernacle of the congregation, and
all the holy vessels that *were* in the
tabernacle, these did the priests *and* the
Lē′vītes bring up.

6 Also king Solomon, and all the congregation of Ĭş′rā-ĕl that were assembled unto him before the ark, sacrificed
sheep and oxen, which could not be
told nor numbered for multitude.

7 And the priests brought in the ark of
the covenant of the LORD unto his place,
to the oracle of the house, into the most
holy *place, even* under the wings of the
cherubim:

8 For the cherubim spread forth *their*
wings over the place of the ark, and the
cherubim covered the ark and the staves
thereof above.

9 And they drew out the staves *of the*
ark, that the ends of the staves were
seen from the ark before the oracle; but

they were not seen without. And there it is unto this day.

10 *There was* nothing in the ark save the two tables which Moses put *therein* at Ho′rĕb, when the LORD made *a covenant* with the children of Ĭṣ′rā-ĕl, when they came out of Egypt.

11 ℂ And it came to pass, when the priests were come out of the holy *place:* (for all the priests *that were* present were sanctified, *and* did not *then* wait by course:

12 Also the Lē′vītes *which were* the singers, all of them of Ā′săph, of Hē′măn, of Jē-dū′thŭn, with their sons and their brethren, *being* arrayed in white linen, having cymbals and psalteries and harps, stood at the east end of the altar, and with them a hundred and twenty priests sounding with trumpets:)

13 It came even to pass, as the trumpeters and singers *were* as one, to make one sound to be heard in praising and thanking the LORD; and when they lifted up *their* voice with the trumpets and cymbals and instruments of music, and praised the LORD, *saying,* For *he is* good; for his mercy *endureth* for ever: that *then* the house was filled with a cloud, *even* the house of the LORD;

14 So that the priests could not stand to minister by reason of the cloud: for the glory of the LORD had filled the house of God.

CHAPTER 6

THEN said Solomon, The LORD hath said that he would dwell in the thick darkness.

2 But I have built a house of habitation for thee, and a place for thy dwelling for ever.

3 And the king turned his face, and blessed the whole congregation of Ĭṣ′rā-ĕl: and all the congregation of Ĭṣ′rā-ĕl stood.

4 And he said, Blessed *be* the LORD God of Ĭṣ′rā-ĕl, who hath with his hands fulfilled *that* which he spake with his mouth to my father David, saying,

5 Since the day that I brought forth my people out of the land of Egypt I chose no city among all the tribes of Ĭṣ′rā-ĕl to build a house in, that my name might be there; neither chose I any man to be a ruler over my people Ĭṣ′rā-ĕl:

6 But I have chosen Jerusalem, that my name might be there; and have chosen David to be over my people Ĭṣ′rā-ĕl.

7 Now it was in the heart of David my father to build a house for the name of the LORD God of Ĭṣ′rā-ĕl.

8 But the LORD said to David my father, Forasmuch as it was in thine heart to build a house for my name, thou didst well in that it was in thine heart:

9 Notwithstanding thou shalt not build the house; but thy son which shall come forth out of thy loins, he shall build the house for my name.

10 The LORD therefore hath performed his word that he hath spoken: for I am risen up in the room of David my father, and am set on the throne of Ĭṣ′rā-ĕl, as the LORD promised, and have built the house for the name of the LORD God of Ĭṣ′rā-ĕl.

11 And in it have I put the ark, wherein *is* the covenant of the LORD, that he made with the children of Ĭṣ′rā-ĕl.

12 ℂ And he stood before the altar of the LORD in the presence of all the congregation of Ĭṣ′rā-ĕl, and spread forth his hands:

13 For Solomon had made a brazen scaffold, of five cubits long, and five cubits broad, and three cubits high, and had set it in the midst of the court: and upon it he stood, and kneeled down upon his knees before all the congregation of Ĭṣ′rā-ĕl, and spread forth his hands toward heaven,

14 And said, O LORD God of Ĭṣ′rā-ĕl, *there is* no God like thee in the heaven, nor in the earth; which keepest covenant, and *showest* mercy unto thy servants, that walk before thee with all their hearts:

15 Thou which hast kept with thy servant David my father that which thou hast promised him; and spakest with thy mouth, and hast fulfilled *it* with thine hand, as *it is* this day.

16 Now therefore, O LORD God of Ĭṣ′rā-ĕl, keep with thy servant David my father that which thou hast promised him, saying, There shall not fail thee a man in my sight to sit upon the throne of Ĭṣ′rā-ĕl; yet so that thy children take heed to their way to walk in my law, as thou hast walked before me.

17 Now then, O LORD God of Ĭṣ′rā-ĕl, let thy word be verified, which thou hast spoken unto thy servant David.

18 But will God in very deed dwell with

men on the earth? Behold, heaven and the heaven of heavens cannot contain thee; how much less this house which I have built!

19 Have respect therefore to the prayer of thy servant, and to his supplication, O LORD my God, to hearken unto the cry and the prayer which thy servant prayeth before thee:

20 That thine eyes may be open upon this house day and night, upon the place whereof thou hast said that thou wouldest put thy name there; to hearken unto the prayer which thy servant prayeth toward this place.

21 Hearken therefore unto the supplications of thy servant, and of thy people Ĭṣ′rā-ĕl, which they shall make toward this place: hear thou from thy dwelling place, *even* from heaven; and when thou hearest, forgive.

22 ¶ If a man sin against his neighbor, and an oath be laid upon him to make him swear, and the oath come before thine altar in this house;

23 Then hear thou from heaven, and do, and judge thy servants, by requiting the wicked, by recompensing his way upon his own head; and by justifying the righteous, by giving him according to his righteousness.

24 ¶ And if thy people Ĭṣ′rā-ĕl be put to the worse before the enemy, because they have sinned against thee; and shall return and confess thy name, and pray and make supplication before thee in this house;

25 Then hear thou from the heavens, and forgive the sin of thy people Ĭṣ′rā-ĕl, and bring them again unto the land which thou gavest to them and to their fathers.

26 ¶ When the heaven is shut up, and there is no rain, because they have sinned against thee; *yet* if they pray toward this place, and confess thy name, and turn from their sin, when thou dost afflict them;

27 Then hear thou from heaven, and forgive the sin of thy servants, and of thy people Ĭṣ′rā-ĕl, when thou hast taught them the good way, wherein they should walk; and send rain upon thy land, which thou hast given unto thy people for an inheritance.

28 ¶ If there be dearth in the land, if there be pestilence, if there be blasting or mildew, locusts or caterpillars; if their enemies besiege them in the cities of their land; whatsoever sore, or whatsoever sickness *there be:*

29 *Then* what prayer *or* what supplication soever shall be made of any man, or of all thy people Ĭṣ′rā-ĕl, when every one shall know his own sore and his own grief, and shall spread forth his hands in this house:

30 Then hear thou from heaven thy dwelling place, and forgive, and render unto every man according unto all his ways, whose heart thou knowest; (for thou only knowest the hearts of the children of men;)

31 That they may fear thee, to walk in thy ways, so long as they live in the land which thou gavest unto our fathers.

32 ¶ Moreover concerning the stranger, which is not of thy people Ĭṣ′rā-ĕl, but is come from a far country for thy great name's sake, and thy mighty hand, and thy stretched out arm; if they come and pray in this house;

33 Then hear thou from the heavens, *even* from thy dwelling place, and do according to all that the stranger calleth to thee for; that all people of the earth may know thy name, and fear thee, as *doth* thy people Ĭṣ′rā-ĕl, and may know that this house which I have built is called by thy name.

34 If thy people go out to war against their enemies by the way that thou shalt send them, and they pray unto thee toward this city which thou hast chosen, and the house which I have built for thy name;

35 Then hear thou from the heavens their prayer and their supplication, and maintain their cause.

36 If they sin against thee, (for *there is* no man which sinneth not,) and thou be angry with them, and deliver them over before *their* enemies, and they carry them away captives unto a land far off or near;

37 Yet *if* they bethink themselves in the land whither they are carried captive, and turn and pray unto thee in the land of their captivity, saying, We have sinned, we have done amiss, and have dealt wickedly;

38 If they return to thee with all their heart and with all their soul in the land of their captivity, whither they have carried them captives, and pray toward their land, which thou gavest unto their

fathers, and *toward* the city which thou hast chosen, and toward the house which I have built for thy name:

39 Then hear thou from the heavens, *even* from thy dwelling place, their prayer and their supplications, and maintain their cause, and forgive thy people which have sinned against thee.

40 Now, my God, let, I beseech thee, thine eyes be open, and *let* thine ears *be* attent unto the prayer *that is made* in this place.

41 Now therefore arise, O LORD God, into thy resting place, thou, and the ark of thy strength: let thy priests, O LORD God, be clothed with salvation, and let thy saints rejoice in goodness.

42 O LORD God, turn not away the face of thine anointed: remember the mercies of David thy servant.

CHAPTER 7

NOW when Solomon had made an end of praying, the fire came down from heaven, and consumed the burnt offering and the sacrifices; and the glory of the LORD filled the house.

2 And the priests could not enter into the house of the LORD, because the glory of the LORD had filled the LORD's house.

3 And when all the children of Ĭş'rā-ĕl saw how the fire came down, and the glory of the LORD upon the house, they bowed themselves with their faces to the ground upon the pavement, and worshipped, and praised the LORD, *saying*, For *he is* good; for his mercy *endureth* for ever.

4 ¶ Then the king and all the people offered sacrifices before the LORD.

5 And king Solomon offered a sacrifice of twenty and two thousand oxen, and a hundred and twenty thousand sheep. So the king and all the people dedicated the house of God.

6 And the priests waited on their offices: the Lē'vītes also with instruments of music of the LORD, which David the king had made to praise the LORD, because his mercy *endureth* for ever, when David praised by their ministry; and the priests sounded trumpets before them, and all Ĭş'rā-ĕl stood.

7 Moreover Solomon hallowed the middle of the court that *was* before the house of the LORD: for there he offered burnt offerings, and the fat of the peace offerings, because the brazen altar which Solomon had made was not able to receive the burnt offerings, and the meat offerings, and the fat.

8 ¶ Also at the same time Solomon kept the feast seven days, and all Ĭş'rā-ĕl with him, a very great congregation, from the entering in of Ha'măth unto the river of Egypt.

9 And in the eighth day they made a solemn assembly: for they kept the dedication of the altar seven days, and the feast seven days.

10 And on the three and twentieth day of the seventh month he sent the people away into their tents, glad and merry in heart for the goodness that the LORD had showed unto David, and to Solomon, and to Ĭş'rā-ĕl his people.

11 Thus Solomon finished the house of the LORD, and the king's house: and all that came into Solomon's heart to make in the house of the LORD, and in his own house, he prosperously effected.

12 ¶ And the LORD appeared to Solomon by night, and said unto him, I have heard thy prayer, and have chosen this place to myself for a house of sacrifice.

13 If I shut up heaven that there be no rain, or if I command the locusts to devour the land, or if I send pestilence among my people;

14 If my people, which are called by my name, shall humble themselves, and pray, and seek my face, and turn from their wicked ways; then will I hear from heaven, and will forgive their sin, and will heal their land.

15 Now mine eyes shall be open, and mine ears attent unto the prayer *that is made* in this place.

16 For now have I chosen and sanctified this house, that my name may be there for ever: and mine eyes and mine heart shall be there perpetually.

17 And as for thee, if thou wilt walk before me, as David thy father walked, and do according to all that I have commanded thee, and shalt observe my statutes and my judgments;

18 Then will I stablish the throne of thy kingdom, according as I have covenanted with David thy father, saying, There shall not fail thee a man *to be* ruler in Ĭş'rā-ĕl.

19 But if ye turn away, and forsake my statutes and my commandments, which

I have set before you, and shall go and serve other gods, and worship them;

20 Then will I pluck them up by the roots out of my land which I have given them; and this house, which I have sanctified for my name, will I cast out of my sight, and will make it *to be* a proverb and a byword among all nations.

21 And this house, which is high, shall be an astonishment to every one that passeth by it; so that he shall say, Why hath the LORD done thus unto this land, and unto this house?

22 And it shall be answered, Because they forsook the LORD God of their fathers, which brought them forth out of the land of Egypt, and laid hold on other gods, and worshipped them, and served them: therefore hath he brought all this evil upon them.

CHAPTER 8

AND it came to pass at the end of twenty years, wherein Solomon had built the house of the LORD, and his own house,

2 That the cities which Hū'răm had restored to Solomon, Solomon built them, and caused the children of Ĭş'rā-ēl to dwell there.

3 And Solomon went to Hā'măth–zō'bȧh, and prevailed against it.

4 And he built Tăd'mŏr in the wilderness, and all the store cities, which he built in Hā'măth.

5 Also he built Bĕth'–hō'rŏn the upper, and Bĕth'–hō'rŏn the nether, fenced cities, with walls, gates, and bars;

6 And Bā'ȧl-ȧth, and all the store cities that Solomon had, and all the chariot cities, and the cities of the horsemen, and all that Solomon desired to build in Jerusalem, and in Lebanon, and throughout all the land of his dominion.

7 ¶ *As for* all the people *that were* left of the Hĭt'tītes, and the Ăm'ō-rītes, and the Pĕr'ĭz-zītes, and the Hī'vītes, and the Jĕb'ū-şītes, which *were* not of Ĭş'rā-ēl,

8 *But* of their children, who were left after them in the land, whom the children of Ĭş'rā-ēl consumed not, them did Solomon make to pay tribute until this day.

9 But of the children of Ĭş'rā-ēl did Solomon make no servants for his work; but they *were* men of war, and chief of his captains, and captains of his chariots and horsemen.

10 And these *were* the chief of king Solomon's officers, *even* two hundred and fifty, that bare rule over the people.

11 ¶ And Solomon brought up the daughter of Phā'raōh out of the city of David unto the house that he had built for her: for he said, My wife shall not dwell in the house of David king of Ĭş'rā-ēl, because *the places are* holy, whereunto the ark of the LORD hath come.

12 ¶ Then Solomon offered burnt offerings unto the LORD on the altar of the LORD, which he had built before the porch,

13 Even after a certain rate every day, offering according to the commandment of Moses, on the sabbaths, and on the new moons, and on the solemn feasts, three times in the year, *even* in the feast of unleavened bread, and in the feast of weeks, and in the feast of tabernacles.

14 ¶ And he appointed, according to the order of David his father, the courses of the priests to their service, and the Lē'vītes to their charges, to praise and minister before the priests, as the duty of every day required: the porters also by their courses at every gate: for so had David the man of God commanded.

15 And they departed not from the commandment of the king unto the priests and Lē'vītes concerning any matter, or concerning the treasures.

16 Now all the work of Solomon was prepared unto the day of the foundation of the house of the LORD, and until it was finished. *So* the house of the LORD was perfected.

17 ¶ Then went Solomon to Ē'zĭ-ŏn–gē'bĕr, and to Ē'lŏth, at the sea side in the land of Ē'dŏm.

18 And Hū'răm sent him, by the hands of his servants, ships, and servants that had knowledge of the sea; and they went with the servants of Solomon to Ō'phĭr, and took thence four hundred and fifty talents of gold, and brought *them* to king Solomon.

CHAPTER 9

AND when the queen of Shē'bȧ heard of the fame of Solomon, she came to prove Solomon with hard questions at Jerusalem, with a very great company, and camels that bare spices, and gold in abundance, and precious stones: and

when she was come to Solomon, she
communed with him of all that was in
her heart.
2 And Solomon told her all her questions: and there was nothing hid from
Solomon which he told her not.
3 And when the queen of Shē'bà had
seen the wisdom of Solomon, and the
house that he had built,
4 And the meat of his table, and the
sitting of his servants, and the attendance of his ministers, and their apparel;
his cupbearers also, and their apparel;
and his ascent by which he went up into
the house of the LORD; there was no
more spirit in her.
5 And she said to the king, *It was* a true
report which I heard in mine own land
of thine acts, and of thy wisdom:
6 Howbeit I believed not their words,
until I came, and mine eyes had seen *it:*
and, behold, the one half of the greatness of thy wisdom was not told me: *for*
thou exceedest the fame that I heard.
7 Happy *are* thy men, and happy *are*
these thy servants, which stand continually before thee, and hear thy wisdom.
8 Blessed be the LORD thy God, which
delighted in thee to set thee on his
throne, *to be* king for the LORD thy God:
because thy God loved Ĭş'rā-ĕl, to estab-
ish them for ever, therefore made he
thee king over them, to do judgment and
justice.
9 And she gave the king a hundred and
twenty talents of gold, and of spices
great abundance, and precious stones:
neither was there any such spice as the
queen of Shē'bà gave king Solomon.
10 And the servants also of Hū'răm,
and the servants of Solomon, which
brought gold from Ō'phīr, brought algum trees and precious stones.
11 And the king made *of* the algum
trees terraces to the house of the LORD,
and to the king's palace, and harps and
psalteries for singers: and there were
none such seen before in the land of
Judah.
12 And king Solomon gave to the queen
of Shē'bà all her desire, whatsoever she
asked, besides *that* which she had
brought unto the king. So she turned,
and went away to her own land, she and
her servants.
13 ¶ Now the weight of gold that came
to Solomon in one year was six hundred
and threescore and six talents of gold;
14 Besides *that which* chapmen and
merchants brought. And all the kings of
Arabia and governors of the country
brought gold and silver to Solomon.
15 ¶ And king Solomon made two hundred targets *of* beaten gold: six hundred
shekels of beaten gold went to one
target.
16 And three hundred shields *made he
of* beaten gold: three hundred *shekels* of
gold went to one shield. And the king
put them in the house of the forest of
Lebanon.
17 Moreover the king made a great
throne of ivory, and overlaid it with pure
gold.
18 And *there were* six steps to the
throne, with a footstool of gold, *which
were* fastened to the throne, and stays
on each side of the sitting place, and two
lions standing by the stays:
19 And twelve lions stood there on the
one side and on the other upon the six
steps. There was not the like made in
any kingdom.
20 ¶ And all the drinking vessels of
king Solomon *were of* gold, and all the
vessels of the house of the forest of
Lebanon *were of* pure gold: none *were
of* silver; it was *not* any thing accounted
of in the days of Solomon.
21 For the king's ships went to Tär'-
shĭsh with the servants of Hū'răm: every
three years once came the ships of Tär'-
shĭsh bringing gold, and silver, ivory, and
apes, and peacocks.
22 And king Solomon passed all the
kings of the earth in riches and wisdom.
23 ¶ And all the kings of the earth
sought the presence of Solomon, to hear
his wisdom, that God had put in his
heart.
24 And they brought every man his
present, vessels of silver, and vessels of
gold, and raiment, harness, and spices,
horses, and mules, a rate year by year.
25 ¶ And Solomon had four thousand
stalls for horses and chariots, and twelve
thousand horsemen; whom he bestowed
in the chariot cities, and with the king at
Jerusalem.
26 ¶ And he reigned over all the kings
from the river even unto the land of the
Phĭ-lĭs'tīneş, and to the border of Egypt.
27 And the king made silver in Jerusalem as stones, and cedar trees made he
as the sycamore trees that *are* in the low
plains in abundance.

28 And they brought unto Solomon horses out of Egypt, and out of all lands.

29 ¶ Now the rest of the acts of Solomon, first and last, *are* they not written in the book of Nathan the prophet, and in the prophecy of Ȧ-hī′jȧh the Shī′lō-nīte, and in the visions of Ĭd′dō the seer against Jĕr′ō-bō′ăm the son of Nē′băt?

30 And Solomon reigned in Jerusalem over all Ĭs̱′rā-ēl forty years.

31 And Solomon slept with his fathers, and he was buried in the city of David his father: and Rē′hō-bō′ăm his son reigned in his stead.

CHAPTER 10

AND Rē′hō-bō′ăm went to Shē′chĕm: for to Shē′chĕm were all Ĭs̱′rā-ĕl come to make him king.

2 And it came to pass, when Jĕr′ō-bō′ăm the son of Nē′băt, who *was* in Egypt, whither he had fled from the presence of Solomon the king, heard *it*, that Jĕr′ō-bō′ăm returned out of Egypt.

3 And they sent and called him. So Jĕr′ō-bō′ăm and all Ĭs̱′rā-ēl came and spake to Rē′hō-bō′ăm, saying,

4 Thy father made our yoke grievous: now therefore ease thou somewhat the grievous servitude of thy father, and his heavy yoke that he put upon us, and we will serve thee.

5 And he said unto them, Come again unto me after three days. And the people departed.

6 ¶ And king Rē′hō-bō′ăm took counsel with the old men that had stood before Solomon his father while he yet lived, saying, What counsel give ye *me* to return answer to this people?

7 And they spake unto him, saying, If thou be kind to this people, and please them, and speak good words to them, they will be thy servants for ever.

8 But he forsook the counsel which the old men gave him, and took counsel with the young men that were brought up with him, that stood before him.

9 And he said unto them, What advice give ye that we may return answer to this people, which have spoken to me, saying, Ease somewhat the yoke that thy father did put upon us?

10 And the young men that were brought up with him spake unto him, saying, Thus shalt thou answer the people that spake unto thee, saying, Thy father made our yoke heavy, but make thou *it* somewhat lighter for us; thus shalt thou say unto them, My little *finger* shall be thicker than my father's loins.

11 For whereas my father put a heavy yoke upon you, I will put more to your yoke: my father chastised you with whips, but I *will chastise you* with scorpions.

12 So Jĕr′ō-bō′ăm and all the people came to Rē′hō-bō′ăm on the third day, as the king bade, saying, Come again to me on the third day.

13 And the king answered them roughly; and king Rē′hō-bō′ăm forsook the counsel of the old men,

14 And answered them after the advice of the young men, saying, My father made your yoke heavy, but I will add thereto: my father chastised you with whips, but I *will chastise you* with scorpions.

15 So the king hearkened not unto the people: for the cause was of God, that the LORD might perform his word, which he spake by the hand of Ȧ-hī′jȧh the Shī′lō-nīte to Jĕr′ō-bō′ăm the son of Nē′băt.

16 ¶ And when all Ĭs̱′rā-ēl *saw* that the king would not hearken unto them, the people answered the king, saying, What portion have we in David? and *we have* none inheritance in the son of Jesse: every man to your tents, O Ĭs̱′rā-ēl: *and* now, David, see to thine own house. So all Ĭs̱′rā-ēl went to their tents.

17 But *as for* the children of Ĭs̱′rā-ēl that dwelt in the cities of Judah, Rē′hō-bō′ăm reigned over them.

18 Then king Rē′hō-bō′ăm sent Hȧ-dō′răm that *was* over the tribute; and the children of Ĭs̱′rā-ēl stoned him with stones, that he died. But king Rē′hō-bō′ăm made speed to get him up to *his* chariot, to flee to Jerusalem.

19 And Ĭs̱′rā-ēl rebelled against the house of David unto this day.

CHAPTER 11

AND when Rē′hō-bō′ăm was come to Jerusalem, he gathered of the house of Judah and Benjamin a hundred and fourscore thousand chosen *men*, which were warriors, to fight against Ĭs̱′rā-ēl, that he might bring the kingdom again to Rē′hō-bō′ăm.

2 But the word of the LORD came to Shē-mā′iȧh the man of God, saying,

3 Speak unto Rē′hō-bō′ăm the son of

Solomon, king of Judah, and to all Ĭş′-
rā-ĕl in Judah and Benjamin, saying,
4 Thus saith the LORD, Ye shall not go
up, nor fight against your brethren: return every man to his house; for this
thing is done of me. And they obeyed
the words of the LORD, and returned
from going against Jĕr′ō-bō′ăm.
5 ¶ And Rē′hō-bō′ăm dwelt in Jerusalem, and built cities for defense in
Judah.
6 He built even Beth-lehem, and Ē′tăm,
and Tē-kō′ȧ,
7 And Bĕth′-zûr′, and Shō′cō, and
Ȧ-dŭl′lăm,
8 And Gath, and Mȧ-rē′shȧh, and
Ziph,
9 And Ăd′ō-rā′ĭm, and Lā′chĭsh, and
Ȧ-zē′kȧh,
10 And Zō′rȧh, and Ăj′ȧ-lŏn, and Hē′-
brȯn, which *are* in Judah and in Benjamin, fenced cities.
11 And he fortified the strongholds,
and put captains in them, and store of
victuals, and of oil and wine.
12 And in every several city *he put*
shields and spears, and made them exceeding strong, having Judah and Benjamin on his side.
13 ¶ And the priests and the Lē′vītes
that *were* in all Ĭş′rā-ĕl resorted to
him out of all their coasts.
14 For the Lē′vītes left their suburbs
and their possession, and came to Judah
and Jerusalem: for Jĕr′ō-bō′ăm and his
sons had cast them off from executing
the priest's office unto the LORD:
15 And he ordained him priests for the
high places, and for the devils, and for
the calves which he had made.
16 And after them, out of all the tribes
of Ĭş-rā-ĕl, such as set their hearts to
seek the LORD God of Ĭş′rā-ĕl came to
Jerusalem, to sacrifice unto the LORD
God of their fathers.
17 So they strengthened the kingdom
of Judah, and made Rē′hō-bō′ăm the
son of Solomon strong, three years: for
three years they walked in the way of
David and Solomon.
18 ¶ And Rē′hō-bō′ăm took him Mā′-
hȧ-lăth the daughter of Jĕr′ĭ-mŏth the
son of David to wife, *and* Ăb′ĭ-hāil the
daughter of Ē-lĭ′ăb the son of Jesse;
19 Which bare him children; Jē′ŭsh,
and Shĕm′ȧ-rī′ȧh, and Zā′hăm.
20 And after her he took Mā′ȧ-chȧh
the daughter of Ăb′sȧ-lŏm; which bare
him Ȧ-bī′jȧh, and Ăt′tā-ī, and Zī′zȧ, and
Shē-lō′mith.
21 And Rē′hō-bō′ăm loved Mā′ȧ-chȧh
the daughter of Ăb′sȧ-lŏm above all his
wives and his concubines: (for he took
eighteen wives, and threescore concubines; and begat twenty and eight sons,
and threescore daughters.)
22 And Rē′hō-bō′ăm made Ȧ-bī′jȧh the
son of Mā′ȧ-chȧh the chief, *to be* ruler
among his brethren: for *he thought* to
make him king.
23 And he dealt wisely, and dispersed
of all his children throughout all the
countries of Judah and Benjamin, unto
every fenced city: and he gave them
victuals in abundance. And he desired
many wives.

CHAPTER 12

AND it came to pass, when Rē′hō-
bō′ăm had established the kingdom, and had strengthened himself, he
forsook the law of the LORD, and all Ĭş′-
rā-ĕl with him.
2 And it came to pass, *that* in the fifth
year of king Rē′hō-bō′ăm, Shī′shăk king
of Egypt came up against Jerusalem, because they had transgressed against the
LORD,
3 With twelve hundred chariots, and
threescore thousand horsemen: and the
people *were* without number that came
with him out of Egypt; the Lū′bĭm, the
Sŭk′kĭ-ĭm, and the Ethiopians.
4 And he took the fenced cities which
pertained to Judah, and came to Jerusalem.
5 ¶ Then came Shē-mā′ịȧh the prophet
to Rē′hō-bō′ăm, and *to* the princes of
Judah, that were gathered together to
Jerusalem because of Shī′shăk, and said
unto them, Thus saith the LORD, Ye
have forsaken me, and therefore have I
also left you in the hand of Shī′shăk.
6 Whereupon the princes of Ĭş′rā-ĕl
and the king humbled themselves; and
they said, The LORD *is* righteous.
7 And when the LORD saw that they
humbled themselves, the word of the
LORD came to Shē-mā′ịȧh, saying, They
have humbled themselves; *therefore* I
will not destroy them, but I will grant
them some deliverance; and my wrath
shall not be poured out upon Jerusalem
by the hand of Shī′shăk.
8 Nevertheless they shall be his servants; that they may know my service,

and the service of the kingdoms of the countries.

9 So Shī′shăk king of Egypt came up against Jerusalem, and took away the treasures of the house of the LORD, and the treasures of the king's house; he took all: he carried away also the shields of gold which Solomon had made.

10 Instead of which king Rē′hō-bō′ăm made shields of brass, and committed *them* to the hands of the chief of the guard, that kept the entrance of the king's house.

11 And when the king entered into the house of the LORD, the guard came and fetched them, and brought them again into the guard chamber.

12 And when he humbled himself, the wrath of the LORD turned from him, that he would not destroy *him* altogether: and also in Judah things went well.

13 ¶ So king Rē′hō-bō′ăm strengthened himself in Jerusalem, and reigned: for Rē′hō-bō′ăm *was* one and forty years old when he began to reign, and he reigned seventeen years in Jerusalem, the city which the LORD had chosen out of all the tribes of Ĭs′rā-ēl, to put his name there. And his mother's name *was* Nā′ȧ-mȧh an Ăm′mŏn-īt′ĕss.

14 And he did evil, because he prepared not his heart to seek the LORD.

15 Now the acts of Rē′hō-bō′ăm, first and last, *are* they not written in the book of Shē-mā′ịȧh the prophet, and of Ĭd′dō the seer concerning genealogies? And *there were* wars between Rē′hō-bō′ăm and Jĕr′ō-bō′ăm continually.

16 And Rē′hō-bō′ăm slept with his fathers, and was buried in the city of David: and Ȧ-bī′jȧh his son reigned in his stead.

CHAPTER 13

NOW in the eighteenth year of king Jĕr′ō-bō′ăm began Ȧ-bī′jȧh to reign over Judah.

2 He reigned three years in Jerusalem. His mother's name also *was* Mī-chā′ịȧh the daughter of Ū′rĭ-ēl of Gĭb′ē-ȧh. And there was war between Ȧ-bī′jȧh and Jĕr′ō-bō′ăm.

3 And Ȧ-bī′jȧh set the battle in array with an army of valiant men of war, *even* four hundred thousand chosen men: Jĕr′ō-bō′ăm also set the battle in array against him with eight hundred thousand chosen men, *being* mighty men of valor.

4 ¶ And Ȧ-bī′jȧh stood up upon mount Zĕm′ȧ-rā′ĭm, which *is* in mount Ē′phrā-ĭm, and said, Hear me, thou Jĕr′ō-bō′ăm, and all Ĭs′rā-ēl;

5 Ought ye not to know that the LORD God of Ĭs′rā-ēl gave the kingdom over Ĭs′rā-ēl to David for ever, *even* to him and to his sons by a covenant of salt?

6 Yet Jĕr′ō-bō′ăm the son of Nē′băt, the servant of Solomon the son of David, is risen up, and hath rebelled against his lord.

7 And there are gathered unto him vain men, the children of Bē′lĭ-ăl, and have strengthened themselves against Rē′hō-bō′ăm the son of Solomon, when Rē′hō-bō′ăm was young and tender-hearted, and could not withstand them.

8 And now ye think to withstand the kingdom of the LORD in the hand of the sons of David; and ye *be* a great multitude, and *there are* with you golden calves, which Jĕr′ō-bō′ăm made you for gods.

9 Have ye not cast out the priests of the LORD, the sons of Aaron, and the Lē′vītes, and have made you priests after the manner of the nations of *other* lands? so that whosoever cometh to consecrate himself with a young bullock and seven rams, *the same* may be a priest of *them that are* no gods.

10 But as for us, the LORD *is* our God, and we have not forsaken him; and the priests, which minister unto the LORD, *are* the sons of Aaron, and the Lē′vītes *wait* upon *their* business:

11 And they burn unto the LORD every morning and every evening burnt sacrifices and sweet incense: the showbread also *set they in order* upon the pure table; and the candlestick of gold with the lamps thereof, to burn every evening: for we keep the charge of the LORD our God; but ye have forsaken him.

12 And, behold, God himself *is* with us for *our* captain, and his priests with sounding trumpets to cry alarm against you. O children of Ĭs′rā-ēl, fight ye not against the LORD God of your fathers; for ye shall not prosper.

13 ¶ But Jĕr′ō-bō′ăm caused an ambushment to come about behind them: so they were before Judah, and the ambushment *was* behind them.

14 And when Judah looked back, behold, the battle *was* before and behind:

and they cried unto the LORD, and the
priests sounded with the trumpets.
15 Then the men of Judah gave a shout:
and as the men of Judah shouted, it
came to pass, that God smote Jĕr′ō-
bō′ăm and all Ĭş′rā-ĕl before Ȧ-bī′jȧh
and Judah.
16 And the children of Ĭş′rā-ĕl fled before Judah: and God delivered them
into their hand.
17 And Ȧ-bī′jȧh and his people slew
them with a great slaughter: so there
fell down slain of Ĭş′rā-ĕl five hundred
thousand chosen men.
18 Thus the children of Ĭş′rā-ĕl were
brought under at that time, and the children of Judah prevailed, because they
relied upon the LORD God of their
fathers.
19 And Ȧ-bī′jȧh pursued after Jĕr′ō-
bō′ăm, and took cities from him, Beth-el
with the towns thereof, and Jĕsh′ȧ-nȧh
with the towns thereof, and Ē′phrā-ĭn
with the towns thereof.
20 Neither did Jĕr′ō-bō′ăm recover
strength again in the days of Ȧ-bī′jȧh:
and the LORD struck him, and he died.
21 ℂ But Ȧ-bī′jȧh waxed mighty, and
married fourteen wives, and begat
twenty and two sons, and sixteen
daughters.
22 And the rest of the acts of Ȧ-bī′jȧh,
and his ways, and his sayings, *are*
written in the story of the prophet
Ĭd′dō.

CHAPTER 14

SO Ȧ-bī′jȧh slept with his fathers, and
they buried him in the city of David:
and Ā′sȧ his son reigned in his stead.
In his days the land was quiet ten years.
2 And Ā′sȧ did *that which was* good and
right in the eyes of the LORD his God:
3 For he took away the altars of the
strange *gods*, and the high places, and
brake down the images, and cut down
the groves:
4 And commanded Judah to seek the
LORD God of their fathers, and to do
the law and the commandment.
5 Also he took away out of all the cities
of Judah the high places and the images:
and the kingdom was quiet before him.
6 ℂ And he built fenced cities in Judah:
for the land had rest, and he had no war
in those years; because the LORD had
given him rest.
7 Therefore he said unto Judah, Let us
build these cities, and make about *them*
walls and towers, gates and bars, *while*
the land *is* yet before us; because we
have sought the LORD our God, we have
sought *him*, and he hath given us rest
on every side. So they built and
prospered.
8 And Ā′sȧ had an army *of men* that
bare targets and spears, out of Judah
three hundred thousand; and out of
Benjamin, that bare shields and drew
bows, two hundred and fourscore thousand: all these *were* mighty men of
valor.
9 ℂ And there came out against them
Zē′rȧh the Ethiopian with a host of a
thousand thousand, and three hundred
chariots; and came unto Mȧ-rē′shȧh.
10 Then Ā′sȧ went out against him, and
they set the battle in array in the valley
of Zĕph′ȧ-thȧh at Mȧ-rē′shȧh.
11 And Ā′sȧ cried unto the LORD his
God, and said, LORD, *it is* nothing with
thee to help, whether with many, or with
them that have no power: help us, O
LORD our God; for we rest on thee, and
in thy name we go against this multitude. O LORD, thou *art* our God; let
not man prevail against thee.
12 So the LORD smote the Ethiopians
before Ā′sȧ, and before Judah; and the
Ethiopians fled.
13 And Ā′sȧ and the people that *were*
with him pursued them unto Gē′rär:
and the Ethiopians were overthrown,
that they could not recover themselves;
for they were destroyed before the
LORD, and before his host; and they
carried away very much spoil.
14 And they smote all the cities round
about Gē′rär; for the fear of the LORD
came upon them: and they spoiled all
the cities; for there was exceeding
much spoil in them.
15 They smote also the tents of cattle,
and carried away sheep and camels in
abundance, and returned to Jerusalem.

CHAPTER 15

AND the Spirit of God came upon
Ăz′ȧ-rī′ȧh the son of Ō′dĕd:
2 And he went out to meet Ā′sȧ, and
said unto him, Hear ye me, Ā′sȧ, and all
Judah and Benjamin; The LORD *is* with
you, while ye be with him; and if ye seek
him, he will be found of you; but if ye
forsake him, he will forsake you.

3 Now for a long season Ĭş′rā-ēl *hath*
been without the true God, and without
a teaching priest, and without law.
4 But when they in their trouble did
turn unto the LORD God of Ĭş′rā-ĕl, and
sought him, he was found of them.
5 And in those times *there was* no
peace to him that went out, nor to him
that came in, but great vexations *were*
upon all the inhabitants of the countries.
6 And nation was destroyed of nation,
and city of city: for God did vex them
with all adversity.
7 Be ye strong therefore, and let not
your hands be weak: for your work shall
be rewarded.
8 And when Ā′sȧ heard these words,
and the prophecy of Ō′dĕd the prophet,
he took courage, and put away the abominable idols out of all the land of Judah
and Benjamin, and out of the cities
which he had taken from mount Ē′phrā-ĭm, and renewed the altar of the LORD,
that *was* before the porch of the LORD.
9 And he gathered all Judah and Benjamin, and the strangers with them out
of Ē′phrā-ĭm and Mȧ-năs′sĕh, and out
of Simeon: for they fell to him out of Ĭş′rā-ĕl in abundance, when they saw that
the LORD his God *was* with him.
10 So they gathered themselves together at Jerusalem in the third month,
in the fifteenth year of the reign of
Ā′sȧ.
11 And they offered unto the LORD the
same time, of the spoil *which* they had
brought, seven hundred oxen and seven
thousand sheep.
12 And they entered into a covenant
to seek the LORD God of their fathers
with all their heart and with all their
soul;
13 That whosoever would not seek the
LORD God of Ĭş′rā-ĕl should be put to
death, whether small or great, whether
man or woman.
14 And they sware unto the LORD with
a loud voice, and with shouting, and
with trumpets, and with cornets.
15 And all Judah rejoiced at the oath:
for they had sworn with all their heart,
and sought him with their whole desire;
and he was found of them: and the LORD
gave them rest round about.
16 ¶ And also *concerning* Mā′ȧ-chăh
the mother of Ā′sȧ the king, he removed
her from *being* queen, because she had
made an idol in a grove: and Ā′sȧ cut
down her idol, and stamped *it,* and
burnt *it* at the brook Kĭd′rŏn.
17 But the high places were not taken
away out of Ĭş′rā-ĕl: nevertheless the
heart of Ā′sȧ was perfect all his days.
18 ¶ And he brought into the house of
God the things that his father had dedicated, and that he himself had dedicated, silver, and gold, and vessels.
19 And there was no *more* war unto the
five and thirtieth year of the reign of
Ā′sȧ.

CHAPTER 16

IN the six and thirtieth year of the
reign of Ā′sȧ, Bā′ȧ-shȧ king of Ĭş′rā-ĕl came up against Judah, and built
Rā′mȧh, to the intent that he might let
none go out or come in to Ā′sȧ king of
Judah.
2 Then Ā′sȧ brought out silver and gold
out of the treasures of the house of the
LORD and of the king's house, and sent
to Bĕn′–hā′dăd king of Syria, that dwelt
at Damascus, saying,
3 *There is* a league between me and
thee, as *there was* between my father
and thy father: behold, I have sent thee
silver and gold; go, break thy league
with Bā′ȧ-shȧ king of Ĭş′rā-ĕl, that he
may depart from me.
4 And Bĕn′–hā′dăd hearkened unto
king Ā′sȧ, and sent the captains of his
armies against the cities of Ĭş′rā-ĕl; and
they smote Ī′jŏn, and Dan, and Ā′bĕl–mā′ĭm, and all the store cities of Năph′tȧ-lī.
5 And it came to pass, when Bā′ȧ-shȧ
heard *it,* that he left off building of Rā′mȧh, and let his work cease.
6 Then Ā′sȧ the king took all Judah;
and they carried away the stones of Rā′mȧh, and the timber thereof, wherewith
Bā′ȧ-shȧ was building; and he built
therewith Gē′bȧ and Mĭz′păh.
7 ¶ And at that time Hȧ-nā′nī the seer
came to Ā′sȧ king of Judah, and said
unto him, Because thou hast relied on
the king of Syria, and not relied on the
LORD thy God, therefore is the host of
the king of Syria escaped out of thine
hand.
8 Were not the Ethiopians and the Lū′bĭm a huge host, with very many chariots and horsemen? yet, because thou
didst rely on the LORD, he delivered
them into thine hand.
9 For the eyes of the LORD run to and

fro throughout the whole earth, to show
himself strong in the behalf of *them*
whose heart *is* perfect toward him.
Herein thou hast done foolishly: therefore from henceforth thou shalt have
wars.
10 Then Ā'sȧ was wroth with the seer,
and put him in a prison house; for *he*
was in a rage with him because of this
thing. And Ā'sȧ oppressed *some* of the
people the same time.
11 ¶ And, behold, the acts of Ā'sȧ,
first and last, lo, they *are* written in the
book of the kings of Judah and Ĭs'rā-ĕl.
12 And Ā'sȧ in the thirty and ninth
year of his reign was diseased in his
feet, until his disease *was* exceeding
great: yet in his disease he sought not
to the LORD, but to the physicians.
13 ¶ And Ā'sȧ slept with his fathers,
and died in the one and fortieth year of
his reign.
14 And they buried him in his own
sepulchres, which he had made for himself in the city of David, and laid him in
the bed which was filled with sweet
odors and divers kinds *of spices* prepared by the apothecaries' art: and they
made a very great burning for him.

CHAPTER 17

AND Jē-hŏsh'ȧ-phăt his son reigned
in his stead, and strengthened
himself against Ĭs'rā-ĕl.
2 And he placed forces in all the fenced
cities of Judah, and set garrisons in the
land of Judah, and in the cities of
Ē'phrā-ĭm which Ā'sȧ his father had
taken.
3 And the LORD was with Jē-hŏsh'ȧ-
phăt, because he walked in the first
ways of his father David, and sought not
unto Bā'ȧ-lĭm;
4 But sought to the *LORD* God of his
father, and walked in his commandments, and not after the doings of
Ĭs'rā-ĕl.
5 Therefore the LORD stablished the
kingdom in his hand; and all Judah
brought to Jē-hŏsh'ȧ-phăt presents; and
he had riches and honor in abundance.
6 And his heart was lifted up in the
ways of the LORD: moreover he took
away the high places and groves out of
Judah.
7 ¶ Also in the third year of his reign
he sent to his princes, *even* to Bĕn'-
hā'ĭl, and to Ō'bȧ-dī'ȧh, and to Zĕch'ȧ-
rī'ȧh, and to Nē-thăn'ē-ĕl, and to Mī-
chā'ịȧh, to teach in the cities of Judah.
8 And with them *he sent* Lē'vītes,
even Shē-mā'ịȧh, and Nĕth'ȧ-nī'ȧh, and
Zĕb'ȧ-dī'ȧh, and Ăs'ȧ-hĕl, and Shē-
mĭr'ȧ-mŏth, and Jē-hŏn'ȧ-thăn, and
Ăd'ō-nī'jȧh, and Tō-bī'jȧh, and Tŏb'-
ăd'ō-nī'jȧh, Lē'vītes; and with them
Ē'lĭsh-ȧ-mä and Jē-hō'răm, priests.
9 And they taught in Judah, and *had*
the book of the law of the LORD with
them, and went about throughout all the
cities of Judah, and taught the people.
10 ¶ And the fear of the LORD fell
upon all the kingdoms of the lands that
were round about Judah, so that they
made no war against Jē-hŏsh'ȧ-phăt.
11 Also *some* of the Phĭ-lĭs'tīneș
brought Jē-hŏsh'ȧ-phăt presents, and
tribute silver; and the Arabians brought
him flocks, seven thousand and seven
hundred rams, and seven thousand and
seven hundred he goats.
12 ¶ And Je-hŏsh'ȧ-phăt waxed great
exceedingly; and he built in Judah castles, and cities of store.
13 And he had much business in the
cities of Judah: and the men of war,
mighty men of valor, *were* in Jerusalem.
14 And these *are* the numbers of them
according to the house of their fathers:
Of Judah, the captains of thousands;
Ăd'nȧh the chief, and with him mighty
men of valor three hundred thousand.
15 And next to him *was* Jē'hō-hā'năn
the captain, and with him two hundred
and fourscore thousand.
16 And next him *was* Ăm'ȧ-sī'ȧh the
son of Zĭch'rī, who willingly offered himself unto the LORD; and with him two
hundred thousand mighty men of valor.
17 And of Benjamin; Ē-lī'ȧ-dȧ a mighty
man of valor, and with him armed men
with bow and shield two hundred
thousand.
18 And next him *was* Jē-hŏz'ȧ-băd,
and with him a hundred and fourscore
thousand ready prepared for the war.
19 These waited on the king, besides
those whom the king put in the fenced
cities throughout all Judah.

CHAPTER 18

NOW Jē-hŏsh'ȧ-phăt had riches and
honor in abundance, and joined
affinity with Ahab.
2 And after *certain* years he went down
to Ahab to Sȧ-mā'rĭ-ȧ. And Ahab killed

sheep and oxen for him in abundance,
and for the people that *he had* with him,
and persuaded him to go up *with him* to
Rā′mŏth–gĭl′ē-ăd.
3 And Ahab king of Ĭş′rā-ēl said unto
Jē-hŏsh′ȧ-phăt king of Judah, Wilt thou
go with me to Rā′mŏth–gĭl′ē-ăd? And he
answered him, I *am* as thou *art*, and my
people as thy people; and *we will be*
with thee in the war.
4 ℂ And Jē-hŏsh′ȧ-phăt said unto the
king of Ĭş′rā-ēl, Inquire, I pray thee, at
the word of the LORD to-day.
5 Therefore the king of Ĭş′rā-ēl gathered together of prophets four hundred
men, and said unto them, Shall we go
to Rā′mŏth–gĭl′ē-ăd to battle, or shall I
forbear? And they said, Go up; for God
will deliver *it* into the king's hand.
6 But Jē-hŏsh′ȧ-phăt said, *Is there* not
here a prophet of the LORD besides,
that we might inquire of him?
7 And the king of Ĭş′rā-ēl said unto
Jē-hŏsh′ȧ-phăt, *There is* yet one man,
by whom we may inquire of the LORD:
but I hate him; for he never prophesied
good unto me, but always evil: the same
is Mī-cā′ịah the son of Ĭm′lȧ. And
Jē-hŏsh′ȧ-phăt said, Let not the king
say so.
8 And the king of Ĭş′rā-ēl called for one
of his officers, and said, Fetch quickly
Mī-cā′ịah the son of Ĭm′lȧ.
9 And the king of Ĭş′rā-ēl and Jē-hŏsh′-
ȧ-phăt king of Judah sat either of them
on his throne, clothed in *their* robes, and
they sat in a void place at the entering
in of the gate of Sȧ-mā′rĭ-ȧ; and all the
prophets prophesied before them.
10 And Zĕd′ē-kī′ȧh the son of Chē-
nā′ȧ-năh had made him horns of iron,
and said, Thus saith the LORD, With
these thou shalt push Syria until they
be consumed.
11 And all the prophets prophesied so,
saying, Go up to Rā′mŏth–gĭl′ē-ăd, and
prosper: for the LORD shall deliver *it*
into the hand of the king.
12 And the messenger that went to call
Mī-cā′ịah spake to him, saying, Behold,
the words of the prophets *declare* good
to the king with one assent; let thy word
therefore, I pray thee, be like one of
theirs, and speak thou good.
13 And Mī-cā′ịah said, *As* the LORD
liveth, even what my God saith, that will
I speak.
14 And when he was come to the king,
the king said unto him, Mī-cā′ịah, shall
we go to Rā′mŏth–gĭl′ē-ăd to battle, or
shall I forbear? And he said, Go ye up,
and prosper, and they shall be delivered
into your hand.
15 And the king said to him, How many
times shall I adjure thee that thou say
nothing but the truth to me in the name
of the LORD?
16 Then he said, I did see all Ĭş′rā-ēl
scattered upon the mountains, as sheep
that have no shepherd: and the LORD
said, These have no master; let them
return *therefore* every man to his house
in peace.
17 And the king of Ĭş′rā-ēl said to Jē-
hŏsh′ȧ-phăt, Did I not tell thee *that* he
would not prophesy good unto me, but
evil?
18 Again he said, Therefore hear the
word of the LORD; I saw the LORD sitting upon his throne, and all the host of
heaven standing on his right hand and
on his left.
19 And the LORD said, Who shall entice Ahab king of Ĭş′rā-ēl, that he may
go up and fall at Rā′mŏth–gĭl′ē-ăd? And
one spake saying after this manner, and
another saying after that manner.
20 Then there came out a spirit, and
stood before the LORD, and said, I will
entice him. And the LORD said unto
him, Wherewith?
21 And he said, I will go out, and be a
lying spirit in the mouth of all his prophets. And *the LORD* said, Thou shalt
entice *him*, and thou shalt also prevail:
go out, and do *even* so.
22 Now therefore, behold, the LORD
hath put a lying spirit in the mouth of
these thy prophets, and the LORD hath
spoken evil against thee.
23 Then Zĕd′ē-kī′ȧh the son of Chē-
nā′ȧ-năh came near, and smote Mī-cā′-
ịah upon the cheek, and said, Which
way went the Spirit of the LORD from
me to speak unto thee?
24 And Mī-cā′ịah said, Behold, thou
shalt see on that day when thou shalt
go into an inner chamber to hide thyself.
25 Then the king of Ĭş′rā-ēl said, Take
ye Mī-cā′ịah, and carry him back to
Ā′mŏn the governor of the city, and to
Jō′ăsh the king's son;
26 And say, Thus saith the king, Put
this *fellow* in the prison, and feed him
with bread of affliction and with water
of affliction, until I return in peace.

27 And Mī-cā'ịah said, If thou certainly
return in peace, *then* hath not the LORD
spoken by me. And he said, Hearken,
all ye people.
28 So the king of Ĭs̱'rā-ĕl and Jē-hŏsh'-
ȧ-phăt the king of Judah went up to Rā'-
mŏth–gĭl'ē-ăd.
29 And the king of Ĭs̱'rā-ĕl said unto
Jē-hŏsh'ȧ-phăt, I will disguise myself,
and will go to the battle; but put thou on
thy robes. So the king of Ĭs̱'rā-ĕl disguised himself; and they went to the
battle.
30 Now the king of Syria had commanded the captains of the chariots that
were with him, saying, Fight ye not
with small or great, save only with the
king of Ĭs̱'rā-ĕl.
31 And it came to pass, when the captains of the chariots saw Jē-hŏsh'ȧ-phăt,
that they said, It *is* the king of Ĭs̱'rā-ĕl.
Therefore they compassed about him to
fight: but Jē-hŏsh'ȧ-phăt cried out, and
the LORD helped him; and God moved
them *to depart* from him.
32 For it came to pass, that, when the
captains of the chariots perceived that
it was not the king of Ĭs̱'rā-ĕl, they
turned back again from pursuing him.
33 And a *certain* man drew a bow at a
venture, and smote the king of Ĭs̱'rā-ĕl
between the joints of the harness: therefore he said to his chariot man, Turn
thine hand, that thou mayest carry me
out of the host; for I am wounded.
34 And the battle increased that day:
howbeit the king of Ĭs̱'rā-ĕl stayed *himself* up in *his* chariot against the Syrians
until the even: and about the time of the
sun going down he died.

CHAPTER 19

AND Jē-hŏsh'ȧ-phăt the king of Judah returned to his house in peace
to Jerusalem.
2 And Jē'hū the son of Hȧ-nā'nī the
seer went out to meet him, and said to
king Jē-hŏsh'ȧ-phăt, Shouldest thou
help the ungodly, and love them that
hate the LORD? therefore *is* wrath upon
thee from before the LORD.
3 Nevertheless, there are good things
found in thee, in that thou hast taken
away the groves out of the land, and
hast prepared thine heart to seek God.
4 And Jē-hŏsh'ȧ-phăt dwelt at Jerusalem: and he went out again through the
people from Bē'ĕr–shē'bȧ to mount
Ē'phrā-ĭm, and brought them back unto
the LORD God of their fathers.
5 ℂ And he set judges in the land
throughout all the fenced cities of Judah, city by city,
6 And said to the judges, Take heed
what ye do: for ye judge not for man,
but for the LORD, who *is* with you in the
judgment.
7 Wherefore now let the fear of the
LORD be upon you; take heed and do *it:*
for *there is* no iniquity with the LORD
our God, nor respect of persons, nor
taking of gifts.
8 ℂ Moreover in Jerusalem did Jē-
hŏsh'ȧ-phăt set of the Lē'vītes, and *of*
the priests, and of the chief of the fathers
of Ĭs̱'rā-ĕl, for the judgment of the LORD,
and for controversies, when they returned to Jerusalem.
9 And he charged them, saying, Thus
shall ye do in the fear of the LORD, faithfully, and with a perfect heart.
10 And what cause soever shall come
to you of your brethren that dwell in
their cities, between blood and blood,
between law and commandment, statutes and judgments, ye shall even warn
them that they trespass not against the
LORD, and *so* wrath come upon you, and
upon your brethren: this do, and ye
shall not trespass.
11 And, behold, Ăm'ȧ-rī'ȧh the chief
priest *is* over you in all matters of the
LORD; and Zĕb'ȧ-dī'ȧh the son of Ĭsh'-
mā-ĕl, the ruler of the house of Judah,
for all the king's matters: also the Lē'-
vītes *shall be* officers before you. Deal
courageously, and the LORD shall be
with the good.

CHAPTER 20

IT came to pass after this also, *that* the
children of Mō'ăb, and the children
of Ammon, and with them *other* besides
the Ammonites, came against Jē-hŏsh'-
ȧ-phăt to battle.
2 Then there came some that told Jē-
hŏsh'ȧ-phăt, saying, There cometh a
great multitude against thee from beyond the sea on this side Syria; and,
behold, they *be* in Hăz'ȧ-zŏn–tā'mȧr,
which *is* Ĕn–gē'dī.
3 And Jē-hŏsh'ȧ-phăt feared, and set
himself to seek the LORD, and proclaimed a fast throughout all Judah.
4 And Judah gathered themselves together, to ask *help* of the LORD: even

out of all the cities of Judah they came to seek the LORD.

5 ¶ And Jē-hŏsh′ȧ-phăt stood in the congregation of Judah and Jerusalem, in the house of the LORD, before the new court,

6 And said, O LORD God of our fathers, *art* not thou God in heaven? and rulest *not* thou over all the kingdoms of the heathen? and in thine hand *is there not* power and might, so that none is able to withstand thee?

7 *Art* not thou our God, *who* didst drive out the inhabitants of this land before thy people Ĭş′rā-ĕl, and gavest it to the seed of Abraham thy friend for ever?

8 And they dwelt therein, and have built thee a sanctuary therein for thy name, saying,

9 If, *when* evil cometh upon us, *as* the sword, judgment, or pestilence, or famine, we stand before this house, and in thy presence, (for thy name *is* in this house,) and cry unto thee in our affliction, then thou wilt hear and help.

10 And now, behold, the children of Ammon and Mō′ăb and mount Sē′ĭr, whom thou wouldest not let Ĭş′rā-ĕl invade, when they came out of the land of Egypt, but they turned from them, and destroyed them not;

11 Behold, *I say, how* they reward us, to come to cast us out of thy possession, which thou hast given us to inherit.

12 O our God, wilt thou not judge them? for we have no might against this great company that cometh against us; neither know we what to do: but our eyes *are* upon thee.

13 And all Judah stood before the LORD, with their little ones, their wives, and their children.

14 ¶ Then upon Jȧ-hā′zĭ-ĕl the son of Zĕch′ȧ-rī′ȧh, the son of Bē-nā′ịȧh, the son of Jē-ī′ĕl, the son of Măt′tȧ-nī′ȧh, a Lē′vīte of the sons of Ā′săph, came the Spirit of the LORD in the midst of the congregation;

15 And he said, Hearken ye, all Judah, and ye inhabitants of Jerusalem, and thou king Jē-hŏsh′ȧ-phăt, Thus saith the LORD unto you, Be not afraid nor dismayed by reason of this great multitude; for the battle *is* not yours, but God's.

16 To-morrow go ye down against them: behold, they come up by the cliff of Zīz; and ye shall find them at the end of the brook, before the wilderness of Jē-rụ′ĕl.

17 Ye shall not *need* to fight in this *battle:* set yourselves, stand ye *still,* and see the salvation of the LORD with you, O Judah and Jerusalem: fear not, nor be dismayed; to-morrow go out against them: for the LORD *will be* with you.

18 And Jē-hŏsh′ȧ-phăt bowed his head with *his* face to the ground: and all Judah and the inhabitants of Jerusalem fell before the LORD, worshipping the LORD.

19 And the Lē′vītes, of the children of the Kō′hăth-ītes, and of the children of the Kôr′hītes, stood up to praise the LORD God of Ĭş′rā-ĕl with a loud voice on high.

20 ¶ And they rose early in the morning, and went forth into the wilderness of Tē-kō′ȧ: and as they went forth, Jē-hŏsh′ȧ-phăt stood and said, Hear me, O Judah, and ye inhabitants of Jerusalem; Believe in the LORD your God, so shall ye be established; believe his prophets, so shall ye prosper.

21 And when he had consulted with the people, he appointed singers unto the LORD, and that should praise the beauty of holiness, as they went out before the army, and to say, Praise the LORD; for his mercy *endureth* for ever.

22 ¶ And when they began to sing and to praise, the LORD set ambushments against the children of Ammon, Mō′ăb, and mount Sē′ĭr, which were come against Judah; and they were smitten.

23 For the children of Ammon and Mō′ăb stood up against the inhabitants of mount Sē′ĭr, utterly to slay and destroy *them:* and when they had made an end of the inhabitants of Sē′ĭr, every one helped to destroy another.

24 And when Judah came toward the watchtower in the wilderness, they looked unto the multitude, and, behold, they *were* dead bodies fallen to the earth, and none escaped.

25 And when Jē-hŏsh′ȧ-phăt and his people came to take away the spoil of them, they found among them in abundance both riches with the dead bodies, and precious jewels, which they stripped off for themselves, more than they could carry away: and they were three days in gathering of the spoil, it was so much.

26 ¶ And on the fourth day they assembled themselves in the valley of Bĕr′ȧ-chȧh; for there they blessed the

LORD: therefore the name of the same place was called, The valley of Bĕr′ȧ-chȧh, unto this day.

27 Then they returned, every man of Judah and Jerusalem, and Jē-hŏsh′ȧ-phăt in the forefront of them, to go again to Jerusalem with joy; for the LORD had made them to rejoice over their enemies.

28 And they came to Jerusalem with psalteries and harps and trumpets unto the house of the LORD.

29 And the fear of God was on all the kingdoms of *those* countries, when they had heard that the LORD fought against the enemies of Ĭş′rā-ĕl.

30 So the realm of Jē-hŏsh′ȧ-phăt was quiet: for his God gave him rest round about.

31 ¶ And Jē-hŏsh′ȧ-phăt reigned over Judah: *he was* thirty and five years old when he began to reign, and he reigned twenty and five years in Jerusalem. And his mother's name *was* Ȧ-zū′bȧh the daughter of Shĭl′hī.

32 And he walked in the way of Ā′sȧ his father, and departed not from it, doing *that which was* right in the sight of the LORD.

33 Howbeit the high places were not taken away: for as yet the people had not prepared their hearts unto the God of their fathers.

34 Now the rest of the acts of Jē-hŏsh′ȧ-phăt, first and last, behold, they *are* written in the book of Jē′hū the son of Hȧ-nā′nī, who *is* mentioned in the book of the kings of Ĭş′rā-ĕl.

35 ¶ And after this did Jē-hŏsh′ȧ-phăt king of Judah join himself with Ā′hȧ-zī′ȧh king of Ĭş′rā-ĕl, who did very wickedly:

36 And he joined himself with him to make ships to go to Tär′shĭsh: and they made the ships in Ē′zĭ-ŏn–gā′bĕr.

37 Then Ĕl′ĭ-ē′zĕr the son of Dō′dȧ-vȧh of Mȧ-rē′shȧh prophesied against Jē-hŏsh′ȧ-phăt, saying, Because thou hast joined thyself with Ā′hȧ-zī′ȧh, the LORD hath broken thy works. And the ships were broken, that they were not able to go to Tär′shĭsh.

CHAPTER 21

NOW Jē-hŏsh′ȧ-phăt slept with his fathers, and was buried with his fathers in the city of David. And Jē-hō′răm his son reigned in his stead.

2 And he had brethren the sons of Jē-hŏsh′ȧ-phăt, Ăz′ȧ-rī′ȧh, and Jē-hī′ĕl, and Zĕch′ȧ-rī′ȧh, and Ăz′ȧ-rī′ȧh, and Mī′chā-ĕl, and Shĕph′ȧ-tī′ȧh: all these *were* the sons of Jē-hŏsh′ȧ-phăt king of Ĭş′rā-ĕl.

3 And their father gave them great gifts of silver, and of gold, and of precious things, with fenced cities in Judah: but the kingdom gave he to Jē-hō′răm; because he *was* the firstborn.

4 Now when Jē-hō′răm was risen up to the kingdom of his father, he strengthened himself, and slew all his brethren with the sword, and *divers* also of the princes of Ĭş′rā-ĕl.

5 ¶ Jē-hō′răm *was* thirty and two years old when he began to reign, and he reigned eight years in Jerusalem.

6 And he walked in the way of the kings of Ĭş′rā-ĕl, like as did the house of Ahab: for he had the daughter of Ahab to wife: and he wrought *that which was* evil in the eyes of the LORD.

7 Howbeit the LORD would not destroy the house of David, because of the covenant that he had made with David, and as he promised to give a light to him and to his sons for ever.

8 ¶ In his days the Ē′dŏm-ītes revolted from under the dominion of Judah, and made themselves a king.

9 Then Jē-hō′răm went forth with his princes, and all his chariots with him: and he rose up by night, and smote the Ē′dŏm-ītes which compassed him in, and the captains of the chariots.

10 So the Ē′dŏm-ītes revolted from under the hand of Judah unto this day. The same time *also* did Lĭb′nȧh revolt from under his hand; because he had forsaken the LORD God of his fathers.

11 Moreover he made high places in the mountains of Judah, and caused the inhabitants of Jerusalem to commit fornication, and compelled Judah *thereto*.

12 ¶ And there came a writing to him from Ē-lī′jȧh the prophet, saying, Thus saith the LORD God of David thy father, Because thou hast not walked in the ways of Jē-hŏsh′ȧ-phăt thy father, nor in the ways of Ā′sȧ king of Judah,

13 But hast walked in the way of the kings of Ĭş′ra-ĕl, and hast made Judah and the inhabitants of Jerusalem to go a whoring, like to the whoredoms of the house of Ahab, and also hast slain thy brethren of thy father's house, *which were* better than thyself:

14 Behold, with a great plague will
the LORD smite thy people, and thy
children, and thy wives, and all thy
goods:
15 And thou *shalt have* great sickness
by disease of thy bowels, until thy bowels fall out by reason of the sickness day
by day.
16 ℂ Moreover the LORD stirred up
against Jē-hō′răm the spirit of the Phĭ-
lĭs′tīneş, and of the Arabians, that *were*
near the Ethiopians:
17 And they came up into Judah, and
brake into it, and carried away all the
substance that was found in the king's
house, and his sons also, and his wives;
so that there was never a son left him,
save Jē-hō′ȧ-hăz, the youngest of his
sons.
18 ℂ And after all this the LORD smote
him in his bowels with an incurable
disease.
19 And it came to pass, that in process
of time, after the end of two years, his
bowels fell out by reason of his sickness:
so he died of sore diseases. And his
people made no burning for him, like
the burning of his fathers.
20 Thirty and two years old was he
when he began to reign, and he reigned
in Jerusalem eight years, and departed
without being desired. Howbeit they
buried him in the city of David, but not
in the sepulchres of the kings.

CHAPTER 22

AND the inhabitants of Jerusalem
made Ā′hȧ-zī′ȧh his youngest son
king in his stead: for the band of men
that came with the Arabians to the camp
had slain all the eldest. So Ā′hȧ-zī′ȧh
the son of Jē-hō′răm king of Judah
reigned.
2 Forty and two years old *was* Ā′hȧ-
zī′ȧh when he began to reign, and he
reigned one year in Jerusalem. His
mother's name also *was* Ăth′ȧ-lī′ȧh the
daughter of Ŏm′rī.
3 He also walked in the ways of the
house of Ahab: for his mother was his
counselor to do wickedly.
4 Wherefore he did evil in the sight of
the LORD like the house of Ahab: for
they were his counselors, after the death
of his father, to his destruction.
5 ℂ He walked also after their counsel, and went with Jē-hō′răm the son of
Ahab king of Ĭş′rā-ĕl to war against
Hăz′ā-ĕl king of Syria at Rā′mŏth-
gĭl′ē-ăd: and the Syrians smote Jō′răm.
6 And he returned to be healed in Jĕz′-
rē-ĕl because of the wounds which were
given him at Rā′mȧh, when he fought
with Hăz′ā-ĕl king of Syria. And Ăz′ȧ-
rī′ȧh the son of Jē-hō′răm king of Judah
went down to see Jē-hō′răm the son
of Ahab at Jĕz′rē-ĕl, because he was
sick.
7 And the destruction of Ā′hȧ-zī′ȧh
was of God by coming to Jō′răm: for
when he was come, he went out with Jē-
hō′răm against Jē′hū the son of Nĭm′-
shī, whom the LORD had anointed to cut
off the house of Ahab.
8 And it came to pass, that, when Jē′hū
was executing judgment upon the house
of Ahab, and found the princes of Judah,
and the sons of the brethren of Ā′hȧ-
zī′ȧh, that ministered to Ā′hȧ-zī′ȧh, he
slew them.
9 And he sought Ā′hȧ-zī′ȧh: and they
caught him, (for he was hid in Sȧ-mā′-
rĭ-ȧ,) and brought him to Jē′hū: and
when they had slain him, they buried
him: Because, said they, he *is* the son of
Jē-hŏsh′ȧ-phăt, who sought the LORD
with all his heart. So the house of Ā′hȧ-
zī′ȧh had no power to keep still the
kingdom.
10 ℂ But when Ăth′ȧ-lī′ȧh the mother
of Ā′hȧ-zī′ȧh saw that her son was dead,
she arose and destroyed all the seed
royal of the house of Judah.
11 But Jē′hō-shăb′ē-ăth, the daughter
of the king, took Jō′ăsh the son of
Ā′hȧ-zī′ȧh, and stole him from among
the king's sons that were slain, and put
him and his nurse in a bedchamber. So
Jē′hō-shăb′ē-ăth, the daughter of king
Jē-hō′răm, the wife of Jē-hoi′ȧ-dȧ the
priest, (for she was the sister of Ā′hȧ-
zī′ȧh,) hid him from Ăth′ȧ-lī′ȧh, so that
she slew him not.
12 And he was with them hid in the
house of God six years: and Ăth′ȧ-lī′ȧh
reigned over the land.

CHAPTER 23

AND in the seventh year Jē-hoi′ȧ-dȧ
strengthened himself, and took the
captains of hundreds, Ăz′ȧ-rī′ȧh the son
of Jē-rō′hăm, and Ĭsh′mā-ĕl the son of
Jē′hō-hā′năn, and Ăz′ȧ-rī′ȧh the son of
Ō′bĕd, and Mā′ȧ-sē′ịah the son of Ȧ-dā′-
ịah and Ē-lĭsh′ȧ-phăt the son of Zĭch′rī,
into covenant with him.

2 And they went about in Judah, and
gathered the Lē′vītes out of all the cities
of Judah, and the chief of the fathers of
Iş′rā-ĕl, and they came to Jerusalem.
3 And all the congregation made a
covenant with the king in the house of
God. And he said unto them, Behold,
the king's son shall reign, as the LORD
hath said of the sons of David.
4 This *is* the thing that ye shall do; A
third part of you entering on the sabbath, of the priests and of the Lē′vītes,
shall be porters of the doors;
5 And a third part *shall be* at the king's
house; and a third part at the gate of the
foundation: and all the people *shall be*
in the courts of the house of the LORD.
6 But let none come into the house of
the LORD, save the priests, and they
that minister of the Lē′vītes; they shall
go in, for they *are* holy: but all the people shall keep the watch of the LORD.
7 And the Lē′vītes shall compass the
king round about, every man with his
weapons in his hand; and whosoever
else cometh into the house, he shall be
put to death: but be ye with the king
when he cometh in, and when he goeth
out.
8 So the Lē′vītes and all Judah did
according to all things that Jē-hoi′ā-dȧ
the priest had commanded, and took
every man his men that were to come in
on the sabbath, with them that were to
go *out* on the sabbath: for Jē-hoi′ā-dȧ
the priest dismissed not the courses.
9 Moreover Jē-hoi′ā-dȧ the priest
delivered to the captains of hundreds
spears, and bucklers, and shields, that
had been king David's, which *were* in
the house of God.
10 And he set all the people, every man
having his weapon in his hand, from the
right side of the temple to the left side
of the temple, along by the altar and the
temple, by the king round about.
11 Then they brought out the king's
son, and put upon him the crown, and
gave him the testimony, and made him
king. And Jē-hoi′ā-dȧ and his sons
anointed him, and said, God save the
king.
12 ¶ Now when Ăth′ā-lī′ăh heard the
noise of the people running and praising
the king, she came to the people into the
house of the LORD:
13 And she looked, and, behold, the
king stood at his pillar at the entering
in, and the princes and the trumpets by
the king: and all the people of the land
rejoiced, and sounded with trumpets,
also the singers with instruments of
music, and such as taught to sing praise.
Then Ăth′ā-lī′ăh rent her clothes, and
said, Treason, treason.
14 Then Jē-hoi′ā-dȧ the priest brought
out the captains of hundreds that were
set over the host, and said unto them,
Have her forth of the ranges: and whoso
followeth her, let him be slain with the
sword. For the priest said, Slay her not
in the house of the LORD.
15 So they laid hands on her; and when
she was come to the entering of the
horse gate by the king's house, they
slew her there.
16 ¶ And Jē-hoi′ā-dȧ made a covenant between him, and between all the
people, and between the king, that they
should be the LORD's people.
17 Then all the people went to the
house of Bā′ăl, and brake it down, and
brake his altars and his images in
pieces, and slew Măt′tăn the priest of
Bā′ăl before the altars.
18 Also Jē-hoi′ā-dȧ appointed the
offices of the house of the LORD by the
hand of the priests the Lē′vītes, whom
David had distributed in the house of
the LORD, to offer the burnt offerings of
the LORD, as *it is* written in the law of
Moses, with rejoicing and with singing,
as it was ordained by David.
19 And he set the porters at the gates
of the house of the LORD, that none
which was unclean in any thing should
enter in.
20 And he took the captains of hundreds, and the nobles, and the governors
of the people, and all the people of the
land, and brought down the king from
the house of the LORD: and they came
through the high gate into the king's
house, and set the king upon the throne
of the kingdom.
21 And all the people of the land rejoiced: and the city was quiet, after
that they had slain Ăth′ā-lī′ăh with the
sword.

CHAPTER 24

JŌ′ĂSH *was* seven years old when he
began to reign, and he reigned forty
years in Jerusalem. His mother's name
also was Zĭb′ĭ-ăh of Bē′ẽr-shē′bȧ.
2 And Jō′ăsh did *that which was* right

in the sight of the LORD all the days of
Jē-hôi'ȧ-dȧ the priest.
3 And Jē-hôi'ȧ-dȧ took for him two
wives; and he begat sons and daughters.
4 ¶ And it came to pass after this, *that*
Jō'ăsh was minded to repair the house
of the LORD.
5 And he gathered together the priests
and the Lē'vītes, and said to them, Go
out unto the cities of Judah, and gather
of all Ĭş'rā-ĕl money to repair the house
of your God from year to year, and see
that ye hasten the matter. Howbeit the
Lē'vītes hastened *it* not.
6 And the king called for Jē-hôi'ȧ-dȧ
the chief, and said unto him, Why hast
thou not required of the Lē'vītes to
bring in out of Judah and out of Jerusalem
the collection, *according to the
commandment* of Moses the servant of
the LORD, and of the congregation of
Ĭş'rā-ĕl, for the tabernacle of witness?
7 For the sons of Ăth'ȧ-lī'ăh, that
wicked woman, had broken up the
house of God; and also all the dedicated
things of the house of the LORD did they
bestow upon Bā'ȧ-lĭm.
8 And at the king's commandment they
made a chest, and set it without at the
gate of the house of the LORD.
9 And they made a proclamation
through Judah and Jerusalem, to bring
in to the LORD the collection *that* Moses
the servant of God *laid* upon Ĭş'rā-ĕl in
the wilderness.
10 And all the princes and all the people
rejoiced, and brought in, and cast into
the chest, until they had made an end.
11 Now it came to pass, that at what
time the chest was brought unto the
king's office by the hand of the Lē'vītes,
and when they saw that *there was* much
money, the king's scribe and the high
priest's officer came and emptied the
chest, and took it, and carried it to his
place again. Thus they did day by day,
and gathered money in abundance.
12 And the king and Jē-hôi'ȧ-dȧ gave
it to such as did the work of the service
of the house of the LORD, and hired
masons and carpenters to repair the
house of the LORD, and also such as
wrought iron and brass to mend the
house of the LORD.
13 So the workmen wrought, and the
work was perfected by them, and they
set the house of God in his state, and
strengthened it.
14 And when they had finished *it*, they
brought the rest of the money before the
king and Jē-hôi'ȧ-dȧ, whereof were
made vessels for the house of the LORD,
even vessels to minister, and to offer
withal, and spoons, and vessels of gold
and silver. And they offered burnt
offerings in the house of the LORD continually
all the days of Jē-hôi'ȧ-dȧ.
15 ¶ But Jē-hôi'ȧ-dȧ waxed old, and
was full of days when he died; a hundred
and thirty years old *was he* when
he died.
16 And they buried him in the city of
David among the kings, because he had
done good in Ĭş'rā-ĕl, both toward God,
and toward his house.
17 Now after the death of Jē-hôi'ȧ-dȧ
came the princes of Judah, and made
obeisance to the king. Then the king
hearkened unto them.
18 And they left the house of the
LORD God of their fathers, and served
groves and idols: and wrath came upon
Judah and Jerusalem for this their
trespass.
19 Yet he sent prophets to them, to
bring them again unto the LORD; and
they testified against them: but they
would not give ear.
20 And the Spirit of God came upon
Zĕch'ȧ-rī'ăh the son of Jē-hôi'ȧ-dȧ the
priest, which stood above the people,
and said unto them, Thus saith God,
Why transgress ye the commandments
of the LORD, that ye cannot prosper? because
ye have forsaken the LORD, he
hath also forsaken you.
21 And they conspired against him,
and stoned him with stones at the commandment
of the king in the court of
the house of the LORD.
22 Thus Jō'ăsh the king remembered
not the kindness which Jē'hôi'ȧ-dȧ his
father had done to him, but slew his
son. And when he died, he said, The
LORD look upon *it*, and require *it*.
23 ¶ And it came to pass at the end of
the year, *that* the host of Syria came up
against him: and they came to Judah
and Jerusalem, and destroyed all the
princes of the people from among the
people, and sent all the spoil of them
unto the king of Damascus.
24 For the army of the Syrians came
with a small company of men, and the
LORD delivered a very great host into
their hand, because they had forsaken

the LORD God of their fathers. So they
executed judgment against Jō′ăsh.
25 And when they were departed from
him, (for they left him in great diseases,)
his own servants conspired against him
for the blood of the sons of Jē-hôi′ȧ-dȧ
the priest, and slew him on his bed, and
he died: and they buried him in the city
of David, but they buried him not in the
sepulchres of the kings.
26 And these are they that conspired
against him; Zā′băd the son of Shĭm′ē-
ăth an Ăm′mŏn-īt′ĕss, and Jē-hŏz′ȧ-
băd the son of Shĭm′rĭth a Mō′ăb-īt′ĕss.
27 ¶ Now *concerning* his sons, and
the greatness of the burdens *laid* upon
him, and the repairing of the house
of God, behold, they *are* written in
the story of the book of the kings.
And Ăm′ȧ-zī′ȧh his son reigned in his
stead.

CHAPTER 25

ĂM′Ȧ-ZĪ′ȦH *was* twenty and five
years old *when* he began to reign,
and he reigned twenty and nine years in
Jerusalem. And his mother's name *was*
Jē′hō-ăd′dăn of Jerusalem.
2 And he did *that which was* right in
the sight of the LORD, but not with a
perfect heart.
3 ¶ Now it came to pass, when the
kingdom was established to him, that he
slew his servants that had killed the
king his father.
4 But he slew not their children, but
did as *it is* written in the law in the book
of Moses, where the LORD commanded,
saying, The fathers shall not die for the
children, neither shall the children die
for the fathers, but every man shall die
for his own sin.
5 ¶ Moreover Ăm′ȧ-zī′ȧh gathered
Judah together, and made them captains over thousands, and captains over
hundreds, according to the houses of
their fathers, throughout all Judah and
Benjamin: and he numbered them from
twenty years old and above, and found
them three hundred thousand choice
men, able to go forth to war, that could
handle spear and shield.
6 He hired also a hundred thousand
mighty men of valor out of Ĭṣ′rā-ĕl for
a hundred talents of silver.
7 But there came a man of God to him,
saying, O king, let not the army of
Ĭṣ′rā-ĕl go with thee; for the LORD *is*
not with Ĭṣ′rā-ĕl, *to wit, with* all the
children of Ē′phrā-ĭm.
8 But if thou wilt go, do *it*, be strong
for the battle: God shall make thee fall
before the enemy: for God hath power
to help, and to cast down.
9 And Ăm′ȧ-zī′ȧh said to the man of
God, But what shall we do for the hundred talents which I have given to the
army of Ĭṣ′rā-ĕl? And the man of God
answered, The LORD is able to give thee
much more than this.
10 Then Ăm′ȧ-zī′ȧh separated them,
to wit, the army that was come to him
out of Ē′phrā-ĭm, to go home again:
wherefore their anger was greatly
kindled against Judah, and they returned home in great anger.
11 ¶ And Ăm′ȧ-zī′ȧh strengthened
himself, and led forth his people, and
went to the valley of salt, and smote of
the children of Sē′ïr ten thousand.
12 And *other* ten thousand *left* alive
did the children of Judah carry away
captive, and brought them unto the top
of the rock, and cast them down from
the top of the rock, that they all were
broken in pieces.
13 ¶ But the soldiers of the army
which Ăm′ȧ-zī′ȧh sent back, that they
should not go with him to battle, fell
upon the cities of Judah, from Sȧ-mā′-
rĭ-ȧ even unto Bĕth′-hō′rŏn, and smote
three thousand of them, and took much
spoil.
14 ¶ Now it came to pass, after that
Ăm′ȧ-zī′ȧh was come from the slaughter
of the Ē′dŏm-ītes, that he brought the
gods of the children of Sē′ïr, and set
them up *to be* his gods, and bowed down
himself before them, and burned incense unto them.
15 Wherefore the anger of the LORD
was kindled against Ăm′ȧ-zī′ȧh, and he
sent unto him a prophet, which said unto
him, Why hast thou sought after the
gods of the people, which could not deliver their own people out of thine hand?
16 And it came to pass, as he talked
with him, that *the king* said unto him, Art
thou made of the king's counsel? forbear; why shouldest thou be smitten?
Then the prophet forbare, and said, I
know that God hath determined to destroy thee, because thou hast done this,
and hast not hearkened unto my
counsel.
17 ¶ Then Ăm′ȧ-zī′ȧh king of Judah

took advice, and sent to Jō′ăsh, the son
of Jē-hō′ȧ-hăz, the son of Jē′hū, king of
Ĭş′rā-ĕl, saying, Come, let us see one
another in the face.
18 And Jō′ăsh king of Ĭş′rā-ĕl sent to
Ăm′ȧ-zī′ȧh king of Judah, saying, The
thistle that *was* in Lebanon sent to the
cedar that *was* in Lebanon, saying, Give
thy daughter to my son to wife: and
there passed by a wild beast that *was* in
Lebanon, and trode down the thistle.
19 Thou sayest, Lo, thou hast smitten
the Ē′dŏm-ītes; and thine heart lifteth
thee up to boast: abide now at home;
why shouldest thou meddle to *thine*
hurt, that thou shouldest fall, *even* thou,
and Judah with thee?
20 But Ăm′ȧ-zī′ȧh would not hear; for
it *came* of God, that he might deliver
them into the hand *of their enemies*, because they sought after the gods of
Ē′dŏm.
21 So Jō′ăsh the king of Ĭş′rā-ĕl went
up; and they saw one another in the
face, *both* he and Ăm′ȧ-zī′ȧh king of
Judah, at Bĕth′–shē′mĕsh, which *belongeth* to Judah.
22 And Judah was put to the worse before Ĭş′rā-ĕl, and they fled every man to
his tent.
23 And Jō′ăsh the king of Ĭş′rā-ĕl took
Ăm′ȧ-zī′ȧh king of Judah, the son of
Jō′ăsh, the son of Jē-hō′ȧ-hăz, at Bĕth′–
shē′mĕsh, and brought him to Jerusalem, and brake down the wall of
Jerusalem from the gate of Ē′phrā-ĭm to
the corner gate, four hundred cubits.
24 And *he took* all the gold and the silver, and all the vessels that were found
in the house of God with Ō′bĕd–ē′dŏm,
and the treasures of the king's house,
the hostages also, and returned to
Sȧ-mā′rĭ-ȧ.
25 ℂ And Ăm′ȧ-zī′ȧh the son of Jō′ăsh
king of Judah lived after the death of
Jō′ăsh son of Jē-hō′ȧ-hăz king of Ĭş′-
rā-ĕl fifteen years.
26 Now the rest of the acts of Ăm′ȧ-
zī′ȧh, first and last, behold, *are* they not
written in the book of the kings of Judah
and Ĭş′rā-ĕl?
27 ℂ Now after the time that Ăm′ȧ-
zī′ȧh did turn away from following the
LORD they made a conspiracy against
him in Jerusalem; and he fled to Lā′-
chĭsh: but they sent to Lā′chĭsh after
him, and slew him there.
28 And they brought him upon horses,
and buried him with his fathers in the
city of Judah.

CHAPTER 26

THEN all the people of Judah took
Ŭz-zī′ȧh, who *was* sixteen years
old, and made him king in the room of
his father Ăm′ȧ-zī′ȧh.
2 He built Ē′lŏth, and restored it to
Judah, after that the king slept with his
fathers.
3 Sixteen years old *was* Ŭz-zī′ȧh when
he began to reign, and he reigned fifty
and two years in Jerusalem. His
mother's name also *was* Jĕc′ō-lī′ȧh of
Jerusalem.
4 And he did *that which was* right in
the sight of the LORD, according to all
that his father Ăm′ȧ-zī′ȧh did.
5 And he sought God in the days of
Zĕch′ȧ-rī′ȧh, who had understanding
in the visions of God: and as long as he
sought the LORD, God made him to
prosper.
6 And he went forth and warred against
the Phĭ-lĭs′tĭneş, and brake down the
wall of Gath, and the wall of Jăb′nĕh,
and the wall of Ashdod, and built cities
about Ashdod, and among the Phĭ-
lĭs′tĭneş.
7 And God helped him against the
Phĭ-lĭs′tĭneş, and against the Arabians
that dwelt in Gûr′–bā′ăl, and the Mē-
hū′nĭm.
8 And the Ammonites gave gifts to
Ŭz-zī′ȧh: and his name spread abroad
even to the entering in of Egypt; for he
strengthened *himself* exceedingly.
9 Moreover Ŭz-zī′ȧh built towers in
Jerusalem at the corner gate, and at the
valley gate, and at the turning *of the
wall*, and fortified them.
10 Also he built towers in the desert,
and digged many wells: for he had much
cattle, both in the low country, and in
the plains; husbandmen *also*, and vinedressers in the mountains, and in Cär′-
mĕl: for he loved husbandry.
11 Moreover Ŭz-zī′ȧh had a host of
fighting men, that went out to war by
bands, according to the number of their
account by the hand of Jē-ī′ĕl the scribe
and Mā′ȧ-sē′ịȧh the ruler, under the
hand of Hăn′ȧ-nī′ȧh, *one* of the king's
captains.
12 The whole number of the chief of
the fathers of the mighty men of valor
were two thousand and six hundred.

13 And under their hand *was* an army, three hundred thousand and seven thousand and five hundred, that made war with mighty power, to help the king against the enemy.

14 And Ŭz-zī′ȧh prepared for them throughout all the host shields, and spears, and helmets, and habergeons, and bows, and slings *to cast* stones.

15 And he made in Jerusalem engines, invented by cunning men, to be on the towers and upon the bulwarks, to shoot arrows and great stones withal. And his name spread far abroad; for he was marvelously helped, till he was strong.

16 ¶ But when he was strong, his heart was lifted up to *his* destruction: for he transgressed against the LORD his God, and went into the temple of the LORD to burn incense upon the altar of incense.

17 And Ăz′ȧ-rī′ȧh the priest went in after him, and with him fourscore priests of the LORD, *that were* valiant men:

18 And they withstood Ŭz-zī′ȧh the king, and said unto him, *It appertaineth* not unto thee, Ŭz-zī′ȧh, to burn incense unto the LORD, but to the priests the sons of Aaron, that are consecrated to burn incense: go out of the sanctuary; for thou hast trespassed; neither *shall it be* for thine honor from the LORD God.

19 Then Ŭz-zī′ȧh was wroth, and *had* a censer in his hand to burn incense: and while he was wroth with the priests, the leprosy even rose up in his forehead before the priests in the house of the LORD, from beside the incense altar.

20 And Ăz′ȧ-rī′ȧh the chief priest, and all the priests, looked upon him, and, behold, he *was* leprous in his forehead, and they thrust him out from thence; yea, himself hasted also to go out, because the LORD had smitten him.

21 And Ŭz-zī′ȧh the king was a leper unto the day of his death, and dwelt in a several house, *being* a leper; for he was cut off from the house of the LORD: and Jō′thăm his son *was* over the king's house, judging the people of the land.

22 ¶ Now the rest of the acts of Ŭz-zī′ȧh, first and last, did Ī-ṣā′iȧh the prophet, the son of Ā′mŏz, write.

23 So Ŭz-zī′ȧh slept with his fathers, and they buried him with his fathers in the field of the burial which *belonged* to the kings; for they said, He *is* a leper: and Jō′thăm his son reigned in his stead.

CHAPTER 27

JŌ′THĂM *was* twenty and five years old when he began to reign, and he reigned sixteen years in Jerusalem. His mother's name also *was* Jē-ru′shȧh, the daughter of Zā′dŏk.

2 And he did *that which was* right in the sight of the LORD, according to all that his father Ŭz-zī′ȧh did: howbeit he entered not into the temple of the LORD. And the people did yet corruptly.

3 He built the high gate of the house of the LORD, and on the wall of Ō′phĕl he built much.

4 Moreover he built cities in the mountains of Judah, and in the forests he built castles and towers.

5 ¶ He fought also with the king of the Ammonites, and prevailed against them. And the children of Ammon gave him the same year a hundred talents of silver, and ten thousand measures of wheat, and ten thousand of barley. So much did the children of Ammon pay unto him, both the second year, and the third.

6 So Jō′thăm became mighty, because he prepared his ways before the LORD his God.

7 ¶ Now the rest of the acts of Jō′thăm, and all his wars, and his ways, lo, they *are* written in the book of the kings of Ĭṣ′rā-ĕl and Judah.

8 He was five and twenty years old when he began to reign, and reigned sixteen years in Jerusalem.

9 ¶ And Jō′thăm slept with his fathers, and they buried him in the city of David: and Ahaz his son reigned in his stead.

CHAPTER 28

AHAZ *was* twenty years old when he began to reign, and he reigned sixteen years in Jerusalem: but he did not *that which was* right in the sight of the LORD, like David his father:

2 For he walked in the ways of the kings of Ĭṣ′rā-ĕl, and made also molten images for Bā′ȧ-lĭm.

3 Moreover he burnt incense in the valley of the son of Hĭn′nŏm, and burnt his children in the fire, after the abominations of the heathen whom the LORD had cast out before the children of Ĭṣ′rā-ĕl.

4 He sacrificed also and burnt incense in the high places, and on the hills, and under every green tree.

5 Wherefore the LORD his God delivered him into the hand of the king of Syria; and they smote him, and carried away a great multitude of them captives, and brought *them* to Damascus. And he was also delivered into the hand of the king of Ĭş'rā-ĕl, who smote him with a great slaughter.

6 ℂ For Pē'kăh the son of Rĕm'ȧ-lī'ȧh slew in Judah a hundred and twenty thousand in one day, *which were* all valiant men; because they had forsaken the LORD God of their fathers.

7 And Zĭch'rī, a mighty man of Ē'phrā-ĭm, slew Mā'ȧ-sē'ịȧh the king's son, and Ăz'rī-kăm the governor of the house, and Ĕl-kā'nȧh *that was* next to the king.

8 And the children of Ĭş'rā-ĕl carried away captive of their brethren two hundred thousand, women, sons, and daughters, and took also away much spoil from them, and brought the spoil to Sȧ-mā'rĭ-ȧ.

9 But a prophet of the LORD was there, whose name *was* Ō'dĕd: and he went out before the host that came to Sȧ-mā'rĭ-ȧ, and said unto them, Behold, because the LORD God of your fathers was wroth with Judah, he hath delivered them into your hand, and ye have slain them in a rage *that* reacheth up unto heaven.

10 And now ye purpose to keep under the children of Judah and Jerusalem for bondmen and bondwomen unto you: *but are there* not with you, even with you, sins against the LORD your God?

11 Now hear me therefore, and deliver the captives again, which ye have taken captive of your brethren: for the fierce wrath of the LORD *is* upon you.

12 Then certain of the heads of the children of Ē'phrā-ĭm, Ăz'ȧ-rī'ȧh the son of Jō-hā'năn, Bĕr'ē-chī'ȧh the son of Mē-shĭl'lē-mŏth, and Jē'hĭz-kī'ȧh the son of Shăl'lŭm, and Ăm'ȧ-sȧ the son of Hăd'laī, stood up against them that came from the war,

13 And said unto them, Ye shall not bring in the captives hither: for whereas we have offended against the LORD *already*, ye intend to add *more* to our sins and to our trespass: for our trespass is great, and *there is* fierce wrath against Ĭş'rā-ĕl.

14 So the armed men left the captives and the spoil before the princes and all the congregation.

15 And the men which were expressed by name rose up, and took the captives, and with the spoil clothed all that were naked among them, and arrayed them, and shod them, and gave them to eat and to drink, and anointed them, and carried all the feeble of them upon asses, and brought them to Jĕr'ī-chō, the city of palm trees, to their brethren: then they returned to Sȧ-mā'rĭ-ȧ.

16 ℂ At that time did king Ahaz send unto the kings of Assyria to help him.

17 For again the Ē'dŏm-ītes had come and smitten Judah, and carried away captives.

18 The Phĭ-lĭs'tĭneş also had invaded the cities of the low country, and of the south of Judah, and had taken Bĕth'–shē'mĕsh, and Ăj'ȧ-lŏn, and Gē-dē'rŏth, and Shō'chō with the villages thereof, and Tĭm'nȧh with the villages thereof, Gĭm'zō also and the villages thereof: and they dwelt there.

19 For the LORD brought Judah low because of Ahaz king of Ĭş'rā-ĕl; for he made Judah naked, and transgressed sore against the LORD.

20 And Tĭl'găth–pĭl-nē'şĕr king of Assyria came unto him, and distressed him, but strengthened him not.

21 For Ahaz took away a portion *out* of the house of the LORD, and *out* of the house of the king, and of the princes, and gave *it* unto the king of Assyria: but he helped him not.

22 ℂ And in the time of his distress did he trespass yet more against the LORD: this *is that* king Ahaz.

23 For he sacrificed unto the gods of Damascus, which smote him: and he said, Because the gods of the kings of Syria help them, *therefore* will I sacrifice to them, that they may help me. But they were the ruin of him, and of all Ĭş'rā-ĕl.

24 And Ahaz gathered together the vessels of the house of God, and cut in pieces the vessels of the house of God, and shut up the doors of the house of the LORD, and he made him altars in every corner of Jerusalem.

25 And in every several city of Judah he made high places to burn incense unto other gods, and provoked to anger the LORD God of his fathers.

26 ℂ Now the rest of his acts and of all his ways, first and last, behold, they *are*

written in the book of the kings of Judah and Ĭs'rā-ĕl.

27 And Ahaz slept with his fathers, and they buried him in the city, *even* in Jerusalem: but they brought him not into the sepulchres of the kings of Ĭs'rā-ĕl: and Hĕz'ē-kī'ȧh his son reigned in his stead.

CHAPTER 29

HĔZ'Ē-KĪ'ȦH began to reign *when he was* five and twenty years old, and he reigned nine and twenty years in Jerusalem. And his mother's name *was* Ȧ-bī'jăh, the daughter of Zĕch'ȧ-rī'ȧh.

2 And he did *that which was* right in the sight of the LORD, according to all that David his father had done.

3 ¶ He in the first year of his reign, in the first month, opened the doors of the house of the LORD, and repaired them.

4 And he brought in the priests and the Lē'vītes, and gathered them together into the east street,

5 And said unto them, Hear me, ye Lē'vītes; sanctify now yourselves, and sanctify the house of the LORD God of your fathers, and carry forth the filthiness out of the holy *place.*

6 For our fathers have trespassed, and done *that which was* evil in the eyes of the LORD our God, and have forsaken him, and have turned away their faces from the habitation of the LORD, and turned *their* backs.

7 Also they have shut up the doors of the porch, and put out the lamps, and have not burned incense nor offered burnt offerings in the holy *place* unto the God of Ĭs'rā-ĕl.

8 Wherefore the wrath of the LORD was upon Judah and Jerusalem, and he hath delivered them to trouble, to astonishment, and to hissing, as ye see with your eyes.

9 For, lo, our fathers have fallen by the sword, and our sons and our daughters and our wives *are* in captivity for this.

10 Now *it is* in mine heart to make a covenant with the LORD God of Ĭs'rā-ĕl, that his fierce wrath may turn away from us.

11 My sons, be not now negligent: for the LORD hath chosen you to stand before him, to serve him, and that ye should minister unto him, and burn incense.

12 ¶ Then the Lē'vītes arose, Mā'hăth the son of Ȧ-măs'ā-ī, and Joel the son of Ăz'ȧ-rī'ȧh, of the sons of the Kō'hăth-ītes: and of the sons of Mē-rā'rī; Kish the son of Ăb'dī, and Ăz'ȧ-rī'ȧh the son of Jē-hăl'ē-lĕl: and of the Gēr'shŏn-ītes; Jō'ȧh the son of Zĭm'mȧh, and Ē'den the son of Jō'ȧh:

13 And of the sons of Ĕl'ĭ-zā'phăn; Shĭm'rī, and Jē-ī'ĕl: and of the sons of Ā'săph; Zĕch'ȧ-rī'ȧh, and Măt'tȧ-nī'ȧh:

14 And of the sons of Hē'măn; Jē-hī'ĕl, and Shĭm'ē-ī: and of the sons of Jē-dū'thŭn; Shē-mā'ịah, and Ŭz-zī'ĕl.

15 And they gathered their brethren, and sanctified themselves, and came, according to the commandment of the king, by the words of the LORD, to cleanse the house of the LORD.

16 And the priests went into the inner part of the house of the LORD, to cleanse *it,* and brought out all the uncleanness that they found in the temple of the LORD into the court of the house of the LORD. And the Lē'vītes took *it,* to carry *it* out abroad into the brook Kĭd'rŏn.

17 Now they began on the first *day* of the first month to sanctify, and on the eighth day of the month came they to the porch of the LORD: so they sanctified the house of the LORD in eight days; and in the sixteenth day of the first month they made an end.

18 Then they went in to Hĕz'ē-kī'ȧh the king, and said, We have cleansed all the house of the LORD, and the altar of burnt offering, with all the vessels thereof, and the showbread table, with all the vessels thereof.

19 Moreover all the vessels, which king Ahaz in his reign did cast away in his transgression, have we prepared and sanctified, and, behold, they *are* before the altar of the LORD.

20 ¶ Then Hĕz'ē-kī'ȧh the king rose early, and gathered the rulers of the city, and went up to the house of the LORD.

21 And they brought seven bullocks, and seven rams, and seven lambs, and seven he goats, for a sin offering for the kingdom, and for the sanctuary, and for Judah. And he commanded the priests the sons of Aaron to offer *them* on the altar of the LORD.

22 So they killed the bullocks, and the priests received the blood, and sprin-

kled *it* on the altar: likewise, when they
had killed the rams, they sprinkled the
blood upon the altar: they killed also the
lambs, and they sprinkled the blood
upon the altar.
23 And they brought forth the he goats
for the sin offering before the king and
the congregation; and they laid their
hands upon them:
24 And the priests killed them, and
they made reconciliation with their
blood upon the altar, to make an atonement for all Ĭş'rā-ĕl: for the king commanded *that* the burnt offering and the
sin offering *should be made* for all
Ĭş'rā-ĕl.
25 And he set the Lē'vītes in the house
of the LORD with cymbals, with psalteries, and with harps, according to the
commandment of David, and of Gad the
king's seer, and Nathan the prophet:
for *so was* the commandment of the
LORD by his prophets.
26 And the Lē'vītes stood with the instruments of David, and the priests with
the trumpets.
27 And Hĕz'ē-kī'ȧh commanded to
offer the burnt offering upon the altar.
And when the burnt offering began, the
song of the LORD began *also* with the
trumpets, and with the instruments
ordained by David king of Ĭş'rā-ĕl.
28 And all the congregation worshipped, and the singers sang, and the
trumpeters sounded: *and* all *this continued* until the burnt offering was
finished.
29 And when they had made an end of
offering, the king and all that were
present with him bowed themselves,
and worshipped.
30 Moreover Hĕz'ē-kī'ȧh the king and
the princes commanded the Lē'vītes to
sing praise unto the LORD with the words
of David, and of Ā'săph the seer. And
they sang praises with gladness, and
they bowed their heads and worshipped.
31 Then Hĕz'ē-kī'ȧh answered and
said, Now ye have consecrated yourselves unto the LORD, come near and
bring sacrifices and thank offerings into
the house of the LORD. And the congregation brought in sacrifices and
thank offerings; and as many as were of
a free heart, burnt offerings.
32 And the number of the burnt offerings, which the congregation brought,
was threescore and ten bullocks, a hundred rams, *and* two hundred lambs: all
these *were* for a burnt offering to the
LORD.
33 And the consecrated things *were*
six hundred oxen and three thousand
sheep.
34 But the priests were too few, so that
they could not flay all the burnt offerings: wherefore their brethren the Lē'-
vītes did help them, till the work was
ended, and until the *other* priests had
sanctified themselves: for the Lē'vītes
were more upright in heart to sanctify
themselves than the priests.
35 And also the burnt offerings *were*
in abundance, with the fat of the peace
offerings, and the drink offerings for
every burnt offering. So the service of
the house of the LORD was set in order.
36 And Hĕz'ē-kī'ȧh rejoiced, and all the
people, that God had prepared the people: for the thing was *done* suddenly.

CHAPTER 30

AND Hĕz'ē-kī'ȧh sent to all Ĭş'rā-ĕl
and Judah, and wrote letters also
to Ē'phrā-ĭm and Mȧ-năs'sĕh, that they
should come to the house of the LORD
at Jerusalem, to keep the passover unto
the LORD God of Ĭş'rā-ĕl.
2 For the king had taken counsel, and
his princes, and all the congregation in
Jerusalem, to keep the passover in the
second month.
3 For they could not keep it at that time,
because the priests had not sanctified
themselves sufficiently, neither had the
people gathered themselves together to
Jerusalem.
4 And the thing pleased the king and
all the congregation.
5 So they established a decree to make
proclamation throughout all Ĭş'rā-ĕl,
from Bē'ĕr-shē'bȧ even to Dan, that
they should come to keep the passover
unto the LORD God of Ĭş'rā-ĕl at Jerusalem: for they had not done *it* of a long
time in such sort as it was written.
6 So the posts went with the letters
from the king and his princes throughout all Ĭş'rā-ĕl and Judah, and according to the commandment of the king,
saying, Ye children of Ĭş'rā-ĕl, turn
again unto the LORD God of Abraham,
Isaac, and Ĭş'rā-ĕl, and he will return to
the remnant of you, that are escaped
out of the hand of the kings of Assyria.
7 And be not ye like your fathers, and

like your brethren, which trespassed
against the LORD God of their fathers,
who therefore gave them up to desolation, as ye see.
8 Now be ye not stiffnecked, as your
fathers *were, but* yield yourselves unto
the LORD, and enter into his sanctuary,
which he hath sanctified for ever: and
serve the LORD your God, that the
fierceness of his wrath may turn away
from you.
9 For if ye turn again unto the LORD,
your brethren and your children *shall
find* compassion before them that lead
them captive, so that they shall come
again into this land: for the LORD your
God *is* gracious and merciful, and will
not turn away *his* face from you, if ye
return unto him.
10 So the posts passed from city to
city, through the country of Ē′phrā-ĭm
and Mȧ-năs′sĕh, even unto Zĕb′ū-lŭn:
but they laughed them to scorn, and
mocked them.
11 Nevertheless, divers of Ăsh′ẽr and
Mȧ-năs′sĕh and of Zĕb′ū-lŭn humbled
themselves, and came to Jerusalem.
12 Also in Judah the hand of God
was to give them one heart to do the
commandment of the king and of the
princes, by the word of the LORD.
13 ¶ And there assembled at Jerusalem much people to keep the feast of
unleavened bread in the second month,
a very great congregation.
14 And they arose and took away the
altars that *were* in Jerusalem, and all
the altars for incense took they away,
and cast *them* into the brook Kĭd′rŏn.
15 Then they killed the passover on
the fourteenth *day* of the second month:
and the priests and the Lē′vītes were
ashamed, and sanctified themselves,
and brought in the burnt offerings into
the house of the LORD.
16 And they stood in their place after
their manner, according to the law of
Moses the man of God: the priests
sprinkled the blood, *which they received* of the hand of the Lē′vītes.
17 For *there were* many in the congregation that were not sanctified: therefore the Lē′vītes had the charge of the
killing of the passovers for every one
that was not clean, to sanctify *them* unto
the LORD.
18 For a multitude of the people, *even*
many of Ē′phrā-ĭm and Mȧ-năs′sĕh,
Ĭs′sȧ-chär and Zĕb′ū-lŭn, had not
cleansed themselves, yet did they eat
the passover otherwise than it was
written. But Hĕz′ē-kī′ȧh prayed for
them, saying, The good LORD pardon
every one
19 *That* prepareth his heart to seek
God, the LORD God of his fathers, though
he be not *cleansed* according to the
purification of the sanctuary.
20 And the LORD hearkened to Hĕz′ē-
kī′ȧh, and healed the people.
21 And the children of Ĭş′rā-ĕl that
were present at Jerusalem kept the
feast of unleavened bread seven days
with great gladness: and the Lē′vītes
and the priests praised the LORD day by
day, *singing* with loud instruments unto
the LORD.
22 And Hĕz′ē-kī′ȧh spake comfortably unto all the Lē′vītes that taught the
good knowledge of the LORD: and they
did eat throughout the feast seven days,
offering peace offerings, and making
confession to the LORD God of their
fathers.
23 And the whole assembly took counsel to keep other seven days: and they
kept *other* seven days with gladness.
24 For Hĕz′ē-kī′ȧh king of Judah did
give to the congregation a thousand bullocks and seven thousand sheep; and
the princes gave to the congregation a
thousand bullocks and ten thousand
sheep: and a great number of priests
sanctified themselves.
25 And all the congregation of Judah,
with the priests and the Lē′vītes, and
all the congregation that came out of
Ĭş′rā-ĕl, and the strangers that came out
of the land of Ĭş′rā-ĕl, and that dwelt in
Judah, rejoiced.
26 So there was great joy in Jerusalem:
for since the time of Solomon the son of
David king of Ĭş′rā-ĕl *there was* not the
like in Jerusalem.
27 ¶ Then the priests the Lē′vītes
arose and blessed the people: and their
voice was heard, and their prayer came
up to his holy dwelling place, *even* unto
heaven.

CHAPTER 31

NOW when all this was finished, all
Ĭş′rā-ĕl that were present went out
to the cities of Judah, and brake the
images in pieces, and cut down the
groves, and threw down the high places

and the altars out of all Judah and Benjamin, in Ē′phrā-ĭm also and Mȧ-năs′sĕh, until they had utterly destroyed them all. Then all the children of Ĭs′rā-ĕl returned, every man to his possession, into their own cities.
2 ℂ And Hĕz′ē-kī′ȧh appointed the courses of the priests and the Lē′vītes after their courses, every man according to his service, the priests and Lē′vītes for burnt offerings and for peace offerings, to minister, and to give thanks, and to praise in the gates of the tents of the LORD.
3 *He appointed* also the king's portion of his substance for the burnt offerings, *to wit*, for the morning and evening burnt offerings, and the burnt offerings for the sabbaths, and for the new moons, and for the set feasts, as *it is* written in the law of the LORD.
4 Moreover he commanded the people that dwelt in Jerusalem to give the portion of the priests and the Lē′vītes, that they might be encouraged in the law of the LORD.
5 ℂ And as soon as the commandment came abroad, the children of Ĭs′rā-ĕl brought in abundance the firstfruits of corn, wine, and oil, and honey, and of all the increase of the field; and the tithe of all *things* brought they in abundantly.
6 And *concerning* the children of Ĭs′rā-ĕl and Judah, that dwelt in the cities of Judah, they also brought in the tithe of oxen and sheep, and the tithe of holy things which were consecrated unto the LORD their God, and laid *them* by heaps.
7 In the third month they began to lay the foundation of the heaps, and finished *them* in the seventh month.
8 And when Hĕz′ē-kī′ȧh and the princes came and saw the heaps, they blessed the LORD, and his people Ĭs′rā-ĕl.
9 Then Hĕz′ē-kī′ȧh questioned with the priests and the Lē′vītes concerning the heaps.
10 And Ăz′ȧ-rī′ȧh the chief priest of the house of Zā′dŏk answered him, and said, Since *the people* began to bring the offerings into the house of the LORD, we have had enough to eat, and have left plenty: for the LORD hath blessed his people; and that which is left *is* this great store.
11 ℂ Then Hĕz′ē-kī′ȧh commanded to prepare chambers in the house of the LORD; and they prepared *them*,
12 And brought in the offerings and the tithes and the dedicated *things* faithfully: over which Cŏn′ō-nī′ȧh the Lē′vīte *was* ruler, and Shĭm′ē-ī his brother *was* the next.
13 And Jē-hī′ĕl, and Ăz′ȧ-zī′ȧh, and Nā′hăth, and Ās′ȧ-hĕl, and Jĕr′ĭ-mŏth, and Jŏz′ȧ-băd, and Ē′lī-ĕl, and Ĭs′mȧ-chī′ȧh, and Mā′hăth, and Bē-nā′iȧh, *were* overseers under the hand of Cŏn′ō-nī′ȧh and Shĭm′ē-ī his brother, at the commandment of Hĕz′ē-kī′ȧh the king, and Ăz′ȧ-rī′ȧh the ruler of the house of God.
14 And Kō′rē the son of Ĭm′nȧh the Lē′vīte, the porter toward the east, *was* over the freewill offerings of God, to distribute the oblations of the LORD, and the most holy things.
15 And next him *were* Ē′den, and Mĭn′iȧ-mĭn, and Jĕsh′ū-ȧ, and Shē-mā′iȧh, Ăm′ȧ-rī′ȧh, and Shĕc′ȧ-nī′ȧh, in the cities of the priests, in *their* set office, to give to their brethren by courses, as well to the great as to the small:
16 Besides their genealogy of males, from three years old and upward, *even* unto every one that entereth into the house of the LORD, his daily portion for their service in their charges according to their courses;
17 Both to the genealogy of the priests by the house of their fathers, and the Lē′vītes from twenty years old and upward, in their charges by their courses;
18 And to the genealogy of all their little ones, their wives, and their sons, and their daughters, through all the congregation: for in their set office they sanctified themselves in holiness:
19 Also of the sons of Aaron the priests, *which were* in the fields of the suburbs of their cities, in every several city, the men that were expressed by name, to give portions to all the males among the priests, and to all that were reckoned by genealogies among the Lē′vītes.
20 ℂ And thus did Hĕz′ē-kī′ȧh throughout all Judah, and wrought *that which was* good and right and truth before the LORD his God.
21 And in every work that he began in the service of the house of God, and in the law, and in the commandments, to seek his God, he did *it* with all his heart, and prospered.

CHAPTER 32

AFTER these things, and the establishment thereof, Sĕn-năch′ĕr-ĭb king of Assyria came, and entered into Judah, and encamped against the fenced cities, and thought to win them for himself.
2 And when Hĕz′ē-kī′ah saw that Sĕn-năch′ĕr-ĭb was come, and that he was purposed to fight against Jerusalem,
3 He took counsel with his princes and his mighty men to stop the waters of the fountains which *were* without the city: and they did help him.
4 So there was gathered much people together, who stopped all the fountains, and the brook that ran through the midst of the land, saying, Why should the kings of Assyria come, and find much water?
5 Also he strengthened himself, and built up all the wall that was broken, and raised *it* up to the towers, and another wall without, and repaired Mĭl′lō *in* the city of David, and made darts and shields in abundance.
6 And he set captains of war over the people, and gathered them together to him in the street of the gate of the city, and spake comfortably to them, saying,
7 Be strong and courageous, be not afraid nor dismayed for the king of Assyria, nor for all the multitude that *is* with him: for *there be* more with us than with him.
8 With him *is* an arm of flesh; but with us *is* the LORD our God to help us, and to fight our battles. And the people rested themselves upon the words of Hĕz′ē-kī′ah king of Judah.
9 ¶ After this did Sĕn-năch′ĕr-ĭb king of Assyria send his servants to Jerusalem, (but he *himself laid siege* against Lā′chĭsh, and all his power with him,) unto Hĕz′ē-kī′ah king of Judah, and unto all Judah that *were* at Jerusalem, saying,
10 Thus saith Sĕn-năch′ĕr-ĭb king of Assyria, Whereon do ye trust, that ye abide in the siege in Jerusalem?
11 Doth not Hĕz′ē-kī′ah persuade you to give over yourselves to die by famine and by thirst, saying, The LORD our God shall deliver us out of the hand of the king of Assyria?
12 Hath not the same Hĕz′ē-kī′ah taken away his high places and his altars, and commanded Judah and Jerusalem, saying, Ye shall worship before one altar, and burn incense upon it?
13 Know ye not what I and my fathers have done unto all the people of *other* lands? were the gods of the nations of those lands any ways able to deliver their lands out of mine hand?
14 Who *was there* among all the gods of those nations that my fathers utterly destroyed, that could deliver his people out of mine hand, that your God should be able to deliver you out of mine hand?
15 Now therefore let not Hĕz′ē-kī′ah deceive you, nor persuade you on this manner, neither yet believe him: for no god of any nation or kingdom was able to deliver his people out of mine hand, and out of the hand of my fathers: how much less shall your God deliver you out of mine hand?
16 And his servants spake yet *more* against the LORD God, and against his servant Hĕz′ē-kī′ah.
17 He wrote also letters to rail on the LORD God of Ĭs′rā-ĕl, and to speak against him, saying, As the gods of the nations of *other* lands have not delivered their people out of mine hand, so shall not the God of Hĕz′ē-kī′ah deliver his people out of mine hand.
18 Then they cried with a loud voice, in the Jews' speech, unto the people of Jerusalem that *were* on the wall, to affright them, and to trouble them; that they might take the city.
19 And they spake against the God of Jerusalem, as against the gods of the people of the earth, *which were* the work of the hands of man.
20 And for this *cause* Hĕz′ē-kī′ah the king, and the prophet Ī-ṣā′iah the son of Ā′mŏz, prayed and cried to heaven.
21 ¶ And the LORD sent an angel, which cut off all the mighty men of valor, and the leaders and captains in the camp of the king of Assyria. So he returned with shame of face to his own land. And when he was come into the house of his god, they that came forth of his own bowels slew him there with the sword.
22 Thus the LORD saved Hĕz′ē-kī′ah and the inhabitants of Jerusalem from the hand of Sĕn-năch′ĕr-ĭb the king of Assyria, and from the hand of all *other*, and guided them on every side.
23 And many brought gifts unto the LORD to Jerusalem, and presents to Hĕz′ē-kī′ah king of Judah: so that he

was magnified in the sight of all nations
from thenceforth.
24 ¶ In those days Hĕz′ē-kī′ȧh was
sick to the death, and prayed unto the
LORD: and he spake unto him, and he
gave him a sign.
25 But Hĕz′ē-kī′ȧh rendered not again
according to the benefit *done* unto him;
for his heart was lifted up: therefore
there was wrath upon him, and upon
Judah and Jerusalem.
26 Notwithstanding, Hĕz′ē-kī′ȧh humbled himself for the pride of his heart,
both he and the inhabitants of Jerusalem, so that the wrath of the LORD
came not upon them in the days of
Hĕz′ē-kī′ȧh.
27 ¶ And Hĕz′ē-kī′ȧh had exceeding
much riches and honor: and he made
himself treasuries for silver, and for
gold, and for precious stones, and for
spices, and for shields, and for all manner of pleasant jewels;
28 Storehouses also for the increase of
corn, and wine, and oil; and stalls for all
manner of beasts, and cotes for flocks.
29 Moreover he provided him cities,
and possessions of flocks and herds in
abundance: for God had given him substance very much.
30 This same Hĕz′ē-kī′ȧh also stopped
the upper watercourse of Gī′hŏn, and
brought it straight down to the west side
of the city of David. And Hĕz′ē-kī′ȧh
prospered in all his works.
31 ¶ Howbeit, in *the business of* the
ambassadors of the princes of Babylon,
who sent unto him to inquire of the wonder that was *done* in the land, God left
him, to try him, that he might know all
that was in his heart.
32 ¶ Now the rest of the acts of Hĕz′ē-
kī′ȧh, and his goodness, behold, they
are written in the vision of Ī-ṣā′iah the
prophet, the son of Ā′mŏz, *and* in the
book of the kings of Judah and Ĭṣ′rā-ĕl.
33 And Hĕz′ē-kī′ȧh slept with his
fathers, and they buried him in the
chiefest of the sepulchres of the sons of
David: and all Judah and the inhabitants
of Jerusalem did him honor at his death.
And Mȧ-năs′sĕh his son reigned in his
stead.

CHAPTER 33

MȦ-NĂS′SĔH *was* twelve years old
when he began to reign, and he
reigned fifty and five years in Jerusalem:
2 But did *that which was* evil in the
sight of the LORD, like unto the abominations of the heathen, whom the LORD
had cast out before the children of
Ĭṣ′rā-ĕl.
3 ¶ For he built again the high places
which Hĕz′ē-kī′ȧh his father had broken
down, and he reared up altars for Bā′ȧ-
lĭm, and made groves, and worshipped
all the host of heaven, and served them.
4 Also he built altars in the house of
the LORD, whereof the LORD had said,
In Jerusalem shall my name be for ever.
5 And he built altars for all the host of
heaven in the two courts of the house of
the LORD.
6 And he caused his children to pass
through the fire in the valley of the son
of Hĭn′nŏm: also he observed times, and
used enchantments, and used witchcraft, and dealt with a familiar spirit,
and with wizards: he wrought much
evil in the sight of the LORD, to provoke
him to anger.
7 And he set a carved image, the idol
which he had made, in the house of God,
of which God had said to David and to
Solomon his son, In this house, and in
Jerusalem, which I have chosen before
all the tribes of Ĭṣ′rā-ĕl, will I put my
name for ever:
8 Neither will I any more remove the
foot of Ĭṣ′rā-ĕl from out of the land which
I have appointed for your fathers; so
that they will take heed to do all that I
have commanded them, according to the
whole law and the statutes and the ordinances by the hand of Moses.
9 So Mȧ-năs′sĕh made Judah and the
inhabitants of Jerusalem to err, *and* to
do worse than the heathen, whom the
LORD had destroyed before the children
of Ĭṣ′rā-ĕl.
10 And the LORD spake to Mȧ-năs′sĕh,
and to his people: but they would not
hearken.
11 ¶ Wherefore the LORD brought
upon them the captains of the host of
the king of Assyria, which took Mȧ-
năs′sĕh among the thorns, and bound
him with fetters, and carried him to
Babylon.
12 And when he was in affliction, he
besought the LORD his God, and humbled himself greatly before the God of
his fathers,
13 And prayed unto him: and he was
entreated of him, and heard his suppli-

cation, and brought him again to Jerusalem into his kingdom. Then Mȧ-năs′sĕh knew that the LORD he *was* God.
14 Now after this he built a wall without the city of David, on the west side of Gī′hŏn, in the valley, even to the entering in at the fish gate, and compassed about Ō′phĕl, and raised it up a very great height, and put captains of war in all the fenced cities of Judah.
15 And he took away the strange gods, and the idol out of the house of the LORD, and all the altars that he had built in the mount of the house of the LORD, and in Jerusalem, and cast *them* out of the city.
16 And he repaired the altar of the LORD, and sacrificed thereon peace offerings and thank offerings, and commanded Judah to serve the LORD God of Ĭs′rā-ĕl.
17 Nevertheless the people did sacrifice still in the high places, *yet* unto the LORD their God only.
18 ¶ Now the rest of the acts of Mȧ-năs′sĕh, and his prayer unto his God, and the words of the seers that spake to him in the name of the LORD God of Ĭs′rā-ĕl, behold, they *are written* in the book of the kings of Ĭs′rā-ĕl.
19 His prayer also, and *how God* was entreated of him, and all his sins, and his trespass, and the places wherein he built high places, and set up groves and graven images, before he was humbled: behold, they *are* written among the sayings of the seers.
20 ¶ So Mȧ-năs′sĕh slept with his fathers, and they buried him in his own house: and Ā′mŏn his son reigned in his stead.
21 ¶ Ā′mŏn *was* two and twenty years old when he began to reign, and reigned two years in Jerusalem.
22 But he did *that which was* evil in the sight of the LORD, as did Mȧ-năs′sĕh his father: for Ā′mŏn sacrificed unto all the carved images which Mȧ-năs′sĕh his father had made, and served them;
23 And humbled not himself before the LORD, as Mȧ-năs′sĕh his father had humbled himself; but Ā′mŏn trespassed more and more.
24 And his servants conspired against him, and slew him in his own house.
25 ¶ But the people of the land slew all them that had conspired against king Ā′mŏn; and the people of the land made Jō-sī′ȧh his son king in his stead.

CHAPTER 34

JŌ-SĪ′ȦH *was* eight years old when he began to reign, and he reigned in Jerusalem one and thirty years.
2 And he did *that which was* right in the sight of the LORD, and walked in the ways of David his father, and declined *neither* to the right hand, nor to the left.
3 ¶ For in the eighth year of his reign, while he was yet young, he began to seek after the God of David his father: and in the twelfth year he began to purge Judah and Jerusalem from the high places, and the groves, and the carved images, and the molten images.
4 And they brake down the altars of Bā′ȧ-lĭm in his presence; and the images, that *were* on high above them, he cut down; and the groves, and the carved images, and the molten images, he brake in pieces, and made dust *of them*, and strewed *it* upon the graves of them that had sacrificed unto them.
5 And he burnt the bones of the priests upon their altars, and cleansed Judah and Jerusalem.
6 And *so did he* in the cities of Mȧ-năs′sĕh, and Ē′phrā-ĭm, and Simeon, even unto Năph′tȧ-lī, with their mattocks round about.
7 And when he had broken down the altars and the groves, and had beaten the graven images into powder, and cut down all the idols throughout all the land of Ĭs′rā-ĕl, he returned to Jerusalem.
8 ¶ Now in the eighteenth year of his reign, when he had purged the land, and the house, he sent Shā′phăn the son of Ăz′ȧ-lī′ȧh, and Mā′ȧ-sē′ịȧh the governor of the city, and Jō′ȧh the son of Jō′ȧ-hăz the recorder, to repair the house of the LORD his God.
9 And when they came to Hĭl-kī′ȧh the high priest, they delivered the money that was brought into the house of God, which the Lē′vītes that kept the doors had gathered of the hand of Mȧ-năs′sĕh and Ē′phrā-ĭm, and of all the remnant of Ĭs′rā-ĕl, and of all Judah and Benjamin; and they returned to Jerusalem.
10 And they put *it* in the hand of the workmen that had the oversight of the house of the LORD, and they gave it to the workmen that wrought in the house

of the LORD, to repair and amend the house:

11 Even to the artificers and builders gave they *it*, to buy hewn stone, and timber for couplings, and to floor the houses which the kings of Judah had destroyed.

12 And the men did the work faithfully: and the overseers of them *were* Jā'hăth and Ō'bȧ-dī'ȧh, the Lē'vītes, of the sons of Mē-rā'rī; and Zĕch'ȧ-rī'ȧh and Mē-shŭl'lăm, of the sons of the Kō'hăth-ītes, to set *it* forward; and *other of* the Lē'vītes, all that could skill of instruments of music.

13 Also *they were* over the bearers of burdens, and *were* overseers of all that wrought the work in any manner of service: and of the Lē'vītes *there were* scribes, and officers, and porters.

14 ¶ And when they brought out the money that was brought into the house of the LORD, Hĭl-kī'ȧh the priest found a book of the law of the LORD *given* by Moses.

15 And Hĭl-kī'ȧh answered and said to Shā'phăn the scribe, I have found the book of the law in the house of the LORD. And Hĭl-kī'ȧh delivered the book to Shā'phăn.

16 And Shā'phăn carried the book to the king, and brought the king word back again, saying, All that was committed to thy servants, they do *it*.

17 And they have gathered together the money that was found in the house of the LORD, and have delivered it into the hand of the overseers, and to the hand of the workmen.

18 Then Shā'phăn the scribe told the king, saying, Hĭl-kī'ȧh the priest hath given me a book. And Shā'phăn read it before the king.

19 And it came to pass, when the king had heard the words of the law, that he rent his clothes.

20 And the king commanded Hĭl-kī'ȧh, and Ȧ-hī'kăm the son of Shā'phăn, and Ăb'dŏn the son of Mī'cȧh, and Shā'phăn the scribe, and Ȧ-sā'ịȧh a servant of the king's, saying,

21 Go, inquire of the LORD for me, and for them that are left in Ĭş'rā-ĕl and in Judah, concerning the words of the book that is found: for great *is* the wrath of the LORD that is poured out upon us, because our fathers have not kept the word of the LORD, to do after all that is written in this book.

22 And Hĭl-kī'ȧh, and *they* that the king *had appointed*, went to Huldah the prophetess, the wife of Shăl'lŭm the son of Tĭk'vȧth, the son of Hăs'rȧh, keeper of the wardrobe; (now she dwelt in Jerusalem in the college;) and they spake to her to that *effect*.

23 ¶ And she answered them, Thus saith the LORD God of Ĭş'rā-ĕl, Tell ye the man that sent you to me,

24 Thus saith the LORD, Behold, I will bring evil upon this place, and upon the inhabitants thereof, *even* all the curses that are written in the book which they have read before the king of Judah:

25 Because they have forsaken me, and have burned incense unto other gods, that they might provoke me to anger with all the works of their hands; therefore my wrath shall be poured out upon this place, and shall not be quenched.

26 And as for the king of Judah, who sent you to inquire of the LORD, so shall ye say unto him, Thus saith the LORD God of Ĭş'rā-ĕl *concerning* the words which thou hast heard;

27 Because thine heart was tender, and thou didst humble thyself before God, when thou heardest his words against this place, and against the inhabitants thereof, and humbledst thyself before me, and didst rend thy clothes, and weep before me; I have even heard *thee* also, saith the LORD.

28 Behold, I will gather thee to thy fathers, and thou shalt be gathered to thy grave in peace, neither shall thine eyes see all the evil that I will bring upon this place, and upon the inhabitants of the same. So they brought the king word again.

29 ¶ Then the king sent and gathered together all the elders of Judah and Jerusalem.

30 And the king went up into the house of the LORD, and all the men of Judah, and the inhabitants of Jerusalem, and the priests, and the Lē'vītes, and all the people, great and small: and he read in their ears all the words of the book of the covenant that was found in the house of the LORD.

31 And the king stood in his place, and made a covenant before the LORD, to walk after the LORD, and to keep his commandments, and his testimonies, and his statutes, with all his heart, and

with all his soul, to perform the words of
the covenant which are written in this
book.
32 And he caused all that were present
in Jerusalem and Benjamin to stand *to*
it. And the inhabitants of Jerusalem did
according to the covenant of God, the
God of their fathers.
33 And Jō-sī′ȧh took away all the
abominations out of all the countries
that *pertained* to the children of Ĭş′rā-ĕl,
and made all that were present in
Ĭş′rā-ĕl to serve, *even* to serve the LORD
their God. *And* all his days they departed not from following the LORD, the
God of their fathers.

CHAPTER 35

MOREOVER, Jō-sī′ȧh kept a passover unto the LORD in Jerusalem:
and they killed the passover on the fourteenth *day* of the first month.
2 And he set the priests in their
charges, and encouraged them to the
service of the house of the LORD,
3 And said unto the Lē′vītes that
taught all Ĭş′rā-ĕl, which were holy unto
the LORD, Put the holy ark in the house
which Solomon the son of David king of
Ĭş′rā-ĕl did build; *it shall* not *be* a burden upon *your* shoulders: serve now
the LORD your God, and his people
Ĭş′rā-ĕl,
4 And prepare *yourselves* by the
houses of your fathers, after your
courses, according to the writing of
David king of Ĭş′rā-ĕl, and according to
the writing of Solomon his son:
5 And stand in the holy *place* according
to the divisions of the families of the
fathers of your brethren the people, and
after the division of the families of the
Lē′vītes.
6 So kill the passover, and sanctify
yourselves, and prepare your brethren,
that *they* may do according to the word
of the LORD by the hand of Moses.
7 And Jō-sī′ȧh gave to the people, of
the flock, lambs and kids, all for the
passover offerings, for all that were
present, to the number of thirty thousand, and three thousand bullocks:
these *were* of the king's substance.
8 And his princes gave willingly unto
the people, to the priests, and to the
Lē′vītes: Hĭl-kī′ȧh and Zĕch′ȧ-rī′ȧh and
Jē-hī′ĕl, rulers of the house of God, gave
unto the priests for the passover offerings two thousand and six hundred
small cattle, and three hundred oxen.
9 Cŏn′ȧ-nī′ȧh also, and Shē-mā′ịȧh
and Nē-thăn′ē-ĕl, his brethren, and
Hăsh′ȧ-bī′ȧh and Jē-ī′ĕl and Jŏz′ȧ-băd,
chief of the Lē′vītes, gave unto the Lē′-
vītes for passover offerings five thousand *small cattle*, and five hundred
oxen.
10 So the service was prepared, and
the priests stood in their place, and the
Lē′vītes in their courses, according to
the king's commandment.
11 And they killed the passover, and
the priests sprinkled *the blood* from
their hands, and the Lē′vītes flayed
them.
12 And they removed the burnt offerings, that they might give according to
the divisions of the families of the people, to offer unto the LORD, as *it is*
written in the book of Moses. And so
did they with the oxen.
13 And they roasted the passover with
fire according to the ordinance: but the
other holy *offerings* sod they in pots,
and in caldrons, and in pans, and divided
them speedily among all the people.
14 And afterward they made ready for
themselves, and for the priests: because
the priests the sons of Aaron *were*
busied in offering of burnt offerings and
the fat until night; therefore the Lē′-
vītes prepared for themselves, and for
the priests the sons of Aaron.
15 And the singers the sons of Ā′săph
were in their place, according to the
commandment of David, and Ā′săph,
and Hē′măn, and Jē-dū′thŭn the king's
seer; and the porters *waited* at every
gate; they might not depart from their
service; for their brethren the Lē′vītes
prepared for them.
16 So all the service of the LORD was
prepared the same day, to keep the
passover, and to offer burnt offerings
upon the altar of the LORD, according to
the commandment of king Jō-sī′ȧh.
17 And the children of Ĭş′rā-ĕl that
were present kept the passover at that
time, and the feast of unleavened bread
seven days.
18 And there was no passover like to
that kept in Ĭş′rā-ĕl from the days of
Samuel the prophet; neither did all the
kings of Ĭş′rā-ĕl keep such a passover
as Jō-sī′ȧh kept, and the priests, and
the Lē′vītes, and all Judah and Ĭş′rā-ĕl

that were present, and the inhabitants
of Jerusalem.
19 In the eighteenth year of the reign
of Jō-sī′ȧh was this passover kept.
20 ℂ After all this, when Jō-sī′ȧh had
prepared the temple, Nē′chō king of
Egypt came up to fight against Cär′chē-
mĭsh by Eū-phrā′tēs: and Jō-sī′ȧh went
out against him.
21 But he sent ambassadors to him,
saying, What have I to do with thee,
thou king of Judah? *I come* not against
thee this day, but against the house
wherewith I have war: for God commanded me to make haste: forbear thee
from *meddling with* God, who *is* with
me, that he destroy thee not.
22 Nevertheless Jō-sī′ȧh would not
turn his face from him, but disguised
himself, that he might fight with him,
and hearkened not unto the words of
Nē′chō from the mouth of God, and
came to fight in the valley of Mē-gĭd′dō.
23 And the archers shot at king Jō-
sī′ȧh; and the king said to his servants,
Have me away; for I am sore wounded.
24 His servants therefore took him out
of that chariot, and put him in the second
chariot that he had; and they brought
him to Jerusalem, and he died, and was
buried in *one of* the sepulchres of his
fathers. And all Judah and Jerusalem
mourned for Jō-sī′ȧh.
25 ℂ And Jeremiah lamented for
Jō-sī′ȧh: and all the singing men and
the singing women spake of Jō-sī′ȧh in
their lamentations to this day, and made
them an ordinance in Ĭṣ′rā-ĕl: and, behold, they *are* written in the lamentations.
26 Now the rest of the acts of Jō-sī′ȧh,
and his goodness, according to *that
which was* written in the law of the
Lord,
27 And his deeds, first and last, behold, they *are* written in the book of the
kings of Ĭṣ′rā-ĕl and Judah.

CHAPTER 36

THEN the people of the land took
Jē-hō′ȧ-hăz the son of Jō-sī′ȧh, and
made him king in his father's stead in
Jerusalem.
2 Jē-hō′ȧ-hăz *was* twenty and three
years old when he began to reign, and
he reigned three months in Jerusalem.
3 And the king of Egypt put him down
at Jerusalem, and condemned the land
in a hundred talents of silver and a talent of gold.
4 And the king of Egypt made Ē-lī′ȧ-
kĭm his brother king over Judah and
Jerusalem, and turned his name to
Jē-hôī′ȧ-kĭm. And Nē′chō took Jē-hō′-
ȧ-hăz his brother, and carried him to
Egypt.
5 ℂ Jē-hôī′ȧ-kĭm *was* twenty and five
years old when he began to reign, and
he reigned eleven years in Jerusalem:
and he did *that which was* evil in the
sight of the Lord his God.
6 Against him came up Nĕb′ū-chăd-
nĕz′zȧr king of Babylon, and bound him
in fetters, to carry him to Babylon.
7 Nĕb′ū-chăd-nĕz′zȧr also carried of
the vessels of the house of the Lord to
Babylon, and put them in his temple at
Babylon.
8 Now the rest of the acts of Jē-hôī′ȧ-
kĭm, and his abominations which he did,
and that which was found in him, behold, they *are* written in the book of the
kings of Ĭṣ′rā-ĕl and Judah: and Jē-
hôī′ȧ-chĭn his son reigned in his stead.
9 ℂ Jē-hôī′ȧ-chĭn *was* eight years old
when he began to reign, and he reigned
three months and ten days in Jerusalem:
and he did *that which was* evil in the
sight of the Lord.
10 And when the year was expired,
king Nĕb′ū-chăd-nĕz′zȧr sent, and
brought him to Babylon, with the goodly
vessels of the house of the Lord, and
made Zĕd′ē-kī′ȧh his brother king over
Judah and Jerusalem.
11 ℂ Zĕd′ē-kī′ȧh *was* one and twenty
years old when he began to reign, and
reigned eleven years in Jerusalem.
12 And he did *that which was* evil in
the sight of the Lord his God, *and* humbled not himself before Jeremiah the
prophet *speaking* from the mouth of the
Lord.
13 And he also rebelled against king
Nĕb′ū-chăd-nĕz′zȧr, who had made him
swear by God: but he stiffened his
neck, and hardened his heart from turning unto the Lord God of Ĭṣ′rā-ĕl.
14 ℂ Moreover all the chief of the
priests, and the people, transgressed
very much after all the abominations of
the heathen; and polluted the house of
the Lord which he had hallowed in
Jerusalem.
15 And the Lord God of their fathers
sent to them by his messengers, rising

up betimes, and sending; because he
had compassion on his people, and on
his dwelling place:
16 But they mocked the messengers of
God, and despised his words, and mis-
used his prophets, until the wrath of the
LORD arose against his people, till *there
was* no remedy.
17 Therefore he brought upon them
the king of the Chăl'dēeş, who slew
their young men with the sword in the
house of their sanctuary, and had no
compassion upon young man or maiden,
old man, or him that stooped for age: he
gave *them* all into his hand.
18 And all the vessels of the house of
God, great and small, and the treasures
of the house of the LORD, and the treasures of the king, and of his princes; all
these he brought to Babylon.
19 And they burnt the house of God,
and brake down the wall of Jerusalem,
and burnt all the palaces thereof with
fire, and destroyed all the goodly vessels thereof.
20 And them that had escaped from
the sword carried he away to Babylon;
where they were servants to him and
his sons until the reign of the kingdom
of Persia:
21 To fulfil the word of the LORD by
the mouth of Jeremiah, until the land
had enjoyed her sabbaths: *for* as long
as she lay desolate she kept sabbath, to
fulfil threescore and ten years.
22 ¶ Now in the first year of Cyrus
king of Persia, that the word of the
LORD *spoken* by the mouth of Jeremiah
might be accomplished, the LORD
stirred up the spirit of Cyrus king of
Persia, that he made a proclamation
throughout all his kingdom, and *put it*
also in writing, saying,
23 Thus saith Cyrus king of Persia, All
the kingdoms of the earth hath the LORD
God of heaven given me; and he hath
charged me to build him a house in Jerusalem, which *is* in Judah. Who *is there*
among you of all his people? The LORD
his God *be* with him, and let him go up.

EZRA

CHAPTER 1

NOW in the first year of Cyrus king
of Persia, that the word of the
LORD by the mouth of Jeremiah might
be fulfilled, the LORD stirred up the
spirit of Cyrus king of Persia, that
he made a proclamation throughout all
his kingdom, and *put it* also in writing,
saying,
2 Thus saith Cyrus king of Persia,
The LORD God of heaven hath given me
all the kingdoms of the earth; and he
hath charged me to build him a house at
Jerusalem, which *is* in Judah.
3 Who *is there* among you of all his
people? his God be with him, and let
him go up to Jerusalem, which *is* in
Judah, and build the house of the LORD
God of Īş'rā-ĕl, (he *is* the God,) which *is*
in Jerusalem.
4 And whosoever remaineth in any
place where he sojourneth, let the men
of his place help him with silver, and
with gold, and with goods, and with
beasts, besides the freewill offering
for the house of God that *is* in Jerusalem.
5 ¶ Then rose up the chief of the
fathers of Judah and Benjamin, and the
priests, and the Lē'vītes, with all *them*
whose spirit God had raised, to go up to
build the house of the LORD which *is* in
Jerusalem.
6 And all they that *were* about them
strengthened their hands with vessels
of silver, with gold, with goods, and with
beasts, and with precious things, besides all *that* was willingly offered.
7 ¶ Also Cyrus the king brought forth
the vessels of the house of the LORD,
which Nĕb'ū-chăd-nĕz'zär had brought
forth out of Jerusalem, and had put
them in the house of his gods;
8 Even those did Cyrus king of Persia
bring forth by the hand of Mĭth'rē-dăth
the treasurer, and numbered them unto
Shĕsh-băz'zär, the prince of Judah.
9 And this *is* the number of them:
thirty chargers of gold, a thousand
chargers of silver, nine and twenty
knives,
10 Thirty basins of gold, silver basins
of a second *sort* four hundred and ten,
and other vessels a thousand.
11 All the vessels of gold and of silver

were five thousand and four hundred. All *these* did Shĕsh-băz′zȧr bring up with *them of* the captivity that were brought up from Babylon unto Jerusalem.

CHAPTER 2

NOW these *are* the children of the province that went up out of the captivity, of those which had been carried away, whom Nĕb′ū-chăd-nĕz′zȧr the king of Babylon had carried away unto Babylon, and came again unto Jerusalem and Judah, every one unto his city;
2 Which came with Zĕ-rŭb′bȧ-bĕl: Jĕsh′ū-ȧ, Nē′hē-mī′ȧh, Sē-rā′iȧh, Rē-ĕl-ā′iȧh, Môr′dē-cai, Bĭl′shăn, Mĭz′păr, Bĭg′vā-ī, Rē′hŭm, Bā′ȧ-nȧh. The number of the men of the people of Iș′rā-ĕl:
3 The children of Pā′rŏsh, two thousand a hundred seventy and two.
4 The children of Shĕph′ȧ-tī′ȧh, three hundred seventy and two.
5 The children of Ā′rȧh, seven hundred seventy and five.
6 The children of Pā′hăth–mō′ăb, of the children of Jĕsh′ū-ȧ *and* Jō′ăb, two thousand eight hundred and twelve.
7 The children of Ē′lăm, a thousand two hundred fifty and four.
8 The children of Zăt′tū, nine hundred forty and five.
9 The children of Zăc′cā-ī, seven hundred and threescore.
10 The children of Bā′nī, six hundred forty and two.
11 The children of Bĕb′ā-ī, six hundred twenty and three.
12 The children of Ăz′găd, a thousand two hundred twenty and two.
13 The children of Ăd′ō-nī′kăm, six hundred sixty and six.
14 The children of Bĭg′vā-ī, two thousand fifty and six.
15 The children of Ā′dĭn, four hundred fifty and four.
16 The children of Ā′tēr of Hĕz′ē-kī′ȧh, ninety and eight.
17 The children of Bē′zā-ī, three hundred twenty and three.
18 The children of Jō′rȧh, a hundred and twelve.
19 The children of Hā′shŭm, two hundred twenty and three.
20 The children of Gĭb′băr, ninety and five.
21 The children of Beth-lehem, a hundred twenty and three.
22 The men of Nē-tō′phȧh, fifty and six.
23 The men of Ăn′ȧ-thŏth, a hundred twenty and eight.
24 The children of Ăz-mā′vĕth, forty and two.
25 The children of Kĭr′jăth–ā′rĭm, Chē-phī′rȧh, and Bē-ē′rŏth, seven hundred and forty and three.
26 The children of Rā′mȧh and Gā′bȧ, six hundred twenty and one.
27 The men of Mĭch′măs, a hundred twenty and two.
28 The men of Beth-el and Ā′ī, two hundred twenty and three.
29 The children of Nē′bō, fifty and two.
30 The children of Măg′bĭsh, a hundred fifty and six.
31 The children of the other Ē′lăm, a thousand two hundred fifty and four.
32 The children of Hā′rĭm, three hundred and twenty.
33 The children of Lŏd, Hā′dĭd, and Ō′nō, seven hundred twenty and five.
34 The children of Jĕr′ī-chō, three hundred forty and five.
35 The children of Sē-nā′ȧh, three thousand and six hundred and thirty.
36 ¶ The priests: the children of Jē-dā′iȧh, of the house of Jĕsh′ū-ȧ, nine hundred seventy and three.
37 The children of Ĭm′mēr, a thousand fifty and two.
38 The children of Păsh′ŭr, a thousand two hundred forty and seven.
39 The children of Hā′rĭm, a thousand and seventeen.
40 ¶ The Lē′vītes: the children of Jĕsh′ū-ȧ and Kăd′mĭ-ĕl, of the children of Hō′dȧ-vī′ȧh, seventy and four.
41 ¶ The singers: the children of Ā′săph, a hundred twenty and eight.
42 ¶ The children of the porters: the children of Shăl′lŭm, the children of Ā′tēr, the children of Tăl′mŏn, the children of Ăk′kŭb, the children of Hȧ-tī′tȧ, the children of Shō′baī, *in* all a hundred thirty and nine.
43 ¶ The Nĕth′ĭ-nĭm: the children of Zī′hȧ, the children of Hȧ-sū′phȧ, the children of Tȧb-bā′ŏth,
44 The children of Kē′rŏs, the children of Sī′ȧ-hȧ, the children of Pā′dŏn,
45 The children of Lē-bā′nȧh, the children of Hăg′ȧ-băh, the children of Ăk′kŭb,
46 The children of Hā′găb, the children of Shăl′maī, the children of Hā′năn,

47 The children of Gĭd′dĕl, the children
of Gā′här, the children of Rē-ā′ịah,
48 The children of Rē′zĭn, the children
of Nē-kō′dȧ, the children of Găz′zăm,
49 The children of Ŭz′zȧ, the children
of Pȧ-sē′ȧh, the children of Bē′saī,
50 The children of Ȧs′nȧh, the children
of Mē-hū′nĭm, the children of Nē-phū′sĭm,
51 The children of Băk′bŭk, the children of Hȧ-kū′phȧ, the children of
Här′hŭr,
52 The children of Băz′lŭth, the children of Mē-hī′dȧ, the children of
Här′shȧ,
53 The children of Bär′kŏs, the children of Sĭs′ĕr-ȧ, the children of Thā′mȧh,
54 The children of Nē-zī′ȧh, the children of Hȧ-tī′phȧ.
55 ℭ The children of Solomon's servants: the children of Sō′taī, the children
of Sō-phē′rĕth, the children of Pĕ-rụ′dȧ,
56 The children of Jā′ȧ-lȧh, the children of Där′kŏn, the children of Gĭd′dĕl,
57 The children of Shĕph′ȧ-tī′ȧh, the
children of Hăt′tĭl, the children of Pŏch′ē-rĕth of Zē-bā′ĭm, the children of Ā′mī.
58 All the Nĕth′ĭ-nĭm, and the children
of Solomon's servants, *were* three hundred ninety and two.
59 And these *were* they which went up
from Tĕl′-mē′lȧh, Tĕl′-här′sȧ, Chē′rŭb,
Ăd′dăn, *and* Ĭm′mĕr: but they could not
show their father's house, and their
seed, whether they *were* of Ĭș′rā-ĕl:
60 The children of Dē-lā′ịah, the children of Tō-bī′ȧh, the children of Nē-kō′dȧ, six hundred fifty and two.
61 ℭ And of the children of the priests:
the children of Hȧ-bā′ịah, the children
of Kŏz, the children of Bär-zĭl′lā-ī; which
took a wife of the daughters of Bär-zĭl′lā-ī the Gĭl′ē-ăd-īte, and was called
after their name:
62 These sought their register *among*
those that were reckoned by genealogy,
but they were not found: therefore were
they, as polluted, put from the priesthood.
63 And the Tĭr-shā′thȧ said unto them,
that they should not eat of the most holy
things, till there stood up a priest with
Ū′rĭm and with Thŭm′mĭm.
64 ℭ The whole congregation together
was forty and two thousand three hundred *and* threescore,
65 Besides their servants and their
maids, of whom *there were* seven thousand three hundred thirty and seven:
and *there were* among them two hundred singing men and singing women.
66 Their horses *were* seven hundred
thirty and six; their mules, two hundred
forty and five;
67 Their camels, four hundred thirty
and five; *their* asses, six thousand seven
hundred and twenty.
68 ℭ And *some* of the chief of the
fathers, when they came to the house of
the LORD which *is* at Jerusalem, offered
freely for the house of God to set it up
in his place:
69 They gave after their ability unto
the treasure of the work threescore and
one thousand drams of gold, and five
thousand pounds of silver, and one hundred priests' garments.
70 So the priests, and the Lē′vītes, and
some of the people, and the singers, and
the porters, and the Nĕth′ĭ-nĭm, dwelt in
their cities, and all Ĭș′rā-ĕl in their cities.

CHAPTER 3

AND when the seventh month was
come, and the children of Ĭș′rā-ĕl
were in the cities, the people gathered
themselves together as one man to
Jerusalem.
2 Then stood up Jĕsh′ū-ȧ the son of
Jŏz′ȧ-dăk, and his brethren the priests,
and Zĕ-rŭb′bȧ-bĕl the son of Shē-ăl′tĭ-ĕl, and his brethren, and builded the
altar of the God of Ĭș′rā-ĕl, to offer
burnt offerings thereon, as *it is* written
in the law of Moses the man of God.
3 And they set the altar upon his bases;
for fear *was* upon them because of the
people of those countries: and they
offered burnt offerings thereon unto the
LORD, *even* burnt offerings morning and
evening.
4 They kept also the feast of tabernacles, as *it is* written, and *offered* the
daily burnt offerings by number, according to the custom, as the duty of every
day required;
5 And afterward *offered* the continual
burnt offering, both of the new moons,
and of all the set feasts of the LORD that
were consecrated, and of every one that
willingly offered a freewill offering unto
the LORD.
6 From the first day of the seventh
month began they to offer burnt offerings unto the LORD. But the foundation
of the temple of the LORD was not *yet* laid.

7 They gave money also unto the masons, and to the carpenters; and meat,
and drink, and oil, unto them of Zī'dŏn,
and to them of Tȳre, to bring cedar trees
from Lebanon to the sea of Jŏp'pȧ,
according to the grant that they had of
Cyrus king of Persia.
8 ¶ Now in the second year of their
coming unto the house of God at Jerusalem, in the second month, began Zĕ-
rŭb'bȧ-bĕl the son of Shē-ăl'tĭ-ĕl, and
Jĕsh'ū-ȧ the son of Jŏz'ȧ-dăk, and the
remnant of their brethren the priests
and the Lē'vītes, and all they that were
come out of the captivity unto Jerusalem; and appointed the Lē'vītes, from
twenty years old and upward, to set
forward the work of the house of the
LORD.
9 Then stood Jĕsh'ū-ȧ *with* his sons
and his brethren, Kăd'mĭ-ĕl and his
sons, the sons of Judah, together, to set
forward the workmen in the house of
God: the sons of Hĕn'ȧ-dăd, *with* their
sons and their brethren the Lē'vītes.
10 And when the builders laid the
foundation of the temple of the LORD,
they set the priests in their apparel with
trumpets, and the Lē'vītes the sons of
Ā'săph with cymbals, to praise the
LORD, after the ordinance of David king
of Ĭs'rā-ĕl.
11 And they sang together by course in
praising and giving thanks unto the
LORD; because *he is* good, for his mercy
endureth for ever toward Ĭs'rā-ĕl. And
all the people shouted with a great
shout, when they praised the LORD, because the foundation of the house of the
LORD was laid.
12 But many of the priests and Lē'-
vītes and chief of the fathers, *who were*
ancient men, that had seen the first
house, when the foundation of this house
was laid before their eyes, wept with a
loud voice; and many shouted aloud for
joy:
13 So that the people could not discern
the noise of the shout of joy from the
noise of the weeping of the people: for
the people shouted with a loud shout,
and the noise was heard afar off.

CHAPTER 4

NOW when the adversaries of Judah
and Benjamin heard that the children of the captivity builded the temple
unto the LORD God of Ĭs'rā-ĕl;
2 Then they came to Zĕ-rŭb'bȧ-bĕl,
and to the chief of the fathers, and said
unto them, Let us build with you: for
we seek your God, as ye *do;* and we do
sacrifice unto him since the days of
Ē'sär-hăd'dŏn king of Ăs'sŭr, which
brought us up hither.
3 But Zĕ-rŭb'bȧ-bĕl, and Jĕsh'ū-ȧ, and
the rest of the chief of the fathers of
Ĭs'rā-ĕl, said unto them, Ye have nothing to do with us to build a house unto
our God; but we ourselves together will
build unto the LORD God of Ĭs'rā-ĕl,
as king Cyrus the king of Persia hath
commanded us.
4 Then the people of the land weakened the hands of the people of Judah,
and troubled them in building,
5 And hired counselors against them,
to frustrate their purpose, all the days of
Cyrus king of Persia, even until the
reign of Dȧ-rī'ŭs king of Persia.
6 And in the reign of Ȧ-hăs'ū-ē'rŭs,
in the beginning of his reign, wrote they
unto him an accusation against the inhabitants of Judah and Jerusalem.
7 ¶ And in the days of Är'tăx-ĕrx'ēs
wrote Bĭsh'lăm, Mĭth'rē-dăth, Tā'bē-ĕl,
and the rest of their companions, unto
Är'tăx-ĕrx'ēs king of Persia; and the
writing of the letter *was* written in the
Syrian tongue, and interpreted in the
Syrian tongue.
8 Rē'hŭm the chancellor and Shĭm'-
shaī the scribe wrote a letter against
Jerusalem to Är'tăx-ĕrx'ēs the king in
this sort:
9 Then *wrote* Rē'hŭm the chancellor,
and Shĭm'shaī the scribe, and the rest
of their companions; the Dī'nȧ-ītes, the
Ăph'är-săth'chītes, the Tär'pĕl-ītes, the
Ȧ-phär'sītes, the Är'chē-vītes, the
Babylonians, the Sū-săn'chītes, the Dē-
hā'vītes, *and* the Ē'lăm-ītes,
10 And the rest of the nations whom
the great and noble Ăs-năp'pĕr brought
over, and set in the cities of Sȧ-mā'rĭ-ȧ,
and the rest *that are* on this side the
river, and at such a time.
11 ¶ This *is* the copy of the letter that
they sent unto him, *even* unto Är'tăx-
ĕrx'ēs the king; Thy servants the men
on this side the river, and at such a
time.
12 Be it known unto the king, that the
Jews which came up from thee to us are
come unto Jerusalem, building the rebellious and the bad city, and have set

up the walls *thereof,* and joined the foundations.

13 Be it known now unto the king, that, if this city be builded, and the walls set up *again, then* will they not pay toll, tribute, and custom, and *so* thou shalt endamage the revenue of the kings.

14 Now because we have maintenance from *the king's* palace, and it was not meet for us to see the king's dishonor, therefore have we sent and certified the king;

15 That search may be made in the book of the records of thy fathers: so shalt thou find in the book of the records, and know that this city *is* a rebellious city, and hurtful unto kings and provinces, and that they have moved sedition within the same of old time: for which cause was this city destroyed.

16 We certify the king that, if this city be builded *again,* and the walls thereof set up, by this means thou shalt have no portion on this side the river.

17 ¶ *Then* sent the king an answer unto Rē′hŭm the chancellor, and *to* Shĭm′shaī the scribe, and *to* the rest of their companions that dwell in Să-mā′rĭ-ȧ, and *unto* the rest beyond the river, Peace, and at such a time.

18 The letter which ye sent unto us hath been plainly read before me.

19 And I commanded, and search hath been made, and it is found that this city of old time hath made insurrection against kings, and *that* rebellion and sedition have been made therein.

20 There have been mighty kings also over Jerusalem, which have ruled over all *countries* beyond the river; and toll, tribute, and custom, was paid unto them.

21 Give ye now commandment to cause these men to cease, and that this city be not builded, until *another* commandment shall be given from me.

22 Take heed now that ye fail not to do this: why should damage grow to the hurt of the kings?

23 ¶ Now when the copy of king Är′tăx-ĕrx′ēş′ letter *was* read before Rē′hŭm, and Shĭm′shaī the scribe, and their companions, they went up in haste to Jerusalem unto the Jews, and made them to cease by force and power.

24 Then ceased the work of the house of God which *is* at Jerusalem. So it ceased unto the second year of the reign of Dȧ-rī′ŭs king of Persia.

CHAPTER 5

THEN the prophets, Hăg′gā-ī the prophet, and Zĕch′ȧ-rī′ȧh the son of Ĭd′dō, prophesied unto the Jews that *were* in Judah and Jerusalem in the name of the God of Ĭş′rā-ĕl, *even* unto them.

2 Then rose up Zĕ-rŭb′bȧ-bĕl the son of Shē-ăl′tĭ-ĕl, and Jĕsh′ū-ȧ the son of Jŏz′ȧ-dăk, and began to build the house of God which *is* at Jerusalem: and with them *were* the prophets of God helping them.

3 ¶ At the same time came to them Tăt′naī, governor on this side the river, and Shē′thăr-bŏz′naī, and their companions, and said thus unto them, Who hath commanded you to build this house, and to make up this wall?

4 Then said we unto them after this manner, What are the names of the men that make this building?

5 But the eye of their God was upon the elders of the Jews, that they could not cause them to cease, till the matter came to Dȧ-rī′ŭs: and then they returned answer by letter concerning this *matter.*

6 ¶ The copy of the letter that Tăt′naī, governor on this side the river, and Shē′thăr-bŏz′naī, and his companions the Ȧ-phăr′săch-ītes, which *were* on this side the river, sent unto Dȧ-rī′ŭs the king:

7 They sent a letter unto him, wherein was written thus; Unto Dȧ-rī′ŭs the king, all peace.

8 Be it known unto the king, that we went into the province of Judea, to the house of the great God, which is builded with great stones, and timber is laid in the walls, and this work goeth fast on, and prospereth in their hands.

9 Then asked we those elders, *and* said unto them thus, Who commanded you to build this house, and to make up these walls?

10 We asked their names also, to certify thee, that we might write the names of the men that *were* the chief of them.

11 And thus they returned us answer, saying, We are the servants of the God of heaven and earth, and build the house that was builded these many years ago, which a great king of Ĭş′rā-ĕl builded and set up.

12 But after that our fathers had provoked the God of heaven unto wrath, he gave them into the hand of Nĕb′ū-chăd-

nĕz′zȧr the king of Babylon, the Chăl-
dē′ăn, who destroyed this house, and
carried the people away into Babylon.
13 But in the first year of Cyrus the
king of Babylon, *the same* king Cyrus
made a decree to build this house of
God.
14 And the vessels also of gold and silver of the house of God, which Nĕb′ū-
chăd-nĕz′zȧr took out of the temple that
was in Jerusalem, and brought them
into the temple of Babylon, those did
Cyrus the king take out of the temple of
Babylon, and they were delivered unto
one, whose name *was* Shĕsh-băz′zȧr,
whom he had made governor;
15 And said unto him, Take these vessels, go, carry them into the temple that
is in Jerusalem, and let the house of God
be builded in his place.
16 Then came the same Shĕsh-băz′zȧr,
and laid the foundation of the house of
God which *is* in Jerusalem: and since
that time even until now hath it been in
building, and *yet* it is not finished.
17 Now therefore, if *it seem* good to
the king, let there be search made in the
king's treasure house, which *is* there at
Babylon, whether it be *so,* that a decree
was made of Cyrus the king to build this
house of God at Jerusalem, and let the
king send his pleasure to us concerning
this matter.

CHAPTER 6

THEN Dȧ-rī′ŭs the king made a decree, and search was made in the
house of the rolls, where the treasures
were laid up in Babylon.
2 And there was found at Ăch′mē-thȧ,
in the palace that *is* in the province of
the Mēdeș, a roll, and therein *was* a
record thus written:
3 In the first year of Cyrus the king,
the same Cyrus the king made a decree
concerning the house of God at Jerusalem, Let the house be builded, the place
where they offered sacrifices, and let the
foundations thereof be strongly laid; the
height thereof threescore cubits, *and*
the breadth thereof threescore cubits;
4 *With* three rows of great stones, and
a row of new timber: and let the expenses be given out of the king's house:
5 And also let the golden and silver
vessels of the house of God, which Nĕb′ū-
chăd-nĕz′zȧr took forth out of the temple
which *is* at Jerusalem, and brought unto
Babylon, be restored, and brought again
unto the temple which *is* at Jerusalem,
every one to his place, and place *them*
in the house of God.
6 Now *therefore,* Tăt′naī, governor beyond the river, Shē′thär–bŏz′naī, and
your companions the Ȧ-phär′săch-ītes,
which *are* beyond the river, be ye far
from thence:
7 Let the work of this house of God
alone; let the governor of the Jews and
the elders of the Jews build this house
of God in his place.
8 Moreover I make a decree what ye
shall do to the elders of these Jews for
the building of this house of God: that
of the king's goods, *even* of the tribute
beyond the river, forthwith expenses be
given unto these men, that they be not
hindered.
9 And that which they have need of,
both young bullocks, and rams, and
lambs, for the burnt offerings of the God
of heaven, wheat, salt, wine, and oil, according to the appointment of the priests
which *are* at Jerusalem, let it be given
them day by day without fail:
10 That they may offer sacrifices of
sweet savors unto the God of heaven,
and pray for the life of the king, and of
his sons.
11 Also I have made a decree, that
whosoever shall alter this word, let
timber be pulled down from his house,
and being set up, let him be hanged
thereon; and let his house be made a
dunghill for this.
12 And the God that hath caused his
name to dwell there destroy all kings
and people, that shall put to their hand
to alter *and* to destroy this house of God
which *is* at Jerusalem. I Dȧ-rī′ŭs have
made a decree; let it be done with speed.
13 ℂ Then Tăt′naī, governor on this
side the river, Shē′thär–bŏz′naī, and
their companions, according to that
which Dȧ-rī′ŭs the king had sent, so
they did speedily.
14 And the elders of the Jews builded,
and they prospered through the prophesying of Hăg′gā-ī the prophet and Zĕch′-
ȧ-rī′ȧh the son of Ĭd′dō. And they builded, and finished *it,* according to the
commandment of the God of Ĭș′rā-ĕl,
and according to the commandment of
Cyrus, and Dȧ-rī′ŭs, and Är′tăx-ẽrx′ĕș
king of Persia.
15 And this house was finished on the

third day of the month Ȧ-där′, which
was in the sixth year of the reign of Dȧ-
rī′ŭs the king.
16 ℂ And the children of Ĭs̱′rā-ĕl, the
priests, and the Lē′vītes, and the rest of
the children of the captivity, kept the
dedication of this house of God with
joy,
17 And offered at the dedication of this
house of God a hundred bullocks, two
hundred rams, four hundred lambs; and
for a sin offering for all Ĭs̱′rā-ĕl, twelve
he goats, according to the number of the
tribes of Ĭs̱′rā-ĕl.
18 And they set the priests in their
divisions, and the Lē′vītes in their
courses, for the service of God, which *is*
at Jerusalem; as it is written in the book
of Moses.
19 And the children of the captivity
kept the passover upon the fourteenth
day of the first month.
20 For the priests and the Lē′vītes were
purified together, all of them *were* pure,
and killed the passover for all the children of the captivity, and for their brethren the priests, and for themselves.
21 And the children of Ĭs̱′rā-ĕl, which
were come again out of captivity, and
all such as had separated themselves
unto them from the filthiness of the
heathen of the land, to seek the LORD
God of Ĭs̱′rā-ĕl, did eat,
22 And kept the feast of unleavened
bread seven days with joy: for the LORD
had made them joyful, and turned the
heart of the king of Assyria unto them,
to strengthen their hands in the work of
the house of God, the God of Ĭs̱′rā-ĕl.

CHAPTER 7

NOW after these things, in the reign
of Är′tăx-ĕrx′ēs̱ king of Persia,
Ezra the son of Sē-rā′ịah, the son of
Ăz′ȧ-rī′ȧh, the son of Hĭl-kī′ȧh,
2 The son of Shăl′lŭm, the son of Zā′-
dŏk, the son of Ȧ-hī′tŭb,
3 The son of Ăm′ȧ-rī′ȧh, the son of
Ăz′ȧ-rī′ȧh, the son of Mē-rā′ịōth,
4 The son of Zĕr′ȧ-hī′ȧh, the son of
Ŭz′zī, the son of Bŭk′kī,
5 The son of Ȧ-bĭsh′ū-ȧ, the son of
Phĭn′ē-hăs, the son of Ĕl′ē-ā′zȧr, the
son of Aaron the chief priest:
6 This Ezra went up from Babylon; and
he *was* a ready scribe in the law of
Moses, which the LORD God of Ĭs̱′rā-ĕl
had given: and the king granted him all
his request, according to the hand of the
LORD his God upon him.
7 And there went up *some* of the children of Ĭs̱′rā-ĕl, and of the priests, and
the Lē′vītes, and the singers, and the
porters, and the Nĕth′ĭ-nĭm, unto Jerusalem, in the seventh year of Är′tăx-
ĕrx′ēs̱ the king.
8 And he came to Jerusalem in the
fifth month, which *was* in the seventh
year of the king.
9 For upon the first *day* of the first
month began he to go up from Babylon,
and on the first *day* of the fifth month
came he to Jerusalem, according to the
good hand of his God upon him.
10 For Ezra had prepared his heart to
seek the law of the LORD, and to do *it*,
and to teach in Ĭs̱′rā-ĕl statutes and
judgments.
11 ℂ Now this *is* the copy of the letter
that the king Är′tăx-ĕrx′ēs̱ gave unto
Ezra the priest, the scribe, *even* a scribe
of the words of the commandments of
the LORD, and of his statutes to Ĭs̱′rā-ĕl.
12 Är′tăx-ĕrx′ēs̱, king of kings, unto
Ezra the priest, a scribe of the law of
the God of heaven, perfect *peace*, and
at such a time.
13 I make a decree, that all they of the
people of Ĭs̱′rā-ĕl, and *of* his priests and
Lē′vītes, in my realm, which are minded
of their own free will to go up to Jerusalem, go with thee.
14 Forasmuch as thou art sent of the
king, and of his seven counselors, to inquire concerning Judah and Jerusalem,
according to the law of thy God which *is*
in thine hand;
15 And to carry the silver and gold,
which the king and his counselors have
freely offered unto the God of Ĭs̱′rā-ĕl,
whose habitation *is* in Jerusalem,
16 And all the silver and gold that thou
canst find in all the province of Babylon,
with the freewill offering of the people,
and of the priests, offering willingly for
the house of their God which *is* in
Jerusalem:
17 That thou mayest buy speedily with
this money bullocks, rams, lambs, with
their meat offerings and their drink offerings, and offer them upon the altar of the
house of your God which *is* in Jerusalem.
18 And whatsoever shall seem good to
thee, and to thy brethren, to do with the
rest of the silver and the gold, that do
after the will of your God.

19 The vessels also that are given thee
for the service of the house of thy God,
those deliver thou before the God of
Jerusalem.
20 And whatsoever more shall be needful for the house of thy God, which thou
shalt have occasion to bestow, bestow *it*
out of the king's treasure house.
21 And I, *even* I Är´tăx-ĕrx´ēș the king,
do make a decree to all the treasurers
which *are* beyond the river, that whatsoever Ezra the priest, the scribe of the
law of the God of heaven, shall require
of you, it be done speedily,
22 Unto a hundred talents of silver, and
to a hundred measures of wheat, and to
a hundred baths of wine, and to a hundred baths of oil, and salt without pre-
scribing *how much*.
23 Whatsoever is commanded by the
God of heaven, let it be diligently done
for the house of the God of heaven: for
why should there be wrath against the
realm of the king and his sons?
24 Also we certify you, that, touching
any of the priests and Lē´vītes, singers,
porters, Nĕth´ĭ-nĭm, or ministers of this
house of God, it shall not be lawful to im-
pose toll, tribute, or custom, upon them.
25 And thou, Ezra, after the wisdom of
thy God, that *is* in thine hand, set magistrates and judges, which may judge all
the people that *are* beyond the river, all
such as know the laws of thy God; and
teach ye them that know *them* not.
26 And whosoever will not do the law
of thy God, and the law of the king, let
judgment be executed speedily upon
him, whether *it be* unto death, or to
banishment, or to confiscation of goods,
or to imprisonment.
27 ¶ Blessed *be* the LORD God of our
fathers, which hath put *such a thing* as
this in the king's heart, to beautify the
house of the LORD which *is* in Jerusalem:
28 And hath extended mercy unto me
before the king, and his counselors, and
before all the king's mighty princes. And
I was strengthened as the hand of the
LORD my God *was* upon me, and I gathered together out of Ĭș´rā-ĕl chief men
to go up with me.

CHAPTER 8

THESE *are* now the chief of their fathers, and *this is* the genealogy of
them that went up with me from Babylon in the reign of Är´tăx-ĕrx´ēș the king.
2 Of the sons of Phĭn´ē-hăs; Gĕr´shŏm:
of the sons of Ĭth´ȧ-mär; Daniel: of the
sons of David; Hăt´tŭsh.
3 Of the sons of Shĕch´ȧ-nī´ȧh, of the
sons of Phā´rŏsh; Zĕch´ȧ-rī´ȧh: and with
him were reckoned by genealogy of the
males a hundred and fifty.
4 Of the sons of Pā´hăth–mō´ăb; Ĕl´ĭ-
hō-ē´nā-ī the son of Zĕr´ȧ-hī´ȧh, and
with him two hundred males.
5 Of the sons of Shĕch´ȧ-nī´ȧh; the son
of Jȧ-hā´zĭ-ĕl, and with him three hundred males.
6 Of the sons also of Ā´dĭn; Ē´bĕd the
son of Jonathan, and with him fifty
males.
7 And of the sons of Ē´lăm; Jē-shā´ịȧh
the son of Ăth´ȧ-lī´ȧh, and with him
seventy males.
8 And of the sons of Shĕph´ȧ-tī´ȧh;
Zĕb´ȧ-dī´ȧh the son of Mī´chā-ĕl, and
with him fourscore males.
9 Of the sons of Jō´ăb; Ō´bȧ-dī´ȧh the
son of Jē-hī´ĕl, and with him two hundred and eighteen males.
10 And of the sons of Shē-lō´mĭth; the
son of Jŏs´ĭ-phī´ȧh, and with him a hundred and threescore males.
11 And of the sons of Bĕb´ā-ī; Zĕch´ȧ-
rī´ȧh the son of Bĕb´ā-ī, and with him
twenty and eight males.
12 And of the sons of Ăz´găd; Jō-hā´năn
the son of Hăk´kȧ-tăn, and with him a
hundred and ten males.
13 And of the last sons of Ăd´ō-nī´kăm,
whose names *are* these, Ē-lĭph´ē-lĕt,
Jē-ī´ĕl, and Shē-mā´ịȧh, and with them
threescore males.
14 Of the sons also of Bĭg´vā-ī; Ū´thaī,
and Zăb´bŭd, and with them seventy
males.
15 ¶ And I gathered them together to
the river that runneth to Ȧ-hā´vȧ; and
there abode we in tents three days: and
I viewed the people, and the priests, and
found there none of the sons of Levi.
16 Then sent I for Ĕl´ĭ-ē´zĕr, for Ā´rĭ-ĕl,
for Shē-mā´ịȧh, and for Ĕl-nā´thăn, and
for Jā´rĭb, and for Ĕl-nā´thăn, and for
Nathan, and for Zĕch´ȧ-rī´ȧh, and for
Mē-shŭl´lăm, chief men; also for Jŏi´ȧ-
rĭb, and for Ĕl-nā´thăn, men of understanding.
17 And I sent them with commandment unto Ĭd´dō the chief at the place
Cȧ-sĭph´ĭ-ȧ, and I told them what they
should say unto Ĭd´dō, *and* to his brethren the Nĕth´ĭ-nĭm, at the place Cȧ-

sĭph'ĭ-ȧ, that they should bring unto us
ministers for the house of our God.
18 And by the good hand of our God
upon us they brought us a man of understanding,
of the sons of Mäh'lī, the son
of Levi, the son of Ĭṣ'rā-ĕl; and Shĕr'ē-
bī'ȧh, with his sons and his brethren,
eighteen;
19 And Hăsh'ȧ-bī'ȧh, and with him Jē-
shā'ịah of the sons of Mē-rā'rī, his
brethren and their sons, twenty;
20 Also of the Nĕth'ĭ-nĭm, whom David
and the princes had appointed for the
service of the Lē'vītes, two hundred and
twenty Nĕth'ĭ-nĭm: all of them were expressed
by name.
21 ¶ Then I proclaimed a fast there,
at the river of Ȧ-hā'vȧ, that we might
afflict ourselves before our God, to seek
of him a right way for us, and for our
little ones, and for all our substance.
22 For I was ashamed to require of the
king a band of soldiers and horsemen to
help us against the enemy in the way:
because we had spoken unto the king,
saying, The hand of our God *is* upon all
them for good that seek him; but his
power and his wrath *is* against all them
that forsake him.
23 So we fasted and besought our God
for this: and he was entreated of us.
24 ¶ Then I separated twelve of the
chief of the priests, Shĕr'ē-bī'ȧh, Hăsh'ȧ-
bī'ȧh, and ten of their brethren with
them,
25 And weighed unto them the silver,
and the gold, and the vessels, *even* the
offering of the house of our God, which
the king, and his counselors, and his
lords, and all Ĭṣ'rā-ĕl *there* present, had
offered:
26 I even weighed unto their hand six
hundred and fifty talents of silver, and
silver vessels a hundred talents, *and* of
gold a hundred talents;
27 Also twenty basins of gold, of a
thousand drams; and two vessels of fine
copper, precious as gold.
28 And I said unto them, Ye *are* holy
unto the LORD; the vessels *are* holy also;
and the silver and the gold *are* a freewill
offering unto the LORD God of your
fathers.
29 Watch ye, and keep *them*, until ye
weigh *them* before the chief of the
priests and the Lē'vītes, and chief of the
fathers of Ĭṣ'rā-ĕl, at Jerusalem, in the
chambers of the house of the LORD.
30 So took the priests and the Lē'vītes
the weight of the silver, and the gold,
and the vessels, to bring *them* to Jerusalem
unto the house of our God.
31 ¶ Then we departed from the river
of Ȧ-hā'vȧ on the twelfth *day* of the first
month, to go unto Jerusalem: and the
hand of our God was upon us, and he
delivered us from the hand of the enemy,
and of such as lay in wait by the way.
32 And we came to Jerusalem, and
abode there three days.
33 ¶ Now on the fourth day was the
silver and the gold and the vessels
weighed in the house of our God by the
hand of Mĕr'ē-mŏth the son of Ū-rī'ȧh
the priest; and with him *was* Ĕl'ē-ā'zȧr
the son of Phĭn'ē-hăs; and with them
was Jŏz'ȧ-băd the son of Jĕsh'ū-ȧ, and
Nō'ȧ-dī'ȧh the son of Bĭn'nū-ī, Lē'vītes;
34 By number *and* by weight of every
one: and all the weight was written at
that time.
35 *Also* the children of those that had
been carried away, which were come out
of the captivity, offered burnt offerings
unto the God of Ĭṣ'rā-ĕl, twelve bullocks
for all Ĭṣ'rā-ĕl, ninety and six rams,
seventy and seven lambs, twelve he
goats *for* a sin offering: all *this was* a
burnt offering unto the LORD.
36 ¶ And they delivered the king's
commissions unto the king's lieutenants,
and to the governors on this side
the river: and they furthered the people,
and the house of God.

CHAPTER 9

NOW when these things were done,
the princes came to me, saying,
The people of Ĭṣ'rā-ĕl, and the priests,
and the Lē'vītes, have not separated
themselves from the people of the lands,
doing according to their abominations,
even of the Cā'năan-ītes, the Hĭt'tītes, the
Pĕr'iz-zītes, the Jĕb'ū-ṣītes, the Ammonites,
the Mō'ăb-ītes, the Egyptians,
and the Ăm'ō-rītes.
2 For they have taken of their daughters
for themselves, and for their sons:
so that the holy seed have mingled
themselves with the people of *those*
lands: yea, the hand of the princes and
rulers hath been chief in this trespass.
3 And when I heard this thing, I rent
my garment and my mantle, and plucked
off the hair of my head and of my beard,
and sat down astonished.

4 Then were assembled unto me every
one that trembled at the words of the
God of Ĭṣ′rā-ĕl, because of the transgression of those that had been carried
away; and I sat astonished until the
evening sacrifice.
5 ℂ And at the evening sacrifice I arose
up from my heaviness; and having rent
my garment and my mantle, I fell upon
my knees, and spread out my hands
unto the LORD my God,
6 And said, O my God, I am ashamed
and blush to lift up my face to thee, my
God: for our iniquities are increased
over *our* head, and our trespass is grown
up unto the heavens.
7 Since the days of our fathers *have* we
been in a great trespass unto this day;
and for our iniquities have we, our kings,
and our priests, been delivered into the
hand of the kings of the lands, to the
sword, to captivity, and to a spoil, and to
confusion of face, as *it is* this day.
8 And now for a little space grace hath
been *showed* from the LORD our God,
to leave us a remnant to escape, and to
give us a nail in his holy place, that our
God may lighten our eyes, and give us a
little reviving in our bondage.
9 For we *were* bondmen; yet our God
hath not forsaken us in our bondage, but
hath extended mercy unto us in the sight
of the kings of Persia, to give us a reviving, to set up the house of our God,
and to repair the desolations thereof,
and to give us a wall in Judah and in
Jerusalem.
10 And now, O our God, what shall we
say after this? for we have forsaken thy
commandments,
11 Which thou hast commanded by thy
servants the prophets, saying, The land,
unto which ye go to possess it, is an
unclean land with the filthiness of the
people of the lands, with their abominations, which have filled it from one
end to another with their uncleanness.
12 Now therefore give not your daughters unto their sons, neither take their
daughters unto your sons, nor seek their
peace or their wealth for ever: that ye
may be strong, and eat the good of the
land, and leave *it* for an inheritance to
your children for ever.
13 And after all that is come upon us for
our evil deeds, and for our great trespass, seeing that thou our God hast punished us less than our iniquities *deserve*,
and hast given us *such* deliverance as
this;
14 Should we again break thy commandments, and join in affinity with the
people of these abominations? wouldest
not thou be angry with us till thou hadst
consumed *us*, so that *there should be* no
remnant nor escaping?
15 O LORD God of Ĭṣ′rā-ĕl, thou *art*
righteous; for we remain yet escaped,
as *it is* this day: behold, we *are* before
thee in our trespasses; for we cannot
stand before thee because of this.

CHAPTER 10

NOW when Ezra had prayed, and
when he had confessed, weeping
and casting himself down before the
house of God, there assembled unto him
out of Ĭṣ′rā-ĕl a very great congregation
of men and women and children: for the
people wept very sore.
2 And Shĕch′ȧ-nī′ȧh the son of Jē-hī′ĕl,
one of the sons of Ē′lăm, answered and
said unto Ezra, We have trespassed
against our God, and have taken strange
wives of the people of the land: yet now
there is hope in Ĭṣ′rā-ĕl concerning this
thing.
3 Now therefore let us make a covenant
with our God to put away all the wives,
and such as are born of them, according
to the counsel of my lord, and of those
that tremble at the commandment of
our God; and let it be done according to
the law.
4 Arise; for *this* matter *belongeth* unto
thee: we also *will be* with thee: be of
good courage, and do *it*.
5 Then arose Ezra, and made the chief
priests, the Lē′vītes, and all Ĭṣ′rā-ĕl, to
swear that they should do according to
this word. And they sware.
6 ℂ Then Ezra rose up from before the
house of God, and went into the chamber of Jō-hā′năn the son of Ē-lī′ȧ-shĭb:
and *when* he came thither, he did eat no
bread, nor drink water: for he mourned
because of the transgression of them
that had been carried away.
7 And they made proclamation throughout Judah and Jerusalem unto all the
children of the captivity, that they should
gather themselves together unto Jerusalem;
8 And that whosoever would not come
within three days, according to the counsel of the princes and the elders, all his

substance should be forfeited, and himself separated from the congregation of
those that had been carried away.
9 ℂ Then all the men of Judah and
Benjamin gathered themselves together
unto Jerusalem within three days. It
was the ninth month, on the twentieth
day of the month; and all the people sat
in the street of the house of God, trembling because of *this* matter, and for the
great rain.
10 And Ezra the priest stood up, and
said unto them, Ye have transgressed,
and have taken strange wives, to increase the trespass of Ĭş'rā-ĕl.
11 Now therefore make confession unto
the LORD God of your fathers, and do
his pleasure: and separate yourselves
from the people of the land, and from
the strange wives.
12 Then all the congregation answered
and said with a loud voice, As thou hast
said, so must we do.
13 But the people *are* many, and *it is* a
time of much rain, and we are not able
to stand without, neither *is this* a work
of one day or two: for we are many that
have transgressed in this thing.
14 Let now our rulers of all the congregation stand, and let all them which have
taken strange wives in our cities come at
appointed times, and with them the elders of every city, and the judges thereof,
until the fierce wrath of our God for this
matter be turned from us.
15 ℂ Only Jonathan the son of Ăs'à-hĕl
and Jā'hà-zī'āh the son of Tĭk'văh were
employed about this *matter:* and Mē-
shŭl'lăm and Shăb'bē-thaī the Lē'vīte
helped them.
16 And the children of the captivity did
so. And Ezra the priest, *with* certain
chief of the fathers, after the house of
their fathers, and all of them by *their*
names, were separated, and sat down
in the first day of the tenth month to
examine the matter.
17 And they made an end with all the
men that had taken strange wives by the
first day of the first month.
18 ℂ And among the sons of the priests
there were found that had taken strange
wives: *namely,* of the sons of Jĕsh'ū-à
the son of Jŏz'à-dăk, and his brethren;
Mā'à-sē'ịah, and Ĕl'ī-ē'zĕr, and Jā'rĭb,
and Gĕd'à-lī'āh.
19 And they gave their hands that they
would put away their wives; and *being*
guilty, *they offered* a ram of the flock for
their trespass.
20 And of the sons of Ĭm'mĕr; Hà-nā'nī,
and Zĕb'à-dī'āh.
21 And of the sons of Hā'rĭm; Mā'à-sē'-
ịah, and Ē-lī'jàh, and Shē-mā'ịah, and
Jē-hī'ĕl, and Ŭz-zī'āh.
22 And of the sons of Păsh'ŭr; Ē-lī'ō-ē'-
nā-ī, Mā'à-sē'ịah, Ĭsh'mā-ĕl, Nē-thăn'-
ē-ĕl, Jŏz'à-băd, and Ĕl'à-sàh.
23 Also of the Lē'vītes; Jŏz'à-băd, and
Shĭm'ē-ī, and Kē-lā'ịah, (the same *is*
Kĕl'ī-tà,) Pĕth'à-hī'āh, Judah, and Ĕl'ī-
ē'zĕr.
24 Of the singers also; Ē-lī'à-shĭb: and
of the porters; Shăl'lŭm, and Tē'lĕm,
and Ū'rī.
25 Moreover of Ĭş'rā-ĕl: of the sons of
Pā'rŏsh; Rà-mī'āh, and Jē-zī'āh, and
Măl-chī'āh, and Mī'à-mĭn, and Ĕl'ē-
ā'zàr, and Măl-chī'jàh, and Bē-nā'ịah.
26 And of the sons of E'lăm; Măt'tà-
nī'āh, Zĕch'à-rī'āh, and Jē-hī'ĕl, and
Ăb'dī, and Jĕr'ē-mŏth, and Ē-lī'āh.
27 And of the sons of Zăt'tū; Ē-lī'ō-ē'-
nā-ī, Ē-lī'à-shĭb, Măt'tà-nī'āh, and Jĕr'-
ē-mŏth, and Zā'băd, and À-zī'zà.
28 Of the sons also of Bĕb'ā-ī; Jē'hō-
hā'năn, Hăn'à-nī'āh, Zăb'bā-ī, *and*
Ăth'lā-ī.
29 And of the sons of Bā'nī; Mē-shŭl'-
lăm, Măl'lŭch, and À-dā'ịah, Jā'shŭb,
and Shē'ăl, and Rā'mŏth.
30 And of the sons of Pā'hăth-mō'ăb;
Ăd'nà, and Chē'lăl, Bē-nā'ịah, Mā'à-sē'-
ịah, Măt'tà-nī'āh, Bē-zăl'ē-ĕl, and Bĭn'-
nū-ī, and Mà-năs'sĕh.
31 And *of* the sons of Hā'rĭm; Ĕl'ī-ē'-
zĕr, Ī-shī'jàh, Măl-chī'āh, Shē-mā'ịah,
Shĭm'ē-ŏn,
32 Benjamin, Măl'lŭch, *and* Shĕm'à-
rī'āh.
33 Of the sons of Hā'shŭm; Măt'tē-
nā'ī, Măt'tà-thàh, Zā'băd, Ē-lĭph'ē-lĕt,
Jĕr'ē-maī, Mà-năs'sĕh, *and* Shĭm'ē-ī.
34 Of the sons of Bā'nī; Mā'à-dā'ī,
Ăm'răm, and Ū'ĕl,
35 Bē-nā'ịah, Bē-dē'ịah, Chĕl'lŭh,
36 Và-nī'āh, Mĕr'ē-mŏth, Ē-lī'à-shĭb,
37 Măt'tà-nī'āh, Măt'tē-nā'ī, and Jā'-
à-saû,
38 And Bā'nī, and Bĭn'nū-ī, Shĭm'ē-ī,
39 And Shĕl'ē-mī'āh, and Nathan, and
À-dā'ịah,
40 Măch-năd'ē-baī, Shā'shaī, Shà-rā'ī,
41 À-zā'rē-ĕl, and Shĕl'ē-mī'āh, Shĕm'-
ā-rī'āh,
42 Shăl'lŭm, Ăm'à-rī'āh, *and* Joseph.

43 Of the sons of Nē′bō; Jē-ī′ĕl, Măt′tĭ-
thī′ȧh, Zā′băd, Zē-bī′nȧ, Jā′daŭ, and
Joel, Bē-nā′ịȧh.
44 All these had taken strange wives:
and *some* of them had wives by whom
they had children.

THE BOOK OF NEHEMIAH

CHAPTER 1

THE words of Nē′hē-mī′ȧh the son of
Hăch′ȧ-lī′ȧh. And it came to pass
in the month Chĭs′leū, in the twentieth
year, as I was in Shụ′shăn the palace,
2 That Hȧ-nā′nī, one of my brethren,
came, he and *certain* men of Judah; and
I asked them concerning the Jews that
had escaped, which were left of the captivity, and concerning Jerusalem.
3 And they said unto me, The remnant
that are left of the captivity there in the
province *are* in great affliction and reproach: the wall of Jerusalem also *is*
broken down, and the gates thereof are
burned with fire.
4 ¶ And it came to pass, when I heard
these words, that I sat down and wept,
and mourned *certain* days, and fasted,
and prayed before the God of heaven,
5 And said, I beseech thee, O LORD
God of heaven, the great and terrible
God, that keepeth covenant and mercy
for them that love him and observe his
commandments:
6 Let thine ear now be attentive, and
thine eyes open, that thou mayest hear
the prayer of thy servant, which I pray
before thee now, day and night, for the
children of Ĭṣ′rā-ĕl thy servants, and
confess the sins of the children of Ĭṣ′-
rā-ĕl, which we have sinned against thee:
both I and my father's house have
sinned.
7 We have dealt very corruptly against
thee, and have not kept the commandments, nor the statutes, nor the judgments, which thou commandedst thy
servant Moses.
8 Remember, I beseech thee, the word
that thou commandedst thy servant
Moses, saying, *If* ye transgress, I will
scatter you abroad among the nations:
9 But *if* ye turn unto me, and keep my
commandments, and do them; though
there were of you cast out unto the uttermost part of the heaven, *yet* will I gather
them from thence, and will bring them
unto the place that I have chosen to set
my name there.
10 Now these *are* thy servants and
thy people, whom thou hast redeemed
by thy great power, and by thy strong
hand.
11 O Lord, I beseech thee, let now
thine ear be attentive to the prayer of
thy servant, and to the prayer of thy
servants, who desire to fear thy name:
and prosper, I pray thee, thy servant
this day, and grant him mercy in the
sight of this man. For I was the king's
cupbearer.

CHAPTER 2

AND it came to pass in the month
Nī′săn, in the twentieth year of
Ăr′tăx-ērx′ēṣ the king, *that* wine *was* before him: and I took up the wine, and
gave *it* unto the king. Now I had not
been *beforetime* sad in his presence.
2 Wherefore the king said unto me,
Why *is* thy countenance sad, seeing thou
art not sick? this *is* nothing *else* but sorrow of heart. Then I was very sore
afraid,
3 And said unto the king, Let the king
live for ever: why should not my countenance be sad, when the city, the place of
my fathers' sepulchres, *lieth* waste, and
the gates thereof are consumed with
fire?
4 Then the king said unto me, For what
dost thou make request? So I prayed to
the God of heaven.
5 And I said unto the king, If it please
the king, and if thy servant have found
favor in thy sight, that thou wouldest
send me unto Judah, unto the city of my
fathers' sepulchres, that I may build it.
6 And the king said unto me, (the queen
also sitting by him,) For how long shall
thy journey be? and when wilt thou return? So it pleased the king to send me;
and I set him a time.
7 Moreover I said unto the king, If it

please the king, let letters be given me
to the governors beyond the river, that
they may convey me over till I come into
Judah;
8 And a letter unto Ā'săph the keeper
of the king's forest, that he may give me
timber to make beams for the gates of
the palace which *appertained* to the
house, and for the wall of the city, and
for the house that I shall enter into. And
the king granted me, according to the
good hand of my God upon me.
9 ¶ Then I came to the governors beyond the river, and gave them the king's
letters. Now the king had sent captains
of the army and horsemen with me.
10 When Săn-băl'lăt the Hŏr'ō-nīte,
and Tō-bī'ȧh the servant, the Ammonite,
heard *of it,* it grieved them exceedingly
that there was come a man to seek the
welfare of the children of Ĭṣ'rā-ĕl.
11 So I came to Jerusalem, and was
there three days.
12 ¶ And I arose in the night, I and
some few men with me; neither told I *any*
man what my God had put in my heart
to do at Jerusalem: neither *was there*
any beast with me, save the beast that I
rode upon.
13 And I went out by night by the gate
of the valley, even before the dragon
well, and to the dung port, and viewed
the walls of Jerusalem, which were broken down, and the gates thereof were
consumed with fire.
14 Then I went on to the gate of the
fountain, and to the king's pool: but
there was no place for the beast *that was*
under me to pass.
15 Then went I up in the night by the
brook, and viewed the wall, and turned
back, and entered by the gate of the valley, and *so* returned.
16 And the rulers knew not whither I
went, or what I did; neither had I as yet
told *it* to the Jews, nor to the priests, nor
to the nobles, nor to the rulers, nor to
the rest that did the work.
17 ¶ Then said I unto them, Ye see the
distress that we *are* in, how Jerusalem
lieth waste, and the gates thereof are
burned with fire: come, and let us build
up the wall of Jerusalem, that we be no
more a reproach.
18 Then I told them of the hand of my
God which was good upon me; as also
the king's words that he had spoken
unto me. And they said, Let us rise up
and build. So they strengthened their
hands for *this* good *work.*
19 But when Săn-băl'lăt the Hŏr'ō-nīte,
and Tō-bī'ȧh the servant, the Ammonite,
and Gē'shĕm the Arabian, heard *it,* they
laughed us to scorn, and despised us,
and said, What *is* this thing that ye do?
will ye rebel against the king?
20 Then answered I them, and said
unto them, The God of heaven, he will
prosper us; therefore we his servants
will arise and build: but ye have no portion, nor right, nor memorial, in Jerusalem.

CHAPTER 3

THEN Ē-lī'ȧ-shĭb the high priest rose
up with his brethren the priests, and
they builded the sheep gate; they sanctified it, and set up the doors of it; even
unto the tower of Mē'ȧh they sanctified
it, unto the tower of Hȧ-năn'ē-ĕl.
2 And next unto him builded the men
of Jĕr'ī-chō. And next to them builded
Zăc'cŭr the son of Ĭm'rī.
3 But the fish gate did the sons of Hăs-
sē-nā'ȧh build, who *also* laid the beams
thereof, and set up the doors thereof,
the locks thereof, and the bars thereof.
4 And next unto them repaired Mĕr'ē-
mŏth the son of Ū-rī'jȧh, the son of Kŏz.
And next unto them repaired Mē-shŭl'-
lăm the son of Bĕr'ē-chī'ȧh, the son of
Mē-shĕz'ȧ-bēel. And next unto them
repaired Zā'dŏk the son of Bā'ȧ-nȧ.
5 And next unto them the Tē-kō'ītes
repaired; but their nobles put not their
necks to the work of their Lord.
6 Moreover the old gate repaired Jē-
hoi'ȧ-dȧ the son of Pȧ-sē'ȧh, and Mē-
shŭl'lăm the son of Bĕs'ō-dē'ịah; they
laid the beams thereof, and set up the
doors thereof, and the locks thereof, and
the bars thereof.
7 And next unto them repaired Mĕl'ȧ-
tī'ȧh the Gĭb'ē-ȯn-īte, and Jā'dŏn the
Mē-rŏn'ō-thīte, the men of Gĭb'ē-ȯn,
and of Mĭz'păh, unto the throne of the
governor on this side the river.
8 Next unto him repaired Ŭz-zī'ĕl the
son of Här-hā'ịah, of the goldsmiths.
Next unto him also repaired Hăn'ȧ-nī'ȧh
the son of *one of* the apothecaries, and
they fortified Jerusalem unto the broad
wall.
9 And next unto them repaired Rē-phā'-
ịah the son of Hûr, the ruler of the half
part of Jerusalem.

10 And next unto them repaired Jē-dā′-
iah the son of Hȧ-ru′mȧph, even over
against his house. And next unto him
repaired Hăt′tŭsh the son of Hăsh′ăb-
nī′ȧh.
11 Măl-chī′jȧh the son of Hā′rĭm, and
Hā′shŭb the son of Pā′hăth–mō′ăb, repaired the other piece, and the tower of
the furnaces.
12 And next unto him repaired Shăl′-
lŭm the son of Hă-lō′hĕsh, the ruler of
the half part of Jerusalem, he and his
daughters.
13 The valley gate repaired Hā′nŭn, and
the inhabitants of Zȧ-nō′ȧh; they built
it, and set up the doors thereof, the locks
thereof, and the bars thereof, and a thousand cubits on the wall unto the dung
gate.
14 But the dung gate repaired Măl-
chī′ȧh the son of Rē′chăb, the ruler of
part of Bĕth′–hăc′çē-rĕm; he built it, and
set up the doors thereof, the locks thereof, and the bars thereof.
15 But the gate of the fountain repaired
Shăl′lŭn the son of Cŏl–hō′zĕh, the
ruler of part of Mĭz′păh; he built it, and
covered it, and set up the doors thereof,
the locks thereof, and the bars thereof,
and the wall of the pool of Sĭ-lō′ȧh by
the king's garden, and unto the stairs
that go down from the city of David.
16 After him repaired Nē′hē-mī′ȧh the
son of Ăz′bŭk, the ruler of the half part
of Bĕth′–zûr′, unto *the place* over
against the sepulchres of David, and to
the pool that was made, and unto the
house of the mighty.
17 After him repaired the Lē′vītes, Rē′-
hŭm the son of Bā′nī. Next unto him
repaired Hăsh′ȧ-bī′ȧh, the ruler of the
half part of Kē-ī′lȧh, in his part.
18 After him repaired their brethren,
Băv′ā-ī the son of Hĕn′ȧ-dăd, the ruler
of the half part of Kē-ī′lȧh.
19 And next to him repaired Ē′zĕr the
son of Jĕsh′ū-ȧ, the ruler of Mĭz′păh,
another piece over against the going
up to the armory at the turning *of the
wall.*
20 After him Bā′rŭch the son of Zăb′-
bā-ī earnestly repaired the other piece,
from the turning *of the wall* unto the
door of the house of Ē-lī′ȧ-shĭb the high
priest.
21 After him repaired Mĕr′ē-mŏth the
son of Ū-rī′jȧh the son of Kŏz another
piece, from the door of the house of
Ē-lī′ȧ-shĭb even to the end of the house
of Ē-lī′ȧ-shĭb.
22 And after him repaired the priests,
the men of the plain.
23 After him repaired Benjamin and
Hā′shŭb over against their house. After
him repaired Ăz′ȧ-rī′ȧh the son of Mā′ȧ-
sē′iah the son of Ăn′ȧ-nī′ȧh by his house.
24 After him repaired Bĭn′nū-ī the son
of Hĕn′ȧ-dăd another piece, from the
house of Ăz′ȧ-rī′ȧh unto the turning *of
the wall,* even unto the corner.
25 Pā′lăl the son of Ū′zai, over against
the turning *of the wall,* and the tower
which lieth out from the king's high
house, that *was* by the court of the
prison. After him Pē-dā′iah the son of
Pā′rŏsh.
26 Moreover the Nĕth′ĭ-nĭm dwelt in
Ō′phĕl, unto *the place* over against the
water gate toward the east, and the
tower that lieth out.
27 After them the Tē-kō′ītes repaired
another piece, over against the great
tower that lieth out, even unto the wall
of Ō′phĕl.
28 From above the horse gate repaired
the priests, every one over against his
house.
29 After them repaired Zā′dŏk the son
of Ĭm′mĕr over against his house. After
him repaired also Shē-mā′iah the son of
Shĕch′ȧ-nī′ȧh, the keeper of the east
gate.
30 After him repaired Hăn′ȧ-nī′ȧh the
son of Shĕl′ē-mī′ȧh, and Hā′nŭn the
sixth son of Zā′lȧph, another piece. After him repaired Mē-shŭl′lăm the son of
Bĕr′ē-chī′ȧh over against his chamber.
31 After him repaired Măl-chī′ȧh the
goldsmith's son unto the place of the
Nĕth′ĭ-nĭm, and of the merchants, over
against the gate Mĭph′kăd, and to the
going up of the corner.
32 And between the going up of the
corner unto the sheep gate repaired the
goldsmiths and the merchants.

CHAPTER 4

BUT it came to pass, that when Săn-
băl′lăt heard that we builded the
wall, he was wroth, and took great indignation, and mocked the Jews.
2 And he spake before his brethren and
the army of Sȧ-mā′rĭ-ȧ, and said, What
do these feeble Jews? will they fortify
themselves? will they sacrifice? will they
make an end in a day? will they revive

the stones out of the heaps of the rubbish which are burned?

3 Now Tō-bī'ăh the Ammonite *was* by him, and he said, Even that which they build, if a fox go up, he shall even break down their stone wall.

4 Hear, O our God; for we are despised: and turn their reproach upon their own head, and give them for a prey in the land of captivity:

5 And cover not their iniquity, and let not their sin be blotted out from before thee: for they have provoked *thee* to anger before the builders.

6 So built we the wall; and all the wall was joined together unto the half thereof: for the people had a mind to work.

7 ¶ But it came to pass, *that* when Săn-băl'lăt, and Tō-bī'ăh, and the Arabians, and the Ammonites, and the Ăsh'dŏd-ītes, heard that the walls of Jerusalem were made up, *and* that the breaches began to be stopped, then they were very wroth,

8 And conspired all of them together to come *and* to fight against Jerusalem, and to hinder it.

9 Nevertheless we made our prayer unto our God, and set a watch against them day and night, because of them.

10 And Judah said, The strength of the bearers of burdens is decayed, and *there is* much rubbish; so that we are not able to build the wall.

11 And our adversaries said, They shall not know, neither see, till we come in the midst among them, and slay them, and cause the work to cease.

12 And it came to pass, that when the Jews which dwelt by them came, they said unto us ten times, From all places whence ye shall return unto us *they will be upon you.*

13 ¶ Therefore set I in the lower places behind the wall, *and* on the higher places, I even set the people after their families with their swords, their spears, and their bows.

14 And I looked, and rose up, and said unto the nobles, and to the rulers, and to the rest of the people, Be not ye afraid of them: remember the Lord, *which is* great and terrible, and fight for your brethren, your sons, and your daughters, your wives, and your houses.

15 And it came to pass, when our enemies heard that it was known unto us, and God had brought their counsel to nought, that we returned all of us to the wall, every one unto his work.

16 And it came to pass from that time forth, *that* the half of my servants wrought in the work, and the other half of them held both the spears, the shields, and the bows, and the habergeons; and the rulers *were* behind all the house of Judah.

17 They which builded on the wall, and they that bare burdens, with those that laded, *every one* with one of his hands wrought in the work, and with the other *hand* held a weapon.

18 For the builders, every one had his sword girded by his side, and *so* builded. And he that sounded the trumpet *was* by me.

19 ¶ And I said unto the nobles, and to the rulers, and to the rest of the people, The work *is* great and large, and we are separated upon the wall, one far from another.

20 In what place *therefore* ye hear the sound of the trumpet, resort ye thither unto us: our God shall fight for us.

21 So we labored in the work: and half of them held the spears from the rising of the morning till the stars appeared.

22 Likewise at the same time said I unto the people, Let every one with his servant lodge within Jerusalem, that in the night they may be a guard to us, and labor on the day.

23 So neither I, nor my brethren, nor my servants, nor the men of the guard which followed me, none of us put off our clothes, *saving that* every one put them off for washing.

CHAPTER 5

AND there was a great cry of the people and of their wives against their brethren the Jews.

2 For there were that said, We, our sons, and our daughters, *are* many: therefore we take up corn *for them,* that we may eat, and live.

3 *Some* also there were that said, We have mortgaged our lands, vineyards, and houses, that we might buy corn, because of the dearth.

4 There were also that said, We have borrowed money for the king's tribute, *and that upon* our lands and vineyards.

5 Yet now our flesh *is* as the flesh of our brethren, our children as their children: and, lo, we bring into bondage our

sons and our daughters to be servants, and *some* of our daughters are brought into bondage *already:* neither *is it* in our power *to redeem them;* for other men have our lands and vineyards.

6 ¶ And I was very angry when I heard their cry and these words.

7 Then I consulted with myself, and I rebuked the nobles, and the rulers, and said unto them, Ye exact usury, every one of his brother. And I set a great assembly against them.

8 And I said unto them, We, after our ability, have redeemed our brethren the Jews, which were sold unto the heathen; and will ye even sell your brethren? or shall they be sold unto us? Then held they their peace, and found nothing *to answer.*

9 Also I said, It *is* not good that ye do: ought ye not to walk in the fear of our God because of the reproach of the heathen our enemies?

10 I likewise, *and* my brethren, and my servants, might exact of them money and corn: I pray you, let us leave off this usury.

11 Restore, I pray you, to them, even this day, their lands, their vineyards, their oliveyards, and their houses, also the hundredth *part* of the money, and of the corn, the wine, and the oil, that ye exact of them.

12 Then said they, We will restore *them,* and will require nothing of them; so will we do as thou sayest. Then I called the priests, and took an oath of them, that they should do according to this promise.

13 Also I shook my lap, and said, So God shake out every man from his house, and from his labor, that performeth not this promise, even thus be he shaken out, and emptied. And all the congregation said, Amen, and praised the LORD. And the people did according to this promise.

14 ¶ Moreover from the time that I was appointed to be their governor in the land of Judah, from the twentieth year even unto the two and thirtieth year of Ăr′tăx-ĕrx′ēş the king, *that is,* twelve years, I and my brethren have not eaten the bread of the governor.

15 But the former governors that *had been* before me were chargeable unto the people, and had taken of them bread and wine, besides forty shekels of silver; yea, even their servants bare rule over the people: but so did not I, because of the fear of God.

16 Yea, also I continued in the work of this wall, neither bought we any land: and all my servants *were* gathered thither unto the work.

17 Moreover *there were* at my table a hundred and fifty of the Jews and rulers, besides those that came unto us from among the heathen that *are* about us.

18 Now *that* which was prepared *for me* daily *was* one ox *and* six choice sheep; also fowls were prepared for me, and once in ten days store of all sorts of wine: yet for all this required not I the bread of the governor, because the bondage was heavy upon this people.

19 Think upon me, my God, for good, *according* to all that I have done for this people.

CHAPTER 6

NOW it came to pass, when Săn-băl′lăt, and Tō-bī′ah, and Gē′shĕm the Arabian, and the rest of our enemies, heard that I had builded the wall, and *that* there was no breach left therein; (though at that time I had not set up the doors upon the gates;)

2 That Săn-băl′lăt and Gē′shĕm sent unto me, saying, Come, let us meet together in *some one of* the villages in the plain of Ō′nō. But they thought to do me mischief.

3 And I sent messengers unto them, saying, I *am* doing a great work, so that I cannot come down: why should the work cease, whilst I leave it, and come down to you?

4 Yet they sent unto me four times after this sort; and I answered them after the same manner.

5 Then sent Săn-băl′lăt his servant unto me in like manner the fifth time with an open letter in his hand;

6 Wherein *was* written, It is reported among the heathen, and Găsh′mū saith *it, that* thou and the Jews think to rebel: for which cause thou buildest the wall, that thou mayest be their king, according to these words.

7 And thou hast also appointed prophets to preach of thee at Jerusalem, saying, *There is* a king in Judah: and now shall it be reported to the king according to these words. Come now therefore, and let us take counsel together.

8 Then I sent unto him, saying, There
are no such things done as thou sayest,
but thou feignest them out of thine own
heart.
9 For they all made us afraid, saying, Their hands shall be weakened
from the work, that it be not done.
Now therefore, *O God,* strengthen my
hands.
10 Afterward I came unto the house of
Shē-mā'ịah the son of Dē-lā'ịah the son
of Mē-hĕt'ȧ-bēel, who *was* shut up;
and he said, Let us meet together in the
house of God, within the temple, and
let us shut the doors of the temple: for
they will come to slay thee; yea, in the
night will they come to slay thee.
11 And I said, Should such a man as I
flee? and who *is there,* that, *being* as I
am, would go into the temple to save
his life? I will not go in.
12 And, lo, I perceived that God had
not sent him; but that he pronounced
this prophecy against me: for Tō-bī'ȧh
and Săn-băl'lăt had hired him.
13 Therefore *was* he hired, that I
should be afraid, and do so, and sin,
and *that* they might have *matter* for
an evil report, that they might reproach
me.
14 My God, think thou upon Tō-bī'ȧh
and Săn-băl'lăt according to these their
works, and on the prophetess Nō'ȧ-
dī'ȧh, and the rest of the prophets, that
would have put me in fear.
15 ¶ So the wall was finished in the
twenty and fifth *day* of *the month* Ĕ-lụl',
in fifty and two days.
16 And it came to pass, that when all
our enemies heard *thereof,* and all the
heathen that *were* about us saw *these
things,* they were much cast down in
their own eyes: for they perceived that
this work was wrought of our God.
17 ¶ Moreover in those days the
nobles of Judah sent many letters unto
Tō-bī'ȧh, and *the letters* of Tō-bī'ȧh
came unto them.
18 For *there were* many in Judah
sworn unto him, because he *was* the
son-in-law of Shĕch'ȧ-nī'ȧh the son of
Ā'rȧh; and his son Jō-hā'năn had taken
the daughter of Mē-shŭl'lăm the son of
Bĕr'ē-chī'ȧh.
19 Also they reported his good deeds
before me, and uttered my words to
him. *And* Tō-bī'ȧh sent letters to put
me in fear.

CHAPTER 7

NOW it came to pass, when the wall
was built, and I had set up the
doors, and the porters and the singers
and the Lē'vītes were appointed,
2 That I gave my brother Hȧ-nā'nī,
and Hăn'ȧ-nī'ȧh the ruler of the palace,
charge over Jerusalem: for he *was* a
faithful man, and feared God above
many.
3 And I said unto them, Let not the
gates of Jerusalem be opened until the
sun be hot; and while they stand by, let
them shut the doors, and bar *them:* and
appoint watches of the inhabitants of
Jerusalem, every one in his watch, and
every one *to be* over against his house.
4 Now the city *was* large and great: but
the people *were* few therein, and the
houses *were* not builded.
5 ¶ And my God put into mine heart
to gather together the nobles, and the
rulers, and the people, that they might
be reckoned by genealogy. And I found
a register of the genealogy of them
which came up at the first, and found
written therein,
6 These *are* the children of the province, that went up out of the captivity,
of those that had been carried away,
whom Nĕb'ū-chăd-nĕz'zȧr the king of
Babylon had carried away, and came
again to Jerusalem and to Judah, every
one unto his city;
7 Who came with Zĕ-rŭb'bȧ-bĕl, Jĕsh'-
ū-ȧ, Nē'hē-mī'ȧh, Ăz'ȧ-rī'ȧh, Rā'ȧ-
mī'ȧh, Nā'hȧ-mā'nī, Môr'dē-caī, Bĭl'-
shăn, Mĭs'pē-rĕth, Bĭg'vā-ī, Nē'hŭm,
Bā'ȧ-nȧh. The number, *I say,* of the
men of the people of Ĭṣ'rā-ĕl *was this;*
8 The children of Pā'rŏsh, two thousand a hundred seventy and two.
9 The children of Shĕph'ȧ-tī'ȧh, three
hundred seventy and two.
10 The children of Ā'rȧh, six hundred
fifty and two.
11 The children of Pā'hăth-mō'ăb, of the
children of Jĕsh'ū-ȧ and Jō'ăb, two thousand and eight hundred *and* eighteen.
12 The children of Ē'lăm, a thousand
two hundred fifty and four.
13 The children of Zăt'tū, eight hundred forty and five.
14 The children of Zăc'cā-ī, seven hundred and threescore.
15 The children of Bĭn'nū-ī, six hundred forty and eight.

16 The children of Běb'ā-ī, six hundred
twenty and eight.
17 The children of Ăz'găd, two thousand three hundred twenty and two.
18 The children of Ăd'ō-nī'kăm, six
hundred threescore and seven.
19 The children of Bĭg'vā-ī, two thousand threescore and seven.
20 The children of Ā'dĭn, six hundred
fifty and five.
21 The children of Ā'tẽr of Hĕz'ē-
kī'ȧh, ninety and eight.
22 The children of Hā'shŭm, three
hundred twenty and eight.
23 The children of Bē'zā-ī, three hundred twenty and four.
24 The children of Hā'rĭph, a hundred
and twelve.
25 The children of Gĭb'ē-ȯn, ninety
and five.
26 The men of Beth-lehem and Nē-tō'-
phȧh, a hundred fourscore and eight.
27 The men of Ăn'ȧ-thŏth, a hundred
twenty and eight.
28 The men of Bĕth'–ăz-mā'vĕth, forty
and two.
29 The men of Kĭr'jăth–jē'ȧ-rĭm, Chē-
phī'rȧh, and Bē-ē'rŏth, seven hundred
forty and three.
30 The men of Rā'mȧh and Gā'bȧ, six
hundred twenty and one.
31 The men of Mĭch'măs, a hundred
and twenty and two.
32 The men of Beth-el and Ā'ī, a hundred twenty and three.
33 The men of the other Nē'bō, fifty
and two.
34 The children of the other Ē'lăm, a
thousand two hundred fifty and four.
35 The children of Hā'rĭm, three hundred and twenty.
36 The children of Jĕr'ĭ-chō, three
hundred forty and five.
37 The children of Lŏd, Hā'dĭd, and
Ō'nō, seven hundred twenty and one.
38 The children of Sē-nā'ȧh, three
thousand nine hundred and thirty.
39 ℂ The priests: the children of Jē-
dā'ịȧh, of the house of Jĕsh'ū-ȧ, nine
hundred seventy and three.
40 The children of Ĭm'mẽr, a thousand
fifty and two.
41 The children of Păsh'ŭr, a thousand
two hundred forty and seven.
42 The children of Hā'rĭm, a thousand
and seventeen.
43 ℂ The Lē'vītes: the children of
Jĕsh'ū-ȧ, of Kăd'mĭ-ēl, *and* of the
children of Hō-dē'vȧh, seventy and
four.
44 ℂ The singers: the children of
Ā'săph, a hundred forty and eight.
45 ℂ The porters: the children of Shăl'-
lŭm, the children of Ā'tẽr, the children
of Tăl'mŏn, the children of Ăk'kŭb, the
children of Hȧ-tī'tȧ, the children of
Shō'baī, a hundred thirty and eight.
46 ℂ The Nĕth'ĭ-nĭm: the children of
Zī'hȧ, the children of Hȧ-shụ'phȧ, the
children of Tȧb-bā'ŏth,
47 The children of Kē'rŏs, the children
of Sī'ȧ, the children of Pā'dŏn,
48 The children of Lē-bā'nȧ, the children of Hăg'ȧ-bä, the children of
Shăl'maī,
49 The children of Hā'năn, the children of Gĭd'dēl, the children of Gā'här,
50 The children of Rē-ā'ịȧh, the children of Rē'zĭn, the children of Nē-kō'dȧ,
51 The children of Găz'zăm, the children of Ŭz'zȧ, the children of Phȧ-sē'ȧh,
52 The children of Bē'saī, the children of Mē-ū'nĭm, the children of Nē-
phĭsh'ē-sĭm,
53 The children of Băk'bŭk, the children of Hȧ-kū'phȧ, the children of
Här'hŭr,
54 The children of Băz'lĭth, the children of Mē-hī'dȧ, the children of
Här'shȧ,
55 The children of Bär'kŏs, the children
of Sĭs'ẽr-ȧ, the children of Tā'mȧh,
56 The children of Nē-zī'ȧh, the children of Hȧ-tī'phȧ.
57 ℂ The children of Solomon's servants: the children of Sō'taī, the children
of Sō-phē'rĕth, the children of Pē-rī'dȧ,
58 The children of Jā'ȧ-lȧ, the children
of Där'kŏn, the children of Gĭd'dēl,
59 The children of Shĕph'ȧ-tī'ȧh, the
children of Hăt'tĭl, the children of Pŏch'-
ē-rĕth of Zē-bā'ĭm, the children of
Ā'mŏn.
60 All the Nĕth'ĭ-nĭm, and the children
of Solomon's servants, *were* three hundred ninety and two.
61 And these *were* they which went up
also from Tĕl'–mē'lȧh, Tĕl'–hȧ-rē'shȧ,
Chē'rŭb, Ăd'dŏn, and Ĭm'mẽr: but they
could not show their father's house, nor
their seed, whether they *were* of Ĭṣ'rā-ēl.
62 The children of Dē-lā'ịȧh, the children of Tō-bī'ȧh, the children of Nē-
kō'dȧ, six hundred forty and two.
63 ℂ And of the priests: the children
of Hȧ-bā'ịȧh, the children of Kŏz, the

children of Bär-zĭl′lā-ī, which took *one*
of the daughters of Bär-zĭl′lā-ī the
Gĭl′ē-ăd-īte to wife, and was called after
their name.
64 These sought their register *among*
those that were reckoned by genealogy,
but it was not found: therefore were
they, as polluted, put from the priesthood.
65 And the Tĭr-shā′thȧ said unto them,
that they should not eat of the most holy
things, till there stood *up* a priest with
Ū′rĭm and Thŭm′mĭm.
66 ¶ The whole congregation together
was forty and two thousand three hundred and threescore,
67 Besides their manservants and their
maidservants, of whom *there were* seven
thousand three hundred thirty and
seven: and they had two hundred forty
and five singing men and singing
women.
68 Their horses, seven hundred thirty
and six: their mules, two hundred forty
and five:
69 *Their* camels, four hundred thirty
and five: six thousand seven hundred
and twenty asses.
70 ¶ And some of the chief of the
fathers gave unto the work. The Tĭr-
shā′thȧ gave to the treasure a thousand
drams of gold, fifty basins, five hundred
and thirty priests' garments.
71 And *some* of the chief of the fathers
gave to the treasure of the work twenty
thousand drams of gold, and two thousand and two hundred pounds of silver.
72 And *that* which the rest of the people gave *was* twenty thousand drams of
gold, and two thousand pounds of silver, and threescore and seven priests'
garments.
73 So the priests, and the Lē′vītes, and
the porters, and the singers, and *some*
of the people, and the Nĕth′ĭ-nĭm, and
all Ĭṣ′rā-ĕl, dwelt in their cities; and
when the seventh month came, the children of Ĭṣ′rā-ĕl *were* in their cities.

CHAPTER 8

AND all the people gathered themselves together as one man into the
street that *was* before the water gate;
and they spake unto Ezra the scribe to
bring the book of the law of Moses,
which the LORD had commanded to
Ĭṣ′rā-ĕl.
2 And Ezra the priest brought the law
before the congregation both of men
and women, and all that could hear with
understanding, upon the first day of the
seventh month.
3 And he read therein before the street
that *was* before the water gate from the
morning until midday, before the men
and the women, and those that could
understand; and the ears of all the people *were attentive* unto the book of the
law.
4 And Ezra the scribe stood upon a
pulpit of wood, which they had made for
the purpose; and beside him stood
Măt′tĭ-thī′ăh, and Shē′mȧ, and Ăn′ȧ-ī′-
ăh, and Ū-rī′jăh, and Hĭl-kī′ăh, and
Mā′ȧ-sē′ịăh, on his right hand; and on
his left hand, Pē-dā′ịăh, and Mĭsh′ā-ĕl,
and Măl-chī′ăh, and Hā′shŭm, and
Hăsh-băd′ȧ-nȧ, Zĕch′ȧ-rī′ăh, *and* Mē-
shŭl′lăm.
5 And Ezra opened the book in the
sight of all the people; (for he was above
all the people;) and when he opened it,
all the people stood up:
6 And Ezra blessed the LORD, the great
God. And all the people answered,
Amen, Amen, with lifting up their hands:
and they bowed their heads, and worshipped the LORD with *their* faces to the
ground.
7 Also Jĕsh′ū-ȧ, and Bā′nī, and Shĕr′ē-
bī′ăh, Jā′mĭn, Ăk′kŭb, Shăb′bē-thaī,
Hō-dī′jăh, Mā′ȧ-sē′ịăh, Kĕl′ī-tȧ, Ăz′ȧ-
rī′ăh, Jŏz′ȧ-băd, Hā′năn, Pē-lā′ịăh, and
the Lē′vītes, caused the people to understand the law: and the people *stood* in
their place.
8 So they read in the book in the law of
God distinctly, and gave the sense, and
caused *them* to understand the reading.
9 ¶ And Nē′hē-mī′ăh, which *is* the
Tĭr-shā′thȧ, and Ezra the priest the
scribe, and the Lē′vītes that taught the
people, said unto all the people, This
day *is* holy unto the LORD your God;
mourn not, nor weep. For all the people
wept, when they heard the words of the
law.
10 Then he said unto them, Go your
way, eat the fat, and drink the sweet,
and send portions unto them for whom
nothing is prepared: for *this* day *is* holy
unto our Lord: neither be ye sorry; for
the joy of the LORD is your strength.
11 So the Lē′vītes stilled all the people,
saying, Hold your peace, for the day *is*
holy; neither be ye grieved.

12 And all the people went their way
to eat, and to drink, and to send portions,
and to make great mirth, because
they had understood the words that were
declared unto them.
13 ¶ And on the second day were
gathered together the chief of the fathers
of all the people, the priests, and the
Lē′vītes, unto Ezra the scribe, even to
understand the words of the law.
14 And they found written in the law
which the LORD had commanded by
Moses, that the children of Is′rā-ēl
should dwell in booths in the feast of the
seventh month:
15 And that they should publish and
proclaim in all their cities, and in Jerusalem,
saying, Go forth unto the mount,
and fetch olive branches, and pine
branches, and myrtle branches, and
palm branches, and branches of thick
trees, to make booths, as *it is* written.
16 ¶ So the people went forth, and
brought *them*, and made themselves
booths, every one upon the roof of his
house, and in their courts, and in the
courts of the house of God, and in the
street of the water gate, and in the street
of the gate of Ē′phrā-ĭm.
17 And all the congregation of them
that were come again out of the captivity
made booths, and sat under the
booths: for since the days of Jĕsh′ū-ȧ
the son of Nŭn unto that day had not the
children of Is′rā-ēl done so. And there
was very great gladness.
18 Also day by day, from the first day
unto the last day, he read in the book of
the law of God. And they kept the feast
seven days; and on the eighth day *was*
a solemn assembly, according unto the
manner.

CHAPTER 9

NOW in the twenty and fourth day
of this month the children of Is′rā-ēl
were assembled with fasting,
and with sackclothes, and earth upon
them.
2 And the seed of Is′rā-ēl separated
themselves from all strangers, and stood
and confessed their sins, and the iniquities
of their fathers.
3 And they stood up in their place, and
read in the book of the law of the LORD
their God *one* fourth part of the day;
and *another* fourth part they confessed,
and worshipped the LORD their God.
4 ¶ Then stood up upon the stairs, of
the Lē′vītes, Jĕsh′ū-ȧ, and Bā′nī, Kăd′mĭ-ēl,
Shĕb′ȧ-nī′ȧh, Bŭn′nī, Shĕr′ē-bī′ȧh,
Bā′nī, *and* Chē-nā′nī, and cried
with a loud voice unto the LORD their
God.
5 Then the Lē′vītes, Jĕsh′ū-ȧ, and
Kăd′mĭ-ēl, Bā′nī, Hăsh′ăb-nī′ȧh, Shĕr′ē-bī′ȧh,
Hō-dī′jȧh, Shĕb′ȧ-nī′ȧh, *and*
Pĕth′ȧ-hī′ȧh, said, Stand up *and* bless
the LORD your God for ever and ever:
and blessed be thy glorious name, which
is exalted above all blessing and praise.
6 Thou, *even* thou, *art* LORD alone;
thou hast made heaven, the heaven of
heavens, with all their host, the earth,
and all *things* that *are* therein, the seas,
and all that *is* therein, and thou preservest
them all; and the host of heaven
worshippeth thee.
7 Thou *art* the LORD the God, who didst
choose Abram, and broughtest him forth
out of Ûr of the Chăl′dēes, and gavest
him the name of Abraham;
8 And foundest his heart faithful before
thee, and madest a covenant with him
to give the land of the Cā′năan-ītes, the
Hĭt′tītes, the Ăm′ō-rītes, and the Pĕr′ĭz-zītes,
and the Jĕb′ū-sītes, and the
Gĭr′gȧ-shītes, to give *it, I say*, to his
seed, and hast performed thy words; for
thou *art* righteous:
9 And didst see the affliction of our
fathers in Egypt, and heardest their cry
by the Red sea;
10 And showedst signs and wonders
upon Phā′raōh, and on all his servants,
and on all the people of his land: for
thou knewest that they dealt proudly
against them. So didst thou get thee a
name, as *it is* this day.
11 And thou didst divide the sea before
them, so that they went through the
midst of the sea on the dry land; and
their persecutors thou threwest into the
deeps, as a stone into the mighty
waters.
12 Moreover thou leddest them in the
day by a cloudy pillar; and in the night
by a pillar of fire, to give them light in
the way wherein they should go.
13 Thou camest down also upon mount
Sī′naī, and spakest with them from
heaven, and gavest them right judgments,
and true laws, good statutes and
commandments:
14 And madest known unto them thy
holy sabbath, and commandedst them

precepts, statutes, and laws, by the hand of Moses thy servant:

15 And gavest them bread from heaven for their hunger, and broughtest forth water for them out of the rock for their thirst, and promisedst them that they should go in to possess the land which thou hadst sworn to give them.

16 But they and our fathers dealt proudly, and hardened their necks, and hearkened not to thy commandments,

17 And refused to obey, neither were mindful of thy wonders that thou didst among them; but hardened their necks, and in their rebellion appointed a captain to return to their bondage: but thou *art* a God ready to pardon, gracious and merciful, slow to anger, and of great kindness, and forsookest them not.

18 Yea, when they had made them a molten calf, and said, This *is* thy God that brought thee up out of Egypt, and had wrought great provocations;

19 Yet thou in thy manifold mercies forsookest them not in the wilderness: the pillar of the cloud departed not from them by day, to lead them in the way; neither the pillar of fire by night, to show them light, and the way wherein they should go.

20 Thou gavest also thy good Spirit to instruct them, and withheldest not thy manna from their mouth, and gavest them water for their thirst.

21 Yea, forty years didst thou sustain them in the wilderness, *so that* they lacked nothing; their clothes waxed not old, and their feet swelled not.

22 Moreover thou gavest them kingdoms and nations, and didst divide them into corners: so they possessed the land of Sī'hŏn, and the land of the king of Hĕsh'bŏn, and the land of Og king of Bā'shăn.

23 Their children also multipliedst thou as the stars of heaven, and broughtest them into the land, concerning which thou hadst promised to their fathers, that they should go in to possess *it*.

24 So the children went in and possessed the land, and thou subduedst before them the inhabitants of the land, the Cā'năan-ites, and gavest them into their hands, with their kings, and the people of the land, that they might do with them as they would.

25 And they took strong cities, and a fat land, and possessed houses full of all goods, wells digged, vineyards, and oliveyards, and fruit trees in abundance: so they did eat, and were filled, and became fat, and delighted themselves in thy great goodness.

26 Nevertheless they were disobedient, and rebelled against thee, and cast thy law behind their backs, and slew thy prophets which testified against them to turn them to thee, and they wrought great provocations.

27 Therefore thou deliveredst them into the hand of their enemies, who vexed them: and in the time of their trouble, when they cried unto thee, thou heardest *them* from heaven; and according to thy manifold mercies thou gavest them saviours, who saved them out of the hand of their enemies.

28 But after they had rest, they did evil again before thee: therefore leftest thou them in the hand of their enemies, so that they had the dominion over them: yet when they returned, and cried unto thee, thou heardest *them* from heaven; and many times didst thou deliver them according to thy mercies;

29 And testifiedst against them, that thou mightest bring them again unto thy law: yet they dealt proudly, and hearkened not unto thy commandments, but sinned against thy judgments, (which if a man do, he shall live in them;) and withdrew the shoulder, and hardened their neck, and would not hear.

30 Yet many years didst thou forbear them, and testifiedst against them by thy Spirit in thy prophets: yet would they not give ear: therefore gavest thou them into the hand of the people of the lands.

31 Nevertheless for thy great mercies' sake thou didst not utterly consume them, nor forsake them; for thou *art* a gracious and merciful God.

32 Now therefore, our God, the great, the mighty, and the terrible God, who keepest covenant and mercy, let not all the trouble seem little before thee, that hath come upon us, on our kings, on our princes, and on our priests, and on our prophets, and on our fathers, and on all thy people, since the time of the kings of Assyria unto this day.

33 Howbeit thou *art* just in all that is brought upon us; for thou hast done right, but we have done wickedly:

34 Neither have our kings, our princes,

our priests, nor our fathers, kept thy
law, nor hearkened unto thy commandments and thy testimonies, wherewith
thou didst testify against them.
35 For they have not served thee in
their kingdom, and in thy great goodness that thou gavest them, and in the
large and fat land which thou gavest before them, neither turned they from
their wicked works.
36 Behold, we *are* servants this day,
and *for* the land that thou gavest unto
our fathers to eat the fruit thereof and
the good thereof, behold, we *are* servants in it:
37 And it yieldeth much increase unto
the kings whom thou hast set over us
because of our sins: also they have
dominion over our bodies, and over our
cattle, at their pleasure, and we *are* in
great distress.
38 And because of all this we make
a sure *covenant*, and write *it;* and
our princes, Lē′vītes, *and* priests, seal
unto it.

CHAPTER 10

NOW those that sealed *were*, Nē-
hē-mī′ȧh, the Tĩr-shā′thȧ, the son
of Hăch′ȧ-lī′ȧh, and Zĭd-kī′jȧh,
2 Sē-rā′ịȧh, Ăz′ȧ-rī′ȧh, Jeremiah,
3 Păsh′ŭr, Ăm′ȧ-rī′ȧh, Măl-chī′jȧh,
4 Hăt′tŭsh, Shĕb′ȧ-nī′ȧh, Măl′lŭch,
5 Hā′rĭm, Mĕr′ē-mŏth, Ō′bȧ-dī′ȧh,
6 Daniel, Gĭn′nē-thŏn, Bā′rŭch,
7 Mē-shŭl′lăm, Ȧ-bī′jȧh, Mĭj′ȧ-mĭn,
8 Mā′ȧ-zī′ȧh, Bĭl′gā-ī, Shē-mā′ịȧh:
these *were* the priests.
9 And the Lē′vītes: both Jĕsh′ū-ā the
son of Ăz′ȧ-nī′ȧh, Bĭn′nū-ī of the sons of
Hĕn′ȧ-dăd, Kăd′mĭ-ēl;
10 And their brethren, Shĕb′ȧ-nī′ȧh,
Hō-dī′jȧh, Kĕl′ĭ-tȧ, Pē-lā′ịȧh, Hā′năn,
11 Mī′chȧ, Rē′hŏb, Hăsh′ȧ-bī′ȧh,
12 Zăc′cŭr, Shĕr′ē-bī′ȧh, Shĕb′ȧ-nī′ȧh,
13 Hō-dī′jȧh, Bā′nī, Bē-nī′nū.
14 The chief of the people; Pā′rŏsh,
Pā′hăth–mō′ăb, Ē′lăm, Zăt′thū, Bā′nī,
15 Bŭn′nī, Ăz′găd, Bĕb′ā-ī,
16 Ăd′ō-nī′jȧh, Bĭg′vā-ī, Ā′dĭn,
17 Ā′tẽr, Hĭz-kī′jȧh, Ăz′zŭr,
18 Hō-dī′jȧh, Hā′shŭm, Bē′zā-ī,
19 Hā′rĭph, Ăn′ȧ-thŏth, Nē′baī,
20 Măg′pĭ-ăsh, Mē-shŭl′lăm, Hē′zĭr,
21 Mē-shĕz′ȧ-bēel, Zā′dŏk, Jȧd-dū′ȧ,
22 Pĕl′ȧ-tī′ȧh, Hā′năn, Ăn′ȧ-ī′ȧh,
23 Hō-shē′ȧ, Hăn′ȧ-nī′ȧh, Hā′shŭb,
24 Hăl-lō′hĕsh, Pĭl′ē-hä, Shō′bĕk,
25 Rē′hŭm, Hȧ-shăb′nȧh, Mā′ȧ-sē′ịȧh,
26 And Ȧ-hī′jȧh, Hā′năn, Ā′năn,
27 Măl′lŭch, Hā′rĭm, Bā′ȧ-nȧh.
28 ¶ And the rest of the people, the
priests, the Lē′vītes, the porters, the
singers, the Nĕth′ĭ-nĭm, and all they that
had separated themselves from the people of the lands unto the law of God,
their wives, their sons, and their daughters, every one having knowledge, and
having understanding;
29 They clave to their brethren, their
nobles, and entered into a curse, and
into an oath, to walk in God's law, which
was given by Moses the servant of God,
and to observe and do all the commandments of the LORD our Lord, and his
judgments and his statutes;
30 And that we would not give our
daughters unto the people of the land,
nor take their daughters for our sons:
31 And *if* the people of the land bring
ware or any victuals on the sabbath day
to sell, *that* we would not buy it of them
on the sabbath, or on the holy day: and
that we would leave the seventh year,
and the exaction of every debt.
32 Also we made ordinances for us, to
charge ourselves yearly with the third
part of a shekel for the service of the
house of our God;
33 For the showbread, and for the continual meat offering, and for the continual burnt offering, of the sabbaths, of
the new moons, for the set feasts, and
for the holy *things*, and for the sin offerings to make an atonement for Ĭṣ′rā-ĕl,
and *for* all the work of the house of our
God.
34 And we cast the lots among the
priests, the Lē′vītes, and the people, for
the wood offering, to bring *it* into the
house of our God, after the houses of
our fathers, at times appointed year by
year, to burn upon the altar of the LORD
our God, as *it is* written in the law:
35 And to bring the firstfruits of our
ground, and the firstfruits of all fruit of
all trees, year by year, unto the house of
the LORD:
36 Also the firstborn of our sons, and
of our cattle, as *it is* written in the law,
and the firstlings of our herds and of our
flocks, to bring to the house of our God,
unto the priests that minister in the
house of our God:
37 And *that* we should bring the firstfruits of our dough, and our offerings,

and the fruit of all manner of trees, of wine and of oil, unto the priests, to the chambers of the house of our God; and the tithes of our ground unto the Lē′vītes, that the same Lē′vītes might have the tithes in all the cities of our tillage.

38 And the priest the son of Aaron shall be with the Lē′vītes, when the Lē′vītes take tithes: and the Lē′vītes shall bring up the tithe of the tithes unto the house of our God, to the chambers, into the treasure house.

39 For the children of Ĭṣ′rā-ĕl and the children of Levi shall bring the offering of the corn, of the new wine, and the oil, unto the chambers, where *are* the vessels of the sanctuary, and the priests that minister, and the porters, and the singers: and we will not forsake the house of our God.

CHAPTER 11

AND the rulers of the people dwelt at Jerusalem: the rest of the people also cast lots, to bring one of ten to dwell in Jerusalem the holy city, and nine parts *to dwell* in *other* cities.

2 And the people blessed all the men, that willingly offered themselves to dwell at Jerusalem.

3 ¶ Now these *are* the chief of the province that dwelt in Jerusalem: but in the cities of Judah dwelt every one in his possession in their cities, *to wit,* Ĭṣ′rā-ĕl, the priests, and the Lē′vītes, and the Nĕth′ĭ-nĭm, and the children of Solomon's servants.

4 And at Jerusalem dwelt *certain* of the children of Judah, and of the children of Benjamin. Of the children of Judah; Ȧ-thā′ịah the son of Ŭz-zī′ȧh, the son of Zĕch′ȧ-rī′ȧh, the son of Ăm′ȧ-rī′ȧh, the son of Shĕph′ȧ-tī′ȧh, the son of Mȧ-hā′lȧ-lē′ĕl, of the children of Pē′rĕz;

5 And Mā′ȧ-sē′ịah the son of Bā′rŭch, the son of Cŏl–hō′zĕh, the son of Hȧ-zā′ịah, the son of Ȧ-dā′ịah, the son of Jŏī′ȧ-rĭb, the son of Zĕch′ȧ-rī′ȧh, the son of Shī-lō′nī.

6 All the sons of Pē′rĕz that dwelt at Jerusalem *were* four hundred threescore and eight valiant men.

7 And these *are* the sons of Benjamin; Săl′lū the son of Mē-shŭl′lăm, the son of Jō′ĕd, the son of Pē-dā′ịah, the son of Kō-lā′ịah, the son of Mā′ȧ-sē′ịah, the son of Ĭth′ĭ-ĕl, the son of Jē-sā′ịah.

8 And after him Găb′bā-ī, Săl′lā-ī, nine hundred twenty and eight.

9 And Joel the son of Zĭch′rī *was* their overseer: and Judah the son of Sē-nū′ȧh *was* second over the city.

10 Of the priests: Jē-dā′ịah the son of Jŏī′ȧ-rĭb, Jā′chĭn.

11 Sē-rā′ịah the son of Hĭl-kī′ȧh, the son of Mē-shŭl′lăm, the son of Zā′dŏk, the son of Mē-rā′ịōth, the son of Ȧ-hī′tŭb, *was* the ruler of the house of God.

12 And their brethren that did the work of the house *were* eight hundred twenty and two: and Ȧ-dā′ịah the son of Jē-rō′hăm, the son of Pĕl′ȧ-lī′ȧh, the son of Ăm′zī, the son of Zĕch′ȧ′rī′ȧh, the son of Păsh′ŭr, the son of Măl-chī′ȧh,

13 And his brethren, chief of the fathers, two hundred forty and two: and Ȧ-măsh′ā-ī the son of Ȧ-zā′rē-ĕl, the son of Ȧ-hā′saī, the son of Mē-shĭl′lē-mōth, the son of Ĭm′mēr,

14 And the brethren, mighty men of valor, a hundred twenty and eight: and their overseer *was* Zăb′dĭ-ĕl, the son of *one of* the great men.

15 Also of the Lē′vītes: Shē-mā′ịah the son of Hā′shŭb, the son of Ăz′rĭ-kăm, the son of Hăsh′ȧ-bī′ȧh, the son of Bŭn′nī;

16 And Shăb′bē-thaī and Jŏz′ȧ-băd, of the chief of the Lē′vītes, *had* the oversight of the outward business of the house of God.

17 And Măt′tȧ-nī′ȧh the son of Mī′chȧ, the son of Zăb′dī, the son of Ā′săph, *was* the principal to begin the thanksgiving in prayer: and Băk′bū-kī′ȧh the second among his brethren, and Abda the son of Shăm-mū′ȧ, the son of Gā′lăl, the son of Jē-dū′thŭn.

18 All the Lē′vītes in the holy city *were* two hundred fourscore and four.

19 Moreover the porters, Ăk′kŭb, Tăl′mŏn, and their brethren that kept the gates, *were* a hundred seventy and two.

20 ¶ And the residue of Ĭṣ′rā-ĕl, of the priests, *and* the Lē′vītes, *were* in all the cities of Judah, every one in his inheritance.

21 But the Nĕth′ĭ-nĭm dwelt in Ō′phĕl: and Zī′hȧ and Gĭs′pȧ *were* over the Nĕth′ĭ-nĭm.

22 The overseer also of the Lē′vītes at Jerusalem *was* Ŭz′zī the son of Bā′nī, the son of Hăsh′ȧ-bī′ȧh, the son of Măt′tȧ-nī′ȧh, the son of Mī′chȧ. Of the

sons of Ā'săph, the singers *were* over the business of the house of God.

23 For *it was* the king's commandment concerning them, that a certain portion should be for the singers, due for every day.

24 And Pĕth'ȧ-hī'ȧh the son of Mē-shĕz'ȧ-bēel, of the children of Zē'rȧh the son of Judah, *was* at the king's hand in all matters concerning the people.

25 And for the villages, with their fields, *some* of the children of Judah dwelt at Kĭr'jăth-är'bȧ, and *in* the villages thereof, and at Dī'bŏn, and *in* the villages thereof, and at Jē-kăb'zē-ĕl, and *in* the villages thereof,

26 And at Jĕsh'ū-ȧ, and at Mŏl'ȧ-dȧh, and at Bĕth'-phē'lĕt,

27 And at Hā'zär-shu̥'ăl, and at Bē'ẽr-shē'bȧ, and *in* the villages thereof,

28 And at Zĭk'lăg, and at Mē-kō'nȧh, and in the villages thereof,

29 And at Ĕn-rĭm'mŏn, and at Zā'rē-ȧh, and at Jär'mŭth,

30 Zȧ-nō'ȧh, Ȧ-dŭl'lăm, and *in* their villages, at Lā'chĭsh, and the fields thereof, at Ȧ-zē'kȧh, and *in* the villages thereof. And they dwelt from Bē'ẽr-shē'bȧ unto the valley of Hĭn'nŏm.

31 The children also of Benjamin from Gē'bȧ *dwelt* at Mĭch'măsh, and Ā-ī'jȧ, and Beth-el, and *in* their villages,

32 *And* at Ăn'ȧ-thŏth, Nŏb, Ăn'ȧ-nī'ȧh,

33 Hā'zŏr, Rā'mȧh, Gĭt'tā-ĭm,

34 Hā'dĭd, Zē-bō'ĭm, Nē-băl'lăt,

35 Lŏd, and Ō'nō, the valley of craftsmen.

36 And of the Lē'vītes *were* divisions *in* Judah, *and* in Benjamin.

CHAPTER 12

NOW these *are* the priests and the Lē'vītes that went up with Zē-rŭb'bȧ-bĕl the son of Shē-ăl'tĭ-ĕl, and Jĕsh'ū-ȧ: Sē-rā'i̥ȧh, Jeremiah, Ezra,

2 Ăm'ȧ-rī'ȧh, Măl'lŭch, Hăt'tŭsh,

3 Shĕch'ȧ-nī'ȧh, Rē'hŭm, Mĕr'ē-mŏth,

4 Ĭd'dō, Gĭn'nē-thō, Ȧ-bī'jȧh,

5 Mī'ȧ-mĭn, Mā'ȧ-dī'ȧh, Bĭl'gȧh,

6 Shē-mā'i̥ȧh, and Jôi'ȧ-rĭb, Jē-dā'i̥ȧh,

7 Săl'lū, Ā'mŏk, Hĭl-kī'ȧh, Jē-dā'i̥ȧh. These *were* the chief of the priests and of their brethren in the days of Jĕsh'ū-ȧ.

8 Moreover the Lē'vītes: Jĕsh'ū-ȧ, Bĭn'nū-ī, Kăd'mĭ-ĕl, Shĕr'ē-bī'ȧh, Judah, *and* Măt'tȧ-nī'ȧh, *which was* over the thanksgiving, he and his brethren.

9 Also Băk'bū-kī'ȧh and Ŭn'nī, their brethren, *were* over against them in the watches.

10 ¶ And Jĕsh'ū-ȧ begat Jôi'ȧ-kĭm, Jôi'ȧ-kĭm also begat Ē-lī'ȧ-shĭb, and Ē-lī'ȧ-shĭb begat Jôi'ȧ-dȧ,

11 And Jôi'ȧ-dȧ begat Jonathan, and Jonathan begat Jȧd-dū'ȧ.

12 And in the days of Jôi'ȧ-kĭm were priests, the chief of the fathers: of Sē-rā'i̥ȧh, Mē-rā'i̥ȧh; of Jeremiah, Hăn'ȧ-nī'ȧh;

13 Of Ezra, Mē-shŭl'lăm; of Ăm'ȧ-rī'ȧh, Jē'hō-hā'năn;

14 Of Mĕl'ĭ-cū, Jonathan; of Shĕb'ȧ-nī'ȧh, Joseph;

15 Of Hā'rĭm, Ăd'nȧ; of Mē-rā'i̥ŏth, Hĕl'kā-ī;

16 Of Ĭd'dō, Zĕch'ȧ-rī'ȧh; of Gĭn'nē-thŏn, Mē-shŭl'lăm;

17 Of Ȧ-bī'jȧh, Zĭch'rī; of Mĭn'i̥ȧ-mĭn, of Mō'ȧ-dī'ȧh, Pĭl'taī;

18 Of Bĭl'gȧh, Shăm-mū'ȧ; of Shē-mā'i̥ȧh, Jē-hŏn'ȧ-thăn;

19 And of Jôi'ȧ-rĭb, Măt'tē-nā'ī; of Jē-dā'i̥ȧh, Ŭz'zī;

20 Of Săl'lā-ī, Kăl'lā-ī; of Ā'mŏk, Ē'bẽr;

21 Of Hĭl-kī'ȧh, Hăsh'ȧ-bī'ȧh; of Jē-dā'i̥ȧh, Nē-thăn'ē-ĕl.

22 ¶ The Lē'vītes in the days of Ē-lī'ȧ-shĭb, Jôi'ȧ-dȧ, and Jō-hā'năn, and Jȧd-dū'ȧ, *were* recorded chief of the fathers: also the priests, to the reign of Dȧ-rī'ŭs the Persian.

23 The sons of Levi, the chief of the fathers, *were* written in the book of the Chronicles, even until the days of Jō-hā'năn the son of Ē-lī'ȧ-shĭb.

24 And the chief of the Lē'vītes: Hăsh'ȧ-bī'ȧh, Shĕr'ē-bī'ȧh, and Jĕsh'ū-ȧ the son of Kăd'mĭ-ĕl, with their brethren over against them, to praise *and* to give thanks, according to the commandment of David the man of God, ward over against ward.

25 Măt'tȧ-nī'ȧh, and Băk'bū-kī'ȧh, Ō'bȧ-dī'ȧh, Mē-shŭl'lăm, Tăl'mŏn, Ăk'kŭb, *were* porters keeping the ward at the thresholds of the gates.

26 These *were* in the days of Jôi'ȧ-kĭm the son of Jĕsh'ū-ȧ, the son of Jŏz'ȧ-dăk, and in the days of Nē'hē-mī'ȧh the governor, and of Ezra the priest, the scribe.

27 ¶ And at the dedication of the wall of Jerusalem they sought the Lē'vītes out of all their places, to bring them to Jerusalem, to keep the dedication with

gladness, both with thanksgivings, and
with singing, *with* cymbals, psalteries,
and with harps.
28 And the sons of the singers gathered
themselves together, both out of the
plain country round about Jerusalem,
and from the villages of Nē-tŏph'ȧ-thī;
29 Also from the house of Gĭl'găl, and
out of the fields of Gē'bȧ and Ăz-mā'-
vĕth: for the singers had builded them
villages round about Jerusalem.
30 And the priests and the Lē'vītes
purified themselves, and purified the
people, and the gates, and the wall.
31 Then I brought up the princes of
Judah upon the wall, and appointed two
great *companies of them that gave*
thanks, *whereof one* went on the right
hand upon the wall toward the dung gate:
32 And after them went Hō-shā'ịah,
and half of the princes of Judah,
33 And Ăz'ȧ-rī'ȧh, Ezra, and Mē-
shŭl'lăm,
34 Judah, and Benjamin, and Shē-
mā'ịah, and Jeremiah,
35 And *certain* of the priests' sons with
trumpets; *namely,* Zĕch'ȧ-rī'ȧh the son
of Jonathan, the son of Shē-mā'ịah, the
son of Măt'tȧ-nī'ȧh, the son of Mī-
chā'ịah, the son of Zăc'cŭr, the son of
Ā'săph:
36 And his brethren, Shē-mā'iah, and
Ȧ-zā'rā-ĕl, Mĭl'ȧ-lā'ī, Gĭl'ȧ-laī, Mā-ā'ī,
Nē-thăn'ē-ĕl, and Judah, Hȧ-nā'nī, with
the musical instruments of David the
man of God, and Ezra the scribe before
them.
37 And at the fountain gate, which was
over against them, they went up by the
stairs of the city of David, at the going
up of the wall, above the house of David,
even unto the water gate eastward.
38 And the other *company of them*
that gave thanks went over against
them, and I after them, and the half of
the people upon the wall, from beyond
the tower of the furnaces even unto the
broad wall;
39 And from above the gate of Ē'phrā-
ĭm, and above the old gate, and above
the fish gate, and the tower of Hȧ-
năn'ē-ĕl, and the tower of Mē'ȧh, even
unto the sheep gate: and they stood still
in the prison gate.
40 So stood the two *companies of them*
that gave thanks in the house of God,
and I, and the half of the rulers with me:
41 And the priests; Ē-lī'ȧ-kĭm, Mā'ȧ-
sē'ịah, Mĭn'ịȧ-mĭn, Mī-chā'ịah, Ē-lī'ō-
ē'nā-ī, Zĕch'ȧ-rī'ȧh, *and* Hăn'ȧ-nī'ȧh,
with trumpets;
42 And Mā'ȧ-sē'ịah, and Shē-mā'ịah,
and Ĕl'ē-ā'zār, and Ŭz'zī, and Jē'hō-hā'-
năn, and Măl-chī'jah, and Ē'lăm, and
Ē'zĕr. And the singers sang loud, with
Jĕz'rȧ-hī'ȧh *their* overseer.
43 Also that day they offered great
sacrifices, and rejoiced: for God had
made them rejoice with great joy: the
wives also and the children rejoiced: so
that the joy of Jerusalem was heard
even afar off.
44 ℭ And at that time were some appointed over the chambers for the treasures, for the offerings, for the firstfruits,
and for the tithes, to gather into them
out of the fields of the cities the portions
of the law for the priests and Lē'vītes:
for Judah rejoiced for the priests and for
the Lē'vītes that waited.
45 And both the singers and the porters
kept the ward of their God, and the
ward of the purification, according to
the commandment of David, *and* of
Solomon his son.
46 For in the days of David and Ā'săph
of old *there were* chief of the singers,
and songs of praise and thanksgiving
unto God.
47 And all Ĭs'rā-ĕl in the days of Zĕ-
rŭb'bȧ-bĕl, and in the days of Nē'hē-
mī'ȧh, gave the portions of the singers
and the porters, every day his portion:
and they sanctified *holy things* unto the
Lē'vītes; and the Lē'vītes sanctified
them unto the children of Aaron.

CHAPTER 13

ON that day they read in the book of
Moses in the audience of the people; and therein was found written, that
the Ammonite and the Mō'ăb-īte should
not come into the congregation of God
for ever;
2 Because they met not the children of
Ĭs'rā-ĕl with bread and with water, but
hired Bā'lȧam against them, that he
should curse them: howbeit our God
turned the curse into a blessing.
3 Now it came to pass, when they had
heard the law, that they separated from
Ĭs'rā-ĕl all the mixed multitude.
4 ℭ And before this, Ē-lī'ȧ-shĭb the
priest, having the oversight of the chamber of the house of our God, *was* allied
unto Tō-bī'ȧh:

5 And he had prepared for him a great chamber, where aforetime they laid the meat offerings, the frankincense, and the vessels, and the tithes of the corn, the new wine, and the oil, which was commanded *to be given* to the Lē′vītes, and the singers, and the porters; and the offerings of the priests.

6 But in all this *time* was not I at Jerusalem: for in the two and thirtieth year of Är′tăx-ĕrx′ēṣ king of Babylon came I unto the king, and after certain days obtained I leave of the king:

7 And I came to Jerusalem, and understood of the evil that Ē-lī′ȧ-shĭb did for Tō-bī′ȧh, in preparing him a chamber in the courts of the house of God.

8 And it grieved me sore: therefore I cast forth all the household stuff of Tō-bī′ȧh out of the chamber.

9 Then I commanded, and they cleansed the chambers: and thither brought I again the vessels of the house of God, with the meat offering and the frankincense.

10 ¶ And I perceived that the portions of the Lē′vītes had not been given *them:* for the Lē′vītes and the singers, that did the work, were fled every one to his field.

11 Then contended I with the rulers, and said, Why is the house of God forsaken? And I gathered them together, and set them in their place.

12 Then brought all Judah the tithe of the corn and the new wine and the oil unto the treasuries.

13 And I made treasurers over the treasuries, Shĕl′ē-mī′ȧh the priest, and Ză′dŏk the scribe, and of the Lē′vītes, Pē-dā′ịah: and next to them *was* Hā′năn the son of Zăc′cŭr, the son of Măt′tȧ-nī′ȧh: for they were counted faithful, and their office *was* to distribute unto their brethren.

14 Remember me, O my God concerning this, and wipe not out my good deeds that I have done for the house of my God, and for the offices thereof.

15 ¶ In those days saw I in Judah *some* treading winepresses on the sabbath, and bringing in sheaves, and lading asses; as also wine, grapes, and figs, and all *manner of* burdens, which they brought into Jerusalem on the sabbath day: and I testified *against them* in the day wherein they sold victuals.

16 There dwelt men of Tȳre also therein, which brought fish, and all manner of ware, and sold on the sabbath unto the children of Judah, and in Jerusalem.

17 Then I contended with the nobles of Judah, and said unto them, What evil thing *is* this that ye do, and profane the sabbath day?

18 Did not your fathers thus, and did not our God bring all this evil upon us, and upon this city? yet ye bring more wrath upon Ĭṣ′rā-ĕl by profaning the sabbath.

19 And it came to pass, that when the gates of Jerusalem began to be dark before the sabbath, I commanded that the gates should be shut, and charged that they should not be opened till after the sabbath: and *some* of my servants set I at the gates, *that* there should no burden be brought in on the sabbath day.

20 So the merchants and sellers of all kind of ware lodged without Jerusalem once or twice.

21 Then I testified against them, and said unto them, Why lodge ye about the wall? if ye do *so* again, I will lay hands on you. From that time forth came they no *more* on the sabbath.

22 And I commanded the Lē′vītes, that they should cleanse themselves, and *that* they should come *and* keep the gates, to sanctify the sabbath day. Remember me, O my God, *concerning* this also, and spare me according to the greatness of thy mercy.

23 ¶ In those days also saw I Jews *that* had married wives of Ashdod, of Ammon, *and* of Mō′ăb:

24 And their children spake half in the speech of Ashdod, and could not speak in the Jews' language, but according to the language of each people.

25 And I contended with them, and cursed them, and smote certain of them, and plucked off their hair, and made them swear by God, *saying,* Ye shall not give your daughters unto their sons, nor take their daughters unto your sons, or for yourselves.

26 Did not Solomon king of Ĭṣ′rā-ĕl sin by these things? yet among many nations was there no king like him, who was beloved of his God, and God made him king over all Ĭṣ′rā-ĕl: nevertheless even him did outlandish women cause to sin.

27 Shall we then hearken unto you to do all this great evil, to transgress

against our God in marrying strange wives?
28 And *one* of the sons of Jŏi′ȧ-dȧ, the son of Ē-lī′ȧ-shĭb the high priest, *was* son-in-law to Săn-băl′lăt the Hŏr′ō-nīte: therefore I chased him from me.
29 Remember them, O my God, because they have defiled the priesthood, and the covenant of the priesthood, and of the Lē′vītes.
30 Thus cleansed I them from all strangers, and appointed the wards of the priests and the Lē′vītes, every one in his business;
31 And for the wood offering, at times appointed, and for the firstfruits. Remember me, O my God, for good.

THE BOOK OF ESTHER

CHAPTER 1

NOW it came to pass in the days of
Ȧ-hăṣ′ū-ē′rŭs, (this *is* Ȧ-hăṣ′ū-ē′rŭs which reigned from India even unto Ethiopia, *over* a hundred and seven and twenty provinces,)
2 *That* in those days, when the king
Ȧ-hăṣ′ū-ē′rŭs sat on the throne of his kingdom, which *was* in Shụ′shăn the palace,
3 In the third year of his reign, he made
a feast unto all his princes and his servants; the power of Persia and Mē′dĭ-ȧ, the nobles and princes of the provinces, *being* before him:
4 When he showed the riches of his
glorious kingdom and the honor of his excellent majesty many days, *even* a hundred and fourscore days.
5 And when these days were expired,
the king made a feast unto all the people that were present in Shụ′shăn the palace, both unto great and small, seven days, in the court of the garden of the king's palace;
6 *Where were* white, green, and blue
hangings, fastened with cords of fine linen and purple to silver rings and pillars of marble: the beds *were of* gold and silver, upon a pavement of red, and blue, and white, and black marble.
7 And they gave *them* drink in vessels
of gold, (the vessels being diverse one from another,) and royal wine in abundance, according to the state of the king.
8 And the drinking *was* according to
the law; none did compel: for so the king had appointed to all the officers of his house, that they should do according to every man's pleasure.
9 Also Văsh′tī the queen made a feast
for the women *in* the royal house which *belonged* to king Ȧ-hăṣ′ū-ē′rŭs.
10 ℂ On the seventh day, when the
heart of the king was merry with wine, he commanded Mē-hū′măn, Bĭz′thȧ, Här-bō′nȧ, Bĭg′thȧ, and Ȧ-băg′thȧ, Zē′thär, and Cär′căs, the seven chamberlains that served in the presence of Ȧ-hăṣ′ū-ē′rŭs the king,
11 To bring Văsh′tī the queen before
the king with the crown royal, to show the people and the princes her beauty: for she *was* fair to look on.
12 But the queen Văsh′tī refused to
come at the king's commandment by *his* chamberlains: therefore was the king very wroth, and his anger burned in him.
13 ℂ Then the king said to the wise
men, which knew the times, (for so *was* the king's manner toward all that knew law and judgment:
14 And the next unto him *was* Cär-
shē-nȧ, Shē′thär, Ăd′mȧ-thȧ, Tär′shish, Mē′rēs, Mär-sē′nȧ, *and* Mē-mū′căn, the seven princes of Persia and Mē′dĭ-ȧ, which saw the king's face, *and* which sat the first in the kingdom,)
15 What shall we do unto the queen
Văsh′tī according to law, because she hath not performed the commandment of the king Ȧ-hăṣ′ū-ē′rŭs by the chamberlains?
16 And Mē-mū′căn answered before
the king and the princes, Văsh′tī the queen hath not done wrong to the king only, but also to all the princes, and to all the people that *are* in all the provinces of the king Ȧ-hăṣ′ū-ē′rŭs.
17 For *this* deed of the queen shall

come abroad unto all women, so that
they shall despise their husbands in
their eyes, when it shall be reported,
The king Ȧ-hăs̱'ū-ē'rŭs commanded
Văsh'tī the queen to be brought in before him, but she came not.
18 *Likewise* shall the ladies of Persia
and Mē'dĭ-ȧ say this day unto all the
king's princes, which have heard of the
deed of the queen. Thus *shall there
arise* too much contempt and wrath.
19 If it please the king, let there go a
royal commandment from him, and let
it be written among the laws of the Persians and the Mēdes̱, that it be not
altered, That Văsh'tī come no more before king Ȧ-hăs̱'ū-ē'rŭs; and let the
king give her royal estate unto another
that is better than she.
20 And when the king's decree, which
he shall make, shall be published
throughout all his empire, (for it is
great,) all the wives shall give to their
husbands honor, both to great and
small.
21 And the saying pleased the king and
the princes; and the king did according
to the word of Mē-mū'căn:
22 For he sent letters into all the king's
provinces, into every province according to the writing thereof, and to every
people after their language, that every
man should bear rule in his own house,
and that *it* should be published according to the language of every people.

CHAPTER 2

AFTER these things, when the wrath
of king Ȧ-hăs̱'ū-ē'rŭs was appeased, he remembered Văsh'tī, and
what she had done, and what was decreed against her.
2 Then said the king's servants that
ministered unto him, Let there be fair
young virgins sought for the king:
3 And let the king appoint officers in
all the provinces of his kingdom, that
they may gather together all the fair
young virgins unto Shṳ'shăn the palace,
to the house of the women, unto the
custody of Hē'gĕ the king's chamberlain, keeper of the women; and let
their things for purification be given
them:
4 And let the maiden which pleaseth
the king be queen instead of Văsh'tī.
And the thing pleased the king; and he
did so.
5 ¶ *Now* in Shṳ'shăn the palace there
was a certain Jew, whose name *was*
Môr'dē-caī, the son of Jā'ĭr, the son of
Shĭm'ē-ī, the son of Kish, a Benjamite;
6 Who had been carried away from
Jerusalem with the captivity which had
been carried away with Jĕc'ō-nī'ȧh king
of Judah, whom Nĕb'ū-ehăd-nĕz'zȧr the
king of Babylon had carried away.
7 And he brought up Hȧ-dăs'sȧh, that
is, Esther, his uncle's daughter: for she
had neither father nor mother, and the
maid *was* fair and beautiful; whom
Môr'dē-caī, when her father and mother
were dead, took for his own daughter.
8 ¶ So it came to pass, when the king's
commandment and his decree was
heard, and when many maidens were
gathered together unto Shṳ'shăn the
palace, to the custody of Hĕg'ā-ī, that
Esther was brought also unto the king's
house, to the custody of Hĕg'ā-ī, keeper
of the women.
9 And the maiden pleased him, and
she obtained kindness of him; and he
speedily gave her her things for purification, with such things as belonged to
her, and seven maidens, *which were*
meet to be given her, out of the king's
house: and he preferred her and her
maids unto the best *place* of the house
of the women.
10 Esther had not showed her people
nor her kindred: for Môr'dē-caī had
charged her that she should not show *it.*
11 And Môr'dē-caī walked every day
before the court of the women's house,
to know how Esther did, and what
should become of her.
12 ¶ Now when every maid's turn was
come to go in to king Ȧ-hăs̱'ū-ē'rŭs,
after that she had been twelve months,
according to the manner of the women,
(for so were the days of their purifications accomplished, *to wit,* six months
with oil of myrrh, and six months with
sweet odors, and with *other* things for
the purifying of the women,)
13 Then thus came *every* maiden unto
the king; whatsoever she desired was
given her to go with her out of the house
of the women unto the king's house.
14 In the evening she went, and on the
morrow she returned into the second
house of the women, to the custody of
Shā-ăsh'găz, the king's chamberlain,
which kept the concubines: she came in
unto the king no more, except the king

delighted in her, and that she were
called by name.
15 ¶ Now when the turn of Esther, the
daughter of Ăb'ĭ-hāil the uncle of Môr'-
dē-caī, who had taken her for his daughter, was come to go in unto the king, she
required nothing but what Hĕg'ā-ī the
king's chamberlain, the keeper of the
women, appointed. And Esther obtained favor in the sight of all them that
looked upon her.
16 So Esther was taken unto king
Ȧ-hăş'ū-ē'rŭs into his house royal in
the tenth month, which *is* the month
Tē-bĕth', in the seventh year of his
reign.
17 And the king loved Esther above all
the women, and she obtained grace and
favor in his sight more than all the virgins; so that he set the royal crown upon
her head, and made her queen instead
of Văsh'tī.
18 Then the king made a great feast
unto all his princes and his servants,
even Esther's feast; and he made a
release to the provinces, and gave gifts,
according to the state of the king.
19 And when the virgins were gathered
together the second time, then Môr'dē-
caī sat in the king's gate.
20 Esther had not *yet* showed her kindred nor her people, as Môr'dē-caī had
charged her: for Esther did the commandment of Môr'dē-caī, like as when
she was brought up with him.
21 ¶ In those days, while Môr'dē-caī
sat in the king's gate, two of the king's
chamberlains, Bĭg'thȧn and Tē'rĕsh, of
those which kept the door, were wroth,
and sought to lay hand on the king
Ȧ-hăş'ū-ē'rŭs.
22 And the thing was known to Môr'-
dē-caī, who told *it* unto Esther the
queen; and Esther certified the king
thereof in Môr'dē-caī's name.
23 And when inquisition was made of
the matter, it was found out; therefore
they were both hanged on a tree: and it
was written in the book of the chronicles
before the king.

CHAPTER 3

AFTER these things did king Ȧ-hăş'ū-
ē'rŭs promote Hā'măn the son of
Hăm'mē-dā'thȧ the Ā'găg-īte, and advanced him, and set his seat above all
the princes that *were* with him.
2 And all the king's servants, that *were*
in the king's gate, bowed, and rever-
enced Hā'măn: for the king had so
commanded concerning him. But Môr'-
dē-caī bowed not, nor did *him* reverence.
3 Then the king's servants, which *were*
in the king's gate, said unto Môr'dē-caī,
Why transgressest thou the king's commandment?
4 Now it came to pass, when they spake
daily unto him, and he hearkened not
unto them, that they told Hā'măn, to
see whether Môr'dē-caī's matters
would stand: for he had told them that
he *was* a Jew.
5 And when Hā'măn saw that Môr'dē-
caī bowed not, nor did him reverence,
then was Hā'măn full of wrath.
6 And he thought scorn to lay hands on
Môr'dē-caī alone; for they had showed
him the people of Môr'dē-caī: wherefore Hā'măn sought to destroy all the
Jews that *were* throughout the whole
kingdom of Ȧ-hăş'ū-ē'rŭs, *even* the
people of Môr'dē-caī.
7 ¶ In the first month, that *is,* the
month Nī'săn, in the twelfth year of king
Ȧ-hăş'ū-ē'rŭs, they cast Pûr, that *is,*
the lot, before Hā'măn from day to day,
and from month to month, *to* the twelfth
month, that *is,* the month Ȧ-där'.
8 ¶ And Hā'măn said unto king
Ȧ-hăş'ū-ē'rŭs, There is a certain people
scattered abroad and dispersed among
the people in all the provinces of thy
kingdom; and their laws *are* diverse
from all people; neither keep they the
king's laws: therefore it *is* not for the
king's profit to suffer them.
9 If it please the king, let it be written
that they may be destroyed: and I will
pay ten thousand talents of silver to the
hands of those that have the charge of
the business, to bring *it* into the king's
treasuries.
10 And the king took his ring from his
hand, and gave it unto Hā'măn the son
of Hăm'mē-dā'thȧ the Ā'găg-īte, the
Jews' enemy.
11 And the king said unto Hā'măn, The
silver *is* given to thee, the people also,
to do with them as it seemeth good to
thee.
12 Then were the king's scribes called
on the thirteenth day of the first month,
and there was written according to all
that Hā'măn had commanded unto the
king's lieutenants, and to the governors
that *were* over every province, and to the

rulers of every people of every province according to the writing thereof, and *to* every people after their language; in the name of king Ȧ-hăṣ′ū-ē′rŭs was it written, and sealed with the king's ring.

13 And the letters were sent by posts into all the king's provinces, to destroy, to kill, and to cause to perish, all Jews, both young and old, little children and women, in one day, *even* upon the thirteenth *day* of the twelfth month, which *is* the month Ȧ-där′, and *to take* the spoil of them for a prey.

14 The copy of the writing for a commandment to be given in every province was published unto all people, that they should be ready against that day.

15 The posts went out, being hastened by the king's commandment, and the decree was given in Shṳ′shăn the palace. And the king and Hā′măn sat down to drink; but the city Shṳ′shăn was perplexed.

CHAPTER 4

WHEN Môr′dē-caī perceived all that was done, Môr′dē-caī rent his clothes, and put on sackcloth with ashes, and went out into the midst of the city, and cried with a loud and a bitter cry;

2 And came even before the king's gate: for none *might* enter into the king's gate clothed with sackcloth.

3 And in every province, whithersoever the king's commandment and his decree came, *there was* great mourning among the Jews, and fasting, and weeping, and wailing; and many lay in sackcloth and ashes.

4 ℂ So Esther's maids and her chamberlains came and told *it* her. Then was the queen exceedingly grieved; and she sent raiment to clothe Môr′dē-caī, and to take away his sackcloth from him: but he received *it* not.

5 Then called Esther for Hā′tăċh, *one* of the king's chamberlains, whom he had appointed to attend upon her, and gave him a commandment to Môr′dē-caī, to know what it *was*, and why it *was*.

6 So Hā′tăċh went forth to Môr′dē-caī unto the street of the city, which *was* before the king's gate.

7 And Môr′dē-caī told him of all that had happened unto him, and of the sum of the money that Hā′măn had promised to pay to the king's treasuries for the Jews, to destroy them.

8 Also he gave him the copy of the writing of the decree that was given at Shṳ′shăn to destroy them, to show *it* unto Esther, and to declare *it* unto her, and to charge her that she should go in unto the king, to make supplication unto him, and to make request before him for her people.

9 And Hā′tăċh came and told Esther the words of Môr′dē-caī.

10 ℂ Again Esther spake unto Hā′tăċh, and gave him commandment unto Môr′dē-caī;

11 All the king's servants, and the people of the king's provinces, do know, that whosoever, whether man or woman, shall come unto the king into the inner court, who is not called, *there is* one law of his to put *him* to death, except such to whom the king shall hold out the golden sceptre, that he may live: but I have not been called to come in unto the king these thirty days.

12 And they told to Môr′dē-caī Esther's words.

13 Then Môr′dē-caī commanded to answer Esther, Think not with thyself that thou shalt escape in the king's house, more than all the Jews.

14 For if thou altogether holdest thy peace at this time, *then* shall there enlargement and deliverance arise to the Jews from another place; but thou and thy father's house shall be destroyed: and who knoweth whether thou art come to the kingdom for *such* a time as this?

15 ℂ Then Esther bade *them* return Môr′dē-caī *this answer*,

16 Go, gather together all the Jews that are present in Shṳ′shăn, and fast ye for me, and neither eat nor drink three days, night or day: I also and my maidens will fast likewise; and so will I go in unto the king, which *is* not according to the law: and if I perish, I perish.

17 So Môr′dē-caī went his way, and did according to all that Esther had commanded him.

CHAPTER 5

NOW it came to pass on the third day, that Esther put on *her* royal *apparel*, and stood in the inner court of the king's house, over against the king's house: and the king sat upon his royal throne in the royal house, over against the gate of the house.

2 And it was so, when the king saw Esther the queen standing in the court, *that* she obtained favor in his sight: and the king held out to Esther the golden sceptre that *was* in his hand. So Esther drew near, and touched the top of the sceptre.

3 Then said the king unto her, What wilt thou, queen Esther? and what *is* thy request? it shall be even given thee to the half of the kingdom.

4 And Esther answered, If *it seem* good unto the king, let the king and Hā'măn come this day unto the banquet that I have prepared for him.

5 Then the king said, Cause Hā'măn to make haste, that he may do as Esther hath said. So the king and Hā'măn came to the banquet that Esther had prepared.

6 ¶ And the king said unto Esther at the banquet of wine, What *is* thy petition? and it shall be granted thee: and what *is* thy request? even to the half of the kingdom it shall be performed.

7 Then answered Esther, and said, My petition and my request *is;*

8 If I have found favor in the sight of the king, and if it please the king to grant my petition, and to perform my request, let the king and Hā'măn come to the banquet that I shall prepare for them, and I will do to-morrow as the king hath said.

9 ¶ Then went Hā'măn forth that day joyful and with a glad heart: but when Hā'măn saw Môr'dē-caī in the king's gate, that he stood not up, nor moved for him, he was full of indignation against Môr'dē-caī.

10 Nevertheless Hā'măn refrained himself: and when he came home, he sent and called for his friends, and Zē'rĕsh his wife.

11 And Hā'măn told them of the glory of his riches, and the multitude of his children, and all *the things* wherein the king had promoted him, and how he had advanced him above the princes and servants of the king.

12 Hā'măn said moreover, Yea, Esther the queen did let no man come in with the king unto the banquet that she had prepared but myself; and to-morrow am I invited unto her also with the king.

13 Yet all this availeth me nothing, so long as I see Môr'dē-caī the Jew sitting at the king's gate.

14 ¶ Then said Zē'rĕsh his wife and all his friends unto him, Let a gallows be made of fifty cubits high, and to-morrow speak thou unto the king that Môr'dē-caī may be hanged thereon: then go thou in merrily with the king unto the banquet. And the thing pleased Hā'măn; and he caused the gallows to be made.

CHAPTER 6

ON that night could not the king sleep, and he commanded to bring the book of records of the chronicles; and they were read before the king.

2 And it was found written, that Môr'dē-caī had told of Bĭg-thā'nȧ and Tē'rĕsh, two of the king's chamberlains, the keepers of the door, who sought to lay hand on the king Ȧ-hăṣ'ū-ē'rŭs.

3 And the king said, What honor and dignity hath been done to Môr'dē-caī for this? Then said the king's servants that ministered unto him, There is nothing done for him.

4 ¶ And the king said, Who *is* in the court? Now Hā'măn was come into the outward court of the king's house, to speak unto the king to hang Môr'dē-caī on the gallows that he had prepared for him.

5 And the king's servants said unto him, Behold, Hā'măn standeth in the court. And the king said, Let him come in.

6 So Hā'măn came in. And the king said unto him, What shall be done unto the man whom the king delighteth to honor? Now Hā'măn thought in his heart, To whom would the king delight to do honor more than to myself?

7 And Hā'măn answered the king, For the man whom the king delighteth to honor,

8 Let the royal apparel be brought which the king *useth* to wear, and the horse that the king rideth upon, and the crown royal which is set upon his head:

9 And let this apparel and horse be delivered to the hand of one of the king's most noble princes, that they may array the man *withal* whom the king delighteth to honor, and bring him on horseback through the street of the city, and proclaim before him, Thus shall it be done

to the man whom the king delighteth to
honor.
10 Then the king said to Hā'măn,
Make haste, *and* take the apparel and
the horse, as thou hast said, and do even
so to Môr'dē-caī the Jew, that sitteth at
the king's gate: let nothing fail of all
that thou hast spoken.
11 Then took Hā'măn the apparel and
the horse, and arrayed Môr'dē-caī, and
brought him on horseback through the
street of the city, and proclaimed before
him, Thus shall it be done unto the man
whom the king delighteth to honor.
12 ¶ And Môr'dē-caī came again to
the king's gate. But Hā'măn hasted to
his house mourning, and having his
head covered.
13 And Hā'măn told Zē'rĕsh his wife
and all his friends every *thing* that had
befallen him. Then said his wise men
and Zē'rĕsh his wife unto him, If Môr'-
dē-caī *be* of the seed of the Jews, before
whom thou hast begun to fall, thou shalt
not prevail against him, but shalt surely
fall before him.
14 And while they *were* yet talking with
him, came the king's chamberlains, and
hasted to bring Hā'măn unto the banquet that Esther had prepared.

CHAPTER 7

So the king and Hā'măn came to banquet with Esther the queen.
2 And the king said again unto Esther
on the second day at the banquet of
wine, What *is* thy petition, queen Esther? and it shall be granted thee: and
what *is* thy request? and it shall be performed, *even* to the half of the kingdom.
3 Then Esther the queen answered and
said, If I have found favor in thy sight,
O king, and if it please the king, let my
life be given me at my petition, and my
people at my request:
4 For we are sold, I and my people, to
be destroyed, to be slain, and to perish.
But if we had been sold for bondmen
and bondwomen, I had held my tongue,
although the enemy could not countervail the king's damage.
5 ¶ Then the king Ȧ-hăs̱'ū-ē'rŭs answered and said unto Esther the queen,
Who is he, and where is he, that durst
presume in his heart to do so?
6 And Esther said, The adversary and
enemy *is* this wicked Hā'măn. Then
Hā'măn was afraid before the king and
the queen.
7 ¶ And the king arising from the banquet of wine in his wrath *went* into the
palace garden: and Hā'măn stood up to
make request for his life to Esther the
queen; for he saw that there was evil
determined against him by the king.
8 Then the king returned out of the
palace garden into the place of the banquet of wine; and Hā'măn was fallen
upon the bed whereon Esther *was*.
Then said the king, Will he force the
queen also before me in the house? As
the word went out of the king's mouth,
they covered Hā'măn's face.
9 And Här-bō'nȧh, one of the chamberlains, said before the king, Behold also
the gallows fifty cubits high, which
Hā'măn had made for Môr'dē-caī, who
had spoken good for the king, standeth
in the house of Hā'măn. Then the king
said, Hang him thereon.
10 So they hanged Hā'măn on the
gallows that he had prepared for Môr'-
dē-caī. Then was the king's wrath
pacified.

CHAPTER 8

On that day did the king Ȧ-hăs̱'ū-ē'-
rŭs give the house of Hā'măn the
Jews' enemy unto Esther the queen.
And Môr'dē-caī came before the king;
for Esther had told what he *was* unto
her.
2 And the king took off his ring, which
he had taken from Hā'măn, and gave it
unto Môr'dē-caī. And Esther set Môr'-
dē-caī over the house of Hā'măn.
3 ¶ And Esther spake yet again before
the king, and fell down at his feet, and
besought him with tears to put away the
mischief of Hā'măn the Ā'găg-īte, and
his device that he had devised against
the Jews.
4 Then the king held out the golden
sceptre toward Esther. So Esther
arose, and stood before the king,
5 And said, If it please the king, and if
I have found favor in his sight, and the
thing *seem* right before the king, and I
be pleasing in his eyes, let it be written
to reverse the letters devised by Hā'-
măn the son of Hăm'mē-dā'thȧ the
Ā'găg-īte, which he wrote to destroy the
Jews which *are* in all the king's provinces:
6 For how can I endure to see the evil

that shall come unto my people? or how
can I endure to see the destruction of
my kindred?
7 ¶ Then the king Ȧ-hăş′ū-ē′rŭs said
unto Esther the queen and to Môr′dē-
caī the Jew, Behold, I have given Esther
the house of Hā′măn, and him they have
hanged upon the gallows, because he
laid his hand upon the Jews.
8 Write ye also for the Jews, as it
liketh you, in the king's name, and seal
it with the king's ring: for the writing
which is written in the king's name, and
sealed with the king's ring, may no man
reverse.
9 Then were the king's scribes called
at that time in the third month, that *is*,
the month Sī-vän′, on the three and
twentieth *day* thereof; and it was written
according to all that Môr′dē-caī commanded unto the Jews, and to the lieutenants, and the deputies and rulers of
the provinces which *are* from India unto
Ethiopia, a hundred twenty and seven
provinces, unto every province according to the writing thereof, and unto
every people after their language, and to
the Jews according to their writing, and
according to their language.
10 And he wrote in the king Ȧ-hăş′ū-
ē′rŭs' name, and sealed *it* with the
king's ring, and sent letters by posts on
horseback, *and* riders on mules, camels,
and young dromedaries:
11 Wherein the king granted the Jews
which *were* in every city to gather themselves together, and to stand for their
life, to destroy, to slay, and to cause to
perish, all the power of the people and
province that would assault them, *both*
little ones and women, and *to take* the
spoil of them for a prey,
12 Upon one day in all the provinces of
king Ȧ-hăş′ū-ē′rŭs, *namely*, upon the
thirteenth *day* of the twelfth month,
which *is* the month Ȧ-där′.
13 The copy of the writing for a commandment to be given in every province
was published unto all people, and that
the Jews should be ready against that
day to avenge themselves on their
enemies.
14 *So* the posts that rode upon mules
and camels went out, being hastened
and pressed on by the king's commandment. And the decree was given at
Shụ′shăn the palace.
15 ¶ And Môr′dē-caī went out from
the presence of the king in royal apparel of blue and white, and with a great
crown of gold, and with a garment of
fine linen and purple: and the city of
Shụ′shăn rejoiced and was glad.
16 The Jews had light, and gladness,
and joy, and honor.
17 And in every province, and in every
city, whithersoever the king's commandment and his decree came, the
Jews had joy and gladness, a feast and a
good day. And many of the people of
the land became Jews; for the fear of
the Jews fell upon them.

CHAPTER 9

NOW in the twelfth month, that *is*,
the month Ȧ-där′, on the thirteenth
day of the same, when the king's commandment and his decree drew near to
be put in execution, in the day that the
enemies of the Jews hoped to have power
over them; (though it was turned to the
contrary, that the Jews had rule over
them that hated them,)
2 The Jews gathered themselves together in their cities throughout all the
provinces of the king Ȧ-hăş′ū-ē′rŭs, to
lay hand on such as sought their hurt:
and no man could withstand them; for
the fear of them fell upon all people.
3 And all the rulers of the provinces,
and the lieutenants, and the deputies,
and officers of the king, helped the
Jews; because the fear of Môr′dē-caī
fell upon them.
4 For Môr′dē-caī *was* great in the
king's house, and his fame went out
throughout all the provinces: for this
man Môr′dē-caī waxed greater and
greater.
5 Thus the Jews smote all their enemies with the stroke of the sword, and
slaughter, and destruction, and did what
they would unto those that hated them.
6 And in Shụ′shăn the palace the Jews
slew and destroyed five hundred men.
7 And Pär′shăn-dā′thȧ, and Dăl′phŏn,
and Ăs-pā′thȧ,
8 And Pō-rā′thȧ, and Ȧ-dā′lĭ-ȧ, and
Ȧ-rĭd′ȧ-thȧ,
9 And Pär-măsh′tȧ, and Ȧ-rĭs′ā-ī, and
Ă-rĭd′ā-ī, and Vȧ-jĕz′ȧ-thȧ,
10 The ten sons of Hā′măn the son of
Hăm′mē-dā′thȧ, the enemy of the Jews,
slew they; but on the spoil laid they not
their hand.
11 On that day the number of those

that were slain in Shṳ′shăn the palace was brought before the king.

12 ¶ And the king said unto Esther the queen, The Jews have slain and destroyed five hundred men in Shṳ′shăn the palace, and the ten sons of Hā′măn; what have they done in the rest of the king's provinces? now what *is* thy petition? and it shall be granted thee: or what *is* thy request further? and it shall be done.

13 Then said Esther, If it please the king, let it be granted to the Jews which *are* in Shṳ′shăn to do to-morrow also according unto this day's decree, and let Hā′măn's ten sons be hanged upon the gallows.

14 And the king commanded it so to be done: and the decree was given at Shṳ′shăn; and they hanged Hā′măn's ten sons.

15 For the Jews that *were* in Shṳ′shăn gathered themselves together on the fourteenth day also of the month Ȧ-där′, and slew three hundred men at Shṳ′shăn; but on the prey they laid not their hand.

16 But the other Jews that *were* in the king's provinces gathered themselves together, and stood for their lives, and had rest from their enemies, and slew of their foes seventy and five thousand, but they laid not their hands on the prey,

17 On the thirteenth day of the month Ȧ-där′; and on the fourteenth day of the same rested they, and made it a day of feasting and gladness.

18 But the Jews that *were* at Shṳ′shăn assembled together on the thirteenth *day* thereof, and on the fourteenth thereof; and on the fifteenth *day* of the same they rested, and made it a day of feasting and gladness.

19 Therefore the Jews of the villages, that dwelt in the unwalled towns, made the fourteenth day of the month Ȧ-där′ *a day of* gladness and feasting, and a good day, and of sending portions one to another.

20 ¶ And Môr′dē-caī wrote these things, and sent letters unto all the Jews that *were* in all the provinces of the king Ȧ-hăṣ′ū-ē′rŭs, *both* nigh and far,

21 To establish *this* among them, that they should keep the fourteenth day of the month Ȧ-där′, and the fifteenth day of the same, yearly,

22 As the days wherein the Jews rested from their enemies, and the month which was turned unto them from sorrow to joy, and from mourning into a good day: that they should make them days of feasting and joy, and of sending portions one to another, and gifts to the poor.

23 And the Jews undertook to do as they had begun, and as Môr′dē-caī had written unto them;

24 Because Hā′măn the son of Hăm-mē-dā′thȧ, the Ā′găg-īte, the enemy of all the Jews, had devised against the Jews to destroy them, and had cast Pûr, that *is*, the lot, to consume them, and to destroy them;

25 But when *Esther* came before the king, he commanded by letters that his wicked device, which he devised against the Jews, should return upon his own head, and that he and his sons should be hanged on the gallows.

26 Wherefore they called these days Pū′rĭm after the name of Pûr. Therefore for all the words of this letter, and *of that* which they had seen concerning this matter, and which had come unto them,

27 The Jews ordained, and took upon them, and upon their seed, and upon all such as joined themselves unto them, so as it should not fail, that they would keep these two days according to their writing, and according to their *appointed* time every year;

28 And *that* these days *should be* remembered and kept throughout every generation, every family, every province, and every city; and *that* these days of Pū′rĭm should not fail from among the Jews, nor the memorial of them perish from their seed.

29 Then Esther the queen, the daughter of Ăb′ĭ-hāil, and Môr′dē-caī the Jew, wrote with all authority, to confirm this second letter of Pū′rĭm.

30 And he sent the letters unto all the Jews, to the hundred twenty and seven provinces of the kingdom of Ȧ-hăṣ′ū-ē′rŭs, *with* words of peace and truth,

31 To confirm these days of Pū′rĭm in their times *appointed*, according as Môr′dē-caī the Jew and Esther the queen had enjoined them, and as they had decreed for themselves and for their seed, the matters of the fastings and their cry.

32 And the decree of Esther confirmed these matters of Pū′rĭm; and it was written in the book.

CHAPTER 10

AND the king Ȧ-hăş′ū-ē′rŭs laid a tribute upon the land, and *upon* the isles of the sea.

2 And all the acts of his power and of his might, and the declaration of the greatness of Môr′dē-caī, whereunto the king advanced him, *are* they not written in the book of the chronicles of the kings of Mē′dĭ-ȧ and Persia?

3 For Môr′dē-caī the Jew *was* next unto king Ȧ-hăş′ū-ē′rŭs, and great among the Jews, and accepted of the multitude of his brethren, seeking the wealth of his people, and speaking peace to all his seed.

THE BOOK OF JOB

CHAPTER 1

THERE was a man in the land of Ŭz, whose name *was* Jōb; and that man was perfect and upright, and one that feared God, and eschewed evil.

2 And there were born unto him seven sons and three daughters.

3 His substance also was seven thousand sheep, and three thousand camels, and five hundred yoke of oxen, and five hundred she asses, and a very great household; so that this man was the greatest of all the men of the east.

4 And his sons went and feasted *in their* houses, every one his day; and sent and called for their three sisters to eat and to drink with them.

5 And it was so, when the days of *their* feasting were gone about, that Jōb sent and sanctified them, and rose up early in the morning, and offered burnt offerings *according* to the number of them all: for Jōb said, It may be that my sons have sinned, and cursed God in their hearts. Thus did Jōb continually.

6 ℂ Now there was a day when the sons of God came to present themselves before the LORD, and Satan came also among them.

7 And the LORD said unto Satan, Whence comest thou? Then Satan answered the LORD, and said, From going to and fro in the earth, and from walking up and down in it.

8 And the LORD said unto Satan, Hast thou considered my servant Jōb, that *there is* none like him in the earth, a perfect and an upright man, one that feareth God, and escheweth evil?

9 Then Satan answered the LORD, and said, Doth Jōb fear God for nought?

10 Hast not thou made a hedge about him, and about his house, and about all that he hath on every side? thou hast blessed the work of his hands, and his substance is increased in the land.

11 But put forth thine hand now, and touch all that he hath, and he will curse thee to thy face.

12 And the LORD said unto Satan, Behold, all that he hath *is* in thy power; only upon himself put not forth thine hand. So Satan went forth from the presence of the LORD.

13 ℂ And there was a day when his sons and his daughters *were* eating and drinking wine in their eldest brother's house:

14 And there came a messenger unto Jōb, and said, The oxen were plowing, and the asses feeding beside them:

15 And the Sȧ-bē′ănş fell *upon them,* and took them away; yea, they have slain the servants with the edge of the sword; and I only am escaped alone to tell thee.

16 While he was yet speaking, there came also another, and said, The fire of God is fallen from heaven, and hath burned up the sheep, and the servants, and consumed them; and I only am escaped alone to tell thee.

17 While he was yet speaking, there came also another, and said, The Chăl-dē′ănş made out three bands, and fell upon the camels, and have carried them away, yea, and slain the servants with the edge of the sword; and I only am escaped alone to tell thee.

18 While he was yet speaking, there came also another, and said, Thy sons and thy daughters *were* eating and

drinking wine in their eldest brother's
house:
19 And, behold, there came a great
wind from the wilderness, and smote
the four corners of the house, and it fell
upon the young men, and they are dead;
and I only am escaped alone to tell thee.
20 Then Jōb arose, and rent his mantle, and shaved his head, and fell down
upon the ground, and worshipped,
21 And said, Naked came I out of my
mother's womb, and naked shall I return thither: the LORD gave, and the
LORD hath taken away; blessed be the
name of the LORD.
22 In all this Jōb sinned not, nor
charged God foolishly.

CHAPTER 2

AGAIN there was a day when the
sons of God came to present themselves before the LORD, and Satan came
also among them to present himself before the LORD.
2 And the LORD said unto Satan, From
whence comest thou? And Satan answered the LORD, and said, From going
to and fro in the earth, and from walking
up and down in it.
3 And the LORD said unto Satan, Hast
thou considered my servant Jōb, that
there is none like him in the earth, a perfect and an upright man, one that feareth God, and escheweth evil? and still
he holdeth fast his integrity, although
thou movedst me against him, to destroy
him without cause.
4 And Satan answered the LORD, and
said, Skin for skin, yea, all that a man
hath will he give for his life.
5 But put forth thine hand now, and
touch his bone and his flesh, and he will
curse thee to thy face.
6 And the LORD said unto Satan, Behold, he *is* in thine hand; but save his
life.
7 ¶ So went Satan forth from the presence of the LORD, and smote Jōb with
sore boils from the sole of his foot unto
his crown.
8 And he took him a potsherd to scrape
himself withal; and he sat down among
the ashes.
9 ¶ Then said his wife unto him, Dost
thou still retain thine integrity? curse
God, and die.
10 But he said unto her, Thou speakest
as one of the foolish women speaketh.
What? shall we receive good at the hand
of God, and shall we not receive evil?
In all this did not Jōb sin with his lips.
11 ¶ Now when Jōb's three friends
heard of all this evil that was come upon
him, they came every one from his own
place; Ĕl'ĭ-phăz the Tē'măn-īte, and Bildad the Shṳ'hīte, and Zō'phȧr the Nā'ȧ-
mȧ-thīte′: for they had made an appointment together to come to mourn with
him, and to comfort him.
12 And when they lifted up their eyes
afar off, and knew him not, they lifted up
their voice, and wept; and they rent
every one his mantle, and sprinkled dust
upon their heads toward heaven.
13 So they sat down with him upon the
ground seven days and seven nights, and
none spake a word unto him: for they
saw that *his* grief was very great.

CHAPTER 3

AFTER this opened Jōb his mouth,
and cursed his day.
2 And Jōb spake, and said,
3 Let the day perish wherein I was
born, and the night *in which* it was said,
There is a man child conceived.
4 Let that day be darkness; let not God
regard it from above, neither let the light
shine upon it.
5 Let darkness and the shadow of
death stain it; let a cloud dwell upon it;
let the blackness of the day terrify it.
6 *As for* that night, let darkness seize
upon it; let it not be joined unto the days
of the year; let it not come into the number of the months.
7 Lo, let that night be solitary; let no
joyful voice come therein.
8 Let them curse it that curse the day,
who are ready to raise up their mourning.
9 Let the stars of the twilight thereof
be dark; let it look for light, but *have*
none; neither let it see the dawning of
the day:
10 Because it shut not up the doors of
my *mother's* womb, nor hid sorrow from
mine eyes.
11 Why died I not from the womb? *why*
did I *not* give up the ghost when I came
out of the belly?
12 Why did the knees prevent me? or
why the breasts that I should suck?
13 For now should I have lain still and
been quiet, I should have slept: then had
I been at rest,
14 With kings and counselors of the

earth, which built desolate places for
themselves;
15 Or with princes that had gold, who
filled their houses with silver:
16 Or as a hidden untimely birth I had
not been; as infants *which* never saw
light.
17 There the wicked cease *from* troubling; and there the weary be at rest.
18 *There* the prisoners rest together;
they hear not the voice of the oppressor.
19 The small and great are there; and
the servant *is* free from his master.
20 Wherefore is light given to him that
is in misery, and life unto the bitter *in*
soul;
21 Which long for death, but it *cometh*
not; and dig for it more than for hid
treasures;
22 Which rejoice exceedingly, *and* are
glad, when they can find the grave?
23 *Why is light given* to a man whose
way is hid, and whom God hath hedged
in?
24 For my sighing cometh before I eat,
and my roarings are poured out like the
waters.
25 For the thing which I greatly feared
is come upon me, and that which I was
afraid of is come unto me.
26 I was not in safety, neither had I
rest, neither was I quiet; yet trouble
came.

CHAPTER 4

THEN Ĕl′ĭ-phăz the Tē′măn-īte answered and said,
2 *If* we assay to commune with thee,
wilt thou be grieved? but who can withhold himself from speaking?
3 Behold, thou hast instructed many,
and thou hast strengthened the weak
hands.
4 Thy words have upholden him that
was falling, and thou hast strengthened
the feeble knees.
5 But now it is come upon thee, and
thou faintest; it toucheth thee, and thou
art troubled.
6 *Is* not *this* thy fear, thy confidence,
thy hope, and the uprightness of thy
ways?
7 Remember, I pray thee, who *ever*
perished, being innocent? or where were
the righteous cut off?
8 Even as I have seen, they that plow
iniquity, and sow wickedness, reap the
same.
9 By the blast of God they perish, and
by the breath of his nostrils are they
consumed.
10 The roaring of the lion, and the
voice of the fierce lion, and the teeth of
the young lions, are broken.
11 The old lion perisheth for lack of
prey, and the stout lion's whelps are
scattered abroad.
12 Now a thing was secretly brought
to me, and mine ear received a little
thereof.
13 In thoughts from the visions of the
night, when deep sleep falleth on men,
14 Fear came upon me, and trembling,
which made all my bones to shake.
15 Then a spirit passed before my face;
the hair of my flesh stood up:
16 It stood still, but I could not discern
the form thereof: an image *was* before
mine eyes, *there was* silence, and I
heard a voice, *saying,*
17 Shall mortal man be more just than
God? shall a man be more pure than his
Maker?
18 Behold, he put no trust in his servants; and his angels he charged with
folly:
19 How much less *in* them that dwell
in houses of clay, whose foundation *is* in
the dust, *which* are crushed before the
moth?
20 They are destroyed from morning to
evening: they perish for ever without any
regarding *it.*
21 Doth not their excellency *which is*
in them go away? they die, even without
wisdom.

CHAPTER 5

CALL now, if there be any that will
answer thee; and to which of the
saints wilt thou turn?
2 For wrath killeth the foolish man, and
envy slayeth the silly one.
3 I have seen the foolish taking root:
but suddenly I cursed his habitation.
4 His children are far from safety, and
they are crushed in the gate, neither *is*
there any to deliver *them.*
5 Whose harvest the hungry eateth up,
and taketh it even out of the thorns, and
the robber swalloweth up their substance.
6 Although affliction cometh not forth
of the dust, neither doth trouble spring
out of the ground;
7 Yet man is born unto trouble, as the
sparks fly upward.

8 I would seek unto God, and unto God would I commit my cause:

9 Which doeth great things and unsearchable; marvelous things without number:

10 Who giveth rain upon the earth, and sendeth waters upon the fields:

11 To set up on high those that be low; that those which mourn may be exalted to safety.

12 He disappointeth the devices of the crafty, so that their hands cannot perform *their* enterprise.

13 He taketh the wise in their own craftiness: and the counsel of the froward is carried headlong.

14 They meet with darkness in the daytime, and grope in the noonday as in the night.

15 But he saveth the poor from the sword, from their mouth, and from the hand of the mighty.

16 So the poor hath hope, and iniquity stoppeth her mouth.

17 Behold, happy *is* the man whom God correcteth: therefore despise not thou the chastening of the Almighty:

18 For he maketh sore, and bindeth up: he woundeth, and his hands make whole.

19 He shall deliver thee in six troubles: yea, in seven there shall no evil touch thee.

20 In famine he shall redeem thee from death: and in war from the power of the sword.

21 Thou shalt be hid from the scourge of the tongue: neither shalt thou be afraid of destruction when it cometh.

22 At destruction and famine thou shalt laugh: neither shalt thou be afraid of the beasts of the earth.

23 For thou shalt be in league with the stones of the field: and the beasts of the field shall be at peace with thee.

24 And thou shalt know that thy tabernacle *shall be* in peace; and thou shalt visit thy habitation, and shalt not sin.

25 Thou shalt know also that thy seed *shall be* great, and thine offspring as the grass of the earth.

26 Thou shalt come to *thy* grave in a full age, like as a shock of corn cometh in in his season.

27 Lo this, we have searched it, so it *is;* hear it, and know thou *it* for thy good.

CHAPTER 6

BUT Jōb answered and said,

2 Oh that my grief were thoroughly weighed, and my calamity laid in the balances together!

3 For now it would be heavier than the sand of the sea: therefore my words are swallowed up.

4 For the arrows of the Almighty *are* within me, the poison whereof drinketh up my spirit: the terrors of God do set themselves in array against me.

5 Doth the wild ass bray when he hath grass? or loweth the ox over his fodder?

6 Can that which is unsavory be eaten without salt? or is there *any* taste in the white of an egg?

7 The things *that* my soul refused to touch *are* as my sorrowful meat.

8 Oh that I might have my request; and that God would grant *me* the thing that I long for!

9 Even that it would please God to destroy me; that he would let loose his hand, and cut me off!

10 Then should I yet have comfort; yea, I would harden myself in sorrow: let him not spare; for I have not concealed the words of the Holy One.

11 What *is* my strength, that I should hope? and what *is* mine end, that I should prolong my life?

12 *Is* my strength the strength of stones? or *is* my flesh of brass?

13 *Is* not my help in me? and is wisdom driven quite from me?

14 To him that is afflicted pity *should be showed* from his friend; but he forsaketh the fear of the Almighty.

15 My brethren have dealt deceitfully as a brook, *and* as the stream of brooks they pass away;

16 Which are blackish by reason of the ice, *and* wherein the snow is hid:

17 What time they wax warm, they vanish: when it is hot, they are consumed out of their place.

18 The paths of their way are turned aside; they go to nothing, and perish.

19 The troops of Tē'mȧ looked, the companies of Shē'bȧ waited for them.

20 They were confounded because they had hoped; they came thither, and were ashamed.

21 For now ye are nothing; ye see *my* casting down, and are afraid.

22 Did I say, Bring unto me? or, Give a
reward for me of your substance?
23 Or, Deliver me from the enemy's
hand? or, Redeem me from the hand of
the mighty?
24 Teach me, and I will hold my tongue:
and cause me to understand wherein I
have erred.
25 How forcible are right words! but
what doth your arguing reprove?
26 Do ye imagine to reprove words, and
the speeches of one that is desperate,
which are as wind?
27 Yea, ye overwhelm the fatherless,
and ye dig *a pit* for your friend.
28 Now therefore be content, look
upon me; for *it is* evident unto you
if I lie.
29 Return, I pray you, let it not be iniquity; yea, return again, my righteousness
is in it.
30 Is there iniquity in my tongue? cannot my taste discern perverse things?

CHAPTER 7

IS there not an appointed time to man
upon earth? *are not* his days also like
the days of a hireling?
2 As a servant earnestly desireth the
shadow, and as a hireling looketh for
the reward of his work;
3 So am I made to possess months of
vanity, and wearisome nights are appointed to me.
4 When I lie down, I say, When shall
I arise, and the night be gone? and I am
full of tossings to and fro unto the dawning of the day.
5 My flesh is clothed with worms and
clods of dust; my skin is broken, and
become loathsome.
6 My days are swifter than a weaver's
shuttle, and are spent without hope.
7 O remember that my life *is* wind:
mine eye shall no more see good.
8 The eye of him that hath seen me
shall see me no *more:* thine eyes *are*
upon me, and I *am* not.
9 *As* the cloud is consumed and vanisheth away; so he that goeth down to
the grave shall come up no *more*.
10 He shall return no more to his house,
neither shall his place know him any
more.
11 Therefore I will not refrain my
mouth; I will speak in the anguish of
my spirit; I will complain in the bitterness of my soul.
12 *Am* I a sea, or a whale, that thou
settest a watch over me?
13 When I say, My bed shall comfort
me, my couch shall ease my complaint;
14 Then thou scarest me with dreams,
and terrifiest me through visions:
15 So that my soul chooseth strangling,
and death rather than my life.
16 I loathe *it;* I would not live alway:
let me alone; for my days *are* vanity.
17 What *is* man, that thou shouldest
magnify him? and that thou shouldest
set thine heart upon him?
18 And *that* thou shouldest visit him
every morning, *and* try him every
moment?
19 How long wilt thou not depart from
me, nor let me alone till I swallow down
my spittle?
20 I have sinned; what shall I do unto
thee, O thou preserver of men? why hast
thou set me as a mark against thee, so
that I am a burden to myself?
21 And why dost thou not pardon my
transgression, and take away mine iniquity? for now shall I sleep in the dust;
and thou shalt seek me in the morning,
but I *shall* not *be*.

CHAPTER 8

THEN answered Bildad the Shu'hite,
and said,
2 How long wilt thou speak these
things? and *how long shall* the words of
thy mouth *be like* a strong wind?
3 Doth God pervert judgment? or doth
the Almighty pervert justice?
4 If thy children have sinned against
him, and he have cast them away for
their transgression;
5 If thou wouldest seek unto God betimes, and make thy supplication to the
Almighty;
6 If thou *wert* pure and upright; surely
now he would awake for thee, and make
the habitation of thy righteousness
prosperous.
7 Though thy beginning was small, yet
thy latter end should greatly increase.
8 For inquire, I pray thee, of the former
age, and prepare thyself to the search
of their fathers:
9 (For we *are but of* yesterday, and
know nothing, because our days upon
earth *are* a shadow:)
10 Shall not they teach thee, *and*
tell thee, and utter words out of their
heart?

11 Can the rush grow up without mire?
can the flag grow without water?
12 Whilst it *is* yet in his greenness, *and*
not cut down, it withereth before any
other herb.
13 So *are* the paths of all that forget
God; and the hypocrite's hope shall
perish:
14 Whose hope shall be cut off, and
whose trust *shall be* a spider's web.
15 He shall lean upon his house, but
it shall not stand: he shall hold it fast,
but it shall not endure.
16 He *is* green before the sun, and his
branch shooteth forth in his garden.
17 His roots are wrapped about the
heap, *and* seeth the place of stones.
18 If he destroy him from his place,
then *it* shall deny him, *saying,* I have
not seen thee.
19 Behold, this *is* the joy of his way,
and out of the earth shall others grow.
20 Behold, God will not cast away a
perfect man, neither will he help the evildoers:
21 Till he fill thy mouth with laughing,
and thy lips with rejoicing.
22 They that hate thee shall be clothed
with shame; and the dwelling place of the
wicked shall come to nought.

CHAPTER 9

THEN Jōb answered and said,
2 I know *it is* so of a truth: but how
should man be just with God?
3 If he will contend with him, he cannot answer him one of a thousand.
4 *He is* wise in heart, and mighty in
strength: who hath hardened *himself*
against him, and hath prospered?
5 Which removeth the mountains, and
they know not; which overturneth them
in his anger;
6 Which shaketh the earth out of her
place, and the pillars thereof tremble;
7 Which commandeth the sun, and it
riseth not; and sealeth up the stars;
8 Which alone spreadeth out the heavens, and treadeth upon the waves of the
sea;
9 Which maketh Ärc-tū′rŭs, Ō-rī′ŏn,
and Plē′ia-dēș, and the chambers of the
south;
10 Which doeth great things past finding
out; yea, and wonders without number.
11 Lo, he goeth by me, and I see *him*
not: he passeth on also, but I perceive
him not.
12 Behold, he taketh away, who can
hinder him? who will say unto him,
What doest thou?
13 *If* God will not withdraw his anger, the proud helpers do stoop under
him.
14 How much less shall I answer him,
and choose out my words *to reason* with
him?
15 Whom, though I were righteous, *yet*
would I not answer, *but* I would make
supplication to my judge.
16 If I had called, and he had answered
me; *yet* would I not believe that he had
hearkened unto my voice.
17 For he breaketh me with a tempest,
and multiplieth my wounds without
cause.
18 He will not suffer me to take my
breath, but filleth me with bitterness.
19 If *I speak* of strength, lo, *he is*
strong: and if of judgment, who shall set
me a time *to plead?*
20 If I justify myself, mine own mouth
shall condemn me: *if I say,* I *am* perfect,
it shall also prove me perverse.
21 *Though* I *were* perfect, *yet* would I
not know my soul: I would despise my
life.
22 This *is* one *thing,* therefore I said *it,*
He destroyeth the perfect and the
wicked.
23 If the scourge slay suddenly, he will
laugh at the trial of the innocent.
24 The earth is given into the hand of
the wicked: he covereth the faces of the
judges thereof; if not, where, *and* who
is he?
25 Now my days are swifter than a post:
they flee away, they see no good.
26 They are passed away as the swift
ships: as the eagle *that* hasteth to the
prey.
27 If I say, I will forget my complaint,
I will leave off my heaviness, and comfort *myself;*
28 I am afraid of all my sorrows, I know
that thou wilt not hold me innocent.
29 *If* I be wicked, why then labor I in
vain?
30 If I wash myself with snow water,
and make my hands never so clean;
31 Yet shalt thou plunge me in the
ditch, and mine own clothes shall abhor
me.
32 For *he is* not a man, as I *am, that* I
should answer him, *and* we should come
together in judgment.

33 Neither is there any daysman betwixt us, *that* might lay his hand upon us both.
34 Let him take his rod away from me, and let not his fear terrify me:
35 *Then* would I speak, and not fear him; but *it is* not so with me.

CHAPTER 10

MY soul is weary of my life; I will leave my complaint upon myself; I will speak in the bitterness of my soul.
2 I will say unto God, Do not condemn me; show me wherefore thou contendest with me.
3 *Is it* good unto thee that thou shouldest oppress, that thou shouldest despise the work of thine hands, and shine upon the counsel of the wicked?
4 Hast thou eyes of flesh? or seest thou as man seeth?
5 *Are* thy days as the days of man? *are* thy years as man's days,
6 That thou inquirest after mine iniquity, and searchest after my sin?
7 Thou knowest that I am not wicked; and *there is* none that can deliver out of thine hand.
8 Thine hands have made me and fashioned me together round about; yet thou dost destroy me.
9 Remember, I beseech thee, that thou hast made me as the clay; and wilt thou bring me into dust again?
10 Hast thou not poured me out as milk, and curdled me like cheese?
11 Thou hast clothed me with skin and flesh, and hast fenced me with bones and sinews.
12 Thou hast granted me life and favor, and thy visitation hath preserved my spirit.
13 And these *things* hast thou hid in thine heart: I know that this *is* with thee.
14 If I sin, then thou markest me, and thou wilt not acquit me from mine iniquity.
15 If I be wicked, woe unto me; and *if* I be righteous, *yet* will I not lift up my head. *I am* full of confusion; therefore see thou mine affliction;
16 For it increaseth. Thou huntest me as a fierce lion: and again thou showest thyself marvelous upon me.
17 Thou renewest thy witnesses against me, and increasest thine indignation upon me; changes and war *are* against me.
18 Wherefore then hast thou brought me forth out of the womb? Oh that I had given up the ghost, and no eye had seen me!
19 I should have been as though I had not been; I should have been carried from the womb to the grave.
20 *Are* not my days few? cease *then, and* let me alone, that I may take comfort a little,
21 Before I go *whence* I shall not return, *even* to the land of darkness and the shadow of death;
22 A land of darkness, as darkness *itself; and* of the shadow of death, without any order, and *where* the light *is* as darkness.

CHAPTER 11

THEN answered Zō′phär the Nā′ȧ-mȧ-thīte′, and said,
2 Should not the multitude of words be answered? and should a man full of talk be justified?
3 Should thy lies make men hold their peace? and when thou mockest, shall no man make thee ashamed?
4 For thou hast said, My doctrine *is* pure, and I am clean in thine eyes.
5 But oh that God would speak, and open his lips against thee;
6 And that he would show thee the secrets of wisdom, that *they are* double to that which is! Know therefore that God exacteth of thee *less* than thine iniquity *deserveth.*
7 Canst thou by searching find out God? canst thou find out the Almighty unto perfection?
8 *It is* as high as heaven; what canst thou do? deeper than hell; what canst thou know?
9 The measure thereof *is* longer than the earth, and broader than the sea.
10 If he cut off, and shut up, or gather together, then who can hinder him?
11 For he knoweth vain men: he seeth wickedness also; will he not then consider *it?*
12 For vain man would be wise, though man be born *like* a wild ass's colt.
13 If thou prepare thine heart, and stretch out thine hands toward him;
14 If iniquity *be* in thine hand, put it far away, and let not wickedness dwell in thy tabernacles.

15 For then shalt thou lift up thy face without spot; yea, thou shalt be steadfast, and shalt not fear:

16 Because thou shalt forget *thy* misery, *and* remember *it* as waters *that* pass away:

17 And *thine* age shall be clearer than the noonday; thou shalt shine forth, thou shalt be as the morning.

18 And thou shalt be secure, because there is hope; yea, thou shalt dig *about thee, and* thou shalt take thy rest in safety.

19 Also thou shalt lie down, and none shall make *thee* afraid; yea, many shall make suit unto thee.

20 But the eyes of the wicked shall fail, and they shall not escape, and their hope *shall be as* the giving up of the ghost.

CHAPTER 12

AND Jōb answered and said,

2 No doubt but ye *are* the people, and wisdom shall die with you.

3 But I have understanding as well as you; I *am* not inferior to you: yea, who knoweth not such things as these?

4 I am *as* one mocked of his neighbor, who calleth upon God, and he answereth him: the just upright *man is* laughed to scorn.

5 He that is ready to slip with *his* feet *is as* a lamp despised in the thought of him that is at ease.

6 The tabernacles of robbers prosper, and they that provoke God are secure; into whose hand God bringeth *abundantly*.

7 But ask now the beasts, and they shall teach thee; and the fowls of the air, and they shall tell thee:

8 Or speak to the earth, and it shall teach thee; and the fishes of the sea shall declare unto thee.

9 Who knoweth not in all these that the hand of the LORD hath wrought this?

10 In whose hand *is* the soul of every living thing, and the breath of all mankind.

11 Doth not the ear try words? and the mouth taste his meat?

12 With the ancient *is* wisdom; and in length of days understanding.

13 With him *is* wisdom and strength, he hath counsel and understanding.

14 Behold, he breaketh down, and it cannot be built again: he shutteth up a man, and there can be no opening.

15 Behold, he withholdeth the waters, and they dry up: also he sendeth them out, and they overturn the earth.

16 With him *is* strength and wisdom: the deceived and the deceiver *are* his.

17 He leadeth counselors away spoiled, and maketh the judges fools.

18 He looseth the bond of kings, and girdeth their loins with a girdle.

19 He leadeth princes away spoiled, and overthroweth the mighty.

20 He removeth away the speech of the trusty, and taketh away the understanding of the aged.

21 He poureth contempt upon princes, and weakeneth the strength of the mighty.

22 He discovereth deep things out of darkness, and bringeth out to light the shadow of death.

23 He increaseth the nations, and destroyeth them: he enlargeth the nations, and straiteneth them *again*.

24 He taketh away the heart of the chief of the people of the earth, and causeth them to wander in a wilderness *where there is* no way.

25 They grope in the dark without light, and he maketh them to stagger like a drunken man.

CHAPTER 13

LO, mine eye hath seen all *this*, mine ear hath heard and understood it.

2 What ye know, *the same* do I know also: I *am* not inferior unto you.

3 Surely I would speak to the Almighty, and I desire to reason with God.

4 But ye *are* forgers of lies, ye *are* all physicians of no value.

5 Oh that ye would altogether hold your peace! and it should be your wisdom.

6 Hear now my reasoning, and hearken to the pleadings of my lips.

7 Will ye speak wickedly for God? and talk deceitfully for him?

8 Will ye accept his person? will ye contend for God?

9 Is it good that he should search you out? or as one man mocketh another, do ye *so* mock him?

10 He will surely reprove you, if ye do secretly accept persons.

11 Shall not his excellency make you afraid? and his dread fall upon you?

12 Your remembrances *are* like unto ashes, your bodies to bodies of clay.

13 Hold your peace, let me alone, that

I may speak, and let come on me what
will.
14 Wherefore do I take my flesh in my
teeth, and put my life in mine hand?
15 Though he slay me, yet will I trust
in him: but I will maintain mine own
ways before him.
16 He also *shall be* my salvation: for a
hypocrite shall not come before him.
17 Hear diligently my speech, and my
declaration with your ears.
18 Behold now, I have ordered *my*
cause; I know that I shall be justified.
19 Who *is* he *that* will plead with me?
for now, if I hold my tongue, I shall give
up the ghost.
20 Only do not two *things* unto me;
then will I not hide myself from thee.
21 Withdraw thine hand far from me:
and let not thy dread make me afraid.
22 Then call thou, and I will answer: or
let me speak, and answer thou me.
23 How many *are* mine iniquities and
sins? make me to know my transgression
and my sin.
24 Wherefore hidest thou thy face, and
holdest me for thine enemy?
25 Wilt thou break a leaf driven to and
fro? and wilt thou pursue the dry
stubble?
26 For thou writest bitter things against
me, and makest me to possess the iniquities of my youth.
27 Thou puttest my feet also in the
stocks, and lookest narrowly unto all my
paths; thou settest a print upon the heels
of my feet.
28 And he, as a rotten thing, consumeth, as a garment that is moth-eaten.

CHAPTER 14

MAN *that is* born of a woman *is* of
few days, and full of trouble.
2 He cometh forth like a flower, and is
cut down: he fleeth also as a shadow,
and continueth not.
3 And dost thou open thine eyes upon
such a one, and bringest me into judgment with thee?
4 Who can bring a clean *thing* out of an
unclean? not one.
5 Seeing his days *are* determined, the
number of his months *are* with thee,
thou hast appointed his bounds that he
cannot pass;
6 Turn from him, that he may rest, till
he shall accomplish, as a hireling, his
day.
7 For there is hope of a tree, if it be cut
down, that it will sprout again, and that
the tender branch thereof will not cease.
8 Though the root thereof wax old in
the earth, and the stock thereof die in
the ground;
9 *Yet* through the scent of water it will
bud, and bring forth boughs like a plant.
10 But man dieth, and wasteth away:
yea, man giveth up the ghost, and where
is he?
11 *As* the waters fail from the sea, and
the flood decayeth and drieth up;
12 So man lieth down, and riseth not:
till the heavens *be* no more, they shall
not awake, nor be raised out of their
sleep.
13 Oh that thou wouldest hide me in
the grave, that thou wouldest keep me
secret, until thy wrath be past, that thou
wouldest appoint me a set time, and remember me!
14 If a man die, shall he live *again?* all
the days of my appointed time will I
wait, till my change come.
15 Thou shalt call, and I will answer
thee: thou wilt have a desire to the work
of thine hands.
16 For now thou numberest my steps:
dost thou not watch over my sin?
17 My transgression *is* sealed up in a
bag, and thou sewest up mine iniquity.
18 And surely the mountain falling
cometh to nought, and the rock is removed out of his place.
19 The waters wear the stones: thou
washest away the things which grow *out*
of the dust of the earth; and thou destroyest the hope of man.
20 Thou prevailest for ever against him,
and he passeth: thou changest his countenance, and sendest him away.
21 His sons come to honor, and he
knoweth *it* not; and they are brought
low, but he perceiveth *it* not of them.
22 But his flesh upon him shall have
pain, and his soul within him shall
mourn.

CHAPTER 15

THEN answered Ĕl'ĭ-phăz the Tē'-
măn-īte, and said,
2 Should a wise man utter vain knowledge, and fill his belly with the east
wind?
3 Should he reason with unprofitable
talk? or with speeches wherewith he can
do no good?

4 Yea, thou castest off fear, and re-
strainest prayer before God.
5 For thy mouth uttereth thine iniquity,
and thou choosest the tongue of the
crafty.
6 Thine own mouth condemneth thee,
and not I: yea, thine own lips testify
against thee.
7 *Art* thou the first man *that* was born?
or wast thou made before the hills?
8 Hast thou heard the secret of God?
and dost thou restrain wisdom to thyself?
9 What knowest thou, that we know
not? *what* understandest thou, which *is*
not in us?
10 With us *are* both the grayheaded and
very aged men, much elder than thy
father.
11 *Are* the consolations of God small
with thee? is there any secret thing with
thee?
12 Why doth thine heart carry thee
away? and what do thy eyes wink at,
13 That thou turnest thy spirit against
God, and lettest *such* words go out of
thy mouth?
14 What *is* man, that he should be
clean? and *he which is* born of a woman,
that he should be righteous?
15 Behold, he putteth no trust in his
saints; yea, the heavens are not clean
in his sight.
16 How much more abominable and
filthy *is* man, which drinketh iniquity
like water?
17 I will show thee, hear me; and that
which I have seen I will declare;
18 Which wise men have told from
their fathers, and have not hid *it:*
19 Unto whom alone the earth was
given, and no stranger passed among
them.
20 The wicked man travaileth with pain
all *his* days, and the number of years is
hidden to the oppressor.
21 A dreadful sound *is* in his ears: in
prosperity the destroyer shall come upon
him.
22 He believeth not that he shall return
out of darkness, and he is waited for of
the sword.
23 He wandereth abroad for bread,
saying, Where *is it?* he knoweth that the
day of darkness is ready at his hand.
24 Trouble and anguish shall make him
afraid; they shall prevail against him, as
a king ready to the battle.
25 For he stretcheth out his hand
against God, and strengtheneth himself
against the Almighty.
26 He runneth upon him, *even* on *his*
neck, upon the thick bosses of his
bucklers:
27 Because he covereth his face with
his fatness, and maketh collops of fat
on *his* flanks.
28 And he dwelleth in desolate cities,
and in houses which no man inhabiteth,
which are ready to become heaps.
29 He shall not be rich, neither shall
his substance continue, neither shall he
prolong the perfection thereof upon the
earth.
30 He shall not depart out of darkness;
the flame shall dry up his branches, and
by the breath of his mouth shall he go
away.
31 Let not him that is deceived trust in
vanity: for vanity shall be his recompense.
32 It shall be accomplished before his
time, and his branch shall not be green.
33 He shall shake off his unripe grape
as the vine, and shall cast off his flower
as the olive.
34 For the congregation of hypocrites
shall be desolate, and fire shall consume
the tabernacles of bribery.
35 They conceive mischief, and bring
forth vanity, and their belly prepareth
deceit.

CHAPTER 16

THEN Jōb answered and said,
2 I have heard many such things:
miserable comforters *are* ye all.
3 Shall vain words have an end? or
what emboldeneth thee that thou answerest?
4 I also could speak as ye *do:* if your
soul were in my soul's stead, I could
heap up words against you, and shake
mine head at you.
5 *But* I would strengthen you with my
mouth, and the moving of my lips should
assuage *your grief.*
6 Though I speak, my grief is not assuaged: and *though* I forbear, what am
I eased?
7 But now he hath made me weary:
thou hast made desolate all my company.
8 And thou hast filled me with wrin-
kles, *which* is a witness *against me:* and
my leanness rising up in me beareth witness to my face.
9 He teareth *me* in his wrath, who

hateth me: he gnasheth upon me with
his teeth; mine enemy sharpeneth his
eyes upon me.
10 They have gaped upon me with
their mouth; they have smitten me upon
the cheek reproachfully; they have gathered themselves together against me.
11 God hath delivered me to the ungodly, and turned me over into the hands
of the wicked.
12 I was at ease, but he hath broken me
asunder: he hath also taken *me* by my
neck, and shaken me to pieces, and set
me up for his mark.
13 His archers compass me round
about, he cleaveth my reins asunder,
and doth not spare; he poureth out my
gall upon the ground.
14 He breaketh me with breach upon
breach; he runneth upon me like a giant.
15 I have sewed sackcloth upon my
skin, and defiled my horn in the dust.
16 My face is foul with weeping, and
on my eyelids *is* the shadow of death;
17 Not for *any* injustice in mine hands:
also my prayer *is* pure.
18 O earth, cover not thou my blood,
and let my cry have no place.
19 Also now, behold, my witness *is* in
heaven, and my record *is* on high.
20 My friends scorn me: *but* mine eye
poureth out *tears* unto God.
21 Oh that one might plead for a man
with God, as a man *pleadeth* for his
neighbor!
22 When a few years are come, then I
shall go the way *whence* I shall not
return.

CHAPTER 17

MY breath is corrupt, my days are
extinct, the graves *are ready* for me.
2 *Are there* not mockers with me? and
doth not mine eye continue in their
provocation?
3 Lay down now, put me in a surety
with thee; who *is* he *that* will strike
hands with me?
4 For thou hast hid their heart from
understanding: therefore shalt thou not
exalt *them*.
5 He that speaketh flattery to *his*
friends, even the eyes of his children
shall fail.
6 He hath made me also a byword of
the people; and aforetime I was as a
tabret.
7 Mine eye also is dim by reason of
sorrow, and all my members *are* as a
shadow.
8 Upright *men* shall be astonished at
this, and the innocent shall stir up himself against the hypocrite.
9 The righteous also shall hold on his
way, and he that hath clean hands shall
be stronger and stronger.
10 But as for you all, do ye return, and
come now: for I cannot find *one* wise
man among you.
11 My days are past, my purposes are
broken off, *even* the thoughts of my
heart.
12 They change the night into day: the
light *is* short because of darkness.
13 If I wait, the grave *is* mine house: I
have made my bed in the darkness.
14 I have said to corruption, Thou *art*
my father: to the worm, *Thou art* my
mother, and my sister.
15 And where *is* now my hope? as for
my hope, who shall see it?
16 They shall go down to the bars of the
pit, when *our* rest together *is* in the dust.

CHAPTER 18

THEN answered Bildad the Shụ'hīte,
and said,
2 How long *will it be ere* ye make an
end of words? mark, and afterward we
will speak.
3 Wherefore are we counted as beasts,
and reputed vile in your sight?
4 He teareth himself in his anger: shall
the earth be forsaken for thee? and shall
the rock be removed out of his place?
5 Yea, the light of the wicked shall be
put out, and the spark of his fire shall
not shine.
6 The light shall be dark in his tabernacle, and his candle shall be put out
with him.
7 The steps of his strength shall be
straitened, and his own counsel shall
cast him down.
8 For he is cast into a net by his own
feet, and he walketh upon a snare.
9 The gin shall take *him* by the heel,
and the robber shall prevail against him.
10 The snare *is* laid for him in the
ground, and a trap for him in the way.
11 Terrors shall make him afraid on
every side, and shall drive him to his
feet.
12 His strength shall be hunger-bitten,
and destruction *shall be* ready at his
side.

13 It shall devour the strength of his skin: *even* the firstborn of death shall devour his strength.
14 His confidence shall be rooted out of his tabernacle, and it shall bring him to the king of terrors.
15 It shall dwell in his tabernacle, because *it is* none of his: brimstone shall be scattered upon his habitation.
16 His roots shall be dried up beneath, and above shall his branch be cut off.
17 His remembrance shall perish from the earth, and he shall have no name in the street.
18 He shall be driven from light into darkness, and chased out of the world.
19 He shall neither have son nor nephew among his people, nor any remaining in his dwellings.
20 They that come after *him* shall be astonished at his day, as they that went before were affrighted.
21 Surely such *are* the dwellings of the wicked, and this *is* the place *of him that* knoweth not God.

CHAPTER 19

THEN Jōb answered and said,
2 How long will ye vex my soul, and break me in pieces with words?
3 These ten times have ye reproached me: ye are not ashamed *that* ye make yourselves strange to me.
4 And be it indeed *that* I have erred, mine error remaineth with myself.
5 If indeed ye will magnify *yourselves* against me, and plead against me my reproach;
6 Know now that God hath overthrown me, and hath compassed me with his net.
7 Behold, I cry out of wrong, but I am not heard: I cry aloud, but *there is* no judgment.
8 He hath fenced up my way that I cannot pass, and he hath set darkness in my paths.
9 He hath stripped me of my glory, and taken the crown *from* my head.
10 He hath destroyed me on every side, and I am gone: and mine hope hath he removed like a tree.
11 He hath also kindled his wrath against me, and he counteth me unto him as *one of* his enemies.
12 His troops come together, and raise up their way against me, and encamp round about my tabernacle.
13 He hath put my brethren far from me, and mine acquaintance are verily estranged from me.
14 My kinsfolk have failed, and my familiar friends have forgotten me.
15 They that dwell in mine house, and my maids, count me for a stranger: I am an alien in their sight.
16 I called my servant, and he gave *me* no answer; I entreated him with my mouth.
17 My breath is strange to my wife, though I entreated for the children's *sake* of mine own body.
18 Yea, young children despised me; I arose, and they spake against me.
19 All my inward friends abhorred me: and they whom I loved are turned against me.
20 My bone cleaveth to my skin and to my flesh, and I am escaped with the skin of my teeth.
21 Have pity upon me, have pity upon me, O ye my friends; for the hand of God hath touched me.
22 Why do ye persecute me as God, and are not satisfied with my flesh?
23 Oh that my words were now written! oh that they were printed in a book!
24 That they were graven with an iron pen and lead in the rock for ever!
25 For I know *that* my Redeemer liveth, and *that* he shall stand at the latter *day* upon the earth:
26 And *though* after my skin *worms* destroy this *body*, yet in my flesh shall I see God:
27 Whom I shall see for myself, and mine eyes shall behold, and not another; *though* my reins be consumed within me.
28 But ye should say, Why persecute we him, seeing the root of the matter is found in me?
29 Be ye afraid of the sword: for wrath *bringeth* the punishments of the sword, that ye may know *there is* a judgment.

CHAPTER 20

THEN answered Zō'phär the Nā'ä-mä-thīte', and said,
2 Therefore do my thoughts cause me to answer, and for *this* I make haste.
3 I have heard the check of my reproach, and the spirit of my understanding causeth me to answer.
4 Knowest thou *not* this of old, since man was placed upon earth,
5 That the triumphing of the wicked *is*

short, and the joy of the hypocrite *but*
for a moment?
6 Though his excellency mount up to
the heavens, and his head reach unto the
clouds;
7 *Yet* he shall perish for ever like his
own dung: they which have seen him
shall say, Where *is* he?
8 He shall fly away as a dream, and
shall not be found: yea, he shall be
chased away as a vision of the night.
9 The eye also *which* saw him shall *see*
him no more; neither shall his place any
more behold him.
10 His children shall seek to please the
poor, and his hands shall restore their
goods.
11 His bones are full *of the sin* of his
youth, which shall lie down with him in
the dust.
12 Though wickedness be sweet in his
mouth, *though* he hide it under his
tongue;
13 *Though* he spare it, and forsake it
not, but keep it still within his mouth;
14 *Yet* his meat in his bowels is turned,
it is the gall of asps within him.
15 He hath swallowed down riches, and
he shall vomit them up again: God shall
cast them out of his belly.
16 He shall suck the poison of asps: the
viper's tongue shall slay him.
17 He shall not see the rivers, the
floods, the brooks of honey and butter.
18 That which he labored for shall he
restore, and shall not swallow *it* down:
according to *his* substance *shall* the restitution *be,* and he shall not rejoice
therein.
19 Because he hath oppressed *and* hath
forsaken the poor; *because* he hath violently taken away a house which he
builded not;
20 Surely he shall not feel quietness in
his belly, he shall not save of that which
he desired.
21 There shall none of his meat be left;
therefore shall no man look for his goods.
22 In the fulness of his sufficiency he
shall be in straits: every hand of the
wicked shall come upon him.
23 *When* he is about to fill his belly,
God shall cast the fury of his wrath upon
him, and shall rain *it* upon him while he
is eating.
24 He shall flee from the iron weapon,
and the bow of steel shall strike him
through.
25 It is drawn, and cometh out of the
body; yea, the glittering sword cometh
out of his gall: terrors *are* upon him.
26 All darkness *shall be* hid in his secret places: a fire not blown shall consume him; it shall go ill with him that
is left in his tabernacle.
27 The heaven shall reveal his iniquity;
and the earth shall rise up against him.
28 The increase of his house shall depart, *and his goods* shall flow away in
the day of his wrath.
29 This *is* the portion of a wicked man
from God, and the heritage appointed
unto him by God.

CHAPTER 21

BUT Jōb answered and said,
2 Hear diligently my speech, and
let this be your consolations.
3 Suffer me that I may speak; and after
that I have spoken, mock on.
4 As for me, *is* my complaint to man?
and if *it were so,* why should not my
spirit be troubled?
5 Mark me, and be astonished, and lay
your hand upon *your* mouth.
6 Even when I remember I am afraid,
and trembling taketh hold on my flesh.
7 Wherefore do the wicked live, become old, yea, are mighty in power?
8 Their seed is established in their
sight with them, and their offspring before their eyes.
9 Their houses *are* safe from fear, neither *is* the rod of God upon them.
10 Their bull gendereth, and faileth
not; their cow calveth, and casteth not
her calf.
11 They send forth their little ones like
a flock, and their children dance.
12 They take the timbrel and harp, and
rejoice at the sound of the organ.
13 They spend their days in wealth, and
in a moment go down to the grave.
14 Therefore they say unto God, Depart from us; for we desire not the
knowledge of thy ways.
15 What *is* the Almighty, that we should
serve him? and what profit should we
have, if we pray unto him?
16 Lo, their good *is* not in their hand:
the counsel of the wicked is far from me.
17 How oft is the candle of the wicked
put out! and *how oft* cometh their destruction upon them! *God* distributeth
sorrows in his anger.
18 They are as stubble before the wind,

and as chaff that the storm carrieth
away.
19 God layeth up his iniquity for his
children: he rewardeth him, and he shall
know *it*.
20 His eyes shall see his destruction,
and he shall drink of the wrath of the
Almighty.
21 For what pleasure *hath* he in his
house after him, when the number of his
months is cut off in the midst?
22 Shall *any* teach God knowledge?
seeing he judgeth those that are high.
23 One dieth in his full strength, being
wholly at ease and quiet.
24 His breasts are full of milk, and his
bones are moistened with marrow.
25 And another dieth in the bitterness
of his soul, and never eateth with
pleasure.
26 They shall lie down alike in the dust,
and the worms shall cover them.
27 Behold, I know your thoughts, and
the devices *which* ye wrongfully imagine
against me.
28 For ye say, Where *is* the house of
the prince? and where *are* the dwelling
places of the wicked?
29 Have ye not asked them that go by
the way? and do ye not know their
tokens,
30 That the wicked is reserved to the
day of destruction? they shall be brought
forth to the day of wrath.
31 Who shall declare his way to his
face? and who shall repay him *what* he
hath done?
32 Yet shall he be brought to the grave,
and shall remain in the tomb.
33 The clods of the valley shall be
sweet unto him, and every man shall
draw after him, as *there are* innumerable
before him.
34 How then comfort ye me in vain,
seeing in your answers there remaineth
falsehood?

CHAPTER 22

THEN Ĕl'ĭ-phăz the Tē'măn-īte answered and said,
2 Can a man be profitable unto God, as
he that is wise may be profitable unto
himself?
3 *Is it* any pleasure to the Almighty,
that thou art righteous? or *is it* gain *to*
him, that thou makest thy ways perfect?
4 Will he reprove thee for fear of thee?
will he enter with thee into judgment?
5 *Is* not thy wickedness great? and
thine iniquities infinite?
6 For thou hast taken a pledge from thy
brother for nought, and stripped the
naked of their clothing.
7 Thou hast not given water to the
weary to drink, and thou hast withholden
bread from the hungry.
8 But *as for* the mighty man, he had the
earth; and the honorable man dwelt in it.
9 Thou hast sent widows away empty,
and the arms of the fatherless have been
broken.
10 Therefore snares *are* round about
thee, and sudden fear troubleth thee;
11 Or darkness, *that* thou canst not see;
and abundance of waters cover thee.
12 *Is* not God in the height of heaven?
and behold the height of the stars, how
high they are!
13 And thou sayest, How doth God
know? can he judge through the dark
cloud?
14 Thick clouds *are* a covering to him,
that he seeth not; and he walketh in the
circuit of heaven.
15 Hast thou marked the old way which
wicked men have trodden?
16 Which were cut down out of time,
whose foundation was overflown with a
flood:
17 Which said unto God, Depart from
us: and what can the Almighty do for
them?
18 Yet he filled their houses with good
things: but the counsel of the wicked is
far from me.
19 The righteous see *it*, and are glad:
and the innocent laugh them to scorn.
20 Whereas our substance is not cut
down, but the remnant of them the fire
consumeth.
21 Acquaint now thyself with him, and
be at peace: thereby good shall come
unto thee.
22 Receive, I pray thee, the law from
his mouth, and lay up his words in thine
heart.
23 If thou return to the Almighty, thou
shalt be built up, thou shalt put away
iniquity far from thy tabernacles.
24 Then shalt thou lay up gold as dust,
and the *gold* of Ō'phīr as the stones of
the brooks.
25 Yea, the Almighty shall be thy defense, and thou shalt have plenty of
silver.
26 For then shalt thou have thy delight

in the Almighty, and shalt lift up thy face
unto God.
27 Thou shalt make thy prayer unto
him, and he shall hear thee, and thou
shalt pay thy vows.
28 Thou shalt also decree a thing, and
it shall be established unto thee: and the
light shall shine upon thy ways.
29 When *men* are cast down, then thou
shalt say, *There is* lifting up; and he
shall save the humble person.
30 He shall deliver the island of the
innocent: and it is delivered by the pureness of thine hands.

CHAPTER 23

THEN Jōb answered and said,
2 Even to-day *is* my complaint
bitter: my stroke is heavier than my
groaning.
3 Oh that I knew where I might find
him! *that* I might come *even* to his seat!
4 I would order *my* cause before him,
and fill my mouth with arguments.
5 I would know the words *which* he
would answer me, and understand what
he would say unto me.
6 Will he plead against me with *his*
great power? No; but he would put
strength in me.
7 There the righteous might dispute
with him; so should I be delivered for
ever from my judge.
8 Behold, I go forward, but he *is* not
there; and backward, but I cannot perceive him:
9 On the left hand, where he doth work,
but I cannot behold *him:* he hideth himself on the right hand, that I cannot see
him:
10 But he knoweth the way that I take:
when he hath tried me, I shall come forth
as gold.
11 My foot hath held his steps, his way
have I kept, and not declined.
12 Neither have I gone back from the
commandment of his lips; I have esteemed the words of his mouth more
than my necessary *food.*
13 But he *is* in one *mind,* and who can
turn him? and *what* his soul desireth,
even *that* he doeth.
14 For he performeth *the thing that is*
appointed for me: and many such *things*
are with him.
15 Therefore am I troubled at his presence: when I consider, I am afraid of
him.
16 For God maketh my heart soft, and
the Almighty troubleth me:
17 Because I was not cut off before the
darkness, *neither* hath he covered the
darkness from my face.

CHAPTER 24

WHY, seeing times are not hidden
from the Almighty, do they that
know him not see his days?
2 *Some* remove the landmarks; they
violently take away flocks, and feed
thereof.
3 They drive away the ass of the fatherless, they take the widow's ox for a
pledge.
4 They turn the needy out of the way:
the poor of the earth hide themselves
together.
5 Behold, *as* wild asses in the desert,
go they forth to their work; rising betimes for a prey: the wilderness *yieldeth*
food for them *and* for *their* children.
6 They reap *every one* his corn in the
field: and they gather the vintage of the
wicked.
7 They cause the naked to lodge without clothing, that *they have* no covering
in the cold.
8 They are wet with the showers of the
mountains, and embrace the rock for
want of a shelter.
9 They pluck the fatherless from the
breast, and take a pledge of the poor.
10 They cause *him* to go naked without
clothing, and they take away the sheaf
from the hungry;
11 *Which* make oil within their walls,
and tread *their* winepresses, and suffer
thirst.
12 Men groan from out of the city, and
the soul of the wounded crieth out: yet
God layeth not folly *to them.*
13 They are of those that rebel against
the light; they know not the ways thereof,
nor abide in the paths thereof.
14 The murderer rising with the light
killeth the poor and needy, and in the
night is as a thief.
15 The eye also of the adulterer waiteth
for the twilight, saying, No eye shall see
me: and disguiseth *his* face.
16 In the dark they dig through houses,
which they had marked for themselves
in the daytime: they know not the
light.
17 For the morning *is* to them even as
the shadow of death: if *one* know *them,*

they are in the terrors of the shadow of
death.
18 He *is* swift as the waters; their portion is cursed in the earth: he beholdeth
not the way of the vineyards.
19 Drought and heat consume the snow
waters: *so doth* the grave *those which*
have sinned.
20 The womb shall forget him; the
worm shall feed sweetly on him; he shall
be no more remembered; and wickedness shall be broken as a tree.
21 He evil entreateth the barren *that*
beareth not: and doeth not good to the
widow.
22 He draweth also the mighty with his
power: he riseth up, and no *man* is sure
of life.
23 *Though* it be given him *to be* in
safety, whereon he resteth; yet his eyes
are upon their ways.
24 They are exalted for a little while,
but are gone and brought low; they
are taken out of the way as all *other,*
and cut off as the tops of the ears of
corn.
25 And if *it be* not *so* now, who will
make me a liar, and make my speech
nothing worth?

CHAPTER 25

THEN answered Bildad the Shụ'hīte,
and said,
2 Dominion and fear *are* with him; he
maketh peace in his high places.
3 Is there any number of his armies?
and upon whom doth not his light arise?
4 How then can man be justified with
God? or how can he be clean *that is* born
of a woman?
5 Behold even to the moon, and it
shineth not; yea, the stars are not pure
in his sight.
6 How much less man, *that is* a worm?
and the son of man, *which is* a worm?

CHAPTER 26

BUT Jōb answered and said,
2 How hast thou helped *him that*
is without power? *how* savest thou the
arm *that hath* no strength?
3 How hast thou counseled *him that*
hath no wisdom? and *how* hast thou
plentifully declared the thing as it is?
4 To whom hast thou uttered words?
and whose spirit came from thee?
5 Dead *things* are formed from under
the waters, and the inhabitants thereof.
6 Hell *is* naked before him, and destruction hath no covering.
7 He stretcheth out the north over the
empty place, *and* hangeth the earth upon
nothing.
8 He bindeth up the waters in his thick
clouds; and the cloud is not rent under
them.
9 He holdeth back the face of his
throne, *and* spreadeth his cloud upon it.
10 He hath compassed the waters with
bounds, until the day and night come to
an end.
11 The pillars of heaven tremble, and
are astonished at his reproof.
12 He divideth the sea with his power,
and by his understanding he smiteth
through the proud.
13 By his Spirit he hath garnished the
heavens; his hand hath formed the
crooked serpent.
14 Lo, these *are* parts of his ways; but
how little a portion is heard of him? but
the thunder of his power who can understand?

CHAPTER 27

MOREOVER Jōb continued his parable, and said,
2 *As* God liveth, *who* hath taken away
my judgment; and the Almighty, *who*
hath vexed my soul;
3 All the while my breath *is* in me, and
the spirit of God *is* in my nostrils;
4 My lips shall not speak wickedness,
nor my tongue utter deceit.
5 God forbid that I should justify you:
till I die I will not remove mine integrity
from me.
6 My righteousness I hold fast, and will
not let it go: my heart shall not reproach
me so long as I live.
7 Let mine enemy be as the wicked,
and he that riseth up against me as the
unrighteous.
8 For what *is* the hope of the hypocrite,
though he hath gained, when God taketh
away his soul?
9 Will God hear his cry when trouble
cometh upon him?
10 Will he delight himself in the Almighty? will he always call upon God?
11 I will teach you by the hand of God:
that which *is* with the Almighty will I
not conceal.
12 Behold, all ye yourselves have seen
it; why then are ye thus altogether vain?
13 This *is* the portion of a wicked man

with God, and the heritage of oppressors, *which* they shall receive of the Almighty.
14 If his children be multiplied, *it is* for the sword: and his offspring shall not be satisfied with bread.
15 Those that remain of him shall be buried in death: and his widows shall not weep.
16 Though he heap up silver as the dust, and prepare raiment as the clay;
17 He may prepare *it*, but the just shall put *it* on, and the innocent shall divide the silver.
18 He buildeth his house as a moth, and as a booth *that* the keeper maketh.
19 The rich man shall lie down, but he shall not be gathered: he openeth his eyes, and he *is* not.
20 Terrors take hold on him as waters, a tempest stealeth him away in the night.
21 The east wind carrieth him away, and he departeth: and as a storm hurleth him out of his place.
22 For *God* shall cast upon him, and not spare: he would fain flee out of his hand.
23 *Men* shall clap their hands at him, and shall hiss him out of his place.

CHAPTER 28

SURELY there is a vein for the silver, and a place for gold *where* they fine *it*.
2 Iron is taken out of the earth, and brass *is* molten *out of* the stone.
3 He setteth an end to darkness, and searcheth out all perfection: the stones of darkness, and the shadow of death.
4 The flood breaketh out from the inhabitant; *even the waters* forgotten of the foot: they are dried up, they are gone away from men.
5 *As for* the earth, out of it cometh bread: and under it is turned up as it were fire.
6 The stones of it *are* the place of sapphires: and it hath dust of gold.
7 *There is* a path which no fowl knoweth, and which the vulture's eye hath not seen:
8 The lion's whelps have not trodden it, nor the fierce lion passed by it.
9 He putteth forth his hand upon the rock; he overturneth the mountains by the roots.
10 He cutteth out rivers among the rocks; and his eye seeth every precious thing.
11 He bindeth the floods from overflowing; and *the thing that is* hid bringeth he forth to light.
12 But where shall wisdom be found? and where *is* the place of understanding?
13 Man knoweth not the price thereof; neither is it found in the land of the living.
14 The depth saith, It *is* not in me: and the sea saith, *It is* not with me.
15 It cannot be gotten for gold, neither shall silver be weighed *for* the price thereof.
16 It cannot be valued with the gold of Ō'phīr, with the precious onyx, or the sapphire.
17 The gold and the crystal cannot equal it: and the exchange of it *shall not be for* jewels of fine gold.
18 No mention shall be made of coral, or of pearls: for the price of wisdom *is* above rubies.
19 The topaz of Ethiopia shall not equal it, neither shall it be valued with pure gold.
20 Whence then cometh wisdom? and where *is* the place of understanding?
21 Seeing it is hid from the eyes of all living, and kept close from the fowls of the air.
22 Destruction and death say, We have heard the fame thereof with our ears.
23 God understandeth the way thereof, and he knoweth the place thereof.
24 For he looketh to the ends of the earth, *and* seeth under the whole heaven;
25 To make the weight for the winds; and he weigheth the waters by measure.
26 When he made a decree for the rain, and a way for the lightning of the thunder;
27 Then did he see it, and declare it; he prepared it, yea, and searched it out.
28 And unto man he said, Behold, the fear of the Lord, that *is* wisdom; and to depart from evil *is* understanding.

CHAPTER 29

MOREOVER Jōb continued his parable, and said,
2 Oh that I were as *in* months past, as *in* the days *when* God preserved me;
3 When his candle shined upon my head, *and when* by his light I walked *through* darkness;
4 As I was in the days of my youth,

when the secret of God *was* upon my
tabernacle;
5 When the Almighty *was* yet with me,
when my children *were* about me;
6 When I washed my steps with butter,
and the rock poured me out rivers of
oil;
7 When I went out to the gate through
the city, *when* I prepared my seat in the
street!
8 The young men saw me, and hid
themselves: and the aged arose, *and*
stood up.
9 The princes refrained talking, and
laid *their* hand on their mouth.
10 The nobles held their peace, and
their tongue cleaved to the roof of their
mouth.
11 When the ear heard *me*, then it
blessed me; and when the eye saw *me*,
it gave witness to me:
12 Because I delivered the poor that
cried, and the fatherless, and *him that*
had none to help him.
13 The blessing of him that was ready
to perish came upon me: and I caused
the widow's heart to sing for joy.
14 I put on righteousness, and it
clothed me: my judgment *was* as a robe
and a diadem.
15 I was eyes to the blind, and feet *was*
I to the lame.
16 I *was* a father to the poor: and the
cause *which* I knew not I searched out.
17 And I brake the jaws of the wicked,
and plucked the spoil out of his teeth.
18 Then I said, I shall die in my nest,
and I shall multiply *my* days as the
sand.
19 My root *was* spread out by the waters, and the dew lay all night upon my
branch.
20 My glory *was* fresh in me, and my
bow was renewed in my hand.
21 Unto me *men* gave ear, and waited,
and kept silence at my counsel.
22 After my words they spake not
again; and my speech dropped upon
them.
23 And they waited for me as for the
rain; and they opened their mouth wide
as for the latter rain.
24 *If* I laughed on them, they believed
it not; and the light of my countenance
they cast not down.
25 I chose out their way, and sat chief,
and dwelt as a king in the army, as one
that comforteth the mourners.

CHAPTER 30

BUT now *they that are* younger than
I have me in derision, whose fathers I would have disdained to have set
with the dogs of my flock.
2 Yea, whereto *might* the strength of
their hands *profit* me, in whom old age
was perished?
3 For want and famine *they were* solitary; fleeing into the wilderness in former time desolate and waste:
4 Who cut up mallows by the bushes,
and juniper roots *for* their meat.
5 They were driven forth from among
men, (they cried after them as *after* a
thief,)
6 To dwell in the cliffs of the valleys,
in caves of the earth, and *in* the rocks.
7 Among the bushes they brayed; under
the nettles they were gathered together.
8 *They were* children of fools, yea,
children of base men: they were viler
than the earth.
9 And now am I their song, yea, I am
their byword.
10 They abhor me, they flee far from
me, and spare not to spit in my face.
11 Because he hath loosed my cord,
and afflicted me, they have also let loose
the bridle before me.
12 Upon *my* right *hand* rise the youth;
they push away my feet, and they raise up
against me the ways of their destruction.
13 They mar my path, they set forward
my calamity, they have no helper.
14 They came *upon me* as a wide
breaking in *of waters:* in the desolation
they rolled themselves *upon me*.
15 Terrors are turned upon me: they
pursue my soul as the wind: and my
welfare passeth away as a cloud.
16 And now my soul is poured out upon
me; the days of affliction have taken
hold upon me.
17 My bones are pierced in me in the
night season: and my sinews take no rest.
18 By the great force *of my disease* is
my garment changed: it bindeth me
about as the collar of my coat.
19 He hath cast me into the mire, and
I am become like dust and ashes.
20 I cry unto thee, and thou dost not
hear me: I stand up, and thou regardest
me *not*.
21 Thou art become cruel to me: with
thy strong hand thou opposest thyself
against me.

22 Thou liftest me up to the wind; thou causest me to ride *upon it*, and dissolvest my substance.
23 For I know *that* thou wilt bring me *to* death, and *to* the house appointed for all living.
24 Howbeit he will not stretch out *his* hand to the grave, though they cry in his destruction.
25 Did not I weep for him that was in trouble? was *not* my soul grieved for the poor?
26 When I looked for good, then evil came *unto me:* and when I waited for light, there came darkness.
27 My bowels boiled, and rested not: the days of affliction prevented me.
28 I went mourning without the sun: I stood up, *and* I cried in the congregation.
29 I am a brother to dragons, and a companion to owls.
30 My skin is black upon me, and my bones are burned with heat.
31 My harp also is *turned* to mourning, and my organ into the voice of them that weep.

CHAPTER 31

I MADE a covenant with mine eyes; why then should I think upon a maid?
2 For what portion of God *is there* from above? and *what* inheritance of the Almighty from on high?
3 *Is* not destruction to the wicked? and a strange *punishment* to the workers of iniquity?
4 Doth not he see my ways, and count all my steps?
5 If I have walked with vanity, or if my foot hath hasted to deceit;
6 Let me be weighed in an even balance that God may know mine integrity.
7 If my step hath turned out of the way, and mine heart walked after mine eyes, and if any blot hath cleaved to mine hands;
8 *Then* let me sow, and let another eat; yea, let my offspring be rooted out.
9 If mine heart have been deceived by a woman, or *if* I have laid wait at my neighbor's door;
10 *Then* let my wife grind unto another, and let others bow down upon her.
11 For this *is* a heinous crime; yea, it *is* an iniquity *to be punished by* the judges.
12 For it *is* a fire *that* consumeth to destruction, and would root out all mine increase.
13 If I did despise the cause of my manservant or of my maidservant, when they contended with me;
14 What then shall I do when God riseth up? and when he visiteth, what shall I answer him?
15 Did not he that made me in the womb make him? and did not one fashion us in the womb?
16 If I have withheld the poor from *their* desire, or have caused the eyes of the widow to fail;
17 Or have eaten my morsel myself alone, and the fatherless hath not eaten thereof;
18 (For from my youth he was brought up with me, as *with* a father, and I have guided her from my mother's womb;)
19 If I have seen any perish for want of clothing, or any poor without covering;
20 If his loins have not blessed me, and *if* he were *not* warmed with the fleece of my sheep;
21 If I have lifted up my hand against the fatherless, when I saw my help in the gate:
22 *Then* let mine arm fall from my shoulder blade, and mine arm be broken from the bone.
23 For destruction *from* God *was* a terror to me, and by reason of his highness I could not endure.
24 If I have made gold my hope, or have said to the fine gold, *Thou art* my confidence;
25 If I rejoiced because my wealth *was* great, and because mine hand had gotten much;
26 If I beheld the sun when it shined, or the moon walking *in* brightness;
27 And my heart hath been secretly enticed, or my mouth hath kissed my hand:
28 This also *were* an iniquity *to be punished by* the judge: for I should have denied the God *that is* above.
29 If I rejoiced at the destruction of him that hated me, or lifted up myself when evil found him;
30 (Neither have I suffered my mouth to sin by wishing a curse to his soul.)
31 If the men of my tabernacle said not, Oh that we had of his flesh! we cannot be satisfied.
32 The stranger did not lodge in the street: *but* I opened my doors to the traveler.

33 If I covered my transgressions as Adam, by hiding mine iniquity in my bosom:

34 Did I fear a great multitude, or did the contempt of families terrify me, that I kept silence, *and* went not out of the door?

35 Oh that one would hear me! behold, my desire *is, that* the Almighty would answer me, and *that* mine adversary had written a book.

36 Surely I would take it upon my shoulder, *and* bind it *as* a crown to me.

37 I would declare unto him the number of my steps; as a prince would I go near unto him.

38 If my land cry against me, or that the furrows likewise thereof complain;

39 If I have eaten the fruits thereof without money, or have caused the owners thereof to lose their life:

40 Let thistles grow instead of wheat, and cockle instead of barley. The words of Jōb are ended.

CHAPTER 32

SO these three men ceased to answer Jōb, because he *was* righteous in his own eyes.

2 Then was kindled the wrath of Ē-lī′hū the son of Băr′ă-chĕl the Bŭz′īte, of the kindred of Răm: against Jōb was his wrath kindled, because he justified himself rather than God.

3 Also against his three friends was his wrath kindled, because they had found no answer, and *yet* had condemned Jōb.

4 Now Ē-lī′hū had waited till Jōb had spoken, because they *were* elder than he.

5 When Ē-lī′hū saw that *there was* no answer in the mouth of *these* three men, then his wrath was kindled.

6 And Ē-lī′hū the son of Băr′ă-chĕl the Bŭz′īte answered and said, I *am* young, and ye *are* very old; wherefore I was afraid, and durst not show you mine opinion.

7 I said, Days should speak, and multitude of years should teach wisdom.

8 But *there is* a spirit in man: and the inspiration of the Almighty giveth them understanding.

9 Great men are not *always* wise: neither do the aged understand judgment.

10 Therefore I said, Hearken to me; I also will show mine opinion.

11 Behold, I waited for your words; I gave ear to your reasons, whilst ye searched out what to say.

12 Yea, I attended unto you, and, behold, *there was* none of you that convinced Jōb, *or* that answered his words:

13 Lest ye should say, We have found out wisdom: God thrusteth him down, not man.

14 Now he hath not directed *his* words against me: neither will I answer him with your speeches.

15 They were amazed, they answered no more: they left off speaking.

16 When I had waited, (for they spake not, but stood still, *and* answered no more,)

17 *I said,* I will answer also my part; I also will show mine opinion.

18 For I am full of matter; the spirit within me constraineth me.

19 Behold, my belly *is* as wine *which* hath no vent; it is ready to burst like new bottles.

20 I will speak, that I may be refreshed: I will open my lips and answer.

21 Let me not, I pray you, accept any man's person; neither let me give flattering titles unto man.

22 For I know not to give flattering titles; *in so doing* my Maker would soon take me away.

CHAPTER 33

WHEREFORE, Jōb, I pray thee, hear my speeches, and hearken to all my words.

2 Behold, now I have opened my mouth, my tongue hath spoken in my mouth.

3 My words *shall be of* the uprightness of my heart: and my lips shall utter knowledge clearly.

4 The Spirit of God hath made me, and the breath of the Almighty hath given me life.

5 If thou canst answer me, set *thy words* in order before me, stand up.

6 Behold, I *am* according to thy wish in God's stead: I also am formed out of the clay.

7 Behold, my terror shall not make thee afraid, neither shall my hand be heavy upon thee.

8 Surely thou hast spoken in mine hearing, and I have heard the voice of *thy* words, *saying,*

9 I am clean without transgression, I *am* innocent; neither *is there* iniquity in me.

10 Behold, he findeth occasions against me, he counteth me for his enemy;

11 He putteth my feet in the stocks, he marketh all my paths.

12 Behold, *in* this thou art not just: I will answer thee, that God is greater than man.

13 Why dost thou strive against him? for he giveth not account of any of his matters.

14 For God speaketh once, yea twice, *yet man* perceiveth it not.

15 In a dream, in a vision of the night, when deep sleep falleth upon men, in slumberings upon the bed;

16 Then he openeth the ears of men, and sealeth their instruction,

17 That he may withdraw man *from his* purpose, and hide pride from man.

18 He keepeth back his soul from the pit, and his life from perishing by the sword.

19 He is chastened also with pain upon his bed, and the multitude of his bones with strong *pain:*

20 So that his life abhorreth bread, and his soul dainty meat.

21 His flesh is consumed away, that it cannot be seen; and his bones *that* were not seen stick out.

22 Yea, his soul draweth near unto the grave, and his life to the destroyers.

23 If there be a messenger with him, an interpreter, one among a thousand, to show unto man his uprightness;

24 Then he is gracious unto him, and saith, Deliver him from going down to the pit: I have found a ransom.

25 His flesh shall be fresher than a child's: he shall return to the days of his youth:

26 He shall pray unto God, and he will be favorable unto him: and he shall see his face with joy: for he will render unto man his righteousness.

27 He looketh upon men, and *if any* say, I have sinned, and perverted *that which was* right, and it profited me not;

28 He will deliver his soul from going into the pit, and his life shall see the light.

29 Lo, all these *things* worketh God oftentimes with man,

30 To bring back his soul from the pit, to be enlightened with the light of the living.

31 Mark well, O Jōb, hearken unto me: hold thy peace, and I will speak.

32 If thou hast any thing to say, answer me: speak, for I desire to justify thee.

33 If not, hearken unto me: hold thy peace, and I shall teach thee wisdom.

CHAPTER 34

FURTHERMORE Ē-lī'hū answered and said,

2 Hear my words, O ye wise *men;* and give ear unto me, ye that have knowledge.

3 For the ear trieth words, as the mouth tasteth meat.

4 Let us choose to us judgment: let us know among ourselves what *is* good.

5 For Jōb hath said, I am righteous: and God hath taken away my judgment.

6 Should I lie against my right? my wound *is* incurable without transgression.

7 What man *is* like Jōb, *who* drinketh up scorning like water?

8 Which goeth in company with the workers of iniquity, and walketh with wicked men.

9 For he hath said, It profiteth a man nothing that he should delight himself with God.

10 Therefore hearken unto me, ye men of understanding: far be it from God, *that he should do* wickedness; and *from* the Almighty, *that he should commit* iniquity.

11 For the work of a man shall he render unto him, and cause every man to find according to *his* ways.

12 Yea, surely God will not do wickedly, neither will the Almighty pervert judgment.

13 Who hath given him a charge over the earth? or who hath disposed the whole world?

14 If he set his heart upon man, *if* he gather unto himself his spirit and his breath;

15 All flesh shall perish together, and man shall turn again unto dust.

16 If now *thou hast* understanding, hear this: hearken to the voice of my words.

17 Shall even he that hateth right govern? and wilt thou condemn him that is most just?

18 *Is it fit* to say to a king, *Thou art* wicked? *and* to princes, *Ye are* ungodly?

19 *How much less to him* that accepteth not the persons of princes, nor regardeth the rich more than the poor? for they all *are* the work of his hands.

20 In a moment shall they die, and the people shall be troubled at midnight, and pass away: and the mighty shall be taken away without hand.

21 For his eyes *are* upon the ways of man, and he seeth all his goings.

22 *There is* no darkness, nor shadow of death, where the workers of iniquity may hide themselves.

23 For he will not lay upon man more *than right;* that he should enter into judgment with God.

24 He shall break in pieces mighty men without number, and set others in their stead.

25 Therefore he knoweth their works, and he overturneth *them* in the night, so that they are destroyed.

26 He striketh them as wicked men in the open sight of others;

27 Because they turned back from him, and would not consider any of his ways:

28 So that they cause the cry of the poor to come unto him, and he heareth the cry of the afflicted.

29 When he giveth quietness, who then can make trouble? and when he hideth *his* face, who then can behold him? whether *it be done* against a nation, or against a man only:

30 That the hypocrite reign not, lest the people be ensnared.

31 Surely it is meet to be said unto God, I have borne *chastisement,* I will not offend *any more:*

32 *That which* I see not teach thou me: if I have done iniquity, I will do no more.

33 *Should it be* according to thy mind? he will recompense it, whether thou refuse, or whether thou choose; and not I: therefore speak what thou knowest.

34 Let men of understanding tell me, and let a wise man hearken unto me.

35 Jōb hath spoken without knowledge, and his words *were* without wisdom.

36 My desire *is that* Jōb may be tried unto the end, because of *his* answers for wicked men.

37 For he addeth rebellion unto his sin, he clappeth *his hands* among us, and multiplieth his words against God.

CHAPTER 35

Ē-LĪ'HŪ spake moreover, and said,

2 Thinkest thou this to be right, *that* thou saidst, My righteousness *is* more than God's?

3 For thou saidst, What advantage will it be unto thee? *and,* What profit shall I have, *if I be cleansed* from my sin?

4 I will answer thee, and thy companions with thee.

5 Look unto the heavens, and see; and behold the clouds *which* are higher than thou.

6 If thou sinnest, what doest thou against him? or *if* thy transgressions be multiplied, what doest thou unto him?

7 If thou be righteous, what givest thou him? or what receiveth he of thine hand?

8 Thy wickedness *may hurt* a man as thou *art;* and thy righteousness *may profit* the son of man.

9 By reason of the multitude of oppressions they make *the oppressed* to cry: they cry out by reason of the arm of the mighty.

10 But none saith, Where *is* God my maker, who giveth songs in the night;

11 Who teacheth us more than the beasts of the earth, and maketh us wiser than the fowls of heaven?

12 There they cry, but none giveth answer, because of the pride of evil men.

13 Surely God will not hear vanity, neither will the Almighty regard it.

14 Although thou sayest thou shalt not see him, *yet* judgment *is* before him; therefore trust thou in him.

15 But now, because *it is* not *so,* he hath visited in his anger; yet he knoweth *it* not in great extremity:

16 Therefore doth Jōb open his mouth in vain; he multiplieth words without knowledge.

CHAPTER 36

Ē-LĪ'HŪ also proceeded, and said,

2 Suffer me a little, and I will show thee that *I have* yet to speak on God's behalf.

3 I will fetch my knowledge from afar, and will ascribe righteousness to my Maker.

4 For truly my words *shall* not *be* false: he that is perfect in knowledge *is* with thee.

5 Behold, God *is* mighty, and despiseth not *any: he is* mighty in strength *and* wisdom.

6 He preserveth not the life of the wicked: but giveth right to the poor.

7 He withdraweth not his eyes from the righteous: but with kings *are they* on the throne; yea, he doth establish them for ever, and they are exalted.

8 And if *they be* bound in fetters, *and*
be holden in cords of affliction;
9 Then he showeth them their work,
and their transgressions that they have
exceeded.
10 He openeth also their ear to disci-
pline, and commandeth that they return
from iniquity.
11 If they obey and serve *him,* they
shall spend their days in prosperity, and
their years in pleasures.
12 But if they obey not, they shall perish by the sword, and they shall die
without knowledge.
13 But the hypocrites in heart heap up
wrath: they cry not when he bindeth
them.
14 They die in youth, and their life *is*
among the unclean.
15 He delivereth the poor in his affliction, and openeth their ears in oppression.
16 Even so would he have removed
thee out of the strait *into* a broad place,
where *there is* no straitness; and that
which should be set on thy table *should
be* full of fatness.
17 But thou hast fulfilled the judgment
of the wicked: judgment and justice
take hold *on thee.*
18 Because *there is* wrath, *beware* lest
he take thee away with *his* stroke: then
a great ransom cannot deliver thee.
19 Will he esteem thy riches? *no,* not
gold, nor all the forces of strength.
20 Desire not the night, when people
are cut off in their place.
21 Take heed, regard not iniquity: for
this hast thou chosen rather than
affliction.
22 Behold, God exalteth by his power:
who teacheth like him?
23 Who hath enjoined him his way?
or who can say, Thou hast wrought
iniquity?
24 Remember that thou magnify his
work, which men behold.
25 Every man may see it; man may
behold *it* afar off.
26 Behold, God *is* great, and we know
him not, neither can the number of his
years be searched out.
27 For he maketh small the drops of
water: they pour down rain according to
the vapor thereof;
28 Which the clouds do drop *and*
distil upon man abundantly.
29 Also can *any* understand the spread-
ings of the clouds, *or* the noise of his
tabernacle?
30 Behold, he spreadeth his light upon
it, and covereth the bottom of the sea.
31 For by them judgeth he the people;
he giveth meat in abundance.
32 With clouds he covereth the light;
and commandeth it *not to shine* by *the
cloud* that cometh betwixt.
33 The noise thereof showeth concerning it, the cattle also concerning the
vapor.

CHAPTER 37

AT this also my heart trembleth, and
is moved out of his place.
2 Hear attentively the noise of his
voice, and the sound *that* goeth out of
his mouth.
3 He directeth it under the whole
heaven, and his lightning unto the ends
of the earth.
4 After it a voice roareth: he thundereth with the voice of his excellency; and
he will not stay them when his voice is
heard.
5 God thundereth marvelously with his
voice; great things doeth he, which we
cannot comprehend.
6 For he saith to the snow, Be thou *on*
the earth; likewise to the small rain, and
to the great rain of his strength.
7 He sealeth up the hand of every man;
that all men may know his work.
8 Then the beasts go into dens, and
remain in their places.
9 Out of the south cometh the whirlwind: and cold out of the north.
10 By the breath of God frost is given:
and the breadth of the waters is
straitened.
11 Also by watering he wearieth the
thick cloud: he scattereth his bright
cloud:
12 And it is turned round about by his
counsels: that they may do whatsoever
he commandeth them upon the face of
the world in the earth.
13 He causeth it to come, whether
for correction, or for his land, or for
mercy.
14 Hearken unto this, O Jōb: stand
still, and consider the wondrous works
of God.
15 Dost thou know when God disposed
them, and caused the light of his cloud
to shine?
16 Dost thou know the balancings of

the clouds, the wondrous works of him
which is perfect in knowledge?
17 How thy garments *are* warm, when
he quieteth the earth by the south *wind?*
18 Hast thou with him spread out the
sky, *which is* strong, *and* as a molten
looking-glass?
19 Teach us what we shall say unto
him; *for* we cannot order *our speech* by
reason of darkness.
20 Shall it be told him that I speak?
if a man speak, surely he shall be swallowed up.
21 And now *men* see not the bright
light which *is* in the clouds: but the wind
passeth, and cleanseth them.
22 Fair weather cometh out of the
north: with God *is* terrible majesty.
23 *Touching* the Almighty, we cannot
find him out: *he is* excellent in power,
and in judgment, and in plenty of justice: he will not afflict.
24 Men do therefore fear him: he
respecteth not any *that are* wise of
heart.

CHAPTER 38

THEN the LORD answered Jōb out of
the whirlwind, and said,
2 Who *is* this that darkeneth counsel
by words without knowledge?
3 Gird up now thy loins like a man; for
I will demand of thee, and answer thou
me.
4 Where wast thou when I laid the
foundations of the earth? declare, if
thou hast understanding.
5 Who hath laid the measures thereof,
if thou knowest? or who hath stretched
the line upon it?
6 Whereupon are the foundations
thereof fastened? or who laid the corner
stone thereof;
7 When the morning stars sang together, and all the sons of God shouted
for joy?
8 Or *who* shut up the sea with doors,
when it brake forth, *as if* it had issued
out of the womb?
9 When I made the cloud the garment
thereof, and thick darkness a swaddling
band for it,
10 And brake up for it my decreed
place, and set bars and doors,
11 And said, Hitherto shalt thou come,
but no further: and here shall thy proud
waves be stayed?
12 Hast thou commanded the morning
since thy days; *and* caused the dayspring to know his place;
13 That it might take hold of the ends
of the earth, that the wicked might be
shaken out of it?
14 It is turned as clay *to* the seal; and
they stand as a garment.
15 And from the wicked their light is
withholden, and the high arm shall be
broken.
16 Hast thou entered into the springs
of the sea? or hast thou walked in the
search of the depth?
17 Have the gates of death been
opened unto thee? or hast thou seen the
doors of the shadow of death?
18 Hast thou perceived the breadth of
the earth? declare if thou knowest it all.
19 Where *is* the way *where* light dwelleth? and *as for* darkness, where *is* the
place thereof,
20 That thou shouldest take it to the
bound thereof, and that thou shouldest
know the paths *to* the house thereof?
21 Knowest thou *it,* because thou wast
then born? or *because* the number of
thy days *is* great?
22 Hast thou entered into the treasures
of the snow? or hast thou seen the
treasures of the hail,
23 Which I have reserved against the
time of trouble, against the day of battle
and war?
24 By what way is the light parted,
which scattereth the east wind upon the
earth?
25 Who hath divided a watercourse for
the overflowing of waters, or a way for
the lightning of thunder;
26 To cause it to rain on the earth,
where no man *is; on* the wilderness,
wherein *there is* no man;
27 To satisfy the desolate and waste
ground; and to cause the bud of the
tender herb to spring forth?
28 Hath the rain a father? or who hath
begotten the drops of dew?
29 Out of whose womb came the ice?
and the hoary frost of heaven, who hath
gendered it?
30 The waters are hid as *with* a stone,
and the face of the deep is frozen.
31 Canst thou bind the sweet influences
of Plē′iȧ-dēș, or loose the bands of
Ō-rī′ŏn?
32 Canst thou bring forth Măz′zȧ-rŏth
in his season? or canst thou guide Ărc-
tū′rŭs with his sons?

33 Knowest thou the ordinances of heaven? canst thou set the dominion thereof in the earth?

34 Canst thou lift up thy voice to the clouds, that abundance of waters may cover thee?

35 Canst thou send lightnings, that they may go, and say unto thee, Here we *are?*

36 Who hath put wisdom in the inward parts? or who hath given understanding to the heart?

37 Who can number the clouds in wisdom? or who can stay the bottles of heaven,

38 When the dust groweth into hardness, and the clods cleave fast together?

39 Wilt thou hunt the prey for the lion? or fill the appetite of the young lions,

40 When they couch in *their* dens, *and* abide in the covert to lie in wait?

41 Who provideth for the raven his food? when his young ones cry unto God, they wander for lack of meat.

CHAPTER 39

KNOWEST thou the time when the wild goats of the rock bring forth? *or* canst thou mark when the hinds do calve?

2 Canst thou number the months *that* they fulfil? or knowest thou the time when they bring forth?

3 They bow themselves, they bring forth their young ones, they cast out their sorrows.

4 Their young ones are in good liking, they grow up with corn; they go forth, and return not unto them.

5 Who hath sent out the wild ass free? or who hath loosed the bands of the wild ass?

6 Whose house I have made the wilderness, and the barren land his dwellings.

7 He scorneth the multitude of the city, neither regardeth he the crying of the driver.

8 The range of the mountains *is* his pasture, and he searcheth after every green thing.

9 Will the unicorn be willing to serve thee, or abide by thy crib?

10 Canst thou bind the unicorn with his band in the furrow? or will he harrow the valleys after thee?

11 Wilt thou trust him, because his strength *is* great? or wilt thou leave thy labor to him?

12 Wilt thou believe him, that he will bring home thy seed, and gather *it into* thy barn?

13 *Gavest thou* the goodly wings unto the peacocks? or wings and feathers unto the ostrich?

14 Which leaveth her eggs in the earth, and warmeth them in the dust,

15 And forgetteth that the foot may crush them, or that the wild beast may break them.

16 She is hardened against her young ones, as though *they were* not hers: her labor is in vain without fear;

17 Because God hath deprived her of wisdom, neither hath he imparted to her understanding.

18 What time she lifteth up herself on high, she scorneth the horse and his rider.

19 Hast thou given the horse strength? hast thou clothed his neck with thunder?

20 Canst thou make him afraid as a grasshopper? the glory of his nostrils *is* terrible.

21 He paweth in the valley, and rejoiceth in *his* strength: he goeth on to meet the armed men.

22 He mocketh at fear, and is not affrighted; neither turneth he back from the sword.

23 The quiver rattleth against him, the glittering spear and the shield.

24 He swalloweth the ground with fierceness and rage: neither believeth he that *it is* the sound of the trumpet.

25 He saith among the trumpets, Ha, ha! and he smelleth the battle afar off, the thunder of the captains, and the shouting.

26 Doth the hawk fly by thy wisdom, *and* stretch her wings toward the south?

27 Doth the eagle mount up at thy command, and make her nest on high?

28 She dwelleth and abideth on the rock, upon the crag of the rock, and the strong place.

29 From thence she seeketh the prey, *and* her eyes behold afar off.

30 Her young ones also suck up blood: and where the slain *are,* there *is* she.

CHAPTER 40

MOREOVER the LORD answered Jōb, and said,

2 Shall he that contendeth with the Almighty instruct *him?* he that reproveth God, let him answer it.

3 ¶ Then Jōb answered the LORD, and
said,
4 Behold, I am vile; what shall I answer
thee? I will lay mine hand upon my
mouth.
5 Once have I spoken; but I will not
answer: yea, twice; but I will proceed
no further.
6 ¶ Then answered the LORD unto
Jōb out of the whirlwind, and said,
7 Gird up thy loins now like a man: I
will demand of thee, and declare thou
unto me.
8 Wilt thou also disannul my judgment?
wilt thou condemn me, that thou mayest
be righteous?
9 Hast thou an arm like God? or canst
thou thunder with a voice like him?
10 Deck thyself now *with* majesty and
excellency; and array thyself with glory
and beauty.
11 Cast abroad the rage of thy wrath:
and behold every one *that is* proud, and
abase him.
12 Look on every one *that is* proud,*and*
bring him low; and tread down the
wicked in their place.
13 Hide them in the dust together; *and*
bind their faces in secret.
14 Then will I also confess unto thee
that thine own right hand can save thee.
15 ¶ Behold now behemoth, which I
made with thee; he eateth grass as an
ox.
16 Lo now, his strength *is* in his loins,
and his force *is* in the navel of his
belly.
17 He moveth his tail like a cedar: the
sinews of his stones are wrapped together.
18 His bones *are as* strong pieces of
brass; his bones *are* like bars of iron.
19 He *is* the chief of the ways of God:
he that made him can make his sword to
approach *unto him*.
20 Surely the mountains bring him
forth food, where all the beasts of the
field play.
21 He lieth under the shady trees, in
the covert of the reed, and fens.
22 The shady trees cover him *with* their
shadow; the willows of the brook compass him about.
23 Behold, he drinketh up a river, *and*
hasteth not: he trusteth that he can
draw up Jordan into his mouth.
24 He taketh it with his eyes: *his* nose
pierceth through snares.

CHAPTER 41

CANST thou draw out leviathan with
a hook? or his tongue with a cord
which thou lettest down?
2 Canst thou put a hook into his nose?
or bore his jaw through with a thorn?
3 Will he make many supplications
unto thee? will he speak soft *words* unto
thee?
4 Will he make a covenant with thee?
wilt thou take him for a servant for ever?
5 Wilt thou play with him as *with* a
bird? or wilt thou bind him for thy
maidens?
6 Shall the companions make a banquet of him? shall they part him among
the merchants?
7 Canst thou fill his skin with barbed
irons? or his head with fish spears?
8 Lay thine hand upon him, remember
the battle, do no more.
9 Behold, the hope of him is in vain:
shall not *one* be cast down even at the
sight of him?
10 None *is so* fierce that dare stir him
up: who then is able to stand before me?
11 Who hath prevented me, that I
should repay *him*? *whatsoever is* under
the whole heaven is mine.
12 I will not conceal his parts, nor his
power, nor his comely proportion.
13 Who can discover the face of his
garment? *or* who can come *to him* with
his double bridle?
14 Who can open the doors of his face?
his teeth *are* terrible round about.
15 *His* scales *are his* pride, shut up
together *as with* a close seal.
16 One is so near to another, that no
air can come between them.
17 They are joined one to another, they
stick together, that they cannot be
sundered.
18 By his sneezings a light doth shine,
and his eyes *are* like the eyelids of the
morning.
19 Out of his mouth go burning lamps,
and sparks of fire leap out.
20 Out of his nostrils goeth smoke, as
out of a seething pot or caldron.
21 His breath kindleth coals, and a
flame goeth out of his mouth.
22 In his neck remaineth strength, and
sorrow is turned into joy before him.
23 The flakes of his flesh are joined together: they are firm in themselves;
they cannot be moved.

24 His heart is as firm as a stone; yea,
as hard as a piece of the nether *millstone.*
25 When he raiseth up himself, the
mighty are afraid: by reason of break-
ings they purify themselves.
26 The sword of him that layeth at him
cannot hold: the spear, the dart, nor the
habergeon.
27 He esteemeth iron as straw, *and*
brass as rotten wood.
28 The arrow cannot make him flee:
sling stones are turned with him into
stubble.
29 Darts are counted as stubble: he
laugheth at the shaking of a spear.
30 Sharp stones *are* under him: he
spreadeth sharp pointed things upon
the mire.
31 He maketh the deep to boil like a
pot: he maketh the sea like a pot of
ointment.
32 He maketh a path to shine after
him, *one* would think the deep *to be*
hoary.
33 Upon earth there is not his like, who
is made without fear.
34 He beholdeth all high *things:* he *is* a
king over all the children of pride.

CHAPTER 42

THEN Jōb answered the LORD, and
said,
2 I know that thou canst do every
thing, and *that* no thought can be withholden from thee.
3 Who *is* he that hideth counsel without knowledge? therefore have I uttered
that I understood not; things too wonderful for me, which I knew not.
4 Hear, I beseech thee, and I will
speak: I will demand of thee, and declare thou unto me.
5 I have heard of thee by the hearing
of the ear; but now mine eye seeth thee:
6 Wherefore I abhor *myself,* and repent in dust and ashes.
7 ¶ And it was *so,* that after the LORD
had spoken these words unto Jōb, the
LORD said to Ĕl'ĭ-phăz the Tē'măn-īte,
My wrath is kindled against thee, and
against thy two friends: for ye have not
spoken of me *the thing that is* right, as
my servant Jōb *hath.*
8 Therefore take unto you now seven
bullocks and seven rams, and go to my
servant Jōb, and offer up for yourselves
a burnt offering; and my servant Jōb
shall pray for you: for him will I accept:
lest I deal with you *after your* folly, in
that ye have not spoken of me *the thing
which is* right, like my servant Jōb.
9 So Ĕl'ĭ-phăz the Tē'măn-īte and Bildad the Shu̇'hīte *and* Zō'phȧr the Nā'ȧ-
mȧ-thīte' went, and did according as the
LORD commanded them: the LORD also
accepted Jōb.
10 And the LORD turned the captivity
of Jōb, when he prayed for his friends:
also the LORD gave Jōb twice as much
as he had before.
11 Then came there unto him all his
brethren, and all his sisters, and all they
that had been of his acquaintance before, and did eat bread with him in his
house: and they bemoaned him, and
comforted him over all the evil that the
LORD had brought upon him: every man
also gave him a piece of money, and
every one an earring of gold.
12 So the LORD blessed the latter end
of Jōb more than his beginning: for he
had fourteen thousand sheep, and six
thousand camels, and a thousand yoke
of oxen, and a thousand she asses.
13 He had also seven sons and three
daughters.
14 And he called the name of the first,
Jē-mī'mȧ; and the name of the second,
Kē-zī'ȧ; and the name of the third,
Kĕr'ĕn–hăp'pŭch.
15 And in all the land were no women
found *so* fair as the daughters of Jōb:
and their father gave them inheritance
among their brethren.
16 After this lived Jōb a hundred and
forty years, and saw his sons, and his
sons' sons, *even* four generations.
17 So Jōb died, *being* old and full of
days.

THE BOOK OF PSALMS

PSALM 1

BLESSED *is* the man that walketh not in the counsel of the ungodly, nor standeth in the way of sinners, nor sitteth in the seat of the scornful.
2 But his delight *is* in the law of the LORD; and in his law doth he meditate day and night.
3 And he shall be like a tree planted by the rivers of water, that bringeth forth his fruit in his season; his leaf also shall not wither; and whatsoever he doeth shall prosper.
4 The ungodly *are* not so: but *are* like the chaff which the wind driveth away.
5 Therefore the ungodly shall not stand in the judgment, nor sinners in the congregation of the righteous.
6 For the LORD knoweth the way of the righteous: but the way of the ungodly shall perish.

PSALM 2

WHY do the heathen rage, and the people imagine a vain thing?
2 The kings of the earth set themselves, and the rulers take counsel together, against the LORD, and against his Anointed, *saying*,
3 Let us break their bands asunder, and cast away their cords from us.
4 He that sitteth in the heavens shall laugh: the LORD shall have them in derision.
5 Then shall he speak unto them in his wrath, and vex them in his sore displeasure.
6 Yet have I set my King upon my holy hill of Zion.
7 I will declare the decree: the LORD hath said unto me, Thou *art* my Son; this day have I begotten thee.
8 Ask of me, and I shall give *thee* the heathen *for* thine inheritance, and the uttermost parts of the earth *for* thy possession.
9 Thou shalt break them with a rod of iron; thou shalt dash them in pieces like a potter's vessel.
10 Be wise now therefore, O ye kings: be instructed, ye judges of the earth.
11 Serve the LORD with fear, and rejoice with trembling.
12 Kiss the Son, lest he be angry, and ye perish *from* the way, when his wrath is kindled but a little. Blessed *are* all they that put their trust in him.

PSALM 3

A Psalm of David, when he fled from Ăb′să-lŏm his son.

LORD, how are they increased that trouble me! many *are* they that rise up against me.
2 Many *there be* which say of my soul, *There is* no help for him in God. Sē′lȧh.
3 But thou, O LORD, *art* a shield for me; my glory, and the lifter up of mine head.
4 I cried unto the LORD with my voice, and he heard me out of his holy hill. Sē′lȧh.
5 I laid me down and slept; I awaked; for the LORD sustained me.
6 I will not be afraid of ten thousands of people, that have set *themselves* against me round about.
7 Arise, O LORD; save me, O my God: for thou hast smitten all mine enemies *upon* the cheek bone; thou hast broken the teeth of the ungodly.
8 Salvation *belongeth* unto the LORD: thy blessing *is* upon thy people. Sē′lȧh.

PSALM 4

To the chief Musician on Nĕg′ĭ-nŏth, A Psalm of David.

HEAR me when I call, O God of my righteousness: thou hast enlarged me *when I was* in distress; have mercy upon me, and hear my prayer.
2 O ye sons of men, how long *will ye turn* my glory into shame? *how long* will ye love vanity, *and* seek after leasing? Sē′lȧh.
3 But know that the LORD hath set apart him that is godly for himself: the LORD will hear when I call unto him.
4 Stand in awe, and sin not: commune with your own heart upon your bed, and be still. Sē′lȧh.
5 Offer the sacrifices of righteousness, and put your trust in the LORD.
6 *There be* many that say, Who will show us *any* good? LORD, lift thou up the light of thy countenance upon us.
7 Thou hast put gladness in my heart,

more than in the time *that* their corn and their wine increased.

8 I will both lay me down in peace, and sleep: for thou, LORD, only makest me dwell in safety.

PSALM 5

To the chief Musician upon Nē'hĭ-lŏth, A Psalm of David.

GIVE ear to my words, O LORD; consider my meditation.

2 Hearken unto the voice of my cry, my King, and my God: for unto thee will I pray.

3 My voice shalt thou hear in the morning, O LORD; in the morning will I direct *my prayer* unto thee, and will look up.

4 For thou *art* not a God that hath pleasure in wickedness: neither shall evil dwell with thee.

5 The foolish shall not stand in thy sight: thou hatest all workers of iniquity.

6 Thou shalt destroy them that speak leasing: the LORD will abhor the bloody and deceitful man.

7 But as for me, I will come *into* thy house in the multitude of thy mercy: *and* in thy fear will I worship toward thy holy temple.

8 Lead me, O LORD, in thy righteousness because of mine enemies; make thy way straight before my face.

9 For *there is* no faithfulness in their mouth; their inward part *is* very wickedness; their throat *is* an open sepulchre; they flatter with their tongue.

10 Destroy thou them, O God; let them fall by their own counsels; cast them out in the multitude of their transgressions; for they have rebelled against thee.

11 But let all those that put their trust in thee rejoice: let them ever shout for joy, because thou defendest them: let them also that love thy name be joyful in thee.

12 For thou, LORD, wilt bless the righteous; with favor wilt thou compass him as *with* a shield.

PSALM 6

To the chief Musician on Nĕg'ĭ-nōth upon Shĕm'ĭ-nith, A Psalm of David.

O LORD, rebuke me not in thine anger, neither chasten me in thy hot displeasure.

2 Have mercy upon me, O LORD; for I *am* weak: O LORD, heal me; for my bones are vexed.

3 My soul is also sore vexed: but thou, O LORD, how long?

4 Return, O LORD, deliver my soul: oh save me for thy mercies' sake.

5 For in death *there is* no remembrance of thee: in the grave who shall give thee thanks?

6 I am weary with my groaning; all the night make I my bed to swim; I water my couch with my tears.

7 Mine eye is consumed because of grief; it waxeth old because of all mine enemies.

8 Depart from me, all ye workers of iniquity; for the LORD hath heard the voice of my weeping.

9 The LORD hath heard my supplication; the LORD will receive my prayer.

10 Let all mine enemies be ashamed and sore vexed: let them return *and* be ashamed suddenly.

PSALM 7

Shig-ga'ịŏn of David, which he sang unto the LORD, concerning the words of Cŭsh the Benjamite.

O LORD my God, in thee do I put my trust: save me from all them that persecute me, and deliver me:

2 Lest he tear my soul like a lion, rending *it* in pieces, while *there is* none to deliver.

3 O LORD my God, if I have done this; if there be iniquity in my hands;

4 If I have rewarded evil unto him that was at peace with me; (yea, I have delivered him that without cause is mine enemy;)

5 Let the enemy persecute my soul, and take *it;* yea, let him tread down my life upon the earth, and lay mine honor in the dust. Sē'lăh.

6 Arise, O LORD, in thine anger, lift up thyself because of the rage of mine enemies: and awake for me *to* the judgment *that* thou hast commanded.

7 So shall the congregation of the people compass thee about: for their sakes therefore return thou on high.

8 The LORD shall judge the people: judge me, O LORD, according to my righteousness, and according to mine integrity *that is* in me.

9 Oh let the wickedness of the wicked come to an end; but establish the just: for the righteous God trieth the hearts and reins.

10 My defense *is* of God, which saveth the upright in heart.

11 God judgeth the righteous, and God is angry *with the wicked* every day.
12 If he turn not, he will whet his sword; he hath bent his bow, and made it ready.
13 He hath also prepared for him the instruments of death; he ordaineth his arrows against the persecutors.
14 Behold, he travaileth with iniquity, and hath conceived mischief, and brought forth falsehood.
15 He made a pit, and digged it, and is fallen into the ditch *which* he made.
16 His mischief shall return upon his own head, and his violent dealing shall come down upon his own pate.
17 I will praise the LORD according to his righteousness: and will sing praise to the name of the LORD most high.

PSALM 8

To the chief Musician upon Gĭt'tĭth, A Psalm of David.

O LORD our Lord, how excellent *is* thy name in all the earth! who hast set thy glory above the heavens.
2 Out of the mouth of babes and sucklings hast thou ordained strength because of thine enemies, that thou mightest still the enemy and the avenger.
3 When I consider thy heavens, the work of thy fingers, the moon and the stars, which thou hast ordained;
4 What is man, that thou art mindful of him? and the son of man, that thou visitest him?
5 For thou hast made him a little lower than the angels, and hast crowned him with glory and honor.
6 Thou madest him to have dominion over the works of thy hands; thou hast put all *things* under his feet:
7 All sheep and oxen, yea, and the beasts of the field;
8 The fowl of the air, and the fish of the sea, *and whatsoever* passeth through the paths of the seas.
9 O LORD our Lord, how excellent *is* thy name in all the earth!

PSALM 9

To the chief Musician upon Mŭth-lăb'bĕn, A Psalm of David.

I WILL praise *thee*, O LORD, with my whole heart; I will show forth all thy marvelous works.
2 I will be glad and rejoice in thee: I will sing praise to thy name, O thou Most High.
3 When mine enemies are turned back, they shall fall and perish at thy presence.
4 For thou hast maintained my right and my cause; thou satest in the throne judging right.
5 Thou hast rebuked the heathen, thou hast destroyed the wicked, thou hast put out their name for ever and ever.
6 O thou enemy, destructions are come to a perpetual end: and thou hast destroyed cities; their memorial is perished with them.
7 But the LORD shall endure for ever: he hath prepared his throne for judgment.
8 And he shall judge the world in righteousness, he shall minister judgment to the people in uprightness.
9 The LORD also will be a refuge for the oppressed, a refuge in times of trouble.
10 And they that know thy name will put their trust in thee: for thou, LORD, hast not forsaken them that seek thee.
11 Sing praises to the LORD, which dwelleth in Zion: declare among the people his doings.
12 When he maketh inquisition for blood, he remembereth them: he forgetteth not the cry of the humble.
13 Have mercy upon me, O LORD; consider my trouble *which I suffer* of them that hate me, thou that liftest me up from the gates of death:
14 That I may show forth all thy praise in the gates of the daughter of Zion: I will rejoice in thy salvation.
15 The heathen are sunk down in the pit *that* they made: in the net which they hid is their own foot taken.
16 The LORD is known *by* the judgment *which* he executeth: the wicked is snared in the work of his own hands. Hĭg-gā'ịŏn. Sē'lah.
17 The wicked shall be turned into hell, *and* all the nations that forget God.
18 For the needy shall not always be forgotten: the expectation of the poor shall *not* perish for ever.
19 Arise, O LORD; let not man prevail: let the heathen be judged in thy sight.
20 Put them in fear, O LORD: *that* the nations may know themselves *to be but* men. Sē'lah.

PSALM 10

WHY standest thou afar off, O LORD? *why* hidest thou *thyself* in times of trouble?

2 The wicked in *his* pride doth persecute the poor: let them be taken in the devices that they have imagined.

3 For the wicked boasteth of his heart's desire, and blesseth the covetous, *whom* the LORD abhorreth.

4 The wicked, through the pride of his countenance, will not seek *after God:* God *is* not in all his thoughts.

5 His ways are always grievous; thy judgments *are* far above out of his sight: *as for* all his enemies, he puffeth at them.

6 He hath said in his heart, I shall not be moved: for *I shall* never *be* in adversity.

7 His mouth is full of cursing and deceit and fraud: under his tongue *is* mischief and vanity.

8 He sitteth in the lurking places of the villages: in the secret places doth he murder the innocent: his eyes are privily set against the poor.

9 He lieth in wait secretly as a lion in his den: he lieth in wait to catch the poor: he doth catch the poor, when he draweth him into his net.

10 He croucheth, *and* humbleth himself, that the poor may fall by his strong ones.

11 He hath said in his heart, God hath forgotten: he hideth his face; he will never see *it*.

12 Arise, O LORD; O God, lift up thine hand: forget not the humble.

13 Wherefore doth the wicked contemn God? he hath said in his heart, Thou wilt not require *it*.

14 Thou hast seen *it;* for thou beholdest mischief and spite, to requite *it* with thy hand: the poor committeth himself unto thee; thou art the helper of the fatherless.

15 Break thou the arm of the wicked and the evil *man:* seek out his wickedness *till* thou find none.

16 The LORD *is* King for ever and ever: the heathen are perished out of his land.

17 LORD, thou hast heard the desire of the humble: thou wilt prepare their heart, thou wilt cause thine ear to hear:

18 To judge the fatherless and the oppressed, that the man of the earth may no more oppress.

PSALM 11

To the chief Musician, *A Psalm* of David.

IN the LORD put I my trust: how say ye to my soul, Flee *as* a bird to your mountain?

2 For, lo, the wicked bend *their* bow, they make ready their arrow upon the string, that they may privily shoot at the upright in heart.

3 If the foundations be destroyed, what can the righteous do?

4 The LORD *is* in his holy temple, the LORD's throne *is* in heaven: his eyes behold, his eyelids try, the children of men.

5 The LORD trieth the righteous: but the wicked and him that loveth violence his soul hateth.

6 Upon the wicked he shall rain snares, fire and brimstone, and a horrible tempest: *this shall be* the portion of their cup.

7 For the righteous LORD loveth righteousness; his countenance doth behold the upright.

PSALM 12

To the chief Musician upon Shĕm'ĭ-nĭth, A Psalm of David.

HELP, LORD; for the godly man ceaseth; for the faithful fail from among the children of men.

2 They speak vanity every one with his neighbor: *with* flattering lips *and* with a double heart do they speak.

3 The LORD shall cut off all flattering lips, *and* the tongue that speaketh proud things:

4 Who have said, With our tongue will we prevail; our lips *are* our own: who *is* lord over us?

5 For the oppression of the poor, for the sighing of the needy, now will I arise, saith the LORD; I will set *him* in safety *from him that* puffeth at him.

6 The words of the LORD *are* pure words: *as* silver tried in a furnace of earth, purified seven times.

7 Thou shalt keep them, O LORD, thou shalt preserve them from this generation for ever.

8 The wicked walk on every side, when the vilest men are exalted.

PSALM 13

To the chief Musician, A Psalm of David.

HOW long wilt thou forget me, O LORD? for ever? how long wilt thou hide thy face from me?

2 How long shall I take counsel in my
soul, *having* sorrow in my heart daily?
how long shall mine enemy be exalted
over me?
3 Consider *and* hear me, O LORD my
God: lighten mine eyes, lest I sleep the
sleep of death;
4 Lest mine enemy say, I have prevailed against him; *and* those that
trouble me rejoice when I am moved.
5 But I have trusted in thy mercy; my
heart shall rejoice in thy salvation.
6 I will sing unto the LORD, because he
hath dealt bountifully with me.

PSALM 14

To the chief Musician, *A Psalm* of David.

THE fool hath said in his heart, *There
is* no God. They are corrupt, they
have done abominable works, *there is*
none that doeth good.
2 The LORD looked down from heaven
upon the children of men, to see if there
were any that did understand, *and* seek
God.
3 They are all gone aside, they are *all*
together become filthy: *there is* none
that doeth good, no, not one.
4 Have all the workers of iniquity no
knowledge? who eat up my people *as*
they eat bread, and call not upon the
LORD.
5 There were they in great fear: for God
is in the generation of the righteous.
6 Ye have shamed the counsel of the
poor, because the LORD *is* his refuge.
7 Oh that the salvation of Ĭş′rā-ĕl *were
come* out of Zion! when the LORD bringeth back the captivity of his people,
Jacob shall rejoice, *and* Ĭş′rā-ĕl shall be
glad.

PSALM 15

A Psalm of David.

LORD, who shall abide in thy tabernacle? who shall dwell in thy holy
hill?
2 He that walketh uprightly, and worketh righteousness, and speaketh the
truth in his heart.
3 *He that* backbiteth not with his
tongue, nor doeth evil to his neighbor,
nor taketh up a reproach against his
neighbor.
4 In whose eyes a vile person is contemned; but he honoreth them that fear
the LORD. *He that* sweareth to *his own*
hurt, and changeth not.
5 *He that* putteth not out his money to
usury, nor taketh reward against the
innocent. He that doeth these *things*
shall never be moved.

PSALM 16

Mĭch′tăm of David.

PRESERVE me, O God: for in thee
do I put my trust.
2 *O my soul,* thou hast said unto the
LORD, Thou *art* my Lord: my goodness
extendeth not to thee;
3 *But* to the saints that *are* in the earth,
and *to* the excellent, in whom *is* all my
delight.
4 Their sorrows shall be multiplied
that hasten *after* another *god:* their
drink offerings of blood will I not offer,
nor take up their names into my lips.
5 The LORD *is* the portion of mine inheritance and of my cup: thou main-
tainest my lot.
6 The lines are fallen unto me in pleasant *places;* yea, I have a goodly heritage.
7 I will bless the LORD, who hath given
me counsel: my reins also instruct me
in the night seasons.
8 I have set the LORD always before
me: because *he is* at my right hand, I
shall not be moved.
9 Therefore my heart is glad, and my
glory rejoiceth: my flesh also shall rest
in hope.
10 For thou wilt not leave my soul in
hell; neither wilt thou suffer thine Holy
One to see corruption.
11 Thou wilt show me the path of life:
in thy presence *is* fulness of joy; at thy
right hand *there are* pleasures for evermore.

PSALM 17

A Prayer of David.

HEAR the right, O LORD, attend
unto my cry; give ear unto my
prayer, *that goeth* not out of feigned
lips.
2 Let my sentence come forth from thy
presence; let thine eyes behold the
things that are equal.
3 Thou hast proved mine heart; thou
hast visited *me* in the night; thou hast
tried me, *and* shalt find nothing: I am
purposed *that* my mouth shall not
transgress.
4 Concerning the works of men, by the
word of thy lips I have kept *me from*
the paths of the destroyer.

5 Hold up my goings in thy paths, *that*
my footsteps slip not.
6 I have called upon thee, for thou wilt
hear me, O God: incline thine ear unto
me, *and* hear my speech.
7 Show thy marvelous loving-kindness,
O thou that savest by thy right hand
them which put their trust *in thee* from
those that rise up *against them.*
8 Keep me as the apple of the eye; hide
me under the shadow of thy wings,
9 From the wicked that oppress me,
from my deadly enemies, *who* compass
me about.
10 They are inclosed in their own fat:
with their mouth they speak proudly.
11 They have now compassed us in our
steps: they have set their eyes bowing
down to the earth;
12 Like as a lion *that* is greedy of his
prey, and as it were a young lion lurking
in secret places.
13 Arise, O LORD, disappoint him, cast
him down: deliver my soul from the
wicked, *which is* thy sword:
14 From men *which are* thy hand, O
LORD, from men of the world, *which
have* their portion in *this* life, and whose
belly thou fillest with thy hid *treasure:*
they are full of children, and leave the
rest of their *substance* to their babes.
15 As for me, I will behold thy face in
righteousness: I shall be satisfied, when
I awake, with thy likeness.

PSALM 18

To the chief Musician, *A Psalm* of David, the servant of the LORD, who spake unto the LORD the words of this song in the day *that* the LORD delivered him from the hand of all his enemies, and from the hand of Saul: And he said,

I WILL love thee, O LORD, my
strength.
2 The LORD *is* my rock, and my fortress, and my deliverer; my God, my
strength, in whom I will trust; my buckler, and the horn of my salvation, *and*
my high tower.
3 I will call upon the LORD, *who is
worthy* to be praised: so shall I be saved
from mine enemies.
4 The sorrows of death compassed me,
and the floods of ungodly men made me
afraid.
5 The sorrows of hell compassed me
about: the snares of death prevented
me.
6 In my distress I called upon the
LORD, and cried unto my God: he heard
my voice out of his temple, and my cry
came before him, *even* into his ears.
7 Then the earth shook and trembled;
the foundations also of the hills moved
and were shaken, because he was wroth.
8 There went up a smoke out of his
nostrils, and fire out of his mouth devoured: coals were kindled by it.
9 He bowed the heavens also, and came
down: and darkness *was* under his feet.
10 And he rode upon a cherub, and did
fly: yea, he did fly upon the wings of
the wind.
11 He made darkness his secret place;
his pavilion round about him *were* dark
waters *and* thick clouds of the skies.
12 At the brightness *that was* before
him his thick clouds passed, hail *stones*
and coals of fire.
13 The LORD also thundered in the
heavens, and the Highest gave his voice;
hail *stones* and coals of fire.
14 Yea, he sent out his arrows, and
scattered them; and he shot out lightnings, and discomfited them.
15 Then the channels of waters were
seen, and the foundations of the world
were discovered at thy rebuke, O LORD,
at the blast of the breath of thy nostrils.
16 He sent from above, he took me, he
drew me out of many waters.
17 He delivered me from my strong
enemy, and from them which hated me:
for they were too strong for me.
18 They prevented me in the day of my
calamity: but the LORD was my stay.
19 He brought me forth also into a large
place; he delivered me, because he
delighted in me.
20 The LORD rewarded me according
to my righteousness; according to the
cleanness of my hands hath he recompensed me.
21 For I have kept the ways of the
LORD, and have not wickedly departed
from my God.
22 For all his judgments *were* before
me, and I did not put away his statutes
from me.
23 I was also upright before him, and I
kept myself from mine iniquity.
24 Therefore hath the LORD recompensed me according to my righteousness, according to the cleanness of my
hands in his eyesight.
25 With the merciful thou wilt show
thyself merciful; with an upright man
thou wilt show thyself upright;

26 With the pure thou wilt show thyself pure; and with the froward thou wilt show thyself froward.
27 For thou wilt save the afflicted people; but wilt bring down high looks.
28 For thou wilt light my candle: the LORD my God will enlighten my darkness.
29 For by thee I have run through a troop; and by my God have I leaped over a wall.
30 *As for* God, his way *is* perfect: the word of the LORD is tried: he *is* a buckler to all those that trust in him.
31 For who *is* God save the LORD? or who *is* a rock save our God?
32 *It is* God that girdeth me with strength, and maketh my way perfect.
33 He maketh my feet like hinds' *feet*, and setteth me upon my high places.
34 He teacheth my hands to war, so that a bow of steel is broken by mine arms.
35 Thou hast also given me the shield of thy salvation: and thy right hand hath holden me up, and thy gentleness hath made me great.
36 Thou hast enlarged my steps under me, that my feet did not slip.
37 I have pursued mine enemies, and overtaken them: neither did I turn again till they were consumed.
38 I have wounded them that they were not able to rise: they are fallen under my feet.
39 For thou hast girded me with strength unto the battle: thou hast subdued under me those that rose up against me.
40 Thou hast also given me the necks of mine enemies; that I might destroy them that hate me.
41 They cried, but *there was* none to save *them: even* unto the LORD, but he answered them not.
42 Then did I beat them small as the dust before the wind: I did cast them out as the dirt in the streets.
43 Thou hast delivered me from the strivings of the people; *and* thou hast made me the head of the heathen: a people *whom* I have not known shall serve me.
44 As soon as they hear of me, they shall obey me: the strangers shall submit themselves unto me.
45 The strangers shall fade away, and be afraid out of their close places.
46 The LORD liveth; and blessed *be* my Rock; and let the God of my salvation be exalted.
47 *It is* God that avengeth me, and subdueth the people under me.
48 He delivereth me from mine enemies: yea, thou liftest me up above those that rise up against me: thou hast delivered me from the violent man.
49 Therefore will I give thanks unto thee, O LORD, among the heathen, and sing praises unto thy name.
50 Great deliverance giveth he to his king; and showeth mercy to his anointed, to David, and to his seed for evermore.

PSALM 19

To the chief Musician, A Psalm of David.

THE heavens declare the glory of God; and the firmament showeth his handiwork.
2 Day unto day uttereth speech, and night unto night showeth knowledge.
3 *There is* no speech nor language, *where* their voice is not heard.
4 Their line is gone out through all the earth, and their words to the end of the world. In them hath he set a tabernacle for the sun,
5 Which *is* as a bridegroom coming out of his chamber, *and* rejoiceth as a strong man to run a race.
6 His going forth *is* from the end of the heaven, and his circuit unto the ends of it: and there is nothing hid from the heat thereof.
7 The law of the LORD *is* perfect, converting the soul: the testimony of the LORD *is* sure, making wise the simple.
8 The statutes of the LORD *are* right, rejoicing the heart: the commandment of the LORD *is* pure, enlightening the eyes.
9 The fear of the LORD *is* clean, enduring for ever: the judgments of the LORD *are* true *and* righteous altogether.
10 More to be desired *are they* than gold, yea, than much fine gold: sweeter also than honey and the honeycomb.
11 Moreover by them is thy servant warned: *and* in keeping of them *there is* great reward.
12 Who can understand *his* errors? cleanse thou me from secret *faults*.
13 Keep back thy servant also from presumptuous *sins;* let them not have dominion over me: then shall I be up-

right, and I shall be innocent from the
great transgression.
14 Let the words of my mouth, and the
meditation of my heart, be acceptable in
thy sight, O LORD, my strength, and my
redeemer.

PSALM 20

To the chief Musician, A Psalm of David.

THE LORD hear thee in the day of
trouble; the name of the God of
Jacob defend thee;
2 Send thee help from the sanctuary,
and strengthen thee out of Zion;
3 Remember all thy offerings, and accept thy burnt sacrifice; Sē′lăh.
4 Grant thee according to thine own
heart, and fulfil all thy counsel.
5 We will rejoice in thy salvation, and
in the name of our God we will set up
our banners: the LORD fulfil all thy
petitions.
6 Now know I that the LORD saveth his
anointed; he will hear him from his holy
heaven with the saving strength of his
right hand.
7 Some *trust* in chariots, and some in
horses: but we will remember the name
of the LORD our God.
8 They are brought down and fallen:
but we are risen, and stand upright.
9 Save, LORD: let the king hear us
when we call.

PSALM 21

To the chief Musician, A Psalm of David.

THE king shall joy in thy strength,
O LORD; and in thy salvation how
greatly shall he rejoice!
2 Thou hast given him his heart's desire, and hast not withholden the request
of his lips. Sē′lăh.
3 For thou preventest him with the
blessings of goodness: thou settest a
crown of pure gold on his head.
4 He asked life of thee, *and* thou gavest
it him, *even* length of days for ever and
ever.
5 His glory *is* great in thy salvation:
honor and majesty hast thou laid upon
him.
6 For thou hast made him most blessed
for ever: thou hast made him exceeding
glad with thy countenance.
7 For the king trusteth in the LORD,
and through the mercy of the Most
High he shall not be moved.
8 Thine hand shall find out all thine
enemies: thy right hand shall find out
those that hate thee.
9 Thou shalt make them as a fiery oven
in the time of thine anger: the LORD
shall swallow them up in his wrath, and
the fire shall devour them.
10 Their fruit shalt thou destroy from
the earth, and their seed from among the
children of men.
11 For they intended evil against thee:
they imagined a mischievous device,
which they are not able *to perform*.
12 Therefore shalt thou make them
turn their back, *when* thou shalt make
ready *thine arrows* upon thy strings
against the face of them.
13 Be thou exalted, LORD, in thine own
strength: *so* will we sing and praise thy
power.

PSALM 22

To the chief Musician upon Ā′jē-lĕth Shā′hăr, A Psalm of David.

MY God, my God, why hast thou for
saken me? *why art thou so* far
from helping me, *and from* the words of
my roaring?
2 O my God, I cry in the daytime, but
thou hearest not; and in the night season, and am not silent.
3 But thou *art* holy, *O thou* that in-
habitest the praises of Ĭs′rā-ĕl.
4 Our fathers trusted in thee: they
trusted, and thou didst deliver them.
5 They cried unto thee, and were delivered: they trusted in thee, and were
not confounded.
6 But I *am* a worm, and no man; a
reproach of men, and despised of the
people.
7 All they that see me laugh me to
scorn: they shoot out the lip, they shake
the head, *saying*,
8 He trusted on the LORD *that* he would
deliver him: let him deliver him, seeing
he delighted in him.
9 But thou *art* he that took me out of
the womb: thou didst make me hope
when I was upon my mother's breasts.
10 I was cast upon thee from the womb:
thou *art* my God from my mother's
belly.
11 Be not far from me; for trouble *is*
near; for *there is* none to help.
12 Many bulls have compassed me:
strong *bulls* of Ba′shăn have beset me
round.
13 They gaped upon me *with* their

mouths, *as* a ravening and a roaring
lion.
14 I am poured out like water, and all
my bones are out of joint: my heart is
like wax; it is melted in the midst of
my bowels.
15 My strength is dried up like a potsherd; and my tongue cleaveth to my
jaws; and thou hast brought me into the
dust of death.
16 For dogs have compassed me: the
assembly of the wicked have inclosed
me: they pierced my hands and my
feet.
17 I may tell all my bones: they look
and stare upon me.
18 They part my garments among
them, and cast lots upon my vesture.
19 But be not thou far from me, O
LORD: O my strength, haste thee to help
me.
20 Deliver my soul from the sword; my
darling from the power of the dog.
21 Save me from the lion's mouth: for
thou hast heard me from the horns of
the unicorns.
22 I will declare thy name unto my
brethren: in the midst of the congregation will I praise thee.
23 Ye that fear the LORD, praise him;
all ye the seed of Jacob, glorify him; and
fear him, all ye the seed of Ĭs'rā-ĕl.
24 For he hath not despised nor abhorred the affliction of the afflicted;
neither hath he hid his face from him;
but when he cried unto him, he heard.
25 My praise *shall be* of thee in the
great congregation: I will pay my vows
before them that fear him.
26 The meek shall eat and be satisfied:
they shall praise the LORD that seek
him: your heart shall live for ever.
27 All the ends of the world shall remember and turn unto the LORD: and
all the kindreds of the nations shall worship before thee.
28 For the kingdom *is* the LORD's: and
he *is* the governor among the nations.
29 All *they that be* fat upon earth shall
eat and worship: all they that go down
to the dust shall bow before him: and
none can keep alive his own soul.
30 A seed shall serve him; it shall be
accounted to the LORD for a generation.
31 They shall come, and shall declare
his righteousness unto a people that
shall be born, that he hath done *this*.

PSALM 23

A Psalm of David.

THE LORD *is* my shepherd; I shall
not want.
2 He maketh me to lie down in green
pastures: he leadeth me beside the still
waters.
3 He restoreth my soul: he leadeth me
in the paths of righteousness for his
name's sake.
4 Yea, though I walk through the valley
of the shadow of death, I will fear no
evil: for thou *art* with me; thy rod and
thy staff they comfort me.
5 Thou preparest a table before me in
the presence of mine enemies: thou
anointest my head with oil; my cup runneth over.
6 Surely goodness and mercy shall follow me all the days of my life: and I will
dwell in the house of the LORD for ever.

PSALM 24

A Psalm of David.

THE earth *is* the LORD's, and the fulness thereof; the world, and they
that dwell therein.
2 For he hath founded it upon the seas,
and established it upon the floods.
3 Who shall ascend into the hill of the
LORD? or who shall stand in his holy
place?
4 He that hath clean hands, and a pure
heart; who hath not lifted up his soul
unto vanity, nor sworn deceitfully.
5 He shall receive the blessing from
the LORD, and righteousness from the
God of his salvation.
6 This *is* the generation of them that seek
him, that seek thy face, O Jacob. Sē'lȧh.
7 Lift up your heads, O ye gates; and
be ye lifted up, ye everlasting doors; and
the King of glory shall come in.
8 Who *is* this King of glory? The LORD
strong and mighty, the LORD mighty in
battle.
9 Lift up your heads, O ye gates; even
lift *them* up, ye everlasting doors; and
the King of glory shall come in.
10 Who is this King of glory? The LORD
of hosts, he *is* the King of glory. Sē'lȧh.

PSALM 25

A Psalm of David.

UNTO thee, O LORD, do I lift up my
soul.
2 O my God, I trust in thee: let me not

be ashamed, let not mine enemies triumph over me.
3 Yea, let none that wait on thee be
ashamed: let them be ashamed which
transgress without cause.
4 Show me thy ways, O LORD; teach
me thy paths.
5 Lead me in thy truth, and teach me:
for thou *art* the God of my salvation; on
thee do I wait all the day.
6 Remember, O LORD, thy tender
mercies and thy loving-kindnesses; for
they *have been* ever of old.
7 Remember not the sins of my youth,
nor my transgressions: according to thy
mercy remember thou me for thy goodness' sake, O LORD.
8 Good and upright *is* the LORD: therefore will he teach sinners in the way.
9 The meek will he guide in judgment:
and the meek will he teach his way.
10 All the paths of the LORD *are* mercy
and truth unto such as keep his covenant and his testimonies.
11 For thy name's sake, O LORD, pardon mine iniquity; for it *is* great.
12 What man *is* he that feareth the
LORD? him shall he teach in the way
that he shall choose.
13 His soul shall dwell at ease; and his
seed shall inherit the earth.
14 The secret of the LORD *is* with them
that fear him; and he will show them his
covenant.
15 Mine eyes *are* ever toward the LORD;
for he shall pluck my feet out of the net.
16 Turn thee unto me, and have mercy
upon me; for I *am* desolate and afflicted.
17 The troubles of my heart are enlarged: *O* bring thou me out of my
distresses.
18 Look upon mine affliction and my
pain; and forgive all my sins.
19 Consider mine enemies; for they are
many; and they hate me with cruel hatred.
20 O keep my soul, and deliver me: let
me not be ashamed; for I put my trust
in thee.
21 Let integrity and uprightness preserve me; for I wait on thee.
22 Redeem Ĭş'rā-ĕl, O God, out of all
his troubles.

PSALM 26

A Psalm of David.

JUDGE me, O LORD; for I have
walked in mine integrity: I have
trusted also in the LORD; *therefore* I
shall not slide.
2 Examine me, O LORD, and prove me;
try my reins and my heart.
3 For thy loving-kindness *is* before
mine eyes: and I have walked in thy
truth.
4 I have not sat with vain persons,
neither will I go in with dissemblers.
5 I have hated the congregation of evildoers; and will not sit with the wicked.
6 I will wash mine hands in innocency:
so will I compass thine altar, O LORD:
7 That I may publish with the voice of
thanksgiving, and tell of all thy wondrous works.
8 LORD, I have loved the habitation of
thy house, and the place where thine
honor dwelleth.
9 Gather not my soul with sinners, nor
my life with bloody men:
10 In whose hands *is* mischief, and
their right hand is full of bribes.
11 But as for me, I will walk in mine
integrity: redeem me, and be merciful
unto me.
12 My foot standeth in an even place:
in the congregations will I bless the
LORD.

PSALM 27

A Psalm of David.

THE LORD *is* my light and my salvation: whom shall I fear? the LORD *is*
the strength of my life; of whom shall I
be afraid?
2 When the wicked, *even* mine enemies and my foes, came upon me to eat
up my flesh, they stumbled and fell.
3 Though a host should encamp against
me, my heart shall not fear: though war
should rise against me, in this *will* I *be*
confident.
4 One *thing* have I desired of the LORD,
that will I seek after; that I may dwell
in the house of the LORD all the days
of my life, to behold the beauty of the
LORD, and to inquire in his temple.
5 For in the time of trouble he shall
hide me in his pavilion: in the secret of
his tabernacle shall he hide me; he shall
set me up upon a rock.
6 And now shall mine head be lifted up
above mine enemies round about me:
therefore will I offer in his tabernacle
sacrifices of joy; I will sing, yea, I will
sing praises unto the LORD.
7 Hear, O LORD, *when* I cry with my
voice: have mercy also upon me, and
answer me.

8 *When thou saidst,* Seek ye my face; my heart said unto thee, Thy face, LORD, will I seek.

9 Hide not thy face *far* from me; put not thy servant away in anger: thou hast been my help; leave me not, neither forsake me, O God of my salvation.

10 When my father and my mother forsake me, then the LORD will take me up.

11 Teach me thy way, O LORD, and lead me in a plain path, because of mine enemies.

12 Deliver me not over unto the will of mine enemies: for false witnesses are risen up against me, and such as breathe out cruelty.

13 *I had fainted,* unless I had believed to see the goodness of the LORD in the land of the living.

14 Wait on the LORD: be of good courage, and he shall strengthen thine heart: wait, I say, on the LORD.

PSALM 28

A Psalm of David.

UNTO thee will I cry, O LORD my rock; be not silent to me: lest, *if* thou be silent to me, I become like them that go down into the pit.

2 Hear the voice of my supplications, when I cry unto thee, when I lift up my hands toward thy holy oracle.

3 Draw me not away with the wicked, and with the workers of iniquity, which speak peace to their neighbors, but mischief *is* in their hearts.

4 Give them according to their deeds, and according to the wickedness of their endeavors: give them after the work of their hands; render to them their desert.

5 Because they regard not the works of the LORD, nor the operation of his hands, he shall destroy them, and not build them up.

6 Blessed *be* the LORD, because he hath heard the voice of my supplications.

7 The LORD *is* my strength and my shield; my heart trusted in him, and I am helped: therefore my heart greatly rejoiceth; and with my song will I praise him.

8 The LORD *is* their strength, and he *is* the saving strength of his anointed.

9 Save thy people, and bless thine inheritance: feed them also, and lift them up for ever.

PSALM 29

A Psalm of David.

GIVE unto the LORD, O ye mighty, give unto the LORD glory and strength.

2 Give unto the LORD the glory due unto his name; worship the LORD in the beauty of holiness.

3 The voice of the LORD *is* upon the waters: the God of glory thundereth: the LORD *is* upon many waters.

4 The voice of the LORD *is* powerful; the voice of the LORD *is* full of majesty.

5 The voice of the LORD breaketh the cedars; yea, the LORD breaketh the cedars of Lebanon.

6 He maketh them also to skip like a calf; Lebanon and Sĭ′rĭ-ŏn like a young unicorn.

7 The voice of the LORD divideth the flames of fire.

8 The voice of the LORD shaketh the wilderness; the LORD shaketh the wilderness of Kā′dĕsh.

9 The voice of the LORD maketh the hinds to calve, and discovereth the forests: and in his temple doth every one speak of *his* glory.

10 The LORD sitteth upon the flood; yea, the LORD sitteth King for ever.

11 The LORD will give strength unto his people; the LORD will bless his people with peace.

PSALM 30

A Psalm *and* Song *at* the dedication of the house of David.

I WILL extol thee, O LORD; for thou hast lifted me up, and hast not made my foes to rejoice over me.

2 O LORD my God, I cried unto thee, and thou hast healed me.

3 O LORD, thou hast brought up my soul from the grave: thou hast kept me alive, that I should not go down to the pit.

4 Sing unto the LORD, O ye saints of his, and give thanks at the remembrance of his holiness.

5 For his anger *endureth but* a moment; in his favor *is* life: weeping may endure for a night, but joy *cometh* in the morning.

6 And in my prosperity I said, I shall never be moved.

7 LORD, by thy favor thou hast made my mountain to stand strong: thou didst hide thy face, *and* I was troubled.

8 I cried to thee, O LORD; and unto the
LORD I made supplication.
9 What profit *is there* in my blood
when I go down to the pit? Shall the
dust praise thee? shall it declare thy
truth?
10 Hear, O LORD, and have mercy
upon me: LORD, be thou my helper.
11 Thou hast turned for me my mourning into dancing: thou hast put off my
sackcloth, and girded me with gladness;
12 To the end that *my* glory may
sing praise to thee, and not be silent.
O LORD my God, I will give thanks unto
thee for ever.

PSALM 31

To the chief Musician, A Psalm of David.

IN thee, O LORD, do I put my trust;
let me never be ashamed: deliver me
in thy righteousness.
2 Bow down thine ear to me; deliver me
speedily: be thou my strong rock, for a
house of defense to save me.
3 For thou *art* my rock and my fortress;
therefore for thy name's sake lead me,
and guide me.
4 Pull me out of the net that they have
laid privily for me: for thou *art* my
strength.
5 Into thine hand I commit my spirit:
thou hast redeemed me, O LORD God of
truth.
6 I have hated them that regard lying
vanities: but I trust in the LORD.
7 I will be glad and rejoice in thy
mercy: for thou hast considered my
trouble; thou hast known my soul in
adversities;
8 And hast not shut me up into the
hand of the enemy: thou hast set my
feet in a large room.
9 Have mercy upon me, O LORD, for I
am in trouble: mine eye is consumed
with grief, *yea,* my soul and my belly.
10 For my life is spent with grief, and
my years with sighing: my strength
faileth because of mine iniquity, and my
bones are consumed.
11 I was a reproach among all mine
enemies, but especially among my
neighbors, and a fear to mine acquaintance: they that did see me without fled
from me.
12 I am forgotten as a dead man out of
mind: I am like a broken vessel.
13 For I have heard the slander of
many: fear *was* on every side: while
they took counsel together against me,
they devised to take away my life.
14 But I trusted in thee, O LORD: I
said, Thou *art* my God.
15 My times *are* in thy hand: deliver
me from the hand of mine enemies, and
from them that persecute me.
16 Make thy face to shine upon thy
servant: save me for thy mercies' sake.
17 Let me not be ashamed, O LORD;
for I have called upon thee: let the
wicked be ashamed, *and* let them be
silent in the grave.
18 Let the lying lips be put to silence;
which speak grievous things proudly and
contemptuously against the righteous.
19 *Oh* how great *is* thy goodness, which
thou hast laid up for them that fear thee;
which thou hast wrought for them that
trust in thee before the sons of men!
20 Thou shalt hide them in the secret
of thy presence from the pride of man:
thou shalt keep them secretly in a
pavilion from the strife of tongues.
21 Blessed *be* the LORD: for he hath
showed me his marvelous kindness in a
strong city.
22 For I said in my haste, I am cut off
from before thine eyes: nevertheless
thou heardest the voice of my supplications when I cried unto thee.
23 O love the LORD, all ye his saints:
for the LORD preserveth the faithful, and
plentifully rewardeth the proud doer.
24 Be of good courage, and he shall
strengthen your heart, all ye that hope
in the LORD.

PSALM 32

A Psalm of David, Măs'chĭl.

BLESSED *is he whose* transgression
is forgiven, *whose* sin *is* covered.
2 Blessed *is* the man unto whom the
LORD imputeth not iniquity, and in
whose spirit *there is* no guile.
3 When I kept silence, my bones waxed
old through my roaring all the day long.
4 For day and night thy hand was
heavy upon me: my moisture is turned
into the drought of summer. Sē'lȧh.
5 I acknowledged my sin unto thee,
and mine iniquity have I not hid. I said,
I will confess my transgressions unto
the LORD; and thou forgavest the iniquity of my sin. Sē'lȧh.
6 For this shall every one that is godly
pray unto thee in a time when thou mayest be found: surely in the floods of

great waters they shall not come nigh unto him.
7 Thou *art* my hiding place; thou shalt preserve me from trouble; thou shalt compass me about with songs of deliverance. Sē′lăh.
8 I will instruct thee and teach thee in the way which thou shalt go: I will guide thee with mine eye.
9 Be ye not as the horse, *or* as the mule, *which* have no understanding: whose mouth must be held in with bit and bridle, lest they come near unto thee.
10 Many sorrows *shall be* to the wicked: but he that trusteth in the LORD, mercy shall compass him about.
11 Be glad in the LORD, and rejoice, ye righteous: and shout for joy, all *ye that are* upright in heart.

PSALM 33

REJOICE in the LORD, O ye righteous: *for* praise is comely for the upright.
2 Praise the LORD with harp: sing unto him with the psaltery *and* an instrument of ten strings.
3 Sing unto him a new song; play skilfully with a loud noise.
4 For the word of the LORD *is* right; and all his works *are done* in truth.
5 He loveth righteousness and judgment: the earth is full of the goodness of the LORD.
6 By the word of the LORD were the heavens made; and all the host of them by the breath of his mouth.
7 He gathereth the waters of the sea together as a heap: he layeth up the depth in storehouses.
8 Let all the earth fear the LORD: let all the inhabitants of the world stand in awe of him.
9 For he spake, and it was *done;* he commanded, and it stood fast.
10 The LORD bringeth the counsel of the heathen to nought: he maketh the devices of the people of none effect.
11 The counsel of the LORD standeth for ever, the thoughts of his heart to all generations.
12 Blessed *is* the nation whose God *is* the LORD; *and* the people *whom* he hath chosen for his own inheritance.
13 The LORD looketh from heaven; he beholdeth all the sons of men.
14 From the place of his habitation he looketh upon all the inhabitants of the earth.
15 He fashioneth their hearts alike; he considereth all their works.
16 There is no king saved by the multitude of a host: a mighty man is not delivered by much strength.
17 A horse *is* a vain thing for safety: neither shall he deliver *any* by his great strength.
18 Behold, the eye of the LORD *is* upon them that fear him, upon them that hope in his mercy;
19 To deliver their soul from death, and to keep them alive in famine.
20 Our soul waiteth for the LORD: he *is* our help and our shield.
21 For our heart shall rejoice in him, because we have trusted in his holy name.
22 Let thy mercy, O LORD, be upon us, according as we hope in thee.

PSALM 34

A Psalm of David, when he changed his behavior before Ă-bĭm′-ĕlĕch; who drove him away, and he departed.

I WILL bless the LORD at all times: his praise *shall* continually *be* in my mouth.
2 My soul shall make her boast in the LORD: the humble shall hear *thereof,* and be glad.
3 O magnify the LORD with me, and let us exalt his name together.
4 I sought the LORD, and he heard me, and delivered me from all my fears.
5 They looked unto him, and were lightened: and their faces were not ashamed.
6 This poor man cried, and the LORD heard *him,* and saved him out of all his troubles.
7 The angel of the LORD encampeth round about them that fear him, and delivereth them.
8 O taste and see that the LORD *is* good: blessed *is* the man *that* trusteth in him.
9 O fear the LORD, ye his saints: for *there is* no want to them that fear him.
10 The young lions do lack, and suffer hunger: but they that seek the LORD shall not want any good *thing.*
11 Come, ye children, hearken unto me: I will teach you the fear of the LORD.
12 What man *is he that* desireth life,

and loveth *many* days, that he may see good?
13 Keep thy tongue from evil, and thy lips from speaking guile.
14 Depart from evil, and do good; seek peace, and pursue it.
15 The eyes of the LORD *are* upon the righteous, and his ears *are open* unto their cry.
16 The face of the LORD *is* against them that do evil, to cut off the remembrance of them from the earth.
17 *The righteous* cry, and the LORD heareth, and delivereth them out of all their troubles.
18 The LORD *is* nigh unto them that are of a broken heart; and saveth such as be of a contrite spirit.
19 Many *are* the afflictions of the righteous: but the LORD delivereth him out of them all.
20 He keepeth all his bones: not one of them is broken.
21 Evil shall slay the wicked: and they that hate the righteous shall be desolate.
22 The LORD redeemeth the soul of his servants: and none of them that trust in him shall be desolate.

PSALM 35

A Psalm of David.

PLEAD *my cause*, O LORD, with them that strive with me: fight against them that fight against me.
2 Take hold of shield and buckler, and stand up for mine help.
3 Draw out also the spear, and stop *the way* against them that persecute me: say unto my soul, I *am* thy salvation.
4 Let them be confounded and put to shame that seek after my soul: let them be turned back and brought to confusion that devise my hurt.
5 Let them be as chaff before the wind: and let the angel of the LORD chase *them*.
6 Let their way be dark and slippery: and let the angel of the LORD persecute them.
7 For without cause have they hid for me their net *in* a pit, *which* without cause they have digged for my soul.
8 Let destruction come upon him at unawares; and let his net that he hath hid catch himself: into that very destruction let him fall.
9 And my soul shall be joyful in the LORD: it shall rejoice in his salvation.
10 All my bones shall say, LORD, who *is* like unto thee, which deliverest the poor from him that is too strong for him, yea, the poor and the needy from him that spoileth him?
11 False witnesses did rise up; they laid to my charge *things* that I knew not.
12 They rewarded me evil for good *to* the spoiling of my soul.
13 But as for me, when they were sick, my clothing *was* sackcloth: I humbled my soul with fasting; and my prayer returned into mine own bosom.
14 I behaved myself as though *he had been* my friend *or* brother: I bowed down heavily, as one that mourneth *for his* mother.
15 But in mine adversity they rejoiced, and gathered themselves together: *yea*, the abjects gathered themselves together against me, and I knew *it* not; they did tear *me*, and ceased not:
16 With hypocritical mockers in feasts, they gnashed upon me with their teeth.
17 LORD, how long wilt thou look on? rescue my soul from their destructions, my darling from the lions.
18 I will give thee thanks in the great congregation: I will praise thee among much people.
19 Let not them that are mine enemies wrongfully rejoice over me: *neither* let them wink with the eye that hate me without a cause.
20 For they speak not peace: but they devise deceitful matters against *them that are* quiet in the land.
21 Yea, they opened their mouth wide against me, *and* said, Aha, aha, our eye hath seen *it*.
22 *This* thou hast seen, O LORD: keep not silence: O LORD, be not far from me.
23 Stir up thyself, and awake to my judgment, *even* unto my cause, my God and my Lord.
24 Judge me, O LORD my God, according to thy righteousness; and let them not rejoice over me.
25 Let them not say in their hearts, Ah, so would we have it: let them not say, We have swallowed him up.
26 Let them be ashamed and brought to confusion together that rejoice at mine hurt: let them be clothed with shame and dishonor that magnify *themselves* against me.
27 Let them shout for joy, and be glad, that favor my righteous cause: yea, let

them say continually, Let the LORD be magnified, which hath pleasure in the prosperity of his servant.

28 And my tongue shall speak of thy righteousness *and* of thy praise all the day long.

PSALM 36

To the chief Musician, *A Psalm* of David the servant of the LORD.

THE transgression of the wicked saith within my heart, *that there is* no fear of God before his eyes.

2 For he flattereth himself in his own eyes, until his iniquity be found to be hateful.

3 The words of his mouth *are* iniquity and deceit: he hath left off to be wise, *and* to do good.

4 He deviseth mischief upon his bed; he setteth himself in a way *that is* not good; he abhorreth not evil.

5 Thy mercy, O LORD, *is* in the heavens; *and* thy faithfulness *reacheth* unto the clouds.

6 Thy righteousness *is* like the great mountains; thy judgments *are* a great deep: O LORD, thou preservest man and beast.

7 How excellent *is* thy loving-kindness, O God! therefore the children of men put their trust under the shadow of thy wings.

8 They shall be abundantly satisfied with the fatness of thy house; and thou shalt make them drink of the river of thy pleasures.

9 For with thee *is* the fountain of life: in thy light shall we see light.

10 O continue thy loving-kindness unto them that know thee; and thy righteousness to the upright in heart.

11 Let not the foot of pride come against me, and let not the hand of the wicked remove me.

12 There are the workers of iniquity fallen: they are cast down, and shall not be able to rise.

PSALM 37

A Psalm of David.

FRET not thyself because of evildoers, neither be thou envious against the workers of iniquity.

2 For they shall soon be cut down like the grass, and wither as the green herb.

3 Trust in the LORD, and do good; *so* shalt thou dwell in the land, and verily thou shalt be fed.

4 Delight thyself also in the LORD; and he shall give thee the desires of thine heart.

5 Commit thy way unto the LORD; trust also in him; and he shall bring *it* to pass.

6 And he shall bring forth thy righteousness as the light, and thy judgment as the noonday.

7 Rest in the LORD, and wait patiently for him: fret not thyself because of him who prospereth in his way, because of the man who bringeth wicked devices to pass.

8 Cease from anger, and forsake wrath: fret not thyself in any wise to do evil.

9 For evildoers shall be cut off: but those that wait upon the LORD, they shall inherit the earth.

10 For yet a little while, and the wicked *shall* not *be:* yea, thou shalt diligently consider his place, and it *shall* not *be*.

11 But the meek shall inherit the earth; and shall delight themselves in the abundance of peace.

12 The wicked plotteth against the just, and gnasheth upon him with his teeth.

13 The LORD shall laugh at him: for he seeth that his day is coming.

14 The wicked have drawn out the sword, and have bent their bow, to cast down the poor and needy, *and* to slay such as be of upright conversation.

15 Their sword shall enter into their own heart, and their bows shall be broken.

16 A little that a righteous man hath *is* better than the riches of many wicked.

17 For the arms of the wicked shall be broken: but the LORD upholdeth the righteous.

18 The LORD knoweth the days of the upright: and their inheritance shall be for ever.

19 They shall not be ashamed in the evil time: and in the days of famine they shall be satisfied.

20 But the wicked shall perish, and the enemies of the LORD *shall be* as the fat of lambs: they shall consume; into smoke shall they consume away.

21 The wicked borroweth, and payeth not again: but the righteous showeth mercy, and giveth.

22 For *such as be* blessed of him shall inherit the earth; and *they that be* cursed of him shall be cut off.

23 The steps of a *good* man are ordered by the LORD: and he delighteth in his way.
24 Though he fall, he shall not be utterly cast down: for the LORD upholdeth *him with* his hand.
25 I have been young, and *now* am old; yet have I not seen the righteous forsaken, nor his seed begging bread.
26 *He is* ever merciful, and lendeth; and his seed *is* blessed.
27 Depart from evil, and do good; and dwell for evermore.
28 For the LORD loveth judgment, and forsaketh not his saints; they are preserved for ever: but the seed of the wicked shall be cut off.
29 The righteous shall inherit the land, and dwell therein for ever.
30 The mouth of the righteous speaketh wisdom, and his tongue talketh of judgment.
31 The law of his God *is* in his heart; none of his steps shall slide.
32 The wicked watcheth the righteous, and seeketh to slay him.
33 The LORD will not leave him in his hand, nor condemn him when he is judged.
34 Wait on the LORD, and keep his way, and he shall exalt thee to inherit the land: when the wicked are cut off, thou shalt see *it*.
35 I have seen the wicked in great power, and spreading himself like a green bay tree.
36 Yet he passed away, and, lo, he *was* not: yea, I sought him, but he could not be found.
37 Mark the perfect *man*, and behold the upright: for the end of *that* man *is* peace.
38 But the transgressors shall be destroyed together: the end of the wicked shall be cut off.
39 But the salvation of the righteous *is* of the LORD: *he is* their strength in the time of trouble.
40 And the LORD shall help them, and deliver them: he shall deliver them from the wicked, and save them, because they trust in him.

PSALM 38

A Psalm of David, to bring to remembrance.

O LORD, rebuke me not in thy wrath: neither chasten me in thy hot displeasure.
2 For thine arrows stick fast in me, and thy hand presseth me sore.
3 *There is* no soundness in my flesh because of thine anger; neither *is there any* rest in my bones because of my sin
4 For mine iniquities are gone over mine head: as a heavy burden they are too heavy for me.
5 My wounds stink *and* are corrupt because of my foolishness.
6 I am troubled; I am bowed down greatly; I go mourning all the day long.
7 For my loins are filled with a loathsome *disease:* and *there is* no soundness in my flesh.
8 I am feeble and sore broken: I have roared by reason of the disquietness of my heart.
9 Lord, all my desire *is* before thee; and my groaning is not hid from thee.
10 My heart panteth, my strength faileth me: as for the light of mine eyes, it also is gone from me.
11 My lovers and my friends stand aloof from my sore; and my kinsmen stand afar off.
12 They also that seek after my life lay snares *for me;* and they that seek my hurt speak mischievous things, and imagine deceits all the day long.
13 But I, as a deaf *man,* heard not; and *I was* as a dumb man *that* openeth not his mouth.
14 Thus I was as a man that heareth not, and in whose mouth *are* no reproofs.
15 For in thee, O LORD, do I hope: thou wilt hear, O Lord my God.
16 For I said, *Hear me,* lest *otherwise* they should rejoice over me: when my foot slippeth, they magnify *themselves* against me.
17 For I *am* ready to halt, and my sorrow *is* continually before me.
18 For I will declare mine iniquity; I will be sorry for my sin.
19 But mine enemies *are* lively, *and* they are strong: and they that hate me wrongfully are multiplied.
20 They also that render evil for good are mine adversaries; because I follow *the thing that* good *is*.
21 Forsake me not, O LORD: O my God, be not far from me.
22 Make haste to help me, O Lord my salvation.

PSALM 39

To the chief Musician, *even* to Jē-dū'thŭn, A Psalm of David.

I SAID, I will take heed to my ways, that I sin not with my tongue: I will keep my mouth with a bridle, while the wicked is before me.

2 I was dumb with silence, I held my peace, *even* from good; and my sorrow was stirred.

3 My heart was hot within me; while I was musing the fire burned: *then* spake I with my tongue,

4 LORD, make me to know mine end, and the measure of my days, what it *is; that* I may know how frail I *am*.

5 Behold, thou hast made my days *as* a handbreadth; and mine age *is* as nothing before thee: verily every man at his best state *is* altogether vanity. Sē'lȧh.

6 Surely every man walketh in a vain show: surely they are disquieted in vain: he heapeth up *riches*, and knoweth not who shall gather them.

7 And now, Lord, what wait I for? my hope *is* in thee.

8 Deliver me from all my transgressions: make me not the reproach of the foolish.

9 I was dumb, I opened not my mouth; because thou didst *it*.

10 Remove thy stroke away from me: I am consumed by the blow of thine hand.

11 When thou with rebukes dost correct man for iniquity, thou makest his beauty to consume away like a moth: surely every man *is* vanity. Sē'lȧh.

12 Hear my prayer, O LORD, and give ear unto my cry; hold not thy peace at my tears: for I *am* a stranger with thee, *and* a sojourner, as all my fathers *were*.

13 O spare me, that I may recover strength, before I go hence, and be no more.

PSALM 40

To the chief Musician, A Psalm of David.

I WAITED patiently for the LORD; and he inclined unto me, and heard my cry.

2 He brought me up also out of a horrible pit, out of the miry clay, and set my feet upon a rock, *and* established my goings.

3 And he hath put a new song in my mouth, *even* praise unto our God: many shall see *it*, and fear, and shall trust in the LORD.

4 Blessed *is* that man that maketh the LORD his trust, and respecteth not the proud, nor such as turn aside to lies.

5 Many, O LORD my God, *are* thy wonderful works *which* thou hast done, and thy thoughts *which are* to us-ward: they cannot be reckoned up in order unto thee: *if* I would declare and speak *of them*, they are more than can be numbered.

6 Sacrifice and offering thou didst not desire; mine ears hast thou opened: burnt offering and sin offering hast thou not required.

7 Then said I, Lo, I come: in the volume of the book *it is* written of me,

8 I delight to do thy will, O my God: yea, thy law *is* within my heart.

9 I have preached righteousness in the great congregation: lo, I have not refrained my lips, O LORD, thou knowest.

10 I have not hid thy righteousness within my heart; I have declared thy faithfulness and thy salvation: I have not concealed thy loving-kindness and thy truth from the great congregation.

11 Withhold not thou thy tender mercies from me, O LORD: let thy lovingkindness and thy truth continually preserve me.

12 For innumerable evils have compassed me about: mine iniquities have taken hold upon me, so that I am not able to look up; they are more than the hairs of mine head: therefore my heart faileth me.

13 Be pleased, O LORD, to deliver me: O LORD, make haste to help me.

14 Let them be ashamed and confounded together that seek after my soul to destroy it; let them be driven backward and put to shame that wish me evil.

15 Let them be desolate for a reward of their shame that say unto me, Aha, aha.

16 Let all those that seek thee rejoice and be glad in thee: let such as love thy salvation say continually, The LORD be magnified.

17 But I *am* poor and needy; *yet* the Lord thinketh upon me: thou *art* my help and my deliverer; make no tarrying, O my God.

PSALM 41

To the chief Musician, A Psalm of David.

BLESSED *is* he that considereth the poor: the LORD will deliver him in time of trouble.

2 The LORD will preserve him, and keep him alive; *and* he shall be blessed upon the earth: and thou wilt not deliver him unto the will of his enemies.

3 The LORD will strengthen him upon the bed of languishing: thou wilt make all his bed in his sickness.

4 I said, LORD, be merciful unto me: heal my soul; for I have sinned against thee.

5 Mine enemies speak evil of me, When shall he die, and his name perish?

6 And if he come to see *me,* he speaketh vanity: his heart gathereth iniquity to itself; *when* he goeth abroad, he telleth *it.*

7 All that hate me whisper together against me: against me do they devise my hurt.

8 An evil disease, *say they,* cleaveth fast unto him: and *now* that he lieth he shall rise up no more.

9 Yea, minc own familiar friend, in whom I trusted, which did eat of my bread, hath lifted up *his* heel against me.

10 But thou, O LORD, be merciful unto me, and raise me up, that I may requite them.

11 By this I know that thou favorest me, because mine enemy doth not triumph over me.

12 And as for me, thou upholdest me in mine integrity, and settest me before thy face for ever.

13 Blessed *be* the LORD God of Ĭṣ′rā-ĕl from everlasting, and to everlasting. Amen, and Amen.

PSALM 42

To the chief Musician, Măs′chĭl, for the sons of Kō′răh.

AS the hart panteth after the water brooks, so panteth my soul after thee, O God.

2 My soul thirsteth for God, for the living God: when shall I come and appear before God?

3 My tears have been my meat day and night, while they continually say unto me, Where *is* thy God?

4 When I remember these *things,* I pour out my soul in me: for I had gone with the multitude, I went with them to the house of God, with the voice of joy and praise, with a multitude that kept holyday.

5 Why art thou cast down, O my soul? and *why* art thou disquieted in me? hope thou in God: for I shall yet praise him *for* the help of his countenance.

6 O my God, my soul is cast down within me: therefore will I remember thee from the land of Jordan, and of the Hermonites, from the hill Mī′zär.

7 Deep calleth unto deep at the noise of thy waterspouts: all thy waves and thy billows are gone over me.

8 *Yet* the LORD will command his loving-kindness in the daytime, and in the night his song *shall be* with me, *and* my prayer unto the God of my life.

9 I will say unto God my rock, Why hast thou forgotten me? why go I mourning because of the oppression of the enemy?

10 *As* with a sword in my bones, mine enemies reproach me; while they say daily unto me, Where *is* thy God?

11 Why art thou cast down, O my soul? and why art thou disquieted within me? hope thou in God: for I shall yet praise him, *who is* the health of my countenance, and my God.

PSALM 43

JUDGE me, O God, and plead my cause against an ungodly nation: O deliver me from the deceitful and unjust man.

2 For thou *art* the God of my strength: why dost thou cast me off? why go I mourning because of the oppression of the enemy?

3 O send out thy light and thy truth: let them lead me; let them bring me unto thy holy hill, and to thy tabernacles.

4 Then will I go unto the altar of God, unto God my exceeding joy: yea, upon the harp will I praise thee, O God my God.

5 Why art thou cast down, O my soul? and why art thou disquieted within me? hope in God: for I shall yet praise him, *who is* the health of my countenance, and my God.

PSALM 44

To the chief Musician for the sons of Kō′răh, Măs′chĭl.

WE have heard with our ears, O God, our fathers have told us, *what* work thou didst in their days, in the times of old.

2 *How* thou didst drive out the heathen with thy hand, and plantedst them; *how* thou didst afflict the people, and cast them out.

3 For they got not the land in possession
by their own sword, neither did their
own arm save them: but thy right hand,
and thine arm, and the light of thy countenance, because thou hadst a favor
unto them.
4 Thou art my King, O God: command
deliverances for Jacob.
5 Through thee will we push down
our enemies: through thy name will
we tread them under that rise up
against us.
6 For I will not trust in my bow, neither
shall my sword save me.
7 But thou hast saved us from our enemies, and hast put them to shame that
hated us.
8 In God we boast all the day long, and
praise thy name for ever. Sē'lȧh.
9 But thou hast cast off, and put us to
shame; and goest not forth with our
armies.
10 Thou makest us to turn back from
the enemy: and they which hate us
spoil for themselves.
11 Thou hast given us like sheep *appointed* for meat; and hast scattered us
among the heathen.
12 Thou sellest thy people for nought,
and dost not increase *thy wealth* by
their price.
13 Thou makest us a reproach to our
neighbors, a scorn and a derision to
them that are round about us.
14 Thou makest us a byword among
the heathen, a shaking of the head
among the people.
15 My confusion *is* continually before
me, and the shame of my face hath covered me,
16 For the voice of him that reproacheth and blasphemeth; by reason of the
enemy and avenger.
17 All this is come upon us; yet have
we not forgotten thee, neither have we
dealt falsely in thy covenant.
18 Our heart is not turned back, neither have our steps declined from thy
way;
19 Though thou hast sore broken us in
the place of dragons, and covered us
with the shadow of death.
20 If we have forgotten the name of
our God, or stretched out our hands to a
strange god;
21 Shall not God search this out? for he
knoweth the secrets of the heart.
22 Yea, for thy sake are we killed all
the day long; we are counted as sheep
for the slaughter.
23 Awake, why sleepest thou, O Lord?
arise, cast *us* not off for ever.
24 Wherefore hidest thou thy face, *and*
forgettest our affliction and our oppression?
25 For our soul is bowed down to the
dust: our belly cleaveth unto the earth.
26 Arise for our help, and redeem us
for thy mercies' sake.

PSALM 45

To the chief Musician upon Shō-shăn'nĭm, for the sons of Kō'rȧh, Măs'chĭl. A Song of loves.

MY heart is inditing a good matter:
I speak of the things which I have
made touching the King: my tongue *is*
the pen of a ready writer.
2 Thou art fairer than the children of
men: grace is poured into thy lips: therefore God hath blessed thee for ever.
3 Gird thy sword upon *thy* thigh, O
most Mighty, with thy glory and thy
majesty.
4 And in thy majesty ride prosperously,
because of truth and meekness *and*
righteousness; and thy right hand shall
teach thee terrible things.
5 Thine arrows *are* sharp in the heart
of the King's enemies; *whereby* the
people fall under thee.
6 Thy throne, O God, *is* for ever and
ever: the sceptre of thy kingdom *is* a
right sceptre.
7 Thou lovest righteousness, and hatest wickedness: therefore God, thy God,
hath anointed thee with the oil of gladness above thy fellows.
8 All thy garments *smell* of myrrh, and
aloes, *and* cassia, out of the ivory palaces, whereby they have made thee glad.
9 Kings' daughters *were* among thy
honorable women: upon thy right hand
did stand the queen in gold of Ō'phĭr.
10 Hearken, O daughter, and consider,
and incline thine ear; forget also thine
own people, and thy father's house;
11 So shall the King greatly desire thy
beauty: for he *is* thy Lord; and worship
thou him.
12 And the daughter of Tȳre *shall be*
there with a gift; *even* the rich among
the people shall entreat thy favor.
13 The King's daughter *is* all glorious
within: her clothing *is* of wrought gold.
14 She shall be brought unto the King
in raiment of needlework: the virgins

her companions that follow her shall be
brought unto thee.
15 With gladness and rejoicing shall
they be brought: they shall enter into
the King's palace.
16 Instead of thy fathers shall be thy
children, whom thou mayest make
princes in all the earth.
17 I will make thy name to be remembered in all generations: therefore
shall the people praise thee for ever
and ever.

PSALM 46

To the chief Musician for the sons of Kō'rah, A Song upon Ăl'ă-mōth.

GOD *is* our refuge and strength, a
very present help in trouble.
2 Therefore will not we fear, though
the earth be removed, and though the
mountains be carried into the midst of
the sea;
3 *Though* the waters thereof roar *and*
be troubled, *though* the mountains
shake with the swelling thereof. Sē'lah.
4 *There is* a river, the streams whereof
shall make glad the city of God, the holy
place of the tabernacles of the Most
High.
5 God *is* in the midst of her; she shall
not be moved: God shall help her, *and*
that right early.
6 The heathen raged, the kingdoms
were moved: he uttered his voice, the
earth melted.
7 The LORD of hosts *is* with us; the
God of Jacob *is* our refuge. Sē'lah.
8 Come, behold the works of the LORD,
what desolations he hath made in the
earth.
9 He maketh wars to cease unto the
end of the earth; he breaketh the bow,
and cutteth the spear in sunder; he
burneth the chariot in the fire.
10 Be still, and know that I *am* God: I
will be exalted among the heathen, I
will be exalted in the earth.
11 The LORD of hosts *is* with us; the
God of Jacob *is* our refuge. Sē'lah.

PSALM 47

To the chief Musician, A Psalm for the sons of Kō'rah.

O CLAP your hands, all ye people;
shout unto God with the voice of
triumph.
2 For the LORD most high *is* terrible;
he is a great King over all the earth.
3 He shall subdue the people under us,
and the nations under our feet.
4 He shall choose our inheritance for
us, the excellency of Jacob whom he
loved. Se'lah.
5 God is gone up with a shout, the
LORD with the sound of a trumpet.
6 Sing praises to God, sing praises:
sing praises unto our King, sing praises.
7 For God *is* the King of all the earth:
sing ye praises with understanding.
8 God reigneth over the heathen:
God sitteth upon the throne of his
holiness.
9 The princes of the people are gathered together, *even* the people of the
God of Abraham: for the shields of the
earth *belong* unto God: he is greatly
exalted.

PSALM 48

A Song *and* Psalm for the sons of Kō'rah.

GREAT *is* the LORD, and greatly to
be praised in the city of our God,
in the mountain of his holiness.
2 Beautiful for situation, the joy of the
whole earth, *is* mount Zion, *on* the sides
of the north, the city of the great King.
3 God is known in her palaces for a
refuge.
4 For, lo, the kings were assembled,
they passed by together.
5 They saw *it, and* so they marveled;
they were troubled, *and* hasted away.
6 Fear took hold upon them there, *and*
pain, as of a woman in travail.
7 Thou breakest the ships of Tär'shish
with an east wind.
8 As we have heard, so have we seen in
the city of the LORD of hosts, in the city
of our God: God will establish it for
ever. Sē'lah.
9 We have thought of thy loving-kindness, O God, in the midst of thy temple.
10 According to thy name, O God, so
is thy praise unto the ends of the earth:
thy right hand is full of righteousness.
11 Let mount Zion rejoice, let the
daughters of Judah be glad, because of
thy judgments.
12 Walk about Zion, and go round
about her: tell the towers thereof.
13 Mark ye well her bulwarks, consider her palaces; that ye may tell *it* to
the generation following.
14 For this God *is* our God for ever and
ever: he will be our guide *even* unto
death.

PSALM 49

To the chief Musician, A Psalm for the sons of
Kō'răh.

HEAR this, all *ye* people; give ear,
all *ye* inhabitants of the world:
2 Both low and high, rich and poor,
together.
3 My mouth shall speak of wisdom;
and the meditation of my heart *shall be*
of understanding.
4 I will incline mine ear to a parable:
I will open my dark saying upon the harp.
5 Wherefore should I fear in the days
of evil, *when* the iniquity of my heels
shall compass me about?
6 They that trust in their wealth, and
boast themselves in the multitude of
their riches;
7 None *of them* can by any means
redeem his brother, nor give to God a
ransom for him:
8 (For the redemption of their soul *is*
precious, and it ceaseth for ever:)
9 That he should still live for ever, *and*
not see corruption.
10 For he seeth *that* wise men die, likewise the fool and the brutish person perish, and leave their wealth to others.
11 Their inward thought *is, that* their
houses *shall continue* for ever, *and* their
dwelling places to all generations; they
call *their* lands after their own names.
12 Nevertheless man *being* in honor
abideth not: he is like the beasts *that*
perish.
13 This their way *is* their folly: yet their
posterity approve their sayings. Sē'lăh.
14 Like sheep they are laid in the grave;
death shall feed on them; and the upright shall have dominion over them in
the morning; and their beauty shall consume in the grave from their dwelling.
15 But God will redeem my soul from
the power of the grave: for he shall receive me. Sē'lăh.
16 Be not thou afraid when one is made
rich, when the glory of his house is increased;
17 For when he dieth he shall carry
nothing away: his glory shall not descend after him.
18 Though while he lived he blessed
his soul, (and *men* will praise thee, when
thou doest well to thyself,)
19 He shall go to the generation of his
fathers; they shall never see light.
20 Man *that is* in honor, and understandeth not, is like the beasts *that*
perish.

PSALM 50

A Psalm of Ā'săph.

THE mighty God, *even* the LORD,
hath spoken, and called the earth
from the rising of the sun unto the going
down thereof.
2 Out of Zion, the perfection of beauty,
God hath shined.
3 Our God shall come, and shall not
keep silence: a fire shall devour before
him, and it shall be very tempestuous
round about him.
4 He shall call to the heavens from
above, and to the earth, that he may
judge his people.
5 Gather my saints together unto me;
those that have made a covenant with
me by sacrifice.
6 And the heavens shall declare his
righteousness: for God *is* judge himself.
Sē'lăh.
7 Hear, O my people, and I will speak;
O Ĭṣ'rā-ĕl, and I will testify against thee:
I *am* God, *even* thy God.
8 I will not reprove thee for thy sacrifices or thy burnt offerings, *to have been*
continually before me.
9 I will take no bullock out of thy
house, *nor* he goats out of thy folds:
10 For every beast of the forest *is* mine,
and the cattle upon a thousand hills.
11 I know all the fowls of the mountains: and the wild beasts of the field
are mine.
12 If I were hungry, I would not tell
thee: for the world *is* mine, and the fulness thereof.
13 Will I eat the flesh of bulls, or drink
the blood of goats?
14 Offer unto God thanksgiving; and
pay thy vows unto the Most High:
15 And call upon me in the day of
trouble: I will deliver thee, and thou
shalt glorify me.
16 But unto the wicked God saith,
What hast thou to do to declare my statutes, or *that* thou shouldest take my
covenant in thy mouth?
17 Seeing thou hatest instruction, and
castest my words behind thee.
18 When thou sawest a thief, then
thou consentedst with him, and hast
been partaker with adulterers.
19 Thou givest thy mouth to evil, and
thy tongue frameth deceit.

20 Thou sittest *and* speakest against thy brother; thou slanderest thine own mother's son.

21 These *things* hast thou done, and I kept silence; thou thoughtest that I was altogether *such a one* as thyself: *but* I will reprove thee, and set *them* in order before thine eyes.

22 Now consider this, ye that forget God, lest I tear *you* in pieces, and *there be* none to deliver.

23 Whoso offereth praise glorifieth me: and to him that ordereth *his* conversation *aright* will I show the salvation of God.

PSALM 51

To the chief Musician, A Psalm of David, when Nathan the prophet came unto him, after he had gone in to Băth'-shē'bȧ.

HAVE mercy upon me, O God, according to thy loving-kindness: according unto the multitude of thy tender mercies blot out my transgressions.

2 Wash me thoroughly from mine iniquity, and cleanse me from my sin.

3 For I acknowledge my transgressions: and my sin *is* ever before me.

4 Against thee, thee only, have I sinned, and done *this* evil in thy sight: that thou mightest be justified when thou speakest, *and* be clear when thou judgest.

5 Behold, I was shapen in iniquity; and in sin did my mother conceive me.

6 Behold, thou desirest truth in the inward parts: and in the hidden *part* thou shalt make me to know wisdom.

7 Purge me with hyssop, and I shall be clean: wash me, and I shall be whiter than snow.

8 Make me to hear joy and gladness; *that* the bones *which* thou hast broken may rejoice.

9 Hide thy face from my sins, and blot out all mine iniquities.

10 Create in me a clean heart, O God; and renew a right spirit within me.

11 Cast me not away from thy presence; and take not thy Holy Spirit from me.

12 Restore unto me the joy of thy salvation; and uphold me *with thy* free Spirit.

13 *Then* will I teach transgressors thy ways; and sinners shall be converted unto thee.

14 Deliver me from bloodguiltiness, O God, thou God of my salvation: *and* my tongue shall sing aloud of thy righteousness.

15 O Lord, open thou my lips; and my mouth shall show forth thy praise.

16 For thou desirest not sacrifice; else would I give *it:* thou delightest not in burnt offering.

17 The sacrifices of God *are* a broken spirit: a broken and a contrite heart, O God, thou wilt not despise.

18 Do good in thy good pleasure unto Zion: build thou the walls of Jerusalem.

19 Then shalt thou be pleased with the sacrifices of righteousness, with burnt offering and whole burnt offering: then shall they offer bullocks upon thine altar.

PSALM 52

To the chief Musician, Măs'chĭl, *A Psalm* of David, when Dō'ĕg the Ē'dŏm-īte came and told Saul, and said unto him, David is come to the house of Ă-hĭm'ē-lĕch.

WHY boastest thou thyself in mischief, O mighty man? the goodness of God *endureth* continually.

2 Thy tongue deviseth mischiefs; like a sharp razor, working deceitfully.

3 Thou lovest evil more than good; *and* lying rather than to speak righteousness. Sē'lȧh.

4 Thou lovest all devouring words, O *thou* deceitful tongue.

5 God shall likewise destroy thee for ever, he shall take thee away, and pluck thee out of *thy* dwelling place, and root thee out of the land of the living. Sē'lȧh.

6 The righteous also shall see, and fear, and shall laugh at him:

7 Lo, *this is* the man *that* made not God his strength; but trusted in the abundance of his riches, *and* strengthened himself in his wickedness.

8 But I *am* like a green olive tree in the house of God: I trust in the mercy of God for ever and ever.

9 I will praise thee for ever, because thou hast done *it:* and I will wait on thy name; for *it is* good before thy saints.

PSALM 53

To the chief Musician upon Mā'hȧ-lăth, Măs'chĭl, *A Psalm* of David.

THE fool hath said in his heart, *There is* no God. Corrupt are they, and have done abominable iniquity: *there is* none that doeth good.

2 God looked down from heaven upon the children of men, to see if there were *any* that did understand, that did seek God.

3 Every one of them is gone back: they are altogether become filthy; *there is* none that doeth good, no, not one.

4 Have the workers of iniquity no knowledge? who eat up my people *as* they eat bread: they have not called upon God.

5 There were they in great fear, *where* no fear was: for God hath scattered the bones of him that encampeth *against* thee: thou hast put *them* to shame, because God hath despised them.

6 Oh that the salvation of Ĭṣ'rā-ĕl *were come* out of Zion! When God bringeth back the captivity of his people, Jacob shall rejoice, *and* Ĭṣ'rā-ĕl shall be glad.

PSALM 54

To the chief Musician on Nĕg'ĭ-nōth, Măs'chĭl, *A Psalm* of David, when the Ziph'ĭm came and said to Saul, Doth not David hide himself with us?

SAVE me, O God, by thy name, and judge me by thy strength.

2 Hear my prayer, O God; give ear to the words of my mouth.

3 For strangers are risen up against me, and oppressors seek after my soul: they have not set God before them. Sē'lȧh.

4 Behold, God *is* mine helper: the Lord *is* with them that uphold my soul.

5 He shall reward evil unto mine enemies: cut them off in thy truth.

6 I will freely sacrifice unto thee: I will praise thy name, O LORD; for *it is* good.

7 For he hath delivered me out of all trouble: and mine eye hath seen *his desire* upon mine enemies.

PSALM 55

To the chief Musician on Nĕg'ĭ-nōth, Măs'chĭl, *A Psalm* of David.

GIVE ear to my prayer, O God; and hide not thyself from my supplication.

2 Attend unto me, and hear me: I mourn in my complaint, and make a noise;

3 Because of the voice of the enemy, because of the oppression of the wicked: for they cast iniquity upon me, and in wrath they hate me.

4 My heart is sore pained within me: and the terrors of death are fallen upon me.

5 Fearfulness and trembling are come upon me, and horror hath overwhelmed me.

6 And I said, Oh that I had wings like a dove! *for then* would I fly away, and be at rest.

7 Lo, *then* would I wander far off, *and* remain in the wilderness. Sē'lȧh.

8 I would hasten my escape from the windy storm *and* tempest.

9 Destroy, O Lord, *and* divide their tongues: for I have seen violence and strife in the city.

10 Day and night they go about it upon the walls thereof: mischief also and sorrow *are* in the midst of it.

11 Wickedness *is* in the midst thereof: deceit and guile depart not from her streets.

12 For *it was* not an enemy *that* reproached me; then I could have borne *it:* neither *was it* he that hated me *that* did magnify *himself* against me; then I would have hid myself from him:

13 But *it was* thou, a man mine equal, my guide, and mine acquaintance.

14 We took sweet counsel together, *and* walked unto the house of God in company.

15 Let death seize upon them, *and* let them go down quick into hell: for wickedness *is* in their dwellings, *and* among them.

16 As for me, I will call upon God; and the LORD shall save me.

17 Evening, and morning, and at noon, will I pray, and cry aloud: and he shall hear my voice.

18 He hath delivered my soul in peace from the battle *that was* against me: for there were many with me.

19 God shall hear, and afflict them, even he that abideth of old. Sē'lȧh. Because they have no changes, therefore they fear not God.

20 He hath put forth his hands against such as be at peace with him: he hath broken his covenant.

21 *The words* of his mouth were smoother than butter, but war *was* in his heart: his words were softer than oil, yet *were* they drawn swords.

22 Cast thy burden upon the LORD, and he shall sustain thee: he shall never suffer the righteous to be moved.

23 But thou, O God, shalt bring them down into the pit of destruction: bloody and deceitful men shall not live out half their days; but I will trust in thee.

PSALM 56

To the chief Musician upon Jō'năth-ē'lĕm-rē-chō'kīm, Mĭch'tăm of David, when the Phi-lis'tines took him in Gath.

BE merciful unto me, O God: for man
would swallow me up; he fighting
daily oppresseth me.
2 Mine enemies would daily swallow
me up: for *they be* many that fight
against me, O thou Most High.
3 What time I am afraid, I will trust in
thee.
4 In God I will praise his word, in God
I have put my trust; I will not fear what
flesh can do unto me.
5 Every day they wrest my words: all
their thoughts *are* against me for evil.
6 They gather themselves together,
they hide themselves, they mark my
steps, when they wait for my soul.
7 Shall they escape by iniquity? in
thine anger cast down the people, O God.
8 Thou tellest my wanderings: put thou
my tears into thy bottle: *are they* not in
thy book?
9 When I cry *unto thee,* then shall
mine enemies turn back: this I know;
for God *is* for me.
10 In God will I praise *his* word: in the
LORD will I praise *his* word.
11 In God have I put my trust: I will
not be afraid what man can do unto me.
12 Thy vows *are* upon me, O God: I
will render praises unto thee.
13 For thou hast delivered my soul from
death: *wilt* not *thou deliver* my feet from
falling, that I may walk before God in
the light of the living?

PSALM 57

To the chief Musician, Ăl-tăs'chīth, Mĭch'tăm of David, when he fled from Saul in the cave.

BE merciful unto me, O God, be
merciful unto me: for my soul trusteth in thee: yea, in the shadow of thy
wings will I make my refuge, until *these*
calamities be overpast.
2 I will cry unto God most high; unto
God that performeth *all things* for me.
3 He shall send from heaven, and save
me *from* the reproach of him that would
swallow me up. Sē'lăh. God shall send
forth his mercy and his truth.
4 My soul *is* among lions: *and* I lie
even among them that are set on fire,
even the sons of men, whose teeth *are*
spears and arrows, and their tongue a
sharp sword.
5 Be thou exalted, O God, above the
heavens; *let* thy glory *be* above all the
earth.
6 They have prepared a net for my
steps; my soul is bowed down: they
have digged a pit before me, into the
midst whereof they are fallen *themselves.* Sē'lăh.
7 My heart is fixed, O God, my heart
is fixed: I will sing and give praise.
8 Awake up, my glory; awake, psaltery
and harp: I *myself* will awake early.
9 I will praise thee, O Lord among the
people: I will sing unto thee among the
nations.
10 For thy mercy *is* great unto the
heavens, and thy truth unto the clouds.
11 Be thou exalted, O God, above the
heavens: *let* thy glory *be* above all the
earth.

PSALM 58

To the chief Musician, Ăl-tăs'chīth, Mĭch'tăm of David.

DO ye indeed speak righteousness,
O congregation? do ye judge uprightly, O ye sons of men?
2 Yea, in heart ye work wickedness; ye
weigh the violence of your hands in the
earth.
3 The wicked are estranged from the
womb: they go astray as soon as they be
born, speaking lies.
4 Their poison *is* like the poison of a
serpent: *they are* like the deaf adder
that stoppeth her ear;
5 Which will not hearken to the voice
of charmers, charming never so wisely.
6 Break their teeth, O God, in their
mouth: break out the great teeth of the
young lions, O LORD.
7 Let them melt away as waters *which*
run continually: *when* he bendeth *his
bow to shoot* his arrows, let them be as
cut in pieces.
8 As a snail *which* melteth, let *every
one of them* pass away: *like* the untimely
birth of a woman, *that* they may not see
the sun.
9 Before your pots can feel the thorns,
he shall take them away as with a whirlwind, both living, and in *his* wrath.
10 The righteous shall rejoice when he
seeth the vengeance: he shall wash his
feet in the blood of the wicked.
11 So that a man shall say, Verily *there
is* a reward for the righteous: verily he
is a God that judgeth in the earth.

PSALM 59

To the chief Musician, Ăl-tăs'chĭth, Mĭch'tăm of
David; when Saul sent, and they watched the
house to kill him.

DELIVER me from mine enemies,
O my God: defend me from them
that rise up against me.
2 Deliver me from the workers of iniquity, and save me from bloody men.
3 For, lo, they lie in wait for my soul:
the mighty are gathered against me; not
for my transgression, nor *for* my sin,
O LORD.
4 They run and prepare themselves
without *my* fault: awake to help me, and
behold.
5 Thou therefore, O LORD God of hosts,
the God of Ĭs'rā-ĕl, awake to visit all the
heathen: be not merciful to any wicked
transgressors. Sē'lȧh.
6 They return at evening: they make a
noise like a dog, and go round about the
city.
7 Behold, they belch out with their
mouth: swords *are* in their lips: for who,
say they, doth hear?
8 But thou, O LORD, shalt laugh at
them; thou shalt have all the heathen in
derision.
9 *Because of* his strength will I wait
upon thee: for God *is* my defense.
10 The God of my mercy shall prevent
me: God shall let me see *my desire* upon
mine enemies.
11 Slay them not, lest my people forget: scatter them by thy power; and
bring them down, O Lord our shield.
12 *For* the sin of their mouth *and* the
words of their lips let them even be
taken in their pride: and for cursing and
lying *which* they speak.
13 Consume *them* in wrath, consume
them, that they *may* not *be*: and let
them know that God ruleth in Jacob
unto the ends of the earth. Sē'lȧh.
14 And at evening let them return; *and*
let them make a noise like a dog, and go
round about the city.
15 Let them wander up and down for
meat, and grudge if they be not satisfied.
16 But I will sing of thy power; yea, I
will sing aloud of thy mercy in the morning: for thou hast been my defense and
refuge in the day of my trouble.
17 Unto thee, O my strength, will I
sing: for God *is* my defense, *and* the
God of my mercy.

PSALM 60

To the chief Musician upon Shụ'shăn-ē'dŭth,
Mĭch'tăm of David, to teach; when he strove
with Ā'răm-nă'hȧ-rā'ĭm and with Ā'răm-zō-
bȧh, when Jō'ăb returned, and smote of Ē'dŏm
in the valley of salt twelve thousand.

O GOD, thou hast cast us off, thou
hast scattered us, thou hast been
displeased; O turn thyself to us again.
2 Thou hast made the earth to tremble;
thou hast broken it: heal the breaches
thereof; for it shaketh.
3 Thou hast showed thy people hard
things: thou hast made us to drink the
wine of astonishment.
4 Thou hast given a banner to them
that fear thee, that it may be displayed
because of the truth. Sē'lȧh.
5 That thy beloved may be delivered;
save *with* thy right hand, and hear me.
6 God hath spoken in his holiness; I
will rejoice, I will divide Shē'chĕm, and
mete out the valley of Sŭc'cŏth.
7 Gĭl'ē-ăd *is* mine, and Mȧ-năs'sĕh *is*
mine; Ē'phrā-ĭm also *is* the strength of
mine head; Judah *is* my lawgiver;
8 Mō'ăb *is* my washpot; over Ē'dŏm
will I cast out my shoe: Phĭ-lĭs'tĭ-ȧ, triumph thou because of me.
9 Who will bring me *into* the strong
city? who will lead me into Ē'dŏm?
10 *Wilt* not thou, O God, *which* hadst
cast us off? and *thou,* O God, *which*
didst not go out with our armies?
11 Give us help from trouble: for vain
is the help of man.
12 Through God we shall do valiantly:
for he *it is that* shall tread down our
enemies.

PSALM 61

To the chief Musician upon Nĕg'ĭ-năh, *A Psalm* of
David.

HEAR my cry, O God; attend unto
my prayer.
2 From the end of the earth will I cry
unto thee, when my heart is overwhelmed: lead me to the rock *that* is
higher than I.
3 For thou hast been a shelter for me,
and a strong tower from the enemy.
4 I will abide in thy tabernacle for
ever: I will trust in the covert of thy
wings. Sē'lȧh.
5 For thou, O God, hast heard my
vows: thou hast given *me* the heritage
of those that fear thy name.
6 Thou wilt prolong the king's life: *and*
his years as many generations.

7 He shall abide before God for ever:
O prepare mercy and truth, *which* may
preserve him.
8 So will I sing praise unto thy name
for ever, that I may daily perform my
vows.

PSALM 62

To the chief Musician, to Jē-dū'thŭn, A Psalm of David.

TRULY my soul waiteth upon God:
from him *cometh* my salvation.
2 He only *is* my rock and my salvation;
he is my defense; I shall not be greatly
moved.
3 How long will ye imagine mischief
against a man? ye shall be slain all of
you: as a bowing wall *shall ye be, and as*
a tottering fence.
4 They only consult to cast *him* down
from his excellency: they delight in lies:
they bless with their mouth, but they
curse inwardly. Sē'lăh.
5 My soul, wait thou only upon God;
for my expectation *is* from him.
6 He only *is* my rock and my salvation: *he is* my defense; I shall not be
moved.
7 In God *is* my salvation and my glory:
the rock of my strength, *and* my refuge,
is in God.
8 Trust in him at all times; ye people,
pour out your heart before him: God *is*
a refuge for us. Sē'lăh.
9 Surely men of low degree *are* vanity,
and men of high degree *are* a lie: to be
laid in the balance, they *are* altogether
lighter than vanity.
10 Trust not in oppression, and become not vain in robbery: if riches
increase, set not your heart *upon them.*
11 God hath spoken once; twice have
I heard this; that power *belongeth* unto
God.
12 Also unto thee, O Lord, *belongeth*
mercy: for thou renderest to every man
according to his work.

PSALM 63

A Psalm of David, when he was in the wilderness of Judah.

O GOD, thou *art* my God; early
will I seek thee: my soul thirsteth
for thee, my flesh longeth for thee
in a dry and thirsty land, where no
water is;
2 To see thy power and thy glory, so *as*
I have seen thee in the sanctuary.
3 Because thy loving-kindness *is* better
than life, my lips shall praise thee.
4 Thus will I bless thee while I live: I
will lift up my hands in thy name.
5 My soul shall be satisfied as *with*
marrow and fatness; and my mouth
shall praise *thee* with joyful lips:
6 When I remember thee upon my bed,
and meditate on thee in the *night*
watches.
7 Because thou hast been my help,
therefore in the shadow of thy wings will
I rejoice.
8 My soul followeth hard after thee:
thy right hand upholdeth me.
9 But those *that* seek my soul, to destroy *it,* shall go into the lower parts of
the earth.
10 They shall fall by the sword: they
shall be a portion for foxes.
11 But the king shall rejoice in God;
every one that sweareth by him shall
glory: but the mouth of them that speak
lies shall be stopped.

PSALM 64

To the chief Musician, A Psalm of David.

HEAR my voice, O God, in my
prayer: preserve my life from fear
of the enemy.
2 Hide me from the secret counsel of
the wicked; from the insurrection of the
workers of iniquity:
3 Who whet their tongue like a sword,
and bend *their bows to shoot* their arrows, *even* bitter words:
4 That they may shoot in secret at the
perfect: suddenly do they shoot at him,
and fear not.
5 They encourage themselves *in* an
evil matter: they commune of laying
snares privily; they say, Who shall see
them?
6 They search out iniquities; they accomplish a diligent search: both the inward *thought* of every one *of them,* and
the heart, *is* deep.
7 But God shall shoot at them *with* an
arrow; suddenly shall they be wounded.
8 So they shall make their own tongue
to fall upon themselves: all that see
them shall flee away.
9 And all men shall fear, and shall declare the work of God; for they shall
wisely consider of his doing.
10 The righteous shall be glad in the
LORD, and shall trust in him; and all
the upright in heart shall glory.

PSALM 65

To the chief Musician, A Psalm *and* Song of David.

PRAISE waiteth for thee, O God, in Zion: and unto thee shall the vow be performed.
2 O thou that hearest prayer, unto thee shall all flesh come.
3 Iniquities prevail against me: *as for* our transgressions, thou shalt purge them away.
4 Blessed *is the man whom* thou choosest, and causest to approach *unto thee, that* he may dwell in thy courts: we shall be satisfied with the goodness of thy house, *even* of thy holy temple.
5 *By* terrible things in righteousness wilt thou answer us, O God of our salvation; *who art* the confidence of all the ends of the earth, and of them that are afar off *upon* the sea:
6 Which by his strength setteth fast the mountains: *being* girded with power:
7 Which stilleth the noise of the seas, the noise of their waves, and the tumult of the people.
8 They also that dwell in the uttermost parts are afraid at thy tokens: thou makest the outgoings of the morning and evening to rejoice.
9 Thou visitest the earth, and waterest it: thou greatly enrichest it with the river of God, *which* is full of water: thou preparest them corn, when thou hast so provided for it.
10 Thou waterest the ridges thereof abundantly: thou settlest the furrows thereof: thou makest it soft with showers: thou blessest the springing thereof.
11 Thou crownest the year with thy goodness; and thy paths drop fatness.
12 They drop *upon* the pastures of the wilderness: and the little hills rejoice on every side.
13 The pastures are clothed with flocks; the valleys also are covered over with corn; they shout for joy, they also sing.

PSALM 66

To the chief Musician, a Song *or* Psalm.

MAKE a joyful noise unto God, all ye lands:
2 Sing forth the honor of his name: make his praise glorious.
3 Say unto God, How terrible *art thou in* thy works! through the greatness of thy power shall thine enemies submit themselves unto thee.
4 All the earth shall worship thee, and shall sing unto thee; they shall sing *to* thy name. Sē'lȧh.
5 Come and see the works of God: *he is* terrible *in his* doing toward the children of men.
6 He turned the sea into dry *land:* they went through the flood on foot: there did we rejoice in him.
7 He ruleth by his power for ever; his eyes behold the nations: let not the rebellious exalt themselves. Sē'lȧh.
8 O bless our God, ye people, and make the voice of his praise to be heard:
9 Which holdeth our soul in life, and suffereth not our feet to be moved.
10 For thou, O God, hast proved us: thou hast tried us, as silver is tried.
11 Thou broughtest us into the net; thou laidst affliction upon our loins.
12 Thou hast caused men to ride over our heads; we went through fire and through water: but thou broughtest us out into a wealthy *place.*
13 I will go into thy house with burnt offerings: I will pay thee my vows,
14 Which my lips have uttered, and my mouth hath spoken, when I was in trouble.
15 I will offer unto thee burnt sacrifices of fatlings, with the incense of rams: I will offer bullocks with goats. Sē'lȧh.
16 Come *and* hear, all ye that fear God, and I will declare what he hath done for my soul.
17 I cried unto him with my mouth, and he was extolled with my tongue.
18 If I regard iniquity in my heart, the Lord will not hear *me:*
19 *But* verily God hath heard *me;* he hath attended to the voice of my prayer.
20 Blessed *be* God, which hath not turned away my prayer, nor his mercy from me.

PSALM 67

To the chief Musician on Nĕg'ĭ-nŏth, A Psalm *or* Song.

GOD be merciful unto us, and bless us; *and* cause his face to shine upon us; Sē'lȧh.
2 That thy way may be known upon earth, thy saving health among all nations.
3 Let the people praise thee, O God; let all the people praise thee.
4 O let the nations be glad and sing for joy: for thou shalt judge the people

righteously, and govern the nations
upon earth. Sē'lăh.
5 Let the people praise thee, O God;
let all the people praise thee.
6 *Then* shall the earth yield her increase; *and* God, *even* our own God,
shall bless us.
7 God shall bless us; and all the ends
of the earth shall fear him.

PSALM 68

To the chief Musician, A Psalm *or* Song of David.

LET God arise, let his enemies be
scattered: let them also that hate
him flee before him.
2 As smoke is driven away, *so* drive
them away: as wax melteth before the
fire, *so* let the wicked perish at the presence of God.
3 But let the righteous be glad; let
them rejoice before God: yea, let them
exceedingly rejoice.
4 Sing unto God, sing praises to his
name: extol him that rideth upon the
heavens by his name JAH, and rejoice
before him.
5 A father of the fatherless, and a
judge of the widows, *is* God in his holy
habitation.
6 God setteth the solitary in families:
he bringeth out those which are bound
with chains: but the rebellious dwell in
a dry *land*.
7 O God, when thou wentest forth before thy people, when thou didst march
through the wilderness; Sē'lăh:
8 The earth shook, the heavens also
dropped at the presence of God: *even*
Sī'naī itself *was moved* at the presence
of God, the God of Ĭs̱'rā-ĕl.
9 Thou, O God, didst send a plentiful
rain, whereby thou didst confirm thine
inheritance, when it was weary.
10 Thy congregation hath dwelt therein: thou, O God, hast prepared of thy
goodness for the poor.
11 The LORD gave the word: great *was*
the company of those that published *it*.
12 Kings of armies did flee apace: and
she that tarried at home divided the
spoil.
13 Though ye have lain among the
pots, *yet shall ye be as* the wings of a
dove covered with silver, and her feathers with yellow gold.
14 When the Almighty scattered kings
in it, it was *white* as snow in Săl'mŏn.
15 The hill of God *is as* the hill of Bā'-
shăn; a high hill *as* the hill of Bā'shăn.
16 Why leap ye, ye high hills? *this is*
the hill *which* God desireth to dwell in;
yea, the LORD will dwell *in it* for ever.
17 The chariots of God *are* twenty
thousand, *even* thousands of angels:
the LORD *is* among them, *as in* Sī'naī, in
the holy *place*.
18 Thou hast ascended on high, thou
hast led captivity captive: thou hast received gifts for men; yea, *for* the rebellious also, that the LORD God might
dwell *among them*.
19 Blessed *be* the LORD, *who* daily
loadeth us *with benefits, even* the God
of our salvation. Sē'lăh.
20 *He that is* our God *is* the God of
salvation; and unto God the LORD
belong the issues from death.
21 But God shall wound the head of
his enemies, *and* the hairy scalp of such
a one as goeth on still in his trespasses.
22 The LORD said, I will bring again
from Bā'shăn, I will bring *my people*
again from the depths of the sea:
23 That thy foot may be dipped in the
blood of *thine* enemies, *and* the tongue
of thy dogs in the same.
24 They have seen thy goings, O God;
even the goings of my God, my King, in
the sanctuary.
25 The singers went before, the players
on instruments *followed* after; among
them were the damsels playing with
timbrels.
26 Bless ye God in the congregations,
even the LORD, from the fountain of
Ĭs̱'rā-ĕl.
27 There *is* little Benjamin *with* their
ruler, the princes of Judah *and* their
council, the princes of Zĕb'ū-lŭn, *and*
the princes of Năph'tă-lī.
28 Thy God hath commanded thy
strength: strengthen, O God, that which
thou hast wrought for us.
29 Because of thy temple at Jerusalem
shall kings bring presents unto thee.
30 Rebuke the company of spearmen,
the multitude of the bulls, with the
calves of the people, *till every one* submit himself with pieces of silver: scatter
thou the people *that* delight in war.
31 Princes shall come out of Egypt;
Ethiopia shall soon stretch out her hands
unto God.
32 Sing unto God, ye kingdoms of the
earth; O sing praises unto the Lord;
Sē'lăh:

33 To him that rideth upon the heavens of heavens, *which were* of old; lo, he doth send out his voice, *and that* a mighty voice.

34 Ascribe ye strength unto God: his excellency *is* over Ĭṣ′rā-ĕl, and his strength *is* in the clouds.

35 O God, *thou art* terrible out of thy holy places: the God of Ĭṣ′rā-ĕl *is* he that giveth strength and power unto *his* people. Blessed *be* God.

PSALM 69

To the chief Musician upon Shō-shăn′nĭm, *A Psalm* of David.

SAVE me, O God; for the waters are come in unto *my* soul.

2 I sink in deep mire, where *there is* no standing: I am come into deep waters, where the floods overflow me.

3 I am weary of my crying: my throat is dried: mine eyes fail while I wait for my God.

4 They that hate me without a cause are more than the hairs of mine head: they that would destroy me, *being* mine enemies wrongfully, are mighty: then I restored *that* which I took not away.

5 O God, thou knowest my foolishness; and my sins are not hid from thee.

6 Let not them that wait on thee, O Lord GOD of hosts, be ashamed for my sake: let not those that seek thee be confounded for my sake, O God of Ĭṣ′rā-ĕl.

7 Because for thy sake I have borne reproach; shame hath covered my face.

8 I am become a stranger unto my brethren, and an alien unto my mother's children.

9 For the zeal of thine house hath eaten me up; and the reproaches of them that reproached thee are fallen upon me.

10 When I wept, *and chastened* my soul with fasting, that was to my reproach.

11 I made sackcloth also my garment; and I became a proverb to them.

12 They that sit in the gate speak against me; and I *was* the song of the drunkards.

13 But as for me, my prayer *is* unto thee, O LORD, *in* an acceptable time: O God, in the multitude of thy mercy hear me, in the truth of thy salvation.

14 Deliver me out of the mire, and let me not sink: let me be delivered from them that hate me, and out of the deep waters.

15 Let not the waterflood overflow me, neither let the deep swallow me up, and let not the pit shut her mouth upon me.

16 Hear me, O LORD; for thy lovingkindness *is* good: turn unto me according to the multitude of thy tender mercies.

17 And hide not thy face from thy servant; for I am in trouble: hear me speedily.

18 Draw nigh unto my soul, *and* redeem it: deliver me because of mine enemies.

19 Thou hast known my reproach, and my shame, and my dishonor: mine adversaries *are* all before thee.

20 Reproach hath broken my heart; and I am full of heaviness: and I looked *for some* to take pity, but *there was* none; and for comforters, but I found none.

21 They gave me also gall for my meat; and in my thirst they gave me vinegar to drink.

22 Let their table become a snare before them: and *that which should have been* for *their* welfare, *let it become* a trap.

23 Let their eyes be darkened, that they see not; and make their loins continually to shake.

24 Pour out thine indignation upon them, and let thy wrathful anger take hold of them.

25 Let their habitation be desolate; *and* let none dwell in their tents.

26 For they persecute *him* whom thou hast smitten; and they talk to the grief of those whom thou hast wounded.

27 Add iniquity unto their iniquity: and let them not come into thy righteousness.

28 Let them be blotted out of the book of the living, and not be written with the righteous.

29 But I *am* poor and sorrowful: let thy salvation, O God, set me up on high.

30 I will praise the name of God with a song, and will magnify him with thanksgiving.

31 *This* also shall please the LORD better than an ox *or* bullock that hath horns and hoofs.

32 The humble shall see *this, and* be glad: and your heart shall live that seek God.

33 For the LORD heareth the poor, and despiseth not his prisoners.

34 Let the heaven and earth praise

him, the seas, and every thing that moveth therein.
35 For God will save Zion, and will
build the cities of Judah: that they may
dwell there, and have it in possession.
36 The seed also of his servants shall
inherit it: and they that love his name
shall dwell therein.

PSALM 70

To the chief Musician, *A Psalm* of David, to
bring to remembrance.

M*AKE haste,* O God, to deliver me;
make haste to help me, O LORD.
2 Let them be ashamed and confounded
that seek after my soul: let them be
turned backward, and put to confusion,
that desire my hurt.
3 Let them be turned back for a reward
of their shame that say, Aha, aha.
4 Let all those that seek thee rejoice
and be glad in thee: and let such as love
thy salvation say continually, Let God be
magnified.
5 But I *am* poor and needy; make haste
unto me, O God: thou *art* my help and
my deliverer; O LORD, make no tarrying.

PSALM 71

IN thee, O LORD, do I put my trust:
let me never be put to confusion.
2 Deliver me in thy righteousness, and
cause me to escape: incline thine ear
unto me, and save me.
3 Be thou my strong habitation, whereunto I may continually resort: thou hast
given commandment to save me; for
thou *art* my rock and my fortress.
4 Deliver me, O my God, out of the
hand of the wicked, out of the hand of
the unrighteous and cruel man.
5 For thou *art* my hope, O Lord GOD:
thou art my trust from my youth.
6 By thee have I been holden up from
the womb: thou art he that took me out
of my mother's bowels: my praise *shall
be* continually of thee.
7 I am as a wonder unto many; but thou
art my strong refuge.
8 Let my mouth be filled *with* thy praise
and with thy honor all the day.
9 Cast me not off in the time of old
age; forsake me not when my strength
faileth.
10 For mine enemies speak against me;
and they that lay wait for my soul take
counsel together,
11 Saying, God hath forsaken him:
persecute and take him; for *there is*
none to deliver *him*.
12 O God, be not far from me: O my
God, make haste for my help.
13 Let them be confounded *and* consumed that are adversaries to my soul;
let them be covered *with* reproach and
dishonor that seek my hurt.
14 But I will hope continually, and will
yet praise thee more and more.
15 My mouth shall show forth thy
righteousness *and* thy salvation all the
day; for I know not the numbers *thereof*.
16 I will go in the strength of the Lord
GOD: I will make mention of thy righteousness, *even* of thine only.
17 O God, thou hast taught me from
my youth: and hitherto have I declared
thy wondrous works.
18 Now also when I am old and grayheaded, O God, forsake me not; until I
have showed thy strength unto *this* generation, *and* thy power to every one *that*
is to come.
19 Thy righteousness also, O God, *is*
very high, who hast done great things:
O God, who *is* like unto thee!
20 *Thou,* which hast showed me great
and sore troubles, shalt quicken me
again, and shalt bring me up again from
the depths of the earth.
21 Thou shalt increase my greatness,
and comfort me on every side.
22 I will also praise thee with the
psaltery, *even* thy truth, O my God:
unto thee will I sing with the harp, O
thou Holy One of Iş'rā-ĕl.
23 My lips shall greatly rejoice when I
sing unto thee; and my soul, which thou
hast redeemed.
24 My tongue also shall talk of thy
righteousness all the day long: for they
are confounded, for they are brought
unto shame, that seek my hurt.

PSALM 72

A Psalm for Solomon.

GIVE the king thy judgments, O God,
and thy righteousness unto the
king's son.
2 He shall judge thy people with righteousness, and thy poor with judgment.
3 The mountains shall bring peace to
the people, and the little hills, by righteousness.
4 He shall judge the poor of the people,
he shall save the children of the needy,
and shall break in pieces the oppressor.

5 They shall fear thee as long as the sun and moon endure, throughout all generations.
6 He shall come down like rain upon the mown grass: as showers *that* water the earth.
7 In his days shall the righteous flourish; and abundance of peace so long as the moon endureth.
8 He shall have dominion also from sea to sea, and from the river unto the ends of the earth.
9 They that dwell in the wilderness shall bow before him; and his enemies shall lick the dust.
10 The kings of Tär′shĭsh and of the isles shall bring presents: the kings of Shē′bȧ and Sē′bȧ shall offer gifts.
11 Yea, all kings shall fall down before him: all nations shall serve him.
12 For he shall deliver the needy when he crieth; the poor also, and *him* that hath no helper.
13 He shall spare the poor and needy, and shall save the souls of the needy.
14 He shall redeem their soul from deceit and violence: and precious shall their blood be in his sight.
15 And he shall live, and to him shall be given of the gold of Shē′bȧ: prayer also shall be made for him continually; *and* daily shall he be praised.
16 There shall be a handful of corn in the earth upon the top of the mountains; the fruit thereof shall shake like Lebanon: and *they* of the city shall flourish like grass of the earth.
17 His name shall endure for ever: his name shall be continued as long as the sun: and *men* shall be blessed in him: all nations shall call him blessed.
18 Blessed *be* the LORD God, the God of Ĭṣ′rā-ĕl, who only doeth wondrous things.
19 And blessed *be* his glorious name for ever: and let the whole earth be filled *with* his glory. Amen, and Amen.
20 The prayers of David the son of Jesse are ended.

PSALM 73

A Psalm of Ā′săph.

TRULY God *is* good to Ĭṣ′rā-ĕl, *even* to such as are of a clean heart.
2 But as for me, my feet were almost gone; my steps had well-nigh slipped.
3 For I was envious at the foolish, *when* I saw the prosperity of the wicked.
4 For *there are* no bands in their death: but their strength *is* firm.
5 They *are* not in trouble *as other* men; neither are they plagued like *other* men.
6 Therefore pride compasseth them about as a chain; violence covereth them *as* a garment.
7 Their eyes stand out with fatness: they have more than heart could wish.
8 They are corrupt, and speak wickedly *concerning* oppression: they speak loftily.
9 They set their mouth against the heavens, and their tongue walketh through the earth.
10 Therefore his people return hither: and waters of a full *cup* are wrung out to them.
11 And they say, How doth God know? and is there knowledge in the Most High?
12 Behold, these *are* the ungodly, who prosper in the world; they increase *in* riches.
13 Verily I have cleansed my heart *in* vain, and washed my hands in innocency.
14 For all the day long have I been plagued, and chastened every morning.
15 If I say, I will speak thus; behold, I should offend *against* the generation of thy children.
16 When I thought to know this, it *was* too painful for me;
17 Until I went into the sanctuary of God; *then* understood I their end.
18 Surely thou didst set them in slippery places: thou castedst them down into destruction.
19 How are they *brought* into desolation, as in a moment! they are utterly consumed with terrors.
20 As a dream when *one* awaketh; *so*, O Lord, when thou awakest, thou shalt despise their image.
21 Thus my heart was grieved, and I was pricked in my reins.
22 So foolish *was* I, and ignorant: I was *as* a beast before thee.
23 Nevertheless I *am* continually with thee: thou hast holden *me* by my right hand.
24 Thou shalt guide me with thy counsel, and afterward receive me *to* glory.
25 Whom have I in heaven *but thee?* and *there is* none upon earth *that* I desire besides thee.
26 My flesh and my heart faileth: *but*

God *is* the strength of my heart, and my portion for ever.

27 For, lo, they that are far from thee shall perish: thou hast destroyed all them that go a whoring from thee.

28 But *it is* good for me to draw near to God: I have put my trust in the Lord GOD, that I may declare all thy works.

PSALM 74

Măs′chĭl of Ā′săph.

O GOD, why hast thou cast *us* off for ever? *why* doth thine anger smoke against the sheep of thy pasture?

2 Remember thy congregation, *which* thou hast purchased of old; the rod of thine inheritance, *which* thou hast redeemed; this mount Zion, wherein thou hast dwelt.

3 Lift up thy feet unto the perpetual desolations; *even* all *that* the enemy hath done wickedly in the sanctuary.

4 Thine enemies roar in the midst of thy congregations; they set up their ensigns *for* signs.

5 *A man* was famous according as he had lifted up axes upon the thick trees.

6 But now they break down the carved work thereof at once with axes and hammers.

7 They have cast fire into thy sanctuary, they have defiled *by casting down* the dwelling place of thy name to the ground.

8 They said in their hearts, Let us destroy them together: they have burned up all the synagogues of God in the land.

9 We see not our signs: *there is* no more any prophet: neither *is there* among us any that knoweth how long.

10 O God, how long shall the adversary reproach? shall the enemy blaspheme thy name for ever?

11 Why withdrawest thou thy hand, even thy right hand? pluck *it* out of thy bosom.

12 For God *is* my King of old, working salvation in the midst of the earth.

13 Thou didst divide the sea by thy strength: thou brakest the heads of the dragons in the waters.

14 Thou brakest the heads of leviathan in pieces, *and* gavest him *to be* meat to the people inhabiting the wilderness.

15 Thou didst cleave the fountain and the flood: thou driedst up mighty rivers.

16 The day *is* thine, the night also *is* thine: thou hast prepared the light and the sun.

17 Thou hast set all the borders of the earth: thou hast made summer and winter.

18 Remember this, *that* the enemy hath reproached, O LORD, and *that* the foolish people have blasphemed thy name.

19 O deliver not the soul of thy turtledove unto the multitude *of the wicked:* forget not the congregation of thy poor for ever.

20 Have respect unto the covenant: for the dark places of the earth are full of the habitations of cruelty.

21 O let not the oppressed return ashamed: let the poor and needy praise thy name.

22 Arise, O God, plead thine own cause: remember how the foolish man reproacheth thee daily.

23 Forget not the voice of thine enemies: the tumult of those that rise up against thee increaseth continually.

PSALM 75

To the chief Musician, Ăl-tăs′chĭth, A Psalm *or* Song of Ā′săph.

UNTO thee, O God, do we give thanks, *unto thee* do we give thanks: for *that* thy name is near thy wondrous works declare.

2 When I shall receive the congregation I will judge uprightly.

3 The earth and all the inhabitants thereof are dissolved: I bear up the pillars of it. Sē′lăh.

4 I said unto the fools, Deal not foolishly: and to the wicked, Lift not up the horn:

5 Lift not up your horn on high: speak *not* with a stiff neck.

6 For promotion *cometh* neither from the east, nor from the west, nor from the south.

7 But God *is* the judge: he putteth down one, and setteth up another.

8 For in the hand of the LORD *there is* a cup, and the wine is red; it is full of mixture; and he poureth out of the same: but the dregs thereof, all the wicked of the earth shall wring *them* out, *and* drink *them.*

9 But I will declare for ever; I will sing praises to the God of Jacob.

10 All the horns of the wicked also will I cut off; *but* the horns of the righteous shall be exalted.

PSALM 76

To the chief Musician on Nĕg′ĭ-nōth, A Psalm *or* Song of Ā′săph.

IN Judah *is* God known: his name *is* great in Is̱′rā-ĕl.

2 In Sā′lĕm also is his tabernacle, and his dwelling place in Zion.

3 There brake he the arrows of the bow, the shield, and the sword, and the battle. Sē′lăh.

4 Thou *art* more glorious *and* excellent than the mountains of prey.

5 The stout-hearted are spoiled, they have slept their sleep: and none of the men of might have found their hands.

6 At thy rebuke, O God of Jacob, both the chariot and horse are cast into a dead sleep.

7 Thou, *even* thou, *art* to be feared: and who may stand in thy sight when once thou art angry?

8 Thou didst cause judgment to be heard from heaven; the earth feared, and was still,

9 When God arose to judgment, to save all the meek of the earth. Sē′lăh.

10 Surely the wrath of man shall praise thee: the remainder of wrath shalt thou restrain.

11 Vow, and pay unto the LORD your God: let all that be round about him bring presents unto him that ought to be feared.

12 He shall cut off the spirit of princes: *he is* terrible to the kings of the earth.

PSALM 77

To the chief Musician, to Jē-dū′thŭn, A Psalm of Ā′săph.

I CRIED unto God with my voice, *even* unto God with my voice; and he gave ear unto me.

2 In the day of my trouble I sought the Lord: my sore ran in the night, and ceased not: my soul refused to be comforted.

3 I remembered God, and was troubled: I complained, and my spirit was overwhelmed. Sē′lăh.

4 Thou holdest mine eyes waking: I am so troubled that I cannot speak.

5 I have considered the days of old, the years of ancient times.

6 I call to remembrance my song in the night: I commune with mine own heart: and my spirit made diligent search.

7 Will the Lord cast off for ever? and will he be favorable no more?

8 Is his mercy clean gone for ever? doth *his* promise fail for evermore?

9 Hath God forgotten to be gracious? hath he in anger shut up his tender mercies? Sē′lăh.

10 And I said, This *is* my infirmity: *but I will remember* the years of the right hand of the Most High.

11 I will remember the works of the LORD: surely I will remember thy wonders of old.

12 I will meditate also of all thy work, and talk of thy doings.

13 Thy way, O God, *is* in the sanctuary: who *is so* great a God as *our* God?

14 Thou *art* the God that doest wonders: thou hast declared thy strength among the people.

15 Thou hast with *thine* arm redeemed thy people, the sons of Jacob and Joseph. Sē′lăh.

16 The waters saw thee, O God, the waters saw thee; they were afraid: the depths also were troubled.

17 The clouds poured out water: the skies sent out a sound: thine arrows also went abroad.

18 The voice of thy thunder *was* in the heaven: the lightnings lightened the world: the earth trembled and shook.

19 Thy way *is* in the sea, and thy path in the great waters, and thy footsteps are not known.

20 Thou leddest thy people like a flock by the hand of Moses and Aaron.

PSALM 78

Măs′chĭl of Ā′săph.

GIVE ear, O my people, *to* my law: incline your ears to the words of my mouth.

2 I will open my mouth in a parable: I will utter dark sayings of old:

3 Which we have heard and known, and our fathers have told us.

4 We will not hide *them* from their children, showing to the generation to come the praises of the LORD, and his strength, and his wonderful works that he hath done.

5 For he established a testimony in Jacob, and appointed a law in Is̱′rā-ĕl, which he commanded our fathers, that they should make them known to their children:

6 That the generation to come might know *them, even* the children *which*

should be born; *who* should arise and
declare *them* to their children:
7 That they might set their hope in God,
and not forget the works of God, but
keep his commandments:
8 And might not be as their fathers, a
stubborn and rebellious generation; a
generation *that* set not their heart aright,
and whose spirit was not steadfast with
God.
9 The children of Ē'phrā-ĭm, *being*
armed, *and* carrying bows, turned back
in the day of battle.
10 They kept not the covenant of God,
and refused to walk in his law;
11 And forgat his works, and his wonders that he had showed them.
12 Marvelous things did he in the sight
of their fathers, in the land of Egypt, *in*
the field of Zō'ăn.
13 He divided the sea, and caused them
to pass through; and he made the waters to stand as a heap.
14 In the daytime also he led them with
a cloud, and all the night with a light of
fire.
15 He clave the rocks in the wilderness,
and gave *them* drink as *out of* the great
depths.
16 He brought streams also out of the
rock, and caused waters to run down like
rivers.
17 And they sinned yet more against
him by provoking the Most High in the
wilderness.
18 And they tempted God in their heart
by asking meat for their lust.
19 Yea, they spake against God; they
said, Can God furnish a table in the
wilderness?
20 Behold, he smote the rock, that the
waters gushed out, and the streams
overflowed; can he give bread also? can
he provide flesh for his people?
21 Therefore the LORD heard *this,*
and was wroth: so a fire was kindled
against Jacob, and anger also came up
against Ĭs̱'rā-ĕl;
22 Because they believed not in God,
and trusted not in his salvation:
23 Though he had commanded the
clouds from above, and opened the doors
of heaven,
24 And had rained down manna upon
them to eat, and had given them of the
corn of heaven.
25 Man did eat angels' food: he sent
them meat to the full.
26 He caused an east wind to blow in
the heaven: and by his power he brought
in the south wind.
27 He rained flesh also upon them as
dust, and feathered fowls like as the
sand of the sea:
28 And he let *it* fall in the midst of their
camp, round about their habitations.
29 So they did eat, and were well filled:
for he gave them their own desire;
30 They were not estranged from their
lust: but while their meat *was* yet in
their mouths,
31 The wrath of God came upon them,
and slew the fattest of them, and smote
down the chosen *men* of Ĭs̱'rā-ĕl.
32 For all this they sinned still, and believed not for his wondrous works.
33 Therefore their days did he consume
in vanity, and their years in trouble.
34 When he slew them, then they
sought him: and they returned and inquired early after God.
35 And they remembered that God *was*
their rock, and the high God their redeemer.
36 Nevertheless they did flatter him
with their mouth, and they lied unto him
with their tongues.
37 For their heart was not right with
him, neither were they steadfast in his
covenant.
38 But he, *being* full of compassion,
forgave *their* iniquity, and destroyed
them not: yea, many a time turned he
his anger away, and did not stir up all
his wrath.
39 For he remembered that they *were*
but flesh; a wind that passeth away, and
cometh not again.
40 How oft did they provoke him in the
wilderness, *and* grieve him in the desert!
41 Yea, they turned back and tempted
God, and limited the Holy One of
Ĭs̱'rā-ĕl.
42 They remembered not his hand, *nor*
the day when he delivered them from
the enemy:
43 How he had wrought his signs in
Egypt, and his wonders in the field of
Zō'ăn:
44 And had turned their rivers into
blood; and their floods, that they could
not drink.
45 He sent divers sorts of flies among
them, which devoured them; and frogs,
which destroyed them.
46 He gave also their increase unto the

caterpillar, and their labor unto the
locust.
47 He destroyed their vines with hail,
and their sycamore trees with frost.
48 He gave up their cattle also to the
hail, and their flocks to hot thunder-
bolts.
49 He cast upon them the fierceness of
his anger, wrath, and indignation, and
trouble, by sending evil angels *among
them.*
50 He made a way to his anger; he
spared not their soul from death, but
gave their life over to the pestilence;
51 And smote all the firstborn in Egypt;
the chief of *their* strength in the tabernacles of Ham:
52 But made his own people to go forth
like sheep, and guided them in the wilderness like a flock.
53 And he led them on safely, so that
they feared not: but the sea overwhelmed
their enemies.
54 And he brought them to the border
of his sanctuary, *even to* this mountain,
which his right hand had purchased.
55 He cast out the heathen also before
them, and divided them an inheritance
by line, and made the tribes of Ĭş'rā-ĕl
to dwell in their tents.
56 Yet they tempted and provoked the
most high God, and kept not his testimonies:
57 But turned back, and dealt unfaith-
fully like their fathers: they were turned
aside like a deceitful bow.
58 For they provoked him to anger with
their high places, and moved him to
jealousy with their graven images.
59 When God heard *this*, he was wroth,
and greatly abhorred Ĭş'rā-ĕl:
60 So that he forsook the tabernacle of
Shī'lōh, the tent *which* he placed among
men;
61 And delivered his strength into captivity, and his glory into the enemy's
hand.
62 He gave his people over also unto
the sword; and was wroth with his inheritance.
63 The fire consumed their young men;
and their maidens were not given to
marriage.
64 Their priests fell by the sword; and
their widows made no lamentation.
65 Then the Lord awaked as one out of
sleep, *and* like a mighty man that shout-
eth by reason of wine.
66 And he smote his enemies in the
hinder parts: he put them to a perpetual
reproach.
67 Moreover he refused the tabernacle
of Joseph, and chose not the tribe of
Ē'phrā-ĭm:
68 But chose the tribe of Judah, the
mount Zion which he loved.
69 And he built his sanctuary like high
palaces, like the earth which he hath
established for ever.
70 He chose David also his servant,
and took him from the sheepfolds:
71 From following the ewes great with
young he brought him to feed Jacob his
people, and Ĭş'rā-ĕl his inheritance.
72 So he fed them according to the integrity of his heart; and guided them by
the skilfulness of his hands.

PSALM 79

A Psalm of Ā'săph.

O GOD, the heathen are come into
thine inheritance; thy holy temple
have they defiled; they have laid Jerusalem on heaps.
2 The dead bodies of thy servants have
they given *to be* meat unto the fowls of
the heaven, the flesh of thy saints unto
the beasts of the earth.
3 Their blood have they shed like water
round about Jerusalem; and *there was*
none to bury *them*.
4 We are become a reproach to our
neighbors, a scorn and derision to them
that are round about us.
5 How long, LORD? wilt thou be angry
for ever? shall thy jealousy burn like
fire?
6 Pour out thy wrath upon the heathen
that have not known thee, and upon the
kingdoms that have not called upon thy
name.
7 For they have devoured Jacob, and
laid waste his dwelling place.
8 O remember not against us former
iniquities: let thy tender mercies speedily prevent us; for we are brought very
low.
9 Help us, O God of our salvation, for
the glory of thy name: and deliver us,
and purge away our sins, for thy name's
sake.
10 Wherefore should the heathen say,
Where *is* their God? let him be known
among the heathen in our sight *by* the
revenging of the blood of thy servants
which is shed.

11 Let the sighing of the prisoner come before thee; according to the greatness of thy power preserve thou those that are appointed to die;

12 And render unto our neighbors sevenfold into their bosom their reproach, wherewith they have reproached thee, O Lord.

13 So we thy people and sheep of thy pasture will give thee thanks for ever: we will show forth thy praise to all generations.

PSALM 80

To the chief Musician upon Shō-shăn'nĭm-Ē dūth, A Psalm of Ā'săph.

GIVE ear, O Shepherd of Ĭs'rā-ĕl, thou that leadest Joseph like a flock; thou that dwellest *between* the cherubim, shine forth.

2 Before Ē'phrā-ĭm and Benjamin and Mȧ-năs'sĕh stir up thy strength, and come *and* save us.

3 Turn us again, O God, and cause thy face to shine; and we shall be saved.

4 O LORD God of hosts, how long wilt thou be angry against the prayer of thy people?

5 Thou feedest them with the bread of tears; and givest them tears to drink in great measure.

6 Thou makest us a strife unto our neighbors: and our enemies laugh among themselves.

7 Turn us again, O God of hosts, and cause thy face to shine; and we shall be saved.

8 Thou hast brought a vine out of Egypt: thou hast cast out the heathen, and planted it.

9 Thou preparedst *room* before it, and didst cause it to take deep root, and it filled the land.

10 The hills were covered with the shadow of it, and the boughs thereof *were like* the goodly cedars.

11 She sent out her boughs unto the sea, and her branches unto the river.

12 Why hast thou *then* broken down her hedges, so that all they which pass by the way do pluck her?

13 The boar out of the wood doth waste it, and the wild beast of the field doth devour it.

14 Return, we beseech thee, O God of hosts: look down from heaven, and behold, and visit this vine;

15 And the vineyard which thy right hand hath planted, and the branch *that* thou madest strong for thyself.

16 *It is* burned with fire, *it is* cut down: they perish at the rebuke of thy countenance.

17 Let thy hand be upon the man of thy right hand, upon the son of man *whom* thou madest strong for thyself.

18 So will not we go back from thee: quicken us, and we will call upon thy name.

19 Turn us again, O LORD God of hosts, cause thy face to shine; and we shall be saved.

PSALM 81

To the chief Musician upon Gĭt'tĭth, *A Psalm* of Ā'săph.

SING aloud unto God our strength: make a joyful noise unto the God of Jacob.

2 Take a psalm, and bring hither the timbrel, the pleasant harp with the psaltery.

3 Blow up the trumpet in the new moon, in the time appointed, on our solemn feast day.

4 For this *was* a statute for Ĭs'rā-ĕl, *and* a law of the God of Jacob.

5 This he ordained in Joseph *for* a testimony, when he went out through the land of Egypt: *where* I heard a language *that* I understood not.

6 I removed his shoulder from the burden: his hands were delivered from the pots.

7 Thou calledst in trouble, and I delivered thee; I answered thee in the secret place of thunder: I proved thee at the waters of Mĕr'ĭ-băh. Sē'lȧh.

8 Hear, O my people, and I will testify unto thee: O Ĭs'rā-ĕl, if thou wilt hearken unto me;

9 There shall no strange god be in thee; neither shalt thou worship any strange god.

10 I *am* the LORD thy God, which brought thee out of the land of Egypt: open thy mouth wide, and I will fill it.

11 But my people would not hearken to my voice; and Ĭs'rā-ĕl would none of me.

12 So I gave them up unto their own hearts' lust: *and* they walked in their own counsels.

13 Oh that my people had hearkened unto me, *and* Ĭs'rā-ĕl had walked in my ways!

14 I should soon have subdued their enemies, and turned my hand against their adversaries.

15 The haters of the LORD should have submitted themselves unto him: but their time should have endured for ever.

16 He should have fed them also with the finest of the wheat: and with honey out of the rock should I have satisfied thee.

PSALM 82

A Psalm of Ā'săph.

GOD standeth in the congregation of the mighty; he judgeth among the gods.

2 How long will ye judge unjustly, and accept the persons of the wicked? Sē'lăh.

3 Defend the poor and fatherless: do justice to the afflicted and needy.

4 Deliver the poor and needy: rid *them* out of the hand of the wicked.

5 They know not, neither will they understand; they walk on in darkness: all the foundations of the earth are out of course.

6 I have said, Ye *are* gods; and all of you *are* children of the Most High.

7 But ye shall die like men, and fall like one of the princes.

8 Arise, O God, judge the earth: for thou shalt inherit all nations.

PSALM 83

A Song *or* Psalm of Ā'săph.

KEEP not thou silence, O God: hold not thy peace, and be not still, O God.

2 For, lo, thine enemies make a tumult: and they that hate thee have lifted up the head.

3 They have taken crafty counsel against thy people, and consulted against thy hidden ones.

4 They have said, Come, and let us cut them off from *being* a nation; that the name of Ĭş'rā-ĕl may be no more in remembrance.

5 For they have consulted together with one consent: they are confederate against thee:

6 The tabernacles of Ē'dŏm, and the Ĭsh'mā-ĕl-ītes; of Mō'ăb, and the Hā'gȧr-ēneş';

7 Gē'băl, and Ammon, and Ăm'ȧ-lĕk; the Phĭ-lĭs'tĭneş with the inhabitants of Tȳre;

8 Ăs'sŭr also is joined with them: they have helped the children of Lot. Sē'lăh.

9 Do unto them as *unto* the Mĭd'ĭ-ăn-ītes; as *to* Sĭs'ĕr-ȧ, as *to* Jā'bĭn, at the brook of Kī'sŏn:

10 *Which* perished at Ĕn'-dôr: they became *as* dung for the earth.

11 Make their nobles like Ō'rĕb, and like Zē'ĕb: yea, all their princes as Zē'băh, and as Zăl-mŭn'nȧ:

12 Who said, Let us take to ourselves the houses of God in possession.

13 O my God, make them like a wheel; as the stubble before the wind.

14 As the fire burneth a wood, and as the flame setteth the mountains on fire;

15 So persecute them with thy tempest, and make them afraid with thy storm.

16 Fill their faces with shame; that they may seek thy name, O LORD.

17 Let them be confounded and troubled for ever; yea, let them be put to shame, and perish:

18 That *men* may know that thou, whose name alone *is* JEHOVAH, *art* the Most High over all the earth.

PSALM 84

To the chief Musician upon Gĭt'tĭth, A Psalm for the sons of Kō'răh.

HOW amiable *are* thy tabernacles, O LORD of hosts!

2 My soul longeth, yea, even fainteth for the courts of the LORD: my heart and my flesh crieth out for the living God.

3 Yea, the sparrow hath found a house, and the swallow a nest for herself, where she may lay her young, *even* thine altars, O LORD of hosts, my King, and my God.

4 Blessed *are* they that dwell in thy house: they will be still praising thee. Sē'lăh.

5 Blessed *is* the man whose strength *is* in thee; in whose heart *are* the ways *of them*.

6 *Who* passing through the valley of Bā'cȧ make it a well; the rain also filleth the pools.

7 They go from strength to strength, *every one of them* in Zion appeareth before God.

8 O LORD God of hosts, hear my prayer: give ear, O God of Jacob. Sē'lăh.

9 Behold, O God our shield, and look upon the face of thine anointed.

10 For a day in thy courts *is* better than a thousand. I had rather be a door-

keeper in the house of my God, than to dwell in the tents of wickedness.

11 For the LORD God *is* a sun and shield: the LORD will give grace and glory: no good *thing* will he withhold from them that walk uprightly.

12 O LORD of hosts, blessed *is* the man that trusteth in thee.

PSALM 85

To the chief Musician, A Psalm for the sons of Kō′răh.

LORD, thou hast been favorable unto thy land: thou hast brought back the captivity of Jacob.

2 Thou hast forgiven the iniquity of thy people; thou hast covered all their sin. Sē′lăh.

3 Thou hast taken away all thy wrath: thou hast turned *thyself* from the fierceness of thine anger.

4 Turn us, O God of our salvation, and cause thine anger toward us to cease.

5 Wilt thou be angry with us for ever? wilt thou draw out thine anger to all generations?

6 Wilt thou not revive us again: that thy people may rejoice in thee?

7 Show us thy mercy, O LORD, and grant us thy salvation.

8 I will hear what God the LORD will speak: for he will speak peace unto his people, and to his saints: but let them not turn again to folly.

9 Surely his salvation *is* nigh them that fear him; that glory may dwell in our land.

10 Mercy and truth are met together; righteousness and peace have kissed *each other.*

11 Truth shall spring out of the earth; and righteousness shall look down from heaven.

12 Yea, the LORD shall give *that which is* good; and our land shall yield her increase.

13 Righteousness shall go before him; and shall set *us* in the way of his steps.

PSALM 86

A Prayer of David.

BOW down thine ear, O LORD, hear me: for I *am* poor and needy.

2 Preserve my soul; for I *am* holy: O thou my God, save thy servant that trusteth in thee.

3 Be merciful unto me, O Lord: for I cry unto thee daily.

4 Rejoice the soul of thy servant: for unto thee, O Lord, do I lift up my soul.

5 For thou, Lord, *art* good, and ready to forgive; and plenteous in mercy unto all them that call upon thee.

6 Give ear, O LORD, unto my prayer; and attend to the voice of my supplications.

7 In the day of my trouble I will call upon thee: for thou wilt answer me.

8 Among the gods *there is* none like unto thee, O Lord; neither *are there any works* like unto thy works.

9 All nations whom thou hast made shall come and worship before thee, O Lord; and shall glorify thy name.

10 For thou *art* great, and doest wondrous things: thou *art* God alone.

11 Teach me thy way, O LORD; I will walk in thy truth: unite my heart to fear thy name.

12 I will praise thee, O Lord my God, with all my heart: and I will glorify thy name for evermore.

13 For great *is* thy mercy toward me: and thou hast delivered my soul from the lowest hell.

14 O God, the proud are risen against me, and the assemblies of violent *men* have sought after my soul; and have not set thee before them.

15 But thou, O Lord, *art* a God full of compassion, and gracious, long-suffering, and plenteous in mercy and truth.

16 O turn unto me, and have mercy upon me; give thy strength unto thy servant, and save the son of thine handmaid.

17 Show me a token for good; that they which hate me may see *it,* and be ashamed: because thou, LORD, hast helped me, and comforted me.

PSALM 87

A Psalm *or* Song for the sons of Kō′răh.

HIS foundation *is* in the holy mountains.

2 The LORD loveth the gates of Zion more than all the dwellings of Jacob.

3 Glorious things are spoken of thee, O city of God. Sē′lăh.

4 I will make mention of Rā′hăb and Babylon to them that know me: behold Phĭ-lĭs′tĭ-ȧ, and Tȳre, with Ethiopia; this *man* was born there.

5 And of Zion it shall be said, This and that man was born in her: and the Highest himself shall establish her.

6 The LORD shall count, when he writ-
eth up the people, *that* this *man* was
born there. Sē′lăh.
7 As well the singers as the players on
instruments *shall be there:* all my
springs *are* in thee.

PSALM 88

A Song *or* Psalm for the sons of Kō′răh, to the chief Musician upon Mā′hă-lăth Lē-ăn′nŏth, Măs′chĭl of Hē′măn the Ĕz′ră-hīte.

O LORD God of my salvation, I have
cried day *and* night before thee:
2 Let my prayer come before thee: incline thine ear unto my cry;
3 For my soul is full of troubles: and my
life draweth nigh unto the grave.
4 I am counted with them that go down
into the pit: I am as a man *that hath* no
strength:
5 Free among the dead, like the slain
that lie in the grave, whom thou rememberest no more: and they are cut off
from thy hand.
6 Thou hast laid me in the lowest pit,
in darkness, in the deeps.
7 Thy wrath lieth hard upon me, and
thou hast afflicted *me* with all thy waves.
Sē′lăh.
8 Thou hast put away mine acquaintance far from me; thou hast made me
an abomination unto them: *I am* shut
up, and I cannot come forth.
9 Mine eye mourneth by reason of
affliction: LORD, I have called daily upon
thee, I have stretched out my hands
unto thee.
10 Wilt thou show wonders to the dead?
shall the dead arise *and* praise thee?
Sē′lăh.
11 Shall thy loving-kindness be declared in the grave? *or* thy faithfulness in
destruction?
12 Shall thy wonders be known in the
dark? and thy righteousness in the land
of forgetfulness?
13 But unto thee have I cried, O LORD;
and in the morning shall my prayer prevent thee.
14 LORD, why castest thou off my
soul? *why* hidest thou thy face from
me?
15 I *am* afflicted and ready to die from
my youth up: *while* I suffer thy terrors
I am distracted.
16 Thy fierce wrath goeth over me;
thy terrors have cut me off.
17 They came round about me daily
like water; they compassed me about
together.
18 Lover and friend hast thou put far
from me, *and* mine acquaintance into
darkness.

PSALM 89

Măs′chĭl of Ē′thăn the Ĕz′ră-hīte.

I WILL sing of the mercies of the
LORD for ever: with my mouth will I
make known thy faithfulness to all
generations.
2 For I have said, Mercy shall be built
up for ever: thy faithfulness shalt thou
establish in the very heavens.
3 I have made a covenant with my
chosen, I have sworn unto David my
servant,
4 Thy seed will I establish for ever, and
build up thy throne to all generations.
Sē′lăh.
5 And the heavens shall praise thy
wonders, O LORD: thy faithfulness also
in the congregation of the saints.
6 For who in the heaven can be compared unto the LORD? *who* among the
sons of the mighty can be likened unto
the LORD?
7 God is greatly to be feared in the
assembly of the saints, and to be had in
reverence of all *them that are* about
him.
8 O LORD God of hosts, who *is* a strong
LORD like unto thee? or to thy faithfulness round about thee?
9 Thou rulest the raging of the sea:
when the waves thereof arise, thou
stillest them.
10 Thou hast broken Rā′hăb in pieces,
as one that is slain; thou hast scattered
thine enemies with thy strong arm.
11 The heavens *are* thine, the earth
also *is* thine: *as for* the world and the
fulness thereof, thou hast founded them.
12 The north and the south thou hast
created them: Tā′bŏr and Hermon shall
rejoice in thy name.
13 Thou hast a mighty arm: strong is
thy hand, *and* high is thy right hand.
14 Justice and judgment *are* the habitation of thy throne: mercy and truth
shall go before thy face.
15 Blessed *is* the people that know the
joyful sound: they shall walk, O LORD,
in the light of thy countenance.
16 In thy name shall they rejoice all
the day: and in thy righteousness shall
they be exalted.

17 For thou *art* the glory of their strength: and in thy favor our horn shall be exalted.

18 For the LORD *is* our defense; and the Holy One of Ĭs̱'rā-ĕl *is* our King.

19 Then thou spakest in vision to thy holy one, and saidst, I have laid help upon *one that is* mighty; I have exalted *one* chosen out of the people.

20 I have found David my servant; with my holy oil have I anointed him:

21 With whom my hand shall be established: mine arm also shall strengthen him.

22 The enemy shall not exact upon him; nor the son of wickedness afflict him.

23 And I will beat down his foes before his face, and plague them that hate him.

24 But my faithfulness and my mercy *shall be* with him: and in my name shall his horn be exalted.

25 I will set his hand also in the sea, and his right hand in the rivers.

26 He shall cry unto me, Thou *art* my father, my God, and the rock of my salvation.

27 Also I will make him *my* firstborn, higher than the kings of the earth.

28 My mercy will I keep for him for evermore, and my covenant shall stand fast with him.

29 His seed also will I make *to endure* for ever, and his throne as the days of heaven.

30 If his children forsake my law, and walk not in my judgments;

31 If they break my statutes, and keep not my commandments;

32 Then will I visit their transgression with the rod, and their iniquity with stripes.

33 Nevertheless my loving-kindness will I not utterly take from him, nor suffer my faithfulness to fail.

34 My covenant will I not break, nor alter the thing that is gone out of my lips.

35 Once have I sworn by my holiness that I will not lie unto David.

36 His seed shall endure for ever, and his throne as the sun before me.

37 It shall be established for ever as the moon, and *as* a faithful witness in heaven. Sē'lȧh.

38 But thou hast cast off and abhorred, thou hast been wroth with thine anointed.

39 Thou hast made void the covenant of thy servant: thou hast profaned his crown *by casting it* to the ground.

40 Thou hast broken down all his hedges; thou hast brought his strongholds to ruin.

41 All that pass by the way spoil him: he is a reproach to his neighbors.

42 Thou hast set up the right hand of his adversaries; thou hast made all his enemies to rejoice.

43 Thou hast also turned the edge of his sword, and hast not made him to stand in the battle.

44 Thou hast made his glory to cease, and cast his throne down to the ground.

45 The days of his youth hast thou shortened: thou hast covered him with shame. Sē'lȧh.

46 How long, LORD? wilt thou hide thyself for ever? shall thy wrath burn like fire?

47 Remember how short my time is: wherefore hast thou made all men in vain?

48 What man *is he that* liveth, and shall not see death? shall he deliver his soul from the hand of the grave? Sē'lȧh.

49 Lord, where *are* thy former loving-kindnesses, *which* thou swarest unto David in thy truth?

50 Remember, Lord, the reproach of thy servants; *how* I do bear in my bosom *the reproach of* all the mighty people;

51 Wherewith thine enemies have reproached, O LORD; wherewith they have reproached the footsteps of thine anointed.

52 Blessed *be* the LORD for evermore. Amen, and Amen.

PSALM 90

A Prayer of Moses the man of God.

LORD, thou hast been our dwelling place in all generations.

2 Before the mountains were brought forth, or ever thou hadst formed the earth and the world, even from everlasting to everlasting, thou *art* God.

3 Thou turnest man to destruction; and sayest, Return, ye children of men.

4 For a thousand years in thy sight *are but* as yesterday when it is past, and *as* a watch in the night.

5 Thou carriest them away as with a flood; they are *as* a sleep: in the morning *they are* like grass *which* groweth up.

6 In the morning it flourisheth, and

groweth up; in the evening it is cut down, and withereth.

7 For we are consumed by thine anger, and by thy wrath are we troubled.

8 Thou hast set our iniquities before thee, our secret *sins* in the light of thy countenance.

9 For all our days are passed away in thy wrath: we spend our years as a tale *that is told*.

10 The days of our years *are* threescore years and ten; and if by reason of strength *they be* fourscore years, yet *is* their strength labor and sorrow; for it is soon cut off, and we fly away.

11 Who knoweth the power of thine anger? even according to thy fear, *so is* thy wrath.

12 So teach *us* to number our days, that we may apply *our* hearts unto wisdom.

13 Return, O LORD, how long? and let it repent thee concerning thy servants.

14 O satisfy us early with thy mercy; that we may rejoice and be glad all our days.

15 Make us glad according to the days *wherein* thou hast afflicted us, *and* the years *wherein* we have seen evil.

16 Let thy work appear unto thy servants, and thy glory unto their children.

17 And let the beauty of the LORD our God be upon us: and establish thou the work of our hands upon us; yea, the work of our hands establish thou it.

PSALM 91

HE that dwelleth in the secret place of the Most High shall abide under the shadow of the Almighty.

2 I will say of the LORD, *He is* my refuge and my fortress: my God; in him will I trust.

3 Surely he shall deliver thee from the snare of the fowler, *and* from the noisome pestilence.

4 He shall cover thee with his feathers, and under his wings shalt thou trust: his truth *shall be thy* shield and buckler.

5 Thou shalt not be afraid for the terror by night; *nor* for the arrow *that* flieth by day;

6 *Nor* for the pestilence *that* walketh in darkness; *nor* for the destruction *that* wasteth at noonday.

7 A thousand shall fall at thy side, and ten thousand at thy right hand; *but* it shall not come nigh thee.

8 Only with thine eyes shalt thou behold and see the reward of the wicked.

9 Because thou hast made the LORD, *which is* my refuge, *even* the Most High, thy habitation;

10 There shall no evil befall thee, neither shall any plague come nigh thy dwelling.

11 For he shall give his angels charge over thee, to keep thee in all thy ways.

12 They shall bear thee up in *their* hands, lest thou dash thy foot against a stone.

13 Thou shalt tread upon the lion and adder: the young lion and the dragon shalt thou trample under feet.

14 Because he hath set his love upon me, therefore will I deliver him: I will set him on high, because he hath known my name.

15 He shall call upon me, and I will answer him: I *will be* with him in trouble; I will deliver him, and honor him.

16 With long life will I satisfy him, and show him my salvation.

PSALM 92

A Psalm *or* Song for the sabbath day.

IT *is* a good thing to give thanks unto the LORD, and to sing praises unto thy name, O Most High:

2 To show forth thy loving-kindness in the morning, and thy faithfulness every night,

3 Upon an instrument of ten strings, and upon the psaltery; upon the harp with a solemn sound.

4 For thou, LORD, hast made me glad through thy work: I will triumph in the works of thy hands.

5 O LORD, how great are thy works! *and* thy thoughts are very deep.

6 A brutish man knoweth not; neither doth a fool understand this.

7 When the wicked spring as the grass, and when all the workers of iniquity do flourish; *it is* that they shall be destroyed for ever:

8 But thou, LORD, *art most* high for evermore.

9 For, lo, thine enemies, O LORD, for, lo, thine enemies shall perish; all the workers of iniquity shall be scattered.

10 But my horn shalt thou exalt like *the horn of* a unicorn: I shall be anointed with fresh oil.

11 Mine eye also shall see *my desire* on mine enemies, *and* mine ears shall

hear *my desire* of the wicked that rise up against me.

12 The righteous shall flourish like the palm tree: he shall grow like a cedar in Lebanon.

13 Those that be planted in the house of the LORD shall flourish in the courts of our God.

14 They shall still bring forth fruit in old age; they shall be fat and flourishing;

15 To show that the LORD *is* upright: *he is* my rock, and *there is* no unrighteousness in him.

PSALM 93

THE LORD reigneth, he is clothed with majesty; the LORD is clothed with strength, *wherewith* he hath girded himself: the world also is stablished, that it cannot be moved.

2 Thy throne *is* established of old: thou *art* from everlasting.

3 The floods have lifted up, O LORD, the floods have lifted up their voice; the floods lift up their waves.

4 The LORD on high *is* mightier than the noise of many waters, *yea, than* the mighty waves of the sea.

5 Thy testimonies are very sure: holiness becometh thine house, O LORD, for ever.

PSALM 94

O LORD God, to whom vengeance belongeth; O God, to whom vengeance belongeth, show thyself.

2 Lift up thyself, thou judge of the earth: render a reward to the proud.

3 LORD, how long shall the wicked, how long shall the wicked triumph?

4 *How long* shall they utter *and* speak hard things? *and* all the workers of iniquity boast themselves?

5 They break in pieces thy people, O LORD, and afflict thine heritage.

6 They slay the widow and the stranger, and murder the fatherless.

7 Yet they say, The LORD shall not see, neither shall the God of Jacob regard *it*.

8 Understand, ye brutish among the people: and *ye* fools, when will ye be wise?

9 He that planted the ear, shall he not hear? he that formed the eye, shall he not see?

10 He that chastiseth the heathen, shall not he correct? he that teacheth man knowledge, *shall not he know?*

11 The LORD knoweth the thoughts of man, that they *are* vanity.

12 Blessed *is* the man whom thou chastenest, O LORD, and teachest him out of thy law;

13 That thou mayest give him rest from the days of adversity, until the pit be digged for the wicked.

14 For the LORD will not cast off his people, neither will he forsake his inheritance.

15 But judgment shall return unto righteousness: and all the upright in heart shall follow it.

16 Who will rise up for me against the evildoers? *or* who will stand up for me against the workers of iniquity?

17 Unless the LORD *had been* my help, my soul had almost dwelt in silence.

18 When I said, My foot slippeth; thy mercy, O LORD, held me up.

19 In the multitude of my thoughts within me thy comforts delight my soul.

20 Shall the throne of iniquity have fellowship with thee, which frameth mischief by a law?

21 They gather themselves together against the soul of the righteous, and condemn the innocent blood.

22 But the LORD is my defense; and my God *is* the rock of my refuge.

23 And he shall bring upon them their own iniquity, and shall cut them off in their own wickedness; *yea,* the LORD our God shall cut them off.

PSALM 95

O COME, let us sing unto the LORD: let us make a joyful noise to the rock of our salvation.

2 Let us come before his presence with thanksgiving, and make a joyful noise unto him with psalms.

3 For the LORD *is* a great God, and a great King above all gods.

4 In his hand *are* the deep places of the earth: the strength of the hills *is* his also.

5 The sea *is* his, and he made it: and his hands formed the dry *land*.

6 O come, let us worship and bow down: let us kneel before the LORD our maker.

7 For he *is* our God; and we *are* the people of his pasture, and the sheep of his hand. To-day if ye will hear his voice,

8 Harden not your heart, as in the

provocation, *and* as *in* the day of temptation in the wilderness:
9 When your fathers tempted me,
proved me, and saw my work.
10 Forty years long was I grieved with
this generation, and said, It *is* a people
that do err in their heart, and they have
not known my ways:
11 Unto whom I sware in my wrath
that they should not enter into my rest.

PSALM 96

O SING unto the LORD a new song:
sing unto the LORD, all the earth.
2 Sing unto the LORD, bless his name;
show forth his salvation from day to
day.
3 Declare his glory among the heathen,
his wonders among all people.
4 For the LORD *is* great, and greatly to
be praised: he *is* to be feared above all
gods.
5 For all the gods of the nations
are idols: but the LORD made the
heavens.
6 Honor and majesty *are* before him:
strength and beauty *are* in his sanctuary.
7 Give unto the LORD, O ye kindreds
of the people, give unto the LORD glory
and strength.
8 Give unto the LORD the glory *due*
unto his name: bring an offering, and
come into his courts.
9 O worship the LORD in the beauty
of holiness: fear before him, all the
earth.
10 Say among the heathen *that* the
LORD reigneth: the world also shall be
established that it shall not be moved:
he shall judge the people righteously.
11 Let the heavens rejoice, and let the
earth be glad; let the sea roar, and the
fulness thereof.
12 Let the field be joyful, and all that
is therein: then shall all the trees of the
wood rejoice
13 Before the LORD: for he cometh, for
he cometh to judge the earth: he shall
judge the world with righteousness,
and the people with his truth.

PSALM 97

THE LORD reigneth; let the earth
rejoice; let the multitude of isles be
glad *thereof*.
2 Clouds and darkness *are* round about
him: righteousness and judgment *are*
the habitation of his throne.
3 A fire goeth before him, and burneth
up his enemies round about.
4 His lightnings enlightened the world:
the earth saw, and trembled.
5 The hills melted like wax at the presence of the LORD, at the presence of the
Lord of the whole earth.
6 The heavens declare his righteousness, and all the people see his glory.
7 Confounded be all they that serve
graven images, that boast themselves of
idols: worship him, all *ye* gods.
8 Zion heard, and was glad; and the
daughters of Judah rejoiced because of
thy judgments, O LORD.
9 For thou, LORD, *art* high above all
the earth: thou art exalted far above all
gods.
10 Ye that love the LORD, hate evil:
he preserveth the souls of his saints; he
delivereth them out of the hand of the
wicked.
11 Light is sown for the righteous, and
gladness for the upright in heart.
12 Rejoice in the LORD, ye righteous;
and give thanks at the remembrance of
his holiness.

PSALM 98

A Psalm.

O SING unto the LORD a new song;
for he hath done marvelous things:
his right hand, and his holy arm, hath
gotten him the victory.
2 The LORD hath made known his salvation: his righteousness hath he openly
showed in the sight of the heathen.
3 He hath remembered his mercy and
his truth toward the house of Ĭş′rā-ĕl:
all the ends of the earth have seen the
salvation of our God.
4 Make a joyful noise unto the LORD,
all the earth: make a loud noise, and
rejoice, and sing praise.
5 Sing unto the LORD with the harp;
with the harp, and the voice of a psalm.
6 With trumpets and sound of cornet
make a joyful noise before the LORD,
the King.
7 Let the sea roar, and the fulness
thereof; the world, and they that dwell
therein.
8 Let the floods clap *their* hands: let
the hills be joyful together
9 Before the LORD; for he cometh to
judge the earth: with righteousness
shall he judge the world, and the people
with equity.

PSALM 99

THE LORD reigneth; let the people tremble: he sitteth *between* the cherubim; let the earth be moved.
2 The LORD *is* great in Zion; and he *is* high above all the people.
3 Let them praise thy great and terrible name; *for* it *is* holy.
4 The king's strength also loveth judgment; thou dost establish equity, thou executest judgment and righteousness in Jacob.
5 Exalt ye the LORD our God, and worship at his footstool; *for* he *is* holy.
6 Moses and Aaron among his priests, and Samuel among them that call upon his name; they called upon the LORD, and he answered them.
7 He spake unto them in the cloudy pillar: they kept his testimonies, and the ordinance *that* he gave them.
8 Thou answeredst them, O LORD our God: thou wast a God that forgavest them, though thou tookest vengeance of their inventions.
9 Exalt the LORD our God, and worship at his holy hill; for the LORD our God *is* holy.

PSALM 100

A Psalm of praise.

MAKE a joyful noise unto the LORD, all ye lands.
2 Serve the LORD with gladness: come before his presence with singing.
3 Know ye that the LORD he *is* God: *it is* he *that* hath made us, and not we ourselves; *we are* his people, and the sheep of his pasture.
4 Enter into his gates with thanksgiving, *and* into his courts with praise: be thankful unto him, *and* bless his name.
5 For the LORD *is* good; his mercy *is* everlasting; and his truth *endureth* to all generations.

PSALM 101

A Psalm of David.

I WILL sing of mercy and judgment: unto thee, O LORD, will I sing.
2 I will behave myself wisely in a perfect way. O when wilt thou come unto me? I will walk within my house with a perfect heart.
3 I will set no wicked thing before mine eyes: I hate the work of them that turn aside; *it* shall not cleave to me.
4 A froward heart shall depart from me: I will not know a wicked *person*.
5 Whoso privily slandereth his neighbor, him will I cut off: him that hath a high look and a proud heart will not I suffer.
6 Mine eyes *shall be* upon the faithful of the land, that they may dwell with me: he that walketh in a perfect way, he shall serve me.
7 He that worketh deceit shall not dwell within my house: he that telleth lies shall not tarry in my sight.
8 I will early destroy all the wicked of the land; that I may cut off all wicked doers from the city of the LORD.

PSALM 102

A Prayer of the afflicted, when he is overwhelmed, and poureth out his complaint before the LORD.

HEAR my prayer, O LORD, and let my cry come unto thee.
2 Hide not thy face from me in the day *when* I am in trouble; incline thine ear unto me: in the day *when* I call answer me speedily.
3 For my days are consumed like smoke, and my bones are burned as a hearth.
4 My heart is smitten, and withered like grass; so that I forget to eat my bread.
5 By reason of the voice of my groaning my bones cleave to my skin.
6 I am like a pelican of the wilderness: I am like an owl of the desert.
7 I watch, and am as a sparrow alone upon the housetop.
8 Mine enemies reproach me all the day; *and* they that are mad against me are sworn against me.
9 For I have eaten ashes like bread, and mingled my drink with weeping,
10 Because of thine indignation and thy wrath: for thou hast lifted me up, and cast me down.
11 My days *are* like a shadow that declineth; and I am withered like grass.
12 But thou, O LORD, shalt endure for ever; and thy remembrance unto all generations.
13 Thou shalt arise, *and* have mercy upon Zion: for the time to favor her, yea, the set time, is come.
14 For thy servants take pleasure in her stones, and favor the dust thereof.
15 So the heathen shall fear the name

of the LORD, and all the kings of the earth thy glory.

16 When the LORD shall build up Zion, he shall appear in his glory.

17 He will regard the prayer of the destitute, and not despise their prayer.

18 This shall be written for the generation to come: and the people which shall be created shall praise the LORD.

19 For he hath looked down from the height of his sanctuary; from heaven did the LORD behold the earth;

20 To hear the groaning of the prisoner; to loose those that are appointed to death;

21 To declare the name of the LORD in Zion, and his praise in Jerusalem;

22 When the people are gathered together, and the kingdoms, to serve the LORD.

23 He weakened my strength in the way; he shortened my days.

24 I said, O my God, take me not away in the midst of my days: thy years *are* throughout all generations.

25 Of old hast thou laid the foundation of the earth: and the heavens *are* the work of thy hands.

26 They shall perish, but thou shalt endure: yea, all of them shall wax old like a garment; as a vesture shalt thou change them, and they shall be changed:

27 But thou *art* the same, and thy years shall have no end.

28 The children of thy servants shall continue, and their seed shall be established before thee.

PSALM 103

A Psalm of David.

BLESS the LORD, O my soul: and all that is within me, *bless* his holy name.

2 Bless the LORD, O my soul, and forget not all his benefits:

3 Who forgiveth all thine iniquities; who healeth all thy diseases;

4 Who redeemeth thy life from destruction; who crowneth thee with loving-kindness and tender mercies;

5 Who satisfieth thy mouth with good *things; so that* thy youth is renewed like the eagle's.

6 The LORD executeth righteousness and judgment for all that are oppressed.

7 He made known his ways unto Moses, his acts unto the children of Is'rā-ĕl.

8 The LORD *is* merciful and gracious, slow to anger, and plenteous in mercy.

9 He will not always chide: neither will he keep *his anger* for ever.

10 He hath not dealt with us after our sins; nor rewarded us according to our iniquities.

11 For as the heaven is high above the earth, *so* great is his mercy toward them that fear him.

12 As far as the east is from the west, *so* far hath he removed our transgressions from us.

13 Like as a father pitieth *his* children, *so* the LORD pitieth them that fear him.

14 For he knoweth our frame; he remembereth that we *are* dust.

15 *As for* man, his days *are* as grass: as a flower of the field, so he flourisheth.

16 For the wind passeth over it, and it is gone; and the place thereof shall know it no more.

17 But the mercy of the LORD *is* from everlasting to everlasting upon them that fear him, and his righteousness unto children's children;

18 To such as keep his covenant, and to those that remember his commandments to do them.

19 The LORD hath prepared his throne in the heavens; and his kingdom ruleth over all.

20 Bless the LORD, ye his angels, that excel in strength, that do his commandments, hearkening unto the voice of his word.

21 Bless ye the LORD, all *ye* his hosts; *ye* ministers of his, that do his pleasure.

22 Bless the LORD, all his works in all places of his dominion: bless the LORD, O my soul.

PSALM 104

BLESS the LORD, O my soul. O LORD my God, thou art very great; thou art clothed with honor and majesty:

2 Who coverest *thyself* with light as *with* a garment: who stretchest out the heavens like a curtain:

3 Who layeth the beams of his chambers in the waters: who maketh the clouds his chariot: who walketh upon the wings of the wind:

4 Who maketh his angels spirits; his ministers a flaming fire:

5 *Who* laid the foundations of the earth, *that* it should not be removed for ever.

6 Thou coveredst it with the deep as
with a garment: the waters stood above
the mountains.
7 At thy rebuke they fled; at the voice
of thy thunder they hasted away.
8 They go up by the mountains; they
go down by the valleys unto the place
which thou hast founded for them.
9 Thou hast set a bound that they may
not pass over; that they turn not again
to cover the earth.
10 He sendeth the springs into the valleys, *which* run among the hills.
11 They give drink to every beast of
the field: the wild asses quench their
thirst.
12 By them shall the fowls of the
heaven have their habitation, *which*
sing among the branches.
13 He watereth the hills from his
chambers: the earth is satisfied with the
fruit of thy works.
14 He causeth the grass to grow for the
cattle, and herb for the service of man:
that he may bring forth food out of the
earth;
15 And wine *that* maketh glad the heart
of man, *and* oil to make *his* face to shine,
and bread *which* strengtheneth man's
heart.
16 The trees of the LORD are full *of*
sap; the cedars of Lebanon, which he
hath planted;
17 Where the birds make their nests: *as*
for the stork, the fir trees *are* her house.
18 The high hills *are* a refuge for the
wild goats; *and* the rocks for the conies.
19 He appointed the moon for seasons:
the sun knoweth his going down.
20 Thou makest darkness, and it is
night: wherein all the beasts of the forest do creep *forth*.
21 The young lions roar after their
prey, and seek their meat from God.
22 The sun ariseth, they gather themselves together, and lay them down in
their dens.
23 Man goeth forth unto his work and
to his labor until the evening.
24 O LORD, how manifold are thy
works! in wisdom hast thou made them
all: the earth is full of thy riches.
25 *So is* this great and wide sea, wherein *are* things creeping innumerable,
both small and great beasts.
26 There go the ships: *there is* that
leviathan, *whom* thou hast made to play
therein.
27 These wait all upon thee; that thou
mayest give *them* their meat in due
season.
28 *That* thou givest them they gather:
thou openest thine hand, they are filled
with good.
29 Thou hidest thy face, they are
troubled: thou takest away their breath,
they die, and return to their dust.
30 Thou sendest forth thy spirit, they
are created: and thou renewest the face
of the earth.
31 The glory of the LORD shall endure
for ever: the LORD shall rejoice in his
works.
32 He looketh on the earth, and it
trembleth: he toucheth the hills, and
they smoke.
33 I will sing unto the LORD as long as
I live: I will sing praise to my God while
I have my being.
34 My meditation of him shall be
sweet: I will be glad in the LORD.
35 Let the sinners be consumed out of
the earth, and let the wicked be no
more. Bless thou the LORD, O my soul.
Praise ye the LORD.

PSALM 105

O GIVE thanks unto the LORD; call
upon his name: make known his
deeds among the people.
2 Sing unto him, sing psalms unto him:
talk ye of all his wondrous works.
3 Glory ye in his holy name: let the
heart of them rejoice that seek the
LORD.
4 Seek the LORD, and his strength:
seek his face evermore.
5 Remember his marvelous works that
he hath done; his wonders, and the
judgments of his mouth;
6 O ye seed of Abraham his servant,
ye children of Jacob his chosen.
7 He *is* the LORD our God: his judgments *are* in all the earth.
8 He hath remembered his covenant
for ever, the word *which* he commanded
to a thousand generations.
9 Which *covenant* he made with Abraham, and his oath unto Isaac;
10 And confirmed the same unto Jacob
for a law, *and* to Ĭş'rā-ĕl *for* an everlasting covenant:
11 Saying, Unto thee will I give the
land of Cā'năan, the lot of your inheritance:

12 When they were *but* a few men in
number; yea, very few, and strangers
in it.
13 When they went from one nation to
another, from *one* kingdom to another
people;
14 He suffered no man to do them
wrong: yea, he reproved kings for their
sakes;
15 *Saying,* Touch not mine anointed,
and do my prophets no harm.
16 Moreover he called for a famine
upon the land: he brake the whole staff
of bread.
17 He sent a man before them, *even*
Joseph, *who* was sold for a servant:
18 Whose feet they hurt with fetters:
he was laid in iron:
19 Until the time that his word came:
the word of the LORD tried him.
20 The king sent and loosed him; *even*
the ruler of the people, and let him go
free.
21 He made him lord of his house, and
ruler of all his substance:
22 To bind his princes at his pleasure;
and teach his senators wisdom.
23 Ĭş'rā-ĕl also came into Egypt; and
Jacob sojourned in the land of Ham.
24 And he increased his people greatly;
and made them stronger than their
enemies.
25 He turned their heart to hate his
people, to deal subtilely with his
servants.
26 He sent Moses his servant; *and*
Aaron whom he had chosen.
27 They showed his signs among them,
and wonders in the land of Ham.
28 He sent darkness, and made it
dark; and they rebelled not against his
word.
29 He turned their waters into blood,
and slew their fish.
30 Their land brought forth frogs in
abundance, in the chambers of their
kings.
31 He spake, and there came divers
sorts of flies, *and* lice in all their coasts.
32 He gave them hail for rain, *and*
flaming fire in their land.
33 He smote their vines also and their
fig trees; and brake the trees of their
coasts.
34 He spake, and the locusts came,
and caterpillars, and that without
number,
35 And did eat up all the herbs in their
land, and devoured the fruit of their
ground.
36 He smote also all the firstborn
in their land, the chief of all their
strength.
37 He brought them forth also with silver and gold: and *there was* not one
feeble *person* among their tribes.
38 Egypt was glad when they departed:
for the fear of them fell upon them.
39 He spread a cloud for a covering;
and fire to give light in the night.
40 *The people* asked, and he brought
quails, and satisfied them with the
bread of heaven.
41 He opened the rock, and the waters
gushed out; they ran in the dry places
like a river.
42 For he remembered his holy promise, *and* Abraham his servant.
43 And he brought forth his people
with joy, *and* his chosen with gladness:
44 And gave them the lands of the
heathen: and they inherited the labor of
the people;
45 That they might observe his statutes, and keep his laws. Praise ye the
LORD.

PSALM 106

PRAISE ye the LORD. O give thanks
unto the LORD; for *he is* good: for
his mercy *endureth* for ever.
2 Who can utter the mighty acts of
the LORD? *who* can show forth all his
praise?
3 Blessed *are* they that keep judgment,
and he that doeth righteousness at all
times.
4 Remember me, O LORD, with the
favor *that thou bearest unto* thy people:
O visit me with thy salvation;
5 That I may see the good of thy
chosen, that I may rejoice in the gladness of thy nation, that I may glory with
thine inheritance.
6 We have sinned with our fathers, we
have committed iniquity, we have done
wickedly.
7 Our fathers understood not thy wonders in Egypt; they remembered not
the multitude of thy mercies; but provoked *him* at the sea, *even* at the Red
sea.
8 Nevertheless he saved them for his
name's sake, that he might make his
mighty power to be known.
9 He rebuked the Red sea also, and it

was dried up: so he led them through the depths, as through the wilderness.

10 And he saved them from the hand of him that hated *them,* and redeemed them from the hand of the enemy.

11 And the waters covered their enemies: there was not one of them left.

12 Then believed they his words; they sang his praise.

13 They soon forgat his works; they waited not for his counsel:

14 But lusted exceedingly in the wilderness, and tempted God in the desert.

15 And he gave them their request; but sent leanness into their soul.

16 They envied Moses also in the camp, *and* Aaron the saint of the LORD.

17 The earth opened and swallowed up Dā'thăn, and covered the company of Ȧ-bī'răm.

18 And a fire was kindled in their company; the flame burned up the wicked.

19 They made a calf in Hō'rĕb, and worshipped the molten image.

20 Thus they changed their glory into the similitude of an ox that eateth grass.

21 They forgat God their saviour, which had done great things in Egypt;

22 Wondrous works in the land of Ham, *and* terrible things by the Red sea.

23 Therefore he said that he would destroy them, had not Moses his chosen stood before him in the breach, to turn away his wrath, lest he should destroy *them.*

24 Yea, they despised the pleasant land, they believed not his word:

25 But murmured in their tents, *and* hearkened not unto the voice of the LORD.

26 Therefore he lifted up his hand against them, to overthrow them in the wilderness:

27 To overthrow their seed also among the nations, and to scatter them in the lands.

28 They joined themselves also unto Bā'ăl–pē'ŏr, and ate the sacrifices of the dead.

29 Thus they provoked *him* to anger with their inventions: and the plague brake in upon them.

30 Then stood up Phĭn'ē-hăs, and executed judgment: and *so* the plague was stayed.

31 And that was counted unto him for righteousness unto all generations for evermore.

32 They angered *him* also at the waters of strife, so that it went ill with Moses for their sakes:

33 Because they provoked his spirit, so that he spake unadvisedly with his lips.

34 They did not destroy the nations, concerning whom the LORD commanded them:

35 But were mingled among the heathen, and learned their works.

36 And they served their idols: which were a snare unto them.

37 Yea, they sacrificed their sons and their daughters unto devils,

38 And shed innocent blood, *even* the blood of their sons and of their daughters, whom they sacrificed unto the idols of Cā'năan: and the land was polluted with blood.

39 Thus were they defiled with their own works, and went a whoring with their own inventions.

40 Therefore was the wrath of the LORD kindled against his people, insomuch that he abhorred his own inheritance.

41 And he gave them into the hand of the heathen; and they that hated them ruled over them.

42 Their enemies also oppressed them, and they were brought into subjection under their hand.

43 Many times did he deliver them; but they provoked *him* with their counsel, and were brought low for their iniquity.

44 Nevertheless he regarded their affliction, when he heard their cry:

45 And he remembered for them his covenant, and repented according to the multitude of his mercies.

46 He made them also to be pitied of all those that carried them captives.

47 Save us, O LORD our God, and gather us from among the heathen, to give thanks unto thy holy name, *and* to triumph in thy praise.

48 Blessed *be* the LORD God of Ĭṣ'rā-ĕl from everlasting to everlasting: and let all the people say, Amen. Praise ye the LORD.

PSALM 107

O GIVE thanks unto the LORD, for *he is* good: for his mercy *endureth* for ever.

2 Let the redeemed of the LORD say *so,* whom he hath redeemed from the hand of the enemy;

3 And gathered them out of the lands, from the east, and from the west, from the north, and from the south.

4 They wandered in the wilderness in a solitary way; they found no city to dwell in.

5 Hungry and thirsty, their soul fainted in them.

6 Then they cried unto the LORD in their trouble, *and* he delivered them out of their distresses.

7 And he led them forth by the right way, that they might go to a city of habitation.

8 Oh that *men* would praise the LORD *for* his goodness, and *for* his wonderful works to the children of men!

9 For he satisfieth the longing soul, and filleth the hungry soul with goodness.

10 Such as sit in darkness and in the shadow of death, *being* bound in affliction and iron;

11 Because they rebelled against the words of God, and contemned the counsel of the Most High:

12 Therefore he brought down their heart with labor; they fell down, and *there was* none to help.

13 Then they cried unto the LORD in their trouble, *and* he saved them out of their distresses.

14 He brought them out of darkness and the shadow of death, and brake their bands in sunder.

15 Oh that *men* would praise the LORD *for* his goodness, and *for* his wonderful works to the children of men!

16 For he hath broken the gates of brass, and cut the bars of iron in sunder.

17 Fools, because of their transgression, and because of their iniquities, are afflicted.

18 Their soul abhorreth all manner of meat; and they draw near unto the gates of death.

19 Then they cry unto the LORD in their trouble, *and* he saveth them out of their distresses.

20 He sent his word, and healed them, and delivered *them* from their destructions.

21 Oh that *men* would praise the LORD *for* his goodness, and *for* his wonderful works to the children of men!

22 And let them sacrifice the sacrifices of thanksgiving, and declare his works with rejoicing.

23 They that go down to the sea in ships, that do business in great waters;

24 These see the works of the LORD, and his wonders in the deep.

25 For he commandeth, and raiseth the stormy wind, which lifteth up the waves thereof.

26 They mount up to the heaven, they go down again to the depths: their soul is melted because of trouble.

27 They reel to and fro, and stagger like a drunken man, and are at their wit's end.

28 Then they cry unto the LORD in their trouble, and he bringeth them out of their distresses.

29 He maketh the storm a calm, so that the waves thereof are still.

30 Then are they glad because they be quiet; so he bringeth them unto their desired haven.

31 Oh that *men* would praise the LORD *for* his goodness, and *for* his wonderful works to the children of men!

32 Let them exalt him also in the congregation of the people, and praise him in the assembly of the elders.

33 He turneth rivers into a wilderness, and the watersprings into dry ground;

34 A fruitful land into barrenness, for the wickedness of them that dwell therein.

35 He turneth the wilderness into a standing water, and dry ground into watersprings.

36 And there he maketh the hungry to dwell, that they may prepare a city for habitation;

37 And sow the fields, and plant vineyards, which may yield fruits of increase.

38 He blesseth them also, so that they are multiplied greatly; and suffereth not their cattle to decrease.

39 Again, they are minished and brought low through oppression, affliction, and sorrow.

40 He poureth contempt upon princes, and causeth them to wander in the wilderness, *where there is* no way.

41 Yet setteth he the poor on high from affliction, and maketh *him* families like a flock.

42 The righteous shall see *it*, and rejoice: and all iniquity shall stop her mouth.

43 Whoso *is* wise, and will observe these *things*, even they shall understand the loving-kindness of the LORD.

PSALM 108

A Song *or* Psalm of David.

O GOD, my heart is fixed; I will sing and give praise, even with my glory.
2 Awake, psaltery and harp: I *myself* will awake early.
3 I will praise thee, O LORD, among the people: and I will sing praises unto thee among the nations.
4 For thy mercy *is* great above the heavens: and thy truth *reacheth* unto the clouds.
5 Be thou exalted, O God, above the heavens: and thy glory above all the earth;
6 That thy beloved may be delivered: save *with* thy right hand, and answer me.
7 God hath spoken in his holiness; I will rejoice, I will divide Shē'chĕm, and mete out the valley of Sŭc'cōth.
8 Gĭl'ē-ăd *is* mine; Mȧ-năs'sĕh *is* mine; Ē'phrā-ĭm also *is* the strength of mine head; Judah *is* my lawgiver;
9 Mō'ăb *is* my washpot; over Ē'dŏm will I cast out my shoe; over Phĭ-lĭs'tĭ-ȧ will I triumph.
10 Who will bring me into the strong city? who will lead me into Ē'dŏm?
11 *Wilt* not *thou,* O God, *who* hast cast us off? and wilt not thou, O God, go forth with our hosts?
12 Give us help from trouble: for vain *is* the help of man.
13 Through God we shall do valiantly: for he *it is that* shall tread down our enemies.

PSALM 109

To the chief Musician, A Psalm of David.

HOLD not thy peace, O God of my praise;
2 For the mouth of the wicked and the mouth of the deceitful are opened against me: they have spoken against me with a lying tongue.
3 They compassed me about also with words of hatred; and fought against me without a cause.
4 For my love they are my adversaries: but I *give myself unto* prayer.
5 And they have rewarded me evil for good, and hatred for my love.
6 Set thou a wicked man over him: and let Satan stand at his right hand.
7 When he shall be judged, let him be condemned: and let his prayer become sin.
8 Let his days be few; *and* let another take his office.
9 Let his children be fatherless, and his wife a widow.
10 Let his children be continually vagabonds, and beg: let them seek *their bread* also out of their desolate places.
11 Let the extortioner catch all that he hath; and let the strangers spoil his labor.
12 Let there be none to extend mercy unto him: neither let there be any to favor his fatherless children.
13 Let his posterity be cut off; *and* in the generation following let their name be blotted out.
14 Let the iniquity of his fathers be remembered with the LORD; and let not the sin of his mother be blotted out.
15 Let them be before the LORD continually, that he may cut off the memory of them from the earth.
16 Because that he remembered not to show mercy, but persecuted the poor and needy man, that he might even slay the broken in heart.
17 As he loved cursing, so let it come unto him: as he delighted not in blessing, so let it be far from him.
18 As he clothed himself with cursing like as with his garment, so let it come into his bowels like water, and like oil into his bones.
19 Let it be unto him as the garment *which* covereth him, and for a girdle wherewith he is girded continually.
20 *Let* this *be* the reward of mine adversaries from the LORD, and of them that speak evil against my soul.
21 But do thou for me, O God the LORD, for thy name's sake: because thy mercy *is* good, deliver thou me.
22 For I *am* poor and needy, and my heart is wounded within me.
23 I am gone like the shadow when it declineth: I am tossed up and down as the locust.
24 My knees are weak through fasting; and my flesh faileth of fatness.
25 I became also a reproach unto them: *when* they looked upon me they shook their heads.
26 Help me, O LORD my God: O save me according to thy mercy:
27 That they may know that this *is* thy hand; *that* thou, LORD, hast done it.
28 Let them curse, but bless thou:

when they arise, let them be ashamed; but let thy servant rejoice.

29 Let mine adversaries be clothed with shame; and let them cover themselves with their own confusion, as with a mantle.

30 I will greatly praise the LORD with my mouth; yea, I will praise him among the multitude.

31 For he shall stand at the right hand of the poor, to save *him* from those that condemn his soul.

PSALM 110

A Psalm of David.

THE LORD said unto my Lord, Sit thou at my right hand, until I make thine enemies thy footstool.

2 The LORD shall send the rod of thy strength out of Zion: rule thou in the midst of thine enemies.

3 Thy people *shall be* willing in the day of thy power, in the beauties of holiness from the womb of the morning: thou hast the dew of thy youth.

4 The LORD hath sworn, and will not repent, Thou *art* a priest for ever after the order of Měl-chĭz′ē-děk.

5 The Lord at thy right hand shall strike through kings in the day of his wrath.

6 He shall judge among the heathen, he shall fill *the places* with the dead bodies; he shall wound the heads over many countries.

7 He shall drink of the brook in the way: therefore shall he lift up the head.

PSALM 111

PRAISE ye the LORD. I will praise the LORD with *my* whole heart, in the assembly of the upright, and *in* the congregation.

2 The works of the LORD *are* great, sought out of all them that have pleasure therein.

3 His work *is* honorable and glorious: and his righteousness endureth for ever.

4 He hath made his wonderful works to be remembered: the LORD *is* gracious and full of compassion.

5 He hath given meat unto them that fear him: he will ever be mindful of his covenant.

6 He hath showed his people the power of his works, that he may give them the heritage of the heathen.

7 The works of his hands *are* verity and judgment; all his commandments *are* sure.

8 They stand fast for ever and ever, *and are* done in truth and uprightness.

9 He sent redemption unto his people: he hath commanded his covenant for ever: holy and reverend *is* his name.

10 The fear of the LORD *is* the beginning of wisdom: a good understanding have all they that do *his commandments:* his praise endureth for ever.

PSALM 112

PRAISE ye the LORD. Blessed *is* the man *that* feareth the LORD, *that* delighteth greatly in his commandments.

2 His seed shall be mighty upon earth: the generation of the upright shall be blessed.

3 Wealth and riches *shall be* in his house: and his righteousness endureth for ever.

4 Unto the upright there ariseth light in the darkness: *he is* gracious, and full of compassion, and righteous.

5 A good man showeth favor, and lendeth: he will guide his affairs with discretion.

6 Surely he shall not be moved for ever: the righteous shall be in everlasting remembrance.

7 He shall not be afraid of evil tidings: his heart is fixed, trusting in the LORD.

8 His heart *is* established, he shall not be afraid, until he see *his desire* upon his enemies.

9 He hath dispersed, he hath given to the poor; his righteousness endureth for ever; his horn shall be exalted with honor.

10 The wicked shall see *it,* and be grieved; he shall gnash with his teeth, and melt away: the desire of the wicked shall perish.

PSALM 113

PRAISE ye the LORD. Praise, O ye servants of the LORD, praise the name of the LORD.

2 Blessed be the name of the LORD from this time forth and for evermore.

3 From the rising of the sun unto the going down of the same the LORD's name *is* to be praised.

4 The LORD *is* high above all nations, *and* his glory above the heavens.

5 Who *is* like unto the LORD our God, who dwelleth on high,

6 Who humbleth *himself* to behold *the*
things that are in heaven, and in the
earth!
7 He raiseth up the poor out of the dust,
and lifteth the needy out of the dunghill;
8 That he may set *him* with princes,
even with the princes of his people.
9 He maketh the barren woman to keep
house, *and to be* a joyful mother of
children. Praise ye the LORD.

PSALM 114

WHEN Ĭş′rā-ĕl went out of Egypt,
the house of Jacob from a people
of strange language;
2 Judah was his sanctuary, *and* Ĭş′rā-ĕl
his dominion.
3 The sea saw *it,* and fled: Jordan was
driven back.
4 The mountains skipped like rams,
and the little hills like lambs.
5 What *ailed* thee, O thou sea, that
thou fleddest? thou Jordan, *that* thou
wast driven back?
6 Ye mountains, *that* ye skipped like
rams; *and* ye little hills, like lambs?
7 Tremble, thou earth, at the presence
of the Lord, at the presence of the God
of Jacob;
8 Which turned the rock *into* a standing
water, the flint into a fountain of waters.

PSALM 115

NOT unto us, O LORD, not unto us,
but unto thy name give glory, for
thy mercy, *and* for thy truth's sake.
2 Wherefore should the heathen say,
Where *is* now their God?
3 But our God *is* in the heavens: he
hath done whatsoever he hath pleased.
4 Their idols *are* silver and gold, the
work of men's hands.
5 They have mouths, but they speak
not: eyes have they, but they see not:
6 They have ears, but they hear not:
noses have they, but they smell not:
7 They have hands, but they handle
not: feet have they, but they walk not:
neither speak they through their throat.
8 They that make them are like unto
them; *so is* every one that trusteth in
them.
9 O Ĭş′rā-ĕl, trust thou in the LORD: he
is their help and their shield.
10 O house of Aaron, trust in the LORD:
he *is* their help and their shield.
11 Ye that fear the LORD, trust in the
LORD: he *is* their help and their shield.
12 The LORD hath been mindful of us:
he will bless *us;* he will bless the house
of Ĭş′rā-ĕl; he will bless the house of
Aaron.
13 He will bless them that fear the
LORD, *both* small and great.
14 The LORD shall increase you more
and more, you and your children.
15 Ye *are* blessed of the LORD which
made heaven and earth.
16 The heaven, *even* the heavens, *are*
the LORD's: but the earth hath he given
to the children of men.
17 The dead praise not the LORD, neither any that go down into silence.
18 But we will bless the LORD from
this time forth and for evermore. Praise
the LORD.

PSALM 116

I LOVE the LORD, because he hath
heard my voice *and* my supplications.
2 Because he hath inclined his ear unto
me, therefore will I call upon *him* as
long as I live.
3 The sorrows of death compassed me,
and the pains of hell gat hold upon me:
I found trouble and sorrow.
4 Then called I upon the name of the
LORD; O LORD, I beseech thee, deliver
my soul.
5 Gracious *is* the LORD, and righteous;
yea, our God *is* merciful.
6 The LORD preserveth the simple: I
was brought low, and he helped me.
7 Return unto thy rest, O my soul; for
the LORD hath dealt bountifully with
thee.
8 For thou hast delivered my soul from
death, mine eyes from tears, *and* my
feet from falling.
9 I will walk before the LORD in the
land of the living.
10 I believed, therefore have I spoken:
I was greatly afflicted:
11 I said in my haste, All men *are* liars.
12 What shall I render unto the LORD
for all his benefits toward me?
13 I will take the cup of salvation, and
call upon the name of the LORD.
14 I will pay my vows unto the LORD
now in the presence of all his people.
15 Precious in the sight of the LORD *is*
the death of his saints.
16 O LORD, truly I *am* thy servant; I
am thy servant, *and* the son of thine
handmaid: thou hast loosed my bonds.
17 I will offer to thee the sacrifice of

thanksgiving, and will call upon the
name of the LORD.
18 I will pay my vows unto the LORD
now in the presence of all his people,
19 In the courts of the LORD's house,
in the midst of thee, O Jerusalem.
Praise ye the LORD.

PSALM 117

O PRAISE the LORD, all ye nations:
praise him, all ye people.
2 For his merciful kindness is great toward us: and the truth of the LORD *endureth* for ever. Praise ye the LORD.

PSALM 118

O GIVE thanks unto the LORD; for *he
is* good: because his mercy *endureth* for ever.
2 Let Ĭş'rā-ĕl now say, that his mercy
endureth for ever.
3 Let the house of Aaron now say, that
his mercy *endureth* for ever.
4 Let them now that fear the LORD say,
that his mercy *endureth* for ever.
5 I called upon the LORD in distress:
the LORD answered me, *and set me* in a
large place.
6 The LORD *is* on my side; I will not
fear: what can man do unto me?
7 The LORD taketh my part with them
that help me: therefore shall I see *my
desire* upon them that hate me.
8 *It is* better to trust in the LORD than
to put confidence in man.
9 *It is* better to trust in the LORD than
to put confidence in princes.
10 All nations compassed me about:
but in the name of the LORD will I destroy them.
11 They compassed me about; yea,
they compassed me about: but in the
name of the LORD I will destroy them.
12 They compassed me about like
bees; they are quenched as the fire of
thorns: for in the name of the LORD I
will destroy them.
13 Thou hast thrust sore at me that I
might fall: but the LORD helped me.
14 The LORD *is* my strength and song,
and is become my salvation.
15 The voice of rejoicing and salvation
is in the tabernacles of the righteous:
the right hand of the LORD doeth valiantly.
16 The right hand of the LORD is exalted: the right hand of the LORD doeth
valiantly.
17 I shall not die, but live, and declare
the works of the LORD.
18 The LORD hath chastened me sore:
but he hath not given me over unto
death.
19 Open to me the gates of righteousness: I will go into them, *and* I will
praise the LORD:
20 This gate of the LORD, into which
the righteous shall enter.
21 I will praise thee: for thou hast
heard me, and art become my salvation.
22 The stone *which* the builders refused
is become the head *stone* of the corner.
23 This is the LORD's doing; it *is* marvelous in our eyes.
24 This *is* the day *which* the LORD hath
made; we will rejoice and be glad in it.
25 Save now, I beseech thee, O LORD:
O LORD, I beseech thee, send now
prosperity.
26 Blessed *be* he that cometh in the
name of the LORD: we have blessed you
out of the house of the LORD.
27 God *is* the LORD, which hath showed
us light: bind the sacrifice with cords,
even unto the horns of the altar.
28 Thou *art* my God, and I will praise
thee: *thou art* my God, I will exalt thee.
29 O give thanks unto the LORD; for
he is good: for his mercy *endureth* for
ever.

PSALM 119

ALEPH

BLESSED *are* the undefiled in the
way, who walk in the law of the
LORD.
2 Blessed *are* they that keep his testimonies, *and that* seek him with the
whole heart.
3 They also do no iniquity: they walk
in his ways.
4 Thou hast commanded *us* to keep thy
precepts diligently.
5 O that my ways were directed to
keep thy statutes!
6 Then shall I not be ashamed, when I
have respect unto all thy commandments.
7 I will praise thee with uprightness of
heart, when I shall have learned thy
righteous judgments.
8 I will keep thy statutes: O forsake
me not utterly.

BETH

9 Wherewithal shall a young man
cleanse his way? by taking heed *thereto*
according to thy word.

10 With my whole heart have I sought thee: O let me not wander from thy commandments.
11 Thy word have I hid in mine heart, that I might not sin against thee.
12 Blessed *art* thou, O LORD: teach me thy statutes.
13 With my lips have I declared all the judgments of thy mouth.
14 I have rejoiced in the way of thy testimonies, as *much as* in all riches.
15 I will meditate in thy precepts, and have respect unto thy ways.
16 I will delight myself in thy statutes: I will not forget thy word.

GIMEL

17 Deal bountifully with thy servant, *that* I may live, and keep thy word.
18 Open thou mine eyes, that I may behold wondrous things out of thy law.
19 I *am* a stranger in the earth: hide not thy commandments from me.
20 My soul breaketh for the longing *that it hath* unto thy judgments at all times.
21 Thou hast rebuked the proud *that are* cursed, which do err from thy commandments.
22 Remove from me reproach and contempt; for I have kept thy testimonies.
23 Princes also did sit *and* speak against me: *but* thy servant did meditate in thy statutes.
24 Thy testimonies also *are* my delight, *and* my counselors.

DALETH

25 My soul cleaveth unto the dust: quicken thou me according to thy word.
26 I have declared my ways, and thou heardest me: teach me thy statutes.
27 Make me to understand the way of thy precepts: so shall I talk of thy wondrous works.
28 My soul melteth for heaviness: strengthen thou me according unto thy word.
29 Remove from me the way of lying: and grant me thy law graciously.
30 I have chosen the way of truth: thy judgments have I laid *before me*.
31 I have stuck unto thy testimonies: O LORD, put me not to shame.
32 I will run the way of thy commandments, when thou shalt enlarge my heart.

HE

33 Teach me, O LORD, the way of thy statutes; and I shall keep it *unto* the end.
34 Give me understanding, and I shall keep thy law; yea, I shall observe it with *my* whole heart.
35 Make me to go in the path of thy commandments; for therein do I delight.
36 Incline my heart unto thy testimonies, and not to covetousness.
37 Turn away mine eyes from beholding vanity; *and* quicken thou me in thy way.
38 Stablish thy word unto thy servant, who *is devoted* to thy fear.
39 Turn away my reproach which I fear: for thy judgments *are* good.
40 Behold, I have longed after thy precepts: quicken me in thy righteousness.

VAU

41 Let thy mercies come also unto me, O LORD, *even* thy salvation, according to thy word.
42 So shall I have wherewith to answer him that reproacheth me: for I trust in thy word.
43 And take not the word of truth utterly out of my mouth; for I have hoped in thy judgments.
44 So shall I keep thy law continually for ever and ever.
45 And I will walk at liberty: for I seek thy precepts.
46 I will speak of thy testimonies also before kings, and will not be ashamed.
47 And I will delight myself in thy commandments, which I have loved.
48 My hands also will I lift up unto thy commandments, which I have loved; and I will meditate in thy statutes.

ZAIN

49 Remember the word unto thy servant, upon which thou hast caused me to hope.
50 This *is* my comfort in my affliction: for thy word hath quickened me.
51 The proud have had me greatly in derision: *yet* have I not declined from thy law.
52 I remembered thy judgments of old, O LORD; and have comforted myself.
53 Horror hath taken hold upon me because of the wicked that forsake thy law.
54 Thy statutes have been my songs in the house of my pilgrimage.

55 I have remembered thy name,
O LORD, in the night, and have kept thy
law.
56 This I had, because I kept thy precepts.

CHETH

57 *Thou art* my portion, O LORD: I
have said that I would keep thy words.
58 I entreated thy favor with *my* whole
heart: be merciful unto me according to
thy word.
59 I thought on my ways, and turned
my feet unto thy testimonies.
60 I made haste, and delayed not to
keep thy commandments.
61 The bands of the wicked have
robbed me: *but* I have not forgotten thy
law.
62 At midnight I will rise to give thanks
unto thee because of thy righteous judgments.
63 I *am* a companion of all *them* that
fear thee, and of them that keep thy
precepts.
64 The earth, O LORD, is full of thy
mercy: teach me thy statutes.

TETH

65 Thou hast dealt well with thy servant, O LORD, according unto thy word.
66 Teach me good judgment and
knowledge: for I have believed thy
commandments.
67 Before I was afflicted I went astray:
but now have I kept thy word.
68 Thou *art* good, and doest good:
teach me thy statutes.
69 The proud have forged a lie against
me: *but* I will keep thy precepts with *my*
whole heart.
70 Their heart is as fat as grease: *but* I
delight in thy law.
71 *It is* good for me that I have been
afflicted; that I might learn thy statutes.
72 The law of thy mouth *is* better unto
me than thousands of gold and silver.

JOD

73 Thy hands have made me and fashioned me: give me understanding, that
I may learn thy commandments.
74 They that fear thee will be glad
when they see me; because I have hoped
in thy word.
75 I know, O LORD, that thy judgments
are right, and *that* thou in faithfulness
hast afflicted me.
76 Let, I pray thee, thy merciful kindness be for my comfort, according to thy
word unto thy servant.
77 Let thy tender mercies come unto
me, that I may live: for thy law *is* my
delight.
78 Let the proud be ashamed; for they
dealt perversely with me without a
cause: *but* I will meditate in thy precepts.
79 Let those that fear thee turn unto
me, and those that have known thy
testimonies.
80 Let my heart be sound in thy statutes; that I be not ashamed.

CAPH

81 My soul fainteth for thy salvation:
but I hope in thy word.
82 Mine eyes fail for thy word, saying,
When wilt thou comfort me?
83 For I am become like a bottle in the
smoke; *yet* do I not forget thy statutes.
84 How many *are* the days of thy servant? when wilt thou execute judgment
on them that persecute me?
85 The proud have digged pits for me,
which *are* not after thy law.
86 All thy commandments *are* faithful:
they persecute me wrongfully; help
thou me.
87 They had almost consumed me upon
earth; but I forsook not thy precepts.
88 Quicken me after thy loving-kindness; so shall I keep the testimony of
thy mouth.

LAMED

89 For ever, O LORD, thy word is settled in heaven.
90 Thy faithfulness *is* unto all generations: thou hast established the earth,
and it abideth.
91 They continue this day according to
thine ordinances: for all *are* thy servants.
92 Unless thy law *had been* my delights, I should then have perished in
mine affliction.
93 I will never forget thy precepts: for
with them thou hast quickened me.
94 I *am* thine, save me; for I have
sought thy precepts.
95 The wicked have waited for me to
destroy me: *but* I will consider thy testimonies.
96 I have seen an end of all perfection:
but thy commandment *is* exceeding
broad.

MEM

97 O how love I thy law! it *is* my meditation all the day.

98 Thou through thy commandments hast made me wiser than mine enemies: for they *are* ever with me.
99 I have more understanding than all my teachers: for thy testimonies *are* my meditation.
100 I understand more than the ancients, because I keep thy precepts.
101 I have refrained my feet from every evil way, that I might keep thy word.
102 I have not departed from thy judgments: for thou hast taught me.
103 How sweet are thy words unto my taste! *yea, sweeter* than honey to my mouth.
104 Through thy precepts I get understanding: therefore I hate every false way.

NUN

105 Thy word *is* a lamp unto my feet, and a light unto my path.
106 I have sworn, and I will perform *it*, that I will keep thy righteous judgments.
107 I am afflicted very much: quicken me, O LORD, according unto thy word.
108 Accept, I beseech thee, the freewill offerings of my mouth, O LORD, and teach me thy judgments.
109 My soul *is* continually in my hand: yet do I not forget thy law.
110 The wicked have laid a snare for me: yet I erred not from thy precepts.
111 Thy testimonies have I taken as a heritage for ever: for they *are* the rejoicing of my heart.
112 I have inclined mine heart to perform thy statutes always, *even unto* the end.

SAMECH

113 I hate *vain* thoughts: but thy law do I love.
114 Thou *art* my hiding place and my shield: I hope in thy word.
115 Depart from me, ye evildoers: for I will keep the commandments of my God.
116 Uphold me according unto thy word, that I may live: and let me not be ashamed of my hope.
117 Hold thou me up, and I shall be safe: and I will have respect unto thy statutes continually.
118 Thou hast trodden down all them that err from thy statutes: for their deceit *is* falsehood.
119 Thou puttest away all the wicked of the earth *like* dross: therefore I love thy testimonies.
120 My flesh trembleth for fear of thee; and I am afraid of thy judgments.

AIN

121 I have done judgment and justice: leave me not to mine oppressors.
122 Be surety for thy servant for good: let not the proud oppress me.
123 Mine eyes fail for thy salvation, and for the word of thy righteousness.
124 Deal with thy servant according unto thy mercy, and teach me thy statutes.
125 I *am* thy servant; give me understanding, that I may know thy testimonies.
126 *It is* time for *thee*, LORD, to work: *for* they have made void thy law.
127 Therefore I love thy commandments above gold; yea, above fine gold.
128 Therefore I esteem all *thy* precepts *concerning* all *things to be* right; *and* I hate every false way.

PE

129 Thy testimonies *are* wonderful: therefore doth my soul keep them.
130 The entrance of thy words giveth light; it giveth understanding unto the simple.
131 I opened my mouth, and panted: for I longed for thy commandments.
132 Look thou upon me, and be merciful unto me, as thou usest to do unto those that love thy name.
133 Order my steps in thy word: and let not any iniquity have dominion over me.
134 Deliver me from the oppression of man: so will I keep thy precepts.
135 Make thy face to shine upon thy servant; and teach me thy statutes.
136 Rivers of waters run down mine eyes, because they keep not thy law.

TZADDI

137 Righteous *art* thou, O LORD, and upright *are* thy judgments.
138 Thy testimonies *that* thou hast commanded *are* righteous and very faithful.
139 My zeal hath consumed me, because mine enemies have forgotten thy words.
140 Thy word *is* very pure: therefore thy servant loveth it.
141 I *am* small and despised: *yet* do not I forget thy precepts.

142 Thy righteousness *is* an everlasting righteousness, and thy law *is* the truth.
143 Trouble and anguish have taken hold on me: *yet* thy commandments *are* my delights.
144 The righteousness of thy testimonies *is* everlasting: give me understanding, and I shall live.

KOPH

145 I cried with *my* whole heart; hear me, O LORD: I will keep thy statutes.
146 I cried unto thee; save me, and I shall keep thy testimonies.
147 I prevented the dawning of the morning, and cried: I hoped in thy word.
148 Mine eyes prevent the *night* watches, that I might meditate in thy word.
149 Hear my voice according unto thy loving-kindness: O LORD, quicken me according to thy judgment.
150 They draw nigh that follow after mischief: they are far from thy law.
151 Thou *art* near, O LORD; and all thy commandments *are* truth.
152 Concerning thy testimonies, I have known of old that thou hast founded them for ever.

RESH

153 Consider mine affliction, and deliver me: for I do not forget thy law.
154 Plead my cause, and deliver me: quicken me according to thy word.
155 Salvation *is* far from the wicked: for they seek not thy statutes.
156 Great *are* thy tender mercies, O LORD: quicken me according to thy judgments.
157 Many *are* my persecutors and mine enemies; *yet* do I not decline from thy testimonies.
158 I beheld the transgressors, and was grieved; because they kept not thy word.
159 Consider how I love thy precepts: quicken me, O LORD, according to thy loving-kindness.
160 Thy word *is* true *from* the beginning: and every one of thy righteous judgments *endureth* for ever.

SCHIN

161 Princes have persecuted me without a cause: but my heart standeth in awe of thy word.
162 I rejoice at thy word, as one that findeth great spoil.
163 I hate and abhor lying: *but* thy law do I love.
164 Seven times a day do I praise thee, because of thy righteous judgments.
165 Great peace have they which love thy law: and nothing shall offend them.
166 LORD, I have hoped for thy salvation, and done thy commandments.
167 My soul hath kept thy testimonies; and I love them exceedingly.
168 I have kept thy precepts and thy testimonies: for all my ways *are* before thee.

TAU

169 Let my cry come near before thee, O LORD: give me understanding according to thy word.
170 Let my supplication come before thee: deliver me according to thy word.
171 My lips shall utter praise, when thou hast taught me thy statutes.
172 My tongue shall speak of thy word: for all thy commandments *are* righteousness.
173 Let thine hand help me; for I have chosen thy precepts.
174 I have longed for thy salvation, O LORD; and thy law *is* my delight.
175 Let my soul live, and it shall praise thee; and let thy judgments help me.
176 I have gone astray like a lost sheep: seek thy servant; for I do not forget thy commandments.

PSALM 120

A Song of degrees.

IN my distress I cried unto the LORD, and he heard me.
2 Deliver my soul, O LORD, from lying lips, *and* from a deceitful tongue.
3 What shall be given unto thee? or what shall be done unto thee, thou false tongue?
4 Sharp arrows of the mighty, with coals of juniper.
5 Woe is me, that I sojourn in Mē′sĕch, *that* I dwell in the tents of Kē′dar!
6 My soul hath long dwelt with him that hateth peace.
7 I *am for* peace: but when I speak, they *are* for war.

PSALM 121

A Song of degrees.

I WILL lift up mine eyes unto the hills, from whence cometh my help.
2 My help *cometh* from the LORD, which made heaven and earth.

3 He will not suffer thy foot to be
moved: he that keepeth thee will not
slumber.
4 Behold, he that keepeth Ĭṣ′rā-ĕl shall
neither slumber nor sleep.
5 The LORD *is* thy keeper: the LORD *is*
thy shade upon thy right hand.
6 The sun shall not smite thee by day,
nor the moon by night.
7 The LORD shall preserve thee from
all evil: he shall preserve thy soul.
8 The LORD shall preserve thy going
out and thy coming in from this time
forth, and even for evermore.

PSALM 122

A Song of degrees of David.

I WAS glad when they said unto
me, Let us go into the house of the
LORD.
2 Our feet shall stand within thy gates,
O Jerusalem.
3 Jerusalem is builded as a city that is
compact together:
4 Whither the tribes go up, the tribes
of the LORD, unto the testimony of Ĭṣ′-
rā-ĕl, to give thanks unto the name of
the LORD.
5 For there are set thrones of judgment, the thrones of the house of
David.
6 Pray for the peace of Jerusalem: they
shall prosper that love thee.
7 Peace be within thy walls, *and* prosperity within thy palaces.
8 For my brethren and companions'
sakes, I will now say, Peace *be* within
thee.
9 Because of the house of the LORD
our God I will seek thy good.

PSALM 123

A Song of degrees.

UNTO thee lift I up mine eyes,
O thou that dwellest in the
heavens.
2 Behold, as the eyes of servants *look*
unto the hand of their masters, *and* as
the eyes of a maiden unto the hand of
her mistress; so our eyes *wait* upon the
LORD our God, until that he have mercy
upon us.
3 Have mercy upon us, O LORD, have
mercy upon us: for we are exceedingly
filled with contempt.
4 Our soul is exceedingly filled with the
scorning of those that are at ease, *and*
with the contempt of the proud.

PSALM 124

A Song of degrees of David.

IF *it had* not *been* the LORD who was
on our side, now may Ĭṣ′rā-ĕl say;
2 If *it had* not *been* the LORD who was
on our side, when men rose up against us:
3 Then they had swallowed us up quick,
when their wrath was kindled against us:
4 Then the waters had overwhelmed
us, the stream had gone over our soul:
5 Then the proud waters had gone over
our soul.
6 Blessed *be* the LORD, who hath not
given us *as* a prey to their teeth.
7 Our soul is escaped as a bird out of
the snare of the fowlers: the snare is
broken, and we are escaped.
8 Our help *is* in the name of the LORD,
who made heaven and earth.

PSALM 125

A Song of degrees.

THEY that trust in the LORD *shall be*
as mount Zion, *which* cannot be removed, *but* abideth for ever.
2 *As* the mountains *are* round about
Jerusalem, so the LORD *is* round about
his people from henceforth even for
ever.
3 For the rod of the wicked shall not
rest upon the lot of the righteous; lest
the righteous put forth their hands unto
iniquity.
4 Do good, O LORD, unto *those that be*
good, and to *them that are* upright in
their hearts.
5 As for such as turn aside unto their
crooked ways, the LORD shall lead them
forth with the workers of iniquity: *but*
peace *shall be* upon Ĭṣ′rā-ĕl.

PSALM 126

A Song of degrees.

WHEN the LORD turned again the
captivity of Zion, we were like
them that dream.
2 Then was our mouth filled with laughter, and our tongue with singing: then
said they among the heathen, The LORD
hath done great things for them.
3 The LORD hath done great things for
us; *whereof* we are glad.
4 Turn again our captivity, O LORD, as
the streams in the south.
5 They that sow in tears shall reap in
joy.
6 He that goeth forth and weepeth,

bearing precious seed, shall doubtless come again with rejoicing, bringing his sheaves *with him*.

PSALM 127

A Song of degrees for Solomon.

EXCEPT the LORD build the house, they labor in vain that build it: except the LORD keep the city, the watchman waketh *but* in vain.
2 *It is* vain for you to rise up early, to sit up late, to eat the bread of sorrows: *for* so he giveth his beloved sleep.
3 Lo, children *are* a heritage of the LORD: *and* the fruit of the womb *is his* reward.
4 As arrows *are* in the hand of a mighty man; so *are* children of the youth.
5 Happy *is* the man that hath his quiver full of them: they shall not be ashamed, but they shall speak with the enemies in the gate.

PSALM 128

A Song of degrees.

BLESSED *is* every one that feareth the LORD; that walketh in his ways.
2 For thou shalt eat the labor of thine hands: happy *shalt* thou *be*, and *it shall be* well with thee.
3 Thy wife *shall be* as a fruitful vine by the sides of thine house: thy children like olive plants round about thy table.
4 Behold, that thus shall the man be blessed that feareth the LORD.
5 The LORD shall bless thee out of Zion: and thou shalt see the good of Jerusalem all the days of thy life.
6 Yea, thou shalt see thy children's children, *and* peace upon Ĭş'rā-ĕl.

PSALM 129

A Song of degrees.

MANY a time have they afflicted me from my youth, may Ĭş'rā-ĕl now say:
2 Many a time have they afflicted me from my youth: yet they have not prevailed against me.
3 The plowers plowed upon my back: they made long their furrows.
4 The LORD *is* righteous: he hath cut asunder the cords of the wicked.
5 Let them all be confounded and turned back that hate Zion.
6 Let them be as the grass *upon* the housetops, which withereth afore it groweth up:
7 Wherewith the mower filleth not his hand; nor he that bindeth sheaves his bosom.
8 Neither do they which go by say, The blessing of the LORD *be* upon you: we bless you in the name of the LORD.

PSALM 130

A Song of degrees.

OUT of the depths have I cried unto thee, O LORD.
2 Lord, hear my voice: let thine ears be attentive to the voice of my supplications.
3 If thou, LORD, shouldest mark iniquities, O Lord, who shall stand?
4 But *there is* forgiveness with thee, that thou mayest be feared.
5 I wait for the LORD, my soul doth wait, and in his word do I hope.
6 My soul *waiteth* for the Lord more than they that watch for the morning: *I say, more than* they that watch for the morning.
7 Let Ĭş'rā-ĕl hope in the LORD: for with the LORD *there is* mercy, and with him *is* plenteous redemption.
8 And he shall redeem Ĭş'rā-ĕl from all his iniquities.

PSALM 131

A Song of degrees of David.

LORD, my heart is not haughty, nor mine eyes lofty: neither do I exercise myself in great matters, or in things too high for me.
2 Surely I have behaved and quieted myself, as a child that is weaned of his mother: my soul *is* even as a weaned child.
3 Let Ĭş'rā-ĕl hope in the LORD from henceforth and for ever.

PSALM 132

A Song of degrees.

LORD, remember David, *and* all his afflictions:
2 How he sware unto the LORD, *and* vowed unto the mighty *God* of Jacob;
3 Surely I will not come into the tabernacle of my house, nor go up into my bed;
4 I will not give sleep to mine eyes, *or* slumber to mine eyelids,
5 Until I find out a place for the LORD, a habitation for the mighty *God* of Jacob.
6 Lo, we heard of it at Ĕph'rā-tāh: we found it in the fields of the wood.

7 We will go into his tabernacles: we will worship at his footstool.
8 Arise, O LORD, into thy rest; thou, and the ark of thy strength.
9 Let thy priests be clothed with righteousness; and let thy saints shout for joy.
10 For thy servant David's sake turn not away the face of thine anointed.
11 The LORD hath sworn *in* truth unto David; he will not turn from it; Of the fruit of thy body will I set upon thy throne.
12 If thy children will keep my covenant and my testimony that I shall teach them, their children shall also sit upon thy throne for evermore.
13 For the LORD hath chosen Zion; he hath desired *it* for his habitation.
14 This *is* my rest for ever: here will I dwell; for I have desired it.
15 I will abundantly bless her provision: I will satisfy her poor with bread.
16 I will also clothe her priests with salvation: and her saints shall shout aloud for joy.
17 There will I make the horn of David to bud: I have ordained a lamp for mine anointed.
18 His enemies will I clothe with shame: but upon himself shall his crown flourish.

PSALM 133

A Song of degrees of David.

BEHOLD, how good and how pleasant *it is* for brethren to dwell together in unity!
2 *It is* like the precious ointment upon the head, that ran down upon the beard, *even* Aaron's beard: that went down to the skirts of his garments;
3 As the dew of Hermon, *and as the dew* that descended upon the mountains of Zion: for there the LORD commanded the blessing, *even* life for evermore.

PSALM 134

A Song of degrees.

BEHOLD, bless ye the LORD, all *ye* servants of the LORD, which by night stand in the house of the LORD.
2 Lift up your hands *in* the sanctuary, and bless the LORD.
3 The LORD that made heaven and earth bless thee out of Zion.

PSALM 135

PRAISE ye the LORD. Praise ye the name of the LORD; praise *him*, O ye servants of the LORD.
2 Ye that stand in the house of the LORD, in the courts of the house of our God,
3 Praise the LORD; for the LORD *is* good: sing praises unto his name; for *it is* pleasant.
4 For the LORD hath chosen Jacob unto himself, *and* Ĭṣ'rā-ĕl for his peculiar treasure.
5 For I know that the LORD *is* great, and *that* our Lord *is* above all gods.
6 Whatsoever the LORD pleased, *that* did he in heaven, and in earth, in the seas, and all deep places.
7 He causeth the vapors to ascend from the ends of the earth; he maketh lightnings for the rain; he bringeth the wind out of his treasuries.
8 Who smote the firstborn of Egypt, both of man and beast.
9 *Who* sent tokens and wonders into the midst of thee, O Egypt, upon Phā'raōh, and upon all his servants.
10 Who smote great nations, and slew mighty kings;
11 Sī'hŏn king of the Ăm'ō-rītes, and Og king of Bā'shăn, and all the kingdoms of Cā'năan:
12 And gave their land *for* a heritage, a heritage unto Ĭṣ'rā-ĕl his people.
13 Thy name, O LORD, *endureth* for ever; *and* thy memorial, O LORD, throughout all generations.
14 For the LORD will judge his people, and he will repent himself concerning his servants.
15 The idols of the heathen *are* silver and gold, the work of men's hands.
16 They have mouths, but they speak not; eyes have they, but they see not;
17 They have ears, but they hear not; neither is there *any* breath in their mouths.
18 They that make them are like unto them: *so is* every one that trusteth in them.
19 Bless the LORD, O house of Ĭṣ'rā-ĕl: bless the LORD, O house of Aaron:
20 Bless the LORD, O house of Levi: ye that fear the LORD, bless the LORD.
21 Blessed be the LORD out of Zion, which dwelleth at Jerusalem. Praise ye the LORD.

PSALM 136

O GIVE thanks unto the LORD; for *he is* good: for his mercy *endureth* for ever.

2 O give thanks unto the God of gods: for his mercy *endureth* for ever.

3 O give thanks to the Lord of lords: for his mercy *endureth* for ever.

4 To him who alone doeth great wonders: for his mercy *endureth* for ever.

5 To him that by wisdom made the heavens: for his mercy *endureth* for ever.

6 To him that stretched out the earth above the waters: for his mercy *endureth* for ever.

7 To him that made great lights: for his mercy *endureth* for ever:

8 The sun to rule by day: for his mercy *endureth* for ever:

9 The moon and stars to rule by night: for his mercy *endureth* for ever.

10 To him that smote Egypt in their firstborn: for his mercy *endureth* for ever:

11 And brought out Ĭṣ′rā-ĕl from among them: for his mercy *endureth* for ever:

12 With a strong hand, and with a stretched out arm: for his mercy *endureth* for ever.

13 To him which divided the Red sea into parts: for his mercy *endureth* for ever:

14 And made Ĭs′rā-ĕl to pass through the midst of it: for his mercy *endureth* for ever:

15 But overthrew Phā′raōh and his host in the Red sea: for his mercy *endureth* for ever.

16 To him which led his people through the wilderness: for his mercy *endureth* for ever.

17 To him which smote great kings: for his mercy *endureth* for ever:

18 And slew famous kings: for his mercy *endureth* for ever:

19 Sī′hŏn king of the Ăm′ō-rītes: for his mercy *endureth* for ever:

20 And Og the king of Bā′shăn: for his mercy *endureth* for ever:

21 And gave their land for a heritage: for his mercy *endureth* for ever:

22 *Even* a heritage unto Ĭs′rā-ĕl his servant: for his mercy *endureth* for ever.

23 Who remembered us in our low estate: for his mercy *endureth* for ever:

24 And hath redeemed us from our enemies: for his mercy *endureth* for ever.

25 Who giveth food to all flesh: for his mercy *endureth* for ever.

26 O give thanks unto the God of heaven: for his mercy *endureth* for ever.

PSALM 137

BY the rivers of Babylon, there we sat down, yea, we wept, when we remembered Zion.

2 We hanged our harps upon the willows in the midst thereof.

3 For there they that carried us away captive required of us a song; and they that wasted us *required of us* mirth, *saying,* Sing us *one* of the songs of Zion.

4 How shall we sing the LORD's song in a strange land?

5 If I forget thee, O Jerusalem, let my right hand forget *her cunning.*

6 If I do not remember thee, let my tongue cleave to the roof of my mouth; if I prefer not Jerusalem above my chief joy.

7 Remember, O LORD, the children of Ē′dŏm in the day of Jerusalem; who said, Rase *it,* rase *it, even* to the foundation thereof.

8 O daughter of Babylon, who art to be destroyed; happy *shall he be,* that rewardeth thee as thou hast served us.

9 Happy *shall he be,* that taketh and dasheth thy little ones against the stones.

PSALM 138

A Psalm of David.

I WILL praise thee with my whole heart: before the gods will I sing praise unto thee.

2 I will worship toward thy holy temple, and praise thy name for thy lovingkindness and for thy truth: for thou hast magnified thy word above all thy name.

3 In the day when I cried thou answeredst me, *and* strengthenedst me *with* strength in my soul.

4 All the kings of the earth shall praise thee, O LORD, when they hear the words of thy mouth.

5 Yea, they shall sing in the ways of the LORD: for great *is* the glory of the LORD.

6 Though the LORD *be* high, yet hath he respect unto the lowly: but the proud he knoweth afar off.

7 Though I walk in the midst of trouble, thou wilt revive me: thou shalt stretch forth thine hand against the wrath of mine enemies, and thy right hand shall save me.

8 The LORD will perfect *that which* concerneth me: thy mercy, O LORD, *endureth* for ever: forsake not the works of thine own hands.

PSALM 139

To the chief Musician, A Psalm of David.

O LORD, thou hast searched me, and known *me*.

2 Thou knowest my downsitting and mine uprising; thou understandest my thought afar off.

3 Thou compassest my path and my lying down, and art acquainted *with* all my ways.

4 For *there is* not a word in my tongue, *but*, lo, O LORD, thou knowest it altogether.

5 Thou hast beset me behind and before, and laid thine hand upon me.

6 *Such* knowledge *is* too wonderful for me; it is high, I cannot *attain* unto it.

7 Whither shall I go from thy Spirit? or whither shall I flee from thy presence?

8 If I ascend up into heaven, thou *art* there: if I make my bed in hell, behold, thou *art there*.

9 *If* I take the wings of the morning, *and* dwell in the uttermost parts of the sea;

10 Even there shall thy hand lead me, and thy right hand shall hold me.

11 If I say, Surely the darkness shall cover me; even the night shall be light about me.

12 Yea, the darkness hideth not from thee; but the night shineth as the day: the darkness and the light *are* both alike *to thee*.

13 For thou hast possessed my reins: thou hast covered me in my mother's womb.

14 I will praise thee; for I am fearfully *and* wonderfully made: marvelous *are* thy works; and *that* my soul knoweth right well.

15 My substance was not hid from thee when I was made in secret, *and* curiously wrought in the lowest parts of the earth.

16 Thine eyes did see my substance, yet being unperfect; and in thy book all *my members* were written, *which* in continuance were fashioned, when *as yet there was* none of them.

17 How precious also are thy thoughts unto me, O God! how great is the sum of them!

18 *If* I should count them, they are more in number than the sand: when I awake, I am still with thee.

19 Surely thou wilt slay the wicked, O God: depart from me therefore, ye bloody men.

20 For they speak against thee wickedly, *and* thine enemies take *thy name* in vain.

21 Do not I hate them, O LORD, that hate thee? and am not I grieved with those that rise up against thee?

22 I hate them with perfect hatred: I count them mine enemies.

23 Search me, O God, and know my heart: try me, and know my thoughts:

24 And see if *there be any* wicked way in me, and lead me in the way everlasting.

PSALM 140

To the chief Musician, A Psalm of David.

DELIVER me, O LORD, from the evil man: preserve me from the violent man;

2 Which imagine mischiefs in *their* heart; continually are they gathered together *for* war.

3 They have sharpened their tongues like a serpent; adders' poison *is* under their lips. Sē'lăh.

4 Keep me, O LORD, from the hands of the wicked; preserve me from the violent man; who have purposed to overthrow my goings.

5 The proud have hid a snare for me, and cords; they have spread a net by the wayside; they have set gins for me. Sē'lăh.

6 I said unto the LORD, Thou *art* my God: hear the voice of my supplications, O LORD.

7 O GOD the Lord, the strength of my salvation, thou hast covered my head in the day of battle.

8 Grant not, O LORD, the desires of the wicked: further not his wicked device; *lest* they exalt themselves. Sē'lăh.

9 *As for* the head of those that compass me about, let the mischief of their own lips cover them

10 Let burning coals fall upon them:

let them be cast into the fire; into deep pits, that they rise not up again.
11 Let not an evil speaker be established in the earth: evil shall hunt the violent man to overthrow *him*.
12 I know that the LORD will maintain the cause of the afflicted, *and* the right of the poor.
13 Surely the righteous shall give thanks unto thy name: the upright shall dwell in thy presence.

PSALM 141

A Psalm of David.

LORD, I cry unto thee: make haste unto me; give ear unto my voice, when I cry unto thee.
2 Let my prayer be set forth before thee *as* incense; *and* the lifting up of my hands *as* the evening sacrifice.
3 Set a watch, O LORD, before my mouth; keep the door of my lips.
4 Incline not my heart to *any* evil thing, to practise wicked works with men that work iniquity: and let me not eat of their dainties.
5 Let the righteous smite me; *it shall be* a kindness: and let him reprove me; *it shall be* an excellent oil, *which* shall not break my head: for yet my prayer also *shall be* in their calamities.
6 When their judges are overthrown in stony places, they shall hear my words; for they are sweet.
7 Our bones are scattered at the grave's mouth, as when one cutteth and cleaveth *wood* upon the earth.
8 But mine eyes *are* unto thee, O GOD the Lord: in thee is my trust; leave not my soul destitute.
9 Keep me from the snares *which* they have laid for me, and the gins of the workers of iniquity.
10 Let the wicked fall into their own nets, whilst that I withal escape.

PSALM 142

Măs'chĭl of David; A Prayer when he was in the cave.

I CRIED unto the LORD with my voice; with my voice unto the LORD did I make my supplication.
2 I poured out my complaint before him; I showed before him my trouble.
3 When my spirit was overwhelmed within me, then thou knewest my path. In the way wherein I walked have they privily laid a snare for me.
4 I looked on *my* right hand, and beheld, but *there was* no man that would know me: refuge failed me; no man cared for my soul.
5 I cried unto thee, O LORD: I said, Thou *art* my refuge *and* my portion in the land of the living.
6 Attend unto my cry; for I am brought very low: deliver me from my persecutors; for they are stronger than I.
7 Bring my soul out of prison, that I may praise thy name: the righteous shall compass me about; for thou shalt deal bountifully with me.

PSALM 143

A Psalm of David.

HEAR my prayer, O LORD, give ear to my supplications: in thy faithfulness answer me, *and* in thy righteousness.
2 And enter not into judgment with thy servant: for in thy sight shall no man living be justified.
3 For the enemy hath persecuted my soul; he hath smitten my life down to the ground; he hath made me to dwell in darkness, as those that have been long dead.
4 Therefore is my spirit overwhelmed within me; my heart within me is desolate.
5 I remember the days of old; I meditate on all thy works; I muse on the work of thy hands.
6 I stretch forth my hands unto thee: my soul *thirsteth* after thee, as a thirsty land. Sē'lăh.
7 Hear me speedily, O LORD; my spirit faileth: hide not thy face from me, lest I be like unto them that go down into the pit.
8 Cause me to hear thy loving-kindness in the morning; for in thee do I trust: cause me to know the way wherein I should walk; for I lift up my soul unto thee.
9 Deliver me, O LORD, from mine enemies: I flee unto thee to hide me.
10 Teach me to do thy will; for thou *art* my God: thy Spirit *is* good; lead me into the land of uprightness.
11 Quicken me, O LORD, for thy name's sake: for thy righteousness' sake bring my soul out of trouble.
12 And of thy mercy cut off mine enemies, and destroy all them that afflict my soul: for I *am* thy servant.

PSALM 144

A Psalm of David.

BLESSED *be* the LORD my strength, which teacheth my hands to war, *and* my fingers to fight:

2 My goodness, and my fortress; my high tower, and my deliverer; my shield, and *he* in whom I trust; who subdueth my people under me.

3 LORD, what *is* man, that thou takest knowledge of him! *or* the son of man, that thou makest account of him!

4 Man is like to vanity: his days *are* as a shadow that passeth away.

5 Bow thy heavens, O LORD, and come down: touch the mountains, and they shall smoke.

6 Cast forth lightning, and scatter them: shoot out thine arrows, and destroy them.

7 Send thine hand from above; rid me, and deliver me out of great waters, from the hand of strange children;

8 Whose mouth speaketh vanity, and their right hand *is* a right hand of falsehood.

9 I will sing a new song unto thee, O God: upon a psaltery *and* an instrument of ten strings will I sing praises unto thee.

10 *It is he* that giveth salvation unto kings: who delivereth David his servant from the hurtful sword.

11 Rid me, and deliver me from the hand of strange children, whose mouth speaketh vanity, and their right hand *is* a right hand of falsehood:

12 That our sons *may be* as plants grown up in their youth; *that* our daughters *may be* as corner stones, polished *after* the similitude of a palace:

13 *That* our garners *may be* full, affording all manner of store; *that* our sheep may bring forth thousands and ten thousands in our streets:

14 *That* our oxen *may be* strong to labor; *that there be* no breaking in, nor going out; that *there be* no complaining in our streets.

15 Happy *is that* people, that is in such a case: *yea,* happy *is that* people, whose God *is* the LORD.

PSALM 145

David's *Psalm* of praise.

I WILL extol thee, my God, O King; and I will bless thy name for ever and ever.

2 Every day will I bless thee; and I will praise thy name for ever and ever.

3 Great *is* the LORD, and greatly to be praised; and his greatness *is* unsearchable.

4 One generation shall praise thy works to another, and shall declare thy mighty acts.

5 I will speak of the glorious honor of thy majesty, and of thy wondrous works.

6 And *men* shall speak of the might of thy terrible acts: and I will declare thy greatness.

7 They shall abundantly utter the memory of thy great goodness, and shall sing of thy righteousness.

8 The LORD *is* gracious, and full of compassion; slow to anger, and of great mercy.

9 The LORD *is* good to all: and his tender mercies *are* over all his works.

10 All thy works shall praise thee, O LORD; and thy saints shall bless thee.

11 They shall speak of the glory of thy kingdom, and talk of thy power;

12 To make known to the sons of men his mighty acts, and the glorious majesty of his kingdom.

13 Thy kingdom *is* an everlasting kingdom, and thy dominion *endureth* throughout all generations.

14 The LORD upholdeth all that fall, and raiseth up all *those that be* bowed down.

15 The eyes of all wait upon thee; and thou givest them their meat in due season.

16 Thou openest thine hand, and satisfiest the desire of every living thing.

17 The LORD *is* righteous in all his ways, and holy in all his works.

18 The LORD *is* nigh unto all them that call upon him, to all that call upon him in truth.

19 He will fulfil the desire of them that fear him: he also will hear their cry, and will save them.

20 The LORD preserveth all them that love him: but all the wicked will he destroy.

21 My mouth shall speak the praise of the LORD: and let all flesh bless his holy name for ever and ever.

PSALM 146

PRAISE ye the LORD. Praise the LORD, O my soul.

2 While I live will I praise the LORD: I

will sing praises unto my God while I
have any being.
3 Put not your trust in princes, *nor* in
the son of man, in whom *there is* no help.
4 His breath goeth forth, he returneth
to his earth; in that very day his thoughts
perish.
5 Happy *is he* that *hath* the God of
Jacob for his help, whose hope *is* in the
LORD his God:
6 Which made heaven, and earth, the
sea, and all that therein *is:* which keepeth truth for ever:
7 Which executeth judgment for the oppressed: which giveth food to the hungry. The LORD looseth the prisoners:
8 The LORD openeth *the eyes of* the
blind: the LORD raiseth them that are
bowed down: the LORD loveth the
righteous:
9 The LORD preserveth the strangers;
he relieveth the fatherless and widow:
but the way of the wicked he turneth
upside down.
10 The LORD shall reign for ever, *even*
thy God, O Zion, unto all generations.
Praise ye the LORD.

PSALM 147

PRAISE ye the LORD: for *it is* good to
sing praises unto our God; for *it is*
pleasant; *and* praise is comely.
2 The LORD doth build up Jerusalem:
he gathereth together the outcasts of
Ĭṣ'rā-ĕl.
3 He healeth the broken in heart, and
bindeth up their wounds.
4 He telleth the number of the stars; he
calleth them all by *their* names.
5 Great *is* our Lord, and of great power:
his understanding *is* infinite.
6 The LORD lifteth up the meek: he
casteth the wicked down to the ground.
7 Sing unto the LORD with thanksgiving; sing praise upon the harp unto
our God:
8 Who covereth the heaven with clouds,
who prepareth rain for the earth, who
maketh grass to grow upon the mountains.
9 He giveth to the beast his food, *and*
to the young ravens which cry.
10 He delighteth not in the strength of
the horse: he taketh not pleasure in the
legs of a man.
11 The LORD taketh pleasure in them
that fear him, in those that hope in his
mercy.
12 Praise the LORD, O Jerusalem;
praise thy God, O Zion.
13 For he hath strengthened the bars
of thy gates; he hath blessed thy children within thee.
14 He maketh peace *in* thy borders,
and filleth thee with the finest of the
wheat.
15 He sendeth forth his commandment
upon earth: his word runneth very
swiftly.
16 He giveth snow like wool: he scattereth the hoar frost like ashes.
17 He casteth forth his ice like morsels:
who can stand before his cold?
18 He sendeth out his word, and melteth them: he causeth his wind to blow,
and the waters flow.
19 He showeth his word unto Jacob,
his statutes and his judgments unto
Ĭṣ'rā-ĕl.
20 He hath not dealt so with any nation: and *as for his* judgments, they have
not known them. Praise ye the LORD.

PSALM 148

PRAISE ye the LORD. Praise ye the
LORD from the heavens: praise him
in the heights.
2 Praise ye him, all his angels: praise
ye him, all his hosts.
3 Praise ye him, sun and moon: praise
him, all ye stars of light.
4 Praise him, ye heavens of heavens,
and ye waters that *be* above the heavens.
5 Let them praise the name of the
LORD: for he commanded, and they
were created.
6 He hath also stablished them for ever
and ever: he hath made a decree which
shall not pass.
7 Praise the LORD from the earth, ye
dragons, and all deeps:
8 Fire, and hail; snow, and vapor;
stormy wind fulfilling his word:
9 Mountains, and all hills; fruitful
trees, and all cedars:
10 Beasts, and all cattle; creeping
things, and flying fowl:
11 Kings of the earth, and all people;
princes, and all judges of the earth:
12 Both young men, and maidens; old
men, and children:
13 Let them praise the name of the
LORD: for his name alone is excellent;
his glory *is* above the earth and heaven.
14 He also exalteth the horn of his
people, the praise of all his saints; *even*

of the children of Ĭş'rā-ĕl, a people near unto him. Praise ye the LORD.

PSALM 149

PRAISE ye the LORD. Sing unto the LORD a new song, *and* his praise in the congregation of saints.

2 Let Ĭş'rā-ĕl rejoice in him that made him: let the children of Zion be joyful in their King.

3 Let them praise his name in the dance: let them sing praises unto him with the timbrel and harp.

4 For the LORD taketh pleasure in his people: he will beautify the meek with salvation.

5 Let the saints be joyful in glory: let them sing aloud upon their beds.

6 *Let* the high *praises* of God *be* in their mouth, and a two-edged sword in their hand;

7 To execute vengeance upon the heathen, *and* punishments upon the people;

8 To bind their kings with chains, and their nobles with fetters of iron;

9 To execute upon them the judgment written: this honor have all his saints. Praise ye the LORD.

PSALM 150

PRAISE ye the LORD. Praise God in his sanctuary: praise him in the firmament of his power.

2 Praise him for his mighty acts: praise him according to his excellent greatness.

3 Praise him with the sound of the trumpet: praise him with the psaltery and harp.

4 Praise him with the timbrel and dance: praise him with stringed instruments and organs.

5 Praise him upon the loud cymbals: praise him upon the high sounding cymbals.

6 Let every thing that hath breath praise the LORD. Praise ye the LORD.

THE PROVERBS

CHAPTER 1

THE Proverbs of Solomon the son of
David, king of Iṣ'rā-ĕl;
2 To know wisdom and instruction; to
perceive the words of understanding;
3 To receive the instruction of wisdom,
justice, and judgment, and equity;
4 To give subtilty to the simple, to the
young man knowledge and discretion.
5 A wise *man* will hear, and will increase learning; and a man of understanding shall attain unto wise counsels:
6 To understand a proverb, and the interpretation; the words of the wise, and
their dark sayings.
7 ¶ The fear of the LORD *is* the beginning of knowledge: *but* fools despise wisdom and instruction.
8 My son, hear the instruction of thy
father, and forsake not the law of thy
mother:
9 For they *shall be* an ornament of
grace unto thy head, and chains about
thy neck.
10 ¶ My son, if sinners entice thee,
consent thou not.
11 If they say, Come with us, let us lay
wait for blood, let us lurk privily for the
innocent without cause:
12 Let us swallow them up alive as the
grave; and whole, as those that go down
into the pit:
13 We shall find all precious substance,
we shall fill our houses with spoil:
14 Cast in thy lot among us; let us all
have one purse:
15 My son, walk not thou in the way
with them; refrain thy foot from their
path:
16 For their feet run to evil, and make
haste to shed blood.
17 Surely in vain the net is spread in
the sight of any bird.
18 And they lay wait for their *own*
blood; they lurk privily for their *own*
lives.
19 So *are* the ways of every one that is
greedy of gain; *which* taketh away the
life of the owners thereof.
20 ¶ Wisdom crieth without; she uttereth her voice in the streets:
21 She crieth in the chief place of concourse, in the openings of the gates: in
the city she uttereth her words, *saying*,
22 How long, ye simple ones, will ye
love simplicity? and the scorners delight
in their scorning, and fools hate knowledge?
23 Turn you at my reproof: behold, I
will pour out my spirit unto you, I will
make known my words unto you.
24 ¶ Because I have called, and ye refused; I have stretched out my hand, and
no man regarded;
25 But ye have set at nought all my
counsel, and would none of my reproof:
26 I also will laugh at your calamity; I
will mock when your fear cometh;
27 When your fear cometh as desolation, and your destruction cometh as a
whirlwind; when distress and anguish
cometh upon you.
28 Then shall they call upon me, but I
will not answer; they shall seek me
early, but they shall not find me:
29 For that they hated knowledge, and
did not choose the fear of the LORD:
30 They would none of my counsel:
they despised all my reproof.
31 Therefore shall they eat of the fruit
of their own way, and be filled with their
own devices.
32 For the turning away of the simple
shall slay them, and the prosperity of
fools shall destroy them.
33 But whoso hearkeneth unto me shall
dwell safely, and shall be quiet from fear
of evil.

CHAPTER 2

MY son, if thou wilt receive my
words, and hide my commandments with thee;
2 So that thou incline thine ear unto
wisdom, *and* apply thine heart to understanding;
3 Yea, if thou criest after knowledge,
and liftest up thy voice for understanding;
4 If thou seekest her as silver, and
searchest for her as *for* hid treasures;
5 Then shalt thou understand the fear
of the LORD, and find the knowledge of
God.
6 For the LORD giveth wisdom: out of
his mouth *cometh* knowledge and understanding.
7 He layeth up sound wisdom for the

righteous: *he is* a buckler to them that walk uprightly.

8 He keepeth the paths of judgment, and preserveth the way of his saints.

9 Then shalt thou understand righteousness, and judgment, and equity; *yea,* every good path.

10 ¶ When wisdom entereth into thine heart, and knowledge is pleasant unto thy soul;

11 Discretion shall preserve thee, understanding shall keep thee:

12 To deliver thee from the way of the evil *man,* from the man that speaketh froward things;

13 Who leave the paths of uprightness, to walk in the ways of darkness;

14 Who rejoice to do evil, *and* delight in the frowardness of the wicked;

15 Whose ways *are* crooked, and *they* froward in their paths:

16 To deliver thee from the strange woman, *even* from the stranger *which* flattereth with her words;

17 Which forsaketh the guide of her youth, and forgetteth the covenant of her God.

18 For her house inclineth unto death, and her paths unto the dead.

19 None that go unto her return again, neither take they hold of the paths of life.

20 That thou mayest walk in the way of good *men,* and keep the paths of the righteous.

21 For the upright shall dwell in the land, and the perfect shall remain in it.

22 But the wicked shall be cut off from the earth, and the transgressors shall be rooted out of it.

CHAPTER 3

MY son, forget not my law; but let thine heart keep my commandments:

2 For length of days, and long life, and peace, shall they add to thee.

3 Let not mercy and truth forsake thee: bind them about thy neck; write them upon the table of thine heart:

4 So shalt thou find favor and good understanding in the sight of God and man.

5 ¶ Trust in the LORD with all thine heart; and lean not unto thine own understanding.

6 In all thy ways acknowledge him, and he shall direct thy paths.

7 ¶ Be not wise in thine own eyes: fear the LORD, and depart from evil.

8 It shall be health to thy navel, and marrow to thy bones.

9 Honor the LORD with thy substance, and with the firstfruits of all thine increase:

10 So shall thy barns be filled with plenty, and thy presses shall burst out with new wine.

11 ¶ My son, despise not the chastening of the LORD; neither be weary of his correction:

12 For whom the LORD loveth he correcteth; even as a father the son *in whom* he delighteth.

13 ¶ Happy *is* the man *that* findeth wisdom, and the man *that* getteth understanding:

14 For the merchandise of it *is* better than the merchandise of silver, and the gain thereof than fine gold.

15 She *is* more precious than rubies: and all the things thou canst desire are not to be compared unto her.

16 Length of days *is* in her right hand; *and* in her left hand riches and honor.

17 Her ways *are* ways of pleasantness, and all her paths *are* peace.

18 She *is* a tree of life to them that lay hold upon her: and happy *is every one* that retaineth her.

19 The LORD by wisdom hath founded the earth; by understanding hath he established the heavens.

20 By his knowledge the depths are broken up, and the clouds drop down the dew.

21 ¶ My son, let not them depart from thine eyes: keep sound wisdom and discretion:

22 So shall they be life unto thy soul, and grace to thy neck.

23 Then shalt thou walk in thy way safely, and thy foot shall not stumble.

24 When thou liest down, thou shalt not be afraid: yea, thou shalt lie down, and thy sleep shall be sweet.

25 Be not afraid of sudden fear, neither of the desolation of the wicked, when it cometh.

26 For the LORD shall be thy confidence, and shall keep thy foot from being taken.

27 ¶ Withhold not good from them to whom it is due, when it is in the power of thine hand to do *it.*

28 Say not unto thy neighbor, Go, and

come again, and to-morrow I will give;
when thou hast it by thee.
29 Devise not evil against thy neighbor,
seeing he dwelleth securely by thee.
30 ¶ Strive not with a man without
cause, if he have done thee no harm.
31 ¶ Envy thou not the oppressor, and
choose none of his ways.
32 For the froward *is* abomination to
the LORD: but his secret *is* with the
righteous.
33 ¶ The curse of the LORD *is* in the
house of the wicked: but he blesseth the
habitation of the just.
34 Surely he scorneth the scorners: but
he giveth grace unto the lowly.
35 The wise shall inherit glory: but
shame shall be the promotion of fools.

CHAPTER 4

HEAR, ye children, the instruction of
a father, and attend to know
understanding.
2 For I give you good doctrine, forsake
ye not my law.
3 For I was my father's son, tender and
only *beloved* in the sight of my mother.
4 He taught me also, and said unto me,
Let thine heart retain my words: keep
my commandments, and live.
5 Get wisdom, get understanding: forget *it* not; neither decline from the words
of my mouth.
6 Forsake her not, and she shall preserve thee: love her, and she shall keep
thee.
7 Wisdom *is* the principal thing; *therefore* get wisdom: and with all thy getting
get understanding.
8 Exalt her, and she shall promote thee:
she shall bring thee to honor, when thou
dost embrace her.
9 She shall give to thine head an ornament of grace: a crown of glory shall she
deliver to thee.
10 Hear, O my son, and receive my
sayings; and the years of thy life shall be
many.
11 I have taught thee in the way of
wisdom; I have led thee in right paths.
12 When thou goest, thy steps shall
not be straitened; and when thou run-
nest, thou shalt not stumble.
13 Take fast hold of instruction; let *her*
not go: keep her; for she *is* thy life.
14 ¶ Enter not into the path of the
wicked, and go not in the way of evil
men.
15 Avoid it, pass not by it, turn from
it, and pass away.
16 For they sleep not, except they have
done mischief; and their sleep is taken
away, unless they cause *some* to fall.
17 For they eat the bread of wickedness, and drink the wine of violence.
18 But the path of the just *is* as the
shining light, that shineth more and
more unto the perfect day.
19 The way of the wicked *is* as darkness: they know not at what they
stumble.
20 ¶ My son, attend to my words; incline thine ear unto my sayings.
21 Let them not depart from thine
eyes; keep them in the midst of thine
heart.
22 For they *are* life unto those that find
them, and health to all their flesh.
23 ¶ Keep thy heart with all diligence;
for out of it *are* the issues of life.
24 Put away from thee a froward
mouth, and perverse lips put far from
thee.
25 Let thine eyes look right on, and let
thine eyelids look straight before thee.
26 Ponder the path of thy feet, and let
all thy ways be established.
27 Turn not to the right hand nor to the
left: remove thy foot from evil.

CHAPTER 5

MY son, attend unto my wisdom, *and*
bow thine ear to my understanding:
2 That thou mayest regard discretion,
and *that* thy lips may keep knowledge.
3 ¶ For the lips of a strange woman
drop *as* a honeycomb, and her mouth *is*
smoother than oil:
4 But her end is bitter as wormwood,
sharp as a two-edged sword.
5 Her feet go down to death; her steps
take hold on hell.
6 Lest thou shouldest ponder the path
of life, her ways are movable, *that* thou
canst not know *them*.
7 Hear me now therefore, O ye children, and depart not from the words of
my mouth.
8 Remove thy way far from her, and
come not nigh the door of her house:
9 Lest thou give thine honor unto
others, and thy years unto the cruel:
10 Lest strangers be filled with thy
wealth; and thy labors *be* in the house
of a stranger;

11 And thou mourn at the last, when
thy flesh and thy body are consumed,
12 And say, How have I hated instruction, and my heart despised reproof;
13 And have not obeyed the voice of
my teachers, nor inclined mine ear to
them that instructed me!
14 I was almost in all evil in the midst
of the congregation and assembly.
15 ¶ Drink waters out of thine own
cistern, and running waters out of thine
own well.
16 Let thy fountains be dispersed
abroad, *and* rivers of waters in the
streets.
17 Let them be only thine own, and
not strangers' with thee.
18 Let thy fountain be blessed: and
rejoice with the wife of thy youth.
19 *Let her be as* the loving hind and
pleasant roe; let her breasts satisfy thee
at all times; and be thou ravished always
with her love.
20 And why wilt thou, my son, be
ravished with a strange woman, and embrace the bosom of a stranger?
21 For the ways of man *are* before the
eyes of the LORD, and he pondereth all
his goings.
22 ¶ His own iniquities shall take the
wicked himself, and he shall be holden
with the cords of his sins.
23 He shall die without instruction; and
in the greatness of his folly he shall go
astray.

CHAPTER 6

MY son, if thou be surety for thy
friend, *if* thou hast stricken thy
hand with a stranger,
2 Thou art snared with the words of thy
mouth, thou art taken with the words of
thy mouth.
3 Do this now, my son, and deliver thyself, when thou art come into the hand
of thy friend; go, humble thyself, and
make sure thy friend.
4 Give not sleep to thine eyes, nor
slumber to thine eyelids.
5 Deliver thyself as a roe from the hand
of the hunter, and as a bird from the
hand of the fowler.
6 ¶ Go to the ant, thou sluggard; consider her ways, and be wise:
7 Which having no guide, overseer, or
ruler,
8 Provideth her meat in the summer,
and gathereth her food in the harvest.
9 How long wilt thou sleep, O sluggard?
when wilt thou arise out of thy sleep?
10 *Yet* a little sleep, a little slumber, a
little folding of the hands to sleep:
11 So shall thy poverty come as one
that traveleth, and thy want as an armed
man.
12 ¶ A naughty person, a wicked man,
walketh with a froward mouth.
13 He winketh with his eyes, he speaketh with his feet, he teacheth with his
fingers;
14 Frowardness *is* in his heart, he deviseth mischief continually; he soweth
discord.
15 Therefore shall his calamity come
suddenly; suddenly shall he be broken
without remedy.
16 ¶ These six *things* doth the LORD
hate; yea, seven *are* an abomination
unto him:
17 A proud look, a lying tongue, and
hands that shed innocent blood,
18 A heart that deviseth wicked imaginations, feet that be swift in running to
mischief,
19 A false witness *that* speaketh lies,
and he that soweth discord among
brethren.
20 ¶ My son, keep thy father's commandment, and forsake not the law of
thy mother:
21 Bind them continually upon thine
heart, *and* tie them about thy neck.
22 When thou goest, it shall lead thee;
when thou sleepest, it shall keep thee;
and *when* thou awakest, it shall talk
with thee.
23 For the commandment *is* a lamp;
and the law *is* light; and reproofs of instruction *are* the way of life:
24 To keep thee from the evil woman,
from the flattery of the tongue of a
strange woman.
25 Lust not after her beauty in thine
heart; neither let her take thee with her
eyelids.
26 For by means of a whorish woman *a
man is brought* to a piece of bread: and
the adulteress will hunt for the precious
life.
27 Can a man take fire in his bosom,
and his clothes not be burned?
28 Can one go upon hot coals, and his
feet not be burned?
29 So he that goeth in to his neighbor's
wife; whosoever toucheth her shall not
be innocent.

30 *Men* do not despise a thief, if he steal to satisfy his soul when he is hungry;

31 But *if* he be found, he shall restore sevenfold; he shall give all the substance of his house.

32 *But* whoso committeth adultery with a woman lacketh understanding: he *that* doeth it destroyeth his own soul.

33 A wound and dishonor shall he get; and his reproach shall not be wiped away.

34 For jealousy *is* the rage of a man: therefore he will not spare in the day of vengeance.

35 He will not regard any ransom; neither will he rest content, though thou givest many gifts.

CHAPTER 7

MY son, keep my words, and lay up my commandments with thee.

2 Keep my commandments, and live; and my law as the apple of thine eye.

3 Bind them upon thy fingers, write them upon the table of thine heart.

4 Say unto wisdom, Thou *art* my sister; and call understanding *thy* kinswoman:

5 That they may keep thee from the strange woman, from the stranger *which* flattereth with her words.

6 ¶ For at the window of my house I looked through my casement,

7 And beheld among the simple ones, I discerned among the youths, a young man void of understanding,

8 Passing through the street near her corner; and he went the way to her house,

9 In the twilight, in the evening, in the black and dark night:

10 And, behold, there met him a woman *with* the attire of a harlot, and subtile of heart.

11 (She *is* loud and stubborn; her feet abide not in her house:

12 Now *is she* without, now in the streets, and lieth in wait at every corner.)

13 So she caught him, and kissed him, *and* with an impudent face said unto him,

14 *I have* peace offerings with me; this day have I paid my vows.

15 Therefore came I forth to meet thee, diligently to seek thy face, and I have found thee.

16 I have decked my bed with coverings of tapestry, with carved *works*, with fine linen of Egypt.

17 I have perfumed my bed with myrrh, aloes, and cinnamon.

18 Come, let us take our fill of love until the morning: let us solace ourselves with loves.

19 For the goodman *is* not at home, he is gone a long journey:

20 He hath taken a bag of money with him, *and* will come home at the day appointed.

21 With her much fair speech she caused him to yield, with the flattering of her lips she forced him.

22 He goeth after her straightway, as an ox goeth to the slaughter, or as a fool to the correction of the stocks;

23 Till a dart strike through his liver; as a bird hasteth to the snare, and knoweth not that it *is* for his life.

24 ¶ Hearken unto me now therefore, O ye children, and attend to the words of my mouth.

25 Let not thine heart decline to her ways, go not astray in her paths.

26 For she hath cast down many wounded: yea, many strong *men* have been slain by her.

27 Her house *is* the way to hell, going down to the chambers of death.

CHAPTER 8

DOTH not wisdom cry? and understanding put forth her voice?

2 She standeth in the top of high places, by the way in the places of the paths.

3 She crieth at the gates, at the entry of the city, at the coming in at the doors:

4 Unto you, O men, I call; and my voice *is* to the sons of man.

5 O ye simple, understand wisdom: and, ye fools, be ye of an understanding heart.

6 Hear; for I will speak of excellent things; and the opening of my lips *shall be* right things.

7 For my mouth shall speak truth; and wickedness *is* an abomination to my lips.

8 All the words of my mouth *are* in righteousness; *there is* nothing froward or perverse in them.

9 They *are* all plain to him that understandeth, and right to them that find knowledge.

10 Receive my instruction, and not sil-

ver; and knowledge rather than choice gold.

11 For wisdom *is* better than rubies; and all the things that may be desired are not to be compared to it.

12 I wisdom dwell with prudence, and find out knowledge of witty inventions.

13 The fear of the LORD *is* to hate evil: pride, and arrogancy, and the evil way, and the froward mouth, do I hate.

14 Counsel *is* mine, and sound wisdom: I *am* understanding; I have strength.

15 By me kings reign, and princes decree justice.

16 By me princes rule, and nobles, *even* all the judges of the earth.

17 I love them that love me; and those that seek me early shall find me.

18 Riches and honor *are* with me; *yea,* durable riches and righteousness.

19 My fruit *is* better than gold, yea, than fine gold; and my revenue than choice silver.

20 I lead in the way of righteousness, in the midst of the paths of judgment:

21 That I may cause those that love me to inherit substance; and I will fill their treasures.

22 The LORD possessed me in the beginning of his way, before his works of old.

23 I was set up from everlasting, from the beginning, or ever the earth was.

24 When *there were* no depths, I was brought forth; when *there were* no fountains abounding with water.

25 Before the mountains were settled, before the hills was I brought forth:

26 While as yet he had not made the earth, nor the fields, nor the highest part of the dust of the world.

27 When he prepared the heavens, I *was* there: when he set a compass upon the face of the depth:

28 When he established the clouds above: when he strengthened the fountains of the deep:

29 When he gave to the sea his decree, that the waters should not pass his commandment: when he appointed the foundations of the earth:

30 Then I was by him, *as* one brought up *with him:* and I was daily *his* delight, rejoicing always before him;

31 Rejoicing in the habitable part of his earth; and my delights *were* with the sons of men.

32 Now therefore hearken unto me, O ye children: for blessed *are they that* keep my ways.

33 Hear instruction, and be wise, and refuse it not.

34 Blessed *is* the man that heareth me, watching daily at my gates, waiting at the posts of my doors.

35 For whoso findeth me findeth life, and shall obtain favor of the LORD.

36 But he that sinneth against me wrongeth his own soul: all they that hate me love death.

CHAPTER 9

WISDOM hath builded her house, she hath hewn out her seven pillars:

2 She hath killed her beasts; she hath mingled her wine; she hath also furnished her table.

3 She hath sent forth her maidens: she crieth upon the highest places of the city,

4 Whoso *is* simple, let him turn in hither: *as for* him that wanteth understanding, she saith to him,

5 Come, eat of my bread, and drink of the wine *which* I have mingled.

6 Forsake the foolish, and live; and go in the way of understanding.

7 He that reproveth a scorner getteth to himself shame: and he that rebuketh a wicked *man getteth* himself a blot.

8 Reprove not a scorner, lest he hate thee: rebuke a wise man, and he will love thee.

9 Give *instruction* to a wise *man,* and he will be yet wiser: teach a just *man,* and he will increase in learning.

10 The fear of the LORD *is* the beginning of wisdom: and the knowledge of the Holy *is* understanding.

11 For by me thy days shall be multiplied, and the years of thy life shall be increased.

12 If thou be wise, thou shalt be wise for thyself: but *if* thou scornest, thou alone shalt bear *it.*

13 ℂ A foolish woman *is* clamorous: *she is* simple, and knoweth nothing.

14 For she sitteth at the door of her house, on a seat in the high places of the city,

15 To call passengers who go right on their ways:

16 Whoso *is* simple, let him turn in hither: and *as for* him that wanteth understanding, she saith to him,

17 Stolen waters are sweet, and bread *eaten* in secret is pleasant.

18 But he knoweth not that the dead *are* there; *and that* her guests *are* in the depths of hell.

CHAPTER 10

THE Proverbs of Solomon. A wise son maketh a glad father: but a foolish son *is* the heaviness of his mother.

2 Treasures of wickedness profit nothing: but righteousness delivereth from death.

3 The LORD will not suffer the soul of the righteous to famish: but he casteth away the substance of the wicked.

4 He becometh poor that dealeth *with* a slack hand: but the hand of the diligent maketh rich.

5 He that gathereth in summer *is* a wise son: *but* he that sleepeth in harvest *is* a son that causeth shame.

6 Blessings *are* upon the head of the just: but violence covereth the mouth of the wicked.

7 The memory of the just *is* blessed: but the name of the wicked shall rot.

8 The wise in heart will receive commandments: but a prating fool shall fall.

9 He that walketh uprightly walketh surely: but he that perverteth his ways shall be known.

10 He that winketh with the eye causeth sorrow: but a prating fool shall fall.

11 The mouth of a righteous *man is* a well of life: but violence covereth the mouth of the wicked.

12 Hatred stirreth up strifes: but love covereth all sins.

13 In the lips of him that hath understanding wisdom is found: but a rod *is* for the back of him that is void of understanding.

14 Wise *men* lay up knowledge: but the mouth of the foolish *is* near destruction.

15 The rich man's wealth *is* his strong city: the destruction of the poor *is* their poverty.

16 The labor of the righteous *tendeth* to life: the fruit of the wicked to sin.

17 He *is in* the way of life that keepeth instruction: but he that refuseth reproof erreth.

18 He that hideth hatred *with* lying lips, and he that uttereth a slander, *is* a fool.

19 In the multitude of words there wanteth not sin: but he that refraineth his lips *is* wise.

20 The tongue of the just *is as* choice silver: the heart of the wicked *is* little worth.

21 The lips of the righteous feed many: but fools die for want of wisdom.

22 The blessing of the LORD, it maketh rich, and he addeth no sorrow with it.

23 *It is* as sport to a fool to do mischief: but a man of understanding hath wisdom.

24 The fear of the wicked, it shall come upon him: but the desire of the righteous shall be granted.

25 As the whirlwind passeth, so *is* the wicked no *more:* but the righteous *is* an everlasting foundation.

26 As vinegar to the teeth, and as smoke to the eyes, so *is* the sluggard to them that send him.

27 The fear of the LORD prolongeth days: but the years of the wicked shall be shortened.

28 The hope of the righteous *shall be* gladness: but the expectation of the wicked shall perish.

29 The way of the LORD *is* strength to the upright: but destruction *shall be* to the workers of iniquity.

30 The righteous shall never be removed: but the wicked shall not inhabit the earth.

31 The mouth of the just bringeth forth wisdom: but the froward tongue shall be cut out.

32 The lips of the righteous know what is acceptable: but the mouth of the wicked *speaketh* frowardness.

CHAPTER 11

A FALSE balance *is* abomination to the LORD: but a just weight *is* his delight.

2 *When* pride cometh, then cometh shame: but with the lowly *is* wisdom.

3 The integrity of the upright shall guide them: but the perverseness of transgressors shall destroy them.

4 Riches profit not in the day of wrath: but righteousness delivereth from death.

5 The righteousness of the perfect shall direct his way: but the wicked shall fall by his own wickedness.

6 The righteousness of the upright shall deliver them: but transgressors shall be taken in *their own* naughtiness.

7 When a wicked man dieth, *his* expectation shall perish: and the hope of
unjust *men* perisheth.
8 The righteous is delivered out of
trouble, and the wicked cometh in his
stead.
9 A hypocrite with *his* mouth destroyeth his neighbor: but through knowledge
shall the just be delivered.
10 When it goeth well with the righteous, the city rejoiceth: and when the
wicked perish, *there is* shouting.
11 By the blessing of the upright the
city is exalted: but it is overthrown by
the mouth of the wicked.
12 He that is void of wisdom despiseth
his neighbor: but a man of understanding holdeth his peace.
13 A talebearer revealeth secrets: but
he that is of a faithful spirit concealeth
the matter.
14 Where no counsel *is*, the people fall:
but in the multitude of counselors *there*
is safety.
15 He that is surety for a stranger shall
smart *for it:* and he that hateth surety-
ship is sure.
16 A gracious woman retaineth honor:
and strong *men* retain riches.
17 The merciful man doeth good to his
own soul: but *he that is* cruel troubleth
his own flesh.
18 The wicked worketh a deceitful
work: but to him that soweth righteousness *shall be* a sure reward.
19 As righteousness *tendeth* to life; so
he that pursueth evil *pursueth it* to his
own death.
20 They that are of a froward heart *are*
abomination to the LORD: but *such as*
are upright in *their* way *are* his delight.
21 *Though* hand *join* in hand, the
wicked shall not be unpunished: but the
seed of the righteous shall be delivered.
22 *As* a jewel of gold in a swine's snout,
so is a fair woman which is without
discretion.
23 The desire of the righteous *is* only
good: *but* the expectation of the wicked
is wrath.
24 There is that scattereth, and yet increaseth; and *there is* that withholdeth
more than is meet, but *it tendeth* to
poverty.
25 The liberal soul shall be made fat:
and he that watereth shall be watered
also himself.
26 He that withholdeth corn, the people
shall curse him: but blessing *shall*
be upon the head of him that selleth *it*.
27 He that diligently seeketh good pro-
cureth favor: but he that seeketh mischief, it shall come unto him.
28 He that trusteth in his riches shall
fall: but the righteous shall flourish as
a branch.
29 He that troubleth his own house
shall inherit the wind: and the fool *shall*
be servant to the wise of heart.
30 The fruit of the righteous *is* a tree
of life; and he that winneth souls *is* wise.
31 Behold, the righteous shall be recompensed in the earth: much more the
wicked and the sinner.

CHAPTER 12

WHOSO loveth instruction loveth
knowledge: but he that hateth
reproof *is* brutish.
2 A good *man* obtaineth favor of the
LORD: but a man of wicked devices will
he condemn.
3 A man shall not be established by
wickedness: but the root of the righteous
shall not be moved.
4 A virtuous woman *is* a crown to her
husband: but she that maketh ashamed
is as rottenness in his bones.
5 The thoughts of the righteous *are*
right: *but* the counsels of the wicked *are*
deceit.
6 The words of the wicked *are* to lie in
wait for blood: but the mouth of the upright shall deliver them.
7 The wicked are overthrown, and *are*
not: but the house of the righteous shall
stand.
8 A man shall be commended according to his wisdom: but he that is of a
perverse heart shall be despised.
9 *He that is* despised, and hath a
servant, *is* better than he that honoreth
himself, and lacketh bread.
10 A righteous *man* regardeth the life
of his beast: but the tender mercies of
the wicked *are* cruel.
11 He that tilleth his land shall be
satisfied with bread: but he that followeth vain *persons is* void of understanding.
12 The wicked desireth the net of evil
men: but the root of the righteous yieldeth *fruit*.
13 The wicked is snared by the transgression of *his* lips: but the just shall
come out of trouble.

14 A man shall be satisfied with good by the fruit of *his* mouth: and the recompense of a man's hands shall be rendered unto him.
15 The way of a fool *is* right in his own eyes: but he that hearkeneth unto counsel *is* wise.
16 A fool's wrath is presently known: but a prudent *man* covereth shame.
17 *He that* speaketh truth showeth forth righteousness: but a false witness deceit.
18 There is that speaketh like the piercings of a sword: but the tongue of the wise *is* health.
19 The lip of truth shall be established for ever: but a lying tongue *is* but for a moment.
20 Deceit *is* in the heart of them that imagine evil: but to the counselors of peace *is* joy.
21 There shall no evil happen to the just: but the wicked shall be filled with mischief.
22 Lying lips *are* abomination to the LORD: but they that deal truly *are* his delight.
23 A prudent man concealeth knowledge: but the heart of fools proclaimeth foolishness.
24 The hand of the diligent shall bear rule: but the slothful shall be under tribute.
25 Heaviness in the heart of man maketh it stoop: but a good word maketh it glad.
26 The righteous *is* more excellent than his neighbor: but the way of the wicked seduceth them.
27 The slothful *man* roasteth not that which he took in hunting: but the substance of a diligent man *is* precious.
28 In the way of righteousness *is* life; and *in* the pathway *thereof there is* no death.

CHAPTER 13

A WISE son *heareth* his father's instruction: but a scorner heareth not rebuke.
2 A man shall eat good by the fruit of *his* mouth: but the soul of the transgressors *shall eat* violence.
3 He that keepeth his mouth keepeth his life: *but* he that openeth wide his lips shall have destruction.
4 The soul of the sluggard desireth, and *hath* nothing: but the soul of the diligent shall be made fat.
5 A righteous *man* hateth lying: but a wicked *man* is loathsome, and cometh to shame.
6 Righteousness keepeth *him that is* upright in the way: but wickedness overthroweth the sinner.
7 There is that maketh himself rich, yet *hath* nothing: *there is* that maketh himself poor, yet *hath* great riches.
8 The ransom of a man's life *are* his riches: but the poor heareth not rebuke.
9 The light of the righteous rejoiceth: but the lamp of the wicked shall be put out.
10 Only by pride cometh contention: but with the well advised *is* wisdom.
11 Wealth *gotten* by vanity shall be diminished: but he that gathereth by labor shall increase.
12 Hope deferred maketh the heart sick: but *when* the desire cometh, *it is* a tree of life.
13 Whoso despiseth the word shall be destroyed: but he that feareth the commandment shall be rewarded.
14 The law of the wise *is* a fountain of life, to depart from the snares of death.
15 Good understanding giveth favor: but the way of transgressors *is* hard.
16 Every prudent *man* dealeth with knowledge: but a fool layeth open *his* folly.
17 A wicked messenger falleth into mischief: but a faithful ambassador *is* health.
18 Poverty and shame *shall be to* him that refuseth instruction: but he that regardeth reproof shall be honored.
19 The desire accomplished is sweet to the soul: but *it is* abomination to fools to depart from evil.
20 He that walketh with wise *men* shall be wise: but a companion of fools shall be destroyed.
21 Evil pursueth sinners: but to the righteous good shall be repaid.
22 A good *man* leaveth an inheritance to his children's children: and the wealth of the sinner *is* laid up for the just.
23 Much food *is in* the tillage of the poor: but there is *that is* destroyed for want of judgment.
24 He that spareth his rod hateth his son: but he that loveth him chasteneth him betimes.

25 The righteous eateth to the satisfying of his soul: but the belly of the wicked shall want.

CHAPTER 14

EVERY wise woman buildeth her house: but the foolish plucketh it down with her hands.

2 He that walketh in his uprightness feareth the LORD: but *he that is* perverse in his ways despiseth him.

3 In the mouth of the foolish *is* a rod of pride: but the lips of the wise shall preserve them.

4 Where no oxen *are*, the crib *is* clean: but much increase *is* by the strength of the ox.

5 A faithful witness will not lie: but a false witness will utter lies.

6 A scorner seeketh wisdom, and *findeth it* not: but knowledge *is* easy unto him that understandeth.

7 Go from the presence of a foolish man, when thou perceivest not *in him* the lips of knowledge.

8 The wisdom of the prudent *is* to understand his way: but the folly of fools *is* deceit.

9 Fools make a mock at sin: but among the righteous *there is* favor.

10 The heart knoweth his own bitterness; and a stranger doth not intermeddle with his joy.

11 The house of the wicked shall be overthrown: but the tabernacle of the upright shall flourish.

12 There is a way which seemeth right unto a man; but the end thereof *are* the ways of death.

13 Even in laughter the heart is sorrowful; and the end of that mirth *is* heaviness.

14 The backslider in heart shall be filled with his own ways: and a good man *shall be satisfied* from himself.

15 The simple believeth every word: but the prudent *man* looketh well to his going.

16 A wise *man* feareth, and departeth from evil: but the fool rageth, and is confident.

17 *He that is* soon angry dealeth foolishly: and a man of wicked devices is hated.

18 The simple inherit folly: but the prudent are crowned with knowledge.

19 The evil bow before the good; and the wicked at the gates of the righteous.

20 The poor is hated even of his own neighbor: but the rich *hath* many friends.

21 He that despiseth his neighbor sinneth: but he that hath mercy on the poor, happy *is* he.

22 Do they not err that devise evil? but mercy and truth *shall be* to them that devise good.

23 In all labor there is profit: but the talk of the lips *tendeth* only to penury.

24 The crown of the wise *is* their riches: *but* the foolishness of fools *is* folly.

25 A true witness delivereth souls: but a deceitful *witness* speaketh lies.

26 In the fear of the LORD *is* strong confidence: and his children shall have a place of refuge.

27 The fear of the LORD *is* a fountain of life, to depart from the snares of death.

28 In the multitude of people *is* the king's honor: but in the want of people *is* the destruction of the prince.

29 *He that is* slow to wrath *is* of great understanding: but *he that is* hasty of spirit exalteth folly.

30 A sound heart *is* the life of the flesh: but envy the rottenness of the bones.

31 He that oppresseth the poor reproacheth his Maker: but he that honoreth him hath mercy on the poor.

32 The wicked is driven away in his wickedness: but the righteous hath hope in his death.

33 Wisdom resteth in the heart of him that hath understanding: but *that which is* in the midst of fools is made known.

34 Righteousness exalteth a nation: but sin *is* a reproach to any people.

35 The king's favor *is* toward a wise servant: but his wrath is *against* him that causeth shame.

CHAPTER 15

A SOFT answer turneth away wrath: but grievous words stir up anger.

2 The tongue of the wise useth knowledge aright: but the mouth of fools poureth out foolishness.

3 The eyes of the LORD *are* in every place, beholding the evil and the good.

4 A wholesome tongue *is* a tree of life: but perverseness therein *is* a breach in the spirit.

5 A fool despiseth his father's instruction: but he that regardeth reproof is prudent.

6 In the house of the righteous *is* much treasure: but in the revenues of the wicked is trouble.

7 The lips of the wise disperse knowledge: but the heart of the foolish *doeth* not so.

8 The sacrifice of the wicked *is* an abomination to the LORD: but the prayer of the upright *is* his delight.

9 The way of the wicked *is* an abomination unto the LORD: but he loveth him that followeth after righteousness.

10 Correction *is* grievous unto him that forsaketh the way: *and* he that hateth reproof shall die.

11 Hell and destruction *are* before the LORD: how much more then the hearts of the children of men?

12 A scorner loveth not one that reproveth him: neither will he go unto the wise.

13 A merry heart maketh a cheerful countenance: but by sorrow of the heart the spirit is broken.

14 The heart of him that hath understanding seeketh knowledge: but the mouth of fools feedeth on foolishness.

15 All the days of the afflicted *are* evil: but he that is of a merry heart *hath* a continual feast.

16 Better *is* little with the fear of the LORD, than great treasure and trouble therewith.

17 Better *is* a dinner of herbs where love is, than a stalled ox and hatred therewith.

18 A wrathful man stirreth up strife: but *he that is* slow to anger appeaseth strife.

19 The way of the slothful *man is* as a hedge of thorns: but the way of the righteous *is* made plain.

20 A wise son maketh a glad father: but a foolish man despiseth his mother.

21 Folly *is* joy to *him that is* destitute of wisdom: but a man of understanding walketh uprightly.

22 Without counsel purposes are disappointed: but in the multitude of counselors they are established.

23 A man hath joy by the answer of his mouth: and a word *spoken* in due season, how good *is it!*

24 The way of life *is* above to the wise, that he may depart from hell beneath.

25 The LORD will destroy the house of the proud: but he will establish the border of the widow.

26 The thoughts of the wicked *are* an abomination to the LORD: but *the words* of the pure *are* pleasant words.

27 He that is greedy of gain troubleth his own house; but he that hateth gifts shall live.

28 The heart of the righteous studieth to answer: but the mouth of the wicked poureth out evil things.

29 The LORD *is* far from the wicked: but he heareth the prayer of the righteous.

30 The light of the eyes rejoiceth the heart: *and* a good report maketh the bones fat.

31 The ear that heareth the reproof of life abideth among the wise.

32 He that refuseth instruction despiseth his own soul: but he that heareth reproof getteth understanding.

33 The fear of the LORD *is* the instruction of wisdom; and before honor *is* humility.

CHAPTER 16

THE preparations of the heart in man, and the answer of the tongue, *is* from the LORD.

2 All the ways of a man *are* clean in his own eyes; but the LORD weigheth the spirits.

3 Commit thy works unto the LORD, and thy thoughts shall be established.

4 The LORD hath made all *things* for himself: yea, even the wicked for the day of evil.

5 Every one *that is* proud in heart *is* an abomination to the LORD: *though* hand *join* in hand, he shall not be unpunished.

6 By mercy and truth iniquity is purged: and by the fear of the LORD *men* depart from evil.

7 When a man's ways please the LORD, he maketh even his enemies to be at peace with him.

8 Better *is* a little with righteousness, than great revenues without right.

9 A man's heart deviseth his way: but the LORD directeth his steps.

10 A divine sentence *is* in the lips of the king: his mouth transgresseth not in judgment.

11 A just weight and balance *are* the LORD'S: all the weights of the bag *are* his work.

12 *It is* an abomination to kings to commit wickedness: for the throne is established by righteousness.

13 Righteous lips *are* the delight of kings; and they love him that speaketh right.

14 The wrath of a king *is as* messengers of death: but a wise man will pacify it.

15 In the light of the king's countenance *is* life; and his favor *is* as a cloud of the latter rain.

16 How much better *is it* to get wisdom than gold! and to get understanding rather to be chosen than silver!

17 The highway of the upright *is* to depart from evil: he that keepeth his way preserveth his soul.

18 Pride *goeth* before destruction, and a haughty spirit before a fall.

19 Better *it is to be* of an humble spirit with the lowly, than to divide the spoil with the proud.

20 He that handleth a matter wisely shall find good: and whoso trusteth in the LORD, happy *is* he.

21 The wise in heart shall be called prudent: and the sweetness of the lips increaseth learning.

22 Understanding *is* a wellspring of life unto him that hath it: but the instruction of fools *is* folly.

23 The heart of the wise teacheth his mouth, and addeth learning to his lips.

24 Pleasant words *are as* a honeycomb, sweet to the soul, and health to the bones.

25 There is a way that seemeth right unto a man; but the end thereof *are* the ways of death.

26 He that laboreth, laboreth for himself; for his mouth craveth it of him.

27 An ungodly man diggeth up evil: and in his lips *there is* as a burning fire.

28 A froward man soweth strife: and a whisperer separateth chief friends.

29 A violent man enticeth his neighbor, and leadeth him into the way *that is* not good.

30 He shutteth his eyes to devise froward things: moving his lips he bringeth evil to pass.

31 The hoary head *is* a crown of glory, *if* it be found in the way of righteousness.

32 *He that is* slow to anger *is* better than the mighty; and he that ruleth his spirit than he that taketh a city.

33 The lot is cast into the lap; but the whole disposing thereof *is* of the LORD.

CHAPTER 17

BETTER *is* a dry morsel, and quietness therewith, than a house full of sacrifices *with* strife.

2 A wise servant shall have rule over a son that causeth shame, and shall have part of the inheritance among the brethren.

3 The fining pot *is* for silver, and the furnace for gold: but the LORD trieth the hearts.

4 A wicked doer giveth heed to false lips; *and* a liar giveth ear to a naughty tongue.

5 Whoso mocketh the poor reproacheth his Maker: *and* he that is glad at calamities shall not be unpunished.

6 Children's children *are* the crown of old men; and the glory of children *are* their fathers.

7 Excellent speech becometh not a fool: much less do lying lips a prince.

8 A gift *is as* a precious stone in the eyes of him that hath it: whithersoever it turneth, it prospereth.

9 He that covereth a transgression seeketh love; but he that repeateth a matter separateth *very* friends.

10 A reproof entereth more into a wise man than a hundred stripes into a fool.

11 An evil *man* seeketh only rebellion: therefore a cruel messenger shall be sent against him.

12 Let a bear robbed of her whelps meet a man, rather than a fool in his folly.

13 Whoso rewardeth evil for good, evil shall not depart from his house.

14 The beginning of strife *is as* when one letteth out water: therefore leave off contention, before it be meddled with.

15 He that justifieth the wicked, and he that condemneth the just, even they both *are* abomination to the LORD.

16 Wherefore *is there* a price in the hand of a fool to get wisdom, seeing *he hath* no heart *to it?*

17 A friend loveth at all times, and a brother is born for adversity.

18 A man void of understanding striketh hands, *and* becometh surety in the presence of his friend.

19 He loveth transgression that loveth strife: *and* he that exalteth his gate seeketh destruction.

20 He that hath a froward heart findeth no good: and he that hath a perverse tongue falleth into mischief.

21 He that begetteth a fool *doeth it* to his sorrow: and the father of a fool hath no joy.

22 A merry heart doeth good *like* a medicine: but a broken spirit drieth the bones.

23 A wicked *man* taketh a gift out of the bosom to pervert the ways of judgment.

24 Wisdom *is* before him that hath understanding; but the eyes of a fool *are* in the ends of the earth.

25 A foolish son *is* a grief to his father, and bitterness to her that bare him.

26 Also to punish the just *is* not good, *nor* to strike princes for equity.

27 He that hath knowledge spareth his words: *and* a man of understanding is of an excellent spirit.

28 Even a fool, when he holdeth his peace, is counted wise: *and* he that shutteth his lips *is esteemed* a man of understanding.

CHAPTER 18

THROUGH desire a man, having separated himself, seeketh *and* intermeddleth with all wisdom.

2 A fool hath no delight in understanding, but that his heart may discover itself.

3 When the wicked cometh, *then* cometh also contempt, and with ignominy reproach.

4 The words of a man's mouth *are as* deep waters, *and* the wellspring of wisdom *as* a flowing brook.

5 *It is* not good to accept the person of the wicked, to overthrow the righteous in judgment.

6 A fool's lips enter into contention, and his mouth calleth for strokes.

7 A fool's mouth *is* his destruction, and his lips *are* the snare of his soul.

8 The words of a talebearer *are* as wounds, and they go down into the innermost parts of the belly.

9 He also that is slothful in his work is brother to him that is a great waster.

10 The name of the LORD *is* a strong tower: the righteous runneth into it, and is safe.

11 The rich man's wealth *is* his strong city, and as a high wall in his own conceit.

12 Before destruction the heart of man is haughty; and before honor *is* humility.

13 He that answereth a matter before he heareth *it*, it *is* folly and shame unto him.

14 The spirit of a man will sustain his infirmity; but a wounded spirit who can bear?

15 The heart of the prudent getteth knowledge; and the ear of the wise seeketh knowledge.

16 A man's gift maketh room for him, and bringeth him before great men.

17 *He that is* first in his own cause *seemeth* just; but his neighbor cometh and searcheth him.

18 The lot causeth contentions to cease, and parteth between the mighty.

19 A brother offended *is harder to be won* than a strong city: and *their* contentions *are* like the bars of a castle.

20 A man's belly shall be satisfied with the fruit of his mouth: *and* with the increase of his lips shall he be filled.

21 Death and life *are* in the power of the tongue: and they that love it shall eat the fruit thereof.

22 *Whoso* findeth a wife findeth a good *thing*, and obtaineth favor of the LORD.

23 The poor useth entreaties; but the rich answereth roughly.

24 A man *that hath* friends must show himself friendly: and there is a friend *that* sticketh closer than a brother.

CHAPTER 19

BETTER *is* the poor that walketh in his integrity, than *he that is* perverse in his lips, and is a fool.

2 Also, *that* the soul *be* without knowledge, *it is* not good; and he that hasteth with *his* feet sinneth.

3 The foolishness of man perverteth his way: and his heart fretteth against the LORD.

4 Wealth maketh many friends; but the poor is separated from his neighbor.

5 A false witness shall not be unpunished; and *he that* speaketh lies shall not escape.

6 Many will entreat the favor of the prince: and every man *is* a friend to him that giveth gifts.

7 All the brethren of the poor do hate him: how much more do his friends go far from him? he pursueth *them with* words, *yet* they *are* wanting *to him.*

8 He that getteth wisdom loveth his own soul: he that keepeth understanding shall find good.

9 A false witness shall not be unpunished

ished; and *he that* speaketh lies shall
perish.
10 Delight is not seemly for a fool;
much less for a servant to have rule over
princes.
11 The discretion of a man deferreth
his anger; and *it is* his glory to pass over
a transgression.
12 The king's wrath *is* as the roaring
of a lion; but his favor *is* as dew upon
the grass.
13 A foolish son *is* the calamity of his
father: and the contentions of a wife *are*
a continual dropping.
14 House and riches *are* the inheritance of fathers: and a prudent wife *is*
from the LORD.
15 Slothfulness casteth into a deep
sleep; and an idle soul shall suffer
hunger.
16 He that keepeth the commandment
keepeth his own soul; *but* he that despiseth his ways shall die.
17 He that hath pity upon the poor
lendeth unto the LORD; and that which
he hath given will he pay him again.
18 Chasten thy son while there is hope,
and let not thy soul spare for his crying.
19 A man of great wrath shall suffer
punishment: for if thou deliver *him*, yet
thou must do it again.
20 Hear counsel, and receive instruction, that thou mayest be wise in thy
latter end.
21 *There are* many devices in a man's
heart; nevertheless the counsel of the
LORD, that shall stand.
22 The desire of a man *is* his kindness:
and a poor man *is* better than a liar.
23 The fear of the LORD *tendeth* to
life: and *he that hath it* shall abide satisfied; he shall not be visited with evil.
24 A slothful *man* hideth his hand in
his bosom, and will not so much as bring
it to his mouth again.
25 Smite a scorner, and the simple will
beware: and reprove one that hath
understanding, *and* he will understand
knowledge.
26 He that wasteth *his* father, *and*
chaseth away *his* mother, *is* a son that
causeth shame, and bringeth reproach.
27 Cease, my son, to hear the instruction *that causeth* to err from the words
of knowledge.
28 An ungodly witness scorneth judgment: and the mouth of the wicked devoureth iniquity.
29 Judgments are prepared for scorners, and stripes for the back of fools.

CHAPTER 20

WINE *is* a mocker, strong drink *is*
raging: and whosoever is deceived thereby is not wise.
2 The fear of a king *is* as the roaring
of a lion: *whoso* provoketh him to anger
sinneth *against* his own soul.
3 *It is* an honor for a man to cease from
strife: but every fool will be meddling.
4 The sluggard will not plow by reason
of the cold; *therefore* shall he beg in
harvest, and *have* nothing.
5 Counsel in the heart of man *is like*
deep water; but a man of understanding
will draw it out.
6 Most men will proclaim every one his
own goodness: but a faithful man who
can find?
7 The just *man* walketh in his integrity:
his children *are* blessed after him.
8 A king that sitteth in the throne of
judgment scattereth away all evil with
his eyes.
9 Who can say, I have made my heart
clean, I am pure from my sin?
10 Divers weights, *and* divers measures, both of them *are* alike abomination
to the LORD.
11 Even a child is known by his doings,
whether his work *be* pure, and whether
it be right.
12 The hearing ear, and the seeing eye,
the LORD hath made even both of them.
13 Love not sleep, lest thou come to
poverty: open thine eyes, *and* thou shalt
be satisfied with bread.
14 *It is* naught, *it is* naught, saith the
buyer: but when he is gone his way,
then he boasteth.
15 There is gold, and a multitude of
rubies: but the lips of knowledge *are* a
precious jewel.
16 Take his garment that is surety *for*
a stranger: and take a pledge of him for
a strange woman.
17 Bread of deceit *is* sweet to a man;
but afterward his mouth shall be filled
with gravel.
18 *Every* purpose is established by
counsel: and with good advice make
war.
19 He that goeth about *as* a talebearer
revealeth secrets: therefore meddle not
with him that flattereth with his lips.
20 Whoso curseth his father or his

mother, his lamp shall be put out in obscure darkness.

21 An inheritance *may be* gotten hastily at the beginning; but the end thereof shall not be blessed.

22 Say not thou, I will recompense evil; *but* wait on the LORD, and he shall save thee.

23 Divers weights *are* an abomination unto the LORD; and a false balance *is* not good.

24 Man's goings *are* of the LORD; how can a man then understand his own way?

25 *It is* a snare to the man *who* devoureth *that which is* holy, and after vows to make inquiry.

26 A wise king scattereth the wicked, and bringeth the wheel over them.

27 The spirit of man *is* the candle of the LORD, searching all the inward parts of the belly.

28 Mercy and truth preserve the king: and his throne is upholden by mercy.

29 The glory of young men *is* their strength: and the beauty of old men *is* the gray head.

30 The blueness of a wound cleanseth away evil: so *do* stripes the inward parts of the belly.

CHAPTER 21

THE king's heart *is* in the hand of the LORD, *as* the rivers of water: he turneth it whithersoever he will.

2 Every way of a man *is* right in his own eyes: but the LORD pondereth the hearts.

3 To do justice and judgment *is* more acceptable to the LORD than sacrifice.

4 A high look, and a proud heart, *and* the plowing of the wicked, *is* sin.

5 The thoughts of the diligent *tend* only to plenteousness; but of every one *that is* hasty only to want.

6 The getting of treasures by a lying tongue *is* a vanity tossed to and fro of them that seek death.

7 The robbery of the wicked shall destroy them; because they refuse to do judgment.

8 The way of man *is* froward and strange: but *as for* the pure, his work *is* right.

9 *It is* better to dwell in a corner of the housetop, than with a brawling woman in a wide house.

10 The soul of the wicked desireth evil: his neighbor findeth no favor in his eyes.

11 When the scorner is punished, the simple is made wise: and when the wise is instructed, he receiveth knowledge.

12 The righteous *man* wisely considereth the house of the wicked: *but God* overthroweth the wicked for *their* wickedness.

13 Whoso stoppeth his ears at the cry of the poor, he also shall cry himself, but shall not be heard.

14 A gift in secret pacifieth anger: and a reward in the bosom, strong wrath.

15 *It is* joy to the just to do judgment: but destruction *shall be* to the workers of iniquity.

16 The man that wandereth out of the way of understanding shall remain in the congregation of the dead.

17 He that loveth pleasure *shall be* a poor man: he that loveth wine and oil shall not be rich.

18 The wicked *shall be* a ransom for the righteous, and the transgressor for the upright.

19 *It is* better to dwell in the wilderness, than with a contentious and an angry woman.

20 *There is* treasure to be desired and oil in the dwelling of the wise; but a foolish man spendeth it up.

21 He that followeth after righteousness and mercy findeth life, righteousness, and honor.

22 A wise *man* scaleth the city of the mighty, and casteth down the strength of the confidence thereof.

23 Whoso keepeth his mouth and his tongue, keepeth his soul from troubles.

24 Proud *and* haughty scorner *is* his name, who dealeth in proud wrath.

25 The desire of the slothful killeth him; for his hands refuse to labor.

26 He coveteth greedily all the day long: but the righteous giveth and spareth not.

27 The sacrifice of the wicked *is* abomination: how much more, *when* he bringeth it with a wicked mind?

28 A false witness shall perish: but the man that heareth speaketh constantly.

29 A wicked man hardeneth his face: but *as for* the upright, he directeth his way.

30 *There is* no wisdom nor understanding nor counsel against the LORD.

31 The horse *is* prepared against the day of battle: but safety *is* of the LORD.

CHAPTER 22

A *GOOD* name *is* rather to be chosen
than great riches, *and* loving favor
rather than silver and gold.
2 The rich and poor meet together: the
LORD *is* the maker of them all.
3 A prudent *man* foreseeth the evil, and
hideth himself: but the simple pass on,
and are punished.
4 By humility *and* the fear of the LORD
are riches, and honor, and life.
5 Thorns *and* snares *are* in the way of
the froward: he that doth keep his soul
shall be far from them.
6 Train up a child in the way he should
go: and when he is old, he will not depart from it.
7 The rich ruleth over the poor, and
the borrower *is* servant to the lender.
8 He that soweth iniquity shall reap
vanity: and the rod of his anger shall fail.
9 He that hath a bountiful eye shall be
blessed; for he giveth of his bread to the
poor.
10 Cast out the scorner, and contention shall go out; yea, strife and reproach shall cease.
11 He that loveth pureness of heart,
for the grace of his lips the king *shall be*
his friend.
12 The eyes of the LORD preserve
knowledge; and he overthroweth the
words of the transgressor.
13 The slothful *man* saith, *There is* a
lion without, I shall be slain in the
streets.
14 The mouth of strange women *is* a
deep pit: he that is abhorred of the
LORD shall fall therein.
15 Foolishness *is* bound in the heart of
a child; *but* the rod of correction shall
drive it far from him.
16 He that oppresseth the poor to increase his *riches*, *and* he that giveth to
the rich, *shall* surely *come* to want.
17 Bow down thine ear, and hear the
words of the wise, and apply thine heart
unto my knowledge.
18 For *it is* a pleasant thing if thou
keep them within thee; they shall withal
be fitted in thy lips.
19 That thy trust may be in the LORD,
I have made known to thee this day,
even to thee.
20 Have not I written to thee excellent
things in counsels and knowledge,
21 That I might make thee know the
certainty of the words of truth; that thou
mightest answer the words of truth to
them that send unto thee?
22 Rob not the poor, because he *is*
poor: neither oppress the afflicted in the
gate:
23 For the LORD will plead their cause,
and spoil the soul of those that spoiled
them.
24 Make no friendship with an angry
man; and with a furious man thou shalt
not go;
25 Lest thou learn his ways, and get a
snare to thy soul.
26 Be not thou *one* of them that strike
hands, *or* of them that are sureties for
debts.
27 If thou hast nothing to pay, why
should he take away thy bed from under
thee?
28 Remove not the ancient landmark, which thy fathers have set.
29 Seest thou a man diligent in his
business? he shall stand before kings;
he shall not stand before mean *men*.

CHAPTER 23

WHEN thou sittest to eat with a
ruler, consider diligently what *is*
before thee:
2 And put a knife to thy throat, if thou
be a man given to appetite.
3 Be not desirous of his dainties: for
they *are* deceitful meat.
4 Labor not to be rich: cease from thine
own wisdom.
5 Wilt thou set thine eyes upon that
which is not? for *riches* certainly make
themselves wings; they fly away as an
eagle toward heaven.
6 Eat thou not the bread of *him that*
hath an evil eye, neither desire thou his
dainty meats:
7 For as he thinketh in his heart, so *is*
he: Eat and drink, saith he to thee; but
his heart *is* not with thee.
8 The morsel *which* thou hast eaten
shalt thou vomit up, and lose thy sweet
words.
9 Speak not in the ears of a fool: for he
will despise the wisdom of thy words.
10 Remove not the old landmark; and
enter not into the fields of the fatherless:
11 For their Redeemer *is* mighty; he
shall plead their cause with thee.
12 Apply thine heart unto instruction,
and thine ears to the words of knowledge.

13 Withhold not correction from the child: for *if* thou beatest him with the rod, he shall not die.

14 Thou shalt beat him with the rod, and shalt deliver his soul from hell.

15 My son, if thine heart be wise, my heart shall rejoice, even mine.

16 Yea, my reins shall rejoice, when thy lips speak right things.

17 Let not thine heart envy sinners; but *be thou* in the fear of the LORD all the day long.

18 For surely there is an end; and thine expectation shall not be cut off.

19 Hear thou, my son, and be wise, and guide thine heart in the way.

20 Be not among winebibbers; among riotous eaters of flesh:

21 For the drunkard and the glutton shall come to poverty: and drowsiness shall clothe *a man* with rags.

22 Hearken unto thy father that begat thee, and despise not thy mother when she is old.

23 Buy the truth, and sell *it* not; *also* wisdom, and instruction, and understanding.

24 The father of the righteous shall greatly rejoice: and he that begetteth a wise *child* shall have joy of him.

25 Thy father and thy mother shall be glad, and she that bare thee shall rejoice.

26 My son, give me thine heart, and let thine eyes observe my ways.

27 For a whore *is* a deep ditch; and a strange woman *is* a narrow pit.

28 She also lieth in wait as *for* a prey, and increaseth the transgressors among men.

29 Who hath woe? who hath sorrow? who hath contentions? who hath babbling? who hath wounds without cause? who hath redness of eyes?

30 They that tarry long at the wine; they that go to seek mixed wine.

31 Look not thou upon the wine when it is red, when it giveth his color in the cup, *when* it moveth itself aright.

32 At the last it biteth like a serpent, and stingeth like an adder.

33 Thine eyes shall behold strange women, and thine heart shall utter perverse things.

34 Yea, thou shalt be as he that lieth down in the midst of the sea, or as he that lieth upon the top of a mast.

35 They have stricken me, *shalt thou say, and* I was not sick; they have beaten me, *and* I felt *it* not: when shall I awake? I will seek it yet again.

CHAPTER 24

BE not thou envious against evil men, neither desire to be with them:

2 For their heart studieth destruction, and their lips talk of mischief.

3 Through wisdom is a house builded; and by understanding it is established:

4 And by knowledge shall the chambers be filled with all precious and pleasant riches.

5 A wise man *is* strong; yea, a man of knowledge increaseth strength.

6 For by wise counsel thou shalt make thy war: and in multitude of counselors *there is* safety.

7 Wisdom *is* too high for a fool: he openeth not his mouth in the gate.

8 He that deviseth to do evil shall be called a mischievous person.

9 The thought of foolishness *is* sin: and the scorner *is* an abomination to men.

10 *If* thou faint in the day of adversity, thy strength *is* small.

11 If thou forbear to deliver *them that are* drawn unto death, and *those that are* ready to be slain;

12 If thou sayest, Behold, we knew it not; doth not he that pondereth the heart consider *it?* and he that keepeth thy soul, doth *not* he know *it?* and shall *not* he render to *every* man according to his works?

13 My son, eat thou honey, because *it is* good; and the honeycomb, *which is* sweet to thy taste:

14 So *shall* the knowledge of wisdom *be* unto thy soul: when thou hast found *it,* then there shall be a reward, and thy expectation shall not be cut off.

15 Lay not wait, O wicked *man,* against the dwelling of the righteous; spoil not his resting place:

16 For a just *man* falleth seven times, and riseth up again: but the wicked shall fall into mischief.

17 Rejoice not when thine enemy falleth, and let not thine heart be glad when he stumbleth:

18 Lest the LORD see *it,* and it displease him, and he turn away his wrath from him.

19 Fret not thyself because of evil *men,* neither be thou envious at the wicked;

20 For there shall be no reward to the evil *man;* the candle of the wicked shall be put out.

21 My son, fear thou the LORD and the king: *and* meddle not with them that are given to change:

22 For their calamity shall rise suddenly; and who knoweth the ruin of them both?

23 These *things* also *belong* to the wise. *It is* not good to have respect of persons in judgment.

24 He that saith unto the wicked, Thou *art* righteous; him shall the people curse, nations shall abhor him:

25 But to them that rebuke *him* shall be delight, and a good blessing shall come upon them.

26 *Every man* shall kiss *his* lips that giveth a right answer.

27 Prepare thy work without, and make it fit for thyself in the field; and afterward build thine house.

28 Be not a witness against thy neighbor without cause; and deceive *not* with thy lips.

29 Say not, I will do so to him as he hath done to me: I will render to the man according to his work.

30 I went by the field of the slothful, and by the vineyard of the man void of understanding;

31 And, lo, it was all grown over with thorns, *and* nettles had covered the face thereof, and the stone wall thereof was broken down.

32 Then I saw, *and* considered *it* well: I looked upon *it, and* received instruction.

33 *Yet* a little sleep, a little slumber, a little folding of the hands to sleep:

34 So shall thy poverty come *as* one that traveleth; and thy want as an armed man.

CHAPTER 25

THESE *are* also proverbs of Solomon, which the men of Hĕz′ē-kī′ȧh king of Judah copied out.

2 *It is* the glory of God to conceal a thing: but the honor of kings *is* to search out a matter.

3 The heaven for height, and the earth for depth, and the heart of kings *is* unsearchable.

4 Take away the dross from the silver, and there shall come forth a vessel for the finer.

5 Take away the wicked *from* before the king, and his throne shall be established in righteousness.

6 Put not forth thyself in the presence of the king, and stand not in the place of great *men:*

7 For better *it is* that it be said unto thee, Come up hither; than that thou shouldest be put lower in the presence of the prince whom thine eyes have seen.

8 Go not forth hastily to strive, lest *thou know not* what to do in the end thereof, when thy neighbor hath put thee to shame.

9 Debate thy cause with thy neighbor *himself;* and discover not a secret to another:

10 Lest he that heareth *it* put thee to shame, and thine infamy turn not away.

11 A word fitly spoken *is like* apples of gold in pictures of silver.

12 *As* an earring of gold, and an ornament of fine gold, *so is* a wise reprover upon an obedient ear.

13 As the cold of snow in the time of harvest, *so is* a faithful messenger to them that send him: for he refresheth the soul of his masters.

14 Whoso boasteth himself of a false gift *is like* clouds and wind without rain.

15 By long forbearing is a prince persuaded, and a soft tongue breaketh the bone.

16 Hast thou found honey? eat so much as is sufficient for thee, lest thou be filled therewith, and vomit it.

17 Withdraw thy foot from thy neighbor's house; lest he be weary of thee, and *so* hate thee.

18 A man that beareth false witness against his neighbor *is* a maul, and a sword, and a sharp arrow.

19 Confidence in an unfaithful man in time of trouble *is like* a broken tooth, and a foot out of joint.

20 *As* he that taketh away a garment in cold weather, *and as* vinegar upon nitre, so *is* he that singeth songs to a heavy heart.

21 If thine enemy be hungry, give him bread to eat; and if he be thirsty, give him water to drink:

22 For thou shalt heap coals of fire upon his head, and the LORD shall reward thee.

23 The north wind driveth away rain: so *doth* an angry countenance a backbiting tongue.

24 *It is* better to dwell in the corner
of the housetop, than with a brawling
woman and in a wide house.
25 *As* cold waters to a thirsty soul, so
is good news from a far country.
26 A righteous man falling down before
the wicked *is as* a troubled fountain,
and a corrupt spring.
27 *It is* not good to eat much honey: so
for men to search their own glory *is not*
glory.
28 He that *hath* no rule over his own
spirit *is like* a city *that is* broken down,
and without walls.

CHAPTER 26

AS snow in summer, and as rain in
harvest, so honor is not seemly for
a fool.
2 As the bird by wandering, as the
swallow by flying, so the curse causeless
shall not come.
3 A whip for the horse, a bridle for the
ass, and a rod for the fool's back.
4 Answer not a fool according to his
folly, lest thou also be like unto him.
5 Answer a fool according to his folly,
lest he be wise in his own conceit.
6 He that sendeth a message by the
hand of a fool cutteth off the feet, *and*
drinketh damage.
7 The legs of the lame are not equal:
so *is* a parable in the mouth of fools.
8 As he that bindeth a stone in a
sling, so *is* he that giveth honor to a
fool.
9 *As* a thorn goeth up into the hand of
a drunkard, so *is* a parable in the
mouth of fools.
10 The great *God* that formed all
things both rewardeth the fool, and
rewardeth transgressors.
11 As a dog returneth to his vomit, *so*
a fool returneth to his folly.
12 Seest thou a man wise in his own
conceit? *there is* more hope of a fool
than of him.
13 The slothful *man* saith, *There is* a
lion in the way; a lion *is* in the streets.
14 *As* the door turneth upon his hinges,
so *doth* the slothful upon his bed.
15 The slothful hideth his hand in *his*
bosom; it grieveth him to bring it again
to his mouth.
16 The sluggard *is* wiser in his own
conceit than seven men that can render
a reason.
17 He that passeth by, *and* meddleth
with strife *belonging* not to him, *is like*
one that taketh a dog by the ears.
18 As a mad *man* who casteth firebrands, arrows, and death,
19 So *is* the man *that* deceiveth his
neighbor, and saith, Am not I in sport?
20 Where no wood is, *there* the fire
goeth out: so where *there is* no talebearer, the strife ceaseth.
21 *As* coals *are* to burning coals, and
wood to fire; so *is* a contentious man to
kindle strife.
22 The words of a talebearer *are* as
wounds, and they go down into the innermost parts of the belly.
23 Burning lips and a wicked heart *are*
like a potsherd covered with silver dross.
24 He that hateth dissembleth with his
lips, and layeth up deceit within him;
25 When he speaketh fair, believe him
not: for *there are* seven abominations
in his heart.
26 *Whose* hatred is covered by deceit,
his wickedness shall be showed before
the *whole* congregation.
27 Whoso diggeth a pit shall fall therein: and he that rolleth a stone, it will
return upon him.
28 A lying tongue hateth *those that are*
afflicted by it; and a flattering mouth
worketh ruin.

CHAPTER 27

BOAST not thyself of to-morrow; for
thou knowest not what a day may
bring forth.
2 Let another man praise thee, and not
thine own mouth; a stranger, and not
thine own lips.
3 A stone *is* heavy, and the sand
weighty; but a fool's wrath *is* heavier
than them both.
4 Wrath *is* cruel, and anger *is* out-
rageous; but who *is* able to stand before
envy?
5 Open rebuke *is* better than secret
love.
6 Faithful *are* the wounds of a friend;
but the kisses of an enemy *are* deceitful.
7 The full soul loatheth a honeycomb;
but to the hungry soul every bitter
thing is sweet.
8 As a bird that wandereth from her
nest, so *is* a man that wandereth from
his place.
9 Ointment and perfume rejoice the
heart: so *doth* the sweetness of a man's
friend by hearty counsel.

10 Thine own friend, and thy father's friend, forsake not; neither go into thy brother's house in the day of thy calamity: *for* better *is* a neighbor *that is* near than a brother far off.

11 My son, be wise, and make my heart glad, that I may answer him that reproacheth me.

12 A prudent *man* foreseeth the evil, *and* hideth himself; *but* the simple pass on, *and* are punished.

13 Take his garment that is surety for a stranger, and take a pledge of him for a strange woman.

14 He that blesseth his friend with a loud voice, rising early in the morning, it shall be counted a curse to him.

15 A continual dropping in a very rainy day and a contentious woman are alike.

16 Whosoever hideth her hideth the wind, and the ointment of his right hand, *which* bewrayeth *itself.*

17 Iron sharpeneth iron; so a man sharpeneth the countenance of his friend.

18 Whoso keepeth the fig tree shall eat the fruit thereof: so he that waiteth on his master shall be honored.

19 As in water face *answereth* to face, so the heart of man to man.

20 Hell and destruction are never full; so the eyes of man are never satisfied.

21 *As* the fining pot for silver, and the furnace for gold; so *is* a man to his praise.

22 Though thou shouldest bray a fool in a mortar among wheat with a pestle, *yet* will not his foolishness depart from him.

23 Be thou diligent to know the state of thy flocks, *and* look well to thy herds:

24 For riches *are* not for ever: and doth the crown *endure* to every generation?

25 The hay appeareth, and the tender grass showeth itself, and herbs of the mountains are gathered.

26 The lambs *are* for thy clothing, and the goats *are* the price of the field.

27 And *thou shalt have* goats' milk enough for thy food, for the food of thy household, and *for* the maintenance for thy maidens.

CHAPTER 28

THE wicked flee when no man pursueth: but the righteous are bold as a lion.

2 For the transgression of a land many *are* the princes thereof: but by a man of understanding *and* knowledge the state *thereof* shall be prolonged.

3 A poor man that oppresseth the poor *is like* a sweeping rain which leaveth no food.

4 They that forsake the law praise the wicked: but such as keep the law contend with them.

5 Evil men understand not judgment: but they that seek the LORD understand all *things.*

6 Better *is* the poor that walketh in his uprightness, than *he that is* perverse *in his* ways, though he *be* rich.

7 Whoso keepeth the law *is* a wise son: but he that is a companion of riotous *men* shameth his father.

8 He that by usury and unjust gain increaseth his substance, he shall gather it for him that will pity the poor.

9 He that turneth away his ear from hearing the law, even his prayer *shall be* abomination.

10 Whoso causeth the righteous to go astray in an evil way, he shall fall himself into his own pit: but the upright shall have good *things* in possession.

11 The rich man *is* wise in his own conceit; but the poor that hath understanding searcheth him out.

12 When righteous *men* do rejoice, *there is* great glory: but when the wicked rise, a man is hidden.

13 He that covereth his sins shall not prosper: but whoso confesseth and forsaketh *them* shall have mercy.

14 Happy *is* the man that feareth always: but he that hardeneth his heart shall fall into mischief.

15 *As* a roaring lion, and a ranging bear; *so is* a wicked ruler over the poor people.

16 The prince that wanteth understanding *is* also a great oppressor: *but* he that hateth covetousness shall prolong *his* days.

17 A man that doeth violence to the blood of *any* person shall flee to the pit; let no man stay him.

18 Whoso walketh uprightly shall be saved: but *he that is* perverse *in his* ways shall fall at once.

19 He that tilleth his land shall have plenty of bread: but he that followeth after vain *persons* shall have poverty enough.

20 A faithful man shall abound with

blessings: but he that maketh haste to be rich shall not be innocent.

21 To have respect of persons *is* not good: for, for a piece of bread *that* man will transgress.

22 He that hasteth to be rich *hath* an evil eye, and considereth not that poverty shall come upon him.

23 He that rebuketh a man, afterward shall find more favor than he that flattereth with the tongue.

24 Whoso robbeth his father or his mother, and saith, *It is* no transgression; the same *is* the companion of a destroyer.

25 He that is of a proud heart stirreth up strife: but he that putteth his trust in the LORD shall be made fat.

26 He that trusteth in his own heart is a fool: but whoso walketh wisely, he shall be delivered.

27 He that giveth unto the poor shall not lack: but he that hideth his eyes shall have many a curse.

28 When the wicked rise, men hide themselves: but when they perish, the righteous increase.

CHAPTER 29

HE, that being often reproved hardeneth *his* neck, shall suddenly be destroyed, and that without remedy.

2 When the righteous are in authority, the people rejoice: but when the wicked beareth rule, the people mourn.

3 Whoso loveth wisdom rejoiceth his father: but he that keepeth company with harlots spendeth *his* substance.

4 The king by judgment establisheth the land: but he that receiveth gifts overthroweth it.

5 A man that flattereth his neighbor spreadeth a net for his feet.

6 In the transgression of an evil man *there is* a snare: but the righteous doth sing and rejoice.

7 The righteous considereth the cause of the poor: *but* the wicked regardeth not to know *it*.

8 Scornful men bring a city into a snare: but wise *men* turn away wrath.

9 *If* a wise man contendeth with a foolish man, whether he rage or laugh, *there is* no rest.

10 The bloodthirsty hate the upright: but the just seek his soul.

11 A fool uttereth all his mind: but a wise *man* keepeth it in till afterward.

12 If a ruler hearken to lies, all his servants *are* wicked.

13 The poor and the deceitful man meet together: the LORD lighteneth both their eyes.

14 The king that faithfully judgeth the poor, his throne shall be established for ever.

15 The rod and reproof give wisdom: but a child left *to himself* bringeth his mother to shame.

16 When the wicked are multiplied, transgression increaseth: but the righteous shall see their fall.

17 Correct thy son, and he shall give thee rest; yea, he shall give delight unto thy soul.

18 Where *there is* no vision, the people perish: but he that keepeth the law, happy *is* he.

19 A servant will not be corrected by words: for though he understand he will not answer.

20 Seest thou a man *that is* hasty in his words? *there is* more hope of a fool than of him.

21 He that delicately bringeth up his servant from a child shall have him become *his* son at the length.

22 An angry man stirreth up strife, and a furious man aboundeth in transgression.

23 A man's pride shall bring him low: but honor shall uphold the humble in spirit.

24 Whoso is partner with a thief hateth his own soul: he heareth cursing, and bewrayeth *it* not.

25 The fear of man bringeth a snare: but whoso putteth his trust in the LORD shall be safe.

26 Many seek the ruler's favor; but *every* man's judgment *cometh* from the LORD.

27 An unjust man *is* an abomination to the just: and *he that is* upright in the way *is* abomination to the wicked.

CHAPTER 30

THE words of Ā′gŭr the son of Jā′kĕh, *even* the prophecy: the man spake unto Ĭth′ĭ-ĕl, even unto Ĭth′ĭ-ĕl and Ū′căl,

2 Surely I *am* more brutish than *any* man, and have not the understanding of a man.

3 I neither learned wisdom, nor have the knowledge of the holy.

4 Who hath ascended up into heaven,
or descended? who hath gathered the
wind in his fists? who hath bound the
waters in a garment? who hath established all the ends of the earth? what *is*
his name, and what *is* his son's name,
if thou canst tell?
5 Every word of God *is* pure: he *is* a
shield unto them that put their trust in
him.
6 Add thou not unto his words, lest he
reprove thee, and thou be found a liar.
7 Two *things* have I required of thee;
deny me *them* not before I die:
8 Remove far from me vanity and lies;
give me neither poverty nor riches; feed
me with food convenient for me:
9 Lest I be full, and deny *thee*, and say,
Who *is* the LORD? or lest I be poor, and
steal, and take the name of my God *in
vain*.
10 Accuse not a servant unto his master, lest he curse thee, and thou be
found guilty.
11 *There is* a generation *that* curseth
their father, and doth not bless their
mother.
12 *There is* a generation *that are* pure
in their own eyes, and *yet* is not washed
from their filthiness.
13 *There is* a generation, O how lofty
are their eyes! and their eyelids are
lifted up.
14 *There is* a generation, whose teeth
are as swords, and their jaw teeth *as*
knives, to devour the poor from off
the earth, and the needy from *among*
men.
15 The horseleech hath two daughters,
crying, Give, give. There are three
things that are never satisfied, *yea*, four
things say not, *It is* enough:
16 The grave; and the barren womb;
the earth *that* is not filled with water;
and the fire *that* saith not, *It is* enough.
17 The eye *that* mocketh at *his* father,
and despiseth to obey *his* mother, the
ravens of the valley shall pick it out, and
the young eagles shall eat it.
18 There be three *things which* are too
wonderful for me, yea, four which I
know not:
19 The way of an eagle in the air; the
way of a serpent upon a rock; the way
of a ship in the midst of the sea; and the
way of a man with a maid.
20 Such *is* the way of an adulterous
woman; she eateth, and wipeth her
mouth, and saith, I have done no
wickedness.
21 For three *things* the earth is disquieted, and for four *which* it cannot
bear:
22 For a servant when he reigneth; and
a fool when he is filled with meat;
23 For an odious *woman* when she is
married; and a handmaid that is heir to
her mistress.
24 There be four *things which are* little
upon the earth, but they *are* exceeding
wise:
25 The ants *are* a people not strong, yet
they prepare their meat in the summer;
26 The conies *are but* a feeble folk, yet
make they their houses in the rocks;
27 The locusts have no king, yet go
they forth all of them by bands;
28 The spider taketh hold with her
hands, and is in kings' palaces.
29 There be three *things* which go well,
yea, four are comely in going:
30 A lion, *which is* strongest among
beasts, and turneth not away for any;
31 A greyhound; a he goat also; and a
king, against whom *there is* no rising up.
32 If thou hast done foolishly in lifting
up thyself, or if thou hast thought evil,
lay thine hand upon thy mouth.
33 Surely the churning of milk bringeth forth butter, and the wringing of the
nose bringeth forth blood: so the forcing
of wrath bringeth forth strife.

CHAPTER 31

THE words of king Lemuel, the prophecy that his mother taught him.
2 What, my son? and what, the son of
my womb? and what, the son of my
vows?
3 Give not thy strength unto women,
nor thy ways to that which destroyeth
kings.
4 *It is* not for kings, O Lemuel, *it is* not
for kings to drink wine; nor for princes
strong drink:
5 Lest they drink, and forget the law,
and pervert the judgment of any of the
afflicted.
6 Give strong drink unto him that is
ready to perish, and wine unto those
that be of heavy hearts.
7 Let him drink, and forget his poverty,
and remember his misery no more.
8 Open thy mouth for the dumb in the
cause of all such as are appointed to
destruction.

9 Open thy mouth, judge righteously, and plead the cause of the poor and needy.

10 ℂ Who can find a virtuous woman? for her price *is* far above rubies.

11 The heart of her husband doth safely trust in her, so that he shall have no need of spoil.

12 She will do him good and not evil all the days of her life.

13 She seeketh wool, and flax, and worketh willingly with her hands.

14 She is like the merchants' ships; she bringeth her food from afar.

15 She riseth also while it is yet night, and giveth meat to her household, and a portion to her maidens.

16 She considereth a field, and buyeth it: with the fruit of her hands she planteth a vineyard.

17 She girdeth her loins with strength, and strengtheneth her arms.

18 She perceiveth that her merchandise *is* good: her candle goeth not out by night.

19 She layeth her hands to the spindle, and her hands hold the distaff.

20 She stretcheth out her hand to the poor; yea, she reacheth forth her hands to the needy.

21 She is not afraid of the snow for her household: for all her household *are* clothed with scarlet.

22 She maketh herself coverings of tapestry; her clothing *is* silk and purple.

23 Her husband is known in the gates, when he sitteth among the elders of the land.

24 She maketh fine linen, and selleth *it;* and delivereth girdles unto the merchant.

25 Strength and honor *are* her clothing; and she shall rejoice in time to come.

26 She openeth her mouth with wisdom; and in her tongue *is* the law of kindness.

27 She looketh well to the ways of her household, and eateth not the bread of idleness.

28 Her children arise up, and call her blessed; her husband *also,* and he praiseth her.

29 Many daughters have done virtuously, but thou excellest them all.

30 Favor *is* deceitful, and beauty *is* vain: *but* a woman *that* feareth the LORD, she shall be praised.

31 Give her of the fruit of her hands; and let her own works praise her in the gates.

ECCLESIASTES

OR, THE PREACHER

CHAPTER 1

THE words of the Preacher, the son of David, king in Jerusalem.

2 Vanity of vanities, saith the Preacher, vanity of vanities; all *is* vanity.

3 What profit hath a man of all his labor which he taketh under the sun?

4 *One* generation passeth away, and *another* generation cometh: but the earth abideth for ever.

5 The sun also ariseth, and the sun goeth down, and hasteth to his place where he arose.

6 The wind goeth toward the south, and turneth about unto the north; it whirleth about continually, and the wind returneth again according to his circuits.

7 All the rivers run into the sea; yet the sea *is* not full: unto the place from whence the rivers come, thither they return again.

8 All things *are* full of labor; man cannot utter *it:* the eye is not satisfied with seeing, nor the ear filled with hearing.

9 The thing that hath been, it *is that* which shall be; and that which is done *is* that which shall be done: and *there is* no new *thing* under the sun.

10 Is there *any* thing whereof it may be said, See, this *is* new? it hath been already of old time, which was before us.

11 *There is* no remembrance of former *things;* neither shall there be *any* remembrance of *things* that are to come with *those* that shall come after.

12 ℂ I the Preacher was king over Ĭs'rā-ēl in Jerusalem.

13 And I gave my heart to seek and

search out by wisdom concerning all *things* that are done under heaven: this sore travail hath God given to the sons of man to be exercised therewith.

14 I have seen all the works that are done under the sun; and, behold, all *is* vanity and vexation of spirit.

15 *That which is* crooked cannot be made straight: and that which is wanting cannot be numbered.

16 I communed with mine own heart, saying, Lo, I am come to great estate, and have gotten more wisdom than all *they* that have been before me in Jerusalem: yea, my heart had great experience of wisdom and knowledge.

17 And I gave my heart to know wisdom, and to know madness and folly: I perceived that this also is vexation of spirit.

18 For in much wisdom *is* much grief: and he that increaseth knowledge increaseth sorrow.

CHAPTER 2

I SAID in mine heart, Go to now, I will prove thee with mirth; therefore enjoy pleasure: and, behold, this also *is* vanity.

2 I said of laughter, *It is* mad: and of mirth, What doeth it?

3 I sought in mine heart to give myself unto wine, yet acquainting mine heart with wisdom; and to lay hold on folly, till I might see what *was* that good for the sons of men, which they should do under the heaven all the days of their life.

4 I made me great works; I builded me houses; I planted me vineyards:

5 I made me gardens and orchards, and I planted trees in them of all *kind of* fruits:

6 I made me pools of water, to water therewith the wood that bringeth forth trees:

7 I got *me* servants and maidens, and had servants born in my house; also I had great possessions of great and small cattle above all that were in Jerusalem before me:

8 I gathered me also silver and gold, and the peculiar treasure of kings and of the provinces: I gat me men singers and women singers, and the delights of the sons of men, *as* musical instruments, and that of all sorts.

9 So I was great, and increased more than all that were before me in Jerusalem: also my wisdom remained with me.

10 And whatsoever mine eyes desired I kept not from them, I withheld not my heart from any joy; for my heart rejoiced in all my labor: and this was my portion of all my labor.

11 Then I looked on all the works that my hands had wrought, and on the labor that I had labored to do: and, behold, all *was* vanity and vexation of spirit, and *there was* no profit under the sun.

12 ℂ And I turned myself to behold wisdom, and madness, and folly: for what *can* the man *do* that cometh after the king? *even* that which hath been already done.

13 Then I saw that wisdom excelleth folly, as far as light excelleth darkness.

14 The wise man's eyes *are* in his head; but the fool walketh in darkness: and I myself perceived also that one event happeneth to them all.

15 Then said I in my heart, As it happeneth to the fool, so it happeneth even to me; and why was I then more wise? Then I said in my heart, that this also *is* vanity.

16 For *there is* no remembrance of the wise more than of the fool for ever; seeing that which now *is* in the days to come shall all be forgotten. And how dieth the wise *man?* as the fool.

17 Therefore I hated life; because the work that is wrought under the sun *is* grievous unto me: for all *is* vanity and vexation of spirit.

18 ℂ Yea, I hated all my labor which I had taken under the sun: because I should leave it unto the man that shall be after me.

19 And who knoweth whether he shall be a wise *man* or a fool? yet shall he have rule over all my labor wherein I have labored, and wherein I have showed myself wise under the sun. This *is* also vanity.

20 Therefore I went about to cause my heart to despair of all the labor which I took under the sun.

21 For there is a man whose labor *is* in wisdom, and in knowledge, and in equity; yet to a man that hath not labored therein shall he leave it *for* his portion. This also *is* vanity and a great evil.

22 For what hath man of all his labor,

and of the vexation of his heart, wherein he hath labored under the sun?

23 For all his days *are* sorrows, and his travail grief; yea, his heart taketh not rest in the night. This is also vanity.

24 ¶ *There is* nothing better for a man, *than* that he should eat and drink, and *that* he should make his soul enjoy good in his labor. This also I saw, that it *was* from the hand of God.

25 For who can eat, or who else can hasten *hereunto,* more than I?

26 For *God* giveth to a man that *is* good in his sight, wisdom, and knowledge, and joy: but to the sinner he giveth travail, to gather and to heap up, that he may give to *him that is* good before God. This also *is* vanity and vexation of spirit.

CHAPTER 3

TO every *thing there is* a season, and a time to every purpose under the heaven:

2 A time to be born, and a time to die; a time to plant, and a time to pluck up *that which is* planted;

3 A time to kill, and a time to heal; a time to break down, and a time to build up;

4 A time to weep, and a time to laugh; a time to mourn, and a time to dance;

5 A time to cast away stones, and a time to gather stones together; a time to embrace, and a time to refrain from embracing;

6 A time to get, and a time to lose; a time to keep, and a time to cast away;

7 A time to rend, and a time to sew; a time to keep silence, and a time to speak;

8 A time to love, and a time to hate; a time of war, and a time of peace.

9 What profit hath he that worketh in that wherein he laboreth?

10 I have seen the travail, which God hath given to the sons of men to be exercised in it.

11 He hath made every *thing* beautiful in his time: also he hath set the world in their heart, so that no man can find out the work that God maketh from the beginning to the end.

12 I know that *there is* no good in them, but for *a man* to rejoice, and to do good in his life.

13 And also that every man should eat and drink, and enjoy the good of all his labor, it *is* the gift of God.

14 I know that, whatsoever God doeth, it shall be for ever: nothing can be put to it, nor any thing taken from it: and God doeth *it,* that *men* should fear before him.

15 That which hath been is now; and that which is to be hath already been; and God requireth that which is past.

16 ¶ And moreover I saw under the sun the place of judgment, *that* wickedness *was* there; and the place of righteousness, *that* iniquity *was* there.

17 I said in mine heart, God shall judge the righteous and the wicked: for *there is* a time there for every purpose and for every work.

18 I said in mine heart concerning the estate of the sons of men, that God might manifest them, and that they might see that they themselves are beasts.

19 For that which befalleth the sons of men befalleth beasts; even one thing befalleth them: as the one dieth, so dieth the other; yea, they have all one breath; so that a man hath no preeminence above a beast: for all *is* vanity.

20 All go unto one place; all are of the dust, and all turn to dust again.

21 Who knoweth the spirit of man that goeth upward, and the spirit of the beast that goeth downward to the earth?

22 Wherefore I perceive that *there is* nothing better, than that a man should rejoice in his own works; for that *is* his portion: for who shall bring him to see what shall be after him?

CHAPTER 4

SO I returned, and considered all the oppressions that are done under the sun: and behold the tears of *such as were* oppressed, and they had no comforter; and on the side of their oppressors *there was* power; but they had no comforter.

2 Wherefore I praised the dead which are already dead, more than the living which are yet alive.

3 Yea, better *is he* than both they, which hath not yet been, who hath not seen the evil work that is done under the sun.

4 ¶ Again, I considered all travail, and every right work, that for this a man is envied of his neighbor. This *is* also vanity and vexation of spirit.

5 The fool foldeth his hands together, and eateth his own flesh.

6 Better *is* a handful *with* quietness,
than both the hands full *with* travail and
vexation of spirit.
7 ¶ Then I returned, and I saw vanity
under the sun.
8 There is one *alone,* and *there is* not
a second; yea, he hath neither child nor
brother: yet *is there* no end of all his labor; neither is his eye satisfied with
riches; neither *saith he,* For whom do I
labor, and bereave my soul of good?
This *is* also vanity, yea, it *is* a sore
travail.
9 ¶ Two *are* better than one; because
they have a good reward for their labor.
10 For if they fall, the one will lift up
his fellow: but woe to him *that is* alone
when he falleth; for *he hath* not another
to help him up.
11 Again, if two lie together, then they
have heat: but how can one be warm
alone?
12 And if one prevail against him, two
shall withstand him; and a threefold
cord is not quickly broken.
13 ¶ Better *is* a poor and a wise child,
than an old and foolish king, who will no
more be admonished.
14 For out of prison he cometh to reign;
whereas also *he that is* born in his kingdom becometh poor.
15 I considered all the living which
walk under the sun, with the second
child that shall stand up in his stead.
16 *There is* no end of all the people,
even of all that have been before them:
they also that come after shall not rejoice in him. Surely this also *is* vanity
and vexation of spirit.

CHAPTER 5

KEEP thy foot when thou goest to
the house of God, and be more
ready to hear, than to give the sacrifice
of fools: for they consider not that they
do evil.
2 Be not rash with thy mouth, and let
not thine heart be hasty to utter *any*
thing before God: for God *is* in heaven,
and thou upon earth: therefore let thy
words be few.
3 For a dream cometh through the
multitude of business; and a fool's voice
is known by multitude of words.
4 When thou vowest a vow unto God,
defer not to pay it; for *he hath* no pleasure in fools: pay that which thou hast
vowed.
5 Better *is it* that thou shouldest not
vow, than that thou shouldest vow and
not pay.
6 Suffer not thy mouth to cause thy
flesh to sin; neither say thou before the
angel, that it *was* an error: wherefore
should God be angry at thy voice, and
destroy the work of thine hands?
7 For in the multitude of dreams and
many words *there are* also *divers* vanities: but fear thou God.
8 ¶ If thou seest the oppression of the
poor, and violent perverting of judgment
and justice in a province, marvel not at
the matter: for *he that is* higher than the
highest regardeth; and *there be* higher
than they.
9 ¶ Moreover the profit of the earth
is for all: the king *himself* is served by
the field.
10 He that loveth silver shall not be
satisfied with silver; nor he that loveth
abundance with increase: this *is* also
vanity.
11 When goods increase, they are increased that eat them: and what good *is*
there to the owners thereof, saving the
beholding *of them* with their eyes?
12 The sleep of a laboring man *is*
sweet, whether he eat little or much: but
the abundance of the rich will not suffer
him to sleep.
13 There is a sore evil *which* I have
seen under the sun, *namely,* riches kept
for the owners thereof to their hurt.
14 But those riches perish by evil travail: and he begetteth a son, and *there is*
nothing in his hand.
15 As he came forth of his mother's
womb, naked shall he return to go as he
came, and shall take nothing of his labor, which he may carry away in his
hand.
16 And this also *is* a sore evil, *that* in all
points as he came, so shall he go: and
what profit hath he that hath labored
for the wind?
17 All his days also he eateth in darkness, and *he hath* much sorrow and
wrath with his sickness.
18 ¶ Behold *that* which I have seen:
it is good and comely *for one* to eat and
to drink, and to enjoy the good of all his
labor that he taketh under the sun all
the days of his life, which God giveth
him: for it *is* his portion.
19 Every man also to whom God hath
given riches and wealth, and hath given

him power to eat thereof, and to take his portion, and to rejoice in his labor; this *is* the gift of God.

20 For he shall not much remember the days of his life; because God answereth *him* in the joy of his heart.

CHAPTER 6

THERE is an evil which I have seen under the sun, and it *is* common among men:

2 A man to whom God hath given riches, wealth, and honor, so that he wanteth nothing for his soul of all that he desireth, yet God giveth him not power to eat thereof, but a stranger eateth it: this *is* vanity, and it *is* an evil disease.

3 ¶ If a man beget a hundred *children*, and live many years, so that the days of his years be many, and his soul be not filled with good, and also *that* he have no burial; I say, *that* an untimely birth *is* better than he.

4 For he cometh in with vanity, and departeth in darkness, and his name shall be covered with darkness.

5 Moreover he hath not seen the sun, nor known *any thing:* this hath more rest than the other.

6 ¶ Yea, though he live a thousand years twice *told,* yet hath he seen no good: do not all go to one place?

7 All the labor of man *is* for his mouth, and yet the appetite is not filled.

8 For what hath the wise more than the fool? what hath the poor, that knoweth to walk before the living?

9 ¶ Better *is* the sight of the eyes than the wandering of the desire: this *is* also vanity and vexation of spirit.

10 That which hath been is named already, and it is known that it *is* man: neither may he contend with him that is mightier than he.

11 ¶ Seeing there be many things that increase vanity, what *is* man the better?

12 For who knoweth what *is* good for man in *this* life, all the days of his vain life which he spendeth as a shadow? for who can tell a man what shall be after him under the sun?

CHAPTER 7

A GOOD name *is* better than precious ointment; and the day of death than the day of one's birth.

2 ¶ *It is* better to go to the house of mourning, than to go to the house of feasting: for that *is* the end of all men; and the living will lay *it* to his heart.

3 Sorrow *is* better than laughter: for by the sadness of the countenance the heart is made better.

4 The heart of the wise *is* in the house of mourning; but the heart of fools *is* in the house of mirth.

5 *It is* better to hear the rebuke of the wise, than for a man to hear the song of fools.

6 For as the crackling of thorns under a pot, so *is* the laughter of the fool: this also *is* vanity.

7 ¶ Surely oppression maketh a wise man mad; and a gift destroyeth the heart.

8 Better *is* the end of a thing than the beginning thereof: *and* the patient in spirit *is* better than the proud in spirit.

9 Be not hasty in thy spirit to be angry: for anger resteth in the bosom of fools.

10 Say not thou, What is *the cause* that the former days were better than these? for thou dost not inquire wisely concerning this.

11 ¶ Wisdom *is* good with an inheritance: and *by it there is* profit to them that see the sun.

12 For wisdom *is* a defense, *and* money *is* a defense: but the excellency of knowledge *is, that* wisdom giveth life to them that have it.

13 Consider the work of God: for who can make *that* straight, which he hath made crooked?

14 In the day of prosperity be joyful, but in the day of adversity consider: God also hath set the one over against the other, to the end that man should find nothing after him.

15 All *things* have I seen in the days of my vanity: there is a just *man* that perisheth in his righteousness, and there is a wicked *man* that prolongeth *his life* in his wickedness.

16 Be not righteous over much, neither make thyself over wise: why shouldest thou destroy thyself?

17 Be not over much wicked, neither be thou foolish: why shouldest thou die before thy time?

18 *It is* good that thou shouldest take hold of this; yea, also from this withdraw not thine hand: for he that feareth God shall come forth of them all.

19 Wisdom strengtheneth the wise more than ten mighty *men* which are in the city.

20 For *there is* not a just man upon earth, that doeth good, and sinneth not.

21 Also take no heed unto all words that are spoken; lest thou hear thy servant curse thee:

22 For oftentimes also thine own heart knoweth that thou thyself likewise hast cursed others.

23 ¶ All this have I proved by wisdom: I said, I will be wise; but it *was* far from me.

24 That which is far off, and exceeding deep, who can find it out?

25 I applied mine heart to know, and to search, and to seek out wisdom, and the reason *of things,* and to know the wickedness of folly, even of foolishness *and* madness:

26 And I find more bitter than death the woman, whose heart *is* snares and nets, *and* her hands *as* bands: whoso pleaseth God shall escape from her; but the sinner shall be taken by her.

27 Behold, this have I found, saith the Preacher, *counting* one by one, to find out the account;

28 Which yet my soul seeketh, but I find not: one man among a thousand have I found; but a woman among all those have I not found.

29 Lo, this only have I found, that God hath made man upright; but they have sought out many inventions.

CHAPTER 8

WHO *is* as the wise *man?* and who knoweth the interpretation of a thing? a man's wisdom maketh his face to shine, and the boldness of his face shall be changed.

2 I *counsel thee* to keep the king's commandment, and *that* in regard of the oath of God.

3 Be not hasty to go out of his sight: stand not in an evil thing; for he doeth whatsoever pleaseth him.

4 Where the word of a king *is, there is* power: and who may say unto him, What doest thou?

5 Whoso keepeth the commandment shall feel no evil thing: and a wise man's heart discerneth both time and judgment.

6 ¶ Because to every purpose there is time and judgment, therefore the misery of man *is* great upon him.

7 For he knoweth not that which shall be: for who can tell him when it shall be?

8 *There is* no man that hath power over the spirit to retain the spirit; neither *hath he* power in the day of death: and *there is* no discharge in *that* war; neither shall wickedness deliver those that are given to it.

9 All this have I seen, and applied my heart unto every work that is done under the sun: *there is* a time wherein one man ruleth over another to his own hurt.

10 And so I saw the wicked buried, who had come and gone from the place of the holy, and they were forgotten in the city where they had so done: this *is* also vanity.

11 Because sentence against an evil work is not executed speedily, therefore the heart of the sons of men is fully set in them to do evil.

12 ¶ Though a sinner do evil a hundred times, and his *days* be prolonged, yet surely I know that it shall be well with them that fear God, which fear before him:

13 But it shall not be well with the wicked, neither shall he prolong *his* days, *which are* as a shadow; because he feareth not before God.

14 There is a vanity which is done upon the earth; that there be just *men,* unto whom it happeneth according to the work of the wicked; again, there be wicked *men,* to whom it happeneth according to the work of the righteous: I said that this also *is* vanity.

15 Then I commended mirth, because a man hath no better thing under the sun, than to eat, and to drink, and to be merry: for that shall abide with him of his labor the days of his life, which God giveth him under the sun.

16 ¶ When I applied mine heart to know wisdom, and to see the business that is done upon the earth: (for also *there is that* neither day nor night seeth sleep with his eyes:)

17 Then I beheld all the work of God, that a man cannot find out the work that is done under the sun: because though a man labor to seek *it* out, yet he shall not find *it;* yea further; though a wise *man* think to know *it,* yet shall he not be able to find *it.*

CHAPTER 9

FOR all this I considered in my heart even to declare all this, that the righteous, and the wise, and their works, *are* in the hand of God: no man knoweth either love or hatred *by* all *that is* before them.

2 All *things come* alike to all: *there is* one event to the righteous, and to the wicked; to the good and to the clean, and to the unclean; to him that sacrificeth, and to him that sacrificeth not: as *is* the good, so *is* the sinner; *and* he that sweareth, as *he* that feareth an oath.

3 This *is* an evil among all *things* that are done under the sun, that *there is* one event unto all: yea, also the heart of the sons of men is full of evil, and madness *is* in their heart while they live, and after that *they go* to the dead.

4 ¶ For to him that is joined to all the living there is hope: for a living dog is better than a dead lion.

5 For the living know that they shall die: but the dead know not any thing, neither have they any more a reward; for the memory of them is forgotten.

6 Also their love, and their hatred, and their envy, is now perished; neither have they any more a portion for ever in any *thing* that is done under the sun.

7 ¶ Go thy way, eat thy bread with joy, and drink thy wine with a merry heart; for God now accepteth thy works.

8 Let thy garments be always white; and let thy head lack no ointment.

9 Live joyfully with the wife whom thou lovest all the days of the life of thy vanity, which he hath given thee under the sun, all the days of thy vanity: for that *is* thy portion in *this* life, and in thy labor which thou takest under the sun.

10 Whatsoever thy hand findeth to do, do *it* with thy might; for *there is* no work, nor device, nor knowledge, nor wisdom, in the grave, whither thou goest.

11 ¶ I returned, and saw under the sun, that the race *is* not to the swift, nor the battle to the strong, neither yet bread to the wise, nor yet riches to men of understanding, nor yet favor to men of skill; but time and chance happeneth to them all.

12 For man also knoweth not his time: as the fishes that are taken in an evil net, and as the birds that are caught in the snare; so *are* the sons of men snared in an evil time, when it falleth suddenly upon them.

13 ¶ This wisdom have I seen also under the sun, and it *seemed* great unto me:

14 *There was* a little city, and few men within it; and there came a great king against it, and besieged it, and built great bulwarks against it.

15 Now there was found in it a poor wise man, and he by his wisdom delivered the city; yet no man remembered that same poor man.

16 Then said I, Wisdom *is* better than strength: nevertheless the poor man's wisdom *is* despised, and his words are not heard.

17 The words of wise *men are* heard in quiet more than the cry of him that ruleth among fools.

18 Wisdom *is* better than weapons of war: but one sinner destroyeth much good.

CHAPTER 10

DEAD flies cause the ointment of the apothecary to send forth a stinking savor: *so doth* a little folly him that is in reputation for wisdom *and* honor.

2 A wise man's heart *is* at his right hand; but a fool's heart at his left.

3 Yea also, when he that is a fool walketh by the way, his wisdom faileth *him*, and he saith to every one *that* he *is* a fool.

4 If the spirit of the ruler rise up against thee, leave not thy place; for yielding pacifieth great offenses.

5 There is an evil *which* I have seen under the sun, as an error *which* proceedeth from the ruler:

6 Folly is set in great dignity, and the rich sit in low place.

7 I have seen servants upon horses, and princes walking as servants upon the earth.

8 He that diggeth a pit shall fall into it; and whoso breaketh a hedge, a serpent shall bite him.

9 Whoso removeth stones shall be hurt therewith; *and* he that cleaveth wood shall be endangered thereby.

10 If the iron be blunt, and he do not whet the edge, then must he put to more strength: but wisdom *is* profitable to direct.

11 Surely the serpent will bite without enchantment; and a babbler is no better.

12 The words of a wise man's mouth *are* gracious; but the lips of a fool will swallow up himself.

13 The beginning of the words of his mouth *is* foolishness: and the end of his talk *is* mischievous madness.

14 A fool also is full of words: a man cannot tell what shall be; and what shall be after him, who can tell him?

15 The labor of the foolish wearieth every one of them, because he knoweth not how to go to the city.

16 ¶ Woe to thee, O land, when thy king *is* a child, and thy princes eat in the morning!

17 Blessed *art* thou, O land, when thy king *is* the son of nobles, and thy princes eat in due season, for strength, and not for drunkenness!

18 ¶ By much slothfulness the building decayeth; and through idleness of the hands the house droppeth through.

19 ¶ A feast is made for laughter, and wine maketh merry: but money answereth all *things*.

20 ¶ Curse not the king, no not in thy thought; and curse not the rich in thy bedchamber: for a bird of the air shall carry the voice, and that which hath wings shall tell the matter.

CHAPTER 11

CAST thy bread upon the waters: for thou shalt find it after many days.

2 Give a portion to seven, and also to eight; for thou knowest not what evil shall be upon the earth.

3 If the clouds be full of rain, they empty *themselves* upon the earth: and if the tree fall toward the south, or toward the north, in the place where the tree falleth, there it shall be.

4 He that observeth the wind shall not sow; and he that regardeth the clouds shall not reap.

5 As thou knowest not what *is* the way of the spirit, *nor* how the bones *do grow* in the womb of her that is with child: even so thou knowest not the works of God who maketh all.

6 In the morning sow thy seed, and in the evening withhold not thine hand: for thou knowest not whether shall prosper, either this or that, or whether they both *shall be* alike good.

7 ¶ Truly the light *is* sweet, and a pleasant *thing it is* for the eyes to behold the sun:

8 But if a man live many years, *and* rejoice in them all; yet let him remember the days of darkness; for they shall be many. All that cometh *is* vanity.

9 ¶ Rejoice, O young man, in thy youth; and let thy heart cheer thee in the days of thy youth, and walk in the ways of thine heart, and in the sight of thine eyes: but know thou, that for all these *things* God will bring thee into judgment.

10 Therefore remove sorrow from thy heart, and put away evil from thy flesh: for childhood and youth *are* vanity.

CHAPTER 12

REMEMBER now thy Creator in the days of thy youth, while the evil days come not, nor the years draw nigh, when thou shalt say, I have no pleasure in them;

2 While the sun, or the light, or the moon, or the stars, be not darkened, nor the clouds return after the rain:

3 In the day when the keepers of the house shall tremble, and the strong men shall bow themselves, and the grinders cease because they are few, and those that look out of the windows be darkened,

4 And the doors shall be shut in the streets, when the sound of the grinding is low, and he shall rise up at the voice of the bird, and all the daughters of music shall be brought low;

5 Also *when* they shall be afraid of *that which is* high, and fears *shall be* in the way, and the almond tree shall flourish, and the grasshopper shall be a burden, and desire shall fail: because man goeth to his long home, and the mourners go about the streets:

6 Or ever the silver cord be loosed, or the golden bowl be broken, or the pitcher be broken at the fountain, or the wheel broken at the cistern.

7 Then shall the dust return to the earth as it was: and the spirit shall return unto God who gave it.

8 ¶ Vanity of vanities, saith the Preacher; all *is* vanity.

9 And moreover, because the Preacher was wise, he still taught the people knowledge; yea, he gave good heed, and sought out, *and* set in order many proverbs.

10 The Preacher sought to find out

acceptable words: and *that which was* written *was* upright, *even* words of truth.

11 The words of the wise *are* as goads, and as nails fastened *by* the masters of assemblies, *which* are given from one shepherd.

12 And further, by these, my son, be admonished: of making many books *there is* no end; and much study *is* a weariness of the flesh.

13 ¶ Let us hear the conclusion of the whole matter: Fear God, and keep his commandments: for this *is* the whole *duty* of man.

14 For God shall bring every work into judgment, with every secret thing, whether *it be* good, or whether *it be* evil.

THE SONG OF SOLOMON

CHAPTER 1

THE Song of songs, which *is* Solomon's.

2 Let him kiss me with the kisses of his mouth: for thy love *is* better than wine.

3 Because of the savor of thy good ointments thy name *is as* ointment poured forth, therefore do the virgins love thee.

4 Draw me, we will run after thee: the King hath brought me into his chambers: we will be glad and rejoice in thee, we will remember thy love more than wine: the upright love thee.

5 I *am* black, but comely, O ye daughters of Jerusalem, as the tents of Kē'dȧr, as the curtains of Solomon.

6 Look not upon me, because I *am* black, because the sun hath looked upon me: my mother's children were angry with me; they made me the keeper of the vineyards; *but* mine own vineyard have I not kept.

7 Tell me, O thou whom my soul loveth, where thou feedest, where thou makest *thy flock* to rest at noon: for why should I be as one that turneth aside by the flocks of thy companions?

8 ¶ If thou know not, O thou fairest among women, go thy way forth by the footsteps of the flock, and feed thy kids beside the shepherds' tents.

9 I have compared thee, O my love, to a company of horses in Phā'raōh's chariots.

10 Thy cheeks are comely with rows *of jewels*, thy neck with chains *of gold*.

11 We will make thee borders of gold with studs of silver.

12 ¶ While the King *sitteth* at his table, my spikenard sendeth forth the smell thereof.

13 A bundle of myrrh *is* my wellbeloved unto me; he shall lie all night betwixt my breasts.

14 My beloved *is* unto me *as* a cluster of camphire in the vineyards of Ĕn–gē'dĭ.

15 Behold, thou *art* fair, my love; behold, thou *art* fair; thou *hast* doves' eyes.

16 Behold, thou *art* fair, my beloved, yea, pleasant: also our bed *is* green.

17 The beams of our house *are* cedar, *and* our rafters of fir.

CHAPTER 2

I AM the rose of Shăr'ŏn, *and* the lily of the valleys.

2 As the lily among thorns, so *is* my love among the daughters.

3 As the apple tree among the trees of the wood, so *is* my beloved among the sons. I sat down under his shadow with great delight, and his fruit *was* sweet to my taste.

4 He brought me to the banqueting house, and his banner over me *was* love.

5 Stay me with flagons, comfort me with apples: for I *am* sick of love.

6 His left hand *is* under my head, and his right hand doth embrace me.

7 I charge you, O ye daughters of Jerusalem, by the roes, and by the hinds of the field, that ye stir not up, nor awake *my* love, till he please.

8 ¶ The voice of my beloved! behold, he cometh leaping upon the mountains, skipping upon the hills.

9 My beloved is like a roe or a young hart: behold, he standeth behind our

wall, he looketh forth at the windows, showing himself through the lattice.

10 My beloved spake, and said unto me, Rise up, my love, my fair one, and come away.

11 For, lo, the winter is past, the rain is over *and* gone;

12 The flowers appear on the earth; the time of the singing *of birds* is come, and the voice of the turtle is heard in our land;

13 The fig tree putteth forth her green figs, and the vines *with* the tender grape give a *good* smell. Arise, my love, my fair one, and come away.

14 ¶ O my dove, *that art* in the clefts of the rock, in the secret *places* of the stairs, let me see thy countenance, let me hear thy voice; for sweet *is* thy voice, and thy countenance *is* comely.

15 Take us the foxes, the little foxes, that spoil the vines: for our vines *have* tender grapes.

16 ¶ My beloved *is* mine, and I *am* his: he feedeth among the lilies.

17 Until the day break, and the shadows flee away, turn, my beloved, and be thou like a roe or a young hart upon the mountains of Bē'thĕr.

CHAPTER 3

BY night on my bed I sought him whom my soul loveth: I sought him, but I found him not.

2 I will rise now, and go about the city in the streets, and in the broad ways I will seek him whom my soul loveth: I sought him, but I found him not.

3 The watchmen that go about the city found me: *to whom I said,* Saw ye him whom my soul loveth?

4 *It was* but a little that I passed from them, but I found him whom my soul loveth: I held him, and would not let him go, until I had brought him into my mother's house, and into the chamber of her that conceived me.

5 I charge you, O ye daughters of Jerusalem, by the roes, and by the hinds of the field, that ye stir not up, nor awake *my* love, till he please.

6 ¶ Who *is* this that cometh out of the wilderness like pillars of smoke, perfumed with myrrh and frankincense, with all powders of the merchant?

7 Behold his bed, which *is* Solomon's; threescore valiant men *are* about it, of the valiant of Ĭş'ră-ĕl.

8 They all hold swords, *being* expert in war: every man *hath* his sword upon his thigh because of fear in the night.

9 King Solomon made himself a chariot of the wood of Lebanon.

10 He made the pillars thereof *of* silver, the bottom thereof *of* gold, the covering of it *of* purple, the midst thereof being paved *with* love, for the daughters of Jerusalem.

11 Go forth, O ye daughters of Zion, and behold king Solomon with the crown wherewith his mother crowned him in the day of his espousals, and in the day of the gladness of his heart.

CHAPTER 4

BEHOLD, thou *art* fair, my love; behold, thou *art* fair; thou *hast* doves' eyes within thy locks: thy hair *is* as a flock of goats, that appear from mount Gĭl'ē-ăd.

2 Thy teeth *are* like a flock *of sheep that are even* shorn, which came up from the washing; whereof every one bear twins, and none *is* barren among them.

3 Thy lips *are* like a thread of scarlet, and thy speech *is* comely: thy temples *are* like a piece of a pomegranate within thy locks.

4 Thy neck *is* like the tower of David builded for an armory, whereon there hang a thousand bucklers, all shields of mighty men.

5 Thy two breasts *are* like two young roes that are twins, which feed among the lilies.

6 Until the day break, and the shadows flee away, I will get me to the mountain of myrrh, and to the hill of frankincense.

7 Thou *art* all fair, my love; *there is* no spot in thee.

8 ¶ Come with me from Lebanon, *my* spouse, with me from Lebanon: look from the top of Ăm'ȧ-nȧ, from the top of Shē'nĭr and Hermon, from the lions' dens, from the mountains of the leopards.

9 Thou hast ravished my heart, my sister, *my* spouse; thou hast ravished my heart with one of thine eyes, with one chain of thy neck.

10 How fair is thy love, my sister, *my* spouse! how much better is thy love than wine! and the smell of thine ointments than all spices!

11 Thy lips, O *my* spouse, drop *as* the

honeycomb: honey and milk *are* under
thy tongue; and the smell of thy garments *is* like the smell of Lebanon.
12 A garden inclosed *is* my sister, *my*
spouse; a spring shut up, a fountain
sealed.
13 Thy plants *are* an orchard of pomegranates, with pleasant fruits; camphire,
with spikenard,
14 Spikenard and saffron; calamus and
cinnamon, with all trees of frankincense;
myrrh and aloes, with all the chief spices:
15 A fountain of gardens, a well of living waters, and streams from Lebanon.
16 ¶ Awake, O north wind; and come,
thou south; blow upon my garden, *that*
the spices thereof may flow out. Let my
beloved come into his garden, and eat
his pleasant fruits.

CHAPTER 5

I AM come into my garden, my sister,
my spouse: I have gathered my
myrrh with my spice; I have eaten my
honeycomb with my honey; I have drunk
my wine with my milk: eat, O friends;
drink, yea, drink abundantly, O beloved.
2 ¶ I sleep, but my heart waketh: *it is*
the voice of my beloved that knocketh,
saying, Open to me, my sister, my love,
my dove, my undefiled: for my head is
filled with dew, *and* my locks with the
drops of the night.
3 I have put off my coat; how shall I
put it on? I have washed my feet; how
shall I defile them?
4 My beloved put in his hand by the
hole *of the door,* and my bowels were
moved for him.
5 I rose up to open to my beloved; and
my hands dropped *with* myrrh, and my
fingers *with* sweet smelling myrrh, upon
the handles of the lock.
6 I opened to my beloved; but my beloved had withdrawn himself, *and* was
gone: my soul failed when he spake: I
sought him, but I could not find him; I
called him, but he gave me no answer.
7 The watchmen that went about the
city found me, they smote me, they
wounded me; the keepers of the walls
took away my veil from me.
8 I charge you, O daughters of Jerusalem, if ye find my beloved, that ye tell
him, that I *am* sick of love.
9 ¶ What *is* thy beloved more than
another beloved, O thou fairest among
women? what *is* thy beloved more than
another beloved, that thou dost so charge
us?
10 My beloved *is* white and ruddy, the
chiefest among ten thousand.
11 His head *is as* the most fine gold;
his locks *are* bushy, *and* black as a
raven:
12 His eyes *are* as *the eyes* of doves by
the rivers of waters, washed with milk,
and fitly set:
13 His cheeks *are* as a bed of spices, *as*
sweet flowers: his lips *like* lilies, dropping sweet smelling myrrh:
14 His hands *are as* gold rings set with
the beryl: his belly *is as* bright ivory
overlaid *with* sapphires:
15 His legs *are as* pillars of marble, set
upon sockets of fine gold: his countenance *is* as Lebanon, excellent as the
cedars:
16 His mouth *is* most sweet: yea, he *is*
altogether lovely. This *is* my beloved,
and this *is* my friend, O daughters of
Jerusalem.

CHAPTER 6

WHITHER is thy beloved gone,
O thou fairest among women?
whither is thy beloved turned aside?
that we may seek him with thee.
2 My beloved is gone down into his
garden, to the beds of spices, to feed in
the gardens, and to gather lilies.
3 I *am* my beloved's, and my beloved *is*
mine: he feedeth among the lilies.
4 ¶ Thou *art* beautiful, O my love, as
Tĭr′zăh, comely as Jerusalem, terrible as
an army with banners.
5 Turn away thine eyes from me, for
they have overcome me: thy hair *is* as a
flock of goats that appear from Gĭl′ē-ăd:
6 Thy teeth *are* as a flock of sheep
which go up from the washing, whereof
every one beareth twins, and *there is*
not one barren among them.
7 As a piece of a pomegranate *are* thy
temples within thy locks.
8 There are threescore queens, and
fourscore concubines, and virgins without number.
9 My dove, my undefiled, is *but* one;
she *is* the *only* one of her mother, she *is*
the choice *one* of her that bare her. The
daughters saw her, and blessed her;
yea, the queens and the concubines, and
they praised her.
10 ¶ Who *is* she *that* looketh forth as
the morning, fair as the moon, clear as

the sun, *and* terrible as *an army* with banners?

11 I went down into the garden of nuts to see the fruits of the valley, *and* to see whether the vine flourished, *and* the pomegranates budded.

12 Or ever I was aware, my soul made me *like* the chariots of Ăm′mĭ–nā′dĭb.

13 Return, return, O Shü′lăm-ïte; return, return, that we may look upon thee. What will ye see in the Shü′lăm-ïte? As it were the company of two armies.

CHAPTER 7

HOW beautiful are thy feet with shoes, O prince's daughter! the joints of thy thighs *are* like jewels, the work of the hands of a cunning workman.

2 Thy navel *is like* a round goblet, *which* wanteth not liquor: thy belly *is like* a heap of wheat set about with lilies.

3 Thy two breasts *are* like two young roes *that are* twins.

4 Thy neck *is* as a tower of ivory; thine eyes *like* the fishpools in Hĕsh′bŏn, by the gate of Băth′–răb′bĭm: thy nose *is* as the tower of Lebanon which looketh toward Damascus.

5 Thine head upon thee *is* like Cär′mĕl, and the hair of thine head like purple; the King *is* held in the galleries.

6 How fair and how pleasant art thou, O love, for delights!

7 This thy stature is like to a palm tree, and thy breasts to clusters *of grapes*.

8 I said, I will go up to the palm tree, I will take hold of the boughs thereof: now also thy breasts shall be as clusters of the vine, and the smell of thy nose like apples;

9 And the roof of thy mouth like the best wine for my beloved, that goeth *down* sweetly, causing the lips of those that are asleep to speak.

10 ¶ I *am* my beloved's, and his desire *is* toward me.

11 Come, my beloved, let us go forth into the field; let us lodge in the villages.

12 Let us get up early to the vineyards; let us see if the vine flourish, *whether* the tender grape appear, *and* the pomegranates bud forth: there will I give thee my loves.

13 The mandrakes give a smell, and at our gates *are* all manner of pleasant *fruits*, new and old, *which* I have laid up for thee, O my beloved.

CHAPTER 8

O THAT thou *wert* as my brother, that sucked the breasts of my mother! *when* I should find thee without, I would kiss thee; yea, I should not be despised.

2 I would lead thee, *and* bring thee into my mother's house, *who* would instruct me: I would cause thee to drink of spiced wine of the juice of my pomegranate.

3 His left hand *should be* under my head, and his right hand should embrace me.

4 I charge you, O daughters of Jerusalem, that ye stir not up, nor awake *my* love, until he please.

5 Who *is* this that cometh up from the wilderness, leaning upon her beloved? I raised thee up under the apple tree: there thy mother brought thee forth; there she brought thee forth *that* bare thee.

6 ¶ Set me as a seal upon thine heart, as a seal upon thine arm: for love *is* strong as death; jealousy *is* cruel as the grave: the coals thereof *are* coals of fire, *which hath* a most vehement flame.

7 Many waters cannot quench love, neither can the floods drown it: if a man would give all the substance of his house for love, it would utterly be contemned.

8 ¶ We have a little sister, and she hath no breasts: what shall we do for our sister in the day when she shall be spoken for?

9 If she *be* a wall, we will build upon her a palace of silver: and if she *be* a door, we will inclose her with boards of cedar.

10 I *am* a wall, and my breasts like towers: then was I in his eyes as one that found favor.

11 Solomon had a vineyard at Bā′ăl–hā′mŏn; he let out the vineyard unto keepers; every one for the fruit thereof was to bring a thousand *pieces* of silver.

12 My vineyard, which *is* mine, *is* before me: thou, O Solomon, *must have* a thousand, and those that keep the fruit thereof two hundred.

13 Thou that dwellest in the gardens, the companions hearken to thy voice: cause me to hear *it*.

14 ¶ Make haste, my beloved, and be thou like to a roe or to a young hart upon the mountains of spices.

THE BOOK OF THE PROPHET

ISAIAH

CHAPTER 1

THE vision of Ī-ṣā′ịȧh the son of Ā′mŏz, which he saw concerning Judah and Jerusalem in the days of Ŭz-zī′ȧh, Jō′thăm, Ahaz, *and* Hĕz′ē-kī′ȧh, kings of Judah.

2 Hear, O heavens, and give ear, O earth: for the LORD hath spoken; I have nourished and brought up children, and they have rebelled against me.

3 The ox knoweth his owner, and the ass his master's crib: *but* Ĭṣ′rā-ĕl doth not know, my people doth not consider.

4 Ah sinful nation, a people laden with iniquity, a seed of evildoers, children that are corrupters: they have forsaken the LORD, they have provoked the Holy One of Ĭṣ′rā-ĕl unto anger, they are gone away backward.

5 ¶ Why should ye be stricken any more? ye will revolt more and more: the whole head is sick, and the whole heart faint.

6 From the sole of the foot even unto the head *there is* no soundness in it; *but* wounds, and bruises, and putrifying sores: they have not been closed, neither bound up, neither mollified with ointment.

7 Your country *is* desolate, your cities *are* burned with fire: your land, strangers devour it in your presence, and *it is* desolate, as overthrown by strangers.

8 And the daughter of Zion is left as a cottage in a vineyard, as a lodge in a garden of cucumbers, as a besieged city.

9 Except the LORD of hosts had left unto us a very small remnant, we should have been as Sŏd′ŏm, *and* we should have been like unto Gō-mŏr′rȧh.

10 ¶ Hear the word of the LORD, ye rulers of Sŏd′ŏm; give ear unto the law of our God, ye people of Gō-mŏr′rȧh.

11 To what purpose *is* the multitude of your sacrifices unto me? saith the LORD: I am full of the burnt offerings of rams, and the fat of fed beasts; and I delight not in the blood of bullocks, or of lambs, or of he goats.

12 When ye come to appear before me, who hath required this at your hand, to tread my courts?

13 Bring no more vain oblations; incense is an abomination unto me; the new moons and sabbaths, the calling of assemblies, I cannot away with; *it is* iniquity, even the solemn meeting.

14 Your new moons and your appointed feasts my soul hateth: they are a trouble unto me; I am weary to bear *them*.

15 And when ye spread forth your hands, I will hide mine eyes from you; yea, when ye make many prayers, I will not hear: your hands are full of blood.

16 ¶ Wash ye, make you clean; put away the evil of your doings from before mine eyes; cease to do evil;

17 Learn to do well; seek judgment, relieve the oppressed, judge the fatherless, plead for the widow.

18 Come now, and let us reason together, saith the LORD: though your sins be as scarlet, they shall be as white as snow; though they be red like crimson, they shall be as wool.

19 If ye be willing and obedient, ye shall eat the good of the land:

20 But if ye refuse and rebel, ye shall be devoured with the sword: for the mouth of the LORD hath spoken *it*.

21 ¶ How is the faithful city become a harlot! it was full of judgment; righteousness lodged in it; but now murderers.

22 Thy silver is become dross, thy wine mixed with water:

23 Thy princes *are* rebellious, and companions of thieves: every one loveth gifts, and followeth after rewards: they judge not the fatherless, neither doth the cause of the widow come unto them.

24 Therefore saith the Lord, the LORD of hosts, the Mighty One of Ĭṣ′rā-ĕl, Ah, I will ease me of mine adversaries, and avenge me of mine enemies.

25 ¶ And I will turn my hand upon thee, and purely purge away thy dross, and take away all thy tin:

26 And I will restore thy judges as at the first, and thy counselors as at the beginning: afterward thou shalt be called, The city of righteousness, the faithful city.

27 Zion shall be redeemed with judg-

ment, and her converts with righteousness.
28 ¶ And the destruction of the transgressors and of the sinners *shall be* together, and they that forsake the LORD
shall be consumed.
29 For they shall be ashamed of the
oaks which ye have desired, and ye shall
be confounded for the gardens that ye
have chosen.
30 For ye shall be as an oak whose leaf
fadeth, and as a garden that hath no
water.
31 And the strong shall be as tow, and
the maker of it as a spark, and they shall
both burn together, and none shall
quench *them*.

CHAPTER 2

THE word that Ī-ṣā'iah the son of
Ā'mŏz saw concerning Judah and
Jerusalem.
2 And it shall come to pass in the last
days, *that* the mountain of the LORD's
house shall be established in the top of
the mountains, and shall be exalted
above the hills; and all nations shall flow
unto it.
3 And many people shall go and say,
Come ye, and let us go up to the mountain of the LORD, to the house of the God
of Jacob; and he will teach us of his
ways, and we will walk in his paths: for
out of Zion shall go forth the law, and
the word of the LORD from Jerusalem.
4 And he shall judge among the nations, and shall rebuke many people:
and they shall beat their swords into
plowshares, and their spears into pruning hooks: nation shall not lift up sword
against nation, neither shall they learn
war any more.
5 O house of Jacob, come ye, and let us
walk in the light of the LORD.
6 ¶ Therefore thou hast forsaken thy
people the house of Jacob, because they
be replenished from the east, and *are*
soothsayers like the Phĭ-lĭs'tīneṣ, and
they please themselves in the children
of strangers.
7 Their land also is full of silver and
gold, neither *is there any* end of their
treasures; their land is also full of horses,
neither *is there any* end of their chariots:
8 Their land also is full of idols; they
worship the work of their own hands,
that which their own fingers have made:
9 And the mean man boweth down, and
the great man humbleth himself: therefore forgive them not.
10 ¶ Enter into the rock, and hide thee
in the dust, for fear of the LORD, and for
the glory of his majesty.
11 The lofty looks of man shall be humbled, and the haughtiness of men shall
be bowed down; and the LORD alone
shall be exalted in that day.
12 For the day of the LORD of hosts
shall be upon every *one that is* proud and
lofty, and upon every *one that is* lifted
up; and he shall be brought low:
13 And upon all the cedars of Lebanon,
that are high and lifted up, and upon all
the oaks of Bā'shăn,
14 And upon all the high mountains,
and upon all the hills *that are* lifted up,
15 And upon every high tower, and
upon every fenced wall,
16 And upon all the ships of Tär'shĭsh,
and upon all pleasant pictures.
17 And the loftiness of man shall be
bowed down, and the haughtiness of
men shall be made low; and the LORD
alone shall be exalted in that day.
18 And the idols he shall utterly abolish.
19 And they shall go into the holes of
the rocks, and into the caves of the
earth, for fear of the LORD, and for the
glory of his majesty, when he ariseth to
shake terribly the earth.
20 In that day a man shall cast his idols
of silver, and his idols of gold, which
they made *each one* for himself to worship, to the moles and to the bats;
21 To go into the clefts of the rocks, and
into the tops of the ragged rocks, for fear
of the LORD, and for the glory of his
majesty, when he ariseth to shake terribly the earth.
22 Cease ye from man, whose breath *is*
in his nostrils: for wherein is he to be
accounted of?

CHAPTER 3

FOR, behold, the Lord, the LORD of
hosts, doth take away from Jerusalem and from Judah the stay and the
staff, the whole stay of bread, and the
whole stay of water,
2 The mighty man, and the man of war,
the judge, and the prophet, and the prudent, and the ancient,
3 The captain of fifty, and the honorable man, and the counselor, and
the cunning artificer, and the eloquent
orator.

4 And I will give children *to be* their princes, and babes shall rule over them.

5 And the people shall be oppressed, every one by another, and every one by his neighbor: the child shall behave himself proudly against the ancient, and the base against the honorable.

6 When a man shall take hold of his brother of the house of his father, *saying,* Thou hast clothing, be thou our ruler, and *let* this ruin *be* under thy hand:

7 In that day shall he swear, saying, I will not be a healer; for in my house *is* neither bread nor clothing: make me not a ruler of the people.

8 For Jerusalem is ruined, and Judah is fallen: because their tongue and their doings *are* against the LORD, to provoke the eyes of his glory.

9 ℭ The show of their countenance doth witness against them; and they declare their sin as Sŏd′ŏm, they hide *it* not. Woe unto their soul! for they have rewarded evil unto themselves.

10 Say ye to the righteous, that *it shall be* well *with him:* for they shall eat the fruit of their doings.

11 Woe unto the wicked! *it shall be* ill *with him:* for the reward of his hands shall be given him.

12 ℭ *As for* my people, children *are* their oppressors, and women rule over them. O my people, they which lead thee cause *thee* to err, and destroy the way of thy paths.

13 The LORD standeth up to plead, and standeth to judge the people.

14 The LORD will enter into judgment with the ancients of his people, and the princes thereof: for ye have eaten up the vineyard; the spoil of the poor *is* in your houses.

15 What mean ye *that* ye beat my people to pieces, and grind the faces of the poor? saith the Lord GOD of hosts.

16 ℭ Moreover the LORD saith, Because the daughters of Zion are haughty, and walk with stretched forth necks and wanton eyes, walking and mincing *as* they go, and making a tinkling with their feet:

17 Therefore the Lord will smite with a scab the crown of the head of the daughters of Zion, and the LORD will discover their secret parts.

18 In that day the Lord will take away the bravery of *their* tinkling ornaments *about their feet,* and *their* cauls, and *their* round tires like the moon,

19 The chains, and the bracelets, and the mufflers,

20 The bonnets, and the ornaments of the legs, and the headbands, and the tablets, and the earrings,

21 The rings, and nose jewels,

22 The changeable suits of apparel, and the mantles, and the wimples, and the crisping pins,

23 The glasses, and the fine linen, and the hoods, and the veils.

24 And it shall come to pass, *that* instead of sweet smell there shall be stink; and instead of a girdle a rent; and instead of well set hair baldness; and instead of a stomacher a girding of sackcloth; *and* burning instead of beauty.

25 Thy men shall fall by the sword, and thy mighty in the war.

26 And her gates shall lament and mourn; and she *being* desolate shall sit upon the ground.

CHAPTER 4

AND in that day seven women shall take hold of one man, saying, We will eat our own bread, and wear our own apparel; only let us be called by thy name, to take away our reproach.

2 In that day shall the branch of the LORD be beautiful and glorious, and the fruit of the earth *shall be* excellent and comely for them that are escaped of Ĭṣ′rā-ĕl.

3 And it shall come to pass, *that he that is* left in Zion, and *he that* remaineth in Jerusalem, shall be called holy, *even* every one that is written among the living in Jerusalem:

4 When the Lord shall have washed away the filth of the daughters of Zion, and shall have purged the blood of Jerusalem from the midst thereof by the spirit of judgment, and by the spirit of burning.

5 And the LORD will create upon every dwelling place of mount Zion, and upon her assemblies, a cloud and smoke by day, and the shining of a flaming fire by night: for upon all the glory *shall be* a defense.

6 And there shall be a tabernacle for a shadow in the daytime from the heat, and for a place of refuge, and for a covert from storm and from rain.

CHAPTER 5

NOW will I sing to my well-beloved
a song of my beloved touching his
vineyard. My well-beloved hath a vineyard in a very fruitful hill:
2 And he fenced it, and gathered out
the stones thereof, and planted it with
the choicest vine, and built a tower in
the midst of it, and also made a winepress therein: and he looked that it
should bring forth grapes, and it brought
forth wild grapes.
3 And now, O inhabitants of Jerusalem,
and men of Judah, judge, I pray you,
betwixt me and my vineyard.
4 What could have been done more to
my vineyard, that I have not done in it?
wherefore, when I looked that it should
bring forth grapes, brought it forth wild
grapes?
5 And now go to; I will tell you what I
will do to my vineyard: I will take away
the hedge thereof, and it shall be eaten
up; *and* break down the wall thereof, and
it shall be trodden down:
6 And I will lay it waste: it shall not be
pruned, nor digged; but there shall come
up briers and thorns: I will also command the clouds that they rain no rain
upon it.
7 For the vineyard of the LORD of hosts
is the house of Ĭṣ′rā-ĕl, and the men of
Judah his pleasant plant: and he looked
for judgment, but behold oppression;
for righteousness, but behold a cry.
8 ¶Woe unto them that join house to
house, *that* lay field to field, till *there be*
no place, that they may be placed alone
in the midst of the earth!
9 In mine ears *said* the LORD of hosts,
Of a truth many houses shall be desolate, *even* great and fair, without inhabitant.
10 Yea, ten acres of vineyard shall yield
one bath, and the seed of a homer shall
yield an ē′phăh.
11 ¶Woe unto them that rise up early
in the morning, *that* they may follow
strong drink; that continue until night,
till wine inflame them!
12 And the harp and the viol, the tabret,
and pipe, and wine, are in their feasts:
but they regard not the work of the
LORD, neither consider the operation of
his hands.
13 ¶Therefore my people are gone
into captivity, because *they have* no
knowledge: and their honorable men *are*
famished, and their multitude dried up
with thirst.
14 Therefore hell hath enlarged herself, and opened her mouth without
measure: and their glory, and their multitude, and their pomp, and he that rejoiceth, shall descend into it.
15 And the mean man shall be brought
down, and the mighty man shall be humbled, and the eyes of the lofty shall be
humbled:
16 But the LORD of hosts shall be exalted in judgment, and God that is holy
shall be sanctified in righteousness.
17 Then shall the lambs feed after their
manner, and the waste places of the fat
ones shall strangers eat.
18 Woe unto them that draw iniquity
with cords of vanity, and sin as it were
with a cart rope:
19 That say, Let him make speed, *and*
hasten his work, that we may see *it:* and
let the counsel of the Holy One of Ĭṣ′-
rā-ĕl draw nigh and come, that we may
know *it!*
20 ¶ Woe unto them that call evil good,
and good evil; that put darkness for
light, and light for darkness; that put
bitter for sweet, and sweet for bitter!
21 Woe unto *them that are* wise in their
own eyes, and prudent in their own sight!
22 Woe unto *them that are* mighty
to drink wine, and men of strength to
mingle strong drink:
23 Which justify the wicked for reward, and take away the righteousness
of the righteous from him!
24 Therefore as the fire devoureth the
stubble, and the flame consumeth the
chaff, *so* their root shall be as rottenness, and their blossom shall go up as
dust: because they have cast away the
law of the LORD of hosts, and despised
the word of the Holy One of Ĭṣ′rā-ĕl.
25 Therefore is the anger of the LORD
kindled against his people, and he hath
stretched forth his hand against them,
and hath smitten them: and the hills did
tremble, and their carcasses *were* torn
in the midst of the streets. For all this
his anger is not turned away, but his
hand *is* stretched out still.
26 ¶ And he will lift up an ensign to
the nations from far, and will hiss unto
them from the end of the earth: and,
behold, they shall come with speed
swiftly:

27 None shall be weary nor stumble
among them; none shall slumber nor
sleep; neither shall the girdle of their
loins be loosed, nor the latchet of their
shoes be broken:
28 Whose arrows *are* sharp, and all
their bows bent, their horses' hoofs shall
be counted like flint, and their wheels
like a whirlwind:
29 Their roaring *shall be* like a lion,
they shall roar like young lions; yea,
they shall roar, and lay hold of the
prey, and shall carry *it* away safe, and
none shall deliver *it*.
30 And in that day they shall roar
against them like the roaring of the sea:
and if *one* look unto the land, behold
darkness *and* sorrow; and the light is
darkened in the heavens thereof.

CHAPTER 6

IN the year that king Ŭz-zī′ȧh died I
saw also the Lord sitting upon a
throne, high and lifted up, and his train
filled the temple.
2 Above it stood the seraphim: each
one had six wings; with twain he covered his face, and with twain he covered
his feet, and with twain he did fly.
3 And one cried unto another, and said,
Holy, holy, holy, *is* the LORD of hosts:
the whole earth *is* full of his glory.
4 And the posts of the door moved at
the voice of him that cried, and the
house was filled with smoke.
5 ¶ Then said I, Woe *is* me! for I am
undone; because I *am* a man of unclean
lips, and I dwell in the midst of a people
of unclean lips: for mine eyes have seen
the King, the LORD of hosts.
6 Then flew one of the seraphim unto
me, having a live coal in his hand, *which*
he had taken with the tongs from off
the altar:
7 And he laid *it* upon my mouth, and
said, Lo, this hath touched thy lips; and
thine iniquity is taken away, and thy
sin purged.
8 Also I heard the voice of the Lord,
saying, Whom shall I send, and who
will go for us? Then said I, Here *am* I;
send me.
9 ¶ And he said, Go, and tell this people, Hear ye indeed, but understand
not; and see ye indeed, but perceive not.
10 Make the heart of this people fat,
and make their ears heavy, and shut
their eyes; lest they see with their eyes,
and hear with their ears, and understand
with their heart, and convert, and be
healed.
11 Then said I, Lord, how long? And
he answered, Until the cities be wasted
without inhabitant, and the houses without man, and the land be utterly desolate,
12 And the LORD have removed men
far away, and *there be* a great forsaking
in the midst of the land.
13 ¶ But yet in it *shall be* a tenth, and
it shall return, and shall be eaten: as a
teil tree, and as an oak, whose substance
is in them, when they cast *their leaves:*
so the holy seed *shall be* the substance
thereof.

CHAPTER 7

AND it came to pass in the days of
Ahaz the son of Jō′thăm, the son of
Ŭz-zī′ȧh, king of Judah, *that* Rē′zĭn the
king of Syria, and Pē′kăh the son of
Rĕm′ȧ-lī′ȧh, king of Ĭṣ′rā-ĕl, went up
toward Jerusalem to war against it, but
could not prevail against it.
2 And it was told the house of David,
saying, Syria is confederate with Ē′phrā-
ĭm. And his heart was moved, and the
heart of his people, as the trees of the
wood are moved with the wind.
3 Then said the LORD unto Ī-ṣā′ịăh,
Go forth now to meet Ahaz, thou, and
Shē′är–jā′shŭb thy son, at the end of
the conduit of the upper pool, in the
highway of the fuller's field;
4 And say unto him, Take heed, and be
quiet; fear not, neither be faint-hearted
for the two tails of these smoking firebrands, for the fierce anger of Rē′zĭn
with Syria, and of the son of Rĕm′ȧ-
lī′ȧh.
5 Because Syria, Ē′phrā-ĭm, and the
son of Rĕm′ȧ-lī′ȧh, have taken evil
counsel against thee, saying,
6 Let us go up against Judah, and vex
it, and let us make a breach therein for
us, and set a king in the midst of it,
even the son of Tā′bē-ăl:
7 Thus saith the Lord GOD, It shall
not stand, neither shall it come to
pass.
8 For the head of Syria *is* Damascus,
and the head of Damascus *is* Rē′zĭn;
and within threescore and five years
shall Ē′phrā-ĭm be broken, that it be
not a people.
9 And the head of Ē′phrā-ĭm *is* Sȧ-

mā′rĭ-ȧ, and the head of Sȧ-mā′rĭ-ȧ *is* Rĕm′ȧ-lī′ȧh's son. If ye will not believe, surely ye shall not be established.

10 ¶ Moreover the LORD spake again unto Ahaz, saying,

11 Ask thee a sign of the LORD thy God; ask it either in the depth, or in the height above.

12 But Ahaz said, I will not ask, neither will I tempt the LORD.

13 And he said, Hear ye now, O house of David; *Is it* a small thing for you to weary men, but will ye weary my God also?

14 Therefore the Lord himself shall give you a sign; Behold, a virgin shall conceive, and bear a son, and shall call his name Ĭm-măn′ū-ĕl.

15 Butter and honey shall he eat, that he may know to refuse the evil, and choose the good.

16 For before the child shall know to refuse the evil, and choose the good, the land that thou abhorrest shall be forsaken of both her kings.

17 ¶ The LORD shall bring upon thee, and upon thy people, and upon thy father's house, days that have not come, from the day that Ē′phrā-ĭm departed from Judah; *even* the king of Assyria.

18 And it shall come to pass in that day, *that* the LORD shall hiss for the fly that *is* in the uttermost part of the rivers of Egypt, and for the bee that *is* in the land of Assyria.

19 And they shall come, and shall rest all of them in the desolate valleys, and in the holes of the rocks, and upon all thorns, and upon all bushes.

20 In the same day shall the Lord shave with a razor that is hired, *namely*, by them beyond the river, by the king of Assyria, the head, and the hair of the feet: and it shall also consume the beard.

21 And it shall come to pass in that day, *that* a man shall nourish a young cow and two sheep;

22 And it shall come to pass, for the abundance of milk *that* they shall give, he shall eat butter: for butter and honey shall every one eat that is left in the land.

23 And it shall come to pass in that day, *that* every place shall be, where there were a thousand vines at a thousand silverlings, it shall *even* be for briers and thorns.

24 With arrows and with bows shall *men* come thither; because all the land shall become briers and thorns.

25 And *on* all hills that shall be digged with the mattock, there shall not come thither the fear of briers and thorns: but it shall be for the sending forth of oxen, and for the treading of lesser cattle.

CHAPTER 8

MOREOVER the LORD said unto me, Take thee a great roll, and write in it with a man's pen concerning Mā′hĕr-shăl′ăl-hăsh′-băz′.

2 And I took unto me faithful witnesses to record, Ū-rī′ȧh the priest, and Zĕch′ȧ-rī′ȧh the son of Jē-bĕr′ĕ-chī′ȧh.

3 And I went unto the prophetess; and she conceived, and bare a son. Then said the LORD to me, Call his name Mā′hĕr-shăl′ăl-hăsh′-băz′.

4 For before the child shall have knowledge to cry, My father, and my mother, the riches of Damascus and the spoil of Sȧ-mā′rĭ-ȧ shall be taken away before the king of Assyria.

5 ¶ The LORD spake also unto me again, saying,

6 Forasmuch as this people refuseth the waters of Shĭ-lō′ȧh that go softly, and rejoice in Rē′zĭn and Rĕm′ȧ-lī′ȧh's son:

7 Now therefore, behold, the Lord bringeth up upon them the waters of the river, strong and many, *even* the king of Assyria, and all his glory: and he shall come up over all his channels, and go over all his banks:

8 And he shall pass through Judah; he shall overflow and go over, he shall reach *even* to the neck; and the stretching out of his wings shall fill the breadth of thy land, O Ĭm-măn′ū-ĕl.

9 ¶ Associate yourselves, O ye people, and ye shall be broken in pieces; and give ear, all ye of far countries: gird yourselves, and ye shall be broken in pieces; gird yourselves, and ye shall be broken in pieces.

10 Take counsel together, and it shall come to nought; speak the word, and it shall not stand: for God *is* with us.

11 ¶ For the LORD spake thus to me with a strong hand, and instructed me that I should not walk in the way of this people, saying,

12 Say ye not, A confederacy, to all *them to* whom this people shall say, A

confederacy; neither fear ye their fear,
nor be afraid.
13 Sanctify the LORD of hosts himself;
and *let* him *be* your fear, and *let* him *be*
your dread.
14 And he shall be for a sanctuary; but
for a stone of stumbling and for a rock
of offense to both the houses of Ĭs̱'rā-ĕl,
for a gin and for a snare to the inhabitants of Jerusalem.
15 And many among them shall stumble, and fall, and be broken, and be
snared, and be taken.
16 Bind up the testimony, seal the law
among my disciples.
17 And I will wait upon the LORD, that
hideth his face from the house of Jacob,
and I will look for him.
18 Behold, I and the children whom
the LORD hath given me *are* for signs
and for wonders in Ĭs̱'rā-ĕl from the
LORD of hosts, which dwelleth in mount
Zion.
19 ¶ And when they shall say unto you,
Seek unto them that have familiar
spirits, and unto wizards that peep and
that mutter: should not a people seek
unto their God? for the living to the
dead?
20 To the law and to the testimony: if
they speak not according to this word,
it is because *there is* no light in them.
21 And they shall pass through it,
hardly bestead and hungry: and it shall
come to pass, that when they shall be
hungry, they shall fret themselves, and
curse their king and their God, and look
upward.
22 And they shall look unto the earth;
and behold trouble and darkness, dimness of anguish; and *they shall be*
driven to darkness.

CHAPTER 9

NEVERTHELESS the dimness *shall*
not *be* such as *was* in her vexation,
when at the first he lightly afflicted the
land of Zĕb'ū-lŭn, and the land of
Năph'tȧ-lī, and afterward did more
grievously afflict *her by* the way of the
sea, beyond Jordan, in Galilee of the
nations.
2 The people that walked in darkness
have seen a great light: they that dwell
in the land of the shadow of death, upon
them hath the light shined.
3 Thou hast multiplied the nation, *and*
not increased the joy: they joy before
thee according to the joy in harvest, *and*
as *men* rejoice when they divide the
spoil.
4 For thou hast broken the yoke of his
burden, and the staff of his shoulder,
the rod of his oppressor, as in the day
of Mĭd'ĭ-ăn.
5 For every battle of the warrior *is* with
confused noise, and garments rolled in
blood; but *this* shall be with burning *and*
fuel of fire.
6 For unto us a child is born, unto us a
son is given: and the government shall
be upon his shoulder: and his name
shall be called Wonderful, Counselor,
The mighty God, The everlasting Father, The Prince of Peace.
7 Of the increase of *his* government
and peace *there shall be* no end, upon
the throne of David, and upon his kingdom, to order it, and to establish it with
judgment and with justice from henceforth even for ever. The zeal of the
LORD of hosts will perform this.
8 ¶ The Lord sent a word into Jacob,
and it hath lighted upon Ĭs̱'rā-ĕl.
9 And all the people shall know, *even*
Ē'phrā-ĭm and the inhabitant of Sȧ-
mā'rĭ-ȧ, that say in the pride and stout-
ness of heart,
10 The bricks are fallen down, but we
will build with hewn stones: the syca-
mores are cut down, but we will change
them into cedars.
11 Therefore the LORD shall set up the
adversaries of Rē'zĭn against him, and
join his enemies together;
12 The Syrians before, and the Phĭ-
lĭs'tĭnes̱ behind; and they shall devour
Ĭs̱'rā-ĕl with open mouth. For all this
his anger is not turned away, but his
hand *is* stretched out still.
13 ¶ For the people turneth not unto
him that smiteth them, neither do they
seek the LORD of hosts.
14 Therefore the LORD will cut off from
Ĭs̱'rā-ĕl head and tail, branch and rush,
in one day.
15 The ancient and honorable, he *is*
the head; and the prophet that teacheth
lies, he *is* the tail.
16 For the leaders of this people cause
them to err; and *they that are* led of
them *are* destroyed.
17 Therefore the LORD shall have no
joy in their young men, neither shall
have mercy on their fatherless and
widows: for every one *is* a hypocrite and

an evildoer, and every mouth speaketh
folly. For all this his anger is not turned
away, but his hand *is* stretched out still.
18 ¶ For wickedness burneth as the
fire: it shall devour the briers and
thorns, and shall kindle in the thickets
of the forest, and they shall mount up
like the lifting up of smoke.
19 Through the wrath of the LORD
of hosts is the land darkened, and the
people shall be as the fuel of the fire:
no man shall spare his brother.
20 And he shall snatch on the right
hand, and be hungry; and he shall eat
on the left hand, and they shall not be
satisfied: they shall eat every man the
flesh of his own arm:
21 Mȧ-năs'sĕh, Ē'phrā-ĭm; and Ē'phrā-
ĭm, Mȧ-năs'sĕh: *and* they together *shall
be* against Judah. For all this his
anger is not turned away, but his hand
is stretched out still.

CHAPTER 10

WOE unto them that decree unrighteous decrees, and that write
grievousness *which* they have pre-
scribed;
2 To turn aside the needy from judgment, and to take away the right from
the poor of my people, that widows may
be their prey, and *that* they may rob the
fatherless!
3 And what will ye do in the day of
visitation, and in the desolation *which*
shall come from far? to whom will ye
flee for help? and where will ye leave
your glory?
4 Without me they shall bow down
under the prisoners, and they shall fall
under the slain. For all this his anger is
not turned away, but his hand *is*
stretched out still.
5 ¶ O Assyrian, the rod of mine anger,
and the staff in their hand is mine
indignation.
6 I will send him against a hypocritical
nation, and against the people of my
wrath will I give him a charge, to take
the spoil, and to take the prey, and to
tread them down like the mire of the
streets.
7 Howbeit he meaneth not so, neither
doth his heart think so; but *it is* in his
heart to destroy and cut off nations not
a few.
8 For he saith, *Are* not my princes altogether kings?
9 *Is* not Căl'nō as Cär'chē-mĭsh? *is* not
Hā'măth as Är'păd? *is* not Sȧ-mā'rĭ-ȧ
as Damascus?
10 As my hand hath found the kingdoms of the idols, and whose graven
images did excel them of Jerusalem and
of Sȧ-mā'rĭ-ȧ;
11 Shall I not, as I have done unto
Sȧ-mā'rĭ-ȧ and her idols, so do to Jerusalem and her idols?
12 Wherefore it shall come to pass,
that, when the Lord hath performed his
whole work upon mount Zion and on
Jerusalem, I will punish the fruit of the
stout heart of the king of Assyria, and
the glory of his high looks.
13 For he saith, By the strength of my
hand I have done *it*, and by my wisdom;
for I am prudent: and I have removed
the bounds of the people, and have
robbed their treasures, and I have put
down the inhabitants like a valiant *man:*
14 And my hand hath found as a nest
the riches of the people: and as one
gathereth eggs *that are* left, have I
gathered all the earth; and there was
none that moved the wing, or opened
the mouth, or peeped.
15 Shall the axe boast itself against
him that heweth therewith? *or* shall the
saw magnify itself against him that
shaketh it? as if the rod should shake *itself* against them that lift it up, *or* as if
the staff should lift up *itself, as if it
were* no wood.
16 Therefore shall the Lord, the Lord
of hosts, send among his fat ones leanness; and under his glory he shall kindle
a burning like the burning of a fire.
17 And the light of Ĭş'rā-ĕl shall be for
a fire, and his Holy One for a flame: and
it shall burn and devour his thorns and
his briers in one day;
18 And shall consume the glory of his
forest, and of his fruitful field, both soul
and body: and they shall be as when a
standardbearer fainteth.
19 And the rest of the trees of his forest
shall be few, that a child may write them.
20 ¶ And it shall come to pass in that
day, *that* the remnant of Ĭş'rā-ĕl, and
such as are escaped of the house of
Jacob, shall no more again stay upon
him that smote them; but shall stay upon the LORD, the Holy One of Ĭş'rā-ĕl,
in truth.
21 The remnant shall return, *even* the
remnant of Jacob, unto the mighty God.

22 For though thy people Ĭs'rā-ēl be as the sand of the sea, *yet* a remnant of them shall return: the consumption decreed shall overflow with righteousness.

23 For the Lord GOD of hosts shall make a consumption, even determined, in the midst of all the land.

24 ¶ Therefore thus saith the Lord GOD of hosts, O my people that dwellest in Zion, be not afraid of the Assyrian: he shall smite thee with a rod, and shall lift up his staff against thee, after the manner of Egypt.

25 For yet a very little while, and the indignation shall cease, and mine anger in their destruction.

26 And the LORD of hosts shall stir up a scourge for him according to the slaughter of Mĭd'ĭ-ăn at the rock of Ō'rĕb: and *as* his rod *was* upon the sea, so shall he lift it up after the manner of Egypt.

27 And it shall come to pass in that day, *that* his burden shall be taken away from off thy shoulder, and his yoke from off thy neck, and the yoke shall be destroyed because of the anointing.

28 He is come to Ā-ī'ăth, he is passed to Mĭg'rŏn; at Mĭch'măsh he hath laid up his carriages:

29 They are gone over the passage: they have taken up their lodging at Gē'bȧ; Rā'mȧh is afraid; Gĭb'ē-ȧh of Saul is fled.

30 Lift up thy voice, O daughter of Găl'lĭm: cause it to be heard unto Lā'ĭsh, O poor Ăn'ȧ-thŏth.

31 Măd-mē'nȧh is removed; the inhabitants of Gē'bĭm gather themselves to flee.

32 As yet shall he remain at Nŏb that day: he shall shake his hand *against* the mount of the daughter of Zion, the hill of Jerusalem.

33 Behold, the Lord, the LORD of hosts, shall lop the bough with terror: and the high ones of stature *shall be* hewn down, and the haughty shall be humbled.

34 And he shall cut down the thickets of the forest with iron, and Lebanon shall fall by a mighty one.

CHAPTER 11

AND there shall come forth a rod out of the stem of Jesse, and a Branch shall grow out of his roots:

2 And the Spirit of the LORD shall rest upon him, the spirit of wisdom and understanding, the spirit of counsel and might, the spirit of knowledge and of the fear of the LORD;

3 And shall make him of quick understanding in the fear of the LORD: and he shall not judge after the sight of his eyes, neither reprove after the hearing of his ears:

4 But with righteousness shall he judge the poor, and reprove with equity for the meek of the earth: and he shall smite the earth with the rod of his mouth, and with the breath of his lips shall he slay the wicked.

5 And righteousness shall be the girdle of his loins, and faithfulness the girdle of his reins.

6 The wolf also shall dwell with the lamb, and the leopard shall lie down with the kid; and the calf and the young lion and the fatling together; and a little child shall lead them.

7 And the cow and the bear shall feed; their young ones shall lie down together: and the lion shall eat straw like the ox.

8 And the sucking child shall play on the hole of the asp, and the weaned child shall put his hand on the cockatrice' den.

9 They shall not hurt nor destroy in all my holy mountain: for the earth shall be full of the knowledge of the LORD, as the waters cover the sea.

10 ¶ And in that day there shall be a root of Jesse, which shall stand for an ensign of the people; to it shall the Ġĕn'tīles seek: and his rest shall be glorious.

11 And it shall come to pass in that day, *that* the Lord shall set his hand again the second time to recover the remnant of his people, which shall be left, from Assyria, and from Egypt, and from Păth'rŏs, and from Cŭsh, and from Ē'lăm, and from Shī'năr, and from Hā'măth, and from the islands of the sea.

12 And he shall set up an ensign for the nations, and shall assemble the outcasts of Ĭs'rā-ēl, and gather together the dispersed of Judah from the four corners of the earth.

13 The envy also of Ē'phrā-ĭm shall depart, and the adversaries of Judah shall be cut off: Ē'phrā-ĭm shall not envy Judah, and Judah shall not vex Ē'phrā-ĭm.

14 But they shall fly upon the shoulders of the Phĭ-lĭs'tīnes toward the west; they shall spoil them of the east

together: they shall lay their hand upon
Ē'dŏm and Mō'ăb; and the children of
Ammon shall obey them.
15 And the LORD shall utterly destroy
the tongue of the Egyptian sea; and with
his mighty wind shall he shake his hand
over the river, and shall smite it in the
seven streams, and make *men* go over
dry-shod.
16 And there shall be a highway for
the remnant of his people, which shall
be left, from Assyria; like as it was to
Ĭs'rā-ĕl in the day that he came up out
of the land of Egypt.

CHAPTER 12

AND in that day thou shalt say, O
LORD, I will praise thee: though
thou wast angry with me, thine anger
is turned away, and thou comfortedst
me.
2 Behold, God *is* my salvation; I will
trust, and not be afraid: for the LORD
JEHOVAH *is* my strength and *my* song;
he also is become my salvation.
3 Therefore with joy shall ye draw
water out of the wells of salvation.
4 And in that day shall ye say, Praise
the LORD, call upon his name, declare
his doings among the people, make
mention that his name is exalted.
5 Sing unto the LORD; for he hath done
excellent things: this *is* known in all the
earth.
6 Cry out and shout, thou inhabitant
of Zion: for great *is* the Holy One of
Ĭs'rā-ĕl in the midst of thee.

CHAPTER 13

THE burden of Babylon, which
Ī-sā'iah the son of Ā'mŏz did see.
2 Lift ye up a banner upon the high
mountain, exalt the voice unto them,
shake the hand, that they may go into
the gates of the nobles.
3 I have commanded my sanctified
ones, I have also called my mighty ones
for mine anger, *even* them that rejoice
in my highness.
4 The noise of a multitude in the mountains, like as of a great people; a tumultuous noise of the kingdoms of nations gathered together: the LORD of
hosts mustereth the host of the battle.
5 They come from a far country, from
the end of heaven, *even* the LORD, and
the weapons of his indignation, to destroy the whole land.
6 ¶ Howl ye; for the day of the LORD
is at hand; it shall come as a destruction from the Almighty.
7 Therefore shall all hands be faint,
and every man's heart shall melt:
8 And they shall be afraid: pangs and
sorrows shall take hold of them; they
shall be in pain as a woman that
travaileth: they shall be amazed one at
another; their faces *shall be as* flames.
9 Behold, the day of the LORD cometh,
cruel both with wrath and fierce anger,
to lay the land desolate: and he shall
destroy the sinners thereof out of it.
10 For the stars of heaven and the con-
stellations thereof shall not give their
light: the sun shall be darkened in his
going forth, and the moon shall not cause
her light to shine.
11 And I will punish the world for *their*
evil, and the wicked for their iniquity;
and I will cause the arrogancy of the
proud to cease, and will lay low the
haughtiness of the terrible.
12 I will make a man more precious
than fine gold; even a man than the
golden wedge of Ō'phīr.
13 Therefore I will shake the heavens,
and the earth shall remove out of her
place, in the wrath of the LORD of hosts,
and in the day of his fierce anger.
14 And it shall be as the chased roe,
and as a sheep that no man taketh up:
they shall every man turn to his own
people, and flee every one into his own
land.
15 Every one that is found shall be
thrust through; and every one that is
joined *unto them* shall fall by the sword.
16 Their children also shall be dashed
to pieces before their eyes; their houses
shall be spoiled, and their wives
ravished.
17 Behold, I will stir up the Mēdes
against them, which shall not regard
silver; and *as for* gold, they shall not
delight in it.
18 *Their* bows also shall dash the
young men to pieces; and they shall
have no pity on the fruit of the womb;
their eye shall not spare children.
19 ¶ And Babylon, the glory of kingdoms, the beauty of the Chăl'dēes' excellency, shall be as when God overthrew Sŏd'ŏm and Gō-mŏr'rah.
20 It shall never be inhabited, neither
shall it be dwelt in from generation to
generation: neither shall the Arabian

pitch tent there; neither shall the shepherds make their fold there.

21 But wild beasts of the desert shall lie there; and their houses shall be full of doleful creatures; and owls shall dwell there, and satyrs shall dance there.

22 And the wild beasts of the islands shall cry in their desolate houses, and dragons in *their* pleasant palaces: and her time *is* near to come, and her days shall not be prolonged.

CHAPTER 14

FOR the LORD will have mercy on Jacob, and will yet choose Ĭş'rā-ĕl, and set them in their own land: and the strangers shall be joined with them, and they shall cleave to the house of Jacob.

2 And the people shall take them, and bring them to their place: and the house of Ĭş'rā-ĕl shall possess them in the land of the LORD for servants and handmaids: and they shall take them captives, whose captives they were; and they shall rule over their oppressors.

3 And it shall come to pass in the day that the LORD shall give thee rest from thy sorrow, and from thy fear, and from the hard bondage wherein thou wast made to serve,

4 ℂ That thou shalt take up this proverb against the king of Babylon, and say, How hath the oppressor ceased! the golden city ceased!

5 The LORD hath broken the staff of the wicked, *and* the sceptre of the rulers.

6 He who smote the people in wrath with a continual stroke, he that ruled the nations in anger, is persecuted, *and* none hindereth.

7 The whole earth is at rest, *and* is quiet: they break forth into singing.

8 Yea, the fir trees rejoice at thee, *and* the cedars of Lebanon, *saying,* Since thou art laid down, no feller is come up against us.

9 Hell from beneath is moved for thee to meet *thee* at thy coming: it stirreth up the dead for thee, *even* all the chief ones of the earth; it hath raised up from their thrones all the kings of the nations.

10 All they shall speak and say unto thee, Art thou also become weak as we? art thou become like unto us?

11 Thy pomp is brought down to the grave, *and* the noise of thy viols: the worm is spread under thee, and the worms cover thee.

12 How art thou fallen from heaven, O Lucifer, son of the morning! *how* art thou cut down to the ground, which didst weaken the nations!

13 For thou hast said in thine heart, I will ascend into heaven, I will exalt my throne above the stars of God: I will sit also upon the mount of the congregation, in the sides of the north:

14 I will ascend above the heights of the clouds; I will be like the Most High.

15 Yet thou shalt be brought down to hell, to the sides of the pit.

16 They that see thee shall narrowly look upon thee, *and* consider thee, *saying, Is* this the man that made the earth to tremble, that did shake kingdoms;

17 *That* made the world as a wilderness, and destroyed the cities thereof; *that* opened not the house of his prisoners?

18 All the kings of the nations, *even* all of them, lie in glory, every one in his own house.

19 But thou art cast out of thy grave like an abominable branch, *and as* the raiment of those that are slain, thrust through with a sword, that go down to the stones of the pit; as a carcass trodden under feet.

20 Thou shalt not be joined with them in burial, because thou hast destroyed thy land, *and* slain thy people: the seed of evildoers shall never be renowned.

21 Prepare slaughter for his children for the iniquity of their fathers; that they do not rise, nor possess the land, nor fill the face of the world with cities.

22 For I will rise up against them, saith the LORD of hosts, and cut off from Babylon the name, and remnant, and son, and nephew, saith the LORD.

23 I will also make it a possession for the bittern, and pools of water: and I will sweep it with the besom of destruction, saith the LORD of hosts.

24 ℂ The LORD of hosts hath sworn, saying, Surely as I have thought, so shall it come to pass; and as I have purposed, *so* shall it stand:

25 That I will break the Assyrian in my land, and upon my mountains tread him under foot: then shall his yoke depart from off them, and his burden depart from off their shoulders.

26 This *is* the purpose that is purposed upon the whole earth: and this *is* the

hand that is stretched out upon all the
nations.
27 For the LORD of hosts hath purposed, and who shall disannul *it?* and
his hand *is* stretched out, and who shall
turn it back?
28 In the year that king Ahaz died was
this burden.
29 ℂ Rejoice not thou, whole Păl′ĕs-
tī′nȧ, because the rod of him that smote
thee is broken: for out of the serpent's
root shall come forth a cockatrice, and
his fruit *shall be* a fiery flying serpent.
30 And the firstborn of the poor shall
feed, and the needy shall lie down in
safety: and I will kill thy root with
famine, and he shall slay thy remnant.
31 Howl, O gate; cry, O city; thou,
whole Păl′ĕs-tī′nȧ, *art* dissolved: for
there shall come from the north a
smoke, and none *shall be* alone in his
appointed times.
32 What shall *one* then answer the
messengers of the nation? That the
LORD hath founded Zion, and the poor
of his people shall trust in it.

CHAPTER 15

THE burden of Mō′ăb. Because in
the night Är of Mō′ăb is laid waste,
and brought to silence; because in the
night Kĭr of Mō′ăb is laid waste, *and*
brought to silence:
2 He is gone up to Bā′jĭth, and to Dī′-
bŏn, the high places, to weep: Mō′ăb
shall howl over Nē′bō, and over Mĕd′ē-
bȧ: on all their heads *shall be* baldness,
and every beard cut off.
3 In their streets they shall gird themselves with sackcloth: on the tops of
their houses, and in their streets, every
one shall howl, weeping abundantly.
4 And Hĕsh′bŏn shall cry, and Ē′l′ē-ā′-
lĕh; their voice shall be heard *even*
unto Jā′hăz: therefore the armed soldiers of Mō′ăb shall cry out; his life
shall be grievous unto him.
5 My heart shall cry out for Mō′ăb; his
fugitives *shall flee* unto Zō′ăr, a heifer of
three years old: for by the mounting up
of Lū′hĭth with weeping shall they go it
up; for in the way of Hŏr′ō-nā′ĭm they
shall raise up a cry of destruction.
6 For the waters of Nĭm′rĭm shall be
desolate: for the hay is withered away,
the grass faileth, there is no green thing.
7 Therefore the abundance they have
gotten, and that which they have laid
up, shall they carry away to the brook of
the willows.
8 For the cry is gone round about the
borders of Mō′ăb; the howling thereof
unto Ĕg′lā-ĭm, and the howling thereof
unto Bē′ĕr–ē′lĭm.
9 For the waters of Dī′mŏn shall be full
of blood: for I will bring more upon Dī′-
mŏn, lions upon him that escapeth of
Mō′ăb, and upon the remnant of the
land.

CHAPTER 16

SEND ye the lamb to the ruler of the
land from Sē′lȧ to the wilderness,
unto the mount of the daughter of Zion.
2 For it shall be, *that*, as a wandering
bird cast out of the nest, *so* the daughters of Mō′ăb shall be at the fords of
Är′nŏn.
3 Take counsel, execute judgment;
make thy shadow as the night in the
midst of the noonday; hide the outcasts;
bewray not him that wandereth.
4 Let mine outcasts dwell with thee,
Mō′ăb; be thou a covert to them from
the face of the spoiler: for the extortioner is at an end, the spoiler ceaseth,
the oppressors are consumed out of the
land.
5 And in mercy shall the throne be
established: and he shall sit upon it in
truth in the tabernacle of David, judging, and seeking judgment, and hasting
righteousness.
6 ℂ We have heard of the pride of
Mō′ăb; *he is* very proud: *even* of his
haughtiness, and his pride, and his
wrath: *but* his lies *shall* not *be* so.
7 Therefore shall Mō′ăb howl for
Mō′ăb, every one shall howl: for the
foundations of Kĭr′–hăr′ē-sĕth shall ye
mourn; surely *they are* stricken.
8 For the fields of Hĕsh′bŏn languish,
and the vine of Sĭb′mȧh: the lords of the
heathen have broken down the principal
plants thereof, they are come *even* unto
Jā′zēr, they wandered *through* the wilderness: her branches are stretched
out, they are gone over the sea.
9 ℂ Therefore I will bewail with the
weeping of Jā′zēr the vine of Sĭb′mȧh:
I will water thee with my tears, O Hĕsh′-
bŏn, and Ē′l′ē-ā′lĕh: for the shouting for
thy summer fruits and for thy harvest
is fallen.
10 And gladness is taken away, and
joy out of the plentiful field; and in the

vineyards there shall be no singing, neither shall there be shouting: the treaders shall tread out no wine in *their* presses; I have made *their vintage* shouting to cease.
11 Wherefore my bowels shall sound like a harp for Mō′ăb, and mine inward parts for Kĭr′-hā′rĕsh.
12 ℭ And it shall come to pass, when it is seen that Mō′ăb is weary on the high place, that he shall come to his sanctuary to pray; but he shall not prevail.
13 This *is* the word that the LORD hath spoken concerning Mō′ăb since that time.
14 But now the LORD hath spoken, saying, Within three years, as the years of a hireling, and the glory of Mō′ăb shall be contemned, with all that great multitude; and the remnant *shall be* very small *and* feeble.

CHAPTER 17

THE burden of Damascus. Behold, Damascus is taken away from *being* a city, and it shall be a ruinous heap.
2 The cities of Ȧ-rō′ĕr *are* forsaken: they shall be for flocks, which shall lie down, and none shall make *them* afraid.
3 The fortress also shall cease from Ē′phrā-ĭm, and the kingdom from Damascus, and the remnant of Syria: they shall be as the glory of the children of Ĭş′rā-ĕl, saith the LORD of hosts.
4 And in that day it shall come to pass, *that* the glory of Jacob shall be made thin, and the fatness of his flesh shall wax lean.
5 And it shall be as when the harvestman gathereth the corn, and reapeth the ears with his arm; and it shall be as he that gathereth ears in the valley of Rĕph′ā-ĭm.
6 ℭ Yet gleaning grapes shall be left in it, as the shaking of an olive tree, two *or* three berries in the top of the uppermost bough, four *or* five in the outmost fruitful branches thereof, saith the LORD God of Ĭş′rā-ĕl.
7 At that day shall a man look to his Maker, and his eyes shall have respect to the Holy One of Ĭş′rā-ĕl.
8 And he shall not look to the altars, the work of his hands, neither shall respect *that* which his fingers have made, either the groves, or the images.
9 ℭ In that day shall his strong cities
be as a forsaken bough, and an uppermost branch, which they left because of the children of Ĭş′rā-ĕl: and there shall be desolation.
10 Because thou hast forgotten the God of thy salvation, and hast not been mindful of the Rock of thy strength, therefore shalt thou plant pleasant plants, and shalt set it with strange slips:
11 In the day shalt thou make thy plant to grow, and in the morning shalt thou make thy seed to flourish: *but* the harvest *shall be* a heap in the day of grief and of desperate sorrow.
12 ℭ Woe to the multitude of many people, *which* make a noise like the noise of the seas; and to the rushing of nations, *that* make a rushing like the rushing of mighty waters!
13 The nations shall rush like the rushing of many waters: but *God* shall rebuke them, and they shall flee far off, and shall be chased as the chaff of the mountains before the wind, and like a rolling thing before the whirlwind.
14 And behold at eveningtide trouble; *and* before the morning he *is* not. This *is* the portion of them that spoil us, and the lot of them that rob us.

CHAPTER 18

WOE to the land shadowing with wings, which *is* beyond the rivers of Ethiopia:
2 That sendeth ambassadors by the sea, even in vessels of bulrushes upon the waters, *saying*, Go, ye swift messengers, to a nation scattered and peeled, to a people terrible from their beginning hitherto; a nation meted out and trodden down, whose land the rivers have spoiled!
3 All ye inhabitants of the world, and dwellers on the earth, see ye, when he lifteth up an ensign on the mountains; and when he bloweth a trumpet, hear ye.
4 For so the LORD said unto me, I will take my rest, and I will consider in my dwelling place like a clear heat upon herbs, *and* like a cloud of dew in the heat of harvest.
5 For afore the harvest, when the bud is perfect, and the sour grape is ripening in the flower, he shall both cut off the sprigs with pruning hooks, and take away *and* cut down the branches.
6 They shall be left together unto the

fowls of the mountains, and to the beasts of the earth: and the fowls shall summer upon them, and all the beasts of the earth shall winter upon them.

7 ℂ In that time shall the present be brought unto the LORD of hosts of a people scattered and peeled, and from a people terrible from their beginning hitherto; a nation meted out and trodden under foot, whose land the rivers have spoiled, to the place of the name of the LORD of hosts, the mount Zion.

CHAPTER 19

THE burden of Egypt. Behold, the LORD rideth upon a swift cloud, and shall come into Egypt: and the idols of Egypt shall be moved at his presence, and the heart of Egypt shall melt in the midst of it.

2 And I will set the Egyptians against the Egyptians: and they shall fight every one against his brother, and every one against his neighbor; city against city, *and* kingdom against kingdom.

3 And the spirit of Egypt shall fail in the midst thereof; and I will destroy the counsel thereof: and they shall seek to the idols, and to the charmers, and to them that have familiar spirits, and to the wizards.

4 And the Egyptians will I give over into the hand of a cruel lord; and a fierce king shall rule over them, saith the Lord, the LORD of hosts.

5 And the waters shall fail from the sea, and the river shall be wasted and dried up.

6 And they shall turn the rivers far away; *and* the brooks of defense shall be emptied and dried up: the reeds and flags shall wither.

7 The paper reeds by the brooks, by the mouth of the brooks, and every thing sown by the brooks, shall wither, be driven away, and be no *more*.

8 The fishers also shall mourn, and all they that cast angle into the brooks shall lament, and they that spread nets upon the waters shall languish.

9 Moreover they that work in fine flax, and they that weave networks, shall be confounded.

10 And they shall be broken in the purposes thereof, all that make sluices *and* ponds for fish.

11 ℂ Surely the princes of Zō'ăn *are* fools, the counsel of the wise counselors of Phā'raōh is become brutish: how say ye unto Phā'raōh, I *am* the son of the wise, the son of ancient kings?

12 Where *are* they? where *are* thy wise *men?* and let them tell thee now, and let them know what the LORD of hosts hath purposed upon Egypt.

13 The princes of Zō'ăn are become fools, the princes of Nŏph are deceived; they have also seduced Egypt, *even they that are* the stay of the tribes thereof.

14 The LORD hath mingled a perverse spirit in the midst thereof: and they have caused Egypt to err in every work thereof, as a drunken *man* staggereth in his vomit.

15 Neither shall there be *any* work for Egypt, which the head or tail, branch or rush, may do.

16 In that day shall Egypt be like unto women: and it shall be afraid and fear because of the shaking of the hand of the LORD of hosts, which he shaketh over it.

17 And the land of Judah shall be a terror unto Egypt, every one that maketh mention thereof shall be afraid in himself, because of the counsel of the LORD of hosts, which he hath determined against it.

18 ℂ In that day shall five cities in the land of Egypt speak the language of Cā'năan, and swear to the LORD of hosts; one shall be called, The city of destruction.

19 In that day shall there be an altar to the LORD in the midst of the land of Egypt, and a pillar at the border thereof to the LORD.

20 And it shall be for a sign and for a witness unto the LORD of hosts in the land of Egypt: for they shall cry unto the LORD because of the oppressors, and he shall send them a saviour, and a great one, and he shall deliver them.

21 And the LORD shall be known to Egypt, and the Egyptians shall know the LORD in that day, and shall do sacrifice and oblation; yea, they shall vow a vow unto the LORD, and perform *it*.

22 And the LORD shall smite Egypt: he shall smite and heal *it:* and they shall return *even* to the LORD, and he shall be entreated of them, and shall heal them.

23 ℂ In that day shall there be a highway out of Egypt to Assyria, and the Assyrian shall come into Egypt, and the

Egyptian into Assyria, and the Egyptians
shall serve with the Assyrians.
24 In that day shall Ĭş′rā-ĕl be the third
with Egypt and with Assyria, *even* a
blessing in the midst of the land:
25 Whom the LORD of hosts shall bless,
saying, Blessed *be* Egypt my people,
and Assyria the work of my hands, and
Ĭş′rā-ĕl mine inheritance.

CHAPTER 20

IN the year that Tär′tăn came unto
Ashdod, (when Sär′gŏn the king of
Assyria sent him,) and fought against
Ashdod, and took it;
2 At the same time spake the LORD by
Ī-şā′ịȧh the son of Ā′mŏz, saying, Go
and loose the sackcloth from off thy
loins, and put off thy shoe from thy foot.
And he did so, walking naked and barefoot.
3 And the LORD said, Like as my servant Ī-şā′ịȧh hath walked naked and
barefoot three years *for* a sign and wonder upon Egypt and upon Ethiopia;
4 So shall the king of Assyria lead away
the Egyptians prisoners, and the Ethiopians captives, young and old, naked
and barefoot, even with *their* buttocks
uncovered, to the shame of Egypt.
5 And they shall be afraid and ashamed
of Ethiopia their expectation, and of
Egypt their glory.
6 And the inhabitant of this isle shall
say in that day, Behold, such *is* our expectation, whither we flee for help to be
delivered from the king of Assyria: and
how shall we escape?

CHAPTER 21

THE burden of the desert of the sea.
As whirlwinds in the south pass
through; *so* it cometh from the desert,
from a terrible land.
2 A grievous vision is declared unto
me; The treacherous dealer dealeth
treacherously, and the spoiler spoileth.
Go up, O Ē′lăm: besiege, O Mē′dĭ-ȧ: all
the sighing thereof have I made to cease.
3 Therefore are my loins filled with
pain: pangs have taken hold upon me,
as the pangs of a woman that travaileth:
I was bowed down at the hearing *of it;*
I was dismayed at the seeing *of it.*
4 My heart panted, fearfulness affrighted me: the night of my pleasure
hath he turned into fear unto me.
5 Prepare the table, watch in the
watchtower, eat, drink: arise, ye princes,
and anoint the shield.
6 For thus hath the Lord said unto me,
Go, set a watchman, let him declare
what he seeth.
7 And he saw a chariot *with* a couple
of horsemen, a chariot of asses, *and* a
chariot of camels; and he hearkened
diligently with much heed:
8 And he cried, A lion: My lord, I stand
continually upon the watchtower in the
daytime, and I am set in my ward whole
nights:
9 And, behold, here cometh a chariot of
men, *with* a couple of horsemen. And
he answered and said, Babylon is fallen,
is fallen; and all the graven images of her
gods he hath broken unto the ground.
10 O my threshing, and the corn of my
floor: that which I have heard of the
LORD of hosts, the God of Ĭş′rā-ĕl, have
I declared unto you.
11 ℂ The burden of Dū′mȧh. He calleth to me out of Sē′ïr, Watchman, what
of the night? Watchman, what of the
night?
12 The watchman said, The morning
cometh, and also the night: if ye will inquire, inquire ye: return, come.
13 ℂ The burden upon Arabia. In the
forest in Arabia shall ye lodge, O ye
traveling companies of Dĕd′ȧ-nĭm.
14 The inhabitants of the land of Tē′mȧ
brought water to him that was thirsty,
they prevented with their bread him
that fled.
15 For they fled from the swords, from
the drawn sword, and from the bent
bow, and from the grievousness of war.
16 For thus hath the Lord said unto
me, Within a year, according to the
years of a hireling, and all the glory of
Kē′dȧr shall fail:
17 And the residue of the number of
archers, the mighty men of the children
of Kē′dȧr, shall be diminished: for the
LORD God of Ĭş′rā-ĕl hath spoken *it.*

CHAPTER 22

THE burden of the valley of vision.
What aileth thee now, that thou art
wholly gone up to the housetops?
2 Thou that art full of stirs, a tumultuous city, a joyous city: thy slain *men*
are not slain with the sword, nor dead
in battle.
3 All thy rulers are fled together, they
are bound by the archers: all that are

found in thee are bound together, *which*
have fled from far.
4 Therefore said I, Look away from me;
I will weep bitterly, labor not to comfort me, because of the spoiling of the
daughter of my people.
5 For *it is* a day of trouble, and of
treading down, and of perplexity by the
Lord GOD of hosts in the valley of
vision, breaking down the walls, and of
crying to the mountains.
6 And Ē'lăm bare the quiver with
chariots of men *and* horsemen, and Kĭr
uncovered the shield.
7 And it shall come to pass, *that* thy
choicest valleys shall be full of chariots,
and the horsemen shall set themselves
in array at the gate.
8 ¶ And he discovered the covering
of Judah, and thou didst look in that day
to the armor of the house of the forest.
9 Ye have seen also the breaches of the
city of David, that they are many: and
ye gathered together the waters of the
lower pool.
10 And ye have numbered the houses
of Jerusalem, and the houses have ye
broken down to fortify the wall.
11 Ye made also a ditch between the
two walls for the water of the old pool:
but ye have not looked unto the maker
thereof, neither had respect unto him
that fashioned it long ago.
12 And in that day did the Lord GOD of
hosts call to weeping, and to mourning,
and to baldness, and to girding with
sackcloth:
13 And behold joy and gladness, slaying oxen, and killing sheep, eating
flesh, and drinking wine: let us eat and
drink; for to-morrow we shall die.
14 And it was revealed in mine ears by
the LORD of hosts, Surely this iniquity
shall not be purged from you till ye die,
saith the Lord GOD of hosts.
15 ¶ Thus saith the Lord GOD of
hosts, Go, get thee unto this treasurer,
even unto Shĕb'nȧ, which *is* over the
house, *and say,*
16 What hast thou here, and whom
hast thou here, that thou hast hewed
thee out a sepulchre here, *as* he that
heweth him out a sepulchre on high,
and that graveth a habitation for himself in a rock?
17 Behold, the LORD will carry thee
away with a mighty captivity, and will
surely cover thee.
18 He will surely violently turn and
toss thee *like* a ball into a large country:
there shalt thou die, and there the
chariots of thy glory *shall be* the shame
of thy lord's house.
19 And I will drive thee from thy sta-
tion, and from thy state shall he pull
thee down.
20 ¶ And it shall come to pass in that
day, that I will call my servant Ē-lī'ȧ-
kĭm the son of Hĭl-kī'āh:
21 And I will clothe him with thy robe,
and strengthen him with thy girdle, and
I will commit thy government into his
hand: and he shall be a father to the inhabitants of Jerusalem, and to the
house of Judah.
22 And the key of the house of David
will I lay upon his shoulder; so he shall
open, and none shall shut; and he shall
shut, and none shall open.
23 And I will fasten him *as* a nail in a
sure place; and he shall be for a glorious throne to his father's house.
24 And they shall hang upon him all
the glory of his father's house, the offspring and the issue, all vessels of small
quantity, from the vessels of cups, even
to all the vessels of flagons.
25 In that day, saith the LORD of hosts,
shall the nail that is fastened in the
sure place be removed, and be cut
down, and fall; and the burden that *was*
upon it shall be cut off: for the LORD
hath spoken *it*.

CHAPTER 23

THE burden of Tȳre. Howl, ye ships
of Tär'shĭsh; for it is laid waste, so
that there is no house, no entering in:
from the land of Chĭt'tĭm it is revealed
to them.
2 Be still, ye inhabitants of the isle;
thou whom the merchants of Zī'dŏn,
that pass over the sea, have replenished.
3 And by great waters the seed of
Sī'hôr, the harvest of the river, *is* her
revenue; and she is a mart of nations.
4 Be thou ashamed, O Zī'dŏn: for the
sea hath spoken, *even* the strength of
the sea, saying, I travail not, nor bring
forth children, neither do I nourish up
young men, *nor* bring up virgins.
5 As at the report concerning Egypt, *so*
shall they be sorely pained at the report
of Tȳre.
6 Pass ye over to Tär'shĭsh; howl, ye
inhabitants of the isle.

7 *Is* this your joyous *city*, whose antiquity *is* of ancient days? her own feet shall carry her afar off to sojourn.

8 Who hath taken this counsel against Tȳre, the crowning *city*, whose merchants *are* princes, whose traffickers *are* the honorable of the earth?

9 The LORD of hosts hath purposed it, to stain the pride of all glory, *and* to bring into contempt all the honorable of the earth.

10 Pass through thy land as a river, O daughter of Tär′shĭsh: *there is* no more strength.

11 He stretched out his hand over the sea, he shook the kingdoms: the LORD hath given a commandment against the merchant *city*, to destroy the strongholds thereof.

12 And he said, Thou shalt no more rejoice, O thou oppressed virgin, daughter of Zī′dŏn: arise, pass over to Chĭt′tĭm; there also shalt thou have no rest.

13 Behold the land of the Chăl-dē′ăns; this people was not, *till* the Assyrian founded it for them that dwell in the wilderness: they set up the towers thereof, they raised up the palaces thereof; *and* he brought it to ruin.

14 Howl, ye ships of Tär′shĭsh: for your strength is laid waste.

15 And it shall come to pass in that day, that Tȳre shall be forgotten seventy years, according to the days of one king: after the end of seventy years shall Tȳre sing as a harlot.

16 Take a harp, go about the city, thou harlot that hast been forgotten; make sweet melody, sing many songs, that thou mayest be remembered.

17 ¶ And it shall come to pass after the end of seventy years, that the LORD will visit Tȳre, and she shall turn to her hire, and shall commit fornication with all the kingdoms of the world upon the face of the earth.

18 And her merchandise and her hire shall be holiness to the LORD: it shall not be treasured nor laid up; for her merchandise shall be for them that dwell before the LORD, to eat sufficiently, and for durable clothing.

CHAPTER 24

BEHOLD, the LORD maketh the earth empty, and maketh it waste, and turneth it upside down, and scattereth abroad the inhabitants thereof.

2 And it shall be, as with the people, so with the priest; as with the servant, so with his master; as with the maid, so with her mistress; as with the buyer, so with the seller; as with the lender, so with the borrower; as with the taker of usury, so with the giver of usury to him.

3 The land shall be utterly emptied, and utterly spoiled: for the LORD hath spoken this word.

4 The earth mourneth *and* fadeth away, the world languisheth *and* fadeth away, the haughty people of the earth do languish.

5 The earth also is defiled under the inhabitants thereof; because they have transgressed the laws, changed the ordinance, broken the everlasting covenant.

6 Therefore hath the curse devoured the earth, and they that dwell therein are desolate: therefore the inhabitants of the earth are burned, and few men left.

7 The new wine mourneth, the vine languisheth, all the merry-hearted do sigh.

8 The mirth of tabrets ceaseth, the noise of them that rejoice endeth, the joy of the harp ceaseth.

9 They shall not drink wine with a song; strong drink shall be bitter to them that drink it.

10 The city of confusion is broken down: every house is shut up, that no man may come in.

11 *There is* a crying for wine in the streets; all joy is darkened, the mirth of the land is gone.

12 In the city is left desolation, and the gate is smitten with destruction.

13 ¶ When thus it shall be in the midst of the land among the people, *there shall be* as the shaking of an olive tree, *and* as the gleaning grapes when the vintage is done.

14 They shall lift up their voice, they shall sing for the majesty of the LORD, they shall cry aloud from the sea.

15 Wherefore glorify ye the LORD in the fires, *even* the name of the LORD God of Ĭs′rā-ĕl in the isles of the sea.

16 ¶ From the uttermost part of the earth have we heard songs, *even* glory to the righteous. But I said, My leanness, my leanness, woe unto me! the treacherous dealers have dealt treach-

erously; yea, the treacherous dealers have dealt very treacherously.

17 Fear, and the pit, and the snare, *are* upon thee, O inhabitant of the earth.

18 And it shall come to pass, *that* he who fleeth from the noise of the fear shall fall into the pit; and he that cometh up out of the midst of the pit shall be taken in the snare: for the windows from on high are open, and the foundations of the earth do shake.

19 The earth is utterly broken down, the earth is clean dissolved, the earth is moved exceedingly.

20 The earth shall reel to and fro like a drunkard, and shall be removed like a cottage; and the transgression thereof shall be heavy upon it; and it shall fall, and not rise again.

21 And it shall come to pass in that day, *that* the LORD shall punish the host of the high ones *that are* on high, and the kings of the earth upon the earth.

22 And they shall be gathered together, *as* prisoners are gathered in the pit, and shall be shut up in the prison, and after many days shall they be visited.

23 Then the moon shall be confounded, and the sun ashamed, when the LORD of hosts shall reign in mount Zion, and in Jerusalem, and before his ancients gloriously.

CHAPTER 25

O LORD, thou *art* my God; I will exalt thee, I will praise thy name; for thou hast done wonderful *things; thy* counsels of old *are* faithfulness *and* truth.

2 For thou hast made of a city a heap; *of* a defensed city a ruin: a palace of strangers to be no city; it shall never be built.

3 Therefore shall the strong people glorify thee, the city of the terrible nations shall fear thee.

4 For thou hast been a strength to the poor, a strength to the needy in his distress, a refuge from the storm, a shadow from the heat, when the blast of the terrible ones *is* as a storm *against* the wall.

5 Thou shalt bring down the noise of strangers, as the heat in a dry place; *even* the heat with the shadow of a cloud: the branch of the terrible ones shall be brought low.

6 ¶ And in this mountain shall the LORD of hosts make unto all people a feast of fat things; a feast of wines on the lees, of fat things full of marrow, of wines on the lees well refined.

7 And he will destroy in this mountain the face of the covering cast over all people, and the veil that is spread over all nations.

8 He will swallow up death in victory; and the Lord GOD will wipe away tears from off all faces; and the rebuke of his people shall he take away from off all the earth: for the LORD hath spoken *it*.

9 ¶ And it shall be said in that day, Lo, this *is* our God; we have waited for him, and he will save us: this *is* the LORD; we have waited for him, we will be glad and rejoice in his salvation.

10 For in this mountain shall the hand of the LORD rest, and Mō'ăb shall be trodden down under him, even as straw is trodden down for the dunghill.

11 And he shall spread forth his hands in the midst of them, as he that swimmeth spreadeth forth *his hands* to swim: and he shall bring down their pride together with the spoils of their hands.

12 And the fortress of the high fort of thy walls shall he bring down, lay low, *and* bring to the ground, *even* to the dust.

CHAPTER 26

IN that day shall this song be sung in the land of Judah; We have a strong city; salvation will *God* appoint *for* walls and bulwarks.

2 Open ye the gates, that the righteous nation which keepeth the truth may enter in.

3 Thou wilt keep *him* in perfect peace, *whose* mind *is* stayed *on thee:* because he trusteth in thee.

4 Trust ye in the LORD for ever: for in the LORD JEHOVAH *is* everlasting strength.

5 ¶ For he bringeth down them that dwell on high; the lofty city, he layeth it low; he layeth it low, *even* to the ground; he bringeth it *even* to the dust.

6 The foot shall tread it down, *even* the feet of the poor, *and* the steps of the needy.

7 The way of the just *is* uprightness: thou, most upright, dost weigh the path of the just.

8 Yea, in the way of thy judgments, O LORD, have we waited for thee; the

desire of *our* soul *is* to thy name, and to
the remembrance of thee.
9 With my soul have I desired thee in
the night; yea, with my spirit within me
will I seek thee early: for when thy
judgments *are* in the earth, the inhabitants of the world will learn
righteousness.
10 Let favor be showed to the wicked,
yet will he not learn righteousness: in
the land of uprightness will he deal unjustly, and will not behold the majesty
of the LORD.
11 LORD, *when* thy hand is lifted up,
they will not see: *but* they shall see, and
be ashamed for *their* envy at the people;
yea, the fire of thine enemies shall
devour them.
12 ¶ LORD, thou wilt ordain peace for
us: for thou also hast wrought all our
works in us.
13 O LORD our God, *other* lords besides thee have had dominion over us;
but by thee only will we make mention
of thy name.
14 *They are* dead, they shall not live;
they are deceased, they shall not rise:
therefore hast thou visited and destroyed them, and made all their
memory to perish.
15 Thou hast increased the nation, O
LORD, thou hast increased the nation;
thou art glorified: thou hadst removed
it far *unto* all the ends of the earth.
16 LORD, in trouble have they visited
thee; they poured out a prayer *when* thy
chastening *was* upon them.
17 Like as a woman with child, *that*
draweth near the time of her delivery, is
in pain, *and* crieth out in her pangs; so
have we been in thy sight, O LORD.
18 We have been with child, we have
been in pain, we have as it were brought
forth wind; we have not wrought any
deliverance in the earth; neither have
the inhabitants of the world fallen.
19 Thy dead *men* shall live, *together*
with my dead body shall they arise.
Awake and sing, ye that dwell in dust:
for thy dew *is as* the dew of herbs, and
the earth shall cast out the dead.
20 ¶ Come, my people, enter thou into thy chambers, and shut thy doors
about thee: hide thyself as it were for a
little moment, until the indignation be
overpast.
21 For, behold, the LORD cometh out of
his place to punish the inhabitants of
the earth for their iniquity: the earth
also shall disclose her blood, and shall
no more cover her slain.

CHAPTER 27

IN that day the LORD with his sore and
great and strong sword shall punish
leviathan the piercing serpent, even
leviathan that crooked serpent; and he
shall slay the dragon that *is* in the sea.
2 In that day sing ye unto her, A vineyard of red wine.
3 I the LORD do keep it; I will water it
every moment: lest *any* hurt it, I will
keep it night and day.
4 Fury *is* not in me: who would set the
briers *and* thorns against me in battle?
I would go through them, I would burn
them together.
5 Or let him take hold of my strength,
that he may make peace with me; *and*
he shall make peace with me.
6 He shall cause them that come of
Jacob to take root: Ĭs′rā-ĕl shall blossom
and bud, and fill the face of the world
with fruit.
7 ¶ Hath he smitten him, as he smote
those that smote him? *or* is he slain according to the slaughter of them that are
slain by him?
8 In measure, when it shooteth forth,
thou wilt debate with it: he stayeth his
rough wind in the day of the east wind.
9 By this therefore shall the iniquity of
Jacob be purged; and this *is* all the fruit
to take away his sin; when he maketh all
the stones of the altar as chalkstones
that are beaten in sunder, the groves and
images shall not stand up.
10 Yet the defensed city *shall be* desolate, *and* the habitation forsaken, and
left like a wilderness: there shall the calf
feed, and there shall he lie down, and
consume the branches thereof.
11 When the boughs thereof are withered, they shall be broken off: the wom-
en come, *and* set them on fire; for it *is* a
people of no understanding: therefore he
that made them will not have mercy on
them, and he that formed them will
show them no favor.
12 ¶ And it shall come to pass in that
day, *that* the LORD shall beat off from
the channel of the river unto the stream
of Egypt, and ye shall be gathered one
by one, O ye children of Ĭs′rā-ĕl.
13 And it shall come to pass in that day,
that the great trumpet shall be blown,

and they shall come which were ready to
perish in the land of Assyria, and the
outcasts in the land of Egypt, and shall
worship the LORD in the holy mount at
Jerusalem.

CHAPTER 28

WOE to the crown of pride, to the
drunkards of Ē′phrā-ĭm, whose
glorious beauty *is* a fading flower, which
are on the head of the fat valleys of
them that are overcome with wine!
2 Behold, the Lord hath a mighty and
strong one, *which* as a tempest of hail
and a destroying storm, as a flood of
mighty waters overflowing, shall cast
down to the earth with the hand.
3 The crown of pride, the drunkards of
Ē′phrā-ĭm, shall be trodden under feet:
4 And the glorious beauty, which *is* on
the head of the fat valley, shall be a fading flower, *and* as the hasty fruit before
the summer; which *when* he that looketh
upon it seeth, while it is yet in his hand
he eateth it up.
5 ¶ In that day shall the LORD of hosts
be for a crown of glory, and for a diadem
of beauty, unto the residue of his people,
6 And for a spirit of judgment to him
that sitteth in judgment, and for strength
to them that turn the battle to the gate.
7 ¶ But they also have erred through
wine, and through strong drink are out
of the way; the priest and the prophet
have erred through strong drink, they
are swallowed up of wine, they are out
of the way through strong drink; they
err in vision, they stumble *in* judgment.
8 For all tables are full of vomit *and*
filthiness, *so that there is* no place *clean.*
9 ¶ Whom shall he teach knowledge?
and whom shall he make to understand
doctrine? *them that are* weaned from the
milk, *and* drawn from the breasts.
10 For precept *must be* upon precept,
precept upon precept; line upon line,
line upon line; here a little, *and* there a
little:
11 For with stammering lips and another
tongue will he speak to this people.
12 To whom he said, This *is* the rest
wherewith ye may cause the weary to
rest; and this *is* the refreshing: yet they
would not hear.
13 But the word of the LORD was unto
them precept upon precept, precept
upon precept; line upon line, line upon
line; here a little, *and* there a little; that
they might go, and fall backward, and be
broken, and snared, and taken.
14 ¶ Wherefore hear the word of the
LORD, ye scornful men, that rule this
people which *is* in Jerusalem.
15 Because ye have said, We have
made a covenant with death, and with
hell are we at agreement; when the overflowing scourge shall pass through, it
shall not come unto us: for we have
made lies our refuge, and under falsehood have we hid ourselves:
16 ¶ Therefore thus saith the Lord
GOD, Behold, I lay in Zion for a foundation a stone, a tried stone, a precious
corner *stone,* a sure foundation: he that
believeth shall not make haste.
17 Judgment also will I lay to the line,
and righteousness to the plummet: and
the hail shall sweep away the refuge of
lies, and the waters shall overflow the
hiding place.
18 ¶ And your covenant with death
shall be disannulled, and your agreement with hell shall not stand; when the
overflowing scourge shall pass through,
then ye shall be trodden down by it.
19 From the time that it goeth forth it
shall take you: for morning by morning
shall it pass over, by day and by night:
and it shall be a vexation only *to* understand the report.
20 For the bed is shorter than that *a*
man can stretch himself *on it:* and the
covering narrower than that he can wrap
himself *in it.*
21 For the LORD shall rise up as *in*
mount Pĕr′ȧ-zĭm, he shall be wroth as *in*
the valley of Gĭb′ē-ŏn, that he may do
his work, his strange work; and bring to
pass his act, his strange act.
22 Now therefore be ye not mockers,
lest your bands be made strong: for I
have heard from the Lord GOD of hosts
a consumption, even determined upon
the whole earth.
23 ¶ Give ye ear, and hear my voice;
hearken, and hear my speech.
24 Doth the plowman plow all day to
sow? doth he open and break the clods
of his ground?
25 When he hath made plain the face
thereof, doth he not cast abroad the
fitches, and scatter the cummin, and
cast in the principal wheat and the appointed barley and the rye in their place?
26 For his God doth instruct him to discretion, *and* doth teach him.

27 For the fitches are not threshed with a threshing instrument, neither is a cart wheel turned about upon the cummin; but the fitches are beaten out with a staff, and the cummin with a rod.

28 Bread *corn* is bruised; because he will not ever be threshing it, nor break *it with* the wheel of his cart, nor bruise it *with* his horsemen.

29 This also cometh forth from the LORD of hosts, *which* is wonderful in counsel, *and* excellent in working.

CHAPTER 29

WOE to Ā′rĭ-ĕl, to Ā′rĭ-ĕl, the city *where* David dwelt! add ye year to year; let them kill sacrifices.

2 Yet I will distress Ā′rĭ-ĕl, and there shall be heaviness and sorrow: and it shall be unto me as Ā′rĭ-ĕl.

3 And I will camp against thee round about, and will lay siege against thee with a mount, and I will raise forts against thee.

4 And thou shalt be brought down, *and* shalt speak out of the ground, and thy speech shall be low out of the dust, and thy voice shall be, as of one that hath a familiar spirit, out of the ground, and thy speech shall whisper out of the dust.

5 Moreover the multitude of thy strangers shall be like small dust, and the multitude of the terrible ones *shall be* as chaff that passeth away: yea, it shall be at an instant suddenly.

6 Thou shalt be visited of the LORD of hosts with thunder, and with earthquake, and great noise, with storm and tempest, and the flame of devouring fire.

7 ¶ And the multitude of all the nations that fight against Ā′rĭ-ĕl, even all that fight against her and her munition, and that distress her, shall be as a dream of a night vision.

8 It shall even be as when a hungry man dreameth, and, behold, he eateth; but he awaketh, and his soul is empty: or as when a thirsty man dreameth, and, behold, he drinketh; but he awaketh, and, behold, *he is* faint, and his soul hath appetite: so shall the multitude of all the nations be, that fight against mount Zion.

9 ¶ Stay yourselves, and wonder; cry ye out, and cry: they are drunken, but not with wine; they stagger, but not with strong drink.

10 For the LORD hath poured out upon you the spirit of deep sleep, and hath closed your eyes: the prophets and your rulers, the seers hath he covered.

11 And the vision of all is become unto you as the words of a book that is sealed, which *men* deliver to one that is learned, saying, Read this, I pray thee: and he saith, I cannot; for it *is* sealed:

12 And the book is delivered to him that is not learned, saying, Read this, I pray thee: and he saith, I am not learned.

13 ¶ Wherefore the Lord said, Forasmuch as this people draw near *me* with their mouth, and with their lips do honor me, but have removed their heart far from me, and their fear toward me is taught by the precept of men:

14 Therefore, behold, I will proceed to do a marvelous work among this people, *even* a marvelous work and a wonder: for the wisdom of their wise *men* shall perish, and the understanding of their prudent *men* shall be hid.

15 Woe unto them that seek deep to hide their counsel from the LORD, and their works are in the dark, and they say, Who seeth us? and who knoweth us?

16 Surely your turning of things upside down shall be esteemed as the potter's clay: for shall the work say of him that made it, He made me not? or shall the thing framed say of him that framed it, He had no understanding?

17 *Is* it not yet a very little while, and Lebanon shall be turned into a fruitful field, and the fruitful field shall be esteemed as a forest?

18 ¶ And in that day shall the deaf hear the words of the book, and the eyes of the blind shall see out of obscurity, and out of darkness.

19 The meek also shall increase *their* joy in the LORD, and the poor among men shall rejoice in the Holy One of Ĭş′rā-ĕl.

20 For the terrible one is brought to nought, and the scorner is consumed, and all that watch for iniquity are cut off:

21 That make a man an offender for a word, and lay a snare for him that reproveth in the gate, and turn aside the just for a thing of nought.

22 Therefore thus saith the LORD, who redeemed Abraham, concerning the house of Jacob, Jacob shall not now be

ashamed, neither shall his face now wax pale.

23 But when he seeth his children, the work of mine hands, in the midst of him, they shall sanctify my name, and sanctify the Holy One of Jacob, and shall fear the God of Ĭs′rā-ĕl.

24 They also that erred in spirit shall come to understanding, and they that murmured shall learn doctrine.

CHAPTER 30

WOE to the rebellious children, saith the LORD, that take counsel, but not of me; and that cover with a covering, but not of my Spirit, that they may add sin to sin:

2 That walk to go down into Egypt, and have not asked at my mouth; to strengthen themselves in the strength of Phā′raōh, and to trust in the shadow of Egypt!

3 Therefore shall the strength of Phā′raōh be your shame, and the trust in the shadow of Egypt *your* confusion.

4 For his princes were at Zō′ăn, and his ambassadors came to Hā′nēs̩.

5 They were all ashamed of a people *that* could not profit them, nor be a help nor profit, but a shame, and also a reproach.

6 The burden of the beasts of the south: Into the land of trouble and anguish, from whence *come* the young and old lion, the viper and fiery flying serpent, they will carry their riches upon the shoulders of young asses, and their treasures upon the bunches of camels, to a people *that* shall not profit *them*.

7 For the Egyptians shall help in vain, and to no purpose: therefore have I cried concerning this, Their strength *is* to sit still.

8 ¶ Now go, write it before them in a table, and note it in a book, that it may be for the time to come for ever and ever:

9 That this *is* a rebellious people, lying children, children *that* will not hear the law of the LORD:

10 Which say to the seers, See not; and to the prophets, Prophesy not unto us right things, speak unto us smooth things, prophesy deceits:

11 Get you out of the way, turn aside out of the path, cause the Holy One of Ĭs′rā-ĕl to cease from before us.

12 Wherefore thus saith the Holy One of Ĭs̩′rā-ĕl, Because ye despise this word, and trust in oppression and perverseness, and stay thereon:

13 Therefore this iniquity shall be to you as a breach ready to fall, swelling out in a high wall, whose breaking cometh suddenly at an instant.

14 And he shall break it as the breaking of the potters' vessel that is broken in pieces; he shall not spare: so that there shall not be found in the bursting of it a sherd to take fire from the hearth, or to take water *withal* out of the pit.

15 For thus saith the Lord GOD, the Holy One of Ĭs̩′rā-ĕl; In returning and rest shall ye be saved; in quietness and in confidence shall be your strength: and ye would not.

16 But ye said, No; for we will flee upon horses; therefore shall ye flee: and, We will ride upon the swift; therefore shall they that pursue you be swift.

17 One thousand *shall flee* at the rebuke of one; at the rebuke of five shall ye flee: till ye be left as a beacon upon the top of a mountain, and as an ensign on a hill.

18 ¶ And therefore will the LORD wait, that he may be gracious unto you, and therefore will he be exalted, that he may have mercy upon you: for the LORD *is* a God of judgment: blessed *are* all they that wait for him.

19 For the people shall dwell in Zion at Jerusalem: thou shalt weep no more: he will be very gracious unto thee at the voice of thy cry; when he shall hear it, he will answer thee.

20 And *though* the Lord give you the bread of adversity, and the water of affliction, yet shall not thy teachers be removed into a corner any more, but thine eyes shall see thy teachers:

21 And thine ears shall hear a word behind thee, saying, This *is* the way, walk ye in it, when ye turn to the right hand, and when ye turn to the left.

22 Ye shall defile also the covering of thy graven images of silver, and the ornament of thy molten images of gold: thou shalt cast them away as a menstruous cloth; thou shalt say unto it, Get thee hence.

23 Then shall he give the rain of thy seed, that thou shalt sow the ground withal; and bread of the increase of the earth, and it shall be fat and plenteous: in that day shall thy cattle feed in large pastures.

24 The oxen likewise and the young asses that ear the ground shall eat clean provender, which hath been winnowed with the shovel and with the fan.

25 And there shall be upon every high mountain, and upon every high hill, rivers *and* streams of waters in the day of the great slaughter, when the towers fall.

26 Moreover the light of the moon shall be as the light of the sun, and the light of the sun shall be sevenfold, as the light of seven days, in the day that the LORD bindeth up the breach of his people, and healeth the stroke of their wound.

27 ¶ Behold, the name of the LORD cometh from far, burning *with* his anger, and the burden *thereof is* heavy: his lips are full of indignation, and his tongue as a devouring fire:

28 And his breath, as an overflowing stream, shall reach to the midst of the neck, to sift the nations with the sieve of vanity: and *there shall be* a bridle in the jaws of the people, causing *them* to err.

29 Ye shall have a song, as in the night *when* a holy solemnity is kept; and gladness of heart, as when one goeth with a pipe to come into the mountain of the LORD, to the Mighty One of Ĭṣ′rā-ĕl.

30 And the LORD shall cause his glorious voice to be heard, and shall show the lighting down of his arm, with the indignation of *his* anger, and *with* the flame of a devouring fire, *with* scattering, and tempest, and hailstones.

31 For through the voice of the LORD shall the Assyrian be beaten down, *which* smote with a rod.

32 And *in* every place where the grounded staff shall pass, which the LORD shall lay upon him, *it* shall be with tabrets and harps: and in battles of shaking will he fight with it.

33 For Tō′phĕt *is* ordained of old; yea, for the king it is prepared; he hath made *it* deep *and* large: the pile thereof *is* fire and much wood; the breath of the LORD, like a stream of brimstone, doth kindle it.

CHAPTER 31

WOE to them that go down to Egypt for help; and stay on horses, and trust in chariots, because *they are* many; and in horsemen, because they are very strong; but they look not unto the Holy One of Ĭṣ′rā-ĕl, neither seek the LORD!

2 Yet he also *is* wise, and will bring evil, and will not call back his words: but will arise against the house of the evildoers, and against the help of them that work iniquity.

3 Now the Egyptians *are* men, and not God; and their horses flesh, and not spirit. When the LORD shall stretch out his hand, both he that helpeth shall fall, and he that is helped shall fall down, and they all shall fail together.

4 For thus hath the LORD spoken unto me, Like as the lion and the young lion roaring on his prey, when a multitude of shepherds is called forth against him, *he* will not be afraid of their voice, nor abase himself for the noise of them: so shall the LORD of hosts come down to fight for mount Zion, and for the hill thereof.

5 As birds flying, so will the LORD of hosts defend Jerusalem; defending also he will deliver *it; and* passing over he will preserve *it*.

6 ¶ Turn ye unto *him from* whom the children of Ĭṣ′rā-ĕl have deeply revolted.

7 For in that day every man shall cast away his idols of silver, and his idols of gold, which your own hands have made unto you *for* a sin.

8 ¶ Then shall the Assyrian fall with the sword, not of a mighty man; and the sword, not of a mean man, shall devour him: but he shall flee from the sword, and his young men shall be discomfited.

9 And he shall pass over to his stronghold for fear, and his princes shall be afraid of the ensign, saith the LORD, whose fire *is* in Zion, and his furnace in Jerusalem.

CHAPTER 32

BEHOLD, a King shall reign in righteousness, and princes shall rule in judgment.

2 And a man shall be as a hiding place from the wind, and a covert from the tempest; as rivers of water in a dry place, as the shadow of a great rock in a weary land.

3 And the eyes of them that see shall not be dim, and the ears of them that hear shall hearken.

4 The heart also of the rash shall understand knowledge, and the tongue of the stammerers shall be ready to speak plainly.

5 The vile person shall be no more

called liberal, nor the churl said *to be*
bountiful.
6 For the vile person will speak villainy,
and his heart will work iniquity, to practise hypocrisy, and to utter error against
the LORD, to make empty the soul of the
hungry; and he will cause the drink of
the thirsty to fail.
7 The instruments also of the churl *are*
evil: he deviseth wicked devices to destroy the poor with lying words, even
when the needy speaketh right.
8 But the liberal deviseth liberal
things; and by liberal things shall he
stand.
9 ¶ Rise up, ye women that are at
ease; hear my voice, ye careless daughters; give ear unto my speech.
10 Many days and years shall ye be
troubled, ye careless women: for the
vintage shall fail, the gathering shall not
come.
11 Tremble, ye women that are at ease;
be troubled, ye careless ones: strip you,
and make you bare, and gird *sackcloth*
upon *your* loins.
12 They shall lament for the teats,
for the pleasant fields, for the fruitful
vine.
13 Upon the land of my people shall
come up thorns *and* briers; yea, upon
all the houses of joy *in* the joyous
city:
14 Because the palaces shall be forsaken; the multitude of the city shall be
left; the forts and towers shall be for
dens for ever, a joy of wild asses, a pasture of flocks;
15 Until the Spirit be poured upon us
from on high, and the wilderness be a
fruitful field, and the fruitful field be
counted for a forest.
16 Then judgment shall dwell in the
wilderness, and righteousness remain in
the fruitful field.
17 And the work of righteousness
shall be peace; and the effect of righteousness, quietness and assurance for
ever.
18 And my people shall dwell in a
peaceable habitation, and in sure dwellings, and in quiet resting places;
19 When it shall hail, coming down on
the forest; and the city shall be low in a
low place.
20 Blessed *are* ye that sow beside all
waters, that send forth *thither* the feet
of the ox and the ass.

CHAPTER 33

WOE to thee that spoilest, and thou
wast not spoiled; and dealest
treacherously, and they dealt not treacherously with thee! when thou shalt cease
to spoil, thou shalt be spoiled; *and* when
thou shalt make an end to deal treacherously, they shall deal treacherously with
thee.
2 O LORD, be gracious unto us; we
have waited for thee: be thou their arm
every morning, our salvation also in the
time of trouble.
3 At the noise of the tumult the people
fled; at the lifting up of thyself the nations were scattered.
4 And your spoil shall be gathered *like*
the gathering of the caterpillar: as the
running to and fro of locusts shall he run
upon them.
5 The LORD is exalted; for he dwelleth
on high: he hath filled Zion with judgment and righteousness.
6 And wisdom and knowledge shall be
the stability of thy times, *and* strength
of salvation: the fear of the LORD *is* his
treasure.
7 Behold, their valiant ones shall cry
without: the ambassadors of peace shall
weep bitterly.
8 The highways lie waste, the wayfaring man ceaseth: he hath broken the
covenant, he hath despised the cities, he
regardeth no man.
9 The earth mourneth *and* languisheth:
Lebanon is ashamed *and* hewn down:
Shăr′ŏn is like a wilderness; and Bā′-
shăn and Cär′mĕl shake off *their fruits*.
10 Now will I rise, saith the LORD; now
will I be exalted; now will I lift up myself.
11 Ye shall conceive chaff, ye shall
bring forth stubble: your breath, *as* fire,
shall devour you.
12 And the people shall be *as* the burnings of lime: *as* thorns cut up shall they
be burned in the fire.
13 ¶ Hear, ye *that are* far off, what I
have done; and, ye *that are* near, acknowledge my might.
14 The sinners in Zion are afraid; fearfulness hath surprised the hypocrites.
Who among us shall dwell with the devouring fire? who among us shall dwell
with everlasting burnings?
15 He that walketh righteously, and
speaketh uprightly; he that despiseth
the gain of oppressions, that shaketh his

hands from holding of bribes, that stoppeth his ears from hearing of blood, and
shutteth his eyes from seeing evil;
16 He shall dwell on high; his place of
defense *shall be* the munitions of rocks:
bread shall be given him; his waters
shall be sure.
17 Thine eyes shall see the King in his
beauty: they shall behold the land that
is very far off.
18 Thine heart shall meditate terror.
Where *is* the scribe? where *is* the re-
ceiver? where *is* he that counted the
towers?
19 Thou shalt not see a fierce people, a
people of a deeper speech than thou
canst perceive; of a stammering tongue,
that thou canst not understand.
20 Look upon Zion, the city of our solemnities: thine eyes shall see Jerusalem
a quiet habitation, a tabernacle *that*
shall not be taken down; not one of the
stakes thereof shall ever be removed,
neither shall any of the cords thereof be
broken.
21 But there the glorious LORD *will be*
unto us a place of broad rivers *and*
streams; wherein shall go no galley with
oars, neither shall gallant ship pass
thereby.
22 For the LORD *is* our judge, the LORD
is our lawgiver, the LORD *is* our King; he
will save us.
23 Thy tacklings are loosed; they could
not well strengthen their mast; they
could not spread the sail: then is the
prey of a great spoil divided; the lame
take the prey.
24 And the inhabitant shall not say, I
am sick: the people that dwell therein
shall be forgiven *their* iniquity.

CHAPTER 34

COME near, ye nations, to hear; and
hearken, ye people: let the earth
hear, and all that is therein; the world,
and all things that come forth of it.
2 For the indignation of the LORD *is*
upon all nations, and *his* fury upon all
their armies: he hath utterly destroyed
them, he hath delivered them to the
slaughter.
3 Their slain also shall be cast out, and
their stink shall come up out of their
carcasses, and the mountains shall be
melted with their blood.
4 And all the host of heaven shall be
dissolved, and the heavens shall be
rolled together as a scroll: and all their
host shall fall down, as the leaf falleth
off from the vine, and as a falling *fig*
from the fig tree.
5 For my sword shall be bathed in
heaven: behold, it shall come down upon
Ĭd′ū-mē′ȧ, and upon the people of my
curse, to judgment.
6 The sword of the LORD is filled with
blood, it is made fat with fatness, *and*
with the blood of lambs and goats, with
the fat of the kidneys of rams: for the
LORD hath a sacrifice in Bŏz′rȧh, and a
great slaughter in the land of Ĭd′ū-mē′ȧ.
7 And the unicorns shall come down
with them, and the bullocks with the
bulls; and their land shall be soaked
with blood, and their dust made fat with
fatness.
8 For *it is* the day of the LORD's
vengeance, *and* the year of recompenses
for the controversy of Zion.
9 And the streams thereof shall be
turned into pitch, and the dust thereof
into brimstone, and the land thereof
shall become burning pitch.
10 It shall not be quenched night nor
day; the smoke thereof shall go up for
ever: from generation to generation it
shall lie waste; none shall pass through
it for ever and ever.
11 ¶ But the cormorant and the bittern shall possess it; the owl also and
the raven shall dwell in it: and he shall
stretch out upon it the line of confusion,
and the stones of emptiness.
12 They shall call the nobles thereof to
the kingdom, but none *shall be* there,
and all her princes shall be nothing.
13 And thorns shall come up in her
palaces, nettles and brambles in the
fortresses thereof: and it shall be a habitation of dragons, *and* a court for owls.
14 The wild beasts of the desert shall
also meet with the wild beasts of the
island, and the satyr shall cry to his fellow; the screech owl also shall rest there,
and find for herself a place of rest.
15 There shall the great owl make her
nest, and lay, and hatch, and gather under her shadow: there shall the vultures
also be gathered, every one with her
mate.
16 ¶ Seek ye out of the book of the
LORD, and read: no one of these shall
fail, none shall want her mate: for my
mouth it hath commanded, and his
spirit it hath gathered them.

17 And he hath cast the lot for them,
and his hand hath divided it unto them
by line: they shall possess it for ever,
from generation to generation shall they
dwell therein.

CHAPTER 35

THE wilderness and the solitary
place shall be glad for them; and
the desert shall rejoice, and blossom as
the rose.
2 It shall blossom abundantly, and rejoice even with joy and singing: the
glory of Lebanon shall be given unto it,
the excellency of Cär'mĕl and Shär'ŏn;
they shall see the glory of the LORD, *and*
the excellency of our God.
3 ¶ Strengthen ye the weak hands, and
confirm the feeble knees.
4 Say to them *that are* of a fearful heart,
Be strong, fear not: behold, your God
will come *with* vengeance, *even* God
with a recompense; he will come and
save you.
5 Then the eyes of the blind shall be
opened, and the ears of the deaf shall
be unstopped.
6 Then shall the lame *man* leap as a
hart, and the tongue of the dumb sing:
for in the wilderness shall waters break
out, and streams in the desert.
7 And the parched ground shall become a pool, and the thirsty land springs
of water: in the habitation of dragons,
where each lay, *shall be* grass with reeds
and rushes.
8 And a highway shall be there, and a
way, and it shall be called The way of
holiness; the unclean shall not pass over
it; but it *shall be* for those: the wayfaring
men, though fools, shall not err *therein.*
9 No lion shall be there, nor *any* ravenous beast shall go up thereon, it shall
not be found there; but the redeemed
shall walk *there:*
10 And the ransomed of the LORD shall
return, and come to Zion with songs and
everlasting joy upon their heads: they
shall obtain joy and gladness, and sorrow and sighing shall flee away.

CHAPTER 36

NOW it came to pass in the fourteenth year of king Hĕz'ē-kī'ăh,
that Sĕn-năch'ĕr-ĭb king of Assyria came
up against all the defensed cities of Judah, and took them.
2 And the king of Assyria sent Răb'-
shá-kĕh from Lā'chĭsh to Jerusalem unto
king Hĕz'ē-kī'ăh with a great army. And
he stood by the conduit of the upper
pool in the highway of the fuller's field.
3 Then came forth unto him Ē-lī'ă-
kĭm, Hĭl-kī'ăh's son, which was over
the house, and Shĕb'nȧ the scribe, and
Jō'ăh, Ā'săph's son, the recorder.
4 ¶ And Răb'shȧ-kĕh said unto them,
Say ye now to Hĕz'ē-kī'ăh, Thus saith
the great king, the king of Assyria, What
confidence *is* this wherein thou trustest?
5 I say, *sayest thou,* (but *they are but*
vain words) *I have* counsel and strength
for war: now on whom dost thou trust,
that thou rebellest against me?
6 Lo, thou trustest in the staff of this
broken reed, on Egypt; whereon if a
man lean, it will go into his hand, and
pierce it: so *is* Phā'raōh king of Egypt to
all that trust in him.
7 But if thou say to me, We trust in the
LORD our God: *is it* not he, whose high
places and whose altars Hĕz'ē-kī'ăh
hath taken away, and said to Judah and
to Jerusalem, Ye shall worship before
this altar?
8 Now therefore give pledges, I pray
thee, to my master the king of Assyria,
and I will give thee two thousand horses,
if thou be able on thy part to set riders
upon them.
9 How then wilt thou turn away the
face of one captain of the least of my
master's servants, and put thy trust on
Egypt for chariots and for horsemen?
10 And am I now come up without the
LORD against this land to destroy it? the
LORD said unto me, Go up against this
land, and destroy it.
11 ¶ Then said Ē-lī'ă-kĭm and Shĕb'nȧ
and Jō'ăh unto Răb'shȧ-kĕh, Speak, I
pray thee, unto thy servants in the Syrian
language; for we understand *it:* and
speak not to us in the Jews' language,
in the ears of the people that *are* on the
wall.
12 ¶ But Răb'shȧ-kĕh said, Hath my
master sent me to thy master and to thee
to speak these words? *hath he* not *sent*
me to the men that sit upon the wall,
that they may eat their own dung, and
drink their own piss with you?
13 Then Răb'shȧ-kĕh stood, and cried
with a loud voice in the Jews' language,
and said, Hear ye the words of the great
king, the king of Assyria.
14 Thus saith the king, Let not Hĕz'ē-

kī′ȧh deceive you: for he shall not be able to deliver you.

15 Neither let Hĕz′ē-kī′ȧh make you trust in the LORD, saying, The LORD will surely deliver us: this city shall not be delivered into the hand of the king of Assyria.

16 Hearken not to Hĕz′ē-kī′ȧh: for thus saith the king of Assyria, Make *an agreement* with me *by* a present, and come out to me: and eat ye every one of his vine, and every one of his fig tree, and drink ye every one the waters of his own cistern;

17 Until I come and take you away to a land like your own land, a land of corn and wine, a land of bread and vineyards.

18 *Beware* lest Hĕz′ē-kī′ȧh persuade you, saying, The LORD will deliver us. Hath any of the gods of the nations delivered his land out of the hand of the king of Assyria?

19 Where *are* the gods of Hā′măth and Är′phăd? where *are* the gods of Sĕph′är-vā′ĭm? and have they delivered Sȧ-mā′rĭ-ȧ out of my hand?

20 Who *are they* among all the gods of these lands, that have delivered their land out of my hand, that the LORD should deliver Jerusalem out of my hand?

21 But they held their peace, and answered him not a word: for the king's commandment was, saying, Answer him not.

22 ℭ Then came Ē-lī′ȧ-kĭm, the son of Hĭl-kī′ȧh, that *was* over the household, and Shĕb′nȧ the scribe, and Jō′ȧh, the son of Ā′săph, the recorder, to Hĕz′ē-kī′ȧh with *their* clothes rent, and told him the words of Răb′shȧ-kĕh.

CHAPTER 37

AND it came to pass, when king Hĕz′ē-kī′ȧh heard *it*, that he rent his clothes, and covered himself with sackcloth, and went into the house of the LORD.

2 And he sent Ē-lī′ȧ-kĭm, who *was* over the household, and Shĕb′nȧ the scribe, and the elders of the priests, covered with sackcloth, unto Ī-ṣā′ịȧh the prophet the son of Ā′mŏz.

3 And they said unto him, Thus saith Hĕz′ē-kī′ȧh, This day *is* a day of trouble, and of rebuke, and of blasphemy: for the children are come to the birth, and *there is* not strength to bring forth.

4 It may be the LORD thy God will hear the words of Răb′shȧ-kĕh, whom the king of Assyria his master hath sent to reproach the living God, and will reprove the words which the LORD thy God hath heard: wherefore lift up *thy* prayer for the remnant that is left.

5 So the servants of king Hĕz′ē-kī′ȧh came to Ī-ṣā′ịȧh.

6 ℭ And Ī-ṣā′ịȧh said unto them, Thus shall ye say unto your master, Thus saith the LORD, Be not afraid of the words that thou hast heard, wherewith the servants of the king of Assyria have blasphemed me.

7 Behold, I will send a blast upon him, and he shall hear a rumor, and return to his own land; and I will cause him to fall by the sword in his own land.

8 ℭ So Răb′shȧ-kĕh returned, and found the king of Assyria warring against Lĭb′nȧh: for he had heard that he was departed from Lā′chĭsh.

9 And he heard say concerning Tĭr-hā′kȧh king of Ethiopia, He is come forth to make war with thee. And when he heard *it*, he sent messengers to Hĕz′ē-kī′ȧh, saying,

10 Thus shall ye speak to Hĕz′ē-kī′ȧh king of Judah, saying, Let not thy God, in whom thou trustest, deceive thee, saying, Jerusalem shall not be given into the hand of the king of Assyria.

11 Behold, thou hast heard what the kings of Assyria have done to all lands by destroying them utterly; and shalt thou be delivered?

12 Have the gods of the nations delivered them which my fathers have destroyed, *as* Gō′zăn, and Hā′răn, and Rē′zĕph, and the children of Ē′den which *were* in Tē-lăs′sȧr?

13 Where *is* the king of Hā′măth, and the king of Är′phăd, and the king of the city of Sĕph′är-vā′ĭm, Hē′nȧ, and Ī′vȧh?

14 ℭ And Hĕz′ē-kī′ȧh received the letter from the hand of the messengers, and read it: and Hĕz′ē-kī′ȧh went up unto the house of the LORD, and spread it before the LORD.

15 And Hĕz′ē-kī′ȧh prayed unto the LORD, saying,

16 O LORD of hosts, God of Ĭṣ′rā-ĕl, that dwellest *between* the cherubim, thou *art* the God, *even* thou alone, of all the kingdoms of the earth: thou hast made heaven and earth.

17 Incline thine ear, O LORD, and hear;

open thine eyes, O LORD, and see: and
hear all the words of Sĕn-năch′ĕr-ĭb,
which hath sent to reproach the living
God.
18 Of a truth, LORD, the kings of Assyria have laid waste all the nations, and their countries,
19 And have cast their gods into the fire: for they *were* no gods, but the work of men's hands, wood and stone: therefore they have destroyed them.
20 Now therefore, O LORD our God, save us from his hand, that all the kingdoms of the earth may know that thou *art* the LORD, *even* thou only.
21 ¶ Then Ī-ṣā′ịah the son of Ā′mŏz sent unto Hĕz′ē-kī′ah, saying, Thus saith the LORD God of Ĭṣ′rā-ĕl, Whereas thou hast prayed to me against Sĕn-năch′ĕr-ĭb king of Assyria:
22 This *is* the word which the LORD hath spoken concerning him; The virgin, the daughter of Zion, hath despised thee, *and* laughed thee to scorn; the daughter of Jerusalem hath shaken her head at thee.
23 Whom hast thou reproached and blasphemed? and against whom hast thou exalted *thy* voice, and lifted up thine eyes on high? *even* against the Holy One of Ĭṣ′rā-ĕl.
24 By thy servants hast thou reproached the Lord, and hast said, By the multitude of my chariots am I come up to the height of the mountains, to the sides of Lebanon; and I will cut down the tall cedars thereof, *and* the choice fir trees thereof: and I will enter into the height of his border, *and* the forest of his Cär′mĕl.
25 I have digged, and drunk water; and with the sole of my feet have I dried up all the rivers of the besieged places.
26 Hast thou not heard long ago, *how* I have done it; *and* of ancient times, that I have formed it? now have I brought it to pass, that thou shouldest be to lay waste defensed cities *into* ruinous heaps.
27 Therefore their inhabitants *were* of small power, they were dismayed and confounded: they were *as* the grass of the field, and *as* the green herb, *as* the grass on the housetops, and *as corn* blasted before it be grown up.
28 But I know thy abode, and thy going out, and thy coming in, and thy rage against me.
29 Because thy rage against me, and thy tumult, is come up into mine ears, therefore will I put my hook in thy nose, and my bridle in thy lips, and I will turn thee back by the way by which thou camest.
30 And this *shall be* a sign unto thee, Ye shall eat *this* year such as groweth of itself; and the second year that which springeth of the same: and in the third year sow ye, and reap, and plant vineyards, and eat the fruit thereof.
31 And the remnant that is escaped of the house of Judah shall again take root downward, and bear fruit upward:
32 For out of Jerusalem shall go forth a remnant, and they that escape out of mount Zion: the zeal of the LORD of hosts shall do this.
33 Therefore thus saith the LORD concerning the king of Assyria, He shall not come into this city, nor shoot an arrow there, nor come before it with shields, nor cast a bank against it.
34 By the way that he came, by the same shall he return, and shall not come into this city, saith the LORD.
35 For I will defend this city to save it for mine own sake, and for my servant David's sake.
36 Then the angel of the LORD went forth, and smote in the camp of the Assyrians a hundred and fourscore and five thousand: and when they arose early in the morning, behold, they *were* all dead corpses.
37 ¶ So Sĕn-năch′ĕr-ĭb king of Assyria departed, and went and returned, and dwelt at Nĭn′ē-vĕh.
38 And it came to pass, as he was worshipping in the house of Nĭs′rŏch his god, that Ā-drăm′mē-lĕch and Shā-rē′zĕr his sons smote him with the sword; and they escaped into the land of Armenia: and Ē′sär–hăd′dȯn his son reigned in his stead.

CHAPTER 38

IN those days was Hĕz′ē-kī′ah sick unto death. And Ī-ṣā′ịah the prophet the son of Ā′mŏz came unto him, and said unto him, Thus saith the LORD, Set thine house in order: for thou shalt die, and not live.
2 Then Hĕz′ē-kī′ah turned his face toward the wall, and prayed unto the LORD,
3 And said, Remember now, O LORD, I beseech thee, how I have walked

before thee in truth and with a perfect
heart, and have done *that which is* good
in thy sight. And Hĕz′ē-kī′ăh wept sore.
4 ¶ Then came the word of the LORD
to Ī-ṣā′ịăh, saying,
5 Go, and say to Hĕz′ē-kī′ăh, Thus
saith the LORD, the God of David thy
father, I have heard thy prayer, I have
seen thy tears: behold, I will add unto
thy days fifteen years.
6 And I will deliver thee and this city
out of the hand of the king of Assyria:
and I will defend this city.
7 And this *shall be* a sign unto thee from
the LORD, that the LORD will do this
thing that he hath spoken;
8 Behold, I will bring again the shadow
of the degrees, which is gone down in
the sun dial of Ahaz, ten degrees backward. So the sun returned ten degrees,
by which degrees it was gone down.
9 ¶ The writing of Hĕz′ē-kī′ăh king of
Judah, when he had been sick, and was
recovered of his sickness:
10 I said in the cutting off of my days,
I shall go to the gates of the grave: I am
deprived of the residue of my years.
11 I said, I shall not see the LORD, *even*
the LORD, in the land of the living: I
shall behold man no more with the inhabitants of the world.
12 Mine age is departed, and is removed from me as a shepherd's tent: I
have cut off like a weaver my life: he
will cut me off with pining sickness:
from day *even* to night wilt thou make
an end of me.
13 I reckoned till morning, *that*, as a
lion, so will he break all my bones: from
day *even* to night wilt thou make an end
of me.
14 Like a crane *or* a swallow, so did I
chatter: I did mourn as a dove: mine
eyes fail *with looking* upward: O LORD,
I am oppressed; undertake for me.
15 What shall I say? he hath both spoken unto me, and himself hath done *it:* I
shall go softly all my years in the bitterness of my soul.
16 O Lord, by these *things men* live,
and in all these *things is* the life of my
spirit: so wilt thou recover me, and make
me to live.
17 Behold, for peace I had great bitterness; but thou hast in love to my soul
delivered it from the pit of corruption:
for thou hast cast all my sins behind thy
back.
18 For the grave cannot praise thee,
death cannot celebrate thee: they that
go down into the pit cannot hope for thy
truth.
19 The living, the living, he shall praise
thee, as I *do* this day: the father to the
children shall make known thy truth.
20 The LORD *was ready* to save me:
therefore we will sing my songs to the
stringed instruments all the days of our
life in the house of the LORD.
21 For Ī-ṣā′ịăh had said, Let them take
a lump of figs, and lay *it* for a plaster
upon the boil, and he shall recover.
22 Hĕz′ē-kī′ăh also had said, What *is*
the sign that I shall go up to the house
of the LORD?

CHAPTER 39

AT that time Mē-rō′dăch–băl′ă-dăn,
the son of Băl′ă-dăn, king of Babylon, sent letters and a present to Hĕz′ē-
kī′ăh: for he had heard that he had been
sick, and was recovered.
2 And Hĕz′ē-kī′ăh was glad of them,
and showed them the house of his precious things, the silver, and the gold, and
the spices, and the precious ointment,
and all the house of his armor, and all
that was found in his treasures: there
was nothing in his house, nor in all his
dominion, that Hĕz′ē-kī′ăh showed them
not.
3 ¶ Then came Ī-ṣā′ịăh the prophet
unto king Hĕz′ē-kī′ăh, and said unto
him, What said these men? and from
whence came they unto thee? And
Hĕz′ē-kī′ăh said, They are come from
a far country unto me, *even* from
Babylon.
4 Then said he, What have they seen
in thine house? And Hĕz′ē-kī′ăh answered, All that *is* in mine house have
they seen: there is nothing among my
treasures that I have not showed them.
5 Then said Ī-ṣā′ịăh to Hĕz′ē-kī′ăh,
Hear the word of the LORD of hosts:
6 Behold, the days come, that all that
is in thine house, and *that* which thy
fathers have laid up in store until this
day, shall be carried to Babylon: nothing
shall be left, saith the LORD.
7 And of thy sons that shall issue from
thee, which thou shalt beget, shall they
take away; and they shall be eunuchs in
the palace of the king of Babylon.
8 Then said Hĕz′ē-kī′ăh to Ī-ṣā′ịăh,
Good *is* the word of the LORD which

thou hast spoken. He said moreover,
For there shall be peace and truth in
my days.

CHAPTER 40

COMFORT ye, comfort ye my people,
saith your God.
2 Speak ye comfortably to Jerusalem,
and cry unto her, that her warfare is
accomplished, that her iniquity is pardoned:
for she hath received of the
LORD's hand double for all her sins.
3 ¶ The voice of him that crieth in the
wilderness, Prepare ye the way of the
LORD, make straight in the desert a
highway for our God.
4 Every valley shall be exalted, and
every mountain and hill shall be made
low: and the crooked shall be made
straight, and the rough places plain:
5 And the glory of the LORD shall be revealed,
and all flesh shall see *it* together:
for the mouth of the LORD hath spoken *it*.
6 The voice said, Cry. And he said,
What shall I cry? All flesh *is* grass, and
all the goodliness thereof *is* as the
flower of the field:
7 The grass withereth, the flower
fadeth; because the spirit of the LORD
bloweth upon it: surely the people *is*
grass.
8 The grass withereth, the flower
fadeth: but the word of our God shall
stand for ever.
9 ¶ O Zion, that bringest good tidings,
get thee up into the high mountain; O
Jerusalem, that bringest good tidings,
lift up thy voice with strength; lift *it* up,
be not afraid; say unto the cities of
Judah, Behold your God!
10 Behold, the Lord GOD will come with
strong *hand*, and his arm shall rule for
him: behold, his reward *is* with him, and
his work before him.
11 He shall feed his flock like a shepherd:
he shall gather the lambs with his
arm, and carry *them* in his bosom, *and*
shall gently lead those that are with
young.
12 ¶ Who hath measured the waters
in the hollow of his hand, and meted
out heaven with the span, and comprehended
the dust of the earth in a
measure, and weighed the mountains in
scales, and the hills in a balance?
13 Who hath directed the Spirit of the
LORD, or *being* his counselor hath
taught him?
14 With whom took he counsel, and
who instructed him, and taught him in
the path of judgment, and taught him
knowledge, and showed to him the way
of understanding?
15 Behold, the nations *are* as a drop of
a bucket, and are counted as the small
dust of the balance: behold, he taketh
up the isles as a very little thing.
16 And Lebanon *is* not sufficient to
burn, nor the beasts thereof sufficient
for a burnt offering.
17 All nations before him *are* as nothing;
and they are counted to him less
than nothing, and vanity.
18 ¶ To whom then will ye liken God?
or what likeness will ye compare unto
him?
19 The workman melteth a graven
image, and the goldsmith spreadeth it
over with gold, and casteth silver chains.
20 He that *is* so impoverished that he
hath no oblation chooseth a tree *that*
will not rot; he seeketh unto him a cunning
workman to prepare a graven
image, *that* shall not be moved.
21 Have ye not known? have ye not
heard? hath it not been told you from
the beginning? have ye not understood
from the foundations of the earth?
22 *It is* he that sitteth upon the circle
of the earth, and the inhabitants thereof
are as grasshoppers; that stretcheth
out the heavens as a curtain, and
spreadeth them out as a tent to dwell in:
23 That bringeth the princes to nothing;
he maketh the judges of the earth as
vanity.
24 Yea, they shall not be planted; yea,
they shall not be sown; yea, their stock
shall not take root in the earth: and he
shall also blow upon them, and they
shall wither, and the whirlwind shall
take them away as stubble.
25 To whom then will ye liken me, or
shall I be equal? saith the Holy One.
26 Lift up your eyes on high, and behold
who hath created these *things*, that
bringeth out their host by number: he
calleth them all by names by the greatness
of his might, for that *he is* strong
in power; not one faileth.
27 Why sayest thou, O Jacob, and
speakest, O Ĭs'rā-ĕl, My way is hid
from the LORD, and my judgment is
passed over from my God?
28 ¶ Hast thou not known? hast thou
not heard, *that* the everlasting God, the

LORD, the Creator of the ends of the
earth, fainteth not, neither is weary?
there is no searching of his understanding.
29 He giveth power to the faint; and to
them that have no might he increaseth
strength.
30 Even the youths shall faint and be
weary, and the young men shall utterly
fall:
31 But they that wait upon the LORD
shall renew *their* strength; they shall
mount up with wings as eagles; they
shall run, and not be weary; *and* they
shall walk, and not faint.

CHAPTER 41

KEEP silence before me, O islands;
and let the people renew *their*
strength: let them come near; then let
them speak: let us come near together
to judgment.
2 Who raised up the righteous *man*
from the east, called him to his foot,
gave the nations before him, and made
him rule over kings? he gave *them* as
the dust to his sword, *and* as driven
stubble to his bow.
3 He pursued them, *and* passed safely;
even by the way *that* he had not gone
with his feet.
4 Who hath wrought and done *it*, calling the generations from the beginning?
I the LORD, the first, and with the last; I
am he.
5 The isles saw *it*, and feared; the ends
of the earth were afraid, drew near, and
came.
6 They helped every one his neighbor;
and *every one* said to his brother, Be of
good courage.
7 So the carpenter encouraged the
goldsmith, *and* he that smootheth *with*
the hammer him that smote the anvil,
saying, It *is* ready for the soldering: and
he fastened it with nails, *that* it should
not be moved.
8 But thou, Ĭş′rā-ĕl, *art* my servant,
Jacob whom I have chosen, the seed of
Abraham my friend.
9 *Thou* whom I have taken from the
ends of the earth, and called thee from
the chief men thereof, and said unto
thee, Thou *art* my servant; I have chosen
thee, and not cast thee away.
10 ¶ Fear thou not; for I *am* with thee:
be not dismayed; for I *am* thy God: I
will strengthen thee; yea, I will help
thee; yea, I will uphold thee with the
right hand of my righteousness.
11 Behold, all they that were incensed
against thee shall be ashamed and confounded: they shall be as nothing; and
they that strive with thee shall perish.
12 Thou shalt seek them, and shalt not
find them, *even* them that contended
with thee: they that war against thee
shall be as nothing, and as a thing of
nought.
13 For I the LORD thy God will hold
thy right hand, saying unto thee, Fear
not; I will help thee.
14 Fear not, thou worm Jacob, *and* ye
men of Ĭş′rā-ĕl; I will help thee, saith
the LORD, and thy Redeemer, the Holy
One of Ĭş′rā-ĕl.
15 Behold, I will make thee a new sharp
threshing instrument having teeth: thou
shalt thresh the mountains, and beat
them small, and shalt make the hills as
chaff.
16 Thou shalt fan them, and the wind
shall carry them away, and the whirlwind shall scatter them: and thou shalt
rejoice in the LORD, *and* shalt glory in
the Holy One of Ĭş′rā-ĕl.
17 *When* the poor and needy seek water, and *there is* none, *and* their tongue
faileth for thirst, I the LORD will hear
them, *I* the God of Ĭş′rā-ĕl will not forsake them.
18 I will open rivers in high places, and
fountains in the midst of the valleys: I
will make the wilderness a pool of water, and the dry land springs of water.
19 I will plant in the wilderness the
cedar, the shittah tree, and the myrtle,
and the oil tree; I will set in the desert
the fir tree, *and* the pine, and the box
tree together:
20 That they may see, and know, and
consider, and understand together, that
the hand of the LORD hath done this,
and the Holy One of Ĭş′rā-ĕl hath
created it.
21 Produce your cause, saith the LORD;
bring forth your strong *reasons*, saith
the King of Jacob.
22 Let them bring *them* forth, and
show us what shall happen: let them
show the former things, what they *be*,
that we may consider them, and know
the latter end of them; or declare us
things for to come.
23 Show the things that are to come
hereafter, that we may know that ye

are gods: yea, do good, or do evil, that
we may be dismayed, and behold *it*
together.
24 Behold, ye *are* of nothing, and your
work of nought: an abomination *is he*
that chooseth you.
25 I have raised up *one* from the north,
and he shall come: from the rising of the
sun shall he call upon my name: and he
shall come upon princes as *upon* mortar,
and as the potter treadeth clay.
26 Who hath declared from the beginning,
that we may know? and beforetime,
that we may say, *He is* righteous?
yea, *there is* none that showeth, yea,
there is none that declareth, yea, *there*
is none that heareth your words.
27 The first *shall say* to Zion, Behold,
behold them: and I will give to Jerusalem
one that bringeth good tidings.
28 For I beheld, and *there was* no man;
even among them, and *there was* no
counselor, that, when I asked of them,
could answer a word.
29 Behold, they *are* all vanity; their
works *are* nothing: their molten images
are wind and confusion.

CHAPTER 42

BEHOLD my servant, whom I uphold;
mine elect, *in whom* my soul
delighteth; I have put my Spirit upon
him: he shall bring forth judgment to
the Gĕn'tīles.
2 He shall not cry, nor lift up, nor
cause his voice to be heard in the street.
3 A bruised reed shall he not break,
and the smoking flax shall he not
quench: he shall bring forth judgment
unto truth.
4 He shall not fail nor be discouraged,
till he have set judgment in the earth:
and the isles shall wait for his law.
5 ¶ Thus saith God the LORD, he that
created the heavens, and stretched
them out; he that spread forth the earth,
and that which cometh out of it; he that
giveth breath unto the people upon it,
and spirit to them that walk therein:
6 I the LORD have called thee in righteousness,
and will hold thine hand, and
will keep thee, and give thee for a covenant
of the people, for a light of the
Gĕn'tīles;
7 To open the blind eyes, to bring out
the prisoners from the prison, *and* them
that sit in darkness out of the prison
house.
8 I *am* the LORD; that *is* my name: and
my glory will I not give to another,
neither my praise to graven images.
9 Behold, the former things are come
to pass, and new things do I declare:
before they spring forth I tell you of
them.
10 Sing unto the LORD a new song,
and his praise from the end of the earth,
ye that go down to the sea, and all that
is therein; the isles, and the inhabitants
thereof.
11 Let the wilderness and the cities
thereof lift up *their voice,* the villages
that Kē'dȧr doth inhabit: let the inhabitants
of the rock sing, let them
shout from the top of the mountains.
12 Let them give glory unto the LORD,
and declare his praise in the islands.
13 The LORD shall go forth as a mighty
man, he shall stir up jealousy like a man
of war: he shall cry, yea, roar; he shall
prevail against his enemies.
14 I have long time holden my peace;
I have been still, *and* refrained myself:
now will I cry like a travailing woman;
I will destroy and devour at once.
15 I will make waste mountains and
hills, and dry up all their herbs; and I
will make the rivers islands, and I will
dry up the pools.
16 And I will bring the blind by a way
that they knew not; I will lead them in
paths *that* they have not known: I will
make darkness light before them, and
crooked things straight. These things will
I do unto them, and not forsake them.
17 ¶ They shall be turned back, they
shall be greatly ashamed, that trust in
graven images, that say to the molten
images, Ye *are* our gods.
18 Hear, ye deaf; and look, ye blind,
that ye may see.
19 Who *is* blind, but my servant? or
deaf, as my messenger *that* I sent? who
is blind as *he that is* perfect, and blind
as the LORD's servant?
20 Seeing many things, but thou observest
not; opening the ears, but he
heareth not.
21 The LORD is well pleased for his
righteousness' sake; he will magnify the
law, and make *it* honorable.
22 But this *is* a people robbed and
spoiled; *they are* all of them snared in
holes, and they are hid in prison houses:
they are for a prey, and none delivereth;
for a spoil, and none saith, Restore.

23 Who among you will give ear to this?
who will hearken and hear for the time
to come?
24 Who gave Jacob for a spoil, and
Ĭs′rā-ĕl to the robbers? did not the
LORD, he against whom we have
sinned? for they would not walk in his
ways, neither were they obedient unto
his law.
25 Therefore he hath poured upon him
the fury of his anger, and the strength of
battle: and it hath set him on fire round
about, yet he knew not; and it burned
him, yet he laid *it* not to heart.

CHAPTER 43

BUT now thus saith the LORD that
created thee, O Jacob, and he that
formed thee, O Ĭs′rā-ĕl, Fear not: for I
have redeemed thee, I have called *thee*
by thy name; thou *art* mine.
2 When thou passest through the waters, I *will be* with thee; and through the
rivers, they shall not overflow thee:
when thou walkest through the fire,
thou shalt not be burned; neither shall
the flame kindle upon thee.
3 For I *am* the LORD thy God, the Holy
One of Ĭs′rā-ĕl, thy Saviour: I gave
Egypt *for* thy ransom, Ethiopia and
Sē′bȧ for thee.
4 Since thou wast precious in my sight,
thou hast been honorable, and I have
loved thee: therefore will I give men for
thee, and people for thy life.
5 Fear not; for I *am* with thee: I will
bring thy seed from the east, and gather
thee from the west:
6 I will say to the north, Give up; and
to the south, Keep not back: bring my
sons from far, and my daughters from
the ends of the earth;
7 *Even* every one that is called by my
name: for I have created him for my
glory, I have formed him; yea, I have
made him.
8 ¶ Bring forth the blind people that
have eyes, and the deaf that have
ears.
9 Let all the nations be gathered together, and let the people be assembled: who among them can declare this,
and show us former things? let them
bring forth their witnesses, that they
may be justified: or let them hear, and
say, *It is* truth.
10 Ye *are* my witnesses, saith the
LORD, and my servant whom I have
chosen; that ye may know and believe
me, and understand that I *am* he: before me there was no God formed,
neither shall there be after me.
11 I, *even* I, *am* the LORD; and beside
me *there is* no saviour.
12 I have declared, and have saved,
and I have showed, when *there was* no
strange *god* among you: therefore ye *are*
my witnesses, saith the LORD, that I *am*
God.
13 Yea, before the day *was* I *am* he;
and *there is* none that can deliver out
of my hand: I will work, and who shall
let it?
14 ¶ Thus saith the LORD, your Redeemer, the Holy One of Ĭs′rā-ĕl; For
your sake I have sent to Babylon, and
have brought down all their nobles, and
the Chăl-dē′ăns, whose cry *is* in the
ships.
15 I *am* the LORD, your Holy One, the
Creator of Ĭs′rā-ĕl, your King.
16 Thus saith the LORD, which maketh
a way in the sea, and a path in the
mighty waters;
17 Which bringeth forth the chariot
and horse, the army and the power; they
shall lie down together, they shall not
rise: they are extinct, they are quenched
as tow.
18 ¶ Remember ye not the former
things, neither consider the things of
old.
19 Behold, I will do a new thing; now
it shall spring forth; shall ye not know
it? I will even make a way in the wilderness, *and* rivers in the desert.
20 The beast of the field shall honor
me, the dragons and the owls: because
I give waters in the wilderness, *and*
rivers in the desert, to give drink to my
people, my chosen.
21 This people have I formed for myself; they shall show forth my praise.
22 ¶ But thou hast not called upon me,
O Jacob; but thou hast been weary of
me, O Ĭs′rā-ĕl.
23 Thou hast not brought me the small
cattle of thy burnt offerings; neither
hast thou honored me with thy sacrifices. I have not caused thee to serve
with an offering, nor wearied thee with
incense.
24 Thou hast bought me no sweet cane
with money, neither hast thou filled me
with the fat of thy sacrifices: but thou
hast made me to serve with thy sins,

thou hast wearied me with thine iniquities.

25 I, *even* I, *am* he that blotteth out thy transgressions for mine own sake, and will not remember thy sins.

26 Put me in remembrance: let us plead together: declare thou, that thou mayest be justified.

27 Thy first father hath sinned, and thy teachers have transgressed against me.

28 Therefore I have profaned the princes of the sanctuary, and have given Jacob to the curse, and Ĭş′rā-ĕl to reproaches.

CHAPTER 44

YET now hear, O Jacob my servant; and Ĭş′rā-ĕl, whom I have chosen:

2 Thus saith the LORD that made thee, and formed thee from the womb, *which* will help thee; Fear not, O Jacob, my servant; and thou, Jĕsh′ū-rŭn, whom I have chosen.

3 For I will pour water upon him that is thirsty, and floods upon the dry ground: I will pour my Spirit upon thy seed, and my blessing upon thine offspring:

4 And they shall spring up *as* among the grass, as willows by the water-courses.

5 One shall say, I *am* the LORD's; and another shall call *himself* by the name of Jacob; and another shall subscribe *with* his hand unto the LORD, and surname *himself* by the name of Ĭş′rā-ĕl.

6 Thus saith the LORD the King of Ĭş′rā-ĕl, and his Redeemer the LORD of hosts; I *am* the first, and I *am* the last; and besides me *there is* no God.

7 And who, as I, shall call, and shall declare it, and set it in order for me, since I appointed the ancient people? and the things that are coming, and shall come, let them show unto them.

8 Fear ye not, neither be afraid: have not I told thee from that time, and have declared *it?* ye *are* even my witnesses. Is there a God besides me? yea, *there is* no God; I know not *any.*

9 ¶ They that make a graven image *are* all of them vanity; and their delectable things shall not profit; and they *are* their own witnesses; they see not, nor know; that they may be ashamed.

10 Who hath formed a god, or molten a graven image *that* is profitable for nothing?

11 Behold, all his fellows shall be ashamed; and the workmen, they *are* of men: let them all be gathered together, let them stand up; *yet* they shall fear, *and* they shall be ashamed together.

12 The smith with the tongs both worketh in the coals, and fashioneth it with hammers, and worketh it with the strength of his arms: yea, he is hungry, and his strength faileth: he drinketh no water, and is faint.

13 The carpenter stretcheth out *his* rule; he marketh it out with a line; he fitteth it with planes, and he marketh it out with the compass, and maketh it after the figure of a man, according to the beauty of a man; that it may remain in the house.

14 He heweth him down cedars, and taketh the cypress and the oak, which he strengtheneth for himself among the trees of the forest: he planteth an ash, and the rain doth nourish *it.*

15 Then shall it be for a man to burn: for he will take thereof, and warm himself; yea, he kindleth *it,* and baketh bread; yea, he maketh a god, and worshippeth *it;* he maketh it a graven image, and falleth down thereto.

16 He burneth part thereof in the fire; with part thereof he eateth flesh; he roasteth roast, and is satisfied: yea, he warmeth *himself,* and saith, Aha, I am warm, I have seen the fire:

17 And the residue thereof he maketh a god, *even* his graven image: he falleth down unto it, and worshippeth *it,* and prayeth unto it, and saith, Deliver me; for thou *art* my god.

18 They have not known nor understood: for he hath shut their eyes, that they cannot see; *and* their hearts, that they cannot understand.

19 And none considereth in his heart, neither *is there* knowledge nor understanding to say, I have burned part of it in the fire; yea, also I have baked bread upon the coals thereof; I have roasted flesh, and eaten *it:* and shall I make the residue thereof an abomination? shall I fall down to the stock of a tree?

20 He feedeth on ashes: a deceived heart hath turned him aside, that he cannot deliver his soul, nor say, *Is there* not a lie in my right hand?

21 ¶ Remember these, O Jacob and Ĭş′rā-ĕl; for thou *art* my servant: I have formed thee; thou *art* my servant: O

Ĭṣ′rā-ĕl, thou shalt not be forgotten of
me.
22 I have blotted out, as a thick cloud,
thy transgressions, and, as a cloud, thy
sins: return unto me; for I have redeemed thee.
23 Sing, O ye heavens; for the LORD
hath done *it:* shout, ye lower parts of
the earth: break forth into singing, ye
mountains, O forest, and every tree
therein: for the LORD hath redeemed
Jacob, and glorified himself in Ĭṣ′rā-ĕl.
24 Thus saith the LORD, thy Redeemer,
and he that formed thee from the
womb, I *am* the LORD that maketh all
things; that stretcheth forth the heavens
alone; that spreadeth abroad the earth
by myself;
25 That frustrateth the tokens of the
liars, and maketh diviners mad; that
turneth wise *men* backward, and maketh their knowledge foolish;
26 That confirmeth the word of his
servant, and performeth the counsel of
his messengers; that saith to Jerusalem,
Thou shalt be inhabited; and to the
cities of Judah, Ye shall be built, and I
will raise up the decayed places thereof:
27 That saith to the deep, Be dry, and
I will dry up thy rivers:
28 That saith of Cyrus, *He is* my shepherd, and shall perform all my pleasure:
even saying to Jerusalem, Thou shalt be
built; and to the temple, Thy foundation
shall be laid.

CHAPTER 45

THUS saith the LORD to his anointed,
to Cyrus, whose right hand I have
holden, to subdue nations before him;
and I will loose the loins of kings, to
open before him the two-leaved gates;
and the gates shall not be shut;
2 I will go before thee, and make the
crooked places straight: I will break in
pieces the gates of brass, and cut in
sunder the bars of iron:
3 And I will give thee the treasures of
darkness, and hidden riches of secret
places, that thou mayest know that I,
the LORD, which call *thee* by thy name,
am the God of Ĭṣ′rā-ĕl.
4 For Jacob my servant's sake, and
Ĭṣ′rā-ĕl mine elect, I have even called
thee by thy name: I have surnamed
thee, though thou hast not known me.
5 ¶ I *am* the LORD, and *there is* none
else, *there is* no God besides me: I
girded thee, though thou hast not
known me;
6 That they may know from the rising
of the sun, and from the west, that *there
is* none besides me. I *am* the LORD, and
there is none else.
7 I form the light, and create darkness:
I make peace, and create evil: I the
LORD do all these *things*.
8 Drop down, ye heavens, from above,
and let the skies pour down righteousness: let the earth open, and let them
bring forth salvation, and let righteousness spring up together; I the LORD
have created it.
9 Woe unto him that striveth with his
Maker! *Let* the potsherd *strive* with
the potsherds of the earth. Shall the
clay say to him that fashioneth it, What
makest thou? or thy work, He hath no
hands?
10 Woe unto him that saith unto *his*
father, What begettest thou? or to the
woman, What hast thou brought forth?
11 Thus saith the LORD, the Holy One
of Ĭṣ′rā-ĕl, and his Maker, Ask me of
things to come concerning my sons, and
concerning the work of my hands command ye me.
12 I have made the earth, and created
man upon it: I, *even* my hands, have
stretched out the heavens, and all their
host have I commanded.
13 I have raised him up in righteousness, and I will direct all his ways: he
shall build my city, and he shall let go
my captives, not for price nor reward,
saith the LORD of hosts.
14 Thus saith the LORD, The labor of
Egypt, and merchandise of Ethiopia and
of the Să-bē′ăns, men of stature, shall
come over unto thee, and they shall be
thine: they shall come after thee; in
chains they shall come over, and they
shall fall down unto thee, they shall
make supplication unto thee, *saying*,
Surely God *is* in thee; and *there is* none
else, *there is* no God.
15 Verily thou *art* a God that hidest
thyself, O God of Ĭṣ′rā-ĕl, the Saviour.
16 They shall be ashamed, and also
confounded, all of them: they shall go
to confusion together *that are* makers of
idols.
17 *But* Ĭṣ′rā-ĕl shall be saved in the
LORD with an everlasting salvation: ye
shall not be ashamed nor confounded
world without end.

18 For thus saith the LORD that created
the heavens; God himself that formed
the earth and made it; he hath established it, he created it not in vain, he
formed it to be inhabited: I *am* the
LORD, and *there is* none else.
19 I have not spoken in secret, in a
dark place of the earth: I said not unto
the seed of Jacob, Seek ye me in vain:
I the LORD speak righteousness, I declare things that are right.
20 ℂ Assemble yourselves and come;
draw near together, ye *that are* escaped
of the nations: they have no knowledge
that set up the wood of their graven
image, and pray unto a god *that* cannot
save.
21 Tell ye, and bring *them* near; yea,
let them take counsel together: who hath
declared this from ancient time? *who*
hath told it from that time? *have* not I
the LORD? and *there is* no God else beside me; a just God and a Saviour; *there*
is none beside me.
22 Look unto me, and be ye saved, all
the ends of the earth: for I *am* God, and
there is none else.
23 I have sworn by myself, the word is
gone out of my mouth *in* righteousness,
and shall not return, That unto me every
knee shall bow, every tongue shall
swear.
24 Surely shall *one* say, In the LORD
have I righteousness and strength: *even*
to him shall *men* come; and all that are
incensed against him shall be ashamed.
25 In the LORD shall all the seed of
Ĭṣ′rā-ĕl be justified, and shall glory.

CHAPTER 46

BEL boweth down, Nē′bō stoopeth;
their idols were upon the beasts,
and upon the cattle: your carriages *were*
heavy laden; *they are* a burden to the
weary *beast*.
2 They stoop, they bow down together;
they could not deliver the burden, but
themselves are gone into captivity.
3 ℂ Hearken unto me, O house of
Jacob, and all the remnant of the house
of Ĭṣ′rā-ĕl, which are borne *by me* from
the belly, which are carried from the
womb:
4 And *even* to *your* old age I *am* he;
and *even* to hoar hairs will I carry *you*:
I have made, and I will bear; even I
will carry, and will deliver *you*.
5 ℂ To whom will ye liken me, and
make *me* equal, and compare me, that
we may be like?
6 They lavish gold out of the bag, and
weigh silver in the balance, *and* hire a
goldsmith; and he maketh it a god: they
fall down, yea, they worship.
7 They bear him upon the shoulder,
they carry him, and set him in his place,
and he standeth; from his place shall he
not remove: yea, *one* shall cry unto him,
yet can he not answer, nor save him out
of his trouble.
8 Remember this, and show yourselves
men: bring *it* again to mind, O ye
transgressors.
9 Remember the former things of old:
for I *am* God, and *there is* none else; *I*
am God, and *there is* none like me,
10 Declaring the end from the beginning, and from ancient times *the things*
that are not *yet* done, saying, My counsel shall stand, and I will do all my
pleasure:
11 Calling a ravenous bird from the
east, the man that executeth my counsel from a far country: yea, I have
spoken *it*, I will also bring it to pass; I
have purposed *it*, I will also do it.
12 ℂ Hearken unto me, ye stout-
hearted, that *are* far from righteousness:
13 I bring near my righteousness; it
shall not be far off, and my salvation
shall not tarry: and I will place salvation
in Zion for Ĭṣ′rā-ĕl my glory.

CHAPTER 47

COME down, and sit in the dust, O
virgin daughter of Babylon, sit on
the ground: *there is* no throne, O daughter of the Chăl-dē′ănṣ: for thou shalt no
more be called tender and delicate.
2 Take the millstones, and grind meal:
uncover thy locks, make bare the leg,
uncover the thigh, pass over the rivers.
3 Thy nakedness shall be uncovered,
yea, thy shame shall be seen: I will take
vengeance, and I will not meet *thee as*
a man.
4 *As for* our Redeemer, the LORD of
hosts *is* his name, the Holy One of
Ĭṣ′rā-ĕl.
5 Sit thou silent, and get thee into
darkness, O daughter of the Chăl-dē′-
ănṣ: for thou shalt no more be called,
The lady of kingdoms.
6 ℂ I was wroth with my people, I
have polluted mine inheritance, and
given them into thine hand: thou didst

show them no mercy; upon the ancient hast thou very heavily laid thy yoke.

7 ¶ And thou saidst, I shall be a lady for ever: *so* that thou didst not lay these *things* to thy heart, neither didst remember the latter end of it.

8 Therefore hear now this, *thou that art* given to pleasures, that dwellest carelessly, that sayest in thine heart, I *am,* and none else besides me; I shall not sit *as* a widow, neither shall I know the loss of children:

9 But these two *things* shall come to thee in a moment in one day, the loss of children, and widowhood: they shall come upon thee in their perfection for the multitude of thy sorceries, *and* for the great abundance of thine enchantments.

10 ¶ For thou hast trusted in thy wickedness: thou hast said, None seeth me. Thy wisdom and thy knowledge, it hath perverted thee; and thou hast said in thine heart, I *am,* and none else besides me.

11 ¶ Therefore shall evil come upon thee; thou shalt not know from whence it riseth: and mischief shall fall upon thee; thou shalt not be able to put it off: and desolation shall come upon thee suddenly, *which* thou shalt not know.

12 Stand now with thine enchantments, and with the multitude of thy sorceries, wherein thou hast labored from thy youth; if so be thou shalt be able to profit, if so be thou mayest prevail.

13 Thou art wearied in the multitude of thy counsels. Let now the astrologers, the stargazers, the monthly prognosticators, stand up, and save thee from *these things* that shall come upon thee.

14 Behold, they shall be as stubble; the fire shall burn them; they shall not deliver themselves from the power of the flame: *there shall* not *be* a coal to warm at, *nor* fire to sit before it.

15 Thus shall they be unto thee with whom thou hast labored, *even* thy merchants, from thy youth: they shall wander every one to his quarter; none shall save thee.

CHAPTER 48

HEAR ye this, O house of Jacob, which are called by the name of Ĭṣ′rā-ĕl, and are come forth out of the waters of Judah, which swear by the name of the LORD, and make mention of the God of Ĭṣ′rā-ĕl, *but* not in truth, nor in righteousness.

2 For they call themselves of the holy city, and stay themselves upon the God of Ĭṣ′rā-ĕl: The LORD of hosts *is* his name.

3 I have declared the former things from the beginning; and they went forth out of my mouth, and I showed them; I did *them* suddenly, and they came to pass.

4 Because I knew that thou *art* obstinate, and thy neck *is* an iron sinew, and thy brow brass;

5 I have even from the beginning declared *it* to thee; before it came to pass I showed *it* thee: lest thou shouldest say, Mine idol hath done them; and my graven image, and my molten image, hath commanded them.

6 Thou hast heard, see all this; and will not ye declare *it?* I have showed thee new things from this time, even hidden things, and thou didst not know them.

7 They are created now, and not from the beginning; even before the day when thou heardest them not; lest thou shouldest say, Behold, I knew them.

8 Yea, thou heardest not; yea, thou knewest not; yea, from that time *that* thine ear was not opened: for I knew that thou wouldest deal very treacherously, and wast called a transgressor from the womb.

9 ¶ For my name's sake will I defer mine anger, and for my praise will I refrain for thee, that I cut thee not off.

10 Behold, I have refined thee, but not with silver; I have chosen thee in the furnace of affliction.

11 For mine own sake, *even* for mine own sake, will I do *it:* for how should *my name* be polluted? and I will not give my glory unto another.

12 ¶ Hearken unto me, O Jacob and Ĭṣ′rā-ĕl, my called; I *am* he; I *am* the first, I also *am* the last.

13 Mine hand also hath laid the foundation of the earth, and my right hand hath spanned the heavens: *when* I call unto them, they stand up together.

14 All ye, assemble yourselves, and hear; which among them hath declared these *things?* The LORD hath loved him: he will do his pleasure on Babylon, and his arm *shall be on* the Chăl-dē′ăns.

15 I, *even* I, have spoken; yea, I have

called him: I have brought him, and he shall make his way prosperous.

16 ¶ Come ye near unto me, hear ye this; I have not spoken in secret from the beginning; from the time that it was, there *am* I: and now the Lord GOD, and his Spirit, hath sent me.

17 Thus saith the LORD, thy Redeemer, the Holy One of Ĭs′rā-ĕl; I *am* the LORD thy God which teacheth thee to profit, which leadeth thee by the way *that* thou shouldest go.

18 O that thou hadst hearkened to my commandments! then had thy peace been as a river, and thy righteousness as the waves of the sea:

19 Thy seed also had been as the sand, and the offspring of thy bowels like the gravel thereof; his name should not have been cut off nor destroyed from before me.

20 ¶ Go ye forth of Babylon, flee ye from the Chăl-dē′ănṣ, with a voice of singing declare ye, tell this, utter it *even* to the end of the earth; say ye, The LORD hath redeemed his servant Jacob.

21 And they thirsted not *when* he led them through the deserts: he caused the waters to flow out of the rock for them: he clave the rock also, and the waters gushed out.

22 *There is* no peace, saith the LORD, unto the wicked.

CHAPTER 49

LISTEN, O isles, unto me; and hearken, ye people, from far; The LORD hath called me from the womb; from the bowels of my mother hath he made mention of my name.

2 And he hath made my mouth like a sharp sword; in the shadow of his hand hath he hid me, and made me a polished shaft; in his quiver hath he hid me;

3 And said unto me, Thou *art* my servant, O Ĭṣ′rā-ĕl, in whom I will be glorified.

4 Then I said, I have labored in vain, I have spent my strength for nought, and in vain: *yet* surely my judgment *is* with the LORD, and my work with my God.

5 ¶ And now, saith the LORD that formed me from the womb *to be* his servant, to bring Jacob again to him, Though Ĭs′rā-ĕl be not gathered, yet shall I be glorious in the eyes of the LORD, and my God shall be my strength.

6 And he said, It is a light thing that thou shouldest be my servant to raise up the tribes of Jacob, and to restore the preserved of Ĭs′rā-ĕl: I will also give thee for a light to the Ḡĕn′tīleṣ, that thou mayest be my salvation unto the end of the earth.

7 Thus saith the LORD, the Redeemer of Ĭs′rā-ĕl, *and* his Holy One, to him whom man despiseth, to him whom the nation abhorreth, to a servant of rulers, Kings shall see and arise, princes also shall worship, because of the LORD that is faithful, *and* the Holy One of Ĭṣ′rā-ĕl, and he shall choose thee.

8 Thus saith the LORD, In an acceptable time have I heard thee, and in a day of salvation have I helped thee: and I will preserve thee, and give thee for a covenant of the people, to establish the earth, to cause to inherit the desolate heritages;

9 That thou mayest say to the prisoners, Go forth; to them that *are* in darkness, Show yourselves. They shall feed in the ways, and their pastures *shall be* in all high places.

10 They shall not hunger nor thirst; neither shall the heat nor sun smite them: for he that hath mercy on them shall lead them, even by the springs of water shall he guide them.

11 And I will make all my mountains a way, and my highways shall be exalted.

12 Behold, these shall come from far: and lo, these from the north and from the west; and these from the land of Sī′nĭm.

13 ¶ Sing, O heavens; and be joyful, O earth; and break forth into singing, O mountains: for the LORD hath comforted his people, and will have mercy upon his afflicted.

14 But Zion said, The LORD hath forsaken me, and my Lord hath forgotten me.

15 Can a woman forget her sucking child, that she should not have compassion on the son of her womb? yea, they may forget, yet will I not forget thee.

16 Behold, I have graven thee upon the palms of *my* hands; thy walls *are* continually before me.

17 Thy children shall make haste; thy destroyers and they that made thee waste shall go forth of thee.

18 ¶ Lift up thine eyes round about,

and behold: all these gather themselves
together, *and* come to thee. *As* I live,
saith the LORD, thou shalt surely clothe
thee with them all, as with an ornament,
and bind them *on thee*, as a bride *doeth*.
19 For thy waste and thy desolate
places, and the land of thy destruction,
shall even now be too narrow by reason
of the inhabitants, and they that swallowed thee up shall be far away.
20 The children which thou shalt have,
after thou hast lost the other, shall say
again in thine ears, The place *is* too
strait for me: give place to me that I may
dwell.
21 Then shalt thou say in thine heart,
Who hath begotten me these, seeing I
have lost my children, and am desolate,
a captive, and removing to and fro? and
who hath brought up these? Behold, I
was left alone; these, where *had* they
been?
22 Thus saith the Lord GOD, Behold,
I will lift up mine hand to the Gĕn′tīleş,
and set up my standard to the people:
and they shall bring thy sons in *their*
arms, and thy daughters shall be carried upon *their* shoulders.
23 And kings shall be thy nursing
fathers, and their queens thy nursing
mothers: they shall bow down to thee
with *their* face toward the earth, and
lick up the dust of thy feet; and thou
shalt know that I *am* the LORD: for they
shall not be ashamed that wait for me.
24 ¶ Shall the prey be taken from the
mighty, or the lawful captive delivered?
25 But thus saith the LORD, Even the
captives of the mighty shall be taken
away, and the prey of the terrible shall
be delivered: for I will contend with him
that contendeth with thee, and I will
save thy children.
26 And I will feed them that oppress
thee with their own flesh; and they shall
be drunken with their own blood, as
with sweet wine: and all flesh shall know
that I the LORD *am* thy Saviour and thy
Redeemer, the Mighty One of Jacob.

CHAPTER 50

THUS saith the LORD, Where *is* the
bill of your mother's divorcement,
whom I have put away? or which of my
creditors *is it* to whom I have sold you?
Behold, for your iniquities have ye sold
yourselves, and for your transgressions
is your mother put away.
2 Wherefore, when I came, *was there*
no man? when I called, *was there* none
to answer? Is my hand shortened at all,
that it cannot redeem? or have I no
power to deliver? behold, at my rebuke
I dry up the sea, I make the rivers a
wilderness: their fish stinketh, because
there is no water, and dieth for thirst.
3 I clothe the heavens with blackness,
and I make sackcloth their covering.
4 The Lord GOD hath given me the
tongue of the learned, that I should
know how to speak a word in season to
him that is weary: he wakeneth morning by morning, he wakeneth mine ear
to hear as the learned.
5 ¶ The Lord GOD hath opened mine
ear, and I was not rebellious, neither
turned away back.
6 I gave my back to the smiters, and
my cheeks to them that plucked off the
hair: I hid not my face from shame and
spitting.
7 ¶ For the Lord GOD will help me;
therefore shall I not be confounded:
therefore have I set my face like a flint,
and I know that I shall not be ashamed.
8 *He is* near that justifieth me; who
will contend with me? let us stand together: who *is* mine adversary? let him
come near to me.
9 Behold, the Lord GOD will help me;
who *is* he *that* shall condemn me? lo,
they all shall wax old as a garment; the
moth shall eat them up.
10 ¶ Who *is* among you that feareth
the LORD, that obeyeth the voice of his
servant, that walketh *in* darkness, and
hath no light? let him trust in the name
of the LORD, and stay upon his God.
11 Behold, all ye that kindle a fire, that
compass *yourselves* about with sparks:
walk in the light of your fire, and in the
sparks *that* ye have kindled. This shall
ye have of mine hand; ye shall lie down
in sorrow.

CHAPTER 51

HEARKEN to me, ye that follow
after righteousness, ye that seek
the LORD: look unto the rock *whence*
ye are hewn, and to the hole of the pit
whence ye are digged.
2 Look unto Abraham your father, and
unto Sarah *that* bare you: for I called
him alone, and blessed him, and increased him.
3 For the LORD shall comfort Zion: he

will comfort all her waste places; and
he will make her wilderness like Ē'den,
and her desert like the garden of the
LORD; joy and gladness shall be found
therein, thanksgiving, and the voice of
melody.
4 ¶ Hearken unto me, my people; and
give ear unto me, O my nation: for a
law shall proceed from me, and I will
make my judgment to rest for a light of
the people.
5 My righteousness *is* near; my salvation is gone forth, and mine arms shall
judge the people; the isles shall wait
upon me, and on mine arm shall they
trust.
6 Lift up your eyes to the heavens, and
look upon the earth beneath: for the
heavens shall vanish away like smoke,
and the earth shall wax old like a garment, and they that dwell therein shall
die in like manner: but my salvation
shall be for ever, and my righteousness
shall not be abolished.
7 ¶ Hearken unto me, ye that know
righteousness, the people in whose
heart *is* my law; fear ye not the reproach
of men, neither be ye afraid of their
revilings.
8 For the moth shall eat them up like a
garment, and the worm shall eat them
like wool: but my righteousness shall be
for ever, and my salvation from generation to generation.
9 ¶ Awake, awake, put on strength, O
arm of the LORD; awake, as in the ancient days, in the generations of old.
Art thou not it that hath cut Rā'hăb, *and*
wounded the dragon?
10 *Art* thou not it which hath dried the
sea, the waters of the great deep; that
hath made the depths of the sea a way
for the ransomed to pass over?
11 Therefore the redeemed of the
LORD shall return, and come with singing unto Zion; and everlasting joy *shall*
be upon their head: they shall obtain
gladness and joy; *and* sorrow and
mourning shall flee away.
12 I, *even* I, *am* he that comforteth
you: who *art* thou, that thou shouldest
be afraid of a man *that* shall die, and of
the son of man *which* shall be made *as*
grass;
13 And forgettest the LORD thy Maker,
that hath stretched forth the heavens,
and laid the foundations of the earth;
and hast feared continually every day
because of the fury of the oppressor, as
if he were ready to destroy? and where
is the fury of the oppressor?
14 The captive exile hasteneth that he
may be loosed, and that he should not
die in the pit, nor that his bread should
fail.
15 But I *am* the LORD thy God, that
divided the sea, whose waves roared:
The LORD of hosts *is* his name.
16 And I have put my words in thy
mouth, and I have covered thee in the
shadow of mine hand, that I may plant
the heavens, and lay the foundations of
the earth, and say unto Zion, Thou *art*
my people.
17 ¶ Awake, awake, stand up, O Jerusalem, which hast drunk at the hand
of the LORD the cup of his fury; thou
hast drunken the dregs of the cup of
trembling, *and* wrung *them* out.
18 *There is* none to guide her among
all the sons *whom* she hath brought
forth; neither *is there any* that taketh
her by the hand of all the sons *that* she
hath brought up.
19 These two *things* are come unto
thee; who shall be sorry for thee? desolation, and destruction, and the famine,
and the sword: by whom shall I comfort
thee?
20 Thy sons have fainted, they lie at
the head of all the streets, as a wild bull
in a net: they are full of the fury of the
LORD, the rebuke of thy God.
21 ¶ Therefore hear now this, thou
afflicted, and drunken, but not with
wine:
22 Thus saith thy Lord the LORD, and
thy God *that* pleadeth the cause of his
people, Behold, I have taken out of
thine hand the cup of trembling, *even*
the dregs of the cup of my fury; thou
shalt no more drink it again:
23 But I will put it into the hand of
them that afflict thee: which have said
to thy soul, Bow down, that we may go
over: and thou hast laid thy body as the
ground, and as the street, to them that
went over.

CHAPTER 52

AWAKE, awake, put on thy strength,
O Zion; put on thy beautiful garments, O Jerusalem, the holy city: for
henceforth there shall no more come into
thee the uncircumcised and the unclean.
2 Shake thyself from the dust; arise,

and sit down, O Jerusalem: loose thyself from the bands of thy neck, O captive daughter of Zion.

3 For thus saith the LORD, Ye have sold yourselves for nought; and ye shall be redeemed without money.

4 For thus saith the Lord GOD, My people went down aforetime into Egypt to sojourn there; and the Assyrian oppressed them without cause.

5 Now therefore, what have I here, saith the LORD, that my people is taken away for nought? they that rule over them make them to howl, saith the LORD; and my name continually every day *is* blasphemed.

6 Therefore my people shall know my name: therefore *they shall know* in that day that I *am* he that doth speak: behold, *it is* I.

7 ¶ How beautiful upon the mountains are the feet of him that bringeth good tidings, that publisheth peace; that bringeth good tidings of good, that publisheth salvation; that saith unto Zion, Thy God reigneth!

8 Thy watchmen shall lift up the voice; with the voice together shall they sing: for they shall see eye to eye, when the LORD shall bring again Zion.

9 ¶ Break forth into joy, sing together, ye waste places of Jerusalem: for the LORD hath comforted his people, he hath redeemed Jerusalem.

10 The LORD hath made bare his holy arm in the eyes of all the nations; and all the ends of the earth shall see the salvation of our God.

11 ¶ Depart ye, depart ye, go ye out from thence, touch no unclean *thing;* go ye out of the midst of her; be ye clean, that bear the vessels of the LORD.

12 For ye shall not go out with haste, nor go by flight: for the LORD will go before you; and the God of Ĭṣ′rā-ĕl *will be* your rearward.

13 ¶ Behold, my servant shall deal prudently, he shall be exalted and extolled, and be very high.

14 As many were astonished at thee; his visage was so marred more than any man, and his form more than the sons of men:

15 So shall he sprinkle many nations; the kings shall shut their mouths at him: for *that* which had not been told them shall they see; and *that* which they had not heard shall they consider.

CHAPTER 53

WHO hath believed our report? and to whom is the arm of the LORD revealed?

2 For he shall grow up before him as a tender plant, and as a root out of a dry ground: he hath no form nor comeliness; and when we shall see him, *there is* no beauty that we should desire him.

3 He is despised and rejected of men; a man of sorrows, and acquainted with grief: and we hid as it were *our* faces from him; he was despised, and we esteemed him not.

4 ¶ Surely he hath borne our griefs, and carried our sorrows: yet we did esteem him stricken, smitten of God, and afflicted.

5 But he *was* wounded for our transgressions, *he was* bruised for our iniquities: the chastisement of our peace *was* upon him; and with his stripes we are healed.

6 All we like sheep have gone astray; we have turned every one to his own way; and the LORD hath laid on him the iniquity of us all.

7 He was oppressed, and he was afflicted, yet he opened not his mouth: he is brought as a lamb to the slaughter, and as a sheep before her shearers is dumb, so he openeth not his mouth.

8 He was taken from prison and from judgment: and who shall declare his generation? for he was cut off out of the land of the living: for the transgression of my people was he stricken.

9 And he made his grave with the wicked, and with the rich in his death; because he had done no violence, neither *was any* deceit in his mouth.

10 ¶ Yet it pleased the LORD to bruise him; he hath put *him* to grief: when thou shalt make his soul an offering for sin, he shall see *his* seed, he shall prolong *his* days, and the pleasure of the LORD shall prosper in his hand.

11 He shall see of the travail of his soul, *and* shall be satisfied: by his knowledge shall my righteous servant justify many; for he shall bear their iniquities.

12 Therefore will I divide him *a portion* with the great, and he shall divide the spoil with the strong; because he hath poured out his soul unto death: and he was numbered with the transgressors;

and he bare the sin of many, and made intercession for the transgressors.

CHAPTER 54

SING, O barren, thou *that* didst not bear; break forth into singing, and cry aloud, thou *that* didst not travail with child: for more *are* the children of the desolate than the children of the married wife, saith the LORD.

2 Enlarge the place of thy tent, and let them stretch forth the curtains of thine habitations: spare not, lengthen thy cords, and strengthen thy stakes;

3 For thou shalt break forth on the right hand and on the left; and thy seed shall inherit the Gĕn′tīleṣ, and make the desolate cities to be inhabited.

4 Fear not; for thou shalt not be ashamed: neither be thou confounded; for thou shalt not be put to shame: for thou shalt forget the shame of thy youth, and shalt not remember the reproach of thy widowhood any more.

5 For thy Maker *is* thine husband; The LORD of hosts *is* his name; and thy Redeemer the Holy One of Ĭs′rā-ĕl; The God of the whole earth shall he be called.

6 For the LORD hath called thee as a woman forsaken and grieved in spirit, and a wife of youth, when thou wast refused, saith thy God.

7 For a small moment have I forsaken thee; but with great mercies will I gather thee.

8 In a little wrath I hid my face from thee for a moment; but with everlasting kindness will I have mercy on thee, saith the LORD thy Redeemer.

9 For this *is as* the waters of Noah unto me: for *as* I have sworn that the waters of Noah should no more go over the earth; so have I sworn that I would not be wroth with thee, nor rebuke thee.

10 For the mountains shall depart, and the hills be removed; but my kindness shall not depart from thee, neither shall the covenant of my peace be removed, saith the LORD that hath mercy on thee.

11 ¶ O thou afflicted, tossed with tempest, *and* not comforted, behold, I will lay thy stones with fair colors, and lay thy foundations with sapphires.

12 And I will make thy windows of agates, and thy gates of carbuncles, and all thy borders of pleasant stones.

13 And all thy children *shall be* taught of the LORD; and great *shall be* the peace of thy children.

14 In righteousness shalt thou be established: thou shalt be far from oppression; for thou shalt not fear: and from terror; for it shall not come near thee.

15 Behold, they shall surely gather together, *but* not by me: whosoever shall gather together against thee shall fall for thy sake.

16 Behold, I have created the smith that bloweth the coals in the fire, and that bringeth forth an instrument for his work; and I have created the waster to destroy.

17 ¶ No weapon that is formed against thee shall prosper; and every tongue *that* shall rise against thee in judgment thou shalt condemn. This *is* the heritage of the servants of the LORD, and their righteousness *is* of me, saith the LORD.

CHAPTER 55

HO, every one that thirsteth, come ye to the waters, and he that hath no money; come ye, buy, and eat; yea, come, buy wine and milk without money and without price.

2 Wherefore do ye spend money for *that which is* not bread? and your labor for *that which* satisfieth not? hearken diligently unto me, and eat ye *that which is* good, and let your soul delight itself in fatness.

3 Incline your ear, and come unto me: hear, and your soul shall live; and I will make an everlasting covenant with you, *even* the sure mercies of David.

4 Behold, I have given him *for* a witness to the people, a leader and commander to the people.

5 Behold, thou shalt call a nation *that* thou knowest not, and nations *that* knew not thee shall run unto thee, because of the LORD thy God, and for the Holy One of Ĭṣ′rā-ĕl; for he hath glorified thee.

6 ¶ Seek ye the LORD while he may be found, call ye upon him while he is near:

7 Let the wicked forsake his way, and the unrighteous man his thoughts: and let him return unto the LORD, and he will have mercy upon him; and to our God, for he will abundantly pardon.

8 ¶ For my thoughts *are* not your
thoughts, neither *are* your ways my
ways, saith the LORD.
9 For *as* the heavens are higher than
the earth, so are my ways higher than
your ways, and my thoughts than your
thoughts.
10 For as the rain cometh down, and
the snow from heaven, and returneth
not thither, but watereth the earth, and
maketh it bring forth and bud, that
it may give seed to the sower, and
bread to the eater:
11 So shall my word be that goeth
forth out of my mouth: it shall not
return unto me void, but it shall accomplish that which I please, and it
shall prosper *in the thing* whereto I
sent it.
12 For ye shall go out with joy, and be
led forth with peace: the mountains
and the hills shall break forth before
you into singing, and all the trees of the
field shall clap *their* hands.
13 Instead of the thorn shall come up
the fir tree, and instead of the brier
shall come up the myrtle tree: and it
shall be to the LORD for a name, for
an everlasting sign *that* shall not be
cut off.

CHAPTER 56

THUS saith the LORD, Keep ye
judgment, and do justice: for my
salvation *is* near to come, and my righteousness to be revealed.
2 Blessed *is* the man *that* doeth this,
and the son of man *that* layeth hold on
it; that keepeth the sabbath from polluting it, and keepeth his hand from
doing any evil.
3 ¶ Neither let the son of the stranger,
that hath joined himself to the LORD,
speak, saying, The LORD hath utterly
separated me from his people: neither
let the eunuch say, Behold, I *am* a dry
tree.
4 For thus saith the LORD unto the
eunuchs that keep my sabbaths, and
choose *the things* that please me, and
take hold of my covenant;
5 Even unto them will I give in mine
house and within my walls a place and
a name better than of sons and of
daughters: I will give them an everlasting name, that shall not be cut off.
6 Also the sons of the stranger, that
join themselves to the LORD, to serve
him, and to love the name of the LORD,
to be his servants, every one that keepeth the sabbath from polluting it, and
taketh hold of my covenant;
7 Even them will I bring to my holy
mountain, and make them joyful in my
house of prayer: their burnt offerings
and their sacrifices *shall be* accepted
upon mine altar; for mine house shall
be called a house of prayer for all
people.
8 The Lord GOD which gathereth the
outcasts of Ĭṣ′rā-ĕl saith, Yet will I
gather *others* to him, besides those that
are gathered unto him.
9 ¶ All ye beasts of the field, come to
devour, *yea,* all ye beasts in the forest.
10 His watchmen *are* blind: they are
all ignorant, they *are* all dumb dogs,
they cannot bark; sleeping, lying down,
loving to slumber.
11 Yea, *they are* greedy dogs *which*
can never have enough, and they *are*
shepherds *that* cannot understand: they
all look to their own way, every one for
his gain, from his quarter.
12 Come ye, *say they,* I will fetch wine,
and we will fill ourselves with strong
drink; and to-morrow shall be as this
day, *and* much more abundant.

CHAPTER 57

THE righteous perisheth, and no
man layeth *it* to heart: and merciful
men *are* taken away, none considering
that the righteous is taken away from
the evil *to come.*
2 He shall enter into peace: they shall
rest in their beds, *each one* walking *in*
his uprightness.
3 ¶ But draw near hither, ye sons of
the sorceress, the seed of the adulterer
and the whore.
4 Against whom do ye sport yourselves? against whom make ye a wide
mouth, *and* draw out the tongue? *are* ye
not children of transgression, a seed of
falsehood,
5 Inflaming yourselves with idols under
every green tree, slaying the children
in the valleys under the clefts of the
rocks?
6 Among the smooth *stones* of the
stream *is* thy portion; they, they *are* thy
lot: even to them hast thou poured a
drink offering, thou hast offered a meat
offering. Should I receive comfort in
these?

7 Upon a lofty and high mountain hast
thou set thy bed: even thither wentest
thou up to offer sacrifice.
8 Behind the doors also and the posts
hast thou set up thy remembrance: for
thou hast discovered *thyself to another*
than me, and art gone up; thou hast
enlarged thy bed, and made thee *a*
covenant with them; thou lovedst their
bed where thou sawest *it*.
9 And thou wentest to the king with
ointment, and didst increase thy per-
fumes, and didst send thy messengers
far off, and didst debase *thyself even*
unto hell.
10 Thou art wearied in the greatness
of thy way; *yet* saidst thou not, There
is no hope: thou hast found the life of
thine hand; therefore thou wast not
grieved.
11 And of whom hast thou been afraid
or feared, that thou hast lied, and hast
not remembered me, nor laid *it* to thy
heart? have not I held my peace even
of old, and thou fearest me not?
12 I will declare thy righteousness,
and thy works; for they shall not profit
thee.
13 ¶ When thou criest, let thy companies deliver thee; but the wind shall
carry them all away; vanity shall take
them: but he that putteth his trust in
me shall possess the land, and shall
inherit my holy mountain;
14 And shall say, Cast ye up, cast ye
up, prepare the way, take up the
stumblingblock out of the way of my
people.
15 For thus saith the high and lofty
One that inhabiteth eternity, whose
name *is* Holy; I dwell in the high and
holy *place*, with him also *that is* of a
contrite and humble spirit, to revive
the spirit of the humble, and to revive
the heart of the contrite ones.
16 For I will not contend for ever,
neither will I be always wroth: for the
spirit should fail before me, and the
souls *which* I have made.
17 For the iniquity of his covetousness
was I wroth, and smote him: I hid me,
and was wroth, and he went on fro-
wardly in the way of his heart.
18 I have seen his ways, and will heal
him: I will lead him also, and restore
comforts unto him and to his mourners.
19 I create the fruit of the lips; Peace,
peace to *him that is* far off, and to *him*
that is near, saith the LORD; and I will
heal him.
20 But the wicked *are* like the troubled
sea, when it cannot rest, whose waters
cast up mire and dirt.
21 *There is* no peace, saith my God,
to the wicked.

CHAPTER 58

CRY aloud, spare not, lift up thy
voice like a trumpet, and show my
people their transgression, and the house
of Jacob their sins.
2 Yet they seek me daily, and delight
to know my ways, as a nation that did
righteousness, and forsook not the ordinance of their God: they ask of me
the ordinances of justice; they take
delight in approaching to God.
3 ¶ Wherefore have we fasted, *say*
they, and thou seest not? *wherefore*
have we afflicted our soul, and thou
takest no knowledge? Behold, in the
day of your fast ye find pleasure, and
exact all your labors.
4 Behold, ye fast for strife and debate,
and to smite with the fist of wickedness:
ye shall not fast as *ye do this* day, to
make your voice to be heard on high.
5 Is it such a fast that I have chosen?
a day for a man to afflict his soul? *is it*
to bow down his head as a bulrush, and
to spread sackcloth and ashes *under*
him? wilt thou call this a fast, and an
acceptable day to the LORD?
6 *Is* not this the fast that I have chosen?
to loose the bands of wickedness, to
undo the heavy burdens, and to let the
oppressed go free, and that ye break
every yoke?
7 *Is it* not to deal thy bread to the
hungry, and that thou bring the poor
that are cast out to thy house? when
thou seest the naked, that thou cover
him; and that thou hide not thyself
from thine own flesh?
8 ¶ Then shall thy light break forth
as the morning, and thine health shall
spring forth speedily: and thy righteousness shall go before thee; the glory of
the LORD shall be thy rearward.
9 Then shalt thou call, and the LORD
shall answer; thou shalt cry, and he
shall say, Here I *am*. If thou take away
from the midst of thee the yoke, the
putting forth of the finger, and speaking
vanity;
10 And *if* thou draw out thy soul to the

hungry, and satisfy the afflicted soul;
then shall thy light rise in obscurity,
and thy darkness *be* as the noonday:
11 And the LORD shall guide thee continually, and satisfy thy soul in drought,
and make fat thy bones: and thou shalt
be like a watered garden, and like a
spring of water, whose waters fail not.
12 And *they that shall be* of thee shall
build the old waste places: thou shalt
raise up the foundations of many generations; and thou shalt be called, The
repairer of the breach, The restorer of
paths to dwell in.
13 ¶ If thou turn away thy foot from
the sabbath, *from* doing thy pleasure on
my holy day; and call the sabbath a
delight, the holy of the LORD, honorable; and shalt honor him, not doing
thine own ways, nor finding thine own
pleasure, nor speaking *thine own* words:
14 Then shalt thou delight thyself in
the LORD; and I will cause thee to ride
upon the high places of the earth, and
feed thee with the heritage of Jacob
thy father: for the mouth of the LORD
hath spoken *it*.

CHAPTER 59

BEHOLD, the LORD'S hand is not
shortened, that it cannot save;
neither his ear heavy, that it cannot hear:
2 But your iniquities have separated
between you and your God, and your
sins have hid *his* face from you, that he
will not hear.
3 For your hands are defiled with
blood, and your fingers with iniquity;
your lips have spoken lies, your tongue
hath muttered perverseness.
4 None calleth for justice, nor *any*
pleadeth for truth: they trust in vanity,
and speak lies; they conceive mischief,
and bring forth iniquity.
5 They hatch cockatrice' eggs, and
weave the spider's web: he that eateth
of their eggs dieth, and that which is
crushed breaketh out into a viper.
6 Their webs shall not become garments, neither shall they cover themselves with their works: their works *are*
works of iniquity, and the act of violence
is in their hands.
7 Their feet run to evil, and they make
haste to shed innocent blood: their
thoughts *are* thoughts of iniquity; wasting and destruction *are* in their paths.
8 The way of peace they know not; and
there is no judgment in their goings:
they have made them crooked paths;
whosoever goeth therein shall not know
peace.
9 ¶ Therefore is judgment far from
us, neither doth justice overtake us: we
wait for light, but behold obscurity; for
brightness, *but* we walk in darkness.
10 We grope for the wall like the blind,
and we grope as if *we had* no eyes: we
stumble at noonday as in the night; *we
are* in desolate places as dead *men*.
11 We roar all like bears, and mourn
sore like doves: we look for judgment,
but *there is* none; for salvation, *but* it
is far off from us.
12 For our transgressions are multiplied before thee, and our sins testify
against us: for our transgressions *are*
with us; and *as for* our iniquities, we
know them;
13 In transgressing and lying against
the LORD, and departing away from our
God, speaking oppression and revolt,
conceiving and uttering from the heart
words of falsehood.
14 And judgment is turned away backward, and justice standeth afar off: for
truth is fallen in the street, and equity
cannot enter.
15 Yea, truth faileth; and he *that*
departeth from evil maketh himself a
prey: and the LORD saw *it*, and it displeased him that *there was* no judgment.
16 ¶ And he saw that *there was* no
man, and wondered that *there was* no
intercessor: therefore his arm brought
salvation unto him; and his righteousness, it sustained him.
17 For he put on righteousness as a
breastplate, and a helmet of salvation
upon his head; and he put on the garments of vengeance *for* clothing, and
was clad with zeal as a cloak.
18 According to *their* deeds, accord-
ingly he will repay, fury to his adversaries, recompense to his enemies; to
the islands he will repay recompense.
19 Sc shall they fear the name of the
LORD from the west, and his glory from
the rising of the sun. When the enemy
shall come in like a flood, the Spirit of
the LORD shall lift up a standard against
him.
20 ¶ And the Redeemer shall come to
Zion, and unto them that turn from
transgression in Jacob, saith the LORD.
21 As for me, this *is* my covenant with

them, saith the LORD; My Spirit that *is* upon thee, and my words which I have put in thy mouth, shall not depart out of thy mouth, nor out of the mouth of thy seed, nor out of the mouth of thy seed's seed, saith the LORD, from henceforth and for ever.

CHAPTER 60

ARISE, shine; for thy light is come, and the glory of the LORD is risen upon thee.

2 For, behold, the darkness shall cover the earth, and gross darkness the people: but the LORD shall arise upon thee, and his glory shall be seen upon thee.

3 And the Ġĕn′tīleṣ shall come to thy light, and kings to the brightness of thy rising.

4 Lift up thine eyes round about, and see: all they gather themselves together, they come to thee: thy sons shall come from far, and thy daughters shall be nursed at *thy* side.

5 Then thou shalt see, and flow together, and thine heart shall fear, and be enlarged; because the abundance of the sea shall be converted unto thee, the forces of the Ġĕn′tīleṣ shall come unto thee.

6 The multitude of camels shall cover thee, the dromedaries of Mĭd′ĭ-ăn and Ē′phȧh; all they from Shē′bȧ shall come: they shall bring gold and incense; and they shall show forth the praises of the LORD.

7 All the flocks of Kē′dȧr shall be gathered together unto thee, the rams of Nē-bā′ịŏth shall minister unto thee: they shall come up with acceptance on mine altar, and I will glorify the house of my glory.

8 Who *are* these *that* fly as a cloud, and as the doves to their windows?

9 Surely the isles shall wait for me, and the ships of Tär′shĭsh first, to bring thy sons from far, their silver and their gold with them, unto the name of the LORD thy God, and to the Holy One of Ĭs′rā-ĕl, because he hath glorified thee.

10 And the sons of strangers shall build up thy walls, and their kings shall minister unto thee: for in my wrath I smote thee, but in my favor have I had mercy on thee.

11 Therefore thy gates shall be open continually; they shall not be shut day nor night; that *men* may bring unto thee the forces of the Ġĕn′tīleṣ, and *that* their kings *may be* brought.

12 For the nation and kingdom that will not serve thee shall perish; yea, *those* nations shall be utterly wasted.

13 The glory of Lebanon shall come unto thee, the fir tree, the pine tree, and the box together, to beautify the place of my sanctuary; and I will make the place of my feet glorious.

14 The sons also of them that afflicted thee shall come bending unto thee; and all they that despised thee shall bow themselves down at the soles of thy feet; and they shall call thee, The city of the LORD, The Zion of the Holy One of Ĭs′rā-ĕl.

15 Whereas thou hast been forsaken and hated, so that no man went through *thee*, I will make thee an eternal excellency, a joy of many generations.

16 Thou shalt also suck the milk of the Ġĕn′tīleṣ, and shalt suck the breast of kings: and thou shalt know that I the LORD *am* thy Saviour and thy Redeemer, the Mighty One of Jacob.

17 For brass I will bring gold, and for iron I will bring silver, and for wood brass, and for stones iron: I will also make thy officers peace, and thine exactors righteousness.

18 Violence shall no more be heard in thy land, wasting nor destruction within thy borders; but thou shalt call thy walls Salvation, and thy gates Praise.

19 The sun shall be no more thy light by day; neither for brightness shall the moon give light unto thee: but the LORD shall be unto thee an everlasting light, and thy God thy glory.

20 Thy sun shall no more go down; neither shall thy moon withdraw itself: for the LORD shall be thine everlasting light, and the days of thy mourning shall be ended.

21 Thy people also *shall be* all righteous: they shall inherit the land for ever, the branch of my planting, the work of my hands, that I may be glorified.

22 A little one shall become a thousand, and a small one a strong nation: I the LORD will hasten it in his time.

CHAPTER 61

THE Spirit of the Lord GOD *is* upon me; because the LORD hath anointed me to preach good tidings unto the

meek; he hath sent me to bind up the
broken-hearted, to proclaim liberty to
the captives, and the opening of the
prison to *them that are* bound;
2 To proclaim the acceptable year of
the LORD, and the day of vengeance of
our God; to comfort all that mourn;
3 To appoint unto them that mourn in
Zion, to give unto them beauty for
ashes, the oil of joy for mourning, the
garment of praise for the spirit of
heaviness; that they might be called
Trees of righteousness, The planting
of the LORD, that he might be glorified.
4 ¶ And they shall build the old
wastes, they shall raise up the former
desolations, and they shall repair the
waste cities, the desolations of many
generations.
5 And strangers shall stand and feed
your flocks, and the sons of the alien
shall be your plowmen and your vinedressers.
6 But ye shall be named The priests
of the LORD: *men* shall call you The
ministers of our God: ye shall eat the
riches of the Gĕn′tīles, and in their
glory shall ye boast yourselves.
7 ¶ For your shame *ye shall have*
double; and *for* confusion they shall
rejoice in their portion: therefore in
their land they shall possess the double:
everlasting joy shall be unto them.
8 For I the LORD love judgment, I
hate robbery for burnt offering; and
I will direct their work in truth, and I
will make an everlasting covenant with
them.
9 And their seed shall be known among
the Gĕn′tīles, and their offspring among
the people: all that see them shall
acknowledge them, that they *are* the
seed *which* the LORD hath blessed.
10 I will greatly rejoice in the LORD,
my soul shall be joyful in my God; for
he hath clothed me with the garments
of salvation, he hath covered me with
the robe of righteousness, as a bridegroom decketh *himself* with ornaments,
and as a bride adorneth *herself* with her
jewels.
11 For as the earth bringeth forth her
bud, and as the garden causeth the
things that are sown in it to spring
forth; so the Lord GOD will cause
righteousness and praise to spring
forth before all the nations.

CHAPTER 62

FOR Zion's sake will I not hold
my peace, and for Jerusalem's sake
I will not rest, until the righteousness thereof go forth as brightness, and
the salvation thereof as a lamp *that*
burneth.
2 And the Gĕn′tīles shall see thy
righteousness, and all kings thy glory:
and thou shalt be called by a new
name, which the mouth of the LORD
shall name.
3 Thou shalt also be a crown of glory
in the hand of the LORD, and a royal
diadem in the hand of thy God.
4 Thou shalt no more be termed Forsaken; neither shall thy land any more
be termed Desolate: but thou shalt be
called Hĕph′zĭ-bah, and thy land Beu-
lah: for the LORD delighteth in thee,
and thy land shall be married.
5 ¶ For *as* a young man marrieth a
virgin, *so* shall thy sons marry thee:
and *as* the bridegroom rejoiceth over the
bride, *so* shall thy God rejoice over thee.
6 I have set watchmen upon thy walls,
O Jerusalem, *which* shall never hold
their peace day nor night: ye that
make mention of the LORD, keep not
silence,
7 And give him no rest, till he establish, and till he make Jerusalem a
praise in the earth.
8 The LORD hath sworn by his right
hand, and by the arm of his strength,
Surely I will no more give thy corn *to be*
meat for thine enemies; and the sons
of the stranger shall not drink thy wine,
for the which thou hast labored:
9 But they that have gathered it shall
eat it, and praise the LORD; and they
that have brought it together shall
drink it in the courts of my holiness.
10 ¶ Go through, go through the
gates; prepare ye the way of the people;
cast up, cast up the highway; gather
out the stones; lift up a standard for
the people.
11 Behold, the LORD hath proclaimed
unto the end of the world, Say ye to
the daughter of Zion, Behold, thy salvation cometh; behold, his reward *is*
with him, and his work before him.
12 And they shall call them, The holy
people, The redeemed of the LORD:
and thou shalt be called, Sought out, A
city not forsaken.

CHAPTER 63

WHO *is* this that cometh from Ē'dŏm, with dyed garments from Bŏz'râh? this *that is* glorious in his apparel, traveling in the greatness of his strength? I that speak in righteousness, mighty to save.

2 Wherefore *art thou* red in thine apparel, and thy garments like him that treadeth in the winevat?

3 I have trodden the winepress alone; and of the people *there was* none with me: for I will tread them in mine anger, and trample them in my fury; and their blood shall be sprinkled upon my garments, and I will stain all my raiment.

4 For the day of vengeance *is* in mine heart, and the year of my redeemed is come.

5 And I looked, and *there was* none to help; and I wondered that *there was* none to uphold: therefore mine own arm brought salvation unto me; and my fury, it upheld me.

6 And I will tread down the people in mine anger, and make them drunk in my fury, and I will bring down their strength to the earth.

7 ¶ I will mention the loving-kindnesses of the LORD, *and* the praises of the LORD, according to all that the LORD hath bestowed on us, and the great goodness toward the house of Ĭṣ'rā-ĕl, which he hath bestowed on them according to his mercies, and according to the multitude of his loving-kindnesses.

8 For he said, Surely they *are* my people, children *that* will not lie: so he was their Saviour.

9 In all their affliction he was afflicted, and the Angel of his presence saved them: in his love and in his pity he redeemed them; and he bare them, and carried them all the days of old.

10 ¶ But they rebelled, and vexed his Holy Spirit: therefore he was turned to be their enemy, *and* he fought against them.

11 Then he remembered the days of old, Moses, *and* his people, *saying*, Where *is* he that brought them up out of the sea with the shepherd of his flock? where *is* he that put his Holy Spirit within him?

12 That led *them* by the right hand of Moses with his glorious arm, dividing the water before them, to make himself an everlasting name?

13 That led them through the deep, as a horse in the wilderness, *that* they should not stumble?

14 As a beast goeth down into the valley, the Spirit of the LORD caused him to rest; so didst thou lead thy people, to make thyself a glorious name.

15 ¶ Look down from heaven, and behold from the habitation of thy holiness and of thy glory: where *is* thy zeal and thy strength, the sounding of thy bowels and of thy mercies toward me? are they restrained?

16 Doubtless thou *art* our Father, though Abraham be ignorant of us, and Ĭṣ'rā-ĕl acknowledge us not: thou, O LORD, *art* our Father, our Redeemer; thy name *is* from everlasting.

17 ¶ O LORD, why hast thou made us to err from thy ways, *and* hardened our heart from thy fear? Return for thy servants' sake, the tribes of thine inheritance.

18 The people of thy holiness have possessed *it* but a little while: our adversaries have trodden down thy sanctuary.

19 We are *thine:* thou never barest rule over them; they were not called by thy name.

CHAPTER 64

OH that thou wouldest rend the heavens, that thou wouldest come down, that the mountains might flow down at thy presence,

2 As *when* the melting fire burneth, the fire causeth the waters to boil, to make thy name known to thine adversaries, *that* the nations may tremble at thy presence!

3 When thou didst terrible things *which* we looked not for, thou camest down, the mountains flowed down at thy presence.

4 For since the beginning of the world *men* have not heard, nor perceived by the ear, neither hath the eye seen, O God, besides thee, *what* he hath prepared for him that waiteth for him.

5 Thou meetest him that rejoiceth and worketh righteousness, *those that* remember thee in thy ways: behold, thou art wroth; for we have sinned: in those is continuance, and we shall be saved.

6 But we are all as an unclean *thing*, and all our righteousnesses *are* as filthy rags; and we all do fade as a leaf; and

our iniquities, like the wind, have taken
us away.
7 And *there is* none that calleth upon
thy name, that stirreth up himself to
take hold of thee: for thou hast hid thy
face from us, and hast consumed us,
because of our iniquities.
8 But now, O LORD, thou *art* our
Father; we *are* the clay, and thou our
potter; and we all *are* the work of thy
hand.
9 ¶ Be not wroth very sore, O LORD,
neither remember iniquity for ever: behold, see, we beseech thee, we *are* all
thy people.
10 Thy holy cities are a wilderness,
Zion is a wilderness, Jerusalem a
desolation.
11 Our holy and our beautiful house,
where our fathers praised thee, is
burned up with fire: and all our pleasant
things are laid waste.
12 Wilt thou refrain thyself for these
things, O LORD? wilt thou hold thy
peace, and afflict us very sore?

CHAPTER 65

I AM sought of *them that* asked not
for me; I am found of *them that*
sought me not: I said, Behold me,
behold me, unto a nation *that* was not
called by my name.
2 I have spread out my hands all the
day unto a rebellious people, which
walketh in a way *that was* not good,
after their own thoughts;
3 A people that provoketh me to anger
continually to my face; that sacrificeth
in gardens, and burneth incense upon
altars of brick;
4 Which remain among the graves,
and lodge in the monuments; which eat
swine's flesh, and broth of abominable
things is in their vessels;
5 Which say, Stand by thyself, come
not near to me; for I am holier than
thou. These *are* a smoke in my nose,
a fire that burneth all the day.
6 Behold, *it is* written before me: I
will not keep silence, but will recompense, even recompense into their
bosom,
7 Your iniquities, and the iniquities of
your fathers together, saith the LORD,
which have burned incense upon the
mountains, and blasphemed me upon
the hills: therefore will I measure their
former work into their bosom.
8 ¶ Thus saith the LORD, As the new
wine is found in the cluster, and *one*
saith, Destroy it not; for a blessing *is*
in it: so will I do for my servants' sake,
that I may not destroy them all.
9 And I will bring forth a seed out of
Jacob, and out of Judah an inheritor
of my mountains: and mine elect shall
inherit it, and my servants shall dwell
there.
10 And Shăr'ŏn shall be a fold of
flocks, and the valley of Ā'chŏr a place
for the herds to lie down in, for my people
that have sought me.
11 ¶ But ye *are* they that forsake the
LORD, that forget my holy mountain,
that prepare a table for that troop, and
that furnish the drink offering unto that
number.
12 Therefore will I number you to the
sword, and ye shall all bow down to the
slaughter: because when I called, ye
did not answer; when I spake, ye did
not hear; but did evil before mine eyes,
and did choose *that* wherein I delighted
not.
13 Therefore thus saith the Lord GOD,
Behold, my servants shall eat, but ye
shall be hungry: behold, my servants
shall drink, but ye shall be thirsty: behold, my servants shall rejoice, but ye
shall be ashamed:
14 Behold, my servants shall sing for
joy of heart, but ye shall cry for sorrow
of heart, and shall howl for vexation of
spirit.
15 And ye shall leave your name for a
curse unto my chosen: for the Lord GOD
shall slay thee, and call his servants by
another name:
16 That he who blesseth himself in the
earth shall bless himself in the God of
truth; and he that sweareth in the earth
shall swear by the God of truth; because
the former troubles are forgotten, and
because they are hid from mine eyes.
17 ¶ For, behold, I create new heavens
and a new earth: and the former shall
not be remembered, nor come into
mind.
18 But be ye glad and rejoice for ever
in that which I create: for, behold, I
create Jerusalem a rejoicing, and her
people a joy.
19 And I will rejoice in Jerusalem, and
joy in my people: and the voice of
weeping shall be no more heard in her,
nor the voice of crying.

20 There shall be no more thence an infant of days, nor an old man that hath not filled his days: for the child shall die a hundred years old; but the sinner *being* a hundred years old shall be accursed.

21 And they shall build houses, and inhabit *them;* and they shall plant vineyards, and eat the fruit of them.

22 They shall not build, and another inhabit; they shall not plant, and another eat: for as the days of a tree *are* the days of my people, and mine elect shall long enjoy the work of their hands.

23 They shall not labor in vain, nor bring forth for trouble; for they *are* the seed of the blessed of the LORD, and their offspring with them.

24 And it shall come to pass, that before they call, I will answer; and while they are yet speaking, I will hear.

25 The wolf and the lamb shall feed together, and the lion shall eat straw like the bullock: and dust *shall be* the serpent's meat. They shall not hurt nor destroy in all my holy mountain, saith the LORD.

CHAPTER 66

THUS saith the LORD, The heaven *is* my throne, and the earth *is* my footstool: where *is* the house that ye build unto me? and where *is* the place of my rest?

2 For all those *things* hath mine hand made, and all those *things* have been, saith the LORD: but to this *man* will I look, *even* to *him that is* poor and of a contrite spirit, and trembleth at my word.

3 He that killeth an ox *is as if* he slew a man; he that sacrificeth a lamb, *as if* he cut off a dog's neck; he that offereth an oblation, *as if he offered* swine's blood; he that burneth incense, *as if* he blessed an idol. Yea, they have chosen their own ways, and their soul delighteth in their abominations.

4 I also will choose their delusions, and will bring their fears upon them; because when I called, none did answer; when I spake, they did not hear: but they did evil before mine eyes, and chose *that* in which I delighted not.

5 ¶ Hear the word of the LORD, ye that tremble at his word; Your brethren that hated you, that cast you out for my name's sake, said, Let the LORD be glorified: but he shall appear to your joy, and they shall be ashamed.

6 A voice of noise from the city, a voice from the temple, a voice of the LORD that rendereth recompense to his enemies.

7 Before she travailed, she brought forth; before her pain came, she was delivered of a man child.

8 Who hath heard such a thing? who hath seen such things? Shall the earth be made to bring forth in one day? *or* shall a nation be born at once? for as soon as Zion travailed, she brought forth her children.

9 Shall I bring to the birth, and not cause to bring forth? saith the LORD: shall I cause to bring forth, and shut *the womb?* saith thy God.

10 Rejoice ye with Jerusalem, and be glad with her, all ye that love her: rejoice for joy with her, all ye that mourn for her:

11 That ye may suck, and be satisfied with the breasts of her consolations; that ye may milk out, and be delighted with the abundance of her glory.

12 For thus saith the LORD, Behold, I will extend peace to her like a river, and the glory of the Gĕn′tīles like a flowing stream: then shall ye suck, ye shall be borne upon *her* sides, and be dandled upon *her* knees.

13 As one whom his mother comforteth, so will I comfort you; and ye shall be comforted in Jerusalem.

14 And when ye see *this,* your heart shall rejoice, and your bones shall flourish like an herb: and the hand of the LORD shall be known toward his servants, and *his* indignation toward his enemies.

15 For, behold, the LORD will come with fire, and with his chariots like a whirlwind, to render his anger with fury, and his rebuke with flames of fire.

16 For by fire and by his sword will the LORD plead with all flesh: and the slain of the LORD shall be many.

17 They that sanctify themselves, and purify themselves in the gardens behind one *tree* in the midst, eating swine's flesh, and the abomination, and the mouse, shall be consumed together, saith the LORD.

18 For I *know* their works and their thoughts: it shall come, that I will

gather all nations and tongues; and
they shall come, and see my glory.
19 And I will set a sign among them,
and I will send those that escape of
them unto the nations, *to* Tär'shĭsh,
Pŭl, and Lŭd, that draw the bow, *to*
Tū'băl and Jā'văn, *to* the isles afar
off, that have not heard my fame,
neither have seen my glory; and they
shall declare my glory among the
Ġĕn'tīleş.
20 And they shall bring all your
brethren *for* an offering unto the LORD
out of all nations upon horses, and in
chariots, and in litters, and upon mules,
and upon swift beasts, to my holy
mountain Jerusalem, saith the LORD,
as the children of Ĭş'rā-ĕl bring an
offering in a clean vessel into the house
of the LORD.
21 And I will also take of them for
priests *and* for Lē'vītes, saith the LORD.
22 For as the new heavens and the
new earth, which I will make, shall
remain before me, saith the LORD, so
shall your seed and your name remain.
23 And it shall come to pass, *that* from
one new moon to another, and from one
sabbath to another, shall all flesh come
to worship before me, saith the LORD.
24 And they shall go forth, and look
upon the carcasses of the men that have
transgressed against me: for their worm
shall not die, neither shall their fire be
quenched; and they shall be an ab-
horring unto all flesh.

THE BOOK OF THE PROPHET JEREMIAH

CHAPTER 1

THE words of Jeremiah the son of
Hĭl-kī'ah, of the priests that *were*
in Ăn'ȧ-thŏth in the land of Benjamin:
2 To whom the word of the LORD came
in the days of Jō-sī'ȧh the son of
Ā'mŏn king of Judah, in the thirteenth
year of his reign.
3 It came also in the days of Jē-hoi'ȧ-
kĭm the son of Jō-sī'ȧh king of Judah,
unto the end of the eleventh year of
Zĕd'ē-kī'ȧh the son of Jō-sī'ȧh king of
Judah, unto the carrying away of Jerusalem captive in the fifth month.
4 Then the word of the LORD came
unto me, saying,
5 Before I formed thee in the belly I
knew thee; and before thou camest
forth out of the womb I sanctified thee,
and I ordained thee a prophet unto the
nations.
6 Then said I, Ah, Lord GOD! behold,
I cannot speak: for I *am* a child.
7 ¶ But the LORD said unto me, Say
not, I *am* a child: for thou shalt go to
all that I shall send thee, and whatsoever I command thee thou shalt speak.
8 Be not afraid of their faces: for I *am*
with thee to deliver thee, saith the LORD.
9 Then the LORD put forth his hand,
and touched my mouth. And the LORD
said unto me, Behold, I have put my
words in thy mouth.
10 See, I have this day set thee over
the nations and over the kingdoms, to
root out, and to pull down, and to
destroy, and to throw down, to build,
and to plant.
11 ¶ Moreover the word of the LORD
came unto me, saying, Jeremiah, what
seest thou? And I said, I see a rod of
an almond tree.
12 Then said the LORD unto me, Thou
hast well seen: for I will hasten my
word to perform it.
13 And the word of the LORD came
unto me the second time, saying, What
seest thou? And I said, I see a seething
pot; and the face thereof *is* toward the
north.
14 Then the LORD said unto me, Out
of the north an evil shall break forth
upon all the inhabitants of the land.
15 For, lo, I will call all the families of
the kingdoms of the north, saith the
LORD; and they shall come, and they
shall set every one his throne at the
entering of the gates of Jerusalem, and
against all the walls thereof round about,
and against all the cities of Judah.
16 And I will utter my judgments

against them touching all their wickedness, who have forsaken me, and have
burned incense unto other gods, and
worshipped the works of their own
hands.
17 ¶ Thou therefore gird up thy loins,
and arise, and speak unto them all that
I command thee: be not dismayed at
their faces, lest I confound thee before
them.
18 For, behold, I have made thee this
day a defensed city, and an iron pillar,
and brazen walls against the whole land,
against the kings of Judah, against the
princes thereof, against the priests
thereof, and against the people of the
land.
19 And they shall fight against thee;
but they shall not prevail against thee;
for I *am* with thee, saith the LORD, to
deliver thee.

CHAPTER 2

MOREOVER the word of the LORD
came to me, saying,
2 Go and cry in the ears of Jerusalem,
saying, Thus saith the LORD; I remember
thee, the kindness of thy youth, the love
of thine espousals, when thou wentest
after me in the wilderness, in a land *that*
was not sown.
3 Ĭş′rā-ĕl *was* holiness unto the LORD,
and the firstfruits of his increase: all
that devour him shall offend; evil shall
come upon them, saith the LORD.
4 Hear ye the word of the LORD, O
house of Jacob, and all the families of
the house of Ĭş′rā-ĕl:
5 ¶ Thus saith the LORD, What iniquity have your fathers found in me,
that they are gone far from me, and
have walked after vanity, and are become vain?
6 Neither said they, Where *is* the LORD
that brought us up out of the land of
Egypt, that led us through the wilderness, through a land of deserts and of
pits, through a land of drought, and of
the shadow of death, through a land
that no man passed through, and where
no man dwelt?
7 And I brought you into a plentiful
country, to eat the fruit thereof and the
goodness thereof; but when ye entered,
ye defiled my land, and made mine
heritage an abomination.
8 The priests said not, Where *is* the
LORD? and they that handle the law
knew me not: the pastors also transgressed against me, and the prophets
prophesied by Bā′ăl, and walked after
things that do not profit.
9 ¶ Wherefore I will yet plead with
you, saith the LORD, and with your
children's children will I plead.
10 For pass over the isles of Chĭt′tĭm,
and see; and send unto Kē′dȧr, and
consider diligently, and see if there be
such a thing.
11 Hath a nation changed *their* gods,
which *are* yet no gods? but my people
have changed their glory for *that which*
doth not profit.
12 Be astonished, O ye heavens, at
this, and be horribly afraid, be ye very
desolate, saith the LORD.
13 For my people have committed two
evils; they have forsaken me the fountain of living waters, *and* hewed them
out cisterns, broken cisterns, that can
hold no water.
14 ¶ *Is* Ĭş′rā-ĕl a servant? *is* he a
homeborn *slave?* why is he spoiled?
15 The young lions roared upon him,
and yelled, and they made his land
waste: his cities are burned without
inhabitant.
16 Also the children of Nŏph and
Tȧ-hăp′ȧ-nēş have broken the crown
of thy head.
17 Hast thou not procured this unto
thyself, in that thou hast forsaken the
LORD thy God, when he led thee by the
way?
18 And now what hast thou to do in
the way of Egypt, to drink the waters
of Sī′hôr? or what hast thou to do in the
way of Assyria, to drink the waters of
the river?
19 Thine own wickedness shall correct
thee, and thy backslidings shall reprove
thee: know therefore and see that *it is*
an evil *thing* and bitter, that thou hast
forsaken the LORD thy God, and that
my fear *is* not in thee, saith the Lord
GOD of hosts.
20 ¶ For of old time I have broken thy
yoke, *and* burst thy bands; and thou
saidst, I will not transgress; when upon
every high hill and under every green
tree thou wanderest, playing the harlot.
21 Yet I had planted thee a noble vine,
wholly a right seed: how then art thou
turned into the degenerate plant of a
strange vine unto me?
22 For though thou wash thee with

nitre, and take thee much soap, *yet* thine iniquity is marked before me, saith the Lord GOD.

23 How canst thou say, I am not polluted, I have not gone after Bā'ă-lĭm? See thy way in the valley, know what thou hast done: *thou art* a swift dromedary traversing her ways;

24 A wild ass used to the wilderness, *that* snuffeth up the wind at her pleasure; in her occasion who can turn her away? all they that seek her will not weary themselves; in her month they shall find her.

25 Withhold thy foot from being unshod, and thy throat from thirst: but thou saidst, There is no hope: no; for I have loved strangers, and after them will I go.

26 As the thief is ashamed when he is found, so is the house of Ĭs'rā-ĕl ashamed; they, their kings, their princes, and their priests, and their prophets,

27 Saying to a stock, Thou *art* my father; and to a stone, Thou hast brought me forth: for they have turned *their* back unto me, and not *their* face: but in the time of their trouble they will say, Arise, and save us.

28 But where *are* thy gods that thou hast made thee? let them arise, if they can save thee in the time of thy trouble: for *according to* the number of thy cities are thy gods, O Judah.

29 Wherefore will ye plead with me? ye all have transgressed against me, saith the LORD.

30 In vain have I smitten your children; they received no correction: your own sword hath devoured your prophets, like a destroying lion.

31 ¶ O generation, see ye the word of the LORD. Have I been a wilderness unto Ĭs'rā-ĕl? a land of darkness? wherefore say my people, We are lords; we will come no more unto thee?

32 Can a maid forget her ornaments, *or* a bride her attire? yet my people have forgotten me days without number.

33 Why trimmest thou thy way to seek love? therefore hast thou also taught the wicked ones thy ways.

34 Also in thy skirts is found the blood of the souls of the poor innocents: I have not found it by secret search, but upon all these.

35 Yet thou sayest, Because I am innocent, surely his anger shall turn from me. Behold, I will plead with thee, because thou sayest, I have not sinned.

36 Why gaddest thou about so much to change thy way? thou also shalt be ashamed of Egypt, as thou wast ashamed of Assyria.

37 Yea, thou shalt go forth from him, and thine hands upon thine head: for the LORD hath rejected thy confidences, and thou shalt not prosper in them.

CHAPTER 3

THEY say, If a man put away his wife, and she go from him, and become another man's, shall he return unto her again? shall not that land be greatly polluted? but thou hast played the harlot with many lovers; yet return again to me, saith the LORD.

2 Lift up thine eyes unto the high places, and see where thou hast not been lain with. In the ways hast thou sat for them, as the Arabian in the wilderness; and thou hast polluted the land with thy whoredoms and with thy wickedness.

3 Therefore the showers have been withholden, and there hath been no latter rain; and thou hadst a whore's forehead, thou refusedst to be ashamed.

4 Wilt thou not from this time cry unto me, My father, thou *art* the guide of my youth?

5 Will he reserve *his anger* for ever? will he keep *it* to the end? Behold, thou hast spoken and done evil things as thou couldest.

6 ¶ The LORD said also unto me in the days of Jō-sī'ăh the king, Hast thou seen *that* which backsliding Ĭs'rā-ĕl hath done? she is gone up upon every high mountain and under every green tree, and there hath played the harlot.

7 And I said after she had done all these *things*, Turn thou unto me. But she returned not. And her treacherous sister Judah saw *it*.

8 And I saw, when for all the causes whereby backsliding Ĭs'rā-ĕl committed adultery, I had put her away, and given her a bill of divorce; yet her treacherous sister Judah feared not, but went and played the harlot also.

9 And it came to pass through the lightness of her whoredom, that she defiled the land, and committed adultery with stones and with stocks.

10 And yet for all this her treacherous

sister Judah hath not turned unto me with her whole heart, but feignedly, saith the LORD.

11 And the LORD said unto me, The backsliding Ĭṣ′rā-ĕl hath justified herself more than treacherous Judah.

12 ¶ Go and proclaim these words toward the north, and say, Return, thou backsliding Ĭṣ′rā-ĕl, saith the LORD; *and* I will not cause mine anger to fall upon you: for I *am* merciful, saith the LORD, *and* I will not keep *anger* for ever.

13 Only acknowledge thine iniquity, that thou hast transgressed against the LORD thy God, and hast scattered thy ways to the strangers under every green tree, and ye have not obeyed my voice, saith the LORD.

14 Turn, O backsliding children, saith the LORD; for I am married unto you: and I will take you one of a city, and two of a family, and I will bring you to Zion:

15 And I will give you pastors according to mine heart, which shall feed you with knowledge and understanding.

16 And it shall come to pass, when ye be multiplied and increased in the land, in those days, saith the LORD, they shall say no more, The ark of the covenant of the LORD: neither shall it come to mind; neither shall they remember it; neither shall they visit *it;* neither shall *that* be done any more.

17 At that time they shall call Jerusalem the throne of the LORD; and all the nations shall be gathered unto it, to the name of the LORD, to Jerusalem: neither shall they walk any more after the imagination of their evil heart.

18 In those days the house of Judah shall walk with the house of Ĭṣ′rā-ĕl, and they shall come together out of the land of the north to the land that I have given for an inheritance unto your fathers.

19 But I said, How shall I put thee among the children, and give thee a pleasant land, a goodly heritage of the hosts of nations? and I said, Thou shalt call me, My father; and shalt not turn away from me.

20 ¶ Surely *as* a wife treacherously departeth from her husband, so have ye dealt treacherously with me, O house of Ĭṣ′rā-ĕl, saith the LORD.

21 A voice was heard upon the high places, weeping *and* supplications of the children of Ĭṣ′rā-ĕl: for they have perverted their way, *and* they have forgotten the LORD their God.

22 Return, ye backsliding children, *and* I will heal your backslidings. Behold, we come unto thee; for thou *art* the LORD our God.

23 Truly in vain *is salvation hoped for* from the hills, *and from* the multitude of mountains: truly in the LORD our God *is* the salvation of Ĭṣ′rā-ĕl.

24 For shame hath devoured the labor of our fathers from our youth; their flocks and their herds, their sons and their daughters.

25 We lie down in our shame, and our confusion covereth us: for we have sinned against the LORD our God, we and our fathers, from our youth even unto this day, and have not obeyed the voice of the LORD our God.

CHAPTER 4

IF thou wilt return, O Ĭṣ′rā-ĕl, saith the LORD, return unto me: and if thou wilt put away thine abominations out of my sight, then shalt thou not remove.

2 And thou shalt swear, The LORD liveth, in truth, in judgment, and in righteousness; and the nations shall bless themselves in him, and in him shall they glory.

3 ¶ For thus saith the LORD to the men of Judah and Jerusalem, Break up your fallow ground, and sow not among thorns.

4 Circumcise yourselves to the LORD, and take away the foreskins of your heart, ye men of Judah and inhabitants of Jerusalem; lest my fury come forth like fire, and burn that none can quench *it,* because of the evil of your doings.

5 Declare ye in Judah, and publish in Jerusalem; and say, Blow ye the trumpet in the land: cry, gather together, and say, Assemble yourselves, and let us go into the defensed cities.

6 Set up the standard toward Zion: retire, stay not; for I will bring evil from the north, and a great destruction.

7 The lion is come up from his thicket, and the destroyer of the Gĕn′tīleṣ is on his way; he is gone forth from his place to make thy land desolate; *and* thy cities shall be laid waste, without an inhabitant.

8 For this gird you with sackcloth,

lament and howl: for the fierce anger
of the LORD is not turned back from us.
9 And it shall come to pass at that
day, saith the LORD, *that* the heart of
the king shall perish, and the heart of
the princes; and the priests shall be
astonished, and the prophets shall
wonder.
10 Then said I, Ah, Lord GOD! surely
thou hast greatly deceived this people
and Jerusalem, saying, Ye shall have
peace; whereas the sword reacheth
unto the soul.
11 At that time shall it be said to this
people and to Jerusalem, A dry wind of
the high places in the wilderness toward
the daughter of my people, not to fan,
nor to cleanse,
12 *Even* a full wind from those *places*
shall come unto me: now also will I
give sentence against them.
13 Behold, he shall come up as clouds,
and his chariots *shall be* as a whirlwind:
his horses are swifter than eagles. Woe
unto us! for we are spoiled.
14 O Jerusalem, wash thine heart
from wickedness, that thou mayest be
saved. How long shall thy vain thoughts
lodge within thee?
15 For a voice declareth from Dan,
and publisheth affliction from mount
Ē′phrā-ĭm.
16 Make ye mention to the nations;
behold, publish against Jerusalem, *that*
watchers come from a far country, and
give out their voice against the cities of
Judah.
17 As keepers of a field, are they
against her round about; because she
hath been rebellious against me, saith
the LORD.
18 Thy way and thy doings have procured these *things* unto thee; this *is* thy
wickedness, because it is bitter, because
it reacheth unto thine heart.
19 ¶ My bowels, my bowels! I am
pained at my very heart; my heart
maketh a noise in me; I cannot hold my
peace, because thou hast heard, O my
soul, the sound of the trumpet, the
alarm of war.
20 Destruction upon destruction is
cried; for the whole land is spoiled:
suddenly are my tents spoiled, *and* my
curtains in a moment.
21 How long shall I see the standard,
and hear the sound of the trumpet?
22 For my people *is* foolish, they have
not known me; they *are* sottish children,
and they have none understanding: they
are wise to do evil, but to do good they
have no knowledge.
23 I beheld the earth, and, lo, *it was*
without form, and void; and the heavens,
and they *had* no light.
24 I beheld the mountains, and, lo,
they trembled, and all the hills moved
lightly.
25 I beheld, and, lo, *there was* no man,
and all the birds of the heavens were
fled.
26 I beheld, and, lo, the fruitful place
was a wilderness, and all the cities
thereof were broken down at the presence of the LORD, *and* by his fierce
anger.
27 For thus hath the LORD said, The
whole land shall be desolate; yet will I
not make a full end.
28 For this shall the earth mourn, and
the heavens above be black: because I
have spoken *it*, I have purposed *it*, and
will not repent, neither will I turn back
from it.
29 The whole city shall flee for the
noise of the horsemen and bowmen;
they shall go into thickets, and climb
up upon the rocks: every city *shall be*
forsaken, and not a man dwell therein.
30 And *when* thou *art* spoiled, what
wilt thou do? Though thou clothest thyself with crimson, though thou deckest
thee with ornaments of gold, though
thou rentest thy face with painting, in
vain shalt thou make thyself fair; *thy*
lovers will despise thee, they will seek
thy life.
31 For I have heard a voice as of a
woman in travail, *and* the anguish as
of her that bringeth forth her first child,
the voice of the daughter of Zion, *that*
bewaileth herself, *that* spreadeth her
hands, *saying*, Woe *is* me now! for my
soul is wearied because of murderers.

CHAPTER 5

RUN ye to and fro through the streets
of Jerusalem, and see now, and
know, and seek in the broad places
thereof, if ye can find a man, if there
be *any* that executeth judgment, that
seeketh the truth; and I will pardon it.
2 And though they say, The LORD
liveth; surely they swear falsely.
3 O LORD, *are* not thine eyes upon the
truth? thou hast stricken them, but they

have not grieved; thou hast consumed
them, *but* they have refused to receive
correction: they have made their faces
harder than a rock; they have refused
to return.
4 Therefore I said, Surely these *are*
poor; they are foolish: for they know
not the way of the LORD, *nor* the
judgment of their God.
5 I will get me unto the great men,
and will speak unto them; for they have
known the way of the LORD, *and* the
judgment of their God: but these have
altogether broken the yoke, *and* burst
the bonds.
6 Wherefore a lion out of the forest
shall slay them, *and* a wolf of the evenings shall spoil them, a leopard shall
watch over their cities: every one that
goeth out thence shall be torn in pieces:
because their transgressions are many,
and their backslidings are increased.
7 ℂ How shall I pardon thee for this?
thy children have forsaken me, and
sworn by *them that are* no gods: when
I had fed them to the full, they then
committed adultery, and assembled
themselves by troops in the harlots'
houses.
8 They were *as* fed horses in the
morning: every one neighed after his
neighbor's wife.
9 Shall I not visit for these *things?*
saith the LORD: and shall not my soul
be avenged on such a nation as this?
10 ℂ Go ye up upon her walls, and
destroy; but make not a full end: take
away her battlements; for they *are* not
the LORD's.
11 For the house of Ĭş'rā-ĕl and the
house of Judah have dealt very treacherously against me, saith the LORD.
12 They have belied the LORD, and
said, *It is* not he; neither shall evil come
upon us; neither shall we see sword nor
famine:
13 And the prophets shall become
wind, and the word *is* not in them: thus
shall it be done unto them.
14 Wherefore thus saith the LORD
God of hosts, Because ye speak this
word, behold, I will make my words in
thy mouth fire, and this people wood,
and it shall devour them.
15 Lo, I will bring a nation upon you
from far, O house of Ĭş'rā-ĕl, saith the
LORD: it *is* a mighty nation, it *is* an
ancient nation, a nation whose language
thou knowest not, neither understandest what they say.
16 Their quiver *is* as an open sepulchre, they *are* all mighty men.
17 And they shall eat up thine harvest
and thy bread, *which* thy sons and thy
daughters should eat: they shall eat up
thy flocks and thine herds: they shall
eat up thy vines and thy fig trees: they
shall impoverish thy fenced cities,
wherein thou trustedst, with the sword.
18 Nevertheless in those days, saith
the LORD, I will not make a full end
with you.
19 ℂ And it shall come to pass, when
ye shall say, Wherefore doeth the LORD
our God all these *things* unto us? then
shalt thou answer them, Like as ye
have forsaken me, and served strange
gods in your land, so shall ye serve
strangers in a land *that is* not yours.
20 Declare this in the house of Jacob,
and publish it in Judah, saying,
21 Hear now this, O foolish people,
and without understanding; which have
eyes, and see not; which have ears, and
hear not:
22 Fear ye not me? saith the LORD: will
ye not tremble at my presence, which
have placed the sand *for* the bound of
the sea by a perpetual decree, that it
cannot pass it: and though the waves
thereof toss themselves, yet can they
not prevail; though they roar, yet can
they not pass over it?
23 But this people hath a revolting and
a rebellious heart; they are revolted and
gone.
24 Neither say they in their heart, Let
us now fear the LORD our God, that
giveth rain, both the former and the
latter, in his season: he reserveth unto
us the appointed weeks of the harvest.
25 ℂ Your iniquities have turned away
these *things*, and your sins have withholden good *things* from you.
26 For among my people are found
wicked *men:* they lay wait, as he that
setteth snares; they set a trap, they
catch men.
27 As a cage is full of birds, so *are*
their houses full of deceit: therefore
they are become great, and waxen
rich.
28 They are waxen fat, they shine:
yea, they overpass the deeds of the
wicked: they judge not the cause, the
cause of the fatherless, yet they pros-

per; and the right of the needy do they not judge.

29 Shall I not visit for these *things?* saith the LORD: shall not my soul be avenged on such a nation as this?

30 ¶ A wonderful and horrible thing is committed in the land;

31 The prophets prophesy falsely, and the priests bear rule by their means; and my people love *to have it* so: and what will ye do in the end thereof?

CHAPTER 6

O YE children of Benjamin, gather yourselves to flee out of the midst of Jerusalem, and blow the trumpet in Tē-kō′ȧ, and set up a sign of fire in Běth′-hăc′çē-rěm: for evil appeareth out of the north, and great destruction.

2 I have likened the daughter of Zion to a comely and delicate *woman*.

3 The shepherds with their flocks shall come unto her; they shall pitch *their* tents against her round about; they shall feed every one in his place.

4 Prepare ye war against her; arise, and let us go up at noon. Woe unto us! for the day goeth away, for the shadows of the evening are stretched out.

5 Arise, and let us go by night, and let us destroy her palaces.

6 ¶ For thus hath the LORD of hosts said, Hew ye down trees, and cast a mount against Jerusalem: this *is* the city to be visited; she *is* wholly oppression in the midst of her.

7 As a fountain casteth out her waters, so she casteth out her wickedness: violence and spoil is heard in her; before me continually *is* grief and wounds.

8 Be thou instructed, O Jerusalem, lest my soul depart from thee; lest I make thee desolate, a land not inhabited.

9 ¶ Thus saith the LORD of hosts, They shall thoroughly glean the remnant of Ĭs′rā-ēl as a vine: turn back thine hand as a grape gatherer into the baskets.

10 To whom shall I speak, and give warning, that they may hear? Behold, their ear *is* uncircumcised, and they cannot hearken: behold, the word of the LORD is unto them a reproach; they have no delight in it.

11 Therefore I am full of the fury of the LORD; I am weary with holding in: I will pour it out upon the children abroad, and upon the assembly of young men together: for even the husband with the wife shall be taken, the aged with *him that is* full of days.

12 And their houses shall be turned unto others, *with their* fields and wives together: for I will stretch out my hand upon the inhabitants of the land, saith the LORD.

13 For from the least of them even unto the greatest of them every one *is* given to covetousness; and from the prophet even unto the priest every one dealeth falsely.

14 They have healed also the hurt of the daughter of my people slightly, saying, Peace, peace; when *there is* no peace.

15 Were they ashamed when they had committed abomination? nay, they were not at all ashamed, neither could they blush; therefore they shall fall among them that fall: at the time *that* I visit them they shall be cast down, saith the LORD.

16 Thus saith the LORD, Stand ye in the ways, and see, and ask for the old paths, where *is* the good way, and walk therein, and ye shall find rest for your souls. But they said, We will not walk *therein*.

17 Also I set watchmen over you, *saying*, Hearken to the sound of the trumpet. But they said, We will not hearken.

18 ¶ Therefore hear, ye nations, and know, O congregation, what *is* among them.

19 Hear, O earth: behold, I will bring evil upon this people, *even* the fruit of their thoughts, because they have not hearkened unto my words, nor to my law, but rejected it.

20 To what purpose cometh there to me incense from Shē′bȧ, and the sweet cane from a far country? your burnt offerings *are* not acceptable, nor your sacrifices sweet unto me.

21 Therefore thus saith the LORD, Behold, I will lay stumblingblocks before this people, and the fathers and the sons together shall fall upon them; the neighbor and his friend shall perish.

22 Thus saith the LORD, Behold, a people cometh from the north country, and a great nation shall be raised from the sides of the earth.

23 They shall lay hold on bow and

spear; they *are* cruel, and have no mercy; their voice roareth like the sea; and they ride upon horses, set in array as men for war against thee, O daughter of Zion.

24 We have heard the fame thereof: our hands wax feeble: anguish hath taken hold of us, *and* pain, as of a woman in travail.

25 Go not forth into the field, nor walk by the way; for the sword of the enemy *and* fear *is* on every side.

26 ¶ O daughter of my people, gird *thee* with sackcloth, and wallow thyself in ashes: make thee mourning, *as for* an only son, most bitter lamentation: for the spoiler shall suddenly come upon us.

27 I have set thee *for* a tower *and* a fortress among my people, that thou mayest know and try their way.

28 They *are* all grievous revolters, walking with slanders: *they are* brass and iron; they *are* all corrupters.

29 The bellows are burned, the lead is consumed of the fire; the founder melteth in vain: for the wicked are not plucked away.

30 Reprobate silver shall *men* call them, because the LORD hath rejected them.

CHAPTER 7

THE word that came to Jeremiah from the LORD, saying,

2 Stand in the gate of the LORD's house, and proclaim there this word, and say, Hear the word of the LORD, all *ye of* Judah, that enter in at these gates to worship the LORD.

3 Thus saith the LORD of hosts, the God of Ĭṣ'rā-ĕl, Amend your ways and your doings, and I will cause you to dwell in this place.

4 Trust ye not in lying words, saying, The temple of the LORD, The temple of the LORD, The temple of the LORD, *are* these.

5 For if ye thoroughly amend your ways and your doings; if ye thoroughly execute judgment between a man and his neighbor;

6 *If* ye oppress not the stranger, the fatherless, and the widow, and shed not innocent blood in this place, neither walk after other gods to your hurt;

7 Then will I cause you to dwell in this place, in the land that I gave to your fathers, for ever and ever.

8 ¶ Behold, ye trust in lying words, that cannot profit.

9 Will ye steal, murder, and commit adultery, and swear falsely, and burn incense unto Ba'äl, and walk after other gods whom ye know not;

10 And come and stand before me in this house, which is called by my name, and say, We are delivered to do all these abominations?

11 Is this house, which is called by my name, become a den of robbers in your eyes? Behold, even I have seen *it,* saith the LORD.

12 But go ye now unto my place which *was* in Shī'lōh, where I set my name at the first, and see what I did to it for the wickedness of my people Ĭs'rā-ĕl.

13 And now, because ye have done all these works, saith the LORD, and I spake unto you, rising up early and speaking, but ye heard not; and I called you, but ye answered not;

14 Therefore will I do unto *this* house, which is called by my name, wherein ye trust, and unto the place which I gave to you and to your fathers, as I have done to Shī'lōh.

15 And I will cast you out of my sight, as I have cast out all your brethren, *even* the whole seed of Ē'phrā-ĭm.

16 Therefore pray not thou for this people, neither lift up cry nor prayer for them, neither make intercession to me: for I will not hear thee.

17 ¶ Seest thou not what they do in the cities of Judah and in the streets of Jerusalem?

18 The children gather wood, and the fathers kindle the fire, and the women knead *their* dough, to make cakes to the queen of heaven, and to pour out drink offerings unto other gods, that they may provoke me to anger.

19 Do they provoke me to anger? saith the LORD: *do they* not *provoke* themselves to the confusion of their own faces?

20 Therefore thus saith the Lord GOD; Behold, mine anger and my fury shall be poured out upon this place, upon man, and upon beast, and upon the trees of the field, and upon the fruit of the ground; and it shall burn, and shall not be quenched.

21 ¶ Thus saith the LORD of hosts, the God of Ĭṣ'rā-ĕl; Put your burnt offerings unto your sacrifices, and eat flesh.

22 For I spake not unto your fathers, nor commanded them in the day that I brought them out of the land of Egypt, concerning burnt offerings or sacrifices:

23 But this thing commanded I them, saying, Obey my voice, and I will be your God, and ye shall be my people: and walk ye in all the ways that I have commanded you, that it may be well unto you.

24 But they hearkened not, nor inclined their ear, but walked in the counsels *and* in the imagination of their evil heart, and went backward, and not forward.

25 Since the day that your fathers came forth out of the land of Egypt unto this day, I have even sent unto you all my servants the prophets, daily rising up early and sending *them:*

26 Yet they hearkened not unto me, nor inclined their ear, but hardened their neck: they did worse than their fathers.

27 Therefore thou shalt speak all these words unto them; but they will not hearken to thee: thou shalt also call unto them; but they will not answer thee.

28 But thou shalt say unto them, This *is* a nation that obeyeth not the voice of the LORD their God, nor receiveth correction: truth is perished, and is cut off from their mouth.

29 ¶ Cut off thine hair, *O Jerusalem,* and cast *it* away, and take up a lamentation on high places; for the LORD hath rejected and forsaken the generation of his wrath.

30 For the children of Judah have done evil in my sight, saith the LORD: they have set their abominations in the house which is called by my name, to pollute it.

31 And they have built the high places of Tō'phĕt, which *is* in the valley of the son of Hĭn'nŏm, to burn their sons and their daughters in the fire; which I commanded *them* not, neither came it into my heart.

32 ¶ Therefore, behold, the days come, saith the LORD, that it shall no more be called Tō'phĕt, nor The valley of the son of Hĭn'nŏm, but The valley of slaughter: for they shall bury in Tō'phĕt, till there be no place.

33 And the carcasses of this people shall be meat for the fowls of the heaven, and for the beasts of the earth; and none shall fray *them* away.

34 Then will I cause to cease from the cities of Judah, and from the streets of Jerusalem, the voice of mirth, and the voice of gladness, the voice of the bridegroom, and the voice of the bride: for the land shall be desolate.

CHAPTER 8

AT that time, saith the LORD, they shall bring out the bones of the kings of Judah, and the bones of his princes, and the bones of the priests, and the bones of the prophets, and the bones of the inhabitants of Jerusalem, out of their graves:

2 And they shall spread them before the sun, and the moon, and all the host of heaven, whom they have loved, and whom they have served, and after whom they have walked, and whom they have sought, and whom they have worshipped: they shall not be gathered, nor be buried; they shall be for dung upon the face of the earth.

3 And death shall be chosen rather than life by all the residue of them that remain of this evil family, which remain in all the places whither I have driven them, saith the LORD of hosts.

4 ¶ Moreover thou shalt say unto them, Thus saith the LORD: Shall they fall, and not arise? shall he turn away, and not return?

5 Why *then* is this people of Jerusalem slidden back by a perpetual backsliding? they hold fast deceit, they refuse to return.

6 I hearkened and heard, *but* they spake not aright: no man repented him of his wickedness, saying, What have I done? every one turned to his course, as the horse rusheth into the battle.

7 Yea, the stork in the heaven knoweth her appointed times; and the turtle and the crane and the swallow observe the time of their coming; but my people know not the judgment of the LORD.

8 How do ye say, We *are* wise, and the law of the LORD *is* with us? Lo, certainly in vain made he *it;* the pen of the scribes *is* in vain.

9 The wise *men* are ashamed, they are dismayed and taken: lo, they have rejected the word of the LORD; and what wisdom *is* in them?

10 Therefore will I give their wives unto others, *and* their fields to them

that shall inherit *them;* for every one from the least even unto the greatest is given to covetousness, from the prophet even unto the priest every one dealeth falsely.

11 For they have healed the hurt of the daughter of my people slightly, saying, Peace, peace; when *there is* no peace.

12 Were they ashamed when they had committed abomination? nay, they were not at all ashamed, neither could they blush; therefore shall they fall among them that fall: in the time of their visitation they shall be cast down, saith the LORD.

13 ¶ I will surely consume them, saith the LORD: *there shall be* no grapes on the vine, nor figs on the fig tree, and the leaf shall fade; and *the things that* I have given them shall pass away from them.

14 Why do we sit still? assemble yourselves, and let us enter into the defensed cities, and let us be silent there: for the LORD our God hath put us to silence, and given us water of gall to drink, because we have sinned against the LORD.

15 We looked for peace, but no good *came; and* for a time of health, and behold trouble!

16 The snorting of his horses was heard from Dan: the whole land trembled at the sound of the neighing of his strong ones; for they are come, and have devoured the land, and all that is in it; the city, and those that dwell therein.

17 For, behold, I will send serpents, cockatrices, among you, which *will* not *be* charmed, and they shall bite you, saith the LORD.

18 ¶ *When* I would comfort myself against sorrow, my heart *is* faint in me.

19 Behold the voice of the cry of the daughter of my people because of them that dwell in a far country: *Is* not the LORD in Zion? *is* not her king in her? Why have they provoked me to anger with their graven images, *and* with strange vanities?

20 The harvest is past, the summer is ended, and we are not saved.

21 For the hurt of the daughter of my people am I hurt; I am black; astonishment hath taken hold on me.

22 *Is there* no balm in Gĭl'ē-ăd? *is there* no physician there? why then is not the health of the daughter of my people recovered?

CHAPTER 9

OH that my head were waters, and mine eyes a fountain of tears, that I might weep day and night for the slain of the daughter of my people!

2 Oh that I had in the wilderness a lodging place of wayfaring men; that I might leave my people, and go from them! for they *be* all adulterers, an assembly of treacherous men.

3 And they bend their tongues *like* their bow *for* lies: but they are not valiant for the truth upon the earth; for they proceed from evil to evil, and they know not me, saith the LORD.

4 Take ye heed every one of his neighbor, and trust ye not in any brother: for every brother will utterly supplant, and every neighbor will walk with slanders.

5 And they will deceive every one his neighbor, and will not speak the truth: they have taught their tongue to speak lies, *and* weary themselves to commit iniquity.

6 Thine habitation *is* in the midst of deceit; through deceit they refuse to know me, saith the LORD.

7 Therefore thus saith the LORD of hosts, Behold, I will melt them, and try them; for how shall I do for the daughter of my people?

8 Their tongue *is as* an arrow shot out; it speaketh deceit: *one* speaketh peaceably to his neighbor with his mouth, but in heart he layeth his wait.

9 ¶ Shall I not visit them for these *things?* saith the LORD: shall not my soul be avenged on such a nation as this?

10 For the mountains will I take up a weeping and wailing, and for the habitations of the wilderness a lamentation, because they are burned up, so that none can pass through *them;* neither can *men* hear the voice of the cattle: both the fowl of the heavens and the beast are fled; they are gone.

11 And I will make Jerusalem heaps, *and* a den of dragons; and I will make the cities of Judah desolate, without an inhabitant.

12 ¶ Who *is* the wise man, that may understand this? and *who is he* to whom the mouth of the LORD hath spoken, that he may declare it, for what the land perisheth *and* is burned up like a wilderness, that none passeth through?

13 And the LORD saith, Because they

have forsaken my law which I set before them, and have not obeyed my voice, neither walked therein;
14 But have walked after the imagination of their own heart, and after Bā'ă-lĭm, which their fathers taught them:
15 Therefore thus saith the LORD of hosts, the God of Ĭṣ'rā-ĕl; Behold, I will feed them, *even* this people, with wormwood, and give them water of gall to drink.
16 I will scatter them also among the heathen, whom neither they nor their fathers have known: and I will send a sword after them, till I have consumed them.
17 ¶ Thus saith the LORD of hosts, Consider ye, and call for the mourning women, that they may come; and send for cunning *women*, that they may come:
18 And let them make haste, and take up a wailing for us, that our eyes may run down with tears, and our eyelids gush out with waters.
19 For a voice of wailing is heard out of Zion, How are we spoiled! we are greatly confounded, because we have forsaken the land, because our dwellings have cast *us* out.
20 Yet hear the word of the LORD, O ye women, and let your ear receive the word of his mouth, and teach your daughters wailing, and every one her neighbor lamentation.
21 For death is come up into our windows, *and* is entered into our palaces, to cut off the children from without, *and* the young men from the streets.
22 Speak, Thus saith the LORD, Even the carcasses of men shall fall as dung upon the open field, and as the handful after the harvestman, and none shall gather *them*.
23 ¶ Thus saith the LORD, Let not the wise *man* glory in his wisdom, neither let the mighty *man* glory in his might, let not the rich *man* glory in his riches:
24 But let him that glorieth glory in this, that he understandeth and knoweth me, that I *am* the LORD which exercise loving-kindness, judgment, and righteousness, in the earth: for in these *things* I delight, saith the LORD.
25 ¶ Behold, the days come, saith the LORD, that I will punish all *them which are* circumcised with the uncircumcised;
26 Egypt, and Judah, and Ē'dŏm, and the children of Ammon, and Mō'ăb, and all *that are* in the utmost corners, that dwell in the wilderness: for all *these* nations *are* uncircumcised, and all the house of Ĭṣ'rā-ĕl *are* uncircumcised in the heart.

CHAPTER 10

HEAR ye the word which the LORD speaketh unto you, O house of Ĭṣ'rā-ĕl:
2 Thus saith the LORD, Learn not the way of the heathen, and be not dismayed at the signs of heaven; for the heathen are dismayed at them.
3 For the customs of the people *are* vain: for *one* cutteth a tree out of the forest, the work of the hands of the workman, with the axe.
4 They deck it with silver and with gold; they fasten it with nails and with hammers, that it move not.
5 They *are* upright as the palm tree, but speak not: they must needs be borne, because they cannot go. Be not afraid of them; for they cannot do evil, neither also *is it* in them to do good.
6 Forasmuch as *there is* none like unto thee, O LORD; thou *art* great, and thy name *is* great in might.
7 Who would not fear thee, O King of nations? for to thee doth it appertain: forasmuch as among all the wise *men* of the nations, and in all their kingdoms, *there is* none like unto thee.
8 But they are altogether brutish and foolish: the stock *is* a doctrine of vanities.
9 Silver spread into plates is brought from Tär'shĭsh, and gold from Ū'phăz, the work of the workman, and of the hands of the founder: blue and purple *is* their clothing: they *are* all the work of cunning *men*.
10 But the LORD *is* the true God, he *is* the living God, and an everlasting King: at his wrath the earth shall tremble, and the nations shall not be able to abide his indignation.
11 Thus shall ye say unto them, The gods that have not made the heavens and the earth, *even* they shall perish from the earth, and from under these heavens.
12 He hath made the earth by his power, he hath established the world by his wisdom, and hath stretched out the heavens by his discretion.

13 When he uttereth his voice, *there is*
a multitude of waters in the heavens,
and he causeth the vapors to ascend
from the ends of the earth; he maketh
lightnings with rain, and bringeth forth
the wind out of his treasures.
14 Every man is brutish in *his* knowledge:
every founder is confounded by
the graven image: for his molten image *is*
falsehood, and *there is* no breath in them.
15 They *are* vanity, *and* the work of
errors: in the time of their visitation
they shall perish.
16 The portion of Jacob *is* not like
them: for he *is* the former of all *things;*
and Ĭş'rā-ĕl *is* the rod of his inheritance:
The LORD of hosts *is* his name.
17 ¶ Gather up thy wares out of the
land, O inhabitant of the fortress.
18 For thus saith the LORD, Behold, I
will sling out the inhabitants of the land
at this once, and will distress them, that
they may find *it so.*
19 ¶ Woe is me for my hurt! my wound
is grievous: but I said, Truly this *is* a
grief, and I must bear it.
20 My tabernacle is spoiled, and all
my cords are broken: my children are
gone forth of me, and they *are* not:
there is none to stretch forth my tent
any more, and to set up my curtains.
21 For the pastors are become brutish,
and have not sought the LORD: therefore
they shall not prosper, and all their
flocks shall be scattered.
22 Behold, the noise of the bruit is
come, and a great commotion out of the
north country, to make the cities of
Judah desolate, *and* a den of dragons.
23 ¶ O LORD, I know that the way of
man *is* not in himself: *it is* not in man
that walketh to direct his steps.
24 O LORD, correct me, but with judgment;
not in thine anger, lest thou
bring me to nothing.
25 Pour out thy fury upon the heathen
that know thee not, and upon the families
that call not on thy name: for they
have eaten up Jacob, and devoured
him, and consumed him, and have made
his habitation desolate.

CHAPTER 11

THE word that came to Jeremiah
from the LORD, saying,
2 Hear ye the words of this covenant,
and speak unto the men of Judah, and
to the inhabitants of Jerusalem;
3 And say thou unto them, Thus saith
the LORD God of Ĭş'rā-ĕl; Cursed *be* the
man that obeyeth not the words of this
covenant,
4 Which I commanded your fathers in
the day *that* I brought them forth out of
the land of Egypt, from the iron furnace,
saying, Obey my voice, and do
them, according to all which I command
you: so shall ye be my people, and I will
be your God:
5 That I may perform the oath which I
have sworn unto your fathers, to give
them a land flowing with milk and
honey, as *it is* this day. Then answered
I, and said, So be it, O LORD.
6 Then the LORD said unto me, Proclaim
all these words in the cities of
Judah, and in the streets of Jerusalem,
saying, Hear ye the words of this covenant,
and do them.
7 For I earnestly protested unto your
fathers in the day *that* I brought them
up out of the land of Egypt, *even* unto
this day, rising early and protesting,
saying, Obey my voice.
8 Yet they obeyed not, nor inclined
their ear, but walked every one in the
imagination of their evil heart: therefore
I will bring upon them all the
words of this covenant, which I commanded
them to do; but they did *them*
not.
9 And the LORD said unto me, A conspiracy
is found among the men of
Judah, and among the inhabitants of
Jerusalem.
10 They are turned back to the iniquities
of their forefathers, which refused
to hear my words; and they went after
other gods to serve them: the house of
Ĭş'rā-ĕl and the house of Judah have
broken my covenant which I made with
their fathers.
11 ¶ Therefore thus saith the LORD,
Behold, I will bring evil upon them,
which they shall not be able to escape;
and though they shall cry unto me, I will
not hearken unto them.
12 Then shall the cities of Judah and
inhabitants of Jerusalem go, and cry
unto the gods unto whom they offer incense:
but they shall not save them at
all in the time of their trouble.
13 For *according to* the number of thy
cities were thy gods, O Judah; and
according to the number of the streets of
Jerusalem have ye set up altars to *that*

shameful thing, *even* altars to burn incense unto Bā'ăl.
14 Therefore pray not thou for this
people, neither lift up a cry or prayer
for them: for I will not hear *them* in the
time that they cry unto me for their
trouble.
15 What hath my beloved to do in mine
house, *seeing* she hath wrought lewdness with many, and the holy flesh is
passed from thee? when thou doest evil,
then thou rejoicest.
16 The LORD called thy name, A green
olive tree, fair, *and* of goodly fruit: with
the noise of a great tumult he hath
kindled fire upon it, and the branches
of it are broken.
17 For the LORD of hosts, that planted
thee, hath pronounced evil against thee,
for the evil of the house of Ĭṣ'rā-ĕl and
of the house of Judah, which they have
done against themselves to provoke me
to anger in offering incense unto Bā'ăl.
18 ¶ And the LORD hath given me
knowledge *of it,* and I know *it:* then
thou showedst me their doings.
19 But I *was* like a lamb *or* an ox *that*
is brought to the slaughter; and I knew
not that they had devised devices
against me, *saying,* Let us destroy the
tree with the fruit thereof, and let us cut
him off from the land of the living, that
his name may be no more remembered.
20 But, O LORD of hosts, that judgest
righteously, that triest the reins and the
heart, let me see thy vengeance on them:
for unto thee have I revealed my cause.
21 Therefore thus saith the LORD of
the men of Ăn'ȧ-thŏth, that seek thy life,
saying, Prophesy not in the name of the
LORD, that thou die not by our hand:
22 Therefore thus saith the LORD of
hosts, Behold, I will punish them: the
young men shall die by the sword; their
sons and their daughters shall die by
famine:
23 And there shall be no remnant of
them: for I will bring evil upon the men
of Ăn'ȧ-thŏth, *even* the year of their
visitation.

CHAPTER 12

RIGHTEOUS *art* thou, O LORD,
when I plead with thee: yet let me
talk with thee of *thy* judgments: Wherefore doth the way of the wicked prosper?
wherefore are all they happy that deal
very treacherously?
2 Thou hast planted them, yea, they
have taken root: they grow, yea, they
bring forth fruit: thou *art* near in their
mouth, and far from their reins.
3 But thou, O LORD, knowest me: thou
hast seen me, and tried mine heart toward thee: pull them out like sheep for
the slaughter, and prepare them for the
day of slaughter.
4 How long shall the land mourn, and
the herbs of every field wither, for the
wickedness of them that dwell therein?
the beasts are consumed, and the birds;
because they said, He shall not see our
last end.
5 ¶ If thou hast run with the footmen,
and they have wearied thee, then how
canst thou contend with horses? and *if*
in the land of peace, *wherein* thou
trustedst, *they wearied thee,* then how
wilt thou do in the swelling of Jordan?
6 For even thy brethren, and the house
of thy father, even they have dealt
treacherously with thee; yea, they have
called a multitude after thee: believe
them not, though they speak fair words
unto thee.
7 ¶ I have forsaken mine house, I have
left mine heritage; I have given the
dearly beloved of my soul into the hand
of her enemies.
8 Mine heritage is unto me as a lion in
the forest; it crieth out against me:
therefore have I hated it.
9 Mine heritage *is* unto me *as* a
speckled bird, the birds round about *are*
against her; come ye, assemble all the
beasts of the field, come to devour.
10 Many pastors have destroyed my
vineyard, they have trodden my portion
under foot, they have made my pleasant
portion a desolate wilderness.
11 They have made it desolate, *and*
being desolate it mourneth unto me; the
whole land is made desolate, because
no man layeth *it* to heart.
12 The spoilers are come upon all high
places through the wilderness: for the
sword of the LORD shall devour from the
one end of the land even to the *other*
end of the land: no flesh shall have
peace.
13 They have sown wheat, but shall
reap thorns: they have put themselves
to pain, *but* shall not profit: and they
shall be ashamed of your revenues because of the fierce anger of the LORD.
14 ¶ Thus saith the LORD against all

mine evil neighbors, that touch the inheritance which I have caused my people Ĭs̱'rā-ĕl to inherit; Behold, I will pluck them out of their land, and pluck out the house of Judah from among them.

15 And it shall come to pass, after that I have plucked them out I will return, and have compassion on them, and will bring them again, every man to his heritage, and every man to his land.

16 And it shall come to pass, if they will diligently learn the ways of my people, to swear by my name, The LORD liveth; as they taught my people to swear by Bā'ăl; then shall they be built in the midst of my people.

17 But if they will not obey, I will utterly pluck up and destroy that nation, saith the LORD.

CHAPTER 13

THUS saith the LORD unto me, Go and get thee a linen girdle, and put it upon thy loins, and put it not in water.

2 So I got a girdle according to the word of the LORD, and put *it* on my loins.

3 And the word of the LORD came unto me the second time, saying,

4 Take the girdle that thou hast got, which *is* upon thy loins, and arise, go to Eū-phrā'tēs̱, and hide it there in a hole of the rock.

5 So I went, and hid it by Eū-phrā'tēs̱, as the LORD commanded me.

6 And it came to pass after many days, that the LORD said unto me, Arise, go to Eū-phrā'tēs̱, and take the girdle from thence, which I commanded thee to hide there.

7 Then I went to Eū-phrā'tēs̱, and digged, and took the girdle from the place where I had hid it: and, behold, the girdle was marred, it was profitable for nothing.

8 Then the word of the LORD came unto me, saying,

9 Thus saith the LORD, After this manner will I mar the pride of Judah, and the great pride of Jerusalem.

10 This evil people, which refuse to hear my words, which walk in the imagination of their heart, and walk after other gods, to serve them, and to worship them, shall even be as this girdle, which is good for nothing.

11 For as the girdle cleaveth to the loins of a man, so have I caused to cleave unto me the whole house of Ĭs̱'rā-ĕl and the whole house of Judah, saith the LORD; that they might be unto me for a people, and for a name, and for a praise, and for a glory: but they would not hear.

12 ¶ Therefore thou shalt speak unto them this word; Thus saith the LORD God of Ĭs̱'rā-ĕl, Every bottle shall be filled with wine: and they shall say unto thee, Do we not certainly know that every bottle shall be filled with wine?

13 Then shalt thou say unto them, Thus saith the LORD, Behold, I will fill all the inhabitants of this land, even the kings that sit upon David's throne, and the priests, and the prophets, and all the inhabitants of Jerusalem, with drunkenness.

14 And I will dash them one against another, even the fathers and the sons together, saith the LORD: I will not pity, nor spare, nor have mercy, but destroy them.

15 ¶ Hear ye, and give ear; be not proud: for the LORD hath spoken.

16 Give glory to the LORD your God, before he cause darkness, and before your feet stumble upon the dark mountains, and, while ye look for light, he turn it into the shadow of death, *and* make *it* gross darkness.

17 But if ye will not hear it, my soul shall weep in secret places for *your* pride; and mine eye shall weep sore, and run down with tears, because the LORD's flock is carried away captive.

18 Say unto the king and to the queen, Humble yourselves, sit down: for your principalities shall come down, *even* the crown of your glory.

19 The cities of the south shall be shut up, and none shall open *them:* Judah shall be carried away captive all of it, it shall be wholly carried away captive.

20 Lift up your eyes, and behold them that come from the north: where *is* the flock *that* was given thee, thy beautiful flock?

21 What wilt thou say when he shall punish thee? for thou hast taught them *to be* captains, *and* as chief over thee: shall not sorrows take thee, as a woman in travail?

22 ¶ And if thou say in thine heart, Wherefore come these things upon me?

For the greatness of thine iniquity are thy skirts discovered, *and* thy heels made bare.

23 Can the Ethiopian change his skin, or the leopard his spots? *then* may ye also do good, that are accustomed to do evil.

24 Therefore will I scatter them as the stubble that passeth away by the wind of the wilderness.

25 This *is* thy lot, the portion of thy measures from me, saith the LORD; because thou hast forgotten me, and trusted in falsehood.

26 Therefore will I discover thy skirts upon thy face, that thy shame may appear.

27 I have seen thine adulteries, and thy neighings, the lewdness of thy whoredom, *and* thine abominations on the hills in the fields. Woe unto thee, O Jerusalem! wilt thou not be made clean? when *shall it* once *be?*

CHAPTER 14

THE word of the LORD that came to Jeremiah concerning the dearth.

2 Judah mourneth, and the gates thereof languish; they are black unto the ground; and the cry of Jerusalem is gone up.

3 And their nobles have sent their little ones to the waters: they came to the pits, *and* found no water; they returned with their vessels empty; they were ashamed and confounded, and covered their heads.

4 Because the ground is chapped, for there was no rain in the earth, the plowmen were ashamed, they covered their heads.

5 Yea, the hind also calved in the field, and forsook *it,* because there was no grass.

6 And the wild asses did stand in the high places, they snuffed up the wind like dragons; their eyes did fail, because *there was* no grass.

7 ¶ O LORD, though our iniquities testify against us, do thou *it* for thy name's sake: for our backslidings are many; we have sinned against thee.

8 O the hope of Ĭṣ′rā-ĕl, the Saviour thereof in time of trouble, why shouldest thou be as a stranger in the land, and as a wayfaring man *that* turneth aside to tarry for a night?

9 Why shouldest thou be as a man astonished, as a mighty man *that* cannot save? yet thou, O LORD, *art* in the midst of us, and we are called by thy name; leave us not.

10 ¶ Thus saith the LORD unto this people, Thus have they loved to wander, they have not refrained their feet, therefore the LORD doth not accept them; he will now remember their iniquity, and visit their sins.

11 Then said the LORD unto me, Pray not for this people for *their* good.

12 When they fast, I will not hear their cry; and when they offer burnt offering and an oblation, I will not accept them: but I will consume them by the sword, and by the famine, and by the pestilence.

13 ¶ Then said I, Ah, Lord GOD! behold, the prophets say unto them, Ye shall not see the sword, neither shall ye have famine; but I will give you assured peace in this place.

14 Then the LORD said unto me, The prophets prophesy lies in my name: I sent them not, neither have I commanded them, neither spake unto them: they prophesy unto you a false vision and divination, and a thing of nought, and the deceit of their heart.

15 Therefore thus saith the LORD concerning the prophets that prophesy in my name, and I sent them not, yet they say, Sword and famine shall not be in this land; By sword and famine shall those prophets be consumed.

16 And the people to whom they prophesy shall be cast out in the streets of Jerusalem, because of the famine and the sword; and they shall have none to bury them, them, their wives, nor their sons, nor their daughters: for I will pour their wickedness upon them.

17 ¶ Therefore thou shalt say this word unto them; Let mine eyes run down with tears night and day, and let them not cease: for the virgin daughter of my people is broken with a great breach, with a very grievous blow.

18 If I go forth into the field, then behold the slain with the sword! and if I enter into the city, then behold them that are sick with famine! yea, both the prophet and the priest go about into a land that they know not.

19 Hast thou utterly rejected Judah? hath thy soul loathed Zion? why hast thou smitten us, and *there is* no healing

for us? we looked for peace, and *there is*
no good; and for the time of healing, and
behold trouble!
20 We acknowledge, O LORD, our
wickedness, *and* the iniquity of our
fathers: for we have sinned against
thee.
21 Do not abhor *us*, for thy name's
sake; do not disgrace the throne of thy
glory: remember, break not thy covenant with us.
22 Are there *any* among the vanities of
the Ġĕn'tīleș that can cause rain? or can
the heavens give showers? *Art* not
thou he, O LORD our God? therefore we
will wait upon thee: for thou hast made
all these *things*.

CHAPTER 15

THEN said the LORD unto me,
Though Moses and Samuel stood
before me, *yet* my mind *could* not *be*
toward this people: cast *them* out of my
sight, and let them go forth.
2 And it shall come to pass, if they say
unto thee, Whither shall we go forth?
then thou shalt tell them, Thus saith the
LORD; Such as *are* for death, to death;
and such as *are* for the sword, to the
sword; and such as *are* for the famine,
to the famine; and such as *are* for the
captivity, to the captivity.
3 And I will appoint over them four
kinds, saith the LORD: the sword to
slay, and the dogs to tear, and the fowls
of the heaven, and the beasts of the
earth, to devour and destroy.
4 And I will cause them to be removed
into all kingdoms of the earth, because
of Mȧ-năs'sĕh the son of Hĕz'ē-kī'ȧh
king of Judah, for *that* which he did in
Jerusalem.
5 For who shall have pity upon thee, O
Jerusalem? or who shall bemoan thee?
or who shall go aside to ask how thou
doest?
6 Thou hast forsaken me, saith the
LORD, thou art gone backward: therefore will I stretch out my hand against
thee, and destroy thee; I am weary with
repenting.
7 And I will fan them with a fan in the
gates of the land; I will bereave *them* of
children, I will destroy my people, *since*
they return not from their ways.
8 Their widows are increased to me
above the sand of the seas: I have
brought upon them against the mother
of the young men a spoiler at noonday:
I have caused *him* to fall upon it suddenly, and terrors upon the city.
9 She that hath borne seven languisheth: she hath given up the ghost; her
sun is gone down while *it was* yet day:
she hath been ashamed and confounded: and the residue of them will I
deliver to the sword before their enemies, saith the LORD.
10 ¶ Woe is me, my mother, that thou
hast borne me a man of strife and a man
of contention to the whole earth! I have
neither lent on usury, nor men have lent
to me on usury; *yet* every one of them
doth curse me.
11 The LORD said, Verily it shall be
well with thy remnant; verily I will
cause the enemy to entreat thee *well*
in the time of evil and in the time of
affliction.
12 Shall iron break the northern iron
and the steel?
13 Thy substance and thy treasures
will I give to the spoil without price, and
that for all thy sins, even in all thy
borders.
14 And I will make *thee* to pass with
thine enemies into a land *which* thou
knowest not: for a fire is kindled in mine
anger, *which* shall burn upon you.
15 ¶ O LORD, thou knowest: remember me, and visit me, and revenge me of
my persecutors; take me not away in thy
long-suffering: know that for thy sake I
have suffered rebuke.
16 Thy words were found, and I did
eat them; and thy word was unto me the
joy and rejoicing of mine heart: for I am
called by thy name, O LORD God of
hosts.
17 I sat not in the assembly of the
mockers, nor rejoiced; I sat alone because of thy hand: for thou hast filled me
with indignation.
18 Why is my pain perpetual, and my
wound incurable, *which* refuseth to be
healed? wilt thou be altogether unto me
as a liar, *and as* waters *that* fail?
19 ¶ Therefore thus saith the LORD,
If thou return, then will I bring thee
again, *and* thou shalt stand before me:
and if thou take forth the precious from
the vile, thou shalt be as my mouth: let
them return unto thee; but return not
thou unto them.
20 And I will make thee unto this
people a fenced brazen wall: and they

shall fight against thee, but they shall
not prevail against thee: for I *am* with
thee to save thee and to deliver thee,
saith the LORD.
21 And I will deliver thee out of the
hand of the wicked, and I will redeem
thee out of the hand of the terrible.

CHAPTER 16

THE word of the LORD came also
unto me, saying,
2 Thou shalt not take thee a wife,
neither shalt thou have sons nor daughters in this place.
3 For thus saith the LORD concerning
the sons and concerning the daughters
that are born in this place, and concerning their mothers that bare them, and
concerning their fathers that begat them
in this land;
4 They shall die of grievous deaths;
they shall not be lamented; neither shall
they be buried; *but* they shall be as dung
upon the face of the earth: and they
shall be consumed by the sword, and by
famine; and their carcasses shall be
meat for the fowls of heaven, and for
the beasts of the earth.
5 For thus saith the LORD, Enter not
into the house of mourning, neither go
to lament nor bemoan them: for I have
taken away my peace from this people,
saith the LORD, *even* loving-kindness
and mercies.
6 Both the great and the small shall die
in this land: they shall not be buried,
neither shall *men* lament for them, nor
cut themselves, nor make themselves
bald for them:
7 Neither shall *men* tear *themselves*
for them in mourning, to comfort them
for the dead; neither shall *men* give
them the cup of consolation to drink for
their father or for their mother.
8 Thou shalt not also go into the house
of feasting, to sit with them to eat and to
drink.
9 For thus saith the LORD of hosts, the
God of Ĭṣ'rā-ĕl; Behold, I will cause to
cease out of this place in your eyes, and
in your days, the voice of mirth, and the
voice of gladness, the voice of the bridegroom, and the voice of the bride.
10 ℂ And it shall come to pass, when
thou shalt show this people all these
words, and they shall say unto thee,
Wherefore hath the LORD pronounced
all this great evil against us? or what *is*
our iniquity? or what *is* our sin that we
have committed against the LORD our
God?
11 Then shalt thou say unto them, Because your fathers have forsaken me,
saith the LORD, and have walked after
other gods, and have served them, and
have worshipped them, and have forsaken me, and have not kept my law;
12 And ye have done worse than your
fathers; for, behold, ye walk every one
after the imagination of his evil heart,
that they may not hearken unto me:
13 Therefore will I cast you out of this
land into a land that ye know not,
neither ye nor your fathers; and there
shall ye serve other gods day and night;
where I will not show you favor.
14 ℂ Therefore, behold, the days
come, saith the LORD, that it shall no
more be said, The LORD liveth, that
brought up the children of Ĭṣ'rā-ĕl out
of the land of Egypt;
15 But, The LORD liveth, that brought
up the children of Ĭṣ'rā-ĕl from the land
of the north, and from all the lands
whither he had driven them: and I will
bring them again into their land that I
gave unto their fathers.
16 ℂ Behold, I will send for many
fishers, saith the LORD, and they shall
fish them; and after will I send for many
hunters, and they shall hunt them from
every mountain, and from every hill,
and out of the holes of the rocks.
17 For mine eyes *are* upon all their
ways: they are not hid from my face,
neither is their iniquity hid from mine
eyes.
18 And first I will recompense their
iniquity and their sin double; because
they have defiled my land, they have
filled mine inheritance with the carcasses of their detestable and abominable things.
19 O LORD, my strength, and my fortress, and my refuge in the day of affliction, the Ġĕn'tīleṣ shall come unto thee
from the ends of the earth, and shall
say, Surely our fathers have inherited
lies, vanity, and *things* wherein *there is*
no profit.
20 Shall a man make gods unto himself, and they *are* no gods?
21 Therefore, behold, I will this once
cause them to know, I will cause them to
know mine hand and my might; and they
shall know that my name *is* The LORD.

CHAPTER 17

THE sin of Judah *is* written with a
pen of iron, *and* with the point of a
diamond: *it is* graven upon the table of
their heart, and upon the horns of your
altars;
2 Whilst their children remember their
altars and their groves by the green
trees upon the high hills.
3 O my mountain in the field, I will
give thy substance *and* all thy treasures
to the spoil, *and* thy high places for sin,
throughout all thy borders.
4 And thou, even thyself, shalt discon-
tinue from thine heritage that I gave
thee; and I will cause thee to serve
thine enemies in the land which thou
knowest not: for ye have kindled a fire
in mine anger, *which* shall burn for ever.
5 ¶ Thus saith the LORD; Cursed *be*
the man that trusteth in man, and maketh flesh his arm, and whose heart
departeth from the LORD.
6 For he shall be like the heath in the
desert, and shall not see when good
cometh; but shall inhabit the parched
places in the wilderness, *in* a salt land
and not inhabited.
7 Blessed *is* the man that trusteth in
the LORD, and whose hope the LORD is.
8 For he shall be as a tree planted by
the waters, and *that* spreadeth out her
roots by the river, and shall not see when
heat cometh, but her leaf shall be green;
and shall not be careful in the year of
drought, neither shall cease from yielding fruit.
9 ¶ The heart *is* deceitful above all
things, and desperately wicked: who
can know it?
10 I the LORD search the heart, *I* try
the reins, even to give every man according to his ways, *and* according to
the fruit of his doings.
11 *As* the partridge sitteth *on eggs*,
and hatcheth *them* not; *so* he that getteth riches, and not by right, shall leave
them in the midst of his days, and at his
end shall be a fool.
12 ¶ A glorious high throne from the
beginning *is* the place of our sanctuary.
13 O LORD, the hope of Is'rā-ĕl, all
that forsake thee shall be ashamed, *and*
they that depart from me shall be written in the earth, because they have forsaken the LORD, the fountain of living
waters.
14 Heal me, O LORD, and I shall be
healed; save me, and I shall be saved:
for thou *art* my praise.
15 ¶ Behold, they say unto me, Where
is the word of the LORD? let it come
now.
16 As for me, I have not hastened from
being a pastor to follow thee: neither
have I desired the woeful day; thou
knowest: that which came out of my
lips was *right* before thee.
17 Be not a terror unto me: thou *art*
my hope in the day of evil.
18 Let them be confounded that persecute me, but let not me be confounded: let them be dismayed, but let
not me be dismayed: bring upon them
the day of evil, and destroy them with
double destruction.
19 ¶ Thus said the LORD unto me; Go
and stand in the gate of the children of
the people, whereby the kings of Judah
come in, and by the which they go out,
and in all the gates of Jerusalem;
20 And say unto them, Hear ye the
word of the LORD, ye kings of Judah,
and all Judah, and all the inhabitants
of Jerusalem, that enter in by these
gates:
21 Thus saith the LORD; Take heed to
yourselves, and bear no burden on the
sabbath day, nor bring *it* in by the gates
of Jerusalem;
22 Neither carry forth a burden out of
your houses on the sabbath day, neither
do ye any work, but hallow ye the sabbath day, as I commanded your fathers.
23 But they obeyed not, neither inclined their ear, but made their neck
stiff, that they might not hear, nor
receive instruction.
24 And it shall come to pass, if ye
diligently hearken unto me, saith the
LORD, to bring in no burden through
the gates of this city on the sabbath
day, but hallow the sabbath day, to do
no work therein;
25 Then shall there enter into the
gates of this city kings and princes sitting upon the throne of David, riding in
chariots and on horses, they, and their
princes, the men of Judah, and the
inhabitants of Jerusalem: and this city
shall remain for ever.
26 And they shall come from the cities
of Judah, and from the places about
Jerusalem, and from the land of Benjamin, and from the plain, and from the

mountains, and from the south, bringing burnt offerings, and sacrifices, and
meat offerings, and incense, and bringing sacrifices of praise, unto the house
of the LORD.
27 But if ye will not hearken unto me
to hallow the sabbath day, and not to
bear a burden, even entering in at the
gates of Jerusalem on the sabbath day;
then will I kindle a fire in the gates
thereof, and it shall devour the palaces
of Jerusalem, and it shall not be
quenched.

CHAPTER 18

THE word which came to Jeremiah
from the LORD, saying,
2 Arise, and go down to the potter's
house, and there I will cause thee to
hear my words.
3 Then I went down to the potter's
house, and, behold, he wrought a work
on the wheels.
4 And the vessel that he made of clay
was marred in the hand of the potter:
so he made it again another vessel, as
seemed good to the potter to make *it*.
5 Then the word of the LORD came to
me, saying,
6 O house of Ĭṣ'rā-ĕl, cannot I do with
you as this potter? saith the LORD. Behold, as the clay *is* in the potter's hand,
so *are* ye in mine hand, O house of
Ĭṣ'rā-ĕl.
7 *At what* instant I shall speak concerning a nation, and concerning a
kingdom, to pluck up, and to pull down,
and to destroy *it;*
8 If that nation, against whom I have
pronounced, turn from their evil, I will
repent of the evil that I thought to do
unto them.
9 And *at what* instant I shall speak
concerning a nation, and concerning a
kingdom, to build and to plant *it;*
10 If it do evil in my sight, that it obey
not my voice, then I will repent of the
good, wherewith I said I would benefit
them.
11 ℂ Now therefore go to, speak to
the men of Judah, and to the inhabitants of Jerusalem, saying, Thus saith
the LORD; Behold, I frame evil against
you, and devise a device against you:
return ye now every one from his evil
way, and make your ways and your
doings good.
12 And they said, There is no hope:
but we will walk after our own devices,
and we will every one do the imagination of his evil heart.
13 Therefore thus saith the LORD; Ask
ye now among the heathen, who hath
heard such things: the virgin of Ĭṣ'rā-ĕl
hath done a very horrible thing.
14 Will *a man* leave the snow of
Lebanon *which cometh* from the rock
of the field? *or* shall the cold flowing
waters that come from another place be
forsaken?
15 Because my people hath forgotten
me, they have burned incense to vanity,
and they have caused them to stumble
in their ways *from* the ancient paths, to
walk in paths, *in* a way not cast up;
16 To make their land desolate, *and* a
perpetual hissing; every one that passeth thereby shall be astonished, and
wag his head.
17 I will scatter them as with an east
wind before the enemy; I will show
them the back, and not the face, in the
day of their calamity.
18 ℂ Then said they, Come, and let
us devise devices against Jeremiah; for
the law shall not perish from the priest,
nor counsel from the wise, nor the word
from the prophet. Come, and let us
smite him with the tongue, and let us
not give heed to any of his words.
19 Give heed to me, O LORD, and
hearken to the voice of them that contend with me.
20 Shall evil be recompensed for good?
for they have digged a pit for my soul.
Remember that I stood before thee to
speak good for them, *and* to turn away
thy wrath from them.
21 Therefore deliver up their children
to the famine, and pour out their *blood*
by the force of the sword; and let their
wives be bereaved of their children, and
be widows; and let their men be put to
death; *let* their young men *be* slain by
the sword in battle.
22 Let a cry be heard from their
houses, when thou shalt bring a troop
suddenly upon them: for they have
digged a pit to take me, and hid snares
for my feet.
23 Yet, LORD, thou knowest all their
counsel against me to slay *me:* forgive
not their iniquity, neither blot out their
sin from thy sight, but let them be
overthrown before thee; deal *thus* with
them in the time of thine anger.

CHAPTER 19

THUS saith the LORD, Go and get a potter's earthen bottle, and *take* of the ancients of the people, and of the ancients of the priests;

2 And go forth unto the valley of the son of Hĭn'nŏm, which *is* by the entry of the east gate, and proclaim there the words that I shall tell thee:

3 And say, Hear ye the word of the LORD, O kings of Judah, and inhabitants of Jerusalem; Thus saith the LORD of hosts, the God of Ĭş'rā-ĕl; Behold, I will bring evil upon this place, the which whosoever heareth, his ears shall tingle.

4 Because they have forsaken me, and have estranged this place, and have burned incense in it unto other gods, whom neither they nor their fathers have known, nor the kings of Judah, and have filled this place with the blood of innocents;

5 They have built also the high places of Bā'ăl, to burn their sons with fire *for* burnt offerings unto Bā'ăl, which I commanded not, nor spake *it*, neither came *it* into my mind:

6 Therefore, behold, the days come, saith the LORD, that this place shall no more be called Tō'phĕt, nor The valley of the son of Hĭn'nŏm, but The valley of slaughter.

7 And I will make void the counsel of Judah and Jerusalem in this place; and I will cause them to fall by the sword before their enemies, and by the hands of them that seek their lives: and their carcasses will I give to be meat for the fowls of the heaven, and for the beasts of the earth.

8 And I will make this city desolate, and a hissing; every one that passeth thereby shall be astonished and hiss, because of all the plagues thereof.

9 And I will cause them to eat the flesh of their sons and the flesh of their daughters, and they shall eat every one the flesh of his friend in the siege and straitness, wherewith their enemies, and they that seek their lives, shall straiten them.

10 Then shalt thou break the bottle in the sight of the men that go with thee,

11 And shalt say unto them, Thus saith the LORD of hosts; Even so will I break this people and this city, as *one* breaketh a potter's vessel, that cannot be made whole again: and they shall bury *them* in Tō'phĕt, till *there be* no place to bury.

12 Thus will I do unto this place, saith the LORD, and to the inhabitants thereof, and *even* make this city as Tō'phĕt:

13 And the houses of Jerusalem, and the houses of the kings of Judah, shall be defiled as the place of Tō'phĕt, because of all the houses upon whose roofs they have burned incense unto all the host of heaven, and have poured out drink offerings unto other gods.

14 Then came Jeremiah from Tō'phĕt, whither the LORD had sent him to prophesy; and he stood in the court of the LORD's house, and said to all the people,

15 Thus saith the LORD of hosts, the God of Ĭş'rā-ĕl; Behold, I will bring upon this city and upon all her towns all the evil that I have pronounced against it, because they have hardened their necks, that they might not hear my words.

CHAPTER 20

NOW Păsh'ŭr the son of Ĭm'mĕr the priest, who *was* also chief governor in the house of the LORD, heard that Jeremiah prophesied these things.

2 Then Păsh'ŭr smote Jeremiah the prophet, and put him in the stocks that *were* in the high gate of Benjamin, which *was* by the house of the LORD.

3 And it came to pass on the morrow, that Păsh'ŭr brought forth Jeremiah out of the stocks. Then said Jeremiah unto him, The LORD hath not called thy name Păsh'ŭr, but Mā'gŏr-mĭs'sȧ-bĭb.

4 For thus saith the LORD, Behold, I will make thee a terror to thyself, and to all thy friends: and they shall fall by the sword of their enemies, and thine eyes shall behold *it:* and I will give all Judah into the hand of the king of Babylon, and he shall carry them captive into Babylon, and shall slay them with the sword.

5 Moreover I will deliver all the strength of this city, and all the labors thereof, and all the precious things thereof, and all the treasures of the kings of Judah will I give into the hand of their enemies, which shall spoil them, and take them, and carry them to Babylon.

6 And thou, Păsh′ŭr, and all that dwell in thine house, shall go into captivity: and thou shalt come to Babylon, and there thou shalt die, and shalt be buried there, thou, and all thy friends, to whom thou hast prophesied lies.

7 ¶ O LORD, thou hast deceived me, and I was deceived: thou art stronger than I, and hast prevailed: I am in derision daily, every one mocketh me.

8 For since I spake, I cried out, I cried violence and spoil; because the word of the LORD was made a reproach unto me, and a derision, daily.

9 Then I said, I will not make mention of him, nor speak any more in his name. But *his word* was in mine heart as a burning fire shut up in my bones, and I was weary with forbearing, and I could not *stay*.

10 ¶ For I heard the defaming of many, fear on every side. Report, *say they*, and we will report it. All my familiars watched for my halting, *saying*, Peradventure he will be enticed, and we shall prevail against him, and we shall take our revenge on him.

11 But the LORD *is* with me as a mighty terrible one: therefore my persecutors shall stumble, and they shall not prevail: they shall be greatly ashamed; for they shall not prosper: *their* everlasting confusion shall never be forgotten.

12 But, O LORD of hosts, that triest the righteous, *and* seest the reins and the heart, let me see thy vengeance on them: for unto thee have I opened my cause.

13 Sing unto the LORD, praise ye the LORD: for he hath delivered the soul of the poor from the hand of evildoers.

14 ¶ Cursed *be* the day wherein I was born: let not the day wherein my mother bare me be blessed.

15 Cursed *be* the man who brought tidings to my father, saying, A man child is born unto thee; making him very glad.

16 And let that man be as the cities which the LORD overthrew, and repented not: and let him hear the cry in the morning, and the shouting at noontide;

17 Because he slew me not from the womb; or that my mother might have been my grave, and her womb *to be* always great *with me*.

18 Wherefore came I forth out of the womb to see labor and sorrow, that my days should be consumed with shame?

CHAPTER 21

THE word which came unto Jeremiah from the LORD, when king Zĕd′ē-kī′ȧh sent unto him Păsh′ŭr the son of Mĕl-chī′ȧh, and Zĕph′ȧ-nī′ȧh the son of Mā′ȧ-sē′ịah the priest, saying,

2 Inquire, I pray thee, of the LORD for us; for Nĕb′ū-chăd-rĕz′zȧr king of Babylon maketh war against us; if so be that the LORD will deal with us according to all his wondrous works, that he may go up from us.

3 ¶ Then said Jeremiah unto them, Thus shall ye say to Zĕd′ē-kī′ȧh:

4 Thus saith the LORD God of Ĭs̨′rā-ĕl; Behold, I will turn back the weapons of war that *are* in your hands, wherewith ye fight against the king of Babylon, and *against* the Chăl-dē′ăns̨, which besiege you without the walls, and I will assemble them into the midst of this city.

5 And I myself will fight against you with an outstretched hand and with a strong arm, even in anger, and in fury, and in great wrath.

6 And I will smite the inhabitants of this city, both man and beast: they shall die of a great pestilence.

7 And afterward, saith the LORD, I will deliver Zĕd′ē-kī′ȧh king of Judah, and his servants, and the people, and such as are left in this city from the pestilence, from the sword, and from the famine, into the hand of Nĕb′ū-chăd-rĕz′zȧr king of Babylon, and into the hand of their enemies, and into the hand of those that seek their life: and he shall smite them with the edge of the sword; he shall not spare them, neither have pity, nor have mercy.

8 ¶ And unto this people thou shalt say, Thus saith the LORD; Behold, I set before you the way of life, and the way of death.

9 He that abideth in this city shall die by the sword, and by the famine, and by the pestilence: but he that goeth out, and falleth to the Chăl-dē′ăns̨ that besiege you, he shall live, and his life shall be unto him for a prey.

10 For I have set my face against this city for evil, and not for good, saith the LORD: it shall be given into the hand of

the king of Babylon, and he shall burn
it with fire.
11 ¶ And touching the house of the
king of Judah, *say,* Hear ye the word
of the LORD;
12 O house of David, thus saith the
LORD; Execute judgment in the morning, and deliver *him that is* spoiled out
of the hand of the oppressor, lest my
fury go out like fire, and burn that none
can quench *it,* because of the evil of
your doings.
13 Behold, I *am* against thee, O inhabitant of the valley, *and* rock of the
plain, saith the LORD; which say, Who
shall come down against us? or who
shall enter into our habitations?
14 But I will punish you according to
the fruit of your doings, saith the LORD:
and I will kindle a fire in the forest
thereof, and it shall devour all things
round about it.

CHAPTER 22

THUS saith the LORD; Go down to
the house of the king of Judah,
and speak there this word,
2 And say, Hear the word of the LORD,
O king of Judah, that sittest upon the
throne of David, thou, and thy servants,
and thy people that enter in by these
gates:
3 Thus saith the LORD; Execute ye
judgment and righteousness, and deliver the spoiled out of the hand of the
oppressor: and do no wrong, do no
violence to the stranger, the fatherless,
nor the widow, neither shed innocent
blood in this place.
4 For if ye do this thing indeed, then
shall there enter in by the gates of this
house kings sitting upon the throne of
David, riding in chariots and on horses,
he, and his servants, and his people.
5 But if ye will not hear these words,
I swear by myself, saith the LORD, that
this house shall become a desolation.
6 For thus saith the LORD unto the
king's house of Judah; Thou *art* Gĭl'ē-ăd
unto me, *and* the head of Lebanon: *yet*
surely I will make thee a wilderness,
and cities *which* are not inhabited.
7 And I will prepare destroyers against
thee, every one with his weapons: and
they shall cut down thy choice cedars,
and cast *them* into the fire.
8 And many nations shall pass by this
city, and they shall say every man to
his neighbor, Wherefore hath the LORD
done thus unto this great city?
9 Then they shall answer, Because
they have forsaken the covenant of the
LORD their God, and worshipped other
gods, and served them.
10 ¶ Weep ye not for the dead, neither
bemoan him; *but* weep sore for him
that goeth away: for he shall return no
more, nor see his native country.
11 For thus saith the LORD touching
Shăl'lŭm the son of Jō-sī'ăh king of
Judah, which reigned instead of Jō-
sī'ăh his father, which went forth out
of this place; He shall not return
thither any more:
12 But he shall die in the place whither
they have led him captive, and shall
see this land no more.
13 ¶ Woe unto him that buildeth his
house by unrighteousness, and his
chambers by wrong; *that* useth his
neighbor's service without wages, and
giveth him not for his work;
14 That saith, I will build me a wide
house and large chambers, and cutteth
him out windows; and *it is* ceiled with
cedar, and painted with vermilion.
15 Shalt thou reign, because thou
closest *thyself* in cedar? did not thy father eat and drink, and do judgment and
justice, *and* then *it was* well with him?
16 He judged the cause of the poor
and needy; then *it was* well *with him:*
was not this to know me? saith the
LORD.
17 But thine eyes and thine heart *are*
not but for thy covetousness, and for
to shed innocent blood, and for oppression, and for violence, to do *it.*
18 Therefore thus saith the LORD concerning Jē-hoi'ă-kĭm the son of Jō-
sī'ăh king of Judah; They shall not
lament for him, *saying,* Ah my brother!
or, Ah sister! they shall not lament for
him, *saying,* Ah lord! or, Ah his glory!
19 He shall be buried with the burial
of an ass, drawn and cast forth beyond
the gates of Jerusalem.
20 ¶ Go up to Lebanon, and cry; and
lift up thy voice in Bā'shăn, and cry
from the passages: for all thy lovers are
destroyed.
21 I spake unto thee in thy prosperity;
but thou saidst, I will not hear. This
hath been thy manner from thy youth,
that thou obeyedst not my voice.
22 The wind shall eat up all thy

pastors, and thy lovers shall go into
captivity: surely then shalt thou be
ashamed and confounded for all thy
wickedness.
23 O inhabitant of Lebanon, that makest thy nest in the cedars, how gracious
shalt thou be when pangs come upon
thee, the pain as of a woman in travail!
24 *As* I live, saith the LORD, though
Cō-nī'ȧh the son of Jē-hoi'ȧ-kim king
of Judah were the signet upon my right
hand, yet would I pluck thee thence;
25 And I will give thee into the hand
of them that seek thy life, and into the
hand *of them* whose face thou fearest,
even into the hand of Nĕb'ū-chăd-
rĕz'zȧr king of Babylon, and into the
hand of the Chăl-dē'ăns.
26 And I will cast thee out, and thy
mother that bare thee, into another
country, where ye were not born; and
there shall ye die.
27 But to the land whereunto they
desire to return, thither shall they not
return.
28 *Is* this man Cō-nī'ȧh a despised
broken idol? *is he* a vessel wherein *is*
no pleasure? wherefore are they cast
out, he and his seed, and are cast into
a land which they know not?
29 O earth, earth, earth, hear the word
of the LORD.
30 Thus saith the LORD, Write ye this
man childless, a man *that* shall not
prosper in his days: for no man of his
seed shall prosper, sitting upon the
throne of David, and ruling any more
in Judah.

CHAPTER 23

WOE be unto the pastors that
destroy and scatter the sheep of
my pasture! saith the LORD.
2 Therefore thus saith the LORD God
of Ĭs'rā-ĕl against the pastors that feed
my people; Ye have scattered my flock,
and driven them away, and have not
visited them: behold, I will visit upon
you the evil of your doings, saith the
LORD.
3 And I will gather the remnant of my
flock out of all countries whither I have
driven them, and will bring them again
to their folds; and they shall be fruitful
and increase.
4 And I will set up shepherds over
them which shall feed them: and they
shall fear no more, nor be dismayed,
neither shall they be lacking, saith the
LORD.
5 ℂ Behold, the days come, saith the
LORD, that I will raise unto David a
righteous Branch, and a King shall
reign and prosper, and shall execute
judgment and justice in the earth.
6 In his days Judah shall be saved,
and Ĭs'rā-ĕl shall dwell safely: and this
is his name whereby he shall be called,
THE LORD OUR RIGHTEOUSNESS.
7 Therefore, behold, the days come,
saith the LORD, that they shall no more
say, The LORD liveth, which brought
up the children of Ĭs'rā-ĕl out of the
land of Egypt;
8 But, The LORD liveth, which brought
up and which led the seed of the house
of Ĭs'rā-ĕl out of the north country, and
from all countries whither I had driven
them; and they shall dwell in their own
land.
9 ℂ Mine heart within me is broken
because of the prophets; all my bones
shake: I am like a drunken man, and
like a man whom wine hath overcome,
because of the LORD, and because of
the words of his holiness.
10 For the land is full of adulterers;
for because of swearing the land
mourneth; the pleasant places of the
wilderness are dried up, and their
course is evil, and their force *is* not
right.
11 For both prophet and priest are
profane; yea, in my house have I found
their wickedness, saith the LORD.
12 Wherefore their way shall be unto
them as slippery *ways* in the darkness:
they shall be driven on, and fall therein:
for I will bring evil upon them, *even* the
year of their visitation, saith the LORD.
13 And I have seen folly in the prophets
of Sȧ-mā'rĭ-ȧ; they prophesied in Bā'ăl,
and caused my people Ĭs'rā-ĕl to err.
14 I have seen also in the prophets of
Jerusalem a horrible thing: they commit adultery, and walk in lies: they
strengthen also the hands of evildoers,
that none doth return from his wickedness: they are all of them unto me as
Sŏd'ŏm, and the inhabitants thereof as
Gō-mŏr'rȧh.
15 Therefore thus saith the LORD of
hosts concerning the prophets; Behold,
I will feed them with wormwood, and
make them drink the water of gall: for
from the prophets of Jerusalem is

profaneness gone forth into all the land.
16 Thus saith the LORD of hosts,
Hearken not unto the words of the
prophets that prophesy unto you; they
make you vain: they speak a vision of
their own heart, *and* not out of the
mouth of the LORD.
17 They say still unto them that
despise me, The LORD hath said, Ye
shall have peace; and they say unto
every one that walketh after the imagination of his own heart, No evil shall
come upon you.
18 For who hath stood in the counsel
of the LORD, and hath perceived and
heard his word? who hath marked his
word, and heard *it?*
19 Behold, a whirlwind of the LORD is
gone forth in fury, even a grievous
whirlwind: it shall fall grievously upon
the head of the wicked.
20 The anger of the LORD shall not
return, until he have executed, and till
he have performed the thoughts of his
heart: in the latter days ye shall consider it perfectly.
21 I have not sent these prophets, yet
they ran: I have not spoken to them,
yet they prophesied.
22 But if they had stood in my counsel,
and had caused my people to hear my
words, then they should have turned
them from their evil way, and from the
evil of their doings.
23 *Am* I a God at hand, saith the LORD,
and not a God afar off?
24 Can any hide himself in secret
places that I shall not see him? saith
the LORD. Do not I fill heaven and
earth? saith the LORD.
25 I have heard what the prophets
said, that prophesy lies in my name,
saying, I have dreamed, I have dreamed.
26 How long shall *this* be in the heart
of the prophets that prophesy lies? yea,
they are prophets of the deceit of their
own heart;
27 Which think to cause my people to
forget my name by their dreams, which
they tell every man to his neighbor, as
their fathers have forgotten my name
for Bā′ăl.
28 The prophet that hath a dream, let
him tell a dream; and he that hath my
word, let him speak my word faithfully.
What *is* the chaff to the wheat? saith
the LORD.
29 *Is* not my word like as a fire? saith
the LORD; and like a hammer *that*
breaketh the rock in pieces?
30 Therefore, behold, I *am* against the
prophets, saith the LORD, that steal my
words every one from his neighbor.
31 Behold, I *am* against the prophets,
saith the LORD, that use their tongues,
and say, He saith.
32 Behold, I *am* against them that
prophesy false dreams, saith the LORD,
and do tell them, and cause my people
to err by their lies, and by their lightness; yet I sent them not, nor commanded them: therefore they shall not
profit this people at all, saith the LORD.
33 ℂ And when this people, or the
prophet, or a priest, shall ask thee,
saying, What *is* the burden of the LORD?
thou shalt then say unto them, What
burden? I will even forsake you, saith
the LORD.
34 And *as for* the prophet, and the
priest, and the people, that shall say,
The burden of the LORD, I will even
punish that man and his house.
35 Thus shall ye say every one to his
neighbor, and every one to his brother,
What hath the LORD answered? and,
What hath the LORD spoken?
36 And the burden of the LORD shall
ye mention no more; for every man's
word shall be his burden: for ye have
perverted the words of the living God,
of the LORD of hosts our God.
37 Thus shalt thou say to the prophet,
What hath the LORD answered thee?
and, What hath the LORD spoken?
38 But since ye say, The burden of the
LORD; therefore thus saith the LORD;
Because ye say this word, The burden
of the LORD, and I have sent unto you,
saying, Ye shall not say, The burden of
the LORD;
39 Therefore, behold, I, even I, will
utterly forget you, and I will forsake
you, and the city that I gave you and
your fathers, *and cast you* out of my
presence:
40 And I will bring an everlasting reproach upon you, and a perpetual
shame, which shall not be forgotten.

CHAPTER 24

THE LORD showed me, and, behold,
two baskets of figs *were* set before
the temple of the LORD, after that
Něb′ū-chăd-rěz′zär king of Babylon had
carried away captive Jěc′ō-nī′ăh the son

of Jē-hoi'ă-kĭm king of Judah, and the
princes of Judah, with the carpenters
and smiths, from Jerusalem, and had
brought them to Babylon.
2 One basket *had* very good figs, *even*
like the figs *that are* first ripe: and the
other basket *had* very naughty figs,
which could not be eaten, they were so
bad.
3 Then said the LORD unto me, What
seest thou, Jeremiah? And I said, Figs;
the good figs, very good; and the evil,
very evil, that cannot be eaten, they are
so evil.
4 ¶ Again the word of the LORD came
unto me, saying,
5 Thus saith the LORD, the God of
Ĭs'rā-ĕl; Like these good figs, so will I
acknowledge them that are carried
away captive of Judah, whom I have
sent out of this place into the land of
the Chăl-dē'ăns for *their* good.
6 For I will set mine eyes upon them
for good, and I will bring them again to
this land: and I will build them, and
not pull *them* down; and I will plant
them, and not pluck *them* up.
7 And I will give them a heart to know
me, that I *am* the LORD; and they shall
be my people, and I will be their God:
for they shall return unto me with their
whole heart.
8 ¶ And as the evil figs, which cannot
be eaten, they are so evil; surely thus
saith the LORD, So will I give Zĕd'ē-
kī'ăh the king of Judah, and his princes,
and the residue of Jerusalem, that remain in this land, and them that dwell
in the land of Egypt:
9 And I will deliver them to be removed into all the kingdoms of the
earth for *their* hurt, *to be* a reproach
and a proverb, a taunt and a curse, in
all places whither I shall drive them.
10 And I will send the sword, the
famine, and the pestilence, among
them, till they be consumed from off
the land that I gave unto them and to
their fathers.

CHAPTER 25

THE word that came to Jeremiah
concerning all the people of Judah,
in the fourth year of Jē-hoi'ă-kĭm the
son of Jō-sī'ăh king of Judah, that *was*
the first year of Nĕb'ū-chăd-rĕz'zăr
king of Babylon;
2 The which Jeremiah the prophet
spake unto all the people of Judah,
and to all the inhabitants of Jerusalem,
saying,
3 From the thirteenth year of Jō-sī'ăh
the son of Ā'mŏn king of Judah, even
unto this day, that *is* the three and
twentieth year, the word of the LORD
hath come unto me, and I have spoken
unto you, rising early and speaking;
but ye have not hearkened.
4 And the LORD hath sent unto you all
his servants the prophets, rising early
and sending *them;* but ye have not
hearkened, nor inclined your ear to
hear.
5 They said, Turn ye again now every
one from his evil way, and from the
evil of your doings, and dwell in the
land that the LORD hath given unto you
and to your fathers for ever and ever:
6 And go not after other gods to serve
them, and to worship them, and provoke
me not to anger with the works of your
hands; and I will do you no hurt.
7 Yet ye have not hearkened unto me,
saith the LORD; that ye might provoke
me to anger with the works of your
hands to your own hurt.
8 ¶ Therefore thus saith the LORD of
hosts; Because ye have not heard my
words,
9 Behold, I will send and take all the
families of the north, saith the LORD,
and Nĕb'ū-chăd-rĕz'zăr the king of
Babylon, my servant, and will bring
them against this land, and against the
inhabitants thereof, and against all
these nations round about, and will
utterly destroy them, and make them
an astonishment, and a hissing, and
perpetual desolations.
10 Moreover I will take from them the
voice of mirth, and the voice of gladness, the voice of the bridegroom, and
the voice of the bride, the sound of the
millstones, and the light of the candle.
11 And this whole land shall be a
desolation, *and* an astonishment; and
these nations shall serve the king of
Babylon seventy years.
12 ¶ And it shall come to pass, when
seventy years are accomplished, *that* I
will punish the king of Babylon, and
that nation, saith the LORD, for their
iniquity, and the land of the Chăl-
dē'ăns, and will make it perpetual
desolations.
13 And I will bring upon that land all

my words which I have pronounced against it, *even* all that is written in this book, which Jeremiah hath prophesied against all the nations.

14 For many nations and great kings shall serve themselves of them also: and I will recompense them according to their deeds, and according to the works of their own hands.

15 ℭ For thus saith the LORD God of Ĭṣ′rā-ĕl unto me; Take the winecup of this fury at my hand, and cause all the nations, to whom I send thee, to drink it.

16 And they shall drink, and be moved, and be mad, because of the sword that I will send among them.

17 Then took I the cup at the LORD's hand, and made all the nations to drink, unto whom the LORD had sent me:

18 *To wit,* Jerusalem, and the cities of Judah, and the kings thereof, and the princes thereof, to make them a desolation, an astonishment, a hissing, and a curse; as *it is* this day;

19 Phā′raōh king of Egypt, and his servants, and the princes, and all his people;

20 And all the mingled people, and all the kings of the land of Ŭz, and all the kings of the land of the Phĭ-lĭs′tīneṣ, and Ăsh′kē-lŏn, and Ăz′zȧh, and Ĕk′rŏn, and the remnant of Ashdod,

21 Ē′dŏm, and Mō′ăb, and the children of Ammon,

22 And all the kings of Tȳ′rŭs, and all the kings of Zī′dŏn, and the kings of the isles which *are* beyond the sea,

23 Dē′dăn, and Tē′mȧ, and Bŭz, and all *that are* in the utmost corners,

24 And all the kings of Arabia, and all the kings of the mingled people that dwell in the desert,

25 And all the kings of Zĭm′rī, and all the kings of Ē′lăm, and all the kings of the Mēdeṣ,

26 And all the kings of the north, far and near, one with another, and all the kingdoms of the world, which *are* upon the face of the earth: and the king of Shē′shăch shall drink after them.

27 Therefore thou shalt say unto them, Thus saith the LORD of hosts, the God of Ĭṣ′rā-ĕl; Drink ye, and be drunken, and spew, and fall, and rise no more, because of the sword which I will send among you.

28 And it shall be, if they refuse to take the cup at thine hand to drink, then shalt thou say unto them, Thus saith the LORD of hosts; Ye shall certainly drink.

29 For, lo, I begin to bring evil on the city which is called by my name, and should ye be utterly unpunished? Ye shall not be unpunished: for I will call for a sword upon all the inhabitants of the earth, saith the LORD of hosts.

30 Therefore prophesy thou against them all these words, and say unto them, The LORD shall roar from on high, and utter his voice from his holy habitation; he shall mightily roar upon his habitation; he shall give a shout, as they that tread *the grapes,* against all the inhabitants of the earth.

31 A noise shall come *even* to the ends of the earth; for the LORD hath a controversy with the nations: he will plead with all flesh; he will give them *that are* wicked to the sword, saith the LORD.

32 Thus saith the LORD of hosts, Behold, evil shall go forth from nation to nation, and a great whirlwind shall be raised up from the coasts of the earth.

33 And the slain of the LORD shall be at that day from *one* end of the earth even unto the *other* end of the earth: they shall not be lamented, neither gathered, nor buried; they shall be dung upon the ground.

34 ℭ Howl, ye shepherds, and cry; and wallow yourselves *in the ashes,* ye principal of the flock: for the days of your slaughter and of your dispersions are accomplished; and ye shall fall like a pleasant vessel.

35 And the shepherds shall have no way to flee, nor the principal of the flock to escape.

36 A voice of the cry of the shepherds, and a howling of the principal of the flock, *shall be heard:* for the LORD hath spoiled their pasture.

37 And the peaceable habitations are cut down because of the fierce anger of the LORD.

38 He hath forsaken his covert, as the lion: for their land is desolate because of the fierceness of the oppressor, and because of his fierce anger.

CHAPTER 26

IN the beginning of the reign of Jē-hōi′ȧ-kĭm the son of Jō-sī′ȧh king of Judah came this word from the LORD, saying,

2 Thus saith the LORD; Stand in the court of the LORD's house, and speak unto all the cities of Judah, which come to worship in the LORD's house, all the words that I command thee to speak unto them; diminish not a word:

3 If so be they will hearken, and turn every man from his evil way, that I may repent me of the evil, which I purpose to do unto them because of the evil of their doings.

4 And thou shalt say unto them, Thus saith the LORD; If ye will not hearken to me, to walk in my law, which I have set before you,

5 To hearken to the words of my servants the prophets, whom I sent unto you, both rising up early, and sending *them,* but ye have not hearkened;

6 Then will I make this house like Shī'lōh, and will make this city a curse to all the nations of the earth.

7 So the priests and the prophets and all the people heard Jeremiah speaking these words in the house of the LORD.

8 ¶ Now it came to pass, when Jeremiah had made an end of speaking all that the LORD had commanded *him* to speak unto all the people, that the priests and the prophets and all the people took him, saying, Thou shalt surely die.

9 Why hast thou prophesied in the name of the LORD, saying, This house shall be like Shī'lōh, and this city shall be desolate without an inhabitant? And all the people were gathered against Jeremiah in the house of the LORD.

10 ¶ When the princes of Judah heard these things, then they came up from the king's house unto the house of the LORD, and sat down in the entry of the new gate of the LORD's *house*.

11 Then spake the priests and the prophets unto the princes and to all the people, saying, This man *is* worthy to die; for he hath prophesied against this city, as ye have heard with your ears.

12 ¶ Then spake Jeremiah unto all the princes and to all the people, saying, The LORD sent me to prophesy against this house and against this city all the words that ye have heard.

13 Therefore now amend your ways and your doings, and obey the voice of the LORD your God; and the LORD will repent him of the evil that he hath pronounced against you.

14 As for me, behold, I *am* in your hand: do with me as seemeth good and meet unto you.

15 But know ye for certain, that if ye put me to death, ye shall surely bring innocent blood upon yourselves, and upon this city, and upon the inhabitants thereof: for of a truth the LORD hath sent me unto you to speak all these words in your ears.

16 ¶ Then said the princes and all the people unto the priests and to the prophets; This man *is* not worthy to die: for he hath spoken to us in the name of the LORD our God.

17 Then rose up certain of the elders of the land, and spake to all the assembly of the people, saying,

18 Mī'cȧh the Mō-răs'thīte prophesied in the days of Hĕz'ē-kī'ȧh king of Judah, and spake to all the people of Judah, saying, Thus saith the LORD of hosts; Zion shall be plowed *like* a field, and Jerusalem shall become heaps, and the mountain of the house as the high places of a forest.

19 Did Hĕz'ē-kī'ȧh king of Judah and all Judah put him at all to death? did he not fear the LORD, and besought the LORD, and the LORD repented him of the evil which he had pronounced against them? Thus might we procure great evil against our souls.

20 And there was also a man that prophesied in the name of the LORD, Ū-rī'jȧh the son of Shē-mā'ịȧh of Kĭr'jăth–jē'ȧ-rĭm, who prophesied against this city and against this land according to all the words of Jeremiah:

21 And when Jē-hôi'ȧ-kĭm the king, with all his mighty men, and all the princes, heard his words, the king sought to put him to death: but when Ū-rī'jȧh heard it, he was afraid, and fled, and went into Egypt;

22 And Jē-hôi'ȧ-kĭm the king sent men into Egypt, *namely,* Ĕl-nā'thăn the son of Ăch'bŏr, and *certain* men with him into Egypt.

23 And they fetched forth Ū-rī'jȧh out of Egypt, and brought him unto Jē-hôi'ȧ-kĭm the king; who slew him with the sword, and cast his dead body into the graves of the common people.

24 Nevertheless, the hand of Ȧ-hī'kăm the son of Shā'phăn was with Jeremiah, that they should not give him into the hand of the people to put him to death.

CHAPTER 27

IN the beginning of the reign of
Jē-hôi'ā-kim the son of Jō-sī'ăh king
of Judah came this word unto Jeremiah
from the LORD, saying,
2 Thus saith the LORD to me; Make
thee bonds and yokes, and put them
upon thy neck,
3 And send them to the king of Ē'dŏm,
and to the king of Mō'ăb, and to the
king of the Ammonites, and to the king
of Tȳ'rŭs, and to the king of Zī'dŏn, by
the hand of the messengers which come
to Jerusalem unto Zĕd'ē-kī'ăh king of
Judah;
4 And command them to say unto
their masters, Thus saith the LORD of
hosts, the God of Is'ra-ĕl; Thus shall
ye say unto your masters;
5 I have made the earth, the man and
the beast that *are* upon the ground, by
my great power and by my outstretched
arm, and have given it unto whom it
seemed meet unto me.
6 And now have I given all these lands
into the hand of Nĕb'ū-chăd-nĕz'zar
the king of Babylon, my servant; and
the beasts of the field have I given him
also to serve him.
7 And all nations shall serve him, and
his son, and his son's son, until the very
time of his land come: and then many
nations and great kings shall serve
themselves of him.
8 And it shall come to pass, *that* the
nation and kingdom which will not
serve the same Nĕb'ū-chăd-nĕz'zar the
king of Babylon, and that will not put
their neck under the yoke of the king
of Babylon, that nation will I punish,
saith the LORD, with the sword, and with
the famine, and with the pestilence,
until I have consumed them by his hand.
9 Therefore hearken not ye to your
prophets, nor to your diviners, nor to
your dreamers, nor to your enchanters,
nor to your sorcerers, which speak unto
you, saying, Ye shall not serve the king
of Babylon:
10 For they prophesy a lie unto you,
to remove you far from your land; and
that I should drive you out, and ye
should perish.
11 But the nations that bring their
neck under the yoke of the king of
Babylon, and serve him, those will I let
remain still in their own land, saith the
LORD; and they shall till it, and dwell
therein.
12 ¶ I spake also to Zĕd'ē-kī'ăh king
of Judah according to all these words,
saying, Bring your necks under the yoke
of the king of Babylon, and serve him
and his people, and live.
13 Why will ye die, thou and thy
people, by the sword, by the famine,
and by the pestilence, as the LORD hath
spoken against the nation that will not
serve the king of Babylon?
14 Therefore hearken not unto the
words of the prophets that speak unto
you, saying, Ye shall not serve the king
of Babylon: for they prophesy a lie
unto you.
15 For I have not sent them, saith the
LORD, yet they prophesy a lie in my
name; that I might drive you out, and
that ye might perish, ye, and the
prophets that prophesy unto you.
16 Also I spake to the priests and to
all this people, saying, Thus saith the
LORD; Hearken not to the words of
your prophets that prophesy unto you,
saying, Behold, the vessels of the
LORD's house shall now shortly be
brought again from Babylon: for they
prophesy a lie unto you.
17 Hearken not unto them; serve the
king of Babylon, and live: wherefore
should this city be laid waste?
18 But if they *be* prophets, and if the
word of the LORD be with them, let
them now make intercession to the
LORD of hosts, that the vessels which
are left in the house of the LORD, and
in the house of the king of Judah, and
at Jerusalem, go not to Babylon.
19 ¶ For thus saith the LORD of hosts
concerning the pillars, and concerning
the sea, and concerning the bases, and
concerning the residue of the vessels
that remain in this city,
20 Which Nĕb'ū-chăd-nĕz'zar king of
Babylon took not, when he carried
away captive Jĕc'ō-nī'ăh the son of
Jē-hôi'ā-kim king of Judah from Jerusalem to Babylon, and all the nobles of
Judah and Jerusalem;
21 Yea, thus saith the LORD of hosts,
the God of Is'ra-ĕl, concerning the
vessels that remain *in* the house of the
LORD, and *in* the house of the king of
Judah and of Jerusalem;
22 They shall be carried to Babylon,
and there shall they be until the day

that I visit them, saith the LORD; then will I bring them up, and restore them to this place.

CHAPTER 28

AND it came to pass the same year, in the beginning of the reign of Zĕd′ē-kī′ȧh king of Judah, in the fourth year, *and* in the fifth month, *that* Hăn′ȧ-nī′ȧh the son of Ā′zŭr the prophet, which *was* of Gĭb′ē-ȯn, spake unto me in the house of the LORD, in the presence of the priests and of all the people, saying,
2 Thus speaketh the LORD of hosts, the God of Ĭs′rā-ĕl, saying, I have broken the yoke of the king of Babylon.
3 Within two full years will I bring again into this place all the vessels of the LORD's house, that Nĕb′ū-chăd-nĕz′zȧr king of Babylon took away from this place, and carried them to Babylon:
4 And I will bring again to this place Jĕc′ō-nī′ȧh the son of Jē-hôi′ȧ-kĭm king of Judah, with all the captives of Judah, that went into Babylon, saith the LORD: for I will break the yoke of the king of Babylon.
5 ¶ Then the prophet Jeremiah said unto the prophet Hăn′ȧ-nī′ȧh in the presence of the priests, and in the presence of all the people that stood in the house of the LORD,
6 Even the prophet Jeremiah said, Amen: the LORD do so: the LORD perform thy words which thou hast prophesied, to bring again the vessels of the LORD's house, and all that is carried away captive, from Babylon into this place.
7 Nevertheless, hear thou now this word that I speak in thine ears, and in the ears of all the people;
8 The prophets that have been before me and before thee of old prophesied both against many countries, and against great kingdoms, of war, and of evil, and of pestilence.
9 The prophet which prophesieth of peace, when the word of the prophet shall come to pass, *then* shall the prophet be known, that the LORD hath truly sent him.
10 ¶ Then Hăn′ȧ-nī′ȧh the prophet took the yoke from off the prophet Jeremiah's neck, and brake it.
11 And Hăn′ȧ-nī′ȧh spake in the presence of all the people, saying, Thus saith the LORD; Even so will I break the yoke of Nĕb′ū-chăd-nĕz′zȧr king of Babylon from the neck of all nations within the space of two full years. And the prophet Jeremiah went his way.
12 ¶ Then the word of the LORD came unto Jeremiah *the prophet*, after that Hăn′ȧ-nī′ȧh the prophet had broken the yoke from off the neck of the prophet Jeremiah, saying,
13 Go and tell Hăn′ȧ-nī′ȧh, saying, Thus saith the LORD; Thou hast broken the yokes of wood; but thou shalt make for them yokes of iron.
14 For thus saith the LORD of hosts, the God of Ĭs′rā-ĕl; I have put a yoke of iron upon the neck of all these nations, that they may serve Nĕb′ū-chăd-nĕz′zȧr king of Babylon; and they shall serve him: and I have given him the beasts of the field also.
15 ¶ Then said the prophet Jeremiah unto Hăn′ȧ-nī′ȧh the prophet, Hear now, Hăn′ȧ-nī′ȧh; the LORD hath not sent thee; but thou makest this people to trust in a lie.
16 Therefore thus saith the LORD; Behold, I will cast thee from off the face of the earth: this year thou shalt die, because thou hast taught rebellion against the LORD.
17 So Hăn′ȧ-nī′ȧh the prophet died the same year in the seventh month.

CHAPTER 29

NOW these *are* the words of the letter that Jeremiah the prophet sent from Jerusalem unto the residue of the elders which were carried away captives, and to the priests, and to the prophets, and to all the people whom Nĕb′ū-chăd-nĕz′zȧr had carried away captive from Jerusalem to Babylon;
2 (After that Jĕc′ō-nī′ȧh the king, and the queen, and the eunuchs, the princes of Judah and Jerusalem, and the carpenters, and the smiths, were departed from Jerusalem;)
3 By the hand of Ĕl′ȧ-sȧh the son of Shā′phăn, and Gĕm′ȧ-rī′ȧh the son of Hĭl-kī′ȧh, (whom Zĕd′ē-kī′ȧh king of Judah sent unto Babylon to Nĕb′ū-chăd-nĕz′zȧr king of Babylon) saying,
4 Thus saith the LORD of hosts, the God of Ĭs′rā-ĕl, unto all that are carried away captives, whom I have caused to be carried away from Jerusalem unto Babylon;

5 Build ye houses, and dwell *in them;* and plant gardens, and eat the fruit of them;

6 Take ye wives, and beget sons and daughters; and take wives for your sons, and give your daughters to husbands, that they may bear sons and daughters; that ye may be increased there, and not diminished.

7 And seek the peace of the city whither I have caused you to be carried away captives, and pray unto the LORD for it: for in the peace thereof shall ye have peace.

8 ¶ For thus saith the LORD of hosts, the God of Ĭṣ′rā-ĕl; Let not your prophets and your diviners, that *be* in the midst of you, deceive you, neither hearken to your dreams which ye cause to be dreamed.

9 For they prophesy falsely unto you in my name: I have not sent them, saith the LORD.

10 ¶ For thus saith the LORD, That after seventy years be accomplished at Babylon I will visit you, and perform my good word toward you, in causing you to return to this place.

11 For I know the thoughts that I think toward you, saith the LORD, thoughts of peace, and not of evil, to give you an expected end.

12 Then shall ye call upon me, and ye shall go and pray unto me, and I will hearken unto you.

13 And ye shall seek me, and find *me,* when ye shall search for me with all your heart.

14 And I will be found of you, saith the LORD: and I will turn away your captivity, and I will gather you from all the nations, and from all the places whither I have driven you, saith the LORD; and I will bring you again into the place whence I caused you to be carried away captive.

15 ¶ Because ye have said, The LORD hath raised us up prophets in Babylon;

16 *Know* that thus saith the LORD of the king that sitteth upon the throne of David, and of all the people that dwelleth in this city, *and* of your brethren that are not gone forth with you into captivity;

17 Thus saith the LORD of hosts; Behold, I will send upon them the sword, the famine, and the pestilence, and will make them like vile figs, that cannot be eaten, they are so evil.

18 And I will persecute them with the sword, with the famine, and with the pestilence, and will deliver them to be removed to all the kingdoms of the earth, to be a curse, and an astonishment, and a hissing, and a reproach, among all the nations whither I have driven them:

19 Because they have not hearkened to my words, saith the LORD, which I sent unto them by my servants the prophets, rising up early and sending *them;* but ye would not hear, saith the LORD.

20 ¶ Hear ye therefore the word of the LORD, all ye of the captivity, whom I have sent from Jerusalem to Babylon:

21 Thus saith the LORD of hosts, the God of Ĭṣ′rā-ĕl, of Ahab the son of Kō-lā′ịah, and of Zĕd′ē-kī′ăh the son of Mā′ȧ-sē′ịah, which prophesy a lie unto you in my name; Behold, I will deliver them into the hand of Nĕb′ū-chăd-rĕz′zär king of Babylon; and he shall slay them before your eyes;

22 And of them shall be taken up a curse by all the captivity of Judah which *are* in Babylon, saying, The LORD make thee like Zĕd′ē-kī′ăh and like Ahab, whom the king of Babylon roasted in the fire;

23 Because they have committed villainy in Ĭṣ′rā-ĕl, and have committed adultery with their neighbors' wives, and have spoken lying words in my name, which I have not commanded them; even I know, and *am* a witness, saith the LORD.

24 ¶ *Thus* shalt thou also speak to Shē-mā′ịah the Nē-hĕl′ȧ-mīte, saying,

25 Thus speaketh the LORD of hosts, the God of Ĭṣ′rā-ĕl, saying, Because thou hast sent letters in thy name unto all the people that *are* at Jerusalem, and to Zĕph′ȧ-nī′ăh the son of Mā′ȧ-sē′ịah the priest, and to all the priests, saying,

26 The LORD hath made thee priest in the stead of Jē-hoi′ȧ-dȧ the priest, that ye should be officers in the house of the LORD, for every man *that is* mad, and maketh himself a prophet, that thou shouldest put him in prison, and in the stocks.

27 Now therefore why hast thou not reproved Jeremiah of Ăn′ȧ-thŏth, which maketh himself a prophet to you?

28 For therefore he sent unto us *in*
Babylon, saying, This *captivity is* long:
build ye houses, and dwell *in them;*
and plant gardens, and eat the fruit of
them.
29 And Zĕph′á-nī′áh the priest read
this letter in the ears of Jeremiah the
prophet.
30 ¶ Then came the word of the LORD
unto Jeremiah, saying,
31 Send to all them of the captivity,
saying, Thus saith the LORD concerning
Shē-mā′ịah the Nē-hĕl′á-mīte; Because
that Shē-mā′ịah hath prophesied unto
you, and I sent him not, and he caused
you to trust in a lie:
32 Therefore thus saith the LORD;
Behold, I will punish Shē-mā′ịah the
Nē-hĕl′á-mīte, and his seed: he shall
not have a man to dwell among this
people; neither shall he behold the
good that I will do for my people, saith
the LORD; because he hath taught
rebellion against the LORD.

CHAPTER 30

THE word that came to Jeremiah
from the LORD, saying,
2 Thus speaketh the LORD God of
Ĭṣ′rā-ĕl, saying, Write thee all the
words that I have spoken unto thee in
a book.
3 For, lo, the days come, saith the
LORD, that I will bring again the captivity of my people Ĭṣ′rā-ĕl and Judah,
saith the LORD: and I will cause them
to return to the land that I gave to their
fathers, and they shall possess it.
4 ¶ And these *are* the words that the
LORD spake concerning Ĭṣ′rā-ĕl and
concerning Judah.
5 For thus saith the LORD; We have
heard a voice of trembling, of fear, and
not of peace.
6 Ask ye now, and see whether a man
doth travail with child? wherefore do I
see every man with his hands on his
loins, as a woman in travail, and all
faces are turned into paleness?
7 Alas! for that day *is* great, so that
none *is* like it: it *is* even the time of
Jacob's trouble; but he shall be saved
out of it.
8 For it shall come to pass in that day,
saith the LORD of hosts, *that* I will
break his yoke from off thy neck, and
will burst thy bonds, and strangers shall
no more serve themselves of him:
9 But they shall serve the LORD their
God, and David their king, whom I will
raise up unto them.
10 ¶ Therefore fear thou not, O my
servant Jacob, saith the LORD; neither
be dismayed, O Ĭṣ′rā-ĕl: for, lo, I will
save thee from afar, and thy seed from
the land of their captivity; and Jacob
shall return, and shall be in rest, and
be quiet, and none shall make *him*
afraid.
11 For I *am* with thee, saith the LORD,
to save thee: though I make a full end
of all nations whither I have scattered
thee, yet will I not make a full end of
thee; but I will correct thee in measure,
and will not leave thee altogether unpunished.
12 For thus saith the LORD, Thy
bruise *is* incurable, *and* thy wound *is*
grievous.
13 *There is* none to plead thy cause,
that thou mayest be bound up: thou
hast no healing medicines.
14 All thy lovers have forgotten thee;
they seek thee not; for I have wounded
thee with the wound of an enemy, with
the chastisement of a cruel one, for the
multitude of thine iniquity; *because* thy
sins were increased.
15 Why criest thou for thine affliction?
thy sorrow *is* incurable for the multitude
of thine iniquity: *because* thy sins were
increased, I have done these things
unto thee.
16 Therefore all they that devour thee
shall be devoured; and all thine adversaries, every one of them, shall go
into captivity; and they that spoil thee
shall be a spoil, and all that prey upon
thee will I give for a prey.
17 For I will restore health unto thee,
and I will heal thee of thy wounds, saith
the LORD; because they called thee an
Outcast, *saying*, This *is* Zion, whom no
man seeketh after.
18 ¶ Thus saith the LORD; Behold, I
will bring again the captivity of Jacob's
tents, and have mercy on his dwelling
places; and the city shall be builded
upon her own heap, and the palace shall
remain after the manner thereof.
19 And out of them shall proceed
thanksgiving and the voice of them that
make merry: and I will multiply them,
and they shall not be few; I will also
glorify them, and they shall not be
small.

20 Their children also shall be as
aforetime, and their congregation shall
be established before me, and I will
punish all that oppress them.
21 And their nobles shall be of themselves, and their governor shall proceed
from the midst of them; and I will
cause him to draw near, and he shall
approach unto me: for who *is* this that
engaged his heart to approach unto me?
saith the LORD.
22 And ye shall be my people, and I
will be your God.
23 Behold, the whirlwind of the LORD
goeth forth with fury, a continuing
whirlwind: it shall fall with pain upon
the head of the wicked.
24 The fierce anger of the LORD shall
not return, until he have done *it*, and
until he have performed the intents of
his heart: in the latter days ye shall
consider it.

CHAPTER 31

AT the same time, saith the LORD,
will I be the God of all the families
of Ĭṣ'rā-ĕl, and they shall be my people.
2 Thus saith the LORD, The people
which were left of the sword found grace
in the wilderness; *even* Ĭṣ'rā-ĕl, when
I went to cause him to rest.
3 The LORD hath appeared of old unto
me, *saying*, Yea, I have loved thee with
an everlasting love: therefore with loving-kindness have I drawn thee.
4 Again I will build thee, and thou
shalt be built, O virgin of Ĭṣ'rā-ĕl: thou
shalt again be adorned with thy tabrets,
and shalt go forth in the dances of them
that make merry.
5 Thou shalt yet plant vines upon the
mountains of Sȧ-mā'rĭ-ȧ: the planters
shall plant, and shall eat *them* as common things.
6 For there shall be a day, *that* the
watchmen upon the mount Ē'phrā-ĭm
shall cry, Arise ye, and let us go up to
Zion unto the LORD our God.
7 For thus saith the LORD; Sing with
gladness for Jacob, and shout among
the chief of the nations: publish ye,
praise ye, and say, O LORD, save thy
people, the remnant of Ĭṣ'rā-ĕl.
8 Behold, I will bring them from the
north country, and gather them from
the coasts of the earth, *and* with them
the blind and the lame, the woman with
child and her that travaileth with child
together: a great company shall return
thither.
9 They shall come with weeping, and
with supplications will I lead them: I
will cause them to walk by the rivers of
waters in a straight way, wherein they
shall not stumble: for I am a father to
Ĭṣ'rā-ĕl, and Ē'phrā-ĭm *is* my firstborn.
10 ¶ Hear the word of the LORD, O
ye nations, and declare *it* in the isles
afar off, and say, He that scattered
Ĭṣ'rā-ĕl will gather him, and keep him,
as a shepherd *doth* his flock.
11 For the LORD hath redeemed Jacob,
and ransomed him from the hand of
him that was stronger than he.
12 Therefore they shall come and sing
in the height of Zion, and shall flow
together to the goodness of the LORD,
for wheat, and for wine, and for oil,
and for the young of the flock and of
the herd: and their soul shall be as a
watered garden; and they shall not
sorrow any more at all.
13 Then shall the virgin rejoice in the
dance, both young men and old together:
for I will turn their mourning into joy,
and will comfort them, and make them
rejoice from their sorrow.
14 And I will satiate the soul of the
priests with fatness, and my people
shall be satisfied with my goodness, saith
the LORD.
15 ¶ Thus saith the LORD; A voice
was heard in Rā'mȧh, lamentation, *and*
bitter weeping; Rachel weeping for her
children refused to be comforted for
her children, because they *were* not.
16 Thus saith the LORD; Refrain thy
voice from weeping, and thine eyes
from tears: for thy work shall be rewarded, saith the LORD; and they shall
come again from the land of the enemy.
17 And there is hope in thine end,
saith the LORD, that thy children shall
come again to their own border.
18 ¶ I have surely heard Ē'phrā-ĭm
bemoaning himself *thus;* Thou hast
chastised me, and I was chastised, as a
bullock unaccustomed *to the yoke:* turn
thou me, and I shall be turned; for thou
art the LORD my God.
19 Surely after that I was turned, I
repented; and after that I was instructed, I smote upon *my* thigh: I
was ashamed, yea, even confounded,
because I did bear the reproach of my
youth.

20 *Is* Ē′phrā-ĭm my dear son? *is he* a pleasant child? for since I spake against him, I do earnestly remember him still: therefore my bowels are troubled for him; I will surely have mercy upon him, saith the LORD.

21 Set thee up waymarks, make thee high heaps: set thine heart toward the highway, *even* the way *which* thou wentest: turn again, O virgin of Ĭş′rā-ĕl, turn again to these thy cities.

22 ¶ How long wilt thou go about, O thou backsliding daughter? for the LORD hath created a new thing in the earth, A woman shall compass a man.

23 Thus saith the LORD of hosts, the God of Ĭş′rā-ĕl, As yet they shall use this speech in the land of Judah and in the cities thereof, when I shall bring again their captivity; The LORD bless thee, O habitation of justice, *and* mountain of holiness.

24 And there shall dwell in Judah itself, and in all the cities thereof together, husbandmen, and they *that* go forth with flocks.

25 For I have satiated the weary soul, and I have replenished every sorrowful soul.

26 Upon this I awaked, and beheld; and my sleep was sweet unto me.

27 ¶ Behold, the days come, saith the LORD, that I will sow the house of Ĭş′rā-ĕl and the house of Judah with the seed of man, and with the seed of beast.

28 And it shall come to pass, *that* like as I have watched over them, to pluck up, and to break down, and to throw down, and to destroy, and to afflict; so will I watch over them, to build, and to plant, saith the LORD.

29 In those days they shall say no more, The fathers have eaten a sour grape, and the children's teeth are set on edge.

30 But every one shall die for his own iniquity: every man that eateth the sour grape, his teeth shall be set on edge.

31 ¶ Behold, the days come, saith the LORD, that I will make a new covenant with the house of Ĭş′rā-ĕl, and with the house of Judah:

32 Not according to the covenant that I made with their fathers, in the day *that* I took them by the hand to bring them out of the land of Egypt; which my covenant they brake, although I was a husband unto them, saith the LORD:

33 But this *shall be* the covenant that I will make with the house of Ĭş′rā-ĕl; After those days, saith the LORD, I will put my law in their inward parts, and write it in their hearts; and will be their God, and they shall be my people.

34 And they shall teach no more every man his neighbor, and every man his brother, saying, Know the LORD: for they shall all know me, from the least of them unto the greatest of them, saith the LORD: for I will forgive their iniquity, and I will remember their sin no more.

35 ¶ Thus saith the LORD, which giveth the sun for a light by day, *and* the ordinances of the moon and of the stars for a light by night, which divideth the sea when the waves thereof roar; The LORD of hosts *is* his name:

36 If those ordinances depart from before me, saith the LORD, *then* the seed of Ĭş′rā-ĕl also shall cease from being a nation before me for ever.

37 Thus saith the LORD; If heaven above can be measured, and the foundations of the earth searched out beneath, I will also cast off all the seed of Ĭş′rā-ĕl for all that they have done, saith the LORD.

38 ¶ Behold, the days come, saith the LORD, that the city shall be built to the LORD from the tower of Hȧ-năn′ē-ĕl unto the gate of the corner.

39 And the measuring line shall yet go forth over against it upon the hill Gā′rĕb, and shall compass about to Gō′ăth.

40 And the whole valley of the dead bodies, and of the ashes, and all the fields unto the brook of Kĭd′rŏn, unto the corner of the horse gate toward the east, *shall be* holy unto the LORD; it shall not be plucked up, nor thrown down any more for ever.

CHAPTER 32

THE word that came to Jeremiah from the LORD in the tenth year of Zĕd′ē-kī′ȧh king of Judah, which *was* the eighteenth year of Nĕb′ū-chăd-rĕz′zȧr.

2 For then the king of Babylon's army besieged Jerusalem: and Jeremiah the prophet was shut up in the court of the

prison, which *was* in the king of Judah's
house.
3 For Zĕd′ē-kī′ȧh king of Judah had
shut him up, saying, Wherefore dost
thou prophesy, and say, Thus saith the
LORD, Behold, I will give this city into
the hand of the king of Babylon, and he
shall take it;
4 And Zĕd′ē-kī′ȧh king of Judah shall
not escape out of the hand of the
Chăl-dē′ăns, but shall surely be delivered into the hand of the king of
Babylon, and shall speak with him
mouth to mouth, and his eyes shall
behold his eyes;
5 And he shall lead Zĕd′ē-kī′ȧh to
Babylon, and there shall he be until I
visit him, saith the LORD: though ye
fight with the Chăl-dē′ăns, ye shall not
prosper?
6 ¶ And Jeremiah said, The word of
the LORD came unto me, saying,
7 Behold, Hȧ-năm′ē-ĕl the son of
Shăl′lŭm thine uncle shall come unto
thee, saying, Buy thee my field that *is*
in Ăn′ȧ-thŏth: for the right of redemption *is* thine to buy *it*.
8 So Hȧ-năm′ē-ĕl mine uncle's son
came to me in the court of the prison
according to the word of the LORD, and
said unto me, Buy my field, I pray thee,
that *is* in Ăn′ȧ-thŏth, which *is* in the
country of Benjamin: for the right of
inheritance *is* thine, and the redemption *is* thine; buy *it* for thyself. Then I
knew that this *was* the word of the
LORD.
9 And I bought the field of Hȧ-năm′ē-
ĕl my uncle's son, that *was* in Ăn′ȧ-
thŏth, and weighed him the money,
even seventeen shekels of silver.
10 And I subscribed the evidence, and
sealed *it*, and took witnesses, and
weighed *him* the money in the balances.
11 So I took the evidence of the purchase, *both* that which was sealed *according* to the law and custom, and
that which was open:
12 And I gave the evidence of the
purchase unto Bā′rŭch the son of
Nē-rī′ȧh, the son of Mā′ȧ-sē′ịȧh, in the
sight of Hȧ-năm′ē-ĕl mine uncle's *son*,
and in the presence of the witnesses
that subscribed the book of the purchase, before all the Jews that sat in
the court of the prison.
13 ¶ And I charged Bā′rŭch before
them, saying,
14 Thus saith the LORD of hosts, the
God of Ĭs′rā-ĕl; Take these evidences,
this evidence of the purchase, both
which is sealed, and this evidence which
is open; and put them in an earthen
vessel, that they may continue many
days.
15 For thus saith the LORD of hosts,
the God of Ĭs′rā-ĕl; Houses and fields
and vineyards shall be possessed again
in this land.
16 ¶ Now when I had delivered the
evidence of the purchase unto Bā′rŭch
the son of Nē-rī′ȧh, I prayed unto the
LORD, saying,
17 Ah Lord GOD! behold, thou hast
made the heaven and the earth by thy
great power and stretched out arm, *and*
there is nothing too hard for thee:
18 Thou showest loving-kindness unto
thousands, and recompensest the iniquity of the fathers into the bosom of
their children after them: The Great,
The Mighty God, The LORD of hosts,
is his name;
19 Great in counsel, and mighty in
work: for thine eyes *are* open upon all
the ways of the sons of men, to give
every one according to his ways, and
according to the fruit of his doings:
20 Which hast set signs and wonders
in the land of Egypt, *even* unto this
day, and in Ĭs′rā-ĕl, and among *other*
men; and hast made thee a name, as
at this day;
21 And hast brought forth thy people
Ĭs′rā-ĕl out of the land of Egypt with
signs, and with wonders, and with a
strong hand, and with a stretched out
arm, and with great terror;
22 And hast given them this land,
which thou didst swear to their fathers
to give them, a land flowing with milk
and honey;
23 And they came in, and possessed
it; but they obeyed not thy voice, neither
walked in thy law; they have done
nothing of all that thou commandedst them to do: therefore thou hast
caused all this evil to come upon
them.
24 Behold the mounts, they are come
unto the city to take it; and the city is
given into the hand of the Chăl-dē′ăns
that fight against it, because of the
sword, and of the famine, and of the
pestilence: and what thou hast spoken is
come to pass; and, behold, thou seest *it*.

25 And thou hast said unto me, O Lord
GOD, Buy thee the field for money, and
take witnesses; for the city is given into
the hand of the Chăl-dē′ănṣ.
26 ¶ Then came the word of the LORD
unto Jeremiah, saying,
27 Behold, I *am* the LORD, the God of
all flesh: is there any thing too hard for
me?
28 Therefore thus saith the LORD; Behold, I will give this city into the hand
of the Chăl-dē′ănṣ, and into the hand
of Nĕb′ū-chăd-rĕz′zȧr king of Babylon,
and he shall take it:
29 And the Chăl-dē′ănṣ, that fight
against this city, shall come and set
fire on this city, and burn it with the
houses, upon whose roofs they have
offered incense unto Bā′ăl, and poured
out drink offerings unto other gods, to
provoke me to anger.
30 For the children of Ĭṣ′rā-ĕl and the
children of Judah have only done evil
before me from their youth: for the
children of Ĭṣ′rā-ĕl have only provoked
me to anger with the work of their
hands, saith the LORD.
31 For this city hath been to me *as* a
provocation of mine anger and of my
fury from the day that they built it even
unto this day, that I should remove it
from before my face;
32 Because of all the evil of the children of Ĭṣ′rā-ĕl and of the children of
Judah, which they have done to provoke
me to anger, they, their kings, their
princes, their priests, and their prophets,
and the men of Judah, and the inhabitants of Jerusalem.
33 And they have turned unto me the
back, and not the face: though I taught
them, rising up early and teaching *them*,
yet they have not hearkened to receive
instruction.
34 But they set their abominations in
the house, which is called by my name,
to defile it.
35 And they built the high places of
Bā′ăl, which *are* in the valley of the
son of Hĭn′nŏm, to cause their sons
and their daughters to pass through *the*
fire unto Mō′lĕch; which I commanded
them not, neither came it into my mind,
that they should do this abomination,
to cause Judah to sin.
36 ¶ And now therefore thus saith
the LORD, the God of Ĭṣ′rā-ĕl, concerning this city, whereof ye say, It shall be
delivered into the hand of the king of
Babylon by the sword, and by the
famine, and by the pestilence;
37 Behold, I will gather them out of
all countries, whither I have driven
them in mine anger, and in my fury,
and in great wrath; and I will bring
them again unto this place, and I will
cause them to dwell safely:
38 And they shall be my people, and
I will be their God:
39 And I will give them one heart, and
one way, that they may fear me for
ever, for the good of them, and of their
children after them:
40 And I will make an everlasting
covenant with them, that I will not turn
away from them, to do them good; but
I will put my fear in their hearts, that
they shall not depart from me.
41 Yea, I will rejoice over them to do
them good, and I will plant them in this
land assuredly with my whole heart and
with my whole soul.
42 For thus saith the LORD; Like as I
have brought all this great evil upon
this people, so will I bring upon them
all the good that I have promised them.
43 And fields shall be bought in this
land, whereof ye say, *It is* desolate
without man or beast; it is given into
the hand of the Chăl-dē′ănṣ.
44 Men shall buy fields for money,
and subscribe evidences, and seal *them*,
and take witnesses in the land of Benjamin, and in the places about Jerusalem, and in the cities of Judah, and
in the cities of the mountains, and in
the cities of the valley, and in the cities
of the south: for I will cause their captivity to return, saith the LORD.

CHAPTER 33

MOREOVER the word of the LORD
came unto Jeremiah the second
time, while he was yet shut up in the
court of the prison, saying,
2 Thus saith the LORD the maker
thereof, the LORD that formed it, to
establish it; the LORD *is* his name;
3 Call unto me, and I will answer
thee, and show thee great and mighty
things, which thou knowest not.
4 For thus saith the LORD, the God of
Ĭṣ′rā-ĕl, concerning the houses of this
city, and concerning the houses of the
kings of Judah, which are thrown down
by the mounts, and by the sword;

5 They come to fight with the Chal-
dē'ăns, but *it is* to fill them with the
dead bodies of men, whom I have slain
in mine anger and in my fury, and for
all whose wickedness I have hid my
face from this city.
6 Behold, I will bring it health and
cure, and I will cure them, and will
reveal unto them the abundance of
peace and truth.
7 And I will cause the captivity of
Judah and the captivity of Ĭs'rā-ĕl to return, and will build them, as at the first.
8 And I will cleanse them from all
their in quity, whereby they have sinned
against me; and I will pardon all their
iniquities, whereby they have sinned,
and whereby they have transgressed
against me.
9 ¶ And it shall be to me a name of
joy, a praise and an honor before all
the nations of the earth, which shall
hear all the good that I do unto them:
and they shall fear and tremble for all
the goodness and for all the prosperity
that I procure unto it.
10 Thus saith the LORD; Again there
shall be heard in this place, which ye
say *shall be* desolate without man and
without beast, *even* in the cities of
Judah, and in the streets of Jerusalem,
that are desolate, without man, and
without inhabitant, and without beast,
11 The voice of joy, and the voice of
gladness, the voice of the bridegroom,
and the voice of the bride, the voice of
them that shall say, Praise the LORD of
hosts: for the LORD *is* good; for his
mercy *endureth* for ever: *and* of them
that shall bring the sacrifice of praise
into the house of the LORD. For I will
cause to return the captivity of the land,
as at first, saith the LORD.
12 Thus saith the LORD of hosts;
Again in this place, which is desolate
without man and without beast, and in
all the cities thereof, shall be a habitation of shepherds causing *their* flocks
to lie down.
13 In the cities of the mountains, in
the cities of the vale, and in the cities
of the south, and in the land of Benjamin, and in the places about Jerusalem, and in the cities of Judah, shall
the flocks pass again under the hands
of him that telleth *them*, saith the LORD.
14 Behold, the days come, saith the
LORD, that I will perform that good thing
which I have promised unto the house
of Ĭs'rā-ĕl and to the house of Judah.
15 ¶ In those days, and at that time,
will I cause the Branch of righteousness
to grow up unto David; and he shall
execute judgment and righteousness in
the land.
16 In those days shall Judah be saved,
and Jerusalem shall dwell safely: and
this *is the name* wherewith she shall
be called, The LORD our righteousness.
17 ¶ For thus saith the LORD; David
shall never want a man to sit upon the
throne of the house of Ĭs'rā-ĕl;
18 Neither shall the priests the Lē'vītes
want a man before me to offer burnt
offerings, and to kindle meat offerings,
and to do sacrifice continually.
19 ¶ And the word of the LORD came
unto Jeremiah, saying,
20 Thus saith the LORD; If ye can
break my covenant of the day, and my
covenant of the night, and that there
should not be day and night in their
season;
21 *Then* may also my covenant be
broken with David my servant, that he
should not have a son to reign upon his
throne; and with the Lē'vītes the priests,
my ministers.
22 As the host of heaven cannot be
numbered, neither the sand of the sea
measured; so will I multiply the seed
of David my servant, and the Lē'vītes
that minister unto me.
23 Moreover the word of the LORD
came to Jeremiah, saying,
24 Considerest thou not what this
people have spoken, saying, The two
families which the LORD hath chosen,
he hath even cast them off? thus they
have despised my people, that they
should be no more a nation before them.
25 Thus saith the LORD; If my covenant *be* not with day and night, *and if* I
have not appointed the ordinances of
heaven and earth;
26 Then will I cast away the seed of
Jacob, and David my servant, *so* that I
will not take *any* of his seed *to be* rulers
over the seed of Abraham, Isaac, and
Jacob: for I will cause their captivity to
return, and have mercy on them.

CHAPTER 34

THE word which came unto Jeremiah
from the LORD, when Nĕb'ū-chăd-
nĕz'zăr king of Babylon, and all his army,

and all the kingdoms of the earth of his
dominion, and all the people, fought
against Jerusalem, and against all the
cities thereof, saying,
2 Thus saith the LORD, the God of
Ĭș'rā-ĕl; Go and speak to Zĕd'ē-kī'ȧh
king of Judah, and tell him, Thus saith
the LORD; Behold, I will give this city
into the hand of the king of Babylon, and
he shall burn it with fire:
3 And thou shalt not escape out of his
hand, but shalt surely be taken, and
delivered into his hand; and thine eyes
shall behold the eyes of the king of
Babylon, and he shall speak with thee
mouth to mouth, and thou shalt go to
Babylon.
4 Yet hear the word of the LORD, O
Zĕd'ē-kī'ȧh king of Judah; Thus saith
the LORD of thee, Thou shalt not die by
the sword;
5 *But* thou shalt die in peace: and with
the burnings of thy fathers, the former
kings which were before thee, so shall
they burn *odors* for thee; and they will
lament thee, *saying*, Ah lord! for I have
pronounced the word, saith the LORD.
6 Then Jeremiah the prophet spake all
these words unto Zĕd'ē-kī'ȧh king of
Judah in Jerusalem,
7 When the king of Babylon's army
fought against Jerusalem, and against
all the cities of Judah that were left,
against Lā'chĭsh, and against Ȧ-zē'kȧh:
for these defensed cities remained of
the cities of Judah.
8 ¶ *This is* the word that came unto
Jeremiah from the LORD, after that the
king Zĕd'ē-kī'ȧh had made a covenant
with all the people which *were* at Jerusalem, to proclaim liberty unto them;
9 That every man should let his manservant, and every man his maidservant,
being a Hebrew or a Hebrewess, go
free; that none should serve himself of
them, *to wit*, of a Jew his brother.
10 Now when all the princes, and all
the people, which had entered into the
covenant, heard that every one should
let his manservant, and every one his
maidservant, go free, that none should
serve themselves of them any more;
then they obeyed, and let *them* go.
11 But afterwards they turned, and
caused the servants and the handmaids,
whom they had let go free, to return,
and brought them into subjection for
servants and for handmaids.
12 ¶ Therefore the word of the LORD
came to Jeremiah from the LORD, saying,
13 Thus saith the LORD, the God of
Ĭș'rā-ĕl; I made a covenant with your
fathers in the day that I brought them
forth out of the land of Egypt, out of the
house of bondmen, saying,
14 At the end of seven years let ye go
every man his brother a Hebrew, which
hath been sold unto thee; and when he
hath served thee six years, thou shalt
let him go free from thee: but your
fathers hearkened not unto me, neither
inclined their ear.
15 And ye were now turned, and had
done right in my sight, in proclaiming
liberty every man to his neighbor; and
ye had made a covenant before me in the
house which is called by my name:
16 But ye turned and polluted my
name, and caused every man his servant, and every man his handmaid, whom
he had set at liberty at their pleasure, to
return, and brought them into subjection, to be unto you for servants and for
handmaids.
17 Therefore thus saith the LORD; Ye
have not hearkened unto me, in proclaiming liberty, every one to his
brother, and every man to his neighbor:
behold, I proclaim a liberty for you,
saith the LORD, to the sword, to the
pestilence, and to the famine; and I will
make you to be removed into all the
kingdoms of the earth.
18 And I will give the men that have
transgressed my covenant, which have
not performed the words of the covenant
which they had made before me, when
they cut the calf in twain, and passed
between the parts thereof,
19 The princes of Judah, and the
princes of Jerusalem, the eunuchs, and
the priests, and all the people of the
land, which passed between the parts of
the calf;
20 I will even give them into the hand
of their enemies, and into the hand of
them that seek their life: and their dead
bodies shall be for meat unto the fowls
of the heaven, and to the beasts of the
earth.
21 And Zĕd'ē-kī'ȧh king of Judah and
his princes will I give into the hand of
their enemies, and into the hand of them
that seek their life, and into the hand of
the king of Babylon's army, which are
gone up from you.

22 Behold, I will command, saith the
LORD, and cause them to return to this
city; and they shall fight against it, and
take it, and burn it with fire: and I will
make the cities of Judah a desolation
without an inhabitant.

CHAPTER 35

THE word which came unto Jeremiah
from the LORD, in the days of Jē-
hôi′ȧ-kĭm the son of Jō-sī′ȧh king of
Judah, saying,
2 Go unto the house of the Rĕch′ȧb-
ītes, and speak unto them, and bring
them into the house of the LORD, into
one of the chambers, and give them wine
to drink.
3 Then I took Jā-ăz′ȧ-nī′ȧh the son of
Jeremiah, the son of Hăb′ȧ-zĭ-nī′ȧh, and
his brethren, and all his sons, and the
whole house of the Rĕch′ȧb-ītes;
4 And I brought them into the house of
the LORD, into the chamber of the sons
of Hā′năn, the son of Ĭg′dȧ-lī′ȧh, a man
of God, which *was* by the chamber of the
princes, which *was* above the chamber
of Mā′ȧ-sē′iȧh the son of Shăl′lŭm, the
keeper of the door:
5 And I set before the sons of the house
of the Rĕch′ȧb-ītes pots full of wine, and
cups; and I said unto them, Drink ye
wine.
6 But they said, We will drink no wine:
for Jŏn′ȧ-dăb the son of Rē′chăb our
father commanded us, saying, Ye shall
drink no wine, *neither* ye, nor your sons
for ever:
7 Neither shall ye build house, nor sow
seed, nor plant vineyard, nor have *any:*
but all your days ye shall dwell in tents;
that ye may live many days in the land
where ye *be* strangers.
8 Thus have we obeyed the voice of
Jŏn′ȧ-dăb the son of Rē′chăb our father
in all that he hath charged us, to drink
no wine all our days, we, our wives, our
sons, nor our daughters;
9 Nor to build houses for us to dwell in;
neither have we vineyard, nor field, nor
seed:
10 But we have dwelt in tents, and have
obeyed, and done according to all that
Jŏn′ȧ-dăb our father commanded us.
11 But it came to pass, when Nĕb′ū-
chăd-rĕz′zȧr king of Babylon came up
into the land, that we said, Come, and
let us go to Jerusalem for fear of the
army of the Chăl-dē′ăns, and for fear of
the army of the Syrians: so we dwell at
Jerusalem.
12 ¶ Then came the word of the LORD
unto Jeremiah, saying,
13 Thus saith the LORD of hosts, the
God of Ĭs′rā-ĕl; Go and tell the men of
Judah and the inhabitants of Jerusalem, Will ye not receive instruction to
hearken to my words? saith the LORD.
14 The words of Jŏn′ȧ-dăb the son of
Rē′chăb, that he commanded his sons
not to drink wine, are performed; for
unto this day they drink none, but obey
their father's commandment: notwithstanding I have spoken unto you, rising
early and speaking; but ye hearkened
not unto me.
15 I have sent also unto you all my
servants the prophets, rising up early
and sending *them,* saying, Return ye
now every man from his evil way, and
amend your doings, and go not after
other gods to serve them, and ye shall
dwell in the land which I have given to
you and to your fathers: but ye have not
inclined your ear, nor hearkened unto
me.
16 Because the sons of Jŏn′ȧ-dăb the
son of Rē′chăb have performed the commandment of their father, which he commanded them; but this people hath not
hearkened unto me:
17 Therefore thus saith the LORD God
of hosts, the God of Ĭs′rā-ĕl; Behold, I
will bring upon Judah and upon all the
inhabitants of Jerusalem all the evil
that I have pronounced against them:
because I have spoken unto them, but
they have not heard; and I have called
unto them, but they have not answered.
18 ¶ And Jeremiah said unto the
house of the Rĕch′ȧb-ītes, Thus saith
the LORD of hosts, the God of Ĭs′rā-ĕl;
Because ye have obeyed the commandment of Jŏn′ȧ-dăb your father, and kept
all his precepts, and done according
unto all that he hath commanded you;
19 Therefore thus saith the LORD of
hosts, the God of Ĭs′rā-ĕl; Jŏn′ȧ-dăb the
son of Rē′chăb shall not want a man to
stand before me for ever.

CHAPTER 36

AND it came to pass in the fourth year
of Jē-hôi′ȧ-kĭm the son of Jō-sī′ȧh
king of Judah, *that* this word came unto
Jeremiah from the LORD, saying,
2 Take thee a roll of a book, and write

therein all the words that I have spoken
unto thee against Ĭṣ′rā-ĕl, and against
Judah, and against all the nations, from
the day I spake unto thee, from the days
of Jō-sī′ȧh, even unto this day.
3 It may be that the house of Judah will
hear all the evil which I purpose to do
unto them; that they may return every
man from his evil way; that I may forgive
their iniquity and their sin.
4 Then Jeremiah called Bā′rŭch the
son of Nē-rī′ȧh: and Bā′rŭch wrote from
the mouth of Jeremiah all the words of
the LORD, which he had spoken unto
him, upon a roll of a book.
5 And Jeremiah commanded Bā′rŭch,
saying, I *am* shut up; I cannot go into
the house of the LORD:
6 Therefore go thou, and read in the
roll, which thou hast written from my
mouth, the words of the LORD in the ears
of the people in the LORD's house upon
the fasting day: and also thou shalt read
them in the ears of all Judah that come
out of their cities.
7 It may be they will present their supplication before the LORD, and will
return every one from his evil way: for
great *is* the anger and the fury that the
LORD hath pronounced against this
people.
8 And Bā′rŭch the son of Nē-rī′ȧh did
according to all that Jeremiah the
prophet commanded him, reading in the
book the words of the LORD in the
LORD's house.
9 And it came to pass in the fifth year
of Jē-hôi′ȧ-kĭm the son of Jō-sī′ȧh king
of Judah, in the ninth month, *that* they
proclaimed a fast before the LORD to all
the people in Jerusalem, and to all the
people that came from the cities of
Judah unto Jerusalem.
10 Then read Bā′rŭch in the book the
words of Jeremiah in the house of the
LORD, in the chamber of Gĕm′ȧ-rī′ȧh the
son of Shā′phăn the scribe, in the
higher court, at the entry of the new gate
of the LORD's house, in the ears of all
the people.
11 ¶ When Mī-chā′ịȧh the son of
Gĕm′ȧ-rī′ȧh, the son of Shā′phăn, had
heard out of the book all the words of
the LORD,
12 Then he went down into the king's
house, into the scribe's chamber: and,
lo, all the princes sat there, *even* Ē-lĭsh′-
ȧ-mä the scribe, and Dē-lā′ịȧh the son
of Shē-mā′ịȧh, and Ĕl-nā′thăn the son
of Ăch′bôr, and Gĕm′ȧ-rī′ȧh the son of
Shā′phăn, and Zĕd′ē-kī′ȧh the son of
Hăn′ȧ-nī′ȧh, and all the princes.
13 Then Mī-chā′ịȧh declared unto them
all the words that he had heard, when
Bā′rŭch read the book in the ears of
the people.
14 Therefore all the princes sent
Jē-hū′dī the son of Nĕth′ȧ-nī′ȧh, the son
of Shĕl′ē-mī′ȧh, the son of Cū′shī, unto
Bā′rŭch, saying, Take in thine hand the
roll wherein thou hast read in the ears of
the people, and come. So Bā′rŭch the
son of Nē-rī′ȧh took the roll in his hand,
and came unto them.
15 And they said unto him, Sit down
now, and read it in our ears. So Bā′rŭch
read *it* in their ears.
16 Now it came to pass, when they had
heard all the words, they were afraid
both one and other, and said unto Bā′-
rŭch, We will surely tell the king of all
these words.
17 And they asked Bā′rŭch, saying,
Tell us now, How didst thou write all
these words at his mouth?
18 Then Bā′rŭch answered them, He
pronounced all these words unto me
with his mouth, and I wrote *them* with
ink in the book.
19 Then said the princes unto Bā′rŭch,
Go, hide thee, thou and Jeremiah; and
let no man know where ye be.
20 ¶ And they went in to the king into
the court, but they laid up the roll in
the chamber of Ē-lĭsh′ȧ-mä the scribe,
and told all the words in the ears of the
king.
21 So the king sent Jē-hū′dī to fetch
the roll; and he took it out of Ē-lĭsh′ȧ-mä
the scribe's chamber. And Jē-hū′dī read
it in the ears of the king, and in the ears
of all the princes which stood beside the
king.
22 Now the king sat in the winter house
in the ninth month: and *there was a fire*
on the hearth burning before him.
23 And it came to pass, *that* when
Jē-hū′dī had read three or four leaves,
he cut it with the penknife, and cast *it*
into the fire that *was* on the hearth, until
all the roll was consumed in the fire
that *was* on the hearth.
24 Yet they were not afraid, nor rent
their garments, *neither* the king, nor any
of his servants that heard all these
words.

25 Nevertheless Ĕl-nā'thăn and Dē-
lā'ịah and Gĕm'ȧ-rī'ȧh had made intercession to the king that he would not
burn the roll; but he would not hear them.
26 But the king commanded Jē-răh'-
mē-ĕl the son of Hăm'mē-lĕch, and
Sē-rā'ịah the son of Ăz'rī-ĕl, and Shĕl'ē-
mī'ȧh the son of Ăb'dē-ĕl, to take Bā'-
rŭch the scribe and Jeremiah the
prophet: but the LORD hid them.
27 ¶ Then the word of the LORD came
to Jeremiah, after that the king had
burned the roll, and the words which Bā'-
rŭch wrote at the mouth of Jeremiah,
saying,
28 Take thee again another roll, and
write in it all the former words that were
in the first roll, which Jē-hôi'ȧ-kĭm the
king of Judah hath burned.
29 And thou shalt say to Jē-hôi'ȧ-kĭm
king of Judah, Thus saith the LORD;
Thou hast burned this roll, saying, Why
hast thou written therein, saying, The
king of Babylon shall certainly come and
destroy this land, and shall cause to
cease from thence man and beast?
30 Therefore thus saith the LORD of
Jē-hôi'ȧ-kĭm king of Judah; He shall
have none to sit upon the throne of
David: and his dead body shall be cast
out in the day to the heat, and in the
night to the frost.
31 And I will punish him and his seed
and his servants for their iniquity; and
I will bring upon them, and upon the
inhabitants of Jerusalem, and upon the
men of Judah, all the evil that I have
pronounced against them; but they
hearkened not.
32 ¶ Then took Jeremiah another roll,
and gave it to Bā'rŭch the scribe, the son
of Nē-rī'ȧh; who wrote therein from the
mouth of Jeremiah all the words of the
book which Jē-hôi'ȧ-kĭm king of Judah
had burned in the fire: and there were
added besides unto them many like
words.

CHAPTER 37

AND king Zĕd'ē-kī'ȧh the son of Jō-
sī'ȧh reigned instead of Cō-nī'ȧh
the son of Jē-hôi'ȧ-kĭm, whom Nĕb'ū-
chăd-rĕz'zȧr king of Babylon made
king in the land of Judah.
2 But neither he, nor his servants, nor
the people of the land, did hearken unto
the words of the LORD, which he spake
by the prophet Jeremiah.
3 And Zĕd'ē-kī'ȧh the king sent Jē-
hū'căl the son of Shĕl'ē-mī'ȧh and
Zĕph'ȧ-nī'ȧh the son of Mā'ȧ-sē'ịah
the priest to the prophet Jeremiah,
saying, Pray now unto the LORD our
God for us.
4 Now Jeremiah came in and went out
among the people: for they had not put
him into prison.
5 Then Phā'raōh's army was come
forth out of Egypt: and when the Chăl-
dē'ănṣ that besieged Jerusalem heard
tidings of them, they departed from
Jerusalem.
6 ¶ Then came the word of the LORD
unto the prophet Jeremiah, saying,
7 Thus saith the LORD, the God of
Iṣ'rā-ĕl; Thus shall ye say to the king of
Judah, that sent you unto me to inquire
of me; Behold, Phā'raōh's army, which
is come forth to help you, shall return to
Egypt into their own land.
8 And the Chăl-dē'ănṣ shall come
again, and fight against this city, and
take it, and burn it with fire.
9 Thus saith the LORD; Deceive not
yourselves, saying, The Chăl-dē'ănṣ
shall surely depart from us: for they
shall not depart.
10 For though ye had smitten the whole
army of the Chăl-dē'ănṣ that fight
against you, and there remained *but*
wounded men among them, *yet* should
they rise up every man in his tent, and
burn this city with fire.
11 ¶ And it came to pass, that when
the army of the Chăl-dē'ănṣ was broken
up from Jerusalem for fear of Phā'-
raōh's army,
12 Then Jeremiah went forth out of
Jerusalem to go into the land of Benjamin, to separate himself thence in the
midst of the people.
13 And when he was in the gate of
Benjamin, a captain of the ward *was*
there, whose name *was* Ī-rī'jȧh, the son
of Shĕl'ē-mī'ȧh, the son of Hăn'ȧ-nī'ȧh;
and he took Jeremiah the prophet, saying, Thou fallest away to the Chăl-
dē'ănṣ.
14 Then said Jeremiah, *It is* false; I
fall not away to the Chăl-dē'ănṣ. But
he hearkened not to him: so Ī-rī'-
jȧh took Jeremiah, and brought him to
the princes.
15 Wherefore the princes were wroth
with Jeremiah, and smote him, and put
him in prison in the house of Jonathan

the scribe; for they had made that the prison.

16 ¶ When Jeremiah was entered into the dungeon, and into the cabins, and Jeremiah had remained there many days;

17 Then Zĕd′ē-kī′ȧh the king sent, and took him out; and the king asked him secretly in his house, and said, Is there *any* word from the LORD? And Jeremiah said, There is: for, said he, thou shalt be delivered into the hand of the king of Babylon.

18 Moreover Jeremiah said unto king Zĕd′ē-kī′ȧh, What have I offended against thee, or against thy servants, or against this people, that ye have put me in prison?

19 Where *are* now your prophets which prophesied unto you, saying, The king of Babylon shall not come against you, nor against this land?

20 Therefore hear now, I pray thee, O my lord the king: let my supplication, I pray thee, be accepted before thee; that thou cause me not to return to the house of Jonathan the scribe, lest I die there.

21 Then Zĕd′ē-kī′ȧh the king commanded that they should commit Jeremiah into the court of the prison, and that they should give him daily a piece of bread out of the bakers' street, until all the bread in the city were spent. Thus Jeremiah remained in the court of the prison.

CHAPTER 38

THEN Shĕph′ȧ-tī′ȧh the son of Măt′tăn, and Gĕd′ȧ-lī′ȧh the son of Păsh′ŭr, and Jṳ′căl the son of Shĕl′ē-mī′ȧh, and Păsh′ŭr the son of Măl-ehī′ȧh, heard the words that Jeremiah had spoken unto all the people, saying,

2 Thus saith the LORD, He that remaineth in this city shall die by the sword, by the famine, and by the pestilence: but he that goeth forth to the Chăl-dē′ănṣ shall live; for he shall have his life for a prey, and shall live.

3 Thus saith the LORD, This city shall surely be given into the hand of the king of Babylon's army, which shall take it.

4 Therefore the princes said unto the king, We beseech thee, let this man be put to death: for thus he weakeneth the hands of the men of war that remain in this city, and the hands of all the people, in speaking such words unto them: for this man seeketh not the welfare of this people, but the hurt.

5 Then Zĕd′ē-kī′ȧh the king said, Behold, he *is* in your hand: for the king *is* not *he that* can do *any* thing against you.

6 Then took they Jeremiah, and cast him into the dungeon of Măl-chī′ȧh the son of Hăm′mē-lĕch, that *was* in the court of the prison: and they let down Jeremiah with cords. And in the dungeon *there was* no water, but mire: so Jeremiah sunk in the mire.

7 ¶ Now when Ē′bĕd–mē′lĕch the Ethiopian, one of the eunuchs which was in the king's house, heard that they had put Jeremiah in the dungeon; the king then sitting in the gate of Benjamin;

8 Ē′bĕd–mē′lĕch went forth out of the king's house, and spake to the king, saying,

9 My lord the king, these men have done evil in all that they have done to Jeremiah the prophet, whom they have cast into the dungeon; and he is like to die for hunger in the place where he is: for *there is* no more bread in the city.

10 Then the king commanded Ē′bĕd–mē′lĕch the Ethiopian, saying, Take from hence thirty men with thee, and take up Jeremiah the prophet out of the dungeon, before he die.

11 So Ē′bĕd–mē′lĕch took the men with him, and went into the house of the king under the treasury, and took thence old cast clouts and old rotten rags, and let them down by cords into the dungeon to Jeremiah.

12 And Ē′bĕd–mē′lĕch the Ethiopian said unto Jeremiah, Put now *these* old cast clouts and rotten rags under thine armholes under the cords. And Jeremiah did so.

13 So they drew up Jeremiah with cords, and took him up out of the dungeon: and Jeremiah remained in the court of the prison.

14 ¶ Then Zĕd′ē-kī′ȧh the king sent, and took Jeremiah the prophet unto him into the third entry that *is* in the house of the LORD: and the king said unto Jeremiah, I will ask thee a thing; hide nothing from me.

15 Then Jeremiah said unto Zĕd′ē-kī′ȧh, If I declare *it* unto thee, wilt thou not surely put me to death? and if I give thee counsel, wilt thou not hearken unto me?

16 So Zĕd′ē-kī′ȧh the king sware secretly unto Jeremiah, saying, *As* the
LORD liveth, that made us this soul, I
will not put thee to death, neither will I
give thee into the hand of these men
that seek thy life.
17 Then said Jeremiah unto Zĕd′ē-
kī′ȧh, Thus saith the LORD, the God of
hosts, the God of Ĭs′rā-ĕl; If thou wilt
assuredly go forth unto the king of
Babylon's princes, then thy soul shall
live, and this city shall not be burned
with fire; and thou shalt live, and thine
house:
18 But if thou wilt not go forth to the
king of Babylon's princes, then shall this
city be given into the hand of the
Chăl-dē′ăns̱, and they shall burn it with
fire, and thou shalt not escape out of
their hand.
19 And Zĕd′ē-kī′ȧh the king said unto
Jeremiah, I am afraid of the Jews that
are fallen to the Chăl-dē′ăns, lest they
deliver me into their hand, and they
mock me.
20 But Jeremiah said, They shall not
deliver *thee*. Obey, I beseech thee, the
voice of the LORD, which I speak unto
thee: so it shall be well unto thee, and
thy soul shall live.
21 But if thou refuse to go forth, this *is*
the word that the LORD hath showed
me:
22 And, behold, all the women that are
left in the king of Judah's house *shall be*
brought forth to the king of Babylon's
princes, and those *women* shall say,
Thy friends have set thee on, and have
prevailed against thee: thy feet are
sunk in the mire, *and* they are turned
away back.
23 So they shall bring out all thy wives
and thy children to the Chăl-dē′ăns̱:
and thou shalt not escape out of their
hand, but shalt be taken by the hand of
the king of Babylon: and thou shalt
cause this city to be burned with fire.
24 ¶ Then said Zĕd′ē-kī′ȧh unto Jeremiah, Let no man know of these words,
and thou shalt not die.
25 But if the princes hear that I have
talked with thee, and they come unto
thee, and say unto thee, Declare unto us
now what thou hast said unto the king,
hide it not from us, and we will not put
thee to death; also what the king said
unto thee:
26 Then thou shalt say unto them, I
presented my supplication before the
king, that he would not cause me
to return to Jonathan's house, to die
there.
27 Then came all the princes unto
Jeremiah, and asked him: and he told
them according to all these words that
the king had commanded. So they left
off speaking with him; for the matter
was not perceived.
28 So Jeremiah abode in the court of
the prison until the day that Jerusalem
was taken: and he was *there* when
Jerusalem was taken.

CHAPTER 39

IN the ninth year of Zĕd′ē-kī′ȧh king
of Judah, in the tenth month, came
Nĕb′ū-chăd-rĕz′zȧr king of Babylon
and all his army against Jerusalem, and
they besieged it.
2 *And* in the eleventh year of Zĕd′ē-
kī′ȧh, in the fourth month, the ninth
day of the month, the city was broken up.
3 And all the princes of the king of
Babylon came in, and sat in the middle
gate, *even* Nĕr′găl–shȧ-rē′zĕr, Săm′-
găr–nē′bō, Sär′sē-chĭm, Răb′–sȧ-rĭs,
Nĕr′găl–shȧ-rē′zĕr, Răb′–măg, with all
the residue of the princes of the king of
Babylon.
4 ¶ And it came to pass, *that* when
Zĕd′ē-kī′ȧh the king of Judah saw them,
and all the men of war, then they fled,
and went forth out of the city by night,
by the way of the king's garden, by the
gate betwixt the two walls: and he went
out the way of the plain.
5 But the Chăl-dē′ăns̱' army pursued
after them, and overtook Zĕd′ē-kī′ȧh in
the plains of Jĕr′ĭ-chō: and when they
had taken him, they brought him up to
Nĕb′ū-chăd-nĕz′zȧr king of Babylon to
Rĭb′lȧh in the land of Hā′măth, where
he gave judgment upon him.
6 Then the king of Babylon slew the
sons of Zĕd′ē-kī′ȧh in Rĭb′lȧh before his
eyes: also the king of Babylon slew all
the nobles of Judah.
7 Moreover he put out Zĕd′ē-kī′ȧh's
eyes, and bound him with chains, to
carry him to Babylon.
8 ¶ And the Chăl-dē′ăns̱ burned the
king's house, and the houses of the people, with fire, and brake down the walls
of Jerusalem.
9 Then Nĕb′ū-zär–ā′dăn the captain of

the guard carried away captive into Babylon the remnant of the people that remained in the city, and those that fell away, that fell to him, with the rest of the people that remained.

10 But Nĕb′ū-zär–ā′dăn the captain of the guard left of the poor of the people, which had nothing, in the land of Judah, and gave them vineyards and fields at the same time.

11 ¶ Now Nĕb′ū-ehăd-rĕz′zȧr king of Babylon gave charge concerning Jeremiah to Nĕb′ū-zär–ā′dăn the captain of the guard, saying,

12 Take him, and look well to him, and do him no harm; but do unto him even as he shall say unto thee.

13 So Nĕb′ū-zär–ā′dăn the captain of the guard sent, and Nĕb′ū-shăs′băn, Răb′–sȧ-rĭs, and Nĕr′gäl–shȧ-rē′zĕr, Răb′–măg, and all the king of Babylon's princes;

14 Even they sent, and took Jeremiah out of the court of the prison, and committed him unto Gĕd′ȧ-lī′ȧh the son of Ȧ-hī′kăm the son of Shā′phăn, that he should carry him home: so he dwelt among the people.

15 ¶ Now the word of the LORD came unto Jeremiah, while he was shut up in the court of the prison, saying,

16 Go and speak to Ē′bĕd–mē′lĕeh the Ethiopian, saying, Thus saith the LORD of hosts, the God of Ĭs′rā-ĕl; Behold, I will bring my words upon this city for evil, and not for good; and they shall be *accomplished* in that day before thee.

17 But I will deliver thee in that day, saith the LORD; and thou shalt not be given into the hand of the men of whom thou *art* afraid.

18 For I will surely deliver thee, and thou shalt not fall by the sword, but thy life shall be for a prey unto thee; because thou hast put thy trust in me, saith the LORD.

CHAPTER 40

THE word which came to Jeremiah from the LORD, after that Nĕb′ū-zär–ā′dăn the captain of the guard had let him go from Rā′mȧh, when he had taken him being bound in chains among all that were carried away captive of Jerusalem and Judah, which were carried away captive unto Babylon.

2 And the captain of the guard took Jeremiah, and said unto him, The LORD thy God hath pronounced this evil upon this place.

3 Now the LORD hath brought *it*, and done according as he hath said: because ye have sinned against the LORD, and have not obeyed his voice, therefore this thing is come upon you.

4 And now, behold, I loose thee this day from the chains which *were* upon thine hand. If it seem good unto thee to come with me into Babylon, come; and I will look well unto thee: but if it seem ill unto thee to come with me into Babylon, forbear: behold, all the land *is* before thee: whither it seemeth good and convenient for thee to go, thither go.

5 Now while he was not yet gone back, *he said,* Go back also to Gĕd′ȧ-lī′ȧh the son of Ȧ-hī′kăm the son of Shā′phăn, whom the king of Babylon hath made governor over the cities of Judah, and dwell with him among the people: or go wheresoever it seemeth convenient unto thee to go. So the captain of the guard gave him victuals and a reward, and let him go.

6 Then went Jeremiah unto Gĕd′ȧ-lī′ȧh the son of Ȧ-hī′kăm to Mĭz′päh; and dwelt with him among the people that were left in the land.

7 ¶ Now when all the captains of the forces which *were* in the fields, *even* they and their men, heard that the king of Babylon had made Gĕd′ȧ-lī′ȧh the son of Ȧ-hī′kăm governor in the land, and had committed unto him men, and women, and children, and of the poor of the land, of them that were not carried away captive to Babylon;

8 Then they came to Gĕd′ȧ-lī′ȧh to Mĭz′päh, even Ĭsh′mā-ĕl the son of Nĕth′ȧ-nī′ȧh, and Jō-hā′năn and Jonathan the sons of Kȧ-rē′ȧh, and Sē-rā′ịah the son of Tăn-hū′mĕth, and the sons of Ē′phaī the Nē-tŏph′ȧ-thīte, and Jĕz′ȧ-nī′ȧh the son of a Mā-ăch′ȧ-thīte, they and their men.

9 And Gĕd′ȧ-lī′ȧh the son of Ȧ-hī′kăm the son of Shā′phăn sware unto them and to their men, saying, Fear not to serve the Chăl-dē′ănș: dwell in the land, and serve the king of Babylon, and it shall be well with you.

10 As for me, behold, I will dwell at Mĭz′päh, to serve the Chăl-dē′ănș, which will come unto us: but ye, gather

ye wine, and summer fruits, and oil, and
put *them* in your vessels, and dwell in
your cities that ye have taken.
11 Likewise when all the Jews that
were in Mō'ăb, and among the Ammonites,
and in Ē'dŏm, and that *were* in
all the countries, heard that the king of
Babylon had left a remnant of Judah,
and that he had set over them Gĕd'ȧ-lī'ȧh
the son of Ȧ-hī'kăm the son of
Shā'phăn;
12 Even all the Jews returned out of all
places whither they were driven, and
came to the land of Judah, to Gĕd'ȧ-lī'ȧh,
unto Mĭz'päh, and gathered wine
and summer fruits very much.
13 ¶ Moreover Jō-hā'năn the son of
Kȧ-rē'ȧh, and all the captains of the
forces that *were* in the fields, came to
Gĕd'ȧ-lī'ȧh to Mĭz'päh,
14 And said unto him, Dost thou certainly
know that Bā'ȧ-lĭs the king of the
Ammonites hath sent Ĭsh'mā-ĕl the son
of Nĕth'ȧ-nī'ȧh to slay thee? But Gĕd'ȧ-lī'ȧh
the son of Ȧ-hī'kăm believed them
not.
15 Then Jō-hā'năn the son of Kȧ-rē'ȧh
spake to Gĕd'ȧ-lī'ȧh in Mĭz'päh
secretly, saying, Let me go, I pray thee,
and I will slay Ĭsh'mā-ĕl the son of
Nĕth'ȧ-nī'ȧh, and no man shall know *it:*
wherefore should he slay thee, that all
the Jews which are gathered unto thee
should be scattered, and the remnant in
Judah perish?
16 But Gĕd'ȧ-lī'ȧh the son of Ȧ-hī'kăm
said unto Jō-hā'năn the son of Kȧ-rē'ȧh,
Thou shalt not do this thing: for
thou speakest falsely of Ĭsh'mā-ĕl.

CHAPTER 41

NOW it came to pass in the seventh
month, *that* Ĭsh'mā-ĕl the son of
Nĕth'ȧ-nī'ȧh the son of Ē-lĭsh'ȧ-mä, of
the seed royal, and the princes of the
king, even ten men with him, came
unto Gĕd'ȧ-lī'ȧh the son of Ȧ-hī'kăm to
Mĭz'päh; and there they did eat bread
together in Mĭz'päh.
2 Then arose Ĭsh'mā-ĕl the son of
Nĕth'ȧ-nī'ȧh, and the ten men that were
with him, and smote Gĕd'ȧ-lī'ȧh the son
of Ȧ-hī'kăm the son of Shā'phăn with
the sword, and slew him, whom the king
of Babylon had made governor over the
land.
3 Ĭsh'mā-ĕl also slew all the Jews that
were with him, *even* with Gĕd'ȧ-lī'ȧh, at
Mĭz'päh, and the Chăl-dē'ănș that were
found there, *and* the men of war.
4 And it came to pass the second day
after he had slain Gĕd'ȧ-lī'ȧh, and no
man knew *it,*
5 That there came certain from Shē'chĕm,
from Shī'lōh, and from Sȧ-mā'rĭ-ȧ,
even fourscore men, having their
beards shaven, and their clothes rent,
and having cut themselves, with offerings
and incense in their hand, to bring
them to the house of the LORD.
6 And Ĭsh'mā-ĕl the son of Nĕth'ȧ-nī'ȧh
went forth from Mĭz'päh to meet
them, weeping all along as he went: and
it came to pass, as he met them, he said
unto them, Come to Gĕd'ȧ-lī'ȧh the son
of Ȧ-hī'kăm.
7 And it was *so,* when they came into
the midst of the city, that Ĭsh'mā-ĕl the
son of Nĕth'ȧ-nī'ȧh slew them, *and cast
them* into the midst of the pit, he, and
the men that *were* with him.
8 But ten men were found among them
that said unto Ĭsh'mā-ĕl, Slay us not:
for we have treasures in the field, of
wheat, and of barley, and of oil, and of
honey. So he forbare, and slew them
not among their brethren.
9 Now the pit wherein Ĭsh'mā-ĕl had
cast all the dead bodies of the men,
whom he had slain because of Gĕd'ȧ-lī'ȧh,
was it which Ā'sȧ the king had
made for fear of Bā'ȧ-shȧ king of Ĭs'rā-ĕl:
and Ĭsh'mā-ĕl the son of Nĕth'ȧ-nī'ȧh
filled it with *them that were* slain.
10 Then Ĭsh'mā-ĕl carried away captive
all the residue of the people that
were in Mĭz'päh, *even* the king's daughters,
and all the people that remained in
Mĭz'päh, whom Nĕb'ū-zär-ă'dăn the
captain of the guard had committed to
Gĕd'ȧ-lī'ȧh the son of Ȧ-hī'kăm: and
Ĭsh'mā-ĕl the son of Nĕth'ȧ-nī'ȧh carried
them away captive, and departed
to go over to the Ammonites.
11 ¶ But when Jō-hā'năn the son of
Kȧ-rē'ȧh, and all the captains of the
forces that *were* with him, heard of all
the evil that Ĭsh'mā-ĕl the son of Nĕth'ȧ-nī'ȧh
had done,
12 Then they took all the men, and
went to fight with Ĭsh'mā-ĕl the son of
Nĕth'ȧ-nī'ȧh, and found him by the
great waters that *are* in Gĭb'ē-ŏn.
13 Now it came to pass, *that* when all
the people which *were* with Ĭsh'mā-ĕl
saw Jō-hā'năn the son of Kȧ-rē'ȧh, and

all the captains of the forces that *were*
with him, then they were glad.
14 So all the people that Ĭsh′mā-ĕl had
carried away captive from Mĭz′pah cast
about and returned, and went unto Jō-
hā′năn the son of Kȧ-rē′ȧh.
15 But Ĭsh′mā-ĕl the son of Nĕth′ȧ-
nī′ȧh escaped from Jō-hā′năn with eight
men, and went to the Ammonites.
16 Then took Jō-hā′năn the son of
Kȧ-rē′ȧh, and all the captains of the
forces that *were* with him, all the remnant of the people whom he had recovered from Ĭsh′mā-ĕl the son of
Nĕth′ȧ-nī′ȧh, from Mĭz′päh, after *that*
he had slain Gĕd′ȧ-lī′ȧh the son of
Ȧ-hī′kăm, *even* mighty men of war, and
the women, and the children, and the
eunuchs, whom he had brought again
from Gĭb′ē-ȯn:
17 And they departed, and dwelt in the
habitation of Chĭm′hăm, which is by
Beth-lehem, to go to enter into Egypt,
18 Because of the Chăl-dē′ăns: for
they were afraid of them, because Ĭsh′-
mā-ĕl the son of Nĕth′ȧ-nī′ȧh had slain
Gĕd′ȧ-lī′ȧh the son of Ȧ-hī′kăm, whom
the king of Babylon made governor in
the land.

CHAPTER 42

THEN all the captains of the forces,
and Jō-hā′năn the son of Kȧ-rē′ȧh,
and Jĕz′ȧ-nī′ȧh the son of Hō-shā′ịah,
and all the people from the least even
unto the greatest, came near,
2 And said unto Jeremiah the prophet,
Let, we beseech thee, our supplication
be accepted before thee, and pray for us
unto the LORD thy God, *even* for all this
remnant; (for we are left *but* a few of
many, as thine eyes do behold us:)
3 That the LORD thy God may show us
the way wherein we may walk, and the
thing that we may do.
4 Then Jeremiah the prophet said unto
them, I have heard *you;* behold, I will
pray unto the LORD your God according
to your words; and it shall come to pass,
that whatsoever thing the LORD shall
answer you, I will declare *it* unto you;
I will keep nothing back from you.
5 Then they said to Jeremiah, The
LORD be a true and faithful witness between us, if we do not even according to
all things for the which the LORD thy
God shall send thee to us.
6 Whether *it be* good, or whether *it be*
evil, we will obey the voice of the LORD
our God, to whom we send thee; that it
may be well with us, when we obey the
voice of the LORD our God.
7 ℂ And it came to pass after ten days,
that the word of the LORD came unto
Jeremiah.
8 Then called he Jō-hā′năn the son of
Kȧ-rē′ȧh, and all the captains of the
forces which *were* with him, and all the
people from the least even to the
greatest,
9 And said unto them, Thus saith the
LORD, the God of Ĭş′rā-ĕl, unto whom ye
sent me to present your supplication
before him;
10 If ye will still abide in this land, then
will I build you, and not pull *you* down;
and I will plant you, and not pluck *you*
up: for I repent me of the evil that I
have done unto you.
11 Be not afraid of the king of Babylon,
of whom ye are afraid; be not afraid of
him, saith the LORD: for I *am* with you
to save you, and to deliver you from his
hand.
12 And I will show mercies unto you,
that he may have mercy upon you, and
cause you to return to your own land.
13 ℂ But if ye say, We will not dwell
in this land, neither obey the voice of
the LORD your God,
14 Saying, No; but we will go into the
land of Egypt, where we shall see no
war, nor hear the sound of the trumpet,
nor have hunger of bread; and there
will we dwell:
15 And now therefore hear the word
of the LORD, ye remnant of Judah; Thus
saith the LORD of hosts, the God of
Ĭş′rā-ĕl; If ye wholly set your faces to
enter into Egypt and go to sojourn
there;
16 Then it shall come to pass, *that* the
sword, which ye feared, shall overtake
you there in the land of Egypt; and the
famine, whereof ye were afraid, shall
follow close after you there in Egypt;
and there ye shall die.
17 So shall it be with all the men that
set their faces to go into Egypt to sojourn there; they shall die by the sword,
by the famine, and by the pestilence:
and none of them shall remain or escape
from the evil that I will bring upon them.
18 For thus saith the LORD of hosts, the
God of Ĭş′rā-ĕl; As mine anger and my
fury hath been poured forth upon the in-

habitants of Jerusalem; so shall my fury
be poured forth upon you, when ye shall
enter into Egypt: and ye shall be an
execration, and an astonishment, and a
curse, and a reproach; and ye shall see
this place no more.
19 ¶ The LORD hath said concerning
you, O ye remnant of Judah; Go ye not
into Egypt: know certainly that I have
admonished you this day.
20 For ye dissembled in your hearts,
when ye sent me unto the LORD your
God, saying, Pray for us unto the LORD
our God; and according unto all that the
LORD our God shall say, so declare unto
us, and we will do *it*.
21 And *now* I have this day declared *it*
to you; but ye have not obeyed the voice
of the LORD your God, nor any *thing* for
the which he hath sent me unto you.
22 Now therefore know certainly that
ye shall die by the sword, by the famine,
and by the pestilence, in the place
whither ye desire to go *and* to sojourn.

CHAPTER 43

AND it came to pass, *that* when Jeremiah had made an end of speaking
unto all the people all the words of the
LORD their God, for which the LORD
their God had sent him to them, *even*
all these words,
2 Then spake Ăz′ȧ-rī′ȧh the son of
Hō-shā′ịȧh, and Jō-hā′năn the son of
Kȧ-rē′ȧh, and all the proud men, saying
unto Jeremiah, Thou speakest falsely:
the LORD our God hath not sent thee to
say, Go not into Egypt to sojourn there:
3 But Bā′rŭch the son of Nē-rī′ȧh
setteth thee on against us, for to deliver
us into the hand of the Chăl-dē′ănṣ,
that they might put us to death, and
carry us away captives into Babylon.
4 So Jō-hā′năn the son of Kȧ-rē′ȧh,
and all the captains of the forces, and
all the people, obeyed not the voice of
the LORD, to dwell in the land of Judah.
5 But Jō-hā′năn the son of Kȧ-rē′ȧh,
and all the captains of the forces, took
all the remnant of Judah, that were returned from all nations, whither they
had been driven, to dwell in the land of
Judah;
6 *Even* men, and women, and children,
and the king's daughters, and every person that Nĕb′ū-zär-ā′dăn the captain of
the guard had left with Gĕd′ȧ-lī′ȧh the
son of Ȧ-hī′kăm the son of Shā′phăn,
and Jeremiah the prophet, and Bā′rŭch
the son of Nē-rī′ȧh.
7 So they came into the land of Egypt:
for they obeyed not the voice of the
LORD: thus came they *even* to Täh′-
păn-hēṣ.
8 ¶ Then came the word of the LORD
unto Jeremiah in Tär′păn-hēṣ, saying,
9 Take great stones in thine hand, and
hide them in the clay in the brickkiln,
which *is* at the entry of Phā′raōh's house
in Täh′păn-hēṣ, in the sight of the men
of Judah;
10 And say unto them, Thus saith the
LORD of hosts, the God of Ĭṣ′rā-ĕl;
Behold, I will send and take Nĕb′ū-
chăd-rĕz′zȧr the king of Babylon, my
servant, and will set his throne upon
these stones that I have hid; and he
shall spread his royal pavilion over them.
11 And when he cometh, he shall smite
the land of Egypt, *and deliver* such *as
are* for death to death; and such *as are*
for captivity to captivity; and such *as
are* for the sword to the sword.
12 And I will kindle a fire in the houses
of the gods of Egypt; and he shall burn
them, and carry them away captives:
and he shall array himself with the land
of Egypt, as a shepherd putteth on his
garment; and he shall go forth from
thence in peace.
13 He shall break also the images of
Bĕth′–shē′mĕsh, that *is* in the land of
Egypt; and the houses of the gods of the
Egyptians shall he burn with fire.

CHAPTER 44

THE word that came to Jeremiah
concerning all the Jews which dwell
in the land of Egypt, which dwell at
Mĭg′dōl, and at Täh′păn-hēṣ, and at
Nōph, and in the country of Păth′rōs,
saying,
2 Thus saith the LORD of hosts, the
God of Ĭṣ′rā-ĕl; Ye have seen all the
evil that I have brought upon Jerusalem,
and upon all the cities of Judah; and,
behold, this day they *are* a desolation,
and no man dwelleth therein;
3 Because of their wickedness which
they have committed to provoke me to
anger, in that they went to burn incense, *and* to serve other gods, whom
they knew not, *neither* they, ye, nor
your fathers.
4 Howbeit I sent unto you all my
servants the prophets, rising early and

sending *them,* saying, Oh, do not this
abominable thing that I hate.
5 But they hearkened not, nor inclined
their ear to turn from their wickedness,
to burn no incense unto other gods.
6 Wherefore my fury and mine anger
was poured forth, and was kindled in
the cities of Judah and in the streets of
Jerusalem; and they are wasted *and*
desolate, as at this day.
7 Therefore now thus saith the LORD,
the God of hosts, the God of Ĭṣ′rā-ĕl;
Wherefore commit ye *this* great evil
against your souls, to cut off from you
man and woman, child and suckling,
out of Judah, to leave you none to
remain;
8 In that ye provoke me unto wrath
with the works of your hands, burning
incense unto other gods in the land of
Egypt, whither ye be gone to dwell, that
ye might cut yourselves off, and that ye
might be a curse and a reproach among
all the nations of the earth?
9 Have ye forgotten the wickedness of
your fathers, and the wickedness of the
kings of Judah, and the wickedness of
their wives, and your own wickedness,
and the wickedness of your wives, which
they have committed in the land of
Judah, and in the streets of Jerusalem?
10 They are not humbled *even* unto
this day, neither have they feared, nor
walked in my law, nor in my statutes,
that I set before you and before your
fathers.
11 ¶ Therefore thus saith the LORD
of hosts, the God of Ĭṣ′rā-ĕl; Behold, I
will set my face against you for evil, and
to cut off all Judah.
12 And I will take the remnant of Judah, that have set their faces to go into
the land of Egypt to sojourn there, and
they shall all be consumed, *and* fall in
the land of Egypt; they shall *even* be
consumed by the sword *and* by the
famine: they shall die, from the least
even unto the greatest, by the sword and
by the famine: and they shall be an execration, *and* an astonishment, and a
curse, and a reproach.
13 For I will punish them that dwell in
the land of Egypt, as I have punished
Jerusalem, by the sword, by the famine,
and by the pestilence:
14 So that none of the remnant of
Judah, which are gone into the land of
Egypt to sojourn there, shall escape or
remain, that they should return into the
land of Judah, to the which they have a
desire to return to dwell there: for none
shall return but such as shall escape.
15 ¶ Then all the men which knew
that their wives had burned incense unto
other gods, and all the women that stood
by, a great multitude, even all the people that dwelt in the land of Egypt, in
Păth′rŏs, answered Jeremiah, saying,
16 *As for* the word that thou hast
spoken unto us in the name of the
LORD, we will not hearken unto thee.
17 But we will certainly do whatsoever
thing goeth forth out of our own mouth,
to burn incense unto the queen of
heaven, and to pour out drink offerings
unto her, as we have done, we, and our
fathers, our kings, and our princes, in
the cities of Judah, and in the streets of
Jerusalem: for *then* had we plenty of
victuals, and were well, and saw no evil.
18 But since we left off to burn incense
to the queen of heaven, and to pour out
drink offerings unto her, we have wanted
all *things,* and have been consumed by
the sword and by the famine.
19 And when we burned incense to the
queen of heaven, and poured out drink
offerings unto her, did we make her
cakes to worship her, and pour out drink
offerings unto her, without our men?
20 ¶ Then Jeremiah said unto all the
people, to the men, and to the women,
and to all the people which had given
him *that* answer, saying,
21 The incense that ye burned in the
cities of Judah, and in the streets of
Jerusalem, ye and your fathers, your
kings and your princes, and the people
of the land, did not the LORD remember
them, and came it *not* into his mind?
22 So that the LORD could no longer
bear, because of the evil of your doings,
and because of the abominations which
ye have committed; therefore is your
land a desolation, and an astonishment,
and a curse, without an inhabitant, as at
this day.
23 Because ye have burned incense,
and because ye have sinned against the
LORD, and have not obeyed the voice of
the LORD, nor walked in his law, nor in
his statutes, nor in his testimonies;
therefore this evil is happened unto you,
as at this day.
24 Moreover Jeremiah said unto all
the people, and to all the women, Hear

the word of the LORD, all Judah that *are*
in the land of Egypt:
25 Thus saith the LORD of hosts, the
God of Iṣ'rā-ēl, saying; Ye and your
wives have both spoken with your
mouths, and fulfilled with your hand,
saying, We will surely perform our
vows that we have vowed, to burn incense to the queen of heaven, and to
pour out drink offerings unto her: ye
will surely accomplish your vows, and
surely perform your vows.
26 Therefore hear ye the word of the
LORD, all Judah that dwell in the land
of Egypt; Behold, I have sworn by my
great name, saith the LORD, that my
name shall no more be named in the
mouth of any man of Judah in all the
land of Egypt, saying, The Lord GOD
liveth.
27 Behold, I will watch over them for
evil, and not for good: and all the men
of Judah that *are* in the land of Egypt
shall be consumed by the sword and by
the famine, until there be an end of
them.
28 Yet a small number that escape the
sword shall return out of the land of
Egypt into the land of Judah; and all the
remnant of Judah, that are gone into the
land of Egypt to sojourn there, shall
know whose words shall stand, mine, or
theirs.
29 ¶ And this *shall be* a sign unto you,
saith the LORD, that I will punish you in
this place, that ye may know that my
words shall surely stand against you for
evil:
30 Thus saith the LORD; Behold, I will
give Phā'raōh–hŏph'rȧ king of Egypt
into the hand of his enemies, and into
the hand of them that seek his life; as I
gave Zĕd'ē-kī'ȧh king of Judah into the
hand of Nĕb'ū-chăd-rĕz'zȧr king of
Babylon, his enemy, and that sought his
life.

CHAPTER 45

THE word that Jeremiah the prophet
spake unto Bā'rŭch the son of
Nē-rī'ȧh, when he had written these
words in a book at the mouth of Jeremiah, in the fourth year of Jē-hoi'ȧ-kĭm
the son of Jō-sī'ȧh king of Judah,
saying,
2 Thus saith the LORD, the God of
Iṣ'rā-ēl, unto thee, O Bā'rŭch;
3 Thou didst say, Woe is me now! for
the LORD hath added grief to my sorrow; I fainted in my sighing, and I find
no rest.
4 ¶ Thus shalt thou say unto him, The
LORD saith thus; Behold, *that* which I
have built will I break down, and that
which I have planted I will pluck up,
even this whole land.
5 And seekest thou great things for thyself? seek *them* not: for, behold, I will
bring evil upon all flesh, saith the LORD:
but thy life I will give unto thee for a
prey in all places whither thou goest.

CHAPTER 46

THE word of the LORD which came
to Jeremiah the prophet against the
Gĕn'tīleṣ;
2 Against Egypt, against the army of
Phā'raōh–nē'chō king of Egypt, which
was by the river Eū-phrā'tēṣ in Cär'-
chē-mĭsh, which Nĕb'ū-chăd-rĕz'zȧr
king of Babylon smote in the fourth year
of Jē-hoi'ȧ-kĭm the son of Jō-sī'ȧh king
of Judah.
3 Order ye the buckler and shield, and
draw near to battle.
4 Harness the horses; and get up, ye
horsemen, and stand forth with *your*
helmets; furbish the spears, *and* put on
the brigandines.
5 Wherefore have I seen them dismayed *and* turned away back? and their
mighty ones are beaten down, and are
fled apace, and look not back: *for* fear
was round about, saith the LORD.
6 Let not the swift flee away, nor the
mighty man escape; they shall stumble,
and fall toward the north by the river
Eū-phrā'tēṣ.
7 Who *is* this *that* cometh up as a
flood, whose waters are moved as the
rivers?
8 Egypt riseth up like a flood, and *his*
waters are moved like the rivers; and he
saith, I will go up, *and* will cover the
earth; I will destroy the city and the inhabitants thereof.
9 Come up, ye horses; and rage, ye
chariots; and let the mighty men come
forth; the Ethiopians and the Libyans,
that handle the shield; and the Lydians,
that handle *and* bend the bow.
10 For this *is* the day of the Lord GOD
of hosts, a day of vengeance, that he may
avenge him of his adversaries: and the
sword shall devour, and it shall be satiate and made drunk with their blood:

for the Lord GOD of hosts hath a sacrifice in the north country by the river Eū-phrā'tēş.
11 Go up into Gĭl'ē-ăd, and take balm, O virgin, the daughter of Egypt: in vain shalt thou use many medicines; *for* thou shalt not be cured.
12 The nations have heard of thy shame, and thy cry hath filled the land: for the mighty man hath stumbled against the mighty, *and* they are fallen both together.
13 ℂ The word that the LORD spake to Jeremiah the prophet, how Něb'ū-chăd-rěz'zär king of Babylon should come *and* smite the land of Egypt.
14 Declare ye in Egypt, and publish in Mĭg'dŏl, and publish in Nŏph and in Täh'păn-hēş: say ye, Stand fast, and prepare thee; for the sword shall devour round about thee.
15 Why are thy valiant *men* swept away? they stood not, because the LORD did drive them.
16 He made many to fall, yea, one fell upon another: and they said, Arise, and let us go again to our own people, and to the land of our nativity, from the oppressing sword.
17 They did cry there, Phā'raōh king of Egypt *is but* a noise; he hath passed the time appointed.
18 *As* I live, saith the King, whose name *is* The LORD of hosts, Surely as Tā'bŏr *is* among the mountains, and as Cär'měl by the sea, *so* shall he come.
19 O thou daughter dwelling in Egypt, furnish thyself to go into captivity: for Nŏph shall be waste and desolate without an inhabitant.
20 Egypt *is like* a very fair heifer, *but* destruction cometh; it cometh out of the north.
21 Also her hired men *are* in the midst of her like fatted bullocks; for they also are turned back, *and* are fled away together: they did not stand, because the day of their calamity was come upon them, *and* the time of their visitation.
22 The voice thereof shall go like a serpent; for they shall march with an army, and come against her with axes, as hewers of wood.
23 They shall cut down her forest, saith the LORD, though it cannot be searched; because they are more than the grasshoppers, and *are* innumerable.
24 The daughter of Egypt shall be confounded; she shall be delivered into the hand of the people of the north.
25 The LORD of hosts, the God of Ĭş'rā-ĕl, saith; Behold, I will punish the multitude of No, and Phā'raōh, and Egypt, with their gods, and their kings; even Phā'raōh, and *all* them that trust in him:
26 And I will deliver them into the hand of those that seek their lives, and into the hand of Něb'ū-chăd-rěz'zär king of Babylon, and into the hand of his servants: and afterward it shall be inhabited, as in the days of old, saith the LORD.
27 ℂ But fear not thou, O my servant Jacob, and be not dismayed, O Ĭş'rā-ĕl: for, behold, I will save thee from afar off, and thy seed from the land of their captivity; and Jacob shall return, and be in rest and at ease, and none shall make *him* afraid.
28 Fear thou not, O Jacob my servant, saith the LORD: for I *am* with thee; for I will make a full end of all the nations whither I have driven thee: but I will not make a full end of thee, but correct thee in measure; yet will I not leave thee wholly unpunished.

CHAPTER 47

THE word of the LORD that came to Jeremiah the prophet against the Phĭ-lĭs'tĭneş before that Phā'raōh smote Gā'zȧ.
2 Thus saith the LORD; Behold, waters rise up out of the north, and shall be an overflowing flood, and shall overflow the land, and all that is therein; the city, and them that dwell therein: then the men shall cry, and all the inhabitants of the land shall howl.
3 At the noise of the stamping of the hoofs of his strong *horses*, at the rushing of his chariots, *and at* the rumbling of his wheels, the fathers shall not look back to *their* children for feebleness of hands;
4 Because of the day that cometh to spoil all the Phĭ-lĭs'tĭneş, *and* to cut off from Tȳ'rŭs and Zī'dŏn every helper that remaineth: for the LORD will spoil the Phĭ-lĭs'tĭneş, the remnant of the country of Căph'tŏr.
5 Baldness is come upon Gā'zȧ; Ăsh'kē-lŏn is cut off *with* the remnant of their valley: how long wilt thou cut thyself?
6 O thou sword of the LORD, how long

will it be ere thou be quiet? put up thyself into thy scabbard, rest, and be still.
7 How can it be quiet, seeing the LORD
hath given it a charge against Ăsh′kĕ-
lŏn, and against the seashore? there
hath he appointed it.

CHAPTER 48

AGAINST Mō′ăb thus saith the LORD
of hosts, the God of Ĭs′rā-ĕl; Woe
unto Nē′bō! for it is spoiled: Kĭr′ĭ-ȧ-
thā′ĭm is confounded *and* taken: Mĭs′-
găb is confounded and dismayed.
2 *There shall be* no more praise of
Mō′ăb: in Hĕsh′bŏn they have devised
evil against it; come, and let us cut it off
from *being* a nation. Also thou shalt be
cut down, O Madmen; the sword shall
pursue thee.
3 A voice of crying *shall be* from Hŏr′ō-
nā′ĭm, spoiling and great destruction.
4 Mō′ăb is destroyed; her little ones
have caused a cry to be heard.
5 For in the going up of Lū′hĭth continual weeping shall go up; for in the
going down of Hŏr′ō-nā′ĭm the enemies
have heard a cry of destruction.
6 Flee, save your lives, and be like the
heath in the wilderness.
7 ¶ For because thou hast trusted in
thy works and in thy treasures, thou
shalt also be taken: and Chē′mŏsh shall
go forth into captivity *with* his priests
and his princes together.
8 And the spoiler shall come upon every
city, and no city shall escape: the valley
also shall perish, and the plain shall be
destroyed, as the LORD hath spoken.
9 Give wings unto Mō′ăb, that it may
flee and get away: for the cities thereof
shall be desolate, without any to dwell
therein.
10 Cursed *be* he that doeth the work
of the LORD deceitfully, and cursed *be*
he that keepeth back his sword from
blood.
11 ¶ Mō′ăb hath been at ease from his
youth, and he hath settled on his lees,
and hath not been emptied from vessel
to vessel, neither hath he gone into captivity: therefore his taste remained in
him, and his scent is not changed.
12 Therefore, behold, the days come,
saith the LORD, that I will send unto him
wanderers, that shall cause him to wander, and shall empty his vessels, and
break their bottles.
13 And Mō′ăb shall be ashamed of
Chē′mŏsh, as the house of Ĭs′rā-ĕl was
ashamed of Beth-el their confidence.
14 ¶ How say ye, We *are* mighty and
strong men for the war?
15 Mō′ăb is spoiled, and gone up *out of*
her cities, and his chosen young men
are gone down to the slaughter, saith the
King, whose name *is* The LORD of hosts.
16 The calamity of Mō′ăb *is* near to
come, and his affliction hasteth fast.
17 All ye that are about him, bemoan
him; and all ye that know his name, say,
How is the strong staff broken, *and* the
beautiful rod!
18 Thou daughter that dost inhabit
Dī′bŏn, come down from *thy* glory, and
sit in thirst; for the spoiler of Mō′ăb
shall come upon thee, *and* he shall
destroy thy strongholds.
19 O inhabitant of Ȧ-rō′ēr, stand by the
way, and espy; ask him that fleeth, and
her that escapeth, *and* say, What is
done?
20 Mō′ăb is confounded; for it is
broken down: howl and cry; tell ye it in
Är′nŏn, that Mō′ăb is spoiled,
21 And judgment is come upon the
plain country; upon Hō′lŏn, and upon
Jȧ-hā′zȧh, and upon Mĕph′ȧ-ăth,
22 And upon Dī′bŏn, and upon Nē′bō,
and upon Bĕth′-dĭb′lȧ-thā′ĭm,
23 And upon Kĭr′ĭ-ȧ-thā′ĭm, and upon
Bĕth′-gā′mŭl, and upon Bĕth′-mē′ŏn,
24 And upon Kē′rĭ-ŏth, and upon Bŏz′-
rȧh, and upon all the cities of the land of
Mō′ăb, far or near.
25 The horn of Mō′ăb is cut off, and his
arm is broken, saith the LORD.
26 ¶ Make ye him drunken; for he
magnified *himself* against the LORD:
Mō′ăb also shall wallow in his vomit,
and he also shall be in derision.
27 For was not Ĭs′rā-ĕl a derision unto
thee? was he found among thieves? for
since thou spakest of him, thou skip-
pedst for joy.
28 O ye that dwell in Mō′ăb, leave the
cities, and dwell in the rock, and be like
the dove *that* maketh her nest in the
sides of the hole's mouth.
29 We have heard the pride of Mō′ăb,
(he is exceeding proud,) his loftiness,
and his arrogancy, and his pride, and
the haughtiness of his heart.
30 I know his wrath, saith the LORD;
but *it shall* not *be* so; his lies shall not
so effect *it*.
31 Therefore will I howl for Mō′ăb, and

I will cry out for all Mō′ăb; *mine heart*
shall mourn for the men of Kĭr′–hē′rĕs.
32 O vine of Sĭb′mȧh, I will weep for
thee with the weeping of Jā′zẽr: thy
plants are gone over the sea, they reach
even to the sea of Jā′zẽr: the spoiler is
fallen upon thy summer fruits and upon
thy vintage.
33 And joy and gladness is taken from
the plentiful field, and from the land of
Mō′ăb; and I have caused wine to fail
from the winepresses: none shall tread
with shouting; *their* shouting *shall be* no
shouting.
34 From the cry of Hĕsh′bŏn *even* unto
Ĕl′ē-ā′lĕh, *and even* unto Jā′hăz, have
they uttered their voice, from Zō′ȧr
even unto Hŏr′ō-nā′ĭm, *as* a heifer of
three years old: for the waters also of
Nĭm′rĭm shall be desolate.
35 Moreover I will cause to cease in
Mō′ăb, saith the LORD, him that offereth in the high places, and him that
burneth incense to his gods.
36 Therefore mine heart shall sound
for Mō′ăb like pipes, and mine heart
shall sound like pipes for the men of
Kĭr′–hē′rĕs: because the riches *that* he
hath gotten are perished.
37 For every head *shall be* bald, and
every beard clipped: upon all the hands
shall be cuttings, and upon the loins
sackcloth.
38 *There shall be* lamentation generally upon all the housetops of Mō′ăb,
and in the streets thereof: for I have
broken Mō′ăb like a vessel wherein *is*
no pleasure, saith the LORD.
39 They shall howl, *saying,* How is it
broken down! how hath Mō′ăb turned
the back with shame! so shall Mō′ăb be
a derision and a dismaying to all them
about him.
40 For thus saith the LORD; Behold, he
shall fly as an eagle, and shall spread his
wings over Mō′ăb.
41 Kē′rĭ-ŏth is taken, and the strongholds are surprised, and the mighty
men's hearts in Mō′ăb at that day shall
be as the heart of a woman in her
pangs.
42 And Mō′ăb shall be destroyed from
being a people, because he hath magnified *himself* against the LORD.
43 Fear, and the pit, and the snare,
shall be upon thee, O inhabitant of
Mō′ăb, saith the LORD.
44 He that fleeth from the fear shall
fall into the pit; and he that getteth up
out of the pit shall be taken in the snare:
for I will bring upon it, *even* upon
Mō′ăb, the year of their visitation, saith
the LORD.
45 They that fled stood under the
shadow of Hĕsh′bŏn because of the
force: but a fire shall come forth out of
Hĕsh′bŏn, and a flame from the midst of
Sī′hŏn, and shall devour the corner of
Mō′ăb, and the crown of the head of the
tumultuous ones.
46 Woe be unto thee, O Mō′ăb! the
people of Chē′mŏsh perisheth: for thy
sons are taken captives, and thy daughters captives.
47 ¶ Yet will I bring again the captivity of Mō′ăb in the latter days, saith
the LORD. Thus far *is* the judgment of
Mō′ăb.

CHAPTER 49

CONCERNING the Ammonites, thus
saith the LORD; Hath Ĭs′rā-ĕl no
sons? hath he no heir? why *then* doth
their king inherit Gad, and his people
dwell in his cities?
2 Therefore, behold, the days come,
saith the LORD, that I will cause an
alarm of war to be heard in Răb′bȧh of
the Ammonites; and it shall be a desolate heap, and her daughters shall be
burned with fire: then shall Ĭs′rā-ĕl be
heir unto them that were his heirs, saith
the LORD.
3 Howl, O Hĕsh′bŏn, for Ā′ī is spoiled:
cry, ye daughters of Răb′bȧh, gird you
with sackcloth; lament, and run to and
fro by the hedges; for their king shall
go into captivity, *and* his priests and his
princes together.
4 Wherefore gloriest thou in the valleys, thy flowing valley, O backsliding
daughter? that trusted in her treasures,
saying, Who shall come unto me?
5 Behold, I will bring a fear upon thee,
saith the Lord GOD of hosts, from all
those that be about thee; and ye shall
be driven out every man right forth;
and none shall gather up him that
wandereth.
6 And afterward I will bring again the
captivity of the children of Ammon,
saith the LORD.
7 ¶ Concerning Ē′dŏm, thus saith the
LORD of hosts; *Is* wisdom no more in
Tē′măn? is counsel perished from the
prudent? is their wisdom vanished?

8 Flee ye, turn back, dwell deep, O
inhabitants of Dē'dăn; for I will bring
the calamity of Ē'saû upon him, the
time *that* I will visit him.
9 If grape gatherers come to thee,
would they not leave *some* gleaning
grapes? if thieves by night, they will
destroy till they have enough.
10 But I have made Ē'saû bare, I have
uncovered his secret places, and he
shall not be able to hide himself: his
seed is spoiled, and his brethren, and
his neighbors, and he *is* not.
11 Leave thy fatherless children, I
will preserve *them* alive; and let thy
widows trust in me.
12 For thus saith the LORD; Behold,
they whose judgment *was* not to drink
of the cup have assuredly drunken; and
art thou he *that* shall altogether go unpunished? thou shalt not go unpunished,
but thou shalt surely drink *of it*.
13 For I have sworn by myself, saith
the LORD, that Bŏz'rȧh shall become a
desolation, a reproach, a waste, and a
curse; and all the cities thereof shall be
perpetual wastes.
14 I have heard a rumor from the
LORD, and an ambassador is sent unto
the heathen, *saying*, Gather ye together, and come against her, and rise
up to the battle.
15 For, lo, I will make thee small
among the heathen, *and* despised
among men.
16 Thy terribleness hath deceived
thee, *and* the pride of thine heart, O
thou that dwellest in the clefts of the
rock, that holdest the height of the hill:
though thou shouldest make thy nest as
high as the eagle, I will bring thee down
from thence, saith the LORD.
17 Also Ē'dŏm shall be a desolation:
every one that goeth by it shall be
astonished, and shall hiss at all the
plagues thereof.
18 As in the overthrow of Sŏd'ŏm and
Gō-mŏr'rȧh and the neighbor *cities*
thereof, saith the LORD, no man shall
abide there, neither shall a son of man
dwell in it.
19 Behold, he shall come up like a lion
from the swelling of Jordan against the
habitation of the strong: but I will suddenly make him run away from her:
and who *is* a chosen *man, that* I may
appoint over her? for who *is* like me?
and who will appoint me the time? and
who *is* that shepherd that will stand
before me?
20 Therefore hear the counsel of the
LORD, that he hath taken against Ē'dŏm;
and his purposes, that he hath purposed
against the inhabitants of Tē'măn:
Surely the least of the flock shall draw
them out; surely he shall make their
habitations desolate with them.
21 The earth is moved at the noise of
their fall; at the cry the noise thereof
was heard in the Red sea.
22 Behold, he shall come up and fly as
the eagle, and spread his wings over
Bŏz'rȧh: and at that day shall the heart
of the mighty men of Ē'dŏm be as
the heart of a woman in her pangs.
23 ¶ Concerning Damascus. Hā'măth
is confounded, and Är'păd; for they
have heard evil tidings: they are faint-
hearted; *there is* sorrow on the sea; it
cannot be quiet.
24 Damascus is waxed feeble, *and*
turneth herself to flee, and fear hath
seized on *her:* anguish and sorrows have
taken her, as a woman in travail.
25 How is the city of praise not left, the
city of my joy!
26 Therefore her young men shall fall
in her streets, and all the men of war
shall be cut off in that day, saith the
LORD of hosts.
27 And I will kindle a fire in the wall
of Damascus, and it shall consume the
palaces of Bĕn'-hā'dăd.
28 ¶ Concerning Kē'dȧr, and concerning the kingdoms of Hā'zŏr, which
Nĕb'ū-chăd-rĕz'zȧr king of Babylon
shall smite, thus saith the LORD; Arise
ye, go up to Kē'dȧr, and spoil the men
of the east.
29 Their tents and their flocks shall
they take away: they shall take to themselves their curtains, and all their vessels, and their camels; and they shall
cry unto them, Fear *is* on every side.
30 ¶ Flee, get you far off, dwell deep,
O ye inhabitants of Hā'zŏr, saith the
LORD; for Nĕb'ū-chăd-rĕz'zȧr king of
Babylon hath taken counsel against you,
and hath conceived a purpose against
you.
31 Arise, get you up unto the wealthy
nation, that dwelleth without care, saith
the LORD, which have neither gates nor
bars, *which* dwell alone.
32 And their camels shall be a booty,
and the multitude of their cattle a spoil:

and I will scatter into all winds them
that are in the utmost corners; and I
will bring their calamity from all sides
thereof, saith the LORD.
33 And Hā'zŏr shall be a dwelling for
dragons, *and* a desolation for ever:
there shall no man abide there, nor *any*
son of man dwell in it.
34 ¶ The word of the LORD that came
to Jeremiah the prophet against Ē'lăm
in the beginning of the reign of Zĕd'ē-
kī'ah king of Judah, saying,
35 Thus saith the LORD of hosts; Behold, I will break the bow of Ē'lăm,
the chief of their might.
36 And upon Ē'lăm will I bring the
four winds from the four quarters of
heaven, and will scatter them toward
all those winds; and there shall be no
nation whither the outcasts of Ē'lăm
shall not come.
37 For I will cause Ē'lăm to be dismayed before their enemies, and before
them that seek their life: and I will
bring evil upon them, *even* my fierce
anger, saith the LORD; and I will send
the sword after them, till I have consumed them:
38 And I will set my throne in Ē'lăm,
and will destroy from thence the king
and the princes, saith the LORD.
39 ¶ But it shall come to pass in the
latter days, *that* I will bring again the
captivity of Ē'lăm, saith the LORD.

CHAPTER 50

THE word that the LORD spake
against Babylon *and* against the
land of the Chăl-dē'ăns by Jeremiah the
prophet.
2 Declare ye among the nations, and
publish, and set up a standard; publish,
and conceal not: say, Babylon is taken,
Bel is confounded, Mē-rō'dăch is
broken in pieces; her idols are confounded, her images are broken in
pieces.
3 For out of the north there cometh
up a nation against her, which shall
make her land desolate, and none shall
dwell therein: they shall remove, they
shall depart, both man and beast.
4 ¶ In those days, and in that time,
saith the LORD, the children of Ĭs'rā-ĕl
shall come, they and the children of
Judah together, going and weeping:
they shall go, and seek the LORD their
God.
5 They shall ask the way to Zion with
their faces thitherward, *saying*, Come,
and let us join ourselves to the LORD
in a perpetual covenant *that* shall not
be forgotten.
6 My people hath been lost sheep:
their shepherds have caused them to
go astray, they have turned them away
on the mountains: they have gone from
mountain to hill, they have forgotten
their resting place.
7 All that found them have devoured
them: and their adversaries said, We
offend not, because they have sinned
against the LORD, the habitation of
justice, even the LORD, the hope of
their fathers.
8 Remove out of the midst of Babylon,
and go forth out of the land of the
Chăl-dē'ăns, and be as the he goats
before the flocks.
9 ¶ For, lo, I will raise and cause to
come up against Babylon an assembly
of great nations from the north country:
and they shall set themselves in array
against her; from thence she shall be
taken: their arrows *shall be* as of a
mighty expert man; none shall return
in vain.
10 And Chăl-dē'a shall be a spoil: all
that spoil her shall be satisfied, saith
the LORD.
11 Because ye were glad, because ye
rejoiced, O ye destroyers of mine heritage, because ye are grown fat as the
heifer at grass, and bellow as bulls;
12 Your mother shall be sore confounded; she that bare you shall be
ashamed: behold, the hindermost of
the nations *shall be* a wilderness, a dry
land, and a desert.
13 Because of the wrath of the LORD
it shall not be inhabited, but it shall be
wholly desolate: every one that goeth
by Babylon shall be astonished, and
hiss at all her plagues.
14 Put yourselves in array against
Babylon round about: all ye that bend
the bow, shoot at her, spare no arrows:
for she hath sinned against the LORD.
15 Shout against her round about: she
hath given her hand: her foundations
are fallen, her walls are thrown down:
for it *is* the vengeance of the LORD: take
vengeance upon her; as she hath done,
do unto her.
16 Cut off the sower from Babylon,
and him that handleth the sickle in the

time of harvest: for fear of the oppressing sword they shall turn every one to his people, and they shall flee every one to his own land.

17 ¶ Ĭs′rā-ĕl *is* a scattered sheep; the lions have driven *him* away: first the king of Assyria hath devoured him; and last this Nĕb′ū-chăd-rĕz′zär king of Babylon hath broken his bones.

18 Therefore thus saith the LORD of hosts, the God of Ĭs′rā-ĕl; Behold, I will punish the king of Babylon and his land, as I have punished the king of Assyria.

19 And I will bring Ĭs′rā-ĕl again to his habitation, and he shall feed on Cär′mĕl and Bā′shăn, and his soul shall be satisfied upon mount Ē′phrā-ĭm and Gĭl′ē-ăd.

20 In those days, and in that time, saith the LORD, the iniquity of Ĭs′rā-ĕl shall be sought for, and *there shall be* none; and the sins of Judah, and they shall not be found: for I will pardon them whom I reserve.

21 ¶ Go up against the land of Mĕr′ă-thā′ĭm, *even* against it, and against the inhabitants of Pē′kŏd: waste and utterly destroy after them, saith the LORD, and do according to all that I have commanded thee.

22 A sound of battle *is* in the land, and of great destruction.

23 How is the hammer of the whole earth cut asunder and broken! how is Babylon become a desolation among the nations!

24 I have laid a snare for thee, and thou art also taken, O Babylon, and thou wast not aware: thou art found, and also caught, because thou hast striven against the LORD.

25 The LORD hath opened his armory, and hath brought forth the weapons of his indignation: for this *is* the work of the Lord GOD of hosts in the land of the Chăl-dē′ănṣ.

26 Come against her from the utmost border, open her storehouses: cast her up as heaps, and destroy her utterly: let nothing of her be left.

27 Slay all her bullocks; let them go down to the slaughter: woe unto them! for their day is come, the time of their visitation.

28 The voice of them that flee and escape out of the land of Babylon, to declare in Zion the vengeance of the LORD our God, the vengeance of his temple.

29 Call together the archers against Babylon: all ye that bend the bow, camp against it round about; let none thereof escape: recompense her according to her work; according to all that she hath done, do unto her: for she hath been proud against the LORD, against the Holy One of Ĭs′rā-ĕl.

30 Therefore shall her young men fall in the streets, and all her men of war shall be cut off in that day, saith the LORD.

31 Behold, I *am* against thee, *O thou* most proud, saith the Lord GOD of hosts: for thy day is come, the time *that* I will visit thee.

32 And the most proud shall stumble and fall, and none shall raise him up: and I will kindle a fire in his cities, and it shall devour all round about him.

33 ¶ Thus saith the LORD of hosts; The children of Ĭs′rā-ĕl and the children of Judah *were* oppressed together: and all that took them captives held them fast; they refused to let them go.

34 Their Redeemer *is* strong; The LORD of hosts *is* his name: he shall thoroughly plead their cause, that he may give rest to the land, and disquiet the inhabitants of Babylon.

35 ¶ A sword *is* upon the Chăl-dē′ănṣ, saith the LORD, and upon the inhabitants of Babylon, and upon her princes, and upon her wise *men*.

36 A sword *is* upon the liars; and they shall dote: a sword *is* upon her mighty men; and they shall be dismayed.

37 A sword *is* upon their horses, and upon their chariots, and upon all the mingled people that *are* in the midst of her; and they shall become as women: a sword *is* upon her treasures; and they shall be robbed.

38 A drought *is* upon her waters; and they shall be dried up: for it *is* the land of graven images, and they are mad upon *their* idols.

39 Therefore the wild beasts of the desert with the wild beasts of the islands shall dwell *there*, and the owls shall dwell therein: and it shall be no more inhabited for ever; neither shall it be dwelt in from generation to generation.

40 As God overthrew Sŏd′ŏm and Gō-mŏr′răh and the neighbor *cities*

thereof, saith the LORD; *so* shall no man abide there, neither shall any son of man dwell therein.

41 Behold, a people shall come from the north, and a great nation, and many kings shall be raised up from the coasts of the earth.

42 They shall hold the bow and the lance: they *are* cruel, and will not show mercy: their voice shall roar like the sea, and they shall ride upon horses, *every one* put in array, like a man to the battle, against thee, O daughter of Babylon.

43 The king of Babylon hath heard the report of them, and his hands waxed feeble: anguish took hold of him, *and* pangs as of a woman in travail.

44 Behold, he shall come up like a lion from the swelling of Jordan unto the habitation of the strong: but I will make them suddenly run away from her: and who *is* a chosen *man, that* I may appoint over her? for who *is* like me? and who will appoint me the time? and who *is* that shepherd that will stand before me?

45 Therefore hear ye the counsel of the LORD, that he hath taken against Babylon; and his purposes, that he hath purposed against the land of the Chăl-dē'ăns: Surely the least of the flock shall draw them out: surely he shall make *their* habitation desolate with them.

46 At the noise of the taking of Babylon the earth is moved, and the cry is heard among the nations.

CHAPTER 51

THUS saith the LORD; Behold, I will raise up against Babylon, and against them that dwell in the midst of them that rise up against me, a destroying wind;

2 And will send unto Babylon fanners, that shall fan her, and shall empty her land: for in the day of trouble they shall be against her round about.

3 Against *him that* bendeth let the archer bend his bow, and against *him that* lifteth himself up in his brigandine: and spare ye not her young men; destroy ye utterly all her host.

4 Thus the slain shall fall in the land of the Chăl-dē'ănṣ, and *they that are* thrust through in her streets.

5 For Iṣ'rā-ĕl *hath* not *been* forsaken, nor Judah of his God, of the LORD of hosts; though their land was filled with sin against the Holy One of Iṣ'rā-ĕl.

6 Flee out of the midst of Babylon, and deliver every man his soul: be not cut off in her iniquity; for this *is* the time of the LORD's vengeance; he will render unto her a recompense.

7 Babylon *hath been* a golden cup in the LORD's hand, that made all the earth drunken: the nations have drunken of her wine; therefore the nations are mad.

8 Babylon is suddenly fallen and destroyed: howl for her; take balm for her pain, if so be she may be healed.

9 We would have healed Babylon, but she is not healed: forsake her, and let us go every one into his own country: for her judgment reacheth unto heaven, and is lifted up *even* to the skies.

10 The LORD hath brought forth our righteousness: come, and let us declare in Zion the work of the LORD our God.

11 Make bright the arrows; gather the shields: the LORD hath raised up the spirit of the kings of the Mēdeṣ: for his device *is* against Babylon, to destroy it; because it *is* the vengeance of the LORD, the vengeance of his temple.

12 Set up the standard upon the walls of Babylon, make the watch strong, set up the watchmen, prepare the ambushes: for the LORD hath both devised and done that which he spake against the inhabitants of Babylon.

13 O thou that dwellest upon many waters, abundant in treasures, thine end is come, *and* the measure of thy covetousness.

14 The LORD of hosts hath sworn by himself, *saying,* Surely I will fill thee with men, as with caterpillars; and they shall lift up a shout against thee.

15 He hath made the earth by his power, he hath established the world by his wisdom, and hath stretched out the heaven by his understanding.

16 When he uttereth *his* voice, *there is* a multitude of waters in the heavens; and he causeth the vapors to ascend from the ends of the earth: he maketh lightnings with rain, and bringeth forth the wind out of his treasures.

17 Every man is brutish by *his* knowledge; every founder is confounded by the graven image: for his molten image

is falsehood, and *there is* no breath in
them.
18 They *are* vanity, the work of errors:
in the time of their visitation they shall
perish.
19 The portion of Jacob *is* not like
them; for he *is* the former of all things:
and *Israel is* the rod of his inheritance:
the LORD of hosts *is* his name.
20 Thou *art* my battle-axe *and* weapons
of war: for with thee will I break in
pieces the nations, and with thee will I
destroy kingdoms;
21 And with thee will I break in pieces
the horse and his rider; and with thee
will I break in pieces the chariot and
his rider;
22 With thee also will I break in pieces
man and woman; and with thee will I
break in pieces old and young; and with
thee will I break in pieces the young
man and the maid;
23 I will also break in pieces with thee
the shepherd and his flock; and with
thee will I break in pieces the husbandman and his yoke of oxen; and with thee
will I break in pieces captains and rulers.
24 And I will render unto Babylon and
to all the inhabitants of Chăl-dē′ȧ all
their evil that they have done in Zion in
your sight, saith the LORD.
25 Behold, I *am* against thee, O destroying mountain, saith the LORD,
which destroyest all the earth: and I
will stretch out mine hand upon thee,
and roll thee down from the rocks, and
will make thee a burnt mountain.
26 And they shall not take of thee a
stone for a corner, nor a stone for foundations; but thou shalt be desolate for
ever, saith the LORD.
27 Set ye up a standard in the land,
blow the trumpet among the nations,
prepare the nations against her, call
together against her the kingdoms of
Ăr′ȧ-răt, Mĭn′nī, and Ăsh′chē-năz; appoint a captain against her; cause the
horses to come up as the rough caterpillars.
28 Prepare against her the nations
with the kings of the Mēdes, the captains thereof, and all the rulers thereof,
and all the land of his dominion.
29 And the land shall tremble and
sorrow: for every purpose of the LORD
shall be performed against Babylon, to
make the land of Babylon a desolation
without an inhabitant.
30 The mighty men of Babylon have
forborne to fight, they have remained
in *their* holds: their might hath failed;
they became as women: they have
burned her dwelling places; her bars
are broken.
31 One post shall run to meet another,
and one messenger to meet another, to
show the king of Babylon that his city
is taken at *one* end,
32 And that the passages are stopped,
and the reeds they have burned with
fire, and the men of war are affrighted.
33 For thus saith the LORD of hosts,
the God of Ĭş′rā-ĕl;. The daughter of
Babylon *is* like a threshingfloor, *it is*
time to thresh her: yet a little while,
and the time of her harvest shall come.
34 Nĕb′ū-chăd-rĕz′zȧr the king of
Babylon hath devoured me, he hath
crushed me, he hath made me an empty
vessel, he hath swallowed me up like a
dragon, he hath filled his belly with my
delicates, he hath cast me out.
35 The violence done to me and to my
flesh *be* upon Babylon, shall the inhabitant of Zion say; and my blood upon
the inhabitants of Chăl-dē′ȧ, shall Jerusalem say.
36 Therefore thus saith the LORD;
Behold, I will plead thy cause, and take
vengeance for thee; and I will dry up
her sea, and make her springs dry.
37 And Babylon shall become heaps,
a dwelling place for dragons, an astonishment, and a hissing, without an
inhabitant.
38 They shall roar together like lions:
they shall yell as lions' whelps.
39 In their heat I will make their
feasts, and I will make them drunken,
that they may rejoice, and sleep a
perpetual sleep, and not wake, saith
the LORD.
40 I will bring them down like lambs
to the slaughter, like rams with he
goats.
41 How is Shē′shăch taken! and how
is the praise of the whole earth surprised! how is Babylon become an
astonishment among the nations!
42 The sea is come up upon Babylon:
she is covered with the multitude of the
waves thereof.
43 Her cities are a desolation, a dry
land, and a wilderness, a land wherein
no man dwelleth, neither doth *any* son
of man pass thereby.

44 And I will punish Bel in Babylon, and I will bring forth out of his mouth that which he hath swallowed up: and the nations shall not flow together any more unto him; yea, the wall of Babylon shall fall.

45 My people, go ye out of the midst of her, and deliver ye every man his soul from the fierce anger of the LORD.

46 And lest your heart faint, and ye fear for the rumor that shall be heard in the land; a rumor shall both come *one* year, and after that in *another* year *shall come* a rumor, and violence in the land, ruler against ruler.

47 Therefore, behold, the days come, that I will do judgment upon the graven images of Babylon: and her whole land shall be confounded, and all her slain shall fall in the midst of her.

48 Then the heaven and the earth, and all that *is* therein, shall sing for Babylon: for the spoilers shall come unto her from the north, saith the LORD.

49 As Babylon *hath caused* the slain of Ĭs'rā-ĕl to fall, so at Babylon shall fall the slain of all the earth.

50 Ye that have escaped the sword, go away, stand not still: remember the LORD afar off, and let Jerusalem come into your mind.

51 We are confounded, because we have heard reproach: shame hath covered our faces; for strangers are come into the sanctuaries of the LORD's house.

52 Wherefore, behold, the days come, saith the LORD, that I will do judgment upon her graven images: and through all her land the wounded shall groan.

53 Though Babylon should mount up to heaven, and though she should fortify the height of her strength, *yet* from me shall spoilers come unto her, saith the LORD.

54 A sound of a cry *cometh* from Babylon, and great destruction from the land of the Chăl-dē'ăns:

55 Because the LORD hath spoiled Babylon, and destroyed out of her the great voice; when her waves do roar like great waters, a noise of their voice is uttered:

56 Because the spoiler is come upon her, *even* upon Babylon, and her mighty men are taken, every one of their bows is broken: for the LORD God of recompenses shall surely requite.

57 And I will make drunk her princes, and her wise *men*, her captains, and her rulers, and her mighty men: and they shall sleep a perpetual sleep, and not wake, saith the King, whose name *is* The LORD of hosts.

58 Thus saith the LORD of hosts; The broad walls of Babylon shall be utterly broken, and her high gates shall be burned with fire; and the people shall labor in vain, and the folk in the fire, and they shall be weary.

59 ¶ The word which Jeremiah the prophet commanded Sē-rā'ịah the son of Nē-rī'ah, the son of Mā'a-sē'ịah, when he went with Zĕd'ē-kī'ah the king of Judah into Babylon in the fourth year of his reign. And *this* Sē-rā'ịah *was* a quiet prince.

60 So Jeremiah wrote in a book all the evil that should come upon Babylon, *even* all these words that are written against Babylon.

61 And Jeremiah said to Sē-rā'ịah, When thou comest to Babylon, and shalt see, and shalt read all these words;

62 Then shalt thou say, O LORD, thou hast spoken against this place, to cut it off, that none shall remain in it, neither man nor beast, but that it shall be desolate for ever.

63 And it shall be, when thou hast made an end of reading this book, *that* thou shalt bind a stone to it, and cast it into the midst of Eū-phrā'tēs:

64 And thou shalt say, Thus shall Babylon sink, and shalt not rise from the evil that I will bring upon her: and they shall be weary. Thus far *are* the words of Jeremiah.

CHAPTER 52

ZĔD'Ē-KĪ'AH *was* one and twenty years old when he began to reign, and he reigned eleven years in Jerusalem. And his mother's name *was* Ha-mū'tăl the daughter of Jeremiah of Lĭb'nah.

2 And he did *that which was* evil in the eyes of the LORD, according to all that Jē-hôi'a-kĭm had done.

3 For through the anger of the LORD it came to pass in Jerusalem and Judah, till he had cast them out from his presence, that Zĕd'ē-kī'ah rebelled against the king of Babylon.

4 ¶ And it came to pass in the ninth year of his reign, in the tenth month,

in the tenth *day* of the month, *that*
Nĕb'ū-chăd-rĕz'zär king of Babylon
came, he and all his army, against
Jerusalem, and pitched against it, and
built forts against it round about.
5 So the city was besieged unto the
eleventh year of king Zĕd'ē-kī'ăh.
6 And in the fourth month, in the ninth
day of the month, the famine was sore
in the city, so that there was no bread
for the people of the land.
7 Then the city was broken up, and all
the men of war fled, and went forth out
of the city by night by the way of the
gate between the two walls, which *was*
by the king's garden; (now the Chăl-
dē'ăns *were* by the city round about:)
and they went by the way of the plain.
8 ¶ But the army of the Chăl-dē'ăns
pursued after the king, and overtook
Zĕd'ē-kī'ăh in the plains of Jĕr'ĭ-chō;
and all his army was scattered from him.
9 Then they took the king, and carried
him up unto the king of Babylon to
Rĭb'lăh in the land of Hā'măth; where
he gave judgment upon him.
10 And the king of Babylon slew the
sons of Zĕd'ē-kī'ăh before his eyes: he
slew also all the princes of Judah in
Rĭb'lăh.
11 Then he put out the eyes of Zĕd'ē-
kī'ăh; and the king of Babylon bound
him in chains, and carried him to Babylon, and put him in prison till the day
of his death.
12 ¶ Now in the fifth month, in the
tenth *day* of the month, which *was* the
nineteenth year of Nĕb'ū-chăd-rĕz'zär
king of Babylon, came Nĕb'ū-zär–ā'dăn,
captain of the guard, *which* served the
king of Babylon, into Jerusalem.
13 And burned the house of the LORD,
and the king's house; and all the houses
of Jerusalem, and all the houses of
the great *men,* burned he with fire:
14 And all the army of the Chăl-dē'ăns,
that *were* with the captain of the guard,
brake down all the walls of Jerusalem
round about.
15 Then Nĕb'ū-zär–ā'dăn the captain
of the guard carried away captive *certain*
of the poor of the people, and the residue
of the people that remained in the city,
and those that fell away, that fell to the
king of Babylon, and the rest of the
multitude.
16 But Nĕb'ū-zär–ā'dăn the captain of
the guard left *certain* of the poor of the
land for vinedressers and for husbandmen.
17 Also the pillars of brass that *were*
in the house of the LORD, and the bases,
and the brazen sea that *was* in the
house of the LORD, the Chăl-dē'ăns
brake, and carried all the brass of them
to Babylon.
18 The caldrons also, and the shovels,
and the snuffers, and the bowls, and
the spoons, and all the vessels of brass
wherewith they ministered, took they
away.
19 And the basins, and the firepans,
and the bowls, and the caldrons, and
the candlesticks, and the spoons, and
the cups; *that* which *was* of gold *in* gold,
and *that* which *was* of silver *in* silver,
took the captain of the guard away.
20 The two pillars, one sea, and twelve
brazen bulls that *were* under the bases,
which king Solomon had made in the
house of the LORD: the brass of all
these vessels was without weight.
21 And *concerning* the pillars, the
height of one pillar *was* eighteen cubits;
and a fillet of twelve cubits did compass
it; and the thickness thereof *was* four
fingers: *it was* hollow.
22 And a chapiter of brass *was* upon
it; and the height of one chapiter *was*
five cubits, with network and pomegranates upon the chapiters round
about, all *of* brass. The second pillar
also and the pomegranates *were* like
unto these.
23 And there were ninety and six
pomegranates on a side; *and* all the
pomegranates upon the network *were*
a hundred round about.
24 ¶ And the captain of the guard
took Sĕ-rā'ịăh the chief priest, and
Zĕph'ă-nī'ăh the second priest, and the
three keepers of the door:
25 He took also out of the city a
eunuch, which had the charge of the
men of war; and seven men of them
that were near the king's person, which
were found in the city; and the principal scribe of the host, who mustered
the people of the land; and threescore
men of the people of the land, that
were found in the midst of the city.
26 So Nĕb'ū-zär–ā'dăn the captain of
the guard took them, and brought them
to the king of Babylon to Rĭb'lăh.
27 And the king of Babylon smote
them, and put them to death in Rĭb'lăh

in the land of Hā′măth. Thus Judah
was carried away captive out of his
own land.
28 This *is* the people whom Nĕb′ū-
chăd-rĕz′zȧr carried away captive: in
the seventh year three thousand Jews
and three and twenty:
29 In the eighteenth year of Nĕb′ū-
chăd-rĕz′zȧr he carried away captive
from Jerusalem eight hundred thirty
and two persons:
30 In the three and twentieth year
of Nĕb′ū-chăd-rĕz′zȧr, Nĕb′ū-zär–ā′dăn
the captain of the guard carried away
captive of the Jews seven hundred
forty and five persons: all the persons
were four thousand and six hundred.
31 ¶ And it came to pass in the seven
and thirtieth year of the captivity of
Jē-hôi′ȧ-chĭn king of Judah, in the
twelfth month, in the five and twentieth
day of the month, *that* Ē′vĭl–mē-rō′dăch
king of Babylon, in the *first* year of his
reign, lifted up the head of Jē-hôi′ȧ-chĭn
king of Judah, and brought him forth
out of prison,
32 And spake kindly unto him, and set
his throne above the throne of the kings
that *were* with him in Babylon,
33 And changed his prison garments:
and he did continually eat bread before
him all the days of his life.
34 And *for* his diet, there was a continual diet given him of the king of
Babylon, every day a portion until the
day of his death, all the days of his life.

THE LAMENTATIONS OF JEREMIAH

CHAPTER 1

HOW doth the city sit solitary, *that*
was full of people! *how* is she
become as a widow! she *that was* great
among the nations, *and* princess among
the provinces, *how* is she become tributary!
2 She weepeth sore in the night, and
her tears *are* on her cheeks: among all
her lovers she hath none to comfort *her:*
all her friends have dealt treacherously
with her, they are become her enemies.
3 Judah is gone into captivity because
of affliction, and because of great servitude: she dwelleth among the heathen,
she findeth no rest: all her persecutors
overtook her between the straits.
4 The ways of Zion do mourn, because
none come to the solemn feasts: all her
gates are desolate: her priests sigh, her
virgins are afflicted, and she *is* in
bitterness.
5 Her adversaries are the chief, her
enemies prosper; for the LORD hath
afflicted her for the multitude of her
transgressions: her children are gone
into captivity before the enemy.
6 And from the daughter of Zion all
her beauty is departed: her princes are
become like harts *that* find no pasture,
and they are gone without strength
before the pursuer.
7 Jerusalem remembered in the days
of her affliction and of her miseries all
her pleasant things that she had in the
days of old, when her people fell into
the hand of the enemy, and none did
help her: the adversaries saw her, *and*
did mock at her sabbaths.
8 Jerusalem hath grievously sinned;
therefore she is removed: all that honored her despise her, because they have
seen her nakedness: yea, she sigheth,
and turneth backward.
9 Her filthiness *is* in her skirts; she
remembereth not her last end; therefore she came down wonderfully: she
had no comforter. O LORD, behold my
affliction: for the enemy hath magnified
himself.
10 The adversary hath spread out his
hand upon all her pleasant things: for
she hath seen *that* the heathen entered
into her sanctuary, whom thou didst
command *that* they should not enter
into thy congregation.
11 All her people sigh, they seek bread;
they have given their pleasant things
for meat to relieve the soul: see, O
LORD, and consider; for I am become
vile.
12 ¶ *Is it* nothing to you, all ye that
pass by? behold, and see if there be
any sorrow like unto my sorrow, which
is done unto me, wherewith the LORD

hath afflicted *me* in the day of his fierce anger.

13 From above hath he sent fire into my bones, and it prevaileth against them: he hath spread a net for my feet, he hath turned me back: he hath made me desolate *and* faint all the day.

14 The yoke of my transgressions is bound by his hand: they are wreathed, *and* come up upon my neck: he hath made my strength to fall, the Lord hath delivered me into *their* hands, *from whom* I am not able to rise up.

15 The Lord hath trodden under foot all my mighty *men* in the midst of me: he hath called an assembly against me to crush my young men: the Lord hath trodden the virgin, the daughter of Judah, *as* in a winepress.

16 For these *things* I weep; mine eye, mine eye runneth down with water, because the comforter that should relieve my soul is far from me: my children are desolate, because the enemy prevailed.

17 Zion spreadeth forth her hands, *and there is* none to comfort her: the LORD hath commanded concerning Jacob, *that* his adversaries *should be* round about him: Jerusalem is as a menstruous woman among them.

18 ¶ The LORD is righteous; for I have rebelled against his commandment: hear, I pray you, all people, and behold my sorrow: my virgins and my young men are gone into captivity.

19 I called for my lovers, *but* they deceived me: my priests and mine elders gave up the ghost in the city, while they sought their meat to relieve their souls.

20 Behold, O LORD; for I *am* in distress: my bowels are troubled; mine heart is turned within me; for I have grievously rebelled: abroad the sword bereaveth, at home *there is* as death.

21 They have heard that I sigh; *there is* none to comfort me: all mine enemies have heard of my trouble; they are glad that thou hast done *it*: thou wilt bring the day *that* thou hast called, and they shall be like unto me.

22 Let all their wickedness come before thee; and do unto them, as thou hast done unto me for all my transgressions: for my sighs *are* many, and my heart *is* faint.

CHAPTER 2

HOW hath the Lord covered the daughter of Zion with a cloud in his anger, *and* cast down from heaven unto the earth the beauty of Ĭṣ′rā-ĕl, and remembered not his footstool in the day of his anger!

2 The Lord hath swallowed up all the habitations of Jacob, and hath not pitied: he hath thrown down in his wrath the strongholds of the daughter of Judah; he hath brought *them* down to the ground: he hath polluted the kingdom and the princes thereof.

3 He hath cut off in *his* fierce anger all the horn of Ĭṣ′rā-ĕl: he hath drawn back his right hand from before the enemy, and he burned against Jacob like a flaming fire, *which* devoureth round about.

4 He hath bent his bow like an enemy: he stood with his right hand as an adversary, and slew all *that were* pleasant to the eye in the tabernacle of the daughter of Zion: he poured out his fury like fire.

5 The Lord was as an enemy: he hath swallowed up Ĭṣ′rā-ĕl, he hath swallowed up all her palaces: he hath destroyed his strongholds, and hath increased in the daughter of Judah mourning and lamentation.

6 And he hath violently taken away his tabernacle, as *if it were of* a garden; he hath destroyed his places of the assembly: the LORD hath caused the solemn feasts and sabbaths to be forgotten in Zion, and hath despised in the indignation of his anger the king and the priest.

7 The Lord hath cast off his altar, he hath abhorred his sanctuary, he hath given up into the hand of the enemy the walls of her palaces; they have made a noise in the house of the LORD, as in the day of a solemn feast.

8 The LORD hath purposed to destroy the wall of the daughter of Zion: he hath stretched out a line, he hath not withdrawn his hand from destroying: therefore he made the rampart and the wall to lament; they languished together.

9 Her gates are sunk into the ground; he hath destroyed and broken her bars: her king and her princes *are* among the Ġĕn′tīleṣ: the law *is* no *more;* her prophets also find no vision from the LORD.

10 The elders of the daughter of Zion

sit upon the ground, *and* keep silence: they have cast up dust upon their heads; they have girded themselves with sackcloth: the virgins of Jerusalem hang down their heads to the ground.

11 Mine eyes do fail with tears, my bowels are troubled, my liver is poured upon the earth, for the destruction of the daughter of my people; because the children and the sucklings swoon in the streets of the city.

12 They say to their mothers, Where *is* corn and wine? when they swooned as the wounded in the streets of the city, when their soul was poured out into their mothers' bosom.

13 What thing shall I take to witness for thee? what thing shall I liken to thee, O daughter of Jerusalem? what shall I equal to thee, that I may comfort thee, O virgin daughter of Zion? for thy breach *is* great like the sea: who can heal thee?

14 Thy prophets have seen vain and foolish things for thee: and they have not discovered thine iniquity, to turn away thy captivity; but have seen for thee false burdens and causes of banishment.

15 All that pass by clap *their* hands at thee; they hiss and wag their head at the daughter of Jerusalem, *saying*, *Is* this the city that *men* call The perfection of beauty, The joy of the whole earth?

16 All thine enemies have opened their mouth against thee: they hiss and gnash the teeth: they say, We have swallowed *her* up; certainly this *is* the day that we looked for; we have found, we have seen *it*.

17 The LORD hath done *that* which he had devised; he hath fulfilled his word that he had commanded in the days of old: he hath thrown down, and hath not pitied: and he hath caused *thine* enemy to rejoice over thee, he hath set up the horn of thine adversaries.

18 Their heart cried unto the Lord, O wall of the daughter of Zion, let tears run down like a river day and night: give thyself no rest; let not the apple of thine eye cease.

19 Arise, cry out in the night: in the beginning of the watches pour out thine heart like water before the face of the Lord: lift up thy hands toward him for the life of thy young children, that faint for hunger in the top of every street.

20 ℂ Behold, O LORD, and consider to whom thou hast done this. Shall the women eat their fruit, *and* children of a span long? shall the priest and the prophet be slain in the sanctuary of the Lord?

21 The young and the old lie on the ground in the streets: my virgins and my young men are fallen by the sword; thou hast slain *them* in the day of thine anger; thou hast killed, *and* not pitied.

22 Thou hast called as in a solemn day my terrors round about, so that in the day of the LORD's anger none escaped nor remained: those that I have swaddled and brought up hath mine enemy consumed.

CHAPTER 3

I *AM* the man *that* hath seen affliction by the rod of his wrath.

2 He hath led me, and brought *me into* darkness, but not *into* light.

3 Surely against me is he turned; he turneth his hand *against me* all the day.

4 My flesh and my skin hath he made old; he hath broken my bones.

5 He hath builded against me, and compassed *me* with gall and travail.

6 He hath set me in dark places, as *they that be* dead of old.

7 He hath hedged me about, that I cannot get out: he hath made my chain heavy.

8 Also when I cry and shout, he shutteth out my prayer.

9 He hath inclosed my ways with hewn stone; he hath made my paths crooked.

10 He *was* unto me *as* a bear lying in wait, *and as* a lion in secret places.

11 He hath turned aside my ways, and pulled me in pieces: he hath made me desolate.

12 He hath bent his bow, and set me as a mark for the arrow.

13 He hath caused the arrows of his quiver to enter into my reins.

14 I was a derision to all my people; *and* their song all the day.

15 He hath filled me with bitterness, he hath made me drunken with wormwood.

16 He hath also broken my teeth with gravel stones, he hath covered me with ashes.

17 And thou hast removed my soul far off from peace: I forgat prosperity.

18 And I said, My strength and my
hope is perished from the LORD:
19 Remembering mine affliction and
my misery, the wormwood and the gall.
20 My soul hath *them* still in remembrance, and is humbled in me.
21 This I recall to my mind, therefore
have I hope.
22 ℭ *It is of* the LORD's mercies that
we are not consumed, because his compassions fail not.
23 *They are* new every morning: great
is thy faithfulness.
24 The LORD *is* my portion, saith my
soul; therefore will I hope in him.
25 The LORD *is* good unto them that
wait for him, to the soul *that* seeketh
him.
26 *It is* good that *a man* should both
hope and quietly wait for the salvation
of the LORD.
27 *It is* good for a man that he bear the
yoke in his youth.
28 He sitteth alone and keepeth silence, because he hath borne *it* upon
him.
29 He putteth his mouth in the dust;
if so be there may be hope.
30 He giveth *his* cheek to him that
smiteth him: he is filled full with
reproach.
31 For the Lord will not cast off for
ever:
32 But though he cause grief, yet will
he have compassion according to the
multitude of his mercies.
33 For he doth not afflict willingly, nor
grieve the children of men.
34 To crush under his feet all the
prisoners of the earth,
35 To turn aside the right of a man before the face of the Most High,
36 To subvert a man in his cause, the
Lord approveth not.
37 ℭ Who *is* he *that* saith, and it cometh to pass, *when* the Lord commandeth
it not?
38 Out of the mouth of the Most High
proceedeth not evil and good?
39 Wherefore doth a living man complain, a man for the punishment of his
sins?
40 Let us search and try our ways, and
turn again to the LORD.
41 Let us lift up our heart with *our*
hands unto God in the heavens.
42 We have transgressed and have
rebelled: thou hast not pardoned.
43 Thou hast covered with anger, and
persecuted us: thou hast slain, thou hast
not pitied.
44 Thou hast covered thyself with a
cloud, that *our* prayer should not pass
through.
45 Thou hast made us *as* the offscouring and refuse in the midst of the
people.
46 All our enemies have opened their
mouths against us.
47 Fear and a snare is come upon us,
desolation and destruction.
48 Mine eye runneth down with rivers
of water for the destruction of the
daughter of my people.
49 Mine eye trickleth down, and ceaseth not, without any intermission,
50 Till the LORD look down, and behold
from heaven.
51 Mine eye affecteth mine heart, because of all the daughters of my city.
52 Mine enemies chased me sore, like
a bird, without cause.
53 They have cut off my life in the
dungeon, and cast a stone upon me.
54 Waters flowed over mine head;
then I said, I am cut off.
55 ℭ I called upon thy name, O LORD,
out of the low dungeon.
56 Thou hast heard my voice: hide not
thine ear at my breathing, at my cry.
57 Thou drewest near in the day *that*
I called upon thee: thou saidst, Fear
not.
58 O Lord, thou hast pleaded the
causes of my soul; thou hast redeemed
my life.
59 O LORD, thou hast seen my wrong:
judge thou my cause.
60 Thou hast seen all their vengeance
and all their imaginations against me.
61 Thou hast heard their reproach, O
LORD, *and* all their imaginations against
me;
62 The lips of those that rose up
against me, and their device against me
all the day.
63 Behold their sitting down, and their
rising up; I *am* their music.
64 ℭ Render unto them a recompense,
O LORD, according to the work of their
hands.
65 Give them sorrow of heart, thy curse
unto them.
66 Persecute and destroy them in
anger from under the heavens of the
LORD.

CHAPTER 4

HOW is the gold become dim! *how* is the most fine gold changed! the stones of the sanctuary are poured out in the top of every street.

2 The precious sons of Zion, comparable to fine gold, how are they esteemed as earthen pitchers, the work of the hands of the potter!

3 Even the sea monsters draw out the breast, they give suck to their young ones: the daughter of my people *is become* cruel, like the ostriches in the wilderness.

4 The tongue of the sucking child cleaveth to the roof of his mouth for thirst: the young children ask bread, *and* no man breaketh *it* unto them.

5 They that did feed delicately are desolate in the streets: they that were brought up in scarlet embrace dunghills.

6 For the punishment of the iniquity of the daughter of my people is greater than the punishment of the sin of Sŏd′ŏm, that was overthrown as in a moment, and no hands stayed on her.

7 Her Nazarites were purer than snow, they were whiter than milk, they were more ruddy in body than rubies, their polishing *was* of sapphire:

8 Their visage is blacker than a coal; they are not known in the streets: their skin cleaveth to their bones; it is withered, it is become like a stick.

9 *They that be* slain with the sword are better than *they that be* slain with hunger: for these pine away, stricken through for *want of* the fruits of the field.

10 The hands of the pitiful women have sodden their own children: they were their meat in the destruction of the daughter of my people.

11 The LORD hath accomplished his fury; he hath poured out his fierce anger, and hath kindled a fire in Zion, and it hath devoured the foundations thereof.

12 The kings of the earth, and all the inhabitants of the world, would not have believed that the adversary and the enemy should have entered into the gates of Jerusalem.

13 ℂ For the sins of her prophets, *and* the iniquities of her priests, that have shed the blood of the just in the midst of her,

14 They have wandered *as* blind *men* in the streets, they have polluted themselves with blood, so that men could not touch their garments.

15 They cried unto them, Depart ye; *it is* unclean; depart, depart, touch not: when they fled away and wandered, they said among the heathen, They shall no more sojourn *there*.

16 The anger of the LORD hath divided them; he will no more regard them: they respected not the persons of the priests, they favored not the elders.

17 As for us, our eyes as yet failed for our vain help: in our watching we have watched for a nation *that* could not save *us*.

18 They hunt our steps, that we cannot go in our streets: our end is near, our days are fulfilled; for our end is come.

19 Our persecutors are swifter than the eagles of the heaven: they pursued us upon the mountains, they laid wait for us in the wilderness.

20 The breath of our nostrils, the anointed of the LORD, was taken in their pits, of whom we said, Under his shadow we shall live among the heathen.

21 ℂ Rejoice and be glad, O daughter of Ē′dŏm, that dwellest in the land of Ŭz; the cup also shall pass through unto thee: thou shalt be drunken, and shalt make thyself naked.

22 ℂ The punishment of thine iniquity is accomplished, O daughter of Zion; he will no more carry thee away into captivity: he will visit thine iniquity, O daughter of Ē′dŏm; he will discover thy sins.

CHAPTER 5

REMEMBER, O LORD, what is come upon us: consider, and behold our reproach.

2 Our inheritance is turned to strangers, our houses to aliens.

3 We are orphans and fatherless, our mothers *are* as widows.

4 We have drunken our water for money; our wood is sold unto us.

5 Our necks *are* under persecution: we labor, *and* have no rest.

6 We have given the hand *to* the Egyptians, *and to* the Assyrians, to be satisfied with bread.

7 Our fathers have sinned, and *are* not; and we have borne their iniquities.

8 Servants have ruled over us: *there is* none that doth deliver *us* out of their hand.

9 We gat our bread with *the peril of*
our lives, because of the sword of the
wilderness.
10 Our skin was black like an oven, because of the terrible famine.
11 They ravished the women in Zion,
and the maids in the cities of Judah.
12 Princes are hanged up by their
hand: the faces of elders were not
honored.
13 They took the young men to grind,
and the children fell under the wood.
14 The elders have ceased from the
gate, the young men from their music.
15 The joy of our heart is ceased; our
dance is turned into mourning.
16 The crown is fallen *from* our head:
woe unto us, that we have sinned!
17 For this our heart is faint; for these
things our eyes are dim.
18 Because of the mountain of Zion,
which is desolate, the foxes walk upon it.
19 Thou, O LORD, remainest for ever;
thy throne from generation to generation.
20 Wherefore dost thou forget us for
ever, *and* forsake us so long time?
21 Turn thou us unto thee, O LORD,
and we shall be turned; renew our days
as of old.
22 But thou hast utterly rejected us;
thou art very wroth against us.

THE BOOK OF THE PROPHET

EZEKIEL

CHAPTER 1

NOW it came to pass in the thirtieth
year, in the fourth *month,* in the
fifth *day* of the month, as I *was* among
the captives by the river of Chē'bär, *that*
the heavens were opened, and I saw
visions of God.
2 In the fifth *day* of the month, which
was the fifth year of king Jē-hôi'á-chĭn's
captivity,
3 The word of the LORD came expressly unto Ē-zē'kĭ-ĕl the priest, the
son of Bū'zī, in the land of the Chăl-
dē'ănș by the river Chē'bär; and the
hand of the LORD was there upon him.
4 ¶ And I looked, and, behold, a whirlwind came out of the north, a great
cloud, and a fire infolding itself, and a
brightness *was* about it, and out of the
midst thereof as the color of amber, out
of the midst of the fire.
5 Also out of the midst thereof *came*
the likeness of four living creatures.
And this *was* their appearance; they had
the likeness of a man.
6 And every one had four faces, and
every one had four wings.
7 And their feet *were* straight feet; and
the sole of their feet *was* like the sole of
a calf's foot: and they sparkled like the
color of burnished brass.
8 And *they had* the hands of a man
under their wings on their four sides;
and they four had their faces and their
wings.
9 Their wings *were* joined one to
another; they turned not when they
went; they went every one straight forward.
10 As for the likeness of their faces,
they four had the face of a man, and the
face of a lion, on the right side: and they
four had the face of an ox on the left
side; they four also had the face of an
eagle.
11 Thus *were* their faces: and their
wings *were* stretched upward; two *wings*
of every one *were* joined one to another,
and two covered their bodies.
12 And they went every one straight
forward: whither the spirit was to go,
they went; *and* they turned not when
they went.
13 As for the likeness of the living
creatures, their appearance *was* like
burning coals of fire, *and* like the appearance of lamps: it went up and down
among the living creatures; and the fire
was bright, and out of the fire went forth
lightning.
14 And the living creatures ran and
returned as the appearance of a flash of
lightning.
15 ¶ Now as I beheld the living creatures, behold one wheel upon the earth
by the living creatures, with his four
faces.

16 The appearance of the wheels and their work *was* like unto the color of a beryl: and they four had one likeness: and their appearance and their work *was* as it were a wheel in the middle of a wheel.

17 When they went, they went upon their four sides: *and* they turned not when they went.

18 As for their rings, they were so high that they were dreadful; and their rings *were* full of eyes round about them four.

19 And when the living creatures went, the wheels went by them: and when the living creatures were lifted up from the earth, the wheels were lifted up.

20 Whithersoever the spirit was to go, they went, thither *was their* spirit to go; and the wheels were lifted up over against them: for the spirit of the living creature *was* in the wheels.

21 When those went, *these* went; and when those stood, *these* stood; and when those were lifted up from the earth, the wheels were lifted up over against them: for the spirit of the living creature *was* in the wheels.

22 And the likeness of the firmament upon the heads of the living creature *was* as the color of the terrible crystal, stretched forth over their heads above.

23 And under the firmament *were* their wings straight, the one toward the other: every one had two, which covered on this side, and every one had two, which covered on that side, their bodies.

24 And when they went, I heard the noise of their wings, like the noise of great waters, as the voice of the Almighty, the voice of speech, as the noise of a host: when they stood, they let down their wings.

25 And there was a voice from the firmament that *was* over their heads, when they stood, *and* had let down their wings.

26 ¶ And above the firmament that *was* over their heads *was* the likeness of a throne, as the appearance of a sapphire stone: and upon the likeness of the throne *was* the likeness as the appearance of a man above upon it.

27 And I saw as the color of amber, as the appearance of fire round about within it, from the appearance of his loins even upward, and from the appearance of his loins even downward, I saw as it were the appearance of fire, and it had brightness round about.

28 As the appearance of the bow that is in the cloud in the day of rain, so *was* the appearance of the brightness round about. This *was* the appearance of the likeness of the glory of the LORD. And when I saw *it*, I fell upon my face, and I heard a voice of one that spake.

CHAPTER 2

AND he said unto me, Son of man, stand upon thy feet, and I will speak unto thee.

2 And the spirit entered into me when he spake unto me, and set me upon my feet, that I heard him that spake unto me.

3 And he said unto me, Son of man, I send thee to the children of Ĭs′rā-ēl, to a rebellious nation that hath rebelled against me: they and their fathers have transgressed against me, *even* unto this very day.

4 For *they are* impudent children and stiffhearted. I do send thee unto them; and thou shalt say unto them, Thus saith the Lord GOD.

5 And they, whether they will hear, or whether they will forbear, (for they *are* a rebellious house,) yet shall know that there hath been a prophet among them.

6 ¶ And thou, son of man, be not afraid of them, neither be afraid of their words, though briers and thorns *be* with thee, and thou dost dwell among scorpions: be not afraid of their words, nor be dismayed at their looks, though they *be* a rebellious house.

7 And thou shalt speak my words unto them, whether they will hear, or whether they will forbear: for they *are* most rebellious.

8 But thou, son of man, hear what I say unto thee; Be not thou rebellious like that rebellious house: open thy mouth, and eat that I give thee.

9 ¶ And when I looked, behold, a hand *was* sent unto me; and, lo, a roll of a book *was* therein;

10 And he spread it before me; and it *was* written within and without: and *there was* written therein lamentations, and mourning, and woe.

CHAPTER 3

MOREOVER he said unto me, Son of man, eat that thou findest; eat this roll, and go speak unto the house of Ĭs′rā-ēl.

2 So I opened my mouth, and he caused
me to eat that roll.
3 And he said unto me, Son of man,
cause thy belly to eat, and fill thy bowels
with this roll that I give thee. Then did
I eat *it;* and it was in my mouth as honey
for sweetness.
4 ¶ And he said unto me, Son of man,
go, get thee unto the house of Ĭs′rā-ĕl,
and speak with my words unto them.
5 For thou *art* not sent to a people of a
strange speech and of a hard language,
but to the house of Ĭs′rā-ĕl;
6 Not to many people of a strange
speech and of a hard language, whose
words thou canst not understand.
Surely, had I sent thee to them, they
would have hearkened unto thee.
7 But the house of Ĭs′rā-ĕl will not
hearken unto thee; for they will not
hearken unto me: for all the house of
Ĭs′rā-ĕl *are* impudent and hard-hearted.
8 Behold, I have made thy face strong
against their faces, and thy forehead
strong against their foreheads.
9 As an adamant harder than flint have
I made thy forehead: fear them not,
neither be dismayed at their looks,
though they *be* a rebellious house.
10 Moreover he said unto me, Son of
man, all my words that I shall speak
unto thee receive in thine heart, and
hear with thine ears.
11 And go, get thee to them of the
captivity, unto the children of thy people, and speak unto them, and tell them,
Thus saith the Lord GOD; whether
they will hear, or whether they will
forbear.
12 Then the spirit took me up, and I
heard behind me a voice of a great rushing, *saying,* Blessed *be* the glory of the
LORD from his place.
13 *I heard* also the noise of the wings
of the living creatures that touched one
another, and the noise of the wheels
over against them, and a noise of a
great rushing.
14 So the spirit lifted me up, and took
me away, and I went in bitterness, in
the heat of my spirit; but the hand of the
LORD was strong upon me.
15 ¶ Then I came to them of the captivity at Tĕl′-ā′bĭb, that dwelt by the
river of Chē′bär, and I sat where they
sat, and remained there astonished
among them seven days.
16 And it came to pass at the end of
seven days, that the word of the LORD
came unto me, saying,
17 Son of man, I have made thee a
watchman unto the house of Ĭs′rā-ĕl:
therefore hear the word at my mouth,
and give them warning from me.
18 When I say unto the wicked, Thou
shalt surely die; and thou givest him not
warning, nor speakest to warn the
wicked from his wicked way, to save
his life; the same wicked *man* shall die
in his iniquity; but his blood will I require at thine hand.
19 Yet if thou warn the wicked, and he
turn not from his wickedness, nor from
his wicked way, he shall die in his iniquity; but thou hast delivered thy soul.
20 Again, When a righteous *man* doth
turn from his righteousness, and commit iniquity, and I lay a stumblingblock
before him, he shall die: because thou
hast not given him warning, he shall die
in his sin, and his righteousness which
he hath done shall not be remembered;
but his blood will I require at thine
hand.
21 Nevertheless, if thou warn the righteous *man,* that the righteous sin not, and
he doth not sin, he shall surely live,
because he is warned; also thou hast
delivered thy soul.
22 ¶ And the hand of the LORD was
there upon me; and he said unto me,
Arise, go forth into the plain, and I will
there talk with thee.
23 Then I arose, and went forth into
the plain: and, behold, the glory of the
LORD stood there, as the glory which I
saw by the river of Chē′bär: and I fell on
my face.
24 Then the spirit entered into me, and
set me upon my feet, and spake with
me, and said unto me, Go, shut thyself
within thine house.
25 But thou, O son of man, behold,
they shall put bands upon thee, and
shall bind thee with them, and thou shalt
not go out among them:
26 And I will make thy tongue cleave
to the roof of thy mouth, that thou shalt
be dumb, and shalt not be to them a
reprover: for they *are* a rebellious house.
27 But when I speak with thee, I will
open thy mouth, and thou shalt say unto
them, Thus saith the Lord GOD; He that
heareth, let him hear; and he that forbeareth, let him forbear: for they *are* a
rebellious house.

CHAPTER 4

THOU also, son of man, take thee a tile, and lay it before thee, and portray upon it the city, *even* Jerusalem:

2 And lay siege against it, and build a fort against it, and cast a mount against it; set the camp also against it, and set *battering* rams against it round about.

3 Moreover take thou unto thee an iron pan, and set it *for* a wall of iron between thee and the city: and set thy face against it, and it shall be besieged, and thou shalt lay siege against it. This *shall be* a sign to the house of Ĭs′rā-ĕl.

4 Lie thou also upon thy left side, and lay the iniquity of the house of Ĭs′rā-ĕl upon it: *according* to the number of the days that thou shalt lie upon it thou shalt bear their iniquity.

5 For I have laid upon thee the years of their iniquity, according to the number of the days, three hundred and ninety days: so shalt thou bear the iniquity of the house of Ĭs′rā-ĕl.

6 And when thou hast accomplished them, lie again on thy right side, and thou shalt bear the iniquity of the house of Judah forty days: I have appointed thee each day for a year.

7 Therefore thou shalt set thy face toward the siege of Jerusalem, and thine arm *shall be* uncovered, and thou shalt prophesy against it.

8 And, behold, I will lay bands upon thee, and thou shalt not turn thee from one side to another, till thou hast ended the days of thy siege.

9 ¶ Take thou also unto thee wheat, and barley, and beans, and lentils, and millet, and fitches, and put them in one vessel, and make thee bread thereof, *according* to the number of the days that thou shalt lie upon thy side; three hundred and ninety days shalt thou eat thereof.

10 And thy meat which thou shalt eat *shall be* by weight, twenty shekels a day: from time to time shalt thou eat it.

11 Thou shalt drink also water by measure, the sixth part of a hin: from time to time shalt thou drink.

12 And thou shalt eat it *as* barley cakes, and thou shalt bake it with dung that cometh out of man, in their sight.

13 And the LORD said, Even thus shall the children of Ĭs′rā-ĕl eat their defiled bread among the Gĕn′tīleş, whither I will drive them.

14 Then said I, Ah Lord GOD! behold, my soul hath not been polluted: for from my youth up even till now have I not eaten of that which dieth of itself, or is torn in pieces; neither came there abominable flesh into my mouth.

15 Then he said unto me, Lo, I have given thee cow's dung for man's dung, and thou shalt prepare thy bread therewith.

16 Moreover he said unto me, Son of man, behold, I will break the staff of bread in Jerusalem: and they shall eat bread by weight, and with care; and they shall drink water by measure, and with astonishment:

17 That they may want bread and water, and be astonished one with another, and consume away for their iniquity.

CHAPTER 5

AND thou, son of man, take thee a sharp knife, take thee a barber's razor, and cause *it* to pass upon thine head and upon thy beard: then take thee balances to weigh, and divide the *hair*.

2 Thou shalt burn with fire a third part in the midst of the city, when the days of the siege are fulfilled: and thou shalt take a third part, *and* smite about it with a knife: and a third part thou shalt scatter in the wind; and I will draw out a sword after them.

3 Thou shalt also take thereof a few in number, and bind them in thy skirts.

4 Then take of them again, and cast them into the midst of the fire, and burn them in the fire; *for* thereof shall a fire come forth into all the house of Ĭs′rā-ĕl.

5 ¶ Thus saith the Lord GOD; This *is* Jerusalem: I have set it in the midst of the nations and countries *that are* round about her.

6 And she hath changed my judgments into wickedness more than the nations, and my statutes more than the countries that *are* round about her: for they have refused my judgments and my statutes, they have not walked in them.

7 Therefore thus saith the Lord GOD; Because ye multiplied more than the nations that *are* round about you, *and* have not walked in my statutes, neither have kept my judgments, neither have

done according to the judgments of the
nations that *are* round about you;
8 Therefore thus saith the Lord GOD;
Behold, I, even I, *am* against thee, and
will execute judgments in the midst of
thee in the sight of the nations.
9 And I will do in thee that which I
have not done, and whereunto I will not
do any more the like, because of all
thine abominations.
10 Therefore the fathers shall eat the
sons in the midst of thee, and the sons
shall eat their fathers; and I will execute judgments in thee, and the whole
remnant of thee will I scatter into all
the winds.
11 Wherefore, *as* I live, saith the Lord
GOD; Surely, because thou hast defiled
my sanctuary with all thy detestable
things, and with all thine abominations,
therefore will I also diminish *thee;*
neither shall mine eye spare, neither
will I have any pity.
12 ¶ A third part of thee shall die with
the pestilence, and with famine shall
they be consumed in the midst of thee:
and a third part shall fall by the sword
round about thee; and I will scatter a
third part into all the winds, and I will
draw out a sword after them.
13 Thus shall mine anger be accomplished, and I will cause my fury to rest
upon them, and I will be comforted: and
they shall know that I the LORD have
spoken *it* in my zeal, when I have accomplished my fury in them.
14 Moreover I will make thee waste,
and a reproach among the nations that
are round about thee, in the sight of all
that pass by.
15 So it shall be a reproach and a taunt,
an instruction and an astonishment unto
the nations that *are* round about thee,
when I shall execute judgments in thee
in anger and in fury and in furious
rebukes. I the LORD have spoken *it*.
16 When I shall send upon them the
evil arrows of famine, which shall be for
their destruction, *and* which I will send
to destroy you: and I will increase the
famine upon you, and will break your
staff of bread:
17 So will I send upon you famine and
evil beasts, and they shall bereave thee;
and pestilence and blood shall pass
through thee; and I will bring the
sword upon thee. I the LORD have
spoken *it*.

CHAPTER 6

AND the word of the LORD came unto
me, saying,
2 Son of man, set thy face toward the
mountains of Ĭṣ′rā-ĕl, and prophesy
against them,
3 And say, Ye mountains of Ĭṣ′rā-ĕl,
hear the word of the Lord GOD; Thus
saith the Lord GOD to the mountains and
to the hills, to the rivers and to the valleys; Behold, I, *even* I, will bring a
sword upon you, and I will destroy your
high places.
4 And your altars shall be desolate,
and your images shall be broken: and I
will cast down your slain *men* before
your idols.
5 And I will lay the dead carcasses of
the children of Ĭṣ′rā-ĕl before their
idols; and I will scatter your bones
round about your altars.
6 In all your dwelling places the cities
shall be laid waste, and the high places
shall be desolate; that your altars may
be laid waste and made desolate, and
your idols may be broken and cease, and
your images may be cut down, and your
works may be abolished.
7 And the slain shall fall in the midst
of you, and ye shall know that I *am* the
LORD.
8 ¶ Yet will I leave a remnant, that
ye may have *some* that shall escape the
sword among the nations, when ye shall
be scattered through the countries.
9 And they that escape of you shall
remember me among the nations
whither they shall be carried captives,
because I am broken with their whorish
heart, which hath departed from me, and
with their eyes, which go a whoring after
their idols: and they shall loathe themselves for the evils which they have
committed in all their abominations.
10 And they shall know that I *am* the
LORD, *and that* I have not said in vain
that I would do this evil unto them.
11 ¶ Thus saith the Lord GOD; Smite
with thine hand, and stamp with thy
foot, and say, Alas for all the evil abominations of the house of Ĭṣ′rā-ĕl! for they
shall fall by the sword, by the famine,
and by the pestilence.
12 He that is far off shall die of the
pestilence; and he that is near shall fall
by the sword; and he that remaineth and
is besieged shall die by the famine: thus

will I accomplish my fury upon them.
13 Then shall ye know that I *am* the
LORD, when their slain *men* shall be
among their idols round about their
altars, upon every high hill, in all the
tops of the mountains, and under every
green tree, and under every thick oak,
the place where they did offer sweet
savor to all their idols.
14 So will I stretch out my hand upon
them, and make the land desolate, yea,
more desolate than the wilderness toward Dĭb'lăth, in all their habitations:
and they shall know that I *am* the LORD.

CHAPTER 7

MOREOVER the word of the LORD
came unto me, saying,
2 Also, thou son of man, thus saith the
Lord GOD unto the land of Ĭs'rā-ĕl; An
end, the end is come upon the four corners of the land.
3 Now *is* the end *come* upon thee, and
I will send mine anger upon thee, and
will judge thee according to thy ways,
and will recompense upon thee all thine
abominations.
4 And mine eye shall not spare thee,
neither will I have pity: but I will recompense thy ways upon thee, and thine
abominations shall be in the midst of
thee: and ye shall know that I *am* the
LORD.
5 Thus saith the Lord GOD; An evil, an
only evil, behold, is come.
6 An end is come, the end is come: it
watcheth for thee; behold, it is come.
7 The morning is come unto thee, O
thou that dwellest in the land: the time
is come, the day of trouble *is* near, and
not the sounding again of the mountains.
8 Now will I shortly pour out my fury
upon thee, and accomplish mine anger
upon thee: and I will judge thee according to thy ways, and will recompense
thee for all thine abominations.
9 And mine eye shall not spare, neither
will I have pity: I will recompense thee
according to thy ways and thine abominations *that* are in the midst of thee; and
ye shall know that I *am* the LORD that
smiteth.
10 Behold the day, behold, it is come:
the morning is gone forth; the rod hath
blossomed, pride hath budded.
11 Violence is risen up into a rod of
wickedness: none of them *shall remain*,
nor of their multitude, nor of any of
theirs: neither *shall there be* wailing
for them.
12 The time is come, the day draweth
near: let not the buyer rejoice, nor the
seller mourn: for wrath *is* upon all the
multitude thereof.
13 For the seller shall not return to that
which is sold, although they were yet
alive: for the vision *is* touching the whole
multitude thereof, *which* shall not return; neither shall any strengthen himself in the iniquity of his life.
14 They have blown the trumpet, even
to make all ready; but none goeth to the
battle: for my wrath *is* upon all the multitude thereof.
15 The sword *is* without, and the pestilence and the famine within: he that *is*
in the field shall die with the sword; and
he that *is* in the city, famine and pestilence shall devour him.
16 ¶ But they that escape of them
shall escape, and shall be on the mountains like doves of the valleys, all of
them mourning, every one for his
iniquity.
17 All hands shall be feeble, and all
knees shall be weak *as* water.
18 They shall also gird *themselves*
with sackcloth, and horror shall cover
them; and shame *shall be* upon all faces,
and baldness upon all their heads.
19 They shall cast their silver in the
streets, and their gold shall be removed:
their silver and their gold shall not be
able to deliver them in the day of the
wrath of the LORD: they shall not satisfy
their souls, neither fill their bowels: because it is the stumblingblock of their
iniquity.
20 ¶ As for the beauty of his ornament, he set it in majesty: but they
made the images of their abominations
and of their detestable things therein:
therefore have I set it far from them.
21 And I will give it into the hands of
the strangers for a prey, and to the
wicked of the earth for a spoil; and they
shall pollute it.
22 My face will I turn also from them,
and they shall pollute my secret *place*:
for the robbers shall enter into it, and
defile it.
23 ¶ Make a chain: for the land is full
of bloody crimes, and the city is full of
violence.
24 Wherefore I will bring the worst of
the heathen, and they shall possess

their houses: I will also make the pomp
of the strong to cease; and their holy
places shall be defiled.
25 Destruction cometh; and they shall
seek peace, and *there shall be* none.
26 Mischief shall come upon mischief, and rumor shall be upon rumor;
then shall they seek a vision of the
prophet; but the law shall perish from
the priest, and counsel from the ancients.
27 The king shall mourn, and the prince
shall be clothed with desolation, and the
hands of the people of the land shall be
troubled: I will do unto them after their
way, and according to their deserts will
I judge them; and they shall know that
I *am* the LORD.

CHAPTER 8

AND it came to pass in the sixth year,
in the sixth *month,* in the fifth *day*
of the month, *as* I sat in mine house, and
the elders of Judah sat before me, that
the hand of the Lord GOD fell there upon
me.
2 Then I beheld, and lo a likeness as
the appearance of fire: from the appearance of his loins even downward, fire;
and from his loins even upward, as the
appearance of brightness, as the color
of amber.
3 And he put forth the form of a hand,
and took me by a lock of mine head;
and the spirit lifted me up between the
earth and the heaven, and brought me
in the visions of God to Jerusalem, to
the door of the inner gate that looketh
toward the north; where *was* the seat of
the image of jealousy, which provoketh
to jealousy.
4 And, behold, the glory of the God
of Ĭṣ′rā-ĕl *was* there, according to the
vision that I saw in the plain.
5 ¶ Then said he unto me, Son of man,
lift up thine eyes now the way toward
the north. So I lifted up mine eyes the
way toward the north, and behold northward at the gate of the altar this image
of jealousy in the entry.
6 He said furthermore unto me, Son
of man, seest thou what they do? *even*
the great abominations that the house of
Ĭṣ′rā-ĕl committeth here, that I should
go far off from my sanctuary? but turn
thee yet again, *and* thou shalt see
greater abominations.
7 ¶ And he brought me to the door of
the court; and when I looked, behold a
hole in the wall.
8 Then said he unto me, Son of man,
dig now in the wall: and when I had
digged in the wall, behold a door.
9 And he said unto me, Go in, and behold the wicked abominations that they
do here.
10 So I went in and saw; and behold
every form of creeping things, and
abominable beasts, and all the idols of
the house of Ĭṣ′rā-ĕl, portrayed upon
the wall round about.
11 And there stood before them seventy
men of the ancients of the house of
Ĭṣ′rā-ĕl, and in the midst of them stood
Jā-ăz′ȧ-nī′ȧh the son of Shā′phăn, with
every man his censer in his hand; and
a thick cloud of incense went up.
12 Then said he unto me, Son of man,
hast thou seen what the ancients of the
house of Ĭṣ′rā-ĕl do in the dark, every
man in the chambers of his imagery? for
they say, The LORD seeth us not; the
LORD hath forsaken the earth.
13 ¶ He said also unto me, Turn thee
yet again, *and* thou shalt see greater
abominations that they do.
14 Then he brought me to the door of
the gate of the LORD's house which *was*
toward the north; and, behold, there sat
women weeping for Tăm′mŭz.
15 ¶ Then said he unto me, Hast thou
seen *this,* O son of man? turn thee yet
again, *and* thou shalt see greater abominations than these.
16 And he brought me into the inner
court of the LORD's house, and, behold,
at the door of the temple of the LORD,
between the porch and the altar, *were*
about five and twenty men, with their
backs toward the temple of the LORD,
and their faces toward the east; and
they worshipped the sun toward the
east.
17 ¶ Then he said unto me, Hast thou
seen *this,* O son of man? Is it a light
thing to the house of Judah that they
commit the abominations which they
commit here? for they have filled the
land with violence, and have returned
to provoke me to anger: and, lo, they put
the branch to their nose.
18 Therefore will I also deal in fury:
mine eye shall not spare, neither will I
have pity: and though they cry in mine
ears with a loud voice, *yet* will I not
hear them.

CHAPTER 9

HE cried also in mine ears with a
loud voice, saying, Cause them
that have charge over the city to draw
near, even every man *with* his destroying weapon in his hand.
2 And, behold, six men came from the
way of the higher gate, which lieth toward the north, and every man a slaughter weapon in his hand; and one man
among them *was* clothed with linen,
with a writer's inkhorn by his side: and
they went in, and stood beside the
brazen altar.
3 And the glory of the God of Ĭṣ′rā-ĕl
was gone up from the cherub, whereupon he was, to the threshold of the
house. And he called to the man clothed
with linen, which *had* the writer's inkhorn by his side;
4 And the LORD said unto him, Go
through the midst of the city, through
the midst of Jerusalem, and set a mark
upon the foreheads of the men that sigh
and that cry for all the abominations
that be done in the midst thereof.
5 ¶ And to the others he said in mine
hearing, Go ye after him through the
city, and smite: let not your eye spare,
neither have ye pity:
6 Slay utterly old *and* young, both
maids, and little children, and women:
but come not near any man upon whom
is the mark; and begin at my sanctuary.
Then they began at the ancient men
which *were* before the house.
7 And he said unto them, Defile the
house, and fill the courts with the slain:
go ye forth. And they went forth, and
slew in the city.
8 ¶ And it came to pass, while they
were slaying them, and I was left, that
I fell upon my face, and cried, and said,
Ah Lord GOD! wilt thou destroy all the
residue of Ĭṣ′rā-ĕl in thy pouring out of
thy fury upon Jerusalem?
9 Then said he unto me, The iniquity
of the house of Ĭṣ′rā-ĕl and Judah *is*
exceeding great, and the land is full of
blood, and the city full of perverseness:
for they say, The LORD hath forsaken
the earth, and the LORD seeth not.
10 And as for me also, mine eye shall
not spare, neither will I have pity, *but* I
will recompense their way upon their
head.
11 And, behold, the man clothed with
linen, which *had* the inkhorn by his side,
reported the matter, saying, I have done
as thou hast commanded me.

CHAPTER 10

THEN I looked, and, behold, in the
firmament that was above the head
of the cherubim there appeared over
them as it were a sapphire stone, as the
appearance of the likeness of a throne.
2 And he spake unto the man clothed
with linen, and said, Go in between the
wheels, *even* under the cherub, and fill
thine hand with coals of fire from between the cherubim, and scatter *them*
over the city. And he went in in my
sight.
3 Now the cherubim stood on the right
side of the house, when the man went
in; and the cloud filled the inner court.
4 Then the glory of the LORD went up
from the cherub, *and stood* over the
threshold of the house; and the house
was filled with the cloud, and the court
was full of the brightness of the LORD's
glory.
5 And the sound of the cherubim's
wings was heard *even* to the outer court,
as the voice of the Almighty God when
he speaketh.
6 And it came to pass, *that* when he
had commanded the man clothed with
linen, saying, Take fire from between
the wheels, from between the cherubim;
then he went in, and stood beside the
wheels.
7 And *one* cherub stretched forth his
hand from between the cherubim unto
the fire that *was* between the cherubim,
and took *thereof*, and put *it* into the
hands of *him that was* clothed with
linen; who took *it*, and went out.
8 ¶ And there appeared in the cherubim the form of a man's hand under
their wings.
9 And when I looked, behold the four
wheels by the cherubim, one wheel by
one cherub, and another wheel by another cherub: and the appearance of the
wheels *was* as the color of a beryl stone.
10 And *as for* their appearances, they
four had one likeness, as if a wheel
had been in the midst of a wheel.
11 When they went, they went upon
their four sides; they turned not as they
went, but to the place whither the head
looked they followed it; they turned not
as they went.

12 And their whole body, and their
backs, and their hands, and their wings,
and the wheels, *were* full of eyes round
about, *even* the wheels that they four
had.
13 As for the wheels, it was cried unto
them in my hearing, O wheel.
14 And every one had four faces: the
first face *was* the face of a cherub, and
the second face *was* the face of a man,
and the third the face of a lion, and the
fourth the face of an eagle.
15 And the cherubim were lifted up.
This *is* the living creature that I saw by
the river of Chē′bär.
16 And when the cherubim went, the
wheels went by them: and when the
cherubim lifted up their wings to mount
up from the earth, the same wheels also
turned not from beside them.
17 When they stood, *these* stood; and
when they were lifted up, *these* lifted up
themselves *also:* for the spirit of the
living creature *was* in them.
18 Then the glory of the LORD departed
from off the threshold of the house, and
stood over the cherubim.
19 And the cherubim lifted up their
wings, and mounted up from the earth
in my sight: when they went out, the
wheels also *were* beside them, and
every one stood at the door of the east
gate of the LORD's house; and the glory
of the God of Ĭṣ′rā-ĕl *was* over them
above.
20 This *is* the living creature that I saw
under the God of Ĭṣ′rā-ĕl by the river
of Chē′bär; and I knew that they *were*
the cherubim.
21 Every one had four faces apiece,
and every one four wings; and the likeness of the hands of a man *was* under
their wings.
22 And the likeness of their faces *was*
the same faces which I saw by the river
of Chē′bär, their appearances and themselves: they went every one straight
forward.

CHAPTER 11

MOREOVER the spirit lifted me up,
and brought me unto the east gate
of the LORD's house, which looketh eastward: and behold at the door of the gate
five and twenty men; among whom I saw
Jā-ăz′ȧ-nī′ăh the son of Ā′zŭr, and
Pĕl′ȧ-tī′ăh the son of Bē-nā′ịăh, princes
of the people.
2 Then said he unto me, Son of man,
these *are* the men that devise mischief,
and give wicked counsel in this city:
3 Which say, *It is* not near; let us build
houses: this *city is* the caldron, and we
be the flesh.
4 ℂ Therefore prophesy against them,
prophesy, O son of man.
5 And the Spirit of the LORD fell upon
me, and said unto me, Speak; Thus saith
the LORD; Thus have ye said, O house
of Ĭs′rā-ĕl: for I know the things that
come into your mind, *every one of* them.
6 Ye have multiplied your slain in
this city, and ye have filled the streets
thereof with the slain.
7 Therefore thus saith the Lord GOD;
Your slain whom ye have laid in the
midst of it, they *are* the flesh, and this
city is the caldron: but I will bring you
forth out of the midst of it.
8 Ye have feared the sword; and I will
bring a sword upon you, saith the Lord
GOD.
9 And I will bring you out of the midst
thereof, and deliver you into the hands
of strangers, and will execute judgments
among you.
10 Ye shall fall by the sword; I will
judge you in the border of Ĭṣ′rā-ĕl; and
ye shall know that I *am* the LORD.
11 This *city* shall not be your caldron,
neither shall ye be the flesh in the midst
thereof; *but* I will judge you in the border of Ĭṣ′rā-ĕl:
12 And ye shall know that I *am* the
LORD: for ye have not walked in my
statutes, neither executed my judgments, but have done after the manners
of the heathen that *are* round about you.
13 ℂ And it came to pass, when I
prophesied, that Pĕl′ȧ-tī′ăh the son of
Bē-nā′ịăh died. Then fell I down upon
my face, and cried with a loud voice, and
said, Ah Lord GOD! wilt thou make a full
end of the remnant of Ĭṣ′rā-ĕl?
14 Again the word of the LORD came
unto me, saying,
15 Son of man, thy brethren, *even* thy
brethren, the men of thy kindred, and
all the house of Ĭṣ′rā-ĕl wholly, *are* they
unto whom the inhabitants of Jerusalem
have said, Get you far from the LORD:
unto us is this land given in possession.
16 Therefore say, Thus saith the Lord
GOD; Although I have cast them far off
among the heathen, and although I have
scattered them among the countries, yet

will I be to them as a little sanctuary in
the countries where they shall come.
17 Therefore say, Thus saith the Lord
GOD; I will even gather you from the
people, and assemble you out of the
countries where ye have been scattered,
and I will give you the land of Ĭṣ′rā-ĕl.
18 And they shall come thither, and
they shall take away all the detestable
things thereof and all the abominations
thereof from thence.
19 And I will give them one heart, and
I will put a new spirit within you; and I
will take the stony heart out of their
flesh, and will give them a heart of flesh:
20 That they may walk in my statutes,
and keep mine ordinances, and do them:
and they shall be my people, and I will
be their God.
21 But *as for them* whose heart walketh
after the heart of their detestable things
and their abominations, I will recompense their way upon their own heads,
saith the Lord GOD.
22 ¶ Then did the cherubim lift up
their wings, and the wheels beside them;
and the glory of the God of Ĭṣ′rā-ĕl *was*
over them above.
23 And the glory of the LORD went up
from the midst of the city, and stood
upon the mountain which *is* on the east
side of the city.
24 ¶ Afterward the spirit took me up,
and brought me in a vision by the Spirit
of God into Chăl-dē′ȧ, to them of the
captivity. So the vision that I had seen
went up from me.
25 Then I spake unto them of the captivity all the things that the LORD had
showed me.

CHAPTER 12

THE word of the LORD also came
unto me, saying,
2 Son of man, thou dwellest in the
midst of a rebellious house, which have
eyes to see, and see not; they have ears
to hear, and hear not: for they *are* a
rebellious house.
3 Therefore, thou son of man, prepare
thee stuff for removing, and remove by
day in their sight; and thou shalt remove
from thy place to another place in their
sight: it may be they will consider,
though they *be* a rebellious house.
4 Then shalt thou bring forth thy stuff
by day in their sight, as stuff for removing: and thou shalt go forth at even in
their sight, as they that go forth into
captivity.
5 Dig thou through the wall in their
sight, and carry out thereby.
6 In their sight shalt thou bear *it* upon
thy shoulders, *and* carry *it* forth in the
twilight: thou shalt cover thy face, that
thou see not the ground: for I have set
thee *for* a sign unto the house of Ĭṣ′rā-ĕl.
7 And I did so as I was commanded:
I brought forth my stuff by day, as stuff
for captivity, and in the even I digged
through the wall with mine hand; I
brought *it* forth in the twilight, *and* I
bare *it* upon *my* shoulder in their sight.
8 ¶ And in the morning came the word
of the LORD unto me, saying,
9 Son of man, hath not the house of
Ĭṣ′rā-ĕl, the rebellious house, said unto
thee, What doest thou?
10 Say thou unto them, Thus saith the
Lord GOD; This burden *concerneth* the
prince in Jerusalem, and all the house
of Ĭṣ′rā-ĕl that *are* among them.
11 Say, I *am* your sign: like as I have
done, so shall it be done unto them: they
shall remove *and* go into captivity.
12 And the prince that *is* among them
shall bear upon *his* shoulder in the twilight, and shall go forth: they shall dig
through the wall to carry out thereby:
he shall cover his face, that he see not
the ground with *his* eyes.
13 My net also will I spread upon him,
and he shall be taken in my snare: and
I will bring him to Babylon *to* the land of
the Chăl-dē′ănṣ; yet shall he not see it,
though he shall die there.
14 And I will scatter toward every wind
all that *are* about him to help him, and
all his bands; and I will draw out the
sword after them.
15 And they shall know that I *am* the
LORD, when I shall scatter them among
the nations, and disperse them in the
countries.
16 But I will leave a few men of them
from the sword, from the famine, and
from the pestilence; that they may declare all their abominations among the
heathen whither they come; and they
shall know that I *am* the LORD.
17 ¶ Moreover the word of the LORD
came to me, saying,
18 Son of man, eat thy bread with
quaking, and drink thy water with
trembling and with carefulness;
19 And say unto the people of the land,

Thus saith the Lord GOD of the inhabitants of Jerusalem, *and* of the land
of Ĭş'rā-ĕl; They shall eat their bread
with carefulness, and drink their water
with astonishment, that her land may
be desolate from all that is therein, because of the violence of all them that
dwell therein.
20 And the cities that are inhabited
shall be laid waste, and the land shall
be desolate; and ye shall know that I
am the LORD.
21 ¶ And the word of the LORD came
unto me, saying,
22 Son of man, what *is* that proverb
that ye have in the land of Ĭş'rā-ĕl, saying, The days are prolonged, and every
vision faileth?
23 Tell them therefore, Thus saith the
Lord GOD; I will make this proverb to
cease, and they shall no more use it as
a proverb in Ĭş'rā-ĕl; but say unto them,
The days are at hand, and the effect of
every vision.
24 For there shall be no more any vain
vision nor flattering divination within
the house of Ĭş'rā-ĕl.
25 For I *am* the LORD: I will speak, and
the word that I shall speak shall come
to pass; it shall be no more prolonged:
for in your days, O rebellious house, will
I say the word, and will perform it,
saith the Lord GOD.
26 ¶ Again the word of the LORD came
to me, saying,
27 Son of man, behold, *they of* the
house of Ĭş'rā-ĕl say, The vision that he
seeth *is* for many days *to come*, and he
prophesieth of the times *that are* far off.
28 Therefore say unto them, Thus saith
the Lord GOD; There shall none of my
words be prolonged any more, but the
word which I have spoken shall be done,
saith the Lord GOD.

CHAPTER 13

AND the word of the LORD came unto
me, saying,
2 Son of man, prophesy against the
prophets of Ĭş'rā-ĕl that prophesy, and
say thou unto them that prophesy out of
their own hearts, Hear ye the word of
the LORD;
3 Thus saith the Lord GOD; Woe
unto the foolish prophets, that follow
their own spirit and have seen nothing!
4 O Ĭş'rā-ĕl, thy prophets are like the
foxes in the deserts.
5 Ye have not gone up into the gaps,
neither made up the hedge for the house
of Ĭş'rā-ĕl to stand in the battle in the
day of the LORD.
6 They have seen vanity and lying
divination, saying, The LORD saith: and
the LORD hath not sent them: and they
have made *others* to hope that they
would confirm the word.
7 Have ye not seen a vain vision, and
have ye not spoken a lying divination,
whereas ye say, The LORD saith *it;*
albeit I have not spoken?
8 Therefore thus saith the Lord GOD;
Because ye have spoken vanity, and
seen lies, therefore, behold, I *am* against
you, saith the Lord GOD.
9 And mine hand shall be upon the
prophets that see vanity, and that divine
lies: they shall not be in the assembly of
my people, neither shall they be written
in the writing of the house of Ĭş'rā-ĕl,
neither shall they enter into the land of
Ĭş'rā-ĕl; and ye shall know that I *am*
the Lord GOD.
10 ¶ Because, even because they have
seduced my people, saying, Peace; and
there was no peace; and one built up a
wall, and, lo, others daubed it with untempered *mortar:*
11 Say unto them which daub *it* with
untempered *mortar*, that it shall fall:
there shall be an overflowing shower;
and ye, O great hailstones, shall fall;
and a stormy wind shall rend *it*.
12 Lo, when the wall is fallen, shall it
not be said unto you, Where *is* the daub-
ing wherewith ye have daubed *it?*
13 Therefore thus saith the Lord GOD;
I will even rend *it* with a stormy wind in
my fury; and there shall be an overflowing shower in mine anger, and great
hailstones in *my* fury to consume *it*.
14 So will I break down the wall that
ye have daubed with untempered *mortar*, and bring it down to the ground, so
that the foundation thereof shall be discovered, and it shall fall, and ye shall be
consumed in the midst thereof: and ye
shall know that I *am* the LORD.
15 Thus will I accomplish my wrath
upon the wall, and upon them that have
daubed it with untempered *mortar*, and
will say unto you, The wall *is* no *more*,
neither they that daubed it;
16 *To wit*, the prophets of Ĭş'rā-ĕl
which prophesy concerning Jerusalem,
and which see visions of peace for her,

and *there is* no peace, saith the Lord
GOD.
17 ¶ Likewise, thou son of man, set
thy face against the daughters of thy
people, which prophesy out of their own
heart; and prophesy thou against them,
18 And say, Thus saith the Lord GOD;
Woe to the *women* that sew pillows to
all armholes, and make kerchiefs upon
the head of every stature to hunt souls!
Will ye hunt the souls of my people, and
will ye save the souls alive *that come*
unto you?
19 And will ye pollute me among my
people for handfuls of barley and for
pieces of bread, to slay the souls that
should not die, and to save the souls
alive that should not live, by your lying
to my people that hear *your* lies?
20 Wherefore thus saith the Lord GOD;
Behold, I *am* against your pillows,
wherewith ye there hunt the souls to
make *them* fly, and I will tear them
from your arms, and will let the souls
go, *even* the souls that ye hunt to make
them fly.
21 Your kerchiefs also will I tear, and
deliver my people out of your hand, and
they shall be no more in your hand to be
hunted; and ye shall know that I *am* the
LORD.
22 Because with lies ye have made the
heart of the righteous sad, whom I have
not made sad; and strengthened the
hands of the wicked, that he should not
return from his wicked way, by promis-
ing him life;
23 Therefore ye shall see no more
vanity, nor divine divinations: for I will
deliver my people out of your hand: and
ye shall know that I *am* the LORD.

CHAPTER 14

THEN came certain of the elders of
Ĭṣ′rā-ĕl unto me, and sat before me.
2 And the word of the LORD came unto
me, saying,
3 Son of man, these men have set up
their idols in their heart, and put the
stumblingblock of their iniquity before
their face: should I be inquired of at all
by them?
4 Therefore speak unto them, and say
unto them, Thus saith the Lord GOD;
Every man of the house of Ĭṣ′rā-ĕl that
setteth up his idols in his heart, and putteth the stumblingblock of his iniquity
before his face, and cometh to the
prophet; I the LORD will answer him
that cometh, according to the multitude
of his idols;
5 That I may take the house of Ĭṣ′rā-ĕl
in their own heart, because they are all
estranged from me through their idols.
6 ¶ Therefore say unto the house of
Ĭṣ′rā-ĕl, Thus saith the Lord GOD; Repent, and turn *yourselves* from your
idols; and turn away your faces from all
your abominations.
7 For every one of the house of Ĭṣ′rā-ĕl,
or of the stranger that sojourneth in
Ĭṣ′rā-ĕl, which separateth himself from
me, and setteth up his idols in his heart,
and putteth the stumblingblock of his
iniquity before his face, and cometh to a
prophet to inquire of him concerning me;
I the LORD will answer him by myself:
8 And I will set my face against that
man, and will make him a sign and a
proverb, and I will cut him off from the
midst of my people; and ye shall know
that I *am* the LORD.
9 And if the prophet be deceived when
he hath spoken a thing, I the LORD have
deceived that prophet, and I will stretch
out my hand upon him, and will destroy him from the midst of my people
Ĭṣ′rā-ĕl.
10 And they shall bear the punishment
of their iniquity: the punishment of the
prophet shall be even as the punishment
of him that seeketh *unto him;*
11 That the house of Ĭṣ′rā-ĕl may go
no more astray from me, neither be
polluted any more with all their transgressions; but that they may be my
people, and I may be their God, saith
the Lord GOD.
12 ¶ The word of the LORD came again
to me, saying,
13 Son of man, when the land sinneth
against me by trespassing grievously,
then will I stretch out mine hand upon
it, and will break the staff of the bread
thereof, and will send famine upon it,
and will cut off man and beast from it:
14 Though these three men, Noah,
Daniel, and Jōb, were in it, they should
deliver *but* their own souls by their
righteousness, saith the Lord GOD.
15 ¶ If I cause noisome beasts to pass
through the land, and they spoil it, so
that it be desolate, that no man may
pass through because of the beasts:
16 *Though* these three men *were* in it,
as I live, saith the Lord GOD, they shall

deliver neither sons nor daughters; they only shall be delivered, but the land shall be desolate.

17 ¶ Or *if* I bring a sword upon that land, and say, Sword, go through the land; so that I cut off man and beast from it:

18 Though these three men *were* in it, *as* I live, saith the Lord GOD, they shall deliver neither sons nor daughters, but they only shall be delivered themselves.

19 ¶ Or *if* I send a pestilence into that land, and pour out my fury upon it in blood, to cut off from it man and beast:

20 Though Noah, Daniel, and Jōb, *were* in it, *as* I live, saith the Lord GOD, they shall deliver neither son nor daughter; they shall *but* deliver their own souls by their righteousness.

21 For thus saith the Lord GOD; How much more when I send my four sore judgments upon Jerusalem, the sword, and the famine, and the noisome beast, and the pestilence, to cut off from it man and beast?

22 ¶ Yet, behold, therein shall be left a remnant that shall be brought forth, *both* sons and daughters: behold, they shall come forth unto you, and ye shall see their way and their doings: and ye shall be comforted concerning the evil that I have brought upon Jerusalem, *even* concerning all that I have brought upon it.

23 And they shall comfort you, when ye see their ways and their doings: and ye shall know that I have not done without cause all that I have done in it, saith the Lord GOD.

CHAPTER 15

AND the word of the LORD came unto me, saying,

2 Son of man, What is the vine tree more than any tree, *or than* a branch which is among the trees of the forest?

3 Shall wood be taken thereof to do any work? or will *men* take a pin of it to hang any vessel thereon?

4 Behold, it is cast into the fire for fuel; the fire devoureth both the ends of it, and the midst of it is burned. Is it meet for *any* work?

5 Behold, when it was whole, it was meet for no work: how much less shall it be meet yet for *any* work, when the fire hath devoured it, and it is burned?

6 ¶ Therefore thus saith the Lord GOD, As the vine tree among the trees of the forest, which I have given to the fire for fuel, so will I give the inhabitants of Jerusalem.

7 And I will set my face against them; they shall go out from *one* fire, and *another* fire shall devour them; and ye shall know that I *am* the LORD, when I set my face against them.

8 And I will make the land desolate, because they have committed a trespass, saith the Lord GOD.

CHAPTER 16

AGAIN the word of the LORD came unto me, saying,

2 Son of man, cause Jerusalem to know her abominations,

3 And say, Thus saith the Lord GOD unto Jerusalem; Thy birth and thy nativity *is* of the land of Cā'năan; thy father *was* an Ăm'ō-rīte, and thy mother a Hĭt'tīte.

4 And *as for* thy nativity, in the day thou wast born thy navel was not cut, neither wast thou washed in water to supple *thee;* thou wast not salted at all, nor swaddled at all.

5 None eye pitied thee, to do any of these unto thee, to have compassion upon thee; but thou wast cast out in the open field, to the loathing of thy person, in the day that thou wast born.

6 ¶ And when I passed by thee, and saw thee polluted in thine own blood, I said unto thee *when thou wast* in thy blood, Live; yea, I said unto thee *when thou wast* in thy blood, Live.

7 I have caused thee to multiply as the bud of the field, and thou hast increased and waxen great, and thou art come to excellent ornaments: *thy* breasts are fashioned, and thine hair is grown, whereas thou *wast* naked and bare.

8 Now when I passed by thee, and looked upon thee, behold, thy time *was* the time of love; and I spread my skirt over thee, and covered thy nakedness: yea, I sware unto thee, and entered into a covenant with thee, saith the Lord GOD, and thou becamest mine.

9 Then washed I thee with water; yea, I thoroughly washed away thy blood from thee, and I anointed thee with oil.

10 I clothed thee also with broidered work, and shod thee with badgers' skin, and I girded thee about with fine linen, and I covered thee with silk.

11 I decked thee also with ornaments,
and I put bracelets upon thy hands, and
a chain on thy neck.
12 And I put a jewel on thy forehead,
and earrings in thine ears, and a beautiful crown upon thine head.
13 Thus wast thou decked with gold
and silver; and thy raiment *was of* fine
linen, and silk, and broidered work;
thou didst eat fine flour, and honey, and
oil; and thou wast exceeding beautiful,
and thou didst prosper into a kingdom.
14 And thy renown went forth among
the heathen for thy beauty: for it *was*
perfect through my comeliness, which I
had put upon thee, saith the Lord GOD.
15 ℂ But thou didst trust in thine own
beauty, and playedst the harlot because
of thy renown, and pouredst out thy
fornications on every one that passed
by; his it was.
16 And of thy garments thou didst
take, and deckedst thy high places with
divers colors, and playedst the harlot
thereupon: *the like things* shall not
come, neither shall it be *so*.
17 Thou hast also taken thy fair jewels
of my gold and of my silver, which I had
given thee, and madest to thyself images
of men, and didst commit whoredom
with them,
18 And tookest thy broidered garments,
and coveredst them: and thou hast set
mine oil and mine incense before them.
19 My meat also which I gave thee,
fine flour, and oil, and honey, *wherewith*
I fed thee, thou hast even set it before
them for a sweet savor: and *thus* it was,
saith the Lord GOD.
20 Moreover thou hast taken thy sons
and thy daughters, whom thou hast
borne unto me, and these hast thou
sacrificed unto them to be devoured.
Is this of thy whoredoms a small matter,
21 That thou hast slain my children,
and delivered them to cause them to
pass through *the fire* for them?
22 And in all thine abominations and
thy whoredoms thou hast not remembered the days of thy youth, when thou
wast naked and bare, *and* wast polluted
in thy blood.
23 And it came to pass after all thy
wickedness, (woe, woe unto thee! saith
the Lord GOD,)
24 *That* thou hast also built unto thee
an eminent place, and hast made thee a
high place in every street.
25 Thou hast built thy high place at
every head of the way, and hast made
thy beauty to be abhorred, and hast
opened thy feet to every one that passed
by, and multiplied thy whoredoms.
26 Thou hast also committed fornication with the Egyptians thy neighbors,
great of flesh; and hast increased thy
whoredoms, to provoke me to anger.
27 Behold, therefore I have stretched
out my hand over thee, and have
diminished thine ordinary *food*, and delivered thee unto the will of them that
hate thee, the daughters of the Phĭ-
lĭs′tĭneș, which are ashamed of thy lewd
way.
28 Thou hast played the whore also
with the Assyrians, because thou wast
unsatiable; yea, thou hast played the
harlot with them, and yet couldest not
be satisfied.
29 Thou hast moreover multiplied thy
fornication in the land of Cā′năan unto
Chăl-dē′á; and yet thou wast not satisfied herewith.
30 How weak is thine heart, saith the
Lord GOD, seeing thou doest all these
things, the work of an imperious whorish woman;
31 In that thou buildest thine eminent
place in the head of every way, and
makest thine high place in every street;
and hast not been as a harlot, in that
thou scornest hire;
32 *But as* a wife that committeth
adultery, *which* taketh strangers instead of her husband!
33 They give gifts to all whores: but
thou givest thy gifts to all thy lovers, and
hirest them, that they may come unto
thee on every side for thy whoredom.
34 And the contrary is in thee from
other women in thy whoredoms, whereas none followeth thee to commit whoredoms: and in that thou givest a reward,
and no reward is given unto thee,
therefore thou art contrary.
35 ℂ Wherefore, O harlot, hear the
word of the LORD:
36 Thus saith the Lord GOD; Because
thy filthiness was poured out, and thy
nakedness discovered through thy
whoredoms with thy lovers, and with
all the idols of thy abominations, and
by the blood of thy children, which thou
didst give unto them;
37 Behold, therefore I will gather all
thy lovers, with whom thou hast taken

pleasure, and all *them* that thou hast loved, with all *them* that thou hast hated; I will even gather them round about against thee, and will discover thy nakedness unto them, that they may see all thy nakedness.

38 And I will judge thee, as women that break wedlock and shed blood are judged; and I will give thee blood in fury and jealousy.

39 And I will also give thee into their hand, and they shall throw down thine eminent place, and shall break down thy high places: they shall strip thee also of thy clothes, and shall take thy fair jewels, and leave thee naked and bare.

40 They shall also bring up a company against thee, and they shall stone thee with stones, and thrust thee through with their swords.

41 And they shall burn thine houses with fire, and execute judgments upon thee in the sight of many women: and I will cause thee to cease from playing the harlot, and thou also shalt give no hire any more.

42 So will I make my fury toward thee to rest, and my jealousy shall depart from thee, and I will be quiet, and will be no more angry.

43 Because thou hast not remembered the days of thy youth, but hast fretted me in all these *things;* behold, therefore I also will recompense thy way upon *thine* head, saith the Lord GOD: and thou shalt not commit this lewdness above all thine abominations.

44 ℂ Behold, every one that useth proverbs shall use *this* proverb against thee, saying, As *is* the mother, *so is* her daughter.

45 Thou *art* thy mother's daughter, that loatheth her husband and her children; and thou *art* the sister of thy sisters, which loathed their husbands and their children: your mother *was* a Hĭt′tīte, and your father an Ăm′ō-rīte.

46 And thine elder sister *is* Sȧ-mā′rĭ-ȧ, she and her daughters that dwell at thy left hand: and thy younger sister, that dwelleth at thy right hand, *is* Sŏd′ȯm and her daughters.

47 Yet hast thou not walked after their ways, nor done after their abominations: but, as *if that were* a very little *thing,* thou wast corrupted more than they in all thy ways.

48 *As* I live, saith the Lord GOD, Sŏd′ȯm thy sister hath not done, she nor her daughters, as thou hast done, thou and thy daughters.

49 Behold, this was the iniquity of thy sister Sŏd′ȯm, pride, fulness of bread, and abundance of idleness was in her and in her daughters, neither did she strengthen the hand of the poor and needy.

50 And they were haughty, and committed abomination before me: therefore I took them away as I saw *good.*

51 Neither hath Sȧ-mā′rĭ-ȧ committed half of thy sins; but thou hast multiplied thine abominations more than they, and hast justified thy sisters in all thine abominations which thou hast done.

52 Thou also, which hast judged thy sisters, bear thine own shame for thy sins that thou hast committed more abominable than they: they are more righteous than thou: yea, be thou confounded also, and bear thy shame, in that thou hast justified thy sisters.

53 When I shall bring again their captivity, the captivity of Sŏd′ȯm and her daughters, and the captivity of Sȧ-mā′rĭ-ȧ and her daughters, then *will I bring again* the captivity of thy captives in the midst of them:

54 That thou mayest bear thine own shame, and mayest be confounded in all that thou hast done, in that thou art a comfort unto them.

55 When thy sisters, Sŏd′ȯm and her daughters, shall return to their former estate, and Sȧ-mā′rĭ-ȧ and her daughters shall return to their former estate, then thou and thy daughters shall return to your former estate.

56 For thy sister Sŏd′ȯm was not mentioned by thy mouth in the day of thy pride,

57 Before thy wickedness was discovered, as at the time of *thy* reproach of the daughters of Syria, and all *that are* round about her, the daughters of the Phĭ-lĭs′tīneş, which despise thee round about.

58 Thou hast borne thy lewdness and thine abominations, saith the LORD.

59 For thus saith the Lord GOD; I will even deal with thee as thou hast done, which hast despised the oath in breaking the covenant.

60 ℂ Nevertheless, I will remember my covenant with thee in the days of

thy youth, and I will establish unto thee
an everlasting covenant.
61 Then thou shalt remember thy
ways, and be ashamed, when thou shalt
receive thy sisters, thine elder and thy
younger: and I will give them unto thee
for daughters, but not by thy covenant.
62 And I will establish my covenant
with thee; and thou shalt know that I
am the LORD:
63 That thou mayest remember, and
be confounded, and never open thy
mouth any more because of thy shame,
when I am pacified toward thee for all
that thou hast done, saith the Lord GOD.

CHAPTER 17

AND the word of the LORD came unto
me, saying,
2 Son of man, put forth a riddle, and
speak a parable unto the house of
Iṣ'rā-ĕl;
3 And say, Thus saith the Lord GOD;
A great eagle with great wings, long-
winged, full of feathers, which had
divers colors, came unto Lebanon, and
took the highest branch of the cedar:
4 He cropped off the top of his young
twigs, and carried it into a land of
traffic; he set it in a city of merchants.
5 He took also of the seed of the land,
and planted it in a fruitful field; he
placed *it* by great waters, *and* set it *as*
a willow tree.
6 And it grew, and became a spreading
vine of low stature, whose branches
turned toward him, and the roots thereof were under him: so it became a vine,
and brought forth branches, and shot
forth sprigs.
7 There was also another great eagle
with great wings and many feathers:
and, behold, this vine did bend her
roots toward him, and shot forth her
branches toward him, that he might
water it by the furrows of her plantation.
8 It was planted in a good soil by
great waters, that it might bring forth
branches, and that it might bear fruit,
that it might be a goodly vine.
9 Say thou, Thus saith the Lord GOD;
Shall it prosper? shall he not pull up
the roots thereof, and cut off the fruit
thereof, that it wither? it shall wither in
all the leaves of her spring, even without great power or many people to pluck
it up by the roots thereof.
10 Yea, behold, *being* planted, shall it
prosper? shall it not utterly wither,
when the east wind toucheth it? it shall
wither in the furrows where it grew.
11 ¶ Moreover the word of the LORD
came unto me, saying,
12 Say now to the rebellious house,
Know ye not what these *things mean?*
tell *them,* Behold, the king of Babylon
is come to Jerusalem, and hath taken
the king thereof, and the princes thereof, and led them with him to Babylon;
13 And hath taken of the king's seed,
and made a covenant with him, and
hath taken an oath of him: he hath also
taken the mighty of the land:
14 That the kingdom might be base,
that it might not lift itself up, *but* that
by keeping of his covenant it might
stand.
15 But he rebelled against him in
sending his ambassadors into Egypt,
that they might give him horses and
much people. Shall he prosper? shall
he escape that doeth such *things?* or
shall he break the covenant, and be
delivered?
16 *As* I live, saith the Lord GOD, surely
in the place *where* the king *dwelleth*
that made him king, whose oath he
despised, and whose covenant he brake,
even with him in the midst of Babylon
he shall die.
17 Neither shall Phā'raōh with *his*
mighty army and great company make
for him in the war, by casting up
mounts, and building forts, to cut off
many persons:
18 Seeing he despised the oath by
breaking the covenant, when, lo, he
had given his hand, and hath done all
these *things,* he shall not escape.
19 Therefore thus saith the Lord GOD;
As I live, surely mine oath that he hath
despised, and my covenant that he hath
broken, even it will I recompense upon
his own head.
20 And I will spread my net upon him,
and he shall be taken in my snare, and
I will bring him to Babylon, and will
plead with him there for his trespass
that he hath trespassed against me.
21 And all his fugitives with all his
bands shall fall by the sword, and they
that remain shall be scattered toward
all winds: and ye shall know that I the
LORD have spoken *it.*
22 ¶ Thus saith the Lord GOD; I will
also take of the highest branch of the

high cedar, and will set *it;* I will crop
off from the top of his young twigs a
tender one, and will plant *it* upon a
high mountain and eminent:
23 In the mountain of the height of
Ĭş'rā-ĕl will I plant it: and it shall bring
forth boughs, and bear fruit, and be a
goodly cedar: and under it shall dwell
all fowl of every wing; in the shadow of
the branches thereof shall they dwell.
24 And all the trees of the field shall
know that I the LORD have brought
down the high tree, have exalted the
low tree, have dried up the green tree,
and have made the dry tree to flourish:
I the LORD have spoken and have done *it*.

CHAPTER 18

THE word of the LORD came unto me
again, saying,
2 What mean ye, that ye use this
proverb concerning the land of Ĭş'rā-ĕl,
saying, The fathers have eaten sour
grapes, and the children's teeth are set
on edge?
3 *As* I live, saith the Lord GOD, ye
shall not have *occasion* any more to use
this proverb in Ĭş'rā-ĕl.
4 Behold, all souls are mine; as the
soul of the father, so also the soul of the
son is mine: the soul that sinneth, it
shall die.
5 ¶ But if a man be just, and do that
which is lawful and right,
6 *And* hath not eaten upon the mountains, neither hath lifted up his eyes to
the idols of the house of Ĭs'rā-ĕl, neither
hath defiled his neighbor's wife, neither
hath come near to a menstruous woman,
7 And hath not oppressed any, *but*
hath restored to the debtor his pledge,
hath spoiled none by violence, hath
given his bread to the hungry, and hath
covered the naked with a garment;
8 He *that* hath not given forth upon
usury, neither hath taken any increase,
that hath withdrawn his hand from
iniquity, hath executed true judgment
between man and man,
9 Hath walked in my statutes, and
hath kept my judgments, to deal truly;
he *is* just, he shall surely live, saith the
Lord GOD.
10 ¶ If he beget a son *that is* a robber,
a shedder of blood, and *that* doeth the
like to *any* one of these *things*,
11 And that doeth not any of those
duties, but even hath eaten upon the
mountains, and defiled his neighbor's
wife,
12 Hath oppressed the poor and needy,
hath spoiled by violence, hath not restored the pledge, and hath lifted up
his eyes to the idols, hath committed
abomination,
13 Hath given forth upon usury, and
hath taken increase: shall he then live?
he shall not live: he hath done all these
abominations; he shall surely die; his
blood shall be upon him.
14 ¶ Now, lo, *if* he beget a son, that
seeth all his father's sins which he hath
done, and considereth, and doeth not
such like,
15 *That* hath not eaten upon the
mountains, neither hath lifted up his
eyes to the idols of the house of Ĭş'rā-ĕl,
hath not defiled his neighbor's wife,
16 Neither hath oppressed any, hath
not withholden the pledge, neither
hath spoiled by violence, *but* hath given
his bread to the hungry, and hath covered the naked with a garment,
17 *That* hath taken off his hand from
the poor, *that* hath not received usury
nor increase, hath executed my judgments, hath walked in my statutes; he
shall not die for the iniquity of his
father, he shall surely live.
18 *As for* his father, because he cruelly
oppressed, spoiled his brother by violence, and did *that* which *is* not good
among his people, lo, even he shall die
in his iniquity.
19 ¶ Yet say ye, Why? doth not the
son bear the iniquity of the father?
When the son hath done that which is
lawful and right, *and* hath kept all my
statutes, and hath done them, he shall
surely live.
20 The soul that sinneth, it shall die.
The son shall not bear the iniquity of
the father, neither shall the father bear
the iniquity of the son: the righteousness
of the righteous shall be upon him, and
the wickedness of the wicked shall be
upon him.
21 But if the wicked will turn from all
his sins that he hath committed, and
keep all my statutes, and do that which
is lawful and right, he shall surely live,
he shall not die.
22 All his transgressions that he hath
committed, they shall not be mentioned
unto him: in his righteousness that he
hath done he shall live.

23 Have I any pleasure at all that the
wicked should die? saith the Lord God:
and not that he should return from his
ways, and live?
24 ¶ But when the righteous turneth
away from his righteousness, and committeth iniquity, *and* doeth according to
all the abominations that the wicked
man doeth, shall he live? All his righteousness that he hath done shall not be
mentioned: in his trespass that he hath
trespassed, and in his sin that he hath
sinned, in them shall he die.
25 ¶ Yet ye say, The way of the Lord
is not equal. Hear now, O house of
Ĭş'rā-ĕl; Is not my way equal? are not
your ways unequal?
26 When a righteous *man* turneth
away from his righteousness, and committeth iniquity, and dieth in them; for
his iniquity that he hath done shall he
die.
27 Again, when the wicked *man* turneth away from his wickedness that he
hath committed, and doeth that which
is lawful and right, he shall save his
soul alive.
28 Because he considereth, and turneth away from all his transgressions that
he hath committed, he shall surely live,
he shall not die.
29 Yet saith the house of Ĭş'rā-ĕl, The
way of the Lord is not equal. O house
of Ĭş'rā-ĕl, are not my ways equal?
are not your ways unequal?
30 Therefore I will judge you, O house
of Ĭş'rā-ĕl, every one according to his
ways, saith the Lord God. Repent, and
turn *yourselves* from all your transgressions; so iniquity shall not be your
ruin.
31 ¶ Cast away from you all your
transgressions, whereby ye have transgressed; and make you a new heart and
a new spirit: for why will ye die, O
house of Ĭş'rā-ĕl?
32 For I have no pleasure in the death
of him that dieth, saith the Lord God:
wherefore turn *yourselves*, and live ye.

CHAPTER 19

MOREOVER, take thou up a lamentation for the princes of Ĭş'rā-ĕl,
2 And say, What *is* thy mother? A
lioness: she lay down among lions, she
nourished her whelps among young
lions.
3 And she brought up one of her
whelps: it became a young lion, and it
learned to catch the prey; it devoured
men.
4 The nations also heard of him; he
was taken in their pit, and they brought
him with chains unto the land of Egypt.
5 Now when she saw that she had
waited, *and* her hope was lost, then she
took another of her whelps, *and* made
him a young lion.
6 And he went up and down among
the lions, he became a young lion, and
learned to catch the prey, *and* devoured
men.
7 And he knew their desolate palaces,
and he laid waste their cities; and the
land was desolate, and the fulness
thereof, by the noise of his roaring.
8 Then the nations set against him on
every side from the provinces, and
spread their net over him: he was taken
in their pit.
9 And they put him in ward in chains,
and brought him to the king of Babylon:
they brought him into holds, that his
voice should no more be heard upon
the mountains of Ĭş'rā-ĕl.
10 ¶ Thy mother *is* like a vine in thy
blood, planted by the waters: she was
fruitful and full of branches by reason
of many waters.
11 And she had strong rods for the
sceptres of them that bare rule, and
her stature was exalted among the
thick branches, and she appeared in
her height with the multitude of her
branches.
12 But she was plucked up in fury, she
was cast down to the ground, and the
east wind dried up her fruit: her strong
rods were broken and withered; the
fire consumed them.
13 And now she *is* planted in the wilderness, in a dry and thirsty ground.
14 And fire is gone out of a rod of her
branches, *which* hath devoured her
fruit, so that she hath no strong rod *to
be* a sceptre to rule. This *is* a lamentation, and shall be for a lamentation.

CHAPTER 20

AND it came to pass in the seventh
year, in the fifth *month*, the tenth
day of the month, *that* certain of the
elders of Ĭş'rā-ĕl came to inquire of the
Lord, and sat before me.
2 Then came the word of the Lord
unto me, saying,

3 Son of man, speak unto the elders
of Ĭṣ′rā-ĕl, and say unto them, Thus
saith the Lord GOD; Are ye come to
inquire of me? *As* I live, saith the Lord
GOD, I will not be inquired of by you.
4 Wilt thou judge them, son of man,
wilt thou judge *them?* cause them to
know the abominations of their fathers:
5 ℂ And say unto them, Thus saith
the Lord GOD; In the day when I chose
Ĭṣ′rā-ĕl, and lifted up mine hand unto
the seed of the house of Jacob, and
made myself known unto them in the
land of Egypt, when I lifted up mine
hand unto them, saying, I *am* the LORD
your God;
6 In the day *that* I lifted up mine hand
unto them, to bring them forth of the
land of Egypt into a land that I had
espied for them, flowing with milk and
honey, which *is* the glory of all lands:
7 Then said I unto them, Cast ye away
every man the abominations of his eyes,
and defile not yourselves with the idols
of Egypt: I *am* the LORD your God.
8 But they rebelled against me, and
would not hearken unto me: they did
not every man cast away the abominations of their eyes, neither did they
forsake the idols of Egypt: then I said,
I will pour out my fury upon them, to
accomplish my anger against them in
the midst of the land of Egypt.
9 But I wrought for my name's sake,
that it should not be polluted before the
heathen, among whom they *were,* in
whose sight I made myself known unto
them, in bringing them forth out of the
land of Egypt.
10 ℂ Wherefore I caused them to go
forth out of the land of Egypt, and
brought them into the wilderness.
11 And I gave them my statutes, and
showed them my judgments, which *if* a
man do, he shall even live in them.
12 Moreover also I gave them my
sabbaths, to be a sign between me and
them, that they might know that I *am*
the LORD that sanctify them.
13 But the house of Ĭṣ′rā-ĕl rebelled
against me in the wilderness: they
walked not in my statutes, and they
despised my judgments, which *if* a
man do, he shall even live in them; and
my sabbaths they greatly polluted: then
I said, I would pour out my fury upon
them in the wilderness, to consume
them.
14 But I wrought for my name's sake,
that it should not be polluted before the
heathen, in whose sight I brought them
out.
15 Yet also I lifted up my hand unto
them in the wilderness, that I would
not bring them into the land which I
had given *them,* flowing with milk and
honey, which *is* the glory of all lands;
16 Because they despised my judgments, and walked not in my statutes,
but polluted my sabbaths: for their
heart went after their idols.
17 Nevertheless mine eye spared them
from destroying them, neither did I
make an end of them in the wilderness.
18 But I said unto their children in the
wilderness, Walk ye not in the statutes
of your fathers, neither observe their
judgments, nor defile yourselves with
their idols:
19 I *am* the LORD your God; walk in
my statutes, and keep my judgments,
and do them;
20 And hallow my sabbaths; and they
shall be a sign between me and you,
that ye may know that I *am* the LORD
your God.
21 Notwithstanding, the children rebelled against me: they walked not in
my statutes, neither kept my judgments
to do them, which *if* a man do, he shall
even live in them; they polluted my
sabbaths: then I said, I would pour out
my fury upon them, to accomplish my
anger against them in the wilderness.
22 Nevertheless I withdrew mine hand,
and wrought for my name's sake, that
it should not be polluted in the sight of
the heathen, in whose sight I brought
them forth.
23 I lifted up mine hand unto them
also in the wilderness, that I would
scatter them among the heathen, and
disperse them through the countries;
24 Because they had not executed my
judgments, but had despised my statutes, and had polluted my sabbaths, and
their eyes were after their fathers' idols.
25 Wherefore I gave them also statutes *that were* not good, and judgments
whereby they should not live;
26 And I polluted them in their own
gifts, in that they caused to pass through
the fire all that openeth the womb, that
I might make them desolate, to the end
that they might know that I *am* the
LORD.

27 ¶ Therefore, son of man, speak
unto the house of Ĭş'rā-ĕl, and say unto
them, Thus saith the Lord GOD; Yet in
this your fathers have blasphemed me,
in that they have committed a trespass
against me.
28 *For* when I had brought them into
the land, *for* the which I lifted up mine
hand to give it to them, then they saw
every high hill, and all the thick trees,
and they offered there their sacrifices,
and there they presented the provocation
of their offering: there also they
made their sweet savor, and poured out
there their drink offerings.
29 Then I said unto them, What *is* the
high place whereunto ye go? And the
name thereof is called Bä'mäh unto this
day.
30 Wherefore say unto the house of
Ĭş'rā-ĕl, Thus saith the Lord GOD; Are
ye polluted after the manner of your
fathers? and commit ye whoredom after
their abominations?
31 For when ye offer your gifts, when
ye make your sons to pass through the
fire, ye pollute yourselves with all your
idols, even unto this day: and shall I be
inquired of by you, O house of Ĭş'rā-ĕl?
As I live, saith the Lord GOD, I will not
be inquired of by you.
32 And that which cometh into your
mind shall not be at all, that ye say, We
will be as the heathen, as the families of
the countries, to serve wood and stone.
33 ¶ *As* I live, saith the Lord GOD,
surely with a mighty hand, and with a
stretched out arm, and with fury poured
out, will I rule over you:
34 And I will bring you out from the
people, and will gather you out of the
countries wherein ye are scattered, with
a mighty hand, and with a stretched out
arm, and with fury poured out.
35 And I will bring you into the wilderness
of the people, and there will I plead
with you face to face.
36 Like as I pleaded with your fathers
in the wilderness of the land of Egypt,
so will I plead with you, saith the Lord
GOD.
37 And I will cause you to pass under
the rod, and I will bring you into the
bond of the covenant:
38 And I will purge out from among
you the rebels, and them that transgress
against me: I will bring them forth
out of the country where they sojourn,
and they shall not enter into the land of
Ĭş'rā-ĕl: and ye shall know that I *am*
the LORD.
39 As for you, O house of Ĭş'rā-ĕl,
thus saith the Lord GOD; Go ye, serve
ye every one his idols, and hereafter
also, if ye will not hearken unto me:
but pollute ye my holy name no more
with your gifts, and with your idols.
40 For in mine holy mountain, in the
mountain of the height of Ĭş'rā-ĕl, saith
the Lord GOD, there shall all the house
of Ĭş'rā-ĕl, all of them in the land, serve
me: there will I accept them, and there
will I require your offerings, and the
firstfruits of your oblations, with all
your holy things.
41 I will accept you with your sweet
savor, when I bring you out from the
people, and gather you out of the countries
wherein ye have been scattered;
and I will be sanctified in you before
the heathen.
42 And ye shall know that I *am* the
LORD, when I shall bring you into the
land of Ĭş'rā-ĕl, into the country *for*
the which I lifted up mine hand to give
it to your fathers.
43 And there shall ye remember your
ways, and all your doings, wherein ye
have been defiled; and ye shall loathe
yourselves in your own sight for all
your evils that ye have committed.
44 And ye shall know that I *am* the
LORD, when I have wrought with you
for my name's sake, not according to
your wicked ways, nor according to your
corrupt doings, O ye house of Ĭş'rā-ĕl,
saith the Lord GOD.
45 ¶ Moreover the word of the LORD
came unto me, saying,
46 Son of man, set thy face toward the
south, and drop *thy word* toward the
south, and prophesy against the forest
of the south field;
47 And say to the forest of the south,
Hear the word of the LORD; Thus saith
the Lord GOD; Behold, I will kindle a
fire in thee, and it shall devour every
green tree in thee, and every dry tree:
the flaming flame shall not be quenched,
and all faces from the south to the
north shall be burned therein.
48 And all flesh shall see that I the
LORD have kindled it: it shall not be
quenched.
49 Then said I, Ah Lord GOD! they
say of me, Doth he not speak parables?

CHAPTER 21

AND the word of the LORD came unto me, saying,

2 Son of man, set thy face toward Jerusalem, and drop *thy word* toward the holy places, and prophesy against the land of Ĭş′rā-ĕl,

3 And say to the land of Ĭş′rā-ĕl, Thus saith the LORD; Behold, I *am* against thee, and will draw forth my sword out of his sheath, and will cut off from thee the righteous and the wicked.

4 Seeing then that I will cut off from thee the righteous and the wicked, therefore shall my sword go forth out of his sheath against all flesh from the south to the north:

5 That all flesh may know that I the LORD have drawn forth my sword out of his sheath: it shall not return any more.

6 Sigh therefore, thou son of man, with the breaking of *thy* loins; and with bitterness sigh before their eyes.

7 And it shall be, when they say unto thee, Wherefore sighest thou? that thou shalt answer, For the tidings, because it cometh: and every heart shall melt, and all hands shall be feeble, and every spirit shall faint, and all knees shall be weak *as* water: behold, it cometh, and shall be brought to pass, saith the Lord GOD.

8 ¶ Again the word of the LORD came unto me saying,

9 Son of man, prophesy, and say, Thus saith the LORD; Say, A sword, a sword is sharpened, and also furbished:

10 It is sharpened to make a sore slaughter; it is furbished that it may glitter: should we then make mirth? it contemneth the rod of my son, *as* every tree.

11 And he hath given it to be furbished, that it may be handled: this sword is sharpened, and it is furbished, to give it into the hand of the slayer.

12 Cry and howl, son of man; for it shall be upon my people, it *shall be* upon all the princes of Ĭş′rā-ĕl: terrors by reason of the sword shall be upon my people: smite therefore upon *thy* thigh.

13 Because *it is* a trial, and what if *the sword* contemn even the rod? it shall be no *more,* saith the Lord GOD.

14 Thou therefore, son of man, prophesy, and smite *thine* hands together, and let the sword be doubled the third time, the sword of the slain: it *is* the sword of the great *men that are* slain, which entereth into their privy chambers.

15 I have set the point of the sword against all their gates, that *their* heart may faint, and *their* ruins be multiplied: ah! *it is* made bright, *it is* wrapped up for the slaughter.

16 Go thee one way or other, *either* on the right hand, *or* on the left, whithersoever thy face *is* set.

17 I will also smite mine hands together, and I will cause my fury to rest: I the LORD have said *it.*

18 ¶ The word of the LORD came unto me again, saying,

19 Also, thou son of man, appoint thee two ways, that the sword of the king of Babylon may come: both twain shall come forth out of one land: and choose thou a place, choose *it* at the head of the way to the city.

20 Appoint a way, that the sword may come to Răb′bȧth of the Ammonites, and to Judah in Jerusalem the defensed.

21 For the king of Babylon stood at the parting of the way, at the head of the two ways, to use divination: he made *his* arrows bright, he consulted with images, he looked in the liver.

22 At his right hand was the divination for Jerusalem, to appoint captains, to open the mouth in the slaughter, to lift up the voice with shouting, to appoint *battering* rams against the gates, to cast a mount, *and* to build a fort.

23 And it shall be unto them as a false divination in their sight, to them that have sworn oaths: but he will call to remembrance the iniquity that they may be taken.

24 Therefore thus saith the Lord GOD; Because ye have made your iniquity to be remembered, in that your transgressions are discovered, so that in all your doings your sins do appear; because, *I say,* that ye are come to remembrance, ye shall be taken with the hand.

25 ¶ And thou, profane wicked prince of Ĭş′rā-ĕl, whose day is come, when iniquity *shall have* an end,

26 Thus saith the Lord GOD; Remove the diadem, and take off the crown: this *shall* not *be* the same: exalt *him that is* low, and abase *him that is* high.

27 I will overturn, overturn, overturn
it: and it shall be no *more,* until he
come whose right it is; and I will give
it *him.*
28 ℂ And thou, son of man, prophesy
and say, Thus saith the Lord GOD concerning
the Ammonites, and concerning
their reproach; even say thou, The
sword, the sword *is* drawn: for the
slaughter *it is* furbished, to consume
because of the glittering:
29 While they see vanity unto thee,
while they divine a lie unto thee, to
bring thee upon the necks of *them that
are* slain, of the wicked, whose day is
come, when their iniquity *shall have* an
end.
30 Shall I cause *it* to return into his
sheath? I will judge thee in the place
where thou wast created, in the land of
thy nativity.
31 And I will pour out mine indignation
upon thee; I will blow against thee
in the fire of my wrath, and deliver thee
into the hand of brutish men, *and* skilful
to destroy.
32 Thou shalt be for fuel to the fire;
thy blood shall be in the midst of the
land; thou shalt be no *more* remembered:
for I the LORD have spoken *it.*

CHAPTER 22

MOREOVER the word of the LORD
came unto me, saying,
2 Now, thou son of man, wilt thou
judge, wilt thou judge the bloody city?
yea, thou shalt show her all her abominations.
3 Then say thou, Thus saith the Lord
GOD; The city sheddeth blood in the
midst of it, that her time may come,
and maketh idols against herself to
defile herself.
4 Thou art become guilty in thy blood
that thou hast shed; and hast defiled
thyself in thine idols which thou hast
made; and thou hast caused thy days
to draw near, and art come *even* unto
thy years: therefore have I made thee
a reproach unto the heathen, and a
mocking to all countries.
5 *Those that be* near, and *those that be*
far from thee, shall mock thee, *which
art* infamous *and* much vexed.
6 Behold, the princes of Ĭș′rā-ĕl, every
one were in thee to their power to shed
blood.
7 In thee have they set light by father
and mother: in the midst of thee have
they dealt by oppression with the
stranger: in thee have they vexed the
fatherless and the widow.
8 Thou hast despised mine holy
things, and hast profaned my sabbaths.
9 In thee are men that carry tales to
shed blood: and in thee they eat upon
the mountains: in the midst of thee
they commit lewdness.
10 In thee have they discovered their
fathers' nakedness: in thee have they
humbled her that was set apart for
pollution.
11 And one hath committed abomination
with his neighbor's wife; and another
hath lewdly defiled his daughter-in-law;
and another in thee hath humbled
his sister, his father's daughter.
12 In thee have they taken gifts to
shed blood; thou hast taken usury and
increase, and thou hast greedily gained
of thy neighbors by extortion, and hast
forgotten me, saith the Lord GOD.
13 ℂ Behold, therefore I have smitten
mine hand at thy dishonest gain which
thou hast made, and at thy blood which
hath been in the midst of thee.
14 Can thine heart endure, or can
thine hands be strong, in the days that
I shall deal with thee? I the LORD have
spoken *it,* and will do *it.*
15 And I will scatter thee among the
heathen, and disperse thee in the countries,
and will consume thy filthiness
out of thee.
16 And thou shalt take thine inheritance
in thyself in the sight of the
heathen, and thou shalt know that I
am the LORD.
17 And the word of the LORD came
unto me, saying,
18 Son of man, the house of Ĭș′rā-ĕl is
to me become dross: all they *are* brass,
and tin, and iron, and lead, in the midst
of the furnace; they are *even* the dross
of silver.
19 Therefore thus saith the Lord GOD;
Because ye are all become dross, behold,
therefore I will gather you into
the midst of Jerusalem.
20 *As* they gather silver, and brass,
and iron, and lead, and tin, into the
midst of the furnace, to blow the fire
upon it, to melt *it;* so will I gather *you*
in mine anger and in my fury, and I
will leave *you there,* and melt you.
21 Yea, I will gather you, and blow

upon you in the fire of my wrath, and
ye shall be melted in the midst thereof.
22 As silver is melted in the midst of
the furnace, so shall ye be melted in
the midst thereof; and ye shall know
that I the LORD have poured out my
fury upon you.
23 ℂ And the word of the LORD came
unto me, saying,
24 Son of man, say unto her, Thou
art the land that is not cleansed,
nor rained upon in the day of indignation.
25 *There is* a conspiracy of her prophets
in the midst thereof, like a roaring lion
ravening the prey: they have devoured
souls; they have taken the treasure and
precious things; they have made her
many widows in the midst thereof.
26 Her priests have violated my law,
and have profaned mine holy things:
they have put no difference between
the holy and profane, neither have they
showed *difference* between the unclean
and the clean, and have hid their eyes
from my sabbaths, and I am profaned
among them.
27 Her princes in the midst thereof *are*
like wolves ravening the prey, to shed
blood, *and* to destroy souls, to get
dishonest gain.
28 And her prophets have daubed
them with untempered *mortar*, seeing
vanity, and divining lies unto them,
saying, Thus saith the Lord GOD, when
the LORD hath not spoken.
29 The people of the land have used
oppression, and exercised robbery, and
have vexed the poor and needy: yea,
they have oppressed the stranger
wrongfully.
30 And I sought for a man among
them, that should make up the hedge,
and stand in the gap before me for the
land, that I should not destroy it: but I
found none.
31 Therefore have I poured out mine
indignation upon them; I have consumed
them with the fire of my wrath: their
own way have I recompensed upon
their heads, saith the Lord GOD.

CHAPTER 23

THE word of the LORD came again
unto me, saying,
2 Son of man, there were two women,
the daughters of one mother:
3 And they committed whoredoms in
Egypt; they committed whoredoms in
their youth: there were their breasts
pressed, and there they bruised the
teats of their virginity.
4 And the names of them *were* Ȧ-hō'lȧh
the elder, and Ȧ-hŏl'ĭ-bȧh her sister:
and they were mine, and they bare
sons and daughters. Thus *were* their
names; Sȧ-mā'rĭ-ȧ *is* Ȧ-hō'lȧh, and
Jerusalem Ȧ-hŏl'ĭ-bȧh.
5 And Ȧ-hō'lȧh played the harlot when
she was mine; and she doted on her
lovers, on the Assyrians *her* neighbors,
6 *Which were* clothed with blue, captains and rulers, all of them desirable
young men, horsemen riding upon
horses.
7 Thus she committed her whoredoms
with them, with all them *that were* the
chosen men of Assyria, and with all on
whom she doted: with all their idols she
defiled herself.
8 Neither left she her whoredoms
brought from Egypt: for in her youth
they lay with her, and they bruised the
breasts of her virginity, and poured
their whoredom upon her.
9 Wherefore I have delivered her into
the hand of her lovers, into the hand of
the Assyrians, upon whom she doted.
10 These discovered her nakedness:
they took her sons and her daughters,
and slew her with the sword: and she
became famous among women; for they
had executed judgment upon her.
11 And when her sister Ȧ-hŏl'ĭ-bȧh
saw *this*, she was more corrupt in her
inordinate love than she, and in her
whoredoms more than her sister in *her*
whoredoms.
12 She doted upon the Assyrians *her*
neighbors, captains and rulers clothed
most gorgeously, horsemen riding upon
horses, all of them desirable young
men.
13 Then I saw that she was defiled,
that they *took* both one way,
14 And *that* she increased her whoredoms: for when she saw men portrayed
upon the wall, the images of the Chăl-
dē'ănş portrayed with vermilion,
15 Girded with girdles upon their
loins, exceeding in dyed attire upon
their heads, all of them princes to look
to, after the manner of the Babylonians
of Chăl-dē'ȧ, the land of their nativity:
16 And as soon as she saw them with
her eyes, she doted upon them, and

sent messengers unto them into Chăl-
dē'ȧ.
17 And the Babylonians came to her
into the bed of love, and they defiled
her with their whoredom, and she was
polluted with them, and her mind was
alienated from them.
18 So she discovered her whoredoms,
and discovered her nakedness: then my
mind was alienated from her, like as my
mind was alienated from her sister.
19 Yet she multiplied her whoredoms,
in calling to remembrance the days of
her youth, wherein she had played the
harlot in the land of Egypt.
20 For she doted upon their paramours,
whose flesh *is as* the flesh of asses, and
whose issue *is like* the issue of horses.
21 Thus thou calledst to remembrance
the lewdness of thy youth, in bruising
thy teats by the Egyptians for the paps
of thy youth.
22 ¶ Therefore, O Ȧ-hŏl'ĭ-bȧh, thus
saith the Lord GOD; Behold, I will raise
up thy lovers against thee, from whom
thy mind is alienated, and I will bring
them against thee on every side;
23 The Babylonians, and all the
Chăl-dē'ăns, Pē'kŏd, and Shō'ȧ, and
Kō'ȧ, *and* all the Assyrians with them:
all of them desirable young men, captains and rulers, great lords and renowned, all of them riding upon horses.
24 And they shall come against thee
with chariots, wagons, and wheels, and
with an assembly of people, *which* shall
set against thee buckler and shield and
helmet round about: and I will set
judgment before them, and they shall
judge thee according to their judgments.
25 And I will set my jealousy against
thee, and they shall deal furiously with
thee: they shall take away thy nose and
thine ears; and thy remnant shall fall
by the sword: they shall take thy sons
and thy daughters; and thy residue
shall be devoured by the fire.
26 They shall also strip thee out of
thy clothes, and take away thy fair
jewels.
27 Thus will I make thy lewdness to
cease from thee, and thy whoredom
brought from the land of Egypt: so that
thou shalt not lift up thine eyes unto
them, nor remember Egypt any more.
28 For thus saith the Lord GOD; Behold, I will deliver thee into the hand
of them whom thou hatest, into the
hand *of them* from whom thy mind is
alienated:
29 And they shall deal with thee hate-
fully, and shall take away all thy labor,
and shall leave thee naked and bare:
and the nakedness of thy whoredoms
shall be discovered, both thy lewdness
and thy whoredoms.
30 I will do these *things* unto thee,
because thou hast gone a whoring after
the heathen, *and* because thou art polluted with their idols.
31 Thou hast walked in the way of thy
sister; therefore will I give her cup into
thine hand.
32 Thus saith the Lord GOD; Thou
shalt drink of thy sister's cup deep and
large: thou shalt be laughed to scorn
and had in derision; it containeth much.
33 Thou shalt be filled with drunkenness and sorrow, with the cup of astonishment and desolation, with the cup
of thy sister Sȧ-mā'rĭ-ȧ.
34 Thou shalt even drink it and suck
it out, and thou shalt break the sherds
thereof, and pluck off thine own breasts:
for I have spoken *it,* saith the Lord GOD.
35 Therefore thus saith the Lord GOD;
Because thou hast forgotten me, and
cast me behind thy back, therefore bear
thou also thy lewdness and thy whoredoms.
36 ¶ The Lord said moreover unto
me; Son of man, wilt thou judge
Ȧ-hō'lȧh and Ȧ-hŏl'ĭ-bȧh? yea, declare
unto them their abominations;
37 That they have committed adultery,
and blood *is* in their hands, and with
their idols have they committed adultery, and have also caused their sons,
whom they bare unto me, to pass for
them through *the fire,* to devour *them.*
38 Moreover this they have done unto
me: they have defiled my sanctuary in
the same day, and have profaned my
sabbaths.
39 For when they had slain their children to their idols, then they came the
same day into my sanctuary to profane
it; and, lo, thus have they done in the
midst of mine house.
40 And furthermore, that ye have sent
for men to come from far, unto whom a
messenger *was* sent; and, lo, they came:
for whom thou didst wash thyself,
paintedst thy eyes, and deckedst thyself with ornaments,
41 And satest upon a stately bed, and

a table prepared before it, whereupon
thou hast set mine incense and mine oil.
42 And a voice of a multitude being at
ease *was* with her: and with the men of
the common sort *were* brought Să-
bē'ăns from the wilderness, which put
bracelets upon their hands, and beautiful crowns upon their heads.
43 Then said I unto *her that was* old
in adulteries, Will they now commit
whoredoms with her, and she *with
them?*
44 Yet they went in unto her, as they
go in unto a woman that playeth the
harlot: so went they in unto Ȧ-hō'lȧh
and unto Ȧ-hŏl'ĭ-bȧh, the lewd women.
45 ¶ And the righteous men, they
shall judge them after the manner of
adulteresses, and after the manner of
women that shed blood; because they
are adulteresses, and blood *is* in their
hands.
46 For thus saith the Lord GOD; I will
bring up a company upon them, and
will give them to be removed and
spoiled.
47 And the company shall stone them
with stones, and dispatch them with
their swords; they shall slay their sons
and their daughters, and burn up their
houses with fire.
48 Thus will I cause lewdness to cease
out of the land, that all women may be
taught not to do after your lewdness.
49 And they shall recompense your
lewdness upon you, and ye shall bear
the sins of your idols: and ye shall
know that I *am* the Lord GOD.

CHAPTER 24

AGAIN in the ninth year, in the tenth
month, in the tenth *day* of the
month, the word of the LORD came
unto me, saying,
2 Son of man, write thee the name of
the day, *even* of this same day: the
king of Babylon set himself against
Jerusalem this same day.
3 And utter a parable unto the rebellious house, and say unto them, Thus
saith the Lord GOD; Set on a pot, set
it on, and also pour water into it:
4 Gather the pieces thereof into it,
even every good piece, the thigh, and
the shoulder; fill *it* with the choice
bones.
5 Take the choice of the flock, and
burn also the bones under it, *and* make
it boil well, and let them seethe the
bones of it therein.
6 ¶ Wherefore thus saith the Lord
GOD; Woe to the bloody city, to the
pot whose scum *is* therein, and whose
scum is not gone out of it! bring it out
piece by piece; let no lot fall upon it.
7 For her blood is in the midst of her;
she set it upon the top of a rock; she
poured it not upon the ground, to cover
it with dust;
8 That it might cause fury to come up
to take vengeance; I have set her blood
upon the top of a rock, that it should
not be covered.
9 Therefore thus saith the Lord GOD;
Woe to the bloody city! I will even
make the pile for fire great.
10 Heap on wood, kindle the fire,
consume the flesh, and spice it well,
and let the bones be burned.
11 Then set it empty upon the coals
thereof, that the brass of it may be
hot, and may burn, and *that* the filthiness of it may be molten in it, *that* the
scum of it may be consumed.
12 She hath wearied *herself* with lies,
and her great scum went not forth
out of her: her scum *shall be* in the
fire.
13 In thy filthiness *is* lewdness: because I have purged thee, and thou
wast not purged, thou shalt not be
purged from thy filthiness any more,
till I have caused my fury to rest upon
thee.
14 I the LORD have spoken *it:* it shall
come to pass, and I will do *it;* I will not
go back, neither will I spare, neither
will I repent; according to thy ways,
and according to thy doings, shall they
judge thee, saith the Lord GOD.
15 ¶ Also the word of the LORD came
unto me, saying,
16 Son of man, behold, I take away
from thee the desire of thine eyes with
a stroke: yet neither shalt thou mourn
nor weep, neither shall thy tears run
down.
17 Forbear to cry, make no mourning
for the dead, bind the tire of thine head
upon thee, and put on thy shoes upon
thy feet, and cover not *thy* lips, and eat
not the bread of men.
18 So I spake unto the people in the
morning: and at even my wife died;
and I did in the morning as I was
commanded.

19 ¶ And the people said unto me, Wilt thou not tell us what these *things are* to us, that thou doest *so?*

20 Then I answered them, The word of the LORD came unto me, saying,

21 Speak unto the house of Ĭṣ′rā-ĕl, Thus saith the Lord GOD; Behold, I will profane my sanctuary, the excellency of your strength, the desire of your eyes, and that which your soul pitieth; and your sons and your daughters whom ye have left shall fall by the sword.

22 And ye shall do as I have done: ye shall not cover *your* lips, nor eat the bread of men.

23 And your tires *shall be* upon your heads, and your shoes upon your feet: ye shall not mourn nor weep; but ye shall pine away for your iniquities, and mourn one toward another.

24 Thus Ē-zē′kĭ-ĕl is unto you a sign: according to all that he hath done shall ye do: and when this cometh, ye shall know that I *am* the Lord GOD.

25 Also, thou son of man, *shall it* not *be* in the day when I take from them their strength, the joy of their glory, the desire of their eyes, and that whereupon they set their minds, their sons and their daughters,

26 *That* he that escapeth in that day shall come unto thee, to cause *thee* to hear *it* with *thine* ears?

27 In that day shall thy mouth be opened to him which is escaped, and thou shalt speak, and be no more dumb: and thou shalt be a sign unto them; and they shall know that I *am* the LORD.

CHAPTER 25

THE word of the LORD came again unto me, saying,

2 Son of man, set thy face against the Ammonites, and prophesy against them;

3 And say unto the Ammonites, Hear the word of the Lord GOD; Thus saith the Lord GOD; Because thou saidst, Aha, against my sanctuary, when it was profaned; and against the land of Ĭṣ′rā-ĕl, when it was desolate; and against the house of Judah, when they went into captivity;

4 Behold, therefore I will deliver thee to the men of the east for a possession, and they shall set their palaces in thee, and make their dwellings in thee: they shall eat thy fruit, and they shall drink thy milk.

5 And I will make Răb′bȧh a stable for camels, and the Ammonites a couching place for flocks: and ye shall know that I *am* the LORD.

6 For thus saith the Lord GOD; Because thou hast clapped *thine* hands, and stamped with the feet, and rejoiced in heart with all thy despite against the land of Ĭṣ′rā-ĕl;

7 Behold, therefore I will stretch out mine hand upon thee, and will deliver thee for a spoil to the heathen; and I will cut thee off from the people, and I will cause thee to perish out of the countries: I will destroy thee; and thou shalt know that I *am* the LORD.

8 ¶ Thus saith the Lord GOD; Because that Mō′ăb and Sē′ĭr do say, Behold, the house of Judah *is* like unto all the heathen;

9 Therefore, behold, I will open the side of Mō′ăb from the cities, from his cities *which are* on his frontiers, the glory of the country, Bĕth′-jĕsh′ĭ-mŏth, Bā′ăl-mē′ŏn, and Kĭr′ĭ-ȧ-thā′ĭm,

10 Unto the men of the east with the Ammonites, and will give them in possession, that the Ammonites may not be remembered among the nations.

11 And I will execute judgments upon Mō′ăb; and they shall know that I *am* the LORD.

12 ¶ Thus saith the Lord GOD; Because that Ē′dŏm hath dealt against the house of Judah by taking vengeance, and hath greatly offended, and revenged himself upon them;

13 Therefore thus saith the Lord GOD; I will also stretch out mine hand upon Ē′dŏm, and will cut off man and beast from it; and I will make it desolate from Tē′măn; and they of Dē′dăn shall fall by the sword.

14 And I will lay my vengeance upon Ē′dŏm by the hand of my people Ĭṣ′rā-ĕl: and they shall do in Ē′dŏm according to mine anger and according to my fury; and they shall know my vengeance, saith the Lord GOD.

15 ¶ Thus saith the Lord GOD; Because the Phĭ-lĭs′tĭneṣ have dealt by revenge, and have taken vengeance with a despiteful heart, to destroy *it* for the old hatred;

16 Therefore thus saith the Lord GOD; Behold, I will stretch out mine hand

upon the Phĭ-lĭs'tīnes, and I will cut off
the Chĕr'ē-thĭm, and destroy the remnant of the seacoast.
17 And I will execute great vengeance
upon them with furious rebukes; and
they shall know that I *am* the LORD,
when I shall lay my vengeance upon
them.

CHAPTER 26

AND it came to pass in the eleventh
year, in the first *day* of the month,
that the word of the LORD came unto
me, saying,
2 Son of man, because that Tȳ'rŭs
hath said against Jerusalem, Aha, she
is broken *that was* the gates of the people; she is turned unto me; I shall be
replenished, *now* she is laid waste:
3 Therefore thus saith the Lord GOD;
Behold, I *am* against thee, O Tȳ'rŭs,
and will cause many nations to come up
against thee, as the sea causeth his
waves to come up.
4 And they shall destroy the walls of
Tȳ'rŭs, and break down her towers: I
will also scrape her dust from her, and
make her like the top of a rock.
5 It shall be *a place for* the spreading
of nets in the midst of the sea: for I
have spoken *it,* saith the Lord GOD:
and it shall become a spoil to the
nations.
6 And her daughters which *are* in the
field shall be slain by the sword; and
they shall know that I *am* the LORD.
7 ¶ For thus saith the Lord GOD;
Behold, I will bring upon Tȳ'rŭs
Nĕb'ū-chăd-rĕz'zär king of Babylon, a
king of kings, from the north, with
horses, and with chariots, and with
horsemen, and companies, and much
people.
8 He shall slay with the sword thy
daughters in the field: and he shall
make a fort against thee, and cast a
mount against thee, and lift up the
buckler against thee.
9 And he shall set engines of war
against thy walls, and with his axes
he shall break down thy towers.
10 By reason of the abundance of his
horses their dust shall cover thee: thy
walls shall shake at the noise of the
horsemen, and of the wheels, and of
the chariots, when he shall enter into
thy gates, as men enter into a city
wherein is made a breach.
11 With the hoofs of his horses shall
he tread down all thy streets: he shall
slay thy people by the sword, and thy
strong garrisons shall go down to the
ground.
12 And they shall make a spoil of thy
riches, and make a prey of thy merchandise: and they shall break down
thy walls, and destroy thy pleasant
houses: and they shall lay thy stones
and thy timber and thy dust in the
midst of the water.
13 And I will cause the noise of thy
songs to cease; and the sound of thy
harps shall be no more heard.
14 And I will make thee like the top
of a rock: thou shalt be *a place* to
spread nets upon; thou shalt be built
no more: for I the LORD have spoken
it, saith the Lord GOD.
15 ¶ Thus saith the Lord GOD to
Tȳ'rŭs; Shall not the isles shake at the
sound of thy fall, when the wounded
cry, when the slaughter is made in the
midst of thee?
16 Then all the princes of the sea shall
come down from their thrones, and lay
away their robes, and put off their
broidered garments: they shall clothe
themselves with trembling; they shall
sit upon the ground, and shall tremble
at *every* moment, and be astonished at
thee.
17 And they shall take up a lamentation for thee, and say to thee, How art
thou destroyed, *that wast* inhabited of
seafaring men, the renowned city, which
wast strong in the sea, she and her
inhabitants, which cause their terror *to
be* on all that haunt it!
18 Now shall the isles tremble in the
day of thy fall; yea, the isles that *are* in
the sea shall be troubled at thy departure.
19 For thus saith the Lord GOD; When
I shall make thee a desolate city, like
the cities that are not inhabited; when
I shall bring up the deep upon thee,
and great waters shall cover thee;
20 When I shall bring thee down with
them that descend into the pit, with the
people of old time, and shall set thee
in the low parts of the earth, in places
desolate of old, with them that go down
to the pit, that thou be not inhabited;
and I shall set glory in the land of the
living;
21 I will make thee a terror, and thou

shalt be no *more:* though thou be sought
for, yet shalt thou never be found again,
saith the Lord GOD.

CHAPTER 27

THE word of the LORD came again
unto me, saying,
2 Now, thou son of man, take up a
lamentation for Tȳ'rŭs;
3 And say unto Tȳ'rŭs, O thou that
art situate at the entry of the sea,
which art a merchant of the people for
many isles, Thus saith the Lord GOD;
O Tȳ'rŭs, thou hast said, I *am* of perfect beauty.
4 Thy borders *are* in the midst of the
seas, thy builders have perfected thy
beauty.
5 They have made all thy *ship* boards
of fir trees of Sē'nĭr: they have taken
cedars from Lebanon to make masts for
thee.
6 *Of* the oaks of Bā'shăn have they
made thine oars; the company of the
Ăsh'ŭr-ītes have made thy benches *of*
ivory, *brought* out of the isles of Chĭt'tĭm.
7 Fine linen with broidered work from
Egypt was that which thou spreadest
forth to be thy sail; blue and purple from
the isles of Ē-lī'shȧh was that which
covered thee.
8 The inhabitants of Zī'dŏn and Är'văd
were thy mariners: thy wise *men,* O
Tȳ'rŭs, *that* were in thee, were thy pilots.
9 The ancients of Gē'băl and the wise
men thereof were in thee thy calkers:
all the ships of the sea with their
mariners were in thee to occupy thy
merchandise.
10 They of Persia and of Lŭd and
of Phŭt were in thine army, thy men
of war: they hanged the shield and
helmet in thee; they set forth thy
comeliness.
11 The men of Är'văd with thine army
were upon thy walls round about, and
the Găm'mȧ-dĭm were in thy towers:
they hanged their shields upon thy
walls round about; they have made thy
beauty perfect.
12 Tär'shĭsh *was* thy merchant by
reason of the multitude of all *kind of*
riches; with silver, iron, tin, and lead,
they traded in thy fairs.
13 Jā'văn, Tū'băl, and Mē'shĕch, they
were thy merchants: they traded the
persons of men and vessels of brass in
thy market.
14 They of the house of Tō-gär'mȧh
traded in thy fairs with horses and
horsemen and mules.
15 The men of Dē'dăn *were* thy merchants; many isles *were* the merchandise of thine hand: they brought thee *for*
a present, horns of ivory and ebony.
16 Syria *was* thy merchant by reason of
the multitude of the wares of thy making: they occupied in thy fairs with
emeralds, purple, and broidered work,
and fine linen, and coral, and agate.
17 Judah, and the land of Ĭṣ'rā-ĕl, they
were thy merchants: they traded in thy
market wheat of Mĭn'nĭth, and Păn'năg,
and honey, and oil, and balm.
18 Damascus *was* thy merchant in the
multitude of the wares of thy making,
for the multitude of all riches; in the
wine of Hĕl'bŏn, and white wool.
19 Dan also and Jā'văn going to and fro
occupied in thy fairs: bright iron, cassia,
and calamus, were in thy market.
20 Dē'dăn *was* thy merchant in precious clothes for chariots.
21 Arabia, and all the princes of Kē'dar,
they occupied with thee in lambs, and
rams, and goats: in these *were they* thy
merchants.
22 The merchants of Shē'bȧ and Rā'ȧ-
mȧh, they *were* thy merchants: they
occupied in thy fairs with chief of all
spices, and with all precious stones, and
gold.
23 Hā'răn, and Căn'nĕh, and Ē'den,
the merchants of Shē'bȧ, Ăṣsh'ŭr, *and*
Chĭl'măd, *were* thy merchants.
24 These *were* thy merchants in all
sorts *of things,* in blue clothes, and
broidered work, and in chests of rich
apparel, bound with cords, and made of
cedar, among thy merchandise.
25 The ships of Tär'shĭsh did sing of
thee in thy market: and thou wast replenished, and made very glorious in
the midst of the seas.
26 ℂ Thy rowers have brought thee
into great waters: the east wind hath
broken thee in the midst of the seas.
27 Thy riches, and thy fairs, thy merchandise, thy mariners, and thy pilots,
thy calkers, and the occupiers of thy merchandise, and all thy men of war, that *are*
in thee, and in all thy company which *is*
in the midst of thee, shall fall into the
midst of the seas in the day of thy ruin.
28 The suburbs shall shake at the
sound of the cry of thy pilots.

29 And all that handle the oar, the mariners, *and* all the pilots of the sea, shall come down from their ships, they shall stand upon the land;

30 And shall cause their voice to be heard against thee, and shall cry bitterly, and shall cast up dust upon their heads, they shall wallow themselves in the ashes:

31 And they shall make themselves utterly bald for thee, and gird them with sackcloth, and they shall weep for thee with bitterness of heart *and* bitter wailing.

32 And in their wailing they shall take up a lamentation for thee, and lament over thee, *saying,* What *city is* like Tȳ'rŭs, like the destroyed in the midst of the sea?

33 When thy wares went forth out of the seas, thou filledst many people; thou didst enrich the kings of the earth with the multitude of thy riches and of thy merchandise.

34 In the time *when* thou shalt be broken by the seas in the depths of the waters, thy merchandise and all thy company in the midst of thee shall fall.

35 All the inhabitants of the isles shall be astonished at thee, and their kings shall be sore afraid, they shall be troubled in *their* countenance.

36 The merchants among the people shall hiss at thee; thou shalt be a terror, and never *shalt be* any more.

CHAPTER 28

THE word of the LORD came again unto me, saying,

2 Son of man, say unto the prince of Tȳ'rŭs, Thus saith the Lord GOD; Because thine heart *is* lifted up, and thou hast said, I *am* a god, I sit *in* the seat of God, in the midst of the seas; yet thou *art* a man, and not God, though thou set thine heart as the heart of God:

3 Behold, thou *art* wiser than Daniel; there is no secret that they can hide from thee:

4 With thy wisdom and with thine understanding thou hast gotten thee riches, and hast gotten gold and silver into thy treasures:

5 By thy great wisdom *and* by thy traffic hast thou increased thy riches, and thine heart is lifted up because of thy riches:

6 Therefore thus saith the Lord GOD; Because thou hast set thine heart as the heart of God;

7 Behold, therefore I will bring strangers upon thee, the terrible of the nations: and they shall draw their swords against the beauty of thy wisdom, and they shall defile thy brightness.

8 They shall bring thee down to the pit, and thou shalt die the deaths of *them that are* slain in the midst of the seas.

9 Wilt thou yet say before him that slayeth thee, I *am* God? but thou *shalt be* a man, and no God, in the hand of him that slayeth thee.

10 Thou shalt die the deaths of the uncircumcised by the hand of strangers: for I have spoken *it,* saith the Lord GOD.

11 ℭ Moreover the word of the LORD came unto me, saying,

12 Son of man, take up a lamentation upon the king of Tȳ'rŭs, and say unto him, Thus saith the Lord GOD; Thou sealest up the sum, full of wisdom, and perfect in beauty.

13 Thou hast been in Ē'den the garden of God; every precious stone *was* thy covering, the sardius, topaz, and the diamond, the beryl, the onyx, and the jasper, the sapphire, the emerald, and the carbuncle, and gold: the workmanship of thy tabrets and of thy pipes was prepared in thee in the day that thou wast created.

14 Thou *art* the anointed cherub that covereth; and I have set thee *so:* thou wast upon the holy mountain of God; thou hast walked up and down in the midst of the stones of fire.

15 Thou *wast* perfect in thy ways from the day that thou wast created, till iniquity was found in thee.

16 By the multitude of thy merchandise they have filled the midst of thee with violence, and thou hast sinned: therefore I will cast thee as profane out of the mountain of God: and I will destroy thee, O covering cherub, from the midst of the stones of fire.

17 Thine heart was lifted up because of thy beauty, thou hast corrupted thy wisdom by reason of thy brightness: I will cast thee to the ground, I will lay thee before kings, that they may behold thee.

18 Thou hast defiled thy sanctuaries by the multitude of thine iniquities, by the iniquity of thy traffic; therefore will I bring forth a fire from the midst of thee, it shall devour thee, and I will bring thee

to ashes upon the earth in the sight of all them that behold thee.

19 All they that know thee among the people shall be astonished at thee: thou shalt be a terror, and never *shalt* thou *be* any more.

20 ℂ Again the word of the LORD came unto me, saying,

21 Son of man, set thy face against Zī'dŏn, and prophesy against it,

22 And say, Thus saith the Lord GOD; Behold, I *am* against thee, O Zī'dŏn; and I will be glorified in the midst of thee: and they shall know that I *am* the LORD, when I shall have executed judgments in her, and shall be sanctified in her.

23 For I will send into her pestilence, and blood into her streets; and the wounded shall be judged in the midst of her by the sword upon her on every side; and they shall know that I *am* the LORD.

24 ℂ And there shall be no more a pricking brier unto the house of Ĭṣ'rā-ĕl, nor *any* grieving thorn of all *that are* round about them, that despised them; and they shall know that I *am* the Lord GOD.

25 Thus saith the Lord GOD; When I shall have gathered the house of Ĭṣ'rā-ĕl from the people among whom they are scattered, and shall be sanctified in them in the sight of the heathen, then shall they dwell in their land that I have given to my servant Jacob.

26 And they shall dwell safely therein, and shall build houses, and plant vineyards; yea, they shall dwell with confidence, when I have executed judgments upon all those that despise them round about them; and they shall know that I *am* the LORD their God.

CHAPTER 29

IN the tenth year, in the tenth *month*, in the twelfth *day* of the month, the word of the LORD came unto me, saying,

2 Son of man, set thy face against Phā'raōh king of Egypt, and prophesy against him, and against all Egypt:

3 Speak, and say, Thus saith the Lord GOD; Behold, I *am* against thee, Phā'raōh king of Egypt, the great dragon that lieth in the midst of his rivers, which hath said, My river *is* mine own, and I have made *it* for myself.

4 But I will put hooks in thy jaws, and I will cause the fish of thy rivers to stick unto thy scales, and I will bring thee up out of the midst of thy rivers, and all the fish of thy rivers shall stick unto thy scales.

5 And I will leave thee *thrown* into the wilderness, thee and all the fish of thy rivers: thou shalt fall upon the open fields; thou shalt not be brought together, nor gathered: I have given thee for meat to the beasts of the field and to the fowls of the heaven.

6 And all the inhabitants of Egypt shall know that I *am* the LORD, because they have been a staff of reed to the house of Ĭṣ'rā-ĕl.

7 When they took hold of thee by thy hand, thou didst break, and rend all their shoulder: and when they leaned upon thee, thou brakest, and madest all their loins to be at a stand.

8 ℂ Therefore thus saith the Lord GOD; Behold, I will bring a sword upon thee, and cut off man and beast out of thee.

9 And the land of Egypt shall be desolate and waste; and they shall know that I *am* the LORD: because he hath said, The river *is* mine, and I have made *it*.

10 Behold, therefore I *am* against thee, and against thy rivers, and I will make the land of Egypt utterly waste *and* desolate, from the tower of Sȳ-ē'nē even unto the border of Ethiopia.

11 No foot of man shall pass through it, nor foot of beast shall pass through it, neither shall it be inhabited forty years.

12 And I will make the land of Egypt desolate in the midst of the countries *that are* desolate, and her cities among the cities *that are* laid waste shall be desolate forty years: and I will scatter the Egyptians among the nations, and will disperse them through the countries.

13 ℂ Yet thus saith the Lord GOD; At the end of forty years will I gather the Egyptians from the people whither they were scattered:

14 And I will bring again the captivity of Egypt, and will cause them to return *into* the land of Păth'rŏs, into the land of their habitation; and they shall be there a base kingdom.

15 It shall be the basest of the kingdoms; neither shall it exalt itself any more above the nations: for I will diminish them, that they shall no more rule over the nations.

16 And it shall be no more the confidence of the house of Ĭş'rā-ĕl, which
bringeth *their* iniquity to remembrance,
when they shall look after them: but
they shall know that I *am* the Lord GOD.
17 ¶ And it came to pass in the seven
and twentieth year, in the first *month,* in
the first *day* of the month, the word of
the LORD came unto me, saying,
18 Son of man, Nĕb'ū-chăd-rĕz'zȧr
king of Babylon caused his army to
serve a great service against Tȳ'rŭs:
every head *was* made bald, and every
shoulder *was* peeled: yet had he no
wages, nor his army, for Tȳ'rŭs, for the
service that he had served against it:
19 Therefore thus saith the Lord GOD;
Behold, I will give the land of Egypt
unto Nĕb'ū-chăd-rĕz'zȧr king of Babylon; and he shall take her multitude, and
take her spoil, and take her prey; and
it shall be the wages for his army.
20 I have given him the land of Egypt
for his labor wherewith he served
against it, because they wrought for me,
saith the Lord GOD.
21 ¶ In that day will I cause the horn
of the house of Ĭş'rā-ĕl to bud forth, and
I will give thee the opening of the mouth
in the midst of them; and they shall
know that I *am* the LORD.

CHAPTER 30

THE word of the LORD came again
unto me, saying,
2 Son of man, prophesy and say, Thus
saith the Lord GOD; Howl ye, Woe worth
the day!
3 For the day *is* near, even the day of
the LORD *is* near, a cloudy day; it shall
be the time of the heathen.
4 And the sword shall come upon
Egypt, and great pain shall be in
Ethiopia, when the slain shall fall in
Egypt, and they shall take away her
multitude, and her foundations shall be
broken down.
5 Ethiopia, and Libya, and Lydia, and
all the mingled people, and Chŭb, and
the men of the land that is in league,
shall fall with them by the sword.
6 Thus saith the LORD; They also that
uphold Egypt shall fall; and the pride of
her power shall come down: from the
tower of Sȳ-ē'nē shall they fall in it by
the sword, saith the Lord GOD.
7 And they shall be desolate in the
midst of the countries *that are* desolate,
and her cities shall be in the midst of the
cities *that are* wasted.
8 And they shall know that I *am* the
LORD, when I have set a fire in Egypt,
and *when* all her helpers shall be
destroyed.
9 In that day shall messengers go forth
from me in ships to make the careless
Ethiopians afraid, and great pain shall
come upon them, as in the day of Egypt:
for, lo, it cometh.
10 Thus saith the Lord GOD; I will also
make the multitude of Egypt to cease by
the hand of Nĕb'ū-chăd-rĕz'zȧr king of
Babylon.
11 He and his people with him, the
terrible of the nations, shall be brought
to destroy the land: and they shall draw
their swords against Egypt, and fill the
land with the slain.
12 And I will make the rivers dry, and
sell the land into the hand of the wicked:
and I will make the land waste, and all
that is therein, by the hand of strangers:
I the LORD have spoken *it.*
13 Thus saith the Lord GOD; I will also
destroy the idols, and I will cause *their*
images to cease out of Nŏph; and there
shall be no more a prince of the land of
Egypt: and I will put a fear in the land
of Egypt.
14 And I will make Păth'rŏs desolate,
and will set fire in Zō'ăn, and will execute judgments in No.
15 And I will pour my fury upon Sin,
the strength of Egypt; and I will cut off
the multitude of No.
16 And I will set fire in Egypt: Sin shall
have great pain, and No shall be rent
asunder, and Nŏph *shall have* distresses
daily.
17 The young men of Ā'vĕn and of
Pī'-bē'sĕth shall fall by the sword: and
these *cities* shall go into captivity.
18 At Tē-hăph'nē-hēş also the day
shall be darkened, when I shall break
there the yokes of Egypt: and the pomp
of her strength shall cease in her: as for
her, a cloud shall cover her, and her
daughters shall go into captivity.
19 Thus will I execute judgments in
Egypt: and they shall know that I *am*
the LORD.
20 ¶ And it came to pass in the
eleventh year, in the first *month,* in the
seventh *day* of the month, *that* the word
of the LORD came unto me, saying,
21 Son of man, I have broken the arm

of Phā′raōh king of Egypt; and, lo, it
shall not be bound up to be healed, to
put a roller to bind it, to make it strong
to hold the sword.
22 Therefore thus saith the Lord GOD;
Behold, I *am* against Phā′raōh king of
Egypt, and will break his arms, the
strong, and that which was broken; and
I will cause the sword to fall out of his
hand.
23 And I will scatter the Egyptians
among the nations, and will disperse
them through the countries.
24 And I will strengthen the arms of
the king of Babylon, and put my sword
in his hand: but I will break Phā′raōh's
arms, and he shall groan before him
with the groanings of a deadly wounded
man.
25 But I will strengthen the arms of the
king of Babylon, and the arms of Phā′-
raōh shall fall down; and they shall know
that I *am* the LORD, when I shall put my
sword into the hand of the king of Babylon, and he shall stretch it out upon the
land of Egypt.
26 And I will scatter the Egyptians
among the nations, and disperse them
among the countries; and they shall
know that I *am* the LORD.

CHAPTER 31

AND it came to pass in the eleventh
year, in the third *month*, in the
first *day* of the month, *that* the word of
the LORD came unto me, saying,
2 Son of man, speak unto Phā′raōh
king of Egypt, and to his multitude;
Whom art thou like in thy greatness?
3 ¶ Behold, the Assyrian *was* a cedar
in Lebanon with fair branches, and with
a shadowing shroud, and of a high stature; and his top was among the thick
boughs.
4 The waters made him great, the deep
set him up on high with her rivers running round about his plants, and sent
out her little rivers unto all the trees of
the field.
5 Therefore his height was exalted
above all the trees of the field, and
his boughs were multiplied, and his
branches became long because of the
multitude of waters, when he shot
forth.
6 All the fowls of heaven made their
nests in his boughs, and under his
branches did all the beasts of the field
bring forth their young, and under his
shadow dwelt all great nations.
7 Thus was he fair in his greatness, in
the length of his branches: for his root
was by great waters.
8 The cedars in the garden of God could
not hide him: the fir trees were not like
his boughs, and the chestnut trees were
not like his branches; not any tree in the
garden of God was like unto him in his
beauty.
9 I have made him fair by the multitude
of his branches; so that all the trees of
Ē′den, that *were* in the garden of God,
envied him.
10 ¶ Therefore thus saith the Lord
GOD; Because thou hast lifted up thyself
in height, and he hath shot up his top
among the thick boughs, and his heart
is lifted up in his height;
11 I have therefore delivered him into
the hand of the mighty one of the
heathen; he shall surely deal with him:
I have driven him out for his wickedness.
12 And strangers, the terrible of the
nations, have cut him off, and have left
him: upon the mountains and in all the
valleys his branches are fallen, and his
boughs are broken by all the rivers of
the land; and all the people of the earth
are gone down from his shadow, and
have left him.
13 Upon his ruin shall all the fowls of
the heaven remain, and all the beasts of
the field shall be upon his branches:
14 To the end that none of all the trees
by the waters exalt themselves for their
height, neither shoot up their top among
the thick boughs, neither their trees
stand up in their height, all that drink
water: for they are all delivered unto
death, to the nether parts of the earth,
in the midst of the children of men, with
them that go down to the pit.
15 Thus saith the Lord GOD; In the
day when he went down to the grave I
caused a mourning: I covered the deep
for him, and I restrained the floods
thereof, and the great waters were
stayed: and I caused Lebanon to mourn
for him, and all the trees of the field
fainted for him.
16 I made the nations to shake at the
sound of his fall, when I cast him down
to hell with them that descend into the
pit: and all the trees of Ē′den, the choice
and best of Lebanon, all that drink

water, shall be comforted in the nether
parts of the earth.
17 They also went down into hell with
him, unto *them that be* slain with the
sword; and *they that were* his arm, *that*
dwelt under his shadow in the midst of
the heathen.
18 ¶ To whom art thou thus like in
glory and in greatness among the trees
of Ē′den? yet shalt thou be brought down
with the trees of Ē′den unto the nether
parts of the earth: thou shalt lie in the
midst of the uncircumcised with *them
that be* slain by the sword. This *is* Phā′-
raōh and all his multitude, saith the
Lord GOD.

CHAPTER 32

AND it came to pass in the twelfth
year, in the twelfth month, in the
first *day* of the month, *that* the word of
the LORD came unto me, saying,
2 Son of man, take up a lamentation
for Pha′raoh king of Egypt, and say unto
him, Thou art like a young lion of the
nations, and thou *art* as a whale in the
seas: and thou camest forth with thy
rivers, and troubledst the waters with
thy feet, and fouledst their rivers.
3 Thus saith the Lord GOD; I will therefore spread out my net over thee with
a company of many people; and they
shall bring thee up in my net.
4 Then will I leave thee upon the land,
I will cast thee forth upon the open
field, and will cause all the fowls of the
heaven to remain upon thee, and I will
fill the beasts of the whole earth with
thee.
5 And I will lay thy flesh upon the
mountains, and fill the valleys with thy
height.
6 I will also water with thy blood the
land wherein thou swimmest, *even* to
the mountains; and the rivers shall be
full of thee.
7 And when I shall put thee out, I will
cover the heaven, and make the stars
thereof dark; I will cover the sun with
a cloud, and the moon shall not give her
light.
8 All the bright lights of heaven will I
make dark over thee, and set darkness
upon thy land, saith the Lord GOD.
9 I will also vex the hearts of many
people, when I shall bring thy destruction among the nations, into the countries which thou hast not known.
10 Yea, I will make many people
amazed at thee, and their kings shall be
horribly afraid for thee, when I shall
brandish my sword before them; and
they shall tremble at *every* moment,
every man for his own life, in the day of
thy fall.
11 ¶ For thus saith the Lord GOD; The
sword of the king of Babylon shall come
upon thee.
12 By the swords of the mighty will I
cause thy multitude to fall, the terrible
of the nations, all of them: and they
shall spoil the pomp of Egypt, and all
the multitude thereof shall be destroyed.
13 I will destroy also all the beasts
thereof from beside the great waters;
neither shall the foot of man trouble
them any more, nor the hoofs of beasts
trouble them.
14 Then will I make their waters deep,
and cause their rivers to run like oil,
saith the Lord GOD.
15 When I shall make the land of
Egypt desolate, and the country shall be
destitute of that whereof it was full,
when I shall smite all them that dwell
therein, then shall they know that I *am*
the LORD.
16 This *is* the lamentation wherewith
they shall lament her: the daughters of
the nations shall lament her: they shall
lament for her, *even* for Egypt, and for
all her multitude, saith the Lord GOD.
17 ¶ It came to pass also in the twelfth
year, in the fifteenth *day* of the month,
that the word of the LORD came unto me,
saying,
18 Son of man, wail for the multitude
of Egypt, and cast them down, *even* her,
and the daughters of the famous nations, unto the nether parts of the earth,
with them that go down into the pit.
19 Whom dost thou pass in beauty? go
down, and be thou laid with the uncircumcised.
20 They shall fall in the midst of *them
that are* slain by the sword: she is delivered to the sword: draw her and all
her multitudes.
21 The strong among the mighty shall
speak to him out of the midst of hell
with them that help him: they are gone
down, they lie uncircumcised, slain by
the sword.
22 Ăṣsh′ŭr *is* there and all her company: his graves *are* about him: all of
them slain, fallen by the sword:

23 Whose graves are set in the sides of
the pit, and her company is round about
her grave; all of them slain, fallen by the
sword, which caused terror in the land of
the living.
24 There *is* Ē'lăm and all her multitude
round about her grave; all of them slain,
fallen by the sword, which are gone
down uncircumcised into the nether
parts of the earth, which caused their
terror in the land of the living; yet have
they borne their shame with them that
go down to the pit.
25 They have set her a bed in the midst
of the slain with all her multitude: her
graves *are* round about him: all of them
uncircumcised, slain by the sword:
though their terror was caused in the
land of the living, yet have they borne
their shame with them that go down to
the pit: he is put in the midst of *them
that be* slain.
26 There *is* Mē'shĕch, Tū'băl, and all
her multitude: her graves *are* round
about him: all of them uncircumcised,
slain by the sword, though they caused
their terror in the land of the living.
27 And they shall not lie with the
mighty *that are* fallen of the uncircumcised, which are gone down to hell with
their weapons of war: and they have laid
their swords under their heads, but their
iniquities shall be upon their bones,
though *they were* the terror of the
mighty in the land of the living.
28 Yea, thou shalt be broken in the
midst of the uncircumcised, and shalt
lie with *them that are* slain with the
sword.
29 There *is* Ē'dŏm, her kings, and all
her princes, which with their might are
laid by *them that were* slain by the
sword: they shall lie with the uncircumcised, and with them that go down
to the pit.
30 There *be* the princes of the north,
all of them, and all the Zī-dō'nĭ-ăns,
which are gone down with the slain;
with their terror they are ashamed of
their might; and they lie uncircumcised
with *them that be* slain by the sword,
and bear their shame with them that go
down to the pit.
31 Phā'raōh shall see them, and shall
be comforted over all his multitude, *even*
Phā'raōh and all his army slain by the
sword, saith the Lord GOD.
32 For I have caused my terror in the
land of the living: and he shall be laid
in the midst of the uncircumcised with
them that are slain with the sword, *even*
Phā'raōh and all his multitude, saith the
Lord GOD.

CHAPTER 33

AGAIN the word of the LORD came
unto me, saying,
2 Son of man, speak to the children of
thy people, and say unto them, When
I bring the sword upon a land, if the
people of the land take a man of their
coasts, and set him for their watchman:
3 If when he seeth the sword come
upon the land, he blow the trumpet, and
warn the people;
4 Then whosoever heareth the sound
of the trumpet, and taketh not warning; if the sword come, and take him
away, his blood shall be upon his own
head.
5 He heard the sound of the trumpet,
and took not warning; his blood shall
be upon him. But he that taketh warning shall deliver his soul.
6 But if the watchman see the sword
come, and blow not the trumpet, and
the people be not warned; if the sword
come, and take *any* person from among
them, he is taken away in his iniquity;
but his blood will I require at the
watchman's hand.
7 ¶ So thou, O son of man, I have set
thee a watchman unto the house of
Is'rā-ĕl; therefore thou shalt hear the
word at my mouth, and warn them from
me.
8 When I say unto the wicked, O
wicked *man*, thou shalt surely die; if
thou dost not speak to warn the wicked
from his way, that wicked *man* shall die
in his iniquity; but his blood will I require at thine hand.
9 Nevertheless, if thou warn the wicked
of his way to turn from it; if he do not
turn from his way, he shall die in his
iniquity; but thou hast delivered thy
soul.
10 Therefore, O thou son of man, speak
unto the house of Is'rā-ĕl; Thus ye
speak, saying, If our transgressions and
our sins *be* upon us, and we pine away
in them, how should we then live?
11 Say unto them, *As* I live, saith the
Lord GOD, I have no pleasure in the
death of the wicked; but that the wicked
turn from his way and live: turn ye,

turn ye from your evil ways; for why will ye die, O house of Ĭṣ′rā-ĕl?

12 Therefore, thou son of man, say unto the children of thy people, The righteousness of the righteous shall not deliver him in the day of his transgression: as for the wickedness of the wicked, he shall not fall thereby in the day that he turneth from his wickedness; neither shall the righteous be able to live for his *righteousness* in the day that he sinneth.

13 When I shall say to the righteous, *that* he shall surely live; if he trust to his own righteousness, and commit iniquity, all his righteousnesses shall not be remembered; but for his iniquity that he hath committed, he shall die for it.

14 Again, when I say unto the wicked, Thou shalt surely die; if he turn from his sin, and do that which is lawful and right;

15 *If* the wicked restore the pledge, give again that he had robbed, walk in the statutes of life, without committing iniquity; he shall surely live, he shall not die.

16 None of his sins that he hath committed shall be mentioned unto him: he hath done that which is lawful and right; he shall surely live.

17 ℂ Yet the children of thy people say, The way of the Lord is not equal: but as for them, their way is not equal.

18 When the righteous turneth from his righteousness, and committeth iniquity, he shall even die thereby.

19 But if the wicked turn from his wickedness, and do that which is lawful and right, he shall live thereby.

20 ℂ Yet ye say, The way of the Lord is not equal. O ye house of Ĭṣ′rā-ĕl, I will judge you every one after his ways.

21 ℂ And it came to pass in the twelfth year of our captivity, in the tenth *month,* in the fifth *day* of the month, *that* one that had escaped out of Jerusalem came unto me, saying, The city is smitten.

22 Now the hand of the LORD was upon me in the evening, afore he that was escaped came; and had opened my mouth, until he came to me in the morning; and my mouth was opened, and I was no more dumb.

23 Then the word of the LORD came unto me, saying,

24 Son of man, they that inhabit those wastes of the land of Ĭṣ′rā-ĕl speak, saying, Abraham was one, and he inherited the land: but we *are* many; the land is given us for inheritance.

25 Wherefore say unto them, Thus saith the Lord GOD; Ye eat with the blood, and lift up your eyes toward your idols, and shed blood: and shall ye possess the land?

26 Ye stand upon your sword, ye work abomination, and ye defile every one his neighbor's wife: and shall ye possess the land?

27 Say thou thus unto them, Thus saith the Lord GOD; *As* I live, surely they that *are* in the wastes shall fall by the sword, and him that *is* in the open field will I give to the beasts to be devoured, and they that *be* in the forts and in the caves shall die of the pestilence.

28 For I will lay the land most desolate, and the pomp of her strength shall cease; and the mountains of Ĭṣ′rā-ĕl shall be desolate, that none shall pass through.

29 Then shall they know that I *am* the LORD, when I have laid the land most desolate, because of all their abominations which they have committed.

30 ℂ Also, thou son of man, the children of thy people still are talking against thee by the walls and in the doors of the houses, and speak one to another, every one to his brother, saying, Come, I pray you, and hear what is the word that cometh forth from the LORD.

31 And they come unto thee as the people cometh, and they sit before thee *as* my people, and they hear thy words, but they will not do them: for with their mouth they show much love, *but* their heart goeth after their covetousness.

32 And, lo, thou *art* unto them as a very lovely song of one that hath a pleasant voice, and can play well on an instrument: for they hear thy words, but they do them not.

33 And when this cometh to pass, (lo, it will come,) then shall they know that a prophet hath been among them.

CHAPTER 34

AND the word of the LORD came unto me, saying,

2 Son of man, prophesy against the shepherds of Ĭṣ′rā-ĕl, prophesy, and say unto them, Thus saith the Lord GOD

unto the shepherds; Woe *be* to the shepherds of Ĭṣʹrā-ĕl that do feed themselves! should not the shepherds feed
the flocks?
3 Ye eat the fat, and ye clothe you with
the wool, ye kill them that are fed: *but*
ye feed not the flock.
4 The diseased have ye not strengthened, neither have ye healed that which
was sick, neither have ye bound up *that
which was* broken, neither have ye
brought again that which was driven
away, neither have ye sought that which
was lost; but with force and with cruelty
have ye ruled them.
5 And they were scattered, because
there is no shepherd: and they became
meat to all the beasts of the field, when
they were scattered.
6 My sheep wandered through all the
mountains, and upon every high hill:
yea, my flock was scattered upon all the
face of the earth, and none did search
or seek *after them*.
7 ¶ Therefore, ye shepherds, hear the
word of the LORD;
8 *As* I live, saith the Lord GOD, surely
because my flock became a prey, and
my flock became meat to every beast of
the field, because *there was* no shepherd, neither did my shepherds search
for my flock, but the shepherds fed
themselves, and fed not my flock;
9 Therefore, O ye shepherds, hear the
word of the LORD;
10 Thus saith the Lord GOD; Behold,
I *am* against the shepherds; and I will
require my flock at their hand, and
cause them to cease from feeding the
flock; neither shall the shepherds feed
themselves any more; for I will deliver
my flock from their mouth, that they
may not be meat for them.
11 ¶ For thus saith the Lord GOD; Behold, I, *even* I, will both search my
sheep, and seek them out.
12 As a shepherd seeketh out his flock
in the day that he is among his sheep
that are scattered; so will I seek out my
sheep, and will deliver them out of all
places where they have been scattered
in the cloudy and dark day.
13 And I will bring them out from the
people, and gather them from the countries, and will bring them to their own
land, and feed them upon the mountains
of Ĭṣʹrā-ĕl by the rivers, and in all the
inhabited places of the country.
14 I will feed them in a good pasture,
and upon the high mountains of Ĭṣʹrā-ĕl
shall their fold be: there shall they lie in
a good fold, and *in* a fat pasture shall
they feed upon the mountains of Ĭṣʹrā-ĕl.
15 I will feed my flock, and I will cause
them to lie down, saith the Lord GOD.
16 I will seek that which was lost, and
bring again that which was driven away,
and will bind up *that which was* broken,
and will strengthen that which was sick:
but I will destroy the fat and the strong;
I will feed them with judgment.
17 And *as for* you, O my flock, thus
saith the Lord GOD; Behold, I judge between cattle and cattle, between the
rams and the he goats.
18 *Seemeth it* a small thing unto you
to have eaten up the good pasture, but
ye must tread down with your feet the
residue of your pastures? and to have
drunk of the deep waters, but ye must
foul the residue with your feet?
19 And *as for* my flock, they eat that
which ye have trodden with your feet;
and they drink that which ye have
fouled with your feet.
20 ¶ Therefore thus saith the Lord
GOD unto them; Behold, I, *even* I, will
judge between the fat cattle and between the lean cattle.
21 Because ye have thrust with side
and with shoulder, and pushed all the
diseased with your horns, till ye have
scattered them abroad;
22 Therefore will I save my flock, and
they shall no more be a prey; and I will
judge between cattle and cattle.
23 And I will set up one shepherd over
them, and he shall feed them, *even* my
servant David; he shall feed them, and
he shall be their shepherd.
24 And I the LORD will be their God,
and my servant David a prince among
them; I the LORD have spoken *it*.
25 And I will make with them a covenant of peace, and will cause the evil
beasts to cease out of the land: and they
shall dwell safely in the wilderness, and
sleep in the woods.
26 And I will make them and the places
round about my hill a blessing; and I
will cause the shower to come down in
his season; there shall be showers of
blessing.
27 And the tree of the field shall yield
her fruit, and the earth shall yield her
increase, and they shall be safe in their

land, and shall know that I *am* the LORD, when I have broken the bands of their yoke, and delivered them out of the hand of those that served themselves of them.

28 And they shall no more be a prey to the heathen, neither shall the beast of the land devour them; but they shall dwell safely, and none shall make *them* afraid.

29 And I will raise up for them a plant of renown, and they shall be no more consumed with hunger in the land, neither bear the shame of the heathen any more.

30 Thus shall they know that I the LORD their God *am* with them, and *that* they, *even* the house of Ĭs′rā-ĕl, *are* my people, saith the Lord GOD.

31 And ye my flock, the flock of my pasture, *are* men, *and* I *cm* your God, saith the Lord GOD.

CHAPTER 35

MOREOVER the word of the LORD came unto me, saying,

2 Son of man, set thy face against mount Sē′ĭr, and prophesy against it,

3 And say unto it, Thus saith the Lord GOD; Behold, O mount Sē′ĭr, I *am* against thee, and I will stretch out mine hand against thee, and I will make thee most desolate.

4 I will lay thy cities waste, and thou shalt be desolate, and thou shalt know that I *am* the LORD.

5 Because thou hast had a perpetual hatred, and hast shed *the blood of* the children of Ĭs′rā-ĕl by the force of the sword in the time of their calamity, in the time *that their* iniquity *had* an end:

6 Therefore, *as* I live, saith the Lord GOD, I will prepare thee unto blood, and blood shall pursue thee: since thou hast not hated blood, even blood shall pursue thee.

7 Thus will I make mount Sē′ĭr most desolate, and cut off from it him that passeth out and him that returneth.

8 And I will fill his mountains with his slain *men:* in thy hills, and in thy valleys, and in all thy rivers, shall they fall that are slain with the sword.

9 I will make thee perpetual desolations, and thy cities shall not return: and ye shall know that I *am* the LORD.

10 Because thou hast said, These two nations and these two countries shall be mine, and we will possess it; whereas the LORD was there:

11 Therefore, *as* I live, saith the Lord GOD, I will even do according to thine anger, and according to thine envy, which thou hast used out of thy hatred against them; and I will make myself known among them, when I have judged thee.

12 And thou shalt know that I *am* the LORD, *and that* I have heard all thy blasphemies which thou hast spoken against the mountains of Ĭs′rā-ĕl, saying, They are laid desolate, they are given us to consume.

13 Thus with your mouth ye have boasted against me, and have multiplied your words against me: I have heard *them.*

14 Thus saith the Lord GOD; When the whole earth rejoiceth, I will make thee desolate.

15 As thou didst rejoice at the inheritance of the house of Ĭs′rā-ĕl, because it was desolate, so will I do unto thee: thou shalt be desolate, O mount Sē′ĭr, and all Ĭd′ū-mē′ȧ, *even* all of it: and they shall know that I *am* the LORD.

CHAPTER 36

ALSO, thou son of man, prophesy unto the mountains of Ĭs′rā-ĕl, and say, Ye mountains of Ĭs′rā-ĕl, hear the word of the LORD:

2 Thus saith the Lord GOD; Because the enemy hath said against you, Aha, even the ancient high places are ours in possession:

3 Therefore prophesy and say, Thus saith the Lord GOD; Because they have made *you* desolate, and swallowed you up on every side, that ye might be a possession unto the residue of the heathen, and ye are taken up in the lips of talkers, and *are* an infamy of the people:

4 Therefore, ye mountains of Ĭs′rā-ĕl, hear the word of the Lord GOD; Thus saith the Lord GOD to the mountains and to the hills, to the rivers and to the valleys, to the desolate wastes and to the cities that are forsaken, which became a prey and derision to the residue of the heathen that *are* round about;

5 Therefore thus saith the Lord GOD; Surely in the fire of my jealousy have I spoken against the residue of the heathen, and against all Ĭd′ū-mē′ȧ,

which have appointed my land into their
possession with the joy of all *their* heart,
with despiteful minds, to cast it out for
a prey.
6 Prophesy therefore concerning the
land of Ĭs'rā-ĕl, and say unto the mountains and to the hills, to the rivers and
to the valleys, Thus saith the Lord GOD;
Behold, I have spoken in my jealousy
and in my fury, because ye have borne
the shame of the heathen:
7 Therefore thus saith the Lord GOD;
I have lifted up mine hand, Surely the
heathen that *are* about you, they shall
bear their shame.
8 ℭ But ye, O mountains of Ĭs'rā-ĕl,
ye shall shoot forth your branches, and
yield your fruit to my people of Ĭs'rā-ĕl;
for they are at hand to come.
9 For, behold, I *am* for you, and I will
turn unto you, and ye shall be tilled and
sown:
10 And I will multiply men upon you,
all the house of Ĭs'rā-ĕl, *even* all of it:
and the cities shall be inhabited, and
the wastes shall be builded:
11 And I will multiply upon you man
and beast; and they shall increase and
bring fruit: and I will settle you after
your old estates, and will do better *unto
you* than at your beginnings: and ye
shall know that I *am* the LORD.
12 Yea, I will cause men to walk upon
you, *even* my people Ĭs'rā-ĕl; and they
shall possess thee, and thou shalt be
their inheritance, and thou shalt no more
henceforth bereave them *of men*.
13 Thus saith the Lord GOD; Because
they say unto you, Thou *land* devourest
up men, and hast bereaved thy nations;
14 Therefore thou shalt devour men no
more, neither bereave thy nations any
more, saith the Lord GOD.
15 Neither will I cause *men* to hear in
thee the shame of the heathen any more,
neither shalt thou bear the reproach of
the people any more, neither shalt thou
cause thy nations to fall any more, saith
the Lord GOD.
16 ℭ Moreover the word of the LORD
came unto me, saying,
17 Son of man, when the house of
Ĭs'rā-ĕl dwelt in their own land, they
defiled it by their own way and by their
doings: their way was before me as the
uncleanness of a removed woman.
18 Wherefore I poured my fury upon
them for the blood that they had shed
upon the land, and for their idols *wherewith* they had polluted it:
19 And I scattered them among the
heathen, and they were dispersed
through the countries: according to their
way and according to their doings I
judged them.
20 And when they entered unto the
heathen, whither they went, they profaned my holy name, when they said to
them, These *are* the people of the LORD,
and are gone forth out of his land.
21 ℭ But I had pity for mine holy
name, which the house of Ĭs'rā-ĕl had
profaned among the heathen, whither
they went.
22 Therefore say unto the house of
Ĭs'rā-ĕl, Thus saith the Lord GOD; I do
not *this* for your sakes, O house of
Ĭs'rā-ĕl, but for mine holy name's sake,
which ye have profaned among the
heathen, whither ye went.
23 And I will sanctify my great name,
which was profaned among the heathen,
which ye have profaned in the midst of
them; and the heathen shall know that I
am the LORD, saith the Lord GOD, when
I shall be sanctified in you before their
eyes.
24 For I will take you from among the
heathen, and gather you out of all countries, and will bring you into your own
land.
25 ℭ Then will I sprinkle clean water
upon you, and ye shall be clean: from
all your filthiness, and from all your
idols, will I cleanse you.
26 A new heart also will I give you, and
a new spirit will I put within you: and I
will take away the stony heart out of
your flesh, and I will give you a heart of
flesh.
27 And I will put my Spirit within you,
and cause you to walk in my statutes,
and ye shall keep my judgments, and do
them.
28 And ye shall dwell in the land that
I gave to your fathers; and ye shall be
my people, and I will be your God.
29 I will also save you from all your
uncleannesses: and I will call for the
corn, and will increase it, and lay no
famine upon you.
30 And I will multiply the fruit of the
tree, and the increase of the field, that
ye shall receive no more reproach of
famine among the heathen.
31 Then shall ye remember your own

evil ways, and your doings that *were* not
good, and shall loathe yourselves in your
own sight for your iniquities and for
your abominations.
32 Not for your sakes do I *this*, saith
the Lord GOD, be it known unto you:
be ashamed and confounded for your
own ways, O house of Ĭṣ′rā-ĕl.
33 Thus saith the Lord GOD; In the day
that I shall have cleansed you from all
your iniquities I will also cause *you* to
dwell in the cities, and the wastes shall
be builded.
34 And the desolate land shall be tilled,
whereas it lay desolate in the sight of all
that passed by.
35 And they shall say, This land that
was desolate is become like the garden
of Ē′den; and the waste and desolate
and ruined cities *are become* fenced,
and are inhabited.
36 Then the heathen that are left round
about you shall know that I the LORD
build the ruined *places, and* plant that
that was desolate: I the LORD have
spoken *it*, and I will do *it*.
37 Thus saith the Lord GOD; I will yet
for this be inquired of by the house of
Ĭṣ′rā-ĕl, to do *it* for them; I will increase
them with men like a flock.
38 As the holy flock, as the flock of
Jerusalem in her solemn feasts; so shall
the waste cities be filled with flocks of
men: and they shall know that I *am* the
LORD.

CHAPTER 37

THE hand of the LORD was upon me,
and carried me out in the Spirit of
the LORD, and set me down in the midst
of the valley which *was* full of bones,
2 And caused me to pass by them round
about: and, behold, *there were* very
many in the open valley; and, lo, *they
were* very dry.
3 And he said unto me, Son of man, can
these bones live? And I answered, O
Lord GOD, thou knowest.
4 Again he said unto me, Prophesy
upon these bones, and say unto them, O
ye dry bones, hear the word of the
LORD.
5 Thus saith the Lord GOD unto these
bones; Behold, I will cause breath to
enter into you, and ye shall live:
6 And I will lay sinews upon you, and
will bring up flesh upon you, and cover
you with skin, and put breath in you,
and ye shall live; and ye shall know that
I *am* the LORD.
7 So I prophesied as I was commanded:
and as I prophesied, there was a noise,
and behold a shaking, and the bones
came together, bone to his bone.
8 And when I beheld, lo, the sinews
and the flesh came up upon them, and
the skin covered them above: but *there
was* no breath in them.
9 Then said he unto me, Prophesy unto
the wind, prophesy, son of man, and say
to the wind, Thus saith the Lord GOD;
Come from the four winds, O breath,
and breathe upon these slain, that they
may live.
10 So I prophesied as he commanded
me, and the breath came into them, and
they lived, and stood up upon their feet,
an exceeding great army.
11 ¶ Then he said unto me, Son of
man, these bones are the whole house of
Ĭṣ′rā-ĕl: behold, they say, Our bones are
dried, and our hope is lost: we are cut
off for our parts.
12 Therefore prophesy and say unto
them, Thus saith the Lord GOD; Behold, O my people, I will open your
graves, and cause you to come up out
of your graves, and bring you into the
land of Ĭṣ′rā-ĕl.
13 And ye shall know that I *am* the
LORD, when I have opened your graves,
O my people, and brought you up out of
your graves,
14 And shall put my Spirit in you, and
ye shall live, and I shall place you in
your own land: then shall ye know that
I the LORD have spoken *it*, and performed *it*, saith the LORD.
15 ¶ The word of the LORD came again
unto me, saying,
16 Moreover, thou son of man, take
thee one stick, and write upon it, For
Judah, and for the children of Ĭṣ′rā-ĕl his
companions: then take another stick,
and write upon it, For Joseph, the stick
of Ē′phrā-ĭm, and *for* all the house of
Ĭṣ′rā-ĕl his companions:
17 And join them one to another into
one stick; and they shall become one in
thine hand.
18 ¶ And when the children of thy
people shall speak unto thee, saying,
Wilt thou not show us what thou *meanest* by these?
19 Say unto them, Thus saith the Lord
GOD; Behold, I will take the stick of

Joseph, which *is* in the hand of Ē'phrā-
ĭm, and the tribes of Ĭṣ'rā-ĕl his fellows,
and will put them with him, *even* with the
stick of Judah, and make them one stick,
and they shall be one in mine hand.
20 ¶ And the sticks whereon thou
writest shall be in thine hand before
their eyes.
21 And say unto them, Thus saith the
Lord GOD; Behold, I will take the children of Ĭṣ'rā-ĕl from among the heathen,
whither they be gone, and will gather
them on every side, and bring them into
their own land:
22 And I will make them one nation in
the land upon the mountains of Ĭṣ'rā-ĕl;
and one king shall be king to them all:
and they shall be no more two nations,
neither shall they be divided into two
kingdoms any more at all:
23 Neither shall they defile themselves
any more with their idols, nor with their
detestable things, nor with any of their
transgressions: but I will save them out
of all their dwelling places, wherein they
have sinned, and will cleanse them: so
shall they be my people, and I will be
their God.
24 And David my servant *shall be* king
over them; and they all shall have one
shepherd: they shall also walk in my
judgments, and observe my statutes,
and do them.
25 And they shall dwell in the land that
I have given unto Jacob my servant,
wherein your fathers have dwelt; and
they shall dwell therein, *even* they, and
their children, and their children's children for ever: and my servant David
shall be their prince for ever.
26 Moreover I will make a covenant
of peace with them; it shall be an everlasting covenant with them: and I will
place them, and multiply them, and will
set my sanctuary in the midst of them
for evermore.
27 My tabernacle also shall be with
them: yea, I will be their God, and they
shall be my people.
28 And the heathen shall know that I
the LORD do sanctify Ĭṣ'rā-ĕl, when my
sanctuary shall be in the midst of them
for evermore.

CHAPTER 38

AND the word of the LORD came unto
me, saying,
2 Son of man, set thy face against Gog,
the land of Mā'gŏg, the chief prince of
Mē'shĕch and Tū'băl, and prophesy
against him,
3 And say, Thus saith the Lord GOD;
Behold, I *am* against thee, O Gog, the
chief prince of Mē'shĕch and Tū'băl:
4 And I will turn thee back, and put
hooks into thy jaws, and I will bring thee
forth, and all thine army, horses and
horsemen, all of them clothed with all
sorts *of armor*, *even* a great company
with bucklers and shields, all of them
handling swords:
5 Persia, Ethiopia, and Libya with
them; all of them with shield and helmet:
6 Gō'mẽr, and all his bands; the house
of Tō-gär'mȧh of the north quarters, and
all his bands: *and* many people with
thee.
7 Be thou prepared, and prepare for
thyself, thou, and all thy company that
are assembled unto thee, and be thou a
guard unto them.
8 ¶ After many days thou shalt be
visited: in the latter years thou shalt
come into the land *that is* brought back
from the sword, *and is* gathered out of
many people, against the mountains
of Ĭṣ'rā-ĕl, which have been always
waste: but it is brought forth out of the
nations, and they shall dwell safely all
of them.
9 Thou shalt ascend and come like a
storm, thou shalt be like a cloud to cover
the land, thou, and all thy bands, and
many people with thee.
10 Thus saith the Lord GOD; It shall
also come to pass, *that* at the same time
shall things come into thy mind, and
thou shalt think an evil thought:
11 And thou shalt say, I will go up to
the land of unwalled villages; I will go
to them that are at rest, that dwell
safely, all of them dwelling without
walls, and having neither bars nor
gates,
12 To take a spoil, and to take a prey;
to turn thine hand upon the desolate
places *that are now* inhabited, and upon
the people *that are* gathered out of the
nations, which have gotten cattle and
goods, that dwell in the midst of the
land.
13 Shē'bȧ, and Dē'dăn, and the merchants of Tär'shĭsh, with all the young
lions thereof, shall say unto thee, Art
thou come to take a spoil? hast thou

gathered thy company to take a prey?
to carry away silver and gold, to take
away cattle and goods, to take a great
spoil?
14 ¶ Therefore, son of man, prophesy
and say unto Gog, Thus saith the Lord
GOD; In that day when my people of
Ĭs′rā-ĕl dwelleth safely, shalt thou not
know *it?*
15 And thou shalt come from thy place
out of the north parts, thou, and many
people with thee, all of them riding upon
horses, a great company, and a mighty
army:
16 And thou shalt come up against my
people of Ĭs′rā-ĕl, as a cloud to cover the
land; it shall be in the latter days, and I
will bring thee against my land, that the
heathen may know me, when I shall be
sanctified in thee, O Gog, before their
eyes.
17 Thus saith the Lord GOD; *Art* thou
he of whom I have spoken in old time
by my servants the prophets of Ĭs′rā-ĕl,
which prophesied in those days *many*
years, that I would bring thee against
them?
18 And it shall come to pass at the
same time when Gog shall come against
the land of Ĭs′rā-ĕl, saith the Lord GOD,
that my fury shall come up in my face.
19 For in my jealousy *and* in the fire of
my wrath have I spoken, Surely in that
day there shall be a great shaking in the
land of Ĭs′rā-ĕl;
20 So that the fishes of the sea, and the
fowls of the heaven, and the beasts of
the field, and all creeping things that
creep upon the earth, and all the men
that *are* upon the face of the earth, shall
shake at my presence, and the mountains shall be thrown down, and the
steep places shall fall, and every wall
shall fall to the ground.
21 And I will call for a sword against
him throughout all my mountains, saith
the Lord GOD: every man's sword shall
be against his brother.
22 And I will plead against him with
pestilence and with blood; and I will
rain upon him, and upon his bands, and
upon the many people that *are* with him,
an overflowing rain, and great hailstones, fire, and brimstone.
23 Thus will I magnify myself, and
sanctify myself; and I will be known in
the eyes of many nations, and they shall
know that I *am* the LORD.

CHAPTER 39

THEREFORE, thou son of man,
prophesy against Gog, and say,
Thus saith the Lord GOD; Behold, I *am*
against thee, O Gog, the chief prince of
Mē′shĕch and Tū′băl:
2 And I will turn thee back, and leave
but the sixth part of thee, and will cause
thee to come up from the north parts,
and will bring thee upon the mountains
of Ĭs′rā-ĕl:
3 And I will smite thy bow out of thy
left hand, and will cause thine arrows to
fall out of thy right hand.
4 Thou shalt fall upon the mountains of
Ĭs′rā-ĕl, thou, and all thy bands, and the
people that *is* with thee: I will give thee
unto the ravenous birds of every sort,
and *to* the beasts of the field, to be
devoured.
5 Thou shalt fall upon the open field:
for I have spoken *it*, saith the Lord GOD.
6 And I will send a fire on Mā′gŏg, and
among them that dwell carelessly in the
isles: and they shall know that I *am* the
LORD.
7 So will I make my holy name known in
the midst of my people Ĭs′rā-ĕl; and I will
not *let them* pollute my holy name any
more: and the heathen shall know that I
am the LORD, the Holy One in Ĭs′rā-ĕl.
8 ¶ Behold, it is come, and it is done,
saith the Lord GOD; this *is* the day
whereof I have spoken.
9 And they that dwell in the cities of
Ĭs′rā-ĕl shall go forth, and shall set on
fire and burn the weapons, both the
shields and the bucklers, the bows and
the arrows, and the handstaves, and the
spears, and they shall burn them with
fire seven years:
10 So that they shall take no wood
out of the field, neither cut down *any*
out of the forests; for they shall burn
the weapons with fire: and they shall
spoil those that spoiled them, and rob
those that robbed them, saith the Lord
GOD.
11 ¶ And it shall come to pass in that
day, *that* I will give unto Gog a place
there of graves in Ĭs′rā-ĕl, the valley of
the passengers on the east of the sea;
and it shall stop the *noses* of the passengers: and there shall they bury Gog and
all his multitude: and they shall call *it*,
The valley of Hā′mŏn-gŏg.
12 And seven months shall the house

of Ĭş′rā-ĕl be burying of them, that they may cleanse the land.

13 Yea, all the people of the land shall bury *them;* and it shall be to them a renown the day that I shall be glorified, saith the Lord GOD.

14 And they shall sever out men of continual employment, passing through the land, to bury with the passengers those that remain upon the face of the earth, to cleanse it: after the end of seven months shall they search.

15 And the passengers *that* pass through the land, when *any* seeth a man's bone, then shall he set up a sign by it, till the buriers have buried it in the valley of Hā′mŏn-gŏg.

16 And also the name of the city *shall be* Hȧ-mō′nȧh. Thus shall they cleanse the land.

17 ¶ And, thou son of man, thus saith the Lord GOD; Speak unto every feathered fowl, and to every beast of the field, Assemble yourselves, and come; gather yourselves on every side to my sacrifice that I do sacrifice for you, *even* a great sacrifice upon the mountains of Ĭş′rā-ĕl, that ye may eat flesh, and drink blood.

18 Ye shall eat the flesh of the mighty, and drink the blood of the princes of the earth, of rams, of lambs, and of goats, of bullocks, all of them fatlings of Bā′shăn.

19 And ye shall eat fat till ye be full, and drink blood till ye be drunken, of my sacrifice which I have sacrificed for you.

20 Thus ye shall be filled at my table with horses and chariots, with mighty men, and with all men of war, saith the Lord GOD.

21 And I will set my glory among the heathen, and all the heathen shall see my judgment that I have executed, and my hand that I have laid upon them.

22 So the house of Ĭş′rā-ĕl shall know that I *am* the LORD their God from that day and forward.

23 ¶ And the heathen shall know that the house of Ĭş′rā-ĕl went into captivity for their iniquity: because they trespassed against me, therefore hid I my face from them, and gave them into the hand of their enemies; so fell they all by the sword.

24 According to their uncleanness and according to their transgressions have I done unto them, and hid my face from them.

25 Therefore thus saith the Lord GOD; Now will I bring again the captivity of Jacob, and have mercy upon the whole house of Ĭş′rā-ĕl, and will be jealous for my holy name;

26 After that they have borne their shame, and all their trespasses whereby they have trespassed against me, when they dwelt safely in their land, and none made *them* afraid.

27 When I have brought them again from the people, and gathered them out of their enemies' lands, and am sanctified in them in the sight of many nations;

28 Then shall they know that I *am* the LORD their God, which caused them to be led into captivity among the heathen: but I have gathered them unto their own land, and have left none of them any more there.

29 Neither will I hide my face any more from them: for I have poured out my Spirit upon the house of Ĭş′rā-ĕl, saith the Lord GOD.

CHAPTER 40

IN the five and twentieth year of our captivity, in the beginning of the year, in the tenth *day* of the month, in the fourteenth year after that the city was smitten, in the selfsame day the hand of the LORD was upon me, and brought me thither.

2 In the visions of God brought he me into the land of Ĭş′rā-ĕl, and set me upon a very high mountain, by which *was* as the frame of a city on the south.

3 And he brought me thither, and, behold, *there was* a man, whose appearance *was* like the appearance of brass, with a line of flax in his hand, and a measuring reed; and he stood in the gate.

4 And the man said unto me, Son of man, behold with thine eyes, and hear with thine ears, and set thine heart upon all that I shall show thee; for to the intent that I might show *them* unto thee *art* thou brought hither: declare all that thou seest to the house of Ĭş′rā-ĕl.

5 And behold a wall on the outside of the house round about, and in the man's hand a measuring reed of six cubits *long* by the cubit and a handbreadth: so he measured the breadth of the building, one reed; and the height, one reed.

6 ¶ Then came he unto the gate which looketh toward the east, and went up

the stairs thereof, and measured the
threshold of the gate, *which was* one
reed broad; and the other threshold *of*
the gate, which was one reed broad.
7 And *every* little chamber *was* one
reed long, and one reed broad; and between the little chambers *were* five cubits; and the threshold of the gate by the
porch of the gate within *was* one reed.
8 He measured also the porch of the
gate within, one reed.
9 Then measured he the porch of the
gate, eight cubits; and the posts thereof,
two cubits; and the porch of the gate *was*
inward.
10 And the little chambers of the gate
eastward *were* three on this side, and
three on that side; they three *were* of
one measure: and the posts had one
measure on this side and on that side.
11 And he measured the breadth of the
entry of the gate, ten cubits; *and* the
length of the gate, thirteen cubits.
12 The space also before the little
chambers *was* one cubit *on this side,*
and the space *was* one cubit on that
side: and the little chambers *were* six
cubits on this side, and six cubits on
that side.
13 He measured then the gate from the
roof of *one* little chamber to the roof of
another: the breadth *was* five and
twenty cubits, door against door.
14 He made also posts of threescore
cubits, even unto the post of the court
round about the gate.
15 And from the face of the gate of the
entrance unto the face of the porch of
the inner gate *were* fifty cubits.
16 And *there were* narrow windows to
the little chambers, and to their posts
within the gate round about, and likewise to the arches: and windows *were*
round about inward: and upon *each* post
were palm trees.
17 Then brought he me into the outward court, and, lo, *there were* chambers, and a pavement made for the
court round about: thirty chambers *were*
upon the pavement.
18 And the pavement by the side of the
gates over against the length of the
gates *was* the lower pavement.
19 Then he measured the breadth from
the forefront of the lower gate unto the
forefront of the inner court without, a
hundred cubits eastward and northward.
20 ¶ And the gate of the outward court
that looked toward the north, he measured the length thereof, and the breadth
thereof.
21 And the little chambers thereof *were*
three on this side and three on that side;
and the posts thereof and the arches
thereof were after the measure of the
first gate: the length thereof *was* fifty
cubits, and the breadth five and twenty
cubits.
22 And their windows, and their arches,
and their palm trees, *were* after the
measure of the gate that looketh toward
the east; and they went up unto it by
seven steps; and the arches thereof
were before them.
23 And the gate of the inner court *was*
over against the gate toward the north,
and toward the east; and he measured
from gate to gate a hundred cubits.
24 ¶ After that he brought me toward
the south, and behold a gate toward the
south: and he measured the posts thereof, and the arches thereof, according to
these measures.
25 And *there were* windows in it and
in the arches thereof round about, like
those windows: the length *was* fifty
cubits, and the breadth five and twenty
cubits.
26 And *there were* seven steps to go up
to it, and the arches thereof *were* before them: and it had palm trees, one on
this side, and another on that side, upon
the posts thereof.
27 And *there was* a gate in the inner
court toward the south: and he measured from gate to gate toward the south
a hundred cubits.
28 And he brought me to the inner
court by the south gate: and he measured the south gate according to these
measures;
29 And the little chambers thereof, and
the posts thereof, and the arches thereof, according to these measures: and
there were windows in it and in the
arches thereof round about: *it was* fifty
cubits long, and five and twenty cubits
broad.
30 And the arches round about *were*
five and twenty cubits long, and five
cubits broad.
31 And the arches thereof *were* toward
the outer court; and palm trees *were*
upon the posts thereof: and the going up
to it *had* eight steps.

32 ¶ And he brought me into the inner court toward the east: and he measured the gate according to these measures.

33 And the little chambers thereof, and the posts thereof, and the arches thereof, *were* according to these measures: and *there were* windows therein and in the arches thereof round about: *it was* fifty cubits long, and five and twenty cubits broad.

34 And the arches thereof *were* toward the outward court; and palm trees *were* upon the posts thereof, on this side, and on that side: and the going up to it *had* eight steps.

35 ¶ And he brought me to the north gate, and measured *it* according to these measures;

36 The little chambers thereof, the posts thereof, and the arches thereof, and the windows to it round about: the length *was* fifty cubits, and the breadth five and twenty cubits.

37 And the posts thereof *were* toward the outer court; and palm trees *were* upon the posts thereof, on this side, and on that side: and the going up to it *had* eight steps.

38 And the chambers and the entries thereof *were* by the posts of the gates, where they washed the burnt offering.

39 ¶ And in the porch of the gate *were* two tables on this side, and two tables on that side, to slay thereon the burnt offering and the sin offering and the trespass offering.

40 And at the side without, as one goeth up to the entry of the north gate, *were* two tables; and on the other side, which *was* at the porch of the gate, *were* two tables.

41 Four tables *were* on this side, and four tables on that side, by the side of the gate; eight tables, whereupon they slew *their sacrifices*.

42 And the four tables *were* of hewn stone for the burnt offering, of a cubit and a half long, and a cubit and a half broad, and one cubit high: whereupon also they laid the instruments wherewith they slew the burnt offering and the sacrifice.

43 And within *were* hooks, a hand broad, fastened round about: and upon the tables *was* the flesh of the offering.

44 ¶ And without the inner gate *were* the chambers of the singers in the inner court, which *was* at the side of the north gate; and their prospect *was* toward the south: one at the side of the east gate *having* the prospect toward the north.

45 And he said unto me, This chamber, whose prospect *is* toward the south, *is* for the priests, the keepers of the charge of the house.

46 And the chamber whose prospect *is* toward the north *is* for the priests, the keepers of the charge of the altar: these *are* the sons of Zā'dŏk among the sons of Levi, which come near to the LORD to minister unto him.

47 So he measured the court, a hundred cubits long, and a hundred cubits broad, foursquare; and the altar *that was* before the house.

48 ¶ And he brought me to the porch of the house, and measured *each* post of the porch, five cubits on this side, and five cubits on that side: and the breadth of the gate *was* three cubits on this side, and three cubits on that side.

49 The length of the porch *was* twenty cubits, and the breadth eleven cubits; and *he brought me* by the steps whereby they went up to it: and *there were* pillars by the posts, one on this side, and another on that side.

CHAPTER 41

AFTERWARD he brought me to the temple, and measured the posts, six cubits broad on the one side, and six cubits broad on the other side, *which was* the breadth of the tabernacle.

2 And the breadth of the door *was* ten cubits; and the sides of the door *were* five cubits on the one side, and five cubits on the other side: and he measured the length thereof, forty cubits, and the breadth, twenty cubits.

3 Then went he inward, and measured the post of the door, two cubits; and the door, six cubits; and the breadth of the door, seven cubits.

4 So he measured the length thereof, twenty cubits; and the breadth, twenty cubits, before the temple: and he said unto me, This *is* the most holy *place*.

5 After he measured the wall of the house, six cubits; and the breadth of *every* side chamber, four cubits, round about the house on every side.

6 And the side chambers *were* three, one over another, and thirty in order; and they entered into the wall which *was* of the house for the side chambers

round about, that they might have hold,
but they had not hold in the wall of the
house.
7 And *there was* an enlarging, and a
winding about still upward to the side
chambers: for the winding about of the
house went still upward round about the
house: therefore the breadth of the
house *was still* upward, and so increased
from the lowest *chamber* to the highest
by the midst.
8 I saw also the height of the house
round about: the foundations of the side
chambers *were* a full reed of six great
cubits.
9 The thickness of the wall, which *was*
for the side chamber without, *was* five
cubits: and *that* which *was* left *was* the
place of the side chambers that *were*
within.
10 And between the chambers *was* the
wideness of twenty cubits round about
the house on every side.
11 And the doors of the side chambers
were toward *the place that was* left, one
door toward the north, and another door
toward the south: and the breadth of the
place that was left *was* five cubits round
about.
12 Now the building that *was* before
the separate place at the end toward the
west *was* seventy cubits broad; and the
wall of the building *was* five cubits thick
round about, and the length thereof
ninety cubits.
13 So he measured the house, a hundred cubits long; and the separate place,
and the building, with the walls thereof,
a hundred cubits long;
14 Also the breadth of the face of the
house, and of the separate place toward
the east, a hundred cubits.
15 And he measured the length of the
building over against the separate place
which *was* behind it, and the galleries
thereof on the one side and on the other
side, a hundred cubits, with the inner
temple, and the porches of the court;
16 The doorposts, and the narrow windows, and the galleries round about on
their three stories, over against the door,
ceiled with wood round about, and from
the ground up to the windows, and the
windows *were* covered;
17 To that above the door, even unto
the inner house, and without, and by all
the wall round about within and without, by measure.
18 And *it was* made with cherubim and
palm trees, so that a palm tree *was* between a cherub and a cherub; and *every*
cherub had two faces;
19 So that the face of a man *was* toward the palm tree on the one side, and
the face of a young lion toward the palm
tree on the other side: *it was* made
through all the house round about.
20 From the ground unto above the
door *were* cherubim and palm trees
made, and *on* the wall of the temple.
21 The posts of the temple *were*
squared, *and* the face of the sanctuary;
the appearance *of the one* as the appearance *of the other.*
22 The altar of wood *was* three cubits
high, and the length thereof two cubits;
and the corners thereof, and the length
thereof, and the walls thereof, *were* of
wood: and he said unto me, This *is* the
table that *is* before the LORD.
23 And the temple and the sanctuary
had two doors.
24 And the doors had two leaves
apiece, two turning leaves; two *leaves*
for the one door, and two leaves for the
other *door.*
25 And *there were* made on them, on
the doors of the temple, cherubim and
palm trees, like as *were* made upon the
walls; and *there were* thick planks upon
the face of the porch without.
26 And *there were* narrow windows
and palm trees on the one side and on
the other side, on the sides of the porch,
and *upon* the side chambers of the
house, and thick planks.

CHAPTER 42

THEN he brought me forth into the
outer court, the way toward the
north: and he brought me into the chamber that *was* over against the separate
place, and which *was* before the building toward the north.
2 Before the length of a hundred cubits
was the north door, and the breadth *was*
fifty cubits.
3 Over against the twenty *cubits* which
were for the inner court, and over
against the pavement which *was* for the
outer court, *was* gallery against gallery
in three *stories.*
4 And before the chambers *was* a walk
of ten cubits breadth inward, a way of
one cubit; and their doors toward the
north.

5 Now the upper chambers *were*
shorter: for the galleries were higher
than these, than the lower, and than the
middlemost of the building.
6 For they *were* in three *stories*, but
had not pillars as the pillars of the
courts: therefore *the building* was
straitened more than the lowest and the
middlemost from the ground.
7 And the wall that *was* without over
against the chambers, toward the outer
court on the forepart of the chambers,
the length thereof *was* fifty cubits.
8 For the length of the chambers that
were in the outer court *was* fifty cubits:
and, lo, before the temple *were* a hundred cubits.
9 And from under these chambers *was*
the entry on the east side, as one goeth
into them from the outer court.
10 The chambers *were* in the thickness
of the wall of the court toward the east,
over against the separate place, and
over against the building.
11 And the way before them *was* like
the appearance of the chambers which
were toward the north, as long as they,
and as broad as they: and all their goings out *were* both according to their
fashions, and according to their doors.
12 And according to the doors of the
chambers that *were* toward the south
was a door in the head of the way, *even*
the way directly before the wall toward
the east, as one entereth into them.
13 ¶ Then said he unto me, The north
chambers *and* the south chambers,
which *are* before the separate place,
they *be* holy chambers, where the priests
that approach unto the LORD shall eat
the most holy things: there shall they
lay the most holy things, and the meat
offering, and the sin offering, and the
trespass offering; for the place *is* holy.
14 When the priests enter therein, then
shall they not go out of the holy *place*
into the outer court, but there they shall
lay their garments wherein they minister; for they *are* holy; and shall put on
other garments, and shall approach to
those things which *are* for the people.
15 Now when he had made an end of
measuring the inner house, he brought
me forth toward the gate whose prospect *is* toward the east, and measured
it round about.
16 He measured the east side with the
measuring reed, five hundred reeds,
with the measuring reed round about.
17 He measured the north side, five
hundred reeds, with the measuring reed
round about.
18 He measured the south side, five
hundred reeds, with the measuring reed.
19 ¶ He turned about to the west side,
and measured five hundred reeds, with
the measuring reed.
20 He measured it by the four sides:
it had a wall round about, five hundred
reeds long, and five hundred broad, to
make a separation between the sanctuary and the profane place.

CHAPTER 43

AFTERWARD he brought me to the
gate, *even* the gate that looketh
toward the east:
2 And, behold, the glory of the God of
Ĭṣ′rā-ĕl came from the way of the east:
and his voice *was* like a noise of many
waters: and the earth shined with his
glory.
3 And *it was* according to the appearance of the vision which I saw, *even*
according to the vision that I saw when
I came to destroy the city: and the visions *were* like the vision that I saw by
the river Chē′bär; and I fell upon my
face.
4 And the glory of the LORD came into
the house by the way of the gate whose
prospect *is* toward the east.
5 So the spirit took me up, and brought
me into the inner court; and, behold, the
glory of the LORD filled the house.
6 And I heard *him* speaking unto me
out of the house; and the man stood by
me.
7 ¶ And he said unto me, Son of man,
the place of my throne, and the place of
the soles of my feet, where I will dwell
in the midst of the children of Ĭṣ′rā-ĕl
for ever, and my holy name, shall the
house of Ĭṣ′rā-ĕl no more defile, *neither*
they, nor their kings, by their whoredom,
nor by the carcasses of their kings in
their high places.
8 In their setting of their threshold by
my thresholds, and their post by my
posts, and the wall between me and
them, they have even defiled my holy
name by their abominations that they
have committed: wherefore I have consumed them in mine anger.
9 Now let them put away their whoredom, and the carcasses of their kings,

far from me, and I will dwell in the
midst of them for ever.
10 ¶ Thou son of man, show the house
to the house of Ĭṣ′rā-ĕl, that they may
be ashamed of their iniquities: and let
them measure the pattern.
11 And if they be ashamed of all that
they have done, show them the form of
the house, and the fashion thereof, and
the goings out thereof, and the comings
in thereof, and all the forms thereof, and
all the ordinances thereof, and all the
forms thereof, and all the laws thereof:
and write *it* in their sight, that they may
keep the whole form thereof, and all the
ordinances thereof, and do them.
12 This *is* the law of the house; Upon
the top of the mountain the whole limit
thereof round about *shall be* most holy.
Behold, this *is* the law of the house.
13 ¶ And these *are* the measures of
the altar after the cubits: The cubit *is* a
cubit and a handbreadth; even the bottom *shall be* a cubit, and the breadth a
cubit, and the border thereof by the
edge thereof round about *shall be* a
span; and this *shall be* the higher place
of the altar.
14 And from the bottom *upon* the
ground *even* to the lower settle *shall be*
two cubits, and the breadth one cubit;
and from the lesser settle *even* to the
greater settle *shall be* four cubits, and
the breadth *one* cubit.
15 So the altar *shall be* four cubits; and
from the altar and upward *shall be* four
horns.
16 And the altar *shall be* twelve *cubits*
long, twelve broad, square in the four
squares thereof.
17 And the settle *shall be* fourteen
cubits long and fourteen broad in the
four squares thereof; and the border
about it *shall be* half a cubit; and the
bottom thereof *shall be* a cubit about;
and his stairs shall look toward the east.
18 ¶ And he said unto me, Son of man,
thus saith the Lord GOD; These *are* the
ordinances of the altar in the day when
they shall make it, to offer burnt offerings thereon, and to sprinkle blood
thereon.
19 And thou shalt give to the priests
the Lē′vītes that be of the seed of Zā′-
dŏk, which approach unto me, to minister unto me, saith the Lord GOD, a
young bullock for a sin offering.
20 And thou shalt take of the blood
thereof, and put *it* on the four horns of
it, and on the four corners of the settle,
and upon the border round about: thus
shalt thou cleanse and purge it.
21 Thou shalt take the bullock also of
the sin offering, and he shall burn it in
the appointed place of the house, without the sanctuary.
22 And on the second day thou shalt
offer a kid of the goats without blemish
for a sin offering; and they shall cleanse
the altar, as they did cleanse *it* with the
bullock.
23 When thou hast made an end of
cleansing *it*, thou shalt offer a young
bullock without blemish, and a ram out
of the flock without blemish.
24 And thou shalt offer them before
the LORD, and the priests shall cast salt
upon them, and they shall offer them up
for a burnt offering unto the LORD.
25 Seven days shalt thou prepare every
day a goat *for* a sin offering: they shall
also prepare a young bullock, and a ram
out of the flock, without blemish.
26 Seven days shall they purge the
altar and purify it; and they shall consecrate themselves.
27 And when these days are expired,
it shall be, *that* upon the eighth day, and
so forward, the priests shall make your
burnt offerings upon the altar, and your
peace offerings; and I will accept you,
saith the Lord GOD.

CHAPTER 44

THEN he brought me back the way
of the gate of the outward sanctuary
which looketh toward the east; and it
was shut.
2 Then said the LORD unto me; This
gate shall be shut, it shall not be opened,
and no man shall enter in by it; because
the LORD the God of Ĭṣ′rā-ĕl hath entered in by it, therefore it shall be shut.
3 *It is* for the prince; the prince, he
shall sit in it to eat bread before the
LORD; he shall enter by the way of the
porch of *that* gate, and shall go out by
the way of the same.
4 ¶ Then brought he me the way of
the north gate before the house: and I
looked, and, behold, the glory of the
LORD filled the house of the LORD: and
I fell upon my face.
5 And the LORD said unto me, Son of
man, mark well, and behold with thine
eyes, and hear with thine ears all that I

say unto thee concerning all the ordinances of the house of the LORD, and
all the laws thereof; and mark well the
entering in of the house, with every
going forth of the sanctuary.
6 And thou shalt say to the rebellious,
even to the house of Ĭs'rā-ĕl, Thus saith
the Lord GOD; O ye house of Ĭs'rā-ĕl,
let it suffice you of all your abominations,
7 In that ye have brought *into my sanctuary* strangers, uncircumcised in heart,
and uncircumcised in flesh, to be in my
sanctuary, to pollute it, *even* my house,
when ye offer my bread, the fat and the
blood, and they have broken my covenant because of all your abominations.
8 And ye have not kept the charge of
mine holy things: but ye have set keepers of my charge in my sanctuary for
yourselves.
9 ¶ Thus saith the Lord GOD; No
stranger, uncircumcised in heart, nor
uncircumcised in flesh, shall enter into
my sanctuary, of any stranger that *is*
among the children of Ĭs'rā-ĕl.
10 And the Lē'vītes that are gone away
far from me, when Ĭs'rā-ĕl went astray,
which went astray away from me after
their idols; they shall even bear their
iniquity.
11 Yet they shall be ministers in my
sanctuary, *having* charge at the gates of
the house, and ministering to the house:
they shall slay the burnt offering and
the sacrifice for the people, and they
shall stand before them to minister unto
them.
12 Because they ministered unto them
before their idols, and caused the house
of Ĭs'rā-ĕl to fall into iniquity; therefore
have I lifted up mine hand against
them, saith the Lord GOD, and they
shall bear their iniquity.
13 And they shall not come near unto
me, to do the office of a priest unto me,
nor to come near to any of my holy
things, in the most holy *place:* but they
shall bear their shame, and their
abominations which they have committed.
14 But I will make them keepers of the
charge of the house, for all the service
thereof, and for all that shall be done
therein.
15 ¶ But the priests the Lē'vītes, the
sons of Zā'dŏk, that kept the charge of
my sanctuary when the children of
Ĭs'rā-ĕl went astray from me, they shall
come near to me to minister unto me,
and they shall stand before me to offer
unto me the fat and the blood, saith the
Lord GOD:
16 They shall enter into my sanctuary,
and they shall come near to my table, to
minister unto me, and they shall keep
my charge.
17 ¶ And it shall come to pass, *that*
when they enter in at the gates of the
inner court, they shall be clothed with
linen garments; and no wool shall come
upon them, while they minister in the
gates of the inner court, and within.
18 They shall have linen bonnets upon
their heads, and shall have linen
breeches upon their loins; they shall not
gird *themselves* with any thing that
causeth sweat.
19 And when they go forth into the
outer court, *even* into the outer court to
the people, they shall put off their garments wherein they ministered, and lay
them in the holy chambers, and they
shall put on other garments; and they
shall not sanctify the people with their
garments.
20 Neither shall they shave their
heads, nor suffer their locks to grow long;
they shall only poll their heads.
21 Neither shall any priest drink wine,
when they enter into the inner court.
22 Neither shall they take for their
wives a widow, nor her that is put away:
but they shall take maidens of the seed
of the house of Ĭs'rā-ĕl, or a widow that
had a priest before.
23 And they shall teach my people *the
difference* between the holy and profane, and cause them to discern between
the unclean and the clean.
24 And in controversy they shall stand
in judgment; *and* they shall judge it
according to my judgments: and they
shall keep my laws and my statutes in
all mine assemblies; and they shall
hallow my sabbaths.
25 And they shall come at no dead person to defile themselves: but for father,
or for mother, or for son, or for daughter, for brother, or for sister that hath had
no husband, they may defile themselves.
26 And after he is cleansed, they shall
reckon unto him seven days.
27 And in the day that he goeth into
the sanctuary, unto the inner court, to
minister in the sanctuary, he shall offer
his sin offering, saith the Lord GOD.

28 And it shall be unto them for an inheritance; I *am* their inheritance: and ye shall give them no possession in Ĭṣ′rā-ēl; I *am* their possession.

29 They shall eat the meat offering, and the sin offering, and the trespass offering; and every dedicated thing in Ĭṣ′rā-ēl shall be theirs.

30 And the first of all the firstfruits of all *things,* and every oblation of all, of every *sort* of your oblations, shall be the priest's: ye shall also give unto the priest the first of your dough, that he may cause the blessing to rest in thine house.

31 The priests shall not eat of any thing that is dead of itself, or torn, whether it be fowl or beast.

CHAPTER 45

MOREOVER, when ye shall divide by lot the land for inheritance, ye shall offer an oblation unto the LORD, a holy portion of the land: the length *shall be* the length of five and twenty thousand *reeds,* and the breadth *shall be* ten thousand. This *shall be* holy in all the borders thereof round about.

2 Of this there shall be for the sanctuary five hundred *in length,* with five hundred *in breadth,* square round about; and fifty cubits round about for the suburbs thereof.

3 And of this measure shalt thou measure the length of five and twenty thousand, and the breadth of ten thousand: and in it shall be the sanctuary *and* the most holy *place.*

4 The holy *portion* of the land shall be for the priests the ministers of the sanctuary, which shall come near to minister unto the LORD: and it shall be a place for their houses, and a holy place for the sanctuary.

5 And the five and twenty thousand of length, and the ten thousand of breadth, shall also the Lē′vītes, the ministers of the house, have for themselves, for a possession for twenty chambers.

6 ¶ And ye shall appoint the possession of the city five thousand broad, and five and twenty thousand long, over against the oblation of the holy *portion:* it shall be for the whole house of Ĭṣ′rā-ēl.

7 ¶ And *a portion shall be* for the prince on the one side and on the other side of the oblation of the holy *portion,* and of the possession of the city, before the oblation of the holy *portion,* and before the possession of the city, from the west side westward, and from the east side eastward: and the length *shall be* over against one of the portions, from the west border unto the east border.

8 In the land shall be his possession in Ĭṣ′rā-ēl: and my princes shall no more oppress my people; and *the rest of* the land shall they give to the house of Ĭṣ′rā-ēl according to their tribes.

9 ¶ Thus saith the Lord GOD; Let it suffice you, O princes of Ĭṣ′rā-ēl: remove violence and spoil, and execute judgment and justice, take away your exactions from my people, saith the Lord GOD.

10 Ye shall have just balances, and a just ē′phȧh, and a just bath.

11 The ē′phȧh and the bath shall be of one measure, that the bath may contain the tenth part of a homer, and the ē′phȧh the tenth part of a homer: the measure thereof shall be after the homer.

12 And the shekel *shall be* twenty gē′rȧhs: twenty shekels, five and twenty shekels, fifteen shekels, shall be your maneh.

13 This *is* the oblation that ye shall offer; the sixth part of an ē′phȧh of a homer of wheat, and ye shall give the sixth part of an ē′phȧh of a homer of barley:

14 Concerning the ordinance of oil, the bath of oil, *ye shall offer* the tenth part of a bath out of the cor, *which is* a homer of ten baths; for ten baths *are* a homer:

15 And one lamb out of the flock, out of two hundred, out of the fat pastures of Ĭṣ′rā-ēl; for a meat offering, and for a burnt offering, and for peace offerings, to make reconciliation for them, saith the Lord GOD.

16 All the people of the land shall give this oblation for the prince in Ĭṣ′rā-ēl.

17 And it shall be the prince's part *to give* burnt offerings, and meat offerings, and drink offerings, in the feasts, and in the new moons, and in the sabbaths, in all solemnities of the house of Ĭṣ′rā-ēl: he shall prepare the sin offering, and the meat offering, and the burnt offering, and the peace offerings, to make reconciliation for the house of Ĭṣ′rā-ēl.

18 Thus saith the Lord GOD; In the

first *month,* in the first *day* of the month, thou shalt take a young bullock without blemish, and cleanse the sanctuary:

19 And the priest shall take of the blood of the sin offering, and put *it* upon the posts of the house, and upon the four corners of the settle of the altar, and upon the posts of the gate of the inner court.

20 And so thou shalt do the seventh *day* of the month for every one that erreth, and for *him that is* simple: so shall ye reconcile the house.

21 In the first *month,* in the fourteenth day of the month, ye shall have the passover, a feast of seven days; unleavened bread shall be eaten.

22 And upon that day shall the prince prepare for himself and for all the people of the land a bullock *for* a sin offering.

23 And seven days of the feast he shall prepare a burnt offering to the LORD, seven bullocks and seven rams without blemish daily the seven days; and a kid of the goats daily *for* a sin offering.

24 And he shall prepare a meat offering of an ē'phȧh for a bullock, and an ē'phȧh for a ram, and a hin of oil for an ē'phȧh.

25 In the seventh *month,* in the fifteenth day of the month, shall he do the like in the feast of the seven days, according to the sin offering, according to the burnt offering, and according to the meat offering, and according to the oil.

CHAPTER 46

THUS saith the Lord GOD; The gate of the inner court that looketh toward the east shall be shut the six working days; but on the sabbath it shall be opened, and in the day of the new moon it shall be opened.

2 And the prince shall enter by the way of the porch of *that* gate without, and shall stand by the post of the gate, and the priests shall prepare his burnt offering and his peace offerings, and he shall worship at the threshold of the gate: then he shall go forth; but the gate shall not be shut until the evening.

3 Likewise the people of the land shall worship at the door of this gate before the LORD in the sabbaths and in the new moons.

4 And the burnt offering that the prince shall offer unto the LORD in the sabbath day *shall be* six lambs without blemish, and a ram without blemish.

5 And the meat offering *shall be* an ē'phȧh for a ram, and the meat offering for the lambs as he shall be able to give, and a hin of oil to an ē'phȧh.

6 And in the day of the new moon *it shall be* a young bullock without blemish, and six lambs, and a ram: they shall be without blemish.

7 And he shall prepare a meat offering, an ē'phȧh for a bullock, and an ē'phȧh for a ram, and for the lambs according as his hand shall attain unto, and a hin of oil to an ē'phȧh.

8 And when the prince shall enter, he shall go in by the way of the porch of *that* gate, and he shall go forth by the way thereof.

9 ¶ But when the people of the land shall come before the LORD in the solemn feasts, he that entereth in by the way of the north gate to worship shall go out by the way of the south gate; and he that entereth by the way of the south gate shall go forth by the way of the north gate: he shall not return by the way of the gate whereby he came in, but shall go forth over against it.

10 And the prince in the midst of them, when they go in, shall go in; and when they go forth, shall go forth.

11 And in the feasts and in the solemnities the meat offering shall be an ē'phȧh to a bullock, and an ē'phȧh to a ram, and to the lambs as he is able to give, and a hin of oil to an ē'phȧh.

12 Now when the prince shall prepare a voluntary burnt offering or peace offerings voluntarily unto the LORD, *one* shall then open him the gate that looketh toward the east, and he shall prepare his burnt offering and his peace offerings, as he did on the sabbath day: then he shall go forth; and after his going forth *one* shall shut the gate.

13 Thou shalt daily prepare a burnt offering unto the LORD *of* a lamb of the first year without blemish: thou shalt prepare it every morning.

14 And thou shalt prepare a meat offering for it every morning, the sixth part of an ē'phȧh, and the third part of a hin of oil, to temper with the fine flour; a meat offering continually by a perpetual ordinance unto the LORD.

15 Thus shall they prepare the lamb,

and the meat offering, and the oil, every
morning *for* a continual burnt offering.
16 ¶ Thus saith the Lord GOD; If the
prince give a gift unto any of his sons,
the inheritance thereof shall be his
sons'; it *shall be* their possession by
inheritance.
17 But if he give a gift of his inheritance to one of his servants, then it shall
be his to the year of liberty; after, it
shall return to the prince: but his inheritance shall be his sons' for them.
18 Moreover the prince shall not take
of the people's inheritance by oppression, to thrust them out of their possession; *but* he shall give his sons inheritance out of his own possession; that my
people be not scattered every man from
his possession.
19 ¶ After he brought me through the
entry, which *was* at the side of the gate,
into the holy chambers of the priests,
which looked toward the north: and,
behold, there *was* a place on the two
sides westward.
20 Then said he unto me, This *is* the
place where the priests shall boil the
trespass offering and the sin offering,
where they shall bake the meat offering;
that they bear *them* not out into the
outer court, to sanctify the people.
21 Then he brought me forth into the
outer court, and caused me to pass by
the four corners of the court; and, behold, in every corner of the court *there*
was a court.
22 In the four corners of the court
there were courts joined of forty *cubits*
long and thirty broad: these four corners *were* of one measure.
23 And *there was* a row *of building*
round about in them, round about them
four, and *it was* made with boiling
places under the rows round about.
24 Then said he unto me, These *are*
the places of them that boil, where the
ministers of the house shall boil the
sacrifice of the people.

CHAPTER 47

AFTERWARD he brought me again
unto the door of the house; and,
behold, waters issued out from under
the threshold of the house eastward: for
the forefront of the house *stood toward*
the east, and the waters came down
from under, from the right side of the
house, at the south *side* of the altar.
2 Then brought he me out of the way
of the gate northward, and led me about
the way without unto the outer gate by
the way that looketh eastward; and, behold, there ran out waters on the right
side.
3 And when the man that had the line
in his hand went forth eastward, he
measured a thousand cubits, and he
brought me through the waters; the
waters *were* to the ankles.
4 Again he measured a thousand, and
brought me through the waters; the
waters *were* to the knees. Again he
measured a thousand, and brought me
through; the waters *were* to the loins.
5 Afterward he measured a thousand;
and it was a river that I could not pass
over: for the waters were risen, waters
to swim in, a river that could not be
passed over.
6 ¶ And he said unto me, Son of man,
hast thou seen *this?* Then he brought
me, and caused me to return to the
brink of the river.
7 Now when I had returned, behold, at
the bank of the river *were* very many
trees on the one side and on the other.
8 Then said he unto me, These waters
issue out toward the east country, and
go down into the desert, and go into the
sea: *which being* brought forth into the
sea, the waters shall be healed.
9 And it shall come to pass, *that* every
thing that liveth, which moveth, whithersoever the rivers shall come, shall
live: and there shall be a very great
multitude of fish, because these waters
shall come thither: for they shall be
healed; and every thing shall live
whither the river cometh.
10 And it shall come to pass, *that* the
fishers shall stand upon it from Ĕn-
gē'dī even unto Ĕn–ĕg'lā-ĭm; they shall
be a *place* to spread forth nets; their fish
shall be according to their kinds, as the
fish of the great sea, exceeding many.
11 But the miry places thereof and the
marshes thereof shall not be healed;
they shall be given to salt.
12 And by the river upon the bank
thereof, on this side and on that side,
shall grow all trees for meat, whose leaf
shall not fade, neither shall the fruit
thereof be consumed: it shall bring forth
new fruit according to his months, because their waters they issued out of the
sanctuary: and the fruit thereof shall be

for meat, and the leaf thereof for
medicine.
13 ¶ Thus saith the Lord GOD; This
shall be the border, whereby ye shall
inherit the land according to the twelve
tribes of Ĭs'rā-ĕl: Joseph *shall have two*
portions.
14 And ye shall inherit it, one as well
as another: *concerning* the which I lifted
up mine hand to give it unto your
fathers: and this land shall fall unto you
for inheritance.
15 And this *shall be* the border of the
land toward the north side, from the
great sea, the way of Hĕth'lŏn, as men
go to Zē'dăd;
16 Hā'măth, Bē-rō'thȧh, Sĭb-rā'ĭm,
which *is* between the border of Damascus and the border of Hā'măth: Hā'zär–
hăt'tĭ-cŏn, which *is* by the coast of
Hau'răn.
17 And the border from the sea shall
be Hā'zär–ē'năn, the border of Damascus, and the north northward, and the
border of Hā'măth. And *this is* the
north side.
18 And the east side ye shall measure
from Hau'răn, and from Damascus, and
from Gĭl'ē-ăd, and from the land of
Ĭs'rā-ĕl *by* Jordan, from the border unto
the east sea. And *this is* the east side.
19 And the south side southward, from
Tā'mȧr *even* to the waters of strife *in*
Kā'dĕsh, the river to the great sea. And
this is the south side southward.
20 The west side also *shall be* the great
sea from the border, till a man come over
against Hā'măth. This *is* the west side.
21 So shall ye divide this land unto
you according to the tribes of Ĭs'rā-ĕl.
22 ¶ And it shall come to pass, *that* ye
shall divide it by lot for an inheritance
unto you, and to the strangers that sojourn among you, which shall beget
children among you: and they shall be
unto you as born in the country among
the children of Ĭs'rā-ĕl; they shall have
inheritance with you among the tribes
of Ĭs'rā-ĕl.
23 And it shall come to pass, *that* in
what tribe the stranger sojourneth, there
shall ye give *him* his inheritance, saith
the Lord GOD.

CHAPTER 48

NOW these *are* the names of the
tribes. From the north end to the
coast of the way of Hĕth'lŏn, as one
goeth to Hā'măth, Hā'zär–ē'năn, the
border of Damascus northward, to the
coast of Hā'măth; for these are his sides
east *and* west; a *portion for* Dan.
2 And by the border of Dan, from the
east side unto the west side, a *portion*
for Ăsh'ẽr.
3 And by the border of Ăsh'ẽr, from
the east side even unto the west side, a
portion for Năph'tȧ-lī.
4 And by the border of Năph'tȧ-lī, from
the east side unto the west side, a *por-*
tion for Mȧ-năs'sĕh.
5 And by the border of Mȧ-năs'sĕh,
from the east side unto the west side,
a *portion for* Ē'phrā-ĭm.
6 And by the border of Ē'phrā-ĭm,
from the east side even unto the west
side, a *portion for* Reuben.
7 And by the border of Reuben, from
the east side unto the west side, a
portion for Judah.
8 ¶ And by the border of Judah, from
the east side unto the west side, shall
be the offering which ye shall offer of
five and twenty thousand *reeds in*
breadth, and *in* length as one of the
other parts, from the east side unto the
west side: and the sanctuary shall be
in the midst of it.
9 The oblation that ye shall offer unto
the LORD *shall be* of five and twenty
thousand in length, and of ten thousand
in breadth.
10 And for them, *even* for the priests,
shall be *this* holy oblation; toward the
north five and twenty thousand *in*
length, and toward the west ten thousand in breadth, and toward the east
ten thousand in breadth, and toward
the south five and twenty thousand in
length: and the sanctuary of the LORD
shall be in the midst thereof.
11 *It shall be* for the priests that are
sanctified of the sons of Zā'dŏk; which
have kept my charge, which went not
astray when the children of Ĭs'rā-ĕl
went astray, as the Lē'vītes went astray.
12 And *this* oblation of the land that
is offered shall be unto them a thing
most holy by the border of the Lē'vītes.
13 And over against the border of the
priests, the Lē'vītes *shall have* five
and twenty thousand in length, and ten
thousand in breadth: all the length *shall*
be five and twenty thousand, and the
breadth ten thousand.
14 And they shall not sell of it, neither

exchange, nor alienate the firstfruits of
the land: for *it is* holy unto the LORD.
15 ¶ And the five thousand, that are
left in the breadth over against the five
and twenty thousand, shall be a profane
place for the city, for dwelling, and for
suburbs: and the city shall be in the
midst thereof.
16 And these *shall be* the measures
thereof; the north side four thousand
and five hundred, and the south side
four thousand and five hundred, and
on the east side four thousand and five
hundred, and the west side four thousand and five hundred.
17 And the suburbs of the city shall
be toward the north two hundred and
fifty, and toward the south two hundred
and fifty, and toward the east two hundred and fifty, and toward the west two
hundred and fifty.
18 And the residue in length over
against the oblation of the holy *portion*
shall be ten thousand eastward, and ten
thousand westward: and it shall be over
against the oblation of the holy *portion;*
and the increase thereof shall be for food
unto them that serve the city.
19 And they that serve the city shall
serve it out of all the tribes of Ĭs'rā-ĕl.
20 All the oblation *shall be* five and
twenty thousand by five and twenty
thousand: ye shall offer the holy oblation foursquare, with the possession of
the city.
21 ¶ And the residue *shall be* for the
prince, on the one side and on the
other of the holy oblation, and of the
possession of the city, over against the
five and twenty thousand of the oblation toward the east border, and westward over against the five and twenty
thousand toward the west border, over
against the portions for the prince: and
it shall be the holy oblation; and the
sanctuary of the house *shall be* in the
midst thereof.
22 Moreover, from the possession of
the Lē'vītes, and from the possession of
the city, *being* in the midst *of that*
which is the prince's, between the
border of Judah and the border of
Benjamin, shall be for the prince.
23 As for the rest of the tribes, from
the east side unto the west side, Benjamin *shall have* a *portion.*
24 And by the border of Benjamin,
from the east side unto the west side,
Simeon *shall have* a *portion.*
25 And by the border of Simeon, from
the east side unto the west side, Ĭs'sȧ-
chär a *portion.*
26 And by the border of Ĭs'sȧ-chär,
from the east side unto the west side,
Zĕb'ū-lŭn a *portion.*
27 And by the border of Zĕb'ū-lŭn,
from the east side unto the west side,
Gad a *portion.*
28 And by the border of Gad, at the
south side southward, the border shall
be even from Tā'mȧr *unto* the waters of
strife *in* Kā'dĕsh, *and* to the river
toward the great sea.
29 This *is* the land which ye shall
divide by lot unto the tribes of Ĭs'rā-ĕl
for inheritance, and these *are* their
portions, saith the Lord GOD.
30 ¶ And these *are* the goings out of
the city on the north side, four thousand
and five hundred measures.
31 And the gates of the city *shall be*
after the names of the tribes of Ĭs'rā-ĕl:
three gates northward; one gate of
Reuben, one gate of Judah, one gate of
Levi.
32 And at the east side four thousand
and five hundred: and three gates; and
one gate of Joseph, one gate of Benjamin, one gate of Dan.
33 And at the south side four thousand
and five hundred measures: and three
gates; one gate of Simeon, one gate
of Ĭs'sȧ-chär, one gate of Zĕb'ū-lŭn.
34 At the west side four thousand and
five hundred, *with* their three gates;
one gate of Gad, one gate of Ăsh'ēr, one
gate of Năph'tȧ-lī.
35 *It was* round about eighteen thousand *measures:* and the name of the city
from *that* day *shall be,* The LORD *is* there.

THE BOOK OF DANIEL

CHAPTER 1

IN the third year of the reign of Jē-hôi′ȧ-kĭm king of Judah came Nĕb′ū-chăd-nĕz′zȧr king of Babylon unto Jerusalem, and besieged it.

2 And the Lord gave Jē-hôi′ȧ-kĭm king of Judah into his hand, with part of the vessels of the house of God: which he carried into the land of Shī′när to the house of his god; and he brought the vessels into the treasure house of his god.

3 ¶ And the king spake unto Ăsh′pē-năz the master of his eunuchs, that he should bring *certain* of the children of Ĭṣ′rā-ĕl, and of the king's seed, and of the princes;

4 Children in whom *was* no blemish, but well-favored, and skilful in all wisdom, and cunning in knowledge, and understanding science, and such as *had* ability in them to stand in the king's palace, and whom they might teach the learning and the tongue of the Chăl-dē′ănṣ.

5 And the king appointed them a daily provision of the king's meat, and of the wine which he drank: so nourishing them three years, that at the end thereof they might stand before the king.

6 Now among these were of the children of Judah, Daniel, Hăn′ȧ-nī′ȧh, Mĭsh′ā-ĕl, and Ăz′ȧ-rī′ȧh:

7 Unto whom the prince of the eunuchs gave names: for he gave unto Daniel *the name* of Bĕl′tē-shăz′zȧr; and to Hăn′ȧ-nī′ȧh, of Shā′drăch; and to Mĭsh′ā-ĕl, of Mē′shăch; and to Ăz′ȧ-rī′ȧh, of Ȧ-bĕd′–nē-gō.

8 ¶ But Daniel purposed in his heart that he would not defile himself with the portion of the king's meat, nor with the wine which he drank: therefore he requested of the prince of the eunuchs that he might not defile himself.

9 Now God had brought Daniel into favor and tender love with the prince of the eunuchs.

10 And the prince of the eunuchs said unto Daniel, I fear my lord the king, who hath appointed your meat and your drink: for why should he see your faces worse liking than the children which *are* of your sort? then shall ye make *me* endanger my head to the king.

11 Then said Daniel to Mĕl′zär, whom the prince of the eunuchs had set over Daniel, Hăn′ȧ-nī′ȧh, Mĭsh′ā-ĕl, and Ăz′ȧ-rī′ȧh,

12 Prove thy servants, I beseech thee, ten days; and let them give us pulse to eat, and water to drink.

13 Then let our countenances be looked upon before thee, and the countenance of the children that eat of the portion of the king's meat: and as thou seest, deal with thy servants.

14 So he consented to them in this matter, and proved them ten days.

15 And at the end of ten days their countenances appeared fairer and fatter in flesh than all the children which did eat the portion of the king's meat.

16 Thus Mĕl′zär took away the portion of their meat, and the wine that they should drink; and gave them pulse.

17 ¶ As for these four children, God gave them knowledge and skill in all learning and wisdom: and Daniel had understanding in all visions and dreams.

18 Now at the end of the days that the king had said he should bring them in, then the prince of the eunuchs brought them in before Nĕb′ū-chăd-nĕz′zȧr.

19 And the king communed with them; and among them all was found none like Daniel, Hăn′ȧ-nī′ȧh, Mĭsh′ā-ĕl, and Ăz′ȧ-rī′ȧh: therefore stood they before the king.

20 And in all matters of wisdom *and* understanding, that the king inquired of them, he found them ten times better than all the magicians *and* astrologers that *were* in all his realm.

21 And Daniel continued *even* unto the first year of king Cyrus.

CHAPTER 2

AND in the second year of the reign of Nĕb′ū-chăd-nĕz′zȧr, Nĕb′ū-chăd-nĕz′zȧr dreamed dreams, wherewith his spirit was troubled, and his sleep brake from him.

2 Then the king commanded to call the magicians, and the astrologers, and the sorcerers, and the Chăl-dē′ănṣ, for to show the king his dreams. So they came and stood before the king.

3 And the king said unto them, I have

dreamed a dream, and my spirit was troubled to know the dream.

4 Then spake the Chăl-dē′ăns to the king in Sўr′ĭ-ăc, O king, live for ever: tell thy servants the dream, and we will show the interpretation.

5 The king answered and said to the Chăl-dē′ăns, The thing is gone from me: if ye will not make known unto me the dream, with the interpretation thereof, ye shall be cut in pieces, and your houses shall be made a dunghill.

6 But if ye show the dream, and the interpretation thereof, ye shall receive of me gifts and rewards and great honor: therefore show me the dream, and the interpretation thereof.

7 They answered again and said, Let the king tell his servants the dream, and we will show the interpretation of it.

8 The king answered and said, I know of certainty that ye would gain the time, because ye see the thing is gone from me.

9 But if ye will not make known unto me the dream, *there is but* one decree for you: for ye have prepared lying and corrupt words to speak before me, till the time be changed: therefore tell me the dream, and I shall know that ye can show me the interpretation thereof.

10 ¶ The Chăl-dē′ăns answered before the king, and said, There is not a man upon the earth that can show the king's matter: therefore *there is* no king, lord, nor ruler, *that* asked such things at any magician, or astrologer, or Chăl-dē′ăn.

11 And *it is* a rare thing that the king requireth, and there is none other that can show it before the king, except the gods, whose dwelling is not with flesh.

12 For this cause the king was angry and very furious, and commanded to destroy all the wise *men* of Babylon.

13 And the decree went forth that the wise *men* should be slain; and they sought Daniel and his fellows to be slain.

14 ¶ Then Daniel answered with counsel and wisdom to Ăr′ĭ-ŏch the captain of the king's guard, which was gone forth to slay the wise *men* of Babylon:

15 He answered and said to Ăr′ĭ-ŏch the king's captain, Why *is* the decree *so* hasty from the king? Then Ăr′ĭ-ŏch made the thing known to Daniel.

16 Then Daniel went in, and desired of the king that he would give him time, and that he would show the king the interpretation.

17 Then Daniel went to his house, and made the thing known to Hăn′ȧ-nī′ȧh, Mĭsh′ā-ĕl, and Ăz′ȧ-rī′ȧh, his companions:

18 That they would desire mercies of the God of heaven concerning this secret; that Daniel and his fellows should not perish with the rest of the wise *men* of Babylon.

19 ¶ Then was the secret revealed unto Daniel in a night vision. Then Daniel blessed the God of heaven.

20 Daniel answered and said, Blessed be the name of God for ever and ever: for wisdom and might are his:

21 And he changeth the times and the seasons: he removeth kings, and setteth up kings: he giveth wisdom unto the wise, and knowledge to them that know understanding:

22 He revealeth the deep and secret things: he knoweth what *is* in the darkness, and the light dwelleth with him.

23 I thank thee, and praise thee, O thou God of my fathers, who hast given me wisdom and might, and hast made known unto me now what we desired of thee: for thou hast *now* made known unto us the king's matter.

24 ¶ Therefore Daniel went in unto Ăr′ĭ-ŏch, whom the king had ordained to destroy the wise *men* of Babylon: he went and said thus unto him; Destroy not the wise *men* of Babylon: bring me in before the king, and I will show unto the king the interpretation.

25 Then Ăr′ĭ-ŏch brought in Daniel before the king in haste, and said thus unto him, I have found a man of the captives of Judah, that will make known unto the king the interpretation.

26 The king answered and said to Daniel, whose name *was* Bĕl′tē-shăz′zȧr, Art thou able to make known unto me the dream which I have seen, and the interpretation thereof?

27 Daniel answered in the presence of the king, and said, The secret which the king hath demanded cannot the wise *men*, the astrologers, the magicians, the soothsayers, show unto the king;

28 But there is a God in heaven that revealeth secrets, and maketh known to the king Nĕb′ū-chăd-nĕz′zȧr what

shall be in the latter days. Thy dream,
and the visions of thy head upon thy
bed, are these;
29 As for thee, O king, thy thoughts
came *into thy mind* upon thy bed, what
should come to pass hereafter: and he
that revealeth secrets maketh known
to thee what shall come to pass.
30 But as for me, this secret is not
revealed to me for *any* wisdom that I
have more than any living, but for *their*
sakes that shall make known the interpretation to the king, and that thou
mightest know the thoughts of thy
heart.
31 ¶ Thou, O king, sawest, and behold
a great image. This great image, whose
brightness *was* excellent, stood before
thee; and the form thereof *was* terrible.
32 This image's head *was* of fine gold,
his breast and his arms of silver, his
belly and his thighs of brass,
33 His legs of iron, his feet part of
iron and part of clay.
34 Thou sawest till that a stone was
cut out without hands, which smote the
image upon his feet *that were* of iron
and clay, and brake them to pieces.
35 Then was the iron, the clay, the
brass, the silver, and the gold, broken
to pieces together, and became like the
chaff of the summer threshingfloors;
and the wind carried them away, that
no place was found for them: and the
stone that smote the image became a
great mountain, and filled the whole
earth.
36 ¶ This *is* the dream; and we will
tell the interpretation thereof before the
king.
37 Thou, O king, *art* a king of kings:
for the God of heaven hath given thee a
kingdom, power, and strength, and glory.
38 And wheresoever the children of
men dwell, the beasts of the field and
the fowls of the heaven hath he given
into thine hand, and hath made thee
ruler over them all. Thou *art* this head
of gold.
39 And after thee shall arise another
kingdom inferior to thee, and another
third kingdom of brass, which shall
bear rule over all the earth.
40 And the fourth kingdom shall be
strong as iron: forasmuch as iron breaketh in pieces and subdueth all *things:*
and as iron that breaketh all these,
shall it break in pieces and bruise.
41 And whereas thou sawest the feet
and toes, part of potters' clay, and part
of iron, the kingdom shall be divided;
but there shall be in it of the strength
of the iron, forasmuch as thou sawest
the iron mixed with miry clay.
42 And *as* the toes of the feet *were*
part of iron, and part of clay, *so* the
kingdom shall be partly strong, and
partly broken.
43 And whereas thou sawest iron
mixed with miry clay, they shall mingle
themselves with the seed of men: but
they shall not cleave one to another,
even as iron is not mixed with clay.
44 And in the days of these kings shall
the God of heaven set up a kingdom,
which shall never be destroyed: and
the kingdom shall not be left to other
people, *but* it shall break in pieces and
consume all these kingdoms, and it
shall stand for ever.
45 Forasmuch as thou sawest that the
stone was cut out of the mountain without hands, and that it brake in pieces
the iron, the brass, the clay, the silver,
and the gold; the great God hath made
known to the king what shall come to
pass hereafter: and the dream *is* certain, and the interpretation thereof
sure.
46 ¶ Then the king Nĕb'ū-chăd-
nĕz'zȧr fell upon his face, and worshipped Daniel, and commanded that
they should offer an oblation and sweet
odors unto him.
47 The king answered unto Daniel,
and said, Of a truth *it is,* that your God
is a God of gods, and a Lord of kings,
and a revealer of secrets, seeing thou
couldest reveal this secret.
48 Then the king made Daniel a great
man, and gave him many great gifts,
and made him ruler over the whole
province of Babylon, and chief of the
governors over all the wise *men* of
Babylon.
49 Then Daniel requested of the king,
and he set Shā'drăch, Mē'shăch, and
Ȧ-bĕd'-nē-gō, over the affairs of the
province of Babylon: but Daniel *sat* in
the gate of the king.

CHAPTER 3

NĔB'Ū-CHĂD-NĔZ'ZȦR the king
made an image of gold, whose
height *was* threescore cubits, *and* the
breadth thereof six cubits: he set it up

in the plain of Dū′rȧ, in the province of
Babylon.
2 Then Nĕb′ū-chăd-nĕz′zȧr the king
sent to gather together the princes, the
governors, and the captains, the judges,
the treasurers, the counselors, the
sheriffs, and all the rulers of the provinces, to come to the dedication of the
image which Nĕb′ū-chăd-nĕz′zȧr the
king had set up.
3 Then the princes, the governors,
and captains, the judges, the treasurers,
the counselors, the sheriffs, and all the
rulers of the provinces, were gathered
together unto the dedication of the
image that Nĕb′ū-chăd-nĕz′zȧr the king
had set up; and they stood before the
image that Nĕb′ū-chăd-nĕz′zȧr had set
up.
4 Then a herald cried aloud, To you it
is commanded, O people, nations, and
languages,
5 *That* at what time ye hear the sound
of the cornet, flute, harp, sackbut,
psaltery, dulcimer, and all kinds of
music, ye fall down and worship the
golden image that Nĕb′ū-chăd-nĕz′zȧr
the king hath set up:
6 And whoso falleth not down and
worshippeth shall the same hour be
cast into the midst of a burning fiery
furnace.
7 Therefore at that time, when all the
people heard the sound of the cornet,
flute, harp, sackbut, psaltery, and all
kinds of music, all the people, the
nations, and the languages, fell down
and worshipped the golden image that
Nĕb′ū-chăd-nĕz′zȧr the king had set up.
8 ¶ Wherefore at that time certain
Chăl-dē′ăns came near, and accused
the Jews.
9 They spake and said to the king
Nĕb′ū-chăd-nĕz′zȧr, O king, live for
ever.
10 Thou, O king, hast made a decree,
that every man that shall hear the sound
of the cornet, flute, harp, sackbut,
psaltery, and dulcimer, and all kinds of
music, shall fall down and worship the
golden image:
11 And whoso falleth not down and
worshippeth, *that* he should be cast
into the midst of a burning fiery furnace.
12 There are certain Jews whom thou
hast set over the affairs of the province
of Babylon, Shā′drăch, Mē′shăch, and
Ȧ-bĕd′–nē-gō; these men, O king, have
not regarded thee: they serve not thy
gods, nor worship the golden image
which thou hast set up.
13 ¶ Then Nĕb′ū-chăd-nĕz′zȧr in *his*
rage and fury commanded to bring
Shā′drăch, Mē′shăch, and Ȧ-bĕd′–nē-
gō. Then they brought these men before the king.
14 Nĕb′ū-chăd-nĕz′zȧr spake and said
unto them, *Is it* true, O Shā′drăch,
Mē′shăch, and Ȧ-bĕd′–nē-gō? do not
ye serve my gods, nor worship the
golden image which I have set up?
15 Now if ye be ready that at what
time ye hear the sound of the cornet,
flute, harp, sackbut, psaltery, and dulcimer, and all kinds of music, ye fall
down and worship the image which I
have made; *well:* but if ye worship not,
ye shall be cast the same hour into the
midst of a burning fiery furnace; and
who *is* that God that shall deliver you
out of my hands?
16 Shā′drăch, Mē′shăch, and Ȧ-bĕd′–
nē-gō, answered and said to the king,
O Nĕb′ū-chăd-nĕz′zȧr, we *are* not careful to answer thee in this matter.
17 If it be *so,* our God whom we serve
is able to deliver us from the burning
fiery furnace, and he will deliver *us*
out of thine hand, O king.
18 But if not, be it known unto thee,
O king, that we will not serve thy gods,
nor worship the golden image which
thou hast set up.
19 ¶ Then was Nĕb′ū-chăd-nĕz′zȧr
full of fury, and the form of his visage
was changed against Shā′drăch, Mē′-
shăch, and Ȧ-bĕd′–nē-gō: *therefore* he
spake, and commanded that they should
heat the furnace one seven times more
than it was wont to be heated.
20 And he commanded the most
mighty men that *were* in his army to
bind Shā′drăch, Mē′shăch, and Ȧ-bĕd′–
nē-gō, *and* to cast *them* into the burning
fiery furnace.
21 Then these men were bound in
their coats, their hose, and their hats,
and their *other* garments, and were
cast into the midst of the burning fiery
furnace.
22 Therefore because the king's commandment was urgent, and the furnace
exceeding hot, the flame of the fire
slew those men that took up Shā′drăch,
Mē′shăch, and Ȧ-bĕd′–nē-gō.
23 And these three men, Shā′drăch,

Mē′shăꞓh, and Ȧ-bĕd′–nē-gō, fell down
bound into the midst of the burning
fiery furnace.
24 Then Nĕb′ū-ꞓhăd-nĕz′zȧr the king
was astonished, and rose up in haste,
and spake, and said unto his counselors, Did not we cast three men bound
into the midst of the fire? They answered and said unto the king, True,
O king.
25 He answered and said, Lo, I see
four men loose, walking in the midst of
the fire, and they have no hurt; and the
form of the fourth is like the Son of
God.
26 ¶ Then Nĕb′ū-ꞓhăd-nĕz′zȧr came
near to the mouth of the burning fiery
furnace, *and* spake, and said, Shā′drăꞓh,
Mē′shăꞓh, and Ȧ-bĕd′–nē-gō, ye servants of the most high God, come forth,
and come *hither*. Then Shā′drăꞓh,
Mē′shăꞓh, and Ȧ-bĕd′–nē-gō, came
forth of the midst of the fire.
27 And the princes, governors, and
captains, and the king's counselors,
being gathered together, saw these men,
upon whose bodies the fire had no
power, nor was a hair of their head
singed, neither were their coats changed,
nor the smell of fire had passed on
them.
28 *Then* Nĕb′ū-ꞓhăd-nĕz′zȧr spake,
and said, Blessed *be* the God of Shā′-
drăꞓh, Mē′shăꞓh, and Ȧ-bĕd′–nē-gō, who
hath sent his angel, and delivered his
servants that trusted in him, and have
changed the king's word, and yielded
their bodies, that they might not serve
nor worship any god, except their own
God.
29 Therefore I make a decree, That
every people, nation, and language,
which speak any thing amiss against
the God of Shā′drăꞓh, Mē′shăꞓh, and
Ȧ-bĕd′–nē-gō, shall be cut in pieces,
and their houses shall be made a dunghill; because there is no other God that
can deliver after this sort.
30 Then the king promoted Shā′drăꞓh,
Mē′shăꞓh, and Ȧ-bĕd′–nē-gō, in the
province of Babylon.

CHAPTER 4

NĔB′Ū-ꞒHĂD-NĔZ′ZȦR the king,
unto all people, nations, and
languages, that dwell in all the earth;
Peace be multiplied unto you.
2 I thought it good to show the signs
and wonders that the high God hath
wrought toward me.
3 How great *are* his signs! and how
mighty *are* his wonders! his kingdom *is*
an everlasting kingdom, and his dominion *is* from generation to generation.
4 ¶ I Nĕb′ū-ꞓhăd-nĕz′zȧr was at rest
in mine house, and flourishing in my
palace:
5 I saw a dream which made me
afraid, and the thoughts upon my bed
and the visions of my head troubled me.
6 Therefore made I a decree to bring
in all the wise *men* of Babylon before
me, that they might make known unto
me the interpretation of the dream.
7 Then came in the magicians, the
astrologers, the Ꞓhăl-dē′ăns̤, and the
soothsayers: and I told the dream
before them; but they did not make
known unto me the interpretation
thereof.
8 ¶ But at the last Daniel came in before
me, whose name *was* Bĕl′tē-shăz′zȧr,
according to the name of my god, and
in whom *is* the spirit of the holy
gods: and before him I told the dream,
saying,
9 O Bĕl′tē-shăz′zȧr, master of the
magicians, because I know that the
spirit of the holy gods *is* in thee, and
no secret troubleth thee, tell me the
visions of my dream that I have seen,
and the interpretation thereof.
10 Thus *were* the visions of mine head
in my bed; I saw, and behold a tree in
the midst of the earth, and the height
thereof *was* great.
11 The tree grew, and was strong, and
the height thereof reached unto heaven,
and the sight thereof to the end of all
the earth:
12 The leaves thereof *were* fair, and
the fruit thereof much, and in it *was*
meat for all: the beasts of the field had
shadow under it, and the fowls of the
heaven dwelt in the boughs thereof,
and all flesh was fed of it.
13 I saw in the visions of my head
upon my bed, and, behold, a watcher
and a holy one came down from heaven;
14 He cried aloud, and said thus, Hew
down the tree, and cut off his branches,
shake off his leaves, and scatter his
fruit: let the beasts get away from under
it, and the fowls from his branches:
15 Nevertheless, leave the stump of
his roots in the earth, even with a band

of iron and brass, in the tender grass
of the field; and let it be wet with the
dew of heaven, and *let* his portion *be*
with the beasts in the grass of the earth:
16 Let his heart be changed from
man's, and let a beast's heart be given
unto him; and let seven times pass over
him.
17 This matter *is* by the decree of the
watchers, and the demand by the word
of the holy ones: to the intent that the
living may know that the Most High
ruleth in the kingdom of men, and giveth it to whomsoever he will, and setteth
up over it the basest of men.
18 This dream I king Něb'ū-chăd-
něz'zār have seen. Now thou, O Běl'tē-
shăz'zār, declare the interpretation
thereof, forasmuch as all the wise *men*
of my kingdom are not able to make
known unto me the interpretation: but
thou *art* able; for the spirit of the holy
gods *is* in thee.
19 ¶ Then Daniel, whose name *was*
Běl'tē-shăz'zār, was astonished for one
hour, and his thoughts troubled him.
The king spake, and said, Běl'tē-shăz'-
zār, let not the dream, or the interpretation thereof, trouble thee. Běl'tē-
shăz'zār answered and said, My lord,
the dream *be* to them that hate thee,
and the interpretation thereof to thine
enemies.
20 The tree that thou sawest, which
grew, and was strong, whose height
reached unto the heaven, and the sight
thereof to all the earth;
21 Whose leaves *were* fair, and the
fruit thereof much, and in it *was* meat
for all; under which the beasts of the
field dwelt, and upon whose branches
the fowls of the heaven had their habitation:
22 It *is* thou, O king, that art grown and
become strong: for thy greatness is
grown, and reacheth unto heaven, and
thy dominion to the end of the earth.
23 And whereas the king saw a watcher
and a holy one coming down from heav-
en, and saying, Hew the tree down, and
destroy it; yet leave the stump of the
roots thereof in the earth, even with a
band of iron and brass, in the tender
grass of the field; and let it be wet with
the dew of heaven, and *let* his portion *be*
with the beasts of the field, till seven
times pass over him;
24 This *is* the interpretation, O king,
and this *is* the decree of the Most High,
which is come upon my lord the king:
25 That they shall drive thee from men,
and thy dwelling shall be with the beasts
of the field, and they shall make thee to
eat grass as oxen, and they shall wet
thee with the dew of heaven, and seven
times shall pass over thee, till thou know
that the Most High ruleth in the kingdom of men, and giveth it to whomsoever he will.
26 And whereas they commanded to
leave the stump of the tree roots; thy
kingdom shall be sure unto thee, after
that thou shalt have known that the
heavens do rule.
27 Wherefore, O king, let my counsel
be acceptable unto thee, and break off
thy sins by righteousness, and thine
iniquities by showing mercy to the poor;
if it may be a lengthening of thy tran-
quillity.
28 ¶ All this came upon the king
Něb'ū-chăd-něz'zār.
29 At the end of twelve months he
walked in the palace of the kingdom of
Babylon.
30 The king spake, and said, Is not this
great Babylon, that I have built for the
house of the kingdom by the might of
my power, and for the honor of my
majesty?
31 While the word *was* in the king's
mouth, there fell a voice from heaven,
saying, O king Něb'ū-chăd-něz'zār, to
thee it is spoken; The kingdom is departed from thee.
32 And they shall drive thee from men,
and thy dwelling *shall be* with the beasts
of the field: they shall make thee to eat
grass as oxen, and seven times shall
pass over thee, until thou know that the
Most High ruleth in the kingdom of
men, and giveth it to whomsoever he
will.
33 The same hour was the thing fulfilled upon Něb'ū-chăd-něz'zār: and he
was driven from men, and did eat grass
as oxen, and his body was wet with the
dew of heaven, till his hairs were grown
like eagles' *feathers*, and his nails like
birds' *claws*.
34 And at the end of the days I Něb'ū-
chăd-něz'zār lifted up mine eyes unto
heaven, and mine understanding returned unto me, and I blessed the Most
High, and I praised and honored him
that liveth for ever, whose dominion *is*

an everlasting dominion, and his kingdom *is* from generation to generation:

35 And all the inhabitants of the earth *are* reputed as nothing: and he doeth according to his will in the army of heaven, and *among* the inhabitants of the earth: and none can stay his hand, or say unto him, What doest thou?

36 At the same time my reason returned unto me; and for the glory of my kingdom, mine honor and brightness returned unto me; and my counselors and my lords sought unto me; and I was established in my kingdom, and excellent majesty was added unto me.

37 Now I Nĕb′ ū-ehăd-nĕz′zȧr praise and extol and honor the King of heaven, all whose works *are* truth, and his ways judgment: and those that walk in pride he is able to abase.

CHAPTER 5

BĔL-SHĂZ′ZȦR the king made a great feast to a thousand of his lords, and drank wine before the thousand.

2 Bĕl-shăz′zȧr, while he tasted the wine, commanded to bring the golden and silver vessels which his father Nĕb′ ū-ehăd-nĕz′zȧr had taken out of the temple which *was* in Jerusalem; that the king and his princes, his wives and his concubines, might drink therein.

3 Then they brought the golden vessels that were taken out of the temple of the house of God which *was* at Jerusalem; and the king and his princes, his wives and his concubines, drank in them.

4 They drank wine, and praised the gods of gold, and of silver, of brass, of iron, of wood, and of stone.

5 ℂ In the same hour came forth fingers of a man's hand, and wrote over against the candlestick upon the plaster of the wall of the king's palace: and the king saw the part of the hand that wrote.

6 Then the king's countenance was changed, and his thoughts troubled him, so that the joints of his loins were loosed, and his knees smote one against another.

7 The king cried aloud to bring in the astrologers, the Ehăl-dē′ăns, and the soothsayers. *And* the king spake, and said to the wise *men* of Babylon, Whosoever shall read this writing, and show me the interpretation thereof, shall be clothed with scarlet, and *have* a chain of gold about his neck, and shall be the third ruler in the kingdom.

8 Then came in all the king's wise *men:* but they could not read the writing, nor make known to the king the interpretation thereof.

9 Then was king Bĕl-shăz′zȧr greatly troubled, and his countenance was changed in him, and his lords were astonished.

10 ℂ *Now* the queen, by reason of the words of the king and his lords, came into the banquet house: *and* the queen spake and said, O king, live for ever: let not thy thoughts trouble thee, nor let thy countenance be changed:

11 There is a man in thy kingdom, in whom *is* the spirit of the holy gods; and in the days of thy father light and understanding and wisdom, like the wisdom of the gods, was found in him; whom the king Nĕb′ ū-ehăd-nĕz′zȧr thy father, the king, *I say*, thy father, made master of the magicians, astrologers, Ehăl-dē′ăns, *and* soothsayers;

12 Forasmuch as an excellent spirit, and knowledge, and understanding, interpreting of dreams, and showing of hard sentences, and dissolving of doubts, were found in the same Daniel, whom the king named Bĕl′tē-shăz′zȧr: now let Daniel be called, and he will show the interpretation.

13 Then was Daniel brought in before the king. *And* the king spake and said unto Daniel, *Art* thou that Daniel, which *art* of the children of the captivity of Judah, whom the king my father brought out of Jewry?

14 I have even heard of thee, that the spirit of the gods *is* in thee, and *that* light and understanding and excellent wisdom is found in thee.

15 And now the wise *men*, the astrologers, have been brought in before me, that they should read this writing, and make known unto me the interpretation thereof: but they could not show the interpretation of the thing:

16 And I have heard of thee, that thou canst make interpretations, and dissolve doubts: now if thou canst read the writing, and make known to me the interpretation thereof, thou shalt be clothed with scarlet, and *have* a chain of gold about thy neck, and shalt be the third ruler in the kingdom.

17 ¶ Then Daniel answered and said before the king, Let thy gifts be to thyself, and give thy rewards to another; yet I will read the writing unto the king and make known to him the interpretation.

18 O thou king, the most high God gave Nĕb′ū-chăd-nĕz′zȧr thy father a kingdom, and majesty, and glory, and honor:

19 And for the majesty that he gave him, all people, nations, and languages, trembled and feared before him: whom he would he slew; and whom he would he kept alive; and whom he would he set up; and whom he would he put down.

20 But when his heart was lifted up, and his mind hardened in pride, he was deposed from his kingly throne, and they took his glory from him:

21 And he was driven from the sons of men; and his heart was made like the beasts, and his dwelling *was* with the wild asses: they fed him with grass like oxen, and his body was wet with the dew of heaven; till he knew that the most high God ruled in the kingdom of men, and *that* he appointeth over it whomsoever he will.

22 And thou his son, O Bĕl-shăz′zȧr, hast not humbled thine heart, though thou knewest all this;

23 But hast lifted up thyself against the Lord of heaven; and they have brought the vessels of his house before thee, and thou and thy lords, thy wives and thy concubines, have drunk wine in them; and thou hast praised the gods of silver, and gold, of brass, iron, wood, and stone, which see not, nor hear, nor know: and the God in whose hand thy breath *is,* and whose *are* all thy ways, hast thou not glorified:

24 Then was the part of the hand sent from him; and this writing was written.

25 ¶ And this *is* the writing that was written, MĔ′NE, MĔ′NE, TĔ′KĔL, U-PHÄR′SĬN.

26 This *is* the interpretation of the thing: MĔ′NE; God hath numbered thy kingdom, and finished it.

27 TĔ′KĔL; Thou art weighed in the balances, and art found wanting.

28 PĒ′RĒS; Thy kingdom is divided, and given to the Mēdes and Persians.

29 Then commanded Bĕl-shăz′zȧr, and they clothed Daniel with scarlet, and *put* a chain of gold about his neck, and made a proclamation concerning him, that he should be the third ruler in the kingdom.

30 ¶ In that night was Bĕl-shăz′zȧr the king of the Chăl-dē′ăns slain.

31 And Dȧ-rī′ŭs the Mē′dĭ-ăn took the kingdom, *being* about threescore and two years old.

CHAPTER 6

IT pleased Dȧ-rī′ŭs to set over the kingdom a hundred and twenty princes, which should be over the whole kingdom;

2 And over these three presidents; of whom Daniel *was* first: that the princes might give accounts unto them, and the king should have no damage.

3 Then this Daniel was preferred above the presidents and princes, because an excellent spirit *was* in him; and the king thought to set him over the whole realm.

4 ¶ Then the presidents and princes sought to find occasion against Daniel concerning the kingdom; but they could find none occasion nor fault; forasmuch as he *was* faithful, neither was there any error or fault found in him.

5 Then said these men, We shall not find any occasion against this Daniel, except we find *it* against him concerning the law of his God.

6 Then these presidents and princes assembled together to the king, and said thus unto him, King Dȧ-rī′ŭs, live for ever.

7 All the presidents of the kingdom, the governors, and the princes, the counselors, and the captains, have consulted together to establish a royal statute, and to make a firm decree, that whosoever shall ask a petition of any God or man for thirty days, save of thee, O king, he shall be cast into the den of lions.

8 Now, O king, establish the decree, and sign the writing, that it be not changed, according to the law of the Mēdes and Persians, which altereth not.

9 Wherefore king Dȧ-rī′ŭs signed the writing and the decree.

10 ¶ Now when Daniel knew that the writing was signed, he went into his house; and, his windows being open in his chamber toward Jerusalem, he kneeled upon his knees three times a day, and prayed, and gave thanks before his God, as he did aforetime.

11 Then these men assembled, and

found Daniel praying and making supplication before his God.
12 Then they came near, and spake
before the king concerning the king's
decree; Hast thou not signed a decree,
that every man that shall ask *a petition*
of any God or man within thirty days,
save of thee, O king, shall be cast into
the den of lions? The king answered
and said, The thing *is* true, according to
the law of the Mēdes̱ and Persians,
which altereth not.
13 Then answered they and said before the king, That Daniel, which *is* of
the children of the captivity of Judah,
regardeth not thee, O king, nor the decree that thou hast signed, but maketh
his petition three times a day.
14 Then the king, when he heard *these*
words, was sore displeased with himself, and set *his* heart on Daniel to deliver him: and he labored till the going
down of the sun to deliver him.
15 Then these men assembled unto
the king, and said unto the king, Know,
O king, that the law of the Mēdes̱ and
Persians *is,* That no decree nor statute
which the king establisheth may be
changed.
16 Then the king commanded, and
they brought Daniel, and cast *him* into
the den of lions. *Now* the king spake
and said unto Daniel, Thy God whom
thou servest continually, he will deliver
thee.
17 And a stone was brought, and laid
upon the mouth of the den; and the
king sealed it with his own signet, and
with the signet of his lords; that the purpose might not be changed concerning
Daniel.
18 ¶ Then the king went to his palace,
and passed the night fasting: neither
were instruments of music brought before him: and his sleep went from him.
19 Then the king arose very early in
the morning, and went in haste unto the
den of lions.
20 And when he came to the den, he
cried with a lamentable voice unto
Daniel: *and* the king spake and said to
Daniel, O Daniel, servant of the living
God, is thy God, whom thou servest
continually, able to deliver thee from
the lions?
21 Then said Daniel unto the king,
O king, live for ever.
22 My God hath sent his angel, and
hath shut the lions' mouths, that they
have not hurt me: forasmuch as before
him innocency was found in me; and
also before thee, O king, have I done
no hurt.
23 Then was the king exceeding glad
for him, and commanded that they
should take Daniel up out of the den.
So Daniel was taken up out of the den,
and no manner of hurt was found upon
him, because he believed in his God.
24 ¶ And the king commanded, and
they brought those men which had accused Daniel, and they cast *them* into
the den of lions, them, their children,
and their wives; and the lions had the
mastery of them, and brake all their
bones in pieces or ever they came at the
bottom of the den.
25 ¶ Then king Dȧ-rī′ŭs wrote unto
all people, nations, and languages, that
dwell in all the earth; Peace be multiplied unto you.
26 I make a decree, That in every
dominion of my kingdom men tremble
and fear before the God of Daniel: for
he *is* the living God, and steadfast for
ever, and his kingdom *that* which shall
not be destroyed, and his dominion *shall*
be even unto the end.
27 He delivereth and rescueth, and he
worketh signs and wonders in heaven
and in earth, who hath delivered Daniel
from the power of the lions.
28 So this Daniel prospered in the
reign of Dȧ-rī′ŭs, and in the reign of
Cyrus the Persian.

CHAPTER 7

IN the first year of Bĕl-shăz′zär king
of Babylon, Daniel had a dream and
visions of his head upon his bed: then
he wrote the dream, *and* told the sum of
the matters.
2 Daniel spake and said, I saw in my
vision by night, and, behold, the four
winds of the heaven strove upon the
great sea.
3 And four great beasts came up from
the sea, diverse one from another.
4 The first *was* like a lion, and had
eagle's wings: I beheld till the wings
thereof were plucked, and it was lifted
up from the earth, and made stand upon
the feet as a man, and a man's heart was
given to it.
5 And behold another beast, a second,
like to a bear, and it raised up itself on

one side, and *it had* three ribs in the
mouth of it between the teeth of it: and
they said thus unto it, Arise, devour
much flesh.
6 After this I beheld, and lo another,
like a leopard, which had upon the back
of it four wings of a fowl; the beast had
also four heads; and dominion was given
to it.
7 After this I saw in the night visions,
and behold a fourth beast, dreadful and
terrible, and strong exceedingly; and it
had great iron teeth: it devoured and
brake in pieces, and stamped the residue with the feet of it: and it *was* diverse
from all the beasts that *were* before it;
and it had ten horns.
8 I considered the horns, and, behold,
there came up among them another
little horn, before whom there were
three of the first horns plucked up by the
roots: and, behold, in this horn *were*
eyes like the eyes of man, and a mouth
speaking great things.
9 ¶ I beheld till the thrones were cast
down, and the Ancient of days did sit,
whose garment *was* white as snow, and
the hair of his head like the pure wool:
his throne *was like* the fiery flame, *and*
his wheels *as* burning fire.
10 A fiery stream issued and came forth
from before him: thousand thousands
ministered unto him, and ten thousand
times ten thousand stood before him:
the judgment was set, and the books
were opened.
11 I beheld then, because of the voice
of the great words which the horn
spake: I beheld *even* till the beast was
slain, and his body destroyed, and given
to the burning flame.
12 As concerning the rest of the beasts,
they had their dominion taken away:
yet their lives were prolonged for a season and time.
13 I saw in the night visions, and, behold, *one* like the Son of man came with
the clouds of heaven, and came to the
Ancient of days, and they brought him
near before him.
14 And there was given him dominion,
and glory, and a kingdom, that all people, nations, and languages, should
serve him: his dominion *is* an everlasting
dominion, which shall not pass away,
and his kingdom *that* which shall not be
destroyed.
15 ¶ I Daniel was grieved in my spirit
in the midst of *my* body, and the visions
of my head troubled me.
16 I came near unto one of them that
stood by, and asked him the truth of all
this. So he told me, and made me know
the interpretation of the things.
17 These great beasts, which are four,
are four kings, *which* shall arise out of
the earth.
18 But the saints of the Most High
shall take the kingdom, and possess the
kingdom for ever, even for ever and
ever.
19 Then I would know the truth of the
fourth beast, which was diverse from all
the others, exceeding dreadful, whose
teeth *were of* iron, and his nails *of*
brass; *which* devoured, brake in pieces,
and stamped the residue with his feet;
20 And of the ten horns that *were* in
his head, and *of* the other which came
up, and before whom three fell; even *of*
that horn that had eyes, and a mouth
that spake very great things, whose look
was more stout than his fellows.
21 I beheld, and the same horn made
war with the saints, and prevailed
against them;
22 Until the Ancient of days came, and
judgment was given to the saints of the
Most High; and the time came that the
saints possessed the kingdom.
23 Thus he said, The fourth beast shall
be the fourth kingdom upon earth,
which shall be diverse from all kingdoms, and shall devour the whole earth,
and shall tread it down, and break it in
pieces.
24 And the ten horns out of this kingdom *are* ten kings *that* shall arise: and
another shall rise after them; and he
shall be diverse from the first, and he
shall subdue three kings.
25 And he shall speak *great* words
against the Most High, and shall wear
out the saints of the Most High, and
think to change times and laws: and
they shall be given into his hand until
a time and times and the dividing of
time.
26 But the judgment shall sit, and they
shall take away his dominion, to consume and to destroy *it* unto the end.
27 And the kingdom and dominion, and
the greatness of the kingdom under the
whole heaven, shall be given to the
people of the saints of the Most High,
whose kingdom *is* an everlasting king-

dom, and all dominions shall serve and obey him.

28 Hitherto *is* the end of the matter. As for me Daniel, my cogitations much troubled me, and my countenance changed in me: but I kept the matter in my heart.

CHAPTER 8

IN the third year of the reign of king Bĕl-shăz′zȧr a vision appeared unto me, *even unto* me Daniel, after that which appeared unto me at the first.

2 And I saw in a vision; and it came to pass, when I saw, that I *was* at Shu̥′shăn *in* the palace, which *is* in the province of Ē′lăm; and I saw in a vision, and I was by the river of Ū′laī.

3 Then I lifted up mine eyes, and saw, and, behold, there stood before the river a ram which had *two* horns: and the *two* horns *were* high; but one *was* higher than the other, and the higher came up last.

4 I saw the ram pushing westward, and northward, and southward; so that no beasts might stand before him, neither *was there any* that could deliver out of his hand; but he did according to his will, and became great.

5 And as I was considering, behold, a he goat came from the west on the face of the whole earth, and touched not the ground: and the goat *had* a notable horn between his eyes.

6 And he came to the ram that had *two* horns, which I had seen standing before the river, and ran unto him in the fury of his power.

7 And I saw him come close unto the ram, and he was moved with choler against him, and smote the ram, and brake his two horns: and there was no power in the ram to stand before him, but he cast him down to the ground, and stamped upon him: and there was none that could deliver the ram out of his hand.

8 Therefore the he goat waxed very great: and when he was strong, the great horn was broken; and for it came up four notable ones toward the four winds of heaven.

9 And out of one of them came forth a little horn, which waxed exceeding great, toward the south, and toward the east, and toward the pleasant *land*.

10 And it waxed great, *even* to the host of heaven; and it cast down *some* of the host and of the stars to the ground, and stamped upon them.

11 Yea, he magnified *himself* even to the prince of the host, and by him the daily *sacrifice* was taken away, and the place of his sanctuary was cast down.

12 And a host was given *him* against the daily *sacrifice* by reason of transgression, and it cast down the truth to the ground; and it practised, and prospered.

13 ¶ Then I heard one saint speaking, and another saint said unto that certain *saint* which spake, How long *shall be* the vision *concerning* the daily *sacrifice*, and the transgression of desolation, to give both the sanctuary and the host to be trodden under foot?

14 And he said unto me, Unto two thousand and three hundred days; then shall the sanctuary be cleansed.

15 ¶ And it came to pass, when I, *even* I Daniel, had seen the vision, and sought for the meaning, then, behold, there stood before me as the appearance of a man.

16 And I heard a man's voice between *the banks of* Ū′laī, which called, and said, Gā′brĭ-ĕl, make this *man* to understand the vision.

17 So he came near where I stood: and when he came, I was afraid, and fell upon my face: but he said unto me, Understand, O son of man: for at the time of the end *shall be* the vision.

18 Now as he was speaking with me, I was in a deep sleep on my face toward the ground: but he touched me, and set me upright.

19 And he said, Behold, I will make thee know what shall be in the last end of the indignation: for at the time appointed the end *shall be*.

20 The ram which thou sawest having *two* horns *are* the kings of Mē′dĭ-ȧ and Persia.

21 And the rough goat *is* the king of Grē′çĭ-ȧ: and the great horn that *is* between his eyes *is* the first king.

22 Now that being broken, whereas four stood up for it, four kingdoms shall stand up out of the nation, but not in his power.

23 And in the latter time of their kingdom, when the transgressors are come to the full, a king of fierce countenance, and understanding dark sentences, shall stand up.

24 And his power shall be mighty, but not by his own power: and he shall destroy wonderfully, and shall prosper, and practise, and shall destroy the mighty and the holy people.

25 And through his policy also he shall cause craft to prosper in his hand; and he shall magnify *himself* in his heart, and by peace shall destroy many: he shall also stand up against the Prince of princes; but he shall be broken without hand.

26 And the vision of the evening and the morning which was told *is* true: wherefore shut thou up the vision; for it *shall be* for many days.

27 And I Daniel fainted, and was sick *certain* days; afterward I rose up, and did the king's business; and I was astonished at the vision, but none understood *it*.

CHAPTER 9

IN the first year of Dȧ-rī'ŭs the son of Ȧ-hăs̱'ū-ē'rŭs, of the seed of the Mēdeṣ, which was made king over the realm of the Chăl-dē'ănṣ;

2 In the first year of his reign, I Daniel understood by books the number of the years, whereof the word of the LORD came to Jeremiah the prophet, that he would accomplish seventy years in the desolations of Jerusalem.

3 ¶ And I set my face unto the Lord God, to seek by prayer and supplications, with fasting, and sackcloth, and ashes:

4 And I prayed unto the LORD my God, and made my confession, and said, O Lord, the great and dreadful God, keeping the covenant and mercy to them that love him, and to them that keep his commandments;

5 We have sinned, and have committed iniquity, and have done wickedly, and have rebelled, even by departing from thy precepts and from thy judgments:

6 Neither have we hearkened unto thy servants the prophets, which spake in thy name to our kings, our princes, and our fathers, and to all the people of the land.

7 O Lord, righteousness *belongeth* unto thee, but unto us confusion of faces, as at this day; to the men of Judah, and to the inhabitants of Jerusalem, and unto all Ĭṣ'rā-ĕl, *that are* near, and *that are* far off, through all the countries whither thou hast driven them, because of their trespass that they have trespassed against thee.

8 O Lord, to us *belongeth* confusion of face, to our kings, to our princes, and to our fathers, because we have sinned against thee.

9 To the Lord our God *belong* mercies and forgivenesses, though we have rebelled against him;

10 Neither have we obeyed the voice of the LORD our God, to walk in his laws, which he set before us by his servants the prophets.

11 Yea, all Ĭṣ'rā-ĕl have transgressed thy law, even by departing, that they might not obey thy voice; therefore the curse is poured upon us, and the oath that *is* written in the law of Moses the servant of God, because we have sinned against him.

12 And he hath confirmed his words, which he spake against us, and against our judges that judged us, by bringing upon us a great evil: for under the whole heaven hath not been done as hath been done upon Jerusalem.

13 As *it is* written in the law of Moses, all this evil is come upon us: yet made we not our prayer before the LORD our God, that we might turn from our iniquities, and understand thy truth.

14 Therefore hath the LORD watched upon the evil, and brought it upon us: for the LORD our God *is* righteous in all his works which he doeth: for we obeyed not his voice.

15 And now, O Lord our God, that hast brought thy people forth out of the land of Egypt with a mighty hand, and hast gotten thee renown, as at this day; we have sinned, we have done wickedly.

16 ¶ O Lord, according to all thy righteousness, I beseech thee, let thine anger and thy fury be turned away from thy city Jerusalem, thy holy mountain: because for our sins, and for the iniquities of our fathers, Jerusalem and thy people *are become* a reproach to all *that are* about us.

17 Now therefore, O our God, hear the prayer of thy servant, and his supplications, and cause thy face to shine upon thy sanctuary that is desolate, for the Lord's sake.

18 O my God, incline thine ear, and hear; open thine eyes, and behold our desolations, and the city which is called

by thy name: for we do not present our
supplications before thee for our righteousnesses, but for thy great mercies.
19 O Lord, hear; O Lord, forgive; O
Lord, hearken and do; defer not, for
thine own sake, O my God: for thy
city and thy people are called by thy
name.
20 ¶ And while I was speaking, and
praying, and confessing my sin and the
sin of my people Ĭṣ′rā-ĕl, and presenting
my supplication before the LORD my
God for the holy mountain of my God;
21 Yea, while I *was* speaking in prayer,
even the man Gā′brĭ-ĕl, whom I had
seen in the vision at the beginning, being caused to fly swiftly, touched me
about the time of the evening oblation.
22 And he informed *me,* and talked
with me, and said, O Daniel, I am now
come forth to give thee skill and understanding.
23 At the beginning of thy supplications
the commandment came forth, and I am
come to show *thee;* for thou *art* greatly
beloved: therefore understand the matter, and consider the vision.
24 Seventy weeks are determined upon
thy people and upon thy holy city, to
finish the transgression, and to make an
end of sins, and to make reconciliation
for iniquity, and to bring in everlasting
righteousness, and to seal up the vision
and prophecy, and to anoint the Most
Holy.
25 Know therefore and understand,
that from the going forth of the commandment to restore and to build Jerusalem, unto the Mĕs-sī′áh the Prince,
shall be seven weeks, and threescore
and two weeks: the street shall be built
again, and the wall, even in troublous
times.
26 And after threescore and two weeks
shall Mĕs-sī′áh be cut off, but not for
himself: and the people of the prince
that shall come shall destroy the city and
the sanctuary; and the end thereof *shall
be* with a flood, and unto the end of the
war desolations are determined.
27 And he shall confirm the covenant
with many for one week: and in the
midst of the week he shall cause the
sacrifice and the oblation to cease, and
for the overspreading of abominations
he shall make *it* desolate, even until the
consummation, and that determined
shall be poured upon the desolate.

CHAPTER 10

IN the third year of Cyrus king of
Persia a thing was revealed unto
Daniel, whose name was called Bĕl′tē-
shăz′zár; and the thing *was* true, but the
time appointed *was* long: and he understood the thing, and had understanding
of the vision.
2 In those days I Daniel was mourning
three full weeks.
3 I ate no pleasant bread, neither came
flesh nor wine in my mouth, neither did
I anoint myself at all, till three whole
weeks were fulfilled.
4 And in the four and twentieth day of
the first month, as I was by the side of
the great river, which *is* Hĭd′dē-kĕl;
5 Then I lifted up mine eyes, and
looked, and behold a certain man
clothed in linen, whose loins *were* girded
with fine gold of Ū′phăz:
6 His body also *was* like the beryl, and
his face as the appearance of lightning,
and his eyes as lamps of fire, and his
arms and his feet like in color to polished brass, and the voice of his words
like the voice of a multitude.
7 And I Daniel alone saw the vision:
for the men that were with me saw not
the vision; but a great quaking fell upon
them, so that they fled to hide themselves.
8 Therefore I was left alone, and saw
this great vision, and there remained no
strength in me: for my comeliness was
turned in me into corruption, and I
retained no strength.
9 Yet heard I the voice of his words:
and when I heard the voice of his words,
then was I in a deep sleep on my face,
and my face toward the ground.
10 ¶ And, behold, a hand touched me,
which set me upon my knees and *upon*
the palms of my hands.
11 And he said unto me, O Daniel, a
man greatly beloved, understand the
words that I speak unto thee, and stand
upright: for unto thee am I now sent.
And when he had spoken this word unto
me, I stood trembling.
12 Then said he unto me, Fear not, Daniel: for from the first day that thou didst
set thine heart to understand, and to
chasten thyself before thy God, thy words
were heard, and I am come for thy words.
13 But the prince of the kingdom of
Persia withstood me one and twenty

days: but, lo, Mī′chā-ĕl, one of the chief
princes, came to help me; and I remained there with the kings of Persia.
14 Now I am come to make thee understand what shall befall thy people in the
latter days: for yet the vision *is* for *many*
days.
15 And when he had spoken such
words unto me, I set my face toward the
ground, and I became dumb.
16 And, behold, *one* like the similitude
of the sons of men touched my lips:
then I opened my mouth, and spake,
and said unto him that stood before me,
O my lord, by the vision my sorrows are
turned upon me, and I have retained no
strength.
17 For how can the servant of this my
lord talk with this my lord? for as for
me, straightway there remained no
strength in me, neither is there breath
left in me.
18 Then there came again and touched
me *one* like the appearance of a man,
and he strengthened me,
19 And said, O man greatly beloved,
fear not: peace *be* unto thee; be strong,
yea, be strong. And when he had
spoken unto me, I was strengthened,
and said, Let my lord speak; for thou
hast strengthened me.
20 Then said he, Knowest thou wherefore I come unto thee? and now will I
return to fight with the prince of Persia:
and when I am gone forth, lo, the prince
of Grē′çi-ȧ shall come.
21 But I will show thee that which is
noted in the Scripture of truth: and *there
is* none that holdeth with me in these
things, but Mī′chā-ĕl your prince.

CHAPTER 11

ALSO I in the first year of Dȧ-rī′ŭs the
Mede, *even* I, stood to confirm and
to strengthen him.
2 And now will I show thee the truth.
Behold, there shall stand up yet three
kings in Persia; and the fourth shall be
far richer than *they* all: and by his
strength through his riches he shall stir
up all against the realm of Grē′çi-ȧ.
3 And a mighty king shall stand up,
that shall rule with great dominion, and
do according to his will.
4 And when he shall stand up, his kingdom shall be broken, and shall be divided toward the four winds of heaven;
and not to his posterity, nor according to
his dominion which he ruled: for his
kingdom shall be plucked up, even for
others besides those.
5 ¶ And the king of the south shall be
strong, and *one* of his princes; and he
shall be strong above him, and have
dominion; his dominion *shall be* a great
dominion.
6 And in the end of years they shall
join themselves together; for the king's
daughter of the south shall come to the
king of the north to make an agreement:
but she shall not retain the power of the
arm; neither shall he stand, nor his arm:
but she shall be given up, and they that
brought her, and he that begat her, and
he that strengthened her in *these* times.
7 But out of a branch of her roots shall
one stand up in his estate, which shall
come with an army, and shall enter
into the fortress of the king of the north,
and shall deal against them, and shall
prevail:
8 And shall also carry captives into
Egypt their gods, with their princes, *and*
with their precious vessels of silver and
of gold; and he shall continue *more*
years than the king of the north.
9 So the king of the south shall come
into *his* kingdom, and shall return into
his own land.
10 But his sons shall be stirred up, and
shall assemble a multitude of great
forces: and *one* shall certainly come, and
overflow, and pass through: then shall
he return, and be stirred up, *even* to his
fortress.
11 And the king of the south shall be
moved with choler, and shall come forth
and fight with him, *even* with the king of
the north: and he shall set forth a great
multitude; but the multitude shall be
given into his hand.
12 *And* when he hath taken away the
multitude, his heart shall be lifted up;
and he shall cast down *many* ten thousands: but he shall not be strengthened
by it.
13 For the king of the north shall return, and shall set forth a multitude
greater than the former, and shall certainly come after certain years with a
great army and with much riches.
14 And in those times there shall many
stand up against the king of the south:
also the robbers of thy people shall exalt
themselves to establish the vision; but
they shall fall.

15 So the king of the north shall come,
and cast up a mount, and take the
most fenced cities: and the arms of the
south shall not withstand, neither his
chosen people, neither *shall there be*
any strength to withstand.
16 But he that cometh against him
shall do according to his own will, and
none shall stand before him: and he
shall stand in the glorious land, which by
his hand shall be consumed.
17 He shall also set his face to enter
with the strength of his whole kingdom,
and upright ones with him; thus shall he
do: and he shall give him the daughter
of women, corrupting her: but she shall
not stand *on his side*, neither be for
him.
18 After this shall he turn his face unto
the isles, and shall take many: but a
prince for his own behalf shall cause the
reproach offered by him to cease; without his own reproach he shall cause *it* to
turn upon him.
19 Then he shall turn his face toward
the fort of his own land: but he shall
stumble and fall, and not be found.
20 Then shall stand up in his estate a
raiser of taxes *in* the glory of the kingdom: but within few days he shall be
destroyed, neither in anger, nor in
battle.
21 And in his estate shall stand up a
vile person, to whom they shall not give
the honor of the kingdom: but he shall
come in peaceably, and obtain the kingdom by flatteries.
22 And with the arms of a flood shall
they be overflown from before him, and
shall be broken; yea, also the prince of
the covenant.
23 And after the league *made* with him
he shall work deceitfully: for he shall
come up, and shall become strong with
a small people.
24 He shall enter peaceably even upon
the fattest places of the province; and
he shall do *that* which his fathers have
not done, nor his fathers' fathers; he
shall scatter among them the prey, and
spoil, and riches: *yea*, and he shall forecast his devices against the strongholds,
even for a time.
25 And he shall stir up his power and
his courage against the king of the south
with a great army; and the king of the
south shall be stirred up to battle with a
very great and mighty army; but he shall
not stand: for they shall forecast devices
against him.
26 Yea, they that feed of the portion of
his meat shall destroy him, and his army
shall overflow: and many shall fall down
slain.
27 And both these kings' hearts *shall be*
to do mischief, and they shall speak lies
at one table; but it shall not prosper:
for yet the end *shall be* at the time
appointed.
28 Then shall he return into his land
with great riches; and his heart *shall be*
against the holy covenant; and he shall
do *exploits*, and return to his own land.
29 At the time appointed he shall
return, and come toward the south; but
it shall not be as the former, or as the
latter.
30 ¶ For the ships of Chĭt'tĭm shall
come against him: therefore he shall be
grieved, and return, and have indignation against the holy covenant: so shall
he do; he shall even return, and have
intelligence with them that forsake the
holy covenant.
31 And arms shall stand on his part,
and they shall pollute the sanctuary of
strength, and shall take away the daily
sacrifice, and they shall place the abomination that maketh desolate.
32 And such as do wickedly against the
covenant shall he corrupt by flatteries:
but the people that do know their God
shall be strong, and do *exploits*.
33 And they that understand among
the people shall instruct many: yet they
shall fall by the sword, and by flame, by
captivity, and by spoil, *many* days.
34 Now when they shall fall, they shall
be helped with a little help: but many
shall cleave to them with flatteries.
35 And *some* of them of understanding
shall fall, to try them, and to purge, and
to make *them* white, *even* to the time of
the end: because *it is* yet for a time
appointed.
36 And the king shall do according to
his will; and he shall exalt himself, and
magnify himself above every god, and
shall speak marvelous things against the
God of gods, and shall prosper till the
indignation be accomplished: for that
that is determined shall be done.
37 Neither shall he regard the God of
his fathers, nor the desire of women, nor
regard any god: for he shall magnify
himself above all.

38 But in his estate shall he honor the
God of forces: and a god whom his fathers knew not shall he honor with gold, and silver, and with precious stones, and pleasant things.
39 Thus shall he do in the most strongholds with a strange god, whom he shall acknowledge *and* increase with glory: and he shall cause them to rule over many, and shall divide the land for gain.
40 And at the time of the end shall the
king of the south push at him: and the king of the north shall come against him like a whirlwind, with chariots, and with horsemen, and with many ships; and he shall enter into the countries, and shall overflow and pass over.
41 He shall enter also into the glorious
land, and many *countries* shall be overthrown: but these shall escape out of his hand, *even* Ē'dŏm, and Mō'ăb, and the chief of the children of Ammon.
42 He shall stretch forth his hand also
upon the countries: and the land of Egypt shall not escape.
43 But he shall have power over the
treasures of gold and of silver, and over all the precious things of Egypt: and the Libyans and the Ethiopians *shall be* at his steps.
44 But tidings out of the east and out
of the north shall trouble him: therefore he shall go forth with great fury to destroy, and utterly to make away many.
45 And he shall plant the tabernacles
of his palace between the seas in the glorious holy mountain; yet he shall come to his end, and none shall help him.

CHAPTER 12

AND at that time shall Mī'chā-ĕl stand up, the great prince which standeth for the children of thy people: and there shall be a time of trouble, such as never was since there was a nation *even* to that same time: and at that time thy people shall be delivered, every one that shall be found written in the book.
2 And many of them that sleep in the
dust of the earth shall awake, some to everlasting life, and some to shame *and* everlasting contempt.
3 And they that be wise shall shine as
the brightness of the firmament; and they that turn many to righteousness, as the stars for ever and ever.
4 But thou, O Daniel, shut up the
words, and seal the book, *even* to the time of the end: many shall run to and fro, and knowledge shall be increased.
5 ¶ Then I Daniel looked, and, behold,
there stood other two, the one on this side of the bank of the river, and the other on that side of the bank of the river.
6 And *one* said to the man clothed in
linen, which *was* upon the waters of the river, How long *shall it be* to the end of these wonders?
7 And I heard the man clothed in linen,
which *was* upon the waters of the river, when he held up his right hand and his left hand unto heaven, and sware by him that liveth for ever, that *it shall be* for a time, times, and a half; and when he shall have accomplished to scatter the power of the holy people, all these *things* shall be finished.
8 And I heard, but I understood not:
then said I, O my Lord, what *shall be* the end of these *things?*
9 And he said, Go thy way, Daniel: for
the words *are* closed up and sealed till the time of the end.
10 Many shall be purified, and made
white, and tried; but the wicked shall do wickedly: and none of the wicked shall understand; but the wise shall understand.
11 And from the time *that* the daily
sacrifice shall be taken away, and the abomination that maketh desolate set up, *there shall be* a thousand two hundred and ninety days.
12 Blessed *is* he that waiteth, and
cometh to the thousand three hundred and five and thirty days.
13 But go thou thy way till the end *be:*
for thou shalt rest, and stand in thy lot at the end of the days.

HOSEA

CHAPTER 1

THE word of the LORD that came
unto Hō-ṣē′ȧ, the son of Bē-ē′rī, in
the days of Ŭz-zī′ȧh, Jō′thăm, Ahaz, *and*
Hĕz′ē-kī′ȧh, kings of Judah, and in the
days of Jĕr′ō-bō′ăm the son of Jō′ăsh,
king of Ĭṣ′rā-ĕl.
2 The beginning of the word of the
LORD by Hō-ṣē′ȧ. And the LORD said to
Hō-ṣē′ȧ, Go, take unto thee a wife of
whoredoms and children of whoredoms:
for the land hath committed great
whoredom, *departing* from the LORD.
3 So he went and took Gō′mĕr the
daughter of Dĭb-lā′ĭm; which conceived,
and bare him a son.
4 And the LORD said unto him, Call his
name Jĕz′rē-ĕl; for yet a little *while,* and
I will avenge the blood of Jĕz′rē-ĕl upon
the house of Jē′hū, and will cause to
cease the kingdom of the house of
Ĭṣ′rā-ĕl.
5 And it shall come to pass at that day,
that I will break the bow of Ĭṣ′rā-ĕl in
the valley of Jĕz′rē-ĕl.
6 ¶ And she conceived again, and
bare a daughter. And *God* said unto
him, Call her name Lō′–rụ-hā′mȧh: for
I will no more have mercy upon the
house of Ĭṣ′rā-ĕl; but I will utterly take
them away.
7 But I will have mercy upon the house
of Judah, and will save them by the
LORD their God, and will not save them
by bow, nor by sword, nor by battle, by
horses, nor by horsemen.
8 ¶ Now when she had weaned Lō′–rụ-
hā′mȧh, she conceived, and bare a son.
9 Then said *God,* Call his name Lō–
ăm′mī: for ye *are* not my people, and I
will not be your *God.*
10 ¶ Yet the number of the children
of Ĭṣ′rā-ĕl shall be as the sand of the
sea, which cannot be measured nor
numbered; and it shall come to pass,
that in the place where it was said unto
them, Ye *are* not my people, *there* it
shall be said unto them, *Ye are* the sons
of the living God.
11 Then shall the children of Judah
and the children of Ĭṣ′rā-ĕl be gathered
together, and appoint themselves one
head, and they shall come up out of the
land: for great *shall be* the day of
Jĕz′rē-ĕl.

CHAPTER 2

SAY ye unto your brethren, Ăm′mī;
and to your sisters, Rụ-hā′mȧh.
2 Plead with your mother, plead; for
she *is* not my wife, neither *am* I her
husband: let her therefore put away her
whoredoms out of her sight, and her
adulteries from between her breasts;
3 Lest I strip her naked, and set her as
in the day that she was born, and make
her as a wilderness, and set her like a
dry land, and slay her with thirst.
4 And I will not have mercy upon her
children; for they *be* the children of
whoredoms.
5 For their mother hath played the
harlot: she that conceived them hath
done shamefully; for she said, I will go
after my lovers, that give *me* my bread
and my water, my wool and my flax,
mine oil and my drink.
6 ¶ Therefore, behold, I will hedge up
thy ways with thorns, and make a wall,
that she shall not find her paths.
7 And she shall follow after her lovers,
but she shall not overtake them; and
she shall seek them, but shall not find
them: then shall she say, I will go and
return to my first husband; for then *was*
it better with me than now.
8 For she did not know that I gave her
corn, and wine, and oil, and multiplied
her silver and gold, *which* they prepared
for Bā′ăl.
9 Therefore will I return, and take away
my corn in the time thereof, and my
wine in the season thereof, and will
recover my wool and my flax *given* to
cover her nakedness.
10 And now will I discover her lewdness in the sight of her lovers, and none
shall deliver her out of mine hand.
11 I will also cause all her mirth to
cease, her feast days, her new moons,
and her sabbaths, and all her solemn
feasts.
12 And I will destroy her vines and her
fig trees, whereof she hath said, These
are my rewards that my lovers have
given me: and I will make them a forest,
and the beasts of the field shall eat
them.
13 And I will visit upon her the days of
Bā′ȧ-lĭm, wherein she burned incense
to them, and she decked herself with

her earrings and her jewels, and she went after her lovers, and forgat me, saith the LORD.

14 ¶ Therefore, behold, I will allure her, and bring her into the wilderness, and speak comfortably unto her.

15 And I will give her her vineyards from thence, and the valley of Ā'chŏr for a door of hope: and she shall sing there, as in the days of her youth, and as in the day when she came up out of the land of Egypt.

16 And it shall be at that day, saith the LORD, *that* thou shalt call me Ĭsh'ī; and shalt call me no more Bā'ă-lī.

17 For I will take away the names of Bā'ă-lĭm out of her mouth, and they shall no more be remembered by their name.

18 And in that day will I make a covenant for them with the beasts of the field, and with the fowls of heaven, and *with* the creeping things of the ground: and I will break the bow and the sword and the battle out of the earth, and will make them to lie down safely.

19 And I will betroth thee unto me for ever; yea, I will betroth thee unto me in righteousness, and in judgment, and in loving-kindness, and in mercies.

20 I will even betroth thee unto me in faithfulness: and thou shalt know the LORD.

21 And it shall come to pass in that day, I will hear, saith the LORD, I will hear the heavens, and they shall hear the earth;

22 And the earth shall hear the corn, and the wine, and the oil; and they shall hear Jĕz'rē-ĕl.

23 And I will sow her unto me in the earth; and I will have mercy upon her that had not obtained mercy; and I will say to *them which were* not my people, Thou *art* my people; and they shall say, *Thou art* my God.

CHAPTER 3

THEN said the LORD unto me, Go yet, love a woman beloved of *her* friend, yet an adulteress, according to the love of the LORD toward the children of Ĭş'rā-ĕl, who look to other gods, and love flagons of wine.

2 So I bought her to me for fifteen *pieces* of silver, and *for* a homer of barley, and a half homer of barley:

3 And I said unto her, Thou shalt abide for me many days; thou shalt not play the harlot, and thou shalt not be for *another* man: so *will* I also *be* for thee.

4 For the children of Ĭş'rā-ĕl shall abide many days without a king, and without a prince, and without a sacrifice, and without an image, and without an ĕph'ŏd, and *without* teraphim:

5 Afterward shall the children of Ĭş'rā-ĕl return, and seek the LORD their God, and David their king; and shall fear the LORD and his goodness in the latter days.

CHAPTER 4

HEAR the word of the LORD, ye children of Ĭş'rā-ĕl: for the LORD hath a controversy with the inhabitants of the land, because *there is* no truth, nor mercy, nor knowledge of God in the land.

2 By swearing, and lying, and killing, and stealing, and committing adultery, they break out, and blood toucheth blood.

3 Therefore shall the land mourn, and every one that dwelleth therein shall languish, with the beasts of the field, and with the fowls of heaven; yea, the fishes of the sea also shall be taken away.

4 Yet let no man strive, nor reprove another: for thy people *are* as they that strive with the priest.

5 Therefore shalt thou fall in the day, and the prophet also shall fall with thee in the night, and I will destroy thy mother.

6 ¶ My people are destroyed for lack of knowledge: because thou hast rejected knowledge, I will also reject thee, that thou shalt be no priest to me: seeing thou hast forgotten the law of thy God, I will also forget thy children.

7 As they were increased, so they sinned against me: *therefore* will I change their glory into shame.

8 They eat up the sin of my people, and they set their heart on their iniquity.

9 And there shall be, like people, like priest: and I will punish them for their ways, and reward them their doings.

10 For they shall eat, and not have enough: they shall commit whoredom, and shall not increase: because they have left off to take heed to the LORD.

11 Whoredom and wine and new wine take away the heart.

12 ¶ My people ask counsel at their stocks, and their staff declareth unto them: for the spirit of whoredoms hath caused *them* to err, and they have gone a whoring from under their God.

13 They sacrifice upon the tops of the mountains, and burn incense upon the hills, under oaks and poplars and elms, because the shadow thereof *is* good: therefore your daughters shall commit whoredom, and your spouses shall commit adultery.

14 I will not punish your daughters when they commit whoredom, nor your spouses when they commit adultery: for themselves are separated with whores, and they sacrifice with harlots: therefore the people *that* doth not understand shall fall.

15 ¶ Though thou, Ĭṣ'rā-ĕl, play the harlot, *yet* let not Judah offend; and come not ye unto Gĭl'găl, neither go ye up to Bĕth'-ā'vĕn, nor swear, The LORD liveth.

16 For Ĭṣ'rā-ĕl slideth back as a backsliding heifer: now the LORD will feed them as a lamb in a large place.

17 Ē'phrā-ĭm *is* joined to idols: let him alone.

18 Their drink is sour: they have committed whoredom continually: her rulers *with* shame do love, Give ye.

19 The wind hath bound her up in her wings, and they shall be ashamed because of their sacrifices.

CHAPTER 5

HEAR ye this, O priests; and hearken, ye house of Ĭṣ'rā-ĕl; and give ye ear, O house of the king; for judgment *is* toward you, because ye have been a snare on Mĭz'păh, and a net spread upon Tā'bŏr.

2 And the revolters are profound to make slaughter, though I *have been* a rebuker of them all.

3 I know Ē'phrā-ĭm, and Ĭṣ'rā-ĕl is not hid from me: for now, O Ē'phrā-ĭm, thou committest whoredom, *and* Ĭṣ'rā-ĕl is defiled.

4 They will not frame their doings to turn unto their God: for the spirit of whoredoms *is* in the midst of them, and they have not known the LORD.

5 And the pride of Ĭṣ'rā-ĕl doth testify to his face: therefore shall Ĭṣ'rā-ĕl and Ē'phrā-ĭm fall in their iniquity; Judah also shall fall with them.

6 They shall go with their flocks and with their herds to seek the LORD; but they shall not find *him;* he hath withdrawn himself from them.

7 They have dealt treacherously against the LORD; for they have begotten strange children: now shall a month devour them with their portions.

8 Blow ye the cornet in Gĭb'ē-āh, *and* the trumpet in Rā'māh: cry aloud *at* Bĕth'-ā'vĕn, after thee, O Benjamin.

9 Ē'phrā-ĭm shall be desolate in the day of rebuke: among the tribes of Ĭṣ'rā-ĕl have I made known that which shall surely be.

10 The princes of Judah were like them that remove the bound: *therefore* I will pour out my wrath upon them like water.

11 Ē'phrā-ĭm *is* oppressed *and* broken in judgment, because he willingly walked after the commandment.

12 Therefore *will* I *be* unto Ē'phrā-ĭm as a moth, and to the house of Judah as rottenness.

13 When Ē'phrā-ĭm saw his sickness, and Judah *saw* his wound, then went Ē'phrā-ĭm to the Assyrian, and sent to king Jā'rĕb: yet could he not heal you, nor cure you of your wound.

14 For I *will be* unto Ē'phrā-ĭm as a lion, and as a young lion to the house of Judah: I, *even* I, will tear and go away; I will take away, and none shall rescue *him*.

15 ¶ I will go *and* return to my place, till they acknowledge their offense, and seek my face: in their affliction they will seek me early.

CHAPTER 6

COME, and let us return unto the LORD: for he hath torn, and he will heal us; he hath smitten, and he will bind us up.

2 After two days will he revive us: in the third day he will raise us up, and we shall live in his sight.

3 Then shall we know, *if* we follow on to know the LORD: his going forth is prepared as the morning; and he shall come unto us as the rain, as the latter *and* former rain unto the earth.

4 ¶ O Ē'phrā-ĭm, what shall I do unto thee? O Judah, what shall I do unto thee? for your goodness *is* as a morning cloud, and as the early dew it goeth away.

5 Therefore have I hewed *them* by the prophets; I have slain them by the words of my mouth: and thy judgments *are as* the light *that* goeth forth.

6 For I desired mercy, and not sacrifice; and the knowledge of God more than burnt offerings.

7 But they like men have transgressed the covenant: there have they dealt treacherously against me.

8 Gĭl′ē-ăd *is* a city of them that work iniquity, *and is* polluted with blood.

9 And as troops of robbers wait for a man, *so* the company of priests murder in the way by consent: for they commit lewdness.

10 I have seen a horrible thing in the house of Ĭs′rā-ĕl: there *is* the whoredom of Ē′phrā-ĭm, Ĭs′rā-ĕl is defiled.

11 Also, O Judah, he hath set a harvest for thee, when I returned the captivity of my people.

CHAPTER 7

WHEN I would have healed Ĭs′rā-ĕl, then the iniquity of Ē′phrā-ĭm was discovered, and the wickedness of Sȧ-mā′rĭ-ȧ: for they commit falsehood; and the thief cometh in, *and* the troop of robbers spoileth without.

2 And they consider not in their hearts *that* I remember all their wickedness: now their own doings have beset them about; they are before my face.

3 They make the king glad with their wickedness, and the princes with their lies.

4 They *are* all adulterers, as an oven heated by the baker, *who* ceaseth from raising after he hath kneaded the dough, until it be leavened.

5 In the day of our king, the princes have made *him* sick with bottles of wine; he stretched out his hand with scorners.

6 For they have made ready their heart like an oven, while they lie in wait: their baker sleepeth all the night; in the morning it burneth as a flaming fire.

7 They are all hot as an oven, and have devoured their judges; all their kings are fallen: *there is* none among them that calleth unto me.

8 Ē′phrā-ĭm, he hath mixed himself among the people; Ē′phrā-ĭm is a cake not turned.

9 Strangers have devoured his strength, and he knoweth *it* not: yea, gray hairs are here and there upon him, yet he knoweth not.

10 And the pride of Ĭs′rā-ĕl testifieth to his face: and they do not return to the LORD their God, nor seek him for all this.

11 ¶ Ē′phrā-ĭm also is like a silly dove without heart: they call to Egypt, they go to Assyria.

12 When they shall go, I will spread my net upon them; I will bring them down as the fowls of the heaven; I will chastise them, as their congregation hath heard.

13 Woe unto them! for they have fled from me: destruction unto them! because they have transgressed against me: though I have redeemed them, yet they have spoken lies against me.

14 And they have not cried unto me with their heart, when they howled upon their beds: they assemble themselves for corn and wine, *and* they rebel against me.

15 Though I have bound *and* strengthened their arms, yet do they imagine mischief against me.

16 They return, *but* not to the Most High: they are like a deceitful bow: their princes shall fall by the sword for the rage of their tongue: this *shall be* their derision in the land of Egypt.

CHAPTER 8

SET the trumpet to thy mouth. *He shall come* as an eagle against the house of the LORD, because they have transgressed my covenant, and trespassed against my law.

2 Ĭs′rā-ĕl shall cry unto me, My God, we know thee.

3 Ĭs′rā-ĕl hath cast off *the thing that is* good: the enemy shall pursue him.

4 They have set up kings, but not by me: they have made princes, and I knew *it* not: of their silver and their gold have they made them idols, that they may be cut off.

5 ¶ Thy calf, O Sȧ-mā′rĭ-ȧ, hath cast *thee* off; mine anger is kindled against them: how long *will it be* ere they attain to innocency?

6 For from Ĭs′rā-ĕl *was* it also: the workman made it; therefore it *is* not God: but the calf of Sȧ-mā′rĭ-ȧ shall be broken in pieces.

7 For they have sown the wind, and they shall reap the whirlwind: it hath no

stalk: the bud shall yield no meal: if so
be it yield, the strangers shall swallow
it up.
8 Ĭs′rā-ĕl is swallowed up: now shall
they be among the Gĕn′tīles as a vessel
wherein *is* no pleasure.
9 For they are gone up to Assyria, a
wild ass alone by himself: Ē′phrā-ĭm
hath hired lovers.
10 Yea, though they have hired among
the nations, now will I gather them, and
they shall sorrow a little for the burden
of the king of princes.
11 Because Ē′phrā-ĭm hath made many
altars to sin, altars shall be unto him
to sin.
12 I have written to him the great
things of my law, *but* they were counted
as a strange thing.
13 They sacrifice flesh *for* the sacrifices of mine offerings, and eat *it: but*
the LORD accepteth them not; now will
he remember their iniquity, and visit
their sins: they shall return to Egypt.
14 For Ĭs′rā-ĕl hath forgotten his
Maker, and buildeth temples; and
Judah hath multiplied fenced cities: but
I will send a fire upon his cities, and it
shall devour the palaces thereof.

CHAPTER 9

REJOICE not, O Ĭs′rā-ĕl, for joy, as
other people: for thou hast gone
a whoring from thy God, thou hast loved
a reward upon every cornfloor.
2 The floor and the winepress shall not
feed them, and the new wine shall fail
in her.
3 They shall not dwell in the LORD's
land; but Ē′phrā-ĭm shall return to
Egypt, and they shall eat unclean *things*
in Assyria.
4 They shall not offer wine *offerings* to
the LORD, neither shall they be pleasing
unto him: their sacrifices *shall be* unto
them as the bread of mourners; all that
eat thereof shall be polluted: for their
bread for their soul shall not come into
the house of the LORD.
5 What will ye do in the solemn day,
and in the day of the feast of the LORD?
6 For, lo, they are gone because of
destruction; Egypt shall gather them up,
Memphis shall bury them: the pleasant
places for their silver, nettles shall possess them: thorns *shall be* in their tabernacles.
7 The days of visitation are come, the
days of recompense are come; Ĭs′rā-ĕl
shall know *it:* the prophet *is* a fool, the
spiritual man *is* mad, for the multitude
of thine iniquity, and the great hatred.
8 The watchman of Ē′phrā-ĭm *was*
with my God: *but* the prophet *is* a snare
of a fowler in all his ways, *and* hatred in
the house of his God.
9 They have deeply corrupted *themselves,* as in the days of Gĭb′ē-ȧh: *therefore* he will remember their iniquity, he
will visit their sins.
10 I found Ĭs′rā-ĕl like grapes in the
wilderness; I saw your fathers as the
first ripe in the fig tree at her first time:
but they went to Bā′ăl–pē′ŏr, and separated themselves unto *that* shame; and
their abominations were according as
they loved.
11 *As for* Ē′phrā-ĭm, their glory shall
fly away like a bird, from the birth, and
from the womb, and from the conception.
12 Though they bring up their children,
yet will I bereave them, *that there shall*
not *be* a man *left:* yea, woe also to them
when I depart from them!
13 Ē′phrā-ĭm, as I saw Tȳ′rŭs, *is*
planted in a pleasant place: but Ē′phrā-
ĭm shall bring forth his children to the
murderer.
14 Give them, O LORD: what wilt thou
give? give them a miscarrying womb and
dry breasts.
15 All their wickedness *is* in Gĭl′găl:
for there I hated them: for the wickedness of their doings I will drive them out
of mine house, I will love them no more:
all their princes *are* revolters.
16 Ē′phrā-ĭm is smitten, their root is
dried up, they shall bear no fruit: yea,
though they bring forth, yet will I slay
even the beloved *fruit* of their womb.
17 My God will cast them away, because they did not hearken unto him:
and they shall be wanderers among the
nations.

CHAPTER 10

ĬS′RĀ-ĔL *is* an empty vine, he bringeth forth fruit unto himself: according to the multitude of his fruit he hath
increased the altars; according to the
goodness of his land they have made
goodly images.
2 Their heart is divided; now shall they
be found faulty: he shall break down
their altars, he shall spoil their images.

3 For now they shall say, We have no
king, because we feared not the LORD;
what then should a king do to us?
4 They have spoken words, swearing
falsely in making a covenant: thus
judgment springeth up as hemlock in
the furrows of the field.
5 The inhabitants of Sȧ-mā'rĭ-ȧ shall
fear because of the calves of Bĕth'–
ā'vĕn: for the people thereof shall
mourn over it, and the priests thereof
that rejoiced on it, for the glory thereof,
because it is departed from it.
6 It shall be also carried unto Assyria
for a present to king Jā'rĕb: Ē'phrā-ĭm
shall receive shame, and Ĭṣ'rā-ĕl shall
be ashamed of his own counsel.
7 *As for* Sȧ-mā'rĭ-ȧ, her king is cut off
as the foam upon the water.
8 The high places also of Ā'vĕn, the sin
of Ĭṣ'rā-ĕl, shall be destroyed: the thorn
and the thistle shall come up on their
altars; and they shall say to the mountains, Cover us; and to the hills, Fall
on us.
9 O Ĭṣ'rā-ĕl, thou hast sinned from the
days of Gĭb'ē-ȧh: there they stood: the
battle in Gĭb'ē-ȧh against the children
of iniquity did not overtake them.
10 *It is* in my desire that I should chastise them; and the people shall be
gathered against them, when they shall
bind themselves in their two furrows.
11 And Ē'phrā-ĭm *is as* a heifer *that is*
taught, *and* loveth to tread out *the corn;*
but I passed over upon her fair neck: I
will make Ē'phrā-ĭm to ride; Judah shall
plow, *and* Jacob shall break his clods.
12 Sow to yourselves in righteousness,
reap in mercy; break up your fallow
ground: for *it is* time to seek the LORD,
till he come and rain righteousness upon
you.
13 Ye have plowed wickedness, ye
have reaped iniquity; ye have eaten the
fruit of lies: because thou didst trust in
thy way, in the multitude of thy mighty
men.
14 Therefore shall a tumult arise
among thy people, and all thy fortresses
shall be spoiled, as Shăl'măn spoiled
Bĕth'–är'bĕl in the day of battle: the
mother was dashed in pieces upon *her*
children.
15 So shall Beth-el do unto you because
of your great wickedness: in a morning shall the king of Ĭṣ'rā-ĕl utterly be
cut off.

CHAPTER 11

WHEN Ĭṣ'rā-ĕl *was* a child, then I
loved him, and called my son out
of Egypt.
2 *As* they called them, so they went
from them: they sacrificed unto Bā'ȧ-
lĭm, and burned incense to graven
images.
3 I taught Ē'phrā-ĭm also to go, taking
them by their arms; but they knew not
that I healed them.
4 I drew them with cords of a man, with
bands of love: and I was to them as they
that take off the yoke on their jaws, and
I laid meat unto them.
5 ¶ He shall not return into the land
of Egypt, but the Assyrian shall be his
king, because they refused to return.
6 And the sword shall abide on his
cities, and shall consume his branches,
and devour *them*, because of their own
counsels.
7 And my people are bent to backsliding from me: though they called
them to the Most High, none at all
would exalt *him*.
8 How shall I give thee up, Ē'phrā-
ĭm? *how* shall I deliver thee, Ĭṣ'rā-ĕl?
how shall I make thee as Ăd'mȧh? *how*
shall I set thee as Zē-bō'ĭm? mine heart
is turned within me, my repentings are
kindled together.
9 I will not execute the fierceness of
mine anger, I will not return to destroy
Ē'phrā-ĭm: for I *am* God, and not man;
the Holy One in the midst of thee: and I
will not enter into the city.
10 They shall walk after the LORD: he
shall roar like a lion: when he shall roar,
then the children shall tremble from the
west.
11 They shall tremble as a bird out of
Egypt, and as a dove out of the land of
Assyria: and I will place them in their
houses, saith the LORD.
12 Ē'phrā-ĭm compasseth me about
with lies, and the house of Ĭṣ'rā-ĕl with
deceit: but Judah yet ruleth with God,
and is faithful with the saints.

CHAPTER 12

Ē'PHRĀ-ĬM feedeth on wind, and
followeth after the east wind: he
daily increaseth lies and desolation; and
they do make a covenant with the Assyrians, and oil is carried into Egypt.
2 The LORD hath also a controversy

with Judah, and will punish Jacob according to his ways; according to his
doings will he recompense him.
3 ¶ He took his brother by the heel in
the womb, and by his strength he had
power with God:
4 Yea, he had power over the angel,
and prevailed: he wept, and made supplication unto him: he found him *in*
Beth-el, and there he spake with us;
5 Even the LORD God of hosts; the
LORD *is* his memorial.
6 Therefore turn thou to thy God: keep
mercy and judgment, and wait on thy
God continually.
7 ¶ *He is* a merchant, the balances of
deceit *are* in his hand: he loveth to
oppress.
8 And Ē′phrā-ĭm said, Yet I am become rich, I have found me out substance: *in* all my labors they shall find
none iniquity in me that *were* sin.
9 And I *that am* the LORD thy God from
the land of Egypt will yet make thee to
dwell in tabernacles, as in the days of
the solemn feast.
10 I have also spoken by the prophets,
and I have multiplied visions, and used
similitudes, by the ministry of the
prophets.
11 *Is there* iniquity *in* Gĭl′ē-ăd? surely
they are vanity: they sacrifice bullocks
in Gĭl′găl; yea, their altars *are* as heaps
in the furrows of the fields.
12 And Jacob fled into the country of
Syria, and Ĭs′rā-ĕl served for a wife, and
for a wife he kept *sheep*.
13 And by a prophet the LORD brought
Ĭs′rā-ĕl out of Egypt, and by a prophet
was he preserved.
14 Ē′phrā-ĭm provoked *him* to anger
most bitterly: therefore shall he leave
his blood upon him, and his reproach
shall his Lord return unto him.

CHAPTER 13

WHEN Ē′phrā-ĭm spake trembling,
he exalted himself in Ĭs′rā-ĕl;
but when he offended in Bā′ăl, he died.
2 And now they sin more and more,
and have made them molten images
of their silver, *and* idols according to
their own understanding, all of it the
work of the craftsmen: they say of
them, Let the men that sacrifice kiss
the calves.
3 Therefore they shall be as the morning cloud, and as the early dew that
passeth away, as the chaff *that* is driven
with the whirlwind out of the floor, and
as the smoke out of the chimney.
4 Yet I *am* the LORD thy God from the
land of Egypt, and thou shalt know no
god but me: for *there is* no saviour beside me.
5 ¶ I did know thee in the wilderness,
in the land of great drought.
6 According to their pasture, so were
they filled; they were filled, and their
heart was exalted; therefore have they
forgotten me.
7 Therefore I will be unto them as a
lion: as a leopard by the way will I
observe *them:*
8 I will meet them as a bear *that is*
bereaved *of her whelps*, and will rend
the caul of their heart, and there will I
devour them like a lion: the wild beast
shall tear them.
9 ¶ O Ĭs′rā-ĕl, thou hast destroyed
thyself; but in me *is* thine help.
10 I will be thy king: where *is any*
other that may save thee in all thy cities?
and thy judges of whom thou saidst,
Give me a king and princes?
11 I gave thee a king in mine anger,
and took *him* away in my wrath.
12 The iniquity of Ē′phrā-ĭm *is* bound
up; his sin *is* hid.
13 The sorrows of a travailing woman
shall come upon him: he *is* an unwise
son; for he should not stay long in *the*
place of the breaking forth of children.
14 I will ransom them from the power
of the grave; I will redeem them from
death: O death, I will be thy plagues; O
grave, I will be thy destruction: repentance shall be hid from mine eyes.
15 ¶ Though he be fruitful among *his*
brethren, an east wind shall come, the
wind of the LORD shall come up from
the wilderness, and his spring shall become dry, and his fountain shall be
dried up: he shall spoil the treasure of
all pleasant vessels.
16 Sȧ-mā′rĭ-ȧ shall become desolate;
for she hath rebelled against her God:
they shall fall by the sword: their infants shall be dashed in pieces, and their
women with child shall be ripped up.

CHAPTER 14

O ĬS′RĀ-ĔL, return unto the LORD
thy God; for thou hast fallen by
thine iniquity.
2 Take with you words, and turn to the

LORD: say unto him, Take away all iniquity, and receive *us* graciously: so will
we render the calves of our lips.
3 Ȧsh′ŭr shall not save us; we will not
ride upon horses: neither will we say
any more to the work of our hands, *Ye*
are our gods: for in thee the fatherless
findeth mercy.
4 ¶ I will heal their backsliding, I will
love them freely: for mine anger is
turned away from him.
5 I will be as the dew unto Ĭṣ′rā-ĕl: he
shall grow as the lily, and cast forth his
roots as Lebanon.
6 His branches shall spread, and his
beauty shall be as the olive tree, and his
smell as Lebanon.
7 They that dwell under his shadow
shall return; they shall revive *as* the
corn, and grow as the vine: the scent
thereof *shall be* as the wine of Lebanon.
8 Ē′phrā-ĭm *shall say,* What have I to
do any more with idols? I have heard
him, and observed him: I *am* like a
green fir tree. From me is thy fruit found.
9 Who *is* wise, and he shall understand
these *things?* prudent, and he shall know
them? for the ways of the LORD *are*
right, and the just shall walk in them:
but the transgressors shall fall therein.

JOEL

CHAPTER 1

THE word of the LORD that came to
Joel the son of Pē-thū′ĕl.
2 Hear this, ye old men, and give ear,
all ye inhabitants of the land. Hath this
been in your days, or even in the days
of your fathers?
3 Tell ye your children of it, and *let*
your children *tell* their children, and
their children another generation.
4 That which the palmerworm hath
left hath the locust eaten; and that which
the locust hath left hath the cankerworm
eaten; and that which the cankerworm
hath left hath the caterpillar eaten.
5 Awake, ye drunkards, and weep; and
howl, all ye drinkers of wine, because of
the new wine; for it is cut off from your
mouth.
6 For a nation is come up upon my
land, strong, and without number, whose
teeth *are* the teeth of a lion, and he hath
the cheek teeth of a great lion.
7 He hath laid my vine waste, and
barked my fig tree: he hath made it
clean bare, and cast *it* away; the
branches thereof are made white.
8 ¶ Lament like a virgin girded with
sackcloth for the husband of her youth.
9 The meat offering and the drink
offering is cut off from the house of the
LORD; the priests, the LORD's ministers, mourn.
10 The field is wasted, the land mourneth; for the corn is wasted: the new wine
is dried up, the oil languisheth.
11 Be ye ashamed, O ye husbandmen;
howl, O ye vinedressers, for the wheat
and for the barley; because the harvest
of the field is perished.
12 The vine is dried up, and the fig
tree languisheth; the pomegranate tree,
the palm tree also, and the apple tree,
even all the trees of the field, are
withered: because joy is withered away
from the sons of men.
13 Gird yourselves, and lament, ye
priests: howl, ye ministers of the altar:
come, lie all night in sackcloth, ye ministers of my God: for the meat offering
and the drink offering is withholden
from the house of your God.
14 ¶ Sanctify ye a fast, call a solemn
assembly, gather the elders *and* all the
inhabitants of the land *into* the house of
the LORD your God, and cry unto the
LORD,
15 Alas for the day! for the day of the
LORD *is* at hand, and as a destruction
from the Almighty shall it come.
16 Is not the meat cut off before our
eyes, *yea,* joy and gladness from the
house of our God?
17 The seed is rotten under their clods,
the garners are laid desolate, the barns
are broken down; for the corn is
withered.
18 How do the beasts groan! the herds
of cattle are perplexed, because they
have no pasture; yea, the flocks of sheep
are made desolate.
19 O LORD, to thee will I cry: for the
fire hath devoured the pastures of the
wilderness, and the flame hath burned
all the trees of the field.
20 The beasts of the field cry also unto
thee: for the rivers of water are dried

up, and the fire hath devoured the pastures of the wilderness.

CHAPTER 2

BLOW ye the trumpet in Zion, and sound an alarm in my holy mountain: let all the inhabitants of the land tremble: for the day of the LORD cometh, for *it is* nigh at hand;

2 A day of darkness and of gloominess, a day of clouds and of thick darkness, as the morning spread upon the mountains: a great people and a strong; there hath not been ever the like, neither shall be any more after it, *even* to the years of many generations.

3 A fire devoureth before them; and behind them a flame burneth: the land *is* as the garden of Ē′den before them, and behind them a desolate wilderness; yea, and nothing shall escape them.

4 The appearance of them *is* as the appearance of horses; and as horsemen, so shall they run.

5 Like the noise of chariots on the tops of mountains shall they leap, like the noise of a flame of fire that devoureth the stubble, as a strong people set in battle array.

6 Before their face the people shall be much pained: all faces shall gather blackness.

7 They shall run like mighty men; they shall climb the wall like men of war; and they shall march every one on his ways, and they shall not break their ranks:

8 Neither shall one thrust another; they shall walk every one in his path: and *when* they fall upon the sword, they shall not be wounded.

9 They shall run to and fro in the city; they shall run upon the wall, they shall climb up upon the houses; they shall enter in at the windows like a thief.

10 The earth shall quake before them; the heavens shall tremble: the sun and the moon shall be dark, and the stars shall withdraw their shining:

11 And the LORD shall utter his voice before his army: for his camp *is* very great: for *he is* strong that executeth his word: for the day of the LORD *is* great and very terrible; and who can abide it?

12 ¶ Therefore also now, saith the LORD, turn ye *even* to me with all your heart, and with fasting, and with weeping, and with mourning:

13 And rend your heart, and not your garments, and turn unto the LORD your God: for he *is* gracious and merciful, slow to anger, and of great kindness, and repenteth him of the evil.

14 Who knoweth *if* he will return and repent, and leave a blessing behind him; *even* a meat offering and a drink offering unto the LORD your God?

15 ¶ Blow the trumpet in Zion, sanctify a fast, call a solemn assembly:

16 Gather the people, sanctify the congregation, assemble the elders, gather the children, and those that suck the breasts: let the bridegroom go forth of his chamber, and the bride out of her closet.

17 Let the priests, the ministers of the LORD, weep between the porch and the altar, and let them say, Spare thy people, O LORD, and give not thine heritage to reproach, that the heathen should rule over them: wherefore should they say among the people, Where *is* their God?

18 ¶ Then will the LORD be jealous for his land, and pity his people.

19 Yea, the LORD will answer and say unto his people, Behold, I will send you corn, and wine, and oil, and ye shall be satisfied therewith: and I will no more make you a reproach among the heathen:

20 But I will remove far off from you the northern *army*, and will drive him into a land barren and desolate, with his face toward the east sea, and his hinder part toward the utmost sea, and his stink shall come up, and his ill savor shall come up, because he hath done great things.

21 ¶ Fear not, O land; be glad and rejoice: for the LORD will do great things.

22 Be not afraid, ye beasts of the field: for the pastures of the wilderness do spring, for the tree beareth her fruit, the fig tree and the vine do yield their strength.

23 Be glad then, ye children of Zion, and rejoice in the LORD your God: for he hath given you the former rain moderately, and he will cause to come down for you the rain, the former rain, and the latter rain in the first *month*.

24 And the floors shall be full of wheat, and the vats shall overflow with wine and oil.

25 And I will restore to you the years
that the locust hath eaten, the cankerworm, and the caterpillar, and the
palmerworm, my great army which I
sent among you.
26 And ye shall eat in plenty, and be
satisfied, and praise the name of the
LORD your God, that hath dealt wondrously with you: and my people shall
never be ashamed.
27 And ye shall know that I *am* in the
midst of Iș'rā-ĕl, and *that* I *am* the
LORD your God, and none else: and my
people shall never be ashamed.
28 ¶ And it shall come to pass afterward, *that* I will pour out my Spirit upon
all flesh; and your sons and your daughters shall prophesy, your old men shall
dream dreams, your young men shall
see visions:
29 And also upon the servants and
upon the handmaids in those days will I
pour out my Spirit.
30 And I will show wonders in the
heavens and in the earth, blood, and
fire, and pillars of smoke.
31 The sun shall be turned into darkness, and the moon into blood, before
the great and the terrible day of the
LORD come.
32 And it shall come to pass, *that* whosoever shall call on the name of the
LORD shall be delivered: for in mount
Zion and in Jerusalem shall be deliverance, as the LORD hath said, and in the
remnant whom the LORD shall call.

CHAPTER 3

FOR, behold, in those days, and in
that time, when I shall bring again
the captivity of Judah and Jerusalem,
2 I will also gather all nations, and will
bring them down into the valley of
Jē-hŏsh'ȧ-phăt, and will plead with
them there for my people and *for* my
heritage Iș'rā-ĕl, whom they have scattered among the nations, and parted my
land.
3 And they have cast lots for my people; and have given a boy for a harlot,
and sold a girl for wine, that they might
drink.
4 Yea, and what have ye to do with me,
O Tȳre, and Zī'dŏn, and all the coasts of
Păl'ĕs-tīne? will ye render me a recompense? and if ye recompense me,
swiftly *and* speedily will I return your
recompense upon your own head;
5 Because ye have taken my silver and
my gold, and have carried into your
temples my goodly pleasant things:
6 The children also of Judah and the
children of Jerusalem have ye sold unto
the Grecians, that ye might remove
them far from their border.
7 Behold, I will raise them out of the
place whither ye have sold them, and
will return your recompense upon your
own head:
8 And I will sell your sons and your
daughters into the hand of the children
of Judah, and they shall sell them to the
Sȧ-bē'ănș, to a people far off: for the
LORD hath spoken *it*.
9 ¶ Proclaim ye this among the Ġĕn'-
tīleș; Prepare war, wake up the mighty
men, let all the men of war draw near;
let them come up:
10 Beat your plowshares into swords,
and your pruning hooks into spears:
let the weak say, I *am* strong.
11 Assemble yourselves, and come, all
ye heathen, and gather yourselves together round about: thither cause thy
mighty ones to come down, O LORD.
12 Let the heathen be wakened, and
come up to the valley of Jē-hŏsh'ȧ-phăt:
for there will I sit to judge all the
heathen round about.
13 Put ye in the sickle, for the harvest
is ripe: come, get you down; for the
press is full, the vats overflow; for their
wickedness *is* great.
14 Multitudes, multitudes in the valley
of decision: for the day of the LORD *is*
near in the valley of decision.
15 The sun and the moon shall be
darkened, and the stars shall withdraw
their shining.
16 The LORD also shall roar out of
Zion, and utter his voice from Jerusalem; and the heavens and the earth
shall shake: but the LORD *will be* the
hope of his people, and the strength of
the children of Iș'rā-ĕl.
17 So shall ye know that I *am* the
LORD your God dwelling in Zion, my
holy mountain: then shall Jerusalem be
holy, and there shall no strangers pass
through her any more.
18 ¶ And it shall come to pass in that
day, *that* the mountains shall drop down
new wine, and the hills shall flow with
milk, and all the rivers of Judah shall
flow with waters, and a fountain shall
come forth of the house of the LORD,

and shall water the valley of Shĭt′tĭm.
19 Egypt shall be a desolation, and
Ē′dŏm shall be a desolate wilderness,
for the violence *against* the children of
Judah, because they have shed innocent
blood in their land.
20 But Judah shall dwell for ever, and
Jerusalem from generation to generation.
21 For I will cleanse their blood *that*
I have not cleansed: for the LORD dwelleth in Zion.

AMOS

CHAPTER 1

THE words of Amos, who was among
the herdmen of Tē-kō′ȧ, which he
saw concerning Ĭş′rā-ĕl in the days of
Ŭz-zī′ȧh king of Judah, and in the days
of Jĕr′ō-bō′ăm the son of Jō′ăsh king of
Ĭş′rā-ĕl, two years before the earthquake.
2 And he said, The LORD will roar from
Zion, and utter his voice from Jerusalem; and the habitations of the shepherds shall mourn, and the top of
Cär′mĕl shall wither.
3 Thus saith the LORD; For three transgressions of Damascus, and for four,
I will not turn away *the punishment*
thereof; because they have threshed Gĭl′-
ē-ăd with threshing instruments of iron:
4 But I will send a fire into the house
of Hăz′ā-ĕl, which shall devour the
palaces of Bĕn′-hā′dăd.
5 I will break also the bar of Damascus,
and cut off the inhabitant from the plain
of Ā′vĕn, and him that holdeth the
sceptre from the house of Ē′den: and
the people of Syria shall go into captivity unto Kĭr, saith the LORD.
6 ¶ Thus saith the LORD; For three
transgressions of Gā′zȧ, and for four, I
will not turn away *the punishment*
thereof; because they carried away captive the whole captivity, to deliver *them*
up to Ē′dŏm:
7 But I will send a fire on the wall of
Gā′zȧ, which shall devour the palaces
thereof:
8 And I will cut off the inhabitant from
Ashdod, and him that holdeth the sceptre from Ăsh′kē-lŏn, and I will turn
mine hand against Ĕk′rŏn: and the remnant of the Phĭ-lĭs′tĭneş shall perish,
saith the Lord GOD.
9 ¶ Thus saith the LORD; For three
transgressions of Tȳ′rŭs, and for four,
I will not turn away *the punishment*
thereof; because they delivered up the
whole captivity to Ē′dŏm, and remembered not the brotherly covenant:
10 But I will send a fire on the wall of
Tȳ′rŭs, which shall devour the palaces
thereof.
11 ¶ Thus saith the LORD; For three
transgressions of Ē′dŏm, and for four,
I will not turn away *the punishment*
thereof; because he did pursue his
brother with the sword, and did cast off
all pity, and his anger did tear perpetually, and he kept his wrath for ever:
12 But I will send a fire upon Tē′-
măn, which shall devour the palaces of
Bŏz′rȧh.
13 ¶ Thus saith the LORD; For three
transgressions of the children of Ammon, and for four, I will not turn away
the punishment thereof; because they
have ripped up the women with child,
of Gĭl′ē-ăd, that they might enlarge
their border:
14 But I will kindle a fire in the wall of
Răb′bȧh, and it shall devour the palaces
thereof, with shouting in the day of
battle, with a tempest in the day of the
whirlwind:
15 And their king shall go into captivity, he and his princes together, saith
the LORD.

CHAPTER 2

THUS saith the LORD; For three
transgressions of Mō′ăb, and for
four, I will not turn away *the punishment* thereof; because he burned the
bones of the king of Ē′dŏm into lime:
2 But I will send a fire upon Mō′ăb,
and it shall devour the palaces of Kĭr′ĭ-
ŏth: and Mō′ăb shall die with tumult,
with shouting, *and* with the sound of
the trumpet:
3 And I will cut off the judge from the
midst thereof, and will slay all the
princes thereof with him, saith the
LORD.
4 ¶ Thus saith the LORD; For three

transgressions of Judah, and for four,
I will not turn away *the punishment*
thereof; because they have despised the
law of the LORD, and have not kept his
commandments, and their lies caused
them to err, after the which their fathers
have walked:
5 But I will send a fire upon Judah, and
it shall devour the palaces of Jerusalem.
6 ¶ Thus saith the LORD; For three
transgressions of Ĭş'rā-ĕl, and for four,
I will not turn away *the punishment*
thereof; because they sold the righteous
for silver, and the poor for a pair of
shoes;
7 That pant after the dust of the earth
on the head of the poor, and turn aside
the way of the meek: and a man and his
father will go in unto the *same* maid, to
profane my holy name:
8 And they lay *themselves* down upon
clothes laid to pledge by every altar, and
they drink the wine of the condemned
in the house of their god.
9 ¶ Yet destroyed I the Ăm'ō-rīte before them, whose height *was* like the
height of the cedars, and he *was* strong
as the oaks; yet I destroyed his fruit
from above, and his roots from beneath.
10 Also I brought you up from the land
of Egypt, and led you forty years through
the wilderness, to possess the land of
the Ăm'ō-rīte.
11 And I raised up of your sons for
prophets, and of your young men for
Nazarites. *Is it* not even thus, O ye
children of Ĭş'rā-ĕl? saith the LORD.
12 But ye gave the Nazarites wine to
drink; and commanded the prophets,
saying, Prophesy not.
13 Behold, I am pressed under you, as
a cart is pressed *that is* full of sheaves.
14 Therefore the flight shall perish
from the swift, and the strong shall not
strengthen his force, neither shall the
mighty deliver himself:
15 Neither shall he stand that handleth
the bow; and *he that is* swift of foot shall
not deliver *himself:* neither shall he that
rideth the horse deliver himself.
16 And *he that is* courageous among
the mighty shall flee away naked in that
day, saith the LORD.

CHAPTER 3

HEAR this word that the LORD
hath spoken against you, O children of Ĭş'rā-ĕl, against the whole family
which I brought up from the land of
Egypt, saying,
2 You only have I known of all the
families of the earth: therefore I will
punish you for all your iniquities.
3 Can two walk together, except they
be agreed?
4 Will a lion roar in the forest, when
he hath no prey? will a young lion
cry out of his den, if he have taken
nothing?
5 Can a bird fall in a snare upon the
earth, where no gin *is* for him? shall *one*
take up a snare from the earth, and
have taken nothing at all?
6 Shall a trumpet be blown in the city,
and the people not be afraid? shall there
be evil in a city, and the LORD hath not
done *it?*
7 Surely the Lord GOD will do nothing,
but he revealeth his secret unto his
servants the prophets.
8 The lion hath roared, who will not
fear? the Lord GOD hath spoken, who
can but prophesy?
9 ¶ Publish in the palaces at Ashdod,
and in the palaces in the land of Egypt,
and say, Assemble yourselves upon the
mountains of Să-mā'rĭ-ȧ, and behold
the great tumults in the midst thereof,
and the oppressed in the midst thereof.
10 For they know not to do right, saith
the LORD, who store up violence and
robbery in their palaces.
11 Therefore thus saith the Lord GOD;
An adversary *there shall be* even round
about the land; and he shall bring down
thy strength from thee, and thy palaces
shall be spoiled.
12 Thus saith the LORD; As the shepherd taketh out of the mouth of the lion
two legs, or a piece of an ear; so shall
the children of Ĭş'rā-ĕl be taken out that
dwell in Să-mā'rĭ-ȧ in the corner of a
bed, and in Damascus *in* a couch.
13 Hear ye, and testify in the house of
Jacob, saith the Lord GOD, the God of
hosts,
14 That, in the day that I shall visit
the transgressions of Ĭş'rā-ĕl upon him,
I will also visit the altars of Beth-el: and
the horns of the altar shall be cut off,
and fall to the ground.
15 And I will smite the winter house
with the summer house; and the houses
of ivory shall perish, and the great
houses shall have an end, saith the
LORD.

CHAPTER 4

HEAR this word, ye kine of Bā'shăn, that *are* in the mountain of Sȧ-mā'rĭ-ȧ, which oppress the poor, which crush the needy, which say to their masters, Bring, and let us drink.

2 The Lord GOD hath sworn by his holiness, that, lo, the days shall come upon you, that he will take you away with hooks, and your posterity with fishhooks.

3 And ye shall go out at the breaches, every *cow at that which is* before her; and ye shall cast *them* into the palace, saith the LORD.

4 ¶ Come to Beth-el, and transgress; at Gĭl'găl multiply transgression; and bring your sacrifices every morning, *and* your tithes after three years:

5 And offer a sacrifice of thanksgiving with leaven, and proclaim *and* publish the free offerings: for this liketh you, O ye children of Ĭs̱'rā-ĕl, saith the Lord GOD.

6 ¶ And I also have given you cleanness of teeth in all your cities, and want of bread in all your places: yet have ye not returned unto me, saith the LORD.

7 And also I have withholden the rain from you, when *there were* yet three months to the harvest: and I caused it to rain upon one city, and caused it not to rain upon another city: one piece was rained upon, and the piece whereupon it rained not withered.

8 So two *or* three cities wandered unto one city, to drink water; but they were not satisfied: yet have ye not returned unto me saith the LORD.

9 I have smitten you with blasting and mildew: when your gardens and your vineyards and your fig trees and your olive trees increased, the palmerworm devoured *them:* yet have ye not returned unto me, saith the LORD.

10 I have sent among you the pestilence after the manner of Egypt: your young men have I slain with the sword, and have taken away your horses; and I have made the stink of your camps to come up unto your nostrils: yet have ye not returned unto me, saith the LORD.

11 I have overthrown *some* of you, as God overthrew Sŏd'ŏm and Gō-mŏr'rȧh, and ye were as a firebrand plucked out of the burning: yet have ye not returned unto me, saith the LORD.

12 Therefore thus will I do unto thee, O Ĭs̱'rā-ĕl: *and* because I will do this unto thee, prepare to meet thy God, O Ĭs̱'rā-ĕl.

13 For, lo, he that formeth the mountains, and createth the wind, and declareth unto man what *is* his thought, that maketh the morning darkness, and treadeth upon the high places of the earth, The LORD, The God of hosts, *is* his name.

CHAPTER 5

HEAR ye this word which I take up against you, *even* a lamentation, O house of Ĭs̱'rā-ĕl.

2 The virgin of Ĭs̱'rā-ĕl is fallen; she shall no more rise: she is forsaken upon her land; *there is* none to raise her up.

3 For thus saith the Lord GOD; The city that went out *by* a thousand shall leave a hundred, and that which went forth *by* a hundred shall leave ten, to the house of Ĭs̱'rā-ĕl.

4 ¶ For thus saith the LORD unto the house of Ĭs̱'rā-ĕl, Seek ye me, and ye shall live:

5 But seek not Beth-el, nor enter into Gĭl'găl, and pass not to Bē'ẽr–shē'bȧ: for Gĭl'găl shall surely go into captivity, and Beth-el shall come to nought.

6 Seek the LORD, and ye shall live; lest he break out like fire in the house of Joseph, and devour *it,* and *there be* none to quench *it* in Beth-el.

7 Ye who turn judgment to wormwood, and leave off righteousness in the earth,

8 *Seek him* that maketh the seven stars and Ō-rī'ŏn, and turneth the shadow of death into the morning, and maketh the day dark with night: that calleth for the waters of the sea, and poureth them out upon the face of the earth: The LORD *is* his name:

9 That strengtheneth the spoiled against the strong, so that the spoiled shall come against the fortress.

10 They hate him that rebuketh in the gate, and they abhor him that speaketh uprightly.

11 Forasmuch therefore as your treading *is* upon the poor, and ye take from him burdens of wheat: ye have built houses of hewn stone, but ye shall not dwell in them; ye have planted pleasant vineyards, but ye shall not drink wine of them.

12 For I know your manifold transgressions and your mighty sins: they

afflict the just, they take a bribe, and
they turn aside the poor in the gate *from*
their right.
13 Therefore the prudent shall keep
silence in that time; for it *is* an evil
time.
14 Seek good, and not evil, that ye
may live: and so the LORD, the God of
hosts, shall be with you, as ye have
spoken.
15 Hate the evil, and love the good, and
establish judgment in the gate: it may
be that the LORD God of hosts will be
gracious unto the remnant of Joseph.
16 Therefore the LORD, the God of
hosts, the Lord, saith thus; Wailing
shall be in all streets; and they shall say
in all the highways, Alas! alas! and they
shall call the husbandman to mourning,
and such as are skilful of lamentation
to wailing.
17 And in all vineyards *shall be* wailing: for I will pass through thee, saith
the LORD.
18 Woe unto you that desire the day of
the LORD! to what end *is* it for you? the
day of the LORD *is* darkness, and not
light.
19 As if a man did flee from a lion, and
a bear met him; or went into the house,
and leaned his hand on the wall, and a
serpent bit him.
20 *Shall* not the day of the LORD *be*
darkness, and not light? even very dark,
and no brightness in it?
21 ¶ I hate, I despise your feast days,
and I will not smell in your solemn
assemblies.
22 Though ye offer me burnt offerings
and your meat offerings, I will not accept
them; neither will I regard the peace
offerings of your fat beasts.
23 Take thou away from me the noise
of thy songs; for I will not hear the
melody of thy viols.
24 But let judgment run down as waters, and righteousness as a mighty
stream.
25 Have ye offered unto me sacrifices
and offerings in the wilderness forty
years, O house of Ĭṣ'rā-ĕl?
26 But ye have borne the tabernacle of
your Mō'lŏch and Chī'ŭn your images,
the star of your god, which ye made to
yourselves.
27 Therefore will I cause you to go into
captivity beyond Damascus, saith the
LORD, whose name *is* The God of hosts.

CHAPTER 6

WOE to them *that are* at ease in
Zion, and trust in the mountain
of Sȧ-mā'rĭ-ȧ, *which are* named chief of
the nations, to whom the house of
Ĭṣ'rā-ĕl came!
2 Pass ye unto Căl'nĕh, and see; and
from thence go ye to Hā'măth the great:
then go down to Gath of the Phĭ-lĭs'-
tīneṣ: *be they* better than these kingdoms? or their border greater than your
border?
3 Ye that put far away the evil day, and
cause the seat of violence to come near;
4 That lie upon beds of ivory, and
stretch themselves upon their couches,
and eat the lambs out of the flock, and
the calves out of the midst of the stall;
5 That chant to the sound of the viol,
and invent to themselves instruments of
music, like David;
6 That drink wine in bowls, and anoint
themselves with the chief ointments:
but they are not grieved for the affliction
of Joseph.
7 ¶ Therefore now shall they go captive with the first that go captive, and
the banquet of them that stretched
themselves shall be removed.
8 The Lord GOD hath sworn by himself,
saith the LORD the God of hosts, I abhor
the excellency of Jacob, and hate his
palaces: therefore will I deliver up the
city with all that is therein.
9 And it shall come to pass, if there
remain ten men in one house, that they
shall die.
10 And a man's uncle shall take him
up, and he that burneth him, to bring
out the bones out of the house, and shall
say unto him that *is* by the sides of the
house, *Is there* yet *any* with thee? and
he shall say, No. Then shall he say,
Hold thy tongue: for we may not make
mention of the name of the LORD.
11 For, behold, the LORD commandeth,
and he will smite the great house with
breaches, and the little house with
clefts.
12 ¶ Shall horses run upon the rock?
will *one* plow *there* with oxen? for ye
have turned judgment into gall, and the
fruit of righteousness into hemlock:
13 Ye which rejoice in a thing of
nought, which say, Have we not taken
to us horns by our own strength?
14 But, behold, I will raise up against

you a nation, O house of Ĭş′rā-ĕl, saith
the LORD the God of hosts; and they
shall afflict you from the entering in of
Hā′măth unto the river of the wilderness.

CHAPTER 7

THUS hath the Lord GOD showed
unto me; and, behold, he formed
grasshoppers in the beginning of the
shooting up of the latter growth; and,
lo, *it was* the latter growth after the
king's mowings.
2 And it came to pass, *that* when they
had made an end of eating the grass of
the land, then I said, O Lord GOD, forgive, I beseech thee: by whom shall
Jacob arise? for he *is* small.
3 The LORD repented for this: It shall
not be, saith the LORD.
4 ¶ Thus hath the Lord GOD showed
unto me: and, behold, the Lord GOD
called to contend by fire, and it devoured
the great deep, and did eat up a part.
5 Then said I, O Lord GOD, cease, I
beseech thee: by whom shall Jacob
arise? for he *is* small.
6 The LORD repented for this: This
also shall not be, saith the Lord GOD.
7 ¶ Thus he showed me: and, behold,
the Lord stood upon a wall *made* by
a plumbline, with a plumbline in his
hand.
8 And the LORD said unto me, Amos,
what seest thou? And I said, A plumbline. Then said the Lord, Behold, I will
set a plumbline in the midst of my
people Ĭş′rā-ĕl: I will not again pass
by them any more:
9 And the high places of Isaac shall be
desolate, and the sanctuaries of Ĭş′rā-ĕl
shall be laid waste; and I will rise
against the house of Jĕr′ō-bō′ăm with
the sword.
10 ¶ Then Ăm′ȧ-zī′ȧh the priest of
Beth-el sent to Jĕr′ō-bō′ăm king of
Ĭş′rā-ĕl, saying, Amos hath conspired
against thee in the midst of the house of
Ĭş′rā-ĕl: the land is not able to bear all
his words.
11 For thus Amos saith, Jĕr′ō-bō′ăm
shall die by the sword, and Ĭş′rā-ĕl
shall surely be led away captive out
of their own land.
12 Also Ăm′ȧ-zī′ȧh said unto Amos, O
thou seer, go, flee thee away into the
land of Judah, and there eat bread, and
prophesy there:
13 But prophesy not again any more
at Beth-el: for it *is* the king's chapel,
and it *is* the king's court.
14 ¶ Then answered Amos, and said
to Ăm′ȧ-zī′ȧh, I *was* no prophet, neither
was I a prophet's son; but I *was* a herd-
man, and a gatherer of sycamore fruit:
15 And the LORD took me as I followed
the flock, and the LORD said unto me,
Go, prophesy unto my people Ĭş′rā-ĕl.
16 ¶ Now therefore hear thou the
word of the LORD: Thou sayest, Prophesy not against Ĭş′rā-ĕl, and drop not
thy word against the house of Isaac.
17 Therefore thus saith the LORD; Thy
wife shall be a harlot in the city, and thy
sons and thy daughters shall fall by the
sword, and thy land shall be divided by
line; and thou shalt die in a polluted
land: and Ĭş′rā-ĕl shall surely go into
captivity forth of his land.

CHAPTER 8

THUS hath the Lord GOD showed
unto me: and behold a basket of
summer fruit.
2 And he said, Amos, what seest thou?
And I said, A basket of summer fruit.
Then said the LORD unto me, The end
is come upon my people of Ĭş′rā-ĕl; I
will not again pass by them any more.
3 And the songs of the temple shall be
howlings in that day, saith the Lord
GOD: *there shall be* many dead bodies
in every place; they shall cast *them*
forth with silence.
4 ¶ Hear this, O ye that swallow up
the needy, even to make the poor of the
land to fail,
5 Saying, When will the new moon be
gone, that we may sell corn? and the
sabbath, that we may set forth wheat,
making the ē′phȧh small, and the shekel
great, and falsifying the balances by
deceit?
6 That we may buy the poor for silver,
and the needy for a pair of shoes; *yea*,
and sell the refuse of the wheat?
7 The LORD hath sworn by the excellency of Jacob, Surely I will never forget any of their works.
8 Shall not the land tremble for this,
and every one mourn that dwelleth
therein? and it shall rise up wholly as a
flood; and it shall be cast out and
drowned, as *by* the flood of Egypt.
9 And it shall come to pass in that day,
saith the Lord GOD, that I will cause the

sun to go down at noon, and I will darken the earth in the clear day:

10 And I will turn your feasts into mourning, and all your songs into lamentation; and I will bring up sackcloth upon all loins, and baldness upon every head; and I will make it as the mourning of an only *son,* and the end thereof as a bitter day.

11 ¶ Behold, the days come, saith the Lord GOD, that I will send a famine in the land, not a famine of bread, nor a thirst for water, but of hearing the words of the LORD:

12 And they shall wander from sea to sea, and from the north even to the east, they shall run to and fro to seek the word of the LORD, and shall not find *it.*

13 In that day shall the fair virgins and young men faint for thirst.

14 They that swear by the sin of Să-mā'rĭ-ȧ, and say, Thy god, O Dan, liveth; and, The manner of Bē'ēr–shē'bȧ liveth; even they shall fall, and never rise up again.

CHAPTER 9

I SAW the Lord standing upon the altar: and he said, Smite the lintel of the door, that the posts may shake: and cut them in the head, all of them; and I will slay the last of them with the sword: he that fleeth of them shall not flee away, and he that escapeth of them shall not be delivered.

2 Though they dig into hell, thence shall mine hand take them; though they climb up to heaven, thence will I bring them down:

3 And though they hide themselves in the top of Cär'mĕl, I will search and take them out thence; and though they be hid from my sight in the bottom of the sea, thence will I command the serpent, and he shall bite them:

4 And though they go into captivity before their enemies, thence will I command the sword, and it shall slay them: and I will set mine eyes upon them for evil, and not for good.

5 And the Lord GOD of hosts *is* he that toucheth the land, and it shall melt, and all that dwell therein shall mourn: and it shall rise up wholly like a flood; and shall be drowned, as *by* the flood of Egypt.

6 *It is* he that buildeth his stories in the heaven, and hath founded his troop in the earth; he that calleth for the waters of the sea, and poureth them out upon the face of the earth: The LORD *is* his name.

7 *Are* ye not as children of the Ethiopians unto me, O children of Ĭs'rā-ĕl? saith the LORD. Have not I brought up Ĭs'rā-ĕl out of the land of Egypt? and the Phĭ-lĭs'tĭnes from Căph'tŏr, and the Syrians from Kïr?

8 Behold, the eyes of the Lord GOD *are* upon the sinful kingdom, and I will destroy it from off the face of the earth; saving that I will not utterly destroy the house of Jacob, saith the LORD.

9 For, lo, I will command, and I will sift the house of Ĭs'rā-ĕl among all nations, like as *corn* is sifted in a sieve, yet shall not the least grain fall upon the earth.

10 All the sinners of my people shall die by the sword, which say, The evil shall not overtake nor prevent us.

11 ¶ In that day will I raise up the tabernacle of David that is fallen, and close up the breaches thereof; and I will raise up his ruins, and I will build it as in the days of old:

12 That they may possess the remnant of Ē'dŏm, and of all the heathen, which are called by my name, saith the LORD that doeth this.

13 Behold, the days come, saith the LORD, that the plowman shall overtake the reaper, and the treader of grapes him that soweth seed; and the mountains shall drop sweet wine, and all the hills shall melt.

14 And I will bring again the captivity of my people of Ĭs'rā-ĕl, and they shall build the waste cities, and inhabit *them;* and they shall plant vineyards, and drink the wine thereof; they shall also make gardens, and eat the fruit of them.

15 And I will plant them upon their land, and they shall no more be pulled up out of their land which I have given them, saith the LORD thy God.

OBADIAH

THE vision of Ō′bȧ-dī′ȧh. Thus saith the Lord GOD concerning Ē′dŏm; We have heard a rumor from the LORD, and an ambassador is sent among the heathen, Arise ye, and let us rise up against her in battle.

2 Behold, I have made thee small among the heathen: thou art greatly despised.

3 ¶ The pride of thine heart hath deceived thee, thou that dwellest in the clefts of the rock, whose habitation *is* high; that saith in his heart, Who shall bring me down to the ground?

4 Though thou exalt *thyself* as the eagle, and though thou set thy nest among the stars, thence will I bring thee down, saith the LORD.

5 If thieves came to thee, if robbers by night, (how art thou cut off!) would they not have stolen till they had enough? if the grape gatherers came to thee, would they not leave *some* grapes?

6 How are *the things* of Ē′sa͡u searched out! *how* are his hidden things sought up!

7 All the men of thy confederacy have brought thee *even* to the border: the men that were at peace with thee have deceived thee, *and* prevailed against thee; *they that eat* thy bread have laid a wound under thee: *there is* none understanding in him.

8 Shall I not in that day, saith the LORD, even destroy the wise *men* out of Ē′dŏm, and understanding out of the mount of Ē′sa͡u?

9 And thy mighty *men,* O Tē′măn, shall be dismayed, to the end that every one of the mount of Ē′sa͡u may be cut off by slaughter.

10 ¶ For *thy* violence against thy brother Jacob shame shall cover thee, and thou shalt be cut off for ever.

11 In the day that thou stoodest on the other side, in the day that the strangers carried away captive his forces, and foreigners entered into his gates, and cast lots upon Jerusalem, even thou *wast* as one of them.

12 But thou shouldest not have looked on the day of thy brother in the day that he became a stranger; neither shouldest thou have rejoiced over the children of Judah in the day of their destruction; neither shouldest thou have spoken proudly in the day of distress.

13 Thou shouldest not have entered into the gate of my people in the day of their calamity; yea, thou shouldest not have looked on their affliction in the day of their calamity, nor have laid *hands* on their substance in the day of their calamity;

14 Neither shouldest thou have stood in the crossway, to cut off those of his that did escape; neither shouldest thou have delivered up those of his that did remain in the day of distress.

15 For the day of the LORD *is* near upon all the heathen: as thou hast done, it shall be done unto thee: thy reward shall return upon thine own head.

16 For as ye have drunk upon my holy mountain, *so* shall all the heathen drink continually; yea, they shall drink, and they shall swallow down, and they shall be as though they had not been.

17 ¶ But upon mount Zion shall be deliverance, and there shall be holiness; and the house of Jacob shall possess their possessions.

18 And the house of Jacob shall be a fire, and the house of Joseph a flame, and the house of Ē′sa͡u for stubble, and they shall kindle in them, and devour them; and there shall not be *any* remaining of the house of Ē′sa͡u; for the LORD hath spoken *it.*

19 And *they of* the south shall possess the mount of Ē′sa͡u; and *they of* the plain, the Phĭ-lĭs′tīneṣ: and they shall possess the fields of Ē′phrā-ĭm, and the fields of Sȧ-mā′rĭ-ȧ: and Benjamin *shall possess* Gĭl′ē-ăd.

20 And the captivity of this host of the children of Ĭṣ′rā-ĕl *shall possess* that of the Cā′năan-ītes, *even* unto Zăr′ē-phȧth; and the captivity of Jerusalem, which *is* in Sē-phā′răd, shall possess the cities of the south.

21 And saviours shall come up on mount Zion to judge the mount of Ē′sa͡u; and the kingdom shall be the LORD'S.

JONAH

CHAPTER 1

NOW the word of the LORD came
unto Jonah the son of Ȧ mĭt′taī,
saying,
2 Arise, go to Nĭn′ē-vĕh, that great
city, and cry against it; for their wickedness is come up before me.
3 But Jonah rose up to flee unto Tär′-
shĭsh from the presence of the LORD,
and went down to Jŏp′pȧ; and he found
a ship going to Tär′shĭsh: so he paid the
fare thereof, and went down into it, to
go with them unto Tär′shĭsh from the
presence of the LORD.
4 ¶ But the LORD sent out a great
wind into the sea, and there was a
mighty tempest in the sea, so that the
ship was like to be broken.
5 Then the mariners were afraid, and
cried every man unto his god, and cast
forth the wares that *were* in the ship
into the sea, to lighten *it* of them. But
Jonah was gone down into the sides of
the ship; and he lay, and was fast
asleep.
6 So the shipmaster came to him, and
said unto him, What meanest thou, O
sleeper? arise, call upon thy God, if so
be that God will think upon us, that we
perish not.
7 And they said every one to his fellow,
Come, and let us cast lots, that we may
know for whose cause this evil *is* upon
us. So they cast lots, and the lot fell
upon Jonah.
8 Then said they unto him, Tell us, we
pray thee, for whose cause this evil *is*
upon us; What *is* thine occupation? and
whence comest thou? what *is* thy country? and of what people *art* thou?
9 And he said unto them, I *am* a Hebrew; and I fear the LORD, the God of
heaven, which hath made the sea and
the dry *land*.
10 Then were the men exceedingly
afraid, and said unto him, Why hast thou
done this? For the men knew that he
fled from the presence of the LORD, because he had told them.
11 ¶ Then said they unto him, What
shall we do unto thee, that the sea may
be calm unto us? for the sea wrought,
and was tempestuous.
12 And he said unto them, Take me
up, and cast me forth into the sea; so
shall the sea be calm unto you: for I
know that for my sake this great tempest *is* upon you.
13 Nevertheless the men rowed hard
to bring *it* to the land; but they could
not: for the sea wrought, and was
tempestuous against them.
14 Wherefore they cried unto the
LORD, and said, We beseech thee, O
LORD, we beseech thee, let us not perish for this man's life, and lay not upon
us innocent blood: for thou, O LORD,
hast done as it pleased thee.
15 So they took up Jonah, and cast
him forth into the sea: and the sea
ceased from her raging.
16 Then the men feared the LORD exceedingly, and offered a sacrifice unto
the LORD, and made vows.
17 ¶ Now the LORD had prepared a
great fish to swallow up Jonah. And
Jonah was in the belly of the fish three
days and three nights.

CHAPTER 2

THEN Jonah prayed unto the LORD
his God out of the fish's belly,
2 And said, I cried by reason of mine
affliction unto the LORD, and he heard
me; out of the belly of hell cried I, *and*
thou heardest my voice.
3 For thou hadst cast me into the deep,
in the midst of the seas; and the floods
compassed me about: all thy billows
and thy waves passed over me.
4 Then I said, I am cast out of thy
sight; yet I will look again toward thy
holy temple.
5 The waters compassed me about,
even to the soul: the depth closed me
round about, the weeds were wrapped
about my head.
6 I went down to the bottoms of the
mountains; the earth with her bars *was*
about me for ever: yet hast thou brought
up my life from corruption, O LORD my
God.
7 When my soul fainted within me I
remembered the LORD: and my prayer
came in unto thee, into thine holy
temple.
8 They that observe lying vanities forsake their own mercy.
9 But I will sacrifice unto thee with the

voice of thanksgiving; I will pay *that* that I have vowed. Salvation *is* of the LORD.

10 ¶ And the LORD spake unto the fish, and it vomited out Jonah upon the dry *land*.

CHAPTER 3

AND the word of the LORD came unto Jonah the second time, saying,

2 Arise, go unto Nĭn'ē-vĕh, that great city, and preach unto it the preaching that I bid thee.

3 So Jonah arose, and went unto Nĭn'ē-vĕh, according to the word of the LORD. Now Nĭn'ē-vĕh was an exceeding great city of three days' journey.

4 And Jonah began to enter into the city a day's journey, and he cried, and said, Yet forty days, and Nĭn'ē-vĕh shall be overthrown.

5 ¶ So the people of Nĭn'ē-vĕh believed God, and proclaimed a fast, and put on sackcloth, from the greatest of them even to the least of them.

6 For word came unto the king of Nĭn'ē-vĕh, and he arose from his throne, and he laid his robe from him, and covered *him* with sackcloth, and sat in ashes.

7 And he caused *it* to be proclaimed and published through Nĭn'ē-vĕh by the decree of the king and his nobles, saying, Let neither man nor beast, herd nor flock, taste any thing: let them not feed, nor drink water:

8 But let man and beast be covered with sackcloth, and cry mightily unto God: yea, let them turn every one from his evil way, and from the violence that *is* in their hands.

9 Who can tell *if* God will turn and repent, and turn away from his fierce anger, that we perish not?

10 ¶ And God saw their works, that they turned from their evil way; and God repented of the evil, that he had said that he would do unto them; and he did *it* not.

CHAPTER 4

BUT it displeased Jonah exceedingly, and he was very angry.

2 And he prayed unto the LORD, and said, I pray thee, O LORD, *was* not this my saying, when I was yet in my country? Therefore I fled before unto Tär'shĭsh: for I knew that thou *art* a gracious God, and merciful, slow to anger, and of great kindness, and repentest thee of the evil.

3 Therefore now, O LORD, take, I beseech thee, my life from me; for *it is* better for me to die than to live.

4 ¶ Then said the LORD, Doest thou well to be angry?

5 So Jonah went out of the city, and sat on the east side of the city, and there made him a booth, and sat under it in the shadow, till he might see what would become of the city.

6 And the LORD God prepared a gourd, and made *it* to come up over Jonah, that it might be a shadow over his head, to deliver him from his grief. So Jonah was exceeding glad of the gourd.

7 But God prepared a worm when the morning rose the next day, and it smote the gourd that it withered.

8 And it came to pass, when the sun did arise, that God prepared a vehement east wind; and the sun beat upon the head of Jonah, that he fainted, and wished in himself to die, and said, *It is* better for me to die than to live.

9 And God said to Jonah, Doest thou well to be angry for the gourd? And he said, I do well to be angry, *even* unto death.

10 Then said the LORD, Thou hast had pity on the gourd, for the which thou hast not labored, neither madest it grow; which came up in a night, and perished in a night:

11 And should not I spare Nĭn'ē-vĕh, that great city, wherein are more than sixscore thousand persons that cannot discern between their right hand and their left hand; and *also* much cattle?

MICAH

CHAPTER 1

THE word of the LORD that came to
Mī'cah the Mō-răs'thīte in the
days of Jō'thăm, Ahaz, *and* Hĕz'ē-kī'ah,
kings of Judah, which he saw concerning
Sa-mā'rĭ-a and Jerusalem.
2 Hear, all ye people; hearken, O
earth, and all that therein is: and let
the Lord GOD be witness against you,
the Lord from his holy temple.
3 For, behold, the LORD cometh forth
out of his place, and will come down, and
tread upon the high places of the earth.
4 And the mountains shall be molten
under him, and the valleys shall be cleft,
as wax before the fire, *and* as the waters
that are poured down a steep place.
5 For the transgression of Jacob *is* all
this, and for the sins of the house of
Ĭş'rā-ĕl. What *is* the transgression of
Jacob? *is it* not Sa-mā'rĭ-a? and what
are the high places of Judah? *are they*
not Jerusalem?
6 Therefore I will make Sa-mā'rĭ-a as
a heap of the field, *and* as plantings of
a vineyard: and I will pour down the
stones thereof into the valley, and I will
discover the foundations thereof.
7 And all the graven images thereof
shall be beaten to pieces, and all the
hires thereof shall be burned with the
fire, and all the idols thereof will I lay
desolate: for she gathered *it* of the hire
of a harlot, and they shall return to the
hire of a harlot.
8 Therefore I will wail and howl, I will
go stripped and naked: I will make a
wailing like the dragons, and mourning
as the owls.
9 For her wound *is* incurable; for it is
come unto Judah; he is come unto the
gate of my people, *even* to Jerusalem.
10 ¶ Declare ye *it* not at Gath, weep
ye not at all: in the house of Ăph'rah
roll thyself in the dust.
11 Pass ye away, thou inhabitant of
Sā'phĭr, having thy shame naked: the
inhabitant of Zā'a-năn came not forth in
the mourning of Bĕth'-ē'zĕl; he shall
receive of you his standing.
12 For the inhabitant of Măr'ŏth
waited carefully for good: but evil came
down from the LORD unto the gate of
Jerusalem.
13 O thou inhabitant of Lā'chĭsh, bind
the chariot to the swift beast: she *is* the
beginning of the sin to the daughter of
Zion: for the transgressions of Ĭş'rā-ĕl
were found in thee.
14 Therefore shalt thou give presents
to Mō'rĕsh-ĕth-găth': the houses of
Ăch'zĭb *shall be* a lie to the kings of
Ĭş'rā-ĕl.
15 Yet will I bring an heir unto thee, O
inhabitant of Ma-rē'shah: he shall come
unto A-dŭl'lăm the glory of Ĭş'rā-ĕl.
16 Make thee bald, and poll thee for
thy delicate children; enlarge thy baldness
as the eagle; for they are gone into
captivity from thee.

CHAPTER 2

WOE to them that devise iniquity,
and work evil upon their beds!
when the morning is light, they practise
it, because it is in the power of their
hand.
2 And they covet fields, and take *them*
by violence; and houses, and take *them*
away: so they oppress a man and his
house, even a man and his heritage.
3 Therefore thus saith the LORD; Behold,
against this family do I devise an
evil, from which ye shall not remove
your necks; neither shall ye go haughtily:
for this time *is* evil.
4 ¶ In that day shall *one* take up a
parable against you, and lament with
a doleful lamentation, *and* say, We be
utterly spoiled: he hath changed the
portion of my people: how hath he removed
it from me! turning away he
hath divided our fields.
5 Therefore thou shalt have none that
shall cast a cord by lot in the congregation
of the LORD.
6 Prophesy ye not, *say they to them*
that prophesy: they shall not prophesy
to them, *that* they shall not take shame.
7 ¶ O *thou that art* named the house
of Jacob, is the Spirit of the LORD
straitened? *are* these his doings? do not
my words do good to him that walketh
uprightly?
8 Even of late my people is risen up as
an enemy: ye pull off the robe with the
garment from them that pass by securely
as men averse from war.
9 The women of my people have ye

cast out from their pleasant houses;
from their children have ye taken away
my glory for ever.
10 Arise ye, and depart; for this *is* not
your rest: because it is polluted, it shall
destroy *you,* even with a sore destruction.
11 If a man walking in the spirit and
falsehood do lie, *saying,* I will prophesy
unto thee of wine and of strong drink;
he shall even be the prophet of this
people.
12 ¶ I will surely assemble, O Jacob,
all of thee; I will surely gather the remnant of Ĭṣ′rā-ĕl; I will put them together
as the sheep of Bŏz′rȧh, as the flock in
the midst of their fold: they shall make
great noise by reason of *the multitude
of* men.
13 The breaker is come up before
them: they have broken up, and have
passed through the gate, and are gone
out by it; and their king shall pass before them, and the LORD on the head of
them.

CHAPTER 3

AND I said, Hear, I pray you, O heads
of Jacob, and ye princes of the
house of Ĭṣ′rā-ĕl; *Is it* not for you to
know judgment?
2 Who hate the good, and love the
evil; who pluck off their skin from off
them, and their flesh from off their
bones;
3 Who also eat the flesh of my people,
and flay their skin from off them; and
they break their bones, and chop them
in pieces, as for the pot, and as flesh
within the caldron.
4 Then shall they cry unto the LORD,
but he will not hear them: he will even
hide his face from them at that time, as
they have behaved themselves ill in
their doings.
5 ¶ Thus saith the LORD concerning
the prophets that make my people err,
that bite with their teeth, and cry,
Peace; and he that putteth not into their
mouths, they even prepare war against
him:
6 Therefore night *shall be* unto you,
that ye shall not have a vision; and it
shall be dark unto you, that ye shall not
divine; and the sun shall go down over
the prophets, and the day shall be dark
over them.
7 Then shall the seers be ashamed,
and the diviners confounded: yea, they
shall all cover their lips; for *there is* no
answer of God.
8 ¶ But truly I am full of power by the
Spirit of the LORD, and of judgment, and
of might, to declare unto Jacob his
transgression, and to Ĭṣ′rā-ĕl his sin.
9 Hear this, I pray you, ye heads of
the house of Jacob, and princes of the
house of Ĭṣ′rā-ĕl, that abhor judgment,
and pervert all equity.
10 They build up Zion with blood, and
Jerusalem with iniquity.
11 The heads thereof judge for reward,
and the priests thereof teach for hire,
and the prophets thereof divine for
money: yet will they lean upon the
LORD, and say, *Is* not the LORD among
us? none evil can come upon us.
12 Therefore shall Zion for your sake
be plowed *as* a field, and Jerusalem
shall become heaps, and the mountain
of the house as the high places of the
forest.

CHAPTER 4

BUT in the last days it shall come to
pass, *that* the mountain of the house
of the LORD shall be established in the
top of the mountains, and it shall be exalted above the hills; and people shall
flow unto it.
2 And many nations shall come, and
say, Come, and let us go up to the mountain of the LORD, and to the house of the
God of Jacob; and he will teach us of his
ways, and we will walk in his paths: for
the law shall go forth of Zion, and the
word of the LORD from Jerusalem.
3 ¶ And he shall judge among many
people, and rebuke strong nations afar
off; and they shall beat their swords
into plowshares, and their spears into
pruning hooks: nation shall not lift up a
sword against nation, neither shall they
learn war any more.
4 But they shall sit every man under
his vine and under his fig tree; and none
shall make *them* afraid: for the mouth
of the LORD of hosts hath spoken *it.*
5 For all people will walk every one in
the name of his god, and we will walk
in the name of the LORD our God for
ever and ever.
6 In that day, saith the LORD, will I
assemble her that halteth, and I will
gather her that is driven out, and her
that I have afflicted;

7 And I will make her that halted a
remnant, and her that was cast far off a
strong nation: and the LORD shall reign
over them in mount Zion from henceforth, even for ever.
8 ¶ And thou, O tower of the flock,
the stronghold of the daughter of Zion,
unto thee shall it come, even the first
dominion; the kingdom shall come to
the daughter of Jerusalem.
9 Now why dost thou cry out aloud?
is there no king in thee? is thy counselor perished? for pangs have taken
thee as a woman in travail.
10 Be in pain, and labor to bring forth,
O daughter of Zion, like a woman in
travail: for now shalt thou go forth out
of the city, and thou shalt dwell in the
field, and thou shalt go *even* to Babylon;
there shalt thou be delivered; there the
LORD shall redeem thee from the hand
of thine enemies.
11 ¶ Now also many nations are
gathered against thee, that say, Let her
be defiled, and let our eye look upon
Zion.
12 But they know not the thoughts of
the LORD, neither understand they his
counsel: for he shall gather them as the
sheaves into the floor.
13 Arise and thresh, O daughter of
Zion; for I will make thine horn iron,
and I will make thy hoofs brass: and
thou shalt beat in pieces many people:
and I will consecrate their gain unto the
LORD, and their substance unto the
Lord of the whole earth.

CHAPTER 5

NOW gather thyself in troops, O
daughter of troops: he hath laid
siege against us: they shall smite the
judge of Ĭş′rā-ēl with a rod upon the
cheek.
2 But thou, Beth-lehem Ĕph′rȧ-täh,
though thou be little among the thousands of Judah, *yet* out of thee shall he
come forth unto me *that is* to be ruler in
Ĭş′rā-ĕl; whose goings forth *have been*
from of old, from everlasting.
3 Therefore will he give them up, until
the time *that* she which travaileth hath
brought forth: then the remnant of his
brethren shall return unto the children
of Ĭş′rā-ĕl.
4 ¶ And he shall stand and feed in the
strength of the LORD, in the majesty of
the name of the LORD his God; and they
shall abide: for now shall he be great
unto the ends of the earth.
5 And this *man* shall be the peace,
when the Assyrian shall come into our
land: and when he shall tread in our
palaces, then shall we raise against him
seven shepherds, and eight principal
men.
6 And they shall waste the land of
Assyria with the sword, and the land of
Nimrod in the entrances thereof: thus
shall he deliver *us* from the Assyrian,
when he cometh into our land, and when
he treadeth within our borders.
7 And the remnant of Jacob shall be in
the midst of many people as a dew from
the LORD, as the showers upon the
grass, that tarrieth not for man, nor
waiteth for the sons of men.
8 ¶ And the remnant of Jacob shall be
among the Ġĕn′tīleş in the midst of
many people, as a lion among the beasts
of the forest, as a young lion among the
flocks of sheep: who, if he go through,
both treadeth down, and teareth in
pieces, and none can deliver.
9 Thine hand shall be lifted up upon
thine adversaries, and all thine enemies
shall be cut off.
10 And it shall come to pass in that day,
saith the LORD, that I will cut off thy
horses out of the midst of thee, and I
will destroy thy chariots:
11 And I will cut off the cities of thy
land, and throw down all thy strongholds:
12 And I will cut off witchcrafts out of
thine hand; and thou shalt have no *more*
soothsayers:
13 Thy graven images also will I cut
off, and thy standing images out of the
midst of thee; and thou shalt no more
worship the work of thine hands.
14 And I will pluck up thy groves out
of the midst of thee: so will I destroy thy
cities.
15 And I will execute vengeance in
anger and fury upon the heathen, such
as they have not heard.

CHAPTER 6

HEAR ye now what the LORD saith;
Arise, contend thou before the
mountains, and let the hills hear thy
voice.
2 Hear ye, O mountains, the LORD's
controversy, and ye strong foundations
of the earth: for the LORD hath a con-

troversy with his people, and he will
plead with Ĭs'rā-ĕl.
3 O my people, what have I done unto
thee? and wherein have I wearied thee?
testify against me.
4 For I brought thee up out of the land
of Egypt, and redeemed thee out of the
house of servants; and I sent before
thee Moses, Aaron, and Miriam.
5 O my people, remember now what
Bā'lăk king of Mō'ăb consulted, and
what Bā'laam the son of Bē'ŏr answered
him from Shĭt'tĭm unto Gĭl'găl; that ye
may know the righteousness of the
LORD.
6 ℂ Wherewith shall I come before
the LORD, *and* bow myself before the
high God? shall I come before him with
burnt offerings, with calves of a year
old?
7 Will the LORD be pleased with thousands of rams, *or* with ten thousands of
rivers of oil? shall I give my firstborn
for my transgression, the fruit of my
body *for* the sin of my soul?
8 He hath showed thee, O man, what
is good; and what doth the LORD require
of thee, but to do justly, and to love
mercy, and to walk humbly with thy
God?
9 The LORD's voice crieth unto the
city, and *the man of* wisdom shall see
thy name: hear ye the rod, and who hath
appointed it.
10 ℂ Are there yet the treasures of
wickedness in the house of the wicked,
and the scant measure *that is* abominable?
11 Shall I count *them* pure with the
wicked balances, and with the bag of
deceitful weights?
12 For the rich men thereof are full of
violence, and the inhabitants thereof
have spoken lies, and their tongue *is*
deceitful in their mouth.
13 Therefore also will I make *thee* sick
in smiting thee, in making *thee* desolate
because of thy sins.
14 Thou shalt eat, but not be satisfied;
and thy casting down *shall be* in the
midst of thee; and thou shalt take hold,
but shalt not deliver; and *that* which
thou deliverest will I give up to the
sword.
15 Thou shalt sow, but thou shalt not
reap; thou shalt tread the olives, but
thou shalt not anoint thee with oil; and
sweet wine, but shalt not drink wine.
16 ℂ For the statutes of Ŏm'rī are
kept, and all the works of the house of
Ahab, and ye walk in their counsels;
that I should make thee a desolation,
and the inhabitants thereof a hissing:
therefore ye shall bear the reproach of
my people.

CHAPTER 7

WOE is me! for I am as when they
have gathered the summer fruits,
as the grape gleanings of the vintage:
there is no cluster to eat: my soul desired the first ripe fruit.
2 The good *man* is perished out of the
earth; and *there is* none upright among
men: they all lie in wait for blood;
they hunt every man his brother with
a net.
3 ℂ That they may do evil with both
hands earnestly, the prince asketh, and
the judge *asketh* for a reward; and the
great *man*, he uttereth his mischievous
desire: so they wrap it up.
4 The best of them *is* as a brier: the
most upright *is sharper* than a thorn
hedge: the day of thy watchmen *and* thy
visitation cometh; now shall be their
perplexity.
5 ℂ Trust ye not in a friend, put ye not
confidence in a guide: keep the doors of
thy mouth from her that lieth in thy
bosom.
6 For the son dishonoreth the father,
the daughter riseth up against her
mother, the daughter-in-law against
her mother-in-law; a man's enemies *are*
the men of his own house.
7 Therefore I will look unto the LORD;
I will wait for the God of my salvation:
my God will hear me.
8 ℂ Rejoice not against me, O mine
enemy: when I fall, I shall arise; when
I sit in darkness, the LORD *shall be* a
light unto me.
9 I will bear the indignation of the
LORD, because I have sinned against
him, until he plead my cause, and execute judgment for me: he will bring me
forth to the light, *and* I shall behold his
righteousness.
10 Then *she that is* mine enemy shall
see *it*, and shame shall cover her which
said unto me, Where is the LORD thy
God? mine eyes shall behold her: now
shall she be trodden down as the mire
of the streets.
11 *In* the day that thy walls are to be

built, *in* that day shall the decree be far
removed.
12 *In* that day *also* he shall come even
to thee from Assyria, and *from* the fortified cities, and from the fortress even to
the river, and from sea to sea, and *from*
mountain to mountain.
13 Notwithstanding, the land shall be
desolate because of them that dwell
therein, for the fruit of their doings.
14 ℂ Feed thy people with thy rod,
the flock of thine heritage, which dwell
solitarily *in* the wood, in the midst of
Cär′mĕl: let them feed *in* Bā′shăn and
Gĭl′ē-ăd, as in the days of old.
15 According to the days of thy coming
out of the land of Egypt will I show unto
him marvelous *things*.
16 ℂ The nations shall see and be confounded at all their might: they shall lay
their hand upon *their* mouth, their ears
shall be deaf.
17 They shall lick the dust like a serpent, they shall move out of their holes
like worms of the earth: they shall be
afraid of the LORD our God, and shall
fear because of thee.
18 Who *is* a God like unto thee, that
pardoneth iniquity, and passeth by the
transgression of the remnant of his
heritage? he retaineth not his anger for
ever, because he delighteth *in* mercy.
19 He will turn again, he will have compassion upon us; he will subdue our
iniquities; and thou wilt cast all their
sins into the depths of the sea.
20 Thou wilt perform the truth to
Jacob, *and* the mercy to Abraham, which
thou hast sworn unto our fathers from
the days of old.

NAHUM

CHAPTER 1

THE burden of Nĭn′ē-vĕh. The book
of the vision of Nā′hŭm the Ĕl′-
kŏsh-īte.
2 God *is* jealous, and the LORD revengeth; the LORD revengeth, and *is*
furious; the LORD will take vengeance
on his adversaries, and he reserveth
wrath for his enemies.
3 The LORD *is* slow to anger, and great
in power, and will not at all acquit *the*
wicked: the LORD *hath* his way in the
whirlwind and in the storm, and the
clouds *are* the dust of his feet.
4 He rebuketh the sea, and maketh
it dry, and drieth up all the rivers:
Bā′shăn languisheth, and Cär′mĕl, and
the flower of Lebanon languisheth.
5 The mountains quake at him, and the
hills melt, and the earth is burned at his
presence, yea, the world, and all that
dwell therein.
6 Who can stand before his indignation? and who can abide in the fierceness of his anger? his fury is poured out
like fire, and the rocks are thrown down
by him.
7 The LORD *is* good, a stronghold in
the day of trouble; and he knoweth them
that trust in him.
8 But with an overrunning flood he
will make an utter end of the place
thereof, and darkness shall pursue his
enemies.
9 What do ye imagine against the
LORD? he will make an utter end:
affliction shall not rise up the second
time.
10 For while *they be* folden together *as*
thorns, and while they are drunken *as*
drunkards, they shall be devoured as
stubble fully dry.
11 There is *one* come out of thee, that
imagineth evil against the LORD, a
wicked counselor.
12 Thus saith the LORD; Though *they*
be quiet, and likewise many, yet thus
shall they be cut down, when he shall
pass through. Though I have afflicted
thee, I will afflict thee no more.
13 For now will I break his yoke from
off thee, and will burst thy bonds in
sunder.
14 And the LORD hath given a commandment concerning thee, *that* no
more of thy name be sown: out of the
house of thy gods will I cut off the graven
image and the molten image: I will make
thy grave; for thou art vile.
15 Behold upon the mountains the feet
of him that bringeth good tidings, that
publisheth peace! O Judah, keep thy
solemn feasts, perform thy vows: for
the wicked shall no more pass through
thee; he is utterly cut off.

CHAPTER 2

HE that dasheth in pieces is come up before thy face: keep the munition, watch the way, make *thy* loins strong, fortify *thy* power mightily.

2 For the LORD hath turned away the excellency of Jacob, as the excellency of Ĭs′rā-ēl: for the emptiers have emptied them out, and marred their vine branches.

3 The shield of his mighty men is made red, the valiant men *are* in scarlet: the chariots *shall be* with flaming torches in the day of his preparation, and the fir trees shall be terribly shaken.

4 The chariots shall rage in the streets, they shall justle one against another in the broad ways: they shall seem like torches, they shall run like the lightnings.

5 He shall recount his worthies: they shall stumble in their walk; they shall make haste to the wall thereof, and the defense shall be prepared.

6 The gates of the rivers shall be opened, and the palace shall be dissolved.

7 And Hŭz′zăb shall be led away captive, she shall be brought up, and her maids shall lead *her* as with the voice of doves, taboring upon their breasts.

8 But Nĭn′ē-vĕh *is* of old like a pool of water: yet they shall flee away. Stand, stand, *shall they cry;* but none shall look back.

9 Take ye the spoil of silver, take the spoil of gold: for *there is* none end of the store *and* glory out of all the pleasant furniture.

10 She is empty, and void, and waste: and the heart melteth, and the knees smite together, and much pain *is* in all loins, and the faces of them all gather blackness.

11 Where *is* the dwelling of the lions, and the feeding place of the young lions, where the lion, *even* the old lion, walked, *and* the lion's whelp, and none made *them* afraid?

12 The lion did tear in pieces enough for his whelps, and strangled for his lionesses, and filled his holes with prey, and his dens with ravin.

13 Behold, I *am* against thee, saith the LORD of hosts, and I will burn her chariots in the smoke, and the sword shall devour thy young lions: and I will cut off thy prey from the earth, and the voice of thy messengers shall no more be heard.

CHAPTER 3

WOE to the bloody city! it *is* all full of lies *and* robbery; the prey departeth not;

2 The noise of a whip, and the noise of the rattling of the wheels, and of the prancing horses, and of the jumping chariots.

3 The horseman lifteth up both the bright sword and the glittering spear: and *there is* a multitude of slain, and a great number of carcasses; and *there is* none end of *their* corpses; they stumble upon their corpses:

4 Because of the multitude of the whoredoms of the well-favored harlot, the mistress of witchcrafts, that selleth nations through her whoredoms, and families through her witchcrafts.

5 Behold, I *am* against thee, saith the LORD of hosts; and I will discover thy skirts upon thy face, and I will show the nations thy nakedness, and the kingdoms thy shame.

6 And I will cast abominable filth upon thee, and make thee vile, and will set thee as a gazingstock.

7 And it shall come to pass, *that* all they that look upon thee shall flee from thee, and say, Nĭn′ē-vĕh is laid waste: who will bemoan her? whence shall I seek comforters for thee?

8 Art thou better than populous No, that was situate among the rivers, *that had* the waters round about it, whose rampart *was* the sea, *and* her wall *was* from the sea?

9 Ethiopia and Egypt *were* her strength, and *it was* infinite; Pŭt and Lū′bĭm were thy helpers.

10 Yet *was* she carried away, she went into captivity: her young children also were dashed in pieces at the top of all the streets: and they cast lots for her honorable men, and all her great men were bound in chains.

11 Thou also shalt be drunken: thou shalt be hid, thou also shalt seek strength because of the enemy.

12 All thy strongholds *shall be like* fig trees with the first ripe figs: if they be shaken, they shall even fall into the mouth of the eater.

13 Behold, thy people in the midst of thee *are* women: the gates of thy land shall be set wide open unto thine enemies: the fire shall devour thy bars.

14 Draw thee waters for the siege, fortify thy strongholds: go into clay, and tread the mortar, make strong the brickkiln.
15 There shall the fire devour thee; the sword shall cut thee off, it shall eat thee up like the cankerworm: make thy self many as the cankerworm, make thyself many as the locusts.
16 Thou hast multiplied thy merchants above the stars of heaven: the cankerworm spoileth, and fleeth away.
17 Thy crowned *are* as the locusts, and thy captains as the great grasshoppers, which camp in the hedges in the cold day, *but* when the sun ariseth they flee away, and their place is not known where they *are*.
18 Thy shepherds slumber, O king of Assyria: thy nobles shall dwell *in the dust:* thy people is scattered upon the mountains, and no man gathereth *them*.
19 *There is* no healing of thy bruise; thy wound is grievous: all that hear the bruit of thee shall clap the hands over thee: for upon whom hath not thy wickedness passed continually?

HABAKKUK

CHAPTER 1

THE burden which Hȧ-băk′kŭk the prophet did see.
2 O LORD, how long shall I cry, and thou wilt not hear! *even* cry out unto thee *of* violence, and thou wilt not save!
3 Why dost thou show me iniquity, and cause *me* to behold grievance? for spoiling and violence *are* before me: and there are *that* raise up strife and contention.
4 Therefore the law is slacked, and judgment doth never go forth: for the wicked doth compass about the righteous; therefore wrong judgment proceedeth.
5 ¶ Behold ye among the heathen, and regard, and wonder marvelously: for I will work a work in your days, *which* ye will not believe, though it be told *you*.
6 For, lo, I raise up the Chăl-dē′ăns, *that* bitter and hasty nation, which shall march through the breadth of the land, to possess the dwelling places *that are* not theirs.
7 They *are* terrible and dreadful: their judgment and their dignity shall proceed of themselves.
8 Their horses also are swifter than the leopards, and are more fierce than the evening wolves: and their horsemen shall spread themselves, and their horsemen shall come from far; they shall fly as the eagle *that* hasteth to eat.
9 They shall come all for violence: their faces shall sup up *as* the east wind, and they shall gather the captivity as the sand.
10 And they shall scoff at the kings, and the princes shall be a scorn unto them: they shall deride every stronghold; for they shall heap dust, and take it.
11 Then shall *his* mind change, and he shall pass over, and offend, *imputing* this his power unto his god.
12 ¶ *Art* thou not from everlasting, O LORD my God, mine Holy One? We shall not die. O LORD, thou hast ordained them for judgment; and, O mighty God, thou hast established them for correction.
13 *Thou art* of purer eyes than to behold evil, and canst not look on iniquity: wherefore lookest thou upon them that deal treacherously, *and* holdest thy tongue when the wicked devoureth *the man that is* more righteous than he?
14 And makest men as the fishes of the sea, as the creeping things, *that have* no ruler over them?
15 They take up all of them with the angle, they catch them in their net, and gather them in their drag: therefore they rejoice and are glad.
16 Therefore they sacrifice unto their net, and burn incense unto their drag; because by them their portion *is* fat, and their meat plenteous.
17 Shall they therefore empty their net, and not spare continually to slay the nations?

CHAPTER 2

I WILL stand upon my watch, and set me upon the tower, and will watch to see what he will say unto me, and what I shall answer when I am reproved.

2 And the LORD answered me, and
said, Write the vision, and make *it* plain
upon tables, that he may run that readeth it.
3 For the vision *is* yet for an appointed
time, but at the end it shall speak, and
not lie: though it tarry, wait for it; because it will surely come, it will not tarry.
4 Behold, his soul *which* is lifted up is
not upright in him: but the just shall live
by his faith.
5 ¶ Yea also, because he transgresseth
by wine, *he is* a proud man, neither
keepeth at home, who enlargeth his
desire as hell, and *is* as death, and cannot be satisfied, but gathereth unto him
all nations, and heapeth unto him all
people:
6 Shall not all these take up a parable
against him, and a taunting proverb
against him, and say, Woe to him that
increaseth *that which is* not his! how
long? and to him that ladeth himself with
thick clay!
7 Shall they not rise up suddenly that
shall bite thee, and awake that shall vex
thee, and thou shalt be for booties unto
them?
8 Because thou hast spoiled many
nations, all the remnant of the people
shall spoil thee; because of men's blood,
and *for* the violence of the land, of the
city, and of all that dwell therein.
9 ¶ Woe to him that coveteth an evil
covetousness to his house, that he may
set his nest on high, that he may be
delivered from the power of evil!
10 Thou hast consulted shame to thy
house by cutting off many people, and
hast sinned *against* thy soul.
11 For the stone shall cry out of the
wall, and the beam out of the timber
shall answer it.
12 ¶ Woe to him that buildeth a town
with blood, and establisheth a city by
iniquity!
13 Behold, *is it* not of the LORD of
hosts that the people shall labor in the
very fire, and the people shall weary
themselves for very vanity?
14 For the earth shall be filled with the
knowledge of the glory of the LORD, as
the waters cover the sea.
15 ¶ Woe unto him that giveth his
neighbor drink, that puttest thy bottle to
him, and makest *him* drunken also, that
thou mayest look on their nakedness!
16 Thou art filled with shame for glory:
drink thou also, and let thy foreskin be
uncovered: the cup of the LORD's right
hand shall be turned unto thee, and
shameful spewing *shall be* on thy glory.
17 For the violence of Lebanon shall
cover thee, and the spoil of beasts,
which made them afraid, because of
men's blood, and for the violence of the
land, of the city, and of all that dwell
therein.
18 ¶ What profiteth the graven image
that the maker thereof hath graven it;
the molten image, and a teacher of lies,
that the maker of his work trusteth
therein, to make dumb idols?
19 Woe unto him that saith to the wood,
Awake; to the dumb stone, Arise, it
shall teach! Behold, it *is* laid over with
gold and silver, and *there is* no breath
at all in the midst of it.
20 But the LORD *is* in his holy temple:
let all the earth keep silence before him.

CHAPTER 3

A PRAYER of Hȧ-băk′kŭk the prophet
upon Shĭg′ĭ-ō′nŏth.
2 O LORD, I have heard thy speech,
and was afraid: O LORD, revive thy
work in the midst of the years, in the
midst of the years make known; in
wrath remember mercy.
3 God came from Tē′măn, and the
Holy One from mount Pā′răn. Sē′lȧh.
His glory covered the heavens, and the
earth was full of his praise.
4 And *his* brightness was as the light;
he had horns *coming* out of his hand:
and there *was* the hiding of his power.
5 Before him went the pestilence, and
burning coals went forth at his feet.
6 He stood, and measured the earth:
he beheld, and drove asunder the nations; and the everlasting mountains
were scattered, the perpetual hills did
bow: his ways *are* everlasting.
7 I saw the tents of Cū′shăn in affliction: *and* the curtains of the land of
Mĭd′ĭ-ăn did tremble.
8 Was the LORD displeased against
the rivers? *was* thine anger against the
rivers? *was* thy wrath against the sea,
that thou didst ride upon thine horses
and thy chariots of salvation?
9 Thy bow was made quite naked,
according to the oaths of the tribes, *even*
thy word. Sē′lȧh. Thou didst cleave
the earth with rivers.
10 The mountains saw thee, *and* they

trembled: the overflowing of the water passed by: the deep uttered his voice, *and* lifted up his hands on high.

11 The sun *and* moon stood still in their habitation: at the light of thine arrows they went, *and* at the shining of thy glittering spear.

12 Thou didst march through the land in indignation, thou didst thresh the heathen in anger.

13 Thou wentest forth for the salvation of thy people, *even* for salvation with thine anointed; thou woundedst the head out of the house of the wicked, by discovering the foundation unto the neck. Sē′lȧh.

14 Thou didst strike through with his staves the head of his villages: they came out as a whirlwind to scatter me: their rejoicing *was* as to devour the poor secretly.

15 Thou didst walk through the sea with thine horses, *through* the heap of great waters.

16 When I heard, my belly trembled; my lips quivered at the voice: rottenness entered into my bones, and I trembled in myself, that I might rest in the day of trouble: when he cometh up unto the people, he will invade them with his troops.

17 ¶ Although the fig tree shall not blossom, neither *shall* fruit *be* in the vines; the labor of the olive shall fail, and the fields shall yield no meat; the flock shall be cut off from the fold, and *there shall be* no herd in the stalls:

18 Yet I will rejoice in the LORD, I will joy in the God of my salvation.

19 The LORD God *is* my strength, and he will make my feet like hinds' *feet*, and he will make me to walk upon mine high places. To the chief singer on my stringed instruments.

ZEPHANIAH

CHAPTER 1

THE word of the LORD which came unto Zĕph′ȧ-nī′ȧh the son of Cū′shī, the son of Gĕd′ȧ-lī′ȧh, the son of Ăm′ȧ-rī′ȧh, the son of Hĭz-kī′ȧh, in the days of Jō-sī′ȧh the son of Ā′mŏn, king of Judah.

2 I will utterly consume all *things* from off the land, saith the LORD.

3 I will consume man and beast; I will consume the fowls of the heaven, and the fishes of the sea, and the stumbling-blocks with the wicked; and I will cut off man from off the land, saith the LORD.

4 I will also stretch out mine hand upon Judah, and upon all the inhabitants of Jerusalem; and I will cut off the remnant of Bā′ăl from this place, *and* the name of the Chĕm′ȧ-rĭm with the priests;

5 And them that worship the host of heaven upon the housetops; and them that worship *and* that swear by the LORD, and that swear by Măl′chăm;

6 And them that are turned back from the LORD; and *those* that have not sought the LORD, nor inquired for him.

7 Hold thy peace at the presence of the Lord GOD: for the day of the LORD *is* at hand: for the LORD hath prepared a sacrifice, he hath bid his guests.

8 And it shall come to pass in the day of the LORD's sacrifice, that I will punish the princes, and the king's children, and all such as are clothed with strange apparel.

9 In the same day also will I punish all those that leap on the threshold, which fill their masters' houses with violence and deceit.

10 And it shall come to pass in that day, saith the LORD, *that there shall be* the noise of a cry from the fish gate, and a howling from the second, and a great crashing from the hills.

11 Howl, ye inhabitants of Măk′tĕsh, for all the merchant people are cut down; all they that bear silver are cut off.

12 And it shall come to pass at that time, *that* I will search Jerusalem with candles, and punish the men that are settled on their lees: that say in their heart, The LORD will not do good, neither will he do evil.

13 Therefore, their goods shall become a booty, and their houses a desolation: they shall also build houses, but not inhabit *them;* and they shall plant vineyards, but not drink the wine thereof.

14 The great day of the LORD *is* near, *it is* near, and hasteth greatly, *even* the

voice of the day of the LORD: the mighty man shall cry there bitterly.

15 That day *is* a day of wrath, a day of trouble and distress, a day of wasteness and desolation, a day of darkness and gloominess, a day of clouds and thick darkness,

16 A day of the trumpet and alarm against the fenced cities, and against the high towers.

17 And I will bring distress upon men, that they shall walk like blind men, because they have sinned against the LORD: and their blood shall be poured out as dust, and their flesh as the dung.

18 Neither their silver nor their gold shall be able to deliver them in the day of the LORD's wrath; but the whole land shall be devoured by the fire of his jealousy: for he shall make even a speedy riddance of all them that dwell in the land.

CHAPTER 2

GATHER yourselves together, yea, gather together, O nation not desired;

2 Before the decree bring forth, *before* the day pass as the chaff, before the fierce anger of the LORD come upon you, before the day of the LORD's anger come upon you.

3 Seek ye the LORD, all ye meek of the earth, which have wrought his judgment; seek righteousness, seek meekness: it may be ye shall be hid in the day of the LORD's anger.

4 ¶ For Gā'zȧ shall be forsaken, and Ăsh'kē-lŏn a desolation: they shall drive out Ashdod at the noonday, and Ĕk'rŏn shall be rooted up.

5 Woe unto the inhabitants of the seacoast, the nation of the Chĕr'ē-thītes! the word of the LORD *is* against you; O Cā'năan, the land of the Phĭ-lĭs'tīneṣ, I will even destroy thee, that there shall be no inhabitant.

6 And the seacoast shall be dwellings *and* cottages for shepherds, and folds for flocks.

7 And the coast shall be for the remnant of the house of Judah; they shall feed thereupon: in the houses of Ăsh'kē-lŏn shall they lie down in the evening: for the LORD their God shall visit them, and turn away their captivity.

8 ¶ I have heard the reproach of Mō'ăb, and the revilings of the children of Ammon, whereby they have reproached my people, and magnified *themselves* against their border.

9 Therefore, *as* I live, saith the LORD of hosts, the God of Ĭṣ'rā-ĕl, Surely Mō'ăb shall be as Sŏd'ŏm, and the children of Ammon as Gō-mŏr'rȧh, *even* the breeding of nettles, and saltpits, and a perpetual desolation: the residue of my people shall spoil them, and the remnant of my people shall possess them.

10 This shall they have for their pride, because they have reproached and magnified *themselves* against the people of the LORD of hosts.

11 The LORD *will be* terrible unto them: for he will famish all the gods of the earth; and *men* shall worship him, every one from his place, *even* all the isles of the heathen.

12 ¶ Ye Ethiopians also, ye *shall be* slain by my sword.

13 And he will stretch out his hand against the north, and destroy Assyria; and will make Nĭn'ē-vĕh a desolation, *and* dry like a wilderness.

14 And flocks shall lie down in the midst of her, all the beasts of the nations: both the cormorant and the bittern shall lodge in the upper lintels of it; *their* voice shall sing in the windows; desolation *shall be* in the thresholds: for he shall uncover the cedar work.

15 This *is* the rejoicing city that dwelt carelessly, that said in her heart, I *am*, and *there is* none besides me: how is she become a desolation, a place for beasts to lie down in! every one that passeth by her shall hiss, *and* wag his hand.

CHAPTER 3

WOE to her that is filthy and polluted, to the oppressing city!

2 She obeyed not the voice; she received not correction; she trusted not in the LORD; she drew not near to her God.

3 Her princes within her *are* roaring lions; her judges *are* evening wolves; they gnaw not the bones till the morrow.

4 Her prophets *are* light *and* treacherous persons: her priests have polluted the sanctuary, they have done violence to the law.

5 The just LORD *is* in the midst thereof; he will not do iniquity: every morning doth he bring his judgment to light,

he faileth not; but the unjust knoweth
no shame.
6 I have cut off the nations: their
towers are desolate; I made their streets
waste, that none passeth by: their cities
are destroyed, so that there is no man,
that there is none inhabitant.
7 I said, Surely, thou wilt fear me, thou
wilt receive instruction; so their dwelling should not be cut off, howsoever I
punished them: but they rose early, *and*
corrupted all their doings.
8 ¶ Therefore wait ye upon me, saith
the LORD, until the day that I rise up to
the prey: for my determination *is* to
gather the nations, that I may assemble
the kingdoms, to pour upon them mine
indignation, *even* all my fierce anger:
for all the earth shall be devoured with
the fire of my jealousy.
9 For then will I turn to the people a
pure language, that they may all call
upon the name of the LORD, to serve
him with one consent.
10 From beyond the rivers of Ethiopia
my suppliants, *even* the daughter of my
dispersed, shall bring mine offering.
11 In that day shalt thou not be
ashamed for all thy doings, wherein
thou hast transgressed against me: for
then I will take away out of the midst of
thee them that rejoice in thy pride, and
thou shalt no more be haughty because
of my holy mountain.
12 I will also leave in the midst of thee
an afflicted and poor people, and they
shall trust in the name of the LORD.
13 The remnant of Ĭṣ′rā-ĕl shall not do
iniquity, nor speak lies; neither shall a
deceitful tongue be found in their
mouth: for they shall feed and lie down,
and none shall make *them* afraid.
14 ¶ Sing, O daughter of Zion; shout,
O Ĭṣ′rā-ĕl; be glad and rejoice with all
the heart, O daughter of Jerusalem.
15 The LORD hath taken away thy
judgments, he hath cast out thine
enemy: the King of Ĭṣ′rā-ĕl, *even* the
LORD, *is* in the midst of thee: thou
shalt not see evil any more.
16 In that day it shall be said to Jerusalem, Fear thou not: *and to* Zion, Let
not thine hands be slack.
17 The LORD thy God in the midst of
thee *is* mighty; he will save, he will
rejoice over thee with joy; he will rest
in his love, he will joy over thee with
singing.
18 I will gather *them that are* sorrowful
for the solemn assembly, *who* are of
thee, *to whom* the reproach of it *was* a
burden.
19 Behold, at that time I will undo all
that afflict thee: and I will save her that
halteth, and gather her that was driven
out; and I will get them praise and fame
in every land where they have been put
to shame.
20 At that time will I bring you *again*,
even in the time that I gather you: for I
will make you a name and a praise
among all people of the earth, when I
turn back your captivity before your
eyes, saith the LORD.

HAGGAI

CHAPTER 1

IN the second year of Dȧ-rī′ŭs the
king, in the sixth month, in the first
day of the month, came the word of the
LORD by Hăg′gā-ī the prophet unto
Zĕ-rŭb′bȧ-bĕl the son of Shē-ăl′tĭ-ĕl,
governor of Judah, and to Joshua the
son of Jŏs′ē-dĕch, the high priest, saying,
2 Thus speaketh the LORD of hosts,
saying, This people say, The time is not
come, the time that the LORD's house
should be built.
3 Then came the word of the LORD by
Hăg′gā-ī the prophet, saying,
4 *Is it* time for you, O ye, to dwell in
your ceiled houses, and this house *lie*
waste?
5 Now therefore thus saith the LORD
of hosts; Consider your ways.
6 Ye have sown much, and bring in
little; ye eat, but ye have not enough;
ye drink, but ye are not filled with drink;
ye clothe you, but there is none warm;
and he that earneth wages, earneth
wages *to put it* into a bag with holes.
7 ¶ Thus saith the LORD of hosts;
Consider your ways.
8 Go up to the mountain, and bring
wood, and build the house; and I will
take pleasure in it, and I will be glorified, saith the LORD.

9 Ye looked for much, and, lo, *it came*
to little; and when ye brought *it* home,
I did blow upon it. Why? saith the LORD
of hosts. Because of mine house that *is*
waste, and ye run every man unto his
own house.
10 Therefore the heaven over you is
stayed from dew, and the earth is stayed
from her fruit.
11 And I called for a drought upon the
land, and upon the mountains, and upon
the corn, and upon the new wine, and
upon the oil, and upon *that* which the
ground bringeth forth, and upon men,
and upon cattle, and upon all the labor
of the hands.
12 ¶ Then Zĕ-rŭb′bȧ-bĕl the son of
Shē-ăl′tĭ-ĕl, and Joshua the son of Jŏs′ē-
dĕch, the high priest, with all the remnant of the people, obeyed the voice of
the LORD their God, and the words of
Hăg′gā-ī the prophet, as the LORD their
God had sent him, and the people did
fear before the LORD.
13 Then spake Hăg′gā-ī the LORD's
messenger in the LORD's message unto
the people, saying, I *am* with you, saith
the LORD.
14 And the LORD stirred up the spirit
of Zĕ-rŭb′bȧ-bĕl the son of Shē-ăl′tĭ-ĕl,
governor of Judah, and the spirit of
Joshua the son of Jŏs′ē-dĕch, the high
priest, and the spirit of all the remnant
of the people; and they came and did
work in the house of the LORD of hosts,
their God,
15 In the four and twentieth day of the
sixth month, in the second year of
Dȧ-rī′ŭs the king.

CHAPTER 2

IN the seventh *month*, in the one and
twentieth *day* of the month, came
the word of the LORD by the prophet
Hăg′gā-ī, saying,
2 Speak now to Zĕ-rŭb′bȧ-bĕl the son
of Shē-ăl′tĭ-ĕl, governor of Judah, and
to Joshua the son of Jŏs′ē-dĕch, the
high priest, and to the residue of the
people, saying,
3 Who *is* left among you that saw this
house in her first glory? and how do ye
see it now? *is it* not in your eyes in comparison of it as nothing?
4 Yet now be strong, O Zĕ-rŭb′bȧ-bĕl,
saith the LORD; and be strong, O
Joshua, son of Jŏs′ē-dĕch, the high
priest; and be strong, all ye people of
the land, saith the LORD, and work: for
I *am* with you, saith the LORD of hosts:
5 *According to* the word that I covenanted with you when ye came out of
Egypt, so my Spirit remaineth among
you: fear ye not.
6 For thus saith the LORD of hosts;
Yet once, it *is* a little while, and I will
shake the heavens, and the earth, and
the sea, and the dry *land;*
7 And I will shake all nations, and the
Desire of all nations shall come: and I
will fill this house with glory, saith the
LORD of hosts.
8 The silver *is* mine, and the gold *is*
mine, saith the LORD of hosts.
9 The glory of this latter house shall be
greater than of the former, saith the
LORD of hosts: and in this place will I
give peace, saith the LORD of hosts.
10 ¶ In the four and twentieth *day* of
the ninth *month*, in the second year of
Dȧ-rī′ŭs, came the word of the LORD by
Hăg′gā-ī the prophet, saying,
11 Thus saith the LORD of hosts; Ask
now the priests *concerning* the law,
saying,
12 If one bear holy flesh in the skirt of
his garment, and with his skirt do touch
bread, or pottage, or wine, or oil, or any
meat, shall it be holy? And the priests
answered and said, No.
13 Then said Hăg′gā-ī, If *one that is*
unclean by a dead body touch any of
these, shall it be unclean? And the
priests answered and said, It shall be
unclean.
14 Then answered Hăg′gā-ī, and said,
So *is* this people, and so *is* this nation
before me, saith the LORD; and so *is*
every work of their hands; and that
which they offer there *is* unclean.
15 And now, I pray you, consider from
this day and upward, from before a
stone was laid upon a stone in the temple of the LORD:
16 Since those *days* were, when *one*
came to a heap of twenty *measures*,
there were *but* ten: when *one* came to
the pressvat for to draw out fifty *vessels*
out of the press, there were *but* twenty.
17 I smote you with blasting and with
mildew and with hail in all the labors of
your hands; yet ye *turned* not to me,
saith the LORD.
18 Consider now from this day and
upward, from the four and twentieth
day of the ninth *month*, *even* from the

day that the foundation of the LORD's
temple was laid, consider *it*.
19 Is the seed yet in the barn? yea, as
yet the vine, and the fig tree, and the
pomegranate, and the olive tree, hath
not brought forth: from this day will I
bless *you*.
20 ℂ And again the word of the LORD
came unto Hăg'gā-ī in the four and
twentieth *day* of the month, saying,
21 Speak to Zĕ-rŭb'bà-bĕl, governor of
Judah, saying, I will shake the heavens
and the earth;
22 And I will overthrow the throne
of kingdoms, and I will destroy the
strength of the kingdoms of the heathen;
and I will overthrow the chariots, and
those that ride in them; and the horses
and their riders shall come down, every
one by the sword of his brother.
23 In that day, saith the LORD of hosts,
will I take thee, O Zĕ-rŭb'bà-bĕl, my
servant, the son of Shē-ăl'tĭ-ĕl, saith
the LORD, and will make thee as a signet: for I have chosen thee, saith the
LORD of hosts.

ZECHARIAH

CHAPTER 1

IN the eighth month, in the second
year of Dà-rī'ŭs, came the word of
the LORD unto Zĕch'à-rī'àh, the son
of Bĕr'ē-chī'àh, the son of Ĭd'dō the
prophet, saying,
2 The LORD hath been sore displeased
with your fathers.
3 Therefore say thou unto them, Thus
saith the LORD of hosts; Turn ye unto
me, saith the LORD of hosts, and I will
turn unto you, saith the LORD of hosts.
4 Be ye not as your fathers, unto whom
the former prophets have cried, saying,
Thus saith the LORD of hosts; Turn ye
now from your evil ways, and *from* your
evildoings: but they did not hear, nor
hearken unto me, saith the LORD.
5 Your fathers, where *are* they? and
the prophets, do they live for ever?
6 But my words and my statutes, which
I commanded my servants the prophets,
did they not take hold of your fathers?
and they returned and said, Like as the
LORD of hosts thought to do unto us,
according to our ways, and according to
our doings, so hath he dealt with us.
7 ℂ Upon the four and twentieth day
of the eleventh month, which *is* the month
Sē-băt', in the second year of Dà-rī'ŭs,
came the word of the LORD unto Zĕch'à-
rī'àh, the son of Bĕr'ē-chī'àh, the son
of Ĭd'dō the prophet, saying,
8 I saw by night, and behold a man
riding upon a red horse, and he stood
among the myrtle trees that *were* in the
bottom; and behind him *were there* red
horses, speckled, and white.
9 Then said I, O my lord, what *are*
these? And the angel that talked with
me said unto me, I will show thee what
these *be*.
10 And the man that stood among the
myrtle trees answered and said, These
are they whom the LORD hath sent to
walk to and fro through the earth.
11 And they answered the angel of the
LORD that stood among the myrtle trees,
and said, We have walked to and fro
through the earth, and, behold, all the
earth sitteth still, and is at rest.
12 ℂ Then the angel of the LORD
answered and said, O LORD of hosts,
how long wilt thou not have mercy on
Jerusalem and on the cities of Judah,
against which thou hast had indignation
these threescore and ten years?
13 And the LORD answered the angel
that talked with me *with* good words
and comfortable words.
14 So the angel that communed with
me said unto me, Cry thou, saying, Thus
saith the LORD of hosts; I am jealous
for Jerusalem and for Zion with a great
jealousy.
15 And I am very sore displeased with
the heathen *that are* at ease: for I was
but a little displeased, and they helped
forward the affliction.
16 Therefore thus saith the LORD; I
am returned to Jerusalem with mercies:
my house shall be built in it, saith the
LORD of hosts, and a line shall be
stretched upon Jerusalem.
17 Cry yet, saying, Thus saith the
LORD of hosts; My cities through prosperity shall yet be spread abroad; and
the LORD shall yet comfort Zion, and
shall yet choose Jerusalem.

18 ℂ Then lifted I up mine eyes, and saw, and behold four horns.

19 And I said unto the angel that talked with me, What *be* these? And he answered me, These *are* the horns which have scattered Judah, Ĭş'rā-ĕl, and Jerusalem.

20 And the LORD showed me four carpenters.

21 Then said I, What come these to do? And he spake, saying, These *are* the horns which have scattered Judah, so that no man did lift up his head: but these are come to fray them, to cast out the horns of the Ġĕn'tīleş, which lifted up *their* horn over the land of Judah to scatter it.

CHAPTER 2

I LIFTED up mine eyes again, and looked, and behold a man with a measuring line in his hand.

2 Then said I, Whither goest thou? And he said unto me, To measure Jerusalem, to see what *is* the breadth thereof, and what *is* the length thereof.

3 And, behold, the angel that talked with me went forth, and another angel went out to meet him,

4 And said unto him, Run, speak to this young man, saying, Jerusalem shall be inhabited *as* towns without walls for the multitude of men and cattle therein:

5 For I, saith the LORD, will be unto her a wall of fire round about, and will be the glory in the midst of her.

6 ℂ Ho, ho, *come forth,* and flee from the land of the north, saith the LORD: for I have spread you abroad as the four winds of the heaven, saith the LORD.

7 Deliver thyself, O Zion, that dwellest *with* the daughter of Babylon.

8 For thus saith the LORD of hosts; After the glory hath he sent me unto the nations which spoiled you: for he that toucheth you, toucheth the apple of his eye.

9 For, behold, I will shake mine hand upon them, and they shall be a spoil to their servants: and ye shall know that the LORD of hosts hath sent me.

10 ℂ Sing and rejoice, O daughter of Zion: for, lo, I come, and I will dwell in the midst of thee, saith the LORD.

11 And many nations shall be joined to the LORD in that day, and shall be my people: and I will dwell in the midst of thee, and thou shalt know that the LORD of hosts hath sent me unto thee.

12 And the LORD shall inherit Judah his portion in the holy land, and shall choose Jerusalem again.

13 Be silent, O all flesh, before the LORD: for he is raised up out of his holy habitation.

CHAPTER 3

AND he showed me Joshua the high priest standing before the angel of the LORD, and Satan standing at his right hand to resist him.

2 And the LORD said unto Satan, The LORD rebuke thee, O Satan; even the LORD that hath chosen Jerusalem rebuke thee: *is* not this a brand plucked out of the fire?

3 Now Joshua was clothed with filthy garments, and stood before the angel.

4 And he answered and spake unto those that stood before him, saying, Take away the filthy garments from him. And unto him he said, Behold, I have caused thine iniquity to pass from thee, and I will clothe thee with change of raiment.

5 And I said, Let them set a fair mitre upon his head. So they set a fair mitre upon his head, and clothed him with garments. And the angel of the LORD stood by.

6 And the angel of the LORD protested unto Joshua, saying,

7 Thus saith the LORD of hosts; If thou wilt walk in my ways, and if thou wilt keep my charge, then thou shalt also judge my house, and shalt also keep my courts, and I will give thee places to walk among these that stand by.

8 Hear now, O Joshua the high priest, thou, and thy fellows that sit before thee: for they *are* men wondered at: for, behold, I will bring forth my servant the BRANCH.

9 For behold the stone that I have laid before Joshua; upon one stone *shall be* seven eyes: behold, I will engrave the graving thereof, saith the LORD of hosts, and I will remove the iniquity of that land in one day.

10 In that day, saith the LORD of hosts, shall ye call every man his neighbor under the vine and under the fig tree.

CHAPTER 4

AND the angel that talked with me came again, and waked me, as a man that is wakened out of his sleep,

2 And said unto me, What seest thou?
And I said, I have looked, and behold a
candlestick all *of* gold, with a bowl upon
the top of it, and his seven lamps thereon, and seven pipes to the seven lamps,
which *are* upon the top thereof:
3 And two olive trees by it, one upon
the right *side* of the bowl, and the other
upon the left *side* thereof.
4 So I answered and spake to the angel
that talked with me, saying, What *are*
these, my lord?
5 Then the angel that talked with me
answered and said unto me, Knowest
thou not what these be? And I said, No,
my lord.
6 Then he answered and spake unto
me, saying, This *is* the word of the
LORD unto Zĕ-rŭb'bȧ-bĕl, saying, Not
by might, nor by power, but by my
Spirit, saith the LORD of hosts.
7 Who *art* thou, O great mountain?
before Zĕ-rŭb'bȧ-bĕl *thou shalt become*
a plain: and he shall bring forth the
headstone *thereof with* shoutings, *crying,* Grace, grace unto it.
8 Moreover the word of the LORD
came unto me, saying,
9 The hands of Zĕ-rŭb'bȧ-bĕl have
laid the foundation of this house; his
hands shall also finish it; and thou shalt
know that the LORD of hosts hath sent
me unto you.
10 For who hath despised the day of
small things? for they shall rejoice, and
shall see the plummet in the hand of
Zĕ-rŭb'bȧ-bĕl *with* those seven; they
are the eyes of the LORD, which run to
and fro through the whole earth.
11 ¶ Then answered I, and said unto
him, What *are* these two olive trees upon
the right *side* of the candlestick and
upon the left *side* thereof?
12 And I answered again, and said unto
him, What *be these* two olive branches,
which through the two golden pipes
empty the golden *oil* out of themselves?
13 And he answered me and said,
Knowest thou not what these *be?* And
I said, No, my lord.
14 Then said he, These *are* the two
anointed ones, that stand by the Lord
of the whole earth.

CHAPTER 5

THEN I turned, and lifted up mine
eyes, and looked, and behold a
flying roll.
2 And he said unto me, What seest
thou? And I answered, I see a flying
roll; the length thereof *is* twenty cubits,
and the breadth thereof ten cubits.
3 Then said he unto me, This *is* the
curse that goeth forth over the face of
the whole earth: for every one that
stealeth shall be cut off *as* on this side
according to it; and every one that
sweareth shall be cut off *as* on that side
according to it.
4 I will bring it forth, saith the LORD of
hosts, and it shall enter into the house
of the thief, and into the house of him
that sweareth falsely by my name: and
it shall remain in the midst of his house,
and shall consume it with the timber
thereof and the stones thereof.
5 ¶ Then the angel that talked with
me went forth, and said unto me, Lift
up now thine eyes, and see what *is* this
that goeth forth.
6 And I said, What *is* it? And he said,
This *is* an ē'phȧh that goeth forth. He
said moreover, This *is* their resemblance
through all the earth.
7 And, behold, there was lifted up a
talent of lead: and this *is* a woman that
sitteth in the midst of the ē'phȧh.
8 And he said, This *is* wickedness. And
he cast it into the midst of the ē'phȧh;
and he cast the weight of lead upon the
mouth thereof.
9 Then lifted I up mine eyes, and
looked, and, behold, there came out two
women, and the wind *was* in their wings;
for they had wings like the wings of a
stork: and they lifted up the ē'phȧh between the earth and the heaven.
10 Then said I to the angel that talked
with me, Whither do these bear the
ē'phȧh?
11 And he said unto me, To build it a
house in the land of Shī'när: and it shall
be established, and set there upon her
own base.

CHAPTER 6

AND I turned, and lifted up mine
eyes, and looked, and, behold,
there came four chariots out from between two mountains; and the mountains *were* mountains of brass.
2 In the first chariot *were* red horses;
and in the second chariot black horses;
3 And in the third chariot white horses;
and in the fourth chariot grizzled and
bay horses.

4 Then I answered and said unto the angel that talked with me, What *are* these, my lord?

5 And the angel answered and said unto me, These *are* the four spirits of the heavens, which go forth from standing before the Lord of all the earth.

6 The black horses which *are* therein go forth into the north country; and the white go forth after them; and the grizzled go forth toward the south country.

7 And the bay went forth, and sought to go that they might walk to and fro through the earth: and he said, Get you hence, walk to and fro through the earth. So they walked to and fro through the earth.

8 Then cried he upon me, and spake unto me, saying, Behold, these that go toward the north country have quieted my spirit in the north country.

9 ¶ And the word of the LORD came unto me, saying,

10 Take of *them of* the captivity, *even* of Hĕl′dā-ī, of Tō-bī′jȧh, and of Jē-dā′ịȧh, which are come from Babylon, and come thou the same day, and go into the house of Jō-sī′ȧh the son of Zĕph′ȧ-nī′ȧh;

11 Then take silver and gold, and make crowns, and set *them* upon the head of Joshua the son of Jŏs′ē-dĕch, the high priest;

12 And speak unto him, saying, Thus speaketh the LORD of hosts, saying, Behold the man whose name *is* The BRANCH; and he shall grow up out of his place, and he shall build the temple of the LORD:

13 Even he shall build the temple of the LORD; and he shall bear the glory, and shall sit and rule upon his throne; and he shall be a priest upon his throne: and the counsel of peace shall be between them both.

14 And the crowns shall be to Hē′lĕm, and to Tō-bī′jȧh, and to Jē-dā′ịȧh, and to Hen the son of Zĕph′ȧ-nī′ȧh, for a memorial in the temple of the LORD.

15 And they *that are* far off shall come and build in the temple of the LORD, and ye shall know that the LORD of hosts hath sent me unto you. And *this* shall come to pass, if ye will diligently obey the voice of the LORD your God.

CHAPTER 7

AND it came to pass in the fourth year of king Dȧ-rī′ŭs, *that* the word of the LORD came unto Zĕch′ȧ-rī′ȧh in the fourth *day* of the ninth month, *even* in Chĭs′leū;

2 When they had sent unto the house of God Shē-rē′zĕr and Rē′gĕm–mē′lĕch, and their men, to pray before the LORD,

3 *And* to speak unto the priests which *were* in the house of the LORD of hosts, and to the prophets, saying, Should I weep in the fifth month, separating myself, as I have done these so many years?

4 ¶ Then came the word of the LORD of hosts unto me, saying,

5 Speak unto all the people of the land, and to the priests, saying, When ye fasted and mourned in the fifth and seventh *month*, even those seventy years, did ye at all fast unto me, *even* to me?

6 And when ye did eat, and when ye did drink, did not ye eat *for yourselves*, and drink *for yourselves?*

7 *Should ye* not *hear* the words which the LORD hath cried by the former prophets, when Jerusalem was inhabited and in prosperity, and the cities thereof round about her, when *men* inhabited the south and the plain?

8 ¶ And the word of the LORD came unto Zĕch′ȧ-rī′ȧh, saying,

9 Thus speaketh the LORD of hosts, saying, Execute true judgment, and show mercy and compassions every man to his brother:

10 And oppress not the widow, nor the fatherless, the stranger, nor the poor; and let none of you imagine evil against his brother in your heart.

11 But they refused to hearken, and pulled away the shoulder, and stopped their ears, that they should not hear.

12 Yea, they made their hearts *as* an adamant stone, lest they should hear the law, and the words which the LORD of hosts hath sent in his Spirit by the former prophets: therefore came a great wrath from the LORD of hosts.

13 Therefore it is come to pass, *that* as he cried, and they would not hear; so they cried, and I would not hear, saith the LORD of hosts:

14 But I scattered them with a whirlwind among all the nations whom they

knew not. Thus the land was desolate after them, that no man passed through nor returned: for they laid the pleasant land desolate.

CHAPTER 8

AGAIN the word of the LORD of hosts came *to me,* saying,

2 Thus saith the LORD of hosts; I was jealous for Zion with great jealousy, and I was jealous for her with great fury.

3 Thus saith the LORD; I am returned unto Zion, and will dwell in the midst of Jerusalem: and Jerusalem shall be called A city of truth; and the mountain of the LORD of hosts, The holy mountain.

4 Thus saith the LORD of hosts; There shall yet old men and old women dwell in the streets of Jerusalem, and every man with his staff in his hand for very age.

5 And the streets of the city shall be full of boys and girls playing in the streets thereof.

6 Thus saith the LORD of hosts; If it be marvelous in the eyes of the remnant of this people in these days, should it also be marvelous in mine eyes? saith the LORD of hosts.

7 Thus saith the LORD of hosts; Behold, I will save my people from the east country, and from the west country;

8 And I will bring them, and they shall dwell in the midst of Jerusalem: and they shall be my people, and I will be their God, in truth and in righteousness.

9 ℂ Thus saith the LORD of hosts; Let your hands be strong, ye that hear in these days these words by the mouth of the prophets, which *were* in the day *that* the foundation of the house of the LORD of hosts was laid, that the temple might be built.

10 For before these days there was no hire for man, nor any hire for beast; neither *was there any* peace to him that went out or came in because of the affliction: for I set all men every one against his neighbor.

11 But now I *will* not *be* unto the residue of this people as in the former days, saith the LORD of hosts.

12 For the seed *shall be* prosperous; the vine shall give her fruit, and the ground shall give her increase, and the heavens shall give their dew; and I will cause the remnant of this people to possess all these *things.*

13 And it shall come to pass, *that* as ye were a curse among the heathen, O house of Judah, and house of Ĭş′rā-ĕl; so will I save you, and ye shall be a blessing: fear not, *but* let your hands be strong.

14 For thus saith the LORD of hosts; As I thought to punish you, when your fathers provoked me to wrath, saith the LORD of hosts, and I repented not:

15 So again have I thought in these days to do well unto Jerusalem and to the house of Judah: fear ye not.

16 ℂ These *are* the things that ye shall do; Speak ye every man the truth to his neighbor; execute the judgment of truth and peace in your gates:

17 And let none of you imagine evil in your hearts against his neighbor; and love no false oath: for all these *are things* that I hate, saith the LORD.

18 ℂ And the word of the LORD of hosts came unto me, saying,

19 Thus saith the LORD of hosts; The fast of the fourth *month,* and the fast of the fifth, and the fast of the seventh, and the fast of the tenth, shall be to the house of Judah joy and gladness, and cheerful feasts; therefore love the truth and peace.

20 Thus saith the LORD of hosts; *It shall* yet *come to pass,* that there shall come people, and the inhabitants of many cities:

21 And the inhabitants of one *city* shall go to another, saying, Let us go speedily to pray before the LORD, and to seek the LORD of hosts: I will go also.

22 Yea, many people and strong nations shall come to seek the LORD of hosts in Jerusalem, and to pray before the LORD.

23 Thus saith the LORD of hosts; In those days *it shall come to pass,* that ten men shall take hold out of all languages of the nations, even shall take hold of the skirt of him that is a Jew, saying, We will go with you: for we have heard *that* God *is* with you.

CHAPTER 9

THE burden of the word of the LORD in the land of Hā′drăch, and Damascus *shall be* the rest thereof: when the eyes of man, as of all the tribes of Ĭş′rā-ĕl, *shall be* toward the LORD.

2 And Hā′măth also shall border there-

by; Tȳ'rŭs, and Zī'dŏn, though it be very
wise.
3 And Tȳ'rŭs did build herself a stronghold, and heaped up silver as the
dust, and fine gold as the mire of the
streets.
4 Behold, the Lord will cast her out,
and he will smite her power in the sea;
and she shall be devoured with fire.
5 Ăsh'kē-lŏn shall see *it,* and fear;
Gā'zȧ also *shall see it,* and be very sorrowful, and Ĕk'rŏn; for her expectation
shall be ashamed; and the king shall
perish from Gā'zȧ, and Ăsh'kē-lŏn shall
not be inhabited.
6 And a bastard shall dwell in Ashdod,
and I will cut off the pride of the
Phĭ-lĭs'tīnes.
7 And I will take away his blood out of
his mouth, and his abominations from
between his teeth: but he that remaineth, even he, *shall be* for our God, and
he shall be as a governor in Judah, and
Ĕk'rŏn as a Jĕb'ŭ-sīte.
8 And I will encamp about mine house
because of the army, because of him
that passeth by, and because of him that
returneth: and no oppressor shall pass
through them any more: for now have I
seen with mine eyes.
9 ¶ Rejoice greatly, O daughter of
Zion; shout, O daughter of Jerusalem:
behold, thy King cometh unto thee: he
is just, and having salvation; lowly, and
riding upon an ass, and upon a colt the
foal of an ass.
10 And I will cut off the chariot from
Ē'phrā-ĭm, and the horse from Jerusalem, and the battle bow shall be cut
off: and he shall speak peace unto the
heathen: and his dominion *shall be* from
sea *even* to sea, and from the river *even*
to the ends of the earth.
11 As for thee also, by the blood of thy
covenant I have sent forth thy prisoners
out of the pit wherein *is* no water.
12 ¶ Turn you to the stronghold, ye
prisoners of hope: even to-day do I
declare *that* I will render double unto
thee;
13 When I have bent Judah for me,
filled the bow with Ē'phrā-ĭm, and
raised up thy sons, O Zion, against thy
sons, O Greece, and made thee as the
sword of a mighty man.
14 And the LORD shall be seen over
them, and his arrow shall go forth as
the lightning: and the Lord GOD shall
blow the trumpet, and shall go with
whirlwinds of the south.
15 The LORD of hosts shall defend
them; and they shall devour, and subdue with sling stones; and they shall
drink, *and* make a noise as through
wine; and they shall be filled like bowls,
and as the corners of the altar.
16 And the LORD their God shall save
them in that day as the flock of his people: for *they shall be as* the stones of a
crown, lifted up as an ensign upon his
land.
17 For how great *is* his goodness, and
how great *is* his beauty! corn shall make
the young men cheerful, and new wine
the maids.

CHAPTER 10

ASK ye of the LORD rain in the time
of the latter rain; *so* the LORD shall
make bright clouds, and give them
showers of rain, to every one grass in
the field.
2 For the idols have spoken vanity, and
the diviners have seen a lie, and have
told false dreams; they comfort in vain:
therefore they went their way as a
flock, they were troubled, because *there
was* no shepherd.
3 Mine anger was kindled against the
shepherds, and I punished the goats:
for the LORD of hosts hath visited his
flock the house of Judah, and hath
made them as his goodly horse in the
battle.
4 Out of him came forth the corner,
out of him the nail, out of him the battle
bow, out of him every oppressor together.
5 ¶ And they shall be as mighty *men,*
which tread down *their enemies* in the
mire of the streets in the battle: and
they shall fight, because the LORD *is*
with them, and the riders on horses
shall be confounded.
6 And I will strengthen the house of
Judah, and I will save the house of
Joseph, and I will bring them again to
place them; for I have mercy upon them:
and they shall be as though I had not
cast them off: for I *am* the LORD their
God, and will hear them.
7 And *they of* Ē'phrā-ĭm shall be like a
mighty *man,* and their heart shall
rejoice as through wine: yea, their children shall see *it,* and be glad; their
heart shall rejoice in the LORD.

8 I will hiss for them, and gather them; for I have redeemed them: and they shall increase as they have increased.

9 And I will sow them among the people: and they shall remember me in far countries; and they shall live with their children, and turn again.

10 I will bring them again also out of the land of Egypt, and gather them out of Assyria; and I will bring them into the land of Gĭl'ē-ăd and Lebanon; and *place* shall not be found for them.

11 And he shall pass through the sea with affliction, and shall smite the waves in the sea, and all the deeps of the river shall dry up: and the pride of Assyria shall be brought down, and the sceptre of Egypt shall depart away.

12 And I will strengthen them in the LORD; and they shall walk up and down in his name, saith the LORD.

CHAPTER 11

OPEN thy doors, O Lebanon, that the fire may devour thy cedars.

2 Howl, fir tree; for the cedar is fallen; because the mighty are spoiled: howl, O ye oaks of Bā'shăn; for the forest of the vintage is come down.

3 ¶ *There is* a voice of the howling of the shepherds; for their glory is spoiled: a voice of the roaring of young lions; for the pride of Jordan is spoiled.

4 Thus saith the LORD my God; Feed the flock of the slaughter;

5 Whose possessors slay them, and hold themselves not guilty: and they that sell them say, Blessed *be* the LORD; for I am rich: and their own shepherds pity them not.

6 For I will no more pity the inhabitants of the land, saith the LORD: but, lo, I will deliver the men every one into his neighbor's hand, and into the hand of his king: and they shall smite the land, and out of their hand I will not deliver *them*.

7 And I will feed the flock of slaughter, *even* you, O poor of the flock. And I took unto me two staves; the one I called Beauty, and the other I called Bands; and I fed the flock.

8 Three shepherds also I cut off in one month; and my soul loathed them, and their soul also abhorred me.

9 Then said I, I will not feed you: that that dieth, let it die; and that that is to be cut off, let it be cut off; and let the rest eat every one the flesh of another.

10 ¶ And I took my staff, *even* Beauty, and cut it asunder, that I might break my covenant which I had made with all the people.

11 And it was broken in that day: and so the poor of the flock that waited upon me knew that it *was* the word of the LORD.

12 And I said unto them, If ye think good, give *me* my price; and if not, forbear. So they weighed for my price thirty *pieces* of silver.

13 And the LORD said unto me, Cast it unto the potter: a goodly price that I was prized at of them. And I took the thirty *pieces* of silver, and cast them to the potter in the house of the LORD.

14 Then I cut asunder mine other staff, *even* Bands, that I might break the brotherhood between Judah and Ĭş'rā-ĕl.

15 ¶ And the LORD said unto me, Take unto thee yet the instruments of a foolish shepherd.

16 For, lo, I will raise up a shepherd in the land, *which* shall not visit those that be cut off, neither shall seek the young one, nor heal that that is broken, nor feed that that standeth still: but he shall eat the flesh of the fat, and tear their claws in pieces.

17 Woe to the idol shepherd that leaveth the flock! the sword *shall be* upon his arm, and upon his right eye: his arm shall be clean dried up, and his right eye shall be utterly darkened.

CHAPTER 12

THE burden of the word of the LORD for Ĭş'rā-ĕl, saith the LORD, which stretcheth forth the heavens, and layeth the foundation of the earth, and formeth the spirit of man within him.

2 Behold, I will make Jerusalem a cup of trembling unto all the people round about, when they shall be in the siege both against Judah *and* against Jerusalem.

3 ¶ And in that day will I make Jerusalem a burdensome stone for all people: all that burden themselves with it shall be cut in pieces, though all the people of the earth be gathered together against it.

4 In that day, saith the LORD, I will smite every horse with astonishment, and his rider with madness: and I will

open mine eyes upon the house of Judah, and will smite every horse of the people with blindness.
5 And the governors of Judah shall say in their heart, The inhabitants of Jerusalem *shall be* my strength in the LORD of hosts their God.
6 ℂ In that day will I make the governors of Judah like a hearth of fire among the wood, and like a torch of fire in a sheaf; and they shall devour all the people round about, on the right hand and on the left: and Jerusalem shall be inhabited again in her own place, *even* in Jerusalem.
7 The LORD also shall save the tents of Judah first, that the glory of the house of David and the glory of the inhabitants of Jerusalem do not magnify *themselves* against Judah.
8 In that day shall the LORD defend the inhabitants of Jerusalem; and he that is feeble among them at that day shall be as David; and the house of David *shall be* as God, as the angel of the LORD before them.
9 ℂ And it shall come to pass in that day, *that* I will seek to destroy all the nations that come against Jerusalem.
10 And I will pour upon the house of David, and upon the inhabitants of Jerusalem, the spirit of grace and of supplications: and they shall look upon me whom they have pierced, and they shall mourn for him, as one mourneth for *his* only *son,* and shall be in bitterness for him, as one that is in bitterness for *his* firstborn.
11 In that day shall there be a great mourning in Jerusalem, as the mourning of Hă′dăd-rĭm′mŏn in the valley of Mē-gĭd′dŏn.
12 And the land shall mourn, every family apart; the family of the house of David apart, and their wives apart; the family of the house of Nathan apart, and their wives apart;
13 The family of the house of Levi apart, and their wives apart; the family of Shĭm′ē-ī apart, and their wives apart;
14 All the families that remain, every family apart, and their wives apart.

CHAPTER 13

IN that day there shall be a fountain opened to the house of David and to the inhabitants of Jerusalem for sin and for uncleanness.
2 ℂ And it shall come to pass in that day, saith the LORD of hosts, *that* I will cut off the names of the idols out of the land, and they shall no more be remembered: and also I will cause the prophets and the unclean spirit to pass out of the land.
3 And it shall come to pass, *that* when any shall yet prophesy, then his father and his mother that begat him shall say unto him, Thou shalt not live; for thou speakest lies in the name of the LORD: and his father and his mother that begat him shall thrust him through when he prophesieth.
4 And it shall come to pass in that day, *that* the prophets shall be ashamed every one of his vision, when he hath prophesied; neither shall they wear a rough garment to deceive:
5 But he shall say, I *am* no prophet, I *am* a husbandman; for man taught me to keep cattle from my youth.
6 And *one* shall say unto him, What *are* these wounds in thine hands? Then he shall answer, *Those* with which I was wounded *in* the house of my friends.
7 ℂ Awake, O sword, against my shepherd, and against the man *that is* my fellow, saith the LORD of hosts: smite the shepherd, and the sheep shall be scattered: and I will turn mine hand upon the little ones.
8 And it shall come to pass, *that* in all the land, saith the LORD, two parts therein shall be cut off *and* die; but the third shall be left therein.
9 And I will bring the third part through the fire, and will refine them as silver is refined, and will try them as gold is tried: they shall call on my name, and I will hear them: I will say, It *is* my people: and they shall say, The LORD *is* my God.

CHAPTER 14

BEHOLD, the day of the LORD cometh, and thy spoil shall be divided in the midst of thee.
2 For I will gather all nations against Jerusalem to battle; and the city shall be taken, and the houses rifled, and the women ravished; and half of the city shall go forth into captivity, and the residue of the people shall not be cut off from the city.
3 Then shall the LORD go forth, and

fight against those nations, as when he
fought in the day of battle.
4 ¶ And his feet shall stand in that
day upon the mount of Olives, which *is*
before Jerusalem on the east, and the
mount of Olives shall cleave in the
midst thereof toward the east and toward the west, *and there shall be* a very
great valley; and half of the mountain
shall remove toward the north, and
half of it toward the south.
5 And ye shall flee *to* the valley of the
mountains; for the valley of the mountains shall reach unto Ā'zăl: yea, ye
shall flee, like as ye fled from before
the earthquake in the days of Ŭz-zī'ȧh
king of Judah: and the LORD my God
shall come, *and* all the saints with thee.
6 And it shall come to pass in that
day, *that* the light shall not be clear,
nor dark:
7 But it shall be one day which shall
be known to the LORD, not day, nor
night: but it shall come to pass, *that* at
evening time it shall be light.
8 And it shall be in that day, *that* living waters shall go out from Jerusalem;
half of them toward the former sea, and
half of them toward the hinder sea: in
summer and in winter shall it be.
9 And the LORD shall be King over all
the earth: in that day shall there be one
LORD, and his name one.
10 All the land shall be turned as a
plain from Gē'bȧ to Rĭm'mŏn south of
Jerusalem: and it shall be lifted up, and
inhabited in her place, from Benjamin's
gate unto the place of the first gate,
unto the corner gate, and *from* the
tower of Hȧ-năn'ē-ĕl unto the king's
winepresses.
11 And *men* shall dwell in it, and there
shall be no more utter destruction; but
Jerusalem shall be safely inhabited.
12 ¶ And this shall be the plague
wherewith the LORD will smite all the
people that have fought against Jerusalem; Their flesh shall consume away
while they stand upon their feet, and
their eyes shall consume away in their
holes, and their tongue shall consume
away in their mouth.
13 And it shall come to pass in that
day, *that* a great tumult from the LORD
shall be among them; and they shall
lay hold every one on the hand of his
neighbor, and his hand shall rise up
against the hand of his neighbor.
14 And Judah also shall fight at Jerusalem; and the wealth of all the heathen
round about shall be gathered together,
gold, and silver, and apparel, in great
abundance.
15 And so shall be the plague of the
horse, of the mule, of the camel, and
of the ass, and of all the beasts that
shall be in these tents, as this plague.
16 ¶ And it shall come to pass, *that*
every one that is left of all the nations
which came against Jerusalem, shall
even go up from year to year to worship
the King, the LORD of hosts, and to
keep the feast of tabernacles.
17 And it shall be, *that* whoso will not
come up of *all* the families of the earth
unto Jerusalem to worship the King,
the LORD of hosts, even upon them
shall be no rain.
18 And if the family of Egypt go not
up, and come not, that *have* no *rain;*
there shall be the plague, wherewith
the LORD will smite the heathen that
come not up to keep the feast of tabernacles.
19 This shall be the punishment of
Egypt, and the punishment of all nations that come not up to keep the feast
of tabernacles.
20 ¶ In that day shall there be upon
the bells of the horses, HOLINESS
UNTO THE LORD; and the pots in
the LORD's house shall be like the
bowls before the altar.
21 Yea, every pot in Jerusalem and in
Judah shall be holiness unto the LORD
of hosts: and all they that sacrifice shall
come and take of them, and seethe
therein: and in that day there shall be
no more the Cā'năan-īte in the house of
the LORD of hosts.

MALACHI

CHAPTER 1

THE burden of the word of the
LORD to Ĭs'rā-ĕl by Măl'ā-chī.
2 I have loved you, saith the LORD.
Yet ye say, Wherein hast thou loved us?
Was not Ē'sau Jacob's brother? saith
the LORD: yet I loved Jacob,
3 And I hated Ē'sau, and laid his
mountains and his heritage waste for
the dragons of the wilderness.
4 Whereas Ē'dŏm saith, We are impoverished, but we will return and
build the desolate places; thus saith
the LORD of hosts, They shall build,
but I will throw down; and they shall
call them, The border of wickedness,
and, The people against whom the
LORD hath indignation for ever.
5 And your eyes shall see, and ye shall
say, The LORD will be magnified from
the border of Ĭs'rā-ĕl.
6 ¶ A son honoreth *his* father, and a
servant his master: if then I *be* a father,
where *is* mine honor? and if I *be* a
master, where *is* my fear? saith the
LORD of hosts unto you, O priests, that
despise my name. And ye say, Wherein
have we despised thy name?
7 Ye offer polluted bread upon mine
altar; and ye say, Wherein have we
polluted thee? In that ye say, The
table of the LORD *is* contemptible.
8 And if ye offer the blind for sacrifice,
is it not evil? and if ye offer the lame
and sick, *is it* not evil? offer it now unto
thy governor; will he be pleased with
thee, or accept thy person? saith the
LORD of hosts.
9 And now, I pray you, beseech God
that he will be gracious unto us: this
hath been by your means: will he regard
your persons? saith the LORD of hosts.
10 Who *is there* even among you that
would shut the doors *for nought?*
neither do ye kindle *fire* on mine altar
for nought. I have no pleasure in you,
saith the LORD of hosts, neither will I
accept an offering at your hand.
11 For, from the rising of the sun even
unto the going down of the same, my
name *shall be* great among the Gĕn'-
tīleṣ; and in every place incense *shall be*
offered unto my name, and a pure offering: for my name *shall be* great among
the heathen, saith the LORD of hosts.
12 ¶ But ye have profaned it, in that
ye say, The table of the LORD *is* polluted; and the fruit thereof, *even* his
meat, *is* contemptible.
13 Ye said also, Behold, what a weariness *is it!* and ye have snuffed at it,
saith the LORD of hosts; and ye brought
that which was torn, and the lame, and
the sick; thus ye brought an offering:
should I accept this of your hand? saith
the LORD.
14 But cursed *be* the deceiver, which
hath in his flock a male, and voweth,
and sacrificeth unto the Lord a corrupt
thing: for I *am* a great King, saith the
LORD of hosts, and my name *is* dreadful among the heathen.

CHAPTER 2

AND now, O ye priests, this commandment *is* for you.
2 If ye will not hear, and if ye will not
lay *it* to heart, to give glory unto my
name, saith the LORD of hosts, I will
even send a curse upon you, and I will
curse your blessings: yea, I have cursed
them already, because ye do not lay *it*
to heart.
3 Behold, I will corrupt your seed, and
spread dung upon your faces, *even* the
dung of your solemn feasts; and *one*
shall take you away with it.
4 And ye shall know that I have sent
this commandment unto you, that my
covenant might be with Levi, saith the
LORD of hosts.
5 My covenant was with him of life
and peace; and I gave them to him *for*
the fear wherewith he feared me, and
was afraid before my name.
6 The law of truth was in his mouth,
and iniquity was not found in his lips:
he walked with me in peace and equity,
and did turn many away from iniquity.
7 For the priest's lips should keep
knowledge, and they should seek the
law at his mouth: for he *is* the messenger of the LORD of hosts.
8 But ye are departed out of the way;
ye have caused many to stumble at the
law; ye have corrupted the covenant of
Levi, saith the LORD of hosts.
9 Therefore have I also made you contemptible and base before all the people,

according as ye have not kept my ways, but have been partial in the law.

10 Have we not all one father? hath not one God created us? why do we deal treacherously every man against his brother, by profaning the covenant of our fathers?

11 ¶ Judah hath dealt treacherously, and an abomination is committed in Ĭs′rā-ĕl and in Jerusalem; for Judah hath profaned the holiness of the LORD which he loved, and hath married the daughter of a strange god.

12 The LORD will cut off the man that doeth this, the master and the scholar, out of the tabernacles of Jacob, and him that offereth an offering unto the LORD of hosts.

13 And this have ye done again, covering the altar of the LORD with tears, with weeping, and with crying out, insomuch that he regardeth not the offering any more, or receiveth *it* with good will at your hand.

14 ¶ Yet ye say, Wherefore? Because the LORD hath been witness between thee and the wife of thy youth, against whom thou hast dealt treacherously: yet *is* she thy companion, and the wife of thy covenant.

15 And did not he make one? Yet had he the residue of the Spirit. And wherefore one? That he might seek a godly seed. Therefore take heed to your spirit, and let none deal treacherously against the wife of his youth.

16 For the LORD, the God of Ĭs′rā-ĕl, saith that he hateth putting away: for *one* covereth violence with his garment, saith the LORD of hosts: therefore take heed to your spirit, that ye deal not treacherously.

17 ¶ Ye have wearied the LORD with your words. Yet ye say, Wherein have we wearied *him?* When ye say, Every one that doeth evil *is* good in the sight of the LORD, and he delighteth in them; or, Where *is* the God of judgment?

CHAPTER 3

BEHOLD, I will send my messenger, and he shall prepare the way before me: and the Lord, whom ye seek, shall suddenly come to his temple, even the messenger of the covenant, whom ye delight in: behold, he shall come, saith the LORD of hosts.

2 But who may abide the day of his coming? and who shall stand when he appeareth? for he *is* like a refiner's fire, and like fullers' soap:

3 And he shall sit *as* a refiner and purifier of silver: and he shall purify the sons of Levi, and purge them as gold and silver, that they may offer unto the LORD an offering in righteousness.

4 Then shall the offering of Judah and Jerusalem be pleasant unto the LORD, as in the days of old, and as in former years.

5 And I will come near to you to judgment; and I will be a swift witness against the sorcerers, and against the adulterers, and against false swearers, and against those that oppress the hireling in *his* wages, the widow, and the fatherless, and that turn aside the stranger *from his right,* and fear not me, saith the LORD of hosts.

6 For I *am* the LORD, I change not; therefore ye sons of Jacob are not consumed.

7 ¶ Even from the days of your fathers ye are gone away from mine ordinances, and have not kept *them.* Return unto me, and I will return unto you, saith the LORD of hosts. But ye said, Wherein shall we return?

8 ¶ Will a man rob God? Yet ye have robbed me. But ye say, Wherein have we robbed thee? In tithes and offerings.

9 Ye *are* cursed with a curse: for ye have robbed me, *even* this whole nation.

10 Bring ye all the tithes into the storehouse, that there may be meat in mine house, and prove me now herewith, saith the LORD of hosts, if I will not open you the windows of heaven, and pour you out a blessing, that *there shall* not *be room* enough *to receive it.*

11 And I will rebuke the devourer for your sakes, and he shall not destroy the fruits of your ground; neither shall your vine cast her fruit before the time in the field, saith the LORD of hosts.

12 And all nations shall call you blessed: for ye shall be a delightsome land, saith the LORD of hosts.

13 ¶ Your words have been stout against me, saith the LORD. Yet ye say, What have we spoken *so much* against thee?

14 Ye have said, It *is* vain to serve God: and what profit *is it* that we have kept his ordinance, and that we have

walked mournfully before the LORD of hosts?

15 And now we call the proud happy; yea, they that work wickedness are set up; yea, *they that* tempt God are even delivered.

16 ¶ Then they that feared the LORD spake often one to another: and the LORD hearkened, and heard *it*, and a book of remembrance was written before him for them that feared the LORD, and that thought upon his name.

17 And they shall be mine, saith the LORD of hosts, in that day when I make up my jewels; and I will spare them, as a man spareth his own son that serveth him.

18 Then shall ye return, and discern between the righteous and the wicked, between him that serveth God and him that serveth him not.

CHAPTER 4

FOR, behold, the day cometh, that shall burn as an oven; and all the proud, yea, and all that do wickedly, shall be stubble: and the day that cometh shall burn them up, saith the LORD of hosts, that it shall leave them neither root nor branch.

2 ¶ But unto you that fear my name shall the Sun of righteousness arise with healing in his wings; and ye shall go forth, and grow up as calves of the stall.

3 And ye shall tread down the wicked; for they shall be ashes under the soles of your feet in the day that I shall do *this*, saith the LORD of hosts.

4 ¶ Remember ye the law of Moses my servant, which I commanded unto him in Hō'rĕb for all Ĭs'rā-ĕl, *with* the statutes and judgments.

5 ¶ Behold, I will send you Ē-lī'jah the prophet before the coming of the great and dreadful day of the LORD:

6 And he shall turn the heart of the fathers to the children, and the heart of the children to their fathers, lest I come and smite the earth with a curse.

THE

NEW TESTAMENT

OF

OUR LORD AND SAVIOUR JESUS CHRIST

TRANSLATED OUT OF THE ORIGINAL GREEK
AND WITH THE FORMER TRANSLATIONS
DILIGENTLY COMPARED & REVISED

THE GOSPEL ACCORDING TO

ST. MATTHEW

CHAPTER 1

THE book of the generation of Jesus
Christ, the son of David, the son
of Abraham.
2 Abraham begat Isaac; and Isaac begat Jacob; and Jacob begat Judas and
his brethren;
3 And Judas begat Phā′rēs̱ and Zā′rȧ
of Thā′mär; and Phā′rēs̱ begat Ĕs′rŏm;
and Ĕs′rŏm begat Ā′răm;
4 And Ā′răm begat Ȧ-mĭn′ȧ-dăb; and
Ȧ-mĭn′ȧ-dăb begat Nā-ăs′sŏn; and Nā-
ăs′sŏn begat Săl′mŏn;
5 And Săl′mŏn begat Bō′ŏz of Rā′chăb;
and Bō′ŏz begat Ō′bĕd of Ruth; and
Ō′bĕd begat Jesse;
6 And Jesse begat David the king; and
David the king begat Solomon of her
that had been the wife of Ū-rī′ăs;
7 And Solomon begat Rō-bō′ăm; and
Rō-bō′ăm begat Ȧ-bī′ȧ; and Ȧ-bī′ȧ begat Ā′sȧ;
8 And Ā′sȧ begat Jŏs′ȧ-phăt; and Jŏs′ȧ-
phăt begat Jō′răm; and Jō′răm begat
Ō-zī′ăs;
9 And Ō-zī′ăs begat Jō′ȧ-thăm; and
Jō′ȧ-thăm begat Ā′chăz; and Ā′chăz begat Ĕz′ē-kī′ăs;
10 And Ĕz′ē-kī′ăs begat Mȧ-năs′sēs̱;
and Mȧ-năs′sēs̱ begat Ā′mŏn; and
Ā′mŏn begat Jō-sī′ăs;
11 And Jō-sī′ăs begat Jĕch′ō-nī′ăs and
his brethren, about the time they were
carried away to Babylon:
12 And after they were brought to
Babylon, Jĕch′ō-nī′ăs begat Sȧ-lā′thĭ-ĕl;
and Sȧ-lā′thĭ-ĕl begat Zō-rŏb′ȧ-bĕl;
13 And Zō-rŏb′ȧ-bĕl begat Ȧ-bī′ŭd;
and Ȧ-bī′ŭd begat Ē-lī′ȧ-kĭm; and Ē-lī′-
ȧ-kĭm begat Ā′zŏr;
14 And Ā′zŏr begat Sā′dŏc; and Sā′dŏc
begat Ā′chĭm; and Ā′chĭm begat Ē-lī′ŭd;
15 And Ē-lī′ŭd begat Ĕl′ē-ā′zȧr; and
Ĕl′ē-ā′zȧr begat Măt′thăn; and Măt′thăn
begat Jacob;
16 And Jacob begat Joseph the husband of Mary, of whom was born Jesus,
who is called Christ.
17 So all the generations from Abraham
to David *are* fourteen generations; and
from David until the carrying away into
Babylon *are* fourteen generations; and
from the carrying away into Babylon
unto Christ *are* fourteen generations.
18 ¶ Now the birth of Jesus Christ was
on this wise: When as his mother Mary
was espoused to Joseph, before they
came together, she was found with child
of the Holy Ghost.
19 Then Joseph her husband, being a
just *man*, and not willing to make her a
public example, was minded to put her
away privily.
20 But while he thought on these
things, behold, the angel of the Lord
appeared unto him in a dream, saying,
Joseph, thou son of David, fear not to
take unto thee Mary thy wife: for that
which is conceived in her is of the Holy
Ghost.
21 And she shall bring forth a son, and
thou shalt call his name JESUS: for he
shall save his people from their sins.
22 Now all this was done, that it might
be fulfilled which was spoken of the
Lord by the prophet, saying,
23 Behold, a virgin shall be with child,
and shall bring forth a son, and they
shall call his name Ĕm-măn′ū-ĕl, which
being interpreted is, God with us.
24 Then Joseph being raised from sleep
did as the angel of the Lord had bidden
him, and took unto him his wife:
25 And knew her not till she had
brought forth her firstborn son: and he
called his name JESUS.

CHAPTER 2

NOW when Jesus was born in
Bethlehem of Judea in the days
of Hĕr′ȯd the king, behold, there came
wis̱e men from the east to Jerusalem,
2 Saying, Where is he that is born
King of the Jews? for we have seen his
star in the east, and are come to worship
him.
3 When Hĕr′ȯd the king had heard
these things, he was troubled, and all
Jerusalem with him.
4 And when he had gathered all the
chief priests and scribes of the people
together, he demanded of them where
Christ should be born.

5 And they said unto him, In Bethlehem of Judea: for thus it is written by
the prophet,
6 And thou Bethlehem, *in* the land of
Ju̦′dȧ, art not the least among the
princes of Ju̦′dȧ: for out of thee shall
come a Governor, that shall rule my
people Ĭs′rā-ĕl.
7 Then Hĕr′ȯd, when he had privily
called the wise men, inquired of them
diligently what time the star appeared.
8 And he sent them to Bethlehem, and
said, Go and search diligently for the
young child; and when ye have found
him, bring me word again, that I may
come and worship him also.
9 When they had heard the king, they
departed; and, lo, the star, which they
saw in the east, went before them, till
it came and stood over where the young
child was.
10 When they saw the star, they rejoiced with exceeding great joy.
11 ℭ And when they were come into
the house, they saw the young child
with Mary his mother, and fell down,
and worshipped him: and when they
had opened their treasures, they presented unto him gifts; gold, and frankincense, and myrrh.
12 And being warned of God in a dream
that they should not return to Hĕr′ȯd,
they departed into their own country
another way.
13 And when they were departed, behold, the angel of the Lord appeareth
to Joseph in a dream, saying, Arise, and
take the young child and his mother, and
flee into Egypt, and be thou there until
I bring thee word: for Hĕr′ȯd will seek
the young child to destroy him.
14 When he arose, he took the young
child and his mother by night, and departed into Egypt:
15 And was there until the death of
Hĕr′ȯd: that it might be fulfilled which
was spoken of the Lord by the prophet,
saying, Out of Egypt have I called my son.
16 ℭ Then Hĕr′ȯd, when he saw that
he was mocked of the wise men, was
exceeding wroth, and sent forth, and
slew all the children that were in Bethlehem, and in all the coasts thereof, from
two years old and under, according to
the time which he had diligently inquired of the wise men.
17 Then was fulfilled that which was
spoken by Jĕr′ē-mȳ̆ the prophet, saying,
18 In Rā′mȧ was there a voice heard,
lamentation, and weeping, and great
mourning, Rachel weeping *for* her children, and would not be comforted, because they are not.
19 ℭ But when Hĕr′ȯd was dead,
behold, an angel of the Lord appeareth
in a dream to Joseph in Egypt,
20 Saying, Arise, and take the young
child and his mother, and go into the
land of Ĭs′rā-ĕl: for they are dead which
sought the young child's life.
21 And he arose, and took the young
child and his mother, and came into the
land of Ĭs′rā-ĕl.
22 But when he heard that Är′ehē-lā′ŭs
did reign in Judea in the room of his
father Hĕr′ȯd, he was afraid to go
thither: notwithstanding, being warned
of God in a dream, he turned aside into
the parts of Galilee:
23 And he came and dwelt in a city
called Nazareth: that it might be fulfilled which was spoken by the prophets, He shall be called a Nazarene.

CHAPTER 3

IN those days came John the Baptist,
preaching in the wilderness of
Judea,
2 And saying, Repent ye: for the kingdom of heaven is at hand.
3 For this is he that was spoken of by
the prophet Ē-sā′ịăs, saying, The voice
of one crying in the wilderness, Prepare
ye the way of the Lord, make his paths
straight.
4 And the same John had his raiment
of camel's hair, and a leathern girdle
about his loins; and his meat was locusts
and wild honey.
5 Then went out to him Jerusalem, and
all Judea, and all the region round about
Jordan,
6 And were baptized of him in Jordan,
confessing their sins.
7 ℭ But when he saw many of the
Phăr′ĭ-sēeș and Săd′dū-çēeș come to
his baptism, he said unto them, O generation of vipers, who hath warned you
to flee from the wrath to come?
8 Bring forth therefore fruits meet for
repentance:
9 And think not to say within yourselves, We have Abraham to *our* father:
for I say unto you, that God is able of
these stones to raise up children unto
Abraham.

10 And now also the axe is laid unto the root of the trees: therefore every tree which bringeth not forth good fruit is hewn down, and cast into the fire.

11 I indeed baptize you with water unto repentance: but he that cometh after me is mightier than I, whose shoes I am not worthy to bear: he shall baptize you with the Holy Ghost, and *with* fire:

12 Whose fan *is* in his hand, and he will thoroughly purge his floor, and gather his wheat into the garner; but he will burn up the chaff with unquenchable fire.

13 ¶ Then cometh Jesus from Galilee to Jordan unto John, to be baptized of him.

14 But John forbade him, saying, I have need to be baptized of thee, and comest thou to me?

15 And Jesus answering said unto him, Suffer *it to be so* now: for thus it becometh us to fulfil all righteousness. Then he suffered him.

16 And Jesus, when he was baptized, went up straightway out of the water: and, lo, the heavens were opened unto him, and he saw the Spirit of God descending like a dove, and lighting upon him:

17 And lo a voice from heaven, saying, This is my beloved Son, in whom I am well pleased.

CHAPTER 4

THEN was Jesus led up of the Spirit into the wilderness to be tempted of the devil.

2 And when he had fasted forty days and forty nights, he was afterward ahungered.

3 And when the tempter came to him, he said, If thou be the Son of God, command that these stones be made bread.

4 But he answered and said, It is written, Man shall not live by bread alone, but by every word that proceedeth out of the mouth of God.

5 Then the devil taketh him up into the holy city, and setteth him on a pinnacle of the temple,

6 And saith unto him, If thou be the Son of God, cast thyself down: for it is written, He shall give his angels charge concerning thee: and in *their* hands they shall bear thee up, lest at any time thou dash thy foot against a stone.

7 Jesus said unto him, It is written again, Thou shalt not tempt the Lord thy God.

8 Again, the devil taketh him up into an exceeding high mountain, and showeth him all the kingdoms of the world, and the glory of them;

9 And saith unto him, All these things will I give thee, if thou wilt fall down and worship me.

10 Then saith Jesus unto him, Get thee hence, Satan: for it is written, Thou shalt worship the Lord thy God, and him only shalt thou serve.

11 Then the devil leaveth him, and, behold, angels came and ministered unto him.

12 ¶ Now when Jesus had heard that John was cast into prison, he departed into Galilee;

13 And leaving Nazareth, he came and dwelt in Cȧ-pĕr'nā-ŭm, which is upon the seacoast, in the borders of Zăb'ū-lŏn and Nĕph'thȧ-lĭm:

14 That it might be fulfilled which was spoken by Ē-sā'ịăs the prophet, saying,

15 The land of Zăb'ū-lŏn, and the land of Nĕph'thȧ-lĭm, *by* the way of the sea, beyond Jordan, Galilee of the Gĕn'tīles;

16 The people which sat in darkness saw great light; and to them which sat in the region and shadow of death light is sprung up.

17 ¶ From that time Jesus began to preach, and to say, Repent: for the kingdom of heaven is at hand.

18 ¶ And Jesus, walking by the sea of Galilee, saw two brethren, Simon called Peter, and Andrew his brother, casting a net into the sea: for they were fishers.

19 And he saith unto them, Follow me, and I will make you fishers of men.

20 And they straightway left *their* nets, and followed him.

21 And going on from thence, he saw other two brethren, James *the son* of Zĕb'ē-dēe, and John his brother, in a ship with Zĕb'ē-dēe their father, mending their nets; and he called them.

22 And they immediately left the ship and their father, and followed him.

23 ¶ And Jesus went about all Galilee, teaching in their synagogues, and preaching the gospel of the kingdom, and healing all manner of sickness and all manner of disease among the people.

24 And his fame went throughout all Syria: and they brought unto him all

sick people that were taken with divers
diseases and torments, and those which
were possessed with devils, and those
which were lunatic, and those that had
the palsy; and he healed them.
25 And there followed him great multitudes of people from Galilee, and *from*
Dē-căp′ō-lĭs, and *from* Jerusalem, and
from Judea, and *from* beyond Jordan.

CHAPTER 5

AND seeing the multitudes, he went
up into a mountain: and when he
was set, his disciples came unto him:
2 And he opened his mouth, and
taught them, saying,
3 Blessed *are* the poor in spirit: for
theirs is the kingdom of heaven.
4 Blessed *are* they that mourn: for
they shall be comforted.
5 Blessed *are* the meek: for they shall
inherit the earth.
6 Blessed *are* they which do hunger
and thirst after righteousness: for they
shall be filled.
7 Blessed *are* the merciful: for they
shall obtain mercy.
8 Blessed *are* the pure in heart: for
they shall see God.
9 Blessed *are* the peacemakers: for
they shall be called the children of
God.
10 Blessed *are* they which are persecuted for righteousness' sake: for theirs
is the kingdom of heaven.
11 Blessed are ye, when *men* shall
revile you, and persecute *you*, and shall
say all manner of evil against you falsely,
for my sake.
12 Rejoice, and be exceeding glad: for
great *is* your reward in heaven: for so
persecuted they the prophets which
were before you.
13 ℂ Ye are the salt of the earth: but
if the salt have lost his savor, wherewith
shall it be salted? it is thenceforth good
for nothing, but to be cast out, and to be
trodden under foot of men.
14 Ye are the light of the world. A city
that is set on a hill cannot be hid.
15 Neither do men light a candle, and
put it under a bushel, but on a candlestick; and it giveth light unto all that are
in the house.
16 Let your light so shine before men,
that they may see your good works, and
glorify your Father which is in heaven.
17 ℂ Think not that I am come to
destroy the law, or the prophets: I am
not come to destroy, but to fulfil.
18 For verily I say unto you, Till heaven
and earth pass, one jot or one tittle shall
in no wise pass from the law, till all be
fulfilled.
19 Whosoever therefore shall break
one of these least commandments, and
shall teach men so, he shall be called
the least in the kingdom of heaven: but
whosoever shall do and teach *them*, the
same shall be called great in the kingdom of heaven.
20 For I say unto you, That except your
righteousness shall exceed *the righteousness* of the scribes and Phăr′ĭ-sēeş,
ye shall in no case enter into the kingdom of heaven.
21 ℂ Ye have heard that it was said by
them of old time, Thou shalt not kill;
and whosoever shall kill shall be in danger of the judgment:
22 But I say unto you, That whosoever
is angry with his brother without a cause
shall be in danger of the judgment: and
whosoever shall say to his brother,
Rā′cȧ, shall be in danger of the council:
but whosoever shall say, Thou fool, shall
be in danger of hell fire.
23 Therefore if thou bring thy gift to
the altar, and there rememberest that
thy brother hath aught against thee;
24 Leave there thy gift before the altar,
and go thy way; first be reconciled to
thy brother, and then come and offer
thy gift.
25 Agree with thine adversary quickly,
while thou art in the way with him; lest
at any time the adversary deliver thee
to the judge, and the judge deliver thee
to the officer, and thou be cast into
prison.
26 Verily I say unto thee, Thou shalt
by no means come out thence, till thou
hast paid the uttermost farthing.
27 ℂ Ye have heard that it was said by
them of old time, Thou shalt not commit adultery:
28 But I say unto you, That whosoever
looketh on a woman to lust after her
hath committed adultery with her already in his heart.
29 And if thy right eye offend thee,
pluck it out, and cast *it* from thee: for it
is profitable for thee that one of thy
members should perish, and not *that*
thy whole body should be cast into hell.
30 And if thy right hand offend thee,

cut it off, and cast *it* from thee: for it is
profitable for thee that one of thy members should perish, and not *that* thy
whole body should be cast into hell.
31 It hath been said, Whosoever shall
put away his wife, let him give her a
writing of divorcement:
32 But I say unto you, That whosoever
shall put away his wife, saving for the
cause of fornication, causeth her to commit adultery: and whosoever shall marry
her that is divorced committeth adultery.
33 ¶ Again, ye have heard that it hath
been said by them of old time, Thou
shalt not forswear thyself, but shalt
perform unto the Lord thine oaths:
34 But I say unto you, Swear not at all;
neither by heaven; for it is God's throne:
35 Nor by the earth; for it is his footstool: neither by Jerusalem; for it is the
city of the great King.
36 Neither shalt thou swear by thy
head, because thou canst not make one
hair white or black.
37 But let your communication be, Yea,
yea; Nay, nay: for whatsoever is more
than these cometh of evil.
38 ¶ Ye have heard that it hath been
said, An eye for an eye, and a tooth for
a tooth:
39 But I say unto you, That ye resist
not evil: but whosoever shall smite thee
on thy right cheek, turn to him the other
also.
40 And if any man will sue thee at the
law, and take away thy coat, let him
have *thy* cloak also.
41 And whosoever shall compel thee
to go a mile, go with him twain.
42 Give to him that asketh thee, and
from him that would borrow of thee
turn not thou away.
43 ¶ Ye have heard that it hath been
said, Thou shalt love thy neighbor, and
hate thine enemy.
44 But I say unto you, Love your enemies, bless them that curse you, do
good to them that hate you, and pray for
them which despitefully use you, and
persecute you;
45 That ye may be the children of your
Father which is in heaven: for he maketh his sun to rise on the evil and on the
good, and sendeth rain on the just and
on the unjust.
46 For if ye love them which love you,
what reward have ye? do not even the
publicans the same?
47 And if ye salute your brethren only,
what do ye more *than others?* do not
even the publicans so?
48 Be ye therefore perfect, even as
your Father which is in heaven is perfect.

CHAPTER 6

TAKE heed that ye do not your alms
before men, to be seen of them:
otherwise ye have no reward of your
Father which is in heaven.
2 Therefore when thou doest *thine*
alms, do not sound a trumpet before
thee, as the hypocrites do in the synagogues and in the streets, that they may
have glory of men. Verily I say unto
you, They have their reward.
3 But when thou doest alms, let not
thy left hand know what thy right hand
doeth:
4 That thine alms may be in secret:
and thy Father which seeth in secret
himself shall reward thee openly.
5 ¶ And when thou prayest, thou shalt
not be as the hypocrites *are:* for they
love to pray standing in the synagogues
and in the corners of the streets, that
they may be seen of men. Verily I say
unto you, They have their reward.
6 But thou, when thou prayest, enter
into thy closet, and when thou hast shut
thy door, pray to thy Father which is in
secret; and thy Father which seeth in
secret shall reward thee openly.
7 But when ye pray, use not vain repe-
titions, as the heathen *do:* for they think
that they shall be heard for their much
speaking.
8 Be not ye therefore like unto them:
for your Father knoweth what things ye
have need of, before ye ask him.
9 After this manner therefore pray ye:
Our Father which art in heaven, Hallowed be thy name.
10 Thy kingdom come. Thy will be
done in earth, as *it is* in heaven.
11 Give us this day our daily bread.
12 And forgive us our debts, as we forgive our debtors.
13 And lead us not into temptation,
but deliver us from evil: For thine is the
kingdom, and the power, and the glory,
for ever. Amen.
14 For if ye forgive men their trespasses, your heavenly Father will also
forgive you:
15 But if ye forgive not men their tres-

passes, neither will your Father forgive
your trespasses.
16 ¶ Moreover when ye fast, be not,
as the hypocrites, of a sad countenance:
for they disfigure their faces, that they
may appear unto men to fast. Verily I
say unto you, They have their reward.
17 But thou, when thou fastest, anoint
thine head, and wash thy face;
18 That thou appear not unto men to
fast, but unto thy Father which is in
secret: and thy Father which seeth in
secret shall reward thee openly.
19 ¶ Lay not up for yourselves treasures upon earth, where moth and rust
doth corrupt, and where thieves break
through and steal:
20 But lay up for yourselves treasures
in heaven, where neither moth nor rust
doth corrupt, and where thieves do not
break through nor steal:
21 For where your treasure is, there
will your heart be also.
22 The light of the body is the eye: if
therefore thine eye be single, thy whole
body shall be full of light.
23 But if thine eye be evil, thy whole
body shall be full of darkness. If therefore the light that is in thee be darkness,
how great *is* that darkness!
24 ¶ No man can serve two masters:
for either he will hate the one, and love
the other; or else he will hold to the one,
and despise the other. Ye cannot serve
God and mammon.
25 Therefore I say unto you, Take no
thought for your life, what ye shall eat,
or what ye shall drink; nor yet for your
body, what ye shall put on. Is not the
life more than meat, and the body than
raiment?
26 Behold the fowls of the air: for they
sow not, neither do they reap, nor gather
into barns; yet your heavenly Father
feedeth them. Are ye not much better
than they?
27 Which of you by taking thought can
add one cubit unto his stature?
28 And why take ye thought for raiment? Consider the lilies of the field,
how they grow; they toil not, neither do
they spin:
29 And yet I say unto you, That even
Solomon in all his glory was not arrayed
like one of these.
30 Wherefore, if God so clothe the
grass of the field, which to-day is, and
to-morrow is cast into the oven, *shall he*
not much more *clothe* you, O ye of little
faith?
31 Therefore take no thought, saying,
What shall we eat? or, What shall we
drink? or, Wherewithal shall we be
clothed?
32 (For after all these things do the
Ġĕn'tīleş seek:) for your heavenly
Father knoweth that ye have need of all
these things.
33 But seek ye first the kingdom of
God, and his righteousness; and all
these things shall be added unto you.
34 Take therefore no thought for the
morrow: for the morrow shall take
thought for the things of itself. Sufficient unto the day *is* the evil thereof.

CHAPTER 7

JUDGE not, that ye be not judged.
2 For with what judgment ye judge,
ye shall be judged: and with what
measure ye mete, it shall be measured
to you again.
3 And why beholdest thou the mote
that is in thy brother's eye, but considerest not the beam that is in thine own
eye?
4 Or how wilt thou say to thy brother,
Let me pull out the mote out of thine
eye; and, behold, a beam *is* in thine own
eye?
5 Thou hypocrite, first cast out the
beam out of thine own eye; and then
shalt thou see clearly to cast out the
mote out of thy brother's eye.
6 ¶ Give not that which is holy unto
the dogs, neither cast ye your pearls
before swine, lest they trample them
under their feet, and turn again and
rend you.
7 ¶ Ask, and it shall be given you;
seek, and ye shall find; knock, and it
shall be opened unto you:
8 For every one that asketh receiveth;
and he that seeketh findeth; and to him
that knocketh it shall be opened.
9 Or what man is there of you, whom
if his son ask bread, will he give him a
stone?
10 Or if he ask a fish, will he give him
a serpent?
11 If ye then, being evil, know how to
give good gifts unto your children, how
much more shall your Father which is
in heaven give good things to them that
ask him?
12 Therefore all things whatsoever ye

would that men should do to you, do ye
even so to them: for this is the law and
the prophets.
13 ¶ Enter ye in at the strait gate: for
wide *is* the gate, and broad *is* the way,
that leadeth to destruction, and many
there be which go in thereat:
14 Because strait *is* the gate, and narrow *is* the way, which leadeth unto life,
and few there be that find it.
15 ¶ Beware of false prophets, which
come to you in sheep's clothing, but inwardly they are ravening wolves.
16 Ye shall know them by their fruits.
Do men gather grapes of thorns, or figs
of thistles?
17 Even so every good tree bringeth
forth good fruit; but a corrupt tree
bringeth forth evil fruit.
18 A good tree cannot bring forth evil
fruit, neither *can* a corrupt tree bring
forth good fruit.
19 Every tree that bringeth not forth
good fruit is hewn down, and cast into
the fire.
20 Wherefore by their fruits ye shall
know them.
21 ¶ Not every one that saith unto me,
Lord, Lord, shall enter into the kingdom of heaven; but he that doeth the
will of my Father which is in heaven.
22 Many will say to me in that day,
Lord, Lord, have we not prophesied in
thy name? and in thy name have cast
out devils? and in thy name done many
wonderful works?
23 And then will I profess unto them,
I never knew you: depart from me, ye
that work iniquity.
24 ¶ Therefore whosoever heareth
these sayings of mine, and doeth them,
I will liken him unto a wise man, which
built his house upon a rock:
25 And the rain descended, and the
floods came, and the winds blew, and
beat upon that house; and it fell not: for
it was founded upon a rock.
26 And every one that heareth these
sayings of mine, and doeth them not,
shall be likened unto a foolish man,
which built his house upon the sand:
27 And the rain descended, and the
floods came, and the winds blew, and
beat upon that house; and it fell: and
great was the fall of it.
28 And it came to pass, when Jesus had
ended these sayings, the people were
astonished at his doctrine:
29 For he taught them as *one* having
authority, and not as the scribes.

CHAPTER 8

WHEN he was come down from
the mountain, great multitudes
followed him.
2 And, behold, there came a leper and
worshipped him, saying, Lord, if thou
wilt, thou canst make me clean.
3 And Jesus put forth *his* hand, and
touched him, saying, I will; be thou
clean. And immediately his leprosy was
cleansed.
4 And Jesus saith unto him, See thou tell
no man; but go thy way, show thyself to
the priest, and offer the gift that Moses
commanded, for a testimony unto them.
5 ¶ And when Jesus was entered into
Cȧ-pĕr′nā-ŭm, there came unto him a
centurion, beseeching him,
6 And saying, Lord, my servant lieth
at home sick of the palsy, grievously
tormented.
7 And Jesus saith unto him, I will come
and heal him.
8 The centurion answered and said,
Lord, I am not worthy that thou shouldest come under my roof: but speak the
word only, and my servant shall be
healed.
9 For I am a man under authority, having soldiers under me: and I say to this
man, Go, and he goeth; and to another,
Come, and he cometh; and to my servant, Do this, and he doeth *it*.
10 When Jesus heard *it*, he marveled,
and said to them that followed, Verily I
say unto you, I have not found so great
faith, no, not in Ĭs′rā-ĕl.
11 And I say unto you, That many shall
come from the east and west, and shall
sit down with Abraham, and Isaac, and
Jacob, in the kingdom of heaven:
12 But the children of the kingdom
shall be cast out into outer darkness:
there shall be weeping and gnashing of
teeth.
13 And Jesus said unto the centurion,
Go thy way; and as thou hast believed,
so be it done unto thee. And his servant
was healed in the selfsame hour.
14 ¶ And when Jesus was come into
Peter's house, he saw his wife's mother
laid, and sick of a fever.
15 And he touched her hand, and the
fever left her: and she arose, and ministered unto them.

16 ℂ When the even was come, they
brought unto him many that were possessed with devils: and he cast out the
spirits with *his* word, and healed all
that were sick:
17 That it might be fulfilled which was
spoken by Ē-ṣā'ịăs the prophet, saying,
Himself took our infirmities, and bare
our sicknesses.
18 ℂ Now when Jesus saw great multitudes about him, he gave commandment to depart unto the other side.
19 And a certain scribe came, and said
unto him, Master, I will follow thee
whithersoever thou goest.
20 And Jesus saith unto him, The foxes
have holes, and the birds of the air *have*
nests; but the Son of man hath not
where to lay *his* head.
21 And another of his disciples said
unto him, Lord, suffer me first to go
and bury my father.
22 But Jesus said unto him, Follow me;
and let the dead bury their dead.
23 ℂ And when he was entered into a
ship, his disciples followed him.
24 And, behold, there arose a great
tempest in the sea, insomuch that the
ship was covered with the waves: but
he was asleep.
25 And his disciples came to *him*, and
awoke him, saying, Lord, save us: we
perish.
26 And he saith unto them, Why are ye
fearful, O ye of little faith? Then he
arose, and rebuked the winds and the
sea; and there was a great calm.
27 But the men marveled, saying, What
manner of man is this, that even the
winds and the sea obey him!
28 ℂ And when he was come to the
other side into the country of the Gĕr'-
gē-sēneṣ, there met him two possessed
with devils, coming out of the tombs, exceeding fierce, so that no man might
pass by that way.
29 And, behold, they cried out, saying,
What have we to do with thee, Jesus,
thou Son of God? art thou come hither
to torment us before the time?
30 And there was a good way off from
them a herd of many swine feeding.
31 So the devils besought him, saying,
If thou cast us out, suffer us to go away
into the herd of swine.
32 And he said unto them, Go. And
when they were come out, they went
into the herd of swine: and, behold, the
whole herd of swine ran violently down
a steep place into the sea, and perished
in the waters.
33 And they that kept them fled, and
went their ways into the city, and told
every thing, and what was befallen to
the possessed of the devils.
34 And, behold, the whole city came
out to meet Jesus: and when they saw
him, they besought *him* that he would
depart out of their coasts.

CHAPTER 9

AND he entered into a ship, and
passed over, and came into his
own city.
2 And, behold, they brought to him a
man sick of the palsy, lying on a bed:
and Jesus seeing their faith said unto
the sick of the palsy; Son, be of good
cheer; thy sins be forgiven thee.
3 And, behold, certain of the scribes
said within themselves, This *man* blasphemeth.
4 And Jesus knowing their thoughts
said, Wherefore think ye evil in your
hearts?
5 For whether is easier, to say, *Thy*
sins be forgiven thee; or to say, Arise,
and walk?
6 But that ye may know that the Son of
man hath power on earth to forgive sins,
(then saith he to the sick of the palsy,)
Arise, take up thy bed, and go unto
thine house.
7 And he arose, and departed to his
house.
8 But when the multitudes saw *it*, they
marveled, and glorified God, which had
given such power unto men.
9 ℂ And as Jesus passed forth from
thence, he saw a man, named Matthew,
sitting at the receipt of custom: and he
saith unto him, Follow me. And he
arose, and followed him.
10 ℂ And it came to pass, as Jesus sat
at meat in the house, behold, many
publicans and sinners came and sat
down with him and his disciples.
11 And when the Phăr'ĭ-sēeṣ saw *it*,
they said unto his disciples, Why
eateth your master with publicans and
sinners?
12 But when Jesus heard *that*, he said
unto them, They that be whole need not
a physician, but they that are sick.
13 But go ye and learn what *that*
meaneth, I will have mercy, and not

sacrifice: for I am not come to call the
righteous, but sinners to repentance.
14 ¶ Then came to him the disciples of
John, saying, Why do we and the Phăr′ĭ-
sēeṣ fast oft, but thy disciples fast
not?
15 And Jesus said unto them, Can the
children of the bridechamber mourn, as
long as the bridegroom is with them?
but the days will come, when the bridegroom shall be taken from them, and
then shall they fast.
16 No man putteth a piece of new cloth
unto an old garment; for that which is
put in to fill it up taketh from the garment, and the rent is made worse.
17 Neither do men put new wine into
old bottles: else the bottles break, and
the wine runneth out, and the bottles
perish: but they put new wine into new
bottles, and both are preserved.
18 ¶ While he spake these things unto
them, behold, there came a certain ruler,
and worshipped him, saying, My daughter is even now dead: but come and
lay thy hand upon her, and she shall
live.
19 And Jesus arose, and followed him,
and *so did* his disciples.
20 ¶ And, behold, a woman, which
was diseased with an issue of blood
twelve years, came behind *him*, and
touched the hem of his garment:
21 For she said within herself, If I
may but touch his garment, I shall be
whole.
22 But Jesus turned him about, and
when he saw her, he said, Daughter, be
of good comfort; thy faith hath made
thee whole. And the woman was made
whole from that hour.
23 And when Jesus came into the
ruler's house, and saw the minstrels and
the people making a noise,
24 He said unto them, Give place: for
the maid is not dead, but sleepeth. And
they laughed him to scorn.
25 But when the people were put forth,
he went in, and took her by the hand,
and the maid arose.
26 And the fame hereof went abroad
into all that land.
27 ¶ And when Jesus departed thence,
two blind men followed him, crying,
and saying, *Thou* Son of David, have
mercy on us.
28 And when he was come into the
house, the blind men came to him: and
Jesus saith unto them, Believe ye that
I am able to do this? They said unto
him, Yea, Lord.
29 Then touched he their eyes, saying,
According to your faith be it unto you.
30 And their eyes were opened; and
Jesus straitly charged them, saying, See
that no man know *it*.
31 But they, when they were departed,
spread abroad his fame in all that country.
32 ¶ As they went out, behold, they
brought to him a dumb man possessed
with a devil.
33 And when the devil was cast out,
the dumb spake: and the multitudes
marveled, saying, It was never so seen
in Ĭṣ′rā-ĕl.
34 But the Phăr′ĭ-sēeṣ said, He casteth
out devils through the prince of the
devils.
35 And Jesus went about all the cities
and villages, teaching in their synagogues, and preaching the gospel of the
kingdom, and healing every sickness
and every disease among the people.
36 ¶ But when he saw the multitudes, he was moved with compassion on
them, because they fainted, and were
scattered abroad, as sheep having no
shepherd.
37 Then saith he unto his disciples,
The harvest truly *is* plenteous, but the
laborers *are* few;
38 Pray ye therefore the Lord of the
harvest, that he will send forth laborers
into his harvest.

CHAPTER 10

AND when he had called unto *him* his
twelve disciples, he gave them
power *against* unclean spirits, to cast
them out, and to heal all manner of
sickness and all manner of disease.
2 Now the names of the twelve apostles
are these; The first, Simon, who is called
Peter, and Andrew his brother; James
the son of Zĕb′ē-dēe, and John his
brother;
3 Philip, and Bartholomew; Thomas,
and Matthew the publican; James *the
son* of Alpheus, and Lĕb-bē′ŭs, whose
surname was Thăd′dē-ŭs;
4 Simon the Că′năan-īte, and Judas
Ĭs-căr′ĭ-ŏt, who also betrayed him.
5 These twelve Jesus sent forth, and
commanded them, saying, Go not into
the way of the Ġĕn′tīleṣ, and into *any*

city of the Să-măr'ĭ-tăns enter ye not:
6 But go rather to the lost sheep of the
house of Ĭs'rā-ĕl.
7 And as ye go, preach, saying, The
kingdom of heaven is at hand.
8 Heal the sick, cleanse the lepers,
raise the dead, cast out devils: freely ye
have received, freely give.
9 Provide neither gold, nor silver, nor
brass in your purses;
10 Nor scrip for *your* journey, neither
two coats, neither shoes, nor yet staves:
for the workman is worthy of his meat.
11 And into whatsoever city or town ye
shall enter, inquire who in it is worthy;
and there abide till ye go thence.
12 And when ye come into a house,
salute it.
13 And if the house be worthy, let your
peace come upon it: but if it be not
worthy, let your peace return to you.
14 And whosoever shall not receive
you, nor hear your words, when ye depart out of that house or city, shake off
the dust of your feet.
15 Verily I say unto you, It shall be
more tolerable for the land of Sŏd'ŏm
and Gō-mŏr'răh in the day of judgment,
than for that city.
16 ¶ Behold, I send you forth as sheep
in the midst of wolves: be ye therefore
wise as serpents, and harmless as doves.
17 But beware of men: for they will
deliver you up to the councils, and they
will scourge you in their synagogues;
18 And ye shall be brought before governors and kings for my sake, for a testimony against them and the Gĕn'tīleș.
19 But when they deliver you up, take
no thought how or what ye shall speak:
for it shall be given you in that same
hour what ye shall speak.
20 For it is not ye that speak, but the
Spirit of your Father which speaketh in
you.
21 And the brother shall deliver up the
brother to death, and the father the
child: and the children shall rise up
against *their* parents, and cause them
to be put to death.
22 And ye shall be hated of all *men* for
my name's sake: but he that endureth to
the end shall be saved.
23 But when they persecute you in this
city, flee ye into another: for verily I say
unto you, Ye shall not have gone over
the cities of Ĭș'rā-ĕl, till the Son of man
be come.
24 The disciple is not above *his* master,
nor the servant above his lord.
25 It is enough for the disciple that he
be as his master, and the servant as his
lord. If they have called the master of
the house Bē-ĕl'zē-bŭb, how much more
shall they call them of his household?
26 Fear them not therefore: for there is
nothing covered, that shall not be revealed; and hid, that shall not be known.
27 What I tell you in darkness, *that*
speak ye in light: and what ye hear in
the ear, *that* preach ye upon the housetops.
28 And fear not them which kill the
body, but are not able to kill the soul:
but rather fear him which is able to destroy both soul and body in hell.
29 Are not two sparrows sold for a
farthing? and one of them shall not fall
on the ground without your Father.
30 But the very hairs of your head are
all numbered.
31 Fear ye not therefore, ye are of more
value than many sparrows.
32 Whosoever therefore shall confess
me before men, him will I confess also
before my Father which is in heaven.
33 But whosoever shall deny me before
men, him will I also deny before my
Father which is in heaven.
34 Think not that I am come to send
peace on earth: I came not to send
peace, but a sword.
35 For I am come to set a man at vari-
ance against his father, and the daughter
against her mother, and the daughter-
in-law against her mother-in-law.
36 And a man's foes *shall be* they of his
own household.
37 He that loveth father or mother
more than me is not worthy of me: and
he that loveth son or daughter more than
me is not worthy of me.
38 And he that taketh not his cross, and
followeth after me, is not worthy of me.
39 He that findeth his life shall lose it:
and he that loseth his life for my sake
shall find it.
40 ¶ He that receiveth you receiveth
me; and he that receiveth me receiveth
him that sent me.
41 He that receiveth a prophet in the
name of a prophet shall receive a prophet's reward; and he that receiveth a
righteous man in the name of a righteous man shall receive a righteous man's
reward.

42 And whosoever shall give to drink unto one of these little ones a cup of cold *water* only in the name of a disciple, verily I say unto you, he shall in no wise lose his reward.

CHAPTER 11

AND it came to pass, when Jesus had made an end of commanding his twelve disciples, he departed thence to teach and to preach in their cities.

2 Now when John had heard in the prison the works of Christ, he sent two of his disciples,

3 And said unto him, Art thou he that should come, or do we look for another?

4 Jesus answered and said unto them, Go and show John again those things which ye do hear and see:

5 The blind receive their sight, and the lame walk, the lepers are cleansed, and the deaf hear, the dead are raised up, and the poor have the gospel preached to them.

6 And blessed is *he,* whosoever shall not be offended in me.

7 ¶ And as they departed, Jesus began to say unto the multitudes concerning John, What went ye out into the wilderness to see? A reed shaken with the wind?

8 But what went ye out for to see? A man clothed in soft raiment? behold, they that wear soft *clothing* are in kings' houses.

9 But what went ye out for to see? A prophet? yea, I say unto you, and more than a prophet.

10 For this is *he,* of whom it is written, Behold, I send my messenger before thy face, which shall prepare thy way before thee.

11 Verily I say unto you, Among them that are born of women there hath not risen a greater than John the Baptist: notwithstanding, he that is least in the kingdom of heaven is greater than he.

12 And from the days of John the Baptist until now the kingdom of heaven suffereth violence, and the violent take it by force.

13 For all the prophets and the law prophesied until John.

14 And if ye will receive *it,* this is Ē-lī'ăs, which was for to come.

15 He that hath ears to hear, let him hear.

16 ¶ But whereunto shall I liken this generation? It is like unto children sitting in the markets, and calling unto their fellows,

17 And saying, We have piped unto you, and ye have not danced; we have mourned unto you, and ye have not lamented.

18 For John came neither eating nor drinking, and they say, He hath a devil.

19 The Son of man came eating and drinking, and they say, Behold a man gluttonous, and a winebibber, a friend of publicans and sinners. But wisdom is justified of her children.

20 ¶ Then began he to upbraid the cities wherein most of his mighty works were done, because they repented not:

21 Woe unto thee, Chō-rā'zĭn! woe unto thee, Běth'sā'ĭ-dȧ! for if the mighty works, which were done in you, had been done in Tȳre and Sī'dŏn, they would have repented long ago in sackcloth and ashes.

22 But I say unto you, It shall be more tolerable for Tȳre and Sī'dŏn at the day of judgment, than for you.

23 And thou, Cȧ-pẽr'nā-ŭm, which art exalted unto heaven, shalt be brought down to hell: for if the mighty works, which have been done in thee, had been done in Sŏd'ŏm, it would have remained until this day.

24 But I say unto you, That it shall be more tolerable for the land of Sŏd'ŏm in the day of judgment, than for thee.

25 ¶ At that time Jesus answered and said, I thank thee, O Father, Lord of heaven and earth, because thou hast hid these things from the wise and prudent, and hast revealed them unto babes.

26 Even so, Father; for so it seemed good in thy sight.

27 All things are delivered unto me of my Father: and no man knoweth the Son, but the Father; neither knoweth any man the Father, save the Son, and *he* to whomsoever the Son will reveal *him.*

28 ¶ Come unto me, all *ye* that labor and are heavy laden, and I will give you rest.

29 Take my yoke upon you, and learn of me; for I am meek and lowly in heart: and ye shall find rest unto your souls.

30 For my yoke *is* easy, and my burden is light.

CHAPTER 12

AT that time Jesus went on the sabbath day through the corn; and his
disciples were ahungered, and began to
pluck the ears of corn, and to eat.
2 But when the Phăr'ĭ-sēeş saw *it,* they
said unto him, Behold, thy disciples do
that which is not lawful to do upon the
sabbath day.
3 But he said unto them, Have ye not
read what David did, when he was ahungered, and they that were with him;
4 How he entered into the house of
God, and did eat the showbread, which
was not lawful for him to eat, neither
for them which were with him, but only
for the priests?
5 Or have ye not read in the law, how
that on the sabbath days the priests in
the temple profane the sabbath, and are
blameless?
6 But I say unto you, That in this place
is *one* greater than the temple.
7 But if ye had known what *this* meaneth, I will have mercy, and not sacrifice,
ye would not have condemned the guiltless.
8 For the Son of man is Lord even of
the sabbath day.
9 And when he was departed thence,
he went into their synagogue:
10 ¶ And, behold, there was a man
which had *his* hand withered. And they
asked him, saying, Is it lawful to heal
on the sabbath days? that they might
accuse him.
11 And he said unto them, What man
shall there be among you, that shall
have one sheep, and if it fall into a pit
on the sabbath day, will he not lay hold
on it, and lift *it* out?
12 How much then is a man better
than a sheep? Wherefore it is lawful to
do well on the sabbath days.
13 Then saith he to the man, Stretch
forth thine hand. And he stretched *it*
forth; and it was restored whole, like as
the other.
14 ¶ Then the Phăr'ĭ-sēeş went out,
and held a council against him, how they
might destroy him.
15 But when Jesus knew *it,* he withdrew himself from thence: and great
multitudes followed him, and he healed
them all;
16 And charged them that they should
not make him known:
17 That it might be fulfilled which was
spoken by Ē-ṣā'ịăs the prophet, saying,
18 Behold my servant, whom I have
chosen; my beloved, in whom my soul
is well pleased: I will put my Spirit upon
him, and he shall show judgment to the
Ġĕn'tīleş.
19 He shall not strive, nor cry; neither
shall any man hear his voice in the
streets.
20 A bruised reed shall he not break,
and smoking flax shall he not quench,
till he send forth judgment unto victory.
21 And in his name shall the Ġĕn'tīleş
trust.
22 ¶ Then was brought unto him one
possessed with a devil, blind, and dumb:
and he healed him, insomuch that the
blind and dumb both spake and saw.
23 And all the people were amazed, and
said, Is not this the Son of David?
24 But when the Phăr'ĭ-sēeş heard *it,*
they said, This *fellow* doth not cast out
devils, but by Bē-ĕl'zē-bŭb the prince
of the devils.
25 And Jesus knew their thoughts, and
said unto them, Every kingdom divided
against itself is brought to desolation;
and every city or house divided against
itself shall not stand:
26 And if Satan cast out Satan, he is
divided against himself; how shall then
his kingdom stand?
27 And if I by Bē-ĕl'zē-bŭb cast out
devils, by whom do your children cast
them out? therefore they shall be your
judges.
28 But if I cast out devils by the Spirit
of God, then the kingdom of God is
come unto you.
29 Or else, how can one enter into a
strong man's house, and spoil his goods,
except he first bind the strong man? and
then he will spoil his house.
30 He that is not with me is against me;
and he that gathereth not with me scattereth abroad.
31 ¶ Wherefore I say unto you, All
manner of sin and blasphemy shall be
forgiven unto men: but the blasphemy
against the *Holy* Ghost shall not be forgiven unto men.
32 And whosoever speaketh a word
against the Son of man, it shall be forgiven him: but whosoever speaketh
against the Holy Ghost, it shall not be
forgiven him, neither in this world,
neither in the *world* to come.

33 Either make the tree good, and his fruit good; or else make the tree corrupt, and his fruit corrupt: for the tree is known by *his* fruit.

34 O generation of vipers, how can ye, being evil, speak good things? for out of the abundance of the heart the mouth speaketh.

35 A good man out of the good treasure of the heart bringeth forth good things: and an evil man out of the evil treasure bringeth forth evil things.

36 But I say unto you, That every idle word that men shall speak, they shall give account thereof in the day of judgment.

37 For by thy words thou shalt be justified, and by thy words thou shalt be condemned.

38 ¶ Then certain of the scribes and of the Phăr′ĭ-sēeş answered, saying, Master, we would see a sign from thee.

39 But he answered and said unto them, An evil and adulterous generation seeketh after a sign; and there shall no sign be given to it, but the sign of the prophet Jō′nȧs:

40 For as Jō′nȧs was three days and three nights in the whale's belly; so shall the Son of man be three days and three nights in the heart of the earth.

41 The men of Nĭn′ē-vĕh shall rise in judgment with this generation, and shall condemn it: because they repented at the preaching of Jō′nȧs; and, behold, a greater than Jō′nȧs *is* here.

42 The queen of the south shall rise up in the judgment with this generation, and shall condemn it: for she came from the uttermost parts of the earth to hear the wisdom of Solomon; and, behold, a greater than Solomon *is* here.

43 When the unclean spirit is gone out of a man, he walketh through dry places, seeking rest, and findeth none.

44 Then he saith, I will return into my house from whence I came out; and when he is come, he findeth *it* empty, swept, and garnished.

45 Then goeth he, and taketh with himself seven other spirits more wicked than himself, and they enter in and dwell there: and the last *state* of that man is worse than the first. Even so shall it be also unto this wicked generation.

46 ¶ While he yet talked to the people, behold, *his* mother and his brethren stood without, desiring to speak with him.

47 Then one said unto him, Behold, thy mother and thy brethren stand without, desiring to speak with thee.

48 But he answered and said unto him that told him, Who is my mother? and who are my brethren?

49 And he stretched forth his hand toward his disciples, and said, Behold my mother and my brethren!

50 For whosoever shall do the will of my Father which is in heaven, the same is my brother, and sister, and mother.

CHAPTER 13

THE same day went Jesus out of the house, and sat by the sea side.

2 And great multitudes were gathered together unto him, so that he went into a ship, and sat; and the whole multitude stood on the shore.

3 And he spake many things unto them in parables, saying, Behold, a sower went forth to sow;

4 And when he sowed, some *seeds* fell by the wayside, and the fowls came and devoured them up:

5 Some fell upon stony places, where they had not much earth: and forthwith they sprung up, because they had no deepness of earth:

6 And when the sun was up, they were scorched; and because they had no root, they withered away.

7 And some fell among thorns; and the thorns sprung up, and choked them:

8 But other fell into good ground, and brought forth fruit, some a hundredfold, some sixtyfold, some thirtyfold.

9 Who hath ears to hear, let him hear.

10 And the disciples came, and said unto him, Why speakest thou unto them in parables?

11 He answered and said unto them, Because it is given unto you to know the mysteries of the kingdom of heaven, but to them it is not given.

12 For whosoever hath, to him shall be given, and he shall have more abundance: but whosoever hath not, from him shall be taken away even that he hath.

13 Therefore speak I to them in parables: because they seeing see not; and hearing they hear not, neither do they understand.

14 And in them is fulfilled the prophecy

of Ē-ṣā'ịās, which saith, By hearing ye shall hear, and shall not understand; and seeing ye shall see, and shall not perceive:

15 For this people's heart is waxed gross, and *their* ears are dull of hearing, and their eyes they have closed; lest at any time they should see with *their* eyes, and hear with *their* ears, and should understand with *their* heart, and should be converted, and I should heal them.

16 But blessed *are* your eyes, for they see: and your ears, for they hear.

17 For verily I say unto you, That many prophets and righteous *men* have desired to see *those things* which ye see, and have not seen *them;* and to hear *those things* which ye hear, and have not heard *them.*

18 ¶ Hear ye therefore the parable of the sower.

19 When any one heareth the word of the kingdom, and understandeth *it* not, then cometh the wicked one, and catcheth away that which was sown in his heart. This is he which received seed by the wayside.

20 But he that received the seed into stony places, the same is he that heareth the word, and anon with joy receiveth it;

21 Yet hath he not root in himself, but dureth for a while: for when tribulation or persecution ariseth because of the word, by and by he is offended.

22 He also that received seed among the thorns is he that heareth the word; and the care of this world, and the deceitfulness of riches, choke the word, and he becometh unfruitful.

23 But he that received seed into the good ground is he that heareth the word, and understandeth *it;* which also beareth fruit, and bringeth forth, some a hundredfold, some sixty, some thirty.

24 ¶ Another parable put he forth unto them, saying, The kingdom of heaven is likened unto a man which sowed good seed in his field:

25 But while men slept, his enemy came and sowed tares among the wheat, and went his way.

26 But when the blade was sprung up, and brought forth fruit, then appeared the tares also.

27 So the servants of the householder came and said unto him, Sir, didst not thou sow good seed in thy field? from whence then hath it tares?

28 He said unto them, An enemy hath done this. The servants said unto him, Wilt thou then that we go and gather them up?

29 But he said, Nay; lest while ye gather up the tares, ye root up also the wheat with them.

30 Let both grow together until the harvest: and in the time of harvest I will say to the reapers, Gather ye together first the tares, and bind them in bundles to burn them: but gather the wheat into my barn.

31 ¶ Another parable put he forth unto them, saying, The kingdom of heaven is like to a grain of mustard seed, which a man took, and sowed in his field:

32 Which indeed is the least of all seeds: but when it is grown, it is the greatest among herbs, and becometh a tree, so that the birds of the air come and lodge in the branches thereof.

33 ¶ Another parable spake he unto them; The kingdom of heaven is like unto leaven, which a woman took, and hid in three measures of meal, till the whole was leavened.

34 All these things spake Jesus unto the multitude in parables; and without a parable spake he not unto them:

35 That it might be fulfilled which was spoken by the prophet, saying, I will open my mouth in parables; I will utter things which have been kept secret from the foundation of the world.

36 Then Jesus sent the multitude away, and went into the house: and his disciples came unto him, saying, Declare unto us the parable of the tares of the field.

37 He answered and said unto them, He that soweth the good seed is the Son of man;

38 The field is the world; the good seed are the children of the kingdom; but the tares are the children of the wicked one;

39 The enemy that sowed them is the devil; the harvest is the end of the world; and the reapers are the angels.

40 As therefore the tares are gathered and burned in the fire; so shall it be in the end of this world.

41 The Son of man shall send forth his angels, and they shall gather out of his

kingdom all things that offend, and them
which do iniquity;
42 And shall cast them into a furnace
of fire: there shall be wailing and gnashing of teeth.
43 Then shall the righteous shine forth
as the sun in the kingdom of their
Father. Who hath ears to hear, let him
hear.
44 ¶ Again, the kingdom of heaven is
like unto treasure hid in a field; the
which when a man hath found, he
hideth, and for joy thereof goeth and
selleth all that he hath, and buyeth
that field.
45 ¶ Again, the kingdom of heaven is
like unto a merchantman, seeking
goodly pearls:
46 Who, when he had found one pearl
of great price, went and sold all that he
had, and bought it.
47 ¶ Again, the kingdom of heaven
is like unto a net, that was cast into
the sea, and gathered of every kind:
48 Which, when it was full, they drew
to shore, and sat down, and gathered
the good into vessels, but cast the bad
away.
49 So shall it be at the end of the world:
the angels shall come forth, and sever
the wicked from among the just,
50 And shall cast them into the furnace
of fire: there shall be wailing and gnashing of teeth.
51 Jesus saith unto them, Have ye
understood all these things? They say
unto him, Yea, Lord.
52 Then said he unto them, Therefore
every scribe *which is* instructed unto the
kingdom of heaven, is like unto a man
that is a householder, which bringeth
forth out of his treasure *things* new and
old.
53 ¶ And it came to pass, *that* when
Jesus had finished these parables, he
departed thence.
54 And when he was come into his own
country, he taught them in their synagogue, insomuch that they were astonished, and said, Whence hath this *man*
this wisdom, and *these* mighty works?
55 Is not this the carpenter's son? is
not his mother called Mary? and his
brethren, James, and Jō'sēş, and Simon,
and Judas?
56 And his sisters, are they not all with
us? Whence then hath this *man* all
these things?
57 And they were offended in him.
But Jesus said unto them, A prophet is
not without honor, save in his own country, and in his own house.
58 And he did not many mighty works
there because of their unbelief.

CHAPTER 14

AT that time Hĕr'ŏd the tetrarch
heard of the fame of Jesus,
2 And said unto his servants, This is
John the Baptist; he is risen from the
dead; and therefore mighty works do
show forth themselves in him.
3 ¶ For Hĕr'ŏd had laid hold on John,
and bound him, and put *him* in prison
for Hē-rō'dĭ-ăs' sake, his brother
Philip's wife.
4 For John said unto him, It is not
lawful for thee to have her.
5 And when he would have put him to
death, he feared the multitude, because
they counted him as a prophet.
6 But when Hĕr'ŏd's birthday was
kept, the daughter of Hē-rō'dĭ-ăs
danced before them, and pleased
Hĕr'ŏd.
7 Whereupon he promised with an
oath to give her whatsoever she would
ask.
8 And she, being before instructed of
her mother, said, Give me here John
Baptist's head in a charger.
9 And the king was sorry: nevertheless
for the oath's sake, and them which sat
with him at meat, he commanded *it* to
be given *her*.
10 And he sent, and beheaded John in
the prison.
11 And his head was brought in a
charger, and given to the damsel: and
she brought *it* to her mother.
12 And his disciples came, and took
up the body, and buried it, and went
and told Jesus.
13 ¶ When Jesus heard *of it*, he departed thence by ship into a desert
place apart: and when the people had
heard *thereof*, they followed him on
foot out of the cities.
14 And Jesus went forth, and saw a
great multitude, and was moved with
compassion toward them, and he healed
their sick.
15 ¶ And when it was evening, his
disciples came to him, saying, This is a
desert place, and the time is now past;
send the multitude away, that they may

go into the villages, and buy themselves victuals.
16 But Jesus said unto them, They need not depart; give ye them to eat.
17 And they say unto him, We have here but five loaves, and two fishes.
18 He said, Bring them hither to me.
19 And he commanded the multitude to sit down on the grass, and took the five loaves, and the two fishes, and looking up to heaven, he blessed, and brake, and gave the loaves to *his* disciples, and the disciples to the multitude.
20 And they did all eat, and were filled: and they took up of the fragments that remained twelve baskets full.
21 And they that had eaten were about five thousand men, beside women and children.
22 ¶ And straightway Jesus constrained his disciples to get into a ship, and to go before him unto the other side, while he sent the multitudes away.
23 And when he had sent the multitudes away, he went up into a mountain apart to pray: and when the evening was come, he was there alone.
24 But the ship was now in the midst of the sea, tossed with waves: for the wind was contrary.
25 And in the fourth watch of the night Jesus went unto them, walking on the sea.
26 And when the disciples saw him walking on the sea, they were troubled, saying, It is a spirit; and they cried out for fear.
27 But straightway Jesus spake unto them, saying, Be of good cheer; it is I; be not afraid.
28 And Peter answered him and said, Lord, if it be thou, bid me come unto thee on the water.
29 And he said, Come. And when Peter was come down out of the ship, he walked on the water, to go to Jesus.
30 But when he saw the wind boisterous, he was afraid; and beginning to sink, he cried, saying, Lord, save me.
31 And immediately Jesus stretched forth *his* hand, and caught him, and said unto him, O thou of little faith, wherefore didst thou doubt?
32 And when they were come into the ship, the wind ceased.
33 Then they that were in the ship came and worshipped him, saying, Of a truth thou art the Son of God.
34 ¶ And when they were gone over, they came into the land of Gĕn-nĕs′ȧ-rĕt.
35 And when the men of that place had knowledge of him, they sent out into all that country round about, and brought unto him all that were diseased;
36 And besought him that they might only touch the hem of his garment: and as many as touched were made perfectly whole.

CHAPTER 15

THEN came to Jesus scribes and Phăr′ĭ-sēeș, which were of Jerusalem, saying,
2 Why do thy disciples transgress the tradition of the elders? for they wash not their hands when they eat bread.
3 But he answered and said unto them, Why do ye also transgress the commandment of God by your tradition?
4 For God commanded, saying, Honor thy father and mother: and, He that curseth father or mother, let him die the death.
5 But ye say, Whosoever shall say to *his* father or *his* mother, *It is* a gift, by whatsoever thou mightest be profited by me;
6 And honor not his father or his mother, *he shall be free*. Thus have ye made the commandment of God of none effect by your tradition.
7 *Ye* hypocrites, well did Ē-ṣā′ịăs prophesy of you, saying,
8 This people draweth nigh unto me with their mouth, and honoreth me with *their* lips; but their heart is far from me.
9 But in vain they do worship me, teaching *for* doctrines the commandments of men.
10 ¶ And he called the multitude, and said unto them, Hear, and understand:
11 Not that which goeth into the mouth defileth a man; but that which cometh out of the mouth, this defileth a man.
12 Then came his disciples, and said unto him, Knowest thou that the Phăr′ĭ-sēeș were offended, after they heard this saying?
13 But he answered and said, Every plant, which my heavenly Father hath not planted, shall be rooted up.
14 Let them alone: they be blind leaders of the blind. And if the blind lead the blind, both shall fall into the ditch.

15 Then answered Peter and said unto
him, Declare unto us this parable.
16 And Jesus said, Are ye also yet without understanding?
17 Do not ye yet understand, that whatsoever entereth in at the mouth goeth
into the belly, and is cast out into the
draught?
18 But those things which proceed out
of the mouth come forth from the heart;
and they defile the man.
19 For out of the heart proceed evil
thoughts, murders, adulteries, fornications, thefts, false witness, blasphemies:
20 These are *the things* which defile a
man: but to eat with unwashen hands
defileth not a man.
21 ¶ Then Jesus went thence, and
departed into the coasts of Tȳre and
Sī′dŏn.
22 And, behold, a woman of Cā′năan
came out of the same coasts, and cried
unto him, saying, Have mercy on me,
O Lord, *thou* Son of David; my daughter is grievously vexed with a devil.
23 But he answered her not a word.
And his disciples came and besought
him, saying, Send her away; for she
crieth after us.
24 But he answered and said, I am not
sent but unto the lost sheep of the house
of Ĭṣ′rā-ĕl.
25 Then came she and worshipped him,
saying, Lord, help me.
26 But he answered and said, It is not
meet to take the children's bread, and
to cast *it* to dogs.
27 And she said, Truth, Lord: yet the
dogs eat of the crumbs which fall from
their masters' table.
28 Then Jesus answered and said unto
her, O woman, great *is* thy faith: be it
unto thee even as thou wilt. And her
daughter was made whole from that
very hour.
29 And Jesus departed from thence,
and came nigh unto the sea of Galilee;
and went up into a mountain, and sat
down there.
30 And great multitudes came unto
him, having with them *those that were*
lame, blind, dumb, maimed, and many
others, and cast them down at Jesus'
feet; and he healed them:
31 Insomuch that the multitude wondered, when they saw the dumb to
speak, the maimed to be whole, the lame
to walk, and the blind to see: and they
glorified the God of Ĭṣ′rā-ĕl.
32 ¶ Then Jesus called his disciples
unto him, and said, I have compassion
on the multitude, because they continue
with me now three days, and have nothing to eat: and I will not send them away
fasting, lest they faint in the way.
33 And his disciples say unto him,
Whence should we have so much bread
in the wilderness, as to fill so great a
multitude?
34 And Jesus saith unto them, How
many loaves have ye? And they said,
Seven, and a few little fishes.
35 And he commanded the multitude
to sit down on the ground.
36 And he took the seven loaves and
the fishes, and gave thanks, and brake
them, and gave to his disciples, and the
disciples to the multitude.
37 And they did all eat, and were filled:
and they took up of the broken *meat*
that was left seven baskets full.
38 And they that did eat were four
thousand men, beside women and
children.
39 And he sent away the multitude,
and took ship, and came into the coasts
of Măg′dȧ-lȧ.

CHAPTER 16

THE Phăr′ĭ-sēeṣ also with the Săd′-
dū-çēeṣ came, and tempting desired
him that he would show them a sign
from heaven.
2 He answered and said unto them,
When it is evening, ye say, *It will be*
fair weather: for the sky is red.
3 And in the morning, *It will be* foul
weather to-day: for the sky is red and
lowering. O *ye* hypocrites, ye can discern the face of the sky; but can ye not
discern the signs of the times?
4 A wicked and adulterous generation
seeketh after a sign; and there shall no
sign be given unto it, but the sign of the
prophet Jō′nȧs. And he left them, and
departed.
5 And when his disciples were come to
the other side, they had forgotten to take
bread.
6 ¶ Then Jesus said unto them, Take
heed and beware of the leaven of the
Phăr′ĭ-sēeṣ and of the Săd′dū-çēeṣ.
7 And they reasoned among themselves, saying, *It is* because we have
taken no bread.

8 *Which* when Jesus perceived, he said
unto them, O ye of little faith, why
reason ye among yourselves, because
ye have brought no bread?
9 Do ye not yet understand, neither
remember the five loaves of the five
thousand, and how many baskets ye
took up?
10 Neither the seven loaves of the four
thousand, and how many baskets ye
took up?
11 How is it that ye do not understand
that I spake *it* not to you concerning
bread, that ye should beware of the
leaven of the Phăr'ĭ-sēe̤s and of the
Săd'dū-çēe̤s?
12 Then understood they how that he
bade *them* not beware of the leaven of
bread, but of the doctrine of the Phăr'ĭ-
sēe̤s and of the Săd'dū-çēe̤s.
13 ℂ When Jesus came into the coasts
of Çæs'ȧ-rē'ȧ Phĭ-lĭp'pī, he asked his
disciples, saying, Whom do men say
that I, the Son of man, am?
14 And they said, Some *say that thou*
art John the Baptist; some, Ē-lī'ăs; and
others, Jĕr'ē-mī'ăs, or one of the
prophets.
15 He saith unto them, But whom say
ye that I am?
16 And Simon Peter answered and
said, Thou art the Christ, the Son of the
living God.
17 And Jesus answered and said unto
him, Blessed art thou, Simon Bär'-jō'nȧ:
for flesh and blood hath not revealed *it*
unto thee, but my Father which is in
heaven.
18 And I say also unto thee, That thou
art Peter, and upon this rock I will build
my church; and the gates of hell shall
not prevail against it.
19 And I will give unto thee the keys
of the kingdom of heaven: and whatsoever thou shalt bind on earth shall
be bound in heaven; and whatsoever
thou shalt loose on earth shall be loosed
in heaven.
20 Then charged he his disciples that
they should tell no man that he was
Jesus the Christ.
21 ℂ From that time forth began Jesus
to show unto his disciples, how that he
must go unto Jerusalem, and suffer
many things of the elders and chief
priests and scribes, and be killed, and
be raised again the third day.
22 Then Peter took him, and began to
rebuke him, saying, Be it far from thee,
Lord: this shall not be unto thee.
23 But he turned, and said unto Peter,
Get thee behind me, Satan: thou art an
offense unto me: for thou savorest not
the things that be of God, but those
that be of men.
24 ℂ Then said Jesus unto his disciples, If any *man* will come after me, let
him deny himself, and take up his cross,
and follow me.
25 For whosoever will save his life
shall lose it: and whosoever will lose
his life for my sake shall find it.
26 For what is a man profited, if he
shall gain the whole world, and lose his
own soul? or what shall a man give in
exchange for his soul?
27 For the Son of man shall come in the
glory of his Father with his angels; and
then he shall reward every man according to his works.
28 Verily I say unto you, There be some
standing here, which shall not taste of
death, till they see the Son of man
coming in his kingdom.

CHAPTER 17

AND after six days Jesus taketh Peter,
James, and John his brother, and
bringeth them up into a high mountain
apart,
2 And was transfigured before them:
and his face did shine as the sun, and
his raiment was white as the light.
3 And, behold, there appeared unto
them Moses and Ē-lī'ăs talking with
him.
4 Then answered Peter, and said unto
Jesus, Lord, it is good for us to be here:
if thou wilt, let us make here three
tabernacles; one for thee, and one for
Moses, and one for Ē-lī'ăs.
5 While he yet spake, behold, a bright
cloud overshadowed them: and behold
a voice out of the cloud, which said,
This is my beloved Son, in whom I am
well pleased; hear ye him.
6 And when the disciples heard *it*, they
fell on their face, and were sore afraid.
7 And Jesus came and touched them,
and said, Arise, and be not afraid.
8 And when they had lifted up their
eyes, they saw no man, save Jesus only.
9 And as they came down from the
mountain, Jesus charged them, saying,
Tell the vision to no man, until the Son
of man be risen again from the dead.

10 And his disciples asked him, saying, Why then say the scribes that Ē-lī'ăs must first come?
11 And Jesus answered and said unto them, Ē-lī'ăs truly shall first come, and restore all things.
12 But I say unto you, That Ē-lī'ăs is come already, and they knew him not, but have done unto him whatsoever they listed. Likewise shall also the Son of man suffer of them.
13 Then the disciples understood that he spake unto them of John the Baptist.
14 ¶ And when they were come to the multitude, there came to him a *certain* man, kneeling down to him, and saying,
15 Lord, have mercy on my son; for he is lunatic, and sore vexed: for ofttimes he falleth into the fire, and oft into the water.
16 And I brought him to thy disciples, and they could not cure him.
17 Then Jesus answered and said, O faithless and perverse generation, how long shall I be with you? how long shall I suffer you? bring him hither to me.
18 And Jesus rebuked the devil; and he departed out of him: and the child was cured from that very hour.
19 Then came the disciples to Jesus apart, and said, Why could not we cast him out?
20 And Jesus said unto them, Because of your unbelief: for verily I say unto you, If ye have faith as a grain of mustard seed, ye shall say unto this mountain, Remove hence to yonder place; and it shall remove: and nothing shall be impossible unto you.
21 Howbeit this kind goeth not out but by prayer and fasting.
22 ¶ And while they abode in Galilee, Jesus said unto them, The Son of man shall be betrayed into the hands of men:
23 And they shall kill him, and the third day he shall be raised again. And they were exceeding sorry.
24 ¶ And when they were come to Cȧ-pĕr'nā-ŭm, they that received tribute *money* came to Peter, and said, Doth not your master pay tribute?
25 He saith, Yes. And when he was come into the house, Jesus prevented him, saying, What thinkest thou, Simon? of whom do the kings of the earth take custom or tribute? of their own children, or of strangers?
26 Peter saith unto him, Of strangers. Jesus saith unto him, Then are the children free.
27 Notwithstanding, lest we should offend them, go thou to the sea, and cast a hook, and take up the fish that first cometh up; and when thou hast opened his mouth, thou shalt find a piece of money: that take, and give unto them for me and thee.

CHAPTER 18

AT the same time came the disciples unto Jesus, saying, Who is the greatest in the kingdom of heaven?
2 And Jesus called a little child unto him, and set him in the midst of them,
3 And said, Verily I say unto you, Except ye be converted, and become as little children, ye shall not enter into the kingdom of heaven.
4 Whosoever therefore shall humble himself as this little child, the same is greatest in the kingdom of heaven.
5 And whoso shall receive one such little child in my name receiveth me.
6 But whoso shall offend one of these little ones which believe in me, it were better for him that a millstone were hanged about his neck, and *that* he were drowned in the depth of the sea.
7 ¶ Woe unto the world because of offenses! for it must needs be that offenses come; but woe to that man by whom the offense cometh!
8 Wherefore if thy hand or thy foot offend thee, cut them off, and cast *them* from thee: it is better for thee to enter into life halt or maimed, rather than having two hands or two feet to be cast into everlasting fire.
9 And if thine eye offend thee, pluck it out, and cast *it* from thee: it is better for thee to enter into life with one eye, rather than having two eyes to be cast into hell fire.
10 Take heed that ye despise not one of these little ones; for I say unto you, That in heaven their angels do always behold the face of my Father which is in heaven.
11 For the Son of man is come to save that which was lost.
12 How think ye? if a man have a hundred sheep, and one of them be gone astray, doth he not leave the ninety and nine, and goeth into the mountains, and seeketh that which is gone astray?
13 And if so be that he find it, verily I

say unto you, he rejoiceth more of that *sheep*, than of the ninety and nine which went not astray.

14 Even so it is not the will of your Father which is in heaven, that one of these little ones should perish.

15 ¶ Moreover if thy brother shall trespass against thee, go and tell him his fault between thee and him alone: if he shall hear thee, thou hast gained thy brother.

16 But if he will not hear *thee, then* take with thee one or two more, that in the mouth of two or three witnesses every word may be established.

17 And if he shall neglect to hear them, tell *it* unto the church: but if he neglect to hear the church, let him be unto thee as a heathen man and a publican.

18 Verily I say unto you, Whatsoever ye shall bind on earth shall be bound in heaven; and whatsoever ye shall loose on earth shall be loosed in heaven.

19 Again I say unto you, That if two of you shall agree on earth as touching any thing that they shall ask, it shall be done for them of my Father which is in heaven.

20 For where two or three are gathered together in my name, there am I in the midst of them.

21 ¶ Then came Peter to him, and said, Lord, how oft shall my brother sin against me, and I forgive him? till seven times?

22 Jesus saith unto him, I say not unto thee, Until seven times: but, Until seventy times seven.

23 ¶ Therefore is the kingdom of heaven likened unto a certain king, which would take account of his servants.

24 And when he had begun to reckon, one was brought unto him, which owed him ten thousand talents.

25 But forasmuch as he had not to pay, his lord commanded him to be sold, and his wife, and children, and all that he had, and payment to be made.

26 The servant therefore fell down, and worshipped him, saying, Lord, have patience with me, and I will pay thee all.

27 Then the lord of that servant was moved with compassion, and loosed him, and forgave him the debt.

28 But the same servant went out, and found one of his fellow servants, which owed him a hundred pence: and he laid hands on him, and took *him* by the throat, saying, Pay me that thou owest.

29 And his fellow servant fell down at his feet, and besought him, saying, Have patience with me, and I will pay thee all.

30 And he would not: but went and cast him into prison, till he should pay the debt.

31 So when his fellow servants saw what was done, they were very sorry, and came and told unto their lord all that was done.

32 Then his lord, after that he had called him, said unto him, O thou wicked servant, I forgave thee all that debt, because thou desiredst me:

33 Shouldest not thou also have had compassion on thy fellow servant, even as I had pity on thee?

34 And his lord was wroth, and delivered him to the tormentors, till he should pay all that was due unto him.

35 So likewise shall my heavenly Father do also unto you, if ye from your hearts forgive not every one his brother their trespasses.

CHAPTER 19

AND it came to pass, *that* when Jesus had finished these sayings, he departed from Galilee, and came into the coasts of Judea beyond Jordan;

2 And great multitudes followed him; and he healed them there.

3 ¶ The Phăr′i-sēeș also came unto him, tempting him, and saying unto him, Is it lawful for a man to put away his wife for every cause?

4 And he answered and said unto them, Have ye not read, that he which made *them* at the beginning made them male and female,

5 And said, For this cause shall a man leave father and mother, and shall cleave to his wife: and they twain shall be one flesh?

6 Wherefore they are no more twain, but one flesh. What therefore God hath joined together, let not man put asunder.

7 They say unto him, Why did Moses then command to give a writing of divorcement, and to put her away?

8 He saith unto them, Moses because of the hardness of your hearts suffered you to put away your wives: but from the beginning it was not so.

9 And I say unto you, Whosoever shall put away his wife, except *it be* for forni-

cation, and shall marry another, committeth adultery: and whoso marrieth
her which is put away doth commit
adultery.
10 ¶ His disciples say unto him, If the
case of the man be so with *his* wife, it
is not good to marry.
11 But he said unto them, All *men* cannot receive this saying, save *they* to
whom it is given.
12 For there are some eunuchs, which
were so born from *their* mother's womb:
and there are some eunuchs, which were
made eunuchs of men: and there be
eunuchs, which have made themselves
eunuchs for the kingdom of heaven's
sake. He that is able to receive *it,* let
him receive *it.*
13 ¶ Then were there brought unto
him little children, that he should put
his hands on them, and pray: and the
disciples rebuked them.
14 But Jesus said, Suffer little children,
and forbid them not, to come unto me;
for of such is the kingdom of heaven.
15 And he laid *his* hands on them, and
departed thence.
16 ¶ And, behold, one came and said
unto him, Good Master, what good thing
shall I do, that I may have eternal life?
17 And he said unto him, Why callest
thou me good? *there is* none good but
one, *that is,* God: but if thou wilt enter
into life, keep the commandments.
18 He saith unto him, Which? Jesus
said, Thou shalt do no murder, Thou
shalt not commit adultery, Thou shalt
not steal, Thou shalt not bear false witness,
19 Honor thy father and *thy* mother:
and, Thou shalt love thy neighbor as
thyself.
20 The young man saith unto him, All
these things have I kept from my youth
up: what lack I yet?
21 Jesus said unto him, If thou wilt
be perfect, go *and* sell that thou hast,
and give to the poor, and thou shalt have
treasure in heaven: and come *and* follow me.
22 But when the young man heard
that saying, he went away sorrowful: for
he had great possessions.
23 ¶ Then said Jesus unto his disciples, Verily I say unto you, That a rich
man shall hardly enter into the kingdom
of heaven.
24 And again I say unto you, It is easier
for a camel to go through the eye of a
needle, than for a rich man to enter into
the kingdom of God.
25 When his disciples heard *it,* they
were exceedingly amazed, saying, Who
then can be saved?
26 But Jesus beheld *them,* and said
unto them, With men this is impossible;
but with God all things are possible.
27 ¶ Then answered Peter and said
unto him, Behold, we have forsaken all,
and followed thee; what shall we have
therefore?
28 And Jesus said unto them, Verily
I say unto you, That ye which have followed me, in the regeneration when the
Son of man shall sit in the throne of his
glory, ye also shall sit upon twelve
thrones, judging the twelve tribes of
Ĭṣ′rā-ĕl.
29 And every one that hath forsaken
houses, or brethren, or sisters, or father,
or mother, or wife, or children, or lands,
for my name's sake, shall receive a hundredfold, and shall inherit everlasting
life.
30 But many *that are* first shall be last;
and the last *shall be* first.

CHAPTER 20

FOR the kingdom of heaven is like
unto a man *that is* a householder,
which went out early in the morning to
hire laborers into his vineyard.
2 And when he had agreed with the
laborers for a penny a day, he sent them
into his vineyard.
3 And he went out about the third hour,
and saw others standing idle in the
market place,
4 And said unto them; Go ye also into
the vineyard, and whatsoever is right I
will give you. And they went their way.
5 Again he went out about the sixth
and ninth hour, and did likewise.
6 And about the eleventh hour he went
out, and found others standing idle, and
saith unto them, Why stand ye here all
the day idle?
7 They say unto him, Because no man
hath hired us. He saith unto them, Go
ye also into the vineyard; and whatsoever is right, *that* shall ye receive.
8 So when even was come, the lord of
the vineyard saith unto his steward,
Call the laborers, and give them *their*
hire, beginning from the last unto the
first.

9 And when they came that *were hired*
about the eleventh hour, they received
every man a penny.
10 But when the first came, they supposed that they should have received
more; and they likewise received every
man a penny.
11 And when they had received *it*, they
murmured against the goodman of the
house,
12 Saying, These last have wrought
but one hour, and thou hast made them
equal unto us, which have borne the
burden and heat of the day.
13 But he answered one of them, and
said, Friend, I do thee no wrong: didst
not thou agree with me for a penny?
14 Take *that* thine *is*, and go thy way: I
will give unto this last, even as unto thee.
15 Is it not lawful for me to do what I
will with mine own? Is thine eye evil,
because I am good?
16 So the last shall be first, and the
first last: for many be called, but few
chosen.
17 ¶ And Jesus going up to Jerusalem
took the twelve disciples apart in the
way, and said unto them,
18 Behold, we go up to Jerusalem; and
the Son of man shall be betrayed unto
the chief priests and unto the scribes,
and they shall condemn him to death,
19 And shall deliver him to the Ġĕn′-
tileṣ to mock, and to scourge, and to crucify *him:* and the third day he shall rise
again.
20 ¶ Then came to him the mother of
Zĕb′ē-dēe's children with her sons, worshipping *him,* and desiring a certain
thing of him.
21 And he said unto her, What wilt
thou? She saith unto him, Grant that
these my two sons may sit, the one on
thy right hand, and the other on the left,
in thy kingdom.
22 But Jesus answered and said, Ye
know not what ye ask. Are ye able to
drink of the cup that I shall drink of,
and to be baptized with the baptism
that I am baptized with? They say unto
him, We are able.
23 And he saith unto them, Ye shall
drink indeed of my cup, and be baptized
with the baptism that I am baptized
with: but to sit on my right hand, and on
my left, is not mine to give, but *it shall
be given to them* for whom it is prepared
of my Father.
24 And when the ten heard *it,* they
were moved with indignation against the
two brethren.
25 But Jesus called them *unto him,*
and said, Ye know that the princes of
the Ġĕn′tīleṣ exercise dominion over
them, and they that are great exercise
authority upon them.
26 But it shall not be so among you:
but whosoever will be great among you,
let him be your minister;
27 And whosoever will be chief among
you, let him be your servant:
28 Even as the Son of man came not to
be ministered unto, but to minister, and
to give his life a ransom for many.
29 And as they departed from Jĕr′ĭ-chō,
a great multitude followed him.
30 ¶ And, behold, two blind men sitting by the wayside, when they heard
that Jesus passed by, cried out, saying,
Have mercy on us, O Lord, *thou* Son of
David.
31 And the multitude rebuked them,
because they should hold their peace:
but they cried the more, saying, Have
mercy on us, O Lord, *thou* Son of David.
32 And Jesus stood still, and called
them, and said, What will ye that I shall
do unto you?
33 They say unto him, Lord, that our
eyes may be opened.
34 So Jesus had compassion *on them,*
and touched their eyes: and immediately their eyes received sight, and
they followed him.

CHAPTER 21

AND when they drew nigh unto Jerusalem, and were come to Bĕth′-
phȧ-ġē, unto the mount of Olives, then
sent Jesus two disciples,
2 Saying unto them, Go into the village
over against you, and straightway ye
shall find an ass tied, and a colt with
her: loose *them,* and bring *them* unto
me.
3 And if any *man* say aught unto you,
ye shall say, The Lord hath need of
them; and straightway he will send
them.
4 All this was done, that it might be
fulfilled which was spoken by the
prophet, saying,
5 Tell ye the daughter of Sī′ŏn, Behold,
thy King cometh unto thee, meek, and
sitting upon an ass, and a colt the foal
of an ass.

6 And the disciples went, and did as
Jesus commanded them,
7 And brought the ass, and the colt,
and put on them their clothes, and they
set *him* thereon.
8 And a very great multitude spread
their garments in the way; others cut
down branches from the trees, and
strewed *them* in the way.
9 And the multitudes that went before,
and that followed, cried, saying, Hosanna
to the Son of David: Blessed *is* he
that cometh in the name of the Lord;
Hosanna in the highest.
10 And when he was come into Jerusalem,
all the city was moved, saying,
Who is this?
11 And the multitude said, This is
Jesus the prophet of Nazareth of
Galilee.
12 ¶ And Jesus went into the temple
of God, and cast out all them that sold
and bought in the temple, and overthrew
the tables of the money changers,
and the seats of them that sold doves,
13 And said unto them, It is written,
My house shall be called the house of
prayer; but ye have made it a den of
thieves.
14 And the blind and the lame came to
him in the temple; and he healed them.
15 And when the chief priests and
scribes saw the wonderful things that
he did, and the children crying in the
temple, and saying, Hosanna to the Son
of David; they were sore displeased,
16 And said unto him, Hearest thou
what these say? And Jesus saith unto
them, Yea; have ye never read, Out of
the mouth of babes and sucklings thou
hast perfected praise?
17 ¶ And he left them, and went out
of the city into Bethany; and he lodged
there.
18 Now in the morning, as he returned
into the city, he hungered.
19 And when he saw a fig tree in the
way, he came to it, and found nothing
thereon, but leaves only, and said unto
it, Let no fruit grow on thee henceforward
for ever. And presently the fig
tree withered away.
20 And when the disciples saw *it*, they
marveled, saying, How soon is the fig
tree withered away!
21 Jesus answered and said unto them,
Verily I say unto you, If ye have faith,
and doubt not, ye shall not only do this
which is done to the fig tree, but also if
ye shall say unto this mountain, Be thou
removed, and be thou cast into the sea;
it shall be done.
22 And all things, whatsoever ye shall
ask in prayer, believing, ye shall receive.
23 ¶ And when he was come into the
temple, the chief priests and the elders
of the people came unto him as he was
teaching, and said, By what authority
doest thou these things? and who gave
thee this authority?
24 And Jesus answered and said unto
them, I also will ask you one thing,
which if ye tell me, I in like wise
will tell you by what authority I do these
things.
25 The baptism of John, whence was
it? from heaven, or of men? And they
reasoned with themselves, saying, If
we shall say, From heaven; he will say
unto us, Why did ye not then believe
him?
26 But if we shall say, Of men; we fear
the people; for all hold John as a
prophet.
27 And they answered Jesus, and said,
We cannot tell. And he said unto them,
Neither tell I you by what authority I do
these things.
28 ¶ But what think ye? A *certain* man
had two sons; and he came to the first,
and said, Son, go work to-day in my
vineyard.
29 He answered and said, I will not;
but afterward he repented, and went.
30 And he came to the second, and
said likewise. And he answered and
said, I *go*, sir; and went not.
31 Whether of them twain did the will
of *his* father? They say unto him, The
first. Jesus saith unto them, Verily I
say unto you, That the publicans and
the harlots go into the kingdom of God
before you.
32 For John came unto you in the way
of righteousness, and ye believed him
not; but the publicans and the harlots
believed him: and ye, when ye had seen
it, repented not afterward, that ye
might believe him.
33 ¶ Hear another parable: There was
a certain householder, which planted a
vineyard, and hedged it round about,
and digged a winepress in it, and built a
tower, and let it out to husbandmen, and
went into a far country:
34 And when the time of the fruit drew

near, he sent his servants to the husbandmen, that they might receive the fruits of it.
35 And the husbandmen took his servants, and beat one, and killed another, and stoned another.
36 Again, he sent other servants more than the first: and they did unto them likewise.
37 But last of all he sent unto them his son, saying, They will reverence my son.
38 But when the husbandmen saw the son, they said among themselves, This is the heir; come, let us kill him, and let us seize on his inheritance.
39 And they caught him, and cast *him* out of the vineyard, and slew *him*.
40 When the lord therefore of the vineyard cometh, what will he do unto those husbandmen?
41 They say unto him, He will miserably destroy those wicked men, and will let out *his* vineyard unto other husbandmen, which shall render him the fruits in their seasons.
42 Jesus saith unto them, Did ye never read in the Scriptures, The stone which the builders rejected, the same is become the head of the corner: this is the Lord's doing, and it is marvelous in our eyes?
43 Therefore say I unto you, The kingdom of God shall be taken from you, and given to a nation bringing forth the fruits thereof.
44 And whosoever shall fall on this stone shall be broken: but on whomsoever it shall fall, it will grind him to powder.
45 And when the chief priests and Phăr'ĭ-sēes̱ had heard his parables, they perceived that he spake of them.
46 But when they sought to lay hands on him, they feared the multitude, because they took him for a prophet.

CHAPTER 22

AND Jesus answered and spake unto them again by parables, and said,
2 The kingdom of heaven is like unto a certain king, which made a marriage for his son,
3 And sent forth his servants to call them that were bidden to the wedding: and they would not come.
4 Again, he sent forth other servants, saying, Tell them which are bidden, Behold, I have prepared my dinner: my oxen and *my* fatlings *are* killed, and all things *are* ready: come unto the marriage.
5 But they made light of *it*, and went their ways, one to his farm, another to his merchandise:
6 And the remnant took his servants, and entreated *them* spitefully, and slew *them*.
7 But when the king heard *thereof*, he was wroth: and he sent forth his armies, and destroyed those murderers, and burned up their city.
8 Then saith he to his servants, The wedding is ready, but they which were bidden were not worthy.
9 Go ye therefore into the highways, and as many as ye shall find, bid to the marriage.
10 So those servants went out into the highways, and gathered together all as many as they found, both bad and good: and the wedding was furnished with guests.
11 ℭ And when the king came in to see the guests, he saw there a man which had not on a wedding garment:
12 And he saith unto him, Friend, how camest thou in hither not having a wedding garment? And he was speechless.
13 Then said the king to the servants, Bind him hand and foot, and take him away, and cast *him* into outer darkness; there shall be weeping and gnashing of teeth.
14 For many are called, but few *are* chosen.
15 ℭ Then went the Phăr'ĭ-sēes̱, and took counsel how they might entangle him in *his* talk.
16 And they sent out unto him their disciples with the Hē-rō'dĭ-ăns̱, saying, Master, we know that thou art true, and teachest the way of God in truth, neither carest thou for any *man:* for thou regardest not the person of men.
17 Tell us therefore, What thinkest thou? Is it lawful to give tribute unto Cæsar, or not?
18 But Jesus perceived their wickedness, and said, Why tempt ye me, *ye* hypocrites?
19 Show me the tribute money. And they brought unto him a penny.
20 And he saith unto them, Whose *is* this image and superscription?
21 They say unto him, Cæsar's. Then

saith he unto them, Render therefore
unto Cæsar the things which are Cæsar's; and unto God the things that are
God's.
22 When they had heard *these words,*
they marveled, and left him, and went
their way.
23 ¶ The same day came to him the
Săd'dū-çēeș, which say that there is no
resurrection, and asked him,
24 Saying, Master, Moses said, If a
man die, having no children, his brother
shall marry his wife, and raise up seed
unto his brother.
25 Now there were with us seven
brethren: and the first, when he had
married a wife, deceased, and, having
no issue, left his wife unto his brother:
26 Likewise the second also, and the
third, unto the seventh.
27 And last of all the woman died
also.
28 Therefore in the resurrection, whose
wife shall she be of the seven? for they
all had her.
29 Jesus answered and said unto them,
Ye do err, not knowing the Scriptures,
nor the power of God.
30 For in the resurrection they neither
marry, nor are given in marriage, but
are as the angels of God in heaven.
31 But as touching the resurrection of
the dead, have ye not read that which
was spoken unto you by God, saying,
32 I am the God of Abraham, and the
God of Isaac, and the God of Jacob?
God is not the God of the dead, but of
the living.
33 And when the multitude heard *this,*
they were astonished at his doctrine.
34 ¶ But when the Phăr'ĭ-sēeș had
heard that he had put the Săd'dū-çēeș
to silence, they were gathered together.
35 Then one of them, *which was* a
lawyer, asked *him a question*, tempting
him, and saying,
36 Master, which *is* the great commandment in the law?
37 Jesus said unto him, Thou shalt
love the Lord thy God with all thy
heart, and with all thy soul, and with all
thy mind.
38 This is the first and great commandment.
39 And the second *is* like unto it, Thou
shalt love thy neighbor as thyself.
40 On these two commandments hang
all the law and the prophets.
41 ¶ While the Phăr'ĭ-sēeș were
gathered together, Jesus asked them,
42 Saying, What think ye of Christ?
whose son is he? They say unto him,
The son of David.
43 He saith unto them, How then doth
David in spirit call him Lord, saying,
44 The LORD said unto my Lord, Sit
thou on my right hand, till I make thine
enemies thy footstool?
45 If David then call him Lord, how
is he his son?
46 And no man was able to answer him
a word, neither durst any *man* from
that day forth ask him any more *questions.*

CHAPTER 23

THEN spake Jesus to the multitude,
and to his disciples,
2 Saying, The scribes and the Phăr'ĭ-
sēeș sit in Moses' seat:
3 All therefore whatsoever they bid
you observe, *that* observe and do; but
do not ye after their works: for they say,
and do not.
4 For they bind heavy burdens and
grievous to be borne, and lay *them* on
men's shoulders; but they *themselves*
will not move them with one of their
fingers.
5 But all their works they do for to be
seen of men: they make broad their
phylacteries, and enlarge the borders
of their garments,
6 And love the uppermost rooms at
feasts, and the chief seats in the synagogues,
7 And greetings in the markets, and to
be called of men, Răb'bī, Răb'bī.
8 But be not ye called Răb'bī: for one
is your Master, *even* Christ; and all ye
are brethren.
9 And call no *man* your father upon the
earth: for one is your Father, which is
in heaven.
10 Neither be ye called masters: for
one is your Master, *even* Christ.
11 But he that is greatest among you
shall be your servant.
12 And whosoever shall exalt himself
shall be abased; and he that shall humble himself shall be exalted.
13 ¶ But woe unto you, scribes and
Phăr'ĭ-sēeș, hypocrites! for ye shut up
the kingdom of heaven against men: for
ye neither go in *yourselves,* neither
suffer ye them that are entering to go in.

14 Woe unto you, scribes and Phăr′ĭ-sēeş, hypocrites! for ye devour widows' houses, and for a pretense make long prayer: therefore ye shall receive the greater damnation.

15 Woe unto you, scribes and Phăr′ĭ-sēeş, hypocrites! for ye compass sea and land to make one proselyte; and when he is made, ye make him twofold more the child of hell than yourselves.

16 Woe unto you, *ye* blind guides, which say, Whosoever shall swear by the temple, it is nothing; but whosoever shall swear by the gold of the temple, he is a debtor!

17 *Ye* fools and blind: for whether is greater, the gold, or the temple that sanctifieth the gold?

18 And, Whosoever shall swear by the altar, it is nothing; but whosoever sweareth by the gift that is upon it, he is guilty.

19 *Ye* fools and blind: for whether *is* greater, the gift, or the altar that sanctifieth the gift?

20 Whoso therefore shall swear by the altar, sweareth by it, and by all things thereon.

21 And whoso shall swear by the temple, sweareth by it, and by him that dwelleth therein.

22 And he that shall swear by heaven, sweareth by the throne of God, and by him that sitteth thereon.

23 Woe unto you, scribes and Phăr′ĭ-sēeş, hypocrites! for ye pay tithe of mint and anise and cummin, and have omitted the weightier *matters* of the law, judgment, mercy, and faith: these ought ye to have done, and not to leave the other undone.

24 *Ye* blind guides, which strain at a gnat, and swallow a camel.

25 Woe unto you, scribes and Phăr′ĭ-sēeş, hypocrites! for ye make clean the outside of the cup and of the platter, but within they are full of extortion and excess.

26 *Thou* blind Phăr′ĭ-sēe, cleanse first that *which is* within the cup and platter, that the outside of them may be clean also.

27 Woe unto you, scribes and Phăr′ĭ-sēeş, hypocrites! for ye are like unto whited sepulchres, which indeed appear beautiful outward, but are within full of dead *men's* bones, and of all uncleanness.

28 Even so ye also outwardly appear righteous unto men, but within ye are full of hypocrisy and iniquity.

29 Woe unto you, scribes and Phăr′ĭ-sēeş, hypocrites! because ye build the tombs of the prophets, and garnish the sepulchres of the righteous,

30 And say, If we had been in the days of our fathers, we would not have been partakers with them in the blood of the prophets.

31 Wherefore ye be witnesses unto yourselves, that ye are the children of them which killed the prophets.

32 Fill ye up then the measure of your fathers.

33 *Ye* serpents, *ye* generation of vipers, how can ye escape the damnation of hell?

34 ℂ Wherefore, behold, I send unto you prophets, and wise men, and scribes: and *some* of them ye shall kill and crucify; and *some* of them shall ye scourge in your synagogues, and persecute *them* from city to city:

35 That upon you may come all the righteous blood shed upon the earth, from the blood of righteous Abel unto the blood of Zăch′ȧ-rī′ȧs son of Băr′ȧ-chī′ȧs, whom ye slew between the temple and the altar.

36 Verily I say unto you, All these things shall come upon this generation.

37 O Jerusalem, Jerusalem, *thou* that killest the prophets, and stonest them which are sent unto thee, how often would I have gathered thy children together, even as a hen gathereth her chickens under *her* wings, and ye would not!

38 Behold, your house is left unto you desolate.

39 For I say unto you, Ye shall not see me henceforth, till ye shall say, Blessed *is* he that cometh in the name of the Lord.

CHAPTER 24

AND Jesus went out, and departed from the temple: and his disciples came to *him* for to show him the buildings of the temple.

2 And Jesus said unto them, See ye not all these things? verily I say unto you, There shall not be left here one stone upon another, that shall not be thrown down.

3 ℂ And as he sat upon the mount of Olives, the disciples came unto him pri-

vately, saying, Tell us, when shall these
things be? and what *shall be* the sign of
thy coming, and of the end of the world?
4 And Jesus answered and said unto
them, Take heed that no man deceive
you.
5 For many shall come in my name,
saying, I am Christ; and shall deceive
many.
6 And ye shall hear of wars and rumors
of wars: see that ye be not troubled: for
all *these things* must come to pass, but
the end is not yet.
7 For nation shall rise against nation,
and kingdom against kingdom: and
there shall be famines, and pestilences,
and earthquakes, in divers places.
8 All these *are* the beginning of sorrows.
9 Then shall they deliver you up to be
afflicted, and shall kill you: and ye shall
be hated of all nations for my name's
sake.
10 And then shall many be offended,
and shall betray one another, and shall
hate one another.
11 And many false prophets shall rise,
and shall deceive many.
12 And because iniquity shall abound,
the love of many shall wax cold.
13 But he that shall endure unto the
end, the same shall be saved.
14 And this gospel of the kingdom shall
be preached in all the world for a witness unto all nations; and then shall the
end come.
15 When ye therefore shall see the
abomination of desolation, spoken of by
Daniel the prophet, stand in the holy
place, (whoso readeth, let him understand,)
16 Then let them which be in Judea
flee into the mountains:
17 Let him which is on the housetop
not come down to take any thing out of
his house:
18 Neither let him which is in the field
return back to take his clothes.
19 And woe unto them that are with
child, and to them that give suck in
those days!
20 But pray ye that your flight be not
in the winter, neither on the sabbath
day:
21 For then shall be great tribulation,
such as was not since the beginning
of the world to this time, no, nor ever
shall be.
22 And except those days should be
shortened, there should no flesh be
saved: but for the elect's sake those
days shall be shortened.
23 Then if any man shall say unto you,
Lo, here *is* Christ, or there; believe *it* not.
24 For there shall arise false Christs,
and false prophets, and shall show great
signs and wonders; insomuch that, if *it
were* possible, they shall deceive the
very elect.
25 Behold, I have told you before.
26 Wherefore if they shall say unto
you, Behold, he is in the desert; go not
forth: behold, *he is* in the secret chambers; believe *it* not.
27 For as the lightning cometh out of
the east, and shineth even unto the west;
so shall also the coming of the Son of
man be.
28 For wheresoever the carcass is,
there will the eagles be gathered together.
29 ℂ Immediately after the tribulation
of those days shall the sun be darkened,
and the moon shall not give her light,
and the stars shall fall from heaven, and
the powers of the heavens shall be
shaken:
30 And then shall appear the sign of
the Son of man in heaven: and then
shall all the tribes of the earth mourn,
and they shall see the Son of man coming in the clouds of heaven with power
and great glory.
31 And he shall send his angels with a
great sound of a trumpet, and they shall
gather together his elect from the four
winds, from one end of heaven to the
other.
32 Now learn a parable of the fig tree;
When his branch is yet tender, and putteth forth leaves, ye know that summer
is nigh:
33 So likewise ye, when ye shall see all
these things, know that it is near, *even*
at the doors.
34 Verily I say unto you, This generation shall not pass, till all these things
be fulfilled.
35 Heaven and earth shall pass away,
but my words shall not pass away.
36 ℂ But of that day and hour knoweth no *man*, no, not the angels of heaven,
but my Father only.
37 But as the days of Nō'ē *were*,
so shall also the coming of the Son of
man be.

38 For as in the days that were before the flood they were eating and drinking, marrying and giving in marriage, until the day that Nō'ē entered into the ark,

39 And knew not until the flood came, and took them all away; so shall also the coming of the Son of man be.

40 Then shall two be in the field; the one shall be taken, and the other left.

41 Two *women shall be* grinding at the mill; the one shall be taken, and the other left.

42 ℂ Watch therefore; for ye know not what hour your Lord doth come.

43 But know this, that if the goodman of the house had known in what watch the thief would come, he would have watched, and would not have suffered his house to be broken up.

44 Therefore be ye also ready: for in such an hour as ye think not the Son of man cometh.

45 Who then is a faithful and wise servant, whom his lord hath made ruler over his household, to give them meat in due season?

46 Blessed *is* that servant, whom his lord when he cometh shall find so doing.

47 Verily I say unto you, That he shall make him ruler over all his goods.

48 But and if that evil servant shall say in his heart, My lord delayeth his coming;

49 And shall begin to smite *his* fellow servants, and to eat and drink with the drunken;

50 The lord of that servant shall come in a day when he looketh not for *him,* and in an hour that he is not aware of,

51 And shall cut him asunder, and appoint *him* his portion with the hypocrites: there shall be weeping and gnashing of teeth.

CHAPTER 25

THEN shall the kingdom of heaven be likened unto ten virgins, which took their lamps, and went forth to meet the bridegroom.

2 And five of them were wise, and five *were* foolish.

3 They that *were* foolish took their lamps, and took no oil with them:

4 But the wise took oil in their vessels with their lamps.

5 While the bridegroom tarried, they all slumbered and slept.

6 And at midnight there was a cry made, Behold, the bridegroom cometh; go ye out to meet him.

7 Then all those virgins arose, and trimmed their lamps.

8 And the foolish said unto the wise, Give us of your oil; for our lamps are gone out.

9 But the wise answered, saying, *Not so;* lest there be not enough for us and you: but go ye rather to them that sell, and buy for yourselves.

10 And while they went to buy, the bridegroom came; and they that were ready went in with him to the marriage: and the door was shut.

11 Afterward came also the other virgins, saying, Lord, Lord, open to us.

12 But he answered and said, Verily I say unto you, I know you not.

13 Watch therefore; for ye know neither the day nor the hour wherein the Son of man cometh.

14 ℂ For *the kingdom of heaven is* as a man traveling into a far country, *who* called his own servants, and delivered unto them his goods.

15 And unto one he gave five talents, to another two, and to another one; to every man according to his several ability; and straightway took his journey.

16 Then he that had received the five talents went and traded with the same, and made *them* other five talents.

17 And likewise he that *had received* two, he also gained other two.

18 But he that had received one went and digged in the earth, and hid his lord's money.

19 After a long time the lord of those servants cometh, and reckoneth with them.

20 And so he that had received five talents came and brought other five talents, saying, Lord, thou deliveredst unto me five talents: behold, I have gained beside them five talents more.

21 His lord said unto him, Well done, *thou* good and faithful servant: thou hast been faithful over a few things, I will make thee ruler over many things: enter thou into the joy of thy lord.

22 He also that had received two talents came and said, Lord, thou deliveredst unto me two talents: behold, I have gained two other talents beside them.

23 His lord said unto him, Well done,

good and faithful servant; thou hast
been faithful over a few things, I will
make thee ruler over many things: enter
thou into the joy of thy lord.
24 Then he which had received the one
talent came and said, Lord, I knew thee
that thou art a hard man, reaping where
thou hast not sown, and gathering where
thou hast not strewed:
25 And I was afraid, and went and hid
thy talent in the earth: lo, *there* thou
hast *that is* thine.
26 His lord answered and said unto
him, *Thou* wicked and slothful servant,
thou knewest that I reap where I sowed
not, and gather where I have not
strewed:
27 Thou oughtest therefore to have
put my money to the exchangers, and
then at my coming I should have received mine own with usury.
28 Take therefore the talent from him,
and give *it* unto him which hath ten
talents.
29 For unto every one that hath shall
be given, and he shall have abundance:
but from him that hath not shall be
taken away even that which he hath.
30 And cast ye the unprofitable servant into outer darkness: there shall be
weeping and gnashing of teeth.
31 ¶ When the Son of man shall come
in his glory, and all the holy angels with
him, then shall he sit upon the throne of
his glory:
32 And before him shall be gathered
all nations: and he shall separate them
one from another, as a shepherd divideth *his* sheep from the goats:
33 And he shall set the sheep on his
right hand, but the goats on the left.
34 Then shall the King say unto them
on his right hand, Come, ye blessed of
my Father, inherit the kingdom prepared for you from the foundation of the
world:
35 For I was ahungered, and ye gave
me meat: I was thirsty, and ye gave me
drink: I was a stranger, and ye took me
in:
36 Naked, and ye clothed me: I was
sick, and ye visited me: I was in prison,
and ye came unto me.
37 Then shall the righteous answer
him, saying, Lord, when saw we thee
ahungered, and fed *thee?* or thirsty, and
gave *thee* drink?
38 When saw we thee a stranger, and
took *thee* in? or naked, and clothed
thee?
39 Or when saw we thee sick, or in
prison, and came unto thee?
40 And the King shall answer and say
unto them, Verily I say unto you, Inasmuch as ye have done *it* unto one of the
least of these my brethren, ye have done
it unto me.
41 Then shall he say also unto them on
the left hand, Depart from me, ye
cursed, into everlasting fire, prepared
for the devil and his angels:
42 For I was ahungered, and ye gave
me no meat: I was thirsty, and ye gave
me no drink:
43 I was a stranger, and ye took me
not in: naked, and ye clothed me not:
sick, and in prison, and ye visited me
not.
44 Then shall they also answer him,
saying, Lord, when saw we thee ahungered, or athirst, or a stranger, or naked,
or sick, or in prison, and did not minister unto thee?
45 Then shall he answer them, saying,
Verily I say unto you, Inasmuch as ye
did *it* not to one of the least of these, ye
did *it* not to me.
46 And these shall go away into everlasting punishment: but the righteous
into life eternal.

CHAPTER 26

AND it came to pass, when Jesus had
finished all these sayings, he said
unto his disciples,
2 Ye know that after two days is *the
feast of* the passover, and the Son of
man is betrayed to be crucified.
3 Then assembled together the chief
priests, and the scribes, and the elders
of the people, unto the palace of the
high priest, who was called Cā'ịa-phăs,
4 And consulted that they might take
Jesus by subtilty, and kill *him.*
5 But they said, Not on the feast *day,*
lest there be an uproar among the
people.
6 ¶ Now when Jesus was in Bethany,
in the house of Simon the leper,
7 There came unto him a woman having an alabaster box of very precious
ointment, and poured it on his head, as
he sat at meat.
8 But when his disciples saw *it,* they
had indignation, saying, To what purpose *is* this waste?

9 For this ointment might have been
sold for much, and given to the poor.
10 When Jesus understood *it,* he said
unto them, Why trouble ye the woman?
for she hath wrought a good work upon
me.
11 For ye have the poor always with
you; but me ye have not always.
12 For in that she hath poured this
ointment on my body, she did *it* for my
burial.
13 Verily I say unto you, Wheresoever
this gospel shall be preached in the
whole world, *there* shall also this, that
this woman hath done, be told for a
memorial of her.
14 ¶ Then one of the twelve, called
Judas Ĭs-căr′ĭ-ŏt, went unto the chief
priests,
15 And said *unto them,* What will ye
give me, and I will deliver him unto you?
And they covenanted with him for thirty
pieces of silver.
16 And from that time he sought opportunity to betray him.
17 ¶ Now the first *day* of the *feast of*
unleavened bread the disciples came to
Jesus, saying unto him, Where wilt
thou that we prepare for thee to eat the
passover?
18 And he said, Go into the city to such
a man, and say unto him, The Master
saith, My time is at hand; I will keep the
passover at thy house with my disciples.
19 And the disciples did as Jesus had
appointed them; and they made ready
the passover.
20 Now when the even was come, he
sat down with the twelve.
21 And as they did eat, he said, Verily
I say unto you, that one of you shall
betray me.
22 And they were exceeding sorrowful,
and began every one of them to say unto
him, Lord, is it I?
23 And he answered and said, He that
dippeth *his* hand with me in the dish,
the same shall betray me.
24 The Son of man goeth as it is written of him: but woe unto that man by
whom the Son of man is betrayed! it had
been good for that man if he had not
been born.
25 Then Judas, which betrayed him,
answered and said, Master, is it I? He
said unto him, Thou hast said.
26 ¶ And as they were eating, Jesus
took bread, and blessed *it,* and brake
it, and gave *it* to the disciples, and said,
Take, eat; this is my body.
27 And he took the cup, and gave
thanks, and gave *it* to them, saying,
Drink ye all of it;
28 For this is my blood of the new testament, which is shed for many for the
remission of sins.
29 But I say unto you, I will not drink
henceforth of this fruit of the vine, until
that day when I drink it new with you
in my Father's kingdom.
30 And when they had sung a hymn,
they went out into the mount of Olives.
31 Then saith Jesus unto them, All ye
shall be offended because of me this
night: for it is written, I will smite the
shepherd, and the sheep of the flock
shall be scattered abroad.
32 But after I am risen again, I will go
before you into Galilee.
33 Peter answered and said unto him,
Though all *men* shall be offended because of thee, *yet* will I never be
offended.
34 Jesus said unto him, Verily I say
unto thee, That this night, before the
cock crow, thou shalt deny me thrice.
35 Peter said unto him, Though I
should die with thee, yet will I not deny
thee. Likewise also said all the disciples.
36 ¶ Then cometh Jesus with them
unto a place called Gĕth-sĕm′ȧ-nē, and
saith unto the disciples, Sit ye here,
while I go and pray yonder.
37 And he took with him Peter and the
two sons of Zĕb′ē-dēe, and began to be
sorrowful and very heavy.
38 Then saith he unto them, My soul
is exceeding sorrowful, even unto death:
tarry ye here, and watch with me.
39 And he went a little further, and fell
on his face, and prayed, saying, O my
Father, if it be possible, let this cup pass
from me: nevertheless, not as I will, but
as thou *wilt.*
40 And he cometh unto the disciples,
and findeth them asleep, and saith unto
Peter, What, could ye not watch with
me one hour?
41 Watch and pray, that ye enter not
into temptation: the spirit indeed *is*
willing, but the flesh *is* weak.
42 He went away again the second
time, and prayed, saying, O my Father,
if this cup may not pass away from me,
except I drink it, thy will be done.

43 And he came and found them asleep again: for their eyes were heavy.

44 And he left them, and went away again, and prayed the third time, saying the same words.

45 Then cometh he to his disciples, and saith unto them, Sleep on now, and take *your* rest: behold, the hour is at hand, and the Son of man is betrayed into the hands of sinners.

46 Rise, let us be going: behold, he is at hand that doth betray me.

47 ¶ And while he yet spake, lo, Judas, one of the twelve, came, and with him a great multitude with swords and staves, from the chief priests and elders of the people.

48 Now he that betrayed him gave them a sign, saying, Whomsoever I shall kiss, that same is he; hold him fast.

49 And forthwith he came to Jesus, and said, Hail, Master; and kissed him.

50 And Jesus said unto him, Friend, wherefore art thou come? Then came they, and laid hands on Jesus, and took him.

51 And, behold, one of them which were with Jesus stretched out *his* hand, and drew his sword, and struck a servant of the high priest, and smote off his ear.

52 Then said Jesus unto him, Put up again thy sword into his place: for all they that take the sword shall perish with the sword.

53 Thinkest thou that I cannot now pray to my Father, and he shall presently give me more than twelve legions of angels?

54 But how then shall the Scriptures be fulfilled, that thus it must be?

55 In that same hour said Jesus to the multitudes, Are ye come out as against a thief with swords and staves for to take me? I sat daily with you teaching in the temple, and ye laid no hold on me.

56 But all this was done, that the Scriptures of the prophets might be fulfilled. Then all the disciples forsook him, and fled.

57 ¶ And they that had laid hold on Jesus led *him* away to Ca′ia-phas the high priest, where the scribes and the elders were assembled.

58 But Peter followed him afar off unto the high priest's palace, and went in, and sat with the servants, to see the end.

59 Now the chief priests, and elders, and all the council, sought false witness against Jesus, to put him to death;

60 But found none: yea, though many false witnesses came, *yet* found they none. At the last came two false witnesses,

61 And said, This *fellow* said, I am able to destroy the temple of God, and to build it in three days.

62 And the high priest arose, and said unto him, Answerest thou nothing? what *is it which* these witness against thee?

63 But Jesus held his peace. And the high priest answered and said unto him, I adjure thee by the living God, that thou tell us whether thou be the Christ, the Son of God.

64 Jesus saith unto him, Thou hast said: nevertheless I say unto you, Hereafter shall ye see the Son of man sitting on the right hand of power, and coming in the clouds of heaven.

65 Then the high priest rent his clothes, saying, He hath spoken blasphemy; what further need have we of witnesses? behold, now ye have heard his blasphemy.

66 What think ye? They answered and said, He is guilty of death.

67 Then did they spit in his face, and buffeted him; and others smote *him* with the palms of their hands,

68 Saying, Prophesy unto us, thou Christ, Who is he that smote thee?

69 ¶ Now Peter sat without in the palace: and a damsel came unto him, saying, Thou also wast with Jesus of Galilee.

70 But he denied before *them* all, saying, I know not what thou sayest.

71 And when he was gone out into the porch, another *maid* saw him, and said unto them that were there, This *fellow* was also with Jesus of Nazareth.

72 And again he denied with an oath, I do not know the man.

73 And after a while came unto *him* they that stood by, and said to Peter, Surely thou also art *one* of them; for thy speech bewrayeth thee.

74 Then began he to curse and to swear, *saying*, I know not the man. And immediately the cock crew.

75 And Peter remembered the word of Jesus, which said unto him, Before the cock crow, thou shalt deny me thrice. And he went out, and wept bitterly.

CHAPTER 27

WHEN the morning was come, all
the chief priests and elders of the
people took counsel against Jesus to
put him to death:
2 And when they had bound him, they
led *him* away, and delivered him to
Pŏn'ti-ŭs Pilate the governor.
3 ¶ Then Judas, which had betrayed
him, when he saw that he was condemned, repented himself, and brought
again the thirty pieces of silver to the
chief priests and elders,
4 Saying, I have sinned in that I have
betrayed the innocent blood. And they
said, What *is that* to us? see thou *to that*.
5 And he cast down the pieces of silver
in the temple, and departed, and went
and hanged himself.
6 And the chief priests took the silver
pieces, and said, It is not lawful for to
put them into the treasury, because it is
the price of blood.
7 And they took counsel, and bought
with them the potter's field, to bury
strangers in.
8 Wherefore that field was called, The
field of blood, unto this day.
9 Then was fulfilled that which was
spoken by Jĕr'ē-mȳ the prophet, saying, And they took the thirty pieces of
silver, the price of him that was valued,
whom they of the children of Ĭs'rā-ĕl
did value;
10 And gave them for the potter's field,
as the Lord appointed me.
11 And Jesus stood before the governor: and the governor asked him, saying, Art thou the King of the Jews? And
Jesus said unto him, Thou sayest.
12 And when he was accused of the chief
priests and elders, he answered nothing.
13 Then said Pilate unto him, Hearest
thou not how many things they witness
against thee?
14 And he answered him to never a
word; insomuch that the governor marveled greatly.
15 Now at *that* feast the governor was
wont to release unto the people a prisoner, whom they would.
16 And they had then a notable prisoner, called Bär-ăb'băs.
17 Therefore when they were gathered
together, Pilate said unto them, Whom
will ye that I release unto you? Bär-ăb'-
băs, or Jesus which is called Christ?
18 For he knew that for envy they had
delivered him.
19 ¶ When he was set down on the
judgment seat, his wife sent unto him,
saying, Have thou nothing to do with
that just man: for I have suffered many
things this day in a dream because of
him.
20 But the chief priests and elders persuaded the multitude that they should
ask Bär-ăb'băs, and destroy Jesus.
21 The governor answered and said
unto them, Whether of the twain will
ye that I release unto you? They said,
Bär-ăb'băs.
22 Pilate saith unto them, What shall
I do then with Jesus which is called
Christ? *They* all say unto him, Let him
be crucified.
23 And the governor said, Why, what
evil hath he done? But they cried out
the more, saying, Let him be crucified.
24 ¶ When Pilate saw that he could
prevail nothing, but *that* rather a tumult was made, he took water, and
washed *his* hands before the multitude,
saying, I am innocent of the blood of
this just person: see ye *to it*.
25 Then answered all the people, and
said, His blood *be* on us, and on our
children.
26 ¶ Then released he Bär-ăb'băs
unto them: and when he had scourged
Jesus, he delivered *him* to be crucified.
27 Then the soldiers of the governor
took Jesus into the common hall, and
gathered unto him the whole band *of
soldiers*.
28 And they stripped him, and put on
him a scarlet robe.
29 ¶ And when they had platted a
crown of thorns, they put *it* upon his
head, and a reed in his right hand: and
they bowed the knee before him, and
mocked him, saying, Hail, King of the
Jews!
30 And they spit upon him, and took
the reed, and smote him on the head.
31 And after that they had mocked
him, they took the robe off from him,
and put his own raiment on him, and
led him away to crucify *him*.
32 And as they came out, they found a
man of Çȳ-rē'nē, Simon by name: him
they compelled to bear his cross.
33 And when they were come unto a
place called Gŏl'gō-thȧ, that is to say, a
place of a skull,

34 ℂ They gave him vinegar to drink
mingled with gall: and when he had
tasted *thereof,* he would not drink.
35 And they crucified him, and parted
his garments, casting lots: that it might
be fulfilled which was spoken by the
prophet, They parted my garments
among them, and upon my vesture did
they cast lots.
36 And sitting down they watched him
there;
37 And set up over his head his accusation written, THIS IS JESUS THE KING
OF THE JEWS.
38 Then were there two thieves crucified with him; one on the right hand,
and another on the left.
39 ℂ And they that passed by reviled
him, wagging their heads,
40 And saying, Thou that destroyest
the temple, and buildest *it* in three
days, save thyself. If thou be the Son of
God, come down from the cross.
41 Likewise also the chief priests
mocking *him,* with the scribes and
elders, said,
42 He saved others; himself he cannot
save. If he be the King of Ĭş'rā-ĕl, let
him now come down from the cross,
and we will believe him.
43 He trusted in God; let him deliver
him now, if he will have him: for he
said, I am the Son of God.
44 The thieves also, which were crucified with him, cast the same in his teeth.
45 Now from the sixth hour there was
darkness over all the land unto the
ninth hour.
46 And about the ninth hour Jesus
cried with a loud voice, saying, E'lĭ, E'lĭ,
lä'mä sä-băch'thä-nĭ'? that is to say, My
God, my God, why hast thou forsaken
me?
47 Some of them that stood there, when
they heard *that,* said, This *man* calleth
for Ē-lī'ăs.
48 And straightway one of them ran,
and took a sponge, and filled *it* with
vinegar, and put *it* on a reed, and gave
him to drink.
49 The rest said, Let be, let us see
whether Ē-lī'ăs will come to save him.
50 ℂ Jesus, when he had cried again
with a loud voice, yielded up the ghost.
51 And, behold, the veil of the temple
was rent in twain from the top to the
bottom; and the earth did quake, and
the rocks rent;
52 And the graves were opened; and
many bodies of the saints which slept
arose,
53 And came out of the graves after
his resurrection, and went into the holy
city, and appeared unto many.
54 Now when the centurion, and they
that were with him, watching Jesus,
saw the earthquake, and those things
that were done, they feared greatly, saying, Truly this was the Son of God.
55 And many women were there beholding afar off, which followed Jesus
from Galilee, ministering unto him:
56 Among which was Mary Măg'dȧ-
lēne, and Mary the mother of James and
Jō'sēş, and the mother of Zĕb'ē-dēe's
children.
57 When the even was come, there
came a rich man of Ăr'ĭ-mȧ-thē'ȧ,
named Joseph, who also himself was
Jesus' disciple:
58 He went to Pilate, and begged the
body of Jesus. Then Pilate commanded
the body to be delivered.
59 And when Joseph had taken the
body, he wrapped it in a clean linen
cloth,
60 And laid it in his own new tomb,
which he had hewn out in the rock: and
he rolled a great stone to the door of the
sepulchre, and departed.
61 And there was Mary Măg'dȧ-lēne,
and the other Mary, sitting over against
the sepulchre.
62 ℂ Now the next day, that followed
the day of the preparation, the chief
priests and Phăr'ĭ-sēeş came together
unto Pilate,
63 Saying, Sir, we remember that that
deceiver said, while he was yet alive,
After three days I will rise again.
64 Command therefore that the sepulchre be made sure until the third day,
lest his disciples come by night, and
steal him away, and say unto the people,
He is risen from the dead: so the last
error shall be worse than the first.
65 Pilate said unto them, Ye have a
watch: go your way, make *it* as sure as
ye can.
66 So they went, and made the sepulchre sure, sealing the stone, and setting
a watch.

CHAPTER 28

IN the end of the sabbath, as it began
to dawn toward the first *day* of the

week, came Mary Măg′dȧ-lēne and the
other Mary to see the sepulchre.
2 And, behold, there was a great earthquake: for the angel of the Lord descended from heaven, and came and
rolled back the stone from the door, and
sat upon it.
3 His countenance was like lightning,
and his raiment white as snow:
4 And for fear of him the keepers did
shake, and became as dead *men*.
5 And the angel answered and said
unto the women, Fear not ye: for I know
that ye seek Jesus, which was crucified.
6 He is not here: for he is risen, as he
said. Come, see the place where the
Lord lay.
7 And go quickly, and tell his disciples
that he is risen from the dead; and, behold, he goeth before you into Galilee;
there shall ye see him: lo, I have told
you.
8 And they departed quickly from the
sepulchre with fear and great joy; and
did run to bring his disciples word.
9 ¶ And as they went to tell his disciples, behold, Jesus met them, saying,
All hail. And they came and held him
by the feet, and worshipped him.
10 Then said Jesus unto them, Be not
afraid: go tell my brethren that they go
into Galilee, and there shall they see
me.
11 ¶ Now when they were going, behold, some of the watch came into the
city, and showed unto the chief priests
all the things that were done.
12 And when they were assembled with
the elders, and had taken counsel, they
gave large money unto the soldiers,
13 Saying, Say ye, His disciples came
by night, and stole him *away* while we
slept.
14 And if this come to the governor's
ears, we will persuade him, and secure
you.
15 So they took the money, and did as
they were taught: and this saying is
commonly reported among the Jews
until this day.
16 ¶ Then the eleven disciples went
away into Galilee, into a mountain
where Jesus had appointed them.
17 And when they saw him, they worshipped him: but some doubted.
18 And Jesus came and spake unto
them, saying, All power is given unto
me in heaven and in earth.
19 ¶ Go ye therefore, and teach all
nations, baptizing them in the name of
the Father, and of the Son, and of the
Holy Ghost:
20 Teaching them to observe all things
whatsoever I have commanded you:
and, lo, I am with you alway, *even* unto
the end of the world. Amen.

THE GOSPEL ACCORDING TO

ST. MARK

CHAPTER 1

THE beginning of the gospel of Jesus
Christ, the Son of God;
2 As it is written in the prophets, Behold,
I send my messenger before thy face,
which shall prepare thy way before thee.
3 The voice of one crying in the wilderness,
Prepare ye the way of the
Lord, make his paths straight.
4 John did baptize in the wilderness,
and preach the baptism of repentance
for the remission of sins.
5 And there went out unto him all the
land of Judea, and they of Jerusalem,
and were all baptized of him in the river
of Jordan, confessing their sins.
6 And John was clothed with camel's
hair, and with a girdle of a skin about
his loins; and he did eat locusts and
wild honey;
7 And preached, saying, There cometh
one mightier than I after me, the latchet
of whose shoes I am not worthy to stoop
down and unloose.
8 I indeed have baptized you with water:
but he shall baptize you with the
Holy Ghost.
9 And it came to pass in those days,
that Jesus came from Nazareth of Galilee,
and was baptized of John in Jordan.
10 And straightway coming up out of
the water, he saw the heavens opened,
and the Spirit like a dove descending
upon him:
11 And there came a voice from heaven,
saying, Thou art my beloved Son, in
whom I am well pleased.
12 And immediately the Spirit driveth
him into the wilderness.
13 And he was there in the wilderness
forty days tempted of Satan; and was
with the wild beasts; and the angels
ministered unto him.
14 Now after that John was put in
prison, Jesus came into Galilee, preaching
the gospel of the kingdom of God,
15 And saying, The time is fulfilled,
and the kingdom of God is at hand: repent
ye, and believe the gospel.
16 Now as he walked by the sea of
Galilee, he saw Simon and Andrew his
brother casting a net into the sea: for
they were fishers.
17 And Jesus said unto them, Come ye
after me, and I will make you to become
fishers of men.
18 And straightway they forsook their
nets, and followed him.
19 And when he had gone a little further
thence, he saw James the *son* of
Zĕb'ē-dēe, and John his brother, who
also were in the ship mending their nets.
20 And straightway he called them:
and they left their father Zĕb'ē-dēe in
the ship with the hired servants, and
went after him.
21 And they went into Cȧ-pĕr'nā-ŭm;
and straightway on the sabbath day he
entered into the synagogue, and taught.
22 And they were astonished at his
doctrine: for he taught them as one that
had authority, and not as the scribes.
23 And there was in their synagogue a
man with an unclean spirit; and he cried
out,
24 Saying, Let *us* alone; what have we
to do with thee, thou Jesus of Nazareth?
art thou come to destroy us? I know
thee who thou art, the Holy One of God.
25 And Jesus rebuked him, saying,
Hold thy peace, and come out of him.
26 And when the unclean spirit had
torn him, and cried with a loud voice, he
came out of him.
27 And they were all amazed, insomuch
that they questioned among themselves,
saying, What thing is this? what new
doctrine *is* this? for with authority commandeth
he even the unclean spirits,
and they do obey him.
28 And immediately his fame spread
abroad throughout all the region round
about Galilee.
29 And forthwith, when they were
come out of the synagogue, they entered
into the house of Simon and Andrew,
with James and John.
30 But Simon's wife's mother lay sick
of a fever; and anon they tell him of her.
31 And he came and took her by the
hand, and lifted her up; and immediately
the fever left her, and she ministered
unto them.

32 And at even, when the sun did set, they brought unto him all that were diseased, and them that were possessed with devils.
33 And all the city was gathered together at the door.
34 And he healed many that were sick of divers diseases, and cast out many devils; and suffered not the devils to speak, because they knew him.
35 And in the morning, rising up a great while before day, he went out, and departed into a solitary place, and there prayed.
36 And Simon and they that were with him followed after him.
37 And when they had found him, they said unto him, All *men* seek for thee.
38 And he said unto them, Let us go into the next towns, that I may preach there also: for therefore came I forth.
39 And he preached in their synagogues throughout all Galilee, and cast out devils.
40 And there came a leper to him, beseeching him, and kneeling down to him, and saying unto him, If thou wilt, thou canst make me clean.
41 And Jesus, moved with compassion, put forth *his* hand, and touched him, and saith unto him, I will; be thou clean.
42 And as soon as he had spoken, immediately the leprosy departed from him, and he was cleansed.
43 And he straitly charged him, and forthwith sent him away;
44 And saith unto him, See thou say nothing to any man: but go thy way, show thyself to the priest, and offer for thy cleansing those things which Moses commanded, for a testimony unto them.
45 But he went out, and began to publish *it* much, and to blaze abroad the matter, insomuch that Jesus could no more openly enter into the city, but was without in desert places: and they came to him from every quarter.

CHAPTER 2

AND again he entered into Cȧ-pĕr′nā-ŭm after *some* days; and it was noised that he was in the house.
2 And straightway many were gathered together, insomuch that there was no room to receive *them*, no, not so much as about the door: and he preached the word unto them.
3 And they come unto him, bringing one sick of the palsy, which was borne of four.
4 And when they could not come nigh unto him for the press, they uncovered the roof where he was: and when they had broken *it* up, they let down the bed wherein the sick of the palsy lay.
5 When Jesus saw their faith, he said unto the sick of the palsy, Son, thy sins be forgiven thee.
6 But there were certain of the scribes sitting there, and reasoning in their hearts,
7 Why doth this *man* thus speak blasphemies? who can forgive sins but God only?
8 And immediately, when Jesus perceived in his spirit that they so reasoned within themselves, he said unto them, Why reason ye these things in your hearts?
9 Whether is it easier to say to the sick of the palsy, *Thy* sins be forgiven thee; or to say, Arise, and take up thy bed, and walk?
10 But that ye may know that the Son of man hath power on earth to forgive sins, (he saith to the sick of the palsy,)
11 I say unto thee, Arise, and take up thy bed, and go thy way into thine house.
12 And immediately he arose, took up the bed, and went forth before them all; insomuch that they were all amazed, and glorified God, saying, We never saw it on this fashion.
13 And he went forth again by the sea side; and all the multitude resorted unto him, and he taught them.
14 And as he passed by, he saw Levi the *son* of Alpheus sitting at the receipt of custom, and said unto him, Follow me. And he arose and followed him.
15 And it came to pass, that, as Jesus sat at meat in his house, many publicans and sinners sat also together with Jesus and his disciples; for there were many, and they followed him.
16 And when the scribes and Phăr′ĭ-sēeș saw him eat with publicans and sinners, they said unto his disciples, How is it that he eateth and drinketh with publicans and sinners?
17 When Jesus heard *it,* he saith unto them, They that are whole have no need of the physician, but they that are sick: I came not to call the righteous, but sinners to repentance.
18 And the disciples of John and of the

Phăr′ĭ-sēeș used to fast: and they come
and say unto him, Why do the disciples
of John and of the Phăr′ĭ-sēeș fast, but
thy disciples fast not?
19 And Jesus said unto them, Can the
children of the bridechamber fast, while
the bridegroom is with them? as long as
they have the bridegroom with them,
they cannot fast.
20 But the days will come, when the
bridegroom shall be taken away from
them, and then shall they fast in those
days.
21 No man also seweth a piece of new
cloth on an old garment; else the new
piece that filled it up taketh away from
the old, and the rent is made worse.
22 And no man putteth new wine into
old bottles; else the new wine doth burst
the bottles, and the wine is spilled, and
the bottles will be marred: but new wine
must be put into new bottles.
23 And it came to pass, that he went
through the corn fields on the sabbath
day; and his disciples began, as they
went, to pluck the ears of corn.
24 And the Phăr′ĭ-sēeș said unto him,
Behold, why do they on the sabbath day
that which is not lawful?
25 And he said unto them, Have ye
never read what David did, when he had
need, and was ahungered, he, and they
that were with him?
26 How he went into the house of God
in the days of Ȧ-bī′ȧ-thär the high priest,
and did eat the showbread, which is not
lawful to eat but for the priests, and
gave also to them which were with him?
27 And he said unto them, The sabbath
was made for man, and not man for the
sabbath:
28 Therefore the Son of man is Lord
also of the sabbath.

CHAPTER 3

AND he entered again into the synagogue; and there was a man there
which had a withered hand.
2 And they watched him, whether he
would heal him on the sabbath day;
that they might accuse him.
3 And he saith unto the man which had
the withered hand, Stand forth.
4 And he saith unto them, Is it lawful
to do good on the sabbath days, or to do
evil? to save life, or to kill? But they
held their peace.
5 And when he had looked round about
on them with anger, being grieved for
the hardness of their hearts, he saith
unto the man, Stretch forth thine hand.
And he stretched *it* out: and his hand
was restored whole as the other.
6 And the Phăr′ĭ-sēeș went forth, and
straightway took counsel with the Hē-
rō′dĭ-ănș against him, how they might
destroy him.
7 But Jesus withdrew himself with his
disciples to the sea: and a great multitude from Galilee followed him, and
from Judea,
8 And from Jerusalem, and from Ĭd′ū-
mē′ȧ, and *from* beyond Jordan; and they
about Tȳre and Sī′dŏn, a great multitude, when they had heard what great
things he did, came unto him.
9 And he spake to his disciples, that a
small ship should wait on him because
of the multitude, lest they should throng
him.
10 For he had healed many; insomuch
that they pressed upon him for to touch
him, as many as had plagues.
11 And unclean spirits, when they saw
him, fell down before him, and cried,
saying, Thou art the Son of God.
12 And he straitly charged them that
they should not make him known.
13 And he goeth up into a mountain,
and calleth *unto him* whom he would:
and they came unto him.
14 And he ordained twelve, that they
should be with him, and that he might
send them forth to preach,
15 And to have power to heal sicknesses, and to cast out devils:
16 And Simon he surnamed Peter;
17 And James the *son* of Zĕb′ē-dēe,
and John the brother of James; and he
surnamed them Bō′ȧ-nēr′ġēș, which is,
The sons of thunder:
18 And Andrew, and Philip, and Bartholomew, and Matthew, and Thomas,
and James the *son* of Alpheus, and
Thăd′dē-ŭs, and Simon the Cā′năan-īte,
19 And Judas Ĭs-căr′ĭ-ŏt, which also
betrayed him: and they went into a
house.
20 And the multitude cometh together
again, so that they could not so much as
eat bread.
21 And when his friends heard *of it*,
they went out to lay hold on him: for
they said, He is beside himself.
22 ℂ And the scribes which came down
from Jerusalem said, He hath Bē-ĕl′

zē-bŭb, and by the prince of the devils
casteth he out devils.
23 And he called them *unto him,* and
said unto them in parables, How can
Satan cast out Satan?
24 And if a kingdom be divided against
itself, that kingdom cannot stand.
25 And if a house be divided against
itself, that house cannot stand.
26 And if Satan rise up against himself, and be divided, he cannot stand,
but hath an end.
27 No man can enter into a strong
man's house, and spoil his goods, except he will first bind the strong man;
and then he will spoil his house.
28 Verily I say unto you, All sins shall
be forgiven unto the sons of men, and
blasphemies wherewith soever they
shall blaspheme:
29 But he that shall blaspheme against
the Holy Ghost hath never forgiveness,
but is in danger of eternal damnation:
30 Because they said, He hath an unclean spirit.
31 ¶ There came then his brethren
and his mother, and, standing without,
sent unto him, calling him.
32 And the multitude sat about him,
and they said unto him, Behold, thy
mother and thy brethren without seek
for thee.
33 And he answered them, saying,
Who is my mother, or my brethren?
34 And he looked round about on them
which sat about him, and said, Behold
my mother and my brethren!
35 For whosoever shall do the will of
God, the same is my brother, and my
sister, and mother.

CHAPTER 4

AND he began again to teach by the
sea side: and there was gathered
unto him a great multitude, so that he
entered into a ship, and sat in the sea;
and the whole multitude was by the sea
on the land.
2 And he taught them many things by
parables, and said unto them in his
doctrine,
3 Hearken; Behold, there went out a
sower to sow:
4 And it came to pass, as he sowed,
some fell by the wayside, and the fowls
of the air came and devoured it up.
5 And some fell on stony ground, where
it had not much earth; and immediately
it sprang up, because it had no depth of
earth:
6 But when the sun was up, it was
scorched; and because it had no root, it
withered away.
7 And some fell among thorns, and the
thorns grew up, and choked it, and it
yielded no fruit.
8 And other fell on good ground, and
did yield fruit that sprang up and increased, and brought forth, some thirty,
and some sixty, and some a hundred.
9 And he said unto them, He that hath
ears to hear, let him hear.
10 And when he was alone, they that
were about him with the twelve asked
of him the parable.
11 And he said unto them, Unto you
it is given to know the mystery of the
kingdom of God: but unto them that are
without, all *these* things are done in
parables:
12 That seeing they may see, and not
perceive; and hearing they may hear,
and not understand; lest at any time
they should be converted, and *their* sins
should be forgiven them.
13 And he said unto them, Know ye
not this parable? and how then will ye
know all parables?
14 ¶ The sower soweth the word.
15 And these are they by the wayside,
where the word is sown; but when they
have heard, Satan cometh immediately,
and taketh away the word that was sown
in their hearts.
16 And these are they likewise which
are sown on stony ground; who, when
they have heard the word, immediately
receive it with gladness;
17 And have no root in themselves,
and so endure but for a time: afterward,
when affliction or persecution ariseth
for the word's sake, immediately they
are offended.
18 And these are they which are sown
among thorns; such as hear the word,
19 And the cares of this world, and the
deceitfulness of riches, and the lusts of
other things entering in, choke the word,
and it becometh unfruitful.
20 And these are they which are sown
on good ground; such as hear the word,
and receive *it,* and bring forth fruit,
some thirtyfold, some sixty, and some a
hundred.
21 ¶ And he said unto them, Is a candle brought to be put under a bushel, or

under a bed? and not to be set on a candlestick?
22 For there is nothing hid, which shall not be manifested; neither was any thing kept secret, but that it should come abroad.
23 If any man have ears to hear, let him hear.
24 And he said unto them, Take heed what ye hear. With what measure ye mete, it shall be measured to you; and unto you that hear shall more be given.
25 For he that hath, to him shall be given; and he that hath not, from him shall be taken even that which he hath.
26 ℂ And he said, So is the kingdom of God, as if a man should cast seed into the ground;
27 And should sleep, and rise night and day, and the seed should spring and grow up, he knoweth not how.
28 For the earth bringeth forth fruit of herself; first the blade, then the ear, after that the full corn in the ear.
29 But when the fruit is brought forth, immediately he putteth in the sickle, because the harvest is come.
30 ℂ And he said, Whereunto shall we liken the kingdom of God? or with what comparison shall we compare it?
31 *It is* like a grain of mustard seed, which, when it is sown in the earth, is less than all the seeds that be in the earth:
32 But when it is sown, it groweth up, and becometh greater than all herbs, and shooteth out great branches; so that the fowls of the air may lodge under the shadow of it.
33 And with many such parables spake he the word unto them, as they were able to hear *it*.
34 But without a parable spake he not unto them: and when they were alone, he expounded all things to his disciples.
35 And the same day, when the even was come, he saith unto them, Let us pass over unto the other side.
36 And when they had sent away the multitude, they took him even as he was in the ship. And there were also with him other little ships.
37 And there arose a great storm of wind, and the waves beat into the ship, so that it was now full.
38 And he was in the hinder part of the ship, asleep on a pillow: and they awake him, and say unto him, Master, carest thou not that we perish?
39 And he arose, and rebuked the wind, and said unto the sea, Peace, be still. And the wind ceased, and there was a great calm.
40 And he said unto them, Why are ye so fearful? how is it that ye have no faith?
41 And they feared exceedingly, and said one to another, What manner of man is this, that even the wind and the sea obey him?

CHAPTER 5

AND they came over unto the other side of the sea, into the country of the Găd′ă-rēneş′.
2 And when he was come out of the ship, immediately there met him out of the tombs a man with an unclean spirit,
3 Who had *his* dwelling among the tombs; and no man could bind him, no, not with chains:
4 Because that he had been often bound with fetters and chains, and the chains had been plucked asunder by him, and the fetters broken in pieces: neither could any *man* tame him.
5 And always, night and day, he was in the mountains, and in the tombs, crying, and cutting himself with stones.
6 But when he saw Jesus afar off, he ran and worshipped him,
7 And cried with a loud voice, and said, What have I to do with thee, Jesus, *thou* Son of the most high God? I adjure thee by God, that thou torment me not.
8 For he said unto him, Come out of the man, *thou* unclean spirit.
9 And he asked him, What *is* thy name? And he answered, saying, My name *is* Legion: for we are many.
10 And he besought him much that he would not send them away out of the country.
11 Now there was there nigh unto the mountains a great herd of swine feeding.
12 And all the devils besought him, saying, Send us into the swine, that we may enter into them.
13 And forthwith Jesus gave them leave. And the unclean spirits went out, and entered into the swine; and the herd ran violently down a steep place into the sea, (they were about two thousand,) and were choked in the sea.
14 And they that fed the swine fled,

and told *it* in the city, and in the country. And they went out to see what it
was that was done.
15 And they come to Jesus, and see
him that was possessed with the devil,
and had the legion, sitting, and clothed,
and in his right mind; and they were
afraid.
16 And they that saw *it* told them how
it befell to him that was possessed
with the devil, and *also* concerning the
swine.
17 And they began to pray him to depart out of their coasts.
18 And when he was come into the
ship, he that had been possessed with
the devil prayed him that he might be
with him.
19 Howbeit Jesus suffered him not,
but saith unto him, Go home to thy
friends, and tell them how great things
the Lord hath done for thee, and hath
had compassion on thee.
20 And he departed, and began to publish in Dē-căp′ō-lĭs how great things
Jesus had done for him: and all *men* did
marvel.
21 And when Jesus was passed over
again by ship unto the other side, much
people gathered unto him; and he was
nigh unto the sea.
22 And, behold, there cometh one of
the rulers of the synagogue, Jā′ĭ-rŭs by
name; and when he saw him, he fell at
his feet,
23 And besought him greatly, saying,
My little daughter lieth at the point of
death: *I pray thee,* come and lay thy
hands on her, that she may be healed;
and she shall live.
24 And *Jesus* went with him; and much
people followed him, and thronged him.
25 And a certain woman, which had an
issue of blood twelve years,
26 And had suffered many things of
many physicians, and had spent all that
she had, and was nothing bettered, but
rather grew worse,
27 When she had heard of Jesus, came
in the press behind, and touched his
garment.
28 For she said, If I may touch but his
clothes, I shall be whole.
29 And straightway the fountain of her
blood was dried up; and she felt in *her*
body that she was healed of that plague.
30 And Jesus, immediately knowing in
himself that virtue had gone out of him,
turned him about in the press, and said,
Who touched my clothes?
31 And his disciples said unto him,
Thou seest the multitude thronging
thee, and sayest thou, Who touched me?
32 And he looked round about to see
her that had done this thing.
33 But the woman fearing and trembling, knowing what was done in her,
came and fell down before him, and
told him all the truth.
34 And he said unto her, Daughter, thy
faith hath made thee whole; go in peace,
and be whole of thy plague.
35 While he yet spake, there came
from the ruler of the synagogue's *house*
certain which said, Thy daughter is
dead; why troublest thou the Master
any further?
36 As soon as Jesus heard the word
that was spoken, he saith unto the ruler
of the synagogue, Be not afraid, only
believe.
37 And he suffered no man to follow
him, save Peter, and James, and John
the brother of James.
38 And he cometh to the house of the
ruler of the synagogue, and seeth the
tumult, and them that wept and wailed
greatly.
39 And when he was come in, he saith
unto them, Why make ye this ado, and
weep? the damsel is not dead, but
sleepeth.
40 And they laughed him to scorn.
But when he had put them all out, he
taketh the father and the mother of the
damsel, and them that were with him,
and entereth in where the damsel was
lying.
41 And he took the damsel by the hand,
and said unto her, Tȧ-lĭ′thȧ cu̢′mĭ;
which is, being interpreted, Damsel, (I
say unto thee,) arise.
42 And straightway the damsel arose,
and walked; for she was *of the age* of
twelve years. And they were astonished
with a great astonishment.
43 And he charged them straitly that
no man should know it; and commanded
that something should be given her to
eat.

CHAPTER 6

AND he went out from thence, and
came into his own country; and his
disciples follow him.
2 And when the sabbath day was come,

he began to teach in the synagogue: and
many hearing *him* were astonished, saying,
From whence hath this *man* these
things? and what wisdom *is* this which
is given unto him, that even such mighty
works are wrought by his hands?
3 Is not this the carpenter, the son of
Mary, the brother of James, and Jō'sēs,
and of Ju'dȧ, and Simon? and are
not his sisters here with us? And they
were offended at him.
4 But Jesus said unto them, A prophet
is not without honor, but in his own
country, and among his own kin, and in
his own house.
5 And he could there do no mighty
work, save that he laid his hands upon
a few sick folk, and healed *them.*
6 And he marveled because of their unbelief.
And he went round about the
villages, teaching.
7 ¶ And he called *unto him* the twelve,
and began to send them forth by two
and two; and gave them power over unclean
spirits;
8 And commanded them that they
should take nothing for *their* journey,
save a staff only; no scrip, no bread, no
money in *their* purse:
9 But *be* shod with sandals; and not
put on two coats.
10 And he said unto them, In what
place soever ye enter into a house, there
abide till ye depart from that place.
11 And whosoever shall not receive
you, nor hear you, when ye depart
thence, shake off the dust under your
feet for a testimony against them.
Verily I say unto you, It shall be more
tolerable for Sŏd'ŏm and Gō-mŏr'rȧh
in the day of judgment, than for that
city.
12 And they went out, and preached
that men should repent.
13 And they cast out many devils, and
anointed with oil many that were sick,
and healed *them.*
14 And king Hĕr'ŏd heard *of him;* (for
his name was spread abroad;) and he
said, That John the Baptist was risen
from the dead, and therefore mighty
works do show forth themselves in him.
15 Others said, That it is Ē-lī'ăs. And
others said, That it is a prophet, or as
one of the prophets.
16 But when Hĕr'ŏd heard *thereof,* he
said, It is John, whom I beheaded: he is
risen from the dead.
17 For Hĕr'ŏd himself had sent forth
and laid hold upon John, and bound him
in prison for Hē-rō'dĭ-ăs' sake, his
brother Philip's wife; for he had married
her.
18 For John had said unto Hĕr'ŏd, It
is not lawful for thee to have thy
brother's wife.
19 Therefore Hē-rō'dĭ-ăs had a quarrel
against him, and would have killed him;
but she could not:
20 For Hĕr'ŏd feared John, knowing
that he was a just man and a holy, and
observed him; and when he heard him, he
did many things, and heard him gladly.
21 And when a convenient day was
come, that Hĕr'ŏd on his birthday made
a supper to his lords, high captains, and
chief *estates* of Galilee;
22 And when the daughter of the said
Hē-rō'dĭ-ăs came in, and danced, and
pleased Hĕr'ŏd and them that sat with
him, the king said unto the damsel, Ask
of me whatsoever thou wilt, and I will
give *it* thee.
23 And he sware unto her, Whatsoever
thou shalt ask of me, I will give *it* thee,
unto the half of my kingdom.
24 And she went forth, and said unto
her mother, What shall I ask? And she
said, The head of John the Baptist.
25 And she came in straightway with
haste unto the king, and asked, saying,
I will that thou give me by and by in a
charger the head of John the Baptist.
26 And the king was exceeding sorry;
yet for his oath's sake, and for their
sakes which sat with him, he would not
reject her.
27 And immediately the king sent an
executioner, and commanded his head
to be brought: and he went and beheaded
him in the prison,
28 And brought his head in a charger,
and gave it to the damsel; and the damsel
gave it to her mother.
29 And when his disciples heard *of it,*
they came and took up his corpse, and
laid it in a tomb.
30 And the apostles gathered themselves
together unto Jesus, and told
him all things, both what they had done,
and what they had taught.
31 And he said unto them, Come ye
yourselves apart into a desert place, and
rest a while: for there were many coming
and going, and they had no leisure
so much as to eat.

32 And they departed into a desert
place by ship privately.
33 And the people saw them departing,
and many knew him, and ran afoot
thither out of all cities, and outwent
them, and came together unto him.
34 And Jesus, when he came out, saw
much people, and was moved with compassion toward them, because they were
as sheep not having a shepherd: and he
began to teach them many things.
35 And when the day was now far
spent, his disciples came unto him, and
said, This is a desert place, and now the
time *is* far passed:
36 Send them away, that they may go
into the country round about, and into
the villages, and buy themselves bread:
for they have nothing to eat.
37 He answered and said unto them,
Give ye them to eat. And they say unto
him, Shall we go and buy two hundred
pennyworth of bread, and give them to
eat?
38 He saith unto them, How many
loaves have ye? go and see. And when
they knew, they say, Five, and two
fishes.
39 And he commanded them to make
all sit down by companies upon the
green grass.
40 And they sat down in ranks, by
hundreds, and by fifties.
41 And when he had taken the five
loaves and the two fishes, he looked up
to heaven, and blessed, and brake the
loaves, and gave *them* to his disciples to
set before them; and the two fishes
divided he among them all.
42 And they did all eat, and were filled.
43 And they took up twelve baskets
full of the fragments, and of the fishes.
44 And they that did eat of the loaves
were about five thousand men.
45 And straightway he constrained his
disciples to get into the ship, and to go
to the other side before unto Bĕth′sā-
ĭ-dȧ, while he sent away the people.
46 And when he had sent them away,
he departed into a mountain to pray.
47 And when even was come, the ship
was in the midst of the sea, and he alone
on the land.
48 And he saw them toiling in rowing;
for the wind was contrary unto them:
and about the fourth watch of the night
he cometh unto them, walking upon the
sea, and would have passed by them.
49 But when they saw him walking
upon the sea, they supposed it had been
a spirit, and cried out:
50 For they all saw him, and were
troubled. And immediately he talked
with them, and saith unto them, Be of
good cheer: it is I; be not afraid.
51 And he went up unto them into the
ship; and the wind ceased: and they
were sore amazed in themselves beyond measure, and wondered.
52 For they considered not *the miracle*
of the loaves; for their heart was hardened.
53 And when they had passed over,
they came into the land of Gĕn-nĕs′ȧ-
rĕt, and drew to the shore.
54 And when they were come out of
the ship, straightway they knew him,
55 And ran through that whole region
round about, and began to carry about
in beds those that were sick, where they
heard he was.
56 And whithersoever he entered, into
villages, or cities, or country, they laid
the sick in the streets, and besought
him that they might touch if it were but
the border of his garment: and as many
as touched him were made whole.

CHAPTER 7

THEN came together unto him the
Phăr′ĭ-sēeș, and certain of the
scribes, which came from Jerusalem.
2 And when they saw some of his disciples eat bread with defiled, that is to say,
with unwashen hands, they found fault.
3 For the Phăr′ĭ-sēeș, and all the Jews,
except they wash *their* hands oft, eat
not, holding the tradition of the elders.
4 And *when they come* from the market, except they wash, they eat not.
And many other things there be, which
they have received to hold, *as* the washing of cups, and pots, brazen vessels,
and of tables.
5 Then the Phăr′ĭ-sēeș and scribes
asked him, Why walk not thy disciples
according to the tradition of the elders,
but eat bread with unwashen hands?
6 He answered and said unto them,
Well hath Ē-șā′ịȧs prophesied of you
hypocrites, as it is written, This people
honoreth me with *their* lips, but their
heart is far from me.
7 Howbeit in vain do they worship me,
teaching *for* doctrines the commandments of men.

8 For laying aside the commandment of God, ye hold the tradition of men, *as* the washing of pots and cups: and many other such like things ye do.

9 And he said unto them, Full well ye reject the commandment of God, that ye may keep your own tradition.

10 For Moses said, Honor thy father and thy mother; and, Whoso curseth father or mother, let him die the death:

11 But ye say, If a man shall say to his father or mother, *It is* Corban, that is to say, a gift, by whatsoever thou mightest be profited by me; *he shall be free.*

12 And ye suffer him no more to do aught for his father or his mother;

13 Making the word of God of none effect through your tradition, which ye have delivered: and many such like things do ye.

14 ¶ And when he had called all the people *unto him,* he said unto them, Hearken unto me every one *of you,* and understand:

15 There is nothing from without a man, that entering into him can defile him: but the things which come out of him, those are they that defile the man.

16 If any man have ears to hear, let him hear.

17 And when he was entered into the house from the people, his disciples asked him concerning the parable.

18 And he saith unto them, Are ye so without understanding also? Do ye not perceive, that whatsoever thing from without entereth into the man, *it* cannot defile him;

19 Because it entereth not into his heart, but into the belly, and goeth out into the draught, purging all meats?

20 And he said, That which cometh out of the man, that defileth the man.

21 For from within, out of the heart of men, proceed evil thoughts, adulteries, fornications, murders,

22 Thefts, covetousness, wickedness, deceit, lasciviousness, an evil eye, blasphemy, pride, foolishness:

23 All these evil things come from within, and defile the man.

24 ¶ And from thence he arose, and went into the borders of Tȳre and Sī′dŏn, and entered into a house, and would have no man know *it:* but he could not be hid.

25 For a *certain* woman, whose young daughter had an unclean spirit, heard of him, and came and fell at his feet:

26 The woman was a Greek, a Sȳ′rō-phē-nĭ′çiăn by nation; and she besought him that he would cast forth the devil out of her daughter.

27 But Jesus said unto her, Let the children first be filled: for it is not meet to take the children's bread, and to cast *it* unto the dogs.

28 And she answered and said unto him, Yes, Lord: yet the dogs under the table eat of the children's crumbs.

29 And he said unto her, For this saying go thy way; the devil is gone out of thy daughter.

30 And when she was come to her house, she found the devil gone out, and her daughter laid upon the bed.

31 ¶ And again, departing from the coasts of Tȳre and Sī′dŏn, he came unto the sea of Galilee, through the midst of the coasts of Dē-căp′ō-lis.

32 And they bring unto him one that was deaf, and had an impediment in his speech; and they beseech him to put his hand upon him.

33 And he took him aside from the multitude, and put his fingers into his ears, and he spit, and touched his tongue;

34 And looking up to heaven, he sighed, and saith unto him, Ĕph′phȧ-thȧ, that is, Be opened.

35 And straightway his ears were opened, and the string of his tongue was loosed, and he spake plain.

36 And he charged them that they should tell no man: but the more he charged them, so much the more a great deal they published *it;*

37 And were beyond measure astonished, saying, He hath done all things well: he maketh both the deaf to hear, and the dumb to speak.

CHAPTER 8

IN those days the multitude being very great, and having nothing to eat, Jesus called his disciples *unto him,* and saith unto them,

2 I have compassion on the multitude, because they have now been with me three days, and have nothing to eat:

3 And if I send them away fasting to their own houses, they will faint by the way: for divers of them came from far.

4 And his disciples answered him,
From whence can a man satisfy these
men with bread here in the wilderness?
5 And he asked them, How many
loaves have ye? And they said, Seven.
6 And he commanded the people to sit
down on the ground: and he took the
seven loaves, and gave thanks, and
brake, and gave to his disciples to set
before *them;* and they did set *them* before the people.
7 And they had a few small fishes: and
he blessed, and commanded to set them
also before *them.*
8 So they did eat, and were filled: and
they took up of the broken *meat* that
was left seven baskets.
9 And they that had eaten were about
four thousand: and he sent them away.
10 ¶ And straightway he entered into
a ship with his disciples, and came into
the parts of Dăl′mȧ-nū′thȧ.
11 And the Phăr′ĭ-sēeṣ came forth, and
began to question with him, seeking of
him a sign from heaven, tempting him.
12 And he sighed deeply in his spirit,
and saith, Why doth this generation seek
after a sign? verily I say unto you, There
shall no sign be given unto this generation.
13 And he left them, and entering into
the ship again departed to the other
side.
14 ¶ Now *the disciples* had forgotten
to take bread, neither had they in the
ship with them more than one loaf.
15 And he charged them, saying, Take
heed, beware of the leaven of the Phăr′-
ĭ-sēeṣ, and *of* the leaven of Hĕr′ŏd.
16 And they reasoned among themselves, saying, *It is* because we have no
bread.
17 And when Jesus knew *it,* he saith
unto them, Why reason ye, because ye
have no bread? perceive ye not yet,
neither understand? have ye your heart
yet hardened?
18 Having eyes, see ye not? and having
ears, hear ye not? and do ye not remember?
19 When I brake the five loaves among
five thousand, how many baskets full of
fragments took ye up? They say unto
him, Twelve.
20 And when the seven among four
thousand, how many baskets full of
fragments took ye up? And they said,
Seven.
21 And he said unto them, How is it
that ye do not understand?
22 ¶ And he cometh to Bĕth′sā′ĭ-dȧ;
and they bring a blind man unto him,
and besought him to touch him.
23 And he took the blind man by the
hand, and led him out of the town; and
when he had spit on his eyes, and put
his hands upon him, he asked him if he
saw aught.
24 And he looked up, and said, I see
men as trees, walking.
25 After that he put *his* hands again
upon his eyes, and made him look up;
and he was restored, and saw every man
clearly.
26 And he sent him away to his house,
saying, Neither go into the town, nor
tell *it* to any in the town.
27 ¶ And Jesus went out, and his disciples, into the towns of Çæ̆s′ȧ-rē′ȧ
Phĭ-lĭp′pī: and by the way he asked his
disciples, saying unto them, Whom do
men say that I am?
28 And they answered, John the Baptist: but some *say,* Ē-lī′ăs; and others,
One of the prophets.
29 And he saith unto them, But whom
say ye that I am? And Peter answereth
and saith unto him, Thou art the Christ.
30 And he charged them that they
should tell no man of him.
31 And he began to teach them, that
the Son of man must suffer many things,
and be rejected of the elders, and *of* the
chief priests, and scribes, and be killed,
and after three days rise again.
32 And he spake that saying openly.
And Peter took him, and began to rebuke him.
33 But when he had turned about and
looked on his disciples, he rebuked
Peter, saying, Get thee behind me, Satan: for thou savorest not the things that
be of God, but the things that be of
men.
34 ¶ And when he had called the people *unto him* with his disciples also, he
said unto them, Whosoever will come
after me, let him deny himself, and take
up his cross, and follow me.
35 For whosoever will save his life
shall lose it; but whosoever shall lose
his life for my sake and the gospel's, the
same shall save it.
36 For what shall it profit a man, if he
shall gain the whole world, and lose his
own soul?

37 Or what shall a man give in exchange for his soul?
38 Whosoever therefore shall be
ashamed of me and of my words, in this
adulterous and sinful generation, of him
also shall the Son of man be ashamed,
when he cometh in the glory of his
Father with the holy angels.

CHAPTER 9

AND he said unto them, Verily I say
unto you, That there be some of
them that stand here, which shall not
taste of death, till they have seen the
kingdom of God come with power.
2 ¶ And after six days Jesus taketh
with him Peter, and James, and John,
and leadeth them up into a high mountain apart by themselves: and he was
transfigured before them.
3 And his raiment became shining, exceeding white as snow; so as no fuller
on earth can white them.
4 And there appeared unto them
Ē-lī'ăs with Moses: and they were
talking with Jesus.
5 And Peter answered and said to
Jesus, Master, it is good for us to be
here: and let us make three tabernacles;
one for thee, and one for Moses, and
one for Ē-lī'ăs.
6 For he wist not what to say; for they
were sore afraid.
7 And there was a cloud that overshadowed them: and a voice came out of
the cloud, saying, This is my beloved
Son: hear him.
8 And suddenly, when they had looked
round about, they saw no man any more,
save Jesus only with themselves.
9 And as they came down from the
mountain, he charged them that they
should tell no man what things they had
seen, till the Son of man were risen from
the dead.
10 And they kept that saying with
themselves, questioning one with another what the rising from the dead
should mean.
11 ¶ And they asked him, saying,
Why say the scribes that Ē-lī'ăs must
first come?
12 And he answered and told them,
Ē-lī'ăs verily cometh first, and restoreth
all things; and how it is written of the
Son of man, that he must suffer many
things, and be set at nought.
13 But I say unto you, That Ē-lī'ăs is
indeed come, and they have done unto
him whatsoever they listed, as it is written of him.
14 ¶ And when he came to *his* disciples, he saw a great multitude about
them, and the scribes questioning with
them.
15 And straightway all the people,
when they beheld him, were greatly
amazed, and running to *him* saluted
him.
16 And he asked the scribes, What
question ye with them?
17 And one of the multitude answered
and said, Master, I have brought unto
thee my son, which hath a dumb spirit;
18 And wheresoever he taketh him, he
teareth him; and he foameth, and gnasheth with his teeth, and pineth away: and
I spake to thy disciples that they should
cast him out; and they could not.
19 He answereth him, and saith, O
faithless generation, how long shall I be
with you? how long shall I suffer you?
bring him unto me.
20 And they brought him unto him:
and when he saw him, straightway the
spirit tare him; and he fell on the
ground, and wallowed foaming.
21 And he asked his father, How long
is it ago since this came unto him? And
he said, Of a child.
22 And ofttimes it hath cast him into
the fire, and into the waters, to destroy
him: but if thou canst do any thing, have
compassion on us, and help us.
23 Jesus said unto him, If thou canst
believe, all things *are* possible to him
that believeth.
24 And straightway the father of the
child cried out, and said with tears,
Lord, I believe; help thou mine unbelief.
25 When Jesus saw that the people
came running together, he rebuked the
foul spirit, saying unto him, *Thou* dumb
and deaf spirit, I charge thee, come out
of him, and enter no more into him.
26 And *the spirit* cried, and rent him
sore, and came out of him: and he was
as one dead; insomuch that many said,
He is dead.
27 But Jesus took him by the hand, and
lifted him up; and he arose.
28 And when he was come into the
house, his disciples asked him privately,
Why could not we cast him out?
29 And he said unto them, This kind

can come forth by nothing, but by
prayer and fasting.
30 ¶ And they departed thence, and
passed through Galilee; and he would
not that any man should know *it*.
31 For he taught his disciples, and said
unto them, The Son of man is delivered
into the hands of men, and they shall
kill him; and after that he is killed, he
shall rise the third day.
32 But they understood not that saying, and were afraid to ask him.
33 ¶ And he came to Cȧ-pĕr′nā-ŭm:
and being in the house he asked them,
What was it that ye disputed among
yourselves by the way?
34 But they held their peace: for by
the way they had disputed among themselves, who *should be* the greatest.
35 And he sat down, and called the
twelve, and saith unto them, If any man
desire to be first, *the same* shall be
last of all, and servant of all.
36 And he took a child, and set him in
the midst of them: and when he had
taken him in his arms, he said unto
them,
37 Whosoever shall receive one of
such children in my name, receiveth
me; and whosoever shall receive me,
receiveth not me, but him that sent me.
38 ¶ And John answered him, saying,
Master, we saw one casting out devils
in thy name, and he followeth not us;
and we forbade him, because he followeth not us.
39 But Jesus said, Forbid him not: for
there is no man which shall do a miracle
in my name, that can lightly speak evil
of me.
40 For he that is not against us is on
our part.
41 For whosoever shall give you a cup
of water to drink in my name, because
ye belong to Christ, verily I say unto
you, he shall not lose his reward.
42 And whosoever shall offend one of
these little ones that believe in me, it is
better for him that a millstone were
hanged about his neck, and he were cast
into the sea.
43 And if thy hand offend thee, cut it
off: it is better for thee to enter into life
maimed, than having two hands to go
into hell, into the fire that never shall
be quenched:
44 Where their worm dieth not, and
the fire is not quenched.
45 And if thy foot offend thee, cut it
off: it is better for thee to enter halt into
life, than having two feet to be cast into
hell, into the fire that never shall be
quenched:
46 Where their worm dieth not, and
the fire is not quenched.
47 And if thine eye offend thee, pluck
it out: it is better for thee to enter into
the kingdom of God with one eye, than
having two eyes to be cast into hell fire:
48 Where their worm dieth not, and
the fire is not quenched.
49 For every one shall be salted with
fire, and every sacrifice shall be salted
with salt.
50 Salt *is* good: but if the salt have lost
his saltness, wherewith will ye season
it? Have salt in yourselves, and have
peace one with another.

CHAPTER 10

AND he arose from thence, and cometh into the coasts of Judea by the
farther side of Jordan: and the people
resort unto him again; and, as he was
wont, he taught them again.
2 ¶ And the Phăr′ĭ-sēe̱s came to him,
and asked him, Is it lawful for a man to
put away *his* wife? tempting him.
3 And he answered and said unto them,
What did Moses command you?
4 And they said, Moses suffered to
write a bill of divorcement, and to put
her away.
5 And Jesus answered and said unto
them, For the hardness of your heart he
wrote you this precept.
6 But from the beginning of the creation God made them male and female.
7 For this cause shall a man leave his
father and mother, and cleave to his
wife;
8 And they twain shall be one flesh: so
then they are no more twain, but one
flesh.
9 What therefore God hath joined together, let not man put asunder.
10 And in the house his disciples asked
him again of the same *matter*.
11 And he saith unto them, Whosoever
shall put away his wife, and marry
another, committeth adultery against
her.
12 And if a woman shall put away her
husband, and be married to another,
she committeth adultery.
13 ¶ And they brought young children

to him, that he should touch them; and
his disciples rebuked those that brought
them.
14 But when Jesus saw *it*, he was much
displeased, and said unto them, Suffer
the little children to come unto me, and
forbid them not; for of such is the kingdom of God.
15 Verily I say unto you, Whosoever
shall not receive the kingdom of God as
a little child, he shall not enter therein.
16 And he took them up in his arms,
put *his* hands upon them, and blessed
them.
17 ℂ And when he was gone forth into
the way, there came one running, and
kneeled to him, and asked him, Good
Master, what shall I do that I may inherit eternal life?
18 And Jesus said unto him, Why callest thou me good? *there is* none good
but one, *that is*, God.
19 Thou knowest the commandments,
Do not commit adultery, Do not kill, Do
not steal, Do not bear false witness,
Defraud not, Honor thy father and
mother.
20 And he answered and said unto him,
Master, all these have I observed from
my youth.
21 Then Jesus beholding him loved
him, and said unto him, One thing thou
lackest: go thy way, sell whatsoever
thou hast, and give to the poor, and
thou shalt have treasure in heaven: and
come, take up the cross, and follow me.
22 And he was sad at that saying, and
went away grieved: for he had great
possessions.
23 ℂ And Jesus looked round about,
and saith unto his disciples, How hardly
shall they that have riches enter into
the kingdom of God!
24 And the disciples were astonished
at his words. But Jesus answereth
again, and saith unto them, Children,
how hard is it for them that trust in
riches to enter into the kingdom of God!
25 It is easier for a camel to go through
the eye of a needle, than for a rich man
to enter into the kingdom of God.
26 And they were astonished out of
measure, saying among themselves,
Who then can be saved?
27 And Jesus looking upon them saith,
With men *it is* impossible, but not with
God: for with God all things are possible.
28 ℂ Then Peter began to say unto
him, Lo, we have left all, and have followed thee.
29 And Jesus answered and said,
Verily I say unto you, There is no man
that hath left house, or brethren, or
sisters, or father, or mother, or wife, or
children, or lands, for my sake, and the
gospel's,
30 But he shall receive a hundredfold
now in this time, houses, and brethren,
and sisters, and mothers, and children,
and lands, with persecutions; and in the
world to come eternal life.
31 But many *that are* first shall be last;
and the last first.
32 ℂ And they were in the way going
up to Jerusalem; and Jesus went before
them: and they were amazed; and as
they followed, they were afraid. And
he took again the twelve, and began to
tell them what things should happen
unto him,
33 *Saying*, Behold, we go up to Jerusalem; and the Son of man shall be delivered unto the chief priests, and unto
the scribes; and they shall condemn
him to death, and shall deliver him to
the Ġĕn′tīleṣ:
34 And they shall mock him, and shall
scourge him, and shall spit upon him,
and shall kill him; and the third day he
shall rise again.
35 ℂ And James and John, the sons of
Zĕb′ē-dēe, come unto him, saying,
Master, we would that thou shouldest
do for us whatsoever we shall desire.
36 And he said unto them, What would
ye that I should do for you?
37 They said unto him, Grant unto us
that we may sit, one on thy right hand,
and the other on thy left hand, in thy
glory.
38 But Jesus said unto them, Ye know
not what ye ask: can ye drink of the
cup that I drink of? and be baptized
with the baptism that I am baptized
with?
39 And they said unto him, We can.
And Jesus said unto them, Ye shall indeed drink of the cup that I drink of;
and with the baptism that I am baptized
withal shall ye be baptized:
40 But to sit on my right hand and on
my left hand is not mine to give; but *it
shall be given to them* for whom it is
prepared.
41 And when the ten heard *it*, they be-

gan to be much displeased with James and John.

42 But Jesus called them *to him,* and saith unto them, Ye know that they which are accounted to rule over the Gĕn′tīleṣ exercise lordship over them; and their great ones exercise authority upon them.

43 But so shall it not be among you: but whosoever will be great among you, shall be your minister:

44 And whosoever of you will be the chiefest, shall be servant of all.

45 For even the Son of man came not to be ministered unto, but to minister, and to give his life a ransom for many.

46 ¶ And they came to Jĕr′ĭ-chō: and as he went out of Jĕr′ĭ-chō with his disciples and a great number of people, blind Bär′tĭ-mē′ŭs, the son of Tī-mē′ŭs, sat by the highway side begging.

47 And when he heard that it was Jesus of Nazareth, he began to cry out, and say, Jesus, *thou* Son of David, have mercy on me.

48 And many charged him that he should hold his peace: but he cried the more a great deal, *Thou* Son of David, have mercy on me.

49 And Jesus stood still, and commanded him to be called. And they call the blind man, saying unto him, Be of good comfort, rise; he calleth thee.

50 And he, casting away his garment, rose, and came to Jesus.

51 And Jesus answered and said unto him, What wilt thou that I should do unto thee? The blind man said unto him, Lord, that I might receive my sight.

52 And Jesus said unto him, Go thy way; thy faith hath made thee whole. And immediately he received his sight, and followed Jesus in the way.

CHAPTER 11

AND when they came nigh to Jerusalem, unto Bĕth′phȧ-ġē and Bethany, at the mount of Olives, he sendeth forth two of his disciples,

2 And saith unto them, Go your way into the village over against you: and as soon as ye be entered into it, ye shall find a colt tied, whereon never man sat; loose him, and bring *him.*

3 And if any man say unto you, Why do ye this? say ye that the Lord hath need of him; and straightway he will send him hither.

4 And they went their way, and found the colt tied by the door without in a place where two ways met; and they loose him.

5 And certain of them that stood there said unto them, What do ye, loosing the colt?

6 And they said unto them even as Jesus had commanded: and they let them go.

7 And they brought the colt to Jesus, and cast their garments on him; and he sat upon him.

8 And many spread their garments in the way; and others cut down branches off the trees, and strewed *them* in the way.

9 And they that went before, and they that followed, cried, saying, Hosanna; Blessed *is* he that cometh in the name of the Lord:

10 Blessed *be* the kingdom of our father David, that cometh in the name of the Lord: Hosanna in the highest.

11 And Jesus entered into Jerusalem, and into the temple: and when he had looked round about upon all things, and now the eventide was come, he went out unto Bethany with the twelve.

12 ¶ And on the morrow, when they were come from Bethany, he was hungry:

13 And seeing a fig tree afar off having leaves, he came, if haply he might find any thing thereon: and when he came to it, he found nothing but leaves; for the time of figs was not *yet.*

14 And Jesus answered and said unto it, No man eat fruit of thee hereafter for ever. And his disciples heard *it.*

15 ¶ And they come to Jerusalem: and Jesus went into the temple, and began to cast out them that sold and bought in the temple, and overthrew the tables of the money changers, and the seats of them that sold doves;

16 And would not suffer that any man should carry *any* vessel through the temple.

17 And he taught, saying unto them, Is it not written, My house shall be called of all nations the house of prayer? but ye have made it a den of thieves.

18 And the scribes and chief priests heard *it,* and sought how they might destroy him: for they feared him, be-

cause all the people was astonished at
his doctrine.
19 And when even was come, he went
out of the city.
20 ¶ And in the morning, as they
passed by, they saw the fig tree dried
up from the roots.
21 And Peter calling to remembrance
saith unto him, Master, behold, the fig
tree which thou cursedst is withered
away.
22 And Jesus answering saith unto
them, Have faith in God.
23 For verily I say unto you, That whosoever shall say unto this mountain,
Be thou removed, and be thou cast into
the sea; and shall not doubt in his heart,
but shall believe that those things which
he saith shall come to pass; he shall have
whatsoever he saith.
24 Therefore I say unto you, What
things soever ye desire, when ye pray,
believe that ye receive *them*, and ye
shall have *them*.
25 And when ye stand praying, forgive,
if ye have aught against any; that your
Father also which is in heaven may forgive you your trespasses.
26 But if ye do not forgive, neither will
your Father which is in heaven forgive
your trespasses.
27 ¶ And they come again to Jerusalem: and as he was walking in the temple, there come to him the chief priests,
and the scribes, and the elders,
28 And say unto him, By what authority doest thou these things? and who
gave thee this authority to do these
things?
29 And Jesus answered and said unto them, I will also ask of you one
question, and answer me, and I will
tell you by what authority I do these
things.
30 The baptism of John, was *it* from
heaven, or of men? answer me.
31 And they reasoned with themselves,
saying, If we shall say, From heaven; he
will say, Why then did ye not believe
him?
32 But if we shall say, Of men; they
feared the people: for all *men* counted
John, that he was a prophet indeed.
33 And they answered and said unto
Jesus, We cannot tell. And Jesus answering saith unto them, Neither do I
tell you by what authority I do these
things.

CHAPTER 12

AND he began to speak unto them by
parables. A *certain* man planted a
vineyard, and set a hedge about *it*, and
digged *a place for* the winevat, and built
a tower, and let it out to husbandmen,
and went into a far country.
2 And at the season he sent to the husbandmen a servant, that he might receive from the husbandmen of the fruit
of the vineyard.
3 And they caught *him*, and beat him,
and sent *him* away empty.
4 And again he sent unto them another
servant; and at him they cast stones,
and wounded *him* in the head, and sent
him away shamefully handled.
5 And again he sent another; and him
they killed, and many others; beating
some, and killing some.
6 Having yet therefore one son, his
well-beloved, he sent him also last unto
them, saying, They will reverence my son.
7 But those husbandmen said among
themselves, This is the heir; come, let us
kill him, and the inheritance shall be ours.
8 And they took him, and killed *him*,
and cast *him* out of the vineyard.
9 What shall therefore the lord of the
vineyard do? he will come and destroy
the husbandmen, and will give the vineyard unto others.
10 And have ye not read this Scripture;
The stone which the builders rejected
is become the head of the corner:
11 This was the Lord's doing, and it is
marvelous in our eyes?
12 And they sought to lay hold on him,
but feared the people; for they knew
that he had spoken the parable against
them: and they left him, and went their
way.
13 ¶ And they send unto him certain
of the Phăr'ĭ-sēeṣ and of the Hē-rō'-
dĭ-ănṣ, to catch him in *his* words.
14 And when they were come, they say
unto him, Master, we know that thou
art true, and carest for no man; for thou
regardest not the person of men, but
teachest the way of God in truth: Is it
lawful to give tribute to Cæsar, or not?
15 Shall we give, or shall we not give?
But he, knowing their hypocrisy, said
unto them, Why tempt ye me? bring me
a penny, that I may see *it*.
16 And they brought *it*. And he saith
unto them, Whose *is* this image and

superscription? And they said unto him,
Cæsar's.
17 And Jesus answering said unto
them, Render to Cæsar the things that
are Cæsar's, and to God the things that
are God's. And they marveled at him.
18 ℭ Then come unto him the Săd'-
dū-çēes̱, which say there is no resurrection; and they asked him, saying,
19 Master, Moses wrote unto us, If a
man's brother die, and leave *his* wife
behind him, and leave no children, that
his brother should take his wife, and
raise up seed unto his brother.
20 Now there were seven brethren:
and the first took a wife, and dying left
no seed.
21 And the second took her, and died,
neither left he any seed: and the third
likewise.
22 And the seven had her, and left no
seed: last of all the woman died also.
23 In the resurrection therefore, when
they shall rise, whose wife shall she be
of them? for the seven had her to wife.
24 And Jesus answering said unto
them, Do ye not therefore err, because
ye know not the Scriptures, neither the
power of God?
25 For when they shall rise from the
dead, they neither marry, nor are given
in marriage; but are as the angels which
are in heaven.
26 And as touching the dead, that they
rise; have ye not read in the book of
Moses, how in the bush God spake unto
him, saying, I *am* the God of Abraham,
and the God of Isaac, and the God of
Jacob?
27 He is not the God of the dead, but
the God of the living: ye therefore do
greatly err.
28 ℭ And one of the scribes came, and
having heard them reasoning together,
and perceiving that he had answered
them well, asked him, Which is the first
commandment of all?
29 And Jesus answered him, The first
of all the commandments *is,* Hear, O
Is̱'rā-ĕl; The Lord our God is one Lord:
30 And thou shalt love the Lord thy God
with all thy heart, and with all thy soul,
and with all thy mind, and with all thy
strength: this *is* the first commandment.
31 And the second *is* like, *namely* this,
Thou shalt love thy neighbor as thyself.
There is none other commandment
greater than these.
32 And the scribe said unto him, Well,
Master, thou hast said the truth: for
there is one God; and there is none
other but he:
33 And to love him with all the heart,
and with all the understanding, and
with all the soul, and with all the
strength, and to love *his* neighbor as
himself, is more than all whole burnt
offerings and sacrifices.
34 And when Jesus saw that he answered discreetly, he said unto him,
Thou art not far from the kingdom of
God. And no man after that durst ask
him *any question.*
35 ℭ And Jesus answered and said,
while he taught in the temple, How say
the scribes that Christ is the son of
David?
36 For David himself said by the Holy
Ghost, The LORD said to my Lord, Sit
thou on my right hand, till I make thine
enemies thy footstool.
37 David therefore himself calleth him
Lord; and whence is he *then* his son?
And the common people heard him
gladly.
38 ℭ And he said unto them in his doctrine, Beware of the scribes, which love
to go in long clothing, and *love* saluta-
tions in the market places,
39 And the chief seats in the synagogues, and the uppermost rooms at
feasts:
40 Which devour widows' houses, and
for a pretense make long prayers: these
shall receive greater damnation.
41 ℭ And Jesus sat over against the
treasury, and beheld how the people
cast money into the treasury: and many
that were rich cast in much.
42 And there came a certain poor widow, and she threw in two mites, which
make a farthing.
43 And he called *unto him* his disciples, and saith unto them, Verily I say
unto you, That this poor widow hath
cast more in, than all they which have
cast into the treasury:
44 For all *they* did cast in of their
abundance; but she of her want did cast
in all that she had, *even* all her living.

CHAPTER 13

AND as he went out of the temple,
one of his disciples saith unto him,
Master, see what manner of stones and
what buildings *are here!*

2 And Jesus answering said unto him,
Seest thou these great buildings? there
shall not be left one stone upon another,
that shall not be thrown down.
3 And as he sat upon the mount of
Olives, over against the temple, Peter
and James and John and Andrew asked
him privately,
4 Tell us, when shall these things be?
and what *shall be* the sign when all
these things shall be fulfilled?
5 And Jesus answering them began to
say, Take heed lest any *man* deceive you:
6 For many shall come in my name,
saying, I am *Christ;* and shall deceive
many.
7 And when ye shall hear of wars and
rumors of wars, be ye not troubled: for
such things must needs be; but the end
shall not *be* yet.
8 For nation shall rise against nation,
and kingdom against kingdom: and
there shall be earthquakes in divers
places, and there shall be famines and
troubles: these *are* the beginnings of
sorrows.
9 ¶ But take heed to yourselves: for
they shall deliver you up to councils;
and in the synagogues ye shall be
beaten: and ye shall be brought before
rulers and kings for my sake, for a testimony against them.
10 And the gospel must first be published among all nations.
11 But when they shall lead *you*, and
deliver you up, take no thought beforehand what ye shall speak, neither do
ye premeditate: but whatsoever shall be
given you in that hour, that speak ye:
for it is not ye that speak, but the Holy
Ghost.
12 Now the brother shall betray the
brother to death, and the father the
son; and children shall rise up against
their parents, and shall cause them to
be put to death.
13 And ye shall be hated of all *men* for
my name's sake: but he that shall endure unto the end, the same shall be
saved.
14 ¶ But when ye shall see the
abomination of desolation, spoken of
by Daniel the prophet, standing where
it ought not, (let him that readeth understand,) then let them that be in Judea
flee to the mountains:
15 And let him that is on the housetop
not go down into the house, neither enter
therein, to take any thing out of his
house:
16 And let him that is in the field not
turn back again for to take up his garment.
17 But woe to them that are with child,
and to them that give suck in those
days!
18 And pray ye that your flight be not
in the winter.
19 For *in* those days shall be affliction,
such as was not from the beginning of
the creation which God created unto
this time, neither shall be.
20 And except that the Lord had
shortened those days, no flesh should
be saved: but for the elect's sake, whom
he hath chosen, he hath shortened the
days.
21 And then if any man shall say to
you, Lo, here *is* Christ; or, lo, *he is* there;
believe *him* not:
22 For false Christs and false prophets
shall rise, and shall show signs and wonders, to seduce, if *it were* possible, even
the elect.
23 But take ye heed: behold, I have
foretold you all things.
24 ¶ But in those days, after that
tribulation, the sun shall be darkened,
and the moon shall not give her light,
25 And the stars of heaven shall fall,
and the powers that are in heaven shall
be shaken.
26 And then shall they see the Son of
man coming in the clouds with great
power and glory.
27 And then shall he send his angels,
and shall gather together his elect from
the four winds, from the uttermost part
of the earth to the uttermost part of
heaven.
28 Now learn a parable of the fig tree:
When her branch is yet tender, and
putteth forth leaves, ye know that summer is near:
29 So ye in like manner, when ye shall
see these things come to pass, know
that it is nigh, *even* at the doors.
30 Verily I say unto you, that this generation shall not pass, till all these
things be done.
31 Heaven and earth shall pass away:
but my words shall not pass away.
32 ¶ But of that day and *that* hour
knoweth no man, no, not the angels
which are in heaven, neither the Son,
but the Father.

33 Take ye heed, watch and pray: for ye know not when the time is.

34 *For the Son of man is* as a man taking a far journey, who left his house, and gave authority to his servants, and to every man his work, and commanded the porter to watch.

35 Watch ye therefore: for ye know not when the master of the house cometh, at even, or at midnight, or at the cockcrowing, or in the morning:

36 Lest coming suddenly he find you sleeping.

37 And what I say unto you I say unto all, Watch.

CHAPTER 14

AFTER two days was *the feast of* the passover, and of unleavened bread: and the chief priests and the scribes sought how they might take him by craft, and put *him* to death.

2 But they said, Not on the feast *day,* lest there be an uproar of the people.

3 ¶ And being in Bethany, in the house of Simon the leper, as he sat at meat, there came a woman having an alabaster box of ointment of spikenard very precious; and she brake the box, and poured *it* on his head.

4 And there were some that had indignation within themselves, and said, Why was this waste of the ointment made?

5 For it might have been sold for more than three hundred pence, and have been given to the poor. And they murmured against her.

6 And Jesus said, Let her alone; why trouble ye her? she hath wrought a good work on me.

7 For ye have the poor with you always, and whensoever ye will ye may do them good: but me ye have not always.

8 She hath done what she could: she is come aforehand to anoint my body to the burying.

9 Verily I say unto you, Wheresoever this gospel shall be preached throughout the whole world, *this* also that she hath done shall be spoken of for a memorial of her.

10 ¶ And Judas Ĭs-căr′ĭ-ŏt, one of the twelve, went unto the chief priests, to betray him unto them.

11 And when they heard *it*, they were glad, and promised to give him money. And he sought how he might conveniently betray him.

12 ¶ And the first day of unleavened bread, when they killed the passover, his disciples said unto him, Where wilt thou that we go and prepare that thou mayest eat the passover?

13 And he sendeth forth two of his disciples, and saith unto them, Go ye into the city, and there shall meet you a man bearing a pitcher of water: follow him.

14 And wheresoever he shall go in, say ye to the goodman of the house, The Master saith, Where is the guest chamber, where I shall eat the passover with my disciples?

15 And he will show you a large upper room furnished *and* prepared: there make ready for us.

16 And his disciples went forth, and came into the city, and found as he had said unto them: and they made ready the passover.

17 And in the evening he cometh with the twelve.

18 And as they sat and did eat, Jesus said, Verily I say unto you, One of you which eateth with me shall betray me.

19 And they began to be sorrowful, and to say unto him one by one, *Is* it I? and another *said, Is* it I?

20 And he answered and said unto them, *It is* one of the twelve, that dippeth with me in the dish.

21 The Son of man indeed goeth, as it is written of him: but woe to that man by whom the Son of man is betrayed! good were it for that man if he had never been born.

22 ¶ And as they did eat, Jesus took bread, and blessed, and brake *it,* and gave to them, and said, Take, eat; this is my body.

23 And he took the cup, and when he had given thanks, he gave *it* to them: and they all drank of it.

24 And he said unto them, This is my blood of the new testament, which is shed for many.

25 Verily I say unto you, I will drink no more of the fruit of the vine, until that day that I drink it new in the kingdom of God.

26 ¶ And when they had sung a hymn, they went out into the mount of Olives.

27 And Jesus saith unto them, All ye shall be offended because of me this night: for it is written, I will smite the

shepherd, and the sheep shall be
scattered.
28 But after that I am risen, I will go
before you into Galilee.
29 But Peter said unto him, Although
all shall be offended, yet *will* not I.
30 And Jesus saith unto him, Verily I
say unto thee, That this day, *even* in
this night, before the cock crow twice,
thou shalt deny me thrice.
31 But he spake the more vehemently,
If I should die with thee, I will not deny
thee in any wise. Likewise also said
they all.
32 And they came to a place which
was named Gĕth-sĕm′á-nē: and he saith
to his disciples, Sit ye here, while I shall
pray.
33 And he taketh with him Peter and
James and John, and began to be sore
amazed, and to be very heavy;
34 And saith unto them, My soul is
exceeding sorrowful unto death: tarry
ye here, and watch.
35 And he went forward a little, and
fell on the ground, and prayed that, if
it were possible, the hour might pass
from him.
36 And he said, Abba, Father, all
things *are* possible unto thee; take away
this cup from me: nevertheless, not
what I will, but what thou wilt.
37 And he cometh, and findeth them
sleeping, and saith unto Peter, Simon,
sleepest thou? couldest not thou watch
one hour?
38 Watch ye and pray, lest ye enter
into temptation. The spirit truly *is*
ready, but the flesh *is* weak.
39 And again he went away, and
prayed, and spake the same words.
40 And when he returned, he found
them asleep again, (for their eyes were
heavy,) neither wist they what to
answer him.
41 And he cometh the third time, and
saith unto them, Sleep on now, and take
your rest: it is enough, the hour is come;
behold, the Son of man is betrayed into
the hands of sinners.
42 Rise up, let us go; lo, he that betrayeth me is at hand.
43 ℂ And immediately, while he yet
spake, cometh Judas, one of the twelve,
and with him a great multitude with
swords and staves, from the chief
priests and the scribes and the elders.
44 And he that betrayed him had given
them a token, saying, Whomsoever I
shall kiss, that same is he; take him,
and lead *him* away safely.
45 And as soon as he was come, he
goeth straightway to him, and saith,
Master, Master; and kissed him.
46 ℂ And they laid their hands on him,
and took him.
47 And one of them that stood by drew
a sword, and smote a servant of the
high priest, and cut off his ear.
48 And Jesus answered and said unto
them, Are ye come out, as against a
thief, with swords and *with* staves to
take me?
49 I was daily with you in the temple
teaching, and ye took me not: but the
Scriptures must be fulfilled.
50 And they all forsook him, and
fled.
51 And there followed him a certain
young man, having a linen cloth cast
about *his* naked *body;* and the young
men laid hold on him:
52 And he left the linen cloth, and fled
from them naked.
53 ℂ And they led Jesus away to the
high priest: and with him were assembled all the chief priests and the elders
and the scribes.
54 And Peter followed him afar off,
even into the palace of the high priest:
and he sat with the servants, and
warmed himself at the fire.
55 And the chief priests and all the
council sought for witness against Jesus
to put him to death; and found none.
56 For many bare false witness against
him, but their witness agreed not together.
57 And there arose certain, and bare
false witness against him, saying,
58 We heard him say, I will destroy
this temple that is made with hands,
and within three days I will build another made without hands.
59 But neither so did their witness
agree together.
60 And the high priest stood up in the
midst, and asked Jesus, saying, Answerest thou nothing? what *is it which*
these witness against thee?
61 But he held his peace, and answered
nothing. Again the high priest asked
him, and said unto him, Art thou the
Christ, the Son of the Blessed?
62 And Jesus said, I am: and ye shall
see the Son of man sitting on the right

hand of power, and coming in the clouds
of heaven.
63 Then the high priest rent his clothes,
and saith, What need we any further
witnesses?
64 Ye have heard the blasphemy: what
think ye? And they all condemned him
to be guilty of death.
65 And some began to spit on him, and
to cover his face, and to buffet him, and
to say unto him, Prophesy: and the
servants did strike him with the palms
of their hands.
66 ℂ And as Peter was beneath in the
palace, there cometh one of the maids
of the high priest:
67 And when she saw Peter warming
himself, she looked upon him, and said,
And thou also wast with Jesus of Nazareth.
68 But he denied, saying, I know not,
neither understand I what thou sayest.
And he went out into the porch; and the
cock crew.
69 And a maid saw him again, and began to say to them that stood by, This
is *one* of them.
70 And he denied it again. And a little
after, they that stood by said again to
Peter, Surely thou art *one* of them: for
thou art a Galilean, and thy speech
agreeth *thereto*.
71 But he began to curse and to swear,
saying, I know not this man of whom ye
speak.
72 And the second time the cock crew.
And Peter called to mind the word that
Jesus said unto him, Before the cock
crow twice, thou shalt deny me thrice.
And when he thought thereon, he wept.

CHAPTER 15

AND straightway in the morning the
chief priests held a consultation
with the elders and scribes and the
whole council, and bound Jesus, and
carried *him* away, and delivered *him*
to Pilate.
2 And Pilate asked him, Art thou the
King of the Jews? And he answering
said unto him, Thou sayest *it*.
3 And the chief priests accused him of
many things; but he answered nothing.
4 And Pilate asked him again, saying,
Answerest thou nothing? behold how
many things they witness against thee.
5 But Jesus yet answered nothing; so
that Pilate marveled.
6 Now at *that* feast he released unto
them one prisoner, whomsoever they
desired.
7 And there was *one* named Bär-ăb'-
băs, *which lay* bound with them that
had made insurrection with him, who
had committed murder in the insurrection.
8 And the multitude crying aloud began
to desire *him to do* as he had ever done
unto them.
9 But Pilate answered them, saying,
Will ye that I release unto you the King
of the Jews?
10 For he knew that the chief priests
had delivered him for envy.
11 But the chief priests moved the
people, that he should rather release
Bär-ăb'băs unto them.
12 And Pilate answered and said again
unto them, What will ye then that I shall
do *unto him* whom ye call the King of
the Jews?
13 And they cried out again, Crucify
him.
14 Then Pilate said unto them, Why,
what evil hath he done? And they cried
out the more exceedingly, Crucify him.
15 ℂ And *so* Pilate, willing to content
the people, released Bär-ăb'băs unto
them, and delivered Jesus, when he had
scourged *him*, to be crucified.
16 And the soldiers led him away into
the hall, called Prē-tō'rĭ-ŭm; and they
call together the whole band.
17 And they clothed him with purple,
and platted a crown of thorns, and put
it about his *head*,
18 And began to salute him, Hail, King
of the Jews!
19 And they smote him on the head
with a reed, and did spit upon him, and
bowing *their* knees worshipped him.
20 And when they had mocked him,
they took off the purple from him, and
put his own clothes on him, and led him
out to crucify him.
21 And they compel one Simon a Çȳ-
rē'nĭ-ăn, who passed by, coming out of
the country, the father of Alexander and
Rufus, to bear his cross.
22 And they bring him unto the place
Gŏl'gō-thȧ, which is, being interpreted,
The place of a skull.
23 And they gave him to drink wine
mingled with myrrh: but he received *it*
not.
24 And when they had crucified him,

they parted his garments, casting lots
upon them, what every man should take.
25 And it was the third hour, and they
crucified him.
26 And the superscription of his accusation was written over, THE KING
OF THE JEWS.
27 And with him they crucify two
thieves; the one on his right hand, and
the other on his left.
28 And the Scripture was fulfilled,
which saith, And he was numbered with
the transgressors.
29 And they that passed by railed on
him, wagging their heads, and saying,
Ah, thou that destroyest the temple, and
buildest *it* in three days,
30 Save thyself, and come down from
the cross.
31 Likewise also the chief priests
mocking said among themselves with
the scribes, He saved others; himself he
cannot save.
32 Let Christ the King of Ĭş′rā-ĕl descend now from the cross, that we may
see and believe. And they that were
crucified with him reviled him.
33 And when the sixth hour was come,
there was darkness over the whole land
until the ninth hour.
34 And at the ninth hour Jesus cried
with a loud voice, saying, E̱′loï, E̱′loï,
lä′mä sä-băch′thä-nï′? which is, being
interpreted, My God, my God, why hast
thou forsaken me?
35 And some of them that stood by,
when they heard *it*, said, Behold, he
calleth Ē-lī′ăs.
36 And one ran and filled a sponge full
of vinegar, and put *it* on a reed, and
gave him to drink, saying, Let alone;
let us see whether Ē-lī′ăs will come to
take him down.
37 And Jesus cried with a loud voice,
and gave up the ghost.
38 And the veil of the temple was rent
in twain from the top to the bottom.
39 ¶ And when the centurion, which
stood over against him, saw that he so
cried out, and gave up the ghost, he
said, Truly this man was the Son of
God.
40 There were also women looking on
afar off: among whom was Mary Măg′-
dȧ-lēne, and Mary the mother of James
the less and of Jō′sēş, and Sȧ-lō′mē;
41 Who also, when he was in Galilee,
followed him, and ministered unto him;
and many other women which came up
with him unto Jerusalem.
42 ¶ And now when the even was
come, because it was the preparation,
that is, the day before the sabbath,
43 Joseph of Ăr′ĭ-mȧ-thē′ȧ, an honorable counselor, which also waited for the
kingdom of God, came, and went in
boldly unto Pilate, and craved the body
of Jesus.
44 And Pilate marveled if he were already dead: and calling *unto him* the
centurion, he asked him whether he had
been any while dead.
45 And when he knew *it* of the centurion, he gave the body to Joseph.
46 And he bought fine linen, and took
him down, and wrapped him in the
linen, and laid him in a sepulchre which
was hewn out of a rock, and rolled a
stone unto the door of the sepulchre.
47 And Mary Măg′dȧ-lēne and Mary
the mother of Jō′sēş beheld where he
was laid.

CHAPTER 16

AND when the sabbath was past,
Mary Măg′dȧ-lēne, and Mary the
mother of James, and Sȧ-lō′mē, had
bought sweet spices, that they might
come and anoint him.
2 And very early in the morning, the
first *day* of the week, they came unto
the sepulchre at the rising of the sun.
3 And they said among themselves,
Who shall roll us away the stone from
the door of the sepulchre?
4 And when they looked, they saw that
the stone was rolled away: for it was
very great.
5 And entering into the sepulchre, they
saw a young man sitting on the right
side, clothed in a long white garment;
and they were affrighted.
6 And he saith unto them, Be not
affrighted: ye seek Jesus of Nazareth,
which was crucified: he is risen; he is
not here: behold the place where they
laid him.
7 But go your way, tell his disciples
and Peter that he goeth before you into
Galilee: there shall ye see him, as he
said unto you.
8 And they went out quickly, and fled
from the sepulchre; for they trembled
and were amazed: neither said they any
thing to any *man;* for they were afraid.
9 ¶ Now when *Jesus* was risen early

the first *day* of the week, he appeared
first to Mary Măg′dȧ-lēne, out of whom
he had cast seven devils.
10 *And* she went and told them that
had been with him, as they mourned
and wept.
11 And they, when they had heard
that he was alive, and had been seen of
her, believed not.
12 ¶ After that he appeared in another
form unto two of them, as they walked,
and went into the country.
13 And they went and told *it* unto the
residue: neither believed they them.
14 ¶ Afterward he appeared unto the
eleven as they sat at meat, and up-
braided them with their unbelief and
hardness of heart, because they believed not them which had seen him
after he was risen.
15 And he said unto them, Go ye into
all the world, and preach the gospel to
every creature.
16 He that believeth and is baptized
shall be saved; but he that believeth not
shall be damned.
17 And these signs shall follow them
that believe; In my name shall they cast
out devils; they shall speak with new
tongues;
18 They shall take up serpents; and if
they drink any deadly thing, it shall not
hurt them; they shall lay hands on the
sick, and they shall recover.
19 ¶ So then, after the Lord had
spoken unto them, he was received up
into heaven, and sat on the right hand
of God.
20 And they went forth, and preached
every where, the Lord working with
them, and confirming the word with
signs following. Amen.

THE GOSPEL ACCORDING TO

ST. LUKE

CHAPTER 1

FORASMUCH as many have taken in hand to set forth in order a declaration of those things which are most surely believed among us,

2 Even as they delivered them unto us, which from the beginning were eyewitnesses, and ministers of the word;

3 It seemed good to me also, having had perfect understanding of all things from the very first, to write unto thee in order, most excellent Thē-ŏph′ĭ-lŭs,

4 That thou mightest know the certainty of those things, wherein thou hast been instructed.

5 ¶ THERE was in the days of Hĕr′ŏd, the king of Judea, a certain priest named Zăch′ȧ-rī′ȧs, of the course of Ȧ-bī′ȧ: and his wife *was* of the daughters of Aaron, and her name *was* Elisabeth.

6 And they were both righteous before God, walking in all the commandments and ordinances of the Lord blameless.

7 And they had no child, because that Elisabeth was barren; and they both were *now* well stricken in years.

8 And it came to pass, that, while he executed the priest's office before God in the order of his course,

9 According to the custom of the priest's office, his lot was to burn incense when he went into the temple of the Lord.

10 And the whole multitude of the people were praying without at the time of incense.

11 And there appeared unto him an angel of the Lord standing on the right side of the altar of incense.

12 And when Zăch′ȧ-rī′ȧs saw *him*, he was troubled, and fear fell upon him.

13 But the angel said unto him, Fear not, Zăch′ȧ-rī′ȧs: for thy prayer is heard; and thy wife Elisabeth shall bear thee a son, and thou shalt call his name John.

14 And thou shalt have joy and gladness; and many shall rejoice at his birth.

15 For he shall be great in the sight of the Lord, and shall drink neither wine nor strong drink; and he shall be filled with the Holy Ghost, even from his mother's womb.

16 And many of the children of Ĭṣ′rā-ĕl shall he turn to the Lord their God.

17 And he shall go before him in the spirit and power of Ē-lī′ȧs, to turn the hearts of the fathers to the children, and the disobedient to the wisdom of the just; to make ready a people prepared for the Lord.

18 And Zăch′ȧ-rī′ȧs said unto the angel, Whereby shall I know this? for I am an old man, and my wife well stricken in years.

19 And the angel answering said unto him, I am Gā′brĭ-ĕl, that stand in the presence of God; and am sent to speak unto thee, and to show thee these glad tidings.

20 And, behold, thou shalt be dumb, and not able to speak, until the day that these things shall be performed, because thou believest not my words, which shall be fulfilled in their season.

21 And the people waited for Zăch′ȧ-rī′ȧs, and marveled that he tarried so long in the temple.

22 And when he came out, he could not speak unto them: and they perceived that he had seen a vision in the temple; for he beckoned unto them, and remained speechless.

23 And it came to pass, that, as soon as the days of his ministration were accomplished, he departed to his own house.

24 And after those days his wife Elisabeth conceived, and hid herself five months, saying,

25 Thus hath the Lord dealt with me in the days wherein he looked on *me*, to take away my reproach among men.

26 And in the sixth month the angel Gā′brĭ-ĕl was sent from God unto a city of Galilee, named Nazareth,

27 To a virgin espoused to a man whose name was Joseph, of the house of David; and the virgin's name *was* Mary.

28 And the angel came in unto her, and said, Hail, *thou that art* highly favored, the Lord *is* with thee: blessed *art* thou among women.

29 And when she saw *him*, she was troubled at his saying, and cast in her mind what manner of salutation this should be.
30 And the angel said unto her, Fear not, Mary: for thou hast found favor with God.
31 And, behold, thou shalt conceive in thy womb, and bring forth a son, and shalt call his name JESUS.
32 He shall be great, and shall be called the Son of the Highest; and the Lord God shall give unto him the throne of his father David:
33 And he shall reign over the house of Jacob for ever; and of his kingdom there shall be no end.
34 Then said Mary unto the angel, How shall this be, seeing I know not a man?
35 And the angel answered and said unto her, The Holy Ghost shall come upon thee, and the power of the Highest shall overshadow thee: therefore also that holy thing which shall be born of thee shall be called the Son of God.
36 And, behold, thy cousin Elisabeth, she hath also conceived a son in her old age; and this is the sixth month with her, who was called barren.
37 For with God nothing shall be impossible.
38 And Mary said, Behold the handmaid of the Lord; be it unto me according to thy word. And the angel departed from her.
39 And Mary arose in those days, and went into the hill country with haste, into a city of Jṳ′dȧ;
40 And entered into the house of Zăch′ȧ-rī′ȧs, and saluted Elisabeth.
41 And it came to pass, that, when Elisabeth heard the salutation of Mary, the babe leaped in her womb; and Elisabeth was filled with the Holy Ghost:
42 And she spake out with a loud voice, and said, Blessed *art* thou among women, and blessed *is* the fruit of thy womb.
43 And whence *is* this to me, that the mother of my Lord should come to me?
44 For, lo, as soon as the voice of thy salutation sounded in mine ears, the babe leaped in my womb for joy.
45 And blessed *is* she that believed: for there shall be a performance of those things which were told her from the Lord.
46 And Mary said, My soul doth magnify the Lord,
47 And my spirit hath rejoiced in God my Saviour.
48 For he hath regarded the low estate of his handmaiden: for, behold, from henceforth all generations shall call me blessed.
49 For he that is mighty hath done to me great things; and holy *is* his name.
50 And his mercy *is* on them that fear him from generation to generation.
51 He hath showed strength with his arm; he hath scattered the proud in the imagination of their hearts.
52 He hath put down the mighty from *their* seats, and exalted them of low degree.
53 He hath filled the hungry with good things; and the rich he hath sent empty away.
54 He hath holpen his servant Ĭs̱′rā-ĕl, in remembrance of *his* mercy;
55 As he spake to our fathers, to Abraham, and to his seed for ever.
56 And Mary abode with her about three months, and returned to her own house.
57 Now Elisabeth's full time came that she should be delivered; and she brought forth a son.
58 And her neighbors and her cousins heard how the Lord had showed great mercy upon her; and they rejoiced with her.
59 And it came to pass, that on the eighth day they came to circumcise the child; and they called him Zăch′ȧ-rī′ȧs, after the name of his father.
60 And his mother answered and said, Not *so;* but he shall be called John.
61 And they said unto her, There is none of thy kindred that is called by this name.
62 And they made signs to his father, how he would have him called.
63 And he asked for a writing table, and wrote, saying, His name is John. And they marveled all.
64 And his mouth was opened immediately, and his tongue *loosed,* and he spake, and praised God.
65 And fear came on all that dwelt round about them: and all these sayings were noised abroad throughout all the hill country of Judea.
66 And all they that heard *them* laid *them* up in their hearts, saying, What

manner of child shall this be? And the
hand of the Lord was with him.
67 And his father Zăch'ă-rī'ăs was
filled with the Holy Ghost, and prophesied, saying,
68 Blessed *be* the Lord God of Ĭş'rā-ĕl;
for he hath visited and redeemed his
people,
69 And hath raised up a horn of salvation for us in the house of his servant
David;
70 As he spake by the mouth of his
holy prophets, which have been since
the world began:
71 That we should be saved from our
enemies, and from the hand of all that
hate us;
72 To perform the mercy *promised* to
our fathers, and to remember his holy
covenant;
73 The oath which he sware to our
father Abraham,
74 That he would grant unto us, that
we, being delivered out of the hand of
our enemies, might serve him without
fear,
75 In holiness and righteousness before him, all the days of our life.
76 And thou, child, shalt be called the
prophet of the Highest: for thou shalt
go before the face of the Lord to prepare his ways;
77 To give knowledge of salvation unto
his people by the remission of their sins,
78 Through the tender mercy of our
God; whereby the dayspring from on
high hath visited us,
79 To give light to them that sit in
darkness and *in* the shadow of death, to
guide our feet into the way of peace.
80 And the child grew, and waxed
strong in spirit, and was in the deserts
till the day of his showing unto Ĭş'rā-ĕl.

CHAPTER 2

AND it came to pass in those days,
that there went out a decree from
Cæsar Augustus, that all the world
should be taxed.
2 (*And* this taxing was first made when
Cȳ-rē'nĭ-ŭs was governor of Syria.)
3 And all went to be taxed, every one
into his own city.
4 And Joseph also went up from Galilee, out of the city of Nazareth, into
Judea, unto the city of David, which is
called Bethlehem, (because he was of
the house and lineage of David,)
5 To be taxed with Mary his espoused
wife, being great with child.
6 And so it was, that, while they were
there, the days were accomplished that
she should be delivered.
7 And she brought forth her firstborn
son, and wrapped him in swaddling
clothes, and laid him in a manger; because there was no room for them in
the inn.
8 And there were in the same country
shepherds abiding in the field, keeping
watch over their flock by night.
9 And, lo, the angel of the Lord came
upon them, and the glory of the Lord
shone round about them; and they were
sore afraid.
10 And the angel said unto them, Fear
not: for, behold, I bring you good tidings
of great joy, which shall be to all people.
11 For unto you is born this day in the
city of David a Saviour, which is Christ
the Lord.
12 And this *shall be* a sign unto you;
Ye shall find the babe wrapped in
swaddling clothes, lying in a manger.
13 And suddenly there was with the
angel a multitude of the heavenly host
praising God, and saying,
14 Glory to God in the highest, and on
earth peace, good will toward men.
15 And it came to pass, as the angels
were gone away from them into heaven,
the shepherds said one to another, Let
us now go even unto Bethlehem, and
see this thing which is come to pass,
which the Lord hath made known unto
us.
16 And they came with haste, and
found Mary and Joseph, and the babe
lying in a manger.
17 And when they had seen *it*, they
made known abroad the saying which
was told them concerning this child.
18 And all they that heard *it* wondered
at those things which were told them by
the shepherds.
19 But Mary kept all these things, and
pondered *them* in her heart.
20 And the shepherds returned, glorifying and praising God for all the things
that they had heard and seen, as it was
told unto them.
21 And when eight days were accomplished for the circumcising of the child,
his name was called JESUS, which was
so named of the angel before he was
conceived in the womb.

22 And when the days of her purification according to the law of Moses were
accomplished, they brought him to Jerusalem, to present *him* to the Lord;
23 (As it is written in the law of the
Lord, Every male that openeth the
womb shall be called holy to the Lord;)
24 And to offer a sacrifice according to
that which is said in the law of the
Lord, A pair of turtledoves, or two
young pigeons.
25 And, behold, there was a man in
Jerusalem, whose name *was* Simeon;
and the same man *was* just and devout,
waiting for the consolation of Ĭş′rā-ĕl:
and the Holy Ghost was upon him.
26 And it was revealed unto him by the
Holy Ghost, that he should not see
death, before he had seen the Lord's
Christ.
27 And he came by the Spirit into the
temple: and when the parents brought
in the child Jesus, to do for him after
the custom of the law,
28 Then took he him up in his arms,
and blessed God, and said,
29 Lord, now lettest thou thy servant
depart in peace, according to thy word:
30 For mine eyes have seen thy salvation,
31 Which thou hast prepared before
the face of all people;
32 A light to lighten the Ġĕn′tīleş, and
the glory of thy people Ĭş′rā-ĕl.
33 And Joseph and his mother marveled at those things which were spoken
of him.
34 And Simeon blessed them, and said
unto Mary his mother, Behold, this
child is set for the fall and rising again
of many in Ĭş′rā-ĕl; and for a sign which
shall be spoken against;
35 (Yea, a sword shall pierce through
thy own soul also;) that the thoughts of
many hearts may be revealed.
36 And there was one Anna, a prophetess, the daughter of Phȧ-nū′ĕl, of the
tribe of Ā′sēr: she was of a great age,
and had lived with a husband seven
years from her virginity;
37 And she *was* a widow of about fourscore and four years, which departed
not from the temple, but served *God*
with fastings and prayers night and day.
38 And she coming in that instant gave
thanks likewise unto the Lord, and
spake of him to all them that looked for
redemption in Jerusalem.
39 And when they had performed all
things according to the law of the
Lord, they returned into Galilee, to
their own city Nazareth.
40 And the child grew, and waxed
strong in spirit, filled with wisdom; and
the grace of God was upon him.
41 Now his parents went to Jerusalem
every year at the feast of the passover.
42 And when he was twelve years old,
they went up to Jerusalem after the custom of the feast.
43 And when they had fulfilled the
days, as they returned, the child Jesus
tarried behind in Jerusalem; and Joseph
and his mother knew not *of it.*
44 But they, supposing him to have
been in the company, went a day's journey; and they sought him among *their*
kinsfolk and acquaintance.
45 And when they found him not, they
turned back again to Jerusalem, seeking him.
46 And it came to pass, that after three
days they found him in the temple, sitting in the midst of the doctors, both
hearing them, and asking them questions.
47 And all that heard him were astonished at his understanding and answers.
48 And when they saw him, they were
amazed: and his mother said unto him,
Son, why hast thou thus dealt with us?
behold, thy father and I have sought
thee sorrowing.
49 And he said unto them, How is it
that ye sought me? wist ye not that I
must be about my Father's business?
50 And they understood not the saying
which he spake unto them.
51 And he went down with them, and
came to Nazareth, and was subject unto
them: but his mother kept all these sayings in her heart.
52 And Jesus increased in wisdom and
stature, and in favor with God and man.

CHAPTER 3

NOW in the fifteenth year of the
reign of Tī-bē′rĭ-ŭs Cæsar, Pŏn′-
ţĭ-ŭs Pilate being governor of Judea,
and Hĕr′ȯd being tetrarch of Galilee,
and his brother Philip tetrarch of Ĭt′ū-
rē′ȧ and of the region of Trăch′ō-nī′tĭs,
and Lȳ-sā′nĭ-ăs the tetrarch of Ăb′ĭ-lē′nē,
2 Annas and Cā′ịȧ-phăs being the high

priests, the word of God came unto
John the son of Zăch'á-rī'ás in the wilderness.
3 And he came into all the country
about Jordan, preaching the baptism of
repentance for the remission of sins;
4 As it is written in the book of the
words of Ē-ṣā'ịăs the prophet, saying,
The voice of one crying in the wilderness,
Prepare ye the way of the Lord,
make his paths straight.
5 Every valley shall be filled, and every
mountain and hill shall be brought low;
and the crooked shall be made straight,
and the rough ways *shall be* made
smooth;
6 And all flesh shall see the salvation
of God.
7 Then said he to the multitude that
came forth to be baptized of him, O
generation of vipers, who hath warned
you to flee from the wrath to come?
8 Bring forth therefore fruits worthy of
repentance, and begin not to say within
yourselves, We have Abraham to *our*
father: for I say unto you, That God is
able of these stones to raise up children
unto Abraham.
9 And now also the axe is laid unto the
root of the trees: every tree therefore
which bringeth not forth good fruit is
hewn down, and cast into the fire.
10 And the people asked him, saying,
What shall we do then?
11 He answereth and saith unto them,
He that hath two coats, let him impart
to him that hath none; and he that hath
meat, let him do likewise.
12 Then came also publicans to be baptized,
and said unto him, Master, what
shall we do?
13 And he said unto them, Exact no
more than that which is appointed you.
14 And the soldiers likewise demanded
of him, saying, And what shall we do?
And he said unto them, Do violence to
no man, neither accuse *any* falsely; and
be content with your wages.
15 And as the people were in expectation,
and all men mused in their hearts
of John, whether he were the Christ, or
not;
16 John answered, saying unto *them*
all, I indeed baptize you with water;
but one mightier than I cometh, the
latchet of whose shoes I am not worthy
to unloose: he shall baptize you with the
Holy Ghost and with fire:
17 Whose fan *is* in his hand, and he will
thoroughly purge his floor, and will
gather the wheat into his garner; but
the chaff he will burn with fire unquenchable.
18 And many other things in his exhortation
preached he unto the people.
19 But Hĕr'ŏd the tetrarch, being reproved
by him for Hē-rō'dĭ-ăs his
brother Philip's wife, and for all the
evils which Hĕr'ŏd had done,
20 Added yet this above all, that he
shut up John in prison.
21 Now when all the people were baptized,
it came to pass, that Jesus also
being baptized, and praying, the heaven
was opened,
22 And the Holy Ghost descended in a
bodily shape like a dove upon him, and
a voice came from heaven, which said,
Thou art my beloved Son; in thee I am
well pleased.
23 And Jesus himself began to be
about thirty years of age, being (as was
supposed) the son of Joseph, which was
the son of Hē'lī,
24 Which was *the son* of Măt'thăt,
which was *the son* of Levi, which was
the son of Mĕl'chī, which was *the son* of
Jăn'nȧ, which was *the son* of Joseph,
25 Which was *the son* of Măt'tȧ-thī'ăs,
which was *the son* of Amos, which was
the son of Nā'ŭm, which was *the son* of
Ĕs'lī, which was *the son* of Năg'gē,
26 Which was *the son* of Mā'ăth, which
was *the son* of Măt'tȧ-thī'ăs, which was
the son of Sĕm'ē-ī, which was *the son* of
Joseph, which was *the son* of Jụ'dȧ,
27 Which was *the son* of Jō-ăn'nȧ,
which was *the son* of Rhē'sȧ, which was
the son of Zō-rŏb'ȧ-bĕl, which was *the
son* of Sȧ-lā'thĭ-ĕl, which was *the son*
of Ne'rı,
28 Which was *the son* of Mĕl'chī, which
was *the son* of Ăd'dī, which was *the son*
of Cō'săm, which was *the son* of Ĕl-mō'dăm,
which was *the son* of Ēr,
29 Which was *the son* of Jō'sē, which
was *the son* of Ĕl'ĭ-ē'zēr, which was *the
son* of Jō'rĭm, which was *the son* of
Măt'thăt, which was *the son* of Levi,
30 Which was *the son* of Simeon, which
was *the son* of Jụ'dȧ, which was *the son*
of Joseph, which was *the son* of Jō'năn,
which was *the son* of Ē-lī'ȧ-kĭm,
31 Which was *the son* of Mē'lē-ȧ,
which was *the son* of Mē'năn, which
was *the son* of Măt'tȧ-thȧ, which was

the son of Nathan, which was *the son* of
David,
32 Which was *the son* of Jesse, which
was *the son* of Ō'bĕd, which was *the
son* of Bō'ŏz, which was *the son* of
Săl'mŏn, which was *the son* of Nā-
ăs'sŏn,
33 Which was *the son* of A-mĭn'a-dăb,
which was *the son* of Ā'răm, which was
the son of Ĕs'rŏm, which was *the son* of
Phā'rēs, which was *the son* of Jụ'dȧ,
34 Which was *the son* of Jacob, which
was *the son* of Isaac, which was *the son*
of Abraham, which was *the son* of
Thā'rȧ, which was *the son* of Nā'chŏr,
35 Which was *the son* of Sā'rŭch,
which was *the son* of Rā'gau, which was
the son of Phā'lĕc, which was *the son*
of Hē'bĕr, which was *the son* of Sā'lȧ,
36 Which was *the son* of Cā-ī'nan,
which was *the son* of Är-phăx'ăd, which
was *the son* of Sĕm, which was *the son*
of Nō'ē, which was *the son* of Lā'mĕch,
37 Which was *the son* of Mȧ-thū'-
sȧ-lȧ, which was *the son* of Enoch,
which was *the son* of Jā'rĕd, which was
the son of Mȧ-lē'lē-ĕl, which was *the
son* of Cā-ī'năn,
38 Which was *the son* of Ē'nŏs, which
was *the son* of Seth, which was *the son*
of Adam, which was *the son* of God.

CHAPTER 4

AND Jesus being full of the Holy
Ghost returned from Jordan, and
was led by the Spirit into the wilderness,
2 Being forty days tempted of the devil.
And in those days he did eat nothing:
and when they were ended, he afterward hungered.
3 And the devil said unto him, If thou
be the Son of God, command this stone
that it be made bread.
4 And Jesus answered him, saying, It
is written, That man shall not live by
bread alone, but by every word of God.
5 And the devil, taking him up into a
high mountain, showed unto him all the
kingdoms of the world in a moment of
time.
6 And the devil said unto him, All this
power will I give thee, and the glory of
them: for that is delivered unto me; and
to whomsoever I will, I give it.
7 If thou therefore wilt worship me, all
shall be thine.
8 And Jesus answered and said unto
him, Get thee behind me, Satan: for it
is written, Thou shalt worship the Lord
thy God, and him only shalt thou serve.
9 And he brought him to Jerusalem,
and set him on a pinnacle of the temple,
and said unto him, If thou be the Son
of God, cast thyself down from hence:
10 For it is written, He shall give his
angels charge over thee, to keep thee:
11 And in *their* hands they shall bear
thee up, lest at any time thou dash thy
foot against a stone.
12 And Jesus answering said unto him,
It is said, Thou shalt not tempt the
Lord thy God.
13 And when the devil had ended all
the temptation, he departed from him
for a season.
14 ¶ And Jesus returned in the power
of the Spirit into Galilee: and there went
out a fame of him through all the region
round about.
15 And he taught in their synagogues,
being glorified of all.
16 ¶ And he came to Nazareth, where
he had been brought up: and, as his
custom was, he went into the synagogue
on the sabbath day, and stood up for
to read.
17 And there was delivered unto him
the book of the prophet Ē-ṣā'ịăs. And
when he had opened the book, he found
the place where it was written,
18 The Spirit of the Lord *is* upon me,
because he hath anointed me to preach
the gospel to the poor; he hath sent me
to heal the broken-hearted, to preach
deliverance to the captives, and recov-
ering of sight to the blind, to set at
liberty them that are bruised,
19 To preach the acceptable year of
the Lord.
20 And he closed the book, and he gave
it again to the minister, and sat down.
And the eyes of all them that were in the
synagogue were fastened on him.
21 And he began to say unto them,
This day is this Scripture fulfilled in
your ears.
22 And all bare him witness, and wondered at the gracious words which proceeded out of his mouth. And they
said, Is not this Joseph's son?
23 And he said unto them, Ye will
surely say unto me this proverb, Physician, heal thyself: whatsoever we have
heard done in Cȧ-pĕr'nā-ŭm, do also
here in thy country.

24 And he said, Verily I say unto you,
No prophet is accepted in his own
country.
25 But I tell you of a truth, many
widows were in Ĭṣ'rā-ĕl in the days of
Ē-lī'ăs, when the heaven was shut up
three years and six months, when great
famine was throughout all the land;
26 But unto none of them was Ē-lī'ăs
sent, save unto Să-rĕp'tă, *a city* of Sī-
dŏn, unto a woman *that was* a widow.
27 And many lepers were in Ĭṣ'rā-ĕl
in the time of Ĕl'ĭ-sē'ŭs the prophet;
and none of them was cleansed, saving
Nā'ă-măn the Syrian.
28 And all they in the synagogue, when
they heard these things, were filled
with wrath,
29 And rose up, and thrust him out of
the city, and led him unto the brow of
the hill whereon their city was built,
that they might cast him down headlong.
30 But he, passing through the midst
of them, went his way,
31 And came down to Că-pĕr'nā-ŭm,
a city of Galilee, and taught them on the
sabbath days.
32 And they were astonished at his
doctrine: for his word was with power.
33 ℭ And in the synagogue there was
a man, which had a spirit of an unclean
devil, and cried out with a loud voice,
34 Saying, Let *us* alone; what have we
to do with thee, *thou* Jesus of Nazareth?
art thou come to destroy us? I know
thee who thou art; the Holy One of
God.
35 And Jesus rebuked him, saying,
Hold thy peace, and come out of him.
And when the devil had thrown him in
the midst, he came out of him, and hurt
him not.
36 And they were all amazed, and
spake among themselves, saying, What
a word *is* this! for with authority and
power he commandeth the unclean
spirits, and they come out.
37 And the fame of him went out into
every place of the country round about.
38 ℭ And he arose out of the synagogue, and entered into Simon's house.
And Simon's wife's mother was taken
with a great fever; and they besought
him for her.
39 And he stood over her, and rebuked
the fever; and it left her: and immediately she arose and ministered unto
them.
40 ℭ Now when the sun was setting,
all they that had any sick with divers
diseases brought them unto him; and
he laid his hands on every one of them,
and healed them.
41 And devils also came out of many,
crying out, and saying, Thou art Christ
the Son of God. And he rebuking *them*
suffered them not to speak: for they
knew that he was Christ.
42 And when it was day, he departed
and went into a desert place: and the
people sought him, and came unto him,
and stayed him, that he should not depart from them.
43 And he said unto them, I must
preach the kingdom of God to other
cities also: for therefore am I sent.
44 And he preached in the synagogues
of Galilee.

CHAPTER 5

AND it came to pass, that, as the
people pressed upon him to hear
the word of God, he stood by the lake
of Gĕn-nĕs'ă-rĕt,
2 And saw two ships standing by the
lake: but the fishermen were gone out
of them, and were washing *their* nets.
3 And he entered into one of the ships,
which was Simon's, and prayed him
that he would thrust out a little from the
land. And he sat down, and taught the
people out of the ship.
4 Now when he had left speaking, he
said unto Simon, Launch out into the
deep, and let down your nets for a
draught.
5 And Simon answering said unto him,
Master, we have toiled all the night,
and have taken nothing: nevertheless
at thy word I will let down the net.
6 And when they had this done, they
inclosed a great multitude of fishes: and
their net brake.
7 And they beckoned unto *their* part-
ners, which were in the other ship, that
they should come and help them. And
they came, and filled both the ships, so
that they began to sink.
8 When Simon Peter saw *it*, he fell
down at Jesus' knees, saying, Depart
from me; for I am a sinful man, O Lord.
9 For he was astonished, and all that
were with him, at the draught of the
fishes which they had taken:
10 And so *was* also James, and John,
the sons of Zĕb'ē-dēe, which were part-

ners with Simon. And Jesus said unto Simon, Fear not; from henceforth thou shalt catch men.

11 And when they had brought their ships to land, they forsook all, and followed him.

12 ¶ And it came to pass, when he was in a certain city, behold a man full of leprosy; who seeing Jesus fell on *his* face, and besought him, saying, Lord, if thou wilt, thou canst make me clean.

13 And he put forth *his* hand, and touched him, saying, I will: be thou clean. And immediately the leprosy departed from him.

14 And he charged him to tell no man: but go, and show thyself to the priest, and offer for thy cleansing, according as Moses commanded, for a testimony unto them.

15 But so much the more went there a fame abroad of him: and great multitudes came together to hear, and to be healed by him of their infirmities.

16 ¶ And he withdrew himself into the wilderness, and prayed.

17 And it came to pass on a certain day, as he was teaching, that there were Phăr'ĭ-sēeş and doctors of the law sitting by, which were come out of every town of Galilee, and Judea, and Jerusalem: and the power of the Lord was *present* to heal them.

18 ¶ And, behold, men brought in a bed a man which was taken with a palsy: and they sought *means* to bring him in, and to lay *him* before him.

19 And when they could not find by what *way* they might bring him in because of the multitude, they went upon the housetop, and let him down through the tiling with *his* couch into the midst before Jesus.

20 And when he saw their faith, he said unto him, Man, thy sins are forgiven thee.

21 And the scribes and the Phăr'ĭ-sēeş began to reason, saying, Who is this which speaketh blasphemies? Who can forgive sins, but God alone?

22 But when Jesus perceived their thoughts, he answering said unto them, What reason ye in your hearts?

23 Whether is easier, to say, Thy sins be forgiven thee; or to say, Rise up and walk?

24 But that ye may know that the Son of man hath power upon earth to forgive sins, (he said unto the sick of the palsy,) I say unto thee, Arise, and take up thy couch, and go into thine house.

25 And immediately he rose up before them, and took up that whereon he lay, and departed to his own house, glorifying God.

26 And they were all amazed, and they glorified God, and were filled with fear, saying, We have seen strange things to-day.

27 ¶ And after these things he went forth, and saw a publican, named Levi, sitting at the receipt of custom: and he said unto him, Follow me.

28 And he left all, rose up, and followed him.

29 And Levi made him a great feast in his own house: and there was a great company of publicans and of others that sat down with them.

30 But their scribes and Phăr'ĭ-sēeş murmured against his disciples, saying, Why do ye eat and drink with publicans and sinners?

31 And Jesus answering said unto them, They that are whole need not a physician; but they that are sick.

32 I came not to call the righteous, but sinners to repentance.

33 ¶ And they said unto him, Why do the disciples of John fast often, and make prayers, and likewise *the disciples* of the Phăr'ĭ-sēeş; but thine eat and drink?

34 And he said unto them, Can ye make the children of the bridechamber fast, while the bridegroom is with them?

35 But the days will come, when the bridegroom shall be taken away from them, and then shall they fast in those days.

36 ¶ And he spake also a parable unto them; No man putteth a piece of a new garment upon an old; if otherwise, then both the new maketh a rent, and the piece that was *taken* out of the new agreeth not with the old.

37 And no man putteth new wine into old bottles; else the new wine will burst the bottles, and be spilled, and the bottles shall perish.

38 But new wine must be put into new bottles; and both are preserved.

39 No man also having drunk old *wine* straightway desireth new; for he saith, The old is better.

CHAPTER 6

AND it came to pass on the second
sabbath after the first, that he went
through the corn fields; and his disciples plucked the ears of corn, and did
eat, rubbing *them* in *their* hands.
2 And certain of the Phăr′ĭ-sēes̱ said
unto them, Why do ye that which is not
lawful to do on the sabbath days?
3 And Jesus answering them said,
Have ye not read so much as this, what
David did, when himself was ahungered, and they which were with him;
4 How he went into the house of God,
and did take and eat the showbread,
and gave also to them that were with
him; which it is not lawful to eat but for
the priests alone?
5 And he said unto them, That the
Son of man is Lord also of the sabbath.
6 And it came to pass also on another
sabbath, that he entered into the synagogue and taught: and there was a man
whose right hand was withered.
7 And the scribes and Phăr′ĭ-sēes̱
watched him, whether he would heal on
the sabbath day; that they might find
an accusation against him.
8 But he knew their thoughts, and said
to the man which had the withered hand,
Rise up, and stand forth in the midst.
And he arose and stood forth.
9 Then said Jesus unto them, I will ask
you one thing; Is it lawful on the sabbath days to do good, or to do evil? to
save life, or to destroy *it?*
10 And looking round about upon them
all, he said unto the man, Stretch forth
thy hand. And he did so: and his hand
was restored whole as the other.
11 And they were filled with madness;
and communed one with another what
they might do to Jesus.
12 And it came to pass in those days,
that he went out into a mountain to pray,
and continued all night in prayer to God.
13 ¶ And when it was day, he called
unto him his disciples: and of them he
chose twelve, whom also he named
apostles;
14 Simon, (whom he also named
Peter,) and Andrew his brother, James
and John, Philip and Bartholomew,
15 Matthew and Thomas, James the
son of Alpheus, and Simon called
Zē-lō′tēs̱,
16 And Judas *the brother* of James,
and Judas Ĭs-căr′ĭ-ŏt, which also was
the traitor.
17 ¶ And he came down with them,
and stood in the plain, and the company
of his disciples, and a great multitude of
people out of all Judea and Jerusalem,
and from the seacoast of Tȳre and
Sī′dŏn, which came to hear him, and to
be healed of their diseases;
18 And they that were vexed with unclean spirits: and they were healed.
19 And the whole multitude sought to
touch him: for there went virtue out of
him, and healed *them* all.
20 ¶ And he lifted up his eyes on his
disciples, and said, Blessed *be ye* poor:
for yours is the kingdom of God.
21 Blessed *are ye* that hunger now: for
ye shall be filled. Blessed *are ye* that
weep now: for ye shall laugh.
22 Blessed are ye, when men shall
hate you, and when they shall separate
you *from their company,* and shall reproach *you,* and cast out your name as
evil, for the Son of man's sake.
23 Rejoice ye in that day, and leap for
joy: for, behold, your reward *is* great in
heaven: for in the like manner did their
fathers unto the prophets.
24 But woe unto you that are rich! for
ye have received your consolation.
25 Woe unto you that are full! for ye
shall hunger. Woe unto you that laugh
now! for ye shall mourn and weep.
26 Woe unto you, when all men shall
speak well of you! for so did their
fathers to the false prophets.
27 ¶ But I say unto you which hear,
Love your enemies, do good to them
which hate you,
28 Bless them that curse you, and pray
for them which despitefully use you.
29 And unto him that smiteth thee on
the *one* cheek offer also the other; and
him that taketh away thy cloak forbid
not *to take thy* coat also.
30 Give to every man that asketh of
thee; and of him that taketh away thy
goods ask *them* not again.
31 And as ye would that men should
do to you, do ye also to them likewise.
32 For if ye love them which love you,
what thank have ye? for sinners also
love those that love them.
33 And if ye do good to them which do
good to you, what thank have ye? for
sinners also do even the same.
34 And if ye lend *to them* of whom ye

hope to receive, what thank have ye? for
sinners also lend to sinners, to receive
as much again.
35 But love ye your enemies, and do
good, and lend, hoping for nothing again;
and your reward shall be great, and ye
shall be the children of the Highest: for
he is kind unto the unthankful and *to*
the evil.
36 Be ye therefore merciful, as your
Father also is merciful.
37 Judge not, and ye shall not be
judged: condemn not, and ye shall not
be condemned: forgive, and ye shall be
forgiven:
38 Give, and it shall be given unto you;
good measure, pressed down, and
shaken together, and running over, shall
men give into your bosom. For with
the same measure that ye mete withal
it shall be measured to you again.
39 And he spake a parable unto them;
Can the blind lead the blind? shall they
not both fall into the ditch?
40 The disciple is not above his master:
but every one that is perfect shall be as
his master.
41 And why beholdest thou the mote
that is in thy brother's eye, but perceivest
not the beam that is in thine
own eye?
42 Either how canst thou say to thy
brother, Brother, let me pull out the
mote that is in thine eye, when thou
thyself beholdest not the beam that is
in thine own eye? Thou hypocrite, cast
out first the beam out of thine own eye,
and then shalt thou see clearly to pull
out the mote that is in thy brother's
eye.
43 For a good tree bringeth not forth
corrupt fruit; neither doth a corrupt tree
bring forth good fruit.
44 For every tree is known by his own
fruit. For of thorns men do not gather
figs, nor of a bramble bush gather they
grapes.
45 A good man out of the good treasure
of his heart bringeth forth that which is
good; and an evil man out of the evil
treasure of his heart bringeth forth that
which is evil: for of the abundance of
the heart his mouth speaketh.
46 ¶ And why call ye me, Lord,
Lord, and do not the things which I say?
47 Whosoever cometh to me, and heareth
my sayings, and doeth them, I will
show you to whom he is like:
48 He is like a man which built a
house, and digged deep, and laid the
foundation on a rock: and when the
flood arose, the stream beat vehemently
upon that house, and could not shake it;
for it was founded upon a rock.
49 But he that heareth, and doeth not,
is like a man that without a foundation
built a house upon the earth; against
which the stream did beat vehemently,
and immediately it fell; and the ruin of
that house was great.

CHAPTER 7

NOW when he had ended all his
sayings in the audience of the
people, he entered into Cȧ-pĕr'nā-ŭm.
2 And a certain centurion's servant,
who was dear unto him, was sick, and
ready to die.
3 And when he heard of Jesus, he sent
unto him the elders of the Jews, beseeching
him that he would come and
heal his servant.
4 And when they came to Jesus, they
besought him instantly, saying, That
he was worthy for whom he should do
this:
5 For he loveth our nation, and he
hath built us a synagogue.
6 Then Jesus went with them. And
when he was now not far from the
house, the centurion sent friends to
him, saying unto him, Lord, trouble
not thyself; for I am not worthy that
thou shouldest enter under my roof:
7 Wherefore neither thought I myself
worthy to come unto thee: but say in a
word, and my servant shall be healed.
8 For I also am a man set under authority,
having under me soldiers, and
I say unto one, Go, and he goeth;
and to another, Come, and he cometh;
and to my servant, Do this, and he
doeth *it*.
9 When Jesus heard these things, he
marveled at him, and turned him about,
and said unto the people that followed
him, I say unto you, I have not found so
great faith, no, not in Ĭṣ'rā-ĕl.
10 And they that were sent, returning
to the house, found the servant whole
that had been sick.
11 ¶ And it came to pass the day after,
that he went into a city called Nā'ĭn;
and many of his disciples went with
him, and much people.
12 Now when he came nigh to the gate

of the city, behold, there was a dead
man carried out, the only son of his
mother, and she was a widow: and much
people of the city was with her.
13 And when the Lord saw her, he
had compassion on her, and said unto
her, Weep not.
14 And he came and touched the bier:
and they that bare *him* stood still. And
he said, Young man, I say unto thee,
Arise.
15 And he that was dead sat up, and
began to speak. And he delivered him
to his mother.
16 And there came a fear on all: and
they glorified God, saying, That a great
prophet is risen up among us; and, That
God hath visited his people.
17 And this rumor of him went forth
throughout all Judea, and throughout
all the region round about.
18 And the disciples of John showed
him of all these things.
19 ¶ And John calling *unto him* two
of his disciples sent *them* to Jesus, saying, Art thou he that should come? or
look we for another?
20 When the men were come unto him,
they said, John Baptist hath sent us
unto thee, saying, Art thou he that
should come? or look we for another?
21 And in that same hour he cured
many of *their* infirmities and plagues,
and of evil spirits; and unto many *that
were* blind he gave sight.
22 Then Jesus answering said unto
them, Go your way, and tell John what
things ye have seen and heard; how
that the blind see, the lame walk, the
lepers are cleansed, the deaf hear, the
dead are raised, to the poor the gospel
is preached.
23 And blessed is *he,* whosoever shall
not be offended in me.
24 ¶ And when the messengers of
John were departed, he began to speak
unto the people concerning John, What
went ye out into the wilderness for to
see? A reed shaken with the wind?
25 But what went ye out for to see?
A man clothed in soft raiment? Behold,
they which are gorgeously appareled,
and live delicately, are in kings' courts.
26 But what went ye out for to see? A
prophet? Yea, I say unto you, and
much more than a prophet.
27 This is *he,* of whom it is written,
Behold, I send my messenger before
thy face, which shall prepare thy way
before thee.
28 For I say unto you, Among those
that are born of women there is not a
greater prophet than John the Baptist:
but he that is least in the kingdom of
God is greater than he.
29 And all the people that heard *him,*
and the publicans, justified God, being
baptized with the baptism of John.
30 But the Phăr'ĭ-sēeş and lawyers
rejected the counsel of God against
themselves, being not baptized of him.
31 ¶ And the Lord said, Whereunto
then shall I liken the men of this generation? and to what are they like?
32 They are like unto children sitting
in the market place, and calling one to
another, and saying, We have piped
unto you, and ye have not danced; we
have mourned to you, and ye have not
wept.
33 For John the Baptist came neither
eating bread nor drinking wine; and ye
say, He hath a devil.
34 The Son of man is come eating and
drinking; and ye say, Behold a gluttonous man, and a winebibber, a friend
of publicans and sinners!
35 But wisdom is justified of all her
children.
36 ¶ And one of the Phăr'ĭ-sēeş desired him that he would eat with him.
And he went into the Phăr'ĭ-sēe'ş house,
and sat down to meat.
37 And, behold, a woman in the city,
which was a sinner, when she knew that
Jesus sat at meat in the Phăr'ĭ-sēe'ş
house, brought an alabaster box of
ointment,
38 And stood at his feet behind *him*
weeping, and began to wash his feet
with tears, and did wipe *them* with the
hairs of her head, and kissed his feet,
and anointed *them* with the ointment.
39 Now when the Phăr'ĭ-sēe which had
bidden him saw *it,* he spake within
himself, saying, This man, if he were a
prophet, would have known who and
what manner of woman *this is* that
toucheth him; for she is a sinner.
40 And Jesus answering said unto him,
Simon, I have somewhat to say unto
thee. And he saith, Master, say on.
41 There was a certain creditor which
had two debtors: the one owed five hundred pence, and the other fifty.
42 And when they had nothing to pay,

he frankly forgave them both. Tell me therefore, which of them will love him most?
43 Simon answered and said, I suppose that *he,* to whom he forgave most. And he said unto him, Thou hast rightly judged.
44 And he turned to the woman, and said unto Simon, Seest thou this woman? I entered into thine house, thou gavest me no water for my feet: but she hath washed my feet with tears, and wiped *them* with the hairs of her head.
45 Thou gavest me no kiss: but this woman, since the time I came in, hath not ceased to kiss my feet.
46 My head with oil thou didst not anoint: but this woman hath anointed my feet with ointment.
47 Wherefore I say unto thee, Her sins, which are many, are forgiven; for she loved much: but to whom little is forgiven, *the same* loveth little.
48 And he said unto her, Thy sins are forgiven.
49 And they that sat at meat with him began to say within themselves, Who is this that forgiveth sins also?
50 And he said to the woman, Thy faith hath saved thee; go in peace.

CHAPTER 8

AND it came to pass afterward, that he went throughout every city and village, preaching and showing the glad tidings of the kingdom of God: and the twelve *were* with him,
2 And certain women, which had been healed of evil spirits and infirmities, Mary called Măg′dȧ-lēne, out of whom went seven devils,
3 And Jō-ăn′nȧ the wife of Chū′zȧ Hĕr′ŏd's steward, and Susanna, and many others, which ministered unto him of their substance.
4 ¶ And when much people were gathered together, and were come to him out of every city, he spake by a parable:
5 A sower went out to sow his seed: and as he sowed, some fell by the wayside; and it was trodden down, and the fowls of the air devoured it.
6 And some fell upon a rock; and as soon as it was sprung up, it withered away, because it lacked moisture.
7 And some fell among thorns; and the thorns sprang up with it, and choked it.
8 And other fell on good ground, and sprang up, and bare fruit a hundredfold. And when he had said these things, he cried, He that hath ears to hear, let him hear.
9 And his disciples asked him, saying, What might this parable be?
10 And he said, Unto you it is given to know the mysteries of the kingdom of God: but to others in parables; that seeing they might not see, and hearing they might not understand.
11 Now the parable is this: The seed is the word of God.
12 Those by the wayside are they that hear; then cometh the devil, and taketh away the word out of their hearts, lest they should believe and be saved.
13 They on the rock *are they,* which, when they hear, receive the word with joy; and these have no root, which for a while believe, and in time of temptation fall away.
14 And that which fell among thorns are they, which, when they have heard, go forth, and are choked with cares and riches and pleasures of *this* life, and bring no fruit to perfection.
15 But that on the good ground are they, which in an honest and good heart, having heard the word, keep *it,* and bring forth fruit with patience.
16 ¶ No man, when he hath lighted a candle, covereth it with a vessel, or putteth *it* under a bed; but setteth *it* on a candlestick, that they which enter in may see the light.
17 For nothing is secret, that shall not be made manifest; neither *any thing* hid, that shall not be known and come abroad.
18 Take heed therefore how ye hear: for whosoever hath, to him shall be given; and whosoever hath not, from him shall be taken even that which he seemeth to have.
19 ¶ Then came to him *his* mother and his brethren, and could not come at him for the press.
20 And it was told him *by certain* which said, Thy mother and thy brethren stand without, desiring to see thee.
21 And he answered and said unto them, My mother and my brethren are these which hear the word of God, and do it.

22 ¶ Now it came to pass on a certain day, that he went into a ship with his disciples: and he said unto them, Let us go over unto the other side of the lake. And they launched forth.

23 But as they sailed, he fell asleep: and there came down a storm of wind on the lake; and they were filled *with water*, and were in jeopardy.

24 And they came to him, and awoke him, saying, Master, Master, we perish. Then he arose, and rebuked the wind and the raging of the water: and they ceased, and there was a calm.

25 And he said unto them, Where is your faith? And they being afraid wondered, saying one to another, What manner of man is this! for he commandeth even the winds and water, and they obey him.

26 ¶ And they arrived at the country of the Găd-ȧ-rēneș′, which is over against Galilee.

27 And when he went forth to land, there met him out of the city a certain man, which had devils long time, and ware no clothes, neither abode in *any* house, but in the tombs.

28 When he saw Jesus, he cried out, and fell down before him, and with a loud voice said, What have I to do with thee, Jesus, *thou* Son of God most high? I beseech thee, torment me not.

29 (For he had commanded the unclean spirit to come out of the man. For oftentimes it had caught him: and he was kept bound with chains and in fetters; and he brake the bands, and was driven of the devil into the wilderness.)

30 And Jesus asked him, saying, What is thy name? And he said, Legion: because many devils were entered into him.

31 And they besought him that he would not command them to go out into the deep.

32 And there was there a herd of many swine feeding on the mountain: and they besought him that he would suffer them to enter into them. And he suffered them.

33 Then went the devils out of the man, and entered into the swine: and the herd ran violently down a steep place into the lake, and were choked.

34 When they that fed *them* saw what was done, they fled, and went and told *it* in the city and in the country.

35 Then they went out to see what was done; and came to Jesus, and found the man, out of whom the devils were departed, sitting at the feet of Jesus, clothed, and in his right mind: and they were afraid.

36 They also which saw *it* told them by what means he that was possessed of the devils was healed.

37 ¶ Then the whole multitude of the country of the Găd-ȧ-rēneș′ round about besought him to depart from them; for they were taken with great fear: and he went up into the ship, and returned back again.

38 Now the man, out of whom the devils were departed, besought him that he might be with him: but Jesus sent him away, saying,

39 Return to thine own house, and show how great things God hath done unto thee. And he went his way, and published throughout the whole city how great things Jesus had done unto him.

40 And it came to pass, that, when Jesus was returned, the people *gladly* received him: for they were all waiting for him.

41 ¶ And, behold, there came a man named Jā′ĭ-rŭs, and he was a ruler of the synagogue; and he fell down at Jesus' feet, and besought him that he would come into his house:

42 For he had one only daughter, about twelve years of age, and she lay a dying. But as he went the people thronged him.

43 ¶ And a woman having an issue of blood twelve years, which had spent all her living upon physicians, neither could be healed of any,

44 Came behind *him*, and touched the border of his garment: and immediately her issue of blood stanched.

45 And Jesus said, Who touched me? When all denied, Peter and they that were with him said, Master, the multitude throng thee and press *thee*, and sayest thou, Who touched me?

46 And Jesus said, Somebody hath touched me: for I perceive that virtue is gone out of me.

47 And when the woman saw that she was not hid, she came trembling, and falling down before him, she declared unto him before all the people for what cause she had touched him, and how she was healed immediately.

48 And he said unto her, Daughter,
be of good comfort: thy faith hath made
thee whole; go in peace.

49 ¶ While he yet spake, there cometh
one from the ruler of the synagogue's
house, saying to him, Thy daughter is
dead; trouble not the Master.

50 But when Jesus heard *it,* he answered him, saying, Fear not: believe
only, and she shall be made whole.

51 And when he came into the house,
he suffered no man to go in, save Peter,
and James, and John, and the father
and the mother of the maiden.

52 And all wept, and bewailed her: but
he said, Weep not; she is not dead, but
sleepeth.

53 And they laughed him to scorn,
knowing that she was dead.

54 And he put them all out, and took
her by the hand, and called, saying,
Maid, arise.

55 And her spirit came again, and she
arose straightway: and he commanded
to give her meat.

56 And her parents were astonished:
but he charged them that they should
tell no man what was done.

CHAPTER 9

THEN he called his twelve disciples
together, and gave them power and
authority over all devils, and to cure
diseases.

2 And he sent them to preach the kingdom of God, and to heal the sick.

3 And he said unto them, Take nothing
for *your* journey, neither staves, nor
scrip, neither bread, neither money;
neither have two coats apiece.

4 And whatsoever house ye enter into,
there abide, and thence depart.

5 And whosoever will not receive you,
when ye go out of that city, shake off
the very dust from your feet for a testimony against them.

6 And they departed, and went through
the towns, preaching the gospel, and
healing every where.

7 ¶ Now Hĕr'ŏd the tetrarch heard of
all that was done by him: and he was
perplexed, because that it was said of
some, that John was risen from the
dead;

8 And of some, that Ē-lī'ăs had appeared; and of others, that one of the
old prophets was risen again.

9 And Hĕr'ŏd said, John have I beheaded; but who is this, of whom I hear
such things? And he desired to see him.

10 ¶ And the apostles, when they were
returned, told him all that they had
done. And he took them, and went aside
privately into a desert place belonging
to the city called Bĕth'sā'ĭ-dȧ.

11 And the people, when they knew *it,*
followed him: and he received them, and
spake unto them of the kingdom of God,
and healed them that had need of healing.

12 And when the day began to wear
away, then came the twelve, and said
unto him, Send the multitude away, that
they may go into the towns and country
round about, and lodge, and get victuals: for we are here in a desert place.

13 But he said unto them, Give ye
them to eat. And they said, We have no
more but five loaves and two fishes; except we should go and buy meat for all
this people.

14 For they were about five thousand
men. And he said to his disciples, Make
them sit down by fifties in a company.

15 And they did so, and made them all
sit down.

16 Then he took the five loaves and
the two fishes, and looking up to heaven,
he blessed them, and brake, and gave
to the disciples to set before the multitude.

17 And they did eat, and were all filled:
and there was taken up of fragments
that remained to them twelve baskets.

18 ¶ And it came to pass, as he was
alone praying, his disciples were with
him; and he asked them, saying, Whom
say the people that I am?

19 They answering said, John the Baptist; but some *say,* Ē-lī'ăs; and others
say, that one of the old prophets is
risen again.

20 He said unto them, But whom say
ye that I am? Peter answering said,
The Christ of God.

21 And he straitly charged them, and
commanded *them* to tell no man that
thing;

22 Saying, The Son of man must suffer
many things, and be rejected of the
elders and chief priests and scribes, and
be slain, and be raised the third day.

23 ¶ And he said to *them* all, If any
man will come after me, let him deny
himself, and take up his cross daily, and
follow me.

24 For whosoever will save his life
shall lose it: but whosoever will lose his
life for my sake, the same shall save it.
25 For what is a man advantaged, if
he gain the whole world, and lose himself, or be cast away?
26 For whosoever shall be ashamed of
me and of my words, of him shall the
Son of man be ashamed, when he shall
come in his own glory, and *in his*
Father's, and of the holy angels.
27 But I tell you of a truth, there be
some standing here, which shall not
taste of death, till they see the kingdom
of God.
28 ¶ And it came to pass about an
eight days after these sayings, he took
Peter and John and James, and went
up into a mountain to pray.
29 And as he prayed, the fashion of his
countenance was altered, and his raiment *was* white *and* glistering.
30 And, behold, there talked with him
two men, which were Moses and
Ē-lī'ăs:
31 Who appeared in glory, and spake
of his decease which he should accomplish at Jerusalem.
32 But Peter and they that were with
him were heavy with sleep: and when
they were awake, they saw his glory,
and the two men that stood with him.
33 And it came to pass, as they departed from him, Peter said unto Jesus,
Master, it is good for us to be here: and
let us make three tabernacles; one for
thee, and one for Moses, and one for
Ē-lī'ăs: not knowing what he said.
34 While he thus spake, there came a
cloud, and overshadowed them: and
they feared as they entered into the
cloud.
35 And there came a voice out of the
cloud, saying, This is my beloved Son:
hear him.
36 And when the voice was past, Jesus
was found alone. And they kept *it*
close, and told no man in those days
any of those things which they had
seen.
37 ¶ And it came to pass, that on the
next day, when they were come down
from the hill, much people met him.
38 And, behold, a man of the company
cried out, saying, Master, I beseech
thee, look upon my son; for he is mine
only child.
39 And, lo, a spirit taketh him, and he
suddenly crieth out; and it teareth him
that he foameth again, and bruising
him, hardly departeth from him.
40 And I besought thy disciples to cast
him out; and they could not.
41 And Jesus answering said, O faithless and perverse generation, how long
shall I be with you, and suffer you?
Bring thy son hither.
42 And as he was yet a coming, the
devil threw him down, and tare *him*.
And Jesus rebuked the unclean spirit,
and healed the child, and delivered him
again to his father.
43 ¶ And they were all amazed at the
mighty power of God. But while they
wondered every one at all things which
Jesus did, he said unto his disciples,
44 Let these sayings sink down into
your ears: for the Son of man shall be
delivered into the hands of men.
45 But they understood not this saying,
and it was hid from them, that they perceived it not: and they feared to ask him
of that saying.
46 ¶ Then there arose a reasoning
among them, which of them should be
greatest.
47 And Jesus, perceiving the thought
of their heart, took a child, and set him
by him,
48 And said unto them, Whosoever
shall receive this child in my name receiveth me; and whosoever shall receive me, receiveth him that sent me:
for he that is least among you all, the
same shall be great.
49 ¶ And John answered and said,
Master, we saw one casting out devils
in thy name; and we forbade him, because he followeth not with us.
50 And Jesus said unto him, Forbid
him not: for he that is not against us is
for us.
51 ¶ And it came to pass, when the
time was come that he should be received up, he steadfastly set his face to
go to Jerusalem,
52 And sent messengers before his
face: and they went, and entered into a
village of the Să-măr'ĭ-tănș, to make
ready for him.
53 And they did not receive him, because his face was as though he would
go to Jerusalem.
54 And when his disciples James and
John saw *this*, they said, Lord, wilt
thou that we command fire to come

down from heaven, and consume them,
even as Ē-lī'ăs did?
55 But he turned, and rebuked them,
and said, Ye know not what manner of
spirit ye are of.
56 For the Son of man is not come to
destroy men's lives, but to save *them*.
And they went to another village.
57 ℂ And it came to pass, that, as
they went in the way, a certain *man* said
unto him, Lord, I will follow thee
whithersoever thou goest.
58 And Jesus said unto him, Foxes
have holes, and birds of the air *have*
nests; but the Son of man hath not
where to lay *his* head.
59 And he said unto another, Follow
me. But he said, Lord, suffer me first
to go and bury my father.
60 Jesus said unto him, Let the dead
bury their dead: but go thou and preach
the kingdom of God.
61 And another also said, Lord, I will
follow thee; but let me first go bid them
farewell, which are at home at my
house.
62 And Jesus said unto him, No man,
having put his hand to the plow, and
looking back, is fit for the kingdom of
God.

CHAPTER 10

AFTER these things the Lord appointed other seventy also, and
sent them two and two before his face
into every city and place, whither he
himself would come.
2 Therefore said he unto them, The
harvest truly *is* great, but the laborers
are few: pray ye therefore the Lord of
the harvest, that he would send forth
laborers into his harvest.
3 Go your ways: behold, I send you
forth as lambs among wolves.
4 Carry neither purse, nor scrip, nor
shoes: and salute no man by the way.
5 And into whatsoever house ye enter,
first say, Peace *be* to this house.
6 And if the son of peace be there, your
peace shall rest upon it: if not, it shall
turn to you again.
7 And in the same house remain, eating and drinking such things as they
give: for the laborer is worthy of his
hire. Go not from house to house.
8 And into whatsoever city ye enter,
and they receive you, eat such things
as are set before you:
9 And heal the sick that are therein,
and say unto them, The kingdom of God
is come nigh unto you.
10 But into whatsoever city ye enter,
and they receive you not, go your ways
out into the streets of the same, and
say,
11 Even the very dust of your city,
which cleaveth on us, we do wipe off
against you: notwithstanding, be ye
sure of this, that the kingdom of God is
come nigh unto you.
12 But I say unto you, that it shall be
more tolerable in that day for Sŏd'ŏm,
than for that city.
13 Woe unto thee, Chō-rā'zĭn! woe
unto thee, Běth'sā'ĭ-dȧ! for if the mighty
works had been done in Tȳre and Sī'-
dŏn, which have been done in you, they
had a great while ago repented, sitting
in sackcloth and ashes.
14 But it shall be more tolerable for
Tȳre and Sī'dŏn at the judgment, than
for you.
15 And thou, Cȧ-pĕr'nā-ŭm, which art
exalted to heaven, shalt be thrust down
to hell.
16 He that heareth you heareth me;
and he that despiseth you despiseth me;
and he that despiseth me despiseth him
that sent me.
17 ℂ And the seventy returned again
with joy, saying, Lord, even the devils
are subject unto us through thy name.
18 And he said unto them, I beheld
Satan as lightning fall from heaven.
19 Behold, I give unto you power to
tread on serpents and scorpions, and
over all the power of the enemy; and
nothing shall by any means hurt you.
20 Notwithstanding, in this rejoice not,
that the spirits are subject unto you;
but rather rejoice, because your names
are written in heaven.
21 ℂ In that hour Jesus rejoiced in
spirit, and said, I thank thee, O Father,
Lord of heaven and earth, that thou
hast hid these things from the wise and
prudent, and hast revealed them unto
babes: even so, Father; for so it seemed
good in thy sight.
22 All things are delivered to me of my
Father: and no man knoweth who the
Son is, but the Father; and who the
Father is, but the Son, and *he* to whom
the Son will reveal *him*.
23 ℂ And he turned him unto *his* disciples, and said privately, Blessed *are*

the eyes which see the things that ye
see:
24 For I tell you, that many prophets
and kings have desired to see those
things which ye see, and have not seen
them; and to hear those things which ye
hear, and have not heard *them.*
25 ℂ And, behold, a certain lawyer
stood up, and tempted him, saying,
Master, what shall I do to inherit eternal
life?
26 He said unto him, What is written
in the law? how readest thou?
27 And he answering said, Thou shalt
love the Lord thy God with all thy heart,
and with all thy soul, and with all thy
strength, and with all thy mind; and
thy neighbor as thyself.
28 And he said unto him, Thou hast
answered right: this do, and thou shalt
live.
29 But he, willing to justify himself,
said unto Jesus, And who is my neighbor?
30 And Jesus answering said, A certain *man* went down from Jerusalem to
Jĕr'ĭ-chō, and fell among thieves, which
stripped him of his raiment, and
wounded *him,* and departed, leaving
him half dead.
31 And by chance there came down a
certain priest that way; and when he
saw him, he passed by on the other side.
32 And likewise a Lē'vīte, when he
was at the place, came and looked *on
him,* and passed by on the other side.
33 But a certain Să-măr'ĭ-tăn, as he
journeyed, came where he was; and
when he saw him, he had compassion
on him,
34 And went to *him,* and bound up his
wounds, pouring in oil and wine, and
set him on his own beast, and brought
him to an inn, and took care of him.
35 And on the morrow when he departed, he took out two pence, and gave
them to the host, and said unto him,
Take care of him: and whatsoever thou
spendest more, when I come again, I
will repay thee.
36 Which now of these three, thinkest
thou, was neighbor unto him that fell
among the thieves?
37 And he said, He that showed mercy
on him. Then said Jesus unto him, Go,
and do thou likewise.
38 ℂ Now it came to pass, as they
went, that he entered into a certain
village: and a certain woman named
Martha received him into her house.
39 And she had a sister called Mary,
which also sat at Jesus' feet, and heard
his word.
40 But Martha was cumbered about
much serving, and came to him, and
said, Lord, dost thou not care that my
sister hath left me to serve alone? bid
her therefore that she help me.
41 And Jesus answered and said unto
her, Martha, Martha, thou art careful
and troubled about many things:
42 But one thing is needful; and Mary
hath chosen that good part, which shall
not be taken away from her.

CHAPTER 11

AND it came to pass, that, as he was
praying in a certain place, when he
ceased, one of his disciples said unto
him, Lord, teach us to pray, as John
also taught his disciples.
2 And he said unto them, When ye
pray, say, Our Father which art in
heaven, Hallowed be thy name. Thy
kingdom come. Thy will be done, as in
heaven, so in earth.
3 Give us day by day our daily bread.
4 And forgive us our sins; for we also
forgive every one that is indebted to us.
And lead us not into temptation; but
deliver us from evil.
5 And he said unto them, Which of
you shall have a friend, and shall go
unto him at midnight, and say unto him,
Friend, lend me three loaves;
6 For a friend of mine in his journey is
come to me, and I have nothing to set
before him?
7 And he from within shall answer and
say, Trouble me not: the door is now
shut, and my children are with me in
bed; I cannot rise and give thee.
8 I say unto you, Though he will not
rise and give him, because he is his
friend, yet because of his importunity
he will rise and give him as many as he
needeth.
9 And I say unto you, Ask, and it
shall be given you; seek, and ye shall
find; knock, and it shall be opened unto
you.
10 For every one that asketh receiveth;
and he that seeketh findeth; and to him
that knocketh it shall be opened.
11 If a son shall ask bread of any of
you that is a father, will he give him a

stone? or if *he ask* a fish, will he for a
fish give him a serpent?
12 Or if he shall ask an egg, will he
offer him a scorpion?
13 If ye then, being evil, know how to
give good gifts unto your children; how
much more shall *your* heavenly Father
give the Holy Spirit to them that ask
him?
14 ℂ And he was casting out a devil,
and it was dumb. And it came to pass,
when the devil was gone out, the dumb
spake; and the people wondered.
15 But some of them said, He casteth
out devils through Bē-ĕl′zē-bŭb the
chief of the devils.
16 And others, tempting *him*, sought
of him a sign from heaven.
17 But he, knowing their thoughts,
said unto them, Every kingdom divided
against itself is brought to desolation;
and a house *divided* against a house
falleth.
18 If Satan also be divided against
himself, how shall his kingdom stand?
because ye say that I cast out devils
through Bē-ĕl′zē-bŭb.
19 And if I by Bē-ĕl′zē-bŭb cast out
devils, by whom do your sons cast *them*
out? therefore shall they be your judges.
20 But if I with the finger of God cast
out devils, no doubt the kingdom of God
is come upon you.
21 When a strong man armed keepeth
his palace, his goods are in peace:
22 But when a stronger than he shall
come upon him, and overcome him, he
taketh from him all his armor wherein
he trusted, and divideth his spoils.
23 He that is not with me is against me;
and he that gathereth not with me
scattereth.
24 When the unclean spirit is gone out
of a man, he walketh through dry places,
seeking rest; and finding none, he saith,
I will return unto my house whence I
came out.
25 And when he cometh, he findeth *it*
swept and garnished.
26 Then goeth he, and taketh *to him*
seven other spirits more wicked than
himself; and they enter in, and dwell
there: and the last *state* of that man is
worse than the first.
27 ℂ And it came to pass, as he spake
these things, a certain woman of the
company lifted up her voice, and said
unto him, Blessed *is* the womb that
bare thee, and the paps which thou hast
sucked.
28 But he said, Yea, rather, blessed
are they that hear the word of God, and
keep it.
29 ℂ And when the people were gathered thick together, he began to say,
This is an evil generation: they seek a
sign; and there shall no sign be given
it, but the sign of Jō′nȧs the prophet.
30 For as Jō′nȧs was a sign unto the
Nĭn′ē-vītes, so shall also the Son of man
be to this generation.
31 The queen of the south shall rise
up in the judgment with the men of this
generation, and condemn them: for she
came from the utmost parts of the earth
to hear the wisdom of Solomon; and,
behold, a greater than Solomon *is* here.
32 The men of Nĭn′ē-vĕh shall rise up
in the judgment with this generation,
and shall condemn it: for they repented
at the preaching of Jō′nȧs; and, behold,
a greater than Jō′nȧs *is* here.
33 No man, when he hath lighted a
candle, putteth *it* in a secret place,
neither under a bushel, but on a candlestick, that they which come in may see
the light.
34 The light of the body is the eye:
therefore when thine eye is single, thy
whole body also is full of light; but when
thine eye is evil, thy body also *is* full of
darkness.
35 Take heed therefore, that the light
which is in thee be not darkness.
36 If thy whole body therefore *be* full
of light, having no part dark, the whole
shall be full of light, as when the bright
shining of a candle doth give thee light.
37 ℂ And as he spake, a certain Phăr′-
ĭ-sēe besought him to dine with him:
and he went in, and sat down to meat.
38 And when the Phăr′ĭ-sēe saw *it*, he
marveled that he had not first washed
before dinner.
39 And the Lord said unto him, Now
do ye Phăr′ĭ-sēeş make clean the outside of the cup and the platter; but your
inward part is full of ravening and
wickedness.
40 *Ye* fools, did not he, that made that
which is without, make that which is
within also?
41 But rather give alms of such things
as ye have; and, behold, all things are
clean unto you.
42 But woe unto you, Phăr′ĭ-sēeş! for

ye tithe mint and rue and all manner
of herbs, and pass over judgment and
the love of God: these ought ye to
have done, and not to leave the other
undone.
43 Woe unto you, Phăr′ĭ-sēeṣ! for ye
love the uppermost seats in the synagogues, and greetings in the markets.
44 Woe unto you, scribes and Phăr′ĭ-
sēeṣ, hypocrites! for ye are as graves
which appear not, and the men that
walk over *them* are not aware *of them*.
45 ¶ Then answered one of the lawyers, and said unto him, Master, thus
saying thou reproachest us also.
46 And he said, Woe unto you also, *ye*
lawyers! for ye lade men with burdens
grievous to be borne, and ye yourselves
touch not the burdens with one of your
fingers.
47 Woe unto you! for ye build the
sepulchres of the prophets, and your
fathers killed them.
48 Truly ye bear witness that ye allow
the deeds of your fathers: for they indeed killed them, and ye build their
sepulchres.
49 Therefore also said the wisdom of
God, I will send them prophets and
apostles, and *some* of them they shall
slay and persecute:
50 That the blood of all the prophets,
which was shed from the foundation of
the world, may be required of this
generation;
51 From the blood of Abel unto the
blood of Zăch′ȧ-rī′ȧs, which perished
between the altar and the temple: verily
I say unto you, It shall be required of
this generation.
52 Woe unto you, lawyers! for ye have
taken away the key of knowledge: ye
entered not in yourselves, and them
that were entering in ye hindered.
53 And as he said these things unto
them, the scribes and the Phăr′ĭ-sēeṣ
began to urge *him* vehemently, and to
provoke him to speak of many things:
54 Laying wait for him, and seeking to
catch something out of his mouth, that
they might accuse him.

CHAPTER 12

IN the mean time, when there were
gathered together an innumerable
multitude of people, insomuch that
they trode one upon another, he began
to say unto his disciples first of all, Beware ye of the leaven of the Phăr′ĭ-sēeṣ,
which is hypocrisy.
2 For there is nothing covered, that
shall not be revealed; neither hid, that
shall not be known.
3 Therefore, whatsoever ye have
spoken in darkness shall be heard in
the light; and that which ye have spoken
in the ear in closets shall be proclaimed
upon the housetops.
4 And I say unto you my friends,
Be not afraid of them that kill the body,
and after that have no more that they
can do.
5 But I will forewarn you whom ye
shall fear: Fear him, which after he hath
killed hath power to cast into hell; yea,
I say unto you, Fear him.
6 Are not five sparrows sold for two
farthings, and not one of them is forgotten before God?
7 But even the very hairs of your head
are all numbered. Fear not therefore:
ye are of more value than many sparrows.
8 Also I say unto you, Whosoever shall
confess me before men, him shall the
Son of man also confess before the
angels of God:
9 But he that denieth me before men
shall be denied before the angels of
God.
10 And whosoever shall speak a word
against the Son of man, it shall be
forgiven him: but unto him that blasphemeth against the Holy Ghost it shall
not be forgiven.
11 And when they bring you unto the
synagogues, and *unto* magistrates, and
powers, take ye no thought how or what
thing ye shall answer, or what ye shall
say:
12 For the Holy Ghost shall teach you
in the same hour what ye ought to
say.
13 ¶ And one of the company said
unto him, Master, speak to my brother,
that he divide the inheritance with me.
14 And he said unto him, Man, who
made me a judge or a divider over you?
15 And he said unto them, Take heed,
and beware of covetousness: for a man's
life consisteth not in the abundance of
the things which he possesseth.
16 And he spake a parable unto them,
saying, The ground of a certain rich
man brought forth plentifully:
17 And he thought within himself,

saying, What shall I do, because I have
no room where to bestow my fruits?
18 And he said, This will I do: I will
pull down my barns, and build greater;
and there will I bestow all my fruits and
my goods.
19 And I will say to my soul, Soul, thou
hast much goods laid up for many years;
take thine ease, eat, drink, *and* be
merry.
20 But God said unto him, *Thou* fool,
this night thy soul shall be required of
thee: then whose shall those things be,
which thou hast provided?
21 So *is* he that layeth up treasure for
himself, and is not rich toward God.
22 ¶ And he said unto his disciples,
Therefore I say unto you, Take no
thought for your life, what ye shall eat;
neither for the body, what ye shall put
on.
23 The life is more than meat, and the
body *is more* than raiment.
24 Consider the ravens: for they
neither sow nor reap; which neither
have storehouse nor barn; and God
feedeth them: how much more are ye
better than the fowls?
25 And which of you with taking
thought can add to his stature one
cubit?
26 If ye then be not able to do that
thing which is least, why take ye
thought for the rest?
27 Consider the lilies how they grow:
they toil not, they spin not; and yet I
say unto you, that Solomon in all his
glory was not arrayed like one of these.
28 If then God so clothe the grass,
which is to-day in the field, and to-
morrow is cast into the oven; how much
more *will he clothe* you, O ye of little
faith?
29 And seek not ye what ye shall eat,
or what ye shall drink, neither be ye of
doubtful mind.
30 For all these things do the nations
of the world seek after: and your
Father knoweth that ye have need of
these things.
31 ¶ But rather seek ye the kingdom
of God; and all these things shall be
added unto you.
32 Fear not, little flock; for it is your
Father's good pleasure to give you the
kingdom.
33 Sell that ye have, and give alms;
provide yourselves bags which wax not
old, a treasure in the heavens that
faileth not, where no thief approacheth,
neither moth corrupteth.
34 For where your treasure is, there
will your heart be also.
35 Let your loins be girded about, and
your lights burning;
36 And ye yourselves like unto men
that wait for their lord, when he will
return from the wedding; that, when he
cometh and knocketh, they may open
unto him immediately.
37 Blessed *are* those servants, whom
the lord when he cometh shall find
watching: verily I say unto you, that he
shall gird himself, and make them to
sit down to meat, and will come forth
and serve them.
38 And if he shall come in the second
watch, or come in the third watch, and
find *them* so, blessed are those servants.
39 And this know, that if the goodman
of the house had known what hour the
thief would come, he would have
watched, and not have suffered his
house to be broken through.
40 Be ye therefore ready also: for the
Son of man cometh at an hour when ye
think not.
41 ¶ Then Peter said unto him, Lord,
speakest thou this parable unto us, or
even to all?
42 And the Lord said, Who then is
that faithful and wise steward, whom
his lord shall make ruler over his household, to give *them their* portion of meat
in due season?
43 Blessed *is* that servant, whom his
lord when he cometh shall find so doing.
44 Of a truth I say unto you, that he
will make him ruler over all that he hath.
45 But and if that servant say in his
heart, My lord delayeth his coming;
and shall begin to beat the menservants and maidens, and to eat and drink,
and to be drunken;
46 The lord of that servant will come
in a day when he looketh not for *him*,
and at an hour when he is not aware, and
will cut him in sunder, and will appoint
him his portion with the unbelievers.
47 And that servant, which knew his
lord's will, and prepared not *himself*,
neither did according to his will, shall
be beaten with many *stripes*.
48 But he that knew not, and did commit things worthy of stripes, shall be
beaten with few *stripes*. For unto

whomsoever much is given, of him shall
be much required; and to whom men
have committed much, of him they will
ask the more.
49 ℭ I am come to send fire on the
earth; and what will I, if it be already
kindled?
50 But I have a baptism to be baptized
with; and how am I straitened till it be
accomplished!
51 Suppose ye that I am come to give
peace on earth? I tell you, Nay; but
rather division:
52 For from henceforth there shall be
five in one house divided, three against
two, and two against three.
53 The father shall be divided against
the son, and the son against the father;
the mother against the daughter, and
the daughter against the mother; the
mother-in-law against her daughter-in-law, and the daughter-in-law against
her mother-in-law.
54 ℭ And he said also to the people,
When ye see a cloud rise out of the
west, straightway ye say, There cometh
a shower; and so it is.
55 And when *ye see* the south wind
blow, ye say, There will be heat; and it
cometh to pass.
56 *Ye* hypocrites, ye can discern the
face of the sky and of the earth; but
how is it that ye do not discern this
time?
57 Yea, and why even of yourselves
judge ye not what is right?
58 ℭ When thou goest with thine
adversary to the magistrate, *as thou art*
in the way, give diligence that thou
mayest be delivered from him; lest he
hale thee to the judge, and the judge
deliver thee to the officer, and the
officer cast thee into prison.
59 I tell thee, thou shalt not depart
thence, till thou hast paid the very last
mite.

CHAPTER 13

THERE were present at that season
some that told him of the Galileans,
whose blood Pilate had mingled with
their sacrifices.
2 And Jesus answering said unto them,
Suppose ye that these Galileans were
sinners above all the Galileans, because
they suffered such things?
3 I tell you, Nay: but, except ye repent,
ye shall all likewise perish.
4 Or those eighteen, upon whom the
tower in Sĭ-lō'ăm fell, and slew them,
think ye that they were sinners above
all men that dwelt in Jerusalem?
5 I tell you, Nay: but, except ye
repent, ye shall all likewise perish.
6 ℭ He spake also this parable; A certain *man* had a fig tree planted in his
vineyard; and he came and sought fruit
thereon, and found none.
7 Then said he unto the dresser of his
vineyard, Behold, these three years I
come seeking fruit on this fig tree, and
find none: cut it down; why cumbereth
it the ground?
8 And he answering said unto him,
Lord, let it alone this year also, till I
shall dig about it, and dung *it:*
9 And if it bear fruit, *well:* and if not,
then after that thou shalt cut it down.
10 And he was teaching in one of the
synagogues on the sabbath.
11 ℭ And, behold, there was a woman
which had a spirit of infirmity eighteen
years, and was bowed together, and
could in no wise lift up *herself.*
12 And when Jesus saw her, he called
her to him, and said unto her, Woman,
thou art loosed from thine infirmity.
13 And he laid *his* hands on her: and
immediately she was made straight,
and glorified God.
14 And the ruler of the synagogue
answered with indignation, because that
Jesus had healed on the sabbath day,
and said unto the people, There are six
days in which men ought to work: in
them therefore come and be healed, and
not on the sabbath day.
15 The Lord then answered him, and
said, *Thou* hypocrite, doth not each one
of you on the sabbath loose his ox or *his*
ass from the stall, and lead *him* away to
watering?
16 And ought not this woman, being a
daughter of Abraham, whom Satan hath
bound, lo, these eighteen years, be
loosed from this bond on the sabbath
day?
17 And when he had said these things,
all his adversaries were ashamed: and
all the people rejoiced for all the glorious
things that were done by him.
18 ℭ Then said he, Unto what is the
kingdom of God like? and whereunto
shall I resemble it?
19 It is like a grain of mustard seed,
which a man took, and cast into his

garden; and it grew, and waxed a great
tree; and the fowls of the air lodged in
the branches of it.
20 And again he said, Whereunto shall
I liken the kingdom of God?
21 It is like leaven, which a woman
took and hid in three measures of meal,
till the whole was leavened.
22 And he went through the cities and
villages, teaching, and journeying toward Jerusalem.
23 Then said one unto him, Lord, are
there few that be saved? And he said
unto them,
24 ℂ Strive to enter in at the strait
gate: for many, I say unto you, will seek
to enter in, and shall not be able.
25 When once the master of the house
is risen up, and hath shut to the door,
and ye begin to stand without, and to
knock at the door, saying, Lord, Lord,
open unto us; and he shall answer and
say unto you, I know you not whence
ye are:
26 Then shall ye begin to say, We have
eaten and drunk in thy presence, and
thou hast taught in our streets.
27 But he shall say, I tell you, I know
you not whence ye are; depart from me,
all *ye* workers of iniquity.
28 There shall be weeping and gnashing of teeth, when ye shall see Abraham,
and Isaac, and Jacob, and all the prophets, in the kingdom of God, and you
yourselves thrust out.
29 And they shall come from the east,
and *from* the west, and from the north,
and *from* the south, and shall sit down
in the kingdom of God.
30 And, behold, there are last which
shall be first; and there are first which
shall be last.
31 ℂ The same day there came certain
of the Phăr′ĭ-sēes, saying unto him,
Get thee out, and depart hence; for
Hĕr′ŏd will kill thee.
32 And he said unto them, Go ye, and
tell that fox, Behold, I cast out devils,
and I do cures to-day and to-morrow,
and the third *day* I shall be perfected.
33 Nevertheless I must walk to-day,
and to-morrow, and the *day* following:
for it cannot be that a prophet perish
out of Jerusalem.
34 O Jerusalem, Jerusalem, which
killest the prophets, and stonest them
that are sent unto thee; how often would
I have gathered thy children together,
as a hen *doth gather* her brood under
her wings, and ye would not!
35 Behold, your house is left unto you
desolate: and verily I say unto you, Ye
shall not see me, until *the time* come
when ye shall say, Blessed *is* he that
cometh in the name of the Lord.

CHAPTER 14

AND it came to pass, as he went into
the house of one of the chief
Phăr′ĭ-sēes to eat bread on the sabbath
day, that they watched him.
2 And, behold, there was a certain man
before him which had the dropsy.
3 And Jesus answering spake unto the
lawyers and Phăr′ĭ-sēes, saying, Is it
lawful to heal on the sabbath day?
4 And they held their peace. And he
took *him*, and healed him, and let him
go;
5 And answered them, saying, Which
of you shall have an ass or an ox fallen
into a pit, and will not straightway pull
him out on the sabbath day?
6 And they could not answer him again
to these things.
7 ℂ And he put forth a parable to
those which were bidden, when he
marked how they chose out the chief
rooms; saying unto them,
8 When thou art bidden of any *man* to
a wedding, sit not down in the highest
room; lest a more honorable man than
thou be bidden of him;
9 And he that bade thee and him come
and say to thee, Give this man place;
and thou begin with shame to take the
lowest room.
10 But when thou art bidden, go and
sit down in the lowest room; that when
he that bade thee cometh, he may say
unto thee, Friend, go up higher: then
shalt thou have worship in the presence
of them that sit at meat with thee.
11 For whosoever exalteth himself
shall be abased; and he that humbleth
himself shall be exalted.
12 ℂ Then said he also to him that
bade him, When thou makest a dinner
or a supper, call not thy friends, nor
thy brethren, neither thy kinsmen, nor
thy rich neighbors; lest they also bid
thee again, and a recompense be made
thee.
13 But when thou makest a feast, call
the poor, the maimed, the lame, the
blind:

14 And thou shalt be blessed; for they
cannot recompense thee: for thou shalt
be recompensed at the resurrection of
the just.
15 ¶ And when one of them that sat
at meat with him heard these things, he
said unto him, Blessed *is* he that shall
eat bread in the kingdom of God.
16 Then said he unto him, A certain
man made a great supper, and bade
many:
17 And sent his servant at supper time
to say to them that were bidden, Come;
for all things are now ready.
18 And they all with one *consent* began
to make excuse. The first said unto him,
I have bought a piece of ground, and I
must needs go and see it: I pray thee
have me excused.
19 And another said, I have bought
five yoke of oxen, and I go to prove
them: I pray thee have me excused.
20 And another said, I have married a
wife, and therefore I cannot come.
21 So that servant came, and showed
his lord these things. Then the master
of the house being angry said to his
servant, Go out quickly into the streets
and lanes of the city, and bring in hither
the poor, and the maimed, and the halt,
and the blind.
22 And the servant said, Lord, it is
done as thou hast commanded, and yet
there is room.
23 And the lord said unto the servant,
Go out into the highways and hedges,
and compel *them* to come in, that my
house may be filled.
24 For I say unto you, That none of
those men which were bidden shall
taste of my supper.
25 ¶ And there went great multitudes
with him: and he turned, and said unto
them,
26 If any *man* come to me, and hate not
his father, and mother, and wife, and
children, and brethren, and sisters, yea,
and his own life also, he cannot be my
disciple.
27 And whosoever doth not bear his
cross, and come after me, cannot be my
disciple.
28 For which of you, intending to build
a tower, sitteth not down first, and
counteth the cost, whether he have
sufficient to finish *it?*
29 Lest haply, after he hath laid the
foundation, and is not able to finish
it, all that behold *it* begin to mock
him,
30 Saying, This man began to build,
and was not able to finish.
31 Or what king, going to make war
against another king, sitteth not down
first, and consulteth whether he be able
with ten thousand to meet him that
cometh against him with twenty thousand?
32 Or else, while the other is yet a
great way off, he sendeth an ambassage,
and desireth conditions of peace.
33 So likewise, whosoever he be of you
that forsaketh not all that he hath, he
cannot be my disciple.
34 ¶ Salt *is* good: but if the salt have
lost his savor, wherewith shall it be
seasoned?
35 It is neither fit for the land, nor yet
for the dunghill; *but* men cast it out.
He that hath ears to hear, let him hear.

CHAPTER 15

THEN drew near unto him all the
publicans and sinners for to hear
him.
2 And the Phăr'ĭ-sēeş and scribes murmured, saying, This man receiveth sinners, and eateth with them.
3 ¶ And he spake this parable unto
them, saying,
4 What man of you, having a hundred
sheep, if he lose one of them, doth not
leave the ninety and nine in the wilderness, and go after that which is lost,
until he find it?
5 And when he hath found *it,* he layeth
it on his shoulders, rejoicing.
6 And when he cometh home, he calleth
together *his* friends and neighbors, saying unto them, Rejoice with me; for I
have found my sheep which was lost.
7 I say unto you, that likewise joy shall
be in heaven over one sinner that repenteth, more than over ninety and nine
just persons, which need no repentance.
8 ¶ Either what woman having ten
pieces of silver, if she lose one piece,
doth not light a candle, and sweep the
house, and seek diligently till she find *it?*
9 And when she hath found *it,* she
calleth *her* friends and *her* neighbors
together, saying, Rejoice with me; for
I have found the piece which I had lost.
10 Likewise, I say unto you, there is
joy in the presence of the angels of God
over one sinner that repenteth.

11 ℂ And he said, A certain man had
two sons:
12 And the younger of them said to *his*
father, Father, give me the portion of
goods that falleth *to me*. And he divided
unto them *his* living.
13 And not many days after the
younger son gathered all together, and
took his journey into a far country, and
there wasted his substance with riotous
living.
14 And when he had spent all, there
arose a mighty famine in that land; and
he began to be in want.
15 And he went and joined himself to
a citizen of that country; and he sent
him into his fields to feed swine.
16 And he would fain have filled his
belly with the husks that the swine did
eat: and no man gave unto him.
17 And when he came to himself, he
said, How many hired servants of my
father's have bread enough and to
spare, and I perish with hunger!
18 I will arise and go to my father, and
will say unto him, Father, I have sinned
against heaven, and before thee,
19 And am no more worthy to be called
thy son: make me as one of thy hired
servants.
20 And he arose, and came to his
father. But when he was yet a great
way off, his father saw him, and had
compassion, and ran, and fell on his
neck, and kissed him.
21 And the son said unto him, Father,
I have sinned against heaven, and in
thy sight, and am no more worthy to be
called thy son.
22 But the father said to his servants,
Bring forth the best robe, and put *it* on
him; and put a ring on his hand, and
shoes on *his* feet:
23 And bring hither the fatted calf, and
kill *it;* and let us eat, and be merry:
24 For this my son was dead, and is
alive again; he was lost, and is found.
And they began to be merry.
25 Now his elder son was in the field:
and as he came and drew nigh to the
house, he heard music and dancing.
26 And he called one of the servants,
and asked what these things meant.
27 And he said unto him, Thy brother
is come; and thy father hath killed the
fatted calf, because he hath received
him safe and sound.
28 And he was angry, and would not
go in: therefore came his father out,
and entreated him.
29 And he answering said to *his* father,
Lo, these many years do I serve thee,
neither transgressed I at any time thy
commandment; and yet thou never
gavest me a kid, that I might make
merry with my friends:
30 But as soon as this thy son was
come, which hath devoured thy living
with harlots, thou hast killed for him the
fatted calf.
31 And he said unto him, Son, thou
art ever with me, and all that I have is
thine.
32 It was meet that we should make
merry, and be glad: for this thy brother
was dead, and is alive again; and was
lost, and is found.

CHAPTER 16

AND he said also unto his disciples,
There was a certain rich man,
which had a steward; and the same
was accused unto him that he had
wasted his goods.
2 And he called him, and said unto
him, How is it that I hear this of thee?
give an account of thy stewardship; for
thou mayest be no longer steward.
3 Then the steward said within himself, What shall I do? for my lord taketh
away from me the stewardship: I cannot dig; to beg I am ashamed.
4 I am resolved what to do, that, when
I am put out of the stewardship, they
may receive me into their houses.
5 So he called every one of his lord's
debtors *unto him,* and said unto the
first, How much owest thou unto my
lord?
6 And he said, A hundred measures of
oil. And he said unto him, Take thy
bill, and sit down quickly, and write
fifty.
7 Then said he to another, And how
much owest thou? And he said, A hundred measures of wheat. And he said
unto him, Take thy bill, and write fourscore.
8 And the lord commended the unjust
steward, because he had done wisely:
for the children of this world are in their
generation wiser than the children of
light.
9 And I say unto you, Make to yourselves friends of the mammon of unrighteousness; that, when ye fail, they

may receive you into everlasting habitations.
10 He that is faithful in that which is
least is faithful also in much: and he
that is unjust in the least is unjust also
in much.
11 If therefore ye have not been faithful
in the unrighteous mammon, who will
commit to your trust the true *riches?*
12 And if ye have not been faithful in
that which is another man's, who shall
give you that which is your own?
13 ¶ No servant can serve two masters: for either he will hate the one, and
love the other; or else he will hold to
the one, and despise the other. Ye cannot serve God and mammon.
14 And the Phăr′ĭ-sēeş also, who were
covetous, heard all these things: and
they derided him.
15 And he said unto them, Ye are they
which justify yourselves before men;
but God knoweth your hearts: for that
which is highly esteemed among men is
abomination in the sight of God.
16 The law and the prophets *were* until
John: since that time the kingdom of
God is preached, and every man presseth into it.
17 And it is easier for heaven and earth
to pass, than one tittle of the law to
fail.
18 Whosoever putteth away his wife,
and marrieth another, committeth adultery: and whosoever marrieth her that
is put away from *her* husband committeth adultery.
19 ¶ There was a certain rich man,
which was clothed in purple and fine
linen, and fared sumptuously every
day:
20 And there was a certain beggar
named Lazarus, which was laid at his
gate, full of sores,
21 And desiring to be fed with the
crumbs which fell from the rich man's
table: moreover the dogs came and
licked his sores.
22 And it came to pass, that the beggar
died, and was carried by the angels into
Abraham's bosom: the rich man also
died, and was buried;
23 And in hell he lifted up his eyes,
being in torments, and seeth Abraham
afar off, and Lazarus in his bosom.
24 And he cried and said, Father
Abraham, have mercy on me, and send
Lazarus, that he may dip the tip of his
finger in water, and cool my tongue; for
I am tormented in this flame.
25 But Abraham said, Son, remember
that thou in thy lifetime receivedst thy
good things, and likewise Lazarus evil
things: but now he is comforted, and
thou art tormented.
26 And beside all this, between us and
you there is a great gulf fixed: so that
they which would pass from hence to
you cannot; neither can they pass to us,
that *would come* from thence.
27 Then he said, I pray thee therefore,
father, that thou wouldest send him to
my father's house:
28 For I have five brethren; that he
may testify unto them, lest they also
come into this place of torment.
29 Abraham saith unto him, They have
Moses and the prophets; let them hear
them.
30 And he said, Nay, father Abraham:
but if one went unto them from the
dead, they will repent.
31 And he said unto him, If they hear
not Moses and the prophets, neither
will they be persuaded, though one rose
from the dead.

CHAPTER 17

THEN said he unto the disciples,
It is impossible but that offenses
will come: but woe *unto him,* through
whom they come!
2 It were better for him that a millstone
were hanged about his neck, and he
cast into the sea, than that he should
offend one of these little ones.
3 ¶ Take heed to yourselves: If thy
brother trespass against thee, rebuke
him; and if he repent, forgive him.
4 And if he trespass against thee seven
times in a day, and seven times in a day
turn again to thee, saying, I repent;
thou shalt forgive him.
5 And the apostles said unto the Lord,
Increase our faith.
6 And the Lord said, If ye had faith as
a grain of mustard seed, ye might say
unto this sycamine tree, Be thou
plucked up by the root, and be thou
planted in the sea; and it should obey
you.
7 But which of you, having a servant
plowing or feeding cattle, will say unto
him by and by, when he is come from
the field, Go and sit down to meat?
8 And will not rather say unto him,

Make ready wherewith I may sup, and
gird thyself, and serve me, till I have
eaten and drunken; and afterward thou
shalt eat and drink?
9 Doth he thank that servant because
he did the things that were commanded
him? I trow not.
10 So likewise ye, when ye shall have
done all those things which are commanded you, say, We are unprofitable
servants: we have done that which was
our duty to do.
11 ¶ And it came to pass, as he went
to Jerusalem, that he passed through
the midst of Sȧ-mā'rĭ-ȧ and Galilee.
12 And as he entered into a certain
village, there met him ten men that
were lepers, which stood afar off:
13 And they lifted up *their* voices, and
said, Jesus, Master, have mercy on
us.
14 And when he saw *them,* he said
unto them, Go show yourselves unto
the priests. And it came to pass, that,
as they went, they were cleansed.
15 And one of them, when he saw that
he was healed, turned back, and with a
loud voice glorified God,
16 And fell down on *his* face at his
feet, giving him thanks: and he was a
Sȧ-măr'ĭ-tăn.
17 And Jesus answering said, Were
there not ten cleansed? but where *are*
the nine?
18 There are not found that returned
to give glory to God, save this stranger.
19 And he said unto him, Arise, go thy
way: thy faith hath made thee whole.
20 ¶ And when he was demanded of
the Phăr'ĭ-sēeş, when the kingdom of
God should come, he answered them
and said, The kingdom of God cometh
not with observation:
21 Neither shall they say, Lo here! or,
lo there! for, behold, the kingdom of
God is within you.
22 And he said unto the disciples, The
days will come, when ye shall desire to
see one of the days of the Son of man,
and ye shall not see *it*.
23 And they shall say to you, See here;
or, see there: go not after *them,* nor
follow *them*.
24 For as the lightning, that lighteneth
out of the one *part* under heaven,
shineth unto the other *part* under
heaven; so shall also the Son of man be
in his day.
25 But first must he suffer many things,
and be rejected of this generation.
26 And as it was in the days of Nō'ē,
so shall it be also in the days of the Son
of man.
27 They did eat, they drank, they married wives, they were given in marriage,
until the day that Nō'ē entered into the
ark, and the flood came, and destroyed
them all.
28 Likewise also as it was in the days
of Lot; they did eat, they drank, they
bought, they sold, they planted, they
builded;
29 But the same day that Lot went out
of Sŏd'ȯm it rained fire and brimstone
from heaven, and destroyed *them* all.
30 Even thus shall it be in the day when
the Son of man is revealed.
31 In that day, he which shall be upon
the housetop, and his stuff in the house,
let him not come down to take it away:
and he that is in the field, let him likewise not return back.
32 Remember Lot's wife.
33 Whosoever shall seek to save his
life shall lose it; and whosoever shall
lose his life shall preserve it.
34 I tell you, in that night there shall
be two *men* in one bed; the one shall be
taken, and the other shall be left.
35 Two *women* shall be grinding together; the one shall be taken, and the
other left.
36 Two *men* shall be in the field;
the one shall be taken, and the other
left.
37 And they answered and said unto
him, Where, Lord? And he said unto
them, Wheresoever the body *is,* thither
will the eagles be gathered together.

CHAPTER 18

AND he spake a parable unto them
to this end, that men ought always to pray, and not to faint;
2 Saying, There was in a city a judge,
which feared not God, neither regarded
man:
3 And there was a widow in that city;
and she came unto him, saying, Avenge
me of mine adversary.
4 And he would not for a while: but
afterward he said within himself,
Though I fear not God, nor regard man;
5 Yet because this widow troubleth
me, I will avenge her, lest by her continual coming she weary me.

6 And the Lord said, Hear what the unjust judge saith.

7 And shall not God avenge his own elect, which cry day and night unto him, though he bear long with them?

8 I tell you that he will avenge them speedily. Nevertheless, when the Son of man cometh, shall he find faith on the earth?

9 And he spake this parable unto certain which trusted in themselves that they were righteous, and despised others:

10 Two men went up into the temple to pray; the one a Phăr′ĭ-sēe, and the other a publican.

11 The Phăr′ĭ-sēe stood and prayed thus with himself, God, I thank thee, that I am not as other men *are,* extortioners, unjust, adulterers, or even as this publican.

12 I fast twice in the week, I give tithes of all that I possess.

13 And the publican, standing afar off, would not lift up so much as *his* eyes unto heaven, but smote upon his breast, saying, God be merciful to me a sinner.

14 I tell you, this man went down to his house justified *rather* than the other: for every one that exalteth himself shall be abased; and he that humbleth himself shall be exalted.

15 And they brought unto him also infants, that he would touch them: but when *his* disciples saw *it,* they rebuked them.

16 But Jesus called them *unto him,* and said, Suffer little children to come unto me, and forbid them not: for of such is the kingdom of God.

17 Verily I say unto you, Whosoever shall not receive the kingdom of God as a little child shall in no wise enter therein.

18 And a certain ruler asked him, saying, Good Master, what shall I do to inherit eternal life?

19 And Jesus said unto him, Why callest thou me good? none *is* good, save one, *that is,* God.

20 Thou knowest the commandments, Do not commit adultery, Do not kill, Do not steal, Do not bear false witness, Honor thy father and thy mother.

21 And he said, All these have I kept from my youth up.

22 Now when Jesus heard these things, he said unto him, Yet lackest thou one thing: sell all that thou hast, and distribute unto the poor, and thou shalt have treasure in heaven: and come, follow me.

23 And when he heard this, he was very sorrowful: for he was very rich.

24 And when Jesus saw that he was very sorrowful, he said, How hardly shall they that have riches enter into the kingdom of God!

25 For it is easier for a camel to go through a needle's eye, than for a rich man to enter into the kingdom of God.

26 And they that heard *it* said, Who then can be saved?

27 And he said, The things which are impossible with men are possible with God.

28 Then Peter said, Lo, we have left all, and followed thee.

29 And he said unto them, Verily I say unto you, There is no man that hath left house, or parents, or brethren, or wife, or children, for the kingdom of God's sake,

30 Who shall not receive manifold more in this present time, and in the world to come life everlasting.

31 ¶ Then he took *unto him* the twelve, and said unto them, Behold, we go up to Jerusalem, and all things that are written by the prophets concerning the Son of man shall be accomplished.

32 For he shall be delivered unto the Gĕn′tīleş, and shall be mocked, and spitefully entreated, and spitted on:

33 And they shall scourge *him,* and put him to death; and the third day he shall rise again.

34 And they understood none of these things: and this saying was hid from them, neither knew they the things which were spoken.

35 ¶ And it came to pass, that as he was come nigh unto Jĕr′ĭ-chō, a certain blind man sat by the wayside begging:

36 And hearing the multitude pass by, he asked what it meant.

37 And they told him, that Jesus of Nazareth passeth by.

38 And he cried, saying, Jesus, *thou* Son of David, have mercy on me.

39 And they which went before rebuked him, that he should hold his peace: but he cried so much the more, *Thou* Son of David, have mercy on me.

40 And Jesus stood, and commanded

him to be brought unto him: and when
he was come near, he asked him,
41 Saying, What wilt thou that I shall
do unto thee? And he said, Lord, that
I may receive my sight.
42 And Jesus said unto him, Receive
thy sight: thy faith hath saved thee.
43 And immediately he received his
sight, and followed him, glorifying God:
and all the people, when they saw *it*,
gave praise unto God.

CHAPTER 19

AND *Jesus* entered and passed
through Jĕr′ĭ-chō.
2 And, behold, *there was* a man
named Zăc-chē′ŭs, which was the chief
among the publicans, and he was rich.
3 And he sought to see Jesus who he
was; and could not for the press, because he was little of stature.
4 And he ran before, and climbed up
into a sycamore tree to see him; for he
was to pass that *way*.
5 And when Jesus came to the place,
he looked up, and saw him, and said
unto him, Zăc-chē′ŭs, make haste, and
come down; for to-day I must abide at
thy house.
6 And he made haste, and came down,
and received him joyfully.
7 And when they saw *it*, they all murmured, saying, That he was gone to be
guest with a man that is a sinner.
8 And Zăc-chē′ŭs stood, and said unto
the Lord; Behold, Lord, the half of
my goods I give to the poor; and if I
have taken any thing from any man by
false accusation, I restore *him* fourfold.
9 And Jesus said unto him, This day
is salvation come to this house, forasmuch as he also is a son of Abraham.
10 For the Son of man is come to seek
and to save that which was lost.
11 And as they heard these things, he
added and spake a parable, because
he was nigh to Jerusalem, and because
they thought that the kingdom of God
should immediately appear.
12 He said therefore, A certain nobleman went into a far country to receive
for himself a kingdom, and to return.
13 And he called his ten servants, and
delivered them ten pounds, and said
unto them, Occupy till I come.
14 But his citizens hated him, and sent
a message after him, saying, We will
not have this *man* to reign over us.
15 And it came to pass, that when he
was returned, having received the kingdom, then he commanded these servants to be called unto him, to whom he
had given the money, that he might
know how much every man had gained
by trading.
16 Then came the first, saying, Lord,
thy pound hath gained ten pounds.
17 And he said unto him, Well, thou
good servant: because thou hast been
faithful in a very little, have thou
authority over ten cities.
18 And the second came, saying, Lord,
thy pound hath gained five pounds.
19 And he said likewise to him, Be
thou also over five cities.
20 And another came, saying, Lord,
behold, *here is* thy pound, which I have
kept laid up in a napkin:
21 For I feared thee, because thou art
an austere man: thou takest up that
thou layedst not down, and reapest that
thou didst not sow.
22 And he saith unto him, Out of thine
own mouth will I judge thee, *thou*
wicked servant. Thou knewest that I
was an austere man, taking up that I
laid not down, and reaping that I did
not sow:
23 Wherefore then gavest not thou my
money into the bank, that at my coming
I might have required mine own with
usury?
24 And he said unto them that stood
by, Take from him the pound, and give
it to him that hath ten pounds.
25 (And they said unto him, Lord, he
hath ten pounds.)
26 For I say unto you, That unto every
one which hath shall be given; and from
him that hath not, even that he hath
shall be taken away from him.
27 But those mine enemies, which
would not that I should reign over them,
bring hither, and slay *them* before me.
28 ¶ And when he had thus spoken,
he went before, ascending up to Jerusalem.
29 And it came to pass, when he was
come nigh to Bĕth′phȧ-ġē and Bethany,
at the mount called *the mount* of Olives,
he sent two of his disciples,
30 Saying, Go ye into the village over
against *you;* in the which at your entering ye shall find a colt tied, whereon yet
never man sat: loose him, and bring *him*
hither.

31 And if any man ask you, Why do
ye loose *him?* thus shall ye say unto
him, Because the Lord hath need of
him.
32 And they that were sent went their
way, and found even as he had said
unto them.
33 And as they were loosing the colt,
the owners thereof said unto them, Why
loose ye the colt?
34 And they said, The Lord hath need
of him.
35 And they brought him to Jesus: and
they cast their garments upon the colt,
and they set Jesus thereon.
36 And as he went, they spread their
clothes in the way.
37 And when he was come nigh, even
now at the descent of the mount of
Olives, the whole multitude of the disciples
began to rejoice and praise God
with a loud voice for all the mighty
works that they had seen;
38 Saying, Blessed *be* the King that
cometh in the name of the Lord: peace
in heaven, and glory in the highest.
39 And some of the Phăr'ĭ-sēeș from
among the multitude said unto him,
Master, rebuke thy disciples.
40 And he answered and said unto
them, I tell you that, if these should
hold their peace, the stones would immediately
cry out.
41 ¶ And when he was come near, he
beheld the city, and wept over it,
42 Saying, If thou hadst known, even
thou, at least in this thy day, the things
which belong unto thy peace! but now
they are hid from thine eyes.
43 For the days shall come upon thee,
that thine enemies shall cast a trench
about thee, and compass thee round,
and keep thee in on every side,
44 And shall lay thee even with the
ground, and thy children within thee;
and they shall not leave in thee one
stone upon another; because thou
knewest not the time of thy visitation.
45 And he went into the temple, and
began to cast out them that sold therein,
and them that bought;
46 Saying unto them, It is written, My
house is the house of prayer; but ye have
made it a den of thieves.
47 And he taught daily in the temple.
But the chief priests and the scribes and
the chief of the people sought to destroy
him,
48 And could not find what they might
do: for all the people were very attentive
to hear him.

CHAPTER 20

AND it came to pass, *that* on one of
those days, as he taught the people
in the temple, and preached the
gospel, the chief priests and the scribes
came upon *him* with the elders,
2 And spake unto him, saying, Tell us,
by what authority doest thou these
things? or who is he that gave thee this
authority?
3 And he answered and said unto them,
I will also ask you one thing; and answer
me:
4 The baptism of John, was it from
heaven, or of men?
5 And they reasoned with themselves,
saying, If we shall say, From heaven;
he will say, Why then believed ye him
not?
6 But and if we say, Of men; all the
people will stone us: for they be persuaded
that John was a prophet.
7 And they answered, that they could
not tell whence *it was.*
8 And Jesus said unto them, Neither
tell I you by what authority I do these
things.
9 Then began he to speak to the people
this parable; A certain man planted a
vineyard, and let it forth to husbandmen,
and went into a far country for a
long time.
10 And at the season he sent a servant
to the husbandmen, that they should
give him of the fruit of the vineyard: but
the husbandmen beat him, and sent *him*
away empty.
11 And again he sent another servant:
and they beat him also, and entreated
him shamefully, and sent *him* away
empty.
12 And again he sent a third: and they
wounded him also, and cast *him* out.
13 Then said the lord of the vineyard,
What shall I do? I will send my beloved
son: it may be they will reverence *him*
when they see him.
14 But when the husbandmen saw
him, they reasoned among themselves,
saying, This is the heir: come, let us
kill him, that the inheritance may be
ours.
15 So they cast him out of the vineyard,
and killed *him.* What therefore shall

the lord of the vineyard do unto them?
16 He shall come and destroy these husbandmen, and shall give the vineyard to others. And when they heard *it,* they said, God forbid.
17 And he beheld them, and said, What is this then that is written, The stone which the builders rejected, the same is become the head of the corner?
18 Whosoever shall fall upon that stone shall be broken; but on whomsoever it shall fall, it will grind him to powder.
19 ¶ And the chief priests and the scribes the same hour sought to lay hands on him; and they feared the people: for they perceived that he had spoken this parable against them.
20 And they watched *him,* and sent forth spies, which should feign themselves just men, that they might take hold of his words, that so they might deliver him unto the power and authority of the governor.
21 And they asked him, saying, Master, we know that thou sayest and teachest rightly, neither acceptest thou the person *of any,* but teachest the way of God truly:
22 Is it lawful for us to give tribute unto Cæsar, or no?
23 But he perceived their craftiness, and said unto them, Why tempt ye me?
24 Show me a penny. Whose image and superscription hath it? They answered and said, Cæsar's.
25 And he said unto them, Render therefore unto Cæsar the things which be Cæsar's, and unto God the things which be God's.
26 And they could not take hold of his words before the people: and they marveled at his answer, and held their peace.
27 ¶ Then came to *him* certain of the Săd'dū-çēeș, which deny that there is any resurrection; and they asked him,
28 Saying, Master, Moses wrote unto us, If any man's brother die, having a wife, and he die without children, that his brother should take his wife, and raise up seed unto his brother.
29 There were therefore seven brethren: and the first took a wife, and died without children.
30 And the second took her to wife, and he died childless.
31 And the third took her; and in like manner the seven also: and they left no children, and died.
32 Last of all the woman died also.
33 Therefore in the resurrection whose wife of them is she? for seven had her to wife.
34 And Jesus answering said unto them, The children of this world marry, and are given in marriage:
35 But they which shall be accounted worthy to obtain that world, and the resurrection from the dead, neither marry, nor are given in marriage:
36 Neither can they die any more: for they are equal unto the angels; and are the children of God, being the children of the resurrection.
37 Now that the dead are raised, even Moses showed at the bush, when he calleth the Lord the God of Abraham, and the God of Isaac, and the God of Jacob.
38 For he is not a God of the dead, but of the living: for all live unto him.
39 ¶ Then certain of the scribes answering said, Master, thou hast well said.
40 And after that they durst not ask him any *question at all.*
41 And he said unto them, How say they that Christ is David's son?
42 And David himself saith in the book of Psalms, The LORD said unto my Lord, Sit thou on my right hand,
43 Till I make thine enemies thy footstool.
44 David therefore calleth him Lord, how is he then his son?
45 ¶ Then in the audience of all the people he said unto his disciples,
46 Beware of the scribes, which desire to walk in long robes, and love greetings in the markets, and the highest seats in the synagogues, and the chief rooms at feasts;
47 Which devour widows' houses, and for a show make long prayers: the same shall receive greater damnation.

CHAPTER 21

AND he looked up, and saw the rich men casting their gifts into the treasury.
2 And he saw also a certain poor widow casting in thither two mites.
3 And he said, Of a truth I say unto you, that this poor widow hath cast in more than they all:

4 For all these have of their abundance
cast in unto the offerings of God: but
she of her penury hath cast in all the
living that she had.
5 ℂ And as some spake of the temple,
how it was adorned with goodly stones
and gifts, he said,
6 *As for* these things which ye behold,
the days will come, in the which there
shall not be left one stone upon another,
that shall not be thrown down.
7 And they asked him, saying, Master,
but when shall these things be? and
what sign *will there be* when these
things shall come to pass?
8 And he said, Take heed that ye be
not deceived: for many shall come in my
name, saying, I am *Christ;* and the time
draweth near: go ye not therefore after
them.
9 But when ye shall hear of wars and
commotions, be not terrified: for these
things must first come to pass; but the
end *is* not by and by.
10 Then said he unto them, Nation
shall rise against nation, and kingdom
against kingdom:
11 And great earthquakes shall be in
divers places, and famines, and pestilences; and fearful sights and great
signs shall there be from heaven.
12 But before all these, they shall lay
their hands on you, and persecute *you,*
delivering *you* up to the synagogues, and
into prisons, being brought before kings
and rulers for my name's sake.
13 And it shall turn to you for a testimony.
14 Settle *it* therefore in your hearts, not
to meditate before what ye shall answer:
15 For I will give you a mouth and wisdom, which all your adversaries shall
not be able to gainsay nor resist.
16 And ye shall be betrayed both by
parents, and brethren, and kinsfolk,
and friends; and *some* of you shall they
cause to be put to death.
17 And ye shall be hated of all *men* for
my name's sake.
18 But there shall not a hair of your
head perish.
19 In your patience possess ye your
souls.
20 And when ye shall see Jerusalem
compassed with armies, then know that
the desolation thereof is nigh.
21 Then let them which are in Judea
flee to the mountains; and let them
which are in the midst of it depart out;
and let not them that are in the countries enter thereinto.
22 For these be the days of vengeance,
that all things which are written may be
fulfilled.
23 But woe unto them that are with
child, and to them that give suck, in
those days! for there shall be great distress in the land, and wrath upon this
people.
24 And they shall fall by the edge of the
sword, and shall be led away captive
into all nations: and Jerusalem shall be
trodden down of the Ġĕn′tīleș, until the
times of the Ġĕn′tīleș be fulfilled.
25 ℂ And there shall be signs in the
sun, and in the moon, and in the stars;
and upon the earth distress of nations,
with perplexity; the sea and the waves
roaring;
26 Men's hearts failing them for fear,
and for looking after those things which
are coming on the earth: for the powers
of heaven shall be shaken.
27 And then shall they see the Son of
man coming in a cloud with power and
great glory.
28 And when these things begin to
come to pass, then look up, and lift up
your heads; for your redemption draweth nigh.
29 And he spake to them a parable;
Behold the fig tree, and all the trees;
30 When they now shoot forth, ye see
and know of your own selves that summer is now nigh at hand.
31 So likewise ye, when ye see these
things come to pass, know ye that the
kingdom of God is nigh at hand.
32 Verily I say unto you, This generation shall not pass away, till all be fulfilled.
33 Heaven and earth shall pass away;
but my words shall not pass away.
34 ℂ And take heed to yourselves, lest
at any time your hearts be overcharged
with surfeiting, and drunkenness, and
cares of this life, and *so* that day come
upon you unawares.
35 For as a snare shall it come on all
them that dwell on the face of the whole
earth.
36 Watch ye therefore, and pray always, that ye may be accounted worthy
to escape all these things that shall
come to pass, and to stand before the
Son of man.

37 And in the daytime he was teaching
in the temple; and at night he went out,
and abode in the mount that is called
the mount of Olives.
38 And all the people came early in
the morning to him in the temple, for to
hear him.

CHAPTER 22

NOW the feast of unleavened bread
drew nigh, which is called the
passover.
2 And the chief priests and scribes
sought how they might kill him; for they
feared the people.
3 ¶ Then entered Satan into Judas
surnamed Ĭs-căr′ĭ-ŏt, being of the number of the twelve.
4 And he went his way, and communed
with the chief priests and captains, how
he might betray him unto them.
5 And they were glad, and covenanted
to give him money.
6 And he promised, and sought opportunity to betray him unto them in the
absence of the multitude.
7 ¶ Then came the day of unleavened
bread, when the passover must be
killed.
8 And he sent Peter and John, saying,
Go and prepare us the passover, that we
may eat.
9 And they said unto him, Where wilt
thou that we prepare?
10 And he said unto them, Behold,
when ye are entered into the city, there
shall a man meet you, bearing a pitcher
of water; follow him into the house
where he entereth in.
11 And ye shall say unto the goodman
of the house, The Master saith unto
thee, Where is the guest chamber,
where I shall eat the passover with my
disciples?
12 And he shall show you a large upper
room furnished: there make ready.
13 And they went, and found as he had
said unto them: and they made ready
the passover.
14 And when the hour was come, he sat
down, and the twelve apostles with him.
15 And he said unto them, With desire
I have desired to eat this passover with
you before I suffer:
16 For I say unto you, I will not any
more eat thereof, until it be fulfilled in
the kingdom of God.
17 And he took the cup, and gave
thanks, and said, Take this, and divide
it among yourselves:
18 For I say unto you, I will not drink
of the fruit of the vine, until the kingdom
of God shall come.
19 ¶ And he took bread, and gave
thanks, and brake *it*, and gave unto
them, saying, This is my body which is
given for you: this do in remembrance
of me.
20 Likewise also the cup after supper,
saying, This cup *is* the new testament
in my blood, which is shed for you.
21 ¶ But, behold, the hand of him
that betrayeth me *is* with me on the
table.
22 And truly the Son of man goeth, as
it was determined: but woe unto that
man by whom he is betrayed!
23 And they began to inquire among
themselves, which of them it was that
should do this thing.
24 ¶ And there was also a strife among
them, which of them should be accounted the greatest.
25 And he said unto them, The kings
of the Ġĕn′tīleş exercise lordship over
them; and they that exercise authority
upon them are called benefactors.
26 But ye *shall* not *be* so: but he that is
greatest among you, let him be as the
younger; and he that is chief, as he that
doth serve.
27 For whether *is* greater, he that
sitteth at meat, or he that serveth? *is*
not he that sitteth at meat? but I am
among you as he that serveth.
28 Ye are they which have continued
with me in my temptations.
29 And I appoint unto you a kingdom,
as my Father hath appointed unto me;
30 That ye may eat and drink at my
table in my kingdom, and sit on thrones
judging the twelve tribes of Ĭş′rā-ēl.
31 ¶ And the Lord said, Simon,
Simon, behold, Satan hath desired *to
have* you, that he may sift *you* as wheat:
32 But I have prayed for thee, that thy
faith fail not: and when thou art converted, strengthen thy brethren.
33 And he said unto him, Lord, I am
ready to go with thee, both into prison,
and to death.
34 And he said, I tell thee, Peter, the
cock shall not crow this day, before
that thou shalt thrice deny that thou
knowest me.
35 And he said unto them, When I sent

you without purse, and scrip, and shoes,
lacked ye any thing? And they said,
Nothing.
36 Then said he unto them, But now,
he that hath a purse, let him take *it*,
and likewise *his* scrip: and he that hath
no sword, let him sell his garment, and
buy one.
37 For I say unto you, that this that is
written must yet be accomplished in me,
And he was reckoned among the transgressors: for the things concerning me
have an end.
38 And they said, Lord, behold, here
are two swords. And he said unto them,
It is enough.
39 ¶ And he came out, and went, as
he was wont, to the mount of Olives;
and his disciples also followed him.
40 And when he was at the place, he
said unto them, Pray that ye enter not
into temptation.
41 And he was withdrawn from them
about a stone's cast, and kneeled down,
and prayed,
42 Saying, Father, if thou be willing,
remove this cup from me: nevertheless,
not my will, but thine, be done.
43 And there appeared an angel unto
him from heaven, strengthening him.
44 And being in an agony he prayed
more earnestly: and his sweat was as it
were great drops of blood falling down
to the ground.
45 And when he rose up from prayer,
and was come to his disciples, he found
them sleeping for sorrow,
46 And said unto them, Why sleep ye?
rise and pray, lest ye enter into temptation.
47 ¶ And while he yet spake, behold
a multitude, and he that was called
Judas, one of the twelve, went before
them, and drew near unto Jesus to kiss
him.
48 But Jesus said unto him, Judas,
betrayest thou the Son of man with a
kiss?
49 When they which were about him
saw what would follow, they said unto
him, Lord, shall we smite with the
sword?
50 ¶ And one of them smote the servant of the high priest, and cut off his
right ear.
51 And Jesus answered and said,
Suffer ye thus far. And he touched his
ear, and healed him.
52 Then Jesus said unto the chief
priests, and captains of the temple, and
the elders, which were come to him,
Be ye come out, as against a thief, with
swords and staves?
53 When I was daily with you in the
temple, ye stretched forth no hands
against me: but this is your hour, and
the power of darkness.
54 ¶ Then took they him, and led
him, and brought him into the high
priest's house. And Peter followed afar
off.
55 And when they had kindled a fire
in the midst of the hall, and were set
down together, Peter sat down among
them.
56 But a certain maid beheld him as
he sat by the fire, and earnestly looked
upon him, and said, This man was also
with him.
57 And he denied him, saying, Woman,
I know him not.
58 And after a little while another saw
him, and said, Thou art also of them.
And Peter said, Man, I am not.
59 And about the space of one hour
after another confidently affirmed, saying, Of a truth this *fellow* also was with
him; for he is a Galilean.
60 And Peter said, Man, I know not
what thou sayest. And immediately,
while he yet spake, the cock crew.
61 And the Lord turned, and looked
upon Peter. And Peter remembered
the word of the Lord, how he had said
unto him, Before the cock crow, thou
shalt deny me thrice.
62 And Peter went out, and wept
bitterly.
63 ¶ And the men that held Jesus
mocked him, and smote *him*.
64 And when they had blindfolded
him, they struck him on the face, and
asked him, saying, Prophesy, who is it
that smote thee?
65 And many other things blasphe-
mously spake they against him.
66 ¶ And as soon as it was day, the
elders of the people and the chief priests
and the scribes came together, and led
him into their council, saying,
67 Art thou the Christ? tell us. And he
said unto them, If I tell you, ye will not
believe:
68 And if I also ask *you*, ye will not
answer me, nor let *me* go.
69 Hereafter shall the Son of man sit

on the right hand of the power of God.
70 Then said they all, Art thou then
the Son of God? And he said unto them,
Ye say that I am.
71 And they said, What need we any
further witness? for we ourselves have
heard of his own mouth.

CHAPTER 23

AND the whole multitude of them
arose, and led him unto Pilate.
2 And they began to accuse him, saying, We found this *fellow* perverting
the nation, and forbidding to give tribute
to Cæsar, saying that he himself is
Christ a king.
3 And Pilate asked him, saying, Art
thou the King of the Jews? And he
answered him and said, Thou sayest *it*.
4 Then said Pilate to the chief priests
and *to* the people, I find no fault in this
man.
5 And they were the more fierce, saying, He stirreth up the people, teaching
throughout all Jewry, beginning from
Galilee to this place.
6 When Pilate heard of Galilee, he
asked whether the man were a Galilean.
7 And as soon as he knew that he belonged unto Hĕr'ŏd's jurisdiction, he
sent him to Hĕr'ŏd, who himself also
was at Jerusalem at that time.
8 ℭ And when Hĕr'ŏd saw Jesus, he
was exceeding glad: for he was desirous
to see him of a long *season*, because he
had heard many things of him; and he
hoped to have seen some miracle done
by him.
9 Then he questioned with him in
many words; but he answered him
nothing.
10 And the chief priests and scribes
stood and vehemently accused him.
11 And Hĕr'ŏd with his men of war set
him at nought, and mocked *him*, and
arrayed him in a gorgeous robe, and
sent him again to Pilate.
12 ℭ And the same day Pilate and
Hĕr'ŏd were made friends together; for
before they were at enmity between
themselves.
13 ℭ And Pilate, when he had called
together the chief priests and the rulers
and the people,
14 Said unto them, Ye have brought
this man unto me, as one that perverteth the people; and, behold, I, having
examined *him* before you, have found
no fault in this man touching those
things whereof ye accuse him:
15 No, nor yet Hĕr'ŏd: for I sent you
to him; and, lo, nothing worthy of death
is done unto him.
16 I will therefore chastise him, and
release *him*.
17 (For of necessity he must release
one unto them at the feast.)
18 And they cried out all at once, saying, Away with this *man*, and release
unto us Bär-ăb'băs:
19 (Who for a certain sedition made in
the city, and for murder, was cast into
prison.)
20 Pilate therefore, willing to release
Jesus, spake again to them.
21 But they cried, saying, Crucify *him*,
crucify him.
22 And he said unto them the third
time, Why, what evil hath he done? I
have found no cause of death in him:
I will therefore chastise him, and let
him go.
23 And they were instant with loud
voices, requiring that he might be crucified: and the voices of them and of the
chief priests prevailed.
24 And Pilate gave sentence that it
should be as they required.
25 And he released unto them him
that for sedition and murder was cast
into prison, whom they had desired; but
he delivered Jesus to their will.
26 And as they led him away, they laid
hold upon one Simon, a Cȳ-rē'nĭ-ăn,
coming out of the country, and on him
they laid the cross, that he might bear
it after Jesus.
27 ℭ And there followed him a great
company of people, and of women,
which also bewailed and lamented
him.
28 But Jesus turning unto them said,
Daughters of Jerusalem, weep not for
me, but weep for yourselves, and for
your children.
29 For, behold, the days are coming,
in the which they shall say, Blessed *are*
the barren, and the wombs that never
bare, and the paps which never gave
suck.
30 Then shall they begin to say to the
mountains, Fall on us; and to the hills,
Cover us.
31 For if they do these things in a green
tree, what shall be done in the dry?
32 And there were also two others,

malefactors, led with him to be put to
death.
33 And when they were come to the
place, which is called Calvary, there
they crucified him, and the malefactors,
one on the right hand, and the other on
the left.
34 ¶ Then said Jesus, Father, forgive
them; for they know not what they do.
And they parted his raiment, and cast
lots.
35 And the people stood beholding.
And the rulers also with them derided
him, saying, He saved others; let him
save himself, if he be Christ, the chosen
of God.
36 And the soldiers also mocked him,
coming to him, and offering him vinegar,
37 And saying, If thou be the King of
the Jews, save thyself.
38 And a superscription also was written over him in letters of Greek, and
Latin, and Hebrew, THIS IS THE KING
OF THE JEWS.
39 ¶ And one of the malefactors which
were hanged railed on him, saying, If
thou be Christ, save thyself and us.
40 But the other answering rebuked
him, saying, Dost not thou fear God,
seeing thou art in the same condemnation?
41 And we indeed justly; for we receive
the due reward of our deeds: but this
man hath done nothing amiss.
42 And he said unto Jesus, Lord,
remember me when thou comest into
thy kingdom.
43 And Jesus said unto him, Verily I
say unto thee, To-day shalt thou be
with me in paradise.
44 And it was about the sixth hour, and
there was a darkness over all the earth
until the ninth hour.
45 And the sun was darkened, and the
veil of the temple was rent in the midst.
46 ¶ And when Jesus had cried with
a loud voice, he said, Father, into thy
hands I commend my spirit: and having
said thus, he gave up the ghost.
47 Now when the centurion saw what
was done, he glorified God, saying, Certainly this was a righteous man.
48 And all the people that came together to that sight, beholding the things
which were done, smote their breasts,
and returned.
49 And all his acquaintance, and the
women that followed him from Galilee,
stood afar off, beholding these things.
50 ¶ And, behold, *there was* a man
named Joseph, a counselor; *and he was*
a good man, and a just:
51 (The same had not consented to the
counsel and deed of them:) *he was* of
Ăr′ĭ-mȧ-thē′ȧ, a city of the Jews; who
also himself waited for the kingdom of
God.
52 This *man* went unto Pilate, and
begged the body of Jesus.
53 And he took it down, and wrapped
it in linen, and laid it in a sepulchre
that was hewn in stone, wherein never
man before was laid.
54 And that day was the preparation,
and the sabbath drew on.
55 And the women also, which came
with him from Galilee, followed after,
and beheld the sepulchre, and how his
body was laid.
56 And they returned, and prepared
spices and ointments; and rested the
sabbath day according to the commandment.

CHAPTER 24

NOW upon the first *day* of the
week, very early in the morning,
they came unto the sepulchre, bringing the spices which they had prepared,
and certain *others* with them.
2 And they found the stone rolled away
from the sepulchre.
3 And they entered in, and found not
the body of the Lord Jesus.
4 And it came to pass, as they were
much perplexed thereabout, behold,
two men stood by them in shining garments:
5 And as they were afraid, and bowed
down *their* faces to the earth, they said
unto them, Why seek ye the living
among the dead?
6 He is not here, but is risen: remember how he spake unto you when he was
yet in Galilee,
7 Saying, The Son of man must be
delivered into the hands of sinful men,
and be crucified, and the third day rise
again.
8 And they remembered his words,
9 And returned from the sepulchre,
and told all these things unto the eleven,
and to all the rest.
10 It was Mary Măg′dȧ-lēne, and Jō-
ăn′nȧ, and Mary *the mother* of James,
and other *women that were* with them,

which told these things unto the
apostles.
11 And their words seemed to them as
idle tales, and they believed them not.
12 Then arose Peter, and ran unto the
sepulchre; and stooping down, he beheld the linen clothes laid by themselves, and departed, wondering in
himself at that which was come to pass.
13 ℂ And, behold, two of them went
that same day to a village called Ĕm-
mā'ŭs, which was from Jerusalem *about*
threescore furlongs.
14 And they talked together of all
these things which had happened.
15 And it came to pass, that, while
they communed *together* and reasoned,
Jesus himself drew near, and went with
them.
16 But their eyes were holden that
they should not know him.
17 And he said unto them, What manner of communications *are* these that
ye have one to another, as ye walk, and
are sad?
18 And the one of them, whose name
was Clē'ō-păs, answering said unto him,
Art thou only a stranger in Jerusalem,
and hast not known the things which are
come to pass there in these days?
19 And he said unto them, What
things? And they said unto him, Concerning Jesus of Nazareth, which was a
prophet mighty in deed and word before
God and all the people:
20 And how the chief priests and our
rulers delivered him to be condemned to
death, and have crucified him.
21 But we trusted that it had been he
which should have redeemed Ĭs'rā-ĕl:
and beside all this, to-day is the third
day since these things were done.
22 Yea, and certain women also of our
company made us astonished, which
were early at the sepulchre;
23 And when they found not his body,
they came, saying, that they had also
seen a vision of angels, which said that
he was alive.
24 And certain of them which were
with us went to the sepulchre, and found
it even so as the women had said: but
him they saw not.
25 Then he said unto them, O fools,
and slow of heart to believe all that the
prophets have spoken:
26 Ought not Christ to have suffered
these things, and to enter into his glory?
27 And beginning at Moses and all the
prophets, he expounded unto them in
all the Scriptures the things concerning
himself.
28 And they drew nigh unto the village,
whither they went: and he made as
though he would have gone further.
29 But they constrained him, saying,
Abide with us; for it is toward evening,
and the day is far spent. And he went
in to tarry with them.
30 And it came to pass, as he sat at
meat with them, he took bread, and
blessed *it*, and brake, and gave to them.
31 And their eyes were opened, and
they knew him; and he vanished out of
their sight.
32 And they said one to another, Did
not our heart burn within us, while he
talked with us by the way, and while he
opened to us the Scriptures?
33 And they rose up the same hour, and
returned to Jerusalem, and found the
eleven gathered together, and them that
were with them,
34 Saying, The Lord is risen indeed,
and hath appeared to Simon.
35 And they told what things *were
done* in the way, and how he was known
of them in breaking of bread.
36 ℂ And as they thus spake, Jesus
himself stood in the midst of them, and
saith unto them, Peace *be* unto you.
37 But they were terrified and affrighted, and supposed that they had
seen a spirit.
38 And he said unto them, Why are ye
troubled? and why do thoughts arise in
your hearts?
39 Behold my hands and my feet, that
it is I myself: handle me, and see; for a
spirit hath not flesh and bones, as ye
see me have.
40 And when he had thus spoken, he
showed them *his* hands and *his* feet.
41 And while they yet believed not for
joy, and wondered, he said unto them,
Have ye here any meat?
42 And they gave him a piece of a
broiled fish, and of a honeycomb.
43 And he took *it*, and did eat before
them.
44 And he said unto them, These *are*
the words which I spake unto you, while
I was yet with you, that all things must
be fulfilled, which were written in the
law of Moses, and *in* the prophets, and
in the psalms, concerning me.

45 Then opened he their understanding, that they might understand the Scriptures,
46 And said unto them, Thus it is written, and thus it behooved Christ to suffer, and to rise from the dead the third day:
47 And that repentance and remission of sins should be preached in his name among all nations, beginning at Jerusalem.
48 And ye are witnesses of these things.
49 ¶ And, behold, I send the promise of my Father upon you: but tarry ye in the city of Jerusalem, until ye be endued with power from on high.
50 ¶ And he led them out as far as to Bethany, and he lifted up his hands, and blessed them.
51 And it came to pass, while he blessed them, he was parted from them, and carried up into heaven.
52 And they worshipped him, and returned to Jerusalem with great joy:
53 And were continually in the temple, praising and blessing God. Amen.

THE GOSPEL ACCORDING TO

ST. JOHN

CHAPTER 1

IN the beginning was the Word, and
the Word was with God, and the
Word was God.
2 The same was in the beginning with
God.
3 All things were made by him; and
without him was not any thing made
that was made.
4 In him was life; and the life was the
light of men.
5 And the light shineth in darkness;
and the darkness comprehended it not.
6 ¶ There was a man sent from God,
whose name *was* John.
7 The same came for a witness, to bear
witness of the Light, that all *men*
through him might believe.
8 He was not that Light, but *was sent*
to bear witness of that Light.
9 *That* was the true Light, which
lighteth every man that cometh into the
world.
10 He was in the world, and the world
was made by him, and the world knew
him not.
11 He came unto his own, and his own
received him not.
12 But as many as received him, to
them gave he power to become the sons
of God, *even* to them that believe on his
name:
13 Which were born, not of blood, nor
of the will of the flesh, nor of the will of
man, but of God.
14 And the Word was made flesh, and
dwelt among us, (and we beheld his
glory, the glory as of the only begotten
of the Father,) full of grace and truth.
15 ¶ John bare witness of him, and
cried, saying, This was he of whom I
spake, He that cometh after me is preferred before me; for he was before me.
16 And of his fulness have all we received, and grace for grace.
17 For the law was given by Moses, *but*
grace and truth came by Jesus Christ.
18 No man hath seen God at any time;
the only begotten Son, which is in the
bosom of the Father, he hath declared
him.
19 ¶ And this is the record of John,
when the Jews sent priests and Lē′vītes
from Jerusalem to ask him, Who art
thou?
20 And he confessed, and denied not;
but confessed, I am not the Christ.
21 And they asked him, What then?
Art thou Ē-lī′ăs? And he saith, I am
not. Art thou that Prophet? And he
answered, No.
22 Then said they unto him, Who art
thou? that we may give an answer to them
that sent us. What sayest thou of thyself?
23 He said, I *am* the voice of one crying in the wilderness, Make straight the
way of the Lord, as said the prophet
Ē-ṣā′ịăs.
24 And they which were sent were of
the Phăr′ĭ-sēeṣ.
25 And they asked him, and said unto
him, Why baptizest thou then, if thou
be not that Christ, nor Ē-lī′ăs, neither
that Prophet?
26 John answered them, saying, I
baptize with water: but there standeth
one among you, whom ye know not;
27 He it is, who coming after me is preferred before me, whose shoe-latchet I
am not worthy to unloose.
28 These things were done in Bĕth′-
ăb′ȧ-rȧ beyond Jordan, where John was
baptizing.
29 ¶ The next day John seeth Jesus
coming unto him, and saith, Behold the
Lamb of God, which taketh away the
sin of the world!
30 This is he of whom I said, After me
cometh a man which is preferred before
me; for he was before me.
31 And I knew him not: but that he
should be made manifest to Ĭṣ′rā-ĕl,
therefore am I come baptizing with
water.
32 And John bare record, saying, I saw
the Spirit descending from heaven like
a dove, and it abode upon him.
33 And I knew him not: but he that
sent me to baptize with water, the same
said unto me, Upon whom thou shalt
see the Spirit descending, and remaining on him, the same is he which baptizeth with the Holy Ghost.

34 And I saw, and bare record that
this is the Son of God.
35 ¶ Again the next day after, John
stood, and two of his disciples;
36 And looking upon Jesus as he walked,
he saith, Behold the Lamb of God!
37 And the two disciples heard him
speak, and they followed Jesus.
38 Then Jesus turned, and saw them
following, and saith unto them, What
seek ye? They said unto him, Răb′bī,
(which is to say, being interpreted,
Master,) where dwellest thou?
39 He saith unto them, Come and see.
They came and saw where he dwelt,
and abode with him that day: for it
was about the tenth hour.
40 One of the two which heard John
speak, and followed him, was Andrew,
Simon Peter's brother.
41 He first findeth his own brother
Simon, and saith unto him, We have
found the Mĕs-sī′ăs, which is, being interpreted, the Christ.
42 And he brought him to Jesus. And
when Jesus beheld him, he said, Thou
art Simon the son of Jō′nȧ: thou shalt be
called Çē′phăs, which is by interpretation, A stone.
43 ¶ The day following Jesus would
go forth into Galilee, and findeth Philip,
and saith unto him, Follow me.
44 Now Philip was of Bĕth′sā′ĭ-dȧ, the
city of Andrew and Peter.
45 Philip findeth Nȧ-thăn′ā-ĕl, and
saith unto him, We have found him, of
whom Moses in the law, and the prophets, did write, Jesus of Nazareth, the
son of Joseph.
46 And Nȧ-thăn′ā-ĕl said unto him,
Can there any good thing come out of
Nazareth? Philip saith unto him, Come
and see.
47 Jesus saw Nȧ-thăn′ā-ĕl coming to
him, and saith of him, Behold an Ĭṣ′rā-
ĕl-īte indeed, in whom is no guile!
48 Nȧ-thăn′ā-ĕl saith unto him,
Whence knowest thou me? Jesus answered and said unto him, Before that
Philip called thee, when thou wast
under the fig tree, I saw thee.
49 Nȧ-thăn′ā-ĕl answered and saith
unto him, Răb′bī, thou art the Son of
God; thou art the King of Ĭṣ′rā-ĕl.
50 Jesus answered and said unto him,
Because I said unto thee, I saw thee
under the fig tree, believest thou? thou
shalt see greater things than these.
51 And he saith unto him, Verily,
verily, I say unto you, Hereafter ye
shall see heaven open, and the angels of
God ascending and descending upon
the Son of man.

CHAPTER 2

AND the third day there was a marriage in Cā′nȧ of Galilee; and
the mother of Jesus was there:
2 And both Jesus was called, and his
disciples, to the marriage.
3 And when they wanted wine, the
mother of Jesus saith unto him, They
have no wine.
4 Jesus saith unto her, Woman, what
have I to do with thee? mine hour is not
yet come.
5 His mother saith unto the servants,
Whatsoever he saith unto you, do *it.*
6 And there were set there six water-
pots of stone, after the manner of the
purifying of the Jews, containing two or
three firkins apiece.
7 Jesus saith unto them, Fill the water-
pots with water. And they filled them
up to the brim.
8 And he saith unto them, Draw out
now, and bear unto the governor of the
feast. And they bare *it.*
9 When the ruler of the feast had tasted
the water that was made wine, and knew
not whence it was, (but the servants
which drew the water knew,) the governor of the feast called the bridegroom,
10 And saith unto him, Every man at
the beginning doth set forth good wine;
and when men have well drunk, then
that which is worse: *but* thou hast kept
the good wine until now.
11 This beginning of miracles did Jesus
in Cā′nȧ of Galilee, and manifested
forth his glory; and his disciples believed on him.
12 ¶ After this he went down to Cȧ-
pĕr′nā-ŭm, he, and his mother, and his
brethren, and his disciples; and they
continued there not many days.
13 ¶ And the Jews' passover was at
hand, and Jesus went up to Jerusalem,
14 And found in the temple those that
sold oxen and sheep and doves, and
the changers of money sitting:
15 And when he had made a scourge
of small cords, he drove them all out of
the temple, and the sheep, and the oxen;
and poured out the changers money,
and overthrew the tables;

16 And said unto them that sold doves,
Take these things hence; make not
my Father's house a house of merchandise.
17 And his disciples remembered that
it was written, The zeal of thine house
hath eaten me up.
18 ℭ Then answered the Jews and
said unto him, What sign showest thou
unto us, seeing that thou doest these
things?
19 Jesus answered and said unto them,
Destroy this temple, and in three days
I will raise it up.
20 Then said the Jews, Forty and six
years was this temple in building, and
wilt thou rear it up in three days?
21 But he spake of the temple of his
body.
22 When therefore he was risen from
the dead, his disciples remembered
that he had said this unto them; and
they believed the Scripture, and the
word which Jesus had said.
23 ℭ Now when he was in Jerusalem
at the passover, in the feast *day*, many
believed in his name, when they saw
the miracles which he did.
24 But Jesus did not commit himself
unto them, because he knew all *men*,
25 And needed not that any should
testify of man; for he knew what was in
man.

CHAPTER 3

THERE was a man of the Phăr′ĭ-
sēeș, named Nĭc′ō-dē′mŭs, a ruler
of the Jews:
2 The same came to Jesus by night,
and said unto him, Răb′bī, we know
that thou art a teacher come from God:
for no man can do these miracles that
thou doest, except God be with him.
3 Jesus answered and said unto him,
Verily, verily, I say unto thee, Except a
man be born again, he cannot see the
kingdom of God.
4 Nĭc′ō-dē′mŭs saith unto him, How
can a man be born when he is old? can
he enter the second time into his
mother's womb, and be born?
5 Jesus answered, Verily, verily, I say
unto thee, Except a man be born of
water and *of* the Spirit, he cannot enter
into the kingdom of God.
6 That which is born of the flesh is
flesh; and that which is born of the
Spirit is spirit.
7 Marvel not that I said unto thee, Ye
must be born again.
8 The wind bloweth where it listeth,
and thou hearest the sound thereof, but
canst not tell whence it cometh, and
whither it goeth: so is every one that is
born of the Spirit.
9 Nĭc′ō-dē′mŭs answered and said
unto him, How can these things be?
10 Jesus answered and said unto him,
Art thou a master of Ĭș′rā-ĕl, and knowest not these things?
11 Verily, verily, I say unto thee, We
speak that we do know, and testify that
we have seen; and ye receive not our
witness.
12 If I have told you earthly things,
and ye believe not, how shall ye believe,
if I tell you *of* heavenly things?
13 And no man hath ascended up to
heaven, but he that came down from
heaven, *even* the Son of man which is
in heaven.
14 ℭ And as Moses lifted up the serpent in the wilderness, even so must
the Son of man be lifted up:
15 That whosoever believeth in him
should not perish, but have eternal life.
16 ℭ For God so loved the world, that
he gave his only begotten Son, that
whosoever believeth in him should not
perish, but have everlasting life.
17 For God sent not his Son into
the world to condemn the world; but
that the world through him might be
saved.
18 ℭ He that believeth on him is not
condemned: but he that believeth not
is condemned already, because he hath
not believed in the name of the only begotten Son of God.
19 And this is the condemnation, that
light is come into the world, and men
loved darkness rather than light, because their deeds were evil.
20 For every one that doeth evil hateth
the light, neither cometh to the light,
lest his deeds should be reproved.
21 But he that doeth truth cometh
to the light, that his deeds may be
made manifest, that they are wrought
in God.
22 ℭ After these things came Jesus
and his disciples into the land of Judea;
and there he tarried with them, and
baptized.
23 ℭ And John also was baptizing in
Æ′nŏn near to Sā′lĭm, because there

was much water there: and they came,
and were baptized.
24 For John was not yet cast into
prison.
25 ¶ Then there arose a question between *some* of John's disciples and the
Jews about purifying.
26 And they came unto John, and said
unto him, Răb'bī, he that was with thee
beyond Jordan, to whom thou barest
witness, behold, the same baptizeth,
and all *men* come to him.
27 John answered and said, A man can
receive nothing, except it be given him
from heaven.
28 Ye yourselves bear me witness,
that I said, I am not the Christ, but that
I am sent before him.
29 He that hath the bride is the bridegroom: but the friend of the bridegroom,
which standeth and heareth him, rejoiceth greatly because of the bridegroom's voice: this my joy therefore is
fulfilled.
30 He must increase, but I *must*
decrease.
31 He that cometh from above is above
all: he that is of the earth is earthly,
and speaketh of the earth: he that
cometh from heaven is above all.
32 And what he hath seen and heard,
that he testifieth; and no man receiveth
his testimony.
33 He that hath received his testimony
hath set to his seal that God is true.
34 For he whom God hath sent speaketh the words of God: for God giveth
not the Spirit by measure *unto him*.
35 The Father loveth the Son, and hath
given all things into his hand.
36 He that believeth on the Son hath
everlasting life: and he that believeth
not the Son shall not see life; but the
wrath of God abideth on him.

CHAPTER 4

WHEN therefore the Lord knew
how the Phăr'ĭ-sēeṣ had heard
that Jesus made and baptized more
disciples than John,
2 (Though Jesus himself baptized not,
but his disciples,)
3 He left Judea, and departed again
into Galilee.
4 And he must needs go through
Sȧ-mā'rĭ-ȧ.
5 Then cometh he to a city of Sȧ-mā'rĭ-ȧ, which is called Sȳ'chăr, near to the
parcel of ground that Jacob gave to his
son Joseph.
6 Now Jacob's well was there. Jesus
therefore, being wearied with *his* journey, sat thus on the well: *and* it was
about the sixth hour.
7 There cometh a woman of Sȧ-mā'rĭ-ȧ to draw water: Jesus saith unto her,
Give me to drink.
8 (For his disciples were gone away
unto the city to buy meat.)
9 Then saith the woman of Sȧ-mā'rĭ-ȧ unto him, How is it that thou, being
a Jew, askest drink of me, which am a
woman of Sȧ-mā'rĭ-ȧ? for the Jews have
no dealings with the Sȧ-măr'ĭ-tănṣ.
10 Jesus answered and said unto her,
If thou knewest the gift of God, and who
it is that saith to thee, Give me to drink;
thou wouldest have asked of him, and
he would have given thee living water.
11 The woman saith unto him, Sir,
thou hast nothing to draw with, and the
well is deep: from whence then hast
thou that living water?
12 Art thou greater than our father
Jacob, which gave us the well, and
drank thereof himself, and his children,
and his cattle?
13 Jesus answered and said unto her,
Whosoever drinketh of this water shall
thirst again:
14 But whosoever drinketh of the water that I shall give him shall never
thirst; but the water that I shall give
him shall be in him a well of water
springing up into everlasting life.
15 The woman saith unto him, Sir,
give me this water, that I thirst not,
neither come hither to draw.
16 Jesus saith unto her, Go, call thy
husband, and come hither.
17 The woman answered and said, I
have no husband. Jesus said unto her,
Thou hast well said, I have no husband:
18 For thou hast had five husbands;
and he whom thou now hast is not thy
husband: in that saidst thou truly.
19 The woman saith unto him, Sir, I
perceive that thou art a prophet.
20 Our fathers worshipped in this
mountain; and ye say, that in Jerusalem
is the place where men ought to worship.
21 Jesus saith unto her, Woman, believe me, the hour cometh, when ye
shall neither in this mountain, nor yet
at Jerusalem, worship the Father.

22 Ye worship ye know not what: we
know what we worship; for salvation is
of the Jews.
23 But the hour cometh, and now is,
when the true worshippers shall worship the Father in spirit and in truth:
for the Father seeketh such to worship
him.
24 God *is* a Spirit: and they that worship him must worship *him* in spirit and
in truth.
25 The woman saith unto him, I know
that Mĕs-sī'ăs cometh, which is called
Christ: when he is come, he will tell us
all things.
26 Jesus saith unto her, I that speak
unto thee am *he*.
27 ¶ And upon this came his disciples,
and marveled that he talked with the
woman: yet no man said, What seekest
thou? or, Why talkest thou with her?
28 The woman then left her waterpot,
and went her way into the city, and saith
to the men,
29 Come, see a man, which told me all
things that ever I did: is not this the
Christ?
30 Then they went out of the city, and
came unto him.
31 ¶ In the mean while his disciples
prayed him, saying, Master, eat.
32 But he said unto them, I have meat
to eat that ye know not of.
33 Therefore said the disciples one to
another, Hath any man brought him
aught to eat?
34 Jesus saith unto them, My meat is
to do the will of him that sent me, and
to finish his work.
35 Say not ye, There are yet four
months, and *then* cometh harvest? behold, I say unto you, Lift up your eyes,
and look on the fields; for they are white
already to harvest.
36 And he that reapeth receiveth
wages, and gathereth fruit unto life
eternal: that both he that soweth and he
that reapeth may rejoice together.
37 And herein is that saying true, One
soweth, and another reapeth.
38 I sent you to reap that whereon ye
bestowed no labor: other men labored,
and ye are entered into their labors.
39 ¶ And many of the Să-măr'ĭ-tănş
of that city believed on him for the saying of the woman, which testified, He
told me all that ever I did.
40 So when the Să-măr'ĭ-tănş were
come unto him, they besought him that
he would tarry with them: and he abode
there two days.
41 And many more believed because of
his own word;
42 And said unto the woman, Now we
believe, not because of thy saying: for
we have heard *him* ourselves, and know
that this is indeed the Christ, the Saviour of the world.
43 ¶ Now after two days he departed
thence, and went into Galilee.
44 For Jesus himself testified, that a
prophet hath no honor in his own
country.
45 Then when he was come into Galilee, the Galileans received him, having
seen all the things that he did at Jerusalem at the feast: for they also went
unto the feast.
46 So Jesus came again into Cā'nȧ of
Galilee, where he made the water wine.
And there was a certain nobleman,
whose son was sick at Cȧ-pẽr'nā-ŭm.
47 When he heard that Jesus was come
out of Judea into Galilee, he went unto
him, and besought him that he would
come down, and heal his son: for he was
at the point of death.
48 Then said Jesus unto him, Except
ye see signs and wonders, ye will not
believe.
49 The nobleman saith unto him, Sir,
come down ere my child die.
50 Jesus saith unto him, Go thy way;
thy son liveth. And the man believed
the word that Jesus had spoken unto
him, and he went his way.
51 And as he was now going down, his
servants met him, and told *him*, saying,
Thy son liveth.
52 Then inquired he of them the hour
when he began to amend. And they
said unto him, Yesterday at the seventh
hour the fever left him.
53 So the father knew that *it was* at
the same hour, in the which Jesus said
unto him, Thy son liveth: and himself
believed, and his whole house.
54 This *is* again the second miracle
that Jesus did, when he was come out
of Judea into Galilee.

CHAPTER 5

AFTER this there was a feast of the
Jews; and Jesus went up to
Jerusalem.
2 Now there is at Jerusalem by the

sheep *market* a pool, which is called in
the Hebrew tongue Bē-thē̦s′dȧ, having
five porches.
3 In these lay a great multitude of
impotent folk, of blind, halt, withered,
waiting for the moving of the water.
4 For an angel went down at a certain
season into the pool, and troubled the
water: whosoever then first after the
troubling of the water stepped in was
made whole of whatsoever disease he
had.
5 And a certain man was there, which
had an infirmity thirty and eight years.
6 When Jesus saw him lie, and knew
that he had been now a long time *in
that case,* he saith unto him, Wilt thou
be made whole?
7 The impotent man answered him,
Sir, I have no man, when the water is
troubled, to put me into the pool: but
while I am coming, another steppeth
down before me.
8 Jesus saith unto him, Rise, take up
thy bed, and walk.
9 And immediately the man was made
whole, and took up his bed, and walked:
and on the same day was the sabbath.
10 ℂ The Jews therefore said unto him
that was cured, It is the sabbath day:
it is not lawful for thee to carry *thy* bed.
11 He answered them, He that made
me whole, the same said unto me, Take
up thy bed, and walk.
12 Then asked they him, What man is
that which said unto thee, Take up thy
bed, and walk?
13 And he that was healed wist not who
it was: for Jesus had conveyed himself
away, a multitude being in *that* place.
14 Afterward Jesus findeth him in the
temple, and said unto him, Behold,
thou art made whole: sin no more, lest
a worse thing come unto thee.
15 The man departed, and told the
Jews that it was Jesus, which had made
him whole.
16 And therefore did the Jews persecute Jesus, and sought to slay him, because he had done these things on the
sabbath day.
17 ℂ But Jesus answered them, My
Father worketh hitherto, and I work.
18 Therefore the Jews sought the more
to kill him, because he not only had
broken the sabbath, but said also that
God was his Father, making himself
equal with God.
19 Then answered Jesus and said unto
them, Verily, verily, I say unto you, The
Son can do nothing of himself, but what
he seeth the Father do: for what things
soever he doeth, these also doeth the
Son likewise.
20 For the Father loveth the Son, and
showeth him all things that himself
doeth: and he will show him greater
works than these, that ye may marvel.
21 For as the Father raiseth up the
dead, and quickeneth *them;* even so the
Son quickeneth whom he will.
22 For the Father judgeth no man, but
hath committed all judgment unto the
Son:
23 That all *men* should honor the Son,
even as they honor the Father. He that
honoreth not the Son honoreth not the
Father which hath sent him.
24 Verily, verily, I say unto you, He
that heareth my word, and believeth on
him that sent me, hath everlasting life,
and shall not come into condemnation;
but is passed from death unto life.
25 Verily, verily, I say unto you, The
hour is coming, and now is, when the
dead shall hear the voice of the Son of
God: and they that hear shall live.
26 For as the Father hath life in himself; so hath he given to the Son to have
life in himself;
27 And hath given him authority to
execute judgment also, because he is
the Son of man.
28 Marvel not at this: for the hour is
coming, in the which all that are in the
graves shall hear his voice,
29 And shall come forth; they that
have done good, unto the resurrection
of life; and they that have done evil,
unto the resurrection of damnation.
30 I can of mine own self do nothing:
as I hear, I judge: and my judgment is
just; because I seek not mine own will,
but the will of the Father which hath
sent me.
31 If I bear witness of myself, my witness is not true.
32 ℂ There is another that beareth
witness of me; and I know that the witness which he witnesseth of me is true.
33 Ye sent unto John, and he bare
witness unto the truth.
34 But I receive not testimony from
man: but these things I say, that ye
might be saved.
35 He was a burning and a shining

light: and ye were willing for a season
to rejoice in his light.
36 ¶ But I have greater witness than
that of John: for the works which the
Father hath given me to finish, the same
works that I do, bear witness of me, that
the Father hath sent me.
37 And the Father himself, which hath
sent me, hath borne witness of me. Ye
have neither heard his voice at any time,
nor seen his shape.
38 And ye have not his word abiding
in you: for whom he hath sent, him ye
believe not.
39 ¶ Search the Scriptures; for in
them ye think ye have eternal life: and
they are they which testify of me.
40 And ye will not come to me, that ye
might have life.
41 I receive not honor from men.
42 But I know you, that ye have not the
love of God in you.
43 I am come in my Father's name, and
ye receive me not: if another shall come
in his own name, him ye will receive.
44 How can ye believe, which receive
honor one of another, and seek not the
honor that *cometh* from God only?
45 Do not think that I will accuse you
to the Father: there is *one* that accuseth
you, *even* Moses, in whom ye trust.
46 For had ye believed Moses, ye
would have believed me: for he wrote of
me.
47 But if ye believe not his writings,
how shall ye believe my words?

CHAPTER 6

AFTER these things Jesus went over
the sea of Galilee, which is *the*
sea of Tī-bē′rĭ-ăs.
2 And a great multitude followed him,
because they saw his miracles which he
did on them that were diseased.
3 And Jesus went up into a mountain,
and there he sat with his disciples.
4 And the passover, a feast of the Jews,
was nigh.
5 ¶ When Jesus then lifted up *his*
eyes, and saw a great company come
unto him, he saith unto Philip, Whence
shall we buy bread, that these may eat?
6 And this he said to prove him: for
he himself knew what he would do.
7 Philip answered him, Two hundred
pennyworth of bread is not sufficient for
them, that every one of them may take a
little.
8 One of his disciples, Andrew, Simon
Peter's brother, saith unto him,
9 There is a lad here, which hath five
barley loaves, and two small fishes: but
what are they among so many?
10 And Jesus said, Make the men sit
down. Now there was much grass in the
place. So the men sat down, in number
about five thousand.
11 And Jesus took the loaves; and
when he had given thanks, he distributed to the disciples, and the disciples
to them that were set down; and likewise
of the fishes as much as they would.
12 When they were filled, he said unto
his disciples, Gather up the fragments
that remain, that nothing be lost.
13 Therefore they gathered *them* together, and filled twelve baskets with
the fragments of the five barley loaves,
which remained over and above unto
them that had eaten.
14 Then those men, when they had
seen the miracle that Jesus did, said,
This is of a truth that Prophet that
should come into the world.
15 ¶ When Jesus therefore perceived
that they would come and take him by
force, to make him a king, he departed
again into a mountain himself alone.
16 And when even was *now* come, his
disciples went down unto the sea,
17 And entered into a ship, and went
over the sea toward Cȧ-pĕr′nā-ŭm.
And it was now dark, and Jesus was
not come to them.
18 And the sea arose by reason of a
great wind that blew.
19 So when they had rowed about five
and twenty or thirty furlongs, they see
Jesus walking on the sea, and drawing
nigh unto the ship: and they were
afraid.
20 But he saith unto them, It is I; be
not afraid.
21 Then they willingly received him
into the ship: and immediately the ship
was at the land whither they went.
22 ¶ The day following, when the
people, which stood on the other side of
the sea, saw that there was none other
boat there, save that one whereinto his
disciples were entered, and that Jesus
went not with his disciples into the
boat, but *that* his disciples were gone
away alone;
23 (Howbeit there came other boats
from Tī-bē′rĭ-ăs nigh unto the place

where they did eat bread, after that
the Lord had given thanks:)
24 When the people therefore saw
that Jesus was not there, neither his
disciples, they also took shipping, and
came to Cȧ-pẽr′nā-ŭm, seeking for
Jesus.
25 And when they had found him on
the other side of the sea, they said unto
him, Răb′bī, when camest thou hither?
26 Jesus answered them and said,
Verily, verily, I say unto you, Ye seek
me, not because ye saw the miracles,
but because ye did eat of the loaves, and
were filled.
27 Labor not for the meat which perisheth,
but for that meat which endureth
unto everlasting life, which the Son of
man shall give unto you: for him hath
God the Father sealed.
28 Then said they unto him, What shall
we do, that we might work the works of
God?
29 Jesus answered and said unto them,
This is the work of God, that ye believe
on him whom he hath sent.
30 They said therefore unto him, What
sign showest thou then, that we may see,
and believe thee? what dost thou work?
31 Our fathers did eat manna in the
desert; as it is written, He gave them
bread from heaven to eat.
32 Then Jesus said unto them, Verily,
verily, I say unto you, Moses gave you
not that bread from heaven; but my
Father giveth you the true bread from
heaven.
33 For the bread of God is he which
cometh down from heaven, and giveth
life unto the world.
34 Then said they unto him, Lord,
evermore give us this bread.
35 And Jesus said unto them, I am the
bread of life: he that cometh to me shall
never hunger; and he that believeth on
me shall never thirst.
36 But I said unto you, That ye also
have seen me, and believe not.
37 All that the Father giveth me shall
come to me; and him that cometh to me
I will in no wise cast out.
38 For I came down from heaven, not
to do mine own will, but the will of him
that sent me.
39 And this is the Father's will which
hath sent me, that of all which he hath
given me I should lose nothing, but
should raise it up again at the last day.
40 And this is the will of him that sent
me, that every one which seeth the Son,
and believeth on him, may have everlasting
life: and I will raise him up at
the last day.
41 The Jews then murmured at him,
because he said, I am the bread which
came down from heaven.
42 And they said, Is not this Jesus, the
son of Joseph, whose father and mother
we know? how is it then that he saith, I
came down from heaven?
43 Jesus therefore answered and said
unto them, Murmur not among yourselves.
44 No man can come to me, except the
Father which hath sent me draw him:
and I will raise him up at the last day.
45 It is written in the prophets, And
they shall be all taught of God. Every
man therefore that hath heard, and hath
learned of the Father, cometh unto me.
46 Not that any man hath seen the
Father, save he which is of God, he
hath seen the Father.
47 Verily, verily, I say unto you, He
that believeth on me hath everlasting
life.
48 I am that bread of life.
49 Your fathers did eat manna in the
wilderness, and are dead.
50 This is the bread which cometh
down from heaven, that a man may eat
thereof, and not die.
51 I am the living bread which came
down from heaven: if any man eat of
this bread, he shall live for ever: and
the bread that I will give is my flesh,
which I will give for the life of the world.
52 The Jews therefore strove among
themselves, saying, How can this man
give us *his* flesh to eat?
53 Then Jesus said unto them, Verily,
verily, I say unto you, Except ye eat the
flesh of the Son of man, and drink his
blood, ye have no life in you.
54 Whoso eateth my flesh, and drinketh
my blood, hath eternal life; and I
will raise him up at the last day.
55 For my flesh is meat indeed, and
my blood is drink indeed.
56 He that eateth my flesh, and drinketh
my blood, dwelleth in me, and I in
him.
57 As the living Father hath sent me,
and I live by the Father; so he that eateth
me, even he shall live by me.
58 This is that bread which came down

from heaven: not as your fathers did eat
manna, and are dead: he that eateth of
this bread shall live for ever.
59 These things said he in the synagogue, as he taught in Cȧ-pĕr′nā-ŭm.
60 Many therefore of his disciples,
when they had heard *this*, said, This is
a hard saying; who can hear it?
61 When Jesus knew in himself that
his disciples murmured at it, he said
unto them, Doth this offend you?
62 *What* and if ye shall see the Son of
man ascend up where he was before?
63 It is the Spirit that quickeneth; the
flesh profiteth nothing: the words that I
speak unto you, *they* are spirit, and
they are life.
64 But there are some of you that believe not. For Jesus knew from the
beginning who they were that believed
not, and who should betray him.
65 And he said, Therefore said I unto
you, that no man can come unto me,
except it were given unto him of my
Father.
66 ¶ From that *time* many of his disciples went back, and walked no more
with him.
67 Then said Jesus unto the twelve,
Will ye also go away?
68 Then Simon Peter answered him,
Lord, to whom shall we go? thou hast
the words of eternal life.
69 And we believe and are sure that
thou art that Christ, the Son of the living
God.
70 Jesus answered them, Have not I
chosen you twelve, and one of you is a
devil?
71 He spake of Judas Ĭs-căr′ĭ-ŏt *the
son* of Simon: for he it was that should
betray him, being one of the twelve.

CHAPTER 7

AFTER these things Jesus walked in
Galilee: for he would not walk in
Jewry, because the Jews sought to kill
him.
2 Now the Jews' feast of tabernacles
was at hand.
3 His brethren therefore said unto him,
Depart hence, and go into Judea, that
thy disciples also may see the works
that thou doest.
4 For *there is* no man *that* doeth any
thing in secret, and he himself seeketh
to be known openly. If thou do these
things, show thyself to the world.
5 For neither did his brethren believe
in him.
6 Then Jesus said unto them, My time
is not yet come: but your time is always
ready.
7 The world cannot hate you; but me
it hateth, because I testify of it, that
the works thereof are evil.
8 Go ye up unto this feast: I go not up
yet unto this feast; for my time is not
yet full come.
9 When he had said these words unto
them, he abode *still* in Galilee.
10 ¶ But when his brethren were
gone up, then went he also up unto the
feast, not openly, but as it were in
secret.
11 Then the Jews sought him at the
feast, and said, Where is he?
12 And there was much murmuring
among the people concerning him: for
some said, He is a good man: others
said, Nay; but he deceiveth the people.
13 Howbeit no man spake openly of
him for fear of the Jews.
14 ¶ Now about the midst of the feast
Jesus went up into the temple, and
taught.
15 And the Jews marveled, saying,
How knoweth this man letters, having
never learned?
16 Jesus answered them, and said, My
doctrine is not mine, but his that sent
me.
17 If any man will do his will, he shall
know of the doctrine, whether it be of
God, or *whether* I speak of myself.
18 He that speaketh of himself seeketh
his own glory: but he that seeketh his
glory that sent him, the same is true,
and no unrighteousness is in him.
19 Did not Moses give you the law,
and *yet* none of you keepeth the law?
Why go ye about to kill me?
20 The people answered and said,
Thou hast a devil: who goeth about to
kill thee?
21 Jesus answered and said unto them,
I have done one work, and ye all marvel.
22 Moses therefore gave unto you circumcision; (not because it is of Moses,
but of the fathers;) and ye on the sabbath day circumcise a man.
23 If a man on the sabbath day receive
circumcision, that the law of Moses
should not be broken; are ye angry at
me, because I have made a man every
whit whole on the sabbath day?

24 Judge not according to the appearance, but judge righteous judgment.
25 Then said some of them of Jerusalem, Is not this he, whom they seek to
kill?
26 But, lo, he speaketh boldly, and
they say nothing unto him. Do the
rulers know indeed that this is the very
Christ?
27 Howbeit we know this man whence
he is: but when Christ cometh, no man
knoweth whence he is.
28 Then cried Jesus in the temple as
he taught, saying, Ye both know me, and
ye know whence I am: and I am not
come of myself, but he that sent me is
true, whom ye know not.
29 But I know him; for I am from him,
and he hath sent me.
30 Then they sought to take him: but
no man laid hands on him, because his
hour was not yet come.
31 And many of the people believed
on him, and said, When Christ cometh,
will he do more miracles than these
which this *man* hath done?
32 ¶ The Phăr′ĭ-sēeş heard that the
people murmured such things concerning him; and the Phăr′ĭ-sēeş and the
chief priests sent officers to take him.
33 Then said Jesus unto them, Yet a
little while am I with you, and *then* I go
unto him that sent me.
34 Ye shall seek me, and shall not find
me: and where I am, *thither* ye cannot
come.
35 Then said the Jews among themselves, Whither will he go, that we shall
not find him? will he go unto the dispersed among the Ġĕn′tīleş, and teach
the Ġĕn′tīleş?
36 What *manner of* saying is this that
he said, Ye shall seek me, and shall not
find *me:* and where I am, *thither* ye
cannot come?
37 In the last day, that great *day* of the
feast, Jesus stood and cried, saying, If
any man thirst, let him come unto me,
and drink.
38 He that believeth on me, as the
Scripture hath said, out of his belly shall
flow rivers of living water.
39 (But this spake he of the Spirit,
which they that believe on him should
receive: for the Holy Ghost was not yet
given; because that Jesus was not yet
glorified.)
40 ¶ Many of the people therefore,
when they heard this saying, said, Of a
truth this is the Prophet.
41 Others said, This is the Christ.
But some said, Shall Christ come out of
Galilee?
42 Hath not the Scripture said, That
Christ cometh of the seed of David, and
out of the town of Bethlehem, where
David was?
43 So there was a division among the
people because of him.
44 And some of them would have taken
him; but no man laid hands on him.
45 ¶ Then came the officers to the
chief priests and Phăr′ĭ-sēeş; and they
said unto them, Why have ye not
brought him?
46 The officers answered, Never man
spake like this man.
47 Then answered them the Phăr′ĭ-
sēeş, Are ye also deceived?
48 Have any of the rulers or of the
Phăr′ĭ-sēeş believed on him?
49 But this people who knoweth not
the law are cursed.
50 Nĭc′ō-dē′mŭs saith unto them, (he
that came to Jesus by night, being one
of them,)
51 Doth our law judge *any* man, before
it hear him, and know what he doeth?
52 They answered and said unto him,
Art thou also of Galilee? Search, and
look: for out of Galilee ariseth no
prophet.
53 And every man went unto his own
house.

CHAPTER 8

JESUS went unto the mount of Olives.
2 And early in the morning he came
again into the temple, and all the
people came unto him; and he sat down,
and taught them.
3 And the scribes and Phăr′ĭ-sēeş
brought unto him a woman taken in
adultery; and when they had set her in
the midst,
4 They say unto him, Master, this
woman was taken in adultery, in the
very act.
5 Now Moses in the law commanded
us, that such should be stoned: but what
sayest thou?
6 This they said, tempting him, that
they might have to accuse him. But
Jesus stooped down, and with *his* finger
wrote on the ground, *as though he heard
them not.*

7 So when they continued asking him, he lifted up himself, and said unto them, He that is without sin among you, let him first cast a stone at her.

8 And again he stooped down, and wrote on the ground.

9 And they which heard *it,* being convicted by *their own* conscience, went out one by one, beginning at the eldest, *even* unto the last: and Jesus was left alone, and the woman standing in the midst.

10 When Jesus had lifted up himself, and saw none but the woman, he said unto her, Woman, where are those thine accusers? hath no man condemned thee?

11 She said, No man, Lord. And Jesus said unto her, Neither do I condemn thee: go, and sin no more.

12 ¶ Then spake Jesus again unto them, saying, I am the light of the world: he that followeth me shall not walk in darkness, but shall have the light of life.

13 The Phăr'ĭ-sēes̱ therefore said unto him, Thou bearest record of thyself; thy record is not true.

14 Jesus answered and said unto them, Though I bear record of myself, *yet* my record is true: for I know whence I came, and whither I go; but ye cannot tell whence I come, and whither I go.

15 Ye judge after the flesh; I judge no man.

16 And yet if I judge, my judgment is true: for I am not alone, but I and the Father that sent me.

17 It is also written in your law, that the testimony of two men is true.

18 I am one that bear witness of myself, and the Father that sent me beareth witness of me.

19 Then said they unto him, Where is thy Father? Jesus answered, Ye neither know me, nor my Father: if ye had known me, ye should have known my Father also.

20 These words spake Jesus in the treasury, as he taught in the temple: and no man laid hands on him; for his hour was not yet come.

21 Then said Jesus again unto them, I go my way, and ye shall seek me, and shall die in your sins: whither I go, ye cannot come.

22 Then said the Jews, Will he kill himself? because he saith, Whither I go, ye cannot come.

23 And he said unto them, Ye are from beneath; I am from above: ye are of this world; I am not of this world.

24 I said therefore unto you, that ye shall die in your sins: for if ye believe not that I am *he,* ye shall die in your sins.

25 Then said they unto him, Who art thou? And Jesus saith unto them, Even *the same* that I said unto you from the beginning.

26 I have many things to say and to judge of you: but he that sent me is true; and I speak to the world those things which I have heard of him.

27 They understood not that he spake to them of the Father.

28 Then said Jesus unto them, When ye have lifted up the Son of man, then shall ye know that I am *he,* and *that* I do nothing of myself; but as my Father hath taught me, I speak these things.

29 And he that sent me is with me: the Father hath not left me alone; for I do always those things that please him.

30 As he spake these words, many believed on him.

31 Then said Jesus to those Jews which believed on him, If ye continue in my word, *then* are ye my disciples indeed;

32 And ye shall know the truth, and the truth shall make you free.

33 ¶ They answered him, We be Abraham's seed, and were never in bondage to any man: how sayest thou, Ye shall be made free?

34 Jesus answered them, Verily, verily, I say unto you, Whosoever committeth sin is the servant of sin.

35 And the servant abideth not in the house for ever: *but* the Son abideth ever.

36 If the Son therefore shall make you free, ye shall be free indeed.

37 I know that ye are Abraham's seed; but ye seek to kill me, because my word hath no place in you.

38 I speak that which I have seen with my Father: and ye do that which ye have seen with your father.

39 They answered and said unto him, Abraham is our father. Jesus saith unto them, If ye were Abraham's children, ye would do the works of Abraham.

40 But now ye seek to kill me, a man that hath told you the truth, which I have heard of God: this did not Abraham.

41 Ye do the deeds of your father.
Then said they to him, We be not born
of fornication; we have one Father,
even God.
42 Jesus said unto them, If God were
your Father, ye would love me: for I
proceeded forth and came from God;
neither came I of myself, but he sent me.
43 Why do ye not understand my
speech? *even* because ye cannot hear
my word.
44 Ye are of *your* father the devil, and
the lusts of your father ye will do: he
was a murderer from the beginning,
and abode not in the truth, because
there is no truth in him. When he
speaketh a lie, he speaketh of his own:
for he is a liar, and the father of it.
45 And because I tell *you* the truth, ye
believe me not.
46 Which of you convinceth me of sin?
And if I say the truth, why do ye not
believe me?
47 He that is of God heareth God's
words: ye therefore hear *them* not, because ye are not of God.
48 Then answered the Jews, and said
unto him, Say we not well that thou art
a Sȧ-măr'ĭ-tăn, and hast a devil?
49 Jesus answered, I have not a devil;
but I honor my Father, and ye do dishonor me.
50 And I seek not mine own glory:
there is one that seeketh and judgeth.
51 Verily, verily, I say unto you, If a
man keep my saying, he shall never see
death.
52 Then said the Jews unto him, Now
we know that thou hast a devil. Abraham is dead, and the prophets; and thou
sayest, If a man keep my saying, he
shall never taste of death.
53 Art thou greater than our father
Abraham, which is dead? and the prophets are dead: whom makest thou thyself?
54 Jesus answered, If I honor myself,
my honor is nothing: it is my Father
that honoreth me; of whom ye say, that
he is your God:
55 Yet ye have not known him; but I
know him: and if I should say, I know
him not, I shall be a liar like unto you:
but I know him, and keep his saying.
56 Your father Abraham rejoiced to see
my day: and he saw *it*, and was glad.
57 Then said the Jews unto him, Thou
art not yet fifty years old, and hast thou
seen Abraham?
58 Jesus said unto them, Verily, verily,
I say unto you, Before Abraham was, I
am.
59 Then took they up stones to cast at
him: but Jesus hid himself, and went
out of the temple, going through the
midst of them, and so passed by.

CHAPTER 9

AND as *Jesus* passed by, he saw a
man which was blind from *his*
birth.
2 And his disciples asked him, saying,
Master, who did sin, this man, or his
parents, that he was born blind?
3 Jesus answered, Neither hath this
man sinned, nor his parents: but that
the works of God should be made manifest in him.
4 I must work the works of him that
sent me, while it is day: the night cometh, when no man can work.
5 As long as I am in the world, I am
the light of the world.
6 When he had thus spoken, he spat
on the ground, and made clay of the
spittle, and he anointed the eyes of the
blind man with the clay.
7 And said unto him, Go, wash in the
pool of Sĭ-lō'ăm, (which is by interpretation, Sent.) He went his way therefore, and washed, and came seeing.
8 ¶ The neighbors therefore, and they
which before had seen him that he was
blind, said, Is not this he that sat and
begged?
9 Some said, This is he: others *said*,
He is like him: *but* he said, I am *he*.
10 Therefore said they unto him, How
were thine eyes opened?
11 He answered and said, A man that
is called Jesus made clay, and anointed
mine eyes, and said unto me, Go to the
pool of Sĭ-lō'ăm, and wash: and I went
and washed, and I received sight.
12 Then said they unto him, Where is
he? He said, I know not.
13 ¶ They brought to the Phăr'ĭ-sēeș
him that aforetime was blind.
14 And it was the sabbath day when
Jesus made the clay, and opened his
eyes.
15 Then again the Phăr'ĭ-sēeș also
asked him how he had received his
sight. He said unto them, He put clay
upon mine eyes, and I washed, and do
see.
16 Therefore said some of the Phăr'ĭ-

sēeș, This man is not of God, because
he keepeth not the sabbath day. Others
said, How can a man that is a sinner do
such miracles? And there was a division
among them.
17 They say unto the blind man again,
What sayest thou of him, that he hath
opened thine eyes? He said, He is a
prophet.
18 But the Jews did not believe concerning him, that he had been blind,
and received his sight, until they called
the parents of him that had received his
sight.
19 And they asked them, saying, Is
this your son, who ye say was born
blind? how then doth he now see?
20 His parents answered them and
said, We know that this is our son, and
that he was born blind:
21 But by what means he now seeth,
we know not; or who hath opened his
eyes, we know not: he is of age; ask
him: he shall speak for himself.
22 These *words* spake his parents, because they feared the Jews: for the Jews
had agreed already, that if any man did
confess that he was Christ, he should be
put out of the synagogue.
23 Therefore said his parents, He is of
age; ask him.
24 Then again called they the man that
was blind, and said unto him, Give God
the praise: we know that this man is a
sinner.
25 He answered and said, Whether he
be a sinner *or no,* I know not: one thing
I know, that, whereas I was blind, now
I see.
26 Then said they to him again, What
did he to thee? how opened he thine
eyes?
27 He answered them, I have told you
already, and ye did not hear: wherefore
would ye hear *it* again? will ye also be
his disciples?
28 Then they reviled him, and said,
Thou art his disciple; but we are Moses'
disciples.
29 We know that God spake unto
Moses: *as for* this *fellow,* we know not
from whence he is.
30 The man answered and said unto
them, Why herein is a marvelous thing,
that ye know not from-whence he is, and
yet he hath opened mine eyes.
31 Now we know that God heareth not
sinners: but if any man be a worshipper
of God, and doeth his will, him he
heareth.
32 Since the world began was it not
heard that any man opened the eyes of
one that was born blind.
33 If this man were not of God, he
could do nothing.
34 They answered and said unto him,
Thou wast altogether born in sins, and
dost thou teach us? And they cast him out.
35 Jesus heard that they had cast him
out; and when he had found him, he
said unto him, Dost thou believe on the
Son of God?
36 He answered and said, Who is he,
Lord, that I might believe on him?
37 And Jesus said unto him, Thou hast
both seen him, and it is he that talketh
with thee.
38 And he said, Lord, I believe. And
he worshipped him.
39 ℂ And Jesus said, For judgment I
am come into this world, that they which
see not might see; and that they which
see might be made blind.
40 And *some* of the Phăr'ĭ-sēeș which
were with him heard these words, and
said unto him, Are we blind also?
41 Jesus said unto them, If ye were
blind, ye should have no sin: but now
ye say, We see; therefore your sin
remaineth.

CHAPTER 10

VERILY, verily, I say unto you, He
that entereth not by the door into
the sheepfold, but climbeth up some
other way, the same is a thief and a
robber.
2 But he that entereth in by the door is
the shepherd of the sheep.
3 To him the porter openeth; and the
sheep hear his voice: and he calleth his
own sheep by name, and leadeth them
out.
4 And when he putteth forth his own
sheep, he goeth before them, and the
sheep follow him: for they know his
voice.
5 And a stranger will they not follow,
but will flee from him; for they know
not the voice of strangers.
6 This parable spake Jesus unto them;
but they understood not what things
they were which he spake unto them.
7 Then said Jesus unto them again,
Verily, verily, I say unto you, I am the
door of the sheep.

8 All that ever came before me are thieves and robbers: but the sheep did not hear them.
9 I am the door: by me if any man enter in, he shall be saved, and shall go in and out, and find pasture.
10 The thief cometh not, but for to steal, and to kill, and to destroy: I am come that they might have life, and that they might have *it* more abundantly.
11 I am the good shepherd: the good shepherd giveth his life for the sheep.
12 But he that is a hireling, and not the shepherd, whose own the sheep are not, seeth the wolf coming, and leaveth the sheep, and fleeth; and the wolf catcheth them, and scattereth the sheep.
13 The hireling fleeth, because he is a hireling, and careth not for the sheep.
14 I am the good shepherd, and know my *sheep,* and am known of mine.
15 As the Father knoweth me, even so know I the Father: and I lay down my life for the sheep.
16 And other sheep I have, which are not of this fold: them also I must bring, and they shall hear my voice; and there shall be one fold, *and* one shepherd.
17 Therefore doth my Father love me, because I lay down my life, that I might take it again.
18 No man taketh it from me, but I lay it down of myself. I have power to lay it down, and I have power to take it again. This commandment have I received of my Father.
19 ¶ There was a division therefore again among the Jews for these sayings.
20 And many of them said, He hath a devil, and is mad; why hear ye him?
21 Others said, These are not the words of him that hath a devil. Can a devil open the eyes of the blind?
22 ¶ And it was at Jerusalem the feast of the dedication, and it was winter.
23 And Jesus walked in the temple in Solomon's porch.
24 Then came the Jews round about him, and said unto him, How long dost thou make us to doubt? If thou be the Christ, tell us plainly.
25 Jesus answered them, I told you, and ye believed not: the works that I do in my Father's name, they bear witness of me.
26 But ye believe not, because ye are not of my sheep, as I said unto you.
27 My sheep hear my voice, and I know them, and they follow me:
28 And I give unto them eternal life; and they shall never perish, neither shall any *man* pluck them out of my hand.
29 My Father, which gave *them* me, is greater than all; and no *man* is able to pluck *them* out of my Father's hand.
30 I and *my* Father are one.
31 Then the Jews took up stones again to stone him.
32 Jesus answered them, Many good works have I showed you from my Father; for which of those works do ye stone me?
33 The Jews answered him, saying, For a good work we stone thee not; but for blasphemy; and because that thou, being a man, makest thyself God.
34 Jesus answered them, Is it not written in your law, I said, Ye are gods?
35 If he called them gods, unto whom the word of God came, and the Scripture cannot be broken;
36 Say ye of him, whom the Father hath sanctified, and sent into the world, Thou blasphemest; because I said, I am the Son of God?
37 If I do not the works of my Father, believe me not.
38 But if I do, though ye believe not me, believe the works; that ye may know, and believe, that the Father *is* in me, and I in him.
39 Therefore they sought again to take him; but he escaped out of their hand,
40 And went away again beyond Jordan into the place where John at first baptized; and there he abode.
41 And many resorted unto him, and said, John did no miracle: but all things that John spake of this man were true.
42 And many believed on him there.

CHAPTER 11

NOW a certain *man* was sick, *named* Lazarus, of Bethany, the town of Mary and her sister Martha.
2 (It was *that* Mary which anointed the Lord with ointment, and wiped his feet with her hair, whose brother Lazarus was sick.)
3 Therefore his sisters sent unto him, saying, Lord, behold, he whom thou lovest is sick.
4 When Jesus heard *that,* he said, This sickness is not unto death, but for

the glory of God, that the Son of God
might be glorified thereby.
5 Now Jesus loved Martha, and her
sister, and Lazarus.
6 When he had heard therefore that he
was sick, he abode two days still in the
same place where he was.
7 Then after that saith he to *his* disciples,
Let us go into Judea again.
8 *His* disciples say unto him, Master,
the Jews of late sought to stone thee;
and goest thou thither again?
9 Jesus answered, Are there not twelve
hours in the day? If any man walk in
the day, he stumbleth not, because he
seeth the light of this world.
10 But if a man walk in the night, he
stumbleth, because there is no light in
him.
11 These things said he: and after
that he saith unto them, Our friend
Lazarus sleepeth; but I go, that I may
awake him out of sleep.
12 Then said his disciples, Lord, if he
sleep, he shall do well.
13 Howbeit Jesus spake of his death:
but they thought that he had spoken of
taking of rest in sleep.
14 Then said Jesus unto them plainly,
Lazarus is dead.
15 And I am glad for your sakes that I
was not there, to the intent ye may
believe; nevertheless let us go unto
him.
16 Then said Thomas, which is called
Dĭd'ȳ-mŭs, unto his fellow disciples,
Let us also go, that we may die with
him.
17 Then when Jesus came, he found
that he had *lain* in the grave four days
already.
18 Now Bethany was nigh unto Jerusalem,
about fifteen furlongs off:
19 And many of the Jews came to
Martha and Mary, to comfort them concerning
their brother.
20 Then Martha, as soon as she heard
that Jesus was coming, went and met
him: but Mary sat *still* in the house.
21 Then said Martha unto Jesus,
Lord, if thou hadst been here, my
brother had not died.
22 But I know, that even now, whatsoever
thou wilt ask of God, God will
give *it* thee.
23 Jesus saith unto her, Thy brother
shall rise again.
24 Martha saith unto him, I know that
he shall rise again in the resurrection at
the last day.
25 Jesus said unto her, I am the resurrection,
and the life: he that believeth
in me, though he were dead, yet shall
he live:
26 And whosoever liveth and believeth
in me shall never die. Believest thou
this?
27 She saith unto him, Yea, Lord: I
believe that thou art the Christ, the Son
of God, which should come into the
world.
28 And when she had so said, she went
her way, and called Mary her sister
secretly, saying, The Master is come,
and calleth for thee.
29 As soon as she heard *that*, she arose
quickly, and came unto him.
30 Now Jesus was not yet come into
the town, but was in that place where
Martha met him.
31 The Jews then which were with her
in the house, and comforted her, when
they saw Mary, that she rose up hastily
and went out, followed her, saying, She
goeth unto the grave to weep there.
32 Then when Mary was come where
Jesus was, and saw him, she fell down
at his feet, saying unto him, Lord, if
thou hadst been here, my brother had
not died.
33 When Jesus therefore saw her
weeping, and the Jews also weeping
which came with her, he groaned in the
spirit, and was troubled.
34 And said, Where have ye laid him?
They say unto him, Lord, come and see.
35 Jesus wept.
36 Then said the Jews, Behold how he
loved him!
37 And some of them said, Could not
this man, which opened the eyes of the
blind, have caused that even this man
should not have died?
38 Jesus therefore again groaning in
himself cometh to the grave. It was a
cave, and a stone lay upon it.
39 Jesus said, Take ye away the stone.
Martha, the sister of him that was dead,
saith unto him, Lord, by this time he
stinketh: for he hath been *dead* four
days.
40 Jesus saith unto her, Said I not
unto thee, that, if thou wouldest believe,
thou shouldest see the glory of God?
41 Then they took away the stone
from the place where the dead was laid.

And Jesus lifted up *his* eyes, and said,
Father, I thank thee that thou hast
heard me.
42 And I knew that thou hearest me
always: but because of the people which
stand by I said *it*, that they may believe
that thou hast sent me.
43 And when he thus had spoken, he
cried with a loud voice, Lazarus, come
forth.
44 And he that was dead came forth,
bound hand and foot with graveclothes;
and his face was bound about with a
napkin. Jesus saith unto them, Loose
him, and let him go.
45 Then many of the Jews which came
to Mary, and had seen the things which
Jesus did, believed on him.
46 But some of them went their ways
to the Phăr'ĭ-sēe̦s, and told them what
things Jesus had done.
47 ¶ Then gathered the chief priests
and the Phăr'ĭ-sēe̦s a council, and said,
What do we? for this man doeth many
miracles.
48 If we let him thus alone, all *men*
will believe on him; and the Romans
shall come and take away both our
place and nation.
49 And one of them, *named* Cā'ịă-
phăs, being the high priest that same
year, said unto them, Ye know nothing
at all,
50 Nor consider that it is expedient
for us, that one man should die for the
people, and that the whole nation perish
not.
51 And this spake he not of himself:
but being high priest that year, he
prophesied that Jesus should die for
that nation;
52 And not for that nation only, but
that also he should gather together in
one the children of God that were scattered abroad.
53 Then from that day forth they took
counsel together for to put him to death.
54 Jesus therefore walked no more
openly among the Jews; but went thence
unto a country near to the wilderness,
into a city called Ē'phrā-ĭm, and there
continued with his disciples.
55 ¶ And the Jews' passover was nigh
at hand: and many went out of the
country up to Jerusalem before the
passover, to purify themselves.
56 Then sought they for Jesus, and
spake among themselves, as they stood
in the temple, What think ye, that he
will not come to the feast?
57 Now both the chief priests and the
Phăr'ĭ-sēe̦s had given a commandment,
that, if any man knew where he were,
he should show *it*, that they might take
him.

CHAPTER 12

THEN Jesus six days before the
passover came to Bethany, where
Lazarus was which had been dead,
whom he raised from the dead.
2 There they made him a supper;
and Martha served: but Lazarus was
one of them that sat at the table with
him.
3 Then took Mary a pound of ointment
of spikenard, very costly, and anointed
the feet of Jesus, and wiped his feet
with her hair: and the house was filled
with the odor of the ointment.
4 Then saith one of his disciples, Judas
Ĭs-căr'ĭ-ŏt, Simon's *son*, which should
betray him,
5 Why was not this ointment sold for
three hundred pence, and given to the
poor?
6 This he said, not that he cared for
the poor; but because he was a thief,
and had the bag, and bare what was put
therein.
7 Then said Jesus, Let her alone:
against the day of my burying hath she
kept this.
8 For the poor always ye have with
you; but me ye have not always.
9 Much people of the Jews therefore
knew that he was there: and they came
not for Jesus' sake only, but that they
might see Lazarus also, whom he had
raised from the dead.
10 ¶ But the chief priests consulted
that they might put Lazarus also to
death;
11 Because that by reason of him
many of the Jews went away, and believed on Jesus.
12 ¶ On the next day much people
that were come to the feast, when they
heard that Jesus was coming to Jerusalem,
13 Took branches of palm trees, and
went forth to meet him, and cried,
Hosanna: Blessed *is* the King of Ĭs̱'rā-ĕl
that cometh in the name of the Lord.
14 And Jesus, when he had found a
young ass, sat thereon; as it is written,

15 Fear not, daughter of Sī′ŏn: behold,
thy King cometh, sitting on an ass's
colt.
16 These things understood not his
disciples at the first: but when Jesus
was glorified, then remembered they
that these things were written of him,
and *that* they had done these things unto
him.
17 The people therefore that was with
him when he called Lazarus out of his
grave, and raised him from the dead,
bare record.
18 For this cause the people also met
him, for that they heard that he had
done this miracle.
19 The Phăr′ĭ-sēeş therefore said
among themselves, Perceive ye how ye
prevail nothing? behold, the world is
gone after him.
20 ¶ And there were certain Greeks
among them that came up to worship at
the feast:
21 The same came therefore to Philip,
which was of Bĕth′sā′ĭ-dȧ of Galilee,
and desired him, saying, Sir, we would
see Jesus.
22 Philip cometh and telleth Andrew:
and again Andrew and Philip tell Jesus.
23 ¶ And Jesus answered them, saying, The hour is come, that the Son of
man should be glorified.
24 Verily, verily, I say unto you, Except
a corn of wheat fall into the ground and
die, it abideth alone: but if it die, it
bringeth forth much fruit.
25 He that loveth his life shall lose it;
and he that hateth his life in this world
shall keep it unto life eternal.
26 If any man serve me, let him follow
me; and where I am, there shall also
my servant be: if any man serve me,
him will *my* Father honor.
27 Now is my soul troubled; and what
shall I say? Father, save me from this
hour: but for this cause came I unto this
hour.
28 Father, glorify thy name. Then
came there a voice from heaven, *saying,*
I have both glorified *it,* and will glorify
it again.
29 The people therefore that stood by,
and heard *it,* said that it thundered:
others said, An angel spake to him.
30 Jesus answered and said, This voice
came not because of me, but for your
sakes.
31 Now is the judgment of this world:
now shall the prince of this world be
cast out.
32 And I, if I be lifted up from the
earth, will draw all *men* unto me.
33 This he said, signifying what death
he should die.
34 The people answered him, We have
heard out of the law that Christ abideth
for ever: and how sayest thou, The Son
of man must be lifted up? who is this
Son of man?
35 Then Jesus said unto them, Yet a
little while is the light with you. Walk
while ye have the light, lest darkness
come upon you: for he that walketh in
darkness knoweth not whither he goeth.
36 While ye have light, believe in the
light, that ye may be the children of
light. These things spake Jesus, and
departed, and did hide himself from
them.
37 ¶ But though he had done so many
miracles before them, yet they believed
not on him:
38 That the saying of Ē-şā′ịăs the
prophet might be fulfilled, which he
spake, Lord, who hath believed our
report? and to whom hath the arm of the
Lord been revealed?
39 Therefore they could not believe,
because that Ē-şā′ịăs said again,
40 He hath blinded their eyes, and
hardened their heart; that they should
not see with *their* eyes, nor understand
with *their* heart, and be converted, and
I should heal them.
41 These things said Ē-şā′ịăs, when he
saw his glory, and spake of him.
42 ¶ Nevertheless among the chief
rulers also many believed on him; but
because of the Phăr′ĭ-sēeş they did not
confess *him,* lest they should be put out
of the synagogue:
43 For they loved the praise of men
more than the praise of God.
44 ¶ Jesus cried and said, He that
believeth on me, believeth not on me,
but on him that sent me.
45 And he that seeth me seeth him
that sent me.
46 I am come a light into the world,
that whosoever believeth on me should
not abide in darkness.
47 And if any man hear my words, and
believe not, I judge him not: for I came
not to judge the world, but to save the
world.
48 He that rejecteth me, and receiveth

not my words, hath one that judgeth him: the word that I have spoken, the same shall judge him in the last day.

49 For I have not spoken of myself; but the Father which sent me, he gave me a commandment, what I should say, and what I should speak.

50 And I know that his commandment is life everlasting: whatsoever I speak therefore, even as the Father said unto me, so I speak.

CHAPTER 13

NOW before the feast of the passover, when Jesus knew that his hour was come that he should depart out of this world unto the Father, having loved his own which were in the world, he loved them unto the end.

2 And supper being ended, the devil having now put into the heart of Judas Ĭs-căr'ĭ-ŏt, Simon's *son*, to betray him;

3 Jesus knowing that the Father had given all things into his hands, and that he was come from God, and went to God;

4 He riseth from supper, and laid aside his garments; and took a towel, and girded himself.

5 After that he poureth water into a basin, and began to wash the disciples' feet, and to wipe *them* with the towel wherewith he was girded.

6 Then cometh he to Simon Peter: and Peter saith unto him, Lord, dost thou wash my feet?

7 Jesus answered and said unto him, What I do thou knowest not now; but thou shalt know hereafter.

8 Peter saith unto him, Thou shalt never wash my feet. Jesus answered him, If I wash thee not, thou hast no part with me.

9 Simon Peter saith unto him, Lord, not my feet only, but also *my* hands and *my* head.

10 Jesus saith to him, He that is washed needeth not save to wash *his* feet, but is clean every whit: and ye are clean, but not all.

11 For he knew who should betray him; therefore said he, Ye are not all clean.

12 So after he had washed their feet, and had taken his garments, and was set down again, he said unto them, Know ye what I have done to you?

13 Ye call me Master and Lord: and ye say well; for *so* I am.

14 If I then, *your* Lord and Master, have washed your feet; ye also ought to wash one another's feet.

15 For I have given you an example, that ye should do as I have done to you.

16 Verily, verily, I say unto you, The servant is not greater than his lord; neither he that is sent greater than he that sent him.

17 If ye know these things, happy are ye if ye do them.

18 ¶ I speak not of you all: I know whom I have chosen: but that the Scripture may be fulfilled, He that eateth bread with me hath lifted up his heel against me.

19 Now I tell you before it come, that, when it is come to pass, ye may believe that I am *he*.

20 Verily, verily, I say unto you, He that receiveth whomsoever I send receiveth me; and he that receiveth me receiveth him that sent me.

21 When Jesus had thus said, he was troubled in spirit, and testified, and said, Verily, verily, I say unto you, that one of you shall betray me.

22 Then the disciples looked one on another, doubting of whom he spake.

23 Now there was leaning on Jesus' bosom one of his disciples, whom Jesus loved.

24 Simon Peter therefore beckoned to him, that he should ask who it should be of whom he spake.

25 He then lying on Jesus' breast saith unto him, Lord, who is it?

26 Jesus answered, He it is, to whom I shall give a sop, when I have dipped *it*. And when he had dipped the sop, he gave *it* to Judas Ĭs-căr'ĭ-ŏt, *the son* of Simon.

27 And after the sop Satan entered into him. Then said Jesus unto him, That thou doest, do quickly.

28 Now no man at the table knew for what intent he spake this unto him.

29 For some *of them* thought, because Judas had the bag, that Jesus had said unto him, Buy *those things* that we have need of against the feast; or, that he should give something to the poor.

30 He then, having received the sop, went immediately out; and it was night.

31 ¶ Therefore, when he was gone out, Jesus said, Now is the Son of man glorified, and God is glorified in him.

32 If God be glorified in him, God shall

also glorify him in himself, and shall straightway glorify him.

33 Little children, yet a little while I am with you. Ye shall seek me; and as I said unto the Jews, Whither I go, ye cannot come; so now I say to you.

34 A new commandment I give unto you, That ye love one another; as I have loved you, that ye also love one another.

35 By this shall all *men* know that ye are my disciples, if ye have love one to another.

36 ℂ Simon Peter said unto him, Lord, whither goest thou? Jesus answered him, Whither I go, thou canst not follow me now; but thou shalt follow me afterward.

37 Peter said unto him, Lord, why cannot I follow thee now? I will lay down my life for thy sake.

38 Jesus answered him, Wilt thou lay down thy life for my sake? Verily, verily, I say unto thee, The cock shall not crow, till thou hast denied me thrice.

CHAPTER 14

LET not your heart be troubled: ye believe in God, believe also in me.

2 In my Father's house are many mansions: if *it were* not *so,* I would have told you. I go to prepare a place for you.

3 And if I go and prepare a place for you, I will come again, and receive you unto myself; that where I am, *there* ye may be also.

4 And whither I go ye know, and the way ye know.

5 Thomas saith unto him, Lord, we know not whither thou goest; and how can we know the way?

6 Jesus saith unto him, I am the way, the truth, and the life: no man cometh unto the Father, but by me.

7 If ye had known me, ye should have known my Father also: and from henceforth ye know him, and have seen him.

8 Philip saith unto him, Lord, show us the Father, and it sufficeth us.

9 Jesus saith unto him, Have I been so long time with you, and yet hast thou not known me, Philip? he that hath seen me hath seen the Father; and how sayest thou *then,* Show us the Father?

10 Believest thou not that I am in the Father, and the Father in me? the words that I speak unto you I speak not of myself: but the Father that dwelleth in me, he doeth the works.

11 Believe me that I *am* in the Father, and the Father in me: or else believe me for the very works' sake.

12 Verily, verily, I say unto you, He that believeth on me, the works that I do shall he do also; and greater *works* than these shall he do; because I go unto my Father.

13 And whatsoever ye shall ask in my name, that will I do, that the Father may be glorified in the Son.

14 If ye shall ask any thing in my name, I will do *it.*

15 ℂ If ye love me, keep my commandments.

16 And I will pray the Father, and he shall give you another Comforter, that he may abide with you for ever;

17 *Even* the Spirit of truth; whom the world cannot receive, because it seeth him not, neither knoweth him: but ye know him; for he dwelleth with you, and shall be in you.

18 I will not leave you comfortless: I will come to you.

19 Yet a little while, and the world seeth me no more; but ye see me: because I live, ye shall live also.

20 At that day ye shall know that I *am* in my Father, and ye in me, and I in you.

21 He that hath my commandments, and keepeth them, he it is that loveth me: and he that loveth me shall be loved of my Father, and I will love him, and will manifest myself to him.

22 Judas saith unto him, not Ĭs-căr′ĭ-ŏt, Lord, how is it that thou wilt manifest thyself unto us, and not unto the world?

23 Jesus answered and said unto him, If a man love me, he will keep my words: and my Father will love him, and we will come unto him, and make our abode with him.

24 He that loveth me not keepeth not my sayings: and the word which ye hear is not mine, but the Father's which sent me.

25 These things have I spoken unto you, being *yet* present with you.

26 But the Comforter, *which is* the Holy Ghost, whom the Father will send in my name, he shall teach you all things, and bring all things to your remembrance, whatsoever I have said unto you.

27 Peace I leave with you, my peace I give unto you: not as the world giveth, give I unto you. Let not your heart be troubled, neither let it be afraid.

28 Ye have heard how I said unto you, I go away, and come *again* unto you. If ye loved me, ye would rejoice, because I said, I go unto the Father: for my Father is greater than I.

29 And now I have told you before it come to pass, that, when it is come to pass, ye might believe.

30 Hereafter I will not talk much with you: for the prince of this world cometh, and hath nothing in me.

31 But that the world may know that I love the Father; and as the Father gave me commandment, even so I do. Arise, let us go hence.

CHAPTER 15

I AM the true vine, and my Father is the husbandman.

2 Every branch in me that beareth not fruit he taketh away: and every *branch* that beareth fruit, he purgeth it, that it may bring forth more fruit.

3 Now ye are clean through the word which I have spoken unto you.

4 Abide in me, and I in you. As the branch cannot bear fruit of itself, except it abide in the vine; no more can ye, except ye abide in me.

5 I am the vine, ye *are* the branches. He that abideth in me, and I in him, the same bringeth forth much fruit; for without me ye can do nothing.

6 If a man abide not in me, he is cast forth as a branch, and is withered; and men gather them, and cast *them* into the fire, and they are burned.

7 If ye abide in me, and my words abide in you, ye shall ask what ye will, and it shall be done unto you.

8 Herein is my Father glorified, that ye bear much fruit; so shall ye be my disciples.

9 As the Father hath loved me, so have I loved you: continue ye in my love.

10 If ye keep my commandments, ye shall abide in my love; even as I have kept my Father's commandments, and abide in his love.

11 These things have I spoken unto you, that my joy might remain in you, and *that* your joy might be full.

12 This is my commandment, That ye love one another, as I have loved you.

13 Greater love hath no man than this, that a man lay down his life for his friends.

14 Ye are my friends, if ye do whatsoever I command you.

15 Henceforth I call you not servants; for the servant knoweth not what his lord doeth: but I have called you friends; for all things that I have heard of my Father I have made known unto you.

16 Ye have not chosen me, but I have chosen you, and ordained you, that ye should go and bring forth fruit, and *that* your fruit should remain; that whatsoever ye shall ask of the Father in my name, he may give it you.

17 These things I command you, that ye love one another.

18 If the world hate you, ye know that it hated me before *it hated* you.

19 If ye were of the world, the world would love his own; but because ye are not of the world, but I have chosen you out of the world, therefore the world hateth you.

20 Remember the word that I said unto you, The servant is not greater than his lord. If they have persecuted me, they will also persecute you; if they have kept my saying, they will keep yours also.

21 But all these things will they do unto you for my name's sake, because they know not him that sent me.

22 If I had not come and spoken unto them, they had not had sin; but now they have no cloak for their sin.

23 He that hateth me hateth my Father also.

24 If I had not done among them the works which none other man did, they had not had sin: but now have they both seen and hated both me and my Father.

25 But *this cometh to pass,* that the word might be fulfilled that is written in their law, They hated me without a cause.

26 But when the Comforter is come, whom I will send unto you from the Father, *even* the Spirit of truth, which proceedeth from the Father, he shall testify of me:

27 And ye also shall bear witness, because ye have been with me from the beginning.

CHAPTER 16

THESE things have I spoken unto you, that ye should not be offended.

2 They shall put you out of the synagogues: yea, the time cometh, that whosoever killeth you will think that he doeth God service.
3 And these things will they do unto you, because they have not known the Father, nor me.
4 But these things have I told you, that when the time shall come, ye may remember that I told you of them. And these things I said not unto you at the beginning, because I was with you.
5 But now I go my way to him that sent me; and none of you asketh me, Whither goest thou?
6 But because I have said these things unto you, sorrow hath filled your heart.
7 Nevertheless I tell you the truth; It is expedient for you that I go away: for if I go not away, the Comforter will not come unto you; but if I depart, I will send him unto you.
8 And when he is come, he will reprove the world of sin, and of righteousness, and of judgment:
9 Of sin, because they believe not on me;
10 Of righteousness, because I go to my Father, and ye see me no more;
11 Of judgment, because the prince of this world is judged.
12 I have yet many things to say unto you, but ye cannot bear them now.
13 Howbeit when he, the Spirit of truth, is come, he will guide you into all truth: for he shall not speak of himself; but whatsoever he shall hear, *that* shall he speak: and he will show you things to come.
14 He shall glorify me: for he shall receive of mine, and shall show *it* unto you.
15 All things that the Father hath are mine: therefore said I, that he shall take of mine, and shall show *it* unto you.
16 A little while, and ye shall not see me: and again, a little while, and ye shall see me, because I go to the Father.
17 Then said *some* of his disciples among themselves, What is this that he saith unto us, A little while, and ye shall not see me: and again, a little while, and ye shall see me: and, Because I go to the Father?
18 They said therefore, What is this that he saith, A little while? we cannot tell what he saith.
19 Now Jesus knew that they were desirous to ask him, and said unto them, Do ye inquire among yourselves of that I said, A little while, and ye shall not see me: and again, a little while, and ye shall see me?
20 Verily, verily, I say unto you, That ye shall weep and lament, but the world shall rejoice; and ye shall be sorrowful, but your sorrow shall be turned into joy.
21 A woman when she is in travail hath sorrow, because her hour is come: but as soon as she is delivered of the child, she remembereth no more the anguish, for joy that a man is born into the world.
22 And ye now therefore have sorrow: but I will see you again, and your heart shall rejoice, and your joy no man taketh from you.
23 And in that day ye shall ask me nothing. Verily, verily, I say unto you, Whatsoever ye shall ask the Father in my name, he will give *it* you.
24 Hitherto have ye asked nothing in my name: ask, and ye shall receive, that your joy may be full.
25 These things have I spoken unto you in proverbs: but the time cometh, when I shall no more speak unto you in proverbs, but I shall show you plainly of the Father.
26 At that day ye shall ask in my name: and I say not unto you, that I will pray the Father for you:
27 For the Father himself loveth you, because ye have loved me, and have believed that I came out from God.
28 I came forth from the Father, and am come into the world: again, I leave the world, and go to the Father.
29 His disciples said unto him, Lo, now speakest thou plainly, and speakest no proverb.
30 Now are we sure that thou knowest all things, and needest not that any man should ask thee: by this we believe that thou camest forth from God.
31 Jesus answered them, Do ye now believe?
32 Behold, the hour cometh, yea, is now come, that ye shall be scattered, every man to his own, and shall leave me alone: and yet I am not alone, because the Father is with me.
33 These things I have spoken unto you, that in me ye might have peace. In the world ye shall have tribulation: but be of good cheer; I have overcome the world.

CHAPTER 17

THESE words spake Jesus, and lifted up his eyes to heaven, and said, Father, the hour is come; glorify thy Son, that thy Son also may glorify thee:

2 As thou hast given him power over all flesh, that he should give eternal life to as many as thou hast given him.

3 And this is life eternal, that they might know thee the only true God, and Jesus Christ, whom thou hast sent.

4 I have glorified thee on the earth: I have finished the work which thou gavest me to do.

5 And now, O Father, glorify thou me with thine own self with the glory which I had with thee before the world was.

6 I have manifested thy name unto the men which thou gavest me out of the world: thine they were, and thou gavest them me; and they have kept thy word.

7 Now they have known that all things whatsoever thou hast given me are of thee.

8 For I have given unto them the words which thou gavest me; and they have received *them,* and have known surely that I came out from thee, and they have believed that thou didst send me.

9 I pray for them: I pray not for the world, but for them which thou hast given me; for they are thine.

10 And all mine are thine, and thine are mine; and I am glorified in them.

11 And now I am no more in the world, but these are in the world, and I come to thee. Holy Father, keep through thine own name those whom thou hast given me, that they may be one, as we *are.*

12 While I was with them in the world, I kept them in thy name: those that thou gavest me I have kept, and none of them is lost, but the son of perdition; that the Scripture might be fulfilled.

13 And now come I to thee; and these things I speak in the world, that they might have my joy fulfilled in themselves.

14 I have given them thy word; and the world hath hated them, because they are not of the world, even as I am not of the world.

15 I pray not that thou shouldest take them out of the world, but that thou shouldest keep them from the evil.

16 They are not of the world, even as I am not of the world.

17 Sanctify them through thy truth: thy word is truth.

18 As thou hast sent me into the world, even so have I also sent them into the world.

19 And for their sakes I sanctify myself, that they also might be sanctified through the truth.

20 Neither pray I for these alone, but for them also which shall believe on me through their word;

21 That they all may be one; as thou, Father, *art* in me, and I in thee, that they also may be one in us: that the world may believe that thou hast sent me.

22 And the glory which thou gavest me I have given them; that they may be one, even as we are one:

23 I in them, and thou in me, that they may be made perfect in one; and that the world may know that thou hast sent me, and hast loved them, as thou hast loved me.

24 Father, I will that they also, whom thou hast given me, be with me where I am; that they may behold my glory, which thou hast given me: for thou lovedst me before the foundation of the world.

25 O righteous Father, the world hath not known thee: but I have known thee, and these have known that thou hast sent me.

26 And I have declared unto them thy name, and will declare *it;* that the love wherewith thou hast loved me may be in them, and I in them.

CHAPTER 18

WHEN Jesus had spoken these words, he went forth with his disciples over the brook Çē′drŏn, where was a garden, into the which he entered, and his disciples.

2 And Judas also, which betrayed him, knew the place: for Jesus ofttimes resorted thither with his disciples.

3 Judas then, having received a band *of men* and officers from the chief priests and Phär′i-seeș, cometh thither with lanterns and torches and weapons.

4 Jesus therefore, knowing all things that should come upon him, went forth, and said unto them, Whom seek ye?

5 They answered him, Jesus of Naza-

reth. Jesus saith unto them, I am *he.*
And Judas also, which betrayed him,
stood with them.
6 As soon then as he had said unto
them, I am *he,* they went backward,
and fell to the ground.
7 Then asked he them again, Whom
seek ye? And they said, Jesus of
Nazareth.
8 Jesus answered, I have told you that
I am *he:* if therefore ye seek me, let
these go their way:
9 That the saying might be fulfilled,
which he spake, Of them which thou
gavest me have I lost none.
10 Then Simon Peter having a sword
drew it, and smote the high priest's
servant, and cut off his right ear. The
servant's name was Măl'chŭs.
11 Then said Jesus unto Peter, Put up
thy sword into the sheath: the cup which
my Father hath given me, shall I not
drink it?
12 Then the band and the captain and
officers of the Jews took Jesus, and
bound him,
13 And led him away to Annas first;
for he was father-in-law to Cā'ịa-phăs,
which was the high priest that same
year.
14 Now Cā'ịa-phăs was he, which gave
counsel to the Jews, that it was expedient that one man should die for the
people.
15 ¶ And Simon Peter followed Jesus,
and *so did* another disciple: that disciple was known unto the high priest,
and went in with Jesus into the palace
of the high priest.
16 But Peter stood at the door without.
Then went out that other disciple, which
was known unto the high priest, and
spake unto her that kept the door, and
brought in Peter.
17 Then saith the damsel that kept the
door unto Peter, Art not thou also *one* of
this man's disciples? He saith, I am
not.
18 And the servants and officers stood
there, who had made a fire of coals, for
it was cold; and they warmed themselves: and Peter stood with them, and
warmed himself.
19 ¶ The high priest then asked Jesus
of his disciples, and of his doctrine.
20 Jesus answered him, I spake openly
to the world; I ever taught in the synagogue, and in the temple, whither the
Jews always resort; and in secret have
I said nothing.
21 Why askest thou me? ask them
which heard me, what I have said unto
them: behold, they know what I said.
22 And when he had thus spoken, one
of the officers which stood by struck
Jesus with the palm of his hand, saying,
Answerest thou the high priest so?
23 Jesus answered him, If I have
spoken evil, bear witness of the evil:
but if well, why smitest thou me?
24 Now Annas had sent him bound
unto Cā'ịa-phăs the high priest.
25 And Simon Peter stood and warmed
himself. They said therefore unto him,
Art not thou also *one* of his disciples?
He denied *it,* and said, I am not.
26 One of the servants of the high
priest, being *his* kinsman whose ear
Peter cut off, saith, Did not I see thee
in the garden with him?
27 Peter then denied again; and immediately the cock crew.
28 ¶ Then led they Jesus from Cā'-
ịa-phăs unto the hall of judgment: and
it was early; and they themselves went
not into the judgment hall, lest they
should be defiled; but that they might
eat the passover.
29 Pilate then went out unto them, and
said, What accusation bring ye against
this man?
30 They answered and said unto him,
If he were not a malefactor, we would
not have delivered him up unto thee.
31 Then said Pilate unto them, Take
ye him, and judge him according to your
law. The Jews therefore said unto him,
It is not lawful for us to put any man to
death:
32 That the saying of Jesus might be
fulfilled, which he spake, signifying
what death he should die.
33 Then Pilate entered into the judgment hall again, and called Jesus, and
said unto him, Art thou the King of the
Jews?
34 Jesus answered him, Sayest thou
this thing of thyself, or did others tell it
thee of me?
35 Pilate answered, Am I a Jew?
Thine own nation and the chief priests
have delivered thee unto me: what hast
thou done?
36 Jesus answered, My kingdom is
not of this world: if my kingdom were of
this world, then would my servants

fight, that I should not be delivered to
the Jews: but now is my kingdom not
from hence.
37 Pilate therefore said unto him, Art
thou a king then? Jesus answered,
Thou sayest that I am a king. To this
end was I born, and for this cause came
I into the world, that I should bear witness unto the truth. Every one that is
of the truth heareth my voice.
38 Pilate saith unto him, What is
truth? And when he had said this, he
went out again unto the Jews, and saith
unto them, I find in him no fault *at all.*
39 But ye have a custom, that I should
release unto you one at the passover:
will ye therefore that I release unto you
the King of the Jews?
40 Then cried they all again, saying,
Not this man, but Bär-ăb′băs. Now
Bär-ăb′băs was a robber.

CHAPTER 19

THEN Pilate therefore took Jesus,
and scourged *him.*
2 And the soldiers platted a crown
of thorns, and put *it* on his head, and
they put on him a purple robe,
3 And said, Hail, King of the Jews!
and they smote him with their hands.
4 Pilate therefore went forth again, and
saith unto them, Behold, I bring him
forth to you, that ye may know that I
find no fault in him.
5 Then came Jesus forth, wearing the
crown of thorns, and the purple robe.
And *Pilate* saith unto them, Behold the
man!
6 When the chief priests therefore
and officers saw him, they cried out,
saying, Crucify *him,* crucify *him.* Pilate
saith unto them, Take ye him, and crucify *him:* for I find no fault in him.
7 The Jews answered him, We have a
law, and by our law he ought to die, because he made himself the Son of God.
8 ℂ When Pilate therefore heard that
saying, he was the more afraid;
9 And went again into the judgment
hall, and saith unto Jesus, Whence art
thou? But Jesus gave him no answer.
10 Then saith Pilate unto him, Speakest thou not unto me? knowest thou not
that I have power to crucify thee, and
have power to release thee?
11 Jesus answered, Thou couldest have
no power *at all* against me, except it
were given thee from above: therefore
he that delivered me unto thee hath the
greater sin.
12 And from thenceforth Pilate sought
to release him: but the Jews cried out,
saying, If thou let this man go, thou
art not Cæsar's friend: whosoever
maketh himself a king speaketh against
Cæsar.
13 ℂ When Pilate therefore heard
that saying, he brought Jesus forth, and
sat down in the judgment seat in a place
that is called the Pavement, but in the
Hebrew, Găb′bȧ-thȧ.
14 And it was the preparation of the
passover, and about the sixth hour: and
he saith unto the Jews, Behold your
King!
15 But they cried out, Away with *him,*
away with *him,* crucify him. Pilate saith
unto them, Shall I crucify your King?
The chief priests answered, We have
no king but Cæsar.
16 Then delivered he him therefore
unto them to be crucified. And they
took Jesus, and led *him* away.
17 And he bearing his cross went forth
into a place called *the place* of a skull,
which is called in the Hebrew Gŏl′-
gō-thȧ:
18 Where they crucified him, and two
others with him, on either side one, and
Jesus in the midst.
19 ℂ And Pilate wrote a title, and put
it on the cross. And the writing was,
JESUS OF NAZARETH THE KING OF
THE JEWS.
20 This title then read many of the
Jews; for the place where Jesus was
crucified was nigh to the city: and it was
written in Hebrew, *and* Greek, *and*
Latin.
21 Then said the chief priests of the
Jews to Pilate, Write not, The King of
the Jews; but that he said, I am King
of the Jews.
22 Pilate answered, What I have written I have written.
23 ℂ Then the soldiers, when they
had crucified Jesus, took his garments,
and made four parts, to every soldier a
part; and also *his* coat: now the coat
was without seam, woven from the top
throughout.
24 They said therefore among themselves, Let us not rend it, but cast lots
for it, whose it shall be: that the Scripture might be fulfilled, which saith,
They parted my raiment among them,

and for my vesture they did cast lots.
These things therefore the soldiers did.
25 ℂ Now there stood by the cross of
Jesus his mother, and his mother's sister, Mary the *wife* of Clē'ō-phăs, and
Mary Măg'dȧ-lēne.
26 When Jesus therefore saw his
mother, and the disciple standing by,
whom he loved, he saith unto his
mother, Woman, behold thy son!
27 Then saith he to the disciple, Behold thy mother! And from that hour
that disciple took her unto his own
home.
28 ℂ After this, Jesus knowing that all
things were now accomplished, that the
Scripture might be fulfilled, saith, I
thirst.
29 Now there was set a vessel full of
vinegar: and they filled a sponge with
vinegar, and put *it* upon hyssop, and
put *it* to his mouth.
30 When Jesus therefore had received
the vinegar, he said, It is finished: and
he bowed his head, and gave up the
ghost.
31 The Jews therefore, because it was
the preparation, that the bodies should
not remain upon the cross on the sabbath day, (for that sabbath day was a
high day,) besought Pilate that their
legs might be broken, and *that* they
might be taken away.
32 Then came the soldiers, and brake
the legs of the first, and of the other
which was crucified with him.
33 But when they came to Jesus, and
saw that he was dead already, they
brake not his legs:
34 But one of the soldiers with a spear
pierced his side, and forthwith came
there out blood and water.
35 And he that saw *it* bare record, and
his record is true; and he knoweth that
he saith true, that ye might believe.
36 For these things were done, that the
Scripture should be fulfilled, A bone of
him shall not be broken.
37 And again another Scripture saith,
They shall look on him whom they
pierced.
38 ℂ And after this Joseph of Ăr'ĭ-mȧ-
thē'ȧ, being a disciple of Jesus, but
secretly for fear of the Jews, besought
Pilate that he might take away the body
of Jesus: and Pilate gave *him* leave. He
came therefore, and took the body of
Jesus.
39 And there came also Nĭc'ō-dē'mŭs,
which at the first came to Jesus by
night, and brought a mixture of myrrh
and aloes, about a hundred pound
weight.
40 Then took they the body of Jesus,
and wound it in linen clothes with the
spices, as the manner of the Jews is to
bury.
41 Now in the place where he was
crucified there was a garden; and in the
garden a new sepulchre, wherein was
never man yet laid.
42 There laid they Jesus therefore
because of the Jews' preparation *day;*
for the sepulchre was nigh at hand.

CHAPTER 20

THE first *day* of the week cometh
Mary Măg'dȧ-lēne early, when it
was yet dark, unto the sepulchre, and
seeth the stone taken away from the
sepulchre.
2 Then she runneth, and cometh to
Simon Peter, and to the other disciple,
whom Jesus loved, and saith unto them,
They have taken away the Lord out of
the sepulchre, and we know not where
they have laid him.
3 Peter therefore went forth, and that
other disciple, and came to the sepulchre.
4 So they ran both together: and the
other disciple did outrun Peter, and
came first to the sepulchre.
5 And he stooping down, *and looking
in,* saw the linen clothes lying; yet went
he not in.
6 Then cometh Simon Peter following
him, and went into the sepulchre, and
seeth the linen clothes lie,
7 And the napkin, that was about his
head, not lying with the linen clothes,
but wrapped together in a place by
itself.
8 Then went in also that other disciple, which came first to the sepulchre,
and he saw, and believed.
9 For as yet they knew not the Scripture, that he must rise again from the
dead.
10 Then the disciples went away again
unto their own home.
11 ℂ But Mary stood without at the
sepulchre weeping: and as she wept,
she stooped down, *and looked* into the
sepulchre,
12 And seeth two angels in white sit-

ting, the one at the head, and the other
at the feet, where the body of Jesus had
lain.
13 And they say unto her, Woman,
why weepest thou? She saith unto
them, Because they have taken away
my Lord, and I know not where they
have laid him.
14 And when she had thus said, she
turned herself back, and saw Jesus
standing, and knew not that it was
Jesus.
15 Jesus saith unto her, Woman, why
weepest thou? whom seekest thou?
She, supposing him to be the gardener,
saith unto him, Sir, if thou have borne
him hence, tell me where thou hast laid
him, and I will take him away.
16 Jesus saith unto her, Mary. She
turned herself, and saith unto him,
Răb-bō′nī; which is to say, Master.
17 Jesus saith unto her, Touch me not;
for I am not yet ascended to my Father:
but go to my brethren, and say unto
them, I ascend unto my Father, and
your Father; and *to* my God, and your
God.
18 Mary Măg′dȧ-lēne came and told
the disciples that she had seen the
Lord, and *that* he had spoken these
things unto her.
19 ¶ Then the same day at evening,
being the first *day* of the week, when
the doors were shut where the disciples
were assembled for fear of the Jews,
came Jesus and stood in the midst, and
saith unto them, Peace *be* unto you.
20 And when he had so said, he showed
unto them *his* hands and his side. Then
were the disciples glad, when they saw
the Lord.
21 Then said Jesus to them again,
Peace *be* unto you: as *my* Father hath
sent me, even so send I you.
22 And when he had said this, he
breathed on *them*, and saith unto them,
Receive ye the Holy Ghost:
23 Whosesoever sins ye remit, they
are remitted unto them; *and* whosesoever
sins ye retain, they are retained.
24 ¶ But Thomas, one of the twelve,
called Dĭd′y̆-mŭs, was not with them
when Jesus came.
25 The other disciples therefore said
unto him, We have seen the Lord. But
he said unto them, Except I shall see in
his hands the print of the nails, and put
my finger into the print of the nails, and
thrust my hand into his side, I will not
believe.
26 ¶ And after eight days again his
disciples were within, and Thomas with
them: *then* came Jesus, the doors being
shut, and stood in the midst, and said,
Peace *be* unto you.
27 Then saith he to Thomas, Reach
hither thy finger, and behold my hands;
and reach hither thy hand, and thrust *it*
into my side; and be not faithless, but
believing.
28 And Thomas answered and said
unto him, My Lord and my God.
29 Jesus saith unto him, Thomas, because
thou hast seen me, thou hast believed:
blessed *are* they that have not
seen, and *yet* have believed.
30 ¶ And many other signs truly did
Jesus in the presence of his disciples,
which are not written in this book:
31 But these are written, that ye might
believe that Jesus is the Christ, the Son
of God; and that believing ye might
have life through his name.

CHAPTER 21

AFTER these things Jesus showed
himself again to the disciples at
the sea of Tī-bē′rĭ-ăs; and on this
wise showed he *himself*.
2 There were together Simon Peter,
and Thomas called Dĭd′y̆-mŭs, and Nȧ-thăn′ā-ĕl
of Cā′nȧ in Galilee, and the
sons of Zĕb′ē-dēe, and two other of his
disciples.
3 Simon Peter saith unto them, I go
a fishing. They say unto him, We also
go with thee. They went forth, and
entered into a ship immediately; and
that night they caught nothing.
4 But when the morning was now come,
Jesus stood on the shore; but the disciples
knew not that it was Jesus.
5 Then Jesus saith unto them, Children,
have ye any meat? They answered
him, No.
6 And he said unto them, Cast the net
on the right side of the ship, and ye shall
find. They cast therefore, and now they
were not able to draw it for the multitude
of fishes.
7 Therefore that disciple whom Jesus
loved saith unto Peter, It is the Lord.
Now when Simon Peter heard that it
was the Lord, he girt *his* fisher's coat
unto him, (for he was naked,) and did
cast himself into the sea.

8 And the other disciples came in a
little ship, (for they were not far from
land, but as it were two hundred cubits,)
dragging the net with fishes.
9 As soon then as they were come to
land, they saw a fire of coals there, and
fish laid thereon, and bread.
10 Jesus saith unto them, Bring of the
fish which ye have now caught.
11 Simon Peter went up, and drew the
net to land full of great fishes, a hundred and fifty and three: and for all
there were so many, yet was not the net
broken.
12 Jesus saith unto them, Come *and*
dine. And none of the disciples durst
ask him, Who art thou? knowing that
it was the Lord.
13 Jesus then cometh, and taketh
bread, and giveth them, and fish likewise.
14 This is now the third time that Jesus
showed himself to his disciples, after
that he was risen from the dead.
15 ℭ So when they had dined, Jesus
saith to Simon Peter, Simon *son* of
Jō'nȧs, lovest thou me more than these?
He saith unto him, Yea, Lord; thou
knowest that I love thee. He saith unto
him, Feed my lambs.
16 He saith to him again the second
time, Simon, *son* of Jō'nȧs, lovest thou
me? He saith unto him, Yea, Lord;
thou knowest that I love thee. He saith
unto him, Feed my sheep.
17 He saith unto him the third time,
Simon, *son* of Jō'nȧs, lovest thou me?
Peter was grieved because he said unto
him the third time, Lovest thou me?
And he said unto him, Lord, thou
knowest all things; thou knowest that I
love thee. Jesus saith unto him, Feed
my sheep.
18 Verily, verily, I say unto thee, When
thou wast young, thou girdedst thyself,
and walkedst whither thou wouldest:
but when thou shalt be old, thou shalt
stretch forth thy hands, and another
shall gird thee, and carry *thee* whither
thou wouldest not.
19 This spake he, signifying by what
death he should glorify God. And when
he had spoken this, he saith unto him,
Follow me.
20 Then Peter, turning about, seeth
the disciple whom Jesus loved following; which also leaned on his breast at
supper, and said, Lord, which is he
that betrayeth thee?
21 Peter seeing him saith to Jesus,
Lord, and what *shall* this man *do?*
22 Jesus saith unto him, If I will that
he tarry till I come, what *is that* to thee?
follow thou me.
23 Then went this saying abroad among
the brethren, that that disciple should
not die: yet Jesus said not unto him, He
shall not die; but, If I will that he tarry
till I come, what *is that* to thee?
24 This is the disciple which testifieth
of these things, and wrote these things:
and we know that his testimony is true.
25 And there are also many other
things which Jesus did, the which, if
they should be written every one, I suppose that even the world itself could not
contain the books that should be written.
Amen.

THE ACTS OF THE APOSTLES

CHAPTER 1

THE former treatise have I made,
O Thē-ŏph'ĭ-lŭs, of all that Jesus
began both to do and teach,
2 Until the day in which he was taken
up, after that he through the Holy Ghost
had given commandments unto the
apostles whom he had chosen:
3 To whom also he showed himself
alive after his passion by many infal-
lible proofs, being seen of them forty
days, and speaking of the things pertaining to the kingdom of God:
4 And, being assembled together with
them, commanded them that they
should not depart from Jerusalem, but
wait for the promise of the Father,
which, *saith he,* ye have heard of me.
5 For John truly baptized with water;
but ye shall be baptized with the Holy
Ghost not many days hence.
6 When they therefore were come together, they asked of him, saying,
Lord, wilt thou at this time restore
again the kingdom to Ĭs'rā-ĕl?
7 And he said unto them, It is not for
you to know the times or the seasons,
which the Father hath put in his own
power.
8 But ye shall receive power, after that
the Holy Ghost is come upon you: and
ye shall be witnesses unto me both in
Jerusalem, and in all Judea, and in
Sȧ-mā'rĭ-ȧ, and unto the uttermost part
of the earth.
9 And when he had spoken these
things, while they beheld, he was taken
up; and a cloud received him out of
their sight.
10 And while they looked steadfastly
toward heaven as he went up, behold,
two men stood by them in white apparel;
11 Which also said, Ye men of Galilee,
why stand ye gazing up into heaven?
this same Jesus, which is taken up from
you into heaven, shall so come in like
manner as ye have seen him go into
heaven.
12 Then returned they unto Jerusalem
from the mount called Ŏl'ĭ-vĕt, which
is from Jerusalem a sabbath day's
journey.
13 And when they were come in, they
went up into an upper room, where
abode both Peter, and James, and John,
and Andrew, Philip, and Thomas, Bartholomew, and Matthew, James *the son*
of Alpheus, and Simon Zē-lō'tēs, and
Judas *the brother* of James.
14 These all continued with one accord
in prayer and supplication, with the
women, and Mary the mother of Jesus,
and with his brethren.
15 ¶ And in those days Peter stood up
in the midst of the disciples, and said,
(the number of names together were
about a hundred and twenty,)
16 Men *and* brethren, this Scripture
must needs have been fulfilled, which
the Holy Ghost by the mouth of David
spake before concerning Judas, which
was guide to them that took Jesus.
17 For he was numbered with us, and
had obtained part of this ministry.
18 Now this man purchased a field
with the reward of iniquity; and falling
headlong, he burst asunder in the midst,
and all his bowels gushed out.
19 And it was known unto all the
dwellers at Jerusalem; insomuch as
that field is called, in their proper
tongue, Ȧ-çĕl'dȧ-mȧ, that is to say, The
field of blood.
20 For it is written in the book of
Psalms, Let his habitation be desolate,
and let no man dwell therein: and, His
bishopric let another take.
21 Wherefore of these men which
have companied with us all the time
that the Lord Jesus went in and out
among us,
22 Beginning from the baptism of John,
unto that same day that he was taken
up from us, must one be ordained to be
a witness with us of his resurrection.
23 And they appointed two, Joseph
called Bär'sȧ-băs, who was surnamed
Justus, and Mȧtth-ī'ăs.
24 And they prayed, and said, Thou,
Lord, which knowest the hearts of all
men, show whether of these two thou
hast chosen,
25 That he may take part of this ministry and apostleship, from which Judas
by transgression fell, that he might go
to his own place.
26 And they gave forth their lots; and
the lot fell upon Mȧtth-ī'ăs; and he was
numbered with the eleven apostles.

CHAPTER 2

AND when the day of Pĕn′tē-cŏst was fully come, they were all with one accord in one place.

2 And suddenly there came a sound from heaven as of a rushing mighty wind, and it filled all the house where they were sitting.

3 And there appeared unto them cloven tongues like as of fire, and it sat upon each of them.

4 And they were all filled with the Holy Ghost, and began to speak with other tongues, as the Spirit gave them utterance.

5 And there were dwelling at Jerusalem Jews, devout men, out of every nation under heaven.

6 Now when this was noised abroad, the multitude came together, and were confounded, because that every man heard them speak in his own language.

7 And they were all amazed and marveled, saying one to another, Behold, are not all these which speak Galileans?

8 And how hear we every man in our own tongue, wherein we were born?

9 Pär′thĭ-ănș, and Mēdeș, and Ē′lăm-ītes, and the dwellers in Mĕs′ō-pō-tā′mĭ-ȧ, and in Judea, and Căp′pȧ-dō′çĭ-ȧ, in Pontus, and Asia,

10 Phrȳġ′ĭ-ȧ, and Păm-phȳl′ĭ-ȧ, in Egypt, and in the parts of Libya about Çȳ-rē′nē, and strangers of Rome, Jews and proselytes,

11 Crētes and Arabians, we do hear them speak in our tongues the wonderful works of God.

12 And they were all amazed, and were in doubt, saying one to another, What meaneth this?

13 Others mocking said, These men are full of new wine.

14 ¶ But Peter, standing up with the eleven, lifted up his voice, and said unto them, Ye men of Judea, and all *ye* that dwell at Jerusalem, be this known unto you, and hearken to my words:

15 For these are not drunken, as ye suppose, seeing it is *but* the third hour of the day.

16 But this is that which was spoken by the prophet Joel;

17 And it shall come to pass in the last days, saith God, I will pour out of my Spirit upon all flesh: and your sons and your daughters shall prophesy, and your young men shall see visions, and your old men shall dream dreams:

18 And on my servants and on my handmaidens I will pour out in those days of my Spirit; and they shall prophesy:

19 And I will show wonders in heaven above, and signs in the earth beneath; blood, and fire, and vapor of smoke:

20 The sun shall be turned into darkness, and the moon into blood, before that great and notable day of the Lord come:

21 And it shall come to pass, *that* whosoever shall call on the name of the Lord shall be saved.

22 Ye men of Ĭș′rā-ĕl, hear these words; Jesus of Nazareth, a man approved of God among you by miracles and wonders and signs, which God did by him in the midst of you, as ye yourselves also know:

23 Him, being delivered by the determinate counsel and foreknowledge of God, ye have taken, and by wicked hands have crucified and slain:

24 Whom God hath raised up, having loosed the pains of death: because it was not possible that he should be holden of it.

25 For David speaketh concerning him, I foresaw the Lord always before my face; for he is on my right hand, that I should not be moved:

26 Therefore did my heart rejoice, and my tongue was glad; moreover also my flesh shall rest in hope:

27 Because thou wilt not leave my soul in hell, neither wilt thou suffer thine Holy One to see corruption.

28 Thou hast made known to me the ways of life; thou shalt make me full of joy with thy countenance.

29 Men *and* brethren, let me freely speak unto you of the patriarch David, that he is both dead and buried, and his sepulchre is with us unto this day.

30 Therefore being a prophet, and knowing that God had sworn with an oath to him, that of the fruit of his loins, according to the flesh, he would raise up Christ to sit on his throne;

31 He, seeing this before, spake of the resurrection of Christ, that his soul was not left in hell, neither his flesh did see corruption.

32 This Jesus hath God raised up, whereof we all are witnesses.

33 Therefore being by the right hand

of God exalted, and having received of
the Father the promise of the Holy
Ghost, he hath shed forth this, which ye
now see and hear.
34 For David is not ascended into the
heavens: but he saith himself, The
LORD said unto my Lord, Sit thou on
my right hand,
35 Until I make thy foes thy footstool.
36 Therefore let all the house of
Ĭṣ'rā-ĕl know assuredly, that God hath
made that same Jesus, whom ye have
crucified, both Lord and Christ.
37 ¶ Now when they heard *this*, they
were pricked in their heart, and said
unto Peter and to the rest of the apostles, Men *and* brethren, what shall we do?
38 Then Peter said unto them, Repent,
and be baptized every one of you in the
name of Jesus Christ for the remission
of sins, and ye shall receive the gift of
the Holy Ghost.
39 For the promise is unto you, and to
your children, and to all that are afar
off, *even* as many as the Lord our God
shall call.
40 And with many other words did he
testify and exhort, saying, Save yourselves from this untoward generation.
41 ¶ Then they that gladly received
his word were baptized: and the same
day there were added *unto them* about
three thousand souls.
42 And they continued steadfastly in
the apostles' doctrine and fellowship,
and in breaking of bread, and in prayers.
43 And fear came upon every soul: and
many wonders and signs were done by
the apostles.
44 And all that believed were together,
and had all things common;
45 And sold their possessions and
goods, and parted them to all *men*, as
every man had need.
46 And they, continuing daily with one
accord in the temple, and breaking
bread from house to house, did eat
their meat with gladness and singleness
of heart,
47 Praising God, and having favor with
all the people. And the Lord added to
the church daily such as should be
saved.

CHAPTER 3

NOW Peter and John went up together into the temple at the
hour of prayer, *being* the ninth *hour*.
2 And a certain man lame from his
mother's womb was carried, whom they
laid daily at the gate of the temple which
is called Beautiful, to ask alms of them
that entered into the temple;
3 Who, seeing Peter and John about to
go into the temple, asked an alms.
4 And Peter, fastening his eyes upon
him with John, said, Look on us.
5 And he gave heed unto them, expecting to receive something of them.
6 Then Peter said, Silver and gold have
I none; but such as I have give I thee:
In the name of Jesus Christ of Nazareth
rise up and walk.
7 And he took him by the right hand,
and lifted *him* up: and immediately his
feet and ankle bones received strength.
8 And he leaping up stood, and walked,
and entered with them into the temple,
walking, and leaping, and praising
God.
9 And all the people saw him walking
and praising God:
10 And they knew that it was he which
sat for alms at the Beautiful gate of the
temple: and they were filled with wonder and amazement at that which had
happened unto him.
11 And as the lame man which was
healed held Peter and John, all the
people ran together unto them in the
porch that is called Solomon's, greatly
wondering.
12 ¶ And when Peter saw *it*, he answered unto the people, Ye men of
Ĭṣ'rā-ĕl, why marvel ye at this? or why
look ye so earnestly on us, as though by
our own power or holiness we had made
this man to walk?
13 The God of Abraham, and of Isaac,
and of Jacob, the God of our fathers,
hath glorified his Son Jesus; whom ye
delivered up, and denied him in the
presence of Pilate, when he was determined to let *him* go.
14 But ye denied the Holy One and the
Just, and desired a murderer to be
granted unto you;
15 And killed the Prince of life, whom
God hath raised from the dead; whereof
we are witnesses.
16 And his name, through faith in his
name, hath made this man strong, whom
ye see and know: yea, the faith which is
by him hath given him this perfect
soundness in the presence of you all.
17 And now, brethren, I wot that

through ignorance ye did *it,* as *did* also your rulers.

18 But those things, which God before had showed by the mouth of all his prophets, that Christ should suffer, he hath so fulfilled.

19 ¶ Repent ye therefore, and be converted, that your sins may be blotted out, when the times of refreshing shall come from the presence of the Lord;

20 And he shall send Jesus Christ, which before was preached unto you:

21 Whom the heaven must receive until the times of restitution of all things, which God hath spoken by the mouth of all his holy prophets since the world began.

22 For Moses truly said unto the fathers, A Prophet shall the Lord your God raise up unto you of your brethren, like unto me; him shall ye hear in all things whatsoever he shall say unto you.

23 And it shall come to pass, *that* every soul, which will not hear that Prophet, shall be destroyed from among the people.

24 Yea, and all the prophets from Samuel and those that follow after, as many as have spoken, have likewise foretold of these days.

25 Ye are the children of the prophets, and of the covenant which God made with our fathers, saying unto Abraham, And in thy seed shall all the kindreds of the earth be blessed.

26 Unto you first God, having raised up his Son Jesus, sent him to bless you, in turning away every one of you from his iniquities.

CHAPTER 4

AND as they spake unto the people, the priests, and the captain of the temple, and the Săd'dū-çēeṣ, came upon them,

2 Being grieved that they taught the people, and preached through Jesus the resurrection from the dead.

3 And they laid hands on them, and put *them* in hold unto the next day: for it was now eventide.

4 Howbeit many of them which heard the word believed; and the number of the men was about five thousand.

5 ¶ And it came to pass on the morrow, that their rulers, and elders, and scribes,

6 And Annas the high priest, and Cā'ịa-phăs, and John, and Alexander, and as many as were of the kindred of the high priest, were gathered together at Jerusalem.

7 And when they had set them in the midst, they asked, By what power, or by what name, have ye done this?

8 Then Peter, filled with the Holy Ghost, said unto them, Ye rulers of the people, and elders of Ĭṣ'rā-ĕl,

9 If we this day be examined of the good deed done to the impotent man, by what means he is made whole;

10 Be it known unto you all, and to all the people of Israel, that by the name of Jesus Christ of Nazareth, whom ye crucified, whom God raised from the dead, *even* by him doth this man stand here before you whole.

11 This is the stone which was set at nought of you builders, which is become the head of the corner.

12 Neither is there salvation in any other: for there is none other name under heaven given among men, whereby we must be saved.

13 ¶ Now when they saw the boldness of Peter and John, and perceived that they were unlearned and ignorant men, they marveled; and they took knowledge of them, that they had been with Jesus.

14 And beholding the man which was healed standing with them, they could say nothing against it.

15 But when they had commanded them to go aside out of the council, they conferred among themselves,

16 Saying, What shall we do to these men? for that indeed a notable miracle hath been done by them *is* manifest to all them that dwell in Jerusalem; and we cannot deny *it*.

17 But that it spread no further among the people, let us straitly threaten them, that they speak henceforth to no man in this name.

18 And they called them, and commanded them not to speak at all nor teach in the name of Jesus.

19 But Peter and John answered and said unto them, Whether it be right in the sight of God to hearken unto you more than unto God, judge ye.

20 For we cannot but speak the things which we have seen and heard.

21 So when they had further threatened them, they let them go, finding nothing how they might punish them,

because of the people: for all *men* glorified God for that which was done.
22 For the man was above forty years
old, on whom this miracle of healing
was showed.
23 ¶ And being let go, they went to
their own company, and reported all
that the chief priests and elders had
said unto them.
24 And when they heard that, they
lifted up their voice to God with one
accord, and said, Lord, thou *art* God,
which hast made heaven, and earth, and
the sea, and all that in them is;
25 Who by the mouth of thy servant
David hast said, Why did the heathen
rage, and the people imagine vain
things?
26 The kings of the earth stood up, and
the rulers were gathered together
against the Lord, and against his
Christ.
27 For of a truth against thy holy child
Jesus, whom thou hast anointed, both
Hĕr′ȯd, and Pŏn′ti̯-ŭs Pilate, with the
Ġĕn′tīles̱, and the people of Is̱′rā-ĕl,
were gathered together,
28 For to do whatsoever thy hand and
thy counsel determined before to be
done.
29 And now, Lord, behold their
threatenings: and grant unto thy servants, that with all boldness they may
speak thy word,
30 By stretching forth thine hand to
heal; and that signs and wonders may
be done by the name of thy holy child
Jesus.
31 ¶ And when they had prayed, the
place was shaken where they were assembled together; and they were all
filled with the Holy Ghost, and they
spake the word of God with boldness.
32 And the multitude of them that believed were of one heart and of one soul:
neither said any *of them* that aught of
the things which he possessed was his
own; but they had all things common.
33 And with great power gave the apostles witness of the resurrection of the
Lord Jesus: and great grace was upon
them all.
34 Neither was there any among them
that lacked: for as many as were possessors of lands or houses sold them,
and brought the prices of the things
that were sold,
35 And laid *them* down at the apostles'
feet: and distribution was made unto
every man according as he had need.
36 And Jō′sēs̱, who by the apostles
was surnamed Barnabas, (which is, being interpreted, The son of consolation,)
a Lē′vīte, *and* of the country of Cyprus,
37 Having land, sold *it*, and brought
the money, and laid *it* at the apostles'
feet.

CHAPTER 5

BUT a certain man named Ăn′ȧ-
nī′ăs, with Sȧpph-ī′rȧ his wife, sold
a possession,
2 And kept back *part* of the price, his
wife also being privy *to it*, and brought
a certain part, and laid *it* at the apostles'
feet.
3 But Peter said, Ăn′ȧ-nī′ăs, why hath
Satan filled thine heart to lie to the Holy
Ghost, and to keep back *part* of the
price of the land?
4 While it remained, was it not thine
own? and after it was sold, was it not in
thine own power? why hast thou conceived this thing in thine heart? thou
hast not lied unto men, but unto God.
5 And Ăn′ȧ-nī′ăs hearing these words
fell down, and gave up the ghost: and
great fear came on all them that heard
these things.
6 And the young men arose, wound
him up, and carried *him* out, and buried
him.
7 And it was about the space of three
hours after, when his wife, not knowing
what was done, came in.
8 And Peter answered unto her, Tell
me whether ye sold the land for so
much? And she said, Yea, for so much.
9 Then Peter said unto her, How is it
that ye have agreed together to tempt
the Spirit of the Lord? behold, the feet
of them which have buried thy husband
are at the door, and shall carry thee out.
10 Then fell she down straightway at
his feet, and yielded up the ghost: and
the young men came in, and found her
dead, and, carrying *her* forth, buried *her*
by her husband.
11 And great fear came upon all the
church, and upon as many as heard
these things.
12 ¶ And by the hands of the apostles
were many signs and wonders wrought
among the people; (and they were all
with one accord in Solomon's porch.
13 And of the rest durst no man join

himself to them: but the people magnified them.
14 And believers were the more added
to the Lord, multitudes both of men and
women;)
15 Insomuch that they brought forth
the sick into the streets, and laid *them*
on beds and couches, that at the least
the shadow of Peter passing by might
overshadow some of them.
16 There came also a multitude *out* of
the cities round about unto Jerusalem,
bringing sick folks, and them which
were vexed with unclean spirits: and
they were healed every one.
17 ℂ Then the high priest rose up, and
all they that were with him, (which is
the sect of the Săd'dū-çēeş,) and were
filled with indignation,
18 And laid their hands on the apostles, and put them in the common
prison.
19 But the angel of the Lord by night
opened the prison doors, and brought
them forth, and said,
20 Go, stand and speak in the temple to
the people all the words of this life.
21 And when they heard *that,* they
entered into the temple early in the
morning, and taught. But the high
priest came, and they that were with
him, and called the council together,
and all the senate of the children of
Ĭş'rā-ĕl, and sent to the prison to have
them brought.
22 But when the officers came, and
found them not in the prison, they returned, and told,
23 Saying, The prison truly found we
shut with all safety, and the keepers
standing without before the doors: but
when we had opened, we found no man
within.
24 Now when the high priest and the
captain of the temple and the chief
priests heard these things, they doubted
of them whereunto this would grow.
25 Then came one and told them, saying, Behold, the men whom ye put in
prison are standing in the temple, and
teaching the people.
26 Then went the captain with the
officers, and brought them without violence: for they feared the people, lest
they should have been stoned.
27 And when they had brought them,
they set *them* before the council: and
the high priest asked them,
28 Saying, Did not we straitly command
you that ye should not teach in this
name? and, behold, ye have filled Jerusalem with your doctrine, and intend to
bring this man's blood upon us.
29 ℂ Then Peter and the *other* apostles answered and said, We ought to
obey God rather than men.
30 The God of our fathers raised up
Jesus, whom ye slew and hanged on a
tree.
31 Him hath God exalted with his right
hand *to be* a Prince and a Saviour, for
to give repentance to Ĭş'rā-ĕl, and forgiveness of sins.
32 And we are his witnesses of these
things; and *so is* also the Holy Ghost,
whom God hath given to them that obey
him.
33 ℂ When they heard *that,* they were
cut *to the heart,* and took counsel to
slay them.
34 Then stood there up one in the
council, a Phăr'ĭ-sēe, named Gá-mā'-
lĭ-ĕl, a doctor of the law, had in reputation among all the people, and commanded to put the apostles forth a little
space;
35 And said unto them, Ye men of
Ĭş'rā-ĕl, take heed to yourselves what
ye intend to do as touching these men.
36 For before these days rose up Theū'-
dás, boasting himself to be somebody;
to whom a number of men, about four
hundred, joined themselves: who was
slain; and all, as many as obeyed him,
were scattered, and brought to nought.
37 After this man rose up Judas of
Galilee in the days of the taxing, and
drew away much people after him: he
also perished; and all, *even* as many as
obeyed him, were dispersed.
38 And now I say unto you, Refrain
from these men, and let them alone: for
if this counsel or this work be of men,
it will come to nought:
39 But if it be of God, ye cannot overthrow it; lest haply ye be found even to
fight against God.
40 And to him they agreed: and when
they had called the apostles, and beaten
them, they commanded that they should
not speak in the name of Jesus, and let
them go.
41 ℂ And they departed from the
presence of the council, rejoicing that
they were counted worthy to suffer
shame for his name.

42 And daily in the temple, and in every house, they ceased not to teach and preach Jesus Christ.

CHAPTER 6

AND in those days, when the number of the disciples was multiplied, there arose a murmuring of the Grecians against the Hebrews, because their widows were neglected in the daily ministration.

2 Then the twelve called the multitude of the disciples *unto them*, and said, It is not reason that we should leave the word of God, and serve tables.

3 Wherefore, brethren, look ye out among you seven men of honest report, full of the Holy Ghost and wisdom, whom we may appoint over this business.

4 But we will give ourselves continually to prayer, and to the ministry of the word.

5 ¶ And the saying pleased the whole multitude: and they chose Stephen, a man full of faith and of the Holy Ghost, and Philip, and Prŏch'ō-rŭs, and Nī-cā'nôr, and Tī'mŏn, and Păr'mē-năs, and Nicolas a proselyte of Ăn'tĭ-ŏch;

6 Whom they set before the apostles: and when they had prayed, they laid *their* hands on them.

7 And the word of God increased; and the number of the disciples multiplied in Jerusalem greatly; and a great company of the priests were obedient to the faith.

8 And Stephen, full of faith and power, did great wonders and miracles among the people.

9 ¶ Then there arose certain of the synagogue, which is called *the synagogue* of the Libertines, and Çȳ-rē'nĭ-ăns, and Alexandrians, and of them of Çĭ-lĭ'çĭ-ȧ and of Asia, disputing with Stephen.

10 And they were not able to resist the wisdom and the spirit by which he spake.

11 Then they suborned men, which said, We have heard him speak blasphemous words against Moses, and *against* God.

12 And they stirred up the people, and the elders, and the scribes, and came upon *him*, and caught him, and brought *him* to the council,

13 And set up false witnesses, which said, This man ceaseth not to speak blasphemous words against this holy place, and the law:

14 For we have heard him say, that this Jesus of Nazareth shall destroy this place, and shall change the customs which Moses delivered us.

15 And all that sat in the council, looking steadfastly on him, saw his face as it had been the face of an angel.

CHAPTER 7

THEN said the high priest, Are these things so?

2 And he said, Men, brethren, and fathers, hearken; The God of glory appeared unto our father Abraham, when he was in Mĕs'ō-pō-tā'mĭ-ȧ, before he dwelt in Chăr'răn,

3 And said unto him, Get thee out of thy country, and from thy kindred, and come into the land which I shall show thee.

4 Then came he out of the land of the Chăl-dē'ăns, and dwelt in Chăr'răn: and from thence, when his father was dead, he removed him into this land, wherein ye now dwell.

5 And he gave him none inheritance in it, no, not *so much as* to set his foot on: yet he promised that he would give it to him for a possession, and to his seed after him, when *as yet* he had no child.

6 And God spake on this wise, That his seed should sojourn in a strange land; and that they should bring them into bondage, and entreat *them* evil four hundred years.

7 And the nation to whom they shall be in bondage will I judge, said God: and after that shall they come forth, and serve me in this place.

8 And he gave him the covenant of circumcision: and so *Abraham* begat Isaac, and circumcised him the eighth day; and Isaac *begat* Jacob; and Jacob *begat* the twelve patriarchs.

9 And the patriarchs, moved with envy, sold Joseph into Egypt: but God was with him,

10 And delivered him out of all his afflictions, and gave him favor and wisdom in the sight of Phā'raōh king of Egypt; and he made him governor over Egypt and all his house.

11 Now there came a dearth over all the land of Egypt and Chā'năan, and

great affliction: and our fathers found
no sustenance.
12 But when Jacob heard that there
was corn in Egypt, he sent out our
fathers first.
13 And at the second *time* Joseph was
made known to his brethren; and
Joseph's kindred was made known unto
Phā'raōh.
14 Then sent Joseph, and called his
father Jacob to *him*, and all his kindred,
threescore and fifteen souls.
15 So Jacob went down into Egypt,
and died, he, and our fathers,
16 And were carried over into Sȳ'chĕm,
and laid in the sepulchre that Abraham
bought for a sum of money of the sons of
Ĕm'mŏr, *the father* of Sȳ'chĕm.
17 But when the time of the promise
drew nigh, which God had sworn to
Abraham, the people grew and multiplied in Egypt,
18 Till another king arose, which knew
not Joseph.
19 The same dealt subtilely with our
kindred, and evil entreated our fathers,
so that they cast out their young children, to the end they might not live.
20 In which time Moses was born, and
was exceeding fair, and nourished up in
his father's house three months:
21 And when he was cast out, Phā'-
raōh's daughter took him up, and nourished him for her own son.
22 And Moses was learned in all the
wisdom of the Egyptians, and was
mighty in words and in deeds.
23 And when he was full forty years
old, it came into his heart to visit his
brethren the children of Ĭs'rā-ĕl.
24 And seeing one *of them* suffer
wrong, he defended *him*, and avenged
him that was oppressed, and smote the
Egyptian:
25 For he supposed his brethren would
have understood how that God by his
hand would deliver them; but they
understood not.
26 And the next day he showed himself
unto them as they strove, and would
have set them at one again, saying, Sirs,
ye are brethren; why do ye wrong one to
another?
27 But he that did his neighbor wrong
thrust him away, saying, Who made
thee a ruler and a judge over us?
28 Wilt thou kill me, as thou didst the
Egyptian yesterday?
29 Then fled Moses at this saying, and
was a stranger in the land of Mā'dĭ-ăn,
where he begat two sons.
30 And when forty years were expired,
there appeared to him in the wilderness
of mount Sī'nȧ an angel of the Lord in
a flame of fire in a bush.
31 When Moses saw *it*, he wondered
at the sight: and as he drew near to
behold *it*, the voice of the Lord came
unto him,
32 *Saying*, I *am* the God of thy fathers,
the God of Abraham, and the God of
Isaac, and the God of Jacob. Then
Moses trembled, and durst not behold.
33 Then said the Lord to him, Put off
thy shoes from thy feet: for the place
where thou standest is holy ground.
34 I have seen, I have seen the affliction of my people which is in Egypt, and
I have heard their groaning, and am
come down to deliver them. And now
come, I will send thee into Egypt.
35 This Moses whom they refused,
saying, Who made thee a ruler and a
judge? the same did God send *to be* a
ruler and a deliverer by the hand of the
angel which appeared to him in the
bush.
36 He brought them out, after that he
had showed wonders and signs in the
land of Egypt, and in the Red sea, and
in the wilderness forty years.
37 ¶ This is that Moses, which said
unto the children of Ĭs'rā-ĕl, A Prophet
shall the Lord your God raise up unto
you of your brethren, like unto me; him
shall ye hear.
38 This is he, that was in the church in
the wilderness with the angel which
spake to him in the mount Sī'nȧ, and
with our fathers: who received the lively
oracles to give unto us:
39 To whom our fathers would not
obey, but thrust *him* from them, and in
their hearts turned back again into
Egypt,
40 Saying unto Aaron, Make us gods to
go before us: for *as for* this Moses,
which brought us out of the land of
Egypt, we wot not what is become of
him.
41 And they made a calf in those days,
and offered sacrifice unto the idol, and
rejoiced in the works of their own
hands.
42 Then God turned, and gave them
up to worship the host of heaven; as it

is written in the book of the prophets, O ye house of Ĭş′rā-ĕl, have ye offered to me slain beasts and sacrifices *by the space of* forty years in the wilderness?
43 Yea, ye took up the tabernacle of Mō′lŏch, and the star of your god Rĕm′phăn, figures which ye made to worship them: and I will carry you away beyond Babylon.
44 Our fathers had the tabernacle of witness in the wilderness, as he had appointed, speaking unto Moses, that he should make it according to the fashion that he had seen.
45 Which also our fathers that came after brought in with Jesus into the possession of the Ġĕn′tīleş, whom God drave out before the face of our fathers, unto the days of David;
46 Who found favor before God, and desired to find a tabernacle for the God of Jacob.
47 But Solomon built him a house.
48 Howbeit the Most High dwelleth not in temples made with hands; as saith the prophet,
49 Heaven *is* my throne, and earth *is* my footstool: what house will ye build me? saith the Lord: or what *is* the place of my rest?
50 Hath not my hand made all these things?
51 ℂ Ye stiffnecked and uncircumcised in heart and ears, ye do always resist the Holy Ghost: as your fathers *did,* so *do* ye.
52 Which of the prophets have not your fathers persecuted? and they have slain them which showed before of the coming of the Just One; of whom ye have been now the betrayers and murderers:
53 Who have received the law by the disposition of angels, and have not kept *it.*
54 ℂ When they heard these things, they were cut to the heart, and they gnashed on him with *their* teeth.
55 But he, being full of the Holy Ghost, looked up steadfastly into heaven, and saw the glory of God, and Jesus standing on the right hand of God,
56 And said, Behold, I see the heavens opened, and the Son of man standing on the right hand of God.
57 Then they cried out with a loud voice, and stopped their ears, and ran upon him with one accord,
58 And cast *him* out of the city, and stoned *him:* and the witnesses laid down their clothes at a young man's feet, whose name was Saul.
59 And they stoned Stephen, calling upon *God,* and saying, Lord Jesus, receive my spirit.
60 And he kneeled down, and cried with a loud voice, Lord, lay not this sin to their charge. And when he had said this, he fell asleep.

CHAPTER 8

AND Saul was consenting unto his death. And at that time there was a great persecution against the church which was at Jerusalem; and they were all scattered abroad throughout the regions of Judea and Sȧ-mā′rĭ-ȧ, except the apostles.
2 And devout men carried Stephen *to his burial,* and made great lamentation over him.
3 As for Saul, he made havoc of the church, entering into every house, and haling men and women committed *them* to prison.
4 Therefore they that were scattered abroad went every where preaching the word.
5 Then Philip went down to the city of Sȧ-mā′rĭ-ȧ, and preached Christ unto them.
6 And the people with one accord gave heed unto those things which Philip spake, hearing and seeing the miracles which he did.
7 For unclean spirits, crying with loud voice, came out of many that were possessed *with them:* and many taken with palsies, and that were lame, were healed.
8 And there was great joy in that city.
9 But there was a certain man, called Simon, which beforetime in the same city used sorcery, and bewitched the people of Sȧ-ma′rĭ-ȧ, giving out that himself was some great one:
10 To whom they all gave heed, from the least to the greatest, saying, This man is the great power of God.
11 And to him they had regard, because that of long time he had bewitched them with sorceries.
12 But when they believed Philip preaching the things concerning the kingdom of God, and the name of Jesus Christ, they were baptized, both men and women.

13 Then Simon himself believed also: and when he was baptized, he continued with Philip, and wondered, beholding the miracles and signs which were done.

14 Now when the apostles which were at Jerusalem heard that Sȧ-mā′rĭ-ȧ had received the word of God, they sent unto them Peter and John:

15 Who, when they were come down, prayed for them, that they might receive the Holy Ghost:

16 (For as yet he was fallen upon none of them: only they were baptized in the name of the Lord Jesus.)

17 Then laid they *their* hands on them, and they received the Holy Ghost.

18 And when Simon saw that through laying on of the apostles' hands the Holy Ghost was given, he offered them money,

19 Saying, Give me also this power, that on whomsoever I lay hands, he may receive the Holy Ghost.

20 But Peter said unto him, Thy money perish with thee, because thou hast thought that the gift of God may be purchased with money.

21 Thou hast neither part nor lot in this matter: for thy heart is not right in the sight of God.

22 Repent therefore of this thy wickedness, and pray God, if perhaps the thought of thine heart may be forgiven thee.

23 For I perceive that thou art in the gall of bitterness, and *in* the bond of iniquity.

24 Then answered Simon, and said, Pray ye to the Lord for me, that none of these things which ye have spoken come upon me.

25 And they, when they had testified and preached the word of the Lord, returned to Jerusalem, and preached the gospel in many villages of the Sȧ-măr′ĭ-tăns̡.

26 And the angel of the Lord spake unto Philip, saying, Arise, and go toward the south, unto the way that goeth down from Jerusalem unto Gā′zȧ, which is desert.

27 And he arose and went: and, behold, a man of Ethiopia, a eunuch of great authority under Căn′dȧ-çē queen of the Ethiopians, who had the charge of all her treasure, and had come to Jerusalem for to worship,

28 Was returning, and sitting in his chariot read Ē-ṣā′ịȧs the prophet.

29 Then the Spirit said unto Philip, Go near, and join thyself to this chariot.

30 And Philip ran thither to *him*, and heard him read the prophet Ē-ṣā′ịȧs, and said, Understandest thou what thou readest?

31 And he said, How can I, except some man should guide me? And he desired Philip that he would come up and sit with him.

32 The place of the Scripture which he read was this, He was led as a sheep to the slaughter; and like a lamb dumb before his shearer, so opened he not his mouth:

33 In his humiliation his judgment was taken away: and who shall declare his generation? for his life is taken from the earth.

34 And the eunuch answered Philip, and said, I pray thee, of whom speaketh the prophet this? of himself, or of some other man?

35 Then Philip opened his mouth, and began at the same Scripture, and preached unto him Jesus.

36 And as they went on *their* way, they came unto a certain water: and the eunuch said, See, *here is* water; what doth hinder me to be baptized?

37 And Philip said, If thou believest with all thine heart, thou mayest. And he answered and said, I believe that Jesus Christ is the Son of God.

38 And he commanded the chariot to stand still: and they went down both into the water, both Philip and the eunuch; and he baptized him.

39 And when they were come up out of the water, the Spirit of the Lord caught away Philip, that the eunuch saw him no more: and he went on his way rejoicing.

40 But Philip was found at Ȧ-zō′tŭs: and passing through he preached in all the cities, till he came to Çæ̆s′ȧ-rē′ȧ.

CHAPTER 9

AND Saul, yet breathing out threatenings and slaughter against the disciples of the Lord, went unto the high priest,

2 And desired of him letters to Damascus to the synagogues, that if he found any of this way, whether they were men or women, he might bring them bound unto Jerusalem.

3 And as he journeyed, he came near
Damascus: and suddenly there shined
round about him a light from heaven:
4 And he fell to the earth, and heard a
voice saying unto him, Saul, Saul, why
persecutest thou me?
5 And he said, Who art thou, Lord?
And the Lord said, I am Jesus whom
thou persecutest: *it is* hard for thee to
kick against the pricks.
6 And he trembling and astonished
said, Lord, what wilt thou have me to
do? And the Lord *said* unto him, Arise,
and go into the city, and it shall be told
thee what thou must do.
7 And the men which journeyed with
him stood speechless, hearing a voice,
but seeing no man.
8 And Saul arose from the earth; and
when his eyes were opened, he saw no
man: but they led him by the hand, and
brought *him* into Damascus.
9 And he was three days without sight,
and neither did eat nor drink.
10 ℂ And there was a certain disciple
at Damascus, named Ăn′ȧ-nī′ăs; and to
him said the Lord in a vision, Ăn′ȧ-
nī′ăs. And he said, Behold, I *am here*,
Lord.
11 And the Lord *said* unto him, Arise,
and go into the street which is called
Straight, and inquire in the house of
Judas for *one* called Saul, of Tär′sŭs:
for, behold, he prayeth,
12 And hath seen in a vision a man
named Ăn′ȧ-nī′ăs coming in, and putting
his hand on him, that he might receive
his sight.
13 Then Ăn′ȧ-nī′ăs answered, Lord, I
have heard by many of this man, how
much evil he hath done to thy saints at
Jerusalem:
14 And here he hath authority from
the chief priests to bind all that call on
thy name.
15 But the Lord said unto him, Go
thy way: for he is a chosen vessel
unto me, to bear my name before the
Ġĕn′tīleṣ, and kings, and the children
of Ĭṣ′rā-ĕl:
16 For I will show him how great things
he must suffer for my name's sake.
17 And Ăn′ȧ-nī′ăs went his way, and
entered into the house; and putting his
hands on him said, Brother Saul, the
Lord, *even* Jesus, that appeared unto
thee in the way as thou camest, hath
sent me, that thou mightest receive thy
sight, and be filled with the Holy Ghost.
18 And immediately there fell from his
eyes as it had been scales: and he received sight forthwith, and arose, and
was baptized.
19 And when he had received meat, he
was strengthened. Then was Saul certain days with the disciples which were
at Damascus.
20 And straightway he preached Christ
in the synagogues, that he is the Son of
God.
21 But all that heard *him* were amazed,
and said; Is not this he that destroyed
them which called on this name in Jerusalem, and came hither for that intent,
that he might bring them bound unto the
chief priests?
22 But Saul increased the more in
strength, and confounded the Jews
which dwelt at Damascus, proving that
this is very Christ.
23 ℂ And after that many days were
fulfilled, the Jews took counsel to kill
him:
24 But their laying wait was known of
Saul. And they watched the gates day
and night to kill him.
25 Then the disciples took him by
night, and let *him* down by the wall in a
basket.
26 And when Saul was come to Jerusalem, he assayed to join himself to the
disciples: but they were all afraid of
him, and believed not that he was a
disciple.
27 But Barnabas took him, and
brought *him* to the apostles, and declared unto them how he had seen the
Lord in the way, and that he had spoken
to him, and how he had preached boldly
at Damascus in the name of Jesus.
28 And he was with them coming in
and going out at Jerusalem.
29 And he spake boldly in the name of
the Lord Jesus, and disputed against
the Grecians: but they went about to
slay him.
30 *Which* when the brethren knew,
they brought him down to Çæ̆s′ȧ-rē′ȧ,
and sent him forth to Tär′sŭs.
31 Then had the churches rest throughout all Judea and Galilee and Sȧ-mā′
rĭ-ȧ, and were edified; and walking in
the fear of the Lord, and in the comfort
of the Holy Ghost, were multiplied.
32 ℂ And it came to pass, as Peter
passed throughout all *quarters*, he came

down also to the saints which dwelt at
Lydda.
33 And there he found a certain man
named Ē-nē'ăs, which had kept his bed
eight years, and was sick of the palsy.
34 And Peter said unto him, Ē-nē'ăs,
Jesus Christ maketh thee whole: arise,
and make thy bed. And he arose immediately.
35 And all that dwelt at Lydda and
Sā'rŏn saw him, and turned to the Lord.
36 ℭ Now there was at Jŏp'pȧ a certain disciple named Tăb'ĭ-thȧ, which by
interpretation is called Dorcas: this
woman was full of good works and alms-
deeds which she did.
37 And it came to pass in those days,
that she was sick, and died: whom when
they had washed, they laid *her* in an
upper chamber.
38 And forasmuch as Lydda was nigh
to Jŏp'pȧ, and the disciples had heard
that Peter was there, they sent unto him
two men, desiring *him* that he would
not delay to come to them.
39 Then Peter arose and went with
them. When he was come, they brought
him into the upper chamber: and all
the widows stood by him weeping,
and showing the coats and garments
which Dorcas made, while she was with
them.
40 But Peter put them all forth, and
kneeled down, and prayed; and turning
him to the body said, Tăb'ĭ-thȧ, arise.
And she opened her eyes: and when she
saw Peter, she sat up.
41 And he gave her *his* hand, and lifted
her up; and when he had called the
saints and widows, he presented her
alive.
42 And it was known throughout
all Jŏp'pȧ; and many believed in the
Lord.
43 And it came to pass, that he tarried
many days in Jŏp'pȧ with one Simon a
tanner.

CHAPTER 10

THERE was a certain man in Çæs'ȧ-
rē'ȧ called Cornelius, a centurion of
the band called the Italian *band*,
2 *A* devout *man*, and one that feared
God with all his house, which gave
much alms to the people, and prayed to
God always.
3 He saw in a vision evidently, about
the ninth hour of the day, an angel of
God coming in to him, and saying unto
him, Cornelius.
4 And when he looked on him, he was
afraid, and said, What is it, Lord? And
he said unto him, Thy prayers and thine
alms are come up for a memorial before
God.
5 And now send men to Jŏp'pȧ, and
call for *one* Simon, whose surname is
Peter:
6 He lodgeth with one Simon a tanner,
whose house is by the sea side: he shall
tell thee what thou oughtest to do.
7 And when the angel which spake unto
Cornelius was departed, he called two
of his household servants, and a devout
soldier of them that waited on him continually;
8 And when he had declared all *these*
things unto them, he sent them to
Jŏp'pȧ.
9 ℭ On the morrow, as they went on
their journey, and drew nigh unto the
city, Peter went up upon the housetop to
pray about the sixth hour:
10 And he became very hungry, and
would have eaten: but while they made
ready, he fell into a trance,
11 And saw heaven opened, and a certain vessel descending unto him, as it
had been a great sheet knit at the four
corners, and let down to the earth:
12 Wherein were all manner of four-
footed beasts of the earth, and wild
beasts, and creeping things, and fowls
of the air.
13 And there came a voice to him,
Rise, Peter; kill, and eat.
14 But Peter said, Not so, Lord; for I
have never eaten any thing that is common or unclean.
15 And the voice *spake* unto him again
the second time, What God hath
cleansed, *that* call not thou common.
16 This was done thrice: and the vessel was received up again into heaven.
17 Now while Peter doubted in himself what this vision which he had seen
should mean, behold, the men which
were sent from Cornelius had made inquiry for Simon's house, and stood before the gate,
18 And called, and asked whether
Simon, which was surnamed Peter,
were lodged there.
19 ℭ While Peter thought on the
vision, the Spirit said unto him, Behold,
three men seek thee.

20 Arise therefore, and get thee down,
and go with them, doubting nothing:
for I have sent them.
21 Then Peter went down to the men
which were sent unto him from Cornelius;
and said, Behold, I am he whom
ye seek: what *is* the cause wherefore ye
are come?
22 And they said, Cornelius the centurion,
a just man, and one that feareth
God, and of good report among all the
nation of the Jews, was warned from
God by a holy angel to send for thee into
his house, and to hear words of thee.
23 Then called he them in, and lodged
them. And on the morrow Peter went
away with them, and certain brethren
from Jŏp′pȧ accompanied him.
24 And the morrow after they entered
into Çæs′ȧ-rē′ȧ. And Cornelius waited
for them, and had called together his
kinsmen and near friends.
25 And as Peter was coming in, Cornelius
met him, and fell down at his
feet, and worshipped *him.*
26 But Peter took him up, saying,
Stand up; I myself also am a man.
27 And as he talked with him, he went
in, and found many that were come together.
28 And he said unto them, Ye know
how that it is an unlawful thing for a
man that is a Jew to keep company, or
come unto one of another nation; but
God hath showed me that I should not
call any man common or unclean.
29 Therefore came I *unto you* without
gainsaying, as soon as I was sent for: I
ask therefore for what intent ye have
sent for me?
30 And Cornelius said, Four days ago
I was fasting until this hour; and at the
ninth hour I prayed in my house, and
behold, a man stood before me in bright
clothing,
31 And said, Cornelius, thy prayer is
heard, and thine alms are had in remembrance
in the sight of God.
32 Send therefore to Jŏp′pȧ, and call
hither Simon, whose surname is Peter;
he is lodged in the house of *one* Simon a
tanner by the sea side: who, when he
cometh, shall speak unto thee.
33 Immediately therefore I sent to
thee; and thou hast well done that thou
art come. Now therefore are we all here
present before God, to hear all things
that are commanded thee of God.
34 ¶ Then Peter opened *his* mouth,
and said, Of a truth I perceive that God
is no respecter of persons:
35 But in every nation he that feareth
him, and worketh righteousness, is accepted
with him.
36 The word which *God* sent unto the
children of Iş′rā-ĕl, preaching peace by
Jesus Christ: (he is Lord of all:)
37 That word, *I say,* ye know, which
was published throughout all Judea, and
began from Galilee, after the baptism
which John preached;
38 How God anointed Jesus of Nazareth
with the Holy Ghost and with
power: who went about doing good, and
healing all that were oppressed of the
devil; for God was with him.
39 And we are witnesses of all things
which he did both in the land of the
Jews, and in Jerusalem; whom they
slew and hanged on a tree:
40 Him God raised up the third day,
and showed him openly;
41 Not to all the people, but unto witnesses
chosen before of God, *even* to
us, who did eat and drink with him after
he rose from the dead.
42 And he commanded us to preach
unto the people, and to testify that it is
he which was ordained of God *to be*
the Judge of quick and dead.
43 To him give all the prophets witness,
that through his name whosoever
believeth in him shall receive remission
of sins.
44 ¶ While Peter yet spake these
words, the Holy Ghost fell on all them
which heard the word.
45 And they of the circumcision which
believed were astonished, as many as
came with Peter, because that on the
Ġĕn′tīleş also was poured out the gift of
the Holy Ghost.
46 For they heard them speak with
tongues, and magnify God. Then answered
Peter,
47 Can any man forbid water, that
these should not be baptized, which have
received the Holy Ghost as well as we?
48 And he commanded them to be
baptized in the name of the Lord. Then
prayed they him to tarry certain days.

CHAPTER 11

AND the apostles and brethren that
were in Judea heard that the Ġĕn′tīleş
had also received the word of God.

2 And when Peter was come up to
Jerusalem, they that were of the circumcision contended with him,
3 Saying, Thou wentest in to men un-
circumcised, and didst eat with them.
4 But Peter rehearsed *the matter* from
the beginning, and expounded *it* by order unto them, saying,
5 I was in the city of Jŏp′pȧ praying:
and in a trance I saw a vision, A certain vessel descend, as it had been a great sheet, let down from heaven by four corners; and it came even to me:
6 Upon the which when I had fastened
mine eyes, I considered, and saw fourfooted beasts of the earth, and wild beasts, and creeping things, and fowls of the air.
7 And I heard a voice saying unto me,
Arise, Peter; slay and eat.
8 But I said, Not so, Lord: for nothing
common or unclean hath at any time entered into my mouth.
9 But the voice answered me again
from heaven, What God hath cleansed, *that* call not thou common.
10 And this was done three times: and
all were drawn up again into heaven.
11 And, behold, immediately there
were three men already come unto the house where I was, sent from Çæ̆s′ȧ-rē′ȧ unto me.
12 And the Spirit bade me go with
them, nothing doubting. Moreover these six brethren accompanied me, and we entered into the man's house:
13 And he showed us how he had seen
an angel in his house, which stood and said unto him, Send men to Jŏp′pȧ, and call for Simon, whose surname is Peter;
14 Who shall tell thee words, where-
by thou and all thy house shall be saved.
15 And as I began to speak, the Holy
Ghost fell on them, as on us at the beginning.
16 Then remembered I the word of the
Lord, how that he said, John indeed baptized with water; but ye shall be baptized with the Holy Ghost.
17 Forasmuch then as God gave them
the like gift as *he did* unto us, who believed on the Lord Jesus Christ, what was I, that I could withstand God?
18 When they heard these things, they
held their peace, and glorified God, saying, Then hath God also to the Ġĕn′tīleṣ granted repentance unto life.
19 ℂ Now they which were scattered
abroad upon the persecution that arose about Stephen traveled as far as Phē-nī′çē, and Cyprus, and Ăn′tĭ-ŏch, preaching the word to none but unto the Jews only.
20 And some of them were men of
Cyprus and Çȳ-rē′nē, which, when they were come to Ăn′tĭ-ŏch, spake unto the Grecians, preaching the Lord Jesus.
21 And the hand of the Lord was with
them: and a great number believed, and turned unto the Lord.
22 ℂ Then tidings of these things came
unto the ears of the church which was in Jerusalem: and they sent forth Barnabas, that he should go as far as Ăn′tĭ-ŏch.
23 Who, when he came, and had seen
the grace of God, was glad, and exhorted them all, that with purpose of heart they would cleave unto the Lord.
24 For he was a good man, and full of
the Holy Ghost and of faith: and much people was added unto the Lord.
25 Then departed Barnabas to Tär′sŭs,
for to seek Saul:
26 And when he had found him, he
brought him unto Ăn′tĭ-ŏch. And it came to pass, that a whole year they assembled themselves with the church, and taught much people. And the disciples were called Christians first in Ăn′tĭ-ŏch.
27 ℂ And in these days came prophets
from Jerusalem unto Ăn′tĭ-ŏch.
28 And there stood up one of them
named Ăg′ȧ-bŭs, and signified by the Spirit that there should be great dearth throughout all the world: which came to pass in the days of Claudius Cæsar.
29 Then the disciples, every man
according to his ability, determined to send relief unto the brethren which dwelt in Judea:
30 Which also they did, and sent it to
the elders by the hands of Barnabas and Saul.

CHAPTER 12

NOW about that time Hĕr′ŏd the king stretched forth *his* hands to vex certain of the church.
2 And he killed James the brother of
John with the sword.
3 And because he saw it pleased the
Jews, he proceeded further to take Peter also. (Then were the days of unleavened bread.)

4 And when he had apprehended him,
he put *him* in prison, and delivered *him*
to four quaternions of soldiers to keep
him; intending after Easter to bring him
forth to the people.
5 Peter therefore was kept in prison:
but prayer was made without ceasing of
the church unto God for him.
6 And when Hĕr′ȯd would have
brought him forth, the same night
Peter was sleeping between two soldiers, bound with two chains: and the
keepers before the door kept the prison.
7 And, behold, the angel of the Lord
came upon *him*, and a light shined in
the prison: and he smote Peter on the
side, and raised him up, saying, Arise
up quickly. And his chains fell off from
his hands.
8 And the angel said unto him, Gird
thyself, and bind on thy sandals. And
so he did. And he saith unto him, Cast
thy garment about thee, and follow
me.
9 And he went out, and followed him;
and wist not that it was true which was
done by the angel; but thought he saw a
vision.
10 When they were past the first and
the second ward, they came unto the
iron gate that leadeth unto the city;
which opened to them of his own accord: and they went out, and passed on
through one street; and forthwith the
angel departed from him.
11 And when Peter was come to himself, he said, Now I know of a surety,
that the Lord hath sent his angel, and
hath delivered me out of the hand of
Hĕr′ȯd, and *from* all the expectation of
the people of the Jews.
12 And when he had considered *the
thing*, he came to the house of Mary the
mother of John, whose surname was
Mark; where many were gathered together praying.
13 And as Peter knocked at the door of
the gate, a damsel came to hearken,
named Rhoda.
14 And when she knew Peter's voice,
she opened not the gate for gladness,
but ran in, and told how Peter stood
before the gate.
15 And they said unto her, Thou art
mad. But she constantly affirmed that
it was even so. Then said they, It is his
angel.
16 But Peter continued knocking: and
when they had opened *the door*, and
saw him, they were astonished.
17 But he, beckoning unto them with
the hand to hold their peace, declared
unto them how the Lord had brought
him out of the prison. And he said, Go
show these things unto James, and to
the brethren. And he departed, and
went into another place.
18 Now as soon as it was day, there
was no small stir among the soldiers,
what was become of Peter.
19 And when Hĕr′ȯd had sought for
him, and found him not, he examined
the keepers, and commanded that *they*
should be put to death. And he went
down from Judea to Çæs′ȧ-rē′ȧ, and
there abode.
20 ℂ And Hĕr′ȯd was highly displeased
with them of Tȳre and Sī′dŏn: but they
came with one accord to him, and, having made Blastus the king's chamberlain their friend, desired peace; because
their country was nourished by the
king's *country*.
21 And upon a set day Hĕr′ȯd, arrayed
in royal apparel, sat upon his throne,
and made an oration unto them.
22 And the people gave a shout, *saying, It is* the voice of a god, and not of
a man.
23 And immediately the angel of the
Lord smote him, because he gave not
God the glory: and he was eaten of
worms, and gave up the ghost.
24 ℂ But the word of God grew and
multiplied.
25 And Barnabas and Saul returned
from Jerusalem, when they had fulfilled
their ministry, and took with them John,
whose surname was Mark.

CHAPTER 13

NOW there were in the church that
was at Ăn′tĭ-ŏch certain prophets
and teachers; as Barnabas, and Simeon
that was called Nī′ġẽr, and Lucius of
Çȳ-rē′nē, and Măn′ȧ-ĕn, which had
been brought up with Hĕr′ȯd the tetrarch, and Saul.
2 As they ministered to the Lord, and
fasted, the Holy Ghost said, Separate
me Barnabas and Saul for the work
whereunto I have called them.
3 And when they had fasted and
prayed, and laid *their* hands on them,
they sent *them* away.
4 ℂ So they, being sent forth by the

Holy Ghost, departed unto Sē-leū'çī-ȧ;
and from thence they sailed to Cyprus.
5 And when they were at Săl'ȧ-mĭs,
they preached the word of God in the
synagogues of the Jews: and they had
also John to *their* minister.
6 And when they had gone through the
isle unto Pā'phŏs, they found a certain
sorcerer, a false prophet, a Jew, whose
name *was* Bär'-jē'sŭs:
7 Which was with the deputy of the
country, Sĕr'gĭ-ŭs Paulus, a prudent
man; who called for Barnabas and Saul,
and desired to hear the word of God.
8 But Ĕl'y̆-măs the sorcerer (for so is
his name by interpretation) withstood
them, seeking to turn away the deputy
from the faith.
9 Then Saul, (who also *is called* Paul,)
filled with the Holy Ghost, set his eyes
on him,
10 And said, O full of all subtilty and
all mischief, *thou* child of the devil, *thou*
enemy of all righteousness, wilt thou
not cease to pervert the right ways of
the Lord?
11 And now, behold, the hand of the
Lord *is* upon thee, and thou shalt be
blind, not seeing the sun for a season.
And immediately there fell on him a
mist and a darkness; and he went about
seeking some to lead him by the hand.
12 Then the deputy, when he saw what
was done, believed, being astonished at
the doctrine of the Lord.
13 Now when Paul and his company
loosed from Pā'phŏs, they came to
Pĕr'gȧ in Păm-phy̆l'ĭ-ȧ: and John departing from them returned to Jerusalem.
14 ¶ But when they departed from
Pĕr'gȧ, they came to Ăn'tĭ-ŏch in Pĭ-
sĭd'ĭ-ȧ, and went into the synagogue on
the sabbath day, and sat down.
15 And after the reading of the law and
the prophets, the rulers of the synagogue sent unto them, saying, *Ye* men
and brethren, if ye have any word of
exhortation for the people, say on.
16 Then Paul stood up, and beckoning
with *his* hand said, Men of Ĭş'rā-ĕl, and
ye that fear God, give audience.
17 The God of this people of Ĭş'rā-ĕl
chose our fathers, and exalted the people when they dwelt as strangers in the
land of Egypt, and with a high arm
brought he them out of it.
18 And about the time of forty years
suffered he their manners in the wilderness.
19 And when he had destroyed seven
nations in the land of Chā'năan, he
divided their land to them by lot.
20 And after that he gave *unto them*
judges about the space of four hundred and fifty years, until Samuel the
prophet.
21 And afterward they desired a king:
and God gave unto them Saul the son
of Çĭs, a man of the tribe of Benjamin,
by the space of forty years.
22 And when he had removed him, he
raised up unto them David to be their
king; to whom also he gave testimony,
and said, I have found David the *son* of
Jesse, a man after mine own heart,
which shall fulfil all my will.
23 Of this man's seed hath God, according to *his* promise, raised unto
Ĭş'rā-ĕl a Saviour, Jesus:
24 When John had first preached before his coming the baptism of repentance to all the people of Ĭş'rā-ĕl.
25 And as John fulfilled his course, he
said, Whom think ye that I am? I am
not *he*. But, behold, there cometh one
after me, whose shoes of *his* feet I am
not worthy to loose.
26 Men *and* brethren, children of the
stock of Abraham, and whosoever
among you feareth God, to you is the
word of this salvation sent.
27 For they that dwell at Jerusalem,
and their rulers, because they knew him
not, nor yet the voices of the prophets
which are read every sabbath day,
they have fulfilled *them* in condemning
him.
28 And though they found no cause of
death *in him*, yet desired they Pilate
that he should be slain.
29 And when they had fulfilled all that
was written of him, they took *him* down
from the tree, and laid *him* in a sepulchre.
30 But God raised him from the dead:
31 And he was seen many days of
them which came up with him from
Galilee to Jerusalem, who are his witnesses unto the people.
32 And we declare unto you glad tidings, how that the promise which was
made unto the fathers,
33 God hath fulfilled the same unto us
their children, in that he hath raised up
Jesus again; as it is also written in the

second psalm, Thou art my Son, this
day have I begotten thee.
34 And as concerning that he raised
him up from the dead, *now* no more to
return to corruption, he said on this
wise, I will give you the sure mercies of
David.
35 Wherefore he saith also in another
psalm, Thou shalt not suffer thine Holy
One to see corruption.
36 For David, after he had served his
own generation by the will of God, fell
on sleep, and was laid unto his fathers,
and saw corruption:
37 But he, whom God raised again,
saw no corruption.
38 ¶ Be it known unto you therefore,
men *and* brethren, that through this
man is preached unto you the forgiveness of sins:
39 And by him all that believe are justified from all things, from which ye
could not be justified by the law of
Moses.
40 Beware therefore, lest that come
upon you, which is spoken of in the
prophets;
41 Behold, ye despisers, and wonder,
and perish: for I work a work in your
days, a work which ye shall in no wise
believe, though a man declare it unto
you.
42 And when the Jews were gone out
of the synagogue, the Ġĕn′tīleṣ besought that these words might be
preached to them the next sabbath.
43 Now when the congregation was
broken up, many of the Jews and religious proselytes followed Paul and
Barnabas; who, speaking to them, persuaded them to continue in the grace of
God.
44 ¶ And the next sabbath day came
almost the whole city together to hear
the word of God.
45 But when the Jews saw the multitudes, they were filled with envy, and
spake against those things which were
spoken by Paul, contradicting and
blaspheming.
46 Then Paul and Barnabas waxed
bold, and said, It was necessary that
the word of God should first have been
spoken to you: but seeing ye put it from
you, and judge yourselves unworthy of
everlasting life, lo, we turn to the
Ġĕn′tīleṣ.
47 For so hath the Lord commanded
us, *saying*, I have set thee to be a
light of the Ġĕn′tīleṣ, that thou shouldest be for salvation unto the ends of the
earth.
48 And when the Ġĕn′tīleṣ heard this,
they were glad, and glorified the word
of the Lord: and as many as were ordained to eternal life believed.
49 And the word of the Lord was published throughout all the region.
50 But the Jews stirred up the devout
and honorable women, and the chief
men of the city, and raised persecution
against Paul and Barnabas, and expelled them out of their coasts.
51 But they shook off the dust of their
feet against them, and came unto
Ī-cō′nĭ-ŭm.
52 And the disciples were filled with
joy, and with the Holy Ghost.

CHAPTER 14

AND it came to pass in Ī-cō′nĭ-ŭm,
that they went both together into
the synagogue of the Jews, and so spake,
that a great multitude both of the Jews
and also of the Greeks believed.
2 But the unbelieving Jews stirred up
the Ġĕn′tīleṣ, and made their minds evil
affected against the brethren.
3 Long time therefore abode they
speaking boldly in the Lord, which gave
testimony unto the word of his grace,
and granted signs and wonders to be
done by their hands.
4 But the multitude of the city was
divided: and part held with the Jews,
and part with the apostles.
5 And when there was an assault made
both of the Ġĕn′tīles, and also of the
Jews with their rulers, to use *them*
despitefully, and to stone them,
6 They were ware of *it*, and fled unto
Lȳs′trȧ and Dĕr′bē, cities of Lȳc′ȧ-ō′-
nĭ-ȧ, and unto the region that lieth round
about:
7 And there they preached the gospel.
8 ¶ And there sat a certain man at
Lȳs′trȧ, impotent in his feet, being a
cripple from his mother's womb, who
never had walked:
9 The same heard Paul speak: who
steadfastly beholding him, and perceiving that he had faith to be healed,
10 Said with a loud voice, Stand upright on thy feet. And he leaped and
walked.
11 And when the people saw what

Paul had done, they lifted up their
voices, saying in the speech of Lўc'ȧ-ō'nĭ-ȧ, The gods are come down to us in the likeness of men.
12 And they called Barnabas, Jupiter;
and Paul, Mĕr-cū'rĭ-ŭs, because he was the chief speaker.
13 Then the priest of Jupiter, which
was before their city, brought oxen and garlands unto the gates, and would have done sacrifice with the people.
14 *Which* when the apostles, Barnabas
and Paul, heard *of*, they rent their clothes, and ran in among the people, crying out,
15 And saying, Sirs, why do ye these
things? We also are men of like passions with you, and preach unto you that ye should turn from these vanities unto the living God, which made heaven, and earth, and the sea, and all things that are therein:
16 Who in times past suffered all na-
tions to walk in their own ways.
17 Nevertheless he left not himself
without witness, in that he did good, and gave us rain from heaven, and fruitful seasons, filling our hearts with food and gladness.
18 And with these sayings scarce re-
strained they the people, that they had not done sacrifice unto them.
19 ¶ And there came thither *certain*
Jews from Ăn'tĭ-ŏch and Ī-cō'nĭ-ŭm, who persuaded the people, and, having stoned Paul, drew *him* out of the city, supposing he had been dead.
20 Howbeit, as the disciples stood
round about him, he rose up, and came into the city: and the next day he departed with Barnabas to Dĕr'bē.
21 And when they had preached the
gospel to that city, and had taught many, they returned again to Lўs'trȧ, and *to* Ī-cō'nĭ-ŭm, and Ăn'tĭ-ŏch,
22 Confirming the souls of the disci-
ples, *and* exhorting them to continue in the faith, and that we must through much tribulation enter into the kingdom of God.
23 And when they had ordained them
elders in every church, and had prayed with fasting, they commended them to the Lord, on whom they believed.
24 And after they had passed through-
out Pĭ-sĭd'ĭ-ȧ, they came to Păm-phўl'ĭ-ȧ.
25 And when they had preached the
word in Pĕr'gȧ, they went down into Ăt'tȧ-lī'ȧ:
26 And thence sailed to Ăn'tĭ-ŏch, from
whence they had been recommended to the grace of God for the work which they fulfilled.
27 And when they were come, and had
gathered the church together, they rehearsed all that God had done with them, and how he had opened the door of faith unto the Ġĕn'tīleș.
28 And there they abode long time
with the disciples.

CHAPTER 15

AND certain men which came down
from Judea taught the brethren, *and said*, Except ye be circumcised after the manner of Moses, ye cannot be saved.
2 When therefore Paul and Barnabas
had no small dissension and disputation with them, they determined that Paul and Barnabas, and certain other of them, should go up to Jerusalem unto the apostles and elders about this question.
3 And being brought on their way by
the church, they passed through Phē-nī'çē and Sȧ-mā'rĭ-ȧ, declaring the conversion of the Ġĕn'tīleș: and they caused great joy unto all the brethren.
4 And when they were come to Jeru-
salem, they were received of the church, and *of* the apostles and elders, and they declared all things that God had done with them.
5 But there rose up certain of the sect
of the Phăr'ĭ-sēeș which believed, saying, That it was needful to circumcise them, and to command *them* to keep the law of Moses.
6 ¶ And the apostles and elders came
together for to consider of this matter.
7 And when there had been much dis-
puting, Peter rose up, and said unto them, Men *and* brethren, ye know how that a good while ago God made choice among us, that the Ġĕn'tīleș by my mouth should hear the word of the gospel, and believe.
8 And God, which knoweth the hearts,
bare them witness, giving them the Holy Ghost, even as *he did* unto us;
9 And put no difference between us and
them, purifying their hearts by faith.
10 Now therefore why tempt ye God,
to put a yoke upon the neck of the dis-

ciples, which neither our fathers nor we
were able to bear?
11 But we believe that through the
grace of the Lord Jesus Christ we shall
be saved, even as they.
12 ¶ Then all the multitude kept silence, and gave audience to Barnabas
and Paul, declaring what miracles and
wonders God had wrought among the
Ġĕn′tīleș by them.
13 ¶ And after they had held their
peace, James answered, saying, Men
and brethren, hearken unto me:
14 Simeon hath declared how God at
the first did visit the Ġĕn′tīleș, to take
out of them a people for his name.
15 And to this agree the words of the
prophets; as it is written,
16 After this I will return, and will
build again the tabernacle of David,
which is fallen down; and I will build
again the ruins thereof, and I will set it
up:
17 That the residue of men might seek
after the Lord, and all the Ġĕn′tīleș,
upon whom my name is called, saith the
Lord, who doeth all these things.
18 Known unto God are all his works
from the beginning of the world.
19 Wherefore my sentence is, that we
trouble not them, which from among the
Ġĕn′tīleș are turned to God:
20 But that we write unto them, that
they abstain from pollutions of idols,
and *from* fornication, and *from* things
strangled, and *from* blood.
21 For Moses of old time hath in
every city them that preach him, being
read in the synagogues every sabbath
day.
22 Then pleased it the apostles and
elders, with the whole church, to send
chosen men of their own company to
Ăn′tĭ-ŏch with Paul and Barnabas;
namely, Judas surnamed Bär′sȧ-băs,
and Silas, chief men among the brethren:
23 And they wrote *letters* by them after
this manner; The apostles and elders
and brethren *send* greeting unto the
brethren which are of the Ġĕn′tīleș in
Ăn′tĭ-ŏch and Syria and Çĭ-lĭ′çĭ-ȧ:
24 Forasmuch as we have heard, that
certain which went out from us have
troubled you with words, subverting
your souls, saying, *Ye must* be circumcised, and keep the law; to whom we
gave no *such* commandment:
25 It seemed good unto us, being assembled with one accord, to send chosen
men unto you with our beloved Barnabas and Paul,
26 Men that have hazarded their lives
for the name of our Lord Jesus Christ.
27 We have sent therefore Judas and
Silas, who shall also tell *you* the same
things by mouth.
28 For it seemed good to the Holy
Ghost, and to us, to lay upon you no
greater burden than these necessary
things;
29 That ye abstain from meats offered
to idols, and from blood, and from
things strangled, and from fornication:
from which if ye keep yourselves, ye
shall do well. Fare ye well.
30 So when they were dismissed, they
came to Ăn′tĭ-ŏch: and when they had
gathered the multitude together, they
delivered the epistle:
31 *Which* when they had read, they
rejoiced for the consolation.
32 And Judas and Silas, being prophets also themselves, exhorted the brethren with many words, and confirmed
them.
33 And after they had tarried *there* a
space, they were let go in peace from
the brethren unto the apostles.
34 Notwithstanding it pleased Silas to
abide there still.
35 Paul also and Barnabas continued
in Ăn′tĭ-ŏch, teaching and preaching the
word of the Lord, with many others
also.
36 ¶ And some days after, Paul said
unto Barnabas, Let us go again and visit
our brethren in every city where we
have preached the word of the Lord,
and see how they do.
37 And Barnabas determined to take
with them John, whose surname was
Mark.
38 But Paul thought not good to take
him with them, who departed from them
from Păm-phȳl′ĭ-ȧ, and went not with
them to the work.
39 And the contention was so sharp
between them, that they departed asunder one from the other: and so Barnabas took Mark, and sailed unto Cyprus;
40 And Paul chose Silas, and departed,
being recommended by the brethren
unto the grace of God.
41 And he went through Syria and
Çĭ-lĭ′çĭ-ȧ, confirming the churches.

CHAPTER 16

THEN came he to Dĕr′bē and Ly̆s′trȧ: and, behold, a certain disciple was there, named Tī-mō′thē-ŭs, the son of a certain woman, which was a Jewess, and believed; but his father *was* a Greek:

2 Which was well reported of by the brethren that were at Ly̆s′trȧ and Ī-cō′nĭ-ŭm.

3 Him would Paul have to go forth with him; and took and circumcised him because of the Jews which were in those quarters: for they knew all that his father was a Greek.

4 And as they went through the cities, they delivered them the decrees for to keep, that were ordained of the apostles and elders which were at Jerusalem.

5 And so were the churches established in the faith, and increased in number daily.

6 Now when they had gone throughout Phry̆ġ′ĭ-ȧ and the region of Gȧ-lā′ti̧-ȧ, and were forbidden of the Holy Ghost to preach the word in Asia,

7 After they were come to My̆s̱′ĭ-ȧ, they assayed to go into Bĭ-thy̆n′ĭ-ȧ: but the Spirit suffered them not.

8 And they passing by My̆s̱′ĭ-ȧ came down to Trō′ăs.

9 And a vision appeared to Paul in the night; There stood a man of Macedonia, and prayed him, saying, Come over into Macedonia, and help us.

10 And after he had seen the vision, immediately we endeavored to go into Macedonia, assuredly gathering that the Lord had called us for to preach the gospel unto them.

11 Therefore loosing from Trō′ăs, we came with a straight course to Săm′ō-thrā′çiȧ, and the next *day* to Nē-ăp′ō-lĭs;

12 And from thence to Phĭ-lĭp′pī, which is the chief city of that part of Macedonia, *and* a colony: and we were in that city abiding certain days.

13 And on the sabbath we went out of the city by a river side, where prayer was wont to be made; and we sat down, and spake unto the women which resorted *thither*.

14 ℂ And a certain woman named Lydia, a seller of purple, of the city of Thy̆′ȧ-tī′rȧ, which worshipped God, heard *us:* whose heart the Lord opened, that she attended unto the things which were spoken of Paul.

15 And when she was baptized, and her household, she besought *us*, saying, If ye have judged me to be faithful to the Lord, come into my house, and abide *there*. And she constrained us.

16 ℂ And it came to pass, as we went to prayer, a certain damsel possessed with a spirit of divination met us, which brought her masters much gain by soothsaying:

17 The same followed Paul and us, and cried, saying, These men are the servants of the most high God, which show unto us the way of salvation.

18 And this did she many days. But Paul, being grieved, turned and said to the spirit, I command thee in the name of Jesus Christ to come out of her. And he came out the same hour.

19 ℂ And when her masters saw that the hope of their gains was gone, they caught Paul and Silas, and drew *them* into the market place unto the rulers,

20 And brought them to the magistrates, saying, These men, being Jews, do exceedingly trouble our city,

21 And teach customs, which are not lawful for us to receive, neither to observe, being Romans.

22 And the multitude rose up together against them; and the magistrates rent off their clothes, and commanded to beat *them*.

23 And when they had laid many stripes upon them, they cast *them* into prison, charging the jailer to keep them safely:

24 Who, having received such a charge, thrust them into the inner prison, and made their feet fast in the stocks.

25 ℂ And at midnight Paul and Silas prayed, and sang praises unto God: and the prisoners heard them.

26 And suddenly there was a great earthquake, so that the foundations of the prison were shaken: and immediately all the doors were opened, and every one's bands were loosed.

27 And the keeper of the prison awaking out of his sleep, and seeing the prison doors open, he drew out his sword, and would have killed himself, supposing that the prisoners had been fled.

28 But Paul cried with a loud voice, saying, Do thyself no harm: for we are all here.

29 Then he called for a light, and

sprang in, and came trembling, and fell
down before Paul and Silas,
30 And brought them out, and said,
Sirs, what must I do to be saved?
31 And they said, Believe on the Lord
Jesus Christ, and thou shalt be saved,
and thy house.
32 And they spake unto him the word
of the Lord, and to all that were in his
house.
33 And he took them the same hour of
the night, and washed *their* stripes; and
was baptized, he and all his, straightway.
34 And when he had brought them into
his house, he set meat before them, and
rejoiced, believing in God with all his
house.
35 And when it was day, the magistrates sent the sergeants, saying, Let
those men go.
36 And the keeper of the prison told
this saying to Paul, The magistrates
have sent to let you go: now therefore
depart, and go in peace.
37 But Paul said unto them, They have
beaten us openly uncondemned, being
Romans, and have cast *us* into prison;
and now do they thrust us out privily?
nay verily; but let them come themselves and fetch us out.
38 And the sergeants told these words
unto the magistrates: and they feared,
when they heard that they were Romans.
39 And they came and besought them,
and brought *them* out, and desired *them*
to depart out of the city.
40 And they went out of the prison, and
entered into *the house of* Lydia: and
when they had seen the brethren, they
comforted them, and departed.

CHAPTER 17

NOW when they had passed through
Ăm-phĭp′ō-lĭs and Ăp′ŏl-lō′nĭ-ȧ,
they came to Thĕs′sȧ-lō-nī′cȧ, where
was a synagogue of the Jews:
2 And Paul, as his manner was, went
in unto them, and three sabbath days
reasoned with them out of the Scriptures,
3 Opening and alleging, that Christ
must needs have suffered, and risen
again from the dead; and that this Jesus,
whom I preach unto you, is Christ.
4 And some of them believed, and con-
sorted with Paul and Silas; and of the
devout Greeks a great multitude, and
of the chief women not a few.
5 ¶ But the Jews which believed not,
moved with envy, took unto them certain lewd fellows of the baser sort, and
gathered a company, and set all the city
on an uproar, and assaulted the house
of Jā′sȯn, and sought to bring them out
to the people.
6 And when they found them not, they
drew Jā′sȯn and certain brethren unto
the rulers of the city, crying, These
that have turned the world upside down
are come hither also;
7 Whom Jā′sȯn hath received: and
these all do contrary to the decrees of
Cæsar, saying that there is another
king, *one* Jesus.
8 And they troubled the people and
the rulers of the city, when they heard
these things.
9 And when they had taken security
of Jā′sȯn, and of the others, they let
them go.
10 ¶ And the brethren immediately
sent away Paul and Silas by night unto
Bĕ-rē′ȧ: who coming *thither* went into
the synagogue of the Jews.
11 These were more noble than those
in Thĕs′sȧ-lō-nī′cȧ, in that they received the word with all readiness of
mind, and searched the Scriptures
daily, whether those things were so.
12 Therefore many of them believed;
also of honorable women which were
Greeks, and of men, not a few.
13 But when the Jews of Thĕs′sȧ-lō-
nī′cȧ had knowledge that the word of
God was preached of Paul at Bĕ-rē′ȧ,
they came thither also, and stirred up
the people.
14 And then immediately the brethren
sent away Paul to go as it were to the
sea: but Silas and Tĭ-mō′thē-ŭs abode
there still.
15 And they that conducted Paul
brought him unto Athens: and receiving
a commandment unto Silas and Tĭ-mō′-
thē-ŭs for to come to him with all speed,
they departed.
16 ¶ Now while Paul waited for them
at Athens, his spirit was stirred in him,
when he saw the city wholly given to
idolatry.
17 Therefore disputed he in the synagogue with the Jews, and with the devout persons, and in the market daily
with them that met with him.

18 Then certain philosophers of the
Ĕp′ĭ-cū rē′ănş, and of the Stō′ĭcs, en-
countered him. And some said, What
will this babbler say? other some, He
seemeth to be a setter forth of strange
gods: because he preached unto them
Jesus, and the resurrection.
19 And they took him, and brought him
unto Ăr′ē-ŏp′á-gŭs, saying, May we
know what this new doctrine, whereof
thou speakest, *is?*
20 For thou bringest certain strange
things to our ears: we would know therefore what these things mean.
21 (For all the Athenians, and strangers which were there, spent their time
in nothing else, but either to tell or to
hear some new thing.)
22 ¶ Then Paul stood in the midst of
Märş' hill, and said, *Ye* men of Athens,
I perceive that in all things ye are too
superstitious.
23 For as I passed by, and beheld
your devotions, I found an altar with
this inscription, TO THE UNKNOWN
GOD. Whom therefore ye ignorantly
worship, him declare I unto you.
24 God that made the world and all
things therein, seeing that he is Lord
of heaven and earth, dwelleth not in
temples made with hands;
25 Neither is worshipped with men's
hands, as though he needed any thing,
seeing he giveth to all life, and breath,
and all things;
26 And hath made of one blood all nations of men for to dwell on all the face
of the earth, and hath determined the
times before appointed, and the bounds
of their habitation;
27 That they should seek the Lord, if
haply they might feel after him, and find
him, though he be not far from every
one of us:
28 For in him we live, and move, and
have our being; as certain also of your
own poets have said, For we are also his
offspring.
29 Forasmuch then as we are the offspring of God, we ought not to think
that the Godhead is like unto gold, or
silver, or stone, graven by art and man's
device.
30 And the times of this ignorance God
winked at; but now commandeth all
men every where to repent:
31 Because he hath appointed a day,
in the which he will judge the world in
righteousness by *that* man whom he
hath ordained; *whereof* he hath given
assurance unto all *men*, in that he hath
raised him from the dead.
32 ¶ And when they heard of the resurrection of the dead, some mocked:
and others said, We will hear thee again
of this *matter*.
33 So Paul departed from among
them.
34 Howbeit certain men clave unto
him, and believed: among the which
was Dī′ō-nȳ′şĭ-ŭs the Ăr′ē-ŏp′á-gīte,
and a woman named Dăm′á-rĭs, and
others with them.

CHAPTER 18

AFTER these things Paul departed
from Athens, and came to Corinth;
2 And found a certain Jew named
Ăq′uĭ-lá, born in Pontus, lately come
from Italy, with his wife Priscilla, (because that Claudius had commanded
all Jews to depart from Rome,) and
came unto them.
3 And because he was of the same
craft, he abode with them, and wrought:
(for by their occupation they were tent-
makers.)
4 And he reasoned in the synagogue
every sabbath, and persuaded the Jews
and the Greeks.
5 And when Silas and Tĭ-mō′thē-ŭs
were come from Macedonia, Paul was
pressed in the spirit, and testified to the
Jews *that* Jesus *was* Christ.
6 And when they opposed themselves,
and blasphemed, he shook *his* raiment,
and said unto them, Your blood *be* upon
your own heads; I *am* clean: from henceforth I will go unto the Ġĕn′tīleş.
7 ¶ And he departed thence, and entered into a certain *man's* house, named
Justus, *one* that worshipped God,
whose house joined hard to the synagogue.
8 And Crĭs′pŭs, the chief ruler of the
synagogue, believed on the Lord with
all his house; and many of the Corinthians hearing believed, and were baptized.
9 Then spake the Lord to Paul in the
night by a vision, Be not afraid, but
speak, and hold not thy peace:
10 For I am with thee, and no man
shall set on thee to hurt thee: for I have
much people in this city.
11 And he continued *there* a year and

six months, teaching the word of God
among them.
12 ℂ And when Găl′lĭ-ō was the deputy
of Ȧ-chā′ia, the Jews made insurrection
with one accord against Paul, and
brought him to the judgment seat,
13 Saying, This *fellow* persuadeth men
to worship God contrary to the law.
14 And when Paul was now about to
open *his* mouth, Găl′lĭ-ō said unto the
Jews, If it were a matter of wrong or
wicked lewdness, O *ye* Jews, reason
would that I should bear with you:
15 But if it be a question of words and
names, and *of* your law, look ye *to it;*
for I will be no judge of such *matters.*
16 And he drave them from the
judgment seat.
17 Then all the Greeks took Sŏs′thē-
nēş, the chief ruler of the synagogue,
and beat *him* before the judgment seat.
And Găl′lĭ-ō cared for none of those
things.
18 ℂ And Paul *after this* tarried *there*
yet a good while, and then took his
leave of the brethren, and sailed thence
into Syria, and with him Priscilla and
Ăq′uĭ-lȧ; having shorn *his* head in
Çĕn-chrē′ȧ: for he had a vow.
19 And he came to Ĕph′ē-sŭs, and left
them there: but he himself entered into
the synagogue, and reasoned with the
Jews.
20 When they desired *him* to tarry
longer time with them, he consented
not;
21 But bade them farewell, saying, I
must by all means keep this feast that
cometh in Jerusalem: but I will return
again unto you, if God will. And he
sailed from Ĕph′ē-sŭs.
22 And when he had landed at Çæ̆s′ȧ-
rē′ȧ, and gone up, and saluted the
church, he went down to Ăn′tĭ-ŏch.
23 And after he had spent some time
there, he departed, and went over *all*
the country of Gȧ-lā′ţi-ȧ and Phrȳ̆g′ĭ-ȧ
in order, strengthening all the disciples.
24 ℂ And a certain Jew named Ȧ-pŏl′-
lŏs, born at Alexandria, an eloquent
man, *and* mighty in the Scriptures,
came to Ĕph′ē-sŭs.
25 This man was instructed in the way
of the Lord; and being fervent in the
spirit, he spake and taught diligently
the things of the Lord, knowing only
the baptism of John.
26 And he began to speak boldly in the
synagogue: whom when Ăq′uĭ-lȧ and
Priscilla had heard, they took him unto
them, and expounded unto him the way
of God more perfectly.
27 And when he was disposed to pass
into Ȧ-chā′ia, the brethren wrote, exhorting the disciples to receive him:
who, when he was come, helped them
much which had believed through grace:
28 For he mightily convinced the Jews,
and that publicly, showing by the Scriptures that Jesus was Christ.

CHAPTER 19

AND it came to pass, that, while
Ȧ-pŏl′lŏs was at Corinth, Paul having passed through the upper coasts
came to Ĕph′ē-sŭs; and finding certain
disciples,
2 He said unto them, Have ye received
the Holy Ghost since ye believed? And
they said unto him, We have not so
much as heard whether there be any
Holy Ghost.
3 And he said unto them, Unto what
then were ye baptized? And they said,
Unto John's baptism.
4 Then said Paul, John verily baptized
with the baptism of repentance, saying
unto the people, that they should believe
on him which should come after him,
that is, on Christ Jesus.
5 When they heard *this,* they were baptized in the name of the Lord Jesus.
6 And when Paul had laid *his* hands
upon them, the Holy Ghost came on
them; and they spake with tongues, and
prophesied.
7 And all the men were about twelve.
8 And he went into the synagogue,
and spake boldly for the space of
three months, disputing and persuad-
ing the things concerning the kingdom
of God.
9 But when divers were hardened, and
believed not, but spake evil of that way
before the multitude, he departed from
them, and separated the disciples, disputing daily in the school of one Tȳ-
răn′nŭs.
10 And this continued by the space of
two years; so that all they which dwelt
in Asia heard the word of the Lord
Jesus, both Jews and Greeks.
11 And God wrought special miracles
by the hands of Paul:
12 So that from his body were brought
unto the sick handkerchiefs or aprons,

and the diseases departed from them,
and the evil spirits went out of them.
13 ℂ Then certain of the vagabond
Jews, exorcists, took upon them to call
over them which had evil spirits the
name of the Lord Jesus, saying, We adjure you by Jesus whom Paul preacheth.
14 And there were seven sons of *one*
Sçē′vȧ, a Jew, *and* chief of the priests,
which did so.
15 And the evil spirit answered and
said, Jesus I know, and Paul I know;
but who are ye?
16 And the man in whom the evil
spirit was leaped on them, and overcame them, and prevailed against them,
so that they fled out of that house naked
and wounded.
17 And this was known to all the Jews
and Greeks also dwelling at Ĕph′ē-sŭs;
and fear fell on them all, and the name
of the Lord Jesus was magnified.
18 And many that believed came, and
confessed, and showed their deeds.
19 Many of them also which used
curious arts brought their books together, and burned them before all
men: and they counted the price of
them, and found *it* fifty thousand
pieces of silver.
20 So mightily grew the word of God
and prevailed.
21 ℂ After these things were ended,
Paul purposed in the spirit, when he had
passed through Macedonia and Ȧ-chā′-
ịȧ, to go to Jerusalem, saying, After I
have been there, I must also see Rome.
22 So he sent into Macedonia two of
them that ministered unto him, Tĭ-mō′-
thē-ŭs and Ē-răs′tŭs; but he himself
stayed in Asia for a season.
23 And the same time there arose no
small stir about that way.
24 For a certain *man* named Dē-mē′-
trĭ-ŭs, a silversmith, which made silver
shrines for Diana, brought no small
gain unto the craftsmen;
25 Whom he called together with the
workmen of like occupation, and said,
Sirs, ye know that by this craft we have
our wealth.
26 Moreover ye see and hear, that not
alone at Ĕph′ē-sŭs, but almost throughout all Asia, this Paul hath persuaded
and turned away much people, saying
that they be no gods, which are made
with hands:
27 So that not only this our craft is in
danger to be set at nought; but also that
the temple of the great goddess Diana
should be despised, and her magnifi-
cence should be destroyed, whom all
Asia and the world worshippeth.
28 And when they heard *these sayings*,
they were full of wrath, and cried out,
saying, Great *is* Diana of the Ē-phē′-
ṣiănṣ.
29 And the whole city was filled with
confusion: and having caught Gā′ịŭs
and Ăr′ĭs-tär′chŭs, men of Macedonia,
Paul's companions in travel, they rushed
with one accord into the theatre.
30 And when Paul would have entered
in unto the people, the disciples suffered
him not.
31 And certain of the chief of Asia,
which were his friends, sent unto him,
desiring *him* that he would not adventure himself into the theatre.
32 Some therefore cried one thing,
and some another: for the assembly was
confused; and the more part knew not
wherefore they were come together.
33 And they drew Alexander out of the
multitude, the Jews putting him forward. And Alexander beckoned with
the hand, and would have made his
defense unto the people.
34 But when they knew that he was a
Jew, all with one voice about the space
of two hours cried out, Great *is* Diana
of the Ē-phē′ṣiănṣ.
35 And when the townclerk had appeased the people, he said, *Ye* men
of Ĕph′ē-sŭs, what man is there that
knoweth not how that the city of the
Ē-phē′ṣiănṣ is a worshipper of the great
goddess Diana, and of the *image* which
fell down from Jupiter?
36 Seeing then that these things cannot be spoken against, ye ought to be
quiet, and to do nothing rashly.
37 For ye have brought hither these
men, which are neither robbers of
churches, nor yet blasphemers of your
goddess.
38 Wherefore if Dē-mē′trĭ-ŭs, and the
craftsmen which are with him, have
a matter against any man, the law is
open, and there are deputies: let them
implead one another.
39 But if ye inquire any thing concerning other matters, it shall be determined in a lawful assembly.
40 For we are in danger to be called in
question for this day's uproar, there

being no cause whereby we may give an
account of this concourse.
41 And when he had thus spoken, he
dismissed the assembly.

CHAPTER 20

AND after the uproar was ceased,
Paul called unto *him* the disciples,
and embraced *them*, and departed for
to go into Macedonia.
2 And when he had gone over those
parts, and had given them much exhortation, he came into Greece,
3 And *there* abode three months. And
when the Jews laid wait for him, as he
was about to sail into Syria, he purposed
to return through Macedonia.
4 And there accompanied him into Asia
Sō'pȧ-tẽr of Bĕ-rē'ȧ; and of the Thĕs'-
sȧ-lō'nĭ-ăns, Ăr'ĭs-tär'chŭs and Sē-
cŭn'dŭs; and Gā'ịŭs of Dẽr'bē, and
Tĭ-mō'thē-ŭs; and of Asia, Tўch'ĭ-cŭs
and Trŏph'ĭ-mŭs.
5 These going before tarried for us at
Trō'ăs.
6 And we sailed away from Phĭ-lĭp'pī
after the days of unleavened bread,
and came unto them to Trō'ăs in five
days; where we abode seven days.
7 And upon the first *day* of the week,
when the disciples came together to
break bread, Paul preached unto them,
ready to depart on the morrow; and continued his speech until midnight.
8 And there were many lights in the
upper chamber, where they were gathered together.
9 And there sat in a window a certain
young man named Eū'tў-chŭs, being
fallen into a deep sleep: and as Paul
was long preaching, he sunk down with
sleep, and fell down from the third loft,
and was taken up dead.
10 And Paul went down, and fell on
him, and embracing *him* said, Trouble
not yourselves; for his life is in him.
11 When he therefore was come up
again, and had broken bread, and eaten,
and talked a long while, even till break
of day, so he departed.
12 And they brought the young man
alive, and were not a little comforted.
13 ¶ And we went before to ship, and
sailed unto Ăs'sŏs, there intending to
take in Paul: for so had he appointed,
minding himself to go afoot.
14 And when he met with us at Ăs'sŏs,
we took him in, and came to Mĭt'ў-lē'nē.
15 And we sailed thence, and came
the next *day* over against Chī'ŏs; and
the next *day* we arrived at Sā'mŏs, and
tarried at Trō-ġўl'lĭ-ŭm; and the next
day we came to Mī-lē'tŭs.
16 For Paul had determined to sail by
Ĕph'ē-sŭs, because he would not spend
the time in Asia: for he hasted, if it were
possible for him, to be at Jerusalem the
day of Pĕn'tē-cŏst.
17 ¶ And from Mī-lē'tŭs he sent to
Ĕph'ē-sŭs, and called the elders of the
church.
18 And when they were come to him,
he said unto them, Ye know, from the
first day that I came into Asia, after
what manner I have been with you at all
seasons,
19 Serving the Lord with all humility
of mind, and with many tears, and temptations, which befell me by the lying in
wait of the Jews:
20 *And* how I kept back nothing that
was profitable *unto you*, but have
showed you, and have taught you publicly, and from house to house,
21 Testifying both to the Jews, and
also to the Greeks, repentance toward
God, and faith toward our Lord Jesus
Christ.
22 And now, behold, I go bound in the
spirit unto Jerusalem, not knowing the
things that shall befall me there:
23 Save that the Holy Ghost witnesseth
in every city, saying that bonds and
afflictions abide me.
24 But none of these things move me,
neither count I my life dear unto myself, so that I might finish my course
with joy, and the ministry, which I have
received of the Lord Jesus, to testify
the gospel of the grace of God.
25 And now, behold, I know that ye
all, among whom I have gone preaching
the kingdom of God, shall see my face
no more.
26 Wherefore I take you to record this
day, that I *am* pure from the blood of
all *men*.
27 For I have not shunned to declare
unto you all the counsel of God.
28 ¶ Take heed therefore unto yourselves, and to all the flock, over the
which the Holy Ghost hath made you
overseers, to feed the church of God,
which he hath purchased with his own
blood.
29 For I know this, that after my de-

parting shall grievous wolves enter in
among you, not sparing the flock.
30 Also of your own selves shall men
arise, speaking perverse things, to draw
away disciples after them.
31 Therefore watch, and remember,
that by the space of three years I ceased
not to warn every one night and day
with tears.
32 And now, brethren, I commend you
to God, and to the word of his grace,
which is able to build you up, and to
give you an inheritance among all them
which are sanctified.
33 I have coveted no man's silver, or
gold, or apparel.
34 Yea, ye yourselves know, that these
hands have ministered unto my necessities, and to them that were with me.
35 I have showed you all things, how
that so laboring ye ought to support the
weak, and to remember the words of
the Lord Jesus, how he said, It is more
blessed to give than to receive.
36 ¶ And when he had thus spoken,
he kneeled down, and prayed with them
all.
37 And they all wept sore, and fell on
Paul's neck, and kissed him,
38 Sorrowing most of all for the words
which he spake, that they should see his
face no more. And they accompanied
him unto the ship.

CHAPTER 21

AND it came to pass, that after we
were gotten from them, and had
launched, we came with a straight course
unto Cō'ŏs, and the *day* following unto
Rhodes, and from thence unto Păt'á-rȧ:
2 And finding a ship sailing over unto
Phē-nĭ'çi-ȧ, we went aboard, and set
forth.
3 Now when we had discovered Cyprus,
we left it on the left hand, and sailed
into Syria, and landed at Tȳre: for there
the ship was to unlade her burden.
4 And finding disciples, we tarried
there seven days: who said to Paul
through the Spirit, that he should not go
up to Jerusalem.
5 And when we had accomplished
those days, we departed and went our
way; and they all brought us on our way,
with wives and children, till *we were*
out of the city: and we kneeled down on
the shore, and prayed.
6 And when we had taken our leave one
of another, we took ship; and they returned home again.
7 And when we had finished *our* course
from Tȳre, we came to Ptŏl'ē-mā'ĭs, and
saluted the brethren, and abode with
them one day.
8 And the next *day* we that were of
Paul's company departed, and came
unto Çæ̆s'á-rē'ȧ; and we entered into
the house of Philip the evangelist, which
was *one* of the seven; and abode with
him.
9 And the same man had four daughters, virgins, which did prophesy.
10 And as we tarried *there* many days,
there came down from Judea a certain
prophet, named Ăg'á-bŭs.
11 And when he was come unto us, he
took Paul's girdle, and bound his own
hands and feet, and said, Thus saith the
Holy Ghost, So shall the Jews at Jerusalem bind the man that owneth this
girdle, and shall deliver *him* into the
hands of the Ġĕn'tīleș.
12 And when we heard these things,
both we, and they of that place, besought him not to go up to Jerusalem.
13 Then Paul answered, What mean ye
to weep and to break mine heart? for I
am ready not to be bound only, but also
to die at Jerusalem for the name of the
Lord Jesus.
14 And when he would not be persuaded, we ceased, saying, The will of
the Lord be done.
15 And after those days we took up
our carriages, and went up to Jerusalem.
16 There went with us also *certain* of
the disciples of Çæ̆s'á-rē'ȧ, and brought
with them one Mnā'sŏn of Cyprus, an
old disciple, with whom we should
lodge.
17 And when we were come to Jerusalem, the brethren received us gladly.
18 And the *day* following Paul went in
with us unto James; and all the elders
were present.
19 And when he had saluted them, he
declared particularly what things God
had wrought among the Ġĕn'tīleș by his
ministry.
20 And when they heard *it*, they glorified the Lord, and said unto him, Thou
seest, brother, how many thousands of
Jews there are which believe; and they
are all zealous of the law:
21 And they are informed of thee, that
thou teachest all the Jews which are

among the Ġĕn'tīle̱s to forsake Moses,
saying that they ought not to circumcise
their children, neither to walk after the
customs.
22 What is it therefore? the multitude
must needs come together: for they will
hear that thou art come.
23 Do therefore this that we say to
thee: We have four men which have a
vow on them;
24 Them take, and purify thyself with
them, and be at charges with them,
that they may shave *their* heads: and
all may know that those things, whereof
they were informed concerning thee,
are nothing; but *that* thou thyself also
walkest orderly, and keepest the law.
25 As touching the Ġĕn'tīle̱s which believe, we have written *and* concluded
that they observe no such thing, save
only that they keep themselves from
things offered to idols, and from blood,
and from strangled, and from fornication.
26 Then Paul took the men, and the
next day purifying himself with them
entered into the temple, to signify the
accomplishment of the days of purification, until that an offering should be
offered for every one of them.
27 And when the seven days were
almost ended, the Jews which were of
Asia, when they saw him in the temple,
stirred up all the people, and laid hands
on him,
28 Crying out, Men of Ĭs̱'rā-ĕl, help:
This is the man, that teacheth all *men*
every where against the people, and
the law, and this place: and further
brought Greeks also into the temple,
and hath polluted this holy place.
29 (For they had seen before with him
in the city Trŏph'ĭ-mŭs an Ē-phē'ṣiăn,
whom they supposed that Paul had
brought into the temple.)
30 And all the city was moved, and the
people ran together: and they took
Paul, and drew him out of the temple:
and forthwith the doors were shut.
31 And as they went about to kill him,
tidings came unto the chief captain of
the band, that all Jerusalem was in an
uproar:
32 Who immediately took soldiers and
centurions, and ran down unto them:
and when they saw the chief captain and
the soldiers, they left beating of Paul.
33 Then the chief captain came near,
and took him, and commanded *him* to
be bound with two chains; and demanded who he was, and what he had
done.
34 And some cried one thing, some
another, among the multitude: and when
he could not know the certainty for the
tumult, he commanded him to be carried into the castle.
35 And when he came upon the stairs,
so it was, that he was borne of the soldiers for the violence of the people.
36 For the multitude of the people followed after, crying, Away with him.
37 And as Paul was to be led into the
castle, he said unto the chief captain,
May I speak unto thee? Who said,
Canst thou speak Greek?
38 Art not thou that Egyptian, which
before these days madest an uproar,
and leddest out into the wilderness four
thousand men that were murderers?
39 But Paul said, I am a man *which*
am a Jew of Tär'sŭs, *a city* in Çĭ-lĭ'çi-ȧ,
a citizen of no mean city: and, I beseech
thee, suffer me to speak unto the people.
40 And when he had given him license,
Paul stood on the stairs, and beckoned
with the hand unto the people. And
when there was made a great silence,
he spake unto *them* in the Hebrew
tongue, saying,

CHAPTER 22

MEN, brethren, and fathers, hear ye
my defense *which I make* now
unto you.
2 (And when they heard that he spake
in the Hebrew tongue to them, they
kept the more silence: and he saith,)
3 I am verily a man *which am* a Jew,
born in Tär'sŭs, *a city* in Çĭ-lĭ'çi-ȧ, yet
brought up in this city at the feet of
Gȧ-mā'lĭ-ĕl, *and* taught according to the
perfect manner of the law of the fathers,
and was zealous toward God, as ye all
are this day.
4 And I persecuted this way unto
the death, binding and delivering into
prisons both men and women.
5 As also the high priest doth bear me
witness, and all the estate of the elders:
from whom also I received letters unto
the brethren, and went to Damascus,
to bring them which were there bound
unto Jerusalem, for to be punished.
6 And it came to pass, that, as I made
my journey, and was come nigh unto

Damascus about noon, suddenly there shone from heaven a great light round about me.
7 And I fell unto the ground, and heard a voice saying unto me, Saul, Saul, why persecutest thou me?
8 And I answered, Who art thou, Lord? And he said unto me, I am Jesus of Nazareth, whom thou persecutest.
9 And they that were with me saw indeed the light, and were afraid; but they heard not the voice of him that spake to me.
10 And I said, What shall I do, Lord? And the Lord said unto me, Arise, and go into Damascus; and there it shall be told thee of all things which are appointed for thee to do.
11 And when I could not see for the glory of that light, being led by the hand of them that were with me, I came into Damascus.
12 And one Ăn′á-nī′ăs, a devout man according to the law, having a good report of all the Jews which dwelt *there*,
13 Came unto me, and stood, and said unto me, Brother Saul, receive thy sight. And the same hour I looked up upon him.
14 And he said, The God of our fathers hath chosen thee, that thou shouldest know his will, and see that Just One, and shouldest hear the voice of his mouth.
15 For thou shalt be his witness unto all men of what thou hast seen and heard.
16 And now why tarriest thou? arise, and be baptized, and wash away thy sins, calling on the name of the Lord.
17 And it came to pass, that, when I was come again to Jerusalem, even while I prayed in the temple, I was in a trance;
18 And saw him saying unto me, Make haste, and get thee quickly out of Jerusalem: for they will not receive thy testimony concerning me.
19 And I said, Lord, they know that I imprisoned and beat in every synagogue them that believed on thee:
20 And when the blood of thy martyr Stephen was shed, I also was standing by, and consenting unto his death, and kept the raiment of them that slew him.
21 And he said unto me, Depart: for I will send thee far hence unto the Ġĕn′tīleş.
22 And they gave him audience unto this word, and *then* lifted up their voice, and said, Away with such a *fellow* from the earth: for it is not fit that he should live.
23 And as they cried out, and cast off *their* clothes, and threw dust into the air,
24 The chief captain commanded him to be brought into the castle, and bade that he should be examined by scourging; that he might know wherefore they cried so against him.
25 And as they bound him with thongs, Paul said unto the centurion that stood by, Is it lawful for you to scourge a man that is a Roman, and uncondemned?
26 When the centurion heard *that*, he went and told the chief captain, saying, Take heed what thou doest; for this man is a Roman.
27 Then the chief captain came, and said unto him, Tell me, art thou a Roman? He said, Yea.
28 And the chief captain answered, With a great sum obtained I this freedom. And Paul said, But I was *free*-born.
29 Then straightway they departed from him which should have examined him: and the chief captain also was afraid, after he knew that he was a Roman, and because he had bound him.
30 On the morrow, because he would have known the certainty wherefore he was accused of the Jews, he loosed him from *his* bands, and commanded the chief priests and all their council to appear, and brought Paul down, and set him before them.

CHAPTER 23

AND Paul, earnestly beholding the council, said, Men *and* brethren, I have lived in all good conscience before God until this day.
2 And the high priest Ăn′á-nī′ăs commanded them that stood by him to smite him on the mouth.
3 Then said Paul unto him, God shall smite thee, *thou* whited wall: for sittest thou to judge me after the law, and commandest me to be smitten contrary to the law?
4 And they that stood by said, Revilest thou God's high priest?
5 Then said Paul, I wist not, brethren, that he was the high priest: for it is

written, Thou shalt not speak evil of the ruler of thy people.

6 But when Paul perceived that the one part were Săd′dū-çēeş, and the other Phăr′ĭ-sēeş, he cried out in the council, Men *and* brethren, I am a Phăr′ĭ-sēe, the son of a Phăr′ĭ-sēe: of the hope and resurrection of the dead I am called in question.

7 And when he had so said, there arose a dissension between the Phăr′ĭ-sēeş and the Săd′dū-çēeş: and the multitude was divided.

8 For the Săd′dū-çēeş say that there is no resurrection, neither angel, nor spirit: but the Phăr′ĭ-sēeş confess both.

9 And there arose a great cry: and the scribes *that were* of the Phăr′ĭ-sēeş′ part arose, and strove, saying, We find no evil in this man: but if a spirit or an angel hath spoken to him, let us not fight against God.

10 And when there arose a great dissension, the chief captain, fearing lest Paul should have been pulled in pieces of them, commanded the soldiers to go down, and to take him by force from among them, and to bring *him* into the castle.

11 And the night following the Lord stood by him, and said, Be of good cheer, Paul: for as thou hast testified of me in Jerusalem, so must thou bear witness also at Rome.

12 And when it was day, certain of the Jews banded together, and bound themselves under a curse, saying that they would neither eat nor drink till they had killed Paul.

13 And they were more than forty which had made this conspiracy.

14 And they came to the chief priests and elders, and said, We have bound ourselves under a great curse, that we will eat nothing until we have slain Paul.

15 Now therefore ye with the council signify to the chief captain that he bring him down unto you to-morrow, as though ye would inquire something more perfectly concerning him: and we, or ever he come near, are ready to kill him.

16 And when Paul's sister's son heard of their lying in wait, he went and entered into the castle, and told Paul.

17 Then Paul called one of the centurions unto *him,* and said, Bring this young man unto the chief captain: for he hath a certain thing to tell him.

18 So he took him, and brought *him* to the chief captain, and said, Paul the prisoner called me unto *him,* and prayed me to bring this young man unto thee, who hath something to say unto thee.

19 Then the chief captain took him by the hand, and went *with him* aside privately, and asked *him,* What is that thou hast to tell me?

20 And he said, The Jews have agreed to desire thee that thou wouldest bring down Paul to-morrow into the council, as though they would inquire somewhat of him more perfectly.

21 But do not thou yield unto them: for there lie in wait for him of them more than forty men, which have bound themselves with an oath, that they will neither eat nor drink till they have killed him: and now are they ready, looking for a promise from thee.

22 So the chief captain *then* let the young man depart, and charged *him, See thou* tell no man that thou hast showed these things to me.

23 And he called unto *him* two centurions, saying, Make ready two hundred soldiers to go to Çæs′ȧ-rē′ȧ, and horsemen threescore and ten, and spearmen two hundred, at the third hour of the night;

24 And provide *them* beasts, that they may set Paul on, and bring *him* safe unto Felix the governor.

25 And he wrote a letter after this manner:

26 Claudius Lȳs′ĭ-ăs unto the most excellent governor Felix *sendeth* greeting.

27 This man was taken of the Jews, and should have been killed of them: then came I with an army, and rescued him, having understood that he was a Roman.

28 And when I would have known the cause wherefore they accused him, I brought him forth into their council:

29 Whom I perceived to be accused of questions of their law, but to have nothing laid to his charge worthy of death or of bonds.

30 And when it was told me how that the Jews laid wait for the man, I sent straightway to thee, and gave commandment to his accusers also to say before thee what *they had* against him. Farewell.

31 Then the soldiers, as it was commanded them, took Paul, and brought *him* by night to Ăn-tĭp′ȧ-trĭs.

32 On the morrow they left the horsemen to go with him, and returned to
the castle:
33 Who, when they came to Çæ̆s′ȧ-
rē′ȧ, and delivered the epistle to the
governor, presented Paul also before
him.
34 And when the governor had read
the letter, he asked of what province he
was. And when he understood that *he
was* of Çi-lĭ′çĭ-ȧ;
35 I will hear thee, said he, when thine
accusers are also come. And he commanded him to be kept in Hĕr′ŏd's
judgment hall.

CHAPTER 24

AND after five days Ăn′ȧ-nī′ăs the
high priest descended with the
elders, and *with* a certain orator *named*
Tĕr-tŭl′lŭs, who informed the governor
against Paul.
2 And when he was called forth, Tĕr-
tŭl′lŭs began to accuse *him*, saying,
Seeing that by thee we enjoy great
quietness, and that very worthy deeds
are done unto this nation by thy provi-
dence,
3 We accept *it* always, and in all places,
most noble Felix, with all thankfulness.
4 Notwithstanding, that I be not further
tedious unto thee, I pray thee that thou
wouldest hear us of thy clemency a few
words.
5 For we have found this man *a* pesti-
lent *fellow*, and a mover of sedition
among all the Jews throughout the
world, and a ringleader of the sect of
the Nazarenes:
6 Who also hath gone about to profane
the temple: whom we took, and would
have judged according to our law.
7 But the chief captain Lȳs′ĭ-ăs came
upon us, and with great violence took
him away out of our hands,
8 Commanding his accusers to come
unto thee: by examining of whom thyself mayest take knowledge of all these
things, whereof we accuse him.
9 And the Jews also assented, saying
that these things were so.
10 Then Paul, after that the governor
had beckoned unto him to speak, answered, Forasmuch as I know that thou
hast been of many years a judge unto
this nation, I do the more cheerfully answer for myself:
11 Because that thou mayest understand, that there are yet but twelve days
since I went up to Jerusalem for to worship.
12 And they neither found me in the
temple disputing with any man, neither
raising up the people, neither in the
synagogues, nor in the city:
13 Neither can they prove the things
whereof they now accuse me.
14 But this I confess unto thee, that
after the way which they call heresy, so
worship I the God of my fathers, believing all things which are written in the
law and in the prophets:
15 And have hope toward God, which
they themselves also allow, that there
shall be a resurrection of the dead, both
of the just and unjust.
16 And herein do I exercise myself, to
have always a conscience void of offense
toward God, and *toward* men.
17 Now after many years I came to
bring alms to my nation, and offerings.
18 Whereupon certain Jews from Asia
found me purified in the temple,
neither with multitude, nor with tumult.
19 Who ought to have been here before
thee, and object, if they had aught
against me.
20 Or else let these same *here* say, if
they have found any evildoing in me,
while I stood before the council,
21 Except it be for this one voice, that
I cried standing among them, Touching
the resurrection of the dead I am called
in question by you this day.
22 And when Felix heard these things,
having more perfect knowledge of *that*
way, he deferred them, and said, When
Lȳs′ĭ-ăs the chief captain shall come
down, I will know the uttermost of your
matter.
23 And he commanded a centurion to
keep Paul, and to let *him* have liberty,
and that he should forbid none of his
acquaintance to minister or come unto
him.
24 And after certain days, when Felix
came with his wife Drụ-sĭl′lȧ, which
was a Jewess, he sent for Paul, and
heard him concerning the faith in Christ.
25 And as he reasoned of righteousness, temperance, and judgment to
come, Felix trembled, and answered,
Go thy way for this time; when I have a
convenient season, I will call for thee.
26 He hoped also that money should
have been given him of Paul, that he

might loose him: wherefore he sent for him the oftener, and communed with him.

27 But after two years Pôr'çĭ-ŭs Festus came into Felix' room: and Felix, willing to show the Jews a pleasure, left Paul bound.

CHAPTER 25

NOW when Festus was come into the province, after three days he ascended from Çæ̆s'ȧ-rē'ȧ to Jerusalem.

2 Then the high priest and the chief of the Jews informed him against Paul, and besought him,

3 And desired favor against him, that he would send for him to Jerusalem, laying wait in the way to kill him.

4 But Festus answered, that Paul should be kept at Çæ̆s'ȧ-rē'ȧ, and that he himself would depart shortly *thither*.

5 Let them therefore, said he, which among you are able, go down with *me*, and accuse this man, if there be any wickedness in him.

6 And when he had tarried among them more than ten days, he went down unto Çæ̆s'ȧ-rē'ȧ; and the next day sitting on the judgment seat commanded Paul to be brought.

7 And when he was come, the Jews which came down from Jerusalem stood round about, and laid many and grievous complaints against Paul, which they could not prove.

8 While he answered for himself, Neither against the law of the Jews, neither against the temple, nor yet against Cæsar, have I offended any thing at all.

9 But Festus, willing to do the Jews a pleasure, answered Paul, and said, Wilt thou go up to Jerusalem, and there be judged of these things before me?

10 Then said Paul, I stand at Cæsar's judgment seat, where I ought to be judged: to the Jews have I done no wrong, as thou very well knowest.

11 For if I be an offender, or have committed any thing worthy of death, I refuse not to die: but if there be none of these things whereof these accuse me, no man may deliver me unto them. I appeal unto Cæsar.

12 Then Festus, when he had conferred with the council, answered, Hast thou appealed unto Cæsar? unto Cæsar shalt thou go.

13 And after certain days king Ȧ-grĭp'pȧ and Bĕr-nī'çē came unto Çæ̆s'ȧ-rē'ȧ to salute Festus.

14 And when they had been there many days, Festus declared Paul's cause unto the king, saying, There is a certain man left in bonds by Felix:

15 About whom, when I was at Jerusalem, the chief priests and the elders of the Jews informed *me*, desiring *to have* judgment against him.

16 To whom I answered, It is not the manner of the Romans to deliver any man to die, before that he which is accused have the accusers face to face, and have license to answer for himself concerning the crime laid against him.

17 Therefore, when they were come hither, without any delay on the morrow I sat on the judgment seat, and commanded the man to be brought forth.

18 Against whom when the accusers stood up, they brought none accusation of such things as I supposed:

19 But had certain questions against him of their own superstition, and of one Jesus, which was dead, whom Paul affirmed to be alive.

20 And because I doubted of such manner of questions, I asked *him* whether he would go to Jerusalem, and there be judged of these matters.

21 But when Paul had appealed to be reserved unto the hearing of Augustus, I commanded him to be kept till I might send him to Cæsar.

22 Then Ȧ-grĭp'pȧ said unto Festus, I would also hear the man myself. To-morrow, said he, thou shalt hear him.

23 And on the morrow, when Ȧ-grĭp'pȧ was come, and Bĕr-nī'çē, with great pomp, and was entered into the place of hearing, with the chief captains, and principal men of the city, at Festus' commandment Paul was brought forth.

24 And Festus said, King Ȧ-grĭp'pȧ, and all men which are here present with us, ye see this man, about whom all the multitude of the Jews have dealt with me, both at Jerusalem, and *also* here, crying that he ought not to live any longer.

25 But when I found that he had committed nothing worthy of death, and that he himself hath appealed to Augustus, I have determined to send him.

26 Of whom I have no certain thing to

write unto my lord. Wherefore I have
brought him forth before you, and specially before thee, O king Ȧ-grĭp′pȧ,
that, after examination had, I might
have somewhat to write.
27 For it seemeth to me unreasonable
to send a prisoner, and not withal to
signify the crimes *laid* against him.

CHAPTER 26

THEN Ȧ-grĭp′pȧ said unto Paul,
Thou art permitted to speak for thyself. Then Paul stretched forth the
hand, and answered for himself:
2 I think myself happy, king Ȧ-grĭp′pȧ,
because I shall answer for myself this
day before thee touching all the things
whereof I am accused of the Jews:
3 Especially *because I know* thee to be
expert in all customs and questions
which are among the Jews: wherefore I
beseech thee to hear me patiently.
4 My manner of life from my youth,
which was at the first among mine own
nation at Jerusalem, know all the Jews;
5 Which knew me from the beginning,
if they would testify, that after the most
straitest sect of our religion I lived a
Phăr′ĭ-sēe.
6 And now I stand and am judged for
the hope of the promise made of God
unto our fathers:
7 Unto which *promise* our twelve
tribes, instantly serving *God* day and
night, hope to çome. For which hope's
sake, king Ȧ-grĭp′pȧ, I am accused of
the Jews.
8 Why should it be thought a thing
incredible with you, that God should
raise the dead?
9 I verily thought with myself, that I
ought to do many things contrary to the
name of Jesus of Nazareth.
10 Which thing I also did in Jerusalem:
and many of the saints did I shut up in
prison, having received authority from
the chief priests; and when they were
put to death, I gave my voice against
them.
11 And I punished them oft in every
synagogue, and compelled *them* to
blaspheme; and being exceedingly mad
against them, I persecuted *them* even
unto strange cities.
12 Whereupon as I went to Damascus
with authority and commission from
the chief priests,
13 At midday, O king, I saw in the way
a light from heaven, above the brightness of the sun, shining round about
me and them which journeyed with me.
14 And when we were all fallen to the
earth, I heard a voice speaking unto me,
and saying in the Hebrew tongue, Saul,
Saul, why persecutest thou me? *it is*
hard for thee to kick against the pricks.
15 And I said, Who art thou, Lord?
And he said, I am Jesus whom thou persecutest.
16 But rise, and stand upon thy feet:
for I have appeared unto thee for this
purpose, to make thee a minister and a
witness both of these things which thou
hast seen, and of those things in the
which I will appear unto thee;
17 Delivering thee from the people,
and *from* the Ġĕn′tīleṣ, unto whom now
I send thee,
18 To open their eyes, *and* to turn
them from darkness to light, and *from*
the power of Satan unto God, that they
may receive forgiveness of sins, and inheritance among them which are sanctified by faith that is in me.
19 Whereupon, O king Ȧ-grĭp′pȧ, I
was not disobedient unto the heavenly
vision:
20 But showed first unto them of
Damascus, and at Jerusalem, and
throughout all the coasts of Judea, and
then to the Ġĕn′tīleṣ, that they should
repent and turn to Ġod, and do works
meet for repentance.
21 For these causes the Jews caught
me in the temple, and went about to
kill *me*.
22 Having therefore obtained help of
God, I continue unto this day, witness-
ing both to small and great, saying none
other things than those which the
prophets and Moses did say should
come:
23 That Christ should suffer, *and* that
he should be the first that should rise
from the dead, and should show light
unto the people, and to the Ġĕn′tīleṣ.
24 And as he thus spake for himself,
Festus said with a loud voice, Paul,
thou art beside thyself; much learning
doth make thee mad.
25 But he said, I am not mad, most
noble Festus; but speak forth the words
of truth and soberness.
26 For the king knoweth of these
things, before whom also I speak freely:
for I am persuaded that none of these

things are hidden from him; for this thing was not done in a corner.

27 King Ȧ-grĭp′pȧ, believest thou the prophets? I know that thou believest.

28 Then Ȧ-grĭp′pȧ said unto Paul, Almost thou persuadest me to be a Christian.

29 And Paul said, I would to God, that not only thou, but also all that hear me this day, were both almost, and altogether such as I am, except these bonds.

30 And when he had thus spoken, the king rose up, and the governor, and Bĕr-nī′çē, and they that sat with them:

31 And when they were gone aside, they talked between themselves, saying, This man doeth nothing worthy of death or of bonds.

32 Then said Ȧ-grĭp′pȧ unto Festus, This man might have been set at liberty, if he had not appealed unto Cæsar.

CHAPTER 27

AND when it was determined that we should sail into Italy, they delivered Paul and certain other prisoners unto *one* named Julius, a centurion of Augustus' band.

2 And entering into a ship of Ăd′rȧ-mỹt′tĭ-ŭm, we launched, meaning to sail by the coasts of Asia; *one* Ăr′ĭs-tär′chŭs, a Macedonian of Thĕs′sȧ-lō-nī′cȧ, being with us.

3 And the next *day* we touched at Sī′dŏn. And Julius courteously entreated Paul, and gave *him* liberty to go unto his friends to refresh himself.

4 And when we had launched from thence, we sailed under Cyprus, because the winds were contrary.

5 And when we had sailed over the sea of Çĭ-lĭ′çĭ-ȧ and Păm-phỹl′ĭ-ȧ, we came to Mỹ′rȧ, *a city* of Lỹç′ĭ-ȧ.

6 And there the centurion found a ship of Alexandria sailing into Italy; and he put us therein.

7 And when we had sailed slowly many days, and scarce were come over against Cnī′dŭs, the wind not suffering us, we sailed under Crete, over against Săl-mō′nē;

8 And, hardly passing it, came unto a place which is called the Fair Havens; nigh whereunto was the city *of* Lȧ-sē′ȧ.

9 Now when much time was spent, and when sailing was now dangerous, because the fast was now already past, Paul admonished *them*,

10 And said unto them, Sirs, I perceive that this voyage will be with hurt and much damage, not only of the lading and ship, but also of our lives.

11 Nevertheless the centurion believed the master and the owner of the ship, more than those things which were spoken by Paul.

12 And because the haven was not commodious to winter in, the more part advised to depart thence also, if by any means they might attain to Phē-nī′çē, *and there* to winter; *which is* a haven of Crete, and lieth toward the southwest and northwest.

13 And when the south wind blew softly, supposing that they had obtained *their* purpose, loosing *thence*, they sailed close by Crete.

14 But not long after there arose against it a tempestuous wind, called Eū-rŏc′lỹ-dŏn.

15 And when the ship was caught, and could not bear up into the wind, we let *her* drive.

16 And running under a certain island which is called Clauda, we had much work to come by the boat:

17 Which when they had taken up, they used helps, undergirding the ship; and, fearing lest they should fall into the quicksands, struck sail, and so were driven.

18 And we being exceedingly tossed with a tempest, the next *day* they lightened the ship;

19 And the third *day* we cast out with our own hands the tackling of the ship.

20 And when neither sun nor stars in many days appeared, and no small tempest lay on *us*, all hope that we should be saved was then taken away.

21 But after long abstinence, Paul stood forth in the midst of them, and said, Sirs, ye should have hearkened unto me, and not have loosed from Crete, and to have gained this harm and loss.

22 And now I exhort you to be of good cheer: for there shall be no loss of *any man's* life among you, but of the ship.

23 For there stood by me this night the angel of God, whose I am, and whom I serve,

24 Saying, Fear not, Paul; thou must be brought before Cæsar: and, lo, God hath given thee all them that sail with thee.

25 Wherefore, sirs, be of good cheer: for I believe God, that it shall be even as it was told me.

26 Howbeit we must be cast upon a certain island.

27 But when the fourteenth night was come, as we were driven up and down in Ā'drĭ-ȧ, about midnight the shipmen deemed that they drew near to some country;

28 And sounded, and found *it* twenty fathoms: and when they had gone a little further, they sounded again, and found *it* fifteen fathoms.

29 Then fearing lest we should have fallen upon rocks, they cast four anchors out of the stern, and wished for the day.

30 And as the shipmen were about to flee out of the ship, when they had let down the boat into the sea, under color as though they would have cast anchors out of the foreship,

31 Paul said to the centurion and to the soldiers, Except these abide in the ship, ye cannot be saved.

32 Then the soldiers cut off the ropes of the boat, and let her fall off.

33 And while the day was coming on, Paul besought *them* all to take meat, saying, This day is the fourteenth day that ye have tarried and continued fasting, having taken nothing.

34 Wherefore I pray you to take *some* meat; for this is for your health: for there shall not a hair fall from the head of any of you.

35 And when he had thus spoken, he took bread, and gave thanks to God in presence of them all; and when he had broken *it*, he began to eat.

36 Then were they all of good cheer, and they also took *some* meat.

37 And we were in all in the ship two hundred threescore and sixteen souls.

38 And when they had eaten enough, they lightened the ship, and cast out the wheat into the sea.

39 And when it was day, they knew not the land: but they discovered a certain creek with a shore, into the which they were minded, if it were possible, to thrust in the ship.

40 And when they had taken up the anchors, they committed *themselves* unto the sea, and loosed the rudder bands, and hoisted up the mainsail to the wind, and made toward shore.

41 And falling into a place where two seas met, they ran the ship aground; and the forepart stuck fast, and remained unmovable, but the hinder part was broken with the violence of the waves.

42 And the soldiers' counsel was to kill the prisoners, lest any of them should swim out, and escape.

43 But the centurion, willing to save Paul, kept them from *their* purpose; and commanded that they which could swim should cast *themselves* first *into the sea,* and get to land:

44 And the rest, some on boards, and some on *broken pieces* of the ship. And so it came to pass, that they escaped all safe to land.

CHAPTER 28

AND when they were escaped, then they knew that the island was called Mĕl'ĭ-tȧ.

2 And the barbarous people showed us no little kindness: for they kindled a fire, and received us every one, because of the present rain, and because of the cold.

3 And when Paul had gathered a bundle of sticks, and laid *them* on the fire, there came a viper out of the heat, and fastened on his hand.

4 And when the barbarians saw the *venomous* beast hang on his hand, they said among themselves, No doubt this man is a murderer, whom, though he hath escaped the sea, yet vengeance suffereth not to live.

5 And he shook off the beast into the fire, and felt no harm.

6 Howbeit they looked when he should have swollen, or fallen down dead suddenly: but after they had looked a great while, and saw no harm come to him, they changed their minds, and said that he was a god.

7 In the same quarters were possessions of the chief man of the island, whose name was Pŭb'lĭ-ŭs; who received us, and lodged us three days courteously.

8 And it came to pass, that the father of Pŭb'lĭ-ŭs lay sick of a fever and of a bloody flux: to whom Paul entered in, and prayed, and laid his hands on him, and healed him.

9 So when this was done, others also, which had diseases in the island, came, and were healed:

10 Who also honored us with many
honors; and when we departed, they
laded *us* with such things as were
necessary.
11 And after three months we departed
in a ship of Alexandria, which had win-
tered in the isle, whose sign was Castor
and Pŏl′lŭx.
12 And landing at Syracuse, we tarried *there* three days.
13 And from thence we fetched a compass, and came to Rhē′ġĭ-ŭm: and after
one day the south wind blew, and we
came the next day to Pū-tē′ō-lī:
14 Where we found brethren, and were
desired to tarry with them seven days:
and so we went toward Rome.
15 And from thence, when the brethren
heard of us, they came to meet us as far
as Ăp′pĭ-ī Fō′rŭm, and the Three Tav-
erns; whom when Paul saw, he thanked
God, and took courage.
16 And when we came to Rome, the
centurion delivered the prisoners to the
captain of the guard: but Paul was suffered to dwell by himself with a soldier
that kept him.
17 And it came to pass, that after three
days Paul called the chief of the Jews
together: and when they were come together, he said unto them, Men *and*
brethren, though I have committed
nothing against the people, or customs
of our fathers, yet was I delivered prisoner from Jerusalem into the hands of
the Romans:
18 Who, when they had examined me,
would have let *me* go, because there
was no cause of death in me.
19 But when the Jews spake against *it,*
I was constrained to appeal unto Cæsar;
not that I had aught to accuse my nation of.
20 For this cause therefore have I
called for you, to see *you*, and to speak
with *you:* because that for the hope of
Ĭş′rā-ĕl I am bound with this chain.
21 And they said unto him, We neither
received letters out of Judea concerning
thee, neither any of the brethren that
came showed or spake any harm of
thee.
22 But we desire to hear of thee what
thou thinkest: for as concerning this
sect, we know that every where it is
spoken against.
23 And when they had appointed him
a day, there came many to him into *his*
lodging; to whom he expounded and
testified the kingdom of God, persuad-
ing them concerning Jesus, both out of
the law of Moses, and *out of* the prophets, from morning till evening.
24 And some believed the things which
were spoken, and some believed not.
25 And when they agreed not among
themselves, they departed, after that
Paul had spoken one word, Well spake
the Holy Ghost by Ē-şā′ịăs the prophet
unto our fathers,
26 Saying, Go unto this people, and
say, Hearing ye shall hear, and shall not
understand; and seeing ye shall see,
and not perceive:
27 For the heart of this people is waxed
gross, and their ears are dull of hearing,
and their eyes have they closed; lest
they should see with *their* eyes, and hear
with *their* ears, and understand with
their heart, and should be converted,
and I should heal them.
28 Be it known therefore unto you, that
the salvation of God is sent unto the
Ġĕn′tīleş, and *that* they will hear it.
29 And when he had said these words,
the Jews departed, and had great reasoning among themselves.
30 And Paul dwelt two whole years in
his own hired house, and received all
that came in unto him,
31 Preaching the kingdom of God, and
teaching those things which concern the
Lord Jesus Christ, with all confidence,
no man forbidding him.

THE EPISTLE OF PAUL THE APOSTLE TO THE

ROMANS

CHAPTER 1

PAUL, a servant of Jesus Christ,
called *to be* an apostle, separated
unto the gospel of God,
2 (Which he had promised afore by his
prophets in the holy Scriptures,)
3 Concerning his Son Jesus Christ our
Lord, which was made of the seed of
David according to the flesh;
4 And declared *to be* the Son of God
with power, according to the Spirit of holiness, by the resurrection from the dead:
5 By whom we have received grace
and apostleship, for obedience to the
faith among all nations, for his name:
6 Among whom are ye also the called
of Jesus Christ:
7 To all that be in Rome, beloved of
God, called *to be* saints: Grace to you,
and peace, from God our Father and the
Lord Jesus Christ.
8 First, I thank my God through Jesus
Christ for you all, that your faith is
spoken of throughout the whole world.
9 For God is my witness, whom I serve
with my spirit in the gospel of his Son,
that without ceasing I make mention of
you always in my prayers;
10 Making request, if by any means
now at length I might have a prosperous
journey by the will of God to come unto
you.
11 For I long to see you, that I may impart unto you some spiritual gift, to the
end ye may be established;
12 That is, that I may be comforted
together with you by the mutual faith
both of you and me.
13 Now I would not have you ignorant,
brethren, that oftentimes I purposed to
come unto you, (but was let hitherto,)
that I might have some fruit among you
also, even as among other Gĕn'tīleș.
14 I am debtor both to the Greeks,
and to the Barbarians; both to the wise,
and to the unwise.
15 So, as much as in me is, I am ready
to preach the gospel to you that are at
Rome also.
16 For I am not ashamed of the gospel
of Christ: for it is the power of God unto
salvation to every one that believeth; to
the Jew first, and also to the Greek.
17 For therein is the righteousness of
God revealed from faith to faith: as it
is written, The just shall live by faith.
18 For the wrath of God is revealed
from heaven against all ungodliness and
unrighteousness of men, who hold the
truth in unrighteousness;
19 Because that which may be known
of God is manifest in them; for God
hath showed *it* unto them.
20 For the invisible things of him from
the creation of the world are clearly
seen, being understood by the things
that are made, *even* his eternal power
and Godhead; so that they are without
excuse:
21 Because that, when they knew God,
they glorified *him* not as God, neither
were thankful; but became vain in their
imaginations, and their foolish heart
was darkened.
22 Professing themselves to be wise,
they became fools,
23 And changed the glory of the un-
corruptible God into an image made
like to corruptible man, and to birds,
and four-footed beasts, and creeping
things.
24 Wherefore God also gave them up
to uncleanness, through the lusts of
their own hearts, to dishonor their own
bodies between themselves:
25 Who changed the truth of God into
a lie, and worshipped and served the
creature more than the Creator, who is
blessed for ever. Amen.
26 For this cause God gave them up
unto vile affections: for even their
women did change the natural use into
that which is against nature:
27 And likewise also the men, leaving
the natural use of the woman, burned
in their lust one toward another; men
with men working that which is unseemly, and receiving in themselves
that recompense of their error which
was meet.
28 And even as they did not like to
retain God in *their* knowledge, God
gave them over to a reprobate mind, to

do those things which are not convenient;
29 Being filled with all unrighteousness, fornication, wickedness, covetousness, maliciousness; full of envy, murder,
debate, deceit, malignity; whisperers,
30 Backbiters, haters of God, despiteful, proud, boasters, inventors of evil
things, disobedient to parents,
31 Without understanding, covenant-
breakers, without natural affection, im-
placable, unmerciful:
32 Who, knowing the judgment of God,
that they which commit such things
are worthy of death, not only do the
same, but have pleasure in them that
do them.

CHAPTER 2

THEREFORE thou art inexcusable,
O man, whosoever thou art that
judgest: for wherein thou judgest
another, thou condemnest thyself; for
thou that judgest doest the same things.
2 But we are sure that the judgment of
God is according to truth against them
which commit such things.
3 And thinkest thou this, O man, that
judgest them which do such things, and
doest the same, that thou shalt escape
the judgment of God?
4 Or despisest thou the riches of his
goodness and forbearance and long-
suffering; not knowing that the goodness
of God leadeth thee to repentance?
5 But, after thy hardness and impeni-
tent heart, treasurest up unto thyself
wrath against the day of wrath and
revelation of the righteous judgment of
God;
6 Who will render to every man according to his deeds:
7 To them who by patient continuance
in well doing seek for glory and honor
and immortality, eternal life:
8 But unto them that are contentious,
and do not obey the truth, but obey unrighteousness, indignation and wrath,
9 Tribulation and anguish, upon every
soul of man that doeth evil; of the Jew
first, and also of the Ġĕn′tīle;
10 But glory, honor, and peace, to
every man that worketh good; to the
Jew first, and also to the Ġĕn′tīle:
11 For there is no respect of persons
with God.
12 For as many as have sinned without law shall also perish without law;
and as many as have sinned in the law
shall be judged by the law;
13 (For not the hearers of the law *are*
just before God, but the doers of the
law shall be justified.
14 For when the Ġĕn′tīleş, which have
not the law, do by nature the things contained in the law, these, having not the
law, are a law unto themselves:
15 Which show the work of the law
written in their hearts, their conscience
also bearing witness, and *their* thoughts
the mean while accusing or else excus-
ing one another;)
16 In the day when God shall judge
the secrets of men by Jesus Christ
according to my gospel.
17 Behold, thou art called a Jew, and
restest in the law, and makest thy boast
of God,
18 And knowest *his* will, and approvest
the things that are more excellent, being instructed out of the law;
19 And art confident that thou thyself
art a guide of the blind, a light of them
which are in darkness,
20 An instructor of the foolish, a teacher
of babes, which hast the form of knowledge and of the truth in the law.
21 Thou therefore which teachest another, teachest thou not thyself? thou
that preachest a man should not steal,
dost thou steal?
22 Thou that sayest a man should not
commit adultery, dost thou commit
adultery? thou that abhorrest idols, dost
thou commit sacrilege?
23 Thou that makest thy boast of the
law, through breaking the law dishonor-
est thou God?
24 For the name of God is blasphemed
among the Ġĕn′tīleş through you, as it
is written.
25 For circumcision verily profiteth,
if thou keep the law: but if thou be a
breaker of the law, thy circumcision is
made uncircumcision.
26 Therefore, if the uncircumcision
keep the righteousness of the law, shall
not his uncircumcision be counted for
circumcision?
27 And shall not uncircumcision which
is by nature, if it fulfil the law, judge
thee, who by the letter and circumcision
dost transgress the law?
28 For he is not a Jew, which is one
outwardly; neither *is that* circumcision,
which is outward in the flesh:

29 But he *is* a Jew, which is one inwardly; and circumcision *is that* of the heart, in the spirit, *and* not in the letter; whose praise *is* not of men, but of God.

CHAPTER 3

WHAT advantage then hath the Jew? or what profit *is there* of circumcision?
2 Much every way: chiefly, because that unto them were committed the oracles of God.
3 For what if some did not believe? shall their unbelief make the faith of God without effect?
4 God forbid: yea, let God be true, but every man a liar; as it is written, That thou mightest be justified in thy sayings, and mightest overcome when thou art judged.
5 But if our unrighteousness commend the righteousness of God, what shall we say? *Is* God unrighteous who taketh vengeance? (I speak as a man)
6 God forbid: for then how shall God judge the world?
7 For if the truth of God hath more abounded through my lie unto his glory; why yet am I also judged as a sinner?
8 And not *rather,* (as we be slanderously reported, and as some affirm that we say,) Let us do evil that good may come? whose damnation is just.
9 What then? are we better *than they?* No, in no wise: for we have before proved both Jews and Ġĕn'tīleş, that they are all under sin;
10 As it is written, There is none righteous, no, not one:
11 There is none that understandeth, there is none that seeketh after God.
12 They are all gone out of the way, they are together become unprofitable; there is none that doeth good, no, not one.
13 Their throat *is* an open sepulchre; with their tongues they have used deceit; the poison of asps *is* under their lips:
14 Whose mouth *is* full of cursing and bitterness:
15 Their feet *are* swift to shed blood:
16 Destruction and misery *are* in their ways:
17 And the way of peace have they not known:
18 There is no fear of God before their eyes.
19 Now we know that what things soever the law saith, it saith to them who are under the law: that every mouth may be stopped, and all the world may become guilty before God.
20 Therefore by the deeds of the law there shall no flesh be justified in his sight: for by the law *is* the knowledge of sin.
21 But now the righteousness of God without the law is manifested, being witnessed by the law and the prophets;
22 Even the righteousness of God *which is* by faith of Jesus Christ unto all and upon all them that believe; for there is no difference:
23 For all have sinned, and come short of the glory of God;
24 Being justified freely by his grace through the redemption that is in Christ Jesus:
25 Whom God hath set forth *to be* a propitiation through faith in his blood, to declare his righteousness for the remission of sins that are past, through the forbearance of God;
26 To declare, *I say,* at this time his righteousness: that he might be just, and the justifier of him which believeth in Jesus.
27 Where *is* boasting then? It is excluded. By what law? of works? Nay; but by the law of faith.
28 Therefore we conclude that a man is justified by faith without the deeds of the law.
29 *Is he* the God of the Jews only? *is he* not also of the Ġĕn'tīleş? Yes, of the Ġĕn'tīleş also:
30 Seeing *it is* one God, which shall justify the circumcision by faith, and uncircumcision through faith.
31 Do we then make void the law through faith? God forbid: yea, we establish the law.

CHAPTER 4

WHAT shall we say then that Abraham our father, as pertaining to the flesh, hath found?
2 For if Abraham were justified by works, he hath *whereof* to glory; but not before God.
3 For what saith the Scripture? Abraham believed God, and it was counted unto him for righteousness.
4 Now to him that worketh is the reward not reckoned of grace, but of debt.

5 But to him that worketh not, but believeth on him that justifieth the ungodly, his faith is counted for righteousness.

6 Even as David also describeth the blessedness of the man, unto whom God imputeth righteousness without works,

7 *Saying*, Blessed *are* they whose iniquities are forgiven, and whose sins are covered.

8 Blessed *is* the man to whom the Lord will not impute sin.

9 *Cometh* this blessedness then upon the circumcision *only*, or upon the uncircumcision also? for we say that faith was reckoned to Abraham for righteousness.

10 How was it then reckoned? when he was in circumcision, or in uncircumcision? Not in circumcision, but in uncircumcision.

11 And he received the sign of circumcision, a seal of the righteousness of the faith which *he had yet* being uncircumcised: that he might be the father of all them that believe, though they be not circumcised; that righteousness might be imputed unto them also:

12 And the father of circumcision to them who are not of the circumcision only, but who also walk in the steps of that faith of our father Abraham, which *he had* being *yet* uncircumcised.

13 For the promise, that he should be the heir of the world, *was* not to Abraham, or to his seed, through the law, but through the righteousness of faith.

14 For if they which are of the law *be* heirs, faith is made void, and the promise made of none effect:

15 Because the law worketh wrath: for where no law is, *there is* no transgression.

16 Therefore *it is* of faith, that *it might be* by grace; to the end the promise might be sure to all the seed; not to that only which is of the law, but to that also which is of the faith of Abraham; who is the father of us all,

17 (As it is written, I have made thee a father of many nations,) before him whom he believed, *even* God, who quickeneth the dead, and calleth those things which be not as though they were:

18 Who against hope believed in hope, that he might become the father of many nations, according to that which was spoken, So shall thy seed be.

19 And being not weak in faith, he considered not his own body now dead, when he was about a hundred years old, neither yet the deadness of Sarah's womb:

20 He staggered not at the promise of God through unbelief; but was strong in faith, giving glory to God;

21 And being fully persuaded, that what he had promised, he was able also to perform.

22 And therefore it was imputed to him for righteousness.

23 Now it was not written for his sake alone, that it was imputed to him;

24 But for us also, to whom it shall be imputed, if we believe on him that raised up Jesus our Lord from the dead;

25 Who was delivered for our offenses, and was raised again for our justification.

CHAPTER 5

THEREFORE being justified by faith, we have peace with God through our Lord Jesus Christ:

2 By whom also we have access by faith into this grace wherein we stand, and rejoice in hope of the glory of God.

3 And not only *so*, but we glory in tribulations also; knowing that tribulation worketh patience;

4 And patience, experience; and experience, hope:

5 And hope maketh not ashamed; because the love of God is shed abroad in our hearts by the Holy Ghost which is given unto us.

6 For when we were yet without strength, in due time Christ died for the ungodly.

7 For scarcely for a righteous man will one die: yet peradventure for a good man some would even dare to die.

8 But God commendeth his love toward us, in that, while we were yet sinners, Christ died for us.

9 Much more then, being now justified by his blood, we shall be saved from wrath through him.

10 For if, when we were enemies, we were reconciled to God by the death of his Son; much more, being reconciled, we shall be saved by his life.

11 And not only *so*, but we also joy in God through our Lord Jesus Christ, by whom we have now received the atonement.

12 Wherefore, as by one man sin entered into the world, and death by sin; and so death passed upon all men, for that all have sinned:

13 (For until the law sin was in the world: but sin is not imputed when there is no law.

14 Nevertheless death reigned from Adam to Moses, even over them that had not sinned after the similitude of Adam's transgression, who is the figure of him that was to come.

15 But not as the offense, so also *is* the free gift: for if through the offense of one many be dead, much more the grace of God, and the gift by grace, *which is* by one man, Jesus Christ, hath abounded unto many.

16 And not as *it was* by one that sinned, *so is* the gift: for the judgment *was* by one to condemnation, but the free gift *is* of many offenses unto justification.

17 For if by one man's offense death reigned by one; much more they which receive abundance of grace and of the gift of righteousness shall reign in life by one, Jesus Christ.)

18 Therefore, as by the offense of one *judgment came* upon all men to condemnation; even so by the righteousness of one *the free gift came* upon all men unto justification of life.

19 For as by one man's disobedience many were made sinners, so by the obedience of one shall many be made righteous.

20 Moreover the law entered, that the offense might abound. But where sin abounded, grace did much more abound:

21 That as sin hath reigned unto death, even so might grace reign through righteousness unto eternal life by Jesus Christ our Lord.

CHAPTER 6

WHAT shall we say then? Shall we continue in sin, that grace may abound?

2 God forbid. How shall we, that are dead to sin, live any longer therein?

3 Know ye not, that so many of us as were baptized into Jesus Christ were baptized into his death?

4 Therefore we are buried with him by baptism into death: that like as Christ was raised up from the dead by the glory of the Father, even so we also should walk in newness of life.

5 For if we have been planted together in the likeness of his death, we shall be also *in the likeness* of *his* resurrection:

6 Knowing this, that our old man is crucified with *him,* that the body of sin might be destroyed, that henceforth we should not serve sin.

7 For he that is dead is freed from sin.

8 Now if we be dead with Christ, we believe that we shall also live with him:

9 Knowing that Christ being raised from the dead dieth no more; death hath no more dominion over him.

10 For in that he died, he died unto sin once: but in that he liveth, he liveth unto God.

11 Likewise reckon ye also yourselves to be dead indeed unto sin, but alive unto God through Jesus Christ our Lord.

12 Let not sin therefore reign in your mortal body, that ye should obey it in the lusts thereof.

13 Neither yield ye your members *as* instruments of unrighteousness unto sin: but yield yourselves unto God, as those that are alive from the dead, and your members *as* instruments of righteousness unto God.

14 For sin shall not have dominion over you: for ye are not under the law, but under grace.

15 What then? shall we sin, because we are not under the law, but under grace? God forbid.

16 Know ye not, that to whom ye yield yourselves servants to obey, his servants ye are to whom ye obey; whether of sin unto death, or of obedience unto righteousness?

17 But God be thanked, that ye were the servants of sin, but ye have obeyed from the heart that form of doctrine which was delivered you.

18 Being then made free from sin, ye became the servants of righteousness.

19 I speak after the manner of men because of the infirmity of your flesh: for as ye have yielded your members servants to uncleanness and to iniquity unto iniquity; even so now yield your members servants to righteousness unto holiness.

20 For when ye were the servants of sin, ye were free from righteousness.

21 What fruit had ye then in those things whereof ye are now ashamed? for the end of those things *is* death.

22 But now being made free from sin,
and become servants to God, ye have
your fruit unto holiness, and the end
everlasting life.
23 For the wages of sin *is* death; but
the gift of God *is* eternal life through
Jesus Christ our Lord.

CHAPTER 7

KNOW ye not, brethren, (for I speak
to them that know the law,) how
that the law hath dominion over a man
as long as he liveth?
2 For the woman which hath a husband is bound by the law to *her* husband
so long as he liveth; but if the husband
be dead, she is loosed from the law of
her husband.
3 So then if, while *her* husband liveth,
she be married to another man, she shall
be called an adulteress: but if her husband be dead, she is free from that law;
so that she is no adulteress, though she
be married to another man.
4 Wherefore, my brethren, ye also are
become dead to the law by the body of
Christ; that ye should be married to
another, *even* to him who is raised from
the dead, that we should bring forth
fruit unto God.
5 For when we were in the flesh, the
motions of sins, which were by the law,
did work in our members to bring forth
fruit unto death.
6 But now we are delivered from the
law, that being dead wherein we were
held; that we should serve in newness
of spirit, and not *in* the oldness of the
letter.
7 What shall we say then? *Is* the law
sin? God forbid. Nay, I had not known
sin, but by the law: for I had not known
lust, except the law had said, Thou shalt
not covet.
8 But sin, taking occasion by the commandment, wrought in me all manner of
concupiscence. For without the law sin
was dead.
9 For I was alive without the law once:
but when the commandment came, sin
revived, and I died.
10 And the commandment, which *was*
ordained to life, I found *to be* unto death.
11 For sin, taking occasion by the commandment, deceived me, and by it slew
me.
12 Wherefore the law *is* holy, and the
commandment holy, and just, and good.
13 Was then that which is good made
death unto me? God forbid. But sin,
that it might appear sin, working death
in me by that which is good; that sin by
the commandment might become exceeding sinful.
14 For we know that the law is spiritual: but I am carnal, sold under sin.
15 For that which I do, I allow not: for
what I would, that do I not; but what I
hate, that do I.
16 If then I do that which I would not,
I consent unto the law that *it is* good.
17 Now then it is no more I that do it,
but sin that dwelleth in me.
18 For I know that in me (that is, in my
flesh,) dwelleth no good thing: for to
will is present with me; but *how* to perform that which is good I find not.
19 For the good that I would, I do
not: but the evil which I would not,
that I do.
20 Now if I do that I would not, it is no
more I that do it, but sin that dwelleth
in me.
21 I find then a law, that, when I would
do good, evil is present with me.
22 For I delight in the law of God after
the inward man:
23 But I see another law in my members, warring against the law of my
mind, and bringing me into captivity to
the law of sin which is in my members.
24 O wretched man that I am! who
shall deliver me from the body of this
death?
25 I thank God through Jesus Christ
our Lord. So then with the mind I myself serve the law of God; but with the
flesh the law of sin.

CHAPTER 8

THERE is therefore now no condemnation to them which are in Christ
Jesus, who walk not after the flesh, but
after the Spirit.
2 For the law of the Spirit of life in
Christ Jesus hath made me free from
the law of sin and death.
3 For what the law could not do, in that
it was weak through the flesh, God
sending his own Son in the likeness of
sinful flesh, and for sin, condemned sin
in the flesh:
4 That the righteousness of the law
might be fulfilled in us, who walk not
after the flesh, but after the Spirit.
5 For they that are after the flesh do

mind the things of the flesh; but they that are after the Spirit, the things of the Spirit.

6 For to be carnally minded *is* death; but to be spiritually minded *is* life and peace.

7 Because the carnal mind *is* enmity against God: for it is not subject to the law of God, neither indeed can be.

8 So then they that are in the flesh cannot please God.

9 But ye are not in the flesh, but in the Spirit, if so be that the Spirit of God dwell in you. Now if any man have not the Spirit of Christ, he is none of his.

10 And if Christ *be* in you, the body *is* dead because of sin; but the Spirit *is* life because of righteousness.

11 But if the Spirit of him that raised up Jesus from the dead dwell in you, he that raised up Christ from the dead shall also quicken your mortal bodies by his Spirit that dwelleth in you.

12 Therefore, brethren, we are debtors, not to the flesh, to live after the flesh.

13 For if ye live after the flesh, ye shall die: but if ye through the Spirit do mortify the deeds of the body, ye shall live.

14 For as many as are led by the Spirit of God, they are the sons of God.

15 For ye have not received the spirit of bondage again to fear; but ye have received the Spirit of adoption, whereby we cry, Abba, Father.

16 The Spirit itself beareth witness with our spirit, that we are the children of God:

17 And if children, then heirs; heirs of God, and joint-heirs with Christ; if so be that we suffer with *him*, that we may be also glorified together.

18 For I reckon that the sufferings of this present time *are* not worthy *to be compared* with the glory which shall be revealed in us.

19 For the earnest expectation of the creature waiteth for the manifestation of the sons of God.

20 For the creature was made subject to vanity, not willingly, but by reason of him who hath subjected *the same* in hope;

21 Because the creature itself also shall be delivered from the bondage of corruption into the glorious liberty of the children of God.

22 For we know that the whole creation groaneth and travaileth in pain together until now.

23 And not only *they*, but ourselves also, which have the firstfruits of the Spirit, even we ourselves groan within ourselves, waiting for the adoption, *to wit*, the redemption of our body.

24 For we are saved by hope: but hope that is seen is not hope: for what a man seeth, why doth he yet hope for?

25 But if we hope for that we see not, *then* do we with patience wait for *it*.

26 Likewise the Spirit also helpeth our infirmities: for we know not what we should pray for as we ought: but the Spirit itself maketh intercession for us with groanings which cannot be uttered.

27 And he that searcheth the hearts knoweth what *is* the mind of the Spirit, because he maketh intercession for the saints according to *the will of* God.

28 And we know that all things work together for good to them that love God, to them who are the called according to *his* purpose.

29 For whom he did foreknow, he also did predestinate *to be* conformed to the image of his Son, that he might be the firstborn among many brethren.

30 Moreover, whom he did predestinate, them he also called: and whom he called, them he also justified: and whom he justified, them he also glorified.

31 What shall we then say to these things? If God *be* for us, who *can be* against us?

32 He that spared not his own Son, but delivered him up for us all, how shall he not with him also freely give us all things?

33 Who shall lay any thing to the charge of God's elect? *It is* God that justifieth.

34 Who *is* he that condemneth? *It is* Christ that died, yea rather, that is risen again, who is even at the right hand of God, who also maketh intercession for us.

35 Who shall separate us from the love of Christ? *shall* tribulation, or distress, or persecution, or famine, or nakedness, or peril, or sword?

36 As it is written, For thy sake we are killed all the day long; we are accounted as sheep for the slaughter.

37 Nay, in all these things we are more than conquerors through him that loved us.

38 For I am persuaded, that neither

death, nor life, nor angels, nor principalities, nor powers, nor things present,
nor things to come,
39 Nor height, nor depth, nor any other
creature, shall be able to separate us
from the love of God, which is in Christ
Jesus our Lord.

CHAPTER 9

I SAY the truth in Christ, I lie not,
my conscience also bearing me witness in the Holy Ghost,
2 That I have great heaviness and
continual sorrow in my heart.
3 For I could wish that myself were
accursed from Christ for my brethren,
my kinsmen according to the flesh:
4 Who are Ĭş′rā-ĕl-ītes; to whom *pertaineth* the adoption, and the glory, and
the covenants, and the giving of the
law, and the service *of God,* and the
promises;
5 Whose *are* the fathers, and of whom
as concerning the flesh Christ *came,*
who is over all, God blessed for ever.
Amen.
6 Not as though the word of God hath
taken none effect. For they *are* not all
Ĭş′rā-ĕl, which are of Ĭş′rā-ĕl:
7 Neither, because they are the seed of
Abraham, *are they* all children: but, In
Isaac shall thy seed be called.
8 That is, They which are the children
of the flesh, these *are* not the children
of God: but the children of the promise
are counted for the seed.
9 For this *is* the word of promise, At
this time will I come, and Sarah shall
have a son.
10 And not only *this;* but when Rē-
bĕc′cȧ also had conceived by one, *even*
by our father Isaac,
11 (For *the children* being not yet born,
neither having done any good or evil,
that the purpose of God according to
election might stand, not of works, but
of him that calleth;)
12 It was said unto her, The elder shall
serve the younger.
13 As it is written, Jacob have I loved,
but Ē′saû have I hated.
14 What shall we say then? *Is there*
unrighteousness with God? God forbid.
15 For he saith to Moses, I will have
mercy on whom I will have mercy, and
I will have compassion on whom I will
have compassion.
16 So then *it is* not of him that willeth,
nor of him that runneth, but of God that
showeth mercy.
17 For the Scripture saith unto Phā′-
raōh, Even for this same purpose have I
raised thee up, that I might show my
power in thee, and that my name might
be declared throughout all the earth.
18 Therefore hath he mercy on whom
he will *have mercy,* and whom he will
he hardeneth.
19 Thou wilt say then unto me, Why
doth he yet find fault? For who hath
resisted his will?
20 Nay but, O man, who art thou that
repliest against God? Shall the thing
formed say to him that formed *it,* Why
hast thou made me thus?
21 Hath not the potter power over the
clay, of the same lump to make one
vessel unto honor, and another unto
dishonor?
22 *What* if God, willing to show *his*
wrath, and to make his power known,
endured with much long-suffering the
vessels of wrath fitted to destruction:
23 And that he might make known the
riches of his glory on the vessels of
mercy, which he had afore prepared
unto glory,
24 Even us, whom he hath called, not
of the Jews only, but also of the Ġĕn′-
tīleş?
25 As he saith also in Ō′şēe, I will call
them my people, which were not my
people; and her beloved, which was not
beloved.
26 And it shall come to pass, *that* in
the place where it was said unto them,
Ye *are* not my people; there shall they
be called the children of the living
God.
27 Ē-şā′ịăs also crieth concerning
Ĭş′rā-ĕl, Though the number of the children of Ĭş′rā-ĕl be as the sand of the
sea, a remnant shall be saved:
28 For he will finish the work, and cut
it short in righteousness: because a
short work will the Lord make upon the
earth.
29 And as Ē-şā′ịăs said before, Except
the Lord of Săb′ā-ōth had left us a seed,
we had been as Sŏd′ō-mȧ, and been
made like unto Go-mŏr′rȧh.
30 What shall we say then? That the
Ġĕn′tīleş, which followed not after
righteousness, have attained to righteousness, even the righteousness which
is of faith.

31 But Ĭş'rā-ĕl, which followed after the law of righteousness, hath not attained to the law of righteousness.

32 Wherefore? Because *they sought it* not by faith, but as it were by the works of the law. For they stumbled at that stumblingstone;

33 As it is written, Behold, I lay in Sī'ŏn a stumblingstone and rock of offense: and whosoever believeth on him shall not be ashamed.

CHAPTER 10

BRETHREN, my heart's desire and prayer to God for Ĭş'rā-ĕl is, that they might be saved.

2 For I bear them record that they have a zeal of God, but not according to knowledge.

3 For they, being ignorant of God's righteousness, and going about to establish their own righteousness, have not submitted themselves unto the righteousness of God.

4 For Christ *is* the end of the law for righteousness to every one that believeth.

5 For Moses describeth the righteousness which is of the law, That the man which doeth those things shall live by them.

6 But the righteousness which is of faith speaketh on this wise, Say not in thine heart, Who shall ascend into heaven? (that is, to bring Christ down *from above:*)

7 Or, Who shall descend into the deep? (that is, to bring up Christ again from the dead.)

8 But what saith it? The word is nigh thee, *even* in thy mouth, and in thy heart: that is, the word of faith, which we preach;

9 That if thou shalt confess with thy mouth the Lord Jesus, and shalt believe in thine heart that God hath raised him from the dead, thou shalt be saved.

10 For with the heart man believeth unto righteousness; and with the mouth confession is made unto salvation.

11 For the Scripture saith, Whosoever believeth on him shall not be ashamed.

12 For there is no difference between the Jew and the Greek: for the same Lord over all is rich unto all that call upon him.

13 For whosoever shall call upon the name of the Lord shall be saved.

14 How then shall they call on him in whom they have not believed? and how shall they believe in him of whom they have not heard? and how shall they hear without a preacher?

15 And how shall they preach, except they be sent? as it is written, How beautiful are the feet of them that preach the gospel of peace, and bring glad tidings of good things!

16 But they have not all obeyed the gospel. For Ē-şā'ịăs saith, Lord, who hath believed our report?

17 So then faith *cometh* by hearing, and hearing by the word of God.

18 But I say, Have they not heard? Yes verily, their sound went into all the earth, and their words unto the ends of the world.

19 But I say, Did not Ĭş'rā-ĕl know? First Moses saith, I will provoke you to jealousy by *them that are* no people, *and* by a foolish nation I will anger you.

20 But Ē-şā'ịăs is very bold, and saith, I was found of them that sought me not; I was made manifest unto them that asked not after me.

21 But to Ĭş'rā-ĕl he saith, All day long I have stretched forth my hands unto a disobedient and gainsaying people.

CHAPTER 11

I SAY then, Hath God cast away his people? God forbid. For I also am an Ĭş'rā-ĕl-īte, of the seed of Abraham, *of* the tribe of Benjamin.

2 God hath not cast away his people which he foreknew. Wot ye not what the Scripture saith of Ē-lī'ăs? how he maketh intercession to God against Ĭş'rā-ĕl, saying,

3 Lord, they have killed thy prophets, and digged down thine altars; and I am left alone, and they seek my life.

4 But what saith the answer of God unto him? I have reserved to myself seven thousand men, who have not bowed the knee to *the image of* Bā'ăl.

5 Even so then at this present time also there is a remnant according to the election of grace.

6 And if by grace, then *is it* no more of works: otherwise grace is no more grace. But if *it be* of works, then is it no more grace: otherwise work is no more work.

7 What then? Ĭş'rā-ĕl hath not obtained that which he seeketh for; but

the election hath obtained it, and the
rest were blinded
8 (According as it is written, God hath
given them the spirit of slumber, eyes
that they should not see, and ears that
they should not hear;) unto this day.
9 And David saith, Let their table
be made a snare, and a trap, and a
stumblingblock, and a recompense unto
them:
10 Let their eyes be darkened, that
they may not see, and bow down their
back alway.
11 I say then, Have they stumbled that
they should fall? God forbid: but
rather through their fall salvation *is*
come unto the Ġĕn′tīleş, for to provoke
them to jealousy.
12 Now if the fall of them *be* the riches
of the world, and the diminishing of
them the riches of the Ġĕn′tīleş; how
much more their fulness?
13 For I speak to you Ġĕn′tīleş, inasmuch as I am the apostle of the Ġĕn′-
tīleş, I magnify mine office:
14 If by any means I may provoke to
emulation *them which are* my flesh, and
might save some of them.
15 For if the casting away of them *be*
the reconciling of the world, what *shall*
the receiving *of them be,* but life from
the dead?
16 For if the firstfruit *be* holy, the lump
is also *holy:* and if the root *be* holy, so
are the branches.
17 And if some of the branches be
broken off, and thou, being a wild olive
tree, wert graffed in among them, and
with them partakest of the root and fatness of the olive tree;
18 Boast not against the branches.
But if thou boast, thou bearest not the
root, but the root thee.
19 Thou wilt say then, The branches
were broken off, that I might be graffed
in.
20 Well; because of unbelief they were
broken off, and thou standest by faith.
Be not high-minded, but fear:
21 For if God spared not the natural
branches, *take heed* lest he also spare
not thee.
22 Behold therefore the goodness and
severity of God: on them which fell,
severity; but toward thee, goodness, if
thou continue in *his* goodness: otherwise thou also shalt be cut off.
23 And they also, if they abide not still
in unbelief, shall be graffed in: for God
is able to graff them in again.
24 For if thou wert cut out of the olive
tree which is wild by nature, and wert
graffed contrary to nature into a good
olive tree; how much more shall these,
which be the natural *branches,* be
graffed into their own olive tree?
25 For I would not, brethren, that ye
should be ignorant of this mystery, lest
ye should be wise in your own conceits,
that blindness in part is happened to
Ĭş′rā-ĕl, until the fulness of the Ġĕn′tīleş
be come in.
26 And so all Ĭş′rā-ĕl shall be saved:
as it is written, There shall come out of
Sī′ȯn the Deliverer, and shall turn away
ungodliness from Jacob:
27 For this *is* my covenant unto them,
when I shall take away their sins.
28 As concerning the gospel, *they are*
enemies for your sakes: but as touching
the election, *they are* beloved for the
fathers' sakes.
29 For the gifts and calling of God *are*
without repentance.
30 For as ye in times past have not
believed God, yet have now obtained
mercy through their unbelief:
31 Even so have these also now not believed, that through your mercy they
also may obtain mercy.
32 For God hath concluded them all in
unbelief, that he might have mercy
upon all.
33 O the depth of the riches both of the
wisdom and knowledge of God! how
unsearchable *are* his judgments, and
his ways past finding out!
34 For who hath known the mind of the
Lord? or who hath been his counselor?
35 Or who hath first given to him, and
it shall be recompensed unto him again?
36 For of him, and through him, and to
him, *are* all things: to whom *be* glory for
ever. Amen.

CHAPTER 12

I BESEECH you therefore, brethren,
by the mercies of God, that ye present your bodies a living sacrifice, holy,
acceptable unto God, *which is* your
reasonable service.
2 And be not conformed to this world:
but be ye transformed by the renewing
of your mind, that ye may prove what *is*
that good, and acceptable, and perfect
will of God.

3 For I say, through the grace given
unto me, to every man that is among
you, not to think *of himself* more highly
than he ought to think; but to think
soberly, according as God hath dealt to
every man the measure of faith.
4 For as we have many members in
one body, and all members have not the
same office:
5 So we, *being* many, are one body in
Christ, and every one members one of
another.
6 Having then gifts differing according
to the grace that is given to us, whether
prophecy, *let us prophesy* according
to the proportion of faith;
7 Or ministry, *let us wait* on *our*
ministering; or he that teacheth, on
teaching;
8 Or he that exhorteth, on exhortation:
he that giveth, *let him do it* with simplicity;
he that ruleth, with diligence; he
that showeth mercy, with cheerfulness.
9 *Let* love be without dissimulation.
Abhor that which is evil; cleave to that
which is good.
10 *Be* kindly affectioned one to another
with brotherly love; in honor preferring
one another;
11 Not slothful in business; fervent in
spirit; serving the Lord;
12 Rejoicing in hope; patient in tribulation;
continuing instant in prayer;
13 Distributing to the necessity of
saints; given to hospitality.
14 Bless them which persecute you:
bless, and curse not.
15 Rejoice with them that do rejoice,
and weep with them that weep.
16 *Be* of the same mind one toward
another. Mind not high things, but condescend
to men of low estate. Be not
wise in your own conceits.
17 Recompense to no man evil for
evil. Provide things honest in the sight
of all men.
18 If it be possible, as much as lieth in
you, live peaceably with all men.
19 Dearly beloved, avenge not yourselves,
but *rather* give place unto wrath:
for it is written, Vengeance *is* mine; I
will repay, saith the Lord.
20 Therefore if thine enemy hunger,
feed him; if he thirst, give him drink:
for in so doing thou shalt heap coals of
fire on his head.
21 Be not overcome of evil, but overcome
evil with good.

CHAPTER 13

LET every soul be subject unto the
higher powers. For there is no
power but of God: the powers that be
are ordained of God.
2 Whosoever therefore resisteth the
power, resisteth the ordinance of God:
and they that resist shall receive to
themselves damnation.
3 For rulers are not a terror to good
works, but to the evil. Wilt thou then
not be afraid of the power? do that
which is good, and thou shalt have
praise of the same:
4 For he is the minister of God to thee
for good. But if thou do that which is
evil, be afraid; for he beareth not the
sword in vain: for he is the minister of
God, a revenger to *execute* wrath upon
him that doeth evil.
5 Wherefore *ye* must needs be subject,
not only for wrath, but also for conscience'
sake.
6 For, for this cause pay ye tribute also:
for they are God's ministers, attending
continually upon this very thing.
7 Render therefore to all their dues:
tribute to whom tribute *is due;* custom
to whom custom; fear to whom fear;
honor to whom honor.
8 Owe no man any thing, but to love
one another: for he that loveth another
hath fulfilled the law.
9 For this, Thou shalt not commit
adultery, Thou shalt not kill, Thou shalt
not steal, Thou shalt not bear false witness,
Thou shalt not covet; and if *there*
be any other commandment, it is briefly
comprehended in this saying, namely,
Thou shalt love thy neighbor as thyself.
10 Love worketh no ill to his neighbor:
therefore love *is* the fulfilling of the law.
11 And that, knowing the time, that
now *it is* high time to awake out of
sleep: for now *is* our salvation nearer
than when we believed.
12 The night is far spent, the day is
at hand: let us therefore cast off the
works of darkness, and let us put on the
armor of light.
13 Let us walk honestly, as in the day;
not in rioting and drunkenness, not in
chambering and wantonness, not in
strife and envying:
14 But put ye on the Lord Jesus Christ,
and make not provision for the flesh,
to *fulfil* the lusts *thereof.*

CHAPTER 14

HIM that is weak in the faith receive ye, *but* not to doubtful disputations.

2 For one believeth that he may eat all things: another, who is weak, eateth herbs.

3 Let not him that eateth despise him that eateth not; and let not him which eateth not judge him that eateth: for God hath received him.

4 Who art thou that judgest another man's servant? to his own master he standeth or falleth. Yea, he shall be holden up: for God is able to make him stand.

5 One man esteemeth one day above another: another esteemeth every day *alike*. Let every man be fully persuaded in his own mind.

6 He that regardeth the day, regardeth *it* unto the Lord; and he that regardeth not the day, to the Lord he doth not regard *it*. He that eateth, eateth to the Lord, for he giveth God thanks; and he that eateth not, to the Lord he eateth not, and giveth God thanks.

7 For none of us liveth to himself, and no man dieth to himself.

8 For whether we live, we live unto the Lord; and whether we die, we die unto the Lord: whether we live therefore, or die, we are the Lord's.

9 For to this end Christ both died, and rose, and revived, that he might be Lord both of the dead and living.

10 But why dost thou judge thy brother? or why dost thou set at nought thy brother? for we shall all stand before the judgment seat of Christ.

11 For it is written, *As* I live, saith the Lord, every knee shall bow to me, and every tongue shall confess to God.

12 So then every one of us shall give account of himself to God.

13 Let us not therefore judge one another any more: but judge this rather, that no man put a stumblingblock or an occasion to fall in *his* brother's way.

14 I know, and am persuaded by the Lord Jesus, that *there is* nothing unclean of itself: but to him that esteemeth any thing to be unclean, to him *it is* unclean.

15 But if thy brother be grieved with *thy* meat, now walkest thou not charitably. Destroy not him with thy meat, for whom Christ died.

16 Let not then your good be evil spoken of:

17 For the kingdom of God is not meat and drink; but righteousness, and peace, and joy in the Holy Ghost.

18 For he that in these things serveth Christ *is* acceptable to God, and approved of men.

19 Let us therefore follow after the things which make for peace, and things wherewith one may edify another.

20 For meat destroy not the work of God. All things indeed *are* pure; but *it is* evil for that man who eateth with offense.

21 *It is* good neither to eat flesh, nor to drink wine, nor *any thing* whereby thy brother stumbleth, or is offended, or is made weak.

22 Hast thou faith? have *it* to thyself before God. Happy *is* he that condemneth not himself in that thing which he alloweth.

23 And he that doubteth is damned if he eat, because *he eateth* not of faith: for whatsoever *is* not of faith is sin.

CHAPTER 15

WE then that are strong ought to bear the infirmities of the weak, and not to please ourselves.

2 Let every one of us please *his* neighbor for *his* good to edification.

3 For even Christ pleased not himself; but, as it is written, The reproaches of them that reproached thee fell on me.

4 For whatsoever things were written aforetime were written for our learning, that we through patience and comfort of the Scriptures might have hope.

5 Now the God of patience and consolation grant you to be likeminded one toward another according to Christ Jesus:

6 That ye may with one mind *and* one mouth glorify God, even the Father of our Lord Jesus Christ.

7 Wherefore receive ye one another, as Christ also received us, to the glory of God.

8 Now I say that Jesus Christ was a minister of the circumcision for the truth of God, to confirm the promises *made* unto the fathers:

9 And that the Ġĕn'tileș might glorify God for *his* mercy; as it is written, For this cause I will confess to thee among the Ġĕn'tileș, and sing unto thy name.

10 And again he saith, Rejoice, ye
Ġĕn′tīleş, with his people.
11 And again, Praise the Lord, all ye
Ġĕn′tīleş; and laud him, all ye people.
12 And again, Ē-şā′ịăs saith, There
shall be a root of Jesse, and he that
shall rise to reign over the Ġĕn′tīleş; in
him shall the Ġĕn′tīleş trust.
13 Now the God of hope fill you with
all joy and peace in believing, that ye
may abound in hope, through the power
of the Holy Ghost.
14 And I myself also am persuaded of
you, my brethren, that ye also are full
of goodness, filled with all knowledge,
able also to admonish one another.
15 Nevertheless, brethren, I have
written the more boldly unto you in
some sort, as putting you in mind, because of the grace that is given to me of
God,
16 That I should be the minister of
Jesus Christ to the Ġĕn′tīleş, ministering the gospel of God, that the offering
up of the Ġĕn′tīleş might be acceptable,
being sanctified by the Holy Ghost.
17 I have therefore whereof I may
glory through Jesus Christ in those
things which pertain to God.
18 For I will not dare to speak of any
of those things which Christ hath not
wrought by me, to make the Ġĕn′tīleş
obedient, by word and deed,
19 Through mighty signs and wonders,
by the power of the Spirit of God; so
that from Jerusalem, and round about
unto Ĭl-lỹr′ĭ-cŭm, I have fully preached
the gospel of Christ.
20 Yea, so have I strived to preach the
gospel, not where Christ was named,
lest I should build upon another man's
foundation:
21 But as it is written, To whom he was
not spoken of, they shall see: and they
that have not heard shall understand.
22 For which cause also I have been
much hindered from coming to you.
23 But now having no more place in
these parts, and having a great desire
these many years to come unto you;
24 Whensoever I take my journey into
Spain, I will come to you: for I trust to
see you in my journey, and to be
brought on my way thitherward by you,
if first I be somewhat filled with your
company.
25 But now I go unto Jerusalem to
minister unto the saints.
26 For it hath pleased them of Macedonia and Ȧ-ɕhā′ịȧ to make a certain
contribution for the poor saints which
are at Jerusalem.
27 It hath pleased them verily; and
their debtors they are. For if the Ġĕn′-
tīleş have been made partakers of
their spiritual things, their duty is
also to minister unto them in carnal
things.
28 When therefore I have performed
this, and have sealed to them this fruit,
I will come by you into Spain.
29 And I am sure that, when I come
unto you, I shall come in the fulness of
the blessing of the gospel of Christ.
30 Now I beseech you, brethren, for
the Lord Jesus Christ's sake, and for
the love of the Spirit, that ye strive together with me in *your* prayers to God
for me;
31 That I may be delivered from them
that do not believe in Judea; and that
my service which *I have* for Jerusalem
may be accepted of the saints;
32 That I may come unto you with joy
by the will of God, and may with you be
refreshed.
33 Now the God of peace *be* with you
all. Amen.

CHAPTER 16

I COMMEND unto you Phē′bē our
sister, which is a servant of the
church which is at Çĕn-ɕhrē′ȧ:
2 That ye receive her in the Lord, as
becometh saints, and that ye assist her
in whatsoever business she hath need
of you: for she hath been a succorer of
many, and of myself also.
3 Greet Priscilla and Ăq′uĭ-lȧ, my
helpers in Christ Jesus:
4 Who have for my life laid down their
own necks: unto whom not only I give
thanks, but also all the churches of the
Ġĕn′tīleş.
5 Likewise *greet* the church that is in
their house. Salute my well-beloved
Ē-pē′nē-tŭs, who is the firstfruits of
Ȧ-ɕhā′ịȧ unto Christ.
6 Greet Mary, who bestowed much
labor on us.
7 Salute Ăn′drō-nī′cŭs and Jụ′nĭ-ȧ, my
kinsmen, and my fellow prisoners, who
are of note among the apostles, who
also were in Christ before me.
8 Greet Ăm′plĭ-ăs, my beloved in the
Lord.

9 Salute Ûr′bāne, our helper in Christ, and Stā′chȳs my beloved.

10 Salute Ȧ-pĕl′lēs̱ approved in Christ. Salute them which are of Ăr′ĭs-tō-bū′lŭs′ *household*.

11 Salute Hē-rō′dĭ-ŏn my kinsman. Greet them that be of the *household* of Narcissus, which are in the Lord.

12 Salute Trȳ-phē′nȧ and Trȳ-phō′sȧ, who labor in the Lord. Salute the beloved Pĕr′sĭs, which labored much in the Lord.

13 Salute Rufus chosen in the Lord, and his mother and mine.

14 Salute Ȧ-sȳn′crĭ-tŭs, Phlē′gŏn, Hĕr′măs, Păt′rō-bȧs, Hĕr′mēs̱, and the brethren which are with them.

15 Salute Phĭ-lŏl′ō-gŭs, and Julia, Nē′reūs, and his sister, and Ō-lȳm′păs, and all the saints which are with them.

16 Salute one another with a holy kiss. The churches of Christ salute you.

17 Now I beseech you, brethren, mark them which cause divisions and offenses contrary to the doctrine which ye have learned; and avoid them.

18 For they that are such serve not our Lord Jesus Christ, but their own belly; and by good words and fair speeches deceive the hearts of the simple.

19 For your obedience is come abroad unto all *men*. I am glad therefore on your behalf: but yet I would have you wise unto that which is good, and simple concerning evil.

20 And the God of peace shall bruise Satan under your feet shortly. The grace of our Lord Jesus Christ *be* with you. Amen.

21 Tĭ-mō′thē-ŭs my workfellow, and Lucius, and Jā′sȯn, and Sō-sĭp′ȧ-tĕr, my kinsmen, salute you.

22 I Tĕr′ṭĭ-ŭs, who wrote *this* epistle, salute you in the Lord.

23 Gā′ịŭs mine host, and of the whole church, saluteth you. Ē-răs′tŭs the chamberlain of the city saluteth you, and Quartus a brother.

24 The grace of our Lord Jesus Christ *be* with you all. Amen.

25 Now to him that is of power to stablish you according to my gospel, and the preaching of Jesus Christ, according to the revelation of the mystery, which was kept secret since the world began,

26 But now is made manifest, and by the Scriptures of the prophets, according to the commandment of the everlasting God, made known to all nations for the obedience of faith:

27 To God only wise, *be* glory through Jesus Christ for ever. Amen.

¶ Written to the Romans from Corinthus, *and sent* by Phebe servant of the church at Cenchrea.

THE FIRST EPISTLE OF PAUL THE APOSTLE TO THE

CORINTHIANS

CHAPTER 1

PAUL, called *to be* an apostle of Jesus Christ through the will of God, and Sŏs′thē-nēs̱ *our* brother,

2 Unto the church of God which is at Corinth, to them that are sanctified in Christ Jesus, called *to be* saints, with all that in every place call upon the name of Jesus Christ our Lord, both theirs and ours:

3 Grace *be* unto you, and peace, from God our Father, and *from* the Lord Jesus Christ.

4 I thank my God always on your behalf, for the grace of God which is given you by Jesus Christ;

5 That in every thing ye are enriched by him, in all utterance, and *in* all knowledge;

6 Even as the testimony of Christ was confirmed in you:

7 So that ye come behind in no gift; waiting for the coming of our Lord Jesus Christ:

8 Who shall also confirm you unto the end, *that ye may be* blameless in the day of our Lord Jesus Christ.

9 God *is* faithful, by whom ye were called unto the fellowship of his Son Jesus Christ our Lord.

10 Now I beseech you, brethren, by the name of our Lord Jesus Christ, that ye all speak the same thing, and

that there be no divisions among you;
but *that* ye be perfectly joined together
in the same mind and in the same
judgment.
11 For it hath been declared unto me
of you, my brethren, by them *which are*
of the house of Chlō'ē, that there are
contentions among you.
12 Now this I say, that every one of
you saith, I am of Paul; and I of Ȧ-pŏl'-
lŏs; and I of Çē'phăs; and I of Christ.
13 Is Christ divided? was Paul crucified for you? or were ye baptized in
the name of Paul?
14 I thank God that I baptized none of
you, but Crĭs'pŭs and Gā'i̤ŭs;
15 Lest any should say that I had baptized in mine own name.
16 And I baptized also the household
of Stĕph'ȧ-năs: besides, I know not
whether I baptized any other.
17 For Christ sent me not to baptize,
but to preach the gospel: not with wisdom of words, lest the cross of Christ
should be made of none effect.
18 For the preaching of the cross is to
them that perish, foolishness; but unto
us which are saved, it is the power of God.
19 For it is written, I will destroy the
wisdom of the wise, and will bring to
nothing the understanding of the prudent.
20 Where *is* the wise? where *is* the
scribe? where *is* the disputer of this
world? hath not God made foolish the
wisdom of this world?
21 For after that in the wisdom of God
the world by wisdom knew not God,
it pleased God by the foolishness of
preaching to save them that believe.
22 For the Jews require a sign, and the
Greeks seek after wisdom:
23 But we preach Christ crucified,
unto the Jews a stumblingblock, and
unto the Greeks foolishness;
24 But unto them which are called,
both Jews and Greeks, Christ the power
of God, and the wisdom of God.
25 Because the foolishness of God is
wiser than men; and the weakness of
God is stronger than men.
26 For ye see your calling, brethren,
how that not many wise men after the
flesh, not many mighty, not many noble,
are called:
27 But God hath chosen the foolish
things of the world to confound the
wise; and God hath chosen the weak
things of the world to confound the
things which are mighty;
28 And base things of the world, and
things which are despised, hath God
chosen, *yea,* and things which are not,
to bring to nought things that are:
29 That no flesh should glory in his
presence.
30 But of him are ye in Christ Jesus,
who of God is made unto us wisdom,
and righteousness, and sanctification,
and redemption:
31 That, according as it is written, He
that glorieth, let him glory in the Lord.

CHAPTER 2

AND I, brethren, when I came to you,
came not with excellency of speech
or of wisdom, declaring unto you the
testimony of God.
2 For I determined not to know any
thing among you, save Jesus Christ,
and him crucified.
3 And I was with you in weakness,
and in fear, and in much trembling.
4 And my speech and my preaching
was not with enticing words of man's
wisdom, but in demonstration of the
Spirit and of power:
5 That your faith should not stand in
the wisdom of men, but in the power of
God.
6 Howbeit we speak wisdom among
them that are perfect: yet not the wisdom of this world, nor of the princes of
this world, that come to nought:
7 But we speak the wisdom of God in
a mystery, *even* the hidden *wisdom,*
which God ordained before the world
unto our glory;
8 Which none of the princes of this
world knew: for had they known *it,* they
would not have crucified the Lord of
glory.
9 But as it is written, Eye hath not
seen, nor ear heard, neither have entered into the heart of man, the things
which God hath prepared for them that
love him.
10 But God hath revealed *them* unto
us by his Spirit: for the Spirit searcheth
all things, yea, the deep things of God.
11 For what man knoweth the things
of a man, save the spirit of man which
is in him? even so the things of God
knoweth no man, but the Spirit of God.
12 Now we have received, not the
spirit of the world, but the Spirit which

is of God; that we might know the things
that are freely given to us of God.
13 Which things also we speak, not in
the words which man's wisdom teacheth, but which the Holy Ghost teacheth;
comparing spiritual things with spiritual.
14 But the natural man receiveth not
the things of the Spirit of God: for they
are foolishness unto him: neither can he
know *them,* because they are spiritually
discerned.
15 But he that is spiritual judgeth all
things, yet he himself is judged of no
man.
16 For who hath known the mind of the
Lord, that he may instruct him? But
we have the mind of Christ.

CHAPTER 3

AND I, brethren, could not speak unto
you as unto spiritual, but as unto
carnal, *even* as unto babes in Christ.
2 I have fed you with milk, and not
with meat: for hitherto ye were not able
to bear it, neither yet now are ye able.
3 For ye are yet carnal: for whereas
there is among you envying, and strife,
and divisions, are ye not carnal, and
walk as men?
4 For while one saith, I am of Paul;
and another, I *am* of Ȧ-pŏl′lŏs; are ye
not carnal?
5 Who then is Paul, and who *is* Ȧ-pŏl′-
lŏs, but ministers by whom ye believed,
even as the Lord gave to every man?
6 I have planted, Ȧ-pŏl′lŏs watered;
but God gave the increase.
7 So then neither is he that planteth
any thing, neither he that watereth; but
God that giveth the increase.
8 Now he that planteth and he that
watereth are one: and every man shall
receive his own reward according to his
own labor.
9 For we are laborers together with
God: ye are God's husbandry, *ye are*
God's building.
10 According to the grace of God which
is given unto me, as a wise master-
builder, I have laid the foundation, and
another buildeth thereon. But let every
man take heed how he buildeth thereupon.
11 For other foundation can no man lay
than that is laid, which is Jesus Christ.
12 Now if any man build upon this
foundation gold, silver, precious stones,
wood, hay, stubble;
13 Every man's work shall be made
manifest: for the day shall declare it,
because it shall be revealed by fire; and
the fire shall try every man's work of
what sort it is.
14 If any man's work abide which he
hath built thereupon, he shall receive a
reward.
15 If any man's work shall be burned,
he shall suffer loss: but he himself shall
be saved; yet so as by fire.
16 Know ye not that ye are the temple
of God, and *that* the Spirit of God
dwelleth in you?
17 If any man defile the temple of God,
him shall God destroy; for the temple of
God is holy, which *temple* ye are.
18 Let no man deceive himself. If any
man among you seemeth to be wise in
this world, let him become a fool, that
he may be wise.
19 For the wisdom of this world is
foolishness with God: for it is written,
He taketh the wise in their own craftiness.
20 And again, The Lord knoweth the
thoughts of the wise, that they are
vain.
21 Therefore let no man glory in men:
for all things are yours;
22 Whether Paul, or Ȧ-pŏl′lŏs, or Çē′-
phăs, or the world, or life, or death, or
things present, or things to come; all
are yours;
23 And ye are Christ's; and Christ *is*
God's.

CHAPTER 4

LET a man so account of us, as of the
ministers of Christ, and stewards
of the mysteries of God.
2 Moreover it is required in stewards,
that a man be found faithful.
3 But with me it is a very small thing
that I should be judged of you, or of
man's judgment: yea, I judge not mine
own self.
4 For I know nothing by myself; yet
am I not hereby justified: but he that
judgeth me is the Lord.
5 Therefore judge nothing before the
time, until the Lord come, who both
will bring to light the hidden things of
darkness, and will make manifest the
counsels of the hearts: and then shall
every man have praise of God.
6 And these things, brethren, I have
in a figure transferred to myself and *to*

Ȧ-pŏl'lŏs for your sakes; that ye might
learn in us not to think *of men* above
that which is written, that no one of you
be puffed up for one against another.
7 For who maketh thee to differ *from
another?* and what hast thou that thou
didst not receive? now if thou didst
receive *it,* why dost thou glory, as if thou
hadst not received *it?*
8 Now ye are full, now ye are rich, ye
have reigned as kings without us: and I
would to God ye did reign, that we also
might reign with you.
9 For I think that God hath set forth
us the apostles last, as it were appointed
to death: for we are made a spectacle
unto the world, and to angels, and to
men.
10 We *are* fools for Christ's sake, but
ye *are* wise in Christ; we *are* weak, but
ye *are* strong; ye *are* honorable, but we
are despised.
11 Even unto this present hour we both
hunger, and thirst, and are naked, and
are buffeted, and have no certain dwelling place;
12 And labor, working with our own
hands: being reviled, we bless; being
persecuted, we suffer it:
13 Being defamed, we entreat: we are
made as the filth of the world, *and are*
the offscouring of all things unto this
day.
14 I write not these things to shame
you, but as my beloved sons I warn *you.*
15 For though ye have ten thousand
instructors in Christ, yet *have ye* not
many fathers: for in Christ Jesus I have
begotten you through the gospel.
16 Wherefore I beseech you, be ye
followers of me.
17 For this cause have I sent unto you
Tĭ-mō'thē-ŭs, who is my beloved son,
and faithful in the Lord, who shall
bring you into remembrance of my ways
which be in Christ, as I teach every
where in every church.
18 Now some are puffed up, as though
I would not come to you.
19 But I will come to you shortly, if
the Lord will, and will know, not the
speech of them which are puffed up,
but the power.
20 For the kingdom of God *is* not in
word, but in power.
21 What will ye? shall I come unto you
with a rod, or in love, and *in* the spirit
of meekness?

CHAPTER 5

IT is reported commonly *that there
is* fornication among you, and such
fornication as is not so much as named
among the Ġĕn'tīleş, that one should
have his father's wife.
2 And ye are puffed up, and have not
rather mourned, that he that hath done
this deed might be taken away from
among you.
3 For I verily, as absent in body, but
present in spirit, have judged already,
as though I were present, *concerning*
him that hath so done this deed,
4 In the name of our Lord Jesus
Christ, when ye are gathered together,
and my spirit, with the power of our
Lord Jesus Christ,
5 To deliver such a one unto Satan for
the destruction of the flesh, that the
spirit may be saved in the day of the
Lord Jesus.
6 Your glorying *is* not good. Know ye
not that a little leaven leaveneth the
whole lump?
7 Purge out therefore the old leaven,
that ye may be a new lump, as ye are
unleavened. For even Christ our passover is sacrificed for us:
8 Therefore let us keep the feast, not
with old leaven, neither with the leaven
of malice and wickedness; but with the
unleavened *bread* of sincerity and truth.
9 I wrote unto you in an epistle not to
company with fornicators:
10 Yet not altogether with the fornicators of this world, or with the covetous,
or extortioners, or with idolaters; for
then must ye needs go out of the world.
11 But now I have written unto you not
to keep company, if any man that is
called a brother be a fornicator, or
covetous, or an idolater, or a railer, or a
drunkard, or an extortioner; with such
a one, no, not to eat.
12 For what have I to do to judge them
also that are without? do not ye judge
them that are within?
13 But them that are without God
judgeth. Therefore put away from
among yourselves that wicked person.

CHAPTER 6

DARE any of you, having a matter
against another, go to law before
the unjust, and not before the saints?
2 Do ye not know that the saints shall

judge the world? and if the world shall
be judged by you, are ye unworthy to
judge the smallest matters?
3 Know ye not that we shall judge
angels? how much more things that pertain to this life?
4 If then ye have judgments of things
pertaining to this life, set them to judge
who are least esteemed in the church.
5 I speak to your shame. Is it so, that
there is not a wise man among you? no,
not one that shall be able to judge between his brethren?
6 But brother goeth to law with brother,
and that before the unbelievers.
7 Now therefore there is utterly a fault
among you, because ye go to law one
with another. Why do ye not rather
take wrong? Why do ye not rather *suffer yourselves to* be defrauded?
8 Nay, ye do wrong, and defraud, and
that *your* brethren.
9 Know ye not that the unrighteous
shall not inherit the kingdom of God?
Be not deceived: neither fornicators,
nor idolaters, nor adulterers, nor effemi-
nate, nor abusers of themselves with
mankind,
10 Nor thieves, nor covetous, nor
drunkards, nor revilers, nor extortioners, shall inherit the kingdom of God.
11 And such were some of you: but ye
are washed, but ye are sanctified, but
ye are justified in the name of the Lord
Jesus, and by the Spirit of our God.
12 All things are lawful unto me, but
all things are not expedient: all things
are lawful for me, but I will not be
brought under the power of any.
13 Meats for the belly, and the belly
for meats: but God shall destroy both
it and them. Now the body *is* not for
fornication, but for the Lord; and the
Lord for the body.
14 And God hath both raised up the
Lord, and will also raise up us by his
own power.
15 Know ye not that your bodies are
the members of Christ? shall I then take
the members of Christ, and make *them*
the members of a harlot? God forbid.
16 What! know ye not that he which is
joined to a harlot is one body? for two,
saith he, shall be one flesh.
17 But he that is joined unto the Lord
is one spirit.
18 Flee fornication. Every sin that a
man doeth is without the body; but he
that committeth fornication sinneth
against his own body.
19 What! know ye not that your body
is the temple of the Holy Ghost *which
is* in you, which ye have of God, and ye
are not your own?
20 For ye are bought with a price:
therefore glorify God in your body, and
in your spirit, which are God's.

CHAPTER 7

NOW concerning the things whereof ye wrote unto me: *It is* good for
a man not to touch a woman.
2 Nevertheless, *to avoid* fornication,
let every man have his own wife, and
let every woman have her own husband.
3 Let the husband render unto the wife
due benevolence: and likewise also the
wife unto the husband.
4 The wife hath not power of her own
body, but the husband: and likewise
also the husband hath not power of his
own body, but the wife.
5 Defraud ye not one the other, except
it be with consent for a time, that ye
may give yourselves to fasting and
prayer; and come together again, that
Satan tempt you not for your incon-
tinency.
6 But I speak this by permission, *and*
not of commandment.
7 For I would that all men were even
as I myself. But every man hath his
proper gift of God, one after this manner, and another after that.
8 I say therefore to the unmarried and
widows, It is good for them if they abide
even as I.
9 But if they cannot contain, let them
marry: for it is better to marry than to
burn.
10 And unto the married I command,
yet not I, but the Lord, Let not the wife
depart from *her* husband:
11 But and if she depart, let her remain unmarried, or be reconciled to *her*
husband: and let not the husband put
away *his* wife.
12 But to the rest speak I, not the
Lord: If any brother hath a wife that
believeth not, and she be pleased to
dwell with him, let him not put her
away.
13 And the woman which hath a husband that believeth not, and if he be
pleased to dwell with her, let her not
leave him.

14 For the unbelieving husband is sanctified by the wife, and the unbelieving wife is sanctified by the husband: else were your children unclean; but now are they holy.

15 But if the unbelieving depart, let him depart. A brother or a sister is not under bondage in such *cases:* but God hath called us to peace.

16 For what knowest thou, O wife, whether thou shalt save *thy* husband? or how knowest thou, O man, whether thou shalt save *thy* wife?

17 But as God hath distributed to every man, as the Lord hath called every one, so let him walk. And so ordain I in all churches.

18 Is any man called being circumcised? let him not become uncircumcised. Is any called in uncircumcision? let him not be circumcised.

19 Circumcision is nothing, and uncircumcision is nothing, but the keeping of the commandments of God.

20 Let every man abide in the same calling wherein he was called.

21 Art thou called *being* a servant? care not for it: but if thou mayest be made free, use *it* rather.

22 For he that is called in the Lord, *being* a servant, is the Lord's freeman: likewise also he that is called, *being* free, is Christ's servant.

23 Ye are bought with a price; be not ye the servants of men.

24 Brethren, let every man, wherein he is called, therein abide with God.

25 Now concerning virgins I have no commandment of the Lord: yet I give my judgment, as one that hath obtained mercy of the Lord to be faithful.

26 I suppose therefore that this is good for the present distress, *I say,* that *it is* good for a man so to be.

27 Art thou bound unto a wife? seek not to be loosed. Art thou loosed from a wife? seek not a wife.

28 But and if thou marry, thou hast not sinned; and if a virgin marry, she hath not sinned. Nevertheless such shall have trouble in the flesh: but I spare you.

29 But this I say, brethren, the time *is* short: it remaineth, that both they that have wives be as though they had none;

30 And they that weep, as though they wept not; and they that rejoice, as though they rejoiced not; and they that buy, as though they possessed not;

31 And they that use this world, as not abusing *it:* for the fashion of this world passeth away.

32 But I would have you without carefulness. He that is unmarried careth for the things that belong to the Lord, how he may please the Lord:

33 But he that is married careth for the things that are of the world, how he may please *his* wife.

34 There is difference *also* between a wife and a virgin. The unmarried woman careth for the things of the Lord, that she may be holy both in body and in spirit: but she that is married careth for the things of the world, how she may please *her* husband.

35 And this I speak for your own profit; not that I may cast a snare upon you, but for that which is comely, and that ye may attend upon the Lord without distraction.

36 But if any man think that he behaveth himself uncomely toward his virgin, if she pass the flower of *her* age, and need so require, let him do what he will, he sinneth not: let them marry.

37 Nevertheless he that standeth steadfast in his heart, having no necessity, but hath power over his own will, and hath so decreed in his heart that he will keep his virgin, doeth well.

38 So then he that giveth *her* in marriage doeth well; but he that giveth *her* not in marriage doeth better.

39 The wife is bound by the law as long as her husband liveth; but if her husband be dead, she is at liberty to be married to whom she will; only in the Lord.

40 But she is happier if she so abide, after my judgment: and I think also that I have the Spirit of God.

CHAPTER 8

NOW as touching things offered unto idols, we know that we all have knowledge. Knowledge puffeth up, but charity edifieth.

2 And if any man think that he knoweth any thing, he knoweth nothing yet as he ought to know.

3 But if any man love God, the same is known of him.

4 As concerning therefore the eating

of those things that are offered in sacrifice unto idols, we know that an idol *is* nothing in the world, and that *there is* none other God but one.
5 For though there be that are called gods, whether in heaven or in earth, (as there be gods many, and lords many,)
6 But to us *there is but* one God, the Father, of whom *are* all things, and we in him; and one Lord Jesus Christ, by whom *are* all things, and we by him.
7 Howbeit *there is* not in every man that knowledge: for some with conscience of the idol unto this hour eat *it* as a thing offered unto an idol; and their conscience being weak is defiled.
8 But meat commendeth us not to God: for neither, if we eat, are we the better; neither, if we eat not, are we the worse.
9 But take heed lest by any means this liberty of yours become a stumblingblock to them that are weak.
10 For if any man see thee which hast knowledge sit at meat in the idol's temple, shall not the conscience of him which is weak be emboldened to eat those things which are offered to idols;
11 And through thy knowledge shall the weak brother perish, for whom Christ died?
12 But when ye sin so against the brethren, and wound their weak conscience, ye sin against Christ.
13 Wherefore, if meat make my brother to offend, I will eat no flesh while the world standeth, lest I make my brother to offend.

CHAPTER 9

AM I not an apostle? am I not free? have I not seen Jesus Christ our Lord? are not ye my work in the Lord?
2 If I be not an apostle unto others, yet doubtless I am to you: for the seal of mine apostleship are ye in the Lord.
3 Mine answer to them that do examine me is this:
4 Have we not power to eat and to drink?
5 Have we not power to lead about a sister, a wife, as well as other apostles, and *as* the brethren of the Lord, and Çē'phăs?
6 Or I only and Barnabas, have not we power to forbear working?
7 Who goeth a warfare any time at his own charges? who planteth a vineyard, and eateth not of the fruit thereof? or who feedeth a flock, and eateth not of the milk of the flock?
8 Say I these things as a man? or saith not the law the same also?
9 For it is written in the law of Moses, Thou shalt not muzzle the mouth of the ox that treadeth out the corn. Doth God take care for oxen?
10 Or saith he *it* altogether for our sakes? For our sakes, no doubt, *this* is written: that he that ploweth should plow in hope; and that he that thresheth in hope should be partaker of his hope.
11 If we have sown unto you spiritual things, *is it* a great thing if we shall reap your carnal things?
12 If others be partakers of *this* power over you, *are* not we rather? Nevertheless we have not used this power; but suffer all things, lest we should hinder the gospel of Christ.
13 Do ye not know that they which minister about holy things live *of the things* of the temple? and they which wait at the altar are partakers with the altar?
14 Even so hath the Lord ordained that they which preach the gospel should live of the gospel.
15 But I have used none of these things: neither have I written these things, that it should be so done unto me: for *it were* better for me to die, than that any man should make my glorying void.
16 For though I preach the gospel, I have nothing to glory of: for necessity is laid upon me; yea, woe is unto me, if I preach not the gospel!
17 For if I do this thing willingly, I have a reward: but if against my will, a dispensation *of the gospel* is committed unto me.
18 What is my reward then? *Verily* that, when I preach the gospel, I may make the gospel of Christ without charge, that I abuse not my power in the gospel.
19 For though I be free from all *men*, yet have I made myself servant unto all, that I might gain the more.
20 And unto the Jews I became as a Jew, that I might gain the Jews; to them that are under the law, as under the

law, that I might gain them that are under the law;

21 To them that are without law, as without law, (being not without law to God, but under the law to Christ,) that I might gain them that are without law.

22 To the weak became I as weak, that I might gain the weak: I am made all things to all *men,* that I might by all means save some.

23 And this I do for the gospel's sake, that I might be partaker thereof with *you.*

24 Know ye not that they which run in a race run all, but one receiveth the prize? So run, that ye may obtain.

25 And every man that striveth for the mastery is temperate in all things. Now they *do it* to obtain a corruptible crown; but we an incorruptible.

26 I therefore so run, not as uncertainly; so fight I, not as one that beateth the air:

27 But I keep under my body, and bring *it* into subjection: lest that by any means, when I have preached to others, I myself should be a castaway.

CHAPTER 10

MOREOVER, brethren, I would not that ye should be ignorant, how that all our fathers were under the cloud, and all passed through the sea;

2 And were all baptized unto Moses in the cloud and in the sea;

3 And did all eat the same spiritual meat;

4 And did all drink the same spiritual drink; for they drank of that spiritual Rock that followed them: and that Rock was Christ.

5 But with many of them God was not well pleased: for they were overthrown in the wilderness.

6 Now these things were our examples, to the intent we should not lust after evil things, as they also lusted.

7 Neither be ye idolaters, as *were* some of them; as it is written, The people sat down to eat and drink, and rose up to play.

8 Neither let us commit fornication, as some of them committed, and fell in one day three and twenty thousand.

9 Neither let us tempt Christ, as some of them also tempted, and were destroyed of serpents.

10 Neither murmur ye, as some of them also murmured, and were destroyed of the destroyer.

11 Now all these things happened unto them for ensamples: and they are written for our admonition, upon whom the ends of the world are come.

12 Wherefore let him that thinketh he standeth take heed lest he fall.

13 There hath no temptation taken you but such as is common to man: but God *is* faithful, who will not suffer you to be tempted above that ye are able; but will with the temptation also make a way to escape, that ye may be able to bear *it.*

14 Wherefore, my dearly beloved, flee from idolatry.

15 I speak as to wise men; judge ye what I say.

16 The cup of blessing which we bless, is it not the communion of the blood of Christ? The bread which we break, is it not the communion of the body of Christ?

17 For we *being* many are one bread, *and* one body: for we are all partakers of that one bread.

18 Behold Ĭṣ′rā-ĕl after the flesh: are not they which eat of the sacrifices partakers of the altar?

19 What say I then? that the idol is any thing, or that which is offered in sacrifice to idols is any thing?

20 But *I say,* that the things which the Ġĕn′tīleṣ sacrifice, they sacrifice to devils, and not to God: and I would not that ye should have fellowship with devils.

21 Ye cannot drink the cup of the Lord, and the cup of devils: ye cannot be partakers of the Lord's table, and of the table of devils.

22 Do we provoke the Lord to jealousy? are we stronger than he?

23 All things are lawful for me, but all things are not expedient: all things are lawful for me, but all things edify not.

24 Let no man seek his own, but every man another's *wealth.*

25 Whatsoever is sold in the shambles, *that* eat, asking no question for conscience' sake:

26 For the earth *is* the Lord's, and the fulness thereof.

27 If any of them that believe not bid you *to a feast,* and ye be disposed to go; whatsoever is set before you, eat, asking no question for conscience' sake.

28 But if any man say unto you, This
is offered in sacrifice unto idols, eat not
for his sake that showed it, and for
conscience' sake: for the earth *is* the
Lord's, and the fulness thereof:
29 Conscience, I say, not thine own,
but of the other: for why is my liberty
judged of another *man's* conscience?
30 For if I by grace be a partaker, why
am I evil spoken of for that for which I
give thanks?
31 Whether therefore ye eat, or drink,
or whatsoever ye do, do all to the glory
of God.
32 Give none offense, neither to the
Jews, nor to the Gĕn'tileṣ, nor to the
church of God:
33 Even as I please all *men* in all
things, not seeking mine own profit,
but the *profit* of many, that they may be
saved.

CHAPTER 11

BE ye followers of me, even as I also
am of Christ.
2 Now I praise you, brethren, that
ye remember me in all things, and
keep the ordinances, as I delivered
them to you.
3 But I would have you know, that the
head of every man is Christ; and the
head of the woman *is* the man; and
the head of Christ *is* God.
4 Every man praying or prophesying,
having *his* head covered, dishonoreth
his head.
5 But every woman that prayeth or
prophesieth with *her* head uncovered
dishonoreth her head: for that is even
all one as if she were shaven.
6 For if the woman be not covered, let
her also be shorn: but if it be a shame
for a woman to be shorn or shaven, let
her be covered.
7 For a man indeed ought not to cover
his head, forasmuch as he is the image
and glory of God: but the woman is the
glory of the man.
8 For the man is not of the woman; but
the woman of the man.
9 Neither was the man created for the
woman; but the woman for the man.
10 For this cause ought the woman to
have power on *her* head because of the
angels.
11 Nevertheless neither is the man
without the woman, neither the woman
without the man, in the Lord.
12 For as the woman *is* of the man,
even so *is* the man also by the woman;
but all things of God.
13 Judge in yourselves: is it comely
that a woman pray unto God uncovered?
14 Doth not even nature itself teach
you, that, if a man have long hair, it is
a shame unto him?
15 But if a woman have long hair, it
is a glory to her: for *her* hair is given
her for a covering.
16 But if any man seem to be contentious, we have no such custom, neither
the churches of God.
17 Now in this that I declare *unto
you* I praise *you* not, that ye come together not for the better, but for the
worse.
18 For first of all, when ye come together in the church, I hear that there
be divisions among you; and I partly
believe it.
19 For there must be also heresies
among you, that they which are approved may be made manifest among
you.
20 When ye come together therefore
into one place, *this* is not to eat the
Lord's supper.
21 For in eating every one taketh before *other* his own supper: and one is
hungry, and another is drunken.
22 What! have ye not houses to eat and
to drink in? or despise ye the church of
God, and shame them that have not?
What shall I say to you? shall I praise
you in this? I praise *you* not.
23 For I have received of the Lord
that which also I delivered unto you,
That the Lord Jesus, the *same* night in
which he was betrayed, took bread:
24 And when he had given thanks, he
brake *it*, and said, Take, eat; this is my
body, which is broken for you: this do
in remembrance of me.
25 After the same manner also *he took*
the cup, when he had supped, saying,
This cup is the new testament in my
blood: this do ye, as oft as ye drink *it*,
in remembrance of me.
26 For as often as ye eat this bread,
and drink this cup, ye do show the
Lord's death till he come.
27 Wherefore whosoever shall eat this
bread, and drink *this* cup of the Lord,
unworthily, shall be guilty of the body
and blood of the Lord.
28 But let a man examine himself, and

so let him eat of *that* bread, and drink
of *that* cup.
29 For he that eateth and drinketh
unworthily, eateth and drinketh damnation to himself, not discerning the
Lord's body.
30 For this cause many *are* weak and
sickly among you, and many sleep.
31 For if we would judge ourselves, we
should not be judged.
32 But when we are judged, we are
chastened of the Lord, that we should
not be condemned with the world.
33 Wherefore, my brethren, when ye
come together to eat, tarry one for
another.
34 And if any man hunger, let him eat
at home; that ye come not together unto
condemnation. And the rest will I set
in order when I come.

CHAPTER 12

NOW concerning spiritual *gifts*,
brethren, I would not have you
ignorant.
2 Ye know that ye were Ġĕn'tīleṣ, carried away unto these dumb idols, even
as ye were led.
3 Wherefore I give you to understand,
that no man speaking by the Spirit of
God calleth Jesus accursed: and *that* no
man can say that Jesus is the Lord, but
by the Holy Ghost.
4 Now there are diversities of gifts,
but the same Spirit.
5 And there are differences of administrations, but the same Lord.
6 And there are diversities of operations, but it is the same God which
worketh all in all.
7 But the manifestation of the Spirit
is given to every man to profit withal.
8 For to one is given by the Spirit the
word of wisdom; to another the word of
knowledge by the same Spirit;
9 To another faith by the same Spirit;
to another the gifts of healing by the
same Spirit;
10 To another the working of miracles;
to another prophecy; to another discerning of spirits; to another *divers*
kinds of tongues; to another the interpretation of tongues:
11 But all these worketh that one and
the selfsame Spirit, dividing to every
man severally as he will.
12 For as the body is one, and hath
many members, and all the members of
that one body, being many, are one
body: so also *is* Christ.
13 For by one Spirit are we all baptized into one body, whether *we be*
Jews or Ġĕn'tīleṣ, whether *we be* bond
or free; and have been all made to drink
into one Spirit.
14 For the body is not one member,
but many.
15 If the foot shall say, Because I am
not the hand, I am not of the body; is it
therefore not of the body?
16 And if the ear shall say, Because I
am not the eye, I am not of the body;
is it therefore not of the body?
17 If the whole body *were* an eye,
where *were* the hearing? If the whole
were hearing, where *were* the smelling?
18 But now hath God set the members
every one of them in the body, as it
hath pleased him.
19 And if they were all one member,
where *were* the body?
20 But now *are they* many members,
yet but one body.
21 And the eye cannot say unto the
hand, I have no need of thee: nor again
the head to the feet, I have no need of
you.
22 Nay, much more those members
of the body, which seem to be more
feeble, are necessary:
23 And those *members* of the body,
which we think to be less honorable,
upon these we bestow more abundant
honor; and our uncomely *parts* have
more abundant comeliness.
24 For our comely *parts* have no need:
but God hath tempered the body together, having given more abundant
honor to that *part* which lacked:
25 That there should be no schism in
the body; but *that* the members should
have the same care one for another.
26 And whether one member suffer,
all the members suffer with it; or one
member be honored, all the members
rejoice with it.
27 Now ye are the body of Christ, and
members in particular.
28 And God hath set some in the
church, first apostles, secondarily
prophets, thirdly teachers, after that
miracles, then gifts of healings, helps,
governments, diversities of tongues.
29 *Are* all apostles? *are* all prophets?
are all teachers? *are* all workers of
miracles?

30 Have all the gifts of healing? do all
speak with tongues? do all interpret?
31 But covet earnestly the best gifts:
and yet show I unto you a more excellent way.

CHAPTER 13

THOUGH I speak with the tongues of
men and of angels, and have not
charity, I am become *as* sounding brass,
or a tinkling cymbal.
2 And though I have *the gift of* prophecy, and understand all mysteries, and
all knowledge; and though I have all
faith, so that I could remove mountains,
and have not charity, I am nothing.
3 And though I bestow all my goods to
feed *the poor*, and though I give my
body to be burned, and have not charity, it profiteth me nothing.
4 Charity suffereth long, *and* is kind;
charity envieth not; charity vaunteth
not itself, is not puffed up,
5 Doth not behave itself unseemly,
seeketh not her own, is not easily provoked, thinketh no evil;
6 Rejoiceth not in iniquity, but rejoiceth in the truth;
7 Beareth all things, believeth all
things, hopeth all things, endureth all
things.
8 Charity never faileth: but whether
there be prophecies, they shall fail;
whether *there be* tongues, they shall
cease; whether *there be* knowledge, it
shall vanish away.
9 For we know in part, and we prophesy in part.
10 But when that which is perfect is
come, then that which is in part shall
be done away.
11 When I was a child, I spake as a
child, I understood as a child, I thought
as a child: but when I became a man, I
put away childish things.
12 For now we see through a glass,
darkly; but then face to face: now I
know in part; but then shall I know even
as also I am known.
13 And now abideth faith, hope, charity, these three; but the greatest of
these *is* charity.

CHAPTER 14

FOLLOW after charity, and desire
spiritual *gifts*, but rather that ye
may prophesy.
2 For he that speaketh in an *unknown*
tongue speaketh not unto men, but unto
God: for no man understandeth *him;*
howbeit in the spirit he speaketh
mysteries.
3 But he that prophesieth speaketh
unto men *to* edification, and exhortation, and comfort.
4 He that speaketh in an *unknown*
tongue edifieth himself; but he that
prophesieth edifieth the church.
5 I would that ye all spake with
tongues, but rather that ye prophesied:
for greater *is* he that prophesieth than
he that speaketh with tongues, except
he interpret, that the church may receive edifying.
6 Now, brethren, if I come unto you
speaking with tongues, what shall I
profit you, except I shall speak to you
either by revelation, or by knowledge,
or by prophesying, or by doctrine?
7 And even things without life giving
sound, whether pipe or harp, except
they give a distinction in the sounds,
how shall it be known what is piped or
harped?
8 For if the trumpet give an uncertain
sound, who shall prepare himself to the
battle?
9 So likewise ye, except ye utter by
the tongue words easy to be understood, how shall it be known what is
spoken? for ye shall speak into the
air.
10 There are, it may be, so many kinds
of voices in the world, and none of them
is without signification.
11 Therefore if I know not the meaning of the voice, I shall be unto him
that speaketh a barbarian, and he
that speaketh *shall be* a barbarian
unto me.
12 Even so ye, forasmuch as ye are
zealous of spiritual *gifts*, seek that ye
may excel to the edifying of the church.
13 Wherefore let him that speaketh in
an *unknown* tongue pray that he may
interpret.
14 For if I pray in an *unknown* tongue,
my spirit prayeth, but my understanding is unfruitful.
15 What is it then? I will pray with the
spirit, and I will pray with the understanding also: I will sing with the spirit,
and I will sing with the understanding
also.
16 Else, when thou shalt bless with the
spirit, how shall he that occupieth the

room of the unlearned say Amen at thy
giving of thanks, seeing he understandeth not what thou sayest?
17 For thou verily givest thanks well,
but the other is not edified.
18 I thank my God, I speak with
tongues more than ye all:
19 Yet in the church I had rather speak
five words with my understanding, that
by my voice I might teach others also,
than ten thousand words in an *unknown*
tongue.
20 Brethren, be not children in understanding: howbeit in malice be ye
children, but in understanding be men.
21 In the law it is written, With
men of other tongues and other lips
will I speak unto this people; and yet
for all that will they not hear me, saith
the Lord.
22 Wherefore tongues are for a sign,
not to them that believe, but to them
that believe not: but prophesying
serveth not for them that believe not,
but for them which believe.
23 If therefore the whole church be
come together into one place, and all
speak with tongues, and there come in
those that are unlearned, or unbelievers,
will they not say that ye are mad?
24 But if all prophesy, and there come
in one that believeth not, or *one* unlearned, he is convinced of all, he is
judged of all:
25 And thus are the secrets of his
heart made manifest; and so falling
down on *his* face he will worship
God, and report that God is in you of
a truth.
26 How is it then, brethren? when ye
come together, every one of you hath a
psalm, hath a doctrine, hath a tongue,
hath a revelation, hath an interpretation. Let all things be done unto
edifying.
27 If any man speak in an *unknown*
tongue, *let it be* by two, or at the most
by three, and *that* by course; and let
one interpret.
28 But if there be no interpreter, let
him keep silence in the church; and let
him speak to himself, and to God.
29 Let the prophets speak two or three,
and let the other judge.
30 If *any thing* be revealed to another
that sitteth by, let the first hold his
peace.
31 For ye may all prophesy one by one,
that all may learn, and all may be comforted.
32 And the spirits of the prophets are
subject to the prophets.
33 For God is not *the author* of confusion, but of peace, as in all churches of
the saints.
34 Let your women keep silence in the
churches: for it is not permitted unto
them to speak; but *they are commanded* to be under obedience, as also
saith the law.
35 And if they will learn any thing,
let them ask their husbands at home:
for it is a shame for women to speak in
the church.
36 What! came the word of God out
from you? or came it unto you only?
37 If any man think himself to be a
prophet, or spiritual, let him acknowledge that the things that I write unto
you are the commandments of the
Lord.
38 But if any man be ignorant, let him
be ignorant.
39 Wherefore, brethren, covet to
prophesy, and forbid not to speak with
tongues.
40 Let all things be done decently
and in order.

CHAPTER 15

MOREOVER, brethren, I declare
unto you the gospel which I
preached unto you, which also ye have
received, and wherein ye stand;
2 By which also ye are saved, if ye
keep in memory what I preached unto
you, unless ye have believed in vain.
3 For I delivered unto you first of all
that which I also received, how that
Christ died for our sins according to the
Scriptures;
4 And that he was buried, and that he
rose again the third day according to
the Scriptures:
5 And that he was seen of Cē′phăs,
then of the twelve:
6 After that, he was seen of above
five hundred brethren at once; of whom
the greater part remain unto this present, but some are fallen asleep.
7 After that, he was seen of James;
then of all the apostles.
8 And last of all he was seen of me also,
as of one born out of due time.
9 For I am the least of the apostles,
that am not meet to be called an apostle,

because I persecuted the church of God.

10 But by the grace of God I am what I am: and his grace which *was bestowed* upon me was not in vain; but I labored more abundantly than they all: yet not I, but the grace of God which was with me.

11 Therefore whether *it were* I or they, so we preach, and so ye believed.

12 Now if Christ be preached that he rose from the dead, how say some among you that there is no resurrection of the dead?

13 But if there be no resurrection of the dead, then is Christ not risen:

14 And if Christ be not risen, then *is* our preaching vain, and your faith *is* also vain.

15 Yea, and we are found false witnesses of God; because we have testified of God that he raised up Christ: whom he raised not up, if so be that the dead rise not.

16 For if the dead rise not, then is not Christ raised:

17 And if Christ be not raised, your faith *is* vain; ye are yet in your sins.

18 Then they also which are fallen asleep in Christ are perished.

19 If in this life only we have hope in Christ, we are of all men most miserable.

20 But now is Christ risen from the dead, *and* become the firstfruits of them that slept.

21 For since by man *came* death, by man *came* also the resurrection of the dead.

22 For as in Adam all die, even so in Christ shall all be made alive.

23 But every man in his own order: Christ the firstfruits; afterward they that are Christ's at his coming.

24 Then *cometh* the end, when he shall have delivered up the kingdom to God, even the Father; when he shall have put down all rule, and all authority and power.

25 For he must reign, till he hath put all enemies under his feet.

26 The last enemy *that* shall be destroyed *is* death.

27 For he hath put all things under his feet. But when he saith, All things are put under *him, it is* manifest that he is excepted, which did put all things under him.

28 And when all things shall be subdued unto him, then shall the Son also himself be subject unto him that put all things under him, that God may be all in all.

29 Else what shall they do which are baptized for the dead, if the dead rise not at all? why are they then baptized for the dead?

30 And why stand we in jeopardy every hour?

31 I protest by your rejoicing which I have in Christ Jesus our Lord, I die daily.

32 If after the manner of men I have fought with beasts at Ĕph'ē-sŭs, what advantageth it me, if the dead rise not? let us eat and drink; for to-morrow we die.

33 Be not deceived: evil communications corrupt good manners.

34 Awake to righteousness, and sin not; for some have not the knowledge of God: I speak *this* to your shame.

35 But some *man* will say, How are the dead raised up? and with what body do they come?

36 *Thou* fool, that which thou sowest is not quickened, except it die:

37 And that which thou sowest, thou sowest not that body that shall be, but bare grain, it may chance of wheat, or of some other *grain:*

38 But God giveth it a body as it hath pleased him, and to every seed his own body.

39 All flesh *is* not the same flesh: but *there is* one *kind of* flesh of men, another flesh of beasts, another of fishes, *and* another of birds.

40 *There are* also celestial bodies, and bodies terrestrial: but the glory of the celestial *is* one, and the *glory* of the terrestrial *is* another.

41 *There is* one glory of the sun, and another glory of the moon, and another glory of the stars; for *one* star differeth from *another* star in glory.

42 So also *is* the resurrection of the dead. It is sown in corruption, it is raised in incorruption:

43 It is sown in dishonor, it is raised in glory: it is sown in weakness, it is raised in power:

44 It is sown a natural body, it is raised a spiritual body. There is a natural body, and there is a spiritual body.

45 And so it is written, The first man
Adam was made a living soul; the last
Adam *was made* a quickening spirit.
46 Howbeit that *was* not first which is
spiritual, but that which is natural; and
afterward that which is spiritual.
47 The first man *is* of the earth,
earthy: the second man *is* the Lord
from heaven.
48 As *is* the earthy, such *are* they also
that are earthy: and as *is* the heavenly,
such *are* they also that are heavenly.
49 And as we have borne the image of
the earthy, we shall also bear the image
of the heavenly.
50 Now this I say, brethren, that flesh
and blood cannot inherit the kingdom
of God; neither doth corruption inherit
incorruption.
51 Behold, I show you a mystery; We
shall not all sleep, but we shall all be
changed,
52 In a moment, in the twinkling of an
eye, at the last trump: for the trumpet
shall sound, and the dead shall be
raised incorruptible, and we shall be
changed.
53 For this corruptible must put on incorruption, and this mortal *must* put on
immortality.
54 So when this corruptible shall have
put on incorruption, and this mortal
shall have put on immortality, then shall
be brought to pass the saying that is
written, Death is swallowed up in
victory.
55 O death, where *is* thy sting? O
grave, where *is* thy victory?
56 The sting of death *is* sin; and the
strength of sin *is* the law.
57 But thanks *be* to God, which giveth
us the victory through our Lord Jesus
Christ.
58 Therefore, my beloved brethren,
be ye steadfast, unmovable, always
abounding in the work of the Lord, forasmuch as ye know that your labor is
not in vain in the Lord.

CHAPTER 16

NOW concerning the collection for
the saints, as I have given order
to the churches of Gȧ-lā'ţĭ-ȧ, even so
do ye.
2 Upon the first *day* of the week let
every one of you lay by him in store, as
God hath prospered him, that there be
no gatherings when I come.
3 And when I come, whomsoever ye
shall approve by *your* letters, them will
I send to bring your liberality unto
Jerusalem.
4 And if it be meet that I go also, they
shall go with me.
5 Now I will come unto you, when I
shall pass through Macedonia: for I do
pass through Macedonia.
6 And it may be that I will abide,
yea, and winter with you, that ye may
bring me on my journey whithersoever
I go.
7 For I will not see you now by the
way; but I trust to tarry a while with
you, if the Lord permit.
8 But I will tarry at Ĕph'ē-sŭs until
Pĕn'tē-cŏst.
9 For a great door and effectual is
opened unto me, and *there are* many
adversaries.
10 Now if Tĭ-mŏ'thē-ŭs come, see that
he may be with you without fear: for
he worketh the work of the Lord, as I
also *do*.
11 Let no man therefore despise him:
but conduct him forth in peace, that he
may come unto me: for I look for him
with the brethren.
12 As touching *our* brother Ȧ-pŏl'lŏs,
I greatly desired him to come unto you
with the brethren: but his will was not
at all to come at this time; but he will
come when he shall have convenient
time.
13 Watch ye, stand fast in the faith,
quit you like men, be strong.
14 Let all your things be done with
charity.
15 I beseech you, brethren, (ye know
the house of Stĕph'ȧ-năs, that it is the
firstfruits of Ȧ-chā'ịȧ, and *that* they have
addicted themselves to the ministry of
the saints,)
16 That ye submit yourselves unto
such, and to every one that helpeth with
us, and laboreth.
17 I am glad of the coming of Stĕph'-
ȧ-năs and Fôr'tū-nā'tŭs and Ȧ-chā'ĭ-
cŭs: for that which was lacking on your
part they have supplied.
18 For they have refreshed my spirit
and yours: therefore acknowledge ye
them that are such.
19 The churches of Asia salute you.
Ăq'uĭ-lȧ and Priscilla salute you much
in the Lord, with the church that is in
their house.

20 All the brethren greet you. Greet
ye one another with a holy kiss.
21 The salutation of *me* Paul with
mine own hand.
22 If any man love not the Lord Jesus
Christ, let him be Ȧ-năth'ē-mȧ, Măr'-
ȧn-ăth'ȧ.
23 The grace of our Lord Jesus Christ
be with you.
24 My love *be* with you all in Christ
Jesus. Amen.

¶ The first *epistle* to the Corinthians was written from Philippi by Stephanas, and Fortunatus, and Achaicus, and Timotheus.

THE SECOND EPISTLE OF PAUL THE APOSTLE TO THE CORINTHIANS

CHAPTER 1

PAUL, an apostle of Jesus Christ by
the will of God, and Timothy *our*
brother, unto the church of God which is
at Corinth, with all the saints which are
in all Ȧ-chā'ịȧ:
2 Grace *be* to you, and peace, from God
our Father, and *from* the Lord Jesus
Christ.
3 Blessed *be* God, even the Father of
our Lord Jesus Christ, the Father of
mercies, and the God of all comfort;
4 Who comforteth us in all our tribulation, that we may be able to comfort
them which are in any trouble, by the
comfort wherewith we ourselves are
comforted of God.
5 For as the sufferings of Christ abound
in us, so our consolation also aboundeth
by Christ.
6 And whether we be afflicted, *it is* for
your consolation and salvation, which is
effectual in the enduring of the same
sufferings which we also suffer: or
whether we be comforted, *it is* for your
consolation and salvation.
7 And our hope of you *is* steadfast,
knowing, that as ye are partakers of
the sufferings, so *shall ye be* also of
the consolation.
8 For we would not, brethren, have
you ignorant of our trouble which came
to us in Asia, that we were pressed out
of measure, above strength, insomuch
that we despaired even of life:
9 But we had the sentence of death
in ourselves, that we should not trust in
ourselves, but in God which raiseth the
dead:
10 Who delivered us from so great a
death, and doth deliver: in whom we
trust that he will yet deliver *us;*
11 Ye also helping together by prayer
for us, that for the gift *bestowed* upon
us by the means of many persons
thanks may be given by many on our
behalf.
12 For our rejoicing is this, the testimony of our conscience, that in simplicity and godly sincerity, not with
fleshly wisdom, but by the grace of God,
we have had our conversation in the
world, and more abundantly to you-
ward.
13 For we write none other things unto
you, than what ye read or acknowledge;
and I trust ye shall acknowledge even
to the end;
14 As also ye have acknowledged us
in part, that we are your rejoicing, even
as ye also *are* ours in the day of the
Lord Jesus.
15 And in this confidence I was minded
to come unto you before, that ye might
have a second benefit;
16 And to pass by you into Macedonia,
and to come again out of Macedonia
unto you, and of you to be brought on
my way toward Judea.
17 When I therefore was thus minded,
did I use lightness? or the things that I
purpose, do I purpose according to the
flesh, that with me there should be yea,
yea, and nay, nay?
18 But *as* God *is* true, our word toward
you was not yea and nay.
19 For the Son of God, Jesus Christ,
who was preached among you by us,
even by me and Sĭl-vā'nŭs and Tĭ-mō'-
thē-ŭs, was not yea and nay, but in him
was yea.
20 For all the promises of God in him
are yea, and in him Amen, unto the
glory of God by us.
21 Now he which stablisheth us with

you in Christ, and hath anointed us, *is*
God;
22 Who hath also sealed us, and given
the earnest of the Spirit in our hearts.
23 Moreover I call God for a record
upon my soul, that to spare you I came
not as yet unto Corinth.
24 Not for that we have dominion over
your faith, but are helpers of your joy:
for by faith ye stand.

CHAPTER 2

BUT I determined this with myself,
that I would not come again to
you in heaviness.
2 For if I make you sorry, who is he
then that maketh me glad, but the same
which is made sorry by me?
3 And I wrote this same unto you, lest,
when I came, I should have sorrow
from them of whom I ought to rejoice;
having confidence in you all, that my
joy is *the joy* of you all.
4 For out of much affliction and anguish of heart I wrote unto you with
many tears; not that ye should be
grieved, but that ye might know the love
which I have more abundantly unto you.
5 But if any have caused grief, he hath
not grieved me, but in part: that I may
not overcharge you all.
6 Sufficient to such a man *is* this punishment, which *was inflicted* of many.
7 So that contrariwise ye *ought* rather
to forgive *him*, and comfort *him*, lest
perhaps such a one should be swallowed
up with overmuch sorrow.
8 Wherefore I beseech you that ye
would confirm *your* love toward him.
9 For to this end also did I write, that
I might know the proof of you, whether
ye be obedient in all things.
10 To whom ye forgive any thing, I *forgive* also: for if I forgave any thing, to
whom I forgave *it*, for your sakes *forgave I it* in the person of Christ;
11 Lest Satan should get an advantage
of us: for we are not ignorant of his
devices.
12 Furthermore, when I came to
Trō′ăs to *preach* Christ's gospel, and a
door was opened unto me of the Lord,
13 I had no rest in my spirit, because I
found not Titus my brother; but taking
my leave of them, I went from thence
into Macedonia.
14 Now thanks *be* unto God, which
always causeth us to triumph in Christ,
and maketh manifest the savor of his
knowledge by us in every place.
15 For we are unto God a sweet savor
of Christ, in them that are saved, and in
them that perish:
16 To the one *we are* the savor of
death unto death; and to the other the
savor of life unto life. And who *is* sufficient for these things?
17 For we are not as many, which corrupt the word of God: but as of sincerity, but as of God, in the sight of
God speak we in Christ.

CHAPTER 3

DO we begin again to commend
ourselves? or need we, as some
others, epistles of commendation to
you, or *letters* of commendation from
you?
2 Ye are our epistle written in our
hearts, known and read of all men:
3 *Forasmuch as ye are* manifestly
declared to be the epistle of Christ
ministered by us, written not with ink,
but with the Spirit of the living God; not
in tables of stone, but in fleshly tables
of the heart.
4 And such trust have we through
Christ to God-ward:
5 Not that we are sufficient of ourselves
to think any thing as of ourselves; but
our sufficiency *is* of God;
6 Who also hath made us able ministers
of the new testament; not of the letter,
but of the spirit: for the letter killeth,
but the spirit giveth life.
7 But if the ministration of death,
written *and* engraven in stones, was
glorious, so that the children of Ĭs′rā-ĕl
could not steadfastly behold the face of
Moses for the glory of his countenance;
which *glory* was to be done away;
8 How shall not the ministration of the
spirit be rather glorious?
9 For if the ministration of condemnation *be* glory, much more doth the ministration of righteousness exceed in
glory.
10 For even that which was made
glorious had no glory in this respect, by
reason of the glory that excelleth.
11 For if that which is done away *was*
glorious, much more that which remaineth *is* glorious.
12 Seeing then that we have such hope,
we use great plainness of speech:
13 And not as Moses, *which* put a

veil over his face, that the children of
Iş′rā-ĕl could not steadfastly look to the
end of that which is abolished:
14 But their minds were blinded: for
until this day remaineth the same veil
untaken away in the reading of the old
testament; which *veil* is done away in
Christ.
15 But even unto this day, when Moses
is read, the veil is upon their heart.
16 Nevertheless, when it shall turn to
the Lord, the veil shall be taken away.
17 Now the Lord is that Spirit: and
where the Spirit of the Lord *is*, there
is liberty.
18 But we all, with open face beholding
as in a glass the glory of the Lord, are
changed into the same image from
glory to glory, *even* as by the Spirit of
the Lord.

CHAPTER 4

THEREFORE, seeing we have this
ministry, as we have received
mercy, we faint not;
2 But have renounced the hidden things
of dishonesty, not walking in craftiness,
nor handling the word of God deceitfully; but, by manifestation of the truth,
commending ourselves to every man's
conscience in the sight of God.
3 But if our gospel be hid, it is hid to
them that are lost:
4 In whom the god of this world hath
blinded the minds of them which believe not, lest the light of the glorious
gospel of Christ, who is the image of
God, should shine unto them.
5 For we preach not ourselves, but
Christ Jesus the Lord; and ourselves
your servants for Jesus' sake.
6 For God, who commanded the light
to shine out of darkness, hath shined in
our hearts, to *give* the light of the knowledge of the glory of God in the face of
Jesus Christ.
7 But we have this treasure in earthen
vessels, that the excellency of the power
may be of God, and not of us.
8 *We are* troubled on every side, yet
not distressed; *we are* perplexed, but
not in despair;
9 Persecuted, but not forsaken; cast
down, but not destroyed;
10 Always bearing about in the body
the dying of the Lord Jesus, that the
life also of Jesus might be made manifest in our body.
11 For we which live are alway delivered unto death for Jesus' sake, that
the life also of Jesus might be made
manifest in our mortal flesh.
12 So then death worketh in us, but life
in you.
13 We having the same spirit of faith,
according as it is written, I believed,
and therefore have I spoken; we also
believe, and therefore speak;
14 Knowing that he which raised up
the Lord Jesus shall raise up us also
by Jesus, and shall present *us* with
you.
15 For all things *are* for your sakes,
that the abundant grace might through
the thanksgiving of many redound to the
glory of God.
16 For which cause we faint not; but
though our outward man perish, yet the
inward *man* is renewed day by day.
17 For our light affliction, which is
but for a moment, worketh for us a far
more exceeding *and* eternal weight of
glory;
18 While we look not at the things
which are seen, but at the things which
are not seen: for the things which are
seen *are* temporal; but the things which
are not seen *are* eternal.

CHAPTER 5

FOR we know that, if our earthly
house of *this* tabernacle were dissolved, we have a building of God, a
house not made with hands, eternal in
the heavens.
2 For in this we groan, earnestly desiring to be clothed upon with our house
which is from heaven:
3 If so be that being clothed we shall
not be found naked.
4 For we that are in *this* tabernacle do
groan, being burdened: not for that we
would be unclothed, but clothed upon,
that mortality might be swallowed up of
life.
5 Now he that hath wrought us for
the selfsame thing *is* God, who also
hath given unto us the earnest of the
Spirit.
6 Therefore *we are* always confident,
knowing that, whilst we are at home in
the body, we are absent from the Lord:
7 (For we walk by faith, not by sight:)
8 We are confident, *I say*, and willing
rather to be absent from the body, and
to be present with the Lord.

9 Wherefore we labor, that, whether
present or absent, we may be accepted
of him.
10 For we must all appear before the
judgment seat of Christ; that every one
may receive the things *done* in *his* body,
according to that he hath done, whether
it be good or bad.
11 Knowing therefore the terror of the
Lord, we persuade men; but we are
made manifest unto God; and I trust
also are made manifest in your con-
sciences.
12 For we commend not ourselves
again unto you, but give you occasion to
glory on our behalf, that ye may have
somewhat to *answer* them which glory
in appearance, and not in heart.
13 For whether we be beside ourselves,
it is to God: or whether we be sober, *it
is* for your cause.
14 For the love of Christ constraineth
us; because we thus judge, that if one
died for all, then were all dead:
15 And *that* he died for all, that they
which live should not henceforth live
unto themselves, but unto him which
died for them, and rose again.
16 Wherefore henceforth know we no
man after the flesh: yea, though we have
known Christ after the flesh, yet now
henceforth know we *him* no more.
17 Therefore if any man *be* in Christ,
he is a new creature: old things are
passed away; behold, all things are become new.
18 And all things *are* of God, who hath
reconciled us to himself by Jesus Christ,
and hath given to us the ministry of
reconciliation;
19 To wit, that God was in Christ, reconciling the world unto himself, not imputing their trespasses unto them; and
hath committed unto us the word of
reconciliation.
20 Now then we are ambassadors for
Christ, as though God did beseech *you*
by us: we pray *you* in Christ's stead, be
ye reconciled to God.
21 For he hath made him *to be* sin
for us, who knew no sin; that we might
be made the righteousness of God in
him.

CHAPTER 6

WE then, *as* workers together
with him, beseech *you* also that
ye receive not the grace of God in vain.
2 (For he saith, I have heard thee in a
time accepted, and in the day of salvation have I succored thee: behold, now
is the accepted time; behold, now *is* the
day of salvation.)
3 Giving no offense in any thing, that
the ministry be not blamed:
4 But in all *things* approving ourselves
as the ministers of God, in much patience, in afflictions, in necessities, in
distresses,
5 In stripes, in imprisonments, in
tumults, in labors, in watchings, in
fastings;
6 By pureness, by knowledge, by long-
suffering, by kindness, by the Holy
Ghost, by love unfeigned,
7 By the word of truth, by the power of
God, by the armor of righteousness on
the right hand and on the left,
8 By honor and dishonor, by evil report
and good report: as deceivers, and *yet*
true;
9 As unknown, and *yet* well known; as
dying, and, behold, we live; as chastened, and not killed;
10 As sorrowful, yet alway rejoicing;
as poor, yet making many rich; as having nothing, and *yet* possessing all
things.
11 O *ye* Corinthians, our mouth is
open unto you, our heart is enlarged.
12 Ye are not straitened in us, but ye
are straitened in your own bowels.
13 Now for a recompense in the same,
(I speak as unto *my* children,) be ye also
enlarged.
14 Be ye not unequally yoked together
with unbelievers: for what fellowship
hath righteousness with unrighteousness? and what communion hath light
with darkness?
15 And what concord hath Christ with
Bē'lĭ-ăl? or what part hath he that believeth with an infidel?
16 And what agreement hath the temple of God with idols? for ye are the
temple of the living God; as God hath
said, I will dwell in them, and walk in
them; and I will be their God, and they
shall be my people.
17 Wherefore come out from among
them, and be ye separate, saith the
Lord, and touch not the unclean *thing;*
and I will receive you,
18 And will be a Father unto you, and
ye shall be my sons and daughters, saith
the Lord Almighty.

CHAPTER 7

HAVING therefore these promises,
dearly beloved, let us cleanse
ourselves from all filthiness of the flesh
and spirit, perfecting holiness in the
fear of God.
2 Receive us; we have wronged no man,
we have corrupted no man, we have defrauded no man.
3 I speak not *this* to condemn *you:* for
I have said before, that ye are in our
hearts to die and live with *you.*
4 Great *is* my boldness of speech
toward you, great *is* my glorying of you:
I am filled with comfort, I am exceeding
joyful in all our tribulation.
5 For, when we were come into Macedonia, our flesh had no rest, but we
were troubled on every side; without
were fightings, within *were* fears.
6 Nevertheless God, that comforteth
those that are cast down, comforted us
by the coming of Titus;
7 And not by his coming only, but by
the consolation wherewith he was comforted in you, when he told us your earnest desire, your mourning, your fervent
mind toward me; so that I rejoiced the
more.
8 For though I made you sorry with a
letter, I do not repent, though I did repent: for I perceive that the same epistle hath made you sorry, though *it were*
but for a season.
9 Now I rejoice, not that ye were made
sorry, but that ye sorrowed to repentance: for ye were made sorry after a
godly manner, that ye might receive
damage by us in nothing.
10 For godly sorrow worketh repentance to salvation not to be repented of:
but the sorrow of the world worketh
death.
11 For behold this selfsame thing, that
ye sorrowed after a godly sort, what
carefulness it wrought in you, yea, *what*
clearing of yourselves, yea, *what* indignation, yea, *what* fear, yea, *what* vehement desire, yea, *what* zeal, yea, *what*
revenge! In all *things* ye have approved
yourselves to be clear in this matter.
12 Wherefore, though I wrote unto you,
I did it not for his cause that had done
the wrong, nor for his cause that suffered wrong, but that our care for you in
the sight of God might appear unto you.
13 Therefore we were comforted in
your comfort: yea, and exceedingly the
more joyed we for the joy of Titus, because his spirit was refreshed by you all.
14 For if I have boasted any thing to
him of you, I am not ashamed; but as we
spake all things to you in truth, even so
our boasting, which *I made* before Titus,
is found a truth.
15 And his inward affection is more
abundant toward you, whilst he remembereth the obedience of you all, how
with fear and trembling ye received him.
16 I rejoice therefore that I have confidence in you in all *things.*

CHAPTER 8

MOREOVER, brethren, we do you
to wit of the grace of God bestowed on the churches of Macedonia;
2 How that in a great trial of affliction,
the abundance of their joy and their
deep poverty abounded unto the riches
of their liberality.
3 For to *their* power, I bear record, yea,
and beyond *their* power *they were* willing of themselves;
4 Praying us with much entreaty that
we would receive the gift, and *take upon*
us the fellowship of the ministering to
the saints.
5 And *this they did,* not as we hoped,
but first gave their own selves to the
Lord, and unto us by the will of God.
6 Insomuch that we desired Titus, that
as he had begun, so he would also finish
in you the same grace also.
7 Therefore, as ye abound in every
thing, in faith, and utterance, and
knowledge, and *in* all diligence, and *in*
your love to us, *see* that ye abound in
this grace also.
8 I speak not by commandment, but by
occasion of the forwardness of others,
and to prove the sincerity of your love.
9 For ye know the grace of our Lord
Jesus Christ, that, though he was rich,
yet for your sakes he became poor, that
ye through his poverty might be rich.
10 And herein I give *my* advice: for
this is expedient for you, who have begun before, not only to do, but also to be
forward a year ago.
11 Now therefore perform the doing *of*
it; that as *there was* a readiness to will,
so *there may be* a performance also out
of that which ye have.
12 For if there be first a willing mind,
it is accepted according to that a man

hath, *and* not according to that he hath not.

13 For *I mean* not that other men be eased, and ye burdened:

14 But by an equality, *that* now at this time your abundance *may be a supply* for their want, that their abundance also may be *a supply* for your want; that there may be equality:

15 As it is written, He that *had gathered* much had nothing over; and he that *had gathered* little had no lack.

16 But thanks *be* to God, which put the same earnest care into the heart of Titus for you.

17 For indeed he accepted the exhortation; but being more forward, of his own accord he went unto you.

18 And we have sent with him the brother, whose praise *is* in the gospel throughout all the churches;

19 And not *that* only, but who was also chosen of the churches to travel with us with this grace, which is administered by us to the glory of the same Lord, and *declaration of* your ready mind:

20 Avoiding this, that no man should blame us in this abundance which is administered by us:

21 Providing for honest things, not only in the sight of the Lord, but also in the sight of men.

22 And we have sent with them our brother, whom we have oftentimes proved diligent in many things, but now much more diligent, upon the great confidence which *I have* in you.

23 Whether *any do inquire* of Titus, *he is* my partner and fellow helper concerning you: or our brethren *be inquired of, they are* the messengers of the churches, *and* the glory of Christ.

24 Wherefore show ye to them, and before the churches, the proof of your love, and of our boasting on your behalf.

CHAPTER 9

FOR as touching the ministering to the saints, it is superfluous for me to write to you:

2 For I know the forwardness of your mind, for which I boast of you to them of Macedonia, that Ȧ-chā′ịȧ was ready a year ago; and your zeal hath provoked very many.

3 Yet have I sent the brethren, lest our boasting of you should be in vain in this behalf; that, as I said, ye may be ready:

4 Lest haply if they of Macedonia come with me, and find you unprepared, we (that we say not, ye) should be ashamed in this same confident boasting.

5 Therefore I thought it necessary to exhort the brethren, that they would go before unto you, and make up beforehand your bounty, whereof ye had notice before, that the same might be ready, as *a matter of* bounty, and not as *of* covetousness.

6 But this *I say,* He which soweth sparingly shall reap also sparingly; and he which soweth bountifully shall reap also bountifully.

7 Every man according as he purposeth in his heart, *so let him give;* not grudgingly, or of necessity: for God loveth a cheerful giver.

8 And God *is* able to make all grace abound toward you; that ye, always having all sufficiency in all *things,* may abound to every good work:

9 (As it is written, He hath dispersed abroad; he hath given to the poor: his righteousness remaineth for ever.

10 Now he that ministereth seed to the sower both minister bread for *your* food, and multiply your seed sown, and increase the fruits of your righteousness:)

11 Being enriched in every thing to all bountifulness, which causeth through us thanksgiving to God.

12 For the administration of this service not only supplieth the want of the saints, but is abundant also by many thanksgivings unto God;

13 While by the experiment of this ministration they glorify God for your professed subjection unto the gospel of Christ, and for *your* liberal distribution unto them, and unto all *men;*

14 And by their prayer for you, which long after you for the exceeding grace of God in you.

15 Thanks *be* unto God for his unspeakable gift.

CHAPTER 10

NOW I Paul myself beseech you by the meekness and gentleness of Christ, who in presence *am* base among you, but being absent bold toward you:

2 But I beseech *you,* that I may not be bold when I am present with that confidence, wherewith I think to be bold

against some, which think of us as if we
walked according to the flesh.
3 For though we walk in the flesh, we
do not war after the flesh:
4 (For the weapons of our warfare *are*
not carnal, but mighty through God to
the pulling down of strongholds;)
5 Casting down imaginations, and every
high thing that exalteth itself against
the knowledge of God, and bringing into
captivity every thought to the obedience
of Christ;
6 And having in a readiness to revenge
all disobedience, when your obedience
is fulfilled.
7 Do ye look on things after the outward appearance? If any man trust to
himself that he is Christ's, let him of
himself think this again, that, as he *is*
Christ's, even so *are* we Christ's.
8 For though I should boast somewhat
more of our authority, which the Lord
hath given us for edification, and not
for your destruction, I should not be
ashamed:
9 That I may not seem as if I would
terrify you by letters.
10 For *his* letters, say they, *are* weighty
and powerful; but *his* bodily presence
is weak, and *his* speech contemptible.
11 Let such a one think this, that, such
as we are in word by letters when we
are absent, such *will we be* also in deed
when we are present.
12 For we dare not make ourselves of
the number, or compare ourselves with
some that commend themselves: but
they, measuring themselves by themselves, and comparing themselves
among themselves, are not wise.
13 But we will not boast of things without *our* measure, but according to the
measure of the rule which God hath distributed to us, a measure to reach even
unto you.
14 For we stretch not ourselves beyond
our measure, as though we reached not
unto you; for we are come as far as to you
also in *preaching* the gospel of Christ:
15 Not boasting of things without *our*
measure, *that is,* of other men's labors;
but having hope, when your faith is increased, that we shall be enlarged by
you according to our rule abundantly,
16 To preach the gospel in the *regions*
beyond you, *and* not to boast in another
man's line of things made ready to our
hand.
17 But he that glorieth, let him glory in
the Lord.
18 For not he that commendeth himself is approved, but whom the Lord
commendeth.

CHAPTER 11

WOULD to God ye could bear with
me a little in *my* folly: and indeed
bear with me.
2 For I am jealous over you with godly
jealousy: for I have espoused you to one
husband, that I may present *you as* a
chaste virgin to Christ.
3 But I fear, lest by any means, as the
serpent beguiled Eve through his subtilty, so your minds should be corrupted
from the simplicity that is in Christ.
4 For if he that cometh preacheth
another Jesus, whom we have not
preached, or *if* ye receive another spirit,
which ye have not received, or another
gospel, which ye have not accepted, ye
might well bear with *him.*
5 For I suppose I was not a whit behind the very chiefest apostles.
6 But though *I be* rude in speech, yet
not in knowledge; but we have been
thoroughly made manifest among you
in all things.
7 Have I committed an offense in abas-
ing myself that ye might be exalted, because I have preached to you the gospel
of God freely?
8 I robbed other churches, taking
wages *of them,* to do you service.
9 And when I was present with you,
and wanted, I was chargeable to no man:
for that which was lacking to me the
brethren which came from Macedonia
supplied: and in all *things* I have kept
myself from being burdensome unto
you, and *so* will I keep *myself.*
10 As the truth of Christ is in me, no
man shall stop me of this boasting in the
regions of A-chā'ịȧ.
11 Wherefore? because I love you not?
God knoweth.
12 But what I do, that I will do, that I
may cut off occasion from them which
desire occasion; that wherein they
glory, they may be found even as we.
13 For such *are* false apostles, deceitful
workers, transforming themselves into
the apostles of Christ.
14 And no marvel; for Satan himself is
transformed into an angel of light.
15 Therefore *it is* no great thing if his

ministers also be transformed as the ministers of righteousness; whose end shall be according to their works.
16 I say again, Let no man think me a fool; if otherwise, yet as a fool receive me, that I may boast myself a little.
17 That which I speak, I speak *it* not after the Lord, but as it were foolishly, in this confidence of boasting.
18 Seeing that many glory after the flesh, I will glory also.
19 For ye suffer fools gladly, seeing ye *yourselves* are wise.
20 For ye suffer, if a man bring you into bondage, if a man devour *you*, if a man take *of you*, if a man exalt himself, if a man smite you on the face.
21 I speak as concerning reproach, as though we had been weak. Howbeit, whereinsoever any is bold, (I speak foolishly,) I am bold also.
22 Are they Hebrews? so *am* I. Are they Iṣ′rā-ĕl-ītes? so *am* I. Are they the seed of Abraham? so *am* I.
23 Are they ministers of Christ? (I speak as a fool,) I *am* more; in labors more abundant, in stripes above measure, in prisons more frequent, in deaths oft.
24 Of the Jews five times received I forty *stripes* save one.
25 Thrice was I beaten with rods, once was I stoned, thrice I suffered shipwreck, a night and a day I have been in the deep;
26 *In* journeyings often, *in* perils of waters, *in* perils of robbers, *in* perils by *mine own* countrymen, *in* perils by the heathen, *in* perils in the city, *in* perils in the wilderness, *in* perils in the sea, *in* perils among false brethren;
27 In weariness and painfulness, in watchings often, in hunger and thirst, in fastings often, in cold and nakedness.
28 Beside those things that are without, that which cometh upon me daily, the care of all the churches.
29 Who is weak, and I am not weak? who is offended, and I burn not?
30 If I must needs glory, I will glory of the things which concern mine infirmities.
31 The God and Father of our Lord Jesus Christ, which is blessed for evermore, knoweth that I lie not.
32 In Damascus the governor under Ăr′ē-tăs the king kept the city of the Dăm′á-sçēneṣ with a garrison, desirous to apprehend me:
33 And through a window in a basket was I let down by the wall, and escaped his hands.

CHAPTER 12

It is not expedient for me doubtless to glory. I will come to visions and revelations of the Lord.
2 I knew a man in Christ above fourteen years ago, (whether in the body, I cannot tell; or whether out of the body, I cannot tell: God knoweth;) such a one caught up to the third heaven.
3 And I knew such a man, (whether in the body, or out of the body, I cannot tell: God knoweth;)
4 How that he was caught up into paradise, and heard unspeakable words, which it is not lawful for a man to utter.
5 Of such a one will I glory: yet of myself I will not glory, but in mine infirmities.
6 For though I would desire to glory, I shall not be a fool; for I will say the truth: but *now* I forbear, lest any man should think of me above that which he seeth me *to be*, or *that* he heareth of me.
7 And lest I should be exalted above measure through the abundance of the revelations, there was given to me a thorn in the flesh, the messenger of Satan to buffet me, lest I should be exalted above measure.
8 For this thing I besought the Lord thrice, that it might depart from me.
9 And he said unto me, My grace is sufficient for thee: for my strength is made perfect in weakness. Most gladly therefore will I rather glory in my infirmities, that the power of Christ may rest upon me.
10 Therefore I take pleasure in infirmities, in reproaches, in necessities, in persecutions, in distresses for Christ's sake: for when I am weak, then am I strong.
11 I am become a fool in glorying; ye have compelled me: for I ought to have been commended of you: for in nothing am I behind the very chiefest apostles, though I be nothing.
12 Truly the signs of an apostle were wrought among you in all patience, in signs, and wonders, and mighty deeds.
13 For what is it wherein ye were inferior to other churches, except *it be*

that I myself was not burdensome to
you? forgive me this wrong.
14 Behold, the third time I am ready to
come to you; and I will not be burdensome to you: for I seek not yours, but
you: for the children ought not to lay up
for the parents, but the parents for the
children.
15 And I will very gladly spend and be
spent for you; though the more abundantly I love you, the less I be loved.
16 But be it so, I did not burden you:
nevertheless, being crafty, I caught you
with guile.
17 Did I make a gain of you by any of
them whom I sent unto you?
18 I desired Titus, and with *him* I sent
a brother. Did Titus make a gain of
you? walked we not in the same spirit?
walked we not in the same steps?
19 Again, think ye that we excuse ourselves unto you? we speak before God
in Christ: but *we do* all things, dearly
beloved, for your edifying.
20 For I fear, lest, when I come, I shall
not find you such as I would, and *that* I
shall be found unto you such as ye would
not: lest *there be* debates, envyings,
wraths, strifes, backbitings, whisper-
ings, swellings, tumults:
21 *And* lest, when I come again, my
God will humble me among you, and
that I shall bewail many which have
sinned already, and have not repented
of the uncleanness and fornication and
lasciviousness which they have committed.

CHAPTER 13

THIS *is* the third *time* I am coming
to you. In the mouth of two or
three witnesses shall every word be
established.
2 I told you before, and foretell you, as
if I were present, the second time; and
being absent now I write to them which
heretofore have sinned, and to all other,
that, if I come again, I will not spare:
3 Since ye seek a proof of Christ speaking in me, which to you-ward is not
weak, but is mighty in you.
4 For though he was crucified through
weakness, yet he liveth by the power of
God. For we also are weak in him, but
we shall live with him by the power of
God toward you.
5 Examine yourselves, whether ye be
in the faith; prove your own selves.
Know ye not your own selves, how that
Jesus Christ is in you, except ye be
reprobates?
6 But I trust that ye shall know that we
are not reprobates.
7 Now I pray to God that ye do no evil;
not that we should appear approved, but
that ye should do that which is honest,
though we be as reprobates.
8 For we can do nothing against the
truth, but for the truth.
9 For we are glad, when we are weak,
and ye are strong: and this also we wish,
even your perfection.
10 Therefore I write these things being
absent, lest being present I should use
sharpness, according to the power which
the Lord hath given me to edification,
and not to destruction.
11 Finally, brethren, farewell. Be perfect, be of good comfort, be of one mind,
live in peace; and the God of love and
peace shall be with you.
12 Greet one another with a holy kiss.
13 All the saints salute you.
14 The grace of the Lord Jesus Christ,
and the love of God, and the communion
of the Holy Ghost, *be* with you all.
Amen.

¶ The second *epistle* to the Corinthians was written from Philippi, *a city* of Macedonia, by Titus and Lucas.

THE EPISTLE OF PAUL THE APOSTLE TO THE

GALATIANS

CHAPTER 1

PAUL, an apostle, (not of men, neither by man, but by Jesus Christ, and God the Father, who raised him from the dead;)

2 And all the brethren which are with me, unto the churches of Gȧ-lā′ṭĭ-ȧ:

3 Grace *be* to you, and peace, from God the Father, and *from* our Lord Jesus Christ,

4 Who gave himself for our sins, that he might deliver us from this present evil world, according to the will of God and our Father:

5 To whom *be* glory for ever and ever. Amen.

6 I marvel that ye are so soon removed from him that called you into the grace of Christ unto another gospel:

7 Which is not another; but there be some that trouble you, and would pervert the gospel of Christ.

8 But though we, or an angel from heaven, preach any other gospel unto you than that which we have preached unto you, let him be accursed.

9 As we said before, so say I now again, If any *man* preach any other gospel unto you than that ye have received, let him be accursed.

10 For do I now persuade men, or God? or do I seek to please men? for if I yet pleased men, I should not be the servant of Christ.

11 But I certify you, brethren, that the gospel which was preached of me is not after man.

12 For I neither received it of man, neither was I taught *it*, but by the revelation of Jesus Christ.

13 For ye have heard of my conversation in time past in the Jews' religion, how that beyond measure I persecuted the church of God, and wasted it:

14 And profited in the Jews' religion above many my equals in mine own nation, being more exceedingly zealous of the traditions of my fathers.

15 But when it pleased God, who separated me from my mother's womb, and called *me* by his grace,

16 To reveal his Son in me, that I might preach him among the heathen; immediately I conferred not with flesh and blood:

17 Neither went I up to Jerusalem to them which were apostles before me; but I went into Arabia, and returned again unto Damascus.

18 Then after three years I went up to Jerusalem to see Peter, and abode with him fifteen days.

19 But other of the apostles saw I none, save James the Lord's brother.

20 Now the things which I write unto you, behold, before God, I lie not.

21 Afterward I came into the regions of Syria and Çĭ-lĭ′çĭ-ȧ;

22 And was unknown by face unto the churches of Judea which were in Christ:

23 But they had heard only, That he which persecuted us in times past now preacheth the faith which once he destroyed.

24 And they glorified God in me.

CHAPTER 2

THEN fourteen years after I went up again to Jerusalem with Barnabas, and took Titus with *me* also.

2 And I went up by revelation, and communicated unto them that gospel which I preach among the Ġĕn′tīleş, but privately to them which were of reputation, lest by any means I should run, or had run, in vain.

3 But neither Titus, who was with me, being a Greek, was compelled to be circumcised:

4 And that because of false brethren unawares brought in, who came in privily to spy out our liberty which we have in Christ Jesus, that they might bring us into bondage:

5 To whom we gave place by subjection, no, not for an hour; that the truth of the gospel might continue with you.

6 But of those who seemed to be somewhat, (whatsoever they were, it maketh no matter to me: God accepteth no man's person:) for they who seemed *to be somewhat* in conference added nothing to me:

7 But contrariwise, when they saw that
the gospel of the uncircumcision was
committed unto me, as *the gospel* of the
circumcision *was* unto Peter;
8 (For he that wrought effectually in
Peter to the apostleship of the circumcision, the same was mighty in me toward the Ġĕn'tīleṣ;)
9 And when James, Çē'phăs, and John,
who seemed to be pillars, perceived the
grace that was given unto me, they gave
to me and Barnabas the right hands of
fellowship; that we *should go* unto the
heathen, and they unto the circumcision.
10 Only *they would* that we should
remember the poor; the same which I
also was forward to do.
11 But when Peter was come to Ăn'-
tĭ-ŏch, I withstood him to the face, because he was to be blamed.
12 For before that certain came from
James, he did eat with the Ġĕn'tīleṣ:
but when they were come, he withdrew
and separated himself, fearing them
which were of the circumcision.
13 And the other Jews dissembled likewise with him; insomuch that Barnabas
also was carried away with their dissimulation.
14 But when I saw that they walked
not uprightly according to the truth of
the gospel, I said unto Peter before
them all, If thou, being a Jew, livest
after the manner of Ġĕn'tīleṣ, and not
as do the Jews, why compellest thou the
Ġĕn'tīleṣ to live as do the Jews?
15 We *who are* Jews by nature, and
not sinners of the Ġĕn'tīleṣ,
16 Knowing that a man is not justified
by the works of the law, but by the faith
of Jesus Christ, even we have believed
in Jesus Christ, that we might be justified by the faith of Christ, and not by the
works of the law: for by the works of the
law shall no flesh be justified.
17 But if, while we seek to be justified
by Christ, we ourselves also are found
sinners, *is* therefore Christ the minister
of sin? God forbid.
18 For if I build again the things which
I destroyed, I make myself a transgressor.
19 For I through the law am dead to
the law, that I might live unto God.
20 I am crucified with Christ: nevertheless I live; yet not I, but Christ liveth in
me: and the life which I now live in the
flesh I live by the faith of the Son of God,
who loved me, and gave himself for me.
21 I do not frustrate the grace of God:
for if righteousness *come* by the law,
then Christ is dead in vain.

CHAPTER 3

O FOOLISH Gă-lā'tiănṣ, who hath
bewitched you, that ye should not
obey the truth, before whose eyes Jesus
Christ hath been evidently set forth,
crucified among you?
2 This only would I learn of you, Received ye the Spirit by the works of the
law, or by the hearing of faith?
3 Are ye so foolish? having begun in the
Spirit, are ye now made perfect by the
flesh?
4 Have ye suffered so many things in
vain? if *it be* yet in vain.
5 He therefore that ministereth to you
the Spirit, and worketh miracles among
you, *doeth he it* by the works of the law,
or by the hearing of faith?
6 Even as Abraham believed God, and it
was accounted to him for righteousness.
7 Know ye therefore that they which
are of faith, the same are the children of
Abraham.
8 And the Scripture, foreseeing that
God would justify the heathen through
faith, preached before the gospel unto
Abraham, *saying*, In thee shall all nations be blessed.
9 So then they which be of faith are
blessed with faithful Abraham.
10 For as many as are of the works of
the law are under the curse: for it is
written, Cursed *is* every one that continueth not in all things which are written in the book of the law to do them.
11 But that no man is justified by the
law in the sight of God, *it is* evident: for,
The just shall live by faith.
12 And the law is not of faith: but, The
man that doeth them shall live in them.
13 Christ hath redeemed us from the
curse of the law, being made a curse for
us: for it is written, Cursed *is* every one
that hangeth on a tree:
14 That the blessing of Abraham might
come on the Ġĕn'tīleṣ through Jesus
Christ; that we might receive the promise of the Spirit through faith.
15 Brethren, I speak after the manner
of men; Though *it be* but a man's covenant, yet *if it be* confirmed, no man dis-
annulleth, or addeth thereto.
16 Now to Abraham and his seed were

the promises made. He saith not, And
to seeds, as of many; but as of one, And
to thy seed, which is Christ.
17 And this I say, *that* the covenant,
that was confirmed before of God in
Christ, the law, which was four hundred
and thirty years after, cannot disannul,
that it should make the promise of none
effect.
18 For if the inheritance *be* of the law,
it is no more of promise: but God gave
it to Abraham by promise.
19 Wherefore then *serveth* the law?
It was added because of transgressions,
till the seed should come to whom the
promise was made; *and it was* ordained
by angels in the hand of a mediator.
20 Now a mediator is not *a mediator* of
one, but God is one.
21 *Is* the law then against the promises
of God? God forbid: for if there had
been a law given which could have given
life, verily righteousness should have
been by the law.
22 But the Scripture hath concluded
all under sin, that the promise by faith
of Jesus Christ might be given to them
that believe.
23 But before faith came, we were kept
under the law, shut up unto the faith
which should afterward be revealed.
24 Wherefore the law was our schoolmaster *to bring us* unto Christ, that we
might be justified by faith.
25 But after that faith is come, we are
no longer under a schoolmaster.
26 For ye are all the children of God by
faith in Christ Jesus.
27 For as many of you as have been
baptized into Christ have put on Christ.
28 There is neither Jew nor Greek,
there is neither bond nor free, there is
neither male nor female: for ye are all
one in Christ Jesus.
29 And if ye *be* Christ's, then are ye
Abraham's seed, and heirs according to
the promise.

CHAPTER 4

NOW I say, *That* the heir, as long
as he is a child, differeth nothing
from a servant, though he be lord of all;
2 But is under tutors and governors
until the time appointed of the father.
3 Even so we, when we were children,
were in bondage under the elements of
the world:
4 But when the fulness of the time was
come, God sent forth his Son, made of
a woman, made under the law,
5 To redeem them that were under the
law, that we might receive the adoption
of sons.
6 And because ye are sons, God hath
sent forth the Spirit of his Son into your
hearts, crying, Abba, Father.
7 Wherefore thou art no more a servant, but a son; and if a son, then an heir
of God through Christ.
8 Howbeit then, when ye knew not
God, ye did service unto them which by
nature are no gods.
9 But now, after that ye have known
God, or rather are known of God, how
turn ye again to the weak and beggarly
elements, whereunto ye desire again to
be in bondage?
10 Ye observe days, and months, and
times, and years.
11 I am afraid of you, lest I have bestowed upon you labor in vain.
12 Brethren, I beseech you, be as I *am;*
for I *am* as ye *are*: ye have not injured
me at all.
13 Ye know how through infirmity of
the flesh I preached the gospel unto you
at the first.
14 And my temptation which was in
my flesh ye despised not, nor rejected;
but received me as an angel of God,
even as Christ Jesus.
15 Where is then the blessedness ye
spake of? for I bear you record, that, if
it had been possible, ye would have
plucked out your own eyes, and have
given them to me.
16 Am I therefore become your enemy,
because I tell you the truth?
17 They zealously affect you, *but* not
well; yea, they would exclude you, that
ye might affect them.
18 But *it is* good to be zealously affected
always in *a* good *thing*, and not only
when I am present with you.
19 My little children, of whom I travail
in birth again until Christ be formed in
you,
20 I desire to be present with you now,
and to change my voice; for I stand in
doubt of you.
21 Tell me, ye that desire to be under
the law, do ye not hear the law?
22 For it is written, that Abraham had
two sons, the one by a bondmaid, the
other by a free woman.
23 But he *who was* of the bondwoman

was born after the flesh; but he of the
free woman *was* by promise.
24 Which things are an allegory: for
these are the two covenants; the one
from the mount Sī′naī, which gendereth
to bondage, which is Ā′gär.
25 For this Ā′gär is mount Sī′naī in
Arabia, and answereth to Jerusalem
which now is, and is in bondage with her
children.
26 But Jerusalem which is above is
free, which is the mother of us all.
27 For it is written, Rejoice, thou
barren that bearest not; break forth and
cry, thou that travailest not: for the
desolate hath many more children than
she which hath a husband.
28 Now we, brethren, as Isaac was, are
the children of promise.
29 But as then he that was born after
the flesh persecuted him *that was born*
after the Spirit, even so *it is* now.
30 Nevertheless what saith the Scripture? Cast out the bondwoman and her
son: for the son of the bondwoman shall
not be heir with the son of the free
woman.
31 So then, brethren, we are not children of the bondwoman, but of the free.

CHAPTER 5

STAND fast therefore in the liberty
wherewith Christ hath made us free,
and be not entangled again with the
yoke of bondage.
2 Behold, I Paul say unto you, that if
ye be circumcised, Christ shall profit
you nothing.
3 For I testify again to every man that
is circumcised, that he is a debtor to do
the whole law.
4 Christ is become of no effect unto
you, whosoever of you are justified by
the law; ye are fallen from grace.
5 For we through the Spirit wait for the
hope of righteousness by faith.
6 For in Jesus Christ neither circumcision availeth any thing, nor uncircumcision; but faith which worketh by
love.
7 Ye did run well; who did hinder you
that ye should not obey the truth?
8 This persuasion *cometh* not of him
that calleth you.
9 A little leaven leaveneth the whole
lump.
10 I have confidence in you through the
Lord, that ye will be none otherwise
minded: but he that troubleth you shall
bear his judgment, whosoever he be.
11 And I, brethren, if I yet preach circumcision, why do I yet suffer persecution? then is the offense of the cross
ceased.
12 I would they were even cut off which
trouble you.
13 For, brethren, ye have been called
unto liberty; only *use* not liberty for an
occasion to the flesh, but by love serve
one another.
14 For all the law is fulfilled in one
word, *even* in this; Thou shalt love thy
neighbor as thyself.
15 But if ye bite and devour one another, take heed that ye be not consumed one of another.
16 *This* I say then, Walk in the Spirit,
and ye shall not fulfil the lust of the flesh.
17 For the flesh lusteth against the
Spirit, and the Spirit against the flesh:
and these are contrary the one to the
other; so that ye cannot do the things
that ye would.
18 But if ye be led of the Spirit, ye are
not under the law.
19 Now the works of the flesh are
manifest, which are *these,* Adultery,
fornication, uncleanness, lasciviousness,
20 Idolatry, witchcraft, hatred, vari-
ance, emulations, wrath, strife, sedi-
tions, heresies,
21 Envyings, murders, drunkenness,
revelings, and such like: of the which I
tell you before, as I have also told *you* in
time past, that they which do such things
shall not inherit the kingdom of God.
22 But the fruit of the Spirit is love,
joy, peace, long-suffering, gentleness,
goodness, faith,
23 Meekness, temperance: against
such there is no law.
24 And they that are Christ's have crucified the flesh with the affections and
lusts.
25 If we live in the Spirit, let us also
walk in the Spirit.
26 Let us not be desirous of vainglory,
provoking one another, envying one
another.

CHAPTER 6

BRETHREN, if a man be overtaken
in a fault, ye which are spiritual,
restore such a one in the spirit of meekness; considering thyself, lest thou also
be tempted.

2 Bear ye one another's burdens, and so fulfil the law of Christ.
3 For if a man think himself to be something, when he is nothing, he deceiveth himself.
4 But let every man prove his own work, and then shall he have rejoicing in himself alone, and not in another.
5 For every man shall bear his own burden.
6 Let him that is taught in the word communicate unto him that teacheth in all good things.
7 Be not deceived; God is not mocked: for whatsoever a man soweth, that shall he also reap.
8 For he that soweth to his flesh shall of the flesh reap corruption; but he that soweth to the Spirit shall of the Spirit reap life everlasting.
9 And let us not be weary in well doing: for in due season we shall reap, if we faint not.
10 As we have therefore opportunity, let us do good unto all *men*, especially unto them who are of the household of faith.
11 Ye see how large a letter I have written unto you with mine own hand.
12 As many as desire to make a fair show in the flesh, they constrain you to be circumcised; only lest they should suffer persecution for the cross of Christ.
13 For neither they themselves who are circumcised keep the law; but desire to have you circumcised, that they may glory in your flesh.
14 But God forbid that I should glory, save in the cross of our Lord Jesus Christ, by whom the world is crucified unto me, and I unto the world.
15 For in Christ Jesus neither circumcision availeth any thing, nor uncircumcision, but a new creature.
16 And as many as walk according to this rule, peace *be* on them, and mercy, and upon the Ĭs′rā-ĕl of God.
17 From henceforth let no man trouble me: for I bear in my body the marks of the Lord Jesus.
18 Brethren, the grace of our Lord Jesus Christ *be* with your spirit. Amen.
¶ Unto the Galatians written from Rome.

THE EPISTLE OF PAUL THE APOSTLE TO THE

EPHESIANS

CHAPTER 1

PAUL, an apostle of Jesus Christ by the will of God, to the saints which are at Ĕph′ē-sŭs, and to the faithful in Christ Jesus:
2 Grace *be* to you, and peace, from God our Father, and *from* the Lord Jesus Christ.
3 Blessed *be* the God and Father of our Lord Jesus Christ, who hath blessed us with all spiritual blessings in heavenly *places* in Christ:
4 According as he hath chosen us in him before the foundation of the world, that we should be holy and without blame before him in love:
5 Having predestinated us unto the adoption of children by Jesus Christ to himself, according to the good pleasure of his will,
6 To the praise of the glory of his grace, wherein he hath made us accepted in the beloved:
7 In whom we have redemption through his blood, the forgiveness of sins, according to the riches of his grace;
8 Wherein he hath abounded toward us in all wisdom and prudence;
9 Having made known unto us the mystery of his will, according to his good pleasure which he hath purposed in himself:
10 That in the dispensation of the fulness of times he might gather together in one all things in Christ, both which are in heaven, and which are on earth; *even* in him:
11 In whom also we have obtained an inheritance, being predestinated according to the purpose of him who worketh all things after the counsel of his own will:
12 That we should be to the praise of his glory, who first trusted in Christ.
13 In whom ye also *trusted*, after that ye heard the word of truth, the gospel of your salvation: in whom also, after that

ye believed, ye were sealed with that
Holy Spirit of promise,
14 Which is the earnest of our inheritance until the redemption of the purchased possession, unto the praise of
his glory.
15 Wherefore I also, after I heard of
your faith in the Lord Jesus, and love
unto all the saints,
16 Cease not to give thanks for you,
making mention of you in my prayers;
17 That the God of our Lord Jesus
Christ, the Father of glory, may give
unto you the spirit of wisdom and revelation in the knowledge of him:
18 The eyes of your understanding being enlightened; that ye may know what
is the hope of his calling, and what the
riches of the glory of his inheritance in
the saints,
19 And what *is* the exceeding greatness
of his power to us-ward who believe,
according to the working of his mighty
power,
20 Which he wrought in Christ, when
he raised him from the dead, and set
him at his own right hand in the
heavenly *places,*
21 Far above all principality, and
power, and might, and dominion, and
every name that is named, not only in
this world, but also in that which is to
come:
22 And hath put all *things* under his
feet, and gave him *to be* the head over
all *things* to the church,
23 Which is his body, the fulness of
him that filleth all in all.

CHAPTER 2

AND you *hath he quickened,* who
were dead in trespasses and sins;
2 Wherein in time past ye walked according to the course of this world,
according to the prince of the power
of the air, the spirit that now worketh
in the children of disobedience:
3 Among whom also we all had our conversation in times past in the lusts of
our flesh, fulfilling the desires of the
flesh and of the mind; and were by nature the children of wrath, even as
others.
4 But God, who is rich in mercy, for his
great love wherewith he loved us,
5 Even when we were dead in sins,
hath quickened us together with Christ,
(by grace ye are saved;)
6 And hath raised *us* up together, and
made *us* sit together in heavenly *places*
in Christ Jesus:
7 That in the ages to come he might
show the exceeding riches of his grace,
in *his* kindness toward us, through
Christ Jesus.
8 For by grace are ye saved through
faith; and that not of yourselves: *it is*
the gift of God:
9 Not of works, lest any man should
boast.
10 For we are his workmanship,
created in Christ Jesus unto good works,
which God hath before ordained that
we should walk in them.
11 Wherefore remember, that ye *being*
in time past Gĕn'tīles̤ in the flesh, who
are called Uncircumcision by that which
is called the Circumcision in the flesh
made by hands;
12 That at that time ye were without Christ, being aliens from the com-
monwealth of Ĭs̤'rā-ĕl, and strangers
from the covenants of promise, having no hope, and without God in the
world:
13 But now, in Christ Jesus, ye who
sometime were far off are made nigh by
the blood of Christ.
14 For he is our peace, who hath
made both one, and hath broken down
the middle wall of partition *between*
us;
15 Having abolished in his flesh the enmity, *even* the law of commandments
contained in ordinances; for to make in
himself of twain one new man, *so* making peace;
16 And that he might reconcile both
unto God in one body by the cross, having slain the enmity thereby:
17 And came and preached peace to
you which were afar off, and to them
that were nigh.
18 For through him we both have access by one Spirit unto the Father.
19 Now therefore ye are no more
strangers and foreigners, but fellow citizens with the saints, and of the household of God;
20 And are built upon the foundation
of the apostles and prophets, Jesus
Christ himself being the chief corner
stone;
21 In whom all the building fitly framed
together groweth unto a holy temple in
the Lord:

22 In whom ye also are builded together for a habitation of God through
the Spirit.

CHAPTER 3

FOR this cause I Paul, the prisoner
of Jesus Christ for you Ġĕn'tīleș,
2 If ye have heard of the dispensation
of the grace of God which is given me to
you-ward:
3 How that by revelation he made
known unto me the mystery; (as I wrote
afore in few words;
4 Whereby, when ye read, ye may understand my knowledge in the mystery
of Christ,)
5 Which in other ages was not made
known unto the sons of men, as it is now
revealed unto his holy apostles and
prophets by the Spirit;
6 That the Ġĕn'tīleș should be fellow
heirs, and of the same body, and partakers of his promise in Christ by the
gospel:
7 Whereof I was made a minister, according to the gift of the grace of God
given unto me by the effectual working
of his power.
8 Unto me, who am less than the least
of all saints, is this grace given, that
I should preach among the Ġĕn'tīleș
the unsearchable riches of Christ;
9 And to make all *men* see what *is* the
fellowship of the mystery, which from
the beginning of the world hath been hid
in God, who created all things by Jesus
Christ:
10 To the intent that now unto the
principalities and powers in heavenly
places might be known by the church
the manifold wisdom of God,
11 According to the eternal purpose
which he purposed in Christ Jesus our
Lord:
12 In whom we have boldness and access with confidence by the faith of him.
13 Wherefore I desire that ye faint not
at my tribulations for you, which is your
glory.
14 For this cause I bow my knees unto
the Father of our Lord Jesus Christ,
15 Of whom the whole family in heaven
and earth is named,
16 That he would grant you, according
to the riches of his glory, to be strengthened with might by his Spirit in the
inner man;
17 That Christ may dwell in your hearts
by faith; that ye, being rooted and
grounded in love,
18 May be able to comprehend with all
saints what *is* the breadth, and length,
and depth, and height;
19 And to know the love of Christ,
which passeth knowledge, that ye might
be filled with all the fulness of God.
20 Now unto him that is able to do exceeding abundantly above all that we
ask or think, according to the power that
worketh in us,
21 Unto him *be* glory in the church by
Christ Jesus throughout all ages, world
without end. Amen.

CHAPTER 4

I THEREFORE, the prisoner of the
Lord, beseech you that ye walk
worthy of the vocation wherewith ye are
called,
2 With all lowliness and meekness,
with long-suffering, forbearing one another in love;
3 Endeavoring to keep the unity of the
Spirit in the bond of peace.
4 *There is* one body, and one Spirit,
even as ye are called in one hope of your
calling;
5 One Lord, one faith, one baptism,
6 One God and Father of all, who *is*
above all, and through all, and in you all.
7 But unto every one of us is given
grace according to the measure of the
gift of Christ.
8 Wherefore he saith, When he ascended up on high, he led captivity captive, and gave gifts unto men.
9 (Now that he ascended, what is it
but that he also descended first into the
lower parts of the earth?
10 He that descended is the same also
that ascended up far above all heavens,
that he might fill all things.)
11 And he gave some, apostles; and
some, prophets; and some, evangelists;
and some, pastors and teachers;
12 For the perfecting of the saints, for
the work of the ministry, for the edifying of the body of Christ:
13 Till we all come in the unity of the
faith, and of the knowledge of the Son of
God, unto a perfect man, unto the measure of the stature of the fulness of
Christ:
14 That we *henceforth* be no more children, tossed to and fro, and carried
about with every wind of doctrine, by

the sleight of men, *and* cunning craftiness whereby they lie in wait to deceive;
15 But speaking the truth in love, may
grow up into him in all things, which is
the head, *even* Christ:
16 From whom the whole body fitly
joined together and compacted by that
which every joint supplieth, according
to the effectual working in the measure
of every part, maketh increase of the
body unto the edifying of itself in
love.
17 This I say therefore, and testify in
the Lord, that ye henceforth walk not as
other Ġĕn′tīleş walk, in the vanity of
their mind,
18 Having the understanding darkened, being alienated from the life of
God through the ignorance that is in
them, because of the blindness of their
heart:
19 Who being past feeling have given
themselves over unto lasciviousness, to
work all uncleanness with greediness.
20 But ye have not so learned Christ;
21 If so be that ye have heard him, and
have been taught by him, as the truth
is in Jesus:
22 That ye put off concerning the
former conversation the old man, which
is corrupt according to the deceitful
lusts;
23 And be renewed in the spirit of your
mind;
24 And that ye put on the new man,
which after God is created in righteousness and true holiness.
25 Wherefore putting away lying, speak
every man truth with his neighbor: for
we are members one of another.
26 Be ye angry, and sin not: let not the
sun go down upon your wrath:
27 Neither give place to the devil.
28 Let him that stole steal no more:
but rather let him labor, working with
his hands the thing which is good,
that he may have to give to him that
needeth.
29 Let no corrupt communication proceed out of your mouth, but that which
is good to the use of edifying, that it may
minister grace unto the hearers.
30 And grieve not the Holy Spirit of
God, whereby ye are sealed unto the
day of redemption.
31 Let all bitterness, and wrath, and
anger, and clamor, and evil speaking,
be put away from you, with all malice:
32 And be ye kind one to another, tender-hearted, forgiving one another, even
as God for Christ's sake hath forgiven
you.

CHAPTER 5

BE ye therefore followers of God, as dear children;
2 And walk in love, as Christ also hath
loved us, and hath given himself for
us an offering and a sacrifice to God for
a sweetsmelling savor.
3 But fornication, and all uncleanness,
or covetousness, let it not be once
named among you, as becometh saints;
4 Neither filthiness, nor foolish talking, nor jesting, which are not convenient: but rather giving of thanks.
5 For this ye know, that no whoremonger, nor unclean person, nor covetous man, who is an idolater, hath any
inheritance in the kingdom of Christ and
of God.
6 Let no man deceive you with vain
words: for because of these things cometh the wrath of God upon the children
of disobedience.
7 Be not ye therefore partakers with
them.
8 For ye were sometime darkness, but
now *are ye* light in the Lord: walk as
children of light;
9 (For the fruit of the Spirit *is* in all
goodness and righteousness and truth;)
10 Proving what is acceptable unto the
Lord.
11 And have no fellowship with the
unfruitful works of darkness, but rather
reprove *them*.
12 For it is a shame even to speak of
those things which are done of them in
secret.
13 But all things that are reproved are
made manifest by the light: for whatsoever doth make manifest is light.
14 Wherefore he saith, Awake thou
that sleepest, and arise from the dead,
and Christ shall give thee light.
15 See then that ye walk circumspectly,
not as fools, but as wise,
16 Redeeming the time, because the
days are evil.
17 Wherefore be ye not unwise, but
understanding what the will of the
Lord *is*.
18 And be not drunk with wine, wherein is excess; but be filled with the
Spirit;

19 Speaking to yourselves in psalms
and hymns and spiritual songs, singing
and making melody in your heart to the
Lord;
20 Giving thanks always for all things
unto God and the Father in the name
of our Lord Jesus Christ;
21 Submitting yourselves one to another in the fear of God.
22 Wives, submit yourselves unto your
own husbands, as unto the Lord.
23 For the husband is the head of
the wife, even as Christ is the head of
the church: and he is the saviour of the
body.
24 Therefore as the church is subject
unto Christ, so *let* the wives *be* to their
own husbands in every thing.
25 Husbands, love your wives, even as
Christ also loved the church, and gave
himself for it;
26 That he might sanctify and cleanse
it with the washing of water by the
word,
27 That he might present it to himself a glorious church, not having
spot, or wrinkle, or any such thing;
but that it should be holy and without
blemish.
28 So ought men to love their wives as
their own bodies. He that loveth his
wife loveth himself.
29 For no man ever yet hated his own
flesh; but nourisheth and cherisheth it,
even as the Lord the church:
30 For we are members of his body, of
his flesh, and of his bones.
31 For this cause shall a man leave his
father and mother, and shall be joined
unto his wife, and they two shall be one
flesh.
32 This is a great mystery: but I speak
concerning Christ and the church.
33 Nevertheless, let every one of you
in particular so love his wife even as
himself; and the wife *see* that she reverence *her* husband.

CHAPTER 6

CHILDREN, obey your parents in the
Lord: for this is right.
2 Honor thy father and mother; which
is the first commandment with promise;
3 That it may be well with thee, and
thou mayest live long on the earth.
4 And, ye fathers, provoke not your
children to wrath: but bring them up in
the nurture and admonition of the Lord.
5 Servants, be obedient to them
that are *your* masters according to
the flesh, with fear and trembling,
in singleness of your heart, as unto
Christ;
6 Not with eyeservice, as menpleasers;
but as the servants of Christ, doing the
will of God from the heart;
7 With good will doing service, as to
the Lord, and not to men:
8 Knowing that whatsoever good thing
any man doeth, the same shall he receive of the Lord, whether *he be* bond
or free.
9 And, ye masters, do the same things
unto them, forbearing threatening:
knowing that your Master also is in
heaven; neither is there respect of persons with him.
10 Finally, my brethren, be strong in
the Lord, and in the power of his
might.
11 Put on the whole armor of God, that
ye may be able to stand against the wiles
of the devil.
12 For we wrestle not against flesh and
blood, but against principalities, against
powers, against the rulers of the darkness of this world, against spiritual
wickedness in high *places*.
13 Wherefore take unto you the whole
armor of God, that ye may be able to
withstand in the evil day, and having
done all, to stand.
14 Stand therefore, having your loins
girt about with truth, and having on the
breastplate of righteousness;
15 And your feet shod with the preparation of the gospel of peace;
16 Above all, taking the shield of faith,
wherewith ye shall be able to quench all
the fiery darts of the wicked.
17 And take the helmet of salvation,
and the sword of the Spirit, which is the
word of God:
18 Praying always with all prayer and
supplication in the Spirit, and watching
thereunto with all perseverance and
supplication for all saints;
19 And for me, that utterance may be
given unto me, that I may open my
mouth boldly, to make known the mystery of the gospel,
20 For which I am an ambassador in
bonds; that therein I may speak boldly,
as I ought to speak.
21 But that ye also may know my affairs, *and* how I do, Tўch'ĭ-cŭs, a be-

loved brother and faithful minister in
the Lord, shall make known to you all
things:
22 Whom I have sent unto you for the
same purpose, that ye might know our
affairs, and *that* he might comfort your
hearts.
23 Peace *be* to the brethren, and love
with faith, from God the Father and the
Lord Jesus Christ.
24 Grace *be* with all them that love our
Lord Jesus Christ in sincerity. Amen.

¶ Written from Rome unto the Ephesians by
Tychicus.

THE EPISTLE OF PAUL THE APOSTLE TO THE PHILIPPIANS

CHAPTER 1

PAUL and Tī-mō'thē-ŭs, the servants
of Jesus Christ, to all the saints in
Christ Jesus which are at Phĭ-lĭp'pī,
with the bishops and deacons:
2 Grace *be* unto you, and peace, from
God our Father and *from* the Lord
Jesus Christ.
3 I thank my God upon every remembrance of you,
4 Always in every prayer of mine for
you all making request with joy,
5 For your fellowship in the gospel
from the first day until now;
6 Being confident of this very thing,
that he which hath begun a good work
in you will perform *it* until the day of
Jesus Christ:
7 Even as it is meet for me to think this of
you all, because I have you in my heart;
inasmuch as both in my bonds, and in
the defense and confirmation of the gospel, ye all are partakers of my grace.
8 For God is my record, how greatly I
long after you all in the bowels of Jesus
Christ.
9 And this I pray, that your love may
abound yet more and more in knowledge and *in* all judgment;
10 That ye may approve things that are
excellent; that ye may be sincere and
without offense till the day of Christ;
11 Being filled with the fruits of righteousness, which are by Jesus Christ,
unto the glory and praise of God.
12 But I would ye should understand,
brethren, that the things *which happened* unto me have fallen out rather
unto the furtherance of the gospel;
13 So that my bonds in Christ are manifest in all the palace, and in all other
places;
14 And many of the brethren in the
Lord, waxing confident by my bonds,
are much more bold to speak the word
without fear.
15 Some indeed preach Christ even of
envy and strife; and some also of good
will:
16 The one preach Christ of contention, not sincerely, supposing to add
affliction to my bonds:
17 But the other of love, knowing that
I am set for the defense of the gospel.
18 What then? notwithstanding, every
way, whether in pretense, or in truth,
Christ is preached; and I therein do rejoice, yea, and will rejoice.
19 For I know that this shall turn to
my salvation through your prayer, and
the supply of the Spirit of Jesus Christ,
20 According to my earnest expectation
and *my* hope, that in nothing I shall be
ashamed, but *that* with all boldness, as
always, *so* now also Christ shall be magnified in my body, whether *it be* by life,
or by death.
21 For to me to live *is* Christ, and to die
is gain.
22 But if I live in the flesh, this *is* the
fruit of my labor: yet what I shall choose
I wot not.
23 For I am in a strait betwixt two, having a desire to depart, and to be with
Christ; which is far better:
24 Nevertheless to abide in the flesh *is*
more needful for you.
25 And having this confidence, I know
that I shall abide and continue with you
all for your furtherance and joy of faith;
26 That your rejoicing may be more
abundant in Jesus Christ for me by my
coming to you again.
27 Only let your conversation be as it
becometh the gospel of Christ: that

whether I come and see you, or else be absent, I may hear of your affairs, that ye stand fast in one spirit, with one mind striving together for the faith of the gospel;

28 And in nothing terrified by your adversaries: which is to them an evident token of perdition, but to you of salvation, and that of God.

29 For unto you it is given in the behalf of Christ, not only to believe on him, but also to suffer for his sake;

30 Having the same conflict which ye saw in me, and now hear *to be* in me.

CHAPTER 2

IF *there be* therefore any consolation in Christ, if any comfort of love, if any fellowship of the Spirit, if any bowels and mercies,

2 Fulfil ye my joy, that ye be likeminded, having the same love, *being* of one accord, of one mind.

3 *Let* nothing *be done* through strife or vainglory; but in lowliness of mind let each esteem other better than themselves.

4 Look not every man on his own things, but every man also on the things of others.

5 Let this mind be in you, which was also in Christ Jesus:

6 Who, being in the form of God, thought it not robbery to be equal with God:

7 But made himself of no reputation, and took upon him the form of a servant, and was made in the likeness of men:

8 And being found in fashion as a man, he humbled himself, and became obedient unto death, even the death of the cross.

9 Wherefore God also hath highly exalted him, and given him a name which is above every name:

10 That at the name of Jesus every knee should bow, of *things* in heaven, and *things* in earth, and *things* under the earth;

11 And *that* every tongue should confess that Jesus Christ *is* Lord, to the glory of God the Father.

12 Wherefore, my beloved, as ye have always obeyed, not as in my presence only, but now much more in my absence, work out your own salvation with fear and trembling:

13 For it is God which worketh in you both to will and to do of *his* good pleasure.

14 Do all things without murmurings and disputings:

15 That ye may be blameless and harmless, the sons of God, without rebuke, in the midst of a crooked and perverse nation, among whom ye shine as lights in the world;

16 Holding forth the word of life; that I may rejoice in the day of Christ, that I have not run in vain, neither labored in vain.

17 Yea, and if I be offered upon the sacrifice and service of your faith, I joy, and rejoice with you all.

18 For the same cause also do ye joy, and rejoice with me.

19 But I trust in the Lord Jesus to send Tĭ-mō′thē-ŭs shortly unto you, that I also may be of good comfort, when I know your state.

20 For I have no man likeminded, who will naturally care for your state.

21 For all seek their own, not the things which are Jesus Christ's.

22 But ye know the proof of him, that, as a son with the father, he hath served with me in the gospel.

23 Him therefore I hope to send presently, so soon as I shall see how it will go with me.

24 But I trust in the Lord that I also myself shall come shortly.

25 Yet I supposed it necessary to send to you Ē-păph′rō-dī′tŭs, my brother, and companion in labor, and fellow soldier, but your messenger, and he that ministered to my wants.

26 For he longed after you all, and was full of heaviness, because that ye had heard that he had been sick.

27 For indeed he was sick nigh unto death: but God had mercy on him; and not on him only, but on me also, lest I should have sorrow upon sorrow.

28 I sent him therefore the more carefully, that, when ye see him again, ye may rejoice, and that I may be the less sorrowful.

29 Receive him therefore in the Lord with all gladness; and hold such in reputation:

30 Because for the work of Christ he was nigh unto death, not regarding his life, to supply your lack of service toward me.

CHAPTER 3

FINALLY, my brethren, rejoice in the Lord. To write the same things to you, to me indeed *is* not grievous, but for you *it is* safe.

2 Beware of dogs, beware of evil workers, beware of the concision.

3 For we are the circumcision, which worship God in the spirit, and rejoice in Christ Jesus, and have no confidence in the flesh.

4 Though I might also have confidence in the flesh. If any other man thinketh that he hath whereof he might trust in the flesh, I more:

5 Circumcised the eighth day, of the stock of Ĭş'rā-ĕl, *of* the tribe of Benjamin, a Hebrew of the Hebrews; as touching the law, a Phăr'ĭ-sēe;

6 Concerning zeal, persecuting the church; touching the righteousness which is in the law, blameless.

7 But what things were gain to me, those I counted loss for Christ.

8 Yea doubtless, and I count all things *but* loss for the excellency of the knowledge of Christ Jesus my Lord: for whom I have suffered the loss of all things, and do count them *but* dung, that I may win Christ,

9 And be found in him, not having mine own righteousness, which is of the law, but that which is through the faith of Christ, the righteousness which is of God by faith:

10 That I may know him, and the power of his resurrection, and the fellowship of his sufferings, being made conformable unto his death;

11 If by any means I might attain unto the resurrection of the dead.

12 Not as though I had already attained, either were already perfect: but I follow after, if that I may apprehend that for which also I am apprehended of Christ Jesus.

13 Brethren, I count not myself to have apprehended: but *this* one thing *I do*, forgetting those things which are behind, and reaching forth unto those things which are before,

14 I press toward the mark for the prize of the high calling of God in Christ Jesus.

15 Let us therefore, as many as be perfect, be thus minded: and if in any thing ye be otherwise minded, God shall reveal even this unto you.

16 Nevertheless, whereto we have already attained, let us walk by the same rule, let us mind the same thing.

17 Brethren, be followers together of me, and mark them which walk so as ye have us for an ensample.

18 (For many walk, of whom I have told you often, and now tell you even weeping, *that they are* the enemies of the cross of Christ:

19 Whose end *is* destruction, whose God *is their* belly, and *whose* glory *is* in their shame, who mind earthly things.)

20 For our conversation is in heaven; from whence also we look for the Saviour, the Lord Jesus Christ:

21 Who shall change our vile body, that it may be fashioned like unto his glorious body, according to the working whereby he is able even to subdue all things unto himself.

CHAPTER 4

THEREFORE, my brethren dearly beloved and longed for, my joy and crown, so stand fast in the Lord, *my* dearly beloved.

2 I beseech Eū-ō'dĭ-ăs, and beseech Sy̆n'ty̆-chē, that they be of the same mind in the Lord.

3 And I entreat thee also, true yokefellow, help those women which labored with me in the gospel, with Clement also, and *with* other my fellow laborers, whose names *are* in the book of life.

4 Rejoice in the Lord always: *and* again I say, Rejoice.

5 Let your moderation be known unto all men. The Lord *is* at hand.

6 Be careful for nothing; but in every thing by prayer and supplication with thanksgiving let your requests be made known unto God.

7 And the peace of God, which passeth all understanding, shall keep your hearts and minds through Christ Jesus.

8 Finally, brethren, whatsoever things are true, whatsoever things *are* honest, whatsoever things *are* just, whatsoever things *are* pure, whatsoever things *are* lovely, whatsoever things *are* of good report; if *there be* any virtue, and if *there be* any praise, think on these things.

9 Those things, which ye have both learned, and received, and heard, and

seen in me, do: and the God of peace shall be with you.
10 But I rejoiced in the Lord greatly, that now at the last your care of me hath flourished again; wherein ye were also careful, but ye lacked opportunity.
11 Not that I speak in respect of want: for I have learned, in whatsoever state I am, *therewith* to be content.
12 I know both how to be abased, and I know how to abound: every where and in all things I am instructed both to be full and to be hungry, both to abound and to suffer need.
13 I can do all things through Christ which strengtheneth me.
14 Notwithstanding, ye have well done, that ye did communicate with my affliction.
15 Now ye Phĭ-lĭp′pĭ-ăns know also, that in the beginning of the gospel, when I departed from Macedonia, no church communicated with me as concerning giving and receiving, but ye only.
16 For even in Thĕs′să-lō-nī′că ye sent once and again unto my necessity.
17 Not because I desire a gift: but I desire fruit that may abound to your account.
18 But I have all, and abound: I am full, having received of Ē-păph′rō-dī′tŭs the things *which were sent* from you, an odor of a sweet smell, a sacrifice acceptable, well-pleasing to God.
19 But my God shall supply all your need according to his riches in glory by Christ Jesus.
20 Now unto God and our Father *be* glory for ever and ever. Amen.
21 Salute every saint in Christ Jesus. The brethren which are with me greet you.
22 All the saints salute you, chiefly they that are of Cæsar's household.
23 The grace of our Lord Jesus Christ *be* with you all. Amen.

¶ It was written to the Philippians from Rome by Epaphroditus.

THE EPISTLE OF PAUL THE APOSTLE TO THE

COLOSSIANS

CHAPTER 1

PAUL, an apostle of Jesus Christ by the will of God, and Tĭ-mō′thē-ŭs *our* brother,
2 To the saints and faithful brethren in Christ which are at Cō-lŏs′sē: Grace *be* unto you, and peace, from God our Father and the Lord Jesus Christ.
3 We give thanks to God and the Father of our Lord Jesus Christ, praying always for you,
4 Since we heard of your faith in Christ Jesus, and of the love *which ye have* to all the saints,
5 For the hope which is laid up for you in heaven, whereof ye heard before in the word of the truth of the gospel;
6 Which is come unto you, as *it is* in all the world; and bringeth forth fruit, as *it doth* also in you, since the day ye heard *of it*, and knew the grace of God in truth:
7 As ye also learned of Ĕp′ă-phrăs our dear fellow servant, who is for you a faithful minister of Christ;
8 Who also declared unto us your love in the Spirit.
9 For this cause we also, since the day we heard *it*, do not cease to pray for you, and to desire that ye might be filled with the knowledge of his will in all wisdom and spiritual understanding;
10 That ye might walk worthy of the Lord unto all pleasing, being fruitful in every good work, and increasing in the knowledge of God;
11 Strengthened with all might, according to his glorious power, unto all patience and long-suffering with joyfulness;
12 Giving thanks unto the Father, which hath made us meet to be partakers of the inheritance of the saints in light:
13 Who hath delivered us from the power of darkness, and hath translated *us* into the kingdom of his dear Son:
14 In whom we have redemption through his blood, *even* the forgiveness of sins:

15 Who is the image of the invisible God, the firstborn of every creature:

16 For by him were all things created, that are in heaven, and that are in earth, visible and invisible, whether *they be* thrones, or dominions, or principalities, or powers: all things were created by him, and for him:

17 And he is before all things, and by him all things consist:

18 And he is the head of the body, the church: who is the beginning, the firstborn from the dead; that in all things he might have the preeminence.

19 For it pleased *the Father* that in him should all fulness dwell;

20 And, having made peace through the blood of his cross, by him to reconcile all things unto himself; by him, *I say*, whether *they be* things in earth, or things in heaven.

21 And you, that were sometime alienated and enemies in *your* mind by wicked works, yet now hath he reconciled

22 In the body of his flesh through death, to present you holy and unblamable and unreprovable in his sight:

23 If ye continue in the faith grounded and settled, and *be* not moved away from the hope of the gospel, which ye have heard, *and* which was preached to every creature which is under heaven; whereof I Paul am made a minister;

24 Who now rejoice in my sufferings for you, and fill up that which is behind of the afflictions of Christ in my flesh for his body's sake, which is the church:

25 Whereof I am made a minister, according to the dispensation of God which is given to me for you, to fulfil the word of God;

26 *Even* the mystery which hath been hid from ages and from generations, but now is made manifest to his saints:

27 To whom God would make known what *is* the riches of the glory of this mystery among the Ġĕn′tīleṣ; which is Christ in you, the hope of glory:

28 Whom we preach, warning every man, and teaching every man in all wisdom; that we may present every man perfect in Christ Jesus:

29 Whereunto I also labor, striving according to his working, which worketh in me mightily.

CHAPTER 2

FOR I would that ye knew what great conflict I have for you, and *for* them at Lā-ŏd′ĭ-çē′ȧ, and *for* as many as have not seen my face in the flesh;

2 That their hearts might be comforted, being knit together in love, and unto all riches of the full assurance of understanding, to the acknowledgment of the mystery of God, and of the Father, and of Christ;

3 In whom are hid all the treasures of wisdom and knowledge.

4 And this I say, lest any man should beguile you with enticing words.

5 For though I be absent in the flesh, yet am I with you in the spirit, joying and beholding your order, and the steadfastness of your faith in Christ.

6 As ye have therefore received Christ Jesus the Lord, *so* walk ye in him:

7 Rooted and built up in him, and stablished in the faith, as ye have been taught, abounding therein with thanksgiving.

8 Beware lest any man spoil you through philosophy and vain deceit, after the tradition of men, after the rudiments of the world, and not after Christ.

9 For in him dwelleth all the fulness of the Godhead bodily.

10 And ye are complete in him, which is the head of all principality and power:

11 In whom also ye are circumcised with the circumcision made without hands, in putting off the body of the sins of the flesh by the circumcision of Christ:

12 Buried with him in baptism, wherein also ye are risen with *him* through the faith of the operation of God, who hath raised him from the dead.

13 And you, being dead in your sins and the uncircumcision of your flesh, hath he quickened together with him, having forgiven you all trespasses;

14 Blotting out the handwriting of ordinances that was against us, which was contrary to us, and took it out of the way, nailing it to his cross;

15 *And* having spoiled principalities and powers, he made a show of them openly, triumphing over them in it.

16 Let no man therefore judge you in meat, or in drink, or in respect of a holyday, or of the new moon, or of the sabbath *days:*

17 Which are a shadow of things to come; but the body *is* of Christ.

18 Let no man beguile you of your reward in a voluntary humility and worshipping of angels, intruding into those things which he hath not seen, vainly puffed up by his fleshly mind,

19 And not holding the Head, from which all the body by joints and bands having nourishment ministered, and knit together, increaseth with the increase of God.

20 Wherefore if ye be dead with Christ from the rudiments of the world, why, as though living in the world, are ye subject to ordinances,

21 (Touch not; taste not; handle not;

22 Which all are to perish with the using;) after the commandments and doctrines of men?

23 Which things have indeed a show of wisdom in will-worship, and humility, and neglecting of the body; not in any honor to the satisfying of the flesh.

CHAPTER 3

IF ye then be risen with Christ, seek those things which are above, where Christ sitteth on the right hand of God.

2 Set your affection on things above, not on things on the earth.

3 For ye are dead, and your life is hid with Christ in God.

4 When Christ, *who is* our life, shall appear, then shall ye also appear with him in glory.

5 Mortify therefore your members which are upon the earth; fornication, uncleanness, inordinate affection, evil concupiscence, and covetousness, which is idolatry:

6 For which things' sake the wrath of God cometh on the children of disobedience:

7 In the which ye also walked sometime, when ye lived in them.

8 But now ye also put off all these; anger, wrath, malice, blasphemy, filthy communication out of your mouth.

9 Lie not one to another, seeing that ye have put off the old man with his deeds;

10 And have put on the new *man*, which is renewed in knowledge after the image of him that created him:

11 Where there is neither Greek nor Jew, circumcision nor uncircumcision, Barbarian, Sçy̆th'i-ăn, bond *nor* free: but Christ *is* all, and in all.

12 Put on therefore, as the elect of God, holy and beloved, bowels of mercies, kindness, humbleness of mind, meekness, long-suffering;

13 Forbearing one another, and forgiving one another, if any man have a quarrel against any: even as Christ forgave you, so also *do* ye.

14 And above all these things *put on* charity, which is the bond of perfectness.

15 And let the peace of God rule in your hearts, to the which also ye are called in one body; and be ye thankful.

16 Let the word of Christ dwell in you richly in all wisdom; teaching and admonishing one another in psalms and hymns and spiritual songs, singing with grace in your hearts to the Lord.

17 And whatsoever ye do in word or deed, *do* all in the name of the Lord Jesus, giving thanks to God and the Father by him.

18 Wives, submit yourselves unto your own husbands, as it is fit in the Lord.

19 Husbands, love *your* wives, and be not bitter against them.

20 Children, obey *your* parents in all things: for this is well-pleasing unto the Lord.

21 Fathers, provoke not your children *to anger*, lest they be discouraged.

22 Servants, obey in all things *your* masters according to the flesh; not with eyeservice, as menpleasers; but in singleness of heart, fearing God:

23 And whatsoever ye do, do *it* heartily, as to the Lord, and not unto men;

24 Knowing that of the Lord ye shall receive the reward of the inheritance: for ye serve the Lord Christ.

25 But he that doeth wrong shall receive for the wrong which he hath done: and there is no respect of persons.

CHAPTER 4

MASTERS, give unto *your* servants that which is just and equal; knowing that ye also have a Master in heaven.

2 Continue in prayer, and watch in the same with thanksgiving;

3 Withal praying also for us, that God would open unto us a door of utterance, to speak the mystery of Christ, for which I am also in bonds:

4 That I may make it manifest, as I ought to speak.

5 Walk in wisdom toward them that are without, redeeming the time.
6 Let your speech *be* always with grace, seasoned with salt, that ye may know how ye ought to answer every man.
7 All my state shall Tȳch'ĭ-cŭs declare unto you, *who is* a beloved brother, and a faithful minister and fellow servant in the Lord:
8 Whom I have sent unto you for the same purpose, that he might know your estate, and comfort your hearts;
9 With Ō-nĕs'ĭ-mŭs, a faithful and beloved brother, who is *one* of you. They shall make known unto you all things which *are done* here.
10 Ăr'ĭs-tär'chŭs my fellow prisoner saluteth you, and Marcus, sister's son to Barnabas, (touching whom ye received commandments: if he come unto you, receive him;)
11 And Jesus, which is called Justus, who are of the circumcision. These only *are my* fellow workers unto the kingdom of God, which have been a comfort unto me.
12 Ĕp'ȧ-phrăs, who is *one* of you, a servant of Christ, saluteth you, always laboring fervently for you in prayers, that ye may stand perfect and complete in all the will of God.
13 For I bear him record, that he hath a great zeal for you, and them *that are* in Lā-ŏd'ĭ-çē'ȧ, and them in Hī'ĕr-ăp'ō-lĭs.
14 Luke, the beloved physician, and Dē'măs, greet you.
15 Salute the brethren which are in Lā-ŏd'ĭ-çē'ȧ, and Nȳm'phăs, and the church which is in his house.
16 And when this epistle is read among you, cause that it be read also in the church of the Lā-ŏd'ĭ-çē'ănş; and that ye likewise read the *epistle* from Lā-ŏd'ĭ-çē'ȧ.
17 And say to Är-chĭp'pŭs, Take heed to the ministry which thou hast received in the Lord, that thou fulfil it.
18 The salutation by the hand of me Paul. Remember my bonds. Grace *be* with you. Amen.

¶ Written from Rome to the Colossians by Tychicus and Onesimus.

THE FIRST EPISTLE OF PAUL THE APOSTLE TO THE

THESSALONIANS

CHAPTER 1

PAUL, and Sĭl-vā'nŭs, and Tī-mō'thē-ŭs, unto the church of the Thĕs'sȧ-lō'nĭ-ănş *which is* in God the Father, and *in* the Lord Jesus Christ: Grace *be* unto you, and peace, from God our Father, and the Lord Jesus Christ.
2 We give thanks to God always for you all, making mention of you in our prayers;
3 Remembering without ceasing your work of faith, and labor of love, and patience of hope in our Lord Jesus Christ, in the sight of God and our Father;
4 Knowing, brethren beloved, your election of God.
5 For our gospel came not unto you in word only, but also in power, and in the Holy Ghost, and in much assurance; as ye know what manner of men we were among you for your sake.
6 And ye became followers of us, and of the Lord, having received the word in much affliction, with joy of the Holy Ghost:
7 So that ye were ensamples to all that believe in Macedonia and Ȧ-chā'ịȧ.
8 For from you sounded out the word of the Lord not only in Macedonia and Ȧ-chā'ịȧ, but also in every place your faith to God-ward is spread abroad; so that we need not to speak any thing.
9 For they themselves show of us what manner of entering in we had unto you, and how ye turned to God from idols to serve the living and true God;
10 And to wait for his Son from heaven, whom he raised from the dead, *even* Jesus, which delivered us from the wrath to come.

CHAPTER 2

FOR yourselves, brethren, know our entrance in unto you, that it was not in vain:

2 But even after that we had suffered
before, and were shamefully entreated,
as ye know, at Phĭ-lĭp′pī, we were bold
in our God to speak unto you the gospel
of God with much contention.
3 For our exhortation *was* not of deceit,
nor of uncleanness, nor in guile:
4 But as we were allowed of God to be
put in trust with the gospel, even so we
speak; not as pleasing men, but God,
which trieth our hearts.
5 For neither at any time used we
flattering words, as ye know, nor a cloak
of covetousness; God *is* witness:
6 Nor of men sought we glory, neither
of you, nor *yet* of others, when we might
have been burdensome, as the apostles
of Christ.
7 But we were gentle among you, even
as a nurse cherisheth her children:
8 So being affectionately desirous of
you, we were willing to have imparted
unto you, not the gospel of God only,
but also our own souls, because ye were
dear unto us.
9 For ye remember, brethren, our
labor and travail: for laboring night and
day, because we would not be chargeable
unto any of you, we preached unto you
the gospel of God.
10 Ye *are* witnesses, and God *also*,
how holily and justly and unblamably
we behaved ourselves among you that
believe:
11 As ye know how we exhorted and
comforted and charged every one of you,
as a father *doth* his children,
12 That ye would walk worthy of God,
who hath called you unto his kingdom
and glory.
13 For this cause also thank we God
without ceasing, because, when ye received the word of God which ye heard
of us, ye received *it* not *as* the word of
men, but, as it is in truth, the word of
God, which effectually worketh also in
you that believe.
14 For ye, brethren, became followers
of the churches of God which in Judea
are in Christ Jesus: for ye also have suffered like things of your own countrymen, even as they *have* of the Jews:
15 Who both killed the Lord Jesus,
and their own prophets, and have persecuted us; and they please not God,
and are contrary to all men:
16 Forbidding us to speak to the Ġĕn′-
tīleṣ that they might be saved, to fill up
their sins always: for the wrath is come
upon them to the uttermost.
17 But we, brethren, being taken from
you for a short time in presence, not in
heart, endeavored the more abundantly
to see your face with great desire.
18 Wherefore we would have come unto you, even I Paul, once and again; but
Satan hindered us.
19 For what *is* our hope, or joy, or
crown of rejoicing? *Are* not even ye in
the presence of our Lord Jesus Christ
at his coming?
20 For ye are our glory and joy.

CHAPTER 3

WHEREFORE when we could no
longer forbear, we thought it good
to be left at Athens alone;
2 And sent Tĭ-mō′thē-ŭs, our brother,
and minister of God, and our fellow
laborer in the gospel of Christ, to establish you, and to comfort you concerning
your faith:
3 That no man should be moved by
these afflictions: for yourselves know
that we are appointed thereunto.
4 For verily, when we were with you,
we told you before that we should suffer
tribulation; even as it came to pass, and
ye know.
5 For this cause, when I could no longer
forbear, I sent to know your faith, lest
by some means the tempter have
tempted you, and our labor be in vain.
6 But now when Tĭ-mō′thē-ŭs came
from you unto us, and brought us good
tidings of your faith and charity, and
that ye have good remembrance of us
always, desiring greatly to see us, as we
also *to see* you:
7 Therefore, brethren, we were comforted over you in all our affliction and
distress by your faith:
8 For now we live, if ye stand fast in
the Lord.
9 For what thanks can we render to God
again for you, for all the joy wherewith
we joy for your sakes before our God;
10 Night and day praying exceedingly
that we might see your face, and might
perfect that which is lacking in your
faith?
11 Now God himself and our Father,
and our Lord Jesus Christ, direct our
way unto you.
12 And the Lord make you to increase
and abound in love one toward another,

and toward all *men*, even as we *do* toward you:

13 To the end he may stablish your hearts unblamable in holiness before God, even our Father, at the coming of our Lord Jesus Christ with all his saints.

CHAPTER 4

FURTHERMORE then we beseech you, brethren, and exhort *you* by the Lord Jesus, that as ye have received of us how ye ought to walk and to please God, *so* ye would abound more and more.

2 For ye know what commandments we gave you by the Lord Jesus.

3 For this is the will of God, *even* your sanctification, that ye should abstain from fornication:

4 That every one of you should know how to possess his vessel in sanctification and honor;

5 Not in the lust of concupiscence, even as the Gĕn′tīleş which know not God:

6 That no *man* go beyond and defraud his brother in *any* matter: because that the Lord *is* the avenger of all such, as we also have forewarned you and testified.

7 For God hath not called us unto uncleanness, but unto holiness.

8 He therefore that despiseth, despiseth not man, but God, who hath also given unto us his Holy Spirit.

9 But as touching brotherly love ye need not that I write unto you: for ye yourselves are taught of God to love one another.

10 And indeed ye do it toward all the brethren which are in all Macedonia: but we beseech you, brethren, that ye increase more and more;

11 And that ye study to be quiet, and to do your own business, and to work with your own hands, as we commanded you;

12 That ye may walk honestly toward them that are without, and *that* ye may have lack of nothing.

13 But I would not have you to be ignorant, brethren, concerning them which are asleep, that ye sorrow not, even as others which have no hope.

14 For if we believe that Jesus died and rose again, even so them also which sleep in Jesus will God bring with him.

15 For this we say unto you by the word of the Lord, that we which are alive *and* remain unto the coming of the Lord shall not prevent them which are asleep.

16 For the Lord himself shall descend from heaven with a shout, with the voice of the archangel, and with the trump of God: and the dead in Christ shall rise first:

17 Then we which are alive *and* remain shall be caught up together with them in the clouds, to meet the Lord in the air: and so shall we ever be with the Lord.

18 Wherefore comfort one another with these words.

CHAPTER 5

BUT of the times and the seasons, brethren, ye have no need that I write unto you.

2 For yourselves know perfectly that the day of the Lord so cometh as a thief in the night.

3 For when they shall say, Peace and safety; then sudden destruction cometh upon them, as travail upon a woman with child; and they shall not escape.

4 But ye, brethren, are not in darkness, that that day should overtake you as a thief.

5 Ye are all the children of light, and the children of the day: we are not of the night, nor of darkness.

6 Therefore let us not sleep, as *do* others; but let us watch and be sober.

7 For they that sleep sleep in the night; and they that be drunken are drunken in the night.

8 But let us, who are of the day, be sober, putting on the breastplate of faith and love; and for a helmet, the hope of salvation.

9 For God hath not appointed us to wrath, but to obtain salvation by our Lord Jesus Christ,

10 Who died for us, that, whether we wake or sleep, we should live together with him.

11 Wherefore comfort yourselves together, and edify one another, even as also ye do.

12 And we beseech you, brethren, to know them which labor among you, and are over you in the Lord, and admonish you;

13 And to esteem them very highly in

love for their work's sake. *And* be at peace among yourselves.

14 Now we exhort you, brethren, warn them that are unruly, comfort the feebleminded, support the weak, be patient toward all *men*.

15 See that none render evil for evil unto any *man*, but ever follow that which is good, both among yourselves, and to all *men*.

16 Rejoice evermore.

17 Pray without ceasing.

18 In every thing give thanks: for this is the will of God in Christ Jesus concerning you.

19 Quench not the Spirit.

20 Despise not prophesyings.

21 Prove all things; hold fast that which is good.

22 Abstain from all appearance of evil.

23 And the very God of peace sanctify you wholly; and *I pray God* your whole spirit and soul and body be preserved blameless unto the coming of our Lord Jesus Christ.

24 Faithful *is* he that calleth you, who also will do *it*.

25 Brethren, pray for us.

26 Greet all the brethren with a holy kiss.

27 I charge you by the Lord, that this epistle be read unto all the holy brethren.

28 The grace of our Lord Jesus Christ *be* with you. Amen.

¶ The first *epistle* unto the Thessalonians was written from Athens.

THE SECOND EPISTLE OF PAUL THE APOSTLE TO THE

THESSALONIANS

CHAPTER 1

PAUL, and Sĭl-vā′nŭs, and Tĭ-mō′thē-ŭs, unto the church of the Thĕs sȧ-lō′nĭ-ănṣ in God our Father and the Lord Jesus Christ:

2 Grace unto you, and peace, from God our Father and the Lord Jesus Christ.

3 We are bound to thank God always for you, brethren, as it is meet, because that your faith groweth exceedingly, and the charity of every one of you all toward each other aboundeth;

4 So that we ourselves glory in you in the churches of God, for your patience and faith in all your persecutions and tribulations that ye endure:

5 *Which is* a manifest token of the righteous judgment of God, that ye may be counted worthy of the kingdom of God, for which ye also suffer:

6 Seeing *it is* a righteous thing with God to recompense tribulation to them that trouble you;

7 And to you who are troubled rest with us, when the Lord Jesus shall be revealed from heaven with his mighty angels,

8 In flaming fire taking vengeance on them that know not God, and that obey not the gospel of our Lord Jesus Christ:

9 Who shall be punished with everlasting destruction from the presence of the Lord, and from the glory of his power;

10 When he shall come to be glorified in his saints, and to be admired in all them that believe (because our testimony among you was believed) in that day.

11 Wherefore also we pray always for you, that our God would count you worthy of *this* calling, and fulfil all the good pleasure of *his* goodness, and the work of faith with power:

12 That the name of our Lord Jesus Christ may be glorified in you, and ye in him, according to the grace of our God and the Lord Jesus Christ.

CHAPTER 2

NOW we beseech you, brethren, by the coming of our Lord Jesus Christ, and *by* our gathering together unto him,

2 That ye be not soon shaken in mind, or be troubled, neither by spirit, nor by word, nor by letter as from us, as that the day of Christ is at hand.

3 Let no man deceive you by any means: for *that day shall not come*, except there come a falling away first, and that man of sin be revealed, the son of perdition;

4 Who opposeth and exalteth himself above all that is called God, or that is worshipped; so that he as God sitteth in the temple of God, showing himself that he is God.

5 Remember ye not, that, when I was yet with you, I told you these things?

6 And now ye know what withholdeth that he might be revealed in his time.

7 For the mystery of iniquity doth already work: only he who now letteth *will let,* until he be taken out of the way.

8 And then shall that Wicked be revealed, whom the Lord shall consume with the spirit of his mouth, and shall destroy with the brightness of his coming:

9 *Even him,* whose coming is after the working of Satan with all power and signs and lying wonders,

10 And with all deceivableness of unrighteousness in them that perish; because they received not the love of the truth, that they might be saved.

11 And for this cause God shall send them strong delusion, that they should believe a lie:

12 That they all might be damned who believed not the truth, but had pleasure in unrighteousness.

13 But we are bound to give thanks always to God for you, brethren beloved of the Lord, because God hath from the beginning chosen you to salvation through sanctification of the Spirit and belief of the truth:

14 Whereunto he called you by our gospel, to the obtaining of the glory of our Lord Jesus Christ.

15 Therefore, brethren, stand fast, and hold the traditions which ye have been taught, whether by word, or our epistle.

16 Now our Lord Jesus Christ himself, and God, even our Father, which hath loved us, and hath given *us* everlasting consolation and good hope through grace,

17 Comfort your hearts, and stablish you in every good word and work.

CHAPTER 3

FINALLY, brethren, pray for us, that the word of the Lord may have *free* course, and be glorified, even as *it is* with you:

2 And that we may be delivered from unreasonable and wicked men: for all *men* have not faith.

3 But the Lord is faithful, who shall stablish you, and keep *you* from evil.

4 And we have confidence in the Lord touching you, that ye both do and will do the things which we command you.

5 And the Lord direct your hearts into the love of God, and into the patient waiting for Christ.

6 Now we command you, brethren, in the name of our Lord Jesus Christ, that ye withdraw yourselves from every brother that walketh disorderly, and not after the tradition which he received of us.

7 For yourselves know how ye ought to follow us: for we behaved not ourselves disorderly among you;

8 Neither did we eat any man's bread for nought; but wrought with labor and travail night and day, that we might not be chargeable to any of you:

9 Not because we have not power, but to make ourselves an ensample unto you to follow us.

10 For even when we were with you, this we commanded you, that if any would not work, neither should he eat.

11 For we hear that there are some which walk among you disorderly, working not at all, but are busybodies.

12 Now them that are such we command and exhort by our Lord Jesus Christ, that with quietness they work, and eat their own bread.

13 But ye, brethren, be not weary in well doing.

14 And if any man obey not our word by this epistle, note that man, and have no company with him, that he may be ashamed.

15 Yet count *him* not as an enemy, but admonish *him* as a brother.

16 Now the Lord of peace himself give you peace always by all means. The Lord *be* with you all.

17 The salutation of Paul with mine own hand, which is the token in every epistle: so I write.

18 The grace of our Lord Jesus Christ *be* with you all. Amen.

¶ The second *epistle* to the Thessalonians was written from Athens.

THE FIRST EPISTLE OF PAUL THE APOSTLE TO

TIMOTHY

CHAPTER 1

PAUL, an apostle of Jesus Christ by
the commandment of God our Saviour, and Lord Jesus Christ, *which is*
our hope;
2 Unto Timothy, *my* own son in the
faith: Grace, mercy, *and* peace, from God
our Father, and Jesus Christ our Lord.
3 As I besought thee to abide still at
Ĕph′ē-sŭs, when I went into Macedonia,
that thou mightest charge some that
they teach no other doctrine,
4 Neither give heed to fables and endless genealogies, which minister questions, rather than godly edifying which
is in faith: *so do.*
5 Now the end of the commandment is
charity out of a pure heart, and *of* a good
conscience, and *of* faith unfeigned:
6 From which some having swerved
have turned aside unto vain jangling;
7 Desiring to be teachers of the law;
understanding neither what they say,
nor whereof they affirm.
8 But we know that the law *is* good, if
a man use it lawfully;
9 Knowing this, that the law is not
made for a righteous man, but for the
lawless and disobedient, for the ungodly
and for sinners, for unholy and profane,
for murderers of fathers and murderers
of mothers, for manslayers,
10 For whoremongers, for them that
defile themselves with mankind, for
menstealers, for liars, for perjured persons, and if there be any other thing that
is contrary to sound doctrine;
11 According to the glorious gospel of
the blessed God, which was committed
to my trust.
12 And I thank Christ Jesus our Lord,
who hath enabled me, for that he
counted me faithful, putting me into the
ministry;
13 Who was before a blasphemer, and
a persecutor, and injurious: but I obtained mercy, because I did *it* ignorantly
in unbelief.
14 And the grace of our Lord was exceeding abundant with faith and love
which is in Christ Jesus.
15 This *is* a faithful saying, and worthy
of all acceptation, that Christ Jesus
came into the world to save sinners; of
whom I am chief.
16 Howbeit for this cause I obtained
mercy, that in me first Jesus Christ
might show forth all long-suffering, for
a pattern to them which should hereafter believe on him to life everlasting.
17 Now unto the King eternal, im-
mortal, invisible, the only wise God, *be*
honor and glory for ever and ever.
Amen.
18 This charge I commit unto thee, son
Timothy, according to the prophecies
which went before on thee, that thou by
them mightest war a good warfare;
19 Holding faith, and a good conscience; which some having put away,
concerning faith have made shipwreck:
20 Of whom is Hȳ′mĕn-ē′ŭs and Alexander; whom I have delivered unto
Satan, that they may learn not to blaspheme.

CHAPTER 2

I EXHORT therefore, that, first of all,
supplications, prayers, intercessions,
and giving of thanks, be made for all
men;
2 For kings, and *for* all that are in
authority; that we may lead a quiet and
peaceable life in all godliness and
honesty.
3 For this *is* good and acceptable in the
sight of God our Saviour;
4 Who will have all men to be saved,
and to come unto the knowledge of the
truth.
5 For *there is* one God, and one mediator between God and men, the man
Christ Jesus;
6 Who gave himself a ransom for all,
to be testified in due time.
7 Whereunto I am ordained a preacher,
and an apostle, (I speak the truth in
Christ, *and* lie not,) a teacher of the
Ġĕn′tīleş in faith and verity.
8 I will therefore that men pray every
where, lifting up holy hands, without
wrath and doubting.
9 In like manner also, that women

adorn themselves in modest apparel, with shamefacedness and sobriety; not with braided hair, or gold, or pearls, or costly array;

10 But (which becometh women professing godliness) with good works.

11 Let the woman learn in silence with all subjection.

12 But I suffer not a woman to teach, nor to usurp authority over the man, but to be in silence.

13 For Adam was first formed, then Eve.

14 And Adam was not deceived, but the woman being deceived was in the transgression.

15 Notwithstanding she shall be saved in childbearing, if they continue in faith and charity and holiness with sobriety.

CHAPTER 3

THIS *is* a true saying, If a man desire the office of a bishop, he desireth a good work.

2 A bishop then must be blameless, the husband of one wife, vigilant, sober, of good behavior, given to hospitality, apt to teach;

3 Not given to wine, no striker, not greedy of filthy lucre; but patient, not a brawler, not covetous;

4 One that ruleth well his own house, having his children in subjection with all gravity;

5 (For if a man know not how to rule his own house, how shall he take care of the church of God?)

6 Not a novice, lest being lifted up with pride he fall into the condemnation of the devil.

7 Moreover he must have a good report of them which are without; lest he fall into reproach and the snare of the devil.

8 Likewise *must* the deacons *be* grave, not double-tongued, not given to much wine, not greedy of filthy lucre;

9 Holding the mystery of the faith in a pure conscience.

10 And let these also first be proved; then let them use the office of a deacon, being *found* blameless.

11 Even so *must their* wives *be* grave, not slanderers, sober, faithful in all things.

12 Let the deacons be the husbands of one wife, ruling their children and their own houses well.

13 For they that have used the office of a deacon well purchase to themselves a good degree, and great boldness in the faith which is in Christ Jesus.

14 These things write I unto thee, hoping to come unto thee shortly:

15 But if I tarry long, that thou mayest know how thou oughtest to behave thyself in the house of God, which is the church of the living God, the pillar and ground of the truth.

16 And without controversy great is the mystery of godliness: God was manifest in the flesh, justified in the Spirit, seen of angels, preached unto the Gĕn′tïles, believed on in the world, received up into glory.

CHAPTER 4

NOW the Spirit speaketh expressly, that in the latter times some shall depart from the faith, giving heed to seducing spirits, and doctrines of devils;

2 Speaking lies in hypocrisy; having their conscience seared with a hot iron;

3 Forbidding to marry, *and commanding* to abstain from meats, which God hath created to be received with thanksgiving of them which believe and know the truth.

4 For every creature of God *is* good, and nothing to be refused, if it be received with thanksgiving:

5 For it is sanctified by the word of God and prayer.

6 If thou put the brethren in remembrance of these things, thou shalt be a good minister of Jesus Christ, nourished up in the words of faith and of good doctrine, whereunto thou hast attained.

7 But refuse profane and old wives' fables, and exercise thyself *rather* unto godliness.

8 For bodily exercise profiteth little: but godliness is profitable unto all things, having promise of the life that now is, and of that which is to come.

9 This *is* a faithful saying, and worthy of all acceptation.

10 For therefore we both labor and suffer reproach, because we trust in the living God, who is the Saviour of all men, specially of those that believe.

11 These things command and teach.

12 Let no man despise thy youth; but be thou an example of the believers, in word, in conversation, in charity, in spirit, in faith, in purity.

13 Till I come, give attendance to reading, to exhortation, to doctrine.

14 Neglect not the gift that is in thee, which was given thee by prophecy, with the laying on of the hands of the presbytery.

15 Meditate upon these things; give thyself wholly to them; that thy profiting may appear to all.

16 Take heed unto thyself, and unto the doctrine; continue in them: for in doing this thou shalt both save thyself, and them that hear thee.

CHAPTER 5

REBUKE not an elder, but entreat *him* as a father; *and* the younger men as brethren;

2 The elder women as mothers; the younger as sisters, with all purity.

3 Honor widows that are widows indeed.

4 But if any widow have children or nephews, let them learn first to show piety at home, and to requite their parents: for that is good and acceptable before God.

5 Now she that is a widow indeed, and desolate, trusteth in God, and continueth in supplications and prayers night and day.

6 But she that liveth in pleasure is dead while she liveth.

7 And these things give in charge, that they may be blameless.

8 But if any provide not for his own, and specially for those of his own house, he hath denied the faith, and is worse than an infidel.

9 Let not a widow be taken into the number under threescore years old, having been the wife of one man,

10 Well reported of for good works; if she have brought up children, if she have lodged strangers, if she have washed the saints' feet, if she have relieved the afflicted, if she have diligently followed every good work.

11 But the younger widows refuse: for when they have begun to wax wanton against Christ, they will marry;

12 Having damnation, because they have cast off their first faith.

13 And withal they learn *to be* idle, wandering about from house to house; and not only idle, but tattlers also and busybodies, speaking things which they ought not.

14 I will therefore that the younger women marry, bear children, guide the house, give none occasion to the adversary to speak reproachfully.

15 For some are already turned aside after Satan.

16 If any man or woman that believeth have widows, let them relieve them, and let not the church be charged; that it may relieve them that are widows indeed.

17 Let the elders that rule well be counted worthy of double honor, especially they who labor in the word and doctrine.

18 For the Scripture saith, Thou shalt not muzzle the ox that treadeth out the corn. And, The laborer *is* worthy of his reward.

19 Against an elder receive not an accusation, but before two or three witnesses.

20 Them that sin rebuke before all, that others also may fear.

21 I charge *thee* before God, and the Lord Jesus Christ, and the elect angels, that thou observe these things without preferring one before another, doing nothing by partiality.

22 Lay hands suddenly on no man, neither be partaker of other men's sins: keep thyself pure.

23 Drink no longer water, but use a little wine for thy stomach's sake and thine often infirmities.

24 Some men's sins are open beforehand, going before to judgment; and some *men* they follow after.

25 Likewise also the good works *of some* are manifest beforehand; and they that are otherwise cannot be hid.

CHAPTER 6

LET as many servants as are under the yoke count their own masters worthy of all honor, that the name of God and *his* doctrine be not blasphemed.

2 And they that have believing masters, let them not despise *them*, because they are brethren; but rather do *them* service, because they are faithful and beloved, partakers of the benefit. These things teach and exhort.

3 If any man teach otherwise, and consent not to wholesome words, *even* the words of our Lord Jesus Christ, and to the doctrine which is according to godliness;

4 He is proud, knowing nothing, but
doting about questions and strifes of
words, whereof cometh envy, strife,
railings, evil surmisings,
5 Perverse disputings of men of corrupt minds, and destitute of the truth,
supposing that gain is godliness: from
such withdraw thyself.
6 But godliness with contentment is
great gain.
7 For we brought nothing into *this*
world, *and it is* certain we can carry
nothing out.
8 And having food and raiment, let us
be therewith content.
9 But they that will be rich fall into
temptation and a snare, and *into* many
foolish and hurtful lusts, which drown
men in destruction and perdition.
10 For the love of money is the root of
all evil: which while some coveted after,
they have erred from the faith, and
pierced themselves through with many
sorrows.
11 But thou, O man of God, flee these
things; and follow after righteousness,
godliness, faith, love, patience, meekness.
12 Fight the good fight of faith, lay
hold on eternal life, whereunto thou art
also called, and hast professed a good
profession before many witnesses.
13 I give thee charge in the sight of
God, who quickeneth all things, and *before* Christ Jesus, who before Pŏn'ti-ŭs
Pilate witnessed a good confession;
14 That thou keep *this* commandment
without spot, unrebukable, until the
appearing of our Lord Jesus Christ:
15 Which in his times he shall show,
who is the blessed and only Potentate,
the King of kings, and Lord of lords;
16 Who only hath immortality, dwelling in the light which no man can approach unto; whom no man hath seen,
nor can see: to whom *be* honor and
power everlasting. Amen.
17 Charge them that are rich in this
world, that they be not high-minded, nor
trust in uncertain riches, but in the living God, who giveth us richly all things
to enjoy;
18 That they do good, that they be rich
in good works, ready to distribute, willing to communicate;
19 Laying up in store for themselves a
good foundation against the time to
come, that they may lay hold on eternal
life.
20 O Timothy, keep that which is committed to thy trust, avoiding profane
and vain babblings, and oppositions of
science falsely so called:
21 Which some professing have erred
concerning the faith. Grace *be* with
thee. Amen.

¶ The first to Timothy was written from Laodicea, which is the chiefest city of Phrygia Pacatiana.

THE SECOND EPISTLE OF PAUL THE APOSTLE TO

TIMOTHY

CHAPTER 1

PAUL, an apostle of Jesus Christ by
the will of God, according to the
promise of life which is in Christ Jesus,
2 To Timothy, *my* dearly beloved son:
Grace, mercy, *and* peace, from God the
Father and Christ Jesus our Lord.
3 I thank God, whom I serve from *my*
forefathers with pure conscience, that
without ceasing I have remembrance of
thee in my prayers night and day;
4 Greatly desiring to see thee, being
mindful of thy tears, that I may be filled
with joy;
5 When I call to remembrance the unfeigned faith that is in thee, which dwelt
first in thy grandmother Lois, and thy
mother Eunice; and I am persuaded
that in thee also.
6 Wherefore I put thee in remembrance, that thou stir up the gift of God,
which is in thee by the putting on of my
hands.
7 For God hath not given us the spirit
of fear; but of power, and of love, and of
a sound mind.
8 Be not thou therefore ashamed of the
testimony of our Lord, nor of me his
prisoner: but be thou partaker of the
afflictions of the gospel according to the
power of God;

9 Who hath saved us, and called *us*
with a holy calling, not according to our
works, but according to his own purpose and grace, which was given us in
Christ Jesus before the world began;
10 But is now made manifest by the
appearing of our Saviour Jesus Christ,
who hath abolished death, and hath
brought life and immortality to light
through the gospel:
11 Whereunto I am appointed a
preacher, and an apostle, and a teacher
of the Ġĕn′tīles.
12 For the which cause I also suffer
these things: nevertheless I am not
ashamed; for I know whom I have believed, and am persuaded that he is able
to keep that which I have committed
unto him against that day.
13 Hold fast the form of sound words,
which thou hast heard of me, in faith
and love which is in Christ Jesus.
14 That good thing which was committed unto thee keep by the Holy
Ghost which dwelleth in us.
15 This thou knowest, that all they which
are in Asia be turned away from me; of
whom are Phȳ-ġĕl′lŭs and Hĕr-mŏġ′ē-nēṣ.
16 The Lord give mercy unto the house
of Ŏn′ē-sĭph′ō-rŭs; for he oft refreshed
me, and was not ashamed of my chain:
17 But, when he was in Rome, he sought
me out very diligently, and found *me*.
18 The Lord grant unto him that he
may find mercy of the Lord in that day:
and in how many things he ministered
unto me at Ĕph′ē-sŭs, thou knowest
very well.

CHAPTER 2

THOU therefore, my son, be strong
in the grace that is in Christ Jesus.
2 And the things that thou hast heard
of me among many witnesses, the same
commit thou to faithful men, who shall
be able to teach others also.
3 Thou therefore endure hardness, as
a good soldier of Jesus Christ.
4 No man that warreth entangleth himself with the affairs of *this* life; that he
may please him who hath chosen him to
be a soldier.
5 And if a man also strive for masteries, *yet* is he not crowned, except he
strive lawfully.
6 The husbandman that laboreth must
be first partaker of the fruits.
7 Consider what I say; and the Lord
give thee understanding in all things.
8 Remember that Jesus Christ of the
seed of David was raised from the dead,
according to my gospel:
9 Wherein I suffer trouble, as an evildoer, *even* unto bonds; but the word of
God is not bound.
10 Therefore I endure all things for the
elect's sake, that they may also obtain
the salvation which is in Christ Jesus
with eternal glory.
11 *It is* a faithful saying: For if we be
dead with *him*, we shall also live with
him:
12 If we suffer, we shall also reign
with *him:* if we deny *him*, he also will
deny us:
13 If we believe not, *yet* he abideth
faithful: he cannot deny himself.
14 Of these things put *them* in remembrance, charging *them* before the Lord
that they strive not about words to no
profit, *but* to the subverting of the
hearers.
15 Study to show thyself approved
unto God, a workman that needeth not
to be ashamed, rightly dividing the word
of truth.
16 But shun profane *and* vain babblings: for they will increase unto more
ungodliness.
17 And their word will eat as doth a
canker: of whom is Hȳ′mĕn-ē′ŭs and
Phĭ-lē′tŭs;
18 Who concerning the truth have
erred, saying that the resurrection is
past already; and overthrow the faith
of some.
19 Nevertheless the foundation of God
standeth sure, having this seal, The
Lord knoweth them that are his. And,
Let every one that nameth the name of
Christ depart from iniquity.
20 But in a great house there are not
only vessels of gold and of silver, but
also of wood and of earth; and some to
honor, and some to dishonor.
21 If a man therefore purge himself
from these, he shall be a vessel unto
honor, sanctified, and meet for the
master's use, *and* prepared unto every
good work.
22 Flee also youthful lusts: but follow
righteousness, faith, charity, peace,
with them that call on the Lord out of
a pure heart.
23 But foolish and unlearned questions

avoid, knowing that they do gender
strifes.
24 And the servant of the Lord must
not strive; but be gentle unto all *men,*
apt to teach, patient;
25 In meekness instructing those that
oppose themselves; if God peradventure
will give them repentance to the acknowledging of the truth;
26 And *that* they may recover themselves out of the snare of the devil, who
are taken captive by him at his will.

CHAPTER 3

THIS know also, that in the last days
perilous times shall come.
2 For men shall be lovers of their own
selves, covetous, boasters, proud, blasphemers, disobedient to parents, unthankful, unholy,
3 Without natural affection, truce-
breakers, false accusers, incontinent,
fierce, despisers of those that are good,
4 Traitors, heady, high-minded, lovers
of pleasures more than lovers of God;
5 Having a form of godliness, but denying the power thereof: from such turn
away.
6 For of this sort are they which creep
into houses, and lead captive silly wom-
en laden with sins, led away with divers
lusts,
7 Ever learning, and never able to come
to the knowledge of the truth.
8 Now as Jăn′nēs̱ and Jăm′brēs̱ withstood Moses, so do these also resist the
truth: men of corrupt minds, reprobate
concerning the faith.
9 But they shall proceed no further: for
their folly shall be manifest unto all
men, as theirs also was.
10 But thou hast fully known my doctrine, manner of life, purpose, faith,
long-suffering, charity, patience,
11 Persecutions, afflictions, which
came unto me at Ăn′tĭ-ŏch, at Ī-cō′-
nĭ-ŭm, at Lȳ̆s′trȧ; what persecutions I
endured: but out of *them* all the Lord
delivered me.
12 Yea, and all that will live godly in
Christ Jesus shall suffer persecution.
13 But evil men and seducers shall wax
worse and worse, deceiving, and being
deceived.
14 But continue thou in the things
which thou hast learned and hast been
assured of, knowing of whom thou hast
learned *them;*
15 And that from a child thou hast
known the holy Scriptures, which are
able to make thee wise unto salvation
through faith which is in Christ Jesus.
16 All Scripture *is* given by inspiration
of God, and *is* profitable for doctrine,
for reproof, for correction, for instruction in righteousness:
17 That the man of God may be perfect, thoroughly furnished unto all good
works.

CHAPTER 4

I CHARGE *thee* therefore before God,
and the Lord Jesus Christ, who shall
judge the quick and the dead at his appearing and his kingdom;
2 Preach the word; be instant in season, out of season; reprove, rebuke,
exhort with all long-suffering and doctrine.
3 For the time will come when they will
not endure sound doctrine; but after
their own lusts shall they heap to themselves teachers, having itching ears;
4 And they shall turn away *their* ears
from the truth, and shall be turned unto
fables.
5 But watch thou in all things, endure
afflictions, do the work of an evangelist,
make full proof of thy ministry.
6 For I am now ready to be offered, and
the time of my departure is at hand.
7 I have fought a good fight, I have finished *my* course, I have kept the faith:
8 Henceforth there is laid up for me
a crown of righteousness, which the
Lord, the righteous judge, shall give
me at that day: and not to me only,
but unto all them also that love his appearing.
9 Do thy diligence to come shortly unto
me:
10 For Dē′măs hath forsaken me, having loved this present world, and is
departed unto Thĕs′sȧ-lō-nī′cȧ; Crĕs′-
çĕns̱ to Gȧ-lā′ti̮-ȧ, Titus unto Dăl-
mā′ti̮-ȧ.
11 Only Luke is with me. Take Mark,
and bring him with thee: for he is profitable to me for the ministry.
12 And Tȳ̆ch′ĭ-cŭs have I sent to
Ĕph′e-sŭs.
13 The cloak that I left at Trō′ăs with
Carpus, when thou comest, bring *with
thee,* and the books, *but* especially the
parchments.
14 Alexander the coppersmith did me

much evil: the Lord reward him according to his works:

15 Of whom be thou ware also; for he hath greatly withstood our words.

16 At my first answer no man stood with me, but all *men* forsook me: *I pray God* that it may not be laid to their charge.

17 Notwithstanding the Lord stood with me, and strengthened me; that by me the preaching might be fully known, and *that* all the Ġĕn′tīleṣ might hear: and I was delivered out of the mouth of the lion.

18 And the Lord shall deliver me from every evil work, and will preserve *me* unto his heavenly kingdom: to whom *be* glory for ever and ever. Amen.

19 Salute Prĭs′cȧ and Ăq′uĭ-lȧ, and the household of Ŏn′ē-sĭph′ō-rŭs.

20 Ē-răs′tŭs abode at Corinth: but Trŏph′ĭ-mŭs have I left at Mī-lē′tŭm sick.

21 Do thy diligence to come before winter. Eū-bū′lŭs greeteth thee, and Pū′dĕnṣ, and Lī′nŭs, and Claudia, and all the brethren.

22 The Lord Jesus Christ *be* with thy spirit. Grace *be* with you. Amen.

The second *epistle* unto Timotheus, ordained the first bishop of the church of the Ephesians, was written from Rome, when Paul was brought before Nero the second time.

THE EPISTLE OF PAUL TO

TITUS

CHAPTER 1

PAUL, a servant of God, and an apostle of Jesus Christ, according to the faith of God's elect, and the acknowledging of the truth which is after godliness;

2 In hope of eternal life, which God, that cannot lie, promised before the world began;

3 But hath in due times manifested his word through preaching, which is committed unto me according to the commandment of God our Saviour;

4 To Titus, *mine* own son after the common faith: Grace, mercy, *and* peace, from God the Father and the Lord Jesus Christ our Saviour.

5 For this cause left I thee in Crete, that thou shouldest set in order the things that are wanting, and ordain elders in every city, as I had appointed thee:

6 If any be blameless, the husband of one wife, having faithful children not accused of riot or unruly.

7 For a bishop must be blameless, as the steward of God; not self-willed, not soon angry, not given to wine, no striker, not given to filthy lucre;

8 But a lover of hospitality, a lover of good men, sober, just, holy, temperate;

9 Holding fast the faithful word as he hath been taught, that he may be able by sound doctrine both to exhort and to convince the gainsayers.

10 For there are many unruly and vain talkers and deceivers, specially they of the circumcision:

11 Whose mouths must be stopped, who subvert whole houses, teaching things which they ought not, for filthy lucre's sake.

12 One of themselves, *even* a prophet of their own, said, The Crē′tĭănṣ *are* always liars, evil beasts, slow bellies.

13 This witness is true. Wherefore rebuke them sharply, that they may be sound in the faith;

14 Not giving heed to Jewish fables, and commandments of men, that turn from the truth.

15 Unto the pure all things *are* pure: but unto them that are defiled and unbelieving *is* nothing pure; but even their mind and conscience is defiled.

16 They profess that they know God; but in works they deny *him*, being abominable, and disobedient, and unto every good work reprobate.

CHAPTER 2

BUT speak thou the things which become sound doctrine:

2 That the aged men be sober, grave, temperate, sound in faith, in charity, in patience.

3 The aged women likewise, that *they*
be in behavior as becometh holiness, not
false accusers, not given to much wine,
teachers of good things;
4 That they may teach the young
women to be sober, to love their husbands, to love their children,
5 *To be* discreet, chaste, keepers at
home, good, obedient to their own husbands, that the word of God be not
blasphemed.
6 Young men likewise exhort to be
sober-minded.
7 In all things showing thyself a pattern of good works: in doctrine *showing*
uncorruptness, gravity, sincerity,
8 Sound speech, that cannot be condemned; that he that is of the contrary
part may be ashamed, having no evil
thing to say of you.
9 *Exhort* servants to be obedient
unto their own masters, *and* to please
them well in all things; not answering
again;
10 Not purloining, but showing all
good fidelity; that they may adorn the
doctrine of God our Saviour in all
things.
11 For the grace of God that bringeth
salvation hath appeared to all men,
12 Teaching us that, denying ungodliness and worldly lusts, we should live
soberly, righteously, and godly, in this
present world;
13 Looking for that blessed hope, and
the glorious appearing of the great God
and our Saviour Jesus Christ;
14 Who gave himself for us, that he
might redeem us from all iniquity, and
purify unto himself a peculiar people,
zealous of good works.
15 These things speak, and exhort,
and rebuke with all authority. Let no
man despise thee.

CHAPTER 3

PUT them in mind to be subject to
principalities and powers, to obey
magistrates, to be ready to every good
work,
2 To speak evil of no man, to be no
brawlers, *but* gentle, showing all meekness unto all men.
3 For we ourselves also were sometime foolish, disobedient, deceived,
serving divers lusts and pleasures, living in malice and envy, hateful, *and*
hating one another.
4 But after that the kindness and love
of God our Saviour toward man appeared,
5 Not by works of righteousness which
we have done, but according to his
mercy he saved us, by the washing of
regeneration, and renewing of the Holy
Ghost;
6 Which he shed on us abundantly
through Jesus Christ our Saviour;
7 That being justified by his grace, we
should be made heirs according to the
hope of eternal life.
8 *This is* a faithful saying, and these
things I will that thou affirm constantly,
that they which have believed in God
might be careful to maintain good
works. These things are good and
profitable unto men.
9 But avoid foolish questions, and
genealogies, and contentions, and strivings about the law; for they are unprofitable and vain.
10 A man that is a heretic, after the
first and second admonition, reject;
11 Knowing that he that is such is sub-
verted, and sinneth, being condemned
of himself.
12 When I shall send Ăr′tē-măs unto
thee, or Tȳch′ĭ-cŭs, be diligent to come
unto me to Nī-cŏp′ō-lĭs: for I have determined there to winter.
13 Bring Zē′năs the lawyer and Ȧ-pŏl′-
lŏs on their journey diligently, that
nothing be wanting unto them.
14 And let ours also learn to maintain
good works for necessary uses, that
they be not unfruitful.
15 All that are with me salute thee.
Greet them that love us in the faith.
Grace *be* with you all. Amen.

¶ It was written to Titus, ordained the first bishop of the church of the Cretians, from Nicopolis of Macedonia.

THE EPISTLE OF PAUL TO

PHILEMON

PAUL, a prisoner of Jesus Christ, and Timothy *our* brother, unto Phĭ-lē'mŏn our dearly beloved, and fellow laborer,

2 And to *our* beloved Ăpph'ĭ-ȧ, and Ăr-chĭp'pŭs our fellow soldier, and to the church in thy house:

3 Grace to you, and peace, from God our Father and the Lord Jesus Christ.

4 I thank my God, making mention of thee always in my prayers,

5 Hearing of thy love and faith, which thou hast toward the Lord Jesus, and toward all saints;

6 That the communication of thy faith may become effectual by the acknowledging of every good thing which is in you in Christ Jesus.

7 For we have great joy and consolation in thy love, because the bowels of the saints are refreshed by thee, brother.

8 Wherefore, though I might be much bold in Christ to enjoin thee that which is convenient,

9 Yet for love's sake I rather beseech *thee*, being such a one as Paul the aged, and now also a prisoner of Jesus Christ.

10 I beseech thee for my son Ō-nĕs'ĭ-mŭs, whom I have begotten in my bonds:

11 Which in time past was to thee unprofitable, but now profitable to thee and to me:

12 Whom I have sent again: thou therefore receive him, that is, mine own bowels:

13 Whom I would have retained with me, that in thy stead he might have ministered unto me in the bonds of the gospel:

14 But without thy mind would I do nothing; that thy benefit should not be as it were of necessity, but willingly.

15 For perhaps he therefore departed for a season, that thou shouldest receive him for ever;

16 Not now as a servant, but above a servant, a brother beloved, specially to me, but how much more unto thee, both in the flesh, and in the Lord?

17 If thou count me therefore a partner, receive him as myself.

18 If he hath wronged thee, or oweth *thee* aught, put that on mine account;

19 I Paul have written *it* with mine own hand, I will repay *it:* albeit I do not say to thee how thou owest unto me even thine own self besides.

20 Yea, brother, let me have joy of thee in the Lord: refresh my bowels in the Lord.

21 Having confidence in thy obedience I wrote unto thee, knowing that thou wilt also do more than I say.

22 But withal prepare me also a lodging: for I trust that through your prayers I shall be given unto you.

23 There salute thee Ĕp'ȧ-phrăs, my fellow prisoner in Christ Jesus;

24 Marcus, Ăr'ĭs-tär'chŭs, Dē'măs, Lū'cȧs, my fellow laborers.

25 The grace of our Lord Jesus Christ *be* with your spirit. Amen.

¶ **Written from Rome to Philemon, by Onesimus a servant.**

THE EPISTLE OF PAUL THE APOSTLE TO THE

HEBREWS

CHAPTER 1

GOD, who at sundry times and in
divers manners spake in time past
unto the fathers by the prophets,
2 Hath in these last days spoken unto
us by *his* Son, whom he hath appointed
heir of all things, by whom also he made
the worlds;
3 Who being the brightness of *his*
glory, and the express image of his person, and upholding all things by the
word of his power, when he had by himself purged our sins, sat down on the
right hand of the Majesty on high;
4 Being made so much better than the
angels, as he hath by inheritance obtained a more excellent name than they.
5 For unto which of the angels said he
at any time, Thou art my Son, this day
have I begotten thee? And again, I will
be to him a Father, and he shall be to
me a Son?
6 And again, when he bringeth in the
first-begotten into the world, he saith,
And let all the angels of God worship him.
7 And of the angels he saith, Who maketh his angels spirits, and his ministers
a flame of fire.
8 But unto the Son *he saith,* Thy
throne, O God, *is* for ever and ever: a
sceptre of righteousness *is* the sceptre
of thy kingdom.
9 Thou hast loved righteousness, and
hated iniquity; therefore God, *even* thy
God, hath anointed thee with the oil of
gladness above thy fellows.
10 And, Thou, Lord, in the beginning
hast laid the foundation of the earth;
and the heavens are the works of thine
hands.
11 They shall perish, but thou remainest: and they all shall wax old as doth a
garment;
12 And as a vesture shalt thou fold
them up, and they shall be changed: but
thou art the same, and thy years shall
not fail.
13 But to which of the angels said he
at any time, Sit on my right hand, until
I make thine enemies thy footstool?
14 Are they not all ministering spirits,
sent forth to minister for them who shall
be heirs of salvation?

CHAPTER 2

THEREFORE we ought to give the
more earnest heed to the things
which we have heard, lest at any time
we should let *them* slip.
2 For if the word spoken by angels was
steadfast, and every transgression and
disobedience received a just recompense of reward;
3 How shall we escape, if we neglect
so great salvation; which at the first began to be spoken by the Lord, and was
confirmed unto us by them that heard
him;
4 God also bearing *them* witness, both
with signs and wonders, and with divers
miracles, and gifts of the Holy Ghost,
according to his own will?
5 For unto the angels hath he not put
in subjection the world to come, whereof we speak.
6 But one in a certain place testified,
saying, What is man, that thou art
mindful of him? or the son of man, that
thou visitest him?
7 Thou madest him a little lower than
the angels; thou crownedst him with
glory and honor, and didst set him over
the works of thy hands:
8 Thou hast put all things in subjection
under his feet. For in that he put all in
subjection under him, he left nothing
that is not put under him. But now we
see not yet all things put under him.
9 But we see Jesus, who was made a
little lower than the angels for the suffering of death, crowned with glory and
honor; that he by the grace of God
should taste death for every man.
10 For it became him, for whom *are* all
things, and by whom *are* all things, in
bringing many sons unto glory, to make
the captain of their salvation perfect
through sufferings.
11 For both he that sanctifieth and they
who are sanctified *are* all of one: for
which cause he is not ashamed to call
them brethren,
12 Saying, I will declare thy name unto

my brethren, in the midst of the church
will I sing praise unto thee.
13 And again, I will put my trust in
him. And again, Behold I and the children which God hath given me.
14 Forasmuch then as the children are
partakers of flesh and blood, he also
himself likewise took part of the same;
that through death he might destroy
him that had the power of death, that
is, the devil;
15 And deliver them, who through fear
of death were all their lifetime subject
to bondage.
16 For verily he took not on *him the*
nature of angels; but he took on *him* the
seed of Abraham.
17 Wherefore in all things it behooved
him to be made like unto *his* brethren,
that he might be a merciful and faithful
high priest in things *pertaining* to God,
to make reconciliation for the sins of
the people.
18 For in that he himself hath suffered
being tempted, he is able to succor them
that are tempted.

CHAPTER 3

WHEREFORE, holy brethren, partakers of the heavenly calling,
consider the Apostle and High Priest of
our profession, Christ Jesus;
2 Who was faithful to him that appointed him, as also Moses *was faithful*
in all his house.
3 For this *man* was counted worthy of
more glory than Moses, inasmuch as he
who hath builded the house hath more
honor than the house.
4 For every house is builded by some
man; but he that built all things *is* God.
5 And Moses verily *was* faithful in all
his house as a servant, for a testimony
of those things which were to be spoken
after;
6 But Christ as a son over his own
house; whose house are we, if we hold
fast the confidence and the rejoicing of
the hope firm unto the end.
7 Wherefore as the Holy Ghost saith,
To-day if ye will hear his voice,
8 Harden not your hearts, as in the
provocation, in the day of temptation in
the wilderness:
9 When your fathers tempted me,
proved me, and saw my works forty
years.
10 Wherefore I was grieved with that
generation, and said, They do always
err in *their* heart; and they have not
known my ways.
11 So I sware in my wrath, They shall
not enter into my rest.
12 Take heed, brethren, lest there be
in any of you an evil heart of unbelief,
in departing from the living God.
13 But exhort one another daily, while
it is called To-day; lest any of you be
hardened through the deceitfulness of
sin.
14 For we are made partakers of
Christ, if we hold the beginning of our
confidence steadfast unto the end;
15 While it is said, To-day if ye will
hear his voice, harden not your hearts,
as in the provocation.
16 For some, when they had heard,
did provoke: howbeit not all that came
out of Egypt by Moses.
17 But with whom was he grieved forty
years? *was it* not with them that had
sinned, whose carcasses fell in the
wilderness?
18 And to whom sware he that they
should not enter into his rest, but to
them that believed not?
19 So we see that they could not enter
in because of unbelief.

CHAPTER 4

LET us therefore fear, lest, a promise
being left *us* of entering into his
rest, any of you should seem to come
short of it.
2 For unto us was the gospel preached,
as well as unto them: but the word
preached did not profit them, not being
mixed with faith in them that heard *it*.
3 For we which have believed do enter
into rest, as he said, As I have sworn in
my wrath, if they shall enter into my
rest: although the works were finished
from the foundation of the world.
4 For he spake in a certain place of the
seventh *day* on this wise, And God did
rest the seventh day from all his works.
5 And in this *place* again, If they shall
enter into my rest.
6 Seeing therefore it remaineth that
some must enter therein, and they to
whom it was first preached entered not
in because of unbelief:
7 Again, he limiteth a certain day, saying in David, To-day, after so long a
time; as it is said, To-day if ye will hear
his voice, harden not your hearts.

8 For if Jesus had given them rest,
then would he not afterward have spoken
of another day.
9 There remaineth therefore a rest to
the people of God.
10 For he that is entered into his rest,
he also hath ceased from his own works,
as God *did* from his.
11 Let us labor therefore to enter into
that rest, lest any man fall after the
same example of unbelief.
12 For the word of God *is* quick, and
powerful, and sharper than any two-
edged sword, piercing even to the dividing asunder of soul and spirit, and of
the joints and marrow, and *is* a dis-
cerner of the thoughts and intents of
the heart.
13 Neither is there any creature that
is not manifest in his sight: but all things
are naked and opened unto the eyes of
him with whom we have to do.
14 Seeing then that we have a great
high priest, that is passed into the heavens, Jesus the Son of God, let us hold
fast *our* profession.
15 For we have not a high priest which
cannot be touched with the feeling of
our infirmities; but was in all points
tempted like as *we are, yet* without sin.
16 Let us therefore come boldly unto
the throne of grace, that we may obtain
mercy, and find grace to help in time of
need.

CHAPTER 5

FOR every high priest taken from
among men is ordained for men in
things *pertaining* to God, that he may
offer both gifts and sacrifices for sins:
2 Who can have compassion on the
ignorant, and on them that are out of the
way; for that he himself also is compassed with infirmity.
3 And by reason hereof he ought, as
for the people, so also for himself, to
offer for sins.
4 And no man taketh this honor unto
himself, but he that is called of God, as
was Aaron.
5 So also Christ glorified not himself
to be made a high priest; but he that
said unto him, Thou art my Son, to-day
have I begotten thee.
6 As he saith also in another *place,*
Thou *art* a priest for ever after the order
of Mĕl-chĭṣ′ē-dĕc.
7 Who in the days of his flesh, when
he had offered up prayers and supplications with strong crying and tears unto
him that was able to save him from
death, and was heard in that he feared;
8 Though he were a Son, yet learned
he obedience by the things which he
suffered;
9 And being made perfect, he became
the author of eternal salvation unto all
them that obey him;
10 Called of God a high priest after the
order of Mĕl-chĭṣ′ē-dĕc.
11 Of whom we have many things to
say, and hard to be uttered, seeing ye
are dull of hearing.
12 For when for the time ye ought to
be teachers, ye have need that one
teach you again which *be* the first principles of the oracles of God; and are become such as have need of milk, and
not of strong meat.
13 For every one that useth milk *is*
unskilful in the word of righteousness:
for he is a babe.
14 But strong meat belongeth to them
that are of full age, *even* those who by
reason of use have their senses exercised to discern both good and evil.

CHAPTER 6

THEREFORE leaving the principles
of the doctrine of Christ, let us go
on unto perfection; not laying again the
foundation of repentance from dead
works, and of faith toward God,
2 Of the doctrine of baptisms, and of
laying on of hands, and of resurrection
of the dead, and of eternal judgment.
3 And this will we do, if God permit.
4 For *it is* impossible for those who
were once enlightened, and have tasted
of the heavenly gift, and were made partakers of the Holy Ghost,
5 And have tasted the good word of
God, and the powers of the world to
come,
6 If they shall fall away, to renew them
again unto repentance; seeing they crucify to themselves the Son of God
afresh, and put *him* to an open shame.
7 For the earth which drinketh in the
rain that cometh oft upon it, and bringeth forth herbs meet for them by whom
it is dressed, receiveth blessing from
God:
8 But that which beareth thorns and
briers *is* rejected, and *is* nigh unto cursing; whose end *is* to be burned.

9 But, beloved, we are persuaded better things of you, and things that accompany salvation, though we thus speak.

10 For God *is* not unrighteous to forget your work and labor of love, which ye have showed toward his name, in that ye have ministered to the saints, and do minister.

11 And we desire that every one of you do show the same diligence to the full assurance of hope unto the end:

12 That ye be not slothful, but followers of them who through faith and patience inherit the promises.

13 For when God made promise to Abraham, because he could swear by no greater, he sware by himself,

14 Saying, Surely blessing I will bless thee, and multiplying I will multiply thee.

15 And so, after he had patiently endured, he obtained the promise.

16 For men verily swear by the greater: and an oath for confirmation *is* to them an end of all strife.

17 Wherein God, willing more abundantly to show unto the heirs of promise the immutability of his counsel, confirmed *it* by an oath:

18 That by two immutable things, in which *it was* impossible for God to lie, we might have a strong consolation, who have fled for refuge to lay hold upon the hope set before us:

19 Which *hope* we have as an anchor of the soul, both sure and steadfast, and which entereth into that within the veil;

20 Whither the forerunner is for us entered, *even* Jesus, made a high priest for ever after the order of Mĕl-chĭṣ'ē-dĕc.

CHAPTER 7

FOR this Mĕl-chĭṣ'ē-dĕc, king of Sā'lĕm, priest of the most high God, who met Abraham returning from the slaughter of the kings, and blessed him;

2 To whom also Abraham gave a tenth part of all; first being by interpretation King of righteousness, and after that also King of Sā'lĕm, which is, King of peace;

3 Without father, without mother, without descent, having neither beginning of days, nor end of life; but made like unto the Son of God; abideth a priest continually.

4 Now consider how great this man *was,* unto whom even the patriarch Abraham gave the tenth of the spoils.

5 And verily they that are of the sons of Levi, who receive the office of the priesthood, have a commandment to take tithes of the people according to the law, that is, of their brethren, though they come out of the loins of Abraham:

6 But he whose descent is not counted from them received tithes of Abraham, and blessed him that had the promises.

7 And without all contradiction the less is blessed of the better.

8 And here men that die receive tithes; but there he *receiveth them,* of whom it is witnessed that he liveth.

9 And as I may so say, Levi also, who receiveth tithes, paid tithes in Abraham.

10 For he was yet in the loins of his father, when Mĕl-chĭṣ'ē-dĕc met him.

11 If therefore perfection were by the Lē-vĭt'ĭ-căl priesthood, (for under it the people received the law,) what further need *was there* that another priest should rise after the order of Mĕl-chĭṣ'ē-dĕc, and not be called after the order of Aaron?

12 For the priesthood being changed, there is made of necessity a change also of the law.

13 For he of whom these things are spoken pertaineth to another tribe, of which no man gave attendance at the altar.

14 For *it is* evident that our Lord sprang out of Jụ'dȧ; of which tribe Moses spake nothing concerning priesthood.

15 And it is yet far more evident: for that after the similitude of Mĕl-chĭṣ'ē-dĕc there ariseth another priest,

16 Who is made, not after the law of a carnal commandment, but after the power of an endless life.

17 For he testifieth, Thou *art* a priest for ever after the order of Mĕl-chĭṣ'ē-dĕc.

18 For there is verily a disannulling of the commandment going before for the weakness and unprofitableness thereof.

19 For the law made nothing perfect, but the bringing in of a better hope *did;* by the which we draw nigh unto God.

20 And inasmuch as not without an oath *he was made priest:*

21 (For those priests were made without an oath; but this with an oath by

him that said unto him, The Lord sware
and will not repent, Thou *art* a priest for
ever after the order of Mĕl-chĭş′ē-dĕc:)
22 By so much was Jesus made a surety
of a better testament.
23 And they truly were many priests,
because they were not suffered to continue by reason of death:
24 But this *man,* because he continueth ever, hath an unchangeable priesthood.
25 Wherefore he is able also to save
them to the uttermost that come unto
God by him, seeing he ever liveth to
make intercession for them.
26 For such a high priest became us,
who is holy, harmless, undefiled, separate from sinners, and made higher than
the heavens;
27 Who needeth not daily, as those
high priests, to offer up sacrifice, first
for his own sins, and then for the people's: for this he did once, when he
offered up himself.
28 For the law maketh men high priests
which have infirmity; but the word of the
oath, which was since the law, *maketh*
the Son, who is consecrated for evermore.

CHAPTER 8

NOW of the things which we have
spoken *this is* the sum: We have
such a high priest, who is set on the
right hand of the throne of the Majesty
in the heavens;
2 A minister of the sanctuary, and of
the true tabernacle, which the Lord
pitched, and not man.
3 For every high priest is ordained to
offer gifts and sacrifices: wherefore *it is*
of necessity that this man have somewhat also to offer.
4 For if he were on earth, he should not
be a priest, seeing that there are priests
that offer gifts according to the law:
5 Who serve unto the example and
shadow of heavenly things, as Moses
was admonished of God when he was
about to make the tabernacle: for, See,
saith he, *that* thou make all things
according to the pattern showed to thee
in the mount.
6 But now hath he obtained a more excellent ministry, by how much also he is
the mediator of a better covenant, which
was established upon better promises.
7 For if that first *covenant* had been
faultless, then should no place have
been sought for the second.
8 For finding fault with them, he saith,
Behold, the days come, saith the Lord,
when I will make a new covenant with
the house of Ĭş′rā-ĕl and with the house
of Judah:
9 Not according to the covenant that I
made with their fathers, in the day when
I took them by the hand to lead them
out of the land of Egypt; because they
continued not in my covenant, and I
regarded them not, saith the Lord.
10 For this *is* the covenant that I will
make with the house of Ĭş′rā-ĕl after
those days, saith the Lord; I will put
my laws into their mind, and write them
in their hearts: and I will be to them a
God, and they shall be to me a people:
11 And they shall not teach every man
his neighbor, and every man his brother,
saying, Know the Lord: for all shall
know me, from the least to the greatest.
12 For I will be merciful to their unrighteousness, and their sins and their
iniquities will I remember no more.
13 In that he saith, A new *covenant,*
he hath made the first old. Now that
which decayeth and waxeth old *is* ready
to vanish away.

CHAPTER 9

THEN verily the first *covenant* had
also ordinances of divine service,
and a worldly sanctuary.
2 For there was a tabernacle made; the
first, wherein *was* the candlestick, and
the table, and the showbread; which is
called the sanctuary.
3 And after the second veil, the tabernacle which is called the holiest of all;
4 Which had the golden censer, and
the ark of the covenant overlaid round
about with gold, wherein *was* the golden
pot that had manna, and Aaron's rod
that budded, and the tables of the
covenant;
5 And over it the cherubim of glory
shadowing the mercy seat; of which we
cannot now speak particularly.
6 Now when these things were thus
ordained, the priests went always into
the first tabernacle, accomplishing the
service *of God.*
7 But into the second *went* the high
priest alone once every year, not without blood, which he offered for himself,
and *for* the errors of the people:

8 The Holy Ghost this signifying, that
the way into the holiest of all was not
yet made manifest, while as the first
tabernacle was yet standing:
9 Which *was* a figure for the time then
present, in which were offered both
gifts and sacrifices, that could not make
him that did the service perfect, as pertaining to the conscience;
10 *Which stood* only in meats and
drinks, and divers washings, and carnal
ordinances, imposed *on them* until the
time of reformation.
11 But Christ being come a high priest
of good things to come, by a greater
and more perfect tabernacle, not made
with hands, that is to say, not of this
building;
12 Neither by the blood of goats and
calves, but by his own blood he entered
in once into the holy place, having obtained eternal redemption *for us*.
13 For if the blood of bulls and of goats,
and the ashes of a heifer sprinkling the
unclean, sanctifieth to the purifying of
the flesh;
14 How much more shall the blood of
Christ, who through the eternal Spirit
offered himself without spot to God,
purge your conscience from dead works
to serve the living God?
15 And for this cause he is the mediator
of the new testament, that by means of
death, for the redemption of the transgressions *that were* under the first
testament, they which are called might
receive the promise of eternal inheritance.
16 For where a testament *is*, there must
also of necessity be the death of the
testator.
17 For a testament *is* of force after
men are dead: otherwise it is of no
strength at all while the testator liveth.
18 Whereupon neither the first *testament* was dedicated without blood.
19 For when Moses had spoken every
precept to all the people according to
the law, he took the blood of calves and
of goats, with water, and scarlet wool,
and hyssop, and sprinkled both the
book and all the people,
20 Saying, This *is* the blood of the
testament which God hath enjoined
unto you.
21 Moreover he sprinkled likewise
with blood both the tabernacle, and all
the vessels of the ministry.
22 And almost all things are by the law
purged with blood; and without shed-
ding of blood is no remission.
23 *It was* therefore necessary that the
patterns of things in the heavens should
be purified with these; but the heavenly
things themselves with better sacrifices than these.
24 For Christ is not entered into the
holy places made with hands, *which are*
the figures of the true; but into heaven
itself, now to appear in the presence of
God for us:
25 Nor yet that he should offer himself
often, as the high priest entereth into
the holy place every year with blood of
others;
26 For then must he often have suffered since the foundation of the world:
but now once in the end of the world
hath he appeared to put away sin by the
sacrifice of himself.
27 And as it is appointed unto men once
to die, but after this the judgment:
28 So Christ was once offered to bear
the sins of many; and unto them that
look for him shall he appear the second
time without sin unto salvation.

CHAPTER 10

FOR the law having a shadow of
good things to come, *and* not the
very image of the things, can never with
those sacrifices, which they offered year
by year continually, make the comers
thereunto perfect.
2 For then would they not have ceased
to be offered? because that the worshippers once purged should have had
no more conscience of sins.
3 But in those *sacrifices there is* a
remembrance again *made* of sins every
year.
4 For *it is* not possible that the blood
of bulls and of goats should take away
sins.
5 Wherefore, when he cometh into the
world, he saith, Sacrifice and offering
thou wouldest not, but a body hast thou
prepared me:
6 In burnt offerings and *sacrifices* for
sin thou hast had no pleasure.
7 Then said I, Lo, I come (in the
volume of the book it is written of me)
to do thy will, O God.
8 Above when he said, Sacrifice and
offering and burnt offerings and *offering* for sin thou wouldest not, neither

hadst pleasure *therein;* which are offered by the law;
9 Then said he, Lo, I come to do thy
will, O God. He taketh away the first,
that he may establish the second.
10 By the which will we are sanctified
through the offering of the body of
Jesus Christ once *for all.*
11 And every priest standeth daily
ministering and offering oftentimes the
same sacrifices, which can never take
away sins:
12 But this man, after he had offered
one sacrifice for sins for ever, sat down
on the right hand of God;
13 From henceforth expecting till his
enemies be made his footstool.
14 For by one offering he hath perfected for ever them that are sanctified.
15 *Whereof* the Holy Ghost also is a
witness to us: for after that he had said
before,
16 This *is* the covenant that I will make
with them after those days, saith the
Lord; I will put my laws into their
hearts, and in their minds will I write
them;
17 And their sins and iniquities will I
remember no more.
18 Now where remission of these *is,*
there is no more offering for sin.
19 Having therefore, brethren, boldness to enter into the holiest by the
blood of Jesus,
20 By a new and living way, which he
hath consecrated for us, through the
veil, that is to say, his flesh;
21 And *having* a high priest over the
house of God;
22 Let us draw near with a true heart
in full assurance of faith, having our
hearts sprinkled from an evil conscience,
and our bodies washed with pure water.
23 Let us hold fast the profession of
our faith without wavering; for he *is*
faithful that promised;
24 And let us consider one another to
provoke unto love and to good works:
25 Not forsaking the assembling of ourselves together, as the manner of some
is; but exhorting *one another:* and so
much the more, as ye see the day approaching.
26 For if we sin wilfully after that we
have received the knowledge of the
truth, there remaineth no more sacrifice
for sins,
27 But a certain fearful looking for of
judgment and fiery indignation, which
shall devour the adversaries.
28 He that despised Moses' law died
without mercy under two or three witnesses:
29 Of how much sorer punishment,
suppose ye, shall he be thought worthy,
who hath trodden under foot the Son of
God, and hath counted the blood of the
covenant, wherewith he was sanctified,
an unholy thing, and hath done despite
unto the Spirit of grace?
30 For we know him that hath said,
Vengeance *belongeth* unto me, I will
recompense, saith the Lord. And again,
The Lord shall judge his people.
31 *It is* a fearful thing to fall into the
hands of the living God.
32 But call to remembrance the former
days, in which, after ye were illumi-
nated, ye endured a great fight of
afflictions;
33 Partly, whilst ye were made a
gazingstock both by reproaches and
afflictions; and partly, whilst ye became
companions of them that were so used.
34 For ye had compassion of me in my
bonds, and took joyfully the spoiling of
your goods, knowing in yourselves that
ye have in heaven a better and an
enduring substance.
35 Cast not away therefore your confidence, which hath great recompense of
reward.
36 For ye have need of patience, that,
after ye have done the will of God, ye
might receive the promise.
37 For yet a little while, and he that
shall come will come, and will not tarry.
38 Now the just shall live by faith: but
if *any man* draw back, my soul shall
have no pleasure in him.
39 But we are not of them who draw
back unto perdition; but of them that
believe to the saving of the soul.

CHAPTER 11

NOW faith is the substance of things
hoped for, the evidence of things
not seen.
2 For by it the elders obtained a good
report.
3 Through faith we understand that
the worlds were framed by the word of
God, so that things which are seen were
not made of things which do appear.
4 By faith Abel offered unto God a
more excellent sacrifice than Cain, by

which he obtained witness that he was
righteous, God testifying of his gifts:
and by it he being dead yet speaketh.
5 By faith Enoch was translated that
he should not see death; and was not
found, because God had translated him:
for before his translation he had this
testimony, that he pleased God.
6 But without faith *it is* impossible to
please *him:* for he that cometh to God
must believe that he is, and *that* he is a
rewarder of them that diligently seek
him.
7 By faith Noah, being warned of God
of things not seen as yet, moved with
fear, prepared an ark to the saving of
his house; by the which he condemned
the world, and became heir of the righteousness which is by faith.
8 By faith Abraham, when he was
called to go out into a place which he
should after receive for an inheritance,
obeyed; and he went out, not knowing
whither he went.
9 By faith he sojourned in the land of
promise, as *in* a strange country, dwelling in tabernacles with Isaac and Jacob,
the heirs with him of the same promise:
10 For he looked for a city which hath
foundations, whose builder and maker
is God.
11 Through faith also Sarah herself
received strength to conceive seed, and
was delivered of a child when she was
past age, because she judged him faithful who had promised.
12 Therefore sprang there even of one,
and him as good as dead, *so many* as
the stars of the sky in multitude, and
as the sand which is by the seashore
innumerable.
13 These all died in faith, not having
received the promises, but having seen
them afar off, and were persuaded of
them, and embraced *them,* and confessed that they were strangers and pilgrims on the earth.
14 For they that say such things declare plainly that they seek a country.
15 And truly, if they had been mindful
of that *country* from whence they came
out, they might have had opportunity
to have returned.
16 But now they desire a better *country,* that is, a heavenly: wherefore God
is not ashamed to be called their God:
for he hath prepared for them a city.
17 By faith Abraham, when he was
tried, offered up Isaac: and he that had
received the promises offered up his
only begotten *son,*
18 Of whom it was said, That in Isaac
shall thy seed be called:
19 Accounting that God *was* able to
raise *him* up, even from the dead; from
whence also he received him in a figure.
20 By faith Isaac blessed Jacob and
Ē′sa͡u concerning things to come.
21 By faith Jacob, when he was a dying,
blessed both the sons of Joseph; and
worshipped, *leaning* upon the top of his
staff.
22 By faith Joseph, when he died,
made mention of the departing of the
children of Ĭṣ′rā-ĕl; and gave commandment concerning his bones.
23 By faith Moses, when he was born,
was hid three months of his parents, because they saw *he was* a proper child;
and they were not afraid of the king's
commandment.
24 By faith Moses, when he was come
to years, refused to be called the son of
Phā′raōh's daughter;
25 Choosing rather to suffer affliction
with the people of God, than to enjoy
the pleasures of sin for a season;
26 Esteeming the reproach of Christ
greater riches than the treasures in
Egypt: for he had respect unto the recompense of the reward.
27 By faith he forsook Egypt, not fearing the wrath of the king: for he endured, as seeing him who is invisible.
28 Through faith he kept the passover,
and the sprinkling of blood, lest he that
destroyed the firstborn should touch
them.
29 By faith they passed through the
Red sea as by dry *land:* which the
Egyptians assaying to do were drowned.
30 By faith the walls of Jĕr′ĭ-chō fell
down, after they were compassed about
seven days.
31 By faith the harlot Rā′hăb perished
not with them that believed not, when
she had received the spies with peace.
32 And what shall I more say? for the
time would fail me to tell of Gideon, and
of Bā′răk, and *of* Samson, and *of* Jĕph′-
thăh; *of* David also, and Samuel, and *of*
the prophets:
33 Who through faith subdued kingdoms, wrought righteousness, obtained
promises, stopped the mouths of lions,
34 Quenched the violence of fire,

escaped the edge of the sword, out of weakness were made strong, waxed valiant in fight, turned to flight the armies of the aliens.

35 Women received their dead raised to life again: and others were tortured, not accepting deliverance; that they might obtain a better resurrection:

36 And others had trial of *cruel* mockings and scourgings, yea, moreover of bonds and imprisonment:

37 They were stoned, they were sawn asunder, were tempted, were slain with the sword: they wandered about in sheepskins and goatskins; being destitute, afflicted, tormented;

38 Of whom the world was not worthy: they wandered in deserts, and *in* mountains, and *in* dens and caves of the earth.

39 And these all, having obtained a good report through faith, received not the promise:

40 God having provided some better thing for us, that they without us should not be made perfect.

CHAPTER 12

WHEREFORE, seeing we also are compassed about with so great a cloud of witnesses, let us lay aside every weight, and the sin which doth so easily beset *us,* and let us run with patience the race that is set before us,

2 Looking unto Jesus the author and finisher of *our* faith; who for the joy that was set before him endured the cross, despising the shame, and is set down at the right hand of the throne of God.

3 For consider him that endured such contradiction of sinners against himself, lest ye be wearied and faint in your minds.

4 Ye have not yet resisted unto blood, striving against sin.

5 And ye have forgotten the exhortation which speaketh unto you as unto children, My son, despise not thou the chastening of the Lord, nor faint when thou art rebuked of him:

6 For whom the Lord loveth he chasteneth, and scourgeth every son whom he receiveth.

7 If ye endure chastening, God dealeth with you as with sons; for what son is he whom the father chasteneth not?

8 But if ye be without chastisement, whereof all are partakers, then are ye bastards, and not sons.

9 Furthermore, we have had fathers of our flesh which corrected *us,* and we gave *them* reverence: shall we not much rather be in subjection unto the Father of spirits, and live?

10 For they verily for a few days chastened *us* after their own pleasure; but he for *our* profit, that *we* might be partakers of his holiness.

11 Now no chastening for the present seemeth to be joyous, but grievous: nevertheless, afterward it yieldeth the peaceable fruit of righteousness unto them which are exercised thereby.

12 Wherefore lift up the hands which hang down, and the feeble knees;

13 And make straight paths for your feet, lest that which is lame be turned out of the way; but let it rather be healed.

14 Follow peace with all *men,* and holiness, without which no man shall see the Lord:

15 Looking diligently lest any man fail of the grace of God; lest any root of bitterness springing up trouble *you,* and thereby many be defiled;

16 Lest there *be* any fornicator, or profane person, as Ē′saȗ, who for one morsel of meat sold his birthright.

17 For ye know how that afterward, when he would have inherited the blessing, he was rejected: for he found no place of repentance, though he sought it carefully with tears.

18 For ye are not come unto the mount that might be touched, and that burned with fire, nor unto blackness, and darkness, and tempest,

19 And the sound of a trumpet, and the voice of words; which *voice* they that heard entreated that the word should not be spoken to them any more:

20 (For they could not endure that which was commanded, And if so much as a beast touch the mountain, it shall be stoned, or thrust through with a dart:

21 And so terrible was the sight, *that* Moses said, I exceedingly fear and quake:)

22 But ye are come unto mount Sī′ŏn, and unto the city of the living God, the heavenly Jerusalem, and to an innumerable company of angels,

23 To the general assembly and church of the firstborn, which are written in heaven, and to God the Judge of all, and to the spirits of just men made perfect,

24 And to Jesus the mediator of the
new covenant, and to the blood of
sprinkling, that speaketh better things
than *that of* Abel.
25 See that ye refuse not him that
speaketh: for if they escaped not who
refused him that spake on earth, much
more *shall not* we *escape,* if we turn
away from him that *speaketh* from
heaven:
26 Whose voice then shook the earth:
but now he hath promised, saying, Yet
once more I shake not the earth only,
but also heaven.
27 And this *word,* Yet once more, sig-
nifieth the removing of those things that
are shaken, as of things that are made,
that those things which cannot be
shaken may remain.
28 Wherefore we receiving a kingdom
which cannot be moved, let us have
grace, whereby we may serve God
acceptably with reverence and godly
fear:
29 For our God *is* a consuming fire.

CHAPTER 13

LET brotherly love continue.
2 Be not forgetful to entertain
strangers: for thereby some have enter-
tained angels unawares.
3 Remember them that are in bonds,
as bound with them; *and* them which
suffer adversity, as being yourselves
also in the body.
4 Marriage *is* honorable in all, and the
bed undefiled: but whoremongers and
adulterers God will judge.
5 *Let your* conversation *be* without
covetousness; *and be* content with such
things as ye have: for he hath said, I
will never leave thee, nor forsake thee.
6 So that we may boldly say, The Lord
is my helper, and I will not fear what
man shall do unto me.
7 Remember them which have the rule
over you, who have spoken unto you the
word of God: whose faith follow, considering the end of *their* conversation.
8 Jesus Christ the same yesterday, and
to-day, and for ever.
9 Be not carried about with divers and
strange doctrines: for *it is* a good thing
that the heart be established with grace;
not with meats, which have not profited
them that have been occupied therein.
10 We have an altar, whereof they have
no right to eat which serve the tabernacle.
11 For the bodies of those beasts,
whose blood is brought into the sanctuary by the high priest for sin, are
burned without the camp.
12 Wherefore Jesus also, that he
might sanctify the people with his own
blood, suffered without the gate.
13 Let us go forth therefore unto him
without the camp, bearing his reproach.
14 For here have we no continuing city,
but we seek one to come.
15 By him therefore let us offer the
sacrifice of praise to God continually,
that is, the fruit of *our* lips, giving
thanks to his name.
16 But to do good and to communicate
forget not: for with such sacrifices God
is well pleased.
17 Obey them that have the rule over
you, and submit yourselves: for they
watch for your souls, as they that must
give account, that they may do it with
joy, and not with grief: for that *is* unprofitable for you.
18 Pray for us: for we trust we have a
good conscience, in all things willing to
live honestly.
19 But I beseech *you* the rather to do
this, that I may be restored to you the
sooner.
20 Now the God of peace, that brought
again from the dead our Lord Jesus,
that great shepherd of the sheep,
through the blood of the everlasting
covenant,
21 Make you perfect in every good
work to do his will, working in you that
which is well-pleasing in his sight,
through Jesus Christ; to whom *be* glory
for ever and ever. Amen.
22 And I beseech you, brethren, suffer
the word of exhortation: for I have
written a letter unto you in few words.
23 Know ye that *our* brother Timothy
is set at liberty; with whom, if he come
shortly, I will see you.
24 Salute all them that have the rule
over you, and all the saints. They of
Italy salute you.
25 Grace *be* with you all. Amen.

¶ Written to the Hebrews from Italy by Timothy.

THE GENERAL EPISTLE OF

JAMES

CHAPTER 1

JAMES, a servant of God and of the
Lord Jesus Christ, to the twelve tribes
which are scattered abroad, greeting.
2 My brethren, count it all joy when
ye fall into divers temptations;
3 Knowing *this,* that the trying of your
faith worketh patience.
4 But let patience have *her* perfect
work, that ye may be perfect and entire,
wanting nothing.
5 If any of you lack wisdom, let him ask
of God, that giveth to all *men* liberally,
and upbraideth not; and it shall be given
him.
6 But let him ask in faith, nothing
wavering: for he that wavereth is like a
wave of the sea driven with the wind
and tossed.
7 For let not that man think that he
shall receive any thing of the Lord.
8 A double-minded man *is* unstable in
all his ways.
9 Let the brother of low degree rejoice
in that he is exalted:
10 But the rich, in that he is made low:
because as the flower of the grass he
shall pass away.
11 For the sun is no sooner risen with
a burning heat, but it withereth the
grass, and the flower thereof falleth, and
the grace of the fashion of it perisheth:
so also shall the rich man fade away in
his ways.
12 Blessed *is* the man that endureth
temptation: for when he is tried, he
shall receive the crown of life, which the
Lord hath promised to them that love
him.
13 Let no man say when he is tempted,
I am tempted of God: for God cannot be
tempted with evil, neither tempteth he
any man:
14 But every man is tempted, when he
is drawn away of his own lust, and
enticed.
15 Then when lust hath conceived, it
bringeth forth sin; and sin, when it is
finished, bringeth forth death.
16 Do not err, my beloved brethren.
17 Every good gift and every perfect
gift is from above, and cometh down
from the Father of lights, with whom
is no variableness, neither shadow of
turning.
18 Of his own will begat he us with the
word of truth, that we should be a kind
of firstfruits of his creatures.
19 Wherefore, my beloved brethren,
let every man be swift to hear, slow to
speak, slow to wrath:
20 For the wrath of man worketh not
the righteousness of God.
21 Wherefore lay apart all filthiness
and superfluity of naughtiness, and
receive with meekness the engrafted
word, which is able to save your souls.
22 But be ye doers of the word, and
not hearers only, deceiving your own
selves.
23 For if any be a hearer of the
word, and not a doer, he is like unto a
man beholding his natural face in a
glass:
24 For he beholdeth himself, and goeth
his way, and straightway forgetteth
what manner of man he was.
25 But whoso looketh into the perfect
law of liberty, and continueth *therein,*
he being not a forgetful hearer, but a
doer of the work, this man shall be
blessed in his deed.
26 If any man among you seem to be
religious, and bridleth not his tongue,
but deceiveth his own heart, this man's
religion *is* vain.
27 Pure religion and undefiled before
God and the Father is this, To visit the
fatherless and widows in their affliction,
and to keep himself unspotted from the
world.

CHAPTER 2

MY brethren, have not the faith of
our Lord Jesus Christ, *the Lord* of
glory, with respect of persons.
2 For if there come unto your assembly
a man with a gold ring, in goodly apparel, and there come in also a poor man
in vile raiment;
3 And ye have respect to him that wear-
eth the gay clothing, and say unto him,
Sit thou here in a good place; and say
to the poor, Stand thou there, or sit here
under my footstool:

4 Are ye not then partial in yourselves, and are become judges of evil thoughts?

5 Hearken, my beloved brethren, Hath not God chosen the poor of this world rich in faith, and heirs of the kingdom which he hath promised to them that love him?

6 But ye have despised the poor. Do not rich men oppress you, and draw you before the judgment seats?

7 Do not they blaspheme that worthy name by the which ye are called?

8 If ye fulfil the royal law according to the Scripture, Thou shalt love thy neighbor as thyself, ye do well:

9 But if ye have respect to persons, ye commit sin, and are convinced of the law as transgressors.

10 For whosoever shall keep the whole law, and yet offend in one *point*, he is guilty of all.

11 For he that said, Do not commit adultery, said also, Do not kill. Now if thou commit no adultery, yet if thou kill, thou art become a transgressor of the law.

12 So speak ye, and so do, as they that shall be judged by the law of liberty.

13 For he shall have judgment without mercy, that hath showed no mercy; and mercy rejoiceth against judgment.

14 What *doth it* profit, my brethren, though a man say he hath faith, and have not works? can faith save him?

15 If a brother or sister be naked, and destitute of daily food,

16 And one of you say unto them, Depart in peace, be *ye* warmed and filled; notwithstanding ye give them not those things which are needful to the body; what *doth it* profit?

17 Even so faith, if it hath not works, is dead, being alone.

18 Yea, a man may say, Thou hast faith, and I have works: show me thy faith without thy works, and I will show thee my faith by my works.

19 Thou believest that there is one God; thou doest well: the devils also believe, and tremble.

20 But wilt thou know, O vain man, that faith without works is dead?

21 Was not Abraham our father justified by works, when he had offered Isaac his son upon the altar?

22 Seest thou how faith wrought with his works, and by works was faith made perfect?

23 And the Scripture was fulfilled which saith, Abraham believed God, and it was imputed unto him for righteousness: and he was called the Friend of God.

24 Ye see then how that by works a man is justified, and not by faith only.

25 Likewise also was not Rā'hăb the harlot justified by works, when she had received the messengers, and had sent *them* out another way?

26 For as the body without the spirit is dead, so faith without works is dead also.

CHAPTER 3

MY brethren, be not many masters, knowing that we shall receive the greater condemnation.

2 For in many things we offend all. If any man offend not in word, the same *is* a perfect man, *and* able also to bridle the whole body.

3 Behold, we put bits in the horses' mouths, that they may obey us; and we turn about their whole body.

4 Behold also the ships, which though *they be* so great, and *are* driven of fierce winds, yet are they turned about with a very small helm, whithersoever the governor listeth.

5 Even so the tongue is a little member, and boasteth great things. Behold, how great a matter a little fire kindleth!

6 And the tongue *is* a fire, a world of iniquity: so is the tongue among our members, that it defileth the whole body, and setteth on fire the course of nature; and it is set on fire of hell.

7 For every kind of beasts, and of birds, and of serpents, and of things in the sea, is tamed, and hath been tamed of mankind:

8 But the tongue can no man tame; *it is* an unruly evil, full of deadly poison.

9 Therewith bless we God, even the Father; and therewith curse we men, which are made after the similitude of God.

10 Out of the same mouth proceedeth blessing and cursing. My brethren, these things ought not so to be.

11 Doth a fountain send forth at the same place sweet *water* and bitter?

12 Can the fig tree, my brethren, bear olive berries? either a vine, figs? so *can* no fountain both yield salt water and fresh.

13 Who *is* a wise man and endued with knowledge among you? let him show out of a good conversation his works with meekness of wisdom.

14 But if ye have bitter envying and strife in your hearts, glory not, and lie not against the truth.

15 This wisdom descendeth not from above, but *is* earthly, sensual, devilish.

16 For where envying and strife *is*, there *is* confusion and every evil work.

17 But the wisdom that is from above is first pure, then peaceable, gentle, *and* easy to be entreated, full of mercy and good fruits, without partiality, and without hypocrisy.

18 And the fruit of righteousness is sown in peace of them that make peace.

CHAPTER 4

FROM whence *come* wars and fightings among you? *come they* not hence, *even* of your lusts that war in your members?

2 Ye lust, and have not: ye kill, and desire to have, and cannot obtain: ye fight and war, yet ye have not, because ye ask not.

3 Ye ask, and receive not, because ye ask amiss, that ye may consume *it* upon your lusts.

4 Ye adulterers and adulteresses, know ye not that the friendship of the world is enmity with God? whosoever therefore will be a friend of the world is the enemy of God.

5 Do ye think that the Scripture saith in vain, The spirit that dwelleth in us lusteth to envy?

6 But he giveth more grace. Wherefore he saith, God resisteth the proud, but giveth grace unto the humble.

7 Submit yourselves therefore to God. Resist the devil, and he will flee from you.

8 Draw nigh to God, and he will draw nigh to you. Cleanse *your* hands, *ye* sinners; and purify *your* hearts, *ye* double-minded.

9 Be afflicted, and mourn, and weep: let your laughter be turned to mourning, and *your* joy to heaviness.

10 Humble yourselves in the sight of the Lord, and he shall lift you up.

11 Speak not evil one of another, brethren. He that speaketh evil of *his* brother, and judgeth his brother, speaketh evil of the law, and judgeth the law: but if thou judge the law, thou art not a doer of the law, but a judge.

12 There is one lawgiver, who is able to save and to destroy: who art thou that judgest another?

13 Go to now, ye that say, To-day or to-morrow we will go into such a city, and continue there a year, and buy and sell, and get gain:

14 Whereas ye know not what *shall be* on the morrow. For what *is* your life? It is even a vapor, that appeareth for a little time, and then vanisheth away.

15 For that ye *ought* to say, If the Lord will, we shall live, and do this, or that.

16 But now ye rejoice in your boastings: all such rejoicing is evil.

17 Therefore to him that knoweth to do good, and doeth *it* not, to him it is sin.

CHAPTER 5

GO to now, *ye* rich men, weep and howl for your miseries that shall come upon *you*.

2 Your riches are corrupted, and your garments are moth-eaten.

3 Your gold and silver is cankered; and the rust of them shall be a witness against you, and shall eat your flesh as it were fire. Ye have heaped treasure together for the last days.

4 Behold, the hire of the laborers who have reaped down your fields, which is of you kept back by fraud, crieth: and the cries of them which have reaped are entered into the ears of the Lord of Săb'ā-ŏth.

5 Ye have lived in pleasure on the earth, and been wanton; ye have nourished your hearts, as in a day of slaughter.

6 Ye have condemned *and* killed the just; *and* he doth not resist you.

7 Be patient therefore, brethren, unto the coming of the Lord. Behold, the husbandman waiteth for the precious fruit of the earth, and hath long patience for it, until he receive the early and latter rain.

8 Be ye also patient; stablish your hearts: for the coming of the Lord draweth nigh.

9 Grudge not one against another, brethren, lest ye be condemned: behold, the judge standeth before the door.

10 Take, my brethren, the prophets,

who have spoken in the name of the
Lord, for an example of suffering affliction, and of patience.
11 Behold, we count them happy which
endure. Ye have heard of the patience
of Job, and have seen the end of the
Lord; that the Lord is very pitiful, and
of tender mercy.
12 But above all things, my brethren,
swear not, neither by heaven, neither
by the earth, neither by any other oath:
but let your yea be yea; and *your* nay,
nay; lest ye fall into condemnation.
13 Is any among you afflicted? let him
pray. Is any merry? let him sing
psalms.
14 Is any sick among you? let him call
for the elders of the church; and let
them pray over him, anointing him with
oil in the name of the Lord:
15 And the prayer of faith shall save
the sick, and the Lord shall raise him
up; and if he have committed sins, they
shall be forgiven him.
16 Confess *your* faults one to another,
and pray one for another, that ye may
be healed. The effectual fervent prayer
of a righteous man availeth much.
17 Ē-lī′ăs was a man subject to like
passions as we are, and he prayed
earnestly that it might not rain: and it
rained not on the earth by the space of
three years and six months.
18 And he prayed again, and the
heaven gave rain, and the earth brought
forth her fruit.
19 Brethren, if any of you do err from
the truth, and one convert him;
20 Let him know, that he which converteth the sinner from the error of his
way shall save a soul from death, and
shall hide a multitude of sins.

THE FIRST EPISTLE GENERAL OF

PETER

CHAPTER 1

PETER, an apostle of Jesus Christ,
to the strangers scattered throughout Pontus, Gȧ-lā′t̬i-ȧ, Căp′pȧ-dō′çi-ȧ,
Asia, and Bĭ-thy̆n′ĭ-ȧ,
2 Elect according to the foreknowledge
of God the Father, through sanctification of the Spirit, unto obedience and
sprinkling of the blood of Jesus Christ:
Grace unto you, and peace, be multiplied.
3 Blessed *be* the God and Father of our
Lord Jesus Christ, which according to
his abundant mercy hath begotten us
again unto a lively hope by the resurrection of Jesus Christ from the dead,
4 To an inheritance incorruptible, and
undefiled, and that fadeth not away,
reserved in heaven for you,
5 Who are kept by the power of God
through faith unto salvation ready to be
revealed in the last time.
6 Wherein ye greatly rejoice, though
now for a season, if need be, ye are in
heaviness through manifold temptations:
7 That the trial of your faith, being
much more precious than of gold that
perisheth, though it be tried with fire,
might be found unto praise and honor
and glory at the appearing of Jesus
Christ:
8 Whom having not seen, ye love; in
whom, though now ye see *him* not, yet
believing, ye rejoice with joy unspeakable and full of glory:
9 Receiving the end of your faith, *even*
the salvation of *your* souls.
10 Of which salvation the prophets
have inquired and searched diligently,
who prophesied of the grace *that should
come* unto you:
11 Searching what, or what manner of
time the Spirit of Christ which was in
them did signify, when it testified beforehand the sufferings of Christ, and
the glory that should follow.
12 Unto whom it was revealed, that not
unto themselves, but unto us they did
minister the things, which are now reported unto you by them that have
preached the gospel unto you with the
Holy Ghost sent down from heaven;
which things the angels desire to look
into.

13 Wherefore gird up the loins of your mind, be sober, and hope to the end for the grace that is to be brought unto you at the revelation of Jesus Christ;

14 As obedient children, not fashioning yourselves according to the former lusts in your ignorance:

15 But as he which hath called you is holy, so be ye holy in all manner of conversation;

16 Because it is written, Be ye holy; for I am holy.

17 And if ye call on the Father, who without respect of persons judgeth according to every man's work, pass the time of your sojourning *here* in fear:

18 Forasmuch as ye know that ye were not redeemed with corruptible things, *as* silver and gold, from your vain conversation *received* by tradition from your fathers;

19 But with the precious blood of Christ, as of a lamb without blemish and without spot:

20 Who verily was foreordained before the foundation of the world, but was manifest in these last times for you,

21 Who by him do believe in God, that raised him up from the dead, and gave him glory; that your faith and hope might be in God.

22 Seeing ye have purified your souls in obeying the truth through the Spirit unto unfeigned love of the brethren, *see that ye* love one another with a pure heart fervently:

23 Being born again, not of corruptible seed, but of incorruptible, by the word of God, which liveth and abideth for ever.

24 For all flesh *is* as grass, and all the glory of man as the flower of grass. The grass withereth, and the flower thereof falleth away:

25 But the word of the Lord endureth for ever. And this is the word which by the gospel is preached unto you.

CHAPTER 2

WHEREFORE laying aside all malice, and all guile, and hypocrisies, and envies, and all evil speakings,

2 As newborn babes, desire the sincere milk of the word, that ye may grow thereby:

3 If so be ye have tasted that the Lord *is* gracious.

4 To whom coming, *as unto* a living stone, disallowed indeed of men, but chosen of God, *and* precious,

5 Ye also, as lively stones, are built up a spiritual house, a holy priesthood, to offer up spiritual sacrifices, acceptable to God by Jesus Christ.

6 Wherefore also it is contained in the Scripture, Behold, I lay in Sī′ŏn a chief corner stone, elect, precious: and he that believeth on him shall not be confounded.

7 Unto you therefore which believe *he is* precious: but unto them which be disobedient, the stone which the builders disallowed, the same is made the head of the corner,

8 And a stone of stumbling, and a rock of offense, *even to them* which stumble at the word, being disobedient: whereunto also they were appointed.

9 But ye *are* a chosen generation, a royal priesthood, a holy nation, a peculiar people; that ye should show forth the praises of him who hath called you out of darkness into his marvelous light:

10 Which in time past *were* not a people, but *are* now the people of God: which had not obtained mercy, but now have obtained mercy.

11 Dearly beloved, I beseech *you* as strangers and pilgrims, abstain from fleshly lusts, which war against the soul;

12 Having your conversation honest among the Ğĕn′tīleş: that, whereas they speak against you as evildoers, they may by *your* good works, which they shall behold, glorify God in the day of visitation.

13 Submit yourselves to every ordinance of man for the Lord's sake: whether it be to the king, as supreme;

14 Or unto governors, as unto them that are sent by him for the punishment of evildoers, and for the praise of them that do well.

15 For so is the will of God, that with well doing ye may put to silence the ignorance of foolish men:

16 As free, and not using *your* liberty for a cloak of maliciousness, but as the servants of God.

17 Honor all *men*. Love the brotherhood. Fear God. Honor the king.

18 Servants, *be* subject to *your* masters with all fear; not only to the good and gentle, but also to the froward.

19 For this *is* thankworthy, if a man for

conscience toward God endure grief, suffering wrongfully.

20 For what glory *is it*, if, when ye be buffeted for your faults, ye shall take it patiently? but if, when ye do well, and suffer *for it*, ye take it patiently, this *is* acceptable with God.

21 For even hereunto were ye called: because Christ also suffered for us, leaving us an example, that ye should follow his steps:

22 Who did no sin, neither was guile found in his mouth:

23 Who, when he was reviled, reviled not again; when he suffered, he threatened not; but committed *himself* to him that judgeth righteously:

24 Who his own self bare our sins in his own body on the tree, that we, being dead to sins, should live unto righteousness: by whose stripes ye were healed.

25 For ye were as sheep going astray; but are now returned unto the Shepherd and Bishop of your souls.

CHAPTER 3

LIKEWISE, ye wives, *be* in subjection to your own husbands; that, if any obey not the word, they also may without the word be won by the conversation of the wives;

2 While they behold your chaste conversation *coupled* with fear.

3 Whose adorning, let it not be that outward *adorning* of plaiting the hair, and of wearing of gold, or of putting on of apparel;

4 But *let it be* the hidden man of the heart, in that which is not corruptible, *even the ornament* of a meek and quiet spirit, which is in the sight of God of great price.

5 For after this manner in the old time the holy women also, who trusted in God, adorned themselves, being in subjection unto their own husbands:

6 Even as Sarah obeyed Abraham, calling him lord: whose daughters ye are, as long as ye do well, and are not afraid with any amazement.

7 Likewise, ye husbands, dwell with *them* according to knowledge, giving honor unto the wife, as unto the weaker vessel, and as being heirs together of the grace of life; that your prayers be not hindered.

8 Finally, *be ye* all of one mind, having compassion one of another; love as brethren, *be* pitiful, *be* courteous:

9 Not rendering evil for evil, or railing for railing: but contrariwise blessing; knowing that ye are thereunto called, that ye should inherit a blessing.

10 For he that will love life, and see good days, let him refrain his tongue from evil, and his lips that they speak no guile:

11 Let him eschew evil, and do good; let him seek peace, and ensue it.

12 For the eyes of the Lord *are* over the righteous, and his ears *are open* unto their prayers: but the face of the Lord *is* against them that do evil.

13 And who *is* he that will harm you, if ye be followers of that which is good?

14 But and if ye suffer for righteousness' sake, happy *are ye:* and be not afraid of their terror, neither be troubled;

15 But sanctify the Lord God in your hearts: and *be* ready always to *give* an answer to every man that asketh you a reason of the hope that is in you, with meekness and fear:

16 Having a good conscience; that, whereas they speak evil of you, as of evildoers, they may be ashamed that falsely accuse your good conversation in Christ.

17 For *it is* better, if the will of God be so, that ye suffer for well doing, than for evildoing.

18 For Christ also hath once suffered for sins, the just for the unjust, that he might bring us to God, being put to death in the flesh, but quickened by the Spirit:

19 By which also he went and preached unto the spirits in prison;

20 Which sometime were disobedient, when once the long-suffering of God waited in the days of Noah, while the ark was a preparing, wherein few, that is, eight souls were saved by water.

21 The like figure whereunto *even* baptism doth also now save us, (not the putting away of the filth of the flesh, but the answer of a good conscience toward God,) by the resurrection of Jesus Christ:

22 Who is gone into heaven, and is on the right hand of God; angels and authorities and powers being made subject unto him.

CHAPTER 4

FORASMUCH then as Christ hath suffered for us in the flesh, arm yourselves likewise with the same mind: for he that hath suffered in the flesh hath ceased from sin;

2 That he no longer should live the rest of *his* time in the flesh to the lusts of men, but to the will of God.

3 For the time past of *our* life may suffice us to have wrought the will of the Gĕn'tīleṣ, when we walked in lasciviousness, lusts, excess of wine, revelings, banquetings, and abominable idolatries:

4 Wherein they think it strange that ye run not with *them* to the same excess of riot, speaking evil of *you:*

5 Who shall give account to him that is ready to judge the quick and the dead.

6 For, for this cause was the gospel preached also to them that are dead, that they might be judged according to men in the flesh, but live according to God in the spirit.

7 But the end of all things is at hand: be ye therefore sober, and watch unto prayer.

8 And above all things have fervent charity among yourselves: for charity shall cover the multitude of sins.

9 Use hospitality one to another without grudging.

10 As every man hath received the gift, *even so* minister the same one to another, as good stewards of the manifold grace of God.

11 If any man speak, *let him speak* as the oracles of God; if any man minister, *let him do it* as of the ability which God giveth; that God in all things may be glorified through Jesus Christ: to whom be praise and dominion for ever and ever. Amen.

12 Beloved, think it not strange concerning the fiery trial which is to try you, as though some strange thing happened unto you:

13 But rejoice, inasmuch as ye are partakers of Christ's sufferings; that, when his glory shall be revealed, ye may be glad also with exceeding joy.

14 If ye be reproached for the name of Christ, happy *are ye;* for the Spirit of glory and of God resteth upon you: on their part he is evil spoken of, but on your part he is glorified.

15 But let none of you suffer as a murderer, or *as* a thief, or *as* an evildoer, or as a busybody in other men's matters.

16 Yet if *any man suffer* as a Christian, let him not be ashamed; but let him glorify God on this behalf.

17 For the time *is come* that judgment must begin at the house of God: and if *it* first *begin* at us, what shall the end *be* of them that obey not the gospel of God?

18 And if the righteous scarcely be saved, where shall the ungodly and the sinner appear?

19 Wherefore, let them that suffer according to the will of God commit the keeping of their souls *to him* in well doing, as unto a faithful Creator.

CHAPTER 5

THE elders which are among you I exhort, who am also an elder, and a witness of the sufferings of Christ, and also a partaker of the glory that shall be revealed:

2 Feed the flock of God which is among you, taking the oversight *thereof,* not by constraint, but willingly; not for filthy lucre, but of a ready mind;

3 Neither as being lords over *God's* heritage, but being ensamples to the flock.

4 And when the chief Shepherd shall appear, ye shall receive a crown of glory that fadeth not away.

5 Likewise, ye younger, submit yourselves unto the elder. Yea, all *of you* be subject one to another, and be clothed with humility: for God resisteth the proud, and giveth grace to the humble.

6 Humble yourselves therefore under the mighty hand of God, that he may exalt you in due time:

7 Casting all your care upon him; for he careth for you.

8 Be sober, be vigilant; because your adversary the devil, as a roaring lion, walketh about, seeking whom he may devour:

9 Whom resist steadfast in the faith, knowing that the same afflictions are accomplished in your brethren that are in the world.

10 But the God of all grace, who hath called us unto his eternal glory by Christ Jesus, after that ye have suffered a while, make you perfect, stablish, strengthen, settle *you.*

11 To him *be* glory and dominion for ever and ever. Amen.

12 By Sĭl-vā'nŭs, a faithful brother unto you, as I suppose, I have written briefly, exhorting, and testifying that this is the true grace of God wherein ye stand.

13 The *church that is* at Babylon, elected together with *you,* saluteth you; and *so doth* Marcus my son.

14 Greet ye one another with a kiss of charity. Peace *be* with you all that are in Christ Jesus. Amen.

THE SECOND EPISTLE GENERAL OF

PETER

CHAPTER 1

SIMON Peter, a servant and an apostle of Jesus Christ, to them that have obtained like precious faith with us through the righteousness of God and our Saviour Jesus Christ:

2 Grace and peace be multiplied unto you through the knowledge of God, and of Jesus our Lord,

3 According as his divine power hath given unto us all things that *pertain* unto life and godliness, through the knowledge of him that hath called us to glory and virtue:

4 Whereby are given unto us exceeding great and precious promises; that by these ye might be partakers of the divine nature, having escaped the corruption that is in the world through lust.

5 And besides this, giving all diligence, add to your faith virtue; and to virtue, knowledge;

6 And to knowledge, temperance; and to temperance, patience; and to patience, godliness;

7 And to godliness, brotherly kindness; and to brotherly kindness, charity.

8 For if these things be in you, and abound, they make *you that ye shall* neither *be* barren nor unfruitful in the knowledge of our Lord Jesus Christ.

9 But he that lacketh these things is blind, and cannot see afar off, and hath forgotten that he was purged from his old sins.

10 Wherefore the rather, brethren, give diligence to make your calling and election sure: for if ye do these things, ye shall never fall:

11 For so an entrance shall be ministered unto you abundantly into the everlasting kingdom of our Lord and Saviour Jesus Christ.

12 Wherefore I will not be negligent to put you always in remembrance of these things, though ye know *them,* and be established in the present truth.

13 Yea, I think it meet, as long as I am in this tabernacle, to stir you up by putting *you* in remembrance;

14 Knowing that shortly I must put off *this* my tabernacle, even as our Lord Jesus Christ hath showed me.

15 Moreover I will endeavor that ye may be able after my decease to have these things always in remembrance.

16 For we have not followed cunningly devised fables, when we made known unto you the power and coming of our Lord Jesus Christ, but were eyewitnesses of his majesty.

17 For he received from God the Father honor and glory, when there came such a voice to him from the excellent glory, This is my beloved Son, in whom I am well pleased.

18 And this voice which came from heaven we heard, when we were with him in the holy mount.

19 We have also a more sure word of prophecy; whereunto ye do well that ye take heed, as unto a light that shineth in a dark place, until the day dawn, and the day-star arise in your hearts:

20 Knowing this first, that no prophecy of the Scripture is of any private interpretation.

21 For the prophecy came not in old time by the will of man: but holy men of God spake *as they were* moved by the Holy Ghost.

CHAPTER 2

BUT there were false prophets also among the people, even as there shall be false teachers among you, who

privily shall bring in damnable heresies,
even denying the Lord that bought
them, and bring upon themselves swift
destruction.
2 And many shall follow their perni-
cious ways; by reason of whom the way
of truth shall be evil spoken of.
3 And through covetousness shall they
with feigned words make merchandise
of you: whose judgment now of a long
time lingereth not, and their damnation
slumbereth not.
4 For if God spared not the angels that
sinned, but cast *them* down to hell, and
delivered *them* into chains of darkness,
to be reserved unto judgment;
5 And spared not the old world,
but saved Noah the eighth *person,* a
preacher of righteousness, bringing in
the flood upon the world of the ungodly;
6 And turning the cities of Sŏd'ŏm and
Gō-mŏr'rȧh into ashes condemned *them*
with an overthrow, making *them* an
ensample unto those that after should
live ungodly;
7 And delivered just Lot, vexed with
the filthy conversation of the wicked:
8 (For that righteous man dwelling
among them, in seeing and hearing,
vexed *his* righteous soul from day to
day with *their* unlawful deeds:)
9 The Lord knoweth how to deliver
the godly out of temptation, and to
reserve the unjust unto the day of
judgment to be punished:
10 But chiefly them that walk after the
flesh in the lust of uncleanness, and
despise government. Presumptuous
are they, self-willed, they are not afraid
to speak evil of dignities.
11 Whereas angels, which are greater
in power and might, bring not railing
accusation against them before the
Lord.
12 But these, as natural brute beasts
made to be taken and destroyed, speak
evil of the things that they understand
not; and shall utterly perish in their
own corruption;
13 And shall receive the reward of unrighteousness, *as* they that count it
pleasure to riot in the daytime. Spots
they are and blemishes, sporting themselves with their own deceivings while
they feast with you;
14 Having eyes full of adultery, and
that cannot cease from sin; beguiling
unstable souls: a heart they have exercised with covetous practices; cursed
children:
15 Which have forsaken the right way,
and are gone astray, following the way
of Bā'lăam *the son* of Bō'sŏr, who loved
the wages of unrighteousness;
16 But was rebuked for his iniquity:
the dumb ass speaking with man's voice
forbade the madness of the prophet.
17 These are wells without water,
clouds that are carried with a tempest;
to whom the mist of darkness is reserved
for ever.
18 For when they speak great swelling
words of vanity, they allure through the
lusts of the flesh, *through much* wantonness, those that were clean escaped from
them who live in error.
19 While they promise them liberty,
they themselves are the servants of corruption: for of whom a man is overcome, of the same is he brought in
bondage.
20 For if after they have escaped the
pollutions of the world through the
knowledge of the Lord and Saviour
Jesus Christ, they are again entangled
therein, and overcome, the latter end is
worse with them than the beginning.
21 For it had been better for them not
to have known the way of righteousness,
than, after they have known *it,* to turn
from the holy commandment delivered
unto them.
22 But it is happened unto them according to the true proverb, The dog *is*
turned to his own vomit again; and the
sow that was washed to her wallowing
in the mire.

CHAPTER 3

THIS second epistle, beloved, I now
write unto you; in *both* which I stir
up your pure minds by way of remembrance:
2 That ye may be mindful of the words
which were spoken before by the holy
prophets, and of the commandment of
us the apostles of the Lord and Saviour:
3 Knowing this first, that there shall
come in the last days scoffers, walking
after their own lusts,
4 And saying, Where is the promise of
his coming? for since the fathers fell
asleep, all things continue as *they were*
from the beginning of the creation.
5 For this they willingly are ignorant of,
that by the word of God the heavens

were of old, and the earth standing out
of the water and in the water:
6 Whereby the world that then was,
being overflowed with water, perished:
7 But the heavens and the earth, which
are now, by the same word are kept in
store, reserved unto fire against the day
of judgment and perdition of ungodly
men.
8 But, beloved, be not ignorant of this
one thing, that one day *is* with the Lord
as a thousand years, and a thousand
years as one day.
9 The Lord is not slack concerning his
promise, as some men count slackness;
but is long-suffering to us-ward, not
willing that any should perish, but that
all should come to repentance.
10 But the day of the Lord will come
as a thief in the night; in the which
the heavens shall pass away with a
great noise, and the elements shall melt
with fervent heat, the earth also and
the works that are therein shall be
burned up.
11 *Seeing* then *that* all these things
shall be dissolved, what manner *of persons*
ought ye to be in *all* holy conversation
and godliness,
12 Looking for and hasting unto the
coming of the day of God, wherein the
heavens being on fire shall be dissolved,
and the elements shall melt with fervent
heat?
13 Nevertheless we, according to his
promise, look for new heavens and a
new earth, wherein dwelleth righteousness.
14 Wherefore, beloved, seeing that ye
look for such things, be diligent that ye
may be found of him in peace, without
spot, and blameless.
15 And account *that* the long-suffering
of our Lord *is* salvation; even as our
beloved brother Paul also according to
the wisdom given unto him hath written
unto you;
16 As also in all *his* epistles, speaking
in them of these things; in which are
some things hard to be understood,
which they that are unlearned and unstable
wrest, as *they do* also the other
Scriptures, unto their own destruction.
17 Ye therefore, beloved, seeing ye
know *these things* before, beware lest
ye also, being led away with the error of
the wicked, fall from your own steadfastness.
18 But grow in grace, and *in* the knowledge
of our Lord and Saviour Jesus
Christ. To him *be* glory both now and
for ever. Amen.

THE FIRST EPISTLE GENERAL OF

JOHN

CHAPTER 1

THAT which was from the beginning,
which we have heard, which
we have seen with our eyes, which we
have looked upon, and our hands have
handled, of the Word of life;
2 (For the life was manifested, and we
have seen *it*, and bear witness, and show
unto you that eternal life, which was with
the Father, and was manifested unto us;)
3 That which we have seen and heard
declare we unto you, that ye also may
have fellowship with us: and truly our
fellowship *is* with the Father, and with
his Son Jesus Christ.
4 And these things write we unto you,
that your joy may be full.
5 This then is the message which we
have heard of him, and declare unto
you, that God is light, and in him is no
darkness at all.
6 If we say that we have fellowship
with him, and walk in darkness, we lie,
and do not the truth:
7 But if we walk in the light, as he is in
the light, we have fellowship one with
another, and the blood of Jesus Christ
his Son cleanseth us from all sin.
8 If we say that we have no sin, we
deceive ourselves, and the truth is not
in us.
9 If we confess our sins, he is faithful
and just to forgive us *our* sins, and to
cleanse us from all unrighteousness.
10 If we say that we have not sinned,

we make him a liar, and his word is not in us.

CHAPTER 2

MY little children, these things write I unto you, that ye sin not. And if any man sin, we have an advocate with the Father, Jesus Christ the righteous:

2 And he is the propitiation for our sins: and not for ours only, but also for *the sins of* the whole world.

3 And hereby we do know that we know him, if we keep his commandments.

4 He that saith, I know him, and keepeth not his commandments, is a liar, and the truth is not in him.

5 But whoso keepeth his word, in him verily is the love of God perfected: hereby know we that we are in him.

6 He that saith he abideth in him ought himself also so to walk, even as he walked.

7 Brethren, I write no new commandment unto you, but an old commandment which ye had from the beginning. The old commandment is the word which ye have heard from the beginning.

8 Again, a new commandment I write unto you, which thing is true in him and in you: because the darkness is past, and the true light now shineth.

9 He that saith he is in the light, and hateth his brother, is in darkness even until now.

10 He that loveth his brother abideth in the light, and there is none occasion of stumbling in him.

11 But he that hateth his brother is in darkness, and walketh in darkness, and knoweth not whither he goeth, because that darkness hath blinded his eyes.

12 I write unto you, little children, because your sins are forgiven you for his name's sake.

13 I write unto you, fathers, because ye have known him *that is* from the beginning. I write unto you, young men, because ye have overcome the wicked one. I write unto you, little children, because ye have known the Father.

14 I have written unto you, fathers, because ye have known him *that is* from the beginning. I have written unto you, young men, because ye are strong, and the word of God abideth in you, and ye have overcome the wicked one.

15 Love not the world, neither the things *that are* in the world. If any man love the world, the love of the Father is not in him.

16 For all that *is* in the world, the lust of the flesh, and the lust of the eyes, and the pride of life, is not of the Father, but is of the world.

17 And the world passeth away, and the lust thereof: but he that doeth the will of God abideth for ever.

18 Little children, it is the last time: and as ye have heard that antichrist shall come, even now are there many antichrists; whereby we know that it is the last time.

19 They went out from us, but they were not of us; for if they had been of us, they would *no doubt* have continued with us: but *they went out,* that they might be made manifest that they were not all of us.

20 But ye have an unction from the Holy One, and ye know all things.

21 I have not written unto you because ye know not the truth, but because ye know it, and that no lie is of the truth.

22 Who is a liar but he that denieth that Jesus is the Christ? He is antichrist, that denieth the Father and the Son.

23 Whosoever denieth the Son, the same hath not the Father: [*but*] *he that acknowledgeth the Son hath the Father also.*

24 Let that therefore abide in you, which ye have heard from the beginning. If that which ye have heard from the beginning shall remain in you, ye also shall continue in the Son, and in the Father.

25 And this is the promise that he hath promised us, *even* eternal life.

26 These things have I written unto you concerning them that seduce you.

27 But the anointing which ye have received of him abideth in you, and ye need not that any man teach you: but as the same anointing teacheth you of all things, and is truth, and is no lie, and even as it hath taught you, ye shall abide in him.

28 And now, little children, abide in him; that, when he shall appear, we may have confidence, and not be ashamed before him at his coming.

29 If ye know that he is righteous, ye know that every one that doeth righteousness is born of him.

CHAPTER 3

BEHOLD, what manner of love the
Father hath bestowed upon us, that
we should be called the sons of God:
therefore the world knoweth us not, because it knew him not.
2 Beloved, now are we the sons of God,
and it doth not yet appear what we shall
be: but we know that, when he shall appear, we shall be like him; for we shall
see him as he is.
3 And every man that hath this hope
in him purifieth himself, even as he is
pure.
4 Whosoever committeth sin transgresseth also the law: for sin is the
transgression of the law.
5 And ye know that he was manifested
to take away our sins; and in him is no sin.
6 Whosoever abideth in him sinneth
not: whosoever sinneth hath not seen
him, neither known him.
7 Little children, let no man deceive
you: he that doeth righteousness is
righteous, even as he is righteous.
8 He that committeth sin is of the devil;
for the devil sinneth from the beginning.
For this purpose the Son of God was
manifested, that he might destroy the
works of the devil.
9 Whosoever is born of God doth not
commit sin; for his seed remaineth in
him: and he cannot sin, because he is
born of God.
10 In this the children of God are manifest, and the children of the devil: whosoever doeth not righteousness is not of
God, neither he that loveth not his
brother.
11 For this is the message that ye
heard from the beginning, that we
should love one another.
12 Not as Cain, *who* was of that wicked
one, and slew his brother. And wherefore slew he him? Because his own
works were evil, and his brother's
righteous.
13 Marvel not, my brethren, if the
world hate you.
14 We know that we have passed from
death unto life, because we love the
brethren. He that loveth not *his* brother
abideth in death.
15 Whosoever hateth his brother is a
murderer: and ye know that no murderer hath eternal life abiding in him.
16 Hereby perceive we the love *of*
God, because he laid down his life for
us: and we ought to lay down *our* lives
for the brethren.
17 But whoso hath this world's good,
and seeth his brother have need, and
shutteth up his bowels *of compassion*
from him, how dwelleth the love of God
in him?
18 My little children, let us not love in
word, neither in tongue; but in deed and
in truth.
19 And hereby we know that we are of
the truth, and shall assure our hearts
before him.
20 For if our heart condemn us, God is
greater than our heart, and knoweth all
things.
21 Beloved, if our heart condemn us
not, *then* have we confidence toward
God.
22 And whatsoever we ask, we receive
of him, because we keep his commandments, and do those things that are
pleasing in his sight.
23 And this is his commandment, That
we should believe on the name of his
Son Jesus Christ, and love one another,
as he gave us commandment.
24 And he that keepeth his commandments dwelleth in him, and he in him.
And hereby we know that he abideth in
us, by the Spirit which he hath given us.

CHAPTER 4

BELOVED, believe not every spirit,
but try the spirits whether they
are of God: because many false prophets are gone out into the world.
2 Hereby know ye the Spirit of God:
Every spirit that confesseth that Jesus
Christ is come in the flesh is of God:
3 And every spirit that confesseth not
that Jesus Christ is come in the flesh is
not of God: and this is that *spirit* of antichrist, whereof ye have heard that it
should come; and even now already is it
in the world.
4 Ye are of God, little children, and
have overcome them: because greater is
he that is in you, than he that is in the
world.
5 They are of the world: therefore
speak they of the world, and the world
heareth them.
6 We are of God: he that knoweth God
heareth us; he that is not of God heareth not us. Hereby know we the spirit
of truth, and the spirit of error.

7 Beloved, let us love one another: for
love is of God; and every one that loveth
is born of God, and knoweth God.
8 He that loveth not, knoweth not God;
for God is love.
9 In this was manifested the love of
God toward us, because that God sent
his only begotten Son into the world,
that we might live through him.
10 Herein is love, not that we loved
God, but that he loved us, and sent
his Son *to be* the propitiation for our
sins.
11 Beloved, if God so loved us, we
ought also to love one another.
12 No man hath seen God at any time.
If we love one another, God dwelleth in
us, and his love is perfected in us.
13 Hereby know we that we dwell in
him, and he in us, because he hath given
us of his Spirit.
14 And we have seen and do testify
that the Father sent the Son *to be* the
Saviour of the world.
15 Whosoever shall confess that Jesus
is the Son of God, God dwelleth in him,
and he in God.
16 And we have known and believed
the love that God hath to us. God is
love; and he that dwelleth in love dwelleth in God, and God in him.
17 Herein is our love made perfect,
that we may have boldness in the day of
judgment: because as he is, so are we in
this world.
18 There is no fear in love; but perfect
love casteth out fear: because fear hath
torment. He that feareth is not made
perfect in love.
19 We love him, because he first
loved us.
20 If a man say, I love God, and hateth
his brother, he is a liar: for he that
loveth not his brother whom he hath
seen, how can he love God whom he hath
not seen?
21 And this commandment have we
from him, That he who loveth God love
his brother also.

CHAPTER 5

WHOSOEVER believeth that Jesus
is the Christ is born of God: and
every one that loveth him that begat
loveth him also that is begotten of him.
2 By this we know that we love the
children of God, when we love God, and
keep his commandments.
3 For this is the love of God, that we
keep his commandments: and his commandments are not grievous.
4 For whatsoever is born of God overcometh the world: and this is the victory that overcometh the world, *even*
our faith.
5 Who is he that overcometh the world,
but he that believeth that Jesus is the
Son of God?
6 This is he that came by water and
blood, *even* Jesus Christ; not by water
only, but by water and blood. And it is
the Spirit that beareth witness, because
the Spirit is truth.
7 For there are three that bear record
in heaven, the Father, the Word, and
the Holy Ghost: and these three are one.
8 And there are three that bear witness
in earth, the spirit, and the water, and
the blood: and these three agree in one.
9 If we receive the witness of men, the
witness of God is greater: for this is the
witness of God which he hath testified
of his Son.
10 He that believeth on the Son of God
hath the witness in himself: he that believeth not God hath made him a liar;
because he believeth not the record that
God gave of his Son.
11 And this is the record, that God hath
given to us eternal life, and this life is in
his Son.
12 He that hath the Son hath life; *and*
he that hath not the Son of God hath not
life.
13 These things have I written unto
you that believe on the name of the Son
of God; that ye may know that ye have
eternal life, and that ye may believe on
the name of the Son of God.
14 And this is the confidence that we
have in him, that, if we ask any thing
according to his will, he heareth us:
15 And if we know that he hear us,
whatsoever we ask, we know that we
have the petitions that we desired of
him.
16 If any man see his brother sin a sin
which is not unto death, he shall ask,
and he shall give him life for them that
sin not unto death. There is a sin unto
death: I do not say that he shall pray
for it.
17 All unrighteousness is sin: and there
is a sin not unto death.
18 We know that whosoever is born of
God sinneth not; but he that is begotten

of God keepeth himself, and that wicked
one toucheth him not.
19 *And* we know that we are of God,
and the whole world lieth in wickedness.
20 And we know that the Son of God
is come, and hath given us an understanding, that we may know him that is
true; and we are in him that is true,
even in his Son Jesus Christ. This is
the true God, and eternal life.
21 Little children, keep yourselves
from idols. Amen.

THE SECOND EPISTLE OF JOHN

THE elder unto the elect lady and
her children, whom I love in the
truth; and not I only, but also all they
that have known the truth;
2 For the truth's sake, which dwelleth
in us, and shall be with us for ever.
3 Grace be with you, mercy, *and* peace,
from God the Father, and from the Lord
Jesus Christ, the Son of the Father, in
truth and love.
4 I rejoiced greatly that I found of thy
children walking in truth, as we have
received a commandment from the
Father.
5 And now I beseech thee, lady, not as
though I wrote a new commandment
unto thee, but that which we had
from the beginning, that we love one
another.
6 And this is love, that we walk after
his commandments. This is the commandment, That, as ye have heard from
the beginning, ye should walk in it.
7 For many deceivers are entered into
the world, who confess not that Jesus
Christ is come in the flesh. This is a
deceiver and an antichrist.
8 Look to yourselves, that we lose not
those things which we have wrought,
but that we receive a full reward.
9 Whosoever transgresseth, and abideth not in the doctrine of Christ, hath
not God. He that abideth in the doctrine of Christ, he hath both the Father
and the Son.
10 If there come any unto you, and
bring not this doctrine, receive him not
into *your* house, neither bid him God-
speed:
11 For he that biddeth him God-speed
is partaker of his evil deeds.
12 Having many things to write unto
you, I would not *write* with paper and
ink: but I trust to come unto you, and
speak face to face, that our joy may be
full.
13 The children of thy elect sister
greet thee. Amen.

THE THIRD EPISTLE OF

JOHN

THE elder unto the well-beloved
Gā'ịŭs, whom I love in the truth.
2 Beloved, I wish above all things that
thou mayest prosper and be in health,
even as thy soul prospereth.
3 For I rejoiced greatly, when the
brethren came and testified of the truth
that is in thee, even as thou walkest in
the truth.
4 I have no greater joy than to hear
that my children walk in truth.
5 Beloved, thou doest faithfully whatsoever thou doest to the brethren, and
to strangers;
6 Which have borne witness of thy
charity before the church: whom if thou
bring forward on their journey after a
godly sort, thou shalt do well:
7 Because that for his name's sake
they went forth, taking nothing of the
Ġĕn'tīleṣ.
8 We therefore ought to receive such,
that we might be fellow helpers to the
truth.
9 I wrote unto the church: but Dī-ŏt'-
rē-phēṣ, who loveth to have the preeminence among them, receiveth us not.
10 Wherefore, if I come, I will remember his deeds which he doeth, prating
against us with malicious words: and
not content therewith, neither doth he
himself receive the brethren, and for-
biddeth them that would, and casteth
them out of the church.
11 Beloved, follow not that which is
evil, but that which is good. He that
doeth good is of God: but he that doeth
evil hath not seen God.
12 Dē-mē'trĭ-ŭs hath good report of
all *men*, and of the truth itself: yea, and
we *also* bear record; and ye know that
our record is true.
13 I had many things to write, but I will
not with ink and pen write unto thee:
14 But I trust I shall shortly see thee,
and we shall speak face to face. Peace
be to thee. *Our* friends salute thee.
Greet the friends by name.

THE GENERAL EPISTLE OF

JUDE

JUDE, the servant of Jesus Christ, and brother of James, to them that are sanctified by God the Father, and preserved in Jesus Christ, *and* called:

2 Mercy unto you, and peace, and love, be multiplied.

3 Beloved, when I gave all diligence to write unto you of the common salvation, it was needful for me to write unto you, and exhort *you* that ye should earnestly contend for the faith which was once delivered unto the saints.

4 For there are certain men crept in unawares, who were before of old ordained to this condemnation, ungodly men, turning the grace of our God into lasciviousness, and denying the only Lord God, and our Lord Jesus Christ.

5 I will therefore put you in remembrance, though ye once knew this, how that the Lord, having saved the people out of the land of Egypt, afterward destroyed them that believed not.

6 And the angels which kept not their first estate, but left their own habitation, he hath reserved in everlasting chains under darkness unto the judgment of the great day.

7 Even as Sŏd′ŏm and Gō-mŏr′rȧh, and the cities about them in like manner, giving themselves over to fornication, and going after strange flesh, are set forth for an example, suffering the vengeance of eternal fire.

8 Likewise also these *filthy* dreamers defile the flesh, despise dominion, and speak evil of dignities.

9 Yet Mī′chā-ĕl the archangel, when contending with the devil he disputed about the body of Moses, durst not bring against him a railing accusation, but said, The Lord rebuke thee.

10 But these speak evil of those things which they know not: but what they know naturally, as brute beasts, in those things they corrupt themselves.

11 Woe unto them! for they have gone in the way of Cain, and ran greedily after the error of Bā′lȧam for reward, and perished in the gainsaying of Cō′rē.

12 These are spots in your feasts of charity, when they feast with you, feeding themselves without fear: clouds *they are* without water, carried about of winds; trees whose fruit withereth, without fruit, twice dead, plucked up by the roots;

13 Raging waves of the sea, foaming out their own shame; wandering stars, to whom is reserved the blackness of darkness for ever.

14 And Enoch also, the seventh from Adam, prophesied of these, saying, Behold, the Lord cometh with ten thousands of his saints,

15 To execute judgment upon all, and to convince all that are ungodly among them of all their ungodly deeds which they have ungodly committed, and of all their hard *speeches* which ungodly sinners have spoken against him.

16 These are murmurers, complainers, walking after their own lusts; and their mouth speaketh great swelling *words*, having men's persons in admiration because of advantage.

17 But, beloved, remember ye the words which were spoken before of the apostles of our Lord Jesus Christ;

18 How that they told you there should be mockers in the last time, who should walk after their own ungodly lusts.

19 These be they who separate themselves, sensual, having not the Spirit.

20 But ye, beloved, building up yourselves on your most holy faith, praying in the Holy Ghost,

21 Keep yourselves in the love of God, looking for the mercy of our Lord Jesus Christ unto eternal life.

22 And of some have compassion, making a difference:

23 And others save with fear, pulling *them* out of the fire; hating even the garment spotted by the flesh.

24 Now unto him that is able to keep you from falling, and to present *you* faultless before the presence of his glory with exceeding joy,

25 To the only wise God our Saviour, *be* glory and majesty, dominion and power, both now and ever. **Amen.**

THE REVELATION

OF ST. JOHN THE DIVINE

CHAPTER 1

THE Revelation of Jesus Christ,
which God gave unto him, to show
unto his servants things which must
shortly come to pass; and he sent and
signified *it* by his angel unto his servant
John:
2 Who bare record of the word of God,
and of the testimony of Jesus Christ,
and of all things that he saw.
3 Blessed *is* he that readeth, and they
that hear the words of this prophecy,
and keep those things which are written
therein: for the time *is* at hand.
4 JOHN to the seven churches which
are in Asia: Grace *be* unto you,
and peace, from him which is, and
which was, and which is to come; and
from the seven Spirits which are before
his throne;
5 And from Jesus Christ, *who is* the
faithful witness, *and* the first-begotten
of the dead, and the prince of the kings
of the earth. Unto him that loved us,
and washed us from our sins in his own
blood,
6 And hath made us kings and priests
unto God and his Father; to him *be* glory
and dominion for ever and ever. Amen.
7 Behold, he cometh with clouds; and
every eye shall see him, and they *also*
which pierced him: and all kindreds of
the earth shall wail because of him.
Even so, Amen.
8 I am Alpha and Ō-mē'gȧ, the beginning and the ending, saith the Lord,
which is, and which was, and which is
to come, the Almighty.
9 I John, who also am your brother,
and companion in tribulation, and in
the kingdom and patience of Jesus
Christ, was in the isle that is called
Patmos, for the word of God, and for the
testimony of Jesus Christ.
10 I was in the Spirit on the Lord's
day, and heard behind me a great voice,
as of a trumpet,
11 Saying, I am Alpha and Ō-mē'gȧ,
the first and the last: and, What thou
seest, write in a book, and send *it* unto
the seven churches which are in Asia;
unto Ĕph'ē-sŭs, and unto Smyrna, and
unto Pĕr'gȧ-mŏs, and unto Thȳ'ȧ-tī'rȧ,
and unto Sardis, and unto Philadelphia,
and unto Lā-ŏd'ĭ-çē'ȧ.
12 And I turned to see the voice that
spake with me. And being turned, I saw
seven golden candlesticks;
13 And in the midst of the seven candlesticks *one* like unto the Son of man,
clothed with a garment down to the
foot, and girt about the paps with a
golden girdle.
14 His head and *his* hairs *were* white
like wool, as white as snow; and his
eyes *were* as a flame of fire;
15 And his feet like unto fine brass, as
if they burned in a furnace; and his
voice as the sound of many waters.
16 And he had in his right hand seven
stars: and out of his mouth went a
sharp two-edged sword: and his countenance *was* as the sun shineth in his
strength.
17 And when I saw him, I fell at his
feet as dead. And he laid his right hand
upon me, saying unto me, Fear not; I
am the first and the last:
18 *I am* he that liveth, and was dead;
and, behold, I am alive for evermore,
Amen; and have the keys of hell and of
death.
19 Write the things which thou hast
seen, and the things which are, and the
things which shall be hereafter;
20 The mystery of the seven stars
which thou sawest in my right hand, and
the seven golden candlesticks. The
seven stars are the angels of the seven
churches: and the seven candlesticks
which thou sawest are the seven
churches.

CHAPTER 2

UNTO the angel of the church of
Ĕph'ē-sŭs write; These things
saith he that holdeth the seven stars in
his right hand, who walketh in the midst
of the seven golden candlesticks;
2 I know thy works, and thy labor, and
thy patience, and how thou canst not
bear them which are evil: and thou
hast tried them which say they are

apostles, and are not, and hast found them liars:

3 And hast borne, and hast patience, and for my name's sake hast labored, and hast not fainted.

4 Nevertheless I have *somewhat* against thee, because thou hast left thy first love.

5 Remember therefore from whence thou art fallen, and repent, and do the first works; or else I will come unto thee quickly, and will remove thy candlestick out of his place, except thou repent.

6 But this thou hast, that thou hatest the deeds of the Nĭc′ō-lā′ĭ-tănṣ, which I also hate.

7 He that hath an ear, let him hear what the Spirit saith unto the churches; To him that overcometh will I give to eat of the tree of life, which is in the midst of the paradise of God.

8 And unto the angel of the church in Smyrna write; These things saith the first and the last, which was dead, and is alive;

9 I know thy works, and tribulation, and poverty, (but thou art rich) and *I know* the blasphemy of them which say they are Jews, and are not, but *are* the synagogue of Satan.

10 Fear none of those things which thou shalt suffer: behold, the devil shall cast *some* of you into prison, that ye may be tried; and ye shall have tribulation ten days: be thou faithful unto death, and I will give thee a crown of life.

11 He that hath an ear, let him hear what the Spirit saith unto the churches; He that overcometh shall not be hurt of the second death.

12 And to the angel of the church in Pĕr′gȧ-mŏs write; These things saith he which hath the sharp sword with two edges;

13 I know thy works, and where thou dwellest, *even* where Satan's seat *is:* and thou holdest fast my name, and hast not denied my faith, even in those days wherein Ăn′tĭ-păs *was* my faithful martyr, who was slain among you, where Satan dwelleth.

14 But I have a few things against thee, because thou hast there them that hold the doctrine of Bā′lȧam, who taught Bā′lăk to cast a stumblingblock before the children of Ĭṣ′rā-ĕl, to eat things sacrificed unto idols, and to commit fornication.

15 So hast thou also them that hold the doctrine of the Nĭc′ō-lā′ĭ-tănṣ, which thing I hate.

16 Repent; or else I will come unto thee quickly, and will fight against them with the sword of my mouth.

17 He that hath an ear, let him hear what the Spirit saith unto the churches; To him that overcometh will I give to eat of the hidden manna, and will give him a white stone, and in the stone a new name written, which no man knoweth saving he that receiveth *it.*

18 And unto the angel of the church in Thȳ′ȧ-tī′rȧ write; These things saith the Son of God, who hath his eyes like unto a flame of fire, and his feet *are* like fine brass;

19 I know thy works, and charity, and service, and faith, and thy patience, and thy works; and the last *to be* more than the first.

20 Notwithstanding I have a few things against thee, because thou sufferest that woman Jĕz′ē-bĕl, which calleth herself a prophetess, to teach and to seduce my servants to commit fornication, and to eat things sacrificed unto idols.

21 And I gave her space to repent of her fornication; and she repented not.

22 Behold, I will cast her into a bed, and them that commit adultery with her into great tribulation, except they repent of their deeds.

23 And I will kill her children with death; and all the churches shall know that I am he which searcheth the reins and hearts: and I will give unto every one of you according to your works.

24 But unto you I say, and unto the rest in Thȳ′ȧ-tī′rȧ, as many as have not this doctrine, and which have not known the depths of Satan, as they speak; I will put upon you none other burden.

25 But that which ye have *already,* hold fast till I come.

26 And he that overcometh, and keepeth my works unto the end, to him will I give power over the nations:

27 And he shall rule them with a rod of iron; as the vessels of a potter shall they be broken to shivers: even as I received of my Father.

28 And I will give him the morning star.

29 He that hath an ear, let him hear what the Spirit saith unto the churches.

CHAPTER 3

AND unto the angel of the church in Sardis write; These things saith he that hath the seven Spirits of God, and the seven stars; I know thy works, that thou hast a name that thou livest, and art dead.

2 Be watchful, and strengthen the things which remain, that are ready to die: for I have not found thy works perfect before God.

3 Remember therefore how thou hast received and heard, and hold fast, and repent. If therefore thou shalt not watch, I will come on thee as a thief, and thou shalt not know what hour I will come upon thee.

4 Thou hast a few names even in Sardis which have not defiled their garments; and they shall walk with me in white: for they are worthy.

5 He that overcometh, the same shall be clothed in white raiment; and I will not blot out his name out of the book of life, but I will confess his name before my Father, and before his angels.

6 He that hath an ear, let him hear what the Spirit saith unto the churches.

7 And to the angel of the church in Philadelphia write; These things saith he that is holy, he that is true, he that hath the key of David, he that openeth, and no man shutteth; and shutteth, and no man openeth;

8 I know thy works: behold, I have set before thee an open door, and no man can shut it: for thou hast a little strength, and hast kept my word, and hast not denied my name.

9 Behold, I will make them of the synagogue of Satan, which say they are Jews, and are not, but do lie; behold, I will make them to come and worship before thy feet, and to know that I have loved thee.

10 Because thou hast kept the word of my patience, I also will keep thee from the hour of temptation, which shall come upon all the world, to try them that dwell upon the earth.

11 Behold, I come quickly: hold that fast which thou hast, that no man take thy crown.

12 Him that overcometh will I make a pillar in the temple of my God, and he shall go no more out: and I will write upon him the name of my God, and the name of the city of my God, *which is* new Jerusalem, which cometh down out of heaven from my God: and *I will write upon him* my new name.

13 He that hath an ear, let him hear what the Spirit saith unto the churches.

14 And unto the angel of the church of the Lā-ŏd′ĭ-çē′ănṣ write; These things saith the Amen, the faithful and true witness, the beginning of the creation of God;

15 I know thy works, that thou art neither cold nor hot: I would thou wert cold or hot.

16 So then because thou art lukewarm, and neither cold nor hot, I will spew thee out of my mouth.

17 Because thou sayest, I am rich, and increased with goods, and have need of nothing; and knowest not that thou art wretched, and miserable, and poor, and blind, and naked:

18 I counsel thee to buy of me gold tried in the fire, that thou mayest be rich; and white raiment, that thou mayest be clothed, and *that* the shame of thy nakedness do not appear; and anoint thine eyes with eyesalve, that thou mayest see.

19 As many as I love, I rebuke and chasten: be zealous therefore, and repent.

20 Behold, I stand at the door, and knock: if any man hear my voice, and open the door, I will come in to him, and will sup with him, and he with me.

21 To him that overcometh will I grant to sit with me in my throne, even as I also overcame, and am set down with my Father in his throne.

22 He that hath an ear, let him hear what the Spirit saith unto the churches.

CHAPTER 4

AFTER this I looked, and, behold, a door *was* opened in heaven: and the first voice which I heard *was* as it were of a trumpet talking with me; which said, Come up hither, and I will show thee things which must be hereafter.

2 And immediately I was in the Spirit: and, behold, a throne was set in heaven, and *one* sat on the throne.

3 And he that sat was to look upon like a jasper and a sardine stone: and *there was* a rainbow round about the throne, in sight like unto an emerald.

4 And round about the throne *were* four

and twenty seats: and upon the seats I
saw four and twenty elders sitting,
clothed in white raiment; and they had
on their heads crowns of gold.
5 And out of the throne proceeded
lightnings and thunderings and voices:
and *there were* seven lamps of fire burning before the throne, which are the
seven Spirits of God.
6 And before the throne *there was* a sea
of glass like unto crystal: and in the
midst of the throne, and round about the
throne, *were* four beasts full of eyes before and behind.
7 And the first beast *was* like a lion,
and the second beast like a calf, and the
third beast had a face as a man, and
the fourth beast *was* like a flying eagle.
8 And the four beasts had each of them
six wings about *him;* and *they were* full
of eyes within: and they rest not day and
night, saying, Holy, holy, holy, Lord
God Almighty, which was, and is, and is
to come.
9 And when those beasts give glory and
honor and thanks to him that sat on the
throne, who liveth for ever and ever,
10 The four and twenty elders fall down
before him that sat on the throne, and
worship him that liveth for ever and
ever, and cast their crowns before the
throne, saying,
11 Thou art worthy, O Lord, to receive
glory and honor and power: for thou hast
created all things, and for thy pleasure
they are and were created.

CHAPTER 5

AND I saw in the right hand of him
that sat on the throne a book
written within and on the back side,
sealed with seven seals.
2 And I saw a strong angel proclaiming
with a loud voice, Who is worthy to open
the book, and to loose the seals thereof?
3 And no man in heaven, nor in earth,
neither under the earth, was able to
open the book, neither to look thereon.
4 And I wept much, because no man
was found worthy to open and to read
the book, neither to look thereon.
5 And one of the elders saith unto me,
Weep not: behold, the Lion of the tribe
of Jụ′dȧ, the Root of David, hath prevailed to open the book, and to loose the
seven seals thereof.
6 And I beheld, and, lo, in the midst of
the throne and of the four beasts, and in
the midst of the elders, stood a Lamb as
it had been slain, having seven horns
and seven eyes, which are the seven
Spirits of God sent forth into all the
earth.
7 And he came and took the book out
of the right hand of him that sat upon the
throne.
8 And when he had taken the book, the
four beasts and four *and* twenty elders
fell down before the Lamb, having every
one of them harps, and golden vials full
of odors, which are the prayers of saints.
9 And they sung a new song, saying,
Thou art worthy to take the book, and to
open the seals thereof: for thou wast
slain, and hast redeemed us to God by
thy blood out of every kindred, and
tongue, and people, and nation;
10 And hast made us unto our God
kings and priests: and we shall reign on
the earth.
11 And I beheld, and I heard the voice
of many angels round about the throne,
and the beasts, and the elders: and the
number of them was ten thousand times
ten thousand, and thousands of thousands;
12 Saying with a loud voice, Worthy is
the Lamb that was slain to receive
power, and riches, and wisdom, and
strength, and honor, and glory, and
blessing.
13 And every creature which is in
heaven, and on the earth and under the
earth, and such as are in the sea, and all
that are in them, heard I saying, Blessing, and honor, and glory, and power, *be*
unto him that sitteth upon the throne,
and unto the Lamb for ever and ever.
14 And the four beasts said, Amen.
And the four *and* twenty elders fell
down and worshipped him that liveth
for ever and ever.

CHAPTER 6

AND I saw when the Lamb opened
one of the seals, and I heard, as
it were the noise of thunder, one of the
four beasts saying, Come and see.
2 And I saw, and behold a white horse:
and he that sat on him had a bow; and a
crown was given unto him: and he went
forth conquering, and to conquer.
3 And when he had opened the second
seal, I heard the second beast say, Come
and see.
4 And there went out another horse

that was red: and *power* was given to
him that sat thereon to take peace from
the earth, and that they should kill one
another: and there was given unto him
a great sword.
5 And when he had opened the third
seal, I heard the third beast say, Come
and see. And I beheld, and lo a black
horse; and he that sat on him had a pair
of balances in his hand.
6 And I heard a voice in the midst of
the four beasts say, A measure of wheat
for a penny, and three measures of barley for a penny; and *see* thou hurt not
the oil and the wine.
7 And when he had opened the fourth
seal, I heard the voice of the fourth beast
say, Come and see.
8 And I looked, and behold a pale
horse: and his name that sat on him was
Death, and Hell followed with him. And
power was given unto them over the
fourth part of the earth, to kill with
sword, and with hunger, and with death,
and with the beasts of the earth.
9 And when he had opened the fifth
seal, I saw under the altar the souls of
them that were slain for the word of
God, and for the testimony which they
held:
10 And they cried with a loud voice,
saying, How long, O Lord, holy and
true, dost thou not judge and avenge
our blood on them that dwell on the
earth?
11 And white robes were given unto
every one of them; and it was said unto
them, that they should rest yet for a little
season, until their fellow servants also
and their brethren, that should be killed
as they *were,* should be fulfilled.
12 And I beheld when he had opened
the sixth seal, and, lo, there was a great
earthquake; and the sun became black
as sackcloth of hair, and the moon became as blood;
13 And the stars of heaven fell unto the
earth, even as a fig tree casteth her untimely figs, when she is shaken of a
mighty wind.
14 And the heaven departed as a scroll
when it is rolled together; and every
mountain and island were moved out of
their places.
15 And the kings of the earth, and the
great men, and the rich men, and the
chief captains, and the mighty men, and
every bondman, and every free man, hid
themselves in the dens and in the rocks
of the mountains;
16 And said to the mountains and
rocks, Fall on us, and hide us from the
face of him that sitteth on the throne,
and from the wrath of the Lamb:
17 For the great day of his wrath is
come; and who shall be able to stand?

CHAPTER 7

AND after these things I saw four
angels standing on the four corners
of the earth, holding the four winds of
the earth, that the wind should not blow
on the earth, nor on the sea, nor on any
tree.
2 And I saw another angel ascending
from the east, having the seal of the living God: and he cried with a loud voice
to the four angels, to whom it was given
to hurt the earth and the sea,
3 Saying, Hurt not the earth, neither
the sea, nor the trees, till we have sealed
the servants of our God in their foreheads.
4 And I heard the number of them
which were sealed: *and there were*
sealed a hundred *and* forty *and* four
thousand of all the tribes of the children
of Ĭs̱′rā-ĕl.
5 Of the tribe of Jṳ′dȧ *were* sealed
twelve thousand. Of the tribe of Reuben
were sealed twelve thousand. Of the
tribe of Gad *were* sealed twelve thousand.
6 Of the tribe of Ā′sẽr *were* sealed
twelve thousand. Of the tribe of Nĕph′-
thȧ-lĭm *were* sealed twelve thousand.
Of the tribe of Mȧ-năs′sēs̱ *were* sealed
twelve thousand.
7 Of the tribe of Simeon *were* sealed
twelve thousand. Of the tribe of Levi
were sealed twelve thousand. Of the
tribe of Ĭs′sȧ-chär *were* sealed twelve
thousand.
8 Of the tribe of Zăb′ū-lŏn *were* sealed
twelve thousand. Of the tribe of Joseph
were sealed twelve thousand. Of the
tribe of Benjamin *were* sealed twelve
thousand.
9 After this I beheld, and, lo, a great
multitude, which no man could number,
of all nations, and kindreds, and people,
and tongues, stood before the throne,
and before the Lamb, clothed with white
robes, and palms in their hands;
10 And cried with a loud voice, saying,
Salvation to our God which sitteth upon
the throne, and unto the Lamb.

11 And all the angels stood round about the throne, and *about* the elders and the four beasts, and fell before the throne on their faces, and worshipped God,

12 Saying, Amen: Blessing, and glory, and wisdom, and thanksgiving, and honor, and power, and might, *be* unto our God for ever and ever. Amen.

13 And one of the elders answered, saying unto me, What are these which are arrayed in white robes? and whence came they?

14 And I said unto him, Sir, thou knowest. And he said to me, These are they which came out of great tribulation, and have washed their robes, and made them white in the blood of the Lamb.

15 Therefore are they before the throne of God, and serve him day and night in his temple: and he that sitteth on the throne shall dwell among them.

16 They shall hunger no more, neither thirst any more; neither shall the sun light on them, nor any heat.

17 For the Lamb which is in the midst of the throne shall feed them, and shall lead them unto living fountains of waters: and God shall wipe away all tears from their eyes.

CHAPTER 8

AND when he had opened the seventh seal, there was silence in heaven about the space of half an hour.

2 And I saw the seven angels which stood before God; and to them were given seven trumpets.

3 And another angel came and stood at the altar, having a golden censer; and there was given unto him much incense, that he should offer *it* with the prayers of all saints upon the golden altar which was before the throne.

4 And the smoke of the incense, *which came* with the prayers of the saints, ascended up before God out of the angel's hand.

5 And the angel took the censer, and filled it with fire of the altar, and cast *it* into the earth: and there were voices, and thunderings, and lightnings, and an earthquake.

6 And the seven angels which had the seven trumpets prepared themselves to sound.

7 The first angel sounded, and there followed hail and fire mingled with blood, and they were cast upon the earth: and the third part of trees was burnt up, and all green grass was burnt up.

8 And the second angel sounded, and as it were a great mountain burning with fire was cast into the sea: and the third part of the sea became blood;

9 And the third part of the creatures which were in the sea, and had life, died; and the third part of the ships were destroyed.

10 And the third angel sounded, and there fell a great star from heaven, burning as it were a lamp, and it fell upon the third part of the rivers, and upon the fountains of waters;

11 And the name of the star is called Wormwood: and the third part of the waters became wormwood; and many men died of the waters, because they were made bitter.

12 And the fourth angel sounded, and the third part of the sun was smitten, and the third part of the moon, and the third part of the stars; so as the third part of them was darkened, and the day shone not for a third part of it, and the night likewise.

13 And I beheld, and heard an angel flying through the midst of heaven, saying with a loud voice, Woe, woe, woe, to the inhabiters of the earth by reason of the other voices of the trumpet of the three angels, which are yet to sound!

CHAPTER 9

AND the fifth angel sounded, and I saw a star fall from heaven unto the earth: and to him was given the key of the bottomless pit.

2 And he opened the bottomless pit; and there arose a smoke out of the pit, as the smoke of a great furnace; and the sun and the air were darkened by reason of the smoke of the pit.

3 And there came out of the smoke locusts upon the earth: and unto them was given power, as the scorpions of the earth have power.

4 And it was commanded them that they should not hurt the grass of the earth, neither any green thing, neither any tree; but only those men which have not the seal of God in their foreheads.

5 And to them it was given that they should not kill them, but that they

should be tormented five months: and
their torment *was* as the torment of a
scorpion, when he striketh a man.
6 And in those days shall men seek
death, and shall not find it; and shall
desire to die, and death shall flee from
them.
7 And the shapes of the locusts *were*
like unto horses prepared unto battle;
and on their heads *were* as it were
crowns like gold, and their faces *were* as
the faces of men.
8 And they had hair as the hair of wom-
en, and their teeth were as *the teeth* of
lions.
9 And they had breastplates, as it were
breastplates of iron; and the sound of
their wings *was* as the sound of chariots
of many horses running to battle.
10 And they had tails like unto scorpions, and there were stings in their
tails: and their power *was* to hurt men
five months.
11 And they had a king over them,
which is the angel of the bottomless pit,
whose name in the Hebrew tongue *is*
Ȧ-băd′dȯn, but in the Greek tongue hath
his name Ȧ-pŏl′lȳ-ŏn.
12 One woe is past; *and,* behold, there
come two woes more hereafter.
13 And the sixth angel sounded, and I
heard a voice from the four horns of the
golden altar which is before God,
14 Saying to the sixth angel which
had the trumpet, Loose the four angels
which are bound in the great river Eū-
phrā′tēṣ.
15 And the four angels were loosed,
which were prepared for an hour, and a
day, and a month, and a year, for to slay
the third part of men.
16 And the number of the army of the
horsemen *were* two hundred thousand
thousand: and I heard the number of
them.
17 And thus I saw the horses in the
vision, and them that sat on them, having breastplates of fire, and of jacinth,
and brimstone: and the heads of the
horses *were* as the heads of lions; and
out of their mouths issued fire and
smoke and brimstone.
18 By these three was the third part of
men killed, by the fire, and by the
smoke, and by the brimstone, which
issued out of their mouths.
19 For their power is in their mouth,
and in their tails: for their tails *were* like
unto serpents, and had heads, and with
them they do hurt.
20 And the rest of the men which were
not killed by these plagues yet repented
not of the works of their hands, that they
should not worship devils, and idols of
gold, and silver, and brass, and stone,
and of wood; which neither can see, nor
hear, nor walk:
21 Neither repented they of their murders, nor of their sorceries, nor of their
fornication, nor of their thefts.

CHAPTER 10

AND I saw another mighty angel come
down from heaven, clothed with a
cloud: and a rainbow *was* upon his head,
and his face *was* as it were the sun, and
his feet as pillars of fire:
2 And he had in his hand a little book
open: and he set his right foot upon the
sea, and *his* left *foot* on the earth,
3 And cried with a loud voice, as *when*
a lion roareth: and when he had cried,
seven thunders uttered their voices.
4 And when the seven thunders had
uttered their voices, I was about to
write: and I heard a voice from heaven
saying unto me, Seal up those things
which the seven thunders uttered, and
write them not.
5 And the angel which I saw stand upon
the sea and upon the earth lifted up his
hand to heaven,
6 And sware by him that liveth for ever
and ever, who created heaven, and the
things that therein are, and the earth,
and the things that therein are, and the
sea, and the things which are therein,
that there should be time no longer:
7 But in the days of the voice of the
seventh angel, when he shall begin to
sound, the mystery of God should be finished, as he hath declared to his servants the prophets.
8 And the voice which I heard from
heaven spake unto me again, and said,
Go *and* take the little book which is open
in the hand of the angel which standeth
upon the sea and upon the earth.
9 And I went unto the angel, and said
unto him, Give me the little book. And
he said unto me, Take *it,* and eat it up;
and it shall make thy belly bitter, but it
shall be in thy mouth sweet as honey.
10 And I took the little book out of the
angel's hand, and ate it up; and it was
in my mouth sweet as honey: and as

soon as I had eaten it, my belly was
bitter.
11 And he said unto me, Thou must
prophesy again before many peoples,
and nations, and tongues, and kings.

CHAPTER 11

AND there was given me a reed like
unto a rod: and the angel stood,
saying, Rise, and measure the temple of
God, and the altar, and them that worship therein.
2 But the court which is without the
temple leave out, and measure it not;
for it is given unto the Gĕn′tīleṣ: and the
holy city shall they tread under foot
forty *and* two months.
3 And I will give *power* unto my two
witnesses, and they shall prophesy a
thousand two hundred *and* threescore
days, clothed in sackcloth.
4 These are the two olive trees, and
the two candlesticks standing before the
God of the earth.
5 And if any man will hurt them, fire
proceedeth out of their mouth, and devoureth their enemies: and if any man
will hurt them, he must in this manner
be killed.
6 These have power to shut heaven,
that it rain not in the days of their
prophecy: and have power over waters
to turn them to blood, and to smite the
earth with all plagueṣ, as often as they
will.
7 And when they shall have finished
their testimony, the beast that ascendeth out of the bottomless pit shall make
war against them, and shall overcome
them, and kill them.
8 And their dead bodies *shall lie* in the
street of the great city, which spiritually
is called Sŏd′ŏm and Egypt, where also
our Lord was crucified.
9 And they of the people and kindreds
and tongues and nations shall see their
dead bodies three days and a half, and
shall not suffer their dead bodies to be
put in graves.
10 And they that dwell upon the earth
shall rejoice over them, and make
merry, and shall send gifts one to
another; because these two prophets
tormented them that dwelt on the
earth.
11 And after three days and a half the
Spirit of life from God entered into
them, and they stood upon their feet;
and great fear fell upon them which saw
them.
12 And they heard a great voice from
heaven saying unto them, Come up
hither. And they ascended up to heaven
in a cloud; and their enemies beheld
them.
13 And the same hour was there a great
earthquake, and the tenth part of the
city fell, and in the earthquake were
slain of men seven thousand: and the
remnant were affrighted, and gave glory
to the God of heaven.
14 The second woe is past; *and*, behold, the third woe cometh quickly.
15 And the seventh angel sounded;
and there were great voices in heaven,
saying, The kingdoms of this world are
become *the kingdoms* of our Lord, and
of his Christ; and he shall reign for ever
and ever.
16 And the four and twenty elders,
which sat before God on their seats, fell
upon their faces, and worshipped God,
17 Saying, We give thee thanks, O
Lord God Almighty, which art, and
wast, and art to come; because thou hast
taken to thee thy great power, and hast
reigned.
18 And the nations were angry, and
thy wrath is come, and the time of the
dead, that they should be judged, and
that thou shouldest give reward unto
thy servants the prophets, and to the
saints, and them that fear thy name,
small and great; and shouldest destroy
them which destroy the earth.
19 And the temple of God was opened
in heaven, and there was seen in his
temple the ark of his testament: and
there were lightnings, and voices, and
thunderings, and an earthquake, and
great hail.

CHAPTER 12

AND there appeared a great wonder
in heaven; a woman clothed with
the sun, and the moon under her feet,
and upon her head a crown of twelve
stars:
2 And she being with child cried, travailing in birth, and pained to be delivered.
3 And there appeared another wonder
in heaven; and behold a great red
dragon, having seven heads and ten
horns, and seven crowns upon his heads.
4 And his tail drew the third part of the

stars of heaven, and did cast them to the earth: and the dragon stood before the woman which was ready to be delivered, for to devour her child as soon as it was born.

5 And she brought forth a man child, who was to rule all nations with a rod of iron: and her child was caught up unto God, and *to* his throne.

6 And the woman fled into the wilderness, where she hath a place prepared of God, that they should feed her there a thousand two hundred *and* threescore days.

7 And there was war in heaven: Mī-chā-ĕl and his angels fought against the dragon; and the dragon fought and his angels,

8 And prevailed not; neither was their place found any more in heaven.

9 And the great dragon was cast out, that old serpent, called the Devil, and Satan, which deceiveth the whole world: he was cast out into the earth, and his angels were cast out with him.

10 And I heard a loud voice saying in heaven, Now is come salvation, and strength, and the kingdom of our God, and the power of his Christ: for the accuser of our brethren is cast down, which accused them before our God day and night.

11 And they overcame him by the blood of the Lamb, and by the word of their testimony; and they loved not their lives unto the death.

12 Therefore rejoice, *ye* heavens, and ye that dwell in them. Woe to the inhabiters of the earth and of the sea! for the devil is come down unto you, having great wrath, because he knoweth that he hath but a short time.

13 And when the dragon saw that he was cast unto the earth, he persecuted the woman which brought forth the man *child*.

14 And to the woman were given two wings of a great eagle, that she might fly into the wilderness, into her place, where she is nourished for a time, and times, and half a time, from the face of the serpent.

15 And the serpent cast out of his mouth water as a flood after the woman, that he might cause her to be carried away of the flood.

16 And the earth helped the woman; and the earth opened her mouth, and swallowed up the flood which the dragon cast out of his mouth.

17 And the dragon was wroth with the woman, and went to make war with the remnant of her seed, which keep the commandments of God, and have the testimony of Jesus Christ.

CHAPTER 13

AND I stood upon the sand of the sea, and saw a beast rise up out of the sea, having seven heads and ten horns, and upon his horns ten crowns, and upon his heads the name of blasphemy.

2 And the beast which I saw was like unto a leopard, and his feet were as *the feet* of a bear, and his mouth as the mouth of a lion: and the dragon gave him his power, and his seat, and great authority.

3 And I saw one of his heads as it were wounded to death; and his deadly wound was healed: and all the world wondered after the beast.

4 And they worshipped the dragon which gave power unto the beast: and they worshipped the beast, saying, Who *is* like unto the beast? who is able to make war with him?

5 And there was given unto him a mouth speaking great things and blasphemies; and power was given unto him to continue forty *and* two months.

6 And he opened his mouth in blasphemy against God, to blaspheme his name, and his tabernacle, and them that dwell in heaven.

7 And it was given unto him to make war with the saints, and to overcome them: and power was given him over all kindreds, and tongues, and nations.

8 And all that dwell upon the earth shall worship him, whose names are not written in the book of life of the Lamb slain from the foundation of the world.

9 If any man have an ear, let him hear.

10 He that leadeth into captivity shall go into captivity: he that killeth with the sword must be killed with the sword. Here is the patience and the faith of the saints.

11 And I beheld another beast coming up out of the earth; and he had two horns like a lamb, and he spake as a dragon.

12 And he exerciseth all the power of the first beast before him, and causeth the earth and them which dwell therein

to worship the first beast, whose deadly wound was healed.

13 And he doeth great wonders, so that he maketh fire come down from heaven on the earth in the sight of men,

14 And deceiveth them that dwell on the earth by *the means of* those miracles which he had power to do in the sight of the beast; saying to them that dwell on the earth, that they should make an image to the beast, which had the wound by a sword, and did live.

15 And he had power to give life unto the image of the beast, that the image of the beast should both speak, and cause that as many as would not worship the image of the beast should be killed.

16 And he causeth all, both small and great, rich and poor, free and bond, to receive a mark in their right hand, or in their foreheads:

17 And that no man might buy or sell, save he that had the mark, or the name of the beast, or the number of his name.

18 Here is wisdom. Let him that hath understanding count the number of the beast: for it is the number of a man; and his number *is* Six hundred threescore *and* six.

CHAPTER 14

AND I looked, and, lo, a Lamb stood on the mount Sī'ŏn, and with him a hundred forty *and* four thousand, having his Father's name written in their foreheads.

2 And I heard a voice from heaven, as the voice of many waters, and as the voice of a great thunder: and I heard the voice of harpers harping with their harps:

3 And they sung as it were a new song before the throne, and before the four beasts, and the elders: and no man could learn that song but the hundred *and* forty *and* four thousand, which were redeemed from the earth.

4 These are they which were not defiled with women; for they are virgins. These are they which follow the Lamb whithersoever he goeth. These were redeemed from among men, *being* the firstfruits unto God and to the Lamb.

5 And in their mouth was found no guile: for they are without fault before the throne of God.

6 And I saw another angel fly in the midst of heaven, having the everlasting gospel to preach unto them that dwell on the earth, and to every nation, and kindred, and tongue, and people,

7 Saying with a loud voice, Fear God, and give glory to him; for the hour of his judgment is come: and worship him that made heaven, and earth, and the sea, and the fountains of waters.

8 And there followed another angel, saying, Babylon is fallen, is fallen, that great city, because she made all nations drink of the wine of the wrath of her fornication.

9 And the third angel followed them, saying with a loud voice, If any man worship the beast and his image, and receive *his* mark in his forehead, or in his hand,

10 The same shall drink of the wine of the wrath of God, which is poured out without mixture into the cup of his indignation; and he shall be tormented with fire and brimstone in the presence of the holy angels, and in the presence of the Lamb:

11 And the smoke of their torment ascendeth up for ever and ever: and they have no rest day nor night, who worship the beast and his image, and whosoever receiveth the mark of his name.

12 Here is the patience of the saints: here *are* they that keep the commandments of God, and the faith of Jesus.

13 And I heard a voice from heaven saying unto me, Write, Blessed *are* the dead which die in the Lord from henceforth: Yea, saith the Spirit, that they may rest from their labors; and their works do follow them.

14 And I looked, and behold a white cloud, and upon the cloud *one* sat like unto the Son of man, having on his head a golden crown, and in his hand a sharp sickle.

15 And another angel came out of the temple, crying with a loud voice to him that sat on the cloud, Thrust in thy sickle, and reap: for the time is come for thee to reap; for the harvest of the earth is ripe.

16 And he that sat on the cloud thrust in his sickle on the earth; and the earth was reaped.

17 And another angel came out of the temple which is in heaven, he also having a sharp sickle.

18 And another angel came out from
the altar, which had power over fire;
and cried with a loud cry to him that had
the sharp sickle, saying, Thrust in thy
sharp sickle, and gather the clusters of
the vine of the earth; for her grapes are
fully ripe.
19 And the angel thrust in his sickle
into the earth, and gathered the vine of
the earth, and cast *it* into the great winepress of the wrath of God.
20 And the winepress was trodden
without the city, and blood came out of
the winepress, even unto the horse
bridles, by the space of a thousand *and*
six hundred furlongs.

CHAPTER 15

AND I saw another sign in heaven,
great and marvelous, seven angels
having the seven last plagues; for in
them is filled up the wrath of God.
2 And I saw as it were a sea of glass
mingled with fire: and them that had
gotten the victory over the beast, and
over his image, and over his mark, *and*
over the number of his name, stand on
the sea of glass, having the harps of
God.
3 And they sing the song of Moses the
servant of God, and the song of the
Lamb, saying, Great and marvelous *are*
thy works, Lord God Almighty; just
and true *are* thy ways, thou King of
saints.
4 Who shall not fear thee, O Lord,
and glorify thy name? for *thou* only *art*
holy: for all nations shall come and worship before thee; for thy judgments are
made manifest.
5 And after that I looked, and, behold,
the temple of the tabernacle of the testimony in heaven was opened:
6 And the seven angels came out of the
temple, having the seven plagues,
clothed in pure and white linen, and
having their breasts girded with golden
girdles.
7 And one of the four beasts gave unto
the seven angels seven golden vials full
of the wrath of God, who liveth for ever
and ever.
8 And the temple was filled with
smoke from the glory of God, and
from his power; and no man was
able to enter into the temple, till the
seven plagues of the seven angels were
fulfilled.

CHAPTER 16

AND I heard a great voice out of the
temple saying to the seven angels,
Go your ways, and pour out the vials of
the wrath of God upon the earth.
2 And the first went, and poured out his
vial upon the earth; and there fell a noisome and grievous sore upon the men
which had the mark of the beast, and
upon them which worshipped his image.
3 And the second angel poured out his
vial upon the sea; and it became as the
blood of a dead *man:* and every living
soul died in the sea.
4 And the third angel poured out his
vial upon the rivers and fountains of
waters; and they became blood.
5 And I heard the angel of the waters
say, Thou art righteous, O Lord, which
art, and wast, and shalt be, because thou
hast judged thus.
6 For they have shed the blood of
saints and prophets, and thou hast given
them blood to drink; for they are worthy.
7 And I heard another out of the altar
say, Even so, Lord God Almighty, true
and righteous *are* thy judgments.
8 And the fourth angel poured out his
vial upon the sun; and power was given
unto him to scorch men with fire.
9 And men were scorched with great
heat, and blasphemed the name of God,
which hath power over these plagues:
and they repented not to give him glory.
10 And the fifth angel poured out his
vial upon the seat of the beast; and his
kingdom was full of darkness; and they
gnawed their tongues for pain,
11 And blasphemed the God of heaven
because of their pains and their sores,
and repented not of their deeds.
12 And the sixth angel poured out his
vial upon the great river Eū-phrā'tēs;
and the water thereof was dried up,
that the way of the kings of the east
might be prepared.
13 And I saw three unclean spirits like
frogs *come* out of the mouth of the
dragon, and out of the mouth of the beast,
and out of the mouth of the false prophet.
14 For they are the spirits of devils,
working miracles, *which* go forth unto
the kings of the earth and of the whole
world, to gather them to the battle of
that great day of God Almighty.
15 Behold, I come as a thief. Blessed
is he that watcheth, and keepeth his

garments, lest he walk naked, and they see his shame.

16 And he gathered them together into a place called in the Hebrew tongue Är′mȧ-gĕd′dŏn.

17 And the seventh angel poured out his vial into the air; and there came a great voice out of the temple of heaven, from the throne, saying, It is done.

18 And there were voices, and thunders, and lightnings; and there was a great earthquake, such as was not since men were upon the earth, so mighty an earthquake, *and* so great.

19 And the great city was divided into three parts, and the cities of the nations fell: and great Babylon came in remembrance before God, to give unto her the cup of the wine of the fierceness of his wrath.

20 And every island fled away, and the mountains were not found.

21 And there fell upon men a great hail out of heaven, *every stone* about the weight of a talent: and men blasphemed God because of the plague of the hail; for the plague thereof was exceeding great.

CHAPTER 17

AND there came one of the seven angels which had the seven vials, and talked with me, saying unto me, Come hither; I will show unto thee the judgment of the great whore that sitteth upon many waters;

2 With whom the kings of the earth have committed fornication, and the inhabitants of the earth have been made drunk with the wine of her fornication.

3 So he carried me away in the spirit into the wilderness: and I saw a woman sit upon a scarlet-colored beast, full of names of blasphemy, having seven heads and ten horns.

4 And the woman was arrayed in purple and scarlet color, and decked with gold and precious stones and pearls, having a golden cup in her hand full of abominations and filthiness of her fornication:

5 And upon her forehead *was* a name written, MYSTERY, BABYLON THE GREAT, THE MOTHER OF HARLOTS AND ABOMINATIONS OF THE EARTH.

6 And I saw the woman drunken with the blood of the saints, and with the blood of the martyrs of Jesus: and when I saw her, I wondered with great admiration.

7 And the angel said unto me, Wherefore didst thou marvel? I will tell thee the mystery of the woman, and of the beast that carrieth her, which hath the seven heads and ten horns.

8 The beast that thou sawest was, and is not; and shall ascend out of the bottomless pit, and go into perdition: and they that dwell on the earth shall wonder, whose names were not written in the book of life from the foundation of the world, when they behold the beast that was, and is not, and yet is.

9 And here *is* the mind which hath wisdom. The seven heads are seven mountains, on which the woman sitteth.

10 And there are seven kings: five are fallen, and one is, *and* the other is not yet come; and when he cometh, he must continue a short space.

11 And the beast that was, and is not, even he is the eighth, and is of the seven, and goeth into perdition.

12 And the ten horns which thou sawest are ten kings, which have received no kingdom as yet; but receive power as kings one hour with the beast.

13 These have one mind, and shall give their power and strength unto the beast.

14 These shall make war with the Lamb, and the Lamb shall overcome them: for he is Lord of lords, and King of kings: and they that are with him *are* called, and chosen, and faithful.

15 And he saith unto me, The waters which thou sawest, where the whore sitteth, are peoples, and multitudes, and nations, and tongues.

16 And the ten horns which thou sawest upon the beast, these shall hate the whore, and shall make her desolate and naked, and shall eat her flesh, and burn her with fire.

17 For God hath put in their hearts to fulfil his will, and to agree, and give their kingdom unto the beast, until the words of God shall be fulfilled.

18 And the woman which thou sawest is that great city, which reigneth over the kings of the earth.

CHAPTER 18

AND after these things I saw another angel come down from heaven, having great power; and the earth was lightened with his glory.

2 And he cried mightily with a strong
voice, saying, Babylon the great is fallen,
is fallen, and is become the habitation
of devils, and the hold of every foul
spirit, and a cage of every unclean and
hateful bird.
3 For all nations have drunk of the
wine of the wrath of her fornication, and
the kings of the earth have committed
fornication with her, and the merchants
of the earth are waxed rich through the
abundance of her delicacies.
4 And I heard another voice from
heaven, saying, Come out of her, my
people, that ye be not partakers of her
sins, and that ye receive not of her
plagues.
5 For her sins have reached unto
heaven, and God hath remembered her
iniquities.
6 Reward her even as she rewarded
you, and double unto her double according to her works: in the cup which she
hath filled, fill to her double.
7 How much she hath glorified herself,
and lived deliciously, so much torment
and sorrow give her: for she saith in her
heart, I sit a queen, and am no widow,
and shall see no sorrow.
8 Therefore shall her plagues come in
one day, death, and mourning, and famine; and she shall be utterly burned with
fire: for strong *is* the Lord God who
judgeth her.
9 And the kings of the earth, who have
committed fornication and lived deliciously with her, shall bewail her, and
lament for her, when they shall see the
smoke of her burning,
10 Standing afar off for the fear of her
torment, saying, Alas, alas, that great
city Babylon, that mighty city! for in one
hour is thy judgment come.
11 And the merchants of the earth shall
weep and mourn over her; for no man
buyeth their merchandise any more:
12 The merchandise of gold, and silver,
and precious stones, and of pearls, and
fine linen, and purple, and silk, and scarlet, and all thyine wood, and all manner
vessels of ivory, and all manner vessels
of most precious wood, and of brass, and
iron, and marble,
13 And cinnamon, and odors, and ointments, and frankincense, and wine, and
oil, and fine flour, and wheat, and
beasts, and sheep, and horses, and
chariots, and slaves, and souls of men.
14 And the fruits that thy soul lusted
after are departed from thee, and all
things which were dainty and goodly are
departed from thee, and thou shalt find
them no more at all.
15 The merchants of these things,
which were made rich by her, shall
stand afar off for the fear of her torment,
weeping and wailing,
16 And saying, Alas, alas, that great
city, that was clothed in fine linen,
and purple, and scarlet, and decked
with gold, and precious stones, and
pearls!
17 For in one hour so great riches is
come to nought. And every shipmaster,
and all the company in ships, and
sailors, and as many as trade by sea,
stood afar off,
18 And cried when they saw the smoke
of her burning, saying, What *city is* like
unto this great city!
19 And they cast dust on their heads,
and cried, weeping and wailing, saying,
Alas, alas, that great city, wherein were
made rich all that had ships in the sea
by reason of her costliness! for in one
hour is she made desolate.
20 Rejoice over her, *thou* heaven, and
ye holy apostles and prophets; for God
hath avenged you on her.
21 And a mighty angel took up a stone
like a great millstone, and cast *it* into the
sea, saying, Thus with violence shall
that great city Babylon be thrown down,
and shall be found no more at all.
22 And the voice of harpers, and musi-
cians, and of pipers, and trumpeters,
shall be heard no more at all in thee;
and no craftsman, of whatsoever craft
he be, shall be found any more in thee;
and the sound of a millstone shall be
heard no more at all in thee;
23 And the light of a candle shall shine
no more at all in thee; and the voice of
the bridegroom and of the bride shall be
heard no more at all in thee: for thy
merchants were the great men of the
earth; for by thy sorceries were all nations deceived.
24 And in her was found the blood of
prophets, and of saints, and of all that
were slain upon the earth.

CHAPTER 19

AND after these things I heard a great
voice of much people in heaven,
saying, Ăl′lē-lu̦′ịȧ; Salvation, and glory,

and honor, and power, unto the Lord our
God:
2 For true and righteous *are* his judgments; for he hath judged the great
whore, which did corrupt the earth with
her fornication, and hath avenged the
blood of his servants at her hand.
3 And again they said, Ăl′lē-lṳ′ịȧ. And
her smoke rose up for ever and ever.
4 And the four and twenty elders and
the four beasts fell down and worshipped God that sat on the throne, saying, Amen; Ăl′lē-lṳ′ịȧ.
5 And a voice came out of the throne,
saying, Praise our God, all ye his servants, and ye that fear him, both small
and great.
6 And I heard as it were the voice of a
great multitude, and as the voice of
many waters, and as the voice of mighty
thunderings, saying, Ăl′lē-lṳ′ịȧ: for the
Lord God omnipotent reigneth.
7 Let us be glad and rejoice, and give
honor to him: for the marriage of the
Lamb is come, and his wife hath made
herself ready.
8 And to her was granted that she
should be arrayed in fine linen, clean
and white: for the fine linen is the righteousness of saints.
9 And he saith unto me, Write, Blessed
are they which are called unto the marriage supper of the Lamb. And he saith
unto me, These are the true sayings of
God.
10 And I fell at his feet to worship him.
And he said unto me, See *thou do it* not:
I am thy fellow servant, and of thy
brethren that have the testimony of
Jesus: worship God: for the testimony
of Jesus is the spirit of prophecy.
11 And I saw heaven opened, and behold a white horse; and he that sat upon
him *was* called Faithful and True, and
in righteousness he doth judge and
make war.
12 His eyes *were* as a flame of fire, and
on his head *were* many crowns; and he
had a name written, that no man knew,
but he himself.
13 And he *was* clothed with a vesture
dipped in blood: and his name is called
The Word of God.
14 And the armies *which were* in
heaven followed him upon white horses,
clothed in fine linen, white and clean.
15 And out of his mouth goeth a sharp
sword, that with it he should smite the
nations; and he shall rule them with a
rod of iron: and he treadeth the winepress of the fierceness and wrath of
Almighty God.
16 And he hath on *his* vesture and on
his thigh a name written, KING OF
KINGS, AND LORD OF LORDS.
17 And I saw an angel standing in the
sun; and he cried with a loud voice,
saying to all the fowls that fly in the
midst of heaven, Come and gather yourselves together unto the supper of the
great God;
18 That ye may eat the flesh of kings,
and the flesh of captains, and the flesh
of mighty men, and the flesh of horses,
and of them that sit on them, and the
flesh of all *men, both* free and bond,
both small and great.
19 And I saw the beast, and the kings of
the earth, and their armies, gathered together to make war against him that sat
on the horse, and against his army.
20 And the beast was taken, and with
him the false prophet that wrought
miracles before him, with which he deceived them that had received the mark
of the beast, and them that worshipped
his image. These both were cast alive
into a lake of fire burning with brimstone.
21 And the remnant were slain with
the sword of him that sat upon the
horse, which *sword* proceeded out of his
mouth: and all the fowls were filled with
their flesh.

CHAPTER 20

AND I saw an angel come down from
heaven, having the key of the
bottomless pit and a great chain in his
hand.
2 And he laid hold on the dragon, that
old serpent, which is the Devil, and
Satan, and bound him a thousand years,
3 And cast him into the bottomless pit,
and shut him up, and set a seal upon
him, that he should deceive the nations
no more, till the thousand years should
be fulfilled: and after that he must be
loosed a little season.
4 And I saw thrones, and they sat upon
them, and judgment was given unto
them: and *I saw* the souls of them that
were beheaded for the witness of Jesus,
and for the word of God, and which had
not worshipped the beast, neither his
image, neither had received *his* mark

upon their foreheads, or in their hands; and they lived and reigned with Christ a thousand years.
5 But the rest of the dead lived not again until the thousand years were finished. This *is* the first resurrection.
6 Blessed and holy *is* he that hath part in the first resurrection: on such the second death hath no power, but they shall be priests of God and of Christ, and shall reign with him a thousand years.
7 And when the thousand years are expired, Satan shall be loosed out of his prison,
8 And shall go out to deceive the nations which are in the four quarters of the earth, Gog and Mā'gŏg, to gather them together to battle: the number of whom *is* as the sand of the sea.
9 And they went up on the breadth of the earth, and compassed the camp of the saints about, and the beloved city: and fire came down from God out of heaven, and devoured them.
10 And the devil that deceived them was cast into the lake of fire and brimstone, where the beast and the false prophet *are*, and shall be tormented day and night for ever and ever.
11 And I saw a great white throne, and him that sat on it, from whose face the earth and the heaven fled away; and there was found no place for them.
12 And I saw the dead, small and great, stand before God; and the books were opened: and another book was opened, which is *the book* of life: and the dead were judged out of those things which were written in the books, according to their works.
13 And the sea gave up the dead which were in it; and death and hell delivered up the dead which were in them: and they were judged every man according to their works.
14 And death and hell were cast into the lake of fire. This is the second death.
15 And whosoever was not found written in the book of life was cast into the lake of fire.

CHAPTER 21

AND I saw a new heaven and a new earth: for the first heaven and the first earth were passed away; and there was no more sea.
2 And I John saw the holy city, new Jerusalem, coming down from God out of heaven, prepared as a bride adorned for her husband.
3 And I heard a great voice out of heaven saying, Behold, the tabernacle of God *is* with men, and he will dwell with them, and they shall be his people, and God himself shall be with them, *and be* their God.
4 And God shall wipe away all tears from their eyes; and there shall be no more death, neither sorrow, nor crying, neither shall there be any more pain: for the former things are passed away.
5 And he that sat upon the throne said, Behold, I make all things new. And he said unto me, Write: for these words are true and faithful.
6 And he said unto me, It is done. I am Alpha and Ō-mē'gȧ, the beginning and the end. I will give unto him that is athirst of the fountain of the water of life freely.
7 He that overcometh shall inherit all things; and I will be his God, and he shall be my son.
8 But the fearful, and unbelieving, and the abominable, and murderers, and whoremongers, and sorcerers, and idolaters, and all liars, shall have their part in the lake which burneth with fire and brimstone: which is the second death.
9 And there came unto me one of the seven angels which had the seven vials full of the seven last plagues, and talked with me, saying, Come hither, I will show thee the bride, the Lamb's wife.
10 And he carried me away in the spirit to a great and high mountain, and showed me that great city, the holy Jerusalem, descending out of heaven from God,
11 Having the glory of God: and her light *was* like unto a stone most precious, even like a jasper stone, clear as crystal;
12 And had a wall great and high, *and* had twelve gates, and at the gates twelve angels, and names written thereon, which are *the names* of the twelve tribes of the children of Ĭs'rā-ĕl:
13 On the east three gates; on the north three gates; on the south three gates; and on the west three gates.
14 And the wall of the city had twelve foundations, and in them the names of the twelve apostles of the Lamb.

15 And he that talked with me had a
golden reed to measure the city, and
the gates thereof, and the wall thereof.
16 And the city lieth foursquare, and
the length is as large as the breadth: and
he measured the city with the reed,
twelve thousand furlongs. The length
and the breadth and the height of it are
equal.
17 And he measured the wall thereof,
a hundred *and* forty *and* four cubits,
according to the measure of a man, that
is, of the angel.
18 And the building of the wall of it
was *of* jasper: and the city *was* pure
gold, like unto clear glass.
19 And the foundations of the wall of
the city *were* garnished with all manner
of precious stones. The first foundation
was jasper; the second, sapphire; the
third, a chalcedony; the fourth, an
emerald;
20 The fifth, sardonyx; the sixth, sardius; the seventh, chrysolite; the eighth,
beryl; the ninth, a topaz; the tenth, a
chrysoprasus; the eleventh, a jacinth;
the twelfth, an amethyst.
21 And the twelve gates *were* twelve
pearls; every several gate was of one
pearl: and the street of the city *was*
pure gold, as it were transparent glass.
22 And I saw no temple therein: for the
Lord God Almighty and the Lamb are
the temple of it.
23 And the city had no need of the sun,
neither of the moon, to shine in it: for
the glory of God did lighten it, and the
Lamb *is* the light thereof.
24 And the nations of them which are
saved shall walk in the light of it: and
the kings of the earth do bring their
glory and honor into it.
25 And the gates of it shall not be shut
at all by day: for there shall be no night
there.
26 And they shall bring the glory and
honor of the nations into it.
27 And there shall in no wise enter into
it any thing that defileth, neither *whatsoever* worketh abomination, or *maketh*
a lie: but they which are written in the
Lamb's book of life.

CHAPTER 22

AND he showed me a pure river of
water of life, clear as crystal, pro-
ceeding out of the throne of God and of
the Lamb.
2 In the midst of the street of it, and on
either side of the river, *was there* the
tree of life, which bare twelve *manner
of* fruits, *and* yielded her fruit every
month: and the leaves of the tree *were*
for the healing of the nations.
3 And there shall be no more curse:
but the throne of God and of the Lamb
shall be in it; and his servants shall
serve him:
4 And they shall see his face; and his
name *shall be* in their foreheads.
5 And there shall be no night there;
and they need no candle, neither light
of the sun; for the Lord God giveth
them light: and they shall reign for ever
and ever.
6 And he said unto me, These sayings
are faithful and true: and the Lord God
of the holy prophets sent his angel to
show unto his servants the things which
must shortly be done.
7 Behold, I come quickly: blessed *is* he
that keepeth the sayings of the prophecy
of this book.
8 And I John saw these things, and
heard *them*. And when I had heard and
seen, I fell down to worship before the
feet of the angel which showed me these
things.
9 Then saith he unto me, See *thou do
it* not: for I am thy fellow servant, and of
thy brethren the prophets, and of them
which keep the sayings of this book:
worship God.
10 And he saith unto me, Seal not the
sayings of the prophecy of this book: for
the time is at hand.
11 He that is unjust, let him be unjust
still: and he which is filthy, let him be
filthy still: and he that is righteous, let
him be righteous still: and he that is
holy, let him be holy still.
12 And, behold, I come quickly; and
my reward *is* with me, to give every man
according as his work shall be.
13 I am Alpha and Ō-mē'gȧ, the beginning and the end, the first and the
last.
14 Blessed *are* they that do his commandments, that they may have right
to the tree of life, and may enter in
through the gates into the city.
15 For without *are* dogs, and sorcerers,
and whoremongers, and murderers, and
idolaters, and whosoever loveth and
maketh a lie.
16 I Jesus have sent mine angel to

testify unto you these things in the
churches. I am the root and the offspring of David, *and* the bright and
morning star.
17 And the Spirit and the bride say,
Come. And let him that heareth say,
Come. And let him that is athirst come.
And whosoever will, let him take the
water of life freely.
18 For I testify unto every man that
heareth the words of the prophecy of
this book, If any man shall add unto
these things, God shall add unto him
the plagues that are written in this
book:
19 And if any man shall take away from
the words of the book of this prophecy,
God shall take away his part out of the
book of life, and out of the holy city, and
from the things which are written in
this book.
20 He which testifieth these things
saith, Surely I come quickly: Amen.
Even so, come, Lord Jesus.
21 The grace of our Lord Jesus Christ
be with you all. Amen.

Words Which Have Changed in Meaning

The following list of over 500 archaic and obsolete words and phrases has been prepared in order to help the average reader understand more readily the meaning of the King James Version. Of course, not all of these words and phrases are inappropriate in all contexts and hence each expression is followed by a list of those passages in which misunderstanding is likely to occur.

In each instance the bold-face word or phrase represents the King James text. This is followed by a dash to separate it from the more meaningful alternative. Where there is more than one alternative, each is given and the corresponding passages are listed.

Though this list of archaic and obsolete words is not exhaustive, it does, however, provide the reader with a handy reference to most expressions which are likely to produce difficulty in comprehending the meaning of the King James Version.

abased—humbled, Mt. 23:12; Lk. 14:11; 18:14
abide—await, Acts 20:23
abroad—outside, Deut. 24:11
—in the street, Jer. 6:11
accursed—devoted, Josh. 6:17, 18 (3 times); 7:1 (2 times), 11, 12 (2 times), 13 (2 times), 15; 22:20; 1 Chr. 2:7
accuse—slander, Prov. 30:10
acquaintance—acquaintances, Lk. 2:44; 23:49; Acts 24:23
admiration—wonder, Rev. 17:6
advanced—appointed, 1 Sam. 12:6
advertise—advise, Num. 24:14
—reveal to, Ruth 4:4
affections—passions, Gal. 5:24
again—back, Mt. 27:3; Lk. 14:6
show again—show, Mt. 11:4
against he come—to meet him, Ex. 7:15
agone—ago, 1 Sam. 30:13
allege—prove, Acts 17:3
allow—approve, Lk. 11:48; Rom. 14:22; 1 Thes. 2:4
—accept, Acts 24:15
—know, Rom. 7:15
almost—soon, Ps. 94:17
amazement—terror, 1 Pet. 3:6
ambassage—embassy, Lk. 14:32
amend—mend, Jn. 4:52
ancient(s)—elder(s), Ps. 119:100; Is. 3:2, 5, 14; 9:15; 24:23; 47:6; Jer. 19:1 (2 times); Ezek. 7:26; 8:11, 12; 27:9
anon—immediately, Mt. 13:20
—straightway, Mk. 1:30
answer—defense, 2 Tim. 4:16
apothecary—perfumer, Ex. 30:25, 35; 37:29; Eccl. 10:1
approve—prove, 2 Cor. 6:4; 7:11
armholes—elbows, Ezek. 13:18
artillery—weapons, 1 Sam. 20:40
assay—essay, Acts 9:26; 16:7; Heb. 11:29
assay(ed)—attempt(ed), Deut. 4:34; 1 Sam. 17:39
—ventures, Job 4:2
at—near to, Ex. 19:15; Num. 6:6; Ezek. 44:25
attendance—attention, 1 Tim. 4:13
audience—hearing, Gen. 23:10, 13, 16; 1 Sam. 25:24; Neh. 13:1

badger's skin—sealskin, Ezek. 16:10
bands—pangs, Ps. 73:4
barbarous people—barbarians, Acts 28:2
barren—bereaved, Song 4:2; 6:6
base—lowly, 1 Cor. 1:28; 2 Cor. 10:1
because—that, Mt. 20:31
bed—couch, Song 1:16
—litter, Song 3:7
behaved—stilled, Ps. 131:2
behind—lacking, Col. 1:24
belied—denied, Jer. 5:12
belly—body, Ps. 31:9
bethink themselves—lay it to heart, 1 Kgs. 8:47; 2 Chr. 6:37
betimes—early, Gen. 26:31; 2 Chr. 36:15; Job 8:5; 24:5; Prov. 13:24
bewitch—amaze, Acts 8:9, 11
bewray—betray, Mt. 26:73
bewrayeth—revealeth, Prov. 29:24
bishopric—office, Acts 1:20
bloody—blood-thirsty, Ps. 5:6; 26:9; 139:19
botch—boil, Deut. 28:27, 35
bottle—jar, Ps. 119:83; Jer. 13:12 (2 times)
bottles—wineskins, Mt. 9:17; Mk. 2:22; Lk. 5:37, 38
bottles of wine—wine-skins, Josh. 9:13; 1 Sam. 1:24; 10:3; 16:20; 2 Sam. 16:1; Job 32:19

bottles of wine—heat of wine, Hos. 7:5
bound—landmark, Hos. 5:10
bowels—heart, Gen. 43:30; 1 Kgs. 3:26; Ps. 109:18; Song 5:4; Is. 16:11; 63:15; Jer. 31:20; Lam. 1:20; 2:11; Phlm. 12, 20; 1 Jn. 3:17
—hearts, Col. 3:12; Phlm. 7
—affections, 2 Cor. 6:12; Phil. 2:1
—anguish, Jer. 4:19
—tender mercies, Phil. 1:8
box—jar, Mt. 26:7; Mk. 14:3; Lk. 7:37
branch—song, Is. 25:5
breaking up—breaking in, Ex. 22:2
breeding—possession, Zeph. 2:9
brigandines—coats of mail, Jer. 46:4; 51:3
brought up for—bore unto, 2 Sam. 21:8
bruit—report, Jer. 10:22; Nah. 3:19
bunches—humps, Is. 30:6
by—beside, Num. 6:9
—by reason of, Num. 6:11
—against, 1 Cor. 4:4
by and by—immediately, Mt. 13:21; Mk. 6:25; Lk. 17:7; 21:9
by that—before, Ex. 22:26

careful—anxious, Lk. 10:41; Phil. 4:6
carefully—anxiously, Mic. 1:12
—diligently, Phil. 2:28
carefulness—anxiety, 1 Cor. 7:32; 2 Cor. 7:11
carriage(s)—baggage, Judg. 18:21; 1 Sam. 17:22; Is. 10:28; Acts 21:15
—the things that ye carried about, Is. 46:1
certified—told, Esth. 2:22
certify—advise, 2 Sam. 15:28
chapiter(s)—capital(s), Ex. 36:38; 38:17, 19, 28; 1 Kgs. 7:16 (3 times), 18 (2 times), 19, 20 (2 times), 31, 41 (2 times), 42; 2 Kgs. 25:17 (3 times); 2 Chr. 3:15; 4:12 (2 times); Jer. 52:22 (3 times)
chapmen—traders, 2 Chr. 9:14
chapped—parched, Jer. 14:4
charge—burden, 1 Tim. 5:16
charger—platter, Mt. 14:8, 11; Mk. 6:25, 28
charity—love, 1 Cor. 8:1; 13:1, 2, 3, 4, 8, 13; 14:1; 16:14; Col. 3:14; 1 Thes. 3:6; 2 Thes. 1:3; 1 Tim. 1:5; 2:15; 4:12; 2 Tim. 2:22; 3:10; Tit. 2:2; 1 Pet. 4:8; 5:14; 2 Pet. 1:7; 3 Jn. 6; Jude 12; Rev. 2:19
charitably—in love, Rom. 14:15
check—chastisement, Job 20:3
chief—chiefs, Lk. 19:47; Acts 19:31; 25:2; 28:17
chief men—corners, Is. 41:9
Chronicles—chronicles, 1 Kgs. 14:19, 29; 15:7, 23, 31; 16:5, 14, 20, 28; 22:39, 45; 2 Kgs. 1:18; 8:23; 10:34; 12:19; 13:8, 12; 14:15, 18, 28; 15:6, 11, 15, 21, 26, 31, 36; 16:19; 20:20; 21:17, 25; 23:28; 24:5; 1 Chr. 27:24
clean—completely, Josh. 3:17; 4:1, 11; Ps. 77:8; Is. 24:19
clouted—patched, Josh. 9:5
old cast clouts—worn-out clothes, Jer. 38:11, 12
cockatrice'—adder's, Is. 11:8; 14:29; 59:5; Jer. 8:17
collops of, maketh—gathereth (fat on his loins), Job 15:27
comely—seemly, Ps. 33:1; Eccl. 5:18; 1 Cor. 7:35; 11:13
—stately, Prov. 30:29
comeliness—majesty, Ezek. 16:14
communicate unto—share with, Gal. 6:6; Phil. 4:14, 15; 1 Tim. 6:18; Heb. 13:16
communication—companionship, 1 Cor. 15:33
—fellowship, Phlm. 6
compass—circle, Prov. 8:27
—encompass, Jer. 31:22
compasseth—searchest out, Ps. 139:3
concluded—shut up, Rom. 11:32; Gal. 3:22
confection—spice, Ex. 30:35
conscience—consciousness, 1 Cor. 8:7; Heb. 10:2
consult(ed)—counsel(ed), 1 Kgs. 12:6, 8; 1 Chr. 13:1; 2 Chr. 20:21; Neh. 5:7; Ps. 62:4; 83:3, 5; Ezek. 21:21; Dan. 6:7; Mic. 6:5; Hab. 2:10
consumption—destruction, Is. 28:22
contrary—different, Ezek. 16:34 (2 times)
convenient—needful, Prov. 30:8
—fitting, Rom. 1:28; Eph. 5:4; Phlm. 8
conversation—in the way, Ps. 37:14; 50:23
—citizenship, Phil. 3:20
—life, 1 Pet. 1:15
—way of life, 2 Cor. 1:12; Gal. 1:13; Eph. 2:3; 4:22; Phil. 1:27; 1 Tim. 4:12; Heb. 13:5, 7; Jas. 3:13; 1 Pet. 1:18; 2:12; 3:1, 2, 16; 2 Pet. 2:7; 3:11
convert—turn, Is. 6:10
corn—grain, Gen. 27:37; 41:35, 49, 57; 42:1, 2, 3, 5, 19, 25, 26; 43:2; 44:2; 45:23; 47:14; Ex. 22:6 (2 times); Lev. 2:14 (2 times), 16; 23:14; Num. 18:27; Deut. 7:13; 11:14; 12:17; 14:23; 16:9, 13; 18:4; 23:25 (2 times); 25:4; 28:51; 33:28; Josh. 5:11 (2 times), 12; Judg. 15:5 (2 times); Ruth 2:2, 14; 3:7; 1 Sam. 17:17; 25:18; 2 Sam. 17:19, 28; 2 Kgs. 4:42; 18:32; 19:26; 2 Chr. 31:5; 32:28; Neh. 5:2, 3, 10, 11; 10:39; 13:5, 12; Job 5:26; 24:6, 24; 39:4; Ps. 4:7; 65:9, 13; 72:16; 78:24; Prov. 11:26; Is. 17:5; 21:10; 28:28; 36:17;

37:27; 62:8; Lam. 2:12; Ezek. 36:29; Hos. 2:8, 9, 22; 7:14; 10:11; 14:7; Joel 1:10, 17; 2:19; Amos 8:5; 9:9; Hag. 1:11; Zech. 9:17; Mt. 12:1; Mk. 2:33; 4:28; Lk. 6:1 (2 times); Jn. 12:24; Acts 7:12; 1 Cor. 9:9; 1 Tim. 5:18
—grainfields, Mt. 12:1
cornfloor—grainfloor, Hos. 9:1
cornets—castanets, 2 Sam. 6:5
corrupt, are—scoff, Ps. 73:8
countervail—compensate for, Esth. 7:4
countries—country, Lk. 21:21
country, a—the country, Jn. 11:54
cover with a covering—pour out a drink offering, Is. 30:1
cracknels—cakes, 1 Kgs. 14:3
crouch—prostrate, 1 Sam. 2:36
cuckoo—sea gull, Deut. 14:15
cunning—skilful, Gen. 25:27; Ex. 35:35; 36:8; 38:23; 1 Sam. 16:16, 18; 1 Kgs. 7:14; 1 Chr. 22:15; 25:7; 2 Chr. 2:7 (2 times), 13, 14 (2 times); 26:15; Song 7:1; Is. 40:20; Jer. 9:17; 10:9
curious—skillfully woven, Ex. 28:8, 27, 28; 29:5; 35:32; 39:5, 20, 21; Lev. 8:7
curse—devoted thing, Josh. 6:18

damnation—condemnation, Mt. 23:14; Mk. 12:40; Lk. 20:47; Jn. 5:29; Rom. 3:8; 13:2; 1 Tim. 5:12
—judgment, 1 Cor. 11:29
damned—condemned, Mk. 16:16; Rom. 14:23; 2 Thes. 2:12
darling—dear life, Ps. 22:20; 35:17
darts—weapons, 2 Chr. 32:5
daysman—umpire, Job 9:33
deal—part, Ex. 29:40; Lev. 14:10, 21; 23:13, 17; 24:5; Num. 15:4, 6, 9; 28:9, 12 (2 times), 13, 20 (2 times), 21, 28 (2 times), 29; 29:3 (2 times), 4, 9 (2 times), 10, 14 (2 times), 15
dearth—drought, Jer. 14:1
deceived—enticed, Jer. 20:7 (2 times)
decline—turn aside, Deut. 17:11
decline after many—turn aside after a multitude, Ex. 23:2
defense—gold, Job 22:25
delicately—cheerfully, 1 Sam. 15:32
—luxuriously, Lk. 7:25
delicates—delicacies, Jer. 51:34
deliciously—wantonly, Rev. 18:7, 9
delight—delicate living, Prov. 19:10
denounce—declare, Deut. 30:18
desolate—condemned, Ps. 34:21, 22
—found guilty, Is. 24:6
destroy—hold guilty, Ps. 5:10
devils—satyrs, 2 Chr. 11:15
direct their work—give them their recompense, Is. 61:8
disappoint—confront, Ps. 17:13
discomfited, be—become tributary, Is. 31:8
discover(ed) (eth) (ing)—disclose(d) (th), 1 Sam. 14:8, 11
—strippeth, Ps. 29:9
—reveal, Prov. 18:2
—uncover(ed) (ing), Lev. 20:18; Deut. 22:30; 2 Sam. 22:16; Ps. 18:15; Is. 3:17; 57:8; Jer. 13:26; Ezek. 13:14; 16:57; 23:10, 18 (2 times), 29; Hos. 2:10; Nah. 3:5; Hab. 3:13
—removed, Is. 22:8
ditch—reservoir, Is. 22:11
divide—distribute, Neh. 9:22
doctors—teachers, Lk. 2:46
doctrine—the message, Is. 28:9
dote—be fools, Jer. 50:36
doubtful—anxious, Lk. 12:29
dragons—jackals, Job 30:29; Ps. 44:19; Is. 13:22; 34:13; 35:7; 43:20; Jer. 9:11; 10:22; 14:6; 49:33; 51:37; Mic. 1:8; Mal. 1:3
—sea-monsters, Ps. 148:7
drams—darics, 1 Chr. 29:7; Neh. 7:71, 72
draught—drain, Mt. 15:17; Mk. 7:19
duke(s)—chief(s), Gen. 36:15f, 29f, 40f et al.; Ex. 15:15; 1 Chr. 1:51 et al.
—princes, Josh. 13:21
durable—stately, Is. 23:18

ear(ed) (ing)—plow(ed) (ing), Gen. 45:6; Ex. 34:21; Deut. 21:4; 1 Sam. 8:12; Is. 30:24
early—earnestly, Ps. 63:1; 78:34; Prov. 1:28; 8:17
earnestly—carefully, Lk. 22:56
—steadfastly, Acts 23:1
earring—ring, Gen. 24:22, 30, 47
Easter—the Passover, Acts 12:4
either—each, Lev. 10:1; 2 Chr. 18:9
emerods—tumors, Deut. 28:27; 1 Sam. 5:6, 9, 12; 6:4, 5, 11, 17
ensue—pursue, 1 Pet. 3:11
entreat(ed)—treat(ed), Mt. 22:6; Lk. 18:32; 20:11; Acts 7:6, 19; 27:3; 1 Thes. 2:2
was entreated of—granted his prayer, Gen. 25:21
environ—compass, Josh. 7:9
erred through, have—reel with, Is. 28:7 (2 times)
estate—council, Acts 22:5
estates—men, Mk. 6:21
ever, or—before, Dan. 6:24; Acts 23:15
evidently—openly, Gal. 3:1
—clearly, Acts 10:3
evenings—deserts, Jer. 5:6
evil—trouble, Jon. 1:7
—bad, Jer. 29:17
evil entreated us—dealt ill with us, Deut. 26:6

exactors—taskmasters, Is. 60:17

failed for—failed in looking for, Lam. 4:17
fame—report, Mt. 4:24; 9:26, 31; 14:1; Mk. 1:28; Lk. 4:14, 37; 5:15
fast—close, Ruth 2:8, 21, 23
feeble-minded—fainthearted, 1 Thes. 5:14
feller—hewer, Is. 14:8
fetch(ed) a compass—make (made) a circuit, 2 Sam. 5:23; 2 Kgs. 3:9; Acts 28:13
—turn about, Num. 34:5
fillet—line, Jer. 52:21
fit—appointed, Lev. 16:21
fitches—spelt, Ezek. 4:9
flagons—cakes of raisins, Song 2:5
flagon(s) of wine—cake(s) of raisins, 2 Sam. 6:19; 1 Chr. 16:3; Hos. 3:1
flags—reeds, Ex. 2:3, 5
flanks—loins, Job 15:27
flood—river, Josh. 24:2, 3, 14, 15
floor—the threshing floor, Hos. 9:2; Mic. 4:12
flowers—impurity, Lev. 15:24, 33
folk in—nations for, Jer. 51:58
forward—earnest, 2 Cor. 8:17
—ready, 2 Cor. 8:10
—eager, Gal. 2:10
forwardness—earnestness, 2 Cor. 8:8
—readiness, 2 Cor. 9:2
frankly—freely, Lk. 7:42
fray—frighten, Deut. 28:26; Jer. 7:33
—terrify, Zech. 1:21
free—willing, Ps. 51:12
freely—for nought, Num. 11:5
fretted—raged against, Ezek. 16:43
froward—wayward, Prov. 4:24
—crooked, Prov. 8:8; 17:20
—perverse, Deut. 32:20; 2 Sam. 22:27; Job 5:13; Ps. 18:26 (2 times); 101:4; Prov. 2:12, 15; 3:32; 6:12; 8:13; 10:31; 11:20; 16:28, 30; 17:20; 22:5
frowardness—perverseness, Prov. 2:14; 6:14; 10:32
furnished—filled, Mt. 22:10
furniture—saddle, Gen. 31:34
furrows—transgressions, Hos. 10:10

galleries—in the tresses, Song 7:5
gender—breed, Lev. 19:19
glistering—glistening, 1 Chr. 29:2; Lk. 9:29
go beyond—transgress, 1 Thes. 4:6
good—goods, 1 Jn. 3:17
goodman—my husband, Prov. 7:19
—master, Mt. 20:11; 24:43; Mk. 14:14; Lk. 12:39; 22:11
governor—pilot, Jas. 3:4
graffed—grafted, Rom. 11:17, 19, 23, 24
grasshoppers—locusts, Amos 7:1
grate—grating, Ex. 27:4
grief—sickness, Jer. 6:7
grudge—grumble, Jas. 5:9; 1 Pet. 4:9
—tarry all night, Ps. 59:15
grave—engrave, Ex. 28:9, 36; 2 Chr. 2:7
graved—carved, 1 Kgs. 7:36
graven—engraven, Ex. 39:6
guide—companion, Ps. 55:13
guilty—bound, Mt. 23:18
gutter—watercourse, 2 Sam. 5:8

habergeon(s)—coat(s) of mail, Ex. 28:32; 39:23; 2 Chr. 26:14; Neh. 4:16; Job 41:26
halted—limped, Gen. 32:31
habitations—pastures, Amos 1:2
hap—lot, Ruth 2:3
hardly—with difficulty, Mt. 19:23
hardly bestead—sore distressed, Is. 8:21
harness—armor, 1 Kgs. 20:11; 22:34; 2 Chr. 9:24; 18:33
harnessed—armed, Ex. 13:18
hasted—hastened, Gen. 18:7, Job 31:5
—urged, Ex. 5:13
hasteth—hasteneth, Job 40:23
hasten—watch over, Jer. 1:12
helve—handle, Deut. 19:5
heresies—factions, 1 Cor. 11:19; Gal. 5:20; 2 Pet. 2:1
heretic—factious, Tit. 3:10
honorable—honored, Gen. 34:19
horseleech—leech, Prov. 30:15
hough(ed)—hock(ed), Josh. 11:6, 9; 2 Sam. 8:4; 1 Chr. 18:4
Huzzab—it is decreed, she, Nah. 2:7

imagination—stubbornness, Deut. 29:19; Jer. 7:24; 9:14; 11:8; 13:10; 16:12; 18:12
imagine—devise, Hos. 7:15
influences, sweet—cluster, Job 38:31
instant—insistent, Lk. 23:23
—constant, Rom. 12:12
—urgent, 2 Tim. 4:2
instantly—diligently, Lk. 7:4
—earnestly, Acts 26:7
instrument—weapon, Is. 54:16
intermeddleth—quarrelleth, Prov. 18:1
inward—familiar, Job 19:19
inventions—doings, Ps. 99:8; 106:29, 39
isle(s)—coast-land(s), Is. 20:6; 23:2; 24:15

jeoparded—jeopardized, Judg. 5:18
Jewry—Judea, Lk. 23:5; Jn. 7:1
judgment—justice, Prov. 21:15; Amos 5:15, 24; Mic. 3:9
—by reason of injustice, Prov. 13:23
juniper-roots—broom-roots, Job 30:4
justle—jostle, Nah. 2:4

keep under—buffet, 1 Cor. 9:27
kindle—burn, Jer. 33:18
kine—cows, Gen. 32:15; 41:2, 3 (2 times), 4 (2 times), 18, 19, 20 (2 times), 26, 27; Deut. 7:13; 28:4, 18, 51; 32:14; 1 Sam. 6:7 (2 times), 10, 12, 14; 2 Sam. 17:29; Amos 4:1

lade—load, Lk. 11:46
lamb to—lambs for, Is. 16:1
large—much, Mt. 28:12
lay to—make, Is. 28:17
leasing—lies, Ps. 5:6
—falsehood, Ps. 4:2
length—last, Prov. 29:21
lent—granted, Ex. 12:36
let—loose, Ex. 5:4
—hindered, Rom. 1:13
—restrain, 2 Thes. 2:7
lewd—wicked, Acts 17:5
lewdness—villainy, Acts 18:14
light—lamp, 2 Kgs. 8:19
—vile, Num. 21:5
lightly—easily, Gen. 26:10
lightness—vain boasting, Jer. 23:32
liketh—pleaseth, Deut. 23:16; Amos 4:5
liking, worse—worse looking, Dan. 1:10
liquor—juice, Num. 6:3
listed—would, Mt. 17:12; Mk. 9:13
listeth—willeth, Jn. 3:8; Jas. 3:4
lively—living, Acts 7:38; 1 Pet. 1:3; 2:5
loft—the chamber, 1 Kgs. 17:19
—story, Acts 20:9
Lucifer—Day-star, Is. 14:12
lunatic—epileptic, Mt. 4:24; 17:15

mad—foolish, Eccl. 7:7
maid—virgin, Deut. 22:14, 17; Job 31:1
make away—sweep away, Dan. 11:44
manner, with the—in the act, Num. 5:13
marred—ruined, Mk. 2:22
maul—club, Prov. 25:18
mean—obscure, Prov. 22:29
meat—meal, Ex. 29:41; 30:9; Lev. 2:1, 3, 4, 5, 6, 7, 8, 9, 10, 11, 13 (2 times), 14 (2 times), 15; 5:13; 6:14, 15 (2 times), 20, 21, 23; 7:9, 10, 37; 9:4, 17; 14:10, 20, 21, 31; 23:13, 16, 18, 37; Num. 4:16; 6:15, 17; 7:13, 19, 25, 31, 37, 43, 49, 55; 7:61, 67, 73, 79, 87; 8:8; 15:4, 6, 9, 24; 18:9; 28:5, 8, 9, 12, 13; 29:3, 6 (2 times), 9, 11, 14, 16, 18, 19, 21, 22, 24, 25, 27, 28, 30, 31, 33, 34, 37, 38, 39; Josh. 22:23, 29; Judg. 13:19, 23; 1 Kgs. 8:64 (2 times); 2 Kgs. 3:20; 16:13, 15 (3 times); 1 Chr. 21:23; 23:29; 2 Chr. 7:7; Ezra 7:17; Neh. 10:33; 13:5, 9; Is. 57:6; Jer. 17:26; 33:18; Ezek. 42:13; 44:29; 45:15, 17 (2 times), 24, 25; 46:5, 7, 11, 14 (2 times), 15, 20; Joel 1:9, 13; 2:14; Amos 5:22
—food, Gen. 1:29, 30; Lev. 25:6, 7; Judg. 1:7; 14:14; 2 Sam. 13:5, 7, 10; 1 Kgs. 10:5; 19:8; 2 Chr. 9:4; Job 6:7; 12:11; 20:14, 21; 33:20, 34.3; 36:31; 38:41; Ps. 42:3; 44:11; 59:15; 69:21; 74:14; 78:18, 25, 30; 79:2; 104:21, 27; 107:18; 111:5; 145:15; Prov. 6:8; 23:3; 30:22, 25; 31:15; Is. 62:8; 65:25; Jer. 7:33; 16:4; 19:7; 34:20; Lam. 1:11; 4:10; Ezek. 4:10; 16:19; 29:5; 34:5, 8, 10; 47:12 (2 times); Dan. 1:5, 8, 10, 13, 15, 16; 4:12, 21; 11:26; Hab. 3:17; Mt. 3:4; 6:25; 10:10; 15:37; 24:45; 25:35, 42; Mk. 7:19; 8:8; Lk. 3:11; 8:55; 9:13; 12:23, 42; 24:41; Jn. 4:8, 32, 34; 6:27 (2 times), 55; 21:5; Acts 2:46; 9:19; 16:34; 27:33, 34, 36; Rom. 14:15 (2 times), 17, 20; 1 Cor. 3:2; 6:13 (2 times); 8:8, 13; 10:3; Col. 2:16; 1 Tim. 4:3; Heb. 5:12, 14; 9:10; 12:16; 13:9
—bread, Lev. 22:11, 13; 2 Sam. 13:5
merchantman—merchant, Mt. 13:45
mete—measure, Ex 16:18; Ps. 60:6
meteyard—measure of length, Lev. 19:35
minished—diminished, Ps. 107:39
minister—attendant, Lk. 4:20
minstrels—flute players, Mt. 9:23
moist—fresh, Num. 6:3
month—new moon, Hos. 5:7
motions—passions, Rom. 7:5
mount (of)—the hill country of, Josh. 20:7; Judg. 2:9; 3:27; 4:5; 7:24; 10:1; 12:15; 17:1; 18:2; 19:1, 16, 18; 1 Sam. 1:1; 9:4; 14:22; 2 Sam. 20:21; 1 Kgs. 4:8; 12:25; Jer. 4:15
mount—mound, Ezek. 4:2
munition(s)—stronghold, Is. 29:7; 33:16; Nah. 2:1

naturally—truly, Phil. 2:20
naughty—bad, Jer. 24:2
naughtiness—wickedness, Jas. 1:21
nephews—grandchildren, 1 Tim. 5:4
nether—lower, Deut. 24:6

observed him—kept him safe, Mk. 6:20
observed—kept, Gen. 37:11
occupy (occupied)—trade(d), Lk. 19:13; Ezek. 27:21
occupied in—traded for, Ezek. 27:16, 19, 22
occupiers—dealers in, Ezek. 27:27
occupied—used, Ex. 38:24
offend—be held guilty, Jer. 2:3
oil olive—olive oil, Ex. 27:20; 30:24; Lev. 24:2; 2 Kgs. 18:32
—olive trees, Deut. 8:8
open—frequent, 1 Sam. 3:1
orator, eloquent—skilful enchanter, Is. 3:3
organs—pipe, Ps. 150:4

other (some)—others, Jn. 21:2; Acts 15:2; 17:18; 2 Cor. 13:2; Phil. 2:3
ouches—settings, Ex. 28:11, 13, 14, 25; 39:6, 13, 16, 18
outlandish—foreign, Neh. 13:26
overcharge(d)—overburden(ed), Lk. 21:34; 2 Cor. 2:5
overlaid it—lay upon it, 1 Kgs. 3:19
owl(s)—ostrich(es), Mic. 1:8; Deut. 14:15; Job 30:29; Is. 13:21; 34:13; 43:20; Jer. 50:39
ox, wild—antelope, Deut. 14:15

palace—turret, Song 8:9
part—share, 1 Sam. 30:24 (3 times)
particularly—in detail, Acts 21:19; Heb. 9:5
passengers—to those passing, Prov. 9:15
pastor(s)—ruler(s), Jer. 2:8
—shepherds, Jer. 3:15; 10:21; 12:10; 17:16; 22:22; 23:1
pate—crown, Ps. 7:16
peep(ed)—chirp(ed), Is. 8:19; 10:14
perish—be ruined, Mt. 9:17; Lk. 5:37
pilled—peeled, Gen. 30:37, 38
pitiful—merciful, 1 Pet. 3:8
very pitiful—full of pity, Jas. 5:11
plain—quiet, Gen. 25:27
plat—portion, 2 Kgs. 9:26 (2 times)
platted—plaited, Mt. 27:29; Mk. 15:17; Jn. 19:2
poll(ed)—cut the hair of, 2 Sam. 14:26 (3 times); Ezek. 44:20; Mic. 1:16
polluted (polluting)—profaned (profaning), Is. 47:6; 56:2, 6
pommels—bowls, 2 Chr. 4:12 (2 times), 13
possessed—formed, Ps. 139:13
pots—sheepfolds, Ps. 68:13
power—striven, Gen. 32:28
precious, more—rarer, Is. 13:12
presently—straightway, Mt. 26:53; Phil. 2:23
—immediately, Mt. 21:19
pressed out of—oppressed beyond, 2 Cor. 1:8
presses—vats, Prov. 3:10
prevent(ed)—come before, Job 41:11; Ps. 88:13; Amos 9:10
—receive, Job 3:12
—precede, 1 Thes. 4:15
—spoke first to, Mt. 17:25
—met, Is. 21:14
—came upon, 2 Sam. 22:6, 19; Job 30:27; Ps. 18:5, 18
—anticipate(d), Ps. 119:147, 148
prevent(est)—meet(est), Ps. 21:3; 59:10; 79:8
printed—inscribed, Job 19:23
privily—secretly, Ps. 10:8; 11:2

profited—advanced, Gal. 1:14
profiting—progress, 1 Tim. 4:15
proper—own, Acts 1:19; 1 Cor. 7:7
—beautiful, Heb. 11:23
prove(d)—test(ed), Dan. 1:12, 14
purely—thoroughly, Is. 1:25
purtenance—entrails, Ex. 12:9

quick—alive, Lev. 13:10; Num. 16:30; Ps. 55:15; 124:3
—living, Heb. 4:12
quit—guiltless, Josh. 2:20
quit you—acquit yourselves, 1 Cor. 16:13

raised up—awakened, Song 8:5
ranges—ranks, Lev. 11:35; 2 Kgs. 11:8, 15; 2 Chr. 23:14; Job 39:8
ranging—roaming, Prov. 28:15
reason—reasonable, Acts 6:2
record—witness, Jn. 1:19; Acts 20:26; 2 Cor. 1:23; Phil. 1:8
regard—preserve, Prov. 5:2
relieve—refresh, Lam. 1:11, 19
removed, be—sway, Is. 24:20
—give way, Is. 22:25
removed woman—woman in her impurity, Ezek. 36:17
removing—wandering, Is. 49:21
rentest—rendest, Jer. 4:30
repeateth—harpeth on, Prov. 17:9
reprobate—refuse, Jer. 6:30
reprove—decide, Is. 11:4
residue—rest, Jer. 39:3; 41:10; Ezek. 9:8
respect, had—looked, Heb. 11:26
rest, take my—be silent, Is. 18:4
rest—resting-place, Ps. 132:8
restrain—limit, Job 15:8
ribband—cord, Num. 15:38
right—steadfast, Ps. 51:10
roaring—groaning, Ps. 22:1
robbery—violence, Prov. 21:7
rock—Sela, Is. 42:11
rod—shoot, Is. 11:1
roebuck—gazelle, Deut. 12:15, 22; 14:5; 15:22
room(s)—stead, 1 Kgs. 5:1, 5; 8:20; 20:24; 2 Kgs. 23:34; 1 Chr. 4:41; 2 Chr. 6:10
in the room—instead, 2 Sam. 19:13
—place, Mt. 2:22; Acts 24:27; 1 Cor. 14:16
—place, Lk. 14:9, 10
—seat, Lk. 14:8
rooms—seats, Lk. 14:7

sardine—sardius, Rev. 4:3
satyr(s)—wild goat(s), Is. 13:21; 34:14
savor—fragrance, Song 1:3
scattered—tall, Is. 18:2, 7
—broken, Ps. 60:2

scrip—wallet, 1 Sam. 17:40
—bag, Mt. 10:10; Mk. 6:8; Lk. 9:3; 10:4; 22:35, 36
secondarily—secondly, 1 Cor. 12:28
secret—counsel, Prov. 3:32
seethe—boil, Ex. 16:23 (2 times); 23:19; 29:31; 34:26; Deut. 14:21; 2 Kgs. 4:38; Ezek. 24:5; Zech. 14:21
seething—boiling, 1 Sam. 2:13
senators—elders, Ps. 105:22
sentence—judgment, Acts 15:19
settle—ledge, Ezek. 43:14 (3 times), 17, 20; 45:19
sever—distinguish, Ex. 9:4
several—single, 2 Chr. 28:25; 31:19;
—particular, Mt. 25:15
shamefacedness—propriety, 1 Tim. 2:9
shape—form, Jn. 5:37
shittah—acacia, Is. 41:19
shittim—acacia, Ex. 25:5, 10, 13, 23, 28; 26:15, 26, 32, 37; 27:1, 6; 30:1, 5; 35:7, 24; 36:20, 31, 36; 37:1, 4, 10, 15, 25, 28; 38:1, 6; Deut. 10:3
shoot—pass, Ex. 36:33
should—would, Acts 23:27
show—tell, Gen. 46:31
sides—innermost parts, 1 Sam. 24:3; Jon. 1:5
sincere—pure, 1 Pet. 2:2
singular—hard, Lev. 27:2
situate—situated, 1 Sam. 14:5
skill, can—has skill (could skill—had skill), 1 Kgs. 5:6; 2 Chr. 2:7, 8; 34:12
smell—take no delight in, Amos 5:21
snuffed up the wind—pant for air, Jer. 14:6
sod—boiled, Gen. 25:29; 2 Chr. 35:13
sodden—boiled, Ex. 12:9; Lev. 6:28 (2 times); Num. 6:19; 1 Sam. 2:15
softly—gently, Gen. 33:14
sore—fierce, 1 Sam. 14:52; 2 Sam. 2:17
sorrowful—loathsome, Job 6:7
sorrows—cords, Ps. 18:4, 5
speckled—sorrel, Zech. 1:8
spirit—breath, Is. 40:7
—wind, Eccl. 11:5
spoil, need of—lack of gain, Prov. 31:11
spoiled—plundered, Gen. 34:27, 29
spoiling—bereaving, Ps. 35:12
spouse—bride, Song 4:8, 9, 10, 11; 5:1
stay—rely, Is. 30:12; 31:1; 50:10
—uphold, Prov. 28:17
stem—stock, Is. 11:1
stonesquarers—Gebalites, 1 Kgs. 5:18
strain at—strain out, Mt. 23:24
strait—narrow, 2 Kgs. 6:1
straiten—distress, Jer. 19:9
straitness—distress, Jer. 19:9
strange—foreign, Acts 26:11
strangers of—visitors from, Acts 2:10
strength—rock, Is. 26:4
—stronghold, Ps. 31:4; Is. 23:14; 25:4 (2 times)
strike—put, Ex. 12:7
—touch, Ex. 12:22
string—bond, Mk. 7:35
study—strive, 1 Thes. 4:11; 2 Tim. 2:15
stuff—baggage, 1 Sam. 10:22; 25:13; 30:24
substance—stock, Is. 6:13 (2 times)
all the substance—every living thing, Deut. 11:6
suburbs—the open space, Ezek. 45:2
sycamore—sycomore, Amos 7:14
Syrian—Aramaic, Is. 36:11

table(s)—tablet(s), Lk. 1:63; 2 Cor. 3:3
tablets—armlets, Ex. 35:22
tabret(s)—timbrel(s), Gen. 31:27; 1 Sam. 10:5; 18:6; Job 17:6; Is. 5:12; 24:8; 30:32; Jer. 31:4; Ezek. 28:13
taches—clasps, Ex. 26:6 (2 times), 11 (2 times), 33; 35:11; 36:13 (2 times), 18; 39:33
take no thought—be not anxious, Mt. 6:25, 28, 31, 34; 10:19; Lk. 12:11, 22, 26
take thought for—worry about, 1 Sam. 9:5; Mt. 6:27; Lk. 12:25
tale—number, Ex. 5:8, 18; 1 Sam. 18:27; 1 Chr. 9:28
target—javelin, 1 Sam. 17:6
teil tree—terebinth, Is. 6:13
tell—count, Ps. 22:17
told—counted, 2 Kgs. 12:10, 11; 2 Chr. 2:2
temperance—self-control, Acts 24:25; Gal. 5:23; 2 Pet. 1:6
temperate—self-controlled, 1 Cor. 9:25; Tit. 1:8
tin—alloy, Is. 1:25
Tirshatha—governor, Ezra 2:63; Neh. 7:65, 70; 8:9; 10:1
tokens—signs, Ps. 135:9
toward—from, Jer. 1:13
translate(d)—transfer(red), 2 Sam. 3:10; Col. 1:13; Heb. 11:5
traveleth, one that—a robber, Prov. 24:34
trow—think, Lk. 17:9
turning away—backsliding, Prov. 1:32
turtle(s)—turtledove(s), Lev. 12:8; 15:29; Num. 6:10; Song 2:12; Jer. 8:7

uncomely—unseemly, 1 Cor. 7:36
unicorn(s)—wild ox (oxen), Num. 23:22; 24:8; Deut. 33:17; Job 39:9, 10; Ps. 22:21; 29:6; 92:10; Is. 34:7
unperfect—unformed, Ps. 139:16
upon—beside, Amos 9:1
—before, Nah. 3:5
untoward—crooked, Acts 2:40
usury—interest, Is. 24:2 (2 times); Mt. 25:27; Lk. 19:23

vagabond—wandering, Acts 19:13
vale—lowland, Deut. 1:7
vain—evil, Jer. 4:14
—lying, Ex. 5:9
vanity—falsehood, Ps. 12:2; 24:4; 41:6; Prov. 30:8
—deceit, Ps. 144:8, 11
—destruction, Is. 30:28
—a breath, Is. 57:13
—wickedly, Is. 58:9
vehement—sultry, Jon. 4:8
vengeance—justice, Acts 28:4
victory, in—forever, Is. 25:8
virtue—power, Mk. 5:30; Lk. 6:19; 8:46
void—an open, 1 Kgs. 22:10
volume—roll, Heb. 10:7

wanted—lacked, Jn. 2:3
ware—wary, 2 Tim. 4:15
—aware, Acts 14:6
waster—destroyer, Prov. 18:9
wealth—good, 1 Cor. 10:24
well—good, Mt. 12:12
wench—maidservant, 2 Sam. 17:17
whale—monster, Ezek. 32:2
whole—healed, Josh. 5:8
wine bottles—wine skins, Josh. 9:4 et al.
wist—knew, Ex. 16:15; 34:29; Lev. 5:17, 18; Josh. 2:4; 8:14; Judg. 16:20; Mk. 9:6; 14:40; Lk. 2:49; Jn. 5:13; Acts 12:9; 23:5
wit—know, Gen. 24:21; Ex. 2:4; 2 Cor. 8:1
wot—know, Gen. 21:26; 44:15; Ex. 32:1, 23; Num. 22:6; Josh. 2:5; Acts 3:17; 7:40; Rom. 11:2; Phil. 1:22
wotteth—knoweth, Gen. 39:8
woman—wife, Is. 54:6
wood—forest, Is. 7:2
work—recompense, Is. 40:10; 49:4; 62:11
worship—honor, Lk. 14:10
worthies—nobles, Nah. 2:5
wounds—dainty morsels, Prov. 26:22
wrap—weave together, Mic. 7:3
wrung out to—drained by, Ps. 73:10

yet—surely, Hos. 12:8

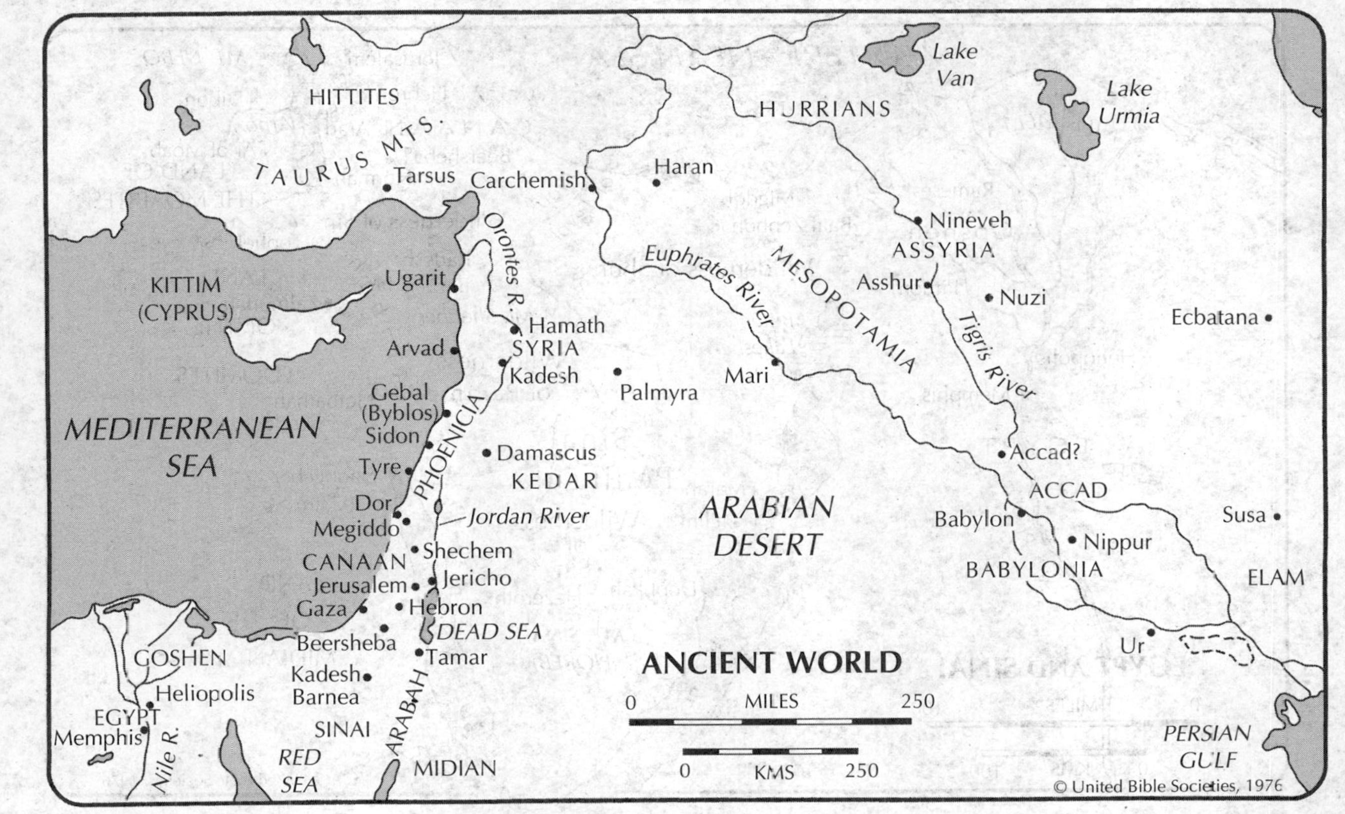
ANCIENT WORLD
HITTITES
TAURUS MTS.
Tarsus
Carchemish
Haran
HURRIANS
Lake Van
Lake Urmia
Nineveh
ASSYRIA
Asshur
Nuzi
Ecbatana
MESOPOTAMIA
Euphrates River
Tigris River
Orontes R.
KITTIM (CYPRUS)
Ugarit
Hamath
Arvad
SYRIA
Kadesh
Palmyra
Mari
Gebal (Byblos)
Sidon
PHOENICIA
MEDITERRANEAN SEA
Damascus
Tyre
KEDAR
Accad?
ACCAD
Dor
Megiddo
Jordan River
ARABIAN DESERT
Babylon
Susa
Nippur
Shechem
CANAAN
Jerusalem
Jericho
BABYLONIA
ELAM
Gaza
Hebron
DEAD SEA
Beersheba
Tamar
Ur
GOSHEN
Kadesh Barnea
Heliopolis
EGYPT
Memphis
Nile R.
SINAI
ARABAH
RED SEA
MIDIAN
0 MILES 250
0 KMS 250
PERSIAN GULF

MEDITERRANEAN SEA
NILE DELTA
Rameses
Goshen
Pithom
Heliopolis
Memphis
EGYPT
Nile River
Migdol
Baal Zephon
Wilderness of Shur
Bitter Lakes
Brook of Egypt
Gaza
Jerusalem
Hebron
CANAAN
Arad
Beersheba
Hormah
Dead Sea
MT. NEBO
Dibon
Arnon
Ar of Moab
LAND OF THE MOABITES
Wilderness of Sin
Tophel
Kadesh Barnea
Mt. Shepher
Arabah
Zalmonah
LAND OF THE EDOMITES
Wilderness of Paran
Jotbathah
Sinai Peninsula
Marah
Elim
Wilderness of Sin
Dophkah
Hazeroth
MT. SINAI (HOREB)
SEA OF REEDS (RED SEA)
GULF OF AQABA
Eziongeber (Elath)
LAND OF MIDIAN
EGYPT AND SINAI
0 MILES 100
0 KMS 100

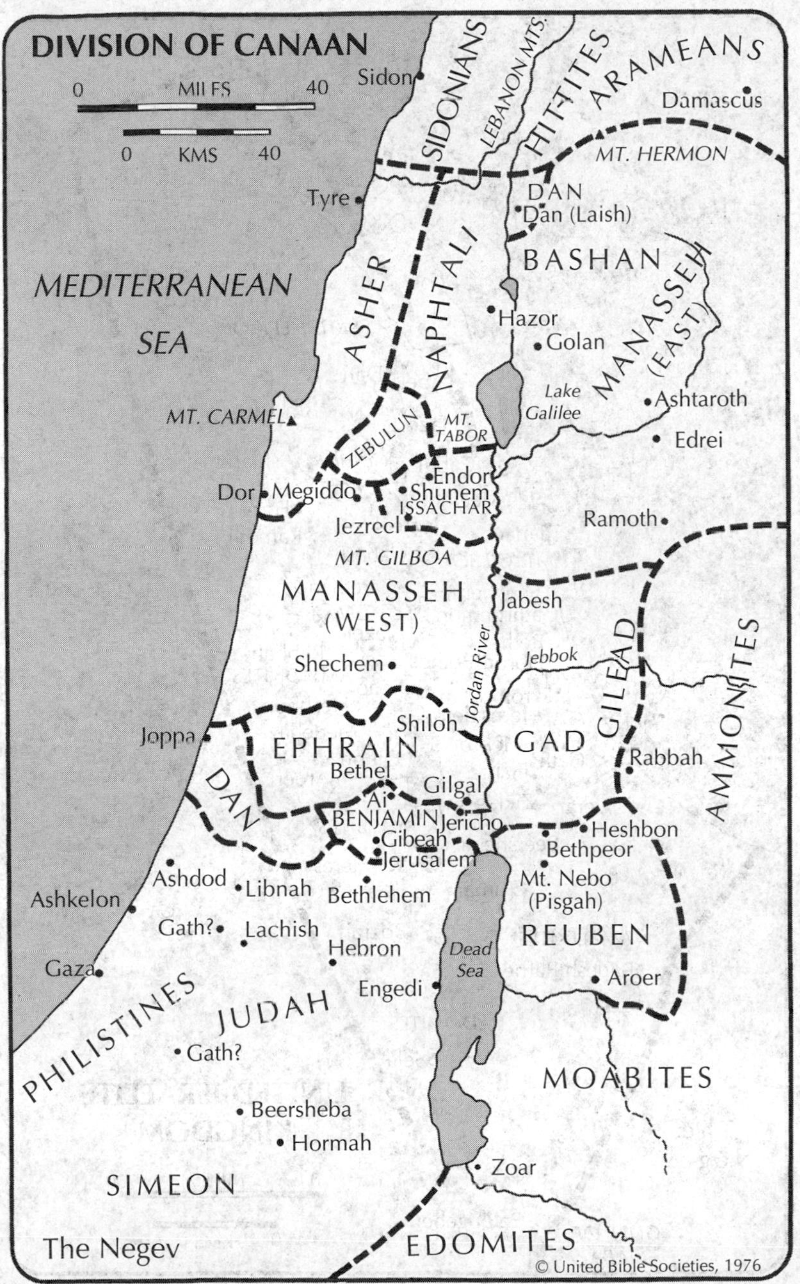
DIVISION OF CANAAN
0 MILES 40
0 KMS 40
Sidon
SIDONIANS
LEBANON MTS.
HITTITES
ARAMEANS
Damascus
MT. HERMON
Tyre
DAN
Dan (Laish)
BASHAN
MEDITERRANEAN SEA
ASHER
NAPHTALI
MANASSEH (EAST)
Hazor
Golan
Lake Galilee
Ashtaroth
MT. CARMEL
ZEBULUN
MT. TABOR
Edrei
Endor
Dor
Megiddo
Shunem
ISSACHAR
Jezreel
Ramoth
MT. GILBOA
MANASSEH (WEST)
Jabesh
Jordan River
Jebbok
GILEAD
AMMONITES
Shechem
Shiloh
Joppa
EPHRAIN
GAD
Rabbah
Bethel
DAN
Gilgal
Ai
BENJAMIN
Jericho
Heshbon
Gibeah
Bethpeor
Jerusalem
Ashdod
Libnah
Bethlehem
Mt. Nebo (Pisgah)
Ashkelon
Gath?
Lachish
REUBEN
Hebron
Dead Sea
Gaza
Aroer
Engedi
PHILISTINES
JUDAH
Gath?
MOABITES
Beersheba
Hormah
Zoar
SIMEON
The Negev
EDOMITES

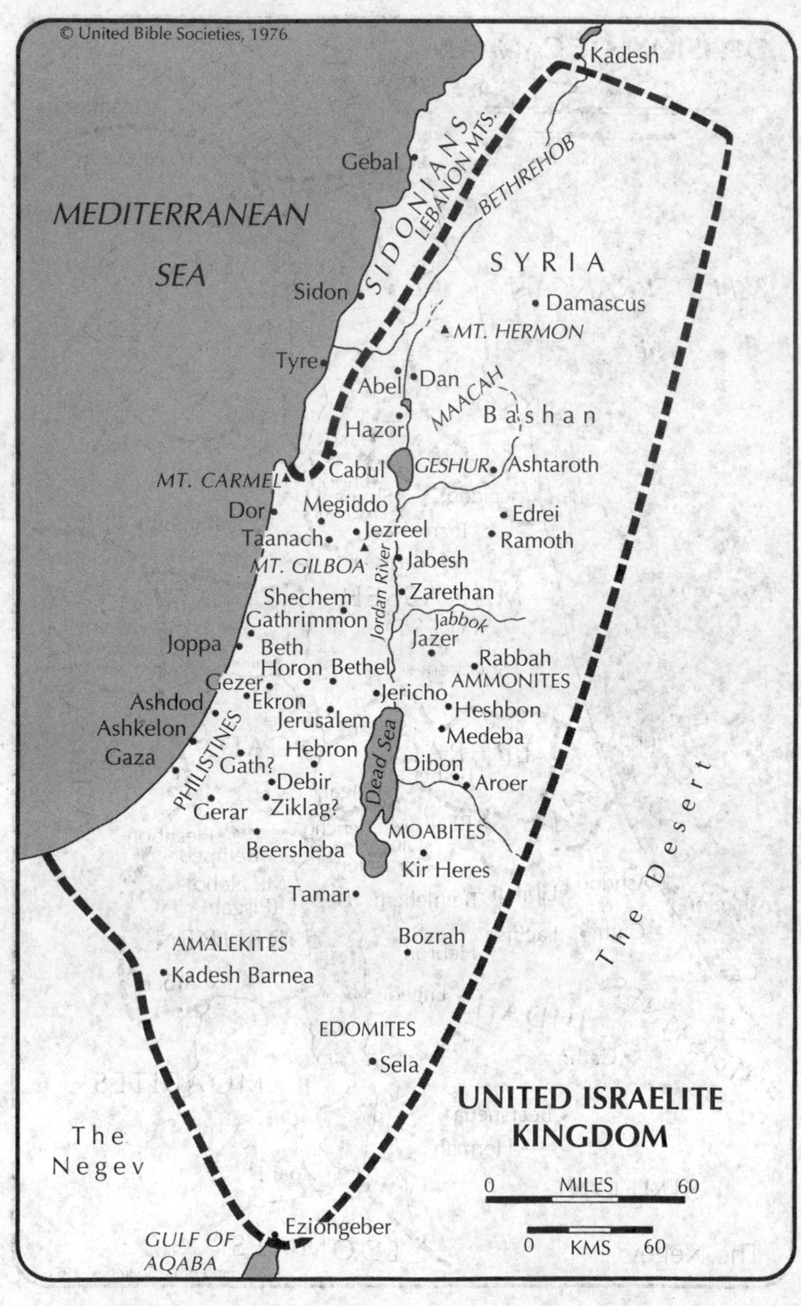
© United Bible Societies, 1976
Kadesh
SIDONIANS
LEBANON MTS.
BETHREHOB
Gebal
MEDITERRANEAN
SEA
SYRIA
Sidon
Damascus
MT. HERMON
Tyre
Abel
Dan
MAACAH
Bashan
Hazor
Cabul
GESHUR
Ashtaroth
MT. CARMEL
Dor
Megiddo
Edrei
Taanach
Jezreel
Ramoth
MT. GILBOA
Jordan River
Jabesh
Zarethan
Shechem
Gathrimmon
Jabbok
Jazer
Joppa
Beth
Horon
Bethel
Rabbah
AMMONITES
Gezer
Ashdod
Ekron
Jericho
Heshbon
Jerusalem
Ashkelon
Medeba
PHILISTINES
Hebron
Gaza
Gath?
Dead Sea
Dibon
Debir
Aroer
Gerar
Ziklag?
MOABITES
Beersheba
Kir Heres
Tamar
The Desert
AMALEKITES
Bozrah
Kadesh Barnea
EDOMITES
Sela
UNITED ISRAELITE
KINGDOM
The
Negev
0
MILES
60
0
KMS
60
Eziongeber
GULF OF
AQABA

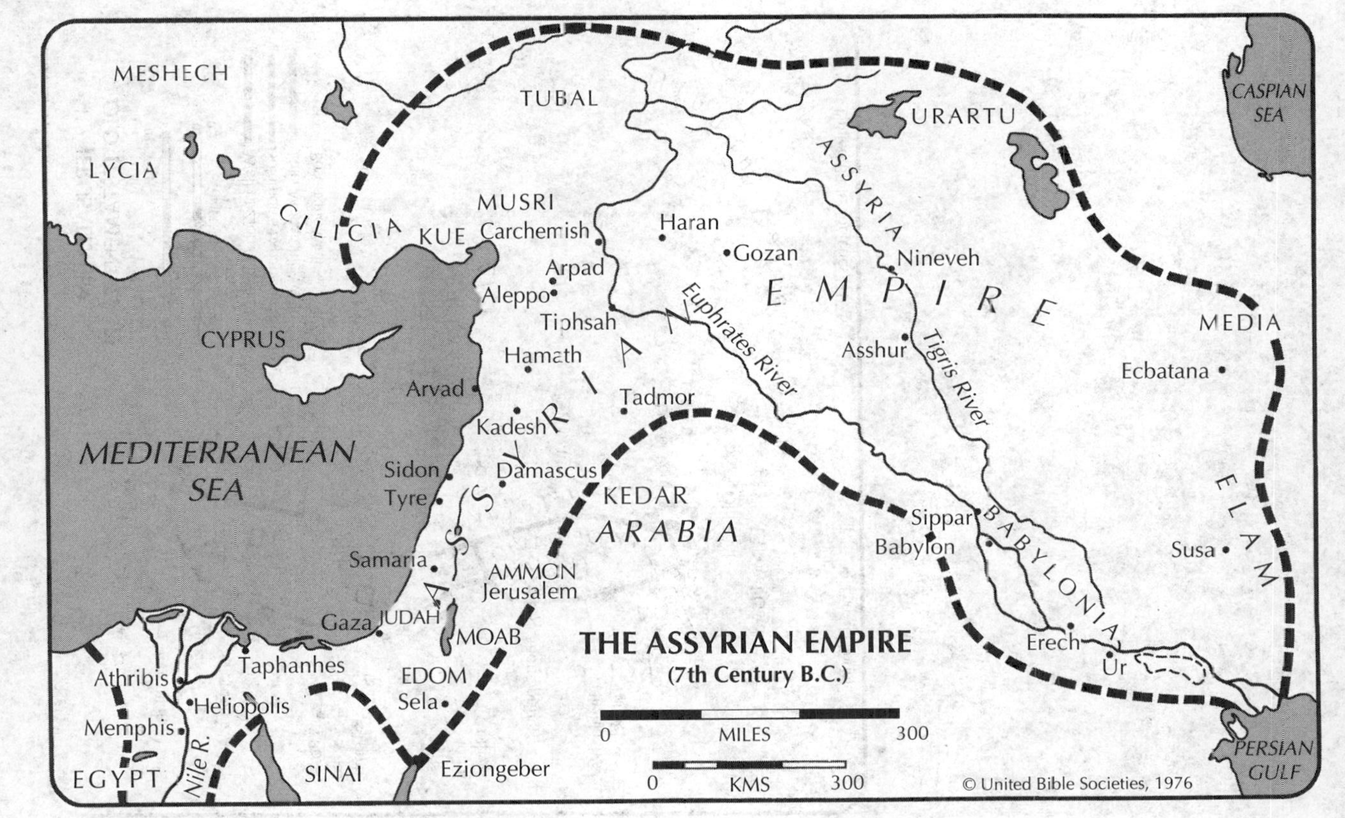
THE ASSYRIAN EMPIRE
(7th Century B.C.)
MESHECH
TUBAL
URARTU
CASPIAN SEA
LYCIA
CILICIA
KUE
MUSRI
Carchemish
Haran
Gozan
ASSYRIA
Nineveh
Arpad
Aleppo
Tiphsah
EMPIRE
MEDIA
CYPRUS
Hamath
ASSYRIAN
Euphrates River
Asshur
Tigris River
Ecbatana
Arvad
Tadmor
Kadesh
MEDITERRANEAN SEA
Sidon
Damascus
Tyre
KEDAR
ARABIA
Sippar
Babylon
BABYLONIA
ELAM
Susa
Samaria
AMMON
Jerusalem
Gaza
JUDAH
MOAB
Erech
Ur
Athribis
Taphanhes
EDOM
Sela
Heliopolis
Memphis
Nile R.
EGYPT
SINAI
Eziongeber
PERSIAN GULF
0 MILES 300
0 KMS 300

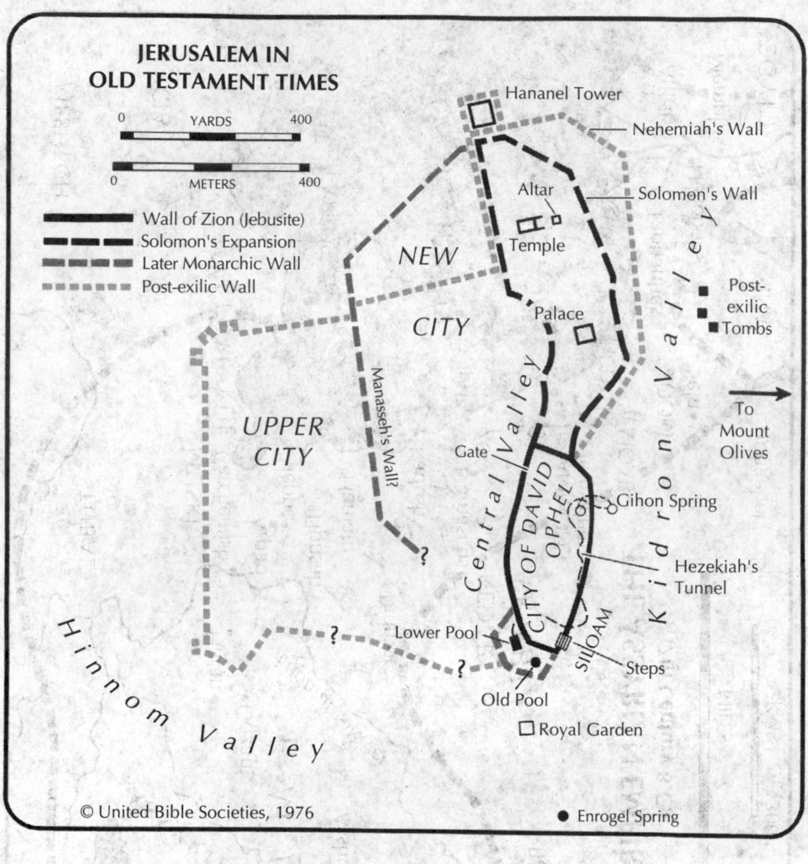
JERUSALEM IN
OLD TESTAMENT TIMES
0 YARDS 400
0 METERS 400
Wall of Zion (Jebusite)
Solomon's Expansion
Later Monarchic Wall
Post-exilic Wall
Hananel Tower
Nehemiah's Wall
Altar
Solomon's Wall
Temple
NEW
CITY
Palace
Post-
exilic
Tombs
Manasseh's Wall?
UPPER
CITY
Central Valley
Kidron Valley
To
Mount
Olives
Gate
CITY OF DAVID
OPHEL
Gihon Spring
Hezekiah's
Tunnel
Lower Pool
SILOAM
Steps
Old Pool
Royal Garden
Hinnom Valley
Enrogel Spring

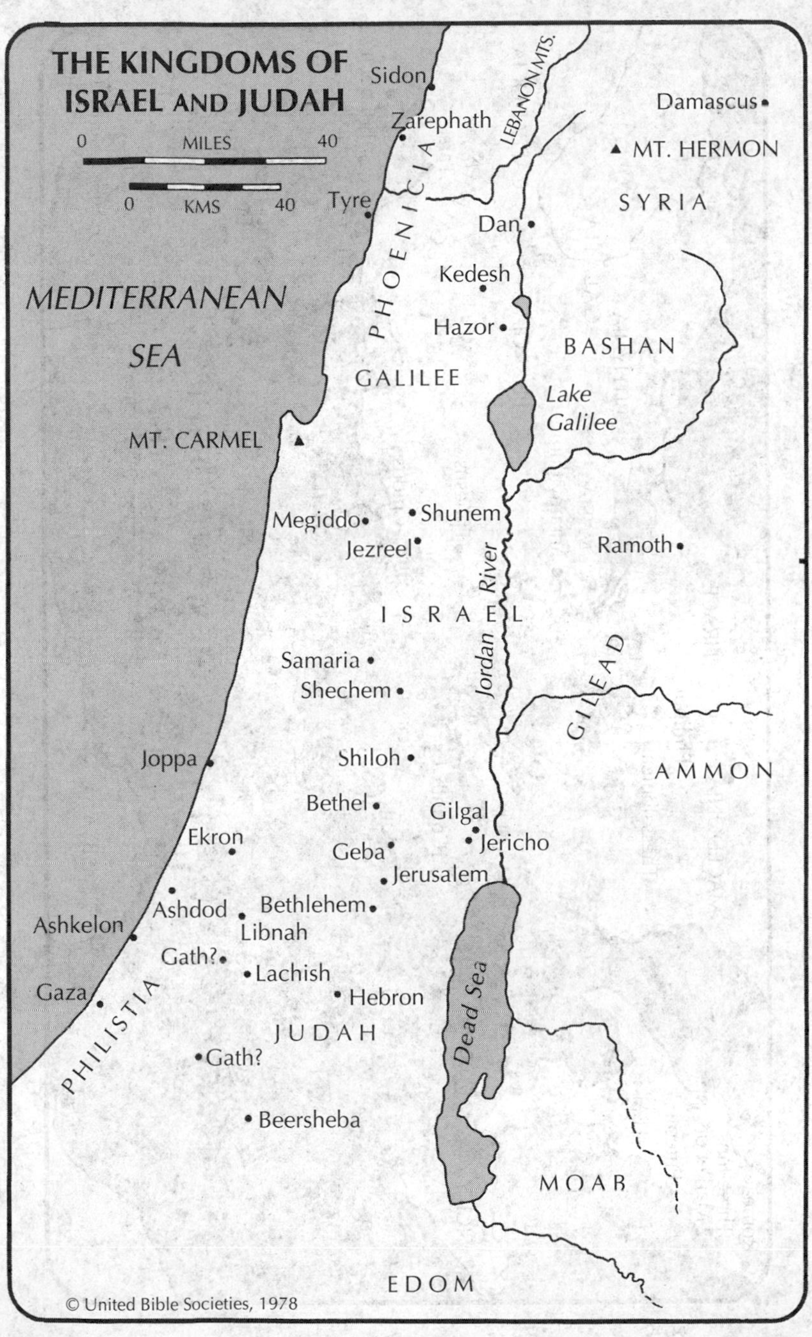
THE KINGDOMS OF ISRAEL AND JUDAH
0 MILES 40
0 KMS 40
Sidon
Zarephath
LEBANON MTS.
Damascus
MT. HERMON
Tyre
PHOENICIA
SYRIA
Dan
Kedesh
MEDITERRANEAN SEA
Hazor
BASHAN
GALILEE
Lake Galilee
MT. CARMEL
Megiddo
Shunem
Jezreel
Ramoth
Jordan River
ISRAEL
Samaria
Shechem
GILEAD
Joppa
Shiloh
AMMON
Bethel
Gilgal
Ekron
Geba
Jericho
Jerusalem
Ashdod
Bethlehem
Ashkelon
Libnah
Gath?
Lachish
Gaza
Hebron
PHILISTIA
JUDAH
Dead Sea
Gath?
Beersheba
MOAB
EDOM

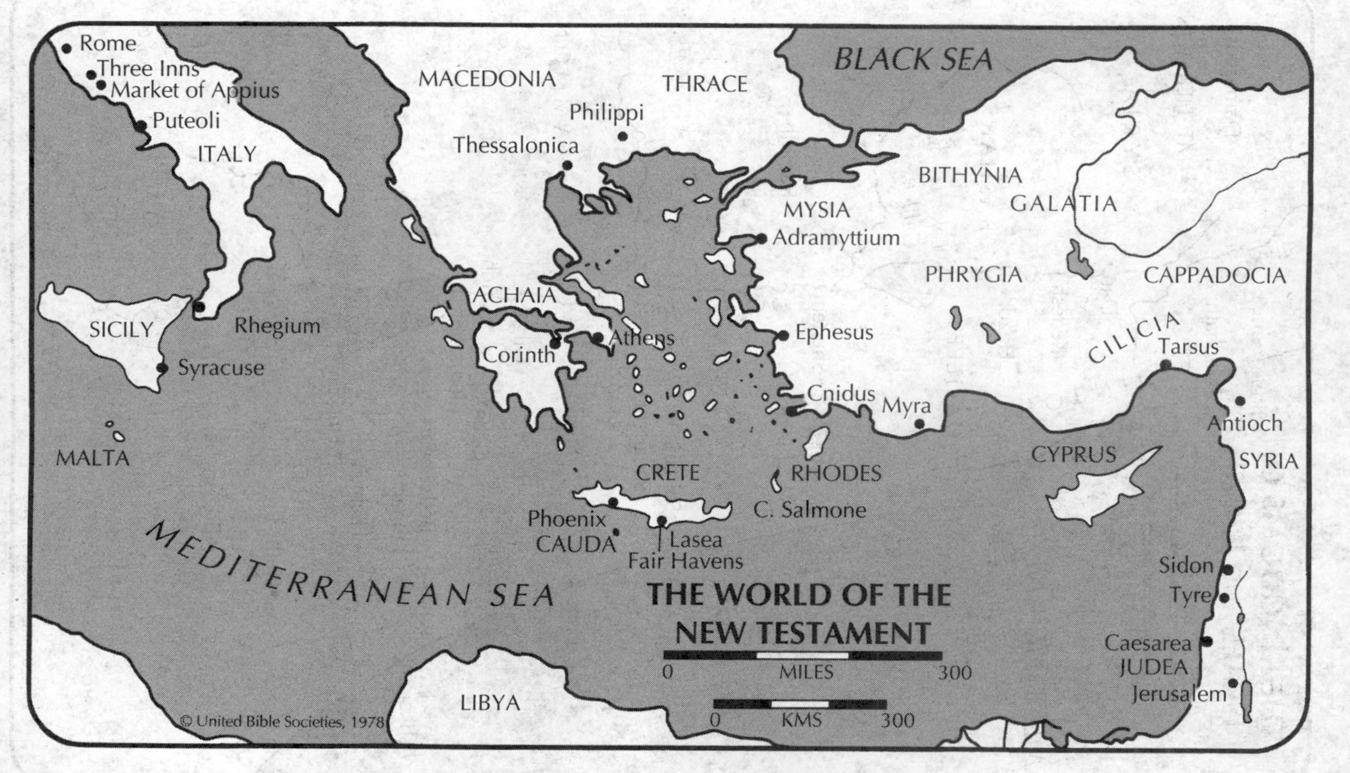

THE WORLD OF THE NEW TESTAMENT
Rome
Three Inns
Market of Appius
Puteoli
ITALY
SICILY
Rhegium
Syracuse
MALTA
MACEDONIA
THRACE
Philippi
Thessalonica
BLACK SEA
BITHYNIA
GALATIA
MYSIA
Adramyttium
PHRYGIA
CAPPADOCIA
ACHAIA
Athens
Corinth
Ephesus
CILICIA
Tarsus
Cnidus
Myra
Antioch
SYRIA
CYPRUS
CRETE
RHODES
C. Salmone
Phoenix
CAUDA
Lasea
Fair Havens
MEDITERRANEAN SEA
Sidon
Tyre
Caesarea
JUDEA
Jerusalem
LIBYA
0 MILES 300
0 KMS 300
© United Bible Societies, 1978

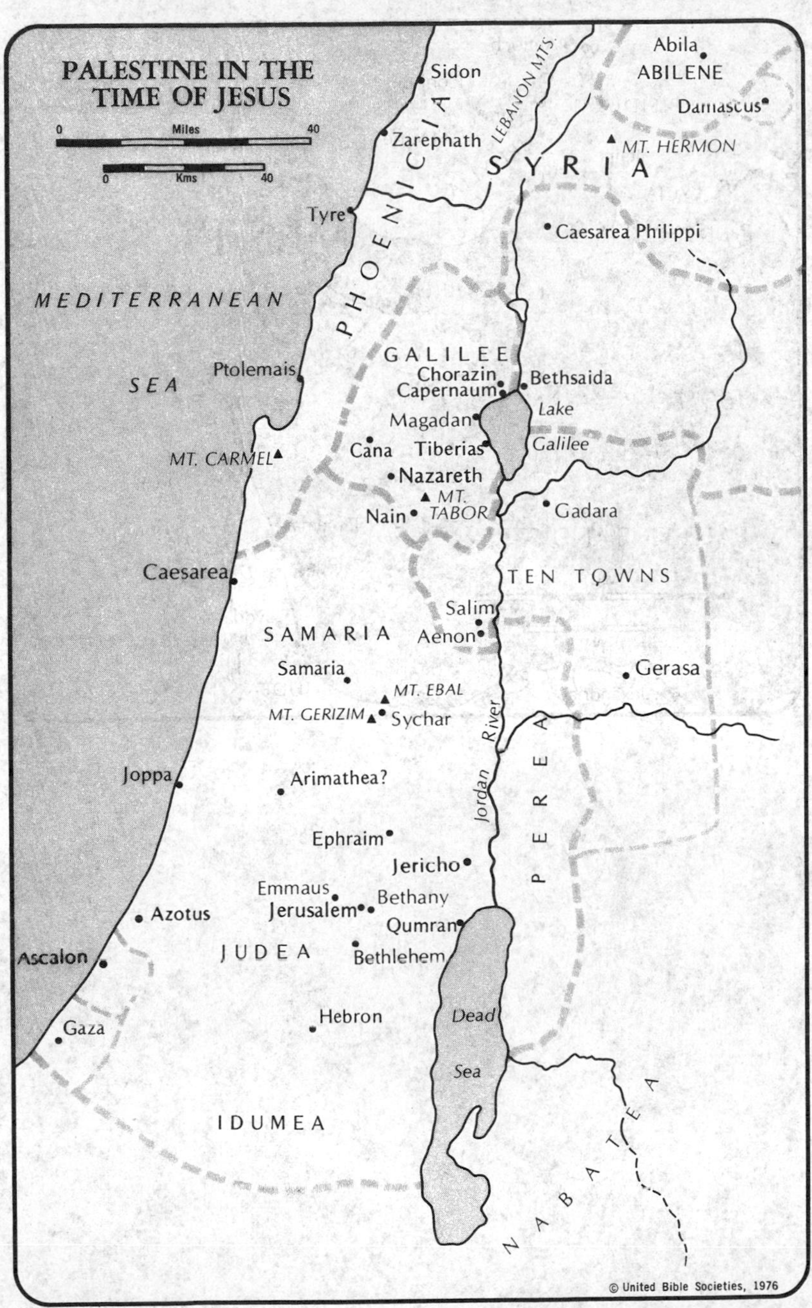
PALESTINE IN THE TIME OF JESUS
0 Miles 40
0 Kms 40
MEDITERRANEAN SEA
Sidon
Zarephath
Tyre
PHOENICIA
LEBANON MTS.
Abila
ABILENE
Damascus
MT. HERMON
SYRIA
Caesarea Philippi
Ptolemais
GALILEE
Chorazin
Capernaum
Bethsaida
Lake Galilee
Magadan
Tiberias
Cana
MT. CARMEL
Nazareth
MT. TABOR
Nain
Gadara
Caesarea
TEN TOWNS
Salim
Aenon
SAMARIA
Samaria
Gerasa
MT. EBAL
MT. GERIZIM
Sychar
Jordan River
PEREA
Joppa
Arimathea?
Ephraim
Jericho
Emmaus
Bethany
Jerusalem
Qumran
Azotus
Ascalon
JUDEA
Bethlehem
Hebron
Dead Sea
Gaza
IDUMEA
NABATEA

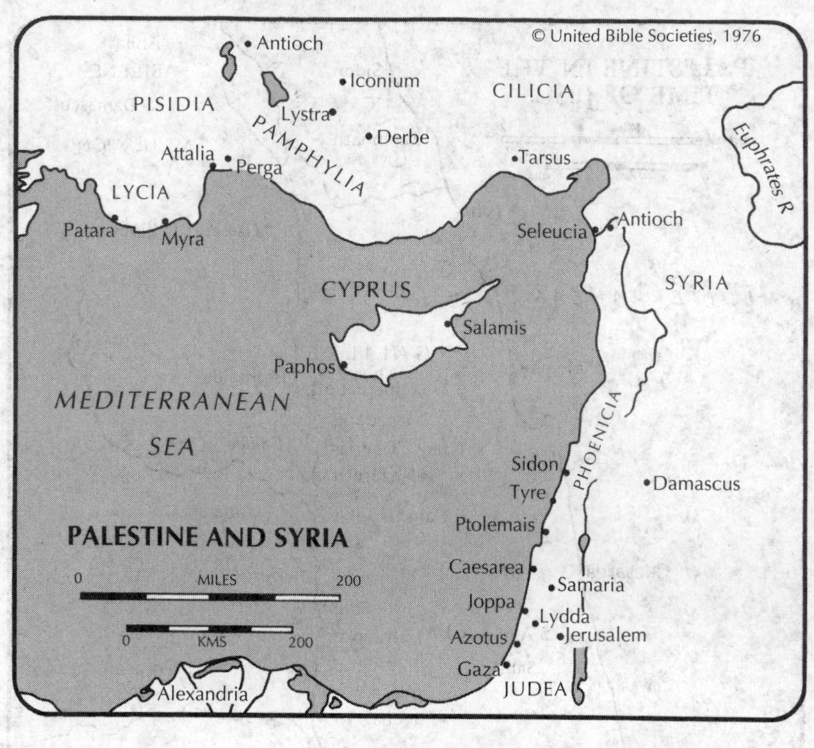
© United Bible Societies, 1976
Antioch
Iconium
CILICIA
PISIDIA
Lystra
PAMPHYLIA
Derbe
Euphrates R
Attalia
Perga
Tarsus
LYCIA
Patara
Myra
Seleucia
Antioch
SYRIA
CYPRUS
Salamis
Paphos
MEDITERRANEAN
SEA
PHOENICIA
Sidon
Tyre
Damascus
Ptolemais
PALESTINE AND SYRIA
0
MILES
200
Caesarea
Samaria
Joppa
Lydda
0
KMS
200
Azotus
Jerusalem
Gaza
Alexandria
JUDEA

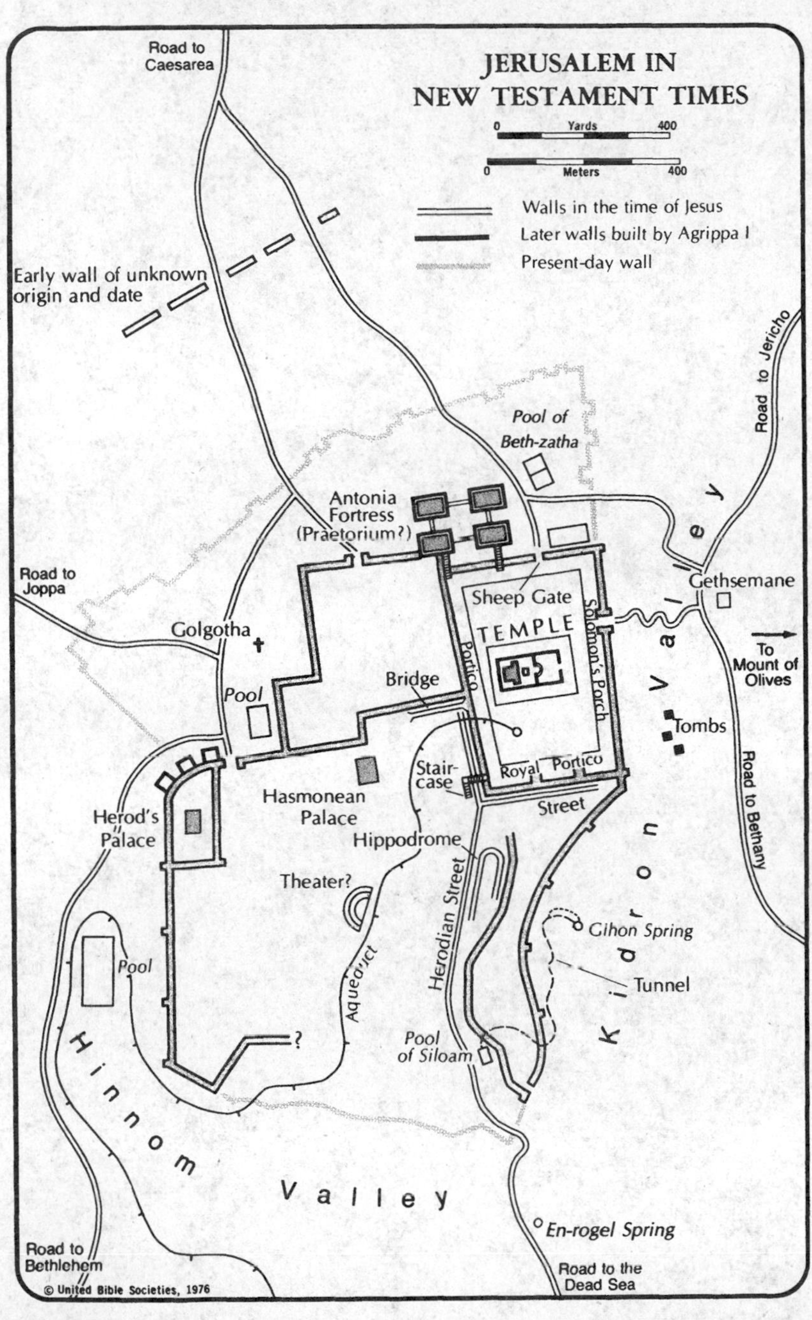
JERUSALEM IN
NEW TESTAMENT TIMES
0 Yards 400
0 Meters 400
Walls in the time of Jesus
Later walls built by Agrippa I
Present-day wall
Road to Caesarea
Early wall of unknown origin and date
Road to Jericho
Pool of Beth-zatha
Antonia Fortress (Praetorium?)
Road to Joppa
Sheep Gate
Gethsemane
Golgotha
TEMPLE
Solomon's Porch
Portico
To Mount of Olives
Bridge
Pool
Tombs
Stair-case
Royal Portico
Hasmonean Palace
Street
Herod's Palace
Hippodrome
Road to Bethany
Theater?
Herodian Street
Kidron Valley
Gihon Spring
Pool
Aqueduct
Tunnel
?
Pool of Siloam
Hinnom Valley
En-rogel Spring
Road to Bethlehem
Road to the Dead Sea
© United Bible Societies, 1976